W. B. SAUNDERS

1999
ICD-9-CM
AND
2000
HCPCS

W.B. SAUNDERS

1999
ICD-9-CM
AND
2000
HCPCS

Carol J. Buck, BS, MS

Program Director, Medical Secretary Program
Northwest Technical College
East Grand Forks, Minnesota

W.B. SAUNDERS COMPANY
A Harcourt Health Sciences Company

Philadelphia   London   Toronto   Montreal   Sydney   Tokyo

W.B. SAUNDERS COMPANY
A Harcourt Health Sciences Company

The Curtis Center
Independence Square West
Philadelphia, Pennsylvania 19106

Library of Congress Cataloging-in-Publication Data

Buck, Carol J.
W.B. Saunders 1999 ICD-9-CM and 2000 HCPCS / Carol J. Buck.

p. cm.

ISBN 0-7216-7787-8

1. Nosology—Code numbers. I. Title.
   [DNLM: 1. Disease—classification. 2. Therapeutics—classification. 3. Disease nomenclature. WB 15B922c 2000]

RB115.B829 2000   616′.001′48—dc21

DNLM/DLC   98-38028

W.B. Saunders 1999 ICD-9-CM and 2000 HCPCS   ISBN 0-7216-7787-8

Printed in the United States of America.

Last digit is the print number: 9   8   7   6   5   4   3   2   1

GUIDE TO USING THE W.B. SAUNDERS 1999 ICD-9-CM AND 2000 HCPCS

Medical coding has long been a part of the health care profession. Through the years medical coding systems have become more complex and extensive. Today, medical coding is an intricate and immense process that is present in every health care setting. The increased use of electronic submissions for health care services only increases the need for coders who understand the coding process.

W.B. Saunders 1999 ICD-9-CM and 2000 HCPCS was developed to help meet the needs of students preparing for a career in medical coding by offering a comprehensive coding text at a reasonable price. This text combines the official coding guidelines, all three volumes of the ICD-9-CM, and HCPCS in one book—three books in one. In addition, the Diagnostic Related Groups (DRGs) list of complications and comorbidities is included for inpatient coding.

All material strictly adheres to the latest government versions available at the time of printing.

ILLUSTRATIONS AND ITEMS

The ICD-9-CM, Volume 1, Tabular List contains illustrations, pictures, and items to assist you in understanding difficult terminology, diseases/conditions, or coding in a specific category. Items are always printed in ▬▬▬ ink so the added material is not mistaken for official notations or instructions. Your ideas on what other descriptions or illustrations should be in future editions of this text are always appreciated.

Annotated

Throughout this text revisions and additions are indicated by the following symbols:

◀▥▶ **Revised:** Revisions within the line or code from the previous edition are indicated by the black arrow.

◀▶ **New:** Additions from the previous edition are indicated by the red triangle.

The revision and addition symbols are the only symbols that appear in the ICD-9-CM indexes.

ICD-9-CM, Volume 1, Tabular List Symbols

● **Not a principal diagnosis:** These codes have a black dot before them. These codes give additional information or describe the circumstances affecting the health care encounter but are unacceptable as principal diagnosis codes.

● **Use additional digit(s):** The red dot cautions you that the code requires additional digit(s) to insure the greatest specificity.

□ **Nonspecific code:** These have a square before the code. Although these codes are valid as a principal diagnosis, they are usually too general to be used as a principal diagnosis for Medicare, and you should continue to seek a code that is more specific.

ICD-9-CM, Volume 3, Tabular List Symbols

● **Use additional digit(s):** The red dot cautions you that the code requires additional digit(s) to insure the greatest specificity.

✖ **Valid O.R. procedure:** The red "x" is placed before a code that is a valid operating room (O.R.) procedure according to the DRG grouper.

In addition to the symbols, the official ICD-9-CM conventions appear throughout the text. Refer to the illustrations of conventions on the following pages and to the Introduction for further information on conventions.

HCPCS Symbols

⊕   **Special coverage instructions** apply to these codes. Usually these special coverage instructions are included in the Medicare Carrier Manual (MCM) select references in Appendix A or in the Coverage Issues Manual (CIM) in Appendix B of this text.

◆   **Not covered by or valid for Medicare** is indicated by the diamond. Usually the reason for the exclusion is included in the Medicare Carrier Manual (MCM) select references in Appendix A or in the Coverage Issues Manual (CIM) in Appendix B of this text.

✳   **Carrier discretion** is an indication that you must contact the individual third-party payors to find out the coverage available for codes identified by this symbol.

W.B.SAUNDERS
1999 ICD-9-CM and 2000 HCPCS

Symbols Used In All Volumes of ICD-9-CM to Identify New or Revised Material

Volume 1, Tabular List

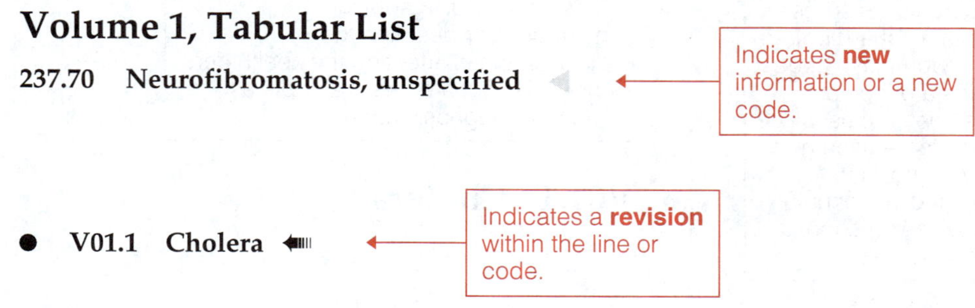

Volume 2, Alphabetic Index

Illness—*see also* Disease
    factitious 300.19
        with
            combined physical and
                psychological symptoms 300.19

Volume 3, Procedures, Index

Biopsy
    peritoneum
        closed 54.24

Volume 3, Procedures, Tabular List

37   **Other operations on heart and pericardium**
      Code also any injection or infusion of platelet
         inhibitor (99.20)

92   **Stereotactic radiosurgery**

Symbols for Volume 1, Tabular List

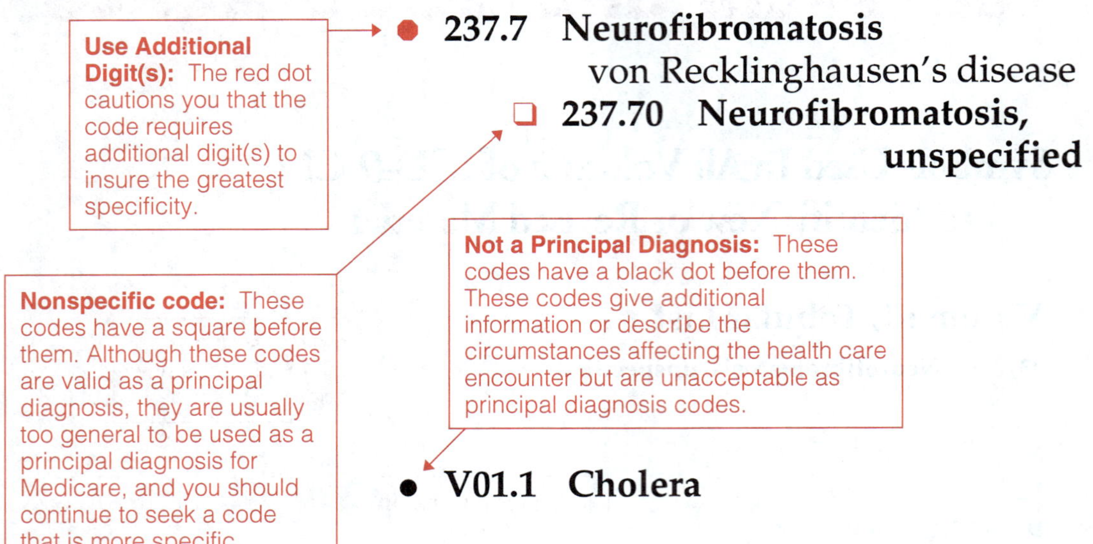

Conventions for Volume 1, Tabular List

2.   NEOPLASMS (140–239)

Notes define terms or give coding instructions.

Notes
1.   Content
This chapter contains the following broad groups:
140–195   Malignant neoplasms, stated or presumed to be primary, of specified sites, except of lymphatic and hematopoietic tissue.

"Use additional digit(s)" directs you to use an additional code to give a more complete picture of the diagnosis.

510   **Empyema**
Use additional code to identify infectious organism (041.0–041.9)

"*Code first*" is used in those categories not intended as the principal diagnosis. In such cases, the code, title, and instructions appear in italics. The note requires that the underlying disease (etiology) be sequenced first.

366.4   **Cataract associated with other disorders**
366.41   *Diabetic cataract*
Code first diabetes (250.5)

474   **Chronic disease of tonsils and adenoids**

"and" indicates a code that can be assigned if either of the conditions is present or if both of the conditions are present.

366.4   **Cataract associated with other disorders**

"with" indicates a code that can only be used if both conditions are present.

The "Includes" note appears immediately under a code to further define, or give example of, the contents of the code.

087   **Relapsing fever**
Includes: recurrent fever

420.0   *Acute pericarditis in disease classified elsewhere*

Italicized type is used for all exclusion notes and to identify those codes that are not usually sequenced as the principal diagnosis.

Terms following the word "Excludes" are to be coded elsewhere. The term "Excludes" means "Do Not Code Here."

150.2   **Abdominal esophagus**
Excludes: *recurrent fever*

244.8   **Other specified acquired hypothyroidism**
Secondary hypothyroidism NEC

NEC means Not Elsewhere Classifiable and is to be used only when the information at hand specifies a condition but there is no more specific code for that condition.

Bold type is used for all codes and titles.

159.0   **Intestinal tract, part unspecified**
Intestine NOS

NOS means Not Otherwise Specified and is the equivalent of "unspecified."

426.89   **Other**
Dissociation:
atrioventricular [AV]

Brackets are used to enclose synonyms, alternative wording, or explanatory phrases.

158.8   **Specified parts of peritoneum**
Cul-de-sac (of Douglas)
Mesentery

Parentheses are used to enclose supplementary words that may be present or absent in the statement of a disease without affecting the code.

628.4   **Of cervical or vaginal origin**
Infertility associated with:
anomaly of cervical mucus
congenital structural anomaly

A colon is used after an incomplete term that needs one or more of the modifiers that follow in order to make it assignable to a given category.

Conventions for Volume 2, Alphabetic Index

Ileus (adynamic) (bowel) (colon) (inhibitory) (intestine) (neurogenic) (paralytic)

Nonessential modifiers are enclosed in parentheses and are words that may be used to clarify the diagnosis but do not affect the code.

Incoordination
  esophageal-pharyngeal (newborn) 787.2

Essential modifiers are NOT enclosed in parentheses and are subterms that DO affect the selection of the appropriate code.

Hereditary—*see* condition

"*see*" is a cross reference directing you to look elsewhere.

Paralysis
  embolic (current episode) (*see also*
    Embolism, brain) 434.1

"*see also*" is a cross reference directing you to look under another main term if all the information being searched for cannot be located under the first main term entry.

Delivery
  completely normal case—*see* category 650

"*see* category" is a cross reference directing you to Volume 1, Tabular List for important information governing the use of the specific code.

Amputation
  traumatic (complete) (partial)

"Notes" are used to define terms and give coding instructions

Note "Complicated" includes traumatic amputation with delayed healing, delayed treatment, foreign body, or major infection.

Adolescence NEC V21.2

NEC means Not Elsewhere Classifiable.

Conventions for Volume 3, Procedures Index

Arthrotomy 80.10

as operative approach—*omit code*

> "*omit code*" identifies procedures or services that are included in another larger procedure or service. For example, an incision that is part of the main surgical procedure is not coded separately.

Ileal

bladder

closed 57.87 [*45.51*]

> For some operative procedures it is necessary to record the individual components of the procedure.
> These procedures are termed **"synchronous procedures"** and are listed together in the Index. The codes are sequenced in the same order as displayed in the Index.

Operation

Thompson

cleft lip repair 27.54

correction of lymphedema 40.9

quadricepsplasty 83.86

> Eponyms are operations named for people and are listed in the Index both under the eponym and under the term "Operation."

Thompson operation

cleft lip repair 27.54

correction of lymphedema 40.9

quadricepsplasty 83.86

Volume 3, Index to Procedures, also contains "*see*," "*see also*," "*see* category," "essential modifiers," "nonessential modifiers," "notes," NEC, and NOS as in Volume 2, Alphabetic Index.

Symbols for Volume 3, Procedures, Tabular List

Use additional digit(s):
The red dot cautions you that the code requires additional digit(s) to insure the greatest specificity.

Valid O.R. procedure:
The red X is placed before a code that is a valid operating room (O.R.) procedure according to the DRG grouper.

● 31.9   **Other operations on larynx and trachea**
✖ 31.91   **Division of laryngeal nerve**

Conventions for Volume 3, Procedures, Tabular List

Bold type is used for all codes and titles.

The "Includes" note appears to further define, or give example of, the contents of the code.

88.4   **Arteriography using contrast material**
Includes: angiography of arteries
    arterial puncture for injection of contrast material
    radiography of arteries (by fluoroscopy)
    retrograde arteriography

The fifth-digit subclassification identifies the site to be viewed, not the site of injection

Terms following the word "Excludes" are to be coded elsewhere. The term means "Do Not Code Here."

Excludes: arteriography using:
    radioisotopes or radionuclides (92.01–92.19)

For some operative procedures it is necessary to record the individual components of the procedure. These procedures are termed "synchronous procedures."

45.5   **Isolation of intestinal segment**
Code also any synchronous:

anastomosis other than end-to-end (45.90–45.94)

enterostomy (46.10–46.39)

Symbols for HCPCS

Special coverage instructions apply to these codes. Usually these instructions are included in the Medicare Carrier Manual (MCM) select references in Appendix A or in the Coverage Issues Manual (CIM) in Appendix B of this text.

L3540 Miscellaneous shoe additions, sole, full
MCM 2079, CIM 70-3

Medicare Carrier Manual (MCM) and Coverage Issues Manual (CIM) give instructions regarding use of the code. MCM and CIM select references are located in the appendices of this text.

Not covered by or valid for Medicare is indicated by the diamond. Usually the reason for the exclusion is included in the Medicare Carrier Manual (MCM) references in Appendix A or in the Coverage Issues Manual (CIM) in Appendix B of this text.

A5074 Pouch, urinary; with faceplate attached; plastic or rubber
MCM 2130

Carrier discretion is an indication that you must contact the individual third-party payors to find out the coverage available for these codes.

A6154 Wound pouch, each

Indicates **new** information or a new code.

A4614 Peak expiratory flow rate meter, hand held

Indicates a **revision** within the line or code.

J0270 Injection alprostadil, per 1.25 mcg

DISCLAIMER

Every effort has been made to make this text complete and accurate, but no guarantee, warranty, or representation is made for its accuracy or completeness.

W.B. Saunders and Carol J. Buck are not providing any legal or professional service/advice in presenting these codes and bear no liability for how the codes are used.

THE PUBLISHER

CLASSIFICATION OF DISEASES AND INJURIES

1. INFECTIOUS AND PARASITIC DISEASES (001–139)
 099 Other venereal diseases
  099.3 Reiter's disease
Add   Use additional code for associated:
    arthropathy (711.1)
    conjunctivitis (372.33)

5. MENTAL DISORDERS (290–319)
Revise **297 Paranoid states** (Delusional disorders)

**6. DISEASES OF THE NERVOUS SYSTEM AND SENSE
ORGANS (320–389)**
 337 Disorders of the autonomic nervous system
New code 337.3 Autonomic dysreflexia
Add   Use additional code to identify the un-
    derlying cause, such as:
    decubitus ulcer (707.0)
    fecal impaction (560.39)
    urinary tract infection (599.0)
 342 Hemiplegia and hemiparesis
Add   **Excludes** *hemiplegia due to late effect of cerebrovascular
    accident (438.20–438.22)*
 344 Other paralytic syndromes
  344.3 Monoplegia of lower limb
Add   **Excludes** *monoplegia of lower limb due to late effect of
    cerebrovascular accident (438.40–438.42)*
  344.4 Monoplegia of upper limb
Add   **Excludes** *monoplegia of upper limb due to late effect of
    cerebrovascular accident (438.30–438.32)*
 357 Inflammatory and toxic neuropathy
  357.8 Other
Add   Chronic inflammatory demyelinating
    polyneuritis
 384 Other disorders of tympanic membrane
  384.2 Perforation of tympanic membrane
Add   **Excludes** *otitis media with perforation of tympanic mem-
    brane (382.00–382.9)*

**7. DISEASES OF THE CIRCULATORY SYSTEM (390–459)
CEREBROVASCULAR DISEASE (430–438)**
 438 Late effects of cerebrovascular disease
Revise Note: This category is to be used to indicate condi-
     tions in 430–437 as the cause of late effects
     ~~themselves classified elsewhere~~. The "late ef-
     fects" include conditions specified as such, as
     sequelae, which may occur at any time after
     the onset of the causal condition.
  438.5 Other paralytic syndrome
Add   Use additional code to identify type of para-
    lytic syndrome, such as:
    locked-in state (344.81)
    quadriplegia (344.00–344.09)
Add   **Excludes** *late effects of cerebrovascular accident with:*
    hemiplegia/hemiparesis (438.20–438.22)
    monoplegia of lower limb (438.40–438.42)
    monoplegia of upper limb (438.30–438.32)
New code   438.53 Other paralytic syndrome, bilateral

 438.8 Other late effects of cerebrovascular disease
  438.89 Other late effects of cerebrovascular
    disease
Add   Use additional code to identify the
    late effect

8. DISEASES OF THE RESPIRATORY SYSTEM (460–519)
 482 Other bacterial pneumonia
New sub- 482.4 Pneumonia due to Staphylococcus
category
New code   482.40 Pneumonia due to Staphylococcus,
     unspecified
New code   482.41 Pneumonia due to Staphylococcus
     aureus
New code   482.49 Other Staphylococcus pneumonia
 493 Asthma
Add   **Excludes** *wheezing NOS (786.07)*
 518 Other disease of lung
  518.5 Pulmonary insufficiency following trauma
    and surgery
Revise   **Excludes** *respiratory failure in other conditions (518.81,
     518.83–518.84)*
  518.8 Other diseases of lung
Revise   518.81 Acute respiratory failure
     Respiratory failure NOS
Delete   ~~Respiratory failure:~~
     ~~acute~~
     ~~acute and chronic (acute on~~
      ~~chronic)~~
     ~~chronic~~
     ~~NOS~~
Add   **Excludes** *acute and chronic respiratory failure (518.84)*
     chronic respiratory failure (518.83)
New code   518.83 Chronic respiratory failure
New code   518.84 Acute and chronic respiratory failure
     Acute on chronic respiratory failure
 519 Other diseases of respiratory system
Revise 519.0 Tracheostomy complications
Delete   ~~Hemorrhage from tracheostomy stoma~~
    ~~Sepsis of stoma~~
    ~~Tracheal stenosis~~
    ~~Tracheoesophageal fistula~~
    ~~Tracheostomy:~~
     ~~hemorrhage~~
     ~~obstruction~~
     ~~sepsis~~
New code   519.00 Tracheostomy complication, unspeci-
     fied
New code   519.01 Infection of tracheostomy
Add   Use additional code to identify type
     of infection, such as abscess or
     cellulitis of neck (682.1)
     septicemia (038.0–038.9)
Add   Use additional code to identify or-
     ganism (041.00–041.9)
New code   519.02 Mechanical complication of tracheos-
     tomy
     Tracheal stenosis due to tracheos-
      tomy
New code   519.09 Other tracheostomy complications
     Hemorrhage due to tracheostomy
     Tracheoesophageal fistula due to
      tracheostomy

9. DISEASES OF THE DIGESTIVE SYSTEM (520–579)

  536 Disorders of function of stomach

New sub-category   **536.4 Gastrostomy complications**

New code   **536.40 Gastrostomy complication, unspecified**

New code   **536.41 Infection of gastrostomy**

Add   Use additional code to specify type of infection, such as:
abscess or cellulitis of abdomen (682.2)
septicemia (038.0–038.9)

Add   Use additional code to identify organism (041.00–041.9)

New code   **536.42 Mechanical complication of gastrostomy**

New code   **536.49 Other gastrostomy complications**

  557 Vascular insufficiency of intestine

  557.0 Acute vascular insufficiency of intestine

Add   Infarction of appendices epiploicae

Add   Necrosis of intestine

  564 Functional digestive disorders, not elsewhere classified

  564.8 Other specified functional disorders of intestine

Delete   ~~Atony of colon~~

New code   **564.81 Neurogenic bowel**

New code   **564.89 Other functional disorders of intestine**
Atony of colon

  569 Other disorders of intestine

  569.6 Colostomy and enterostomy complications

Revise   **569.60 Colostomy and enterostomy complication, unspecified**

  569.61 Infection of colostomy and enterostomy

Delete   ~~Cellulitis or abscess~~

Add   Use additional code to specify type of infection, such as:
abscess or cellulitis of abdomen (682.2)
septicemia (038.0–038.9)

New code   **569.62 Mechanical complication of colostomy and enterostomy**
Malfunction of colostomy and enterostomy

  569.69 Other complication

Delete   ~~Malfunction~~

Add   Fistula

Add   Hernia

Add   Prolapse

11. COMPLICATIONS OF PREGNANCY, CHILDBIRTH, AND THE PUERPERIUM (630–677)

  652 Malposition and malpresentation of fetus

  652.2 Breech presentation without mention of version

Add   Buttocks presentation

Add   Complete breech

Add   Frank breech

Add   **Excludes** *footling presentation (652.8)*

Add   *incomplete breech (652.8)*

  655 Known or suspected fetal abnormality affecting management of mother

  655.5 Suspected damage to fetus from drugs

Delete   **Excludes** ~~*fetal distress in labor and delivery due to drug administration (656.3)*~~

  656 Other fetal and placental problems affecting management of mother

  656.3 Fetal distress

Add   Fetal metabolic acidemia

Delete   ~~Abnormal fetal:~~
~~acid base balance~~
~~heart rate or rhythm~~
~~Fetal:~~
~~bradycardia~~
~~tachycardia~~
~~Meconium in liquor~~

Add   **Excludes** *abnormal fetal acid-base balance (656.8)*
abnormality in fetal heart rate or rhythm (659.7)
fetal bradycardia (659.7)
fetal distress NOS (656.8)
fetal tachycardia (659.7)
meconium in liquor (656.8)

  656.8 Other specified fetal and placental problems

Add   Abnormal acid-base balance
Intrauterine acidosis
Meconium in liquor

  659 Other indications for care or intervention related to labor and delivery, not elsewhere classified

  659.5 Elderly primigravida

Add   [0, 1, 3]   First pregnancy in a woman who will be 35 years of age or older at expected date of delivery

Revise   **Excludes** *supervision only, in pregnancy (V23.81)*

Revise   **659.6 ~~Other advanced maternal age~~ Elderly multigravida**

Add   Second or more pregnancy in a woman who will be 35 years of age or older at expected date of delivery

Add   **Excludes** *supervision only, in pregnancy (V23.82)*

New code
[0, 1, 3]   **659.7 Abnormality in fetal heart rate or rhythm**
[0, 1, 3]   Depressed fetal heart tones
Fetal:
bradycardia
tachycardia
Fetal heart rate decelerations
Non-reassuring fetal heart rate or rhythm

  659.8 Other specified indications for care or intervention related to labor and delivery

Add   Pregnancy in a female less than 16 years old at expected date of delivery

Add   Very young maternal age

15. CERTAIN CONDITIONS ORIGINATING IN THE PERINATAL PERIOD (760–779)

  760 Fetus or newborn affected by maternal conditions which may be unrelated to present pregnancy

  760.6 Surgical operation on mother

Revise   **Excludes** *previous surgery to uterus or pelvic organs (763.89)*

  763 Fetus or newborn affected by other complications of labor and delivery

  763.8 Other specified complications of labor and delivery affecting fetus or newborn

Delete   ~~Fetus or newborn affected by:~~
~~abnormality of maternal soft tissues~~
~~destructive operation on live fetus to facilitate delivery~~
~~induction of labor (medical)~~
~~previous surgery to uterus or pelvic organs~~
~~other conditions classifiable to 650–669~~
~~other procedures used in labor and delivery~~

New code   **763.81 Abnormality in fetal heart rate or rhythm before the onset of labor**

New code   **763.82 Abnormality in fetal heart rate or rhythm during labor**

New code   **763.83 Abnormality in fetal heart rate or rhythm, unspecified as to time of onset**

New code   **763.89 Other specified complications of labor and delivery affecting fetus or newborn**

Add   Fetus or newborn affected by:
                              abnormality of maternal soft tissues
                              destructive operation on live fetus to facilitate delivery
                              induction of labor (medical)
                              previous surgery to uterus or pelvic organs
                              other conditions classifiable to 650–669
                              other procedures used in labor and delivery

768 Intrauterine hypoxia and birth asphyxia
768.2 Fetal distress before onset of labor, in liveborn infant

Add   Fetal metabolic acidemia before onset of labor, in liveborn infant
Delete   ~~Abnormal fetal heart rate or rhythm~~
                              ~~Fetal or intrauterine acidosis~~
                              ~~Fetal or intrauterine anoxia or hypoxia~~
                              ~~Any condition classifiable to 768.4~~

768.3 Fetal distress first noted during labor, in liveborn infant

Add   Fetal metabolic acidemia first noted during labor, in liveborn infant
Delete   ~~Abnormal fetal heart rate or rhythm~~
                              ~~Fetal or intrauterine acidosis~~
                              ~~Fetal or intrauterine anoxia or hypoxia~~
                              ~~Any condition classifiable to 768.4~~

768.4 Fetal distress, unspecified as to time of onset, in liveborn infant

Add   Fetal metabolic acidemia unspecified as to time of onset, in liveborn infant
Delete   ~~Abnormal fetal heart rate or rhythm~~
                              ~~Fetal or intrauterine~~
                                ~~acidosis~~
                                ~~anoxia~~
                                ~~asphyxia~~
                                ~~distress~~
                                ~~hypercapnia~~
                                ~~hypoxia~~

770 Other respiratory conditions of fetus and newborn
770.8 Other respiratory problems after birth

Add   Fetal acidosis affecting newborn
Add   Fetal anoxia affecting newborn
Add   Fetal asphyxia affecting newborn
Add   Fetal hypercapnia affecting newborn
Add   Fetal hypoxia affecting newborn
Add   Respiratory depression of newborn

16.   SYMPTOMS, SIGNS, AND ILL-DEFINED CONDITIONS (780–799)
780 General symptoms
780.7 Malaise and fatigue

Delete   ~~Asthenia NOS~~
                              ~~Lethargy~~
                              ~~Postviral (asthenic) syndrome~~
                              ~~Tiredness~~
New code   **780.71 Chronic fatigue syndrome**
New code   **780.79 Other malaise and fatigue**
                              Asthenia NOS
                              Lethargy
                              Postviral (asthenic) syndrome
                              Tiredness

786 Symptoms involving respiratory system and other chest symptoms
786.0 Dyspnea and respiratory abnormalities
New code   **786.03 Apnea**

Add   **Excludes** *sleep apnea (780.51, 780.53, 780.57)*
New code   **786.04 Cheyne-Stokes respiration**
New code   **786.05 Shortness of breath**

New code   **786.06 Tachypnea**
Add   **Excludes** *transitory tachypnea of newborn (770.6)*
New code   **786.07 Wheezing**
Add   **Excludes** *asthma (493.00–493.91)*
            786.09 Other
Delete   ~~Apnea~~
                              ~~Cheyne-Stokes respiration~~
                              ~~Shortness of breath~~
                              ~~Tachypnea~~
                              ~~Wheezing~~
Revise   **Excludes** *respiratory failure (518.81, 518.83–518.84)*
Delete   **Excludes** *~~sleep apnea (780.51, 780.53, 780.57)~~*
                         ~~transitory tachypnea of newborn (770.6)~~
            786.7 Abnormal chest sounds
Revise   **Excludes** *wheezing (786.07)*
799 Other ill-defined and unknown causes of morbidity and mortality
            799.1 Respiratory arrest
Revise   **Excludes** *respiratory failure (518.81, 518.83–518.84)*
            799.3 Debility, unspecified
Revise   **Excludes** *asthenia (780.79)*

17.   INJURY AND POISONING (800–999)
850 Concussion
Revise   **Excludes** *concussion with:*
Delete   *~~head injury NOS (959.01)~~*
Add   *head injury NOS (959.01)*
873 Other open wound of head
Delete   **Excludes** *~~that with mention of intracranial injury (851.0–854.1)~~*
948 Burns classified according to extent of body surface involved
Add   **Excludes** *sunburn (692.71)*
959 Injury, other and unspecified
            Excludes *injury NOS of:*
Revise   *intracranial sites (854.0–854.1)*
            959.0 Head, face, and neck
            959.01 Head injury, unspecified
Add   **Excludes** *concussion (850.1–850.9)*
                         with head injury NOS (850.1–850.9)
                         specified intracranial injuries (850.0–854.1)
965 Poisoning by analgesics, antipyretics, and antirheumatics
            965.6 Antirheumatics [antiphlogistics]
Delete   ~~Gold salts~~
                              ~~Indomethacin~~
New code   **965.61 Propionic acid derivatives**
                              Fenoprofen
                              Flurbiprofen
                              Ibuprofen
                              Ketoprofen
                              Naproxen
                              Oxaprozin
New code   **965.69 Other antirheumatics**
                              Gold salts
                              Indomethacin
992 Effects of heat and light
Revise   **Excludes** *malignant hyperpyrexia following anesthesia (995.86)*
995 Certain adverse effects not elsewhere classified
            995.5 Child maltreatment syndrome
Revise   Use additional code(s), if applicable, to identify any associated injuries
Revise   **995.8 Other specified adverse effects, not elsewhere classified**
New code   **995.86 Malignant hyperthermia**
                              Malignant hyperpyrexia due to anesthesia

995.89 Other

Delete — ~~Malignant hyperpyrexia or hypothermia due to anesthesia~~

Add — Hypothermia due to anesthesia

996 Complications peculiar to certain specified procedures

996.1 Mechanical complication of other vascular device, implant, and graft

Mechanical complications involving: arteriovenous:

Add — dialysis catheter

Delete — ~~dialysis catheter~~

Add — **Excludes** *peritoneal dialysis catheter (996.56)*

996.5 Mechanical complications of other specified prosthetic device, implant, and graph

996.52 Due to graft of other tissue, not elsewhere classified

Skin graft failure or rejection

Add — **Excludes** *failure of artificial skin graft (996.55)*

Add — *failure of decellularized allodermis (996.55)*

New code — 996.55 Due to artificial skin graft and decellularized allodermis

Dislodgement
Displacement
Failure
Non-adherence
Poor incorporation
Shearing

New code — 996.56 Due to peritoneal dialysis catheter

Add — **Excludes** *mechanical complication arteriovenous dialysis catheter (996.1)*

996.6 Infection and inflammatory reaction due to internal prosthetic device, implant, and graft

Add — Use additional code to identify specified infections

996.64 Due to indwelling urinary catheter

Add — Use additional code to identify specified infections, such as:
Cystitis (595.0–595.9)
Sepsis (038.0–038.9)

New code — 996.68 Due to peritoneal dialysis catheter

Exit-site infection or inflammation

997 Complications affecting specified body systems, not elsewhere classified

997.3 Respiratory complications

Revise — **Excludes** *tracheostomy complications (519.00–519.09)*

997.4 Digestive system complications

Add — **Excludes** *gastrostomy complications (536.40–536.49)*

SUPPLEMENTARY CLASSIFICATION OF FACTORS INFLUENCING HEALTH STATUS AND CONTACT WITH HEALTH SERVICES (V01–V82)

V02 Carrier or suspected carrier of infectious disease

V02.5 Other specified bacterial diseases

Delete — ~~Bacterial disease:~~
~~meningococcal~~
~~staphylococcal~~
~~streptococcal~~

New code — V02.51 Group B streptococcus

New code — V02.52 Other streptococcus

New code — V02.59 Other specified bacterial diseases
Meningococcal
Staphylococcal

V10 Personal history of malignant neoplasm

V10.4 Genital organs

New code — V10.48 Epididymis

V13 Personal history of other diseases

V13.6 Congenital malformations

New code — V13.61 Hypospadias

New code — V13.69 Other congenital malformations

V16 Family history of malignant neoplasm

V16.5 Urinary organs

New code — V16.51 Kidney

New code — V16.59 Other

V18 Family history of certain other specific conditions

V18.6 Kidney diseases

New code — V18.61 Polycystic kidney

New code — V18.69 Other kidney diseases

V23 Supervision of high-risk pregnancy

V23.8 Other high-risk pregnancy

New code — V23.81 Elderly primigravida

First pregnancy in a woman who will be 35 years of age or older at expected date of delivery

Add — **Excludes** *elderly primigravida complicating pregnancy (659.5)*

New code — V23.82 Elderly multigravida

Second or more pregnancy in a woman who will be 35 years of age or older at expected date of delivery

Add — **Excludes** *elderly multigravida complicating pregnancy (659.6)*

New code — V23.83 Young primigravida

First pregnancy in a female less than 16 years old at expected date of delivery

Add — **Excludes** *young primigravida complicating pregnancy (659.8)*

New code — V23.84 Young multigravida

Second or more pregnancy in a female less than 16 years old at expected date of delivery

Add — **Excludes** *young multigravida complicating pregnancy (659.9)*

New code — V23.89 Other high-risk pregnancy

V26 Procreative management

V26.5 Sterilization status

New subcategory —

New code — V26.51 Tubal ligation status

Excludes *infertility not due to previous tubal ligation (628.0–628.9)*

New code — V26.52 Vasectomy status

V29 Observation and evaluation of newborns for suspected condition not found

New code — V29.3 Observation for suspected genetic or metabolic condition

V43 Organ or tissue replaced by other means

V43.8 Organ or tissue replaced by other means

New code — V43.83 Artificial skin

V44 Artificial opening status

V44.5 Cystostomy

New code — V44.50 Cystostomy, unspecified

New code — V44.51 Cutaneous-vesicostomy

New code — V44.52 Appendico-vesicostomy

New code — V44.59 Other cystostomy

V45 Other postsurgical states

V45.6 States following surgery of eye and adnexa

Delete — **Excludes** ~~artificial lens (V43.1)~~

V45.61 Cataract extraction status

Add — Use additional code for associated artificial lens status (V43.1)

V55 Attention to artificial openings

Revise — **Excludes** *complications of external stoma (519.00–519.09)*

V56 Encounter for dialysis and dialysis catheter care

Revise — V56.1 Fitting and adjustment of extracorporeal dialysis catheter

Add — Use additional code for any concurrent extracorporeal dialysis (V56.0)

New code — V56.2 Fitting and adjustment of peritoneal dialysis catheter

Add — Use additional code for any concurrent peritoneal dialysis (V56.8)

V58 Encounter for other and unspecified procedures and aftercare
  V58.6 Long-term (current) drug use
New code   V58.62 Long-term (current) use of antibiotics
  V58.8 Other specified procedures and aftercare
    V58.82 Fitting and adjustment of nonvascular catheter, NEC
Revise   <u>Excludes</u> *fitting and adjustment of peritoneal dialysis catheter (V56.2)*
V76 Special screening for malignant neoplasm
  V76.4 Other sites
New code   V76.44 Prostate
New code   V76.45 Testis
V82 Special screening for other conditions
Revise V82.4 Maternal postnatal screening for chromosomal anomalies

OPERATIONS ON THE CARDIOVASCULAR SYSTEM
36 Operations of vessels of heart

Includes: Sternotomy (medial) (transverse), as operative approach
Thoracotomy, as operative approach
Code also cardiopulmonary bypass, if performed [extracorporeal circulation] [heart-lung machine] (39.61)
Add   Code also any injection or infusion of platelet inhibitor (99.20)
  36.0 Removal of coronary artery obstruction and insertion of stent(s)
    36.04 Intracoronary artery thrombolytic infusion
      That by direct coronary artery injection, infusion, or catheterization
      enzyme infusion
      platelet inhibitor
Revise   <u>Excludes</u> *infusion of platelet inhibitor (99.20)*
      infusion of thrombolytic agent (99.10)
New category   36.3 Other heart revascularization
Delete   ~~Abrasion of epicardium~~
Delete   ~~Cardio-omentopexy~~
Delete   ~~Intrapericardial poudrage~~
Delete   ~~Myocardial graft:~~
Delete   ~~mediastinal fat~~
Delete   ~~omentum~~
Delete   ~~pectoral muscles~~
New code   36.31 Open chest transmyocardial revascularization
New code   36.32 Other transmyocardial revascularization
      Percutaneous transmyocardial revascularization
      Thoracoscopic transmyocardial revascularization
New code   36.39 Other heart revascularization
      Abrasion of epicardium
      Cardio-omentopexy
      Intrapericardial poudrage
      Myocardial graft:
        mediastinal fat
        omentum
        pectoral muscles
37 Other operations on heart and pericardium
Add   Code also any injection or infusion of platelet inhibitor (99.20)
  37.3 Pericardiectomy and excision of lesion of heart
    37.32 Excision of aneurysm of heart
Add   Repair of aneurysm of heart
  37.6 Implantation of heart assist system

New code   37.67 Implantation of cardiomyostimulation system
      Note: Two-step open procedure consisting of transfer of one end of the latissimus dorsi muscle; wrapping it around the heart; rib resection; implantation of epicardial cardiac pacing leads into the right ventricle; tunneling and pocket creation for the cardiomyostimulator.
39 Other operations of vessels
  39.3 Suture of vessel
Add   <u>Excludes</u> *any other vascular puncture closure device—omit code*
  39.5 Other repair of vessels
    39.50 Angioplasty or atherectomy of non-coronary vessel
      Code also any:
        injection or infusion of thrombolytic agent (99.10)

OPERATIONS ON THE DIGESTIVE SYSTEM
46 Other operations on intestine
  46.8 Dilation and manipulation of intestine
    46.80 Intra-abdominal manipulation of intestine, not otherwise specified
Add   <u>Excludes</u> *reduction of intussusception with:*
      fluoroscopy
      ionizing radiation enema 96.29
      ultrasonography guidance 96.29
54 Other operations on abdominal region
  54.2 Diagnostic procedures of abdominal region
    54.23 Biopsy of peritoneum
Add   <u>Excludes</u> *closed biopsy of:*
      omentum (54.24)
      peritoneum (54.24)
    54.24 Closed [percutaneous] [needle] biopsy of intra-abdominal mass
Add   Closed biopsy of:
Add   omentum
Add   peritoneum
    <u>Excludes</u> *that of:*
Delete   *peritoneum (54.23)*
  54.7 Other repair of abdominal wall and peritoneum
    54.74 Other repair of omentum
  <u>Excludes</u> *cardio-omentopexy (36.39)*

OPERATIONS ON THE FEMALE GENITAL ORGANS
67 Operations on cervix
  67.3 Other excisions or destruction of lesion or tissue of cervix
    67.32 Destruction of lesion of cervix by cauterization
Add   LEEP (loop electrosurgical excision procedure)
Add   LLETZ (large loop excision of the transformation zone)

OBSTETRICAL PROCEDURES
75 Other obstetric operations
  75.3 Other intrauterine operations on fetus and amnion
New code   75.37 Amnioinfusion
      Code also injection of antibiotic (99.21)

OPERATIONS ON THE INTEGUMENTARY SYSTEM
    86 Operations on skin and subcutaneous tissue
      86.6 Free skin graft
New code   86.67 Dermal regenerative graft
              Artificial skin, NOS
              Creation of "neodermis"
              Decellularized allodermis
              Integumentary matrix implants
              Prosthetic implant of dermal layer of
                 skin
              Regenerate dermal layer of skin

          Excludes *heterograft to skin (86.65)*
                  homograft to skin (86.66)
      86.8 Other repair and reconstruction of skin and
        subcutaneous tissue
        86.83 Size reduction plastic operation
Add   Liposuction

MISCELLANEOUS DIAGNOSTIC AND THERAPEUTIC PRO-
CEDURES
    92 Nuclear medicine
New category 92.3 Stereotactic radiosurgery
Delete   ~~Gamma irradiation (multisource)~~
Delete   ~~Linear accelerator (single source)~~
Delete   ~~Particle beam radiation (cyclotron)~~
Delete   ~~Stereotactic multisource photon radiosurgery~~

Add   **Excludes:** *stereotactic biopsy*
New code   92.30 Stereotactic radiosurgery, not otherwise
              specified
New code   92.31 Single source photon radiosurgery
              High energy x-rays
              Linear accelerator (LINAC)
New code   92.32 Multi-source photon radiosurgery
              Cobalt 60 radiation
              Gamma irradiation
New code   92.33 Particulate radiosurgery
              Particle beam radiation (cyclotron)
              Proton accelerator
New code   92.39 Stereotactic radiosurgery, not elsewhere
              classified
    96 Nonoperative intubation and irrigation
      96.2 Nonoperative dilation and manipulation
New code   96.29 Reduction of intussusception of alimen-
              tary tract
              With:
                 fluoroscopy
                 ionizing radiation enema
                 ultrasonography guidance
              Hydrostatic reduction
              Pneumatic reduction

          Excludes *intra-abdominal manipulation of intestine, not*
                  otherwise specified (46.80)

      96.3 Nonoperative alimentary tract irrigation, clean-
        ing, and local instillation
        96.39 Other transanal enema
Add   **Excludes** *reduction of intussusception of alimentary tract*
                by ionizing radiation enema (96.29)
    99 Other nonoperative procedures
      99.1 Injection or infusion of therapeutic or prophy-
        lactic substance
New code   99.10 Injection or infusion of thrombolytic
              agent
              Streptokinase
              Tissue plasminogen activator (TPA)
              Urokinase

          Excludes *aspirin—omit code*
                  GP IIB/IIIa platelet inhibitors (99.20)
                  heparin (99.29)
                  single vessel percutaneous transluminal cor-
                  onary angioplasty [PTCA] or coronary
                  atherectomy with mention of throm-
                  bolytic agent (36.02)
                  warfarin—omit code
      99.2 Injection or infusion of other therapeutic or
        prophylactic substances
New code   99.20 Injection or infusion of platelet inhibitor
              Glycoprotein IIB/IIIa inhibitor
              GP IIB/IIIa inhibitor

          Excludes *infusion of heparin (99.29)*
                  injection or infusion of thrombolytic agent
                  (99.10)
        99.28 Injection or infusion of biological re-
              sponse modifier [BRM] as an antineo-
              plastic agent
Add   Tumor vaccine
        99.29 Injection or infusion of other therapeutic
             or prophylactic substance
Add   **Excludes** *injection or infusion of platelet inhibitor (99.20)*
                injection or infusion of thrombolytic agent
                  (99.10)

HCPCS 2000 New/Revised/Deleted Codes and Modifiers

NEW CODES/MODIFIERS

G7	A7005	G0164	J7642	S0011	S2052	S9033
G8	A7006	G0165	J7643	S0012	S2053	S9055
G9	A7007	G0166	J7644	S0014	S2054	S9056
A4280	A7008	G0167	J7648	S0016	S2055	S9075
A4369	A7009	G0168	J7649	S0017	S2109	S9085
A4370	A7010	G0169	J7658	S0020	S2190	S9090
A4371	A7011	G0170	J7659	S0021	S2204	S9122
A4372	A7012	G0171	J7668	S0023	S2205	S9123
A4373	A7013	G0172	J7669	S0024	S2206	S9124
A4374	A7014	J0200	J7680	S0028	S2207	S9125
A4375	A7015	J0456	J7681	S0029	S2208	S9126
A4376	A7016	J1327	J7682	S0030	S2209	S9127
A4377	A7017	J1438	J7683	S0032	S2210	S9128
A4378	A9504	J1450	J7684	S0034	S2300	S9129
A4379	A9900	J1745	J8510	S0039	S2350	S9140
A4380	A9901	J1750	J8520	S0040	S2351	S9141
A4381	E0144	J2352	J8521	S0071	S3645	S9455
A4382	E0590	J2500	J9001	S0072	S3650	S9460
A4383	E0602	J2543	J9355	S0073	S3652	S9465
A4384	E0616	J2780	J9357	S0074	S8035	S9470
A4385	E0779	J3245	K0462	S0077	S8040	S9472
A4386	E0780	J7198	K0531	S0078	S8048	S9473
A4387	E1390	J7199	K0532	S0080	S8049	S9474
A4388	E1900	J7515	K0533	S0081	S8060	S9475
A4389	G0102	J7516	K0534	S0090	S8092	S9480
A4390	G0103	J7517	L3807	S0096	S8095	S9485
A4391	G0129	J7608	L9900	S0097	S8096	S9524
A4392	G0151	J7618	P9023	S0098	S8110	S9527
A4393	G0152	J7619	Q0186	S0601	S8200	S9528
A4394	G0153	J7628	Q0187	S0605	S8205	S9543
A4395	G0154	J7629	Q1001	S0610	S8260	S9990
A5508	G0155	J7631	Q1002	S0612	S8300	S9991
A7000	G0156	J7635	Q1003	S0620	S8950	S9992
A7001	G0159	J7636	Q1004	S0621	S9001	S9994
A7002	G0160	J7637	Q1005	S0800	S9022	S9996
A7003	G0161	J7638	S0009	S0810	S9023	S9999
A7004	G0163	J7639	S0010	S2050	S9024	

REVISED CODES/MODIFIERS

EJ	A4231	A5126	J0290	J3370	K0101	L5988
QS	A4232	A9502	J0690	J7500	K0102	L6693
A4206	A4244	E0155	J1100	J7501	K0104	L8435
A4207	A4245	E0158	J1260	J7504	K0105	M0302
A4208	A4246	E0450	J1820	K0028	K0108	
A4209	A4247	E0781	J1825	K0031	L4392	
A4213	A4550	E0784	J1830	K0065	L4396	
A4215	A4556	J0270	J3030	K0099	L5925	
A4230	A4557	J0275	J3240	K0100	L5968	

DELETED CODES/MODIFIERS

AB	G0097	K0168	K0192	K0423	K0439	K0520
AC	G0098	K0169	K0193	K0424	K0503	K0521
AE	J1760	K0170	K0194	K0425	K0504	K0522
AF	J1770	K0171	K0277	K0426	K0505	K0523
AG	J1780	K0172	K0278	K0427	K0506	K0524
QR	J7196	K0173	K0279	K0428	K0507	K0525
A4363	J7503	K0174	K0284	K0429	K0508	K0526
E0452	K0109	K0175	K0400	K0430	K0509	K0527
E0453	K0119	K0176	K0401	K0431	K0511	K0528
E1400	K0120	K0177	K0412	K0432	K0512	K0530
E1401	K0121	K0178	K0417	K0433	K0513	Q0068
E1402	K0122	K0179	K0418	K0434	K0514	Q0132
E1403	K0123	K0180	K0419	K0435	K0515	
E1404	K0137	K0181	K0420	K0436	K0516	
G0095	K0138	K0190	K0421	K0437	K0518	
G0096	K0139	K0191	K0422	K0438	K0519	

CONTENTS

Part IV Procedures, Volume 3 991

UNIT TWO HCPCS: LEVEL II NATIONAL CODES 1183

ICD-9-CM

Introduction

ICD-9-CM BACKGROUND

The International Classification of Diseases, 9th Revision, Clinical Modification (ICD-9-CM) is based on the official version of the World Health Organization's 9th Revision, International Classification of Diseases (ICD-9). ICD-9 is designed for the classification of morbidity and mortality information for statistical purposes, and for the indexing of hospital records by disease and operation, for data storage and retrieval. The historical background of the International Classification of Diseases may be found in the Introduction to ICD-9 (Manual of the International Classification of Diseases, Injuries, and Causes of Death, World Health Organization, Geneva, Switzerland, 1977).

ICD-9-CM is a clinical modification of the World Health Organization's International Classification of Diseases, 9th Revision (ICD-9). The term "clinical" is used to emphasize the modification's intent: to serve as a useful tool in the area of classification of morbidity data for indexing of medical records, medical care review, and ambulatory and other medical care programs, as well as for basic health statistics. To describe the clinical picture of the patient, the codes must be more precise than those needed only for statistical groupings and trend analysis.

COORDINATION AND MAINTENANCE COMMITTEE

Annual modifications are made to the ICD-9-CM through the ICD-9-CM Coordination and Maintenance Committee (C&M). The Committee is made up of representatives from two Federal Government agencies, the National Center for Health Statistics and the Health Care Financing Administration. The Committee holds meetings twice a year which are open to the public. Modification proposals submitted to the Committee for consideration are presented at the meetings for public discussion. Those modification proposals which are approved are incorporated into the official government version of the ICD-9-CM and become effective for use October 1 of the year following their presentation. The CD-ROM contains the modifications approved from the 1995 C&M cycle.

The CD-ROM is the only official federal government version of the ICD-9-CM. It may be purchased through the Government Printing Office.

CHARACTERISTICS OF ICD-9-CM

ICD-9-CM far exceeds its predecessors in the number of codes provided. The disease classification has been expanded to include health-related conditions and to provide greater specificity at the fifth-digit level of detail. These fifth digits are not optional; they are intended for use in recording the information substantiated in the clinical record.

Volume I of ICD-9-CM contains five appendices:

Appendix A	Morphology of Neoplasms
Appendix B	Glossary of Mental Disorders
Appendix C	Classification of Drugs by American Hospital Formulary Service List Number and Their ICD-9-CM Equivalents
Appendix D	Classification of Industrial Accidents According to Agency
Appendix E	List of Three-Digit Categories

These appendices are included as a reference to the user in order to provide further information about the patient's clinical picture, to further define a diagnostic statement, to aid in classifying new drugs, or to reference three-digit categories.

Volume 2 of ICD-9-CM contains many diagnostic terms which do not appear in Volume 1 since the index includes most diagnostic terms currently in use.

The Disease Classification

ICD-9-CM is totally compatible with its parent system, ICD-9, thus meeting the need for comparability of morbidity and mortality statistics at the international level. A few fourth-digit codes were created in existing three-digit rubrics only when the necessary detail could not be accommodated by the use of a fifth-digit subclassification. To ensure that each rubric of ICD-9-CM collapses back to its ICD-9 counterpart the following specifications governed the ICD-9-CM disease classification:

Specifications for the Tabular List

1. Three-digit rubrics and their contents are unchanged from ICD-9.
2. The sequence of three-digit rubrics is unchanged from ICD-9.
3. Unsubdivided three-digit rubrics are subdivided where necessary to:
   a) Add clinical detail
   b) Isolate terms for clinical accuracy
4. The modification in ICD-9-CM is accomplished by the addition of a fifth digit to existing ICD-9 rubrics.
5. The optional dual classification in ICD-9 is modified.
   a) Duplicate rubrics are deleted:
      1) Four-digit manifestation categories duplicating etiology entries.
      2) Manifestation inclusion terms duplicating etiology entries.
   b) Manifestations of diseases are identified, to the extent possible, by creating five-digit codes in the etiology rubrics.
   c) When the manifestation of a disease cannot be included in the etiology rubrics, provision for its identification is made by retaining the ICD-9 rubrics used for classifying manifestations of disease.
6. The format of ICD-9-CM is revised from that used in ICD-9.
   a) American spelling of medical terms is used.
   b) Inclusion terms are indented beneath the titles of codes.
   c) Codes not to be used for principal tabulation of disease are printed with the notation, "Code first underlying disease."

Specifications for the Alphabetic Index

1. Format of the Alphabetic Index follows the format of ICD-9.
2. When two codes are required to indicate etiology and manifestation, the manifestation code appears in brackets, e.g., diabetic cataract 250.5X [366.41]. The etiology code is always sequenced first followed by the manifestation code.

CONVENTIONS USED IN THE TABULAR LIST

The ICD-9-CM Tabular List for both the Disease and Procedure Classification makes use of certain abbreviations, punctuation, and other conventions which need to be clearly understood.

Abbreviations

NEC Not elsewhere classifiable. The category number for the term including NEC is to be used only when the coder lacks the information necessary to code the term to a more specific category.

NOS Not otherwise specified. This abbreviation is the equivalent of "unspecified."

Punctuation

[ ] Brackets are used to enclose synonyms, alternative wordings, or explanatory phrases.

( ) Parentheses are used to enclose supplementary words which may be present or absent in the statement of a disease or procedure without affecting the code number to which it is assigned.

: Colons are used in the Tabular List after an incomplete term which needs one or more of the modifiers which follow in order to make it assignable to a given category.

Other Conventions

Format: ICD-9-CM uses an indented format for ease in reference.

Instructional Notations

Includes:
   This note appears immediately under a three-digit code title to further define, or give example of, the contents of the category.

Excludes:
   Terms following the word "excludes" are to be coded elsewhere. The term excludes means "DO NOT CODE HERE".

Use additional code

This instruction is placed in the Tabular List in those categories where the user will need to add further information (by using an additional code) to give a more complete picture of the diagnosis or procedure.

Code first underlying disease:

This instructional note is used for those codes not intended to be used as a principal diagnosis, or not to be sequenced before the underlying disease. The note requires that the underlying disease (etiology) be recorded first and the particular manifestation recorded secondarily. This note appears only in the Tabular List.

GUIDANCE IN THE USE OF ICD-9-CM

To code accurately, it is necessary to have a working knowledge of medical terminology and to understand the characteristics, terminology, and conventions of the ICD-9-CM. Transforming verbal descriptions of diseases, injuries, conditions, and procedures into numerical designations (coding) is a complex activity and should not be undertaken without proper training.

Originally, coding was accomplished to provide access to medical records by diagnoses and operations through retrieval for medical research, education, and administration. Medical codes today are utilized to facilitate payment of health services, to evaluate utilization patterns, and to study the appropriateness of health care costs. Coding provides the bases for epidemiological studies and research into the quality of health care.

Coding must be performed correctly and consistently to produce meaningful statistics to aid in the planning for the health needs of the nation.

Basic steps in coding diagnoses/diseases:

1. Always consult Volume 1, Alphabetic Index to ICD-9-CM first.

Locate the main entry term. The Alphabetic Index is arranged by condition. Conditions may be expressed as nouns, adjectives, and eponyms. Some conditions have multiple entries under their synonyms. Select the appropriate code.

2. Refer to Volume 1 of the ICD-9-CM locating the selected code.

Be guided by any exclusion notes or other instructions that would direct the use of a different code from that selected in the Index for a particular diagnosis, condition, or disease.

3. Read and be guided by the conventions used in the Tabular List (Volume 1, ICD-9-CM).

As reference for use by researchers and to maintain comparability with its parent, the ICD-9, a list of three-digit ICD-9-CM categories is given in Appendix E. While these categories form natural statistical groupings, they cannot substitute for the required five-digit ICD-9-CM code.

Questions regarding the use and interpretation of the International Classification of Diseases, 9th Revision, Clinical Modification can be directed to any of the organizations listed below.

Central Office on ICD-9-CM
American Hospital Association
1 North Franklin
Chicago, Illinois 60606

National Center for Health Statistics
Centers for Disease Control and Prevention
Department of Health and Human Services
6525 Belcrest Road
Hyattsville, Maryland 20782

Health Care Financing Administration
Division of Prospective Payment System
Office of Hospital Policy
7500 Security Blvd., C5-06-27
Baltimore, Maryland 21244-185

GUIDELINES

The Public Health Service and the Health Care Financing Administration of the U.S. Department of Health and Human Services present the following guidelines for coding and reporting using the International Classification of Diseases, 9th Revision, Clinical Modification (ICD-9-CM). These guidelines should be used as a companion document to the official versions of the ICD-9-CM.

These guidelines for coding and reporting have been developed and approved by the cooperating parties for ICD-9-CM: American Hospital Association, American Health Information Management Association, Health Care Financing Administration and the National Center for Health Statistics. These guidelines previously appeared in the Coding Clinic for ICD-9-CM, published by the American Hospital Association.

These guidelines have been developed to assist the user in coding and reporting in situations where the ICD-9-CM manual does not provide direction. Coding and sequencing instructions in the three ICD-9-CM manuals take precedence over any guidelines.

These guidelines are not exhaustive. The cooperating parties are continuing to conduct review of these guidelines and develop new guidelines as needed. Users of the ICD-9-CM should be aware that only guidelines approved by the cooperating parties are official. Revision of these guidelines and new guidelines will be published by the U.S. Department of Health and Human Services when they are approved by the cooperating parties.

OFFICIAL GUIDELINES FOR CODING AND REPORTING

TABLE OF CONTENTS

1. GENERAL INPATIENT CODING GUIDELINES

1.1 Use of Both Alphabetic Index and Tabular List

A. Use both the Alphabetic Index and the Tabular List when locating and assigning a code. Reliance on only the Alphabetic Index or the Tabular List leads to errors in code assignments and less specificity in code selection.

B. Locate each term in the Alphabetic Index and verify the code selected in the Tabular List. Read and be guided by instructional notations that appear in both the Alphabetic Index and the Tabular List.

1.2 Level of Specificity in Coding

Diagnostic and procedure codes are to be used at their highest level of specificity:

Assign three-digit codes only if there are no four-digit codes within that code category.

Assign four-digit codes only if there is no fifth-digit subclassification for that category.

Assign the fifth-digit subclassification code for those categories where it exists.

1.3   Other (NEC) and Unspecified (NOS) Code Titles

Codes labeled "other specified" (NEC, not elsewhere classified) or "unspecified" (NOS, not otherwise specified) are used only when neither the diagnostic statement nor a thorough review of the medical record provides adequate information to permit assignment of a more specific code.

Use the code assignment for "other" or NEC when the information at hand specifies a condition but no separate code for that condition is provided.

Use "unspecified" (NOS) when the information at hand does not permit either a more specific or "other" code assignment.

When the Alphabetic Index assigns a code to a category labeled "other (NEC)" or to a category labeled "unspecified (NOS)", refer to the Tabular List and review the titles and inclusion terms in the subdivisions under that particular three-digit category (or subdivision under the four-digit code) to determine if the information at hand can be appropriately assigned to a more specific code.

1.4   Acute and Chronic Conditions

If the same condition is described as both acute (subacute) and chronic and separate subentries exist in the Alphabetic Index at the same indentation level, code both and sequence the acute (subacute) code first.

1.5   Combination Code

A single code used to classify two diagnoses or a diagnosis with an associated secondary process (manifestation) or an associated complication is called a combination code. Combination codes are identified by referring to subterm entries in the Alphabetic Index and by reading the inclusion and exclusion notes in the Tabular List.

A. Assign only the combination code when that code fully identifies the diagnostic conditions involved or when the Alphabetic Index so directs. Multiple coding should not be used when the classification provides a combination code that clearly identifies all of the elements documented in the diagnosis. When the combination code lacks necessary specificity in describing the manifestation or complication, an additional code may be used as a secondary code.

1.6   Multiple Coding of Diagnoses

Multiple coding is required for certain conditions not subject to the rules for combination codes.

Instruction for conditions that require multiple coding appear in the Alphabetic Index and the Tabular List.

A. Alphabetic Index: Codes for both etiology and manifestation of a disease appear following the subentry term, with the second code in brackets. Assign both codes in the same sequence in which they appear in the Alphabetic Index.

B. Tabular List: Instructional terms, such as "Code first…," "Use additional code for any…," and "Note…," indicate when to use more than one code.

"Code first underlying disease"—Assign the codes for both the manifestation and underlying cause. The codes for manifestations cannot be used (designated) as principal diagnosis.

"Use additional code, to identify manifestation, as…"—Assign also the code that identifies the manifestation, such as, but not limited to, the examples listed. The codes for manifestations cannot be used (designated) as principal diagnosis.

C. Apply multiple coding instructions throughout the classification where appropriate, whether or not multiple coding directions appear in the Alphabetic Index or the Tabular List. Avoid indiscriminate multiple coding or irrelevant information, such as symptoms or signs characteristic of the diagnosis.

1.7   Late Effect

A late effect is the residual effect (condition produced) after the acute phase of an illness or injury has terminated. There is no time limit on when a late effect code can be used. The residual may be apparent early, such as in cerebrovascular accident cases, or it may occur months or years later, such as that due to a previous injury.

Coding of late effects requires two codes:

The residual condition or nature of the late effect

The cause of the late effect

The residual condition or nature of the late effect is sequenced first, followed by the cause of the late effect, except in those few instances where the code for late effect is followed by a manifestation code identified in the Tabular List as an italicized code and title.

The code for the acute phase of an illness or injury that led to the late effect is never used with a code for the cause of the late effect.

A. Late Effects of Cerebrovascular Disease

Category 438 is used to indicate conditions classifiable to categories 430-437 as the causes of late effects (neurologic deficits), themselves classified elsewhere. These "late effects" include neurologic deficits that persist after initial onset of conditions classifiable to 430-437. Unlike other late effects, the neurologic deficits caused by cerebrovascular disease are present from the onset rather than arising months later.

Assign code for the specific neurologic deficit (for example, aphasia, dysphagia, and/or hemiplegia) followed by code 438.

Do not assign code 438 when a current diagnosis classifiable to the 430–437 categories is present.

Assign only code 438 when there is no mention of any particular deficits but the diagnosis is stated as "old cerebrovascular accident" (Old CVA).

Assign code V12.59 (and not a code 438) as an additional code for history of cerebrovascular disease when no neurologic deficits are present.

1.8   Uncertain Diagnosis

If the diagnosis documented at the time of discharge is qualified as "probable", "suspected", "likely", "questionable", "possible", or "still to be ruled out", code the condition as if it existed or was established. The bases for this guideline are the diagnostic workup, arrangements for further workup or observation, and initial therapeutic approach that correspond most closely with the established diagnosis.

1.9   Impending or Threatened Condition

Code any condition described at the time of discharge as "impending" or "threatened" as follows:

If it did occur, code as confirmed diagnosis.

If it did not occur, reference the Alphabetic Index to determine if the condition has a subentry term for "impending" or "threatened" and also reference main term entries for Impending and for Threatened.

If the subterms are listed, assign the given code.

If the subterms are not listed, code the existing forerunner condition(s) and not the condition described as impending or threatened.

2. SELECTION OF PRINCIPAL DIAGNOSIS

The circumstances of inpatient admission always govern the selection of principal diagnosis. The principal diagnosis is defined in the Uniform Hospital Discharge Data Set (UHDDS) as "that condition established after study to be chiefly responsible for occasioning the admission of the patient to the hospital for care".

In determining principal diagnosis the coding directives in the ICD-9-CM manuals, Volumes 1, 2, and 3, take precedence over all other guidelines.

The importance of consistent, complete documentation in the medical record cannot be over-emphasized. Without such documentation the application of all coding guidelines is a difficult, if not impossible, task.

2.1   Codes for symptoms, signs, and ill-defined conditions.

Codes for symptoms, signs, and ill-defined conditions from Chapter 16 are not to be used as principal diagnosis when a related definitive diagnosis has been established.

2.2   Codes in brackets.

Codes in brackets in the Alphabetic Index can never be sequenced as principal diagnosis. Coding directives require that the codes in brackets be sequenced in the order as they appear in the Alphabetic Index.

2.3   Acute and chronic conditions.

If the same condition is described as both acute (subacute) and chronic and separate subentries exist in the Alphabetic Index at the same indentation level, code both and sequence the acute (subacute) code first.

2.4   Two or more interrelated conditions, each potentially meeting the definition for principal diagnosis.

When there are two or more interrelated conditions (such as diseases in the same ICD-9-CM chapter or manifestations characteristically associated with a certain disease) potentially meeting the definition of principal diagnosis, either condition may be sequenced first, unless the circumstances of the admission, the therapy provided, the Tabular List, or the Alphabetic Index indicates otherwise.

2.5   Two or more diagnoses that equally meet the definition for principal diagnosis.

In the unusual instance when two or more diagnoses equally meet the criteria for principal diagnosis as determined by the circumstances of admission, diagnostic workup and/or therapy provided, and the Alphabetic Index, Tabular List, or another coding guideline does not provide sequencing direction, any one of the diagnoses may be sequenced first.

2.6   Two or more comparative or contrasting conditions.

In those rare instances when two or more contrasting or comparative diagnoses are documented as "either/or" (or similar terminology), they are coded as if the diagnoses were confirmed and the diagnoses are sequenced according to the circumstances of the admission. If no further determination can be made as to which diagnosis should be principal, either diagnosis may be sequenced first.

2.7   A symptom(s) followed by contrasting/comparative diagnoses.

When a symptom(s) is followed by contrasting/comparative diagnoses, the symptom code is sequenced first. All the contrasting/comparative diagnoses should be coded as suspected conditions.

2.8   Codes from the V71.0-V71.9 series, Observation and evaluation for suspected conditions.

Codes from the V71.0-V71.9 series are assigned as principal diagnoses for encounters or admissions to evaluate the patient's condition when there is some evidence to suggest the existence of an abnormal condition or following an accident or other incident that ordinarily results in a health problem, and where no supporting evidence for the suspected condition is found and no treatment is currently required. The fact that the patient may be scheduled for continuing observation in the office/clinic setting following discharge does not limit the use of this category.

2.9   Original treatment plan not carried out.

Sequence as the principal diagnosis the condition which after study occasioned the admission to the hospital, even though treatment may not have been carried out due to unforeseen circumstances.

2.10 Residual condition or nature of late effect.

The residual condition or nature of the late effect is sequenced first, followed by the late effect code for the cause of the residual condition, except in a few instances where the Alphabetic Index or Tabular List directs otherwise.

2.11 Multiple burns.

Sequence first the code that reflects the highest degree of burn when more than one burn is present. (See also Burns guideline 8.3.)

2.12 Multiple injuries.

When multiple injuries exist, the code for the most severe injury as determined by the attending physician is sequenced first.

2.13 Neoplasms.

A. If the treatment is directed at the malignancy, designate the malignancy as the principal diagnosis, except when the purpose of the encounter or hospital admission is for radiotherapy session(s), V58.0, or for chemotherapy session(s), V58.1, in which instance the malignancy is coded and sequenced second.

B. When a patient is admitted for the purpose of radiotherapy or chemotherapy and develops complications such as uncontrolled nausea and vomiting or dehydration, the principal diagnosis is Encounter for radiotherapy, V58.0, or Encounter for chemotherapy, V58.1.

C. When an episode of inpatient care involves surgical removal of a primary site or secondary site malignancy followed by adjunct chemotherapy or radiotherapy, code the malignancy as the principal diagnosis, using codes in the 140-198 series or where appropriate in the 200-203 series.

D. When the reason for admission is to determine the extent of the malignancy, or for a procedure such as paracentesis or thoracentesis, the primary malignancy or appropriate metastatic site is designated as the principal diagnosis, even though chemotherapy or radiotherapy is administered.

E. When the primary malignancy has been previously excised or eradicated from its site and there is no adjunct treatment directed to that site and no evidence of any remaining malignancy at the primary site, use the appropriate code from the V10 series to indicate the former site of primary malignancy. Any mention of extension, invasion, or metastasis to a nearby structure or organ or to a distant site is coded as a secondary malignant neoplasm to that site and may be the principal diagnosis in the absence of the primary site.

F. When a patient is admitted because of a primary neoplasm with metastasis and treatment is directed toward the secondary site only, the secondary neoplasm is designated as the principal diagnosis even though the primary malignancy is still present.

G. Symptoms, signs, and ill-defined conditions listed in Chapter 16 characteristic of, or associated with, an existing primary or secondary site malignancy cannot be used to replace the malignancy as principal diagnosis, regardless of the number of admissions or encounters for treatment and care of the neoplasm.

H. Coding and sequencing of complications associated with the malignant neoplasm or with the therapy thereof are subject to the following guidelines:

When admission is for management of an anemia associated with the malignancy, and the treatment is only for anemia, the anemia is designated as the principal diagnosis and is followed by the appropriate code(s) for the malignancy.

When the admission is for management of an anemia associated with chemotherapy or radiotherapy and the only treatment is for the anemia, the anemia is designated as the principal diagnosis followed by the appropriate code(s) for the malignancy.

When the admission is for management of dehydration due to the malignancy or the therapy, or a combination of both, and only the dehydration is being treated (intravenous rehydration), the dehydration is designated as the principal diagnosis, followed by the code(s) for the malignancy.

When the admission is for treatment of a complication resulting from a surgical procedure performed for the treatment of an intestinal malignancy, designate the complication as the principal diagnosis if treatment is directed at resolving the complication.

2.14 Poisoning

When coding a poisoning or reaction to the improper use of a medication (e.g., wrong dose, wrong substance, wrong route of administration) the poisoning code is sequenced first, followed by a code for the manifestation. If there is also a diagnosis of drug abuse or dependence to the substance, the abuse or dependence is coded as an additional code.

2.15 Complications of surgery and other medical care.

When the admission is for treatment of a complication resulting from surgery or other medical care, the complication code is sequenced as the principal diagnosis. If the complication is classified to the 996-999 series, an additional code for the specific complication may be assigned.

2.16 Complication of pregnancy.

When a patient is admitted because of a condition that is either a complication of pregnancy or that is complicating the pregnancy, the code for the obstetric complication is the principal diagnosis. An additional code may be assigned as needed to provide specificity.

3. REPORTING OTHER (ADDITIONAL) DIAGNOSES

A joint effort between the attending physician and coder is essential to achieve complete and accurate documentation, code assignment, and reporting of diagnoses and procedures.

These guidelines have been developed and approved by the Cooperating Parties to assure both the physician and the coder in identifying those diagnoses that are to be reported in addition to the principal diagnosis. Hospitals may record other diagnoses as needed for internal data use.

The UHDDS definitions are used by acute care short-term hospitals to report inpatient data elements in a standardized manner. These data elements and their definitions can be found in the July 31, 1985, Federal Register (Vol. 50, No, 147), pp. 31038-40.

The UHDDS item #11-b defines Other Diagnoses as "all conditions that coexist at the time of admission, that develop subsequently, or that affect the treatment received and/or the length of stay. Diagnoses that relate to an earlier episode which have no bearing on the current hospital stay are to be excluded".

GENERAL RULE

For reporting purposes the definition for "other diagnoses" is interpreted as additional conditions that affect patient care in terms of requiring:

clinical evaluation; or
therapeutic treatment; or
diagnostic procedures; or
extended length of hospital stay; or
increased nursing care and/or monitoring.

The following guidelines are to be applied in designating "other diagnoses" when neither the Alphabetic Index nor the Tabular List in ICD-9-CM provides direction.

The listing of the diagnoses on the attestation statement is the responsibility of the attending physician.

3.1   Previous conditions.

If the physician has included a diagnosis in the final diagnostic statement, such as the discharge summary or the face sheet, it should ordinarily be coded. Some physicians include in the diagnostic statement resolved conditions or diagnoses and status-post procedures from previous admission that have no bearing on the current stay. Such conditions are not to be reported and are coded only if required by hospital policy.

However, history codes (V10-V19) may be used as secondary codes if the historical condition or family history has an impact on current care or influences treatment.

3.2   Diagnoses not listed in the final diagnostic statement.

When the physician has documented what appears to be a current diagnosis in the body of the record, but has not included the diagnosis in the final diagnostic statement, the physician should be asked whether the diagnosis should be added.

3.3   Conditions that are an integral part of a disease process.

Conditions that are integral to the disease process should not be assigned as additional codes.

3.4   Conditions that are not an integral part of a disease process.

Additional conditions that may not be associated routinely with a disease process should be coded when present.

3.5   Abnormal findings.

Abnormal findings (laboratory, x-ray, pathologic, and other diagnostic results) are not coded and reported unless the physician indicates their clinical significance. If the findings are outside the normal range and the physician has ordered other tests to evaluate the condition or prescribed treatment, it is appropriate to ask the physician whether the diagnosis should be added.

4.   HYPERTENSION

4.1   Hypertension, Essential, or NOS

Assign hypertension (arterial) (essential) (primary) (systemic) (NOS) to category code 401 with the appropriate fourth digit to indicate malignant (.0), benign (.1), or unspecified (.9). Do not use either .0 malignant or .1 benign unless medical record documentation supports such a designation.

4.2   Hypertension with Heart Disease

Certain heart conditions (425.8, 428, 429.0-429.3, 429.8, 429.9) are assigned to a code from category 402 when a causal relationship is stated (due to hypertension) or implied (hypertensive). Use only the code from category 402.

The same heart conditions (425.8, 428, 429.0-429.3, 429.8, 429.9) with hypertension, but without a stated casual relationship, are coded separately. Sequence according to the circumstances of the admission.

4.3   Hypertensive Renal Disease with Chronic Renal Failure

Assign codes from category 403, Hypertensive renal disease, when conditions classified to categories 585-587 are present. Unlike hypertension with heart disease, ICD-9-CM presumes a cause-and-effect relationship and classifies renal failure with hypertension as hypertensive renal disease.

4.4   Hypertensive Heart and Renal Disease

Assign codes from combination category 404, Hypertensive heart and renal disease, when both hypertensive renal disease and hypertensive heart disease are stated in the diagnosis. Assume a relationship between the hypertension and the renal disease, whether or not the condition is so designated.

4.5   Hypertensive Cerebrovascular Disease.

First assign codes from 430-438, Cerebrovascular disease, then the appropriate hypertension code from categories 401-405.

4.6   Hypertensive Retinopathy

Two codes are necessary to identify the condition. First assign the code from subcategory 362.11, Hypertensive retinopathy, then the appropriate code from categories 401-405 to indicate the type of hypertension.

4.7   Hypertension, Secondary

Two codes are required: one to identify the underlying condition and one from category 405 to identify the hypertension. Sequencing of codes is determined by the reason for admission to the hospital.

4.8   Hypertension, Transient

Assign code 796.2, Elevated blood pressure reading without diagnosis of hypertension, unless patient has an established diagnosis of hypertension. Assign code 642.3X for transient hypertension of pregnancy.

4.9 Hypertension, Controlled

Assign appropriate code from categories 401-405. This diagnostic statement usually refers to an existing state of hypertension under control by therapy.

4.10 Hypertension, Uncontrolled

Uncontrolled hypertension may refer to untreated hypertension or hypertension not responding to current therapeutic regimen. In either case, assign the appropriate code from categories 401-405 to designate the stage and type of hypertension. Code to the type of hypertension.

4.11 Elevated Blood Pressure

For a statement of elevated blood pressure without further specificity, assign code 796.2, Elevated blood pressure reading without diagnosis of hypertension, rather than a code from category 401.

5. OBSTETRICS

Introduction

These guidelines have been developed and approved by the Cooperating Parties in conjunction with the Editorial Advisory Board of Coding Clinic and the American College of Obstetricians and Gynecologists, to assist the coder in coding and reporting obstetric cases. Where feasible, previously published advice has been incorporated. Some advice in these new guidelines may supersede previous advice. The guidelines are provided for reporting purposes. Health care facilities may record additional diagnoses as needed for internal data needs.

5.1 General Rules

A. Obstetric cases require codes from chapter 11, codes in the range 630-677, Complications of Pregnancy, Childbirth, and the Puerperium. Should the physician document that the pregnancy is incidental to the encounter, then code V22.2 should be used in place of any chapter 11 codes. It is the physician's responsibility to state that the condition being treated is not affecting the pregnancy.

B. Chapter 11 codes have sequencing priority over codes from other chapters. Additional codes from other chapters may be used in conjunction with chapter 11 codes to further specify conditions.

C. Chapter 11 codes are to be used only on the maternal record, never on the record of the newborn.

D. An outcome of delivery code, V27.0-V27.9, should be included on every maternal record when a delivery has occurred. These codes are not to be used on subsequent records or on the newborn record.

5.2 Selection of Principal Diagnosis

A. The circumstances of the encounter govern the selection of the principal diagnosis.

B. In episodes when no delivery occurs the principal diagnosis should correspond to the principal complication of the pregnancy which necessitated the encounter. Should more than one complication exist, all of which are treated or monitored, any of the complications codes may be sequenced first.

C. When a delivery occurs the principal diagnosis should correspond to the main circumstances or complication of the delivery. In cases of cesarean deliveries, the principal diagnosis should correspond to the reason the cesarean was performed, unless the reason for admission was unrelated to the condition resulting in the cesarean delivery.

D. For routine prenatal visits when no complications are present codes V22.0, Supervision of normal first pregnancy, and V22.1, Supervision of other normal pregnancy, should be used as principal diagnoses. These codes should not be used in conjunction with chapter 11 codes.

E. For prenatal outpatient visits for patients with high-risk pregnancies, a code from category V23, Supervision of high-risk pregnancy, should be used as the principal diagnosis. Secondary chapter 11 codes may be used in conjunction with these codes if appropriate. A thorough review of any pertinent "excludes" note is necessary to be certain that these V codes are being used properly.

5.3 Chapter 11 Fifth-digits

A. Categories 640-648, 651-676 have required fifth-digits which indicate whether the encounter is antepartum, postpartum and whether a delivery has also occurred.

B. The fifth-digits which are appropriate for each code number are listed in brackets under each code. The fifth-digits on each code should all be consistent with each other. That is, should a delivery occur all of the fifth-digits should indicate the delivery.

5.4   Fetal Conditions Affecting the Management of the Mother.

Codes from category 655, Known or suspected fetal abnormality affecting management of the mother, and category 656, Other fetal and placental problems affecting the management of the mother, are assigned only when the fetal condition is actually responsible for modifying the management of the mother, i.e., by requiring diagnostic studies, additional observation, special care, or termination of pregnancy. The fact that the fetal condition exists does not justify assigning a code from this series to the mother's record.

5.5   Normal Delivery, 650

A. Code 650 is for use in cases when a woman is admitted for a full-term normal delivery and delivers a single, healthy infant without any complications antepartum, during the delivery, or postpartum during the delivery episode.

B. 650 may be used if the patient had a complication at some point during her pregnancy but the complication is not present at the time of the admission for delivery.

C. Code 650 is always a principal diagnosis. It is not to be used if any other code from chapter 11 is needed to describe a current complication of the antenatal, delivery, or perinatal period. Additional codes from other chapters may be used with code 650 if they are not related to or are not in any way complicating the pregnancy.

D. V27.0, Single liveborn, is the only outcome of delivery code appropriate for use with 650.

5.6   Procedure Codes

A. In cases of cesarean delivery, the selection of the principal diagnosis should correspond to the reason the cesarean delivery was performed unless the reason for admission was unrelated to the condition resulting in the cesarean delivery.

B. A delivery procedure code should not be used for a woman who has delivered prior to admission to the hospital. Any postpartum repairs should be coded.

5.7   The Postpartum Period

A. The postpartum period begins immediately after delivery and continues for 6 weeks following delivery.

B. A postpartum complication is any complication occurring within the 6 week period.

C. Chapter 11 codes may also be used to describe pregnancy-related complications after the 6 week period should the physician document that a condition is pregnancy related.

D. Postpartum complications that occur during the same admission as the delivery are identified with a fifth digit of "2". Subsequent admissions for postpartum complications should be identified with a fifth digit of "4".

E. When the mother delivers outside the hospital prior to admission and is admitted for routine postpartum care and no complications are noted, code V24.0, Postpartum care and examination immediately after delivery, should be assigned as the principal diagnosis.

5.8   Abortions

A. Fifth-digits are required for abortion categories 634-637. Fifth-digit 1, incomplete, indicates that all of the products of conception have not been expelled from the uterus. Fifth-digit 2, complete, indicates that all products of conception have been expelled from the uterus prior to the episode of care.

B. Codes from categories 640-648 and 651-657 may be used as additional codes with an abortion code to indicate the complication leading to the abortion.

Fifth digit 3 is assigned with codes from these categories when used with an abortion code because the other fifth digits will not apply. Codes from the 660-669 series are not to be used for complications of abortion.

C. Code 639 is to be used for all complications following abortion. Code 639 cannot be assigned with codes from categories 634-638.

D. Abortion with Liveborn Fetus. When an attempted termination of pregnancy results in a liveborn fetus assign code 644.21, Early onset of delivery, with an appropriate code from category V27, Outcome of Delivery. The procedure code for the attempted termination of pregnancy should also be assigned.

E. Retained Products of Conception following an abortion. Subsequent admissions for retained products of conception following a spontaneous or legally induced abortion are assigned the appropriate code from category 634, Spontaneous abortion, or legally induced abortion, with a fifth digit of "1" (incomplete). This advice is appropriate even when the patient was discharged previously with a discharge diagnosis of complete abortion.

5.9   Code 677, Late effect of complication of pregnancy, childbirth, and the puerperium

A. Code 677, Late effect of complication of pregnancy, childbirth, and the puerperium is for use in those cases when an initial complication of a pregnancy develops a sequela requiring care or treatment at a future date.

B. This code may be used at any time after the initial postpartum period.

C. This code, like all late effect codes, is to be sequenced following the code describing the sequela of the complication.

6. NEWBORN GUIDELINES

Definition

The newborn period is defined as beginning at birth and lasting through the 28th day following birth.

The following guidelines are provided for reporting purposes. Hospitals may record other diagnoses as needed for internal data use.

GENERAL RULE

All clinically significant conditions noted on routine newborn examination should be coded. A condition is clinically significant if it requires:

clinical evaluation; or
therapeutic treatment; or
diagnostic procedures; or
extended length of hospital stay; or
increased nursing care and/or monitoring; or
has implications for future health care needs.

Note: The newborn guidelines listed above are the same as the general coding guidelines for "other diagnoses," except for the final bullet regarding implications for future health care needs. Whether or not a condition is clinically significant can only be determined by the physician.

6.1   Use of Codes V30-V39

When coding the birth of an infant, assign a code from categories V30-V39, according to the type of birth. A code from this series is assigned as a principal diagnosis, and assigned only once to a newborn at the time of birth.

6.2   Newborn Transfers

If the newborn is transferred to another institution, the V30 series is not used.

6.3   Use of Category V29

A. Assign a code from category V29, Observation and evaluation of newborns and infants for suspected conditions not found, to identify those instances when a healthy newborn is evaluated for a suspected condition that is determined after study not to be present. Do not use a code from category V29 when the patient has identified signs or symptoms of a suspected problem; in such cases, code the sign or symptom.

B. A V29 code is to be used as a secondary code after the V30, Outcome of delivery, code. It may also be assigned as a principal code for readmissions or encounters when the V30 code no longer applies. It is for use only for healthy newborns and infants for which no condition after study is found to be present.

6.4   Maternal Causes of Perinatal Morbidity

Codes from categories 760-763, Maternal causes of perinatal morbidity and mortality, are assigned only when the maternal condition has actually affected the fetus or newborn. The fact that the mother has an associated medical condition or experiences some complication of pregnancy, labor or delivery does not justify the routine assignment of codes from these categories to the newborn record.

6.5   Congenital Anomalies

Assign an appropriate code from categories 740-759, Congenital Anomalies, when a specific abnormality is diagnosed for an infant. Such abnormalities may occur as a set of symptoms or multiple malformations. A code should be assigned for each presenting manifestation of the syndrome if the syndrome is not specifically indexed in ICD-9-CM.

6.6   Coding of Other (Additional) Diagnoses

A. Assign codes for conditions that require treatment or further investigation, prolong the length of stay, or require resource utilization.

B. Assign codes for conditions that have been specified by the physician as having implications for future health care needs.

NOTE: This guideline should not be used for adult patients.

C. Assign a code for Newborn conditions originating in the perinatal period (categories 760-779), as well as complications arising during the current episode of care classified in other chapters, only if the diagnoses have been documented by the responsible physician at the time of transfer or discharge as having affected the fetus or newborn.

D. Insignificant conditions or signs or symptoms that resolve without treatment are not coded.

6.7   Prematurity and Fetal Growth Retardation

Codes from categories 764 and 765 should not be assigned based solely on recorded birthweight or estimated gestational age, but upon the attending physician's clinical assessment of maturity of the infant.

NOTE: Since physicians may utilize different criteria in determining prematurity, do not code the diagnosis of prematurity unless the physician documents this condition.

7. SEPTICEMIA AND SEPTIC SHOCK

When the diagnosis of septicemia with shock or the diagnosis of general sepsis with septic shock is documented, code and list the septicemia first and report the septic shock code as a secondary condition. The septicemia code assignment should identify the type of bacteria if it is known.

Sepsis and septic shock associated with abortion, ectopic pregnancy, and molar pregnancy are classified to category codes in Chapter 11 (630-639).

Negative or inconclusive blood cultures do not preclude a diagnosis of septicemia in patients with clinical evidence of the condition.

8. TRAUMA

8.1   Coding for Multiple Injuries

When coding multiple injuries such as fracture of tibia and fibula, assign separate codes for each injury unless a combination code is provided, in which case the combination code is assigned. Multiple injury codes are provided in ICD-9-CM, but should not be assigned unless information for a more specific code is not available.

A. The code for the most serious injury, as determined by the physician, is sequenced first.

B. Superficial injuries such as abrasions or contusions are not coded when associated with more severe injuries of the same site.

C. When a primary injury results in mi-

nor damage to peripheral nerves or blood vessels, the primary injury is sequenced first with additional code(s) from categories 950-957, Injury to nerves and spinal cord, and/or 900-904, Injury to blood vessels. When the primary injury is to the blood vessels or nerves, that injury should be sequenced first.

8.2   Coding for Multiple Fractures

The principle of multiple coding of injuries should be followed in coding multiple fractures. Multiple fractures of specified sites are coded individually by site in accordance with both the provisions within categories 800-829 and the level of detail furnished by medical record content. Combination categories for multiple fractures are provided for use when there is insufficient detail in the medical record (such as trauma cases transferred to another hospital), when the reporting form limits the number of codes that can be used in reporting pertinent clinical data, or when there is insufficient specificity at the fourth-digit or fifth-digit level. More specific guidelines are as follows:

A. Multiple fractures of same limb classifiable to the same three-digit or four-digit category are coded to that category.

B. Multiple unilateral or bilateral fractures of same bone(s) but classified to different fourth-digit subdivisions (bone part) within the same three-digit category are coded individually by site.

C. Multiple fracture categories 819 and 828 classify bilateral fractures of both upper limbs (819) and both lower limbs (828), but without any detail at the fourth-digit level other than open and closed type of fractures.

D. Multiple fractures are sequenced in accordance with the severity of the fracture and the physician should be asked to list the fracture diagnoses in the order of severity.

8.3   Current Burns and Encounters for Late Effects of Burns

Current burns (940-948) are classified by depth, extent and, if desired, by agent (E code). By depth burns are classified as first degree (erythema), second degree (blistering), and third degree (full-thickness involvement).

A. All burns are coded with the highest degree of burn sequenced first.

B. Classify burns of the same local site

(three-digit category level, 940-947) but of different degrees to the subcategory identifying the highest degree recorded in the diagnosis.

C. Non-healing burns are coded as acute burns. Necrosis of burned skin should be coded as a non-healed burn.

D. Assign code 958.3, Posttraumatic wound infection, not elsewhere classified, as an additional code for any documented infected burn site.

E. When coding multiple burns, assign separate codes for each burn site. Category 946 Burns of Multiple specified sites, should only be used if the location[s] of the burns are not documented.

Category 949, Burn, unspecified, is extremely vague and should rarely be used.

F. Assign codes from category 948, Burns classified according to extent of body surface involved, when the site of the burn is not specified or when there is a need for additional data. It is advisable to use category 948 as additional coding when needed to provide data for evaluating burn mortality, such as that needed by burn units. It is also advisable to use category 948 as an additional code for reporting purposes when there is mention of a third-degree burn involving 20 percent or more of the body surface. In assigning a code from category 948:

Fourth-digit codes are used to identify the percentage of total body surface involved in a burn (all degree).

Fifth-digits are assigned to identify the percentage of body surface involved in third-degree burn.

Fifth-digit zero (0) is assigned when less than 10 percent or when no body surface is involved in a third-degree burn.

Category 948 is based on the classic "rule of nines" in estimating body surface involved: head and neck are assigned nine percent, each arm nine percent, each leg 18 percent, the anterior trunk 18 percent, posterior trunk 18 percent, and genitalia one percent. Physicians may change these percentage assignments where necessary to accommodate infants and children who have proportionately larger heads than adults and patients who have large buttocks, thighs, or abdomen that involve burns.

G. Encounters for the treatment of the late effects of burns (i.e., scars or joint contractures) should be coded to the residual condition (sequela) followed by the appropriate late effect code (906.5-906.9). A late effect E code may also be used, if desired.

H. When appropriate, both a sequela with a late effect code, and a current burn code may be assigned on the same record.

8.4 Debridement of Wound, Infection, or Burn

A. For coding purposes, excisional debridement, 86.22, is assigned only when the procedure is performed by a physician.

B. For coding purposes, nonexcisional debridement performed by the physician or nonphysician health care professional is assigned to 86.28. Any "excisional" type procedure performed by a nonphysician is assigned to 86.28.

9. ADVERSE EFFECTS AND POISONING

The properties of certain drugs, medicinal and biological substances or combinations of such substances, may cause toxic reactions. The occurrence of drug toxicity is classified in ICD-9-CM as follows:

9.1 Adverse Effect

When the drug was correctly prescribed and properly administered, code the reaction plus the appropriate code from the E930-E949 series.

Adverse effects of therapeutic substances correctly prescribed and properly administered (toxicity, synergistic reaction, side effect, and idiosyncratic reaction) may be due to (1) differences among patients, such as age, sex, disease, and genetic factors, and (2) drug-related factors, such as type of drug, route of administration, duration of therapy, dosage, and bioavailability.

Codes from the E930-E949 series must be used to identify the causative substance for an adverse effect of drug, medicinal and biological substances, correctly prescribed and properly administered. The effect, such as tachycardia, delirium, gastrointestinal hemorrhaging, vomiting, hypokalemia, hepatitis, renal failure, or respiratory failure, is coded and followed by the appropriate code from the E930-E949 series.

9.2 Poisoning

Poisoning when an error was made in drug prescription or in the administration of the drug by physician, nurse, patient, or other person, use the appropriate code from the 960-979 series. If an overdose of a drug was intentionally taken or administered and resulted in drug toxicity, it would be coded as a poisoning (960-979 series). If a nonprescribed drug or medicinal agent was taken in combination with a correctly prescribed and properly administered drug, any drug toxicity or other reaction resulting from the interaction of the two drugs would be classified as a poisoning.

10. HUMAN IMMUNODEFICIENCY VIRUS (HIV) INFECTIONS

10.1   Code only confirmed cases of HIV infection/illness.

This is an exception to guideline 1.8 which states "If the diagnosis documented at the time of discharge is qualified as 'probable,' 'suspected,' 'likely,' 'questionable,' 'possible,' or 'still to be ruled out,' code the condition as if it existed or was established..."

In this context, "confirmation" does not require documentation of positive serology or culture for HIV; the physician's diagnostic statement that the patient is HIV positive, or has an HIV-related illness is sufficient.

10.2   Selection of HIV code

042   Human Immunodeficiency Virus [HIV] Disease

Patients with an HIV-related illness should be coded to 042, Human Immunodeficiency Virus [HIV] Disease.

V08   Asymptomatic Human Immunodeficiency Virus [HIV] Infection

Patients with physician-documented asymptomatic HIV infections who have never had an HIV-related illness should be coded to V08, Asymptomatic Human Immunodeficiency Virus [HIV] Infection.

795.71   Nonspecific Serologic Evidence of Human Immunodeficiency Virus [HIV]

Code 795.71, Nonspecific serologic evidence of human immunodeficiency virus [HIV], should be used for patients (including infants) with inconclusive HIV test results.

10.3   Previously diagnosed HIV-related illness

Patients with any known prior diagnosis of an HIV-related illness should be coded to 042. Once a patient has developed an HIV-related illness, the patient should always be assigned code 042 on every subsequent admission. Patients previously diagnosed with any HIV illness (042) should never be assigned to 795.71 or V08.

10.4   Sequencing

The sequencing of diagnoses for patients with HIV-related illnesses follows guideline 2 for selection of principal diagnosis. That is, the circumstances of admission govern the selection of principal diagnosis, "that condition established after study to be chiefly responsible for occasioning the admission of the patient to the hospital for care."

Patients who are admitted for an HIV-related illness should be assigned a minimum of two codes: first assign code 042 to identify the HIV disease and then sequence additional codes to identify the other diagnoses. If a patient is admitted for an HIV-related condition, the principal diagnosis should be 042, followed by additional diagnosis codes for all reported HIV-related conditions.

If a patient with HIV disease is admitted for an unrelated condition (such as a traumatic injury), the code for the unrelated condition (e.g., the nature of injury code) should be the principal diagnosis. Other diagnoses would be 042 followed by additional diagnosis codes for all reported HIV-related conditions.

Whether the patient is newly diagnosed or has had previous admissions for HIV conditions (or has expired) is irrelevant to the sequencing decision.

10.5   HIV Infection in Pregnancy, Childbirth and the Puerperium

During pregnancy, childbirth or the puerperium, a patient admitted because of an HIV-related illness should receive a principal diagnosis of 647.8X, Other specified infectious and parasitic diseases in the mother classifiable elsewhere, but complicating the pregnancy, childbirth or the puerperium, followed by 042 and the code(s) for the HIV-related illness(es). This is an exception to the sequencing rule found in 10.4 above.

Patients with asymptomatic HIV infection status admitted during pregnancy, childbirth, or the puerperium should receive codes of 647.8X and V08.

10.6   Asymptomatic HIV Infection

V08, Asymptomatic human immunodeficiency virus [HIV] infection, is to be applied when the patient without any documentation of symptoms is listed as being "HIV positive," "known HIV," "HIV test positive," or similar terminology. Do not use this code if the term "AIDS" is used or if the patient is treated for any HIV-related illness or is described as having any condition(s) resulting from his/her HIV positive status; use 042 in these cases.

10.7 Inconclusive Laboratory Test for HIV

Patients with inconclusive HIV serology, but no definitive diagnosis or manifestations of the illness may be assigned code 795.71, inconclusive serologic test for human immunodeficiency virus [HIV].

10.8 Testing for HIV

If the patient is asymptomatic but wishes to know his/her HIV status, use code V73.89, Screening for other specified viral disease. Use code V69.8, Other problems related to lifestyle, as a secondary code if an asymptomatic patient is in a known high-risk group for HIV. Should a patient with signs or symptoms or illness, or a confirmed HIV-related diagnosis be tested for HIV, code the signs and symptoms or the diagnosis. An additional counseling code V65.44 may be used if counseling is provided during the encounter for the test.

When the patient returns to be informed of his/her HIV test results use code V65.44, HIV counseling, if the results of the test are negative. If the results are positive but the patient is asymptomatic use code V08, Asymptomatic HIV infection. If the results are positive and the patient is symptomatic use code 042, HIV infection, with codes for the HIV-related symptoms or diagnosis. The HIV counseling code may also be used if counseling is provided for patients with positive test results.

11. GUIDELINES FOR CODING EXTERNAL CAUSES OF INJURIES, POISONINGS AND ADVERSE EFFECTS OF DRUGS (E Codes)

Introduction: These guidelines are provided for those who are currently collecting E codes in order that there will be standardization in the process. If your institution plans to begin collect·ing E codes, these guidelines are to be applied. The use of E codes is supplemental to the application of basic ICD-9-CM codes. E codes are never to be recorded as principal diagnosis (first listed in the outpatient setting) and are not required for reporting to the Health Care Financing Administration.

Injuries are a major cause of mortality, morbidity and disability. In the United States, the care of patients who suffer intentional and unintentional injuries and poisonings contributes signifi-cantly to the increase in medical care costs. External causes of injury and poisoning codes (E codes) are intended to provide data for injury research and evaluation of injury prevention strategies. E codes capture how the injury or poisoning happened (cause), the intent (unintentional or accidental; or intentional, such as suicide or assault), and the place where the event occurred. Some major categories of E codes include:

transport accidents
poisoning and adverse effects of drugs, medicinal substances and biologicals
accidental falls
accidents caused by fire and flames
accidents due to natural and environmental factors
late effects of accidents, assaults or self injury
assaults or purposely inflicted injury
suicide or self inflicted injury

These guidelines apply for the coding and collection of E codes from records in hospitals, outpatient clinics, emergency departments, other ambulatory care settings and physician offices except when other specific guidelines apply. (See Reporting Diagnostic Guidelines for Hospital-based Outpatient Services/Reporting Requirements for Physician Billing.)

11.1 GENERAL E CODE CODING GUIDELINES

A. An E code may be used with any code in the range of 001-V82.9 which indicates an injury, poisoning, or adverse effect due to an external cause.

B. Assign the appropriate E code for all initial treatments of an injury, poisoning, or adverse effect of drugs.

C. Use a late effect E code for subsequent visits when a late effect of the initial injury or poisoning is being treated. There is no late effect E code for adverse effects of drugs.

D. Use the full range of E codes to completely describe the cause, the intent and the place of occurrence, if applicable, for all injuries, poisonings, and adverse effects of drugs.

E. Assign as many E codes as necessary to fully explain each cause. If only one E code can be recorded, assign the E code most related to the principal diagnosis.

F. The selection of the appropriate E code is guided by the Index to External Causes which is located after the Alphabetic Index to Diseases and by Inclusion and Exclusion notes in the Tabular List.

G. An E code can never be a principal (first listed) diagnosis.

11.2 PLACE OF OCCURRENCE GUIDELINE

Use an additional code from category E849 to indicate the Place of Occurrence for injuries and poisonings. The Place of Occurrence describes the place where the event occurred and not the patient's activity at the time of the event.

Do not use E849.9 if the place of occurrence is not stated.

11.3 POISONINGS AND ADVERSE EFFECTS OF DRUGS, MEDICINAL AND BIOLOGICAL SUBSTANCES GUIDELINES

A. Do not code directly from the Table of Drugs and Chemicals. Always refer back to the Tabular List.

B. Use as many codes as necessary to describe completely all drugs, medicinal or biological substances.

C. If the same E code would describe the causative agent for more than one adverse reaction, assign the code only once.

D. If two or more drugs, medicinal or biological substances are reported, code each individually unless the combination code is listed in the Table of Drugs and Chemicals. In that case, assign the E code for the combination.

E. When a reaction results from the interaction of a drug(s) and alcohol, use poisoning codes and E codes for both.

F. If the reporting format limits the number of E codes that can be used in reporting clinical data, code the one most related to the principal diagnosis. Include at least one from each category (cause, intent, place) if possible.

If there are different fourth digit codes in the same three digit category, use the code for "Other specified" of that category. If there is no "Other specified" code in that category, use the appropriate "Unspecified" code in that category.

If the codes are in different three digit categories, assign the appropriate E code for other multiple drugs and medicinal substances.

11.4 MULTIPLE CAUSE E CODE CODING GUIDELINES

If two or more events cause separate injuries, an E code should be assigned for each cause. The first listed E code will be selected in the following order:

E codes for child and adult abuse take priority over all other E codes—*see* Child and Adult Abuse guidelines

E codes for cataclysmic events take priority over all other E codes except child and adult abuse

E codes for transport accidents take priority over all other E codes except cataclysmic events and child and adult abuse

The first listed E code should correspond to the cause of the most serious diagnosis due to an assault, accident, or self-harm, following the order of hierarchy listed above.

11.5 CHILD AND ADULT ABUSE GUIDELINES

A. When the cause of an injury or neglect is intentional child or adult abuse, the first listed E code should be assigned from categories E960-E968, Homicide and injury purposely inflicted by other persons (except category E967). An E code from category E967, Child and adult battering and other maltreatment, should be added as an additional code to identify the perpetrator, if known.

B. In cases of neglect when the intent is determined to be accidental E code E904.0, Abandonment or neglect of infant and helpless person, should be the first listed E code.

11.6 UNKNOWN OR SUSPECTED INTENT GUIDELINES

A. If the intent (accident, self-harm, assault) of the cause of an injury or poisoning is unknown or unspecified, code the intent as undetermined E980-E989.

B. If the intent (accident, self-harm, assault) of the cause of an injury or poisoning is questionable, probable or suspected, code the intent as undetermined E980-E989.

11.7 UNDETERMINED CAUSE

When the intent of an injury or poisoning is known, but the cause is unknown, use codes E928.9, Unspecified accident, E958.9, Suicide and self-inflicted injury by unspecified means, and E968.9, Assault by unspecified means.

These E codes should rarely be used as the documentation in the medical record, in both the inpatient and outpatient settings, should normally provide sufficient detail to determine the cause of the injury.

11.8 LATE EFFECTS OF EXTERNAL CAUSE GUIDELINES

    A. Late effect E codes exist for injuries and poisonings but not for adverse effects of drugs, misadventures and surgical complications.

    B. A late effect E code (E929, E959, E969, E977, E989, or E999) should be used with any report of a late effect or sequela resulting from a previous injury or poisoning (905-909).

    C. A late effect E code should never be used with a related current nature of injury code.

11.9 MISADVENTURES AND COMPLICATIONS OF CARE GUIDELINES

    A. Assign a code in the range of E870-E876 if misadventures are stated by the physician.

    B. Assign a code in the range of E878-E879 if the physician attributes an abnormal reaction or later complication to a surgical or medical procedure, but does not mention misadventure at the time of the procedure as the cause of the reaction.

12. DIAGNOSTIC CODING AND REPORTING GUIDELINES FOR OUTPATIENT SERVICES (HOSPITAL-BASED AND PHYSICIAN OFFICE)

    Revised October 1, 1995

Introduction

These revised coding guidelines for outpatient diagnoses have been approved for use by hospitals/physicians in coding and reporting hospital-based outpatient services and physician office visits. These guidelines replace the official guidelines on the October 1, 1994 CD-ROM.

Information about the use of certain abbreviations, punctuation, symbols, and other conventions used in the ICD-9-CM Tabular List (code numbers and titles), can be found in the section at the beginning of the ICD-9-CM on "Conventions Used in the Tabular List." Information about the correct sequence to use in finding a code is described in the Introduction to the Alphabetic Index of ICD-9-CM.

The terms encounter and visit are often used interchangeably in describing outpatient service contacts and, therefore, appear together in these guidelines without distinguishing one from the other.

Coding guidelines for outpatient and physician reporting of diagnoses will vary in a number of instances from those for inpatient diagnoses, recognizing that:

The Uniform Hospital Discharge Data Set (UHDDS) definition of principal diagnosis applies only to inpatients in acute, short-term, general hospitals.

Coding guidelines for inconclusive diagnoses (probable, suspected, rule out, etc.) were developed for inpatient reporting and do not apply to outpatients.

Diagnoses often are not established at the time of the initial encounter/visit. It may take two or more visits before the diagnosis is confirmed.

The most critical rule involves beginning the search for the correct code assignment through the Alphabetic Index. Never begin searching initially in the Tabular List as this will lead to coding errors.

BASIC CODING GUIDELINES FOR OUTPATIENT SERVICES

    A. The appropriate code or codes from 001.0 through V82.9 must be used to identify diagnoses, symptoms, conditions, problems, complaints, or other reason(s) for the encounter/visit.

    B. For accurate reporting of ICD-9-CM diagnosis codes, the documentation should describe the patient's condition, using terminology which includes specific diagnoses as well as symptoms, problems, or reasons for the encounter. There are ICD-9-CM codes to describe all of these.

    C. The selection of codes 001.0 through 999.9 will frequently be used to describe the reason for the encounter. These codes are from the section of ICD-9-CM for the classification of diseases and injuries (e.g., infectious and parasitic diseases; neoplasms; symptoms, signs, and ill-defined conditions, etc.).

    D. Codes that describe symptoms and signs, as opposed to diagnoses, are acceptable for reporting purposes when an established diagnosis has not been diagnosed (confirmed) by the physician. Chapter 16 of ICD-9-CM, Symptoms, Signs, and Ill-defined conditions (codes 780.0-799.9) contains many, but not all codes for symptoms.

    E. ICD-9-CM provides codes to deal with encounters for circumstances other than a disease or injury. The Supplementary Classification of Factors Influencing Health Status and Contact with Health Services (V01.0-V82.9) is provided to deal with occasions when circumstances other than a disease or injury are recorded as diagnosis or problems.

F. ICD-9-CM is composed of codes with either 3, 4, or 5 digits. Codes with 3 digits are included in ICD-9-CM as the heading of a category of codes that may be further subdivided by the use of fourth and/or fifth digits which provide greater specificity.

A three-digit code is to be used only if it is not further subdivided. Where fourth-digit subcategories and/or fifth-digit subclassifications are provided, they must be assigned. A code is invalid if it has not been coded to the full number of digits required for that code.

G. List first the ICD-9-CM code for the diagnosis, condition, problem, or other reason for encounter/visit shown in the medical record to be chiefly responsible for the services provided. List additional codes that describe any coexisting conditions.

H. Do not code diagnoses documented as "probable," "suspected," "questionable," "rule out," or "working diagnosis." Rather, code the condition(s) to the highest degree of certainty for that encounter/visit, such as symptoms, signs, abnormal test results, or other reason for the visit.

Please note: This is contrary to the coding practices used by hospitals and medical record departments for coding the diagnosis of hospital inpatients.

I. Chronic diseases treated on an ongoing basis may be coded and reported as many times as the patient receives treatment and care for the condition(s).

J. Code all documented conditions that coexist at the time of the encounter/visit, and require or affect patient care treatment or management. Do not code conditions that were previously treated and no longer exist. However, history codes (V10-V19) may be used as sec-ondary codes if the historical condition or family history has an impact on current care or influences treatment.

K. For patients receiving diagnostic services only during an encounter/visit, sequence first the diagnosis, condition, problem, or other reason for encounter/visit shown in the medical record to be chiefly responsible for the outpatient services provided during the encounter/visit. Codes for other diagnoses (e.g., chronic conditions) may be sequenced as additional diagnoses.

L. For patients receiving therapeutic services only during an encounter/visit, sequence first the diagnosis, condition, problem, or other reason for encounter/visit shown in the medical record to be chiefly responsible for the outpatient services provided during the encounter/visit. Codes for other diagnoses (e.g., chronic conditions) may be sequenced as additional diagnoses.

The only exception to this rule is that for patients receiving chemotherapy, radiation therapy, or rehabilitation, the appropriate V code for the service is listed first, and the diagnosis or problem for which the service is being performed listed second.

N. For patients receiving preoperative evaluations only, sequence a code from category V72.8, Other specified examinations, to describe the pre-op consultations. Assign a code for the condition to describe the reason for the surgery as an additional diagnosis. Code also any findings related to the pre-op evaluation.

O. For ambulatory surgery, code the diagnosis for which the surgery was performed. If the postoperative diagnosis is known to be different from the preoperative diagnosis at the time the diagnosis is confirmed, select the postoperative diagnosis for coding, since it is the most definitive.

PART II

Alphabetic Index, Volume 2

A

AAV (disease) (illness) (infection) - *see* Human immunodeficiency virus (disease) (illness) (infection)
Abactio - *see* Abortion, induced
Abactus venter - *see* Abortion, induced
Abarognosis 781.9
Abasia (-astasia) 307.9
  atactica 781.3
  choreic 781.3
  hysterical 300.11
  paroxysmal trepidant 781.3
  spastic 781.3
  trembling 781.3
  trepidans 781.3
Abderhalden-Kaufmann-Lignac syndrome (cystinosis) 270.0
Abdomen, abdominal - *see also* condition
  accordion 306.4
  acute 789.0
  angina 557.1
  burst 868.00
  convulsive equivalent (*see also* Epilepsy) 345.5
  heart 746.87
  muscle deficiency syndrome 756.79
  obstipum 756.79
Abdominalgia 789.0
  periodic 277.3
Abduction contracture, hip or other joint - *see* Contraction, joint
Abercrombie's syndrome (amyloid degeneration) 277.3
Aberrant (congenital) - *see also* Malposition, congenital
  adrenal gland 759.1
  blood vessel NEC 747.60
    arteriovenous NEC 747.60
    cerebrovascular 747.81
    gastrointestinal 747.61
    lower limb 747.64
    renal 747.62
    spinal 747.82
    upper limb 747.63
  breast 757.6
  endocrine gland NEC 759.2
  gastrointestinal vessel (peripheral) 747.61
  hepatic duct 751.69
  lower limb vessel (peripheral) 747.64
  pancreas 751.7
  parathyroid gland 759.2
  peripheral vascular vessel NEC 747.60
  pituitary gland (pharyngeal) 759.2
  renal blood vessel 747.62
  sebaceous glands, mucous membrane, mouth 750.26
  spinal vessel 747.82
  spleen 759.0
  testis (descent) 752.51
  thymus gland 759.2
  thyroid gland 759.2
  upper limb vessel (peripheral) 747.63
Aberratio
  lactis 757.6
  testis 752.51
Aberration - *see also* Anomaly
  chromosome - *see* Anomaly, chromosome(s)
  distantial 368.9

Aberration (*Continued*)
  mental (*see also* Disorder, mental, non-psychotic) 300.9
Abetalipoproteinemia 272.5
Abionarce 780.79
Abiotrophy 799.8
Ablatio
  placentae - *see* Placenta, ablatio
  retinae (*see also* Detachment, retina) 361.9
Ablation
  pituitary (gland) (with hypofunction) 253.7
  placenta - *see* Placenta, ablatio
  uterus 621.8
Ablepharia, ablepharon, ablephary 743.62
Ablepsia - *see* Blindness
Ablepsy - *see* Blindness
Ablutomania 300.3
Abnormal, abnormality, abnormalities - *see also* Anomaly
  acid-base balance 276.4
    fetus or newborn - *see* Distress, fetal
  adaptation curve, dark 368.63
  alveolar ridge 525.9
  amnion 658.9
    affecting fetus or newborn 762.9
  anatomical relationship NEC 759.9
  apertures, congenital, diaphragm 756.6
  auditory perception NEC 388.40
  autosomes NEC 758.5
    13 758.1
    18 758.2
    21 or 22 758.0
    D_1 758.1
    E_3 758.2
    G 758.0
  ballistocardiogram 794.39
  basal metabolic rate (BMR) 794.7
  biosynthesis, testicular androgen 257.2
  blood level (of)
    cobalt 790.6
    copper 790.6
    iron 790.6
    lithium 790.6
    magnesium 790.6
    mineral 790.6
    zinc 790.6
  blood pressure
    elevated (without diagnosis of hypertension) 796.2
    low (*see also* Hypotension) 458.9
      reading (incidental) (isolated) (nonspecific) 796.3
  bowel sounds 787.5
  breathing behavior - *see* Respiration
  caloric test 794.19
  cervix (acquired) NEC 622.9
    congenital 752.40
    in pregnancy or childbirth 654.6
      causing obstructed labor 660.2
        affecting fetus or newborn 763.1
  chemistry, blood NEC 790.6
  chest sounds 786.7
  chorion 658.9
    affecting fetus or newborn 762.9
  chromosomal NEC 758.89
    analysis, nonspecific result 795.2
    autosomes (*see also* Abnormal, autosomes NEC) 758.5
    fetal (suspected), affecting management of pregnancy 655.1

Abnormal, abnormality, abnormalities (*Continued*)
  chromosomal NEC (*Continued*)
    sex 758.81
  clinical findings NEC 796.4
  communication - *see* Fistula
  configuration of pupils 379.49
  coronary
    artery 746.85
    vein 746.9
  cortisol-binding globulin 255.8
  course, Eustachian tube 744.24
  dentofacial NEC 524.9
    functional 524.5
    specified type NEC 524.8
  development, developmental NEC 759.9
    bone 756.9
    central nervous system 742.9
  direction, teeth 524.3
  dynia (*see also* Defect, coagulation) 286.9
  Ebstein 746.2
  echocardiogram 793.2
  echoencephalogram 794.01
  echogram NEC - *see* Findings, abnormal, structure
  electrocardiogram (ECG) (EKG) 794.31
  electroencephalogram (EEG) 794.02
  electromyogram (EMG) 794.17
    ocular 794.14
  electro-oculogram (EOG) 794.12
  electroretinogram (ERG) 794.11
  erythrocytes 289.9
    congenital, with perinatal jaundice 282.9 [774.0]
  eustachian valve 746.9
  excitability under minor stress 301.9
  fat distribution 782.9
  feces 787.7
  fetal heart rate - *see* Distress, fetal
  fetus NEC
    affecting management of pregnancy - *see* Pregnancy, management affected by, fetal
    causing disproportion 653.7
      affecting fetus or newborn 763.1
      causing obstructed labor 660.1
        affecting fetus or newborn 763.1
  findings without manifest disease - *see* Findings, abnormal
  fluid
    amniotic 792.3
    cerebrospinal 792.0
    peritoneal 792.9
    pleural 792.9
    synovial 792.9
    vaginal 792.9
  forces of labor NEC 661.9
    affecting fetus or newborn 763.7
  form, teeth 520.2
  function studies
    auditory 794.15
    bladder 794.9
    brain 794.00
    cardiovascular 794.30
    endocrine NEC 794.6
    kidney 794.4
    liver 794.8
    nervous system
      central 794.00
      peripheral 794.19

◀▶ **New Code**   ⬅||| |||➡ **Revised Code**

Abnormal, abnormality, abnormalities
(Continued)
function studies *(Continued)*
  oculomotor 794.14
  pancreas 794.9
  placenta 794.9
  pulmonary 794.2
  retina 794.11
  special senses 794.19
  spleen 794.9
  thyroid 794.5
  vestibular 794.16
gait 781.2
  hysterical 300.11
gastrin secretion 251.5
globulin
  cortisol-binding 255.8
  thyroid-binding 246.8
glucagon secretion 251.4
glucose tolerance test 790.2
  in pregnancy, childbirth, or puerperium 648.8
  fetus or newborn 775.0
gravitational (G) forces or states 994.9
hair NEC 704.2
hard tissue formation in pulp 522.3
head movement 781.0
heart
  rate
    fetus affecting liveborn
      infant
        before the onset of labor 763.81
        during labor 763.82
        unspecified as to time of onset 763.83
      intrauterine
        before the onset of labor 763.81
        during labor 763.82
        unspecified as to time of onset 763.83
      newborn
        before the onset of labor 763.81
        during labor 763.82
        unspecified as to time of onset 763.83
  shadow 793.2
  sounds NEC 785.3
hemoglobin (*see also* Disease, hemoglobin) 282.7
  trait - *see* Trait, hemoglobin, abnormal
hemorrhage, uterus - *see* Hemorrhage, uterus
histology NEC 795.4
increase
  in
    appetite 783.6
    development 783.9
involuntary movement 781.0
jaw closure 524.5
karyotype 795.2
knee jerk 796.1
labor NEC 661.9
  affecting fetus or newborn 763.7
laboratory findings - *see* Findings, abnormal
length, organ or site, congenital - *see* Distortion
loss of weight 783.2
lung shadow 793.1
mammogram 793.8
Mantoux test 795.5

Abnormal, abnormality, abnormalities
(Continued)
membranes (fetal)
  affecting fetus or newborn 762.9
  complicating pregnancy 658.8
menstruation - *see* Menstruation
metabolism (*see also* condition) 783.9
movement 781.0
  disorder NEC 333.90
    specified NEC 333.99
  head 781.0
  involuntary 781.0
  specified type NEC 333.99
muscle contraction, localized 728.85
myoglobin (Aberdeen) (Annapolis) 289.9
narrowness, eyelid 743.62
optokinetic response 379.57
organs or tissues of pelvis NEC
  in pregnancy or childbirth 654.9
    affecting fetus or newborn 763.89
      causing obstructed labor 660.2
        affecting fetus or newborn 763.1
origin - *see* Malposition, congenital
palmar creases 757.2
Papanicolaou (smear)
  cervix 795.0
  other site 795.1
parturition
  affecting fetus or newborn 763.9
  mother - *see* Delivery, complicated
pelvis (bony) - *see* Deformity, pelvis
percussion, chest 786.7
periods (grossly) (*see also* Menstruation) 626.9
phonocardiogram 794.39
placenta - *see* Placenta, abnormal
plantar reflex 796.1
plasma protein - *see* Deficiency, plasma, protein
pleural folds 748.8
position - *see also* Malposition
  gravid uterus 654.4
    causing obstructed labor 660.2
      affecting fetus or newborn 763.1
posture NEC 781.9
presentation (fetus) - *see* Presentation, fetus, abnormal
product of conception NEC 631
puberty - *see* Puberty
pulmonary
  artery 747.3
  function, newborn 770.8
  test results 794.2
  ventilation, newborn 770.8
    hyperventilation 786.01
pulsations in neck 785.1
pupil reflexes 379.40
quality of milk 676.8
radiological examination 793.9
  abdomen NEC 793.6
  biliary tract 793.3
  breast 793.8
  gastrointestinal tract 793.4
  genitourinary organs 793.5
  head 793.0
  intrathoracic organ NEC 793.2
  lung (field) 793.1
  musculoskeletal system 793.7
  retroperitoneum 793.6
  skin and subcutaneous tissue 793.9
  skull 793.0
red blood cells 790.0

Abnormal, abnormality, abnormalities
(Continued)
red blood cells *(Continued)*
  morphology 790.0
  volume 790.0
reflex NEC 796.1
renal function test 794.4
respiration signs - *see* Respiration
response to nerve stimulation 794.10
retinal correspondence 368.34
rhythm, heart - *see also* Arrhythmia
  fetus - *see* Distress, fetal
saliva 792.4
scan
  brain 794.09
  kidney 794.4
  liver 794.8
  lung 794.2
  thyroid 794.5
secretion
  gastrin 251.5
  glucagon 251.4
semen 792.2
serum level (of)
  acid phosphatase 790.5
  alkaline phosphatase 790.5
  amylase 790.5
  enzymes NEC 790.5
  lipase 790.5
shape
  cornea 743.41
  gallbladder 751.69
  gravid uterus 654.4
    affecting fetus or newborn 763.89
      causing obstructed labor 660.2
        affecting fetus or newborn 763.1
  head (*see also* Anomaly, skull) 756.0
  organ or site, congenital NEC - *see* Distortion
sinus venosus 747.40
size
  fetus, complicating delivery 653.5
    causing obstructed labor 660.1
  gallbladder 751.69
  head (*see also* Anomaly, skull) 756.0
  organ or site, congenital NEC - *see* Distortion
  teeth 520.2
skin and appendages, congenital NEC 757.9
soft parts of pelvis - *see* Abnormal, organs or tissues of pelvis
spermatozoa 792.2
sputum (amount) (color) (excessive) (odor) (purulent) 786.4
stool NEC 787.7
  bloody 578.1
    occult 792.1
  bulky 787.7
  color (dark) (light) 792.1
  content (fat) (mucus) (pus) 792.1
  occult blood 792.1
synchondrosis 756.9
test results without manifest disease - *see* Findings, abnormal
thebesian valve 746.9
thermography - *see* Findings, abnormal, structure
threshold, cones or rods (eye) 368.63
thyroid-binding globulin 246.8
thyroid product 246.8
toxicology (findings) NEC 796.0
tracheal cartilage (congenital) 748.3

ICD-9-CM
A
Vol. 2

Abnormal, abnormality, abnormalities
(Continued)
transport protein 273.8
ultrasound results - *see* Findings, abnormal, structure
umbilical cord
affecting fetus or newborn 762.6
complicating delivery 663.9
specified NEC 663.8
union
cricoid cartilage and thyroid cartilage 748.3
larynx and trachea 748.3
thyroid cartilage and hyoid bone 748.3
urination NEC 788.69
psychogenic 306.53
stream
intermittent 788.61
slowing 788.62
splitting 788.61
weak 788.62
urine (constituents) NEC 791.9
uterine hemorrhage (*see also* Hemorrhage, uterus) 626.9
climacteric 627.0
postmenopausal 627.1
vagina (acquired) (congenital)
in pregnancy or childbirth 654.7
affecting fetus or newborn 763.89
causing obstructed labor 660.2
affecting fetus or newborn 763.1
vascular sounds 785.9
vectorcardiogram 794.39
visually evoked potential (VEP) 794.13
vulva (acquired) (congenital)
in pregnancy or childbirth 654.8
affecting fetus or newborn 763.89
causing obstructed labor 660.2
affecting fetus or newborn 763.1
weight
gain 783.1
of pregnancy 646.1
with hypertension - *see* Toxemia, of pregnancy
loss 783.2
x-ray examination - *see* Abnormal, radiological examination
Abnormally formed uterus - *see* Anomaly, uterus
Abnormity (any organ or part) - *see* Anomaly
ABO
hemolytic disease 773.1
incompatibility reaction 999.6
Abocclusion 524.2
Abolition, language 784.69
Aborter, habitual or recurrent NEC
without current pregnancy 629.9
current abortion (*see also* Abortion, spontaneous) 634.9
affecting fetus or newborn 761.8
observation in current pregnancy 646.3
Abortion (complete) (incomplete) (inevitable) (with retained products of conception) 637.9

Note   Use the following fifth-digit subclassification with categories 634-637:

0   unspecified
1   incomplete
2   complete

Abortion *(Continued)*
with
complication(s) (any) following previous abortion - *see* category 639
damage to pelvic organ (laceration) (rupture) (tear) 637.2
embolism (air) (amniotic fluid) (blood clot) (pulmonary) (pyemic) (septic) (soap) 637.6
genital tract and pelvic infection 637.0
hemorrhage, delayed or excessive 637.1
metabolic disorder 637.4
renal failure (acute) 637.3
sepsis (genital tract) (pelvic organ) 637.0
urinary tract 637.7
shock (postoperative) (septic) 637.5
specified complication NEC 637.7
toxemia 637.3
unspecified complication(s) 637.8
urinary tract infection 637.7
accidental - *see* Abortion, spontaneous
artificial - *see* Abortion, induced
attempted (failed) - *see* Abortion, failed
criminal - *see* Abortion, illegal
early - *see* Abortion, spontaneous
elective - *see* Abortion, legal
failed (legal) 638.9
with
damage to pelvic organ (laceration) (rupture) (tear) 638.2
embolism (air) (amniotic fluid) (blood clot) (pulmonary) (pyemic) (septic) (soap) 638.6
genital tract and pelvic infection 638.0
hemorrhage, delayed or excessive 638.1
metabolic disorder 638.4
renal failure (acute) 638.3
sepsis (genital tract) (pelvic organ) 638.0
urinary tract 638.7
shock (postoperative) (septic) 638.5
specified complication NEC 638.7
toxemia 638.3
unspecified complication(s) 638.8
urinary tract infection 638.7
fetal indication - *see* Abortion, legal
fetus 779.6
following threatened abortion - *see* Abortion, by type
habitual or recurrent (care during pregnancy) 646.3
with current abortion (*see also* Abortion, spontaneous) 634.9
affecting fetus or newborn 761.8
without current pregnancy 629.9
homicidal - *see* Abortion, illegal
illegal 636.9
with
damage to pelvic organ (laceration) (rupture) (tear) 636.2
embolism (air) (amniotic fluid) (blood clot) (pulmonary)l (pyemic) (septic) (soap) 636.6
genital tract and pelvic infection 636.0
hemorrhage, delayed or excessive 636.1
metabolic disorder 636.4
renal failure 636.3

Abortion *(Continued)*
illegal *(Continued)*
with *(Continued)*
sepsis (genital tract) (pelvic organ) 636.0
urinary tract 636.7
shock (postoperative) (septic) 636.5
specified complication NEC 636.7
toxemia 636.3
unspecified complication(s) 636.8
urinary tract infection 636.7
fetus 779.6
induced 637.9
illegal - *see* Abortion, illegal
legal indications - *see* Abortion, legal
medical indications - *see* Abortion, legal
therapeutic - *see* Abortion, legal
late - *see* Abortion, spontaneous
legal (legal indication) (medical indication) (under medical supervision) 635.9
with
damage to pelvic organ (laceration) (rupture) (tear) 635.2
embolism (air) (amniotic fluid) (blood clot) (pulmonary) (pyemic) (septic) (soap) 635.6
genital tract and pelvic infection 635.0
hemorrhage, delayed or excessive 635.1
metabolic disorder 635.4
renal failure (acute) 635.3
sepsis (genital tract) (pelvic organ) 635.0
urinary tract 635.7
shock (postoperative) (septic) 635.5
specified complication NEC 635.7
toxemia 635.3
unspecified complication(s) 635.8
urinary tract infection 635.7
fetus 779.6
medical indication - *see* Abortion, legal
mental hygiene problem - *see* Abortion, legal
missed 632
operative - *see* Abortion, legal
psychiatric indication - *see* Abortion, legal
recurrent - *see* Abortion, spontaneous
self-induced - *see* Abortion, illegal
septic - *see* Abortion, by type, with sepsis
spontaneous 634.9
with
damage to pelvic organ (laceration) (rupture) (tear) 634.2
embolism (air) (amniotic fluid) (blood clot) (pulmonary) (pyemic) (septic) (soap) 634.6
genital tract and pelvic infection 634.0
hemorrhage, delayed or excessive 634.1
metabolic disorder 634.4
renal failure 634.3
sepsis (genital tract) (pelvic organ) 634.0
urinary tract 634.7
shock (postoperative) (septic) 634.5
specified complication NEC 634.7
toxemia 634.3

ICD-9-CM

A

Vol. 2

Abortion *(Continued)*
  spontaneous *(Continued)*
    with *(Continued)*
      unspecified complication(s) 634.8
      urinary tract infection 634.7
    fetus 761.8
    threatened 640.0
      affecting fetus or newborn 762.1
  surgical - *see* Abortion, legal
  therapeutic - *see* Abortion, legal
  threatened 640.0
    affecting fetus or newborn 762.1
  tubal - *see* Pregnancy, tubal
  voluntary - *see* Abortion, legal
Abortus fever 023.9
Aboulomania 301.6
Abrachia 755.20
Abrachiatism 755.20
Abrachiocephalia 759.89
Abrachiocephalus 759.89
Abrami's disease (acquired hemolytic jaundice) 283.9
Abramov-Fiedler myocarditis (acute isolated myocarditis) 422.91
Abrasion - *see also* Injury, superficial, by site
  cornea 918.1 ◄
  dental 521.2
  teeth, tooth (dentifrice) (habitual) (hard tissues) (occupational) (ritual) (traditional) (wedge defect) 521.2
Abrikossov's tumor (M9580/0) - *see also* Neoplasm, connective tissue, benign
  malignant (M9580/3) - *see* Neoplasm, connective tissue, malignant
Abrism 988.8
Abruption, placenta - *see* Placenta, abruptio
Abruptio placentae - *see* Placenta, abruptio
Abscess (acute) (chronic) (infectional) (lymphangitic) (metastatic) (multiple) (pyogenic) (septic) (with lymphangitis) (*see also* Cellulitis) 682.9
  abdomen, abdominal
    cavity - *see* Abscess, peritoneum
    wall 682.2
  abdominopelvic - *see* Abscess, peritoneum
  accessory sinus (chronic) (*see also* Sinusitis) 473.9
  adrenal (capsule) (gland) 255.8
  alveolar 522.5
    with sinus 522.7
  amebic 006.3
    bladder 006.8
    brain (with liver or lung abscess) 006.5
    liver (without mention of brain or lung abscess) 006.3
      with
        brain abscess (and lung abscess) 006.5
        lung abscess 006.4
    lung (with liver abscess) 006.4
      with brain abscess 006.5
    seminal vesicle 006.8
    specified site NEC 006.8
    spleen 006.8
  anaerobic 040.0
  ankle 682.6
  anorectal 566
  antecubital space 682.3
  antrum (chronic) (Highmore) (*see also* Sinusitis, maxillary) 473.0

Abscess *(Continued)*
  anus 566
  apical (tooth) 522.5
    with sinus (alveolar) 522.7
  appendix 540.1
  areola (acute) (chronic) (nonpuerperal) 611.0
    puerperal, postpartum 675.1
  arm (any part, above wrist) 682.3
  artery (wall) 447.2
  atheromatous 447.2
  auditory canal (external) 380.10
  auricle (ear) (staphylococcal) (streptococcal) 380.10
  axilla, axillary (region) 682.3
    lymph gland or node 683
  back (any part) 682.2
  Bartholin's gland 616.3
    with
      abortion - *see* Abortion, by type, with sepsis
      ectopic pregnancy (*see also* categories 633.0-633.9) 639.0
      molar pregnancy (*see also* categories 630-632) 639.0
    complicating pregnancy or puerperium 646.6
    following
      abortion 639.0
      ectopic or molar pregnancy 639.0
  bartholinian 616.3
  Bezold's 383.01
  bile, biliary, duct or tract (*see also* Cholecystitis) 576.8
  bilharziasis 120.1
  bladder (wall) 595.89
    amebic 006.8
  bone (subperiosteal) (*see also* Osteomyelitis) 730.0
    accessory sinus (chronic) (*see also* Sinusitis) 473.9
    acute 730.0
    chronic or old 730.1
    jaw (lower) (upper) 526.4
    mastoid - *see* Mastoiditis, acute
    petrous (*see also* Petrositis) 383.20
    spinal (tuberculous) (*see also* Tuberculosis) 015.0 *[730.88]*
      nontuberculous 730.08
  bowel 569.5
  brain (any part) 324.0
    amebic (with liver or lung abscess) 006.5
    cystic 324.0
    late effect - *see* category 326
    otogenic 324.0
    tuberculous (*see also* Tuberculosis) 013.3
  breast (acute) (chronic) (nonpuerperal) 611.0
    newborn 771.5
    puerperal, postpartum 675.1
    tuberculous (*see also* Tuberculosis) 017.9
  broad ligament (chronic) (*see also* Disease, pelvis, inflammatory) 614.4
    acute 614.3
  Brodie's (chronic) (localized) (*see also* Osteomyelitis) 730.1
  bronchus 519.1
  buccal cavity 528.3
  bulbourethral gland 597.0
  bursa 727.89
    pharyngeal 478.29

Abscess *(Continued)*
  buttock 682.5
  canaliculus, breast 611.0
  canthus 372.20
  cartilage 733.99
  cecum 540.1
  cerebellum, cerebellar 324.0
    late effect - *see* category 326
  cerebral (embolic) 324.0
    late effect - *see* category 326
  cervical (neck region) 682.1
    lymph gland or node 683
    stump (*see also* Cervicitis) 616.0
  cervix (stump) (uteri) (*see also* Cervicitis) 616.0
  cheek, external 682.0
    inner 528.3
  chest 510.9
    with fistula 510.0
    wall 682.2
  chin 682.0
  choroid 363.00
  ciliary body 364.3
  circumtonsillar 475
  cold (tuberculous) - *see also* Tuberculosis, abscess
    articular - *see* Tuberculosis, joint
  colon (wall) 569.5
  colostomy or enterostomy 569.61
  conjunctiva 372.00
  connective tissue NEC 682.9
  cornea 370.55
    with ulcer 370.00
  corpus
    cavernosum 607.2
    luteum (*see also* Salpingo-oophoritis) 614.2
  Cowper's gland 597.0
  cranium 324.0
  cul-de-sac (Douglas') (posterior) (*see also* Disease, pelvis, inflammatory) 614.4
    acute 614.3
  dental 522.5
    with sinus (alveolar) 522.7
  dentoalveolar 522.5
    with sinus (alveolar) 522.7
  diaphragm, diaphragmatic - *see* Abscess, peritoneum
  digit NEC 681.9
  Douglas' cul-de-sac or pouch (*see also* Disease, pelvis, inflammatory) 614.4
    acute 614.3
  Dubois' 090.5
  ductless gland 259.8
  ear
    acute 382.00
    external 380.10
    inner 386.30
    middle - *see* Otitis media
  elbow 682.3
  endamebic - *see* Abscess, amebic
  entamebic - *see* Abscess, amebic
  enterostomy 569.61
  epididymis 604.0
  epidural 324.9
    brain 324.0
    late effect - *see* category 326
    spinal cord 324.1
  epiglottis 478.79
  epiploon, epiploic - *see* Abscess, peritoneum
  erysipelatous (*see also* Erysipelas) 035

Abscess *(Continued)*
  esophagus 530.19
  ethmoid (bone) (chronic) (sinus) *(see also* Sinusitis, ethmoidal) 473.2
  external auditory canal 380.10
  extradural 324.9
    brain 324.0
    late effect - *see* category 326
    spinal cord 324.1
  extraperitoneal - *see* Abscess, peritoneum
  eye 360.00
  eyelid 373.13
  face (any part, except eye) 682.0
  fallopian tube *(see also* Salpingo-oophoritis) 614.2
  fascia 728.89
  fauces 478.29
  fecal 569.5
  femoral (region) 682.6
  filaria, filarial *(see also* Infestation, filarial) 125.9
  finger (any) (intrathecal) (periosteal) (subcutaneous) (subcuticular) 681.00
  fistulous NEC 682.9
  flank 682.2
  foot (except toe) 682.7
  forearm 682.3
  forehead 682.0
  frontal (sinus) (chronic) *(see also* Sinusitis, frontal) 473.1
  gallbladder *(see also* Cholecystitis, acute) 575.0
  gastric 535.0
  genital organ or tract NEC
    female 616.9
      with
        abortion - *see* Abortion, by type, with sepsis
        ectopic pregnancy *(see also* categories 633.0-633.9) 639.0
        molar pregnancy *(see also* categories 630-632) 639.0
      following
        abortion 639.0
        ectopic or molar pregnancy 639.0
      puerperal, postpartum, childbirth 670
    male 608.4
  genitourinary system, tuberculous *(see also* Tuberculosis) 016.9
  gingival 523.3
  gland, glandular (lymph) (acute) NEC 683
  glottis 478.79
  gluteal (region) 682.5
  gonorrheal NEC *(see also* Gonococcus) 098.0
  groin 682.2
  gum 523.3
  hand (except finger or thumb) 682.4
  head (except face) 682.8
  heart 429.89
  heel 682.7
  helminthic *(see also* Infestation, by specific parasite) 128.9
  hepatic 572.0
    amebic *(see also* Abscess, liver, amebic) 006.3
    duct 576.8
  hip 682.6
    tuberculous (active) *(see also* Tuberculosis) 015.1

Abscess *(Continued)*
  ileocecal 540.1
  ileostomy (bud) 569.61
  iliac (region) 682.2
    fossa 540.1
  iliopsoas (tuberculous) *(see also* Tuberculosis) 015.0 *[730.88]*
    nontuberculous 728.89
  infraclavicular (fossa) 682.3
  inguinal (region) 682.2
    lymph gland or node 683
  intersphincteric (anus) 566
  intestine, intestinal 569.5
    rectal 566
  intra-abdominal *(see also* Abscess, peritoneum) 567.2
    postoperative 998.59
  intracranial 324.0
    late effect - *see* category 326
  intramammary - *see* Abscess, breast
  intramastoid *(see also* Mastoiditis, acute) 383.00
  intraorbital 376.01
  intraperitoneal - *see* Abscess, peritoneum
  intraspinal 324.1
    late effect - *see* category 326
  intratonsillar 475
  iris 364.3
  ischiorectal 566
  jaw (bone) (lower) (upper) 526.4
    skin 682.0
  joint *(see also* Arthritis, pyogenic) 711.0
    vertebral (tuberculous) *(see also* Tuberculosis) 015.0 *[730.88]*
      nontuberculous 724.8
  kidney 590.2
    with
      abortion - *see* Abortion, by type, with urinary tract infection
      calculus 592.0
      ectopic pregnancy *(see also* categories 633.0-633.9) 639.8
      molar pregnancy *(see also* categories 630-632) 639.8
      complicating pregnancy or puerperium 646.6
        affecting fetus or newborn 760.1
      following
        abortion 639.8
        ectopic or molar pregnancy 639.8
  knee 682.6
    joint 711.06
    tuberculous (active) *(see also* Tuberculosis) 015.2
  labium (majus) (minus) 616.4
    complicating pregnancy, childbirth, or puerperium 646.6
  lacrimal (passages) (sac) *(see also* Dacryocystitis) 375.30
    caruncle 375.30
    gland *(see also* Dacryoadenitis) 375.00
  lacunar 597.0
  larynx 478.79
  lateral (alveolar) 522.5
    with sinus 522.7
  leg, except foot 682.6
  lens 360.00
  lid 373.13
  lingual 529.0
    tonsil 475
  lip 528.5
  Littre's gland 597.0

Abscess *(Continued)*
  liver 572.0
    amebic 006.3
      with
        brain abscess (and lung abscess) 006.5
        lung abscess 006.4
      due to Entamoeba histolytica 006.3
    dysenteric *(see also* Abscess, liver, amebic) 006.3
    pyogenic 572.0
    tropical *(see also* Abscess, liver, amebic) 006.3
  loin (region) 682.2
  lumbar (tuberculous) *(see also* Tuberculosis) 015.0 *[730.88]*
    nontuberculous 682.2
  lung (miliary) (putrid) 513.0
    amebic (with liver abscess) 006.4
      with brain abscess 006.5
  lymph, lymphatic, gland or node (acute) 683
    any site, except mesenteric 683
    mesentery 289.2
  lymphangitic, acute - *see* Cellulitis
  malar 526.4
  mammary gland - *see* Abscess, breast
  marginal (anus) 566
  mastoid (process) *(see also* Mastoiditis, acute) 383.00
    subperiosteal 383.01
  maxilla, maxillary 526.4
    molar (tooth) 522.5
      with sinus 522.7
    premolar 522.5
    sinus (chronic) *(see also* Sinusitis, maxillary) 473.0
  mediastinum 513.1
  meibomian gland 373.12
  meninges *(see also* Meningitis) 320.9
  mesentery, mesenteric - *see* Abscess, peritoneum
  mesosalpinx *(see also* Salpingo-oophoritis) 614.2
  milk 675.1
  Monro's (psoriasis) 696.1
  mons pubis 682.2
  mouth (floor) 528.3
  multiple sites NEC 682.9
  mural 682.2
  muscle 728.89
  myocardium 422.92
  nabothian (follicle) *(see also* Cervicitis) 616.0
  nail (chronic) (with lymphangitis) 681.9
    finger 681.02
    toe 681.11
  nasal (fossa) (septum) 478.1
    sinus (chronic) *(see also* Sinusitis) 473.9
  nasopharyngeal 478.29
  nates 682.5
  navel 682.2
    newborn NEC 771.4
  neck (region) 682.1
    lymph gland or node 683
  nephritic *(see also* Abscess, kidney) 590.2
  nipple 611.0
    puerperal, postpartum 675.0
  nose (septum) 478.1
    external 682.0
  omentum - *see* Abscess, peritoneum
  operative wound 998.59
  orbit, orbital 376.01

ICD-9-CM

A

Vol. 2

Abscess (*Continued*)
 ossifluent - *see* Abscess, bone
 ovary, ovarian (corpus luteum) (*see also* Salpingo-oophoritis) 614.2
 oviduct (*see also* Salpingo-oophoritis) 614.2
 palate (soft) 528.3
  hard 526.4
 palmar (space) 682.4
 pancreas (duct) 577.0
 paradontal 523.3
 parafrenal 607.2
 parametric, parametrium (chronic) (*see also* Disease, pelvis, inflammatory) 614.4
  acute 614.3
 paranephric 590.2
 parapancreatic 577.0
 parapharyngeal 478.22
 pararectal 566
 parasinus (*see also* Sinusitis) 473.9
 parauterine (*see also* Disease, pelvis, inflammatory) 614.4
  acute 614.3
 paravaginal (*see also* Vaginitis) 616.10
 parietal region 682.8
 parodontal 523.3
 parotid (duct) (gland) 527.3
  region 528.3
 parumbilical 682.2
  newborn 771.4
 pectoral (region) 682.2
 pelvirectal - *see* Abscess, peritoneum
 pelvis, pelvic
  female (chronic) (*see also* Disease, pelvis, inflammatory) 614.4
   acute 614.3
  male, peritoneal (cellular tissue) - *see* Abscess, peritoneum
  tuberculous (*see also* Tuberculosis) 016.9
 penis 607.2
  gonococcal (acute) 098.0
   chronic or duration of 2 months or over 098.2
 perianal 566
 periapical 522.5
  with sinus (alveolar) 522.7
 periappendiceal 540.1
 pericardial 420.99
 pericecal 540.1
 pericemental 523.3
 pericholecystic (*see also* Cholecystitis, acute) 575.0
 pericoronal 523.3
 peridental 523.3
 perigastric 535.0
 perimetric (*see also* Disease, pelvis, inflammatory) 614.4
  acute 614.3
 perinephric, perinephritic (*see also* Abscess, kidney) 590.2
 perineum, perineal (superficial) 682.2
  deep (with urethral involvement) 597.0
  urethra 597.0
 periodontal (parietal) 523.3
  apical 522.5
 periosteum, periosteal (*see also* Periostitis) 730.3
  with osteomyelitis (*see also* Osteomyelitis) 730.2
   acute or subacute 730.0
   chronic or old 730.1

Abscess (*Continued*)
 peripleuritic 510.9
  with fistula 510.0
 periproctic 566
 periprostatic 601.2
 perirectal (staphylococcal) 566
 perirenal (tissue) (*see also* Abscess, kidney) 590.2
 perisinuous (nose) (*see also* Sinusitis) 473.9
 peritoneum, peritoneal (perforated) (ruptured) 567.2
  with
   abortion - *see* Abortion, by type, with sepsis
   appendicitis 540.1
   ectopic pregnancy (*see also* categories 633.0-633.9) 639.0
   molar pregnancy (*see also* categories 630-632) 639.0
  following
   abortion 639.0
   ectopic or molar pregnancy 639.0
  pelvic, female (*see also* Disease, pelvis, inflammatory) 614.4
   acute 614.3
  postoperative 998.59
  puerperal, postpartum, childbirth 670
  tuberculous (*see also* Tuberculosis) 014.0
 peritonsillar 475
 perityphlic 540.1
 periureteral 593.89
 periurethral 597.0
  gonococcal (acute) 098.0
   chronic or duration of 2 months or over 098.2
 periuterine (*see also* Disease, pelvis, inflammatory) 614.4
  acute 614.3
 perivesical 595.89
 pernicious NEC 682.9
 petrous bone - *see* Petrositis
 phagedenic NEC 682.9
  chancroid 099.0
 pharynx, pharyngeal (lateral) 478.29
 phlegmonous NEC 682.9
 pilonidal 685.0
 pituitary (gland) 253.8
 pleura 510.9
  with fistula 510.0
 popliteal 682.6
 postanal 566
 postcecal 540.1
 postlaryngeal 478.79
 postnasal 478.1
 postpharyngeal 478.24
 posttonsillar 475
 posttyphoid 002.0
 Pott's (*see also* Tuberculosis) 015.0 [730.88]
 pouch of Douglas (chronic) (*see also* Disease, pelvis, inflammatory) 614.4
 premammary - *see* Abscess, breast
 prepatellar 682.6
 prostate (*see also* Prostatitis) 601.2
  gonococcal (acute) 098.12
   chronic or duration of 2 months or over 098.32
 psoas (tuberculous) (*see also* Tuberculosis) 015.0 [730.88]
  nontuberculous 728.89

Abscess (*Continued*)
 pterygopalatine fossa 682.8
 pubis 682.2
 puerperal - *see* Puerperal, abscess, by site
 pulmonary - *see* Abscess, lung
 pulp, pulpal (dental) 522.0
  finger 681.01
  toe 681.10
 pyemic - *see* Septicemia
 pyloric valve 535.0
 rectovaginal septum 569.5
 rectovesical 595.89
 rectum 566
 regional NEC 682.9
 renal (*see also* Abscess, kidney) 590.2
 retina 363.00
 retrobulbar 376.01
 retrocecal - *see* Abscess, peritoneum
 retrolaryngeal 478.79
 retromammary - *see* Abscess, breast
 retroperineal 682.2
 retroperitoneal - *see* Abscess, peritoneum
 retropharyngeal 478.24
  tuberculous (*see also* Tuberculosis) 012.8
 retrorectal 566
 retrouterine (*see also* Disease, pelvis, inflammatory) 614.4
  acute 614.3
 retrovesical 595.89
 root, tooth 522.5
  with sinus (alveolar) 522.7
 round ligament (*see also* Disease, pelvis, inflammatory) 614.4
  acute 614.3
 rupture (spontaneous) NEC 682.9
 sacrum (tuberculous) (*see also* Tuberculosis) 015.0 [730.88]
  nontuberculous 730.08
 salivary duct or gland 527.3
 scalp (any part) 682.8
 scapular 730.01
 sclera 379.09
 scrofulous (*see also* Tuberculosis) 017.2
 scrotum 608.4
 seminal vesicle 608.0
  amebic 006.8
 septal, dental 522.5
  with sinus (alveolar) 522.7
 septum (nasal) 478.1
 serous (*see also* Periostitis) 730.3
 shoulder 682.3
 side 682.2
 sigmoid 569.5
 sinus (accessory) (chronic) (nasal) (*see also* Sinusitis) 473.9
  intracranial venous (any) 324.0
   late effect - *see* category 326
 Skene's duct or gland 597.0
 skin NEC 682.9
  tuberculous (primary) (*see also* Tuberculosis) 017.0
 sloughing NEC 682.9
 specified site NEC 682.8
  amebic 006.8
 spermatic cord 608.4
 sphenoidal (sinus) (*see also* Sinusitis, sphenoidal) 473.3
 spinal
  cord (any part) (staphylococcal) 324.1
   tuberculous (*see also* Tuberculosis) 013.5
  epidural 324.1

Abscess *(Continued)*
spine (column) (tuberculous) *(see also* Tuberculosis) 015.0 *[730.88]*
  nontuberculous 730.08
spleen 289.59
  amebic 006.8
staphylococcal NEC 682.9
stitch 998.59
stomach (wall) 535.0
strumous (tuberculous) *(see also* Tuberculosis) 017.2
subarachnoid 324.9
  brain 324.0
  cerebral 324.0
  late effect - *see* category 326
  spinal cord 324.1
subareolar - *see also* Abscess, breast
  puerperal, postpartum 675.1
subcecal 540.1
subcutaneous NEC 682.9
subdiaphragmatic - *see* Abscess, peritoneum
subdorsal 682.2
subdural 324.9
  brain 324.0
  late effect - *see* category 326
  spinal cord 324.1
subgaleal 682.8
subhepatic - *see* Abscess, peritoneum
sublingual 528.3
  gland 527.3
submammary - *see* Abscess, breast
submandibular (region) (space) (triangle) 682.0
  gland 527.3
submaxillary (region) 682.0
  gland 527.3
submental (pyogenic) 682.0
  gland 527.3
subpectoral 682.2
subperiosteal - *see* Abscess, bone
subperitoneal - *see* Abscess, peritoneum
subphrenic - *see also* Abscess, peritoneum
  postoperative 998.59
subscapular 682.2
subungual 681.9
suburethral 597.0
sudoriparous 705.89
suppurative NEC 682.9
supraclavicular (fossa) 682.3
suprahepatic - *see* Abscess, peritoneum
suprapelvic *(see also* Disease, pelvis, inflammatory) 614.4
  acute 614.3
suprapubic 682.2
suprarenal (capsule) (gland) 255.8
sweat gland 705.89
syphilitic 095.8
teeth, tooth (root) 522.5
  with sinus (alveolar) 522.7
  supporting structures NEC 523.3
temple 682.0
temporal region 682.0
temporosphenoidal 324.0
  late effect - *see* category 326
tendon (sheath) 727.89
testicle - *see* Orchitis
thecal 728.89
thigh (acquired) 682.6
thorax 510.9
  with fistula 510.0
throat 478.29
thumb (intrathecal) (periosteal) (subcutaneous) (subcuticular) 681.00

Abscess *(Continued)*
thymus (gland) 254.1
thyroid (gland) 245.0
toe (any) (intrathecal) (periosteal) (subcutaneous) (subcuticular) 681.10
tongue (staphylococcal) 529.0
tonsil(s) (lingual) 475
tonsillopharyngeal 475
tooth, teeth (root) 522.5
  with sinus (alveolar) 522.7
  supporting structure NEC 523.3
trachea 478.9
trunk 682.2
tubal *(see also* Salpingo-oophoritis) 614.2
tuberculous - *see* Tuberculosis, abscess
tubo-ovarian *(see also* Salpingo-oophoritis) 614.2
tunica vaginalis 608.4
umbilicus NEC 682.2
  newborn 771.4
upper arm 682.3
upper respiratory 478.9
urachus 682.2
urethra (gland) 597.0
urinary 597.0
uterus, uterine (wall) *(see also* Endometritis) 615.9
  ligament *(see also* Disease, pelvis, inflammatory) 614.4
    acute 614.3
  neck *(see also* Cervicitis) 616.0
uvula 528.3
vagina (wall) *(see also* Vaginitis) 616.10
vaginorectal *(see also* Vaginitis) 616.10
vas deferens 608.4
vermiform appendix 540.1
vertebra (column) (tuberculous) *(see also* Tuberculosis) 015.0 *[730.88]*
  nontuberculous 730.0
vesical 595.89
vesicouterine pouch *(see also* Disease, pelvis, inflammatory) 614.4
vitreous (humor) (pneumococcal) 360.04
vocal cord 478.5
von Bezold's 383.01
vulva 616.4
  complicating pregnancy, childbirth, or puerperium 646.6
vulvovaginal gland *(see also* Vaginitis) 616.3
web-space 682.4
wrist 682.4
Absence (organ or part) (complete or partial)
acoustic nerve 742.8
adrenal (gland) (congenital) 759.1
  acquired 255.8
albumin (blood) 273.8
alimentary tract (complete) (congenital) (partial) 751.8
  lower 751.5
  upper 750.8
alpha-fucosidase 271.8
alveolar process (acquired) 525.8
  congenital 750.26
anus, anal (canal) (congenital) 751.2
aorta (congenital) 747.22
aortic valve (congenital) 746.89
appendix, congenital 751.2

Absence *(Continued)*
arm (acquired) V49.60
  above elbow V49.66
  below elbow V49.65
  congenital *(see also* Deformity, reduction, upper limb) 755.20
    lower - *see* Absence, forearm, congenital
    upper (complete) (partial) (with absence of distal elements, incomplete) 755.24
    with
      complete absence of distal elements 755.21
      forearm (incomplete) 755.23
artery (congenital) (peripheral) NEC *(see also* Anomaly, peripheral vascular system) 747.60
  brain 747.81
  cerebral 747.81
  coronary 746.85
  pulmonary 747.3
  umbilical 747.5
atrial septum 745.69
auditory canal (congenital) (external) 744.01
auricle (ear) (with stenosis or atresia of auditory canal), congenital 744.01
bile, biliary duct (common) or passage (congenital) 751.61
bladder (acquired) 596.8
  congenital 753.8
bone (congenital) NEC 756.9
  marrow 284.9
    acquired (secondary) 284.8
    congenital 284.0
    hereditary 284.0
    idiopathic 284.9
  skull 756.0
bowel sounds 787.5
brain 740.0
  specified part 742.2
breast(s) (acquired) V45.71
  congenital 757.6
broad ligament (congenital) 752.19
bronchus (congenital) 748.3
calvarium, calvaria (skull) 756.0
canaliculus lacrimalis, congenital 743.65
carpal(s) (congenital) (complete) (partial) (with absence of distal elements, incomplete) *(see also* Deformity, reduction, upper limb) 755.28
  with complete absence of distal elements 755.21
cartilage 756.9
caudal spine 756.13
cecum (acquired) (postoperative) (posttraumatic) V45.72
  congenital 751.2
cementum 520.4
cerebellum (congenital) (vermis) 742.2
cervix (acquired) (uteri) 622.8
  congenital 752.49
chin, congenital 744.89
cilia (congenital) 743.63
  acquired 374.89
circulatory system, part NEC 747.89
clavicle 755.51
clitoris (congenital) 752.49
coccyx, congenital 756.13

Absence (*Continued*)
cold sense (*see also* Disturbance, sensation) 782.0
colon (acquired) (postoperative) V45.72
  congenital 751.2
congenital
  lumen - *see* Atresia
  organ or site NEC - *see* Agenesis
  septum - *see* Imperfect, closure
corpus callosum (congenital) 742.2
cricoid cartilage 748.3
diaphragm (congenital) (with hernia) 756.6
  with obstruction 756.6
digestive organ(s) or tract, congenital (complete) (partial) 751.8
  lower 751.5
  upper 750.8
ductus arteriosus 747.89
duodenum (acquired) (postoperative) V45.72
  congenital 751.1
ear, congenital 744.09
  acquired 388.8
  auricle 744.01
  external 744.01
  inner 744.05
  lobe, lobule 744.21
  middle, except ossicles 744.03
    ossicles 744.04
  ossicles 744.04
ejaculatory duct (congenital) 752.8
endocrine gland NEC (congenital) 759.2
epididymis (congenital) 752.8
  acquired 608.89
epiglottis, congenital 748.3
epileptic (atonic) (typical) (*see also* Epilepsy) 345.0
erythrocyte 284.9
erythropoiesis 284.9
  congenital 284.0
esophagus (congenital) 750.3
eustachian tube (congenital) 744.24
extremity (acquired)
  congenital (*see also* Deformity, reduction) 755.4
  lower V49.70
  upper V49.60
extrinsic muscle, eye 743.69
eye (acquired) 360.89
  adnexa (congenital) 743.69
  congenital 743.00
  muscle (congenital) 743.69
eyelid (fold), congenital 743.62
  acquired 374.89
face
  bones NEC 756.0
  specified part NEC 744.89
fallopian tube(s) (acquired) 620.8
  congenital 752.19
femur, congenital (complete) (partial) (with absence of distal elements, incomplete) (*see also* Deformity, reduction, lower limb) 755.34
  with
    complete absence of distal elements 755.31
    tibia and fibula (incomplete) 755.33
fibrin 790.92
fibrinogen (congenital) 286.3
  acquired 286.6

Absence (*Continued*)
fibula, congenital (complete) (partial) (with absence of distal elements, incomplete) (*see also* Deformity, reduction, lower limb) 755.37
  with
    complete absence of distal elements 755.31
    tibia 755.35
     with
      complete absence of distal elements 755.31
      femur (incomplete) 755.33
       with complete absence of distal elements 755.31
finger (acquired) V49.62
  congenital (complete) (partial) (*see also* Deformity, reduction, upper limb) 755.29
  meaning all fingers (complete) (partial) 755.21
  transverse 755.21
fissures of lungs (congenital) 748.5
foot (acquired) V49.73
  congenital (complete) 755.31
forearm (acquired) V49.65
  congenital (complete) (partial) (with absence of distal elements, incomplete) (*see also* Deformity, reduction, upper limb) 755.25
  with
    complete absence of distal elements (hand and fingers) 755.21
    humerus (incomplete) 755.23
fovea centralis 743.55
fucosidase 271.8
gallbladder (acquired) V45.89
  congenital 751.69
gamma globulin (blood) 279.00
genital organs, congenital
  female 752.8
    external 752.49
    internal NEC 752.8
  male 752.8
    penis 752.69
genitourinary organs, congenital NEC 752.8
glottis 748.3
gonadal, congenital NEC 758.6
hair (congenital) 757.4
  acquired - *see* Alopecia
hand (acquired) V49.63
  congenital (complete) (*see also* Deformity, reduction, upper limb) 755.21
heart (congenital) 759.89
  acquired - *see* Status, organ replacement
heat sense (*see also* Disturbance, sensation) 782.0
humerus, congenital (complete) (partial) (with absence of distal elements, incomplete) (*see also* Deformity, reduction, upper limb) 755.24
  with
    complete absence of distal elements 755.21
    radius and ulna (incomplete) 755.23
hymen (congenital) 752.49
ileum (acquired) (postoperative) (posttraumatic) V45.72
  congenital 751.1

Absence (*Continued*)
immunoglobulin, isolated NEC 279.03
  IgA 279.01
  IgG 279.03
  IgM 279.02
incus (acquired) 385.24
  congenital 744.04
internal ear (congenital) 744.05
intestine (acquired) (small) V45.72
  congenital 751.1
  large 751.2
  large V45.72
    congenital 751.2
iris (congenital) 743.45
jaw - *see* Absence, mandible
jejunum (acquired) V45.72
  congenital 751.1
joint, congenital NEC 755.8
kidney(s) (acquired) V45.73
  congenital 753.0
labium (congenital) (majus) (minus) 752.49
labyrinth, membranous 744.05
lacrimal apparatus (congenital) 743.65
larynx (congenital) 748.3
leg (acquired) V49.70
  above knee V49.76
  below knee V49.75
  congenital (partial) (unilateral) (*see also* Deformity, reduction, lower limb) 755.31
  lower (complete) (partial) (with absence of distal elements, incomplete) 755.35
    with
      complete absence of distal elements (foot and toes) 755.31
      thigh (incomplete) 755.33
       with complete absence of distal elements 755.31
  upper - *see* Absence, femur
lens (congenital) 743.35
  acquired 379.31
ligament, broad (congenital) 752.19
limb (acquired)
  congenital (complete) (partial) (*see also* Deformity, reduction) 755.4
  lower 755.30
    complete 755.31
    incomplete 755.32
    longitudinal - *see* Deficiency, lower limb, longitudinal
    transverse 755.31
  upper 755.20
    complete 755.21
    incomplete 755.22
    longitudinal - *see* Deficiency, upper limb, longitudinal
    transverse 755.21
  lower NEC V49.70
  upper NEC V49.60
lip 750.26
liver (congenital) (lobe) 751.69
lumbar (congenital) (vertebra) 756.13
  isthmus 756.11
  pars articularis 756.11
lumen - *see* Atresia
lung (bilateral) (congenital) (fissure) (lobe) (unilateral) 748.5
  acquired (any part) 518.89
mandible (congenital) 524.09
maxilla (congenital) 524.09

Absence (*Continued*)
  menstruation 626.0
  metacarpal(s), congenital (complete)
    (partial) (with absence of distal elements, incomplete) (*see also* Deformity, reduction, upper limb) 755.28
    with all fingers, complete 755.21
  metatarsal(s), congenital (complete)
    (partial) (with absence of distal elements, incomplete) (*see also* Deformity, reduction, lower limb) 755.38
    with complete absence of distal elements 755.31
  muscle (congenital) (pectoral) 756.81
  ocular 743.69
  musculoskeletal system (congenital) NEC 756.9
  nail(s) (congenital) 757.5
  neck, part 744.89
  nerve 742.8
  nervous system, part NEC 742.8
  neutrophil 288.0
  nipple (congenital) 757.6
  nose (congenital) 748.1
    acquired 738.0
  nuclear 742.8
  ocular muscle (congenital) 743.69
  organ
    of Corti (congenital) 744.05
    or site, congenital NEC 759.89
  osseous meatus (ear) 744.03
  ovary (acquired) 620.8
    congenital 752.0
  oviduct (acquired) 620.8
    congenital 752.19
  pancreas (congenital) 751.7
    acquired (postoperative) (posttraumatic) 577.8
  parathyroid gland (congenital) 759.2
  parotid gland(s) (congenital) 750.21
  patella, congenital 755.64
  pelvic girdle (congenital) 755.69
  penis (congenital) 752.69
    acquired 607.89
  pericardium (congenital) 746.89
  perineal body (congenital) 756.81
  phalange(s), congenital 755.4
    lower limb (complete) (intercalary) (partial) (terminal) (*see also* Deformity, reduction, lower limb) 755.39
      meaning all toes (complete) (partial) 755.31
      transverse 755.31
    upper limb (complete) (intercalary) (partial) (terminal) (*see also* Deformity, reduction, upper limb) 755.29
      meaning all digits (complete) (partial) 755.21
      transverse 755.21
  pituitary gland (congenital) 759.2
  postoperative - *see* Absence, by site, acquired
  prostate (congenital) 752.8
    acquired 602.8
  pulmonary
    artery 747.3
    trunk 747.3
    valve (congenital) 746.01
    vein 747.49

Absence (*Continued*)
  punctum lacrimale (congenital) 743.65
  radius, congenital (complete) (partial) (with absence of distal elements, incomplete) 755.26
    with
      complete absence of distal elements 755.21
      ulna 755.25
        with
          complete absence of distal elements 755.21
          humerus (incomplete) 755.23
  ray, congenital 755.4
    lower limb (complete) (partial) (*see also* Deformity, reduction, lower limb) 755.38
      meaning all rays 755.31
      transverse 755.31
    upper limb (complete) (partial) (*see also* Deformity, reduction, upper limb) 755.28
      meaning all rays 755.21
      transverse 755.21
  rectum (congenital) 751.2
    acquired 569.49
  red cell 284.9
    acquired (secondary) 284.8
    congenital 284.0
    hereditary 284.0
    idiopathic 284.9
  respiratory organ (congenital) NEC 748.9
  rib (acquired) 738.3
    congenital 756.3
  roof of orbit (congenital) 742.0
  round ligament (congenital) 752.8
  sacrum, congenital 756.13
  salivary gland(s) (congenital) 750.21
  scapula 755.59
  scrotum, congenital 752.8
  seminal tract or duct (congenital) 752.8
    acquired 608.89
  septum (congenital) - *see also* Imperfect, closure, septum
    atrial 745.69
      and ventricular 745.7
    between aorta and pulmonary artery 745.0
    ventricular 745.3
      and atrial 745.7
  sex chromosomes 758.81
  shoulder girdle, congenital (complete) (partial) 755.59
  skin (congenital) 757.39
  skull bone 756.0
    with
      anencephalus 740.0
      encephalocele 742.0
      hydrocephalus 742.3
        with spina bifida (*see also* Spina bifida) 741.0
      microcephalus 742.1
  spermatic cord (congenital) 752.8
  spinal cord 742.59
  spine, congenital 756.13
  spleen (congenital) 759.0
    acquired 289.59
  sternum, congenital 756.3
  stomach (acquired) (partial) (postoperative) V45.89
    with postgastric surgery syndrome 564.2
    congenital 750.7

Absence (*Continued*)
  submaxillary gland(s) (congenital) 750.21
  superior vena cava (congenital) 747.49
  tarsal(s), congenital (complete) (partial) (with absence of distal elements, incomplete) (*see also* Deformity, reduction, lower limb) 755.38
  teeth, tooth (congenital) 520.0
    with abnormal spacing 524.3
    acquired 525.1
      with malocclusion 524.3
  tendon (congenital) 756.81
  testis (congenital) 752.8
    acquired 608.89
  thigh (acquired) 736.89
  thumb (acquired) V49.61
    congenital 755.29
  thymus gland (congenital) 759.2
  thyroid (gland) (surgical) 246.8
    with hypothyroidism 244.0
    cartilage, congenital 748.3
    congenital 243
  tibia, congenital (complete) (partial) (with absence of distal elements, incomplete) (*see also* Deformity, reduction, lower limb) 755.36
    with
      complete absence of distal elements 755.31
      fibula 755.35
        with
          complete absence of distal elements 755.31
          femur (incomplete) 755.33
            with complete absence of distal elements 755.31
  toe (acquired) V49.72
    congenital (complete) (partial) 755.39
      meaning all toes 755.31
      transverse 755.31
    great V49.71
  tongue (congenital) 750.11
  tooth, teeth (congenital) 520.0
    with abnormal spacing 524.3
    acquired 525.1
      with malocclusion 524.3
  trachea (cartilage) (congenital) (rings) 748.3
  transverse aortic arch (congenital) 747.21
  tricuspid valve 746.1
  ulna, congenital (complete) (partial) (with absence of distal elements, incomplete) (*see also* Deformity, reduction, upper limb) 755.27
    with
      complete absence of distal elements 755.21
      radius 755.25
        with
          complete absence of distal elements 755.21
          humerus (incomplete) 755.23
  umbilical artery (congenital) 747.5
  ureter (congenital) 753.4
    acquired 593.89
  urethra, congenital 753.8
  urinary system, part NEC 753.8
  uterus (acquired) 621.8
    congenital 752.3
  uvula (congenital) 750.26

◀▶   **New Code**   ⬅▥▥▥➡   **Revised Code**

Absence (*Continued*)
vagina, congenital 752.49
vas deferens (congenital) 752.8
  acquired 608.89
vein (congenital) (peripheral) NEC (*see also* Anomaly, peripheral vascular system) 747.60
  brain 747.81
  great 747.49
  portal 747.49
  pulmonary 747.49
vena cava (congenital) (inferior) (superior) 747.49
ventral horn cell 742.59
ventricular septum 745.3
vermis of cerebellum 742.2
vertebra, congenital 756.13
vulva, congenital 752.49
Absentia epileptica (*see also* Epilepsy) 345.0
Absinthemia (*see also* Dependence) 304.6
Absinthism (*see also* Dependence) 304.6
Absorbent system disease 459.89
Absorption
alcohol, through placenta or breast milk 760.71
antibiotics, through placenta or breast milk 760.74
anti-infective, through placenta or breast milk 760.74
chemical NEC 989.9
  specified chemical or substance - *see* Table of Drugs and Chemicals
  through placenta or breast milk (fetus or newborn) 760.70
    alcohol 760.71
    anti-infective agents 760.74
    cocaine 760.75
    "crack" 760.75
    diethylstilbestrol [DES] 760.76
    hallucinogenic agents 760.73
    medicinal agents NEC 760.79
    narcotics 760.72
    obstetric anesthetic or analgesic drug 763.5
    specified agent NEC 760.79
    suspected, affecting management of pregnancy 655.5
cocaine, through placenta or breast milk 760.75
drug NEC (*see also* Reaction, drug)
  through placenta or breast milk (fetus or newborn) 760.70
    alcohol 760.71
    anti-infective agents 760.74
    cocaine 760.75
    "crack" 760.75
    diethylstilbestrol (DES) 760.76
    hallucinogenic agents 760.73
    medicinal agents NEC 760.79
    narcotics 760.72
    obstetric anesthetic or analgesic drug 763.5
    specified agent NEC 760.79
    suspected, affecting management of pregnancy 655.5
fat, disturbance 579.8
hallucinogenic agents, through placenta or breast milk 760.73
immune sera, through placenta or breast milk 760.79
lactose defect 271.3

Absorption (*Continued*)
medicinal agents NEC, through placenta or breast milk 760.79
narcotics, through placenta or breast milk 760.72
noxious substance - *see* Absorption, chemical
protein, disturbance 579.8
pus or septic, general - *see* Septicemia
quinine, through placenta or breast milk 760.74
toxic substance - *see* Absorption, chemical
uremic - *see* Uremia
Abstinence symptoms or syndrome
alcohol 291.81
drug 292.0
Abt-Letterer-Siwe syndrome (acute histiocytosis X) (M9722/3) 202.5
Abulia 799.8
Abulomania 301.6
Abuse
adult 995.80
  emotional 995.82
  multiple forms 995.85
  neglect (nutritional) 995.84
  physical 995.81
  psychological 995.82
  sexual 995.83
alcohol (*see also* Alcoholism) 303.9
  nondependent 305.0
child 995.50
  counseling
    perpetrator
      non-parent V62.83
      parent V61.22
    victim V61.21
  emotional 995.51
  multiple forms 995.59
  neglect (nutritional) 995.52
  physical 995.54
    shaken infant syndrome 995.55
  psychological 995.51
  sexual 995.53
drugs, nondependent 305.9

Note	Use the following fifth-digit subclassification with the following codes: 305.0, 305.2-305.9:
0	unspecified
1	continuous
2	episodic
3	in remission

amphetamine type 305.7
antidepressants 305.8
barbiturates 305.4
caffeine 305.9
cannabis 305.2
cocaine type 305.6
hallucinogens 305.3
hashish 305.2
LSD 305.3
marijuana 305.2
mixed 305.9
morphine type 305.5
opioid type 305.5
phencyclidine (PCP) 305.9
specified NEC 305.9
tranquilizers 305.4
spouse 995.80
tobacco 305.1

Acalcerosis 275.40
Acalcicosis 275.40
Acalculia 784.69
developmental 315.1
Acanthocheilonemiasis 125.4
Acanthocytosis 272.5
Acanthokeratodermia 701.1
Acantholysis 701.8
bullosa 757.39
Acanthoma (benign) (M8070/0) - *see also* Neoplasm, by site, benign
malignant (M8070/3) - *see* Neoplasm, by site, malignant
Acanthosis (acquired) (nigricans) 701.2
adult 701.2
benign (congenital) 757.39
congenital 757.39
glycogenic
  esophagus 530.89
juvenile 701.2
tongue 529.8
Acanthrocytosis 272.5
Acapnia 276.3
Acarbia 276.2
Acardia 759.89
Acardiacus amorphus 759.89
Acardiotrophia 429.1
Acardius 759.89
Acariasis 133.9
sarcoptic 133.0
Acaridiasis 133.9
Acarinosis 133.9
Acariosis 133.9
Acarodermatitis 133.9
urticarioides 133.9
Acarophobia 300.29
Acatalasemia 277.8
Acatalasia 277.8
Acatamathesia 784.69
Acataphasia 784.5
Acathisia 781.0
due to drugs 333.99
Acceleration, accelerated
atrioventricular conduction 426.7
idioventricular rhythm 427.89
Accessory (congenital)
adrenal gland 759.1
anus 751.5
appendix 751.5
atrioventricular conduction 426.7
auditory ossicles 744.04
auricle (ear) 744.1
autosome(s) NEC 758.5
  21 or 22 758.0
biliary duct or passage 751.69
bladder 753.8
blood vessels (peripheral) (congenital) NEC (*see also* Anomaly, peripheral vascular system) 747.60
  cerebral 747.81
  coronary 746.85
bone NEC 756.9
  foot 755.67
breast tissue, axilla 757.6
carpal bones 755.56
cecum 751.5
cervix 752.49
chromosome(s) NEC 758.5
  13-15 758.1
  16-18 758.2
  21 or 22 758.0
  autosome(s) NEC 758.5
  D_1 758.1

Accessory *(Continued)*
  chromosome(s) NEC *(Continued)*
    E$_3$ 758.2
    G 758.0
    sex 758.81
  coronary artery 746.85
  cusp(s), heart valve NEC 746.89
    pulmonary 746.09
  cystic duct 751.69
  digits 755.0
  ear (auricle) (lobe) 744.1
  endocrine gland NEC 759.2
  external os 752.49
  eyelid 743.62
  eye muscle 743.69
  face bone(s) 756.0
  fallopian tube (fimbria) (ostium)
    752.19
  fingers 755.01
  foreskin 605
  frontonasal process 756.0
  gallbladder 751.69
  genital organ(s)
    female 752.8
      external 752.49
      internal NEC 752.8
    male NEC 752.8
      penis 752.69
  genitourinary organs NEC 752.8
  heart 746.89
    valve NEC 746.89
      pulmonary 746.09
  hepatic ducts 751.69
  hymen 752.49
  intestine (large) (small) 751.5
  kidney 753.3
  lacrimal canal 743.65
  leaflet, heart valve NEC 746.89
    pulmonary 746.09
  ligament, broad 752.19
  liver (duct) 751.69
  lobule (ear) 744.1
  lung (lobe) 748.69
  muscle 756.82
  navicular of carpus 755.56
  nervous system, part NEC 742.8
  nipple 757.6
  nose 748.1
  organ or site NEC - *see* Anomaly, spec-
    ified type NEC
  ovary 752.0
  oviduct 752.19
  pancreas 751.7
  parathyroid gland 759.2
  parotid gland (and duct) 750.22
  pituitary gland 759.2
  placental lobe - *see* Placenta, abnor-
    mal
  preauricular appendage 744.1
  prepuce 605
  renal arteries (multiple) 747.62
  rib 756.3
    cervical 756.2
  roots (teeth) 520.2
  salivary gland 750.22
  sesamoids 755.8
  sinus - *see* Condition
  skin tags 757.39
  spleen 759.0
  sternum 756.3
  submaxillary gland 750.22
  tarsal bones 755.67
  teeth, tooth 520.1
    causing crowding 524.3

Accessory *(Continued)*
  tendon 756.89
  thumb 755.01
  thymus gland 759.2
  thyroid gland 759.2
  toes 755.02
  tongue 750.13
  tragus 744.1
  ureter 753.4
  urethra 753.8
  urinary organ or tract NEC 753.8
  uterus 752.2
  vagina 752.49
  valve, heart NEC 746.89
    pulmonary 746.09
  vertebra 756.19
  vocal cords 748.3
  vulva 752.49
Accident, accidental - *see also* Condition
  birth NEC 767.9
  cardiovascular (*see also* Disease, cardio-
    vascular) 429.2
  cerebral (*see also* Disease, cerebrovascu-
    lar, acute) 436
  cerebrovascular (current) (CVA) (*see also*
    Disease, cerebrovascular, acute) 436
    healed or old V12.59
    impending 435.9
    late effect - *see* Late effect(s) (of)
      cerebrovascular disease
  coronary (*see also* Infarct, myocardium)
    410.9
  craniovascular (*see also* Disease, cere-
    brovascular, acute) 436
  during pregnancy, to mother, affecting
    fetus or newborn 760.5
  heart, cardiac (*see also* Infarct, myocar-
    dium) 410.9
  intrauterine 779.8
  vascular - *see* Disease, cerebrovascular,
    acute
Accommodation
  disorder of 367.51
    drug-induced 367.89
    toxic 367.89
  insufficiency of 367.4
  paralysis of 367.51
    hysterical 300.11
  spasm of 367.53
Accouchement - *see* Delivery
Accreta placenta (without hemorrhage)
  667.0
  with hemorrhage 666.0
Accretio cordis (nonrheumatic) 423.1
Accretions on teeth 523.6
Accumulation secretion, prostate 602.8
Acephalia, acephalism, acephaly 740.0
Acephalic 740.0
Acephalobrachia 759.89
Acephalocardia 759.89
Acephalocardius 759.89
Acephalochiria 759.89
Acephalochirus 759.89
Acephalogaster 759.89
Acephalostomus 759.89
Acephalothorax 759.89
Acephalus 740.0
Acetonemia 790.6
  diabetic 250.1
Acetonglycosuria 982.8
Acetonuria 791.6
Achalasia 530.0
  cardia 530.0
  digestive organs, congenital NEC 751.8

Achalasia *(Continued)*
  esophagus 530.0
  pelvirectal 751.3
  psychogenic 306.4
  pylorus 750.5
  sphincteral NEC 564.89
Achard-Thiers syndrome (adrenogenital)
  255.2
Ache(s) - *see* Pain
Acheilia 750.26
Acheiria 755.21
Achilloburitis 726.71
Achillodynia 726.71
Achlorhydria, achlorhydric 536.0
  anemia 280.9
  diarrhea 536.0
  neurogenic 536.0
  postvagotomy 564.2
  psychogenic 306.4
  secondary to vagotomy 564.2
Achroroblepsia 368.52
Achloropsia 368.52
Acholia 575.8
Acholuric jaundice (familial) (splenome-
  galic) (*see also* Spherocytosis) 282.0
  acquired 283.9
Achondroplasia 756.4
Achrestic anemia 281.8
Achroacytosis, lacrimal gland 375.00
  tuberculous (*see also* Tuberculosis)
    017.3
Achroma, cutis 709.00
Achromate (congenital) 368.54
Achromatopia 368.54
Achromatopsia (congenital) 368.54
Achromia
  congenital 270.2
  parasitica 111.0
  unguium 703.8
Achylia
  gastrica 536.8
    neurogenic 536.3
    psychogenic 306.4
  pancreatica 577.1
Achylosis 536.8
Acid
  burn - *see also* Burn, by site
    from swallowing acid - *see* Burn, in-
      ternal organs
  deficiency
    amide nicotinic 265.2
    amino 270.9
    ascorbic 267
    folic 266.2
    nicotinic (amide) 265.2
    pantothenic 266.2
  intoxication 276.2
  peptic disease 536.8
  stomach 536.8
    psychogenic 306.4
Acidemia 276.2
  arginosuccinic 270.6
  fetal
    before onset of labor, in
      liveborn infant 768.2
    during labor, in liveborn infant
      768.3
    intrauterine—*see* Distress fetal
    unspecified as to time of onset,
      in liveborn infant 768.4
  pipecolic 270.7
Acidity, gastric (high) (low) 536.8
  psychogenic 306.4
Acidocytopenia 288.0

Acidocytosis 288.3
Acidopenia 288.0
Acidosis 276.2
  diabetic 250.1
  fetal
    affecting management of
        pregnancy 656.8
    affecting newborn 770.8
  kidney tubular 588.8
  lactic 276.2
  metabolic NEC 276.2
    with respiratory acidosis 276.4
    late, of newborn 775.7
  renal
    hyperchloremic 588.8
    tubular (distal) (proximal) 588.8
  respiratory 276.2
    complicated by
        metabolic acidosis 276.4
        metabolic alkalosis 276.4
Aciduria 791.9
  arginosuccinic 270.6
  beta-aminoisobutyric (BAIB) 277.2
  glycolic 271.8
  organic 270.9
  orotic (congenital) (hereditary) (pyrimidine deficiency) 281.4
Acladiosis 111.8
  skin 111.8
Aclasis
  diaphyseal 756.4
  tarsoepiphyseal 756.59
Acleistocardia 745.5
Aclusion 524.4
Acmesthesia 782.0
Acne (pustular) (vulgaris) 706.1
  agminata (see also Tuberculosis) 017.0
  artificialis 706.1
  atrophica 706.0
  cachecticorum (Hebra) 706.1
  conglobata 706.1
  conjunctiva 706.1
  cystic 706.1
  decalvans 704.09
  erythematosa 695.3
  eyelid 706.1
  frontalis 706.0
  indurata 706.1
  keloid 706.1
  lupoid 706.0
  necrotic, necrotica 706.0
    miliaris 704.8
  nodular 706.1
  occupational 706.1
  papulosa 706.1
  rodens 706.0
  rosacea 695.3
  scorbutica 267
  scrofulosorum (Bazin) (see also Tuberculosis) 017.0
  summer 692.72
  tropical 706.1
  varioliformis 706.0
Acneiform drug eruptions 692.3
Acnitis (primary) (see also Tuberculosis) 017.0
Acomia 704.00
Acontractile bladder 344.61
Aconuresis (see also Incontinence) 788.30
Acosta's disease 993.2
Acousma 780.1
Acoustic - see Condition
Acousticophobia 300.29

Acquired - see Condition
Acquired immune deficiency syndrome - see Human immunodeficiency virus (disease) (illness) (infection)
Acquired immunodeficiency syndrome - see Human immunodeficiency virus (disease) (illness) (infection)
Acragnosis 781.9
Acrania 740.0
Acroagnosis 781.9
Acroasphyxia, chronic 443.89
Acrobrachycephaly 756.0
Acrobystiolith 608.89
Acrobystitis 607.2
Acrocephalopolysyndactyly 755.55
Acrocephalosyndactyly 755.55
Acrocephaly 756.0
Acrochondrohyperplasia 759.82
Acrocyanosis 443.89
  newborn 770.8
Acrodermatitis 686.8
  atrophicans (chronica) 701.8
  continua (Hallopeau) 696.1
  enteropathica 686.8
  Hallopeau's 696.1
  perstans 696.1
  pustulosa continua 696.1
  recalcitrant pustular 696.1
Acrodynia 985.0
Acrodysplasia 755.55
Acrohyperhidrosis 780.8
Acrokeratosis verruciformis 757.39
Acromastitis 611.0
Acromegaly, acromegalia (skin) 253.0
Acromelalgia 443.89
Acromicria, acromikria 756.59
Acronyx 703.0
Acropachy, thyroid (see also Thyrotoxicosis) 242.9
Acropachyderma 757.39
Acroparesthesia 443.89
  simple (Schultz's type) 443.89
  vasomotor (Nothnagel's type) 443.89
Acropathy thyroid (see also Thyrotoxicosis) 242.9
Acrophobia 300.29
Acroposthitis 607.2
Acroscleriasis (see also Scleroderma) 710.1
Acroscleroderma (see also Scleroderma) 710.1
Acrosclerosis (see also Scleroderma) 710.1
Acrosphacelus 785.4
Acrosphenosyndactylia 755.55
Acrospiroma, eccrine (M8402/0) - see Neoplasm, skin, benign
Acrostealgia 732.9
Acrosyndactyly (see also Syndactylism) 755.10
Acrotrophodynia 991.4
Actinic - see also Condition
  cheilitis (due to sun) 692.72
    chronic NEC 692.74
    due to radiation, except from sun 692.82
  conjunctivitis 370.24
  dermatitis (due to sun) (see also Dermatitis, actinic) 692.70
  due to
    roentgen rays or radioactive substance 692.82
    ultraviolet radiation, except from sun 692.82
    sun NEC 692.70
  elastosis solare 692.74

Actinic (Continued)
  granuloma 692.73
  keratitis 370.24
  ophthalmia 370.24
  reticuloid 692.73
Actinobacillosis, general 027.8
Actinobacillus
  lignieresii 027.8
  mallei 024
  muris 026.1
Actinocutitis NEC (see also Dermatitis, actinic) 692.70
Actinodermatitis NEC (see also Dermatitis, actinic) 692.70
Actinomyces
  israelii (infection) - see Actinomycosis
  muris-ratti (infection) 026.1
Actinomycosis, actinomycotic 039.9
  with
    pneumonia 039.1
  abdominal 039.2
  cervicofacial 039.3
  cutaneous 039.0
  pulmonary 039.1
  specified site NEC 039.8
  thoracic 039.1
Actinoneuritis 357.8
Action, heart
  disorder 427.9
    postoperative 997.1
  irregular 427.9
    postoperative 997.1
  psychogenic 306.2
Active - see Condition
Activity decrease, functional 780.9
Acute - see also Condition
  abdomen NEC 789.0
  gallbladder (see also Cholecystitis, acute) 575.0
Acyanoblepsia 368.53
Acyanopsia 368.53
Acystia 753.8
Acystinervia - see Neurogenic, bladder
Acystineuria - see Neurogenic, bladder
Adactylia, adactyly (congenital) 755.4
  lower limb (complete) (intercalary) (partial) (terminal) (see also Deformity, reduction, lower limb) 755.39
    meaning all digits (complete) (partial) 755.31
    transverse (complete) (partial) 755.31
  upper limb (complete) (intercalary) (partial) (terminal) (see also Deformity, reduction, upper limb) 755.29
    meaning all digits (complete) (partial) 755.21
    transverse (complete) (partial) 755.21
Adair-Dighton syndrome (brittle bones and blue sclera, deafness) 756.51
Adamantinoblastoma (M9310/0) - see Ameloblastoma
Adamantinoma (M9310/0) - see Ameloblastoma
Adamantoblastoma (M9310/0) - see Ameloblastoma
Adams-Stokes (-Morgagni) disease or syndrome (syncope with heart block) 426.9
Adaptation reaction (see also Reaction, adjustment) 309.9
Addiction - see also Dependence
  absinthe 304.6

ICD-9-CM
A
Vol. 2

Addiction *(Continued)*
  alcoholic (ethyl) (methyl) (wood) 303.9
    complicating pregnancy, childbirth,
        or puerperium 648.4
      affecting fetus or newborn 760.71
      suspected damage to fetus affecting
        management of pregnancy
        655.4
  drug *(see also* Dependence) 304.9
  ethyl alcohol 303.9
  heroin 304.0
  hospital 301.51
  methyl alcohol 303.9
  methylated spirit 303.9
  morphine (-like substances) 304.0
  nicotine 305.1
  opium 304.0
  tobacco 305.1
  wine 303.9
Addison's
  anemia (pernicious) 281.0
  disease (bronze) (primary adrenal in-
      sufficiency) 255.4
    tuberculous *(see also* Tuberculosis)
      017.6
  keloid (morphea) 701.0
  melanoderma (adrenal cortical hypo-
      function) 255.4
Addison-Biermer anemia (pernicious)
    281.0
Addison-Gull disease - *see* Xanthoma
Addisonian crisis or melanosis (acute
    adrenocortical insufficiency) 255.4
Additional - *see also* Accessory
  chromosome(s) 758.5
    13-15 758.1
    16-18 758.2
    21 758.0
    autosome(s) NEC 758.5
    sex 758.81
**Adduction contracture, hip or other
    joint** - *see* Contraction, joint
Adenasthenia gastrica 536.0
Aden fever 061
Adenitis *(see also* Lymphadenitis) 289.3
  acute, unspecified site 683
    epidemic infectious 075
  axillary 289.3
    acute 683
    chronic or subacute 289.1
  Bartholin's gland 616.8
  bulbourethral gland *(see also* Urethritis)
      597.89
  cervical 289.3
    acute 683
    chronic or subacute 289.1
  chancroid (Ducrey's bacillus) 099.0
  chronic (any lymph node, except mes-
      enteric) 289.1
    mesenteric 289.2
  Cowper's gland *(see also* Urethritis)
      597.89
  epidemic, acute 075
  gangrenous 683
  gonorrheal NEC 098.89
  groin 289.3
    acute 683
    chronic or subacute 289.1
  infectious 075
  inguinal (region) 289.3
    acute 683
    chronic or subacute 289.1
  lymph gland or node, except mesen-
      teric 289.3

Adenitis *(Continued)*
  lymph gland or node *(Continued)*
    acute 683
    chronic or subacute 289.1
    mesenteric (acute) (chronic) (nonspe-
        cific) (subacute) 289.2
  mesenteric (acute) (chronic) (nonspe-
      cific) (subacute) 289.2
    due to Pasteurella multocida (P. sep-
        tica) 027.2
  parotid gland (suppurative) 527.2
  phlegmonous 683
  salivary duct or gland (any) (recur-
      ring) (suppurative) 527.2
  scrofulous *(see also* Tuberculosis)
      017.2
  septic 289.3
  Skene's duct or gland *(see also* Urethri-
      tis) 597.89
  strumous, tuberculous *(see also* Tuber-
      culosis) 017.2
  subacute, unspecified site 289.1
  sublingual gland (suppurative) 527.2
  submandibular gland (suppurative)
      527.2
  submaxillary gland (suppurative)
      527.2
  suppurative 683
  tuberculous - *see* Tuberculosis, lymph
      gland
  urethral gland *(see also* Urethritis)
      597.89
  venereal NEC 099.8
  Wharton's duct (suppurative) 527.2
Adenoacanthoma (M8570/3) - *see* Neo-
    plasm, by site, malignant
Adenoameloblastoma (M9300/0) 213.1
  upper jaw (bone) 213.0
Adenocarcinoma (M8140/3) - *see also*
    Neoplasm, by site, malignant

Note   The list of adjectival modifiers
below is not exhaustive. A description of adenocarcinoma that does not
appear in this list should be coded in
the same manner as carcinoma with
that description. Thus, "mixed acidophil-basophil adenocarcinoma"
should be coded in the same manner
as "mixed acidophil-basophil carcinoma," which appears in the list under "Carcinoma."

Except where otherwise indicated, the
morphological varieties of adenocarcinoma in the list below should be
coded by site as for "Neoplasm, malignant."

  with
    apocrine metaplasia (M8573/3)
    cartilaginous (and osseous) metapla-
        sia (M8571/3)
    osseous (and cartilaginous) metapla-
        sia (M8571/3)
    spindle cell metaplasia (M8572/3)
    squamous metaplasia (M8570/3)
  acidophil (M8280/3)
    specified site - *see* Neoplasm, by site,
        malignant
    unspecified site 194.3
  acinar (M8550/3)
  acinic cell (M8550/3)
  adrenal cortical (M8370/3) 194.0

Adenocarcinoma *(Continued)*
  alveolar (M8251/3)
    and
      epidermoid carcinoma, mixed
          (M8560/3)
      squamous cell carcinoma, mixed
          (M8560/3)
  apocrine (M8401/3)
    breast - *see* Neoplasm, breast, malig-
        nant
    specified site NEC - *see* Neoplasm,
        skin, malignant
    unspecified site 173.9
  basophil (M8300/3)
    specified site - *see* Neoplasm, by site,
        malignant
    unspecified site 194.3
  bile duct type (M8160/3)
    liver 155.1
    specified site NEC - *see* Neoplasm,
        by site, malignant
    unspecified site 155.1
  bronchiolar (M8250/3) - *see* Neoplasm,
      lung, malignant
  ceruminous (M8420/3) 173.2
  chromophobe (M8270/3)
    specified site - *see* Neoplasm, by site,
        malignant
    unspecified site 194.3
  clear cell (mesonephroid type)
      (M8310/3)
  colloid (M8480/3)
  cylindroid type (M8200/3)
  diffuse type (M8145/3)
    specified site - *see* Neoplasm, by site,
        malignant
    unspecified site 151.9
  duct (infiltrating) (M8500/3)
    with Paget's disease (M8541/3) - *see*
        Neoplasm, breast, malignant
    specified site - *see* Neoplasm, by site,
        malignant
    unspecified site 174.9
  embryonal (M9070/3)
  endometrioid (M8380/3) - *see* Neo-
      plasm, by site, malignant
  eosinophil (M8280/3)
    specified site - *see* Neoplasm, by site,
        malignant
    unspecified site 194.3
  follicular (M8330/3)
    and papillary (M8340/3) 193
    moderately differentiated type
        (M8332/3) 193
    pure follicle type (M8331/3) 193
    specified site - *see* Neoplasm, by site,
        malignant
    trabecular type (M8332/3) 193
    unspecified type 193
    well differentiated type (M8331/3)
        193
  gelatinous (M8480/3)
  granular cell (M8320/3)
  Hürthle cell (M8290/3) 193
  in
    adenomatous
      polyp (M8210/3)
      polyposis coli (M8220/3) 153.9
    polypoid adenoma (M8210/3)
    tubular adenoma (M8210/3)
    villous adenoma (M8261/3)
  infiltrating duct (M8500/3)
    with Paget's disease (M8541/3) - *see*
        Neoplasm, breast, malignant

ICD-9-CM

A

Vol. 2

Adenocarcinoma *(Continued)*
  infiltrating duct *(Continued)*
    specified site - *see* Neoplasm, by site,
      malignant
    unspecified site 174.9
    inflammatory (M8530/3)
      specified site - *see* Neoplasm, by site,
        malignant
      unspecified site 174.9
    in situ (M8140/2) - *see* Neoplasm, by
      site, in situ
    intestinal type (M8144/3)
      specified site - *see* Neoplasm, by site,
        malignant
      unspecified site 151.9
    intraductal (noninfiltrating) (M8500/2)
      papillary (M8503/2)
        specified site - *see* Neoplasm, by
          site, in situ
        unspecified site 233.0
      specified site - *see* Neoplasm, by site,
        in situ
      unspecified site 233.0
    islet cell (M8150/3)
      and exocrine, mixed (M8154/3)
        specified site - *see* Neoplasm, by
          site, malignant
        unspecified site 157.9
      pancreas 157.4
      specified site NEC - *see* Neoplasm,
        by site, malignant
      unspecified site 157.4
    lobular (M8520/3)
      specified site - *see* Neoplasm, by site,
        malignant
      unspecified site 174.9
    medullary (M8510/3)
    mesonephric (M9110/3)
    mixed cell (M8323/3)
    mucinous (M8480/3)
    mucin-producing (M8481/3)
    mucoid (M8480/3) - *see also* Neoplasm,
      by site, malignant
      cell (M8300/3)
        specified site - *see* Neoplasm, by
          site, malignant
        unspecified site 194.3
    nonencapsulated sclerosing (M8350/3)
      193
    oncocytic (M8290/3)
    oxyphilic (M8290/3)
    papillary (M8260/3)
      and follicular (M8340/3) 193
      intraductal (noninfiltrating) (M8503/
        2)
        specified site - *see* Neoplasm, by
          site, in situ
        unspecified site 233.0
      serous (M8460/3)
        specified site - *see* Neoplasm, by
          site, malignant
        unspecified site 183.0
    papillocystic (M8450/3)
      specified site - *see* Neoplasm, by site,
        malignant
      unspecified site 183.0
    pseudomucinous (M8470/3)
      specified site - *see* Neoplasm, by site,
        malignant
      unspecified site 183.0
    renal cell (M8312/3) 189.0
    sebaceous (M8410/3)
    serous (M8441/3) - *see also* Neoplasm,
      by site, malignant

Adenocarcinoma *(Continued)*
  serous *(Continued)*
    papillary
      specified site - *see* Neoplasm, by
        site, malignant
      unspecified site 183.0
    signet ring cell (M8490/3)
    superficial spreading (M8143/3)
    sweat gland (M8400/3) - *see* Neo-
      plasm, skin, malignant
    trabecular (M8190/3)
    tubular (M8211/3)
    villous (M8262/3)
    water-clear cell (M8322/3) 194.1
Adenofibroma (M9013/0)
  clear cell (M8313/0) - *see* Neoplasm,
    by site, benign
  endometrioid (M8381/0) 220
    borderline malignancy (M8381/1)
      236.2
    malignant (M8381/3) 183.0
  mucinous (M9015/0)
    specified site - *see* Neoplasm, by site,
      benign
    unspecified site 220
  prostate 600
  serous (M9014/0)
    specified site - *see* Neoplasm, by site,
      benign
    unspecified site 220
  specified site - *see* Neoplasm, by site,
    benign
  unspecified site 220
Adenofibrosis
  breast 610.2
  endometrioid 617.0
Adenoiditis 474.01
  acute 463
  chronic 474.01
    with chronic tonsillitis 474.02
Adenoids (congenital) (of nasal fossa)
  474.9
  hypertrophy 474.12
  vegetations 474.2
Adenolipomatosis (symmetrical)
  272.8
Adenolymphoma (M8561/0)
  specified site - *see* Neoplasm, by site,
    benign
  unspecified 210.2
Adenoma (sessile) (M8140/0) - *see also*
  Neoplasm, by site, benign

> Note   Except where otherwise indi-
> cated, the morphological varieties of
> adenoma in the list below should be
> coded by site as for "Neoplasm, be-
> nign."

  acidophil (M8280/0)
    specified site - *see* Neoplasm, by site,
      benign
    unspecified site 227.3
  acinar (cell) (M8550/0)
  acinic cell (M8550/0)
  adrenal (cortex) (cortical) (functioning)
    (M8370/0) 227.0
    clear cell type (M8373/0) 227.0
    compact cell type (M8371/0)
      227.0
    glomerulosa cell type (M8374/0)
      227.0
    heavily pigmented variant (M8372/
      0) 227.0
    mixed cell type (M8375/0) 227.0

Adenoma *(Continued)*
  alpha cell (M8152/0)
    pancreas 211.7
    specified site NEC - *see* Neoplasm,
      by site, benign
    unspecified site 211.7
  alveolar (M8251/0)
  apocrine (M8401/0)
    breast 217
    specified site NEC - *see* Neoplasm,
      skin, benign
    unspecified site 216.9
  basal cell (M8147/0)
  basophil (M8300/0)
    specified site - *see* Neoplasm, by site,
      benign
    unspecified site 227.3
  beta cell (M8151/0)
    pancreas 211.7
    specified site NEC - *see* Neoplasm,
      by site, benign
    unspecified site 211.7
  bile duct (M8160/0) 211.5
  black (M8372/0) 227.0
  bronchial (M8140/1) 235.7
    carcinoid type (M8240/3) - *see* Neo-
      plasm, lung, malignant
    cylindroid type (M8200/3) - *see*
      Neoplasm, lung, malignant
  ceruminous (M8420/0) 216.2
  chief cell (M8321/0) 227.1
  chromophobe (M8270/0)
    specified site - *see* Neoplasm, by site,
      benign
    unspecified site 227.3
  clear cell (M8310/0)
  colloid (M8334/0)
    specified site - *see* Neoplasm, by site,
      benign
    unspecified site 226
  cylindroid type, bronchus (M8200/3) -
    see Neoplasm, lung, malignant
  duct (M8503/0)
  embryonal (M8191/0)
  endocrine, multiple (M8360/1)
    single specified site - *see* Neoplasm,
      by site, uncertain behavior
    two or more specified sites 237.4
    unspecified site 237.4
  endometrioid (M8380/0) - *see also*
    Neoplasm, by site, benign
    borderline malignancy (M8380/1) -
      see Neoplasm, by site, uncertain
      behavior
  eosinophil (M8280/0)
    specified site - *see* Neoplasm, by site,
      benign
    unspecified site 227.3
  fetal (M8333/0)
    specified site - *see* Neoplasm, by site,
      benign
    unspecified site 226
  follicular (M8330/0)
    specified site - *see* Neoplasm, by site,
      benign
    unspecified site 226
  hepatocellular (M8170/0) 211.5
  Hürthle cell (M8290/0) 226
  intracystic papillary (M8504/0)
  islet cell (functioning) (M8150/0)
    pancreas 211.7
    specified site NEC - *see* Neoplasm,
      by site, benign
    unspecified site 211.7

◀▶   **New Code**   ⬅▮▮ ▮▮➡   **Revised Code**

Adenoma *(Continued)*
  liver cell (M8170/0) 211.5
  macrofollicular (M8334/0)
    specified site NEC - *see* Neoplasm,
      by site, benign
    unspecified site 226
  malignant, malignum (M8140/3) - *see*
    Neoplasm, by site,
    malignant
  mesonephric (M9110/0)
  microfollicular (M8333/0)
    specified site - *see* Neoplasm, by site,
      benign
    unspecified site 226
  mixed cell (M8323/0)
  monomorphic (M8146/0)
  mucinous (M8480/0)
  mucoid cell (M8300/0)
    specified site - *see* Neoplasm, by site,
      benign
    unspecified site 227.3
  multiple endocrine (M8360/1)
    single specified site - *see* Neoplasm,
      by site, uncertain behavior
    two or more specified sites
      237.4
    unspecified site 237.4
  nipple (M8506/0) 217
  oncocytic (M8290/0)
  oxyphilic (M8290/0)
  papillary (M8260/0) - *see also* Neo-
    plasm, by site, benign
    intracystic (M8504/0)
  papillotubular (M8263/0)
  Pick's tubular (M8640/0)
    specified site - *see* Neoplasm, by site,
      benign
    unspecified site
      female 220
      male 222.0
  pleomorphic (M8940/0)
  polypoid (M8210/0)
  prostate (benign) 600
  rete cell 222.0
  sebaceous, sebaceum (gland) (senile)
    (M8410/0) - *see also* Neoplasm,
    skin, benign
    disseminata 759.5
  Sertoli cell (M8640/0)
    specified site - *see* Neoplasm, by site,
      benign
    unspecified site
      female 220
      male 222.0
  skin appendage (M8390/0) - *see* Neo-
    plasm, skin, benign
  sudoriferous gland (M8400/0) - *see* Ne-
    oplasm, skin, benign
  sweat gland or duct (M8400/0) - *see*
    Neoplasm, skin, benign
  testicular (M8640/0)
    specified site - *see* Neoplasm, by site,
      benign
    unspecified site
      female 220
      male 222.0
  thyroid 226
  trabecular (M8190/0)
  tubular (M8211/0) - *see also* Neoplasm,
    by site, benign
    papillary (M8460/3)
    Pick's (M8640/0)
      specified site - *see* Neoplasm, by
        site, benign

Adenoma *(Continued)*
  tubular *(Continued)*
    Pick's *(Continued)*
      unspecified site
        female 220
        male 222.0
  tubulovillous (M8263/0)
  villoglandular (M8263/0)
  villous (M8261/1) - *see* Neoplasm, by
    site, uncertain behavior
  water-clear cell (M8322/0) 227.1
  wolffian duct (M9110/0)
Adenomatosis (M8220/0)
  endocrine (multiple) (M8360/1)
    single specified site - *see* Neoplasm,
      by site, uncertain behavior
    two or more specified sites 237.4
    unspecified site 237.4
  erosive of nipple (M8506/0) 217
  pluriendocrine - *see* Adenomatosis, en-
    docrine
  pulmonary (M8250/1) 235.7
    malignant (M8250/3) - *see* Neo-
      plasm, lung, malignant
  specified site - *see* Neoplasm, by site,
    benign
  unspecified site 211.3
Adenomatous
  cyst, thyroid (gland) - *see* Goiter, nod-
    ular
  goiter (nontoxic) (*see also* Goiter, nodu-
    lar) 241.9
    toxic or with hyperthyroidism 242.3
Adenomyoma (M8932/0) - *see also* Neoplasm, by site, benign
  prostate 600
Adenomyometritis 617.0
Adenomyosis (uterus) (internal) 617.0
Adenopathy (lymph gland) 785.6
  inguinal 785.6
  mediastinal 785.6
  mesentery 785.6
  syphilitic (secondary) 091.4
  tracheobronchial 785.6
    tuberculous (*see also* Tuberculosis)
      012.1
      primary, progressive 010.8
  tuberculous (*see also* Tuberculosis,
    lymph gland) 017.2
    tracheobronchial 012.1
      primary, progressive 010.8
Adenopharyngitis 462
Adenophlegmon 683
Adenosalpingitis 614.1
Adenosarcoma (M8960/3) 189.0
Adenosclerosis 289.3
Adenosis
  breast (sclerosing) 610.2
  vagina, congenital 752.49
Adentia (complete) (partial) (*see also* Absence, teeth) 520.0
Adherent
  labium (minus) 624.4
  pericardium (nonrheumatic) 423.1
    rheumatic 393
  placenta 667.0
    with hemorrhage 666.0
  prepuce 605
  scar (skin) NEC 709.2
  tendon in scar 709.2
Adhesion(s), adhesive (postinfectional)
  (postoperative)
  abdominal (wall) (*see also* Adhesions,
    peritoneum) 568.0

Adhesion(s) *(Continued)*
  amnion to fetus 658.8
    affecting fetus or newborn
      762.8
  appendix 543.9
  arachnoiditis - *see* Meningitis
  auditory tube (Eustachian) 381.89
  bands - *see also* Adhesions, perito-
    neum
    cervix 622.3
    uterus 621.5
  bile duct (any) 576.8
  bladder (sphincter) 596.8
  bowel (*see also* Adhesions, peritoneum)
    568.0
  cardiac 423.1
    rheumatic 398.99
  cecum (*see also* Adhesions, peritoneum)
    568.0
  cervicovaginal 622.3
    congenital 752.49
    postpartal 674.8
    old 622.3
  cervix 622.3
  clitoris 624.4
  colon (*see also* Adhesions, peritoneum)
    568.0
  common duct 576.8
  congenital - *see also* Anomaly, specified
    type NEC
    fingers (*see also* Syndactylism, fin-
      gers) 755.11
    labium (majus) (minus) 752.49
    omental, anomalous 751.4
    ovary 752.0
    peritoneal 751.4
    toes (*see also* Syndactylism, toes)
      755.13
    tongue (to gum or roof of mouth)
      750.12
  conjunctiva (acquired) (localized)
    372.62
    congenital 743.63
    extensive 372.63
  cornea - *see* Opacity, cornea
  cystic duct 575.8
  diaphragm (*see also* Adhesions, peri-
    toneum) 568.0
  due to foreign body - *see* Foreign
    body
  duodenum (*see also* Adhesions, peri-
    toneum) 568.0
    with obstruction 537.3
  ear, middle - *see* Adhesions, middle
    ear
  epididymis 608.89
  epidural - *see* Adhesions, meninges
  epiglottis 478.79
  Eustachian tube 381.89
  eyelid 374.46
    postoperative 997.99
      surgically created V45.69
  gallbladder (*see also* Disease, gallblad-
    der) 575.8
  globe 360.89
  heart 423.1
    rheumatic 398.99
  ileocecal (coil) (*see also* Adhesions,
    peritoneum) 568.0
  ileum (*see also* Adhesions, peritoneum)
    568.0
  intestine (postoperative) (*see also* Adhe-
    sions, peritoneum) 568.0
    with obstruction 560.81

◀▶ New Code　　⬅▬▬▶ Revised Code

◄ ►   **New Code**   ◄▦ ▦►   **Revised Code**

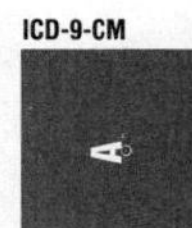

Admission *(Continued)*
  for *(Continued)*
    elective surgery *(Continued)*
      prophylactic organ removal V50.49
        breast V50.41
        ovary V50.42
      repair of scarred tissue (following healed injury or operation) V51
      specified type NEC V50.8
    end-of-life care V66.7
    examination *(see also Examination)* V70.9
      administrative purpose NEC V70.3
      adoption V70.3
      allergy V72.7
      at health care facility V70.0
      athletic team V70.3
      camp V70.3
      cardiovascular, preoperative V72.81
      clinical research investigation V70.7
      dental V72.2
      developmental testing (child) (infant) V20.2
      donor (potential) V70.8
      driver's license V70.3
      ear V72.1
      employment V70.5
      eye V72.0
      follow-up (routine) - *see* Examination, follow-up
      for admission to
        old age home V70.3
        school V70.3
      general V70.9
        specified reason NEC V70.8
      gynecological V72.3
      health supervision (child) (infant) V20.2
      hearing V72.1
      immigration V70.3
      insurance certification V70.3
      laboratory V72.6
      marriage license V70.3
      medical (general) *(see also Examination, medical)* V70.9
      medicolegal reasons V70.4
      naturalization V70.3
      pelvic (annual) (periodic) V72.3
      postpartum checkup V24.2
      pregnancy (possible) (unconfirmed) V72.4
      preoperative V72.84
        cardiovascular V72.81
        respiratory V72.82
        specified NEC V72.83
      prison V70.3
      psychiatric (general) V70.2
        requested by authority V70.1
      radiological NEC V72.5
      respiratory, preoperative V72.82
      school V70.3
      screening - *see* Screening
      skin hypersensitivity V72.7
      specified type NEC V72.85
      sport competition V70.3
      vision V72.0
      well baby and child care V20.2
    exercise therapy V57.1
    face-lift, cosmetic reason V50.1

Admission *(Continued)*
  for *(Continued)*
    fitting (of)
      artificial
        arm (complete) (partial) V52.0
        eye V52.2
        leg (complete) (partial) V52.1
      brain neuropacemaker V53.02
      breast V52.4
        implant V52.4
        prosthesis V52.4
      cardiac pacemaker V53.31
      catheter
        non-vascular V58.82
        vascular V58.81
      cerebral ventricle (communicating) shunt V53.01
      colostomy belt V55.2
      contact lenses V53.1
      cystostomy device V53.6
      dental prosthesis V52.3
      device NEC V53.9
        abdominal V53.5
        cerebral ventricle (communicating) shunt V53.01
        intrauterine contraceptive V25.1
        nervous system V53.09
        orthodontic V53.4
        prosthetic V52.9
          breast V52.4
          dental V52.3
          eye V52.2
        special senses V53.09
        substitution
          auditory V53.09
          nervous system V53.09
          visual V53.09
      diaphragm (contraceptive) V25.02
      hearing aid V53.2
      ileostomy device V55.2
      intestinal appliance or device NEC V53.5
      intrauterine contraceptive device V25.1
      neuropacemaker (brain) (peripheral nerve) (spinal cord) V53.02
      orthodontic device V53.4
      orthopedic (device) V53.7
        brace V53.7
        cast V53.7
        shoes V53.7
      pacemaker
        brain V53.02
        cardiac V53.31
        carotid sinus V53.39
        spinal cord V53.02
      prosthesis V52.9
        arm (complete) (partial) V52.0
        breast V52.4
        dental V52.3
        eye V52.2
        leg (complete) (partial) V52.1
        specified type NEC V52.8
      spectacles V53.1
      wheelchair V53.8
    follow-up examination (routine) (following) V67.9
      cancer chemotherapy V67.2
      chemotherapy V67.2
      high-risk medication NEC V67.51
      injury NEC V67.59
      psychiatric V67.3

Admission *(Continued)*
  for *(Continued)*
    follow-up examination (routine) (following) *(Continued)*
      psychotherapy V67.3
      radiotherapy V67.1
      surgery V67.0
      treatment (for) V67.9
        combined V67.6
        fracture V67.4
        involving high-risk medication NEC V67.51
        mental disorder V67.3
        specified NEC V67.59
    hair transplant, for cosmetic reason V50.0
    health advice, education, or instruction V65.4
    hospice care V66.7
    insertion (of)
      subdermal implantable contraceptive V25.5
    intrauterine device
      insertion V25.1
      management V25.42
    investigation to determine further disposition V63.8
    isolation V07.0
    issue of
      medical certificate NEC V68.0
      repeat prescription NEC V68.1
        contraceptive device NEC V25.49
    kidney dialysis V56.0
    mental health evaluation V70.2
      requested by authority V70.1
    nonmedical reason NEC V68.89
    nursing care evaluation V63.8
    observation (without need for further medical care) *(see also Observation)* V71.9
      accident V71.4
      alleged rape or seduction V71.5
      criminal assault V71.6
      following accident V71.4
        at work V71.3
      foreign body ingestion V71.8
      growth and development variations, childhood V21.0
      inflicted injury NEC V71.6
      ingestion of deleterious agent or foreign body V71.8
      injury V71.6
      malignant neoplasm V71.1
      mental disorder V71.09
      newborn - *see* Observation, suspected, condition, newborn
      rape V71.5
      specified NEC V71.8
      suspected disorder V71.9
        accident V71.4
          at work V71.3
        benign neoplasm V71.8
        cardiovascular V71.7
        heart V71.7
        inflicted injury NEC V71.6
        malignant neoplasm V71.1
        mental NEC V71.09
        specified condition NEC V71.8
        tuberculosis V71.2
      tuberculosis V71.2
    occupational therapy V57.21

Admission *(Continued)*
  for *(Continued)*
    organ transplant, donor - *see* Donor
    ovary, ovarian removal, prophylactic
        V50.42
    palliative care V66.7
    Papanicolaou smear, cervix V76.2
        for suspected malignant neoplasm
            V76.2
        no disease found V71.1
        routine, as part of gynecological
            examination V72.3
    passage of sounds or bougie in arti-
        ficial opening - *see* Attention to,
        artificial, opening
    paternity testing V70.4
    peritoneal dialysis V56.8
    physical therapy NEC V57.1
    plastic surgery
        cosmetic NEC V50.1
        following healed injury or opera-
            tion V51
    postmenopausal hormone replace-
        ment therapy V07.4
    postpartum observation
        immediately after delivery
            V24.0
        routine follow-up V24.2
    poststerilization (for restoration)
        V26.0
    procreative management V26.9
        specified type NEC V26.8
    prophylactic
        administration of
            antibiotics V07.39
            antitoxin, any V07.2
            antivenin V07.2
            chemotherapeutic agent NEC
                V07.39
            chemotherapy NEC V07.39
            diphtheria antitoxin V07.2
            fluoride V07.31
            gamma globulin V07.2
            immune sera (gamma globulin)
                V07.2
            RhoGAM V07.2
            tetanus antitoxin V07.2
        breathing exercises V57.0
        chemotherapy NEC V07.39
            fluoride V07.31
        measure V07.9
            specified type NEC V07.8
        organ removal V50.49
            breast V50.41
            ovary V50.42
    psychiatric examination (general)
        V70.2
        requested by authority V70.1
    radiation management V58.0
    radiotherapy V58.0
    reforming of artificial opening - *see*
        Attention to, artificial, opening
    rehabilitation V57.9
        multiple types V57.89
        occupational V57.21
        orthoptic V57.4
        orthotic V57.81
        physical NEC V57.1
        specified type NEC V57.89
        speech V57.3
        vocational V57.22
    removal of
        cardiac pacemaker V53.31
        cast (plaster) V54.8

Admission *(Continued)*
  for *(Continued)*
    removal of *(Continued)*
        catheter from artificial opening -
            see Attention to, artificial,
            opening
        cerebral ventricle (communicating)
            shunt V53.01
        cystostomy catheter V55.5
        device
            cerebral ventricle (communicat-
                ing) shunt V53.01
            fixation
                external V54.8
                internal V54.0
            intrauterine contraceptive
                V25.42
            traction, external V54.8
        dressing V58.3
        fixation device
            external V54.8
            internal V54.0
        intrauterine contraceptive device
            V25.42
        Kirschner wire V54.8
        neuropacemaker (brain) (peripheral
            nerve) (spinal cord) V53.02
        orthopedic fixation device
            external V54.8
            internal V54.0
        pacemaker device
            brain V53.02
            cardiac V53.31
            carotid sinus V53.39
            nervous system V53.02
        plaster cast V54.8
        plate (fracture) V54.0
        rod V54.0
        screw (fracture) V54.0
        splint, traction V54.8
        Steinmann pin V54.8
        subdermal implantable contracep-
            tive V25.43
        surgical dressing V58.3
        sutures V58.3
        traction device, external V54.8
        ureteral stent V53.6
    repair of scarred tissue (following
        healed injury or operation)
        V51
    reprogramming of cardiac pace-
        maker V53.31
    restoration of organ continuity
        (poststerilization) (tuboplasty)
        (vasoplasty) V26.0
    sensitivity test - *see also* Test, skin
        allergy NEC V72.7
        bacterial disease NEC V74.9
        Dick V74.8
        Kveim V82.8
        Mantoux V74.1
        mycotic infection NEC V75.4
        parasitic disease NEC V75.8
        Schick V74.3
        Schultz-Charlton V74.8
    social service (agency) referral or
        evaluation V63.8
    speech therapy V57.3
    sterilization V25.2
    suspected disorder (ruled out) (with-
        out need for further care) - *see*
        Observation
    terminal care V66.7
    tests only - *see* Test

Admission *(Continued)*
  for *(Continued)*
    therapy
        blood transfusion, without re-
            ported diagnosis V58.2
        breathing exercises V57.0
        chemotherapy V58.1
            prophylactic NEC V07.39
                fluoride V07.31
        dialysis (intermittent) (treatment)
            extracorporeal V56.0
            peritoneal V56.8
            renal V56.0
            specified type NEC V56.8
        exercise (remedial) NEC V57.1
            breathing V57.0
        long-term (current) drug use NEC
            V58.69
            antibiotics V58.62   ◀
            anticoagulant V58.61
        occupational V57.21
        orthoptic V57.4
        physical NEC V57.1
        radiation V58.0
        speech V57.3
        vocational V57.22
    toilet or cleaning
        of artificial opening - *see* Attention
            to, artificial, opening
        of non-vascular catheter V58.82
        of vascular catheter V58.81
    tubal ligation V25.2
    tuboplasty for previous sterilization
        V26.0
    vaccination, prophylactic (against)
        arthropod-borne virus, viral NEC
            V05.1
            disease NEC V05.1
            encephalitis V05.0
        Bacille Calmette Guérin (BCG) V03.2
        BCG V03.2
        chickenpox V05.4
        cholera alone V03.0
            with typhoid-paratyphoid (chol-
                era TAB) V06.0
        common cold V04.7
        dengue V05.1
        diphtheria alone V03.5
        diphtheria-tetanus-pertussis (DTP)
            V06.1
            with
                poliomyelitis (DTP + polio)
                    V06.3
                typhoid-paratyphoid (DTP +
                    TAB) V06.2
        diphtheria-tetanus [Td] without
            pertussis V06.5
        disease (single) NEC V05.9
            bacterial NEC V03.9
                specified type NEC V03.89
            combinations NEC V06.9
                specified type NEC V06.8
            specified type NEC V05.8
        encephalitis, viral, arthropod-
            borne V05.0
        Hemophilus influenzae, type B
            [Hib] V03.81
        hepatitis, viral V05.3
        immune sera (gamma globulin)
            V07.2
        influenza V04.8
            with
                Streptococcus pneumoniae
                    [pneumococcus] V06.6

Admission (*Continued*)
  for (*Continued*)
    vaccination, prophylactic (against)
        arthropod-borne virus, viral
          NEC (*Continued*)
        Leishmaniasis V05.2
        measles alone V04.2
        measles-mumps-rubella (MMR)
            V06.4
        mumps alone V04.6
          with measles and rubella
              (MMR) V06.4
        not done because of contraindica-
            tion V64.0
        pertussis alone V03.6
        plague V03.3
        poliomyelitis V04.0
          with diphtheria-tetanus-pertus-
              sis (DTP + polio) V06.3
        rabies V04.5
        rubella alone V04.3
          with measles and mumps
              (MMR) V06.4
        smallpox V04.1
        specified type NEC V05.8
        Streptococcus pneumoniae [pneu-
            mococcus] V03.82
          with
              influenza V06.6
        tetanus toxoid alone V03.7
          with diphtheria [Td] V06.5
              and pertussis (DTP) V06.1
        tuberculosis (BCG) V03.2
        tularemia V03.4
        typhoid alone V03.1
          with diphtheria-tetanus-pertus-
              sis (TAB + DTP) V06.2
        typhoid-paratyphoid alone (TAB)
            V03.1
        typhus V05.8
        varicella V05.4
        viral encephalitis, arthropod-borne
            V05.0
        viral hepatitis V05.3
        yellow fever V04.4
    vasectomy V25.2
    vasoplasty for previous sterilization
        V26.0
    vision examination V72.0
    vocational therapy V57.22
    waiting period for admission to
        other facility V63.2
      undergoing social agency investi-
          gation V63.8
    well baby and child care V20.2
    x-ray of chest
      for suspected tuberculosis V71.2
      routine V72.5
Adnexitis (suppurative) (*see also* Sal-
    pingo-oophoritis) 614.2
Adolescence NEC V21.2
Adoption
  agency referral V68.89
  examination V70.3
  held for V68.89
Adrenal gland - *see* condition
Adrenalism 255.9
  tuberculous (*see also* Tuberculosis) 017.6
Adrenalitis, adrenitis 255.8
  meningococcal hemorrhagic 036.3
Adrenarche, precocious 259.1
Adrenocortical syndrome 255.2
Adrenogenital syndrome (acquired)
    (congenital) 255.2

Adrenogenital syndrome (*Continued*)
  iatrogenic, fetus or newborn 760.79
Adventitious bursa - *see* Bursitis
Adynamia (episodica) (hereditary) (peri-
    odic) 359.3
Adynamic
  ileus or intestine (*see also* Ileus) 560.1
  ureter 753.22
Aeration lung, imperfect, newborn
    770.5
Aerobullosis 993.3
Aerocele - *see* Embolism, air
Aerodermectasia
  subcutaneous (traumatic) 958.7
    surgical 998.81
  surgical 998.81
Aerodontalgia 993.2
Aeroembolism 993.3
Aerogenes capsulatus infection (*see also*
    Gangrene, gas) 040.0
Aero-otitis media 993.0
Aerophagy, aerophagia 306.4
  psychogenic 306.4
Aerosinusitis 993.1
Aerotitis 993.0
Affection, affections - *see also* Disease
  sacroiliac (joint), old 724.6
  shoulder region NEC 726.2
Afibrinogenemia 286.3
  acquired 286.6
  congenital 286.3
  postpartum 666.3
African
  sleeping sickness 086.5
  tick fever 087.1
  trypanosomiasis 086.5
    Gambian 086.3
    Rhodesian 086.4
Aftercare V58.9
  artificial openings - *see* Attention to,
      artificial, opening
  blood transfusion without reported di-
      agnosis V58.2
  breathing exercise V57.0
  cardiac device V53.39
    defibrillator, automatic implantable
        V53.32
    pacemaker V53.31
      carotid sinus V53.39
  carotid sinus pacemaker V53.39
  cerebral ventricle (communicating)
      shunt V53.01
  chemotherapy session (adjunctive)
      (maintenance) V58.1
  defibrillator, automatic implantable
      cardiac V53.32
  exercise (remedial) (therapeutic) V57.1
    breathing V57.0
  extracorporeal dialysis (intermittent)
      (treatment) V56.0
  following surgery NEC V58.49
    wound closure, planned V58.41
  fracture V54.9
    removal of
        external fixation device V54.8
        internal fixation device V54.0
      specified care NEC V54.8
  gait training V57.1
    for use of artificial limb(s) V57.81
  involving
    dialysis (intermittent) (treatment)
        extracorporeal V56.0
        peritoneal V56.8
        renal V56.0

Aftercare (*Continued*)
  involving (*Continued*)
    gait training V57.1
      for use of artificial limb(s) V57.81
    orthoptic training V57.4
    orthotic training V57.81
    radiotherapy session V58.0
    removal of
        dressings V58.3
        fixation device
          external V54.8
          internal V54.0
        fracture plate V54.0
        pins V54.0
        plaster cast V54.8
        rods V54.0
        screws V54.0
        surgical dressings V58.3
        sutures V58.3
        traction device, external V54.8
    neuropacemaker (brain) (peripheral
        nerve) (spinal cord) V53.02
    occupational therapy V57.21
    orthodontic V58.5
    orthopedic V54.9
      change of external fixation or trac-
          tion device V54.8
      removal of fixation device
          external V54.8
          internal V54.0
      specified care NEC V54.8
    orthoptic training V57.4
    orthotic training V57.81
    pacemaker
      brain V53.02
      cardiac V53.31
      carotid sinus V53.39
      peripheral nerve V53.02
      spinal cord V53.02
    peritoneal dialysis (intermittent) (treat-
        ment) V56.8
    physical therapy NEC V57.1
      breathing exercises V57.0
    radiotherapy session V58.0
    rehabilitation procedure V57.9
      breathing exercises V57.0
      multiple types V57.89
      occupational V57.21
      orthoptic V57.4
      orthotic V57.81
      physical therapy NEC V57.1
      remedial exercises V57.1
      specified type NEC V57.89
      speech V57.3
      therapeutic exercises V57.1
      vocational V57.22
    renal dialysis (intermittent) (treatment)
        V56.0
    specified type NEC V58.89
      removal of non-vascular catheter
          V58.82
      removal of vascular catheter
          V58.81
    speech therapy V57.3
    vocational rehabilitation V57.22
After-cataract 366.50
  obscuring vision 366.53
  specified type, not obscuring vision
      366.52
Agalactia 676.4
Agammaglobulinemia 279.00
  with lymphopenia 279.2
  acquired (primary) (secondary) 279.06
  Bruton's X-linked 279.04

Agammaglobulinemia (*Continued*)
  infantile sex-linked (Bruton's) (congenital) 279.04
  Swiss-type 279.2
Aganglionosis (bowel) (colon) 751.3
Age (old) (*see also* Senile) 797
Agenesis - *see also* Absence, by site, congenital
  acoustic nerve 742.8
  adrenal (gland) 759.1
  alimentary tract (complete) (partial) NEC 751.8
    lower 751.2
    upper 750.8
  anus, anal (canal) 751.2
  aorta 747.22
  appendix 751.2
  arm (complete) (partial) (*see also* Deformity, reduction, upper limb) 755.20
  artery (peripheral) NEC (*see also* Anomaly, peripheral vascular system) 747.60
    brain 747.81
    coronary 746.85
    pulmonary 747.3
    umbilical 747.5
  auditory (canal) (external) 744.01
  auricle (ear) 744.01
  bile, biliary duct or passage 751.61
  bone NEC 756.9
  brain 740.0
    specified part 742.2
  breast 757.6
  bronchus 748.3
  canaliculus lacrimalis 743.65
  carpus NEC (*see also* Deformity, reduction, upper limb) 755.28
  cartilage 756.9
  cecum 751.2
  cerebellum 742.2
  cervix 752.49
  chin 744.89
  cilia 743.63
  circulatory system, part NEC 747.89
  clavicle 755.51
  clitoris 752.49
  coccyx 756.13
  colon 751.2
  corpus callosum 742.2
  cricoid cartilage 748.3
  diaphragm (with hernia) 756.6
  digestive organ(s) or tract (complete) (partial) NEC 751.8
    lower 751.2
    upper 750.8
  ductus arteriosus 747.89
  duodenum 751.1
  ear NEC 744.09
    auricle 744.01
    lobe 744.21
  ejaculatory duct 752.8
  endocrine (gland) NEC 759.2
  epiglottis 748.3
  esophagus 750.3
  Eustachian tube 744.24
  extrinsic muscle, eye 743.69
  eye 743.00
    adnexa 743.69
  eyelid (fold) 743.62
  face
    bones NEC 756.0
    specified part NEC 744.89

Agenesis (*Continued*)
  fallopian tube 752.19
  femur NEC (*see also* Absence, femur, congenital) 755.34
  fibula NEC (*see also* Absence, fibula, congenital) 755.37
  finger NEC (*see also* Absence, finger, congenital) 755.29
  foot (complete) (*see also* Deformity, reduction, lower limb) 755.31
  gallbladder 751.69
  gastric 750.8
  genitalia, genital (organ)
    female 752.8
      external 752.49
      internal NEC 752.8
    male 752.8
      penis 752.69
  glottis 748.3
  gonadal 758.6
  hair 757.4
  hand (complete) (*see also* Deformity, reduction, upper limb) 755.21
  heart 746.89
    valve NEC 746.89
      aortic 746.89
      mitral 746.89
      pulmonary 746.01
  hepatic 751.69
  humerus NEC (*see also* Absence, humerus, congenital) 755.24
  hymen 752.49
  ileum 751.1
  incus 744.04
  intestine (small) 751.1
    large 751.2
  iris (dilator fibers) 743.45
  jaw 524.09
  jejunum 751.1
  kidney(s) (partial) (unilateral) 753.0
  labium (majus) (minus) 752.49
  labyrinth, membranous 744.05
  lacrimal apparatus (congenital) 743.65
  larynx 748.3
  leg NEC (*see also* Deformity, reduction, lower limb) 755.30
  lens 743.35
  limb (complete) (partial) (*see also* Deformity, reduction) 755.4
    lower NEC 755.30
    upper 755.20
  lip 750.26
  liver 751.69
  lung (bilateral) (fissures) (lobe) (unilateral) 748.5
  mandible 524.09
  maxilla 524.09
  metacarpus NEC 755.28
  metatarsus NEC 755.38
  muscle (any) 756.81
  musculoskeletal system NEC 756.9
  nail(s) 757.5
  neck, part 744.89
  nerve 742.8
  nervous system, part NEC 742.8
  nipple 757.6
  nose 748.1
  nuclear 742.8
  organ
    of Corti 744.05
    or site not listed - *see* Anomaly, specified type NEC

Agenesis (*Continued*)
  osseous meatus (ear) 744.03
  ovary 752.0
  oviduct 752.19
  pancreas 751.7
  parathyroid (gland) 759.2
  patella 755.64
  pelvic girdle (complete) (partial) 755.69
  penis 752.69
  pericardium 746.89
  perineal body 756.81
  pituitary (gland) 759.2
  prostate 752.8
  pulmonary
    artery 747.3
    trunk 747.3
    vein 747.49
  punctum lacrimale 743.65
  radioulnar NEC (*see also* Absence, forearm, congenital) 755.25
  radius NEC (*see also* Absence, radius, congenital) 755.26
  rectum 751.2
  renal 753.0
  respiratory organ NEC 748.9
  rib 756.3
  roof of orbit 742.0
  round ligament 752.8
  sacrum 756.13
  salivary gland 750.21
  scapula 755.59
  scrotum 752.8
  seminal duct or tract 752.8
  septum
    atrial 745.69
    between aorta and pulmonary artery 745.0
    ventricular 745.3
  shoulder girdle (complete) (partial) 755.59
  skull (bone) 756.0
    with
      anencephalus 740.0
      encephalocele 742.0
      hydrocephalus 742.3
        with spina bifida (*see also* Spina bifida) 741.0
      microcephalus 742.1
  spermatic cord 752.8
  spinal cord 742.59
  spine 756.13
    lumbar 756.13
      isthmus 756.11
      pars articularis 756.11
  spleen 759.0
  sternum 756.3
  stomach 750.7
  tarsus NEC 755.38
  tendon 756.81
  testicular 752.8
  testis 752.8
  thymus (gland) 759.2
  thyroid (gland) 243
    cartilage 748.3
  tibia NEC (*see also* Absence, tibia, congenital) 755.36
  tibiofibular NEC 755.35
  toe (complete) (partial) (*see also* Absence, toe, congenital) 755.39
  tongue 750.11
  trachea (cartilage) 748.3
  ulna NEC (*see also* Absence, ulna, congenital) 755.27

◀ ▶ **New Code**   ◀▥ ▥▶ **Revised Code**

Agenesis *(Continued)*
  ureter 753.4
  urethra 753.8
  urinary tract NEC 753.8
  uterus 752.3
  uvula 750.26
  vagina 752.49
  vas deferens 752.8
  vein(s) (peripheral) NEC *(see also*
      Anomaly, peripheral vascular sys-
      tem) 747.60
    brain 747.81
    great 747.49
    portal 747.49
    pulmonary 747.49
  vena cava (inferior) (superior) 747.49
  vermis of cerebellum 742.2
  vertebra 756.13
    lumbar 756.13
      isthmus 756.11
        pars articularis 756.11
  vulva 752.49
Ageusia *(see also* Disturbance, sensation)
    781.1
Aggressiveness 301.3
Aggressive outburst *(see also* Distur-
    bance, conduct) 312.0
  in children and adolescents 313.9
Aging skin 701.8
Agitated - *see* condition
Agitation 307.9
  catatonic *(see also* Schizophrenia)
    295.2
Aglossia (congenital) 750.11
Aglycogenosis 271.0
Agnail (finger) (with lymphangitis)
    681.02
Agnosia (body image) (tactile) 784.69
  verbal 784.69
    auditory 784.69
      secondary to organic lesion 784.69
    developmental 315.8
    secondary to organic lesion 784.69
    visual 784.69
      developmental 315.8
      secondary to organic lesion 784.69
  visual 368.16
    developmental 315.31
Agoraphobia 300.22
  with panic attacks 300.21
Agrammatism 784.69
Agranulocytopenia 288.0
Agranulocytosis (angina) (chronic) (cycli-
    cal) (genetic) (infantile) (periodic)
    (pernicious) 288.0
Agraphia (absolute) 784.69
  with alexia 784.61
  developmental 315.39
Agrypnia *(see also* Insomnia) 780.52
Ague *(see also* Malaria) 084.6
  brass-founders' 985.8
  dumb 084.6
  tertian 084.1
Agyria 742.2
Ahumada-del Castillo syndrome (non-
    puerperal galactorrhea and amenor-
    rhea) 253.1
AIDS 042
AIDS-associated retrovirus (disease) (ill-
    ness) 042
  infection - *see* Human immunodefi-
      ciency virus, infection
AIDS-associated virus (disease) (illness)
    042

AIDS-associated virus *(Continued)*
  infection - *see* Human immunodefi-
      ciency virus, infection
AIDS-like disease (illness) (syndrome)
    042
AIDS-related complex 042
AIDS-related conditions 042
AIDS-related virus (disease) (illness) 042
  infection - *see* Human immunodefi-
      ciency virus, infection
AIDS virus (disease) (illness) 042
  infection - *see* Human immunodefi-
      ciency virus, infection
Ailment, heart - *see* Disease, heart
Ailurophobia 300.29
Ainhum (disease) 136.0
Air
  anterior mediastinum 518.1
  compressed, disease 993.3
  embolism (any site) (artery) (cerebral)
      958.0
    with
      abortion - *see* Abortion, by type,
          with embolism
      ectopic pregnancy *(see also* catego-
          ries 633.0-633.9) 639.6
      molar pregnancy *(see also* catego-
          ries 630-632) 639.6
    due to implanted device - *see* Com-
        plications, due to (presence of)
        any device, implant, or graft
        classified to 996.0-996.5 NEC
    following
      abortion 639.6
      ectopic or molar pregnancy 639.6
    infusion, perfusion, or transfusion
        999.1
    in pregnancy, childbirth, or puerpe-
        rium 673.0
    traumatic 958.0
  hunger 786.09
    psychogenic 306.1
  leak (lung) (pulmonary) (thorax) 512.8
    iatrogenic 512.1
    postoperative 512.1
  rarefied, effects of - *see* Effect, adverse,
      high altitude
  sickness 994.6
Airplane sickness 994.6
Akathisia, acathisia 781.0
  due to drugs 333.99
Akinesia algeria 352.6
Akiyami 100.89
Akureyri disease (epidemic neuromyas-
    thenia) 049.8
Alacrima (congenital) 743.65
Alactasia (hereditary) 271.3
Alalia 784.3
  developmental 315.31
    receptive-expressive 315.32
  secondary to organic lesion 784.3
Alaninemia 270.8
Alastrim 050.1
Albarrán's disease (colibacilluria) 599.0
Albers-Schönberg's disease (marble
    bones) 756.52
Albert's disease 726.71
Albinism, albino (choroid) (cutaneous)
    (eye) (generalized) (isolated) (ocular)
    (oculocutaneous) (partial) 270.2
Albinismus 270.2
Albright (-Martin) (-Bantam) disease
    (pseudohypoparathyroidism)
    275.49

Albright (-McCune) (-Sternberg) syn-
    drome (osteitis fibrosa disseminata)
    756.59
Albuminous - *see* condition
Albuminuria, albuminuric (acute)
    (chronic) (subacute) 791.0
  Bence-Jones 791.0
  cardiac 785.9
  complicating pregnancy, childbirth, or
      puerperium 646.2
    with hypertension - *see* Toxemia, of
        pregnancy
    affecting fetus or newborn 760.1
  cyclic 593.6
  gestational 646.2
  gravidarum 646.2
    with hypertension - *see* Toxemia, of
        pregnancy
    affecting fetus or newborn 760.1
  heart 785.9
  idiopathic 593.6
  orthostatic 593.6
  postural 593.6
  pre-eclamptic (mild) 642.4
    affecting fetus or newborn 760.0
    severe 642.5
      affecting fetus or newborn 760.0
  recurrent physiologic 593.6
  scarlatinal 034.1
Albumosuria 791.0
  Bence-Jones 791.0
  myelopathic (M9730/3) 203.0
Alcaptonuria 270.2
Alcohol, alcoholic
  abstinence 291.81
  acute intoxication 305.0
    with dependence 303.0
  addiction *(see also* Alcoholism) 303.9
    maternal
      with suspected fetal damage af-
          fecting management of preg-
          nancy 655.4
      affecting fetus or newborn
          760.71
  amnestic disorder, persisting 291.1
  anxiety 291.89
  brain syndrome, chronic 291.2
  cardiopathy 425.5
  chronic *(see also* Alcoholism) 303.9
  cirrhosis (liver) 571.2
  delirium 291.0
    acute 291.0
    chronic 291.1
    tremens 291.0
    withdrawal 291.0
  dementia NEC 291.2
  deterioration 291.2
  drunkenness (simple) 305.0
  hallucinosis (acute) 291.3
  insanity 291.9
  intoxication (acute) 305.0
    with dependence 303.0
    pathological 291.4
  jealousy 291.5
  Korsakoff's, Korsakov's, Korsakow's
      291.1
  liver NEC 571.3
    acute 571.1
    chronic 571.2
  mania (acute) (chronic) 291.9
  mood 291.89
  paranoia 291.5
  paranoid (type) psychosis 291.5
  pellagra 265.2

Alcohol, alcoholics (*Continued*)
poisoning, accidental (acute) NEC
980.9
specified type of alcohol - *see* Table
of Drugs and Chemicals
psychosis (*see also* Psychosis, alcoholic)
291.9
Korsakoff's, Korsakov's, Korsakow's
291.1
polyneuritic 291.1
with
delusions 291.5
hallucinations 291.3
withdrawal symptoms, syndrome NEC
291.81
delirium 291.0
hallucinosis 291.3
Alcoholism 303.9

Note   Use the following fifth-digit
subclassification with category 303:

0   unspecified
1   continuous
2   episodic
3   in remission

with psychosis (*see also* Psychosis, alcoholic) 291.9
acute 303.0
chronic 303.9
with psychosis 291.9
complicating pregnancy, childbirth, or
puerperium 648.4
affecting fetus or newborn 760.71
history V11.3
Korsakoff's, Korsakov's, Korsakow's
291.1
suspected damage to fetus affecting
management of pregnancy 655.4
Alder's anomaly or syndrome (leukocyte
granulation anomaly) 288.2
Alder-Reilly anomaly (leukocyte granulation) 288.2
Aldosteronism (primary) (secondary)
255.1
congenital 255.1
Aldosteronoma (M8370/1) 237.2
Aldrich (-Wiskott) syndrome (eczema-
thrombocytopenia) 279.12
Aleppo boil 085.1
Aleukemic - *see* condition
Aleukia
congenital 288.0
hemorrhagica 284.9
acquired (secondary) 284.8
congenital 284.0
idiopathic 284.9
splenica 289.4
Alexia (congenital) (developmental) 315.01
secondary to organic lesion 784.61
Algoneurodystrophy 733.7
Algophobia 300.29
Alibert's disease (mycosis fungoides)
(M9700/3) 202.1
Alibert-Bazin disease (M9700/3) 202.1
Alice in Wonderland syndrome 293.89
Alienation, mental (*see also* Psychosis)
298.9
Alkalemia 276.3
Alkalosis 276.3
metabolic 276.3
with respiratory acidosis 276.4
respiratory 276.3
Alkaptonuria 270.2

Allen-Masters syndrome 620.6
**Allergic bronchopulmonary aspergillo-
sis** 518.6
Allergy, allergic (reaction) 995.3
air-borne substance (*see also* Fever,
hay) 477.9
specified allergen NEC 477.8
alveolitis (extrinsic) 495.9
due to
Aspergillus clavatus 495.4
cryptostroma corticale 495.6
organisms (fungal, thermophilic
actinomycete, other) growing
in ventilation (air conditioning systems) 495.7
specified type NEC 495.8
anaphylactic shock 999.4
due to food - *see* Anaphylactic
shock, due to, food
angioneurotic edema 995.1
animal (dander) (epidermal) (hair)
477.8
arthritis (*see also* Arthritis, allergic)
716.2
asthma - *see* Asthma
bee sting (anaphylactic shock) 989.5
biological - *see* Allergy, drug
bronchial asthma - *see* Asthma
conjunctivitis (eczematous) 372.14
dander (animal) 477.8
dandruff 477.8
dermatitis (venenata) - *see* Dermatitis
diathesis V15.0
drug, medicinal substance, and biological (any) (correct medicinal substance properly administered) (external) (internal) 995.2
wrong substance given or taken
NEC 977.9
specified drug or substance - *see*
Table of Drugs and Chemicals
dust (house) (stock) 477.8
eczema - *see* Eczema
endophthalmitis 360.19
epidermal (animal) 477.8
feathers 477.8
food (any) (ingested) 693.1
atopic 691.8
in contact with skin 692.5
gastritis 535.4
gastroenteritis 558.9
gastrointestinal 558.9
grain 477.0
grass (pollen) 477.0
asthma (*see also* Asthma) 493.0
hay fever 477.0
hair (animal) 477.8
hay fever (grass) (pollen) (ragweed)
(tree) (*see also* Fever, hay) 477.9
history (of) V15.0
horse serum - *see* Allergy, serum
inhalant 477.9
dust 477.8
pollen 477.0
specified allergen other than pollen
477.8
kapok 477.8
medicine - *see* Allergy, drug
migraine 346.2
pannus 370.62
pneumonia 518.3
pollen (any) (hay fever) 477.0
asthma (*see also* Asthma) 493.0
primrose 477.0

Allergy, allergic (*Continued*)
primula 477.0
purpura 287.0
ragweed (pollen) (Senecio jacobae)
477.0
asthma (*see also* Asthma) 493.0
hay fever 477.0
respiratory (*see also* Allergy, inhalant)
477.9
due to
drug - *see* Allergy, drug
food - *see* Allergy, food
rhinitis (*see also* Fever, hay) 477.9
rose 477.0
Senecio jacobae 477.0
serum (prophylactic) (therapeutic)
999.5
anaphylactic shock 999.4
shock (anaphylactic) (due to adverse
effect of correct medicinal substance properly administered)
995.0
food - *see* Anaphylactic shock, due
to, food
from serum or immunization 999.5
anaphylactic 999.4
sinusitis (*see also* Fever, hay) 477.9
skin reaction 692.9
specified substance - *see* Dermatitis,
due to
tree (any) (hay fever) (pollen) 477.0
asthma (*see also* Asthma) 493.0
upper respiratory (*see also* Fever, hay)
477.9
urethritis 597.89
urticaria 708.0
vaccine - *see* Allergy, serum
Allescheriosis 117.6
Alligator skin disease (ichthyosis congenita) 757.1
acquired 701.1
Allocheiria, allochiria (*see also* Disturbance, sensation) 782.0
Almeida's disease (Brazilian blastomycosis) 116.1
Alopecia (atrophicans) (pregnancy) (premature) (senile) 704.00
adnata 757.4
areata 704.01
celsi 704.01
cicatrisata 704.09
circumscripta 704.01
congenital, congenitalis 757.4
disseminata 704.01
effluvium (telogen) 704.02
febrile 704.09
generalisata 704.09
hereditaria 704.09
marginalis 704.01
mucinosa 704.09
postinfectional 704.09
seborrheica 704.09
specific 091.82
syphilitic (secondary) 091.82
telogen effluvium 704.02
totalis 704.09
toxica 704.09
universalis 704.09
x-ray 704.09
Alpers' disease 330.8
Alpha-lipoproteinemia 272.4
Alpha thalassemia 282.4
Alphos 696.1
Alpine sickness 993.2

Alport's syndrome (hereditary hematuria-nephropathy-deafness) 759.89
Alteration (of), altered
awareness 780.09
transient 780.02
consciousness 780.09
persistent vegetative state 780.03
transient 780.02
mental status 780.9
Alternaria (infection) 118
Alternating - *see* condition
Altitude, high (effects) - *see* Effect, adverse, high altitude
Aluminosis (of lung) 503
Alvarez syndrome (transient cerebral ischemia) 435.9
Alveolar capillary block syndrome 516.3
Alveolitis
allergic (extrinsic) 495.9
due to organisms (fungal, thermophilic actinomycete, other) growing in ventilation (air conditioning systems) 495.7
specified type NEC 495.8
due to
Aspergillus clavatus 495.4
Cryptostroma corticale 495.6
fibrosing (chronic) (cryptogenic) (lung) 516.3
idiopathic 516.3
rheumatoid 714.81
jaw 526.5
sicca dolorosa 526.5
Alveolus, alveolar - *see* condition
Alymphocytosis (pure) 279.2
Alymphoplasia, thymic 279.2
Alzheimer's
dementia (senile) 331.0 *[294.1]*
disease or sclerosis 331.0
with dementia - *see* Alzheimer's, dementia
Amastia (*see also* Absence, breast) 611.8
Amaurosis (acquired) (congenital) (*see also* Blindness) 369.00
fugax 362.34
hysterical 300.11
Leber's (congenital) 362.76
tobacco 377.34
uremic - *see* Uremia
Amaurotic familial idiocy (infantile) (juvenile) (late) 330.1
Ambisexual 752.7
Amblyopia (acquired) (congenital) (partial) 368.00
color 368.59
acquired 368.55
deprivation 368.02
ex anopsia 368.00
hysterical 300.11
nocturnal 368.60
vitamin A deficiency 264.5
refractive 368.03
strabismic 368.01
suppression 368.01
tobacco 377.34
toxic NEC 377.34
uremic - *see* Uremia
Ameba, amebic (histolytica) - *see also* Amebiasis
abscess 006.3
bladder 006.8
brain (with liver and lung abscess) 006.5

Ameba, amebic (*Continued*)
abscess (*Continued*)
liver 006.3
with
brain abscess (and lung abscess) 006.5
lung abscess 006.4
lung (with liver abscess) 006.4
with brain abscess 006.5
seminal vesicle 006.8
spleen 006.8
carrier (suspected of) V02.2
meningoencephalitis
due to Naegleria (gruberi) 136.2
primary 136.2
Amebiasis NEC 006.9
with
brain abscess (with liver or lung abscess) 006.5
liver abscess (without mention of brain or lung abscess) 006.3
lung abscess (with liver abscess) 006.4
with brain abscess 006.5
acute 006.0
bladder 006.8
chronic 006.1
cutaneous 006.6
cutis 006.6
due to organism other than Entamoeba histolytica 007.8
hepatic (*see also* Abscess, liver, amebic) 006.3
nondysenteric 006.2
seminal vesicle 006.8
specified
organism NEC 007.8
site NEC 006.8
Ameboma 006.8
Amelia 755.4
lower limb 755.31
upper limb 755.21
Ameloblastoma (M9310/0) 213.1
jaw (bone) (lower) 213.1
upper 213.0
long bones (M9261/3) - *see* Neoplasm, bone, malignant
malignant (M9310/3) 170.1
jaw (bone) (lower) 170.1
upper 170.0
mandible 213.1
tibial (M9261/3) 170.7
Amelogenesis imperfecta 520.5
nonhereditaria (segmentalis) 520.4
Amenorrhea (primary) (secondary) 626.0
due to ovarian dysfunction 256.8
hyperhormonal 256.8
Amentia (*see also* Retardation, mental) 319
Meynert's (nonalcoholic) 294.0
alcoholic 291.1
nevoid 759.6
American
leishmaniasis 085.5
mountain tick fever 066.1
trypanosomiasis - *see* Trypanosomiasis, American
Ametropia (*see also* Disorder, accommodation) 367.9
Amianthosis 501
Amimia 784.69

Amino acid
deficiency 270.9
anemia 281.4
metabolic disorder (*see also* Disorder, amino acid) 270.9
Aminoaciduria 270.9
imidazole 270.5
Amnesia (retrograde) 780.9
auditory 784.69
developmental 315.31
secondary to organic lesion 784.69
hysterical or dissociative type 300.12
psychogenic 300.12
transient global 437.7
Amnestic (confabulatory) syndrome 294.0
alcohol-induced 291.1
drug-induced 292.83
posttraumatic 294.0
Amniocentesis screening (for) V28.2
alpha-fetoprotein level, raised V28.1
chromosomal anomalies V28.0
Amnion, amniotic - *see also* condition
nodosum 658.8
Amnionitis (complicating pregnancy) 658.4
affecting fetus or newborn 762.7
Amoral trends 301.7
Amotio retinae (*see also* Detachment, retina) 361.9
Ampulla
lower esophagus 530.89
phrenic 530.89
Amputation
any part of fetus, to facilitate delivery 763.89
cervix (supravaginal) (uteri) 622.8
in pregnancy or childbirth 654.6
affecting fetus or newborn 763.89
clitoris - *see* Wound, open, clitoris
congenital
lower limb 755.31
upper limb 755.21
neuroma (traumatic) - *see also* Injury, nerve, by site
surgical complication (late) 997.61
penis - *see* Amputation, traumatic, penis
status (without complication) - *see* Absence, by site, acquired
stump (surgical) (posttraumatic)
abnormal, painful, or with complication (late) 997.60
healed or old NEC - *see also* Absence, by site, acquired
lower V49.70
upper V49.60
traumatic (complete) (partial)

Note   "Complicated" includes traumatic amputation with delayed healing, delayed treatment, foreign body, or major infection.

arm 887.4
at or above elbow 887.2
complicated 887.3
below elbow 887.0
complicated 887.1
both (bilateral) (any level(s)) 887.6
complicated 887.7

Amputation (*Continued*)
  arm (*Continued*)
    complicated 887.5
    finger(s) (one or both hands) 886.0
      with thumb(s) 885.0
        complicated 885.1
      complicated 886.1
    foot (except toe(s) only) 896.0
      and other leg 897.6
        complicated 897.7
      both (bilateral) 896.2
        complicated 896.3
      complicated 896.1
    toe(s) only (one or both feet) 895.0
      complicated 895.1
  genital organ(s) (external) NEC 878.8
    complicated 878.9
  hand (except finger(s) only) 887.0
    and other arm 887.6
      complicated 887.7
    both (bilateral) 887.6
      complicated 887.7
    complicated 887.1
    finger(s) (one or both hands) 886.0
      with thumb(s) 885.0
        complicated 885.1
      complicated 886.1
    thumb(s) (with fingers of either
      hand) 885.0
      complicated 885.1
  head 874.9
  late effect - *see* Late, effects (of), amputation
  leg 897.4
    and other foot 897.6
      complicated 897.7
    at or above knee 897.2
      complicated 897.3
    below knee 897.0
      complicated 897.1
    both (bilateral) 897.6
      complicated 897.7
    complicated 897.5
  lower limb(s) except toe(s) - *see* Amputation, traumatic, leg
  nose - *see* Wound, open, nose
  penis 878.0
    complicated 878.1
  sites other than limbs - *see* Wound, open, by site
  thumb(s) (with finger(s) of either
    hand) 885.0
    complicated 885.1
  toe(s) (one or both feet) 895.0
    complicated 895.1
  upper limb(s) - *see* Amputation, traumatic, arm
Amputee (bilateral) (old) - *see* Absence, by site, acquired V49.70 ⬅▥
Amusia 784.69
  developmental 315.39
  secondary to organic lesion 784.69
Amyelencephalus 740.0
Amyelia 742.59
Amygdalitis - *see* Tonsillitis
Amygdalolith 474.8
Amyloid disease or degeneration 277.3
  heart 277.3 [425.7]
Amyloidosis (familial) (general) (generalized) (genetic) (primary) (secondary) 277.3
  with lung involvement 277.3 [517.8]
  heart 277.3 [425.7]
  nephropathic 277.3 [583.81]

Amyloidosis (*Continued*)
  neuropathic (Portuguese) (Swiss) 277.3
    [357.4]
  pulmonary 277.3 [517.8]
  systemic, inherited 277.3
Amylopectinosis (brancher enzyme deficiency) 271.0
Amylophagia 307.52
Amyoplasia congenita 756.89
Amyotonia 728.2
  congenita 358.8
Amyotrophia, amyotrophy, amyotrophic 728.2
  congenita 756.89
  diabetic 250.6 [358.1]
  lateral sclerosis (syndrome) 335.20
  neuralgic 353.5
  sclerosis (lateral) 335.20
  spinal progressive 335.21
Anacidity, gastric 536.0
  psychogenic 306.4
Anaerosis of newborn 770.8
Analbuminemia 273.8
Analgesia (*see also* Anesthesia) 782.0
Analphalipoproteinemia 272.5
Anaphylactic shock or reaction (correct substance properly administered) 995.0
  due to
    food 995.60
      additives 995.66
      crustaceans 995.62
      eggs 995.68
      fish 995.65
      fruits 995.63
      milk products 995.67
      nuts (tree) 995.64
      peanuts 995.61
      seeds 995.64,
      specified NEC 995.69
      tree nuts 995.64
      vegetables 995.63
    immunization 999.4
    overdose or wrong substance given
      or taken 977.9
      specified drug - *see* Table of Drugs
        and Chemicals
    serum 999.4
  following sting(s) 989.5
  purpura 287.0
  serum 999.4
Anaphylactoid shock or reaction - *see* Anaphylactic shock
Anaphylaxis - *see* Anaphylactic shock
Anaplasia, cervix 622.1
Anarthria 784.5
Anarthritic rheumatoid disease 446.5
Anasarca 782.3
  cardiac (*see also* Failure, heart, congestive) 428.0
  fetus or newborn 778.0
  lung 514
  nutritional 262
  pulmonary 514
  renal (*see also* Nephrosis) 581.9
Anaspadias 752.62
Anastomosis
  aneurysmal - *see* Aneurysm
  arteriovenous, congenital NEC (*see
    also* Anomaly, arteriovenous)
    747.60
    ruptured, of brain (*see also* Hemorrhage, subarachnoid) 430

Anastomosis (*Continued*)
  intestinal 569.89
    complicated NEC 997.4
      involving urinary tract 997.5
  retinal and choroidal vessels 743.58
    acquired 362.17
Anatomical narrow angle (glaucoma) 365.02
Ancylostoma (infection) (infestation) 126.9
  americanus 126.1
  braziliense 126.2
  caninum 126.8
  ceylanicum 126.3
  duodenale 126.0
  Necator americanus 126.1
Ancylostomiasis (intestinal) 126.9
  Ancylostoma
    americanus 126.1
    caninum 126.8
    ceylanicum 126.3
    duodenale 126.0
  braziliense 126.2
  Necator americanus 126.1
Anders' disease or syndrome (adiposis tuberosa simplex) 272.8
Andersen's glycogen storage disease 271.0
Anderson's disease 272.7
Andes disease 993.2
Andrews' disease (bacterid) 686.8
Androblastoma (M8630/1)
  benign (M8630/0)
    specified site - *see* Neoplasm, by site, benign
    unspecified site
      female 220
      male 222.0
  malignant (M8630/3)
    specified site - *see* Neoplasm, by site, malignant
    unspecified site
      female 183.0
      male 186.9
  specified site - *see* Neoplasm, by site, uncertain behavior
  tubular (M8640/0)
    with lipid storage (M8641/0)
      specified site - *see* Neoplasm, by site, benign
      unspecified site
        female 220
        male 222.0
    specified site - *see* Neoplasm, by site, benign
    unspecified site
      female 220
      male 222.0
  unspecified site
    female 236.2
    male 236.4
Android pelvis 755.69
  with disproportion (fetopelvic) 653.3
    affecting fetus or newborn 763.1
    causing obstructed labor 660.1
      affecting fetus or newborn 763.1
Anectasis, pulmonary (newborn or fetus) 770.5
Anemia 285.9
  with
    disorder of
      anaerobic glycolysis 282.3
      pentose phosphate pathway 282.2
    koilonychia 280.9

Anemia (*Continued*)
6-phosphogluconic dehydrogenase
  deficiency 282.2
achlorhydric 280.9
achrestic 281.8
Addison's (pernicious) 281.0
Addison-Biermer (pernicious) 281.0
agranulocytic 288.0
amino acid deficiency 281.4
aplastic 284.9
  acquired (secondary) 284.8
  congenital 284.0
  constitutional 284.0
  due to
    chronic systemic disease 284.8
    drugs 284.8
    infection 284.8
    radiation 284.8
  idiopathic 284.9
  myxedema 244.9
  of or complicating pregnancy 648.2
  red cell (acquired) (pure) (with thy-
    moma) 284.8
    congenital 284.0
  specified type NEC 284.8
  toxic (paralytic) 284.8
aregenerative 284.9
  congenital 284.0
asiderotic 280.9
atypical (primary) 285.9
autohemolysis of Selwyn and Dacie
  (type I) 282.2
autoimmune hemolytic 283.0
Baghdad Spring 282.2
Balantidium coli 007.0
Biermer's (pernicious) 281.0
blood loss (chronic) 280.0
  acute 285.1
bothriocephalus 123.4
brickmakers' (*see also* Ancylostomiasis)
  126.9
cerebral 437.8
childhood 285.9
chlorotic 280.9
chronica congenita aregenerativa 284.0
chronic simple 281.9
combined system disease NEC 281.0
  [336.2]
  due to dietary deficiency 281.1
    [336.2]
complicating pregnancy or childbirth
  648.2
congenital (following fetal blood loss)
  776.5
  aplastic 284.0
  due to isoimmunization NEC 773.2
  Heinz-body 282.7
  hereditary hemolytic NEC 282.9
  nonspherocytic
    type I 282.2
    type II 282.3
  pernicious 281.0
  spherocytic (*see also* Spherocytosis)
    282.0
Cooley's (erythroblastic) 282.4
crescent - *see* Disease, sickle-cell
cytogenic 281.0
Dacie's (nonspherocytic)
  type I 282.2
  type II 282.3
Davidson's (refractory) 284.9
deficiency 281.9
  2, 3 diphosphoglycurate mutase
    282.3

Anemia (*Continued*)
deficiency (*Continued*)
  2, 3 PG 282.3
  6-PGD 282.2
  6-phosphogluronic dehydrogenase
    282.2
  amino acid 281.4
  combined B$_{12}$ and folate 281.3
  enzyme, drug-induced (hemolytic)
    282.2
  erythrocytic glutathione 282.2
  folate 281.2
    dietary 281.2
    drug-induced 281.2
  folic acid 281.2
    dietary 281.2
    drug-induced 281.2
  G-6-PD 282.2
  GGS-R 282.2
  glucose-6-phosphate dehydrogenase
    (G-6-PD) 282.2
  glucose-phosphate isomerase 282.3
  glutathione peroxidase 282.2
  glutathione reductase 282.2
  glyceraldehyde phosphate dehydro-
    genase 282.3
  GPI 282.3
  G SH 282.2
  hexokinase 282.3
  iron (Fe) 280.9
    specified NEC 280.8
  nutritional 281.9
    with
      poor iron absorption 280.9
      specified deficiency NEC 281.8
    due to inadequate dietary iron in-
      take 280.1
    specified type NEC 281.8
  of or complicating pregnancy 648.2
  pentose phosphate pathway 282.2
  PFK 282.3
  phosphofructo-aldolase 282.3
  phosphofructokinase 282.3
  phosphoglycerate kinase 282.3
  PK 282.3
  protein 281.4
  pyruvate kinase (PK) 282.3
  TPI 282.3
  triosephosphate isomerase 282.3
  vitamin B$_{12}$ NEC 281.1
    dietary 281.1
    pernicious 281.0
Diamond-Blackfan (congenital hypoplastic) 284.0
dibothriocephalus 123.4
dimorphic 281.9
diphasic 281.8
diphtheritic 032.89
Diphyllobothrium 123.4
drepanocytic (*see also* Disease, sickle-
  cell) 282.60
due to
  blood loss (chronic) 280.0
    acute 285.1
  defect of Embden-Meyerhof path-
    way glycolysis 282.3
  disorder of glutathione metabolism
    282.2
  fetal blood loss 776.5
  fish tapeworm (D. latum) infestation
    123.4
  glutathione metabolism disorder 282.2
  hemorrhage (chronic) 280.0
    acute 285.1

Anemia (*Continued*)
due to (*Continued*)
  hexose monophosphate (HMP)
    shunt deficiency 282.2
  impaired absorption 280.9
  loss of blood (chronic) 280.0
    acute 285.1
  myxedema 244.9
  Necator americanus 126.1
  prematurity 776.6
  selective vitamin B$_{12}$ malabsorption
    with proteinuria 281.1
Dyke-Young type (secondary)
  (symptomatic) 283.9
dyserythropoietic (congenital) (types I,
  II, III) 285.8
dyshemopoietic (congenital) 285.8
Egypt (*see also* Ancylostomiasis) 126.9
elliptocytosis (*see also* Elliptocytosis)
  282.1
enzyme deficiency, drug-induced 282.2
epidemic (*see also* Ancylostomiasis)
  126.9
erythroblastic
  familial 282.4
  fetus or newborn (*see also* Disease,
    hemolytic) 773.2
    late 773.5
erythrocytic glutathione deficiency
  282.2
essential 285.9
Faber's (achlorhydric anemia) 280.9
factitious (self-induced bloodletting)
  280.0
familial erythroblastic (microcytic)
  282.4
Fanconi's (congenital pancytopenia)
  284.0
favism 282.2
fetal, following blood loss 776.5
fetus or newborn
  due to
    ABO
      antibodies 773.1
      incompatibility, maternal/fetal
        773.1
      isoimmunization 773.1
    Rh
      antibodies 773.0
      incompatibility, maternal/fetal
        773.0
      isoimmunization 773.0
  following fetal blood loss 776.5
fish tapeworm (D. latum) infestation
  123.4
folate (folic acid) deficiency 281.2
  dietary 281.2
  drug-induced 281.2
folate malabsorption, congenital 281.2
folic acid deficiency 281.2
  dietary 281.2
  drug-induced 281.2
G-6-PD 282.2
general 285.9
glucose-6-phosphate dehydrogenase
  deficiency 282.2
glutathione-reductase deficiency
  282.2
goat's milk 281.2
granulocytic 288.0
Heinz-body, congenital 282.7
hemoglobin deficiency 285.9
hemolytic 283.9
  acquired 283.9

Anemia *(Continued)*
  hemolytic *(Continued)*
    acquired *(Continued)*
      with hemoglobinuria NEC 283.2
      autoimmune (cold type) (idiopathic) (primary) (secondary) (symptomatic) (warm type) 283.0
      due to
        cold reactive antibodies 283.0
        drug exposure 283.0
        warm reactive antibodies 283.0
      fragmentation 283.19
      idiopathic (chronic) 283.9
      infectious 283.19
        autoimmune 283.0
        non-autoimmune 283.10
        toxic 283.19
      traumatic cardiac 283.19
    acute 283.9
      due to enzyme deficiency NEC 282.3
      fetus or newborn (*see also* Disease, hemolytic) 773.2
        late 773.5
      Lederer's (acquired infectious hemolytic anemia) 283.19
    autoimmune (acquired) 283.0
    chronic 282.9
      idiopathic 283.9
    cold type (secondary) (symptomatic) 283.0
    congenital (spherocytic) (*see also* Spherocytosis) 282.0
      nonspherocytic - *see* Anemia, hemolytic, nonspherocytic, congenital
    drug-induced 283.0
      enzyme deficiency 282.2
    due to
      cardiac conditions 283.19
      drugs 283.0
      enzyme deficiency NEC 282.3
        drug-induced 282.2
      presence of shunt or other internal prosthetic device 283.19
      thrombotic thrombocytopenic purpura 446.6
    elliptocytotic (*see also* Elliptocytosis) 282.1
    familial 282.9
    hereditary 282.9
      due to enzyme deficiency NEC 282.3
      specified NEC 282.8
    idiopathic (chronic) 283.9
    infectious (acquired) 283.19
    mechanical 283.19
    microangiopathic 283.19
    nonautoimmune 283.10
    nonspherocytic
      congenital or hereditary NEC 282.3
        glucose-6-phosphate dehydrogenase deficiency 282.2
        pyruvate kinase (PK) deficiency 282.3
        type I 282.2
        type II 282.3
        type I 282.2
        type II 282.3
    of or complicating pregnancy 648.2
    resulting from presence of shunt or other internal prosthetic device 283.19

Anemia *(Continued)*
  hemolytic *(Continued)*
    secondary 283.19
      autoimmune 283.0
    sickle-cell - *see* Disease, sickle-cell
    Stransky-Regala type (Hb-E) (*see also* Disease, hemoglobin) 282.7
    symptomatic 283.19
      autoimmune 283.0
    toxic (acquired) 283.19
    uremic (adult) (child) 283.11
    warm type (secondary) (symptomatic) 283.0
  hemorrhagic (chronic) 280.0
    acute 285.1
  HEMPAS 285.8
  hereditary erythroblast multinuclearity-positive acidified serum test 285.8
  Herrick's (hemoglobin S disease) 282.61
  hexokinase deficiency 282.3
  high A_2 282.4
  hookworm (*see also* Ancylostomiasis) 126.9
  hypochromic (idiopathic) (microcytic) (normoblastic) 280.9
    with iron loading 285.0
    due to blood loss (chronic) 280.0
      acute 285.1
    familial sex linked 285.0
    pyridoxine-responsive 285.0
  hypoplasia, red blood cells 284.8
    congenital or familial 284.0
  hypoplastic (idiopathic) 284.9
    congenital 284.0
    familial 284.0
    of childhood 284.0
  idiopathic 285.9
    hemolytic, chronic 283.9
  infantile 285.9
  infective, infectional 285.9
  intertropical (*see also* Ancylostomiasis) 126.9
  iron (Fe) deficiency 280.9
    due to blood loss (chronic) 280.0
      acute 285.1
    of or complicating pregnancy 648.2
    specified NEC 280.8
  Jaksch's (pseudoleukemia infantum) 285.8
  Joseph-Diamond-Blackfan (congenital hypoplastic) 284.0
  labyrinth 386.50
  Lederer's (acquired infectious hemolytic anemia) 283.19
  leptocytosis (hereditary) 282.4
  leukoerythroblastic 285.8
  macrocytic 281.9
    nutritional 281.2
    of or complicating pregnancy 648.2
    tropical 281.2
  malabsorption (familial), selective B_{12} with proteinuria 281.1
  malarial (*see also* Malaria) 084.6
  malignant (progressive) 281.0
  malnutrition 281.9
  marsh (*see also* Malaria) 084.6
  Mediterranean (with hemoglobinopathy) 282.4
  megaloblastic 281.9
    combined B_{12} and folate deficiency 281.3

Anemia *(Continued)*
  megaloblastic *(Continued)*
    nutritional (of infancy) 281.2
    of infancy 281.2
    of or complicating pregnancy 648.2
    refractory 281.3
    specified NEC 281.3
  megalocytic 281.9
  microangiopathic hemolytic 283.19
  microcytic (hypochromic) 280.9
    due to blood loss (chronic) 280.0
      acute 285.1
    familial 282.4
    hypochromic 280.9
  microdrepanocytosis 282.4
  miners' (*see also* Ancylostomiasis) 126.9
  myelopathic 285.8
  myelophthisic (normocytic) 285.8
  newborn (*see also* Disease, hemolytic) 773.2
    due to isoimmunization (*see also* Disease, hemolytic) 773.2
    late, due to isoimmunization 773.5
    posthemorrhagic 776.5
  nonregenerative 284.9
  nonspherocytic hemolytic - *see* Anemia, hemolytic, nonspherocytic
  normocytic (infectional) (not due to blood loss) 285.9
    due to blood loss (chronic) 280.0
      acute 285.1
    myelophthisic 284.8
  nutritional (deficiency) 281.9
    with
      poor iron absorption 280.9
      specified deficiency NEC 281.8
    due to inadequate dietary iron intake 280.1
    megaloblastic (of infancy) 281.2
  of childhood (*see also* Thalassemia) 282.4
  of or complicating pregnancy 648.2
    affecting fetus or newborn 760.8
  of prematurity 776.6
  orotic aciduric (congenital) (hereditary) 281.4
  osteosclerotic 289.8
  ovalocytosis (hereditary) (*see also* Elliptocytosis) 282.1
  paludal (*see also* Malaria) 084.6
  pentose phosphate pathway deficiency 282.2
  pernicious (combined system disease) (congenital) (dorsolateral spinal degeneration) (juvenile) (myelopathy) (neuropathy) (posterior sclerosis) (primary) (progressive) (spleen) 281.0
    of or complicating pregnancy 648.2
  pleochromic 285.9
    of sprue 281.8
  portal 285.8
  posthemorrhagic (chronic) 280.0
    acute 285.1
    newborn 776.5
  pressure 285.9
  primary 285.9
  profound 285.9
  progressive 285.9
    malignant 281.0
    pernicious 281.0
  protein-deficiency 281.4

Anemia *(Continued)*
pseudoleukemia infantum 285.8
puerperal 648.2
pure red cell 284.8
  congenital 284.0
pyridoxine-responsive (hypochromic) 285.0
pyruvate kinase (PK) deficiency 282.3
refractoria sideroblastica 285.0
refractory (primary) 284.9
  with hemochromatosis 285.0
  megaloblastic 281.3
  sideroblastic 285.0
  sideropenic 280.9
Rietti-Greppi-Micheli (thalassemia minor) 282.4
scorbutic 281.8
secondary (to) 285.9
  blood loss (chronic) 280.0
    acute 285.1
  hemorrhage 280.0
    acute 285.1
    inadequate dietary iron intake 280.1
semiplastic 284.9
septic 285.9
sickle-cell *(see also* Disease, sickle-cell) 282.60
sideroachrestic 285.0
sideroblastic (acquired) (any type) (congenital) (drug-induced) (due to disease) (hereditary) (primary) (refractory) (secondary) (sex-linked hypochromic) (vitamin B$_6$ responsive) 285.0
sideropenic (refractory) 280.9
  due to blood loss (chronic) 280.0
    acute 285.1
simple chronic 281.9
specified type NEC 285.8
spherocytic (hereditary) *(see also* Spherocytosis) 282.0
splenic 285.8
  familial (Gaucher's) 272.7
splenomegalic 285.8
stomatocytosis 282.8
syphilitic 095.8
target cell (oval) 282.4
thalassemia 282.4
thrombocytopenic *(see also* Thrombocytopenia) 287.5
toxic 284.8
triosephosphate isomerase deficiency 282.3
tropical, macrocytic 281.2
tuberculous *(see also* Tuberculosis) 017.9
vegan's 281.1
vitamin
  B$_6$-responsive 285.0
  B$_{12}$ deficiency (dietary) 281.1
    pernicious 281.0
von Jaksch's (pseudoleukemia infantum) 285.8
Witts' (achlorhydric anemia) 280.9
Zuelzer (-Ogden) (nutritional megaloblastic anemia) 281.2
Anencephalus, anencephaly 740.0
fetal, affecting management of pregnancy 655.0
Anergasia *(see also* Psychosis, organic) 294.9
senile 290.0

Anesthesia, anesthetic 782.0
complication or reaction NEC 995.2
due to
  correct substance properly administered 995.2
  overdose or wrong substance given 968.4
  specified anesthetic - *see* Table of Drugs and Chemicals
cornea 371.81
death from
  correct substance properly administered 995.4
  during delivery 668.9
  overdose or wrong substance given 968.4
  specified anesthetic - *see* Table of Drugs and Chemicals
eye 371.81
functional 300.11
hyperesthetic, thalamic 348.8
hysterical 300.11
local skin lesion 782.0
olfactory 781.1
sexual (psychogenic) 302.72
shock
  due to
    correct substance properly administered 995.4
    overdose or wrong substance given 968.4
    specified anesthetic - *see* Table of Drugs and Chemicals
skin 782.0
tactile 782.0
testicular 608.9
thermal 782.0
Anetoderma (maculosum) 701.3
Aneuploidy NEC 758.5
Aneurin deficiency 265.1
Aneurysm (anastomotic) (artery) (cirsoid) (diffuse) (false) (fusiform) (multiple) (ruptured) (saccular) (varicose) 442.9
abdominal (aorta) 441.4
  ruptured 441.3
  syphilitic 093.0
aorta, aortic (nonsyphilitic) 441.9
  abdominal 441.4
    dissecting 441.02
    ruptured 441.3
    syphilitic 093.0
  arch 441.2
    ruptured 441.1
  arteriosclerotic NEC 441.9
    ruptured 441.5
  ascending 441.2
    ruptured 441.1
  congenital 747.29
  descending 441.9
    abdominal 441.4
      ruptured 441.3
    ruptured 441.5
    thoracic 441.2
      functional 441.1
  dissecting 441.00
    abdominal 441.02
    thoracic 441.01
    thoracoabdominal 441.03
  due to coarctation (aorta) 747.10
  ruptured 441.5
  sinus, right 747.29

Aneurysm *(Continued)*
aorta *(Continued)*
  syphilitic 093.0
  thoracoabdominal 441.7
    ruptured 441.6
  thorax, thoracic (arch) (nonsyphilitic) 441.2
    dissecting 441.01
    ruptured 441.1
    syphilitic 093.0
  transverse 441.2
    ruptured 441.1
  valve (heart) *(see also* Endocarditis, aortic) 424.1
arteriosclerotic NEC 442.9
  cerebral 437.3
    ruptured *(see also* Hemorrhage, subarachnoid) 430
arteriovenous (congenital) (peripheral) NEC *(see also* Anomaly, arteriovenous) 747.60
  acquired NEC 447.0
    brain 437.3
      ruptured *(see also* Hemorrhage, subarachnoid) 430
    coronary 414.11
    pulmonary 417.0
  brain (cerebral) 747.81
    ruptured *(see also* Hemorrhage, subarachnoid) 430
  coronary 746.85
  pulmonary 747.3
  retina 743.58
  specified site NEC 747.89
    acquired 447.0
  traumatic *(see also* Injury, blood vessel, by site) 904.9
basal - *see* Aneurysm, brain
berry (congenital) (ruptured) *(see also* Hemorrhage, subarachnoid) 430
brain 437.3
  arteriosclerotic 437.3
    ruptured *(see also* Hemorrhage, subarachnoid) 430
  arteriovenous 747.81
    acquired 437.3
      ruptured *(see also* Hemorrhage, subarachnoid) 430
    ruptured *(see also* Hemorrhage, subarachnoid) 430
  berry (congenital) (ruptured) *(see also* Hemorrhage, subarachnoid) 430
  congenital 747.81
    ruptured *(see also* Hemorrhage, subarachnoid) 430
  meninges 437.3
    ruptured *(see also* Hemorrhage, subarachnoid) 430
  miliary (congenital) (ruptured) *(see also* Hemorrhage, subarachnoid) 430
  mycotic 421.0
    ruptured *(see also* Hemorrhage, subarachnoid) 430
  nonruptured 437.3
  ruptured *(see also* Hemorrhage, subarachnoid) 430
  syphilitic 094.87
  syphilitic (hemorrhage) 094.87
  traumatic - *see* Injury, intracranial
cardiac (false) *(see also* Aneurysm, heart) 414.10

Aneurysm *(Continued)*
  carotid artery (common) (external)
    442.81
    internal (intracranial portion) 437.3
      extracranial portion 442.81
      ruptured into brain (*see also* Hem-
        orrhage, subarachnoid) 430
    syphilitic 093.89
      intracranial 094.87
  cavernous sinus (*see also* Aneurysm,
    brain) 437.3
    arteriovenous 747.81
      ruptured (*see also* Hemorrhage,
        subarachnoid) 430
    congenital 747.81
      ruptured (*see also* Hemorrhage,
        subarachnoid) 430
  celiac 442.84
  central nervous system, syphilitic 094.89
  cerebral - *see* Aneurysm, brain
  chest - *see* Aneurysm, thorax
  circle of Willis (*see also* Aneurysm,
    brain) 437.3
    congenital 747.81
      ruptured (*see also* Hemorrhage,
        subarachnoid) 430
    ruptured (*see also* Hemorrhage, sub-
      arachnoid) 430
  common iliac artery 442.2
  congenital (peripheral) NEC 747.60
    brain 747.81
      ruptured (*see also* Hemorrhage,
        subarachnoid) 430
    cerebral - *see* Aneurysm, brain, con-
      genital
    coronary 746.85
    gastrointestinal 747.61
    lower limb 747.64
    pulmonary 747.3
    renal 747.62
    retina 743.58
    specified site NEC 747.89
    spinal 747.82
    upper limb 747.63
  conjunctiva 372.74
  conus arteriosus (*see also* Aneurysm,
    heart) 414.10
  coronary (arteriosclerotic) (artery) (vein)
    (*see also* Aneurysm, heart) 414.11
    arteriovenous 746.85
    congenital 746.85
    syphilitic 093.89
  cylindrical 441.9
    ruptured 441.5
    syphilitic 093.9
  dissecting 442.9
    aorta 441.00
      abdominal 441.02
      thoracic 441.01
      thoracoabdominal 441.03
    syphilitic 093.9
  ductus arteriosus 747.0
  embolic - *see* Embolism, artery
  endocardial, infective (any valve) 421.0
  femoral 442.3
  gastroduodenal 442.84
  gastroepiploic 442.84
  heart (chronic or with a stated dura-
    tion of over 8 weeks) (infectional)
    (wall) 414.10
    acute or with a stated duration of 8
      weeks or less (*see also* Infarct,
      myocardium) 410.9
    congenital 746.89

Aneurysm *(Continued)*
  heart *(Continued)*
    valve - *see* Endocarditis
  hepatic 442.84
  iliac (common) 442.2
  infective (any valve) 421.0
  innominate (nonsyphilitic) 442.89
    syphilitic 093.89
  interauricular septum (*see also* Aneu-
    rysm, heart) 414.10
  interventricular septum (*see also* Aneu-
    rysm, heart) 414.10
  intracranial - *see* Aneurysm,
    brain
  intrathoracic (nonsyphilitic)
    441.2
    ruptured 441.1
    syphilitic 093.0
  jugular vein 453.8
  lower extremity 442.3
  lung (pulmonary artery) 417.1
  malignant 093.9
  mediastinal (nonsyphilitic) 442.89
    syphilitic 093.89
  miliary (congenital) (ruptured) (*see
    also* Hemorrhage, subarachnoid)
    430
  mitral (heart) (valve) 424.0
  mural (arteriovenous) (heart) (*see also*
    Aneurysm, heart) 414.10
  mycotic, any site 421.0
    ruptured, brain (*see also* Hemor-
      rhage, subarachnoid) 430
  myocardium (*see also* Aneurysm, heart)
    414.10
  neck 442.81
  pancreaticoduodenal 442.84
  patent ductus arteriosus 747.0
  peripheral NEC 442.89
    congenital NEC (*see also* Aneurysm,
      congenital) 747.60
  popliteal 442.3
  pulmonary 417.1
    arteriovenous 747.3
      acquired 417.0
    syphilitic 093.89
    valve (heart) (*see also* Endocarditis,
      pulmonary) 424.3
  racemose 442.9
    congenital (peripheral) NEC
      747.60
  radial 442.0
  Rasmussen's (*see also* Tuberculosis)
    011.2
  renal 442.1
  retinal (acquired) 362.17
    congenital 743.58
    diabetic 250.5 *[362.01]*
  sinus, aortic (of Valsalva) 747.29
  specified site NEC 442.89
  spinal (cord) 442.89
    congenital 747.82
    syphilitic (hemorrhage) 094.89
  spleen, splenic 442.83
  subclavian 442.82
    syphilitic 093.89
  superior mesenteric 442.84
  syphilitic 093.9
    aorta 093.0
    central nervous system 094.89
    congenital 090.5
    spine, spinal 094.89
  thoracoabdominal 441.7
    ruptured 441.6

Aneurysm *(Continued)*
  thorax, thoracic (arch) (nonsyphilitic)
    441.2
    dissecting 441.01
    ruptured 441.1
    syphilitic 093.0
  traumatic (complication) (early) - *see*
    Injury, blood vessel, by site
  tricuspid (heart) (valve) - *see* Endocar-
    ditis, tricuspid
  ulnar 442.0
  upper extremity 442.0
  valve, valvular - *see* Endocarditis
  venous 456.8
    congenital NEC (*see also* Aneurysm,
      congenital) 747.60
  ventricle (arteriovenous) (*see also* An-
    eurysm, heart) 414.10
  visceral artery NEC 442.84
Angiectasis 459.89
Angiectopia 459.9
Angiitis 447.6
  allergic granulomatous 446.4
  hypersensitivity 446.20
    Goodpasture's syndrome 446.21
    specified NEC 446.29
  necrotizing 446.0
  Wegener's (necrotizing respiratory
    granulomatosis) 446.4
Angina (attack) (cardiac) (chest) (effort)
    (heart) (pectoris) (syndrome) (vaso-
    motor) 413.9
  abdominal 557.1
  agranulocytic 288.0
  aphthous 074.0
  catarrhal 462
  crescendo 411.1
  croupous 464.4
  cruris 443.9
    due to atherosclerosis NEC (*see also*
      Arteriosclerosis, extremities)
      440.20
  decubitus 413.0
  diphtheritic (membranous) 032.0
  erysipelatous 034.0
  erythematous 462
  exudative, chronic 476.0
  faucium 478.29
  gangrenous 462
    diphtheritic 032.0
  infectious 462
  initial 411.1
  intestinal 557.1
  ludovici 528.3
  Ludwig's 528.3
  malignant 462
    diphtheritic 032.0
  membranous 464.4
    diphtheritic 032.0
  mesenteric 557.1
  monocytic 075
  nocturnal 413.0
  phlegmonous 475
    diphtheritic 032.0
  preinfarctional 411.1
  Prinzmetal's 413.1
  progressive 411.1
  pseudomembranous 101
  psychogenic 306.2
  pultaceous, diphtheritic 032.0
  scarlatinal 034.1
  septic 034.0
  simple 462
  stable NEC 413.9

ICD-9-CM

A

Vol. 2

Angina *(Continued)*
staphylococcal 462
streptococcal 034.0
stridulous, diphtheritic 032.3
syphilitic 093.9
congenital 090.5
tonsil 475
trachealis 464.4
unstable 411.1
variant 413.1
Vincent's 101
Angioblastoma (M9161/1) - *see* Neoplasm, connective tissue, uncertain behavior
Angiocholecystitis (*see also* Cholecystitis, acute) 575.0
Angiocholitis (*see also* Cholecystitis, acute) 576.1
Angiodysgenesis spinalis 336.1
Angiodysplasia (intestinalis) (intestine) 569.84
with hemorrhage 569.85
duodenum 537.82
with hemorrhage 537.83
stomach 537.82
with hemorrhage 537.83
Angioedema (allergic) (any site) (with urticaria) 995.1
hereditary 277.6
Angioendothelioma (M9130/1) - *see also* Neoplasm, by site, uncertain behavior
benign (M9130/0) (*see also* Hemangioma, by site) 228.00
bone (M9260/3) - *see* Neoplasm, bone, malignant
Ewing's (M9260/3) - *see* Neoplasm, bone, malignant
nervous system (M9130/0) 228.09
Angiofibroma (M9160/0) - *see also* Neoplasm, by site, benign
juvenile (M9160/0) 210.7
specified site - *see* Neoplasm, by site, benign
unspecified site 210.7
Angiohemophilia (A) (B) 286.4
Angioid streaks (choroid) (retina) 363.43
Angiokeratoma (M9141/0) - *see also* Neoplasm, skin, benign
corporis diffusum 272.7
Angiokeratosis
diffuse 272.7
Angioleiomyoma (M8894/0) - *see* Neoplasm, connective tissue, benign
Angioleucitis 683
Angiolipoma (M8861/0) (*see also* Lipoma, by site) 214.9
infiltrating (M8861/1) - *see* Neoplasm, connective tissue, uncertain behavior
Angioma (M9120/0) (*see also* Hemangioma, by site) 228.00
capillary 448.1
hemorrhagicum hereditaria 448.0
malignant (M9120/3) - *see* Neoplasm, connective tissue, malignant
pigmentosum et atrophicum 757.33
placenta - *see* Placenta, abnormal
plexiform (M9131/0) - *see* Hemangioma, by site
senile 448.1
serpiginosum 709.1
spider 448.1
stellate 448.1

Angiomatosis 757.32
bacillary 083.8
corporis diffusum universale 272.7
cutaneocerebral 759.6
encephalocutaneous 759.6
encephalofacial 759.6
encephalotrigeminal 759.6
hemorrhagic familial 448.0
hereditary familial 448.0
heredofamilial 448.0
meningo-oculofacial 759.6
multiple sites 228.09
neuro-oculocutaneous 759.6
retina (Hippel's disease) 759.6
retinocerebellosa 759.6
retinocerebral 759.6
systemic 228.09
Angiomyolipoma (M8860/0)
specified site - *see* Neoplasm, connective tissue, benign
unspecified site 223.0
Angiomyoliposarcoma (M8860/3) - *see* Neoplasm, connective tissue, malignant
Angiomyoma (M8894/0) - *see* Neoplasm, connective tissue, benign
Angiomyosarcoma (M8894/3) - *see* Neoplasm, connective tissue, malignant
Angioneurosis 306.2
Angioneurotic edema (allergic) (any site) (with urticaria) 995.1
hereditary 277.6
Angiopathia, angiopathy 459.9
diabetic (peripheral) 250.7 *[443.81]*
peripheral 443.9
diabetic 250.7 *[443.81]*
specified type NEC 443.89
retinae syphilitica 093.89
retinalis (juvenilis) 362.18
background 362.10
diabetic 250.5 *[362.01]*
proliferative 362.29
tuberculous (*see also* Tuberculosis) 017.3 *[362.18]*
Angiosarcoma (M9120/3) - *see* Neoplasm, connective tissue, malignant
Angiosclerosis - *see* Arteriosclerosis
Angioscotoma, enlarged 368.42
Angiospasm 443.9
brachial plexus 353.0
cerebral 435.9
cervical plexus 353.2
nerve
arm 354.9
axillary 353.0
median 354.1
ulnar 354.2
autonomic (*see also* Neuropathy, peripheral, autonomic) 337.9
axillary 353.0
leg 355.8
plantar 355.6
lower extremity - *see* Angiospasm, nerve, leg
median 354.1
peripheral NEC 355.9
spinal NEC 355.9
sympathetic (*see also* Neuropathy, peripheral, autonomic) 337.9
ulnar 354.2
upper extremity - *see* Angiospasm, nerve, arm
peripheral NEC 443.9

Angiospasm *(Continued)*
traumatic 443.9
foot 443.9
leg 443.9
vessel 443.9
Angiospastic disease or edema 443.9
Anguillulosis 127.2
Angulation
cecum (*see also* Obstruction, intestine) 560.9
coccyx (acquired) 738.6
congenital 756.19
femur (acquired) 736.39
congenital 755.69
intestine (large) (small) (*see also* Obstruction, intestine) 560.9
sacrum (acquired) 738.5
congenital 756.19
sigmoid (flexure) (*see also* Obstruction, intestine) 560.9
spine (*see also* Curvature, spine) 737.9
tibia (acquired) 736.89
congenital 755.69
ureter 593.3
wrist (acquired) 736.09
congenital 755.59
Angulus infectiosus 686.8
Anhedonia 302.72
Anhidrosis (lid) (neurogenic) (thermogenic) 705.0
Anhydration 276.5
with
hypernatremia 276.0
hyponatremia 276.1
Anhydremia 276.5
with
hypernatremia 276.0
hyponatremia 276.1
Anidrosis 705.0
Aniridia (congenital) 743.45
Anisakiasis (infection) (infestation) 127.1
Anisakis larva infestation 127.1
Aniseikonia 367.32
Anisocoria (pupil) 379.41
congenital 743.46
Anisocytosis 790.0
Anisometropia (congenital) 367.31
Ankle - *see* condition
Ankyloblepharon (acquired) (eyelid) 374.46
filiforme (adnatum) (congenital) 743.62
total 743.62
Ankylodactyly (*see also* Syndactylism) 755.10
Ankyloglossia 750.0
Ankylosis (fibrous) (osseous) 718.50
ankle 718.57
any joint, produced by surgical fusion V45.4
cricoarytenoid (cartilage) (joint) (larynx) 478.79
dental 521.6
ear ossicle NEC 385.22
malleus 385.21
elbow 718.52
finger 718.54
hip 718.55
incostapedial joint (infectional) 385.22
joint, produced by surgical fusion NEC V45.4
knee 718.56
lumbosacral (joint) 724.6
malleus 385.21

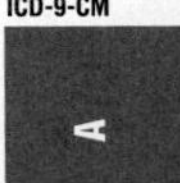

Anomaly, anomalous *(Continued)*
 chromosomes, chromosomal *(Continued)*
  E₃ 758.2
  G 758.0
  mitochondrial 758.9
  mosaics 758.89
  sex 758.81
   complement, XO 758.6
   complement, XXX 758.81
   complement, XXY 758.7
   complement, XYY 758.81
   gonadal dysgenesis 758.6
   Klinefelter's 758.7
   Turner's 758.6
   trisomy 21 758.0
 cilia 743.9
 circulatory system 747.9
  specified type NEC 747.89
 clavicle 755.51
 clitoris 752.40
 coccyx 756.10
 colon 751.5
 common duct 751.60
 communication
  coronary artery 746.85
  left ventricle with right atrium
    745.4
 concha (ear) 744.3
 connection
  renal vessels with kidney
    747.62
  total pulmonary venous 747.41
 connective tissue 756.9
  specified type NEC 756.89
 cornea 743.9
  shape 743.41
  size 743.41
  specified type NEC 743.49
 coronary
  artery 746.85
  vein 746.89
 cranium - *see* Anomaly, skull
 cricoid cartilage 748.3
 cushion, endocardial 745.60
  specified type NEC 745.69
 cystic duct 751.60
 dental arch relationship 524.2
 dentition 520.6
 dentofacial NEC 524.9
  functional 524.5
  specified type NEC 524.8
 dermatoglyphic 757.2
 Descemet's membrane 743.9
  specified type NEC 743.49
 development
  cervix 752.40
  vagina 752.40
  vulva 752.40
 diaphragm, diaphragmatic (apertures)
   NEC 756.6
 digestive organ(s) or system 751.9
  lower 751.5
  specified type NEC 751.8
  upper 750.9
 distribution, coronary artery 746.85
 ductus
  arteriosus 747.0
  Botalli 747.0
 duodenum 751.5
 dura 742.9
  brain 742.4
  spinal cord 742.59
 ear 744.3

Anomaly, anomalous *(Continued)*
 ear *(Continued)*
  causing impairment of hearing
    744.00
   specified type NEC 744.09
  external 744.3
   causing impairment of hearing
     744.02
   specified type NEC 744.29
  inner (causing impairment of hear-
    ing) 744.05
  middle, except ossicles (causing im-
    pairment of hearing) 744.03
   ossicles 744.04
  ossicles 744.04
  prominent auricle 744.29
  specified type NEC 744.29
   with hearing impairment
     744.09
 Ebstein's (heart) 746.2
  tricuspid valve 746.2
 ectodermal 757.9
 Eisenmenger's (ventricular septal defect) 745.4
 ejaculatory duct 752.9
  specified type NEC 752.8
 elbow (joint) 755.50
 endocardial cushion 745.60
  specified type NEC 745.69
 endocrine gland NEC 759.2
 epididymis 752.9
 epiglottis 748.3
 esophagus 750.9
  specified type NEC 750.4
 Eustachian tube 744.3
  specified type NEC 744.24
 eye (any part) 743.9
  adnexa 743.9
   specified type NEC 743.69
  anophthalmos 743.00
  anterior
   chamber and related structures
     743.9
    angle 743.9
     specified type NEC 743.44
    specified type NEC 743.44
   segment 743.9
    combined 743.48
    multiple 743.48
    specified type NEC 743.49
  cataract (*see also* Cataract) 743.30
  glaucoma (*see also* Buphthalmia)
    743.20
  lid 743.9
   specified type NEC 743.63
  microphthalmos (*see also* Mi-
    crophthalmos) 743.10
  posterior segment 743.9
   specified type NEC 743.59
   vascular 743.58
   vitreous 743.9
    specified type NEC 743.51
  ptosis (eyelid) 743.61
  retina 743.9
   specified type NEC 743.59
  sclera 743.9
   specified type NEC 743.47
  specified type NEC 743.8
 eyebrow 744.89
 eyelid 743.9
  specified type NEC 743.63
 face (any part) 744.9
  bone(s) 756.0
  specified type NEC 744.89

Anomaly, anomalous *(Continued)*
 fallopian tube 752.10
  specified type NEC 752.19
 fascia 756.9
  specified type NEC 756.89
 femur 755.60
 fibula 755.60
 finger 755.50
  supernumerary 755.01
  webbed (*see also* Syndactylism, fin-
    gers) 755.11
 fixation, intestine 751.4
 flexion (joint) 755.9
  hip or thigh (*see also* Dislocation,
    hip, congenital) 754.30
 folds, heart 746.9
 foot 755.67
 foramen
  Botalli 745.5
  ovale 745.5
 forearm 755.50
 forehead (*see also* Anomaly, skull)
   756.0
 form, teeth 520.2
 fovea centralis 743.9
 frontal bone (*see also* Anomaly, skull)
   756.0
 gallbladder 751.60
 Gartner's duct 752.11
 gastrointestinal tract 751.9
  specified type NEC 751.8
  vessel 747.61
 genitalia, genital organ(s) or system
   female 752.9
    external 752.40
     specified type NEC 752.49
    internal NEC 752.9
   male (external and internal) 752.9
    epispadias 752.62
    hidden penis 752.65
    hydrocele, congenital 778.6
    hypospadias 752.61
    micropenis 752.64
    testis, undescended 752.51
     retractile 752.52
   specified type NEC 752.8
 genitourinary NEC 752.9
 Gerbode 745.4
 globe (eye) 743.9
 glottis 748.3
 granulation or granulocyte, genetic
   288.2
  constitutional 288.2
  leukocyte 288.2
 gum 750.9
 gyri 742.9
 hair 757.9
  specified type NEC 757.4
 hand 755.50
 hard tissue formation in pulp 522.3
 head (*see also* Anomaly, skull)
   756.0
 heart 746.9
  auricle 746.9
  bands 746.9
  fibroelastosis cordis 425.3
  folds 746.9
  malposition 746.87
  maternal, affecting fetus or newborn
    760.3
  obstructive NEC 746.84
  patent ductus arteriosus (Botalli)
    747.0
  septum 745.9

Anomaly, anomalous *(Continued)*
  heart *(Continued)*
    septum *(Continued)*
      acquired 429.71
      aortic 745.0
      aorticopulmonary 745.0
      atrial 745.5
      auricular 745.5
      between aorta and pulmonary
        artery 745.0
      endocardial cushion type
        745.60
        specified type NEC 745.69
      interatrial 745.5
      interventricular 745.4
        with pulmonary stenosis or
          atresia, dextraposition of
          aorta, and hypertrophy of
          right ventricle 745.2
        acquired 429.71
      specified type NEC 745.8
      ventricular 745.4
        with pulmonary stenosis or
          atresia, dextraposition of
          aorta, and hypertrophy of
          right ventricle 745.2
        acquired 429.71
    specified type NEC 746.89
    tetralogy of Fallot 745.2
    valve NEC 746.9
      aortic 746.9
        atresia 746.89
        bicuspid valve 746.4
        insufficiency 746.4
        specified type NEC 746.89
        stenosis 746.3
          subaortic 746.81
          supravalvular 747.22
      mitral 746.9
        atresia 746.89
        insufficiency 746.6
        specified type NEC 746.89
        stenosis 746.5
      pulmonary 746.00
        atresia 746.01
        insufficiency 746.09
        stenosis 746.02
          infundibular 746.83
          subvalvular 746.83
      tricuspid 746.9
        atresia 746.1
        stenosis 746.1
    ventricle 746.9
  heel 755.67
  Hegglin's 288.2
  hemianencephaly 740.0
  hemicephaly 740.0
  hemicrania 740.0
  hepatic duct 751.60
  hip (joint) 755.63
  hourglass
    bladder 753.8
    gallbladder 751.69
    stomach 750.7
  humerus 755.50
  hymen 752.40
  hypersegmentation of neutrophils, hereditary 288.2
  hypophyseal 759.2
  ileocecal (coil) (valve) 751.5
  ileum (intestine) 751.5
  ilium 755.60
  integument 757.9
    specified type NEC 757.8

Anomaly, anomalous *(Continued)*
  intervertebral cartilage or disc 756.10
  intestine (large) (small) 751.5
    fixational type 751.4
  iris 743.9
    specified type NEC 743.46
  ischium 755.60
  jaw NEC 524.9
    closure 524.5
    size (major) NEC 524.00
    specified type NEC 524.8
  jaw-cranial base relationship 524.10
    specified NEC 524.19
  jejunum 751.5
  joint 755.9
    hip
      dislocation *(see also* Dislocation,
        hip, congenital) 754.30
      predislocation *(see also* Subluxation, congenital, hip) 754.32
      preluxation *(see also* Subluxation, congenital, hip) 754.32
      subluxation *(see also* Subluxation, congenital, hip) 754.32
    lumbosacral 756.10
      spondylolisthesis 756.12
      spondylosis 756.11
    multiple arthrogryposis 754.89
    sacroiliac 755.69
  Jordan's 288.2
  kidney(s) (calyx) (pelvis) 753.9
    vessel 747.62
  Klippel-Feil (brevicollis) 756.16
  knee (joint) 755.64
  labium (majus) (minus) 752.40
  labyrinth, membranous (causing impairment of hearing) 744.05
  lacrimal
    apparatus, duct or passage 743.9
      specified type NEC 743.65
    gland 743.9
      specified type NEC 743.64
  Langdon Down (mongolism) 758.0
  larynx, laryngeal (muscle) 748.3
    web, webbed 748.2
  leg (lower) (upper) 755.60
    reduction NEC *(see also* Deformity, reduction, lower limb) 755.30
  lens 743.9
    shape 743.36
    specified type NEC 743.39
  leukocytes, genetic 288.2
    granulation (constitutional) 288.2
  lid (fold) 743.9
  ligament 756.9
    broad 752.10
    round 752.9
  limb, except reduction deformity 755.8
    lower 755.60
      reduction deformity *(see also* Deformity, reduction, lower limb) 755.30
      specified type NEC 755.69
    upper 755.50
      reduction deformity *(see also* Deformity, reduction, upper limb) 755.20
      specified type NEC 755.59
  lip 750.9
    harelip *(see also* Cleft, lip) 749.10
    specified type NEC 750.26
  liver (duct) 751.60
    atresia 751.69

Anomaly, anomalous *(Continued)*
  lower extremity 755.60
    vessel 747.64
  lumbosacral (joint) (region) 756.10
  lung (fissure) (lobe) NEC 748.60
    agenesis 748.5
    specified type NEC 748.69
  lymphatic system 759.9
  Madelung's (radius) 755.54
  mandible 524.9
    size NEC 524.00
  maxilla 524.90
    size NEC 524.00
  May (-Hegglin) 288.2
  meatus urinarius 753.9
    specified type NEC 753.8
  meningeal bands or folds, constriction of 742.8
  meninges 742.9
    brain 742.4
    spinal 742.59
  meningocele *(see also* Spina bifida) 741.9
  mesentery 751.9
  metacarpus 755.50
  metatarsus 755.67
  middle ear, except ossicles (causing impairment of hearing) 744.03
    ossicles 744.04
  mitral (leaflets) (valve) 746.9
    atresia 746.89
    insufficiency 746.6
    specified type NEC 746.89
    stenosis 746.5
  mouth 750.9
    specified type NEC 750.26
  multiple NEC 759.7
    specified type NEC 759.89
  muscle 756.9
    eye 743.9
      specified type NEC 743.69
    specified type NEC 756.89
  musculoskeletal system, except limbs 756.9
    specified type NEC 756.9
  nail 757.9
    specified type NEC 757.5
  narrowness, eyelid 743.62
  nasal sinus or septum 748.1
  neck (any part) 744.9
    specified type NEC 744.89
  nerve 742.9
    acoustic 742.9
      specified type NEC 742.8
    optic 742.9
      specified type NEC 742.8
    specified type NEC 742.8
  nervous system NEC 742.9
    brain 742.9
      specified type NEC 742.4
    specified type NEC 742.8
  neurological 742.9
  nipple 757.9
  nonteratogenic NEC 754.89
  nose, nasal (bone) (cartilage) (septum) (sinus) 748.1
  ocular muscle 743.9
  omphalomesenteric duct 751.0
  opening, pulmonary veins 747.49
  optic
    disc 743.9
      specified type NEC 743.57
    nerve 742.9

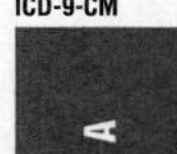

Anomaly, anomalous *(Continued)*
opticociliary vessels 743.9
orbit (eye) 743.9
  specified type NEC 743.66
organ
  of Corti (causing impairment of
      hearing) 744.05
  or site 759.9
    specified type NEC 759.89
origin
  both great arteries from same ventri-
      cle 745.11
  coronary artery 746.85
  innominate artery 747.69
  left coronary artery from pulmonary
      artery 746.85
  pulmonary artery 747.3
  renal vessels 747.62
  subclavian artery (left) (right)
      747.21
osseous meatus (ear) 744.03
ovary 752.0
oviduct 752.10
palate (hard) (soft) 750.9
  cleft (*see also* Cleft, palate) 749.00
pancreas (duct) 751.7
papillary muscles 746.9
parathyroid gland 759.2
paraurethral ducts 753.9
parotid (gland) 750.9
patella 755.64
Pelger-Huët (hereditary hyposegmen-
    tation) 288.2
pelvic girdle 755.60
  specified type NEC 755.69
pelvis (bony) 755.60
  complicating delivery 653.0
  rachitic 268.1
    fetal 756.4
penis (glans) 752.69
pericardium 746.89
peripheral vascular system NEC 747.60
  gastrointestinal 747.61
  lower limb 747.64
  renal 747.62
  specified site NEC 747.69
  spinal 747.82
  upper limb 747.63
Peter's 743.44
pharynx 750.9
  branchial cleft 744.41
  specified type NEC 750.29
Pierre Robin 756.0
pigmentation 709.00
  congenital 757.33
  specified NEC 709.09
pituitary (gland) 759.2
pleural folds 748.8
portal vein 747.40
position tooth, teeth 524.3
preauricular sinus 744.46
prepuce 752.9
prostate 752.9
pulmonary 748.60
  artery 747.3
  circulation 747.3
  specified type NEC 748.69
  valve 746.00
    atresia 746.01
    insufficiency 746.09
    specified type NEC 746.09
    stenosis 746.02
      infundibular 746.83
      subvalvular 746.83

Anomaly, anomalous *(Continued)*
pulmonary *(Continued)*
  vein 747.40
  venous
    connection 747.49
      partial 747.42
      total 747.41
    return 747.49
      partial 747.42
      total (TAPVR) (complete) (sub-
          diaphragmatic) (supradia-
          phragmatic) 747.41
pupil 743.9
pylorus 750.9
  hypertrophy 750.5
  stenosis 750.5
rachitic, fetal 756.4
radius 755.50
rectovaginal (septum) 752.40
rectum 751.5
refraction 367.9
renal 753.9
  vessel 747.62
respiratory system 748.9
  specified type NEC 748.8
rib 756.3
  cervical 756.2
Rieger's 743.44
rings, trachea 748.3
rotation - *see also* Malrotation
  hip or thigh (*see also* Subluxation,
      congenital, hip) 754.32
round ligament 752.9
sacroiliac (joint) 755.69
sacrum 756.10
saddle
  back 754.2
  nose 754.0
    syphilitic 090.5
salivary gland or duct 750.9
  specified type NEC 750.26
scapula 755.50
sclera 743.9
  specified type NEC 743.47
scrotum 752.9
sebaceous gland 757.9
seminal duct or tract 752.9
sense organs 742.9
  specified type NEC 742.8
septum
  heart - *see* Anomaly, heart,
      septum
  nasal 748.1
sex chromosomes NEC (*see also*
    Anomaly, chromosomes)
    758.81
shoulder (girdle) (joint) 755.50
  specified type NEC 755.59
sigmoid (flexure) 751.5
sinus of Valsalva 747.29
site NEC 759.9
skeleton generalized NEC 756.50
skin (appendage) 757.9
  specified type NEC 757.39
skull (bone) 756.0
  with
    anencephalus 740.0
    encephalocele 742.0
    hydrocephalus 742.3
      with spina bifida (*see also* Spina
          bifida) 741.0
    microcephalus 742.1
specified type NEC
  adrenal (gland) 759.1

Anomaly, anomalous *(Continued)*
specified type NEC *(Continued)*
  alimentary tract (complete) (partial)
      751.8
    lower 751.5
    upper 750.8
  ankle 755.69
  anus, anal (canal) 751.5
  aorta, aortic 747.29
    arch 747.21
  appendix 751.5
  arm 755.59
  artery (peripheral) NEC (*see also*
      Anomaly, peripheral vascular
      system) 747.60
    brain 747.81
    coronary 746.85
    eye 743.58
    pulmonary 747.3
    retinal 743.58
    umbilical 747.5
  auditory canal 744.29
    causing impairment of hearing
        744.02
  bile duct or passage 751.69
  bladder 753.8
    neck 753.8
  bone(s) 756.9
    arm 755.59
    face 756.0
    leg 755.69
    pelvic girdle 755.69
    shoulder girdle 755.59
    skull 756.0
      with
        anencephalus 740.0
        encephalocele 742.0
        hydrocephalus 742.3
          with spina bifida (*see
              also* Spina bifida)
              741.0
        microcephalus 742.1
  brain 742.4
  breast 757.6
  broad ligament 752.19
  bronchus 748.3
  canal of Nuck 752.8
  cardiac septal closure 745.8
  carpus 755.59
  cartilaginous 756.9
  cecum 751.5
  cervix 752.49
  chest (wall) 756.3
  chin 744.89
  ciliary body 743.46
  circulatory system 747.89
  clavicle 755.51
  clitoris 752.49
  coccyx 756.19
  colon 751.5
  common duct 751.69
  connective tissue 756.89
  cricoid cartilage 748.3
  cystic duct 751.69
  diaphragm 756.6
  digestive organ(s) or tract
      751.8
    lower 751.5
    upper 750.8
  duodenum 751.5
  ear 744.29
    auricle 744.29
      causing impairment of hearing
          744.02

Anomaly, anomalous (*Continued*)
specified type NEC (*Continued*)
ear (*Continued*)
causing impairment of hearing 744.09
inner (causing impairment of hearing) 744.05
middle, except ossicles 744.03
ossicles 744.04
ejaculatory duct 752.8
endocrine 759.2
epiglottis 748.3
esophagus 750.4
eustachian tube 744.24
eye 743.8
lid 743.63
muscle 743.69
face 744.89
bone(s) 756.0
fallopian tube 752.19
fascia 756.89
femur 755.69
fibula 755.69
finger 755.59
foot 755.67
fovea centralis 743.55
gallbladder 751.69
Gartner's duct 752.8
gastrointestinal tract 751.8
genitalia, genital organ(s)
female 752.8
external 752.49
internal NEC 752.8
male 752.8
penis 752.69
genitourinary tract NEC 752.8
glottis 748.3
hair 757.4
hand 755.59
heart 746.89
valve NEC 746.89
pulmonary 746.09
hepatic duct 751.69
hydatid of Morgagni 752.8
hymen 752.49
integument 757.8
intestine (large) (small) 751.5
fixational type 751.4
iris 743.46
jejunum 751.5
joint 755.8
kidney 753.3
knee 755.64
labium (majus) (minus) 752.49
labyrinth, membranous 744.05
larynx 748.3
leg 755.69
lens 743.39
limb, except reduction deformity 755.8
lower 755.69
reduction deformity (*see also* Deformity, reduction, lower limb) 755.30
upper 755.59
reduction deformity (*see also* Deformity, reduction, upper limb) 755.20
lip 750.26
liver 751.69
lung (fissure) (lobe) 748.69
meatus urinarius 753.8
metacarpus 755.59

Anomaly, anomalous (*Continued*)
specified type NEC (*Continued*)
mouth 750.26
muscle 756.89
eye 743.69
musculoskeletal system, except limbs 756.9
nail 757.5
neck 744.89
nerve 742.8
acoustic 742.8
optic 742.8
nervous system 742.8
nipple 757.6
nose 748.1
organ NEC 759.89
of Corti 744.05
osseous meatus (ear) 744.03
ovary 752.0
oviduct 752.19
pancreas 751.7
parathyroid 759.2
patella 755.64
pelvic girdle 755.69
penis 752.69
pericardium 746.89
peripheral vascular system NEC (*see also* Anomaly, peripheral vascular system) 747.60
pharynx 750.29
pituitary 759.2
prostate 752.8
radius 755.59
rectum 751.5
respiratory system 748.8
rib 756.3
round ligament 752.8
sacrum 756.19
salivary duct or gland 750.26
scapula 755.59
sclera 743.47
scrotum 752.8
seminal duct or tract 752.8
shoulder girdle 755.59
site NEC 759.89
skin 757.39
skull (bone(s)) 756.0
with
anencephalus 740.0
encephalocele 742.0
hydrocephalus 742.3
with spina bifida (*see also* Spina bifida) 741.0
microcephalus 742.1
specified organ or site NEC 759.89
spermatic cord 752.8
spinal cord 742.59
spine 756.19
spleen 759.0
sternum 756.3
stomach 750.7
tarsus 755.67
tendon 756.89
testis 752.8
thorax (wall) 756.3
thymus 759.2
thyroid (gland) 759.2
cartilage 748.3
tibia 755.69
toe 755.66
tongue 750.19
trachea (cartilage) 748.3
ulna 755.59

Anomaly, anomalous (*Continued*)
specified type NEC (*Continued*)
urachus 753.7
ureter 753.4
obstructive 753.29
urethra 753.8
obstructive 753.6
urinary tract 753.8
uterus 752.3
uvula 750.26
vagina 752.49
vascular NEC (*see also* Anomaly, peripheral vascular system) 747.60
brain 747.81
vas deferens 752.8
vein(s) (peripheral) NEC (*see also* Anomaly, peripheral vascular system) 747.60
brain 747.81
great 747.49
portal 747.49
pulmonary 747.49
vena cava (inferior) (superior) 747.49
vertebra 756.19
vulva 752.49
spermatic cord 752.9
spine, spinal 756.10
column 756.10
cord 742.9
meningocele (*see also* Spina bifida) 741.9
specified type NEC 742.59
spina bifida (*see also* Spina bifida) 741.9
vessel 747.82
meninges 742.59
nerve root 742.9
spleen 759.0
Sprengel's 755.52
sternum 756.3
stomach 750.9
specified type NEC 750.7
submaxillary gland 750.9
superior vena cava 747.40
talipes - *see* Talipes
tarsus 755.67
with complete absence of distal elements 755.31
teeth, tooth NEC 520.9
position 524.3
spacing 524.3
tendon 756.9
specified type NEC 756.89
termination
coronary artery 746.85
testis 752.9
thebesian valve 746.9
thigh 755.60
flexion (*see also* Subluxation, congenital, hip) 754.32
thorax (wall) 756.3
throat 750.9
thumb 755.50
supernumerary 755.01
thymus gland 759.2
thyroid (gland) 759.2
cartilage 748.3
tibia 755.60
saber 090.5
toe 755.66
supernumerary 755.02
webbed (*see also* Syndactylism, toes) 755.13

Anomaly, anomalous *(Continued)*
tongue 750.10
  specified type NEC 750.19
trachea, tracheal 748.3
  cartilage 748.3
  rings 748.3
tragus 744.3
transverse aortic arch 747.21
trichromata 368.59
trichromatopsia 368.59
tricuspid (leaflet) (valve) 746.9
  atresia 746.1
  Ebstein's 746.2
  specified type NEC 746.89
  stenosis 746.1
trunk 759.9
Uhl's (hypoplasia of myocardium,
    right ventricle) 746.84
ulna 755.50
umbilicus 759.9
  artery 747.5
union, trachea with larynx 748.3
unspecified site 759.9
upper extremity 755.50
  vessel 747.63
urachus 753.7
  specified type NEC 753.7
ureter 753.9
  obstructive 753.20
  specified type NEC 753.4
    obstructive 753.29
urethra (valve) 753.9
  obstructive 753.6
  specified type NEC 753.8
urinary tract or system (any part, ex-
    cept urachus) 753.9
  specified type NEC 753.8
  urachus 753.7
uterus 752.3
  with only one functioning horn
    752.3
  in pregnancy or childbirth 654.0
    affecting fetus or newborn
      763.89
    causing obstructed labor 660.2
      affecting fetus or newborn
        763.1
uvula 750.9
vagina 752.40
valleculae 748.3
valve (heart) NEC 746.9
  formation, ureter 753.29
  pulmonary 746.00
  specified type NEC 746.89
vascular NEC (*see also* Anomaly,
    peripheral vascular system)
    747.60
  ring 747.21
vas deferens 752.9
vein(s) (peripheral) NEC (*see also*
    Anomaly, peripheral vascular sys-
    tem) 747.60
  brain 747.81
  cerebral 747.81
  coronary 746.89
  great 747.40
    specified type NEC 747.49
  portal 747.40
  pulmonary 747.40
  retina 743.9
vena cava (inferior) (superior) 747.40
venous return (pulmonary) 747.49
  partial 747.42
  total 747.41

Anomaly, anomalous *(Continued)*
ventricle, ventricular (heart) 746.9
  bands 746.9
  folds 746.9
  septa 745.4
vertebra 756.10
vesicourethral orifice 753.9
vessels NEC (*see also* Anomaly, periph-
    eral vascular system) 747.60
  optic papilla 743.9
vitelline duct 751.0
vitreous humor 743.9
  specified type NEC 743.51
vulva 752.40
wrist (joint) 755.50
Anomia 784.69
Anonychia 757.5
  acquired 703.8
Anophthalmos, anophthalmus (clinical)
    (congenital) (globe) 743.00
  acquired 360.89
Anopsia (altitudinal) (quadrant) 368.46
Anorchia 752.8
Anorchism, anorchidism 752.8
Anorexia 783.0
  hysterical 300.11
  nervosa 307.1
Anosmia (*see also* Disturbance, sensation)
    781.1
  hysterical 300.11
  postinfectional 478.9
  psychogenic 306.7
  traumatic 951.8
Anosognosia 780.9
Anosphrasia 781.1
Anosteoplasia 756.50
Anotia 744.09
Anovulatory cycle 628.0
Anoxemia 799.0
  newborn 770.8
Anoxia 799.0
  altitude 993.2
  cerebral 348.1
    with
      abortion - *see* Abortion, by type,
        with specified complication
        NEC
      ectopic pregnancy (*see also* catego-
        ries 633.0-633.9) 639.8
      molar pregnancy (*see also* catego-
        ries 630-632) 639.8
    complicating
      delivery (cesarean) (instrumental)
        669.4
      ectopic or molar pregnancy 639.8
      obstetric anesthesia or sedation
        668.2
    during or resulting from a proce-
      dure 997.01
    following
      abortion 639.8
      ectopic or molar pregnancy 639.8
  newborn (*see also* Distress, fetal,
      liveborn infant) 768.9
  due to drowning 994.1
  fetal, affecting newborn 770.8
  heart - *see* Insufficiency, coronary
  high altitude 993.2
  intrauterine
    fetal death (before onset of labor)
      768.0
      during labor 768.1
    liveborn infant - *see* Distress, fetal,
      liveborn infant

Anoxia *(Continued)*
  myocardial - *see* Insufficiency, coronary
  newborn 768.9
    mild or moderate 768.6
    severe 768.5
  pathological 799.0
Anteflexion - *see* Anteversion
Antenatal
  care, normal pregnancy V22.1
    first V22.0
  screening (for) V28.9
    based on amniocentesis NEC V28.2
      chromosomal anomalies V28.0
      raised alphafetoprotein levels V28.1
    chromosomal anomalies V28.0
    fetal growth retardation using ultra-
      sonics V28.4
    isoimmunization V28.5
    malformations using ultrasonics
      V28.3
    raised alphafetoprotein levels in am-
      niotic fluid V28.1
    specified condition NEC V28.8
    Streptococcus B V28.6
Antepartum - *see* condition
Anterior - *see also* condition
  spinal artery compression syndrome
    721.1
Antero-occlusion 524.2
Anteversion
  cervix (*see also* Anteversion, uterus)
    621.6
  femur (neck), congenital 755.63
  uterus, uterine (cervix) (postinfec-
    tional) (postpartal, old) 621.6
    congenital 752.3
    in pregnancy or childbirth 654.4
      affecting fetus or newborn
        763.89
      causing obstructed labor 660.2
        affecting fetus or newborn 763.1
Anthracosilicosis (occupational) 500
Anthracosis (lung) (occupational) 500
  lingua 529.3
Anthrax 022.9
  with pneumonia 022.1 [484.5]
  colitis 022.2
  cutaneous 022.0
  gastrointestinal 022.2
  intestinal 022.2
  pulmonary 022.1
  respiratory 022.1
  septicemia 022.3
  specified manifestation NEC 022.8
Anthropoid pelvis 755.69
  with disproportion (fetopelvic) 653.2
    affecting fetus or newborn 763.1
    causing obstructed labor 660.1
      affecting fetus or newborn 763.1
Anthropophobia 300.29
Antibioma, breast 611.0
Antibodies
  maternal (blood group) (*see also* Incom-
    patibility) 656.2
    anti-D, cord blood 656.1
      fetus or newborn 773.0
Antibody deficiency syndrome
  agammaglobulinemic 279.00
  congenital 279.04
  hypogammaglobulinemic 279.00
Anticoagulant, circulating (*see also* Cir-
    culating anticoagulants) 286.5
Antimongolism syndrome 758.3
Antimonial cholera 985.4

Apoplexia, apoplexy, apoplectic (Continued)
fit (see also Disease, cerebrovascular, acute) 436
healed or old V12.59
heart (auricle) (ventricle) (see also Infarct, myocardium) 410.9
heat 992.0
hemiplegia (see also Disease, cerebrovascular, acute) 436
hemorrhagic (stroke) (see also Hemorrhage, brain) 432.9
ingravescent (see also Disease, cerebrovascular, acute) 436
late effect - see Late effect(s) (of) cerebrovascular disease
lung - see Embolism, pulmonary
meninges, hemorrhagic (see also Hemorrhage, subarachnoid) 430
neonatorum 767.0
newborn 767.0
pancreatitis 577.0
placenta 641.2
progressive (see also Disease, cerebrovascular, acute) 436
pulmonary (artery) (vein) - see Embolism, pulmonary
sanguineous (see also Disease, cerebrovascular, acute) 436
seizure (see also Disease, cerebrovascular, acute) 436
serous (see also Disease, cerebrovascular, acute) 436
spleen 289.59
stroke (see also Disease, cerebrovascular, acute) 436
thrombotic (see also Thrombosis, brain) 434.0
uremic - see Uremia
uteroplacental 641.2
Appendage
fallopian tube (cyst of Morgagni) 752.11
intestine (epiploic) 751.5
preauricular 744.1
testicular (organ of Morgagni) 752.8
Appendicitis 541
with
perforation, peritonitis (generalized), or rupture 540.0
with peritoneal abscess 540.1
peritoneal abscess 540.1
acute (catarrhal) (fulminating) (gangrenous) (inflammatory) (obstructive) (retrocecal) (suppurative) 540.9
with
perforation, peritonitis, or rupture 540.0
with peritoneal abscess 540.1
peritoneal abscess 540.1
amebic 006.8
chronic (recurrent) 542
exacerbation - see Appendicitis, acute
fulminating - see Appendicitis, acute
gangrenous - see Appendicitis, acute
healed (obliterative) 542
interval 542
neurogenic 542
obstructive 542
pneumococcal 541
recurrent 542
relapsing 542
retrocecal 541

Appendicitis (Continued)
subacute (adhesive) 542
subsiding 542
suppurative - see Appendicitis, acute
tuberculous (see also Tuberculosis) 014.8
Appendiclausis 543.9
Appendicolithiasis 543.9
Appendicopathia oxyurica 127.4
Appendix, appendicular - see also condition
Morgagni (male) 752.8
fallopian tube 752.11
Appetite
depraved 307.52
excessive 783.6
psychogenic 307.51
lack or loss (see also Anorexia) 783.0
nonorganic origin 307.59
perverted 307.52
hysterical 300.11
Apprehension, apprehensiveness (abnormal) (state) 300.00
specified type NEC 300.09
Approximal wear 521.1
Apraxia (classic) (ideational) (ideokinetic) (ideomotor) (motor) 784.69
oculomotor, congenital 379.51
verbal 784.69
Aptyalism 527.7
Arabicum elephantiasis (see also Infestation, filarial) 125.9
Arachnidism 989.5
Arachnitis - see Meningitis
Arachnodactyly 759.82
Arachnoidism 989.5
Arachnoiditis (acute) (adhesive) (basic) (brain) (cerebrospinal) (chiasmal) (chronic) (spinal) (see also Meningitis) 322.9
meningococcal (chronic) 036.0
syphilitic 094.2
tuberculous (see also Tuberculosis, meninges) 013.0
Araneism 989.5
Arboencephalitis, Australian 062.4
Arborization block (heart) 426.6
Arbor virus, arbovirus (infection) NEC 066.9
ARC 042
Arches - see condition
Arcuatus uterus 752.3
Arcus (cornea)
juvenilis 743.43
interfering with vision 743.42
senilis 371.41
Arc-welders' lung 503
Arc-welders' syndrome (photokeratitis) 370.24
Areflexia 796.1
Areola - see condition
Argentaffinoma (M8241/1) - see also Neoplasm, by site, uncertain behavior
benign (M8241/0) - see Neoplasm, by site, benign
malignant (M8241/3) - see Neoplasm, by site, malignant
syndrome 259.2
Argentinian hemorrhagic fever 078.7
Arginosuccinicaciduria 270.6
Argonz-del Castillo syndrome (nonpuerperal galactorrhea and amenorrhea) 253.1

Argyll-Robertson phenomenon, pupil, or syndrome (syphilitic) 094.89
atypical 379.45
nonluetic 379.45
nonsyphilitic 379.45
reversed 379.45
Argyria, argyriasis NEC 985.8
conjunctiva 372.55
cornea 371.16
from drug or medicinal agent
correct substance properly administered 709.09
overdose or wrong substance given or taken 961.2
Arhinencephaly 742.2
Arias-Stella phenomenon 621.3
Ariboflavinosis 266.0
Arizona enteritis 008.1
Arm - see condition
Armenian disease 277.3
Arnold-Chiari obstruction or syndrome (see also Spina bifida) 741.0
type I 348.4
type II (see also Spina bifida) 741.0
type III 742.0
type IV 742.2
Arrest, arrested
active phase of labor 661.1
affecting fetus or newborn 763.7
any plane in pelvis
complicating delivery 660.1
affecting fetus or newborn 763.1
bone marrow (see also Anemia, aplastic) 284.9
cardiac 427.5
with
abortion - see Abortion, by type, with specified complication NEC
ectopic pregnancy (see also categories 633.0-633.9) 639.8
molar pregnancy (see also categories 630-632) 639.8
complicating
anesthesia
correct substance properly administered 427.5
obstetric 668.1
overdose or wrong substance given 968.4
specified anesthetic - see Table of Drugs and Chemicals
delivery (cesarean) (instrumental) 669.4
ectopic or molar pregnancy 639.8
surgery (nontherapeutic) (therapeutic) 997.1
fetus or newborn 779.8
following
abortion 639.8
ectopic or molar pregnancy 639.8
postoperative (immediate) 997.1
long-term effect of cardiac surgery 429.4
cardiorespiratory (see also Arrest, cardiac) 427.5
deep transverse 660.3
affecting fetus or newborn 763.1
development or growth
bone 733.91
child 783.4
fetus 764.9
affecting management of pregnancy 656.5

Arrest, arrested *(Continued)*
  development or growth *(Continued)*
    tracheal rings 748.3
    epiphyseal 733.91
    granulopoiesis 288.0
    heart - *see* Arrest, cardiac
    respiratory 799.1
      newborn 770.8
    sinus 426.6
    transverse (deep) 660.3
      affecting fetus or newborn 763.1
Arrhenoblastoma (M8630/1)
  benign (M8630/0)
    specified site - *see* Neoplasm, by site,
      benign
    unspecified site
      female 220
      male 222.0
  malignant (M8630/3)
    specified site - *see* Neoplasm, by site,
      malignant
    unspecified site
      female 183.0
      male 186.9
  specified site - *see* Neoplasm, by site,
    uncertain behavior
  unspecified site
    female 236.2
    male 236.4
Arrhinencephaly 742.2
  due to
    trisomy 13 (13-15) 758.1
    trisomy 18 (16-18) 758.2
Arrhythmia (auricle) (cardiac) (cordis)
    (gallop rhythm) (juvenile) (nodal)
    (reflex) (sinus) (supraventricular)
    (transitory) (ventricle) 427.9
  bigeminal rhythm 427.89
  block 426.9
  bradycardia 427.89
  contractions, premature 427.60
  coronary sinus 427.89
  ectopic 427.89
  extrasystolic 427.60
  postoperative 997.1
  psychogenic 306.2
  vagal 780.2
Arrillaga-Ayerza syndrome (pulmonary
    artery sclerosis with pulmonary hy-
    pertension) 416.0
Arsenical
  dermatitis 692.4
  keratosis 692.4
  pigmentation 985.1
    from drug or medicinal agent
      correct substance properly admin-
        istered 709.09
      overdose or wrong substance
        given or taken 961.1
Arsenism 985.1
  from drug or medicinal agent
    correct substance properly adminis-
      tered 692.4
    overdose or wrong substance given
      or taken 961.1
Arterial - *see* condition
Arteriectasis 447.8
Arteriofibrosis - *see* Arteriosclerosis
Arteriolar sclerosis - *see* Arteriosclerosis
Arteriolith - *see* Arteriosclerosis
Arteriolitis 447.6
  necrotizing, kidney 447.5
  renal - *see* Hypertension, kidney
Arteriolosclerosis - *see* Arteriosclerosis

Arterionephrosclerosis (*see also* Hyper-
    tension, kidney) 403.90
Arteriopathy 447.9
Arteriosclerosis, arteriosclerotic (artery)
    (deformans) (diffuse) (disease) (end-
    arteritis) (general) (obliterans) (oblit-
    erative) (occlusive) (senile) (with cal-
    cification) 440.9
  with
    gangrene 440.24
    psychosis (*see also* Psychosis, arte-
      riosclerotic) 290.40
    ulceration 440.23
  aorta 440.0
  arteries of extremities - *see* Arterioscle-
    rosis, extremities
  basilar (artery) (*see also* Occlusion, ar-
    tery, basilar) 433.0
  brain 437.0
  bypass graft
    coronary artery 414.05
      autologous artery (gastroepiploic)
        (internal mammary) 414.04
      autologous vein 414.02
      nonautologous biological 414.03
    extremity 440.30
      autologous vein 440.31
      nonautologous biological 440.32
  cardiac - *see* Arteriosclerosis, coronary
  cardiopathy - *see* Arteriosclerosis, coro-
    nary
  cardiorenal (*see also* Hypertension, car-
    diorenal) 404.90
  cardiovascular (*see also* Disease, cardio-
    vascular) 429.2
  carotid (artery) (common) (internal)
    (*see also* Occlusion, artery, carotid)
    433.1
  central nervous system 437.0
  cerebral 437.0
    late effect - *see* Late effect(s) (of)
      cerebrovascular disease
  cerebrospinal 437.0
  cerebrovascular 437.0
  coronary (artery) 414.00
    graft - *see* Arteriosclerosis, bypass
      graft
    native artery 414.01
  extremities (native artery) NEC
    440.20
    bypass graft 440.30
      autologous vein 440.31
      nonautologous biological 440.32
    claudication (intermittent) 440.21
      and
        gangrene 440.24
        rest pain 440.22
          and
            gangrene 440.24
            ulceration 440.23
              and gangrene 440.24
        ulceration 440.23
          and gangrene 440.24
    gangrene 440.24
    rest pain 440.22
      and
        gangrene 440.24
        ulceration 440.23
          and gangrene 440.24
    specified site NEC 440.29
    ulceration 440.23
      and gangrene 440.24
  heart (disease) - *see also* Arteriosclero-
    sis, coronary

Arteriosclerosis, arteriosclerotic *(Contin-
    ued)*
  heart (disease) *(Continued)*
    valve 424.99
      aortic 424.1
      mitral 424.0
      pulmonary 424.3
      tricuspid 424.2
  kidney (*see also* Hypertension, kidney)
    403.90
  labyrinth, labyrinthine 388.00
  medial NEC (*see also* Arteriosclerosis,
    extremities) 440.20
  mesentery (artery) 557.1
  Mönckeberg's (*see also* Arteriosclerosis,
    extremities) 440.20
  myocarditis 429.0
  nephrosclerosis (*see also* Hypertension,
    kidney) 403.90
  peripheral (of extremities) - *see* Arte-
    riosclerosis, extremities
  precerebral 433.9
    specified artery NEC 433.8
  pulmonary (idiopathic) 416.0
  renal (*see also* Hypertension, kidney)
    403.90
    arterioles (*see also* Hypertension, kid-
      ney) 403.90
    artery 440.1
  retinal (vascular) 440.8 [362.13]
  specified artery NEC 440.8
    with gangrene 440.8 [785.4]
  spinal (cord) 437.0
  vertebral (artery) (*see also* Occlusion,
    artery, vertebral) 433.2
Arteriospasm 443.9
Arteriovenous - *see* condition
Arteritis 447.6
  allergic (*see also* Angiitis, hypersensitiv-
    ity) 446.20
  aorta (nonsyphilitic) 447.6
    syphilitic 093.1
  aortic arch 446.7
  brachiocephalica 446.7
  brain 437.4
    syphilitic 094.89
  branchial 446.7
  cerebral 437.4
    late effect - *see* Late effect(s) (of)
      cerebrovascular disease
    syphilitic 094.89
  coronary (artery) - *see also* Arterioscle-
    rosis, coronary
    rheumatic 391.9
      chronic 398.99
    syphilitic 093.89
  cranial (left) (right) 446.5
  deformans - *see* Arteriosclerosis
  giant cell 446.5
  necrosing or necrotizing 446.0
  nodosa 446.0
  obliterans - *see also* Arteriosclerosis
    subclavicocarotica 446.7
  pulmonary 417.8
  retina 362.18
  rheumatic - *see* Fever, rheumatic
  senile - *see* Arteriosclerosis
  suppurative 447.2
  syphilitic (general) 093.89
    brain 094.89
    coronary 093.89
    spinal 094.89
  temporal 446.5
  young female, syndrome 446.7

Artery, arterial - *see* condition
Arthralgia (*see also* Pain, joint)
  719.4
  allergic (*see also* Pain, joint) 719.4
  in caisson disease 993.3
  psychogenic 307.89
  rubella 056.71
  Salmonella 003.23
  temporomandibular joint 524.62
Arthritis, arthritic (acute) (chronic) (subacute) 716.9
  meaning Osteoarthritis - *see* Osteoar-
    throsis

Note Use the following fifth-digit
subclassification with categories 711-
712, 715-716:

  0   site unspecified
  1   shoulder region
  2   upper arm
  3   forearm
  4   hand
  5   pelvic region and thigh
  6   lower leg
  7   ankle and foot
  8   other specified sites
  9   multiple sites

---

allergic 716.2
ankylosing (crippling) (spine) 720.0
  [713.2]
  sites other than spine 716.9
atrophic 714.0
  spine 720.9
back (*see also* Arthritis, spine) 721.90
Bechterew's (ankylosing spondylitis)
  720.0
blennorrhagic 098.50 [711.6]
cervical, cervicodorsal (*see also* Spondylosis, cervical) 721.0
Charcôt's 094.0 [713.5]
  diabetic 250.6 [713.5]
  syringomyelic 336.0 [713.5]
  tabetic 094.0 [713.5]
chylous (*see also* Filariasis) 125.9 [711.7]
climacteric NEC 716.3
coccyx 721.8
cricoarytenoid 478.79
crystal (-induced) - *see* Arthritis, due to
  crystals
deformans (*see also* Osteoarthrosis)
  715.9
  spine 721.90
    with myelopathy 721.91
degenerative (*see also* Osteoarthrosis)
  715.9
  idiopathic 715.09
  polyarticular 715.09
  spine 721.90
    with myelopathy 721.91
dermatoarthritis, lipoid 272.8 [713.0]
due to or associated with
  acromegaly 253.0 [713.0]
  actinomycosis 039.8 [711.4]
  amyloidosis 277.3 [713.7]
  bacterial disease NEC 040.89 [711.4]
  Behçet's syndrome 136.1 [711.2]
  blastomycosis 116.0 [711.6]
  brucellosis (*see also* Brucellosis) 023.9
    [711.4]
  caisson disease 993.3
  coccidioidomycosis 114.3 [711.6]

Arthritis, arthritic (*Continued*)
  due to or associated with (*Continued*)
    coliform (Escherichia coli) 711.0
    colitis, ulcerative - (*see also* Colitis,
      ulcerative) 556.9 [713.1]
    cowpox 051.0 [711.5]
    crystals -(*see also* Gout)
      dicalcium phosphate 275.49 [712.1]
      pyrophosphate 275.49 [712.2]
      specified NEC 275.49 [712.8]
    dermatoarthritis, lipoid 272.8 [713.0]
    dermatological disorder NEC 709.9
      [713.3]
    diabetes 250.6 [713.5]
    diphtheria 032.89 [711.4]
    dracontiasis 125.7 [711.7]
    dysentery 009.0 [711.3]
    endocrine disorder NEC 259.9
      [713.0]
    enteritis NEC 009.1 [711.3]
      infectious (*see also* Enteritis, infec-
        tious) 009.0 [711.3]
        specified organism NEC 008.8
          [711.3]
      regional (*see also* Enteritis, re-
        gional) 555.9 [713.1]
      specified organism NEC 008.8
        [711.3]
    epiphyseal slip, nontraumatic (old)
      716.8
    erysipelas 035 [711.4]
    erythema
      epidemic 026.1
      multiforme 695.1 [713.3]
      nodosum 695.2 [713.3]
    Escherichia coli 711.0
    filariasis NEC 125.9 [711.7]
    gastrointestinal condition NEC 569.9
      [713.1]
    glanders 024 [711.4]
    Gonococcus 098.50
    gout 274.0
    H. influenzae 711.0
    helminthiasis NEC 128.9 [711.7]
    hematological disorder NEC 289.9
      [713.2]
    hemochromatosis 275.0 [713.0]
    hemoglobinopathy NEC (*see also*
      Disease, hemoglobin) 282.7
      [713.2]
    hemophilia (*see also* Hemophilia)
      286.0 [713.2]
    Hemophilus influenzae (H. influen-
      zae) 711.0
    Henoch (-Schönlein) purpura 287.0
      [713.6]
    histoplasmosis NEC (*see also* Histo-
      plasmosis) 115.99 [711.6]
    hyperparathyroidism 252.0 [713.0]
    hypersensitivity reaction NEC 995.3
      [713.6]
    hypogammaglobulinemia (*see also*
      Hypogammaglobulinemia)
      279.00 [713.0]
    hypothyroidism NEC 244.9 [713.0]
    infection (*see also* Arthritis, infec-
      tious) 711.9
    infectious disease NEC 136.9 [711.8]
    leprosy (*see also* Leprosy) 030.9
      [711.4]
    leukemia NEC (M9800/3) 208.9
      [713.2]
    lipoid dermatoarthritis 272.8 [713.0]
    Lyme disease 088.81 [711.8]

Arthritis, arthritic (*Continued*)
  due to or associated with (*Continued*)
    Mediterranean fever, familial 277.3
      [713.7]
    meningococcal infection 036.82
    metabolic disorder NEC 277.9 [713.0]
    multiple myelomatosis (M9730/3)
      203.0 [713.2]
    mumps 072.79 [711.5]
    mycobacteria 031.8 [711.4]
    mycosis NEC 117.9 [711.6]
    neurological disorder NEC 349.9
      [713.5]
    ochronosis 270.2 [713.0]
    O'Nyong Nyong 066.3 [711.5]
    parasitic disease NEC 136.9 [711.8]
    paratyphoid fever (*see also* Fever,
      paratyphoid) 002.9 [711.3]
    Pneumococcus 711.0
    poliomyelitis (*see also* Poliomyelitis)
      045.9 [711.5]
    Pseudomonas 711.0
    psoriasis 696.0
    pyogenic organism (E. coli) (H. in-
      fluenzae) (Pseudomonas) (Strep-
      tococcus) 711.0
    rat-bite fever 026.1 [711.4]
    regional enteritis (*see also* Enteritis,
      regional) 555.9 [713.1]
    Reiter's disease 099.3 [711.1]
    respiratory disorder NEC 519.9
      [713.4]
    reticulosis, malignant (M9720/3)
      202.3 [713.2]
    rubella 056.71
    salmonellosis 003.23
    sarcoidosis 135 [713.7]
    serum sickness 999.5 [713.6]
    Staphylococcus 711.0
    Streptococcus 711.0
    syphilis (*see also* Syphilis) 094.0 [711.4]
    syringomyelia 336.0 [713.5]
    thalassemia 282.4 [713.2]
    tuberculosis (*see also* Tuberculosis,
      arthritis) 015.9 [711.4]
    typhoid fever 002.0 [711.3]
    ulcerative colitis - (*see also* Colitis, ul-
      cerative) 556.9 [713.1]
    urethritis
      nongonococcal (*see also* Urethritis,
        nongonococcal) 099.40 [711.1]
      nonspecific (*see also* Urethritis,
        nongonococcal) 099.40 [711.1]
      Reiter's 099.3 [711.1]
    viral disease NEC 079.99 [711.5]
  erythema epidemic 026.1
  gonococcal 098.50
  gouty (acute) 274.0
  hypertrophic (*see also* Osteoarthrosis)
    715.9
    spine 721.90
      with myelopathy 721.91
  idiopathic, blennorrheal 099.3
  in caisson disease 993.3 [713.8]
  infectious or infective (acute) (chronic)
    (subacute) NEC 711.9
    nonpyogenic 711.9
    spine 720.9
  inflammatory NEC 714.9
  juvenile rheumatoid (chronic) (polyar-
    ticular) 714.30
    acute 714.31
    monoarticular 714.33
    pauciarticular 714.32

Arthritis, arthritic *(Continued)*
  lumbar *(see also* Spondylosis, lumbar)
      721.3
  meningococcal 036.82
  menopausal NEC 716.3
  migratory - *see* Fever, rheumatic
  neuropathic (Charcôt's) 094.0 *[713.5]*
      diabetic 250.6 *[713.5]*
      nonsyphilitic NEC 349.9 *[713.5]*
      syringomyelic 336.0 *[713.5]*
      tabetic 094.0 *[713.5]*
  nodosa *(see also* Osteoarthrosis) 715.9
      spine 721.90
          with myelopathy 721.91
  nonpyogenic NEC 716.9
      spine 721.90
          with myelopathy 721.91
  ochronotic 270.2 *[713.0]*
  palindromic *(see also* Rheumatism, pal-
      indromic) 719.3
  pneumococcal 711.0
  postdysenteric 009.0 *[711.3]*
  postrheumatic, chronic (Jaccoud's) 714.4
  primary progressive 714.0
      spine 720.9
  proliferative 714.0
      spine 720.0
  psoriatic 696.0
  purulent 711.0
  pyogenic or pyemic 711.0
  rheumatic 714.0
      acute or subacute - *see* Fever, rheu-
          matic
      chronic 714.0
      spine 720.9
  rheumatoid (nodular) 714.0
      with
          splenoadenomegaly and leuko-
              penia 714.1
          visceral or systemic involvement
              714.2
      aortitis 714.89
      carditis 714.2
      heart disease 714.2
      juvenile (chronic) (polyarticular)
          714.30
          acute 714.31
          monoarticular 714.33
          pauciarticular 714.32
      spine 720.0
  rubella 056.71
  sacral, sacroiliac, sacrococcygeal *(see
      also* Spondylosis, sacral) 721.3
  scorbutic 267
  senile or senescent *(see also* Osteoar-
      throsis) 715.9
      spine 721.90
          with myelopathy 721.91
  septic 711.0
  serum (nontherapeutic) (therapeutic)
      999.5 *[713.6]*
  specified form NEC 716.8
  spine 721.90
      with myelopathy 721.91
      atrophic 720.9
      degenerative 721.90
          with myelopathy 721.91
      hypertrophic (with deformity) 721.90
          with myelopathy 721.91
      infectious or infective NEC 720.9
      Marie-Strümpell 720.0
      nonpyogenic 721.90
          with myelopathy 721.91
      pyogenic 720.9

Arthritis, arthritic *(Continued)*
  spine *(Continued)*
      rheumatoid 720.0
      traumatic (old) 721.7
      tuberculous *(see also* Tuberculosis)
          015.0 *[720.81]*
  staphylococcal 711.0
  streptococcal 711.0
  suppurative 711.0
  syphilitic 094.0 *[713.5]*
      congenital 090.49 *[713.5]*
  syphilitica deformans (Charcôt) 094.0
      [713.5]
  temporomandibular joint 524.69
  thoracic *(see also* Spondylosis, thoracic)
      721.2
  toxic of menopause 716.3
  transient 716.4
  traumatic (chronic) (old) (post) 716.1
      current injury - *see* Nature of injury
  tuberculous *(see also* Tuberculosis, ar-
      thritis) 015.9 *[711.4]*
  urethritica 099.3 *[711.1]*
  urica, uratic 274.0
  venereal 099.3 *[711.1]*
  vertebral *(see also* Arthritis, spine) 721.90
  villous 716.8
  von Bechterew's 720.0
Arthrocele *(see also* Effusion, joint) 719.0
Arthrochondritis - *see* Arthritis
Arthrodesis status V45.4
Arthrodynia *(see also* Pain, joint) 719.4
  psychogenic 307.89
Arthrodysplasia 755.9
Arthrofibrosis, joint *(see also* Ankylosis)
  718.5
Arthrogryposis 728.3
  multiplex, congenita 754.89
Arthrokatadysis 715.35
Arthrolithiasis 274.0
Arthro-onychodysplasia 756.89
Arthro-osteo-onychodysplasia 756.89
Arthropathy *(see also* Arthritis) 716.9

Note Use the following fifth-digit subclassification with categories 711-712, 716:	
0	site unspecified
1	shoulder region
2	upper arm
3	forearm
4	hand
5	pelvic region and thigh
6	lower leg
7	ankle and foot
8	other specified sites
9	multiple sites

  Behçet's 136.1 *[711.2]*
  Charcôt's 094.0 *[713.5]*
      diabetic 250.6 *[713.5]*
      syringomyelic 336.0 *[713.5]*
      tabetic 094.0 *[713.5]*
  crystal (-induced) - *see* Arthritis, due to
      crystals
  gouty 274.0
  neurogenic, neuropathic (Charcôt's)
      (tabetic) 094.0 *[713.5]*
      diabetic 250.6 *[713.5]*
      nonsyphilitic NEC 349.9 *[713.5]*
      syringomyelic 336.0 *[713.5]*
  postdysenteric NEC 009.0 *[711.3]*
  postrheumatic, chronic (Jaccoud's) 714.4
  psoriatic 696.0

Arthropathy *(Continued)*
  pulmonary 731.2
  specified NEC 716.8
  syringomyelia 336.0 *[713.5]*
  tabes dorsalis 094.0 *[713.5]*
  tabetic 094.0 *[713.5]*
  transient 716.4
  traumatic 716.1
  uric acid 274.0
Arthrophyte *(see also* Loose, body, joint)
  718.1
Arthrophytis 719.80
  ankle 719.87
  elbow 719.82
  foot 719.87
  hand 719.84
  hip 719.85
  knee 719.86
  multiple sites 719.89
  pelvic region 719.85
  shoulder (region) 719.81
  specified site NEC 719.88
  wrist 719.83
Arthropyosis *(see also* Arthritis, pyogenic) 711.0
Arthrosis (deformans) (degenerative) *(see
  also* Osteoarthrosis) 715.9
  Charcôt's 094.0 *[713.5]*
  polyarticular 715.09
  spine *(see also* Spondylosis) 721.90
Arthus' phenomenon 995.2
  due to
      correct substance properly adminis-
          tered 995.2
      overdose or wrong substance given
          or taken 977.9
      specified drug - *see* Table of Drugs
          and Chemicals
  serum 999.5
Articular - *see also* condition
  disc disorder (reducing or non-reduc-
      ing) 524.63
  spondylolisthesis 756.12
Artificial
  device (prosthetic) - *see* Fitting, device
  insemination V26.1
  menopause (states) (symptoms) (syn-
      drome) 627.4
  opening status (functioning) (without
      complication) V44.9
      anus (colostomy) V44.3
      colostomy V44.3
      cystostomy V44.50
          appendico-vesicostomy
              V44.52
          cutaneous-vesicostomy
              V44.51
          specified type NEC V44.59
      enterostomy V44.4
      gastrostomy V44.1
      ileostomy V44.2
      intestinal tract NEC V44.4
      jejunostomy V44.4
      nephrostomy V44.6
      specified site NEC V44.8
      tracheostomy V44.0
      ureterostomy V44.6
      urethrostomy V44.6
      urinary tract NEC V44.6
      vagina V44.7
      vagina status V44.7
ARV (disease) (illness) (infection) - *see*
  Human immunodeficiency virus
  (disease) (illness) (infection)

ICD-9-CM

A

Vol. 2

Arytenoid - *see* condition
Asbestosis (occupational) 501
Asboe-Hansen's disease (incontinentia
   pigmenti) 757.33
Ascariasis (intestinal) (lung) 127.0
Ascaridiasis 127.0
Ascaridosis 127.0
Ascaris 127.0
   lumbricoides (infestation) 127.0
   pneumonia 127.0
Ascending - *see* condition
Aschoff's bodies (*see also* Myocarditis,
   rheumatic) 398.0
Ascites 789.5
   abdominal NEC 789.5
   cancerous (M8000/6) 197.6
   cardiac 428.0
   chylous (nonfilarial) 457.8
     filarial (*see also* Infestation, filarial)
      125.9
   congenital 778.0
   due to S. japonicum 120.2
   fetal, causing fetopelvic disproportion
     653.7
   heart 428.0
   joint (*see also* Effusion, joint) 719.0
   malignant (M8000/6) 197.6
   pseudochylous 789.5
   syphilitic 095.2
   tuberculous (*see also* Tuberculosis)
     014.0
Ascorbic acid (vitamin C) deficiency
   (scurvy) 267
ASCVD (arteriosclerotic cardiovascular
   disease) 429.2
Aseptic - *see* condition
Asherman's syndrome 621.5
Asialia 527.7
Asiatic cholera (*see also* Cholera) 001.9
Asocial personality or trends 301.7
Asomatognosia 781.8
Aspergillosis 117.3
   with pneumonia 117.3 [484.6]
   allergic bronchopulmonary 518.6
   nonsyphilitic NEC 117.3
Aspergillus (flavus) (fumigatus) (infection) (terreus) 117.3
Aspermatogenesis 606.0
Aspermia (testis) 606.0
Asphyxia, asphyxiation (by) 799.0
   antenatal - *see* Distress, fetal
   bedclothes 994.7
   birth (*see also* Asphyxia, newborn) 768.9
   bunny bag 994.7
   carbon monoxide 986
   caul (*see also* Asphyxia, newborn) 768.9
   cave-in 994.7
     crushing - *see* Injury, internal, intra-
      thoracic organs
   constriction 994.7
   crushing - *see* Injury, internal, intratho-
     racic organs
   drowning 994.1
   fetal, affecting newborn 770.8
   food or foreign body (in larynx)
     933.1
     bronchioles 934.8
     bronchus (main) 934.1
     lung 934.8
     nasopharynx 933.0
     nose, nasal passages 932
     pharynx 933.0
     respiratory tract 934.9
      specified part NEC 934.8

Asphyxia, asphyxiation (*Continued*)
   food or foreign body (*Continued*)
     throat 933.0
     trachea 934.0
   gas, fumes, or vapor NEC 987.9
     specified - *see* Table of Drugs and
      Chemicals
   gravitational changes 994.7
   hanging 994.7
   inhalation - *see* Inhalation
   intrauterine
     fetal death (before onset of labor)
      768.0
      during labor 768.1
     liveborn infant - *see* Distress, fetal,
      liveborn infant
   local 443.0
   mechanical 994.7
     during birth (*see also* Distress,
      fetal) 770.8
   mucus 933.1
     bronchus (main) 934.1
     larynx 933.1
     lung 934.8
     nasal passages 932
     newborn 770.1
     pharynx 933.0
     respiratory tract 934.9
      specified part NEC 934.8
     throat 933.0
     trachea 934.0
     vaginal (fetus or newborn) 770.1
   newborn 768.9
     with neurologic involvement 768.5
     blue 768.6
     livida 768.6
     mild or moderate 768.6
     pallida 768.5
     severe 768.5
     white 768.5
   pathological 799.0
   plastic bag 994.7
   postnatal (*see also* Asphyxia, newborn)
     768.9
     mechanical 994.7
   pressure 994.7
   reticularis 782.61
   strangulation 994.7
   submersion 994.1
   traumatic NEC - *see* Injury, internal,
     intrathoracic organs
   vomiting, vomitus - *see* Asphyxia, food
     or foreign body
Aspiration
   acid pulmonary (syndrome) 997.3
     obstetric 668.0
   amniotic fluid 770.1
   bronchitis 507.0
   contents of birth canal 770.1
   fetal pneumonitis 770.1
   food, foreign body, or gasoline (with
     asphyxiation) - *see* Asphyxia, food
     or foreign body
   meconium 770.1
   mucus 933.1
     into
      bronchus (main) 934.1
      lung 934.8
      respiratory tract 934.9
       specified part NEC 934.8
      trachea 934.0
     newborn 770.1
     vaginal (fetus or newborn) 770.1
   newborn 770.1

Aspiration (*Continued*)
   pneumonia 507.0
   pneumonitis 507.0
     fetus or newborn 770.1
     obstetric 668.0
   syndrome of newborn (massive) (me-
     conium) 770.1
   vernix caseosa 770.1
Asplenia 759.0
   with mesocardia 746.87
Assam fever 085.0
Assimilation, pelvis
   with disproportion 653.2
     affecting fetus or newborn 763.1
     causing obstructed labor 660.1
      affecting fetus or newborn 763.1
Assmann's focus (*see also* Tuberculosis)
   011.0
Astasia (-abasia) 307.9
   hysterical 300.11
Asteatosis 706.8
   cutis 706.8
Astereognosis 780.9
Asterixis 781.3
   in liver disease 572.8
Asteroid hyalitis 379.22
Asthenia, asthenic 780.79
   cardiac (*see also* Failure, heart) 428.9
     psychogenic 306.2
   cardiovascular (*see also* Failure, heart)
     428.9
     psychogenic 306.2
   heart (*see also* Failure, heart) 428.9
     psychogenic 306.2
   hysterical 300.11
   myocardial (*see also* Failure, heart) 428.9
     psychogenic 306.2
   nervous 300.5
   neurocirculatory 306.2
   neurotic 300.5
   psychogenic 300.5
   psychoneurotic 300.5
   psychophysiologic 300.5
   reaction, psychoneurotic 300.5
   senile 797
   Stiller's 780.79
   tropical anhidrotic 705.1
Asthenopia 368.13
   accommodative 367.4
   hysterical (muscular) 300.11
   psychogenic 306.7
Asthenospermia 792.2
Asthma, asthmatic (bronchial) (catarrh)
   (spasmodic) 493.9

> Note   Use the following fifth digit
> subclassification with category 493:
>
>   0   without mention of status asth-
>   maticus
>   1   with status asthmaticus

   with
     chronic obstructive pulmonary dis-
      ease (COPD) 493.2
     hay fever 493.0
     rhinitis, allergic 493.0
   allergic 493.9
     stated cause (external allergen)
      493.0
   atopic 493.0
   cardiac (*see also* Failure, ventricular,
     left) 428.1
   cardiobronchial (*see also* Failure, ven-
     tricular, left) 428.1

Asthma, asthmatic *(Continued)*
  cardiorenal *(see also* Hypertension, cardiorenal) 404.90
  childhood 493.0
  Colliers' 500
  croup 493.9
  detergent 507.8
  due to
    detergent 507.8
    inhalation of fumes 506.3
    internal immunological process 493.0
  endogenous (intrinsic) 493.1
  eosinophilic 518.3
  exogenous (cosmetics) (dander or dust) (drugs) (dust) (feathers) (food) (hay) (platinum) (pollen) 493.0
  extrinsic 493.0
  grinders' 502
  hay 493.0
  heart *(see also* Failure, ventricular, left) 428.1
  IgE 493.0
  infective 493.1
  intrinsic 493.1
  Kopp's 254.8
  late-onset 493.1
  meat-wrappers' 506.9
  Millar's (laryngismus stridulus) 478.75
  millstone makers' 502
  miners' 500
  Monday morning 504
  New Orleans (epidemic) 493.0
  platinum 493.0
  pneumoconiotic (occupational) NEC 505
  potters' 502
  psychogenic 316 *[493.9]*
  pulmonary eosinophilic 518.3
  red cedar 495.8
  Rostan's *(see also* Failure, ventricular, left) 428.1
  sandblasters' 502
  sequoiosis 495.8
  stonemasons' 502
  thymic 254.8
  tuberculous *(see also* Tuberculosis, pulmonary) 011.9
  Wichmann's (laryngismus stridulus) 478.75
  wood 495.8
Astigmatism (compound) (congenital) 367.20
  irregular 367.22
  regular 367.21
Astroblastoma (M9430/3)
  nose 748.1
  specified site - *see* Neoplasm, by site, malignant
  unspecified site 191.9
Astrocytoma (cystic) (M9400/3)
  anaplastic type (M9401/3)
    specified site - *see* Neoplasm, by site, malignant
    unspecified site 191.9
  fibrillary (M9420/3)
    specified site - *see* Neoplasm, by site, malignant
    unspecified site 191.9
  fibrous (M9420/3)
    specified site - *see* Neoplasm, by site, malignant
    unspecified site 191.9

Astrocytoma *(Continued)*
  gemistocytic (M9411/3)
    specified site - *see* Neoplasm, by site, malignant
    unspecified site 191.9
  juvenile (M9421/3)
    specified site - *see* Neoplasm, by site, malignant
    unspecified site 191.9
  nose 748.1
  pilocytic (M9421/3)
    specified site - *see* Neoplasm, by site, malignant
    unspecified site 191.9
  piloid (M9421/3)
    specified site - *see* Neoplasm, by site, malignant
    unspecified site 191.9
  protoplasmic (M9410/3)
    specified site - *see* Neoplasm, by site, malignant
    unspecified site 191.9
  specified site - *see* Neoplasm, by site, malignant
  subependymal (M9383/1) 237.5
    giant cell (M9384/1) 237.5
  unspecified site 191.9
Astroglioma (M9400/3)
  nose 748.1
  specified site - *see* Neoplasm, by site, malignant
  unspecified site 191.9
Asymbolia 784.60
Asymmetrical breathing 786.09
Asymmetry - *see also* Distortion
  chest 786.9
  face 754.0
  jaw NEC 524.12
    maxillary 524.11
  pelvis with disproportion 653.0
    affecting fetus or newborn 763.1
    causing obstructed labor 660.1
      affecting fetus or newborn 763.1
Asynergia 781.3
Asynergy 781.3
  ventricular 429.89
Asystole (heart) *(see also* Arrest, cardiac) 427.5
Ataxia, ataxy, ataxic 781.3
  acute 781.3
  brain 331.89
  cerebellar 334.3
    hereditary (Marie's) 334.2
    in
      alcoholism 303.9 *[334.4]*
      myxedema *(see also* Myxedema) 244.9 *[334.4]*
      neoplastic disease NEC 239.9 *[334.4]*
  cerebral 331.89
  family, familial 334.2
    cerebral (Marie's) 334.2
    spinal (Friedreich's) 334.0
  Friedreich's (heredofamilial) (spinal) 334.0
  frontal lobe 781.3
  gait 781.2
    hysterical 300.11
  general 781.3
  hereditary NEC 334.2
    cerebellar 334.2
    spastic 334.1
    spinal 334.0

Ataxia, ataxy, ataxic *(Continued)*
  heredofamilial (Marie's) 334.2
  hysterical 300.11
  locomotor (progressive) 094.0
    diabetic 250.6 *[337.1]*
  Marie's (cerebellar) (heredofamilial) 334.2
  nonorganic origin 307.9
  partial 094.0
  postchickenpox 052.7
  progressive locomotor 094.0
  psychogenic 307.9
  Sanger-Brown's 334.2
  spastic 094.0
    hereditary 334.1
    syphilitic 094.0
  spinal
    hereditary 334.0
    progressive locomotor 094.0
  telangiectasia 334.8
Ataxia-telangiectasia 334.8
Atelectasis (absorption collapse) (complete) (compression) (massive) (partial) (postinfective) (pressure collapse) (pulmonary) (relaxation) 518.0
  newborn (congenital) (partial) 770.5
    primary 770.4
  primary 770.4
  tuberculous *(see also* Tuberculosis, pulmonary) 011.9
Ateleiosis, ateliosis 253.3
Atelia - *see* Distortion
Ateliosis 253.3
Atelocardia 746.9
Atelomyelia 742.59
Athelia 757.6
Atheroembolism - *see* Atherosclerosis
Atheroma, atheromatous *(see also* Arteriosclerosis) 440.9
  aorta, aortic 440.0
    valve *(see also* Endocarditis, aortic) 424.1
  artery - *see* Arteriosclerosis
  basilar (artery) *(see also* Occlusion, artery, basilar) 433.0
  carotid (artery) (common) (internal) *(see also* Occlusion, artery, carotid) 433.1
  cerebral (arteries) 437.0
  coronary (artery) - *see* Arteriosclerosis, coronary
  degeneration - *see* Arteriosclerosis
  heart, cardiac - *see* Arteriosclerosis, coronary
  mitral (valve) 424.0
  myocardium, myocardial - *see* Arteriosclerosis, coronary
  pulmonary valve (heart) *(see also* Endocarditis, pulmonary) 424.3
  skin 706.2
  tricuspid (heart) (valve) 424.2
  valve, valvular - *see* Endocarditis
  vertebral (artery) *(see also* Occlusion, artery, vertebral) 433.2
Atheromatosis - *see also* Arteriosclerosis
  arterial, congenital 272.8
Atherosclerosis - *see* Arteriosclerosis
Athetosis (acquired) 781.0
  bilateral 333.7
  congenital (bilateral) 333.7
  double 333.7
  unilateral 781.0

ICD-9-CM

A

Vol. 2

Athlete's
　foot 110.4
　heart 429.3
Athletic team examination V70.3
Athrepsia 261
Athyrea (acquired) (*see also* Hypothy-
　　roidism) 244.9
　congenital 243
Athyreosis (congenital) 243
　acquired - *see* Hypothyroidism
Athyroidism (acquired) (*see also* Hypo-
　　thyroidism) 244.9
　congenital 243
Atmospheric pyrexia 992.0
Atonia, atony, atonic
　abdominal wall 728.2
　bladder (sphincter) 596.4
　　neurogenic NEC 596.54
　　　with cauda equina syndrome
　　　　344.61
　capillary 448.9
　cecum 564.89
　　psychogenic 306.4
　colon 564.89
　　psychogenic 306.4
　congenital 779.8
　dyspepsia 536.3
　　psychogenic 306.4
　intestine 564.89
　　psychogenic 306.4
　stomach 536.3
　　neurotic or psychogenic 306.4
　　psychogenic 306.4
　uterus 666.1
　　affecting fetus or newborn 763.7
　vesical 596.4
Atopy NEC V15.0
Atransferrinemia, congenital 273.8
Atresia, atretic (congenital) 759.89
　alimentary organ or tract NEC 751.8
　　lower 751.2
　　upper 750.8
　ani, anus, anal (canal) 751.2
　aorta 747.22
　　with hypoplasia of ascending aorta
　　　and defective development of
　　　left ventricle (with mitral valve
　　　atresia) 746.7
　　arch 747.11
　　ring 747.21
　aortic (orifice) (valve) 746.89
　　arch 747.11
　aqueduct of Sylvius 742.3
　　with spina bifida (*see also* Spina bi-
　　　fida) 741.0
　artery NEC (*see also* Atresia, blood ves-
　　　sel) 747.60
　　cerebral 747.81
　　coronary 746.85
　　eye 743.58
　　pulmonary 747.3
　　umbilical 747.5
　auditory canal (external) 744.02
　bile, biliary duct (common) or passage
　　　751.61
　　acquired (*see also* Obstruction, bili-
　　　ary) 576.2
　bladder (neck) 753.6
　blood vessel (peripheral) NEC 747.60
　　cerebral 747.81
　　gastrointestinal 747.61
　　lower limb 747.64
　　pulmonary artery 747.3
　　renal 747.62

Atresia, atretic (*Continued*)
　blood vessel (*Continued*)
　　spinal 747.82
　　upper limb 747.63
　bronchus 748.3
　canal, ear 744.02
　cardiac
　　valve 746.89
　　　aortic 746.89
　　　mitral 746.89
　　　pulmonary 746.01
　　　tricuspid 746.1
　cecum 751.2
　cervix (acquired) 622.4
　　congenital 752.49
　　in pregnancy or childbirth 654.6
　　　affecting fetus or newborn
　　　　763.89
　　　causing obstructed labor 660.2
　　　　affecting fetus or newborn
　　　　　763.1
　choana 748.0
　colon 751.2
　cystic duct 751.61
　　acquired 575.8
　　　with obstruction (*see also* Obstruc-
　　　　tion, gallbladder) 575.2
　digestive organs NEC 751.8
　duodenum 751.1
　ear canal 744.02
　ejaculatory duct 752.8
　epiglottis 748.3
　esophagus 750.3
　Eustachian tube 744.24
　fallopian tube (acquired) 628.2
　　congenital 752.19
　follicular cyst 620.0
　foramen of
　　Luschka 742.3
　　　with spina bifida (*see also* Spina
　　　　bifida) 741.0
　　Magendie 742.3
　　　with spina bifida (*see also* Spina
　　　　bifida) 741.0
　gallbladder 751.69
　genital organ
　　external
　　　female 752.49
　　　male NEC 752.8
　　　　penis 752.69
　　internal
　　　female 752.8
　　　male 752.8
　glottis 748.3
　gullet 750.3
　heart
　　valve NEC 746.89
　　　aortic 746.89
　　　mitral 746.89
　　　pulmonary 746.01
　　　tricuspid 746.1
　hymen 752.42
　　acquired 623.3
　　postinfective 623.3
　ileum 751.1
　intestine (small) 751.1
　　large 751.2
　iris, filtration angle (*see also* Buphthal-
　　　mia) 743.20
　jejunum 751.1
　kidney 753.3
　lacrimal, apparatus 743.65
　　acquired - *see* Stenosis, lacrimal
　larynx 748.3

Atresia, atretic (*Continued*)
　ligament, broad 752.19
　lung 748.5
　meatus urinarius 753.6
　mitral valve 746.89
　　with atresia or hypoplasia of aortic
　　　orifice or valve, with hypoplasia
　　　of ascending aorta and defective
　　　development of left ventricle
　　　746.7
　nares (anterior) (posterior) 748.0
　nasolacrimal duct 743.65
　nasopharynx 748.8
　nose, nostril 748.0
　　acquired 738.0
　organ or site NEC - *see* Anomaly, spec-
　　　ified type NEC
　osseous meatus (ear) 744.03
　oviduct (acquired) 628.2
　　congenital 752.19
　parotid duct 750.23
　　acquired 527.8
　pulmonary (artery) 747.3
　　valve 746.01
　　vein 747.49
　pulmonic 746.01
　pupil 743.46
　rectum 751.2
　salivary duct or gland 750.23
　　acquired 527.8
　sublingual duct 750.23
　　acquired 527.8
　submaxillary duct or gland 750.23
　　acquired 527.8
　trachea 748.3
　tricuspid valve 746.1
　ureter 753.29
　ureteropelvic junction 753.21
　ureterovesical orifice 753.22
　urethra (valvular) 753.6
　urinary tract NEC 753.29
　uterus 752.3
　　acquired 621.8
　vagina (acquired) 623.2
　　congenital 752.49
　　postgonococcal (old) 098.2
　　postinfectional 623.2
　　senile 623.2
　vascular NEC (*see also* Atresia, blood
　　　vessel) 747.60
　　cerebral 747.81
　vas deferens 752.8
　vein NEC (*see also* Atresia, blood ves-
　　　sel) 747.60
　　cardiac 746.89
　　great 747.49
　　portal 747.49
　　pulmonary 747.49
　vena cava (inferior) (superior) 747.49
　vesicourethral orifice 753.6
　vulva 752.49
　　acquired 624.8
Atrichia, atrichosis 704.00
　congenital (universal) 757.4
Atrioventricularis commune 745.69
Atrophia - *see also* Atrophy
　alba 709.09
　cutis 701.8
　　idiopathica progressiva 701.8
　　senilis 701.8
　dermatological, diffuse (idiopathic)
　　　701.8
　flava hepatis (acuta) (subacuta) (*see
　　　also* Necrosis, liver) 570

Atrophia (Continued)
  gyrata of choroid and retina (central)
    363.54
    generalized 363.57
  senilis 797
    dermatological 701.8
  unguium 703.8
    congenita 757.5
Atrophoderma, atrophodermia 701.9
  diffusum (idiopathic) 701.8
  maculatum 701.3
    et striatum 701.3
      due to syphilis 095.8
    syphilitic 091.3
  neuriticum 701.8
  pigmentosum 757.33
  reticulatum symmetricum faciei
    701.8
  senile 701.8
  symmetrical 701.8
  vermiculata 701.8
Atrophy, atrophic
  adrenal (autoimmune) (capsule) (cor-
    tex) (gland) 255.4
    with hypofunction 255.4
  alveolar process or ridge (edentulous)
    525.2
  appendix 543.9
  Aran-Duchenne muscular 335.21
  arm 728.2
  arteriosclerotic - see Arteriosclerosis
  arthritis 714.0
    spine 720.9
  bile duct (any) 576.8
  bladder 596.8
  blanche (of Milian) 701.3
  bone (senile) 733.99
    due to
      disuse 733.7
      infection 733.99
      tabes dorsalis (neurogenic) 094.0
    posttraumatic 733.99
  brain (cortex) (progressive) 331.9
    with dementia 290.10
    Alzheimer's 331.0
      with dementia - see Alzheimer's,
        dementia
    circumscribed (Pick's) 331.1
      with dementia 331.1 [294.1]
    congenital 742.4
    hereditary 331.9
    senile 331.2
  breast 611.4
    puerperal, postpartum 676.3
  buccal cavity 528.9
  cardiac (brown) (senile) (see also De-
    generation, myocardial) 429.1
  cartilage (infectional) (joint) 733.99
  cast, plaster of Paris 728.2
  cerebellar - see Atrophy, brain
  cerebral - see Atrophy, brain
  cervix (endometrium) (mucosa) (my-
    ometrium) (senile) (uteri) 622.8
    menopausal 627.8
  Charcôt-Marie-Tooth 356.1
  choroid 363.40
    diffuse secondary 363.42
    hereditary (see also Dystrophy, cho-
      roid) 363.50
      gyrate
        central 363.54
        diffuse 363.57
        generalized 363.57
    senile 363.41

Atrophy, atrophic (Continued)
  ciliary body 364.57
  colloid, degenerative 701.3
  conjunctiva (senile) 372.8
  corpus cavernosum 607.89
  cortical (see also Atrophy, brain)
    331.9
  Cruveilhier's 335.21
  cystic duct 576.8
  dacryosialadenopathy 710.2
  degenerative
    colloid 701.3
    senile 701.3
  Déjérine-Thomas 333.0
  diffuse idiopathic, dermatological
    701.8
  disuse
    bone 733.7
    muscle 728.2
  Duchenne-Aran 335.21
  ear 388.9
  edentulous alveolar ridge 525.2
  emphysema, lung 492.8
  endometrium (senile) 621.8
    cervix 622.8
  enteric 569.89
  epididymis 608.3
  eyeball, cause unknown 360.41
  eyelid (senile) 374.50
  facial (skin) 701.9
  facioscapulohumeral (Landouzy-Déjér-
    ine) 359.1
  fallopian tube (senile), acquired
    620.3
  fatty, thymus (gland) 254.8
  gallbladder 575.8
  gastric 537.89
  gastritis (chronic) 535.1
  gastrointestinal 569.89
  genital organ, male 608.89
  glandular 289.3
  globe (phthisis bulbi) 360.41
  gum 523.2
  hair 704.2
  heart (brown) (senile) (see also Degen-
    eration, myocardial) 429.1
  hemifacial 754.0
    Romberg 349.89
  hydronephrosis 591
  infantile 261
    paralysis, acute (see also Poliomyeli-
      tis, with paralysis) 045.1
  intestine 569.89
  iris (generalized) (postinfectional) (sec-
    tor shaped) 364.59
    essential 364.51
    progressive 364.51
    sphincter 364.54
  kidney (senile) (see also Sclerosis, renal)
    587
    with hypertension (see also Hyper-
      tension, kidney) 403.90
    congenital 753.0
    hydronephrotic 591
    infantile 753.0
  lacrimal apparatus (primary) 375.13
    secondary 375.14
  Landouzy-Déjérine 359.1
  laryngitis, infection 476.0
  larynx 478.79
  Leber's optic 377.16
  lip 528.5
  liver (acute) (subacute) (see also Necro-
    sis, liver) 570

Atrophy, atrophic (Continued)
  liver (Continued)
    chronic (yellow) 571.8
    yellow (congenital) 570
      with
        abortion - see Abortion, by type,
          with specified complication
          NEC
        ectopic pregnancy (see also cate-
          gories 633.0-633.9) 639.8
        molar pregnancy (see also cate-
          gories 630-632) 639.8
      chronic 571.8
      complicating pregnancy 646.7
      following
        abortion 639.8
        ectopic or molar pregnancy
          639.8
      from injection, inoculation or
        transfusion (onset within 8
        months after administration) -
        see Hepatitis, viral
      healed 571.5
      obstetric 646.7
      postabortal 639.8
      postimmunization - see Hepatitis,
        viral
      posttransfusion - see Hepatitis, vi-
        ral
      puerperal, postpartum 674.8
  lung (senile) 518.89
    congenital 748.69
  macular (dermatological) 701.3
    syphilitic, skin 091.3
      striated 095.8
  muscle, muscular 728.2
    disuse 728.2
    Duchenne-Aran 335.21
    extremity (lower) (upper) 728.2
    familial spinal 335.11
    general 728.2
    idiopathic 728.2
    infantile spinal 335.0
    myelopathic (progressive) 335.10
    myotonic 359.2
    neuritic 356.1
    neuropathic (peroneal) (progressive)
      356.1
    peroneal 356.1
    primary (idiopathic) 728.2
    progressive (familial) (hereditary)
      (pure) 335.21
      adult (spinal) 335.19
      infantile (spinal) 335.0
      juvenile (spinal) 335.11
      spinal 335.10
        adult 335.19
        hereditary or familial 335.11
        infantile 335.0
    pseudohypertrophic 359.1
    spinal (progressive) 335.10
      adult 335.19
      Aran-Duchenne 335.21
      familial 335.11
      hereditary 335.11
      infantile 335.0
      juvenile 335.11
    syphilitic 095.6
  myocardium (see also Degeneration,
    myocardial) 429.1
  myometrium (senile) 621.8
    cervix 622.8
  myotatic 728.2
  myotonia 359.2

Atrophy, atrophic (*Continued*)
nail 703.8
  congenital 757.5
nasopharynx 472.2
nerve - *see also* Disorder, nerve
  abducens 378.54
  accessory 352.4
  acoustic or auditory 388.5
  cranial 352.9
    first (olfactory) 352.0
    second (optic) (*see also* Atrophy,
      optic nerve) 377.10
    third (oculomotor) (partial)
      378.51
      total 378.52
    fourth (trochlear) 378.53
    fifth (trigeminal) 350.8
    sixth (abducens) 378.54
    seventh (facial) 351.8
    eighth (auditory) 388.5
    ninth (glossopharyngeal) 352.2
    tenth (pneumogastric) (vagus)
      352.3
    eleventh (accessory) 352.4
    twelfth (hypoglossal) 352.5
  facial 351.8
  glossopharyngeal 352.2
  hypoglossal 352.5
  oculomotor (partial) 378.51
    total 378.52
  olfactory 352.0
  peripheral 355.9
  pneumogastric 352.3
  trigeminal 350.8
  trochlear 378.53
  vagus (pneumogastric) 352.3
nervous system, congenital 742.8
neuritic (*see also* Disorder, nerve)
  355.9
neurogenic NEC 355.9
  bone
    tabetic 094.0
nutritional 261
old age 797
olivopontocerebellar 333.0
optic nerve (ascending) (descending)
  (infectional) (nonfamilial) (papillo-
  macular bundle) (postretinal) (secondary NEC) (simple) 377.10
  associated with retinal dystrophy
    377.13
  dominant hereditary 377.16
  glaucomatous 377.14
  hereditary (dominant) (Leber's)
    377.16
  Leber's (hereditary) 377.16
  partial 377.15
  postinflammatory 377.12
  primary 377.11
  syphilitic 094.84
    congenital 090.49
    tabes dorsalis 094.0
orbit 376.45
ovary (senile), acquired 620.3
oviduct (senile), acquired 620.3
palsy, diffuse 335.20
pancreas (duct) (senile) 577.8
papillary muscle 429.81
paralysis 355.9
parotid gland 527.0
patches skin 701.3
  senile 701.8
penis 607.89
pharyngitis 472.1

Atrophy, atrophic (*Continued*)
pharynx 478.29
pluriglandular 258.8
polyarthritis 714.0
prostate 602.2
pseudohypertrophic 359.1
renal (*see also* Sclerosis, renal) 587
reticulata 701.8
retina (*see also* Degeneration, retina)
  362.60
  hereditary (*see also* Dystrophy, ret-
    ina) 362.70
rhinitis 472.0
salivary duct or gland 527.0
scar NEC 709.2
sclerosis, lobar (of brain) 331.0
  with dementia 331.0 *[294.1]*
scrotum 608.89
seminal vesicle 608.89
senile 797
  degenerative, of skin 701.3
skin (patches) (senile) 701.8
spermatic cord 608.89
spinal (cord) 336.8
  acute 336.8
  muscular (chronic) 335.10
    adult 335.19
    familial 335.11
    juvenile 335.10
  paralysis 335.10
    acute (*see also* Poliomyelitis, with
      paralysis) 045.1
spine (column) 733.99
spleen (senile) 289.59
spots (skin) 701.3
  senile 701.8
stomach 537.89
striate and macular 701.3
  syphilitic 095.8
subcutaneous 701.9
  due to injection 999.9
sublingual gland 527.0
submaxillary gland 527.0
Sudeck's 733.7
suprarenal (autoimmune) (capsule)
  (gland) 255.4
  with hypofunction 255.4
tarso-orbital fascia, congenital 743.66
testis 608.3
thenar, partial 354.0
throat 478.29
thymus (fat) 254.8
thyroid (gland) 246.8
  with
    cretinism 243
    myxedema 244.9
  congenital 243
tongue (senile) 529.8
  papillae 529.4
  smooth 529.4
trachea 519.1
tunica vaginalis 608.89
turbinate 733.99
tympanic membrane (nonflaccid)
  384.82
  flaccid 384.81
ulcer (*see also* Ulcer, skin) 707.9
upper respiratory tract 478.9
uterus, uterine (acquired) (senile)
  621.8
  cervix 622.8
  due to radiation (intended effect)
    621.8
vagina (senile) 627.3

Atrophy, atrophic (*Continued*)
vascular 459.89
vas deferens 608.89
vertebra (senile) 733.99
vulva (primary) (senile) 624.1
Werdnig-Hoffmann 335.0
yellow (acute) (congenital) (liver) (subacute) (*see also* Necrosis, liver)
  570
  chronic 571.8
  resulting from administration of
    blood, plasma, serum, or other
    biological substance (within 8
    months of administration) - *see*
    Hepatitis, viral
Attack
akinetic (*see also* Epilepsy) 345.0
angina - *see* Angina
apoplectic (*see also* Disease, cerebrovascular, acute) 436
benign shuddering 333.93
bilious - *see* Vomiting
cataleptic 300.11
cerebral (*see also* Disease, cerebrovascular, acute) 436
coronary (*see also* Infarct, myocardium)
  410.9
cyanotic, newborn 770.8
epileptic (*see also* Epilepsy) 345.9
epileptiform 780.39
heart (*see also* Infarct, myocardium)
  410.9
hemiplegia (*see also* Disease, cerebrovascular, acute) 436
hysterical 300.11
jacksonian (*see also* Epilepsy) 345.5
myocardium, myocardial (*see also* Infarct, myocardium) 410.9
myoclonic (*see also* Epilepsy) 345.1
panic 300.01
paralysis (*see also* Disease, cerebrovascular, acute) 436
paroxysmal 780.39
psychomotor (*see also* Epilepsy) 345.4
salaam (*see also* Epilepsy) 345.6
schizophreniform (*see also* Schizophrenia) 295.4
sensory and motor 780.39
syncope 780.2
toxic, cerebral 780.39
transient ischemic (TIA) 435.9
unconsciousness 780.2
  hysterical 300.11
vasomotor 780.2
vasovagal (idiopathic) (paroxysmal)
  780.2
Attention to
artificial
  opening (of) V55.9
    digestive tract NEC V55.4
    specified site NEC V55.8
    urinary tract NEC V55.6
  vagina V55.7
colostomy V55.3
cystostomy V55.5
gastrostomy V55.1
ileostomy V55.2
jejunostomy V55.4
nephrostomy V55.6
surgical dressings V58.3
sutures V58.3
tracheostomy V55.0
ureterostomy V55.6
urethrostomy V55.6

Attrition
  gum 523.2
  teeth (excessive) (hard tissues) 521.1
Atypical - *see also* condition
  distribution, vessel (congenital) (peripheral) NEC 747.60
  endometrium 621.9
  kidney 593.89
Atypism, cervix 622.1
Audible tinnitus (*see also* Tinnitus) 388.30
Auditory - *see* condition
Audry's syndrome (acropachyderma) 757.39
Aujeszky's disease 078.89
Aura, jacksonian (*see also* Epilepsy) 345.5
Aurantiasis, cutis 278.3
Auricle, auricular - *see* condition
Auriculotemporal syndrome 350.8
Australian
  Q fever 083.0
  X disease 062.4
Autism, autistic (child) (infantile) 299.0
Autodigestion 799.8
Autoerythrocyte sensitization 287.2
Autographism 708.3
Autoimmune
  cold sensitivity 283.0
  disease NEC 279.4
  hemolytic anemia 283.0
  thyroiditis 245.2
Autoinfection, septic - *see* Septicemia
Autointoxication 799.8
Automatism 348.8
  epileptic (*see also* Epilepsy) 345.4
  paroxysmal, idiopathic (*see also* Epilepsy) 345.4
Autonomic, autonomous
  bladder 596.54
    neurogenic 596.54
      with cauda equina 344.61
  dysreflexia 337.3 ◀
  faciocephalalgia (*see also* Neuropathy, peripheral, autonomic) 337.9
  hysterical seizure 300.11
  imbalance (*see also* Neuropathy, peripheral, autonomic 337.9
Autophony 388.40
Autosensitivity, erythrocyte 287.2

Autotopagnosia 780.9
Autotoxemia 799.8
Autumn - *see* condition
Avellis' syndrome 344.89
Aviators'
  disease or sickness (*see also* Effect, adverse, high altitude) 993.2
  ear 993.0
  effort syndrome 306.2
Avitaminosis (multiple NEC) (*see also* Deficiency, vitamin) 269.2
  A 264.9
  B 266.9
    with
      beriberi 265.0
      pellagra 265.2
  B_1 265.1
  B_2 266.0
  B_6 266.1
  B_{12} 266.2
  C (with scurvy) 267
  D 268.9
    with
      osteomalacia 268.2
      rickets 268.0
  E 269.1
  G 266.0
  H 269.1
  K 269.0
  multiple 269.2
  nicotinic acid 265.2
  P 269.1
Avulsion (traumatic) 879.8
  blood vessel - *see* Injury, blood vessel, by site
  cartilage - *see also* Dislocation, by site
    knee, current (*see also* Tear, meniscus) 836.2
    symphyseal (inner), complicating delivery 665.6
  complicated 879.9
  diaphragm - *see* Injury, internal, diaphragm
  ear - *see* Wound, open, ear
  epiphysis of bone - *see* Fracture, by site
  external site other than limb - *see* Wound, open, by site
  eye 871.3
  fingernail - *see* Wound, open, finger
  fracture - *see* Fracture, by site

Avulsion (*Continued*)
  genital organs, external - *see* Wound, open, genital organs
  head (intracranial) NEC - *see also* Injury, intracranial, with open intracranial wound
    complete 874.9
    external site NEC 873.8
    complicated 873.9
  internal organ or site - *see* Injury, internal, by site
  joint - *see also* Dislocation, by site
    capsule - *see* Sprain, by site
  ligament - *see* Sprain, by site
  limb - *see also* Amputation, traumatic, by site
    skin and subcutaneous tissue - *see* Wound, open, by site
  muscle - *see* Sprain, by site
  nerve (root) - *see* Injury, nerve, by site
  scalp - *see* Wound, open, scalp
  skin and subcutaneous tissue - *see* Wound, open, by site
  symphyseal cartilage (inner), complicating delivery 665.6
  tendon - *see also* Sprain, by site
    with open wound - *see* Wound, open, by site
  toenail - *see* Wound, open, toe(s)
  tooth 873.63
    complicated 873.73
Awareness of heart beat 785.1
Axe grinders' disease 502
Axenfeld's anomaly or syndrome 743.44
Axilla, axillary - *see also* condition
  breast 757.6
Axonotmesis - *see* Injury, nerve, by site
Ayala's disease 756.89
Ayerza's disease or syndrome (pulmonary artery sclerosis with pulmonary hypertension) 416.0
Azoospermia 606.0
Azotemia 790.6
  meaning uremia (*see also* Uremia) 586
Aztec ear 744.29
Azygos lobe, lung (fissure) 748.69

B

Baader's syndrome (erythema multiforme exucatiuum) 695.1
Baastrup's syndrome 721.5
Babesiasis 088.82
Babesiosis 088.82
Babington's disease (familial hemorrhagic telangiectasia) 448.0
Babinski's syndrome (cardiovascular syphilis) 093.89
Babinski-Fröhlich syndrome (adiposogenital dystrophy) 253.8
Babinski-Nageotte syndrome 344.89
Bacillary - *see* condition
Bacilluria 791.9
  asymptomatic, in pregnancy or puerperium 646.5
  tuberculous (*see also* Tuberculosis) 016.9
Bacillus - *see also* Infection, bacillus
  abortus infection 023.1
  anthracis infection 022.9
  coli
    infection 041.4
      generalized 038.42
      intestinal 008.00
    pyemia 038.42
    septicemia 038.42
  Flexner's 004.1
  fusiformis infestation 101
  mallei infection 024
  Shiga's 004.0
  suipestifer infection (*see also* Infection, Salmonella) 003.9
Back - *see* condition
Backache (postural) 724.5
  psychogenic 307.89
  sacroiliac 724.6
Backflow (pyelovenous) (*see also* Disease, renal) 593.9
Backknee (*see also* Genu, recurvatum) 736.5
Bacteremia 790.7
  with
    sepsis - *see* Septicemia
  during
    labor 659.3
    pregnancy 647.8
  newborn 771.8
Bacteria
  in blood (*see also* Bacteremia) 790.7
  in urine (*see also* Bacteriuria) 791.9
Bacterial - *see* condition
Bactericholia (*see also* Cholecystitis, acute) 575.0
Bacterid, bacteride (Andrews' pustular) 686.8
Bacteriuria, bacteruria 791.9
  with
    urinary tract infection 599.0
  asymptomatic 791.9
    in pregnancy or puerperium 646.5
      affecting fetus or newborn 760.1
Bad
  breath 784.9
  heart - *see* Disease, heart
  trip (*see also* Abuse, drugs, nondependent) 305.3
Baehr-Schiffrin disease (thrombotic thrombocytopenic purpura) 446.6
Baelz's disease (cheilitis glandularis apostematosa) 528.5

Baerensprung's disease (eczema marginatum) 110.3
Bagassosis (occupational) 495.1
Baghdad boil 085.1
Bagratuni's syndrome (temporal arteritis) 446.5
Baker's
  cyst (knee) 727.51
    tuberculous (*see also* Tuberculosis) 015.2
  itch 692.89
Bakwin-Krida syndrome (craniometaphyseal dysplasia) 756.89
Balanitis (circinata) (gangraenosa) (infectious) (vulgaris) 607.1
  amebic 006.8
  candidal 112.2
  chlamydial 099.53
  due to Ducrey's bacillus 099.0
  erosiva circinata et gangraenosa 607.1
  gangrenous 607.1
  gonococcal (acute) 098.0
    chronic or duration of 2 months or over 098.2
  nongonococcal 607.1
  phagedenic 607.1
  venereal NEC 099.8
  xerotica obliterans 607.81
Balanoposthitis 607.1
  chlamydial 099.53
  gonococcal (acute) 098.0
    chronic or duration of 2 months or over 098.2
  ulcerative NEC 099.8
Balanorrhagia - *see* Balanitis
Balantidiasis 007.0
Balantidiosis 007.0
Balbuties, balbutio 307.0
Bald
  patches on scalp 704.00
  tongue 529.4
Baldness (*see also* Alopecia) 704.00
Balfour's disease (chloroma) 205.3
Balint's syndrome (psychic paralysis of visual fixation) 368.16
Balkan grippe 083.0
Ball
  food 938
  hair 938
Ballantyne (-Runge) **syndrome** (postmaturity) 766.2
Balloon disease (*see also* Effect, adverse, high altitude) 993.2
Ballooning posterior leaflet syndrome 424.0
Baló's disease or concentric sclerosis 341.1
Bamberger's disease (hypertrophic pulmonary osteoarthropathy) 731.2
Bamberger-Marie disease (hypertrophic pulmonary osteoarthropathy) 731.2
Bamboo spine 720.0
Bancroft's filariasis 125.0
Band(s)
  adhesive (*see also* Adhesions, peritoneum) 568.0
  amniotic 658.8
    affecting fetus or newborn 762.8
  anomalous or congenital - *see also* Anomaly, specified type NEC
    atrial 746.9
    heart 746.9

Band(s) (*Continued*)
  anomalous or congenital (*Continued*)
    intestine 751.4
    omentum 751.4
    ventricular 746.9
  cervix 622.3
  gallbladder (congenital) 751.69
  intestinal (adhesive) (*see also* Adhesions, peritoneum) 568.0
    congenital 751.4
    obstructive (*see also* Obstruction, intestine) 560.81
  periappendiceal (congenital) 751.4
  peritoneal (adhesive) (*see also* Adhesions, peritoneum) 568.0
    with intestinal obstruction 560.81
    congenital 751.4
  uterus 621.5
  vagina 623.2
Bandl's ring (contraction)
  complicating delivery 661.4
    affecting fetus or newborn 763.7
Bang's disease (Brucella abortus) 023.1
Bangkok hemorrhagic fever 065.4
Bannister's disease 995.1
Bantam-Albright-Martin disease (pseudohypoparathyroidism) 275.49
Banti's disease or syndrome (with cirrhosis) (with portal hypertension) - *see* Cirrhosis, liver
Bar
  calcaneocuboid 755.67
  calcaneonavicular 755.67
  cubonavicular 755.67
  prostate 600
  talocalcaneal 755.67
Baragnosis 780.9
Barasheh, barashek 266.2
Barcoo disease or rot (*see also* Ulcer, skin) 707.9
Bard-Pic syndrome (carcinoma, head of pancreas) 157.0
Bärensprung's disease (eczema marginatum) 110.3
Baritosis 503
Barium lung disease 503
Barlow's syndrome (meaning mitral valve prolapse) 424.0
Barlow (-Möller) **disease or syndrome** (meaning infantile scurvy) 267
Barodontalgia 993.2
Baron Münchausen syndrome 301.51
Barosinusitis 993.1
Barotitis 993.0
Barotrauma 993.2
  odontalgia 993.2
  otitic 993.0
  sinus 993.1
Barraquer's disease or syndrome (progressive lipodystrophy) 272.6
Barré-Guillain syndrome 357.0
Barré-Liéou syndrome (posterior cervical sympathetic) 723.2
Barrel chest 738.3
Barrett's syndrome or ulcer (chronic peptic ulcer of esophagus) 530.2
Bársony-Polgár syndrome (corkscrew esophagus) 530.5
Bársony-Teschendorf syndrome (corkscrew esophagus) 530.5
Bartholin's
  adenitis (*see also* Bartholinitis) 616.8
  gland - *see* condition

ICD-9-CM

B

Vol. 2

Bartholinitis (suppurating) 616.8
  gonococcal (acute) 098.0
    chronic or duration of 2 months or
      over 098.2
Bartonellosis 088.0
Bartter's syndrome (secondary hyperal-
  dosteronism with juxtaglomerular
  hyperplasia) 255.1
Basal - *see* condition
Basan's (hidrotic) ectodermal dysplasia
  757.31
Baseball finger 842.13
Basedow's disease or syndrome (exoph-
  thalmic goiter) 242.0
Basic - *see* condition
Basilar - *see* condition
Bason's (hidrotic) ectodermal dysplasia
  757.31
Basopenia 288.0
Basophilia 288.8
Basophilism (corticoadrenal) (Cushing's)
  (pituitary) (thymic) 255.0
Bassen-Kornzweig syndrome (abetalipo-
  proteinemia) 272.5
Bat ear 744.29
Bateman's
  disease 078.0
  purpura (senile) 287.2
Bathing cramp 994.1
Bathophobia 300.23
Batten's disease, retina 330.1 *[362.71]*
Batten-Mayou disease 330.1 *[362.71]*
Batten-Steinert syndrome 359.2
Battered
  adult (syndrome) 995.81
  baby or child (syndrome) 995.54
  spouse (syndrome) 995.81
Battey mycobacterium infection 031.0
Battledore placenta - *see* Placenta, abnor-
  mal
Battle exhaustion (*see also* Reaction,
  stress, acute) 308.9
Baumgarten-Cruveilhier (cirrhosis) dis-
  ease, or syndrome 571.5
Bauxite
  fibrosis (of lung) 503
  workers' disease 503
Bayle's disease (dementia paralytica)
  094.1
Bazin's disease (primary) (*see also* Tuberculosis) 017.1
Beach ear 380.12
Beaded hair (congenital) 757.4
Beard's disease (neurasthenia) 300.5
Bearn-Kunkel (-Slater) syndrome (lupoid
  hepatitis) 571.49
Beat
  elbow 727.2
  hand 727.2
  knee 727.2
Beats
  ectopic 427.60
  escaped, heart 427.60
    postoperative 997.1
  premature (nodal) 427.60
    atrial 427.61
    auricular 427.61
    postoperative 997.1
    specified type NEC 427.69
    supraventricular 427.61
    ventricular 427.69
Beau's
  disease or syndrome (*see also* Degener-
    ation, myocardial) 429.1

Beau's (*Continued*)
  lines (transverse furrows on finger-
    nails) 703.8
Bechterew's disease (ankylosing spondylitis) 720.0
Bechterew-Strümpell-Marie syndrome
  (ankylosing spondylitis) 720.0
Beck's syndrome (anterior spinal artery
  occlusion) 433.8
Becker's
  disease (idiopathic mural endomyocar-
    dial disease) 425.2
  dystrophy 359.1
Beckwith (-Wiedemann) syndrome
  759.89
**Bedclothes, asphyxiation or suffocation
  by** 994.7
Bednar's aphthae 528.2
Bedsore 707.0
  with gangrene 707.0 *[785.4]*
Bedwetting (*see also* Enuresis)
  788.36
Beer-drinkers' heart (disease) 425.5
Bee sting (with allergic or anaphylactic
  shock) 989.5
Begbie's disease (exophthalmic goiter)
  242.0
Behavior disorder, disturbance - *see also*
  Disturbance, conduct
  antisocial, without manifest psychiatric
    disorder
    adolescent V71.02
    adult V71.01
    child V71.02
  dyssocial, without manifest psychiatric
    disorder
    adolescent V71.02
    adult V71.01
    child V71.02
  high-risk- see problem
Behçet's syndrome 136.1
Behr's disease 362.50
Beigel's disease or morbus (white
  piedra) 111.2
Bejel 104.0
Bekhterev's (Bechterew's) disease (anky-
  losing spondylitis) 720.0
Bekhterev-Strümpell-Marie syndrome
  (ankylosing spondylitis) 720.0
Belching (*see also* Eructation) 787.3
Bell's
  disease (*see also* Psychosis, affective)
    296.0
  mania (*see also* Psychosis, affective)
    296.0
  palsy, paralysis 351.0
    infant 767.5
    newborn 767.5
    syphilitic 094.89
  spasm 351.0
**Bence-Jones albuminuria, albumino-
  suria, or proteinuria** 791.0
Bends 993.3
Benedikt's syndrome (paralysis)
  344.89
Benign - *see also* condition
  prostate
    hyperplasia 600
    neoplasm 222.2
Bennett's
  disease (leukemia) 208.9
  fracture (closed) 815.01
    open 815.11
Benson's disease 379.22

Bent
  back (hysterical) 300.11
  nose 738.0
    congenital 754.0
Bereavement V62.82
  as adjustment reaction 309.0
Berger's paresthesia (lower limb) 782.0
Bergeron's disease (hysteroepilepsy)
  300.11
Beriberi (acute) (atrophic) (chronic) (dry)
  (subacute) (wet) 265.0
  with polyneuropathy 265.0 *[357.4]*
  heart (disease) 265.0 *[425.7]*
  leprosy 030.1
  neuritis 265.0 *[357.4]*
Berlin's disease or edema (traumatic)
  921.3
Berloque dermatitis 692.72
Bernard-Horner syndrome (*see also* Neuropathy, peripheral, autonomic)
  337.9
Bernard-Sergent syndrome (acute adrenocortical insufficiency) 255.4
**Bernard-Soulier disease or thrombopa-
  thy** 287.1
Bernhardt's disease or paresthesia
  355.1
Bernhardt-Roth disease or syndrome
  (paresthesia) 355.1
Bernheim's syndrome (*see also* Failure,
  heart, congestive) 428.0
Bertielliasis 123.8
Bertolotti's syndrome (sacralization of
  fifth lumbar vertebra) 756.15
Berylliosis (acute) (chronic) (lung) (occu-
  pational) 503
Besnier's
  lupus pernio 135
  prurigo (atopic dermatitis) (infantile
    eczema) 691.8
Besnier-Boeck disease or sarcoid 135
Besnier-Boeck-Schaumann disease (sar-
  coidosis) 135
Best's disease 362.76
Bestiality 302.1
**Beta-adrenergic hyperdynamic circula-
  tory state** 429.82
Beta-aminoisobutyric aciduria 277.2
**Beta-mercaptolactate-cysteine disulfidu-
  ria** 270.0
Beta thalassemia (major) (minor)
  (mixed) 282.4
Beurmann's disease (sporotrichosis)
  117.1
Bezoar 938
  intestine 936
  stomach 935.2
Bezold's abscess (*see also* Mastoiditis)
  383.01
Bianchi's syndrome (aphasia-apraxia-
  alexia) 784.69
Bicornuate or bicornis uterus 752.3
  in pregnancy or childbirth 654.0
    with obstructed labor 660.2
      affecting fetus or newborn
        763.1
    affecting fetus or newborn
      763.89
Bicuspid aortic valve 746.4
Biedl-Bardet syndrome 759.89
Bielschowsky's disease 330.1
Bielschowsky-Jansky
  amaurotic familial idiocy 330.1
  disease 330.1

Biemond's syndrome (obesity, polydactyly, and mental retardation) 759.89
Biermer's anemia or disease (pernicious anemia) 281.0
Biett's disease 695.4
Bifid (congenital) - *see also* Imperfect, closure
apex, heart 746.89
clitoris 752.49
epiglottis 748.3
kidney 753.3
nose 748.1
patella 755.64
scrotum 752.8
toe 755.66
tongue 750.13
ureter 753.4
uterus 752.3
uvula 749.02
with cleft lip (*see also* Cleft, palate, with cleft lip) 749.20
Biforis uterus (suprasimplex) 752.3
Bifurcation (congenital) - *see also* Imperfect, closure
gallbladder 751.69
kidney pelvis 753.3
renal pelvis 753.3
rib 756.3
tongue 750.13
trachea 748.3
ureter 753.4
urethra 753.8
uvula 749.02
with cleft lip (*see also* Cleft, palate, with cleft lip) 749.20
vertebra 756.19
Bigeminal pulse 427.89
Bigeminy 427.89
Big spleen syndrome 289.4
Bilateral - *see* condition
Bile duct - *see* condition
Bile pigments in urine 791.4
Bilharziasis (*see also* Schistosomiasis) 120.9
chyluria 120.0
cutaneous 120.3
galacturia 120.0
hematochyluria 120.0
intestinal 120.1
lipemia 120.9
lipuria 120.0
Oriental 120.2
piarhemia 120.9
pulmonary 120.2
tropical hematuria 120.0
vesical 120.0
Biliary - *see* condition
Bilious (attack) - *see also* Vomiting
fever, hemoglobinuric 084.8
Bilirubinuria 791.4
Biliuria 791.4
Billroth's disease
meningocele (*see also* Spina bifida) 741.9
Bilobate placenta - *see* Placenta, abnormal
Bilocular
heart 745.7
stomach 536.8
Bing-Horton syndrome (histamine cephalgia) 346.2
Binswanger's disease or dementia 290.12

Biörck (-Thorson) syndrome (malignant carcinoid) 259.2
Biparta, bipartite - *see also* Imperfect, closure
carpal scaphoid 755.59
patella 755.64
placenta - *see* Placenta, abnormal
vagina 752.49
Bird
face 756.0
fanciers' lung or disease 495.2
Bird's disease (oxaluria) 271.8
Birth
abnormal fetus or newborn 763.9
accident, fetus or newborn - *see* Birth, injury
complications in mother - *see* Delivery, complicated
compression during NEC 767.9
defect - *see* Anomaly
delayed, fetus 763.9
difficult NEC, affecting fetus or newborn 763.9
dry, affecting fetus or newborn 761.1
forced, NEC, affecting fetus or newborn 763.89
forceps, affecting fetus or newborn 763.2
hematoma of sternomastoid 767.8
immature 765.1
extremely 765.0
inattention, after or at 995.52
induced, affecting fetus or newborn 763.89
infant - *see* Newborn
injury NEC 767.9
adrenal gland 767.8
basal ganglia 767.0
brachial plexus (paralysis) 767.6
brain (compression) (pressure) 767.0
cerebellum 767.0
cerebral hemorrhage 767.0
conjunctiva 767.8
eye 767.8
fracture
bone, any except clavicle or spine 767.3
clavicle 767.2
femur 767.3
humerus 767.3
long bone 767.3
radius and ulna 767.3
skeleton NEC 767.3
skull 767.3
spine 767.4
tibia and fibula 767.3
hematoma 767.8
liver (subcapsular) 767.8
mastoid 767.8
skull 767.1
sternomastoid 767.8
testes 767.8
vulva 767.8
intracranial (edema) 767.0
laceration
brain 767.0
by scalpel 767.8
peripheral nerve 767.7
liver 767.8
meninges
brain 767.0
spinal cord 767.4

Birth (*Continued*)
injury NEC (*Continued*)
nerves (cranial, peripheral) 767.7
brachial plexus 767.6
facial 767.5
paralysis 767.7
brachial plexus 767.6
Erb (-Duchenne) 767.6
facial nerve 767.5
Klumpke (-Déjérine) 767.6
radial nerve 767.6
spinal (cord) (hemorrhage) (laceration) (rupture) 767.4
rupture
intracranial 767.0
liver 767.8
spinal cord 767.4
spleen 767.8
viscera 767.8
scalp 767.1
scalpel wound 767.8
skeleton NEC 767.3
specified NEC 767.8
spinal cord 767.4
spleen 767.8
subdural hemorrhage 767.0
tentorial, tear 767.0
testes 767.8
vulva 767.8
instrumental, NEC, affecting fetus or newborn 763.2
lack of care, after or at 995.52
multiple
affected by maternal complications of pregnancy 761.5
healthy liveborn - *see* Newborn, multiple
neglect, after or at 995.52
newborn - *see* Newborn
palsy or paralysis NEC 767.7
precipitate, fetus or newborn 763.6
premature (infant) 765.1
prolonged, affecting fetus or newborn 763.9
retarded, fetus or newborn 763.9
shock, newborn 779.8
strangulation or suffocation
due to aspiration of amniotic fluid 770.1
mechanical 767.8
trauma NEC 767.9
triplet
affected by maternal complications of pregnancy 761.5
healthy liveborn - *see* Newborn, multiple
twin
affected by maternal complications of pregnancy 761.5
healthy liveborn - *see* Newborn, twin
ventouse, affecting fetus or newborn 763.3
Birthmark 757.32
Bisalbuminemia 273.8
Biskra button 085.1
Bite(s)
with intact skin surface - *see* Contusion
animal - *see* Wound, open, by site
intact skin surface - *see* Contusion
centipede 989.5
chigger 133.8
fire ant 989.5

ICD-9-CM

Vol. 2

Blindness *(Continued)*
  legal *(Continued)*
    with impairment of better (less impaired) eye *(Continued)*
      severe 369.21
        with
          lesser eye impairment 369.21
            blind 369.11
            near-total 369.13
            profound 369.14
            severe 369.22
            total 369.12
      total
        with lesser eye impairment
          total 369.01
  mind 784.69
  moderate
    both eyes 369.25
      with impairment of lesser eye (specified as)
        blind, not further specified 369.15
        low vision, not further specified 369.23
        near-total 369.17
        profound 369.18
        severe 369.24
        total 369.16
    one eye 369.74
      with vision of other eye (specified as)
        near-normal 369.75
        normal 369.76
  near-total
    both eyes 369.04
      with impairment of lesser eye (specified as)
        blind, not further specified 369.02
        total 369.03
    one eye 369.64
      with vision of other eye (specified as)
        near-normal 369.65
        normal 369.66
  night 368.60
    acquired 368.62
    congenital (Japanese) 368.61
    hereditary 368.61
    specified type NEC 368.69
    vitamin A deficiency 264.5
  nocturnal - *see* Blindness, night
  one eye 369.60
    with low vision of other eye 369.10
  profound
    both eyes 369.08
      with impairment of lesser eye (specified as)
        blind, not further specified 369.05
        near-total 369.07
        total 369.06
    one eye 369.67
      with vision of other eye (specified as)
        near-normal 369.68
        normal 369.69
  psychic 784.69
  severe
    both eyes 369.22
      with impairment of lesser eye (specified as)
        blind, not further specified 369.11

Blindness *(Continued)*
  severe *(Continued)*
    both eyes *(Continued)*
      with impairment of lesser eye (specified as) *(Continued)*
        low vision, not further specified 369.21
        near-total 369.13
        profound 369.14
        total 369.12
    one eye 369.71
      with vision of other eye (specified as)
        near-normal 369.72
        normal 369.73
  snow 370.24
  sun 363.31
  temporary 368.12
  total
    both eyes 369.01
    one eye 369.61
      with vision of other eye (specified as)
        near-normal 369.62
        normal 369.63
  transient 368.12
  traumatic NEC 950.9
  word (developmental) 315.01
    acquired 784.61
    secondary to organic lesion 784.61
Blister - *see also* Injury, superficial, by site
  beetle dermatitis 692.89
  due to burn - *see* Burn, by site, second degree
  fever 054.9
  multiple, skin, nontraumatic 709.8
Bloating 787.3
Bloch-Siemens syndrome (incontinentia pigmenti) 757.33
Bloch-Stauffer dyshormonal dermatosis 757.33
Bloch-Sulzberger disease or syndrome (incontinentia pigmenti) (melanoblastosis) 757.33
Block
  alveolar capillary 516.3
  arborization (heart) 426.6
  arrhythmic 426.9
  atrioventricular (AV) (incomplete) (partial) 426.10
    with
      2:1 atrioventricular response block 426.13
      atrioventricular dissociation 426.0
    first degree (incomplete) 426.11
    second degree (Mobitz type I) 426.13
      Mobitz (type II) 426.12
    third degree 426.0
    complete 426.0
      congenital 746.86
    congenital 746.86
    Mobitz (incomplete)
      type I (Wenckebach's) 426.13
      type II 426.12
    partial 426.13
  auriculoventricular (*see also* Block, atrioventricular) 426.10
    complete 426.0
      congenital 746.86
    congenital 746.86
  bifascicular (cardiac) 426.53

Block *(Continued)*
  bundle branch (complete) (false) (incomplete) 426.50
    bilateral 426.53
    left (complete) (main stem) 426.3
      with right bundle branch block 426.53
      anterior fascicular 426.2
        with
          posterior fascicular block 426.3
          right bundle branch block 426.52
      hemiblock 426.2
      incomplete 426.2
        with right bundle branch block 426.53
      posterior fascicular 426.2
        with
          anterior fascicular block 426.3
          right bundle branch block 426.51
    right 426.4
      with
        left bundle branch block (incomplete) (main stem) 426.53
        left fascicular block 426.53
          anterior 426.52
          posterior 426.51
    Wilson's type 426.4
  cardiac 426.9
  conduction 426.9
    complete 426.0
  eustachian tube (*see also* Obstruction, Eustachian tube) 381.60
  fascicular (left anterior) (left posterior) 426.2
  foramen Magendie (acquired) 331.3
    congenital 742.3
      with spina bifida (*see also* Spina bifida) 741.0
  heart 426.9
    first degree (atrioventricular) 426.11
    second degree (atrioventricular) 426.13
    third degree (atrioventricular) 426.0
    bundle branch (complete) (false) (incomplete) 426.50
      bilateral 426.53
      left (*see also* Block, bundle branch, left) 426.3
      right (*see also* Block, bundle branch, right) 426.4
    complete (atrioventricular) 426.0
    congenital 746.86
    incomplete 426.13
    intra-atrial 426.6
    intraventricular NEC 426.6
    sinoatrial 426.6
    specified type NEC 426.6
  hepatic vein 453.0
  intraventricular (diffuse) (myofibrillar) 426.6
    bundle branch (complete) (false) (incomplete) 426.50
      bilateral 426.53
      left (*see also* Block, bundle branch, left) 426.3
      right (*see also* Block, bundle branch, right) 426.4
  kidney (*see also* Disease, renal) 593.9
    postcystoscopic 997.5

ICD-9-CM

B

Vol. 2

Block (*Continued*)
  myocardial (*see also* Block, heart)
    426.9
  nodal 426.10
  optic nerve 377.49
  organ or site (congenital) NEC - *see*
    Atresia
  parietal 426.6
  peri-infarction 426.6
  portal (vein) 452
  sinoatrial 426.6
  sinoauricular 426.6
  spinal cord 336.9
  trifascicular 426.54
  tubal 628.2
  vein NEC 453.9
Blocq's disease or syndrome (astasia-
  abasia) 307.9
Blood
  constituents, abnormal NEC 790.6
  disease 289.9
    specified NEC 289.8
  donor V59.01
    other blood components V59.09
    stem cells V59.02
    whole blood V59.01
  dyscrasia 289.9
    with
      abortion - *see* Abortion, by type,
        with hemorrhage, delayed or
        excessive
      ectopic pregnancy (*see also* catego-
        ries 633.0-633.9) 639.1
      molar pregnancy (*see also* catego-
        ries 630-632) 639.1
    fetus or newborn NEC 776.9
    following
      abortion 639.1
      ectopic or molar pregnancy
        639.1
    puerperal, postpartum 666.3
  flukes NEC (*see also* Infestation, Schis-
    tosoma) 120.9
  in
    feces (*see also* Melena) 578.1
      occult 792.1
    urine (*see also* Hematuria) 599.7
  mole 631
  occult 792.1
  poisoning (*see also* Septicemia) 038.9
  pressure
    decreased, due to shock following
      injury 958.4
    fluctuating 796.4
    high (*see also* Hypertension) 401.9
      incidental reading (isolated) (non-
        specific), without diagnosis of
        hypertension 796.2
    low (*see also* Hypotension) 458.9
      incidental reading (isolated) (non-
        specific), without diagnosis of
        hypotension 796.3
  spitting (*see also* Hemoptysis) 786.3
  staining cornea 371.12
  transfusion
    without reported diagnosis V58.2
    donor V59.01
      stem cells V59.02
    reaction or complication - *see* Com-
      plications, transfusion
  tumor - *see* Hematoma
  vessel rupture - *see* Hemorrhage
  vomiting (*see also* Hematemesis)
    578.0

Blood-forming organ disease 289.9
Bloodgood's disease 610.1
Bloodshot eye 379.93
Bloom (-Machacek) (-Torre) syndrome
  757.39
Blotch, palpebral 372.55
Blount's disease (tibia vara) 732.4
Blount-Barber syndrome (tibia vara)
  732.4
Blue
  baby 746.9
  bloater 491.20
    with acute bronchitis or exacerbation
      491.21
  diaper syndrome 270.0
  disease 746.9
  dome cyst 610.0
  drum syndrome 381.02
  sclera 743.47
    with fragility of bone and deafness
      756.51
  toe syndrome - *see* Atherosclerosis
Blueness (*see also* Cyanosis) 782.5
Blurring, visual 368.8
Blushing (abnormal) (excessive) 782.62
Boarder, hospital V65.0
  infant V65.0
Bockhart's impetigo (superficial folliculitis) 704.8
Bodechtel-Guttmann disease (subacute sclerosing panencephalitis)
  046.2
Boder-Sedgwick syndrome (ataxia-telangiectasia) 334.8
Body, bodies
  Aschoff (*see also* Myocarditis, rheu-
    matic) 398.0
  asteroid, vitreous 379.22
  choroid, colloid (degenerative)
    362.57
    hereditary 362.77
  cytoid (retina) 362.82
  drusen (retina) (*see also* Drusen)
    362.57
    optic disc 377.21
  fibrin, pleura 511.0
  foreign - *see* Foreign body
  Hassall-Henle 371.41
  loose
    joint (*see also* Loose, body, joint)
      718.1
      knee 717.6
    knee 717.6
    sheath, tendon 727.82
  Mallory's 034.1
  Mooser 081.0
  Negri 071
  rice (joint) (*see also* Loose, body, joint)
    718.1
    knee 717.6
  rocking 307.3
Boeck's
  disease (sarcoidosis) 135
  lupoid (miliary) 135
  sarcoid 135
Boerhaave's syndrome (spontaneous
  esophageal rupture) 530.4
Boggy
  cervix 622.8
  uterus 621.8
Boil (*see also* Carbuncle) 680.9
  abdominal wall 680.2
  Aleppo 085.1
  ankle 680.6

Boil (*Continued*)
  anus 680.5
  arm (any part, above wrist) 680.3
  auditory canal, external 680.0
  axilla 680.3
  back (any part) 680.2
  Baghdad 085.1
  breast 680.2
  buttock 680.5
  chest wall 680.2
  corpus cavernosum 607.2
  Delhi 085.1
  ear (any part) 680.0
  eyelid 373.13
  face (any part, except eye) 680.0
  finger (any) 680.4
  flank 680.2
  foot (any part) 680.7
  forearm 680.3
  Gafsa 085.1
  genital organ, male 608.4
  gluteal (region) 680.5
  groin 680.2
  hand (any part) 680.4
  head (any part, except face) 680.8
  heel 680.7
  hip 680.6
  knee 680.6
  labia 616.4
  lacrimal (*see also* Dacryocystitis)
    375.30
    gland (*see also* Dacryoadenitis)
      375.00
    passages (duct) (sac) (*see also* Dac-
      ryocystitis) 375.30
  leg, any part, except foot 680.6
  multiple sites 680.9
  Natal 085.1
  neck 680.1
  nose (external) (septum) 680.0
  orbit, orbital 376.01
  partes posteriores 680.5
  pectoral region 680.2
  penis 607.2
  perineum 680.2
  pinna 680.0
  scalp (any part) 680.8
  scrotum 608.4
  seminal vesicle 608.0
  shoulder 680.3
  skin NEC 680.9
  specified site NEC 680.8
  spermatic cord 608.4
  temple (region) 680.0
  testis 608.4
  thigh 680.6
  thumb 680.4
  toe (any) 680.7
  tropical 085.1
  trunk 680.2
  tunica vaginalis 608.4
  umbilicus 680.2
  upper arm 680.3
  vas deferens 608.4
  vulva 616.4
  wrist 680.4
Bold hives (*see also* Urticaria) 708.9
Bolivian hemorrhagic fever 078.7
Bombé, iris 364.74
Bomford-Rhoads anemia (refractory)
  284.9
Bone - *see* condition
Bonnevie-Ullrich syndrome 758.6
Bonnier's syndrome 386.19

◀▶ New Code   ⇐⇛ Revised Code

Bonvale Dam fever 780.79
Bony block of joint 718.80
  ankle 718.87
  elbow 718.82
  foot 718.87
  hand 718.84
  hip 718.85
  knee 718.86
  multiple sites 718.89
  pelvic region 718.85
  shoulder (region) 718.81
  specified site NEC 718.88
  wrist 718.83
Borderline
  intellectual functioning V62.89
  pelvis 653.1
    with obstruction during labor 660.1
      affecting fetus or newborn 763.1
  psychosis (*see also* Schizophrenia) 295.5
    of childhood (*see also* Psychosis, childhood) 299.8
  schizophrenia (*see also* Schizophrenia) 295.5
Borna disease 062.9
Bornholm disease (epidemic pleurodynia) 074.1
Borrelia vincentii (mouth) (pharynx) (tonsils) 101
Bostock's catarrh (*see also* Fever, hay) 477.9
Boston exanthem 048
Botalli, ductus (patent) (persistent) 747.0
Bothriocephalus latus infestation 123.4
Botulism 005.1
Bouba (*see also* Yaws) 102.9
Bouffée délirante 298.3
Bouillaud's disease or syndrome (rheumatic heart disease) 391.9
Bourneville's disease (tuberous sclerosis) 759.5
Boutonneuse fever 082.1
Boutonniere
  deformity (finger) 736.21
  hand (intrinsic) 736.21
Bouveret (-Hoffmann) disease or syndrome (paroxysmal tachycardia) 427.2
Bovine heart - *see* Hypertrophy, cardiac
Bowel - *see* condition
Bowen's
  dermatosis (precancerous) (M8081/2) - *see* Neoplasm, skin, in situ
  disease (M8081/2) - *see* Neoplasm, skin, in situ
  epithelioma (M8081/2) - *see* Neoplasm, skin, in situ
  type
    epidermoid carcinoma in situ (M8081/2) - *see* Neoplasm, skin, in situ
    intraepidermal squamous cell carcinoma (M8081/2) - *see* Neoplasm, skin, in situ
Bowing
  femur 736.89
    congenital 754.42
  fibula 736.89
    congenital 754.43
  forearm 736.09
    away from midline (cubitus valgus) 736.01

Bowing (*Continued*)
  forearm (*Continued*)
    toward midline (cubitus varus) 736.02
  leg(s), long bones, congenital 754.44
  radius 736.09
    away from midline (cubitus valgus) 736.01
    toward midline (cubitus varus) 736.02
  tibia 736.89
    congenital 754.43
Bowleg(s) 736.42
  congenital 754.44
  rachitic 268.1
Boyd's dysentery 004.2
Brachial - *see* condition
Brachman-de Lange syndrome (Amsterdam dwarf, mental retardation, and brachycephaly) 759.89
Brachycardia 427.89
Brachycephaly 756.0
Brachymorphism and ectopia lentis 759.89
Bradley's disease (epidemic vomiting) 078.82
Bradycardia 427.89
  chronic (sinus) 427.81
  newborn 763.83
  nodal 427.89
  postoperative 997.1
  reflex 337.0
  sinoatrial 427.89
    with paroxysmal tachyarrhythmia or tachycardia 427.81
    chronic 427.81
  sinus 427.89
    with paroxysmal tachyarrhythmia or tachycardia 427.81
    chronic 427.81
    persistent 427.81
    severe 427.81
  tachycardia syndrome 427.81
  vagal 427.89
Bradypnea 786.09
Brailsford's disease 732.3
  radial head 732.3
  tarsal scaphoid 732.5
Brailsford-Morquio disease or syndrome (mucopolysaccharidosis IV) 277.5
Brain - *see also* condition
  death 348.8
  syndrome (acute) (chronic) (nonpsychotic) (organic) (with neurotic reaction) (with behavioral reaction) (*see also* Syndrome, brain) 310.9
    with
      presenile brain disease 290.10
      psychosis, psychotic reaction (*see also* Psychosis, organic) 294.9
    congenital (*see also* Retardation, mental) 319
Branched-chain amino-acid disease 270.3
Branchial - *see* condition
Brandt's syndrome (acrodermatitis enteropathica) 686.8
Brash (water) 787.1
Brass-founders' ague 985.8
Bravais-Jacksonian epilepsy (*see also* Epilepsy) 345.5

Braxton Hicks contractions 644.1
Braziers' disease 985.8
Brazilian
  blastomycosis 116.1
  leishmaniasis 085.5
Break
  cardiorenal - *see* Hypertension, cardiorenal
  retina (*see also* Defect, retina) 361.30
Breakbone fever 061
Breakdown
  device, implant, or graft - *see* Complications, mechanical
  nervous (*see also* Disorder, mental, nonpsychotic) 300.9
  perineum 674.2
Breast - *see* condition
Breast feeding difficulties 676.8
Breath
  foul 784.9
  holder, child 312.81
  holding spells 786.9
  shortness 786.05
Breathing
  asymmetrical 786.09
  bronchial 786.09
  exercises V57.0
  labored 786.09
  mouth 784.9
  periodic 786.09
  tic 307.20
Breathlessness 786.09
Breda's disease (*see also* Yaws) 102.9
Breech
  delivery, affecting fetus or newborn 763.0
  extraction, affecting fetus or newborn 763.0
  presentation (buttocks) (complete) (frank) 652.2
    with successful version 652.1
    before labor, affecting fetus or newborn 761.7
    during labor, affecting fetus or newborn 763.0
Breisky's disease (kraurosis vulvae) 624.0
Brennemann's syndrome (acute mesenteric lymphadenitis) 289.2
Brenner's
  tumor (benign) (M9000/0) 220
    borderline malignancy (M9000/1) 236.2
    malignant (M9000/3) 183.0
    proliferating (M9000/1) 236.2
Bretonneau's disease (diphtheritic malignant angina) 032.0
Breus' mole 631
Brevicollis 756.16
Bricklayers' itch 692.89
Brickmakers' anemia 126.9
Bridge
  myocardial 746.85
Bright's
  blindness - *see* Uremia
  disease (*see also* Nephritis) 583.9
    arteriosclerotic (*see also* Hypertension, kidney) 403.90
Brill's disease (recrudescent typhus) 081.1
  flea-borne 081.0
  louse-borne 081.1
Brill-Symmers disease (follicular lymphoma) (M9690/3) 202.0

Bronchitis *(Continued)*
Vincent's 101
viral, acute or subacute 466.0
with bronchospasm or obstruction 466.0
Bronchoalveolitis 485
Bronchoaspergillosis 117.3
Bronchocele
meaning
dilatation of bronchus 519.1
goiter 240.9
Bronchogenic carcinoma 162.9
Bronchohemisporosis 117.9
Broncholithiasis 518.89
tuberculous *(see also* Tuberculosis) 011.3
Bronchomalacia 748.3 ◄
Bronchomoniliasis 112.89
Bronchomycosis 112.89
Bronchonocardiosis 039.1
Bronchopleuropneumonia - *see* Pneumonia, broncho-
Bronchopneumonia - *see* Pneumonia, broncho-
Bronchopneumonitis - *see* Pneumonia, broncho-
Bronchopulmonary - *see* Condition
Bronchopulmonitis - *see* Pneumonia, broncho-
Bronchorrhagia 786.3
newborn 770.3
tuberculous *(see also* Tuberculosis) 011.3
Bronchorrhea (chronic) (purulent) 491.0
acute 466.0
Bronchospasm 519.1
with
asthma - *see* Asthma
bronchiolitis, acute 466.19
due to respiratory syncytial virus 466.11
bronchitis - *see* Bronchitis
chronic obstructive pulmonary disease (COPD) 496
emphysema - *see* Emphysema
due to external agent - *see* Condition, respiratory, acute, due to
Bronchospirochetosis 104.8
Bronchostenosis 519.1
Bronchus - *see* Condition
Bronze, bronzed
diabetes 275.0
disease (Addison's) (skin) 255.4
tuberculous *(see also* Tuberculosis) 017.6
Brooke's disease or tumor (M8100/0) - *see* Neoplasm, skin, benign
Brown's tendon sheath syndrome 378.61
Brown enamel of teeth (hereditary) 520.5
Brown-Séquard's paralysis (syndrome) 344.89
Brow presentation complicating delivery 652.4
causing obstructed labor 660.0
Brucella, brucellosis (infection) 023.9
abortus 023.1
canis 023.3
dermatitis, skin 023.9
melitensis 023.0
mixed 023.8
suis 023.2

Bruck's disease 733.99
Bruck-de Lange disease or syndrome (Amsterdam dwarf, mental retardation, and brachycephaly) 759.89
Brug's filariasis 125.1
Brugsch's syndrome (acropachyderma) 757.39
Bruhl's disease (splenic anemia with fever) 285.8
Bruise (skin surface intact) - *see also* Contusion
with
fracture - *see* Fracture, by site
open wound - *see* Wound, open, by site
internal organ (abdomen, chest, or pelvis) - *see* Injury, internal, by site
umbilical cord 663.6
affecting fetus or newborn 762.6
Bruit 785.9
arterial (abdominal) (carotid) 785.9
supraclavicular 785.9
Brushburn - *see* Injury, superficial, by site
Bruton's X-linked agammaglobulinemia 279.04
Bruxism 306.8
Bubbly lung syndrome 770.7
Bubo 289.3
blennorrhagic 098.89
chancroidal 099.0
climatic 099.1
due to Hemophilus ducreyi 099.0
gonococcal 098.89
indolent NEC 099.8
inguinal NEC 099.8
chancroidal 099.0
climatic 099.1
due to H. ducreyi 099.0
scrofulous *(see also* Tuberculosis) 017.2
soft chancre 099.0
suppurating 683
syphilitic 091.0
congenital 090.0
tropical 099.1
venereal NEC 099.8
virulent 099.0
Bubonic plague 020.0
Bubonocele - *see* Hernia, inguinal
Buccal - *see* Condition
Buchanan's disease (juvenile osteochondrosis of iliac crest) 732.1
Buchem's syndrome (hyperostosis corticalis) 733.3
Buchman's disease (osteochondrosis, juvenile) 732.1
Bucket handle fracture (semilunar cartilage) *(see also* Tear, meniscus) 836.2
Budd-Chiari syndrome (hepatic vein thrombosis) 453.0
Budgerigar-fanciers' disease of lung 495.2
Büdinger-Ludloff-Läwen disease 717.89
Buerger's disease (thromboangiitis obliterans) 443.1
Bulbar - *see* Condition
Bulbus cordis 745.9
persistent (in left ventricle) 745.8
Bulging fontanels (congenital) 756.0
Bulimia 783.6
nonorganic origin 307.51

Bulky uterus 621.2
Bulla(e) 709.8
lung (emphysematous) (solitary) 492.0
Bullet wound - *see also* Wound, open, by site
fracture - *see* Fracture, by site, open
internal organ (abdomen, chest, or pelvis) - *see* Injury, internal, by site, with open wound
intracranial - *see* Laceration, brain, with open wound
Bullis fever 082.8
Bullying *(see also* Disturbance, conduct) 312.0
Bundle
branch block (complete) (false) (incomplete) 426.50
bilateral 426.53
left *(see also* Block, bundle branch, left) 426.3
hemiblock 426.2
right *(see also* Block, bundle branch, right) 426.4
of His - *see* Condition
of Kent syndrome (anomalous atrioventricular excitation) 426.7
Bungpagga 040.81
Bunion 727.1
Bunionette 727.1
Bunyamwera fever 066.3
Buphthalmia, buphthalmos (congenital) 743.20
associated with
keratoglobus, congenital 743.22
megalocornea 743.22
ocular anomalies NEC 743.22
isolated 743.21
simple 743.21
Bürger-Grütz disease or syndrome (essential familial hyperlipemia) 272.3
Buried roots 525.3
Burke's syndrome 577.8
Burkitt's
tumor (M9750/3) 200.2
type (malignant, lymphoma, lymphoblastic, or undifferentiated) (M9750/3) 200.2
Burn (acid) (cathode ray) (caustic) (chemical) (electric heating appliance) (electricity) (fire) (flame) (hot liquid or object) (irradiation) (lime) (radiation) (steam) (thermal) (x-ray) 949.0

Note   Use the following fifth-digit subclassification with category 948 to indicate the percent of body surface with third degree burn:

0	less than 10 percent or unspecified
1	10-19 percent
2	20-29 percent
3	30-39 percent
4	40-49 percent
5	50-59 percent
6	60-69 percent
7	70-79 percent
8	80-89 percent
9	90 percent or more of body surface

ICD-9-CM
B
Vol. 2

Burn (*Continued*)
- with
  - blisters - *see* Burn, by site, second degree
  - erythema - *see* Burn, by site, first degree
  - skin loss (epidermal) - *see also* Burn, by site, second degree
    - full thickness - *see also* Burn, by site, third degree
      - with necrosis of underlying tissues - *see* Burn, by site, third degree, deep
  - first degree - *see* Burn, by site, first degree
  - second degree - *see* Burn, by site, second degree
  - third degree - *see also* Burn, by site, third degree
    - deep - *see* Burn, by site, third degree, deep
- abdomen, abdominal (muscle) (wall) 942.03
  - with
    - trunk - *see* Burn, trunk, multiple sites
  - first degree 942.13
  - second degree 942.23
  - third degree 942.33
    - deep 942.43
      - with loss of body part 942.53
- ankle 945.03
  - with
    - lower limb(s) - *see* Burn, leg, multiple sites
  - first degree 945.13
  - second degree 945.23
  - third degree 945.33
    - deep 945.43
      - with loss of body part 945.53
- anus - *see* Burn, trunk, specified site NEC
- arm(s) 943.00
  - first degree 943.10
  - second degree 943.20
  - third degree 943.30
    - deep 943.40
      - with loss of body part 943.50
  - lower - *see* Burn, forearm(s)
  - multiple sites, except hand(s) or wrist(s) 943.09
    - first degree 943.19
    - second degree 943.29
    - third degree 943.39
      - deep 943.49
        - with loss of body part 943.59
  - upper 943.03
    - first degree 943.13
    - second degree 943.23
    - third degree 943.33
      - deep 943.43
        - with loss of body part 943.53
- auditory canal (external) - *see* Burn, ear
- auricle (ear) - *see* Burn, ear
- axilla 943.04
  - with
    - upper limb(s), except hand(s) or wrist(s) - *see* Burn, arm(s), multiple sites

Burn (*Continued*)
- axilla (*Continued*)
  - first degree 943.14
  - second degree 943.24
  - third degree 943.34
    - deep 943.44
      - with loss of body part 943.54
- back 942.04
  - with
    - trunk - *see* Burn, trunk, multiple sites
  - first degree 942.14
  - second degree 942.24
  - third degree 942.34
    - deep 942.44
      - with loss of body part 942.54
- biceps
  - brachii - *see* Burn, arm(s), upper
  - femoris - *see* Burn, thigh
- breast(s) 942.01
  - with
    - trunk - *see* Burn, trunk, multiple sites
  - first degree 942.11
  - second degree 942.21
  - third degree 942.31
    - deep 942.41
      - with loss of body part 942.51
- brow - *see* Burn, forehead
- buttock(s) - *see* Burn, back
- canthus (eye) 940.1
  - chemical 940.0
- cervix (uteri) 947.4
- cheek (cutaneous) 941.07
  - with
    - face or head - *see* Burn, head, multiple sites
  - first degree 941.17
  - second degree 941.27
  - third degree 941.37
    - deep 941.47
      - with loss of body part 941.57
- chest wall (anterior) 942.02
  - with
    - trunk - *see* Burn, trunk, multiple sites
  - first degree 942.12
  - second degree 942.22
  - third degree 942.32
    - deep 942.42
      - with loss of body part 942.52
- chin 941.04
  - with
    - face or head - *see* Burn, head, multiple sites
  - first degree 941.14
  - second degree 941.24
  - third degree 941.34
    - deep 941.44
      - with loss of body part 941.54
- clitoris - *see* Burn, genitourinary organs, external
- colon 947.3
- conjunctiva (and cornea) 940.4
  - chemical
    - acid 940.3
    - alkaline 940.2
- cornea (and conjunctiva) 940.4
  - chemical
    - acid 940.3
    - alkaline 940.2
- costal region - *see* Burn, chest wall

Burn (*Continued*)
- due to ingested chemical agent - *see* Burn, internal organs
- ear (auricle) (canal) (drum) (external) 941.01
  - with
    - face or head - *see* Burn, head, multiple sites
  - first degree 941.11
  - second degree 941.21
  - third degree 941.31
    - deep 941.41
      - with loss of a body part 941.51
- elbow 943.02
  - with
    - hand(s) and wrist(s) - *see* Burn, multiple specified sites
    - upper limb(s), except hand(s) or wrist(s) - *see also* Burn, arm(s), multiple sites
  - first degree 943.12
  - second degree 943.22
  - third degree 943.32
    - deep 943.42
      - with loss of body part 943.52
- electricity, electric current - *see* Burn, by site
- entire body - *see* Burn, multiple, specified sites
- epididymis - *see* Burn, genitourinary organs, external
- epigastric region - *see* Burn, abdomen
- epiglottis 947.1
- esophagus 947.2
- extent (percent of body surface)
  - less than 10 percent 948.0
  - 10-19 percent 948.1
  - 20-29 percent 948.2
  - 30-39 percent 948.3
  - 40-49 percent 948.4
  - 50-59 percent 948.5
  - 60-69 percent 948.6
  - 70-79 percent 948.7
  - 80-89 percent 948.8
  - 90 percent or more 948.9
- extremity
  - lower - *see* Burn, leg
  - upper - *see* Burn, arm(s)
- eye(s) (and adnexa) (only) 940.9
  - with
    - face, head, or neck 941.02
      - first degree 941.12
      - second degree 941.22
      - third degree 941.32
        - deep 941.42
          - with loss of body part 941.52
    - other sites (classifiable to more than one category in 940-945) - *see* Burn, multiple, specified sites
    - resulting rupture and destruction of eyeball 940.5
    - specified part - *see* Burn, by site
  - eyeball - *see also* Burn, eye
    - with resulting rupture and destruction of eyeball 940.5
  - eyelid(s) 940.1
    - chemical 940.0
- face - *see* Burn, head
- finger (nail) (subungual) 944.01

Burn *(Continued)*
  finger *(Continued)*
    with
      hand(s) - *see* Burn, hand(s), multiple sites
      other sites - *see* Burn, multiple, specified sites
      thumb 944.04
        first degree 944.14
        second degree 944.24
        third degree 944.34
          deep 944.44
            with loss of body part 944.54
    first degree 944.11
    second degree 944.21
    third degree 944.31
      deep 944.41
        with loss of body part 944.51
    multiple (digits) 944.03
      with thumb - *see* Burn, finger, with thumb
      first degree 944.13
      second degree 944.23
      third degree 944.33
        deep 944.43
          with loss of body part 944.53
  flank - *see* Burn, abdomen
  foot 945.02
    with
      lower limb(s) - *see* Burn, leg, multiple sites
    first degree 945.12
    second degree 945.22
    third degree 945.32
      deep 945.42
        with loss of body part 945.52
  forearm(s) 943.01
    with
      upper limb(s), except hand(s) or wrist(s) - *see* Burn, arm(s), multiple sites
    first degree 943.11
    second degree 943.21
    third degree 943.31
      deep 943.41
        with loss of body part 943.51
  forehead 941.07
    with
      face or head - *see* Burn, head, multiple sites
    first degree 941.17
    second degree 941.27
    third degree 941.37
      deep 941.47
        with loss of body part 941.57
  fourth degree - *see* Burn, by site, third degree, deep
  friction - *see* Injury, superficial, by site
  from swallowing caustic or corrosive substance NEC - *see* Burn, internal organs
  full thickness - *see* Burn, by site, third degree
  gastrointestinal tract 947.3
  genitourinary organs
    external 942.05
      with
        trunk - *see* Burn, trunk, multiple sites
      first degree 942.15
      second degree 942.25

Burn *(Continued)*
  genitourinary organs *(Continued)*
    external *(Continued)*
      third degree 942.35
        deep 942.45
          with loss of body part 942.55
      internal 947.8
  globe (eye) - *see* Burn, eyeball
  groin - *see* Burn, abdomen
  gum 947.0
  hand(s) (phalanges) (and wrist) 944.00
    first degree 944.10
    second degree 944.20
    third degree 944.30
      deep 944.40
        with loss of body part 944.50
    back (dorsal surface) 944.06
      first degree 944.16
      second degree 944.26
      third degree 944.36
        deep 944.46
          with loss of body part 944.56
    multiple sites 944.08
      first degree 944.18
      second degree 944.28
      third degree 944.38
        deep 944.48
          with loss of body part 944.58
  head (and face) 941.00
    eye(s) only 940.9
      specified part - *see* Burn, by site
    first degree 941.10
    second degree 941.20
    third degree 941.30
      deep 941.40
        with loss of body part 941.50
    multiple sites 941.09
      with eyes - *see* Burn, eyes, with face, head, or neck
      first degree 941.19
      second degree 941.29
      third degree 941.39
        deep 941.49
          with loss of body part 941.59
  heel - *see* Burn, foot
  hip - *see* Burn, trunk, specified site NEC
  iliac region - *see* Burn, trunk, specified site NEC
  infected 958.3
  inhalation (*see also* Burn, internal organs) 947.9
  internal organs 947.9
    from caustic or corrosive substance (swallowing) NEC 947.9
    specified NEC (*see also* Burn, by site) 947.8
  interscapular region - *see* Burn, back
  intestine (large) (small) 947.3
  iris - *see* Burn, eyeball
  knee 945.05
    with
      lower limb(s) - *see* Burn, leg, multiple sites
    first degree 945.15
    second degree 945.25
    third degree 945.35
      deep 945.45
        with loss of body part 945.55
  labium (majus) (minus) - *see* Burn, genitourinary organs, external

Burn *(Continued)*
  lacrimal apparatus, duct, gland, or sac 940.1
    chemical 940.0
  larynx 947.1
  late effect - *see* Late, effects (of), burn
  leg 945.00
    first degree 945.10
    second degree 945.20
    third degree 945.30
      deep 945.40
        with loss of body part 945.50
    lower 945.04
      with other part(s) of lower limb(s) - *see* Burn, leg, multiple sites
      first degree 945.14
      second degree 945.24
      third degree 945.34
        deep 945.44
          with loss of body part 945.54
    multiple sites 945.09
      first degree 945.19
      second degree 945.29
      third degree 945.39
        deep 945.49
          with loss of body part 945.59
    upper - *see* Burn, thigh
  lightning - *see* Burn, by site
  limb(s)
    lower (including foot or toe(s)) - *see* Burn, leg
    upper (except wrist and hand) - *see* Burn, arm(s)
  lip(s) 941.03
    with
      face or head - *see* Burn, head, multiple sites
    first degree 941.13
    second degree 941.23
    third degree 941.33
      deep 941.43
        with loss of body part 941.53
  lumbar region - *see* Burn, back
  lung 947.1
  malar region - *see* Burn, cheek
  mastoid region - *see* Burn, scalp
  membrane, tympanic - *see* Burn, ear
  midthoracic region - *see* Burn, chest wall
  mouth 947.0
  multiple (*see also* Burn, unspecified) 949.0
    specified sites classifiable to more than one category in 940-945 946.0
      first degree 946.1
      second degree 946.2
      third degree 946.3
        deep 946.4
          with loss of body part 946.5
  muscle, abdominal - *see* Burn, abdomen
  nasal (septum) - *see* Burn, nose
  neck 941.08
    with
      face or head - *see* Burn, head, multiple sites
    first degree 941.18
    second degree 941.28

Burn (*Continued*)
  neck (*Continued*)
    third degree 941.38
      deep 941.48
        with loss of body part 941.58
  nose (septum) 941.05
    with
      face or head - *see* Burn, head, multiple sites
    first degree 941.15
    second degree 941.25
    third degree 941.35
      deep 941.45
        with loss of body part 941.55
  occipital region - *see* Burn, scalp
  orbit region 940.1
    chemical 940.0
  oronasopharynx 947.0
  palate 947.0
  palm(s) 944.05
    with
      hand(s) and wrist(s) - *see* Burn, hand(s), multiple sites
    first degree 944.15
    second degree 944.25
    third degree 944.35
      deep 944.45
        with loss of a body part 944.55
  parietal region - *see* Burn, scalp
  penis - *see* Burn, genitourinary organs, external
  perineum - *see* Burn, genitourinary organs, external
  periocular area 940.1
    chemical 940.0
  pharynx 947.0
  pleura 947.1
  popliteal space - *see* Burn, knee
  prepuce - *see* Burn, genitourinary organs, external
  pubic region - *see* Burn, genitourinary organs, external
  pudenda - *see* Burn, genitourinary organs, external
  rectum 947.3
  sac, lacrimal 940.1
    chemical 940.0
  sacral region - *see* Burn, back
  salivary (ducts) (glands) 947.0
  scalp 941.06
    with
      face or neck - *see* Burn, head, multiple sites
    first degree 941.16
    second degree 941.26
    third degree 941.36
      deep 941.46
        with loss of body part 941.56
  scapular region 943.06
    with
      upper limb(s), except hand(s) or wrist(s) - *see* Burn, arm(s), multiple sites
    first degree 943.16
    second degree 943.26
    third degree 943.36
      deep 943.46
        with loss of body part 943.56
  sclera - *see* Burn, eyeball
  scrotum - *see* Burn, genitourinary organs, external
  septum, nasal - *see* Burn, nose
  shoulder(s) 943.05

Burn (*Continued*)
  shoulder(s) (*Continued*)
    with
      hand(s) and wrist(s) - *see* Burn, multiple, specified sites
      upper limb(s), except hand(s) or wrist(s) - *see* Burn, arm(s), multiple sites
    first degree 943.15
    second degree 943.25
    third degree 943.35
      deep 943.45
        with loss of body part 943.55
  skin NEC (*see also* Burn, unspecified) 949.0
  skull - *see* Burn, head
  small intestine 947.3
  sternal region - *see* Burn, chest wall
  stomach 947.3
  subconjunctival - *see* Burn, conjunctiva
  subcutaneous - *see* Burn, by site, third degree
  submaxillary region - *see* Burn, head
  submental region - *see* Burn, chin
  supraclavicular fossa - *see* Burn, neck
  supraorbital - *see* Burn, forehead
  temple - *see* Burn, scalp
  temporal region - *see* Burn, scalp
  testicle - *see* Burn, genitourinary organs, external
  testis - *see* Burn, genitourinary organs, external
  thigh 945.06
    with
      lower limb(s) - *see* Burn, leg, multiple sites
    first degree 945.16
    second degree 945.26
    third degree 945.36
      deep 945.46
        with loss of body part 945.56
  thorax (external) - *see* Burn, chest wall
  throat 947.0
  thumb(s) (nail) (subungual) 944.02
    with
      finger(s) - *see* Burn, finger, with other sites, thumb
      hand(s) and wrist(s) - *see* Burn, hand(s), multiple sites
    first degree 944.12
    second degree 944.22
    third degree 944.32
      deep 944.42
        with loss of body part 944.52
  toe (nail) (subungual) 945.01
    with
      lower limb(s) - *see* Burn, leg, multiple sites
    first degree 945.11
    second degree 945.21
    third degree 945.31
      deep 945.41
        with loss of body part 945.51
  tongue 947.0
  tonsil 947.0
  trachea 947.1
  trunk 942.00
    first degree 942.10
    second degree 942.20
    third degree 942.30
      deep 942.40
        with loss of body part 942.50

Burn (*Continued*)
  trunk (*Continued*)
    multiple sites 942.09
      first degree 942.19
      second degree 942.29
      third degree 942.39
        deep 942.49
          with loss of body part 942.59
    specified site NEC 942.09
      first degree 942.19
      second degree 942.29
      third degree 942.39
        deep 942.49
          with loss of body part 942.59
  tunica vaginalis - *see* Burn, genitourinary organs, external
  tympanic membrane - *see* Burn, ear
  tympanum - *see* Burn, ear
  unspecified site (multiple) 949.0
    with extent of body surface involved specified
      less than 10 percent 948.0
      10-19 percent 948.1
      20-29 percent 948.2
      30-39 percent 948.3
      40-49 percent 948.4
      50-59 percent 948.5
      60-69 percent 948.6
      70-79 percent 948.7
      80-89 percent 948.8
      90 percent or more 948.9
    first degree 949.1
    second degree 949.2
    third degree 949.3
      deep 949.4
        with loss of body part 949.5
  uterus 947.4
  uvula 947.0
  vagina 947.4
  vulva - *see* Burn, genitourinary organs, external
  wrist(s) 944.07
    with
      hand(s) - *see* Burn, hand(s), multiple sites
    first degree 944.17
    second degree 944.27
    third degree 944.37
      deep 944.47
        with loss of body part 944.57
Burnett's syndrome (milk-alkali) 999.9
Burnier's syndrome (hypophyseal dwarfism) 253.3
Burning
  feet syndrome 266.2
  sensation (*see also* Disturbance, sensation) 782.0
  tongue 529.6
Burns' disease (osteochondrosis, lower ulna) 732.3
Bursa - *see also* condition
  pharynx 478.29
Bursitis NEC 727.3
  Achilles tendon 726.71
  adhesive 726.90
    shoulder 726.0
  ankle 726.79
  buttock 726.5
  calcaneal 726.79
  collateral ligament
    fibular 726.63
    tibial 726.62
  Duplay's 726.2

ICD-9-CM

B

Vol. 2

C

Cacergasia 300.9
Cachexia 799.4
  cancerous (M8000/3) 199.1
  cardiac - *see* Disease, heart
  dehydration 276.5
    with
      hypernatremia 276.0
      hyponatremia 276.1
  due to malnutrition 261
  exophthalmic 242.0
  heart - *see* Disease, heart
  hypophyseal 253.2
  hypopituitary 253.2
  lead 984.9
    specified type of lead - *see* Table of
      Drugs and Chemicals
  malaria 084.9
  malignant (M8000/3) 199.1
  marsh 084.9
  nervous 300.5
  old age 797
  pachydermic - *see* Hypothyroidism
  paludal 084.9
  pituitary (postpartum) 253.2
  renal (*see also* Disease, renal) 593.9
  saturnine 984.9
    specified type of lead - *see* Table of
      Drugs and Chemicals
  senile 797
  Simmonds' (pituitary cachexia) 253.2
  splenica 289.59
  strumipriva (*see also* Hypothyroidism)
    244.9
  tuberculous NEC (*see also* Tuberculo-
    sis) 011.9
Café au lait spots 709.09
Caffey's disease or syndrome (infantile
  cortical hyperostosis) 756.59
Caisson disease 993.3
Caked breast (puerperal, postpartum)
  676.2
Cake kidney 753.3
Calabar swelling 125.2
Calcaneal spur 726.73
Calcaneoapophysitis 732.5
Calcaneonavicular bar 755.67
Calcareous - *see* condition
Calcicosis (occupational) 502
Calciferol (vitamin D) deficiency
  268.9
  with
    osteomalacia 268.2
    rickets (*see also* Rickets) 268.0
Calcification
  adrenal (capsule) (gland) 255.4
    tuberculous (*see also* Tuberculosis)
      017.6
  aorta 440.0
  artery (annular) - *see* Arteriosclerosis
  auricle (ear) 380.89
  bladder 596.8
    due to S. hematobium 120.0
  brain (cortex) - *see* Calcification, cere-
    bral
  bronchus 519.1
  bursa 727.82
  cardiac (*see also* Degeneration, myocar-
    dial) 429.1
  cartilage (postinfectional) 733.99
  cerebral (cortex) 348.8
    artery 437.0
  cervix (uteri) 622.8

Calcification (*Continued*)
  choroid plexus 349.2
  conjunctiva 372.54
  corpora cavernosa (penis) 607.89
  cortex (brain) - *see* Calcification, cere-
    bral
  dental pulp (nodular) 522.2
  dentinal papilla 520.4
  disc, intervertebral 722.90
    cervical, cervicothoracic 722.91
    lumbar, lumbosacral 722.93
    thoracic, thoracolumbar 722.92
  fallopian tube 620.8
  falx cerebri - *see* Calcification, cerebral
  fascia 728.89
  gallbladder 575.8
  general 275.40
  heart (*see also* Degeneration, myocar-
    dial) 429.1
    valve - *see* Endocarditis
  intervertebral cartilage or disc (postin-
    fectional) 722.90
    cervical, cervicothoracic 722.91
    lumbar, lumbosacral 722.93
    thoracic, thoracolumbar 722.92
  intracranial - *see* Calcification, cerebral
  intraspinal ligament 728.89
  joint 719.80
    ankle 719.87
    elbow 719.82
    foot 719.87
    hand 719.84
    hip 719.85
    knee 719.86
    multiple sites 719.89
    pelvic region 719.85
    shoulder (region) 719.81
    specified site NEC 719.88
    wrist 719.83
  kidney 593.89
    tuberculous (*see also* Tuberculosis)
      016.0
  larynx (senile) 478.79
  lens 366.8
  ligament 728.89
    intraspinal 728.89
    knee (medial collateral) 717.89
  lung 518.89
    active 518.89
    postinfectional 518.89
    tuberculous (*see also* Tuberculosis,
      pulmonary) 011.9
  lymph gland or node (postinfectional)
    289.3
    tuberculous (*see also* Tuberculosis,
      lymph gland) 017.2
  massive (paraplegic) 728.10
  medial (*see also* Arteriosclerosis, ex-
    tremities) 440.20
  meninges (cerebral) 349.2
  metastatic 275.40
  Mönckeberg's - *see* Arteriosclerosis
  muscle 728.10
    heterotopic, postoperative 728.13
  myocardium, myocardial (*see also* De-
    generation, myocardial) 429.1
  ovary 620.8
  pancreas 577.8
  penis 607.89
  periarticular 728.89
  pericardium (*see also* Pericarditis) 423.8
  pineal gland 259.8
  pleura 511.0
    postinfectional 518.89

Calcification (*Continued*)
  pleura (*Continued*)
    tuberculous (*see also* Tuberculosis,
      pleura) 012.0
  pulp (dental) (nodular) 522.2
  renal 593.89
  Rider's bone 733.99
  sclera 379.16
  semilunar cartilage 717.89
  spleen 289.59
  subcutaneous 709.3
  suprarenal (capsule) (gland) 255.4
  tendon (sheath) 727.82
    with bursitis, synovitis or tenosyno-
      vitis 727.82
  trachea 519.1
  ureter 593.89
  uterus 621.8
  vitreous 379.29
Calcified - *see also* Calcification
  hematoma NEC 959.9
Calcinosis (generalized) (interstitial) (tu-
  moral) (universalis) 275.49
  circumscripta 709.3
  cutis 709.3
  intervertebralis 275.49 *[722.90]*
  Raynaud's phenomenon sclerodactyly-
    telangiectasis (CRST) 710.1
Calcium
  blood
    high (*see also* Hypercalcemia) 275.42
    low (*see also* Hypocalcemia) 275.41
  deposits - *see also* Calcification, by site
    in bursa 727.82
    in tendon (sheath) 727.82
      with bursitis, synovitis or teno-
        synovitis 727.82
  salts or soaps in vitreous 379.22
Calciuria 791.9
Calculi - *see* Calculus
Calculosis, intrahepatic - *see* Choledocholithiasis
Calculus, calculi, calculous 592.9
  ampulla of Vater - *see* Choledocholi-
    thiasis
  anuria (impacted) (recurrent) 592.0
  appendix 543.9
  bile duct (any) - *see* Choledocholithiasis
  biliary - *see* Cholelithiasis
  bilirubin, multiple - *see* Cholelithiasis
  bladder (encysted) (impacted) (uri-
    nary) 594.1
    diverticulum 594.0
  bronchus 518.89
  calyx (kidney) (renal) 592.0
    congenital 753.3
  cholesterol (pure) (solitary) - *see* Chole-
    lithiasis
  common duct (bile) - *see* Choledocho-
    lithiasis
  conjunctiva 372.54
  cystic 594.1
    duct - *see* Cholelithiasis
  dental 523.6
    subgingival 523.6
    supragingival 523.6
  epididymis 608.89
  gallbladder - *see also* Cholelithiasis
    congenital 751.69
  hepatic (duct) - *see* Choledocholithiasis
  intestine (impaction) (obstruction)
    560.39
  kidney (impacted) (multiple) (pelvis)
    (recurrent) (staghorn) 592.0

Calculus, calculi, calculous *(Continued)*
  kidney *(Continued)*
    congenital 753.3
    lacrimal (passages) 375.57
    liver (impacted) - *see* Choledocholi-
        thiasis
    lung 518.89
    nephritic (impacted) (recurrent) 592.0
    nose 478.1
    pancreas (duct) 577.8
    parotid gland 527.5
    pelvis, encysted 592.0
    prostate 602.0
    pulmonary 518.89
    renal (impacted) (recurrent) 592.0
      congenital 753.3
    salivary (duct) (gland) 527.5
    seminal vesicle 608.89
    staghorn 592.0
    Stensen's duct 527.5
    sublingual duct or gland 527.5
      congenital 750.26
    submaxillary duct, gland, or region
        527.5
    suburethral 594.8
    tonsil 474.8
    tooth, teeth 523.6
    tunica vaginalis 608.89
    ureter (impacted) (recurrent) 592.1
    urethra (impacted) 594.2
    urinary (duct) (impacted) (passage)
        (tract) 592.9
      lower tract NEC 594.9
        specified site 594.8
    vagina 623.8
    vesicle (impacted) 594.1
    Wharton's duct 527.5
Caliectasis 593.89
California
  disease 114.0
  encephalitis 062.5
Caligo cornea 371.03
Callositas, callosity (infected) 700
Callus (infected) 700
  bone 726.91
  excessive, following fracture - *see also*
      Late, effect (of), fracture
Calvé (-Perthes) disease (osteochon-
    drosis, femoral capital) 732.1
Calvities (*see also* Alopecia) 704.00
Cameroon fever (*see also* Malaria) 084.6
Camptocormia 300.11
Camptodactyly (congenital) 755.59
Camurati-Engelmann disease (diaphy-
    seal sclerosis) 756.59
Canal - *see* condition
Canaliculitis (lacrimal) (acute) 375.31
  Actinomyces 039.8
  chronic 375.41
Canavan's disease 330.0
Cancer (M8000/3)-see also Neoplasm, by
    site, malignant

Note   The term "cancer" when modified by an adjective or adjectival
phrase indicating a morphological
type should be coded in the same
manner as "carcinoma" with that adjective or phrase. Thus, "squamous-
cell cancer" should be coded in the
same manner as "squamous-cell carcinoma," which appears in the list
under "Carcinoma."

Cancer *(Continued)*
  bile duct type (M8160/3), liver 155.1
  hepatocellular (M8170/3) 155.0
Cancerous (M8000/3) - *see* Neoplasm, by
    site, malignant
Cancerphobia 300.29
Cancrum oris 528.1
Candidiasis, candidal 112.9
  with pneumonia 112.4
  balanitis 112.2
  congenital 771.7
  disseminated 112.5
  endocarditis 112.81
  esophagus 112.84
  intertrigo 112.3
  intestine 112.85
  lung 112.4
  meningitis 112.83
  mouth 112.0
  nails 112.3
  neonatal 771.7
  onychia 112.3
  otitis externa 112.82
  otomycosis 112.82
  paronychia 112.3
  perionyxis 112.3
  pneumonia 112.4
  pneumonitis 112.4
  skin 112.3
  specified site NEC 112.89
  systemic 112.5
  urogenital site NEC 112.2
  vagina 112.1
  vulva 112.1
  vulvovaginitis 112.1
Candidiosis - *see* Candidiasis
Candiru infection or infestation 136.8
Canities (premature) 704.3
  congenital 757.4
Canker (mouth) (sore) 528.2
  rash 034.1
Cannabinosis 504
Canton fever 081.9
Cap
  cradle 690.11
Capillariasis 127.5
Capillary - *see* condition
Caplan's syndrome 714.81
Caplan-Colinet syndrome 714.81
Capsule - *see* condition
Capsulitis (joint) 726.90
  adhesive (shoulder) 726.0
  labyrinthine 387.8
  thyroid 245.9
Caput
  crepitus 756.0
  medusae 456.8
  succedaneum 767.1
Carapata disease 087.1
Carate - *see* Pinta
Carboxyhemoglobinemia 986
Carbuncle 680.9
  abdominal wall 680.2
  ankle 680.6
  anus 680.5
  arm (any part, above wrist) 680.3
  auditory canal, external 680.0
  axilla 680.3
  back (any part) 680.2
  breast 680.2
  buttock 680.5
  chest wall 680.2
  corpus cavernosum 607.2
  ear (any part) (external) 680.0

Carbuncle *(Continued)*
  eyelid 373.13
  face (any part, except eye) 680.0
  finger (any) 680.4
  flank 680.2
  foot (any part) 680.7
  forearm 680.3
  genital organ (male) 608.4
  gluteal (region) 680.5
  groin 680.2
  hand (any part) 680.4
  head (any part, except face) 680.8
  heel 680.7
  hip 680.6
  kidney (*see also* Abscess, kidney) 590.2
  knee 680.6
  labia 616.4
  lacrimal
    gland (*see also* Dacryoadenitis) 375.00
    passages (duct) (sac) (*see also* Dac-
        ryocystitis) 375.30
  leg, any part except foot 680.6
  lower extremity, any part except foot
      680.6
  malignant 022.0
  multiple sites 680.9
  neck 680.1
  nose (external) (septum) 680.0
  orbit, orbital 376.01
  partes posteriores 680.5
  pectoral region 680.2
  penis 607.2
  perineum 680.2
  pinna 680.0
  scalp (any part) 680.8
  scrotum 608.4
  seminal vesicle 608.0
  shoulder 680.3
  skin NEC 680.9
  specified site NEC 680.8
  spermatic cord 608.4
  temple (region) 680.0
  testis 608.4
  thigh 680.6
  thumb 680.4
  toe (any) 680.7
  trunk 680.2
  tunica vaginalis 608.4
  umbilicus 680.2
  upper arm 680.3
  urethra 597.0
  vas deferens 608.4
  vulva 616.4
  wrist 680.4
Carbunculus (*see also* Carbuncle) 680.9
Carcinoid (tumor) (M8240/1) - *see also*
    Neoplasm, by site, uncertain behavior
    and struma ovarii (M9091/1) 236.2
  argentaffin (M8241/1) - *see* Neoplasm,
      by site, uncertain behavior
    malignant (M8241/3) - *see* Neo-
        plasm, by site, malignant
  benign (M9091/0) 220
  composite (M8244/3) - *see* Neoplasm,
      by site, malignant
  goblet cell (M8243/3) - *see* Neoplasm,
      by site, malignant
  malignant (M8240/3) - *see* Neoplasm,
      by site, malignant
  nonargentaffin (M8242/1) - *see also* Ne-
      oplasm, by site, uncertain behavior
    malignant (M8242/3) - *see* Neo-
        plasm, by site, malignant
  strumal (M9091/1) 236.2

Carcinoid *(Continued)*
   syndrome (intestinal) (metastatic)
      259.2
   type bronchial adenoma (M8240/3) -
      see Neoplasm, lung, malignant
Carcinoidosis 259.2
Carcinoma (M8010/3) - *see also* Neoplasm, by site, malignant

> Note   Except where otherwise indi-
> cated, the morphological varieties of
> carcinoma in the list below should be
> coded by site as for "Neoplasm, ma-
> lignant."

   with
      apocrine metaplasia (M8573/3)
      cartilaginous (and osseous) metapla-
         sia (M8571/3)
      osseous (and cartilaginous) metapla-
         sia (M8571/3)
      productive fibrosis (M8141/3)
      spindle cell metaplasia (M8572/3)
      squamous metaplasia (M8570/3)
   acidophil (M8280/3)
      specified site - *see* Neoplasm, by site,
         malignant
      unspecified site 194.3
   acidophil-basophil, mixed (M8281/3)
      specified site - *see* Neoplasm, by site,
         malignant
      unspecified site 194.3
   acinar (cell) (M8550/3)
   acinic cell (M8550/3)
   adenocystic (M8200/3)
   adenoid
      cystic (M8200/3)
      squamous cell (M8075/3)
   adenosquamous (M8560/3)
   adnexal (skin) (M8390/3) - *see* Neo-
      plasm, skin, malignant
   adrenal cortical (M8370/3) 194.0
   alveolar (M8251/3)
      cell (M8250/3) - *see* Neoplasm, lung,
         malignant
   anaplastic type (M8021/3)
   apocrine (M8401/3)
      breast - *see* Neoplasm, breast, malig-
         nant
      specified site NEC - *see* Neoplasm,
         skin, malignant
      unspecified site 173.9
   basal cell (pigmented) (M8090/3) - *see*
      also Neoplasm, skin, malignant
      fibro-epithelial type (M8093/3) - *see*
         Neoplasm, skin, malignant
      morphea type (M8092/3) - *see* Neo-
         plasm, skin, malignant
      multicentric (M8091/3) - *see* Neo-
         plasm, skin, malignant
   basaloid (M8123/3)
   basal-squamous cell, mixed (M8094/3)
      - *see* Neoplasm, skin, malignant
   basophil (M8300/3)
      specified site - *see* Neoplasm, by site,
         malignant
      unspecified site 194.3
   basophil-acidophil, mixed (M8281/3)
      specified site - *see* Neoplasm, by site,
         malignant
      unspecified site 194.3
   basosquamous (M8094/3) - *see* Neo-
      plasm, skin, malignant
   bile duct type (M8160/3)

Carcinoma *(Continued)*
   bile duct type (M8160/3) *(Continued)*
      and hepatocellular, mixed (M8180/3)
         155.0
      liver 155.1
      specified site NEC - *see* Neoplasm,
         by site, malignant
      unspecified site 155.1
   branchial or branchiogenic 146.8
   bronchial or bronchogenic - *see* Neo-
      plasm, lung, malignant
   bronchiolar (terminal) (M8250/3) - *see*
      Neoplasm, lung, malignant
   bronchiolo-alveolar (M8250/3) - *see*
      Neoplasm, lung, malignant
   bronchogenic (epidermoid) 162.9
   C cell (M8510/3)
      specified site - *see* Neoplasm, by site,
         malignant
      unspecified site 193
   ceruminous (M8420/3) 173.2
   chorionic (M9100/3)
      specified site - *see* Neoplasm, by site,
         malignant
      unspecified site
         female 181
         male 186.9
   chromophobe (M8270/3)
      specified site - *see* Neoplasm, by site,
         malignant
      unspecified site 194.3
   clear cell (mesonephroid type)
      (M8310/3)
   cloacogenic (M8124/3)
      specified site - *see* Neoplasm, by site,
         malignant
      unspecified site 154.8
   colloid (M8480/3)
   cribriform (M8201/3)
   cylindroid type (M8200/3)
   diffuse type (M8145/3)
      specified site - *see* Neoplasm, by site,
         malignant
      unspecified site 151.9
   duct (cell) (M8500/3)
      with Paget's disease (M8541/3) - *see*
         Neoplasm, breast, malignant
      infiltrating (M8500/3)
         specified site - *see* Neoplasm, by
            site, malignant
         unspecified site 174.9
   ductal (M8500/3)
   ductular, infiltrating (M8521/3)
   embryonal (M9070/3)
      and teratoma, mixed (M9081/3)
      combined with choriocarcinoma
         (M9101/3) - *see* Neoplasm, by
         site, malignant
      infantile type (M9071/3)
      liver 155.0
      polyembryonal type (M9072/3)
   endometrioid (M8380/3)
   eosinophil (M8280/3)
      specified site - *see* Neoplasm, by site,
         malignant
      unspecified site 194.3
   epidermoid (M8070/3) - *see also* Carci-
      noma, squamous cell
      and adenocarcinoma, mixed
         (M8560/3)
      in situ, Bowen's type (M8081/2) - *see*
         Neoplasm, skin, in situ
      intradermal - *see* Neoplasm, skin, in
         situ

Carcinoma *(Continued)*
   fibroepithelial type basal cell (M8093/
      3) - *see* Neoplasm, skin, malignant
   follicular (M8330/3)
      and papillary (mixed) (M8340/3) 193
      moderately differentiated type
         (M8332/3) 193
      pure follicle type (M8331/3) 193
      specified site - *see* Neoplasm, by site,
         malignant
      trabecular type (M8332/3) 193
      unspecified site 193
      well differentiated type (M8331/3)
         193
   gelatinous (M8480/3)
   giant cell (M8031/3)
      and spindle cell (M8030/3)
   granular cell (M8320/3)
   granulosa cell (M8620/3) 183.0
   hepatic cell (M8170/3) 155.0
   hepatocellular (M8170/3) 155.0
      and bile duct, mixed (M8180/3)
         155.0
   hepatocholangiolitic (M8180/3) 155.0
   Hürthle cell (thyroid) 193
   hypernephroid (M8311/3)
   in
      adenomatous
         polyp (M8210/3)
         polyposis coli (M8220/3) 153.9
      pleomorphic adenoma (M8940/3)
      polypoid adenoma (M8210/3)
      situ (M8010/3) - *see* Carcinoma, in
         situ
      tubular adenoma (M8210/3)
      villous adenoma (M8261/3)
   infiltrating duct (M8500/3)
      with Paget's disease (M8541/3) - *see*
         Neoplasm, breast, malignant
      specified site - *see* Neoplasm, by site,
         malignant
      unspecified site 174.9
   inflammatory (M8530/3)
      specified site - *see* Neoplasm, by site,
         malignant
      unspecified site 174.9
   in situ (M8010/2) - *see also* Neoplasm,
      by site, in situ
      epidermoid (M8070/2) - *see also*
         Neoplasm, by site, in situ
         with questionable stromal inva-
            sion (M8076/2)
            specified site - *see* Neoplasm, by
               site, in situ
            unspecified site 233.1
         Bowen's type (M8081/2) - *see*
            Neoplasm, skin, in situ
      intraductal (M8500/2)
         specified site - *see* Neoplasm, by
            site, in situ
         unspecified site 233.0
      lobular (M8520/2)
         specified site - *see* Neoplasm, by
            site, in situ
         unspecified site 233.0
      papillary (M8050/2) - *see* Neoplasm,
         by site, in situ
      squamous cell (M8070/2) - *see also*
         Neoplasm, by site, in situ
         with questionable stromal inva-
            sion (M8076/2)
            specified site - *see* Neoplasm, by
               site, in situ
            unspecified site 233.1

◄ ▶   New Code   ⬅▥ ▥➡   Revised Code

Carcinoma (*Continued*)
  in situ (M8010/2) (*Continued*)
    transitional cell (M8120/2) - *see*
      Neoplasm, by site, in situ
  intestinal type (M8144/3)
    specified site - *see* Neoplasm, by site,
      malignant
    unspecified site 151.9
  intraductal (noninfiltrating)
    (M8500/2)
    papillary (M8503/2)
      specified site - *see* Neoplasm, by
        site, in situ
      unspecified site 233.0
    specified site - *see* Neoplasm, by site,
      in situ
    unspecified site 233.0
  intraepidermal (M8070/2) - *see also*
    Neoplasm, skin, in situ
    squamous cell, Bowen's type
      (M8081/2) - *see* Neoplasm, skin,
      in situ
  intraepithelial (M8010/2) - *see also*
    Neoplasm, by site, in situ
    squamous cell (M8072/2) - *see* Neo-
      plasm, by site, in situ
  intraosseous (M9270/3) 170.1
    upper jaw (bone) 170.0
  islet cell (M8150/3)
    and exocrine, mixed (M8154/3)
      specified site - *see* Neoplasm, by
        site, malignant
      unspecified site 157.9
    pancreas 157.4
    specified site NEC - *see* Neoplasm,
      by site, malignant
    unspecified site 157.4
  juvenile, breast (M8502/3) - *see* Neo-
    plasm, breast, malignant
  Kulchitsky's cell (carcinoid tumor of
    intestine) 259.2
  large cell (M8012/3)
    squamous cell, non-keratinizing type
      (M8072/3)
  Leydig cell (testis) (M8650/3)
    specified site - *see* Neoplasm, by site,
      malignant
    unspecified site 186.9
      female 183.0
      male 186.9
  liver cell (M8170/3) 155.0
  lobular (infiltrating) (M8520/3)
    noninfiltrating (M8520/3)
      specified site - *see* Neoplasm, by
        site, in situ
      unspecified site 233.0
    specified site - *see* Neoplasm, by site,
      malignant
    unspecified site 174.9
  lymphoepithelial (M8082/3)
  medullary (M8510/3)
    with
      amyloid stroma (M8511/3)
        specified site - *see* Neoplasm, by
          site, malignant
        unspecified site 193
      lymphoid stroma (M8512/3)
        specified site - *see* Neoplasm, by
          site, malignant
        unspecified site 174.9
  mesometanephric (M9110/3)
  mesonephric (M9110/3)
  metastatic (M8010/6) - *see* Metastasis,
    cancer

Carcinoma (*Continued*)
  metatypical (M8095/3) - *see* Neoplasm,
    skin, malignant
  morphea type basal cell (M8092/3) -
    see Neoplasm, skin, malignant
  mucinous (M8480/3)
  mucin-producing (M8481/3)
  mucin-secreting (M8481/3)
  mucoepidermoid (M8430/3)
  mucoid (M8480/3)
    cell (M8300/3)
      specified site - *see* Neoplasm, by
        site, malignant
      unspecified site 194.3
  mucous (M8480/3)
  nonencapsulated sclerosing (M8350/3)
    193
  noninfiltrating
    intracystic (M8504/2) - *see* Neo-
      plasm, by site, in situ
    intraductal (M8500/2)
      papillary (M8503/2)
        specified site - *see* Neoplasm, by
          site, in situ
        unspecified site 233.0
      specified site - *see* Neoplasm, by
        site, in situ
      unspecified site 233.0
    lobular (M8520/2)
      specified site - *see* Neoplasm, by
        site, in situ
      unspecified site 233.0
  oat cell (M8042/3)
    specified site - *see* Neoplasm, by site,
      malignant
    unspecified site 162.9
  odontogenic (M9270/3) 170.1
    upper jaw (bone) 170.0
  oncocytic (M8290/3)
  oxyphilic (M8290/3)
  papillary (M8050/3)
    and follicular (mixed) (M8340/3) 193
    epidermoid (M8052/3)
    intraductal (noninfiltrating) (M8503/2)
      specified site - *see* Neoplasm, by
        site, in situ
      unspecified site 233.0
    serous (M8460/3)
      specified site - *see* Neoplasm, by
        site, malignant
      surface (M8461/3)
        specified site - *see* Neoplasm, by
          site, malignant
        unspecified site 183.0
      unspecified site 183.0
    squamous cell (M8052/3)
    transitional cell (M8130/3)
  papillocystic (M8450/3)
    specified site - *see* Neoplasm, by site,
      malignant
    unspecified site 183.0
  parafollicular cell (M8510/3)
    specified site - *see* Neoplasm, by site,
      malignant
    unspecified site 193
  pleomorphic (M8022/3)
  polygonal cell (M8034/3)
  prickle cell (M8070/3)
  pseudoglandular, squamous cell
    (M8075/3)
  pseudomucinous (M8470/3)
    specified site - *see* Neoplasm, by site,
      malignant
    unspecified site 183.0

Carcinoma (*Continued*)
  pseudosarcomatous (M8033/3)
  regaud type (M8082/3) - *see* Neo-
    plasm, nasopharynx, malignant
  renal cell (M8312/3) 189.0
  reserve cell (M8041/3)
  round cell (M8041/3)
  Schmincke (M8082/3) - *see* Neoplasm,
    nasopharynx, malignant
  Schneiderian (M8121/3)
    specified site - *see* Neoplasm, by site,
      malignant
    unspecified site 160.0
  scirrhous (M8141/3)
  sebaceous (M8410/3) - *see* Neoplasm,
    skin, malignant
  secondary (M8010/6) - *see* Neoplasm,
    by site, malignant, secondary
  secretory, breast (M8502/3) - *see* Neo-
    plasm, breast, malignant
  serous (M8441/3)
    papillary (M8460/3)
      specified site - *see* Neoplasm, by
        site, malignant
      unspecified site 183.0
    surface, papillary (M8461/3)
      specified site - *see* Neoplasm, by
        site, malignant
      unspecified site 183.0
  Sertoli cell (M8640/3)
    specified site - *see* Neoplasm, by site,
      malignant
    unspecified site 186.9
  signet ring cell (M8490/3)
    metastatic (M8490/6) - *see* Neo-
      plasm, by site, secondary
  simplex (M8231/3)
  skin appendage (M8390/3) - *see* Neo-
    plasm, skin, malignant
  small cell (M8041/3)
    fusiform cell type (M8043/3)
    squamous cell, nonkeratinizing type
      (M8073/3)
  solid (M8230/3)
    with amyloid stroma (M8511/3)
      specified site - *see* Neoplasm, by
        site, malignant
      unspecified site 193
  spheroidal cell (M8035/3)
  spindle cell (M8032/3)
    and giant cell (M8030/3)
  spinous cell (M8070/3)
  squamous (cell) (M8070/3)
    adenoid type (M8075/3)
    and adenocarcinoma, mixed
      (M8560/3)
    intraepidermal, Bowen's type - *see*
      Neoplasm, skin, in situ
    keratinizing type (large cell)
      (M8071/3)
    large cell, nonkeratinizing type
      (M8072/3)
    microinvasive (M8076/3)
      specified site - *see* Neoplasm, by
        site, malignant
      unspecified site 180.9
    nonkeratinizing type (M8072/3)
    papillary (M8052/3)
    pseudoglandular (M8075/3)
    small cell, nonkeratinizing type
      (M8073/3)
    spindle cell type (M8074/3)
    verrucous (M8051/3)
  superficial spreading (M8143/3)

Carcinoma (*Continued*)
  sweat gland (M8400/3) - *see* Neo-
    plasm, skin, malignant
  theca cell (M8600/3) 183.0
  thymic (M8580/3) 164.0
  trabecular (M8190/3)
  transitional (cell) (M8120/3)
    papillary (M8130/3)
    spindle cell type (M8122/3)
  tubular (M8211/3)
  undifferentiated type (M8020/3)
  urothelial (M8120/3)
  ventriculi 151.9
  verrucous (epidermoid) (squamous
    cell) (M8051/3)
  villous (M8262/3)
  water-clear cell (M8322/3) 194.1
  wolffian duct (M9110/3)
Carcinomaphobia 300.29
Carcinomatosis
  peritonei (M8010/6) 197.6
  specified site NEC (M8010/3) - *see*
    Neoplasm, by site, malignant
  unspecified site (M8010/6) 199.0
Carcinosarcoma (M8980/3) - *see also*
  Neoplasm, by site, malignant
  embryonal type (M8981/3) - *see* Neo-
    plasm, by site, malignant
Cardia, cardial - *see* condition
Cardiac - *see also* condition
  death - *see* Disease, heart
  device
    defibrillator, automatic implantable
      V45.02
    in situ NEC V45.00
    pacemaker
      cardiac
        fitting or adjustment V53.31
        in situ V45.01
      carotid sinus
        fitting or adjustment V53.39
        in situ V45.09
  pacemaker - *see* Cardiac, device, pace-
    maker
  tamponade 423.9
Cardialgia (*see also* Pain, precordial)
  786.51
Cardiectasis - *see* Hypertrophy, cardiac
Cardiochalasia 530.81
Cardiomalacia (*see also* Degeneration,
  myocardial) 429.1
Cardiomegalia glycogenica diffusa 271.0
Cardiomegaly (*see also* Hypertrophy, cardiac) 429.3
  congenital 746.89
  glycogen 271.0
  hypertensive (*see also* Hypertension,
    heart) 402.90
  idiopathic 425.4
Cardiomyoliposis (*see also* Degeneration,
  myocardial) 429.1
Cardiomyopathy (congestive) (constrictive) (familial) (infiltrative) (obstructive) (restrictive) (sporadic) 425.4
  alcoholic 425.5
  amyloid 277.3 [425.7]
  beriberi 265.0 [425.7]
  cobalt-beer 425.5
  congenital 425.3
  due to
    amyloidosis 277.3 [425.7]
    beriberi 265.0 [425.7]
    cardiac glycogenosis 271.0 [425.7]
    Chagas' disease 086.0

Cardiomyopathy (*Continued*)
  due to (*Continued*)
    Friedreich's ataxia 334.0 [425.8]
    hypertension - *see* Hypertension,
      with, heart involvement
    mucopolysaccharidosis 277.5
      [425.7]
    myotonia atrophica 359.2 [425.8]
    progressive muscular dystrophy
      359.1 [425.8]
    sarcoidosis 135 [425.8]
  glycogen storage 271.0 [425.7]
  hypertensive - *see* Hypertension, with,
    heart involvement
  hypertrophic
    nonobstructive 425.4
    obstructive 425.1
      congenital 746.84
  idiopathic (concentric) 425.4
  in
    Chagas' disease 086.0
    sarcoidosis 135 [425.8]
  ischemic 414.8
  metabolic NEC 277.9 [425.7]
    amyloid 277.3 [425.7]
    thyrotoxic (*see also* Thyrotoxicosis)
      242.9 [425.7]
    thyrotoxicosis (*see also* Thyrotoxico-
      sis) 242.9 [425.7]
  nutritional 269.9 [425.7]
    beriberi 265.0 [425.7]
  obscure of Africa 425.2
  postpartum 674.8
  primary 425.4
  secondary 425.9
  thyrotoxic (*see also* Thyrotoxicosis)
    242.9 [425.7]
  toxic NEC 425.9
  tuberculous (*see also* Tuberculosis)
    017.9 [425.8]
Cardionephritis - *see* Hypertension, cardiorenal
Cardionephropathy - *see* Hypertension,
  cardiorenal
Cardionephrosis - *see* Hypertension, cardiorenal
Cardioneurosis 306.2
Cardiopathia nigra 416.0
Cardiopathy (*see also* Disease, heart)
  429.9
  hypertensive (*see also* Hypertension,
    heart) 402.90
  idiopathic 425.4
  mucopolysaccharidosis 277.5 [425.7]
Cardiopericarditis (*see also* Pericarditis)
  423.9
Cardiophobia 300.29
Cardioptosis 746.87
Cardiorenal - *see* condition
Cardiorrhexis (*see also* Infarct, myocar-
  dium) 410.9
Cardiosclerosis - *see* Arteriosclerosis, cor-
  onary
Cardiosis - *see* Disease, heart
Cardiospasm (esophagus) (reflex) (stom-
  ach) 530.0
  congenital 750.7
Cardiostenosis - *see* Disease, heart
Cardiosymphysis 423.1
Cardiothyrotoxicosis - *see* Hyperthyroid-
  ism
Cardiovascular - *see* condition
Carditis (acute) (bacterial) (chronic) (sub-
  acute) 429.89

Carditis (*Continued*)
  Coxsackie 074.20
  hypertensive (*see also* Hypertension,
    heart) 402.90
  meningococcal 036.40
  rheumatic - *see* Disease, heart, rheu-
    matic
  rheumatoid 714.2
Care (of)
  child (routine) V20.1
  convalescent following V66.9
    chemotherapy V66.2
    medical NEC V66.5
    psychotherapy V66.3
    radiotherapy V66.1
    surgery V66.0
    surgical NEC V66.0
    treatment (for) V66.5
      combined V66.6
      fracture V66.4
      mental disorder NEC V66.3
      specified type NEC V66.5
  end-of-life V66.7
  family member (handicapped) (sick)
    creating problem for family
    V61.49
    provided away from home for holi-
      day relief V60.5
    unavailable, due to
      absence (person rendering care)
        (sufferer) V60.4
      inability (any reason) of person
        rendering care V60.4
  holiday relief V60.5
  hospice V66.7
  lack of (at or after birth) (infant)
    (child) 995.52
    adult 995.84
  lactation of mother V24.1
  palliative V66.7
  postpartum
    immediately after delivery V24.0
    routine follow-up V24.2
  prenatal V22.1
    first pregnancy V22.0
    high-risk pregnancy V23.9
      specified problem NEC V23.8
  terminal V66.7
  unavailable, due to
    absence of person rendering care
      V60.4
    inability (any reason) of person ren-
      dering care V60.4
  well baby V20.1
Caries (bone) (*see also* Tuberculosis,
  bone) 015.9 [730.8]
  arrested 521.0
  cementum 521.0
  cerebrospinal (tuberculous) 015.0
    [730.88]
  dental (acute) (chronic) (incipient) (in-
    fected) (with pulp exposure) 521.0
  dentin (acute) (chronic) 521.0
  enamel (acute) (chronic) (incipient)
    521.0
  external meatus 380.89
  hip (*see also* Tuberculosis) 015.1
    [730.85]
  knee 015.2 [730.86]
  labyrinth 386.8
  limb NEC 015.7 [730.88]
  mastoid (chronic) (process) 383.1
  middle ear 385.89
  nose 015.7 [730.88]

◄▶   New Code   ⬅▬▶   Revised Code

Caries *(Continued)*
orbit 015.7 *[730.88]*
ossicle 385.24
petrous bone 383.20
sacrum (tuberculous) 015.0 *[730.88]*
spine, spinal (column) (tuberculous)
015.0 *[730.88]*
syphilitic 095.5
congenital 090.0 *[730.8]*
teeth (internal) 521.0
vertebra (column) (tuberculous) 015.0
[730.88]
Carini's syndrome (ichthyosis congenita)
757.1
Carious teeth 521.0
Carneous mole 631
Carnosinemia 270.5
Carotid body or sinus syndrome 337.0
Carotidynia 337.0
Carotinemia (dietary) 278.3
Carotinosis (cutis) (skin) 278.3
Carpal tunnel syndrome 354.0
Carpenter's syndrome 759.89
Carpopedal spasm *(see also* Tetany) 781.7
Carpoptosis 736.05
Carrier (suspected) of
amebiasis V02.2
bacterial disease (meningococcal,
staphylococcal) NEC V02.59 ◄▭▭
cholera V02.0
defective gene V19.8
diphtheria V02.4
dysentery (bacillary) V02.3
amebic V02.2
Entamoeba histolytica V02.2
gastrointestinal pathogens NEC V02.3
genetic defect V19.8
gonorrhea V02.7
group B streptococcus V02.51 ◄
HAA (hepatitis Australian-antigen)
V02.61
hepatitis V02.60
Australian-antigen (HAA) V02.61
B V02.61
C V02.62
specified type NEC V02.69
serum V02.61
viral V02.60
infective organism NEC V02.9
malaria V02.9
paratyphoid V02.3
Salmonella V02.3
typhosa V02.1
serum hepatitis V02.61
Shigella V02.3
Staphylococcus NEC V02.59 ◄▭▭▭
Streptococcus NEC V02.52 ◄
group B V02.51 ◄
typhoid V02.1
venereal disease NEC V02.8
Carrión's disease (Bartonellosis) 088.0
Car sickness 994.6
Carter's
relapsing fever (Asiatic) 087.0
Cartilage - *see* condition
Caruncle (inflamed)
abscess, lacrimal *(see also* Dacryocystitis) 375.30
conjunctiva 372.00
acute 372.00
eyelid 373.00
labium (majus) (minus) 616.8
lacrimal 375.30
urethra (benign) 599.3

Caruncle *(Continued)*
vagina (wall) 616.8
Cascade stomach 537.6
Caseation lymphatic gland *(see also* Tuberculosis) 017.2
Caseous
bronchitis - *see* Tuberculosis, pulmonary
meningitis 013.0
pneumonia - *see* Tuberculosis, pulmonary
Cassidy (-Scholte) syndrome (malignant
carcinoid) 259.2
Castellani's bronchitis 104.8
Castleman's tumor or lymphoma (mediastinal lymph node hyperplasia) 785.6
Castration, traumatic 878.2
complicated 878.3
Casts in urine 791.7
Cat's ear 744.29
Catalepsy 300.11
catatonic (acute) *(see also* Schizophrenia) 295.2
hysterical 300.11
schizophrenic *(see also* Schizophrenia)
295.2
Cataphasia 307.0
Cataplexy (idiopathic) 347
Cataract (anterior cortical) (anterior polar) (black) (capsular) (central) (cortical) (hypermature) (immature) (incipient) (mature) (nuclear) 366.9
anterior
and posterior axial embryonal 743.33
pyramidal 743.31
subcapsular polar
infantile, juvenile, or presenile
366.01
senile 366.13
associated with
calcinosis 275.40 *[366.42]*
craniofacial dysostosis 756.0 *[366.44]*
galactosemia 271.1 *[366.44]*
hypoparathyroidism 252.1 *[366.42]*
myotonic disorders 359.2 *[366.43]*
neovascularization 366.33
blue dot 743.39
cerulean 743.39
complicated NEC 366.30
congenital 743.30
capsular or subcapsular 743.31
cortical 743.32
nuclear 743.33
specified type NEC 743.39
total or subtotal 743.34
zonular 743.32
coronary (congenital) 743.39
acquired 366.12
cupuliform 366.14
diabetic 250.5 *[366.41]*
drug-induced 366.45
due to
chalcosis 360.24 *[366.34]*
chronic choroiditis *(see also* Choroiditis) 363.20 *[366.32]*
degenerative myopia 360.21 *[366.34]*
glaucoma *(see also* Glaucoma) 365.9
[366.31]
infection, intraocular NEC 366.32
inflammatory ocular disorder NEC
366.32
iridocyclitis, chronic 364.10 *[366.33]*
pigmentary retinal dystrophy 362.74
[366.34]
radiation 366.46

Cataract *(Continued)*
electric 366.46
glassblowers' 366.46
heat ray 366.46
heterochromic 366.33
in eye disease NEC 366.30
infantile *(see also* Cataract, juvenile)
366.00
intumescent 366.12
irradiational 366.46
juvenile 366.00
anterior subcapsular polar 366.01
combined forms 366.09
cortical 366.03
lamellar 366.03
nuclear 366.04
posterior subcapsular polar 366.02
specified NEC 366.09
zonular 366.03
lamellar 743.32
infantile juvenile, or presenile 366.03
morgagnian 366.18
myotonic 359.2 *[366.43]*
myxedema 244.9 *[366.44]*
posterior, polar (capsular) 743.31
infantile, juvenile, or presenile
366.02
senile 366.14
presenile *(see also* Cataract, juvenile)
366.00
punctate
acquired 366.12
congenital 743.39
secondary (membrane) 366.50
obscuring vision 366.53
specified type, not obscuring vision
366.52
senile 366.10
anterior subcapsular polar 366.13
combined forms 366.19
cortical 366.15
hypermature 366.18
immature 366.12
incipient 366.12
mature 366.17
nuclear 366.16
posterior subcapsular polar 366.14
specified NEC 366.19
total or subtotal 366.17
snowflake 250.5 *[366.41]*
specified NEC 366.8
subtotal (senile) 366.17
congenital 743.34
sunflower 360.24 *[366.34]*
tetanic NEC 252.1 *[366.42]*
total (mature) (senile) 366.17
congenital 743.34
localized 366.21
traumatic 366.22
toxic 366.45
traumatic 366.20
partially resolved 366.23
total 366.22
zonular (perinuclear) 743.32
infantile, juvenile, or presenile
366.03
Cataracta 366.10
brunescens 366.16
cerulea 743.39
complicata 366.30
congenita 743.30
coralliformis 743.39
coronaria (congenital) 743.39
acquired 366.12

Cellulitis *(Continued)*
pelvis, pelvic *(Continued)*
with *Continued*
ectopic pregnancy *(see also* categories 633.0-633.9) 639.0
molar pregnancy *(see also* categories 630-632) 639.0
female *(see also* Disease, pelvis, inflammatory) 614.4
acute 614.3
following
abortion 639.0
ectopic or molar pregnancy 639.0
male *(see also* Abscess, peritoneum) 567.2
puerperal, postpartum, childbirth 670
penis 607.2
perineal, perineum 682.2
perirectal 566
peritonsillar 475
periurethral 597.0
periuterine *(see also* Disease, pelvis, inflammatory) 614.4
acute 614.3
pharynx 478.21
phlegmonous NEC 682.9
rectum 566
retromammary 611.0
retroperitoneal *(see also* Peritonitis) 567.2
round ligament *(see also* Disease, pelvis, inflammatory) 614.4
acute 614.3
scalp (any part) 682.8
dissecting 704.8
scrotum 608.4
seminal vesicle 608.0
septic NEC 682.9
shoulder 682.3
specified sites NEC 682.8
spermatic cord 608.4
submandibular (region) (space) (triangle) 682.0
gland 527.3
submaxillary 528.3
gland 527.3
submental (pyogenic) 682.0
gland 527.3
suppurative NEC 682.9
testis 608.4
thigh 682.6
thumb (intrathecal) (periosteal) (subcutaneous) (subcuticular) 681.00
toe (intrathecal) (periosteal) (subcutaneous) (subcuticular) 681.10
tonsil 475
trunk 682.2
tuberculous (primary) *(see also* Tuberculosis) 017.0
tunica vaginalis 608.4
umbilical 682.2
newborn NEC 771.4
vaccinal 999.3
vagina - *see* Vaginitis
vas deferens 608.4
vocal cords 478.5
vulva *(see also* Vulvitis) 616.10
wrist 682.4
Cementoblastoma, benign (M9273/0) 213.1
upper jaw (bone) 213.0

Cementoma (M9273/0) 213.1
gigantiform (M9276/0) 213.1
upper jaw (bone) 213.0
upper jaw (bone) 213.0
Cementoperiostitis 523.4
Cephalgia, cephalalgia *(see also* Headache) 784.0
histamine 346.2
nonorganic origin 307.81
psychogenic 307.81
tension 307.81
Cephalhematocele, cephalematocele
due to birth injury 767.1
fetus or newborn 767.1
traumatic *(see also* Contusion, head) 920
Cephalhematoma, cephalematoma (calcified)
due to birth injury 767.1
fetus or newborn 767.1
traumatic *(see also* Contusion, head) 920
Cephalic - *see* condition
Cephalitis - *see* Encephalitis
Cephalocele 742.0
Cephaloma - *see* Neoplasm, by site, malignant
Cephalomenia 625.8
Cephalopelvic - *see* condition
Cercomoniasis 007.3
Cerebellitis - *see* Encephalitis
Cerebellum (cerebellar) - *see* condition
Cerebral - *see* condition
Cerebritis - *see* Encephalitis
Cerebrohepatorenal syndrome 759.89
Cerebromacular degeneration 330.1
Cerebromalacia *(see also* Softening, brain) 434.9
Cerebrosidosis 272.7
Cerebrospasticity - *see* Palsy, cerebral
Cerebrospinal - *see* condition
Cerebrum - *see* condition
Ceroid storage disease 272.7
Cerumen (accumulation) (impacted) 380.4
Cervical - *see also* condition
auricle 744.43
rib 756.2
Cervicalgia 723.1
Cervicitis (acute) (chronic) (nonvenereal) (subacute) (with erosion or ectropion) 616.0
with
abortion - *see* Abortion, by type, with sepsis
ectopic pregnancy *(see also* categories 633.0-633.9) 639.0
molar pregnancy *(see also* categories 630-632) 639.0
ulceration 616.0
chlamydial 099.53
complicating pregnancy or puerperium 646.6
affecting fetus or newborn 760.8
following
abortion 639.0
ectopic or molar pregnancy 639.0
gonococcal (acute) 098.15
chronic or duration of 2 months or more 098.35
senile (atrophic) 616.0
syphilitic 095.8
trichomonal 131.09
tuberculous *(see also* Tuberculosis) 016.7

Cervicoaural fistula 744.49
Cervicocolpitis (emphysematosa) *(see also* Cervicitis) 616.0
Cervix - *see* condition
Cesarean delivery, operation or section NEC 669.7
affecting fetus or newborn 763.4
post mortem, affecting fetus or newborn 761.6
previous, affecting management of pregnancy 654.2
Céstan's syndrome 344.89
Céstan-Chenais paralysis 344.89
Céstan-Raymond syndrome 433.8
Cestode infestation NEC 123.9
specified type NEC 123.8
Cestodiasis 123.9
Chabert's disease 022.9
Chacaleh 266.2
Chafing 709.8
Chagas' disease *(see also* Trypanosomiasis, American) 086.2
with heart involvement 086.0
Chagres fever 084.0
Chalasia (cardiac sphincter) 530.81
Chalazion 373.2
Chalazoderma 757.39
Chalcosis 360.24
cornea 371.15
crystalline lens 360.24 [366.34]
retina 360.24
Chalicosis (occupational) (pulmonum) 502
Chancre (any genital site) (hard) (indurated) (infecting) (primary) (recurrent) 091.0
congenital 090.0
conjunctiva 091.2
Ducrey's 099.0
extragenital 091.2
eyelid 091.2
Hunterian 091.0
lip (syphilis) 091.2
mixed 099.8
nipple 091.2
Nisbet's 099.0
of
carate 103.0
pinta 103.0
yaws 102.0
palate, soft 091.2
phagedenic 099.0
Ricord's 091.0
Rollet's (syphilitic) 091.0
seronegative 091.0
seropositive 091.0
simple 099.0
soft 099.0
bubo 099.0
urethra 091.0
yaws 102.0
Chancriform syndrome 114.1
Chancroid 099.0
anus 099.0
penis (Ducrey's bacillus) 099.0
perineum 099.0
rectum 099.0
scrotum 099.0
urethra 099.0
vulva 099.0
Chandipura fever 066.8
Chandler's disease (osteochondritis dissecans, hip) 732.7

ICD-9-CM

C

Vol. 2

Change(s) (of) - *see also* Removal of
  arteriosclerotic - *see* Arteriosclerosis
  battery
    cardiac pacemaker V53.31
  bone 733.90
    diabetic 250.8 [731.8]
    in disease, unknown cause 733.90
  bowel habits 787.99
  cardiorenal (vascular) (*see also* Hypertension, cardiorenal) 404.90
  cardiovascular - *see* Disease, cardiovascular
  circulatory 459.9
  cognitive or personality change of other type, nonpsychotic 310.1
  color, teeth, tooth
    during formation 520.8
    posteruptive 521.7
  contraceptive device V25.42
  cornea, corneal
    degenerative NEC 371.40
    membrane NEC 371.30
    senile 371.41
  coronary (*see also* Ischemia, heart) 414.9
  degenerative
    chamber angle (anterior) (iris) 364.56
    ciliary body 364.57
    spine or vertebra (*see also* Spondylosis) 721.90
  dental pulp, regressive 522.2
  dressing V58.3
  fixation device V54.8
    external V54.8
    internal V54.0
  heart - *see also* Disease, heart
  hip joint 718.95
  hyperplastic larynx 478.79
  hypertrophic
    nasal sinus (*see also* Sinusitis) 473.9
    turbinate, nasal 478.0
    upper respiratory tract 478.9
  inflammatory - *see* Inflammation
  joint (*see also* Derangement, joint) 718.90
    sacroiliac 724.6
  Kirschner wire V54.8
  knee 717.9
  macular, congenital 743.55
  malignant (M----/3) - *see also* Neoplasm, by site, malignant

> Note   For malignant change occurring in a neoplasm, use the appropriate M code with behavior digit/3 e.g., malignant change in uterine fibroid-M8890/3. For malignant change occurring in a nonneoplastic condition (e.g., gastric ulcer) use the M code M8000/3.

  mental (status) NEC 780.9
    due to or associated with physical condition - *see* Syndrome, brain
  myocardium, myocardial - *see* Degeneration, myocardial
  of life (*see also* Menopause) 627.2
  pacemaker battery (cardiac) V53.31
  peripheral nerve 355.9
  personality (nonpsychotic) NEC 310.1
  plaster cast V54.8
  refractive, transient 367.81
  regressive, dental pulp 522.2
  retina 362.9

Change(s) (*Continued*)
  retina (*Continued*)
    myopic (degenerative) (malignant) 360.21
    vascular appearance 362.13
  sacroiliac joint 724.6
  scleral 379.19
    degenerative 379.16
  senile (*see also* Senility) 797
  sensory (*see also* Disturbance, sensation) 782.0
  skin texture 782.8
  spinal cord 336.9
  splint, external V54.8
  subdermal implantable contraceptive V25.5
  suture V58.3
  traction device V54.8
  trophic 355.9
    arm NEC 354.9
    leg NEC 355.8
    lower extremity NEC 355.8
    upper extremity NEC 354.9
  vascular 459.9
  vasomotor 443.9
  voice 784.49
    psychogenic 306.1
Changing sleep-work schedule, affecting sleep 307.45
Changuinola fever 066.0
Chapping skin 709.8
Character
  depressive 301.12
Charcôt's
  arthropathy 094.0 [713.5]
  cirrhosis - *see* Cirrhosis, biliary
  disease 094.0
    spinal cord 094.0
  fever (biliary) (hepatic) (intermittent) - *see* Choledocholithiasis
  joint (disease) 094.0 [713.5]
    diabetic 250.6 [713.5]
    syringomyelic 336.0 [713.5]
  syndrome (intermittent claudication) 443.9
    due to atherosclerosis 440.21
Charcôt-Marie-Tooth disease, paralysis, or syndrome 356.1
Charleyhorse (quadriceps) 843.8
  muscle, except quadriceps - *see* Sprain, by site
Charlouis' disease (*see also* Yaws) 102.9
Chauffeur's fracture - *see* Fracture, ulna, lower end
Cheadle (-Möller) (-Barlow) disease or syndrome (infantile scurvy) 267
Checking (of)
  contraceptive device (intrauterine) V25.42
  device
    fixation V54.8
      external V54.8
      internal V54.0
    traction V54.8
  Kirschner wire V54.8
  plaster cast V54.8
  splint, external V54.8
Checkup
  following treatment - *see* Examination
  health V70.0
  infant (not sick) V20.2
  pregnancy (normal) V22.1
    first V22.0
    high-risk pregnancy V23.9
      specified problem NEC V23.8

Chédiak-Higashi (-Steinbrinck) anomaly, disease, or syndrome (congenital gigantism of peroxidase granules) 288.2
Cheek - *see also* condition
  biting 528.9
Cheese itch 133.8
Cheese washers' lung 495.8
Cheilitis 528.5
  actinic (due to sun) 692.72
    chronic NEC 692.74
      due to radiation, except from sun 692.82
      due to radiation, except from sun 692.82
  acute 528.5
  angular 528.5
  catarrhal 528.5
  chronic 528.5
  exfoliative 528.5
  gangrenous 528.5
  glandularis apostematosa 528.5
  granulomatosa 351.8
  infectional 528.5
  membranous 528.5
  Miescher's 351.8
  suppurative 528.5
  ulcerative 528.5
  vesicular 528.5
Cheilodynia 528.5
Cheilopalatoschisis (*see also* Cleft, palate, with cleft lip) 749.20
Cheilophagia 528.9
Cheiloschisis (*see also* Cleft, lip) 749.10
Cheilosis 528.5
  with pellagra 265.2
  angular 528.5
  due to
    dietary deficiency 266.0
    vitamin deficiency 266.0
Cheiromegaly 729.89
Cheiropompholyx 705.81
Cheloid (*see also* Keloid) 701.4
Chemical burn - *see also* Burn, by site
  from swallowing chemical - *see* Burn, internal organs
Chemodectoma (M8693/1) - *see* Paraganglioma, nonchromaffin
Chemoprophylaxis NEC V07.39
Chemosis, conjunctiva 372.73
Chemotherapy
  convalescence V66.2
  encounter (for) V58.1
  maintenance V58.1
  prophylactic NEC V07.39
    fluoride V07.31
Cherubism 526.89
Chest - *see* condition
Cheyne-Stokes respiration (periodic) 786.04
Chiari's
  disease or syndrome (hepatic vein thrombosis) 453.0
  malformation
    type I 348.4
    type II (*see also* Spina bifida) 741.0
    type III 742.0
    type IV 742.2
  network 746.89
Chiari-Frommel syndrome 676.6
Chicago disease (North American blastomycosis) 116.0

Chickenpox (*see also* Varicella) 052.9
   vaccination and inoculation (prophylactic) V05.4
Chiclero ulcer 085.4
Chiggers 133.8
Chignon 111.2
   fetus or newborn (from vacuum extraction) 767.1
Chigoe disease 134.1
Chikungunya fever 066.3
Chilaiditi's syndrome (subphrenic displacement, colon) 751.4
Chilblains 991.5
   lupus 991.5
Child
   behavior causing concern V61.20
Childbed fever 670
Childbirth - *see also* Delivery
   puerperal complications - *see* Puerperal
Childhood, period of rapid growth V21.0
Chill(s) 780.9
   with fever 780.6
   congestive 780.9
      in malarial regions 084.6
   septic - *see* Septicemia
   urethral 599.84
Chilomastigiasis 007.8
Chin - *see* condition
Chinese dysentery 004.9
Chiropractic dislocation (*see also* Lesion, nonallopathic, by site) 739.9
Chitral fever 066.0
Chlamydia, chlamydial - *see* condition
Chloasma 709.09
   cachecticorum 709.09
   eyelid 374.52
      congenital 757.33
      hyperthyroid 242.0
   gravidarum 646.8
   idiopathic 709.09
   skin 709.09
   symptomatic 709.09
Chloroma (M9930/3) 205.3
Chlorosis 280.9
   Egyptian (*see also* Ancylostomiasis) 126.9
   miners' (*see also* Ancylostomiasis) 126.9
Chlorotic anemia 280.9
Chocolate cyst (ovary) 617.1
Choked
   disk or disc - *see* Papilledema
   on food, phlegm, or vomitus NEC (*see also* Asphyxia, food) 933.1
   phlegm 933.1
   while vomiting NEC (*see also* Asphyxia, food) 933.1
Chokes (resulting from bends) 993.3
Choking sensation 784.9
Cholangiectasis (*see also* Disease, gallbladder) 575.8
Cholangiocarcinoma (M8160/3)
   and hepatocellular carcinoma, combined (M8180/3) 155.0
   liver 155.1
   specified site NEC - *see* Neoplasm, by site, malignant
   unspecified site 155.1
Cholangiohepatitis 575.8
   due to fluke infestation 121.1
Cholangiohepatoma (M8180/3) 155.0

Cholangiolitis (acute) (chronic) (extrahepatic) (gangrenous) 576.1
   intrahepatic 575.8
   paratyphoidal (*see also* Fever, paratyphoid) 002.9
   typhoidal 002.0
Cholangioma (M8160/0) 211.5
   malignant - *see* Cholangiocarcinoma
Cholangitis (acute) (ascending) (catarrhal) (chronic) (infective) (malignant) (primary) (recurrent) (sclerosing) (secondary) (stenosing) (suppurative) 576.1
   chronic nonsuppurative destructive 571.6
   nonsuppurative destructive (chronic) 571.6
Cholecystdocholithiasis - *see* Choledocholithiasis
Cholecystitis 575.10
   with
      calculus, stones in
         bile duct (common) (hepatic) -see Choledocholithiasis
         gallbladder - *see* Cholelithiasis
   acute 575.0
   acute and chronic 575.12
   chronic 575.11
   emphysematous (acute) (*see also* Cholecystitis, acute) 575.0
   gangrenous (*see also* Cholecystitis, acute) 575.0
   paratyphoidal, current (*see also* Fever, paratyphoid) 002.9
   suppurative (*see also* Cholecystitis, acute) 575.0
   typhoidal 002.0
Choledochitis (suppurative) 576.1
Choledocholith - *see* Choledocholithiasis
Choledocholithiasis 574.5

> Note   Use the following fifth-digit subclassification with category 574:
>
> 0   without mention of obstruction
> 1   with obstruction

   with
      cholecystitis 574.4
         acute 574.3
         chronic 574.4
      cholelithiasis 574.9
         with
            cholecystitis 574.7
               acute 574.6
                  and chronic 574.8
               chronic 574.7
Cholelithiasis (impacted) (multiple) 574.2

> Note   Use the following fifth-digit subclassification with category 574:
>
> 0   without mention of obstruction
> 1   with obstruction

   with
      cholecystitis 574.1
         acute 574.0
         chronic 574.1
      choledocholithiasis 574.9
         with
            cholecystitis 574.7
               acute 574.6
                  and chronic 574.8
               chronic cholecystitis 574.7

Cholemia (*see also* Jaundice) 782.4
   familial 277.4
   Gilbert's (familial nonhemolytic) 277.4
Cholemic gallstone - *see* Cholelithiasis
Choleperitoneum, choleperitonitis (*see also* Disease, gallbladder) 567.8
Cholera (algid) (Asiatic) (asphyctic) (epidemic) (gravis) (Indian) (malignant) (morbus) (pestilential) (spasmodic) 001.9
   antimonial 985.4
   carrier (suspected) of V02.0
   classical 001.0
   contact V01.0
   due to
      Vibrio
         cholerae (Inaba, Ogawa, Hikojima serotypes) 001.0
         el Tor 001.1
   El Tor 001.1
   exposure to V01.0
   vaccination, prophylactic (against) V03.0
Cholerine (*see also* Cholera) 001.9
Cholestasis 576.8
Cholesteatoma (ear) 385.30
   attic (primary) 385.31
   diffuse 385.35
   external ear (canal) 380.21
   marginal (middle ear) 385.32
      with involvement of mastoid cavity 385.33
      secondary (with middle ear involvement) 385.33
   mastoid cavity 385.30
   middle ear (secondary) 385.32
      with involvement of mastoid cavity 385.33
   postmastoidectomy cavity (recurrent) 383.32
   primary 385.31
   recurrent, postmastoidectomy cavity 383.32
   secondary (middle ear) 385.32
      with involvement of mastoid cavity 385.33
Cholesteatosis (middle ear) (*see also* Cholesteatoma) 385.30
   diffuse 385.35
Cholesteremia 272.0
Cholesterin
   granuloma, middle ear 385.82
   in vitreous 379.22
Cholesterol
   deposit
      retina 362.82
      vitreous 379.22
   imbibition of gallbladder (*see also* Disease, gallbladder) 575.6
Cholesterolemia 272.0
   essential 272.0
   familial 272.0
   hereditary 272.0
Cholesterosis, cholesterolosis (gallbladder) 575.6
   with
      cholecystitis - *see* Cholecystitis
      cholelithiasis - *see* Cholelithiasis
   middle ear (*see also* Cholesteatoma) 385.30
Cholocolic fistula (*see also* Fistula, gallbladder) 575.5
Choluria 791.4

Chondritis (purulent) 733.99
  costal 733.6
    Tietze's 733.6
  patella, posttraumatic 717.7
  posttraumatica patellae 717.7
  tuberculous (active) (*see also* Tuberculosis) 015.9
    intervertebral 015.0 *[730.88]*
Chondroangiopathia calcarea seu punctate 756.59
Chondroblastoma (M9230/0) - *see also* Neoplasm, bone, benign
  malignant (M9230/3) - *see* Neoplasm, bone, malignant
Chondrocalcinosis (articular) (crystal deposition) (dihydrate) (*see also* Arthritis, due to, crystals) 275.49 *[712.3]*
  due to
    calcium pyrophosphate 275.49 *[712.2]*
    dicalcium phosphate crystals 275.49 *[712.1]*
    pyrophosphate crystals 275.49 *[712.2]*
Chondrodermatitis nodularis helicis 380.00
Chondrodysplasia 756.4
  angiomatose 756.4
  calcificans congenita 756.59
  epiphysialis punctata 756.59
  hereditary deforming 756.4
Chondrodystrophia (fetalis) 756.4
  calcarea 756.4
  calcificans congenita 756.59
  fetalis hypoplastica 756.59
  hypoplastica calcinosa 756.59
  punctata 756.59
  tarda 277.5
Chondrodystrophy (familial) (hypoplastic) 756.4
Chondroectodermal dysplasia 756.55
Chondrolysis 733.99
Chondroma (M9220/0) - *see also* Neoplasm, cartilage, benign
  juxtacortical (M9221/0) - *see* Neoplasm, bone, benign
  periosteal (M9221/0) - *see* Neoplasm, bone, benign
Chondromalacia 733.92
  epiglottis (congenital) 748.3
  generalized 733.92
  knee 717.7
  larynx (congenital) 748.3
  localized, except patella 733.92
  patella, patellae 717.7
  systemic 733.92
  tibial plateau 733.92
  trachea (congenital) 748.3
Chondromatosis (M9220/1) - *see* Neoplasm, cartilage, uncertain behavior
Chondromyxosarcoma (M9220/3) - *see* Neoplasm, cartilage, malignant
Chondro-osteodysplasia (Morquio-Brailsford type) 277.5
Chondro-osteodystrophy 277.5
Chondro-osteoma (M9210/0) - *see* Neoplasm, bone, benign
Chondropathia tuberosa 733.6
Chondrosarcoma (M9220/3) - *see also* Neoplasm, cartilage, malignant
  juxtacortical (M9221/3) - *see* Neoplasm, bone, malignant
  mesenchymal (M9240/3) - *see* Neoplasm, connective tissue, malignant

Chordae tendineae rupture (chronic) 429.5
Chordee (nonvenereal) 607.89
  congenital 752.63
  gonococcal 098.2
Chorditis (fibrinous) (nodosa) (tuberosa) 478.5
Chordoma (M9370/3) - *see* Neoplasm, by site, malignant
Chorea (gravis) (minor) (spasmodic) 333.5
  with
    heart involvement - *see* Chorea with rheumatic heart disease
    rheumatic heart disease (chronic, inactive, or quiescent) (conditions classifiable to 393-398) - *see* rheumatic heart condition involved
    active or acute (conditions classifiable to 391) 392.0
  acute - *see* Chorea, Sydenham's
  apoplectic (*see also* Disease, cerebrovascular, acute) 436
  chronic 333.4
  electric 049.8
  gravidarum - *see* Eclampsia, pregnancy
  habit 307.22
  hereditary 333.4
  Huntington's 333.4
  posthemiplegic 344.89
  pregnancy - *see* Eclampsia, pregnancy
  progressive 333.4
    chronic 333.4
    hereditary 333.4
  rheumatic (chronic) 392.9
    with heart disease or involvement - *see* Chorea, with rheumatic heart disease
  senile 333.5
  Sydenham's 392.9
    with heart involvement - *see* Chorea, with rheumatic heart disease
    nonrheumatic 333.5
  variabilis 307.23
Choreoathetosis (paroxysmal) 333.5
Chorioadenoma (destruens) (M9100/1) 236.1
Chorioamnionitis 658.4
  affecting fetus or newborn 762.7
Chorioangioma (M9120/0) 219.8
Choriocarcinoma (M9100/3)
  combined with
    embryonal carcinoma (M9101/3) - *see* Neoplasm, by site, malignant
    teratoma (M9101/3) - *see* Neoplasm, by site, malignant
  specified site - *see* Neoplasm, by site, malignant
  unspecified site
    female 181
    male 186.9
Chorioencephalitis, lymphocytic (acute) (serous) 049.0
Chorioepithelioma (M9100/3) - *see* Choriocarcinoma
Choriomeningitis (acute) (benign) (lymphocytic) (serous) 049.0
Chorionepithelioma (M9100/3) - *see* Choriocarcinoma
Chorionitis (*see also* Scleroderma) 710.1

Chorioretinitis 363.20
  disseminated 363.10
    generalized 363.13
    in
      neurosyphilis 094.83
      secondary syphilis 091.51
    peripheral 363.12
    posterior pole 363.11
    tuberculous (*see also* Tuberculosis) 017.3 *[363.13]*
  due to
    histoplasmosis (*see also* Histoplasmosis) 115.92
    toxoplasmosis (acquired) 130.2
      congenital (active) 771.2
  focal 363.00
    juxtapapillary 363.01
    peripheral 363.04
    posterior pole NEC 363.03
  juxtapapillaris, juxtapapillary 363.01
  progressive myopia (degeneration) 360.21
  syphilitic (secondary) 091.51
    congenital (early) 090.0 *[363.13]*
      late 090.5 *[363.13]*
    late 095.8 *[363.13]*
  tuberculous (*see also* Tuberculosis) 017.3 *[363.13]*
Choristoma - *see* Neoplasm, by site, benign
Choroid - *see* condition
Choroideremia, choroidermia (initial stage) (late stage) (partial or total atrophy) 363.55
Choroiditis (*see also* Chorioretinitis) 363.20
  leprous 030.9 *[363.13]*
  senile guttate 363.41
  sympathetic 360.11
  syphilitic (secondary) 091.51
    congenital (early) 090.0 *[363.13]*
      late 090.5 *[363.13]*
    late 095.8 *[363.13]*
  Tay's 363.41
  tuberculous (*see also* Tuberculosis) 017.3 *[363.13]*
Choroidopathy NEC 363.9
  degenerative (*see also* Degeneration, choroid) 363.40
  hereditary (*see also* Dystrophy, choroid) 363.50
  specified type NEC 363.8
Choroidoretinitis - *see* Chorioretinitis
Choroidosis, central serous 362.41
Choroidretinopathy, serous 362.41
Christian's syndrome (chronic histiocytosis X) 277.8
Christian-Weber disease (nodular nonsuppurative panniculitis) 729.30
Christmas disease 286.1
Chromaffinoma (M8700/0) - *see also* Neoplasm, by site, benign
  malignant (M8700/3) - *see* Neoplasm, by site, malignant
Chromatopsia 368.59
Chromhidrosis, chromidrosis 705.89
Chromoblastomycosis 117.2
Chromomycosis 117.2
Chromophytosis 111.0
Chromotrichomycosis 111.8
Chronic - *see* condition
Chyle cyst, mesentery 457.8
Chylocele (nonfilarial) 457.8
  filarial (*see also* Infestation, filarial) 125.9

◀▶ New Code   ◀▦▦▷ Revised Code

Chylocele (*Continued*)
tunica vaginalis (nonfilarial) 608.84
filarial (*see also* Infestation, filarial)
125.9
Chylomicronemia (fasting) (with hyper-prebetalipoproteinemia) 272.3
Chylopericardium (acute) 420.90
Chylothorax (nonfilarial) 457.8
filarial (*see also* Infestation, filarial)
125.9
Chylous
ascites 457.8
cyst of peritoneum 457.8
hydrocele 603.9
hydrothorax (nonfilarial) 457.8
filarial (*see also* Infestation, filarial)
125.9
Chyluria 791.1
bilharziasis 120.0
due to
Brugia (malayi) 125.1
Wuchereria (bancrofti) 125.0
malayi 125.1
filarial (*see also* Infestation, filarial)
125.9
filariasis (*see also* Infestation, filarial)
125.9
nonfilarial 791.1
Cicatricial (deformity) - *see* Cicatrix
Cicatrix (adherent) (contracted) (painful)
(vicious) 709.2
adenoid 474.8
alveolar process 525.8
anus 569.49
auricle 380.89
bile duct (*see also* Disease, biliary)
576.8
bladder 596.8
bone 733.99
brain 348.8
cervix (postoperative) (postpartal)
622.3
in pregnancy or childbirth 654.6
causing obstructed labor 660.2
chorioretinal 363.30
disseminated 363.35
macular 363.32
peripheral 363.34
posterior pole NEC 363.33
choroid - *see* Cicatrix, chorioretinal
common duct (*see also* Disease, biliary)
576.8
congenital 757.39
conjunctiva 372.64
cornea 371.00
tuberculous (*see also* Tuberculosis)
017.3 [371.05]
duodenum (bulb) 537.3
esophagus 530.3
eyelid 374.46
with
ectropion - *see* Ectropion
entropion - *see* Entropion
hypopharynx 478.29
knee, semilunar cartilage 717.5
lacrimal
canaliculi 375.53
duct
acquired 375.56
neonatal 375.55
punctum 375.52
sac 375.54
larynx 478.79
limbus (cystoid) 372.64

Cicatrix (*Continued*)
lung 518.89
macular 363.32
disseminated 363.35
peripheral 363.34
middle ear 385.89
mouth 528.9
muscle 728.89
nasolacrimal duct
acquired 375.56
neonatal 375.55
nasopharynx 478.29
palate (soft) 528.9
penis 607.89
prostate 602.8
rectum 569.49
retina 363.30
disseminated 363.35
macular 363.32
peripheral 363.34
posterior pole NEC 363.33
semilunar cartilage - *see* Derangement,
meniscus
seminal vesicle 608.89
skin 709.2
infected 686.8
postinfectional 709.2
tuberculous (*see also* Tuberculosis)
017.0
specified site NEC 709.2
throat 478.29
tongue 529.8
tonsil (and adenoid) 474.8
trachea 478.9
tuberculous NEC (*see also* Tuberculo-sis) 011.9
ureter 593.89
urethra 599.84
uterus 621.8
vagina 623.4
in pregnancy or childbirth 654.7
causing obstructed labor 660.2
vocal cord 478.5
wrist, constricting (annular) 709.2
**CIN I [cervical intraepithelial neoplasia
I]** 622.1
CIN II [cervical intraepithelial neopla-sia II] 622.1
CIN III [cervical intraepithelial neopla-sia III] 233.1
Cinchonism
correct substance properly adminis-tered 386.9
overdose or wrong substance given or
taken 961.4
Circine herpes 110.5
Circle of Willis - *see* condition
Circular - *see also* condition
hymen 752.49
Circulating anticoagulants 286.5
following childbirth 666.3
postpartum 666.3
Circulation
collateral (venous), any site 459.89
defective 459.9
congenital 747.9
lower extremity 459.89
embryonic 747.9
failure 799.8
fetus or newborn 779.8
peripheral 785.59
fetal, persistent 747.89
heart, incomplete 747.9
Circulatory system - *see* condition

Circulus senilis 371.41
Circumcision
in absence of medical indication
V50.2
ritual V50.2
routine V50.2
Circumscribed - *see* condition
Circumvallata placenta - *see* Placenta,
abnormal
Cirrhosis, cirrhotic 571.5
with alcoholism 571.2
alcoholic (liver) 571.2
atrophic (of liver) - *see* Cirrhosis, por-tal
Baumgarten-Cruveilhier 571.5
biliary (cholangiolitic) (cholangitic)
(cholestatic) (extrahepatic) (hyper-trophic) (intrahepatic) (nonob-structive) (obstructive) (pericho-langiolitic) (posthepatic) (primary)
(secondary) (xanthomatous) 571.6
due to
clonorchiasis 121.1
flukes 121.3
brain 331.9
capsular - *see* Cirrhosis, portal
cardiac 571.5
alcoholic 571.2
central (liver) - *see* Cirrhosis, liver
Charcôt's 571.6
cholangiolitic - *see* Cirrhosis, biliary
cholangitic - *see* Cirrhosis, biliary
cholestatic - *see* Cirrhosis, biliary
clitoris (hypertrophic) 624.2
coarsely nodular 571.5
congestive (liver) - *see* Cirrhosis, car-diac
Cruveilhier-Baumgarten 571.5
cryptogenic (of liver) 571.5
alcoholic 571.2
dietary (*see also* Cirrhosis, portal)
571.5
due to
bronzed diabetes 275.0
congestive hepatomegaly - *see* Cir-rhosis, cardiac
cystic fibrosis 277.00
hemochromatosis 275.0
hepatolenticular degeneration 275.1
passive congestion (chronic) - *see*
Cirrhosis, cardiac
Wilson's disease 275.1
xanthomatosis 272.2
extrahepatic (obstructive) - *see* Cirrho-sis, biliary
fatty 571.8
alcoholic 571.0
florid 571.2
Glisson's - *see* Cirrhosis, portal
Hanot's (hypertrophic) - *see* Cirrhosis,
biliary
hepatic - *see* Cirrhosis, liver
hepatolienal - *see* Cirrhosis, liver
hobnail - *see* Cirrhosis, portal
hypertrophic - *see also* Cirrhosis, liver
biliary - *see* Cirrhosis, biliary
Hanot's - *see* Cirrhosis, biliary
infectious NEC - *see* Cirrhosis, portal
insular - *see* Cirrhosis, portal
intrahepatic (obstructive) (primary)
(secondary) - *see* Cirrhosis, biliary
juvenile (*see also* Cirrhosis, portal)
571.5
kidney (*see also* Sclerosis, renal) 587

ICD-9-CM

C

Vol. 2

Closure *(Continued)*
cranial sutures, premature 756.0
defective or imperfect NEC - *see* Imperfect, closure
fistula, delayed - *see* Fistula
fontanelle, delayed 756.0
foramen ovale, imperfect 745.5
hymen 623.3
interauricular septum, defective 745.5
interventricular septum, defective 745.4
lacrimal duct 375.56
congenital 743.65
neonatal 375.55
nose (congenital) 748.0
acquired 738.0
vagina 623.2
valve - *see* Endocarditis
vulva 624.8
Clot (blood)
artery (obstruction) (occlusion) (*see also* Embolism) 444.9
bladder 596.7
brain (extradural or intradural) (*see also* Thrombosis, brain) 434.0
late effect - *see* Late effect(s) (of) cerebrovascular disease
circulation 444.9
heart (*see also* Infarct, myocardium) 410.9
vein (*see also* Thrombosis) 453.9
Clotting defect NEC (*see also* Defect, coagulation) 286.9
Clouded state 780.09
epileptic (*see also* Epilepsy) 345.9
paroxysmal (idiopathic) (*see also* Epilepsy) 345.9
Clouding
corneal graft 996.51
Cloudy antrum, antra 473.0
Clouston's (hidrotic) ectodermal dysplasia 757.31
Clubbing of fingers 781.5
Clubfinger 736.29
acquired 736.29
congenital 754.89
Clubfoot (congenital) 754.70
acquired 736.71
equinovarus 754.51
paralytic 736.71
Club hand (congenital) 754.89
acquired 736.07
Clubnail (acquired) 703.8
congenital 757.5
Clump kidney 753.3
Clumsiness 781.3
syndrome 315.4
Cluttering 307.0
Clutton's joints 090.5
Coagulation, intravascular (diffuse) (disseminated) (*see also* Fibrinolysis) 286.6
newborn 776.2
Coagulopathy (*see also* Defect, coagulation) 286.9
consumption 286.6
intravascular (disseminated) NEC 286.6
newborn 776.2
Coalition
calcaneoscaphoid 755.67
calcaneus 755.67
tarsal 755.67
Coal miners'
elbow 727.2
lung 500

Coal workers' lung or pneumoconiosis 500
Coarctation
aorta (postductal) (preductal) 747.10
pulmonary artery 747.3
Coated tongue 529.3
Coats' disease 362.12
Cocainism (*see also* Dependence) 304.2
Coccidioidal granuloma 114.3
Coccidioidomycosis 114.9
with pneumonia 114.0
cutaneous (primary) 114.1
disseminated 114.3
extrapulmonary (primary) 114.1
lung 114.5
acute 114.0
chronic 114.4
primary 114.0
meninges 114.2
primary (pulmonary) 114.0
acute 114.0
prostate 114.3
pulmonary 114.5
acute 114.0
chronic 114.4
primary 114.0
specified site NEC 114.3
Coccidioidosis 114.9
lung 114.5
acute 114.0
chronic 114.4
primary 114.0
meninges 114.2
Coccidiosis (colitis) (diarrhea) (dysentery) 007.2
Cocciuria 599.0
Coccus in urine 599.0
Coccydynia 724.79
Coccygodynia 724.79
Coccyx - *see* condition
Cochin-China
diarrhea 579.1
anguilluliasis 127.2
ulcer 085.1
Cock's peculiar tumor 706.2
Cockayne's disease or syndrome (microcephaly and dwarfism) 759.89
Cockayne-Weber syndrome (epidermolysis bullosa) 757.39
Cocked-up toe 735.2
Codman's tumor (benign chondroblastoma) (M9230/0) - *see* Neoplasm, bone, benign
Coenurosis 123.8
Coffee workers' lung 495.8
Cogan's syndrome 370.52
congenital oculomotor apraxia 379.51
nonsyphilitic interstitial keratitis 370.52
Coiling, umbilical cord - *see* Complications, umbilical cord
Coitus, painful (female) 625.0
male 608.89
psychogenic 302.76
Cold 460
with influenza, flu, or grippe 487.1
abscess - *see also* Tuberculosis, abscess
articular - *see* Tuberculosis, joint
agglutinin
disease (chronic) or syndrome 283.0
hemoglobinuria 283.0
paroxysmal (cold) (nocturnal) 283.2
allergic (*see also* Fever, hay) 477.9
bronchus or chest - *see* Bronchitis
with grippe or influenza 487.1

Cold *(Continued)*
common (head) 460
vaccination, prophylactic (against) V04.7
deep 464.10
effects of 991.9
specified effect NEC 991.8
excessive 991.9
specified effect NEC 991.8
exhaustion from 991.8
exposure to 991.9
specified effect NEC 991.8
grippy 487.1
head 460
injury syndrome (newborn) 778.2
intolerance 780.9
on lung - *see* Bronchitis
rose 477.0
sensitivity, autoimmune 283.0
virus 460
Coldsore (*see also* Herpes, simplex) 054.9
Colibacillosis 041.4
generalized 038.42
Colibacilluria 599.0
Colic (recurrent) 789.0
abdomen 789.0
psychogenic 307.89
appendicular 543.9
appendix 543.9
bile duct - *see* Choledocholithiasis
biliary - *see* Cholelithiasis
bilious - *see* Cholelithiasis
common duct - *see* Choledocholithiasis
Devonshire NEC 984.9
specified type of lead - *see* Table of Drugs and Chemicals
flatulent 787.3
gallbladder or gallstone - *see* Cholelithiasis
gastric 536.8
hepatic (duct) - *see* Choledocholithiasis
hysterical 300.11
infantile 789.0
intestinal 789.0
kidney 788.0
lead NEC 984.9
specified type of lead - *see* Table of Drugs and Chemicals
liver (duct) - *see* Choledocholithiasis
mucous 564.1
psychogenic 316 [564.1]
nephritic 788.0
Painter's NEC 984.9
pancreas 577.8
psychogenic 306.4
renal 788.0
saturnine NEC 984.9
specified type of lead - *see* Table of Drugs and Chemicals
spasmodic 789.0
ureter 788.0
urethral 599.84
due to calculus 594.2
uterus 625.8
menstrual 625.3
vermicular 543.9
virus 460
worm NEC 128.9
Colicystitis (*see also* Cystitis) 595.9
Colitis (acute) (catarrhal) (croupous) (cystica superficialis) (exudative) (hemorrhagic) (noninfectious) (phlegmonous) (presumed noninfectious) 558.9

Colitis (*Continued*)
adaptive 564.1
allergic 558.9
amebic (*see also* Amebiasis) 006.9
  nondysenteric 006.2
anthrax 022.2
bacillary (*see also* Infection, Shigella) 004.9
balantidial 007.0
chronic 558.9
  ulcerative (*see also* Colitis, ulcerative) 556.9
coccidial 007.2
dietetic 558.9
due to radiation 558.1
functional 558.9
gangrenous 009.0
giardial 007.1
granulomatous 555.1
gravis (*see also* Colitis, ulcerative) 556.9
infectious (*see also* Enteritis, due to, specific organism) 009.0
  presumed 009.1
ischemic 557.9
  acute 557.0
  chronic 557.1
  due to mesenteric artery insufficiency 557.1
membranous 564.1
  psychogenic 316 [564.1]
mucous 564.1
  psychogenic 316 [564.1]
necrotic 009.0
polyposa (*see also* Colitis, ulcerative) 556.9
protozoal NEC 007.9
pseudomembranous 008.45
pseudomucinous 564.1
regional 555.1
segmental 555.1
septic (*see also* Enteritis, due to, specific organism) 009.0
spastic 564.1
  psychogenic 316 [564.1]
Staphylococcus 008.41
  food 005.0
thromboulcerative 557.0
toxic 558.2
transmural 555.1
trichomonal 007.3
tuberculous (ulcerative) 014.8
ulcerative (chronic) (idiopathic) (nonspecific) 556.9
  entero- 556.0
  fulminant 557.0
  ileo- 556.1
  left-sided 556.5
  procto- 556.2
  proctosigmoid 556.3
  psychogenic 316 [556]
  specified NEC 556.8
  universal 556.6
Collagen disease NEC 710.9
nonvascular 710.9
vascular (allergic) (*see also* Angiitis, hypersensitivity) 446.20
Collagenosis (*see also* Collagen disease) 710.9
cardiovascular 425.4
mediastinal 519.3
Collapse 780.2
adrenal 255.8
cardiorenal (*see also* Hypertension, cardiorenal) 404.90

Collapse (*Continued*)
cardiorespiratory 785.51
  fetus or newborn 779.8
cardiovascular (*see also* Disease, heart) 785.51
  fetus or newborn 779.8
circulatory (peripheral) 785.59
  with
    abortion - *see* Abortion, by type, with shock
    ectopic pregnancy (*see also* categories 633.0-633.9) 639.5
    molar pregnancy (*see also* categories 630-632) 639.5
  during or after labor and delivery 669.1
  fetus or newborn 779.8
  following
    abortion 639.5
    ectopic or molar pregnancy 639.5
during or after labor and delivery 669.1
  fetus or newborn 779.8
external ear canal 380.50
  secondary to
    inflammation 380.53
    surgery 380.52
    trauma 380.51
general 780.2
heart - *see* Disease, heart
heat 992.1
hysterical 300.11
labyrinth, membranous (congenital) 744.05
lung (massive) (*see also* Atelectasis) 518.0
  pressure, during labor 668.0
myocardial - *see* Disease, heart
nervous (*see also* Disorder, mental, nonpsychotic) 300.9
neurocirculatory 306.2
nose 738.0
postoperative (cardiovascular) 998.0
pulmonary (*see also* Atelectasis) 518.0
  fetus or newborn 770.5
    partial 770.5
    primary 770.4
thorax 512.8
  iatrogenic 512.1
  postoperative 512.1
trachea 519.1
valvular - *see* Endocarditis
vascular (peripheral) 785.59
  with
    abortion - *see* Abortion, by type, with shock
    ectopic pregnancy (*see also* categories 633.0-633.9) 639.5
    molar pregnancy (*see also* categories 630-632) 639.5
  cerebral (*see also* Disease, cerebrovascular, acute) 436
  during or after labor and delivery 669.1
  fetus or newborn 779.8
  following
    abortion 639.5
    ectopic or molar pregnancy 639.5
vasomotor 785.59
vertebra 733.13
Collateral - *see also* condition
circulation (venous) 459.89
dilation, veins 459.89

Colles' fracture (closed) (reversed) (separation) 813.41
open 813.51
Collet's syndrome 352.6
Collet-Sicard syndrome 352.6
Colliculitis urethralis (*see also* Urethritis) 597.89
Colliers'
asthma 500
lung 500
phthisis (*see also* Tuberculosis) 011.4
Collodion baby (ichthyosis congenita) 757.1
Colloid milium 709.3
Coloboma NEC 743.49
choroid 743.59
fundus 743.52
iris 743.46
lens 743.36
lids 743.62
optic disc (congenital) 743.57
  acquired 377.23
retina 743.56
sclera 743.47
Coloenteritis - *see* Enteritis
Colon - *see* condition
Coloptosis 569.89
Color
amblyopia NEC 368.59
  acquired 368.55
blindness NEC (congenital) 368.59
  acquired 368.55
Colostomy
attention to V55.3
fitting or adjustment V55.3
malfunctioning 569.62
status V44.3
Colpitis (*see also* Vaginitis) 616.10
Colpocele 618.6
Colpocystitis (*see also* Vaginitis) 616.10
Colporrhexis 665.4
Colpospasm 625.1
Column, spinal, vertebral - *see* condition
Coma 780.01
apoplectic (*see also* Disease, cerebrovascular, acute) 436
diabetic (with ketoacidosis) 250.3
  hyperosmolar 250.2
eclamptic (*see also* Eclampsia) 780.39
epileptic 345.3
hepatic 572.2
hyperglycemic 250.2
hyperosmolar (diabetic) (nonketotic) 250.2
hypoglycemic 251.0
  diabetic 250.3
insulin 250.3
  hyperosmolar 250.2
  nondiabetic 251.0
  organic hyperinsulinism 251.0
Kussmaul's (diabetic) 250.3
liver 572.2
newborn 779.2
prediabetic 250.2
uremic - *see* Uremia
Combat fatigue (*see also* Reaction, stress, acute) 308.9
Combined - *see* condition
Comedo 706.1
Comedocarcinoma (M8501/3) - *see also* Neoplasm, breast, malignant noninfiltrating (M8501/2)

Comedocarcinoma *(Continued)*
noninfiltrating *(Continued)*
specified site - *see* Neoplasm, by site, in situ
unspecified site 233.0
Comedomastitis 610.4
Comedones 706.1
lanugo 757.4
Comma bacillus, carrier (suspected) of V02.3
Comminuted fracture - *see* Fracture, by site
Common
aortopulmonary trunk 745.0
atrioventricular canal (defect) 745.69
atrium 745.69
cold (head) 460
vaccination, prophylactic (against) V04.7
truncus (arteriosus) 745.0
ventricle 745.3
Commotio (current)
cerebri (*see also* Concussion, brain) 850.9
with skull fracture - *see* Fracture, skull, by site
retinae 921.3
spinalis - *see* Injury, spinal, by site
Commotion (current)
brain (without skull fracture) (*see also* Concussion, brain) 850.9
with skull fracture - *see* Fracture, skull, by site
spinal cord - *see* Injury, spinal, by site
Communication
abnormal - *see also* Fistula
between
base of aorta and pulmonary artery 745.0
left ventricle and right atrium 745.4
pericardial sac and pleural sac 748.8
pulmonary artery and pulmonary vein 747.3
congenital, between uterus and anterior abdominal wall 752.3
bladder 752.3
intestine 752.3
rectum 752.3
left ventricular-right atrial 745.4
pulmonary artery-pulmonary vein 747.3
Compensation
broken - *see* Failure, heart, congestive
failure - *see* Failure, heart, congestive
neurosis, psychoneurosis 300.11
Complaint - *see also* Disease
bowel, functional 564.9
psychogenic 306.4
intestine, functional 564.9
psychogenic 306.4
kidney (*see also* Disease, renal) 593.9
liver 573.9
miners' 500
Complete - *see* condition
Complex
cardiorenal (*see also* Hypertension, cardiorenal) 404.90
castration 300.9
Costen's 524.60
ego-dystonic homosexuality 302.0
Eisenmenger's (ventricular septal defect) 745.4

Complex *(Continued)*
homosexual, ego-dystonic 302.0
hypersexual 302.89
inferiority 301.9
jumped process
spine - *see* Dislocation, vertebra
primary, tuberculosis (*see also* Tuberculosis) 010.0
Taussig-Bing (transposition, aorta and overriding pulmonary artery) 745.11
Complications
abortion NEC - *see* categories 634-639
accidental puncture or laceration during a procedure 998.2
amputation stump (late) (surgical) 997.60
traumatic - *see* Amputation, traumatic
anastomosis (and bypass) - *see also* Complications, due to (presence of) any device, implant, or graft classified to 996.0-996.5 NEC
hemorrhage NEC 998.11
intestinal (internal) NEC 997.4
involving urinary tract 997.5
mechanical - *see* Complications, mechanical, graft
urinary tract (involving intestinal tract) 997.5
anesthesia, anesthetic NEC (*see also* Anesthesia, complication) 995.2
in labor and delivery 668.9
affecting fetus or newborn 763.5
cardiac 668.1
central nervous system 668.2
pulmonary 668.0
specified type NEC 668.8
aortocoronary (bypass) graft 996.03
atherosclerosis - *see* Arteriosclerosis, coronary
embolism 996.72
occlusion NEC 996.72
thrombus 996.72
arthroplasty 996.4
artificial opening
cecostomy 569.60
colostomy 569.60
cystostomy 997.5
enterostomy 569.60
gastrostomy 536.40 ◄▥▥
ileostomy 569.60
jejunostomy 569.60
nephrostomy 997.5
tracheostomy 519.00 ◄▥▥
ureterostomy 997.5
urethrostomy 997.5
bile duct implant (prosthetic) NEC 996.79
infection or inflammation 996.69
mechanical 996.59
bleeding (intraoperative) (postoperative) 998.11
blood vessel graft 996.1
aortocoronary 996.03
atherosclerosis - *see* Arteriosclerosis, coronary
embolism 996.72
occlusion NEC 996.72
thrombus 996.72
atherosclerosis - *see* Arteriosclerosis, extremities
embolism 996.74

Complications *(Continued)*
blood vessel graft *(Continued)*
occlusion NEC 996.74
thrombus 996.74
bone growth stimulator NEC 996.78
infection or inflammation 996.67
bone marrow transplant 996.85
breast implant (prosthetic) NEC 996.79
infection or inflammation 996.69
mechanical 996.54
bypass - *see also* Complications, anastomosis
aortocoronary 996.03
atherosclerosis - *see* Arteriosclerosis, coronary
embolism 996.72
occlusion NEC 996.72
thrombus 996.72
carotid artery 996.1
atherosclerosis - *see* Arteriosclerosis, coronary
embolism 996.74
occlusion NEC 996.74
thrombus 996.74
cardiac (*see also* Disease, heart) 429.9
device, implant, or graft NEC 996.72
infection or inflammation 996.61
long-term effect 429.4
mechanical (*see also* Complications, mechanical, by type) 996.00
valve prosthesis 996.71
infection or inflammation 996.61
postoperative NEC 997.1
long-term effect 429.4
cardiorenal (*see also* Hypertension, cardiorenal) 404.90
carotid artery bypass graft 996.1
atherosclerosis - *see* Arteriosclerosis, coronary
embolism 996.74
occlusion NEC 996.74
thrombus 996.74
cataract fragments in eye 998.82
catheter device NEC - *see also* Complications, due to (presence of) any device, implant, or graft classified to 996.0-996.5 NEC
mechanical - *see* Complications, mechanical, catheter
cecostomy 569.60
cesarean section wound 674.3
chin implant (prosthetic) NEC 996.79
infection or inflammation 996.69
mechanical 996.59
colostomy (enterostomy) 569.60
specified type NEC 569.69 ◄
contraceptive device, intrauterine NEC 996.76
infection 996.65
inflammation 996.65
mechanical 996.32
cord (umbilical) - *see* Complications, umbilical cord
cornea
due to
contact lens 371.82
coronary (artery) bypass (graft) NEC 996.03
atherosclerosis - *see* Arteriosclerosis, coronary
embolism 996.72
infection or inflammation 996.61
mechanical 996.03
occlusion NEC 996.72

ICD-9-CM

C

Vol. 2

Complications *(Continued)*
  coronary (artery) bypass (graft) NEC
    (Continued)
    specified type NEC 996.72
    thrombus 996.72
  cystostomy 997.5
  delivery 669.9
    procedure (instrumental) (manual)
      (surgical) 669.4
    specified type NEC 669.8
  dialysis (hemodialysis) (peritoneal) (re-
    nal) NEC 999.9
    catheter NEC - *see also* Complica-
      tions, due to (presence of) any
      device, implant, or graft classi-
      fied to 996.0-996.5 NEC
      infection or inflammation 996.62
        peritoneal 996.68
      mechanical 996.1
        peritoneal 996.56
  due to (presence of) any device, im-
    plant, or graft classified to 996.0-
    996.5 NEC 996.70
    with infection or inflammation - *see*
      Complications, infection or in-
      flammation, due to (presence of)
      any device, implant, or graft
      classified to 996.0-996.5 NEC
    arterial NEC 996.74
      coronary NEC 996.03
        atherosclerosis - *see* Arterioscle-
          rosis, coronary
        embolism 996.72
        occlusion NEC 996.72
        specified type NEC 996.72
        thrombus 996.72
      renal dialysis 996.73
    arteriovenous fistula or shunt NEC
      996.74
    bone growth stimulator 996.78
    breast NEC 996.79
    cardiac NEC 996.72
      defibrillator 996.72
      pacemaker 996.72
      valve prosthesis 996.71
    catheter NEC 996.79
      spinal 996.75
      urinary, indwelling 996.76
      vascular NEC 996.74
        renal dialysis 996.73
      ventricular shunt 996.75
    coronary (artery) bypass (graft) NEC
      996.03
      atherosclerosis - *see* Arteriosclero-
        sis, coronary
      embolism 996.72
      occlusion NEC 996.72
      thrombus 996.72
    electrodes
      brain 996.75
      heart 996.72
    gastrointestinal NEC 996.79
    genitourinary NEC 996.76
    heart valve prosthesis NEC 996.71
    infusion pump 996.74
    internal
      joint prosthesis 996.77
      orthopedic NEC 996.78
      specified type NEC 996.79
    intrauterine contraceptive device
      NEC 996.76
    joint prosthesis, internal NEC 996.77
    mechanical - *see* Complications, me-
      chanical

Complications *(Continued)*
  due to (presence of) any device, im-
    plant, or graft classified to *(Contin-*
    ued)
    nervous system NEC 996.75
    ocular lens NEC 996.79
    orbital NEC 996.79
    orthopedic NEC 996.78
      joint, internal 996.77
    renal dialysis 996.73
    specified type NEC 996.79
    urinary catheter, indwelling 996.76
    vascular NEC 996.74
    ventricular shunt 996.75
  during dialysis NEC 999.9
  ectopic or molar pregnancy NEC 639.9
  electroshock therapy NEC 999.9
  enterostomy 569.60
    specified type NEC 569.69 ◀
  external (fixation) device with internal
    component(s) NEC 996.78
    infection or inflammation 996.67
    mechanical 996.4
  extracorporeal circulation NEC 999.9
  eye implant (prosthetic) NEC 996.79
    infection or inflammation 996.69
    mechanical
      ocular lens 996.53
      orbital globe 996.59
  gastrointestinal, postoperative NEC
    (*see also* Complications, surgical
    procedures) 997.4
  gastrostomy 536.40
    specified type NEC 536.49 ◀
  genitourinary device, implant or graft
    NEC 996.76
    infection or inflammation 996.65
      urinary catheter, indwelling 996.64
    mechanical (*see also* Complications,
      mechanical, by type) 996.30
    specified NEC 996.39
  graft (bypass) (patch) - *see also* Compli-
    cations, due to (presence of) any
    device, implant, or graft classified
    to 996.0-996.5 NEC
    bone marrow 996.85
    corneal NEC 996.79
      infection or inflammation 996.69
      rejection or reaction 996.51
    mechanical - *see* Complications, me-
      chanical, graft
    organ (immune or nonimmune
      cause) (partial) (total) 996.80
      bone marrow 996.85
      heart 996.83
      intestines 996.89
      kidney 996.81
      liver 996.82
      lung 996.84
      pancreas 996.86
      specified NEC 996.89
    skin NEC 996.79
      infection or inflammation 996.69
      rejection 996.52
        artificial 996.55 ◀
        decellularized allodermis
          996.55 ◀
  heart - *see also* Disease, heart trans-
    plant (immune or nonimmune
    cause) 996.83
  hematoma (intraoperative) (postopera-
    tive) 998.12
  hemorrhage (intraoperative) (postoper-
    ative) 998.11

Complications *(Continued)*
  hyperalimentation therapy NEC 999.9
  immunization (procedure) - *see* Com-
    plications, vaccination
  implant - *see also* Complications, due
    to (presence of) any device, im-
    plant, or graft classified to 996.0-
    996.5 NEC
    mechanical - *see* Complications, me-
      chanical, implant
  infection and inflammation
    due to (presence of) any device, im-
      plant or graft classified to 996.0-
      996.5 NEC 996.60
      arterial NEC 996.62
        coronary 996.61
        renal dialysis 996.62
      arteriovenous fistula or shunt
        996.62
      bone growth stimulator 996.67
      breast 996.69
      cardiac 996.61
      catheter NEC 996.69
        peritoneal 996.68
        spinal 996.63
        urinary, indwelling 996.64
        vascular NEC 996.62
        ventricular shunt 996.63
      coronary artery bypass 996.61
      electrodes
        brain 996.63
        heart 996.61
      gastrointestinal NEC 996.69
      genitourinary NEC 996.65
        indwelling urinary catheter
          996.64
      heart valve 996.61
      infusion pump 996.62
      intrauterine contraceptive device
        996.65
      joint prosthesis, internal 996.66
      ocular lens 996.69
      orbital (implant) 996.69
      orthopedic NEC 996.67
        joint, internal 996.66
      specified type NEC 996.69
      urinary catheter, indwelling
        996.64
      ventricular shunt 996.63
  infusion (procedure) 999.9
    blood - *see* Complications, transfusion
    infection NEC 999.3
    sepsis NEC 999.3
  inhalation therapy NEC 999.9
  injection (procedure) 999.9
    drug reaction (*see also* Reaction,
      drug) 995.2
    infection NEC 999.3
    sepsis NEC 999.3
    serum (prophylactic) (therapeutic) -
      see Complications, vaccination
    vaccine (any) - *see* Complications,
      vaccination
  inoculation (any) - *see* Complications,
    vaccination
  internal device (catheter) (electronic)
    (fixation) (prosthetic) - *see also*
    Complications, due to (presence
    of) any device, implant, or graft
    classified to 996.0-996.5 NEC
    mechanical - *see* Complications, me-
      chanical
  intestinal transplant (immune or non-
    immune cause) 996.89

◀▶   New Code   ◀▥ ▥▶   Revised Code

Complications (*Continued*)
  intraoperative bleeding or hemorrhage
      998.11
  intrauterine contraceptive device (*see
      also* Complications, contraceptive
      device) 996.76
    with fetal damage affecting manage-
      ment of pregnancy 655.8
    infection or inflammation 996.65
  jejunostomy 569.60
  kidney transplant (immune or nonim-
      mune cause) 996.81
  labor 669.9
    specified condition NEC 669.8
  liver transplant (immune or nonim-
      mune cause) 996.82
  lumbar puncture 349.0
  mechanical
    anastomosis - *see* Complications, me-
      chanical, graft
    bypass - *see* Complications, mechani-
      cal, graft
    catheter NEC 996.59
      cardiac 996.09
      cystostomy 996.39
      dialysis (hemodialysis)
          996.1
        peritoneal 996.56 ◄
      during a procedure 998.2
      urethral, indwelling 996.31
    colostomy 569.62 ◄
    device NEC 996.59
      balloon (counterpulsation), intra-
          aortic 996.1
      cardiac 996.00
        long-term effect 429.4
        specified NEC 996.09
      contraceptive, intrauterine 996.32
      counterpulsation, intra-aortic 996.1
      fixation, external, with internal
          components 996.4
      fixation, internal (nail, rod, plate)
          996.4
      genitourinary 996.30
        specified NEC 996.39
      nervous system 996.2
      orthopedic, internal 996.4
      prosthetic NEC 996.59
      umbrella, vena cava 996.1
      vascular 996.1
    dorsal column stimulator 996.2
    electrode NEC 996.59
      brain 996.2
      cardiac 996.01
      spinal column 996.2
    enterostomy 569.62 ◄
    fistula, arteriovenous, surgically
        created 996.1
    gastrostomy 536.42 ◄
    graft NEC 996.52
      aortic (bifurcation) 996.1
      aortocoronary bypass 996.03
      blood vessel NEC 996.1
      bone 996.4
      cardiac 996.00
      carotid artery bypass 996.1
      cartilage 996.4
      corneal 996.51
      coronary bypass 996.03
      decellularized allodermis
          996.55 ◄
      genitourinary 996.30
        specified NEC 996.39
      muscle 996.4

Complications (*Continued*)
  mechanical (*Continued*)
    graft NEC (*Continued*)
      nervous system 996.2
      organ (immune or nonimmune
          cause) 996.80
        heart 996.83
        intestines 996.89
        kidney 996.81
        liver 996.82
        lung 996.84
        pancreas 996.86
        specified NEC 996.89
      orthopedic, internal 996.4
      peripheral nerve 996.2
      prosthetic NEC 996.59
      skin 996.52
        artificial 996.55 ◄
      specified NEC 996.59
      tendon 996.4
      tissue NEC 996.52
      tooth 996.59
      ureter, without mention of resec-
          tion 996.39
      vascular 996.1
    heart valve prosthesis 996.02
      long-term effect 429.4
    implant NEC 996.59
      cardiac 996.00
        long-term effect 429.4
        specified NEC 996.09
      electrode NEC 996.59
        brain 996.2
        cardiac 996.01
        spinal column 996.2
      genitourinary 996.30
      nervous system 996.2
      orthopedic, internal 996.4
      prosthetic NEC 996.59
        in
          bile duct 996.59
          breast 996.54
          chin 996.59
          eye
            ocular lens 996.53
            orbital globe 996.59
      vascular 996.1
    nonabsorbable surgical material 996.59
    pacemaker NEC 996.59
      brain 996.2
      cardiac 996.01
      nerve (phrenic) 996.2
    patch - *see* Complications, mechani-
        cal, graft
    prosthesis NEC 996.59
      bile duct 996.59
      breast 996.54
      chin 996.59
      ocular lens 996.53
      reconstruction, vas deferens 996.39
    reimplant NEC 996.59
      extremity (*see also* Complications,
          reattached, extremity) 996.90
      organ (*see also* Complications, trans-
          plant, organ, by site) 996.80
    repair - *see* Complications, mechani-
        cal, graft
    shunt NEC 996.59
      arteriovenous, surgically created
          996.1
      ventricular (communicating) 996.2
    stent NEC 996.59
    tracheostomy 519.02 ◄
    vas deferens reconstruction 996.39

Complications (*Continued*)
  medical care NEC 999.9
    cardiac NEC 997.1
    gastrointestinal NEC 997.4
    nervous system NEC 997.00
    peripheral vascular NEC 997.2
    respiratory NEC 997.3
    urinary NEC 997.5
  nephrostomy 997.5
  nervous system
    device, implant, or graft NEC 349.1
      mechanical 996.2
    postoperative NEC 997.00
  obstetric 669.9
    procedure (instrumental) (manual)
        (surgical) 669.4
    specified NEC 669.8
    surgical wound 674.3
  ocular lens implant NEC 996.79
    infection or inflammation 996.69
    mechanical 996.53
  organ transplant - *see* Complications,
      transplant, organ, by site
  orthopedic device, implant, or graft
    internal (fixation) (nail) (plate) (rod)
        NEC 996.78
      infection or inflammation 996.67
      joint prosthesis 996.77
        infection or inflammation 996.66
      mechanical 996.4
  pacemaker (cardiac) 996.72
    infection or inflammation 996.61
    mechanical 996.01
  pancreas transplant (immune or non-
      immune cause) 996.86
  perfusion NEC 999.9
  perineal repair (obstetrical) 674.3
    disruption 674.2
  pessary (uterus) (vagina) - *see* Compli-
      cations, contraceptive device
  phototherapy 990
  postcystoscopic 997.5
  postmastoidectomy NEC 383.30
  postoperative - *see* Complications, sur-
      gical procedures
  pregnancy NEC 646.9
    affecting fetus or newborn 761.9
  prosthetic device, internal - *see also*
      Complications, due to (presence
      of) any device, implant or graft
      classified to 996.0-996.5 NEC
    mechanical NEC (*see also* Complica-
        tions, mechanical) 996.59
  puerperium NEC (*see also* Puerperal)
      674.9
  puncture, spinal 349.0
  pyelogram 997.5
  radiation 990
  radiotherapy 990
  reattached
    body part, except extremity 996.99
    extremity (infection) (rejection)
        996.90
      arm(s) 996.94
      digit(s) (hand) 996.93
        foot 996.95
      finger(s) 996.93
      foot 996.95
      forearm 996.91
      hand 996.92
      leg 996.96
      lower NEC 996.96
      toe(s) 996.95
      upper NEC 996.94

◄► **New Code**   ◄▌▐▐▌► **Revised Code**

Complications *(Continued)*
  reimplant NEC - *see also* Complications, due to (presence of) any device, implant, or graft classified to 996.0-996.5 NEC
    bone marrow 996.85
    extremity *(see also* Complications, reattached, extremity) 996.90
      due to infection 996.90
    mechanical - *see* Complications, mechanical, reimplant
    organ (immune or nonimmune cause) (partial) (total) *(see also* Complications, transplant, organ, by site)* 996.80
  renal allograft 996.81
  renal dialysis - *see* Complications, dialysis
  respiratory 519.9
    device, implant or graft NEC 996.79
      infection or inflammation 996.69
      mechanical 996.59
    distress syndrome, adult, following trauma or surgery 518.5
    insufficiency, acute, postoperative 518.5
    postoperative NEC 997.3
    therapy NEC 999.9
  sedation during labor and delivery 668.9
    affecting fetus or newborn 763.5
    cardiac 668.1
    central nervous system 668.2
    pulmonary 668.0
    specified type NEC 668.8
  seroma (intraoperative) (postoperative) (noninfected) 998.13
    infected 998.51
  shunt - *see also* Complications, due to (presence of) any device, implant, or graft classified to 996.0-996.5 NEC
    mechanical - *see* Complications, mechanical, shunt
  specified body system NEC
    device, implant, or graft - *see* Complications, due to (presence of) any device, implant, or graft classified to 996.0-996.5 NEC
    postoperative NEC 997.99
  spinal puncture or tap 349.0
  stoma, external
    gastrointestinal tract
      colostomy 569.60
      enterostomy 569.60
      gastrostomy 536.40
    urinary tract 997.5
  surgical procedures 998.9
    accidental puncture or laceration 998.2
    amputation stump (late) 997.60
    anastomosis - *see* Complications, anastomosis
    burst stitches or sutures 998.3
    cardiac 997.1
      long-term effect following cardiac surgery 429.4
    catheter device - *see* Complications, catheter device
    cataract fragments in eye 998.82
    cecostomy malfunction 569.62
    colostomy malfunction 569.62
    cystostomy malfunction 997.5
    dehiscence (of incision) 998.3
    dialysis NEC *(see also* Complications, dialysis) 999.9

Complications *(Continued)*
  surgical procedures *(Continued)*
    disruption
      anastomosis (internal) - *see* Complications, mechanical, graft
      internal suture (line) 998.3
      wound 998.3
    dumping syndrome (postgastrectomy) 564.2
    elephantiasis or lymphedema 997.99
      postmastectomy 457.0
    emphysema (surgical) 998.81
    enterostomy malfunction 569.62
    evisceration 998.3
    fistula (persistent postoperative) 998.6
    foreign body inadvertently left in wound (sponge) (suture) (swab) 998.4
    from nonabsorbable surgical material (Dacron) (mesh) (permanent suture) (reinforcing) (Teflon) - *see* Complications due to (presence of) any device, implant, or graft classified to 996.0-996.5 NEC
    gastrointestinal NEC 997.4
    gastrostomy malfunction 536.42
    hematoma 998.12
    hemorrhage 998.11
    ileostomy malfunction 569.62
    internal prosthetic device NEC *(see also* Complications, internal device)* 996.70
      hemolytic anemia 283.19
      infection or inflammation 996.60
      malfunction - *see* Complications, mechanical
      mechanical complication - *see* Complications, mechanical
      thrombus 996.70
    jejunostomy malfunction 569.62
    nervous system NEC 997.00
    obstruction, internal anastomosis - *see* Complications, mechanical, graft
    other body system NEC 997.99
    peripheral vascular NEC 997.2
    postcardiotomy syndrome 429.4
    postcholecystectomy syndrome 576.0
    postcommissurotomy syndrome 429.4
    postgastrectomy dumping syndrome 564.2
    postmastectomy lymphedema syndrome 457.0
    postmastoidectomy 383.30
      cholesteatoma, recurrent 383.32
      cyst, mucosal 383.31
      granulation 383.33
      inflammation, chronic 383.33
    postvagotomy syndrome 564.2
    postvalvulotomy syndrome 429.4
    reattached extremity (infection) (rejection) *(see also* Complications, reattached, extremity) 996.90
    respiratory NEC 997.3
    seroma 998.13
    shock (endotoxic) (hypovolemic) (septic) 998.0
    shunt, prosthetic (thrombus) - *see also* Complications, due to (presence of) any device, implant, or graft classified to 996.0-996.5 NEC
      hemolytic anemia 283.19

Complications *(Continued)*
  surgical procedures *(Continued)*
    specified complication NEC 998.89
    stitch abscess 998.59
    transplant - *see* Complications, graft
    ureterostomy malfunction 997.5
    urethrostomy malfunction 997.5
    urinary NEC 997.5
    wound infection 998.59
  therapeutic misadventure NEC 999.9
    surgical treatment 998.9
  tracheostomy 519.00
  transfusion (blood) (lymphocytes) (plasma) NEC 999.8
    atrophy, liver, yellow, subacute (within 8 months of administration) - *see* Hepatitis, viral
    bone marrow 996.85
    embolism
      air 999.1
      thrombus 999.2
    hemolysis NEC 999.8
      bone marrow 996.85
    hepatitis (serum) (type B) (within 8 months after administration) - *see* Hepatitis, viral
    incompatibility reaction (ABO) (blood group) 999.6
      Rh (factor) 999.7
    infection 999.3
    jaundice (serum) (within 8 months after administration) - *see* Hepatitis, viral
    sepsis 999.3
    shock or reaction NEC 999.8
      bone marrow 996.85
    subacute yellow atrophy of liver (within 8 months after administration) - *see* Hepatitis, viral
    thromboembolism 999.2
  transplant NEC - *see also* Complications, due to (presence of) any device, implant, or graft classified to 996.0-996.5 NEC
    bone marrow 996.85
    organ (immune or nonimmune cause) (partial) (total) 996.80
      bone marrow 996.85
      heart 996.83
      intestines 996.89
      kidney 996.81
      liver 996.82
      lung 996.84
      pancreas 996.86
      specified NEC 996.89
  trauma NEC (early) 958.8
  ultrasound therapy NEC 999.9
  umbilical cord
    affecting fetus or newborn 762.6
    complicating delivery 663.9
      affecting fetus or newborn 762.6
      specified type NEC 663.8
  urethral catheter NEC 996.76
    infection or inflammation 996.64
    mechanical 996.31
  urinary, postoperative NEC 997.5
  vaccination 999.9
    anaphylaxis NEC 999.4
    cellulitis 999.3
    encephalitis or encephalomyelitis 323.5
    hepatitis (serum) (type B) (within 8 months after administration) - *see* Hepatitis, viral

Complications (*Continued*)
  vaccination (*Continued*)
    infection (general) (local) NEC 999.3
    jaundice (serum) (within 8 months
      after administration) - *see* Hepa-
      titis, viral
    meningitis 997.09 *[321.8]*
    myelitis 323.5
    protein sickness 999.5
    reaction (allergic) 999.5
      Herxheimer's 995.0
      serum 999.5
    sepsis 999.3
    serum intoxication, sickness, rash, or
      other serum reaction NEC
      999.5
    shock (allergic) (anaphylactic)
      999.4
    subacute yellow atrophy of liver
      (within 8 months after adminis-
      tration) - *see* Hepatitis, viral
    vaccinia (generalized) 999.0
      localized 999.3
  vascular
    device, implant, or graft NEC 996.74
      infection or inflammation 996.62
      mechanical NEC 996.1
        cardiac (*see also* Complications,
        mechanical, by type) 996.00
    following infusion, perfusion, or
      transfusion 999.2
    postoperative NEC 997.2
  ventilation therapy NEC 999.9
Compound presentation, complicating
  delivery 652.8
  causing obstructed labor 660.0
Compressed air disease 993.3
Compression
  with injury - *see* specific injury
  arm NEC 354.9
  artery 447.1
    celiac, syndrome 447.4
  brachial plexus 353.0
  brain (stem) 348.4
    due to
      contusion, brain - *see* Contusion,
        brain
      injury NEC - *see also* Hemorrhage,
        brain, traumatic
        birth - *see* Birth, injury, brain
      laceration, brain - *see* Laceration,
        brain
    osteopathic 739.0
  bronchus 519.1
  by cicatrix - *see* Cicatrix
  cardiac 423.9
  cauda equina 344.60
    with neurogenic bladder 344.61
  celiac (artery) (axis) 447.4
  cerebral - *see* Compression, brain
  cervical plexus 353.2
  cord (umbilical) - *see* Compression,
    umbilical cord
  cranial nerve 352.9
    second 377.49
    third (partial) 378.51
      total 378.52
    fourth 378.53
    fifth 350.8
    sixth 378.54
    seventh 351.8
  divers' squeeze 993.3
  duodenum (external) (*see also* Obstruc-
    tion, duodenum) 537.3

Compression (*Continued*)
  during birth 767.9
  esophagus 530.3
    congenital, external 750.3
  Eustachian tube 381.63
  facies (congenital) 754.0
  fracture - *see* Fracture, by site
  heart - *see* Disease, heart
  intestine (*see also* Obstruction, intes-
    tine) 560.9
    with hernia - *see* Hernia, by site,
      with obstruction
  laryngeal nerve, recurrent 478.79
  leg NEC 355.8
  lower extremity NEC 355.8
  lumbosacral plexus 353.1
  lung 518.89
  lymphatic vessel 457.1
  medulla - *see* Compression, brain
  nerve NEC - *see also* Disorder, nerve
    arm NEC 354.9
    autonomic nervous system (*see also*
      Neuropathy, peripheral, auto-
      nomic) 337.9
    axillary 353.0
    cranial NEC 352.9
    due to displacement of intervertebral
      disc 722.2
      with myelopathy 722.70
      cervical 722.0
        with myelopathy 722.71
      lumbar, lumbosacral 722.10
        with myelopathy 722.73
      thoracic, thoracolumbar 722.11
        with myelopathy 722.72
    iliohypogastric 355.79
    ilioinguinal 355.79
    leg NEC 355.8
    lower extremity NEC 355.8
    median (in carpal tunnel) 354.0
    obturator 355.79
    optic 377.49
    plantar 355.6
    posterior tibial (in tarsal tunnel)
      355.5
    root (by scar tissue) NEC 724.9
      cervical NEC 723.4
      lumbar NEC 724.4
      lumbosacral 724.4
      thoracic 724.4
    saphenous 355.79
    sciatic (acute) 355.0
    sympathetic 337.9
    traumatic - *see* Injury, nerve
    ulnar 354.2
    upper extremity NEC 354.9
  peripheral - *see* Compression, nerve
  spinal (cord) (old or nontraumatic)
    336.9
    by displacement of intervertebral
      disc - *see* Displacement, inter-
      vertebral disc
    nerve
      root NEC 724.9
        postoperative 722.80
          cervical region 722.81
          lumbar region 722.83
          thoracic region 722.82
        traumatic - *see* Injury, nerve,
          spinal
    traumatic - *see* Injury, nerve, spi-
      nal
    spondylogenic 721.91
      cervical 721.1

Compression (*Continued*)
  spinal (cord) (*Continued*)
    spondylogenic (*Continued*)
      lumbar, lumbosacral 721.42
      thoracic 721.41
    traumatic - *see also* Injury, spinal, by
      site
      with fracture, vertebra - *see* Frac-
        ture, vertebra, by site, with
        spinal cord injury
    spondylogenic - *see* Compression, spi-
      nal cord, spondylogenic
  subcostal nerve (syndrome) 354.8
  sympathetic nerve NEC 337.9
  syndrome 958.5
  thorax 512.8
    iatrogenic 512.1
    postoperative 512.1
  trachea 519.1
    congenital 748.3
  ulnar nerve (by scar tissue) 354.2
  umbilical cord
    affecting fetus or newborn 762.5
      cord prolapsed 762.4
    complicating delivery 663.2
      cord around neck 663.1
      cord prolapsed 663.0
  upper extremity NEC 354.9
  ureter 593.3
  urethra - *see* Stricture, urethra
  vein 459.2
  vena cava (inferior) (superior) 459.2
  vertebral NEC - *see* Compression, spi-
    nal (cord)
Compulsion, compulsive
  eating 307.51
  neurosis (obsessive) 300.3
  personality 301.4
  states (mixed) 300.3
  swearing 300.3
    in Gilles de la Tourette's syndrome
      307.23
  tics and spasms 307.22
  water drinking NEC (syndrome)
    307.9
Concato's disease (pericardial polyserositis) 423.2
  peritoneal 568.82
  pleural - *see* Pleurisy
Concavity, chest wall 738.3
Concealed
  hemorrhage NEC 459.0
  penis 752.65
Concentric fading 368.12
Concern (normal) about sick person in
  family V61.49
Concrescence (teeth) 520.2
Concretio cordis 423.1
  rheumatic 393
Concretion - *see also* Calculus
  appendicular 543.9
  canaliculus 375.57
  clitoris 624.8
  conjunctiva 372.54
  eyelid 374.56
  intestine (impaction) (obstruction)
    560.39
  lacrimal (passages) 375.57
  prepuce (male) 605
    female (clitoris) 624.8
  salivary gland (any) 527.5
  seminal vesicle 608.89
  stomach 537.89
  tonsil 474.8

ICD-9-CM

Vol. 2

Concussion (current) 850.9
  with
    loss of consciousness 850.5
      brief (less than one hour) 850.1
      moderate (1-24 hours) 850.2
      prolonged (more than 24 hours)
        (with complete recovery)
        (with return to pre-existing
          conscious level) 850.3
      without return to pre-existing
        conscious level 850.4
    mental confusion or disorientation
      (without loss of consciousness)
      850.0
      with loss of consciousness - *see*
        Concussion, with, loss of con-
        sciousness
    without loss of consciousness 850.0
  blast (air) (hydraulic) (immersion) (un-
    derwater) 869.0
    with open wound into cavity
      869.1
  abdomen or thorax - *see* Injury, in-
    ternal, by site
  brain - *see* Concussion, brain
  ear (acoustic nerve trauma) 951.5
    with perforation, tympanic mem-
      brane - *see* Wound, open, ear
      drum
  thorax - *see* Injury, internal, intratho-
    racic organs NEC
  brain or cerebral (without skull frac-
    ture) 850.9
  with
    loss of consciousness 850.5
      brief (less than one hour)
        850.1
      moderate (1-24 hours) 850.2
      prolonged (more than 24 hours)
        (with complete recovery)
        (with return to pre-existing
          conscious level) 850.3
      without return to pre-existing
        conscious level 850.4
    mental confusion or disorientation
      (without loss of conscious-
      ness) 850.0
      with loss of consciousness - *see*
        Concussion, brain, with,
        loss of consciousness
    skull fracture - *see* Fracture, skull,
      by site
    without loss of consciousness
      850.0
  cauda equina 952.4
  cerebral - *see* Concussion, brain
  conus medullaris (spine) 952.4
  hydraulic - *see* Concussion, blast
  internal organs - *see* Injury, internal, by
    site
  labyrinth - *see* Injury, intracranial
  ocular 921.3
  osseous labyrinth - *see* Injury, intracra-
    nial
  spinal (cord) - *see also* Injury, spinal,
    by site
    due to
      broken
        back - *see* Fracture, vertebra,
          by site, with spinal cord
          injury
        neck - *see* Fracture, vertebra,
          cervical, with spinal cord
          injury

Concussion (*Continued*)
  spinal (cord) (*Continued*)
    due to (*Continued*)
      fracture, fracture dislocation, or
        compression fracture of spine
        or vertebra - *see* Fracture, ver-
        tebra, by site, with spinal
        cord injury
  syndrome 310.2
  underwater blast - *see* Concussion,
    blast
Condition - *see also* Disease
  psychiatric 298.9
  respiratory NEC 519.9
    acute or subacute NEC 519.9
      due to
        external agent 508.9
          specified type NEC 508.8
          fumes or vapors (chemical) (in-
          halation) 506.3
          radiation 508.0
    chronic NEC 519.9
      due to
        external agent 508.9
          specified type NEC 508.8
          fumes or vapors (chemical) (in-
          halation) 506.4
          radiation 508.1
    due to
      external agent 508.9
        specified type NEC 508.8
      fumes or vapors (chemical) inhala-
        tion 506.9
Conduct disturbance (*see also* Disturbance, conduct) 312.9
  adjustment reaction 309.3
  hyperkinetic 314.2
Condyloma NEC 078.10
  acuminatum 078.11
  gonorrheal 098.0
  latum 091.3
  syphilitic 091.3
    congenital 090.0
  venereal, syphilitic 091.3
Confinement - *see* Delivery
Conflagration - *see also* Burn, by site
  asphyxia (by inhalation of smoke,
    gases, fumes, or vapors) 987.9
    specified agent - *see* Table of Drugs
      and Chemicals
Conflict
  family V61.9
    specified circumstance NEC V61.8
  interpersonal NEC V62.81
  marital V61.10
    involving divorce or estrangement
      V61.0
  parent-child V61.20
  partner V61.10
Confluent - *see* condition
Confusion, confused (mental) (state) (*see*
  also State, confusional) 298.9
  acute 293.0
  epileptic 293.0
  postoperative 293.9
  psychogenic 298.2
  reactive (from emotional stress, psy-
    chological trauma) 298.2
  subacute 293.1
Congelation 991.9
Congenital - *see also* condition
  aortic septum 747.29
  intrinsic factor deficiency 281.0
  malformation - *see* Anomaly

Congestion, congestive (chronic) (passive)
  asphyxia, newborn 768.9
  bladder 596.8
  bowel 569.89
  brain (*see also* Disease, cerebrovascular
    NEC) 437.8
    malarial 084.9
  breast 611.79
  bronchi 519.1
  bronchial tube 519.1
  catarrhal 472.0
  cerebral - *see* Congestion, brain
  cerebrospinal - *see* Congestion, brain
  chest 514
  chill 780.9
    malarial (*see also* Malaria) 084.6
  circulatory NEC 459.9
  conjunctiva 372.71
  due to disturbance of circulation 459.9
  duodenum 537.3
  enteritis - *see* Enteritis
  eye 372.71
  fibrosis syndrome (pelvic) 625.5
  gastroenteritis - *see* Enteritis
  general 799.8
  glottis 476.0
  heart (*see also* Failure, heart, conges-
    tive) 428.0
  hepatic 573.0
  hypostatic (lung) 514
  intestine 569.89
  intracranial - *see* Congestion, brain
  kidney 593.89
  labyrinth 386.50
  larynx 476.0
  liver 573.0
  lung 514
    active or acute (*see also* Pneumonia)
      486
      congenital 770.0
    chronic 514
    hypostatic 514
    idiopathic, acute 518.5
    passive 514
  malaria, malarial (brain) (fever) (*see*
    also Malaria) 084.6
  medulla - *see* Congestion, brain
  nasal 478.1
  orbit, orbital 376.33
    inflammatory (chronic) 376.10
      acute 376.00
  ovary 620.8
  pancreas 577.8
  pelvic, female 625.5
  pleural 511.0
  prostate (active) 602.1
  pulmonary - *see* Congestion, lung
  renal 593.89
  retina 362.89
  seminal vesicle 608.89
  spinal cord 336.1
  spleen 289.51
    chronic 289.51
  stomach 537.89
  trachea 464.11
  urethra 599.84
  uterus 625.5
    with subinvolution 621.1
  viscera 799.8
Congestive - *see* Congestion
Conical
  cervix 622.6
  cornea 371.60
  teeth 520.2

Conjoined twins 759.4
  causing disproportion (fetopelvic) 653.7
Conjugal maladjustment V61.10
  involving divorce or estrangement V61.0
Conjunctiva - *see* condition
Conjunctivitis (exposure) (infectious) (nondiphtheritic) (pneumococcal) (pustular) (staphylococcal) (streptococcal) NEC 372.30
  actinic 370.24
  acute 372.00
    atopic 372.05
    contagious 372.03
    follicular 372.02
    hemorrhagic (viral) 077.4
  adenoviral (acute) 077.3
  allergic (chronic) 372.14
    with hay fever 372.05
  anaphylactic 372.05
  angular 372.03
  Apollo (viral) 077.4
  atopic 372.05
  blennorrhagic (neonatorum) 098.40
  catarrhal 372.03
  chemical 372.05
  chlamydial 077.98
    due to
      Chlamydia trachomatis - *see* Trachoma
      paratrachoma 077.0
  chronic 372.10
    allergic 372.14
    follicular 372.12
    simple 372.11
    specified type NEC 372.14
    vernal 372.13
  diphtheritic 032.81
  due to
    dust 372.05
    enterovirus type 70 077.4
    erythema multiforme 695.1 [372.33]
    filariasis (*see also* Filariasis) 125.9 [372.15]
    mucocutaneous
      disease NEC 372.33
      leishmaniasis 085.5 [372.15]
    Reiter's disease 099.3 [372.33]
    syphilis 095.8 [372.10]
    toxoplasmosis (acquired) 130.1
      congenital (active) 771.2
    trachoma - *see* Trachoma
  dust 372.05
  eczematous 370.31
  epidemic 077.1
    hemorrhagic 077.4
  follicular (acute) 372.02
    adenoviral (acute) 077.3
    chronic 372.12
  glare 370.24
  gonococcal (neonatorum) 098.40
  granular (trachomatous) 076.1
    late effect 139.1
  hemorrhagic (acute) (epidemic) 077.4
  herpetic (simplex) 054.43
    zoster 053.21
  inclusion 077.0
  infantile 771.6
  influenzal 372.03
  Koch-Weeks 372.03
  light 372.05
  medicamentosa 372.05

Conjunctivitis (*Continued*)
  membranous 372.04
  meningococcic 036.89
  Morax-Axenfeld 372.02
  mucopurulent NEC 372.03
  neonatal 771.6
    gonococcal 098.40
  Newcastle's 077.8
  nodosa 360.14
  of Beal 077.3
  parasitic 372.15
    filariasis (*see also* Filariasis) 125.9 [372.15]
    mucocutaneous leishmaniasis 085.5 [372.15]
  Parinaud's 372.02
  petrificans 372.39
  phlyctenular 370.31
  pseudomembranous 372.04
    diphtheritic 032.81
  purulent 372.03
  Reiter's 099.3 [372.33]
  rosacea 695.3 [372.31]
  serous 372.01
    viral 077.99
  simple chronic 372.11
  specified NEC 372.39
  sunlamp 372.04
  swimming pool 077.0
  trachomatous (follicular) 076.1
    acute 076.0
    late effect 139.1
  traumatic NEC 372.39
  tuberculous (*see also* Tuberculosis) 017.3 [370.31]
  tularemic 021.3
  tularensis 021.3
  vernal 372.13
    limbar 372.13 [370.32]
  viral 077.99
    acute hemorrhagic 077.4
    specified NEC 077.8
Conjunctoblepharitis - *see* Conjunctivitis
Conn (-Louis) syndrome (primary aldosteronism) 255.1
Connective tissue - *see* condition
Conradi (-Hünermann) syndrome or disease (chondrodysplasia calcificans congenita) 756.59
Consanguinity V19.7
Consecutive - *see* condition
Consolidated lung (base) - *see* Pneumonia, lobar
Constipation (atonic) (neurogenic) (simple) (spastic) 564.0
  drug induced
    correct substance properly administered 564.0
    overdose or wrong substance given or taken 977.9
      specified drug - *see* Table of Drugs and Chemicals
  neurogenic 564.0
  psychogenic 306.4
Constitutional - *see also* condition
  arterial hypotension (*see also* Hypotension) 458.9
  obesity 278.00
    morbid 278.01
  psychopathic state 301.9
  short stature 783.4
  state, developmental V21.9
    specified development NEC V21.8
  substandard 301.6

Constitutionally substandard 301.6
Constriction
  anomalous, meningeal bands or folds 742.8
  aortic arch (congenital) 747.10
  asphyxiation or suffocation by 994.7
  bronchus 519.1
  canal, ear (*see also* Stricture, ear canal, acquired) 380.50
  duodenum 537.3
  gallbladder (*see also* Obstruction, gallbladder) 575.2
    congenital 751.69
  intestine (*see also* Obstruction, intestine) 560.9
  larynx 478.74
    congenital 748.3
  meningeal bands or folds, anomalous 742.8
  organ or site, congenital NEC - *see* Atresia
  prepuce (congenital) 605
  pylorus 537.0
    adult hypertrophic 537.0
    congenital or infantile 750.5
    newborn 750.5
  ring (uterus) 661.4
    affecting fetus or newborn 763.7
  spastic - *see also* Spasm
    ureter 593.3
    urethra - *see* Stricture, urethra
  stomach 537.89
  ureter 593.3
  urethra - *see* Stricture, urethra
  visual field (functional) (peripheral) 368.45
Constrictive - *see* condition
Consultation V65.9
  medical - *see also* Counseling, medical
  specified reason NEC V65.8
  without complaint or sickness V65.9
    feared complaint unfounded V65.5
    specified reason NEC V65.8
Consumption - *see* Tuberculosis
Contact
  with
    AIDS virus V01.7
    cholera V01.0
    communicable disease V01.9
      specified type NEC V01.8
      viral NEC V01.7
    German measles V01.4
    gonorrhea V01.6
    HIV V01.7
    human immunodeficiency virus V01.7
    parasitic disease NEC V01.8
    poliomyelitis V01.2
    rabies V01.5
    rubella V01.4
    smallpox V01.3
    syphilis V01.6
    tuberculosis V01.1
    venereal disease V01.6
    viral disease NEC V01.7
  dermatitis - *see* Dermatitis
Contamination, food (*see also* Poisoning, food) 005.9
Contraception, contraceptive
  advice NEC V25.09
    family planning V25.09
    fitting of diaphragm V25.02

ICD-9-CM

C

Vol. 2

Contraction, contracture, contracted
(*Continued*)
stomach 536.8
  hourglass 536.8
    congenital 750.7
    psychogenic 306.4
  psychogenic 306.4
tendon (sheath) (*see also* Short, tendon)
  727.81
toe 735.8
ureterovesical orifice (postinfectional)
  593.3
urethra 599.84
uterus 621.8
  abnormal 661.9
    affecting fetus or newborn 763.7
  clonic, hourglass or tetanic 661.4
    affecting fetus or newborn 763.7
  dyscoordinate 661.4
    affecting fetus or newborn 763.7
  hourglass 661.4
    affecting fetus or newborn 763.7
  hypotonic NEC 661.2
    affecting fetus or newborn 763.7
  incoordinate 661.4
    affecting fetus or newborn 763.7
  inefficient or poor 661.2
    affecting fetus or newborn 763.7
  irregular 661.2
    affecting fetus or newborn 763.7
  tetanic 661.4
    affecting fetus or newborn 763.7
vagina (outlet) 623.2
vesical 596.8
  neck or urethral orifice 596.0
visual field, generalized 368.45
Volkmann's (ischemic) 958.6
Contusion (skin surface intact) 924.9
with
  crush injury - *see* Crush
  dislocation - *see* Dislocation, by site
  fracture - *see* Fracture, by site
  internal injury - *see also* Injury, inter-
    nal, by site
    heart - *see* Contusion, cardiac
    kidney - *see* Contusion, kidney
    liver - *see* Contusion, liver
    lung - *see* Contusion, lung
    spleen - *see* Contusion, spleen
  intracranial injury - *see* Injury, intra-
    cranial
  nerve injury - *see* Injury, nerve
  open wound - *see* Wound, open, by
    site
abdomen, abdominal (muscle) (wall)
  922.2
  organ(s) NEC 868.00
adnexa, eye NEC 921.9
ankle 924.21
  with other parts of foot 924.20
arm 923.9
  lower (with elbow) 923.10
  upper 923.03
    with shoulder or axillary region
      923.09
auditory canal (external) (meatus) (and
  other part(s) of neck, scalp, or
  face, except eye) 920
auricle, ear, (and other part(s) of neck,
  scalp, or face except eye) 920
axilla 923.02
  with shoulder or upper arm 923.09
back 922.31
bone NEC 924.9

Contusion (*Continued*)
brain (cerebral) (membrane) (with
  hemorrhage) 851.8

> Note   Use the following fifth-digit
> subclassification with categories 851-
> 854:
>
> 0   unspecified state of conscious-
>   ness
> 1   with no loss of consciousness
> 2   with brief [less than one hour]
>   loss of consciousness
> 3   with moderate [1-24 hours]
>   loss of consciousness
> 4   with prolonged [more than 24
>   hours] loss of consciousness
>   and return to pre-existing con-
>   scious level
> 5   with prolonged [more than 24
>   hours] loss of consciousness,
>   without return to pre-existing
>   conscious level
>
> Use fifth-digit 5 to designate when a
> patient is unconscious and dies be-
> fore regaining consciousness, regard-
> less of the duration of the loss of con-
> sciousness
>
> 6   with loss of consciousness of
>   unspecified duration
> 9   with concussion, unspecified

  with
    open intracranial wound 851.9
    skull fracture - *see* Fracture, skull,
      by site
  cerebellum 851.4
    with open intracranial wound
      851.5
  cortex 851.0
    with open intracranial wound
      851.1
  occipital lobe 851.4
    with open intracranial wound
      851.5
  stem 851.4
    with open intracranial wound
      851.5
breast 922.0
brow (and other part(s) of neck, scalp,
  or face, except eye) 920
buttock 922.32
canthus 921.1
cardiac 861.01
  with open wound into thorax 861.11
cauda equina (spine) 952.4
cerebellum - *see* Contusion, brain, cerebellum
cerebral - *see* Contusion, brain
cheek(s) (and other part(s) of neck,
  scalp, or face, except eye) 920
chest (wall) 922.1
chin (and other part(s) of neck, scalp,
  or face, except eye) 920
clitoris 922.4
conjunctiva 921.1
conus medullaris (spine) 952.4
cornea 921.3
corpus cavernosum 922.4
cortex (brain) (cerebral) - *see* Contusion, brain, cortex
costal region 922.1
ear (and other part(s) of neck, scalp, or
  face except eye) 920

Contusion (*Continued*)
elbow 923.11
  with forearm 923.10
epididymis 922.4
epigastric region 922.2
eye NEC 921.9
eyeball 921.3
eyelid(s) (and periocular area) 921.1
face (and neck, or scalp, any part, except eye) 920
femoral triangle 922.2
fetus or newborn 772.6
finger(s) (nail) (subungual) 923.3
flank 922.2
foot (with ankle) (excluding toe(s))
  924.20
forearm (and elbow) 923.10
forehead (and other part(s) of neck,
  scalp, or face, except eye) 920
genital organs, external 922.4
globe (eye) 921.3
groin 922.2
gum(s) (and other part(s) of neck,
  scalp, or face, except eye) 920
hand(s) (except fingers alone) 923.20
head (any part, except eye) (and face)
  (and neck) 920
heart - *see* Contusion, cardiac
heel 924.20
hip 924.01
  with thigh 924.00
iliac region 922.2
inguinal region 922.2
internal organs (abdomen, chest, or
  pelvis) NEC - *see* Injury, internal,
  by site
interscapular region 922.33
iris (eye) 921.3
kidney 866.01
  with open wound into cavity 866.11
knee 924.11
  with lower leg 924.10
labium (majus) (minus) 922.4
lacrimal apparatus, gland, or sac 921.1
larynx (and other part(s) of neck,
  scalp, or face, except eye) 920
late effect - *see* Late, effects (of), contusion
leg 924.5
  lower (with knee) 924.10
lens 921.3
lingual (and other part(s) of neck,
  scalp, or face, except eye) 920
lip(s) (and other part(s) of neck, scalp,
  or face, except eye) 920
liver 864.01
  with
    laceration - *see* Laceration, liver
    open wound into cavity 864.11
lower extremity 924.5
  multiple sites 924.4
lumbar region 922.31
lung 861.21
  with open wound into thorax
    861.31
malar region (and other part(s) of
  neck, scalp, or face, except eye)
  920
mandibular joint (and other part(s) of
  neck, scalp, or face, except eye)
  920
mastoid region (and other part(s) of
  neck, scalp, or face, except eye)
  920

ICD-9-CM

Vol. 2

Corbus' disease 607.1
Cord - *see also* condition
  around neck (tightly) (with compression)
    affecting fetus or newborn 762.5
    complicating delivery 663.1
      without compression 663.3
        affecting fetus or newborn 762.6
  bladder NEC 344.61
    tabetic 094.0
  prolapse
    affecting fetus or newborn 762.4
    complicating delivery 663.0
Cord's angiopathy (*see also* Tuberculosis) 017.3 *[362.18]*
Cordis ectopia 746.87
Corditis (spermatic) 608.4
Corectopia 743.46
Cori type glycogen storage disease - *see* Disease, glycogen storage
Cork-handlers' disease or lung 495.3
Corkscrew esophagus 530.5
Corlett's pyosis (impetigo) 684
Corn (infected) 700
Cornea - *see also* condition
  donor V59.5
  guttata (dystrophy) 371.57
  plana 743.41
Cornelia de Lange's syndrome (Amsterdam dwarf, mental retardation, and brachycephaly) 759.89
Cornual gestation or pregnancy - *see* Pregnancy, cornual
Cornu cutaneum 702.8
Coronary (artery) - *see also* condition
  arising from aorta or pulmonary trunk 746.85
Corpora - *see also* condition
  amylacea (prostate) 602.8
  cavernosa - *see* condition
Corpulence (*see* Obesity)
Corpus - *see* condition
Corrigan's disease - *see* Insufficiency, aortic
Corrosive burn - *see* Burn, by site
Corsican fever (*see also* Malaria) 084.6
Cortical - *see also* condition
  blindness 377.75
  necrosis, kidney (bilateral) 583.6
Corticoadrenal - *see* condition
Corticosexual syndrome 255.2
Coryza (acute) 460
  with grippe or influenza 487.1
  syphilitic 095.8
    congenital (chronic) 090.0
Costen's syndrome or complex 524.60
Costiveness (*see also* Constipation) 564.0
Costochondritis 733.6
Cotard's syndrome (paranoia) 297.1
Cot death 798.0
Cotungo's disease 724.3
Cough 786.2
  with hemorrhage (*see also* Hemoptysis) 786.3
  affected 786.2
  bronchial 786.2
    with grippe or influenza 487.1
  chronic 786.2
  epidemic 786.2
  functional 306.1
  hemorrhagic 786.3
  hysterical 300.11
  laryngeal, spasmodic 786.2

Cough (*Continued*)
  nervous 786.2
  psychogenic 306.1
  smokers' 491.0
  tea tasters' 112.89
Counseling NEC V65.40
  without complaint or sickness V65.49
  abuse victim NEC V62.89
    child V61.21
    partner V61.11
    spouse V61.11
  child abuse, maltreatment, or neglect V61.21
  contraceptive NEC V25.09
    device (intrauterine) V25.02
    maintenance V25.40
      intrauterine contraceptive device V25.42
      oral contraceptive (pill) V25.41
      specified type NEC V25.49
      subdermal implantable V25.43
    management NEC V25.9
    oral contraceptive (pill) V25.01
    prescription NEC V25.02
      oral contraceptive (pill) V25.01
        repeat prescription V25.41
      repeat prescription V25.40
    subdermal implantable V25.43
    surveillance NEC V25.40
  dietary V65.3
  exercise V65.41
  explanation of
    investigation finding NEC V65.49
    medication NEC V65.49
  family planning V25.09
  for nonattending third party V65.1
  genetic V26.3
  gonorrhea V65.45
  health (advice) (education) (instruction) NEC V65.49
  HIV V65.44
  human immunodeficiency virus V65.44
  injury prevention V65.43
  marital V61.10
  medical (for) V65.9
    boarding school resident V60.6
    condition not demonstrated V65.5
    feared complaint and no disease found V65.5
    institutional resident V60.1
    on behalf of another V65.1
    person living alone V60.3
  parent-child conflict V61.20
    specified problem NEC V61.29
  partner abuse
    perpetrator V61.12
    victim V61.11
  perpetrator of
    child abuse V62.83
      parental V61.22
    partner abuse V61.12
    spouse abuse V61.12
  procreative V65.49
  sex NEC V65.49
    transmitted disease NEC V65.45
      HIV V65.44
  specified reason NEC V65.49
  spousal abuse
    perpetrator V61.12
    victim V61.11
  substance use and abuse V65.42
  syphilis V65.45

Counseling NEC (*Continued*)
  victim (of)
    abuse NEC V62.89
    child abuse V61.21
    partner abuse V61.11
    spousal abuse V61.11
Coupled rhythm 427.89
Couvelaire uterus (complicating delivery) - *see* Placenta, separation
Cowper's gland - *see* condition
Cowperitis (*see also* Urethritis) 597.89
  gonorrheal (acute) 098.0
    chronic or duration of 2 months or over 098.2
Cowpox (abortive) 051.0
  due to vaccination 999.0
  eyelid 051.0 *[373.5]*
    postvaccination 999.0 *[373.5]*
Coxa
  plana 732.1
  valga (acquired) 736.31
    congenital 755.61
    late effect of rickets 268.1
  vara (acquired) 736.32
    congenital 755.62
    late effect of rickets 268.1
Coxae malum senilis 715.25
Coxalgia (nontuberculous) 719.45
  tuberculous (*see also* Tuberculosis) 015.1 *[730.85]*
Coxalgic pelvis 736.30
Coxitis 716.65
Coxsackie (infection) (virus) 079.2
  central nervous system NEC 048
  endocarditis 074.22
  enteritis 008.67
  meningitis (aseptic) 047.0
  myocarditis 074.23
  pericarditis 074.21
  pharyngitis 074.0
  pleurodynia 074.1
  specific disease NEC 074.8
Crabs, meaning pubic lice 132.2
Crack baby 760.75
Cracked nipple 611.2
  puerperal, postpartum 676.1
Cradle cap 690.11
Craft neurosis 300.89
Craigiasis 007.8
Cramp(s) 729.82
  abdominal 789.0
  bathing 994.1
  colic 789.0
    psychogenic 306.4
  due to immersion 994.1
  extremity (lower) (upper) NEC 729.82
  fireman 992.2
  heat 992.2
  hysterical 300.11
  immersion 994.1
  intestinal 789.0
    psychogenic 306.4
  linotypists' 300.89
    organic 333.84
  muscle (extremity) (general) 729.82
    due to immersion 994.1
    hysterical 300.11
  occupational (hand) 300.89
    organic 333.84
  psychogenic 307.89
  salt depletion 276.1
  stoker 992.2
  stomach 789.0

Cramp(s) *(Continued)*
 telegraphers' 300.89
  organic 333.84
 typists' 300.89
  organic 333.84
 uterus 625.8
  menstrual 625.3
 writers' 300.89
  organic 333.84
Cranial - *see* condition
Cranioclasis, fetal 763.89 ◄
Craniocleidodysostosis 755.59
Craniofenestria (skull) 756.0
Craniolacunia (skull) 756.0
Craniopagus 759.4
Craniopathy, metabolic 733.3
Craniopharyngeal - *see* condition
Craniopharyngioma (M9350/1) 237.0
Craniorachischisis (totalis) 740.1
Cranioschisis 756.0
Craniostenosis 756.0
Craniosynostosis 756.0
Craniotabes (cause unknown) 733.3
 rachitic 268.1
 syphilitic 090.5
Craniotomy, fetal 763.89 ◄▮▮
Cranium - *see* condition
Craw-craw 125.3
Creaking joint 719.60
 ankle 719.67
 elbow 719.62
 foot 719.67
 hand 719.64
 hip 719.65
 knee 719.66
 multiple sites 719.69
 pelvic region 719.65
 shoulder (region) 719.61
 specified site NEC 719.68
 wrist 719.63
Creeping
 eruption 126.9
 palsy 335.21
 paralysis 335.21
Crenated tongue 529.8
Creotoxism 005.9
Crepitus
 caput 756.0
 joint 719.60
  ankle 719.67
  elbow 719.62
  foot 719.67
  hand 719.64
  hip 719.65
  knee 719.66
  multiple sites 719.69
  pelvic region 719.65
  shoulder (region) 719.61
  specified site NEC 719.68
  wrist 719.63
Crescent or conus choroid, congenital
 743.57
Cretin, cretinism (athyrotic) (congenital)
 (endemic) (metabolic) (nongoitrous)
 (sporadic) 243
 goitrous (sporadic) 246.1
 pelvis (dwarf type) (male type) 243
  with disproportion (fetopelvic)
   653.1
   affecting fetus or newborn 763.1
   causing obstructed labor 660.1
    affecting fetus or newborn 763.1
 pituitary 253.3
Cretinoid degeneration 243

Creutzfeldt-Jakob disease (syndrome)
 046.1
 with dementia 046.1 *[294.1]*
Crib death 798.0
Cribriform hymen 752.49
Cri-du-chat syndrome 758.3
Crigler-Najjar disease or syndrome (congenital hyperbilirubinemia) 277.4
Crimean hemorrhagic fever 065.0
Criminalism 301.7
Crisis
 abdomen 789.0
 addisonian (acute adrenocortical insufficiency) 255.4
 adrenal (cortical) 255.4
 asthmatic - *see* Asthma
 brain, cerebral (*see also* Disease, cerebrovascular, acute) 436
 celiac 579.0
 Dietl's 593.4
 emotional NEC 309.29
  acute reaction to stress 308.0
  adjustment reaction 309.9
  specific to childhood and adolescence 313.9
 gastric (tabetic) 094.0
 glaucomatocyclitic 364.22
 heart (*see also* Failure, heart) 428.9
 hypertensive - *see* Hypertension
 nitritoid
  correct substance properly administered 458.2
  overdose or wrong substance given
   or taken 961.1
 oculogyric 378.87
  psychogenic 306.7
 Pel's 094.0
 psychosexual identity 302.6
 rectum 094.0
 renal 593.81
 sickle cell 282.62
 stomach (tabetic) 094.0
 tabetic 094.0
 thyroid (*see also* Thyrotoxicosis) 242.9
 thyrotoxic (*see also* Thyrotoxicosis)
  242.9
 vascular - *see* Disease, cerebrovascular,
  acute
Crocq's disease (acrocyanosis) 443.89
Crohn's disease (*see also* Enteritis, regional) 555.9
Cronkhite-Canada syndrome 211.3
Crooked septum, nasal 470
Cross
 birth (of fetus) complicating delivery
  652.3
  with successful version 652.1
  causing obstructed labor 660.0
 bite, anterior or posterior 524.2
 eye (*see also* Esotropia) 378.00
Crossed ectopia of kidney 753.3
Crossfoot 754.50
Croup, croupous (acute) (angina) (catarrhal) (infective) (inflammatory)
 (laryngeal) (membranous) (nondiphtheritic) (pseudomembranous) 464.4
 asthmatic (*see also* Asthma) 493.9
 bronchial 466.0
 diphtheritic (membranous) 032.3
 false 478.75
 spasmodic 478.75
  diphtheritic 032.3
 stridulous 478.75
  diphtheritic 032.3

Crouzon's disease (craniofacial dysostosis) 756.0
Crowding, teeth 524.3
CRST syndrome (cutaneous systemic
 sclerosis) 710.1
Cruchet's disease (encephalitis lethargica) 049.8
Cruelty in children (*see also* Disturbance,
 conduct) 312.9
Crural ulcer (*see also* Ulcer, lower extremity) 707.1
Crush, crushed, crushing (injury) 929.9
 with
  fracture - *see* Fracture, by site
 abdomen 926.19
  internal - *see* Injury, internal, abdomen
 ankle 928.21
  with other parts of foot 928.20
 arm 927.9
  lower (and elbow) 927.10
  upper 927.03
   with shoulder or axillary region
    927.09
 axilla 927.02
  with shoulder or upper arm 927.09
 back 926.11
 breast 926.19
 buttock 926.12
 cheek 925.1
 chest - *see* Injury, internal, chest
 ear 925.1
 elbow 927.11
  with forearm 927.10
 face 925.1
 finger(s) 927.3
  with hand(s) 927.20
   and wrist(s) 927.21
 flank 926.19
 foot, excluding toe(s) alone (with ankle) 928.20
 forearm (and elbow) 927.10
 genitalia, external (female) (male) 926.0
  internal - *see* Injury, internal, genital
   organ NEC
 hand, except finger(s) alone (and
  wrist) 927.20
 head - *see* Fracture, skull, by site
 heel 928.20
 hip 928.01
  with thigh 928.00
 internal organ (abdomen, chest, or pelvis) - *see* Injury, internal, by site
 knee 928.11
  with leg, lower 928.10
 labium (majus) (minus) 926.0
 larynx 925.2
 late effect - *see* Late, effects (of), crushing
 leg 928.9
  lower 928.10
   and knee 928.11
  upper 928.00
 limb
  lower 928.9
   multiple sites 928.8
  upper 927.9
   multiple sites 927.8
 multiple sites NEC 929.0
 neck 925.2
 nerve - *see* Injury, nerve, by site
 nose 802.0
  open 802.1
 penis 926.0

ICD-9-CM

Vol. 2

Cyst *(Continued)*

> Note   In general, cysts are not neo-
> plastic and are classified to the ap-
> propriate category for disease of the
> specified anatomical site. This gener-
> alization does not apply to certain
> types of cysts which are neoplastic in
> nature, for example, dermoid, nor
> does it apply to cysts of certain struc-
> tures, for example, branchial cleft,
> which are classified as developmental
> anomalies.
>
> The following listing includes some
> of the most frequently reported sites
> of cysts as well as qualifiers which
> indicate the type of cyst. The latter
> qualifiers usually are not repeated
> under the anatomical sites. Since the
> code assignment for a given site may
> vary depending upon the type of
> cyst, the coder should refer to the
> listings under the specified type of
> cyst before consideration is given to
> the site.

accessory, fallopian tube 752.11
adenoid (infected) 474.8
adrenal gland 255.8
   congenital 759.1
air, lung 518.89
allantoic 753.7
alveolar process (jaw bone) 526.2
amnion, amniotic 658.8
anterior chamber (eye) 364.60
   exudative 364.62
   implantation (surgical) (traumatic)
      364.61
   parasitic 360.13
anterior nasopalatine 526.1
antrum 478.1
anus 569.49
apical (periodontal) (tooth) 522.8
appendix 543.9
arachnoid, brain 348.0
arytenoid 478.79
auricle 706.2
Baker's (knee) 727.51
   tuberculous (*see also* Tuberculosis)
      015.2
Bartholin's gland or duct 616.2
bile duct (*see also* Disease, biliary)
   576.8
bladder (multiple) (trigone) 596.8
Blessig's 362.62
blood, endocardial (*see also* Endocarditis) 424.90
blue dome 610.0
bone (local) 733.20
   aneurysmal 733.22
   jaw 526.2
      developmental (odontogenic)
        526.0
      fissural 526.1
      latent 526.89
   solitary 733.21
   unicameral 733.21
brain 348.0
   congenital 742.4
   hydatid (*see also* Echinococcus)
      122.9
   third ventricle (colloid) 742.4
branchial (cleft) 744.42
branchiogenic 744.42

Cyst *(Continued)*

breast (benign) (blue dome) (pedunculated) (solitary) (traumatic) 610.0
   involution 610.4
   sebaceous 610.8
broad ligament (benign) 620.8
   embryonic 752.11
bronchogenic (mediastinal) (sequestration) 518.89
   congenital 748.4
buccal 528.4
bulbourethral gland (Cowper's) 599.89
bursa, bursal 727.49
   pharyngeal 478.26
calcifying odontogenic (M9301/0) 213.1
   upper jaw (bone) 213.0
canal of Nuck (acquired) (serous) 629.1
   congenital 752.41
canthus 372.75
carcinomatous (M8010/3) - *see* Neoplasm, by site, malignant
cartilage (joint) - *see* Derangement,
   joint
cauda equina 336.8
cavum septi pellucidi NEC 348.0
celomic (pericardium) 746.89
cerebellopontine (angle) - *see* Cyst,
   brain
cerebellum - *see* Cyst, brain
cerebral - *see* Cyst, brain
cervical lateral 744.42
cervix 622.8
   embryonal 752.41
   nabothian (gland) 616.0
chamber, anterior (eye) 364.60
   exudative 364.62
   implantation (surgical) (traumatic)
      364.61
   parasitic 360.13
chiasmal, optic NEC (*see also* Lesion,
   chiasmal) 377.54
chocolate (ovary) 617.1
choledochal (congenital) 751.69
   acquired 576.8
choledochus 751.69
chorion 658.8
choroid plexus 348.0
chyle, mesentery 457.8
ciliary body 364.60
   exudative 364.64
   implantation 364.61
   primary 364.63
clitoris 624.8
coccyx (*see also* Cyst, bone) 733.20
colloid
   third ventricle (brain) 742.4
   thyroid gland - *see* Goiter
colon 569.89
common (bile) duct (*see also* Disease,
   biliary) 576.8
congenital NEC 759.89
   adrenal glands 759.1
   epiglottis 748.3
   esophagus 750.4
   fallopian tube 752.11
   kidney 753.10
      multiple 753.19
      single 753.11
   larynx 748.3
   liver 751.62
   lung 748.4
   mediastinum 748.8
   ovary 752.0
   oviduct 752.11

Cyst *(Continued)*

congenital NEC *(Continued)*
   pancreas 751.7
   periurethral (tissue) 753.8
   prepuce NEC 752.69
      penis 752.69
   sublingual 750.26
   submaxillary gland 750.26
   thymus (gland) 759.2
   tongue 750.19
   ureterovesical orifice 753.4
   vulva 752.41
conjunctiva 372.75
cornea 371.23
corpora quadrigemina 348.0
corpus
   albicans (ovary) 620.2
   luteum (ruptured) 620.1
Cowper's gland (benign) (infected)
   599.89
cranial meninges 348.0
craniobuccal pouch 253.8
craniopharyngeal pouch 253.8
cystic duct (*see also* Disease, gallbladder) 575.8
Cysticercus (any site) 123.1
Dandy-Walker 742.3
   with spina bifida (*see also* Spina bi-
      fida) 741.0
dental 522.8
   developmental 526.0
   eruption 526.0
   lateral periodontal 526.0
   primordial (keratocyst) 526.0
   root 522.8
dentigerous 526.0
   mandible 526.0
   maxilla 526.0
dermoid (M9084/0) - *see also* Neoplasm, by site, benign
   with malignant transformation
      (M9084/3) 183.0
   implantation
      external area or site (skin) NEC
        709.8
      iris 364.61
      skin 709.8
      vagina 623.8
      vulva 624.8
   mouth 528.4
   oral soft tissue 528.4
   sacrococcygeal 685.1
      with abscess 685.0
developmental of ovary, ovarian 752.0
dura (cerebral) 348.0
   spinal 349.2
ear (external) 706.2
echinococcal (*see also* Echinococcus)
   122.9
embryonal
   cervix uteri 752.41
   genitalia, female external 752.41
   uterus 752.3
   vagina 752.41
endometrial 621.8
   ectopic 617.9
endometrium (uterus) 621.8
   ectopic - *see* Endometriosis
enteric 751.5
enterogenous 751.5
epidermal (inclusion) (*see also* Cyst,
   skin) 706.2
epidermoid (inclusion) (*see also* Cyst,
   skin) 706.2

Cyst *(Continued)*
  epidermoid *(Continued)*
    mouth 528.4
    not of skin - *see* Cyst, by site
    oral soft tissue 528.4
  epididymis 608.89
  epiglottis 478.79
  epiphysis cerebri 259.8
  epithelial (inclusion) *(see also* Cyst, skin) 706.2
  epoophoron 752.11
  eruption 526.0
  esophagus 530.89
  ethmoid sinus 478.1
  eye (retention) 379.8
    congenital 743.03
    posterior segment, congenital 743.54
  eyebrow 706.2
  eyelid (sebaceous) 374.84
    infected 373.13
    sweat glands or ducts 374.84
  falciform ligament (inflammatory) 573.8
  fallopian tube 620.8
  female genital organs NEC 629.8
  fimbrial (congenital) 752.11
  fissural (oral region) 526.1
  follicle (atretic) (graafian) (ovarian) 620.0
    nabothian (gland) 616.0
  follicular (atretic) (ovarian) 620.0
    dentigerous 526.0
  frontal sinus 478.1
  gallbladder or duct 575.8
  ganglion 727.43
  Gartner's duct 752.11
  gas, of mesentery 568.89
  gingiva 523.8
  gland of moll 374.84
  globulomaxillary 526.1
  graafian follicle 620.0
  granulosal lutein 620.2
  hemangiomatous (M9121/0) *(see also* Hemangioma) 228.00
  hydatid *(see also* Echinococcus) 122.9
    fallopian tube (Morgagni) 752.11
    liver NEC 122.8
    lung NEC 122.9
    Morgagni 752.8
      fallopian tube 752.11
    specified site NEC 122.9
  hymen 623.8
    embryonal 752.41
  hypopharynx 478.26
  hypophysis, hypophyseal (duct) (recurrent) 253.8
    cerebri 253.8
  implantation (dermoid)
    anterior chamber (eye) 364.61
    external area or site (skin) NEC 709.8
    iris 364.61
    vagina 623.8
    vulva 624.8
  incisor, incisive canal 526.1
  inclusion (epidermal) (epithelial) (epidermoid) (mucous) (squamous) *(see also* Cyst, skin) 706.2
    not of skin - *see* Neoplasm, by site, benign
  intestine (large) (small) 569.89
  intracranial - *see* Cyst, brain

Cyst *(Continued)*
  intraligamentous 728.89
    knee 717.89
  intrasellar 253.8
  iris (idiopathic) 364.60
    exudative 364.62
    implantation (surgical) (traumatic) 364.61
    miotic pupillary 364.55
    parasitic 360.13
  Iwanoff's 362.62
  jaw (bone) (aneurysmal) (extravasation) (hemorrhagic) (traumatic) 526.2
    developmental (odontogenic) 526.0
    fissural 526.1
  keratin 706.2
  kidney (congenital) 753.10
    acquired 593.2
    calyceal *(see also* Hydronephrosis) 591
    multiple 753.19
    pyelogenic *(see also* Hydronephrosis) 591
    simple 593.2
    single 753.11
    solitary (not congenital) 593.2
  labium (majus) (minus) 624.8
    sebaceous 624.8
  lacrimal
    apparatus 375.43
    gland or sac 375.12
  larynx 478.79
  lens 379.39
    congenital 743.39
  lip (gland) 528.5
  liver 573.8
    congenital 751.62
    hydatid *(see also* Echinococcus) 122.8
      granulosis 122.0
      multilocularis 122.5
  lung 518.89
    congenital 748.4
    giant bullous 492.0
  lutein 620.1
  lymphangiomatous (M9173/0) 228.1
  lymphoepithelial
    mouth 528.4
    oral soft tissue 528.4
  macula 362.54
  malignant (M8000/3) - *see* Neoplasm, by site, malignant
  mammary gland (sweat gland) *(see also* Cyst, breast) 610.0
  mandible 526.2
    dentigerous 526.0
    radicular 522.8
  maxilla 526.2
    dentigerous 526.0
    radicular 522.8
  median
    anterior maxillary 526.1
    palatal 526.1
  mediastinum (congenital) 748.8
  meibomian (gland) (retention) 373.2
    infected 373.12
  membrane, brain 348.0
  meninges (cerebral) 348.0
    spinal 349.2
  meniscus knee 717.5
  mesentery, mesenteric (gas) 568.89
    chyle 457.8
    gas 568.89

Cyst *(Continued)*
  mesonephric duct 752.8
  mesothelial
    peritoneum 568.89
    pleura (peritoneal) 568.89
  milk 611.5
  miotic pupillary (iris) 364.55
  Morgagni (hydatid) 752.8
    fallopian tube 752.11
  mouth 528.4
  mullerian duct 752.8
  multilocular (ovary) (M8000/1) 239.5
  myometrium 621.8
  nabothian (follicle) (ruptured) 616.0
  nasal sinus 478.1
  nasoalveolar 528.4
  nasolabial 528.4
  nasopalatine (duct) 526.1
    anterior 526.1
  nasopharynx 478.26
  neoplastic (M8000/1) - *see also* Neoplasm, by site, unspecified nature
    benign (M8000/0) - *see* Neoplasm, by site, benign
    uterus 621.8
  nervous system - *see* Cyst, brain
  neuroenteric 742.59
  neuroepithelial ventricle 348.0
  nipple 610.0
  nose 478.1
    skin of 706.2
  odontogenic, developmental 526.0
  omentum (lesser) 568.89
    congenital 751.8
  oral soft tissue (dermoid) (epidermoid) (lymphoepithelial) 528.4
  ora serrata 361.19
  orbit 376.81
  ovary, ovarian (twisted) 620.2
    adherent 620.2
    chocolate 617.1
    corpus
      albicans 620.2
      luteum 620.1
    dermoid (M9084/0) 220
    developmental 752.0
    due to failure of involution NEC 620.2
    endometrial 617.1
    follicular (atretic) (graafian) (hemorrhagic) 620.0
    hemorrhagic 620.2
    in pregnancy or childbirth 654.4
      affecting fetus or newborn 763.89
      causing obstructed labor 660.2
        affecting fetus or newborn 763.1
    multilocular (M8000/1) 239.5
    pseudomucinous (M8470/0) 220
    retention 620.2
    serous 620.2
    theca lutein 620.2
    tuberculous *(see also* Tuberculosis) 016.6
    unspecified 620.2
  oviduct 620.8
  palatal papilla (jaw) 526.1
  palate 526.1
    fissural 526.1
    median (fissural) 526.1
  palatine, of papilla 526.1
  pancreas, pancreatic 577.2
    congenital 751.7

Cystadenocarcinoma *(Continued)*
 papillary *(Continued)*
  pseudomucinous (M8471/3)
   specified site - *see* Neoplasm, by
    site, malignant
   unspecified site 183.0
  serous (M8460/3)
   specified site - *see* Neoplasm, by
    site, malignant
   unspecified site 183.0
  specified site - *see* Neoplasm, by site,
   malignant
  unspecified 183.0
 pseudomucinous (M8470/3)
  papillary (M8471/3)
   specified site - *see* Neoplasm, by
    site, malignant
   unspecified site 183.0
  specified site - *see* Neoplasm, by site,
   malignant
  unspecified site 183.0
 serous (M8441/3)
  papillary (M8460/3)
   specified site - *see* Neoplasm, by
    site, malignant
   unspecified site 183.0
  specified site - *see* Neoplasm, by site,
   malignant
  unspecified site 183.0
Cystadenofibroma (M9013/0)
 clear cell (M8313/0) - *see* Neoplasm,
  by site, benign
 endometrioid (M8381/0) 220
  borderline malignancy (M8381/1)
   236.2
  malignant (M8381/3) 183.0
 mucinous (M9015/0)
  specified site - *see* Neoplasm, by site,
   benign
  unspecified site 220
 serous (M9014/0)
  specified site - *see* Neoplasm, by site,
   benign
  unspecified site 220
 specified site - *see* Neoplasm, by site,
  benign
 unspecified site 220
Cystadenoma (M8440/0) - *see also* Neoplasm, by site, benign
 bile duct (M8161/0) 211.5
 endometrioid (M8380/0) - *see also*
  Neoplasm, by site, benign
  borderline malignancy (M8380/1) -
   see Neoplasm, by site, uncertain
   behavior
 malignant (M8440/3) - *see* Neoplasm,
  by site, malignant
 mucinous (M8470/0)
  borderline malignancy (M8470/1)
   specified site - *see* Neoplasm, by
    site, uncertain behavior
   unspecified site 236.2
  papillary (M8471/0)
   borderline malignancy (M8471/1)
    specified site - *see* Neoplasm, by
     site, uncertain behavior
    unspecified site 236.2
   specified site - *see* Neoplasm, by
    site, benign
   unspecified site 220
  specified site - *see* Neoplasm, by site,
   benign
  unspecified site 220
 papillary (M8450/0)

Cystadenoma *(Continued)*
 papillary *(Continued)*
  borderline malignancy (M8450/1)
   specified site - *see* Neoplasm, by
    site, uncertain behavior
   unspecified site 236.2
  lymphomatosum (M8561/0) 210.2
  mucinous (M8471/0)
   borderline malignancy (M8471/1)
    specified site - *see* Neoplasm, by
     site, uncertain behavior
    unspecified site 236.2
   specified site - *see* Neoplasm, by
    site, benign
   unspecified site 220
  pseudomucinous (M8471/0)
   borderline malignancy (M8471/1)
    specified site - *see* Neoplasm, by
     site, uncertain behavior
    unspecified site 236.2
   specified site - *see* Neoplasm, by
    site, benign
   unspecified site 220
  serous (M8460/0)
   borderline malignancy (M8460/1)
    specified site - *see* Neoplasm, by
     site, uncertain behavior
    unspecified site 236.2
   specified site - *see* Neoplasm, by
    site, benign
   unspecified site 220
 specified site - *see* Neoplasm, by site,
  benign
 unspecified site 220
 pseudomucinous (M8470/0)
  borderline malignancy (M8470/1)
   specified site - *see* Neoplasm, by
    site, uncertain behavior
   unspecified site 236.2
  papillary (M8471/0)
   borderline malignancy (M8471/1)
    specified site - *see* Neoplasm, by
     site, uncertain behavior
    unspecified site 236.2
   specified site - *see* Neoplasm, by
    site, benign
   unspecified site 220
  specified site - *see* Neoplasm, by site,
   benign
  unspecified site 220
 serous (M8441/0)
  borderline malignancy (M8441/1)
   specified site - *see* Neoplasm, by
    site, uncertain behavior
   unspecified site 236.2
  papillary (M8460/0)
   borderline malignancy (M8460/1)
    specified site - *see* Neoplasm, by
     site, uncertain behavior
    unspecified site 236.2
   specified site - *see* Neoplasm, by
    site, benign
   unspecified site 220
  specified site - *see* Neoplasm, by site,
   benign
  unspecified site 220
 thyroid 226
Cystathioninemia 270.4
Cystathioninuria 270.4
Cystic - *see also* condition
 breast, chronic 610.1
 corpora lutea 620.1
 degeneration, congenital
  brain 742.4

Cystic *(Continued)*
 degeneration, congenital *(Continued)*
  kidney (*see also* Cystic, disease, kidney) 753.10
 disease
  breast, chronic 610.1
  kidney, congenital 753.10
   medullary 753.16
   multiple 753.19
   polycystic - *see* Polycystic, kidney
   single 753.11
   specified NEC 753.19
  liver, congenital 751.62
  lung 518.89
   congenital 748.4
  pancreas, congenital 751.7
  semilunar cartilage 717.5
 duct - *see* condition
 eyeball, congenital 743.03
 fibrosis (pancreas) 277.00
 hygroma (M9173/0) 228.1
 kidney, congenital 753.10
  medullary 753.16
  multiple 753.19
  polycystic - *see* Polycystic, kidney
  single 753.11
  specified NEC 753.19
 liver, congenital 751.62
 lung 518.89
  congenital 748.4
 mass - *see* Cyst
 mastitis, chronic 610.1
 ovary 620.2
 pancreas, congenital 751.7
Cysticerciasis 123.1
Cysticercosis (mammary) (subretinal)
  123.1
Cysticercus 123.1
 cellulosae infestation 123.1
Cystinosis (malignant) 270.0
Cystinuria 270.0
Cystitis (bacillary) (colli) (diffuse) (exudative) (hemorrhagic) (purulent) (recurrent) (septic) (suppurative) (ulcerative) 595.9
 with
  abortion - *see* Abortion, by type,
   with urinary tract infection
  ectopic pregnancy (*see also* categories
   633.0-633.9) 639.8
  fibrosis 595.1
  leukoplakia 595.1
  malakoplakia 595.1
  metaplasia 595.1
  molar pregnancy (*see also* categories
   630-632) 639.8
 actinomycotic 039.8 *[595.4]*
 acute 595.0
  of trigone 595.3
 allergic 595.89
 amebic 006.8 *[595.4]*
 bilharzial 120.9 *[595.4]*
 blennorrhagic (acute) 098.11
  chronic or duration of 2 months or
   more 098.31
 bullous 595.89
 calculous 594.1
 chlamydial 099.53
 chronic 595.2
  interstitial 595.1
  of trigone 595.3
 complicating pregnancy, childbirth, or
  puerperium 646.6
  affecting fetus or newborn 760.1

ICD-9-CM

c

Vol. 2

Cystitis *(Continued)*
  cystic(a) 595.81
  diphtheritic 032.84
  echinococcal
    glanulosus 122.3 *[595.4]*
    multilocularis 122.6 *[595.4]*
  emphysematous 595.89
  encysted 595.81
  follicular 595.3
  following
    abortion 639.8
    ectopic or molar pregnancy 639.8
  gangrenous 595.89
  glandularis 595.89
  gonococcal (acute) 098.11
    chronic or duration of 2 months or
      more 098.31
  incrusted 595.89
  interstitial 595.1
  irradiation 595.82
  irritation 595.89
  malignant 595.89
  monilial 112.2
  of trigone 595.3
  panmural 595.1
  polyposa 595.89
  prostatic 601.3
  radiation 595.82
  Reiter's (abacterial) 099.3
  specified NEC 595.89
  subacute 595.2

Cystitis *(Continued)*
  submucous 595.1
  syphilitic 095.8
  trichomoniasis 131.09
  tuberculous *(see also* Tuberculosis)
    016.1
  ulcerative 595.1
Cystocele (-rectocele)
  female (without uterine prolapse)
    618.0
    with uterine prolapse 618.4
      complete 618.3
      incomplete 618.2
  in pregnancy or childbirth 654.4
    affecting fetus or newborn
      763.89
    causing obstructed labor 660.2
      affecting fetus or newborn 763.1
  male 596.8
Cystoid
  cicatrix limbus 372.64
  degeneration, macula 362.53
Cystolithiasis 594.1
Cystoma (M8440/0) - *see also* Neoplasm,
  by site, benign
  endometrial, ovary 617.1
  mucinous (M8470/0)
    specified site - *see* Neoplasm, by site,
      benign
    unspecified site 220
  serous (M8441/0)

Cystoma *(Continued)*
  serous *(Continued)*
    specified site - *see* Neoplasm, by site,
      benign
    unspecified site 220
  simple (ovary) 620.2
Cystoplegia 596.53
Cystoptosis 596.8
Cystopyelitis *(see also* Pyelitis) 590.80
Cystorrhagia 596.8
Cystosarcoma phyllodes (M9020/1)
  238.3
  benign (M9020/0) 217
  malignant (M9020/3) - *see* Neoplasm,
    breast, malignant
Cystostomy status V44.50
  appendico-vesicostomy V44.52
  cutaneous-vesicostomy V44.51
  specified type NEC V44.59
  with complication 997.5
Cystourethritis *(see also* Urethritis) 597.89
Cystourethrocele *(see also* Cystocele)
  female (without uterine prolapse) 618.0
    with uterine prolapse 618.4
      complete 618.3
      incomplete 618.2
  male 596.8
Cytomegalic inclusion disease 078.5
  congenital 771.1
Cytomycosis, reticuloendothelial *(see also*
  Histoplasmosis, American) 115.00

D

Daae (-Finsen) disease (epidemic pleurodynia) 074.1
Dabney's grip 074.1
Da Costa's syndrome (neurocirculatory asthenia) 306.2
Dacryoadenitis, dacryadenitis 375.00
  acute 375.01
  chronic 375.02
Dacryocystitis 375.30
  acute 375.32
  chronic 375.42
  neonatal 771.6
  phlegmonous 375.33
  syphilitic 095.8
    congenital 090.0
  trachomatous, active 076.1
    late effect 139.1
  tuberculous (see also Tuberculosis) 017.3
Dacryocystoblenorrhea 375.42
Dacryocystocele 375.43
Dacryolith, dacryolithiasis 375.57
Dacryoma 375.43
Dacryopericystitis (acute) (subacute) 375.32
  chronic 375.42
Dacryops 375.11
Dacryosialadenopathy, atrophic 710.2
Dacryostenosis 375.56
  congenital 743.65
Dactylitis 686.9
  bone (see also Osteomyelitis) 730.2
  sickle-cell 282.61
  syphilitic 095.5
  tuberculous (see also Tuberculosis) 015.5
Dactylolysis spontanea 136.0
Dactylosymphysis (see also Syndactylism) 755.10
Damage
  arteriosclerotic - see Arteriosclerosis
  brain 348.9
    anoxic, hypoxic 348.1
      during or resulting from a procedure 997.01
    child NEC 343.9
    due to birth injury 767.0
    minimal (child) (see also Hyperkinesia) 314.9
    newborn 767.0
  cardiac - see also Disease, heart
  cardiorenal (vascular) (see also Hypertension, cardiorenal) 404.90
  central nervous system - see Damage, brain
  cerebral NEC - see Damage, brain
  coccyx, complicating delivery 665.6
  coronary (see also Ischemia, heart) 414.9
  eye, birth injury 767.8
  heart - see also Disease, heart
    valve - see Endocarditis
  hypothalamus NEC 348.9
  liver 571.9
    alcoholic 571.3
  myocardium (see also Degeneration, myocardial) 429.1
  pelvic
    joint or ligament, during delivery 665.6

Damage (Continued)
  pelvic (Continued)
    organ NEC
      with
        abortion - see Abortion, by type, with damage to pelvic organs
        ectopic pregnancy (see also categories 633.0-633.9) 639.2
        molar pregnancy (see also categories 630-632) 639.2
      during delivery 665.5
      following
        abortion 639.2
        ectopic or molar pregnancy 639.2
    renal (see also Disease, renal) 593.9
    skin, solar 692.79
      acute 692.72
      chronic 692.74
    subendocardium, subendocardial (see also Degeneration, myocardial) 429.1
    vascular 459.9
Dameshek's syndrome (erythroblastic anemia) 282.4
Dana-Putnam syndrome (subacute combined sclerosis with pernicious anemia) 281.0 [336.2]
Danbolt (-Closs) syndrome (acrodermatitis enteropathica) 686.8
Dandruff 690.18
Dandy fever 061
Dandy-Walker deformity or syndrome (atresia, foramen of Magendie) 742.3
  with spina bifida (see also Spina bifida) 741.0
Dangle foot 736.79
Danielssen's disease (anesthetic leprosy) 030.1
Danlos' syndrome 756.83
Darier's disease (congenital) (keratosis follicularis) 757.39
  due to vitamin A deficiency 264.8
  meaning erythema annulare centrifugum 695.0
Darier-Roussy sarcoid 135
Darling's
  disease (see also Histoplasmosis, American) 115.00
  histoplasmosis (see also Histoplasmosis, American) 115.00
Dartre 054.9
Darwin's tubercle 744.29
Davidson's anemia (refractory) 284.9
Davies' disease 425.0
Davies-Colley syndrome (slipping rib) 733.99
Dawson's encephalitis 046.2
Day blindness (see also Blindness, day) 368.60
Dead
  fetus
    retained (in utero) 656.4
      early pregnancy (death before 22 completed weeks' gestation) 632
      late (death after 22 completed weeks' gestation) 656.4
    syndrome 641.3
  labyrinth 386.50
  ovum, retained 631
Deaf and dumb NEC 389.7

Deaf mutism (acquired) (congenital) NEC 389.7
  endemic 243
  hysterical 300.11
  syphilitic, congenital 090.0
Deafness (acquired) (bilateral) (both ears) (complete) (congenital) (hereditary) (middle ear) (partial) (unilateral) 389.9
  with blue sclera and fragility of bone 756.51
  auditory fatigue 389.9
  aviation 993.0
    nerve injury 951.5
  boilermakers' 951.5
  central 389.14
    with conductive hearing loss 389.2
  conductive (air) 389.00
    with sensorineural hearing loss 389.2
    combined types 389.08
    external ear 389.01
    inner ear 389.04
    middle ear 389.03
    multiple types 389.08
    tympanic membrane 389.02
  emotional (complete) 300.11
  functional (complete) 300.11
  high frequency 389.8
  hysterical (complete) 300.11
  injury 951.5
  low frequency 389.8
  mental 784.69
  mixed conductive and sensorineural 389.2
  nerve 389.12
    with conductive hearing loss 389.2
  neural 389.12
    with conductive hearing loss 389.2
  noise-induced 388.12
    nerve injury 951.5
  nonspeaking 389.7
  perceptive 389.10
    with conductive hearing loss 389.2
    central 389.14
    combined types 389.18
    multiple types 389.18
    neural 389.12
    sensory 389.11
  psychogenic (complete) 306.7
  sensorineural (see also Deafness, perceptive) 389.10
  sensory 389.11
    with conductive hearing loss 389.2
  specified type NEC 389.8
  sudden NEC 388.2
  syphilitic 094.89
  transient ischemic 388.02
  transmission - see Deafness, conductive
  traumatic 951.5
  word (secondary to organic lesion) 784.69
    developmental 315.31
Death
  after delivery (cause not stated) (sudden) 674.9
  anesthetic
    due to
      correct substance properly administered 995.4
      overdose or wrong substance given 968.4
        specified anesthetic - see Table of Drugs and Chemicals
  during delivery 668.9

ICD-9-CM

D

Vol. 2

Death *(Continued)*
  brain 348.8
  cardiac - *see* Disease, heart
  cause unknown 798.2
  cot (infant) 798.0
  crib (infant) 798.0
  fetus, fetal (cause not stated) (intra-
      uterine) 779.9
    early, with retention (before 22 com-
        pleted weeks' gestation) 632
    from asphyxia or anoxia (before la-
        bor) 768.0
      during labor 768.1
    late, affecting management of preg-
        nancy (after 22 completed
        weeks' gestation) 656.4
  from pregnancy NEC 646.9
  instantaneous 798.1
  intrauterine (*see also* Death, fetus) 779.9
    complicating pregnancy 656.4
  maternal, affecting fetus or newborn
      761.6
  neonatal NEC 779.9
  sudden (cause unknown) 798.1
    during delivery 669.9
      under anesthesia NEC 668.9
    infant, syndrome (SIDS) 798.0
    puerperal, during puerperium 674.9
  unattended (cause unknown) 798.9
  under anesthesia NEC
    due to
      correct substance properly admin-
          istered 995.4
      overdose or wrong substance
          given 968.4
        specified anesthetic - *see* Table
            of Drugs and Chemicals
    during delivery 668.9
  violent 798.1
de Beurmann-Gougerot disease (sporo-
    trichosis) 117.1
Debility (general) (infantile) (postinfec-
    tional) 799.3
  with nutritional difficulty 269.9
  congenital or neonatal NEC 779.9
  nervous 300.5
  old age 797
  senile 797
Débove's disease (splenomegaly) 789.2
Decalcification
  bone (*see also* Osteoporosis) 733.00
  teeth 521.8
Decapitation 874.9
  fetal (to facilitate delivery) 763.89
Decapsulation, kidney 593.89
Decay
  dental 521.0
  senile 797
  tooth, teeth 521.0
Decensus, uterus - *see* Prolapse, uterus
Deciduitis (acute)
  with
    abortion - *see* Abortion, by type,
        with sepsis
    ectopic pregnancy (*see also* categories
        633.0-633.9) 639.0
    molar pregnancy (*see also* categories
        630-632) 639.0
  affecting fetus or newborn 760.8
  following
    abortion 639.0
    ectopic or molar pregnancy 639.0
  in pregnancy 646.6
  puerperal, postpartum 670

Deciduoma malignum (M9100/3) 181
Deciduous tooth (retained) 520.6
Decline (general) (*see also* Debility)
    799.3
Decompensation
  cardiac (acute) (chronic) (*see also* Dis-
      ease, heart) 429.9
    failure - *see* Failure, heart, congestive
  cardiorenal (*see also* Hypertension, car-
      diorenal) 404.90
  cardiovascular (*see also* Disease, cardio-
      vascular) 429.2
  heart (*see also* Disease, heart) 429.9
    failure - *see* Failure, heart, congestive
  hepatic 572.2
  myocardial (acute) (chronic) (*see also*
      Disease, heart) 429.9
    failure - *see* Failure, heart, conges-
        tive
  respiratory 519.9
Decompression sickness 993.3
Decrease, decreased
  blood
    platelets (*see also* Thrombocytopenia)
        287.5
    pressure 796.3
      due to shock following
          injury 958.4
          operation 998.0
  cardiac reserve - *see* Disease, heart
  estrogen 256.3
    postablative 256.2
  fetal movements 655.7
  fragility of erythrocytes 289.8
  function
    adrenal (cortex) 255.4
      medulla 255.5
    ovary in hypopituitarism 253.4
    parenchyma of pancreas 577.8
    pituitary (gland) (lobe) (anterior)
        253.2
      posterior (lobe) 253.8
  functional activity 780.9
  glucose 790.2
  haptoglobin (serum) NEC 273.8
  platelets (*see also* Thrombocytopenia)
      287.5
  pulse pressure 785.9
  respiration due to shock following in-
      jury 958.4
  tear secretion NEC 375.15
  tolerance
    fat 579.8
    glucose 790.2
    salt and water 276.9
  vision NEC 369.9
Decubital gangrene 707.0 *[785.4]*
Decubiti (*see also* Decubitus) 707.0
Decubitus (ulcer) 707.0
  with gangrene 707.0 *[785.4]*
Deepening acetabulum 718.85
Defect, defective 759.9
  3-beta-hydroxysteroid dehydrogenase
      255.2
  11-hydroxylase 255.2
  21-hydroxylase 255.2
  abdominal wall, congenital 756.70
  aorticopulmonary septum 745.0
  aortic septal 745.0
  atrial septal (ostium secundum type)
      745.5
    acquired 429.71
    ostium primum type 745.61
    sinus venosus 745.8

Defect, defective *(Continued)*
  atrioventricular
    canal 745.69
    septum 745.4
      acquired 429.71
  atrium secundum 745.5
    acquired 429.71
  auricular septal 745.5
    acquired 429.71
  bilirubin excretion 277.4
  biosynthesis, testicular androgen
      257.2
  bulbar septum 745.0
  butanol-insoluble iodide 246.1
  chromosome - *see* Anomaly, chromo-
      some
  circulation (acquired) 459.9
    congenital 747.9
    newborn 747.9
  clotting NEC (*see also* Defect, coagula-
      tion) 286.9
  coagulation (factor) (*see also* Deficiency,
      coagulation factor) 286.9
    with
      abortion - *see* Abortion, by type,
          with hemorrhage
      ectopic pregnancy (*see also* catego-
          ries 634-638) 639.1
      molar pregnancy (*see also* catego-
          ries 630-632) 639.1
    acquired (any) 286.7
    antepartum or intrapartum 641.3
      affecting fetus or newborn 762.1
    causing hemorrhage of pregnancy or
        delivery 641.3
    due to
      liver disease 286.7
      vitamin K deficiency 286.7
    newborn, transient 776.3
    postpartum 666.3
    specified type NEC 286.3
  conduction (heart) 426.9
    bone (*see also* Deafness, conductive)
        389.00
  congenital, organ or site NEC - *see also*
      Anomaly
    circulation 747.9
    Descemet's membrane 743.9
      specified type NEC 743.49
    diaphragm 756.6
    ectodermal 757.9
    esophagus 750.9
    pulmonic cusps - *see* Anomaly, heart
        valve
    respiratory system 748.9
      specified type NEC 748.8
  cushion endocardial 745.60
  dentin (hereditary) 520.5
  Descemet's membrane (congenital) 743.9
    acquired 371.30
    specific type NEC 743.49
  deutan 368.52
  developmental - *see also* Anomaly, by
      site
    cauda equina 742.59
    left ventricle 746.9
      with atresia or hypoplasia of aor-
          tic orifice or valve, with hy-
          poplasia of ascending aorta
          746.7
      in hypoplastic left heart syndrome
          746.7
    testis 752.9
    vessel 747.9

Defect, defective *(Continued)*
  diaphragm
    with elevation, eventration, or hernia - *see* Hernia, diaphragm
    congenital 756.6
      with elevation, eventration, or hernia 756.6
        gross (with elevation, eventration, or hernia) 756.6
  ectodermal, congenital 757.9
  Eisenmenger's (ventricular septal defect) 745.4
  endocardial cushion 745.60
    specified type NEC 745.69
  esophagus, congenital 750.9
  extensor retinaculum 728.9
  fibrin polymerization (*see also* Defect, coagulation) 286.3
  filling
    biliary tract 793.3
    bladder 793.5
    gallbladder 793.3
    kidney 793.5
    stomach 793.4
    ureter 793.5
  fossa ovalis 745.5
  gene, carrier (suspected) of V19.8
  Gerbode 745.4
  glaucomatous, without elevated tension 365.89
  Hageman (factor) (*see also* Defect, coagulation) 286.3
  hearing (*see also* Deafness) 389.9
  high grade 317
  homogentisic acid 270.2
  interatrial septal 745.5
    acquired 429.71
  interauricular septal 745.5
    acquired 429.71
  interventricular septal 745.4
    with pulmonary stenosis or atresia, dextraposition of aorta, and hypertrophy of right ventricle 745.2
    acquired 429.71
    in tetralogy of Fallot 745.2
  iodide trapping 246.1
  iodotyrosine dehalogenase 246.1
  kynureninase 270.2
  learning, specific 315.2
  mental (*see also* Retardation, mental) 319
  osteochondral NEC 738.8
  ostium
    primum 745.61
    secundum 745.5
  pericardium 746.89
  peroxidase-binding 246.1
  placental blood supply - *see* Placenta, insufficiency
  platelet (qualitative) 287.1
    constitutional 286.4
  postural, spine 737.9
  protan 368.51
  pulmonic cusps, congenital 746.00
  renal pelvis 753.9
    obstructive 753.29
    specified type NEC 753.3
  respiratory system, congenital 748.9
    specified type NEC 748.8
  retina, retinal 361.30
    with detachment (*see also* Detachment, retina, with retinal defect) 361.00

Defect, defective *(Continued)*
  retina, retinal *(Continued)*
    multiple 361.33
      with detachment 361.02
    nerve fiber bundle 362.85
    single 361.30
      with detachment 361.01
  septal (closure) (heart) NEC 745.9
    acquired 429.71
    atrial 745.5
    specified type NEC 745.8
  speech NEC 784.5
    developmental 315.39
    secondary to organic lesion 784.5
  Taussig-Bing (transposition, aorta and overriding pulmonary artery) 745.11
  teeth, wedge 521.2
  thyroid hormone synthesis 246.1
  tritan 368.53
  ureter 753.9
    obstructive 753.29
  vascular (acquired) (local) 459.9
    congenital (peripheral) NEC 747.60
      gastrointestinal 747.61
      lower limb 747.64
      renal 747.62
      specified NEC 747.69
      spinal 747.82
      upper limb 747.63
  ventricular septal 745.4
    with pulmonary stenosis or atresia, dextraposition of aorta, and hypertrophy of right ventricle 745.2
    acquired 429.71
    atrioventricular canal type 745.69
    between infundibulum and anterior portion 745.4
    in tetralogy of Fallot 745.2
    isolated anterior 745.4
  vision NEC 369.9
  visual field 368.40
    arcuate 368.43
    heteronymous, bilateral 368.47
    homonymous, bilateral 368.46
    localized NEC 368.44
    nasal step 368.44
    peripheral 368.44
    sector 368.43
  voice 784.40
  wedge, teeth (abrasion) 521.2
Defeminization syndrome 255.2
Deferentitis 608.4
  gonorrheal (acute) 098.14
    chronic or duration of 2 months or over 098.34
Defibrination syndrome (*see also* Fibrinolysis) 286.6
Deficiency, deficient
  3-beta-hydroxysteroid dehydrogenase 255.2
  6-phosphogluconic dehydrogenase (anemia) 282.2
  11-beta-hydroxylase 255.2
  17-alpha-hydroxylase 255.2
  18-hydroxysteroid dehydrogenase 255.2
  20-alpha-hydroxylase 255.2
  21-hydroxylase 255.2
  abdominal muscle syndrome 756.79
  accelerator globulin (Ac G) (blood) (*see also* Defect, coagulation) 286.3

Deficiency, deficient *(Continued)*
  AC globulin (congenital) (*see also* Defect, coagulation) 286.3
    acquired 286.7
  activating factor (blood) (*see also* Defect, coagulation) 286.3
  adenohypophyseal 253.2
  adenosine deaminase 277.2
  aldolase (hereditary) 271.2
  alpha-1-antitrypsin 277.6
  alpha-1-trypsin inhibitor 277.6
  alpha-fucosidase 271.8
  alpha-lipoprotein 272.5
  alpha-mannosidase 271.8
  amino acid 270.9
  anemia - *see* Anemia, deficiency
  aneurin 265.1
    with beriberi 265.0
  antibody NEC 279.00
  antidiuretic hormone 253.5
  antihemophilic
    factor (A) 286.0
      B 286.1
      C 286.2
    globulin (AHG) NEC 286.0
  antitrypsin 277.6
  argininosuccinate synthetase or lyase 270.6
  ascorbic acid (with scurvy) 267
  autoprothrombin
    I (*see also* Defect, coagulation) 286.3
    II 286.1
    C (*see also* Defect, coagulation) 286.3
  bile salt 579.8
  biotin 266.2
  biotindtdase 277.6
  bradykinase-1 277.6
  brancher enzyme (amylopectinosis) 271.0
  calciferol 268.9
    with
      osteomalacia 268.2
      rickets (*see also* Rickets) 268.0
  calcium 275.40
    dietary 269.3
  calorie, severe 261
  carbamyl phosphate synthetase 270.6
  cardiac (*see also* Insufficiency, myocardial) 428.0
  carnitine palmityl transferase 791.3
  carotene 264.9
  Carr factor (*see also* Defect, coagulation) 286.9
  central nervous system 349.9
  ceruloplasmin 275.1
  cevitamic acid (with scurvy) 267
  choline 266.2
  Christmas factor 286.1
  chromium 269.3
  citrin 269.1
  clotting (blood) (*see also* Defect, coagulation) 286.9
  coagulation factor NEC 286.9
    with
      abortion - *see* Abortion, by type, with hemorrhage
      ectopic pregnancy (*see also* categories 634-638) 639.1
      molar pregnancy (*see also* categories 630-632) 639.1
    acquired (any) 286.7
    antepartum or intrapartum 641.3
      affecting fetus or newborn 762.1

Deficiency, deficient *(Continued)*
luteinizing hormone (LH) 253.4
lysosomal alpha-1, 4 glucosidase 271.0
magnesium 275.2
mannosidase 271.8
melanocyte-stimulating hormone
   (MSH) 253.4
menadione (vitamin K) 269.0
  newborn 776.0
mental (familial) (hereditary) *(see also*
   Retardation, mental) 319
mineral NEC 269.3
molybdenum 269.3
moral 301.7
multiple, syndrome 260
myocardial *(see also* Insufficiency, myocardial) 428.0
myophosphorylase 271.0
NADH (DPNH)-methemoglobin-reduc-
   tase (congenital) 289.7
NADH diaphorase or reductase (congenital) 289.7
neck V48.1
niacin (amide) (-tryptophan) 265.2
nicotinamide 265.2
nicotinic acid (amide) 265.2
nose V48.8
number of teeth *(see also* Anodontia)
   520.0
nutrition, nutritional 269.9
  specified NEC 269.8
ornithine transcarbamylase 270.6
ovarian 256.3
oxygen *(see also* Anoxia) 799.0
pantothenic acid 266.2
parathyroid (gland) 252.1
phenylalanine hydroxylase 270.1
phosphofructokinase 271.2
phosphoglucomutase 271.0
phosphohexosisomerase 271.0
phosphorylase kinase, liver 271.0
pituitary (anterior) 253.2
  posterior 253.5
placenta - *see* Placenta, insufficiency
plasma
  cell 279.00
  protein (paraproteinemia) (pyroglob-
    ulinemia) 273.8
    gamma globulin 279.00
  thromboplastin
    antecedent (PTA) 286.2
    component (PTC) 286.1
platelet NEC 287.1
  constitutional 286.4
polyglandular 258.9
potassium (K) 276.8
proaccelerin (congenital) *(see also* Defect, congenital) 286.3
  acquired 286.7
proconvertin factor (congenital) *(see
   also* Defect, coagulation) 286.3
  acquired 286.7
prolactin 253.4
protein 260
  anemia 281.4
  plasma - *see* Deficiency, plasma, pro-
    tein
prothrombin (congenital) *(see also* Defect, coagulation) 286.3
  acquired 286.7
Prower factor *(see also* Defect, coagulation) 286.3
PRT 277.2
pseudocholinesterase 289.8

Deficiency, deficient *(Continued)*
psychobiological 301.6
PTA 286.2
PTC 286.1
purine nucleoside phosphorylase
   277.2
pyracin (alpha) (beta) 266.1
pyridoxal 266.1
pyridoxamine 266.1
pyridoxine (derivatives) 266.1
pyruvate kinase (PK) 282.3
riboflavin (vitamin B_2) 266.0
saccadic eye movements 379.57
salivation 527.7
salt 276.1
secretion
  ovary 256.3
  salivary gland (any) 527.7
  urine 788.5
selenium 269.3
serum
  antitrypsin, familial 277.6
  protein (congenital) 273.8
smooth pursuit movements (eye)
   379.58
sodium (Na) 276.1
SPCA *(see also* Defect, coagulation)
   286.3
specified NEC 269.8
stable factor (congenital) *(see also* Defect, coagulation) 286.3
  acquired 286.7
Stuart (-Prower) factor *(see also* Defect,
   coagulation) 286.3
sucrase 271.3
sucrase-isomaltase 271.3
sulfite oxidase 270.0
syndrome, multiple 260
thiamine, thiaminic (chloride)
   265.1
thrombokinase *(see also* Defect, coagulation) 286.3
  newborn 776.0
thrombopoieten 287.3
thymolymphatic 279.2
thyroid (gland) 244.9
tocopherol 269.1
toe - *see* Absence, toe
tooth bud *(see also* Anodontia) 520.0
trunk V48.1
UDPG-glycogen transferase 271.0
upper limb V49.0
  congenital 755.20
    with complete absence of distal el-
      ements 755.21
    longitudinal (complete) (partial)
      (with distal deficiencies, in-
      complete) 755.22
      carpal(s) 755.28
      combined humeral, radial, ulnar
        (incomplete) 755.23
      humeral 755.24
      metacarpal(s) 755.28
      phalange(s) 755.29
        meaning all digits 755.21
      radial 755.26
      radioulnar 755.25
      ulnar 755.27
    transverse (complete) (partial)
      755.21
vascular 459.9
vasopressin 253.5
viosterol *(see also* Deficiency, calciferol)
   268.9

Deficiency, deficient *(Continued)*
vitamin (multiple) NEC 269.2
  A 264.9
    with
      Bitôt's spot 264.1
        corneal 264.2
          with corneal ulceration
            264.3
      keratomalacia 264.4
      keratosis, follicular 264.8
      night blindness 264.5
      scar of cornea, xerophthalmic
        264.6
      specified manifestation NEC
        264.8
        ocular 264.7
      xeroderma 264.8
      xerophthalmia 264.7
      xerosis
        conjunctival 264.0
          with Bitôt's spot 264.1
        corneal 264.2
          with corneal ulceration
            264.3
  B (complex) NEC 266.9
    with
      beriberi 265.0
      pellagra 265.2
    specified type NEC 266.2
  B_1 NEC 265.1
    beriberi 265.0
  B_2 266.0
  B_6 266.1
  B_{12} 266.2
  B_C (folic acid) 266.2
  C (ascorbic acid) (with scurvy) 267
  D (calciferol) (ergosterol) 268.9
    with
      osteomalacia 268.2
      rickets *(see also* Rickets) 268.0
  E 269.1
  folic acid 266.2
  G 266.0
  H 266.2
  K 269.0
    of newborn 776.0
  nicotinic acid 265.2
  P 269.1
  PP 265.2
  specified NEC 269.1
  zinc 269.3
Deficient - *see also* Deficiency
blink reflex 374.45
craniofacial axis 756.0
number of teeth *(see also* Anodontia)
   520.0
secretion of urine 788.5
Deficit
neurologic NEC 781.9
  due to
    cerebrovascular lesion *(see also*
      Disease, cerebrovascular,
      acute) 436
      late effect - *see* Late effect(s) (of)
        cerebrovascular disease
    transient ischemic attack 435.9
oxygen 799.0
Deflection
radius 736.09
septum (acquired) (nasal) (nose) 470
spine - *see* Curvature, spine
turbinate (nose) 470
Defluvium
capillorum *(see also* Alopecia) 704.00

ICD-9-CM

Vol. 2

Deformity *(Continued)*
  multiple, congenital NEC *(Continued)*
    specified type NEC 759.89
  muscle (acquired) 728.9
    congenital 756.9
      specified type NEC 756.89
      sternocleidomastoid (due to intra-uterine malposition and pressure) 754.1
  musculoskeletal system, congenital NEC 756.9
    specified type NEC 756.9
  nail (acquired) 703.9
    congenital 757.9
  nasal - *see* Deformity, nose
  neck (acquired) NEC 738.2
    congenital (any part) 744.9
      sternocleidomastoid 754.1
  nervous system (congenital) 742.9
  nipple (congenital) 757.9
    acquired 611.8
  nose, nasal (cartilage) (acquired) 738.0
    bone (turbinate) 738.0
    congenital 748.1
      bent 754.0
      squashed 754.0
    saddle 738.0
      syphilitic 090.5
    septum 470
      congenital 748.1
    sinus (wall) (congenital) 748.1
      acquired 738.0
    syphilitic (congenital) 090.5
      late 095.8
  ocular muscle (congenital) 743.9
    acquired 378.60
  opticociliary vessels (congenital) 743.9
  orbit (congenital) (eye) 743.9
    acquired NEC 376.40
      associated with craniofacial deformities 376.44
      due to
        bone disease 376.43
        surgery 376.47
        trauma 376.47
  organ of Corti (congenital) 744.05
  ovary (congenital) 752.0
    acquired 620.8
  oviduct (congenital) 752.10
    acquired 620.8
  palate (congenital) 750.9
    acquired 526.89
    cleft (congenital) (*see also* Cleft, palate) 749.00
    hard, acquired 526.89
    soft, acquired 528.9
  pancreas (congenital) 751.7
    acquired 577.8
  parachute, mitral valve 746.5
  parathyroid (gland) 759.2
  parotid (gland) (congenital) 750.9
    acquired 527.8
  patella (acquired) 736.6
    congenital 755.64
  pelvis, pelvic (acquired) (bony) 738.6
    with disproportion (fetopelvic) 653.0
      affecting fetus or newborn 763.1
      causing obstructed labor 660.1
        affecting fetus or newborn 763.1
    congenital 755.60
    rachitic (late effect) 268.1
  penis (glans) (congenital) 752.9
    acquired 607.89

Deformity *(Continued)*
  pericardium (congenital) 746.9
    acquired - *see* Pericarditis
  pharynx (congenital) 750.9
    acquired 478.29
  Pierre Robin (congenital) 756.0
  pinna (acquired) 380.32
    congenital 744.3
  pituitary (congenital) 759.2
  pleural folds (congenital) 748.8
  portal vein (congenital) 747.40
  posture - *see* Curvature, spine
  prepuce (congenital) 752.9
    acquired 607.89
  prostate (congenital) 752.9
    acquired 602.8
  pulmonary valve - *see* Endocarditis, pulmonary
  pupil (congenital) 743.9
    acquired 364.75
  pylorus (congenital) 750.9
    acquired 537.89
  rachitic (acquired), healed or old 268.1
  radius (acquired) 736.00
    congenital 755.50
      reduction - *see* Deformity, reduction, upper limb
  rectovaginal septum (congenital) 752.40
    acquired 623.8
  rectum (congenital) 751.5
    acquired 569.49
  reduction (extremity) (limb) 755.4
    brain 742.2
    lower limb 755.30
      with complete absence of distal elements 755.31
      longitudinal (complete) (partial) (with distal deficiencies, incomplete) 755.32
        with complete absence of distal elements 755.31
        combined femoral, tibial, fibular (incomplete) 755.33
        femoral 755.34
        fibular 755.37
        metatarsal(s) 755.38
        phalange(s) 755.39
          meaning all digits 755.31
        tarsal(s) 755.38
        tibia 755.36
        tibiofibular 755.35
      transverse 755.31
    upper limb 755.20
      with complete absence of distal elements 755.21
      longitudinal (complete) (partial) (with distal deficiencies, incomplete) 755.22
        with complete absence of distal elements 755.21
        carpal(s) 755.28
        combined humeral, radial, ulnar (incomplete) 755.23
        humeral 755.24
        metacarpal(s) 755.28
        phalange(s) 755.29
          meaning all digits 755.21
        radial 755.26
        radioulnar 755.25
        ulnar 755.27
      transverse (complete) (partial) 755.21

Deformity *(Continued)*
  renal - *see* Deformity, kidney
  respiratory system (congenital) 748.9
    specified type NEC 748.8
  rib (acquired) 738.3
    congenital 756.3
      cervical 756.2
  rotation (joint) (acquired) 736.9
    congenital 755.9
    hip or thigh 736.39
      congenital (*see also* Subluxation, congenital, hip) 754.32
  sacroiliac joint (congenital) 755.69
    acquired 738.5
  sacrum (acquired) 738.5
    congenital 756.10
  saddle
    back 737.8
    nose 738.0
      syphilitic 090.5
  salivary gland or duct (congenital) 750.9
    acquired 527.8
  scapula (acquired) 736.89
    congenital 755.50
  scrotum (congenital) 752.9
    acquired 608.89
  sebaceous gland, acquired 706.8
  seminal tract or duct (congenital) 752.9
    acquired 608.89
  septum (nasal) (acquired) 470
    congenital 748.1
  shoulder (joint) (acquired) 736.89
    congenital 755.50
      specified type NEC 755.59
    contraction 718.41
  sigmoid (flexure) (congenital) 751.5
    acquired 569.89
  sinus of Valsalva 747.29
  skin (congenital) 757.9
    acquired NEC 709.8
  skull (acquired) 738.19
    congenital 756.0
      with
        anencephalus 740.0
        encephalocele 742.0
        hydrocephalus 742.3
          with spina bifida (*see also* Spina bifida) 741.0
        microcephalus 742.1
      due to intrauterine malposition and pressure 754.0
  soft parts, organs or tissues (of pelvis) in pregnancy or childbirth NEC 654.9
    affecting fetus or newborn 763.89
    causing obstructed labor 660.2
      affecting fetus or newborn 763.1
  spermatic cord (congenital) 752.9
    acquired 608.89
    torsion 608.2
  spinal
    column - *see* Deformity, spine
    cord (congenital) 742.9
      acquired 336.8
      vessel (congenital) 747.82
    nerve root (congenital) 742.9
      acquired 724.9
  spine (acquired) NEC 738.5
    congenital 756.10
      due to intrauterine malposition and pressure 754.2
    kyphoscoliotic (*see also* Kyphoscoliosis) 737.30

Deformity *(Continued)*
    spine (acquired) NEC *(Continued)*
        kyphotic *(see also* Kyphosis) 737.10
        lordotic *(see also* Lordosis) 737.20
        rachitic 268.1
        scoliotic *(see also* Scoliosis) 737.30
    spleen
        acquired 289.59
        congenital 759.0
    Sprengel's (congenital) 755.52
    sternum (acquired) 738.3
        congenital 756.3
    stomach (congenital) 750.9
        acquired 537.89
    submaxillary gland (congenital) 750.9
        acquired 527.8
    swan neck (acquired)
        finger 736.22
        hand 736.09
    talipes - *see* Talipes
    teeth, tooth NEC 520.9
    testis (congenital) 752.9
        acquired 608.89
            torsion 608.2
    thigh (acquired) 736.89
        congenital 755.60
    thorax (acquired) (wall) 738.3
        congenital 754.89
        late effect of rickets 268.1
    thumb (acquired) 736.20
        congenital 755.50
    thymus (tissue) (congenital) 759.2
    thyroid (gland) (congenital) 759.2
        cartilage 748.3
            acquired 478.79
    tibia (acquired) 736.89
        congenital 755.60
        saber 090.5
    toe (acquired) 735.9
        congenital 755.66
        specified NEC 735.8
    tongue (congenital) 750.10
        acquired 529.8
    tooth, teeth NEC 520.9
    trachea (rings) (congenital) 748.3
        acquired 519.1
    transverse aortic arch (congenital)
        747.21
    tricuspid (leaflets) (valve) (congenital)
        746.9
        acquired - *see* Endocarditis, tricuspid
        atresia or stenosis 746.1
        specified type NEC 746.89
    trunk (acquired) 738.3
        congenital 759.9
    ulna (acquired) 736.00
        congenital 755.50
    upper extremity - *see* Deformity, arm
    urachus (congenital) 753.7
    ureter (opening) (congenital) 753.9
        acquired 593.89
    urethra (valve) (congenital) 753.9
        acquired 599.84
    urinary tract or system (congenital)
        753.9
            urachus 753.7
    uterus (congenital) 752.3
        acquired 621.8
    uvula (congenital) 750.9
        acquired 528.9
    vagina (congenital) 752.40
        acquired 623.8
    valve, valvular (heart) (congenital)
        746.9

Deformity *(Continued)*
    valve, valvular *(Continued)*
        acquired - *see* Endocarditis
        pulmonary 746.00
        specified type NEC 746.89
    vascular (congenital) (peripheral) NEC
        747.60
        acquired 459.9
        gastrointestinal 747.61
        lower limb 747.64
        renal 747.62
        specified site NEC 747.69
        spinal 747.82
        upper limb 747.63
    vas deferens (congenital) 752.9
        acquired 608.89
    vein (congenital) NEC *(see also* Defor-
        mity, vascular) 747.60
        brain 747.81
        coronary 746.9
        great 747.40
    vena cava (inferior) (superior) (congen-
        ital) 747.40
    vertebra - *see* Deformity, spine
    vesicourethral orifice (acquired) 596.8
        congenital NEC 753.9
            specified type NEC 753.8
    vessels of optic papilla (congenital)
        743.9
    visual field (contraction) 368.45
    vitreous humor (congenital) 743.9
        acquired 379.29
    vulva (congenital) 752.40
        acquired 624.8
    wrist (joint) (acquired) 736.00
        congenital 755.50
        contraction 718.43
        valgus 736.03
            congenital 755.59
        varus 736.04
            congenital 755.59

Degeneration, degenerative
    adrenal (capsule) (gland) 255.8
        with hypofunction 255.4
        fatty 255.8
        hyaline 255.8
        infectional 255.8
        lardaceous 277.3
    amyloid (any site) (general) 277.3
    anterior cornua, spinal cord 336.8
    aorta, aortic 440.0
        fatty 447.8
        valve (heart) *(see also* Endocarditis,
            aortic) 424.1
    arteriovascular - *see* Arteriosclerosis
    artery, arterial (atheromatous) (calcare-
        ous) - *see also* Arteriosclerosis
        amyloid 277.3
        lardaceous 277.3
        medial NEC *(see also* Arteriosclerosis,
            extremities) 440.20
    articular cartilage NEC *(see also* Disor-
        der, cartilage, articular) 718.0
        elbow 718.02
        knee 717.5
        patella 717.7
        shoulder 718.01
        spine *(see also* Spondylosis)
            721.90
    atheromatous - *see* Arteriosclerosis
    bacony (any site) 277.3
    basal nuclei or ganglia NEC 333.0
    bone 733.90
    brachial plexus 353.0

Degeneration, degenerative *(Continued)*
    brain (cortical) (progressive) 331.9
        arteriosclerotic 437.0
        childhood 330.9
            specified type NEC 330.8
        congenital 742.4
        cystic 348.0
            congenital 742.4
        familial NEC 331.89
        grey matter 330.8
        heredofamilial NEC 331.89
        in
            alcoholism 303.9 *[331.7]*
            beriberi 265.0 *[331.7]*
            cerebrovascular disease 437.9 *[331.7]*
            congenital hydrocephalus 742.3
                [331.7]
                with spina bifida *(see also* Spina
                    bifida) 741.0 *[331.7]*
            Fabry's disease 272.7 *[330.2]*
            Gaucher's disease 272.7 *[330.2]*
            Hunter's disease or syndrome
                277.5 *[330.3]*
            lipidosis
                cerebral *[330.1]*
                generalized 272.7 *[330.2]*
            mucopolysaccharidosis 277.5 *[330.3]*
            myxedema *(see also* Myxedema)
                244.9 *[331.7]*
            neoplastic disease NEC (M8000/1)
                239.9 *[331.7]*
            Niemann-Pick disease 272.7 *[330.2]*
            sphingolipidosis 272.7 *[330.2]*
            vitamin B_{12} deficiency 266.2 *[331.7]*
        motor centers 331.89
        senile 331.2
        specified type NEC 331.89
    breast - *see* Disease, breast
    Bruch's membrane 363.40
    bundle of His 426.50
        left 426.3
        right 426.4
    calcareous NEC 275.49
    capillaries 448.9
        amyloid 277.3
        fatty 448.9
        lardaceous 277.3
    cardiac (brown) (calcareous) (fatty) (fi-
        brous) (hyaline) (mural) (muscu-
        lar) (pigmentary) (senile) (with ar-
        teriosclerosis) *(see also*
        Degeneration, myocardial) 429.1
        valve, valvular - *see* Endocarditis
    cardiorenal *(see also* Hypertension, car-
        diorenal) 404.90
    cardiovascular *(see also* Disease, cardio-
        vascular) 429.2
        renal *(see also* Hypertension, cardio-
            renal) 404.90
    cartilage (joint) - *see* Derangement, joint
    cerebellar NEC 334.9
        primary (hereditary) (sporadic) 334.2
    cerebral - *see* Degeneration, brain
    cerebromacular 330.1
    cerebrovascular 437.1
        due to hypertension 437.2
        late effect - *see* Late effect(s) (of)
            cerebrovascular disease
    cervical plexus 353.2
    cervix 622.8
        due to radiation (intended effect)
            622.8
            adverse effect or misadventure
                622.8

ICD-9-CM

Vol. 2

Degeneration, degenerative (*Continued*)
changes, spine or vertebra (*see also*
    Spondylosis) 721.90
chitinous 277.3
chorioretinal 363.40
    congenital 743.53
    hereditary 363.50
choroid (colloid) (drusen) 363.40
    hereditary 363.50
    senile 363.41
        diffuse secondary 363.42
cochlear 386.8
collateral ligament (knee) (medial)
    717.82
    lateral 717.81
combined (spinal cord) (subacute)
    266.2 [336.2]
    with anemia (pernicious) 281.0
        [336.2]
        due to dietary deficiency 281.1
            [336.2]
        due to vitamin B₁₂ deficiency anemia
            (dietary) 281.1 [336.2]
conjunctiva 372.50
    amyloid 277.3 [372.50]
cornea 371.40
    calcerous 371.44
    familial (hereditary) (*see also* Dystro-
        phy, cornea) 371.50
        macular 371.55
        reticular 371.54
    hyaline (of old scars) 371.41
    marginal (Terrien's) 371.48
    mosaic (shagreen) 371.41
    nodular 371.46
    peripheral 371.48
    senile 371.41
cortical (cerebellar) (parenchymatous)
    334.2
    alcoholic 303.9 [334.4]
    diffuse, due to arteriopathy 437.0
corticostriatal-spinal 334.8
cretinoid 243
cruciate ligament (knee) (posterior)
    717.84
    anterior 717.83
cutis 709.3
    amyloid 277.3
dental pulp 522.2
disc disease - *see* Degeneration, inter-
    vertebral disc
dorsolateral (spinal cord) - *see* Degen-
    eration, combined
endocardial 424.90
extrapyramidal NEC 333.90
eye NEC 360.40
    macular (*see also* Degeneration, mac-
        ula) 362.50
        congenital 362.75
        hereditary 362.76
fatty (diffuse) (general) 272.8
    liver 571.8
        alcoholic 571.0
    localized site - *see* Degeneration, by
        site, fatty
    placenta - *see* Placenta, abnormal
globe (eye) NEC 360.40
    macular - *see* Degeneration, macula
grey matter 330.8
heart (brown) (calcareous) (fatty) (fi-
    brous) (hyaline) (mural) (muscu-
    lar) (pigmentary) (senile) (with ar-
    teriosclerosis) (*see also*
        Degeneration, myocardial) 429.1

Degeneration, degenerative (*Continued*)
heart (*Continued*)
    amyloid 277.3 [425.7]
    atheromatous - *see* Arteriosclerosis,
        coronary
    gouty 274.82
    hypertensive (*see also* Hypertension,
        heart) 402.90
    ischemic 414.9
    valve, valvular - *see* Endocarditis
hepatolenticular (Wilson's) 275.1
hepatorenal 572.4
heredofamilial
    brain NEC 331.89
    spinal cord NEC 336.8
hyaline (diffuse) (generalized) 728.9
    localized - *see also* Degeneration, by
        site
        cornea 371.41
        keratitis 371.41
hypertensive vascular - *see* Hyperten-
    sion
infrapatellar fat pad 729.31
internal semilunar cartilage 717.3
intervertebral disc 722.6
    with myelopathy 722.70
    cervical, cervicothoracic 722.4
        with myelopathy 722.71
    lumbar, lumbosacral 722.52
        with myelopathy 722.73
    thoracic, thoracolumbar 722.51
        with myelopathy 722.72
intestine 569.89
    amyloid 277.3
    lardaceous 277.3
iris (generalized) (*see also* Atrophy, iris)
    364.59
    pigmentary 364.53
    pupillary margin 364.54
ischemic - *see* Ischemia
joint disease (*see also* Osteoarthrosis)
    715.9
    multiple sites 715.09
    spine (*see also* Spondylosis) 721.90
kidney (*see also* Sclerosis, renal) 587
    amyloid 277.3 [583.81]
    cyst, cystic (multiple) (solitary) 593.2
        congenital (*see also* Cystic, disease,
            kidney) 753.10
    fatty 593.89
    fibrocystic (congenital) 753.19
    lardaceous 277.3 [583.81]
    polycystic (congenital) 753.12
        adult type (APKD) 753.13
        autosomal dominant 753.13
        autosomal recessive 753.14
        childhood type (CPKD) 753.14
        infantile type 753.14
    waxy 277.3 [583.81]
Kuhnt-Junius (retina) 362.52
labyrinth, osseous 386.8
lacrimal passages, cystic 375.12
lardaceous (any site) 277.3
lateral column (posterior), spinal cord
    (*see also* Degeneration, combined)
    266.2 [336.2]
lattice 362.63
lens 366.9
    infantile, juvenile, or presenile 366.00
    senile 366.10
lenticular (familial) (progressive) (Wil-
    son's) (with cirrhosis of liver)
    275.1
    striate artery 437.0

Degeneration, degenerative (*Continued*)
lethal ball, prosthetic heart valve
    996.02
ligament
    collateral (knee) (medial) 717.82
        lateral 717.81
    cruciate (knee) (posterior) 717.84
        anterior 717.83
liver (diffuse) 572.8
    amyloid 277.3
    congenital (cystic) 751.62
    cystic 572.8
        congenital 751.62
    fatty 571.8
        alcoholic 571.0
    hypertrophic 572.8
    lardaceous 277.3
    parenchymatous, acute or subacute
        (*see also* Necrosis, liver) 570
    pigmentary 572.8
    toxic (acute) 573.8
    waxy 277.3
lung 518.89
lymph gland 289.3
    hyaline 289.3
    lardaceous 277.3
macula (acquired) (senile) 362.50
    atrophic 362.51
    Best's 362.76
    congenital 362.75
    cystic 362.54
    cystoid 362.53
    disciform 362.52
    dry 362.51
    exudative 362.52
    familial pseudoinflammatory 362.77
    hereditary 362.76
    hole 362.54
    juvenile (Stargardt's) 362.75
    nonexudative 362.51
    pseudohole 362.54
    wet 362.52
medullary - *see* Degeneration, brain
membranous labyrinth, congenital
    (causing impairment of hearing)
    744.05
meniscus - *see* Derangement, joint
microcystoid 362.62
mitral - *see* Insufficiency, mitral
Mönckeberg's (*see also* Arteriosclerosis,
    extremities) 440.20
moral 301.7
motor centers, senile 331.2
mural (*see also* Degeneration, myocar-
    dial) 429.1
    heart, cardiac (*see also* Degeneration,
        myocardial) 429.1
    myocardium, myocardial (*see also*
        Degeneration, myocardial)
        429.1
muscle 728.9
    fatty 728.9
    fibrous 728.9
    heart (*see also* Degeneration, myocar-
        dial) 429.1
    hyaline 728.9
muscular progressive 728.2
myelin, central nervous system NEC
    341.9
myocardium, myocardial (brown) (cal-
    careous) (fatty) (fibrous) (hyaline)
    (mural) (muscular) (pigmentary)
    (senile) (with arteriosclerosis)
    429.1

Degeneration, degenerative *(Continued)*
myocardium, myocardial *(Continued)*
with rheumatic fever (conditions
classifiable to 390) 398.0
active, acute, or subacute 391.2
with chorea 392.0
inactive or quiescent (with chorea)
398.0
amyloid 277.3 *[425.7]*
congenital 746.89
fetus or newborn 779.8
gouty 274.82
hypertensive *(see also* Hypertension,
heart) 402.90
ischemic 414.8
rheumatic *(see also* Degeneration,
myocardium, with rheumatic fever) 398.0
syphilitic 093.82
nasal sinus (mucosa) *(see also* Sinusitis)
473.9
frontal 473.1
maxillary 473.0
nerve - *see* Disorder, nerve
nervous system 349.89
amyloid 277.3 *[357.4]*
autonomic *(see also* Neuropathy, peripheral, autonomic) 337.9
fatty 349.89
peripheral autonomic NEC *(see also*
Neuropathy, peripheral, autonomic) 337.9
nipple 611.9
nose 478.1
oculoacousticocerebral, congenital
(progressive) 743.8
olivopontocerebellar (familial) (hereditary) 333.0
osseous labyrinth 386.8
ovary 620.8
cystic 620.2
microcystic 620.2
pallidal, pigmentary (progressive) 333.0
pancreas 577.8
tuberculous *(see also* Tuberculosis)
017.9
papillary muscle 429.81
paving stone 362.61
penis 607.89
peritoneum 568.89
pigmentary (diffuse) (general)
localized - *see* Degeneration, by site
pallidal (progressive) 333.0
secondary 362.65
pineal gland 259.8
pituitary (gland) 253.8
placenta (fatty) (fibrinoid) (fibroid) -
see Placenta, abnormal
popliteal fat pad 729.31
posterolateral (spinal cord) *(see also*
Degeneration, combined) 266.2
[336.2]
pulmonary valve (heart) *(see also* Endocarditis, pulmonary) 424.3
pulp (tooth) 522.2
pupillary margin 364.54
renal *(see also* Sclerosis, renal) 587
fibrocystic 753.19
polycystic 753.12
adult type (APKD) 753.13
autosomal dominant 753.13
autosomal recessive 753.14
childhood type (CPKD) 753.14
infantile type 753.14

Degeneration, degenerative *(Continued)*
reticuloendothelial system 289.8
retina (peripheral) 362.60
with retinal defect *(see also* Detachment, retina, with retinal defect)
361.00
cystic (senile) 362.50
cystoid 362.53
hereditary *(see also* Dystrophy, retina) 362.70
cerebroretinal 362.71
congenital 362.75
juvenile (Stargardt's) 362.75
macula 362.76
Kuhnt-Junius 362.52
lattice 362.63
macular *(see also* Degeneration, macula) 362.50
microcystoid 362.62
palisade 362.63
paving stone 362.61
pigmentary (primary) 362.74
secondary 362.65
posterior pole *(see also* Degeneration,
macula) 362.50
secondary 362.66
senile 362.60
cystic 362.53
reticular 362.64
saccule, congenital (causing impairment of hearing) 744.05
sacculocochlear 386.8
senile 797
brain 331.2
cardiac, heart, or myocardium *(see also*
Degeneration, myocardial) 429.1
motor centers 331.2
reticule 362.64
retina, cystic 362.50
vascular - *see* Arteriosclerosis
silicone rubber poppet (prosthetic
valve) 996.02
sinus (cystic) *(see also* Sinusitis) 473.9
polypoid 471.1
skin 709.3
amyloid 277.3
colloid 709.3
spinal (cord) 336.8
amyloid 277.3
column 733.90
combined (subacute) *(see also* Degeneration, combined) 266.2 *[336.2]*
with anemia (pernicious) 281.0
[336.2]
dorsolateral *(see also* Degeneration,
combined) 266.2 *[336.2]*
familial NEC 336.8
fatty 336.8
funicular *(see also* Degeneration,
combined) 266.2 *[336.2]*
heredofamilial NEC 336.8
posterolateral *(see also* Degeneration,
combined) 266.2 *[336.2]*
subacute combined - *see* Degeneration, combined
tuberculous *(see also* Tuberculosis)
013.8
spine 733.90
spleen 289.59
amyloid 277.3
lardaceous 277.3
stomach 537.89
lardaceous 277.3
strionigral 333.0

Degeneration, degenerative *(Continued)*
sudoriparous (cystic) 705.89
suprarenal (capsule) (gland) 255.8
with hypofunction 255.4
sweat gland 705.89
synovial membrane (pulpy) 727.9
tapetoretinal 362.74
adult or presenile form 362.50
testis (postinfectional) 608.89
thymus (gland) 254.8
fatty 254.8
lardaceous 277.3
thyroid (gland) 246.8
tricuspid (heart) (valve) - *see* Endocarditis, tricuspid
tuberculous NEC *(see also* Tuberculosis) 011.9
turbinate 733.90
uterus 621.8
cystic 621.8
vascular (senile) - *see also* Arteriosclerosis
hypertensive - *see* Hypertension
vitreoretinal (primary) 362.73
secondary 362.66
vitreous humor (with infiltration)
379.21
wallerian NEC - *see* Disorder, nerve
waxy (any site) 277.3
Wilson's hepatolenticular 275.1
Deglutition
paralysis 784.9
hysterical 300.11
pneumonia 507.0
Degos' disease or syndrome 447.8
**Degradation disorder, branched-chain
amino-acid** 270.3
Dehiscence
anastomosis - *see* Complications, anastomosis
cesarean wound 674.1
episiotomy 674.2
operation wound 998.3
perineal wound (postpartum) 674.2
postoperative 998.3
abdomen 998.3
uterine wound 674.1
Dehydration (cachexia) 276.5
newborn 775.5
Deiters' nucleus syndrome 386.19
Déjérine's disease 356.0
Déjérine-Klumpke paralysis 767.6
Déjérine-Roussy syndrome 348.8
Déjérine-Sottas disease or neuropathy
(hypertrophic) 356.0
Déjérine-Thomas atrophy or syndrome
333.0
de Lange's syndrome (Amsterdam
dwarf, mental retardation, and
brachycephaly) 759.89
Delay, delayed
adaptation, cones or rods 368.63
any plane in pelvis
affecting fetus or newborn 763.1
complicating delivery 660.1
birth or delivery NEC 662.1
affecting fetus or newborn
763.9
second twin, triplet, or multiple
mate 662.3
closure - *see also* Fistula
cranial suture 756.0
fontanel 756.0
coagulation NEC 790.92

Delay, delayed *(Continued)*
conduction (cardiac) (ventricular) 426.9
delivery NEC 662.1
second twin, triplet, etc. 662.3
affecting fetus or newborn 763.89
development 783.4
intellectual NEC 315.9
learning NEC 315.2
physiological 783.4
reading 315.00
sexual 259.0
speech 315.39
associated with hyperkinesis 314.1
spelling 315.09
gastric emptying 536.8
menarche 256.3
due to pituitary hypofunction 253.4
menstruation (cause unknown) 626.8
milestone 783.4
motility - *see* Hypomotility
passage of meconium (newborn) 777.1
primary respiration 768.9
puberty 259.0
sexual maturation, female 259.0
Del Castillo's syndrome (germinal aplasia) 606.0
Deleage's disease 359.8
Delhi (boil) (button) (sore) 085.1
Delinquency (juvenile) 312.9
group (*see also* Disturbance, conduct) 312.2
neurotic 312.4
Delirium, delirious 780.09
acute (psychotic) 293.0
alcoholic 291.0
acute 291.0
chronic 291.1
alcoholicum 291.0
chronic (*see also* Psychosis) 293.89
due to or associated with physical condition - *see* Psychosis, organic
drug-induced 292.81
eclamptic (*see also* Eclampsia) 780.39
exhaustion (*see also* Reaction, stress, acute) 308.9
hysterical 300.11
in
presenile dementia 290.11
senile dementia 290.3
induced by drug 292.81
manic, maniacal (acute) (*see also* Psychosis, affective) 296.0
recurrent episode 296.1
single episode 296.0
puerperal 293.9
senile 290.3
subacute (psychotic) 293.1
thyroid (*see also* Thyrotoxicosis) 242.9
traumatic - *see also* Injury, intracranial
with
lesion, spinal cord - *see* Injury, spinal, by site
shock, spinal - *see* Injury, spinal, by site
tremens (impending) 291.0
uremic - *see* Uremia
withdrawal
alcoholic (acute) 291.0
chronic 291.1
drug 292.0

Delivery

> Note   Use the following fifth-digit subclassification with categories 640-648, 651-676:
>
> 0   unspecified as to episode of care
> 1   delivered, with or without mention of antepartum condition
> 2   delivered, with mention of postpartum complication
> 3   antepartum condition or complication
> 4   postpartum condition or complication

breech (assisted) (spontaneous) 652.2
affecting fetus or newborn 763.0
extraction NEC 669.6
cesarean (for) 669.7
abnormal
cervix 654.6
pelvic organs of tissues 654.9
pelvis (bony) (major) NEC 653.0
presentation or position 652.9
in multiple gestation 652.6
size, fetus 653.5
soft parts (of pelvis) 654.9
uterus, congenital 654.0
vagina 654.7
vulva 654.8
abruptio placentae 641.2
acromion presentation 652.8
affecting fetus or newborn 763.4
anteversion, cervix or uterus 654.4
atony, uterus 666.1
bicornis or bicornuate uterus 654.0
breech presentation 652.2
brow presentation 652.4
cephalopelvic disproportion (normally formed fetus) 653.4
chin presentation 652.4
cicatrix of cervix 654.6
contracted pelvis (general) 653.1
inlet 653.2
outlet 653.3
cord presentation or prolapse 663.0
cystocele 654.4
deformity (acquired) (congenital)
pelvic organs or tissues NEC 654.9
pelvis (bony) NEC 653.0
displacement, uterus NEC 654.4
disproportion NEC 653.9
distress
fetal 656.8
maternal 669.0
eclampsia 642.6
face presentation 652.4
failed
forceps 660.7
trial of labor NEC 660.6
vacuum extraction 660.7
ventouse 660.7
fetal deformity 653.7
fetal-maternal hemorrhage 656.0
fetus, fetal
distress 656.8
prematurity 656.8
fibroid (tumor) (uterus) 654.1
footling 652.8
with successful version 652.1
hemorrhage (antepartum) (intrapartum) NEC 641.9

Delivery *(Continued)*
cesarean (for) *(Continued)*
hydrocephalic fetus 653.6
incarceration of uterus 654.3
incoordinate uterine action 661.4
inertia, uterus 661.2
primary 661.0
secondary 661.1
lateroversion, uterus or cervix 654.4
mal lie 652.9
malposition
fetus 652.9
in multiple gestation 652.6
pelvic organs or tissues NEC 654.9
uterus NEC or cervix 654.4
malpresentation NEC 652.9
in multiple gestation 652.6
maternal
diabetes mellitus 648.0
heart disease NEC 648.6
meconium in liquor 656.8
staining only 792.3
oblique presentation 652.3
oversize fetus 653.5
pelvic tumor NEC 654.9
placental insufficiency 656.5
placenta previa 641.0
with hemorrhage 641.1
poor dilation, cervix 661.0
pre-eclampsia 642.4
severe 642.5
previous
cesarean delivery, section 654.2
surgery (to)
cervix 654.6
gynecological NEC 654.9
uterus NEC 654.9
previous cesarean delivery, section 654.2
vagina 654.7
prolapse
arm or hand 652.7
uterus 654.4
prolonged labor 662.1
rectocele 654.4
retroversion, uterus or cervix 654.3
rigid
cervix 654.6
pelvic floor 654.4
perineum 654.8
vagina 654.7
vulva 654.8
sacculation, pregnant uterus 654.4
scar(s)
cervix 654.6
cesarean delivery, section 654.2
uterus NEC 654.9
due to previous cesarean delivery, section 654.2
Shirodkar suture in situ 654.5
shoulder presentation 652.8
stenosis or stricture, cervix 654.6
transverse presentation or lie 652.3
tumor, pelvic organs or tissues NEC 654.4
umbilical cord presentation or prolapse 663.0
completely normal case - *see* category 650
complicated (by) NEC 669.9
abdominal tumor, fetal 653.7
causing obstructed labor 660.1

ICD-9-CM

Vol. 2

Delivery *(Continued)*
  complicated (by) NEC *(Continued)*
    fetal *(Continued)*
      death (near term) NEC 656.4
        early (before 22 completed
          weeks' gestation) 632
      deformity 653.7
        causing obstructed labor
          660.1
      distress 656.8
      heart rate or rhythm 659.7
    fetopelvic disproportion 653.4
      causing obstructed labor 660.1
    fever during labor 659.2
    fibroid (tumor) (uterus) 654.1
      causing obstructed labor 660.2
    fibromyomata 654.1
      causing obstructed labor 660.2
    forelying umbilical cord 663.0
    fracture of coccyx 665.6
    hematoma 664.5
      broad ligament 665.7
      ischial spine 665.7
      pelvic 665.7
      perineum 664.5
      soft tissues 665.7
      subdural 674.0
      umbilical cord 663.6
      vagina 665.7
      vulva or perineum 664.5
    hemorrhage (uterine) (antepartum)
      (intrapartum) (pregnancy) 641.9
      accidental 641.2
      associated with
        afibrinogenemia 641.3
        coagulation defect 641.3
          hyperfibrinolysis 641.3
          hypofibrinogenemia 641.3
      cerebral 674.0
      due to
        low-lying placenta 641.1
        placenta previa 641.1
        premature separation of pla-
          centa (normally implanted)
          641.2
        retained placenta 666.0
        trauma 641.8
        uterine leiomyoma 641.8
      marginal sinus rupture 641.2
      placenta NEC 641.9
      postpartum (atonic) (immediate)
        (within 24 hours) 666.1
        with retained or trapped pla-
          centa 666.0
        delayed 666.2
        secondary 666.2
        third stage 666.0
    hourglass contraction, uterus 661.4
    hydramnios 657
    hydrocephalic fetus 653.6
      causing obstructed labor 660.1
    hydrops fetalis 653.7
      causing obstructed labor 660.1
    hypertension - *see* Hypertension,
      complicating pregnancy
    hypertonic uterine dysfunction 661.4
    hypotonic uterine dysfunction 661.2
    impacted shoulders 660.4
    incarceration, uterus 654.3
      causing obstructed labor 660.2
    incomplete dilation (cervix) 661.0
    incoordinate uterus 661.4
    indication NEC 659.9
      specified type NEC 659.8

Delivery *(Continued)*
  complicated (by) NEC *(Continued)*
    inertia, uterus 661.2
      hypertonic 661.4
      hypotonic 661.2
      primary 661.0
      secondary 661.1
    infantile
      genitalia 654.4
        causing obstructed labor 660.2
      uterus (os) 654.4
        causing obstructed labor 660.2
    injury (to mother) NEC 665.9
    intrauterine fetal death (near term)
      NEC 656.4
      early (before 22 completed weeks'
        gestation) 632
    inversion, uterus 665.2
    kidney, ectopic 654.4
      causing obstructed labor 660.2
    knot (true), umbilical cord 663.2
    labor, premature (before 37 com-
      pleted weeks' gestation) 644.2
    laceration 664.9
      anus (sphincter) 664.2
        with mucosa 664.3
      bladder (urinary) 665.5
      bowel 665.5
      central 664.4
      cervix (uteri) 665.3
      fourchette 664.0
      hymen 664.0
      labia (majora) (minora) 664.0
      pelvic
        floor 664.1
        organ NEC 665.5
      perineum, perineal 664.4
        first degree 664.0
        second degree 664.1
        third degree 664.2
        fourth degree 664.3
        central 664.4
        extensive NEC 664.4
        muscles 664.1
        skin 664.0
        slight 664.0
      peritoneum 665.5
      periurethral tissue 665.5
      rectovaginal (septum) (without
        perineal laceration) 665.4
        with perineum 664.2
          with anal or rectal mucosa
          664.3
      skin (perineum) 664.0
      specified site or type NEC 664.8
      sphincter ani 664.2
        with mucosa 664.3
      urethra 665.5
      uterus 665.1
        before labor 665.0
      vagina, vaginal (deep) (high) (sul-
        cus) (wall) (without perineal
        laceration) 665.4
        with perineum 664.0
        muscles, with perineum 664.1
      vulva 664.0
    lateroversion, uterus or cervix 654.4
      causing obstructed labor 660.2
    locked mates 660.5
    low implantation of placenta - *see*
      Delivery, complicated, placenta,
      previa
    mal lie 652.9
      causing obstructed labor 660.0

Delivery *(Continued)*
  complicated (by) NEC *(Continued)*
    malposition
      fetus NEC 652.9
        causing obstructed labor 660.0
      pelvic organs or tissues NEC
        654.9
        causing obstructed labor 660.2
      placenta 641.1
        without hemorrhage 641.0
      uterus NEC or cervix 654.4
        causing obstructed labor 660.2
    malpresentation 652.9
      causing obstructed labor 660.0
    marginal sinus (bleeding) (rupture)
      641.2
    maternal hypotension syndrome
      669.2
    meconium in liquor 656.8
    membranes, retained - *see* Delivery,
      complicated, placenta, retained
    mentum presentation 652.4
      causing obstructed labor 660.0
    metrorrhagia (myopathia) - *see* De-
      livery, complicated, hemorrhage
    metrorrhexis - *see* Delivery, compli-
      cated, rupture, uterus
    multiparity (grand) 659.4
    myelomeningocele, fetus 653.7
      causing obstructed labor 660.1
    Nägele's pelvis 653.0
      causing obstructed labor 660.1
    nonengagement, fetal head 652.5
      causing obstructed labor 660.0
    oblique presentation 652.3
      causing obstructed labor 660.0
    obstetric
      shock 669.1
      trauma NEC 665.9
    obstructed labor 660.9
      due to
        abnormality of pelvic organs or
          tissues (conditions classifia-
          ble to 654.0-654.9) 660.2
        deep transverse arrest 660.3
        impacted shoulders 660.4
        locked twins 660.5
        malposition and malpresenta-
          tion of fetus (conditions
          classifiable to 652.0-652.9)
          660.0
        persistent occipitoposterior
          660.3
        shoulder dystocia 660.4
    occult prolapse of umbilical cord
      663.0
    oversize fetus 653.5
      causing obstructed labor 660.1
    pathological retraction ring, uterus
      661.4
    pelvic
      arrest (deep) (high) (of fetal head)
        (transverse) 660.3
      deformity (bone) - *see also* Defor-
        mity, pelvis, with dispropor-
        tion
      soft tissue 654.9
        causing obstructed labor 660.2
      tumor NEC 654.9
        causing obstructed labor 660.2
    penetration, pregnant uterus by in-
      strument 665.1
    perforation - *see* Delivery, compli-
      cated, laceration

Delivery (*Continued*)
  complicated (by) NEC (*Continued*)
    persistent
      hymen 654.8
        causing obstructed labor 660.2
      occipitoposterior 660.3
    placenta, placental
      ablatio 641.2
      abnormality 656.7
        with hemorrhage 641.2
      abruptio 641.2
      accreta 667.0
        with hemorrhage 666.0
      adherent (without hemorrhage)
        667.0
        with hemorrhage 666.0
      apoplexy 641.2
      Battledore - see Placenta, abnor-
        mal
      detachment (premature) 641.2
      disease 656.7
      hemorrhage NEC 641.9
      increta (without hemorrhage) 667.0
        with hemorrhage 666.0
      low (implantation) 641.1
        without hemorrhage 641.0
      malformation 656.7
        with hemorrhage 641.2
      malposition 641.1
        without hemorrhage 641.0
      marginal sinus rupture 641.2
      percreta 667.0
        with hemorrhage 666.0
      premature separation 641.2
      previa (central) (lateral) (marginal)
        (partial) 641.1
        without hemorrhage 641.0
      retained (with hemorrhage) 666.0
        without hemorrhage 667.0
      rupture of marginal sinus 641.2
      separation (premature) 641.2
      trapped 666.0
        without hemorrhage 667.0
      vicious insertion 641.1
    polyhydramnios 657
    polyp, cervix 654.6
      causing obstructed labor 660.2
    precipitate labor 661.3
    premature
      labor (before 37 completed weeks'
        gestation) 644.2
      rupture, membranes 658.1
        delayed delivery following 658.2
    presenting umbilical cord 663.0
    previous
      cesarean delivery, section 654.2
      surgery
        cervix 654.6
          causing obstructed labor 660.2
        gynecological NEC 654.9
          causing obstructed labor 660.2
        perineum 654.8
        uterus NEC 654.9
          due to previous cesarean de-
            livery, section 654.2
        vagina 654.7
          causing obstructed labor 660.2
        vulva 654.8
    primary uterine inertia 661.0
    primipara, elderly or old 659.5
    prolapse
      arm or hand 652.7
        causing obstructed labor 660.0
      cord (umbilical) 663.0

Delivery (*Continued*)
  complicated (by) NEC (*Continued*)
    prolapse (*Continued*)
      fetal extremity 652.8
      foot or leg 652.8
        causing obstructed labor
          660.0
      umbilical cord (complete) (occult)
        (partial) 663.0
      uterus 654.4
        causing obstructed labor
          660.2
    prolonged labor 662.1
      first stage 662.0
      second stage 662.2
      active phase 661.2
      due to
        cervical dystocia 661.0
        contraction ring 661.4
        tetanic uterus 661.4
        uterine inertia 661.2
          primary 661.0
          secondary 661.1
      latent phase 661.0
    pyrexia during labor 659.2
    rachitic pelvis 653.2
      causing obstructed labor 660.1
    rectocele 654.4
      causing obstructed labor 660.2
    retained membranes or portions of
        placenta 666.2
      without hemorrhage 667.1
    retarded (prolonged) birth 662.1
    retention secundines (with hemor-
        rhage) 666.2
      without hemorrhage 667.1
    retroversion, uterus or cervix 654.3
      causing obstructed labor 660.2
    rigid
      cervix 654.6
        causing obstructed labor 660.2
      pelvic floor 654.4
        causing obstructed labor 660.2
      perineum or vulva 654.8
        causing obstructed labor 660.2
      vagina 654.7
        causing obstructed labor 660.2
    Robert's pelvis 653.0
      causing obstructed labor 660.1
    rupture - see also Delivery, compli-
        cated, laceration
      bladder (urinary) 665.5
      cervix 665.3
      marginal sinus 641.2
      membranes, premature 658.1
      pelvic organ NEC 665.5
      perineum (without mention of
          other laceration) - see Deliv-
          ery, complicated, laceration,
          perineum
      peritoneum 665.5
      urethra 665.5
      uterus (during labor) 665.1
        before labor 665.0
    sacculation, pregnant uterus 654.4
    sacral teratomas, fetal 653.7
      causing obstructed labor 660.1
    scar(s)
      cervix 654.6
        causing obstructed labor 660.2
      cesarean delivery, section 654.2
        causing obstructed labor 660.2
      perineum 654.8
        causing obstructed labor 660.2

Delivery (*Continued*)
  complicated (by) NEC (*Continued*)
    scar(s) (*Continued*)
      uterus NEC 654.9
        causing obstructed labor 660.2
        due to previous cesarean deliv-
          ery, section 654.2
      vagina 654.7
        causing obstructed labor 660.2
      vulva 654.8
        causing obstructed labor 660.2
    scoliotic pelvis 653.0
      causing obstructed labor 660.1
    secondary uterine inertia 661.1
    secundines, retained - see Delivery,
        complicated, placenta, retained
    separation
      placenta (premature) 641.2
      pubic bone 665.6
      symphysis pubis 665.6
    septate vagina 654.7
      causing obstructed labor 660.2
    shock (birth) (obstetric) (puerperal)
        669.1
    short cord syndrome 663.4
    shoulder
      girdle dystocia 660.4
      presentation 652.8
        causing obstructed labor 660.0
    Siamese twins 653.7
      causing obstructed labor 660.1
    slow slope active phase 661.2
    spasm
      cervix 661.4
      uterus 661.4
    spondylolisthesis, pelvis 653.3
      causing obstructed labor 660.1
    spondylolysis (lumbosacral) 653.3
      causing obstructed labor 660.1
    spondylosis 653.0
      causing obstructed labor 660.1
    stenosis or stricture
      cervix 654.6
        causing obstructed labor 660.2
      vagina 654.7
        causing obstructed labor 660.2
    sudden death, unknown cause 669.9
    tear (pelvic organ) (see also Delivery,
        complicated, laceration) 664.9
    teratomas, sacral, fetal 653.7
      causing obstructed labor 660.1
    tetanic uterus 661.4
    tipping pelvis 653.0
      causing obstructed labor 660.1
    transverse
      arrest (deep) 660.3
      presentation or lie 652.3
        with successful version 652.1
        causing obstructed labor 660.0
    trauma (obstetrical) NEC 665.9
    tumor
      abdominal, fetal 653.7
        causing obstructed labor 660.1
      pelvic organs or tissues NEC
        654.9
        causing obstructed labor 660.2
    umbilical cord (see also Delivery,
        complicated, cord) 663.9
      around neck tightly, or with com-
        pression 663.1
      entanglement NEC 663.3
        with compression 663.2
      prolapse (complete) (occult) (par-
        tial) 663.0

ICD-9-CM

Vol. 2

Delivery (*Continued*)
  complicated (by) NEC (*Continued*)
    unstable lie 652.0
      causing obstructed labor 660.0
    uterine
      inertia (*see also* Delivery, complicated, inertia, uterus) 661.2
      spasm 661.4
    vasa previa 663.5
    velamentous insertion of cord 663.5
    young maternal age 659.8 ◄
  delayed NEC 662.1
    following rupture of membranes (spontaneous) 658.2
      artificial 658.3
    second twin, triplet, etc. 662.3
  difficult NEC 669.9
    previous, affecting management of pregnancy or childbirth V23.4
    specified type NEC 669.8
  early onset (spontaneous) 644.2 ◄
  footling 652.8 ◄
    with successful version 652.1 ◄
  forceps NEC 669.5
    affecting fetus or newborn 763.2
  missed (at or near term) 656.4
  multiple gestation NEC 651.9
    with fetal loss and retention of one or more fetus(es) 651.6
    specified type NEC 651.8
      with fetal loss and retention of one or more fetus(es) 651.6
  nonviable infant 656.4
  normal - *see* category 650
  precipitate 661.3
    affecting fetus or newborn 763.6
  premature NEC (before 37 completed weeks' gestation) 644.2
    previous, affecting management of pregnancy V23.4
  quadruplet NEC 651.2
    with fetal loss and retention of one or more fetus(es) 651.5
  quintuplet NEC 651.8
    with fetal loss and retention of one or more fetus(es) 651.6
  sextuplet NEC 651.8
    with fetal loss and retention of one or more fetus(es) 651.6
  specified complication NEC 669.8
  stillbirth (near term) NEC 656.4
    early (before 22 completed weeks' gestation) 632
  term pregnancy (live birth) NEC - *see* category 650
    stillbirth NEC 656.4
  threatened premature 644.2
  triplets NEC 651.1
    with fetal loss and retention of one or more fetus(es) 651.4
    delayed delivery (one or more mates) 662.3
    locked mates 660.5
  twins NEC 651.0
    with fetal loss and retention of one fetus 651.3
    delayed delivery (one or more mates) 662.3
    locked mates 660.5
  uncomplicated - *see* category 650
  vacuum extractor NEC 669.5
    affecting fetus or newborn 763.3
  ventouse NEC 669.5
    affecting fetus or newborn 763.3

Dellen, cornea 371.41
Delusions (paranoid) 297.9
  grandiose 297.1
  parasitosis 300.29
  systematized 297.1
Dementia 294.8
  alcoholic (*see also* Psychosis, alcoholic) 291.2
  Alzheimer's - *see* Alzheimer's, dementia
  arteriosclerotic (simple type) (uncomplicated) 290.40
    with
      acute confusional state 290.41
      delirium 290.41
      delusional features 290.42
      depressive features 290.43
    depressed type 290.43
    paranoid type 290.42
  Binswanger's 290.12
  catatonic (acute) (*see also* Schizophrenia) 295.2
  congenital (*see also* Retardation, mental) 319
  degenerative 290.9
    presenile-onset - *see* Dementia, presenile
    senile-onset - *see* Dementia, senile
  developmental (*see also* Schizophrenia) 295.9
  dialysis 294.8
    transient 293.9
  due to or associated with condition(s) classified elsewhere
    multiple sclerosis 340 [294.1]
    polyarteritis nodosa 446.0 [294.1]
  hebephrenic (acute) 295.1
  Heller's (infantile psychosis) (*see also* Psychosis, childhood) 299.1
  idiopathic 290.9
    presenile-onset - *see* Dementia, presenile
    senile-onset - *see* Dementia, senile
  in
    Alzheimer's disease - *see* Alzheimer's, dementia
    arteriosclerotic brain disease 290.40
    cerebral lipidoses 330.1 [294.1]
    epilepsy 345.9 [294.1]
    hepatolenticular degeneration 275.1 [294.1]
    Huntington's chorea 333.4 [294.1]
    Jakob-Creutzfeldt disease 046.1 [294.1]
    multiple sclerosis 340 [294.1]
    neurosyphilis 094.9 [294.1]
    Pelizaeus-Merzbacher disease 333.0 [294.1]
    Pick's disease 331.1 [294.1]
    polyarteritis nodosa 446.0 [294.1]
    senility 290.0
    Wilson's disease 275.1 [294.1]
  induced by drug 292.82
  infantile, infantilia (*see also* Psychosis, childhood) 299.0
  multi-infarct (cerebrovascular) (*see also* Dementia, arteriosclerotic) 290.40
  old age 290.0
  paralytica, paralytic 094.1
    juvenilis 090.40
    syphilitic 094.1
      congenital 090.40
    tabetic form 094.1
  paranoid (*see also* Schizophrenia) 295.3

Dementia (*Continued*)
  paraphrenic (*see also* Schizophrenia) 295.3
  paretic 094.1
  praecox (*see also* Schizophrenia) 295.9
  presenile 290.10
    with
      acute confusional state 290.11
      delirium 290.11
      delusional features 290.12
      depressive features 290.13
    depressed type 290.13
    paranoid type 290.12
    simple type 290.10
    uncomplicated 290.10
  primary (acute) (*see also* Schizophrenia) 295.0
  progressive, syphilitic 094.1
  puerperal - *see* Psychosis, puerperal
  schizophrenic (*see also* Schizophrenia) 295.9
  senile 290.0
    with
      acute confusional state 290.3
      delirium 290.3
      delusional features 290.20
      depressive features 290.21
    depressed type 290.21
    exhaustion 290.0
    paranoid type 290.20
  simple type (acute) (*see also* Schizophrenia) 295.0
  simplex (acute) (*see also* Schizophrenia) 295.0
  syphilitic 094.1
  uremic - *see* Uremia
Demerol dependence (*see also* Dependence) 304.0
Demineralization, ankle (*see also* Osteoporosis) 733.00
Demodex folliculorum (infestation) 133.8
de Morgan's spots (senile angiomas) 448.1
Demyelinating polyneuritis, chronic inflammatory 357.8 ◄
Demyelination, demyelinization
  central nervous system 341.9
    specified NEC 341.8
  corpus callosum (central) 341.8
  global 340
Dengue (fever) 061
  sandfly 061
  vaccination, prophylactic (against) V05.1
  virus hemorrhagic fever 065.4
Dens
  evaginatus 520.2
  in dente 520.2
  invaginatus 520.2
Density
  increased, bone (disseminated) (generalized) (spotted) 733.99
  lung (nodular) 518.89
Dental - *see also* condition
  examination only V72.2
Dentia praecox 520.6
Denticles (in pulp) 522.2
Dentigerous cyst 526.0
Dentin
  irregular (in pulp) 522.3
  opalescent 520.5
  secondary (in pulp) 522.3
  sensitive 521.8
Dentinogenesis imperfecta 520.5
Dentinoma (M9271/0) 213.1
  upper jaw (bone) 213.0

Dentition 520.7
  abnormal 520.6
  anomaly 520.6
  delayed 520.6
  difficult 520.7
  disorder of 520.6
  precocious 520.6
  retarded 520.6
Denture sore (mouth) 528.9
Dependence

> Note   Use the following fifth-digit
> subclassification with category 304:
>
> 0   unspecified
> 1   continuous
> 2   episodic
> 3   in remission

  with
    withdrawal symptoms
      alcohol 291.81
      drug 292.0
  14-hydroxy-dihydromorphinone 304.0
  absinthe 304.6
  acemorphan 304.0
  acetanilid(e) 304.6
  acetophenetidin 304.6
  acetorphine 304.0
  acetyldihydrocodeine 304.0
  acetyldihydrocodeinone 304.0
  Adalin 304.1
  Afghanistan black 304.3
  agrypnal 304.1
  alcohol, alcoholic (ethyl) (methyl)
      (wood) 303.9
    maternal, with suspected fetal dam-
        age affecting management of
        pregnancy 655.4
  allobarbitone 304.1
  allonal 304.1
  allylisopropylacetylurea 304.1
  alphaprodine (hydrochloride) 304.0
  Alurate 304.1
  Alvodine 304.0
  amethocaine 304.6
  amidone 304.0
  amidopyrine 304.6
  aminopyrine 304.6
  amobarbital 304.1
  amphetamine(s) (type) (drugs classifia-
      ble to 969.7) 304.4
  amylene hydrate 304.6
  amylobarbitone 304.1
  amylocaine 304.6
  Amytal (sodium) 304.1
  analgesic (drug) NEC 304.6
    synthetic with morphine-like effect
        304.0
  anesthetic (agent) (drug) (gas) (gen-
      eral) (local) NEC 304.6
  Angel dust 304.6
  anileridine 304.0
  antipyrine 304.6
  aprobarbital 304.1
  aprobarbitone 304.1
  atropine 304.6
  Avertin (bromide) 304.6
  barbenyl 304.1
  barbital(s) 304.1
  barbitone 304.1
  barbiturate(s) (compounds) (drugs
      classifiable to 967.0) 304.1
  barbituric acid (and compounds) 304.1
  benzedrine 304.4

Dependence (*Continued*)
  benzylmorphine 304.0
  Beta-chlor 304.1
  bhang 304.3
  blue velvet 304.0
  Brevital 304.1
  bromal (hydrate) 304.1
  bromide(s) NEC 304.1
  bromine compounds NEC 304.1
  bromisovalum 304.1
  bromoform 304.1
  Bromo-seltzer 304.1
  bromural 304.1
  butabarbital (sodium) 304.1
  butabarpal 304.1
  butallylonal 304.1
  butethal 304.1
  buthalitone (sodium) 304.1
  Butisol 304.1
  butobarbitone 304.1
  butyl chloral (hydrate) 304.1
  caffeine 304.4
  cannabis (indica) (sativa) (resin) (deriv-
      atives) (type) 304.3
  carbamazepine 304.6
  Carbrital 304.1
  carbromal 304.1
  carisoprodol 304.6
  Catha (edulis) 304.4
  chloral (betaine) (hydrate) 304.1
  chloralamide 304.1
  chloralformamide 304.1
  chloralose 304.1
  chlordiazepoxide 304.1
  Chloretone 304.1
  chlorobutanol 304.1
  chlorodyne 304.1
  chloroform 304.6
  Cliradon 304.0
  coca (leaf) and derivatives 304.2
  cocaine 304.2
    hydrochloride 304.2
    salt (any) 304.2
  codeine 304.0
  combination of drugs (excluding mor-
      phine or opioid type drug) NEC
      304.8
    morphine or opioid type drug with
        any other drug 304.7
  croton-chloral 304.1
  cyclobarbital 304.1
  cyclobarbitone 304.1
  dagga 304.3
  Delvinal 304.1
  Demerol 304.0
  desocodeine 304.0
  desomorphine 304.0
  desoxyephedrine 304.4
  DET 304.5
  dexamphetamine 304.4
  dexedrine 304.4
  dextromethorphan 304.0
  dextromoramide 304.0
  dextronorpseudoephedrine 304.4
  dextrorphan 304.0
  diacetylmorphine 304.0
  Dial 304.1
  diallylbarbituric acid 304.1
  diamorphine 304.0
  diazepam 304.1
  dibucaine 304.6
  dichloroethane 304.6
  diethyl barbituric acid 304.1
  diethylsulfone-diethylmethane 304.1

Dependence (*Continued*)
  difencloxazine 304.0
  dihydrocodeine 304.0
  dihydrocodeinone 304.0
  dihydrohydroxycodeinone 304.0
  dihydroisocodeine 304.0
  dihydromorphine 304.0
  dihydromorphinone 304.0
  dihydroxcodeinone 304.0
  Dilaudid 304.0
  dimenhydrinate 304.6
  dimethylmeperidine 304.0
  dimethyltriptamine 304.5
  Dionin 304.0
  diphenoxylate 304.6
  dipipanone 304.0
  d-lysergic acid diethylamide 304.5
  DMT 304.5
  Dolophine 304.0
  DOM 304.2
  doriden 304.1
  dormiral 304.1
  Dormison 304.1
  Dromoran 304.0
  drug NEC 304.9
    analgesic NEC 304.6
    combination (excluding morphine or
        opioid type drug) NEC 304.8
      morphine or opioid type drug
          with any other drug 304.7
    complicating pregnancy, childbirth,
        or puerperium 648.3
      affecting fetus or newborn 779.5
    hallucinogenic 304.5
    hypnotic NEC 304.1
    narcotic NEC 304.9
    psychostimulant NEC 304.4
    sedative 304.1
    soporific NEC 304.1
    specified type NEC 304.6
    suspected damage to fetus affecting
        management of pregnancy
        655.5
    synthetic, with morphine-like effect
        304.0
    tranquilizing 304.1
  duboisine 304.6
  ectylurea 304.1
  Endocaine 304.6
  Equanil 304.1
  Eskabarb 304.1
  ethchlorvynol 304.1
  ether (ethyl) (liquid) (vapor) (vinyl)
      304.6
  ethidene 304.6
  ethinamate 304.1
  ethoheptazine 304.6
  ethyl
    alcohol 303.9
    bromide 304.6
    carbamate 304.6
    chloride 304.6
    morphine 304.0
  ethylene (gas) 304.6
    dichloride 304.6
  ethylidene chloride 304.6
  etilfen 304.1
  etorphine 304.0
  etoval 304.1
  eucodal 304.0
  euneryl 304.1
  Evipal 304.1
  Evipan 304.1
  fentanyl 304.0

Dependence *(Continued)*
ganja 304.3
gardenal 304.1
gardenpanyl 304.1
gelsemine 304.6
Gelsemium 304.6
Gemonil 304.1
glucochloral 304.1
glue (airplane) (sniffing) 304.6
glutethimide 304.1
hallucinogenics 304.5
hashish 304.3
headache powder NEC 304.6
Heavenly Blue 304.5
hedonal 304.1
hemp 304.3
heptabarbital 304.1
Heptalgin 304.0
heptobarbitone 304.1
heroin 304.0
   salt (any) 304.0
hexethal (sodium) 304.1
hexobarbital 304.1
Hycodan 304.0
hydrocodone 304.0
hydromorphinol 304.0
hydromorphinone 304.0
hydromorphone 304.0
hydroxycodeine 304.0
hypnotic NEC 304.1
Indian hemp 304.3
intranarcon 304.1
Kemithal 304.1
ketobemidone 304.0
khat 304.4
kif 304.3
Lactuca (virosa) extract 304.1
lactucarium 304.1
laudanum 304.0
Lebanese red 304.3
Leritine 304.0
lettuce opium 304.1
Levanil 304.1
Levo-Dromoran 304.0
levo-iso-methadone 304.0
levorphanol 304.0
Librium 304.1
Lomotil 304.6
Lotusate 304.1
LSD (-25) (and derivatives) 304.5
Luminal 304.1
lysergic acid 304.5
   amide 304.5
maconha 304.3
magic mushroom 304.5
marihuana 304.3
MDA (methylene dioxyamphetamine)
   304.4
Mebaral 304.1
Medinal 304.1
Medomin 304.1
megahallucinogenics 304.5
meperidine 304.0
mephobarbital 304.1
meprobamate 304.1
mescaline 304.5
methadone 304.0
methamphetamine(s) 304.4
methaqualone 304.1
metharbital 304.1
methitural 304.1
methobarbitone 304.1
methohexital 304.1
methopholine 304.6

Dependence *(Continued)*
methyl
   alcohol 303.9
   bromide 304.6
   morphine 304.0
   sulfonal 304.1
methylated spirit 303.9
methylbutinol 304.6
methyldihydromorphinone 304.0
methylene
   chloride 304.6
   dichloride 304.6
   dioxyamphetamine (MDA) 304.4
methylparafynol 304.1
methylphenidate 304.4
methyprylone 304.1
metopon 304.0
Miltown 304.1
morning glory seeds 304.5,
morphinan(s) 304.0
morphine (sulfate) (sulfite) (type)
      (drugs classifiable to 965.00-965.09)
      304.0
morphine or opioid type drug (drugs
      classifiable to 965.00-965.09) with
      any other drug 304.7
morphinol(s) 304.0
morphinon 304.0
morpholinylethylmorphine 304.0
mylomide 304.1
myristicin 304.5
narcotic (drug) NEC 304.9
nealbarbital 304.1
nealbarbitone 304.1
Nembutal 304.1
Neonal 304.1
Neraval 304.1
Neravan 304.1
neurobarb 304.1
nicotine 305.1
Nisentil 304.0
nitrous oxide 304.6
Noctec 304.1
Noludar 304.1
nonbarbiturate sedatives and tranquil-
      izers with similar effect 304.1
noptil 304.1
normorphine 304.0
noscapine 304.0
Novocaine 304.6
Numorphan 304.0
nunol 304.1
Nupercaine 304.6
Oblivon 304.1
on
   aspirator V46.0
   hyperbaric chamber V46.8
   iron lung V46.1
   machine (enabling) V46.9
      specified type NEC V46.8
   Possum (patient-operated-selector-
      mechanism) V46.8
   renal dialysis machine V45.1
   respirator V46.1
opiate 304.0
opioids 304.0
opioid type drug 304.0
   with any other drug 304.7
opium (alkaloids) (derivatives) (tinc-
      ture) 304.0
ortal 304.1
Oxazepam 304.1
oxycodone 304.0
oxymorphone 304.0

Dependence *(Continued)*
Palfium 304.0
Panadol 304.6
pantopium 304.0
pantopon 304.0
papaverine 304.0
paracetamol 304.6
paracodin 304.0
paraldehyde 304.1
paregoric 304.0
Parzone 304.0
PCP (phencyclidine) 304.6
Pearly Gates 304.5
pentazocine 304.0
pentobarbital 304.1
pentobarbitone (sodium) 304.1
Pentothal 304.1
Percaine 304.6
Percodan 304.0
Perichlor 304.1
Pernocton 304.1
Pernoston 304.1
peronine 304.0
pethidine (hydrochloride) 304.0
petrichloral 304.1
peyote 304.5
Phanodorn 304.1
phenacetin 304.6
phenadoxone 304.0
phenaglycodol 304.1
phenazocine 304.0
phencyclidine 304.6
phenmetrazine 304.4
phenobal 304.1
phenobarbital 304.1
phenobarbitone 304.1
phenomorphan 304.0
phenonyl 304.1
phenoperidine 304.0
pholcodine 304.0
piminodine 304.0
Pipadone 304.0
Pitkin's solution 304.6
Placidyl 304.1
polysubstance 304.8
Pontocaine 304.6
pot 304.3
potassium bromide 304.1
Preludin 304.4
Prinadol 304.0
probarbital 304.1
procaine 304.6
propanal 304.1
propoxyphene 304.6
psilocibin 304.5
psilocin 304.5
psilocybin 304.5
psilocyline 304.5
psilocyn 304.5
psychedelic agents 304.5
psychostimulant NEC 304.4
psychotomimetic agents 304.5
pyrahexyl 304.3
Pyramidon 304.6
quinalbarbitone 304.1
racemoramide 304.0
racemorphan 304.0
Rela 304.6
scopolamine 304.6
secobarbital 304.1
seconal 304.1
sedative NEC 304.1
   nonbarbiturate with barbiturate ef-
      fect 304.1

Dependence *(Continued)*
  Sedormid 304.1
  sernyl 304.1
  sodium bromide 304.1
  Soma 304.6
  Somnal 304.1
  Somnos 304.1
  Soneryl 304.1
  soporific (drug) NEC 304.1
  specified drug NEC 304.6
  speed 304.4
  spinocaine 304.6
  stovaine 304.6
  STP 304.5
  stramonium 304.6
  Sulfonal 304.1
  sulfonethylmethane 304.1
  sulfonmethane 304.1
  Surital 304.1
  synthetic drug with morphine-like effect 304.0
  talbutal 304.1
  tetracaine 304.6
  tetrahydrocannabinol 304.3
  tetronal 304.1
  THC 304.3
  thebacon 304.0
  thebaine 304.0
  thiamil 304.1
  thiamylal 304.1
  thiopental 304.1
  tobacco 305.1
  toluene, toluol 304.6
  tranquilizer NEC 304.1
    nonbarbiturate with barbiturate effect 304.1
  tribromacetaldehyde 304.6
  tribromethanol 304.6
  tribromomethane 304.6
  trichloroethanol 304.6
  trichoroethyl phosphate 304.1
  triclofos 304.1
  Trional 304.1
  Tuinal 304.1
  Turkish green 304.3
  urethan(e) 304.6
  Valium 304.1
  Valmid 304.1
  veganin 304.0
  veramon 304.1
  Veronal 304.1
  versidyne 304.6
  vinbarbital 304.1
  vinbarbitone 304.1
  vinyl bitone 304.1
  vitamin B_6 266.1
  wine 303.9
  Zactane 304.6
Dependency
  passive 301.6
  reactions 301.6
Depersonalization (episode, in neurotic state) (neurotic) (syndrome) 300.6
Depletion
  carbohydrates 271.9
  complement factor 279.8
  extracellular fluid 276.5
  plasma 276.5
  potassium 276.8
    nephropathy 588.8
  salt or sodium 276.1
    causing heat exhaustion or prostration 992.4
    nephropathy 593.9

Depletion *(Continued)*
  volume 276.5
    extracellular fluid 276.5
    plasma 276.5
Deposit
  argentous, cornea 371.16
  bone, in Boeck's sarcoid 135
  calcareous, calcium - *see* Calcification
  cholesterol
    retina 362.82
    skin 709.3
    vitreous (humor) 379.22
  conjunctival 372.56
  cornea, corneal NEC 371.10
    argentous 371.16
    in
      cystinosis 270.0 *[371.15]*
      mucopolysaccharidosis 277.5 *[371.15]*
  crystalline, vitreous (humor) 379.22
  hemosiderin, in old scars of cornea 371.11
  metallic, in lens 366.45
  skin 709.3
  teeth, tooth (betel) (black) (green) (materia alba) (orange) (soft) (tobacco) 523.6
  urate, in kidney (*see also* Disease, renal) 593.9
Depraved appetite 307.52
Depression 311
  acute (*see also* Psychosis, affective) 296.2
    recurrent episode 296.3
    single episode 296.2
  agitated (*see also* Psychosis, affective) 296.2
    recurrent episode 296.3
    single episode 296.2
  anaclitic 309.21
  anxiety 300.4
  arches 734
    congenital 754.61
  autogenous (*see also* Psychosis, affective) 296.2
    recurrent episode 296.3
    single episode 296.2
  basal metabolic rate (BMR) 794.7
  bone marrow 289.9
  central nervous system 799.1
    newborn 779.2
  cerebral 331.9
    newborn 779.2
  cerebrovascular 437.8
    newborn 779.2
  chest wall 738.3
  endogenous (*see also* Psychosis, affective) 296.2
    recurrent episode 296.3
    single episode 296.2
  functional activity 780.9
  hysterical 300.11
  involutional, climacteric, or menopausal (*see also* Psychosis, affective) 296.2
    recurrent episode 296.3
    single episode 296.2
  manic (*see also* Psychosis, affective) 296.80
  medullary 348.8
    newborn 779.2
  mental 300.4
  metatarsal heads - see Depression, arches

Depression *(Continued)*
  metatarsus - see Depression, arches
  monopolar (*see also* Psychosis, affective) 296.2
    recurrent episode 296.3
    single episode 296.2
  nervous 300.4
  neurotic 300.4
  nose 738.0
  postpartum 648.4
  psychogenic 300.4
    reactive 298.0
  psychoneurotic 300.4
  psychotic (*see also* Psychosis, affective) 296.2
    reactive 298.0
    recurrent episode 296.3
    single episode 296.2
  reactive 300.4
    neurotic 300.4
    psychogenic 298.0
    psychoneurotic 300.4
    psychotic 298.0
  recurrent 296.3
  respiratory center 348.8
    newborn 770.8
  scapula 736.89
  senile 290.21
  situational (acute) (brief) 309.0
    prolonged 309.1
  skull 754.0
  sternum 738.3
  visual field 368.40
Depressive reaction - *see also* Reaction, depressive
  acute (transient) 309.0
    with anxiety 309.28
  prolonged 309.1
  situational (acute) 309.0
    prolonged 309.1
Deprivation
  cultural V62.4
  emotional V62.89
    affecting
      adult 995.82
      infant or child 995.51
  food 994.2
    specific substance NEC 269.8
  protein (familial) (kwashiorkor) 260
  social V62.4
    affecting
      adult 995.82
      infant or child 995.51
  symptoms, syndrome
    alcohol 291.81
    drug 292.0
  vitamins (*see also* Deficiency, vitamin) 269.2
  water 994.3
de Quervain's
  disease (tendon sheath) 727.04
  thyroiditis (subacute granulomatous thyroiditis) 245.1
Derangement
  ankle (internal) 718.97
    current injury (*see also* Dislocation, ankle) 837.0
    recurrent 718.37
  cartilage (articular) NEC (*see also* Disorder, cartilage, articular) 718.0
    knee 717.9
      recurrent 718.36
    recurrent 718.3

ICD-9-CM

Vol. 2

Derangement *(Continued)*
  collateral ligament (knee) (medial) (tibial) 717.82
    current injury 844.1
      lateral (fibular) 844.0
    lateral (fibular) 717.81
      current injury 844.0
  cruciate ligament (knee) (posterior) 717.84
    anterior 717.83
      current injury 844.2
    current injury 844.2
  elbow (internal) 718.92
    current injury *(see also* Dislocation, elbow) 832.00
    recurrent 718.32
  gastrointestinal 536.9
  heart - see Disease, heart
  hip (joint) (internal) (old) 718.95
    current injury *(see also* Dislocation, hip) 835.00
    recurrent 718.35
  intervertebral disc - see Displacement, intervertebral disc
  joint (internal) 718.90
    ankle 718.97
    current injury - *see also* Dislocation, by site
      knee, meniscus or cartilage *(see also* Tear, meniscus) 836.2
    elbow 718.92
    foot 718.97
    hand 718.94
    hip 718.95
    knee 717.9
    multiple sites 718.99
    pelvic region 718.95
    recurrent 718.30
      ankle 718.37
      elbow 718.32
      foot 718.37
      hand 718.34
      hip 718.35
      knee 718.36
      multiple sites 718.39
      pelvic region 718.35
      shoulder (region) 718.31
      specified site NEC 718.38
      temporomandibular (old) 524.69
      wrist 718.33
    shoulder (region) 718.91
    specified site NEC 718.98
    spine NEC 724.9
    temporomandibular 524.69
    wrist 718.93
  knee (cartilage) (internal) 717.9
    current injury *(see also* Tear, meniscus) 836.2
    ligament 717.89
      capsular 717.85
      collateral - *see* Derangement, collateral ligament
      cruciate - *see* Derangement, cruciate ligament
      specified NEC 717.85
    recurrent 718.36
  low back NEC 724.9
  meniscus NEC (knee) 717.5
    current injury *(see also* Tear, meniscus) 836.2
    lateral 717.40
      anterior horn 717.42
      posterior horn 717.43
      specified NEC 717.49

Derangement *(Continued)*
  meniscus NEC (knee) *(Continued)*
    medial 717.3
      anterior horn 717.1
      posterior horn 717.2
    recurrent 718.3
    site other than knee - *see* Disorder, cartilage, articular
  mental *(see also* Psychosis) 298.9
  rotator cuff (recurrent) (tear) 726.10
    current 840.4
  sacroiliac (old) 724.6
    current - *see* Dislocation, sacroiliac
  semilunar cartilage (knee) 717.5
    current injury 836.2
      lateral 836.1
      medial 836.0
    recurrent 718.3
  shoulder (internal) 718.91
    current injury *(see also* Dislocation, shoulder) 831.00
    recurrent 718.31
  spine (recurrent) NEC 724.9
    current - *see* Dislocation, spine
  temporomandibular (internal) (joint) (old) 524.69
    current - *see* Dislocation, jaw
Dercum's disease or syndrome (adiposis dolorosa) 272.8
Derealization (neurotic) 300.6
Dermal - *see* condition
Dermaphytid - *see* Dermatophytosis
Dermatergosis - *see* Dermatitis
Dermatitis (allergic) (contact) (occupational) (venenata) 692.9
  ab igne 692.82
  acneiform 692.9
  actinic (due to sun) 692.70
    acute 692.72
    chronic NEC 692.74
    other than from sun NEC 692.82
  ambustionis
    due to
      burn or scald - *see* Burn, by site
      sunburn 692.71
  amebic 006.6
  ammonia 691.0
  anaphylactoid NEC 692.9
  arsenical 692.4
  artefacta 698.4
    psychogenic 316 [698.4]
  asthmatic 691.8
  atopic (allergic) (intrinsic) 691.8
    psychogenic 316 [691.8]
  atrophicans 701.8
    diffusa 701.8
    maculosa 701.3
  berlock, berloque 692.72
  blastomycetic 116.0
  blister beetle 692.89
  Brucella NEC 023.9
  bullosa 694.9
    striata pratensis 692.6
  bullous 694.9
    mucosynechial, atrophic 694.60
      with ocular involvement 694.61
    seasonal 694.8
  calorica
    due to
      burn or scald - *see* Burn, by site
      cold 692.89
      sunburn 692.71
  caterpillar 692.89

Dermatitis *(Continued)*
  cercarial 120.3
  combustionis
    due to
      burn or scald - *see* Burn, by site
      sunburn 692.71
  congelationis 991.5
  contusiformis 695.2
  diabetic 250.8
  diaper 691.0
  diphtheritica 032.85
  due to
    acetone 692.2
    acids 692.4
    adhesive plaster 692.4
    alcohol (skin contact) (substances classifiable to 980.0-980.9) 692.4
      taken internally 693.8
    alkalis 692.4
    allergy NEC 692.9
    ammonia (household) (liquid) 692.4
    arnica 692.3
    arsenic 692.4
      taken internally 693.8
    blister beetle 692.89
    cantharides 692.3
    carbon disulphide 692.2
    caterpillar 692.89
    caustics 692.4
    cereal (ingested) 693.1
      contact with skin 692.5
    chemical(s) NEC 692.4
      internal 693.8
      irritant NEC 692.4
      taken internally 693.8
    chlorocompounds 692.2
    coffee (ingested) 693.1
      contact with skin 692.5
    cold weather 692.89
    cosmetics 692.81
    cyclohexanes 692.2
    deodorant 692.81
    detergents 692.0
    dichromate 692.4
    drugs and medicinals (correct substance properly administered) (internal use) 693.0
      external (in contact with skin) 692.3
        wrong substance given or taken 976.9
        specified substance - *see* Table of Drugs and Chemicals
      wrong substance given or taken 977.9
        specified substance - *see* Table of Drugs and Chemicals
    dyes 692.89
      hair 692.89
    epidermophytosis - *see* Dermatophytosis
    esters 692.2
    external irritant NEC 692.9
      specified agent NEC 692.89
    eye shadow 692.81
    fish (ingested) 693.1
      contact with skin 692.5
    flour (ingested) 693.1
      contact with skin 692.5
    food (ingested) 693.1
      in contact with skin 692.5
    fruit (ingested) 693.1
      contact with skin 692.5
    fungicides 692.3

Dermatitis *(Continued)*
  due to *(Continued)*
    furs 692.89
    glycols 692.2
    greases NEC 692.1
    hair dyes 692.89
    hot
      objects and materials - *see* Burn,
        by site
      weather or places 692.89
    hydrocarbons 692.2
    infrared rays, except from sun
      692.82
      solar NEC (*see also* Dermatitis, due
        to, sun) 692.70
    ingested substance 693.9
      drugs and medicinals (*see also*
        Dermatitis, due to, drugs and
        medicinals) 693.0
      food 693.1
      specified substance NEC 693.8
    ingestion or injection of
      chemical 693.8
      drug (correct substance properly
        administered) 693.0
        wrong substance given or taken
          977.9
          specified substance - *see* Table
            of Drugs and Chemicals
    insecticides 692.4
    internal agent 693.9
      drugs and medicinals (*see also*
        Dermatitis, due to, drugs and
        medicinals) 693.0
      food (ingested) 693.1
        in contact with skin 692.5
      specified agent NEC 693.8
    iodine 692.3
    iodoform 692.3
    irradiation 692.82
    jewelry 692.83
    keratolytics 692.3
    ketones 692.2
    lacquer tree (Rhus verniciflua)
      692.6
    light (sun) NEC (*see also* Dermatitis,
      due to, sun) 692.70
      other 692.82
    low temperature 692.89
    mascara 692.81
    meat (ingested) 693.1
      contact with skin 692.5
    mercury, mercurials 692.3
    metals 692.83
    milk (ingested) 693.1
      contact with skin 692.5
    Neomycin 692.3
    nylon 692.4
    oils NEC 692.1
    paint solvent 692.2
    pediculocides 692.3
    petroleum products (substances clas-
      sifiable to 981) 692.4
    phenol 692.3
    photosensitiveness, photosensitivity
      (sun) 692.72
      other light 692.82
    plants NEC 692.6
    plasters, medicated (any) 692.3
    plastic 692.4
    poison
      ivy (Rhus toxicodendron) 692.6
      oak (Rhus diversiloba) 692.6
      plant or vine 692.6

Dermatitis *(Continued)*
  due to *(Continued)*
    poison *(Continued)*
      sumac (Rhus venenata) 692.6
      vine (Rhus radicans) 692.6
    preservatives 692.89
    primrose (primula) 692.6
    primula 692.6
    radiation 692.82
      sun NEC (*see also* Dermatitis, due
        to, sun) 692.70
    radioactive substance 692.82
    radium 692.82
    ragweed (Senecio jacobae)
      692.6
    Rhus (diversiloba) (radicans) (toxi-
      codendron) (venenata) (vernici-
      flua) 692.6
    rubber 692.4
    scabicides 692.3
    Senecio jacobae 692.6
    solar radiation - *see* Dermatitis, due
      to, sun
    solvents (any) (substances classifia-
      ble to (982.0-982.8) 692.2
      chlorocompound group 692.2
      cyclohexane group 692.2
      ester group 692.2
      glycol group 692.2
      hydrocarbon group 692.2
      ketone group 692.2
      paint 692.2
    specified agent NEC 692.89
    sun 692.70
      acute 692.72
      chronic NEC 692.74
      specified NEC 692.79
    sunburn 692.71
    sunshine NEC (*see also* Dermatitis,
      due to, sun) 692.70
    tetrachlorethylene 692.2
    toluene 692.2
    topical medications 692.3
    turpentine 692.2
    ultraviolet rays, except from sun
      692.82
      sun NEC (*see also* Dermatitis, due
        to, sun) 692.70
    vaccine or vaccination (correct sub-
      stance properly administered)
      693.0
      wrong substance given or taken
        bacterial vaccine 978.8
          specified - *see* Table of Drugs
            and Chemicals
        other vaccines NEC 979.9
          specified - *see* Table of Drugs
            and Chemicals
    varicose veins (*see also* Varicose,
      vein, inflamed or infected)
      454.1
    x-rays 692.82
  dyshydrotic 705.81
  dysmenorrheica 625.8
  eczematoid NEC 692.9
    infectious 690.8
  eczematous NEC 692.9
  epidemica 695.89
  erysipelatosa 695.81
  escharotica - *see* Burn, by site
  exfoliativa, exfoliative 695.89
    generalized 695.89
    infantum 695.81
    neonatorum 695.81

Dermatitis *(Continued)*
  eyelid 373.31
    allergic 373.32
    contact 373.32
    eczematous 373.31
    herpes (zoster) 053.20
      simplex 054.41
    infective 373.5
      due to
        actinomycosis 039.3 *[373.5]*
        herpes
          simplex 054.41
          zoster 053.20
        impetigo 684 *[373.5]*
        leprosy (*see also* Leprosy) 030.0
          [373.4]
        lupus vulgaris (tuberculous) (*see*
          also Tuberculosis) 017.0
          [373.4]
        mycotic dermatitis (*see also* Der-
          matomycosis) 111.9 *[373.5]*
        vaccinia 051.0 *[373.5]*
          postvaccination 999.0 *[373.5]*
        yaws (*see also* Yaws) 102.9 *[373.4]*
  facta, factitia 698.4
    psychogenic 316 *[698.4]*
  ficta 698.4
    psychogenic 316 *[698.4]*
  flexural 691.8
  follicularis 704.8
  friction 709.8
  fungus 111.9
    specified type NEC 111.8
  gangrenosa, gangrenous (infantum)
    (*see also* Gangrene) 785.4
  gestationis 646.8
  gonococcal 098.89
  gouty 274.89
  harvest mite 133.8
  heat 692.89
  herpetiformis (bullous) (erythematous)
    (pustular) (vesicular) 694.0
    juvenile 694.2
    senile 694.5
  hiemalis 692.89
  hypostatic, hypostatica 454.1
    with ulcer 454.2
  impetiginous 684
  infantile (acute) (chronic) (intertrigi-
    nous) (intrinsic) (seborrheic)
    690.12
  infectiosa eczematoides 690.8
  infectious (staphylococcal) (streptococ-
    cal) 686.9
    eczematoid 690.8
  infective eczematoid 690.8
  Jacquet's (diaper dermatitis) 691.0
  leptus 133.8
  lichenified NEC 692.9
  lichenoid, chronic 701.0
  lichenoides purpurica pigmentosa
    709.1
  meadow 692.6
  medicamentosa (correct substance
    properly administered) (internal
    use) (*see also* Dermatitis, due to,
    drugs or medicinals) 693.0
    due to contact with skin 692.3
  mite 133.8
  multiformis 694.0
    juvenile 694.2
    senile 694.5
  napkin 691.0
  neuro 698.3

ICD-9-CM

Vol. 2

Dermatitis *(Continued)*
neurotica 694.0
nummular NEC 692.9
osteatosis, osteatotic 706.8
papillaris capillitii 706.1
pellagrous 265.2
perioral 695.3
perstans 696.1
photosensitivity (sun) 692.72
   other light 692.82
pigmented purpuric lichenoid
   709.1
polymorpha dolorosa 694.0
primary irritant 692.9
pruriginosa 694.0
pruritic NEC 692.9
psoriasiform nodularis 696.2
psychogenic 316
purulent 686.00
pustular contagious 051.2
pyococcal 686.00
pyocyaneus 686.09
pyogenica 686.00
radiation 692.82
repens 696.1
Ritter's (exfoliativa) 695.81
Schamberg's (progressive pigmentary
   dermatosis) 709.09
schistosome 120.3
seasonal bullous 694.8
seborrheic 690.10
   infantile 690.12
sensitization NEC 692.9
septic (*see also* Septicemia) 686.00
   gonococcal 098.89
solar, solare NEC (*see also* Dermatitis,
   due to, sun) 692.70
stasis 459.81
   due to
      postphlebitic syndrome 459.1
      varicose veins - *see* Varicose
   ulcerated or with ulcer (varicose)
      454.2
sunburn 692.71
suppurative 686.00
traumatic NEC 709.8
trophoneurotica 694.0
ultraviolet, except from sun 692.82
   due to sun NEC (*see also* Dermatitis,
      due to, sun) 692.70
varicose 454.1
   with ulcer 454.2
vegetans 686.8
verrucosa 117.2
xerotic 706.8
Dermatoarthritis, lipoid 272.8 *[713.0]*
Dermatochalasia, dermatochalasis
   374.87
Dermatofibroma (lenticulare) (M8832/0)
   - *see also* Neoplasm, skin, benign
   protuberans (M8832/1) - *see* Neo-
      plasm, skin, uncertain behavior
Dermatofibrosarcoma (protuberans)
   (M8832/3) - *see* Neoplasm, skin, ma-
      lignant
Dermatographia 708.3
Dermatolysis (congenital) (exfoliativa)
   757.39
   acquired 701.8
   eyelids 374.34
   palpebrarum 374.34
   senile 701.8
Dermatomegaly NEC 701.8
Dermatomucomyositis 710.3

Dermatomycosis 111.9
   furfuracea 111.0
   specified type NEC 111.8
Dermatomyositis (acute) (chronic) 710.3
Dermatoneuritis of children 985.0
Dermatophiliasis 134.1
Dermatophytide - *see* Dermatophytosis
Dermatophytosis (Epidermophyton) (in-
      fection) (microsporum) (tinea) (Tri-
      chophyton) 110.9
   beard 110.0
   body 110.5
   deep seated 110.6
   fingernails 110.1
   foot 110.4
   groin 110.3
   hand 110.2
   nail 110.1
   perianal (area) 110.3
   scalp 110.0
   scrotal 110.8
   specified site NEC 110.8
   toenails 110.1
   vulva 110.8
Dermatopolyneuritis 985.0
Dermatorrhexis 756.83
   acquired 701.8
Dermatosclerosis (*see also* Scleroderma)
   710.1
   localized 701.0
Dermatosis 709.9
   Andrews' 686.8
   atopic 691.8
   Bowen's (M8081/2) - *see* Neoplasm,
      skin, in situ
   bullous 694.9
      specified type NEC 694.8
   erythematosquamous 690.8
   exfoliativa 695.89
   factitial 698.4
   gonococcal 098.89
   herpetiformis 694.0
      juvenile 694.2
      senile 694.5
   hysterical 300.11
   menstrual NEC 709.8
   neutrophilic, acute febrile 695.89
   occupational (*see also* Dermatitis)
      692.9
   papulosa nigra 709.8
   pigmentary NEC 709.00
      progressive 709.09
      Schamberg's 709.09
      Siemens-Bloch 757.33
   progressive pigmentary 709.09
   psychogenic 316
   pustular subcorneal 694.1
   Schamberg's (progressive pigmentary)
      709.09
   senile NEC 709.3
   specified NEC 702.8
   Unna's (seborrheic dermatitis) 690.10
Dermographia 708.3
Dermographism 708.3
Dermoid (cyst) (M9084/0) - *see also*
      Neoplasm, by site, benign
   with malignant transformation
      (M9084/3) 183.0
Dermopathy
   infiltrative, with thyrotoxicosis 242.0
   senile NEC 709.3
Dermophytosis - *see* Dermatophytosis
Descemet's membrane - *see* condition
Descemetocele 371.72

Descending - *see* condition
Descensus uteri (complete) (incomplete)
      (partial) (without vaginal wall pro-
      lapse) 618.1
   with mention of vaginal wall prolapse
      - *see* Prolapse, uterovaginal
Desensitization to allergens V07.1
Desert
   rheumatism 114.0
   sore (*see also* Ulcer, skin) 707.9
Desertion (child) (newborn) 995.52
   adult 995.84
Desmoid (extra-abdominal) (tumor)
      (M8821/1) - *see also* Neoplasm, con-
      nective tissue, uncertain behavior
   abdominal (M8822/1) - *see* Neoplasm,
      connective tissue, uncertain behav-
      ior
Despondency 300.4
Desquamative dermatitis NEC 695.89
Destruction
   articular facet (*see also* Derangement,
      joint) 718.9
      vertebra 724.9
   bone 733.90
      syphilitic 095.5
   joint (*see also* Derangement, joint) 718.9
      sacroiliac 724.6
   kidney 593.89
   live fetus to facilitate birth NEC
      763.89
   ossicles (ear) 385.24
   rectal sphincter 569.49
   septum (nasal) 478.1
   tuberculous NEC (*see also* Tuberculo-
      sis) 011.9
   tympanic membrane 384.82
   tympanum 385.89
   vertebral disc - *see* Degeneration, inter-
      vertebral disc
Destructiveness (*see also* Disturbance,
      conduct) 312.9
   adjustment reaction 309.3
Detachment
   cartilage - *see also* Sprain, by site
      knee - *see* Tear, meniscus
   cervix, annular 622.8
      complicating delivery 665.3
   choroid (old) (postinfectional) (simple)
      (spontaneous) 363.70
      hemorrhagic 363.72
      serous 363.71
   knee, medial meniscus (old) 717.3
      current injury 836.0
   ligament - *see* Sprain, by site
   placenta (premature) - *see* Placenta,
      separation
   retina (recent) 361.9
      with retinal defect (rhegmatogenous)
         361.00
      giant tear 361.03
      multiple 361.02
      partial
         with
            giant tear 361.03
            multiple defects 361.02
            retinal dialysis (juvenile)
               361.04
            single defect 361.01
         retinal dialysis (juvenile) 361.04
         single 361.01
         subtotal 361.05
         total 361.05
      delimited (old) (partial) 361.06

Detachment *(Continued)*
  retina *(Continued)*
    old
      delimited 361.06
      partial 361.06
      total or subtotal 361.07
    pigment epithelium (RPE) (serous)
        362.42
      exudative 362.42
      hemorrhagic 362.43
    rhegmatogenous *(see also* Detach-
        ment, retina, with retinal defect)
        361.00
    serous (without retinal defect) 361.2
    specified type NEC 361.89
    traction (with vitreoretinal organiza-
        tion) 361.81
  vitreous humor 379.21
Detergent asthma 507.8
Deterioration
  epileptic 345.9 *[294.1]*
  heart, cardiac *(see also* Degeneration,
      myocardial) 429.1
  mental *(see also* Psychosis) 298.9
  myocardium, myocardial *(see also* De-
      generation, myocardial) 429.1
  senile (simple) 797
    transplanted organ - *see* Complica-
        tions, transplant, organ, by site
de Toni-Fanconi syndrome (cystinosis)
    270.0
Deuteranomaly 368.52
Deuteranopia (anomalous trichromat)
    (complete) (incomplete) 368.52
Deutschländer's disease - *see* Fracture,
    foot
Development
  abnormal, bone 756.9
  arrested 783.4
    bone 733.91
    child 783.4
    due to malnutrition (protein-calorie)
        263.2
    fetus or newborn 764.9
    tracheal rings (congenital) 748.3
  defective, congenital - *see also* Anomaly
    cauda equina 742.59
    left ventricle 746.9
      with atresia or hypoplasia of aor-
          tic orifice or valve with hypo-
          plasia of ascending aorta
          746.7
      in hypoplastic left heart syndrome
          746.7
  delayed *(see also* Delay, development)
      783.4
    arithmetical skills 315.1
    language (skills) 315.31
      expressive 315.31
      mixed receptive-expressive
          315.32
    learning skill, specified NEC 315.2
    mixed skills 315.5
    motor coordination 315.4
    reading 315.00
    specified
      learning skill NEC 315.2
      type NEC, except learning 315.8
    speech 315.39
      associated with hyperkinesia
          314.1
      phonological 315.39
    spelling 315.09
    written expression 315.2

Development *(Continued)*
  imperfect, congenital - *see also* Anom-
      aly
    heart 746.9
    lungs 748.60
  improper (fetus or newborn) 764.9
  incomplete (fetus or newborn) 764.9
    affecting management of pregnancy
        656.5
    bronchial tree 748.3
    organ or site not listed - *see* Hypo-
        plasia
    respiratory system 748.9
  sexual, precocious NEC 259.1
  tardy, mental *(see also* Retardation,
      mental) 319
Developmental - *see* condition
Devergie's disease (pityriasis rubra pi-
    laris) 696.4
Deviation
  conjugate (eye) 378.87
    palsy 378.81
    spasm, spastic 378.82
  esophagus 530.89
  eye, skew 378.87
  midline (jaw) (teeth) 524.2
    specified site NEC - *see* Malposition
  organ or site, congenital NEC - *see*
      Malposition, congenital
  septum (acquired) (nasal) 470
    congenital 754.0
  sexual 302.9
    bestiality 302.1
    coprophilia 302.89
    ego-dystonic
      homosexuality 302.0
      lesbianism 302.0
    erotomania 302.89
      Clérambault's 297.8
    exhibitionism (sexual) 302.4
    fetishism 302.81
      transvestic 302.3
    frotteurism 302.89
    homosexuality, ego-dystonic 302.0
      pedophilic 302.2
    lesbianism, ego-dystonic 302.0
    masochism 302.83
    narcissism 302.89
    necrophilia 302.89
    nymphomania 302.89
    pederosis 302.2
    pedophilia 302.2
    sadism 302.84
    sadomasochism 302.84
    satyriasis 302.89
    specified type NEC 302.89
    transvestic fetishism 302.3
    transvestism 302.3
    voyeurism 302.82
    zoophilia (erotica) 302.1
  teeth, midline 524.2
  trachea 519.1
  ureter (congenital) 753.4
Devic's disease 341.0
Device
  cerebral ventricle (communicating) in
      situ V45.2
  contraceptive - *see* Contraceptive, de-
      vice
  drainage, cerebrospinal fluid V45.2
Devil's
  grip 074.1
  pinches (purpura simplex) 287.2
Devitalized tooth 522.9

Devonshire colic 984.9
  specified type of lead - *see* Table of
      Drugs and Chemicals
Dextraposition, aorta 747.21
  with ventricular septal defect, pulmo-
      nary stenosis or atresia, and hy-
      pertrophy of right ventricle
      745.2
  in tetralogy of Fallot 745.2
Dextratransposition, aorta 745.11
Dextrinosis, limit (debrancher enzyme
    deficiency) 271.0
Dextrocardia (corrected) (false) (isolated)
    (secondary) (true) 746.87
  with
    complete transposition of viscera
        759.3
    situs inversus 759.3
Dextroversion, kidney (left) 753.3
Dhobie itch 110.3
Diabetes, diabetic (brittle) (congenital)
    (familial) (mellitus) (severe) (slight)
    (without complication) 250.0

Note   Use the following fifth-digit
subclassification with category 250:

  0   type II [non-insulin dependent
      type] [NIDDM type] [adult-on-
      set type] or unspecified type,
      not stated as uncontrolled

      Fifth-digit 0 is for use for type
      II, adult-onset diabetic patients,
      even if the patient requires in-
      sulin

  1   type I [insulin dependent type]
      [IDDM type] [juvenile type],
      not stated as uncontrolled
  2   type II [non-insulin dependent
      type] [NIDDM type] [adult-on-
      set type] or unspecified type,
      uncontrolled
      Fifth-digit 2 is for use for type
      II, adult-onset diabetic patients,
      even if the patient requires in-
      sulin

  3   type I [insulin dependent type]
      [IDDM type] [juvenile type],
      uncontrolled

  with
    coma (with ketoacidosis) 250.3
      hyperosmolar (nonketotic) 250.2
    complication NEC 250.9
      specified NEC 250.8
    gangrene 250.7 *[785.4]*
    hyperosmolarity 250.2
    ketosis, ketoacidosis 250.1
    osteomyelitis 250.8 *[731.8]*
    specified manifestations NEC 250.8
  acetonemia 250.1
  acidosis 250.1
  amyotrophy 250.6 *[358.1]*
  angiopathy, peripheral 250.7 *[443.81]*
  asymptomatic 790.2
  autonomic neuropathy (peripheral)
      250.6 *[337.1]*
  bone change 250.8 *[731.8]*
  bronze, bronzed 275.0
  cataract 250.5 *[366.41]*
  chemical 790.2
    complicating pregnancy, childbirth,
        or puerperium 648.8

Diabetes, diabetic *(Continued)*
coma (with ketoacidosis) 250.3
hyperglycemic 250.3
hyperosmolar (nonketotic) 250.2
hypoglycemic 250.3
insulin 250.3
complicating pregnancy, childbirth, or
puerperium (maternal)
648.0
affecting fetus or newborn 775.0
complication NEC 250.9
specified NEC 250.8
dorsal sclerosis 250.6 *[340]*
dwarfism-obesity syndrome 258.1
gangrene 250.7 *[785.4]*
gastroparesis 250.6 *[536.3]*
gestational 648.8
complicating pregnancy, childbirth,
or puerperium 648.8
glaucoma 250.5 *[365.44]*
glomerulosclerosis (intercapillary)
250.4 *[581.81]*
glycogenosis, secondary 250.8 *[259.8]*
hemochromatosis 275.0
hyperosmolar coma 250.2
hyperosmolarity 250.2
hypertension-nephrosis syndrome
250.4 *[581.81]*
hypoglycemia 250.8
hypoglycemic shock 250.8
insipidus 253.5
nephrogenic 588.1
pituitary 253.5
vasopressin-resistant 588.1
intercapillary glomerulosclerosis 250.4
[581.81]
iritis 250.5 *[364.42]*
ketosis, ketoacidosis 250.1
Kimmelstiel (-Wilson) disease or syndrome (intercapillary glomerulosclerosis) 250.4 *[581.81]*
Lancereaux's (diabetes mellitus with
marked emaciation) 250.8 *[261]*
latent (chemical) 790.2
complicating pregnancy, childbirth,
or puerperium 648.8
lipoidosis 250.8 *[272.7]*
macular edema 250.5 *[362.01]*
maternal
with manifest disease in the infant
775.1
affecting fetus or newborn 775.0
microaneurysms, retinal 250.5
[362.01]
mononeuropathy 250.6 *[355.9]*
neonatal, transient 775.1
nephropathy 250.4 *[583.81]*
nephrosis (syndrome) 250.4 *[581.81]*
neuralgia 250.6 *[357.2]*
neuritis 250.6 *[357.2]*
neurogenic arthropathy 250.6 *[713.5]*
neuropathy 250.6 *[357.2]*
nonclinical 790.2
osteomyelitis 250.8 *[731.8]*
peripheral autonomic neuropathy 250.6
[337.1]
phosphate 275.3
polyneuropathy 250.6 *[357.2]*
renal (true) 271.4
retinal
edema 250.5 *[362.01]*   ◄▦▦
hemorrhage 250.5 *[362.83]*
microaneurysms 250.5 *[362.01]*
retinitis 250.5 *[362.01]*

Diabetes, diabetic *(Continued)*
retinopathy 250.5 *[362.01]*
background 250.5 *[362.01]*
proliferative 250.5 *[362.02]*
steroid induced
correct substance properly administered 251.8
overdose or wrong substance given
or taken 962.0
stress 790.2
subclinical 790.2
subliminal 790.2
sugar 250.0
ulcer (skin) 250.8 *[707.9]*
lower extremity 250.8 *[707.1]*
specified site NEC 250.8 *[707.8]*
xanthoma 250.8 *[272.2]*
Diacyclothrombopathia 287.1
Diagnosis deferred 799.9
Dialysis (intermittent) (treatment)
anterior retinal (juvenile) (with detachment) 361.04
extracorporeal V56.0
peritoneal V56.8
renal V56.0
status only V45.1
specified type NEC V56.8
Diamond-Blackfan anemia or syndrome
(congenital hypoplastic anemia)
284.0
Diamond-Gardener syndrome (autoerythrocyte sensitization) 287.2
Diaper rash 691.0
Diaphoresis (excessive) NEC 780.8
Diaphragm - *see* condition
Diaphragmalgia 786.52
Diaphragmitis 519.4
Diaphyseal aclasis 756.4
Diaphysitis 733.99
Diarrhea, diarrheal (acute) (autumn)
(bilious) (bloody) (catarrhal) (chole-
raic) (chronic) (gravis) (green) (infantile) (lienteric) (noninfectious)
(presumed noninfectious) (putrefac-
tive) (secondary) (sporadic) (summer) (symptomatic) (thermic)
787.91
achlorhydric 536.0
allergic 558.9
amebic (*see also* Amebiasis) 006.9
with abscess - *see* Abscess, amebic
acute 006.0
chronic 006.1
nondysenteric 006.2
bacillary - *see* Dysentery, bacillary
bacterial NEC 008.5
balantidial 007.0
bile salt-induced 579.8
cachectic NEC 558.9
chilomastix 007.8
choleriformis 001.1
coccidial 007.2
Cochin-China 579.1
anguilluliasis 127.2
psilosis 579.1
Dientamoeba 007.8
dietetic 558.9
due to
achylia gastrica 536.8
Aerobacter aerogenes 008.2
Bacillus coli - *see* Enteritis,
E. coli
bacteria NEC 008.5
bile salts 579.8

Diarrhea, diarrheal *(Continued)*
due to *(Continued)*
Capillaria
hepatica 128.8
philippinensis 127.5
Clostridium perfringens (C) (F)
008.46
Enterobacter aerogenes 008.2
enterococci 008.49
Escherichia coli - *see* Enteritis, E. coli
Giardia lamblia 007.1
Heterophyes heterophyes 121.6
irritating foods 558.9
Metagonimus yokogawai 121.5
Necator americanus 126.1
Paracolobactrum arizonae 008.1
Paracolon bacillus NEC 008.47
Arizona 008.1
Proteus (bacillus) (mirabilis) (Morganii) 008.3
Pseudomonas aeruginosa 008.42
S. japonicum 120.2
specified organism NEC 008.8
bacterial 008.49
viral NEC 008.69
Staphylococcus 008.41
Streptococcus 008.49
anaerobic 008.46
Strongyloides stercoralis 127.2
Trichuris trichiuria 127.3
virus NEC (*see also* Enteritis, viral)
008.69
dysenteric 009.2
due to specified organism NEC 008.8
dyspeptic 558.9
endemic 009.3
due to specified organism NEC 008.8
epidemic 009.2
due to specified organism NEC 008.8
fermentative 558.9
flagellate 007.9
Flexner's (ulcerative) 004.1
functional 564.5
following gastrointestinal surgery
564.4
psychogenic 306.4
giardial 007.1
Giardia lamblia 007.1
hill 579.1
hyperperistalsis (nervous) 306.4
infectious 009.2
due to specified organism NEC 008.8
presumed 009.3
inflammatory 558.9
due to specified organism NEC 008.8
malarial (*see also* Malaria) 084.6
mite 133.8
mycotic 117.9
nervous 306.4
neurogenic 564.5
parenteral NEC 009.2
postgastrectomy 564.4
postvagotomy 564.4
prostaglandin induced 579.8
protozoal NEC 007.9
psychogenic 306.4
septic 009.2
due to specified organism NEC 008.8
specified organism NEC 008.8
bacterial 008.49
viral NEC 008.69
Staphylococcus 008.41
Streptococcus 008.49
anaerobic 008.46

ICD-9-CM

Vol. 2

Diminuta taenia 123.6
Diminution, sense or sensation (cold) (heat) (tactile) (vibratory) (*see also* Disturbance, sensation) 782.0
Dimitri-Sturge-Weber disease (encephalocutaneous angiomatosis) 759.6
Dimple
  parasacral 685.1
    with abscess 685.0
  pilonidal 685.1
    with abscess 685.0
  postanal 685.1
    with abscess 685.0
Dioctophyma renale (infection) (infestation) 128.8
Dipetalonemiasis 125.4
Diphallus 752.69
Diphtheria, diphtheritic (gangrenous) (hemorrhagic) 032.9
  carrier (suspected) of V02.4
  cutaneous 032.85
  cystitis 032.84
  faucial 032.0
  infection of wound 032.85
  inoculation (anti) (not sick) V03.5
  laryngeal 032.3
  myocarditis 032.82
  nasal anterior 032.2
  nasopharyngeal 032.1
  neurological complication 032.89
  peritonitis 032.83
  specified site NEC 032.89
Diphyllobothriasis (intestine) 123.4
  larval 123.5
Diplacusis 388.41
Diplegia (upper limbs) 344.2
  brain or cerebral 437.8
  congenital 343.0
  facial 351.0
    congenital 352.6
  infantile or congenital (cerebral) (spastic) (spinal) 343.0
  lower limbs 344.1
  syphilitic, congenital 090.49
Diplococcus, diplococcal - *see* condition
Diplomyelia 742.59
Diplopia 368.2
  refractive 368.15
Dipsomania (*see also* Alcoholism) 303.9
  with psychosis (*see also* Psychosis, alcoholic) 291.9
Dipylidiasis 123.8
  intestine 123.8
Direction, teeth, abnormal 524.3
Dirt-eating child 307.52
Disability
  heart - *see* Disease, heart
  learning NEC 315.2
  special spelling 315.09
Disarticulation (*see also* Derangement, joint) 718.9
  meaning
    amputation
      status - *see* Absence, by site
      traumatic - *see* Amputation, traumatic
    dislocation, traumatic or congenital - *see* Dislocation
Disaster, cerebrovascular (*see also* Disease, cerebrovascular, acute) 436

Discharge
  anal NEC 787.99
  breast (female) (male) 611.79
  conjunctiva 372.8
  continued locomotor idiopathic (*see also* Epilepsy) 345.5
  diencephalic autonomic idiopathic (*see also* Epilepsy) 345.5
  ear 388.60
    blood 388.69
    cerebrospinal fluid 388.61
  excessive urine 788.42
  eye 379.93
  nasal 478.1
  nipple 611.79
  patterned motor idiopathic (*see also* Epilepsy) 345.5
  penile 788.7
  postnasal - *see* Sinusitis
  sinus, from mediastinum 510.0
  umbilicus 789.9
  urethral 788.7
    bloody 599.84
  vaginal 623.5
Discitis 722.90
  cervical, cervicothoracic 722.91
  lumbar, lumbosacral 722.93
  thoracic, thoracolumbar 722.92
Discogenic syndrome - *see* Displacement, intervertebral disc
Discoid
  kidney 753.3
  meniscus, congenital 717.5
  semilunar cartilage 717.5
Discoloration
  mouth 528.9
  nails 703.8
  teeth 521.7
    due to
      drugs 521.7
      metals (copper) (silver) 521.7
      pulpal bleeding 521.7
    during formation 520.8
    posteruptive 521.7
Discomfort
  chest 786.59
  visual 368.13
Discomycosis - *see* Actinomycosis
Discontinuity, ossicles, ossicular chain 385.23
Discrepancy
  leg length (acquired) 736.81
    congenital 755.30
  uterine size-date 655.8
Discrimination
  political V62.4
  racial V62.4
  religious V62.4
  sex V62.4
Disease, diseased - *see also* Syndrome
  Abrami's (acquired hemolytic jaundice) 283.9
  absorbent system 459.89
  accumulation - *see* Thesaurismosis
  acid-peptic 536.8
  Acosta's 993.2
  Adams-Stokes (-Morgagni) (syncope with heart block) 426.9
  Addison's (bronze) (primary adrenal insufficiency) 255.4
    anemia (pernicious) 281.0
    tuberculous (*see also* Tuberculosis) 017.6

Disease, diseased (*Continued*)
  Addison-Gull - *see* Xanthoma
  adenoids (and tonsils) (chronic) 474.9
  adrenal (gland) (capsule) (cortex) 255.9
    hyperfunction 255.3
    hypofunction 255.4
    specified type NEC 255.8
  ainhum (dactylolysis spontanea) 136.0
  akamushi (scrub typhus) 081.2
  Akureyri (epidemic neuromyasthenia) 049.8
  Albarrán's (colibacilluria) 599.0
  Albers-Schönberg's (marble bones) 756.52
  Albert's 726.71
  Albright (-Martin) (-Bantam) 275.49
  Alibert's (mycosis fungoides) (M9700/3) 202.1
  Alibert-Bazin (M9700/3) 202.1
  alimentary canal 569.9
  alligator skin (ichthyosis congenita) 757.1
    acquired 701.1
  Almeida's (Brazilian blastomycosis) 116.1
  Alpers' 330.8
  alpine 993.2
  altitude 993.2
  alveoli, teeth 525.9
  Alzheimer's - *see* Alzheimer's
  amyloid (any site) 277.3
  anarthritic rheumatoid 446.5
  Anders' (adiposis tuberosa simplex) 272.8
  Andersen's (glycogenosis IV) 271.0
  Anderson's (angiokeratoma corporis diffusum) 272.7
  Andes 993.2
  Andrews' (bacterid) 686.8
  angiopastic, angiospasmodic 443.9
    cerebral 435.9
      with transient neurologic deficit 435.9
    vein 459.89
  anterior
    chamber 364.9
    horn cell 335.9
      specified type NEC 335.8
  antral (chronic) 473.0
    acute 461.0
  anus NEC 569.49
  aorta (nonsyphilitic) 447.9
    syphilitic NEC 093.89
  aortic (heart) (valve) (*see also* Endocarditis, aortic) 424.1
  apollo 077.4
  aponeurosis 726.90
  appendix 543.9
  aqueous (chamber) 364.9
  arc-welders' lung 503
  Armenian 277.3
  Arnold-Chiari (*see also* Spina bifida) 741.0
  arterial 447.9
    occlusive (*see also* Occlusion, by site) 444.22
      with embolus or thrombus - *see* Occlusion, by site
      due to stricture or stenosis 447.1
    specified type NEC 447.8
  arteriocardiorenal (*see also* Hypertension, cardiorenal) 404.90

Disease, diseased (*Continued*)
  arteriolar (generalized) (obliterative) 447.90
    specified type NEC 447.8
  arteriorenal - *see* Hypertension, kidney
  arteriosclerotic - *see also* Arteriosclerosis
    cardiovascular 429.2
    coronary - *see* Arteriosclerosis, coronary
    heart - *see* Arteriosclerosis, coronary
    vascular - *see* Arteriosclerosis
  artery 447.9
    cerebral 437.9
    coronary - *see* Arteriosclerosis, coronary
    specified type NEC 447.8
  arthropod-borne NEC 088.9
    specified type NEC 088.89
  Asboe-Hansen's (incontinentia pigmenti) 757.33
  atticoantral, chronic (with posterior or superior marginal perforation of ear drum) 382.2
  auditory canal, ear 380.9
  Aujeszky's 078.89
  auricle, ear NEC 380.30
  Australian X 062.4
  autoimmune NEC 279.4
    hemolytic (cold type) (warm type) 283.0
    parathyroid 252.1
    thyroid 245.2
  aviators' (*see also* Effect, adverse, high altitude) 993.2
  ax(e)-grinders' 502
  Ayala's 756.89
  Ayerza's (pulmonary artery sclerosis with pulmonary hypertension) 416.0
  Babington's (familial hemorrhagic telangiectasia) 448.0
  back bone NEC 733.90
  bacterial NEC 040.89
    zoonotic NEC 027.9
      specified type NEC 027.8
  Baehr-Schiffrin (thrombotic thrombocytopenic purpura) 446.6
  Baelz's (cheilitis glandularis apostematosa) 528.5
  Baerensprung's (eczema marginatum) 110.3
  Balfour's (chloroma) 205.3
  balloon (*see also* Effect, adverse, high altitude) 993.2
  Baló's 341.1
  Bamberger (-Marie) (hypertrophic pulmonary osteoarthropathy) 731.2
  Bang's (Brucella abortus) 023.1
  Bannister's 995.1
  Banti's (with cirrhosis) (with portal hypertension) - *see* Cirrhosis, liver
  Barcoo (*see also* Ulcer, skin) 707.9
  barium lung 503
  Barlow (-Möller) (infantile scurvy) 267
  barometer makers' 985.0
  Barraquer (-Simons) (progressive lipodystrophy) 272.6
  basal ganglia 333.90
    degenerative NEC 333.0
    specified NEC 333.89
  Basedow's (exophthalmic goiter) 242.0
  basement membrane NEC 583.89

Disease, diseased (*Continued*)
  basement membrane NEC (*Continued*)
    with
      pulmonary hemorrhage (Goodpasture's syndrome) 446.21 [583.81]
  Bateman's 078.0
    purpura (senile) 287.2
  Batten's 330.1 [362.71]
  Batten-Mayou (retina) 330.1 [362.71]
  Batten-Steinert 359.2
  Battey 031.0
  Baumgarten-Cruveilhier (cirrhosis of liver) 571.5
  bauxite-workers' 503
  Bayle's (dementia paralytica) 094.1
  Bazin's (primary) (*see also* Tuberculosis) 017.1
  Beard's (neurasthenia) 300.5
  Beau's (*see also* Degeneration, myocardial) 429.1
  Bechterew's (ankylosing spondylitis) 720.0
  Becker's (idiopathic mural endomyocardial disease) 425.2
  Begbie's (exophthalmic goiter) 242.0
  Behr's 362.50
  Beigel's (white piedra) 111.2
  Bekhterev's (ankylosing spondylitis) 720.0
  Bell's (*see also* Psychosis, affective) 296.0
  Bennett's (leukemia) 208.9
  Benson's 379.22
  Bergeron's (hysteroepilepsy) 300.11
  Berlin's 921.3
  Bernard-Soulier (thrombopathy) 287.1
  Bernhardt (-Roth) 355.1
  beryllium 503
  Besnier-Boeck (-Schaumann) (sarcoidosis) 135
  Best's 362.76
  Beurmann's (sporotrichosis) 117.1
  Bielschowsky (-Jansky) 330.1
  Biermer's (pernicious anemia) 281.0
  Biett's (discoid lupus erythematosus) 695.4
  bile duct (*see also* Disease, biliary) 576.9
  biliary (duct) (tract) 576.9
    with calculus, choledocholithiasis, or stones - *see* Choledocholithiasis
  Billroth's (meningocele) (*see also* Spina bifida) 741.9
  Binswanger's 290.12
  Bird's (oxaluria) 271.8
  bird fanciers' 495.2
  black lung 500
  bladder 596.9
    specified NEC 596.8
  bleeder's 286.0
  Bloch-Sulzberger (incontinentia pigmenti) 757.33
  Blocq's (astasia-abasia) 307.9
  blood (-forming organs) 289.9
    specified NEC 289.8
    vessel 459.9
  Bloodgood's 610.1
  Blount's (tibia vara) 732.4
  blue 746.9
  Bodechtel-Guttmann (subacute sclerosing panencephalitis) 046.2
  Boeck's (sarcoidosis) 135
  bone 733.90
    fibrocystic NEC 733.29
      jaw 526.2

Disease, diseased (*Continued*)
  bone (*Continued*)
    marrow 289.9
    Paget's (osteitis deformans) 731.0
    specified type NEC 733.99
    von Recklinghausen's (osteitis fibrosa cystica) 252.0
  Bonfils' - *see* Disease, Hodgkin's
  Borna 062.9
  Bornholm (epidemic pleurodynia) 074.1
  Bostock's (*see also* Fever, hay) 477.9
  Bouchard's (myopathic dilatation of the stomach) 536.1
  Bouillaud's (rheumatic heart disease) 391.9
  Bourneville (-Brissaud) (tuberous sclerosis) 759.5
  Bouveret (-Hoffmann) (paroxysmal tachycardia) 427.2
  bowel 569.9
    functional 564.9
      psychogenic 306.4
  Bowen's (M8081/2) - *see* Neoplasm, skin, in situ
  Bozzolo's (multiple myeloma) (M9730/3) 203.0
  Bradley's (epidemic vomiting) 078.82
  Brailsford's 732.3
    radius, head 732.3
    tarsal, scaphoid 732.5
  Brailsford-Morquio (mucopolysaccharidosis IV) 277.5
  brain 348.9
    Alzheimer's 331.0
      with dementia - *see* Alzheimer's, dementia
    arterial, artery 437.9
    arteriosclerotic 437.0
    congenital 742.9
    degenerative - *see* Degeneration, brain
    inflammatory - *see also* Encephalitis
      late effect - *see* category 326
    organic 348.9
      arteriosclerotic 437.0
    parasitic NEC 123.9
    Pick's 331.1
      with dementia 331.1 [294.1]
    senile 331.2
  braziers' 985.8
  breast 611.9
    cystic (chronic) 610.1
    fibrocystic 610.1
    inflammatory 611.0
    Paget's (M8540/3) 174.0
    puerperal, postpartum NEC 676.3
    specified NEC 611.8
  Breda's (*see also* Yaws) 102.9
  Breisky's (kraurosis vulvae) 624.0
  Bretonneau's (diphtheritic malignant angina) 032.0
  Bright's (*see also* Nephritis) 583.9
    arteriosclerotic (*see also* Hypertension, kidney) 403.90
  Brill's (recrudescent typhus) 081.1
    flea-borne 081.0
    louse-borne 081.1
  Brill-Symmers (follicular lymphoma) (M9690/3) 202.0
  Brill-Zinsser (recrudescent typhus) 081.1
  Brinton's (leather bottle stomach) (M8142/3) 151.9

Disease, diseased (*Continued*)
  Brion-Kayser (*see also* Fever, paraty-
      phoid) 002.9
  broad
    beta 272.2
    ligament, noninflammatory 620.9
      specified NEC 620.8
  Brocq's 691.8
    meaning
      atopic (diffuse) neurodermatitis
        691.8
      dermatitis herpetiformis 694.0
      lichen simplex chronicus 698.3
      parapsoriasis 696.2
      prurigo 698.2
  Brocq-Duhring (dermatitis herpeti-
      formis) 694.0
  Brodie's (joint) (*see also* Osteomyelitis)
      730.1
  bronchi 519.1
  bronchopulmonary 519.1
  bronze (Addison's) 255.4
    tuberculous (*see also* Tuberculosis)
      017.6
  Brown-Séquard 344.89
  Bruck's 733.99
  Bruck-de Lange (Amsterdam dwarf,
      mental retardation, and brachy-
      cephaly) 759.89
  Bruhl's (splenic anemia with fever)
      285.8
  Bruton's (X-linked agammaglobuline-
      mia) 279.04
  buccal cavity 528.9
  Buchanan's (juvenile osteochondrosis,
      iliac crest) 732.1
  Buchman's (osteochondrosis juvenile)
      732.1
  Budgerigar-Fanciers' 495.2
  Budinger-Ludloff-Läwen 717.89
  Büerger's (thromboangiitis obliterans)
      443.1
  Burger-Grütz (essential familial hyper-
      lipemia) 272.3
  Burns' (lower ulna) 732.3
  bursa 727.9
  Bury's (erythema elevatum diutinum)
      695.89
  Buschke's 710.1
  Busquet's (*see also* Osteomyelitis)
      730.1
  Busse-Buschke (cryptococcosis) 117.5
  C$_2$ (*see also* Alcoholism) 303.9
  Caffey's (infantile cortical hyperostosis)
      756.59
  caisson 993.3
  calculus 592.9
  California 114.0
  Calvé (-Perthes) (osteochondrosis, fem-
      oral capital) 732.1
  Camurati-Engelmann (diaphyseal scle-
      rosis) 756.59
  Canavan's 330.0
  capillaries 448.9
  Carapata 087.1
  cardiac - *see* Disease, heart
  cardiopulmonary, chronic 416.9
  cardiorenal (arteriosclerotic) (hepatic)
      (hypertensive) (vascular) (*see also*
      Hypertension, cardiorenal) 404.90
  cardiovascular (arteriosclerotic) 429.2
    congenital 746.9
    hypertensive (*see also* Hypertension,
        heart) 402.90

Disease, diseased (*Continued*)
  cardiovascular (*Continued*)
    hypertensive (*Continued*)
      benign 402.10
      malignant 402.00
    renal (*see also* Hypertension, cardior-
        enal) 404.90
    syphilitic (asymptomatic) 093.9
  carotid gland 259.8
  Carrión's (Bartonellosis) 088.0
  cartilage NEC 733.90
    specified NEC 733.99
  Castellani's 104.8
  cat-scratch 078.3
  Cavare's (familial periodic paralysis)
      359.3
  Cazenave's (pemphigus) 694.4
  cecum 569.9
  celiac (adult) 579.0
    infantile 579.0
  cellular tissue NEC 709.9
  central core 359.0
  cerebellar, cerebellum - *see* Disease,
      brain
  cerebral (*see also* Disease, brain)
      348.9
    arterial, artery 437.9
    degenerative - *see* Degeneration,
        brain
  cerebrospinal 349.9
  cerebrovascular NEC 437.9
    acute 436
      embolic - *see* Embolism, brain
      late effect - *see* Late effect(s) (of)
          cerebrovascular disease
      puerperal, postpartum, childbirth
          674.0
      thrombotic - *see* Thrombosis, brain
    arteriosclerotic 437.0
    embolic - *see* Embolism, brain
    ischemic, generalized NEC 437.1
    late effect - *see* Late effect(s) (of)
        cerebrovascular disease
    occlusive 437.1
    puerperal, postpartum, childbirth
        674.0
    specified type NEC 437.8
    thrombotic - *see* Thrombosis, brain
  ceroid storage 272.7
  cervix (uteri)
    inflammatory 616.9
      specified NEC 616.8
    noninflammatory 622.9
      specified NEC 622.8
  Chabert's 022.9
  Chagas' (*see also* Trypanosomiasis,
      American) 086.2
  Chandler's (osteochondritis dissecans,
      hip) 732.7
  Charcôt's (joint) 094.0 [713.5]
    spinal cord 094.0
  Charcôt-Marie-Tooth 356.1
  Charlouis' (*see also* Yaws) 102.9
  Cheadle (-Möller) (-Barlow) (infantile
      scurvy) 267
  Chédiak-Steinbrinck (-Higashi) (con-
      genital gigantism of peroxidase
      granules) 288.2
  cheek, inner 528.9
  chest 519.9
  Chiari's (hepatic vein thrombosis)
      453.0
  Chicago (North American blastomy-
      cosis) 116.0

Disease, diseased (*Continued*)
  chignon (white piedra) 111.2
  chigoe, chigo (jigger) 134.1
  childhood granulomatous 288.1
  Chinese liver fluke 121.1
  chlamydial NEC 078.88
  cholecystic (*see also* Disease, gallblad-
      der) 575.9
  choroid 363.9
    degenerative (*see also* Degeneration,
        choroid) 363.40
    hereditary (*see also* Dystrophy, cho-
        roid) 363.50
    specified type NEC 363.8
  Christian's (chronic histiocytosis X)
      277.8
  Christian-Weber (nodular nonsuppura-
      tive panniculitis) 729.30
  Christmas 286.1
  ciliary body 364.9
  circulatory (system) NEC 459.9
    chronic, maternal, affecting fetus or
        newborn 760.3
    specified NEC 459.89
    syphilitic 093.9
      congenital 090.5
  Civatte's (poikiloderma) 709.09
  climacteric 627.2
    male 608.89
  coagulation factor deficiency (congeni-
      tal) (*see also* Defect, coagulation)
      286.9
  Coats' 362.12
  coccidioidal pulmonary 114.5
    acute 114.0
    chronic 114.4
    primary 114.0
    residual 114.4
  Cockayne's (microcephaly and dwarf-
      ism) 759.89
  Cogan's 370.52
  cold
    agglutinin 283.0
      or hemoglobinuria 283.0
        paroxysmal (cold) (nocturnal)
            283.2
    hemagglutinin (chronic) 283.0
  collagen NEC 710.9
    nonvascular 710.9
    specified NEC 710.8
    vascular (allergic) (*see also* Angiitis,
        hypersensitivity) 446.20
  colon 569.9
    functional 564.9
      congenital 751.3
    ischemic 557.0
  combined system (of spinal cord) 266.2
      [336.2]
    with anemia (pernicious) 281.0
        [336.2]
  compressed air 993.3
  Concato's (pericardial polyserositis)
      423.2
    peritoneal 568.82
    pleural - *see* Pleurisy
  congenital NEC 799.8
  conjunctiva 372.9
    chlamydial 077.98
      specified NEC 077.8
    specified type NEC 372.8
    viral 077.99
      specified NEC 077.8
  connective tissue, diffuse (*see also* Dis-
      ease, collagen) 710.9

◀▶ **New Code**   ⬅▮▮▮➡ **Revised Code**

Disease, diseased (*Continued*)
Conor and Bruch's (boutonneuse fever) 082.1
Conradi (-Hünermann) 756.59
Cooley's (erythroblastic anemia) 282.4
Cooper's 610.1
Corbus' 607.1
cork-handlers' 495.3
cornea (*see also* Keratopathy) 371.9
coronary (*see also* Ischemia, heart) 414.9
  congenital 746.85
  ostial, syphilitic 093.20
    aortic 093.22
    mitral 093.21
    pulmonary 093.24
    tricuspid 093.23
Corrigan's - *see* Insufficiency, aortic
Cotugno's 724.3
Coxsackie (virus) NEC 074.8
cranial nerve NEC 352.9
Creutzfeldt-Jakob 046.1
  with dementia 046.1 [294.1]
Crigler-Najjar (congenital hyperbilirubinemia) 277.4
Crocq's (acrocyanosis) 443.89
Crohn's (intestine) (*see also* Enteritis, regional) 555.9
Crouzon's (craniofacial dysostosis) 756.0
Cruchet's (encephalitis lethargica) 049.8
Cruveilhier's 335.21
Cruz-Chagas (*see also* Trypanosomiasis, American) 086.2
crystal deposition (*see also* Arthritis, due to, crystals) 712.9
Csillag's (lichen sclerosus et atrophicus) 701.0
Curschmann's 359.2
Cushing's (pituitary basophilism) 255.0
cystic
  breast (chronic) 610.1
  kidney, congenital (*see also* Cystic, disease, kidney) 753.10
  liver, congenital 751.62
  lung 518.89
    congenital 748.4
  pancreas 577.2
    congenital 751.7
  renal, congenital (*see also* Cystic, disease, kidney) 753.10
  semilunar cartilage 717.5
cysticercus 123.1
cystine storage (with renal sclerosis) 270.0
cytomegalic inclusion (generalized) 078.5
  with
    pneumonia 078.5 [484.1]
  congenital 771.1
Daae (-Finsen) (epidemic pleurodynia) 074.1
dancing 297.8
Danielssen's (anesthetic leprosy) 030.1
Darier's (congenital) (keratosis follicularis) 757.39
  erythema annulare centrifugum 695.0
  vitamin A deficiency 264.8
Darling's (histoplasmosis) (*see also* Histoplasmosis, American) 115.00

Disease, diseased (*Continued*)
Davies' 425.0
de Beurmann-Gougerot (sporotrichosis) 117.1
Débove's (splenomegaly) 789.2
deer fly (*see also* Tularemia) 021.9
deficiency 269.9
degenerative - *see also* Degeneration
  disc - *see* Degeneration, intervertebral disc
Degos' 447.8
Déjérine (-Sottas) 356.0
Déleage's 359.8
demyelinating, demyelinizating (brain stem) (central nervous system) 341.9
  multiple sclerosis 340
  specified NEC 341.8
de Quervain's (tendon sheath) 727.04
  thyroid (subacute granulomatous thyroiditis) 245.1
Dercum's (adiposis dolorosa) 272.8
Deutschländer's - *see* Fracture, foot
Devergie's (pityriasis rubra pilaris) 696.4
Devic's 341.0
diaphorase deficiency 289.7
diaphragm 519.4
diarrheal, infectious 009.2
diatomaceous earth 502
Diaz's (osteochondrosis astragalus) 732.5
digestive system 569.9
Di Guglielmo's (erythemic myelosis) (M9841/3) 207.0
Dimitri-Sturge-Weber (encephalocutaneous angiomatosis) 759.6
disc, degenerative - *see* Degeneration, intervertebral disc
discogenic (*see also* Disease, intervertebral disc) 722.90
diverticular - *see* Diverticula
Down's (mongolism) 758.0
Dubini's (electric chorea) 049.8
Dubois' (thymus gland) 090.5
Duchenne's 094.0
  locomotor ataxia 094.0
  muscular dystrophy 359.1
  paralysis 335.22
  pseudohypertrophy, muscles 359.1
Duchenne-Griesinger 359.1
ductless glands 259.9
Duhring's (dermatitis herpetiformis) 694.0
Dukes (-Filatov) 057.8
duodenum NEC 537.9
  specified NEC 537.89
Duplay's 726.2
Dupré's (meningism) 781.6
Dupuytren's (muscle contracture) 728.6
Durand-Nicolas-Favre (climatic bubo) 099.1
Duroziez's (congenital mitral stenosis) 746.5
Dutton's (trypanosomiasis) 086.9
Eales' 362.18
ear (chronic) (inner) NEC 388.9
  middle 385.9
    adhesive (*see also* Adhesions, middle ear) 385.10
    specified NEC 385.89
Eberth's (typhoid fever) 002.0

Disease, diseased (*Continued*)
Ebstein's
  heart 746.2
  meaning diabetes 250.4 [581.81]
Echinococcus (*see also* Echinococcus) 122.9
ECHO virus NEC 078.89
Economo's (encephalitis lethargica) 049.8
Eddowes' (brittle bones and blue sclera) 756.51
Edsall's 992.2
Eichstedt's (pityriasis versicolor) 111.0
Ellis-van Creveld (chondroectodermal dysplasia) 756.55
endocardium - *see* Endocarditis
endocrine glands or system NEC 259.9
  specified NEC 259.8
endomyocardial, idiopathic mural 425.2
Engel-von Recklinghausen (osteitis fibrosa cystica) 252.0
Engelmann's (diaphyseal sclerosis) 756.59
English (rickets) 268.0
Engman's (infectious eczematoid dermatitis) 690.8
enteroviral, enterovirus NEC 078.89
  central nervous system NEC 048
epidemic NEC 136.9
epididymis 608.9
epigastric, functional 536.9
  psychogenic 306.4
Erb (-Landouzy) 359.1
Erb-Goldflam 358.0
Erichsen's (railway spine) 300.16
esophagus 530.9
  functional 530.5
  psychogenic 306.4
Eulenburg's (congenital paramyotonia) 359.2
Eustachian tube 381.9
Evans' (thrombocytopenic purpura) 287.3
external auditory canal 380.9
extrapyramidal NEC 333.90
eye 379.90
  anterior chamber 364.9
  inflammatory NEC 364.3
  muscle 378.9
eyeball 360.9
eyelid 374.9
eyeworm of Africa 125.2
Fabry's (angiokeratoma corporis diffusum) 272.7
facial nerve (seventh) 351.9
  newborn 767.5
Fahr-Volhard (malignant nephrosclerosis) 403.00
fallopian tube, noninflammatory 620.9
  specified NEC 620.8
familial periodic 277.3
  paralysis 359.3
Fanconi's (congenital pancytopenia) 284.0
Farber's (disseminated lipogranulomatosis) 272.8
fascia 728.9
  inflammatory 728.9
Fauchard's (periodontitis) 523.4
Favre-Durand-Nicolas (climatic bubo) 099.1
Favre-Racouchot (elastoidosis cutanea nodularis) 701.8

ICD-9-CM

Vol. 2

Disease, diseased (*Continued*)
  Fede's 529.0
  Feer's 985.0
  Felix's (juvenile osteochondrosis, hip) 732.1
  Fenwick's (gastric atrophy) 537.89
  Fernels' (aortic aneurysm) 441.9
  fibrocaseous, of lung (*see also* Tuberculosis, pulmonary) 011.9
  fibrocystic - *see also* Fibrocystic, disease
    newborn 277.01
  Fiedler's (leptospiral jaundice) 100.0
  fifth 057.0
  Filatoff's (infectious mononucleosis) 075
  Filatov's (infectious mononucleosis) 075
  file-cutters' 984.9
    specified type of lead - *see* Table of Drugs and Chemicals
  filterable virus NEC 078.89
  fish skin 757.1
    acquired 701.1
  Flajani (-Basedow) (exophthalmic goiter) 242.0
  Flatau-Schilder 341.1
  flax-dressers' 504
  Fleischner's 732.3
  flint 502
  fluke - *see* Infestation, fluke
  Følling's (phenylketonuria) 270.1
  foot and mouth 078.4
  foot process 581.3
  Forbes' (glycogenosis III) 271.0
  Fordyce's (ectopic sebaceous glands) (mouth) 750.26
  Fordyce-Fox (apocrine miliaria) 705.82
  Fothergill's
    meaning scarlatina anginosa 034.1
    neuralgia (*see also* Neuralgia, trigeminal) 350.1
  Fournier's 608.83
  fourth 057.8
  Fox (-Fordyce) (apocrine miliaria) 705.82
  Francis' (*see also* Tularemia) 021.9
  Franklin's (heavy chain) 273.2
  Frei's (climatic bubo) 099.1
  Freiberg's (flattening metatarsal) 732.5
  Friedländer's (endarteritis obliterans) - *see* Arteriosclerosis
  Friedreich's
    combined systemic or ataxia 334.0
    facial hemihypertrophy 756.0
    myoclonia 333.2
  Fröhlich's (adiposogenital dystrophy) 253.8
  Frommel's 676.6
  frontal sinus (chronic) 473.1
    acute 461.1
  Fuller's earth 502
  fungus, fungous NEC 117.9
  Gaisböck's (polycythemia hypertonica) 289.0
  gallbladder 575.9
    congenital 751.60
  Gamna's (siderotic splenomegaly) 289.51
  Gamstorp's (adynamia episodica hereditaria) 359.3
  Gandy-Nanta (siderotic splenomegaly) 289.51

Disease, diseased (*Continued*)
  Gannister (occupational) 502
  Garré's (*see also* Osteomyelitis) 730.1
  gastric (*see also* Disease, stomach) 537.9
  gastrointestinal (tract) 569.9
    amyloid 277.3
    functional 536.9
      psychogenic 306.4
  Gaucher's (adult) (cerebroside lipidosis) (infantile) 272.7
  Gayet's (superior hemorrhagic polioencephalitis) 265.1
  Gee (-Herter) (-Heubner) (-Thaysen) (nontropical sprue) 579.0
  generalized neoplastic (M8000/6) 199.0
  genital organs NEC
    female 629.9
      specified NEC 629.8
    male 608.9
  Gerhardt's (erythromelalgia) 443.89
  Gerlier's (epidemic vertigo) 078.81
  Gibert's (pityriasis rosea) 696.3
  Gibney's (perispondylitis) 720.9
  Gierke's (glycogenosis I) 271.0
  Gilbert's (familial nonhemolytic jaundice) 277.4
  Gilchrist's (North American blastomycosis) 116.0
  Gilford (-Hutchinson) (progeria) 259.8
  Gilles de la Tourette's (motor-verbal tic) 307.23
  Giovannini's 117.9
  gland (lymph) 289.9
  Glanzmann's (hereditary hemorrhagic thrombasthenia) 287.1
  glassblowers' 527.1
  Glénard's (enteroptosis) 569.89
  Glisson's (*see also* Rickets) 268.0
  glomerular
    membranous, idiopathic 581.1
    minimal change 581.3
  glycogen storage (Andersen's) (Cori types 1-7) (Forbes') (McArdle-Schmid-Pearson) (Pompe's) (types I-VII) 271.0
    cardiac 271.0 [425.7]
    generalized 271.0
    glucose-6-phosphatase deficiency 271.0
    heart 271.0 [425.7]
    hepatorenal 271.0
    liver and kidneys 271.0
    myocardium 271.0 [425.7]
    von Gierke's (glycogenosis I) 271.0
  Goldflam-Erb 358.0
  Goldscheider's (epidermolysis bullosa) 757.39
  Goldstein's (familial hemorrhagic telangiectasia) 448.0
  gonococcal NEC 098.0
  Goodall's (epidemic vomiting) 078.82
  Gordon's (exudative enteropathy) 579.8
  Gougerot's (trisymptomatic) 709.1
  Gougerot-Carteaud (confluent reticulate papillomatosis) 701.8
  Gougerot-Hailey-Hailey (benign familial chronic pemphigus) 757.39
  graft-versus-host (bone marrow) 996.85

Disease, diseased (*Continued*)
  graft-versus-host (*Continued*)
    due to organ transplant NEC - *see* Complications, transplant, organ
  grain-handlers' 495.8
  Grancher's (splenopneumonia) - *see* Pneumonia
  granulomatous (childhood) (chronic) 288.1
  graphite lung 503
  Graves' (exophthalmic goiter) 242.0
  Greenfield's 330.0
  green monkey 078.89
  Griesinger's (*see also* Ancylostomiasis) 126.9
  grinders' 502
  Grisel's 723.5
  Gruby's (tinea tonsurans) 110.0
  Guertin's (electric chorea) 049.8
  Guillain-Barré 357.0
  Guinon's (motor-verbal tic) 307.23
  Gull's (thyroid atrophy with myxedema) 244.8
  Gull and Sutton's - *see* Hypertension, kidney
  gum NEC 523.9
  Günther's (congenital erythropoietic porphyria) 277.1
  gynecological 629.9
    specified NEC 629.8
  H 270.0
  Haas' 732.3
  Habermann's (acute parapsoriasis varioliformis) 696.2
  Haff 985.1
  Hageman (congenital factor XII deficiency) (*see also* Defect, congenital) 286.3
  Haglund's (osteochondrosis os tibiale externum) 732.5
  Hagner's (hypertrophic pulmonary osteoarthropathy) 731.2
  Hailey-Hailey (benign familial chronic pemphigus) 757.39
  hair (follicles) NEC 704.9
    specified type NEC 704.8
  Hallervorden-Spatz 333.0
  Hallopeau's (lichen sclerosus et atrophicus) 701.0
  Hamman's (spontaneous mediastinal emphysema) 518.1
  hand, foot, and mouth 074.3
  Hand-Schüller-Christian (chronic histiocytosis X) 277.8
  Hanot's - *see* Cirrhosis, biliary
  Hansen's (leprosy) 030.9
    benign form 030.1
    malignant form 030.0
  Harada's 363.22
  Harley's (intermittent hemoglobinuria) 283.2
  Hart's (pellagra-cerebellar ataxia-renal aminoaciduria) 270.0
  Hartnup (pellagra-cerebellar ataxia-renal aminoaciduria) 270.0
  Hashimoto's (struma lymphomatosa) 245.2
  Hb - *see* Disease, hemoglobin
  heart (organic) 429.9
    with
      acute pulmonary edema (*see also* Failure, ventricular, left) 428.1
        hypertensive 402.91
          with renal failure 404.92

◀▶ **New Code**   ⬛▶ **Revised Code**

Disease, diseased (*Continued*)
heart (*Continued*)
  with (*Continued*)
   acute pulmonary edema (*Continued*)
     hypertensive (*Continued*)
       benign 402.11
         with renal failure 404.12
       malignant 402.01
         with renal failure 404.02
     kidney disease - *see* Hypertension, cardiorenal
     rheumatic fever (conditions classifiable to 390)
       active 391.9
         with chorea 392.0
       inactive or quiescent (with chorea) 398.90
   amyloid 277.3 [425.7]
   aortic (valve) (*see also* Endocarditis, aortic) 424.1
   arteriosclerotic or sclerotic (minimal) (senile) - *see* Arteriosclerosis, coronary
   artery, arterial 414.0 - *see* Arteriosclerosis, coronary
   atherosclerotic 414.0 - *see* Arteriosclerosis, coronary
   beer drinkers' 425.5
   beriberi 265.0 [425.7]
   black 416.0
   congenital NEC 746.9
     cyanotic 746.9
     maternal, affecting fetus or newborn 760.3
     specified type NEC 746.89
   congestive (*see also* Failure, heart, congestive) 428.0
   coronary 414.9
   cryptogenic 429.9
   due to
     amyloidosis 277.3 [425.7]
     beriberi 265.0 [425.7]
     cardiac glycogenosis 271.0 [425.7]
     Friedreich's ataxia 334.0 [425.8]
     gout 274.82
     mucopolysaccharidosis 277.5 [425.7]
     myotonia atrophica 359.2 [425.8]
     progressive muscular dystrophy 359.1 [425.8]
     sarcoidosis 135 [425.8]
   fetal 746.9
     inflammatory 746.89
   fibroid (*see also* Myocarditis) 429.0
   functional 427.9
     postoperative 997.1
     psychogenic 306.2
   glycogen storage 271.0 [425.7]
   gonococcal NEC 098.85
   gouty 274.82
   hypertensive (*see also* Hypertension, heart) 402.90
     benign 402.10
     malignant 402.00
   hyperthyroid (*see also* Hyperthyroidism) 242.9 [425.7]
   incompletely diagnosed - *see* Disease, heart
   ischemic (chronic) (*see also* Ischemia, heart) 414.9
     acute (*see also* Infarct, myocardium) 410.9

Disease, diseased (*Continued*)
heart (*Continued*)
  with (*Continued*)
   ischemic (*Continued*)
     without myocardial infarction 411.89
       with coronary (artery) occlusion 411.81
     asymptomatic 412
     diagnosed on ECG or other special investigation but currently presenting no symptoms 412
   kyphoscoliotic 416.1
   mitral (*see also* Endocarditis, mitral) 394.9
   muscular (*see also* Degeneration, myocardial) 429.1
   postpartum 674.8
   psychogenic (functional) 306.2
   pulmonary (chronic) 416.9
     acute 415.0
     specified NEC 416.8
   rheumatic (chronic) (inactive) (old) (quiescent) (with chorea) 398.90
     active or acute 391.9
       with chorea (active) (rheumatic) (Sydenham's) 392.0
     specified type NEC 391.8
     maternal, affecting fetus or newborn 760.3
   rheumatoid - *see* Arthritis, rheumatoid
   sclerotic - *see* Arteriosclerosis, coronary
   senile (*see also* Myocarditis) 429.0
   specified type NEC 429.89
   syphilitic 093.89
     aortic 093.1
       aneurysm 093.0
     asymptomatic 093.89
     congenital 090.5
   thyroid (gland) (*see also* Hyperthyroidism) 242.9 [425.7]
   thyrotoxic (*see also* Thyrotoxicosis) 242.9 [425.7]
   tuberculous (*see also* Tuberculosis) 017.9 [425.8]
   valve, valvular (obstructive) (regurgitant) - *see also* Endocarditis
     congenital NEC (*see also* Anomaly, heart, valve) 746.9
       pulmonary 746.00
       specified type NEC 746.89
   vascular - *see* Disease, cardiovascular
heavy-chain (gamma G) 273.2
Heberden's 715.04
Hebra's
  dermatitis exfoliativa 695.89
  erythema multiforme exudativum 695.1
  pityriasis
   maculata et circinata 696.3
   rubra 695.89
   pilaris 696.4
  prurigo 698.2
Heerfordt's (uveoparotitis) 135
Heidenhain's 290.10
  with dementia 290.10
Heilmeyer-Schöner (M9842/3) 207.1
Heine-Medin (*see also* Poliomyelitis) 045.9

Disease, diseased (*Continued*)
Heller's (*see also* Psychosis, childhood) 299.1
Heller-Döhle (syphilitic aortitis) 093.1
hematopoietic organs 289.9
hemoglobin (Hb) 282.7
  with thalassemia 282.4
  abnormal (mixed) NEC 282.7
   with thalassemia 282.4
  AS genotype 282.5
  Bart's 282.7
  C (Hb-C) 282.7
   with other abnormal hemoglobin NEC 282.7
   elliptocytosis 282.7
   Hb-S 282.63
   sickle-cell 282.63
   thalassemia 282.4
  constant spring 282.7
  D (Hb-D) 282.7
   with other abnormal hemoglobin NEC 282.7
   Hb-S 282.69
   sickle-cell 282.69
   thalassemia 282.4
  E (Hb-E) 282.7
   with other abnormal hemoglobin NEC 282.7
   Hb-S 282.69
   sickle-cell 282.69
   thalassemia 282.4
  elliptocytosis 282.7
  F (Hb-F) 282.7
  G (Hb-G) 282.7
  H (Hb-H) 282.4
  hereditary persistence, fetal (HPFH) ("Swiss variety") 282.7
  high fetal gene 282.7
  I thalassemia 282.4
  M 289.7
  S - *see* Disease, sickle-cell, Hb-S
  spherocytosis 282.7
  unstable, hemolytic 282.7
  Zurich (Hb-Zurich) 282.7
hemolytic (fetus) (newborn) 773.2
  autoimmune (cold type) (warm type) 283.0
  due to or with
   incompatibility
     ABO (blood group) 773.1
     blood (group) (Duffy) (Kell) (Kidd) (Lewis) (M) (S) NEC 773.2
     Rh (blood group) (factor) 773.0
     Rh negative mother 773.0
  unstable hemoglobin 282.7
hemorrhagic 287.9
  newborn 776.0
Henoch (-Schönlein) (purpura nervosa) 287.0
hepatic - *see* Disease, liver
hepatolenticular 275.1
heredodegenerative NEC
  brain 331.89
  spinal cord 336.8
Hers' (glycogenosis VI) 271.0
Herter (-Gee) (-Heubner) (nontropical sprue) 579.0
Herxheimer's (diffuse idiopathic cutaneous atrophy) 701.8
Heubner's 094.89
Heubner-Herter (nontropical sprue) 579.0

Disease, diseased (*Continued*)
　high fetal gene or hemoglobin thalassemia 282.4
　Hildenbrand's (typhus) 081.9
　hip (joint) NEC 719.95
　　congenital 755.63
　　suppurative 711.05
　　tuberculous (*see also* Tuberculosis) 015.1 [730.85]
　Hippel's (retinocerebral angiomatosis) 759.6
　Hirschfeld's (acute diabetes mellitus) (*see also* Diabetes) 250.0
　Hirschsprung's (congenital megacolon) 751.3
　His (-Werner) (trench fever) 083.1
　HIV 042
　Hodgkin's (M9650/3) 201.9

> Note　Use the following fifth-digit subclassification with category 201:
>
> 0　unspecified site
> 1　lymph nodes of head, face, and neck
> 2　intrathoracic lymph nodes
> 3　intra-abdominal lymph nodes
> 4　lymph nodes of axilla and upper limb
> 5　lymph nodes of inguinal region and lower limb
> 6　intrapelvic lymph nodes
> 7　spleen
> 8　lymph nodes of multiple sites

　　lymphocytic
　　　depletion (M9653/3) 201.7
　　　　diffuse fibrosis (M9654/3) 201.7
　　　　reticular type (M9655/3) 201.7
　　　predominance (M9651/3) 201.4
　　lymphocytic-histiocytic predominance (M9651/3) 201.4
　　mixed cellularity (M9652/3) 201.6
　　nodular sclerosis (M9656/3) 201.5
　　　cellular phase (M9657/3) 201.5
　Hodgson's 441.9
　　ruptured 441.5
　Hoffa (-Kastert) (liposynovitis prepatellaris) 272.8
　Holla (*see also* Spherocytosis) 282.0
　homozygous-Hb-S 282.61
　hoof and mouth 078.4
　hookworm (*see also* Ancylostomiasis) 126.9
　Horton's (temporal arteritis) 446.5
　host-versus-graft (immune or nonimmune cause) 996.80
　　bone marrow 996.85
　　heart 996.83
　　intestines 996.89
　　kidney 996.81
　　liver 996.82
　　lung 996.84
　　pancreas 996.86
　　specified NEC 996.89
　HPFH (hereditary persistence of fetal hemoglobin) ("Swiss variety") 282.7
　Huchard's (continued arterial hypertension) 401.9
　Huguier's (uterine fibroma) 218.9
　human immunodeficiency (virus) 042
　hunger 251.1

Disease, diseased (*Continued*)
　Hunt's
　　dyssynergia cerebellaris myoclonica 334.2
　　herpetic geniculate ganglionitis 053.11
　Huntington's 333.4
　Huppert's (multiple myeloma) (M9730/3) 203.0
　Hurler's (mucopolysaccharidosis I) 277.5
　Hutchinson's, meaning
　　angioma serpiginosum 709.1
　　cheiropompholyx 705.81
　　prurigo estivalis 692.72
　Hutchinson-Boeck (sarcoidosis) 135
　Hutchinson-Gilford (progeria) 259.8
　hyaline (diffuse) (generalized) 728.9
　　membrane (lung) (newborn) 769
　hydatid (*see also* Echinococcus) 122.9
　Hyde's (prurigo nodularis) 698.3
　hyperkinetic (*see also* Hyperkinesia) 314.9
　　heart 429.82
　hypertensive (*see also* Hypertension) 401.9
　hypophysis 253.9
　　hyperfunction 253.1
　　hypofunction 253.2
　Iceland (epidemic neuromyasthenia) 049.8
　I cell 272.7
　ill-defined 799.8
　immunologic NEC 279.9
　immunoproliferative 203.8
　inclusion 078.5
　　salivary gland 078.5
　infancy, early NEC 779.9
　infective NEC 136.9
　inguinal gland 289.9
　internal semilunar cartilage, cystic 717.5
　intervertebral disc 722.90
　　with myelopathy 722.70
　　cervical, cervicothoracic 722.91
　　　with myelopathy 722.71
　　lumbar, lumbosacral 722.93
　　　with myelopathy 722.73
　　thoracic, thoracolumbar 722.92
　　　with myelopathy 722.72
　intestine 569.9
　　functional 564.9
　　　congenital 751.3
　　　psychogenic 306.4
　　lardaceous 277.3
　　organic 569.9
　　protozoal NEC 007.9
　iris 364.9
　iron
　　metabolism 275.0
　　storage 275.0
　Isambert's (*see also* Tuberculosis, larynx) 012.3
　Iselin's (osteochondrosis, fifth metatarsal) 732.5
　island (scrub typhus) 081.2
　itai-itai 985.5
　Jadassohn's (maculopapular erythroderma) 696.2
　Jadassohn-Pellizari's (anetoderma) 701.3
　Jakob-Creutzfeldt 046.1
　　with dementia 046.1 [294.1]
　Jaksch (-Luzet) (pseudoleukemia infantum) 285.8

Disease, diseased (*Continued*)
　Janet's 300.89
　Jansky-Bielschowsky 330.1
　jaw NEC 526.9
　　fibrocystic 526.2
　Jensen's 363.05
　Jeune's (asphyxiating thoracic dystrophy) 756.4
　jigger 134.1
　Johnson-Stevens (erythema multiforme exudativum) 695.1
　joint NEC 719.9
　　ankle 719.97
　　Charcôt 094.0 [713.5]
　　degenerative (*see also* Osteoarthrosis) 715.9
　　　multiple 715.09
　　　spine (*see also* Spondylosis) 721.90
　　elbow 719.92
　　foot 719.97
　　hand 719.94
　　hip 719.95
　　hypertrophic (chronic) (degenerative) (*see also* Osteoarthrosis) 715.9
　　　spine (*see also* Spondylosis) 721.90
　　knee 719.96
　　Luschka 721.90
　　multiple sites 719.99
　　pelvic region 719.95
　　sacroiliac 724.6
　　shoulder (region) 719.91
　　specified site NEC 719.98
　　spine NEC 724.9
　　　pseudarthrosis following fusion 733.82
　　　sacroiliac 724.6
　　wrist 719.93
　Jourdain's (acute gingivitis) 523.0
　Jüngling's (sarcoidosis) 135
　Kahler (-Bozzolo) (multiple myeloma) (M9730/3) 203.0
　Kalischer's 759.6
　Kaposi's 757.33
　　lichen ruber 697.8
　　　acuminatus 696.4
　　　moniliformis 697.8
　　xeroderma pigmentosum 757.33
　Kaschin-Beck (endemic polyarthritis) 716.00
　　ankle 716.07
　　arm 716.02
　　　lower (and wrist) 716.03
　　　upper (and elbow) 716.02
　　foot (and ankle) 716.07
　　forearm (and wrist) 716.03
　　hand 716.04
　　leg 716.06
　　　lower 716.06
　　　upper 716.05
　　multiple sites 716.09
　　pelvic region (hip) (thigh) 716.05
　　shoulder region 716.01
　　specified site NEC 716.08
　Katayama 120.2
　Kawasaki 446.1
　Kedani (scrub typhus) 081.2
　kidney (functional) (pelvis) (*see also* Disease, renal) 593.9
　　cystic (congenital) 753.10
　　　multiple 753.19
　　　single 753.11
　　　specified NEC 753.19
　　fibrocystic (congenital) 753.19

Disease, diseased *(Continued)*
kidney *(Continued)*
in gout 274.10
polycystic (congenital) 753.12
adult type (APKD) 753.13
autosomal dominant 753.13
autosomal recessive 753.14
childhood type (CPKD) 753.14
infantile type 753.14
Kienböck's (carpal lunate) (wrist) 732.3
Kimmelstiel (-Wilson) (intercapillary glomerulosclerosis) 250.4 *[581.81]*
Kinnier Wilson's (hepatolenticular degeneration) 275.1
kissing 075
Kleb's *(see also* Nephritis) 583.9
Klinger's 446.4
Klippel's 723.8
Klippel-Feil (brevicollis) 756.16
Knight's 911.1
Köbner's (epidermolysis bullosa) 757.39
Koenig-Wichmann (pemphigus) 694.4
Köhler's
first (osteoarthrosis juvenilis) 732.5
second (Freiberg's infraction, metatarsal head) 732.5
patellar 732.4
tarsal navicular (bone) (osteoarthrosis juvenilis) 732.5
Köhler-Freiberg (infraction, metatarsal head) 732.5
Köhler-Mouchet (osteoarthrosis juvenilis) 732.5
Köhler-Pellegrini-Stieda (calcification, knee joint) 726.62
König's (osteochondritis dissecans) 732.7
Korsakoff's (nonalcoholic) 294.0
alcoholic 291.1
Kostmann's (infantile genetic agranulocytosis) 288.0
Krabbe's 330.0
Kraepelin-Morel *(see also* Schizophrenia) 295.9
Kraft-Weber-Dimitri 759.6
Kufs' 330.1
Kugelberg-Welander 335.11
Kuhnt-Junius 362.52
Kümmell's (-Verneuil) (spondylitis) 721.7
Kundrat's (lymphosarcoma) 200.1
kuru 046.0
Kussmaul (-Meier) (polyarteritis nodosa) 446.0
Kyasanur Forest 065.2
Kyrle's (hyperkeratosis follicularis in cutem penetrans) 701.1
labia
inflammatory 616.9
specified NEC 616.8
noninflammatory 624.9
specified NEC 624.8
labyrinth, ear 386.8
lacrimal system (apparatus) (passages) 375.9
gland 375.00
specified NEC 375.89
Lafora's 333.2
Lagleyze-von Hippel (retinocerebral angiomatosis) 759.6
Lancereaux-Mathieu (leptospiral jaundice) 100.0

Disease, diseased *(Continued)*
Landry's 357.0
Lane's 569.89
lardaceous (any site) 277.3
Larrey-Weil (leptospiral jaundice) 100.0
Larsen (-Johansson) (juvenile osteopathia patellae) 732.4
larynx 478.70
Lasègue's (persecution mania) 297.9
Leber's 377.16
Lederer's (acquired infectious hemolytic anemia) 283.19
Legg's (capital femoral osteochondrosis) 732.1
Legg-Calvé-Perthes (capital femoral osteochondrosis) 732.1
Legg-Calvé-Waldenström (femoral capital osteochondrosis) 732.1
Legg-Perthes (femoral capital osteochrondosis) 732.1
Legionnaires' 482.84
Leigh's 330.8
Leiner's (exfoliative dermatitis) 695.89
Leloir's (lupus erythematosus) 695.4
Lenegre's 426.0
lens (eye) 379.39
Leriche's (osteoporosis, posttraumatic) 733.7
Letterer-Siwe (acute histiocytosis X) (M9722/3) 202.5
Lev's (acquired complete heart block) 426.0
Lewandowski's *(see also* Tuberculosis) 017.0
Lewandowski-Lutz (epidermodysplasia verruciformis) 078.19
Leyden's (periodic vomiting) 536.2
Libman-Sacks (verrucous endocarditis) 710.0 *[424.91]*
Lichtheim's (subacute combined sclerosis with pernicious anemia) 281.0 *[336.2]*
ligament 728.9
light chain 203.0
Lightwood's (renal tubular acidosis) 588.8
Lignac's (cystinosis) 270.0
Lindau's (retinocerebral angiomatosis) 759.6
Lindau-von Hippel (angiomatosis retinocerebellosa) 759.6
lip NEC 528.5
lipidosis 272.7
lipoid storage NEC 272.7
Lipschütz's 616.50
Little's - *see* Palsy, cerebral
liver 573.9
alcoholic 571.3
acute 571.1
chronic 571.3
chronic 571.9
alcoholic 571.3
cystic, congenital 751.62
drug-induced 573.3
due to
chemicals 573.3
fluorinated agents 573.3
hypersensitivity drugs 573.3
isoniazids 573.3
fibrocystic (congenital) 751.62
glycogen storage 271.0
organic 573.9
polycystic (congenital) 751.62
Lobo's (keloid blastomycosis) 116.2

Disease, diseased *(Continued)*
Lobstein's (brittle bones and blue sclera) 756.51
locomotor system 334.9
Lorain's (pituitary dwarfism) 253.3
Lou Gehrig's 335.20
Lucas-Championnière (fibrinous bronchitis) 466.0
Ludwig's (submaxillary cellulitis) 528.3
luetic - *see* Syphilis
lumbosacral region 724.6
lung NEC 518.89
black 500
congenital 748.60
cystic 518.89
congenital 748.4
fibroid (chronic) *(see also* Fibrosis, lung) 515
fluke 121.2
Oriental 121.2
in
amyloidosis 277.3 *[517.8]*
polymyositis 710.4 *[517.8]*
sarcoidosis 135 *[517.8]*
Sjögren's syndrome 710.2 *[517.8]*
syphilis 095.1
systemic lupus erythematosus 710.0 *[517.8]*
systemic sclerosis 710.1 *[517.2]*
interstitial (chronic) 515
acute 136.3
nonspecific, chronic 496
obstructive (chronic) (COPD) 496
with
acute exacerbation NEC 491.21
alveolitis, allergic *(see also* Alveolitis, allergic) 495.9
asthma (chronic) (obstructive) 493.2
bronchiectasis 494
bronchitis (chronic) 491.20
with acute exacerbation 491.21
emphysema NEC 492.8
diffuse (with fibrosis) 496
polycystic 518.89
asthma (chronic) (obstructive) 493.2
congenital 748.4
purulent (cavitary) 513.0
restrictive 518.89
rheumatoid 714.81
diffuse interstitial 714.81
specified NEC 518.89
Lutembacher's (atrial septal defect with mitral stenosis) 745.5
Lutz-Miescher (elastosis perforans serpiginosa) 701.1
Lutz-Splendore-de Almeida (Brazilian blastomycosis) 116.1
Lyell's (toxic epidermal necrolysis) 695.1
due to drug
correct substance properly administered 695.1
overdose or wrong substance given or taken 977.9
specific drug - *see* Table of Drugs and Chemicals
Lyme 088.81
lymphatic (gland) (system) 289.9
channel (noninfective) 457.9
vessel (noninfective) 457.9
specified NEC 457.8

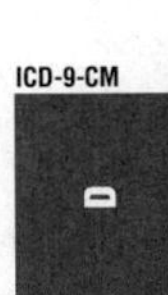

Disease, diseased *(Continued)*
  lymphoproliferative (chronic) (M9970/
      1) 238.7
  Madelung's (lipomatosis) 272.8
  Madura (actinomycotic) 039.9
      mycotic 117.4
  Magitot's 526.4
  Majocchi's (purpura annularis telan-
      giectodes) 709.1
  malarial (*see also* Malaria) 084.6
  Malassez's (cystic) 608.89
  Malibu 919.8
      infected 919.9
  malignant (M8000/3) - *see also* Neo-
      plasm, by site, malignant
      previous, affecting management of
          pregnancy V23.8
  Manson's 120.1
  maple bark 495.6
  maple syrup (urine) 270.3
  Marburg (virus) 078.89
  Marchiafava (-Bignami) 341.8
  Marfan's 090.49
      congenital syphilis 090.49
      meaning Marfan's syndrome
          759.82
  Marie-Bamberger (hypertrophic pul-
      monary osteoarthropathy) (sec-
      ondary) 731.2
      primary or idiopathic (acropachy-
          derma) 757.39
      pulmonary (hypertrophic osteoar-
          thropathy) 731.2
  Marie-Strümpell (ankylosing spondyli-
      tis) 720.0
  Marion's (bladder neck obstruction)
      596.0
  Marsh's (exophthalmic goiter) 242.0
  Martin's 715.27
  mast cell 757.33
      systemic (M9741/3) 202.6
  mastoid (*see also* Mastoiditis) 383.9
      process 385.9
  maternal, unrelated to pregnancy
      NEC, affecting fetus or newborn
      760.9
  Mathieu's (leptospiral jaundice) 100.0
  Mauclaire's 732.3
  Mauriac's (erythema nodosum syphili-
      ticum) 091.3
  Maxcy's 081.0
  McArdle (-Schmid-Pearson) (glycoge-
      nosis V) 271.0
  mediastinum NEC 519.3
  Medin's (*see also* Poliomyelitis) 045.9
  Mediterranean (with hemoglobinopa-
      thy) 282.4
  medullary center (idiopathic) (respira-
      tory) 348.8
  Meige's (chronic hereditary edema)
      757.0
  Meleda 757.39
  Ménétrier's (hypertrophic gastritis)
      535.2
  Méniére's (active) 386.00
      cochlear 386.02
      cochleovestibular 386.01
      inactive 386.04
      in remission 386.04
      vestibular 386.03
  meningeal - *see* Meningitis
  mental (*see also* Psychosis) 298.9
  Merzbacher-Pelizaeus 330.0
  mesenchymal 710.9

Disease, diseased *(Continued)*
  mesenteric embolic 557.0
  metabolic NEC 277.9
  metal polishers' 502
  metastatic - *see* Metastasis
  Mibelli's 757.39
  microdrepanocytic 282.4
  Miescher's 709.3
  Mikulicz's (dryness of mouth, absent
      or decreased lacrimation) 527.1
  Milkman (-Looser) (osteomalacia with
      pseudofractures) 268.2
  Miller's (osteomalacia) 268.2
  Mills' 335.29
  Milroy's (chronic hereditary edema)
      757.0
  Minamata 985.0
  Minor's 336.1
  Minot's (hemorrhagic disease, new-
      born) 776.0
  Minot-von Willebrand-Jürgens (an-
      giohemophilia) 286.4
  Mitchell's (erythromelalgia) 443.89
  mitral - *see* Endocarditis, mitral
  Mljet (mal de Meleda) 757.39
  Möbius', Moebius' 346.8
  Möeller's 267
  Möller (-Barlow) (infantile scurvy) 267
  Mönckeberg's (*see also* Arteriosclerosis,
      extremities) 440.20
  Mondor's (thrombophlebitis of breast)
      451.89
  Monge's 993.2
  Morel-Kraepelin (*see also* Schizophre-
      nia) 295.9
  Morgagni's (syndrome) (hyperostosis
      frontalis interna) 733.3
  Morgagni-Adams-Stokes (syncope with
      heart block) 426.9
  Morquio (-Brailsford) (-Ullrich) (muco-
      polysaccharidosis IV) 277.5
  Morton's (with metatarsalgia) 355.6
  Morvan's 336.0
  motor neuron (bulbar) (mixed type)
      335.20
  Mouchet's (juvenile osteochondrosis,
      foot) 732.5
  mouth 528.9
  Moyamoya 437.5
  Mucha's (acute parapsoriasis varioli-
      formis) 696.2
  mu-chain 273.2
  mucolipidosis (I) (II) (III) 272.7
  Münchmeyer's (exostosis luxurians)
      728.11
  Murri's (intermittent hemoglobinuria)
      283.2
  muscle 359.9
      inflammatory 728.9
      ocular 378.9
  musculoskeletal system 729.9
  mushroom workers' 495.5
  Myà's (congenital dilation, colon)
      751.3
  mycotic 117.9
  myeloproliferative (chronic) (M9960/1)
      238.7
  myocardium, myocardial (*see also* De-
      generation, myocardial) 429.1
      hypertensive (*see also* Hypertension,
          heart) 402.90
      primary (idiopathic) 425.4
  myoneural 358.9
  Naegeli's 287.1

Disease, diseased *(Continued)*
  nail 703.9
      specified type NEC 703.8
  Nairobi sheep 066.1
  nasal 478.1
      cavity NEC 478.1
      sinus (chronic) - *see* Sinusitis
  navel (newborn) NEC 779.8
  nemaline body 359.0
  neoplastic, generalized (M8000/6)
      199.0
  nerve - *see* Disorder, nerve
  nervous system (central) 349.9
      autonomic, peripheral (*see also* Neu-
          ropathy, peripheral, autonomic)
          337.9
      congenital 742.9
      inflammatory - *see* Encephalitis
      parasympathetic (*see also* Neuropa-
          thy, peripheral, autonomic)
          337.9
      peripheral NEC 355.9
      specified NEC 349.89
      sympathetic (*see also* Neuropathy,
          peripheral, autonomic) 337.9
      vegetative (*see also* Neuropathy, pe-
          ripheral, autonomic) 337.9
  Nettleship's (urticaria pigmentosa)
      757.33
  Neumann's (pemphigus vegetans)
      694.4
  neurologic (central) NEC (*see also* Dis-
      ease, nervous system) 349.9
      peripheral NEC 355.9
  neuromuscular system NEC 358.9
  Newcastle 077.8
  Nicolas (-Durand) -Favre (climatic
      bubo) 099.1
  Niemann-Pick (lipid histiocytosis)
      272.7
  nipple 611.9
      Paget's (M8540/3) 174.0
  Nishimoto (-Takeuchi) 437.5
  nonarthropod-borne NEC 078.89
      central nervous system NEC 049.9
      enterovirus NEC 078.89
  nonautoimmune hemolytic NEC 283.10
  Nonne-Milroy-Meige (chronic heredi-
      tary edema) 757.0
  Norrie's (congenital progressive ocu-
      loacousticocerebral degeneration)
      743.8
  nose 478.1
  nucleus pulposus - *see* Disease, inter-
      vertebral disc
  nutritional 269.9
      maternal, affecting fetus or newborn
          760.4
  oasthouse, urine 270.2
  obliterative vascular 447.1
  Odelberg's (juvenile osteochondrosis)
      732.1
  Oguchi's (retina) 368.61
  Ohara's (*see also* Tularemia) 021.9
  Ollier's (chondrodysplasia) 756.4
  Opitz's (congestive splenomegaly)
      289.51
  Oppenheim's 358.8
  Oppenheim-Urbach (necrobiosis li-
      poidica diabeticorum) 250.8
      [709.3]
  optic nerve NEC 377.49
  orbit 376.9
      specified NEC 376.89

Disease, diseased (*Continued*)
Oriental liver fluke 121.1
Oriental lung fluke 121.2
Ormond's 593.4
Osgood's tibia (tubercle) 732.4
Osgood-Schlatter 732.4
Osler (-Vaquez) (polycythemia vera)
   (M9950/1) 238.4
Osler-Rendu (familial hemorrhagic tel-
   angiectasia) 448.0
osteofibrocystic 252.0
Otto's 715.35
outer ear 380.9
ovary (noninflammatory) NEC 620.9
   cystic 620.2
   polycystic 256.4
   specified NEC 620.8
Owren's (congenital) (*see also* Defect,
   coagulation) 286.3
Paas' 756.59
Paget's (osteitis deformans) 731.0
   with infiltrating duct carcinoma of
      the breast (M8541/3) - *see* Neo-
      plasm, breast, malignant
   bone 731.0
      osteosarcoma in (M9184/3) - *see*
         Neoplasm, bone, malignant
   breast (M8540/3) 174.0
   extramammary (M8542/3) - *see also*
      Neoplasm, skin, malignant
      anus 154.3
      skin 173.5
   malignant (M8540/3)
      breast 174.0
      specified site NEC (M8542/3) - *see*
         Neoplasm, skin, malignant
      unspecified site 174.0
   mammary (M8540/3) 174.0
   nipple (M8540/3) 174.0
palate (soft) 528.9
Paltauf-Sternberg 201.9
pancreas 577.9
   cystic 577.2
      congenital 751.7
   fibrocystic 277.00
Panner's 732.3
   capitellum humeri 732.3
   head of humerus 732.3
   tarsal navicular (bone) (osteochon-
      drosis) 732.5
panvalvular - *see* Endocarditis, mitral
parametrium 629.9
parasitic NEC 136.9
   cerebral NEC 123.9
   intestinal NEC 129
   mouth 112.0
   skin NEC 134.9
   specified type - *see* Infestation
   tongue 112.0
parathyroid (gland) 252.9
   specified NEC 252.8
Parkinson's 332.0
parodontal 523.9
Parrot's (syphilitic osteochondritis)
   090.0
Parry's (exophthalmic goiter) 242.0
Parson's (exophthalmic goiter) 242.0
Pavy's 593.6
Paxton's (white piedra) 111.2
Payr's (splenic flexure syndrome)
   569.89
pearl-workers' (chronic osteomyelitis)
   (*see also* Osteomyelitis) 730.1
Pel-Ebstein - *see* Disease, Hodgkin's

Disease, diseased (*Continued*)
Pelizaeus-Merzbacher 330.0
   with dementia 330.0 [*294.1*]
Pellegrini-Stieda (calcification, knee
   joint) 726.62
pelvis, pelvic
   female NEC 629.9
      specified NEC 629.8
   gonococcal (acute) 098.19
      chronic or duration of 2 months
         or over 098.39
   infection (*see also* Disease, pelvis,
      inflammatory) 614.9
   inflammatory (female) (PID) 614.9
      with
         abortion - *see* Abortion, by type,
            with sepsis
         ectopic pregnancy (*see also* cate-
            gories 633.0-633.9) 639.0
         molar pregnancy (*see also* cate-
            gories 630-632) 639.0
      acute 614.3
      chronic 614.4
      complicating pregnancy 646.6
         affecting fetus or newborn 760.8
      following
         abortion 639.0
         ectopic or molar pregnancy
            639.0
      peritonitis (acute) 614.5
         chronic NEC 614.7
      puerperal, postpartum, childbirth
         670
      specified NEC 614.8
   organ, female NEC 629.9
      specified NEC 629.8
   peritoneum, female NEC 629.9
      specified NEC 629.8
penis 607.9
   inflammatory 607.2
peptic NEC 536.9
   acid 536.8
periapical tissues NEC 522.9
pericardium 423.9
   specified type NEC 423.8
perineum
   female
      inflammatory 616.9
         specified NEC 616.8
      noninflammatory 624.9
         specified NEC 624.8
   male (inflammatory) 682.2
periodic (familial) (Reimann's) NEC
   277.3
   paralysis 359.3
periodontal NEC 523.9
   specified NEC 523.8
periosteum 733.90
peripheral
   arterial 443.9
   autonomic nervous system (*see also*
      Neuropathy, autonomic) 337.9
   nerve NEC (*see also* Neuropathy)
      356.9
      multiple - *see* Polyneuropathy
   vascular 443.9
      specified type NEC 443.89
peritoneum 568.9
   pelvic, female 629.9
      specified NEC 629.8
Perrin-Ferraton (snapping hip) 719.65
persistent mucosal (middle ear) (with
   posterior or superior marginal
   perforation of ear drum) 382.2

Disease, diseased (*Continued*)
Perthes' (capital femoral osteochondrosis) 732.1
Petit's (*see also* Hernia, lumbar) 553.8
Peutz-Jeghers 759.6
Peyronie's 607.89
Pfeiffer's (infectious mononucleosis)
   075
pharynx 478.20
Phocas' 610.1
photochromogenic (acid-fast bacilli)
   (pulmonary) 031.0
   nonpulmonary 031.9
Pick's
   brain 331.1
      with dementia 331.1 [*294.1*]
      cerebral atrophy 331.1
         with dementia 331.1 [*294.1*]
   lipid histiocytosis 272.7
   liver (pericardial pseudocirrhosis of
      liver) 423.2
   pericardium (pericardial pseudocir-
      rhosis of liver) 423.2
   polyserositis (pericardial pseudocir-
      rhosis of liver) 423.2
Pierson's (osteochondrosis) 732.1
pigeon fanciers' or breeders' 495.2
pineal gland 259.8
pink 985.0
Pinkus' (lichen nitidus) 697.1
pinworm 127.4
pituitary (gland) 253.9
   hyperfunction 253.1
   hypofunction 253.2
pituitary snuff-takers' 495.8
placenta
   affecting fetus or newborn 762.2
   complicating pregnancy or childbirth
      656.7
pleura (cavity) (*see also* Pleurisy) 511.0
Plummer's (toxic nodular goiter) 242.3
pneumatic
   drill 994.9
   hammer 994.9
policeman's 729.2
Pollitzer's (hidradenitis suppurativa)
   705.83
polycystic (congenital) 759.89
   kidney or renal 753.12
      adult type (APKD) 753.13
      autosomal dominant 753.13
      autosomal recessive 753.14
      childhood type (CPKD) 753.14
      infantile type 753.14
   liver or hepatic 751.62
   lung or pulmonary 518.89
      congenital 748.4
   ovary, ovaries 256.4
   spleen 759.0
Pompe's (glycogenosis II) 271.0
Poncet's (tuberculous rheumatism) (*see
   also* Tuberculosis) 015.9
Posada-Wernicke 114.9
Potain's (pulmonary edema) 514
Pott's (*see also* Tuberculosis) 015.0
   [*730.88*]
   osteomyelitis 015.0 [*730.88*]
   paraplegia 015.0 [*730.88*]
   spinal curvature 015.0 [*737.43*]
   spondylitis 015.0 [*720.81*]
Potter's 753.0
Poulet's 714.2
pregnancy NEC (*see also* Pregnancy)
   646.9

Disease, diseased (*Continued*)
  Preiser's (osteoporosis) 733.09
  Pringle's (tuberous sclerosis) 759.5
  Profichet's 729.9
  prostate 602.9
    specified type NEC 602.8
  protozoal NEC 136.8
    intestine, intestinal NEC 007.9
  pseudo-Hurler's (mucolipidosis III) 272.7
  psychiatric (*see also* Psychosis) 298.9
  psychotic (*see also* Psychosis) 298.9
  Puente's (simple glandular cheilitis) 528.5
  puerperal NEC (*see also* Puerperal) 674.9
  pulmonary - *see also* Disease, lung
    amyloid 277.3 [517.8]
    artery 417.9
    circulation, circulatory 417.9
      specified NEC 417.8
    diffuse obstructive (chronic) 496
      with
        acute exacerbation NEC 491.21
        asthma (chronic) (obstructive) 493.2
    heart (chronic) 416.9
      specified NEC 416.8
    hypertensive (vascular) 416.0
      cardiovascular 416.0
    obstructive diffuse (chronic) 496
      with
        acute exacerbation NEC 491.21
        asthma (chronic) (obstructive) 493.2
        bronchitis (chronic) 491.20
          with acute exacerbation 491.21
    valve (*see also* Endocarditis, pulmonary) 424.3
  pulp (dental) NEC 522.9
  pulseless 446.7
  Putnam's (subacute combined sclerosis with pernicious anemia) 281.0 [336.2]
  Pyle (-Cohn) (craniometaphyseal dysplasia) 756.89
  pyramidal tract 333.90
  Quervain's
    tendon sheath 727.04
    thyroid (subacute granulomatous thyroiditis) 245.1
  Quincke's - *see* Edema, angioneurotic
  Quinquaud (acne decalvans) 704.09
  rag sorters' 022.1
  Raynaud's (paroxysmal digital cyanosis) 443.0
  reactive airway - *see* Asthma
  Recklinghausen's (M9540/1) 237.71
    bone (osteitis fibrosa cystica) 252.0
  Recklinghausen-Applebaum (hemochromatosis) 275.0
  Reclus' (cystic) 610.1
  rectum NEC 569.49
  Refsum's (heredopathia atactica polyneuritiformis) 356.3
  Reichmann's (gastrosuccorrhea) 536.8
  Reimann's (periodic) 277.3
  Reiter's 099.3
  renal (functional) (pelvis) 593.9
    with
      edema (*see also* Nephrosis) 581.9
      exudative nephritis 583.89

Disease, diseased (*Continued*)
  renal (*Continued*)
    with (*Continued*)
      lesion of interstitial nephritis 583.89
      stated generalized cause - *see* Nephritis
    acute - *see* Nephritis, acute
    basement membrane NEC 583.89
      with
        pulmonary hemorrhage (Goodpasture's syndrome) 446.21 [583.81]
    chronic - *see* Nephritis, chronic
    complicating pregnancy or puerperium NEC 646.2
      with hypertension - *see* Toxemia, of pregnancy
      affecting fetus or newborn 760.1
    cystic, congenital (*see also* Cystic, disease, kidney) 753.10
    diabetic 250.4 [583.81]
    due to
      amyloidosis 277.3 [583.81]
      diabetes mellitus 250.4 [583.81]
      systemic lupus erythematosis 710.0 [583.81]
    end-stage 585
    exudative 583.89
    fibrocystic (congenital) 753.19
    gonococcal 098.19 [583.81]
    gouty 274.10
    hypertensive (*see also* Hypertension, kidney) 403.90
    immune complex NEC 583.89
    interstitial (diffuse) (focal) 583.89
    lupus 710.0 [583.81]
    maternal, affecting fetus or newborn 760.1
      hypertensive 760.0
    phosphate-losing (tubular) 588.0
    polycystic (congenital) 753.12
      adult type (APKD) 753.13
      autosomal dominant 753.13
      autosomal recessive 753.14
      childhood type (CPKD) 753.14
      infantile type 753.14
    specified lesion or cause NEC (*see also* Glomerulonephritis) 583.89
    subacute 581.9
    syphilitic 095.4
    tuberculous (*see also* Tuberculosis) 016.0 [583.81]
    tubular (*see also* Nephrosis, tubular) 584.5
  Rendu-Osler-Weber (familial hemorrhagic telangiectasia) 448.0
  renovascular (arteriosclerotic) (*see also* Hypertension, kidney) 403.90
  respiratory (tract) 519.9
    acute or subacute (upper) NEC 465.9
      due to fumes or vapors 506.3
      multiple sites NEC 465.8
      noninfectious 478.9
      streptococcal 034.0
    chronic 519.9
      arising in the perinatal period 770.7
      due to fumes or vapors 506.4
    due to
      aspiration of liquids or solids 508.9
      external agents NEC 508.9
        specified NEC 508.8

Disease, diseased (*Continued*)
  respiratory (*Continued*)
    due to (*Continued*)
      fumes or vapors 506.9
        acute or subacute NEC 506.3
        chronic 506.4
    fetus or newborn NEC 770.9
    obstructive 496
    specified type NEC 519.8
    upper (acute) (infectious) NEC 465.9
      multiple sites NEC 465.8
      noninfectious NEC 478.9
      streptococcal 034.0
  retina, retinal NEC 362.9
    Batten's or Batten-Mayou 330.1 [362.71]
    degeneration 362.89
    vascular lesion 362.17
  rheumatic (*see also* Arthritis) 716.8
    heart - *see* Disease, heart, rheumatic
  rheumatoid (heart) - *see* Arthritis, rheumatoid
  rickettsial NEC 083.9
    specified type NEC 083.8
  Riedel's (ligneous thyroiditis) 245.3
  Riga (-Fede) (cachectic aphthae) 529.0
  Riggs' (compound periodontitis) 523.4
  Ritter's 695.81
  Rivalta's (cervicofacial actinomycosis) 039.3
  Robles' (onchocerciasis) 125.3 [360.13]
  Roger's (congenital interventricular septal defect) 745.4
  Rokitansky's (*see also* Necrosis, liver) 570
  Romberg's 349.89
  Rosenthal's (factor XI deficiency) 286.2
  Rossbach's (hyperchlorhydria) 536.8
    psychogenic 306.4
  Roth (-Bernhardt) 355.1
  Runeberg's (progressive pernicious anemia) 281.0
  Rust's (tuberculous spondylitis) (*see also* Tuberculosis) 015.0 [720.81]
  Rustitskii's (multiple myeloma) (M9730/3) 203.0
  Ruysch's (Hirschsprung's disease) 751.3
  Sachs (-Tay) 330.1
  sacroiliac NEC 724.6
  salivary gland or duct NEC 527.9
    inclusion 078.5
      streptococcal 034.0
    virus 078.5
  Sander's (paranoia) 297.1
  Sandhoff's 330.1
  sandworm 126.9
  Savill's (epidemic exfoliative dermatitis) 695.89
  Schamberg's (progressive pigmentary dermatosis) 709.09
  Schaumann's (sarcoidosis) 135
  Schenck's (sporotrichosis) 117.1
  Scheuermann's (osteochondrosis) 732.0
  Schilder (-Flatau) 341.1
  Schimmelbusch's 610.1
  Schlatter's tibia (tubercle) 732.4
  Schlatter-Osgood 732.4
  Schmorl's 722.30
    cervical 722.39
    lumbar, lumbosacral 722.32
    specified region NEC 722.39
    thoracic, thoracolumbar 722.31
  Scholz's 330.0

ICD-9-CM

Vol. 2

Disease, diseased *(Continued)*
  triglyceride-storage, type I, II, III 272.7
  triple vessel - *see* Arteriosclerosis, coronary
  trisymptomatic, Gougerot's 709.1
  trophoblastic *(see also* Hydatidiform mole) 630
    previous, affecting management of pregnancy V23.1
  tsutsugamushi (scrub typhus) 081.2
  tube (fallopian), noninflammatory 620.9
    specified NEC 620.8
  tuberculous NEC *(see also* Tuberculosis) 011.9
  tubo-ovarian
    inflammatory *(see also* Salpingo-oophoritis) 614.2
    noninflammatory 620.9
      specified NEC 620.8
  tubotympanic, chronic (with anterior perforation of ear drum) 382.1
  tympanum 385.9
  Uhl's 746.84
  umbilicus (newborn) NEC 779.8
  Underwood's (sclerema neonatorum) 778.1
  undiagnosed 799.9
  Unna's (seborrheic dermatitis) 690.18
  unstable hemoglobin hemolytic 282.7
  Unverricht (-Lundborg) 333.2
  Urbach-Oppenheim (necrobiosis lipoidica diabeticorum) 250.8 *[709.3]*
  Urbach-Wiethe (lipoid proteinosis) 272.8
  ureter 593.9
  urethra 599.9
    specified type NEC 599.84
  urinary (tract) 599.9
    bladder 596.9
      specified NEC 596.8
    maternal, affecting fetus or newborn 760.1
  Usher-Senear (pemphigus erythematosus) 694.4
  uterus (organic) 621.9
    infective *(see also* Endometritis) 615.9
    inflammatory *(see also* Endometritis) 615.9
    noninflammatory 621.9
      specified type NEC 621.8
  uveal tract
    anterior 364.9
    posterior 363.9
  vagabonds' 132.1
  vagina, vaginal
    inflammatory 616.9
      specified NEC 616.8
    noninflammatory 623.9
      specified NEC 623.8
  Valsuani's (progressive pernicious anemia, puerperal) 648.2
    complicating pregnancy or puerperium 648.2
  valve, valvular - *see* Endocarditis
  van Bogaert-Nijssen (-Peiffer) 330.0
  van Creveld-von Gierke (glycogenosis I) 271.0
  van den Bergh's (enterogenous cyanosis) 289.7
  van Neck's (juvenile osteochondrosis) 732.1
  Vaquez (-Osler) (polycythemia vera) (M9950/1) 238.4

Disease, diseased *(Continued)*
  vascular 459.9
    arteriosclerotic - *see* Arteriosclerosis
    hypertensive - *see* Hypertension
    obliterative 447.1
      peripheral 443.9
    occlusive 459.9
    peripheral (occlusive) 443.9
      in diabetes mellitus 250.7 *[443.81]*
      specified type NEC 443.89
  vas deferens 608.9
  vasomotor 443.9
  vasospastic 443.9
  vein 459.9
  venereal 099.9
    chlamydial NEC 099.50
      anus 099.52
      bladder 099.53
      cervix 099.53
      epididymis 099.54
      genitourinary NEC 099.55
        lower 099.53
          specified NEC 099.54
      pelvic inflammatory disease 099.54
      perihepatic 099.56
      peritoneum 099.56
      pharynx 099.51
      rectum 099.52
      specified site NEC 099.59
      testis 099.54
      vagina 099.53
      vulva 099.53
    fifth 099.1
    sixth 099.1
    complicating pregnancy, childbirth, or puerperium 647.2
    specified nature or type NEC 099.8
      chlamydial - *see* Disease, venereal, chlamydial
  Verneuil's (syphilitic bursitis) 095.7
  Verse's (calcinosis intervertebralis) 275.49 *[722.90]*
  vertebra, vertebral NEC 733.90
    disc - *see* Disease, Intervertebral disc
  vibration NEC 994.9
  Vidal's (lichen simplex chronicus) 698.3
  Vincent's (trench mouth) 101
  Virchow's 733.99
  virus (filterable) NEC 078.89
    arbovirus NEC 066.9
    arthropod-borne NEC 066.9
    central nervous system NEC 049.9
      specified type NEC 049.8
    complicating pregnancy, childbirth, or puerperium 647.6
    contact (with) V01.7
    exposure to V01.7
    Marburg 078.89
    maternal
      with fetal damage affecting management of pregnancy 655.3
    nonarthropod-borne NEC 078.89
      central nervous system NEC 049.9
        specified NEC 049.8
  vitreous 379.29
  vocal cords NEC 478.5
  Vogt's (Cecile) 333.7
  Vogt-Spielmeyer 330.1
  Volhard-Fahr (malignant nephrosclerosis) 403.00
  Volkmann's
    acquired 958.6

Disease, diseased *(Continued)*
  von Bechterew's (ankylosing spondylitis) 720.0
  von Economo's (encephalitis lethargica) 049.8
  von Eulenburg's (congenital paramyotonia) 359.2
  von Gierke's (glycogenosis I) 271.0
  von Graefe's 378.72
  von Hippel's (retinocerebral angiomatosis) 759.6
  von Hippel-Lindau (angiomatosis retinocerebellosa) 759.6
  von Jaksch's (pseudoleukemia infantum) 285.8
  von Recklinghausen's (M9540/1) 237.71
    bone (osteitis fibrosa cystica) 252.0
  von Recklinghausen-Applebaum (hemochromatosis) 275.0
  von Willebrand (-Jürgens) (angiohemophilia) 286.4
  von Zambusch's (lichen sclerosus et atrophicus) 701.0
  Voorhoeve's (dyschondroplasia) 756.4
  Vrolik's (osteogenesis imperfecta) 756.51
  vulva
    noninflammatory 624.9
      specified NEC 624.8
  Wagner's (colloid milium) 709.3
  Waldenström's (osteochondrosis capital femoral) 732.1
  Wallgren's (obstruction of splenic vein with collateral circulation) 459.89
  Wardrop's (with lymphangitis) 681.9
    finger 681.02
    toe 681.11
  Wassilieff's (leptospiral jaundice) 100.0
  wasting NEC 799.4
    due to malnutrition 261
    paralysis 335.21
  Waterhouse-Friderichsen 036.3
  waxy (any site) 277.3
  Weber-Christian (nodular nonsuppurative panniculitis) 729.30
  Wegner's (syphilitic osteochondritis) 090.0
  Weil's (leptospiral jaundice) 100.0
    of lung 100.0
  Weir Mitchell's (erythromelalgia) 443.89
  Werdnig-Hoffmann 335.0
  Werlhof's *(see also* Purpura, thrombocytopenic) 287.3
  Wermer's 258.0
  Werner's (progeria adultorum) 259.8
  Werner-His (trench fever) 083.1
  Werner-Schultz (agranulocytosis) 288.0
  Wernicke's (superior hemorrhagic polioencephalitis) 265.1
  Wernicke-Posadas 114.9
  Whipple's (intestinal lipodystrophy) 040.2
  whipworm 127.3
  white
    blood cell 288.9
      specified NEC 288.8
    spot 701.0
  White's (congenital) (keratosis follicularis) 757.39
  Whitmore's (melioidosis) 025

Disease, diseased (*Continued*)

Widal-Abrami (acquired hemolytic jaundice) 283.9

Wilkie's 557.1

Wilkinson-Sneddon (subcorneal pustular dermatosis) 694.1

Willis' (diabetes mellitus) (*see also* Diabetes) 250.0

Wilson's (hepatolenticular degeneration) 275.1

Wilson-Brocq (dermatitis exfoliativa) 695.89

winter vomiting 078.82

Wise's 696.2

Wohlfart-Kugelberg-Welander 335.11

Woillez's (acute idiopathic pulmonary congestion) 518.5

Wolman's (primary familial xanthomatosis) 272.7

wool-sorters' 022.1

Zagari's (xerostomia) 527.7

Zahorsky's (exanthem subitum) 057.8

Ziehen-Oppenheim 333.6

zoonotic, bacterial NEC 027.9

specified type NEC 027.8

Disfigurement (due to scar) 709.2

head V48.6

limb V49.4

neck V48.7

trunk V48.7

Disgerminoma - *see* Dysgerminoma

Disinsertion, retina 361.04

Disintegration, complete, of the body 799.8

traumatic 869.1

Disk kidney 753.3

Dislocatable hip, congenital (*see also* Dislocation, hip, congenital) 754.30

Dislocation (articulation) (closed) (displacement) (simple) (subluxation) 839.8

Note

"Closed" includes simple, complete, partial, uncomplicated, and unspecified dislocation.

"Open" includes dislocation specified as infected or compound and dislocation with foreign body.

"Chronic," "habitual," "old," or "recurrent" dislocations should be coded as indicated under the entry "Dislocation, recurrent"; and "pathological" as indicated under the entry "Dislocation, pathological."

For late effect of dislocation see Late, effect, dislocation.

---

with fracture - *see* Fracture, by site

acromioclavicular (joint) (closed) 831.04

open 831.14

anatomical site (closed)

specified NEC 839.69

open 839.79

unspecified or ill-defined 839.8

open 839.9

ankle (scaphoid bone) (closed) 837.0

open 837.1

arm (closed) 839.8

open 839.9

Dislocation (*Continued*)

astragalus (closed) 837.0

open 837.1

atlanto-axial (closed) 839.01

open 839.11

atlas (closed) 839.01

open 839.11

axis (closed) 839.02

open 839.12

back (closed) 839.8

open 839.9

Bell-Dally 723.8

breast bone (closed) 839.61

open 839.71

capsule, joint - *see* Dislocation, by site

carpal (bone) - *see* Dislocation, wrist

carpometacarpal (joint) (closed) 833.04

open 833.14

cartilage (joint) - *see also* Dislocation, by site

knee - *see* Tear, meniscus

cervical, cervicodorsal, or cervicothoracic (spine) (vertebra) - *see* Dislocation, vertebra, cervical

chiropractic (*see also* Lesion, nonallopathic) 739.9

chondrocostal - *see* Dislocation, costochondral

chronic - *see* Dislocation, recurrent

clavicle (closed) 831.04

open 831.14

coccyx (closed) 839.41

open 839.51

collar bone (closed) 831.04

open 831.14

compound (open) NEC 839.9

congenital NEC 755.8

hip (*see also* Dislocation, hip, congenital) 754.30

lens 743.37

rib 756.3

sacroiliac 755.69

spine NEC 756.19

vertebra 756.19

coracoid (closed) 831.09

open 831.19

costal cartilage (closed) 839.69

open 839.79

costochondral (closed) 839.69

open 839.79

cricoarytenoid articulation (closed) 839.69

open 839.79

cricothyroid (cartilage) articulation (closed) 839.69

open 839.79

dorsal vertebrae (closed) 839.21

open 839.31

ear ossicle 385.23

elbow (closed) 832.00

anterior (closed) 832.01

open 832.11

congenital 754.89

divergent (closed) 832.09

open 832.19

lateral (closed) 832.04

open 832.14

medial (closed) 832.03

open 832.13

open 832.10

posterior (closed) 832.02

open 832.12

recurrent 718.32

Dislocation (*Continued*)

elbow (*Continued*)

specified type NEC 832.09

open 832.19

eye 360.81

lateral 376.36

eyeball 360.81

lateral 376.36

femur

distal end (closed) 836.50

anterior 836.52

open 836.62

lateral 836.53

open 836.63

medial 836.54

open 836.64

open 836.60

posterior 836.51

open 836.61

proximal end (closed) 835.00

anterior (pubic) 835.03

open 835.13

obturator 835.02

open 835.12

open 835.10

posterior 835.01

open 835.11

fibula

distal end (closed) 837.0

open 837.1

proximal end (closed) 836.59

open 836.69

finger(s) (phalanx) (thumb) (closed) 834.00

interphalangeal (joint) 834.02

open 834.12

metacarpal (bone), distal end 834.01

open 834.11

metacarpophalangeal (joint) 834.01

open 834.11

recurrent 718.34

foot (closed) 838.00

open 838.10

recurrent 718.37

forearm (closed) 839.8

open 839.9

fracture - *see* Fracture, by site

glenoid (closed) 831.09

open 831.19

habitual - *see* Dislocation, recurrent

hand (closed) 839.8

open 839.9

hip (closed) 835.00

anterior 835.03

obturator 835.02

open 835.12

open 835.13

congenital (unilateral) 754.30

with subluxation of other hip 754.35

bilateral 754.31

open 835.10

posterior 835.01

open 835.11

recurrent 718.35

humerus (closed) 831.00

distal end (*see also* Dislocation, elbow) 832.00

open 831.10

proximal end (closed) 831.00

anterior (subclavicular) (subcoracoid) (subglenoid) (closed) 831.01

Dislocation (*Continued*)
  humerus (*Continued*)
    proximal end (*Continued*)
      anterior (*Continued*)
        open 831.11
        inferior (closed) 831.03
          open 831.13
        open 831.10
        posterior (closed) 831.02
          open 831.12
  implant - *see* Complications, mechanical
  incus 385.23
  infracoracoid (closed) 831.01
    open 831.11
  innominate (pubic junction) (sacral junction) (closed) 839.69
    acetabulum (*see also* Dislocation, hip) 835.00
    open 839.79
  interphalangeal (joint)
    finger or hand (closed) 834.02
      open 834.12
    foot or toe (closed) 838.06
      open 838.16
  jaw (cartilage) (meniscus) (closed) 830.0
    open 830.1
    recurrent 524.69
  joint NEC (closed) 839.8
    open 839.9
    pathological - *see* Dislocation, pathological
    recurrent - *see* Dislocation, recurrent
  knee (closed) 836.50
    anterior 836.51
      open 836.61
    congenital (with genu recurvatum) 754.41
    habitual 718.36
    lateral 836.54
      open 836.64
    medial 836.53
      open 836.63
    old 718.36
    open 836.60
    posterior 836.52
      open 836.62
    recurrent 718.36
    rotatory 836.59
      open 836.69
  lacrimal gland 375.16
  leg (closed) 839.8
    open 839.9
  lens (crystalline) (complete) (partial) 379.32
    anterior 379.33
    congenital 743.37
    ocular implant 996.53
    posterior 379.34
    traumatic 921.3
  ligament - *see* Dislocation, by site
  lumbar (vertebrae) (closed) 839.20
    open 839.30
  lumbosacral (vertebrae) (closed) 839.20
    congenital 756.19
    open 839.30
  mandible (closed) 830.0
    open 830.1
  maxilla (inferior) (closed) 830.0
    open 830.1
  meniscus (knee) - *see also* Tear, meniscus
    other sites - *see* Dislocation, by site

Dislocation (*Continued*)
  metacarpal (bone)
    distal end (closed) 834.01
      open 834.11
    proximal end (closed) 833.05
      open 833.15
  metacarpophalangeal (joint) (closed) 834.01
    open 834.11
  metatarsal (bone) (closed) 838.04
    open 838.14
  metatarsophalangeal (joint) (closed) 838.05
    open 838.15
  midcarpal (joint) (closed) 833.03
    open 833.13
  midtarsal (joint) (closed) 838.02
    open 838.12
  Monteggia's - *see* Dislocation, hip
  multiple locations (except fingers only or toes only) (closed) 839.8
    open 839.9
  navicular (bone) foot (closed) 837.0
    open 837.1
  neck (*see also* Dislocation, vertebra, cervical) 839.00
  Nélaton's - *see* Dislocation, ankle
  nontraumatic (joint) - *see* Dislocation, pathological
  nose (closed) 839.69
    open 839.79
  not recurrent, not current injury - *see* Dislocation, pathological
  occiput from atlas (closed) 839.01
    open 839.11
  old - *see* Dislocation, recurrent
  open (compound) NEC 839.9
  ossicle, ear 385.23
  paralytic (flaccid) (spastic) - *see* Dislocation, pathological
  patella (closed) 836.3
    congenital 755.64
    open 836.4
  pathological NEC 718.20
    ankle 718.27
    elbow 718.22
    foot 718.27
    hand 718.24
    hip 718.25
    knee 718.26
    lumbosacral joint 724.6
    multiple sites 718.29
    pelvic region 718.25
    sacroiliac 724.6
    shoulder (region) 718.21
    specified site NEC 718.28
    spine 724.8
      sacroiliac 724.6
    wrist 718.23
  pelvis (closed) 839.69
    acetabulum (*see also* Dislocation, hip) 835.00
    open 839.79
  phalanx
    foot or toe (closed) 838.09
      open 838.19
    hand or finger (*see also* Dislocation, finger) 834.00
  postpoliomyelitic - *see* Dislocation, pathological
  prosthesis, internal - *see* Complications, mechanical
  radiocarpal (joint) (closed) 833.02
    open 833.12

Dislocation (*Continued*)
  radioulnar (joint)
    distal end (closed) 833.01
      open 833.11
    proximal end (*see also* Dislocation, elbow) 832.00
  radius
    distal end (closed) 833.00
      open 833.10
    proximal end (closed) 832.01
      open 832.11
  recurrent (*see also* Derangement, joint, recurrent) 718.3
    elbow 718.32
    hip 718.35
    joint NEC 718.38
    knee 718.36
    lumbosacral (joint) 724.6
    patella 718.36
    sacroiliac 724.6
    shoulder 718.31
    temporomandibular 524.69
  rib (cartilage) (closed) 839.69
    congenital 756.3
    open 839.79
  sacrococcygeal (closed) 839.42
    open 839.52
  sacroiliac (joint) (ligament) (closed) 839.42
    congenital 755.69
    open 839.52
    recurrent 724.6
  sacrum (closed) 839.42
    open 839.52
  scaphoid (bone)
    ankle or foot (closed) 837.0
      open 837.1
    wrist (closed) (*see also* Dislocation, wrist) 833.00
      open 833.10
  scapula (closed) 831.09
    open 831.19
  semilunar cartilage, knee - *see* Tear, meniscus
  septal cartilage (nose) (closed) 839.69
    open 839.79
  septum (nasal) (old) 470
  sesamoid bone - *see* Dislocation, by site
  shoulder (blade) (ligament) (closed) 831.00
    anterior (subclavicular) (subcoracoid) (subglenoid) (closed) 831.01
      open 831.11
    chronic 718.31
    inferior 831.03
      open 831.13
    open 831.10
    posterior (closed) 831.02
      open 831.12
    recurrent 718.31
  skull - *see* Injury, intracranial
  Smith's - *see* Dislocation, foot
  spine (articular process) (*see also* Dislocation, vertebra) (closed) 839.40
    atlanto-axial (closed) 839.01
      open 839.11
      recurrent 723.8
    cervical, cervicodorsal, cervicothoracic (closed) (*see also* Dislocation, vertebrae, cervical) 839.00
      open 839.10
      recurrent 723.8

Dislocation *(Continued)*
  spine *(Continued)*
    coccyx 839.41
      open 839.51
    congenital 756.19
    due to birth trauma 767.4
    open 839.50
    recurrent 724.9
    sacroiliac 839.42
      recurrent 724.6
    sacrum (sacrococcygeal) (sacroiliac)
        839.42
      open 839.52
    spontaneous - *see* Dislocation, patho-
        logical
    sternoclavicular (joint) (closed)
        839.61
      open 839.71
  sternum (closed) 839.61
    open 839.71
  subastragalar - *see* Dislocation, foot
  subglenoid (closed) 831.01
    open 831.11
  symphysis
    jaw (closed) 830.0
      open 830.1
    mandibular (closed) 830.0
      open 830.1
    pubis (closed) 839.69
      open 839.79
  tarsal (bone) (joint) 838.01
    open 838.11
  tarsometatarsal (joint) 838.03
    open 838.13
  temporomandibular (joint) (closed)
      830.0
    open 830.1
    recurrent 524.69
  thigh
    distal end (*see also* Dislocation, fe-
        mur, distal end) 836.50
    proximal end (*see also* Dislocation,
        hip) 835.00
  thoracic (vertebrae) (closed) 839.21
    open 839.31
  thumb(s) (*see also* Dislocation, finger)
      834.00
  thyroid cartilage (closed) 839.69
    open 839.79
  tibia
    distal end (closed) 837.0
      open 837.1
    proximal end (closed) 836.50
      anterior 836.51
        open 836.61
      lateral 836.54
        open 836.64
      medial 836.53
        open 836.63
      open 836.60
      posterior 836.52
        open 836.62
      rotatory 836.59
        open 836.69
  tibiofibular
    distal (closed) 837.0
      open 837.1
    superior (closed) 836.59
      open 836.69
  toe(s) (closed) 838.09
    open 838.19
  trachea (closed) 839.69
    open 839.79
  ulna

Dislocation *(Continued)*
  ulna *(Continued)*
    distal end (closed) 833.09
      open 833.19
    proximal end - *see* Dislocation, elbow
  vertebra (articular process) (body)
      (closed) 839.40
    cervical, cervicodorsal or cervico-
        thoracic (closed) 839.00
      first (atlas) 839.01
        open 839.11
      second (axis) 839.02
        open 839.12
      third 839.03
        open 839.13
      fourth 839.04
        open 839.14
      fifth 839.05
        open 839.15
      sixth 839.06
        open 839.16
      seventh 839.07
        open 839.17
      congenital 756.19
      multiple sites 839.08
        open 839.18
      open 839.10
    congenital 756.19
    dorsal 839.21
      open 839.31
      recurrent 724.9
    lumbar, lumbosacral 839.20
      open 839.30
    open NEC 839.50
    recurrent 724.9
    specified region NEC 839.49
      open 839.59
    thoracic 839.21
      open 839.31
  wrist (carpal bone) (scaphoid) (semilu-
      nar) (closed) 833.00
    carpometacarpal (joint) 833.04
      open 833.14
    metacarpal bone, proximal end
        833.05
      open 833.15
    midcarpal (joint) 833.03
      open 833.13
    open 833.10
    radiocarpal (joint) 833.02
      open 833.12
    radioulnar (joint) 833.01
      open 833.11
    recurrent 718.33
    specified site NEC 833.09
      open 833.19
  xiphoid cartilage (closed) 839.61
    open 839.71
Dislodgement ◄
  artificial skin graft 996.55 ◄
  decellularized allodermis graft
      996.55 ◄
Disobedience, hostile (covert) (overt)
    (*see also* Disturbance, conduct) 312.0
Disorder - *see also* Disease
  academic underachievement, child-
      hood and adolescence 313.83
  accommodation 367.51
    drug-induced 367.89
    toxic 367.89
  adjustment (*see also* Reaction, adjust-
      ment) 309.9
  adrenal (capsule) (cortex) (gland) 255.9
    specified type NEC 255.8

Disorder *(Continued)*
  adrenogenital 255.2
  affective (*see also* Psychosis, affective)
      296.90
    atypical 296.81
  aggressive, unsocialized (*see also* Dis-
      turbance, conduct) 312.0
  alcohol, alcoholic (*see also* Alcohol) 291.9
  allergic - *see* Allergy
  amino acid (metabolic) (*see also* Distur-
      bance, metabolism, amino acid)
      270.9
    albinism 270.2
    alkaptonuria 270.2
    argininosuccinicaciduria 270.6
    beta-amino-isobutyricaciduria 277.2
    cystathioninuria 270.4
    cystinosis 270.0
    cystinuria 270.0
    glycinuria 270.0
    homocystinuria 270.4
    imidazole 270.5
    maple syrup (urine) disease 270.3
    neonatal, transitory 775.8
    oasthouse urine disease 270.2
    ochronosis 270.2
    phenylketonuria 270.1
    phenylpyruvic oligophrenia 270.1
    purine NEC 277.2
    pyrimidine NEC 277.2
    renal transport NEC 270.0
    specified type NEC 270.8
    transport NEC 270.0
      renal 270.0
    xanthinuria 277.2
  amnestic (*see also* Amnestic syndrome)
      294.0
  anaerobic glycolysis with anemia 282.3
  anxiety (*see also* Anxiety) 300.00
    due to or associated with physical
        condition 293.84 ◄
  arteriole 447.9
    specified type NEC 447.8
  artery 447.9
    specified type NEC 447.8
  articulation - *see* Disorder, joint
  Asperger's 299.8
  attachment of infancy 313.89
  attention deficit 314.00
    with hyperactivity 314.01
    predominantly
    combined hyperactive/inattentive
        314.01
      hyperactive/impulsive 314.01
      inattentive 314.00
    residual type 314.8
  autoimmune NEC 279.4
    hemolytic (cold type) (warm type)
        283.0
    parathyroid 252.1
    thyroid 245.2
  autistic 299.0
  avoidant, childhood or adolescence
      313.21
  balance
    acid-base 276.9
      mixed (with hypercapnia) 276.4
    electrolyte 276.9
    fluid 276.9
  behavior NEC (*see also* Disturbance,
      conduct) 312.9
  bilirubin excretion 277.4
  bipolar (affective) (alternating) (*see also*
      Psychosis, affective) (Type I) 296.7

Disorder *(Continued)*
  bipolar *(Continued)*
    atypical 296.7
    currently
      hypomanic 296.4
      depressed 296.5
      manic 296.4
    mixed 296.6
    type II (recurrent major depressive
      episodes with hypomania) 296.89
  bladder 596.9
    functional NEC 596.59
    specified NEC 596.8
  bone NEC 733.90
    specified NEC 733.99
  brachial plexus 353.0
  branched-chain amino-acid degrada-
    tion 270.3
  breast 611.9
    puerperal, postpartum 676.3
    specified NEC 611.8
  Briquet's 300.81
  bursa 727.9
    shoulder region 726.10
  carbohydrate metabolism, congenital
    271.9
  cardiac, functional 427.9
    postoperative 997.1
    psychogenic 306.2
  cardiovascular, psychogenic 306.2
  cartilage NEC 733.90
    articular 718.00
      ankle 718.07
      elbow 718.02
      foot 718.07
      hand 718.04
      hip 718.05
      knee 717.9
      multiple sites 718.09
      pelvic region 718.05
      shoulder region 718.01
      specified
        site NEC 718.08
        type NEC 733.99
      wrist 718.03
  catatonic—*see* Catatonia ◀
  cervical region NEC 723.9
  cervical root (nerve) NEC 353.2
  character NEC (*see also* Disorder, per-
    sonality) 301.9
  coagulation (factor) (*see also* Defect, co-
    agulation) 286.9
    factor VIII (congenital) (functional)
      286.0
    factor IX (congenital) (functional) 286.1
    neonatal, transitory 776.3
  coccyx 724.70
    specified NEC 724.79
  colon 569.9
    functional 564.9
      congenital 751.3
  cognitive 294.9
  conduct (*see also* Disturbance, conduct)
    312.9
    adjustment reaction 309.3
    adolescent onset type 312.82
    childhood onset type 312.81
    compulsive 312.30
      specified type NEC 312.39
    hyperkinetic 314.2
    socialized (type) 312.20
      aggressive 312.23
      unaggressive 312.21
    specified NEC 312.89

Disorder *(Continued)*
  conduction, heart 426.9
    specified NEC 426.89
  convulsive (secondary) (*see also* Con-
    vulsions) 780.39
    due to injury at birth 767.0
    idiopathic 780.39
  coordination 781.3
  cornea NEC 371.89
    due to contact lens 371.82
  corticosteroid metabolism NEC 255.2
  cranial nerve - *see* Disorder, nerve, cra-
    nial
  cyclothymic 301.13
  degradation, branched-chain amino
    acid 270.3
  delusional 297.9 ◀
  dentition 520.6
  depressive NEC 311
    atypical 296.82
    major (*see also* Psychosis, affective)
      296.2
      recurrent episode 296.3
      single episode 296.2
  development, specific 315.9
    associated with hyperkinesia 314.1
    language 315.31
    learning 315.2
      arithmetical 315.1
      reading 315.00
    mixed 315.5
    motor coordination 315.4
    specified type NEC 315.8
    speech 315.39
  diaphragm 519.4
  digestive 536.9
    fetus or newborn 777.9
      specified NEC 777.8
    psychogenic 306.4
  disintegrative (childhood) 299.1
  dissociative 300.15
    identity 300.14
  dysmorphic body 300.7
  dysthymic 300.4
  ear 388.9
    degenerative NEC 388.00
    external 380.9
      specified 380.89
    pinna 380.30
    specified type NEC 388.8
    vascular NEC 388.00
  eating NEC 307.50
  electrolyte NEC 276.9
    with
      abortion - *see* Abortion, by type,
        with metabolic disorder
      ectopic pregnancy (*see also* catego-
        ries 633.0-633.9) 639.4
      molar pregnancy (*see also* catego-
        ries 630-632) 639.4
    acidosis 276.2
      metabolic 276.2
      respiratory 276.2
    alkalosis 276.3
      metabolic 276.3
      respiratory 276.3
    following
      abortion 639.4
      ectopic or molar pregnancy 639.4
    neonatal, transitory NEC 775.5
  emancipation as adjustment reaction
    309.22
  emotional (*see also* Disorder, mental,
    nonpsychotic) V40.9

Disorder *(Continued)*
  endocrine 259.9
    specified type NEC 259.8
  esophagus 530.9
    functional 530.5
    psychogenic 306.4
  explosive
    intermittent 312.34
    isolated 312.35
  expressive language 315.31
  eye 379.90
    globe - *see* Disorder, globe
    ill-defined NEC 379.99
    limited duction NEC 378.63
    specified NEC 379.8
  eyelid 374.9
    degenerative 374.50
    sensory 374.44
    specified type NEC 374.89
    vascular 374.85
  factitious - *see* Illness, factitious
  factor, coagulation (*see also* Defect, co-
    agulation) 286.9
    VIII (congenital) (functional) 286.0
    IX (congenital) (functional) 286.1
  fascia 728.9
  feeding - *see* Feeding
  female sexual arousal 302.72
  fluid NEC 276.9
  gastric (functional) 536.9
    motility 536.8
    psychogenic 306.4
    secretion 536.8
  gastrointestinal (functional) NEC
    536.9
    newborn (neonatal) 777.9
      specified NEC 777.8
    psychogenic 306.4
  gender (child) 302.6
    adult 302.85
  gender identity (childhood) 302.6
    adult-life 302.85
  genitourinary system, psychogenic
    306.50
  globe 360.9
    degenerative 360.20
      specified NEC 360.29
    specified type NEC 360.89
  hearing - *see also* Deafness
    conductive type (air) (*see also* Deaf-
      ness, conductive) 389.00
    mixed conductive and sensorineural
      389.2
    nerve 389.12
    perceptive (*see also* Deafness, percep-
      tive) 389.10
    sensorineural type NEC (*see also*
      Deafness, perceptive) 389.10
  heart action 427.9
    postoperative 997.1
  hematological, transient neonatal 776.9
    specified type NEC 776.8
  hematopoietic organs 289.9
  hemorrhagic NEC 287.9
    due to circulating anticoagulants
      286.5
    specified type NEC 287.8
  hemostasis (*see also* Defect, coagula-
    tion) 286.9
  homosexual conflict 302.0
  hypomanic (chronic) 301.11
  identity
    childhood and adolescence 313.82
      gender 302.6

Disorder (*Continued*)
immune mechanism (immunity) 279.9
single complement (C_1-C_9) 279.8
specified type NEC 279.8
impulse control (*see also* Disturbance,
conduct, compulsive) 312.30
integument, fetus or newborn 778.9
specified type NEC 778.8
interactional psychotic (childhood) (*see
also* Psychosis, childhood) 299.1
intermittent explosive 312.34
intervertebral disc 722.90
cervical, cervicothoracic 722.91
lumbar, lumbosacral 722.93
thoracic, thoracolumbar 722.92
intestinal 569.9
functional NEC 564.9
congenital 751.3
postoperative 564.4
psychogenic 306.4
introverted, of childhood and adolescence 313.22
iron, metabolism 275.0
isolated explosive 312.35
joint NEC 719.90
ankle 719.97
elbow 719.92
foot 719.97
hand 719.94
hip 719.95
knee 719.96
multiple sites 719.99
pelvic region 719.95
psychogenic 306.0
shoulder (region) 719.91
specified site NEC 719.98
temporomandibular 524.60
specified NEC 524.69
wrist 719.93
kidney 593.9
functional 588.9
specified NEC 588.8
labyrinth, labyrinthine 386.9
specified type NEC 386.8
lactation 676.9
language (developmental) (expressive)
315.31
mixed (receptive) (receptive-expressive) 315.32
ligament 728.9
ligamentous attachments, peripheral -
see also Enthesopathy
spine 720.1
limb NEC 729.9
psychogenic 306.0
lipid
metabolism, congenital 272.9
storage 272.7
lipoprotein deficiency (familial) 272.5
low back NEC 724.9
psychogenic 306.0
lumbosacral
plexus 353.1
root (nerve) NEC 353.4
lymphoproliferative (chronic) NEC
(M9970/1) 238.7
major depressive (*see also* Psychosis, affective) 296.2
recurrent episode 296.3
single episode 296.2
male erectile 302.72
organic origin 607.84
manic (*see also* Psychosis, affective) 296.0
atypical 296.81

Disorder (*Continued*)
meniscus NEC (*see also* Disorder, cartilage, articular) 718.0
menopausal 627.9
specified NEC 627.8
menstrual 626.9
psychogenic 306.52
specified NEC 626.8
mental (nonpsychotic) 300.9
affecting management of pregnancy,
childbirth, or puerperium 648.4
drug-induced 292.9
hallucinogen persisting perception
292.89
specified type NEC 292.89
due to or associated with
alcoholism 291.9
drug consumption NEC 292.9
specified type NEC 292.89
physical condition NEC 293.9 ◄
induced by drug 292.9
specified type NEC 292.89
neurotic (*see also* Neurosis) 300.9
presenile 310.1
psychotic NEC 290.10
previous, affecting management of
pregnancy V23.8
psychoneurotic (*see also* Neurosis)
300.9
psychotic (*see also* Psychosis) 298.9
senile 290.20
specific, following organic brain
damage 310.9
cognitive or personality change of
other type 310.1
frontal lobe syndrome 310.0
postconcussional syndrome 310.2
specified type NEC 310.8
metabolism NEC 277.9
with
abortion - *see* Abortion, by type,
with metabolic disorder
ectopic pregnancy (*see also* categories 633.0-633.9) 639.4
molar pregnancy (*see also* categories 630-632) 639.4
alkaptonuria 270.2
amino acid (*see also* Disorder, amino
acid) 270.9
specified type NEC 270.8
ammonia 270.6
arginine 270.6
argininosuccinic acid 270.6
basal 794.7
bilirubin 277.4
calcium 275.40
carbohydrate 271.9
specified type NEC 271.8
cholesterol 272.9
citrulline 270.6
copper 275.1
corticosteroid 255.2
cystine storage 270.0
cystinuria 270.0
fat 272.9
following
abortion 639.4
ectopic or molar pregnancy 639.4
fructosemia 271.2
fructosuria 271.2
fucosidosis 271.8
galactose-1-phosphate uridyl transferase 271.1
glutamine 270.7

Disorder (*Continued*)
metabolism (*Continued*)
glycine 270.7
glycogen storage NEC 271.0
hepatorenal 271.0
hemochromatosis 275.0
in labor and delivery 669.0
iron 275.0
lactose 271.3
lipid 272.9
specified type NEC 272.8
storage 272.7
lipoprotein - *see also* Hyperlipemia
deficiency (familial) 272.5
lysine 270.7
magnesium 275.2
mannosidosis 271.8
mineral 275.9
specified type NEC 275.8
mucopolysaccharide 277.5
nitrogen 270.9
ornithine 270.6
oxalosis 271.8
pentosuria 271.8
phenylketonuria 270.1
phosphate 275.3
phosphorus 275.3
plasma protein 273.9
specified type NEC 273.8
porphyrin 277.1
purine 277.2
pyrimidine 277.2
serine 270.7
sodium 276.9
specified type NEC 277.8
steroid 255.2
threonine 270.7
urea cycle 270.6
xylose 271.8
micturition NEC 788.69
psychogenic 306.53
misery and unhappiness, of childhood
and adolescence 313.1
mitral valve 424.0 ◄
mood—*see* Psychosis, affective ◄
motor tic 307.20
chronic 307.22
transient, childhood 307.21
movement NEC 333.90
hysterical 300.11
specified type NEC 333.99
stereotypic 307.3
mucopolysaccharide 277.5
muscle 728.9
psychogenic 306.0
specified type NEC 728.3
muscular attachments, peripheral - *see
also* Enthesopathy
spine 720.1
musculoskeletal system NEC 729.9
psychogenic 306.0
myeloproliferative (chronic) NEC
(M9960/1) 238.7
myoneural 358.9
due to lead 358.2
specified type NEC 358.8
toxic 358.2
myotonic 359.2
neck region NEC 723.9
nerve 349.9
abducens NEC 378.54
accessory 352.4
acoustic 388.5
auditory 388.5

Disorder (*Continued*)
nerve (*Continued*)
  auriculotemporal 350.8
  axillary 353.0
  cerebral - *see* Disorder, nerve,
    cranial
  cranial 352.9
    first 352.0
    second 377.49
    third
      partial 378.51
      total 378.52
    fourth 378.53
    fifth 350.9
    sixth 378.54
    seventh NEC 351.9
    eighth 388.5
    ninth 352.2
    tenth 352.3
    eleventh 352.4
    twelfth 352.5
    multiple 352.6
  entrapment - *see* Neuropathy, en-
    trapment
  facial 351.9
    specified NEC 351.8
  femoral 355.2
  glossopharyngeal NEC 352.2
  hypoglossal 352.5
  iliohypogastric 355.79
  ilioinguinal 355.79
  intercostal 353.8
  lateral
    cutaneous of thigh 355.1
    popliteal 355.3
  lower limb NEC 355.8
  medial, popliteal 355.4
  median NEC 354.1
  obturator 355.79
  oculomotor
    partial 378.51
    total 378.52
  olfactory 352.0
  optic 377.49
    ischemic 377.41
    nutritional 377.33
    toxic 377.34
  peroneal 355.3
  phrenic 354.8
  plantar 355.6
  pneumogastric 352.3
  posterior tibial 355.5
  radial 354.3
  recurrent laryngeal 352.3
  root 353.9
    specified NEC 353.8
  saphenous 355.79
  sciatic NEC 355.0
  specified NEC 355.9
    lower limb 355.79
    upper limb 354.8
  spinal 355.9
  sympathetic NEC 337.9
  trigeminal 350.9
    specified NEC 350.8
  trochlear 378.53
  ulnar 354.2
  upper limb NEC 354.9
  vagus 352.3
nervous system NEC 349.9
  autonomic (peripheral) (*see also* Neu-
    ropathy, peripheral, autonomic)
    337.9
  cranial 352.9

Disorder (*Continued*)
nervous system NEC (*Continued*)
  parasympathetic (*see also* Neuropathy,
    peripheral, autonomic) 337.9
  specified type NEC 349.89
  sympathetic (*see also* Neuropathy,
    peripheral, autonomic) 337.9
  vegetative (*see also* Neuropathy, pe-
    ripheral, autonomic) 337.9
neurohypophysis NEC 253.6
neurological NEC 781.9
  peripheral NEC 355.9
neuromuscular NEC 358.9
  hereditary NEC 359.1
  specified NEC 358.8
  toxic 358.2
neurotic 300.9
  specified type NEC 300.89
neutrophil, polymorphonuclear (functional) 288.1
obsessive-compulsive 300.3
oppositional, childhood and adolescence 313.81
optic
  chiasm 377.54
    associated with
      inflammatory disorders
        377.54
      neoplasm NEC 377.52
        pituitary 377.51
      pituitary disorders 377.51
      vascular disorders 377.53
  nerve 377.49
  radiations 377.63
  tracts 377.63
orbit 376.9
  specified NEC 376.89
overanxious, of childhood and adolescence 313.0
pancreas, internal secretion (other than
  diabetes mellitus) 251.9
  specified type NEC 251.8
panic 300.01
  with agoraphobia 300.21
papillary muscle NEC 429.81
paranoid 297.9
  induced 297.3
  shared 297.3
parathyroid 252.9
  specified type NEC 252.8
paroxysmal, mixed 780.39
pentose phosphate pathway with anemia 282.2
personality 301.9
  affective 301.10
  aggressive 301.3
  amoral 301.7
  anancastic, anankastic 301.4
  antisocial 301.7
  asocial 301.7
  asthenic 301.6
  borderline 301.83
  compulsive 301.4
  cyclothymic 301.13
  dependent-passive 301.6
  dyssocial 301.7
  emotional instability 301.59
  epileptoid 301.3
  explosive 301.3
  following organic brain damage
    310.1
  histrionic 301.50
  hyperthymic 301.11
  hypomanic (chronic) 301.11

Disorder (*Continued*)
personality (*Continued*)
  hypothymic 301.12
  hysterical 301.50
  immature 301.89
  inadequate 301.6
  introverted 301.21
  labile 301.59
  moral deficiency 301.7
  obsessional 301.4
  obsessive (-compulsive) 301.4
  overconscientious 301.4
  paranoid 301.0
  passive (-dependent) 301.6
  passive-aggressive 301.84
  pathological NEC 301.9
  pseudosocial 301.7
  psychopathic 301.9
  schizoid 301.20
    introverted 301.21
    schizotypal 301.22
  schizotypal 301.22
  seductive 301.59
  type A 301.4
  unstable 301.59
pervasive developmental, childhood-
  onset 299.8
pigmentation, choroid (congenital)
  743.53
pinna 380.30
  specified type NEC 380.39
pituitary, thalamic 253.9
  anterior NEC 253.4
  iatrogenic 253.7
  postablative 253.7
  specified NEC 253.8
pityriasis-like NEC 696.8
platelets (blood) 287.1
polymorphonuclear neutrophils (functional) 288.1
porphyrin metabolism 277.1
postmenopausal 627.9
  specified type NEC 627.8
posttraumatic stress 309.81
  acute 308.3
  brief 308.3
  chronic 309.81
psoriatic-like NEC 696.8
psychic, with diseases classified elsewhere 316
psychogenic NEC (*see also* condition)
  300.9
  allergic NEC
    respiratory 306.1
  anxiety 300.00
    atypical 300.00
    generalized 300.02
  appetite 307.50
  articulation, joint 306.0
  asthenic 300.5
  blood 306.8
  cardiovascular (system) 306.2
  compulsive 300.3
  cutaneous 306.3
  depressive 300.4
  digestive (system) 306.4
  dysmenorrheic 306.52
  dyspneic 306.1
  eczematous 306.3
  endocrine (system) 306.6
  eye 306.7
  feeding 307.59
  functional NEC 306.9
  gastric 306.4

Disorder *(Continued)*
  psychogenic NEC *(Continued)*
    gastrointestinal (system) 306.4
    genitourinary (system) 306.50
    heart (function) (rhythm) 306.2
    hemic 306.8
    hyperventilatory 306.1
    hypochondriacal 300.7
    hysterical 300.10
    intestinal 306.4
    joint 306.0
    learning 315.2
    limb 306.0
    lymphatic (system) 306.8
    menstrual 306.52
    micturition 306.53
    monoplegic NEC 306.0
    motor 307.9
    muscle 306.0
    musculoskeletal 306.0
    neurocirculatory 306.2
    obsessive 300.3
    occupational 300.89
    organ or part of body NEC 306.9
    organs of special sense 306.7
    paralytic NEC 306.0
    phobic 300.20
    physical NEC 306.9
    pruritic 306.3
    rectal 306.4
    respiratory (system) 306.1
    rheumatic 306.0
    sexual (function) 302.70
      specified type NEC 302.79
    skin (allergic) (eczematous) (pruritic)
      306.3
    sleep 307.40
      initiation or maintenance 307.41
        persistent 307.42
        transient 307.41
      specified type NEC 307.49
    specified part of body NEC 306.8
    stomach 306.4
  psychomotor NEC 307.9
    hysterical 300.11
  psychoneurotic *(see also* Neurosis)
    300.9
    mixed NEC 300.89
  psychophysiologic *(see also* Disorder,
    psychosomatic) 306.9
  psychosexual identity (childhood)
    302.6
    adult-life 302.85
  psychosomatic NEC 306.9
    allergic NEC
      respiratory 306.1
    articulation, joint 306.0
    cardiovascular (system) 306.2
    cutaneous 306.3
    digestive (system) 306.4
    dysmenorrheic 306.52
    dyspneic 306.1
    endocrine (system) 306.6
    eye 306.7
    gastric 306.4
    gastrointestinal (system) 306.4
    genitourinary (system) 306.50
    heart (functional) (rhythm)
      306.2
    hyperventilatory 306.1
    intestinal 306.4
    joint 306.0
    limb 306.0
    lymphatic (system) 306.8

Disorder *(Continued)*
  psychosomatic NEC *(Continued)*
    menstrual 306.52
    micturition 306.53
    monoplegic NEC 306.0
    muscle 306.0
    musculoskeletal 306.0
    neurocirculatory 306.2
    organs of special sense 306.7
    paralytic NEC 306.0
    pruritic 306.3
    rectal 306.4
    respiratory (system) 306.1
    rheumatic 306.0
    sexual (function) 302.70
      specified type NEC 302.79
    skin 306.3
    specified part of body NEC 306.8
    stomach 306.4
  psychotic - *see* Psychosis ◄
  purine metabolism NEC 277.2
  pyrimidine metabolism NEC 277.2
  reactive attachment (of infancy or
    early childhood) 313.89
  reading, developmental 315.00
  reflex 796.1
  renal function, impaired 588.9
    specified type NEC 588.8
  renal transport NEC 588.8
  respiration, respiratory NEC 519.9
    due to
      aspiration of liquids or solids 508.9
      inhalation of fumes or vapors 506.9
    psychogenic 306.1
  retina 362.9
    specified type NEC 362.89
  sacroiliac joint NEC 724.6
  sacrum 724.6
  schizo-affective *(see also* Schizophrenia)
    295.7
  schizophreniform 295.4
  schizoid, childhood or adolescence
    313.22
  schizotypal personality 301.22
  secretion, thyrocalcitonin 246.0
  seizure 780.39
    recurrent 780.39
      epileptic - *see* Epilepsy
  sense of smell 781.1
    psychogenic 306.7
  separation anxiety 309.21
  sexual *(see also* Deviation, sexual) 302.9
    function, psychogenic 302.70
  shyness, of childhood and adolescence
    313.21
  single complement (C$_1$-C$_9$) 279.8
  skin NEC 709.9
    fetus or newborn 778.9
      specified type 778.8
    psychogenic (allergic) (eczematous)
      (pruritic) 306.3
    specified type NEC 709.8
    vascular 709.1
  sleep 780.50
    with apnea - *see* Apnea, sleep
    circadian rhythm 307.45
    initiation or maintenance *(see also* In-
      somnia) 780.52
      nonorganic origin (transient)
        307.41
        persistent 307.42
    nonorganic origin 307.40
      specified type NEC 307.49
    specified NEC 780.59

Disorder *(Continued)*
  social, of childhood and adolescence
    313.22
    specified NEC 780.59
  soft tissue 729.9
  somatization 300.81
  somatoform (atypical) (undifferen-
    tiated) 300.82
    severe 300.81
  speech NEC 784.5
    nonorganic origin 307.9
  spine NEC 724.9
    ligamentous or muscular attach-
      ments, peripheral 720.1
  steroid metabolism NEC 255.2
  stomach (functional) *(see also* Disorder,
    gastric) 536.9
    psychogenic 306.4
  storage, iron 275.0
  stress *(see also* Reaction, stress, acute)
    308.9
    posttraumatic
      acute 308.3
      brief 308.3
      chronic (motor or vocal) 309.81
  substitution 300.11
  suspected - *see* Observation
  synovium 727.9
  temperature regulation, fetus or new-
    born 778.4
  temporomandibular joint NEC
    524.60
    specified NEC 524.69
  tendon 727.9
    shoulder region 726.10
  thoracic root (nerve) NEC 353.3
  thyrocalcitonin secretion 246.0
  thyroid (gland) NEC 246.9
    specified type NEC 246.8
  tic 307.20
    chronic (motor or vocal) 307.22
    motor-verbal 307.23
    organic origin 333.1
    transient of childhood 307.21
  tooth NEC 525.9
    development NEC 520.9
      specified type NEC 520.8
    eruption 520.6
      with abnormal position 524.3
    specified type NEC 525.8
  transport, carbohydrate 271.9
    specified type NEC 271.8
  tubular, phosphate-losing 588.0
  tympanic membrane 384.9
  unaggressive, unsocialized *(see also*
    Disturbance, conduct) 312.1
  undersocialized, unsocialized *(see also*
    Disturbance, conduct)
    aggressive (type) 312.0
    unaggressive (type) 312.1
  vision, visual NEC 368.9
    binocular NEC 368.30
    cortex 377.73
      associated with
        inflammatory disorders 377.73
        neoplasms 377.71
        vascular disorders 377.72
    pathway NEC 377.63
      associated with
        inflammatory disorders 377.63
        neoplasms 377.61
        vascular disorders 377.62
  wakefulness *(see also* Hypersomnia)
    780.54

Disorder (*Continued*)
  wakefulness (*Continued*)
    nonorganic origin (transient) 307.43
     persistent 307.44
Disorganized globe 360.29
Displacement, displaced

> Note   For acquired displacement of
> bones, cartilage, joints, tendons, due
> to injury, *see also* Dislocation.
>
> Displacements at ages under one year
> should be considered congenital, pro-
> vided there is no indication the con-
> dition was acquired after birth.

  acquired traumatic of bone, cartilage,
    joint, tendon NEC (without frac-
    ture) (*see also* Dislocation) 839.8
    with fracture - *see* Fracture, by site
  adrenal gland (congenital) 759.1
  appendix, retrocecal (congenital) 751.5
  auricle (congenital) 744.29
  bladder (acquired) 596.8
    congenital 753.8
  brachial plexus (congenital) 742.8
  brain stem, caudal 742.4
  canaliculus lacrimalis 743.65
  cardia, through esophageal hiatus 750.6
  cerebellum, caudal 742.4
  cervix (*see also* Malposition, uterus)
    621.6
  colon (congenital) 751.4
  device, implant, or graft - *see* Compli-
    cations, mechanical
  epithelium
    columnar of cervix 622.1
    cuboidal, beyond limits of external
     os (uterus) 752.49
  esophageal mucosa into cardia of
    stomach, congenital 750.4
  esophagus (acquired) 530.89
    congenital 750.4
  eyeball (acquired) (old) 376.36
    congenital 743.8
    current injury 871.3
    lateral 376.36
  fallopian tube (acquired) 620.4
    congenital 752.19
    opening (congenital) 752.19
  gallbladder (congenital) 751.69
  gastric mucosa 750.7
    into
      duodenum 750.7
      esophagus 750.7
      Meckel's diverticulum, congenital
       750.7
  globe (acquired) (lateral) (old) 376.36
    current injury 871.3
  graft ◄
    artificial skin graft 996.55 ◄
    decellularized allodermis graft
     996.55 ◄
  heart (congenital) 746.87
    acquired 429.89
  hymen (congenital) (upward) 752.49
  internal prosthesis NEC - *see* Compli-
    cations, mechanical
  intervertebral disc (with neuritis, radi-
    culitis, sciatica, or other pain)
    722.2
    with myelopathy 722.70
    cervical, cervicodorsal, cervicothora-
     cic 722.0
     with myelopathy 722.71

Displacement, displaced (*Continued*)
  intervertebral disc (*Continued*)
    cervical, cervicodorsal, cervicothora-
     cic (*Continued*)
      due to major trauma - *see* Disloca-
       tion, vertebra, cervical
     due to major trauma - *see* Disloca-
      tion, vertebra
    lumbar, lumbosacral 722.10
     with myelopathy 722.73
     due to major trauma - *see* Disloca-
      tion, vertebra, lumbar
    thoracic, thoracolumbar 722.11
     with myelopathy 722.72
     due to major trauma - *see* Disloca-
      tion, vertebra, thoracic
  intrauterine device 996.32
  kidney (acquired) 593.0
    congenital 753.3
  lacrimal apparatus or duct (congenital)
    743.65
  macula (congenital) 743.55
  Meckel's diverticulum (congenital) 751.0
  nail (congenital) 757.5
    acquired 703.8
  opening of Wharton's duct in mouth
    750.26
  organ or site, congenital NEC - *see*
    Malposition, congenital
  ovary (acquired) 620.4
    congenital 752.0
    free in peritoneal cavity (congenital)
     752.0
    into hernial sac 620.4
  oviduct (acquired) 620.4
    congenital 752.19
  parathyroid (gland) 252.8
  parotid gland (congenital) 750.26
  punctum lacrimale (congenital) 743.65
  sacroiliac (congenital) (joint) 755.69
    current injury - *see* Dislocation,
     sacroiliac
    old 724.6
  spine (congenital) 756.19
  spleen, congenital 759.0
  stomach (congenital) 750.7
    acquired 537.89
  subglenoid (closed) 831.01
  sublingual duct (congenital) 750.26
  teeth, tooth 524.3
  tongue (congenital) (downward) 750.19
  trachea (congenital) 748.3
  ureter or ureteric opening or orifice
    (congenital) 753.4
  uterine opening of oviducts or fallo-
    pian tubes 752.19
  uterus, uterine (*see also* Malposition,
    uterus) 621.6
    congenital 752.3
  ventricular septum 746.89
    with rudimentary ventricle 746.89
  xyphoid bone (process) 738.3
Disproportion 653.9
  affecting fetus or newborn 763.1
  caused by
    conjoined twins 653.7
    contraction, pelvis (general) 653.1
     inlet 653.2
     midpelvic 653.8
     midplane 653.8
     outlet 653.3
    fetal
     ascites 653.7
     hydrocephalus 653.6

Disproportion (*Continued*)
  caused by (*Continued*)
    fetal (*Continued*)
     hydrops 653.7
     meningomyelocele 653.7
     sacral teratoma 653.7
     tumor 653.7
    hydrocephalic fetus 653.6
    pelvis, pelvic, abnormality (bony)
     NEC 653.0
    unusually large fetus 653.5
    causing obstructed labor 660.1
  cephalopelvic, normally formed fetus
    653.4
    causing obstructed labor 660.1
  fetal NEC 653.5
    causing obstructed labor 660.1
  fetopelvic, normally formed fetus 653.4
    causing obstructed labor 660.1
  mixed maternal and fetal origin, nor-
    mally, formed fetus 653.4
  pelvis, pelvic (bony) NEC 653.1
    causing obstructed labor 660.1
  specified type NEC 653.8
Disruption
  cesarean wound 674.1
  family V61.0
  gastrointestinal anastomosis 997.4
  ligament(s) - *see also* Sprain
    knee
     current injury - *see* Dislocation,
      knee
     old 717.89
      capsular 717.85
      collateral (medial) 717.82
       lateral 717.81
      cruciate (posterior) 717.84
       anterior 717.83
      specified site NEC 717.85
  marital V61.10
    involving divorce or estrangement
     V61.0
  operation wound 998.3
  organ transplant, anastomosis site - *see*
    Complications, transplant, organ,
    by site
  ossicles, ossicular chain 385.23
    traumatic - *see* Fracture, skull, base
  parenchyma
    liver (hepatic) - *see* Laceration, liver,
     major
    spleen - *see* Laceration, spleen, pa-
     renchyma, massive
  phase-shift, of 24-hour sleep-wake cy-
    cle 780.55
    nonorganic origin 307.45
  sleep-wake cycle (24-hour) 780.55
    circadian rhythm 307.45
    nonorganic origin 307.45
  suture line (external) 998.3
    internal 998.3
  wound
    cesarean operation 674.1
    episiotomy 674.2
    operation 998.3
     cesarean 674.1
    perineal (obstetric) 674.2
    uterine 674.1
Disruptio uteri - *see also* Rupture, uterus
  complicating delivery - *see* Delivery,
    complicated, rupture, uterus
Dissatisfaction with
  employment V62.2
  school environment V62.3

Dissecting - *see* condition
Dissection
aorta 441.00
abdominal 441.02
thoracic 441.01
thoracoabdominal 441.03
vascular 459.9
wound - *see* Wound, open, by site
Disseminated - *see* condition
Dissociated personality NEC 300.15
Dissociation
auriculoventricular or atrioventricular
(any degree) (AV) 426.89
with heart block 426.0
interference 426.89
isorhythmic 426.89
rhythm
atrioventricular (AV) 426.89
interference 426.89
Dissociative
identity disorder 300.14
reaction NEC 300.15
Dissolution, vertebra (*see also* Osteoporosis) 733.00
Distention
abdomen (gaseous) 787.3
bladder 596.8
cecum 569.89
colon 569.89
gallbladder 575.8
gaseous (abdomen) 787.3
intestine 569.89
kidney 593.89
liver 573.9
seminal vesicle 608.89
stomach 536.8
acute 536.1
psychogenic 306.4
ureter 593.5
uterus 621.8
Distichia, distichiasis (eyelid) 743.63
Distoma hepaticum infestation
121.3
Distomiasis 121.9
bile passages 121.3
due to Clonorchis sinensis 121.1
hemic 120.9
hepatic (liver) 121.3
due to Clonorchis sinensis (clonorchiasis) 121.1
intestinal 121.4
liver 121.3
due to Clonorchis sinensis 121.1
lung 121.2
pulmonary 121.2
Distomolar (fourth molar) 520.1
causing crowding 524.3
Disto-occlusion 524.2
Distortion (congenital)
adrenal (gland) 759.1
ankle (joint) 755.69
anus 751.5
aorta 747.29
appendix 751.5
arm 755.59
artery (peripheral) NEC (*see also* Distortion, peripheral vascular system) 747.60
cerebral 747.81
coronary 746.85
pulmonary 747.3
retinal 743.58
umbilical 747.5
auditory canal 744.29

Distortion (*Continued*)
auditory canal (*Continued*)
causing impairment of hearing
744.02
bile duct or passage 751.69
bladder 753.8
brain 742.4
bronchus 748.3
cecum 751.5
cervix (uteri) 752.49
chest (wall) 756.3
clavicle 755.51
clitoris 752.49
coccyx 756.19
colon 751.5
common duct 751.69
cornea 743.41
cricoid cartilage 748.3
cystic duct 751.69
duodenum 751.5
ear 744.29
auricle 744.29
causing impairment of hearing
744.02
causing impairment of hearing
744.09
external 744.29
causing impairment of hearing
744.02
inner 744.05
middle, except ossicles 744.03
ossicles 744.04
ossicles 744.04
endocrine (gland) NEC 759.2
epiglottis 748.3
Eustachian tube 744.24
eye 743.8
adnexa 743.69
face bone(s) 756.0
fallopian tube 752.19
femur 755.69
fibula 755.69
finger(s) 755.59
foot 755.67
gallbladder 751.69
genitalia, genital organ(s)
female 752.8
external 752.49
internal NEC 752.8
male 752.8
penis 752.69
glottis 748.3
gyri 742.4
hand bone(s) 755.59
heart (auricle) (ventricle) 746.89
valve (cusp) 746.89
hepatic duct 751.69
humerus 755.59
hymen 752.49
ileum 751.5
intestine (large) (small) 751.5
with anomalous adhesions,
fixation or malrotation
751.4
jaw NEC 524.8
jejunum 751.5
kidney 753.3
knee (joint) 755.64
labium (majus) (minus) 752.49
larynx 748.3
leg 755.69
lens 743.36
liver 751.69
lumbar spine 756.19

Distortion (*Continued*)
lumbar spine (*Continued*)
with disproportion (fetopelvic) 653.0
affecting fetus or newborn 763.1
causing obstructed labor 660.1
lumbosacral (joint) (region) 756.19
lung (fissures) (lobe) 748.69
nerve 742.8
nose 748.1
organ
of Corti 744.05
of site not listed - *see* Anomaly,
specified type NEC
ossicles, ear 744.04
ovary 752.0
oviduct 752.19
pancreas 751.7
parathyroid (gland) 759.2
patella 755.64
peripheral vascular system NEC 747.60
gastrointestinal 747.61
lower limb 747.64
renal 747.62
spinal 747.82
upper limb 747.63
pituitary (gland) 759.2
radius 755.59
rectum 751.5
rib 756.3
sacroiliac joint 755.69
sacrum 756.19
scapula 755.59
shoulder girdle 755.59
site not listed - *see* Anomaly, specified
type NEC
skull bone(s) 756.0
with
anencephalus 740.0
encephalocele 742.0
hydrocephalus 742.3
with spina bifida (*see also* Spina
bifida) 741.0
microcephalus 742.1
spinal cord 742.59
spine 756.19
spleen 759.0
sternum 756.3
thorax (wall) 756.3
thymus (gland) 759.2
thyroid (gland) 759.2
cartilage 748.3
tibia 755.69
toe(s) 755.66
tongue 750.19
trachea (cartilage) 748.3
ulna 755.59
ureter 753.4
causing obstruction 753.20
urethra 753.8
causing obstruction 753.6
uterus 752.3
vagina 752.49
vein (peripheral) NEC (*see also* Distortion, peripheral vascular system)
747.60
great 747.49
portal 747.49
pulmonary 747.49
vena cava (inferior) (superior) 747.49
vertebra 756.19
visual NEC 368.15
shape or size 368.14
vulva 752.49
wrist (bones) (joint) 755.59

ICD-9-CM

Vol. 2

Distress
  abdomen 789.0
  colon 564.9
  emotional V40.9
  epigastric 789.0
  fetal (syndrome) 768.4
    affecting management of pregnancy or childbirth 656.8 ◄▥▥
    liveborn infant 768.4
      first noted
        before onset of labor 768.2
        during labor or delivery 768.3
    stillborn infant (death before onset of labor) 768.0
      death during labor 768.1
  gastrointestinal (functional) 536.9
    psychogenic 306.4
  intestinal (functional) NEC 564.9
    psychogenic 306.4
  intrauterine - see Distress, fetal ◄▥▥
  leg 729.5
  maternal 669.0
  mental V40.9
  respiratory 786.09
    acute (adult) 518.82
    adult syndrome (following shock, surgery, or trauma) 518.5
      specified NEC 518.82
    fetus or newborn 770.8
    syndrome (idiopathic) (newborn) 769
  stomach 536.9
    psychogenic 306.4
Distribution vessel, atypical NEC 747.60
  coronary artery 746.85
  spinal 747.82
Distichiasis 704.2
Disturbance - see also Disease
  absorption NEC 579.9
    calcium 269.3
    carbohydrate 579.8
    fat 579.8
    protein 579.8
    specified type NEC 579.8
    vitamin (see also Deficiency, vitamin) 269.2
  acid-base equilibrium 276.9
  activity and attention, simple, with hyperkinesis 314.01
  amino acid (metabolic) (see also Disorder, amino acid) 270.9
    imidazole 270.5
    maple syrup (urine) disease 270.3
    transport 270.0
  assimilation, food 579.9
  attention, simple 314.00
    with hyperactivity 314.01
  auditory, nerve, except deafness 388.5
  behavior (see also Disturbance, conduct) 312.9
  blood clotting (hypoproteinemia) (mechanism) (see also Defect, coagulation) 286.9
  central nervous system NEC 349.9
  cerebral nerve NEC 352.9
  circulatory 459.9
  conduct 312.9

Note Use the following fifth-digit subclassification with categories 312.0-312.2:

0	unspecified
1	mild
2	moderate
3	severe

Disturbance (Continued)
  conduct (Continued)
    adjustment reaction 309.3 ◄▶
    adolescent onset type 312.82
    childhood onset type 312.81
    compulsive 312.30
      intermittent explosive disorder 312.34
      isolated explosive disorder 312.35
      kleptomania 312.32
      pathological gambling 312.31
      pyromania 312.33
    hyperkinetic 314.2
    intermittent explosive 312.34
    isolated explosive 312.35
    mixed with emotions 312.4
    socialized (type) 312.20
      aggressive 312.23
      unaggressive 312.21
    specified type NEC 312.89 ◄▥▥
    undersocialized, unsocialized
      aggressive (type) 312.0
      unaggressive (type) 312.1
  coordination 781.3
  cranial nerve NEC 352.9
  deep sensibility - see Disturbance, sensation
  digestive 536.9
    psychogenic 306.4
  electrolyte - see Imbalance, electrolyte
  emotions specific to childhood and adolescence 313.9
    with
      academic underachievement 313.83
      anxiety and fearfulness 313.0
      elective mutism 313.23
      identity disorder 313.82
      jealousy 313.3
      misery and unhappiness 313.1
      oppositional disorder 313.81
      overanxiousness 313.0
      sensitivity 313.21
      shyness 313.21
      social withdrawal 313.22
      withdrawal reaction 313.22
    involving relationship problems 313.3
    mixed 313.89
    specified type NEC 313.89
  endocrine (gland) 259.9
    neonatal, transitory 775.9
      specified NEC 775.8
  equilibrium 780.4
  feeding (elderly) (infant) 783.3
    newborn 779.3
    nonorganic origin NEC 307.59
    psychogenic NEC 307.59
  fructose metabolism 271.2
  gait 781.2
    hysterical 300.11
  gastric (functional) 536.9
    motility 536.8
    psychogenic 306.4
    secretion 536.8
  gastrointestinal (functional) 536.9
    psychogenic 306.4
  habit, child 307.9
  hearing, except deafness 388.40
  heart, functional (conditions classifiable to 426, 427, 428)
    due to presence of (cardiac) prosthesis 429.4
    postoperative (immediate) 997.1

Disturbance (Continued)
  heart, functional (Continued)
    postoperative (Continued)
      long-term effect of cardiac surgery 429.4
    psychogenic 306.2
  hormone 259.9
  innervation uterus, sympathetic, parasympathetic 621.8
  keratinization NEC
    gingiva 523.1
    lip 528.5
    oral (mucosa) (soft tissue) 528.7
    tongue 528.7
  labyrinth, labyrinthine (vestibule) 386.9
  learning, specific NEC 315.2
  memory (see also Amnesia) 780.9
    mild, following organic brain damage 310.1
  mental (see also Disorder, mental) 300.9
    associated with diseases classified elsewhere 316
  metabolism (acquired) (congenital) (see also Disorder, metabolism) 277.9
    with
      abortion - see Abortion, by type, with metabolic disorder
      ectopic pregnancy (see also categories 633.0-633.9) 639.4
      molar pregnancy (see also categories 630-632) 639.4
    amino acid (see also Disorder, amino acid) 270.9
      aromatic NEC 270.2
      branched-chain 270.3
      specified type NEC 270.8
      straight-chain NEC 270.7
      sulfur-bearing 270.4
      transport 270.0
    ammonia 270.6
    arginine 270.6
    argininosuccinic acid 270.6
    carbohydrate NEC 271.9
    cholesterol 272.9
    citrulline 270.6
    cystathionine 270.4
    fat 272.9
    following
      abortion 639.4
      ectopic or molar pregnancy 639.4
    general 277.9
      carbohydrate 271.9
      iron 275.0
      phosphate 275.3
      sodium 276.9
    glutamine 270.7
    glycine 270.7
    histidine 270.5
    homocystine 270.4
    in labor or delivery 669.0
    iron 275.0
    isoleucine 270.3
    leucine 270.3
    lipoid 272.9
      specified type NEC 272.8
    lysine 270.7
    methionine 270.4
    neonatal, transitory 775.9
      specified type NEC 775.8
    nitrogen 788.9
    ornithine 270.6
    phosphate 275.3

Disturbance *(Continued)*
  metabolism *(Continued)*
    phosphatides 272.7
    serine 270.7
    sodium NEC 276.9
    threonine 270.7
    tryptophan 270.2
    tyrosine 270.2
    urea cycle 270.6
    valine 270.3
  motor 796.1
  nervous functional 799.2
  neuromuscular mechanism (eye) due
      to syphilis 094.84
  nutritional 269.9
    nail 703.8
  ocular motion 378.87
    psychogenic 306.7
  oculogyric 378.87
    psychogenic 306.7
  oculomotor NEC 378.87
    psychogenic 306.7
  olfactory nerve 781.1
  optic nerve NEC 377.49
  oral epithelium, including tongue
      528.7
  personality (pattern) (trait) *(see also
      Disorder, personality)* 301.9
    following organic brain damage
        310.1
  polyglandular 258.9
  psychomotor 307.9
  pupillary 379.49
  reflex 796.1
  rhythm, heart 427.9
    postoperative (immediate) 997.1
      long-term effect of cardiac surgery
          429.4
    psychogenic 306.2
  salivary secretion 527.7
  sensation (cold) (heat) (localization)
      (tactile discrimination localization)
      (texture) (vibratory) NEC 782.0
    hysterical 300.11
    skin 782.0
    smell 781.1
    taste 781.1
  sensory *(see also* Disturbance, sensa-
      tion) 782.0
    innervation 782.0
  situational (transient) *(see also* Reaction,
      adjustment) 309.9
    acute 308.3
  sleep 780.50
    with apnea - *see* Apnea, sleep
    initiation or maintenance *(see also* In-
        somnia) 780.52
      nonorganic origin 307.41
    nonorganic origin 307.40
      specified type NEC 307.49
    specified NEC 780.59
      nonorganic origin 307.49
    wakefulness *(see also* Hypersomnia)
        780.54
      nonorganic origin 307.43
  sociopathic 301.7
  speech NEC 784.5
    developmental 315.39
      associated with hyperkinesis 314.1
    secondary to organic lesion 784.5
  stomach (functional) *(see also* Distur-
      bance, gastric) 536.9
  sympathetic (nerve) *(see also* Neuropa-
      thy, peripheral, autonomic) 337.9

Disturbance *(Continued)*
  temperature sense 782.0
    hysterical 300.11
  tooth
    eruption 520.6
    formation 520.4
    structure, hereditary NEC 520.5
  touch *(see also* Disturbance, sensation)
      782.0
  vascular 459.9
    arteriosclerotic - *see* Arteriosclerosis
  vasomotor 443.9
  vasospastic 443.9
  vestibular labyrinth 386.9
  vision, visual NEC 368.9
    psychophysical 368.16
    specified NEC 368.8
    subjective 368.10
  voice 784.40
  wakefulness (initiation or mainte-
      nance) *(see also* Hypersomnia)
      780.54
    nonorganic origin 307.43
**Disulfiduria, beta-mercaptolactate-cyste-
  ine** 270.0
Disuse atrophy, bone 733.7
Ditthomska syndrome 307.81
Diuresis 788.42
Divers'
  palsy or paralysis 993.3
  squeeze 993.3
Diverticula, diverticulosis, diverticulum
    (acute) (multiple) (perforated) (rup-
    tured) 562.10
  with diverticulitis 562.11
  aorta (Kommerell's) 747.21
  appendix (noninflammatory) 543.9
  bladder (acquired) (sphincter) 596.3
    congenital 753.8
  broad ligament 620.8
  bronchus (congenital) 748.3
    acquired 494
  calyx, calyceal (kidney) 593.89
  cardia (stomach) 537.1
  cecum 562.10
    with
      diverticulitis 562.11
        with hemorrhage 562.13
      hemorrhage 562.12
    congenital 751.5
  colon (acquired) 562.10
    with
      diverticulitis 562.11
        with hemorrhage 562.13
      hemorrhage 562.12
    congenital 751.5
  duodenum 562.00
    with
      diverticulitis 562.01
        with hemorrhage 562.03
      hemorrhage 562.02
    congenital 751.5
  epiphrenic (esophagus) 530.6
  esophagus (congenital) 750.4
    acquired 530.6
    epiphrenic 530.6
    pulsion 530.6
    traction 530.6
    Zenker's 530.6
  Eustachian tube 381.89
  fallopian tube 620.8
  gallbladder (congenital) 751.69
  gastric 537.1
  heart (congenital) 746.89

Diverticula, diverticulosis, diverticulum
    (Continued)
  ileum 562.00
    with
      diverticulitis 562.01
        with hemorrhage 562.03
      hemorrhage 562.03
  intestine (large) 562.10
    with
      diverticulitis 562.11
        with hemorrhage 562.13
      hemorrhage 562.12
    congenital 751.5
    small 562.00
      with
        diverticulitis 562.01
          with hemorrhage 562.03
        hemorrhage 562.02
      congenital 751.5
  jejunum 562.00
    with
      diverticulitis 562.01
        with hemorrhage 562.03
      hemorrhage 562.02
  kidney (calyx) (pelvis) 593.89
    with calculus 592.0
  Kommerell's 747.21
  laryngeal ventricle (congenital) 748.3
  Meckel's (displaced) (hypertrophic)
      751.0
  midthoracic 530.6
  organ or site, congenital NEC - *see* Dis-
      tortion
  pericardium (congenital) (cyst) 746.89
    acquired (true) 423.8
  pharyngoesophageal (pulsion) 530.6
  pharynx (congenital) 750.27
  pulsion (esophagus) 530.6
  rectosigmoid 562.10
    with
      diverticulitis 562.11
        with hemorrhage 562.13
      hemorrhage 562.12
    congenital 751.5
  rectum 562.10
    with
      diverticulitis 562.11
        with hemorrhage 562.13
      hemorrhage 562.12
  renal (calyces) (pelvis) 593.89
    with calculus 592.0
  Rokitansky's 530.6
  seminal vesicle 608.0
  sigmoid 562.10
    with
      diverticulitis 562.11
        with hemorrhage 562.13
      hemorrhage 562.12
    congenital 751.5
  small intestine 562.00
    with
      diverticulitis 562.01
        with hemorrhage 562.03
      hemorrhage 562.02
  stomach (cardia) (juxtacardia) (juxtapy-
      loric) (acquired) 537.1
    congenital 750.7
  subdiaphragmatic 530.6
  trachea (congenital) 748.3
    acquired 519.1
  traction (esophagus) 530.6
  ureter (acquired) 593.89
    congenital 753.4
  ureterovesical orifice 593.89

Diverticula, diverticulosis, diverticulum
  (Continued)
  urethra (acquired) 599.2
    congenital 753.8
  ventricle, left (congenital) 746.89
  vesical (urinary) 596.3
    congenital 753.8
  Zenker's (esophagus) 530.6
Diverticulitis (acute) (*see also* Diverticula) 562.11
  with hemorrhage 562.13
  bladder (urinary) 596.3
  cecum (perforated) 562.11
    with hemorrhage 562.13
  colon (perforated) 562.11
    with hemorrhage 562.13
  duodenum 562.01
    with hemorrhage 562.03
  esophagus 530.6
  ileum (perforated) 562.01
    with hemorrhage 562.03
  intestine (large) (perforated) 562.11
    with hemorrhage 562.13
    small 562.01
      with hemorrhage 562.03
  jejunum (perforated) 562.01
    with hemorrhage 562.03
  Meckel's (perforated) 751.0
  pharyngoesophageal 530.6
  rectosigmoid (perforated) 562.11
    with hemorrhage 562.13
  rectum 562.11
    with hemorrhage 562.13
  sigmoid (old) (perforated) 562.11
    with hemorrhage 562.13
  small intestine (perforated) 562.01
    with hemorrhage 562.03
  vesical (urinary) 596.3
Diverticulosis - *see* Diverticula
Division
  cervix uteri 622.8
    external os into two openings by frenum 752.49
  external (cervical) into two openings by frenum 752.49
  glans penis 752.69
  hymen 752.49
  labia minora (congenital) 752.49
  ligament (partial or complete) (current) - *see also* Sprain, by site
    with open wound - *see* Wound, open, by site
  muscle (partial or complete) (current) - *see also* Sprain, by site
    with open wound - *see* Wound, open, by site
  nerve - *see* Injury, nerve, by site
  penis glans 752.69
  spinal cord - *see* Injury, spinal, by site
  vein 459.9
    traumatic - *see* Injury, vascular, by site
Divorce V61.0
Dix-Hallpike neurolabyrinthitis 386.12
Dizziness 780.4
  hysterical 300.11
  psychogenic 306.9
Doan-Wiseman syndrome (primary splenic neutropenia) 288.0
Dog bite - *see* Wound, open, by site
Döhle-Heller aortitis 093.1
Döhle body-panmyelopathic syndrome 288.2
Dolichocephaly, dolichocephalus 754.0

Dolichocolon 751.5
Dolichostenomelia 759.82
Donohue's syndrome (leprechaunism) 259.8
Donor
  blood V59.01
    other blood components V59.09
    stem cells V59.02
    whole blood V59.01
  bone V59.2
    marrow V59.3
  cornea V59.5
  heart V59.8
  kidney V59.4
  liver V59.6
  lung V59.8
  lymphocyte V59.8
  organ V59.9
    specified NEC V59.8
  potential, examination of V70.8
  skin V59.1
  specified organ or tissue NEC V59.8
  stem cells V59.02
  tissue V59.9
    specified type NEC V59.8
Donovanosis (granuloma venereum) 099.2
DOPS (diffuse obstructive pulmonary syndrome) 496
Double
  albumin 273.8
  aortic arch 747.21
  auditory canal 744.29
  auricle (heart) 746.82
  bladder 753.8
  external (cervical) os 752.49
  kidney with double pelvis (renal) 753.3
  larynx 748.3
  meatus urinarius 753.8
  organ or site NEC - *see* Accessory, orifice
    heart valve NEC 746.89
      pulmonary 746.09
  outlet, right ventricle 745.11
  pelvis (renal) with double ureter 753.4
  penis 752.69
  tongue 750.13
  ureter (one or both sides) 753.4
    with double pelvis (renal) 753.4
  urethra 753.8
  urinary meatus 753.8
  uterus (any degree) 752.2
    with doubling of cervix and vagina 752.2
    in pregnancy or childbirth 654.0
      affecting fetus or newborn 763.89 ◄▮▯
  vagina 752.49
    with doubling of cervix and uterus 752.2
  vision 368.2
  vocal cords 748.3
  vulva 752.49
  whammy (syndrome) 360.81
Douglas' pouch, cul-de-sac - *see* condition
Down's disease or syndrome (mongolism) 758.0
Down-growth, epithelial (anterior chamber) 364.61
Dracontiasis 125.7
Dracunculiasis 125.7
Dracunculosis 125.7
Drainage
  abscess (spontaneous) - *see* Abscess

Drainage *(Continued)*
  anomalous pulmonary veins to hepatic veins or right atrium 747.41
  stump (amputation) (surgical) 997.62
  suprapubic, bladder 596.8
Dream state, hysterical 300.13
Drepanocytic anemia (*see also* Disease, sickle cell) 282.60
Dresbach's syndrome (elliptocytosis) 282.1
Dreschlera (infection) 118
  hawaiiensis 117.8
Dressler's syndrome (postmyocardial infarction) 411.0
Dribbling (post-void) 788.35
Drift, ulnar 736.09
Drinking (alcohol) - *see also* Alcoholism
  excessive, to excess NEC (*see also* Abuse, drugs, nondependent) 305.0
    bouts, periodic 305.0
    continual 303.9
    episodic 305.0
    habitual 303.9
    periodic 305.0
Drip, postnasal (chronic) - *see* Sinusitis
Drivers' license examination V70.3
Droop, Cooper's 611.8
Drop
  finger 736.29
  foot 736.79
  toe 735.8
  wrist 736.05
Dropped
  dead 798.1
  heart beats 426.6
Dropsy, dropsical (*see also* Edema) 782.3
  abdomen 789.5
  amnion (*see also* Hydramnios) 657
  brain - *see* Hydrocephalus
  cardiac (*see also* Failure, heart, congestive) 428.0
  cardiorenal (*see also* Hypertension, cardiorenal) 404.90
  chest 511.9
  fetus or newborn 778.0
    due to isoimmunization 773.3
  gangrenous (*see also* Gangrene) 785.4
  heart (*see also* Failure, heart, congestive) 428.0
  hepatic - *see* Cirrhosis, liver
  infantile - *see* Hydrops, fetalis
  kidney (*see also* Nephrosis) 581.9
  liver - *see* Cirrhosis, liver
  lung 514
  malarial (*see also* Malaria) 084.9
  neonatorum - *see* Hydrops, fetalis
  nephritic 581.9
  newborn - *see* Hydrops, fetalis
  nutritional 269.9
  ovary 620.8
  pericardium (*see also* Pericarditis) 423.9
  renal (*see also* Nephrosis) 581.9
  uremic - *see* Uremia
Drowned, drowning 994.1
  lung 518.5
Drowsiness 780.09
Drug - *see also* condition
  addiction (*see also* Dependence) 304.9
  adverse effect NEC, correct substance properly administered 995.2
  dependence (*see also* Dependence) 304.9

Drug (*Continued*)
  habit (*see also* Dependence) 304.9
  overdose - *see* Table of Drugs and Chemicals
  poisoning - *see* Table of Drugs and Chemicals
  therapy (maintenance) status NEC V58.1
    anticoagulant V58.61
    long-term (current) use V58.69
      antibiotics V58.62
  wrong substance given or taken in error - *see* Table of Drugs and Chemicals
Drunkenness (*see also* Abuse, drugs, nondependent) 305.0
  acute in alcoholism (*see also* Alcoholism) 303.0
  chronic (*see also* Alcoholism) 303.9
  pathologic 291.4
  simple (acute) 305.0
    in alcoholism 303.0
  sleep 307.47
Drusen
  optic disc or papilla 377.21
  retina (colloid) (hyaloid degeneration) 362.57
    hereditary 362.77
Drusenfieber 075
Dry, dryness - *see also* condition
  eye 375.15
    syndrome 375.15
  larynx 478.79
  mouth 527.7
  nose 478.1
  skin syndrome 701.1
  socket (teeth) 526.5
  throat 478.29
Duane's retraction syndrome 378.71
Duane-Stilling-Türk syndrome (ocular retraction syndrome) 378.71
Dubin-Johnson disease or syndrome 277.4
Dubini's disease (electric chorea) 049.8
Dubois' abscess or disease 090.5
Duchenne's
  disease 094.0
    locomotor ataxia 094.0
    muscular dystrophy 359.1
    pseudohypertrophy, muscles 359.1
  paralysis 335.22
  syndrome 335.22
Duchenne-Aran myelopathic, muscular atrophy (nonprogressive) (progressive) 335.21
Duchenne-Griesinger disease 359.1
Ducrey's
  bacillus 099.0
  chancre 099.0
  disease (chancroid) 099.0
Duct, ductus - *see* condition
Duengero 061
Duhring's disease (dermatitis herpetiformis) 694.0
Dukes (-Filatov) disease 057.8
Dullness
  cardiac (decreased) (increased) 785.3
Dumb ague (*see also* Malaria) 084.6
Dumbness (*see also* Aphasia) 784.3
Dumdum fever 085.0
Dumping syndrome (postgastrectomy) 564.2
  nonsurgical 536.8

Duodenitis (nonspecific) (peptic) 535.60
  with hemorrhage 535.61
  due to
    strongyloides stercoralis 127.2
Duodenocholangitis 575.8
Duodenum, duodenal - *see* condition
Duplay's disease, periarthritis, or syndrome 726.2
Duplex - *see also* Accessory
  kidney 753.3
  placenta - *see* Placenta, abnormal
  uterus 752.2
Duplication - *see also* Accessory
  anus 751.5
  aortic arch 747.21
  appendix 751.5
  biliary duct (any) 751.69
  bladder 753.8
  cecum 751.5
    and appendix 751.5
  clitoris 752.49
  cystic duct 751.69
  digestive organs 751.8
  duodenum 751.5
  esophagus 750.4
  fallopian tube 752.19
  frontonasal process 756.0
  gallbladder 751.69
  ileum 751.5
  intestine (large) (small) 751.5
  jejunum 751.5
  kidney 753.3
  liver 751.69
  nose 748.1
  pancreas 751.7
  penis 752.69
  respiratory organs NEC 748.9
  salivary duct 750.22
  spinal cord (incomplete) 742.51
  stomach 750.7
  ureter 753.4
  vagina 752.49
  vas deferens 752.8
  vocal cords 748.3
Dupré's disease or syndrome (meningism) 781.6
Dupuytren's
  contraction 728.6
  disease (muscle contracture) 728.6
  fracture (closed) 824.4
    ankle (closed) 824.4
      open 824.5
    fibula (closed) 824.4
      open 824.5
    open 824.5
    radius (closed) 813.42
      open 813.52
  muscle contracture 728.6
Durand-Nicolas-Favre disease (climatic bubo) 099.1
Duroziez's disease (congenital mitral stenosis) 746.5
Dust
  conjunctivitis 372.05
  reticulation (occupational) 504
Dutton's
  disease (trypanosomiasis) 086.9
  relapsing fever (West African) 087.1
Dwarf, dwarfism 259.4
  with infantilism (hypophyseal) 253.3
  achondroplastic 756.4
  Amsterdam 759.89
  bird-headed 759.89
  congenital 259.4

Dwarf, dwarfism (*Continued*)
  constitutional 259.4
  hypophyseal 253.3
  infantile 259.4
  Levi type 253.3
  Lorain-Levi (pituitary) 253.3
  Lorain type (pituitary) 253.3
  metatropic 756.4
  nephrotic-glycosuric, with hypophosphatemic rickets 270.0
  nutritional 263.2
  ovarian 758.6
  pancreatic 577.8
  pituitary 253.3
  polydystrophic 277.5
  primordial 253.3
  psychosocial 259.4
  renal 588.0
    with hypertension - *see* Hypertension, kidney
  Russell's (uterine dwarfism and craniofacial dysostosis) 759.89
Dyke-Young anemia or syndrome (acquired macrocytic hemolytic anemia) (secondary) (symptomatic) 283.9
Dynia abnormality (*see also* Defect, coagulation) 286.9
Dysacousis 388.40
Dysadrenocortism 255.9
  hyperfunction 255.3
  hypofunction 255.4
Dysarthria 784.5
Dysautonomia (*see also* Neuropathy, peripheral, autonomic) 337.9
  familial 742.8
Dysbarism 993.3
Dysbasia 719.7
  angiosclerotica intermittens 443.9
    due to atherosclerosis 440.21
  hysterical 300.11
  lordotica (progressiva) 333.6
  nonorganic origin 307.9
  psychogenic 307.9
Dysbetalipoproteinemia (familial) 272.2
Dyscalculia 315.1
Dyschezia (*see also* Constipation) 564.0
Dyschondroplasia (with hemangiomata) 756.4
  Voorhoeve's 756.4
Dyschondrosteosis 756.59
Dyschromia 709.00
Dyscollagenosis 710.9
Dyscoria 743.41
Dyscraniopyophalangy 759.89
Dyscrasia
  blood 289.9
    with antepartum hemorrhage 641.3
    fetus or newborn NEC 776.9
    hemorrhage, subungual 287.8
    puerperal, postpartum 666.3
  ovary 256.8
  plasma cell 273.9
  pluriglandular 258.9
  polyglandular 258.9
Dysdiadochokinesia 781.3
Dysectasia, vesical neck 596.8
Dysendocrinism 259.9
Dysentery, dysenteric (bilious) (catarrhal) (diarrhea) (epidemic) (gangrenous) (hemorrhagic) (infectious) (sporadic) (tropical) (ulcerative) 009.0
  abscess, liver (*see also* Abscess, amebic) 006.3

ICD-9-CM

D

Vol. 2

Dysfunction *(Continued)*
  thyroid 246.9
    complicating pregnancy, childbirth, or puerperium 648.1
    hyperfunction - *see* Hyperthyroidism
    hypofunction - *see* Hypothyroidism
  uterus, complicating delivery 661.9
    affecting fetus or newborn 763.7
    hypertonic 661.4
    hypotonic 661.2
      primary 661.0
      secondary 661.1
  velopharyngeal (acquired) 528.9
    congenital 750.29
  ventricular 429.9
    with congestive heart failure (*see also* Failure, heart, congestive) 428.0
    due to
      cardiomyopathy - *see* Cardiomyopathy
      hypertension - *see* Hypertension, heart
  vesicourethral NEC 596.59
  vestibular 386.50
    specified type NEC 386.58
Dysgammaglobulinemia 279.06
Dysgenesis
  gonadal (due to chromosomal anomaly) 758.6
    pure 752.7
  kidney(s) 753.0
  ovarian 758.6
  renal 753.0
  reticular 279.2
  seminiferous tubules 758.6
  tidal platelet 287.3
Dysgerminoma (M9060/3)
  specified site - *see* Neoplasm, by site, malignant
  unspecified site
    female 183.0
    male 186.9
Dysgeusia 781.1
Dysgraphia 781.3
Dyshidrosis 705.81
Dysidrosis 705.81
Dysinsulinism 251.8
Dyskaryotic cervical smear 795.0
Dyskeratosis (*see also* Keratosis) 701.1
  bullosa hereditaria 757.39
  cervix 622.1
  congenital 757.39
  follicularis 757.39
    vitamin A deficiency 264.8
  gingiva 523.8
  oral soft tissue NEC 528.7
  tongue 528.7
  uterus NEC 621.8
Dyskinesia 781.3
  biliary 575.8
  esophagus 530.5
  hysterical 300.11
  intestinal 564.89
  nonorganic origin 307.9
  orofacial 333.82
  psychogenic 307.9
  tardive (oral) 333.82
Dyslalia 784.5
  developmental 315.39
Dyslexia 784.61
  developmental 315.02
  secondary to organic lesion 784.61

Dysmaturity (*see also* Immaturity) 765.1
  lung 770.4
  pulmonary 770.4
Dysmenorrhea (essential) (exfoliative) (functional) (intrinsic) (membranous) (primary) (secondary) 625.3
  psychogenic 306.52
Dysmetria 781.3
Dysmorodystrophia mesodermalis congenita 759.82
Dysnomia 784.3
Dysorexia 783.0
  hysterical 300.11
Dysostosis
  cleidocranial, cleidocranialis 755.59
  craniofacial 756.0
  Fairbank's (idiopathic familial generalized osteophytosis) 756.50
  mandibularis 756.0
  mandibulofacial, incomplete 756.0
  multiplex 277.5
  orodigitofacial 759.89
Dyspareunia (female) 625.0
  male 608.89
  psychogenic 302.76
Dyspepsia (allergic) (congenital) (fermentative) (flatulent) (functional) (gastric) (gastrointestinal) (neurogenic) (occupational) (reflex) 536.8
  acid 536.8
  atonic 536.3
    psychogenic 306.4
  diarrhea 558.9
    psychogenic 306.4
  intestinal 564.89
    psychogenic 306.4
  nervous 306.4
  neurotic 306.4
  psychogenic 306.4
Dysphagia 787.2
  functional 300.11
  hysterical 300.11
  nervous 300.11
  psychogenic 306.4
  sideropenic 280.8
  spastica 530.5
Dysphagocytosis, congenital 288.1
Dysphasia 784.5
Dysphonia 784.49
  clericorum 784.49
  functional 300.11
  hysterical 300.11
  psychogenic 306.1
  spastica 478.79
Dyspigmentation - *see also* Pigmentation
  eyelid (acquired) 374.52
Dyspituitarism 253.9
  hyperfunction 253.1
  hypofunction 253.2
  posterior lobe 253.6
Dysplasia - *see also* Anomaly
  artery
    fibromuscular NEC 447.8
      carotid 447.8
      renal 447.3
  bladder 596.8
  bone (fibrous) NEC 733.29
    diaphyseal, progressive 756.59
    jaw 526.89
    monostotic 733.29
    polyostotic 756.54
    solitary 733.29

Dysplasia *(Continued)*
  brain 742.9
  bronchopulmonary, fetus or newborn 770.7
  cervix (uteri) 622.1
    cervical intraepithelial neoplasia I [CIN I] 622.1
    cervical intraepithelial neoplasia II [CIN II] 622.1
    cervical intraepithelial neoplasia III [CIN III] 233.1
    CIN I 622.1
    CIN II 622.1
    CIN III 233.1
  chondroectodermal 756.55
  chondromatose 756.4
  craniocarpotarsal 759.89
  craniometaphyseal 756.89
  dentinal 520.5
  diaphyseal, progressive 756.59
  ectodermal (anhidrotic) (Bason) (Clouston's) (congenital) (Feinmesser) (hereditary) (hidrotic) (Marshall) (Robinson's) 757.31
  epiphysealis 756.9
    multiplex 756.56
    punctata 756.59
  epiphysis 756.9
    multiple 756.56
  epithelial
    epiglottis 478.79
    uterine cervix 622.1
  erythroid NEC 289.8
  eye (*see also* Microphthalmos) 743.10
  familial metaphyseal 756.89
  fibromuscular, artery NEC 447.8
    carotid 447.8
    renal 447.3
  fibrous
    bone NEC 733.29
    diaphyseal, progressive 756.59
    jaw 526.89
    monostotic 733.29
    polyostotic 756.54
    solitary 733.29
  hip (congenital) 755.63
    with dislocation (*see also* Dislocation, hip, congenital) 754.30
  hypohidrotic ectodermal 757.31
  joint 755.8
  kidney 753.15
  leg 755.69
  linguofacialis 759.89
  lung 748.5
  macular 743.55
  mammary (benign) (gland) 610.9
    cystic 610.1
    specified type NEC 610.8
  metaphyseal 756.9
    familial 756.89
  monostotic fibrous 733.29
  muscle 756.89
  myeloid NEC 289.8
  nervous system (general) 742.9
  neuroectodermal 759.6
  oculoauriculovertebral 756.0
  oculodentodigital 759.89
  olfactogenital 253.4
  osteo-onycho-arthro (hereditary) 756.89
  periosteum 733.99
  polyostotic fibrous 756.54
  progressive diaphyseal 756.59
  renal 753.15
  renofacialis 753.0

Dysplasia (*Continued*)
  retinal NEC 743.56
  retrolental 362.21
  spinal cord 742.9
  thymic, with immunodeficiency
      279.2
  vagina 623.0
  vocal cord 478.5
  vulva 624.8
      VIN III 233.3
Dyspnea (nocturnal) (paroxysmal) 786.09
  asthmatic (bronchial) (*see also* Asthma)
      493.9
      with bronchitis (*see also* Asthma)
          493.9
          chronic 491.20
              with acute exacerbation 491.21
  cardiac (*see also* Failure, ventricular,
      left) 428.1
  cardiac (*see also* Failure, ventricular,
      left) 428.1
  functional 300.11
  hyperventilation 786.01
  hysterical 300.11
  Monday morning 504
  newborn 770.8
  psychogenic 306.1
  uremic - *see* Uremia
Dyspraxia 781.3
  syndrome 315.4
Dysproteinemia 273.8
  transient with copper deficiency 281.4
Dysprothrombinemia (constitutional)
      (*see also* Defect, coagulation) 286.3
Dysreflexia, autonomic 337.3 ◀
Dysrhythmia
  cardiac 427.9
      postoperative (immediate) 997.1
          long-term effect of cardiac surgery
              429.4
      specified type NEC 427.89
  cerebral or cortical 348.3
Dyssecretosis, mucoserous 710.2
**Dyssocial reaction, without manifest
    psychiatric disorder**
  adolescent V71.02
  adult V71.01
  child V71.02
Dyssomnia NEC 780.56
  nonorganic origin 307.47
Dyssplenism 289.4
Dyssynergia
  biliary (*see also* Disease, biliary) 576.8
  cerebellaris myoclonica 334.2
  detrusor sphincter (bladder) 596.55
  ventricular 429.89
Dystasia, hereditary areflexic 334.3
Dysthymia 300.4
Dysthymic disorder 300.4
Dysthyroidism 246.9
Dystocia 660.9
  affecting fetus or newborn 763.1
  cervical 661.0
      affecting fetus or newborn 763.7
  contraction ring 661.4
      affecting fetus or newborn 763.7
  fetal 660.9
      abnormal size 653.5
      affecting fetus or newborn 763.1
      deformity 653.7
  maternal 660.9
      affecting fetus or newborn 763.1
  positional 660.0
      affecting fetus or newborn 763.1

Dystocia (*Continued*)
  shoulder (girdle) 660.4
      affecting fetus or newborn 763.1
  uterine NEC 661.4
      affecting fetus or newborn 763.7
Dystonia
  deformans progressiva 333.6
  due to drugs 333.7
  lenticularis 333.6
  musculorum deformans 333.6
  torsion (idiopathic) 333.6
      fragments (of) 333.89
      symptomatic 333.7
Dystonic
  movements 781.0
Dystopia kidney 753.3
Dystrophy, dystrophia 783.9
  adiposogenital 253.8
  asphyxiating thoracic 756.4
  Becker's type 359.1
  brevicollis 756.16
  Bruch's membrane 362.77
  cervical (sympathetic) NEC
      337.0
  chondro-osseus with punctate epiphy-
      seal dysplasia 756.59
  choroid (hereditary) 363.50
      central (areolar) (partial) 363.53
          total (gyrate) 363.54
      circinate 363.53
      circumpapillary (partial) 363.51
          total 363.52
      diffuse
          partial 363.56
          total 363.57
      generalized
          partial 363.56
          total 363.57
      gyrate
          central 363.54
          generalized 363.57
      helicoid 363.52
      peripapillary - *see* Dystrophy, cho-
          roid, circumpapillary
      serpiginous 363.54
  cornea (hereditary) 371.50
      anterior NEC 371.52
      Cogan's 371.52
      combined 371.57
      crystalline 371.56
      endothelial (Fuchs') 371.57
      epithelial 371.50
          juvenile 371.51
          microscopic cystic 371.52
      granular 371.53
      lattice 371.54
      macular 371.55
      marginal (Terrien's) 371.48
      Meesman's 371.51
      microscopic cystic (epithelial)
          371.52
      nodular, Salzmann's 371.46
      polymorphous 371.58
      posterior NEC 371.58
      ring-like 371.52
      Salzmann's nodular 371.46
      stromal NEC 371.56
  dermatochondrocorneal 371.50
  Duchenne's 359.1
  due to malnutrition 263.9
  Erb's 359.1
  familial
      hyperplastic periosteal 756.59
      osseous 277.5

Dystrophy, dystrophia (*Continued*)
  foveal 362.77
  Fuchs', cornea 371.57
  Gowers' muscular 359.1
  hair 704.2
  hereditary, progressive muscular
      359.1
  hypogenital, with diabetic tendency
      759.81
  Landouzy-Déjérine 359.1
  Leyden-Möbius 359.1
  mesodermalis congenita 759.82
  muscular 359.1
      congenital (hereditary) 359.0
          myotonic 359.2
      distal 359.1
      Duchenne's 359.1
      Erb's 359.1
      fascioscapulohumeral 359.1
      Gowers' 359.1
      hereditary (progressive) 359.1
      Landouzy-Déjérine 359.1
      limb-girdle 359.1
      myotonic 359.2
      progressive (hereditary) 359.1
          Charcôt-Marie-Tooth 356.1
      pseudohypertrophic (infantile)
          359.1
  myocardium, myocardial (*see also* De-
      generation, myocardial) 429.1
  myotonic 359.2
  myotonica 359.2
  nail 703.8
      congenital 757.5
  neurovascular (traumatic) (*see also*
      Neuropathy, peripheral, auto-
      nomic) 337.9
  nutritional 263.9
  ocular 359.1
  oculocerebrorenal 270.8
  oculopharyngeal 359.1
  ovarian 620.8
  papillary (and pigmentary) 701.1
  pelvicrural atrophic 359.1
  pigmentary (*see also* Acanthosis)
      701.2
  pituitary (gland) 253.8
  polyglandular 258.8
  posttraumatic sympathetic - *see* Dys-
      trophy, symphatic
  progressive ophthalmoplegic 359.1
  retina, retinal (hereditary) 362.70
      albipunctate 362.74
      Bruch's membrane 362.77
      cone, progressive 362.75
      hyaline 362.77
      in
          Bassen-Kornzweig syndrome 272.5
              [362.72]
          cerebroretinal lipidosis 330.1
              [362.71]
          Refsum's disease 356.3 [362.72]
          systemic lipidosis 272.7 [362.71]
      juvenile (Stargardt's) 362.75
      pigmentary 362.74
      pigment epithelium 362.76
      progressive cone (-rod) 362.75
      pseudoinflammatory foveal 362.77
      rod, progressive 362.75
      sensory 362.75
      vitelliform 362.76
  Salzmann's nodular 371.46
  scapuloperoneal 359.1
  skin NEC 709.9

Dystrophy, dystrophia (*Continued*)
  sympathetic (posttraumatic) (reflex) 337.20
    lower limb 337.22
    specified site NEC 337.29
    upper limb 337.21

Dystrophy, dystrophia (*Continued*)
  tapetoretinal NEC 362.74
  thoracic asphyxiating 756.4
  unguium 703.8
    congenital 757.5
  vitreoretinal (primary) 362.73

Dystrophy, dystrophia (*Continued*)
  vitreoretinal (*Continued*)
    secondary 362.66
  vulva 624.0
Dysuria 788.1
  psychogenic 306.53

E

Eagle-Barrett syndrome 756.71
Eales' disease (syndrome) 362.18
Ear - *see also* condition
  ache 388.70
    otogenic 388.71
    referred 388.72
  lop 744.29
  piercing V50.3
  swimmers' acute 380.12
  tank 380.12
  tropical 111.8 *[380.15]*
  wax 380.4
Earache 388.70
  otogenic 388.71
  referred 388.72
Eaton-Lambert syndrome (*see also* Neoplasm, by site, malignant) 199.1
  [358.1]
Eberth's disease (typhoid fever) 002.0
Ebstein's
  anomaly or syndrome (downward displacement, tricuspid valve into right ventricle) 746.2
  disease (diabetes) 250.4 *[581.81]*
Eccentro-osteochondrodysplasia 277.5
Ecchondroma (M9210/0) - *see* Neoplasm, bone, benign
Ecchondrosis (M9210/1) 238.0
Ecchordosis physaliphora 756.0
Ecchymosis (multiple) 459.89
  conjunctiva 372.72
  eye (traumatic) 921.0
  eyelids (traumatic) 921.1
  newborn 772.6
  spontaneous 782.7
  traumatic - *see* Contusion
Echinococciasis - *see* Echinococcus
Echinococcosis - *see* Echinococcus
Echinococcus (infection) 122.9
  granulosus 122.4
    liver 122.0
    lung 122.1
    orbit 122.3 *[376.13]*
    specified site NEC 122.3
    thyroid 122.2
  liver NEC 122.8
    granulosus 122.0
    multilocularis 122.5
  lung NEC 122.9
    granulosus 122.1
    multilocularis 122.6
  multilocularis 122.7
    liver 122.5
    specified site NEC 122.6
  orbit 122.9 *[376.13]*
    granulosus 122.3 *[376.13]*
    multilocularis 122.6 *[376.13]*
  specified site NEC 122.9
    granulosus 122.3
    multilocularis 122.6 *[376.13]*
  thyroid NEC 122.9
    granulosus 122.2
    multilocularis 122.6
Echinorhynchiasis 127.7
Echinostomiasis 121.8
Echolalia 784.69
ECHO virus infection NEC 079.1
Eclampsia, eclamptic (coma) (convulsions) (delirium) 780.39
  female, child-bearing age NEC - *see* Eclampsia, pregnancy
  gravidarum - *see* Eclampsia, pregnancy

Eclampsia, eclamptic (Continued)
  male 780.39
  not associated with pregnancy or childbirth 780.39
  pregnancy, childbirth, or puerperium 642.6
    with pre-existing hypertension 642.7
    affecting fetus or newborn 760.0
  uremic 586
Eclipse blindness (total) 363.31
Economic circumstance affecting care V60.9
  specified type NEC V60.8
Economo's disease (encephalitis lethargica) 049.8
Ectasia, ectasis
  aorta (*see also* Aneurysm, aorta) 441.9
    ruptured 441.5
  breast 610.4
  capillary 448.9
  cornea (marginal) (postinfectional) 371.71
  duct (mammary) 610.4
  kidney 593.89
  mammary duct (gland) 610.4
  papillary 448.9
  renal 593.89
  salivary gland (duct) 527.8
  scar, cornea 371.71
  sclera 379.11
Ecthyma 686.8
  contagiosum 051.2
  gangrenosum 686.09
  infectiosum 051.2
Ectocardia 746.87
Ectodermal dysplasia, congenital 757.31
Ectodermosis erosiva pluriorificialis 695.1
Ectopic, ectopia (congenital) 759.89
  abdominal viscera 751.8
    due to defect in anterior abdominal wall 756.79
  ACTH syndrome 255.0
  adrenal gland 759.1
  anus 751.5
  auricular beats 427.61
  beats 427.60
  bladder 753.5
  bone and cartilage in lung 748.69
  brain 742.4
  breast tissue 757.6
  cardiac 746.87
  cerebral 742.4
  cordis 746.87
  endometrium 617.9
  gallbladder 751.69
  gastric mucosa 750.7
  gestation - *see* Pregnancy, ectopic
  heart 746.87
  hormone secretion NEC 259.3
  hyperparathyroidism 259.3
  kidney (crossed) (intrathoracic) (pelvis) 753.3
    in pregnancy or childbirth 654.4
      causing obstructed labor 660.2
  lens 743.37
  lentis 743.37
  mole - *see* Pregnancy, ectopic
  organ or site NEC - *see* Malposition, congenital
  ovary 752.0
  pancreas, pancreatic tissue 751.7
  pregnancy - *see* Pregnancy, ectopic
  pupil 364.75

Ectopic, ectopia (Continued)
  renal 753.3
  sebaceous glands of mouth 750.26
  secretion
    ACTH 255.0
    adrenal hormone 259.3
    adrenalin 259.3
    adrenocorticotropin 255.0
    antidiuretic hormone (ADH) 259.3
    epinephrine 259.3
    hormone NEC 259.3
    norepinephrine 259.3
    pituitary (posterior) 259.3
  spleen 759.0
  testis 752.51
  thyroid 759.2
  ureter 753.4
  ventricular beats 427.69
  vesicae 753.5
Ectrodactyly 755.4
  finger (*see also* Absence, finger, congenital) 755.29
  toe (*see also* Absence, toe, congenital) 755.39
Ectromelia 755.4
  lower limb 755.30
  upper limb 755.20
Ectropion 374.10
  anus 569.49
  cervix 622.0
    with mention of cervicitis 616.0
  cicatricial 374.14
  congenital 743.62
  eyelid 374.10
    cicatricial 374.14
    congenital 743.62
    mechanical 374.12
    paralytic 374.12
    senile 374.11
    spastic 374.13
  iris (pigment epithelium) 364.54
  lip (congenital) 750.26
    acquired 528.5
  mechanical 374.12
  paralytic 374.12
  rectum 569.49
  senile 374.11
  spastic 374.13
  urethra 599.84
  uvea 364.54
Eczema (acute) (allergic) (chronic) (erythematous) (fissum) (occupational) (rubrum) (squamous) 692.9
  asteatotic 706.8
  atopic 691.8
  contact NEC 692.9
  dermatitis NEC 692.9
  due to specified cause - *see* Dermatitis, due to
  dyshidrotic 705.81
  external ear 380.22
  flexural 691.8
  gouty 274.89
  herpeticum 054.0
  hypertrophicum 701.8
  hypostatic - *see* Varicose, vein
  impetiginous 684
  infantile (acute) (chronic) (due to any substance) (intertriginous) (seborrheic) 690.12
  intertriginous NEC 692.9
    infantile 690.12
  intrinsic 691.8
  lichenified NEC 692.9

Eczema *(Continued)*
marginatum 110.3
nummular 692.9
pustular 686.8
seborrheic 690.18
infantile 690.12
solare 692.72
stasis (lower extremity) 454.1
ulcerated 454.2
vaccination, vaccinatum 999.0
varicose (lower extremity) - *see* Varicose, vein
verrucosum callosum 698.3
Eczematoid, exudative 691.8
Eddowes' syndrome (brittle bones and blue sclera) 756.51
Edema, edematous 782.3
with nephritis (*see also* Nephrosis) 581.9
allergic 995.1
angioneurotic (allergic) (any site) (with urticaria) 995.1
hereditary 277.6
angiospastic 443.9
Berlin's (traumatic) 921.3
brain 348.5
due to birth injury 767.8
fetus or newborn 767.8
cardiac (*see also* Failure, heart, congestive) 428.0
cardiovascular (*see also* Failure, heart, congestive) 428.0
cerebral - *see* Edema, brain
cerebrospinal vessel - *see* Edema, brain
cervix (acute) (uteri) 622.8
puerperal, postpartum 674.8
chronic hereditary 757.0
circumscribed, acute 995.1
hereditary 277.6
complicating pregnancy (gestational) 646.1
with hypertension - *see* Toxemia, of pregnancy
conjunctiva 372.73
connective tissue 782.3
cornea 371.20
due to contact lenses 371.24
idiopathic 371.21
secondary 371.22
cystoid macular 362.53
due to
lymphatic obstruction - *see* Edema, lymphatic
salt retention 276.0
epiglottis - *see* Edema, glottis
essential, acute 995.1
hereditary 277.6
extremities, lower - *see* Edema, legs
eyelid NEC 374.82
familial, hereditary (legs) 757.0
famine 262
fetus or newborn 778.5
genital organs
female 629.8
male 608.86
gestational 646.1
with hypertension - *see* Toxemia, of pregnancy
glottis, glottic, glottides (obstructive) (passive) 478.6
allergic 995.1
hereditary 277.6
due to external agent - *see* Condition, respiratory, acute, due to specified agent

Edema, edematous *(Continued)*
heart (*see also* Failure, heart, congestive) 428.0
newborn 779.8
heat 992.7
hereditary (legs) 757.0
inanition 262
infectious 782.3
intracranial 348.5
due to injury at birth 767.8
iris 364.8
joint (*see also* Effusion, joint) 719.0
larynx (*see also* Edema, glottis) 478.6
legs 782.3
due to venous obstruction 459.2
hereditary 757.0
localized 782.3
due to venous obstruction 459.2
lower extremity 459.2
lower extremities - *see* Edema, legs
lung 514
acute 518.4
with heart disease or failure (*see also* Failure, ventricular, left) 428.1
congestive 428.0
chemical (due to fumes or vapors) 506.1
due to
external agent(s) NEC 508.9
specified NEC 508.8
fumes and vapors (chemical) (inhalation) 506.1
radiation 508.0
chemical (acute) 506.1
chronic 506.4
chronic 514
chemical (due to fumes or vapors) 506.4
due to
external agent(s) NEC 508.9
specified NEC 508.8
fumes or vapors (chemical) (inhalation) 506.4
radiation 508.1
due to
external agent 508.9
specified NEC 508.8
high altitude 993.2
near drowning 994.1
postoperative 518.4
terminal 514
lymphatic 457.1
due to mastectomy operation 457.0
macula 362.83
cystoid 362.53
diabetic 250.5 *[362.01]*
malignant (*see also* Gangrene, gas) 040.0
Milroy's 757.0
nasopharynx 478.25
neonatorum 778.5
nutritional (newborn) 262
with dyspigmentation, skin and hair 260
optic disc or nerve - *see* Papilledema
orbit 376.33
circulatory 459.89
palate (soft) (hard) 528.9
pancreas 577.8
penis 607.83
periodic 995.1
hereditary 277.6
pharynx 478.25

Edema, edematous *(Continued)*
pitting 782.3
pulmonary - *see* Edema, lung
Quincke's 995.1
hereditary 277.6
renal (*see also* Nephrosis) 581.9
retina (localized) (macular) (peripheral) 362.83
cystoid 362.53
diabetic 250.5 *[362.01]*
salt 276.0
scrotum 608.86
seminal vesicle 608.86
spermatic cord 608.86
spinal cord 336.1
starvation 262
subconjunctival 372.73
subglottic (*see also* Edema, glottis) 478.6
supraglottic (*see also* Edema, glottis) 478.6
testis 608.86
toxic NEC 782.3
traumatic NEC 782.3
tunica vaginalis 608.86
vas deferens 608.86
vocal cord - *see* Edema, glottis
vulva (acute) 624.8
Edentia (complete) (partial) (*see also* Absence, tooth) 520.0
causing malocclusion 524.3
congenital (deficiency of tooth buds) 520.0
due to accident, extraction, or local periodontal disease 525.1
Edsall's disease 992.2
Educational handicap V62.3
Edwards' syndrome 758.2
Effect, adverse NEC
abnormal gravitational (G) forces or states 994.9
air pressure - *see* Effect, adverse, atmospheric pressure
altitude (high) - *see* Effect, adverse, high altitude
anesthetic
in labor and delivery NEC 668.9
affecting fetus or newborn 763.5
antitoxin - *see* Complications, vaccination
atmospheric pressure 993.9
due to explosion 993.4
high 993.3
low - *see* Effect, adverse, high altitude
specified effect NEC 993.8
biological, correct substance properly administered (*see also* Effect, adverse, drug) 995.2
blood (derivatives) (serum) (transfusion) - *see* Complications, transfusion
chemical substance NEC 989.9
specified - *see* Table of Drugs and Chemicals
cobalt, radioactive (*see also* Effect, adverse, radioactive substance) 990
cold (temperature) (weather) 991.9
chilblains 991.5
frostbite - *see* Frostbite
specified effect NEC 991.8
drugs and medicinals NEC 995.2
correct substance properly administered 995.2

Effect, adverse NEC *(Continued)*
  drugs and medicinals NEC *(Continued)*
    overdose or wrong substance given
        or taken 977.9
      specified drug - *see* Table of Drugs
          and Chemicals
  electric current (shock) 994.8
    burn - *see* Burn, by site
  electricity (electrocution) (shock) 994.8
    burn - *see* Burn, by site
  exertion (excessive) 994.5
  exposure 994.9
    exhaustion 994.4
  external cause NEC 994.9
  fallout (radioactive) NEC 990
  fluoroscopy NEC 990
  foodstuffs
    allergic reaction (*see also* Allergy,
        food) 693.1
      anaphylactic shock due to food
          NEC 995.60
    noxious 988.9
      specified type NEC (*see also* Poi-
          soning, by name of noxious
          foodstuff) 988.8
  gases, fumes, or vapors - *see* Table of
      Drugs and Chemicals
  glue (airplane) sniffing 304.6
  heat - *see* Heat
  high altitude NEC 993.2
    anoxia 993.2
    on
      ears 993.0
      sinuses 993.1
    polycythemia 289.0
  hot weather - *see* Heat
  hunger 994.2
  immersion, foot 991.4
  immunization - *see* Complications, vac-
      cination
  immunological agents - *see* Complica-
      tions, vaccination
  implantation (removable) of isotope or
      radium NEC 990
  infrared (radiation) (rays) NEC 990
    burn - *see* Burn, by site
    dermatitis or eczema 692.82
  infusion - *see* Complications, infusion
  ingestion or injection of isotope (thera-
      peutic) NEC 990
  irradiation NEC (*see also* Effect, ad-
      verse, radiation) 990
  isotope (radioactive) NEC 990
  lack of care (child) (infant) (newborn)
      995.52
    adult 995.84
  lightning 994.0
    burn - *see* Burn, by site
  Lirugin - *see* Complications, vaccina-
      tion
  medicinal substance, correct, properly
      administered (*see also* Effect, ad-
      verse, drugs) 995.2
  mesothorium NEC 990
  motion 994.6
  noise, inner ear 388.10
  overheated places - *see* Heat
  polonium NEC 990
  psychosocial, of work environment
      V62.1
  radiation (diagnostic) (fallout) (infra-
      red) (natural source) (therapeutic)
      (tracer) (ultraviolet) (x-ray) NEC
      990

Effect, adverse NEC *(Continued)*
  radiation *(Continued)*
    with pulmonary manifestations
      acute 508.0
      chronic 508.1
    dermatitis or eczema 692.82
      due to sun NEC (*see also* Dermati-
          tis, due to, sun) 692.70
    fibrosis of lungs 508.1
    maternal with suspected damage to
        fetus affecting management of
        pregnancy 655.6
    pneumonitis 508.0
  radioactive substance NEC 990
    dermatitis or eczema 692.82
  radioactivity NEC 990
  radiotherapy NEC 990
    dermatitis or eczema 692.82
  radium NEC 990
  reduced temperature 991.9
    frostbite - *see* Frostbite
    immersion, foot (hand) 991.4
    specified effect NEC 991.8
  roentgenography NEC 990
  roentgenoscopy NEC 990
  roentgen rays NEC 990
  serum (prophylactic) (therapeutic)
      NEC 999.5
  specified NEC 995.89
    external cause NEC 994.9
  strangulation 994.7
  submersion 994.1
  teletherapy NEC 990
  thirst 994.3
  transfusion - *see* Complications, trans-
      fusion
  ultraviolet (radiation) (rays) NEC 990
    burn - *see also* Burn, by site
      from sun 692.71
    dermatitis or eczema 692.82
      due to sun NEC (*see also* Dermati-
          tis, due to, sun) 692.70
  uranium NEC 990
  vaccine (any) - *see* Complications, vac-
      cination
  weightlessness 994.9
  whole blood - *see also* Complications,
      transfusion
    overdose or wrong substance given
        (*see also* Table of Drugs and
        Chemicals) 964.7
  working environment V62.1
  x-rays NEC 990
    dermatitis or eczema 692.82
Effect, remote
  of cancer-*see* condition
Effects, late - *see* Late, effect (of)
Effluvium, telogen 704.02
Effort
  intolerance 306.2
  syndrome (aviators) (psychogenic) 306.2
Effusion
  amniotic fluid (*see also* Rupture, mem-
      branes, premature) 658.1
  brain (serous) 348.5
  bronchial (*see also* Bronchitis) 490
  cerebral 348.5
  cerebrospinal (*see also* Meningitis) 322.9
    vessel 348.5
  chest - *see* Effusion, pleura
  intracranial 348.5
  joint 719.00
    ankle 719.07
    elbow 719.02

Effusion *(Continued)*
  joint *(Continued)*
    foot 719.07
    hand 719.04
    hip 719.05
    knee 719.06
    multiple sites 719.09
    pelvic region 719.05
    shoulder (region) 719.01
    specified site NEC 719.08
    wrist 719.03
  meninges (*see also* Meningitis) 322.9
  pericardium, pericardial (*see also* Peri-
      carditis) 423.9
    acute 420.90
  peritoneal (chronic) 568.82
  pleura, pleurisy, pleuritic, pleuroperi-
      cardial 511.9
    bacterial, nontuberculous 511.1
    fetus or newborn 511.9
    malignant 197.2
    nontuberculous 511.9
      bacterial 511.1
    pneumococcal 511.1
    staphylococcal 511.1
    streptococcal 511.1
    traumatic 862.29 ◄
      with open wound 862.39 ◄
    tuberculous (*see also* Tuberculosis,
        pleura) 012.0
      primary progressive 010.1
  pulmonary - *see* Effusion, pleura
  spinal (*see also* Meningitis) 322.9
  thorax, thoracic - *see* Effusion, pleura
Eggshell nails 703.8
  congenital 757.5
Ego-dystonic
  homosexuality 302.0
  lesbianism 302.0
Egyptian splenomegaly 120.1
Ehlers-Danlos syndrome 756.83
Eichstedt's disease (pityriasis versicolor)
    111.0
Eisenmenger's complex or syndrome
    (ventricular septal defect) 745.4
Ejaculation, semen
  painful 608.89
    psychogenic 306.59
  premature 302.75
Ekbom syndrome (restless legs) 333.99
Ekman's syndrome (brittle bones and
    blue sclera) 756.51
Elastic skin 756.83
  acquired 701.8
Elastofibroma (M8820/0) - *see* Neo-
    plasm, connective tissue, benign
Elastoidosis
  cutanea nodularis 701.8
  cutis cystica et comedonica 701.8
Elastoma 757.39
  juvenile 757.39
  Miescher's (elastosis perforans serpigi-
      nosa) 701.1
Elastomyofibrosis 425.3
Elastosis 701.8
  atrophicans 701.8
  perforans serpiginosa 701.1
  reactive perforating 701.1
  senilis 701.8
  solar (actinic) 692.74
Elbow - *see* condition
Electric
  current, electricity, effects (concussion)
      (fatal) (nonfatal) (shock) 994.8

Electric *(Continued)*
current, electricity, effects *(Continued)*
burn - *see* Burn, by site
feet (foot) syndrome 266.2
Electrocution 994.8
Electrolyte imbalance 276.9
with
abortion - *see* Abortion, by type,
with metabolic disorder
ectopic pregnancy *(see also* categories
633.0-633.9) 639.4
hyperemesis gravidarum (before 22
completed weeks' gestation)
643.1
molar pregnancy *(see also* categories
630-632) 639.4
following
abortion 639.4
ectopic or molar pregnancy 639.4
Elephant man syndrome 237.71 ◄
Elephantiasis (nonfilarial) 457.1
arabicum *(see also* Infestation, filarial)
125.9
congenita hereditaria 757.0
congenital (any site) 757.0
due to
Brugia (malayi) 125.1
mastectomy operation 457.0
Wuchereria (bancrofti) 125.0
malayi 125.1
eyelid 374.83
filarial *(see also* Infestation, filarial) 125.9
filariensis *(see also* Infestation, filarial)
125.9
gingival 523.8
glandular 457.1
graecorum 030.9
lymphangiectatic 457.1
lymphatic vessel 457.1
due to mastectomy operation 457.0
neuromatosa 237.71
postmastectomy 457.0
scrotum 457.1
streptococcal 457.1
surgical 997.99
postmastectomy 457.0
telangiectodes 457.1
vulva (nonfilarial) 624.8
Elevated - *see* Elevation
Elevation
17-ketosteroids 791.9
acid phosphatase 790.5
alkaline phosphatase 790.5
amylase 790.5
antibody titers 795.79
basal metabolic rate (BMR) 794.7
blood pressure *(see also* Hypertension)
401.9
reading (incidental) (isolated) (nonspecific), no diagnosis of hypertension 796.2
body temperature (of unknown origin)
(see also Pyrexia) 780.6
conjugate, eye 378.81
diaphragm, congenital 756.6
immunoglobulin level 795.79
indolacetic acid 791.9
lactic acid dehydrogenase (LDH) level
790.4
lipase 790.5
prostate specific antigen (PSA) 790.93
renin 790.99
in hypertension *(see also* Hypertension, renovascular) 405.91

Elevation *(Continued)*
Rh titer 999.7
scapula, congenital 755.52
sedimentation rate 790.1
SGOT 790.4
SGPT 790.4
transaminase 790.4
vanillylmandelic acid 791.9
venous pressure 459.89
VMA 791.9
Elliptocytosis (congenital) (hereditary)
282.1
Hb-C (disease) 282.7
hemoglobin disease 282.7
sickle-cell (disease) 282.60
trait 282.5
Ellis-van Creveld disease or syndrome
(chondroectodermal dysplasia)
756.55
Ellison-Zollinger syndrome
(gastric hypersecretion with pancreatic
islet cell tumor) 251.5
Elongation, elongated (congenital) - *see
also* Distortion
bone 756.9
cervix (uteri) 752.49
acquired 622.6
hypertrophic 622.6
colon 751.5
common bile duct 751.69
cystic duct 751.69
frenulum, penis 752.69
labia minora, acquired 624.8
ligamentum patellae 756.89
petiolus (epiglottidis) 748.3
styloid bone (process) 733.99
tooth, teeth 520.2
uvula 750.26
acquired 528.9
Elschnig bodies or pearls 366.51
El Tor cholera 001.1
Emaciation (due to malnutrition) 261
Emancipation disorder 309.22
Embadomoniasis 007.8
Embarrassment heart, cardiac - *see* Disease, heart
Embedded tooth, teeth 520.6
with abnormal position (same or adjacent tooth) 524.3
root only 525.3
Embolic - *see* condition
Embolism (septic) 444.9
with
abortion - *see* Abortion, by type,
with embolism
ectopic pregnancy *(see also* categories
633.0-633.9) 639.6
molar pregnancy *(see also* categories
630-632) 639.6
air (any site) 958.0
with
abortion - *see* Abortion, by type,
with embolism
ectopic pregnancy *(see also* categories 633.0-633.9) 639.6
molar pregnancy *(see also* categories 630-632) 639.6
due to implanted device - *see* Complications, due to (presence of)
any device, implant, or graft
classified to 996.0-996.5 NEC
following
abortion 639.6
ectopic or molar pregnancy 639.6

Embolism *(Continued)*
air (any site) *(Continued)*
following *(Continued)*
infusion, perfusion, or transfusion
999.1
in pregnancy, childbirth, or puerperium 673.0
traumatic 958.0
amniotic fluid (pulmonary) 673.1
with
abortion - *see* Abortion, by type,
with embolism
ectopic pregnancy *(see also* categories 633.0-633.9) 639.6
molar pregnancy *(see also* categories 630-632) 639.6
following
abortion 639.6
ectopic or molar pregnancy 639.6
aorta, aortic 444.1
abdominal 444.0
bifurcation 444.0
saddle 444.0
thoracic 444.1
artery 444.9
auditory, internal 433.8
basilar *(see also* Occlusion, artery,
basilar) 433.0
bladder 444.89
carotid (common) (internal) *(see also*
Occlusion, artery, carotid) 433.1
cerebellar (anterior inferior) (posterior inferior) (superior)
433.8
cerebral *(see also* Embolism, brain)
434.1
choroidal (anterior) 433.8
communicating posterior 433.8
coronary *(see also* Infarct, myocardium) 410.9
without myocardial infarction
411.81
extremity 444.22
lower 444.22
upper 444.21
hypophyseal 433.8
mesenteric (with gangrene) 557.0
ophthalmic *(see also* Occlusion, retina) 362.30
peripheral 444.22
pontine 433.8
precerebral NEC - *see* Occlusion, artery, precerebral
pulmonary - *see* Embolism, pulmonary
renal 593.81
retinal *(see also* Occlusion, retina)
362.30
specified site NEC 444.89
vertebral *(see also* Occlusion, artery,
vertebral) 433.2
auditory, internal 433.8
basilar (artery) *(see also* Occlusion, artery, basilar) 433.0
birth, mother - *see* Embolism, obstetrical
blood-clot
with
abortion - *see* Abortion, by type,
with embolism
ectopic pregnancy *(see also* categories 633.0-633.9) 639.6
molar pregnancy *(see also* categories 630-632) 639.6

Embolism (*Continued*)
 vena cava (inferior) (superior) 453.2
 vessels of brain (*see also* Embolism,
  brain) 434.1
Embolization - *see* Embolism
Embolus - *see* Embolism
Embryoma (M9080/1) - *see also* Neoplasm, by site, uncertain behavior
 benign (M9080/0) - *see* Neoplasm, by
  site, benign
 kidney (M8960/3) 189.0
 liver (M8970/3) 155.0
 malignant (M9080/3) - *see also* Neoplasm, by site, malignant
 kidney (M8960/3) 189.0
 liver (M8970/3) 155.0
 testis (M9070/3) 186.9
  undescended 186.0
 testis (M9070/3) 186.9
  undescended 186.0
Embryonic
 circulation 747.9
 heart 747.9
 vas deferens 752.8
Embryopathia NEC 759.9
Embryotomy, fetal 763.89
Embryotoxon 743.43
 interfering with vision 743.42
Emesis - *see also* Vomiting
 gravidarum - *see* Hyperemesis, gravidarum
Emissions, nocturnal (semen) 608.89
Emotional
 crisis - *see* Crisis, emotional
 disorder (*see also* Disorder, mental)
  300.9
 instability (excessive) 301.3
 overlay - *see* Reaction, adjustment
 upset 300.9
Emotionality, pathological 301.3
Emotogenic disease (*see also* Disorder,
  psychogenic) 306.9
Emphysema (atrophic) (centriacinar)
  (centrilobular) (chronic) (diffuse) (essential) (hypertrophic) (interlobular)
  (lung) (obstructive) (panlobular)
  (paracicatricial) (paracinar) (postural)
  (pulmonary) (senile) (subpleural)
  (traction) (unilateral) (unilobular)
  (vesicular) 492.8
 with bronchitis
  acute and chronic 491.21
  chronic 491.20
   with acute bronchitis or acute ex-
    acerbation 491.21
 bullous (giant) 492.0
 cellular tissue 958.7
  surgical 998.81
 compensatory 518.2
 congenital 770.2
 conjunctiva 372.8
 connective tissue 958.7
  surgical 998.81
 due to fumes or vapors 506.4
 eye 376.89
 eyelid 374.85
  surgical 998.81
  traumatic 958.7
 fetus or newborn (interstitial) (mediastinal) (unilobular) 770.2
 heart 416.9
 interstitial 518.1
  congenital 770.2
  fetus or newborn 770.2

Emphysema (*Continued*)
 laminated tissue 958.7
  surgical 998.81
 mediastinal 518.1
  fetus or newborn 770.2
 newborn (interstitial) (mediastinal)
  (unilobular) 770.2
 obstructive diffuse with fibrosis 492.8
 orbit 376.89
 subcutaneous 958.7
  due to trauma 958.7
  nontraumatic 518.1
  surgical 998.81
 surgical 998.81
 thymus (gland) (congenital)
  254.8
 traumatic 958.7
 tuberculous (*see also* Tuberculosis, pulmonary) 011.9
Employment examination (certification)
  V70.5
Empty sella (turcica) syndrome 253.8
Empyema (chest) (diaphragmatic) (double)
  (encapsulated) (general) (interlobar)
  (lung) (medial) (necessitatis) (perforating chest wall) (pleura) (pneumococcal) (residual) (sacculated) (streptococcal) (supradiaphragmatic) 510.9
 with fistula 510.0
 accessory sinus (chronic) (*see also* Sinusitis) 473.9
 acute 510.9
  with fistula 510.0
 antrum (chronic) (*see also* Sinusitis,
  maxillary) 473.0
 brain (any part) (*see also* Abscess,
  brain) 324.0
 ethmoidal (sinus) (chronic) (*see also* Sinusitis, ethmoidal) 473.2
 extradural (*see also* Abscess, extradural)
  324.9
 frontal (sinus) (chronic) (*see also* Sinusitis, frontal) 473.1
 gallbladder (*see also* Cholecystitis,
  acute) 575.0
 mastoid (process) (acute) (*see also* Mastoiditis, acute) 383.00
 maxilla, maxillary 526.4
  sinus (chronic) (*see also* Sinusitis,
   maxillary) 473.0
 nasal sinus (chronic) (*see also* Sinusitis)
  473.9
 sinus (accessory) (nasal) (*see also* Sinusitis) 473.9
 sphenoidal (chronic) (sinus) (*see also* Sinusitis, sphenoidal) 473.3
 subarachnoid (*see also* Abscess, extradural) 324.9
 subdural (*see also* Abscess, extradural)
  324.9
 tuberculous (*see also* Tuberculosis,
  pleura) 012.0
 ureter (*see also* Ureteritis) 593.89
 ventricular (*see also* Abscess, brain)
  324.0
Enameloma 520.2
Encephalitis (bacterial) (chronic) (hemorrhagic) (idiopathic) (nonepidemic)
  (spurious) (subacute) 323.9
 acute - *see also* Encephalitis, viral
  disseminated (postinfectious) NEC
   136.9 [323.6]
  postimmunization or postvaccination 323.5

Encephalitis (*Continued*)
 acute (*Continued*)
  inclusional 049.8
  inclusion body 049.8
  necrotizing 049.8
 arboviral, arbovirus NEC 064
 arthropod-borne (*see also* Encephalitis,
  viral, arthropod-borne) 064
 Australian X 062.4
 Bwamba fever 066.3
 California (virus) 062.5
 Central European 063.2
 Czechoslovakian 063.2
 Dawson's (inclusion body) 046.2
 diffuse sclerosing 046.2
 due to
  actinomycosis 039.8 [323.4]
  cat-scratch disease 078.3 [323.0]
  infectious mononucleosis 075
   [323.0]
  malaria (*see also* Malaria) 084.6
   [323.2]
  Negishi virus 064
  ornithosis 073.7 [323.0]
  prophylactic inoculation against
   smallpox 323.5
  rickettsiosis (*see also* Rickettsiosis)
   083.9 [323.1]
  rubella 056.01
  toxoplasmosis (acquired) 130.0
   congenital (active) 771.2 [323.4]
  typhus (fever) (*see also* Typhus) 081.9
   [323.1]
  vaccination (smallpox) 323.5
 Eastern equine 062.2
 endemic 049.8
 epidemic 049.8
 equine (acute) (infectious) (viral)
  062.9
  eastern 062.2
  Venezuelan 066.2
  western 062.1
 Far Eastern 063.0
 following vaccination or other immunization procedure 323.5
 herpes 054.3
 Ilheus (virus) 062.8
 inclusion body 046.2
 infectious (acute) (virus) NEC 049.8
 influenzal 487.8 [323.4]
  lethargic 049.8
 Japanese (B type) 062.0
 La Crosse 062.5
 Langat 063.8
 late effect - *see* Late, effect, encephalitis
 lead 984.9 [323.7]
 lethargic (acute) (infectious) (influenzal) 049.8
 lethargica 049.8
 louping ill 063.1
 lupus 710.0 [323.8]
 lymphatica 049.0
 Mengo 049.8
 meningococcal 036.1
 mumps 072.2
 Murray Valley 062.4
 myoclonic 049.8
 Negishi virus 064
 otitic NEC 382.4 [323.4]
 parasitic NEC 123.9 [323.4]
 periaxialis (concentrica) (diffusa) 341.1
 postchickenpox 052.0
 postexanthematous NEC 057.9 [323.6]

ICD-9-CM

Vol. 2

Encephalitis *(Continued)*
postimmunization 323.5
postinfectious NEC 136.9 *[323.6]*
postmeasles 055.0
posttraumatic 323.8
postvaccinal (smallpox) 323.5
postvaricella 052.0
postviral NEC 079.99 *[323.6]*
    postexanthematous 057.9 *[323.6]*
        specified NEC 057.8 *[323.6]*
Powassan 063.8
progressive subcortical (Binswanger's)
    290.12
Rio Bravo 049.8
rubella 056.01
Russian
    autumnal 062.0
    spring-summer type (taiga) 063.0
saturnine 984.9 *[323.7]*
Semliki Forest 062.8
serous 048
slow-acting virus NEC 046.8
specified cause NEC 323.8
St. Louis type 062.3
subacute sclerosing 046.2
subcorticalis chronica 290.12
summer 062.0
suppurative 324.0
syphilitic 094.81
    congenital 090.41
tick-borne 063.9
torula, torular 117.5 *[323.4]*
toxic NEC 989.9 *[323.7]*
toxoplasmic (acquired) 130.0
    congenital (active) 771.2 *[323.4]*
trichinosis 124 *[323.4]*
Trypanosomiasis *(see also* Trypanoso-
    miasis) 086.9 *[323.2]*
tuberculous *(see also* Tuberculosis) 013.6
type B (Japanese) 062.0
type C 062.3
van Bogaert's 046.2
Venezuelan 066.2
Vienna type 049.8
viral, virus 049.9
    arthropod-borne NEC 064
        mosquito-borne 062.9
            Australian X disease 062.4
            California virus 062.5
            Eastern equine 062.2
            Ilheus virus 062.8
            Japanese (B type) 062.0
            Murray Valley 062.4
            specified type NEC 062.8
            St. Louis 062.3
            type B 062.0
            type C 062.3
            Western equine 062.1
        tick-borne 063.9
            biundulant 063.2
            Central European 063.2
            Czechoslovakian 063.2
            diphasic meningoencephalitis
                063.2
            Far Eastern 063.0
            Langat 063.8
            louping ill 063.1
            Powassan 063.8
            Russian spring-summer (taiga)
                063.0
            specified type NEC 063.8
        vector unknown 064
    slow acting NEC 046.8
    specified type NEC 049.8

Encephalitis *(Continued)*
    viral, virus *(Continued)*
        vaccination, prophylactic (against)
            V05.0
        von Economo's 049.8
        Western equine 062.1
        West Nile type 066.3
Encephalocele 742.0
    orbit 376.81
Encephalocystocele 742.0
Encephalomalacia (brain) (cerebellar)
    (cerebral) (cerebrospinal) *(see also*
    Softening, brain) 434.9
    due to
        hemorrhage *(see also* Hemorrhage,
            brain) 431
        recurrent spasm of artery
            435.9
    embolic (cerebral) *(see also* Embolism,
        brain) 434.1
    subcorticalis chronicus arteriosclerotica
        290.12
    thrombotic *(see also* Thrombosis, brain)
        434.0
Encephalomeningitis - *see* Meningoen-
    cephalitis
Encephalomeningocele 742.0
Encephalomeningomyelitis - *see* Menin-
    goencephalitis
Encephalomeningopathy *(see also* Menin-
    goencephalitis) 349.9
Encephalomyelitis (chronic) (granuloma-
    tous) (hemorrhagic necrotizing,
    acute) (myalgic, benign) *(see also* En-
    cephalitis) 323.9
    abortive disseminated 049.8
    acute disseminated (postinfectious)
        136.9 *[323.6]*
        postimmunization 323.5
    due to or resulting from vaccination
        (any) 323.5
    equine (acute) (infectious) 062.9
        eastern 062.2
        Venezuelan 066.2
        western 062.1
    funicularis infectiosa 049.8
    late effect - *see* Late, effect, encephalitis
    Munch-Peterson's 049.8
    postchickenpox 052.0
    postimmunization 323.5
    postmeasles 055.0
    postvaccinal (smallpox) 323.5
    rubella 056.01
    specified cause NEC 323.8
    syphilitic 094.81
Encephalomyelocele 742.0
Encephalomyelomeningitis - *see* Menin-
    goencephalitis
Encephalomyeloneuropathy 349.9
Encephalomyelopathy 349.9
    subacute necrotizing (infantile) 330.8
Encephalomyeloradiculitis (acute)
    357.0
Encephalomyeloradiculoneuritis (acute)
    357.0
Encephalomyeloradiculopathy 349.9
Encephalomyocarditis 074.23
Encephalopathia hyperbilirubinemica,
    newborn 774.7
    due to isoimmunization (conditions
        classifiable to 773.0-773.2) 773.4
Encephalopathy (acute) 348.3
    alcoholic 291.2
    anoxic - *see* Damage, brain, anoxic

Encephalopathy *(Continued)*
    arteriosclerotic 437.0
        late effect - *see* Late effect(s) (of)
            cerebrovascular disease
    bilirubin, newborn 774.7
        due to isoimmunization 773.4
    congenital 742.9
    demyelinating (callosal) 341.8
    due to
        birth injury (intracranial) 767.8
        dialysis 294.8
            transient 293.9
        hyperinsulinism - *see* Hyperinsulin-
            ism
        influenza (virus) 487.8
        lack of vitamin *(see also* Deficiency,
            vitamin) 269.2
        nicotinic acid deficiency 291.2
        serum (nontherapeutic) (therapeutic)
            999.5
        syphilis 094.81
        trauma (postconcussional) 310.2
            current *(see also* Concussion, brain)
                850.9
                with skull fracture - *see* Frac-
                    ture, skull, by site, with in-
                    tracranial injury
        vaccination 323.5
    hepatic 572.2
    hyperbilirubinemic, newborn 774.7
        due to isoimmunization (conditions
            classifiable to 773.0-773.2) 773.4
    hypertensive 437.2
    hypoglycemic 251.2
    hypoxic - *see* Damage, brain, anoxic
    infantile cystic necrotizing (congenital)
        341.8
    lead 984.9 *[323.7]*
    leukopolio 330.0
    metabolic (toxic) - *see* Delirium
    necrotizing, subacute 330.8
    pellagrous 265.2
    portal-systemic 572.2
    postcontusional 310.2
    posttraumatic 310.2
    saturnine 984.9 *[323.7]*
    spongioform, subacute (viral) 046.1
    subacute
        necrotizing 330.8
        spongioform 046.1
        viral, spongioform 046.1
    subcortical progressive (Schilder)
        341.1
        chronic (Binswanger's) 290.12
    toxic 349.82
        metabolic - *see* Delirium
    traumatic (postconcussional) 310.2
        current *(see also* Concussion, brain)
            850.9
            with skull fracture - *see* Fracture,
                skull, by site, with intracra-
                nial injury
    vitamin B deficiency NEC 266.9
    Wernicke's (superior hemorrhagic po-
        lioencephalitis) 265.1
Encephalorrhagia *(see also* Hemorrhage,
    brain) 432.9
    healed or old V12.59
    late effect - *see* Late effect(s) (of) cere-
        brovascular disease
Encephalosis, posttraumatic 310.2
Enchondroma (M9220/0) - *see also* Neo-
    plasm, bone, benign
    multiple, congenital 756.4

ICD-9-CM

Vol. 2

Enteritis (*Continued*)
allergic 558.9
amebic (*see also* Amebiasis) 006.9
  with abscess - *see* Abscess, amebic
  acute 006.0
    with abscess - *see* Abscess, amebic
    nondysenteric 006.2
  chronic 006.1
    with abscess - *see* Abscess, amebic
    nondysenteric 006.2
  nondysenteric 006.2
anaerobic (cocci) (gram-negative) (gram-positive) (mixed) NEC 008.46
bacillary NEC 004.9
bacterial NEC 008.5
  specified NEC 008.49
Bacteroides (fragilis) (melaninogenicus) (oralis) 008.46
Butyrivibrio (fibriosolvens) 008.46
Campylobacter 008.43
Candida 112.85
Chilomastix 007.8
choleriformis 001.1
chronic 558.9
  ulcerative (*see also* Colitis, ulcerative) 556.9
cicatrizing (chronic) 555.0
Clostridium
  botulinum 005.1
  difficile 008.45
  haemolyticum 008.46
  novyi 008.46
  perfringens (C) (F) 008.46
  specified type NEC 008.46
coccidial 007.2
dietetic 558.9
due to
  achylia gastrica 536.8
  adenovirus 008.62
  Aerobacter aerogenes 008.2
  anaerobes (*see also* Enteritis, anaerobic) 008.46
  Arizona (bacillus) 008.1
  astrovirus 008.66
  Bacillus coli - *see* Enteritis, E. coli
  bacteria NEC 008.5
    specified NEC 008.49
  Bacteroides (*see also* Enteritis, Bacteroides) 008.46
  Butyrivibrio (fibriosolvens) 008.46
  Calcivirus 008.65
  Campylobacter 008.43
  Clostridium - *see* Enteritis, Clostridium
  Cockle agent 008.64
  Coxsackie (virus) 008.67
  Ditchling agent 008.64
  ECHO virus 008.67
  Enterobacter aerogenes 008.2
  enterococci 008.49
  enterovirus NEC 008.67
  Escherichia coli - *see* Enteritis, E. coli
  Eubacterium 008.46
  Fusobacterium (nucleatum) 008.46
  gram-negative bacteria NEC 008.47
    anaerobic NEC 008.46
  Hawaii agent 008.63
  irritating foods 558.9
  Klebsiella aerogenes 008.47
  Marin County agent 008.66
  Montgomery County agent 008.63
  Norwalk-like agent 008.63
  Norwalk virus 008.63
  Otofuke agent 008.63

Enteritis (*Continued*)
due to (*Continued*)
  Paracolobactrum arizonae 008.1
  paracolon bacillus NEC 008.47
    Arizona 008.1
  Paramatta agent 008.64
  Peptococcus 008.46
  Peptostreptococcus 008.46
  Proprionibacterium 008.46
  Proteus (bacillus) (mirabilis) (morganii) 008.3
  Pseudomonas aeruginosa 008.42
  Rotavirus 008.61
  Sapporo agent 008.63
  small round virus (SRV) NEC 008.64
    featureless NEC 008.63
    structured NEC 008.63
  Snow Mountain (SM) agent 008.63
  specified
    bacteria NEC 008.49
    organism, nonbacterial NEC 008.8
    virus NEC 008.69
  Staphylococcus 008.41
  Streptococcus 008.49
    anaerobic 008.46
  Taunton agent 008.63
  Torovirus 008.69
  Treponema 008.46
  Veillonella 008.46
  virus 008.8
    specified type NEC 008.69
  Wollan (W) agent 008.64
  Yersinia enterocolitica 008.44
dysentery - *see* Dysentery
E. coli 008.00
  enterohemorrhagic 008.04
  enteroinvasive 008.03
  enteropathogenic 008.01
  enterotoxigenic 008.02
  specified type NEC 008.09
El Tor 001.1
embadomonial 007.8
epidemic 009.0
Eubacterium 008.46
fermentative 558.9
fulminant 557.0
Fusobacterium (nucleatum) 008.46
gangrenous (*see also* Enteritis, due to, by organism) 009.0
giardial 007.1
gram-negative bacteria NEC 008.47
  anaerobic NEC 008.46
infectious NEC (*see also* Enteritis, due to, by organism) 009.0
  presumed 009.1
influenzal 487.8
ischemic 557.9
  acute 557.0
  chronic 557.1
  due to mesenteric artery insufficiency 557.1
membranous 564.1
mucous 564.1
myxomembranous 564.1
necrotic (*see also* Enteritis, due to, by organism) 009.0
necroticans 005.2
necrotizing of fetus or newborn 777.5
neurogenic 564.1
newborn 777.8
  necrotizing 777.5
parasitic NEC 129
paratyphoid (fever) (*see also* Fever, paratyphoid) 002.9

Enteritis (*Continued*)
Peptococcus 008.46
Peptostreptococcus 008.46
Proprionibacterium 008.46
protozoal NEC 007.9
regional (of) 555.9
  intestine
    large (bowel, colon, or rectum) 555.1
      with small intestine 555.2
    small (duodenum, ileum, or jejunum) 555.0
      with large intestine 555.2
Salmonella infection 003.0
salmonellosis 003.0
segmental (*see also* Enteritis, regional) 555.9
septic (*see also* Enteritis, due to, by organism) 009.0
Shigella 004.9
simple 558.9
spasmodic 564.1
spastic 564.1
staphylococcal 008.41
  due to food 005.0
streptococcal 008.49
  anaerobic 008.46
toxic 558.2
Treponema (denticola) (macrodentium) 008.46
trichomonal 007.3
tuberculous (*see also* Tuberculosis) 014.8
typhosa 002.0
ulcerative (chronic) (*see also* Colitis, ulcerative) 556.9
Veillonella 008.46
viral 008.8
  adenovirus 008.62
  enterovirus 008.67
  specified virus NEC 008.69
Yersinia enterocolitica 008.44
zymotic 009.0
Enteroarticular syndrome 099.3
Enterobiasis 127.4
Enterobius vermicularis 127.4
Enterocele (*see also* Hernia) 553.9
pelvis, pelvic (acquired) (congenital) 618.6
vagina, vaginal (acquired) (congenital) 618.6
Enterocolitis - *see also* Enteritis
fetus or newborn 777.8
  necrotizing 777.5
fulminant 557.0
granulomatous 555.2
hemorrhagic (acute) 557.0
  chronic 557.1
necrotizing (acute) (membranous) 557.0
primary necrotizing 777.5
pseudomembranous 008.45
radiation 558.1
  newborn 777.5
ulcerative 556.0
Enterocystoma 751.5
Enterogastritis - *see* Enteritis
Enterogenous cyanosis 289.7
Enterolith, enterolithiasis (impaction) 560.39
with hernia - *see also* Hernia, by site, with obstruction
  gangrenous - *see* Hernia, by site, with gangrene

Enteropathy 569.9
  exudative (of Gordon) 579.8
  gluten 579.0
  hemorrhagic, terminal 557.0
  protein-losing 579.8
Enteroperitonitis (*see also* Peritonitis)
  567.9
Enteroptosis 569.89
Enterorrhagia 578.9
Enterospasm 564.1
  psychogenic 306.4
Enterostenosis (*see also* Obstruction, intestine) 560.9
Enterostomy status V44.4
  with complication 569.60
Enthesopathy 726.90
  ankle and tarsus 726.70
  elbow region 726.30
    specified NEC 726.39
  hip 726.5
  knee 726.60
  peripheral NEC 726.8
  shoulder region 726.10
    adhesive 726.0
  spinal 720.1
  wrist and carpus 726.4
Entrance, air into vein - *see* Embolism,
  air
Entrapment, nerve - *see* Neuropathy, entrapment
Entropion (eyelid) 374.00
  cicatricial 374.04
  congenital 743.62
  late effect of trachoma (healed) 139.1
  mechanical 374.02
  paralytic 374.02
  senile 374.01
  spastic 374.03
Enucleation of eye (current) (traumatic)
  871.3
Enuresis 788.30
  habit disturbance 307.6
  nocturnal 788.36
    psychogenic 307.6
  nonorganic origin 307.6
  psychogenic 307.6
Enzymopathy 277.9
Eosinopenia 288.0
Eosinophilia 288.3
  allergic 288.3
  hereditary 288.3
  idiopathic 288.3
  infiltrative 518.3
  Loeffler's 518.3
  myalgia syndrome 710.5
  pulmonary (tropical) 518.3
  secondary 288.3
  tropical 518.3
Eosinophilic - *see also* condition
  fasciitis 728.89
  granuloma (bone) 277.8
  infiltration lung 518.3
Ependymitis (acute) (cerebral) (chronic)
  (granular) (*see also* Meningitis) 322.9
Ependymoblastoma (M9392/3)
  specified site - *see* Neoplasm, by site,
    malignant
  unspecified site 191.9
Ependymoma (epithelial) (malignant)
  (M9391/3)
  anaplastic type (M9392/3)
    specified site - *see* Neoplasm, by site,
      malignant
    unspecified site 191.9

Ependymoma (*Continued*)
  benign (M9391/0)
    specified site - *see* Neoplasm, by site,
      benign
    unspecified site 225.0
  myxopapillary (M9394/1) 237.5
  papillary (M9393/1) 237.5
    specified site - *see* Neoplasm, by site,
      malignant
    unspecified site 191.9
Ependymopathy 349.2
  spinal cord 349.2
Ephelides, ephelis 709.09
Ephemeral fever (*see also* Pyrexia) 780.6
Epiblepharon (congenital) 743.62
Epicanthus, epicanthic fold (congenital)
  (eyelid) 743.63
Epicondylitis (elbow) (lateral) 726.32
  medial 726.31
Epicystitis (*see also* Cystitis) 595.9
Epidemic - *see* condition
Epidermidalization, cervix - *see* condi-
  tion
Epidermidization, cervix - *see* condition
Epidermis, epidermal - *see* condition
Epidermization, cervix - *see* condition
Epidermodysplasia verruciformis 078.19
Epidermoid
  cholesteatoma - *see* Cholesteatoma
  inclusion (*see also* Cyst, skin) 706.2
Epidermolysis
  acuta (combustiformis) (toxica) 695.1
  bullosa 757.39
  necroticans combustiformis 695.1
    due to drug
      correct substance properly admin-
        istered 695.1
      overdose or wrong substance
        given or taken 977.9
      specified drug - *see* Table of
        Drugs and Chemicals
Epidermophytid - *see* Dermatophytosis
Epidermophytosis (infected) - *see* Dermatophytosis
Epidermosis, ear (middle) (*see also* Cholesteatoma) 385.30
Epididymis - *see* condition
Epididymitis (nonvenereal) 604.90
  with abscess 604.0
  acute 604.99
  blennorrhagic (acute) 098.0
    chronic or duration of 2 months or
      over 098.2
  caseous (*see also* Tuberculosis) 016.4
  chlamydial 099.54
  diphtheritic 032.89 *[604.91]*
  filarial 125.9 *[604.91]*
  gonococcal (acute) 098.0
    chronic or duration of 2 months or
      over 098.2
  recurrent 604.99
  residual 604.99
  syphilitic 095.8 *[604.91]*
  tuberculous (*see also* Tuberculosis)
    016.4
Epididymo-orchitis (*see also* Epididymitis) 604.90
  with abscess 604.0
  chlamydial 099.54
  gonococcal (acute) 098.13
    chronic or duration of 2 months or
      over 098.33
Epidural - *see* condition
Epigastritis (*see also* Gastritis) 535.5

Epigastrium, epigastric - *see* condition
Epigastrocele (*see also* Hernia, epigastric)
  553.29
Epiglottiditis (acute) 464.30
  with obstruction 464.31
  chronic 476.1
  viral 464.30
    with obstruction 464.31
Epiglottis - *see* condition
Epiglottitis (acute) 464.30
  with obstruction 464.31
  chronic 476.1
  viral 464.30
    with obstruction 464.31
Epignathus 759.4
Epilepsia
  partialis continua (*see also* Epilepsy)
    345.7
  procursiva (*see also* Epilepsy) 345.8
Epilepsy, epileptic (idiopathic) 345.9

> Note　use the following fifth-digit
> subclassifications with categories
> 345.0, 345.1, 345.4-345.9
>
> 0　without mention of intractable
>   epilepsy
> 1　with intractable epilepsy

  abdominal 345.5
  absence (attack) 345.0
  akinetic 345.0
    psychomotor 345.4
  automatism 345.4
  autonomic diencephalic 345.5
  brain 345.9
  Bravais-Jacksonian 345.5
  cerebral 345.9
  climacteric 345.9
  clonic 345.1
  clouded state 345.9
  coma 345.3
  communicating 345.4
  congenital 345.9
  convulsions 345.9
  cortical (focal) (motor) 345.5
  cursive (running) 345.8
  cysticercosis 123.1
  deterioration 345.9 *[294.1]*
  due to syphilis 094.89
  equivalent 345.5
  fit 345.9
  focal (motor) 345.5
  gelastic 345.8
  generalized 345.9
    convulsive 345.1
    flexion 345.1
    nonconvulsive 345.0
  grand mal (idiopathic) 345.1
  Jacksonian (motor) (sensory) 345.5
  Kojevnikoff's, Kojevnikov's, Kojewni-
    koff's 345.7
  laryngeal 786.2
  limbic system 345.4
  major (motor) 345.1
  minor 345.0
  mixed (type) 345.9
  motor partial 345.5
  musicogenic 345.1
  myoclonus, myoclonic 345.1
    progressive (familial) 333.2
  nonconvulsive, generalized 345.0
  parasitic NEC 123.9

ICD-9-CM

Vol. 2

Eructation 787.3
 nervous 306.4
 psychogenic 306.4
Eruption
 creeping 126.9
 drug - *see* Dermatitis, due to, drug
 Hutchinson, summer 692.72
 Kaposi's varicelliform 054.0
 napkin (psoriasiform) 691.0
 polymorphous
  light (sun) 692.72
   other source 692.82
 psoriasiform, napkin 691.0
 recalcitrant pustular 694.8
 ringed 695.89
 skin (*see also* Dermatitis) 782.1
  creeping (meaning hookworm) 126.9
  due to
   chemical(s) NEC 692.4
    internal use 693.8
   drug - *see* Dermatitis, due to, drug
   prophylactic inoculation or vacci-
     nation against disease - *see*
     Dermatitis, due to, vaccine
    smallpox vaccination NEC - *see*
     Dermatitis, due to, vaccine
  erysipeloid 027.1
  feigned 698.4
  Hutchinson, summer 692.72
  Kaposi's, varicelliform 054.0
   vaccinia 999.0
  lichenoid, axilla 698.3
  polymorphous, due to light 692.72
  toxic NEC 695.0
  vesicular 709.8
 teeth, tooth
  accelerated 520.6
  delayed 520.6
  difficult 520.6
  disturbance of 520.6
  in abnormal sequence 520.6
  incomplete 520.6
  late 520.6
  natal 520.6
  neonatal 520.6
  obstructed 520.6
  partial 520.6
  persistent primary 520.6
  premature 520.6
 vesicular 709.8
Erysipelas (gangrenous) (infantile) (newborn) (phlegmonous) (suppurative)
  035
 external ear 035 [380.13]
 puerperal, postpartum, childbirth 670
Erysipelatoid (Rosenbach's) 027.1
Erysipeloid (Rosenbach's) 027.1
Erythema, erythematous (generalized)
  695.9
 ab igne - *see* Burn, by site, first degree
 annulare (centrifugum) (rheumaticum)
  695.0
 arthriticum epidemicum 026.1
 brucellum (*see also* Brucellosis) 023.9
 bullosum 695.1
 caloricum - *see* Burn, by site, first degree
 chronicum migrans 088.81
 circinatum 695.1
 diaper 691.0
 due to
  chemical (contact) NEC 692.4
   internal 693.8
  drug (internal use) 693.0
   contact 692.3

Erythema, erythematous (*Continued*)
 elevatum diutinum 695.89
 endemic 265.2
 epidemic, arthritic 026.1
 figuratum perstans 695.0
 gluteal 691.0
 gyratum (perstans) (repens) 695.1
 heat - *see* Burn, by site, first degree
 ichthyosiforme congenitum 757.1
 induratum (primary) (scrofulosorum)
   (*see also* Tuberculosis) 017.1
  nontuberculous 695.2
 infantum febrile 057.8
 infectional NEC 695.9
 infectiosum 057.0
 inflammation NEC 695.9
 intertrigo 695.89
 iris 695.1
 lupus (discoid) (localized) (*see also* Lupus, erythematosus) 695.4
 marginatum 695.0
  rheumaticum - *see* Fever, rheumatic
 medicamentosum - *see* Dermatitis, due
   to, drug
 migrans 529.1
  chronicum 088.81
 multiforme 695.1
  bullosum 695.1
  conjunctiva 695.1
  exudativum (Hebra) 695.1
  pemphigoides 694.5
 napkin 691.0
 neonatorum 778.8
 nodosum 695.2
  tuberculous (*see also* Tuberculosis)
   017.1
 nummular, nummulare 695.1
 palmar 695.0
 palmaris hereditarium 695.0
 pernio 991.5
 perstans solare 692.72
 rash, newborn 778.8
 scarlatiniform (exfoliative) (recurrent)
   695.0
 simplex marginatum 057.8
 solare 692.71
 streptogenes 696.5
 toxic, toxicum NEC 695.0
  newborn 778.8
 tuberculous (primary) (*see also* Tuberculosis) 017.0
 venenatum 695.0
Erythematosus - *see* condition
Erythematous - *see* condition
Erythermalgia (primary) 443.89
Erythralgia 443.89
Erythrasma 039.0
Erythredema 985.0
 polyneuritica 985.0
 polyneuropathy 985.0
Erythremia (acute) (M9841/3) 207.0
 chronic (M9842/3) 207.1
 secondary 289.0
Erythroblastopenia (acquired) 284.8
 congenital 284.0
Erythroblastophthisis 284.0
Erythroblastosis (fetalis) (newborn)
  773.2
 due to
  ABO
   antibodies 773.1
   incompatibility, maternal/fetal
    773.1
   isoimmunization 773.1

Erythroblastosis (*Continued*)
 due to (*Continued*)
  Rh
   antibodies 773.0
   incompatibility, maternal/fetal 773.0
   isoimmunization 773.0
Erythrocyanosis (crurum) 443.89
Erythrocythemia - *see* Erythremia
Erythrocytosis (megalosplenic)
 familial 289.6
 oval, hereditary (*see also* Elliptocytosis)
  282.1
 secondary 289.0
 stress 289.0
Erythroderma (*see also* Erythema) 695.9
 desquamativa (in infants) 695.89
 exfoliative 695.89
 ichthyosiform, congenital 757.1
 infantum 695.89
 maculopapular 696.2
 neonatorum 778.8
 psoriaticum 696.1
 secondary 695.9
Erythrogenesis imperfecta 284.0
Erythroleukemia (M9840/3) 207.0
Erythromelalgia 443.89
Erythromelia 701.8
Erythrophagocytosis 289.9
Erythrophobia 300.23
Erythroplakia
 oral mucosa 528.7
 tongue 528.7
Erythroplasia (Queyrat) (M8080/2)
 specified site - *see* Neoplasm, skin, in
  situ
 unspecified site 233.5
Erythropoiesis, idiopathic ineffective
  285.0
Escaped beats, heart 427.60
 postoperative 997.1
Esoenteritis - *see* Enteritis
Esophagalgia 530.89
Esophagectasis 530.89
 due to cardiospasm 530.0
Esophagismus 530.5
Esophagitis (acute) (alkaline) (chemical)
  (chronic) (infectional) (necrotic)
  (postoperative) 530.10
 candidal 112.84
 reflux 530.11
 specified NEC 530.19
 tuberculous (*see also* Tuberculosis) 017.8
Esophagocele 530.6
Esophagodynia 530.89
Esophagomalacia 530.89
Esophagoptosis 530.89
Esophagospasm 530.5
Esophagostenosis 530.3
Esophagostomiasis 127.7
Esophagotracheal - *see* condition
Esophagus - *see* condition
Esophoria 378.41
 convergence, excess 378.84
 divergence, insufficiency 378.85
Esotropia (nonaccommodative) 378.00
 accommodative 378.35
 alternating 378.05
  with
   A pattern 378.06
   specified noncomitancy NEC 378.08
   V pattern 378.07
   X pattern 378.08
   Y pattern 378.08
  intermittent 378.22

ICD-9-CM

Vol. 2

Examination *(Continued)*
preoperative V72.84
cardiovascular V72.81
respiratory V72.82
specified NEC V72.83
psychiatric V70.2
follow-up not needing further care
V67.3
requested by authority V70.1
radiological NEC V72.5
respiratory preoperative V72.82
screening - *see* Screening
sensitization V72.7
skin V72.7
hypersensitivity V72.7
special V72.9
specified type or reason NEC V72.85
preoperative V72.83
specified NEC V72.83
teeth V72.2
victim or culprit following
alleged rape or seduction V71.5
inflicted injury NEC V71.6
vision V72.0
well baby V20.2
Exanthem, exanthema *(see also* Rash)
782.1
Boston 048
epidemic, with meningitis 048
lichenoid psoriasiform 696.2
subitum 057.8
viral, virus NEC 057.9
specified type NEC 057.8
Excess, excessive, excessively
alcohol level in blood 790.3
carbohydrate tissue, localized 278.1
carotene (dietary) 278.3
cold 991.9
specified effect NEC 991.8
convergence 378.84
development, breast 611.1
diaphoresis 780.8
divergence 378.85
drinking (alcohol) NEC *(see also*
Abuse, drugs, nondependent)
305.0
continual *(see also* Alcoholism) 303.9
habitual *(see also* Alcoholism) 303.9
eating 783.6
eyelid fold (congenital) 743.62
fat 278.00
in heart *(see also* Degeneration, myocardial) 429.1
tissue, localized 278.1
foreskin 605
gas 787.3
gastrin 251.5
glucagon 251.4
heat *(see also* Heat) 992.9
large
colon 564.7
congenital 751.3
fetus or infant 766.0
with obstructed labor 660.1
affecting management of pregnancy 656.6
causing disproportion 653.5
newborn (weight of 4500 grams or
more) 766.0
organ or site, congenital NEC - *see*
Anomaly, specified type NEC
lid fold (congenital) 743.62
long
colon 751.5

Excess, excessive, excessively *(Continued)*
long *(Continued)*
organ or site, congenital NEC - *see*
Anomaly, specified type NEC
umbilical cord (entangled)
affecting fetus or newborn 762.5
in pregnancy or childbirth 663.3
with compression 663.2
menstruation 626.2
number of teeth 520.1
causing crowding 524.3
nutrients (dietary) NEC 783.6
potassium (K) 276.7
salivation *(see also* Ptyalism) 527.7
secretion - *see also* Hypersecretion
milk 676.6
sputum 786.4
sweat 780.8
short
organ or site, congenital NEC - *see*
Anomaly, specified type NEC
umbilical cord
affecting fetus or newborn 762.6
in pregnancy or childbirth 663.4
skin NEC 701.9
eyelid 743.62
acquired 374.30
sodium (Na) 276.0
sputum 786.4
sweating 780.8
tearing (ducts) (eye) *(see also* Epiphora)
375.20
thirst 783.5
due to deprivation of water 994.3
vitamin
A (dietary) 278.2
administered as drug (chronic)
(prolonged excessive intake)
278.2
reaction to sudden overdose
963.5
D (dietary) 278.4
administered as drug (chronic)
(prolonged excessive intake)
278.4
reaction to sudden overdose
963.5
weight 278.00
gain 783.1
of pregnancy 646.1
loss 783.2
**Excitability, abnormal, under minor
stress** 309.29
Excitation
catatonic *(see also* Schizophrenia)
295.2
psychogenic 298.1
reactive (from emotional stress, psychological trauma) 298.1
Excitement
manic *(see also* Psychosis, affective)
296.0
recurrent episode 296.1
single episode 296.0
mental, reactive (from emotional
stress, psychological trauma)
298.1
state, reactive (from emotional stress,
psychological trauma) 298.1
Excluded pupils 364.76
Excoriation (traumatic) *(see also* Injury,
superficial, by site) 919.8
neurotic 698.4
Excyclophoria 378.44

Excyclotropia 378.33
Exencephalus, exencephaly 742.0
Exercise
breathing V57.0
remedial NEC V57.1
therapeutic NEC V57.1
**Exfoliation, teeth due to systemic
causes** 525.0
Exfoliative - *see also* condition
dermatitis 695.89
Exhaustion, exhaustive (physical
NEC) 780.79
battle *(see also* Reaction, stress, acute)
308.9
cardiac *(see also* Failure, heart) 428.9
delirium *(see also* Reaction, stress,
acute) 308.9
due to
cold 991.8
excessive exertion 994.5
exposure 994.4
fetus or newborn 779.8
heart *(see also* Failure, heart) 428.9
heat 992.5
due to
salt depletion 992.4
water depletion 992.3
manic *(see also* Psychosis, affective)
296.0
recurrent episode 296.1
single episode 296.0
maternal, complicating delivery 669.8
affecting fetus or newborn
763.89
mental 300.5
myocardium, myocardial *(see also* Failure, heart) 428.9
nervous 300.5
old age 797
postinfectional NEC 780.79
psychogenic 300.5
psychosis *(see also* Reaction, stress,
acute) 308.9
senile 797
dementia 290.0
Exhibitionism (sexual) 302.4
Exomphalos 756.79
Exophoria 378.42
convergence, insufficiency 378.83
divergence, excess 378.85
Exophthalmic
cachexia 242.0
goiter 242.0
ophthalmoplegia 242.0 [376.22]
Exophthalmos 376.30
congenital 743.66
constant 376.31
endocrine NEC 259.9 [376.22]
hyperthyroidism 242.0 [376.21]
intermittent NEC 376.34
malignant 242.0 [376.21]
pulsating 376.35
endocrine NEC 259.9 [376.22]
thyrotoxic 242.0 [376.21]
Exostosis 726.91
cartilaginous (M9210/0) - *see* Neoplasm, bone, benign
congenital 756.4
ear canal, external 380.81
gonococcal 098.89
hip 726.5
intracranial 733.3
jaw (bone) 526.81
luxurians 728.11

◀ ▶ **New Code**   ⬅▥▥ ▥▥➡ **Revised Code**

Exostosis *(Continued)*
  multiple (cancellous) (congenital) (hereditary) 756.4
  nasal bones 726.91
  orbit, orbital 376.42
  osteocartilaginous (M9210/0) - *see* Neoplasm, bone, benign
  spine 721.8
    with spondylosis - *see* Spondylosis
  syphilitic 095.5
  wrist 726.4
Exotropia 378.10
  alternating 378.15
    with
      A pattern 378.16
      specified noncomitancy NEC 378.18
      V pattern 378.17
      X pattern 378.18
      Y pattern 378.18
    intermittent 378.24
  intermittent 378.20
    alternating 378.24
    monocular 378.23
  monocular 378.11
    with
      A pattern 378.12
      specified noncomitancy NEC 378.14
      V pattern 378.13
      X pattern 378.14
      Y pattern 378.14
    intermittent 378.23
Explanation of
  investigation finding V65.4
  medication V65.4
Exposure 994.9
  cold 991.9
    specified effect NEC 991.8
  effects of 994.9
  exhaustion due to 994.4
  to
    AIDS virus V01.7
    asbestos V15.84

Exposure *(Continued)*
  to *(Continued)*
    body fluids (hazardous) V15.85
    cholera V01.0
    communicable disease V01.9
      specified type NEC V01.8
    German measles V01.4
    gonorrhea V01.6
    hazardous body fluids V15.85
    HIV V01.7
    human immunodeficiency virus V01.7
    lead V15.86
    parasitic disease V01.8
    poliomyelitis V01.2
    potentially hazardous body fluids V15.85
    rabies V01.5
    rubella V01.4
    smallpox V01.3
    syphilis V01.6
    tuberculosis V01.1
    venereal disease V01.6
    viral disease NEC V01.7
Exsanguination, fetal 772.0
Exstrophy
  abdominal content 751.8
  bladder (urinary) 753.5
Extensive - *see* condition
Extra - *see also* Accessory
  rib 756.3
    cervical 756.2
Extraction
  with hook 763.89
  breech NEC 669.6
    affecting fetus or newborn 763.0
  cataract postsurgical V45.61
  manual NEC 669.8
    affecting fetus or newborn 763.89
Extrasystole 427.60
  atrial 427.61

Extrasystole *(Continued)*
  postoperative 997.1
  ventricular 427.69
Extrauterine gestation or pregnancy - *see* Pregnancy, ectopic
Extravasation
  blood 459.0
    lower extremity 459.0
  chyle into mesentery 457.8
  pelvicalyceal 593.4
  pyelosinus 593.4
  urine 788.8
    from ureter 788.8
Extremity - *see* condition
Extrophy - *see* Exstrophy
Extroversion
  bladder 753.5
  uterus 618.1
    complicating delivery 665.2
      affecting fetus or newborn 763.89
    postpartal (old) 618.1
Extrusion
  breast implant (prosthetic) 996.54
  device, implant, or graft - *see* Complications, mechanical
  eye implant (ball) (globe) 996.59
  intervertebral disc - *see* Displacement, intervertebral disc
  lacrimal gland 375.43
  mesh (reinforcing) 996.59
  ocular lens implant 996.53
  prosthetic device NEC - *see* Complications, mechanical
  vitreous 379.26
Exudate, pleura - *see* Effusion, pleura
Exudates, retina 362.82
Exudative - *see* condition
Eye, eyeball, eyelid - *see* condition
Eyestrain 368.13
Eyeworm disease of Africa 125.2

ICD-9-CM

Vol. 2

F

Faber's anemia or syndrome (achlorhydric anemia) 280.9
Fabry's disease (angiokeratoma corporis diffusum) 272.7
Face, facial - *see* condition
Facet of cornea 371.44
Faciocephalalgia, autonomic (*see also* Neuropathy, peripheral, autonomic) 337.9
Facioscapulohumeral myopathy 359.1
Factitious disorder, illness - *see* Illness, factitious
Factor
  deficiency - *see* Deficiency, factor
  psychic, associated with diseases classified elsewhere 316
  risk-see problem
Fahr-Volhard disease (malignant nephrosclerosis) 403.00
Failure, failed
  adenohypophyseal 253.2
  attempted abortion (legal) (*see also* Abortion, failed) 638.9
  bone marrow (anemia) 284.9
    acquired (secondary) 284.8
    congenital 284.0
    idiopathic 284.9
  cardiac (*see also* Failure, heart) 428.9
    newborn 779.8
  cardiorenal (chronic) 428.9
    hypertensive (*see also* Hypertension, cardiorenal) 404.93
  cardiorespiratory 799.1
    specified during or due to a procedure 997.1
      long-term effect of cardiac surgery 429.4
  cardiovascular (chronic) 428.9
  cerebrovascular 437.8
  cervical dilatation in labor 661.0
    affecting fetus or newborn 763.7
  circulation, circulatory 799.8
    fetus or newborn 779.8
    peripheral 785.50
  compensation - *see* Disease, heart
  congestive (*see also* Failure, heart, congestive) 428.0
  coronary (*see also* Insufficiency, coronary) 411.89
  descent of head (at term) 652.5
    affecting fetus or newborn 763.1
    in labor 660.0
      affecting fetus or newborn 763.1
  device, implant, or graft - *see* Complications, mechanical
  engagement of head NEC 652.5
    in labor 660.0
  extrarenal 788.9
  fetal head to enter pelvic brim 652.5
    affecting fetus or newborn 763.1
    in labor 660.0
      affecting fetus or newborn 763.1
  forceps NEC 660.7
    affecting fetus or newborn 763.1
  fusion (joint) (spinal) 996.4
  growth 783.4
  heart (acute) (sudden) 428.9
    with
      abortion - *see* Abortion, by type, with specified complication NEC

Failure, failed (*Continued*)
  heart (*Continued*)
    with (*Continued*)
      acute pulmonary edema (*see also* Failure, ventricular, left) 428.1
        with congestion 428.0
      decompensation (*see also* Failure, heart, congestive) 428.0
      dilation - *see* Disease, heart
      ectopic pregnancy (*see also* categories 633.0-633.9) 639.8
      molar pregnancy (*see also* categories 630-632) 639.8
    arteriosclerotic 440.9
    combined left-right sided 428.0
    compensated (*see also* Failure, heart, congestive) 428.0
    complicating
      abortion - *see* Abortion, by type, with specified complication NEC
      delivery (cesarean) (instrumental) 669.4
      ectopic pregnancy (*see also* categories 633.0-633.9) 639.8
      molar pregnancy (*see also* categories 630-632) 639.8
      obstetric anesthesia or sedation 668.1
      surgery 997.1
    congestive (compensated) (decompensated) 428.0
      with rheumatic fever (conditions classifiable to 390)
        active 391.8
        inactive or quiescent (with chorea) 398.91
      fetus or newborn 779.8
      hypertensive (*see also* Hypertension, heart) 402.91
        with renal disease (*see also* Hypertension, cardiorenal) 404.91
          with renal failure 404.93
        benign 402.11
        malignant 402.01
      rheumatic (chronic) (inactive) (with chorea) 398.91
        active or acute 391.8
          with chorea (Sydenham's) 392.0
    decompensated (*see also* Failure, heart, congestive) 428.0
    degenerative (*see also* Degeneration, myocardial) 429.1
    due to presence of (cardiac) prosthesis 429.4
    fetus or newborn 779.8
    following
      abortion 639.8
      cardiac surgery 429.4
      ectopic or molar pregnancy 639.8
    high output NEC 428.9
    hypertensive (*see also* Hypertension, heart) 402.91
      with renal disease (*see also* Hypertension, cardiorenal) 404.91
        with renal failure 404.93
      benign 402.11
      malignant 402.01
    left (ventricular) (*see also* Failure, ventricular, left) 428.1
      with right-sided failure 428.0
    low output (syndrome) NEC 428.9

Failure, failed (*Continued*)
  heart (*Continued*)
    organic - *see* Disease, heart
    postoperative (immediate) 997.1
      long term effect of cardiac surgery 429.4
    rheumatic (chronic) (congestive) (inactive) 398.91
    right (secondary to left heart failure, conditions classifiable to 428.1) (ventricular) (*see also* Failure, heart, congestive) 428.0
    senile 797
    specified during or due to a procedure 997.1
      long-term effect of cardiac surgery 429.4
    thyrotoxic (*see also* Thyrotoxicosis) 242.9 [425.7]
    valvular - *see* Endocarditis
  hepatic 572.8
    acute 570
    due to a procedure 997.4
  hepatorenal 572.4
  hypertensive heart (*see also* Hypertension, heart) 402.91
    benign 402.11
    malignant 402.01
  induction (of labor) 659.1
    abortion (legal) (*see also* Abortion, failed) 638.9
    affecting fetus or newborn 763.89
    by oxytocic drugs 659.1
    instrumental 659.0
    mechanical 659.0
    medical 659.1
    surgical 659.0
  initial alveolar expansion, newborn 770.4
  involution, thymus (gland) 254.8
  kidney - *see* Failure, renal
  lactation 676.4
  Leydig's cell, adult 257.2
  liver 572.8
    acute 570
  medullary 799.8
  mitral - *see* Endocarditis, mitral
  myocardium, myocardial (*see also* Failure, heart) 428.9
    chronic (*see also* Failure, heart, congestive) 428.0
    congestive (*see also* Failure, heart, congestive) 428.0
  ovarian (primary) 256.3
    iatrogenic 256.2
    postablative 256.2
    postirradiation 256.2
    postsurgical 256.2
  ovulation 628.0
  prerenal 788.9
  renal 586
    with
      abortion - *see* Abortion, by type, with renal failure
      ectopic pregnancy (*see also* categories 633.0-633.9) 639.3
      edema (*see also* Nephrosis) 581.9
      hypertension (*see also* Hypertension, kidney) 403.91
      hypertensive heart disease (conditions classifiable to 402) 404.92
        with heart failure 404.93

Failure, failed *(Continued)*
  renal *(Continued)*
    with *(Continued)*
      hypertensive heart disease *(Continued)*
        benign 404.12
          with heart failure 404.13
        malignant 404.02
          with heart failure 404.03
      molar pregnancy *(see also* categories 630-632) 639.3
      tubular necrosis (acute) 584.5
    acute 584.9
      with lesion of
        necrosis
          cortical (renal) 584.6
          medullary (renal) (papillary) 584.7
          tubular 584.5
        specified pathology NEC 584.8
    chronic 585
      hypertensive or with hypertension *(see also* Hypertension, kidney) 403.91
    due to a procedure 997.5
    following
      abortion 639.3
      crushing 958.5
      ectopic or molar pregnancy 639.3
      labor and delivery (acute) 669.3
    hypertensive *(see also* Hypertension, kidney) 403.91
    puerperal, postpartum 669.3
  respiration, respiratory 518.81
    acute 518.81
    acute and chronic 518.84
    center 348.8
      newborn 770.8
    chronic 518.83
    due to trauma, surgery or shock 518.5
    newborn 770.8
  rotation
    cecum 751.4
    colon 751.4
    intestine 751.4
    kidney 753.3
  segmentation - *see also* Fusion
    fingers *(see also* Syndactylism, fingers) 755.11
    toes *(see also* Syndactylism, toes) 755.13
  seminiferous tubule, adult 257.2
  senile (general) 797
    with psychosis 290.20
  testis, primary (seminal) 257.2
  to progress 661.2
  to thrive 783.4
  transplant 996.80
    bone marrow 996.85
    organ (immune or nonimmune cause) 996.80
      bone marrow 996.85
      heart 996.83
      intestines 996.89
      kidney 996.81
      liver 996.82
      lung 996.84
      pancreas 996.86
      specified NEC 996.89
    skin 996.52
      artificial 996.55
      decellularized allodermis 996.55
      temporary allograft or pigskin graft - omit code

Failure, failed *(Continued)*
  trial of labor NEC 660.6
    affecting fetus or newborn 763.1
  urinary 586
  vacuum extraction
    abortion - *see* Abortion, failed
    delivery NEC 660.7
      affecting fetus or newborn 763.1
  ventouse NEC 660.7
    affecting fetus or newborn 763.1
  ventricular *(see also* Failure, heart) 428.9
    left 428.1
      with rheumatic fever (conditions classifiable to 390)
        active 391.8
          with chorea 392.0
        inactive or quiescent (with chorea) 398.91
      hypertensive *(see also* Hypertension, heart) 402.91
        benign 402.11
        malignant 402.01
      rheumatic (chronic) (inactive) (with chorea) 398.91
        active or acute 391.8
          with chorea 392.0
    right *(see also* Failure, heart, congestive) 428.0
  vital centers, fetus or newborn 779.8
  weight gain 783.4
Fainting (fit) (spell) 780.2
Falciform hymen 752.49
Fall, maternal, affecting fetus or newborn 760.5
Fallen arches 734
Falling, any organ or part - *see* Prolapse
Fallopian
  insufflation V26.2
  tube - *see* condition
Fallot's
  pentalogy 745.2
  tetrad or tetralogy 745.2
  triad or trilogy 746.09
Fallout, radioactive (adverse effect) NEC 990
False - *see also* condition
  bundle branch block 426.50
  bursa 727.89
  croup 478.75
  joint 733.82
  labor (pains) 644.1
  opening, urinary, male 752.69
  passage, urethra (prostatic) 599.4
  positive
    serological test for syphilis 795.6
    Wassermann reaction 795.6
  pregnancy 300.11
Family, familial - *see also* condition
  disruption V61.0
  planning advice V25.09
  problem V61.9
    specified circumstance NEC V61.8
Famine 994.2
  edema 262
Fanconi's anemia (congenital pancytopenia) 284.0
Fanconi (-de Toni) (-Debré) syndrome (cystinosis) 270.0
Farber (-Uzman) syndrome or disease (disseminated lipogranulomatosis) 272.8
Farcin 024
Farcy 024

Farmers'
  lung 495.0
  skin 692.74
Farsightedness 367.0
Fascia - *see* condition
Fasciculation 781.0
Fasciculitis optica 377.32
Fasciitis 729.4
  eosinophilic 728.89
  necrotizing 728.86
  nodular 728.79
  perirenal 593.4
  plantar 728.71
  pseudosarcomatous 728.79
  traumatic (old) NEC 728.79
    current - *see* Sprain, by site
Fasciola hepatica infestation 121.3
Fascioliasis 121.3
Fasciolopsiasis (small intestine) 121.4
Fasciolopsis (small intestine) 121.4
Fast pulse 785.0
Fat
  embolism (cerebral) (pulmonary) (systemic) 958.1
    with
      abortion - *see* Abortion, by type, with embolism
      ectopic pregnancy *(see also* categories 633.0-633.9) 639.6
      molar pregnancy *(see also* categories 630-632) 639.6
      complicating delivery or puerperium 673.8
      following
        abortion 639.6
        ectopic or molar pregnancy 639.6
      in pregnancy, childbirth, or the puerperium 673.8
  excessive 278.00
    in heart *(see also* Degeneration, myocardial) 429.1
  general 278.00
  hernia, herniation 729.30
    eyelid 374.34
    knee 729.31
    orbit 374.34
    retro-orbital 374.34
    retropatellar 729.31
    specified site NEC 729.39
  indigestion 579.8
  in stool 792.1
  localized (pad) 278.1
    heart *(see also* Degeneration, myocardial) 429.1
    knee 729.31
    retropatellar 729.31
  necrosis - *see also* Fatty, degeneration
    breast (aseptic) (segmental) 611.3
    mesentery 567.8
    omentum 567.8
  pad 278.1
Fatal syncope 798.1
Fatigue 780.79
  auditory deafness *(see also* Deafness) 389.9
  chronic, syndrome 780.71
  combat *(see also* Reaction, stress, acute) 308.9
  during pregnancy 646.8
  general 780.79
    psychogenic 300.5
  heat (transient) 992.6
  muscle 729.89

Fatigue (*Continued*)
  myocardium (*see also* Failure, heart)
    428.9
  nervous 300.5
  neurosis 300.5
  operational 300.89
  postural 729.89
  posture 729.89
  psychogenic (general) 300.5
  senile 797
  syndrome NEC 300.5
    chronic 780.71
  undue 780.79
  voice 784.49
Fatness 278.00
Fatty - *see also* condition
  apron 278.1
  degeneration (diffuse) (general) NEC
    272.8
    localized - *see* Degeneration, by site,
      fatty
    placenta - *see* Placenta, abnormal
  heart (enlarged) (*see also* Degeneration,
    myocardial) 429.1
  infiltration (diffuse) (general) (*see
    also* Degeneration, by site, fatty)
    272.8
    heart (enlarged) (*see also* Degenera-
      tion, myocardial) 429.1
  liver 571.8
    alcoholic 571.0
  necrosis - *see* Degeneration, fatty
  phanerosis 272.8
Fauces - *see* condition
Fauchard's disease (periodontitis) 523.4
Faucitis 478.29
Faulty - *see also* condition
  position of teeth 524.3
Favism (anemia) 282.2
Favre-Racouchot disease (elastoidosis
  cutanea nodularis) 701.8
Favus 110.9
  beard 110.0
  capitis 110.0
  corporis 110.5
  eyelid 110.8
  foot 110.4
  hand 110.2
  scalp 110.0
  specified site NEC 110.8
Fear, fearfulness (complex) (reaction)
  300.20
  child 313.0
  of
    animals 300.29
    closed spaces 300.29
    crowds 300.29
    eating in public 300.23
    heights 300.29
    open spaces 300.22
      with panic attacks 300.21
    public speaking 300.23
    streets 300.22
      with panic attacks 300.21
    travel 300.22
      with panic attacks 300.21
    washing in public 300.23
  transient 308.0
Feared complaint unfounded V65.5
Febricula (continued) (simple) (*see also*
  Pyrexia) 780.6
Febrile (*see also* Pyrexia) 780.6
  convulsion 780.31
  seizure 780.31

Febris (*see also* Fever) 780.6
  aestiva (*see also* Fever, hay) 477.9
  flava (*see also* Fever, yellow) 060.9
  melitensis 023.0
  pestis (*see also* Plague) 020.9
  puerperalis 672
  recurrens (*see also* Fever, relapsing)
    087.9
    pediculo vestimenti 087.0
  rubra 034.1
  typhoidea 002.0
  typhosa 002.0
Fecal - *see* condition
Fecalith (impaction) 560.39
  with hernia - *see also* Hernia, by site,
    with obstruction
    gangrenous - *see* Hernia, by site,
      with gangrene
  appendix 543.9
  congenital 777.1
Fede's disease 529.0
Feeble-minded 317
**Feeble rapid pulse due to shock follow-
  ing injury** 958.4
Feeding
  faulty (elderly) (infant) 783.3
    newborn 779.3
  formula check V20.2
  improper (elderly) (infant) 783.3
    newborn 779.3
  problem (elderly) (infant) 783.3
    newborn 779.3
    nonorganic origin 307.59
Feer's disease 985.0
Feet - *see* condition
Feigned illness V65.2
Feil-Klippel syndrome (brevicollis)
  756.16
Feinmesser's (hidrotic) ectodermal dys-
  plasia 757.31
Felix's disease (juvenile osteochondrosis,
  hip) 732.1
Felon (any digit) (with lymphangitis)
  681.01
  herpetic 054.6
Felty's syndrome (rheumatoid arthritis
  with splenomegaly and leukopenia)
  714.1
Feminism in boys 302.6
Feminization, testicular 257.8
  with pseudohermaphroditism, male
    257.8
Femoral hernia - *see* Hernia, femoral
Femora vara 736.32
Femur, femoral - *see* condition
Fenestrata placenta - *see* Placenta, abnormal
Fenestration, fenestrated - *see also* Imperfect, closure
  aorta-pulmonary 745.0
  aorticopulmonary 745.0
  aortopulmonary 745.0
  cusps, heart valve NEC 746.89
    pulmonary 746.09
  hymen 752.49
  pulmonic cusps 746.09
Fenwick's disease 537.89
Fermentation (gastric) (gastrointestinal)
  (stomach) 536.8
  intestine 564.89
    psychogenic 306.4
  psychogenic 306.4
Fernell's disease (aortic aneurysm) 441.9
Fertile eunuch syndrome 257.2

Fertility, meaning multiparity - *see*
  Multiparity
Fetal alcohol syndrome 760.71
Fetalis uterus 752.3
Fetid
  breath 784.9
  sweat 705.89
Fetishism 302.81
  transvestic 302.3
Fetomaternal hemorrhage
  affecting management of pregnancy
    656.0
  fetus or newborn 772.0
Fetus, fetal - *see also* condition
  papyraceous 779.8
  type lung tissue 770.4
Fever 780.6
  with chills 780.6
    in malarial regions (*see also* Malaria)
      084.6
  abortus NEC 023.9
  aden 061
  African tick-borne 087.1
  American
    mountain tick 066.1
    spotted 082.0
  and ague (*see also* Malaria) 084.6
  aphthous 078.4
  arbovirus hemorrhagic 065.9
  Assam 085.0
  Australian A or Q 083.0
  Bangkok hemorrhagic 065.4
  biliary, Charcôt's intermittent - *see*
    Choledocholithiasis
  bilious, hemoglobinuric 084.8
  blackwater 084.8
  blister 054.9
  Bonvale Dam 780.79
  boutonneuse 082.1
  brain 323.9
    late effect - *see* category 326
  breakbone 061
  Bullis 082.8
  Bunyamwera 066.3
  Burdwan 085.0
  Bwamba (encephalitis) 066.3
  Cameroon (*see also* Malaria) 084.6
  Canton 081.9
  catarrhal (acute) 460
    chronic 472.0
  cat-scratch 078.3
  cerebral 323.9
    late effect - *see* category 326
  cerebrospinal (meningococcal) (*see
    also* Meningitis, cerebrospinal)
    036.0
  Chagres 084.0
  Chandipura 066.8
  changuinola 066.0
  Charcôt's (biliary) (hepatic) (intermit-
    tent) *see* Choledocholithiasis
  Chikungunya (viral) 066.3
    hemorrhagic 065.4
  childbed 670
  Chitral 066.0
  Colombo (*see also* Fever, paratyphoid)
    002.9
  Colorado tick (virus) 066.1
  congestive
    malarial (*see also* Malaria) 084.6
    remittent (*see also* Malaria) 084.6
  Congo virus 065.0
  continued 780.6
    malarial 084.0

◀ ▶   **New Code**   ◀ ▶   **Revised Code**

Fever *(Continued)*
  Corsican *(see also* Malaria) 084.6
  Crimean hemorrhagic 065.0
  Cyprus *(see also* Brucellosis) 023.9
  dandy 061
  deer fly *(see also* Tularemia) 021.9
  dehydration, newborn 778.4
  dengue (virus) 061
    hemorrhagic 065.4
  desert 114.0
  due to heat 992.0
  Dumdum 085.0
  enteric 002.0
  ephemeral (of unknown origin) *(see also* Pyrexia) 780.6
  epidemic, hemorrhagic of the Far East 065.0
  erysipelatous *(see also* Erysipelas) 035
  estivo-autumnal (malarial) 084.0
  etiocholanolone 277.3
  famine - *see also* Fever, relapsing
    meaning typhus - *see* Typhus
  Far Eastern hemorrhagic 065.0
  five day 083.1
  Fort Bragg 100.89
  gastroenteric 002.0
  gastromalarial *(see also* Malaria) 084.6
  Gibraltar *(see also* Brucellosis) 023.9
  glandular 075
  Guama (viral) 066.3
  Haverhill 026.1
  hay (allergic) (with rhinitis) 477.9
    with
      asthma (bronchial) *(see also* Asthma) 493.0
    due to
      dander 477.8
      dust 477.8
      fowl 477.8
      pollen, any plant or tree 477.0
      specified allergen other than pollen 477.8
  heat (effects) 992.0
  hematuric, bilious 084.8
  hemoglobinuric (malarial) 084.8
    bilious 084.8
  hemorrhagic (arthropod-borne) NEC 065.9
    with renal syndrome 078.6
    arenaviral 078.7
    Argentine 078.7
    Bangkok 065.4
    Bolivian 078.7
    Central Asian 065.0
    chikungunya 065.4
    Crimean 065.0
    dengue (virus) 065.4
    Ebola 065.8
    epidemic 078.6
      of Far East 065.0
    Far Eastern 065.0
    Junin virus 078.7
    Korean 078.6
    Kyasanur forest 065.2
    Machupo virus 078.7
    mite-borne NEC 065.8
    mosquito-borne 065.4
    Omsk 065.1
    Philippine 065.4
    Russian (Yaroslav) 078.6
    Singapore 065.4
    Southeast Asia 065.4
    Thailand 065.4
    tick-borne NEC 065.3

Fever *(Continued)*
  hepatic *(see also* Cholecystitis) 575.8
    intermittent (Charcôt's) - *see* Choledocholithiasis
  herpetic *(see also* Herpes) 054.9
  hyalomma tick 065.0
  icterohemorrhagic 100.0
  inanition 780.6
    newborn 778.4
  infective NEC 136.9
  intermittent (bilious) *(see also* Malaria) 084.6
    hepatic (Charcôt) - *see* Choledocholithiasis
    of unknown origin *(see also* Pyrexia) 780.6
    pernicious 084.0
  iodide
    correct substance properly administered 780.6
    overdose or wrong substance given or taken 975.5
  Japanese river 081.2
  jungle yellow 060.0
  Junin virus, hemorrhagic 078.7
  Katayama 120.2
  Kedani 081.2
  Kenya 082.1
  Korean hemorrhagic 078.6
  Lassa 078.89
  Lone Star 082.8
  lung - *see* Pneumonia
  Machupo virus, hemorrhagic 078.7
  malaria, malarial *(see also* Malaria) 084.6
  Malta *(see also* Brucellosis) 023.9
  Marseilles 082.1
  marsh *(see also* Malaria) 084.6
  Mayaro (viral) 066.3
  Mediterranean *(see also* Brucellosis) 023.9
    familial 277.3
    tick 082.1
  meningeal - *see* Meningitis
  metal fumes NEC 985.8
  Meuse 083.1
  Mexican - *see* Typhus, Mexican
  Mianeh 087.1
  miasmatic *(see also* Malaria) 084.6
  miliary 078.2
  milk, female 672
  mill 504
  mite-borne hemorrhagic 065.8
  Monday 504
  mosquito-borne NEC 066.3
    hemorrhagic NEC 065.4
  mountain 066.1
    meaning
      Rocky Mountain spotted 082.0
      undulant fever *(see also* Brucellosis) 023.9
    tick (American) 066.1
  Mucambo (viral) 066.3
  mud 100.89
  Neapolitan *(see also* Brucellosis) 023.9
  neutropenic 288.0
  nine-mile 083.0
  nonexanthematous tick 066.1
  North Asian tick-borne typhus 082.2
  Omsk hemorrhagic 065.1
  O'nyong nyong (viral) 066.3
  Oropouche (viral) 066.3

Fever *(Continued)*
  Oroya 088.0
  paludal *(see also* Malaria) 084.6
  Panama 084.0
  pappataci 066.0
  paratyphoid 002.9
    A 002.1
    B (Schottmüller's) 002.2
    C (Hirschfeld) 002.3
  parrot 073.9
  periodic 277.3
  pernicious, acute 084.0
  persistent (of unknown origin) *(see also* Pyrexia) 780.6
  petechial 036.0
  pharyngoconjunctival 077.2
    adenoviral type 3 077.2
  Philippine hemorrhagic 065.4
  phlebotomus 066.0
  Piry 066.8
  Pixuna (viral) 066.3
  Plasmodium ovale 084.3
  pleural *(see also* Pleurisy) 511.0
  pneumonic - *see* Pneumonia
  polymer fume 987.8
  postoperative 998.89
    due to infection 998.59
  pretibial 100.89
  puerperal, postpartum 672
  putrid - *see* Septicemia
  pyemic - *see* Septicemia
  Q 083.0
    with pneumonia 083.0 [484.8]
  quadrilateral 083.0
  quartan (malaria) 084.2
  Queensland (coastal) 083.0
    seven-day 100.89
  Quintan (A) 083.1
  quotidian 084.0
  rabbit *(see also* Tularemia) 021.9
  rat-bite 026.9
    due to
      Spirillum minor or minus 026.0
      Spirochaeta morsus muris 026.0
      Streptobacillus moniliformis 026.1
  recurrent - *see* Fever, relapsing
  relapsing 087.9
    Carter's (Asiatic) 087.0
    Dutton's (West African) 087.1
    Koch's 087.9
    louse-borne (epidemic) 087.0
    Novy's (American) 087.1
    Obermeyer's (European) 087.0
    spirillum NEC 087.9
    tick-borne (endemic) 087.1
  remittent (bilious) (congestive) (gastric) *(see also* Malaria) 084.6
  rheumatic (active) (acute) (chronic) (subacute) 390
    with heart involvement 391.9
      carditis 391.9
      endocarditis (aortic) (mitral) (pulmonary) (tricuspid) 391.1
      multiple sites 391.8
      myocarditis 391.2
      pancarditis, acute 391.8
      pericarditis 391.0
      specified type NEC 391.8
      valvulitis 391.1
    inactive or quiescent with
      cardiac hypertrophy 398.99
      carditis 398.90

ICD-9-CM

Vol. 2

Fever *(Continued)*
rheumatic *(Continued)*
inactive or quiescent with *(Continued)*
endocarditis 397.9
aortic (valve) 395.9
with mitral (valve) disease 396.9
mitral (valve) 394.9
with aortic (valve) disease 396.9
pulmonary (valve) 397.1
tricuspid (valve) 397.0
heart conditions (classifiable to 429.3, 429.6, 429.9) 398.99
failure (congestive) (conditions classifiable to 428.0, 428.9) 398.91
left ventricular failure (conditions classifiable to 428.1) 398.91
myocardial degeneration (conditions classifiable to 429.1) 398.0
myocarditis (conditions classifiable to 429.0) 398.0
pancarditis 398.99
pericarditis 393
Rift Valley (viral) 066.3
Rocky Mountain spotted 082.0
rose 477.0
Ross river (viral) 066.3
Russian hemorrhagic 078.6
sandfly 066.0
San Joaquin (valley) 114.0
São Paulo 082.0
scarlet 034.1
septic - *see* Septicemia
seven-day 061
Japan 100.89
Queensland 100.89
shin bone 083.1
Singapore hemorrhagic 065.4
solar 061
sore 054.9
South African tick-bite 087.1
Southeast Asia hemorrhagic 065.4
spinal - *see* Meningitis
spirillary 026.0
splenic *(see also* Anthrax) 022.9
spotted (Rocky Mountain) 082.0
American 082.0
Brazilian 082.0
Colombian 082.0
meaning
cerebrospinal meningitis 036.0
typhus 082.9
spring 309.23
steroid
correct substance properly administered 780.6
overdose or wrong substance given or taken 962.0
streptobacillary 026.1
subtertian 084.0
Sumatran mite 081.2
sun 061
swamp 100.89
sweating 078.2
swine 003.8
sylvatic yellow 060.0
Tahyna 062.5
tertian - *see* Malaria, tertian
Thailand hemorrhagic 065.4
thermic 992.0

Fever *(Continued)*
three day 066.0
with Coxsackie exanthem 074.8
tick
American mountain 066.1
Colorado 066.1
Kemerovo 066.1
Mediterranean 082.1
mountain 066.1
nonexanthematous 066.1
Quaranfil 066.1
tick-bite NEC 066.1
tick-borne NEC 066.1
hemorrhagic NEC 065.3
transitory of newborn 778.4
trench 083.1
tsutsugamushi 081.2
typhogastric 002.0
typhoid (abortive) (ambulant) (any site) (hemorrhagic) (infection) (intermittent) (malignant) (rheumatic) 002.0
typhomalarial *(see also* Malaria) 084.6
typhus - *see* Typhus
undulant *(see also* Brucellosis) 023.9
unknown origin *(see also* Pyrexia) 780.6
uremic - *see* Uremia
uveoparotid 135
valley (Coccidioidomycosis) 114.0
Venezuelan equine 066.2
Volhynian 083.1
Wesselsbron (viral) 066.3
West
African 084.8
Nile (viral) 066.3
Whitmore's 025
Wolhynian 083.1
worm 128.9
Yaroslav hemorrhagic 078.6
yellow 060.9
jungle 060.0
sylvatic 060.0
urban 060.1
vaccination, prophylactic (against) V04.4
Zika (viral) 066.3
Fibrillation
atrial (established) (paroxysmal) 427.31
auricular (atrial) (established) 427.31
cardiac (ventricular) 427.41
coronary *(see also* Infarct, myocardium) 410.9
heart (ventricular) 427.41
muscular 728.9
postoperative 997.1
ventricular 427.41
Fibrin
ball or bodies, pleural (sac) 511.0
chamber, anterior (eye) (gelatinous exudate) 364.04
Fibrinogenolysis (hemorrhagic) - *see* Fibrinolysis
Fibrinogenopenia (congenital) (hereditary) *(see also* Defect, coagulation) 286.3
acquired 286.6
Fibrinolysis (acquired) (hemorrhagic) (pathologic) 286.6
with
abortion - *see* Abortion, by type, with hemorrhage, delayed or excessive

Fibrinolysis *(Continued)*
with *(Continued)*
ectopic pregnancy *(see also* categories 633.0-633.9) 639.1
molar pregnancy *(see also* categories 630-632) 639.1
antepartum or intrapartum 641.3
affecting fetus or newborn 762.1
following
abortion 639.1
ectopic or molar pregnancy 639.1
newborn, transient 776.2
postpartum 666.3
Fibrinopenia (hereditary) *(see also* Defect, coagulation) 286.3
acquired 286.6
Fibrinopurulent - *see* condition
Fibrinous - *see* condition
Fibroadenoma (M9010/0)
cellular intracanalicular (M9020/0) 217
giant (intracanalicular) (M9020/0) 217
intracanalicular (M9011/0)
cellular (M9020/0) 217
giant (M9020/0) 217
specified site - *see* Neoplasm, by site, benign
unspecified site 217
juvenile (M9030/0) 217
pericanicular (M9012/0)
specified site - *see* Neoplasm, by site, benign
unspecified site 217
phyllodes (M9020/0) 217
prostate 600
specified site - *see* Neoplasm, by site, benign
unspecified site 217
Fibroadenosis, breast (chronic) (cystic) (diffuse) (periodic) (segmental) 610.2
Fibroangioma (M9160/0) - *see also* Neoplasm, by site, benign
juvenile (M9160/0)
specified site - *see* Neoplasm, by site, benign
unspecified site 210.7
Fibrocellulitis progressiva ossificans 728.11
Fibrochondrosarcoma (M9220/3) - *see* Neoplasm, cartilage, malignant
Fibrocystic
disease 277.00
bone NEC 733.29
breast 610.1
jaw 526.2
kidney (congenital) 753.19
liver 751.62
lung 518.89
congenital 748.4
pancreas 277.00
kidney (congenital) 753.19
Fibrodysplasia ossificans multiplex (progressiva) 728.11
Fibroelastosis (cordis) (endocardial) (endomyocardial) 425.3
Fibroid (tumor) (M8890/0) - *see also* Neoplasm, connective tissue, benign
disease, lung (chronic) *(see also* Fibrosis, lung) 515
heart (disease) *(see also* Myocarditis) 429.0
induration, lung (chronic) *(see also* Fibrosis, lung) 515

Fibroid (*Continued*)
in pregnancy or childbirth 654.1
 affecting fetus or newborn
  763.89
 causing obstructed labor 660.2
 affecting fetus or newborn
  763.1
liver - *see* Cirrhosis, liver
lung (*see also* Fibrosis, lung) 515
pneumonia (chronic) (*see also* Fibrosis,
 lung) 515
uterus (M8890/0) (*see also* Leiomyoma,
 uterus) 218.9
Fibrolipoma (M8851/0) (*see also* Lipoma,
 by site) 214.9
Fibroliposarcoma (M8850/3) - *see*
 Neoplasm, connective tissue, malignant
Fibroma (M8810/0) - *see also* Neoplasm,
 connective tissue, benign
ameloblastic (M9330/0) 213.1
 upper jaw (bone) 213.0
bone (nonossifying) 733.99
 ossifying (M9262/0) - *see* Neoplasm,
  bone, benign
cementifying (M9274/0) - *see* Neoplasm, bone, benign
chondromyxoid (M9241/0) - *see* Neoplasm, bone, benign
desmoplastic (M8823/1) - *see* Neoplasm, connective tissue, uncertain
 behavior
facial (M8813/0) - *see* Neoplasm, connective tissue, benign
invasive (M8821/1) - *see* Neoplasm,
 connective tissue, uncertain behavior
molle (M8851/0) (*see also* Lipoma, by
 site) 214.9
myxoid (M8811/0) - *see* Neoplasm,
 connective tissue, benign
nasopharynx, nasopharyngeal (juvenile) (M9160/0) 210.7
nonosteogenic (nonossifying) - *see* Dysplasia, fibrous
odontogenic (M9321/0) 213.1
 upper jaw (bone) 213.0
ossifying (M9262/0) - *see* Neoplasm,
 bone, benign
periosteal (M8812/0) - *see* Neoplasm,
 bone, benign
prostate 600
soft (M8851/0) (*see also* Lipoma, by
 site) 214.9
Fibromatosis
abdominal (M8822/1) - *see* Neoplasm,
 connective tissue, uncertain behavior
aggressive (M8821/1) - *see* Neoplasm,
 connective tissue, uncertain behavior
Dupuytren's 728.6
gingival 523.8
plantar fascia 728.71
proliferative 728.79
pseudosarcomatous (proliferative)
 (subcutaneous) 728.79
subcutaneous pseudosarcomatous
 (proliferative) 728.79
Fibromyalgia 729.1
Fibromyoma (M8890/0) - *see also* Neoplasm, connective tissue, benign
uterus (corpus) (*see also* Leiomyoma,
 uterus) 218.9

Fibromyoma (*Continued*)
uterus (*Continued*)
 in pregnancy or childbirth 654.1
  affecting fetus or newborn
   763.89
  causing obstructed labor 660.2
  affecting fetus or newborn
   763.1
Fibromyositis (*see also* Myositis) 729.1
scapulohumeral 726.2
Fibromyxolipoma (M8852/0) (*see also* Lipoma, by site) 214.9
Fibromyxoma (M8811/0) - *see* Neoplasm,
 connective tissue, benign
Fibromyxosarcoma (M8811/3) - *see* Neoplasm, connective tissue, malignant
Fibro-odontoma, ameloblastic (M9290/0)
 213.1
upper jaw (bone) 213.0
Fibro-osteoma (M9262/0) - *see* Neoplasm, bone, benign
Fibroplasia, retrolental 362.21
Fibropurulent - *see* condition
Fibrosarcoma (M8810/3) - *see also* Neoplasm, connective tissue, malignant
ameloblastic (M9330/3) 170.1
 upper jaw (bone) 170.0
congenital (M8814/3) - *see* Neoplasm,
 connective tissue, malignant
fascial (M8813/3) - *see* Neoplasm, connective tissue, malignant
infantile (M8814/3) - *see* Neoplasm,
 connective tissue, malignant
odontogenic (M9330/3) 170.1
 upper jaw (bone) 170.0
periosteal (M8812/3) - *see* Neoplasm,
 bone, malignant
Fibrosclerosis
breast 610.3
corpora cavernosa (penis) 607.89
familial multifocal NEC 710.8
multifocal (idiopathic) NEC 710.8
penis (corpora cavernosa) 607.89
Fibrosis, fibrotic
adrenal (gland) 255.8
alveolar (diffuse) 516.3
amnion 658.8
anal papillae 569.49
anus 569.49
appendix, appendiceal, noninflammatory 543.9
arteriocapillary - *see* Arteriosclerosis
bauxite (of lung) 503
biliary 576.8
 due to Clonorchis sinensis 121.1
bladder 596.8
 interstitial 595.1
 localized submucosal 595.1
 panmural 595.1
bone, diffuse 756.59
breast 610.3
capillary - *see also* Arteriosclerosis
 lung (chronic) (*see also* Fibrosis,
  lung) 515
cardiac (*see also* Myocarditis) 429.0
cervix 622.8
chorion 658.8
corpus cavernosum 607.89
cystic (of pancreas) 277.00
due to (presence of) any device, implant, or graft - *see* Complications,
 due to (presence of) any device,
 implant, or graft classified to
 996.0-996.5 NEC

Fibrosis, fibrotic (*Continued*)
ejaculatory duct 608.89
endocardium (*see also* Endocarditis)
 424.90
endomyocardial (African) 425.0
epididymis 608.89
eye muscle 378.62
graphite (of lung) 503
heart (*see also* Myocarditis) 429.0
hepatic - *see also* Cirrhosis, liver
 due to Clonorchis sinensis 121.1
hepatolienal - *see* Cirrhosis, liver
hepatosplenic - *see* Cirrhosis, liver
infrapatellar fat pad 729.31
interstitial pulmonary, newborn 770.7
intrascrotal 608.89
kidney (*see also* Sclerosis, renal) 587
liver - *see* Cirrhosis, liver
lung (atrophic) (capillary) (chronic)
 (confluent) (massive) (perialveolar)
 (peribronchial) 515
with
 anthracosilicosis (occupational)
  500
 anthracosis (occupational) 500
 asbestosis (occupational) 501
 bagassosis (occupational) 495.1
 bauxite 503
 berylliosis (occupational) 503
 byssinosis (occupational) 504
 calcicosis (occupational) 502
 chalicosis (occupational) 502
 dust reticulation (occupational)
  504
 farmers' lung 495.0
 gannister disease (occupational)
  502
 graphite 503
 pneumonoconiosis (occupational)
  505
 pneumosiderosis (occupational)
  503
 siderosis (occupational) 503
 silicosis (occupational) 502
 tuberculosis (*see also* Tuberculosis)
  011.4
diffuse (idiopathic) (interstitial)
 516.3
due to
 bauxite 503
 fumes or vapors (chemical) (inhalation) 506.4
 graphite 503
following radiation 508.1
postinflammatory 515
silicotic (massive) (occupational) 502
tuberculous (*see also* Tuberculosis)
 011.4
lymphatic gland 289.3
median bar 600
mediastinum (idiopathic) 519.3
meninges 349.2
muscle NEC 728.2
 iatrogenic (from injection) 999.9
myocardium, myocardial (*see also* Myocarditis) 429.0
oral submucous 528.8
ovary 620.8
oviduct 620.8
pancreas 577.8
 cystic 277.00
penis 607.89
periappendiceal 543.9
periarticular (*see also* Ankylosis) 718.5

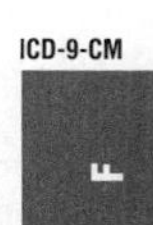

Findings, abnormal, without diagnosis
(Continued)
gallbladder, nonvisualization 793.3
glucose 790.2
tolerance test 790.2
glycosuria 791.5
heart
shadow 793.2
sounds 785.3
hematinuria 791.2
hematocrit
elevated 282.7
low 285.9
hematologic NEC 790.99
hematuria 599.7
hemoglobin
elevated 282.7
low 285.9
hemoglobinuria 791.2
histological NEC 795.4
hormones 259.9
immunoglobulins, elevated 795.79
indolacetic acid, elevated 791.9
iron 790.6
karyotype 795.2
ketonuria 791.6
lactic acid dehydrogenase (LDH) 790.4
lipase 790.5
lipids NEC 272.9
lithium, blood 790.6
lung field (coin lesion) (shadow) 793.1
magnesium, blood 790.6
mammogram 793.8
mediastinal shift 793.2
melanin, urine 791.9
microbiologic NEC 795.3
mineral, blood NEC 790.6
myoglobinuria 791.3
nitrogen derivatives, blood 790.6
nonvisualization of gallbladder 793.3
nose culture, positive 795.3
odor of urine (unusual) NEC 791.9
oxygen saturation 790.91
Papanicolaou (smear) 795.1
cervix (dyskaryotic) 795.0
other site 795.1
peritoneal fluid 792.9
phonocardiogram 794.39
phosphorus 275.3
pleural fluid 792.9
pneumoencephalogram 793.0
PO$_2$-oxygen ratio 790.91
poikilocytosis 790.0
potassium
deficiency 276.8
excess 276.7
PPD 795.5
prostate specific antigen (PSA) 790.93
protein, serum NEC 790.99
proteinuria 791.0
prothrombin time (prolonged) (partial)
(PT) (PTT) 790.92
pyuria 599.0
radiologic (x-ray) 793.9
abdomen 793.6
biliary tract 793.3
breast 793.8
gastrointestinal tract 793.4
genitourinary organs 793.5
head 793.0
intrathoracic organs NEC 793.2
lung 793.1
musculoskeletal 793.7
placenta 793.9

Findings, abnormal, without diagnosis
(Continued)
radiologic *(Continued)*
retroperitoneum 793.6
skin 793.9
skull 793.0
subcutaneous tissue 793.9
red blood cell 790.0
count 790.0
morphology 790.0
sickling 790.0
volume 790.0
saliva 792.4
scan NEC 794.9
bladder 794.9
bone 794.9
brain 794.09
kidney 794.4
liver 794.8
lung 794.2
pancreas 794.9
placental 794.9
spleen 794.9
thyroid 794.5
sedimentation rate, elevated 790.1
semen 792.2
serological (for)
human immunodeficiency virus
(HIV)
inconclusive 795.71
positive V08
syphilis - *see* Findings, serology for
syphilis
serology for syphilis
false positive 795.6
positive 097.1
false 795.6
follow-up of latent syphilis - *see*
Syphilis, latent
only finding - *see* Syphilis, latent
serum 790.99
blood NEC 790.99
enzymes NEC 790.5
proteins 790.99
SGOT 790.4
SGPT 790.4
sickling of red blood cells 790.0
skin test, positive 795.79
tuberculin (without active tuberculosis) 795.5
sodium 790.6
deficiency 276.1
excess 276.0
spermatozoa 792.2
spinal fluid 792.0
culture, positive 792.0
sputum culture, positive 795.3
for acid-fast bacilli 795.3
stool NEC 792.1
bloody 578.1
occult 792.1
color 792.1
culture, positive 792.1
occult blood 792.1
structure, body (echogram) (thermogram) (ultrasound) (x-ray) NEC
793.9
abdomen 793.6
breast 793.8
gastrointestinal tract 793.4
genitourinary organs 793.5
head 793.0
echogram (ultrasound) 794.01
intrathoracic organs NEC 793.2

Findings, abnormal, without diagnosis
(Continued)
structure, body *(Continued)*
lung 793.1
musculoskeletal 793.7
placenta 793.9
retroperitoneum 793.6
skin 793.9
subcutaneous tissue NEC 793.9
synovial fluid 792.9
thermogram - *see* Findings, abnormal,
structure
throat culture, positive 795.3
thyroid (function) 794.5
metabolism (rate) 794.5
scan 794.5
uptake 794.5
total proteins 790.99
toxicology (drugs) (heavy metals) 796.0
transaminase (level) 790.4
triglycerides 272.9
tuberculin skin test (without active tuberculosis) 795.5
ultrasound - *see also* Findings, abnormal, structure
cardiogram 793.2
uric acid, blood 790.6
urine, urinary constituents 791.9
acetone 791.6
albumin 791.0
bacteria 791.9
bile 791.4
blood 599.7
casts or cells 791.7
chyle 791.1
culture, positive 791.9
glucose 791.5
hemoglobin 791.2
ketone 791.6
protein 791.0
pus 599.0
sugar 791.5
vaginal fluid 792.9
vanillylmandelic acid, elevated 791.9
vectorcardiogram (VCG) 793.2
ventriculogram (cerebral) 793.0
VMA, elevated 791.9
Wassermann reaction
false positive 795.6
positive 097.1
follow-up of latent syphilis - *see*
Syphilis, latent
only finding - *see* Syphilis, latent
white blood cell 288.9
count 288.9
elevated 288.8
low 288.0
differential 288.9
morphology 288.9
wound culture 795.3
xerography 793.8
zinc, blood 790.6
Finger - *see* condition
Fire, St. Anthony's (*see also* Erysipelas)
035
Fish
hook stomach 537.89
meal workers' lung 495.8
Fisher's syndrome 357.0
Fissure, fissured
abdominal wall (congenital) 756.79
anus, anal 565.0
congenital 751.5
buccal cavity 528.9

Fissure, fissured (*Continued*)
  clitoris (congenital) 752.49
  ear, lobule (congenital) 744.29
  epiglottis (congenital) 748.3
  larynx 478.79
    congenital 748.3
  lip 528.5
    congenital (*see also* Cleft, lip) 749.10
  nipple 611.2
    puerperal, postpartum 676.1
  palate (congenital) (*see also* Cleft, palate) 749.00
  postanal 565.0
  rectum 565.0
  skin 709.8
    streptococcal 686.9
  spine (congenital) (*see also* Spina bifida) 741.9
  sternum (congenital) 756.3
  tongue (acquired) 529.5
    congenital 750.13
Fistula (sinus) 686.9
  abdomen (wall) 569.81
    bladder 596.2
    intestine 569.81
    ureter 593.82
    uterus 619.2
  abdominorectal 569.81
  abdominosigmoidal 569.81
  abdominothoracic 510.0
  abdominouterine 619.2
    congenital 752.3
  abdominovesical 596.2
  accessory sinuses (*see also* Sinusitis) 473.9
  actinomycotic - *see* Actinomycosis
  alveolar
    antrum (*see also* Sinusitis, maxillary) 473.0
    process 522.7
  anorectal 565.1
  antrobuccal (*see also* Sinusitis, maxillary) 473.0
  antrum (*see also* Sinusitis, maxillary) 473.0
  anus, anal (infectional) (recurrent) 565.1
    congenital 751.5
    tuberculous (*see also* Tuberculosis) 014.8
  aortic sinus 747.29
  aortoduodenal 447.2
  appendix, appendicular 543.9
  arteriovenous (acquired) 447.0
    brain 437.3
      congenital 747.81
        ruptured (*see also* Hemorrhage, subarachnoid) 430
      ruptured (*see also* Hemorrhage, subarachnoid) 430
    cerebral 437.3
      congenital 747.81
    congenital (peripheral) 747.60
      brain - *see* Fistula, arteriovenous, brain, congenital
      coronary 746.85
      gastrointestinal 747.61
      lower limb 747.64
      pulmonary 747.3
      renal 747.62
      specified site NEC 747.69
      upper limb 747.63
    coronary 414.19
      congenital 746.85

Fistula (*Continued*)
  arteriovenous (*Continued*)
    heart 414.19
    pulmonary (vessels) 417.0
      congenital 747.3
    surgically created (for dialysis) V45.1
      complication NEC 996.73
        atherosclerosis - *see* Arteriosclerosis, extremities
        embolism 996.74
        infection or inflammation 996.62
        mechanical 996.1
        occlusion NEC 996.74
        thrombus 996.74
    traumatic - *see* Injury, blood vessel, by site
  artery 447.2
  aural 383.81
    congenital 744.49
  auricle 383.81
    congenital 744.49
  Bartholin's gland 619.8
  bile duct (*see also* Fistula, biliary) 576.4
  biliary (duct) (tract) 576.4
    congenital 751.69
  bladder (neck) (sphincter) 596.2
    into seminal vesicle 596.2
  bone 733.99
  brain 348.8
    arteriovenous - *see* Fistula, arteriovenous, brain
  branchial (cleft) 744.41
  branchiogenous 744.41
  breast 611.0
    puerperal, postpartum 675.1
  bronchial 510.0
  bronchocutaneous, bronchomediastinal, bronchopleural, bronchopleuromediastinal (infective) 510.0
    tuberculous (*see also* Tuberculosis) 011.3
  bronchoesophageal 530.84
    congenital 750.3
  buccal cavity (infective) 528.3
  canal, ear 380.89
  carotid-cavernous
    congenital 747.81
      with hemorrhage 430
    traumatic 900.82
      with hemorrhage (*see also* Hemorrhage, brain, traumatic) 853.0
      late effect 908.3
  cecosigmoidal 569.81
  cecum 569.81
  cerebrospinal (fluid) 349.81
  cervical, lateral (congenital) 744.41
  cervicoaural (congenital) 744.49
  cervicosigmoidal 619.1
  cervicovesical 619.0
  cervix 619.8
  chest (wall) 510.0
  cholecystocolic (*see also* Fistula, gallbladder) 575.5
  cholecystocolonic (*see also* Fistula, gallbladder) 575.5
  cholecystoduodenal (*see also* Fistula, gallbladder) 575.5
  cholecystoenteric (*see also* Fistula, gallbladder) 575.5
  cholecystogastric (*see also* Fistula, gallbladder) 575.5
  cholecystointestinal (*see also* Fistula, gallbladder) 575.5
  choledochoduodenal 576.4

Fistula (*Continued*)
  cholocolic (*see also* Fistula, gallbladder) 575.5
  coccyx 685.1
    with abscess 685.0
  colon 569.81
  colostomy 569.69
  colovaginal (acquired) 619.1
  common duct (bile duct) 576.4
  congenital, NEC - *see* Anomaly, specified type NEC
  cornea, causing hypotony 360.32
  coronary, arteriovenous 414.19
    congenital 746.85
  costal region 510.0
  cul-de-sac, Douglas' 619.8
  cutaneous 686.9
  cystic duct (*see also* Fistula, gallbladder) 575.5
    congenital 751.69
  dental 522.7
  diaphragm 510.0
    bronchovisceral 510.0
    pleuroperitoneal 510.0
    pulmonoperitoneal 510.0
  duodenum 537.4
  ear (canal) (external) 380.89
  enterocolic 569.81
  enterocutaneous 569.81
  enteroenteric 569.81
  entero-uterine 619.1
    congenital 752.3
  enterovaginal 619.1
    congenital 752.49
  enterovesical 596.1
  epididymis 608.89
    tuberculous (*see also* Tuberculosis) 016.4
  esophagobronchial 530.89
    congenital 750.3
  esophagocutaneous 530.89
  esophagopleurocutaneous 530.89
  esophagotracheal 530.84
    congenital 750.3
  esophagus 530.89
    congenital 750.4
  ethmoid (*see also* Sinusitis, ethmoidal) 473.2
  eyeball (cornea) (sclera) 360.32
  eyelid 373.11
  fallopian tube (external) 619.2
  fecal 569.81
    congenital 751.5
  from periapical lesion 522.7
  frontal sinus (*see also* Sinusitis, frontal) 473.1
  gallbladder 575.5
    with calculus, cholelithiasis, stones (*see also* Cholelithiasis) 574.2
    congenital 751.69
  gastric 537.4
  gastrocolic 537.4
    congenital 750.7
    tuberculous (*see also* Tuberculosis) 014.8
  gastroenterocolic 537.4
  gastroesophageal 537.4
  gastrojejunal 537.4
  gastrojejunocolic 537.4
  genital
    organs
      female 619.9
        specified site NEC 619.8
      male 608.89

Fistula *(Continued)*
  genital *(Continued)*
    tract-skin (female) 619.2
  hepatopleural 510.0
  hepatopulmonary 510.0
  horseshoe 565.1
  ileorectal 569.81
  ileosigmoidal 569.81
  ileostomy 569.69
  ileovesical 596.1
  ileum 569.81
  in ano 565.1
    tuberculous *(see also* Tuberculosis)
      014.8
  inner ear *(see also* Fistula, labyrinth)
    386.40
  intestine 569.81
  intestinocolonic (abdominal) 569.81
  intestinoureteral 593.82
  intestinouterine 619.1
  intestinovaginal 619.1
    congenital 752.49
  intestinovesical 596.1
  involving female genital tract 619.9
    digestive-genital 619.1
    genital tract-skin 619.2
    specified site NEC 619.8
    urinary-genital 619.0
  ischiorectal (fossa) 566
  jejunostomy 569.69
  jejunum 569.81
  joint 719.80
    ankle 719.87
    elbow 719.82
    foot 719.87
    hand 719.84
    hip 719.85
    knee 719.86
    multiple sites 719.89
    pelvic region 719.85
    shoulder (region) 719.81
    specified site NEC 719.88
    tuberculous - *see* Tuberculosis, joint
    wrist 719.83
  kidney 593.89
  labium (majus) (minus) 619.8
  labyrinth, labyrinthine NEC 386.40
    combined sites 386.48
    multiple sites 386.48
    oval window 386.42
    round window 386.41
    semicircular canal 386.43
  lacrimal, lachrymal (duct) (gland) (sac)
    375.61
  lacrimonasal duct 375.61
  laryngotracheal 748.3
  larynx 478.79
  lip 528.5
    congenital 750.25
  lumbar, tuberculous *(see also* Tubercu-
    losis) 015.0 *[730.8]*
  lung 510.0
  lymphatic (node) (vessel) 457.8
  mamillary 611.0
  mammary (gland) 611.0
    puerperal, postpartum 675.1
  mastoid (process) (region) 383.1
  maxillary *(see also* Sinusitis, maxillary)
    473.0
  mediastinal 510.0
  mediastinobronchial 510.0
  mediastinocutaneous 510.0
  middle ear 385.89
  mouth 528.3

Fistula *(Continued)*
  nasal 478.1
    sinus *(see also* Sinusitis) 473.9
  nasopharynx 478.29
  nipple - *see* Fistula, breast
  nose 478.1
  oral (cutaneous) 528.3
    maxillary *(see also* Sinusitis, maxil-
      lary) 473.0
    nasal (with cleft palate) *(see also*
      Cleft, palate) 749.00
  orbit, orbital 376.10
  oro-antral *(see also* Sinusitis, maxillary)
    473.0
  oval window (internal ear) 386.42
  oviduct (external) 619.2
  palate (hard) 526.89
    soft 528.9
  pancreatic 577.8
  pancreaticoduodenal 577.8
  parotid (gland) 527.4
    region 528.3
  pelvoabdominointestinal 569.81
  penis 607.89
  perianal 565.1
  pericardium (pleura) (sac) *(see also* Per-
    icarditis) 423.8
  pericecal 569.81
  perineal - *see* Fistula, perineum
  perineorectal 569.81
  perineosigmoidal 569.81
  perineo-urethroscrotal 608.89
  perineum, perineal (with urethral in-
    volvement) NEC 599.1
    tuberculous *(see also* Tuberculosis)
      017.9
    ureter 593.82
  perirectal 565.1
    tuberculous *(see also* Tuberculosis)
      014.8
  peritoneum *(see also* Peritonitis) 567.2
  periurethral 599.1
  pharyngo-esophageal 478.29
  pharynx 478.29
    branchial cleft (congenital) 744.41
  pilonidal (infected) (rectum) 685.1
    with abscess 685.0
  pleura, pleural, pleurocutaneous, pleu-
    roperitoneal 510.0
    stomach 510.0
    tuberculous *(see also* Tuberculosis)
      012.0
  pleuropericardial 423.8
  postauricular 383.81
  postoperative, persistent 998.6
  preauricular (congenital) 744.46
  prostate 602.8
  pulmonary 510.0
    arteriovenous 417.0
      congenital 747.3
    tuberculous *(see also* Tuberculosis,
      pulmonary) 011.9
  pulmonoperitoneal 510.0
  rectolabial 619.1
  rectosigmoid (intercommunicating)
    569.81
  rectoureteral 593.82
  rectourethral 599.1
    congenital 753.8
  rectouterine 619.1
    congenital 752.3
  rectovaginal 619.1
    congenital 752.49
    old, postpartal 619.1

Fistula *(Continued)*
  rectovaginal *(Continued)*
    tuberculous *(see also* Tuberculosis)
      014.8
  rectovesical 596.1
    congenital 753.8
  rectovesicovaginal 619.1
  rectovulvar 619.1
    congenital 752.49
  rectum (to skin) 565.1
    tuberculous *(see also* Tuberculosis)
      014.8
  renal 593.89
  retroauricular 383.81
  round window (internal ear) 386.41
  salivary duct or gland 527.4
    congenital 750.24
  sclera 360.32
  scrotum (urinary) 608.89
    tuberculous *(see also* Tuberculosis)
      016.5
  semicircular canals (internal ear)
    386.43
  sigmoid 569.81
    vesicoabdominal 596.1
  sigmoidovaginal 619.1
    congenital 752.49
  skin 686.9
    ureter 593.82
    vagina 619.2
  sphenoidal sinus *(see also* Sinusitis,
    sphenoidal) 473.3
  splenocolic 289.59
  stercoral 569.81
  stomach 537.4
  sublingual gland 527.4
    congenital 750.24
  submaxillary
    gland 527.4
      congenital 750.24
    region 528.3
  thoracic 510.0
    duct 457.8
  thoracicoabdominal 510.0
  thoracicogastric 510.0
  thoracicointestinal 510.0
  thoracoabdominal 510.0
  thoracogastric 510.0
  thorax 510.0
  thyroglossal duct 759.2
  thyroid 246.8
  trachea (congenital) (external) (inter-
    nal) 748.3
  tracheoesophageal 530.84
    congenital 750.3
    following tracheostomy 519.09
  traumatic
    arteriovenous *(see also* Injury, blood
      vessel, by site) 904.9
    brain - *see* Injury, intracranial
  tuberculous - *see* Tuberculosis, by site
  typhoid 002.0
  umbilical 759.89
  umbilico-urinary 753.8
  urachal, urachus 753.7
  ureter (persistent) 593.82
  ureteroabdominal 593.82
  ureterocervical 593.82
  ureterorectal 593.82
  ureterosigmoido-abdominal 593.82
  ureterovaginal 619.0
  ureterovesical 596.2
  urethra 599.1
    congenital 753.8

Fistula *(Continued)*
  urethra *(Continued)*
    tuberculous *(see also* Tuberculosis)
      016.3
  urethroperineal 599.1
  urethroperineovesical 596.2
  urethrorectal 599.1
    congenital 753.8
  urethroscrotal 608.89
  urethrovaginal 619.0
  urethrovesical 596.2
  urethrovesicovaginal 619.0
  urinary (persistent) (recurrent) 599.1
  uteroabdominal (anterior wall) 619.2
    congenital 752.3
  uteroenteric 619.1
  uterofecal 619.1
  uterointestinal 619.1
    congenital 752.3
  uterorectal 619.1
    congenital 752.3
  uteroureteric 619.0
  uterovaginal 619.8
  uterovesical 619.0
    congenital 752.3
  uterus 619.8
  vagina (wall) 619.8
    postpartal, old 619.8
  vaginocutaneous (postpartal) 619.2
  vaginoileal (acquired) 619.1
  vaginoperineal 619.2
  vesical NEC 596.2
  vesicoabdominal 596.2
  vesicocervicovaginal 619.0
  vesicocolic 596.1
  vesicocutaneous 596.2
  vesicoenteric 596.1
  vesicointestinal 596.1
  vesicometrorectal 619.1
  vesicoperineal 596.2
  vesicorectal 596.1
    congenital 753.8
  vesicosigmoidal 596.1
  vesicosigmoidovaginal 619.1
  vesicoureteral 596.2
  vesicoureterovaginal 619.0
  vesicourethral 596.2
  vesicourethrorectal 596.1
  vesicouterine 619.0
    congenital 752.3
  vesicovaginal 619.0
  vulvorectal 619.1
    congenital 752.49
Fit 780.39
  apoplectic *(see also* Disease, cerebrovascular, acute) 436
    late effect - *see* Late effect(s) (of) cerebrovascular disease
  epileptic *(see also* Epilepsy) 345.9
  fainting 780.2
  hysterical 300.11
  newborn 779.0
Fitting (of)
  artificial
    arm (complete) (partial) V52.0
    breast V52.4
    eye(s) V52.2
    leg(s) (complete) (partial) V52.1
  brain neuropacemaker V53.02
  cardiac pacemaker V53.31
  carotid sinus pacemaker V53.39
  cerebral ventricle (communicating)
    shunt V53.01
  colostomy belt V55.3

Fitting *(Continued)*
  contact lenses V53.1
  cystostomy device V53.6
  defibrillator, automatic implantable
    cardiac V53.32
  dentures V52.3
  device NEC V53.9
    abdominal V53.5
    cardiac
      defibrillator, automatic implantable V53.32
      pacemaker V53.31
      specified NEC V53.39
    cerebral ventricle (communicating)
      shunt V53.01
    intrauterine contraceptive V25.1
    nervous system V53.09
    orthodontic V53.4
    orthoptic V53.1
    prosthetic V52.9
      breast V52.4
      dental V52.3
      eye V52.2
      specified type NEC V52.8
    special senses V53.09
    substitution
      auditory V53.09
      nervous system V53.09
      visual V53.09
    urinary V53.6
  diaphragm (contraceptive) V25.02
  glasses (reading) V53.1
  hearing aid V53.2
  ileostomy device V55.2
  intestinal appliance or device NEC
    V53.5
  intrauterine contraceptive device
    V25.1
  neuropacemaker (brain) (peripheral
    nerve) (spinal cord) V53.02
  orthodontic device V53.4
  orthopedic (device) V53.7
    brace V53.7
    cast V53.7
    corset V53.7
    shoes V53.7
  pacemaker (cardiac) V53.31
    brain V53.02
    carotid sinus V53.39
    peripheral nerve V53.02
    spinal cord V53.02
  prosthesis V52.9
    arm (complete) (partial) V52.0
    breast V52.4
    dental V52.3
    eye V52.2
    leg (complete) (partial) V52.1
    specified type NEC V52.8
  spectacles V53.1
  wheelchair V53.8
Fitz's syndrome (acute hemorrhagic pancreatitis) 577.0
Fitz-Hugh and Curtis syndrome (gonococcal peritonitis) 098.86
Fixation
  joint - *see* Ankylosis
  larynx 478.79
  pupil 364.76
  stapes 385.22
    deafness *(see also* Deafness, conductive) 389.04
  uterus (acquired) - *see* Malposition, uterus
  vocal cord 478.5

Flaccid - *see also* condition
  foot 736.79
  forearm 736.09
  palate, congenital 750.26
Flail
  chest 807.4
    newborn 767.3
  joint (paralytic) 718.80
    ankle 718.87
    elbow 718.82
    foot 718.87
    hand 718.84
    hip 718.85
    knee 718.86
    multiple sites 718.89
    pelvic region 718.85
    shoulder (region) 718.81
    specified site NEC 718.88
    wrist 718.83
Flajani (-Basedow) syndrome or disease
  (exophthalmic goiter) 242.0
Flap, liver 572.8
Flare, anterior chamber (aqueous) (eye)
  364.04
Flashback phenomena (drug) (hallucinogenic) 292.89
Flat
  chamber (anterior) (eye) 360.34
  chest, congenital 754.89
  electroencephalogram (EEG) 348.8
  foot (acquired) (fixed type) (painful)
    (postural) (spastic) 734
    congenital 754.61
      rocker bottom 754.61
      vertical talus 754.61
    rachitic 268.1
    rocker bottom (congenital) 754.61
    vertical talus, congenital 754.61
  organ or site, congenital NEC - *see*
    Anomaly, specified type NEC
  pelvis 738.6
    with disproportion (fetopelvic) 653.2
      affecting fetus or newborn 763.1
      causing obstructed labor 660.1
        affecting fetus or newborn 763.1
    congenital 755.69
Flatau-Schilder disease 341.1
Flattening
  head, femur 736.39
  hip 736.39
  lip (congenital) 744.89
  nose (congenital) 754.0
    acquired 738.0
Flatulence 787.3
Flatus 787.3
  vaginalis 629.8
Flax dressers' disease 504
Flea bite - *see* Injury, superficial, by site
Fleischer (-Kayser) ring (corneal pigmentation) 275.1 [371.14]
Fleischner's disease 732.3
Fleshy mole 631
Flexibilitas cerea (see also Catalepsy) 300.11
Flexion
  cervix *(see also* Malposition, uterus)
    621.6
  contracture, joint *(see also* Contraction,
    joint) 718.4
  deformity, joint *(see also* Contraction,
    joint) 718.4
    hip, congenital *(see also* Subluxation,
      congenital, hip) 754.32
  uterus *(see also* Malposition, uterus)
    621.6

Flexner's
  bacillus 004.1
  diarrhea (ulcerative) 004.1
  dysentery 004.1
Flexner-Boyd dysentery 004.2
Flexure - *see* condition
Floater, vitreous 379.24
Floating
  cartilage (joint) (*see also* Disorder, cartilage, articular) 718.0
    knee 717.6
  gallbladder (congenital) 751.69
  kidney 593.0
    congenital 753.3
  liver (congenital) 751.69
  rib 756.3
  spleen 289.59
Flooding 626.2
Floor - *see* condition
Floppy
  infant NEC 781.9
  valve syndrome (mitral) 424.0
Flu - *see also* Influenza
  gastric NEC 008.8
Fluctuating blood pressure 796.4
Fluid
  abdomen 789.5
  chest (*see also* Pleurisy, with effusion) 511.9
  heart (*see also* Failure, heart, congestive) 428.0
  joint (*see also* Effusion, joint) 719.0
  loss (acute) 276.5
    with
      hypernatremia 276.0
      hyponatremia 276.1
  lung - *see also* Edema, lung
    encysted 511.8
  peritoneal cavity 789.5
  pleural cavity (*see also* Pleurisy, with effusion) 511.9
  retention 276.6
Flukes NEC (*see also* Infestation, fluke) 121.9
  blood NEC (*see also* Infestation, Schistosoma) 120.9
  liver 121.3
Fluor (albus) (vaginalis) 623.5
  trichomonal (Trichomonas vaginalis) 131.00
Fluorosis (dental) (chronic) 520.3
Flushing 782.62
  menopausal 627.2
Flush syndrome 259.2
Flutter
  atrial or auricular 427.32
  heart (ventricular) 427.42
    atrial 427.32
  impure 427.32
  postoperative 997.1
  ventricular 427.42
Flux (bloody) (serosanguineous) 009.0
Focal - *see* condition
Fochier's abscess - *see* Abscess, by site
Focus, Assmann's (*see also* Tuberculosis) 011.0
Fogo selvagem 694.4
Foix-Alajouanine syndrome 336.1
Folds, anomalous - *see also* Anomaly, specified type NEC
  Bowman's membrane 371.31
  Descemet's membrane 371.32
  epicanthic 743.63
  heart 746.89

Folds, anomalous (*Continued*)
  posterior segment of eye, congenital 743.54
Folie deux 297.3
Follicle
  cervix (nabothian) (ruptured) 616.0
  graafian, ruptured, with hemorrhage 620.0
  nabothian 616.0
Folliclis (primary) (*see also* Tuberculosis) 017.0
Follicular - *see also* condition
  cyst (atretic) 620.0
Folliculitis 704.8
  abscedens et suffodiens 704.8
  decalvans 704.09
  gonorrheal (acute) 098.0
    chronic or duration of 2 months or more 098.2
  keloid, keloidalis 706.1
  pustular 704.8
  ulerythematosa reticulata 701.8
Folliculosis, conjunctival 372.02
Foølling's disease (phenylketonuria) 270.1
Follow-up (examination) (routine) (following) V67.9
  cancer chemotherapy V67.2
  chemotherapy V67.2
  fracture V67.4
  high-risk medication V67.51
  injury NEC V67.59
  postpartum
    immediately after delivery V24.0
    routine V24.2
  psychiatric V67.3
  psychotherapy V67.3
  radiotherapy V67.1
  specified condition NEC V67.59
  surgery V67.0
  treatment V67.9
    combined NEC V67.6
    fracture V67.4
    involving high-risk medication NEC V67.51
    mental disorder V67.3
    specified NEC V67.59
Fong's syndrome (hereditary osteoonychodysplasia) 756.89
Food
  allergy 693.1
  anaphylactic shock - *see* Anaphylactic shock, due to food
  asphyxia (from aspiration or inhalation) (*see also* Asphyxia, food) 933.1
  choked on (*see also* Asphyxia, food) 933.1
  deprivation 994.2
    specified kind of food NEC 269.8
  intoxication (*see also* Poisoning, food) 005.9
  lack of 994.2
  poisoning (*see also* Poisoning, food) 005.9
  refusal or rejection NEC 307.59
  strangulation or suffocation (*see also* Asphyxia, food) 933.1
  toxemia (*see also* Poisoning, food) 005.9
Foot - *see also* condition
  and mouth disease 078.4
  process disease 581.3
Foramen ovale (nonclosure) (patent) (persistent) 745.5

Forbes' (glycogen storage) disease 271.0
Forbes-Albright syndrome (nonpuerperal amenorrhea and lactation associated with pituitary tumor) 253.1
Forced birth or delivery NEC 669.8
  affecting fetus or newborn NEC 763.89
Forceps
  delivery NEC 669.5
    affecting fetus or newborn 763.2
Fordyce's disease (ectopic sebaceous glands) (mouth) 750.26
Fordyce-Fox disease (apocrine miliaria) 705.82
Forearm - *see* condition
Foreign body

> Note For foreign body with open wound or other injury, see Wound, open, or the type of injury specified.

  accidentally left during a procedure 998.4
  anterior chamber (eye) 871.6
    magnetic 871.5
      retained or old 360.51
    retained or old 360.61
  ciliary body (eye) 871.6
    magnetic 871.5
      retained or old 360.52
    retained or old 360.62
  entering through orifice (current) (old)
    accessory sinus 932
    air passage (upper) 933.0
      lower 934.8
    alimentary canal 938
    alveolar process 935.0
    antrum (Highmore) 932
    anus 937
    appendix 936
    asphyxia due to (*see also* Asphyxia, food) 933.1
    auditory canal 931
    auricle 931
    bladder 939.0
    bronchioles 934.8
    bronchus (main) 934.1
    buccal cavity 935.0
    canthus (inner) 930.1
    cecum 936
    cervix (canal) uterine 939.1
    coil, ileocecal 936
    colon 936
    conjunctiva 930.1
    conjunctival sac 930.1
    cornea 930.0
    digestive organ or tract NEC 938
    duodenum 936
    ear (external) 931
    esophagus 935.1
    eye (external) 930.9
      combined sites 930.8
      intraocular - *see* Foreign body, by site
      specified site NEC 930.8
    eyeball 930.8
      intraocular - *see* Foreign body, intraocular
    eyelid 930.1
      retained or old 374.86
    frontal sinus 932
    gastrointestinal tract 938

Foreign body *(Continued)*
  entering through orifice *(Continued)*
    genitourinary tract 939.9
    globe 930.8
      penetrating 871.6
        magnetic 871.5
          retained or old 360.50
        retained or old 360.60
    gum 935.0
    Highmore's antrum 932
    hypopharynx 933.0
    ileocecal coil 936
    ileum 936
    inspiration (of) 933.1
    intestine (large) (small) 936
    lacrimal apparatus, duct, gland, or
      sac 930.2
    larynx 933.1
    lung 934.8
    maxillary sinus 932
    mouth 935.0
    nasal sinus 932
    nasopharynx 933.0
    nose (passage) 932
    nostril 932
    oral cavity 935.0
    palate 935.0
    penis 939.3
    pharynx 933.0
    pyriform sinus 933.0
    rectosigmoid 937
      junction 937
    rectum 937
    respiratory tract 934.9
      specified part NEC 934.8
    sclera 930.1
    sinus 932
      accessory 932
      frontal 932
      maxillary 932
      nasal 932
      pyriform 933.0
    small intestine 936
    stomach (hairball) 935.2
    suffocation by *(see also* Asphyxia,
      food) 933.1
    swallowed 938
      tongue 933.0
    tear ducts or glands 930.2
    throat 933.0
    tongue 935.0
      swallowed 933.0
    tonsil, tonsillar 933.0
      fossa 933.0
    trachea 934.0
    ureter 939.0
    urethra 939.0
    uterus (any part) 939.1
    vagina 939.2
    vulva 939.2
    wind pipe 934.0
  granuloma (old) 728.82
    bone 733.99
    in operative wound (inadvertently
      left) 998.4
      due to surgical material intention-
        ally left - *see* Complications,
        due to (presence of) any de-
        vice, implant, or graft classi-
        fied to 996.0-996.5 NEC
    muscle 728.82
    skin 709.4
    soft tissue NEC 709.4
    subcutaneous tissue 709.4

Foreign body *(Continued)*
  in
    bone (residual) 733.99
    open wound - *see* Wound, open, by
      site complicated
    soft tissue (residual) 729.6
  inadvertently left in operation wound
    (causing adhesions, obstruction, or
    perforation) 998.4
  ingestion, ingested NEC 938
  inhalation or inspiration *(see also* As-
    phyxia, food) 933.1
  internal organ, not entering through
    an orifice - *see* Injury, internal, by
    site, with open wound
  intraocular (nonmagnetic) 871.6
    combined sites 871.6
      magnetic 871.5
        retained or old 360.59
      retained or old 360.69
    magnetic 871.5
      retained or old 360.50
    retained or old 360.60
    specified site NEC 871.6
      magnetic 871.5
        retained or old 360.59
      retained or old 360.69
    iris (nonmagnetic) 871.6
      magnetic 871.5
        retained or old 360.52
      retained or old 360.62
    lens (nonmagnetic) 871.6
      magnetic 871.5
        retained or old 360.53
      retained or old 360.63
    lid, eye 930.1
    ocular muscle 870.4
      retained or old 376.6
    old or residual
      bone 733.99
      eyelid 374.86
      middle ear 385.83
      muscle 729.6
        ocular 376.6
      retrobulbar 376.6
      skin 729.6
        with granuloma 709.4
      soft tissue 729.6
        with granuloma 709.4
      subcutaneous tissue 729.6
        with granuloma 709.4
    operation wound, left accidentally 998.4
    orbit 870.4
      retained or old 376.6
    posterior wall, eye 871.6
      magnetic 871.5
        retained or old 360.55
      retained or old 360.65
    respiratory tree 934.9
      specified site NEC 934.8
    retained (old) (nonmagnetic) (in)
      anterior chamber (eye) 360.61
        magnetic 360.51
      ciliary body 360.62
        magnetic 360.52
      eyelid 374.86
      globe 360.60
        magnetic 360.50
      intraocular 360.60
        magnetic 360.50
        specified site NEC 360.69
          magnetic 360.59
      iris 360.62
        magnetic 360.52

Foreign body *(Continued)*
  retained *(Continued)*
    lens 360.63
      magnetic 360.53
    muscle 729.6
    orbit 376.6
    posterior wall of globe 360.65
      magnetic 360.55
    retina 360.65
      magnetic 360.55
    retrobulbar 376.6
    skin 729.6
      with granuloma 709.4
    soft tissue 729.6
      with granuloma 709.4
    subcutaneous tissue 729.6
      with granuloma 709.4
    vitreous 360.64
      magnetic 360.54
  retina 871.6
    magnetic 871.5
      retained or old 360.55
    retained or old 360.65
  superficial, without major open wound
    (see also Injury, superficial, by site)
    919.6
  swallowed NEC 938
  vitreous (humor) 871.6
    magnetic 871.5
      retained or old 360.54
    retained or old 360.64
Forking, aqueduct of Sylvius 742.3
  with spina bifida *(see also* Spina bifida)
    741.0
Formation
  bone in scar tissue (skin) 709.3
  connective tissue in vitreous 379.25
  Elschnig pearls (postcataract extrac-
    tion) 366.51
  hyaline in cornea 371.49
  sequestrum in bone (due to infection)
    (see also Osteomyelitis) 730.1
  valve
    colon, congenital 751.5
    ureter (congenital) 753.29
Formication 782.0
Fort Bragg fever 100.89
Fossa - *see also* condition
  pyriform - *see* condition
Foster-Kennedy syndrome 377.04
Fothergill's
  disease, meaning scarlatina anginosa
    034.1
  neuralgia *(see also* Neuralgia, trigemi-
    nal) 350.1
Foul breath 784.9
Found dead (cause unknown) 798.9
Foundling V20.0
Fournier's disease (idiopathic gangrene)
  608.83
Fourth
  cranial nerve - *see* condition
  disease 057.8
  molar 520.1
Foville's syndrome 344.89
Fox's
  disease (apocrine miliaria) 705.82
  impetigo (contagiosa) 684
Fox-Fordyce disease (apocrine miliaria)
  705.82
Fracture (abduction) (adduction) (avulsion) (compression) (crush) (dislocation) (oblique) (separation) (closed)
  829.0

Fracture *(Continued)*

Note For fracture of any of the following sites with fracture of other bones, *see* Fracture, multiple.

"Closed" includes the following descriptions of fractures, with or without delayed healing, unless they are specified as open or compound:

   comminuted
   depressed
   elevated
   fissured
   greenstick
   impacted
   linear
   march
   simple
   slipped epiphysis
   spiral
   unspecified

"Open" includes the following descriptions of fractures, with or without delayed healing:

   compound
   infected
   missile
   puncture
   with foreign body

For late effect of fracture, *see* Late, effect, fracture, by site.

with
   internal injuries in same region (conditions classifiable to 860-869) - *see also* Injury, internal, by site
   pelvic region - *see* Fracture, pelvis
acetabulum (with visceral injury) (closed) 808.0
   open 808.1
acromion (process) (closed) 811.01
   open 811.11
alveolus (closed) 802.8
   open 802.9
ankle (malleolus) (closed) 824.8
   bimalleolar (Dupuytren's) (Pott's) 824.4
     open 824.5
   bone 825.21
     open 825.31
   lateral malleolus only (fibular) 824.2
     open 824.3
   medial malleolus only (tibial) 824.0
     open 824.1
   open 824.9
   pathologic 733.16
   talus 825.21
     open 825.31
   trimalleolar 824.6
     open 824.7
antrum - *see* Fracture, skull, base
arm (closed) 818.0
   and leg(s) (any bones) 828.0
     open 828.1
   both (any bones) (with rib(s)) (with sternum) 819.0
     open 819.1
   lower 813.80
     open 813.90
   open 818.1
   upper - *see* Fracture, humerus

Fracture *(Continued)*

astragalus (closed) 825.21
   open 825.31
atlas - *see* Fracture, vertebra, cervical, first
axis - *see* Fracture, vertebra, cervical, second
back - *see* Fracture, vertebra, by site
Barton's - *see* Fracture, radius, lower end
basal (skull) - *see* Fracture, skull, base
Bennett's (closed) 815.01
   open 815.11
bimalleolar (closed) 824.4
   open 824.5
bone (closed) NEC 829.0
   birth injury NEC 767.3
   open 829.1
   pathological NEC (*see also* Fracture, pathologic) 733.10
boot top - *see* Fracture, fibula
boxers' - *see* Fracture, metacarpal bone(s)
breast bone - *see* Fracture, sternum
bucket handle (semilunar cartilage) - *see* Tear, meniscus
bursting - *see* Fracture, phalanx, hand, distal
calcaneus (closed) 825.0
   open 825.1
capitate (bone) (closed) 814.07
   open 814.17
capitellum (humerus) (closed) 812.49
   open 812.59
carpal bone(s) (wrist NEC) (closed) 814.00
   open 814.10
   specified site NEC 814.09
     open 814.19
cartilage, knee (semilunar) - *see* Tear, meniscus
cervical - *see* Fracture, vertebra, cervical
chauffeur's - *see* Fracture, ulna, lower end
chisel - *see* Fracture, radius, upper end
clavicle (interligamentous part) (closed) 810.00
   acromial end 810.03
     open 810.13
   due to birth trauma 767.2
   open 810.10
   shaft (middle third) 810.02
     open 810.12
   sternal end 810.01
     open 810.11
clayshovelers' - *see* Fracture, vertebra, cervical
coccyx - *see also* Fracture, vertebra, coccyx
   complicating delivery 665.6
collar bone - *see* Fracture, clavicle
Colles' (reversed) (closed) 813.41
   open 813.51
comminuted - *see* Fracture, by site
compression - *see also* Fracture, by site
   nontraumatic - *see* Fracture, pathologic
congenital 756.9
coracoid process (closed) 811.02
   open 811.12
coronoid process (ulna) (closed) 813.02
   mandible (closed) 802.23
     open 802.33
   open 813.12

Fracture *(Continued)*

costochondral junction - *see* Fracture, rib
costosternal junction - *see* Fracture, rib
cranium - *see* Fracture, skull, by site
cricoid cartilage (closed) 807.5
   open 807.6
cuboid (ankle) (closed) 825.23
   open 825.33
cuneiform
   foot (closed) 825.24
     open 825.34
   wrist (closed) 814.03
     open 814.13
due to
   birth injury - *see* Birth injury, fracture
   gunshot - *see* Fracture, by site, open
   neoplasm - *see* Fracture, pathologic
   osteoporosis - *see* Fracture, pathologic
Dupuytren's (ankle) (fibula) (closed) 824.4
   open 824.5
   radius 813.42
     open 813.52
Duverney's - *see* Fracture, ilium
elbow - *see also* Fracture, humerus, lower end
   olecranon (process) (closed) 813.01
     open 813.11
   supracondylar (closed) 812.41
     open 812.51
ethmoid (bone) (sinus) - *see* Fracture, skull, base
face bone(s) (closed) NEC 802.8
   with
     other bone(s) - *see* Fracture, multiple, skull
     skull - *see also* Fracture, skull
       involving other bones - *see* Fracture, multiple, skull
   open 802.9
fatigue - *see* Fracture, march
femur, femoral (closed) 821.00
   cervicotrochanteric 820.03
     open 820.13
   condyles, epicondyles 821.21
     open 821.31
   distal end - *see* Fracture, femur, lower end
   epiphysis (separation)
     capital 820.01
       open 820.11
     head 820.01
       open 820.11
     lower 821.22
       open 821.32
     trochanteric 820.01
       open 820.11
     upper 820.01
       open 820.11
   head 820.09
     open 820.19
   lower end or extremity (distal end) (closed) 821.20
     condyles, epicondyles 821.21
       open 821.31
     epiphysis (separation) 821.22
       open 821.32
     multiple sites 821.29
       open 821.39
     open 821.30
     specified site NEC 821.29
       open 821.39

Fracture *(Continued)*
  hyperextension - *see* Fracture, radius,
    lower end
  ilium (with visceral injury) (closed)
    808.41
    open 808.51
  impaction, impacted - *see* Fracture, by
    site
  incus - *see* Fracture, skull, base
  innominate bone (with visceral injury)
    (closed) 808.49
    open 808.59
  instep, of one foot (closed) 825.20
    with toe(s) of same foot 827.0
      open 827.1
    open 825.30
  internal
    ear - *see* Fracture, skull, base
    semilunar cartilage, knee - *see* Tear,
      meniscus, medial
  intertrochanteric - *see* Fracture, femur,
    neck, intertrochanteric
  ischium (with visceral injury) (closed)
    808.42
    open 808.52
  jaw (bone) (lower) (closed) *(see also*
    Fracture, mandible) 802.20
    angle 802.25
      open 802.35
    open 802.30
    upper - *see* Fracture, maxilla
  knee
    cap (closed) 822.0
      open 822.1
    cartilage (semilunar) - *see* Tear, me-
      niscus
  labyrinth (osseous) - *see* Fracture, skull,
    base
  larynx (closed) 807.5
    open 807.6
  late effect - *see* Late, effects (of), frac-
    ture
  Le Fort's - *see* Fracture, maxilla
  leg (closed) 827.0
    with rib(s) or sternum 828.0
      open 828.1
    both (any bones) 828.0
      open 828.1
    lower - *see* Fracture, tibia
    open 827.1
    upper - *see* Fracture, femur
  limb
    lower (multiple) (closed) NEC 827.0
      open 827.1
    upper (multiple) (closed) NEC 818.0
      open 818.1
  long bones, due to birth trauma - *see*
    Birth injury, fracture
  lumbar - *see* Fracture, vertebra, lum-
    bar
  lunate bone (closed) 814.02
    open 814.12
  malar bone (closed) 802.4
    open 802.5
  Malgaigne's (closed) 808.43
    open 808.53
  malleolus (closed) 824.8
    bimalleolar 824.4
      open 824.5
    lateral 824.2
      and medial - *see also* Fracture,
        malleolus, bimalleolar
        with lip of tibia - *see* Fracture,
          malleolus, trimalleolar

Fracture *(Continued)*
  malleolus *(Continued)*
    lateral *(Continued)*
      open 824.3
    medial (closed) 824.0
      and lateral - *see also* Fracture, mal-
        leolus, bimalleolar
        with lip of tibia - *see* Fracture,
          malleolus, trimalleolar
      open 824.1
    open 824.9
    trimalleolar (closed) 824.6
      open 824.7
  malleus - *see* Fracture, skull, base
  malunion 733.81
  mandible (closed) 802.20
    angle 802.25
      open 802.35
    body 802.28
      alveolar border 802.27
        open 802.37
        open 802.38
      symphysis 802.26
        open 802.36
    condylar process 802.21
      open 802.31
    coronoid process 802.23
      open 802.33
    multiple sites 802.29
      open 802.39
    open 802.30
    ramus NEC 802.24
      open 802.34
    subcondylar 802.22
      open 802.32
  manubrium - *see* Fracture, sternum
  march (closed) 825.20
    open 825.30
  maxilla, maxillary (superior) (upper
    jaw) (closed) 802.4
    inferior - *see* Fracture, mandible
    open 802.5
  meniscus, knee - *see* Tear, meniscus
  metacarpus, metacarpal (bone(s)), of
    one hand (closed) 815.00
    with phalanx, phalanges, hand (fin-
      ger(s)) (thumb) of same hand
      817.0
      open 817.1
    base 815.02
      first metacarpal 815.01
        open 815.11
      open 815.12
      thumb 815.01
        open 815.11
    multiple sites 815.09
      open 815.19
    neck 815.04
      open 815.14
    open 815.10
    shaft 815.03
      open 815.13
  metatarsus, metatarsal (bone(s)), of one
    foot (closed) 825.25
    with tarsal bone(s) 825.29
      open 825.39
    open 825.35
  Monteggia's (closed) 813.03
    open 813.13
  Moore's - *see* Fracture, radius, lower
    end multangular bone (closed)
    larger 814.05
      open 814.15
    smaller 814.06

Fracture *(Continued)*
  Moore's *(Continued)*
    smaller *(Continued)*
      open 814.16
  multiple (closed) 829.0

> **Note** Multiple fractures of sites clas-
> sifiable to the same three- or four-
> digit category are coded to that cate-
> gory, except for sites classifiable to
> 810-818 or 820-827 in different limbs.
>
> Multiple fractures of sites classifiable
> to different fourth-digit subdivisions
> within the same three-digit category
> should be dealt with according to
> coding rules.
>
> Multiple fractures of sites classifiable
> to different three-digit categories
> (identifiable from the listing under
> "Fracture"), and of sites classifiable to
> 810-818 or 820-827 in different limbs
> should be coded according to the fol-
> lowing list, which should be referred
> to in the following priority order:
> skull or face bones, pelvis or verte-
> bral column, legs, arms.

    arm (multiple bones in same arm
      except in hand alone) (sites clas-
      sifiable to 810-817 with sites
      classifiable to a different three-
      digit category in 810-817 in
      same arm) (closed) 818.0
    open 818.1
    arms, both or arm(s) with rib(s) or
      sternum (sites classifiable to
      810-818 with sites classifiable to
      same range of categories in
      other limb or to 807) (closed)
      819.0
    open 819.1
    bones of trunk NEC (closed) 809.0
      open 809.1
    hand, metacarpal bone(s) with pha-
      lanx or phalanges of same hand
      (sites classifiable to 815 with
      sites classifiable to 816 in same
      hand) (closed) 817.0
    open 817.1
    leg (multiple bones in same leg)
      (sites classifiable to 820-826 with
      sites classifiable to a different
      three-digit category in that
      range in same leg) (closed) 827.0
    open 827.1
    legs, both or leg(s) with arm(s),
      rib(s), or sternum (sites classifia-
      ble to 820-827 with sites classifi-
      able to same range of categories
      in other leg or to 807 or 810-
      819) (closed) 828.0
    open 828.1
    open 829.1
    pelvis with other bones except skull
      or face bones (sites classifiable
      to 808 with sites classifiable to
      805-807 or 810-829) (closed)
      809.0
      open 809.1
    skull, specified or unspecified bones,
      or face bone(s) with any other
      bone(s) (sites classifiable to 800-
      803 with sites classifiable to 805-
      829) (closed) 804.0

Fracture (*Continued*)
  multiple (*Continued*)

> Note   Use the following fifth-digit subclassification with categories 800, 801, 803, and 804:
>
>   0   unspecified state of consciousness
>   1   with no loss of consciousness
>   2   with brief [less than one hour] loss of consciousness
>   3   with moderate [1-24 hours] loss of consciousness
>   4   with prolonged [more than 24 hours] loss of consciousness and return to pre-existing conscious level
>   5   with prolonged [more than 24 hours] loss of consciousness, without return to pre-existing conscious level
>
> Use fifth-digit 5 to designate when a patient is unconscious and dies before regaining consciousness, regardless of the duration of the loss of consciousness
>
>   6   with loss of consciousness of unspecified duration
>   9   with concussion, unspecified

  with
    contusion, cerebral 804.1
    epidural hemorrhage 804.2
    extradural hemorrhage 804.2
    hemorrhage (intracranial) NEC 804.3
    intracranial injury NEC 804.4
    laceration, cerebral 804.1
    subarachnoid hemorrhage 804.2
    subdural hemorrhage 804.2
  open 804.5
    with
      contusion, cerebral 804.6
      epidural hemorrhage 804.7
      extradural hemorrhage 804.7
      hemorrhage (intracranial) NEC 804.8
      intracranial injury NEC 804.9
      laceration, cerebral 804.6
      subarachnoid hemorrhage 804.7
      subdural hemorrhage 804.7
      vertebral column with other bones, except skull or face bones (sites classifiable to 805 or 806 with sites classifiable to 807-808 or 810-829) (closed) 809.0
        open 809.1
  nasal (bone(s)) (closed) 802.0
    open 802.1
    sinus - *see* Fracture, skull, base
  navicular
    carpal (wrist) (closed) 814.01
      open 814.11
    tarsal (ankle) (closed) 825.22
      open 825.32
  neck - *see* Fracture, vertebra, cervical
  neural arch - *see* Fracture, vertebra, by site
  nonunion 733.82
  nose, nasal, (bone) (septum) (closed) 802.0
    open 802.1
  occiput - *see* Fracture, skull, base

Fracture (*Continued*)
  odontoid process - *see* Fracture, vertebra, cervical
  olecranon (process) (ulna) (closed) 813.01
    open 813.11
  open 829.1
  orbit, orbital (bone) (region) (closed) 802.8
    floor (blow-out) 802.6
      open 802.7
    open 802.9
    roof - *see* Fracture, skull, base
    specified part NEC 802.8
      open 802.9
  os
    calcis (closed) 825.0
      open 825.1
    magnum (closed) 814.07
      open 814.17
    pubis (with visceral injury) (closed) 808.2
      open 808.3
    triquetrum (closed) 814.03
      open 814.13
  osseous
    auditory meatus - *see* Fracture, skull, base
    labyrinth - *see* Fracture, skull, base
  ossicles, auditory (incus) (malleus) (stapes) - *see* Fracture, skull, base
  osteoporotic - *see* Fracture, pathologic
  palate (closed) 802.8
    open 802.9
  paratrooper - *see* Fracture, tibia, lower end
  parietal bone - *see* Fracture, skull, vault
  parry - *see* Fracture, Monteggia's
  patella (closed) 822.0
    open 822.1
  pathologic (cause unknown) 733.10
    ankle 733.16
    femur (neck) 733.14
      specified NEC 733.15
    fibula 733.16
    hip 733.14
    humerus 733.11
    radius (distal) 733.12
    specified site NEC 733.19
    tibia 733.16
    ulna 733.12
    vertebrae (collapse) 733.13
    wrist 733.12
  pedicle (of vertebral arch) - *see* Fracture, vertebra, by site
  pelvis, pelvic (bone(s)) (with visceral injury) (closed) 808.8
    multiple (with disruption of pelvic circle) 808.43
      open 808.53
    open 808.9
    rim (closed) 808.49
      open 808.59
  peritrochanteric (closed) 820.20
    open 820.30
  phalanx, phalanges, of one
    foot (closed) 826.0
      with bone(s) of same lower limb 827.0
        open 827.1
      open 826.1
    hand (closed) 816.00

Fracture (*Continued*)
  phalanx, phalanges, of one (*Continued*)
    hand (*Continued*)
      with metacarpal bone(s) of same hand 817.0
        open 817.1
      distal 816.02
        open 816.12
      middle 816.01
        open 816.11
      multiple sites NEC 816.03
        open 816.13
      open 816.10
      proximal 816.01
        open 816.11
  pisiform (closed) 814.04
    open 814.14
  pond - *see* Fracture, skull, vault
  Pott's (closed) 824.4
    open 824.5
  prosthetic device, internal - *see* Complications, mechanical
  pubis (with visceral injury) (closed) 808.2
    open 808.3
  Quervain's (closed) 814.01
    open 814.11
  radius (alone) (closed) 813.81
    with ulna NEC 813.83
      open 813.93
    distal end - *see* Fracture, radius, lower end
    epiphysis
      lower - *see* Fracture, radius, lower end
      upper - *see* Fracture, radius, upper end
    head - *see* Fracture, radius, upper end
    lower end or extremity (distal end) (lower epiphysis) 813.42
      with ulna (lower end) 813.44
        open 813.54
      open 813.52
    neck - *see* Fracture, radius, upper end
    open NEC 813.91
    pathologic 733.12
    proximal end - *see* Fracture, radius, upper end
    shaft (closed) 813.21
      with ulna (shaft) 813.23
        open 813.33
      open 813.31
    upper end 813.07
      with ulna (upper end) 813.08
        open 813.18
      epiphysis 813.05
        open 813.15
      head 813.05
        open 813.15
      multiple sites 813.07
        open 813.17
      neck 813.06
        open 813.17
      specified site NEC 813.07
        open 813.17
  ramus
    inferior or superior (with visceral injury) (closed) 808.2
      open 808.3
    ischium - *see* Fracture, ischium

Fracture (*Continued*)
  ramus (*Continued*)
    mandible 802.24
      open 802.34
  rib(s) (closed) 807.0

Note   Use the following fifth-digit
subclassification with categories
807.0-807.1:

  0   rib(s), unspecified
  1   one rib
  2   two ribs
  3   three ribs
  4   four ribs
  5   five ribs
  6   six ribs
  7   seven ribs
  8   eight or more ribs
  9   multiple ribs, unspecified

---

    with flail chest (open) 807.4
    open 807.1
  root, tooth 873.63
    complicated 873.73
  sacrum - *see* Fracture, vertebra, sacrum
  scaphoid
    ankle (closed) 825.22
      open 825.32
    wrist (closed) 814.01
      open 814.11
  scapula (closed) 811.00
    acromial, acromion (process) 811.01
      open 811.11
    body 811.09
      open 811.19
    coracoid process 811.02
      open 811.12
    glenoid (cavity) (fossa) 811.03
      open 811.13
    neck 811.03
      open 811.13
    open 811.10
  semilunar
    bone, wrist (closed) 814.02
      open 814.12
    cartilage (interior) (knee) - *see* Tear,
      meniscus
  sesamoid bone - *see* Fracture, by site
  Shepherd's (closed) 825.21
    open 825.31
  shoulder - *see also* Fracture, humerus,
    upper end
    blade - *see* Fracture, scapula
  silverfork - *see* Fracture, radius, lower
    end
  sinus (ethmoid) (frontal) (maxillary)
    (nasal) (sphenoidal) - *see* Fracture,
    skull, base
  Skillern's - *see* Fracture, radius, shaft
  skull (multiple NEC) (with face bones)
    (closed) 803.0

Note   Use the following fifth-digit
subclassification with categories 800,
801, 803, and 804:

  0   unspecified state of conscious-
    ness
  1   with no loss of consciousness
  2   with brief [less than one hour]
    loss of consciousness
  3   with moderate [1-24 hours]
    loss of consciousness
  4   with prolonged [more than 24
    hours] loss of consciousness

Fracture (*Continued*)
      and return to pre-existing con-
      scious level
  5   with prolonged [more than 24
    hours] loss of consciousness,
    without return to pre-existing
    conscious level

Use fifth-digit 5 to designate when a
patient is unconscious and dies before regaining consciousness, regardless of the duration of the loss of consciousness

  6   with loss of consciousness of
    unspecified duration
  9   with concussion, unspecified

---

    with
      contusion, cerebral 803.1
      epidural hemorrhage 803.2
      extradural hemorrhage 803.2
      hemorrhage (intracranial) NEC
        803.3
      intracranial injury NEC 803.4
      laceration, cerebral 803.1
      other bones - *see* Fracture, multi-
        ple, skull
      subarachnoid hemorrhage 803.2
      subdural hemorrhage 803.2
    base (antrum) (ethmoid bone) (fossa)
      (internal ear) (nasal sinus) (occi-
      put) (sphenoid) (temporal bone)
      (closed) 801.0
      with
        contusion, cerebral 801.1
        epidural hemorrhage 801.2
        extradural hemorrhage 801.2
        hemorrhage (intracranial) NEC
          801.3
        intracranial injury NEC 801.4
        laceration, cerebral 801.1
        subarachnoid hemorrhage
          801.2
        subdural hemorrhage 801.2
      open 801.5
        with
          contusion, cerebral 801.6
          epidural hemorrhage 801.7
          extradural hemorrhage 801.7
          hemorrhage (intracranial)
            NEC 801.8
          intracranial injury NEC 801.9
          laceration, cerebral 801.6
          subarachnoid hemorrhage
            801.7
          subdural hemorrhage 801.7
    birth injury 767.3
    face bones - *see* Fracture, face bones
    open 803.5
      with
        contusion, cerebral 803.6
        epidural hemorrhage 803.7
        extradural hemorrhage 803.7
        hemorrhage (intracranial) NEC
          803.8
        intracranial injury NEC 803.9
        laceration, cerebral 803.6
        subarachnoid hemorrhage 803.7
        subdural hemorrhage 803.7
    vault (frontal bone) (parietal bone)
      (vertex) (closed) 800.0
      with
        contusion, cerebral 800.1
        epidural hemorrhage 800.2

Fracture (*Continued*)
  skull (*Continued*)
    vault (*Continued*)
      with (*Continued*)
        extradural hemorrhage 800.2
        hemorrhage (intracranial) NEC
          800.3
        intracranial injury NEC 800.4
        laceration, cerebral 800.1
        subarachnoid hemorrhage 800.2
        subdural hemorrhage 800.2
      open 800.5
        with
          contusion, cerebral 800.6
          epidural hemorrhage 800.7
          extradural hemorrhage 800.7
          hemorrhage (intracranial)
            NEC 800.8
          intracranial injury NEC 800.9
          laceration, cerebral 800.6
          subarachnoid hemorrhage
            800.7
          subdural hemorrhage 800.7
  Smith's 813.41
    open 813.51
  sphenoid (bone) (sinus) - *see* Fracture,
    skull, base
  spine - *see also* Fracture, vertebra, by
    site due to birth trauma 767.4
  spinous process - *see* Fracture, verte-
    bra, by site
  spontaneous - *see* Fracture, pathologic
  sprinters' - *see* Fracture, ilium
  stapes - *see* Fracture, skull, base
  stave - *see also* Fracture, metacarpus,
    metacarpal bone(s)
    spine - *see* Fracture, tibia, upper end
  sternum (closed) 807.2
    with flail chest (open) 807.4
    open 807.3
  Stieda's - *see* Fracture, femur, lower
    end
  stress - *see* Fracture, pathologic
  styloid process
    metacarpal (closed) 815.02
      open 815.12
    radius - *see* Fracture, radius, lower
      end
    temporal bone - *see* Fracture, skull,
      base
    ulna - *see* Fracture, ulna, lower end
  supracondylar, elbow 812.41
    open 812.51
  symphysis pubis (with visceral injury)
    (closed) 808.2
    open 808.3
  talus (ankle bone) (closed) 825.21
    open 825.31
  tarsus, tarsal bone(s) (with metatarsus)
    of one foot (closed) NEC 825.29
    open 825.39
  temporal bone (styloid) - *see* Fracture,
    skull, base
  tendon - *see* Sprain, by site
  thigh - *see* Fracture, femur, shaft
  thumb (and finger(s)) of one hand
    (closed) (*see also* Fracture, phalanx,
    hand) 816.00
    with metacarpal bone(s) of same
      hand 817.0
      open 817.1
    metacarpal(s) - *see* Fracture, metacar-
      pus
    open 816.10

Fracture *(Continued)*
  thyroid cartilage (closed) 807.5
    open 807.6
  tibia (closed) 823.80
    with fibula 823.82
      open 823.92
    condyles - *see* Fracture, tibia, upper
      end
    distal end 824.8
      open 824.9
    epiphysis
      lower 824.8
        open 824.9
      upper - *see* Fracture, tibia, upper
        end
    head (involving knee joint) - *see*
      Fracture, tibia, upper end
    intercondyloid eminence - *see* Frac-
      ture, tibia, upper end
    involving ankle 824.0
      open 824.1
    lower end or extremity (anterior lip)
      (posterior lip) 824.8
      open 824.9
    malleolus (internal) (medial) 824.0
      open 824.1
    open NEC 823.90
    pathologic 733.16
    proximal end - *see* Fracture, tibia,
      upper end
    shaft 823.20
      with fibula 823.22
        open 823.32
      open 823.30
    spine - *see* Fracture, tibia, upper end
    tuberosity - *see* Fracture, tibia, upper
      end
    upper end or extremity (condyle)
      (epiphysis) (head) (spine) (prox-
      imal end) (tuberosity)
      823.00
      with fibula 823.02
        open 823.12
      open 823.10
  toe(s), of one foot (closed) 826.0
    with bone(s) of same lower limb
      827.0
      open 827.1
    open 826.1
  tooth (root) 873.63
    complicated 873.73
  trachea (closed) 807.5
    open 807.6
  transverse process - *see* Fracture, verte-
    bra, by site
  trapezium (closed) 814.05
    open 814.15
  trapezoid bone (closed) 814.06
    open 814.16
  trimalleolar (closed) 824.6
    open 824.7
  triquetral (bone) (closed) 814.03
    open 814.13
  trochanter (greater) (lesser) (closed)
    (*see also* Fracture, femur, neck, by
    site) 820.20
    open 820.30
  trunk (bones) (closed) 809.0
    open 809.1
  tuberosity (external) - *see* Fracture, by
    site
  ulna (alone) (closed) 813.82
    with radius NEC 813.83
      open 813.93

Fracture *(Continued)*
  ulna *(Continued)*
    coronoid process (closed) 813.02
      open 813.12
    distal end - *see* Fracture, ulna, lower
      end
    epiphysis
      lower - *see* Fracture, ulna, lower
        end
      upper - *see* Fracture, ulna, upper,
        end
    head - *see* Fracture, ulna, lower end
    lower end (distal end) (head) (lower
      epiphysis) (styloid process)
      813.43
      with radius (lower end)
        813.44
        open 813.54
      open 813.53
    olecranon process (closed)
      813.01
      open 813.11
    open NEC 813.92
    pathologic 733.12
    proximal end - *see* Fracture, ulna,
      upper end
    shaft 813.22
      with radius (shaft) 813.23
        open 813.33
      open 813.32
    styloid process - *see* Fracture, ulna,
      lower end
    transverse - *see* Fracture, ulna, by
      site
    upper end (epiphysis) 813.04
      with radius (upper end)
        813.08
        open 813.18
      multiple sites 813.04
        open 813.14
      open 813.14
      specified site NEC 813.04
        open 813.14
  unciform (closed) 814.08
    open 814.18
  vertebra, vertebral (back) (body) (col-
    umn) (neural arch) (pedicle)
    (spine) (spinous process) (trans-
    verse process) (closed) 805.8
    with
      hematomyelia - *see* Fracture, verte-
        bra, by site, with spinal cord
        injury
      injury to
        cauda equina - *see* Fracture, ver-
          tebra, sacrum, with spinal
          cord injury
        nerve - *see* Fracture, vertebra,
          by site, with spinal cord
          injury
        paralysis - *see* Fracture, vertebra,
          by site, with spinal cord in-
          jury
        paraplegia - *see* Fracture, vertebra,
          by site, with spinal cord in-
          jury
        quadriplegia - *see* Fracture, verte-
          bra, by site, with spinal cord
          injury
        spinal concussion - *see* Fracture,
          vertebra, by site, with spinal
          cord injury
      spinal cord injury (closed) NEC
        806.8

Fracture *(Continued)*
  vertebra, vertebral *(Continued)*
    with *(Continued)*

> Note   Use the following fifth-digit
> subclassification with categories
> 806.0-806.3:
>
> C_1-C_4 or unspecified level and D_1-D_6
> (T_1-T_6) or unspecified level with:
>
>   0   unspecified spinal cord injury
>   1   complete lesion of cord
>   2   anterior cord syndrome
>   3   central cord syndrome
>   4   specified injury NEC
>
> level and D_1-D_{12} level with:
>
>   5   unspecified spinal cord injury
>   6   complete lesion of cord
>   7   anterior cord syndrome
>   8   central cord syndrome
>   9   specified injury NEC

      cervical 806.0
        open 806.1
      dorsal, dorsolumbar 806.2
        open 806.3
      thoracic, thoracolumbar 806.2
        open 806.3
    atlanto-axial - *see* Fracture, vertebra,
      cervical
    cervical (hangman) (teardrop) (closed)
      805.00
      with spinal cord injury - *see* Frac-
        ture, vertebra, with spinal cord
        injury, cervical
      first (atlas) 805.01
        open 805.11
      second (axis) 805.02
        open 805.12
      third 805.03
        open 805.13
      fourth 805.04
        open 805.14
      fifth 805.05
        open 805.15
      sixth 805.06
        open 805.16
      seventh 805.07
        open 805.17
      multiple sites 805.08
        open 805.18
      open 805.10
    coccyx (closed) 805.6
      with spinal cord injury (closed)
        806.60
        cauda equina injury 806.62
          complete lesion 806.61
            open 806.71
          open 806.72
        open 806.70
        specified type NEC 806.69
          open 806.79
      open 805.7
    collapsed 733.13
    compression, not due to trauma
      733.13
    dorsal (closed) 805.2
      with spinal cord injury -
        see Fracture, vertebra, with
        spinal cord injury,
        dorsal
      open 805.3
    dorsolumbar (closed) 805.2

◀▶   New Code   ⬅⮕   Revised Code

Fracture *(Continued)*
coccyx *(Continued)*
dorsolumbar *(Continued)*
with spinal cord injury - *see* Fracture, vertebra, with spinal cord injury, dorsal
open 805.3
due to osteoporosis 733.13
fetus or newborn 767.4
lumbar (closed) 805.4
with spinal cord injury (closed) 806.4
open 806.5
open 805.5
nontraumatic 733.13
open NEC 805.9
pathologic (any site) 733.13
sacrum (closed) 805.6
with spinal cord injury 806.60
cauda equina injury 806.62
complete lesion 806.61
open 806.71
open 806.72
open 806.70
specified type NEC 806.69
open 806.79
open 805.7
site unspecified (closed) 805.8
with spinal cord injury (closed) 806.8
open 806.9
open 805.9
thoracic (closed) 805.2
with spinal cord injury - *see* Fracture, vertebra, with spinal cord injury, thoracic
open 805.3
vertex - *see* Fracture, skull, vault
vomer (bone) 802.0
open 802.1
Wagstaffe's - *see* Fracture, ankle
wrist (closed) 814.00
open 814.10
pathologic 733.12
xiphoid (process) - *see* Fracture, sternum
zygoma (zygomatic arch) (closed) 802.4
open 802.5
Fragile X syndrome 759.83
Fragilitas
crinium 704.2
hair 704.2
ossium 756.51
with blue sclera 756.51
unguium 703.8
congenital 757.5
Fragility
bone 756.51
with deafness and blue sclera 756.51
capillary (hereditary) 287.8
hair 704.2
nails 703.8
Fragmentation - *see* Fracture, by site
Frambesia, frambesial (tropica) *(see also* Yaws)* 102.9
initial lesion or ulcer 102.0
primary 102.0
Frambeside
gummatous 102.4
of early yaws 102.2
Frambesioma 102.1

Franceschetti's syndrome (mandibulofacial dysostosis) 756.0
Francis' disease *(see also* Tularemia) 021.9
Frank's essential thrombocytopenia *(see also* Purpura, thrombocytopenic) 287.3
Franklin's disease (heavy chain) 273.2
Fraser's syndrome 759.89
Freckle 709.09
malignant melanoma in (M8742/3) - *see* Melanoma
melanotic (of Hutchinson) (M8742/2) - *see* Neoplasm, skin, in situ
Freeman-Sheldon syndrome 759.89
Freezing 991.9
specified effect NEC 991.8
Frei's disease (climatic bubo) 099.1
Freiberg's
disease (osteochondrosis, second metatarsal) 732.5
infraction of metatarsal head 732.5
osteochondrosis 732.5
Fremitus, friction, cardiac 785.3
Frenulum linguae 750.0
Frenum
external os 752.49
tongue 750.0
Frequency (urinary) NEC 788.41
micturition 788.41
nocturnal 788.43
polyuria 788.42
psychogenic 306.53
Frey's syndrome (auriculotemporal syndrome) 350.8
Friction
burn *(see also* Injury, superficial, by site) 919.0
fremitus, cardiac 785.3
precordial 785.3
sounds, chest 786.7
Friderichsen-Waterhouse syndrome or disease 036.3
Friedländer's
B (bacillus) NEC *(see also* condition) 041.3
sepsis or septicemia 038.49
disease (endarteritis obliterans) - *see* Arteriosclerosis
Friedreich's
ataxia 334.0
combined systemic disease 334.0
disease 333.2
combined systemic 334.0
myoclonia 333.2
sclerosis (spinal cord) 334.0
Friedrich-Erb-Arnold syndrome (acropachyderma) 757.39
Frigidity 302.72
psychic or psychogenic 302.72
Fröhlich's disease or syndrome (adiposogenital dystrophy) 253.8
Froin's syndrome 336.8
Frommel's disease 676.6
Frommel-Chiari syndrome 676.6
Frontal - *see also* condition
lobe syndrome 310.0
Frostbite 991.3
face 991.0
foot 991.2
hand 991.1
specified site NEC 991.3
Frotteurism 302.89

Frozen 991.9
pelvis 620.8
shoulder 726.0
Fructosemia 271.2
Fructosuria (benign) (essential) 271.2
Fuchs'
black spot (myopic) 360.21
corneal dystrophy (endothelial) 371.57
heterochromic cyclitis 364.21
Fucosidosis 271.8
Fugue 780.9
hysterical (dissociative) 300.13
reaction to exceptional stress (transient) 308.1
Fuller Albright's syndrome (osteitis fibrosa disseminata) 756.59
Fuller's earth disease 502
Fulminant, fulminating - *see* condition
Functional - *see* condition
Fundus - *see also* condition
flavimaculatus 362.76
Fungemia 117.9
Fungus, fungous
cerebral 348.8
disease NEC 117.9
infection - *see* Infection, fungus
testis *(see also* Tuberculosis) 016.5 *[608.81]*
Funiculitis (acute) 608.4
chronic 608.4
endemic 608.4
gonococcal (acute) 098.14
chronic or duration of 2 months or over 098.34
tuberculous *(see also* Tuberculosis) 016.5
FUO *(see also* Pyrexia) 780.6
Funnel
breast (acquired) 738.3
congenital 754.81
late effect of rickets 268.1
chest (acquired) 738.3
congenital 754.81
late effect of rickets 268.1
pelvis (acquired) 738.6
with disproportion (fetopelvic) 653.3
affecting fetus or newborn 763.1
causing obstructed labor 660.1
affecting fetus or newborn 763.1
congenital 755.69
tuberculous *(see also* Tuberculosis) 016.9
Furfur 690.18
microsporon 111.0
Furor, paroxysmal (idiopathic) *(see also* Epilepsy) 345.8
Furriers' lung 495.8
Furrowed tongue 529.5
congenital 750.13
Furrowing nail(s) (transverse) 703.8
congenital 757.5
Furuncle 680.9
abdominal wall 680.2
ankle 680.6
anus 680.5
arm (any part, above wrist) 680.3
auditory canal, external 680.0
axilla 680.3
back (any part) 680.2
breast 680.2
buttock 680.5
chest wall 680.2
corpus cavernosum 607.2
ear (any part) 680.0

G

Gafsa boil 085.1
Gain, weight (abnormal) (excessive) (*see also* Weight, gain) 783.1
Gaisböck's disease or syndrome (polycythemia hypertonica) 289.0
Gait
  abnormality 781.2
    hysterical 300.11
  ataxic 781.2
    hysterical 300.11
  disturbance 781.2
    hysterical 300.11
  paralytic 781.2
  scissor 781.2
  spastic 781.2
  staggering 781.2
    hysterical 300.11
Galactocele (breast) (infected) 611.5
  puerperal, postpartum 676.8
Galactophoritis 611.0
  puerperal, postpartum 675.2
Galactorrhea 676.6
  not associated with childbirth 611.6
Galactosemia (classic) (congenital) 271.1
Galactosuria 271.1
Galacturia 791.1
  bilharziasis 120.0
Galen's vein - *see* condition
Gallbladder - *see also* condition
  acute (*see also* Disease, gallbladder) 575.0
Gall duct - *see* condition
Gallop rhythm 427.89
Gallstone (cholemic) (colic) (impacted) - *see also* Cholelithiasis
  causing intestinal obstruction 560.31
Gambling, pathological 312.31
Gammaloidosis 277.3
Gammopathy 273.9
  macroglobulinemia 273.3
  monoclonal (benign) (essential) (idiopathic) (with lymphoplasmacytic dyscrasia) 273.1
Gamna's disease (siderotic splenomegaly) 289.51
Gampsodactylia (congenital) 754.71
Gamstorp's disease (adynamia episodica hereditaria) 359.3
Gandy-Nanta disease (siderotic splenomegaly) 289.51
Gang activity, without manifest psychiatric disorder V71.09
  adolescent V71.02
  adult V71.01
  child V71.02
Gangliocytoma (M9490/0) - *see* Neoplasm, connective tissue, benign
Ganglioglioma (M9505/1) - *see* Neoplasm, by site, uncertain behavior
Ganglion 727.43
  joint 727.41
  of yaws (early) (late) 102.6
  periosteal (*see also* Periostitis) 730.3
  tendon sheath (compound) (diffuse) 727.42
  tuberculous (*see also* Tuberculosis) 015.9
Ganglioneuroblastoma (M9490/3) - *see* Neoplasm, connective tissue, malignant

Ganglioneuroma (M9490/0) - *see also* Neoplasm, connective tissue, benign
  malignant (M9490/3) - *see* Neoplasm, connective tissue, malignant
Ganglioneuromatosis (M9491/0) - *see* Neoplasm, connective tissue, benign
Ganglionitis
  fifth nerve (*see also* Neuralgia, trigeminal) 350.1
  gasserian 350.1
  geniculate 351.1
    herpetic 053.11
    newborn 767.5
  herpes zoster 053.11
  herpetic geniculate (Hunt's syndrome) 053.11
Gangliosidosis 330.1
Gangosa 102.5
Gangrene, gangrenous (anemia) (artery) (cellulitis) (dermatitis) (dry) (infective) (moist) (pemphigus) (septic) (skin) (stasis) (ulcer) 785.4
  with
    arteriosclerosis (native artery) 440.24
      bypass graft 440.30
        autologous vein 440.31
        nonautologous biological 440.32
    diabetes (mellitus) 250.7 [785.4]
  abdomen (wall) 785.4
    arteriosclerotic 440.29 [785.4]
  adenitis 683
  alveolar 526.5
  angina 462
    diphtheritic 032.0
  anus 569.49
  appendices epiploicae - *see* Gangrene, mesentery
  appendix - *see* Appendicitis, acute
  arteriosclerotic - *see* Arteriosclerosis, with, gangrene
  auricle 785.4
  Bacillus welchii (*see also* Gangrene, gas) 040.0
  bile duct (*see also* Cholangitis) 576.8
  bladder 595.89
  bowel - *see* Gangrene, intestine
  cecum - *see* Gangrene, intestine
  Clostridium perfringens or welchii (*see also* Gangrene, gas) 040.0
  colon - *see* Gangrene, intestine
  connective tissue 785.4
  cornea 371.40
  corpora cavernosa (infective) 607.2
    noninfective 607.89
  cutaneous, spreading 785.4
  decubital 707.0 [785.4]
  diabetic (any site) 250.7 [785.4]
  dropsical 785.4
  emphysematous (*see also* Gangrene, gas) 040.0
  epidemic (ergotized grain) 988.2
  epididymis (infectional) (*see also* Epididymitis) 604.99
  erysipelas (*see also* Erysipelas) 035
  extremity (lower) (upper) 785.4
  gallbladder or duct (*see also* Cholecystitis, acute) 575.0
  gas (bacillus) 040.0
    with
      abortion - *see* Abortion, by type, with sepsis
      ectopic pregnancy (*see also* categories 633.0-633.9) 639.0

Gangrene, gangrenous (*Continued*)
  gas (*Continued*)
    with (*Continued*)
      molar pregnancy (*see also* categories 630-632) 639.0
    following
      abortion 639.0
      ectopic or molar pregnancy 639.0
    puerperal, postpartum, childbirth 670
  glossitis 529.0
  gum 523.8
  hernia - *see* Hernia, by site, with gangrene
  hospital noma 528.1
  intestine, intestinal (acute) (hemorrhagic) (massive) 557.0
    with
      hernia - *see* Hernia, by site, with gangrene
      mesenteric embolism or infarction 557.0
      obstruction (*see also* Obstruction, intestine) 560.9
  laryngitis 464.0
  liver 573.8
  lung 513.0
    spirochetal 104.8
  lymphangitis 457.2
  Meleney's (cutaneous) 686.09
  mesentery 557.0
    with
      embolism or infarction 557.0
      intestinal obstruction (*see also* Obstruction, intestine) 560.9
  mouth 528.1
  noma 528.1
  orchitis 604.90
  ovary (*see also* Salpingo-oophoritis) 614.2
  pancreas 577.0
  penis (infectional) 607.2
    noninfective 607.89
  perineum 785.4
  pharynx 462
    septic 034.0
  pneumonia 513.0
  Pott's 440.24
  presenile 443.1
  pulmonary 513.0
  pulp, tooth 522.1
  quinsy 475
  Raynaud's (symmetric gangrene) 443.0 [785.4]
  rectum 569.49
  retropharyngeal 478.24
  rupture - *see* Hernia, by site, with gangrene
  scrotum 608.4
    noninfective 608.83
  senile 440.24
  sore throat 462
  spermatic cord 608.4
    noninfective 608.89
  spine 785.4
  spirochetal NEC 104.8
  spreading cutaneous 785.4
  stomach 537.89
  stomatitis 528.1
  symmetrical 443.0 [785.4]
  testis (infectional) (*see also* Orchitis) 604.99
    noninfective 608.89

Gangrene, gangrenous *(Continued)*
  throat 462
    diphtheritic 032.0
  thyroid (gland) 246.8
  tonsillitis (acute) 463
  tooth (pulp) 522.1
  tuberculous NEC *(see also* Tuberculosis) 011.9
  tunica vaginalis 608.4
    noninfective 608.89
  umbilicus 785.4
  uterus *(see also* Endometritis) 615.9
  uvulitis 528.3
  vas deferens 608.4
    noninfective 608.89
  vulva *(see also* Vulvitis) 616.10
Gannister disease (occupational) 502
  with tuberculosis - *see* Tuberculosis,
    pulmonary
Ganser's syndrome, hysterical 300.16
Gardner-Diamond syndrome (autoerythrocyte sensitization) 287.2
Gargoylism 277.5
Garré's
  disease *(see also* Osteomyelitis) 730.1
  osteitis (sclerosing) *(see also* Osteomyelitis) 730.1
  osteomyelitis *(see also* Osteomyelitis) 730.1
Garrod's pads, knuckle 728.79
Gartner's duct
  cyst 752.11
  persistent 752.11
Gas
  asphyxia, asphyxiation, inhalation, poisoning, suffocation NEC 987.9
    specified gas - *see* Table of Drugs and Chemicals
  bacillus gangrene or infection - *see* Gas, gangrene
  cyst, mesentery 568.89
  excessive 787.3
  gangrene 040.0
    with
      abortion - *see* Abortion, by type, with sepsis
      ectopic pregnancy *(see also* categories 633.0-633.9) 639.0
      molar pregnancy *(see also* categories 630-632) 639.0
    following
      abortion 639.0
      ectopic or molar pregnancy 639.0
    puerperal, postpartum, childbirth 670
  on stomach 787.3
  pains 787.3
Gastradenitis 535.0
Gastralgia 536.8
  psychogenic 307.89
Gastrectasis, gastrectasia 536.1
  psychogenic 306.4
Gastric - *see* condition
Gastrinoma (M8153/1)
  malignant (M8153/3)
    pancreas 157.4
    specified site NEC - *see* Neoplasm, by site, malignant
    unspecified site 157.4
  specified site - *see* Neoplasm, by site, uncertain behavior
  unspecified site 235.5

Gastritis 535.5

Note   Use the following fifth-digit subclassification for category 535:
0   without mention of hemorrhage
1   with hemorrhage

  acute 535.0
  alcoholic 535.3
  allergic 535.4
  antral 535.4
  atrophic 535.1
  atrophic-hyperplastic 535.1
  bile-induced 535.4
  catarrhal 535.0
  chronic (atrophic) 535.1
  cirrhotic 535.4
  corrosive (acute) 535.4
  dietetic 535.4
  due to diet deficiency 269.9 [535.4]
  eosinophilic 535.4
  erosive 535.4
  follicular 535.4
    chronic 535.1
  giant hypertrophic 535.2
  glandular 535.4
    chronic 535.1
  hypertrophic (mucosa) 535.2
    chronic giant 211.1
  irritant 535.4
  nervous 306.4
  phlegmonous 535.0
  psychogenic 306.4
  sclerotic 535.4
  spastic 536.8
  subacute 535.0
  superficial 535.4
  suppurative 535.0
  toxic 535.4
  tuberculous *(see also* Tuberculosis) 017.9
Gastrocarcinoma (M8010/3) 151.9
Gastrocolic - *see* condition
Gastrocolitis - *see* Enteritis
Gastrodisciasis 121.8
Gastroduodenitis *(see also* Gastritis) 535.5
  catarrhal 535.0
  infectional 535.0
  virus, viral 008.8
    specified type NEC 008.69
Gastrodynia 536.8
Gastroenteritis (acute) (catarrhal) (congestive) (hemorrhagic) (noninfectious) *(see also* Enteritis) 558.9
  aertrycke infection 003.0
  allergic 558.9
  chronic 558.9
    ulcerative *(see also* Colitis, ulcerative) 556.9
  dietetic 558.9
  due to
    food poisoning *(see also* Poisoning, food) 005.9
    radiation 558.1
  epidemic 009.0
  functional 558.9
  infectious *(see also* Enteritis, due to, by organism) 009.0
    presumed 009.1
  salmonella 003.0
  septic *(see also* Enteritis, due to, by organism) 009.0
  toxic 558.2

Gastroenteritis *(Continued)*
  tuberculous *(see also* Tuberculosis) 014.8
  ulcerative *(see also* Colitis, ulcerative) 556.9
  viral NEC 008.8
    specified type NEC 008.69
  zymotic 009.0
Gastroenterocolitis - *see* Enteritis
Gastroenteropathy, protein-losing 579.8
Gastroenteroptosis 569.89
Gastroesophageal laceration-hemorrhage syndrome 530.7
Gastroesophagitis 530.19
Gastrohepatitis *(see also* Gastritis) 535.5
Gastrointestinal - *see* condition
Gastrojejunal - *see* condition
Gastrojejunitis *(see also* Gastritis) 535.5
Gastrojejunocolic - *see* condition
Gastroliths 537.89
Gastromalacia 537.89
Gastroparalysis 536.3
  diabetic 250.6 [536.3]
Gastroparesis 536.3
  diabetic 250.6 [536.3]
Gastropathy, exudative 579.8
Gastroptosis 537.5
Gastrorrhagia 578.0
Gastrorrhea 536.8
  psychogenic 306.4
Gastroschisis (congenital) 756.79
  acquired 569.89
Gastrospasm (neurogenic) (reflex) 536.8
  neurotic 306.4
  psychogenic 306.4
Gastrostaxis 578.0
Gastrostenosis 537.89
Gastrostomy
  attention to V55.1
  complication 536.40
    specified type 536.49
  infection 536.41
  malfunctioning 536.42
  status V44.1
Gastrosuccorrhea (continuous) (intermittent) 536.8
  neurotic 306.4
  psychogenic 306.4
Gaucher's
  disease (adult) (cerebroside lipidosis) (infantile) 272.7
  hepatomegaly 272.7
  splenomegaly (cerebroside lipidosis) 272.7
Gayet's disease (superior hemorrhagic polioencephalitis) 265.1
Gayet-Wernicke's syndrome (superior hemorrhagic polioencephalitis) 265.1
Gee (-Herter) (-Heubner) (-Thaysen) disease or syndrome (nontropical sprue) 579.0
Gélineau's syndrome 347
Gemination, teeth 520.2
Gemistocytoma (M9411/3)
  specified site - *see* Neoplasm, by site, malignant
  unspecified site 191.9
General, generalized - *see* condition
Genital - *see* condition
  warts 078.19
Genito-anorectal syndrome 099.1
Genitourinary system - *see* condition

Genu
  congenital 755.64
  extrorsum (acquired) 736.42
    congenital 755.64
    late effects of rickets 268.1
  introrsum (acquired) 736.41
    congenital 755.64
    late effects of rickets 268.1
  rachitic (old) 268.1
  recurvatum (acquired) 736.5
    congenital 754.40
      with dislocation of knee 754.41
    late effects of rickets 268.1
  valgum (acquired) (knock-knee) 736.41
    congenital 755.64
    late effects of rickets 268.1
  varum (acquired) (bowleg) 736.42
    congenital 755.64
    late effect of rickets 268.1
Geographic tongue 529.1
Geophagia 307.52
Geotrichosis 117.9
  intestine 117.9
  lung 117.9
  mouth 117.9
Gephyrophobia 300.29
Gerbode defect 745.4
Gerhardt's
  disease (erythromelalgia) 443.89
  syndrome (vocal cord paralysis) 478.30
Gerlier's disease (epidemic vertigo)
  078.81
German measles 056.9
  exposure to V01.4
Germinoblastoma (diffuse) (M9614/3)
  202.8
  follicular (M9692/3) 202.0
Germinoma (M9064/3) - *see* Neoplasm,
  by site, malignant
Gerontoxon 371.41
Gerstmann's syndrome (finger agnosia)
  784.69
Gestation (period) - *see also* Pregnancy
  ectopic NEC (*see also* Pregnancy, ec-
    topic) 633.9
Gestational proteinuria 646.2
  with hypertension - *see* Toxemia, of
    pregnancy
Ghon tubercle primary infection (*see*
  also Tuberculosis) 010.0
Ghost
  teeth 520.4
  vessels, cornea 370.64
Ghoul hand 102.3
Giant
  cell
    epulis 523.8
    peripheral (gingiva) 523.8
    tumor, tendon sheath 727.02
  colon (congenital) 751.3
  esophagus (congenital) 750.4
  kidney 753.3
  urticaria 995.1
    hereditary 277.6
Giardia lamblia infestation 007.1
Giardiasis 007.1
Gibert's disease (pityriasis rosea) 696.3
Gibraltar fever - *see* Brucellosis
Giddiness 780.4
  hysterical 300.11
  psychogenic 306.9
Gierke's disease (glycogenosis I) 271.0
Gigantism (cerebral) (hypophyseal) (pituitary) 253.0

Gilbert's disease or cholemia (familial
  nonhemolytic jaundice) 277.4
Gilchrist's disease (North American
  blastomycosis) 116.0
Gilford (-Hutchinson) disease or syndrome (progeria) 259.8
Gilles de la Tourette's disease (motor-
  verbal tic) 307.23
Gillespie's syndrome (dysplasia oculodentodigitalis) 759.89
Gingivitis 523.1
  acute 523.0
    necrotizing 101
  catarrhal 523.0
  chronic 523.1
  desquamative 523.1
  expulsiva 523.4
  hyperplastic 523.1
  marginal, simple 523.1
  necrotizing, acute 101
  pellagrous 265.2
  ulcerative 523.1
    acute necrotizing 101
  Vincent's 101
Gingivoglossitis 529.0
Gingivopericementitis 523.4
Gingivosis 523.1
Gingivostomatitis 523.1
  herpetic 054.2
Giovannini's disease 117.9
Gland, glandular - *see* condition
Glanders 024
Glanzmann (-Naegeli) disease or thrombasthenia 287.1
Glassblowers' disease 527.1
Glaucoma (capsular) (inflammatory)
  (noninflammatory) (primary) 365.9
  with increased episcleral venous pres-
    sure 365.82
  absolute 360.42
  acute 365.22
    narrow angle 365.22
    secondary 365.60
  angle closure 365.20
    acute 365.22
    chronic 365.23
    intermittent 365.21
    interval 365.21
    residual stage 365.24
    subacute 365.21
  borderline 365.00
  chronic 365.11
    noncongestive 365.11
    open angle 365.11
    simple 365.11
  closed angle - *see* Glaucoma, angle clo-
    sure
  congenital 743.20
    associated with other eye anomalies
      743.22
    simple 743.21
  congestive - *see* Glaucoma, narrow an-
    gle
  corticosteroid-induced (glaucomatous
    stage) 365.31
    residual stage 365.32
  hemorrhagic 365.60
  hypersecretion 365.81
  in or with
    aniridia 743.45 [365.42]
    Axenfeld's anomaly 743.44 [365.41]
    concussion of globe 921.3 [365.65]
    congenital syndromes NEC 759.89
      [365.44]

Glaucoma (*Continued*)
  in or with (*Continued*)
    dislocation of lens
      anterior 379.33 [365.59]
      posterior 379.34 [365.59]
    disorder of lens NEC [365.59]
    epithelial down-growth 364.61
      [365.64]
    glaucomatocyclitic crisis 364.22
      [365.62]
    hypermature cataract 366.18 [365.51]
    hyphema 364.41 [365.63]
    inflammation, ocular 365.62
    iridocyclitis 364.3 [365.62]
    iris
      anomalies NEC 743.46 [365.42]
      atrophy, essential 364.51 [365.42]
      bombé 364.74 [365.61]
      rubeosis 364.42 [365.63]
    microcornea 743.41 [365.43]
    neurofibromatosis 237.71 [365.44]
    ocular
      cysts NEC 365.64
      disorders NEC 365.60
      trauma 365.65
      tumors NEC 365.64
    postdislocation of lens
      anterior 379.33 [365.59]
      posterior 379.34 [365.59]
    pseudoexfoliation of capsule 366.11
      [365.52]
    pupillary block or seclusion 364.74
      [365.61]
    recession of chamber angle 364.77
      [365.65]
    retinal vein occlusion 362.35 [365.63]
    Rieger's anomaly or syndrome
      743.44 [365.41]
    rubeosis of iris 364.42 [365.63]
    seclusion of pupil 364.74 [365.61]
    spherophakia 743.36 [365.59]
    Sturge-Weber (-Dimitri) syndrome
      759.6 [365.44]
    systemic syndrome NEC 365.44
    tumor of globe 365.64
    vascular disorders NEC 365.63
  infantile 365.14
    congenital 743.20
      associated with other eye anoma-
        lies 743.22
      simple 743.21
  juvenile 365.14
  low tension 365.12
  malignant 365.20
  narrow angle (primary) 365.20
    acute 365.22
    chronic 365.23
    intermittent 365.21
    interval 365.21
    residual stage 365.24
    subacute 365.21
  newborn 743.20
    associated with other eye anomalies
      743.22
    simple 743.21
  noncongestive (chronic) 365.11
  nonobstructive (chronic) 365.11
  obstructive 365.60
    due to lens changes 365.59
  open angle 365.10
    with
      borderline intraocular pressure
        365.01
      cupping of optic discs 365.01

Glaucoma *(Continued)*
　open angle *(Continued)*
　　primary 365.11
　　residual stage 365.15
　　phacolytic 365.51
　　　with hypermature cataract 366.18 [365.51]
　　pigmentary 365.13
　　postinfectious 365.60
　　pseudoexfoliation 365.52
　　　with pseudoexfoliation of capsule 366.11 [365.52]
　　secondary NEC 365.60
　　simple (chronic) 365.11
　　simplex 365.11
　　steroid responders 365.03
　　suspect 365.00
　　syphilitic 095.8
　　traumatic NEC 365.65
　　　newborn 767.8
　　tuberculous *(see also* Tuberculosis) 017.3 [365.62]
　　wide angle *(see also* Glaucoma, open angle) 365.10
Glaucomatous flecks (subcapsular) 366.31
Glazed tongue 529.4
Gleet 098.2
Glénard's disease or syndrome (enteroptosis) 569.89
Glinski-Simmonds syndrome (pituitary cachexia) 253.2
Glioblastoma (multiforme) (M9440/3)
　with sarcomatous component (M9442/3)
　　specified site - *see* Neoplasm, by site, malignant
　　unspecified site 191.9
　giant cell (M9441/3)
　　specified site - *see* Neoplasm, by site, malignant
　　unspecified site 191.9
　specified site - *see* Neoplasm, by site, malignant
　unspecified site 191.9
Glioma (malignant) (M9380/3)
　astrocytic (M9400/3)
　　specified site - *see* Neoplasm, by site, malignant
　　unspecified site 191.9
　mixed (M9382/3)
　　specified site - *see* Neoplasm, by site, malignant
　　unspecified site 191.9
　nose 748.1
　specified site NEC - *see* Neoplasm, by site, malignant
　subependymal (M9383/1) 237.5
　unspecified site 191.9
Gliomatosis cerebri (M9381/3) 191.0
Glioneuroma (M9505/1) - *see* Neoplasm, by site, uncertain behavior
Gliosarcoma (M9380/3)
　specified site - *see* Neoplasm, by site, malignant
　unspecified site 191.9
Gliosis (cerebral) 349.89
　spinal 336.0
Glisson's
　cirrhosis - *see* Cirrhosis, portal
　disease *(see also* Rickets) 268.0
Glissonitis 573.3
Globinuria 791.2
Globus 306.4
　hystericus 300.11

Glomangioma (M8712/0) *(see also* Hemangioma) 228.00
Glomangiosarcoma (M8710/3) - *see* Neoplasm, connective tissue, malignant
Glomerular nephritis *(see also* Nephritis) 583.9
Glomerulitis *(see also* Nephritis) 583.9
Glomerulonephritis *(see also* Nephritis) 583.9
　with
　　edema *(see also* Nephrosis) 581.9
　　lesion of
　　　exudative nephritis 583.89
　　　interstitial nephritis (diffuse) (focal) 583.89
　　　necrotizing glomerulitis 583.4
　　　　acute 580.4
　　　　chronic 582.4
　　　renal necrosis 583.9
　　　　cortical 583.6
　　　　medullary 583.7
　　　specified pathology NEC 583.89
　　　　acute 580.89
　　　　chronic 582.89
　　necrosis, renal 583.9
　　　cortical 583.6
　　　medullary (papillary) 583.7
　　specified pathology or lesion NEC 583.89
　acute 580.9
　　with
　　　exudative nephritis 580.89
　　　interstitial nephritis (diffuse) (focal) 580.89
　　　necrotizing glomerulitis 580.4
　　extracapillary with epithelial crescents 580.4
　　poststreptococcal 580.0
　　proliferative (diffuse) 580.0
　　rapidly progressive 580.4
　　specified pathology NEC 580.89
　arteriolar *(see also* Hypertension, kidney) 403.90
　arteriosclerotic *(see also* Hypertension, kidney) 403.90
　ascending *(see also* Pyelitis) 590.80
　basement membrane NEC 583.89
　　with
　　　pulmonary hemorrhage (Goodpasture's syndrome) 446.21 [583.81]
　chronic 582.9
　　with
　　　exudative nephritis 582.89
　　　interstitial nephritis (diffuse) (focal) 582.89
　　　necrotizing glomerulitis 582.4
　　　specified pathology or lesion NEC 582.89
　　endothelial 582.2
　　extracapillary with epithelial crescents 582.4
　　hypocomplementemic persistent 582.2
　　lobular 582.2
　　membranoproliferative 582.2
　　membranous 582.1
　　　and proliferative (mixed) 582.2
　　　sclerosing 582.1
　　mesangiocapillary 582.2
　　mixed membranous and proliferative 582.2

Glomerulonephritis *(Continued)*
　chronic *(Continued)*
　　proliferative (diffuse) 582.0
　　rapidly progressive 582.4
　　sclerosing 582.1
　cirrhotic - *see* Sclerosis, renal
　desquamative - *see* Nephrosis
　due to or associated with
　　amyloidosis 277.3 [583.81]
　　　with nephrotic syndrome 277.3 [581.81]
　　　chronic 277.3 [582.81]
　　diabetes mellitus 250.4 [583.81]
　　　with nephrotic syndrome 250.4 [581.81]
　　diphtheria 032.89 [580.81]
　　gonococcal infection (acute) 098.19 [583.81]
　　　chronic or duration of 2 months or over 098.39 [583.81]
　　infectious hepatitis 070.9 [580.81]
　　malaria (with nephrotic syndrome) 084.9 [581.81]
　　mumps 072.79 [580.81]
　　polyarteritis (nodosa) (with nephrotic syndrome) 446.0 [581.81]
　　specified pathology NEC 583.89
　　　acute 580.89
　　　chronic 582.89
　　streptotrichosis 039.8 [583.81]
　　subacute bacterial endocarditis 421.0 [580.81]
　　syphilis (late) 095.4
　　　congenital 090.5 [583.81]
　　　early 091.69 [583.81]
　　systemic lupus erythematosus 710.0 [583.81]
　　　with nephrotic syndrome 710.0 [581.81]
　　　chronic 710.0 [582.81]
　　tuberculosis *(see also* Tuberculosis) 016.0 [583.81]
　　typhoid fever 002.0 [580.81]
　extracapillary with epithelial crescents 583.4
　acute 580.4
　chronic 582.4
　exudative 583.89
　　acute 580.89
　　chronic 582.89
　focal *(see also* Nephritis) 583.9
　　embolic 580.4
　granular 582.89
　granulomatous 582.89
　hydremic *(see also* Nephrosis) 581.9
　hypocomplementemic persistent 583.2
　　with nephrotic syndrome 581.2
　　chronic 582.2
　immune complex NEC 583.89
　infective *(see also* Pyelitis) 590.80
　interstitial (diffuse) (focal) 583.89
　　with nephrotic syndrome 581.89
　　acute 580.89
　　chronic 582.89
　latent or quiescent 582.9
　lobular 583.2
　　with nephrotic syndrome 581.2
　　chronic 582.2
　membranoproliferative 583.2
　　with nephrotic syndrome 581.2
　　chronic 582.2
　membranous 583.1

◀▶　**New Code**　　　⬅▮▮▮➡　**Revised Code**

Glomerulonephritis *(Continued)*
  membranous *(Continued)*
    with nephrotic syndrome 581.1
    and proliferative (mixed) 583.2
      with nephrotic syndrome 581.2
      chronic 582.2
    chronic 582.1
    sclerosing 582.1
      with nephrotic syndrome 581.1
  mesangiocapillary 583.2
    with nephrotic syndrome 581.2
    chronic 582.2
  minimal change 581.3
  mixed membranous and proliferative 583.2
    with nephrotic syndrome 581.2
    chronic 582.2
  necrotizing 583.4
    acute 580.4
    chronic 582.4
  nephrotic *(see also* Nephrosis) 581.9
  old - *see* Glomerulonephritis, chronic
  parenchymatous 581.89
  poststreptococcal 580.0
  proliferative (diffuse) 583.0
    with nephrotic syndrome 581.0
    acute 580.0
    chronic 582.0
  purulent *(see also* Pyelitis) 590.80
  quiescent - *see* Nephritis, chronic
  rapidly progressive 583.4
    acute 580.4
    chronic 582.4
  sclerosing membranous (chronic) 582.1
    with nephrotic syndrome 581.1
  septic *(see also* Pyelitis) 590.80
  specified pathology or lesion NEC 583.89
    with nephrotic syndrome 581.89
    acute 580.89
    chronic 582.89
  suppurative (acute) (disseminated) *(see also* Pyelitis) 590.80
  toxic - *see* Nephritis, acute
  tubal, tubular - *see* Nephrosis, tubular
  type II (Ellis) - *see* Nephrosis
  vascular - *see* Hypertension, kidney
Glomerulosclerosis *(see also* Sclerosis, renal) 587
  focal 582.1
    with nephrotic syndrome 581.1
  intercapillary (nodular) (with diabetes) 250.4 *[581.81]*
Glossagra 529.6
Glossalgia 529.6
Glossitis 529.0
  areata exfoliativa 529.1
  atrophic 529.4
  benign migratory 529.1
  gangrenous 529.0
  Hunter's 529.4
  median rhomboid 529.2
  Moeller's 529.4
  pellagrous 265.2
Glossocele 529.8
Glossodynia 529.6
  exfoliativa 529.4
Glossoncus 529.8
Glossophytia 529.3
Glossoplegia 529.8
Glossoptosis 529.8
Glossopyrosis 529.6
Glossotrichia 529.3
Glossy skin 701.9

Glottis - *see* condition
Glottitis - *see* Glossitis
Glucagonoma (M8152/0)
  malignant (M8152/3)
    pancreas 157.4
    specified site NEC - *see* Neoplasm, by site, malignant
    unspecified site 157.4
  pancreas 211.7
  specified site NEC - *see* Neoplasm, by site, benign
  unspecified site 211.7
Glucoglycinuria 270.7
Glue ear syndrome 381.20
Glue sniffing (airplane glue) *(see also* Dependence) 304.6
Glycinemia (with methylmalonic acidemia) 270.7
Glycinuria (renal) (with ketosis) 270.0
Glycogen
  infiltration *(see also* Disease, glycogen storage) 271.0
  storage disease *(see also* Disease, glycogen storage) 271.0
Glycogenosis *(see also* Disease, glycogen storage) 271.0
  cardiac 271.0 *[425.7]*
  Cori, types I-VII 271.0
  diabetic, secondary 250.8 *[259.8]*
  diffuse (with hepatic cirrhosis) 271.0
  generalized 271.0
  glucose-6-phosphatase deficiency 271.0
  hepatophosphorylase deficiency 271.0
  hepatorenal 271.0
  myophosphorylase deficiency 271.0
Glycopenia 251.2
Glycoprolinuria 270.8
Glycosuria 791.5
  renal 271.4
Gnathostoma (spinigerum) (infection) (infestation) 128.1
  wandering swellings from 128.1
Gnathostomiasis 128.1
Goiter (adolescent) (colloid) (diffuse) (dipping) (due to iodine deficiency) (endemic) (euthyroid) (heart) (hyperplastic) (internal) (intrathoracic) (juvenile) (mixed type) (nonendemic) (parenchymatous) (plunging) (sporadic) (subclavicular) (substernal) 240.9
  with
    hyperthyroidism (recurrent) *(see also* Goiter, toxic) 242.0
    thyrotoxicosis *(see also* Goiter, toxic) 242.0
  adenomatous *(see also* Goiter, nodular) 241.9
  cancerous (M8000/3) 193
  complicating pregnancy, childbirth, or puerperium 648.1
  congenital 246.1
  cystic *(see also* Goiter, nodular) 241.9
  due to enzyme defect in synthesis of thyroid hormone (butane-insoluble iodine) (coupling) (deiodinase) (iodide trapping or organification) (iodotyrosine dehalogenase) (peroxidase) 246.1
  dyshormonogenic 246.1
  exophthalmic *(see also* Goiter, toxic) 242.0
  familial (with deaf-mutism) 243
  fibrous 245.3

Goiter *(Continued)*
  lingual 759.2
  lymphadenoid 245.2
  malignant (M8000/3) 193
  multinodular (nontoxic) 241.1
    toxic or with hyperthyroidism *(see also* Goiter, toxic) 242.2
  nodular (nontoxic) 241.9
    with
      hyperthyroidism *(see also* Goiter, toxic) 242.3
      thyrotoxicosis *(see also* Goiter, toxic) 242.3
    endemic 241.9
    exophthalmic (diffuse) *(see also* Goiter, toxic) 242.0
    multinodular (nontoxic) 241.1
    sporadic 241.9
    toxic *(see also* Goiter, toxic) 242.3
    uninodular (nontoxic) 241.0
  nontoxic (nodular) 241.9
    multinodular 241.1
    uninodular 241.0
  pulsating *(see also* Goiter, toxic) 242.0
  simple 240.0
  toxic 242.0

> Note   Use the following fifth-digit subclassification with category 242:
>
> 0   without mention of thyrotoxic crisis or storm
> 1   with mention of thyrotoxic crisis or storm

  adenomatous 242.3
    multinodular 242.2
    uninodular 242.1
  multinodular 242.2
  nodular 242.3
    multinodular 242.2
    uninodular 242.1
  uninodular 242.1
  uninodular (nontoxic) 241.0
    toxic or with hyperthyroidism *(see also* Goiter, toxic) 242.1
Goldberg (-Maxwell) (-Morris) syndrome (testicular feminization) 257.8
Goldblatt's
  hypertension 440.1
  kidney 440.1
Goldenhar's syndrome (oculoauriculovertebral dysplasia) 756.0
Goldflam-Erb disease or syndrome 358.0
Goldscheider's disease (epidermolysis bullosa) 757.39
Goldstein's disease (familial hemorrhagic telangiectasia) 448.0
Golfer's elbow 726.32
Goltz-Gorlin syndrome (dermal hypoplasia) 757.39
Gonadoblastoma (M9073/1)
  specified site - *see* Neoplasm, by site uncertain behavior
  unspecified site
    female 236.2
    male 236.4
Gonecystitis *(see also* Vesiculitis) 608.0
Gongylonemiasis 125.6
  mouth 125.6
Goniosynechiae 364.73
Gonococcemia 098.89
Gonococcus, gonococcal (disease) (infection) *(see also* condition) 098.0
  anus 098.7

Gonococcus, gonococcal (*Continued*)
  bursa 098.52
  chronic NEC 098.2
  complicating pregnancy, childbirth, or
      puerperium 647.1
    affecting fetus or newborn 760.2
  conjunctiva, conjunctivitis (neonato-
      rum) 098.40
  dermatosis 098.89
  endocardium 098.84
  epididymo-orchitis 098.13
    chronic or duration of 2 months or
        over 098.33
  eye (newborn) 098.40
  fallopian tube (chronic) 098.37
    acute 098.17
  genitourinary (acute) (organ) (system)
      (tract) (*see also* Gonorrhea)
      098.0
    lower 098.0
      chronic 098.2
    upper 098.10
      chronic 098.30
  heart NEC 098.85
  joint 098.50
  keratoderma 098.81
  keratosis (blennorrhagica) 098.81
  lymphatic (gland) (node) 098.89
  meninges 098.82
  orchitis (acute) 098.13
    chronic or duration of 2 months or
        over 098.33
  pelvis (acute) 098.19
    chronic or duration of 2 months or
        over 098.39
  pericarditis 098.83
  peritonitis 098.86
  pharyngitis 098.6
  pharynx 098.6
  proctitis 098.7
  pyosalpinx (chronic) 098.37
    acute 098.17
  rectum 098.7
  septicemia 098.89
  skin 098.89
  specified site NEC 098.89
  synovitis 098.51
  tendon sheath 098.51
  throat 098.6
  urethra (acute) 098.0
    chronic or duration of 2 months or
        over 098.2
  vulva (acute) 098.0
    chronic or duration of 2 months or
        over 098.2
Gonocytoma (M9073/1)
  specified site - *see* Neoplasm, by site,
      uncertain behavior
  unspecified site
    female 236.2
    male 236.4
Gonorrhea 098.0
  acute 098.0
  Bartholin's gland (acute) 098.0
    chronic or duration of 2 months or
        over 098.2
  bladder (acute) 098.11
    chronic or duration of 2 months or
        over 098.31
  carrier (suspected of) V02.7
  cervix (acute) 098.15
    chronic or duration of 2 months or
        over 098.35
  chronic 098.2

Gonorrhea (*Continued*)
  complicating pregnancy, childbirth, or
      puerperium 647.1
    affecting fetus or newborn 760.2
  conjunctiva, conjunctivitis (neonato-
      rum) 098.40
  contact V01.6
  Cowper's gland (acute) 098.0
    chronic or duration of 2 months or
        over 098.2
  duration of 2 months or over 098.2
  exposure to V01.6
  fallopian tube (chronic) 098.37
    acute 098.17
  genitourinary (acute) (organ) (system)
      (tract) 098.0
    chronic 098.2
    duration of 2 months or over 098.2
  kidney (acute) 098.19
    chronic or duration of 2 months or
        over 098.39
  ovary (acute) 098.19
    chronic or duration of 2 months or
        over 098.39
  pelvis (acute) 098.19
    chronic or duration of 2 months or
        over 098.39
  penis (acute) 098.0
    chronic or duration of 2 months or
        over 098.2
  prostate (acute) 098.12
    chronic or duration of 2 months or
        over 098.32
  seminal vesicle (acute) 098.14
    chronic or duration of 2 months or
        over 098.34
  specified site NEC - *see* Gonococcus
  spermatic cord (acute) 098.14
    chronic or duration of 2 months or
        over 098.34
  urethra (acute) 098.0
    chronic or duration of 2 months or
        over 098.2
  vagina (acute) 098.0
    chronic or duration of 2 months or
        over 098.2
  vas deferens (acute) 098.14
    chronic or duration of 2 months or
        over 098.34
  vulva (acute) 098.0
    chronic or duration of 2 months or
        over 098.2
Goodpasture's syndrome (pneumorenal)
    446.21
Gopalan's syndrome (burning feet)
    266.2
Gordon's disease (exudative enteropa-
    thy) 579.8
Gorlin-Chaudhry-Moss syndrome
    759.89
Gougerot's syndrome (trisymptomatic)
    709.1
Gougerot-Blum syndrome (pigmented
    purpuric lichenoid dermatitis) 709.1
Gougerot-Carteaud disease or syndrome
    (confluent reticulate papillomatosis)
    701.8
Gougerot-Hailey-Hailey disease (benign
    familial chronic pemphigus) 757.39
Gougerot (-Houwer)-Sjögren syndrome
    (keratoconjunctivitis sicca) 710.2
Gouley's syndrome (constrictive pericar-
    ditis) 423.2
Goundou 102.6

Gout, gouty 274.9
  with specified manifestations NEC
      274.89
  arthritis (acute) 274.0
  arthropathy 274.0
  degeneration, heart 274.82
  diathesis 274.9
  eczema 274.89
  episcleritis 274.89 [379.09]
  external ear (tophus) 274.81
  glomerulonephritis 274.10
  iritis 274.89 [364.11]
  joint 274.0
  kidney 274.10
  lead 984.9
    specified type of lead - *see* Table of
        Drugs and Chemicals
  nephritis 274.10
  neuritis 274.89 [357.4]
  phlebitis 274.89 [451.9]
  rheumatic 714.0
  saturnine 984.9
    specified type of lead - *see* Table of
        Drugs and Chemicals
  spondylitis 274.0
  synovitis 274.0
  syphilitic 095.8
  tophi 274.0
    ear 274.81
    heart 274.82
    specified site NEC 274.82
Gowers'
  muscular dystrophy 359.1
  syndrome (vasovagal attack) 780.2
Gowers-Paton-Kennedy syndrome 377.04
Gradenigo's syndrome 383.02
Graft-versus-host disease (bone marrow)
    996.85
  due to organ transplant NEC - *see*
      Complications, transplant, organ
Graham Steell's murmur (pulmonic re-
    gurgitation) (*see also* Endocarditis,
    pulmonary) 424.3
Grain-handlers' disease or lung 495.8
Grain mite (itch) 133.8
Grand
  mal (idiopathic) (*see also* Epilepsy)
      345.1
    hysteria of Charcôt 300.11
    nonrecurrent or isolated 780.39
  multipara
    affecting management of labor and
        delivery 659.4
    status only (not pregnant) V61.5
Granite workers' lung 502
Granular - *see also* condition
  inflammation, pharynx 472.1
  kidney (contracting) (*see also* Sclerosis,
      renal) 587
  liver - *see* Cirrhosis, liver
  nephritis - *see* Nephritis
Granulation tissue, abnormal - *see also*
    Granuloma
  abnormal or excessive 701.5
  postmastoidectomy cavity 383.33
  postoperative 701.5
  skin 701.5
Granulocytopenia, granulocytopenic
    (primary) 288.0
  malignant 288.0
Granuloma NEC 686.1
  abdomen (wall) 568.89
    skin (pyogenicum) 686.1
      from residual foreign body 709.4

Granuloma NEC (*Continued*)
  annulare 695.89
  anus 569.49
  apical 522.6
  appendix 543.9
  aural 380.23
  beryllium (skin) 709.4
    lung 503
  bone (*see also* Osteomyelitis) 730.1
    eosinophilic 277.8
    from residual foreign body 733.99
  canaliculus lacrimalis 375.81
  cerebral 348.8
  cholesterin, middle ear 385.82
  coccidioidal (progressive) 114.3
    lung 114.4
    meninges 114.2
    primary (lung) 114.0
  colon 569.89
  conjunctiva 372.61
  dental 522.6
  ear, middle (cholesterin) 385.82
    with otitis media - *see* Otitis media
  eosinophilic 277.8
    bone 277.8
    lung 277.8
    oral mucosa 528.9
  exuberant 701.5
  eyelid 374.89
  facial
    lethal midline 446.3
    malignant 446.3
  faciale 701.8
  fissuratum (gum) 523.8
  foot NEC 686.1
  foreign body (in soft tissue) NEC
    728.82
    bone 733.99
    in operative wound 998.4
    muscle 728.82
    skin 709.4
    subcutaneous tissue 709.4
  fungoides 202.1
  gangraenescens 446.3
  giant cell (central) (jaw) (reparative)
    526.3
    gingiva 523.8
    peripheral (gingiva) 523.8
  gland (lymph) 289.3
  Hodgkin's (M9661/3) 201.1
  ileum 569.89
  infectious NEC 136.9
  inguinale (Donovan) 099.2
    venereal 099.2
  intestine 569.89
  iridocyclitis 364.10
  jaw (bone) 526.3
    reparative giant cell 526.3
  kidney (*see also* Infection, kidney) 590.9
  lacrimal sac 375.81
  larynx 478.79
  lethal midline 446.3
  lipid 277.8
  lipoid 277.8
  liver 572.8
  lung (infectious) (*see also* Fibrosis,
    lung) 515
    coccidioidal 114.4
    eosinophilic 277.8
  lymph gland 289.3
  Majocchi's 110.6
  malignant, face 446.3
  mandible 526.3
  mediastinum 519.3

Granuloma NEC (*Continued*)
  midline 446.3
  monilial 112.3
  muscle 728.82
    from residual foreign body 728.82
  nasal sinus (*see also* Sinusitis) 473.9
  operation wound 998.59
    foreign body 998.4
    stitch (external) 998.89
      internal wound 998.89
    talc 998.7
  oral mucosa, eosinophilic or pyogenic
    528.9
  orbit, orbital 376.11
  paracoccidioidal 116.1
  penis, venereal 099.2
  periapical 522.6
  peritoneum 568.89
    due to ova of helminths NEC (*see
      also* Helminthiasis) 128.9
  postmastoidectomy cavity 383.33
  postoperative - *see* Granuloma, opera-
    tion wound
  prostate 601.8
  pudendi (ulcerating) 099.2
  pudendorum (ulcerative) 099.2
  pulp, internal (tooth) 521.4
  pyogenic, pyogenicum (skin) 686.1
    maxillary alveolar ridge 522.6
    oral mucosa 528.9
  rectum 569.49
  reticulohistiocytic 277.8
  rubrum nasi 705.89
  sarcoid 135
  Schistosoma 120.9
  septic (skin) 686.1
  silica (skin) 709.4
  sinus (accessory) (infectional) (nasal)
    (*see also* Sinusitis) 473.9
  skin (pyogenicum) 686.1
    from foreign body or material
      709.4
  sperm 608.89
  spine
    syphilitic (epidural) 094.89
    tuberculous (*see also* Tuberculosis)
      015.0 [730.88]
  stitch (postoperative) 998.89
    internal wound 998.89
  suppurative (skin) 686.1
  suture (postoperative) 998.89
    internal wound 998.89
  swimming pool 031.1
  talc 728.82
    in operation wound 998.7
  telangiectaticum (skin) 686.1
  trichophyticum 110.6
  tropicum 102.4
  umbilicus 686.1
    newborn 771.4
  urethra 599.84
  uveitis 364.10
  vagina 099.2
  venereum 099.2
  vocal cords 478.5
  Wegener's (necrotizing respiratory
    granulomatosis) 446.4
Granulomatosis NEC 686.1
  disciformis chronica et progressiva
    709.3
  infantiseptica 771.2
  lipoid 277.8
  lipophagic, intestinal 040.2
  miliary 027.0

Granulomatosis NEC (*Continued*)
  necrotizing, respiratory 446.4
  progressive, septic 288.1
  Wegener's (necrotizing respiratory)
    446.4
Granulomatous tissue - *see* Granuloma
Granulosis rubra nasi 705.89
Graphite fibrosis (of lung) 503
Graphospasm 300.89
  organic 333.84
Grating scapula 733.99
Gravel (urinary) (*see also* Calculus)
  592.9
Graves' disease (exophthalmic goiter)
  (*see also* Goiter, toxic) 242.0
Gravis - *see* condition
Grawitz's tumor (hypernephroma)
  (M8312/3) 189.0
Grayness, hair (premature) 704.3
  congenital 757.4
Gray or grey syndrome (chlorampheni-
  col) (newborn) 779.4
Greenfield's disease 330.0
Green sickness 280.9
Greenstick fracture - *see* Fracture, by
  site
Greig's syndrome (hypertelorism) 756.0
Griesinger's disease (*see also* Ancylosto-
  miasis) 126.9
Grinders'
  asthma 502
  lung 502
  phthisis (*see also* Tuberculosis) 011.4
Grinding, teeth 306.8
Grip
  Dabney's 074.1
  devil's 074.1
Grippe, grippal - *see also* Influenza
  Balkan 083.0
  intestinal 487.8
  summer 074.8
Grippy cold 487.1
Grisel's disease 723.5
Groin - *see* condition
Grooved
  nails (transverse) 703.8
  tongue 529.5
    congenital 750.13
Ground itch 126.9
Growing pains, children 781.9
Growth (fungoid) (neoplastic) (new)
  (M8000/1) - *see also* Neoplasm, by
  site, unspecified nature
  adenoid (vegetative) 474.12
  benign (M8000/0) - *see* Neoplasm, by
    site, benign
  fetal, poor 764.9
    affecting management of pregnancy
      656.5
  malignant (M8000/3) - *see* Neoplasm,
    by site, malignant
  rapid, childhood V21.0
  secondary (M8000/6) - *see* Neoplasm,
    by site, malignant, secondary
Gruber's hernia - *see* Hernia, Gruber's
Gruby's disease (tinea tonsurans) 110.0
G-trisomy 758.0
Guama fever 066.3
Gubler (-Millard) paralysis or syndrome
  344.89
Guérin-Stern syndrome (arthrogryposis
  multiplex congenita) 754.89
Guertin's disease (electric chorea)
  049.8

H

Haas' disease (osteochondrosis head of humerus) 732.3
Habermann's disease (acute parapsoriasis varioliformis) 696.2
Habit, habituation
  chorea 307.22
  disturbance, child 307.9
  drug (*see also* Dependence) 304.9
  laxative (*see also* Abuse, drugs, nondependent) 305.9
  spasm 307.20
    chronic 307.22
    transient of childhood 307.21
  tic 307.20
    chronic 307.22
    transient of childhood 307.21
  use of
    nonprescribed drugs (*see also* Abuse, drugs, nondependent) 305.9
    patent medicines (*see also* Abuse, drugs, nondependent) 305.9
  vomiting 536.2
Hadfield-Clarke syndrome (pancreatic infantilism) 577.8
Haff disease 985.1
Hageman factor defect, deficiency, or disease (*see also* Defect, coagulation) 286.3
Haglund's disease (osteochondrosis os tibiale externum) 732.5
Haglund-Läwen-Fründ syndrome 717.89
Hagner's disease (hypertrophic pulmonary osteoarthropathy) 731.2
Hag teeth, tooth 524.3
Hailey-Hailey disease (benign familial chronic pemphigus) 757.39
Hair - *see also* condition
  plucking 307.9
Hairball in stomach 935.2
Hairy black tongue 529.3
Half vertebra 756.14
Halitosis 784.9
Hallermann-Streiff syndrome 756.0
Hallervorden-Spatz disease or syndrome 333.0
Hallopeau's
  acrodermatitis (continua) 696.1
  disease (lichen sclerosis et atrophicus) 701.0
Hallucination (auditory) (gustatory) (olfactory) (tactile) 780.1
  alcoholic 291.3
  drug-induced 292.12
  visual 368.16
Hallucinosis 298.9
  alcoholic (acute) 291.3
  drug-induced 292.12
Hallus - *see* Hallux
Hallux 735.9
  malleus (acquired) 735.3
  rigidus (acquired) 735.2
    congenital 755.66
    late effects of rickets 268.1
  valgus (acquired) 735.0
    congenital 755.66
  varus (acquired) 735.1
    congenital 755.66
Halo, visual 368.15
Hamartoblastoma 759.6

Hamartoma 759.6
  epithelial (gingival), odontogenic, central, or peripheral (M9321/0) 213.1
    upper jaw (bone) 213.0
  vascular 757.32
Hamartosis, hamartoses NEC 759.6
Hamman's disease or syndrome (spontaneous mediastinal emphysema) 518.1
Hamman-Rich syndrome (diffuse interstitial pulmonary fibrosis) 516.3
Hammer toe (acquired) 735.4
  congenital 755.66
  late effects of rickets 268.1
Hand - *see* condition
Hand-Schüller-Christian disease or syndrome (chronic histiocytosis X) 277.8
Hand-foot syndrome 282.61
Hanging (asphyxia) (strangulation) (suffocation) 994.7
Hangnail (finger) (with lymphangitis) 681.02
Hangover (alcohol) (*see also* Abuse, drugs, nondependent) 305.0
Hanot's cirrhosis or disease - *see* Cirrhosis, biliary
Hanot-Chauffard (-Troisier) **syndrome** (bronze diabetes) 275.0
Hansen's disease (leprosy) 030.9
  benign form 030.1
  malignant form 030.0
Harada's disease or syndrome 363.22
Hard chancre 091.0
Hardening
  artery - *see* Arteriosclerosis
  brain 348.8
  liver 571.8
Hare's syndrome (M8010/3) (carcinoma, pulmonary apex) 162.3
Harelip (*see also* Cleft, lip) 749.10
Harkavy's syndrome 446.0
Harlequin (fetus) 757.1
  color change syndrome 779.8
Harley's disease (intermittent hemoglobinuria) 283.2
Harris'
  lines 733.91
  syndrome (organic hyperinsulinism) 251.1
Hart's disease or syndrome (pellagra-cerebellar ataxia-renal aminoaciduria) 270.0
Hartmann's pouch (abnormal sacculation of gallbladder neck) 575.8
Hartnup disease (pellagra-cerebellar ataxia-renal aminoaciduria) 270.0
Harvester lung 495.0
Hashimoto's disease or struma (struma lymphomatosa) 245.2
Hassall-Henle bodies (corneal warts) 371.41
Haut mal (*see also* Epilepsy) 345.1
Haverhill fever 026.1
Hawaiian wood rose dependence 304.5
Hawkins' keloid 701.4
Hay
  asthma (*see also* Asthma) 493.0
  fever (allergic) (with rhinitis) 477.9
    with asthma (bronchial) (*see also* Asthma) 493.0
    allergic, due to grass, pollen, ragweed, or tree 477.0
    conjunctivitis 372.05

Hay (*Continued*)
  fever (*Continued*)
    due to
      dander 477.8
      dust 477.8
      fowl 477.8
      pollen 477.0
      specified allergen other than pollen 477.8
Hayem-Faber syndrome (achlorhydric anemia) 280.9
Hayem-Widal syndrome (acquired hemolytic jaundice) 283.9
Haygarth's nodosities 715.04
Hazard-Crile tumor (M8350/3) 193
Hb (abnormal)
  disease - *see* Disease, hemoglobin
  trait - *see* Trait
H disease 270.0
Head - *see also* condition
  banging 307.3
Headache 784.0
  allergic 346.2
  cluster 346.2
  due to
    loss, spinal fluid 349.0
    lumbar puncture 349.0
    saddle block 349.0
  emotional 307.81
  histamine 346.2
  lumbar puncture 349.0
  menopausal 627.2
  migraine 346.9
  nonorganic origin 307.81
  postspinal 349.0
  psychogenic 307.81
  psychophysiologic 307.81
  sick 346.1
  spinal fluid loss 349.0
  tension 307.81
  vascular 784.0
    migraine type 346.9
  vasomotor 346.9
Health
  advice V65.4
  audit V70.0
  checkup V70.0
  education V65.4
  hazard (*see also* History of) V15.9
    specified cause NEC V15.89
  instruction V65.4
  services provided because (of)
    boarding school residence V60.6
    holiday relief for person providing home care V60.5
    inadequate
      housing V60.1
      resources V60.2
    lack of housing V60.0
    no care available in home V60.4
    person living alone V60.3
    poverty V60.3
    residence in institution V60.6
    specified cause NEC V60.8
    vacation relief for person providing home care V60.5
Healthy
  donor (*see also* Donor) V59.9
  infant or child
    accompanying sick mother V65.0
    receiving care V20.1
  person
    accompanying sick relative V65.0
    admitted for sterilization V25.2

ICD-9-CM

H

Vol. 2

Healthy (*Continued*)
  person (*Continued*)
    receiving prophylactic inoculation or vaccination (*see also* Vaccination, prophylactic) V05.9
Hearing examination V72.1
Heart - *see* condition
Heartburn 787.1
  psychogenic 306.4
Heat (effects) 992.9
  apoplexy 992.0
  burn - *see also* Burn, by site
    from sun 692.71
  collapse 992.1
  cramps 992.2
  dermatitis or eczema 692.89
  edema 992.7
  erythema - *see* Burn, by site
  excessive 992.9
    specified effect NEC 992.8
  exhaustion 992.5
    anhydrotic 992.3
    due to
      salt (and water) depletion 992.4
      water depletion 992.3
  fatigue (transient) 992.6
  fever 992.0
  hyperpyrexia 992.0
  prickly 705.1
  prostration - *see* Heat, exhaustion
  pyrexia 992.0
  rash 705.1
  specified effect NEC 992.8
  stroke 992.0
  sunburn 692.71
  syncope 992.1
Heavy-chain disease 273.2
Heavy-for-dates (fetus or infant) 766.1
  4500 grams or more 766.0
  exceptionally 766.0
Hebephrenia, hebephrenic (acute) (*see also* Schizophrenia) 295.1
  dementia (praecox) (*see also* Schizophrenia) 295.1
  schizophrenia (*see also* Schizophrenia) 295.1
Heberden's
  disease or nodes 715.04
  syndrome (angina pectoris) 413.9
Hebra's disease
  dermatitis exfoliativa 695.89
  erythema multiforme exudativum 695.1
  pityriasis 695.89
    maculata et circinata 696.3
    rubra 695.89
      pilaris 696.4
  prurigo 698.2
Hebra, nose 040.1
Hedinger's syndrome (malignant carcinoid) 259.2
Heel - *see* condition
Heerfordt's disease or syndrome (uveoparotitis) 135
Hegglin's anomaly or syndrome 288.2
Heidenhain's disease 290.10
  with dementia 290.10
Heilmeyer-Schoner disease (M9842/3) 207.1
Heine-Medin disease (*see also* Poliomyelitis) 045.9
Heinz-body anemia, congenital 282.7
Heller's disease or syndrome (infantile psychosis) (*see also* Psychosis, childhood) 299.1

H.E.L.L.P 642.5
Helminthiasis (*see also* Infestation, by specific parasite) 128.9
  Ancylostoma (*see also* Ancylostoma) 126.9
  intestinal 127.9
    mixed types (types classifiable to more than one of the categories 120.0-127.7) 127.8
    specified type 127.7
  mixed types (intestinal) (types classifiable to more than one of the categories 120.0-127.7) 127.8
  Necator americanus 126.1
  specified type NEC 128.8
  Trichinella 124
Heloma 700
Hemangioblastoma (M9161/1) - *see also* Neoplasm, connective tissue, uncertain behavior
  malignant (M9161/3) - *see* Neoplasm, connective tissue, malignant
Hemangioblastomatosis, cerebelloretinal 759.6
Hemangioendothelioma (M9130/1) - *see also* Neoplasm, by site, uncertain behavior
  benign (M9130/0) 228.00
  bone (diffuse) (M9130/3) - *see* Neoplasm, bone, malignant
  malignant (M9130/3) - *see* Neoplasm, connective tissue, malignant
  nervous system (M9130/0) 228.09
Hemangioendotheliosarcoma (M9130/3) - *see* Neoplasm, connective tissue, malignant
Hemangiofibroma (M9160/0) - *see* Neoplasm, by site, benign
Hemangiolipoma (M8861/0) - *see* Lipoma
Hemangioma (M9120/0) 228.00
  arteriovenous (M9123/0) - *see* Hemangioma, by site
  brain 228.02
  capillary (M9131/0) - *see* Hemangioma, by site
  cavernous (M9121/0) - *see* Hemangioma, by site
  central nervous system NEC 228.09
  choroid 228.09
  heart 228.09
  infantile (M9131/0) - *see* Hemangioma, by site
  intra-abdominal structures 228.04
  intracranial structures 228.02
  intramuscular (M9132/0) - *see* Hemangioma, by site
  iris 228.09
  juvenile (M9131/0) - *see* Hemangioma, by site
  malignant (M9120/3) - *see* Neoplasm, connective tissue, malignant
  meninges 228.09
    brain 228.02
    spinal cord 228.09
  peritoneum 228.04
  placenta - *see* Placenta, abnormal
  plexiform (M9131/0) - *see* Hemangioma, by site
  racemose (M9123/0) - *see* Hemangioma, by site
  retina 228.03
  retroperitoneal tissue 228.04
  sclerosing (M8832/0) - *see* Neoplasm, skin, benign

Hemangioma (*Continued*)
  simplex (M9131/0) - *see* Hemangioma, by site
  skin and subcutaneous tissue 228.01
  specified site NEC 228.09
  spinal cord 228.09
  venous (M9122/0) - *see* Hemangioma, by site
  verrucous keratotic (M9142/0) - *see* Hemangioma, by site
Hemangiomatosis (systemic) 757.32
  involving single site - *see* Hemangioma
Hemangiopericytoma (M9150/1) - *see also* Neoplasm, connective tissue, uncertain behavior
  benign (M9150/0) - *see* Neoplasm, connective tissue, benign
  malignant (M9150/3) - *see* Neoplasm, connective tissue, malignant
Hemangiosarcoma (M9120/3) - *see* Neoplasm, connective tissue, malignant
Hemarthrosis (nontraumatic) 719.10
  ankle 719.17
  elbow 719.12
  foot 719.17
  hand 719.14
  hip 719.15
  knee 719.16
  multiple sites 719.19
  pelvic region 719.15
  shoulder (region) 719.11
  specified site NEC 719.18
  traumatic - *see* Sprain, by site
  wrist 719.13
Hematemesis 578.0
  with ulcer - *see* Ulcer, by site, with hemorrhage
  due to S. japonicum 120.2
  Goldstein's (familial hemorrhagic telangiectasia) 448.0
  newborn 772.4
    due to swallowed maternal blood 777.3
Hematidrosis 705.89
Hematinuria (*see also* Hemoglobinuria) 791.2
  malarial 084.8
  paroxysmal 283.2
Hematite miners' lung 503
Hematobilia 576.8
Hematocele (congenital) (diffuse) (idiopathic) 608.83
  broad ligament 620.7
  canal of Nuck 629.0
  cord, male 608.83
  fallopian tube 620.8
  female NEC 629.0
  ischiorectal 569.89
  male NEC 608.83
  ovary 629.0
  pelvis, pelvic
    female 629.0
      with ectopic pregnancy (*see also* Pregnancy, ectopic) 633.9
    male 608.83
  periuterine 629.0
  retrouterine 629.0
  scrotum 608.83
  spermatic cord (diffuse) 608.83
  testis 608.84
  traumatic - *see* Injury, internal, pelvis
  tunica vaginalis 608.83
  uterine ligament 629.0
  uterus 621.4

Hematocele *(Continued)*
  vagina 623.6
  vulva 624.5
Hematocephalus 742.4
Hematochezia *(see also* Melena) 578.1
Hematochyluria *(see also* Infestation, filarial) 125.9
Hematocolpos 626.8
Hematocornea 371.12
Hematogenous - *see* condition
Hematoma (skin surface intact) (traumatic) - *see also* Contusion

> Note   Hematomas are coded according to origin and the nature and site of the hematoma or the accompanying injury. Hematomas of unspecified origin are coded as injuries of the sites involved, except:
>
> (a)   hematomas of genital organs which are coded as diseases of the organ involved unless they complicate pregnancy or delivery
> (b)   hematomas of the eye which are coded as diseases of the eye.
>
> For late effect of hematoma classifiable to 920-924 *see* Late, effect, contusion.

with
  crush injury - *see* Crush
  fracture - *see* Fracture, by site
  injury of internal organs - *see also* Injury, internal, by site
    kidney - *see* Hematoma, kidney, traumatic
    liver - *see* Hematoma, liver, traumatic
    spleen - *see* Hematoma, spleen
  nerve injury - *see* Injury, nerve
  open wound - *see* Wound, open, by site
  skin surface intact - *see* Contusion
abdomen (wall) - *see* Contusion, abdomen
amnion 658.8
aorta, dissecting 441.00
  abdominal 441.02
  thoracic 441.01
  thoracoabdominal 441.03
arterial (complicating trauma) 904.9
  specified site - *see* Injury, blood vessel, by site
auricle (ear) 380.31
birth injury 767.8
  skull 767.1
brain (traumatic) 853.0

> Note   Use the following fifth-digit subclassification with categories 851-854:
>
> 0   unspecified state of consciousness
> 1   with no loss of consciousness
> 2   with brief [less than one hour] loss of consciousness
> 3   with moderate [1-24 hours] loss of consciousness
> 4   with prolonged [more than 24 hours] loss of consciousness and return to pre-existing conscious level
> 5   with prolonged [more than 24 hours] loss of consciousness, without return to pre-existing conscious level
>
> Use fifth-digit 5 to designate when a patient is unconscious and dies before regaining consciousness, regardless of the duration of the loss of consciousness
>
> 6   with loss of consciousness of unspecified duration
> 9   with concussion, unspecified

Hematoma *(Continued)*
  with
    cerebral
      contusion - *see* Contusion, brain
      laceration - *see* Laceration, brain
      open intracranial wound 853.1
      skull fracture - *see* Fracture, skull, by site
    extradural or epidural 852.4
      with open intracranial wound 852.5
      fetus or newborn 767.0
      nontraumatic 432.0
    fetus or newborn NEC 767.0
    nontraumatic (*see also* Hemorrhage, brain) 431
      epidural or extradural 432.0
      newborn NEC 772.8
      subarachnoid, arachnoid, or meningeal (*see also* Hemorrhage, subarachnoid) 430
      subdural (*see also* Hemorrhage, subdural) 432.1
    subarachnoid, arachnoid, or meningeal 852.0
      with open intracranial wound 852.1
      fetus or newborn 772.2
      nontraumatic (*see also* Hemorrhage, subarachnoid) 430
    subdural 852.2
      with open intracranial wound 852.3
      fetus or newborn (localized) 767.0
      nontraumatic (*see also* Hemorrhage, subdural) 432.1
  breast (nontraumatic) 611.8
  broad ligament (nontraumatic) 620.7
    complicating delivery 665.7
    traumatic - *see* Injury, internal, broad ligament
  calcified NEC 959.9
  capitis 920
    due to birth injury 767.1
    newborn 767.1
  cerebral - *see* Hematoma, brain
  cesarean section wound 674.3
  chorion - *see* Placenta, abnormal
  complicating delivery (perineum) (vulva) 664.5
    pelvic 665.7
    vagina 665.7
  corpus
    cavernosum (nontraumatic) 607.82
    luteum (nontraumatic) (ruptured) 620.1
  dura (mater) - *see* Hematoma, brain, subdural
  epididymis (nontraumatic) 608.83
  epidural (traumatic) - *see also* Hematoma, brain, extradural
    spinal - *see* Injury, spinal, by site
  episiotomy 674.3

Hematoma *(Continued)*
  external ear 380.31
  extradural - *see also* Hematoma, brain, extradural
    fetus or newborn 767.0
    nontraumatic 432.0
      fetus or newborn 767.0
  fallopian tube 620.8
  genital organ (nontraumatic)
    female NEC 629.8
    male NEC 608.83
    traumatic (external site) 922.4
      internal - *see* Injury, internal, genital organ
  graafian follicle (ruptured) 620.0
  internal organs (abdomen, chest, or pelvis) - *see also* Injury, internal, by site
    kidney - *see* Hematoma, kidney, traumatic
    liver - *see* Hematoma, liver, traumatic
    spleen - *see* Hematoma, spleen
  intracranial - *see* Hematoma, brain
  kidney, cystic 593.81
    traumatic 866.01
      with open wound into cavity 866.11
  labia (nontraumatic) 624.5
  lingual (and other parts of neck, scalp, or face, except eye) 920
  liver (subcapsular) 573.8
    birth injury 767.8
    fetus or newborn 767.8
    traumatic NEC 864.01
      with
        laceration - *see* Laceration, liver
        open wound into cavity 864.11
  mediastinum - *see* Injury, internal, mediastinum
  meninges, meningeal (brain) - *see also* Hematoma, brain, subarachnoid
  spinal - *see* Injury, spinal, by site
  mesosalpinx (nontraumatic) 620.8
    traumatic - *see* Injury, internal, pelvis
  muscle (traumatic) - *see* Contusion, by site
  nasal (septum) (and other part(s) of neck, scalp, or face, except eye) 920
  obstetrical surgical wound 674.3
  orbit, orbital (nontraumatic) 376.32
    traumatic 921.2
  ovary (corpus luteum) (nontraumatic) 620.1
    traumatic - *see* Injury, internal, ovary
  pelvis (female) (nontraumatic) 629.8
    complicating delivery 665.7
    male 608.83
    traumatic - *see also* Injury, internal, pelvis
      specified organ NEC (*see also* Injury, internal, pelvis) 867.6
  penis (nontraumatic) 607.82
  pericranial (and neck, or face any part, except eye) 920
    due to injury at birth 767.1
  perineal wound (obstetrical) 674.3
    complicating delivery 664.5
  perirenal, cystic 593.81
  pinna 380.31
  placenta - *see* Placenta, abnormal
  postoperative 998.12

ICD-9-CM

H

Vol. 2

Hematoma *(Continued)*
  retroperitoneal (nontraumatic) 568.81
    traumatic - *see* Injury, internal, retroperitoneum
  retropubic, male 568.81
  scalp (and neck, or face any part, except eye) 920
    fetus or newborn 767.1
  scrotum (nontraumatic) 608.83
    traumatic 922.4
  seminal vesicle (nontraumatic) 608.83
    traumatic - *see* Injury, internal, seminal, vesicle
  spermatic cord - *see also* Injury, internal, spermatic cord
    nontraumatic 608.83
  spinal (cord) (meninges) - *see also* Injury, spinal, by site
    fetus or newborn 767.4
    nontraumatic 336.1
  spleen 865.01
    with
      laceration - *see* Laceration, spleen
      open wound into cavity 865.11
  sternocleidomastoid, birth injury 767.8
  sternomastoid, birth injury 767.8
  subarachnoid - *see also* Hematoma, brain, subarachnoid
    fetus or newborn 772.2
    nontraumatic (*see also* Hemorrhage, subarachnoid) 430
    newborn 772.2
  subdural - *see also* Hematoma, brain, subdural
    fetus or newborn (localized) 767.0
    nontraumatic (*see also* Hemorrhage, subdural) 432.1
  subperiosteal (syndrome) 267
    traumatic - *see* Hematoma, by site
  superficial, fetus or newborn 772.6
  syncytium - *see* Placenta, abnormal
  testis (nontraumatic) 608.83
    birth injury 767.8
    traumatic 922.4
  tunica vaginalis (nontraumatic) 608.83
  umbilical cord 663.6
    affecting fetus or newborn 762.6
  uterine ligament (nontraumatic) 620.7
    traumatic - *see* Injury, internal, pelvis
  uterus 621.4
    traumatic - *see* Injury, internal, pelvis
  vagina (nontraumatic) (ruptured) 623.6
    complicating delivery 665.7
    traumatic 922.4
  vas deferens (nontraumatic) 608.83
    traumatic - *see* Injury, internal, vas deferens
  vitreous 379.23
  vocal cord 920
  vulva (nontraumatic) 624.5
    complicating delivery 664.5
    fetus or newborn 767.8
    traumatic 922.4
Hematometra 621.4
Hematomyelia 336.1
  with fracture of vertebra (*see also* Fracture, vertebra, by site, with spinal cord injury) 806.8
  fetus or newborn 767.4
Hematomyelitis 323.9
  late effect - *see* category 326
Hematoperitoneum (*see also* Hemoperitoneum) 568.81

Hematopneumothorax (*see also* Hemothorax) 511.8
Hematoporphyria (acquired) (congenital) 277.1
Hematoporphyrinuria (acquired) (congenital) 277.1
Hematorachis, hematorrhachis 336.1
  fetus or newborn 767.4
Hematosalpinx 620.8
  with
    ectopic pregnancy (*see also* categories 633.0-633.9) 639.2
    molar pregnancy (*see also* categories 630-632) 639.2
    infectional (*see also* Salpingo-oophoritis) 614.2
Hematospermia 608.83
Hematothorax (*see also* Hemothorax) 511.8
Hematotympanum 381.03
Hematuria (benign) (essential) (idiopathic) 599.7
  due to S. hematobium 120.0
  endemic 120.0
  intermittent 599.7
  malarial 084.8
  paroxysmal 599.7
  sulfonamide
    correct substance properly administered 599.7
    overdose or wrong substance given or taken 961.0
  tropical (bilharziasis) 120.0
  tuberculous (*see also* Tuberculosis) 016.9
Hematuric bilious fever 084.8
Hemeralopia 368.60
  meaning day blindness 368.10
  vitamin A deficiency 264.5
Hemiabiotrophy 799.8
Hemi-akinesia 781.8
Hemianalgesia (*see also* Disturbance, sensation) 782.0
Hemianencephaly 740.0
Hemianesthesia (*see also* Disturbance, sensation) 782.0
Hemianopia, hemianopsia (altitudinal) (homonymous) 368.46
  binasal 368.47
  bitemporal 368.47
  heteronymous 368.47
  syphilitic 095.8
Hemiasomatognosia 307.9
Hemiathetosis 781.0
Hemiatrophy 799.8
  cerebellar 334.8
  face 349.89
    progressive 349.89
  fascia 728.9
  leg 728.2
  tongue 529.8
Hemiballism(us) 333.5
Hemiblock (cardiac) (heart) (left) 426.2
Hemicardia 746.89
Hemicephalus, hemicephaly 740.0
Hemichorea 333.5
Hemicrania 346.9
  congenital malformation 740.0
Hemidystrophy - *see* Hemiatrophy
Hemiectromelia 755.4
Hemihypalgesia (*see also* Disturbance, sensation) 782.0
Hemihypertrophy (congenital) 759.89
  cranial 756.0

Hemihypesthesia (*see also* Disturbance, sensation) 782.0
Hemi-inattention 781.8
Hemimelia 755.4
  lower limb 755.30
    paraxial (complete) (incomplete) (intercalary) (terminal) 755.32
      fibula 755.37
      tibia 755.36
    transverse (complete) (partial) 755.31
  upper limb 755.20
    paraxial (complete) (incomplete) (intercalary) (terminal) 755.22
      radial 755.26
      ulnar 755.27
    transverse (complete) (partial) 755.21
Hemiparalysis (*see also* Hemiplegia) 342.9
Hemiparesis (*see also* Hemiplegia) 342.9
Hemiparesthesia (*see also* Disturbance, sensation) 782.0
Hemiplegia 342.9
  acute (*see also* Disease, cerebrovascular, acute) 436
  alternans facialis 344.89
  apoplectic (*see also* Disease, cerebrovascular, acute) 436
    late effect or residual
      affecting
        dominant side 438.21
        nondominant side 438.22
        unspecified side 438.20
  arteriosclerotic 437.0
    late effect or residual
      affecting
        dominant side 438.21
        nondominant side 438.22
        unspecified side 438.20
  ascending (spinal) NEC 344.89
  attack (*see also* Disease, cerebrovascular, acute) 436
  brain, cerebral (current episode) 437.8
    congenital 343.1
  cerebral - *see* Hemiplegia, brain
  congenital (cerebral) (spastic) (spinal) 343.1
  conversion neurosis (hysterical) 300.11
  cortical - *see* Hemiplegia, brain
  due to
    arteriosclerosis 437.0
      late effect or residual
        affecting
          dominant side 438.21
          nondominant side 438.22
          unspecified side 438.20
    cerebrovascular lesion (*see also* Disease, cerebrovascular, acute) 436
      late effect
        affecting
          dominant side 438.21
          nondominant side 438.22
          unspecified side 438.20
  embolic (current) (*see also* Embolism, brain) 434.1
    late effect
      affecting
        dominant side 438.21
        nondominant side 438.22
        unspecified side 438.20
  flaccid 342.0
  hypertensive (current episode) 437.8
  infantile (postnatal) 343.4

Hemiplegia (*Continued*)
late effect
birth injury, intracranial or spinal 343.4
cerebrovascular lesion - *see* Late effect(s) (of) cerebrovascular disease
viral encephalitis 139.0
middle alternating NEC 344.89
newborn NEC 767.0
seizure (current episode) (*see also* Disease, cerebrovascular, acute) 436
spastic 342.1
congenital or infantile 343.1
specified NEC 342.8
thrombotic (current) (*see also* Thrombosis, brain) 434.0
late effect - *see* Late effect(s) (of) cerebrovascular disease
Hemisection, spinal cord - *see* Fracture, vertebra, by site, with spinal cord injury
Hemispasm 781.0
facial 781.0
Hemispatial neglect 781.8
Hemisporosis 117.9
Hemitremor 781.0
Hemivertebra 756.14
Hemobilia 576.8
Hemocholecyst 575.8
Hemochromatosis (acquired) (diabetic) (hereditary) (liver) (myocardium) (primary idiopathic) (secondary) 275.0
with refractory anemia 285.0
Hemodialysis V56.0
Hemoglobin - *see also* condition
abnormal (disease) - *see* Disease, hemoglobin
AS genotype 282.5
fetal, hereditary persistence 282.7
high-oxygen-affinity 289.0
low NEC 285.9
S (Hb-S), heterozygous 282.5
Hemoglobinemia 283.2
due to blood transfusion NEC 999.8
bone marrow 996.85
paroxysmal 283.2
Hemoglobinopathy (mixed) (*see also* Disease, hemoglobin) 282.7
with thalassemia 282.4
sickle-cell 282.60
with thalassemia 282.4
Hemoglobinuria, hemoglobinuric 791.2
with anemia, hemolytic, acquired (chronic) NEC 283.2
cold (agglutinin) (paroxysmal) (with Raynaud's syndrome) 283.2
due to
exertion 283.2
hemolysis (from external causes) NEC 283.2
exercise 283.2
fever (malaria) 084.8
infantile 791.2
intermittent 283.2
malarial 084.8
march 283.2
nocturnal (paroxysmal) 283.2
paroxysmal (cold) (nocturnal) 283.2
Hemolymphangioma (M9175/0) 228.1

Hemolysis
fetal - *see* Jaundice, fetus or newborn
intravascular (disseminated) NEC 286.6
with
abortion - *see* Abortion, by type, with hemorrhage, delayed or excessive
ectopic pregnancy (*see also* categories 633.0-633.9) 639.1
hemorrhage of pregnancy 641.3
affecting fetus or newborn 762.1
molar pregnancy (*see also* categories 630-632) 639.1
acute 283.2
following
abortion 639.1
ectopic or molar pregnancy 639.1
neonatal - *see* Jaundice, fetus or newborn
transfusion NEC 999.8
bone marrow 996.85
Hemolytic - *see also* condition
anemia - *see* Anemia, hemolytic
uremic syndrome 283.11
Hemometra 621.4
Hemopericardium (with effusion) 423.0
newborn 772.8
traumatic (*see also* Hemothorax, traumatic) 860.2
with open wound into thorax 860.3
Hemoperitoneum 568.81
infectional (*see also* Peritonitis) 567.2
traumatic - *see* Injury, internal, peritoneum
Hemophilia (familial) (hereditary) 286.0
A 286.0
B (Leyden) 286.1
C 286.2
calcipriva (*see also* Fibrinolysis) 286.7
classical 286.0
nonfamilial 286.7
vascular 286.4
Hemophilus influenzae NEC 041.5
arachnoiditis (basic) (brain) (spinal) 320.0
late effect - *see* category 326
bronchopneumonia 482.2
cerebral ventriculitis 320.0
late effect - *see* category 326
cerebrospinal inflammation 320.0
late effect - *see* category 326
infection NEC 041.5
leptomeningitis 320.0
late effect - *see* category 326
meningitis (cerebral) (cerebrospinal) (spinal) 320.0
late effect - *see* category 326
meningomyelitis 320.0
late effect - *see* category 326
pachymeningitis (adhesive) (fibrous) (hemorrhagic) (hypertrophic) (spinal) 320.0
late effect - *see* category 326
pneumonia (broncho-) 482.2
Hemophthalmos 360.43
Hemopneumothorax (*see also* Hemothorax) 511.8
traumatic 860.4
with open wound into thorax 860.5
Hemoptysis 786.3
due to Paragonimus (westermani) 121.2
newborn 770.3
tuberculous (*see also* Tuberculosis, pulmonary) 011.9

Hemorrhage, hemorrhagic (nontraumatic) 459.0
abdomen 459.0
accidental (antepartum) 641.2
affecting fetus or newborn 762.1
adenoid 474.8
adrenal (capsule) (gland) (medulla) 255.4
newborn 772.5
after labor - *see* Hemorrhage, postpartum
alveolar
lung, newborn 770.3
process 525.8
alveolus 525.8
amputation stump (surgical) 998.11
secondary, delayed 997.69
anemia (chronic) 280.0
acute 285.1
antepartum - *see* Hemorrhage, pregnancy
anus (sphincter) 569.3
apoplexy (stroke) 432.9
arachnoid - *see* Hemorrhage, subarachnoid
artery NEC 459.0
brain (*see also* Hemorrhage, brain) 431
middle meningeal - *see* Hemorrhage, subarachnoid
basilar (ganglion) (*see also* Hemorrhage, brain) 431
bladder 596.8
blood dyscrasia 289.9
bowel 578.9
newborn 772.4
brain (miliary) (nontraumatic) 431
with
birth injury 767.0
arachnoid - *see* Hemorrhage, subarachnoid
due to
birth injury 767.0
rupture of aneurysm (congenital) (*see also* Hemorrhage, subarachnoid) 430
mycotic 431
syphilis 094.89
epidural or extradural - *see* Hemorrhage, extradural
fetus or newborn (anoxic) (hypoxic) (due to birth trauma) (nontraumatic) 767.0
iatrogenic 997.02
postoperative 997.02
puerperal, postpartum, childbirth 674.0
stem 431
subarachnoid, arachnoid, or meningeal - *see* Hemorrhage, subarachnoid
subdural - *see* Hemorrhage, subdural
traumatic NEC 853.0

Note   Use the following fifth-digit subclassification with categories 851-854:

0   unspecified state of consciousness
1   with no loss of consciousness
2   with brief [less than one hour] loss of consciousness
3   with moderate [1-24 hours] loss of consciousness

Hemorrhage, hemorrhagic *(Continued)*

> 4   with prolonged [more than 24 hours] loss of consciousness and return to pre-existing conscious level
>
> 5   with prolonged [more than 24 hours] loss of consciousness, without return to pre-existing conscious level
>
> Use fifth-digit 5 to designate when a patient is unconscious and dies before regaining consciousness, regardless of the duration of the loss of consciousness
>
> 6   with loss of consciousness of unspecified duration
> 9   with concussion, unspecified

  with
    cerebral
      contusion - *see* Contusion, brain
      laceration - *see* Laceration, brain
    open intracranial wound 853.1
    skull fracture - *see* Fracture, skull, by site
  extradural or epidural 852.4
    with open intracranial wound 852.5
  subarachnoid 852.0
    with open intracranial wound 852.1
  subdural 852.2
    with open intracranial wound 852.3
breast 611.79
bronchial tube - *see* Hemorrhage, lung
bronchopulmonary - *see* Hemorrhage, lung
bronchus (cause unknown) *(see also* Hemorrhage, lung) 786.3
bulbar *(see also* Hemorrhage, brain) 431
bursa 727.89
capillary 448.9
  primary 287.8
capsular - *see* Hemorrhage, brain
cardiovascular 429.89
cecum 578.9
cephalic *(see also* Hemorrhage, brain) 431
cerebellar *(see also* Hemorrhage, brain) 431
cerebellum *(see also* Hemorrhage, brain) 431
cerebral *(see also* Hemorrhage, brain) 431
  fetus or newborn (anoxic) (traumatic) 767.0
cerebromeningeal *(see also* Hemorrhage, brain) 431
cerebrospinal *(see also* Hemorrhage, brain) 431
cerebrum *(see also* Hemorrhage, brain) 431
cervix (stump) (uteri) 622.8
cesarean section wound 674.3
chamber, anterior (eye) 364.41
childbirth - *see* Hemorrhage, complicating, delivery
choroid 363.61
  expulsive 363.62
ciliary body 364.41
cochlea 386.8

Hemorrhage, hemorrhagic *(Continued)*
colon - *see* Hemorrhage, intestine
complicating
  delivery 641.9
    affecting fetus or newborn 762.1
    associated with
      afibrinogenemia 641.3
        affecting fetus or newborn 763.89 ◀▥
      coagulation defect 641.3
        affecting fetus or newborn 763.89 ◀▥
      hyperfibrinolysis 641.3
        affecting fetus or newborn 763.89 ◀▥
      hypofibrinogenemia 641.3
        affecting fetus or newborn 763.89 ◀▥
    due to
      low-lying placenta 641.1
        affecting fetus or newborn 762.0
      placenta previa 641.1
        affecting fetus or newborn 762.0
      premature separation of placenta 641.2
        affecting fetus or newborn 762.1
      retained
        placenta 666.0
        secundines 666.2
      trauma 641.8
        affecting fetus or newborn 763.89 ◀▥
      uterine leiomyoma 641.8
        affecting fetus or newborn 763.89 ◀▥
  surgical procedure 998.11
concealed NEC 459.0
congenital 772.9
conjunctiva 372.72
  newborn 772.8
cord, newborn 772.0
  slipped ligature 772.3
  stump 772.3
corpus luteum (ruptured) 620.1
cortical *(see also* Hemorrhage, brain) 431
cranial 432.9
cutaneous 782.7
  newborn 772.6
cyst, pancreas 577.2
cystitis - *see* Cystitis
delayed
  with
    abortion - *see* Abortion, by type, with hemorrhage, delayed or excessive
    ectopic pregnancy *(see also* categories 633.0-633.9) 639.1
    molar pregnancy *(see also* categories 630-632) 639.1
  following
    abortion 639.1
    ectopic or molar pregnancy 639.1
  postpartum 666.2
diathesis (familial) 287.9
  newborn 776.0
disease 287.9
  newborn 776.0
  specified type NEC 287.8
disorder 287.9
  due to circulating anticoagulants 286.5

Hemorrhage, hemorrhagic *(Continued)*
disorder *(Continued)*
  specified type NEC 287.8
due to
  any device, implant, or graft (presence of) classifiable to 996.0-996.5 - *see* Complications, due to (presence of) any device, implant, or graft classified to 996.0-996.5 NEC
  circulating anticoagulant 286.5
duodenum, duodenal 537.89
  ulcer - *see* Ulcer, duodenum, with hemorrhage
dura mater - *see* Hemorrhage, subdural
endotracheal - *see* Hemorrhage, lung
epidural - *see* Hemorrhage, extradural
episiotomy 674.3
esophagus 530.82
  varix *(see also* Varix, esophagus, bleeding) 456.0
excessive
  with
    abortion - *see* Abortion, by type, with hemorrhage, delayed or excessive
    ectopic pregnancy *(see also* categories 633.0-633.9) 639.1
    molar pregnancy *(see also* categories 630-632) 639.1
  following
    abortion 639.1
    ectopic or molar pregnancy 639.1
external 459.0
extradural (traumatic) - *see also* Hemorrhage, brain, traumatic, extradural
  birth injury 767.0
  fetus or newborn (anoxic) (traumatic) 767.0
  nontraumatic 432.0
eye 360.43
  chamber (anterior) (aqueous) 364.41
  fundus 362.81
eyelid 374.81
fallopian tube 620.8
fetomaternal 772.0
  affecting management of pregnancy or puerperium 656.0
fetus, fetal 772.0
  from
    cut end of co-twin's cord 772.0
    placenta 772.0
    ruptured cord 772.0
    vasa previa 772.0
  into
    co-twin 772.0
    mother's circulation 772.0
      affecting management of pregnancy or puerperium 656.0
fever *(see also* Fever, hemorrhagic) 065.9
  with renal syndrome 078.6
  arthropod-borne NEC 065.9
  Bangkok 065.4
  Crimean 065.0
  dengue virus 065.4
  epidemic 078.6
  Junin virus 078.7
  Korean 078.6
  Machupo virus 078.7
  mite-borne 065.8
  mosquito-borne 065.4
  Philippine 065.4

Hemorrhage, hemorrhagic (*Continued*)
fever (*Continued*)
    Russian (Yaroslav) 078.6
    Singapore 065.4
    Southeast Asia 065.4
    Thailand 065.4
    tick-borne NEC 065.3
fibrinogenolysis (*see also* Fibrinolysis) 286.6
fibrinolytic (acquired) (*see also* Fibrinolysis) 286.6
fontanel 767.1
from tracheostomy stoma 519.09
fundus, eye 362.81
funis
    affecting fetus or newborn 772.0
    complicating delivery 663.8
gastric (*see also* Hemorrhage, stomach) 578.9
gastroenteric 578.9
    newborn 772.4
gastrointestinal (tract) 578.9
    newborn 772.4
genitourinary (tract) NEC 599.89
gingiva 523.8
globe 360.43
gravidarum - *see* Hemorrhage, pregnancy
gum 523.8
heart 429.89
hypopharyngeal (throat) 784.8
intermenstrual 626.6
    irregular 626.6
    regular 626.5
internal (organs) 459.0
    capsule (*see also* Hemorrhage brain) 431
    ear 386.8
    newborn 772.8
intestine 578.9
    congenital 772.4
    newborn 772.4
into
    bladder wall 596.7
    bursa 727.89
    corpus luysii (*see also* Hemorrhage, brain) 431
intra-abdominal 459.0
    during or following surgery 998.11
intra-alveolar, newborn (lung) 770.3
intracerebral (*see also* Hemorrhage, brain) 431
intracranial NEC 432.9
    puerperal, postpartum, childbirth 674.0
    traumatic - *see* Hemorrhage, brain, traumatic
intramedullary NEC 336.1
intraocular 360.43
intraoperative 998.11
intrapartum - *see* Hemorrhage, complicating, delivery
intrapelvic
    female 629.8
    male 459.0
intraperitoneal 459.0
intrapontine (*see also* Hemorrhage, brain) 431
intrauterine 621.4
    complicating delivery - *see* Hemorrhage, complicating, delivery
    in pregnancy or childbirth - *see* Hemorrhage, pregnancy

Hemorrhage, hemorrhagic (*Continued*)
intrauterine (*Continued*)
    postpartum (*see also* Hemorrhage, postpartum) 666.1
intraventricular (*see also* Hemorrhage, brain) 431
    fetus or newborn (anoxic) (traumatic) 772.1
intravesical 596.7
iris (postinfectional) (postinflammatory) (toxic) 364.41
joint (nontraumatic) 719.10
    ankle 719.17
    elbow 719.12
    foot 719.17
    forearm 719.13
    hand 719.14
    hip 719.15
    knee 719.16
    lower leg 719.16
    multiple sites 719.19
    pelvic region 719.15
    shoulder (region) 719.11
    specified site NEC 719.18
    thigh 719.15
    upper arm 719.12
    wrist 719.13
kidney 593.81
knee (joint) 719.16
labyrinth 386.8
leg NEC 459.0
lenticular striate artery (*see also* Hemorrhage, brain) 431
ligature, vessel 998.11
liver 573.8
lower extremity NEC 459.0
lung 786.3
    newborn 770.3
    tuberculous (*see also* Tuberculosis, pulmonary) 011.9
malaria 084.8
marginal sinus 641.2
massive subaponeurotic, birth injury 767.1
maternal, affecting fetus or newborn 762.1
mediastinum 786.3
medulla (*see also* Hemorrhage, brain) 431
membrane (brain) (*see also* Hemorrhage, subarachnoid) 430
    spinal cord - *see* Hemorrhage, spinal cord
meninges, meningeal (brain) (middle) (*see also* Hemorrhage, subarachnoid) 430
    spinal cord - *see* Hemorrhage, spinal cord
mesentery 568.81
metritis 626.8
midbrain (*see also* Hemorrhage, brain) 431
mole 631
mouth 528.9
mucous membrane NEC 459.0
    newborn 772.8
muscle 728.89
nail (subungual) 703.8
nasal turbinate 784.7
    newborn 772.8
nasopharynx 478.29
navel, newborn 772.3
newborn 772.9
    adrenal 772.5

Hemorrhage, hemorrhagic (*Continued*)
newborn (*Continued*)
    alveolar (lung) 770.3
    brain (anoxic) (hypoxic) (due to birth trauma) 767.0
    cerebral (anoxic) (hypoxic) (due to birth trauma) 767.0
    conjunctiva 772.8
    cutaneous 772.6
    diathesis 776.0
    due to vitamin K deficiency 776.0
    gastrointestinal 772.4
    internal (organs) 772.8
    intestines 772.4
    intra-alveolar (lung) 770.3
    intracranial (from any perinatal cause) 767.0
    intraventricular (from any perinatal cause) 772.1
    lung 770.3
    pulmonary (massive) 770.3
    spinal cord, traumatic 767.4
    stomach 772.4
    subaponeurotic (massive) 767.1
    subarachnoid (from any perinatal cause) 772.2
    subconjunctival 772.8
    umbilicus 772.0
        slipped ligature 772.3
        vasa previa 772.0
nipple 611.79
nose 784.7
    newborn 772.8
obstetrical surgical wound 674.3
omentum 568.89
    newborn 772.4
optic nerve (sheath) 377.42
orbit 376.32
ovary 620.1
oviduct 620.8
pancreas 577.8
parathyroid (gland) (spontaneous) 252.8
parturition - *see* Hemorrhage, complicating, delivery
penis 607.82
pericardium, pericarditis 423.0
perineal wound (obstetrical) 674.3
peritoneum, peritoneal 459.0
peritonsillar tissue 474.8
    after operation on tonsils 998.11
    due to infection 475
petechial 782.7
pituitary (gland) 253.8
placenta NEC 641.9
    affecting fetus or newborn 762.1
    from surgical or instrumental damage 641.8
        affecting fetus or newborn 762.1
    previa 641.1
        affecting fetus or newborn 762.0
pleura - *see* Hemorrhage, lung
polioencephalitis, superior 265.1
polymyositis - *see* Polymyositis
pons (*see also* Hemorrhage, brain) 431
pontine (*see also* Hemorrhage, brain) 431
popliteal 459.0
postcoital 626.7
postextraction (dental) 998.11
postmenopausal 627.1
postnasal 784.7
postoperative 998.11

Hemorrhoids *(Continued)*
internal 455.0
with complication NEC 455.2
bleeding, prolapsed, strangulated, or ulcerated 455.2
thrombosed 455.1
residual skin tag 455.9
sentinel pile 455.9
thrombosed NEC 455.7
external 455.4
internal 455.1
Hemosalpinx 620.8
Hemosiderosis 275.0
dietary 275.0
pulmonary (idiopathic) 275.0 [516.1]
transfusion NEC 999.8
bone marrow 996.85
Hemospermia 608.83
Hemothorax 511.8
bacterial, nontuberculous 511.1
newborn 772.8
nontuberculous 511.8
bacterial 511.1
pneumococcal 511.1
postoperative 998.11
staphylococcal 511.1
streptococcal 511.1
traumatic 860.2
with
open wound into thorax 860.3
pneumothorax 860.4
with open wound into thorax 860.5
tuberculous (*see also* Tuberculosis, pleura) 012.0
Hemotympanum 385.89
Hench-Rosenberg syndrome (palindromic arthritis) (*see also* Rheumatism, palindromic) 719.3
Henle's warts 371.41
Henoch (-Schönlein)
disease or syndrome (allergic purpura) 287.0
purpura (allergic) 287.0
Henpue, henpuye 102.6
Heparitinuria 277.5
Hepar lobatum 095.3
Hepatalgia 573.8
Hepatic - *see also* condition
flexure syndrome 569.89
Hepatitis 573.3
acute (*see also* Necrosis, liver) 570
alcoholic 571.1
infective 070.1
with hepatic coma 070.0
alcoholic 571.1
amebic - *see* Abscess, liver, amebic
anicteric (acute) - *see* Hepatitis, viral
antigen-associated (HAA) - *see* Hepatitis, viral, type B
Australian antigen (positive) - *see* Hepatitis, viral, type B
catarrhal (acute) 070.1
with hepatic coma 070.0
chronic 571.40
newborn 070.1
with hepatic coma 070.0
chemical 573.3
cholangiolitic 573.8
cholestatic 573.8
chronic 571.40
active 571.49
viral - *see* Hepatitis, viral

Hepatitis *(Continued)*
chronic *(Continued)*
aggressive 571.49
persistent 571.41
viral - *see* Hepatitis, viral
cytomegalic inclusion virus 078.5 [573.1]
diffuse 573.3
"dirty needle" - *see* Hepatitis, viral
drug-induced 573.3
due to
Coxsackie 074.8 [573.1]
cytomegalic inclusion virus 078.5 [573.1]
infectious mononucleosis 075 [573.1]
malaria 084.9 [573.2]
mumps 072.71
secondary syphilis 091.62
toxoplasmosis (acquired) 130.5
congenital (active) 771.2
epidemic - *see* Hepatitis, viral, type A
fetus or newborn 774.4
fibrous (chronic) 571.49
acute 570
from injection, inoculation, or transfusion (blood) (other substance) (plasma) (serum) (onset within 8 months after administration) - *see* Hepatitis, viral
fulminant (viral) (*see also* Hepatitis, viral) 070.9
with hepatic coma 070.6
type A 070.1
with hepatic coma 070.0
type B - *see* Hepatitis, viral, type B
giant cell (neonatal) 774.4
hemorrhagic 573.8
homologous serum - *see* Hepatitis, viral
hypertrophic (chronic) 571.49
acute 570
infectious, infective (acute) (chronic) (subacute) 070.1
with hepatic coma 070.0
inoculation - *see* Hepatitis, viral
interstitial (chronic) 571.49
acute 570
lupoid 571.49
malarial 084.9 [573.2]
malignant (*see also* Necrosis, liver) 570
neonatal (toxic) 774.4
newborn 774.4
parenchymatous (acute) (*see also* Necrosis, liver) 570
peliosis 573.3
persistent, chronic 571.41
plasma cell 571.49
postimmunization - *see* Hepatitis, viral
postnecrotic 571.49
posttransfusion - *see* Hepatitis, viral
recurrent 571.49
septic 573.3
serum - *see* Hepatitis, viral
carrier (suspected of) V02.61
subacute (*see also* Necrosis, liver) 570
suppurative (diffuse) 572.0
syphilitic (late) 095.3
congenital (early) 090.0 [573.2]
late 090.5 [573.2]
secondary 091.62
toxic (noninfectious) 573.3
fetus or newborn 774.4
tuberculous (*see also* Tuberculosis) 017.9

Hepatitis *(Continued)*
viral (acute) (anicteric) (cholangiolitic) (cholestatic) (chronic) (subacute) 070.9
with hepatic coma 070.6
AU-SH type virus - *see* Hepatitis, viral, type B
Australia antigen - *see* Hepatitis, viral, type B
B-antigen - *see* Hepatitis, viral, type B
Coxsackie 074.8 [573.1]
cytomegalic inclusion 078.5 [573.1]
IH (virus) - *see* Hepatitis, viral, type A
infectious hepatitis virus - *see* Hepatitis, viral, type A
serum hepatitis virus - *see* Hepatitis, viral, type B
SH - *see* Hepatitis, viral, type B
specified type NEC 070.59
with hepatic coma 070.49
type A 070.1
with hepatic coma 070.0
type B (acute) 070.30
with
hepatic coma 070.20
with hepatitis delta 070.21
hepatitis delta 070.31
with hepatic coma 070.21
carrier status V02.61
chronic 070.32
with
hepatic coma 070.22
with hepatitis delta 070.23
hepatitis delta 070.33
with hepatic coma 070.23
type C (acute) 070.51
with hepatic coma 070.41
carrier status V02.62
chronic 070.54
with hepatic coma 070.44
type delta (with hepatitis B carrier state) 070.52
with
active hepatitis B disease - *see* Hepatitis, viral, type B
hepatic coma 070.42
type E 070.53
with hepatic coma 070.43
vaccination and inoculation (prophylactic) V05.3
Waldenström's (lupoid hepatitis) 571.49
Hepatization, lung (acute) - *see also* Pneumonia, lobar
chronic (*see also* Fibrosis, lung) 515
Hepatoblastoma (M8970/3) 155.0
Hepatocarcinoma (M8170/3) 155.0
Hepatocholangiocarcinoma (M8180/3) 155.0
Hepatocholangioma, benign (M8180/0) 211.5
Hepatocholangitis 573.8
Hepatocystitis (*see also* Cholecystitis) 575.10
Hepatodystrophy 570
Hepatolenticular degeneration 275.1
Hepatolithiasis - *see* Choledocholithiasis
Hepatoma (malignant) (M8170/3) 155.0
benign (M8170/0) 211.5
congenital (M8970/3) 155.0
embryonal (M8970/3) 155.0
Hepatomegalia glycogenica diffusa 271.0

ICD-9-CM

Vol. 2

Hepatomegaly (*see also* Hypertrophy,
  liver) 789.1
  congenital 751.69
    syphilitic 090.0
  due to Clonorchis sinensis 121.1
  Gaucher's 272.7
  syphilitic (congenital) 090.0
Hepatoptosis 573.8
Hepatorrhexis 573.8
Hepatosis, toxic 573.8
Hepatosplenomegaly 571.8
  due to S. japonicum 120.2
  hyperlipemic (Burger-Grutz type) 272.3
Herald patch 696.3
Hereditary - *see* condition
Heredodegeneration 330.9
  macular 362.70
Heredopathia atactica polyneuritiformis
  356.3
Heredosyphilis (*see also* Syphilis, congenital) 090.9
Hermaphroditism (true) 752.7
  with specified chromosomal anomaly -
    see Anomaly, chromosomes, sex
Hernia, hernial (acquired) (recurrent)
  553.9
  with
    gangrene (obstructed) NEC 551.9
    obstruction NEC 552.9
      and gangrene 551.9
  abdomen (wall) - *see* Hernia, ventral
  abdominal, specified site NEC 553.8
    with
      gangrene (obstructed) 551.8
      obstruction 552.8
        and gangrene 551.8
  appendix 553.8
    with
      gangrene (obstructed) 551.8
      obstruction 552.8
        and gangrene 551.8
  bilateral (inguinal) - *see* Hernia, ingui-
    nal
  bladder (sphincter)
    congenital (female) (male) 756.71
    female 618.0
    male 596.8
  brain 348.4
    congenital 742.0
  broad ligament 553.8
  cartilage, vertebral - *see* Displacement,
    intervertebral disc
  cerebral 348.4
    congenital 742.0
    endaural 742.0
  ciliary body 364.8
    traumatic 871.1
  colic 553.9
    with
      gangrene (obstructed) 551.9
      obstruction 552.9
        and gangrene 551.9
  colon 553.9
    with
      gangrene (obstructed) 551.9
      obstruction 552.9
        and gangrene 551.9
  colostomy (stoma) 569.69
  Cooper's (retroperitoneal) 553.8
    with
      gangrene (obstructed) 551.8
      obstruction 552.8
        and gangrene 551.8
  crural - *see* Hernia, femoral

Hernia, hernial (*Continued*)
  diaphragm, diaphragmatic 553.3
    with
      gangrene (obstructed) 551.3
      obstruction 552.3
        and gangrene 551.3
    congenital 756.6
    due to gross defect of diaphragm
      756.6
    traumatic 862.0
      with open wound into cavity 862.1
  direct (inguinal) - *see* Hernia, inguinal
  disc, intervertebral - *see* Displacement,
    intervertebral disc
  diverticulum, intestine 553.9
    with
      gangrene (obstructed) 551.9
      obstruction 552.9
        and gangrene 551.9
  double (inguinal) - *see* Hernia, inguinal
  duodenojejunal 553.8
    with
      gangrene (obstructed) 551.8
      obstruction 552.8
        and gangrene 551.8
  en glissade - *see* Hernia, inguinal
  enterostomy (stoma) 569.69
  epigastric 553.29
    with
      gangrene (obstruction) 551.29
      obstruction 552.29
        and gangrene 551.29
    recurrent 553.21
      with
        gangrene (obstructed) 551.21
        obstruction 552.21
          and gangrene 551.21
  esophageal hiatus (sliding) 553.3
    with
      gangrene (obstructed) 551.3
      obstruction 552.3
        and gangrene 551.3
    congenital 750.6
  external (inguinal) - *see* Hernia, inguinal
  fallopian tube 620.4
  fascia 728.89
  fat 729.30
    eyelid 374.34
    orbital 374.34
    pad 729.30
      eye, eyelid 374.34
      knee 729.31
      orbit 374.34
      popliteal (space) 729.31
      specified site NEC 729.39
  femoral (unilateral) 553.00
    with
      gangrene (obstructed) 551.00
      obstruction 552.00
        with gangrene 551.00
    bilateral 553.02
      gangrenous (obstructed) 551.02
      obstructed 552.02
        with gangrene 551.02
      recurrent 553.03
        gangrenous (obstructed)
          551.03
        obstructed 552.03
          with gangrene 551.03
    recurrent (unilateral) 553.01
      bilateral 553.03
        gangrenous (obstructed) 551.03
        obstructed 552.03
          with gangrene 551.03

Hernia, hernial (*Continued*)
  femoral (*Continued*)
    recurrent (*Continued*)
      gangrenous (obstructed) 551.01
      obstructed 552.01
        with gangrene 551.01
  foramen
    Bochdalek 553.3
      with
        gangrene (obstructed) 551.3
        obstruction 552.3
          and gangrene 551.3
      congenital 756.6
    magnum 348.4
    Morgagni, morgagnian 553.3
      with
        gangrene 551.3
        obstruction 552.3
          and gangrene 551.3
      congenital 756.6
  funicular (umbilical) 553.1
    with
      gangrene (obstructed) 551.1
      obstruction 552.1
        and gangrene 551.1
    spermatic cord - *see* Hernia, inguinal
  gangrenous - *see* Hernia, by site, with
    gangrene
  gastrointestinal tract 553.9
    with
      gangrene (obstructed) 551.9
      obstruction 552.9
        and gangrene 551.9
  gluteal - *see* Hernia, femoral
  Gruber's (internal mesogastric) 553.8
    with
      gangrene (obstructed) 551.8
      obstruction 552.8
        and gangrene 551.8
  Hesselbach's 553.8
    with
      gangrene (obstructed) 551.8
      obstruction 552.8
        and gangrene 551.8
  hiatal (esophageal) (sliding) 553.3
    with
      gangrene (obstructed) 551.3
      obstruction 552.3
        and gangrene 551.3
    congenital 750.6
  incarcerated (*see also* Hernia, by site,
    with obstruction) 552.9
    gangrenous (*see also* Hernia, by site,
      with gangrene) 551.9
  incisional 553.21
    with
      gangrene (obstructed) 551.21
      obstruction 552.21
        and gangrene 551.21
    lumbar - *see* Hernia, lumbar
    recurrent 553.21
      with
        gangrene (obstructed) 551.21
        obstruction 552.21
          and gangrene 551.21
  indirect (inguinal) - *see* Hernia, ingui-
    nal
  infantile - *see* Hernia, inguinal
  infrapatellar fat pad 729.31
  inguinal (direct) (double) (encysted)
    (external) (funicular) (indirect) (in-
    fantile) (internal) (interstitial)
    (oblique) (scrotal) (sliding)
    550.9

Hernia, hernial (*Continued*)

> Note   Use the following fifth-digit subclassification with category 550:
>
> 0   unilateral or unspecified (not specified as recurrent)
> 1   unilateral or unspecified, recurrent
> 2   bilateral (not specified as recurrent)
> 3   bilateral, recurrent

   with
      gangrene (obstructed) 550.0
      obstruction 550.1
         and gangrene 550.0
internal 553.8
   with
      gangrene (obstructed) 551.8
      obstruction 552.8
         and gangrene 551.8
   inguinal - *see* Hernia, inguinal
interstitial 553.9
   with
      gangrene (obstructed) 551.9
      obstruction 552.9
         and gangrene 551.9
   inguinal - *see* Hernia, inguinal
intervertebral cartilage or disc - *see* Displacement, intervertebral disc
intestine, intestinal 553.9
   with
      gangrene (obstructed) 551.9
      obstruction 552.9
         and gangrene 551.9
intra-abdominal 553.9
   with
      gangrene (obstructed) 551.9
      obstruction 552.9
         and gangrene 551.9
intraparietal 553.9
   with
      gangrene (obstructed) 551.9
      obstruction 552.9
         and gangrene 551.9
iris 364.8
   traumatic 871.1
irreducible (*see also* Hernia, by site, with obstruction) 552.9
   gangrenous (with obstruction) (*see also* Hernia, by site, with gangrene) 551.9
ischiatic 553.8
   with
      gangrene (obstructed) 551.8
      obstruction 552.8
         and gangrene 551.8
ischiorectal 553.8
   with
      gangrene (obstructed) 551.8
      obstruction 552.8
         and gangrene 551.8
lens 379.32
   traumatic 871.1
linea
   alba - *see* Hernia, epigastric
   semilunaris - *see* Hernia, spigelian
Littre's (diverticular) 553.9
   with
      gangrene (obstructed) 551.9
      obstruction 552.9
         and gangrene 551.9
lumbar 553.8
   with
      gangrene (obstructed) 551.8

Hernia, hernial (*Continued*)

lumbar (*Continued*)
   with (*Continued*)
      obstruction 552.8
         and gangrene 551.8
   intervertebral disc 722.10
lung (subcutaneous) 518.89
   congenital 748.69
mediastinum 519.3
mesenteric (internal) 553.8
   with
      gangrene (obstructed) 551.8
      obstruction 552.8
         and gangrene 551.8
mesocolon 553.8
   with
      gangrene (obstructed) 551.8
      obstruction 552.8
         and gangrene 551.8
muscle (sheath) 728.89
nucleus pulposus - *see* Displacement, intervertebral disc
oblique (inguinal) - *see* Hernia, inguinal
obstructive (*see also* Hernia, by site, with obstruction) 552.9
   gangrenous (with obstruction) (*see also* Hernia, by site, with gangrene) 551.9
obturator 553.8
   with
      gangrene (obstructed) 551.8
      obstruction 552.8
         and gangrene 551.8
omental 553.8
   with
      gangrene (obstructed) 551.8
      obstruction 552.8
         and gangrene 551.8
orbital fat (pad) 374.34
ovary 620.4
oviduct 620.4
paracolostomy (stoma) 569.69
paraduodenal 553.8
   with
      gangrene (obstructed) 551.8
      obstruction 552.8
         and gangrene 551.8
paraesophageal 553.3
   with
      gangrene (obstructed) 551.3
      obstruction 552.3
         and gangrene 551.3
   congenital 750.6
parahiatal 553.3
   with
      gangrene (obstructed) 551.3
      obstruction 552.3
         and gangrene 551.3
paraumbilical 553.1
   with
      gangrene (obstructed) 551.1
      obstruction 552.1
         and gangrene 551.1
parietal 553.9
   with
      gangrene (obstructed) 551.9
      obstruction 552.9
         and gangrene 551.9
perineal 553.8
   with
      gangrene (obstructed) 551.8
      obstruction 552.8
         and gangrene 551.8

Hernia, hernial (*Continued*)

peritoneal sac, lesser 553.8
   with
      gangrene (obstructed) 551.8
      obstruction 552.8
         and gangrene 551.8
popliteal fat pad 729.31
postoperative 553.21
   with
      gangrene (obstructed) 551.21
      obstruction 552.21
         and gangrene 551.21
pregnant uterus 654.4
prevesical 596.8
properitoneal 553.8
   with
      gangrene (obstructed) 551.8
      obstruction 552.8
         and gangrene 551.8
pudendal 553.8
   with
      gangrene (obstructed) 551.8
      obstruction 552.8
         and gangrene 551.8
rectovaginal 618.6
retroperitoneal 553.8
   with
      gangrene (obstructed) 551.8
      obstruction 552.8
         and gangrene 551.8
Richter's (parietal) 553.9
   with
      gangrene (obstructed) 551.9
      obstruction 552.9
         and gangrene 551.9
Rieux's, Riex's (retrocecal) 553.8
   with
      gangrene (obstructed) 551.8
      obstruction 552.8
         and gangrene 551.8
sciatic 553.8
   with
      gangrene (obstructed) 551.8
      obstruction 552.8
         and gangrene 551.8
scrotum, scrotal - *see* Hernia, inguinal
sliding (inguinal) - *see also* Hernia, inguinal
   hiatus - *see* Hernia, hiatal
spigelian 553.29
   with
      gangrene (obstructed) 551.29
      obstruction 552.29
         and gangrene 551.29
spinal (*see also* Spina bifida) 741.9
   with hydrocephalus 741.0
strangulated (*see also* Hernia, by site, with obstruction) 552.9
   gangrenous (with obstruction) (*see also* Hernia, by site, with gangrene) 551.9
supraumbilicus (linea alba) - *see* Hernia, epigastric
tendon 727.9
testis (nontraumatic) 095.8
Treitz's (fossa) 553.8
   with
      gangrene (obstructed) 551.8
      obstruction 552.8
         and gangrene 551.8
tunica
   albuginea 608.89
   vaginalis 752.8

ICD-9-CM

Vol. 2

Hernia, hernial (*Continued*)
umbilicus, umbilical 553.1
with
gangrene (obstructed) 551.1
obstruction 552.1
and gangrene 551.1
ureter 593.89
with obstruction 593.4
uterus 621.8
pregnant 654.4
vaginal (posterior) 618.6
Velpeau's (femoral) (*see also* Hernia,
femoral) 553.00
ventral 553.20
with
gangrene (obstructed) 551.20
obstruction 552.20
and gangrene 551.20
incisional 553.21
recurrent 553.21
with
gangrene (obstructed) 551.21
obstruction 552.21
and gangrene 551.21
vesical
congenital (female) (male) 756.71
female 618.0
male 596.8
vitreous (into anterior chamber) 379.21
traumatic 871.1
Herniation - *see also* Hernia
brain (stem) 348.4
cerebral 348.4
gastric mucosa (into duodenal bulb)
537.89
mediastinum 519.3
nucleus pulposus - *see* Displacement,
intervertebral disc
Herpangina 074.0
Herpes, herpetic 054.9
auricularis (zoster) 053.71
simplex 054.73
blepharitis (zoster) 053.20
simplex 054.41
circinate 110.5
circinatus 110.5
bullous 694.5
conjunctiva (simplex) 054.43
zoster 053.21
cornea (simplex) 054.43
disciform (simplex) 054.43
zoster 053.21
encephalitis 054.3
eye (zoster) 053.29
simplex 054.40
eyelid (zoster) 053.20
simplex 054.41
febrilis 054.9
fever 054.9
geniculate ganglionitis 053.11
genital, genitalis 054.10
specified site NEC 054.19
gestationis 646.8
gingivostomatitis 054.2
iridocyclitis (simplex) 054.44
zoster 053.22
iris (any site) 695.1
iritis (simplex) 054.44
keratitis (simplex) 054.43
dendritic 054.42
disciform 054.43
interstitial 054.43
zoster 053.21
keratoconjunctivitis (simplex) 054.43

Herpes, herpetic (*Continued*)
keratoconjunctivitis (*Continued*)
zoster 053.21
labialis 054.9
meningococcal 036.89
lip 054.9
meningitis (simplex) 054.72
zoster 053.0
ophthalmicus (zoster) 053.20
simplex 054.40
otitis externa (zoster) 053.71
simplex 054.73
penis 054.13
perianal 054.10
pharyngitis 054.79
progenitalis 054.10
scrotum 054.19
septicemia 054.5
simplex 054.9
complicated 054.8
ophthalmic 054.40
specified NEC 054.49
specified NEC 054.79
congenital 771.2
external ear 054.73
keratitis 054.43
dendritic 054.42
meningitis 054.72
neuritis 054.79
specified complication NEC 054.79
ophthalmic 054.49
visceral 054.71
stomatitis 054.2
tonsurans 110.0
maculosus (of Hebra) 696.3
visceral 054.71
vulva 054.12
vulvovaginitis 054.11
whitlow 054.6
zoster 053.9
auricularis 053.71
complicated 053.8
specified NEC 053.79
conjunctiva 053.21
cornea 053.21
ear 053.71
eye 053.29
geniculate 053.11
keratitis 053.21
interstitial 053.21
neuritis 053.10
ophthalmicus(a) 053.20
oticus 053.71
otitis externa 053.71
specified complication NEC 053.79
specified site NEC 053.9
zosteriform, intermediate type 053.9
Herrick's
anemia (hemoglobin S disease) 282.61
syndrome (hemoglobin S disease)
282.61
Hers' disease (glycogenosis VI) 271.0
Herter's infantilism (nontropical sprue)
579.0
Herter (-Gee) disease or syndrome (nontropical sprue) 579.0
Herxheimer's disease (diffuse idiopathic
cutaneous atrophy) 701.8
Herxheimer's reaction 995.0
Hesselbach's hernia - *see* Hernia, Hesselbach's
Heterochromia (congenital) 743.46
acquired 364.53
cataract 366.33

Heterochromia (*Continued*)
cyclitis 364.21
hair 704.3
iritis 364.21
retained metallic foreign body 360.62
magnetic 360.52
uveitis 364.21
Heterophoria 378.40
alternating 378.45
vertical 378.43
Heterophyes, small intestine 121.6
Heterophyiasis 121.6
Heteropsia 368.8
Heterotopia, heterotopic - *see also* Malposition, congenital
cerebralis 742.4
pancreas, pancreatic 751.7
spinalis 742.59
Heterotropia 378.30
intermittent 378.20
vertical 378.31
vertical (constant) (intermittent)
378.31
Heubner's disease 094.89
Heubner-Herter disease or syndrome
(nontropical sprue) 579.0
Hexadactylism 755.00
Heyd's syndrome (hepatorenal) 572.4
Hibernoma (M8880/0) - *see* Lipoma
Hiccough 786.8
epidemic 078.89
psychogenic 306.1
Hiccup (*see also* Hiccough) 786.8
Hicks (-Braxton) contractions 644.1
Hidden penis 752.65
Hidradenitis (axillaris) (suppurative)
705.83
Hidradenoma (nodular) (M8400/0) - *see
also* Neoplasm, skin, benign
clear cell (M8402/0) - *see* Neoplasm,
skin, benign
papillary (M8405/0) - *see* Neoplasm,
skin, benign
Hidrocystoma (M8404/0) - *see* Neoplasm, skin, benign
High
A$_2$ anemia 282.4
altitude effects 993.2
anoxia 993.2
on
ears 993.0
sinuses 993.1
polycythemia 289.0
arch
foot 755.67
palate 750.26
artery (arterial) tension (*see also* Hypertension) 401.9
without diagnosis of hypertension
796.2
basal metabolic rate (BMR) 794.7
blood pressure (*see also* Hypertension)
401.9
incidental reading (isolated) (nonspecific), no diagnosis of hypertension 796.2
compliance bladder 596.4
diaphragm (congenital) 756.6
frequency deafness (congenital) (regional) 389.8
head at term 652.5
affecting fetus or newborn 763.1
causing obstructed labor 660.0
affecting fetus or newborn 763.1

High *(Continued)*
output failure (cardiac) *(see also* Failure, heart) 428.9
oxygen-affinity hemoglobin 289.0
palate 750.26
risk
behavior - *see* problem
family situation V61.9
specified circumstance NEC V61.8
individual NEC V62.89
infant NEC V20.1
patient taking drugs (prescribed) V67.51
nonprescribed *(see also* Abuse, drugs, nondependent) 305.9
pregnancy V23.9
inadequate prenatal care V23.7
specified problem NEC V23.8
temperature (of unknown origin) *(see also* Pyrexia) 780.6
thoracic rib 756.3
Hildenbrand's disease (typhus) 081.9
Hilger's syndrome 337.0
Hill diarrhea 579.1
Hilliard's lupus *(see also* Tuberculosis) 017.0
Hilum - *see* condition
Hip - *see* condition
Hippel's disease (retinocerebral angiomatosis) 759.6
Hippus 379.49
Hirschfeld's disease (acute diabetes mellitus) *(see also* Diabetes) 250.0
Hirschsprung's disease or megacolon (congenital) 751.3
Hirsuties *(see also* Hypertrichosis) 704.1
Hirsutism *(see also* Hypertrichosis) 704.1
Hirudiniasis (external) (internal) 134.2
His-Werner disease (trench fever) 083.1
Hiss-Russell dysentery 004.1
Histamine cephalgia 346.2
Histidinemia 270.5
Histidinuria 270.5
Histiocytoma (M8832/0) - *(see also* Neoplasm, skin, benign)
fibrous (M8830/0) - *(see also* Neoplasm, skin, benign)
atypical (M8830/1) - *see* Neoplasm, connective tissue, uncertain behavior
malignant (M8830/3) - *see* Neoplasm, connective tissue, malignant
Histiocytosis (acute) (chronic) (subacute) 277.8
acute differentiated progressive (M9722/3) 202.5
cholesterol 277.8
essential 277.8
lipid, lipoid (essential) 272.7
lipochrome (familial) 288.1
malignant (M9720/3) 202.3
X (chronic) 277.8
acute (progressive) (M9722/3) 202.5
Histoplasmosis 115.90
with
endocarditis 115.94
meningitis 115.91
pericarditis 115.93
pneumonia 115.95
retinitis 115.92
specified manifestation NEC 115.99
African (due to Histoplasma duboisii) 115.10

Histoplasmosis *(Continued)*
African *(Continued)*
with
endocarditis 115.14
meningitis 115.11
pericarditis 115.13
pneumonia 115.15
retinitis 115.12
specified manifestation NEC 115.19
American (due to Histoplasma capsulatum) 115.00
with
endocarditis 115.04
meningitis 115.01
pericarditis 115.03
pneumonia 115.05
retinitis 115.02
specified manifestation NEC 115.09
Darling's - *see* Histoplasmosis, American
large form *(see also* Histoplasmosis, African) 115.10
lung 115.05
small form *(see also* Histoplasmosis, American) 115.00
History (personal) of
abuse
emotional V15.42
neglect V15.42
physical V15.41
affective psychosis V11.1
alcoholism V11.3
specified as drinking problem *(see also* Abuse, drugs, nondependent) 305.0
allergy to
analgesic agent NEC V14.6
anesthetic NEC V14.4
antibiotic agent NEC V14.1
penicillin V14.0
anti-infective agent NEC V14.3
diathesis V15.0
drug V14.9
specified type NEC V14.8
medicinal agents V14.9
specified type NEC V14.8
narcotic agent NEC V14.5
penicillin V14.0
radiographic dye V15.0
serum V14.7
specified nonmedicinal agents NEC V15.0
sulfa V14.2
sulfonamides V14.2
therapeutic agent NEC V15.0
vaccine V14.7
anemia V12.3
arthritis V13.4
benign neoplasm of brain V12.41
blood disease V12.3
calculi, urinary V13.01
cardiovascular disease V12.50
myocardial infarction 412
child abuse V15.41
cigarette smoking V15.82
circulatory system disease V12.50
myocardial infarction 412
congenital malformation V13.69   ◀▥▥
contraception V15.7
diathesis, allergic V15.0
digestive system disease V12.70
peptic ulcer V12.71
polyps, colonic V12.72
specified NEC V12.79

History *(Continued)*
disease (of) V13.9
blood V12.3
blood-forming organs V12.3
cardiovascular system V12.50
circulatory system V12.50
digestive system V12.70
peptic ulcer V12.71
polyps, colonic V12.72
specified NEC V12.79
infectious V12.00
malaria V12.03
poliomyelitis V12.02
specified NEC V12.09
tuberculosis V12.01
parasitic V12.00
specified NEC V12.09
respiratory system V12.6
skin V13.3
specified site NEC V13.8
subcutaneous tissue V13.3
trophoblastic V13.1
affecting management of pregnancy V23.1
disorder (of) V13.9
endocrine V12.2
genital system V13.2
hematological V12.3
immunity V12.2
mental V11.9
affective type V11.1
manic-depressive V11.1
neurosis V11.2
schizophrenia V11.0
specified type NEC V11.8
metabolic V12.2
musculoskeletal NEC V13.5
nervous system V12.40
specified type NEC V12.49
obstetric V13.2
affecting management of current pregnancy V23.4
sense organs V12.40
specified type NEC V12.49
specified site NEC V13.8
urinary system V13.00
calculi V13.01
specified NEC V13.09
drug use
nonprescribed *(see also* Abuse, drugs, nondependent) 305.9
patent *(see also* Abuse, drugs, nondependent) 305.9
effect NEC of external cause V15.89
embolism (pulmonary) V12.51
emotional abuse V15.42
endocrine disorder V12.2
family
allergy V19.6
anemia V18.2
arteriosclerosis V17.4
arthritis V17.7
asthma V17.5
blindness V19.0
blood disorder NEC V18.3
cardiovascular disease V17.4
cerebrovascular disease V17.1
chronic respiratory condition NEC V17.6
congenital anomalies V19.5
consanguinity V19.7
coronary artery disease V17.3
cystic fibrosis V18.1
deafness V19.2

◀ ▶   **New Code**   ◀‖‖ ‖‖▶   **Revised Code**

History *(Continued)*
  malignant neoplasm *(Continued)*
    urinary organ V10.50
    uterine adnexa V10.44
    uterus V10.42
    vagina V10.44
    vulva V10.44
  manic-depressive psychosis V11.1
  mental disorder V11.9
    affective type V11.1
    manic-depressive V11.1
    neurosis V11.2
    schizophrenia V11.0
    specified type NEC V11.8
  metabolic disorder V12.2
  musculoskeletal disorder NEC V13.5
  myocardial infarction 412
  neglect (emotional) V15.42
  nervous system disorder V12.40
    specified type NEC V12.49
  neurosis V11.2
  noncompliance with medical treatment
    V15.81
  nutritional deficiency V12.1
  obstetric disorder V13.2
    affecting management of current
      pregnancy V23.4
  parasitic disease V12.00
    specified NEC V12.09
  perinatal problems V13.7
  physical abuse V15.41
  poisoning V15.6
  poliomyelitis V12.02
  polyps, colonic V12.72
  poor obstetric V23.4
  psychiatric disorder V11.9
    affective type V11.1
    manic-depressive V11.1
    neurosis V11.2
    schizophrenia V11.0
    specified type NEC V11.8
  psychological trauma V15.49
    emotional abuse V15.42
    neglect V15.42
    physical abuse V15.41
    rape V15.41
  psychoneurosis V11.2
  radiation therapy V15.3
  rape V15.41
  respiratory system disease V12.6
  reticulosarcoma V10.71
  schizophrenia V11.0
  skin disease V13.3
  smoking (tobacco) V15.82
  subcutaneous tissue disease V13.3
  surgery (major) to
    great vessels V15.1
    heart V15.1
    major organs NEC V15.2
  thrombophlebitis V12.52
  thrombosis V12.51
  tobacco use V15.82
  trophoblastic disease V13.1
    affecting management of pregnancy
      V23.1
  tuberculosis V12.01
  ulcer, peptic V12.71
  urinary system disorder V13.00
    calculi V13.01
    specified NEC V13.09
HIV infection (disease) (illness) - *see* Human immunodeficiency virus (disease) (illness) (infection)
Hives (bold) (*see also* Urticaria) 708.9

Hoarseness 784.49
Hobnail liver - *see* Cirrhosis, portal
Hobo, hoboism V60.0
Hodgkin's
  disease (M9650/3) 201.9
    lymphocytic
      depletion (M9653/3) 201.7
        diffuse fibrosis (M9654/3) 201.7
        reticular type (M9655/3) 201.7
      predominance (M9651/3) 201.4
    lymphocytic-histiocytic predominance (M9651/3) 201.4
    mixed cellularity (M9652/3) 201.6
    nodular sclerosis (M9656/3) 201.5
      cellular phase (M9657/3) 201.5
  granuloma (M9661/3) 201.1
  lymphogranulomatosis (M9650/3) 201.9
  lymphoma (M9650/3) 201.9
  lymphosarcoma (M9650/3) 201.9
  paragranuloma (M9660/3) 201.0
  sarcoma (M9662/3) 201.2
Hodgson's disease (aneurysmal dilatation of aorta) 441.9
  ruptured 441.5
Hodi-potsy 111.0
Hoffa (-Kastert) disease or syndrome (liposynovitis prepatellaris) 272.8
Hoffmann's syndrome 244.9 *[359.5]*
Hoffmann-Bouveret syndrome (paroxysmal tachycardia) 427.2
Hole
  macula 362.54
  optic disc, crater-like 377.22
  retina (macula) 362.54
    round 361.31
      with detachment 361.01
Holla disease (*see also* Spherocytosis) 282.0
Holländer-Simons syndrome (progressive lipodystrophy) 272.6
Hollow foot (congenital) 754.71
  acquired 736.73
Holmes' syndrome (visual disorientation) 368.16
Holoprosencephaly 742.2
  due to
    trisomy 13 758.1
    trisomy 18 758.2
Holthouse's hernia - *see* Hernia, inguinal
Homesickness 309.89
Homocystinemia 270.4
Homocystinuria 270.4
Homologous serum jaundice (prophylactic) (therapeutic) - *see* Hepatitis, viral
Homosexuality - omit code
  ego-dystonic 302.0
  pedophilic 302.2
  problems with 302.0
Homozygous Hb-S disease 282.61
Honeycomb lung 518.89
  congenital 748.4
Hong Kong ear 117.3
HOOD (hereditary osteo-onychodysplasia) 756.89
Hooded
  clitoris 752.49
  penis 752.69
Hookworm (anemia) (disease) (infestation) - *see* Ancylostomiasis
Hoppe-Goldflam syndrome 358.0
Hordeolum (external) (eyelid) 373.11
  internal 373.12

Horn
  cutaneous 702.8
    cheek 702.8
    eyelid 702.8
    penis 702.8
  iliac 756.89
  nail 703.8
    congenital 757.5
  papillary 700
Horner's
  syndrome (*see also* Neuropathy, peripheral, autonomic) 337.9
    traumatic 954.0
  teeth 520.4
Horseshoe kidney (congenital) 753.3
Horton's
  disease (temporal arteritis) 446.5
  headache or neuralgia 346.2
Hospice care V66.7
Hospitalism (in children) NEC 309.83
Hourglass contraction, contracture
  bladder 596.8
  gallbladder 575.2
    congenital 751.69
  stomach 536.8
    congenital 750.7
    psychogenic 306.4
  uterus 661.4
    affecting fetus or newborn 763.7
Household circumstance affecting care V60.9
  specified type NEC V60.8
Housemaid's knee 727.2
Housing circumstance affecting care V60.9
  specified type NEC V60.8
Huchard's disease (continued arterial hypertension) 401.9
Hudson-Stähli lines 371.11
Huguier's disease (uterine fibroma) 218.9
Hum, venous - omit code
Human bite (open wound) - (*see also* Wound, open, by site)
  intact skin surface - *see* Contusion
Human immunodeficiency virus (disease) (illness) 042
  infection V08
    with symptoms, symptomatic 042
Human immunodeficiency virus-2 infection 079.53
Human immunovirus (disease) (illness) (infection) - *see* Human immunodeficiency virus (disease) (illness) (infection)
Human papillomavirus 079.4
Human T-cell lymphotrophic virus I infection 079.51
Human T-cell lymphotrophic virus II infection 079.52
Human T-cell lymphotropic virus-III (disease) (illness) (infection) - *see* Human immunodeficiency virus (disease) (illness) (infection)
HTLV-I infection 079.51
HTLV-II infection 079.52
HTLV-III (disease) (illness) (infection) - *see* Human immunodeficiency virus (disease) (illness) (infection)
HTLV-III/LAV (disease) (illness) (infection) - *see* Human immunodeficiency virus (disease) (illness) (infection)
Humpback (acquired) 737.9
  congenital 756.19

ICD-9-CM

Vol. 2

Hunchback (acquired) 737.9
  congenital 756.19
Hunger 994.2
  air, psychogenic 306.1
  disease 251.1
Hunner's ulcer (*see also* Cystitis) 595.1
Hunt's
  neuralgia 053.11
  syndrome (herpetic geniculate gan-
    glionitis) 053.11
    dyssynergia cerebellaris myoclonica
      334.2
Hunter's glossitis 529.4
Hunter (-Hurler) syndrome (mucopolysaccharidosis II) 277.5
Hunterian chancre 091.0
Huntington's
  chorea 333.4
  disease 333.4
Huppert's disease (multiple myeloma)
  (M9730/3) 203.0
Hurler (-Hunter) disease or syndrome
  (mucopolysaccharidosis II) 277.5
Hürthle cell
  adenocarcinoma (M8290/3) 193
  adenoma (M8290/0) 226
  carcinoma (M8290/3) 193
  tumor (M8290/0) 226
Hutchinson's
  disease meaning
    angioma serpiginosum 709.1
    cheiropompholyx 705.81
    prurigo estivalis 692.72
    summer eruption, or summer pru-
      rigo 692.72
  incisors 090.5
  melanotic freckle (M8742/2) - *see also*
    Neoplasm, skin, in situ
    malignant melanoma in (M8742/3) -
      see Melanoma
  teeth or incisors (congenital syphilis)
    090.5
Hutchinson-Boeck disease or syndrome
  (sarcoidosis) 135
**Hutchinson-Gilford disease or syn-
drome** (progeria) 259.8
Hyaline
  degeneration (diffuse) (generalized)
    728.9
    localized - *see* Degeneration, by site
  membrane (disease) (lung) (newborn)
    769
Hyalinosis cutis et mucosae 272.8
Hyalin plaque, sclera, senile 379.16
Hyalitis (asteroid) 379.22
  syphilitic 095.8
Hydatid
  cyst or tumor - *see also* Echinococcus
    fallopian tube 752.11
  mole - *see* Hydatidiform mole
  Morgagni (congenital) 752.8
    fallopian tube 752.11
Hydatidiform mole (benign) (complicating pregnancy) (delivered) (undelivered) 630
  invasive (M9100/1) 236.1
  malignant (M9100/1) 236.1
  previous, affecting management of
    pregnancy V23.1
Hydatidosis - *see* Echinococcus
Hyde's disease (prurigo nodularis) 698.3
Hydradenitis 705.83
Hydradenoma (M8400/0) - *see* Hidradenoma

Hydralazine lupus or syndrome
  correct substance properly adminis-
    tered 695.4
  overdose or wrong substance given or
    taken 972.6
Hydramnios 657
  affecting fetus or newborn 761.3
Hydrancephaly 742.3
  with spina bifida (*see also* Spina bifida)
    741.0
Hydranencephaly 742.3
  with spina bifida (*see also* Spina bifida)
    741.0
Hydrargyrism NEC 985.0
Hydrarthrosis (*see also* Effusion, joint)
  719.0
  gonococcal 098.50
  intermittent (*see also* Rheumatism, pal-
    indromic) 719.3
  of yaws (early) (late) 102.6
  syphilitic 095.8
    congenital 090.5
Hydremia 285.9
Hydrencephalocele (congenital) 742.0
Hydrencephalomeningocele (congenital)
  742.0
Hydroa 694.0
  aestivale 692.72
  gestationis 646.8
  herpetiformis 694.0
  pruriginosa 694.0
  vacciniforme 692.72
Hydroadenitis 705.83
Hydrocalycosis (*see also* Hydronephrosis)
  591
  congenital 753.29
Hydrocalyx (*see also* Hydronephrosis)
  591
Hydrocele (calcified) (chylous) (idiopathic) (infantile) (inguinal canal)
  (recurrent) (senile) (spermatic cord)
  (testis) (tunica vaginalis) 603.9
  canal of Nuck (female) 629.1
    male 603.9
  congenital 778.6
  encysted 603.0
    congenital 778.6
  female NEC 629.8
  infected 603.1
  round ligament 629.8
  specified type NEC 603.8
    congenital 778.6
  spinalis (*see also* Spina bifida) 741.9
  vulva 624.8
Hydrocephalic fetus
  affecting management or pregnancy
    655.0
  causing disproportion 653.6
    with obstructed labor 660.1
      affecting fetus or newborn 763.1
Hydrocephalus (acquired) (external)
  (internal) (malignant) (noncommuni-
  cating) (obstructive) (recurrent)
  331.4
  aqueduct of Sylvius stricture 742.3
    with spina bifida (*see also* Spina
      bifida) 741.0
  chronic 742.3
    with spina bifida (*see also* Spina
      bifida) 741.0
  communicating 331.3
  congenital (external) (internal) 742.3
    with spina bifida (*see also* Spina
      bifida) 741.0

Hydrocephalus (*Continued*)
  due to
    stricture of aqueduct of Sylvius 742.3
      with spina bifida (*see also* Spina
        bifida) 741.0
    toxoplasmosis (congenital) 771.2
  fetal affecting management of preg-
    nancy 655.0
  foramen Magendie block (acquired)
    331.3
    congenital 742.3
      with spina bifida (*see also* Spina
        bifida) 741.0
  newborn 742.3
    with spina bifida (*see also* Spina
      bifida) 741.0
  otitic 331.4
  syphilitic, congenital 090.49
  tuberculous (*see also* Tuberculosis) 013.8
Hydrocolpos (congenital) 623.8
Hydrocystoma (M8404/0) - *see* Neo-
  plasm, skin, benign
Hydroencephalocele (congenital) 742.0
Hydroencephalomeningocele (congenital) 742.0
Hydrohematopneumothorax (*see also* Hemothorax) 511.8
Hydromeningitis - *see* Meningitis
Hydromeningocele (spinal) (*see also*
  Spina bifida) 741.9
  cranial 742.0
Hydrometra 621.8
Hydrometrocolpos 623.8
Hydromicrocephaly 742.1
Hydromphalus (congenital) (since birth)
  757.39
Hydromyelia 742.53
Hydromyelocele (*see also* Spina bifida)
  741.9
Hydronephrosis 591
  atrophic 591
  congenital 753.29
  due to S. hematobium 120.0
  early 591
  functionless (infected) 591
  infected 591
  intermittent 591
  primary 591
  secondary 591
  tuberculous (*see also* Tuberculosis) 016.0
Hydropericarditis (*see also* Pericarditis)
  423.9
Hydropericardium (*see also* Pericarditis)
  423.9
Hydroperitoneum 789.5
Hydrophobia 071
Hydrophthalmos (*see also* Buphthalmia)
  743.20
Hydropneumohemothorax (*see also* Hemothorax) 511.8
Hydropneumopericarditis (*see also* Pericarditis) 423.9
Hydropneumopericardium (*see also* Pericarditis) 423.9
Hydropneumothorax 511.8
  nontuberculous 511.8
    bacterial 511.1
    pneumococcal 511.1
    staphylococcal 511.1
    streptococcal 511.1
  traumatic 860.0
    with open wound into thorax 860.1
  tuberculous (*see also* Tuberculosis,
    pleura) 012.0

ICD-9-CM

Ⅎ

Vol. 2

Hyperesthesia (*Continued*)
  larynx (reflex) 478.79
    hysterical 300.11
  pharynx (reflex) 478.29
Hyperestrinism 256.0
Hyperestrogenism 256.0
Hyperestrogenosis 256.0
Hyperextension, joint 718.80
  ankle 718.87
  elbow 718.82
  foot 718.87
  hand 718.84
  hip 718.85
  knee 718.86
  multiple sites 718.89
  pelvic region 718.85
  shoulder (region) 718.81
  specified site NEC 718.88
  wrist 718.83
Hyperfibrinolysis - *see* Fibrinolysis
Hyperfolliculinism 256.0
Hyperfructosemia 271.2
Hyperfunction
  adrenal (cortex) 255.3
    androgenic, acquired benign 255.3
    medulla 255.6
    virilism 255.2
  corticoadrenal NEC 255.3
  labyrinth - *see* Hyperactive, labyrinth
  medulloadrenal 255.6
  ovary 256.1
    estrogen 256.0
  pancreas 577.8
  parathyroid (gland) 252.0
  pituitary (anterior) (gland) (lobe) 253.1
  testicular 257.0
Hypergammaglobulinemia 289.8
  monoclonal, benign (BMH) 273.1
  polyclonal 273.0
  Waldenström's 273.0
Hyperglobulinemia 273.8
Hyperglycemia 790.6
  maternal
    affecting fetus or newborn 775.0
    manifest diabetes in infant 775.1
  postpancreatectomy (complete) (partial) 251.3
Hyperglyceridemia 272.1
  endogenous 272.1
  essential 272.1
  familial 272.1
  hereditary 272.1
  mixed 272.3
  pure 272.1
Hyperglycinemia 270.7
Hypergonadism
  ovarian 256.1
  testicular (infantile) (primary) 257.0
Hyperheparinemia (*see also* Circulating
  anticoagulants) 286.5
Hyperhidrosis, hyperidrosis 780.8
  psychogenic 306.3
Hyperhistidinemia 270.5
Hyperinsulinism (ectopic) (functional)
  (organic) NEC 251.1
  iatrogenic 251.0
  reactive 251.2
  spontaneous 251.2
  therapeutic misadventure (from administration of insulin) 962.3
Hyperiodemia 276.9
Hyperirritability (cerebral), in newborn
  779.1
Hyperkalemia 276.7

Hyperkeratosis (*see also* Keratosis) 701.1
  cervix 622.1
  congenital 757.39
  cornea 371.89
  due to yaws (early) (late) (palmar or
    plantar) 102.3
  eccentrica 757.39
  figurata centrifuga atrophica 757.39
  follicularis 757.39
    in cutem penetrans 701.1
  limbic (cornea) 371.89
  palmoplantaris climacterica 701.1
  pinta (carate) 103.1
  senile (with pruritus) 702.0
  tongue 528.7
  universalis congenita 757.1
  vagina 623.1
  vocal cord 478.5
  vulva 624.0
Hyperkinesia, hyperkinetic (disease) (reaction) (syndrome) 314.9
  with
    attention deficit - *see* Disorder, attention deficit
    conduct disorder 314.2
    developmental delay 314.1
    simple disturbance of activity and
      attention 314.01
    specified manifestation NEC 314.8
  heart (disease) 429.82
  of childhood or adolescence NEC 314.9
Hyperlacrimation (*see also* Epiphora)
  375.20
Hyperlipemia (*see also* Hyperlipidemia)
  272.4
Hyperlipidemia 272.4
  carbohydrate-induced 272.1
  combined 272.4
  endogenous 272.1
  exogenous 272.3
  fat-induced 272.3
  group
    A 272.0
    B 272.1
    C 272.2
    D 272.3
  mixed 272.2
  specified type NEC 272.4
Hyperlipidosis 272.7
  hereditary 272.7
Hyperlipoproteinemia (acquired) (essential) (familial) (hereditary) (primary)
  (secondary) 272.4
  Fredrickson type
    I 272.3
    IIA 272.0
    IIB 272.2
    III 272.2
    IV 272.1
    V 272.3
  low-density-lipoid-type (LDL) 272.0
  very-low-density-lipoid-type [VLDL]
    272.1
Hyperlucent lung, unilateral 492.8
Hyperluteinization 256.1
Hyperlysinemia 270.7
Hypermagnesemia 275.2
  neonatal 775.5
Hypermaturity (fetus or newborn)
  766.2
Hypermenorrhea 626.2
Hypermetabolism 794.7
Hypermethioninemia 270.4
Hypermetropia (congenital) 367.0

Hypermobility
  cecum 564.1
  coccyx 724.71
  colon 564.1
    psychogenic 306.4
  ileum 564.89
  joint (acquired) 718.80
    ankle 718.87
    elbow 718.82
    foot 718.87
    hand 718.84
    hip 718.85
    knee 718.86
    multiple sites 718.89
    pelvic region 718.85
    shoulder (region) 718.81
    specified site NEC 718.88
    wrist 718.83
  kidney, congenital 753.3
  meniscus (knee) 717.5
  scapula 718.81
  stomach 536.8
    psychogenic 306.4
  syndrome 728.5
  testis, congenital 752.52
  urethral 599.81
Hypermotility
  gastrointestinal 536.8
  intestine 564.1
    psychogenic 306.4
  stomach 536.8
Hypernasality 784.49
Hypernatremia 276.0
  with water depletion 276.0
Hypernephroma (M8312/3) 189.0
Hyperopia 367.0
Hyperorexia 783.6
Hyperornithinemia 270.6
Hyperosmia (*see also* Disturbance, sensation) 781.1
Hyperosmolality 276.0
Hyperosteogenesis 733.99
Hyperostosis 733.99
  calvarial 733.3
  cortical 733.3
    infantile 756.59
  frontal, internal of skull 733.3
  interna frontalis 733.3
  monomelic 733.99
  skull 733.3
    congenital 756.0
  vertebral 721.8
    with spondylosis - *see* Spondylosis
    ankylosing 721.6
Hyperovarianism 256.1
Hyperovarism, hyperovaria 256.1
Hyperoxaluria (primary) 271.8
Hyperoxia 987.8
Hyperparathyroidism 252.0
  ectopic 259.3
  secondary, of renal origin 588.8
Hyperpathia (*see also* Disturbance, sensation) 782.0
  psychogenic 307.80
Hyperperistalsis 787.4
  psychogenic 306.4
Hyperpermeability, capillary 448.9
Hyperphagia 783.6
Hyperphenylalaninemia 270.1
Hyperphoria 378.40
  alternating 378.45
Hyperphosphatemia 275.3
Hyperpiesia (*see also* Hypertension) 401.9
Hyperpiesis (*see also* Hypertension) 401.9

Hyperpigmentation - *see* Pigmentation
Hyperpinealism 259.8
Hyperpipecolatemia 270.7
Hyperpituitarism 253.1
Hyperplasia, hyperplastic
adenoids (lymphoid tissue) 474.12
and tonsils 474.10
adrenal (capsule) (cortex) (gland) 255.8
with
sexual precocity (male) 255.2
virilism, adrenal 255.2
virilization (female) 255.2
congenital 255.2
due to excess ACTH (ectopic) (pituitary) 255.0
medulla 255.8
alpha cells (pancreatic)
with
gastrin excess 251.5
glucagon excess 251.4
appendix (lymphoid) 543.0
artery, fibromuscular NEC 447.8
carotid 447.8
renal 447.3
bone 733.99
marrow 289.9
breast (*see also* Hypertrophy, breast) 611.1
carotid artery 447.8
cementation, cementum (teeth) (tooth) 521.5
cervical gland 785.6
cervix (uteri) 622.1
basal cell 622.1
congenital 752.49
endometrium 622.1
polypoid 622.1
chin 524.05
clitoris, congenital 752.49
dentin 521.5
endocervicitis 616.0
endometrium, endometrial (adenomatous) (atypical) (cystic) (glandular) (polypoid) (uterus) 621.3
cervix 622.1
epithelial 709.8
focal, oral, including tongue 528.7
mouth (focal) 528.7
nipple 611.8
skin 709.8
tongue (focal) 528.7
vaginal wall 623.0
erythroid 289.9
fascialis ossificans (progressiva) 728.11
fibromuscular, artery NEC 447.8
carotid 447.8
renal 447.3
genital
female 629.8
male 608.89
gingiva 523.8
glandularis
cystica uteri 621.3
endometrium (uterus) 621.3
interstitialis uteri 621.3
granulocytic 288.8
gum 523.8
hymen, congenital 752.49
islands of Langerhans 251.1
islet cell (pancreatic) 251.9
alpha cells
with excess
gastrin 251.5
glucagon 251.4
beta cells 251.1

Hyperplasia, hyperplastic (*Continued*)
juxtaglomerular (complex) (kidney) 593.89
kidney (congenital) 753.3
liver (congenital) 751.69
lymph node (gland) 785.6
lymphoid (diffuse) (nodular) 785.6
appendix 543.0
intestine 569.89
mandibular 524.02
alveolar 524.72
unilateral condylar 526.89
Marchand multiple nodular (liver) - *see* Cirrhosis, postnecrotic
maxillary 524.01
alveolar 524.71
medulla, adrenal 255.8
myometrium, myometrial 621.2
nose (lymphoid) (polypoid) 478.1
oral soft tissue (inflammatory) (irritative) (mucosa) NEC 528.9
gingiva 523.8
tongue 529.8
organ or site, congenital NEC - *see* Anomaly, specified type NEC
ovary 620.8
palate, papillary 528.9
pancreatic islet cells 251.9
alpha
with excess
gastrin 251.5
glucagon 251.4
beta 251.1
parathyroid (gland) 252.0
persistent, vitreous (primary) 743.51
pharynx (lymphoid) 478.29
prostate (adenofibromatous) (nodular) 600
renal artery (fibromuscular) 447.3
reticuloendothelial (cell) 289.9
salivary gland (any) 527.1
Schimmelbusch's 610.1
suprarenal (capsule) (gland) 255.8
thymus (gland) (persistent) 254.0
thyroid (*see also* Goiter) 240.9
primary 242.0
secondary 242.2
tonsil (lymphoid tissue) 474.11
and adenoids 474.10
urethrovaginal 599.89
uterus, uterine (myometrium) 621.2
endometrium 621.3
vitreous (humor), primary persistent 743.51
vulva 624.3
zygoma 738.11
Hyperpnea (*see also* Hyperventilation) 786.01
Hyperpotassemia 276.7
Hyperprebetalipoproteinemia 272.1
with chylomicronemia 272.3
familial 272.1
Hyperprolactinemia 253.1
Hyperprolinemia 270.8
Hyperproteinemia 273.8
Hyperprothrombinemia 289.8
Hyperpselaphesia 782.0
Hyperpyrexia 780.6
heat (effects of) 992.0
malarial (*see also* Malaria) 084.6
malignant, due to anesthetic 995.86
rheumatic - *see* Fever, rheumatic
unknown origin (*see also* Pyrexia) 780.6

Hyperreactor, vascular 780.2
Hyperreflexia 796.1
bladder, autonomic 596.54
with cauda equina 344.61
detrusor 344.61
Hypersalivation (*see also* Ptyalism) 527.7
Hypersarcosinemia 270.8
Hypersecretion
ACTH 255.3
androgens (ovarian) 256.1
calcitonin 246.0
corticoadrenal 255.3
cortisol 255.0
estrogen 256.0
gastric 536.8
psychogenic 306.4
gastrin 251.5
glucagon 251.4
hormone
ACTH 255.3
anterior pituitary 253.1
growth NEC 253.0
ovarian androgen 256.1
testicular 257.0
thyroid stimulating 242.8
insulin - *see* Hyperinsulinism
lacrimal glands (*see also* Epiphora) 375.20
medulloadrenal 255.6
milk 676.6
ovarian androgens 256.1
pituitary (anterior) 253.1
salivary gland (any) 527.7
testicular hormones 257.0
thyrocalcitonin 246.0
upper respiratory 478.9
Hypersegmentation, hereditary 288.2
eosinophils 288.2
neutrophil nuclei 288.2
Hypersensitive, hypersensitiveness, hypersensitivity - *see also* Allergy
angiitis 446.20
specified NEC 446.29
carotid sinus 337.0
colon 564.1
psychogenic 306.4
DNA (deoxyribonucleic acid) NEC 287.2
drug (*see also* Allergy, drug) 995.2
esophagus 530.89
insect bites - *see* Injury, superficial, by site
labyrinth 386.58
pain (*see also* Disturbance, sensation) 782.0
pneumonitis NEC 495.9
reaction (*see also* Allergy) 995.3
upper respiratory tract NEC 478.8
stomach (allergic) (nonallergic) 536.8
psychogenic 306.4
Hypersomatotropism (classic) 253.0
Hypersomnia 780.54
with sleep apnea 780.53
nonorganic origin 307.43
persistent (primary) 307.44
transient 307.43
Hypersplenia 289.4
Hypersplenism 289.4
Hypersteatosis 706.3
Hyperstimulation, ovarian 256.1
Hypersuprarenalism 255.3
Hypersusceptibility - *see* Allergy
Hyper-TBG-nemia 246.8
Hypertelorism 756.0
orbit, orbital 376.41

	Malignant	Benign	Unspecified
Hypertension, hypertensive (arterial) (arteriolar) (crisis) (degeneration) (disease) (essential) (fluctuating) (idiopathic) (intermittent) (labile) (low renin) (orthostatic) (paroxysmal) (primary) (systemic) (uncontrolled) (vascular)	401.0	401.1	401.9
with			
heart involvement (conditions classifiable to 425.8, 428, 429.0-429.3, 429.8, 429.9 due to hypertension) (*see also* Hypertension, heart)	402.00	402.10	402.90
with kidney involvement-*see* Hypertension, cardiorenal			
renal involvement (only conditions classifiable to 585, 586, 587) (excludes conditions classifiable to 584) (*see also* Hypertension, kidney)	403.00	403.10	403.90
renal sclerosis or failure	403.00	403.10	403.90
with heart involvement-*see* Hypertension, cardiorenal			
failure (and sclerosis) (*see also* Hypertension, kidney)	403.01	403.11	403.91
sclerosis without failure (*see also* Hypertension, kidney)	403.00	403.10	403.90
accelerated (*see also* Hypertension, by type, malignant)	401.0	-	-
antepartum-see Hypertension, complicating pregnancy, childbirth, or the puerperium			
cardiorenal (disease)	404.00	404.10	404.90
with			
heart failure (congestive)	402.01	404.11	404.91
and renal failure	404.03	404.13	404.93
renal failure	404.02	404.12	404.92
and heart failure (congestive)	404.03	404.13	404.93
cardiovascular disease (arteriosclerotic) (sclerotic)	402.00	402.10	402.90
with			
heart failure (congestive)	402.01	402.11	402.91
renal involvement (conditions classifiable to 403) (*see also* Hypertension, cardiorenal)	404.00	404.10	404.90
cardiovascular renal (disease) (sclerosis) (*see also* Hypertension, cardiorenal)	404.00	404.10	404.90
cerebrovascular disease NEC	437.2	437.2	437.2
complicating pregnancy, childbirth, or the puerperium	642.2	642.0	642.9
with			
albuminuria (and edema) (mild)	-	-	642.4
severe	-	-	642.5
edema (mild)	-	-	642.4
severe	-	-	642.5
heart disease	642.2	642.2	642.2
and renal disease	642.2	642.2	642.2
renal disease	642.2	642.2	642.2
and heart disease	642.2	642.2	642.2
chronic	642.2	642.0	642.0
with pre-eclampsia or eclampsia	642.7	642.7	642.7
fetus or newborn	760.0	760.0	760.0
essential	-	642.0	642.0
with pre-eclampsia or eclampsia	-	642.7	642.7
fetus or newborn	760.0	760.0	760.0
fetus or newborn	760.0	760.0	760.0
gestational	-	-	642.3
pre-existing	642.2	642.0	642.0
with pre-eclampsia or eclampsia	642.7	642.7	642.7
fetus or newborn	760.0	760.0	760.0
secondary to renal disease	642.1	642.1	642.1
with pre-eclampsia or eclampsia	642.7	642.7	642.7
fetus or newborn	760.0	760.0	760.0
transient	-	-	642.3
due to			
aldosteronism, primary	405.09	405.19	405.99
brain tumor	405.09	405.19	405.99
bulbar poliomyelitis	405.09	405.19	405.99
calculus			
kidney	405.09	405.19	405.99
ureter	405.09	405.19	405.99
coarctation, aorta	405.09	405.19	405.99
Cushing's disease	405.09	405.19	405.99
glomerulosclerosis (*see also* Hypertension, kidney)	403.00	403.10	403.90
periarteritis nodosa	405.09	405.19	405.99
pheochromocytoma	405.09	405.19	405.99
polycystic kidney(s)	405.09	405.19	405.99
polycythemia	405.09	405.19	405.99
porphyria	405.09	405.19	405.99
pyelonephritis	405.09	405.19	405.99

◀▶ **New Code**   ◀▥▥▶ **Revised Code**

	Malignant	Benign	Unspecified
Hypertension *(Continued)*			
due to *(Continued)*			
renal (artery)			
aneurysm	405.01	405.11	405.91
anomaly	405.01	405.11	405.91
embolism	405.01	405.11	405.91
fibromuscular hyperplasia	405.01	405.11	405.91
occlusion	405.01	405.11	405.91
stenosis	405.01	405.11	405.91
thrombosis	405.01	405.11	405.91
encephalopathy	437.2	437.2	437.2
gestational (transient) NEC	-	-	642.3
Goldblatt's	440.1	440.1	440.1
heart (disease) (conditions classifiable to 425.8, 428, 429.0-429.3, 429.8, 429.9 due to hypertension)	402.00	402.10	402.90
with			
heart failure	402.01	402.11	402.91
congestive	402.01	402.11	402.91
hypertensive kidney disease (conditions classifiable to 403) (*see also* Hypertension, cardiorenal)	404.00	404.10	404.90
renal sclerosis (*see also* Hypertension, cardiorenal)	404.00	404.10	404.90
intracranial, benign	-	348.2	-
intraocular	-	-	365.04
kidney	403.00	403.10	403.90
with			
heart involvement (conditions classifiable to 425.8, 428, 429.0-429.3, 429.8, 429.9 due to hypertension)			
(*see also* Hypertension, cardiorenal)	404.00	404.10	404.90
hypertensive heart (disease) (conditions classifiable to 402) (*see also* Hypertension, cardiorenal)	404.00	404.10	404.90
renal failure (conditions classifiable to 585, 586)	403.01	403.11	403.91
lesser circulation	-	-	416.0
necrotizing	401.0	-	-
ocular	-	-	365.04
portal (due to chronic liver disease)	-	-	572.3
postoperative			997.91
psychogenic	-	-	306.2
puerperal, postpartum-			
see Hypertension, complicating pregnancy, childbirth, or the puerperium			
pulmonary (artery) (idiopathic) (primary) (solitary)	-	-	416.0
with cor pulmonale (chronic)	-	-	416.8
acute	-	-	415.0
secondary	-	-	416.8
renal (disease) (*see also* Hypertension, kidney)	403.00	403.10	403.90
renovascular NEC	405.01	405.11	405.91
secondary NEC	405.09	405.19	405.99
due to			
aldosteronism, primary	405.09	405.19	405.99
brain tumor	405.09	405.19	405.99
bulbar poliomyelitis	405.09	405.19	405.99
calculus			
kidney	405.09	405.19	405.99
ureter	405.09	405.19	405.99
coarctation, aorta	405.09	405.19	405.99
Cushing's disease	405.09	405.19	405.99
glomerulosclerosis (*see also* Hypertension, kidney)	403.00	403.10	403.90
periarteritis nodosa	405.09	405.19	405.99
pheochromocytoma	405.09	405.19	405.99
polycystic kidney(s)	405.09	405.19	405.99
polycythemia	405.09	405.19	405.99
porphyria	405.09	405.19	405.99
pyelonephritis	405.09	405.19	405.99
renal (artery)			
aneurysm	405.01	405.11	405.91
anomaly	405.01	405.11	405.91
embolism	405.01	405.11	405.91
fibromuscular hyperplasia	405.01	405.11	405.91
occlusion	405.01	405.11	405.91
stenosis	405.01	405.11	405.91
thrombosis	405.01	405.11	405.91
transient	-	-	796.2
of pregnancy	-	-	642.3

Hyperthecosis, ovary 256.8
Hyperthermia (of unknown origin) (*see also* Pyrexia) 780.6
  malignant (due to anesthesia) 995.86
  newborn 778.4
Hyperthymergasia (*see also* Psychosis, affective) 296.0
  reactive (from emotional stress, psychological trauma) 298.1
  recurrent episode 296.1
  single episode 296.0
Hyperthymism 254.8
Hyperthyroid (recurrent) - *see* Hyperthyroidism
Hyperthyroidism (latent) (preadult) (recurrent) (without goiter) 242.9

> Note   Use the following fifth-digit subclassification with category 242:
>
> 0   without mention of thyrotoxic crisis or storm
> 1   with mention of thyrotoxic crisis or storm

  with
    goiter (diffuse) 242.0
      adenomatous 242.3
        multinodular 242.2
        uninodular 242.1
      nodular 242.3
        multinodular 242.2
        uninodular 242.1
      thyroid nodule 242.1
    complicating pregnancy, childbirth, or puerperium 648.1
  neonatal (transient) 775.3
Hypertonia - *see* Hypertonicity
Hypertonicity
  bladder 596.51
  fetus or newborn 779.8
  gastrointestinal (tract) 536.8
  infancy 779.8
    due to electrolyte imbalance 779.8
  muscle 728.85
  stomach 536.8
    psychogenic 306.4
  uterus, uterine (contractions) 661.4
    affecting fetus or newborn 763.7
Hypertony - *see* Hypertonicity
Hypertransaminemia 790.4
Hypertrichosis 704.1
  congenital 757.4
  eyelid 374.54
  lanuginosa 757.4
    acquired 704.1
Hypertriglyceridemia, essential 272.1
Hypertrophy, hypertrophic
  adenoids (infectional) 474.12
    and tonsils (faucial) (infective) (lingual) (lymphoid) 474.10
  adrenal 255.8
  alveolar process or ridge 525.8
  anal papillae 569.49
  apocrine gland 705.82
  artery NEC 447.8
    carotid 447.8
    congenital (peripheral) NEC 747.60
      gastrointestinal 747.61
      lower limb 747.64
      renal 747.62
      specified NEC 747.69
      spinal 747.82
      upper limb 747.63

Hypertrophy, hypertrophic (*Continued*)
  artery NEC (*Continued*)
    renal 447.3
  arthritis (chronic) (*see also* Osteoarthrosis) 715.9
    spine (*see also* Spondylosis) 721.90
  arytenoid 478.79
  asymmetrical (heart) 429.9
  auricular - *see* Hypertrophy, cardiac
  Bartholin's gland 624.8
  bile duct 576.8
  bladder (sphincter) (trigone) 596.8
  blind spot, visual field 368.42
  bone 733.99
  brain 348.8
  breast 611.1
    cystic 610.1
    fetus or newborn 778.7
    fibrocystic 610.1
    massive pubertal 611.1
    puerperal, postpartum 676.3
    senile (parenchymatous) 611.1
  cardiac (chronic) (idiopathic) 429.3
    with
      rheumatic fever (conditions classifiable to 390)
        active 391.8
          with chorea 392.0
        inactive or quiescent (with chorea) 398.99
    congenital NEC 746.89
    fatty (*see also* Degeneration, myocardial) 429.1
    hypertensive (*see also* Hypertension, heart) 402.90
    rheumatic (with chorea) 398.99
      active or acute 391.8
        with chorea 392.0
    valve (*see also* Endocarditis) 424.90
      congenital NEC 746.89
  cartilage 733.99
  cecum 569.89
  cervix (uteri) 622.6
    congenital 752.49
    elongation 622.6
  clitoris (cirrhotic) 624.2
    congenital 752.49
  colon 569.89
    congenital 751.3
  conjunctiva, lymphoid 372.73
  cornea 371.89
  corpora cavernosa 607.89
  duodenum 537.89
  endometrium (uterus) 621.3
    cervix 622.6
  epididymis 608.89
  esophageal hiatus (congenital) 756.6
    with hernia - *see* Hernia, diaphragm
  eyelid 374.30
  falx, skull 733.99
  fat pad 729.30
    infrapatellar 729.31
    knee 729.31
    orbital 374.34
    popliteal 729.31
    prepatellar 729.31
    retropatellar 729.31
    specified site NEC 729.39
  foot (congenital) 755.67
  frenum, frenulum (tongue) 529.8
    linguae 529.8
    lip 528.5
  gallbladder or cystic duct 575.8
  gastric mucosa 535.2

Hypertrophy, hypertrophic (*Continued*)
  gingiva 523.8
  gland, glandular (general) NEC 785.6
  gum (mucous membrane) 523.8
  heart (idiopathic) - *see also* Hypertrophy, cardiac
    valve - *see also* Endocarditis
      congenital NEC 746.89
  hemifacial 754.0
  hepatic - *see* Hypertrophy, liver
  hiatus (esophageal) 756.6
  hilus gland 785.6
  hymen, congenital 752.49
  ileum 569.89
  infrapatellar fat pad 729.31
  intestine 569.89
  jejunum 569.89
  kidney (compensatory) 593.1
    congenital 753.3
  labial frenulum 528.5
  labium (majus) (minus) 624.3
  lacrimal gland, chronic 375.03
  ligament 728.9
    spinal 724.8
  linguae frenulum 529.8
  lingual tonsil (infectional) 474.11
  lip (frenum) 528.5
    congenital 744.81
  liver 789.1
    acute 573.8
    cirrhotic - *see* Cirrhosis, liver
    congenital 751.69
    fatty - *see* Fatty, liver
  lymph gland 785.6
    tuberculous - *see* Tuberculosis, lymph gland
  mammary gland - *see* Hypertrophy, breast
  maxillary frenulum 528.5
  Meckel's diverticulum (congenital) 751.0
  medial meniscus, acquired 717.3
  median bar 600
  mediastinum 519.3
  meibomian gland 373.2
  meniscus, knee, congenital 755.64
  metatarsal head 733.99
  metatarsus 733.99
  mouth 528.9
  mucous membrane
    alveolar process 523.8
    nose 478.1
    turbinate (nasal) 478.0
  muscle 728.9
  muscular coat, artery NEC 447.8
    carotid 447.8
    renal 447.3
  myocardium (*see also* Hypertrophy, cardiac) 429.3
    idiopathic 425.4
  myometrium 621.2
  nail 703.8
    congenital 757.5
  nasal 478.1
    alae 478.1
    bone 738.0
    cartilage 478.1
    mucous membrane (septum) 478.1
    sinus (*see also* Sinusitis) 473.9
    turbinate 478.0
  nasopharynx, lymphoid (infectional) (tissue) (wall) 478.29
  neck, uterus 622.6
  nipple 611.1

◀ ▶   New Code   ◀▥ ▥▶   Revised Code

Hypertrophy, hypertrophic (*Continued*)
  normal aperture diaphragm (congenital) 756.6
  nose (*see also* Hypertrophy, nasal) 478.1
  orbit 376.46
  organ or site, congenital NEC - *see* Anomaly, specified type NEC
  osteoarthropathy (pulmonary) 731.2
  ovary 620.8
  palate (hard) 526.89
    soft 528.9
  pancreas (congenital) 751.7
  papillae
    anal 569.49
    tongue 529.3
  parathyroid (gland) 252.0
  parotid gland 527.1
  penis 607.89
  phallus 607.89
    female (clitoris) 624.2
  pharyngeal tonsil 474.12
  pharyngitis 472.1
  pharynx 478.29
    lymphoid (infectional) (tissue) (wall) 478.29
  pituitary (fossa) (gland) 253.8
  popliteal fat pad 729.31
  preauricular (lymph) gland (Hampstead) 785.6
  prepuce (congenital) 605
    female 624.2
  prostate (adenofibromatous) (asymptomatic) (benign) (early) (recurrent) 600
    congenital 752.8
  pseudoedematous hypodermal 757.0
  pseudomuscular 359.1
  pylorus (muscle) (sphincter) 537.0
    congenital 750.5
    infantile 750.5
  rectal sphincter 569.49
  rectum 569.49
  renal 593.1
  rhinitis (turbinate) 472.0
  salivary duct or gland 527.1
    congenital 750.26
  scaphoid (tarsal) 733.99
  scar 701.4
  scrotum 608.89
  sella turcica 253.8
  seminal vesicle 608.89
  sigmoid 569.89
  skin condition NEC 701.9
  spermatic cord 608.89
  spinal ligament 728.9
  spleen - *see* Splenomegaly
  spondylitis (spine) (*see also* Spondylosis) 721.90
  stomach 537.89
  subaortic stenosis (idiopathic) 425.1
  sublingual gland 527.1
    congenital 750.26
  submaxillary gland 527.1
  suprarenal (gland) 255.8
  tendon 727.9
  testis 608.89
    congenital 752.8
  thymic, thymus (congenital) (gland) 254.0
  thyroid (gland) (*see also* Goiter) 240.9
    primary 242.0
    secondary 242.2
  toe (congenital) 755.65
    acquired 735.8

Hypertrophy, hypertrophic (*Continued*)
  tongue 529.8
    congenital 750.15
    frenum 529.8
    papillae (foliate) 529.3
  tonsil (faucial) (infective) (lingual) (lymphoid) 474.11
    with
      adenoiditis 474.01
      tonsillitis 474.00
        and adenoiditis 474.02
    and adenoids 474.10
  tunica vaginalis 608.89
  turbinate (mucous membrane) 478.0
  ureter 593.89
  urethra 599.84
  uterus 621.2
    puerperal, postpartum 674.8
  uvula 528.9
  vagina 623.8
  vas deferens 608.89
  vein 459.89
  ventricle, ventricular (heart) (left) (right) - *see also* Hypertrophy, cardiac
    congenital 746.89
    due to hypertension (left) (right) (*see also* Hypertension, heart) 402.90
      benign 402.10
      malignant 402.00
    right with ventricular septal defect, pulmonary stenosis or atresia, and dextraposition of aorta 745.2
  verumontanum 599.89
  vesical 596.8
  vocal cord 478.5
  vulva 624.3
    stasis (nonfilarial) 624.3
Hypertropia (intermittent) (periodic) 378.31
Hypertyrosinemia 270.2
Hyperuricemia 790.6
Hypervalinemia 270.3
Hyperventilation (tetany) 786.01
  hysterical 300.11
  psychogenic 306.1
  syndrome 306.1
Hyperviscidosis 277.00
Hyperviscosity (of serum) (syndrome) NEC 273.3
  polycythemic 289.0
  sclerocythemic 282.8
Hypervitaminosis (dietary) NEC 278.8
  A (dietary) 278.2
  D (dietary) 278.4
  from excessive administration or use of vitamin preparations (chronic) 278.8
    reaction to sudden overdose 963.5
  vitamin A 278.2
    reaction to sudden overdose 963.5
  vitamin D 278.4
    reaction to sudden overdose 963.5
  vitamin K
    correct substance properly administered 278.8
    overdose or wrong substance given or taken 964.3
Hypervolemia 276.6
Hypesthesia (*see also* Disturbance, sensation) 782.0
  cornea 371.81

Hyphema (anterior chamber) (ciliary body) (iris) 364.41
  traumatic 921.3
Hyphemia - *see* Hyphema
Hypoacidity, gastric 536.8
  psychogenic 306.4
Hypoactive labyrinth (function) - *see* Hypofunction, labyrinth
Hypoadrenalism 255.4
  tuberculous (*see also* Tuberculosis) 017.6
Hypoadrenocorticism 255.4
  pituitary 253.4
Hypoalbuminemia 273.8
Hypoalphalipoproteinemia 272.5
Hypobarism 993.2
Hypobaropathy 993.2
Hypobetalipoproteinemia (familial) 272.5
Hypocalcemia 275.41
  cow's milk 775.4
  dietary 269.3
  neonatal 775.4
  phosphate-loading 775.4
Hypocalcification, teeth 520.4
Hypochloremia 276.9
Hypochlorhydria 536.8
  neurotic 306.4
  psychogenic 306.4
Hypocholesteremia 272.5
Hypochondria (reaction) 300.7
Hypochondriac 300.7
Hypochondriasis 300.7
Hypochromasia blood cells 280.9
Hypochromic anemia 280.9
  due to blood loss (chronic) 280.0
    acute 285.1
  microcytic 280.9
Hypocoagulability (*see also* Defect, coagulation) 286.9
Hypocomplementemia 279.8
Hypocythemia (progressive) 284.9
Hypodontia (*see also* Anodontia) 520.0
Hypoeosinophilia 288.8
Hypoesthesia (*see also* Disturbance, sensation) 782.0
  cornea 371.81
  tactile 782.0
Hypoestrinism 256.3
Hypoestrogenism 256.3
Hypoferremia 280.9
  due to blood loss (chronic) 280.0
Hypofertility
  female 628.9
  male 606.1
Hypofibrinogenemia 286.3
  acquired 286.6
  congenital 286.3
Hypofunction
  adrenal (gland) 255.4
    cortex 255.4
    medulla 255.5
    specified NEC 255.5
  cerebral 331.9
  corticoadrenal NEC 255.4
  intestinal 564.89
  labyrinth (unilateral) 386.53
    with loss of labyrinthine reactivity 386.55
    bilateral 386.54
      with loss of labyrinthine reactivity 386.56
  Leydig cell 257.2
  ovary 256.3
    postablative 256.2

ICD-9-CM

Vol. 2

Hypoplasia, hypoplasis (*Continued*)
glottis 748.3
hair 757.4
hand 755.21
heart 746.89
  left (complex) (syndrome) 746.7
  valve NEC 746.89
    pulmonary 746.01
humerus (*see also* Absence, humerus, congenital) 755.24
hymen 752.49
intestine (small) 751.1
  large 751.2
iris 743.46
jaw 524.09
kidney(s) 753.0
labium (majus) (minus) 752.49
labyrinth, membranous 744.05
lacrimal duct (apparatus) 743.65
larynx 748.3
leg (*see also* Absence, limb, congenital, lower) 755.30
limb 755.4
  lower (*see also* Absence, limb, congenital, lower) 755.30
  upper (*see also* Absence, limb, congenital, upper) 755.20
liver 751.69
lung (lobe) 748.5
mammary (areolar) 757.6
mandibular 524.04
  alveolar 524.74
  unilateral condylar 526.89
maxillary 524.03
  alveolar 524.73
medullary 284.9
megakaryocytic 287.3
metacarpus (*see also* Absence, metacarpal, congenital) 755.28
metatarsus (*see also* Absence, metatarsal, congenital) 755.38
muscle 756.89
  eye 743.69
myocardium (congenital) (Uhl's anomaly) 746.84
nail(s) 757.5
nasolacrimal duct 743.65
nervous system NEC 742.8
neural 742.8
nose, nasal 748.1
ophthalmic (*see also* Microphthalmos) 743.10
organ
  of Corti 744.05
  or site NEC - *see* Anomaly, by site
osseous meatus (ear) 744.03
ovary 752.0
oviduct 752.19
pancreas 751.7
parathyroid (gland) 759.2
parotid gland 750.26
patella 755.64
pelvis, pelvic girdle 755.69
penis 752.69
peripheral vascular system (congenital) NEC 747.60
  gastrointestinal 747.61
  lower limb 747.64
  renal 747.62
  specified NEC 747.69
  spinal 747.82
  upper limb 747.63
pituitary (gland) 759.2
pulmonary 748.5

Hypoplasia, hypoplasis (*Continued*)
pulmonary (*Continued*)
  arteriovenous 747.3
  artery 747.3
  valve 746.01
punctum lacrimale 743.65
radioulnar (*see also* Absence, radius, congenital, with ulna) 755.25
radius (*see also* Absence, radius, congenital) 755.26
rectum 751.2
respiratory system NEC 748.9
rib 756.3
sacrum 756.19
scapula 755.59
shoulder girdle 755.59
skin 757.39
skull (bone) 756.0
  with
    anencephalus 740.0
    encephalocele 742.0
    hydrocephalus 742.3
      with spina bifida (*see also* Spina bifida) 741.0
    microcephalus 742.1
spinal (cord) (ventral horn cell) 742.59
  vessel 747.82
spine 756.19
spleen 759.0
sternum 756.3
tarsus (*see also* Absence, tarsal, congenital) 755.38
testis, testicle 752.8
thymus (gland) 279.11
thyroid (gland) 243
  cartilage 748.3
tibiofibular (*see also* Absence, tibia, congenital, with fibula) 755.35
toe (*see also* Absence, toe, congenital) 755.39
tongue 750.16
trachea (cartilage) (rings) 748.3
Turner's (tooth) 520.4
ulna (*see also* Absence, ulna, congenital) 755.27
umbilical artery 747.5
ureter 753.29
uterus 752.3
vagina 752.49
vascular (peripheral) NEC (*see also* Hypoplasia, peripheral vascular system) 747.60
  brain 747.81
vein(s) (peripheral) NEC (*see also* Hypoplasia, peripheral vascular system) 747.60
  brain 747.81
  cardiac 746.89
  great 747.49
  portal 747.49
  pulmonary 747.49
vena cava (inferior) (superior) 747.49
vertebra 756.19
vulva 752.49
zonule (ciliary) 743.39
zygoma 738.12
Hypopotassemia 276.8
Hypoproaccelerinemia (*see also* Defect, coagulation) 286.3
Hypoproconvertinemia (congenital) (*see also* Defect, coagulation) 286.3
Hypoproteinemia (essential) (hypermetabolic) (idiopathic) 273.8
Hypoproteinosis 260

Hypoprothrombinemia (congenital) (hereditary) (idiopathic) (*see also* Defect, coagulation) 286.3
acquired 286.7
newborn 776.3
Hypopselaphesia 782.0
Hypopyon (anterior chamber) (eye) 364.05
iritis 364.05
ulcer (cornea) 370.04
Hypopyrexia 780.9
Hyporeflex 796.1
Hyporeninemia, extreme 790.99
in primary aldosteronism 255.1
Hyposecretion
ACTH 253.4
ovary 256.3
  postablative 256.2
salivary gland (any) 527.7
Hyposegmentation of neutrophils, hereditary 288.2
Hyposiderinemia 280.9
Hyposmolality 276.1
syndrome 276.1
Hyposomatotropism 253.3
Hyposomnia (*see also* Insomnia) 780.52
Hypospadias (male) 752.61
female 753.8
Hypospermatogenesis 606.1
Hyposphagma 372.72
Hyposplenism 289.59
Hypostasis, pulmonary 514
Hypostatic - *see* condition
Hyposthenuria 593.89
Hyposuprarenalism 255.4
Hypo-TBG-nemia 246.8
Hypotension (arterial) (constitutional) 458.9
chronic 458.1
iatrogenic 458.2
maternal, syndrome (following labor and delivery) 669.2
orthostatic (chronic) 458.0
  dysautonomic-dyskinetic syndrome 333.0
permanent idiopathic 458.1
postoperative 458.2
postural 458.0
specified type NEC 458.8
transient 796.3
Hypothermia (accidental) 991.6
anesthetic 995.89
newborn NEC 778.3
not associated with low environmental temperature 780.9
Hypothymergasia (*see also* Psychosis, affective) 296.2
recurrent episode 296.3
single episode 296.2
Hypothyroidism (acquired) 244.9
complicating pregnancy, childbirth, or puerperium 648.1
congenital 243
due to
  ablation 244.1
    radioactive iodine 244.1
    surgical 244.0
  iodine (administration) (ingestion) 244.2
    radioactive 244.1
  irradiation therapy 244.1
  p-aminosalicylic acid (PAS) 244.3
  phenylbutazone 244.3
  resorcinol 244.3

I

Iatrogenic syndrome of excess cortisol 255.0
Iceland disease (epidemic neuromyasthenia) 049.8
Ichthyosis (congenita) 757.1
 acquired 701.1
 fetalis gravior 757.1
 follicularis 757.1
 hystrix 757.39
 lamellar 757.1
 lingual 528.6
 palmaris and plantaris 757.39
 simplex 757.1
 vera 757.1
 vulgaris 757.1
Ichthyotoxism 988.0
 bacterial (*see also* Poisoning, food) 005.9
Icteroanemia, hemolytic (acquired) 283.9
 congenital (*see also* Spherocytosis) 282.0
Icterus (*see also* Jaundice) 782.4
 catarrhal - *see* Icterus, infectious
 conjunctiva 782.4
  newborn 774.6
 epidemic - *see* Icterus, infectious
 febrilis - *see* Icterus, infectious
 fetus or newborn - *see* Jaundice, fetus
  or newborn
 gravis (*see also* Necrosis, liver) 570
  complicating pregnancy 646.7
   affecting fetus or newborn 760.8
  fetus or newborn NEC 773.0
  obstetrical 646.7
   affecting fetus or newborn 760.8
 hematogenous (acquired) 283.9
 hemolytic (acquired) 283.9
  congenital (*see also* Spherocytosis)
   282.0
 hemorrhagic (acute) 100.0
  leptospiral 100.0
  newborn 776.0
  spirochetal 100.0
 infectious 070.1
  with hepatic coma 070.0
  leptospiral 100.0
  spirochetal 100.0
 intermittens juvenilis 277.4
 malignant (*see also* Necrosis, liver) 570
 neonatorum (*see also* Jaundice, fetus or
  newborn) 774.6
 pernicious (*see also* Necrosis, liver) 570
 spirochetal 100.0
Ictus solaris, solis 992.0
Identity disorder 313.82
 dissociative 300.14
 gender role (child) 302.6
  adult 302.85
 psychosexual (child) 302.6
  adult 302.85
Idioglossia 307.9
Idiopathic - *see* condition
Idiosyncrasy (*see also* Allergy) 995.3
 drug, medicinal substance, and biological - *see* Allergy, drug
Idiot, idiocy (congenital) 318.2
 amaurotic (Bielschowsky) (-Jansky)
  (family) (infantile (late)) (juvenile
  (late)) (Vogt-Spielmeyer) 330.1
 microcephalic 742.1
 mongolian 758.0
 oxycephalic 756.0
Id reaction (due to bacteria) 692.89
IgE asthma 493.0

Ileitis (chronic) (*see also* Enteritis) 558.9
 infectious 009.0
 noninfectious 558.9
 regional (ulcerative) 555.0
  with large intestine 555.2
 segmental 555.0
  with large intestine 555.2
 terminal (ulcerative) 555.0
  with large intestine 555.2
Ileocolitis (*see also* Enteritis) 558.9
 ulcerative 556.1
 infectious 009.0
 regional 555.2
Ileostomy status V44.2
 with complication 569.60
Ileotyphus 002.0
Ileum - *see* condition
Ileus (adynamic) (bowel) (colon) (inhibitory) (intestine) (neurogenic) (paralytic) 560.1
 arteriomesenteric duodenal 537.2
 due to gallstone (in intestine) 560.31
 duodenal, chronic 537.2
 following gastrointestinal surgery 997.4
 gallstone 560.31
 mechanical (*see also* Obstruction, intestine) 560.9
 meconium 777.1
  due to cystic fibrosis 277.01
 myxedema 564.89 ⬅
 postoperative 997.4
 transitory, newborn 777.4
Iliac - *see* condition
Iliotibial band friction syndrome 728.89 ◄
Ill, louping 063.1
Illegitimacy V61.6
Illness - *see also* Disease
 factitious 300.19 ⬅
  with ◄
   combined physical and psychological symptoms 300.19 ◄
   physical symptoms 300.19 ◄
   psychological symptoms 300.16 ◄
  chronic (with physical symptoms) 301.51
 heart - *see* Disease, heart
 manic-depressive (*see also* Psychosis, affective) 296.80
 mental (*see also* Disorder, mental) 300.9
Imbalance 781.2
 autonomic (*see also* Neuropathy, peripheral, autonomic) 337.9
 electrolyte 276.9
  with
   abortion - *see* Abortion, by type, with metabolic disorder
   ectopic pregnancy (*see also* categories 633.0-633.9) 639.4
   hyperemesis gravidarum (before 22 completed weeks' gestation) 643.1
   molar pregnancy (*see also* categories 630-632) 639.4
  following
   abortion 639.4
   ectopic or molar pregnancy 639.4
  neonatal, transitory NEC 775.5
 endocrine 259.9
 eye muscle NEC 378.9
  heterophoria - *see* Heterophoria
 glomerulotubular NEC 593.89

Imbalance (*Continued*)
 hormone 259.9
 hysterical (*see also* Hysteria) 300.10
 labyrinth NEC 386.50
 posture 729.9
 sympathetic (*see also* Neuropathy, peripheral, autonomic) 337.9
Imbecile, imbecility 318.0
 moral 301.7
 old age 290.9
 senile 290.9
 specified IQ - *see* IQ
 unspecified IQ 318.0
Imbedding, intrauterine device 996.32
Imbibition, cholesterol (gallbladder) 575.6
Imerslund (-Gräsbeck) syndrome (anemia due to familial selective vitamin B_{12} malabsorption) 281.1
Iminoacidopathy 270.8
Iminoglycinuria, familial 270.8
Immature - *see also* Immaturity
 personality 301.89
Immaturity 765.1
 extreme 765.0
 fetus or infant light-for-dates - *see* Light-for-dates
 lung, fetus or newborn 770.4
 organ or site NEC - *see* Hypoplasia
 pulmonary, fetus or newborn 770.4
 reaction 301.89
 sexual (female) (male) 259.0
Immersion 994.1
 foot 991.4
 hand 991.4
Immobile, immobility
 intestine 564.89 ⬅
 joint - *see* Ankylosis
 syndrome (paraplegic) 728.3
Immunization
 ABO
  affecting management of pregnancy 656.2
  fetus or newborn 773.1
 complication - *see* Complications, vaccination
 Rh factor
  affecting management of pregnancy 656.1
  fetus or newborn 773.0
 from transfusion 999.7
Immunodeficiency 279.3
 with
  adenosine-deaminase deficiency 279.2
  defect, predominant
   B-cell 279.00
   T-cell 279.10
  hyperimmunoglobulinemia 279.2
  lymphopenia, hereditary 279.2
  thrombocytopenia and eczema 279.12
  thymic
   aplasia 279.2
   dysplasia 279.2
 autosomal recessive, Swiss-type 279.2
 common variable 279.06
 severe combined (SCID) 279.2
 to Rh factor
  affecting management of pregnancy 656.1
  fetus or newborn 773.0
 X-linked, with increased IgM 279.05
Immunotherapy, prophylactic V07.2

Impaction, impacted
bowel, colon, rectum 560.30
with hernia - *see also* Hernia, by site,
with, obstruction
gangrenous - *see* Hernia, by site,
with gangrene
by
calculus 560.39
gallstone 560.31
fecal 560.39
specified type NEC 560.39
calculus - *see* Calculus
cerumen (ear) (external) 380.4
cuspid 520.6
with abnormal position (same or adjacent tooth) 524.3
dental 520.6
with abnormal position (same or adjacent tooth) 524.3
fecal, feces 560.39
with hernia - *see also* Hernia, by site,
with obstruction
gangrenous - *see* Hernia, by site,
with gangrene
fracture - *see* Fracture, by site
gallbladder - *see* Cholelithiasis
gallstone(s) - *see* Cholelithiasis
in intestine (any part) 560.31
intestine(s) 560.30
with hernia - *see also* Hernia, by site,
with obstruction
gangrenous - *see* Hernia, by site,
with gangrene
by
calculus 560.39
gallstone 560.31
fecal 560.39
specified type NEC 560.39
intrauterine device (IUD) 996.32
molar 520.6
with abnormal position (same or adjacent tooth) 524.3
shoulder 660.4
affecting fetus or newborn 763.1
tooth, teeth 520.6
with abnormal position (same or adjacent tooth) 524.3
turbinate 733.99
Impaired, impairment (function)
arm V49.1
movement, involving
musculoskeletal system V49.1
nervous system V49.2
auditory discrimination 388.43
back V48.3
body (entire) V49.8
hearing (*see also* Deafness) 389.9
heart - *see* Disease, heart
kidney (*see also* Disease, renal)
593.9
disorder resulting from 588.9
specified NEC 588.8
leg V49.1
movement, involving
musculoskeletal system V49.1
nervous system V49.2
limb V49.1
movement, involving
musculoskeletal system V49.1
nervous system V49.2
liver 573.8
mastication 524.9
mobility
ear ossicles NEC 385.22

Impaired, impairment (Continued)
mobility (*Continued*)
incostapedial joint 385.22
malleus 385.21
myocardium, myocardial (*see also* Insufficiency, myocardial) 428.0
neuromusculoskeletal NEC V49.8
back V48.3
head V48.2
limb V49.2
neck V48.3
spine V48.3
trunk V48.3
rectal sphincter 787.99
renal (*see also* Disease, renal) 593.9
disorder resulting from 588.9
specified NEC 588.8
spine V48.3
vision NEC 369.9
both eyes NEC 369.3
moderate 369.74
both eyes 369.25
with impairment of lesser eye
(specified as)
blind, not further specified
369.15
low vision, not further specified 369.23
near-total 369.17
profound 369.18
severe 369.24
total 369.16
one eye 369.74
with vision of other eye (specified as)
near-normal 369.75
normal 369.76
near-total 369.64
both eyes 369.04
with impairment of lesser eye
(specified as)
blind, not further specified
369.02
total 369.03
one eye 369.64
with vision of other eye (specified as)
near-normal 369.65
normal 369.66
one eye 369.60
with low vision of other eye
369.10
profound 369.67
both eyes 369.08
with impairment of lesser eye
(specified as)
blind, not further specified
369.05
near-total 369.07
total 369.06
one eye 369.67
with vision of other eye (specified as)
near-normal 369.68
normal 369.69
severe 369.71
both eyes 369.22
with impairment of lesser eye
(specified as)
blind, not further specified
369.11
low vision, not further specified 369.21
near-total 369.13

Impaired, impairment (Continued)
vision NEC (*Continued*)
severe (*Continued*)
both eyes (*Continued*)
with impairment of lesser eye
(*Continued*)
profound 369.14
total 369.12
one eye 369.71
with vision of other eye (specified as)
near-normal 369.72
normal 369.73
total
both eyes 369.01
one eye 369.61
with vision of other eye (specified as)
near-normal 369.62
normal 369.63
Impaludism - *see* Malaria
Impediment, speech NEC 784.5
psychogenic 307.9
secondary to organic lesion 784.5
Impending
cerebrovascular accident or attack
435.9
coronary syndrome 411.1
delirium tremens 291.0
myocardial infarction 411.1
Imperception, auditory (acquired) (congenital) 389.9
Imperfect
aeration, lung (newborn) 770.5
closure (congenital)
alimentary tract NEC 751.8
lower 751.5
upper 750.8
atrioventricular ostium 745.69
atrium (secundum) 745.5
primum 745.61
branchial cleft or sinus 744.41
choroid 743.59
cricoid cartilage 748.3
cusps, heart valve NEC 746.89
pulmonary 746.09
ductus
arteriosus 747.0
Botallo 747.0
ear drum 744.29
causing impairment of hearing
744.03
endocardial cushion 745.60
epiglottis 748.3
esophagus with communication to
bronchus or trachea 750.3
eustachian valve 746.89
eyelid 743.62
face, facial (*see also* Cleft, lip) 749.10
foramen
Botallo 745.5
ovale 745.5
genitalia, genital organ(s) or system
female 752.8
external 752.49
internal NEC 752.8
uterus 752.3
male 752.8
penis 752.69
glottis 748.3
heart valve (cusps) NEC 746.89
interatrial ostium or septum 745.5
interauricular ostium or septum
745.5

Imperfect (*Continued*)
  closure (*Continued*)
    interventricular ostium or septum
        745.4
    iris 743.46
    kidney 753.3
    larynx 748.3
    lens 743.36
    lip (*see also* Cleft, lip) 749.10
    nasal septum or sinus 748.1
    nose 748.1
    omphalomesenteric duct 751.0
    optic nerve entry 743.57
    organ or site NEC - *see* Anomaly,
        specified type, by site
    ostium
      interatrial 745.5
      interauricular 745.5
      interventricular 745.4
    palate (*see also* Cleft, palate) 749.00
    preauricular sinus 744.46
    retina 743.56
    roof of orbit 742.0
    sclera 743.47
    septum
      aortic 745.0
      aorticopulmonary 745.0
      atrial (secundum) 745.5
        primum 745.61
      between aorta and pulmonary ar-
          tery 745.0
      heart 745.9
      interatrial (secundum) 745.5
        primum 745.61
      interauricular (secundum) 745.5
        primum 745.61
      interventricular 745.4
        with pulmonary stenosis or
            atresia, dextroposition of
            aorta, and hypertrophy of
            right ventricle 745.2
          in tetralogy of Fallot 745.2
      nasal 748.1
      ventricular 745.4
        with pulmonary stenosis or
            atresia, dextroposition of
            aorta, and hypertrophy of
            right ventricle 745.2
          in tetralogy of Fallot 745.2
    skull 756.0
      with
        anencephalus 740.0
        encephalocele 742.0
        hydrocephalus 742.3
          with spina bifida (*see also*
              Spina bifida) 741.0
        microcephalus 742.1
      spine (with meningocele) (*see also*
          Spina bifida) 741.90
    thyroid cartilage 748.3
    trachea 748.3
    tympanic membrane 744.29
      causing impairment of hearing
          744.03
    uterus (with communication to blad-
        der, intestine, or rectum) 752.3
    uvula 749.02
      with cleft lip (*see also* Cleft, palate,
          with cleft lip) 749.20
    vitelline duct 751.0
  development - *see* Anomaly, by site
  erection 607.84
  fusion - *see* Imperfect, closure
  inflation lung (newborn) 770.5

Imperfect (*Continued*)
  intestinal canal 751.5
  poise 729.9
  rotation - *see* Malrotation
  septum, ventricular 745.4
Imperfectly descended testis 752.51
Imperforate (congenital) - *see also* Atresia
  anus 751.2
  bile duct 751.61
  cervix (uteri) 752.49
  esophagus 750.3
  hymen 752.42
  intestine (small) 751.1
    large 751.2
  jejunum 751.1
  pharynx 750.29
  rectum 751.2
  salivary duct 750.23
  urethra 753.6
  urinary meatus 753.6
  vagina 752.49
Impervious (congenital) - *see also* Atresia
  anus 751.2
  bile duct 751.61
  esophagus 750.3
  intestine (small) 751.1
    large 751.5
  rectum 751.2
  urethra 753.6
Impetiginization of other dermatoses
    684
Impetigo (any organism) (any site) (bul-
    lous) (circinate) (contagiosa) (neona-
    torum) (simplex) 684
  Bockhart's (superficial folliculitis) 704.8
  external ear 684 [380.13]
  eyelid 684 [373.5]
  Fox's (contagiosa) 684
  furfuracea 696.5
  herpetiformis 694.3
    nonobstetrical 694.3
  staphylococcal infection 684
  ulcerative 686.8
  vulgaris 684
Impingement, soft tissue between teeth
    524.2
Implant, endometrial 617.9
Implantation
  anomalous - *see also* Anomaly, speci-
      fied type, by site
    ureter 753.4
  cyst
    external area or site (skin) NEC
        709.8
    iris 364.61
    vagina 623.8
    vulva 624.8
  dermoid (cyst)
    external area or site (skin) NEC
        709.8
    iris 364.61
    vagina 623.8
    vulva 624.8
  placenta, low or marginal - *see* Pla-
      centa previa
Impotence (sexual) (psychogenic) 302.72
  organic origin NEC 607.84
Impoverished blood 285.9
Impression, basilar 756.0
Imprisonment V62.5
Improper
  development, infant 764.9
Improperly tied umbilical cord (causing
    hemorrhage) 772.3

Impulses, obsessional 300.3
Impulsive neurosis 300.3
Inaction, kidney (*see also* Disease, renal)
    593.9
Inactive - *see* condition
Inadequate, inadequacy
  biologic 301.6
  cardiac and renal - *see* Hypertension,
      cardiorenal
  constitutional 301.6
  development
    child 783.4
    fetus 764.9
      affecting management of preg-
          nancy 656.5
    genitalia
      after puberty NEC 259.0
      congenital - *see* Hypoplasia, geni-
          talia
    lungs 748.5
    organ or site NEC - *see* Hypoplasia,
        by site
  dietary 269.9
  education V62.3
  environment
    economic problem V60.2
    household condition NEC V60.1
    poverty V60.2
    unemployment V62.0
  functional 301.6
  household care, due to
    family member
      handicapped or ill V60.4
      temporarily away from home V60.4
        on vacation V60.5
    technical defects in home V60.1
    temporary absence from home of
        person rendering care V60.4
  housing (heating) (space) V60.1
  material resources V60.2
  mental (*see also* Retardation, mental)
      319
  nervous system 799.2
  personality 301.6
  prenatal care in current pregnancy
      V23.7
  pulmonary
    function 786.09
      newborn 770.8
    ventilation, newborn 770.8
  respiration 786.09
    newborn 770.8
  social 301.6
Inanition 263.9
  with edema 262
  due to
    deprivation of food 994.2
    malnutrition 263.9
  fever 780.6
Inappropriate secretion
  ACTH 255.0
  antidiuretic hormone (ADH) (exces-
      sive) 253.6
    deficiency 253.5
  ectopic hormone NEC 259.3
  pituitary (posterior) 253.6
Inattention after or at birth 995.52
Inborn errors of metabolism - *see* Disor-
    der, metabolism
Incarceration, incarcerated
  bubonocele - *see also* Hernia, inguinal,
      with obstruction
    gangrenous - *see* Hernia, inguinal,
        with gangrene

ICD-9-CM

—

Vol. 2

Incarceration, incarcerated (Continued)
- colon (by hernia) - see also Hernia, by site with obstruction
  - gangrenous - see Hernia, by site, with gangrene
- enterocele 552.9
  - gangrenous 551.9
- epigastrocele 552.29
  - gangrenous 551.29
- epiplocele 552.9
  - gangrenous 551.9
- exomphalos 552.1
  - gangrenous 551.1
- fallopian tube 620.8
- hernia - see also Hernia, by site, with obstruction
  - gangrenous - see Hernia, by site, with gangrene
- iris, in wound 871.1
- lens, in wound 871.1
- merocele (see also Hernia, femoral, with obstruction) 552.00
- omentum (by hernia) - see also Hernia, by site, with obstruction
  - gangrenous - see Hernia, by site, with gangrene
- omphalocele 756.79
- rupture (meaning hernia) (see also Hernia, by site, with obstruction) 552.9
  - gangrenous (see also Hernia, by site, with gangrene) 551.9
- sarcoepiplocele 552.9
  - gangrenous 551.9
- sarcoepiplomphalocele 552.1
  - with gangrene 551.1
- uterus 621.8
  - gravid 654.3
    - causing obstructed labor 660.2
    - affecting fetus or newborn 763.1

Incident, cerebrovascular (see also Disease, cerebrovascular, acute) 436

Incineration (entire body) (from fire, conflagration, electricity, or lightning) - see Burn, multiple, specified sites

Incised wound
- external - see Wound, open, by site
- internal organs (abdomen, chest, or pelvis) - see Injury, internal, by site, with open wound

Incision, incisional
- hernia - see Hernia, incisional
- surgical, complication - see Complications, surgical procedures
- traumatic
  - external - see Wound, open, by site
  - internal organs (abdomen, chest, or pelvis) - see Injury, internal, by site, with open wound

Inclusion
- azurophilic leukocytic 288.2
- blennorrhea (neonatal) (newborn) 771.6
- cyst - see Cyst, skin
- gallbladder in liver (congenital) 751.69

Incompatibility
- ABO
  - affecting management of pregnancy 656.2
  - fetus or newborn 773.1
  - infusion or transfusion reaction 999.6
- blood (group) (Duffy) (E) (K(ell)) (Kidd) (Lewis) (M) (N) (P) (S) NEC
  - affecting management of pregnancy 656.2

Incompatibility (Continued)
- blood (Continued)
  - fetus or newborn 773.2
  - infusion or transfusion reaction 999.6
- marital V61.10
  - involving divorce or estrangement V61.0
- Rh (blood group) (factor)
  - affecting management of pregnancy 656.1
  - fetus or newborn 773.0
  - infusion or transfusion reaction 999.7
- Rhesus - see Incompatibility, Rh

Incompetency, incompetence, incompetent
- annular
  - aortic (valve) (see also Insufficiency, aortic) 424.1
  - mitral (valve) - (see also Insufficiency, mitral) 424.0
  - pulmonary valve (heart) (see also Endocarditis, pulmonary) 424.3
- aortic (valve) (see also Insufficiency, aortic) 424.1
  - syphilitic 093.22
- cardiac (orifice) 530.0
- valve - see Endocarditis
- cervix, cervical (os) 622.5
  - in pregnancy 654.5
    - affecting fetus or newborn 761.0
- esophagogastric (junction) (sphincter) 530.0
- heart valve, congenital 746.89
- mitral (valve) - see Insufficiency, mitral
- papillary muscle (heart) 429.81
- pelvic fundus 618.8
- pulmonary valve (heart) (see also Endocarditis, pulmonary) 424.3
  - congenital 746.09
- tricuspid (annular) (rheumatic) (valve) (see also Endocarditis, tricuspid) 397.0
- valvular - see Endocarditis
- vein, venous (saphenous) (varicose) (see also Varicose, vein) 454.9
- velopharyngeal (closure)
  - acquired 528.9
  - congenital 750.29

Incomplete - see also condition
- bladder emptying 788.21
- expansion lungs (newborn) 770.5
- gestation (liveborn) - see Immaturity
- rotation - see Malrotation

Incontinence 788.30
- without sensory awareness 788.34
- anal sphincter 787.6
- continuous leakage 788.37
- feces 787.6
  - due to hysteria 300.11
  - nonorganic origin 307.7
- hysterical 300.11
- mixed (male) (female) (urge and stress) 788.33
- overflow 788.39
- paradoxical 788.39
- rectal 787.6
- specified NEC 788.39
- stress (female) 625.6
  - male NEC 788.32
- urethral sphincter 599.84
- urge 788.31
  - and stress (male) (female) 788.33

Incontinence (Continued)
- urine 788.30
  - active 788.30
  - male 788.30
    - stress 788.32
      - and urge 788.33
  - neurogenic 788.39
  - nonorganic origin 307.6
  - stress (female) 625.6
    - male NEC 788.32
  - urge 788.31
    - and stress 788.33

Incontinentia pigmenti 757.33

Incoordinate
- uterus (action) (contractions) 661.4
  - affecting fetus or newborn 763.7

Incoordination
- esophageal-pharyngeal (newborn) 787.2
- muscular 781.3
- papillary muscle 429.81

Increase, increased
- abnormal, in development 783.9
- androgens (ovarian) 256.1
- anticoagulants (antithrombin) (anti-VIIIa) (anti-IXa) (anti-Xa) (anti-XIa) 286.5
  - postpartum 666.3
- cold sense (see also Disturbance, sensation) 782.0
- estrogen 256.0
- function
  - adrenal (cortex) 255.3
    - medulla 255.6
  - pituitary (anterior) (gland) (lobe) 253.1
    - posterior 253.6
- heat sense (see also Disturbance, sensation) 782.0
- intracranial pressure 781.9 ◄▥
  - injury at birth 767.8
- light reflex of retina 362.13
- permeability, capillary 448.9
- pressure
  - intracranial 781.9 ◄▥
    - injury at birth 767.8
  - intraocular 365.00
- pulsations 785.9
- pulse pressure 785.9
- sphericity, lens 743.36
- splenic activity 289.4
- venous pressure 459.89
  - portal 572.3

Incrustation, cornea, lead, or zinc 930.0

Incyclophoria 378.44

Incyclotropia 378.33

Indeterminate sex 752.7

India rubber skin 756.83

Indicanuria 270.2

Indigestion (bilious) (functional) 536.8
- acid 536.8
- catarrhal 536.8
- due to decomposed food NEC 005.9
- fat 579.8
- nervous 306.4
- psychogenic 306.4

Indirect - see condition

Indolent bubo NEC 099.8

Induced
- abortion - see Abortion, induced
- birth, affecting fetus or newborn 763.89
- delivery - see Delivery
- labor - see Delivery

Induration, indurated
brain 348.8
breast (fibrous) 611.79
puerperal, postpartum 676.3
broad ligament 620.8
chancre 091.0
anus 091.1
congenital 090.0
extragenital NEC 091.2
corpora cavernosa (penis) (plastic)
607.89
liver (chronic) 573.8
acute 573.8
lung (black) (brown) (chronic) (fibroid)
(*see also* Fibrosis, lung) 515
essential brown 275.0 [516.1]
penile 607.89
phlebitic - *see* Phlebitis
skin 782.8
stomach 537.89
Induratio penis plastica 607.89
Industrial - *see* condition
Inebriety (*see also* Abuse, drugs, nondependent) 305.0
Inefficiency
kidney (*see also* Disease, renal) 593.9
thyroid (acquired) (gland) 244.9
Inelasticity, skin 782.8
Inequality, leg (acquired) (length) 736.81
congenital 755.30
Inertia
bladder 596.4
neurogenic 596.54
with cauda equina syndrome 344.61
stomach 536.8
psychogenic 306.4
uterus, uterine 661.2
affecting fetus or newborn 763.7
primary 661.0
secondary 661.1
vesical 596.4
neurogenic 596.54
with cauda equina 344.61
Infant - *see also* condition
held for adoption V68.89
newborn - *see* Newborn
syndrome of diabetic mother 775.0
"Infant Hercules" syndrome 255.2
Infantile - *see also* condition
genitalia, genitals 259.0
in pregnancy or childbirth NEC
654.4
affecting fetus or newborn
763.89
causing obstructed labor 660.2
affecting fetus or newborn
763.1
heart 746.9
kidney 753.3
lack of care 995.52
macula degeneration 362.75
melanodontia 521.0
os, uterus (*see also* Infantile, genitalia)
259.0
pelvis 738.6
with disproportion (fetopelvic) 653.1
affecting fetus or newborn 763.1
causing obstructed labor 660.1
affecting fetus or newborn 763.1
penis 259.0
testis 257.2
uterus (*see also* Infantile, genitalia)
259.0
vulva 752.49

Infantilism 259.9
with dwarfism (hypophyseal) 253.3
Brissaud's (infantile myxedema) 244.9
celiac 579.0
Herter's (nontropical sprue) 579.0
hypophyseal 253.3
hypothalamic (with obesity) 253.8
idiopathic 259.9
intestinal 579.0
pancreatic 577.8
pituitary 253.3
renal 588.0
sexual (with obesity) 259.0
Infants, healthy liveborn - *see* Newborn
Infarct, infarction
adrenal (capsule) (gland) 255.4
amnion 658.8
anterior (with contiguous portion of
intraventricular septum) NEC (*see
also* Infarct, myocardium) 410.1
appendices epiploicae 557.0
bowel 557.0
brain (stem) 434.91
embolic (*see also* Embolism, brain)
434.11
healed or old, without residuals
V12.59
iatrogenic 997.02
lacunar 434.91
postoperative 997.02
puerperal, postpartum, childbirth
674.0
thrombotic (*see also* Thrombosis,
brain) 434.01
breast 611.8
Brewer's (kidney) 593.81
cardiac (*see also* Infarct, myocardium)
410.9
cerebellar (*see also* Infarct, brain) 434.91
embolic (*see also* Embolism, brain)
434.11
cerebral (*see also* Infarct, brain) 434.91
embolic (*see also* Embolism, brain)
434.11
chorion 658.8
colon (acute) (agnogenic) (embolic)
(hemorrhagic) (nonocclusive) (nonthrombotic) (occlusive) (segmental)
(thrombotic) (with gangrene) 557.0
coronary artery (*see also* Infarct, myocardium) 410.9
embolic (*see also* Embolism) 444.9
fallopian tube 620.8
gallbladder 575.8
heart (*see also* Infarct, myocardium)
410.9
hepatic 573.4
hypophysis (anterior lobe) 253.8
impending (myocardium) 411.1
intestine (acute) (agnogenic) (embolic)
(hemorrhagic) (nonocclusive)
(nonthrombotic) (occlusive)
(thrombotic) (with gangrene) 557.0
kidney 593.81
lacunar 434.91
liver 573.4
lung (embolic) (thrombotic) 415.19
with
abortion - *see* Abortion, by type,
with, embolism
ectopic pregnancy (*see also* categories 633.0-633.9) 639.6
molar pregnancy (*see also* categories 630-632) 639.6

Infarct, infarction (*Continued*)
lung (*Continued*)
following
abortion 639.6
ectopic or molar pregnancy 639.6
iatrogenic 415.11
in pregnancy, childbirth, or puerperium - *see* Embolism, obstetrical
postoperative 415.11
lymph node or vessel 457.8
medullary (brain) - *see* Infarct, brain
meibomian gland (eyelid) 374.85
mesentary, mesenteric (embolic)
(thrombotic) (with gangrene) 557.0
midbrain - *see* Infarct, brain
myocardium, myocardial (acute or
with a stated duration of 8 weeks
or less) (with hypertension) 410.9

> Note   Use the following fifth-digit
> subclassification with category 410:
>
> 0   episode unspecified
> 1   initial episode
> 2   subsequent episode without re-
>   currence

with symptoms after 8 weeks from
date of infarction 414.8
anterior (wall) (with contiguous portion of intraventricular septum)
NEC 410.1
anteroapical (with contiguous portion of intraventricular septum)
410.1
anterolateral (wall) 410.0
anteroseptal (with contiguous portion of intraventricular septum)
410.1
apical-lateral 410.5
atrial 410.8
basal-lateral 410.5
chronic (with symptoms after 8 weeks
from date of infarction) 414.8
diagnosed on ECG, but presenting
no symptoms 412
diaphragmatic wall (with contiguous
portion of intraventricular septum) 410.4
healed or old, currently presenting
no symptoms 412
high lateral 410.5
impending 411.1
inferior (wall) (with contiguous portion of intraventricular septum)
410.4
inferolateral (wall) 410.2
inferoposterior wall 410.3
lateral wall 410.5
nontransmural 410.7
papillary muscle 410.8
past (diagnosed on ECG or other special investigation, but currently
presenting no symptoms) 412
with symptoms NEC 414.8
posterior (strictly) (true) (wall) 410.6
posterobasal 410.6
posteroinferior 410.3
posterolateral 410.5
previous, currently presenting no
symptoms 412
septal 410.8
specified site NEC 410.8
subendocardial 410.7
syphilitic 093.82

Infarct, infarction *(Continued)*
   nontransmural 410.7
   omentum 557.0
   ovary 620.8
   pancreas 577.8
   papillary muscle *(see also* Infarct, myo-
         cardium) 410.8
   parathyroid gland 252.8
   pituitary (gland) 253.8
   placenta (complicating pregnancy)
         656.7
      affecting fetus or newborn 762.2
   pontine - *see* Infarct, brain
   posterior NEC *(see also* Infarct, myocar-
         dium) 410.6
   prostate 602.8
   pulmonary (artery) (hemorrhagic)
         (vein) 415.19
      with
         abortion - *see* Abortion, by type,
               with embolism
         ectopic pregnancy *(see also* catego-
               ries 633.0-633.9) 639.6
         molar pregnancy *(see also* catego-
               ries 630-632) 639.6
      following
         abortion 639.6
         ectopic or molar pregnancy 639.6
      iatrogenic 415.11
      in pregnancy, childbirth, or puerpe-
            rium - *see* Embolism, obstetrical
      postoperative 415.11
   renal 593.81
      embolic or thrombotic 593.81
   retina, retinal 362.84
      with occlusion - *see* Occlusion, retina
   spinal (acute) (cord) (embolic) (nonem-
         bolic) 336.1
   spleen 289.59
      embolic or thrombotic 444.89
   subchorionic - *see* Infarct, placenta
   subendocardial *(see also* Infarct, myo-
         cardium) 410.7
   suprarenal (capsule) (gland) 255.4
   syncytium - *see* Infarct, placenta
   testis 608.83
   thrombotic *(see also* Thrombosis) 453.9
      artery, arterial - *see* Embolism
   thyroid (gland) 246.3
   ventricle (heart) *(see also* Infarct, myo-
         cardium) 410.9
Infecting - *see* condition
Infection, infected, infective (opportun-
      istic) 136.9
   with lymphangitis - *see* Lymphangitis
   abortion - *see* Abortion, by type, with,
         sepsis
   abscess (skin) - *see* Abscess, by site
   Absidia 117.7
   Acanthocheilonema (perstans) 125.4
      streptocerca 125.6
   accessory sinus (chronic) *(see also* Si-
         nusitis) 473.9
   Achorion - *see* Dermatophytosis
   Acremonium falciforme 117.4
   acromioclavicular (joint) 711.91
   Actinobacillus
      lignieresii 027.8
      mallei 024
      muris 026.1
   Actinomadura - *see* Actinomycosis
   Actinomyces (israelii) - *see also* Actino-
         mycosis
      muris-ratti 026.1

Infection, infected, infective *(Continued)*
   Actinomycetales (Actinomadura) (Acti-
         nomyces) (Nocardia) (Streptomy-
         ces) - *see* Actinomycosis
   actinomycotic NEC *(see also* Actinomy-
         cosis) 039.9
   adenoid (chronic) 474.01
      acute 463
      and tonsil (chronic) 474.02
         acute or subacute 463
   adenovirus NEC 079.0
      in diseases classified elsewhere - *see*
            category 079
      unspecified nature or site 079.0
   Aerobacter aerogenes NEC 041.85
      enteritis 008.2
   Aerogenes capsulatus *(see also* Gan-
         grene, gas) 040.0
   aertrycke *(see also* Infection, Salmo-
         nella) 003.9
   Ajellomyces dermatitidis 116.0
   alimentary canal NEC *(see also* Enteri-
         tis, due to, by organism) 009.0
   Allescheria boydii 117.6
   Alternaria 118
   alveolus, alveolar (process) (pulpal ori-
         gin) 522.4
   ameba, amebic (histolytica) *(see also*
         Amebiasis) 006.9
      acute 006.0
      chronic 006.1
      free-living 136.2
      hartmanni 007.8
      specified
         site NEC 006.8
         type NEC 007.8
   amniotic fluid or cavity 658.4
      affecting fetus or newborn 762.7
   anaerobes (cocci) (gram-negative)
         (gram-positive) (mixed) NEC
         041.84
   anal canal 569.49
   Ancylostoma braziliense 126.2
   Angiostrongylus cantonensis 128.8
   anisakiasis 127.1
   Anisakis larva 127.1
   anthrax *(see also* Anthrax) 022.9
   antrum (chronic) *(see also* Sinusitis,
         maxillary) 473.0
   anus (papillae) (sphincter) 569.49
   arbor virus NEC 066.9
   arbovirus NEC 066.9
   argentophil-rod 027.0
   Ascaris lumbricoides 127.0
   ascomycetes 117.4
   Aspergillus (flavus) (fumigatus) (ter-
         reus) 117.3
   atypical
      acid-fast (bacilli) *(see also* Mycobacte-
            rium, atypical) 031.9
      mycobacteria *(see also* Mycobacte-
            rium, atypical) 031.9
   auditory meatus (circumscribed) (dif-
         fuse) (external) *(see also* Otitis, ex-
         terna) 380.10
   auricle (ear) *(see also* Otitis, externa)
         380.10
   axillary gland 683
   babesiasis 088.82
   babesiosis 088.82
   Bacillus NEC 041.89
      abortus 023.1
      anthracis *(see also* Anthrax) 022.9
      cereus (food poisoning) 005.89

Infection, infected, infective *(Continued)*
   Bacillus NEC *(Continued)*
      coli - *see* Infection, Escherichia coli
      coliform NEC 041.85
      Ducrey's (any location) 099.0
      Flexner's 004.1
      fragilis NEC 041.82
      Friedländer's NEC 041.3
      fusiformis 101
      gas (gangrene) *(see also* Gangrene,
            gas) 040.0
      mallei 024
      melitensis 023.0
      paratyphoid, paratyphosus 002.9
         A 002.1
         B 002.2
         C 002.3
      Schmorl's 040.3
      Shiga 004.0
      suipestifer *(see also* Infection, Salmo-
            nella) 003.9
      swimming pool 031.1
      typhosa 002.0
      welchii *(see also* Gangrene, gas)
            040.0
      Whitmore's 025
   bacterial NEC 041.9
      specified NEC 041.89
         anaerobic NEC 041.84
         gram-negative NEC 041.85
            anaerobic NEC 041.84
   Bacterium
      paratyphosum 002.9
         A 002.1
         B 002.2
         C 002.3
      typhosum 002.9
   Bacteroides (fragilis) (melaninogenicus)
         (oralis) NEC 041.84
   Balantidium coli 007.0
   Bartholin's gland 616.8
   Basidiobolus 117.7
   Bedsonia 079.98
      specified NEC 079.88
   bile duct 576.1
   bladder *(see also* Cystitis) 595.9
   Blastomyces, blastomycotic 116.0
      brasiliensis 116.1
      dermatitidis 116.0
      European 117.5
      loboi 116.2
      North American 116.0
      South American 116.1
   blood stream - *see* Septicemia
   bone 730.9
      specified - *see* Osteomyelitis
   Bordetella 033.9
      bronchiseptica 033.8
      parapertussis 033.1
      pertussis 033.0
   Borrelia
      bergdorfi 088.81
      vincentii (mouth) (pharynx) (tonsil)
            101
   brain *(see also* Encephalitis) 323.9
      late effect - *see* category 326
      membranes - *(see also* Meningitis)
            322.9
      septic 324.0
         late effect - *see* category 326
         meninges *(see also* Meningitis)
               320.9
   branchial cyst 744.42
   breast 611.0

Infection, infected, infective *(Continued)*
  breast *(Continued)*
    puerperal, postpartum 675.2
      with nipple 675.9
        specified type NEC 675.8
      nonpurulent 675.2
      purulent 675.1
  bronchus *(see also* Bronchitis) 490
    fungus NEC 117.9
  Brucella 023.9
    abortus 023.1
    canis 023.3
    melitensis 023.0
    mixed 023.8
    suis 023.2
  Brugia (Wuchereria) malayi 125.1
  bursa - *see* Bursitis
  buttocks (skin) 686.9
  Candida (albicans) (tropicalis) *(see also*
      Candidiasis) 112.9
    congenital 771.7
  Candiru 136.8
  Capillaria
    hepatica 128.8
    philippinensis 127.5
  cartilage 733.99
  cat liver fluke 121.0
  cellulitis - *see* Cellulitis, by site
  Cephalosporum falciforme 117.4
  Cercomonas hominis (intestinal) 007.3
  cerebrospinal *(see also* Meningitis) 322.9
    late effect - *see* category 326
  cervical gland 683
  cervix *(see also* Cervicitis) 616.0
  cesarean section wound 674.3
  Chilomastix (intestinal) 007.8
  Chlamydia 079.98
    specified NEC 079.88
  Cholera *(see also* Cholera) 001.9
  chorionic plate 658.8
  Cladosporium
    bantianum 117.8
    carrionii 117.2
    mansonii 111.1
    trichoides 117.8
    werneckii 111.1
  Clonorchis (sinensis) (liver) 121.1
  Clostridium (haemolyticum) (novyi)
      NEC 041.84
    botulinum 005.1
    congenital 771.8
    histolyticum *(see also* Gangrene, gas)
        040.0
    oedematiens *(see also* Gangrene, gas)
        040.0
    perfringens 041.83
      due to food 005.2
    septicum *(see also* Gangrene, gas)
        040.0
    sordellii *(see also* Gangrene, gas)
        040.0
    welchii *(see also* Gangrene, gas) 040.0
      due to food 005.2
  Coccidioides (immitis) *(see also* Coccid-
      ioidomycosis) 114.9
  coccus NEC 041.89
  colon *(see also* Enteritis, due to, by or-
      ganism) 009.0
    bacillus - *see* Infection, Escherichia coli
  colostomy or enterostomy 569.61
  common duct 576.1
  complicating pregnancy, childbirth, or
      puerperium NEC 647.9
    affecting fetus or newborn 760.2

Infection, infected, infective *(Continued)*
  congenital NEC 771.8
    Candida albicans 771.7
    chronic 771.2
    clostridial 771.8
    cytomegalovirus 771.1
    Escherichia coli 771.8
    hepatitis, viral 771.2
    herpes simplex 771.2
    listeriosis 771.2
    malaria 771.2
    poliomyelitis 771.2
    rubella 771.0
    Salmonella 771.8
    streptococcal 771.8
    toxoplasmosis 771.2
    tuberculosis 771.2
    urinary (tract) 771.8
    vaccinia 771.2
  Conidiobolus 117.7
  corpus luteum *(see also* Salpingo-
      oophoritis) 614.2
  Corynebacterium diphtheriae - *see*
      Diphtheria
  Coxsackie *(see also* Coxsackie) 079.2
    endocardium 074.22
    heart NEC 074.20
    in diseases classified elsewhere - *see*
        category 079
    meninges 047.0
    myocardium 074.23
    pericardium 074.21
    pharynx 074.0
    specified disease NEC 074.8
    unspecified nature or site 079.2
  Cryptococcus neoformans 117.5
  Cryptosporidia 007.4
  Cunninghamella 117.7
  cyst - *see* Cyst
  Cysticercus cellulosae 123.1
  cytomegalovirus 078.5
    congenital 771.1
  dental (pulpal origin) 522.4
  deuteromycetes 117.4
  Dicrocoelium dendriticum 121.8
  Dipetalonema (perstans) 125.4
    streptocerca 125.6
  diphtherial - *see* Diphtheria
  Diphyllobothrium (adult) (latum) (pa-
      cificum) 123.4
    larval 123.5
  Diplogonoporus (grandis) 123.8
  Dipylidium (caninum) 123.8
  Dirofilaria 125.6
  dog tapeworm 123.8
  Dracunculus medinensis 125.7
  Dreschlera 118
    hawaiiensis 117.8
  Ducrey's bacillus (any site) 099.0
  due to or resulting from
    device, implant, or graft (any) (pres-
        ence of) - *see* Complications, in-
        fection and inflammation, due
        to (presence of) any device, im-
        plant, or graft classified to
        996.0-996.5 NEC
    injection, inoculation, infusion,
        transfusion, or vaccination
        (prophylactic) (therapeutic)
        999.3
    injury NEC - *see* Wound, open, by
        site, complicated
    surgery 998.59
  duodenum 535.6

Infection, infected, infective *(Continued)*
  ear - *see also* Otitis
    external *(see also* Otitis, externa)
        380.10
    inner *(see also* Labyrinthitis) 386.30
    middle - *see* Otitis, media
  Eaton's agent NEC 041.81
  Eberthella typhosa 002.0
  Ebola 065.8
  echinococcosis 122.9
  Echinococcus *(see also* Echinococcus)
      122.9
  Echinostoma 121.8
  ECHO virus 079.1
    in diseases classified elsewhere - *see*
        category 079
    unspecified nature or site 079.1
  Endamoeba - *see* Infection, ameba
  endocardium *(see also* Endocarditis) 421.0
  endocervix *(see also* Cervicitis) 616.0
  Entamoeba - *see* Infection, ameba
  enteric *(see also* Enteritis, due to, by
      organism) 009.0
  Enterobacter aerogenes NEC 041.85
  Enterobius vermicularis 127.4
  enterococcus NEC 041.04
  enterovirus NEC 079.89
    central nervous system NEC 048
    enteritis 008.67
    meningitis 047.9
  Entomophthora 117.7
  Epidermophyton - *see* Dermatophytosis
  epidermophytosis - *see* Dermatophytosis
  episiotomy 674.3
  Epstein-Barr virus 075
  erysipeloid 027.1
  Erysipelothrix (insidiosa) (rhusiopa-
      thiae) 027.1
  erythema infectiosum 057.0
  Escherichia coli NEC 041.4
    congenital 771.8
    enteritis - *see* Enteritis, E. coli
    generalized 038.42
    intestinal - *see* Enteritis, E. coli
  ethmoidal (chronic) (sinus) *(see also* Si-
      nusitis, ethmoidal) 473.2
  Eubacterium 041.84
  Eustachian tube (ear) 381.50
    acute 381.51
    chronic 381.52
  exanthema subitum 057.8
  external auditory canal (meatus) *(see
      also* Otitis, externa) 380.10
  eye NEC 360.00
  eyelid 373.9
    specified NEC 373.8
  fallopian tube *(see also* Salpingo-
      oophoritis) 614.2
  fascia 728.89
  Fasciola
    gigantica 121.3
    hepatica 121.3
  Fasciolopsis (buski) 121.4
  fetus (intra-amniotic) - *see* Infection,
      congenital
  filarial - *see* Infestation, filarial
  finger (skin) 686.9
    abscess (with lymphangitis) 681.00
      pulp 681.01
    cellulitis (with lymphangitis) 681.00
    distal closed space (with lymphangi-
        tis) 681.00
    nail 681.02
      fungus 110.1

Infection, infected, infective (*Continued*)
major
  with
    abortion - *see* Abortion, by type,
      with sepsis
    ectopic pregnancy (*see also* catego-
      ries 633.0-633.9) 639.0
    molar pregnancy (*see also* catego-
      ries 630-632) 639.0
  following
    abortion 639.0
    ectopic or molar pregnancy 639.0
  puerperal, postpartum, childbirth
    670
malarial - *see* Malaria
Malassezia furfur 111.0
Malleomyces
  mallei 024
  pseudomallei 025
mammary gland 611.0
  puerperal, postpartum 675.2
Mansonella (ozzardi) 125.5
mastoid (suppurative) - *see* Mastoiditis
maxilla, maxillary 526.4
  sinus (chronic) (*see also* Sinusitis,
    maxillary) 473.0
mediastinum 519.2
medina 125.7
meibomian
  cyst 373.12
  gland 373.12
melioidosis 025
meninges (*see also* Meningitis) 320.9
meningococcal (*see also* condition)
  036.9
  brain 036.1
  cerebrospinal 036.0
  endocardium 036.42
  generalized 036.2
  meninges 036.0
  meningococcemia 036.2
  specified site NEC 036.89
mesenteric lymph nodes or glands
  NEC 289.2
Metagonimus 121.5
metatarsophalangeal 711.97
microorganism resistant to drugs - *see*
  Resistance (to), drugs by microorganisms
Microsporidia 136.8
Microsporum, microsporic - *see* Dermatophytosis
mima polymorpha NEC 041.85
mixed flora NEC 041.89
Monilia (*see also* Candidiasis) 112.9
  neonatal 771.7
Monosporium apiospermum 117.6
mouth (focus) NEC 528.9
  parasitic 136.9
Mucor 117.7
muscle NEC 728.89
mycelium NEC 117.9
mycetoma
  actinomycotic NEC (*see also* Actino-
    mycosis) 039.9
  mycotic NEC 117.4
Mycobacterium, mycobacterial (*see also*
  Mycobacterium) 031.9
mycoplasma NEC 041.81
mycotic NEC 117.9
  pathogenic to compromised host
    only 118
  skin NEC 111.9
  systemic 117.9

Infection, infected, infective (*Continued*)
myocardium NEC 422.90
nail (chronic) (with lymphangitis)
  681.9
  finger 681.02
    fungus 110.1
  ingrowing 703.0
  toe 681.11
    fungus 110.1
nasal sinus (chronic) (*see also* Sinusitis)
  473.9
nasopharynx (chronic) 478.29
  acute 460
navel 686.9
  newborn 771.4
Neisserian - *see* Gonococcus
Neotestudina rosatii 117.4
newborn, generalized 771.8
nipple 611.0
  puerperal, postpartum 675.0
    with breast 675.9
      specified type NEC 675.8
Nocardia - *see* Actinomycosis
nose 478.1
nostril 478.1
obstetrical surgical wound 674.3
Oesophagostomum (apiostomum)
  127.7
Oestrus ovis 134.0
Oidium albicans (*see also* Candidiasis)
  112.9
Onchocerca (volvulus) 125.3
  eye 125.3 [360.13]
  eyelid 125.3 [373.6]
operation wound 998.59
Opisthorchis (felineus) (tenuicollis)
  (viverrini) 121.0
orbit 376.00
  chronic 376.10
ovary (*see also* Salpingo-oophoritis)
  614.2
Oxyuris vermicularis 127.4
pancreas 577.0
Paracoccidioides brasiliensis 116.1
Paragonimus (westermani) 121.2
parainfluenza virus 079.89
parameningococcus NEC 036.9
  with meningitis 036.0
parasitic NEC 136.9
paratyphoid 002.9
  type A 002.1
  type B 002.2
  type C 002.3
paraurethral ducts 597.89
parotid gland 527.2
Pasteurella NEC 027.2
  multocida (cat-bite) (dog-bite) 027.2
  pestis (*see also* Plague) 020.9
  pseudotuberculosis 027.2
  septica (cat-bite) (dog-bite) 027.2
  tularensis (*see also* Tularemia) 021.9
pelvic, female (*see also* Disease, pelvis,
  inflammatory) 614.9
penis (glans) (retention) NEC 607.2
  herpetic 054.13
Peptococcus 041.84
Peptostreptococcus 041.84
periapical (pulpal origin) 522.4
peridental 523.3
perineal wound (obstetrical) 674.3
periodontal 523.3
periorbital 376.00
  chronic 376.10
perirectal 569.49

Infection, infected, infective (*Continued*)
perirenal (*see also* Infection, kidney)
  590.9
peritoneal (*see also* Peritonitis) 567.9
periureteral 593.89
periurethral 597.89
Petriellidium boydii 117.6
pharynx 478.29
  Coxsackie virus 074.0
  phlegmonous 462
  posterior, lymphoid 474.00
Phialophora
  gougerotii 117.8
  jeanselmei 117.8
  verrucosa 117.2
Piedraia hortai 111.3
pinna, acute 380.11
pinta 103.9
  intermediate 103.1
  late 103.2
  mixed 103.3
  primary 103.0
pinworm 127.4
Pityrosporum furfur 111.0
pleuropneumonia-like organisms NEC
  (PPLO) 041.81
pneumococcal NEC 041.2
  generalized (purulent) 038.2
Pneumococcus NEC 041.2
postoperative wound 998.59
posttraumatic NEC 958.3
postvaccinal 999.3
prepuce NEC 607.1
Propionibacterium 041.84
prostate (capsule) (*see also* Prostatitis)
  601.9
Proteus (mirabilis) (morganii) (vulgaris) NEC 041.6
  enteritis 008.3
protozoal NEC 136.8
  intestinal NEC 007.9
Pseudomonas NEC 041.7
  mallei 024
  pneumonia 482.1
  pseudomallei 025
psittacosis 073.9
puerperal, postpartum (major) 670
  minor 646.6
pulmonary - *see* Infection, lung
purulent - *see* Abscess
putrid, generalized - *see* Septicemia
pyemic - *see* Septicemia
Pyrenochaeta romeroi 117.4
Q fever 083.0
rabies 071
rectum (sphincter) 569.49
renal (*see also* Infection, kidney) 590.9
  pelvis and ureter 590.3
resistant to drugs - *see* Resistance (to),
  drugs by microorganisms
respiratory 519.8
  chronic 519.8
  influenzal (acute) (upper) 487.1
  lung 518.89
  rhinovirus 460
  syncytial virus 079.6
  upper (acute) (infectious) NEC 465.9
    with flu, grippe, or influenza 487.1
    influenzal 487.1
    multiple sites NEC 465.8
    streptococcal 034.0
    viral NEC 465.9
respiratory syncytial virus (RSV)
  079.6

ICD-9-CM

Vol. 2

Infection, infected, infective (*Continued*)
resulting from presence of shunt or
    other internal prosthetic device -
    see Complications, infection and
    inflammation, due to (presence of)
    any device, implant, or graft clas-
    sified to 996.0-996.5 NEC
retrovirus 079.50
    human immunodeficiency virus type
        2 [HIV 2] 079.53
    human T-cell lymphotrophic virus
        type I [HTLV-I] 079.51
    human T-cell lymphotrophic virus
        type II [HTLV-II] 079.52
    specified NEC 079.59
Rhinocladium 117.1
Rhinosporidium (seeberi) 117.0,
rhinovirus
    in diseases classified elsewhere - *see*
        category 079
    unspecified nature or site 079.3
Rhizopus 117.7
rickettsial 083.9
rickettsialpox 083.2
rubella (*see also* Rubella) 056.9
    congenital 771.0
Saccharomyces (*see also* Candidiasis)
    112.9
Saksenaea 117.7
salivary duct or gland (any) 527.2
Salmonella (aertrycke) (callinarum)
    (choleraesuis) (enteritidis) (suipes-
    tifer) (typhimurium) 003.9
    with
        arthritis 003.23
        gastroenteritis 003.0
        localized infection 003.20
            specified type NEC 003.29
        meningitis 003.21
        osteomyelitis 003.24
        pneumonia 003.22
        septicemia 003.1
        specified manifestation NEC 003.8
    congenital 771.8
    due to food (poisoning) (any sero-
        type) (*see also* Poisoning, food,
        due to, Salmonella)
    hirschfeldii 002.3
    localized 003.20
        specified type NEC 003.29
    paratyphi 002.9
        A 002.1
        B 002.2
        C 002.3
    schottmuelleri 002.2
    specified type NEC 003.8
    typhi 002.0
    typhosa 002.0
saprophytic 136.8
Sarcocystis, lindemanni 136.5
scabies 133.0
Schistosoma - *see* Infestation, Schisto-
    soma
Schmorl's bacillus 040.3
scratch or other superficial injury - *see*
    Injury, superficial, by site
scrotum (acute) NEC 608.4
secondary, burn or open wound (dislo-
    cation) (fracture) 958.3
seminal vesicle (*see also* Vesiculitis) 608.0
septic
    generalized - *see* Septicemia
    localized, skin (*see also* Abscess)
        682.9

Infection, infected, infective (*Continued*)
septicemic - *see* Septicemia
seroma 998.51
Serratia (marcescens) 041.85
    generalized 038.44
sheep liver fluke 121.3
Shigella 004.9
    boydii 004.2
    dysenteriae 004.0
    Flexneri 004.1
        group
            A 004.0
            B 004.1
            C 004.2
            D 004.3
    Schmitz (-Stutzer) 004.0
    Schmitzii 004.0
    Shiga 004.0
    Sonnei 004.3
    specified type NEC 004.8
Sin Nombre virus 079.81   ◄
sinus (*see also* Sinusitis) 473.9
    pilonidal 685.1
        with abscess 685.0
    skin NEC 686.9
Skene's duct or gland (*see also* Urethri-
    tis) 597.89
skin (local) (staphylococcal) (strepto-
    coccal) NEC 686.9
    abscess - *see* Abscess, by site
    cellulitis - *see* Cellulitis, by site
    due to fungus 111.9
        specified type NEC 111.8
    mycotic 111.9
        specified type NEC 111.8
    ulcer (*see also* Ulcer, skin) 707.9
slow virus 046.9
    specified condition NEC 046.8
Sparganum (mansoni) (proliferum) 123.5
spermatic cord NEC 608.4
sphenoidal (chronic) (sinus) (*see also* Si-
    nusitis, sphenoidal) 473.3
Spherophorus necrophorus 040.3
spinal cord NEC (*see also* Encephalitis)
    323.9
    abscess 324.1
        late effect - *see* category 326
    late effect - *see* category 326
    meninges - *see* Meningitis
    streptococcal 320.2
Spirillum
    minus or minor 026.0
    morsus muris 026.0
    obermeieri 087.0
spirochetal NEC 104.9
    lung 104.8
    specified nature or site NEC 104.8
spleen 289.59
Sporothrix schenckii 117.1
Sporotrichum (schenckii) 117.1
Sporozoa 136.8
staphylococcal NEC 041.10
    aureus 041.11
    food poisoning 005.0
    generalized (purulent) 038.10
        aureus 038.11
        specified organism NEC 038.19
    pneumonia 482.40   ◄▬
        aureus 482.41   ◄
        specified type NEC 482.49   ◄
    septicemia 038.10
        aureus 038.11
        specified organism NEC 038.19
    specified NEC 041.19

Infection, infected, infective (*Continued*)
steatoma 706.2
Stellantchasmus falcatus 121.6
Streptobacillus moniliformis 026.1
streptococcal NEC 041.00
    congenital 771.8
    generalized (purulent) 038.0
    group
        A 041.01
        B 041.02
        C 041.03
        D [enterococcus] 041.04
        G 041.05
    pneumonia - *see* Pneumonia, strepto-
        coccal
    septicemia 038.0
    sore throat 034.0
    specified NEC 041.09
Streptomyces - *see* Actinomycosis
streptotrichosis - *see* Actinomycosis
Strongyloides (stercoralis) 127.2
stump (amputation) (posttraumatic)
    (surgical) 997.62
    traumatic - *see* Amputation, trau-
        matic, by site, complicated
subcutaneous tissue, local NEC 686.9
submaxillary region 528.9
suipestifer (*see also* Infection, Salmo-
    nella) 003.9
swimming pool bacillus 031.1
syphilitic - *see* Syphilis
systemic - *see* Septicemia
Taenia - *see* Infestation, Taenia
Taeniarhynchus saginata 123.2
tapeworm - *see* Infestation, tapeworm
tendon (sheath) 727.89
Ternidens diminutus 127.7
testis (*see also* Orchitis) 604.90
thigh (skin) 686.9
threadworm 127.4
throat 478.29
    pneumococcal 462
    staphylococcal 462
    streptococcal 034.0
    viral NEC (*see also* Pharyngitis) 462
thumb (skin) 686.9
    abscess (with lymphangitis) 681.00
        pulp 681.01
    cellulitis (with lymphangitis) 681.00
    nail 681.02
thyroglossal duct 529.8
toe (skin) 686.9
    abscess (with lymphangitis) 681.10
    cellulitis (with lymphangitis)
        681.10
    nail 681.11
        fungus 110.1
tongue NEC 529.0
    parasitic 112.0
tonsil (faucial) (lingual) (pharyngeal)
    474.00
    acute or subacute 463
    and adenoid 474.02
    tag 474.00
tooth, teeth 522.4
    periapical (pulpal origin) 522.4
    peridental 523.3
    periodontal 523.3
    pulp 522.0
    socket 526.5
Torula histolytica 117.5
Toxocara (cani) (cati) (felis) 128.0
Toxoplasma gondii (*see also* Toxoplas-
    mosis) 130.9

◄▶ **New Code**   ◄▬ ▬▶ **Revised Code**

Infection, infected, infective (*Continued*)
trachea, chronic 491.8
  fungus 117.9
traumatic NEC 958.3
trematode NEC 121.9
trench fever 083.1
Treponema
  denticola 041.84
  macrodenticum 041.84
  pallidum (*see also* Syphilis) 097.9
Trichinella (spiralis) 124
Trichomonas 131.9
  bladder 131.09
  cervix 131.09
  hominis 007.3
  intestine 007.3
  prostate 131.03
  specified site NEC 131.8
  urethra 131.02
  urogenitalis 131.00
  vagina 131.01
  vulva 131.01
Trichophyton, trichophytid - *see* Dermatophytosis
Trichosporon (beigelii) cutaneum 111.2
Trichostrongylus 127.6
Trichuris (trichiura) 127.3
Trombicula (irritans) 133.8
Trypanosoma (*see also* Trypanosomiasis) 086.9
  cruzi 086.2
tubal (*see also* Salpingo-oophoritis) 614.2
tuberculous NEC (*see also* Tuberculosis) 011.9
tubo-ovarian (*see also* Salpingo-oophoritis) 614.2
tunica vaginalis 608.4
tympanic membrane - *see* Myringitis
typhoid (abortive) (ambulant) (bacillus) 002.0
typhus 081.9
  flea-borne (endemic) 081.0
  louse-borne (epidemic) 080
  mite-borne 081.2
  recrudescent 081.1
  tick-borne 082.9
    African 082.1
    North Asian 082.2
umbilicus (septic) 686.9
  newborn NEC 771.4
ureter 593.89
urethra (*see also* Urethritis) 597.80
urinary (tract) NEC 599.0
  with
    abortion - *see* Abortion, by type, with urinary tract infection
    ectopic pregnancy (*see also* categories 633.0-633.9) 639.8
    molar pregnancy (*see also* categories 630-632) 639.8
  candidal 112.2
  complicating pregnancy, childbirth, or puerperium 646.6
    affecting fetus or newborn 760.1
    asymptomatic 646.5
      affecting fetus or newborn 760.1
  diplococcal (acute) 098.0
    chronic 098.2
  due to Trichomonas (vaginalis) 131.00
  following
    abortion 639.8
    ectopic or molar pregnancy 639.8

Infection, infected, infective (*Continued*)
urinary (tract) NEC (*Continued*)
  gonococcal (acute) 098.0
    chronic or duration of 2 months or over 098.2
  newborn 771.8
  trichomonal 131.00
  tuberculous (*see also* Tuberculosis) 016.3
uterus, uterine (*see also* Endometritis) 615.9
utriculus masculinus NEC 597.89
vaccination 999.3
vagina (granulation tissue) (wall) (*see also* Vaginitis) 616.10
varicella 052.9
varicose veins - *see* Varicose, veins
variola 050.9
  major 050.0
  minor 050.1
vas deferens NEC 608.4
Veillonella 041.84
verumontanum 597.89
vesical (*see also* Cystitis) 595.9
Vibrio
  cholerae 001.0
    el Tor 001.1
  parahaemolyticus (food poisoning) 005.4
  vulnificus 041.85
Vincent's (gums) (mouth) (tonsil) 101
virus, viral 079.99
  adenovirus
    in diseases classified elsewhere - *see* category 079
    unspecified nature or site 079.0
  central nervous system NEC 049.9
    enterovirus 048
      meningitis 047.9
        specified type NEC 047.8
    slow virus 046.9
    specified condition NEC 046.8
  chest 519.8
  conjunctivitis 077.99
    specified type NEC 077.89
  Coxsackie (*see also* Infection, Coxsackie) 079.2
  Ebola 065.8
  ECHO
    in diseases classified elsewhere - *see* category 079
    unspecified nature or site 079.1
  encephalitis 049.9
    arthropod-borne NEC 064
    tick-borne 063.9
      specified type NEC 063.8
  enteritis NEC (*see also* Enteritis, viral) 008.8
  exanthem NEC 057.9
  Hantavirus 079.81
  human papilloma 079.4
  in diseases classified elsewhere - *see* category 079
  intestine (*see also* Enteritis, viral) 008.8
  lung - *see* Pneumonia, viral
  respiratory syncytial (RSV) 079.6
  Retrovirus 079.50
  rhinovirus
    in diseases classified elsewhere - *see* category 079
    unspecified nature or site 079.3
  salivary gland disease 078.5
  slow 046.9
    specified condition NEC 046.8

Infection, infected, infective (*Continued*)
virus, viral (*Continued*)
  specified type NEC 079.89
    in diseases classified elsewhere - *see* category 079
  unspecified nature or site 079.99
  warts NEC 078.10
vulva (*see also* Vulvitis) 616.10
whipworm 127.3
Whitmore's bacillus 025
wound (local) (posttraumatic) NEC 958.3
  with
    dislocation - *see* Dislocation, by site, open
    fracture - *see* Fracture, by site, open
    open wound - *see* Wound, open, by site, complicated
  postoperative 998.59
  surgical 998.59
Wuchereria 125.0
  bancrofti 125.0
  malayi 125.1
yaws - *see* Yaws
yeast (*see also* Candidiasis) 112.9
yellow fever (*see also* Fever, yellow) 060.9
Yersinia pestis (*see also* Plague) 020.9
Zeis' gland 373.12
zoonotic bacterial NEC 027.9
Zopfia senegalensis 117.4
Infective, infectious - *see* condition
Inferiority complex 301.9
constitutional psychopathic 301.9
Infertility
female 628.9
  associated with
    adhesions, peritubal 614.6 [628.2]
    anomaly
      cervical mucus 628.4
      congenital
        cervix 628.4
        fallopian tube 628.2
        uterus 628.3
        vagina 628.4
    anovulation 628.0
    dysmucorrhea 628.4
    endometritis, tuberculous (*see also* Tuberculosis) 016.7 [628.3]
    Stein-Leventhal syndrome 256.4 [628.0]
  due to
    adiposogenital dystrophy 253.8 [628.1]
    anterior pituitary disorder NEC 253.4 [628.1]
      hyperfunction 253.1 [628.1]
    cervical anomaly 628.4
    fallopian tube anomaly 628.2
    ovarian failure 256.3 [628.0]
    Stein-Leventhal syndrome 256.4 [628.0]
    uterine anomaly 628.3
    vaginal anomaly 628.4
  nonimplantation 628.3
  origin
    cervical 628.4
    pituitary-hypothalamus NEC 253.8 [628.1]
      anterior pituitary NEC 253.4 [628.1]
        hyperfunction NEC 253.1 [628.1]
      dwarfism 253.3 [628.1]
      panhypopituitarism 253.2 [628.1]

ICD-9-CM

—

Vol. 2

Infertility *(Continued)*
  female *(Continued)*
    origin *(Continued)*
      specified NEC 628.8
      tubal (block) (occlusion) (stenosis)
          628.2
        adhesions 614.6 *[628.2]*
      uterine 628.3
      vaginal 628.4
    previous, requiring supervision of
        pregnancy V23.0
  male 606.9
    absolute 606.0
    due to
      azoospermia 606.0
      drug therapy 606.8
      extratesticular cause NEC 606.8
      germinal cell
        aplasia 606.0
          desquamation 606.1
      hypospermatogenesis 606.1
      infection 606.8
      obstruction, afferent ducts 606.8
      oligospermia 606.1
      radiation 606.8
      spermatogenic arrest (complete)
          606.0
        incomplete 606.1
      systemic disease 606.8
Infestation 134.9
  Acanthocheilonema (perstans) 125.4
    streptocerca 125.6
  Acariasis 133.9
    demodex folliculorum 133.8
    sarcoptes scabiei 133.0
    trombiculae 133.8
  Agamofilaria streptocerca 125.6
  Ancylostoma, Ankylostoma 126.9
    americanum 126.1
    braziliense 126.2
    cannium 126.8
    ceylanicum 126.3
    duodenale 126.0
    new world 126.1
    old world 126.0
  Angiostrongylus cantonensis 128.8
  anisakiasis 127.1
  Anisakis larva 127.1
  arthropod NEC 134.1
  Ascaris lumbricoides 127.0
  Bacillus fusiformis 101
  Balantidium coli 007.0
  beef tapeworm 123.2
  Bothriocephalus (latus) 123.4
    larval 123.5
  broad tapeworm 123.4
    larval 123.5
  Brugia malayi 125.1
  Candiru 136.8
  Capillaria
    hepatica 128.8
    philippinensis 127.5
  cat liver fluke 121.0
  Cercomonas hominis (intestinal) 007.3
  cestodes 123.9
    specified type NEC 123.8
  chigger 133.8
  chigoe 134.1
  Chilomastix 007.8
  Clonorchis (sinensis) (liver) 121.1
  coccidia 007.2
  complicating pregnancy, childbirth, or
      puerperium 647.9
    affecting fetus or newborn 760.8

Infestation *(Continued)*
  Cysticercus cellulosae 123.1
  Demodex folliculorum 133.8
  Dermatobia (hominis) 134.0
  Dibothriocephalus (latus) 123.4
    larval 123.5
  Dicrocoelium dendriticum 121.8
  Diphyllobothrium (adult) (intestinal)
      (latum) (pacificum) 123.4
    larval 123.5
  Diplogonoporus (grandis) 123.8
  Dipylidium (caninum) 123.8
  Distoma hepaticum 121.3
  dog tapeworm 123.8
  Dracunculus medinensis 125.7
  dragon worm 125.7
  dwarf tapeworm 123.6
  Echinococcus *(see also* Echinococcus)
      122.9
  Echinostoma ilocanum 121.8
  Embadomonas 007.8
  Endamoeba (histolytica) - *see* Infection,
      ameba
  Entamoeba (histolytica) - *see* Infection,
      ameba
  Enterobius vermicularis 127.4
  Epidermophyton - *see* Dermatophytosis
  eyeworm 125.2
  Fasciola
    gigantica 121.3
    hepatica 121.3
  Fasciolopsis (buski) (small intestine) 121.4
  filarial 125.9
    due to
      Acanthocheilonema (perstans) 125.4
        streptocerca 125.6
      Brugia (Wuchereria) malayi 125.1
      Dracunculus medinensis 125.7
      guinea worms 125.7
      Mansonella (ozzardi) 125.5
      Onchocerca volvulus 125.3
        eye 125.3 *[360.13]*
        eyelid 125.3 *[373.6]*
      Wuchereria (bancrofti) 125.0
        malayi 125.1
    specified type NEC 125.6
  fish tapeworm 123.4
    larval 123.5
  fluke 121.9
    blood NEC *(see also* Schistosomiasis)
        120.9
    cat liver 121.0
    intestinal (giant) 121.4
    liver (sheep) 121.3
      cat 121.0
      Chinese 121.1
      clonorchiasis 121.1
      fascioliasis 121.3
      Oriental 121.1
    lung (oriental) 121.2
    sheep liver 121.3
  fly larva 134.0
  Gasterophilus (intestinalis) 134.0
  Gastrodiscoides hominis 121.8
  Giardia lamblia 007.1
  Gnathostoma (spinigerum) 128.1
  Gongylonema 125.6
  guinea worm 125.7
  helminth NEC 128.9
    intestinal 127.9
      mixed (types classifiable to more
          than one category in 120.0-
          127.7) 127.8
      specified type NEC 127.7

Infestation *(Continued)*
  helminth NEC *(Continued)*
    specified type NEC 128.8
  Heterophyes heterophyes (small intes-
      tine) 121.6
  hookworm *(see also* Infestation, ancylo-
      stoma) 126.9
  Hymenolepis (diminuta) (nana) 123.6
  intestinal NEC 129
  leeches (aquatic) (land) 134.2
  Leishmania - *see* Leishmaniasis
  lice *(see also* Infestation, pediculus)
      132.9
  Linguatulidae, linguatula (pentastoma)
      (serrata) 134.1
  Loa loa 125.2
    eyelid 125.2 *[373.6]*
  louse *(see also* Infestation, Pediculus)
      132.9
    body 132.1
    head 132.0
    pubic 132.2
  maggots 134.0
  Mansonella (ozzardi) 125.5
  medina 125.7
  Metagonimus yokogawai (small intes-
      tine) 121.5
  Microfilaria streptocerca 125.3
    eye 125.3 *[360.13]*
    eyelid 125.3 *[373.6]*
  Microsporon furfur 111.0
  microsporum - *see* Dermatophytosis
  mites 133.9
    scabic 133.0
    specified type NEC 133.8
  Monilia (albicans) *(see also* Candidiasis)
      112.9
    vagina 112.1
    vulva 112.1
  mouth 112.0
  Necator americanus 126.1
  nematode (intestinal) 127.9
    Ancylostoma *(see also* Ancylostoma)
        126.9
    Ascaris lumbricoides 127.0
    conjunctiva NEC 128.9
    Dioctophyma 128.8
    Enterobius vermicularis 127.4
    Gnathostoma spinigerum 128.1
    Oesophagostomum (apiostomum)
        127.7
    Physaloptera 127.4
    specified type NEC 127.7
    Strongyloides stercoralis 127.2
    Ternidens diminutus 127.7
    Trichinella spiralis 124
    Trichostrongylus 127.6
    Trichuris (trichiura) 127.3
  Oesophagostomum (apiostomum) 127.7
  Oestrus ovis 134.0
  Onchocerca (volvulus) 125.3
    eye 125.3 *[360.13]*
    eyelid 125.3 *[373.6]*
  Opisthorchis (felineus) (tenuicollis)
      (viverrini) 121.0
  Oxyuris vermicularis 127.4
  Paragonimus (westermani) 121.2
  parasite, parasitic NEC 136.9
    eyelid 134.9 *[373.6]*
    intestinal 129
    mouth 112.0
    orbit 376.13
    skin 134.9
    tongue 112.0

Infestation *(Continued)*
pediculus 132.9
  capitis (humanus) (any site) 132.0
  corporis (humanus) (any site) 132.1
  eyelid 132.0 *[373.6]*
  mixed (classifiable to more than one
    category in 132.0-132.2) 132.3
  pubis (any site) 132.2
phthirus (pubis) (any site) 132.2
  with any infestation classifiable to
    132.0 and 132.1 132.3
pinworm 127.4
pork tapeworm (adult) 123.0
protozoal NEC 136.8
pubic louse 132.2
rat tapeworm 123.6
red bug 133.8
roundworm (large) NEC 127.0
sand flea 134.1
saprophytic NEC 136.8
Sarcoptes scabiei 133.0
scabies 133.0
Schistosoma 120.9
  bovis 120.8
  cercariae 120.3
  hematobium 120.0
  intercalatum 120.8
  japonicum 120.2
  mansoni 120.1
  mattheii 120.8
  specified
    site - *see* Schistosomiasis
    type NEC 120.8
  spindale 120.8
screw worms 134.0
skin NEC 134.9
Sparganum (mansoni) (proliferum)
  123.5
  larval 123.5
specified type NEC 134.8
Spirometra larvae 123.5
Sporozoa NEC 136.8
Stellantchasmus falcatus 121.6
Strongyloides 127.2
Strongylus (gibsoni) 127.7
Taenia 123.3
  diminuta 123.6
  Echinococcus (*see also* Echinococcus)
    122.9
  mediocanellata 123.2
  nana 123.6
  saginata (mediocanellata) 123.2
  solium (intestinal form) 123.0
    larval form 123.1
Taeniarhynchus saginatus 123.2
tapeworm 123.9
  beef 123.2
  broad 123.4
    larval 123.5
  dog 123.8
  dwarf 123.6
  fish 123.4
    larval 123.5
  pork 123.0
  rat 123.6
Ternidens diminutus 127.7
Tetranychus molestissimus 133.8
threadworm 127.4
tongue 112.0
Toxocara (cani) (cati) (felis) 128.0
trematode(s) NEC 121.9
Trichina spiralis 124
Trichinella spiralis 124
Trichocephalus 127.3

Infestation *(Continued)*
Trichomonas 131.9
  bladder 131.09
  cervix 131.09
  intestine 007.3
  prostate 131.03
  specified site NEC 131.8
  urethra (female) (male) 131.02
  urogenital 131.00
  vagina 131.01
  vulva 131.01
Trichophyton - *see* Dermatophytosis
Trichostrongylus instabilis 127.6
Trichuris (trichiura) 127.3
Trombicula (irritans) 133.8
Trypanosoma - *see* Trypanosomiasis
Tunga penetrans 134.1
Uncinaria americana 126.1
whipworm 127.3
worms NEC 128.9
  intestinal 127.9
Wuchereria 125.0
  bancrofti 125.0
  malayi 125.1
Infiltrate, infiltration
with an iron compound 275.0
amyloid (any site) (generalized) 277.3
calcareous (muscle) NEC 275.49
  localized - *see* Degeneration, by site
calcium salt (muscle) 275.49
corneal (*see also* Edema, cornea) 371.20
eyelid 373.9
fatty (diffuse) (generalized) 272.8
  localized - *see* Degeneration, by site,
    fatty
glycogen, glycogenic (*see also* Disease,
  glycogen storage) 271.0
heart, cardiac
  fatty (*see also* Degeneration, myocar-
    dial) 429.1
  glycogenic 271.0 *[425.7]*
inflammatory in vitreous 379.29
kidney (*see also* Disease, renal) 593.9
leukemic (M9800/3) - *see* Leukemia
liver 573.8
  fatty - *see* Fatty, liver
  glycogen (*see also* Disease, glycogen
    storage) 271.0
lung (*see also* Infiltrate, pulmonary)
  518.3
  eosinophilic 518.3
x-ray finding only 793.1
lymphatic (*see also* Leukemia, lymphatic) 204.9
  gland, pigmentary 289.3
muscle, fatty 728.9
myelogenous (*see also* Leukemia, myeloid) 205.9
myocardium, myocardial
  fatty (*see also* Degeneration, myocar-
    dial) 429.1
  glycogenic 271.0 *[425.7]*
pulmonary 518.3
  with
    eosinophilia 518.3
    pneumonia - *see* Pneumonia, by
      type
  x-ray finding only 793.1
Ranke's primary (*see also* Tuberculosis)
  010.0
skin, lymphocytic (benign) 709.8
thymus (gland) (fatty) 254.8
urine 788.8
vitreous humor 379.29

Infirmity 799.8
senile 797
Inflammation, inflamed, inflammatory
(with exudation)
abducens (nerve) 378.54
accessory sinus (chronic) (*see also* Sinusitis) 473.9
adrenal (gland) 255.8
alimentary canal - *see* Enteritis
alveoli (teeth) 526.5
  scorbutic 267
amnion - *see* Amnionitis
anal canal 569.49
antrum (chronic) (*see also* Sinusitis,
  maxillary) 473.0
anus 569.49
appendix (*see also* Appendicitis) 541
arachnoid - *see* Meningitis
areola 611.0
  puerperal, postpartum 675.0
areolar tissue NEC 686.9
artery - *see* Arteritis
auditory meatus (external) (*see also* Otitis, externa) 380.10
Bartholin's gland 616.8
bile duct or passage 576.1
bladder (*see also* Cystitis) 595.9
bone - *see* Osteomyelitis
bowel (*see also* Enteritis) 558.9
brain (*see also* Encephalitis) 323.9
  late effect - *see* category 326
  membrane - *see* Meningitis
breast 611.0
  puerperal, postpartum 675.2
broad ligament (*see also* Disease, pelvis,
  inflammatory) 614.4
  acute 614.3
bronchus - *see* Bronchitis
bursa - *see* Bursitis
capsule
  liver 573.3
  spleen 289.59
catarrhal (*see also* Catarrh) 460
  vagina 616.10
cecum (*see also* Appendicitis) 541
cerebral (*see also* Encephalitis) 323.9
  late effect - *see* category 326
  membrane - *see* Meningitis
cerebrospinal (*see also* Meningitis)
  322.9
  late effect - *see* category 326
  meningococcal 036.0
  tuberculous (*see also* Tuberculosis)
    013.6
cervix (uteri) (*see also* Cervicitis) 616.0
chest 519.9
choroid NEC (*see also* Choroiditis)
  363.20
cicatrix (tissue) - *see* Cicatrix
colon (*see also* Enteritis) 558.9
  granulomatous 555.1
  newborn 558.9
connective tissue (diffuse) NEC 728.9
cornea (*see also* Keratitis) 370.9
  with ulcer (*see also* Ulcer, cornea)
    370.00
corpora cavernosa (penis) 607.2
cranial nerve - *see* Disorder, nerve, cranial
diarrhea - *see* Diarrhea
disc (intervertebral) (space) 722.90
  cervical, cervicothoracic 722.91
  lumbar, lumbosacral 722.93
  thoracic, thoracolumbar 722.92

Inflammation, inflamed, inflammatory
(Continued)
Douglas' cul-de-sac or pouch (chronic)
(*see also* Disease, pelvis, inflammatory) 614.4
acute 614.3
due to (presence of) any device, implant, or graft classifiable to 996.0-996.5 - *see* Complications, infection and inflammation, due to (presence of) any device, implant, or graft classified to 996.0-996.5 NEC
duodenum 535.6
dura mater - *see* Meningitis
ear - *see also* Otitis
external (*see also* Otitis, externa) 380.10
inner (*see also* Labyrinthitis) 386.30
middle - *see* Otitis media
esophagus 530.10
ethmoidal (chronic) (sinus) (*see also* Sinusitis, ethmoidal) 473.2
eustachian tube (catarrhal) 381.50
acute 381.51
chronic 381.52
extrarectal 569.49
eye 379.99
eyelid 373.9
specified NEC 373.8
fallopian tube (*see also* Salpingo-oophoritis) 614.2
fascia 728.9
fetal membranes (acute) 658.4
affecting fetus or newborn 762.7
follicular, pharynx 472.1
frontal (chronic) (sinus) (*see also* Sinusitis, frontal) 473.1
gallbladder (*see also* Cholecystitis, acute) 575.0
gall duct (*see also* Cholecystitis) 575.10
gastrointestinal (*see also* Enteritis) 558.9
genital organ (diffuse) (internal)
female 614.9
with
abortion - *see* Abortion, by type, with sepsis
ectopic pregnancy (*see also* categories 633.0-633.9) 639.0
molar pregnancy (*see also* categories 630-632) 639.0
complicating pregnancy, childbirth, or puerperium 646.6
affecting fetus or newborn 760.8
following
abortion 639.0
ectopic or molar pregnancy 639.0
male 608.4
gland (lymph) (*see also* Lymphadenitis) 289.3
glottis (*see also* Laryngitis) 464.0
granular, pharynx 472.1
gum 523.1
heart (*see also* Carditis) 429.89
hepatic duct 576.8
hernial sac - *see* Hernia, by site
ileum (*see also* Enteritis) 558.9
terminal or regional 555.0
with large intestine 555.2
intervertebral disc 722.90
cervical, cervicothoracic 722.91
lumbar, lumbosacral 722.93
thoracic, thoracolumbar 722.92
intestine (*see also* Enteritis) 558.9

Inflammation, inflamed, inflammatory
(Continued)
jaw (acute) (bone) (chronic) (lower) (suppurative) (upper) 526.4
jejunum - *see* Enteritis
joint NEC (*see also* Arthritis) 716.9
sacroiliac 720.2
kidney (*see also* Nephritis) 583.9
knee (joint) 716.66
tuberculous (active) (*see also* Tuberculosis) 015.2
labium (majus) (minus) (*see also* Vulvitis) 616.10
lacrimal
gland (*see also* Dacryoadenitis) 375.00
passages (duct) (sac) (*see also* Dacryocystitis) 375.30
larynx (*see also* Laryngitis) 464.0
diphtheritic 032.3
leg NEC 686.9
lip 528.5
liver (capsule) (*see also* Hepatitis) 573.3
acute 570
chronic 571.40
suppurative 572.0
lung (acute) (*see also* Pneumonia) 486
chronic (interstitial) 518.89
lymphatic vessel (*see also* Lymphangitis) 457.2
lymph node or gland (*see also* Lymphadenitis) 289.3
mammary gland 611.0
puerperal, postpartum 675.2
maxilla, maxillary 526.4
sinus (chronic) (*see also* Sinusitis, maxillary) 473.0
membranes of brain or spinal cord - *see* Meningitis
meninges - *see* Meningitis
mouth 528.0
muscle 728.9
myocardium (*see also* Myocarditis) 429.0
nasal sinus (chronic) (*see also* Sinusitis) 473.9
nasopharynx - *see* Nasopharyngitis
navel 686.9
newborn NEC 771.4
nerve NEC 729.2
nipple 611.0
puerperal, postpartum 675.0
nose 478.1
suppurative 472.0
oculomotor nerve 378.51
optic nerve 377.30
orbit (chronic) 376.10
acute 376.00
chronic 376.10
ovary (*see also* Salpingo-oophoritis) 614.2
oviduct (*see also* Salpingo-oophoritis) 614.2
pancreas - *see* Pancreatitis
parametrium (chronic) (*see also* Disease, pelvis, inflammatory) 614.4
acute 614.3
parotid region 686.9
gland 527.2
pelvis, female (*see also* Disease, pelvis, inflammatory) 614.9
penis (corpora cavernosa) 607.2
perianal 569.49
pericardium (*see also* Pericarditis) 423.9
perineum (female) (male) 686.9

Inflammation, inflamed, inflammatory
(Continued)
perirectal 569.49
peritoneum (*see also* Peritonitis) 567.9
periuterine (*see also* Disease, pelvis, inflammatory) 614.9
perivesical (*see also* Cystitis) 595.9
petrous bone (*see also* Petrositis) 383.20
pharynx (*see also* Pharyngitis) 462
follicular 472.1
granular 472.1
pia mater - *see* Meningitis
pleura - *see* Pleurisy
postmastoidectomy cavity 383.30
chronic 383.33
prostate (*see also* Prostatitis) 601.9
rectosigmoid - *see* Rectosigmoiditis
rectum (*see also* Proctitis) 569.49
respiratory, upper (*see also* Infection, respiratory, upper) 465.9
chronic, due to external agent - *see* Condition, respiratory, chronic, due to, external agent
due to
fumes or vapors (chemical) (inhalation) 506.2
radiation 508.1
retina (*see also* Retinitis) 363.20
retrocecal (*see also* Appendicitis) 541
retroperitoneal (*see also* Peritonitis) 567.9
salivary duct or gland (any) (suppurative) 527.2
scorbutic, alveoli, teeth 267
scrotum 608.4
sigmoid - *see* Enteritis
sinus (*see also* Sinusitis) 473.9
Skene's duct or gland (*see also* Urethritis) 597.89
skin 686.9
spermatic cord 608.4
sphenoidal (sinus) (*see also* Sinusitis, sphenoidal) 473.3
spinal
cord (*see also* Encephalitis) 323.9
late effect - *see* category 326
membrane - *see* Meningitis
nerve - *see* Disorder, nerve
spine (*see also* Spondylitis) 720.9
spleen (capsule) 289.59
stomach - *see* Gastritis
stricture, rectum 569.49
subcutaneous tissue NEC 686.9
suprarenal (gland) 255.8
synovial (fringe) (membrane) - *see* Bursitis
tendon (sheath) NEC 726.90
testis (*see also* Orchitis) 604.90
thigh 686.9
throat (*see also* Sore throat) 462
thymus (gland) 254.8
thyroid (gland) (*see also* Thyroiditis) 245.9
tongue 529.0
tonsil - *see* Tonsillitis
trachea - *see* Tracheitis
trochlear nerve 378.53
tubal (*see also* Salpingo-oophoritis) 614.2
tuberculous NEC (*see also* Tuberculosis) 011.9
tubo-ovarian (*see also* Salpingo-oophoritis) 614.2
tunica vaginalis 608.4

◀ ▶   **New Code**   ⬅ ⇒   **Revised Code**

Inflammation, inflamed, inflammatory
  (Continued)
  tympanic membrane - *see* Myringitis
  umbilicus, umbilical 686.9
    newborn NEC 771.4
  uterine ligament (*see also* Disease, pelvis, inflammatory) 614.4
    acute 614.3
  uterus (catarrhal) (*see also* Endometritis) 615.9
  uveal tract (anterior) (*see also* Iridocyclitis) 364.3
    posterior - *see* Chorioretinitis
    sympathetic 360.11
  vagina (*see also* Vaginitis) 616.10
  vas deferens 608.4
  vein (*see also* Phlebitis) 451.9
    thrombotic 451.9
      cerebral (*see also* Thrombosis, brain) 434.0
      leg 451.2
        deep (vessels) NEC 451.19
        superficial (vessels) 451.0
      lower extremity 451.2
        deep (vessels) NEC 451.19
        superficial (vessels) 451.0
  vocal cord 478.5
  vulva (*see also* Vulvitis) 616.10
Inflation, lung imperfect (newborn) 770.5
Influenza, influenzal 487.1
  with
    bronchitis 487.1
    bronchopneumonia 487.0
    cold (any type) 487.1
    digestive manifestations 487.8
    hemoptysis 487.1
    involvement of
      gastrointestinal tract 487.8
      nervous system 487.8
    laryngitis 487.1
    manifestations NEC 487.8
      respiratory 487.1
        pneumonia 487.0
    pharyngitis 487.1
    pneumonia (any form classifiable to 480-483, 485-486) 487.0
    respiratory manifestations NEC 487.1
    sinusitis 487.1
    sore throat 487.1
    tonsillitis 487.1
    tracheitis 487.1
    upper respiratory infection (acute) 487.1
  abdominal 487.8
  Asian 487.1
  bronchial 487.1
  bronchopneumonia 487.0
  catarrhal 487.1
  epidemic 487.1
  gastric 487.8
  intestinal 487.8
  laryngitis 487.1
  maternal affecting fetus or newborn 760.2
    manifest influenza in infant 771.2
  pharyngitis 487.1
  pneumonia (any form) 487.0
  respiratory (upper) 487.1
  stomach 487.8
  vaccination, prophylactic (against) V04.8
Influenza-like disease 487.1

Infraction, Freiberg's (metatarsal head) 732.5
Infusion complication, misadventure, or reaction - *see* Complication, infusion
Ingestion
  chemical - *see* Table of Drugs and Chemicals
  drug or medicinal substance
    overdose or wrong substance given or taken 977.9
      specified drug - *see* Table of Drugs and Chemicals
  foreign body NEC (*see also* Foreign body) 938
Ingrowing
  hair 704.8
  nail (finger) (toe) (infected) 703.0
Inguinal - *see also* condition
  testis 752.51
Inhalation
  carbon monoxide 986
  flame
    mouth 947.0
    lung 947.1
  food or foreign body (*see also* Asphyxia, food or foreign body) 933.1
  gas, fumes, or vapor (noxious) 987.9
    specified agent - *see* Table of Drugs and Chemicals
  liquid or vomitus (*see also* Asphyxia, food or foreign body) 933.1
    lower respiratory tract NEC 934.9
  meconium (fetus or newborn) 770.1
  mucus (*see also* Asphyxia, mucus) 933.1
  oil (causing suffocation) (*see also* Asphyxia, food or foreign body) 933.1
  pneumonia - *see* Pneumonia, aspiration
  smoke 987.9
  steam 987.9
  stomach contents or secretions (*see also* Asphyxia, food or foreign body) 933.1
    in labor and delivery 668.0
Inhibition, inhibited
  academic as adjustment reaction 309.23
  orgasm
    female 302.73
    male 302.74
  sexual
    desire 302.71
    excitement 302.72
  work as adjustment reaction 309.23
Inhibitor, systemic lupus erythematosus (presence of) 286.5
Iniencephalus, iniencephaly 740.2
Injected eye 372.74
Injury 959.9

> Note For abrasion, insect bite (nonvenomous), blister, or scratch, *see* Injury, superficial.
>
> For laceration, traumatic rupture, tear, or penetrating wound of internal organs, such as heart, lung, liver, kidney, pelvic organs, whether or not accompanied by open wound in the same region, *see* Injury, internal.
>
> For nerve injury, *see* Injury, nerve.
>
> For late effect of injuries classifiable to 850-854, 860-869, 900-919, 950-959, *see* Late, effect, injury, by type.

Injury *(Continued)*
  abdomen, abdominal (viscera) - *see also* Injury, internal, abdomen
    muscle or wall 959.1
  acoustic, resulting in deafness 951.5
  adenoid 959.09
  adrenal (gland) - *see* Injury, internal, adrenal
  alveolar (process) 959.09
  ankle (and foot) (and knee) (and leg, except thigh) 959.7
  anterior chamber, eye 921.3
  anus 959.1
  aorta (thoracic) 901.0
    abdominal 902.0
  appendix - *see* Injury, internal, appendix
  arm, upper (and shoulder) 959.2
  artery (complicating trauma) (*see also* Injury, blood vessel, by site) 904.9
    cerebral or meningeal (*see also* Hemorrhage, brain, traumatic, subarachnoid) 852.0
  auditory canal (external) (meatus) 959.09
  auricle, auris, ear 959.09
  axilla 959.2
  back 959.1
  bile duct - *see* Injury, internal, bile duct
  birth - *see also* Birth, injury
    canal NEC, complicating delivery 665.9
  bladder (sphincter) - *see* Injury, internal, bladder
  blast (air) (hydraulic) (immersion) (underwater) NEC 869.0
    with open wound into cavity NEC 869.1
    abdomen or thorax - *see* Injury, internal, by site
    brain - *see* Concussion, brain
    ear (acoustic nerve trauma) 951.5
      with perforation of tympanic membrane - *see* Wound, open, ear, drum
  blood vessel NEC 904.9
    abdomen 902.9
      multiple 902.87
      specified NEC 902.89
    aorta (thoracic) 901.0
      abdominal 902.0
    arm NEC 903.9
    axillary 903.00
      artery 903.1
      vein 903.02
    azygos vein 901.89
    basilic vein 903.1
    brachial (artery) (vein) 903.1
    bronchial 901.89
    carotid artery 900.00
      common 900.01
      external 900.02
      internal 900.03
    celiac artery 902.20
      specified branch NEC 902.24
    cephalic vein (arm) 903.1
    colica dextra 902.26
    cystic
      artery 902.24
      vein 902.39
    deep plantar 904.6
    digital (artery) (vein) 903.5
    due to accidental puncture or laceration during procedure 998.2

Injury *(Continued)*
  forehead 959.09
  gallbladder - *see* Injury, internal, gall-
    bladder
  gasserian ganglion 951.2
  gastrointestinal tract - *see* Injury, inter-
    nal, gastrointestinal tract
  genital organ(s)
    with
      abortion - *see* Abortion, by type,
        with, damage to pelvic organs
      ectopic pregnancy (*see also* catego-
        ries 633.0-633.9) 639.2
      molar pregnancy (*see also* catego-
        ries 630-632) 639.2
    external 959.1
    following
      abortion 639.2
      ectopic or molar pregnancy 639.2
    internal - *see* Injury, internal, genital
      organs
    obstetrical trauma NEC 665.9
      affecting fetus or newborn
        763.89
  gland
    lacrimal 921.1
      laceration 870.8
    parathyroid 959.09
    salivary 959.09
    thyroid 959.09
  globe (eye) (*see also* Injury, eyeball) 921.3
  grease gun - *see* Wound, open, by site,
    complicated
  groin 959.1
  gum 959.09
  hand(s) (except fingers) 959.4
  head NEC 959.01
    with
      skull fracture - *see* Fracture, skull,
        by site
  heart - *see* Injury, internal, heart
  heel 959.7
  hip (and thigh) 959.6
  hymen 959.1
  hyperextension (cervical) (vertebra)
    847.0
  ileum - *see* Injury, internal, ileum
  iliac region 959.1
  infrared rays NEC 990
  instrumental (during surgery) 998.2
    birth injury - *see* Birth, injury
    nonsurgical (*see also* Injury, by site)
      959.9
    obstetrical 665.9
      affecting fetus or newborn
        763.89
      bladder 665.5
      cervix 665.3
      high vaginal 665.4
      perineal NEC 664.9
      urethra 665.5
      uterus 665.5
  internal 869.0

> Note For injury of internal organ(s)
> by foreign body entering through a
> natural orifice (e.g., inhaled, ingested,
> or swallowed)-*see* Foreign body, en-
> tering through orifice.
>
> For internal injury of any of the fol-
> lowing sites with internal injury of
> any other of the sites-*see* Injury, inter-
> nal, multiple.

Injury *(Continued)*
  internal *(Continued)*
    with
      fracture
        pelvis - *see* Fracture, pelvis
        specified site, except pelvis - *see*
          Injury, internal, by site
      open wound into cavity 869.1
    abdomen, abdominal (viscera) NEC
      868.00
      with
        fracture, pelvis - *see* Fracture,
          pelvis
        open wound into cavity 868.10
      specified site NEC 868.09
        with open wound into cavity
          868.19
    adrenal (gland) 868.01
      with open wound into cavity
        868.11
    aorta (thoracic) 901.0
      abdominal 902.0
    appendix 863.85
      with open wound into cavity
        863.95
    bile duct 868.02
      with open wound into cavity
        868.12
    bladder (sphincter) 867.0
      with
        abortion - *see* Abortion, by type,
          with, damage to pelvic or-
          gans
        ectopic pregnancy (*see also* cate-
          gories 633.0-633.9) 639.2
        molar pregnancy (*see also* cate-
          gories 630-632) 639.2
        open wound into cavity 867.1
      following
        abortion 639.2
        ectopic or molar pregnancy
          639.2
      obstetrical trauma 665.5
        affecting fetus or newborn
          763.89
    blood vessel - *see* Injury, blood ves-
      sel, by site
    broad ligament 867.6
      with open wound into cavity
        867.7
    bronchus, bronchi 862.21
      with open wound into cavity
        862.31
    cecum 863.89
      with open wound into cavity
        863.99
    cervix (uteri) 867.4
      with
        abortion - *see* Abortion, by type,
          with damage to pelvic or-
          gans
        ectopic pregnancy (*see also* cate-
          gories 633.0-633.9) 639.2
        molar pregnancy (*see also* cate-
          gories 630-632) 639.2
        open wound into cavity 867.5
      following
        abortion 639.2
        ectopic or molar pregnancy 639.2
      obstetrical trauma 665.3
        affecting fetus or newborn
          763.89
    chest (*see also* Injury, internal, in-
      trathoracic organs) 862.8

Injury *(Continued)*
  internal *(Continued)*
    chest *(Continued)*
      with open wound into cavity
        862.9
    colon 863.40
      with
        open wound into cavity 863.50
        rectum 863.46
          with open wound into cavity
            863.56
      ascending (right) 863.41
        with open wound into cavity
          863.51
      descending (left) 863.43
        with open wound into cavity
          863.53
      multiple sites 863.46
        with open wound into cavity
          863.56
      sigmoid 863.44
        with open wound into cavity
          863.54
      specified site NEC 863.49
        with open wound into cavity
          863.59
      transverse 863.42
        with open wound into cavity
          863.52
    common duct 868.02
      with open wound into cavity
        868.12
    complicating delivery 665.9
      affecting fetus or newborn
        763.89
    diaphragm 862.0
      with open wound into cavity
        862.1
    duodenum 863.21
      with open wound into cavity
        863.31
    esophagus (intrathoracic) 862.22
      with open wound into cavity
        862.32
      cervical region 874.4
        complicated 874.5
    fallopian tube 867.6
      with open wound into cavity
        867.7
    gallbladder 868.02
      with open wound into cavity
        868.12
    gastrointestinal tract NEC 863.80
      with open wound into cavity
        863.90
    genital organ NEC 867.6
      with open wound into cavity
        867.7
    heart 861.00
      with open wound into thorax
        861.10
    ileum 863.29
      with open wound into cavity
        863.39
    intestine NEC 863.89
      with open wound into cavity
        863.99
    large NEC 863.40
      with open wound into cavity
        863.50
    small NEC 863.20
      with open wound into cavity
        863.30
    intra-abdominal (organ) 868.00

Injury *(Continued)*
 internal *(Continued)*
  intra-abdominal *(Continued)*
   with open wound into cavity
    868.10
   multiple sites 868.09
    with open wound into cavity
     868.19
   specified site NEC 868.09
    with open wound into cavity
     868.19
  intrathoracic organs (multiple) 862.8
   with open wound into cavity
    862.9
   diaphragm (only) - *see* Injury, in-
    ternal, diaphragm
   heart (only) - *see* Injury, internal,
    heart
   lung (only) - *see* Injury, internal,
    lung
   specified site NEC 862.29
    with open wound into cavity
     862.39
  intrauterine *(see also* Injury, internal,
   uterus) 867.4
   with open wound into cavity
    867.5
  jejunum 863.29
   with open wound into cavity
    863.39
  kidney (subcapsular) 866.00
   with
    disruption of parenchyma (com-
     plete) 866.03
     with open wound into cavity
      866.13
    hematoma (without rupture of
     capsule) 866.01
     with open wound into cavity
      866.11
    laceration 866.02
     with open wound into cavity
      866.12
    open wound into cavity 866.10
  liver 864.00
   with
    contusion 864.01
     with open wound into cavity
      864.11
    hematoma 864.01
     with open wound into cavity
      864.11
    laceration 864.05
     with open wound into cavity
      864.15
    major (disruption of hepatic
     parenchyma) 864.04
     with open wound into cav-
      ity 864.14
    minor (capsule only) 864.02
     with open wound into cav-
      ity 864.12
    moderate (involving paren-
     chyma) 864.03
     with open wound into cav-
      ity 864.13
    multiple 864.04
    stellate 864.04
     with open wound into cav-
      ity 864.14
    open wound into cavity 864.10
  lung 861.20
   with open wound into thorax
    861.30

Injury *(Continued)*
 internal *(Continued)*
  lung *(Continued)*
   hemopneumothorax - *see* Hemo-
    pneumothorax, traumatic
   hemothorax - *see* Hemothorax,
    traumatic
   pneumohemothorax - *see* Pneumo-
    hemothorax, traumatic
   pneumothorax - *see* Pneumo-
    thorax, traumatic
  mediastinum 862.29
   with open wound into cavity
    862.39
  mesentery 863.89
   with open wound into cavity
    863.99
  mesosalpinx 867.6
   with open wound into cavity
    867.7
  multiple 869.0

> Note   Multiple internal injuries of
> sites classifiable to the same three- or
> four-digit category should be classi-
> fied to that category.
>
> Multiple injuries classifiable to differ-
> ent fourth-digit subdivisions of 861.-
> (heart and lung injuries) should be
> dealt with according to coding rules.

   internal 869.0
    with open wound into cavity
     869.1
   intra-abdominal organ (sites classi-
    fiable to 863-868)
    with
     intrathoracic organ(s) (sites
      classifiable to 861-862)
      869.0
      with open wound into cav-
       ity 869.1
     other intra-abdominal or-
      gan(s) (sites classifiable to
      863-868, except where
      classifiable to the same
      three-digit category)
      868.09
      with open wound into cav-
       ity 868.19
   intrathoracic organ (sites classifia-
    ble to 861-862)
    with
     intra-abdominal organ(s)
      (sites classifiable to 863-
      868) 869.0
      with open wound into cav-
       ity 869.1
     other intrathoracic organs(s)
      (sites classifiable to 861-862,
      except where classifiable to
      the same three-digit cate-
      gory) 862.8
     with open wound into cavity
      862.9
  myocardium - *see* Injury, internal,
   heart
  ovary 867.6
   with open wound into cavity 867.7
  pancreas (multiple sites) 863.84
   with open wound into cavity 863.94
   body 863.82
    with open wound into cavity
     863.92

Injury *(Continued)*
 internal *(Continued)*
  pancreas *(Continued)*
   head 863.81
    with open wound into cavity
     863.91
   tail 863.83
    with open wound into cavity
     863.93
  pelvis, pelvic (organs) (viscera) 867.8
   with
    fracture, pelvis - *see* Fracture,
     pelvis
    open wound into cavity 867.9
   specified site NEC 867.6
    with open wound into cavity
     867.7
  peritoneum 868.03
   with open wound into cavity
    868.13
  pleura 862.29
   with open wound into cavity
    862.39
  prostate 867.6
   with open wound into cavity
    867.7
  rectum 863.45
   with
    colon 863.46
     with open wound into cavity
      863.56
    open wound into cavity 863.55
  retroperitoneum 868.04
   with open wound into cavity
    868.14
  round ligament 867.6
   with open wound into cavity
    867.7
  seminal vesicle 867.6
   with open wound into cavity
    867.7
  spermatic cord 867.6
   with open wound into cavity
    867.7
   scrotal - *see* Wound, open, sper-
    matic cord
  spleen 865.00
   with
    disruption of parenchyma (mas-
     sive) 865.04
     with open wound into cavity
      865.14
    hematoma (without rupture of
     capsule) 865.01
     with open wound into cavity
      865.11
    open wound into cavity 865.10
    tear, capsular 865.02
     with open wound into cavity
      865.12
     extending into parenchyma
      865.03
      with open wound into cav-
       ity 865.13
  stomach 863.0
   with open wound into cavity 863.1
  suprarenal gland (multiple) 868.01
   with open wound into cavity
    868.11
  thorax, thoracic (cavity) (organs)
   (multiple) *(see also* Injury, internal, intrathoracic organs) 862.8
   with open wound into cavity
    862.9

Injury (*Continued*)
internal (*Continued*)
thymus (gland) 862.29
with open wound into cavity 862.39
trachea (intrathoracic) 862.29
with open wound into cavity 862.39
cervical region (*see also* Wound, open, trachea) 874.02
ureter 867.2
with open wound into cavity 867.3
urethra (sphincter) 867.0
with
abortion - *see* Abortion, by type, with, damage to pelvic organs
ectopic pregnancy (*see also* categories 633.0-633.9) 639.2
molar pregnancy (*see also* categories 630-632) 639.2
open wound into cavity 867.1
following
abortion 639.2
ectopic or molar pregnancy 639.2
obstetrical trauma 665.5
affecting fetus or newborn 763.89 ⬅
uterus 867.4
with
abortion - *see* Abortion, by type, with, damage to pelvic organs
ectopic pregnancy (*see also* categories 633.0-633.9) 639.2
molar pregnancy (*see also* categories 630-632) 639.2
open wound into cavity 867.5
following
abortion 639.2
ectopic or molar pregnancy 639.2
obstetrical trauma NEC 665.5
affecting fetus or newborn - 763.89 ⬅
vas deferens 867.6
with open wound into cavity 867.7
vesical (sphincter) 867.0
with open wound into cavity 867.1
viscera (abdominal) (*see also* Injury, internal, multiple) 868.00
with
fracture, pelvis - *see* Fracture, pelvis
open wound into cavity 868.10
thoracic NEC (*see also* Injury, internal, intrathoracic organs) 862.8
with open wound into cavity 862.9
interscapular region 959.1
intervertebral disc 959.1
intestine - *see* Injury, internal, intestine
intra-abdominal (organs) NEC - *see* Injury, internal, intra-abdominal
intracranial 854.0

Note Use the following fifth-digit subclassification with categories 851-854:

0 unspecified state of consciousness
1 with no loss of consciousness
2 with brief [less than one hour] loss of consciousness

Injury (*Continued*)
intracranial (*Continued*)
3 with moderate [1-24 hours] loss of consciousness
4 with prolonged [more than 24 hours] loss of consciousness and return to pre-existing conscious level
5 with prolonged [more than 24 hours] loss of consciousness, without return to pre-existing conscious level

Use fifth-digit 5 to designate when a patient is unconscious and dies before regaining consciousness, regardless of the duration of the loss of consciousness

6 with loss of consciousness of unspecified duration
9 with concussion, unspecified

with
open intracranial wound 854.1
skull fracture - *see* Fracture, skull, by site
contusion 851.8
with open intracranial wound 851.9
brain stem 851.4
with open intracranial wound 851.5
cerebellum 851.4
with open intracranial wound 851.5
cortex (cerebral) 851.0
with open intracranial wound 851.2
hematoma - *see* Injury, intracranial, hemorrhage
hemorrhage 853.0
with
laceration - *see* Injury, intracranial, laceration
open intracranial wound 853.1
extradural 852.4
with open intracranial wound 852.5
subarachnoid 852.0
with open intracranial wound 852.1
subdural 852.2
with open intracranial wound 852.3
laceration 851.8
with open intracranial wound 851.9
brain stem 851.6
with open intracranial wound 851.7
cerebellum 851.6
with open intracranial wound 851.7
cortex (cerebral) 851.2
with open intracranial wound 851.3
intraocular - *see* Injury, eyeball, penetrating
intrathoracic organs (multiple) - *see* Injury, internal, intrathoracic organs
intrauterine - *see* Injury, internal, intrauterine
iris 921.3
penetrating - *see* Injury, eyeball, penetrating

Injury (*Continued*)
jaw 959.09
jejunum - *see* Injury, internal, jejunum
joint NEC 959.9
old or residual 718.80
ankle 718.87
elbow 718.82
foot 718.87
hand 718.84
hip 718.85
knee 718.86
multiple sites 718.89
pelvic region 718.85
shoulder (region) 718.81
specified site NEC 718.88
wrist 718.83
kidney - *see* Injury, internal, kidney
knee (and ankle) (and foot) (and leg, except thigh) 959.7
labium (majus) (minus) 959.1
labyrinth, ear 959.09
lacrimal apparatus, gland, or sac 921.1
laceration 870.8
larynx 959.09
late effect - *see* Late, effects (of), injury
leg, except thigh (and ankle) (and foot) (and knee) 959.7
upper or thigh 959.6
lens, eye 921.3
penetrating - *see* Injury, eyeball, penetrating
lid, eye - *see* Injury, eyelid
lip 959.09
liver - *see* Injury, internal, liver
lobe, parietal - *see* Injury, intracranial
lumbar (region) 959.1
plexus 953.5
lumbosacral (region) 959.1
plexus 953.5
lung - *see* Injury, internal, lung
malar region 959.09
mastoid region 959.09
maternal, during pregnancy, affecting fetus or newborn 760.5
maxilla 959.09
mediastinum - *see* Injury, internal, mediastinum
membrane
brain (*see also* Injury, intracranial) 854.0
tympanic 959.09
meningeal artery - *see* Hemorrhage, brain, traumatic, subarachnoid
meninges (cerebral) - *see* Injury, intracranial
mesenteric
artery - *see* Injury, blood vessel, mesenteric, artery
plexus, inferior 954.1
vein - *see* Injury, blood vessel, mesenteric, vein
mesentery - *see* Injury, internal, mesentery
mesosalpinx - *see* Injury, internal, mesosalpinx
middle ear 959.09
midthoracic region 959.1
mouth 959.09
multiple (sites not classifiable to the same four-digit category in 959.0-959.7) 959.8
internal 869.0
with open wound into cavity 869.1
musculocutaneous nerve 955.4

Injury (*Continued*)
  nail
    finger 959.5
    toe 959.7
  nasal (septum) (sinus) 959.09
  nasopharynx 959.09
  neck (and face) 959.09
  nerve 957.9
    abducens 951.3
    abducent 951.3
    accessory 951.6
    acoustic 951.5
    ankle and foot 956.9
    anterior crural, femoral 956.1
    arm (*see also* Injury, nerve, upper
      limb) 955.9
    auditory 951.5
    axillary 955.0
    brachial plexus 953.4
    cervical sympathetic 954.0
    cranial 951.9
      first or olfactory 951.8
      second or optic 950.0
      third or oculomotor 951.0
      fourth or trochlear 951.1
      fifth or trigeminal 951.2
      sixth or abducens 951.3
      seventh or facial 951.4
      eighth, acoustic, or auditory 951.5
      ninth or glossopharyngeal 951.8
      tenth, pneumogastric, or vagus
        951.8
      eleventh or accessory 951.6
      twelfth or hypoglossal 951.7
      newborn 767.7
    cutaneous sensory
      lower limb 956.4
      upper limb 955.5
    digital (finger) 955.6
      toe 956.5
    facial 951.4
      newborn 767.5
    femoral 956.1
    finger 955.9
    foot and ankle 956.9
    forearm 955.9
    glossopharyngeal 951.8
    hand and wrist 955.9
    head and neck, superficial 957.0
    hypoglossal 951.7
    involving several parts of body 957.8
    leg (*see also* Injury, nerve, lower
      limb) 956.9
    lower limb 956.9
      multiple 956.8
      specified site NEC 956.5
    lumbar plexus 953.5
    lumbosacral plexus 953.5
    median 955.1
      forearm 955.1
      wrist and hand 955.1
    multiple (in several parts of body)
      (sites not classifiable to the same
      three-digit category) 957.8
    musculocutaneous 955.4
    musculospiral 955.3
      upper arm 955.3
    oculomotor 951.0
    olfactory 951.8
    optic 950.0
    pelvic girdle 956.9
      multiple sites 956.8
      specified site NEC 956.5
    peripheral 957.9

Injury (*Continued*)
  nerve (*Continued*)
    peripheral (*Continued*)
      multiple (in several regions) (sites
        not classifiable to the same
        three-digit category) 957.8
      specified site NEC 957.1
    peroneal 956.3
      ankle and foot 956.3
      lower leg 956.3
    plantar 956.5
    plexus 957.9
      celiac 954.1
      mesenteric, inferior 954.1
      spinal 953.9
        brachial 953.4
        lumbosacral 953.5
        multiple sites 953.8
      sympathetic NEC 954.1
    pneumogastric 951.8
    radial 955.3
      wrist and hand 955.3
    sacral plexus 953.5
    sciatic 956.0
      thigh 956.0
    shoulder girdle 955.9
      multiple 955.8
      specified site NEC 955.7
    specified site NEC 957.1
    spinal 953.9
      plexus - *see* Injury, nerve, plexus,
        spinal
      root 953.9
        cervical 953.0
        dorsal 953.1
        lumbar 953.2
        multiple sites 953.8
        sacral 953.3
    splanchnic 954.1
    sympathetic NEC 954.1
      cervical 954.0
    thigh 956.9
    tibial 956.5
      ankle and foot 956.2
      lower leg 956.5
      posterior 956.2
    toe 956.9
    trigeminal 951.2
    trochlear 951.1
    trunk, excluding shoulder and pelvic
      girdles 954.9
      specified site NEC 954.8
      sympathetic NEC 954.1
    ulnar 955.2
      forearm 955.2
      wrist (and hand) 955.2
    upper limb 955.9
      multiple 955.8
      specified site NEC 955.7
    vagus 951.8
    wrist and hand 955.9
  nervous system, diffuse 957.8
  nose (septum) 959.09
  obstetrical NEC 665.9
    affecting fetus or newborn
      763.89
  occipital (region) (scalp) 959.09
    lobe (*see also* Injury, intracranial)
      854.0
  optic 950.9
    chiasm 950.1
    cortex 950.3
    nerve 950.0
    pathways 950.2

Injury (*Continued*)
  orbit, orbital (region) 921.2
    penetrating 870.3
      with foreign body 870.4
  ovary - *see* Injury, internal, ovary
  paint-gun - *see* Wound, open, by site,
    complicated
  palate (soft) 959.09
  pancreas - *see* Injury, internal, pancreas
  parathyroid (gland) 959.09
  parietal (region) (scalp) 959.09
    lobe - *see* Injury, intracranial
  pelvic
    floor 959.1
      complicating delivery 664.1
        affecting fetus or newborn
          763.89
    joint or ligament, complicating deliv-
      ery 665.6
      affecting fetus or newborn
        763.89
    organs - *see also* Injury, internal, pel-
      vis
      with
        abortion - *see* Abortion, by type,
          with damage to pelvic or-
          gans
        ectopic pregnancy (*see also* cate-
          gories 633.0-633.9) 639.2
        molar pregnancy (*see also* cate-
          gories 633.0-633.9) 639.2
      following
        abortion 639.2
        ectopic or molar pregnancy 639.2
      obstetrical trauma 665.5
        affecting fetus or newborn
          763.89
  pelvis 959.1
  penis 959.1
  perineum 959.1
  peritoneum - *see* Injury, internal, peri-
    toneum
  periurethral tissue
    with
      abortion - *see* Abortion, by type,
        with damage to pelvic organs
      ectopic pregnancy (*see also* catego-
        ries 633.0-633.9) 639.2
      molar pregnancy (*see also* catego-
        ries 630-632) 639.2
    complicating delivery 665.5
      affecting fetus or newborn
        763.89
    following
      abortion 639.2
      ectopic or molar pregnancy 639.2
  phalanges
    foot 959.7
    hand 959.5
  pharynx 959.09
  pleura - *see* Injury, internal, pleura
  popliteal space 959.7
  prepuce 959.1
  prostate - *see* Injury, internal, prostate
  pubic region 959.1
  pudenda 959.1
  radiation NEC 990
  radioactive substance or radium NEC
    990
  rectovaginal septum 959.1
  rectum - *see* Injury, internal, rectum
  retina 921.3
    penetrating - *see* Injury, eyeball, pen-
      etrating

Injury *(Continued)*
  retroperitoneal - *see* Injury, internal,
    retroperitoneum
  roentgen rays NEC 990
  round ligament - *see* Injury, internal,
    round ligament
  sacral (region) 959.1
    plexus 953.5
  sacroiliac ligament NEC 959.1
  sacrum 959.1
  salivary ducts or glands 959.09
  scalp 959.09
    due to birth trauma 767.1
    fetus or newborn 767.1
  scapular region 959.2
  sclera 921.3
    penetrating - *see* Injury, eyeball, pen-
      etrating
    superficial 918.2
  scrotum 959.1
  seminal vesicle - *see* Injury, internal,
    seminal vesicle
  shoulder (and upper arm) 959.2
  sinus
    cavernous (*see also* Injury, intracra-
      nial) 854.0
    nasal 959.09
  skeleton NEC, birth injury 767.3
  skin NEC 959.9
  skull - *see* Fracture, skull, by site
  soft tissue (of external sites) (severe) -
    see Wound, open, by site
  specified site NEC 959.8
  spermatic cord - *see* Injury, internal,
    spermatic cord
  spinal (cord) 952.9
    with fracture, vertebra - *see* Fracture,
      vertebra, by site, with spinal
      cord injury
    cervical (C_1-C_4) 952.00
      with
        anterior cord syndrome 952.02
        central cord syndrome 952.03
        complete lesion of cord 952.01
        incomplete lesion NEC 952.04
        posterior cord syndrome 952.04
      C_5-C_7 level 952.05
        with
          anterior cord syndrome 952.07
          central cord syndrome 952.08
          complete lesion of cord 952.06
          incomplete lesion NEC 952.09
          posterior cord syndrome
            952.09
        specified type NEC 952.09
      specified type NEC 952.04
    dorsal (D_1-D_6) (T_1-T_6) (thoracic)
      952.10
      with
        anterior cord syndrome 952.12
        central cord syndrome 952.13
        complete lesion of cord 952.11
        incomplete lesion NEC 952.14
        posterior cord syndrome 952.14
      D_7-D_{12} level (T_7-T_{12}) 952.15
        with
          anterior cord syndrome 952.17
          central cord syndrome 952.18
          complete lesion of cord 952.16
          incomplete lesion NEC 952.19
          posterior cord syndrome
            952.19
        specified type NEC 952.19
      specified type NEC 952.14

Injury *(Continued)*
  spinal *(Continued)*
    lumbar 952.2
    multiple sites 952.8
    nerve (root) NEC - *see* Injury, nerve,
      spinal, root
    plexus 953.9
      brachial 953.4
      lumbosacral 953.5
      multiple sites 953.8
    sacral 952.3
    thoracic (*see also* Injury, spinal, dor-
      sal) 952.10
  spleen - *see* Injury, internal, spleen
  stellate ganglion 954.1
  sternal region 959.1
  stomach - *see* Injury, internal, stomach
  subconjunctival 921.1
  subcutaneous 959.9
  subdural - *see* Injury, intracranial
  submaxillary region 959.09
  submental region 959.09
  subungual
    fingers 959.5
    toes 959.7
  superficial 919

Note   Use the following fourth-digit
subdivisions with categories 910-919:

  .0   abrasion or friction burn with-
      out mention of infection
  .1   abrasion or friction burn, in-
      fected
  .2   blister without mention of in-
      fection
  .3   blister, infected
  .4   insect bite, nonvenomous,
      without mention of infection
  .5   insect bite, nonvenomous, in-
      fected
  .6   superficial foreign body (splin-
      ter) without major open
      wound and without mention
      of infection
  .7   superficial foreign body (splin-
      ter) without major open
      wound, infected
  .8   other and unspecified superfi-
      cial injury without mention of
      infection
  .9   other and unspecified superfi-
      cial injury, infected

For late effects of superficial injury,
see category 906.2.

---

    abdomen, abdominal (muscle) (wall)
      (and other part(s) of trunk) 911
    ankle (and hip, knee, leg, or thigh)
      916
    anus (and other part(s) of trunk) 911
    arm 913
      upper (and shoulder) 912
    auditory canal (external) (meatus)
      (and other part(s) of face, neck,
      or scalp, except eye) 910
    axilla (and upper arm) 912
    back (and other part(s) of trunk) 911
    breast (and other part(s) of trunk)
      911
    brow (and other part(s) of face,
      neck, or scalp, except eye) 910
    buttock (and other part(s) of trunk)
      911

Injury *(Continued)*
  superficial *(Continued)*
    canthus, eye 918.0
    cheek(s) (and other part(s) of face,
      neck, or scalp, except eye) 910
    chest wall (and other part(s) of
      trunk) 911
    chin (and other part(s) of face, neck,
      or scalp, except eye) 910
    clitoris (and other part(s) of trunk)
      911
    conjunctiva 918.2
    cornea 918.1
      due to contact lens 371.82
    costal region (and other part(s) of
      trunk) 911
    ear(s) (auricle) (canal) (drum) (exter-
      nal) (and other part(s) of face,
      neck, or scalp, except eye) 910
    elbow (and forearm) (and wrist) 913
    epididymis (and other part(s) of
      trunk) 911
    epigastric region (and other part(s)
      of trunk) 911
    epiglottis (and other part(s) of face,
      neck, or scalp, except eye) 910
    eye(s) (and adnexa) NEC 918.9
    eyelid(s) (and periocular area) 918.0
    face (any part(s), except eye) (and
      neck or scalp) 910
    finger(s) (nail) (any) 915
    flank (and other part(s) of trunk) 911
    foot (phalanges) (and toe(s)) 917
    forearm (and elbow) (and wrist) 913
    forehead (and other part(s) of face,
      neck, or scalp, except eye) 910
    globe (eye) 918.9
    groin (and other part(s) of trunk)
      911
    gum(s) (and other part(s) of face,
      neck, or scalp, except eye) 910
    hand(s) (except fingers alone) 914
    head (and other part(s) of face, neck,
      or scalp, except eye) 910
    heel (and foot or toe) 917
    hip (and ankle, knee, leg, or thigh)
      916
    iliac region (and other part(s) of
      trunk) 911
    interscapular region (and other
      part(s) of trunk) 911
    iris 918.9
    knee (and ankle, hip, leg, or thigh)
      916
    labium (majus) (minus) (and other
      part(s) of trunk) 911
    lacrimal (apparatus) (gland) (sac)
      918.0
    leg (lower) (upper) (and ankle, hip,
      knee, or thigh) 916
    lip(s) (and other part(s) of face,
      neck, or scalp, except eye)
      910
    lower extremity (except foot) 916
    lumbar region (and other part(s) of
      trunk) 911
    malar region (and other part(s) of
      face, neck, or scalp, except eye)
      910
    mastoid region (and other part(s) of
      face, neck, or scalp, except eye)
      910
    midthoracic region (and other
      part(s) of trunk) 911

ICD-9-CM

Vol. 2

Injury (*Continued*)
  superficial (*Continued*)
    mouth (and other part(s) of face, neck, or scalp, except eye) 910
    multiple sites (not classifiable to the same three-digit category) 919
    nasal (septum) (and other part(s) of face, neck, or scalp, except eye) 910
    neck (and face or scalp, any part(s), except eye) 910
    nose (septum) (and other part(s) of face, neck, or scalp, except eye) 910
    occipital region (and other part(s) of face, neck, or scalp, except eye) 910
    orbital region 918.0
    palate (soft) (and other part(s) of face, neck, or scalp, except eye) 910
    parietal region (and other part(s) of face, neck, or scalp, except eye) 910
    penis (and other part(s) of trunk) 911
    perineum (and other part(s) of trunk) 911
    periocular area 918.0
    pharynx (and other part(s) of face, neck, or scalp, except eye) 910
    popliteal space (and ankle, hip, leg, or thigh) 916
    prepuce (and other part(s) of trunk) 911
    pubic region (and other part(s) of trunk) 911
    pudenda (and other part(s) of trunk) 911
    sacral region (and other part(s) of trunk) 911
    salivary (ducts) (glands) (and other part(s) of face, neck, or scalp, except eye) 910
    scalp (and other part(s) of face or neck, except eye) 910
    scapular region (and upper arm) 912
    sclera 918.2
    scrotum (and other part(s) of trunk) 911
    shoulder (and upper arm) 912
    skin NEC 919
    specified site(s) NEC 919
    sternal region (and other part(s) of trunk) 911
    subconjunctival 918.2
    subcutaneous NEC 919
    submaxillary region (and other part(s) of face, neck, or scalp, except eye) 910
    submental region (and other part(s) of face, neck, or scalp, except eye) 910
    supraclavicular fossa (and other part(s) of face, neck, or scalp, except eye) 910
    supraorbital 918.0
    temple (and other part(s) of face, neck, or scalp, except eye) 910
    temporal region (and other part(s) of face, neck, or scalp, except eye) 910

Injury (*Continued*)
  superficial (*Continued*)
    testis (and other part(s) of trunk) 911
    thigh (and ankle, hip, knee, or leg) 916
    thorax, thoracic (external) (and other part(s) of trunk) 911
    throat (and other part(s) of face, neck, or scalp, except eye) 910
    thumb(s) (nail) 915
    toe(s) (nail) (subungual) (and foot) 917
    tongue (and other part(s) of face, neck, or scalp, except eye) 910
    tooth, teeth 521.2
    trunk (any part(s)) 911
    tunica vaginalis (and other part(s) of trunk) 911
    tympanum, tympanic membrane (and other part(s) of face, neck, or scalp, except eye) 910
    upper extremity NEC 913
    uvula (and other part(s) of face, neck, or scalp, except eye) 910
    vagina (and other part(s) of trunk) 911
    vulva (and other part(s) of trunk) 911
    wrist (and elbow) (and forearm) 913
  supraclavicular fossa 959.1
  supraorbital 959.09
  surgical complication (external or internal site) 998.2
  symphysis pubis 959.1
    complicating delivery 665.6
      affecting fetus or newborn 763.89 ◀◖▮
  temple 959.09
  temporal region 959.09
  testis 959.1
  thigh (and hip) 959.6
  thorax, thoracic (external) 959.1
    cavity - *see* Injury, internal, thorax
    internal - *see* Injury, internal, intrathoracic organs
  throat 959.09
  thumb(s) (nail) 959.5
  thymus - *see* Injury, internal, thymus
  thyroid (gland) 959.09
  toe (nail) (any) 959.7
  tongue 959.09
  tonsil 959.09
  tooth NEC 873.63
    complicated 873.73
  trachea - *see* Injury, internal, trachea
  trunk 959.1
  tunica vaginalis 959.1
  tympanum, tympanic membrane 959.09
  ultraviolet rays NEC 990
  ureter - *see* Injury, internal, ureter
  urethra (sphincter) - *see* Injury, internal, urethra
  uterus - *see* Injury, internal, uterus
  uvula 959.09
  vagina 959.1
  vascular - *see* Injury, blood vessel
  vas deferens - *see* Injury, internal, vas deferens
  vein (*see also* Injury, blood vessel, by site) 904.9
  vena cava
    inferior 902.10
    superior 901.2

Injury (*Continued*)
  vesical (sphincter) - *see* Injury, internal, vesical
  viscera (abdominal) - *see* Injury, internal, viscera
    with fracture, pelvis - *see* Fracture, pelvis
  visual 950.9
    cortex 950.3
  vitreous (humor) 871.2
  vulva 959.1
  whiplash (cervical spine) 847.0
  wringer - *see* Crush, by site
  wrist (and elbow) (and forearm) 959.3
  x-ray NEC 990
Inoculation - *see also* Vaccination
  complication or reaction - *see* Complication, vaccination
Insanity, insane (*see also* Psychosis) 298.9
  adolescent (*see also* Schizophrenia) 295.9
  alternating (*see also* Psychosis, affective, circular) 296.7
  confusional 298.9
    acute 293.0
    subacute 293.1
  delusional 298.9
  paralysis, general 094.1
    progressive 094.1
  paresis, general 094.1
  senile 290.20
Insect
  bite - *see* Injury, superficial, by site
  venomous, poisoning by 989.5
Insemination, artificial V26.1
Insertion
  cord (umbilical) lateral or velamentous 663.5
    affecting fetus or newborn 762.6
  intrauterine contraceptive device V25.1
  placenta, vicious - *see* Placenta, previa
  subdermal implantable contraceptive V25.5
  velamentous, umbilical cord 663.5
    affecting fetus or newborn 762.6
Insolation 992.0
  meaning sunstroke 992.0
Insomnia 780.52
  with sleep apnea 780.51
  nonorganic origin 307.41
    persistent (primary) 307.42 ◀◖▮
    transient 307.41
  subjective complaint 307.49
Inspiration
  food or foreign body (*see also* Asphyxia, food or foreign body) 933.1
  mucus (*see also* Asphyxia, mucus) 933.1
Inspissated bile syndrome, newborn 774.4
Instability
  detrusor 596.59
  emotional (excessive) 301.3
  joint (posttraumatic) 718.80
    ankle 718.87
    elbow 718.82
    foot 718.87
    hand 718.84
    hip 718.85
    knee 718.86
    lumbosacral 724.6
    multiple sites 718.89
    pelvic region 718.85
    sacroiliac 724.6

Instability (*Continued*)
  joint (*Continued*)
    shoulder (region) 718.81
    specified site NEC 718.88
    wrist 718.83
  lumbosacral 724.6
  nervous 301.89
  personality (emotional) 301.59
  thyroid, paroxysmal 242.9
  urethral 599.83
  vasomotor 780.2
Insufficiency, insufficient
  accommodation 367.4
  adrenal (gland) (acute) (chronic) 255.4
    medulla 255.5
    primary 255.4
    specified site NEC 255.5
  adrenocortical 255.4
  anus 569.49
  aortic (valve) 424.1
    with
      mitral (valve) disease 396.1
        insufficiency, incompetence, or
          regurgitation 396.3
        stenosis or obstruction 396.1
      stenosis or obstruction 424.1
        with mitral (valve) disease
          396.8
    congenital 746.4
    rheumatic 395.1
      with
        mitral (valve) disease 396.1
          insufficiency, incompetence,
            or regurgitation 396.3
          stenosis or obstruction 396.1
        stenosis or obstruction 395.2
          with mitral (valve) disease
            396.8
    specified cause NEC 424.1
    syphilitic 093.22
  arterial 447.1
    basilar artery 435.0
    carotid artery 435.8
    cerebral 437.1
    coronary (acute or subacute)
      411.89
    mesenteric 557.1
    peripheral 443.9
    precerebral 435.9
    vertebrobasilar 435.3
    vertebral artery 435.1
  arteriovenous 459.9
  basilar artery 435.0
  biliary 575.8
  cardiac (*see also* Insufficiency, myocar-
    dial) 428.0
    complicating surgery 997.1
    due to presence of (cardiac) prosthe-
      sis 429.4
    postoperative 997.1
      long-term effect of cardiac surgery
        429.4
    specified during or due to a proce-
      dure 997.1
      long-term effect of cardiac surgery
        429.4
  cardiorenal (*see also* Hypertension, car-
    diorenal) 404.90
  cardiovascular (*see also* Disease, cardio-
    vascular) 429.2
    renal (*see also* Hypertension, cardior-
      enal) 404.90
  carotid artery 435.8
  cerebral (vascular) 437.9

Insufficiency, insufficient (*Continued*)
  cerebrovascular 437.9
    with transient focal neurological
      signs and symptoms 435.9
    acute 437.1
      with transient focal neurological
        signs and symptoms 435.9
  circulatory NEC 459.9
    fetus or newborn 779.8
  convergence 378.83
  coronary (acute or subacute) 411.89
    chronic or with a stated duration of
      over 8 weeks 414.8
  corticoadrenal 255.4
  dietary 269.9
  divergence 378.85
  food 994.2
  gastroesophageal 530.89
  gonadal
    ovary 256.3
    testis 257.2
  gonadotropic hormone secretion
    253.4
  heart - *see also* Insufficiency, myocar-
    dial
    fetus or newborn 779.8
    valve (*see also* Endocarditis)
      424.90
      congenital NEC 746.89
  hepatic 573.8
  idiopathic autonomic 333.0
  kidney (*see also* Disease, renal) 593.9
  labyrinth, labyrinthine (function)
    386.53
    bilateral 386.54
    unilateral 386.53
  lacrimal 375.15
  liver 573.8
  lung (acute) (*see also* Insufficiency, pul-
    monary) 518.82
    following trauma, surgery, or shock
      518.5
    newborn 770.8
  mental (congenital) (*see also* Retarda-
    tion, mental) 319
  mesenteric 557.1
  mitral (valve) 424.0
    with
      aortic (valve) disease 396.3
        insufficiency, incompetence, or
          regurgitation 396.3
        stenosis or obstruction 396.2
      obstruction or stenosis 394.2
        with aortic valve disease 396.8
    congenital 746.6
    rheumatic 394.1
      with
        aortic (valve) disease 396.3
          insufficiency, incompetence,
            or regurgitation 396.3
          stenosis or obstruction 396.2
        obstruction or stenosis 394.2
        with aortic valve disease
          396.8
      active or acute 391.1
        with chorea, rheumatic (Syden-
          ham's) 392.0
    specified cause, except rheumatic
      424.0
  muscle
    heart - *see* Insufficiency, myocardial
    ocular (*see also* Strabismus) 378.9
  myocardial, myocardium (with arterio-
    sclerosis) 428.0

Insufficiency, insufficient (*Continued*)
  myocardial, myocardium (*Continued*)
    with rheumatic fever (conditions
      classifiable to 390)
      active, acute, or subacute 391.2
        with chorea 392.0
      inactive or quiescent (with chorea)
        398.0
    congenital 746.89
    due to presence of (cardiac) prosthe-
      sis 429.4
    fetus or newborn 779.8
    following cardiac surgery 429.4
    hypertensive (*see also* Hypertension,
      heart) 402.91
      benign 402.11
      malignant 402.01
    postoperative 997.1
      long-term effect of cardiac surgery
        429.4
    rheumatic 398.0
      active, acute, or subacute 391.2
        with chorea (Sydenham's) 392.0
    syphilitic 093.82
  nourishment 994.2
  organic 799.8
  ovary 256.3
    postablative 256.2
  pancreatic 577.8
  parathyroid (gland) 252.1
  peripheral vascular (arterial) 443.9
  pituitary (anterior) 253.2
    posterior 253.5
  placental - *see* Placenta, insufficiency
  platelets 287.5
  prenatal care in current pregnancy
    V23.7
  progressive pluriglandular 258.9
  pseudocholinesterase 289.8
  pulmonary (acute) 518.82
    following
      shock 518.5
      surgery 518.5
      trauma 518.5
    newborn 770.8
    valve (*see also* Endocarditis, pulmo-
      nary) 424.3
      congenital 746.09
  pyloric 537.0
  renal 593.9
    due to a procedure 997.5
  respiratory 786.09
    acute 518.82
      following shock, surgery, or
        trauma 518.5
    newborn 770.8
  rotation - *see* Malrotation
  suprarenal 255.4
    medulla 255.5
  tarso-orbital fascia, congenital 743.66
  tear film 375.15
  testis 257.2
  thyroid (gland) (acquired) - *see also*
    Hypothyroidism
    congenital 243
  tricuspid (*see also* Endocarditis, tricus-
    pid) 397.0
    congenital 746.89
    syphilitic 093.23
  urethral sphincter 599.84
  valve, valvular (heart) (*see also* Endo-
    carditis) 424.90
  vascular 459.9
    intestine NEC 557.9

Insufficiency, insufficient *(Continued)*
  vascular *(Continued)*
    mesenteric 557.1
    peripheral 443.9
    renal *(see also* Hypertension, kidney)
      403.90
    velopharyngeal
      acquired 528.9
      congenital 750.29
    venous (peripheral) 459.81
    ventricular - *see* Insufficiency, myocardial
    vertebral artery 435.1
    vertebrobasilar artery 435.3
    weight gain during pregnancy 646.8
    zinc 269.3
Insufflation
  fallopian V26.2
  meconium 770.1
Insular - *see* condition
Insulinoma (M8151/0)
  malignant (M8151/3)
    pancreas 157.4
    specified site - *see* Neoplasm, by site,
      malignant
    unspecified site 157.4
  pancreas 211.7
  specified site - *see* Neoplasm, by site,
    benign
  unspecified site 211.7
Insuloma - *see* Insulinoma
Insult
  brain 437.9
    acute 436
  cerebral 437.9
    acute 436
  cerebrovascular 437.9
    acute 436
  vascular NEC 437.9
    acute 436
Insurance examination (certification)
  V70.3
Intemperance *(see also* Alcoholism) 303.9
Interception of pregnancy (menstrual
  extraction) V25.3
Intermenstrual
  bleeding 626.6
    irregular 626.6
    regular 626.5
  hemorrhage 626.6
    irregular 626.6
    regular 626.5
  pain(s) 625.2
Intermittent - *see* condition
Internal - *see* condition
Interproximal wear 521.1
Interruption
  aortic arch 747.11
  bundle of His 426.50
  fallopian tube (for sterilization)
    V25.2
  phase-shift, sleep cycle 307.45
  repeated REM-sleep 307.48
  sleep
    due to perceived environmental
      disturbances 307.48
    phase-shift, of 24-hour sleep-wake
      cycle 307.45
    repeated REM-sleep type 307.48
  vas deferens (for sterilization) V25.2
Intersexuality 752.7
Interstitial - *see* condition
Intertrigo 695.89
  labialis 528.5

Intervertebral disc - *see* condition
Intestine, intestinal - *see also* condition
  flu 487.8
Intolerance
  carbohydrate NEC 579.8
  cardiovascular exercise, with pain (at
    rest) (with less than ordinary ac-
    tivity) (with ordinary activity)
    V47.2
  cold 780.9
  disaccharide (hereditary) 271.3
  drug
    correct substance properly adminis-
      tered 995.2
    wrong substance given or taken in
      error 977.9
      specified drug - *see* Table of Drugs
        and Chemicals
  effort 306.2
  fat NEC 579.8
  foods NEC 579.8
  fructose (hereditary) 271.2
  glucose (-galactose) (congenital) 271.3
  gluten 579.0
  lactose (hereditary) (infantile) 271.3
  lysine (congenital) 270.7
  milk NEC 579.8
  protein (familial) 270.7
  starch NEC 579.8
  sucrose (-isomaltose) (congenital)
    271.3
Intoxicated NEC *(see also* Alcoholism)
  305.0
Intoxication
  acid 276.2
  acute
    alcoholic 305.0
      with alcoholism 303.0
      hangover effects 305.0
    caffeine 305.9
    hallucinogenic *(see also* Abuse,
      drugs, nondependent) 305.3
  alcohol (acute) 305.0
    with alcoholism 303.0
    hangover effects 305.0
    idiosyncratic 291.4
    pathological 291.4
  alimentary canal 558.2
  ammonia (hepatic) 572.2
  chemical - *see also* Table of Drugs and
    Chemicals
    via placenta or breast milk 760.70
      alcohol 760.71
      anti-infective agents 760.74
      cocaine 760.75
      "crack" 760.75
      hallucinogenic agents NEC 760.73
      medicinal agents NEC 760.79
      narcotics 760.72
      obstetric anesthetic or analgesic
        drug 763.5
      specified agent NEC 760.79
      suspected, affecting management
        of pregnancy 655.5
  cocaine, through placenta or breast
    milk 760.75
  delirium ◀
    alcohol 291.0 ◀
    drug 292.81 ◀
  drug
    correct substance properly adminis-
      tered *(see also* Allergy, drug)
      995.2
      with delirium 292.81 ◀

Intoxication *(Continued)*
  drug *(Continued)*
    newborn 779.4
    obstetric anesthetic or sedation 668.9
      affecting fetus or newborn 763.5
    overdose or wrong substance given
      or taken - *see* Table of Drugs
      and Chemicals
    pathologic 292.2
    specific to newborn 779.4
    via placenta or breast milk 760.70
      alcohol 760.71
      anti-infective agents 760.74
      cocaine 760.75
      "crack" 760.75
      hallucinogenic agents 760.73
      medicinal agents NEC 760.79
      narcotics 760.72
      obstetric anesthetic or analgesic
        drug 763.5
      specified agent NEC 760.79
      suspected, affecting management
        of pregnancy 655.5
  enteric - *see* Intoxication, intestinal
  fetus or newborn, via placenta or
    breast milk 760.70
    alcohol 760.71
    anti-infective agents 760.74
    cocaine 760.75
    "crack" 760.75
    hallucinogenic agents 760.73
    medicinal agents NEC 760.79
    narcotics 760.72
    obstetric anesthetic or analgesic drug
      763.5
    specified agent NEC 760.79
    suspected, affecting management of
      pregnancy 655.5
  food - *see* Poisoning, food
  gastrointestinal 558.2
  hallucinogenic (acute) 305.3
  hepatocerebral 572.2
  idiosyncratic alcohol 291.4
  intestinal 569.89
    due to putrefaction of food 005.9
  methyl alcohol *(see also* Alcoholism)
    305.0
    with alcoholism 303.0
  pathologic 291.4
    drug 292.2
  potassium (K) 276.7
  septic
    with
      abortion - *see* Abortion, by type,
        with sepsis
      ectopic pregnancy *(see also* catego-
        ries 633.0-633.9) 639.0
      molar pregnancy *(see also* catego-
        ries 630-632) 639.0
    during labor 659.3
    following
      abortion 639.0
      ectopic or molar pregnancy 639.0
    generalized - *see* Septicemia
    puerperal, postpartum, childbirth 670
  serum (prophylactic) (therapeutic) 999.5
  uremic - *see* Uremia
  water 276.6
Intracranial - *see* condition
Intrahepatic gallbladder 751.69
Intraligamentous - *see also* condition
  pregnancy - *see* Pregnancy, cornual
Intraocular - *see also* condition
  sepsis 360.00

ICD-9-CM

Vol. 2

Irritation
anus 569.49
axillary nerve 353.0
bladder 596.8
brachial plexus 353.0
brain (traumatic) (*see also* Injury, intracranial) 854.0
nontraumatic - *see* Encephalitis
bronchial (*see also* Bronchitis) 490
cerebral (traumatic) (*see also* Injury, intracranial) 854.0
nontraumatic - *see* Encephalitis
cervical plexus 353.2
cervix (*see also* Cervicitis) 616.0
choroid, sympathetic 360.11
cranial nerve - *see* Disorder, nerve, cranial
digestive tract 536.9
psychogenic 306.4
gastric 536.9
psychogenic 306.4
gastrointestinal (tract) 536.9
functional 536.9
psychogenic 306.4
globe, sympathetic 360.11
intestinal (bowel) 564.1
labyrinth 386.50
lumbosacral plexus 353.1
meninges (traumatic) (*see also* Injury, intracranial) 854.0
nontraumatic - *see* Meningitis
myocardium 306.2
nerve - *see* Disorder, nerve
nervous 799.2
nose 478.1
penis 607.89
perineum 709.9
peripheral
autonomic nervous system (*see also* Neuropathy, peripheral, autonomic) 337.9
nerve - *see* Disorder, nerve
peritoneum (*see also* Peritonitis) 567.9
pharynx 478.29
plantar nerve 355.6
spinal (cord) (traumatic) - *see also* Injury, spinal, by site
nerve - *see also* Disorder, nerve
root NEC 724.9
traumatic - *see* Injury, nerve, spinal
nontraumatic - *see* Myelitis
stomach 536.9
psychogenic 306.4
sympathetic nerve NEC (*see also* Neuropathy, peripheral, autonomic) 337.9
ulnar nerve 354.2
vagina 623.9
Isambert's disease 012.3
Ischemia, ischemic 459.9
basilar artery (with transient neurologic deficit) 435.0
bone NEC 733.40
bowel (transient) 557.9
acute 557.0
chronic 557.1
due to mesenteric artery insufficiency 557.1
brain - *see also* Ischemia, cerebral
recurrent focal 435.9
cardiac (*see also* Ischemia, heart) 414.9

Ischemia, ischemic (*Continued*)
cardiomyopathy 414.8
carotid artery (with transient neurologic deficit) 435.8
cerebral (chronic) (generalized) 437.1
arteriosclerotic 437.0
intermittent (with transient neurologic deficit) 435.9
puerperal, postpartum, childbirth 674.0
recurrent focal (with transient neurologic deficit) 435.9
transient (with transient neurologic deficit) 435.9
colon 557.9
acute 557.0
chronic 557.1
due to mesenteric artery insufficiency 557.1
coronary (chronic) (*see also* Ischemia, heart) 414.8
heart (chronic or with a stated duration of over 8 weeks) 414.9
acute or with a stated duration of 8 weeks or less (*see also* Infarct, myocardium) 410.9
without myocardial infarction 411.89
with coronary (artery) occlusion 411.81
subacute 411.89
intestine (transient) 557.9
acute 557.0
chronic 557.1
due to mesenteric artery insufficiency 557.1
kidney 593.81
labyrinth 386.50
muscles, leg 728.89
myocardium, myocardial (chronic or with a stated duration of over 8 weeks) 414.8
acute (*see also* Infarct, myocardium) 410.9
without myocardial infarction 411.89
with coronary (artery) occlusion 411.81
renal 593.81
retina, retinal 362.84
small bowel 557.9
acute 557.0
chronic 557.1
due to mesenteric artery insufficiency 557.1
spinal cord 336.1
subendocardial (*see also* Insufficiency, coronary) 411.89
vertebral artery (with transient neurologic deficit) 435.1
Ischialgia (*see also* Sciatica) 724.3
Ischiopagus 759.4
Ischium, ischial - *see* condition
Ischomenia 626.8
Ischuria 788.5
Iselin's disease or osteochondrosis 732.5
Islands of
parotid tissue in
lymph nodes 750.26
neck structures 750.26

Islands of (*Continued*)
submaxillary glands in
fascia 750.26
lymph nodes 750.26
neck muscles 750.26
Islet cell tumor, pancreas (M8150/0) 211.7
Isoimmunization NEC (*see also* Incompatibility) 656.2
fetus or newborn 773.2
ABO blood groups 773.1
rhesus (Rh) factor 773.0
Isolation V07.0
social V62.4
Isosporosis 007.2
Issue
medical certificate NEC V68.0
cause of death V68.0
fitness V68.0
incapacity V68.0
repeat prescription NEC V68.1
appliance V68.1
contraceptive V25.40
device NEC V25.49
intrauterine V25.42
specified type NEC V25.49
pill V25.41
glasses V68.1
medicinal substance V68.1
Itch (*see also* Pruritus) 698.9
bakers' 692.89
barbers' 110.0
bricklayers' 692.89
cheese 133.8
clam diggers' 120.3
coolie 126.9
copra 133.8
Cuban 050.1
dew 126.9
dhobie 110.3
eye 379.99
filarial (*see also* Infestation, filarial) 125.9
grain 133.8
grocers' 133.8
ground 126.9
harvest 133.8
jock 110.3
Malabar 110.9
beard 110.0
foot 110.4
scalp 110.0
meaning scabies 133.0
Norwegian 133.0
perianal 698.0
poultrymen's 133.8
sarcoptic 133.0
scrub 134.1
seven year V61.10
meaning scabies 133.0
straw 133.8
swimmers' 120.3
washerwoman's 692.4
water 120.3
winter 698.8
Itsenko-Cushing syndrome (pituitary basophilism) 255.0
Ivemark's syndrome (asplenia with congenital heart disease) 759.0
Ivory bones 756.52
Ixodes 134.8
Ixodiasis 134.8

J

Jaccoud's nodular fibrositis, chronic (Jaccoud's syndrome) 714.4
Jackson's
membrane 751.4
paralysis or syndrome 344.89
veil 751.4
Jacksonian
epilepsy (*see also* Epilepsy) 345.5
seizures (focal) (*see also* Epilepsy) 345.5
Jacob's ulcer (M8090/3) - *see* Neoplasm, skin, malignant, by site
Jacquet's dermatitis (diaper dermatitis) 691.0
Jadassohn's
blue nevus (M8780/0) - *see* Neoplasm, skin, benign
disease (maculopapular erythroderma) 696.2
intraepidermal epithelioma (M8096/0) - *see* Neoplasm, skin, benign
Jadassohn-Lewandowski syndrome (pachyonychia congenita) 757.5
Jadassohn-Pellizari's disease (anetoderma) 701.3
Jadassohn-Tièche nevus (M8780/0) - *see* Neoplasm, skin, benign
Jaffe-Lichtenstein (-Uehlinger) syndrome 252.0
Jahnke's syndrome (encephalocutaneous angiomatosis) 759.6
Jakob-Creutzfeldt disease or syndrome 046.1
with dementia 046.1 [294.1]
Jaksch (-Luzet) disease or syndrome (pseudoleukemia infantum) 285.8
Jamaican
neuropathy 349.82
paraplegic tropical ataxic-spastic syndrome 349.82
Janet's disease (psychasthenia) 300.89
Janiceps 759.4
Jansky-Bielschowsky amaurotic familial idiocy 330.1
Japanese
B-type encephalitis 062.0
river fever 081.2
seven-day fever 100.89
Jaundice (yellow) 782.4
acholuric (familial) (splenomegalic) (*see also* Spherocytosis) 282.0
acquired 283.9
breast milk 774.39
catarrhal (acute) 070.1
with hepatic coma 070.0
chronic 571.9
epidemic - *see* Jaundice, epidemic
cholestatic (benign) 782.4
chronic idiopathic 277.4
epidemic (catarrhal) 070.1
with hepatic coma 070.0
leptospiral 100.0
spirochetal 100.0
febrile (acute) 070.1
with hepatic coma 070.0
leptospiral 100.0
spirochetal 100.0

Jaundice (*Continued*)
fetus or newborn 774.6
due to or associated with
ABO
antibodies 773.1
incompatibility, maternal/fetal 773.1
isoimmunization 773.1
absence or deficiency of enzyme system for bilirubin conjugation (congenital) 774.39
blood group incompatibility NEC 773.2
breast milk inhibitors to conjugation 774.39
associated with preterm delivery 774.2
bruising 774.1
Crigler-Najjar syndrome 277.4 [774.31]
delayed conjugation 774.30
associated with preterm delivery 774.2
development 774.39
drugs or toxins transmitted from mother 774.1
G-6-PD deficiency 282.2 [774.0]
galactosemia 271.1 [774.5]
Gilbert's syndrome 277.4 [774.31]
hepatocellular damage 774.4
hereditary hemolytic anemia (*see also* Anemia, hemolytic) 282.9 [774.0]
hypothyroidism, congenital 243 [774.31]
incompatibility, maternal/fetal NEC 773.2
infection 774.1
inspissated bile syndrome 774.4
isoimmunization NEC 773.2
mucoviscidosis 277.01 [774.5]
obliteration of bile duct, congenital 751.61 [774.5]
polycythemia 774.1
preterm delivery 774.2
red cell defect 282.9 [774.0]
Rh
antibodies 773.0
incompatibility, maternal/fetal 773.0
isoimmunization 773.0
spherocytosis (congenital) 282.0 [774.0]
swallowed maternal blood 774.1
physiological NEC 774.6
from injection, inoculation, infusion, or transfusion (blood) (plasma) (serum) (other substance) (onset within 8 months after administration) - *see* Hepatitis, viral
Gilbert's (familial nonhemolytic) 277.4
hematogenous 283.9
hemolytic (acquired) 283.9
congenital (*see also* Spherocytosis) 282.0
hemorrhagic (acute) 100.0
leptospiral 100.0
newborn 776.0
spirochetal 100.0
hepatocellular 573.8

Jaundice (*Continued*)
homologous (serum) - *see* Hepatitis, viral
idiopathic, chronic 277.4
infectious (acute) (subacute) 070.1
with hepatic coma 070.0
leptospiral 100.0
spirochetal 100.0
leptospiral 100.0
malignant (*see also* Necrosis, liver) 570
newborn (physiological) (*see also* Jaundice, fetus or newborn) 774.6
nonhemolytic, congenital familial (Gilbert's) 277.4
nuclear, newborn (*see also* Kernicterus of newborn) 774.7
obstructive NEC (*see also* Obstruction, biliary) 576.8
postimmunization - *see* Hepatitis, viral
posttransfusion - *see* Hepatitis, viral
regurgitation (*see also* Obstruction, biliary) 576.8
serum (homologous) (prophylactic) (therapeutic) - *see* Hepatitis, viral
spirochetal (hemorrhagic) 100.0
symptomatic 782.4
newborn 774.6
Jaw - *see* condition
Jaw-blinking 374.43
congenital 742.8
Jaw-winking phenomenon or syndrome 742.8
Jealousy
alcoholic 291.5
childhood 313.3
sibling 313.3
Jejunitis (*see also* Enteritis) 558.9
Jejunostomy status V44.4
Jejunum, jejunal - *see* condition
Jensen's disease 363.05
Jericho boil 085.1
Jerks, myoclonic 333.2
Jeune's disease or syndrome (asphyxiating thoracic dystrophy) 756.4
Jigger disease 134.1
Job's syndrome (chronic granulomatous disease) 288.1
Jod-Basedow phenomenon 242.8
Johnson-Stevens disease (erythema multiforme exudativum) 695.1
Joint - *see also* condition
Charcôt's 094.0 [713.5]
false 733.82
flail - *see* Flail, joint
mice - *see* Loose, body, joint, by site
sinus to bone 730.9
von Gies' 095.8
Jordan's anomaly or syndrome 288.2
Josephs-Diamond-Blackfan anemia (congenital hypoplastic) 284.0
Jumpers' knee 727.2
Jungle yellow fever 060.0
Jungling's disease (sarcoidosis) 135
Junin virus hemorrhagic fever 078.7
Juvenile - *see also* condition
delinquent 312.9
group (*see also* Disturbance, conduct) 312.2
neurotic 312.4

ICD-9-CM

Vol. 2

K

Kahler (-Bozzolo) **disease** (multiple myeloma) (M9730/3) 203.0
Kakergasia 300.9
Kakke 265.0
Kala-azar (Indian) (infantile) (Mediterranean) (Sudanese) 085.0
Kalischer's syndrome (encephalocutaneous angiomatosis) 759.6
Kallmann's syndrome (hypogonadotropic hypogonadism with anosmia) 253.4
Kanner's syndrome (autism) (*see also* Psychosis, childhood) 299.0
Kaolinosis 502
Kaposi's
  disease 757.33
    lichen ruber 696.4
      acuminatus 696.4
      moniliformis 697.8
    xeroderma pigmentosum 757.33
  sarcoma (M9140/3) 176.9
    adipose tissue 176.1
    aponeurosis 176.1
    artery 176.1
    blood vessel 176.1
    bursa 176.1
    connective tissue 176.1
    external genitalia 176.8
    fascia 176.1
    fatty tissue 176.1
    fibrous tissue 176.1
    gastrointestinal tract NEC 176.3
    ligament 176.1
    lung 176.4
    lymph
      gland(s) 176.5
      node(s) 176.5
    lymphatic(s) NEC 176.1
    muscle (skeletal) 176.1
    oral cavity NEC 176.8
    palate 176.2
    scrotum 176.8
    skin 176.0
    soft tissue 176.1
    specified site NEC 176.8
    subcutaneous tissue 176.1
    synovia 176.1
    tendon (sheath) 176.1
    vein 176.1
    vessel 176.1
    viscera NEC 176.9
    vulva 176.8
  varicelliform eruption 054.0
  vaccinia 999.0
Kartagener's syndrome or triad (sinusitis, bronchiectasis, situs inversus) 759.3
Kasabach-Merritt syndrome (capillary hemangioma associated with thrombocytopenic purpura) 287.3
Kaschin-Beck disease (endemic polyarthritis) - *see* Disease, Kaschin-Beck
Kast's syndrome (dyschondroplasia with hemangiomas) 756.4
Katatonia- *see* **Catatonia**
Katayama disease or fever 120.2
Kathisophobia 781.0
Kawasaki disease 446.1
Kayser-Fleischer ring (cornea) (pseudosclerosis) 275.1 [371.14]
Kaznelson's syndrome (congenital hypoplastic anemia) 284.0

Kedani fever 081.2
Kelis 701.4
Kelly (-Paterson) **syndrome** (sideropenic dysphagia) 280.8
Keloid, cheloid 701.4
  Addison's (morphea) 701.0
  cornea 371.00
  Hawkins' 701.4
  scar 701.4
Keloma 701.4
Kenya fever 082.1
Keratectasia 371.71
  congenital 743.41
Keratitis (nodular) (nonulcerative) (simple) (zonular) NEC 370.9
  with ulceration (*see also* Ulcer, cornea) 370.00
  actinic 370.24
  arborescens 054.42
  areolar 370.22
  bullosa 370.8
  deep - *see* Keratitis, interstitial
  dendritic(a) 054.42
  desiccation 370.34
  diffuse interstitial 370.52
  disciform(is) 054.43
    varicella 052.7 [370.44]
  epithelialis vernalis 372.13 [370.32]
  exposure 370.34
  filamentary 370.23
  gonococcal (congenital) (prenatal) 098.43
  herpes, herpetic (simplex) NEC 054.43
    zoster 053.21
  hypopyon 370.04
  in
    chickenpox 052.7 [370.44]
    exanthema (*see also* Exanthem) 057.9 [370.44]
    paravaccinia (*see also* Paravaccinia) 051.9 [370.44]
    smallpox (*see also* Smallpox) 050.9 [370.44]
    vernal conjunctivitis 372.13 [370.32]
  interstitial (nonsyphilitic) 370.50
    with ulcer (*see also* Ulcer, cornea) 370.00
    diffuse 370.52
    herpes, herpetic (simplex) 054.43
      zoster 053.21
    syphilitic (congenital) (hereditary) 090.3
    tuberculous (*see also* Tuberculosis) 017.3 [370.59]
  lagophthalmic 370.34
  macular 370.22
  neuroparalytic 370.35
  neurotrophic 370.35
  nummular 370.22
  oyster-shuckers' 370.8
  parenchymatous - *see* Keratitis, interstitial
  petrificans 370.8
  phlyctenular 370.31
  postmeasles 055.71
  punctata, punctate 370.21
    leprosa 030.0 [370.21]
    profunda 090.3
    superficial (Thygeson's) 370.21
  purulent 370.8
  pustuliformis profunda 090.3
  rosacea 695.3 [370.49]
  sclerosing 370.54
  specified type NEC 370.8

Keratitis (*Continued*)
  stellate 370.22
  striate 370.22
  superficial 370.20
    with conjunctivitis (*see also* Keratoconjunctivitis) 370.40
    punctate (Thygeson's) 370.21
  suppurative 370.8
  syphilitic (congenital) (prenatal) 090.3
  trachomatous 076.1
    late effect 139.1
  tuberculous (phlyctenular) (*see also* Tuberculosis) 017.3 [370.31]
  ulcerated (*see also* Ulcer, cornea) 370.00
  vesicular 370.8
  welders' 370.24
  xerotic (*see also* Keratomalacia) 371.45
    vitamin A deficiency 264.4
Keratoacanthoma 238.2
Keratocele 371.72
Keratoconjunctivitis (*see also* Keratitis) 370.40
  adenovirus type 8 077.1
  epidemic 077.1
  exposure 370.34
  gonococcal 098.43
  herpetic (simplex) 054.43
    zoster 053.21
  in
    chickenpox 052.7 [370.44]
    exanthema (*see also* Exanthem) 057.9 [370.44]
    paravaccinia (*see also* Paravaccinia) 051.9 [370.44]
    smallpox (*see also* Smallpox) 050.9 [370.44]
  infectious 077.1
  neurotrophic 370.35
  phlyctenular 370.31
  postmeasles 055.71
  shipyard 077.1
  sicca (Sjögren's syndrome) 710.2
    not in Sjögren's syndrome 370.33
  specified type NEC 370.49
  tuberculous (phlyctenular) (*see also* Tuberculosis) 017.3 [370.31]
Keratoconus 371.60
  acute hydrops 371.62
  congenital 743.41
  stable 371.61
Keratocyst (dental) 526.0
Keratoderma, keratodermia (congenital) (palmaris et plantaris) (symmetrical) 757.39
  acquired 701.1
  blennorrhagica 701.1
    gonococcal 098.81
  climacterium 701.1
  eccentrica 757.39
  gonorrheal 098.81
  punctata 701.1
  tylodes, progressive 701.1
Keratodermatocele 371.72
Keratoglobus 371.70
  congenital 743.41
    associated with buphthalmos 743.22
Keratohemia 371.12
Keratoiritis (*see also* Iridocyclitis) 364.3
  syphilitic 090.3
  tuberculous (*see also* Tuberculosis) 017.3 [364.11]

Keratolysis exfoliativa (congenital) 757.39
  acquired 695.89
  neonatorum 757.39
Keratoma 701.1
  congenital 757.39
  malignum congenitale 757.1
  palmaris et plantaris hereditarium
    757.39
  senile 702.0
Keratomalacia 371.45
  vitamin A deficiency 264.4
Keratomegaly 743.41
Keratomycosis 111.1
  nigricans (palmaris) 111.1
Keratopathy 371.40
  band (*see also* Keratitis) 371.43
  bullous (*see also* Keratitis) 371.23
  degenerative (*see also* Degeneration,
    cornea) 371.40
    hereditary (*see also* Dystrophy, cor-
      nea) 371.50
  discrete colliquative 371.49
Keratoscleritis, tuberculous (*see also* Tu-
    berculosis) 017.3 *[370.31]*
Keratosis 701.1
  actinic 702.0
  arsenical 692.4
  blennorrhagica 701.1
    gonococcal 098.81
  congenital (any type) 757.39
  ear (middle) (*see also* Cholesteatoma)
    385.30
  female genital (external) 629.8
  follicular, vitamin A deficiency 264.8
  follicularis 757.39
    acquired 701.1
    congenital (acneiformis) (Siemens')
      757.39
    spinulosa (decalvans) 757.39
    vitamin A deficiency 264.8
  gonococcal 098.81
  larynx, laryngeal 478.79
  male genital (external) 608.89
  middle ear (*see also* Cholesteatoma)
    385.30
  nigricans 701.2
    congenital 757.39
  obturans 380.21
  palmaris et plantaris (symmetrical)
    757.39
  penile 607.89
  pharyngeus 478.29
  pilaris 757.39
    acquired 701.1
  punctata (palmaris et plantaris) 701.1
  scrotal 608.89
  seborrheic 702.19
    inflamed 702.11
  senilis 702.0
  solar 702.0
  suprafollicularis 757.39
  tonsillaris 478.29
  vagina 623.1
  vegetans 757.39
  vitamin A deficiency 264.8
Kerato-uveitis (*see also* Iridocyclitis) 364.3
Keraunoparalysis 994.0
Kerion (celsi) 110.0
Kernicterus of newborn (not due to iso-
    immunization) 774.7
  due to isoimmunization (conditions
    classifiable to 773.0-773.2) 773.4
Ketoacidosis 276.2
  diabetic 250.1

Ketonuria 791.6
  branched-chain, intermittent 270.3
Ketosis 276.2
  diabetic 250.1
Kidney - *see* condition
Kienböck's
  disease 732.3
    adult 732.8
  osteochondrosis 732.3
Kimmelstiel (-Wilson) disease or syn-
    drome (intercapillary glomeruloscle-
    rosis) 250.4 *[581.81]*
Kink, kinking
  appendix 543.9
  artery 447.1
  cystic duct, congenital 751.61
  hair (acquired) 704.2
  ileum or intestine (*see also* Obstruction,
    intestine) 560.9
  Lane's (*see also* Obstruction, intestine)
    560.9
  organ or site, congenital NEC - *see*
    Anomaly, specified type NEC, by
    site
  ureter (pelvic junction) 593.3
    congenital 753.20
  vein(s) 459.2
    caval 459.2
    peripheral 459.2
Kinnier Wilson's disease (hepatolenticu-
    lar degeneration) 275.1
Kissing
  osteophytes 721.5
  spine 721.5
  vertebra 721.5
Klauder's syndrome (erythema multi-
    forme exudativum) 695.1
Klebs' disease (*see also* Nephritis)
    583.9
Klein-Waardenburg syndrome (ptosis-
    epicanthus) 270.2
Kleine-Levin syndrome 349.89
Kleptomania 312.32
Klinefelter's syndrome 758.7
Klinger's disease 446.4
Klippel's disease 723.8
Klippel-Feil disease or syndrome (brevi-
    collis) 756.16
Klippel-Trenaunay syndrome 759.89
Klumpke (-Déjérine) palsy, paralysis
    (birth) (newborn) 767.6
Kluver-Bucy (-Terzian) syndrome 310.0
Knee - *see* condition
Knifegrinders' rot (*see also* Tuberculosis)
    011.4
Knock-knee (acquired) 736.41
  congenital 755.64
Knot
  intestinal, syndrome (volvulus) 560.2
  umbilical cord (true) 663.2
    affecting fetus or newborn 762.5
Knots, surfer 919.8
  infected 919.9
Knotting (of)
  hair 704.2
  intestine 560.2
Knuckle pads (Garrod's) 728.79
Köbner's disease (epidermolysis bullosa)
    757.39
Koch's
  infection (*see also* Tuberculosis, pulmo-
    nary) 011.9
  relapsing fever 087.9
Koch-Weeks conjunctivitis 372.03

Koenig-Wichman disease (pemphigus)
    694.4
Köhler's disease (osteochondrosis) 732.5
  first (osteochondrosis juvenilis) 732.5
  second (Freiburg's infarction, metatar-
    sal head) 732.5
  patellar 732.4
  tarsal navicular (bone) (osteoarthosis
    juvenilis) 732.5
Köhler-Mouchet disease (osteoarthrosis
    juvenilis) 732.5
**Köhler-Pellegrini-Stieda disease or syn-
    drome** (calcification, knee joint)
    726.62
Koilonychia 703.8
  congenital 757.5
Kojevnikov's, Kojewnikoff's epilepsy
    (*see also* Epilepsy) 345.7
König's
  disease (osteochondritis dissecans)
    732.7
  syndrome 564.89
Koniophthisis (*see also* Tuberculosis)
    011.4
Koplik's spots 055.9
Kopp's asthma 254.8
Korean hemorrhagic fever 078.6
Korsakoff (-Wernicke) disease, psycho-
    sis, or syndrome (nonalcoholic)
    294.0
  alcoholic 291.1
Korsakov's disease - *see* Korsakoff's dis-
    ease
Korsakow's disease - *see* Korsakoff's dis-
    ease
Kostmann's disease or syndrome (infan-
    tile genetic agranulocytosis) 288.0
Krabbe's
  disease (leukodystrophy) 330.0
  syndrome
    congenital muscle hypoplasia 756.89
    cutaneocerebral angioma 759.6
Kraepelin-Morel disease (*see also* Schizo-
    phrenia) 295.9
Kraft-Weber-Dimitri disease 759.6
Kraurosis
  ani 569.49
  penis 607.0
  vagina 623.8
  vulva 624.0
Kreotoxism 005.9
Krukenberg's
  spindle 371.13
  tumor (M8490/6) 198.6
Kufs' disease 330.1
Kugelberg-Welander disease 335.11
Kuhnt-Junius degeneration or disease
    362.52
Kulchitsky's cell carcinoma (carcinoid
    tumor of intestine) 259.2
Kummell's disease or spondylitis 721.7
Kundrat's disease (lymphosarcoma)
    200.1
Kunekune - *see* Dermatophytosis
Kunkel syndrome (lupoid hepatitis)
    571.49
Kupffer cell sarcoma (M9124/3) 155.0
Kuru 046.0
Kussmaul's
  coma (diabetic) 250.3
  disease (polyarteritis nodosa) 446.0
  respiration (air hunger) 786.09
Kwashiorkor (marasmus type) 260
Kyasanur Forest disease 065.2

Kyphoscoliosis, kyphoscoliotic (acquired) (*see also* Scoliosis) 737.30
  congenital 756.19
  due to radiation 737.33
  heart (disease) 416.1
  idiopathic 737.30
    infantile
      progressive 737.32
      resolving 737.31
  late effect of rickets 268.1 [737.43]
  specified NEC 737.39
  thoracogenic 737.34
  tuberculous (*see also* Tuberculosis)
    015.0 [737.43]
Kyphosis, kyphotic (acquired) (postural)
  737.10
  adolescent postural 737.0

Kyphosis, kyphotic (*Continued*)
  congenital 756.19
  dorsalis juvenilis 732.0
  due to or associated with
    Charcôt-Marie-Tooth disease 356.1
      [737.41]
    mucopolysaccharidosis 277.5
      [737.41]
    neurofibromatosis 237.71 [737.41]
    osteitis
      deformans 731.0 [737.41]
      fibrosa cystica 252.0 [737.41]
    osteoporosis (*see also* Osteoporosis)
      733.0 [737.41]
    poliomyelitis (*see also* Poliomyelitis)
      138 [737.41]
    radiation 737.11

Kyphosis, kyphotic (*Continued*)
  due to or associated with (*Continued*)
    tuberculosis (*see also* Tuberculosis)
      015.0 [737.41]
  Kümmell's 721.7
  late effect of rickets 268.1 [737.41]
  Morquio-Brailsford type (spinal) 277.5
    [737.41]
  pelvis 738.6
  postlaminectomy 737.12
  specified cause NEC 737.19
  syphilitic, congenital 090.5 [737.41]
  tuberculous (*see also* Tuberculosis)
    015.0 [737.41]
Kyrle's disease (hyperkeratosis follicularis in cutem penetrans) 701.1

L

Labia, labium - *see* condition
Labiated hymen 752.49
Labile
   blood pressure 796.2
   emotions, emotionality 301.3
   vasomotor system 443.9
Labioglossal paralysis 335.22
Labium leporinum (*see also* Cleft, lip)
   749.10
Labor (*see also* Delivery)
   with complications - *see* Delivery, complicated
   abnormal NEC 661.9
      affecting fetus or newborn 763.7
   arrested active phase 661.1
      affecting fetus or newborn 763.7
   desultory 661.2
      affecting fetus or newborn 763.7
   dyscoordinate 661.4
      affecting fetus or newborn 763.7
   early onset (22-36 weeks gestation)
      644.2
   failed
      induction 659.1
         mechanical 659.0
         medical 659.1
         surgical 659.0
      trial (vaginal delivery) 660.6
   false 644.1
   forced or induced, affecting fetus or
      newborn 763.89
   hypertonic 661.4
      affecting fetus or newborn 763.7
   hypotonic 661.2
      affecting fetus or newborn 763.7
      primary 661.0
         affecting fetus or newborn 763.7
      secondary 661.1
         affecting fetus or newborn 763.7
   incoordinate 661.4
      affecting fetus or newborn 763.7
   irregular 661.2
      affecting fetus or newborn 763.7
   long - *see* Labor, prolonged
   missed (at or near term) 656.4
   obstructed NEC 660.9
      affecting fetus or newborn 763.1
      specified cause NEC 660.8
         affecting fetus or newborn 763.1
   pains, spurious 644.1
   precipitate 661.3
      affecting fetus or newborn 763.6
   premature 644.2
      threatened 644.0
   prolonged or protracted 662.1
      affecting fetus or newborn
         763.89
      first stage 662.0
         affecting fetus or newborn
            763.89
      second stage 662.2
         affecting fetus or newborn
            763.89
   threatened NEC 644.1
   undelivered 644.1
Labored breathing (*see also* Hyperventilation) 786.09
Labyrinthitis (inner ear) (destructive) (latent) 386.30
   circumscribed 386.32
   diffuse 386.31
   focal 386.32

Labyrinthitis (*Continued*)
   purulent 386.33
   serous 386.31
   suppurative 386.33
   syphilitic 095.8
   toxic 386.34
   viral 386.35
Laceration - *see also* Wound, open, by site
   accidental, complicating surgery 998.2
   Achilles tendon 845.09
      with open wound 892.2
   anus (sphincter) 863.89
      with
         abortion - *see* Abortion, by type,
            with damage to pelvic organs
         ectopic pregnancy (*see also* categories 633.0-633.9) 639.2
         molar pregnancy (*see also* categories 630-632) 639.2
      complicating delivery 664.2
         with laceration of anal or rectal
            mucosa 664.3
      following
         abortion 639.2
         ectopic or molar pregnancy 639.2
      nontraumatic, nonpuerperal 565.0
   bladder (urinary)
      with
         abortion - *see* Abortion, by type,
            with damage to pelvic organs
         ectopic pregnancy (*see also* categories 633.0-633.9) 639.2
         molar pregnancy (*see also* categories 630-632) 639.2
      following
         abortion 639.2
         ectopic or molar pregnancy 639.2
      obstetrical trauma 665.5
   blood vessel - *see* Injury, blood vessel,
      by site
   bowel
      with
         abortion - *see* Abortion, by type,
            with damage to pelvic organs
         ectopic pregnancy (*see also* categories 633.0-633.9) 639.2
         molar pregnancy (*see also* categories 630-632) 639.2
      following
         abortion 639.2
         ectopic or molar pregnancy 639.2
      obstetrical trauma 665.5
   brain (cerebral) (membrane) (with
      hemorrhage) 851.8

Note   Use the following fifth-digit subclassification with categories 851-854:

0	unspecified state of consciousness
1	with no loss of consciousness
2	with brief [less than one hour] loss of consciousness
3	with moderate [1-24 hours] loss of consciousness
4	with prolonged [more than 24 hours] loss of consciousness and return to pre-existing conscious level
5	with prolonged [more than 24 hours] loss of consciousness, without return to pre-existing conscious level

---

Laceration (*Continued*)
   brain (*Continued*)
   Use fifth-digit 5 to designate when a patient is unconscious and dies before regaining consciousness, regardless of the duration of the loss of consciousness

6	with loss of consciousness of unspecified duration
9	with concussion, unspecified

      with
         open intracranial wound 851.9
         skull fracture - *see* Fracture, skull,
            by site
      cerebellum 851.6
         with open intracranial wound 851.7
      cortex 851.2
         with open intracranial wound 851.3
      during birth 767.0
      stem 851.6
         with open intracranial wound
            851.7
   broad ligament
      with
         abortion - *see* Abortion, by type,
            with damage to pelvic organs
         ectopic pregnancy (*see also* categories 633.0-633.9) 639.2
         molar pregnancy (*see also* categories 630-632) 639.2
      following
         abortion 639.2
         ectopic or molar pregnancy 639.2
      nontraumatic 620.6
      obstetrical trauma 665.6
      syndrome (nontraumatic) 620.6
   capsule, joint - *see* Sprain, by site
   cardiac - *see* Laceration, heart
   causing eversion of cervix uteri (old)
      622.0
   central, complicating delivery 664.4
   cerebellum - *see* Laceration, brain, cerebellum
   cerebral - *see also* Laceration, brain
      during birth 767.0
   cervix (uteri)
      with
         abortion - *see* Abortion, by type,
            with damage to pelvic organs
         ectopic pregnancy (*see also* categories 633.0-633.9) 639.2
         molar pregnancy (*see also* categories 630-632) 639.2
      following
         abortion 639.2
         ectopic or molar pregnancy 639.2
      nonpuerperal, nontraumatic 622.3
      obstetrical trauma (current) 665.3
      old (postpartal) 622.3
      traumatic - *see* Injury, internal, cervix
   chordae heart 429.5
   complicated 879.9
   cornea - *see* Laceration, eyeball
      superficial 918.1
   cortex (cerebral) - *see* Laceration, brain, cortex
   esophagus 530.89
   eye(s) - *see* Laceration, ocular
   eyeball NEC 871.4
      with prolapse or exposure of intraocular tissue 871.1
      penetrating - *see* Penetrating wound, eyeball

Laceration (*Continued*)
  eyeball NEC (*Continued*)
    specified as without prolapse of intraocular tissue 871.0
  eyelid NEC 870.8
    full thickness 870.1
      involving lacrimal passages 870.2
    skin (and periocular area) 870.0
      penetrating - *see* Penetrating wound, orbit
  fourchette
    with
      abortion - *see* Abortion, by type, with damage to pelvic organs
      ectopic pregnancy (*see also* categories 633.0-633.9) 639.2
      molar pregnancy (*see also* categories 630-632) 639.2
    complicating delivery 664.0
    following
      abortion 639.2
      ectopic or molar pregnancy 639.2
  heart (without penetration of heart chambers) 861.02
    with
      open wound into thorax 861.12
      penetration of heart chambers 861.03
        with open wound into thorax 861.13
  hernial sac - *see* Hernia, by site
  internal organ (abdomen) (chest) (pelvis) NEC - *see* Injury, internal, by site
  kidney (parenchyma) 866.02
    with
      complete disruption of parenchyma (rupture) 866.03
        with open wound into cavity 866.13
      open wound into cavity 866.12
  labia
    complicating delivery 664.0
  ligament - *see also* Sprain, by site
    with open wound - *see* Wound, open, by site
  liver 864.05
    with open wound into cavity 864.15
    major (disruption of hepatic parenchyma) 864.04
      with open wound into cavity 864.14
    minor (capsule only) 864.02
      with open wound into cavity 864.12
    moderate (involving parenchyma without major disruption) 864.03
      with open wound into cavity 864.13
    multiple 864.04
      with open wound into cavity 864.14
    stellate 864.04
      with open wound into cavity 864.14
  lung 861.22
    with open wound into thorax 861.32
  meninges - *see* Laceration, brain
  meniscus (knee) (*see also* Tear, meniscus) 836.2
    old 717.5
    site other than knee - *see also* Sprain, by site
      old NEC (*see also* Disorder, cartilage, articular) 718.0

Laceration (*Continued*)
  muscle - *see also* Sprain, by site
    with open wound - *see* Wound, open, by site
  myocardium - *see* Laceration, heart
  nerve - *see* Injury, nerve, by site
  ocular NEC (*see also* Laceration, eyeball) 871.4
    adnexa NEC 870.8
      penetrating 870.3
        with foreign body 870.4
  orbit (eye) 870.8
    penetrating 870.3
      with foreign body 870.4
  pelvic
    floor (muscles)
      with
        abortion - *see* Abortion, by type, with damage to pelvic organs
        ectopic pregnancy (*see also* categories 633.0-633.9) 639.2
        molar pregnancy (*see also* categories 630-632) 639.2
      complicating delivery 664.1
      following
        abortion 639.2
        ectopic or molar pregnancy 639.2
      nonpuerperal 618.7
      old (postpartal) 618.7
    organ NEC
      with
        abortion - *see* Abortion, by type, with damage to pelvic organs
        ectopic pregnancy (*see also* categories 633.0-633.9) 639.2
        molar pregnancy (*see also* categories 630-632) 639.2
      complicating delivery 665.5
        affecting fetus or newborn 763.89   ⬅
      following
        abortion 639.2
        ectopic or molar pregnancy 639.2
      obstetrical trauma 665.5
  perineum, perineal (old) (postpartal) 618.7
    with
      abortion - *see* Abortion, by type, with damage to pelvic floor
      ectopic pregnancy (*see also* categories 633.0-633.9) 639.2
      molar pregnancy (*see also* categories 630-632) 639.2
    complicating delivery 664.4
      first degree 664.0
      second degree 664.1
      third degree 664.2
      fourth degree 664.3
      central 664.4
      involving
        anal sphincter 664.2
        fourchette 664.0
        hymen 664.0
        labia 664.0
        pelvic floor 664.1
        perineal muscles 664.1
        rectovaginal with septum 664.2
          with anal mucosa 664.3
        skin 664.0
        sphincter (anal) 664.2
          with anal mucosa 664.3
        vagina 664.0

Laceration (*Continued*)
  perineum, perineal (*Continued*)
    complicating delivery (*Continued*)
      involving (*Continued*)
        vaginal muscles 664.1
        vulva 664.0
      secondary 674.2
    following
      abortion 639.2
      ectopic or molar pregnancy 639.2
    male 879.6
      complicated 879.7
    muscles, complicating delivery 664.1
    nonpuerperal, current injury 879.6
      complicated 879.7
    secondary (postpartal) 674.2
  peritoneum
    with
      abortion - *see* Abortion, by type, with damage to pelvic organs
      ectopic pregnancy (*see also* categories 633.0-633.9) 639.2
      molar pregnancy (*see also* categories 630-632) 639.2
    following
      abortion 639.2
      ectopic or molar pregnancy 639.2
    obstetrical trauma 665.5
  periurethral tissue
    with
      abortion - *see* Abortion, by type, with damage to pelvic organs
      ectopic pregnancy (*see also* categories 633.0-633.9) 639.2
      molar pregnancy (*see also* categories 630-632) 639.2
    following
      abortion 639.2
      ectopic or molar pregnancy 639.2
    obstetrical trauma 665.5
  rectovaginal (septum)
    with
      abortion - *see* Abortion, by type, with damage to pelvic organs
      ectopic pregnancy (*see also* categories 633.0-633.9) 639.2
      molar pregnancy (*see also* categories 630-632) 639.2
    complicating delivery 665.4
      with perineum 664.2
        involving anal or rectal mucosa 664.3
    following
      abortion 639.2
      ectopic or molar pregnancy 639.2
    nonpuerperal 623.4
    old (postpartal) 623.4
  spinal cord (meninges) - *see also* Injury, spinal, by site
    due to injury at birth 767.4
    fetus or newborn 767.4
  spleen 865.09
    with
      disruption of parenchyma (massive) 865.04
        with open wound into cavity 865.14
      open wound into cavity 865.19
    capsule (without disruption of parenchyma) 865.02
      with open wound into cavity 865.12
    parenchyma 865.03

Laceration (*Continued*)
  spleen (*Continued*)
    parenchyma (*Continued*)
      with open wound into cavity 865.13
      massive disruption (rupture) 865.04
        with open wound into cavity 865.14
  tendon 848.9
    with open wound - *see* Wound, open, by site
    Achilles 845.09
      with open wound 892.2
    lower limb NEC 844.9
      with open wound NEC 894.2
    upper limb NEC 840.9
      with open wound NEC 884.2
  tentorium cerebelli - *see* Laceration, brain, cerebellum
  tongue 873.64 ◄
    complicated 873.74 ◄
  urethra
    with
      abortion - *see* Abortion, by type, with damage to pelvic organs
      ectopic pregnancy (*see also* categories 633.0-633.9) 639.2
      molar pregnancy (*see also* categories 630-632) 639.2
    following
      abortion 639.2
      ectopic or molar pregnancy 639.2
    nonpuerperal, nontraumatic 599.84
    obstetrical trauma 665.5
  uterus
    with
      abortion - *see* Abortion, by type, with damage to pelvic organs
      ectopic pregnancy (*see also* categories 633.0-633.9) 639.2
      molar pregnancy (*see also* categories 630-632) 639.2
    following
      abortion 639.2
      ectopic or molar pregnancy 639.2
    nonpuerperal, nontraumatic 621.8
    obstetrical trauma NEC 665.1
    old (postpartal) 621.8
  vagina
    with
      abortion - *see* Abortion, by type, with damage to pelvic organs
      ectopic pregnancy (*see also* categories 633.0-633.9) 639.2
      molar pregnancy (*see also* categories 630-632) 639.2
      perineal involvement, complicating delivery 664.0
    complicating delivery 665.4
      first degree 664.0
      second degree 664.1
      third degree 664.2
      fourth degree 664.3
      high 665.4
      muscles 664.1
      sulcus 665.4
      wall 665.4
    following
      abortion 639.2
      ectopic or molar pregnancy 639.2
    nonpuerperal, nontraumatic 623.4
    old (postpartal) 623.4
  valve, heart - *see* Endocarditis

Laceration (*Continued*)
  vulva
    with
      abortion - *see* Abortion, by type, with damage to pelvic organs
      ectopic pregnancy (*see also* categories 633.0-633.9) 639.2
      molar pregnancy (*see also* categories 630-632) 639.2
    complicating delivery 664.0
    following
      abortion 639.2
      ectopic or molar pregnancy 639.2
    nonpuerperal, nontraumatic 624.4
    old (postpartal) 624.4
Lachrymal - *see* condition
Lachrymonasal duct - *see* condition
Lack of
  appetite (*see also* Anorexia) 783.0
  care
    in home V60.4
    of adult 995.84
    of infant (at or after birth) 995.52
  coordination 781.3
  development - *see also* Hypoplasia
    physiological 783.4
  education V62.3
  energy 780.79 ⬅
  financial resources V60.2
  food 994.2
    in environment V60.8
  growth 783.4
  heating V60.1
  housing (permanent) (temporary) V60.0
    adequate V60.1
  material resources V60.2
  medical attention 799.8
  memory (*see also* Amnesia) 780.9
    mild, following organic brain damage 310.1
  ovulation 628.0
  person able to render necessary care V60.4
  physical exercise V69.0
  physiologic development 783.4
  prenatal care in current pregnancy V23.7
  shelter V60.0
  water 994.3
Lacrimal - *see* condition
Lacrimation, abnormal (*see also* Epiphora) 375.20
Lacrimonasal duct - *see* condition
Lactation, lactating (breast) (puerperal) (postpartum)
  defective 676.4
  disorder 676.9
    specified type NEC 676.8
  excessive 676.6
  failed 676.4
  mastitis NEC 675.2
  mother (care and/or examination) V24.1
  nonpuerperal 611.6
  suppressed 676.5
Lacticemia 271.3
  excessive 276.2
Lactosuria 271.3
Lacunar skull 756.0
Laennec's cirrhosis (alcoholic) 571.2
  nonalcoholic 571.5
Lafora's disease 333.2
Lag, lid (nervous) 374.41

Lagleyze-von Hippel disease (retinocerebral angiomatosis) 759.6
Lagophthalmos (eyelid) (nervous) 374.20
  cicatricial 374.23
  keratitis (*see also* Keratitis) 370.34
  mechanical 374.22
  paralytic 374.21
La grippe - *see* Influenza
Lahore sore 085.1
Lakes, venous (cerebral) 437.8
Laki-Lorand factor deficiency (*see also* Defect, coagulation) 286.3
Lalling 307.9
Lambliasis 007.1
Lame back 724.5
Lancereaux's (diabetes, diabetes mellitus with marked emaciation) 250.8 [261]
Landouzy-Déjérine dystrophy (fascioscapulohumeral atrophy) 359.1
Landry's disease or paralysis 357.0
Landry-Guillain-Barré syndrome 357.0
Lane's
  band 751.4
  disease 569.89
  kink (*see also* Obstruction, intestine) 560.9
Langdon Down's syndrome (mongolism) 758.0
Language abolition 784.69
Lanugo (persistent) 757.4
Laparoscopic surgical procedure converted to open procedure V64.4
Lardaceous
  degeneration (any site) 277.3
  disease 277.3
  kidney 277.3 [583.81]
  liver 277.3
Large
  baby (regardless of gestational age) 766.1
    exceptionally (weight of 4500 grams or more) 766.0
    of diabetic mother 775.0
  ear 744.22
  fetus - *see also* Oversize, fetus
    causing disproportion 653.5
      with obstructed labor 660.1
  for dates
    fetus or newborn (regardless of gestational age) 766.1
      affecting management of pregnancy 656.6
      exceptionally (weight of 4500 grams or more) 766.0
  physiological cup 743.57
  waxy liver 277.3
  white kidney - *see* Nephrosis
Larsen's syndrome (flattened facies and multiple congenital dislocations) 755.8
Larsen-Johansson disease (juvenile osteopathia patellae) 732.4
Larva migrans
  cutaneous NEC 126.9
    ancylostoma 126.9
  of Diptera in vitreous 128.0
  visceral NEC 128.0
Laryngeal - *see also* condition
  syncope 786.2
Laryngismus (acute) (infectious) (stridulous) 478.75
  congenital 748.3
  diphtheritic 032.3

Laryngitis (acute) (edematous) (fibrinous) (gangrenous) (infective) (infiltrative) (malignant) (membranous) (phlegmonous) (pneumococcal) (pseudomembranous) (septic) (subglottic) (suppurative) (ulcerative) (viral) 464.0
  with
    influenza, flu, or grippe 487.1
    tracheitis (*see also* Laryngotracheitis) 464.20
      with obstruction 464.21
      acute 464.20
        with obstruction 464.21
      chronic 476.1
  atrophic 476.0
  Borrelia vincentii 101
  catarrhal 476.0
  chronic 476.0
    with tracheitis (chronic) 476.1
    due to external agent - *see* Condition, respiratory, chronic, due to
  diphtheritic (membranous) 032.3
  due to external agent - *see* Inflammation, respiratory, upper, due to
  H. influenzae 464.0
  Hemophilus influenzae 464.0
  hypertrophic 476.0
  influenzal 487.1
  pachydermic 478.79
  sicca 476.0
  spasmodic 478.75
    acute 464.0
  streptococcal 034.0
  stridulous 478.75
  syphilitic 095.8
    congenital 090.5
  tuberculous (*see also* Tuberculosis, larynx) 012.3
  Vincent's 101
Laryngocele (congenital) (ventricular) 748.3
Laryngofissure 478.79
  congenital 748.3
Laryngomalacia (congenital) 748.3
Laryngopharyngitis (acute) 465.0
  chronic 478.9
    due to external agent - *see* Condition, respiratory, chronic, due to
  due to external agent - *see* Inflammation, respiratory, upper, due to
  septic 034.0
Laryngoplegia (*see also* Paralysis, vocal cord) 478.30
Laryngoptosis 478.79
Laryngospasm 478.75
  due to external agent - *see* Condition, respiratory, acute, due to
Laryngostenosis 478.74
  congenital 748.3
Laryngotracheitis (acute) (infectional) (viral) (*see also* Laryngitis) 464.20
  with obstruction 464.21
  atrophic 476.1
  Borrelia vincentii 101
  catarrhal 476.1
  chronic 476.1
    due to external agent - *see* Condition, respiratory, chronic, due to
  diphtheritic (membranous) 032.3
  due to external agent - *see* Inflammation, respiratory, upper, due to
  H. influenzae 464.20
    with obstruction 464.21

Laryngotracheitis (*Continued*)
  hypertrophic 476.1
  influenzal 487.1
  pachydermic 478.75
  sicca 476.1
  spasmodic 478.75
    acute 464.20
      with obstruction 464.21
  streptococcal 034.0
  stridulous 478.75
  syphilitic 095.8
    congenital 090.5
  tuberculous (*see also* Tuberculosis, larynx) 012.3
  Vincent's 101
Laryngotracheobronchitis (*see also* Bronchitis) 490
  acute 466.0
  chronic 491.8
  viral 466.0
Laryngotracheobronchopneumonitis - *see* Pneumonia, broncho-
Larynx, laryngeal - *see* condition
Lasègue's disease (persecution mania) 297.9
Lassa fever 078.89
Lassitude (*see also* Weakness) 780.79
Late - *see also* condition
  effect(s) (of) - *see also* condition
    abscess
      intracranial or intraspinal (conditions classifiable to 324) - *see* category 326
    adverse effect of drug, medicinal or biological substance 909.5
    allergic reaction 909.9
    amputation
      postoperative (late) 997.60
      traumatic (injury classifiable to 885-887 and 895-897) 905.9
    burn (injury classifiable to 948-949) 906.9
      extremities NEC (injury classifiable to 943 or 945) 906.7
      hand or wrist (injury classifiable to 944) 906.6
      eye (injury classifiable to 940) 906.5
      face, head, and neck (injury classifiable to 941) 906.5
      specified site NEC (injury classifiable to 942 and 946-947) 906.8
    cerebrovascular disease (conditions classifiable to 430-437) 438.9
      with
        aphasia 438.11
        apraxia 438.81
        cognitive deficits 438.0
        dysphagia 438.82
        dysphasia 438.12
        hemiplegia/hemiparesis
          affecting
            dominant side 438.21
            nondominant side 438.22
            unspecified side 438.20
        monoplegia of lower limb
          affecting
            dominant side 438.41
            nondominant side 438.42
            unspecified side 438.40
        monoplegia of upper limb
          affecting
            dominant side 438.31
            nondominant side 438.32
            unspecified side 438.30

Late (*Continued*)
  effect(s) (*Continued*)
    cerebrovascular disease (*Continued*)
      with (*Continued*)
        paralytic syndrome NEC affecting
          bilateral 438.53
          dominant side 438.51
          nondominant side 438.52
          unspecified side 438.50
        speech and language deficit 438.10
        specified type NEC 438.19
      specified type NEC 438.89
    childbirth complication(s) 677
    complication(s) of
      childbirth 677
      delivery 677
      pregnancy 677
      puerperium 677
      surgical and medical care (conditions classifiable to 996-999) 909.3
      trauma (conditions classifiable to 958) 908.6
    contusion (injury classifiable to 920-924) 906.3
    crushing (injury classifiable to 925-929) 906.4
    delivery complication(s) 677
    dislocation (injury classifiable to 830-839) 905.6
    encephalitis or encephalomyelitis (conditions classifiable to 323) - *see* category 326
    in infectious diseases 139.8
      viral (conditions classifiable to 049.8, 049.9, 062-064) 139.0
    external cause NEC (conditions classifiable to 995) 909.9
    certain conditions classifiable to categories 991-994 909.4
    foreign body in orifice (injury classifiable to 930-939) 908.5
    fracture (multiple) (injury classifiable to 828-829) 905.5
      extremity
        lower (injury classifiable to 821-827) 905.4
          neck of femur (injury classifiable to 820) 905.3
        upper (injury classifiable to 810-819) 905.2
      face and skull (injury classifiable to 800-804) 905.0
      skull and face (injury classifiable to 800-804) 905.0
      spine and trunk (injury classifiable to 805 and 807-809) 905.1
        with spinal cord lesion (injury classifiable to 806) 907.2
    infection
      pyogenic, intracranial - *see* category 326
    infectious diseases (conditions classifiable to 001-136) NEC 139.8
    injury (injury classifiable to 959) 908.9
      blood vessel 908.3
        abdomen and pelvis (injury classifiable to 902) 908.4
        extremity (injury classifiable to 903-904) 908.3
        head and neck (injury classifiable to 900) 908.3

Leiomyomatosis (intravascular) (M8890/1) - *see* Neoplasm, connective tissue, uncertain behavior
Leiomyosarcoma (M8890/3) - *see also* Neoplasm, connective tissue, malignant
  epithelioid (M8891/3) - *see* Neoplasm, connective tissue, malignant
Leishmaniasis 085.9
  American 085.5
    cutaneous 085.4
    mucocutaneous 085.5
  Asian desert 085.2
  Brazilian 085.5
  cutaneous 085.9
    acute necrotizing 085.2
    American 085.4
    Asian desert 085.2
    diffuse 085.3
    dry form 085.1
    Ethiopian 085.3
    eyelid 085.5 [373.6]
    late 085.1
    lepromatous 085.3
    recurrent 085.1
    rural 085.2
    ulcerating 085.1
    urban 085.1
    wet form 085.2
    zoonotic form 085.2
  dermal - *see also* Leishmaniasis, cutaneous
    post kala-azar 085.0
  eyelid 085.5 [373.6]
  infantile 085.0
  Mediterranean 085.0
  mucocutaneous (American) 085.5
  naso-oral 085.5
  nasopharyngeal 085.5
  Old World 085.1
  tegumentaria diffusa 085.4
  vaccination, prophylactic (against) V05.2
  visceral (Indian) 085.0
Leishmanoid, dermal - *see also* Leishmaniasis, cutaneous
  post kala-azar 085.0
Leloir's disease 695.4
Lenegre's disease 426.0
Lengthening, leg 736.81
Lennox's syndrome (*see also* Epilepsy) 345.0
Lens - *see* condition
Lenticonus (anterior) (posterior) (congenital) 743.36
Lenticular degeneration, progressive 275.1
Lentiglobus (posterior) (congenital) 743.36
Lentigo (congenital) 709.09
  juvenile 709.09
  maligna (M8742/2) - *see also* Neoplasm, skin, in situ
    melanoma (M8742/3) - *see* Melanoma
  senile 709.09
Leonine leprosy 030.0
Leontiasis
  ossium 733.3
  syphilitic 095.8
    congenital 090.5
Léopold-Lévi's syndrome (paroxysmal thyroid instability) 242.9
Lepore hemoglobin syndrome 282.4

Lepothrix 039.0
Lepra 030.9
  Willan's 696.1
Leprechaunism 259.8
Lepromatous leprosy 030.0
Leprosy 030.9
  anesthetic 030.1
  beriberi 030.1
  borderline (group B) (infiltrated) (neuritic) 030.3
  cornea (*see also* Leprosy, by type) 030.9 [371.89]
  dimorphous (group B) (infiltrated) (lepromatous) (neuritic) (tuberculoid) 030.3
  eyelid 030.0 [373.4]
  indeterminate (group I) (macular) (neuritic) (uncharacteristic) 030.2
  leonine 030.0
  lepromatous (diffuse) (infiltrated) (macular) (neuritic) (nodular) (type L) 030.0
  macular (early) (neuritic) (simple) 030.2
  maculoanesthetic 030.1
  mixed 030.0
  neuro 030.1
  nodular 030.0
  primary neuritic 030.3
  specified type or group NEC 030.8
  tubercular 030.1
  tuberculoid (macular) (maculoanesthetic) (major) (minor) (neuritic) (type T) 030.1
Leptocytosis, hereditary 282.4
Leptomeningitis (chronic) (circumscribed) (hemorrhagic) (nonsuppurative) (*see also* Meningitis) 322.9
  aseptic 047.9
    adenovirus 049.1
    Coxsackie virus 047.0
    ECHO virus 047.1
    enterovirus 047.9
    lymphocytic choriomeningitis 049.0
  epidemic 036.0
  late effect - *see* category 326
  meningococcal 036.0
  pneumococcal 320.1
  syphilitic 094.2
  tuberculous (*see also* Tuberculosis, meninges) 013.0
Leptomeningopathy (*see also* Meningitis) 322.9
Leptospiral - *see* condition
Leptospirochetal - *see* condition
Leptospirosis 100.9
  autumnalis 100.89
  canicula 100.89
  grippotyphosa 100.89
  hebdomadis 100.89
  icterohemorrhagica 100.0
  nanukayami 100.89
  pomona 100.89
  Weil's disease 100.0
Leptothricosis - *see* Actinomycosis
Leptothrix infestation - *see* Actinomycosis
Leptotricosis - *see* Actinomycosis
Leptus dermatitis 133.8
Léris pleonosteosis 756.89
Léri-Weill syndrome 756.59
Leriche's syndrome (aortic bifurcation occlusion) 444.0
Lermoyez's syndrome (*see also* Disease, Ménière's) 386.00

Lesbianism - omit code
  ego-dystonic 302.0
  problems with 302.0
Lesch-Nyhan syndrome (hypoxanthine-guanine-phosphoribosyltransferase deficiency) 277.2
Lesion
  abducens nerve 378.54
  alveolar process 525.8
  anorectal 569.49
  aortic (valve) - *see* Endocarditis, aortic
  auditory nerve 388.5
  basal ganglion 333.90
  bile duct (*see also* Disease, biliary) 576.8
  bladder 596.9
  bone 733.90
  brachial plexus 353.0
  brain 348.8
    congenital 742.9
    vascular (*see also* Lesion, cerebrovascular) 437.9
      degenerative 437.1
      healed or old without residuals V12.59
      hypertensive 437.2
      late effect - *see* Late effect(s) (of) cerebrovascular disease
  buccal 528.9
  calcified - *see* Calcification
  canthus 373.9
  carate - *see* Pinta, lesions
  cardia 537.89
  cardiac - *see also* Disease, heart
    congenital 746.9
    valvular - *see* Endocarditis
  cauda equina 344.60
    with neurogenic bladder 344.61
  cecum 569.89
  cerebral - *see* Lesion, brain
  cerebrovascular (*see also* Disease, cerebrovascular NEC) 437.9
    degenerative 437.1
    healed or old without residuals V12.59
    hypertensive 437.2
    specified type NEC 437.8
  cervical root (nerve) NEC 353.2
  chiasmal 377.54
    associated with
      inflammatory disorders 377.54
      neoplasm NEC 377.52
        pituitary 377.51
      pituitary disorders 377.51
      vascular disorders 377.53
  chorda tympani 351.8
  coin, lung 793.1
  colon 569.89
  congenital - *see* Anomaly
  conjunctiva 372.9
  coronary artery (*see also* Ischemia, heart) 414.9
  cranial nerve 352.9
    first 352.0
    second 377.49
    third
      partial 378.51
      total 378.52
    fourth 378.53
    fifth 350.9
    sixth 378.54
    seventh 351.9
    eighth 388.5
    ninth 352.2
    tenth 352.3

Note Use the following fifth-digit
subclassification for categories 203-
208:

  0   without mention of remission
  1   with remission

Leukemia, leukemic (*Continued*)
eosinophilic (M9880/3) 205.1
giant cell (M9910/3) 207.2
granulocytic (M9860/3) 205.9
  acute (M9861/3) 205.0
  aleukemic (M9864/3) 205.8
  blastic (M9861/3) 205.0
  chronic (M9863/3) 205.1
  subacute (M9862/3) 205.2
  subleukemic (M9864/3) 205.8
hairy cell (M9940/3) 202.4
hemoblastic (M9801/3) 208.0
histiocytic (M9890/3) 206.9
lymphatic (M9820/3) 204.9
  acute (M9821/3) 204.0
  aleukemic (M9824/3) 204.8
  chronic (M9823/3) 204.1
  subacute (M9822/3) 204.2
  subleukemic (M9824/3) 204.8
lymphoblastic (M9821/3) 204.0
lymphocytic (M9820/3) 204.9
  acute (M9821/3) 204.0
  aleukemic (M9824/3) 204.8
  chronic (M9823/3) 204.1
  subacute (M9822/3) 204.2
  subleukemic (M9824/3) 204.8
lymphogenous (M9820/3) - *see* Leukemia, lymphoid
lymphoid (M9820/3) 204.9
  acute (M9821/3) 204.0
  aleukemic (M9824/3) 204.8
  blastic (M9821/3) 204.0
  chronic (M9823/3) 204.1
  subacute (M9822/3) 204.2
  subleukemic (M9824/3) 204.8
lymphosarcoma cell (M9850/3) 207.8
mast cell (M9900/3) 207.8
megakaryocytic (M9910/3) 207.2
megakaryocytoid (M9910/3) 207.2
mixed (cell) (M9810/3) 207.8
monoblastic (M9891/3) 206.0
monocytic (Schilling-type) (M9890/3) 206.9
  acute (M9891/3) 206.0
  aleukemic (M9894/3) 206.8
  chronic (M9893/3) 206.1
  Naegeli-type (M9863/3) 205.1
  subacute (M9892/3) 206.2
  subleukemic (M9894/3) 206.8
monocytoid (M9890/3) 206.9
  acute (M9891/3) 206.0
  aleukemic (M9894/3) 206.8
  chronic (M9893/3) 206.1
  myelogenous (M9863/3) 205.1
  subacute (M9892/3) 206.2
  subleukemic (M9894/3) 206.8
monomyelocytic (M9860/3) - *see* Leukemia, myelomonocytic
myeloblastic (M9861/3) 205.0
myelocytic (M9863/3) 205.1
  acute (M9861/3) 205.0
myelogenous (M9860/3) 205.9
  acute (M9861/3) 205.0
  aleukemic (M9864/3) 205.8
  chronic (M9863/3) 205.1
  monocytoid (M9863/3) 205.1
  subacute (M9862/3) 205.2
  subleukemic (M9864) 205.8
myeloid (M9860/3) 205.9
  acute (M9861/3) 205.0
  aleukemic (M9864/3) 205.8
  chronic (M9863/3) 205.1
  subacute (M9862/3) 205.2
  subleukemic (M9864/3) 205.8

Leukemia, leukemic (*Continued*)
myelomonocytic (M9860/3) 205.9
  acute (M9861/3) 205.0
  chronic (M9863/3) 205.1
Naegeli-type monocytic (M9863/3) 205.1
neutrophilic (M9865/3) 205.1
plasma cell (M9830/3) 203.1
plasmacytic (M9830/3) 203.1
prolymphocytic (M9825/3) - *see* Leukemia, lymphoid
promyelocytic, acute (M9866/3) 205.0
Schilling-type monocytic (M9890/3) - *see* Leukemia, monocytic
stem cell (M9801/3) 208.0
subacute NEC (M9802/3) 208.2
subleukemic NEC (M9804/3) 208.8
thrombocytic (M9910/3) 207.2
undifferentiated (M9801/3) 208.0
Leukemoid reaction (lymphocytic) (monocytic) (myelocytic) 288.8
Leukoclastic vasculitis 446.29
Leukocoria 360.44
Leukocythemia - *see* Leukemia
Leukocytosis 288.8
basophilic 288.8
eosinophilic 288.3
lymphocytic 288.8
monocytic 288.8
neutrophilic 288.8
Leukoderma 709.09
syphilitic 091.3
late 095.8
Leukodermia (*see also* Leukoderma) 709.09
Leukodystrophy (cerebral) (globoid cell) (metachromatic) (progressive) (sudanophilic) 330.0
Leukoedema, mouth or tongue 528.7
Leukoencephalitis
acute hemorrhagic (postinfectious) NEC 136.9 [323.6]
  postimmunization or postvaccinal 323.5
subacute sclerosing 046.2
  van Bogaert's 046.2
van Bogaert's (sclerosing) 046.2
Leukoencephalopathy (*see also* Encephalitis) 323.9
acute necrotizing hemorrhagic (postinfectious) 136.9 [323.6]
  postimmunization or postvaccinal 323.5
metachromatic 330.0
multifocal (progressive) 046.3
progressive multifocal 046.3
Leukoerythroblastosis 289.0
Leukoerythrosis 289.0
Leukokeratosis (*see also* Leukoplakia) 702.8
mouth 528.6
nicotina palati 528.7
tongue 528.6
Leukokoria 360.44
Leukokraurosis vulva, vulvae 624.0
Leukolymphosarcoma (M9850/3) 207.8
Leukoma (cornea) (interfering with central vision) 371.03
adherent 371.04
Leukomelanopathy, hereditary 288.2
Leukonychia (punctata) (striata) 703.8
congenital 757.5

Leukopathia
unguium 703.8
congenital 757.5
Leukopenia 288.0
cyclic 288.0
familial 288.0
malignant 288.0
periodic 288.0
transitory neonatal 776.7
Leukopenic - *see* condition
Leukoplakia 702.8
anus 569.49
bladder (postinfectional) 596.8
buccal 528.6
cervix (uteri) 622.2
esophagus 530.83
gingiva 528.6
kidney (pelvis) 593.89
larynx 478.79
lip 528.6
mouth 528.6
oral soft tissue (including tongue) (mucosa) 528.6
palate 528.6
pelvis (kidney) 593.89
penis (infectional) 607.0
rectum 569.49
syphilitic 095.8
tongue 528.6
tonsil 478.29
ureter (postinfectional) 593.89
urethra (postinfectional) 599.84
uterus 621.8
vagina 623.1
vesical 596.8
vocal cords 478.5
vulva 624.0
Leukopolioencephalopathy 330.0
Leukorrhea (vagina) 623.5
due to Trichomonas (vaginalis) 131.00
trichomonal (Trichomonas vaginalis) 131.00
Leukosarcoma (M9850/3) 207.8
Leukosis (M9800/3) - *see* Leukemia
Lev's disease or syndrome (acquired complete heart block) 426.0
Levi's syndrome (pituitary dwarfism) 253.3
Levocardia (isolated) 746.87
with situs inversus 759.3
Levulosuria 271.2
Lewandowski's disease (primary) (*see also* Tuberculosis) 017.0
Lewandowski-Lutz disease (epidermodysplasia verruciformis) 078.19
Leyden's disease (periodic vomiting) 536.2
Leyden-Möbius dystrophy 359.1
Leydig cell
carcinoma (M8650/3)
  specified site - *see* Neoplasm, by site, malignant
  unspecified site
    female 183.0
    male 186.9
tumor (M8650/1)
  benign (M8650/0)
    specified site - *see* Neoplasm, by site, benign
    unspecified site
      female 220
      male 222.0

Leydig cell (*Continued*)
  tumor (*Continued*)
    malignant (M8650/3)
      specified site - *see* Neoplasm, by
        site, malignant
      unspecified site
        female 183.0
        male 186.9
    specified site - *see* Neoplasm, by site,
      uncertain behavior
    unspecified site
      female 236.2
      male 236.4
Leydig-Sertoli cell tumor (M8631/0)
  specified site - *see* Neoplasm, by site,
    benign
  unspecified site
    female 220
    male 222.0
Liar, pathologic 301.7
Libman-Sacks disease or syndrome
  710.0 [*424.91*]
Lice (infestation) 132.9
  body (pediculus corporis) 132.1
  crab 132.2
  head (pediculus capitis) 132.0
  mixed (classifiable to more than one
    of the categories 132.0-132.2)
    132.3
  pubic (pediculus pubis) 132.2
Lichen 697.9
  albus 701.0
  annularis 695.89
  atrophicus 701.0
  corneus obtusus 698.3
  myxedematous 701.8
  nitidus 697.1
  pilaris 757.39
    acquired 701.1
  planopilaris 697.0
  planus (acute) (chronicus) (hyper-
    trophic) (verrucous) 697.0
    morphoeicus 701.0
    sclerosus (et atrophicus) 701.0
  ruber 696.4
    acuminatus 696.4
    moniliformis 697.8
    obtusus corneus 698.3
    of Wilson 697.0
    planus 697.0
  sclerosus (et atrophicus) 701.0
  scrofulosus (primary) (*see also* Tubercu-
    losis) 017.0
  simplex (Vidal's) 698.3
    chronicus 698.3
    circumscriptus 698.3
  spinulosus 757.39
    mycotic 117.9
  striata 697.8
  urticatus 698.2
Lichenification 698.3
  nodular 698.3
Lichenoides tuberculosis (primary) (*see
  also* Tuberculosis) 017.0
Lichtheim's disease or syndrome (subacute combined sclerosis with pernicious anemia) 281.0 [*336.2*]
Lien migrans 289.59
Lientery (*see also* Diarrhea) 558.9
  infectious 009.2
Life circumstance problem NEC
  V62.89
Li-Fraumeni cancer syndrome 758.3
Ligament - *see* condition

Light-for-dates (infant) 764.0
  with signs of fetal malnutrition 764.1
  affecting management of pregnancy
    656.5
Light-headedness 780.4
Lightning (effects) (shock) (stroke)
  (struck by) 994.0
  burn - *see* Burn, by site
  foot 266.2
Lightwood's disease or syndrome (renal
  tubular acidosis) 588.8
Lignac's disease (cystinosis) 270.0
Lignac (-de Toni) (-Fanconi) (-Debré)
  syndrome (cystinosis) 270.0
Lignac (-Fanconi) syndrome (cystinosis)
  270.0
Ligneous thyroiditis 245.3
Likoff's syndrome (angina in meno-
  pausal women) 413.9
Limb - *see* condition
Limitation of joint motion (*see also* Stiff-
  ness, joint) 719.5
  sacroiliac 724.6
Limit dextrinosis 271.0
Limited
  cardiac reserve - *see* Disease, heart
  duction, eye NEC 378.63
Lindau's disease (retinocerebral angio-
  matosis) 759.6
Lindau (-von Hippel) disease (angio-
  matosis retinocerebellosa) 759.6
Linea corneae senilis 371.41
Lines
  Beau's (transverse furrows on finger-
    nails) 703.8
  Harris' 733.91
  Hudson-Stähli 371.11
  Stähli's 371.11
Lingua
  geographical 529.1
  nigra (villosa) 529.3
  plicata 529.5
    congenital 750.13
  tylosis 528.6
Lingual (tongue) - *see also* condition
  thyroid 759.2
Linitis (gastric) 535.4
  plastica (M8142/3) 151.9
Lioderma essentialis (cum melanosis et
  telangiectasia) 757.33
Lip - *see also* condition
  biting 528.9
Lipalgia 272.8
Lipedema - *see* Edema
Lipemia (*see also* Hyperlipidemia)
  272.4
  retina, retinalis 272.3
Lipidosis 272.7
  cephalin 272.7
  cerebral (infantile) (juvenile) (late)
    330.1
  cerebroretinal 330.1 [*362.71*]
  cerebroside 272.7
  cerebrospinal 272.7
  chemically induced 272.7
  cholesterol 272.7
  diabetic 250.8 [*272.7*]
  dystopic (hereditary) 272.7
  glycolipid 272.7
  hepatosplenomegalic 272.3
  hereditary, dystopic 272.7
  sulfatide 330.0
Lipoadenoma (M8324/0 - *see* Neoplasm,
  by site, benign

Lipoblastoma (M8881/0) - *see* Lipoma,
  by site
Lipoblastomatosis (M8881/0) - *see* Li-
  poma, by site
Lipochondrodystrophy 277.5
Lipochrome histiocytosis (familial) 288.1
Lipodystrophia progressiva 272.6
Lipodystrophy (progressive) 272.6
  insulin 272.6
  intestinal 040.2
Lipofibroma (M8851/0) - *see* Lipoma, by
  site
Lipoglycoproteinosis 272.8
Lipogranuloma, sclerosing 709.8
Lipogranulomatosis (disseminated) 272.8
  kidney 272.8
Lipoid - *see also* condition
  histiocytosis 272.7
    essential 272.7
  nephrosis (*see also* Nephrosis) 581.3
  proteinosis of Urbach 272.8
Lipoidemia (*see also* Hyperlipidemia)
  272.4
Lipoidosis (*see also* Lipidosis) 272.7
Lipoma (M8850/0) 214.9
  breast (skin) 214.1
  face 214.0
  fetal (M8881/0) - *see also* Lipoma, by
    site
    fat cell (M8880/0) - *see* Lipoma, by
      site
  infiltrating (M8856/0) - *see* Lipoma, by
    site
  intra-abdominal 214.3
  intramuscular (M8856/0) - *see* Lipoma,
    by site
  intrathoracic 214.2
  kidney 214.3
  mediastinum 214.2
  muscle 214.8
  peritoneum 214.3
  retroperitoneum 214.3
  skin 214.1
    face 214.0
  spermatic cord 214.4
  spindle cell (M8857/0) - *see* Lipoma,
    by site
  stomach 214.3
  subcutaneous tissue 214.1
    face 214.0
  thymus 214.2
  thyroid gland 214.2
Lipomatosis (dolorosa) 272.8
  fetal (M8881/0) - *see* Lipoma, by site
  Launois-Bensaude's 272.8
Lipomyohemangioma (M8860/0)
  specified site - *see* Neoplasm, connec-
    tive tissue, benign
  unspecified site 223.0
Lipomyoma (M8860/0)
  specified site - *see* Neoplasm, connec-
    tive tissue, benign
  unspecified site 223.0
Lipomyxoma (M8852/0) - *see* Lipoma, by
  site
Lipomyxosarcoma (M8852/3) - *see* Neoplasm, connective tissue, malignant
Lipophagocytosis 289.8
Lipoproteinemia (alpha) 272.4
  broad-beta 272.2
  floating-beta 272.2
  hyper-pre-beta 272.1
Lipoproteinosis (Rossle-Urbach-Wiethe)
  272.8

Liposarcoma (M8850/3) - *see also* Neoplasm, connective tissue, malignant
  differentiated type (M8851/3) - *see* Neoplasm, connective tissue, malignant
  embryonal (M8852/3) - *see* Neoplasm, connective tissue, malignant
  mixed type (M8855/3) - *see* Neoplasm, connective tissue, malignant
  myxoid (M8852/3) - *see* Neoplasm, connective tissue, malignant
  pleomorphic (M8854/3) - *see* Neoplasm, connective tissue, malignant
  round cell (M8853/3) - *see* Neoplasm, connective tissue, malignant
  well differentiated type (M8851/3) - *see* Neoplasm, connective tissue, malignant
Liposynovitis prepatellaris 272.8
Lipping
  cervix 622.0
  spine (*see also* Spondylosis) 721.90
  vertebra (*see also* Spondylosis) 721.90
Lip pits (mucus), congenital 750.25
Lipschütz disease or ulcer 616.50
Lipuria 791.1
  bilharziasis 120.0
Liquefaction, vitreous humor 379.21
Lisping 307.9
Lissauer's paralysis 094.1
Lissencephalia, lissencephaly 742.2
Listerellose 027.0
Listeriose 027.0
Listeriosis 027.0
  congenital 771.2
  fetal 771.2
  suspected fetal damage affecting management of pregnancy 655.4
Listlessness 780.79
Lithemia 790.6
Lithiasis - *see also* Calculus
  hepatic (duct) - *see* Choledocholithiasis
  urinary 592.9
Lithopedion 779.9
  affecting management of pregnancy 656.8
Lithosis (occupational) 502
  with tuberculosis - *see* Tuberculosis, pulmonary
Lithuria 791.9
Litigation V62.5
Little
  league elbow 718.82
  stroke syndrome 435.9
Little's disease - *see* Palsy, cerebral
Littre's
  gland - *see* condition
  hernia - *see* Hernia, Littre's
Littritis (*see also* Urethritis) 597.89
Livedo 782.61
  annularis 782.61
  racemose 782.61
  reticularis 782.61
Live flesh 781.0
Liver - *see also* condition
  donor V59.8
Livida, asphyxia
  newborn 768.6
Living
  alone V60.3
    with handicapped person V60.4
Lloyd's syndrome 258.1
Loa loa 125.2
Loasis 125.2

Lobe, lobar - *see* condition
Lobo's disease or blastomycosis 116.2
Lobomycosis 116.2
Lobotomy syndrome 310.0
Lobstein's disease (brittle bones and blue sclera) 756.51
Lobster-claw hand 755.58
Lobulation (congenital) - *see also* Anomaly, specified type NEC, by site
  kidney, fetal 753.3
  liver, abnormal 751.69
  spleen 759.0
Lobule, lobular - *see* condition
Local, localized - *see* condition
Locked bowel or intestine (*see also* Obstruction, intestine) 560.9
Locked-in state 344.81
Locked twins 660.5
  affecting fetus or newborn 763.1
Locking
  joint (*see also* Derangement, joint) 718.90
  knee 717.9
Lockjaw (*see also* Tetanus) 037
Locomotor ataxia (progressive) 094.0
Löffler's
  endocarditis 421.0
  eosinophilia or syndrome 518.3
  pneumonia 518.3
  syndrome (eosinophilic pneumonitis) 518.3
Löfgren's syndrome (sarcoidosis) 135
Loiasis 125.2
  eyelid 125.2 [373.6]
Loneliness V62.89
Lone Star fever 082.8
Long labor 662.1
  affecting fetus or newborn 763.89
  first stage 662.0
  second stage 662.2
Longitudinal stripes or grooves, nails 703.8
  congenital 757.5
Long-term (current) drug use V58.69
  antibiotics V58.62
  anticoagulants V58.61
Loop
  intestine (*see also* Volvulus) 560.2
  intrascleral nerve 379.29
  vascular on papilla (optic) 743.57
Loose - *see also* condition
  body
    in tendon sheath 727.82
    joint 718.10
      ankle 718.17
      elbow 718.12
      foot 718.17
      hand 718.14
      hip 718.15
      knee 717.6
      multiple sites 718.19
      pelvic region 718.15
      prosthetic implant - *see* Complications, mechanical
      shoulder (region) 718.11
      specified site NEC 718.18
      wrist 718.13
    cartilage (joint) (*see also* Loose, body, joint) 718.1
      knee 717.6
    facet (vertebral) 724.9
    prosthetic implant - *see* Complications, mechanical
    sesamoid, joint (*see also* Loose, body, joint) 718.1

Loose (*Continued*)
  tooth, teeth 525.8
Loosening epiphysis 732.9
Looser (-Debray)-Milkman syndrome (osteomalacia with pseudofractures) 268.2
Lop ear (deformity) 744.29
Lorain's disease or syndrome (pituitary dwarfism) 253.3
Lorain-Levi syndrome (pituitary dwarfism) 253.3
Lordosis (acquired) (postural) 737.20
  congenital 754.2
  due to or associated with
    Charcôt-Marie-Tooth disease 356.1 [737.42]
    mucopolysaccharidosis 277.5 [737.42]
    neurofibromatosis 237.71 [737.42]
    osteitis
      deformans 731.0 [737.42]
      fibrosa cystica 252.0 [737.42]
    osteoporosis (*see also* Osteoporosis) 733.00 [737.42]
    poliomyelitis (*see also* Poliomyelitis) 138 [737.42]
    tuberculosis (*see also* Tuberculosis) 015.0 [737.42]
  late effect of rickets 268.1 [737.42]
  postlaminectomy 737.21
  postsurgical NEC 737.22
  rachitic 268.1 [737.42]
  specified NEC 737.29
  tuberculous (*see also* Tuberculosis) 015.0 [737.42]
Loss
  appetite 783.0
    hysterical 300.11
    nonorganic origin 307.59
    psychogenic 307.59
  blood - *see* Hemorrhage
  central vision 368.41
  consciousness 780.09
    transient 780.2
  control, sphincter, rectum 787.6
    nonorganic origin 307.7
  ear ossicle, partial 385.24
  elasticity, skin 782.8
  extremity or member, traumatic, current - *see* Amputation, traumatic
  fluid (acute) 276.5
    with
      hypernatremia 276.0
      hyponatremia 276.1
    fetus or newborn 775.5
  hair 704.00
  hearing - *see also* Deafness
    central 389.14
    conductive (air) 389.00
      with sensorineural hearing loss 389.2
      combined types 389.08
      external ear 389.01
      inner ear 389.04
      middle ear 389.03
      multiple types 389.08
      tympanic membrane 389.02
    mixed type 389.2
    nerve 389.12
    neural 389.12
    noise-induced 388.12
    perceptive NEC (*see also* Loss, hearing, sensorineural) 389.10
    sensorineural 389.10
      with conductive hearing loss 389.2

Loss (Continued)
  hearing (Continued)
    sensorineural (Continued)
      central 389.14
      combined types 389.18
      multiple types 389.18
      neural 389.12
      sensory 389.11
     sensory 389.11
     specified type NEC 389.8
     sudden NEC 388.2
   labyrinthine reactivity (unilateral) 386.55
    bilateral 386.56
  memory (see also Amnesia) 780.9
   mild, following organic brain damage 310.1
  mind (see also Psychosis) 298.9
  organ or part - see Absence, by site, acquired
  sensation 782.0
  sense of
   smell (see also Disturbance, sensation) 781.1
   taste (see also Disturbance, sensation) 781.1
   touch (see also Disturbance, sensation) 781.1
  sight (acquired) (complete) (congenital) - see Blindness
  spinal fluid
   headache 349.0
  substance of
   bone (see also Osteoporosis) 733.00
   cartilage 733.99
    ear 380.32
   vitreous (humor) 379.26
  tooth, teeth, due to accident, extraction, or local periodontal disease 525.1
  vision, visual (see also Blindness) 369.9
   both eyes (see also Blindness, both eyes) 369.3
   complete (see also Blindness, both eyes) 369.00
   one eye 369.8
   sudden 368.11
   transient 368.12
   vitreous 379.26
  voice (see also Aphonia) 784.41
  weight (cause unknown) 783.2
Lou Gehrig's disease 335.20
Louis-Bar syndrome (ataxia-telangiectasia) 334.8
Louping ill 063.1
Lousiness - see Lice
Low
  back syndrome 724.2
  basal metabolic rate (BMR) 794.7
  birthweight 765.1
   extreme (less than 1000 grams) 765.0
   for gestational age 764.0
  bladder compliance 596.52
  blood pressure (see also Hypotension) 458.9
   reading (incidental) (isolated) (nonspecific) 796.3
  cardiac reserve - see Disease, heart
  compliance bladder 596.52
  frequency deafness - see Disorder, hearing
  function - see also Hypofunction
   kidney (see also Disease, renal) 593.9
   liver 573.9

Low (Continued)
  hemoglobin 285.9
  implantation, placenta - see Placenta, previa
  insertion, placenta - see Placenta, previa
  lying
   kidney 593.0
   organ or site, congenital - see Malposition, congenital
   placenta - see Placenta, previa
  output syndrome (cardiac) (see also Failure, heart) 428.9
  platelets (blood) (see also Thrombocytopenia) 287.5
  reserve, kidney (see also Disease, renal) 593.9
  salt syndrome 593.9
  tension glaucoma 365.12
  vision 369.9
   both eyes 369.20
   one eye 369.70
Lowe (-Terrey-MacLachlan) syndrome (oculocerebrorenal dystrophy) 270.8
Lower extremity - see condition
Lown (-Ganong)-Levine syndrome (short P-R interval, normal QRS complex, and paroxysmal supraventricular tachycardia) 426.81
LSD reaction (see also Abuse, drugs, nondependent) 305.3
L-shaped kidney 753.3
Lucas-Championnière disease (fibrinous bronchitis) 466.0
Lucey-Driscoll syndrome (jaundice due to delayed conjugation) 774.30
Ludwig's
  angina 528.3
  disease (submaxillary cellulitis) 528.3
Lues (venerea), luetic - see Syphilis
Luetscher's syndrome (dehydration) 276.5
Lumbago 724.2
  due to displacement, intervertebral disc 722.10
Lumbalgia 724.2
  due to displacement, intervertebral disc 722.10
Lumbar - see condition
Lumbarization, vertebra 756.15
Lumbermen's itch 133.8
Lump - see also Mass
  abdominal 789.3
  breast 611.72
  chest 786.6
  epigastric 789.3
  head 784.2
  kidney 753.3
  liver 789.1
  lung 786.6
  mediastinal 786.6
  neck 784.2
  nose or sinus 784.2
  pelvic 789.3
  skin 782.2
  substernal 786.6
  throat 784.2
  umbilicus 789.3
Lunacy (see also Psychosis) 298.9
Lunatomalacia 732.3
Lung - see also condition
  donor V59.8
  drug addict's 417.8
  mainliners' 417.8
  vanishing 492.0
Lupoid (miliary) of Boeck 135

Lupus 710.0
  Cazenave's (erythematosus) 695.4
  discoid (local) 695.4
  disseminated 710.0
  erythematodes (discoid) (local) 695.4
   disseminated 710.0
  eyelid 373.34
  systemic 710.0
   with
    encephalitis 710.0 [323.8]
    lung involvement 710.0 [517.8]
   inhibitor (presence of) 286.5
  exedens 017.0
  eyelid (see also Tuberculosis) 017.0 [373.4]
  Hilliard's 017.0
  hydralazine
   correct substance properly administered 695.4
   overdose or wrong substance given or taken 972.6
  miliaris disseminatus faciei 017.0
  nephritis 710.0 [583.81]
   acute 710.0 [580.81]
   chronic 710.0 [582.81]
  nontuberculous, not disseminated 695.4
  pernio (Besnier) 135
  tuberculous (see also Tuberculosis) 017.0
   eyelid (see also Tuberculosis) 017.0 [373.4]
  vulgaris 017.0
Luschka's joint disease 721.90
Luteinoma (M8610/0) 220
Lutembacher's disease or syndrome (atrial septal defect with mitral stenosis) 745.5
Luteoma (M8610/0) 220
Lutz-Miescher disease (elastosis perforans serpiginosa) 701.1
Lutz-Splendore-de Almeida disease (Brazilian blastomycosis) 116.1
Luxatio
  bulbi due to birth injury 767.8
  coxae congenita (see also Dislocation, hip, congenital) 754.30
  erecta - see Dislocation, shoulder
  imperfecta - see Sprain, by site
  perinealis - see Dislocation, hip
Luxation - see also Dislocation, by site
  eyeball 360.81
   due to birth injury 767.8
   lateral 376.36
  genital organs (external) NEC - see Wound, open, genital organs
  globe (eye) 360.81
   lateral 376.36
  lacrimal gland (postinfectional) 375.16
  lens (old) (partial) 379.32
   congenital 743.37
    syphilitic 090.49 [379.32]
   Marfan's disease 090.49
   spontaneous 379.32
  penis - see Wound, open, penis
  scrotum - see Wound, open, scrotum
  testis - see Wound, open, testis
L-xyloketosuria 271.8
Lycanthropy (see also Psychosis) 298.9
Lyell's disease or syndrome (toxic epidermal necrolysis) 695.1
  due to drug
   correct substance properly administered 695.1

Lyell's disease or syndrome (*Continued*)
  due to drug (*Continued*)
    overdose or wrong substance given or taken 977.9
      specified drug - *see* Table of Drugs and Chemicals
Lyme disease 088.81
Lymph
  gland or node - *see* condition
  scrotum (*see also* Infestation, filarial) 125.9
Lymphadenitis 289.3
  with
    abortion - *see* Abortion, by type, with sepsis
    ectopic pregnancy (*see also* categories 633.0-633.9) 639.0
    molar pregnancy (*see also* categories 630-632) 639.0
  acute 683
    mesenteric 289.2
  any site, except mesenteric 289.3
    acute 683
    chronic 289.1
    mesenteric (acute) (chronic) (nonspecific) (subacute) 289.2
    subacute 289.1
      mesenteric 289.2
  breast, puerperal, postpartum 675.2
  chancroidal (congenital) 099.0
  chronic 289.1
    mesenteric 289.2
  dermatopathic 695.89
  due to
    anthracosis (occupational) 500
    Brugia (Wuchereria) malayi 125.1
    diphtheria (toxin) 032.89
    lymphogranuloma venereum 099.1
    Wuchereria bancrofti 125.0
  following
    abortion 639.0
    ectopic or molar pregnancy 639.0
  generalized 289.3
  gonorrheal 098.89
  granulomatous 289.1
  infectional 683
  mesenteric (acute) (chronic) (nonspecific) (subacute) 289.2
    due to Bacillus typhi 002.0
    tuberculous (*see also* Tuberculosis) 014.8
  mycobacterial 031.8
  purulent 683
  pyogenic 683
  regional 078.3
  septic 683
  streptococcal 683
  subacute, unspecified site 289.1
  suppurative 683
  syphilitic (early) (secondary) 091.4
    late 095.8
  tuberculous - *see* Tuberculosis, lymph gland
  venereal 099.1
Lymphadenoid goiter 245.2
Lymphadenopathy (general) 785.6
  due to toxoplasmosis (acquired) 130.7
    congenital (active) 771.2
Lymphadenopathy-associated virus (disease) (illness) (infection) - *see* Human immunodeficiency virus (disease) (illness) (infection)
Lymphadenosis 785.6
  acute 075

Lymphangiectasis 457.1
  conjunctiva 372.8
  postinfectional 457.1
  scrotum 457.1
Lymphangiectatic elephantiasis, nonfilarial 457.1
Lymphangioendothelioma (M9170/0) 228.1
  malignant (M9170/3) - *see* Neoplasm, connective tissue, malignant
Lymphangioma (M9170/0) 228.1
  capillary (M9171/0) 228.1
  cavernous (M9172/0) 228.1
  cystic (M9173/0) 228.1
  malignant (M9170/3) - *see* Neoplasm, connective tissue, malignant
Lymphangiomyoma (M9174/0) 228.1
Lymphangiomyomatosis (M9174/1) - *see* Neoplasm, connective tissue, uncertain behavior
Lymphangiosarcoma (M9170/3) - *see* Neoplasm, connective tissue, malignant
Lymphangitis 457.2
  with
    abortion - *see* Abortion, by type, with sepsis
    abscess - *see* Abscess, by site
    cellulitis - *see* Abscess, by site
    ectopic pregnancy (*see also* categories 633.0-633.9) 639.0
    molar pregnancy (*see also* categories 630-632) 639.0
  acute (with abscess or cellulitis) 682.9
    specified site - *see* Abscess, by site
  breast, puerperal, postpartum 675.2
  chancroidal 099.0
  chronic (any site) 457.2
  due to
    Brugia (Wuchereria) malayi 125.1
    Wuchereria bancrofti 125.0
  following
    abortion 639.0
    ectopic or molar pregnancy 639.0
  gangrenous 457.2
  penis
    acute 607.2
    gonococcal (acute) 098.0
      chronic or duration of 2 months or more 098.2
  puerperal, postpartum, childbirth 670
  strumous, tuberculous (*see also* Tuberculosis) 017.2
  subacute (any site) 457.2
  tuberculous - *see* Tuberculosis, lymph gland
Lymphatic (vessel) - *see* condition
Lymphatism 254.8
  scrofulous (*see also* Tuberculosis) 017.2
Lymphectasia 457.1
Lymphedema (*see also* Elephantiasis) 457.1
  acquired (chronic) 457.1
  chronic hereditary 757.0
  congenital 757.0
  idiopathic hereditary 757.0
  praecox 457.1
  secondary 457.1
  surgical NEC 997.99
    postmastectomy (syndrome) 457.0
Lymph-hemangioma (M9120/0) - *see* Hemangioma, by site
Lymphoblastic - *see* condition

Lymphoblastoma (diffuse) (M9630/3) 200.1
  giant follicular (M9690/3) 202.0
  macrofollicular (M9690/3) 202.0
Lymphoblastosis, acute benign 075
Lymphocele 457.8
Lymphocythemia 288.8
Lymphocytic - *see also* condition
  chorioencephalitis (acute) (serous) 049.0
  choriomeningitis (acute) (serous) 049.0
Lymphocytoma (diffuse) (malignant) (M9620/3) 200.1
Lymphocytomatosis (M9620/3) 200.1
Lymphocytopenia 288.8
Lymphocytosis (symptomatic) 288.8
  infectious (acute) 078.89
Lymphoepithelioma (M8082/3) - *see* Neoplasm, by site, malignant
Lymphogranuloma (malignant) (M9650/3) 201.9
  inguinale 099.1
  venereal (any site) 099.1
    with stricture of rectum 099.1
  venereum 099.1
Lymphogranulomatosis (malignant) (M9650/3) 201.9
  benign (Boeck's sarcoid) (Schaumann's) 135
  Hodgkin's (M9650/3) 201.9
Lymphoid - *see* condition
Lympholeukoblastoma (M9850/3) 207.8
Lympholeukosarcoma (M9850/3) 207.8
Lymphoma (malignant) (M9590/3) 202.8

Note   Use the following fifth-digit subclassification with categories 200-202:

0	unspecified site
1	lymph nodes of head, face, and neck
2	intrathoracic lymph nodes
3	intra-abdominal lymph nodes
4	lymph nodes of axilla and upper limb
5	lymph nodes of inguinal region and lower limb
6	intrapelvic lymph nodes
7	spleen
8	lymph nodes of multiple sites

---

  benign (M9590/0) - *see* Neoplasm, by site, benign
  Burkitt's type (lymphoblastic) (undifferentiated) (M9750/3) 200.2
  Castleman's (mediastinal lymph node hyperplasia) 785.6
  centroblastic-centrocytic
    diffuse (M9614/3) 202.8
    follicular (M9692/3) 202.0
  centroblastic type (diffuse) (M9632/3) 202.8
    follicular (M9697/3) 202.0
  centrocytic (M9622/3) 202.8
  compound (M9613/3) 200.8
  convoluted cell type (lymphoblastic) (M9602/3) 202.8
  diffuse NEC (M9590/3) 202.8
  follicular (giant) (M9690/3) 202.0
    center cell (diffuse) (M9615/3) 202.8
      cleaved (diffuse) (M9623/3) 202.8
        follicular (M9695/3) 202.0

Lymphoma *(Continued)*
  follicular *(Continued)*
    center cell *(Continued)*
      non-cleaved (diffuse) (M9633/3)
        202.8
        follicular (M9698/3) 202.0
    centroblastic-centrocytic (M9692/3)
      202.0
    centroblastic type (M9697/3) 202.0
    lymphocytic
      intermediate differentiation
        (M9694/3) 202.0
      poorly differentiated (M9696/3)
        202.0
    mixed (cell type) (lymphocytic-histi-
      ocytic) (small cell and large cell)
      (M9691/3) 202.0
  germinocytic (M9622/3) 202.8
  giant, follicular or follicle (M9690/3)
    202.0
  histiocytic (diffuse) (M9640/3) 200.0
    nodular (M9642/3) 200.0
    pleomorphic cell type (M9641/3)
      200.0
  Hodgkin's (M9650/3) *(see also* Disease,
    Hodgkin's) 201.9
  immunoblastic (type) (M9612/3) 200.8
  large cell (M9640/3) 200.0
    nodular (M9642/3) 200.0
    pleomorphic cell type (M9641/3)
      200.0
  lymphoblastic (diffuse) (M9630/3) 200.1
    Burkitt's type (M9750/3) 200.2
    convoluted cell type (M9602/3)
      202.8
  lymphocytic (cell type) (diffuse)
    (M9620/3) 200.1
    with plasmacytoid differentiation,
      diffuse (M9611/3) 200.8
    intermediate differentiation (diffuse)
      (M9621/3) 200.1
      follicular (M9694/3) 202.0
      nodular (M9694/3) 202.0
    nodular (M9690/3) 202.0
    poorly differentiated (diffuse)
      (M9630/3) 200.1

Lymphoma *(Continued)*
  lymphocytic *(Continued)*
    poorly differentiated *(Continued)*
      follicular (M9696/3) 202.0
      nodular (M9696/3) 202.0
    well differentiated (diffuse) (M9620/
      3) 200.1
      follicular (M9693/3) 202.0
      nodular (M9693/3) 202.0
  lymphocytic-histiocytic, mixed (diffuse)
    (M9613/3) 200.8
    follicular (M9691/3) 202.0
    nodular (M9691/3) 202.0
  lymphoplasmacytoid type (M9611/3)
    200.8
  lymphosarcoma type (M9610/3) 200.1
  macrofollicular (M9690/3) 202.0
  mixed cell type (diffuse) (M9613/3)
    200.8
    follicular (M9691/3) 202.0
    nodular (M9691/3) 202.0
  nodular (M9690/3) 202.0
    histiocytic (M9642/3) 200.0
    lymphocytic (M9690/3) 202.0
      intermediate differentiation
        (M9694/3) 202.0
      poorly differentiated (M9696/3)
        202.0
    mixed (cell type) (lymphocytic-histi-
      ocytic) (small cell and large cell)
      (M9691/3) 202.0
  non-Hodgkin's type NEC (M9591/3)
    202.8
  reticulum cell (type) (M9640/3) 200.0
  small cell and large cell, mixed (dif-
    fuse) (M9613/3) 200.8
    follicular (M9691/3) 202.0
    nodular (9691/3) 202.0
  stem cell (type) (M9601/3) 202.8
  T-cell 202.1
  undifferentiated (cell type) (non-Burk-
    itt's) (M9600/3) 202.8
    Burkitt's type (M9750/3) 200.2
Lymphomatosis (M9590/3) - *see also*
  Lymphoma
  granulomatous 099.1

Lymphopathia
  venereum 099.1
  veneris 099.1
Lymphopenia 288.8
  familial 279.2
Lymphoreticulosis, benign (of inoculation) 078.3
Lymphorrhea 457.8
Lymphosarcoma (M9610/3) 200.1
  diffuse (M9610/3) 200.1
    with plasmacytoid differentiation
      (M9611/3) 200.8
      lymphoplasmacytic (M9611/3)
        200.8
    follicular (giant) (M9690/3) 202.0
      lymphoblastic (M9696/3) 202.0
      lymphocytic, intermediate differenti-
        ation (M9694/3) 202.0
      mixed cell type (M9691/3) 202.0
    giant follicular (M9690/3) 202.0
    Hodgkin's (M9650/3) 201.9
    immunoblastic (M9612/3) 200.8
    lymphoblastic (diffuse) (M9630/3)
      200.1
      follicular (M9696/3) 202.0
      nodular (M9696/3) 202.0
    lymphocytic (diffuse) (M9620/3)
      200.1
      intermediate differentiation (diffuse)
        (M9621/3) 200.1
        follicular (M9694/3) 202.0
        nodular (M9694/3) 202.0
      mixed cell type (diffuse) (M9613/3)
        200.8
        follicular (M9691/3) 202.0
        nodular (M9691/3) 202.0
      nodular (M9690/3) 202.0
        lymphoblastic (M9696/3) 202.0
        lymphocytic, intermediate differenti-
          ation (M9694/3) 202.0
        mixed cell type (M9691/3) 202.0
    prolymphocytic (M9631/3) 200.1
    reticulum cell (M9640/3) 200.0
Lymphostasis 457.8
Lypemania *(see also* Melancholia) 296.2
Lyssa 071

M

Macacus ear 744.29
Maceration
  fetus (cause not stated) 779.9
  wet feet, tropical (syndrome) 991.4
Machupo virus hemorrhagic fever
    078.7
Macleod's syndrome (abnormal trans-
    radiancy, one lung) 492.8
Macrocephalia, macrocephaly 756.0
Macrocheilia (congenital) 744.81
Macrochilia (congenital) 744.81
Macrocolon (congenital) 751.3
Macrocornea 743.41
  associated with buphthalmos 743.22
Macrocytic - *see* condition
Macrocytosis 289.8
Macrodactylia, macrodactylism (fingers)
    (thumbs) 755.57
  toes 755.65
Macrodontia 520.2
Macroencephaly 742.4
Macrogenia 524.05
Macrogenitosomia (female) (male) (prae-
    cox) 255.2
Macrogingivae 523.8
Macroglobulinemia (essential) (idio-
    pathic) (monoclonal) (primary) (syn-
    drome) (Waldenström's) 273.3
Macroglossia (congenital) 750.15
  acquired 529.8
Macrognathia, macrognathism (congeni-
    tal) 524.00
  mandibular 524.02
    alveolar 524.72
  maxillary 524.01
    alveolar 524.71
Macrogyria (congenital) 742.4
Macrohydrocephalus (*see also* Hydro-
    cephalus) 331.4
Macromastia (*see also* Hypertrophy,
    breast) 611.1
Macropsia 368.14
Macrosigmoid 564.7
  congenital 751.3
Macrospondylitis, acromegalic 253.0
Macrostomia (congenital) 744.83
Macrotia (external ear) (congenital)
    744.22
Macula
  cornea, corneal
    congenital 743.43
      interfering with vision 743.42
    interfering with central vision
      371.03
    not interfering with central vision
      371.02
  degeneration (*see also* Degeneration,
    macula) 362.50
    hereditary (*see also* Dystrophy, ret-
      ina) 362.70
  edema, cystoid 362.53
Maculae ceruleae 132.1
Macules and papules 709.8
Maculopathy, toxic 362.55
Madarosis 374.55
Madelung's
  deformity (radius) 755.54
  disease (lipomatosis) 272.8
  lipomatosis 272.8
Madness (*see also* Psychosis) 298.9
  myxedema (acute) 293.0
    subacute 293.1

Madura
  disease (actinomycotic) 039.9
    mycotic 117.4
  foot (actinomycotic) 039.4
    mycotic 117.4
Maduromycosis (actinomycotic) 039.9
  mycotic 117.4
Maffucci's syndrome (dyschondroplasia
    with hemangiomas) 756.4
Magenblase syndrome 306.4
Main en griffe (acquired) 736.06
  congenital 755.59
Maintenance
  chemotherapy regimen or treatment
    V58.1
  dialysis regimen or treatment
    extracorporeal (renal) V56.0
    peritoneal V56.8
    renal V56.0
  drug therapy or regimen V58.1
  external fixation NEC V54.8
  radiotherapy V58.0
  traction NEC V54.8
Majocchi's
  disease (purpura annularis telangiecto-
    des) 709.1
  granuloma 110.6
Major - *see* condition
Mal
  cerebral (idiopathic) (*see also* Epilepsy)
    345.9
  comital (*see also* Epilepsy) 345.9
  de los pintos (*see also* Pinta) 103.9
  de Meleda 757.39
  de mer 994.6
  lie - *see* Presentation, fetal
  perforant (*see also* Ulcer, lower extrem-
    ity) 707.1
Malabar itch 110.9
  beard 110.0
  foot 110.4
  scalp 110.0
Malabsorption 579.9
  calcium 579.8
  carbohydrate 579.8
  disaccharide 271.3
  drug-induced 579.8
  due to bacterial overgrowth 579.8
  fat 579.8
  folate, congenital 281.2
  galactose 271.1
  glucose-galactose (congenital) 271.3
  intestinal 579.9
  isomaltose 271.3
  lactose (hereditary) 271.3
  methionine 270.4
  monosaccharide 271.8
  postgastrectomy 579.3
  postsurgical 579.3
  protein 579.8
  sucrose (-isomaltose) (congenital) 271.3
  syndrome 579.9
    postgastrectomy 579.3
    postsurgical 579.3
Malacia, bone 268.2
  juvenile (*see also* Rickets) 268.0
  Kienböck's (juvenile) (lunate) (wrist)
    732.3
    adult 732.8
Malacoplakia
  bladder 596.8
  colon 569.89
  pelvis (kidney) 593.89
  ureter 593.89

Malacoplakia (*Continued*)
  urethra 599.84
Malacosteon 268.2
  juvenile (*see also* Rickets) 268.0
Maladaptation - *see* Maladjustment
Maladie de Roger 745.4
Maladjustment
  conjugal V61.10
    involving divorce or estrangement
      V61.0
  educational V62.3
  family V61.9
    specified circumstance NEC V61.8
  marital V61.10
    involving divorce or estrangement
      V61.0
  occupational V62.2
  simple, adult (*see also* Reaction, adjust-
    ment) 309.9
  situational acute (*see also* Reaction, ad-
    justment) 309.9
  social V62.4
Malaise 780.79
Malakoplakia - *see* Malacoplakia
Malaria, malarial (fever) 084.6
  algid 084.9
  any type, with
    algid malaria 084.9
    blackwater fever 084.8
    fever
      blackwater 084.8
      hemoglobinuric (bilious) 084.8
    hemoglobinuria, malarial 084.8
    hepatitis 084.9 [573.2]
    nephrosis 084.9 [581.81]
    pernicious complication NEC 084.9
      cardiac 084.9
      cerebral 084.9
  cardiac 084.9
  carrier (suspected) of V02.9
  cerebral 084.9
  complicating pregnancy, childbirth, or
    puerperium 647.4
  congenital 771.2
  congestion, congestive 084.6
    brain 084.9
  continued 084.0
  estivo-autumnal 084.0
  falciparum (malignant tertian) 084.0
  hematinuria 084.8
  hematuria 084.8
  hemoglobinuria 084.8
  hemorrhagic 084.6
  induced (therapeutically) 084.7
    accidental - *see* Malaria, by type
  liver 084.9 [573.2]
  malariae (quartan) 084.2
  malignant (tertian) 084.0
  mixed infections 084.5
  monkey 084.4
  ovale 084.3
  pernicious, acute 084.0
  Plasmodium, P.
    falciparum 084.0
    malariae 084.2
    ovale 084.3
    vivax 084.1
  quartan 084.2
  quotidian 084.0
  recurrent 084.6
    induced (therapeutically) 084.7
      accidental - *see* Malaria, by type
  remittent 084.6
  specified types NEC 084.4

Malaria, malarial (*Continued*)
spleen 084.6
subtertian 084.0
tertian (benign) 084.1
malignant 084.0
tropical 084.0
typhoid 084.6
vivax (benign tertian) 084.1
Malassez's disease (testicular cyst) 608.89
Malassimilation 579.9
Maldescent, testis 752.51
Maldevelopment - *see also* Anomaly, by
site
brain 742.9
colon 751.5
hip (joint) 755.63
congenital dislocation (*see also* Dislocation, hip, congenital) 754.30
mastoid process 756.0
middle ear, except ossicles 744.03
ossicles 744.04
newborn (not malformation) 764.9
ossicles, ear 744.04
spine 756.10
toe 755.66
Male type pelvis 755.69
with disproportion (fetopelvic) 653.2
affecting fetus or newborn 763.1
causing obstructed labor 660.1
affecting fetus or newborn 763.1
Malformation (congenital) - *see also*
Anomaly
bone 756.9
bursa 756.9
Chiari
type I 348.4
type II (*see also* Spina bifida) 741.0
type III 742.0
type IV 742.2
circulatory system NEC 747.9
specified type NEC 747.89
cochlea 744.05
digestive system NEC 751.9
lower 751.5
specified type NEC 751.8
upper 750.9
eye 743.9
gum 750.9
heart NEC 746.9
specified type NEC 746.89
valve 746.9
internal ear 744.05
joint NEC 755.9
specified type NEC 755.8
Mondini's (congenital) (malformation,
cochlea) 744.05
muscle 756.9
nervous system (central) 742.9
pelvic organs or tissues
in pregnancy or childbirth 654.9
affecting fetus or newborn
763.89
causing obstructed labor 660.2
affecting fetus or newborn 763.1
placenta (*see also* Placenta, abnormal)
656.7
respiratory organs 748.9
specified type NEC 748.8
Rieger's 743.44
sense organs NEC 742.9
specified type NEC 742.8
skin 757.9
specified type NEC 757.8
spinal cord 742.9

Malformation (*Continued*)
teeth, tooth NEC 520.9
tendon 756.9
throat 750.9
umbilical cord (complicating delivery)
663.9
affecting fetus or newborn 762.6
umbilicus 759.9
urinary system NEC 753.9
specified type NEC 753.8
Malfunction - *see also* Dysfunction
arterial graft 996.1
cardiac pacemaker 996.01
catheter device - *see* Complications,
mechanical, catheter
colostomy 569.62
cystostomy 997.5
device, implant, or graft NEC - *see*
Complications, mechanical
enteric stoma 569.62
enterostomy 569.62
gastroenteric 536.2
gastrostomy 536.42
nephrostomy 997.5
pacemaker - *see* Complications, mechanical, pacemaker
prosthetic device, internal - *see* Complications, mechanical
tracheostomy 519.02
vascular graft or shunt 996.1
Malgaigne's fracture (closed) 808.43
open 808.53
Malherbe's
calcifying epithelioma (M8110/0) - *see*
Neoplasm, skin, benign
tumor (M8110/0) - *see* Neoplasm, skin,
benign
Malibu disease 919.8
infected 919.9
Malignancy (M8000/3) - *see* Neoplasm,
by site, malignant
Malignant - *see* condition
Malingerer, malingering V65.2
Mallet, finger (acquired) 736.1
congenital 755.59
late effect of rickets 268.1
Malleus 024
Mallory's bodies 034.1
Mallory-Weiss syndrome 530.7
Malnutrition (calorie) 263.9
complicating pregnancy 648.9
degree
first 263.1
second 263.0
third 262
mild 263.1
moderate 263.0
severe 261
protein-calorie 262
fetus 764.2
"light-for-dates" 764.1
following gastrointestinal surgery 579.3
intrauterine or fetal 764.2
fetus or infant "light-for-dates" 764.1
lack of care, or neglect (child) (infant)
995.52
adult 995.84
malignant 260
mild 263.1
moderate 263.0
protein 260
protein-calorie 263.9
severe 262
specified type NEC 263.8

Malnutrition (*Continued*)
severe 261
protein-calorie NEC 262
Malocclusion (teeth) 524.4
due to
abnormal swallowing 524.5
accessory teeth (causing crowding)
524.3
dentofacial abnormality NEC 524.8
impacted teeth (causing crowding)
524.3
missing teeth 524.3
mouth breathing 524.5
supernumerary teeth (causing
crowding) 524.3
thumb sucking 524.5
tongue, lip, or finger habits 524.5
temporomandibular (joint) 524.69
Malposition
cardiac apex (congenital) 746.87
cervix - *see* Malposition, uterus
congenital
adrenal (gland) 759.1
alimentary tract 751.8
lower 751.5
upper 750.8
aorta 747.21
appendix 751.5
arterial trunk 747.29
artery (peripheral) NEC (*see also*
Malposition, congenital, peripheral vascular system) 747.60
coronary 746.85
pulmonary 747.3
auditory canal 744.29
causing impairment of hearing
744.02
auricle (ear) 744.29
causing impairment of hearing
744.02
cervical 744.43
biliary duct or passage 751.69
bladder (mucosa) 753.8
exteriorized or extroverted 753.5
brachial plexus 742.8
brain tissue 742.4
breast 757.6
bronchus 748.3
cardiac apex 746.87
cecum 751.5
clavicle 755.51
colon 751.5
digestive organ or tract NEC 751.8
lower 751.5
upper 750.8
ear (auricle) (external) 744.29
ossicles 744.04
endocrine (gland) NEC 759.2
epiglottis 748.3
eustachian tube 744.24
eye 743.8
facial features 744.89
fallopian tube 752.19
finger(s) 755.59
supernumerary 755.01
foot 755.67
gallbladder 751.69
gastrointestinal tract 751.8
genitalia, genital organ(s) or tract
female 752.8
external 752.49
internal NEC 752.8
male 752.8
penis 752.69

Malposition *(Continued)*
congenital *(Continued)*
glottis 748.3
hand 755.59
heart 746.87
dextrocardia 746.87
with complete transposition of viscera 759.3
hepatic duct 751.69
hip (joint) *(see also* Dislocation, hip, congenital) 754.30
intestine (large) (small) 751.5
with anomalous adhesions, fixation, or malrotation 751.4
joint NEC 755.8
kidney 753.3
larynx 748.3
limb 755.8
lower 755.69
upper 755.59
liver 751.69
lung (lobe) 748.69
nail(s) 757.5
nerve 742.8
nervous system NEC 742.8
nose, nasal (septum) 748.1
organ or site NEC - *see* Anomaly, specified type NEC, by site
ovary 752.0
pancreas 751.7
parathyroid (gland) 759.2
patella 755.64
peripheral vascular system 747.60
gastrointestinal 747.61
lower limb 747.64
renal 747.62
specified NEC 747.69
spinal 747.82
upper limb 747.63
pituitary (gland) 759.2
respiratory organ or system NEC 748.9
rib (cage) 756.3
supernumerary in cervical region 756.2
scapula 755.59
shoulder 755.59
spinal cord 742.59
spine 756.19
spleen 759.0
sternum 756.3
stomach 750.7
symphysis pubis 755.69
testis (undescended)752.51
thymus (gland) 759.2
thyroid (gland) (tissue) 759.2
cartilage 748.3
toe(s) 755.66
supernumerary 755.02
tongue 750.19
trachea 748.3
uterus 752.3
vein(s) (peripheral) NEC *(see also* Malposition, congenital, peripheral vascular system) 747.60
great 747.49
portal 747.49
pulmonary 747.49
vena cava (inferior) (superior) 747.49
device, implant, or graft - *see* Complications, mechanical
fetus NEC *(see also* Presentation, fetal) 652.9
with successful version 652.1
affecting fetus or newborn 763.1

Malposition *(Continued)*
fetus NEC *(Continued)*
before labor, affecting fetus or newborn 761.7
causing obstructed labor 660.0
in multiple gestation (one fetus or more) 652.6
with locking 660.5
causing obstructed labor 660.0
gallbladder *(see also* Disease, gallbladder) 575.8
gastrointestinal tract 569.89
congenital 751.8
heart *(see also* Malposition, congenital, heart) 746.87
intestine 569.89
congenital 751.5
pelvic organs or tissues
in pregnancy or childbirth 654.4
affecting fetus or newborn 763.89 ◄▥
causing obstructed labor 660.2
affecting fetus or newborn 763.1
placenta - *see* Placenta, previa
stomach 537.89
congenital 750.7
tooth, teeth (with impaction) 524.3
uterus or cervix (acquired) (acute) (adherent) (any degree) (asymptomatic) (postinfectional) (postpartal, old) 621.6
anteflexion or anteversion *(see also* Anteversion, uterus) 621.6
congenital 752.3
flexion 621.6
lateral *(see also* Lateroversion, uterus) 621.6
in pregnancy or childbirth 654.4
affecting fetus or newborn 763.89 ◄▥
causing obstructed labor 660.2
affecting fetus or newborn 763.1
inversion 621.6
lateral (flexion) (version) *(see also* Lateroversion, uterus) 621.6
lateroflexion *(see also* Lateroversion, uterus) 621.6
lateroversion *(see also* Lateroversion, uterus) 621.6
retroflexion or retroversion *(see also* Retroversion, uterus) 621.6
Malposture 729.9
Malpresentation, fetus *(see also* Presentation, fetal) 652.9
Malrotation
cecum 751.4
colon 751.4
intestine 751.4
kidney 753.3
Malta fever *(see also* Brucellosis) 023.9
Maltosuria 271.3
Maltreatment (of)
adult 995.80
emotional 995.82
multiple forms 995.85
neglect (nutritional) 995.84
physical 995.81
psychological 995.82
sexual 995.83
child 995.50
emotional 995.51
multiple forms 995.59
neglect (nutritional) 995.52
psychological 995.51

Maltreatment *(Continued)*
child *(Continued)*
physical 995.54
shaken infant syndrome 995.55
sexual 995.53
spouse 995.80 *(see also* Maltreatment, adult)
Malt workers' lung 495.4
Malum coxae senilis 715.25
Malunion, fracture 733.81
Mammillitis *(see also* Mastitis) 611.0
puerperal, postpartum 675.2
Mammitis *(see also* Mastitis) 611.0
puerperal, postpartum 675.2
Mammoplasia 611.1
Management
contraceptive V25.9
specified type NEC V25.8
procreative V26.9
specified type NEC V26.8
Mangled NEC *(see also* nature and site of injury) 959.9
Mania (monopolar) *(see also* Psychosis, affective) 296.0
alcoholic (acute) (chronic) 291.9
Bell's - *see* Mania, chronic
chronic 296.0
recurrent episode 296.1
single episode 296.0
compulsive 300.3
delirious (acute) 296.0
recurrent episode 296.1
single episode 296.0
epileptic *(see also* Epilepsy) 345.4
hysterical 300.10
inhibited 296.89
puerperal (after delivery) 296.0
recurrent episode 296.1
single episode 296.0
recurrent episode 296.1
senile 290.8
single episode 296.0
stupor 296.89
stuporous 296.89
unproductive 296.89
Manic-depressive insanity, psychosis, reaction, or syndrome *(see also* Psychosis, affective) 296.80
circular (alternating) 296.7
currently
depressed 296.5
episode unspecified 296.7
hypomanic, previously depressed 296.4
manic 296.4
mixed 296.6
depressed (type), depressive 296.2
atypical 296.82
recurrent episode 296.3
single episode 296.2
hypomanic 296.0
recurrent episode 296.1
single episode 296.0
manic 296.0
atypical 296.81
recurrent episode 296.1
single episode 296.0
mixed NEC 296.89
perplexed 296.89
stuporous 296.89
Manifestations, rheumatoid
lungs 714.81
pannus - *see* Arthritis, rheumatoid

Manifestations, rheumatoid (*Continued*)
subcutaneous nodules - *see* Arthritis, rheumatoid
Mankowsky's syndrome (familial dysplastic osteopathy) 731.2
Mannoheptulosuria 271.8
Mannosidosis 271.8
Manson's
disease (schistosomiasis) 120.1
pyosis (pemphigus contagiosus) 684
schistosomiasis 120.1
Mansonellosis 125.5
Manual - *see* condition
Maple bark disease 495.6
Maple bark-strippers' lung 495.6
Maple syrup (urine) disease or syndrome 270.3
Marable's syndrome (celiac artery compression) 447.4
Marasmus 261
brain 331.9
due to malnutrition 261
intestinal 569.89
nutritional 261
senile 797
tuberculous NEC (*see also* Tuberculosis) 011.9
Marble
bones 756.52
skin 782.61
Marburg disease (virus) 078.89
March
foot (closed) 825.20
open 825.30
hemoglobinuria 283.2
Marchand multiple nodular hyperplasia (liver) 571.5
Marchesani (-Weill) syndrome (brachymorphism and ectopia lentis) 759.89
Marchiafava (-Bignami) disease or syndrome 341.8
Marchiafava-Micheli syndrome (paroxysmal nocturnal hemoglobinuria) 283.2
Marcus Gunn's syndrome (jaw-winking syndrome) 742.8
Marfan's
congenital syphilis 090.49
disease 090.49
syndrome (arachnodactyly) 759.82
meaning congenital syphilis 090.49
with luxation of lens 090.49
[379.32]
Marginal
implantation, placenta - *see* Placenta, previa
placenta - *see* Placenta, previa
sinus (hemorrhage) (rupture) 641.2
affecting fetus or newborn 762.1
Marie's
cerebellar ataxia 334.2
syndrome (acromegaly) 253.0
Marie-Bamberger disease or syndrome (hypertrophic) (pulmonary) (secondary) 731.2
idiopathic (acropachyderma) 757.39
primary (acropachyderma) 757.39
Marie-Charcôt-Tooth neuropathic atrophy, muscle 356.1
Marie-Strümpell arthritis or disease (ankylosing spondylitis) 720.0
Marihuana, marijuana
abuse (*see also* Abuse, drugs, nondependent) 305.2

Marihuana, marijuana (*Continued*)
dependence (*see also* Dependence) 304.3
Marion's disease (bladder neck obstruction) 596.0
Marital conflict V61.10
Mark
port wine 757.32
raspberry 757.32
strawberry 757.32
stretch 701.3
tattoo 709.09
Maroteaux-Lamy syndrome (mucopolysaccharidosis VI) 277.5
Marriage license examination V70.3
Marrow (bone)
arrest 284.9
megakaryocytic 287.3
poor function 289.9
Marseilles fever 082.1
Marsh's disease (exophthalmic goiter) 242.0
Marshall's (hidrotic) ectodermal dysplasia 757.31
Marsh fever (*see also* Malaria) 084.6
Martin's disease 715.27
Martin-Albright syndrome (pseudohypoparathyroidism) 275.49
Martorell-Fabre syndrome (pulseless disease) 446.7
Masculinization, female, with adrenal hyperplasia 255.2
Masculinovoblastoma (M8670/0) 220
Masochism 302.83
Masons' lung 502
Mass
abdominal 789.3
anus 787.99
bone 733.90
breast 611.72
cheek 784.2
chest 786.6
cystic - *see* Cyst
ear 388.8
epigastric 789.3
eye 379.92
female genital organ 625.8
gum 784.2
head 784.2
intracranial 784.2
joint 719.60
ankle 719.67
elbow 719.62
foot 719.67
hand 719.64
hip 719.65
knee 719.66
multiple sites 719.69
pelvic region 719.65
shoulder (region) 719.61
specified site NEC 719.68
wrist 719.63
kidney (*see also* Disease, kidney) 593.9
lung 786.6
lymph node 785.6
malignant (M8000/3) - *see* Neoplasm, by site, malignant
mediastinal 786.6
mouth 784.2
muscle (limb) 729.89
neck 784.2
nose or sinus 784.2
palate 784.2
pelvis, pelvic 789.3

Mass (*Continued*)
penis 607.89
perineum 625.8
rectum 787.99
scrotum 608.89
skin 782.2
specified organ NEC - *see* Disease of specified organ or site
splenic 789.2
substernal 786.6
thyroid (*see also* Goiter) 240.9
superficial (localized) 782.2
testes 608.89
throat 784.2
tongue 784.2
umbilicus 789.3
uterus 625.8
vagina 625.8
vulva 625.8
Massive - *see* condition
Mastalgia 611.71
psychogenic 307.89
Mast cell
disease 757.33
systemic (M9741/3) 202.6
leukemia (M9900/3) 207.8
sarcoma (M9742/3) 202.6
tumor (M9740/1) 238.5
malignant (M9740/3) 202.6
Masters-Allen syndrome 620.6
Mastitis (acute) (adolescent) (diffuse) (interstitial) (lobular) (nonpuerperal) (nonsuppurative) (parenchymatous) (phlegmonous) (simple) (subacute) (suppurative) 611.0
chronic (cystic) (fibrocystic) 610.1
cystic 610.1
Schimmelbusch's type 610.1
fibrocystic 610.1
infective 611.0
lactational 675.2
lymphangitis 611.0
neonatal (noninfective) 778.7
infective 771.5
periductal 610.4
plasma cell 610.4
puerperal, postpartum, (interstitial) (nonpurulent) (parenchymatous) 675.2
purulent 675.1
stagnation 676.2
puerperalis 675.2
retromammary 611.0
puerperal, postpartum 675.1
submammary 611.0
puerperal, postpartum 675.1
Mastocytoma (M9740/1) 238.5
malignant (M9740/3) 202.6
Mastocytosis 757.33
malignant (M9741/3) 202.6
systemic (M9741/3) 202.6
Mastodynia 611.71
psychogenic 307.89
Mastoid - *see* condition
Mastoidalgia (*see also* Otalgia) 388.70
Mastoiditis (coalescent) (hemorrhagic) (pneumococcal) (streptococcal) (suppurative) 383.9
acute or subacute 383.00
with
Gradenigo's syndrome 383.02
petrositis 383.02
specified complication NEC 383.02
subperiosteal abscess 383.01

Mastoiditis *(Continued)*
  chronic (necrotic) (recurrent) 383.1
  tuberculous *(see also* Tuberculosis) 015.6
Mastopathy, mastopathia 611.9
  chronica cystica 610.1
  diffuse cystic 610.1
  estrogenic 611.8
  ovarian origin 611.8
Mastoplasia 611.1
Masturbation 307.9
Maternal condition, affecting fetus or
    newborn
  acute yellow atrophy of liver 760.8
  albuminuria 760.1
  anesthesia or analgesia 763.5
  blood loss 762.1
  chorioamnionitis 762.7
  circulatory disease, chronic (conditions
      classifiable to 390-459, 745-747)
      760.3
  congenital heart disease (conditions
      classifiable to 745-746) 760.3
  cortical necrosis of kidney 760.1
  death 761.6
  diabetes mellitus 775.0
    manifest diabetes in the infant 775.1
  disease NEC 760.9
    circulatory system, chronic (condi-
        tions classifiable to 390-459, 745-
        747) 760.3
    genitourinary system (conditions
        classifiable to 580-599) 760.1
    respiratory (conditions classifiable to
        490-519, 748) 760.3
  eclampsia 760.0
  hemorrhage NEC 762.1
  hepatitis acute, malignant, or subacute
      760.8
  hyperemesis (gravidarum) 761.8
  hypertension (arising during preg-
      nancy) (conditions classifiable to
      642) 760.0
  infection
    disease classifiable to 001-136 760.2
    genital tract NEC 760.8
    urinary tract 760.1
  influenza 760.2
    manifest influenza in the infant 771.2
  injury (conditions classifiable to 800-
      996) 760.5
  malaria 760.2
    manifest malaria in infant or fetus
        771.2
  malnutrition 760.4
  necrosis of liver 760.8
  nephritis (conditions classifiable to
      580-583) 760.1
  nephrosis (conditions classifiable to
      581) 760.1
  noxious substance transmitted via
      breast milk or placenta 760.70
    alcohol 760.71
    anti-infective agents 760.74
    cocaine 760.75
    "crack" 760.75
    diethylstilbestrol [DES] 760.76
    hallucinogenic agents 760.73
    medicinal agents NEC 760.79
    narcotics 760.72
    obstetric anesthetic or analgesic drug
        760.72
    specified agent NEC 760.79
  nutritional disorder (conditions classifi-
      able to 260-269) 760.4

Maternal condition, affecting fetus or
    newborn *(Continued)*
  operation unrelated to current delivery
      760.6
  pre-eclampsia 760.0
  pyelitis or pyelonephritis, arising dur-
      ing pregnancy (conditions classifi-
      able to 590) 760.1
  renal disease or failure 760.1
  respiratory disease, chronic (conditions
      classifiable to 490-519, 748) 760.3
  rheumatic heart disease (chronic) (con-
      ditions classifiable to 393-398)
      760.3
  rubella (conditions classifiable to 056)
      760.2
    manifest rubella in the infant or fe-
        tus 771.0
  surgery unrelated to current delivery
      760.6
    to uterus or pelvic organs 763.89 ◄▦▦
  syphilis (conditions classifiable to 090-
      097) 760.2
    manifest syphilis in the infant or fe-
        tus 090.0
  thrombophlebitis 760.3
  toxemia (of pregnancy) 760.0
    pre-eclamptic 760.0
  toxoplasmosis (conditions classifiable
      to 130) 760.2
    manifest toxoplasmosis in the infant
        or fetus 771.2
  transmission of chemical substance
      through the placenta 760.70
    alcohol 760.71
    anti-infective 760.74
    cocaine 760.75
    "crack" 760.75
    diethylstilbestrol [DES] 760.76
    hallucinogenic agents 760.73
    narcotics 760.72
    specified substance NEC 760.79
  uremia 760.1
  urinary tract conditions (conditions
      classifiable to 580-599) 760.1
  vomiting (pernicious) (persistent) (vi-
      cious) 761.8
Maternity - *see* Delivery
Matheiu's disease (leptospiral jaundice)
    100.0
Mauclaire's disease or osteochondrosis
    732.3
Maxcy's disease 081.0
Maxilla, maxillary - *see* condition
May (-Hegglin) anomaly or syndrome
    288.2
Mayaro fever 066.3
Mazoplasia 610.8
MBD (minimal brain dysfunction), child
    (see also Hyperkinesia) 314.9
McArdle (-Schmid-Pearson) disease or
    syndrome (glycogenosis V) 271.0
McCune-Albright syndrome (osteitis fi-
    brosa disseminata) 756.59
MCLS (mucocutaneous lymph node syn-
    drome) 446.1
McQuarrie's syndrome (idiopathic famil-
    ial hypoglycemia) 251.2
Measles (black) (hemorrhagic) (sup-
    pressed) 055.9
  with
    encephalitis 055.0
    keratitis 055.71
    keratoconjunctivitis 055.71

Measles *(Continued)*
  with *(Continued)*
    otitis media 055.2
    pneumonia 055.1
  complication 055.8
    specified type NEC 055.79
  encephalitis 055.0
  French 056.9
  German 056.9
  keratitis 055.71
  keratoconjunctivitis 055.71
  liberty 056.9
  otitis media 055.2
  pneumonia 055.1
  specified complications NEC 055.79
  vaccination, prophylactic (against)
      V04.2
Meatitis, urethral *(see also* Urethritis)
    597.89
Meat poisoning - *see* Poisoning, food
Meatus, meatal - *see* condition
Meat-wrappers' asthma 506.9
Meckel's
  diverticulitis 751.0
  diverticulum (displaced) (hyper-
      trophic) 751.0
Meconium
  aspiration 770.1
  delayed passage in newborn 777.1
  ileus 777.1
    due to cystic fibrosis 277.01
  in liquor 792.3
    noted during delivery 656.8 ◄▦▦
  insufflation 770.1
  obstruction
    fetus or newborn 777.1
      in mucoviscidosis 277.01
  passage of 792.3
    noted during delivery - omit
        code
  peritonitis 777.6
  plug syndrome (newborn) NEC 777.1
Median - *see also* condition
  arcuate ligament syndrome 447.4
  bar (prostate) 600
    vesical orifice 600
  rhomboid glossitis 529.2
Mediastinal shift 793.2
Mediastinitis (acute) (chronic) 519.2
  actinomycotic 039.8
  syphilitic 095.8
  tuberculous *(see also* Tuberculosis) 012.8
Mediastinopericarditis *(see also* Pericar-
    ditis) 423.9
  acute 420.90
  chronic 423.8
    rheumatic 393
  rheumatic, chronic 393
Mediastinum, mediastinal - *see* condition
Medical services provided for - *see*
    Health, services provided because
    (of)
Medicine poisoning (by overdose)
    (wrong substance given or taken in
    error) 977.9
  specified drug or substance - *see* Table
      of Drugs and Chemicals
Medin's disease (poliomyelitis) 045.9
Mediterranean
  anemia (with other hemoglobinopathy)
      282.4
  disease or syndrome (hemipathic) 282.4
  fever *(see also* Brucellosis) 023.9
    familial 277.3

Melanoma *(Continued)*
  nodular (M8721/3) - *see* Melanoma, by
      site
  nose, external 172.3
  orbit 190.1
  penis 187.4
  perianal skin 172.5
  perineum 172.5
  pinna 172.2
  popliteal (fossa) (space) 172.7
  prepuce 187.1
  pubes 172.5
  pudendum 184.4
  retina 190.5
  scalp 172.4
  scrotum 187.7
  septum nasal (skin) 172.3
  shoulder 172.6
  skin NEC 172.8
  spindle cell (M8772/3) - *see also* Mela-
      noma, by site
    type A (M8773/3) 190.0
    type B (M8774/3) 190.0
  submammary fold 172.5
  superficial spreading (M8743/3) - *see*
      Melanoma, by site
  temple 172.3
  thigh 172.7
  toe 172.7
  trunk NEC 172.5
  umbilicus 172.5
  upper limb NEC 172.6
  vagina vault 184.0
  vulva 184.4
Melanoplakia 528.9
Melanosarcoma (M8720/3) - *see also* Mel-
    anoma
  epithelioid cell (M8771/3) - *see* Mela-
      noma
Melanosis 709.09
  addisonian (primary adrenal insuffi-
      ciency) 255.4
    tuberculous (*see also* Tuberculosis)
        017.6
  adrenal 255.4
  colon 569.89
  conjunctiva 372.55
    congenital 743.49
  corii degenerativa 757.33
  cornea (presenile) (senile) 371.12
    congenital 743.43
      interfering with vision 743.42
    prenatal 743.43
      interfering with vision 743.42
  eye 372.55
    congenital 743.49
  jute spinners' 709.09
  lenticularis progressiva 757.33
  liver 573.8
  precancerous (M8741/2) - *see also* Neo-
      plasm, skin, in situ
    malignant melanoma in (M8741/3) -
        see Melanoma
  Riehl's 709.09
  sclera 379.19
    congenital 743.47
  suprarenal 255.4
  tar 709.09
  toxic 709.09
Melanuria 791.9
MELAS 758.89
Melasma 709.09
  adrenal (gland) 255.4
  suprarenal (gland) 255.4

Melena 578.1
  due to
    swallowed maternal blood 777.3
    ulcer - *see* Ulcer, by site, with hem-
        orrhage
  newborn 772.4
    due to swallowed maternal blood
        777.3
Meleney's
  gangrene (cutaneous) 686.09
  ulcer (chronic undermining) 686.09
Melioidosis 025
Melitensis, febris 023.0
Melitococcosis 023.0
Melkersson (-Rosenthal) syndrome
    351.8
Mellitus, diabetes - *see* Diabetes
Melorheostosis (bone) (leri) 733.99
Meloschisis 744.83
Melotia 744.29
Membrana
  capsularis lentis posterior 743.39
  epipapillaris 743.57
Membranacea placenta - *see* Placenta,
    abnormal
Membranaceous uterus 621.8
Membrane, membranous - *see also* con-
    dition
  folds, congenital - *see* Web
  Jackson's 751.4
  over face (causing asphyxia), fetus or
      newborn 768.9
  premature rupture - *see* Rupture,
      membranes, premature
  pupillary 364.74
    persistent 743.46
  retained (complicating delivery) (with
      hemorrhage) 666.2
    without hemorrhage 667.1
  secondary (eye) 366.50
  unruptured (causing asphyxia) 768.9
  vitreous humor 379.25
Membranitis, fetal 658.4
  affecting fetus or newborn 762.7
Memory disturbance, loss or lack (*see
    also* Amnesia) 780.9
  mild, following organic brain damage
      310.1
Menadione (vitamin K) deficiency 269.0
Menarche, precocious 259.1
Mendacity, pathologic 301.7
Mende's syndrome (ptosis-epicanthus)
    270.2
Mendelson's syndrome (resulting from a
    procedure) 997.3
  obstetric 668.0
Ménétrier's disease or syndrome (hyper-
    trophic gastritis) 535.2
Ménière's disease, syndrome, or vertigo
    386.00
  cochlear 386.02
  cochleovestibular 386.01
  inactive 386.04
  in remission 386.04
  vestibular 386.03
Meninges, meningeal - *see* condition
Meningioma (M9530/0) - *see also* Neo-
    plasm, meninges, benign
  angioblastic (M9535/0) - *see* Neoplasm,
      meninges, benign
  angiomatous (M9534/0) - *see* Neo-
      plasm, meninges, benign
  endotheliomatous (M9531/0) - *see* Ne-
      oplasm, meninges, benign

Meningioma *(Continued)*
  fibroblastic (M9532/0) - *see* Neoplasm,
      meninges, benign
  fibrous (M9532/0) - *see* Neoplasm, me-
      ninges, benign
  hemangioblastic (M9535/0) - *see* Neo-
      plasm, meninges, benign
  hemangiopericytic (M9536/0) - *see* Ne-
      oplasm, meninges, benign
  malignant (M9530/3) - *see* Neoplasm,
      meninges, malignant
  meningiothelial (M9531/0) - *see* Neo-
      plasm, meninges, benign
  meningotheliomatous (M9531/0) - *see*
      Neoplasm, meninges, benign
  mixed (M9537/0) - *see* Neoplasm, me-
      ninges, benign
  multiple (M9530/1) 237.6
  papillary (M9538/1) 237.6
  psammomatous (M9533/0) - *see* Neo-
      plasm, meninges, benign
  syncytial (M9531/0) - *see* Neoplasm,
      meninges, benign
  transitional (M9537/0) - *see* Neoplasm,
      meninges, benign
Meningiomatosis (diffuse) (M9530/1)
    237.6
Meningism (*see also* Meningismus) 781.6
Meningismus (infectional) (pneumococ-
    cal) 781.6
  due to serum or vaccine 997.09 *[321.8]*
  influenzal NEC 487.8
Meningitis (basal) (basic) (basilar)
    (brain) (cerebral) (cervical) (conges-
    tive) (diffuse) (hemorrhagic) (infan-
    tile) (membranous) (metastatic)
    (nonspecific) (pontine) (progressive)
    (simple) (spinal) (subacute) (sym-
    pathetica) (toxic) 322.9
  abacterial NEC (*see also* Meningitis,
      aseptic) 047.9
  actinomycotic 039.8 *[320.7]*
  adenoviral 049.1
  Aerobacter aerogenes 320.82
  anaerobes (cocci) (gram-negative)
      (gram-positive) (mixed) (NEC)
      320.81
  arbovirus NEC 066.9 *[321.2]*
    specified type NEC 066.8 *[321.2]*
  aseptic (acute) NEC 047.9
    adenovirus 049.1
    Coxsackie virus 047.0
    due to
      adenovirus 049.1
      Coxsackie virus 047.0
      echo virus 047.1
      enterovirus 047.9
      mumps 072.1
      poliovirus (*see also* Poliomyelitis)
          045.2 *[321.2]*
    echo virus 047.1
    herpes (simplex) virus 054.72
      zoster 053.0
    leptospiral 100.81
    lymphocytic choriomeningitis 049.0
    noninfective 322.0
  Bacillus pyocyaneus 320.89
  bacterial NEC 320.9
    anaerobic 320.81
    gram-negative 320.82
      anaerobic 320.81
  Bacteroides (fragilis) (oralis) (melanino-
      genicus) 320.81
  cancerous (M8000/6) 198.4

◀▶ New Code   ⬅▦▦▶ Revised Code

Meningitis (*Continued*)
candidal 112.83
carcinomatous (M8010/6) 198.4
caseous (*see also* Tuberculosis, meninges) 013.0
cerebrospinal (acute) (chronic) (diplococcal) (endemic) (epidemic) (fulminant) (infectious) (malignant) (meningococcal) (sporadic) 036.0
  carrier (suspected) of V02.59
chronic NEC 322.2
clear cerebrospinal fluid NEC 322.0
Clostridium (haemolyticum) (novyi) NEC 320.81
coccidioidomycosis 114.2
Coxsackie virus 047.0
cryptococcal 117.5 [321.0]
diplococcal 036.0
  gram-negative 036.0
  gram-positive 320.1
Diplococcus pneumoniae 320.1
due to
  actinomycosis 039.8 [320.7]
  adenovirus 049.1
  coccidiomycosis 114.2
  enterovirus 047.9
    specified NEC 047.8
  histoplasmosis (*see also* Histoplasmosis) 115.91
  listerosis 027.0 [320.7]
  Lyme disease 088.81 [320.7]
  moniliasis 112.83
  mumps 072.1
  neurosyphilis 094.2
  nonbacterial organisms NEC 321.8
  oidiomycosis 112.83
  poliovirus (*see also* Poliomyelitis) 045.2 [321.2]
  preventive immunization, inoculation, or vaccination 997.09 [321.8]
  sarcoidosis 135 [321.4]
  sporotrichosis 117.1 [321.1]
  syphilis 094.2
    acute 091.81
    congenital 090.42
    secondary 091.81
  trypanosomiasis (*see also* Trypanosomiasis) 086.9 [321.3]
  whooping cough 033.9 [320.7]
E. coli 320.82
ECHO virus 047.1
endothelial-leukocytic, benign, recurrent 047.9
Enterobacter aerogenes 320.82
enteroviral 047.9
  specified type NEC 047.8
enterovirus 047.9
  specified NEC 047.8
eosinophilic 322.1
epidemic NEC 036.0
Escherichia coli (E. coli) 320.82
Eubacterium 320.81
fibrinopurulent NEC 320.9
  specified type NEC 320.89
Friedländer (bacillus) 320.82
fungal NEC 117.9 [321.1]
Fusobacterium 320.81
gonococcal 098.82
gram-negative bacteria NEC 320.82
  anaerobic 320.81
  cocci 036.0
    specified NEC 320.82
gram-negative cocci NEC 036.0

Meningitis (*Continued*)
gram-negative cocci NEC (*Continued*)
  specified NEC 320.82
gram-positive cocci NEC 320.9
H. influenzae 320.0
herpes (simplex) virus 054.72
  zoster 053.0
infectious NEC 320.9
influenzal 320.0
Klebsiella pneumoniae 320.82
late effect - *see* Late, effect, meningitis
leptospiral (aseptic) 100.81
Listerella (monocytogenes) 027.0 [320.7]
Listeria monocytogenes 027.0 [320.7]
lymphocytic (acute) (benign) (serous) 049.0
  choriomeningitis virus 049.0
meningococcal (chronic) 036.0
Mima polymorpha 320.82
Mollaret's 047.9
monilial 112.83
mumps (virus) 072.1
mycotic NEC 117.9 [321.1]
Neisseria 036.0
neurosyphilis 094.2
nonbacterial NEC (*see also* Meningitis, aseptic) 047.9
nonpyogenic NEC 322.0
oidiomycosis 112.83
ossificans 349.2
Peptococcus 320.81
Peptostreptococcus 320.81
pneumococcal 320.1
poliovirus (*see also* Poliomyelitis) 045.2 [321.2]
Propionibacterium 320.81
Proteus morganii 320.82
Pseudomonas (aeruginosa) (pyocyaneus) 320.82
purulent NEC 320.9
  specified organism NEC 320.89
pyogenic NEC 320.9
  specified organism NEC 320.89
Salmonella 003.21
septic NEC 320.9
  specified organism NEC 320.89
serosa circumscripta NEC 322.0
serous NEC (*see also* Meningitis, aseptic) 047.9
  lymphocytic 049.0
  syndrome 348.2
Serratia (marcescens) 320.82
specified organism NEC 320.89
sporadic cerebrospinal 036.0
sporotrichosis 117.1 [321.1]
staphylococcal 320.3
sterile 997.09
streptococcal (acute) 320.2
suppurative 320.9
  specified organism NEC 320.89
syphilitic 094.2
  acute 091.81
  congenital 090.42
  secondary 091.81
torula 117.5 [321.0]
traumatic (complication of injury) 958.8
Treponema (denticola) (macrodenticum) 320.81
trypanosomiasis 086.1 [321.3]
tuberculous (*see also* Tuberculosis, meninges) 013.0
typhoid 002.0 [320.7]

Meningitis (*Continued*)
Veillonella 320.81
Vibrio vulnificus 320.82
viral, virus NEC (*see also* Meningitis, aseptic) 047.9
Wallgren's (*see also* Meningitis, aseptic) 047.9
Meningocele (congenital) (spinal) (*see also* Spina bifida) 741.9
acquired (traumatic) 349.2
cerebral 742.0
cranial 742.0
Meningocerebritis - *see* Meningoencephalitis
Meningococcemia (acute) (chronic) 036.2
Meningococcus, meningococcal (*see also* condition) 036.9
adrenalitis, hemorrhagic 036.3
carditis 036.40
carrier (suspected) of V02.59
cerebrospinal fever 036.0
encephalitis 036.1
endocarditis 036.42
infection NEC 036.9
meningitis (cerebrospinal) 036.0
myocarditis 036.43
optic neuritis 036.81
pericarditis 036.41
septicemia (chronic) 036.2
Meningoencephalitis (*see also* Encephalitis) 323.9
acute NEC 048
bacterial, purulent, pyogenic, or septic - *see* Meningitis
chronic NEC 094.1
diffuse NEC 094.1
diphasic 063.2
due to
  actinomycosis 039.8 [320.7]
  blastomycosis NEC (*see also* Blastomycosis) 116.0 [323.4]
  free-living amebae 136.2
  Listeria monocytogenes 027.0 [320.7]
  Lyme disease 088.81 [320.7]
  mumps 072.2
  Naegleria (amebae) (gruberi) (organisms) 136.2
  rubella 056.01
  sporotrichosis 117.1 [321.1]
  toxoplasmosis (acquired) 130.0
    congenital (active) 771.2 [323.4]
  Trypanosoma 086.1 [323.2]
epidemic 036.0
herpes 054.3
herpetic 054.3
H. influenzae 320.0
infectious (acute) 048
influenzal 320.0
late effect - *see* category 326
Listeria monocytogenes 027.0 [320.7]
lymphocytic (serous) 049.0
mumps 072.2
parasitic NEC 123.9 [323.4]
pneumococcal 320.1
primary ambic 136.2
rubella 056.01
serous 048
  lymphocytic 049.0
specific 094.2
staphylococcal 320.3
streptococcal 320.2
syphilitic 094.2
toxic NEC 989.9 [323.7]

Meningoencephalitis *(Continued)*
  toxic NEC *(Continued)*
    due to
      carbon tetrachloride 987.8
        [323.7]
      hydroxyquinoline derivatives poi-
        soning 961.3 *[323.7]*
      lead 984.9 *[323.7]*
      mercury 985.0 *[323.7]*
      thallium 985.8 *[323.7]*
  toxoplasmosis (acquired) 130.0
  trypanosomic 086.1 *[323.2]*
  tuberculous *(see also* Tuberculosis, me-
    ninges) 013.0
  virus NEC 048
Meningoencephalocele 742.0
  syphilitic 094.89
    congenital 090.49
Meningoencephalomyelitis *(see also* Meningoencephalitis) 323.9
  acute NEC 048
    disseminated (postinfectious) 136.9
      [323.6]
      postimmunization or postvaccina-
        tion 323.5
  due to
    actinomycosis 039.8 *[320.7]*
    torula 117.5 *[323.4]*
    toxoplasma or toxoplasmosis (ac-
      quired) 130.0
      congenital (active) 771.2 *[323.4]*
  late effect - *see* category 326
Meningoencephalomyelopathy *(see also*
  Meningoencephalomyelitis) 349.9
Meningoencephalopathy *(see also* Meningoencephalitis) 348.3
Meningoencephalopoliomyelitis *(see also*
  Poliomyelitis, bulbar) 045.0
  late effect 138
Meningomyelitis *(see also* Meningoencephalitis) 323.9
  blastomycotic NEC *(see also* Blastomy-
    cosis) 116.0 *[323.4]*
  due to
    actinomycosis 039.8 *[320.7]*
    blastomycosis *(see also* Blastomy-
      cosis) 116.0 *[323.4]*
    Meningococcus 036.0
    sporotrichosis 117.1 *[323.4]*
    torula 117.5 *[323.4]*
  late effect - *see* category 326
  lethargic 049.8
  meningococcal 036.0
  syphilitic 094.2
  tuberculous *(see also* Tuberculosis, me-
    ninges) 013.0
Meningomyelocele *(see also* Spina bifida)
  741.9
  syphilitic 094.89
Meningomyeloneuritis - *see* Meningoencephalitis
Meningoradiculitis - *see* Meningitis
Meningovascular - *see* condition
Meniscocytosis 282.60
Menkes' syndrome - *see* Syndrome,
  Menkes'
Menolipsis 626.0
Menometrorrhagia 626.2
Menopause, menopausal (symptoms)
  (syndrome) 627.2
  arthritis (any site) NEC 716.3
  artificial 627.4
  bleeding 627.0
  crisis 627.2

Menopause, menopausal *(Continued)*
  depression *(see also* Psychosis, affec-
    tive) 296.2
    agitated 296.2
      recurrent episode 296.3
      single episode 296.2
    psychotic 296.2
      recurrent episode 296.3
      single episode 296.2
    recurrent episode 296.3
    single episode 296.2
    melancholia *(see also* Psychosis, affec-
      tive) 296.2
      recurrent episode 296.3
      single episode 296.2
  paranoid state 297.2
  paraphrenia 297.2
  postsurgical 627.4
  premature 256.3
    postirradiation 256.2
    postsurgical 256.2
  psychoneurosis 627.2
  psychosis NEC 298.8
  surgical 627.4
  toxic polyarthritis NEC 716.39
Menorrhagia (primary) 626.2
  climacteric 627.0
  menopausal 627.0
  postclimacteric 627.1
  postmenopausal 627.1
  preclimacteric 627.0
  premenopausal 627.0
  puberty (menses retained) 626.3
Menorrhalgia 625.3
Menoschesis 626.8
Menostaxis 626.2
Menses, retention 626.8
Menstrual - *see also* Menstruation
  cycle, irregular 626.4
  disorders NEC 626.9
  extraction V25.3
  fluid, retained 626.8
  molimen 625.4
  period, normal V65.5
  regulation V25.3
Menstruation
  absent 626.0
  anovulatory 628.0
  delayed 626.8
  difficult 625.3
  disorder 626.9
    psychogenic 306.52
    specified NEC 626.8
  during pregnancy 640.8
  excessive 626.2
  frequent 626.2
  infrequent 626.1
  irregular 626.4
  latent 626.8
  membranous 626.8
  painful (primary) (secondary) 625.3
    psychogenic 306.52
  passage of clots 626.2
  precocious 626.8
  protracted 626.8
  retained 626.8
  retrograde 626.8
  scanty 626.1
  suppression 626.8
  vicarious (nasal) 625.8
Mentagra *(see also* Sycosis) 704.8
Mental - *see also* condition
  deficiency *(see also* Retardation, mental)
    319

Mental *(Continued)*
  deterioration *(see also* Psychosis) 298.9
  disorder *(see also* Disorder, mental)
    300.9
  exhaustion 300.5
  insufficiency (congenital) *(see also* Re-
    tardation, mental) 319
  observation without need for further
    medical care NEC V71.09
  retardation *(see also* Retardation, men-
    tal) 319
  subnormality *(see also* Retardation,
    mental) 319
    mild 317
    moderate 318.0
    profound 318.2
    severe 318.1
  upset *(see also* Disorder, mental) 300.9
Meralgia paresthetica 355.1
Mercurial - *see* condition
Mercurialism NEC 985.0
Merergasia 300.9
MERFF 758.89
Merocele *(see also* Hernia, femoral) 553.00
Meromelia 755.4
  lower limb 755.30
    intercalary 755.32
      femur 755.34
        tibiofibular (complete) (incom-
          plete) 755.33
      fibula 755.37
      metatarsal(s) 755.38
      tarsal(s) 755.38
      tibia 755.36
      tibiofibular 755.35
    terminal (complete) (partial) (trans-
      verse) 755.31
      longitudinal 755.32
        metatarsal(s) 755.38
        phalange(s) 755.39
        tarsal(s) 755.38
      transverse 755.31
  upper limb 755.20
    intercalary 755.22
      carpal(s) 755.28
      humeral 755.24
        radioulnar (complete) (incom-
          plete) 755.23
      metacarpal(s) 755.28
      phalange(s) 755.29
      radial 755.26
      radioulnar 755.25
      ulnar 755.27
    terminal (complete) (partial) (trans-
      verse) 755.21
      longitudinal 755.22
        carpal(s) 755.28
        metacarpal(s) 755.28
        phalange(s) 755.29
    transverse 755.21
Merosmia 781.1
Merycism - *see also* Vomiting
  psychogenic 307.53
Merzbacher-Pelizaeus disease 330.0
Mesaortitis - *see* Aortitis
Mesarteritis - *see* Arteritis
Mesencephalitis *(see also* Encephalitis)
  323.9
  late effect - *see* category 326
Mesenchymoma (M8990/1) - *see also* Ne-
  oplasm, connective tissue, uncertain
  behavior
  benign (M8990/0) - *see* Neoplasm, con-
    nective tissue, benign

◀▶ **New Code**   ◀▥ ▥▶ **Revised Code**

Mesenchymoma *(Continued)*
malignant (M8990/3) - *see* Neoplasm, connective tissue, malignant
Mesentery, mesenteric - *see* condition
Mesiodens, mesiodentes 520.1
causing crowding 524.3
Mesio-occlusion 524.2
Mesocardia (with asplenia) 746.87
Mesocolon - *see* condition
Mesonephroma (malignant) (M9110/3) - *see also* Neoplasm, by site, malignant
benign (M9110/0) - *see* Neoplasm, by site, benign
Mesophlebitis - *see* Phlebitis
Mesostromal dysgenesis 743.51
Mesothelioma (malignant) (M9050/3) - *see also* Neoplasm, by site, malignant
benign (M9050/0) - *see* Neoplasm, by site, benign
biphasic type (M9053/3) - *see also* Neoplasm, by site, malignant
benign (M9053/0) - *see* Neoplasm, by site, benign
epithelioid (M9052/3) - *see also* Neoplasm, by site, malignant
benign (M9052/0) - *see* Neoplasm, by site, benign
fibrous (M9051/3) - *see also* Neoplasm, by site, malignant
benign (M9051/0) - *see* Neoplasm, by site, benign
Metabolism disorder 277.9
specified type NEC 277.8
Metagonimiasis 121.5
Metagonimus infestation (small intestine) 121.5
Metal
pigmentation (skin) 709.00
polishers' disease 502
Metalliferous miners' lung 503
Metamorphopsia 368.14
Metaplasia
bone, in skin 709.3
breast 611.8
cervix - omit code
endometrium (squamous) 621.8
intestinal, of gastric mucosa 537.89
kidney (pelvis) (squamous) (*see also* Disease, renal) 593.89
myelogenous 289.8
myeloid (agnogenic) (megakaryocytic) 289.8
spleen 289.59
squamous cell
amnion 658.8
bladder 596.8
cervix - *see* condition
trachea 519.1
tracheobronchial tree 519.1
uterus 621.8
cervix - *see* condition
Metastasis, metastatic
abscess - *see* Abscess
calcification 275.40
cancer, neoplasm, or disease
from specified site (M8000/3) - *see* Neoplasm, by site, malignant
to specified site (M8000/6) - *see* Neoplasm, by site, secondary
deposits (in) (M8000/6) - *see* Neoplasm, by site, secondary
pneumonia 038.8 *[484.8]*

Metastasis, metastatic *(Continued)*
spread (to) (M8000/6) - *see* Neoplasm, by site, secondary
Metatarsalgia 726.70
anterior 355.6
due to Freiberg's disease 732.5
Morton's 355.6
Metatarsus, metatarsal - *see also* condition
abductus varus (congenital) 754.53
adductus valgus (congenital) 754.60
primus varus 754.52
valgus (adductus) (congenital) 754.60
varus (abductus) (congenital) 754.53
primus 754.52
Methemoglobinemia 289.7
acquired (with sulfhemoglobinemia) 289.7
congenital 289.7
enzymatic 289.7
Hb-M disease 289.7
hereditary 289.7
toxic 289.7
Methemoglobinuria (*see also* Hemoglobinuria) 791.2
Methioninemia 270.4
Metritis (catarrhal) (septic) (suppurative) (*see also* endometritis) 615.9
blennorrhagic 098.16
chronic or duration of 2 months or over 098.36
cervical (*see also* Cervicitis) 616.0
gonococcal 098.16
chronic or duration of 2 months or over 098.36
hemorrhagic 626.8
puerperal, postpartum, childbirth 670
tuberculous (*see also* Tuberculosis) 016.7
Metropathia hemorrhagica 626.8
Metroperitonitis (*see also* Peritonitis, pelvic, female) 614.5
Metrorrhagia 626.6
arising during pregnancy - *see* Hemorrhage, pregnancy
postpartum NEC 666.2
primary 626.6
psychogenic 306.59
puerperal 666.2
Metrorrhexis - *see* Rupture, uterus
Metrosalpingitis (*see also* Salpingo-oophoritis) 614.2
Metrostaxis 626.6
Metrovaginitis (*see also* Endometritis) 615.9
gonococcal (acute) 098.16
chronic or duration of 2 months or over 098.36
Mexican fever - *see* Typhus, Mexican
Meyenburg-Altherr-Uehlinger syndrome 733.99
Meyer-Schwickerath and Weyers syndrome (dysplasia oculodentodigitalis) 759.89
Meynert's amentia (nonalcoholic) 294.0
alcoholic 291.1
Mibelli's disease 757.39
Mice, joint (*see also* Loose, body, joint) 718.1
knee 717.6
Micheli-Rietti syndrome (thalassemia minor) 282.4
Michotte's syndrome 721.5
Micrencephalon, micrencephaly 742.1

Microaneurysm, retina 362.14
diabetic 250.5 *[362.01]*
Microangiopathy 443.9
diabetic (peripheral) 250.7 *[443.81]*
retinal 250.5 *[362.01]*
peripheral 443.9
diabetic 250.7 *[443.81]*
retinal 362.18
diabetic 250.5 *[362.01]*
thrombotic 446.6
Moschcowitz's (thrombotic thrombocytopenic purpura) 446.6
Microcephalus, microcephalic, microcephaly 742.1
due to toxoplasmosis (congenital) 771.2
Microcheilia 744.82
Microcolon (congenital) 751.5
Microcornea (congenital) 743.41
Microcytic - *see* condition
Microdontia 520.2
Microdrepanocytosis (thalassemia-Hb-S disease) 282.4
Microembolism, retina 362.33
Microencephalon 742.1
Microfilaria streptocerca infestation 125.3
Microgastria (congenital) 750.7
Microgenia 524.06
Microgenitalia (congenital) 752.8
penis 752.64
Microglioma (M9710/3)
specified site - *see* Neoplasm, by site, malignant
unspecified site 191.9
Microglossia (congenital) 750.16
Micrognathia, micrognathism (congenital) 524.00
mandibular 524.04
alveolar 524.74
maxillary 524.03
alveolar 524.73
Microgyria (congenital) 742.2
Microinfarct, heart (*see also* Insufficiency, coronary) 411.89
Microlithiasis, alveolar, pulmonary 516.2
Micromyelia (congenital) 742.59
Micropenis 752.64
Microphakia (congenital) 743.36
Microphthalmia (congenital) (*see also* Microphthalmos) 743.10
Microphthalmos (congenital) 743.10
associated with eye and adnexal anomalies NEC 743.12
due to toxoplasmosis (congenital) 771.2
isolated 743.11
simple 743.11
syndrome 759.89
Micropsia 368.14
Microsporidiosis 136.8
Microsporosis (*see also* Dermatophytosis) 110.9
nigra 111.1
Microsporum furfur infestation 111.0
Microstomia (congenital) 744.84
Microthelia 757.6
Microthromboembolism - *see* Embolism
Microtia (congenital) (external ear) 744.23
Microtropia 378.34
Micturition
disorder NEC 788.69
psychogenic 306.53
frequency 788.41

Micturition (*Continued*)
　frequency (*Continued*)
　　psychogenic 306.53
　　nocturnal 788.43
　　painful 788.1
　　psychogenic 306.53
Middle
　ear - *see* condition
　lobe (right) syndrome 518.0
Midplane - *see* condition
Miescher's disease 709.3
　cheilitis 351.8
　granulomatosis disciformis 709.3
Miescher-Leder syndrome or granulom-
　　atosis 709.3
Mieten's syndrome 759.89
Migraine (idiopathic) 346.9
　with aura 346.0
　abdominal (syndrome) 346.2
　allergic (histamine) 346.2
　atypical 346.1
　basilar 346.2
　classical 346.0
　common 346.1
　hemiplegic 346.8
　lower-half 346.2
　menstrual 625.4
　ophthalmic 346.8
　ophthalmoplegic 346.8
　retinal 346.2
　variant 346.2
Migrant, social V60.0
Migratory, migrating - *see also* condition
　person V60.0
　testis, congenital 752.52
Mikulicz's disease or syndrome (dry-
　　ness of mouth, absent or decreased
　　lacrimation) 527.1
Milian atrophia blanche 701.3
Miliaria (crystallina) (rubra) (tropicalis)
　　705.1
　apocrine 705.82
Miliary - *see* condition
Milium (*see also* Cyst, sebaceous) 706.2
　colloid 709.3
　eyelid 374.84
Milk
　crust 690.11
　excess secretion 676.6
　fever, female 672
　poisoning 988.8
　retention 676.2
　sickness 988.8
　spots 423.1
Milkers' nodes 051.1
Milk-leg (deep vessels) 671.4
　complicating pregnancy 671.3
　nonpuerperal 451.19
　puerperal, postpartum, childbirth
　　671.4
Milkman (-Looser) disease or syndrome
　　(osteomalacia with pseudofractures)
　　268.2
Milky urine (*see also* Chyluria) 791.1
Millar's asthma (laryngismus stridulus)
　　478.75
Millard-Gubler paralysis or syndrome
　　344.89
Millard-Gubler-Foville paralysis 344.89
Miller's disease (osteomalacia) 268.2
Miller Fisher's syndrome 357.0
Milles' syndrome (encephalocutaneous
　　angiomatosis) 759.6
Mills' disease 335.29

Millstone makers' asthma or lung 502
Milroy's disease (chronic hereditary
　　edema) 757.0
Miners' - *see also* condition
　asthma 500
　elbow 727.2
　knee 727.2
　lung 500
　nystagmus 300.89
　phthisis (*see also* Tuberculosis) 011.4
　tuberculosis (*see also* Tuberculosis)
　　011.4
Minkowski-Chauffard syndrome (*see
　　also* Spherocytosis) 282.0
Minor - *see* condition
Minor's disease 336.1
Minot's disease (hemorrhagic disease,
　　newborn) 776.0
Minot-von Willebrand (-Jurgens) disease
　　or syndrome (angiohemophilia)
　　286.4
Minus (and plus) hand (intrinsic) 736.09
Miosis (persistent) (pupil) 379.42
Mirizzi's syndrome (hepatic duct steno-
　　sis) (*see also* Obstruction, biliary)
　　576.2
　with calculus, cholelithiasis, or stones -
　　see Choledocholithiasis
Mirror writing 315.09
　secondary to organic lesion 784.69
Misadventure (prophylactic) (therapeu-
　　tic) (*see also* Complications) 999.9
　administration of insulin 962.3
　infusion - *see* Complications, infusion
　local applications (of fomentations,
　　plasters, etc.) 999.9
　　burn or scald - *see* Burn, by site
　medical care (early) (late) NEC 999.9
　　adverse effect of drugs or chemicals
　　　- *see* Table of Drugs and Chemi-
　　　cals
　　burn or scald - *see* Burn, by site
　radiation NEC 990
　radiotherapy NEC 990
　surgical procedure (early) (late) - *see*
　　Complications, surgical procedure
　transfusion - *see* Complications, trans-
　　fusion
　vaccination or other immunological
　　procedure - *see* Complications,
　　vaccination
Misanthropy 301.7
Miscarriage - *see* Abortion, spontaneous
Mischief, malicious, child (*see also* Dis-
　　turbance, conduct) 312.0
Mismanagement, feeding 783.3
Misplaced, misplacement
　kidney (*see also* Disease, renal) 593.0
　　congenital 753.3
　organ or site, congenital NEC - *see*
　　Malposition, congenital
Missed
　abortion 632
　delivery (at or near term) 656.4
　labor (at or near term) 656.4
Missing - *see also* Absence
　teeth (acquired) 525.1
　　congenital (*see also* Anodontia)
　　　520.0
　vertebrae (congenital) 756.13
Misuse of drugs NEC (*see also* Abuse,
　　drug, nondependent) 305.9
Mitchell's disease (erythromelalgia)
　　443.89

Mite(s)
　diarrhea 133.8
　grain (itch) 133.8
　hair follicle (itch) 133.8
　in sputum 133.8
Mitral - *see* condition
Mittelschmerz 625.2
Mixed - *see* condition
Mljet disease (mal de Meleda) 757.39
Mobile, mobility
　cecum 751.4
　coccyx 733.99
　excessive - *see* Hypermobility
　gallbladder 751.69
　kidney 593.0
　　congenital 753.3
　organ or site, congenital NEC - *see*
　　Malposition, congenital
　spleen 289.59
Mobitz heart block (atrioventricular)
　　426.10
　type I (Wenckebach's) 426.13
　type II 426.12
Möbius'
　disease 346.8
　syndrome
　　congenital oculofacial paralysis 352.6
　　ophthalmoplegic migraine 346.8
Moeller (-Barlow) disease (infantile
　　scurvy) 267
　glossitis 529.4
Mohr's syndrome (types I and II) 759.89
Mola destruens (M9100/1) 236.1
Molarization, premolars 520.2
Molar pregnancy 631
　hydatidiform (delivered) (undelivered)
　　630
Mold(s) in vitreous 117.9
Molding, head (during birth) 767.3
Mole (pigmented) (M8720/0) - *see also*
　　Neoplasm, skin, benign
　blood 631
　Breus' 631
　cancerous (M8720/3) - *see* Melanoma
　carneous 631
　destructive (M9100/1) 236.1
　ectopic - *see* Pregnancy, ectopic
　fleshy 631
　hemorrhagic 631
　hydatid, hydatidiform (benign) (com-
　　plicating pregnancy) (delivered)
　　(undelivered) (*see also* Hydatidi-
　　form mole) 630
　　invasive (M9100/1) 236.1
　　malignant (M9100/1) 236.1
　　previous, affecting management of
　　　pregnancy V23.1
　invasive (hydatidiform) (M9100/1)
　　236.1
　malignant
　　meaning
　　　malignant hydatidiform mole
　　　　(9100/1) 236.1
　　　melanoma (M8720/3) - *see* Mela-
　　　　noma
　nonpigmented (M8730/0) - *see* Neo-
　　plasm, skin, benign
　pregnancy NEC 631
　skin (M8720/0) - *see* Neoplasm, skin,
　　benign
　tubal - *see* Pregnancy, tubal
　vesicular (*see also* Hydatidiform mole)
　　630
Molimen, molimina (menstrual) 625.4

Mollaret's meningitis 047.9
Mollities (cerebellar) (cerebral) 437.8
  ossium 268.2
Molluscum
  contagiosum 078.0
  epitheliale 078.0
  fibrosum (M8851/0) - *see* Lipoma, by
    site
  pendulum (M8851/0) - *see* Lipoma, by
    site
Mönckeberg's arteriosclerosis, degener-
  ation, disease, or sclerosis (*see also*
  Arteriosclerosis, extremities) 440.20
Monday fever 504
Monday morning dyspnea or asthma
  504
Mondini's malformation (cochlea) 744.05
Mondor's disease (thrombophlebitis of
  breast) 451.89
Mongolian, mongolianism, mongolism,
  mongoloid 758.0
  spot 757.33
Monilethrix (congenital) 757.4
Monilia infestation - *see* Candidiasis
Moniliasis - *see also* Candidiasis
  neonatal 771.7
  vulvovaginitis 112.1
Monoarthritis 716.60
  ankle 716.67
  arm 716.62
    lower (and wrist) 716.63
    upper (and elbow) 716.62
  foot (and ankle) 716.67
  forearm (and wrist) 716.63
  hand 716.64
  leg 716.66
    lower 716.66
    upper 716.65
  pelvic region (hip) (thigh) 716.65
  shoulder (region) 716.61
  specified site NEC 716.68
Monoblastic - *see* condition
Monochromatism (cone) (rod) 368.54
Monocytic - *see* condition
Monocytosis (symptomatic) 288.8
Monofixation syndrome 378.34
Monomania (*see also* Psychosis) 298.9
Mononeuritis 355.9
  cranial nerve - *see* Disorder, nerve, cra-
    nial
  femoral nerve 355.2
  lateral
    cutaneous nerve of thigh 355.1
    popliteal nerve 355.3
  lower limb 355.8
    specified nerve NEC 355.79
  medial popliteal nerve 355.4
  median nerve 354.1
  multiplex 354.5
  plantar nerve 355.6
  posterior tibial nerve 355.5
  radial nerve 354.3
  sciatic nerve 355.0
  ulnar nerve 354.2
  upper limb 354.9
    specified nerve NEC 354.8
  vestibular 388.5
Mononeuropathy (*see also* Mononeuritis)
  355.9
  diabetic NEC 250.6 *[355.9]*
    lower limb 250.6 *[355.8]*
    upper limb 250.6 *[354.9]*
  iliohypogastric nerve 355.79
  ilioinguinal nerve 355.79

Mononeuropathy (*Continued*)
  obturator nerve 355.79
  saphenous nerve 355.79
Mononucleosis, infectious 075
  with hepatitis 075 *[573.1]*
Monoplegia 344.5
  brain (current episode) (*see also* Paraly-
    sis, brain) 437.8
    fetus or newborn 767.8
  cerebral (current episode) (*see also* Pa-
    ralysis, brain) 437.8
  congenital or infantile (cerebral) (spas-
    tic) (spinal) 343.3
  embolic (current) (*see also* Embolism,
    brain) 434.1
    late effect - *see* Late effect(s) (of)
      cerebrovascular disease
  infantile (cerebral) (spastic) (spinal) 343.3
  lower limb 344.30
    affecting
      dominant side 344.31
      nondominant side 344.32
    due to late effect of cerebrovascular
      accident - *see* Late effect(s) (of)
      cerebrovascular accident ◄
  newborn 767.8
  psychogenic 306.0
    specified as conversion reaction
      300.11
  thrombotic (current) (*see also* Thrombo-
    sis, brain) 434.0
    late effect - *see* Late effect(s) (of)
      cerebrovascular disease
  transient 781.4
  upper limb 344.40
    affecting
      dominant side 344.41
      nondominant side 344.42
    due to late effect of cerebrovascular
      accident - *see* Late effect(s) (of)
      cerebrovascular accident ◄
Monorchism, monorchidism 752.8
Monteggia's fracture (closed) 813.03
  open 813.13
Mood swings
  brief compensatory 296.99
  rebound 296.99
Moore's syndrome (*see also* Epilepsy) 345.5
Mooren's ulcer (cornea) 370.07
Mooser-Neill reaction 081.0
Mooser bodies 081.0
Moral
  deficiency 301.7
  imbecility 301.7
Morax-Axenfeld conjunctivitis 372.03
Morbilli (*see also* Measles) 055.9
Morbus
  anglicus, anglorum 268.0
  Beigel 111.2
  caducus (*see also* Epilepsy) 345.9
  caeruleus 746.89
  celiacus 579.0
  comitialis (*see also* Epilepsy) 345.9
  cordis - *see also* Disease, heart
    valvulorum - *see* Endocarditis
  coxae 719.95
    tuberculous (*see also* Tuberculosis)
      015.1
  hemorrhagicus neonatorum 776.0
  maculosus neonatorum 772.6
  renum 593.0
  senilis (*see also* Osteoarthrosis) 715.9
Morel-Kraepelin disease (*see also* Schizophrenia) 295.9

Morel-Moore syndrome (hyperostosis
  frontalis interna) 733.3
Morel-Morgagni syndrome (hyperostosis
  frontalis interna) 733.3
Morgagni
  cyst, organ, hydatid, or appendage
    752.8
    fallopian tube 752.11
  disease or syndrome (hyperostosis
    frontalis interna) 733.3
Morgagni-Adams-Stokes syndrome
  (syncope with heart block) 426.9
Morgagni-Stewart-Morel syndrome (hy-
  perostosis frontalis interna) 733.3
Moria (*see also* Psychosis) 298.9
Morning sickness 643.0
Moron 317
Morphea (guttate) (linear) 701.0
Morphine dependence (*see also* Depen-
  dence) 304.0
Morphinism (*see also* Dependence) 304.0
Morphinomania (*see also* Dependence)
  304.0
Morphoea 701.0
Morquio (-Brailsford) (-Ullrich) disease
  or syndrome (mucopolysaccharidosis
  IV) 277.5
  kyphosis 277.5
Morris syndrome (testicular feminization) 257.8
Morsus humanus (open wound) - *see*
  also Wound, open, by site
  skin surface intact - *see* Contusion
Mortification (dry) (moist) (*see also* Gangrene) 785.4
Morton's
  disease 355.6
  foot 355.6
  metatarsalgia (syndrome) 355.6
  neuralgia 355.6
  neuroma 355.6
  syndrome (metatarsalgia) (neuralgia)
    355.6
  toe 355.6
Morvan's disease 336.0
Mosaicism, mosaic (chromosomal) 758.9
  autosomal 758.5
  sex 758.81
Moschcowitz's syndrome (thrombotic
  thrombocytopenic purpura) 446.6
Mother yaw 102.0
Motion sickness (from travel, any vehicle) (from roundabouts or swings)
  994.6
Mottled teeth (enamel) (endemic) (nonendemic) 520.3
Mottling enamel (endemic) (nonendemic) (teeth) 520.3
Mouchet's disease 732.5
Mould(s) (in vitreous) 117.9
Moulders'
  bronchitis 502
  tuberculosis (*see also* Tuberculosis) 011.4
Mounier-Kuhn syndrome 494
Mountain
  fever - *see* Fever, mountain
  sickness 993.2
    with polycythemia, acquired 289.0
    acute 289.0
  tick fever 066.1
Mouse, joint (*see also* Loose, body, joint)
  718.1
  knee 717.6
Mouth - *see* condition

Movable
coccyx 724.71
kidney (*see also* Disease, renal) 593.0
congenital 753.3
organ or site, congenital NEC - *see*
Malposition, congenital
spleen 289.59
Movement
abnormal (dystonic) (involuntary)
781.0
decreased fetal 655.7
paradoxical facial 374.43
Moya Moya disease 437.5
Mozart's ear 744.29
Mucha's disease (acute parapsoriasis
varioliformis) 696.2
Mucha-Haberman syndrome (acute
parapsoriasis varioliformis) 696.2
Mu-chain disease 273.2
Mucinosis (cutaneous) (papular) 701.8
Mucocele
appendix 543.9
buccal cavity 528.9
gallbladder (*see also* Disease, gallbladder) 575.3
lacrimal sac 375.43
orbit (eye) 376.81
salivary gland (any) 527.6
sinus (accessory) (nasal) 478.1
turbinate (bone) (middle) (nasal) 478.1
uterus 621.8
Mucocutaneous lymph node syndrome
(acute) (febrile) (infantile) 446.1
Mucoenteritis 564.1
Mucolipidosis I, II, III 272.7
Mucopolysaccharidosis (types 1-6)
277.5
cardiopathy 277.5 [425.7]
Mucormycosis (lung) 117.7
Mucositis - *see also* Inflammation, by site
necroticans agranulocytica 288.0
Mucous - *see also* condition
patches (syphilitic) 091.3
congenital 090.0
Mucoviscidosis 277.00
with meconium obstruction 277.01
Mucus
asphyxia or suffocation (*see also* Asphyxia, mucus) 933.1
newborn 770.1
in stool 792.1
plug (*see also* Asphyxia, mucus) 933.1
aspiration, of newborn 770.1
tracheobronchial 519.1
newborn 770.1
Muguet 112.0
Mulberry molars 090.5
Mullerian mixed tumor (M8950/3) - *see*
Neoplasm, by site, malignant
Multicystic kidney 753.19
Multilobed placenta - *see* Placenta, abnormal
Multiparity V61.5
affecting
fetus or newborn 763.89
management of
labor and delivery 659.4
pregnancy V23.3
requiring contraceptive management
(*see also* Contraception) V25.9
Multipartita placenta - *see* Placenta, abnormal
Multiple, multiplex - *see also* condition
birth

Multiple, multiplex (*Continued*)
birth (*Continued*)
affecting fetus or newborn 761.5
healthy liveborn - *see* Newborn,
multiple
digits (congenital) 755.00
fingers 755.01
toes 755.02
organ or site NEC - *see* Accessory
personality 300.14
renal arteries 747.62
Mumps 072.9
with complication 072.8
specified type NEC 072.79
encephalitis 072.2
hepatitis 072.71
meningitis (aseptic) 072.1
meningoencephalitis 072.2
oophoritis 072.79
orchitis 072.0
pancreatitis 072.3
polyneuropathy 072.72
vaccination, prophylactic (against)
V04.6
Mumu (*see also* Infestation, filarial) 125.9
Münchausen syndrome 301.51
Münchmeyer's disease or syndrome (exostosis luxurians) 728.11
Mural - *see* condition
Murmur (cardiac) (heart) (nonorganic)
(organic) 785.2
abdominal 787.5
aortic (valve) (*see also* Endocarditis,
aortic) 424.1
benign - omit code
cardiorespiratory 785.2
diastolic - *see* condition
Flint (*see also* Endocarditis, aortic) 424.1
functional - omit code
Graham Steell (pulmonic regurgitation)
(*see also* Endocarditis, pulmonary)
424.3
innocent - omit code
insignificant - omit code
midsystolic 785.2
mitral (valve) - *see* Stenosis
physiologic - *see* condition
presystolic, mitral - *see* Insufficiency,
mitral
pulmonic (valve) (*see also* Endocarditis,
pulmonary) 424.3
Still's (vibratory) - omit code
systolic (valvular) - *see* condition
tricuspid (valve) - *see* Endocarditis, tricuspid
undiagnosed 785.2
valvular - *see* condition
vibratory - omit code
Murri's disease (intermittent hemoglobinuria) 283.2
Muscae volitantes 379.24
Muscle, muscular - *see* condition
Musculoneuralgia 729.1
Mushrooming hip 718.95
Mushroom workers' (pickers') lung
495.5
Mutism (*see also* Aphasia) 784.3
akinetic 784.3
deaf (acquired) (congenital) 389.7
elective (selective) 313.23
adjustment reaction 309.83
hysterical 300.11
Myà's disease (congenital dilation, colon) 751.3

Myalgia (intercostal) 729.1
eosinophilia syndrome 710.5
epidemic 074.1
cervical 078.89
psychogenic 307.89
traumatic NEC 959.9
Myasthenia, myasthenic 358.0
cordis - *see* Failure, heart
gravis 358.0
neonatal 775.2
pseudoparalytica 358.0
stomach 536.8
psychogenic 306.4
syndrome
in
botulism 005.1 [358.1]
diabetes mellitus 250.6 [358.1]
hypothyroidism (*see also* Hypothyroidism) 244.9 [358.1]
malignant neoplasm NEC 199.1
[358.1]
pernicious anemia 281.0 [358.1]
thyrotoxicosis (*see also* Thyrotoxicosis) 242.9 [358.1]
Mycelium infection NEC 117.9
Mycetismus 988.1
Mycetoma (actinomycotic) 039.9
bone 039.8
mycotic 117.4
foot 039.4
mycotic 117.4
madurae 039.9
mycotic 117.4
maduromycotic 039.9
mycotic 117.4
mycotic 117.4
nocardial 039.9
Mycobacteriosis - *see* Mycobacterium
Mycobacterium, mycobacterial (infection) 031.9
acid-fast (bacilli) 031.9
anonymous (*see also* Mycobacterium,
atypical) 031.9
atypical (acid-fast bacilli) 031.9
cutaneous 031.1
pulmonary 031.0
tuberculous (*see also* Tuberculosis,
pulmonary) 011.9
specified site NEC 031.8
avium 031.0
intracellulare complex bacteremia
(MAC) 031.2
balnei 031.1
Battey 031.0
cutaneous 031.1
disseminated 031.2
avium-intracellulare complex
(DMAC) 031.2
fortuitum 031.0
intracellulare (Battey bacillus) 031.0
kakerifu 031.8
kansasii 031.0
kasongo 031.8
leprae - *see* Leprosy
luciflavum 031.0
marinum 031.1
pulmonary 031.0
tuberculous (*see also* Tuberculosis,
pulmonary) 011.9
scrofulaceum 031.1
tuberculosis (human, bovine) - *see also*
Tuberculosis
avian type 031.0
ulcerans 031.1

Mycobacterium, mycobacterial (Continued)
xenopi 031.0
Mycosis, mycotic 117.9
cutaneous NEC 111.9
ear 111.8 [380.15]
fungoides (M9700/3) 202.1
mouth 112.0
pharynx 117.9
skin NEC 111.9
stomatitis 112.0
systemic NEC 117.9
tonsil 117.9
vagina, vaginitis 112.1
Mydriasis (persistent) (pupil) 379.43
Myelatelia 742.59
Myelinoclasis, perivascular, acute (post-infectious) NEC 136.9 [323.6]
postimmunization or postvaccinal 323.5
Myelinosis, central pontine 341.8
Myelitis (acute) (ascending) (cerebellar) (childhood) (chronic) (descending) (diffuse) (disseminated) (pressure) (progressive) (spinal cord) (subacute) (transverse) (see also Encephalitis) 323.9
late effect - see category 326
optic neuritis in 341.0
postchickenpox 052.7
postvaccinal 323.5
syphilitic (transverse) 094.89
tuberculous (see also Tuberculosis) 013.6
virus 049.9
Myeloblastic - see condition
Myelocele (see also Spina bifida) 741.9
with hydrocephalus 741.0
Myelocystocele (see also Spina bifida) 741.9
Myelocytic - see condition
Myelocytoma 205.1
Myelodysplasia (spinal cord) 742.59
meaning myelodysplastic syndrome - see Syndrome, myelodysplastic
Myeloencephalitis - see Encephalitis
Myelofibrosis (osteosclerosis) 289.8
Myelogenous - see condition
Myeloid - see condition
Myelokathexis 288.0
Myeloleukodystrophy 330.0
Myelolipoma (M8870/0) - see Neoplasm, by site, benign
Myeloma (multiple) (plasma cell) (plasmacytic) (M9730/3) 203.0
monostotic (M9731/1) 238.6
solitary (M9731/1) 238.6
Myelomalacia 336.8
Myelomata, multiple (M9730/3) 203.0
Myelomatosis (M9730/3) 203.0
Myelomeningitis - see Meningoencephalitis
Myelomeningocele (spinal cord) (see also Spina bifida) 741.9
fetal, causing fetopelvic disproportion 653.7
Myelo-osteo-musculodysplasia hereditaria 756.89
Myelopathic - see condition
Myelopathy (spinal cord) 336.9
cervical 721.1
diabetic 250.6 [336.3]
drug-induced 336.8
due to or with
carbon tetrachloride 987.8 [323.7]

Myelopathy (Continued)
due to or with (Continued)
degeneration or displacement, intervertebral disc 722.70
cervical, cervicothoracic 722.71
lumbar, lumbosacral 722.73
thoracic, thoracolumbar 722.72
hydroxyquinoline derivatives 961.3 [323.7]
infection - see Encephalitis
intervertebral disc disorder 722.70
cervical, cervicothoracic 722.71
lumbar, lumbosacral 722.73
thoracic, thoracolumbar 722.72
lead 984.9 [323.7]
mercury 985.0 [323.7]
neoplastic disease (see also Neoplasm, by site) 239.9 [336.3]
pernicious anemia 281.0 [336.3]
spondylosis 721.91
cervical 721.1
lumbar, lumbosacral 721.42
thoracic 721.41
thallium 985.8 [323.7]
lumbar, lumbosacral 721.42
necrotic (subacute) 336.1
radiation-induced 336.8
spondylogenic NEC 721.91
cervical 721.1
lumbar, lumbosacral 721.42
thoracic 721.41
thoracic 721.41
toxic NEC 989.9 [323.7]
transverse (see also Encephalitis) 323.9
vascular 336.1
Myeloproliferative disease (M9960/1) 238.7
Myeloradiculitis (see also Polyneuropathy) 357.0
Myeloradiculodysplasia (spinal) 742.59
Myelosarcoma (M9930/3) 205.3
Myelosclerosis 289.8
with myeloid metaplasia (M9961/1) 238.7
disseminated, of nervous system 340
megakaryocytic (M9961/1) 238.7
Myelosis (M9860/3) (see also Leukemia, myeloid) 205.9
acute (M9861/3) 205.0
aleukemic (M9864/3) 205.8
chronic (M9863/3) 205.1
erythremic (M9840/3) 207.0
acute (M9841/3) 207.0
megakaryocytic (M9920/3) 207.2
nonleukemic (chronic) 288.8
subacute (M9862/3) 205.2
Myesthenia - see Myasthenia
Myiasis (cavernous) 134.0
orbit 134.0 [376.13]
Myoadenoma, prostate 600
Myoblastoma
granular cell (M9580/0) - see also Neoplasm, connective tissue, benign
malignant (M9580/3) - see Neoplasm, connective tissue, malignant
tongue (M9580/0) 210.1
Myocardial - see condition
Myocardiopathy (congestive) (constrictive) (familial) (hypertrophic nonobstructive) (idiopathic) (infiltrative) (obstructive) (primary) (restrictive) (sporadic) 425.4
alcoholic 425.5

Myocardiopathy (Continued)
amyloid 277.3 [425.7]
beriberi 265.0 [425.7]
cobalt-beer 425.5
due to
amyloidosis 277.3 [425.7]
beriberi 265.0 [425.7]
cardiac glycogenosis 271.0 [425.7]
Chagas' disease 086.0
Friedreich's ataxia 334.0 [425.8]
influenza 487.8 [425.8]
mucopolysaccharidosis 277.5 [425.7]
myotonia atrophica 359.2 [425.8]
progressive muscular dystrophy 359.1 [425.8]
sarcoidosis 135 [425.8]
glycogen storage 271.0 [425.7]
hypertrophic obstructive 425.1
metabolic NEC 277.9 [425.7]
nutritional 269.9 [425.7]
obscure (African) 425.2
postpartum 674.8
secondary 425.9
thyrotoxic (see also Thyrotoxicosis) 242.9 [425.7]
toxic NEC 425.9
Myocarditis (fibroid) (interstitial) (old) (progressive) (senile) (with arteriosclerosis) 429.0
with
rheumatic fever (conditions classifiable to 390) 398.0
active (see also Myocarditis, acute, rheumatic) 391.2
inactive or quiescent (with chorea) 398.0
active (nonrheumatic) 422.90
rheumatic 391.2
with chorea (acute) (rheumatic) (Sydenham's) 392.0
acute or subacute (interstitial) 422.90
due to Streptococcus (beta-hemolytic) 391.2
idiopathic 422.91
rheumatic 391.2
with chorea (acute) (rheumatic) (Sydenham's) 392.0
specified type NEC 422.99
aseptic of newborn 074.23
bacterial (acute) 422.92
chagasic 086.0
chronic (interstitial) 429.0
congenital 746.89
constrictive 425.4
Coxsackie (virus) 074.23
diphtheritic 032.82
due to or in
Coxsackie (virus) 074.23
diphtheria 032.82
epidemic louse-borne typhus 080 [422.0]
influenza 487.8 [422.0]
Lyme disease 088.81 [422.0]
scarlet fever 034.1 [422.0]
toxoplasmosis (acquired) 130.3
tuberculosis (see also Tuberculosis) 017.9 [422.0]
typhoid 002.0 [422.0]
typhus NEC 081.9 [422.0]
eosinophilic 422.91
epidemic of newborn 074.23
Fiedler's (acute) (isolated) (subacute) 422.91
giant cell (acute) (subacute) 422.91

Myocarditis *(Continued)*
gonococcal 098.85
granulomatous (idiopathic) (isolated)
(nonspecific) 422.91
hypertensive *(see also* Hypertension,
heart) 402.90
idiopathic 422.91
granulomatous 422.91
infective 422.92
influenzal 487.8 *[422.0]*
isolated (diffuse) (granulomatous)
422.91
malignant 422.99
meningococcal 036.43
nonrheumatic, active 422.90
parenchymatous 422.90
pneumococcal (acute) (subacute)
422.92
rheumatic (chronic) (inactive) (with
chorea) 398.0
active or acute 391.2
with chorea (acute) (rheumatic)
(Sydenham's) 392.0
septic 422.92
specific (giant cell) (productive)
422.91
staphylococcal (acute) (subacute)
422.92
suppurative 422.92
syphilitic (chronic) 093.82
toxic 422.93
rheumatic *(see also* Myocarditis,
acute rheumatic) 391.2
tuberculous *(see also* Tuberculosis)
017.9 *[422.0]*
typhoid 002.0 *[422.0]*
valvular - *see* Endocarditis
viral, except Coxsackie 422.91
Coxsackie 074.23
of newborn (Coxsackie) 074.23
Myocardium, myocardial - *see* condition
Myocardosis *(see also* Cardiomyopathy)
425.4
Myoclonia (essential) 333.2
epileptica 333.2
Friedrich's 333.2
massive 333.2
Myoclonic
epilepsy, familial (progressive) 333.2
jerks 333.2
Myoclonus (familial essential) (multifocal) (simplex) 333.2
facial 351.8
massive (infantile) 333.2
pharyngeal 478.29
Myodiastasis 728.84
Myoendocarditis - *see also* Endocarditis
acute or subacute 421.9
Myoepithelioma (M8982/0) - *see* Neoplasm, by site, benign
Myofascitis (acute) 729.1
low back 724.2
Myofibroma (M8890/0) - *see also* Neoplasm, connective tissue, benign
uterus (cervix) (corpus) *(see also* Leiomyoma) 218.9
Myofibrosis 728.2
heart *(see also* Myocarditis) 429.0
humeroscapular region 726.2
scapulohumeral 726.2
Myofibrositis *(see also* Myositis) 729.1
scapulohumeral 726.2
Myogelosis (occupational) 728.89
Myoglobinuria 791.3

Myoglobulinuria, primary 791.3
Myokymia - *see also* Myoclonus
facial 351.8
Myolipoma (M8860/0)
specified site - *see* Neoplasm, connective tissue, benign
unspecified site 223.0
Myoma (M8895/0) - *see also* Neoplasm,
connective tissue, benign
cervix (stump) (uterus) *(see also* Leiomyoma) 218.9
malignant (M8895/3) - *see* Neoplasm,
connective tissue, malignant
prostate 600
uterus (cervix) (corpus) *(see also* Leiomyoma) 218.9
in pregnancy or childbirth 654.1
affecting fetus or newborn
763.89 ◀▥▥▶
causing obstructed labor 660.2
affecting fetus or newborn
763.1
Myomalacia 728.9
cordis, heart *(see also* Degeneration,
myocardial) 429.1
Myometritis *(see also* Endometritis)
615.9
Myometrium - *see* condition
Myonecrosis, clostridial 040.0
Myopathy 359.9
alcoholic 359.4
amyloid 277.3 *[359.6]*
benign, congenital 359.0
central core 359.0
centronuclear 359.0
congenital (benign) 359.0
distal 359.1
due to drugs 359.4
endocrine 259.9 *[359.5]*
specified type NEC 259.8 *[359.5]*
extraocular muscles 376.82
facioscapulohumeral 359.1
in
Addison's disease 255.4 *[359.5]*
amyloidosis 277.3 *[359.6]*
cretinism 243 *[359.5]*
Cushing's syndrome 255.0 *[359.5]*
disseminated lupus erythematosus
710.0 *[359.6]*
giant cell arteritis 446.5 *[359.6]*
hyperadrenocorticism NEC 255.3
[359.5]
hyperparathyroidism 252.0 *[359.5]*
hypopituitarism 253.2 *[359.5]*
hypothyroidism *(see also* Hypothyroidism) 244.9 *[359.5]*
malignant neoplasm NEC (M8000/3)
199.1 *[359.6]*
myxedema *(see also* Myxedema)
244.9 *[359.5]*
polyarteritis nodosa 446.0 *[359.6]*
rheumatoid arthritis 714.0 *[359.6]*
sarcoidosis 135 *[359.6]*
scleroderma 710.1 *[359.6]*
Sjögren's disease 710.2 *[359.6]*
thyrotoxicosis *(see also* Thyrotoxicosis) 242.9 *[359.5]*
inflammatory 359.8
limb-girdle 359.1
myotubular 359.0
nemaline 359.0
ocular 359.1
oculopharyngeal 359.1
primary 359.8

Myopathy *(Continued)*
progressive NEC 359.8
rod body 359.0
scapulohumeral 359.1
specified type NEC 359.8
toxic 359.4
Myopericarditis *(see also* Pericarditis)
423.9
Myopia (axial) (congenital) (increased
curvature or refraction, nucleus of
lens) 367.1
degenerative, malignant 360.21
malignant 360.21
progressive high (degenerative)
360.21
Myosarcoma (M8895/3) - *see* Neoplasm,
connective tissue, malignant
Myosis (persistent) 379.42
stromal (endolymphatic) (M8931/1)
236.0
Myositis 729.1
clostridial 040.0
due to posture 729.1
epidemic 074.1
fibrosa or fibrous (chronic) 728.2
Volkmann's (complicating trauma)
958.6
infective 728.0
interstitial 728.81
multiple - *see* Polymyositis
occupational 729.1
orbital, chronic 376.12
ossificans 728.12
circumscribed 728.12
progressive 728.11
traumatic 728.12
progressive fibrosing 728.11
purulent 728.0
rheumatic 729.1
rheumatoid 729.1
suppurative 728.0
syphilitic 095.6
traumatic (old) 729.1
Myospasia impulsiva 307.23
Myotonia (acquisita) (intermittens)
728.85
atrophica 359.2
congenita 359.2
dystrophica 359.2
Myotonic pupil 379.46
Myriapodiasis 134.1
Myringitis
with otitis media - *see* Otitis media
acute 384.00
specified type NEC 384.09
bullosa hemorrhagica 384.01
bullous 384.01
chronic 384.1
Mysophobia 300.29
Mytilotoxism 988.0
Myxadenitis labialis 528.5
Myxedema (adult) (idiocy) (infantile) (juvenile) (thyroid gland) *(see also* Hypothyroidism) 244.9
circumscribed 242.9
congenital 243
cutis 701.8
localized (pretibial) 242.9
madness (acute) 293.0
subacute 293.1
papular 701.8
pituitary 244.8
postpartum 674.8
pretibial 242.9

Myxedema *(Continued)*
  primary 244.9
Myxochondrosarcoma (M9220/3) - *see*
  Neoplasm, cartilage, malignant
Myxofibroma (M8811/0) - *see also* Neoplasm, connective tissue, benign
  odontogenic (M9320/0) 213.1
  upper jaw (bone) 213.0

Myxofibrosarcoma (M8811/3) - *see*
  Neoplasm, connective tissue, malig-
  nant
Myxolipoma (M8852/0) (*see also* Lipoma,
  by site) 214.9
Myxoliposarcoma (M8852/3) - *see*
  Neoplasm, connective tissue, malig-
  nant

Myxoma (M8840/0) - *see also* Neoplasm,
  connective tissue, benign
  odontogenic (M9320/0) 213.1
  upper jaw (bone) 213.0
Myxosarcoma (M8840/3) - *see* Neoplasm,
  connective tissue, malignant

ICD-9-CM

M

Vol. 2

N

Naegeli's
 disease (hereditary hemorrhagic
  thrombasthenia 287.1
 leukemia, monocytic (M9863/3)
  205.1
 syndrome (incontinentia pigmenti)
  757.33
Naffziger's syndrome 353.0
Naga sore (*see also* Ulcer, skin) 707.9
Nägele's pelvis 738.6
 with disproportion (fetopelvic) 653.0
  affecting fetus or newborn 763.1
  causing obstructed labor 660.1
   affecting fetus or newborn 763.1
Nager-de Reynier syndrome (dysostosis
  mandibularis) 756.0
Nail - *see also* condition
 biting 307.9
 patella syndrome (hereditary osteoonychodysplasia) 756.89
Nanism, nanosomia (*see also* Dwarfism)
  259.4
 hypophyseal 253.3
 pituitary 253.3
 renis, renalis 588.0
Nanukayami 100.89
Napkin rash 691.0
Narcissism 301.81
Narcolepsy 347
Narcosis
 carbon dioxide (respiratory)
  786.09
 due to drug
  correct substance properly administered 780.09
  overdose or wrong substance given
   or taken 977.9
   specified drug - *see* Table of Drugs
    and Chemicals
Narcotism (chronic) (*see also* Dependence) 304.9
 acute
  correct substance properly administered 349.82
  overdose or wrong substance given
   or taken 967.8
   specified drug - *see* Table of Drugs
    and Chemicals
Narrow
 anterior chamber angle 365.02
 pelvis (inlet) (outlet) - *see* Contraction,
  pelvis
Narrowing
 artery NEC 447.1
  auditory, internal 433.8
  basilar 433.0
   with other precerebral artery
    433.3
   bilateral 433.3
  carotid 433.1
   with other precerebral artery
    433.3
   bilateral 433.3
  cerebellar 433.8
  choroidal 433.8
  communicating posterior 433.8
  coronary - *see also* Arteriosclerosis,
   coronary
   congenital 746.85
    due to syphilis 090.5
  hypophyseal 433.8
  pontine 433.8

Narrowing (*Continued*)
 artery NEC (*Continued*)
  precerebral NEC 433.9
   multiple or bilateral 433.3
   specified NEC 433.8
  vertebral 433.2
   with other precerebral artery
    433.3
   bilateral 433.3
 auditory canal (external) (*see also*
  Stricture, ear canal, acquired)
  380.50
 cerebral arteries 437.0
 cicatricial - *see* Cicatrix
 congenital - *see* Anomaly, congenital
 coronary artery - *see* Narrowing, artery, coronary
 ear, middle 385.22
 Eustachian tube (*see also* Obstruction,
  Eustachian tube) 381.60
 eyelid 374.46
  congenital 743.62
 intervertebral disc or space NEC - *see*
  Degeneration, intervertebral disc
 joint space, hip 719.85
 larynx 478.74
 lids 374.46
  congenital 743.62
 mesenteric artery (with gangrene)
  557.0
 palate 524.8
 palpebral fissure 374.46
 retinal artery 362.13
 ureter 593.3
 urethra (*see also* Stricture, urethra)
  598.9
Narrowness, abnormal, eyelid 743.62
Nasal - *see* condition
Nasolacrimal - *see* condition
Nasopharyngeal - *see also* condition
 bursa 478.29
 pituitary gland 759.2
 torticollis 723.5
Nasopharyngitis (acute) (infective) (subacute) 460
 chronic 472.2
  due to external agent - *see* Condition, respiratory, chronic, due to
 due to external agent - *see* Condition,
  respiratory, due to
 septic 034.0
 streptococcal 034.0
 suppurative (chronic) 472.2
 ulcerative (chronic) 472.2
Nasopharynx, nasopharyngeal - *see* condition
Natal tooth, teeth 520.6
Nausea (*see also* Vomiting) 787.02
 with vomiting 787.01
 epidemic 078.82
 gravidarum - *see* Hyperemesis, gravidarum
 marina 994.6
Naval - *see* condition
Neapolitan fever (*see also* Brucellosis)
  023.9
Near-syncope 780.2
Nearsightedness 367.1
Nebécourt's syndrome 253.3
Nebula, cornea (eye) 371.01
 congenital 743.43
  interfering with vision 743.42
Necator americanus infestation 126.1
Necatoriasis 126.1

Neck - *see* condition
Necrencephalus (*see also* Softening,
  brain) 437.8
Necrobacillosis 040.3
Necrobiosis 799.8
 brain or cerebral (*see also* Softening,
  brain) 437.8
 lipoidica 709.3
  diabeticorum 250.8 [709.3]
Necrodermolysis 695.1
Necrolysis, toxic epidermal 695.1
 due to drug
  correct substance properly administered 695.1
  overdose or wrong substance given
   or taken 977.9
   specified drug - *see* Table of Drugs
    and Chemicals
Necrophilia 302.89
Necrosis, necrotic
 adrenal (capsule) (gland) 255.8
 antrum, nasal sinus 478.1
 aorta (hyaline) (*see also* Aneurysm,
  aorta) 441.9
  cystic medial 441.00
   abdominal 441.02
   thoracic 441.01
   thoracoabdominal 441.03
  ruptured 441.5
 arteritis 446.0
 artery 447.5
 aseptic, bone 733.40
  femur (head) (neck) 733.42
   medial condyle 733.43
  humoral head 733.41
  medial femoral condyle 733.43
  specific site NEC 733.49
  talus 733.44
 avascular, bone NEC (*see also* Necrosis,
  aseptic, bone) 733.40
 bladder (aseptic) (sphincter) 596.8
 bone (*see also* Osteomyelitis) 730.1
  acute 730.0
  aseptic or avascular 733.40
   femur (head) (neck) 733.42
    medial condyle 733.43
   humoral head 733.41
   medial femoral condyle 733.43
   specified site NEC 733.49
   talus 733.44
  ethmoid 478.1
  ischemic 733.40
  jaw 526.4
  marrow 289.8
  Paget's (osteitis deformans) 731.0
  tuberculous - *see* Tuberculosis,
   bone
 brain (softening) (*see also* Softening,
  brain) 437.8
 breast (aseptic) (fat) (segmental)
  611.3
 bronchus, bronchi 519.1
 central nervous system NEC (*see also*
  Softening, brain) 437.8
 cerebellar (*see also* Softening, brain)
  437.8
 cerebral (softening) (*see also* Softening,
  brain) 437.8
 cerebrospinal (softening) (*see also* Softening, brain) 437.8
 cornea (*see also* Keratitis) 371.40
 cortical, kidney 583.6
 cystic medial (aorta) 441.00
  abdominal 441.02

Necrosis, necrotic *(Continued)*
cystic medial *(Continued)*
    thoracic 441.01
    thoracoabdominal 441.03
dental 521.0
    pulp 522.1
due to swallowing corrosive substance
    - *see* Burn, by site
ear (ossicle) 385.24
esophagus 530.89
ethmoid (bone) 478.1
eyelid 374.50
fat, fatty (generalized) *(see also* Degen-
    eration, fatty) 272.8
    breast (aseptic) (segmental) 611.3
    intestine 569.89
    localized - *see* Degeneration, by site,
        fatty
    mesentery 567.8
    omentum 567.8
    pancreas 577.8
    peritoneum 567.8
    skin (subcutaneous) 709.3
        newborn 778.1
femur (aseptic) (avascular) 733.42
    head 733.42
    medial condyle 733.43
    neck 733.42
gallbladder *(see also* Cholecystitis,
    acute) 575.0
gangrenous 785.4
gastric 537.89
glottis 478.79
heart (myocardium) - *see* Infarct, myo-
    cardium
hepatic *(see also* Necrosis, liver) 570
hip (aseptic) (avascular) 733.42
intestine (acute) (hemorrhagic) (mas-
    sive) 557.0
ischemic 785.4
jaw 526.4
kidney (bilateral) 583.9
    acute 584.9
    cortical 583.6
        acute 584.6
            with
                abortion - *see* Abortion, by
                    type, with renal failure
                ectopic pregnancy *(see also*
                    categories 633.0-633.9)
                    639.3
                molar pregnancy *(see also* cat-
                    egories 630-632) 639.3
            complicating pregnancy 646.2
                affecting fetus or newborn
                    760.1
            following labor and delivery
                669.3
    medullary (papillary) *(see also* Pyeli-
        tis) 590.80
        in
            acute renal failure 584.7
            nephritis, nephropathy 583.7
    papillary *(see also* Pyelitis) 590.80
        in
            acute renal failure 584.7
            nephritis, nephropathy 583.7
    tubular 584.5
        with

Necrosis, necrotic *(Continued)*
kidney *(Continued)*
    tubular *(Continued)*
        with *(Continued)*
            abortion - *see* Abortion, by type,
                with renal failure
            ectopic pregnancy *(see also* cate-
                gories 633.0-633.9) 639.3
            molar pregnancy *(see also* cate-
                gories 630-632) 639.3
        complicating
            abortion 639.3
            ectopic or molar pregnancy
                639.3
            pregnancy 646.2
                affecting fetus or newborn
                    760.1
        following labor and delivery 669.3
        traumatic 958.5
larynx 478.79
liver (acute) (congenital) (diffuse)
    (massive) (subacute) 570
    with
        abortion - *see* Abortion, by type,
            with specified complication
            NEC
        ectopic pregnancy *(see also* catego-
            ries 633.0-633.9) 639.8
        molar pregnancy *(see also* catego-
            ries 630-632) 639.8
    complicating pregnancy 646.7
        affecting fetus or newborn 760.8
    following
        abortion 639.8
        ectopic or molar pregnancy 639.8
    obstetrical 646.7
    postabortal 639.8
    puerperal, postpartum 674.8
    toxic 573.3
lung 513.0
lymphatic gland 683
mammary gland 611.3
mastoid (chronic) 383.1
mesentery 557.0
    fat 567.8
mitral valve - *see* Insufficiency, mitral
myocardium, myocardial - *see* Infarct,
    myocardium
nose (septum) 478.1
omentum 557.0
    with mesenteric infarction 557.0
    fat 567.8
orbit, orbital 376.10
ossicles, ear (aseptic) 385.24
ovary *(see also* Salpingo-oophoritis)
    614.2
pancreas (aseptic) (duct) (fat) 577.8
    acute 577.0
    infective 577.0
papillary, kidney *(see also* Pyelitis)
    590.80
peritoneum 557.0
    with mesenteric infarction 557.0
    fat 567.8
pharynx 462
    in granulocytopenia 288.0
phosphorus 983.9
pituitary (gland) (postpartum) (Shee-
    han) 253.2

Necrosis, necrotic *(Continued)*
placenta *(see also* Placenta, abnormal)
    656.7
pneumonia 513.0
pulmonary 513.0
pulp (dental) 522.1
pylorus 537.89
radiation - *see* Necrosis, by site
radium - *see* Necrosis, by site
renal - *see* Necrosis, kidney
sclera 379.19
scrotum 608.89
skin or subcutaneous tissue 709.8
    due to burn - *see* Burn, by site
    gangrenous 785.4
spine, spinal (column) 730.18
    acute 730.18
    cord 336.1
spleen 289.59
stomach 537.89
stomatitis 528.1
subcutaneous fat 709.3
    fetus or newborn 778.1
subendocardial - *see* Infarct, myocar-
    dium
suprarenal (capsule) (gland) 255.8
teeth, tooth 521.0
testis 608.89
thymus (gland) 254.8
tonsil 474.8
trachea 519.1
tuberculous NEC - *see* Tuberculosis
tubular (acute) (anoxic) (toxic)
    584.5
    due to a procedure 997.5
umbilical cord, affecting fetus or new-
    born 762.6
vagina 623.8
vertebra (lumbar) 730.18
    acute 730.18
    tuberculous *(see also* Tuberculosis)
        015.0 *[730.8]*
vesical (aseptic) (bladder) 596.8
x-ray - *see* Necrosis, by site
Necrospermia 606.0
Necrotizing angiitis 446.0
Negativism 301.7
Neglect (child) (newborn) NEC
    995.52
    adult 995.84
    after or at birth 995.52
    hemispatial 781.8
    left-sided 781.8
    sensory 781.8
    visuospatial 781.8
Negri bodies 071
    Neill-Dingwall syndrome (microceph-
        aly and dwarfism) 759.89
Neisserian infection NEC - *see* Gonococ-
    cus
Nematodiasis NEC *(see also* Infestation,
    Nematode) 127.9
    ancylostoma *(see also* Ancylostomiasis)
        126.9
Neoformans cryptococcus infection
    117.5
Neonatal - *see also* condition
    teeth, tooth 520.6
Neonatorum - *see* condition

| | Malignant | | | | | |
	Primary	Secondary	Ca in situ	Benign	Uncertain Behavior	Unspecified
Neoplasm, neoplastic	199.1	199.1	234.9	229.9	238.9	239.9

Notes — 1. The list below gives the code numbers for neoplasms by anatomical site. For each site there are six possible code numbers according to whether the neoplasm in question is malignant, benign, in situ, of uncertain behavior, or of unspecified nature. The description of the neoplasm will often indicate which of the six columns is appropriate; e.g., malignant melanoma of skin, benign fibroadenoma of breast, carcinoma in situ of cervix uteri.

Where such descriptors are not present, the remainder of the Index should be consulted where guidance is given to the appropriate column for each morphological (histological) variety listed; e.g., Mesonephroma—*see* Neoplasm, malignant; Embryoma—*see also* Neoplasm, uncertain behavior; Disease, Bowen's—*see* Neoplasm, skin, in situ. However, the guidance in the Index can be overridden if one of the descriptors mentioned above is present; e.g., malignant adenoma of colon is coded to 153.9 and not to 211.3 as the adjective "malignant" overrides the Index entry "Adenoma—*see also* Neoplasm, benign."

2. Sites marked with the sign * (e.g., face NEC*) should be classified to malignant neoplasm of skin of these sites if the variety of neoplasm is a squamous cell carcinoma or an epidermoid carcinoma and to benign neoplasm of skin of these sites if the variety of neoplasm is a papilloma (any type).

	Primary	Secondary	Ca in situ	Benign	Uncertain Behavior	Unspecified
abdomen, abdominal	195.2	198.89	234.8	229.8	238.8	239.8
cavity	195.2	198.89	234.8	229.8	238.8	239.8
organ	195.2	198.89	234.8	229.8	238.8	239.8
viscera	195.2	198.89	234.8	229.8	238.8	239.8
wall	173.5	198.2	232.5	216.5	238.2	239.2
connective tissue	171.5	198.89	—	215.5	238.1	239.2
abdominopelvic	195.8	198.89	234.8	229.8	238.8	239.8
accessory sinus-*see* Neoplasm, sinus						
acoustic nerve	192.0	198.4	—	225.1	237.9	239.7
acromion (process)	170.4	198.5	—	213.4	238.0	239.2
adenoid (pharynx) (tissue)	147.1	198.89	230.0	210.7	235.1	239.0
adipose tissue (*see also* Neoplasm, connective tissue)	171.9	198.89	—	215.9	238.1	239.2
adnexa (uterine)	183.9	198.82	233.3	221.8	236.3	239.5
adrenal (cortex) (gland) (medulla)	194.0	198.7	234.8	227.0	237.2	239.7
ala nasi (external)	173.3	198.2	232.3	216.3	238.2	239.2
alimentary canal or tract NEC	159.9	197.8	230.9	211.9	235.5	239.0
alveolar	143.9	198.89	230.0	210.4	235.1	239.0
mucosa	143.9	198.89	230.0	210.4	235.1	239.0
lower	143.1	198.89	230.0	210.4	235.1	239.0
upper	143.0	198.89	230.0	210.4	235.1	239.0
ridge or process	170.1	198.5	—	213.1	238.0	239.2
carcinoma	143.9	—	—	—	—	—
lower	143.1	—	—	—	—	—
upper	143.0	—	—	—	—	—
lower	170.1	198.5	—	213.1	238.0	239.2
mucosa	143.9	198.89	230.0	210.4	235.1	239.0
lower	143.1	198.89	230.0	210.4	235.1	239.0
upper	143.0	198.89	230.0	210.4	235.1	239.0
upper	170.0	198.5	—	213.0	238.0	239.2
sulcus	145.1	198.89	230.0	210.4	235.1	239.0
alveolus	143.9	198.89	230.0	210.4	235.1	239.0
lower	143.1	198.89	230.0	210.4	235.1	239.0
upper	143.0	198.89	230.0	210.4	235.1	239.0
ampulla of Vater	156.2	197.8	230.8	211.5	235.3	239.0
ankle NEC*	195.5	198.89	232.7	229.8	238.8	239.8
anorectum, anorectal (junction)	154.8	197.5	230.7	211.4	235.2	239.0
antecubital fossa or space*	195.4	198.89	232.6	229.8	238.8	239.8
antrum (Highmore) (maxillary)	160.2	197.3	231.8	212.0	235.9	239.1
pyloric	151.2	197.8	230.2	211.1	235.2	239.0
tympanicum	160.1	197.3	231.8	212.0	235.9	239.1
anus, anal	154.3	197.5	230.6	211.4	235.5	239.0
canal	154.2	197.5	230.5	211.4	235.5	239.0
contiguous sites with rectosigmoid junction or rectum	154.8	—	—	—	—	—
margin	173.5	198.2	232.5	216.5	238.2	239.2
skin	173.5	198.2	232.5	216.5	238.2	239.2
sphincter	154.2	197.5	230.5	211.4	235.5	239.0
aorta (thoracic)	171.4	198.89	—	215.4	238.1	239.2
abdominal	171.5	198.89	—	215.5	238.1	239.2
aortic body	194.6	198.89	—	227.6	237.3	239.7
aponeurosis	171.9	198.89	—	215.9	238.1	239.2
palmar	171.2	198.89	—	215.2	238.1	239.2
plantar	171.3	198.89	—	215.3	238.1	239.2

	Malignant					
	Primary	Secondary	Ca in situ	Benign	Uncertain Behavior	Unspecified
Neoplasm (*Continued*)						
appendix	153.5	197.5	230.3	211.3	235.2	239.0
arachnoid (cerebral)	192.1	198.4	—	225.2	237.6	239.7
spinal	192.3	198.4	—	225.4	237.6	239.7
areola (female)	174.0	198.81	233.0	217	238.3	239.3
male	175.0	198.81	233.0	217	238.3	239.3
arm NEC*	195.4	198.89	232.6	229.8	238.8	239.8
artery-*see* Neoplasm, connective tissue						
aryepiglottic fold	148.2	198.89	230.0	210.8	235.1	239.0
hypopharyngeal aspect	148.2	198.89	230.0	210.8	235.1	239.0
laryngeal aspect	161.1	197.3	231.0	212.1	235.6	239.1
marginal zone	148.2	198.89	230.0	210.8	235.1	239.0
arytenoid (cartilage)	161.3	197.3	231.0	212.1	235.6	239.1
fold-*see* Neoplasm, aryepiglottic						
atlas	170.2	198.5	—	213.2	238.0	239.2
atrium, cardiac	164.1	198.89	—	212.7	238.8	239.8
auditory						
canal (external) (skin)	173.2	198.2	232.2	216.2	238.2	239.2
internal	160.1	197.3	231.8	212.0	235.9	239.1
nerve	192.0	198.4	—	225.1	237.9	239.7
tube	160.1	197.3	231.8	212.0	235.9	239.1
opening	147.2	198.89	230.0	210.7	235.1	239.0
auricle, ear	173.2	198.2	232.2	216.2	238.2	239.2
cartilage	171.0	198.89	—	215.0	238.1	239.2
auricular canal (external)	173.2	198.2	232.2	216.2	238.2	239.2
internal	160.1	197.3	231.8	212.0	235.9	239.1
autonomic nerve or nervous system NEC	171.9	198.89	—	215.9	238.1	239.2
axilla, axillary	195.1	198.89	234.8	229.8	238.8	239.8
fold	173.5	198.2	232.5	216.5	238.2	239.2
back NEC*	195.8	198.89	232.5	229.8	238.8	239.8
Bartholin's gland	184.1	198.82	233.3	221.2	236.3	239.5
basal ganglia	191.0	198.3	—	225.0	237.5	239.6
basis pedunculi	191.7	198.3	—	225.0	237.5	239.6
bile or biliary (tract)	156.9	197.8	230.8	211.5	235.3	239.0
canaliculi (biliferi) (intrahepatic)	155.1	197.8	230.8	211.5	235.3	239.0
canals, interlobular	155.1	197.8	230.8	211.5	235.3	239.0
contiguous sites	156.8	—	—	—	—	—
duct or passage (common) (cystic) (extrahepatic)	156.1	197.8	230.8	211.5	235.3	239.0
contiguous sites						
with gallbladder	156.8	—	—	—	—	—
interlobular	155.1	197.8	230.8	211.5	235.3	239.0
intrahepatic	155.1	197.8	230.8	211.5	235.3	239.0
and extrahepatic	156.9	197.8	230.8	211.5	235.3	239.0
bladder (urinary)	188.9	198.1	233.7	223.3	236.7	239.4
contiguous sites	188.8	—	—	—	—	—
dome	188.1	198.1	233.7	223.3	236.7	239.4
neck	188.5	198.1	233.7	223.3	236.7	239.4
orifice	188.9	198.1	233.7	223.3	236.7	239.4
ureteric	188.6	198.1	233.7	223.3	236.7	239.4
urethral	188.5	198.1	233.7	223.3	236.7	239.4
sphincter	188.8	198.1	233.7	223.3	236.7	239.4
trigone	188.0	198.1	233.7	223.3	236.7	239.4
urachus	188.7	—	233.7	223.3	236.7	239.4
wall	188.9	198.1	233.7	223.3	236.7	239.4
anterior	188.3	198.1	233.7	223.3	236.7	239.4
lateral	188.2	198.1	233.7	223.3	236.7	239.4
posterior	188.4	198.1	233.7	223.3	236.7	239.4
blood vessel-*see* Neoplasm, connective tissue						
bone (periosteum)	170.9	198.5	—	213.9	238.0	239.2

Note-Carcinomas and adenocarcinomas, of any type other than intraosseous or odontogenic, of the sites listed under "Neoplasm, bone" should be considered as constituting metastatic spread from an unspecified primary site and coded to 198.5 for morbidity coding and to 199.1 for underlying cause of death coding.

acetabulum	170.6	198.5	—	213.6	238.0	239.2

◄▶ **New Code**   ◄▥▥ ▥▥▶ **Revised Code**

	Malignant					
	Primary	Secondary	Ca in stiu	Benign	Uncertain Behavior	Unspecified
Neoplasm *(Continued)*						
bone *(Continued)*						
acromion (process)	170.4	198.5	—	213.4	238.0	239.2
ankle	170.8	198.5	—	213.8	238.0	239.2
arm NEC	170.4	198.5	—	213.4	238.0	239.2
astragalus	170.8	198.5	—	213.8	238.0	239.2
atlas	170.2	198.5	—	213.2	238.0	239.2
axis	170.2	198.5	—	213.2	238.0	239.2
back NEC	170.2	198.5	—	213.2	238.0	239.2
calcaneus	170.8	198.5	—	213.8	238.0	239.2
calvarium	170.0	198.5	—	213.0	238.0	239.2
carpus (any)	170.5	198.5	—	213.5	238.0	239.2
cartilage NEC	170.9	198.5	—	213.9	238.0	239.2
clavicle	170.3	198.5	—	213.3	238.0	239.2
clivus	170.0	198.5	—	213.0	238.0	239.2
coccygeal vertebra	170.6	198.5	—	213.6	238.0	239.2
coccyx	170.6	198.5	—	213.6	238.0	239.2
costal cartilage	170.3	198.5	—	213.3	238.0	239.2
costovertebral joint	170.3	198.5	—	213.3	238.0	239.2
cranial	170.0	198.5	—	213.0	238.0	239.2
cuboid	170.8	198.5	—	213.8	238.0	239.2
cuneiform	170.9	198.5	—	213.9	238.0	239.2
ankle	170.8	198.5	—	213.8	238.0	239.2
wrist	170.5	198.5	—	213.5	238.0	239.2
digital	170.9	198.5	—	213.9	238.0	239.2
finger	170.5	198.5	—	213.5	238.0	239.2
toe	170.8	198.5	—	213.8	238.0	239.2
elbow	170.4	198.5	—	213.4	238.0	239.2
ethmoid (labyrinth)	170.0	198.5	—	213.0	238.0	239.2
face	170.0	198.5	—	213.0	238.0	239.2
lower jaw	170.1	198.5	—	213.1	238.0	239.2
femur (any part)	170.7	198.5	—	213.7	238.0	239.2
fibula (any part)	170.7	198.5	—	213.7	238.0	239.2
finger (any)	170.5	198.5	—	213.5	238.0	239.2
foot	170.8	198.5	—	213.8	238.0	239.2
forearm	170.4	198.5	—	213.4	238.0	239.2
frontal	170.0	198.5	—	213.0	238.0	239.2
hand	170.5	198.5	—	213.5	238.0	239.2
heel	170.8	198.5	—	213.8	238.0	239.2
hip	170.6	198.5	—	213.6	238.0	239.2
humerus (any part)	170.4	198.5	—	213.4	238.0	239.2
hyoid	170.0	198.5	—	213.0	238.0	239.2
ilium	170.6	198.5	—	213.6	238.0	239.2
innominate	170.6	198.5	—	213.6	238.0	239.2
intervertebral cartilage or disc	170.2	198.5	—	213.2	238.0	239.2
ischium	170.6	198.5	—	213.6	238.0	239.2
jaw (lower)	170.1	198.5	—	213.1	238.0	239.2
upper	170.0	198.5	—	213.0	238.0	239.2
knee	170.7	198.5	—	213.7	238.0	239.2
leg NEC	170.7	198.5	—	213.7	238.0	239.2
limb NEC	170.9	198.5	—	213.9	238.0	239.2
lower (long bones)	170.7	198.5	—	213.7	238.0	239.2
short bones	170.8	198.5	—	213.8	238.0	239.2
upper (long bones)	170.4	198.5	—	213.4	238.0	239.2
short bones	170.5	198.5	—	213.5	238.0	239.2
long	170.9	198.5	—	213.9	238.0	239.2
lower limbs NEC	170.7	198.5	—	213.7	238.0	239.2
upper limbs NEC	170.4	198.5	—	213.4	238.0	239.2
malar	170.0	198.5	—	213.0	238.0	239.2
mandible	170.1	198.5	—	213.1	238.0	239.2
marrow NEC	202.9	198.5	—	—	—	238.7
mastoid	170.0	198.5	—	213.0	238.0	239.2
maxilla, maxillary (superior)	170.0	198.5	—	213.0	238.0	239.2
inferior	170.1	198.5	—	213.1	238.0	239.2

◀▶ **New Code**   ◀▥▥▥ ▥▥▥▶ **Revised Code**

	Malignant					
	Primary	Secondary	Ca in stiu	Benign	Uncertain Behavior	Unspecified
Neoplasm *(Continued)*						
bone *(Continued)*						
metacarpus (any)	170.5	198.5	—	213.5	238.0	239.2
metatarsus (any)	170.8	198.5	—	213.8	238.0	239.2
navicular (ankle)	170.8	198.5	—	213.8	238.0	239.2
hand	170.5	198.5	—	213.5	238.0	239.2
nose, nasal	170.0	198.5	—	213.0	238.0	239.2
occipital	170.0	198.5	—	213.0	238.0	239.2
orbit	170.0	198.5	—	213.0	238.0	239.2
parietal	170.0	198.5	—	213.0	238.0	239.2
patella	170.8	198.5	—	213.8	238.0	239.2
pelvic	170.6	198.5	—	213.6	238.0	239.2
phalanges	170.9	198.5	—	213.9	238.0	239.2
foot	170.8	198.5	—	213.8	238.0	239.2
hand	170.5	198.5	—	213.5	238.0	239.2
pubic	170.6	198.5	—	213.6	238.0	239.2
radius (any part)	170.4	198.5	—	213.4	238.0	239.2
rib	170.3	198.5	—	213.3	238.0	239.2
sacral vertebra	170.6	198.5	—	213.6	238.0	239.2
sacrum	170.6	198.5	—	213.6	238.0	239.2
scaphoid (of hand)	170.5	198.5	—	213.5	238.0	239.2
of ankle	170.8	198.5	—	213.8	238.0	239.2
scapula (any part)	170.4	198.5	—	213.4	238.0	239.2
sella turcica	170.0	198.5	—	213.0	238.0	239.2
short	170.9	198.5	—	213.9	238.0	239.2
lower limb	170.8	198.5	—	213.8	238.0	239.2
upper limb	170.5	198.5	—	213.5	238.0	239.2
shoulder	170.4	198.5	—	213.4	238.0	239.2
skeleton, skeletal NEC	170.9	198.5	—	213.9	238.0	239.2
skull	170.0	198.5	—	213.0	238.0	239.2
sphenoid	170.0	198.5	—	213.0	238.0	239.2
spine, spinal (column)	170.2	198.5	—	213.2	238.0	239.2
coccyx	170.6	198.5	—	213.6	238.0	239.2
sacrum	170.6	198.5	—	213.6	238.0	239.2
sternum	170.3	198.5	—	213.3	238.0	239.2
tarsus (any)	170.8	198.5	—	213.8	238.0	239.2
temporal	170.0	198.5	—	213.0	238.0	239.2
thumb	170.5	198.5	—	213.5	238.0	239.2
tibia (any part)	170.7	198.5	—	213.7	238.0	239.2
toe (any)	170.8	198.5	—	213.8	238.0	239.2
trapezium	170.5	198.5	—	213.5	238.0	239.2
trapezoid	170.5	198.5	—	213.5	238.0	239.2
turbinate	170.0	198.5	—	213.0	238.0	239.2
ulna (any part)	170.4	198.5	—	213.4	238.0	239.2
unciform	170.5	198.5	—	213.5	238.0	239.2
vertebra (column)	170.2	198.5	—	213.2	238.0	239.2
coccyx	170.6	198.5	—	213.6	238.0	239.2
sacrum	170.6	198.5	—	213.6	238.0	239.2
vomer	170.0	198.5	—	213.0	238.0	239.2
wrist	170.5	198.5	—	213.5	238.0	239.2
xiphoid process	170.3	198.5	—	213.3	238.0	239.2
zygomatic	170.0	198.5	—	213.0	238.0	239.2
book-leaf (mouth)	145.8	198.89	230.0	210.4	235.1	239.0
bowel - *see* Neoplasm, intestine						
brachial plexus	171.2	198.89	—	215.2	238.1	239.2
brain NEC	191.9	198.3	—	225.0	237.5	239.6
basal ganglia	191.0	198.3	—	225.0	237.5	239.6
cerebellopontine angle	191.6	198.3	—	225.0	237.5	239.6
cerebellum NOS	191.6	198.3	—	225.0	237.5	239.6
cerebrum	191.0	198.3	—	225.0	237.5	239.6
choroid plexus	191.5	198.3	—	225.0	237.5	239.6
contiguous sites	191.8	—	—	—	—	—
corpus callosum	191.8	198.3	—	225.0	237.5	239.6
corpus striatum	191.0	198.3	—	225.0	237.5	239.6

◄▶ **New Code**   ◄▥ ▥▶ **Revised Code**

	Malignant					
	Primary	Secondary	Ca in stiu	Benign	Uncertain Behavior	Unspecified
Neoplasm *(Continued)*						
brain *(Continued)*						
cortex (cerebral)	191.0	198.3	—	225.0	237.5	239.6
frontal lobe	191.1	198.3	—	225.0	237.5	239.6
globus pallidus	191.0	198.3	—	225.0	237.5	239.6
hippocampus	191.2	198.3	—	225.0	237.5	239.6
hypothalamus	191.0	198.3	—	225.0	237.5	239.6
internal capsule	191.0	198.3	—	225.0	237.5	239.6
medulla oblongata	191.7	198.3	—	225.0	237.5	239.6
meninges	192.1	198.4	—	225.2	237.6	239.7
midbrain	191.7	198.3	—	225.0	237.5	239.6
occipital lobe	191.4	198.3	—	225.0	237.5	239.6
parietal lobe	191.3	198.3	—	225.0	237.5	239.6
peduncle	191.7	198.3	—	225.0	237.5	239.6
pons	191.7	198.3	—	225.0	237.5	239.6
stem	191.7	198.3	—	225.0	237.5	239.6
tapetum	191.8	198.3	—	225.0	237.5	239.6
temporal lobe	191.2	198.3	—	225.0	237.5	239.6
thalamus	191.0	198.3	—	225.0	237.5	239.6
uncus	191.2	198.3	—	225.0	237.5	239.6
ventricle (floor)	191.5	198.3	—	225.0	237.5	239.6
branchial (cleft) (vestiges)	146.8	198.89	230.0	210.6	235.1	239.0
breast (connective tissue) (female) (glandular tissue) (soft parts)	174.9	198.81	233.0	217	238.3	239.3
areola	174.0	198.81	233.0	217	238.3	239.3
male	175.0	198.81	233.0	217	238.3	239.3
axillary tail	174.6	198.81	233.0	217	238.3	239.3
central portion	174.1	198.81	233.0	217	238.3	239.3
contiguous sites	174.8	—	—	—	—	—
ectopic sites	174.8	198.81	233.0	217	238.3	239.3
inner	174.8	198.81	233.0	217	238.3	239.3
lower	174.8	198.81	233.0	217	238.3	239.3
lower-inner quadrant	174.3	198.81	233.0	217	238.3	239.3
lower-outer quadrant	174.5	198.81	233.0	217	238.3	239.3
male	175.9	198.81	233.0	217	238.3	239.3
areola	175.0	198.81	233.0	217	238.3	239.3
ectopic tissue	175.9	198.81	233.0	217	238.3	239.3
nipple	175.0	198.81	233.0	217	238.3	239.3
mastectomy site (skin)	173.5	198.2	—	—	—	—
specified as breast tissue	174.8	198.81	—	—	—	—
midline	174.8	198.81	233.0	217	238.3	239.3
nipple	174.0	198.81	233.0	217	238.3	239.3
male	175.0	198.81	233.0	217	238.3	239.3
outer	174.8	198.81	233.0	217	238.3	239.3
skin	173.5	198.2	232.5	216.5	238.2	239.2
tail (axillary)	174.6	198.81	233.0	217	238.3	239.3
upper	174.8	198.81	233.0	217	238.3	239.3
upper-inner quadrant	174.2	198.81	233.0	217	238.3	239.3
upper-outer quadrant	174.4	198.81	233.0	217	238.3	239.3
broad ligament	183.3	198.82	233.3	221.0	236.3	239.5
bronchiogenic, bronchogenic (lung)	162.9	197.0	231.2	212.3	235.7	239.1
bronchiole	162.9	197.0	231.2	212.3	235.7	239.1
bronchus	162.9	197.0	231.2	212.3	235.7	239.1
carina	162.2	197.0	231.2	212.3	235.7	239.1
contiguous sites with lung or trachea	162.8	—	—	—	—	—
lower lobe of lung	162.5	197.0	231.2	212.3	235.7	239.1
main	162.2	197.0	231.2	212.3	235.7	239.1
middle lobe of lung	162.4	197.0	231.2	212.3	235.7	239.1
upper lobe of lung	162.3	197.0	231.2	212.3	235.7	239.1
brow	173.3	198.2	232.3	216.3	238.2	239.2
buccal (cavity)	145.9	198.89	230.0	210.4	235.1	239.0
commissure	145.0	198.89	230.0	210.4	235.1	239.0
groove (lower) (upper)	145.1	198.89	230.0	210.4	235.1	239.0
mucosa	145.0	198.89	230.0	210.4	235.1	239.0
sulcus (lower) (upper)	145.1	198.89	230.0	210.4	235.1	239.0

	Malignant					
	Primary	Secondary	Ca in stiu	Benign	Uncertain Behavior	Unspecified
Neoplasm *(Continued)*						
bulbourethral gland	189.3	198.1	233.9	223.81	236.99	239.5
bursa-*see* Neoplasm, connective tissue						
buttock NEC*	195.3	198.89	232.5	229.8	238.8	239.8
calf*	195.5	198.89	232.7	229.8	238.8	239.8
calvarium	170.0	198.5	—	213.0	238.0	239.2
calyx, renal	189.1	198.0	233.9	223.1	236.91	239.5
canal						
anal	154.2	197.5	230.5	211.4	235.5	239.0
auditory (external)	173.2	198.2	232.2	216.2	238.2	239.2
auricular (external)	173.2	198.2	232.2	216.2	238.2	239.2
canaliculi, biliary (biliferi) (intrahepatic)	155.1	197.8	230.8	211.5	235.3	239.0
canthus (eye) (inner) (outer)	173.1	198.2	232.1	216.1	238.2	239.2
capillary-*see* Neoplasm, connective tissue						
caput coli	153.4	197.5	230.3	211.3	235.2	239.0
cardia (gastric)	151.0	197.8	230.2	211.1	235.2	239.0
cardiac orifice (stomach)	151.0	197.8	230.2	211.1	235.2	239.0
cardio-esophageal junction	151.0	197.8	230.2	211.1	235.2	239.0
cardio-esophagus	151.0	197.8	230.2	211.1	235.2	239.0
carina (bronchus) (trachea)	162.2	197.0	231.2	212.3	235.7	239.1
carotid (artery)	171.0	198.89	—	215.0	238.1	239.2
body	194.5	198.89	—	227.5	237.3	239.7
carpus (any bone)	170.5	198.5	—	213.5	238.0	239.2
cartilage (articular) (joint) NEC-*see also* Neoplasm, bone	170.9	198.5	—	213.9	238.0	239.2
arytenoid	161.3	197.3	231.0	212.1	235.6	239.1
auricular	171.0	198.89	—	215.0	238.1	239.2
bronchi	162.2	197.3	—	212.3	235.7	239.1
connective tissue-*see* Neoplasm, connective tissue						
costal	170.3	198.5	—	213.3	238.0	239.2
cricoid	161.3	197.3	231.0	212.1	235.6	239.1
cuneiform	161.3	197.3	231.0	212.1	235.6	239.1
ear (external)	171.0	198.89	—	215.0	238.1	239.2
ensiform	170.3	198.5	—	213.3	238.0	239.2
epiglottis	161.1	197.3	231.0	212.1	235.6	239.1
anterior surface	146.4	198.89	230.0	210.6	235.1	239.0
eyelid	171.0	198.89	—	215.0	238.1	239.2
intervertebral	170.2	198.5	—	213.2	238.0	239.2
larynx, laryngeal	161.3	197.3	231.0	212.1	235.6	239.1
nose, nasal	160.0	197.3	231.8	212.0	235.9	239.1
pinna	171.0	198.89	—	215.0	238.1	239.2
rib	170.3	198.5	—	213.3	238.0	239.2
semilunar (knee)	170.7	198.5	—	213.7	238.0	239.2
thyroid	161.3	197.3	231.0	212.1	235.6	239.1
trachea	162.0	197.3	231.1	212.2	235.7	239.1
cauda equina	192.2	198.3	—	225.3	237.5	239.7
cavity						
buccal	145.9	198.89	230.0	210.4	235.1	239.0
nasal	160.0	197.3	231.8	212.0	235.9	239.1
oral	145.9	198.89	230.0	210.4	235.1	239.0
peritoneal	158.9	197.6	—	211.8	235.4	239.0
tympanic	160.1	197.3	231.8	212.0	235.9	239.1
cecum	153.4	197.5	230.3	211.3	235.2	239.0
central nervous system-*see* Neoplasm,						
white matter	191.0	198.3	—	225.0	237.5	239.6
cerebellopontine (angle)	191.6	198.3	—	225.0	237.5	239.6
cerebellum, cerebellar	191.6	198.3	—	225.0	237.5	239.6
cerebrum, cerebral (cortex) (hemisphere) (white matter)	191.0	198.3	—	225.0	237.5	239.6
meninges	192.1	198.4	—	225.2	237.6	239.7
peduncle	191.7	198.3	—	225.0	237.5	239.6
ventricle (any)	191.5	198.3	—	225.0	237.5	239.6
cervical region	195.0	198.89	234.8	229.8	238.8	239.8
cervix (cervical) (uteri) (uterus)	180.9	198.82	233.1	219.0	236.0	239.5

◄▶ **New Code**   ◄▥▥▶ **Revised Code**

	Malignant			Benign	Uncertain Behavior	Unspecified
	Primary	Secondary	Ca in stiu			
Neoplasm *(Continued)*						
cervix *(Continued)*						
canal	180.0	198.82	233.1	219.0	236.0	239.5
contiguous sites	180.8	—		—	—	—
endocervix (canal) (gland)	180.0	198.82	233.1	219.0	236.0	239.5
exocervix	180.1	198.82	233.1	219.0	236.0	239.5
external os	180.1	198.82	233.1	219.0	236.0	239.5
internal os	180.0	198.82	233.1	219.0	236.0	239.5
nabothian gland	180.0	198.82	233.1	219.0	236.0	239.5
squamocolumnar junction	180.8	198.82	233.1	219.0	236.0	239.5
stump	180.8	198.82	233.1	219.0	236.0	239.5
cheek	195.0	198.89	234.8	229.8	238.8	239.8
external	173.3	198.2	232.3	216.3	238.2	239.2
inner aspect	145.0	198.89	230.0	210.4	235.1	239.0
internal	145.0	198.89	230.0	210.4	235.1	239.0
mucosa	145.0	198.89	230.0	210.4	235.1	239.0
chest (wall) NEC	195.1	198.89	234.8	229.8	238.8	239.8
chiasma opticum	192.0	198.4	—	225.1	237.9	239.7
chin	173.3	198.2	232.3	216.3	238.2	239.2
choana	147.3	198.89	230.0	210.7	235.1	239.0
cholangiole	155.1	197.8	230.8	211.5	235.3	239.0
choledochal duct	156.1	197.8	230.8	211.5	235.3	239.0
choroid	190.6	198.4	234.0	224.6	238.8	239.8
plexus	191.5	198.3	—	225.0	237.5	239.6
ciliary body	190.0	198.4	234.0	224.0	238.8	239.8
clavicle	170.3	198.5	—	213.3	238.0	239.2
clitoris	184.3	198.82	233.3	221.2	236.3	239.5
clivus	170.0	198.5	—	213.0	238.0	239.2
cloacogenic zone	154.8	197.5	230.7	211.4	235.5	239.0
coccygeal						
body or glomus	194.6	198.89	—	227.6	237.3	239.7
vertebra	170.6	198.5	—	213.6	238.0	239.2
coccyx	170.6	198.5	—	213.6	238.0	239.2
colon-*see also* Neoplasm, intestine,						
large and rectum	154.0	197.5	230.4	211.4	235.2	239.0
column, spinal-*see* Neoplasm, spine						
columnella	173.3	198.2	232.3	216.3	238.2	239.2
commissure						
labial, lip	140.6	198.89	230.0	210.4	235.1	239.0
laryngeal	161.0	197.3	231.0	212.1	235.6	239.1
common (bile) duct	156.1	197.8	230.8	211.5	235.3	239.0
concha	173.2	198.2	232.2	216.2	238.2	239.2
nose	160.0	197.3	231.8	212.0	235.9	239.1
conjunctiva	190.3	198.4	234.0	224.3	238.8	239.8
connective tissue NEC	171.9	198.89	—	215.9	238.1	239.2

Note-For neoplasms of connective tissue (blood vessel, bursa, fascia, ligament, muscle, peripheral nerves, sympathetic and parasympathetic nerves and ganglia, synovia, tendon, etc.) or of morphological types that indicate connective tissue, code according to the list under "Neoplasm, connective tissue;" for sites that do not appear in this list, code to neoplasm of that site; e.g.,

liposarcoma, shoulder	171.2					
leiomyosarcoma, stomach	151.9					
neurofibroma, chest wall	215.4					

Morphological types that indicate connective tissue appear in their proper place in the alphabetic index with the instruction "*see* Neoplasm, connective tissue ...."

abdomen	171.5	198.89	—	215.5	238.1	239.2
abdominal wall	171.5	198.89	—	215.5	238.1	239.2
ankle	171.3	198.89	—	215.3	238.1	239.2
antecubital fossa or space	171.2	198.89	—	215.2	238.1	239.2
arm	171.2	198.89	—	215.2	238.1	239.2
auricle (ear)	171.0	198.89	—	215.0	238.1	239.2
axilla	171.4	198.89	—	215.4	238.1	239.2
back	171.7	198.89	—	215.7	238.1	239.2
breast (female) (*see also* Neoplasm, breast)	174.9	198.81	233.0	217	238.3	239.3
male	175.9	198.81	233.0	217	238.3	239.3

◄▶ **New Code**   ◄▦ ▦▶ **Revised Code**

	Malignant			Benign	Uncertain Behavior	Unspecified
	Primary	Secondary	Ca in stiu			
Neoplasm *(Continued)*						
connective tissue NEC *(Continued)*						
buttock	171.6	198.89	—	215.6	238.1	239.2
calf	171.3	198.89	—	215.3	238.1	239.2
cervical region	171.0	198.89	—	215.0	238.1	239.2
cheek	171.0	198.89	—	215.0	238.1	239.2
chest (wall)	171.4	198.89	—	215.4	238.1	239.2
chin	171.0	198.89	—	215.0	238.1	239.2
contiguous sites	171.8	—	—	—	—	—
diaphragm	171.4	198.89	—	215.4	238.1	239.2
ear (external)	171.0	198.89	—	215.0	238.1	239.2
elbow	171.2	198.89	—	215.2	238.1	239.2
extrarectal	171.6	198.89	—	215.6	238.1	239.2
extremity	171.8	198.89	—	215.8	238.1	239.2
lower	171.3	198.89	—	215.3	238.1	239.2
upper	171.2	198.89	—	215.2	238.1	239.2
eyelid	171.0	198.89	—	215.0	238.1	239.2
face	171.0	198.89	—	215.0	238.1	239.2
finger	171.2	198.89	—	215.2	238.1	239.2
flank	171.7	198.89	—	215.7	238.1	239.2
foot	171.3	198.89	—	215.3	238.1	239.2
forearm	171.2	198.89	—	215.2	238.1	239.2
forehead	171.0	198.89	—	215.0	238.1	239.2
gluteal region	171.6	198.89	—	215.6	238.1	239.2
great vessels NEC	171.4	198.89	—	215.4	238.1	239.2
groin	171.6	198.89	—	215.6	238.1	239.2
hand	171.2	198.89	—	215.2	238.1	239.2
head	171.0	198.89	—	215.0	238.1	239.2
heel	171.3	198.89	—	215.3	238.1	239.2
hip	171.3	198.89	—	215.3	238.1	239.2
hypochondrium	171.5	198.89	—	215.5	238.1	239.2
iliopsoas muscle	171.6	198.89	—	215.5	238.1	239.2
infraclavicular region	171.4	198.89	—	215.4	238.1	239.2
inguinal (canal) (region)	171.6	198.89	—	215.6	238.1	239.2
intrathoracic	171.4	198.89	—	215.4	238.1	239.2
ischorectal fossa	171.6	198.89	—	215.6	238.1	239.2
jaw	143.9	198.89	230.0	210.4	235.1	239.0
knee	171.3	198.89	—	215.3	238.1	239.2
leg	171.3	198.89	—	215.3	238.1	239.2
limb NEC	171.9	198.89	—	215.8	238.1	239.2
lower	171.3	198.89	—	215.3	238.1	239.2
upper	171.2	198.89	—	215.2	238.1	239.2
nates	171.6	198.89	—	215.6	238.1	239.2
neck	171.0	198.89	—	215.0	238.1	239.2
orbit	190.1	198.4	234.0	224.1	238.8	239.8
pararectal	171.6	198.89	—	215.6	238.1	239.2
para-urethral	171.6	198.89	—	215.6	238.1	239.2
paravaginal	171.6	198.89	—	215.6	238.1	239.2
pelvis (floor)	171.6	198.89	—	215.6	238.1	239.2
pelvo-abdominal	171.8	198.89	—	215.8	238.1	239.2
perineum	171.6	198.89	—	215.6	238.1	239.2
perirectal (tissue)	171.6	198.89	—	215.6	238.1	239.2
periurethral (tissue)	171.6	198.89	—	215.6	238.1	239.2
popliteal fossa or space	171.3	198.89	—	215.3	238.1	239.2
presacral	171.6	198.89	—	215.6	238.1	239.2
psoas muscle	171.5	198.89	—	215.5	238.1	239.2
pterygoid fossa	171.0	198.89	—	215.0	238.1	239.2
rectovaginal septum or wall	171.6	198.89	—	215.6	238.1	239.2
rectovesical	171.6	198.89	—	215.6	238.1	239.2
retroperitoneum	158.0	197.6	—	211.8	235.4	239.0
sacrococcygeal region	171.6	198.89	—	215.6	238.1	239.2
scalp	171.0	198.89	—	215.0	238.1	239.2
scapular region	171.4	198.89	—	215.4	238.1	239.2
shoulder	171.2	198.89	—	215.2	238.1	239.2

◀▶ **New Code**   ◀▦▦▶ **Revised Code**

ICD-9-CM

Vol. 2

	Malignant			Benign	Uncertain Behavior	Unspecified
	Primary	Secondary	Ca in situ			
Neoplasm *(Continued)*						
connective tissue NEC *(Continued)*						
skin (dermis) NEC	173.9	198.2	232.9	216.9	238.2	239.2
submental	171.0	198.89	—	215.0	238.1	239.2
supraclavicular region	171.0	198.89	—	215.0	238.1	239.2
temple	171.0	198.89	—	215.0	238.1	239.2
temporal region	171.0	198.89	—	215.0	238.1	239.2
thigh	171.3	198.89	—	215.3	238.1	239.2
thoracic (duct) (wall)	171.4	198.89	—	215.4	238.1	239.2
thorax	171.4	198.89	—	215.4	238.1	239.2
thumb	171.2	198.89	—	215.2	238.1	239.2
toe	171.3	198.89	—	215.3	238.1	239.2
trunk	171.7	198.89	—	215.7	238.1	239.2
umbilicus	171.5	198.89	—	215.5	238.1	239.2
vesicorectal	171.6	198.89	—	215.6	238.1	239.2
wrist	171.2	198.89	—	215.2	238.1	239.2
conus medullaris	192.2	198.3	—	225.3	237.5	239.7
cord (true) (vocal)	161.0	197.3	231.0	212.1	235.6	239.1
false	161.1	197.3	231.0	212.1	235.6	239.1
spermatic	187.6	198.82	233.6	222.8	236.6	239.5
spinal (cervical) (lumbar) (thoracic)	192.2	198.3	—	225.3	237.5	239.7
cornea (limbus)	190.4	198.4	234.0	224.4	238.8	239.8
corpus						
albicans	183.0	198.6	233.3	220	236.2	239.5
callosum, brain	191.8	198.3	—	225.0	237.5	239.6
cavernosum	187.3	198.82	233.5	222.1	236.6	239.5
gastric	151.4	197.8	230.2	211.1	235.2	239.0
penis	187.3	198.82	233.5	222.1	236.6	239.5
striatum, cerebrum	191.0	198.3	—	225.0	237.5	239.6
uteri	182.0	198.82	233.2	219.1	236.0	239.5
isthmus	182.1	198.82	233.2	219.1	236.0	239.5
cortex						
adrenal	194.0	198.7	234.8	227.0	237.2	239.7
cerebral	191.0	198.3	—	225.0	237.5	239.6
costal cartilage	170.3	198.5	—	213.3	238.0	239.2
costovertebral joint	170.3	198.5	—	213.3	238.0	239.2
Cowper's gland	189.3	198.1	233.9	223.81	236.99	239.5
cranial (fossa, any)	191.9	198.3	—	225.0	237.5	239.6
meninges	192.1	198.4	—	225.2	237.6	239.7
nerve (any)	192.0	198.4	—	225.1	237.9	239.7
craniobuccal pouch	194.3	198.89	234.8	227.3	237.0	239.7
craniopharyngeal (duct) (pouch)	194.3	198.89	234.8	227.3	237.0	239.7
cricoid	148.0	198.89	230.0	210.8	235.1	239.0
cartilage	161.3	197.3	231.0	212.1	235.6	239.1
cricopharynx	148.0	198.89	230.0	210.8	235.1	239.0
crypt of Morgagni	154.8	197.5	230.7	211.4	235.2	239.0
crystalline lens	190.0	198.4	234.0	224.0	238.8	239.8
cul-de-sac (Douglas')	158.8	197.6	—	211.8	235.4	239.0
cuneiform cartilage	161.3	197.3	231.0	212.1	235.6	239.1
cutaneous-*see* Neoplasm, skin						
cutis-*see* Neoplasm, skin						
cystic (bile) duct (common)	156.1	197.8	230.8	211.5	235.3	239.0
dermis-*see* Neoplasm, skin						
diaphragm	171.4	198.89	—	215.4	238.1	239.2
digestive organs, system, tube, or tract NEC	159.9	197.8	230.9	211.9	235.5	239.0
contiguous sites with peritoneum	159.8	—				
disc, intervertebral	170.2	198.5	—	213.2	238.0	239.2
disease, generalized	199.0	199.0	234.9	229.9	238.9	199.0
disseminated	199.0	199.0	234.9	229.9	238.9	199.0
Douglas' cul-de-sac or pouch	158.8	197.6	—	211.8	235.4	239.0
duodenojejunal junction	152.8	197.4	230.7	211.2	235.2	239.0
duodenum	152.0	197.4	230.7	211.2	235.2	239.0
dura (cranial) (mater)	192.1	198.4	—	225.2	237.6	239.7

	Malignant					
	Primary	**Secondary**	**Ca in stiu**	**Benign**	**Uncertain Behavior**	**Unspecified**
Neoplasm *(Continued)*						
dura *(Continued)*						
cerebral	192.1	198.4	—	225.2	237.6	239.7
spinal	192.3	198.4	—	225.4	237.6	239.7
ear (external)	173.2	198.2	232.2	216.2	238.2	239.2
auricle or auris	173.2	198.2	232.2	216.2	238.2	239.2
canal, external	173.2	198.2	232.2	216.2	238.2	239.2
cartilage	171.0	198.89	—	215.0	238.1	239.2
external meatus	173.2	198.2	232.2	216.2	238.2	239.2
inner	160.1	197.3	231.8	212.0	235.9	239.1
lobule	173.2	198.2	232.2	216.2	238.2	239.2
middle	160.1	197.3	231.8	212.0	235.9	239.1
contiguous sites with accessory sinuses or nasal cavities	160.8	—	—	—	—	—
skin	173.2	198.2	232.2	216.2	238.2	239.2
earlobe	173.2	198.2	232.2	216.2	238.2	239.2
ejaculatory duct	187.8	198.82	233.6	222.8	236.6	239.5
elbow NEC*	195.4	198.89	232.6	229.8	238.8	239.8
endocardium	164.1	198.89	—	212.7	238.8	239.8
endocervix (canal) (gland)	180.0	198.82	233.1	219.0	236.0	239.5
endocrine gland NEC	194.9	198.89	—	227.9	237.4	239.7
pluriglandular NEC	194.8	198.89	234.8	227.8	237.4	239.7
endometrium (gland) (stroma)	182.0	198.82	233.2	219.1	236.0	239.5
ensiform cartilage	170.3	198.5	—	213.3	238.0	239.2
enteric—*see* Neoplasm, intestine						
ependyma (brain)	191.5	198.3	—	225.0	237.5	239.6
epicardium	164.1	198.89	—	212.7	238.8	239.8
epididymis	187.5	198.82	233.6	222.3	236.6	239.5
epidural	192.9	198.4	—	225.9	237.9	239.7
epiglottis	161.1	197.3	231.0	212.1	235.6	239.1
anterior aspect or surface	146.4	198.89	230.0	210.6	235.1	239.0
cartilage	161.3	197.3	231.0	212.1	235.6	239.1
free border (margin)	146.4	198.89	230.0	210.6	235.1	239.0
junctional region	146.5	198.89	230.0	210.6	235.1	239.0
posterior (laryngeal) surface	161.1	197.3	231.0	212.1	235.6	239.1
suprahyoid portion	161.1	197.3	231.0	212.1	235.6	239.1
esophagogastric junction	151.0	197.8	230.2	211.1	235.2	239.0
esophagus	150.9	197.8	230.1	211.0	235.5	239.0
abdominal	150.2	197.8	230.1	211.0	235.5	239.0
cervical	150.0	197.8	230.1	211.0	235.5	239.0
contiguous sites	150.8	—	—	—	—	—
distal (third)	150.5	197.8	230.1	211.0	235.5	239.0
lower (third)	150.5	197.8	230.1	211.0	235.5	239.0
middle (third)	150.4	197.8	230.1	211.0	235.5	239.0
proximal (third)	150.3	197.8	230.1	211.0	235.5	239.0
specified part NEC	150.8	197.8	230.1	211.0	235.5	239.0
thoracic	150.1	197.8	230.1	211.0	235.5	239.0
upper (third)	150.3	197.8	230.1	211.0	235.5	239.0
ethmoid (sinus)	160.3	197.3	231.8	212.0	235.9	239.1
bone or labyrinth	170.0	198.5	—	213.0	238.0	239.2
Eustachian tube	160.1	197.3	231.8	212.0	235.9	239.1
exocervix	180.1	198.82	233.1	219.0	236.0	239.5
external						
meatus (ear)	173.2	198.2	232.2	216.2	238.2	239.2
os, cervix uteri	180.1	198.82	233.1	219.0	236.0	239.5
extradural	192.9	198.4	—	225.9	237.9	239.7
extrahepatic (bile) duct	156.1	197.8	230.8	211.5	235.3	239.0
contiguous sites with gallbladder	156.8	—	—	—	—	—
extraocular muscle	190.1	198.4	234.0	224.1	238.8	239.8
extrarectal	195.3	198.89	234.8	229.8	238.8	239.8
extremity*	195.8	198.89	232.8	229.8	238.8	239.8
lower*	195.5	198.89	232.7	229.8	238.8	239.8
upper*	195.4	198.89	232.6	229.8	238.8	239.8
eye NEC	190.9	198.4	234.0	224.9	238.8	239.8

ICD-9-CM

Vol. 2

	Malignant					
	Primary	Secondary	Ca in situ	Benign	Uncertain Behavior	Unspecified
Neoplasm *(Continued)*						
eye NEC *(Continued)*						
contiguous sites	190.8	—	—	—	—	—
specified sites NEC	190.8	198.4	234.0	224.8	238.8	239.8
eyeball	190.0	198.4	234.0	224.0	238.8	239.8
eyebrow	173.3	198.2	232.3	216.3	238.2	239.2
eyelid (lower) (skin) (upper)	173.1	198.2	232.1	216.1	238.2	239.2
cartilage	171.0	198.89	—	215.0	238.1	239.2
face NEC*	195.0	198.89	232.3	229.8	238.8	239.8
Fallopian tube (accessory)	183.2	198.82	233.3	221.0	236.3	239.5
falx (cerebella) (cerebri)	192.1	198.4	—	225.2	237.6	239.7
fascia-*see also* Neoplasm, connective tissue						
palmar	171.2	198.89	—	215.2	238.1	239.2
plantar	171.3	198.89	—	215.3	238.1	239.2
fatty tissue-*see* Neoplasm, connective tissue						
fauces, faucial NEC	146.9	198.89	230.0	210.6	235.1	239.0
pillars	146.2	198.89	230.0	210.6	235.1	239.0
tonsil	146.0	198.89	230.0	210.5	235.1	239.0
femur (any part)	170.7	198.5	—	213.7	238.0	239.2
fetal membrane	181	198.82	233.2	219.8	236.1	239.5
fibrous tissue-*see* Neoplasm, connective tissue						
fibula (any part)	170.7	198.5	—	213.7	238.0	239.2
filum terminale	192.2	198.3	—	225.3	237.5	239.7
finger NEC*	195.4	198.89	232.6	229.8	238.8	239.8
flank NEC*	195.8	198.89	232.5	229.8	238.8	239.8
follicle, nabothian	180.0	198.82	233.1	219.0	236.0	239.5
foot NEC*	195.5	198.89	232.7	229.8	238.8	239.8
forearm NEC*	195.4	198.89	232.6	229.8	238.8	239.8
forehead (skin)	173.3	198.2	232.3	216.3	238.2	239.2
foreskin	187.1	198.82	233.5	222.1	236.6	239.5
fornix						
pharyngeal	147.3	198.89	230.0	210.7	235.1	239.0
vagina	184.0	198.82	233.3	221.1	236.3	239.5
fossa (of)						
anterior (cranial)	191.9	198.3	—	225.0	237.5	239.6
cranial	191.9	198.3	—	225.0	237.5	239.6
ischiorectal	195.3	198.89	234.8	229.8	238.8	239.8
middle (cranial)	191.9	198.3	—	225.0	237.5	239.6
pituitary	194.3	198.89	234.8	227.3	237.0	239.7
posterior (cranial)	191.9	198.3	—	225.0	237.5	239.6
pterygoid	171.0	198.89	—	215.0	238.1	239.2
pyriform	148.1	198.89	230.0	210.8	235.1	239.0
Rosenmüller	147.2	198.89	230.0	210.7	235.1	239.0
tonsillar	146.1	198.89	230.0	210.6	235.1	239.0
fourchette	184.4	198.82	233.3	221.2	236.3	239.5
frenulum						
labii-*see* Neoplasm, lip, internal						
linguae	141.3	198.89	230.0	210.1	235.1	239.0
frontal						
bone	170.0	198.5	—	213.0	238.0	239.2
lobe, brain	191.1	198.3	—	225.0	237.5	239.6
meninges	192.1	198.4	—	225.2	237.6	239.7
pole	191.1	198.3	—	225.0	237.5	239.6
sinus	160.4	197.3	231.8	212.0	235.9	239.1
fundus						
stomach	151.3	197.8	230.2	211.1	235.2	239.0
uterus	182.0	198.82	233.2	219.1	236.0	239.5
gall duct (extrahepatic)	156.1	197.8	230.8	211.5	235.3	239.0
intrahepatic	155.1	197.8	230.8	211.5	235.3	239.0
gallbladder	156.0	197.8	230.8	211.5	235.3	239.0
contiguous sites with extrahepatic bile ducts	156.8	—		—	—	—
ganglia (*see also* Neoplasm, connective tissue)	171.9	198.89	—	215.9	238.1	239.2
basal	191.0	198.3	—	225.0	237.5	239.6

	Malignant					
	Primary	Secondary	Ca in stiu	Benign	Uncertain Behavior	Unspecified
Neoplasm *(Continued)*						
ganglion (*see also* Neoplasm, connective tissue)	171.9	198.89	—	215.9	238.1	239.2
cranial nerve	192.0	198.4	—	225.1	237.9	239.7
Gartner's duct	184.0	198.82	233.3	221.1	236.3	239.5
gastric-*see* Neoplasm, stomach						
gastrocolic	159.8	197.8	230.9	211.9	235.5	239.0
gastroesophageal junction	151.0	197.8	230.2	211.1	235.2	239.0
gastrointestinal (tract) NEC	159.9	197.8	230.9	211.9	235.5	239.0
generalized	199.0	199.0	234.9	229.9	238.9	199.0
genital organ or tract						
female NEC	184.9	198.82	233.3	221.9	236.3	239.5
contiguous sites	184.8					
specified site NEC	184.8	198.82	233.3	221.8	236.3	239.5
male NEC	187.9	198.82	233.6	222.9	236.6	239.5
contiguous sites	187.8	—	—	—	—	—
specified site NEC	187.8	198.82	233.6	222.8	236.6	239.5
genitourinary tract						
female	184.9	198.82	233.3	221.9	236.3	239.5
male	187.9	198.82	233.6	222.9	236.6	239.5
gingiva (alveolar) (marginal)	143.9	198.89	230.0	210.4	235.1	239.0
lower	143.1	198.89	230.0	210.4	235.1	239.0
mandibular	143.1	198.89	230.0	210.4	235.1	239.0
maxillary	143.0	198.89	230.0	210.4	235.1	239.0
upper	143.0	198.89	230.0	210.4	235.1	239.0
gland, glandular (lymphatic) (system)-*see also* Neoplasm, lymph gland						
endocrine NEC	194.9	198.89	—	227.9	237.4	239.7
salivary-*see* Neoplasm, salivary, gland						
glans penis	187.2	198.82	233.5	222.1	236.6	239.5
globus pallidus	191.0	198.3	—	225.0	237.5	239.6
glomus						
coccygeal	194.6	198.89	—	227.6	237.3	239.7
jugularis	194.6	198.89	—	227.6	237.3	239.7
glosso-epiglottic fold(s)	146.4	198.89	230.0	210.6	235.1	239.0
glossopalatine fold	146.2	198.89	230.0	210.6	235.1	239.0
glossopharyngeal sulcus	146.1	198.89	230.0	210.6	235.1	239.0
glottis	161.0	197.3	231.0	212.1	235.6	239.1
gluteal region*	195.3	198.89	232.5	229.8	238.8	239.8
great vessels NEC	171.4	198.89	—	215.4	238.1	239.2
groin NEC	195.3	198.89	232.5	229.8	238.8	239.8
gum	143.9	198.89	230.0	210.4	235.1	239.0
contiguous sites	143.8	—	—	—	—	—
lower	143.1	198.89	230.0	210.4	235.1	239.0
upper	143.0	198.89	230.0	210.4	235.1	239.0
hand NEC*	195.4	198.89	232.6	229.8	238.8	239.8
head NEC*	195.0	198.89	232.4	229.8	238.8	239.8
heart	164.1	198.89	—	212.7	238.8	239.8
contiguous sites with mediastinum or thymus	164.8	—	—	—	—	—
heel NEC*	195.5	198.89	232.7	229.8	238.8	239.8
helix	173.2	198.2	232.2	216.2	238.2	239.2
hematopoietic, hemopoietic tissue NEC	202.8	198.89	—	—	—	238.7
hemisphere, cerebral	191.0	198.3	—	225.0	237.5	239.6
hemorrhoidal zone	154.2	197.5	230.5	211.4	235.5	239.0
hepatic	155.2	197.7	230.8	211.5	235.3	239.0
duct (bile)	156.1	197.8	230.8	211.5	235.3	239.0
flexure (colon)	153.0	197.5	230.3	211.3	235.2	239.0
primary	155.0	—				
hilus of lung	162.2	197.0	231.2	212.3	235.7	239.1
hip NEC*	195.5	198.89	232.7	229.8	238.8	239.8
hippocampus, brain	191.2	198.3	—	225.0	237.5	239.6
humerus (any part)	170.4	198.5	—	213.4	238.0	239.2
hymen	184.0	198.82	233.3	221.1	236.3	239.5
hypopharynx, hypopharyngeal NEC	148.9	198.89	230.0	210.8	235.1	239.0
contiguous sites	148.8	—	—	—	—	—

ICD-9-CM

N

Vol. 2

	Malignant					
	Primary	Secondary	Ca in situ	Benign	Uncertain Behavior	Unspecified
Neoplasm *(Continued)*						
hypopharynx, hypopharyngeal NEC *(Continued)*						
postcricoid region	148.0	198.89	230.0	210.8	235.1	239.0
posterior wall	148.3	198.89	230.0	210.8	235.1	239.0
pyriform fossa (sinus)	148.1	198.89	230.0	210.8	235.1	239.0
specified site NEC	148.8	198.89	230.0	210.8	235.1	239.0
wall	148.9	198.89	230.0	210.8	235.1	239.0
posterior	148.3	198.89	230.0	210.8	235.1	239.0
hypophysis	194.3	198.89	234.8	227.3	237.0	239.7
hypothalamus	191.0	198.3	—	225.0	237.5	239.6
ileocecum, ileocecal (coil) (junction) (valve)	153.4	197.5	230.3	211.3	235.2	239.0
ileum	152.2	197.4	230.7	211.2	235.2	239.0
ilium	170.6	198.5	—	213.6	238.0	239.2
immunoproliferative NEC	203.8	—	—	—	—	—
infraclavicular (region)*	195.1	198.89	232.5	229.8	238.8	239.8
inguinal (region)*	195.3	198.89	232.5	229.8	238.8	239.8
insula	191.0	198.3	—	225.0	237.5	239.6
insular tissue (pancreas)	157.4	197.8	230.9	211.7	235.5	239.0
brain	191.0	198.3	—	225.0	237.5	239.6
interarytenoid fold	148.2	198.89	230.0	210.8	235.1	239.0
hypopharyngeal aspect	148.2	198.89	230.0	210.8	235.1	239.0
laryngeal aspect	161.1	197.3	231.0	212.1	235.6	239.1
marginal zone	148.2	198.89	230.0	210.8	235.1	239.0
interdental papillae	143.9	198.89	230.0	210.4	235.1	239.0
lower	143.1	198.89	230.0	210.4	235.1	239.0
upper	143.0	198.89	230.0	210.4	235.1	239.0
internal						
capsule	191.0	198.3	—	225.0	237.5	239.6
os (cervix)	180.0	198.82	233.1	219.0	236.0	239.5
intervertebral cartilage or disc	170.2	198.5	—	213.2	238.0	239.2
intestine, intestinal	159.0	197.8	230.7	211.9	235.2	239.0
large	153.9	197.5	230.3	211.3	235.2	239.0
appendix	153.5	197.5	230.3	211.3	235.2	239.0
caput coli	153.4	197.5	230.3	211.3	235.2	239.0
cecum	153.4	197.5	230.3	211.3	235.2	239.0
colon	153.9	197.5	230.3	211.3	235.2	239.0
and rectum	154.0	197.5	230.4	211.4	235.2	239.0
ascending	153.6	197.5	230.3	211.3	235.2	239.0
caput	153.4	197.5	230.3	211.3	235.2	239.0
contiguous sites	153.8	—	—	—	—	—
descending	153.2	197.5	230.3	211.3	235.2	239.0
distal	153.2	197.5	230.3	211.3	235.2	239.0
left	153.2	197.5	230.3	211.3	235.2	239.0
pelvic	153.3	197.5	230.3	211.3	235.2	239.0
right	153.6	197.5	230.3	211.3	235.2	239.0
sigmoid (flexure)	153.3	197.5	230.3	211.3	235.2	239.0
transverse	153.1	197.5	230.3	211.3	235.2	239.0
contiguous sites	153.8	—	—	—	—	—
hepatic flexure	153.0	197.5	230.3	211.3	235.2	239.0
ileocecum, ileocecal (coil) (valve)	153.4	197.5	230.3	211.3	235.2	239.0
sigmoid flexure (lower) (upper)	153.3	197.5	230.3	211.3	235.2	239.0
splenic flexure	153.7	197.5	230.3	211.3	235.2	239.0
small	152.9	197.4	230.7	211.2	235.2	239.0
contiguous sites	152.8	—	—	—	—	—
duodenum	152.0	197.4	230.7	211.2	235.2	239.0
ileum	152.2	197.4	230.7	211.2	235.2	239.0
jejunum	152.1	197.4	230.7	211.2	235.2	239.0
tract NEC	159.0	197.8	230.7	211.9	235.2	239.0
intra-abdominal	195.2	198.89	234.8	229.8	238.8	239.8
intracranial NEC	191.9	198.3	—	225.0	237.5	239.6
intrahepatic (bile) duct	155.1	197.8	230.8	211.5	235.3	239.0
intraocular	190.0	198.4	234.0	224.0	238.8	239.8
intraorbital	190.1	198.4	234.0	224.1	238.8	239.8

◀▶ **New Code**   ◀▥ ▥▶ **Revised Code**

	Malignant					
	Primary	Secondary	Ca in situ	Benign	Uncertain Behavior	Unspecified
Neoplasm *(Continued)*						
intrasellar	194.3	198.89	234.8	227.3	237.0	239.7
intrathoracic (cavity) (organs NEC)	195.1	198.89	234.8	229.8	238.8	239.8
contiguous sites with respiratory organs	165.8	—	—	—	—	—
iris	190.0	198.4	234.0	224.0	238.8	239.8
ischiorectal (fossa)	195.3	198.89	234.8	229.8	238.8	239.8
ischium	170.6	198.5	—	213.6	238.0	239.2
island of Reil	191.0	198.3	—	225.0	237.5	239.6
islands or islets of Langerhans	157.4	197.8	230.9	211.7	235.5	239.0
isthmus uteri	182.1	198.82	233.2	219.1	236.0	239.5
jaw	195.0	198.89	234.8	229.8	238.8	239.8
bone	170.1	198.5	—	213.1	238.0	239.2
carcinoma	143.9	—	—	—	—	—
lower	143.1	—	—	—	—	—
upper	143.0	—	—	—	—	—
lower	170.1	198.5	—	213.1	238.0	239.2
upper	170.0	198.5	—	213.0	238.0	239.2
carcinoma (any type) (lower) (upper)	195.0	—	—	—	—	—
skin	173.3	198.2	232.3	216.3	238.2	239.2
soft tissues	143.9	198.89	230.0	210.4	235.1	239.0
lower	143.1	198.89	230.0	210.4	235.1	239.0
upper	143.0	198.89	230.0	210.4	235.1	239.0
jejunum	152.1	197.4	230.7	211.2	235.2	239.0
joint NEC (*see also* Neoplasm, bone)	170.9	198.5	—	213.9	238.0	239.2
acromioclavicular	170.4	198.5	—	213.4	238.0	239.2
bursa or synovial membrane-*see* Neoplasm, connective tissue						
costovertebral	170.3	198.5	—	213.3	238.0	239.2
sternocostal	170.3	198.5	—	213.3	238.0	239.2
temporomandibular	170.1	198.5	—	213.1	238.0	239.2
junction						
anorectal	154.8	197.5	230.7	211.4	235.5	239.0
cardioesophageal	151.0	197.8	230.2	211.1	235.2	239.0
esophagogastric	151.0	197.8	230.2	211.1	235.2	239.0
gastroesophageal	151.0	197.8	230.2	211.1	235.2	239.0
hard and soft palate	145.5	198.89	230.0	210.4	235.1	239.0
ileocecal	153.4	197.5	230.3	211.3	235.2	239.0
pelvirectal	154.0	197.5	230.4	211.4	235.2	239.0
pelviureteric	189.1	198.0	233.9	223.1	236.91	239.5
rectosigmoid	154.0	197.5	230.4	211.4	235.2	239.0
squamocolumnar, of cervix	180.8	198.82	233.1	219.0	236.0	239.5
kidney (parenchymal)	189.0	198.0	233.9	223.0	236.91	239.5
calyx	189.1	198.0	233.9	223.1	236.91	239.5
hilus	189.1	198.0	233.9	223.1	236.91	239.5
pelvis	189.1	198.0	233.9	223.1	236.91	239.5
knee NEC*	195.5	198.89	232.7	229.8	238.8	239.8
labia (skin)	184.4	198.82	233.3	221.2	236.3	239.5
majora	184.1	198.82	233.3	221.2	236.3	239.5
minora	184.2	198.82	233.3	221.2	236.3	239.5
labial-*see also* Neoplasm, lip sulcus (lower) (upper)	145.1	198.89	230.0	210.4	235.1	239.0
labium (skin)	184.4	198.82	233.3	221.2	236.3	239.5
majus	184.1	198.82	233.3	221.2	236.3	239.5
minus	184.2	198.82	233.3	221.2	236.3	239.5
lacrimal						
canaliculi	190.7	198.4	234.0	224.7	238.8	239.8
duct (nasal)	190.7	198.4	234.0	224.7	238.8	239.8
gland	190.2	198.4	234.0	224.2	238.8	239.8
punctum	190.7	198.4	234.0	224.7	238.8	239.8
sac	190.7	198.4	234.0	224.7	238.8	239.8
Langerhans, islands or islets	157.4	197.8	230.9	211.7	235.5	239.0
laryngopharynx	148.9	198.89	230.0	210.8	235.1	239.0
larynx, laryngeal NEC	161.9	197.3	231.0	212.1	235.6	239.1
aryepiglottic fold	161.1	197.3	231.0	212.1	235.6	239.1
cartilage (arytenoid) (cricoid) (cuneiform) (thyroid)	161.3	197.3	231.0	212.1	235.6	239.1

ICD-9-CM

N

Vol. 2

◀▶ **New Code**   ◀▥ ▥▶ **Revised Code**

	Malignant			Benign	Uncertain Behavior	Unspecified
	Primary	Secondary	Ca in situ	Benign	Uncertain Behavior	Unspecified
Neoplasm *(Continued)*						
larynx, laryngeal NEC *(Continued)*						
commissure (anterior) (posterior)	161.0	197.3	231.0	212.1	235.6	239.1
contiguous sites	161.8	—	—	—	—	—
extrinsic NEC	161.1	197.3	231.0	212.1	235.6	239.1
meaning hypopharynx	148.9	198.89	230.0	210.8	235.1	239.0
interarytenoid fold	161.1	197.3	231.0	212.1	235.6	239.1
intrinsic	161.0	197.3	231.0	212.1	235.6	239.1
ventricular band	161.1	197.3	231.0	212.1	235.6	239.1
leg NEC*	195.5	198.89	232.7	229.8	238.8	239.8
lens, crystalline	190.0	198.4	234.0	224.0	238.8	239.8
lid (lower) (upper)	173.1	198.2	232.1	216.1	238.2	239.2
ligament-*see also* Neoplasm, connective tissue						
broad	183.3	198.82	233.3	221.0	236.3	239.5
Mackenrodt's	183.8	198.82	233.3	221.8	236.3	239.5
non-uterine-*see* Neoplasm, connective tissue						
round	183.5	198.82	—	221.0	236.3	239.5
sacro-uterine	183.4	198.82	—	221.0	236.3	239.5
uterine	183.4	198.82	—	221.0	236.3	239.5
utero-ovarian	183.8	198.82	233.3	221.8	236.3	239.5
uterosacral	183.4	198.82	—	221.0	236.3	239.5
limb*	195.8	198.89	232.8	229.8	238.8	239.8
lower*	195.5	198.89	232.7	229.8	238.8	239.8
upper*	195.4	198.89	232.6	229.8	238.8	239.8
limbus of cornea	190.4	198.4	234.0	224.4	238.8	239.8
lingual NEC (*see also* Neoplasm, tongue)	141.9	198.89	230.0	210.1	235.1	239.0
lingula, lung	162.3	197.0	231.2	212.3	235.7	239.1
lip (external) (lipstick area) (vermillion border)	140.9	198.89	230.0	210.0	235.1	239.0
buccal aspect-*see* Neoplasm, lip, internal						
commissure	140.6	198.89	230.0	210.4	235.1	239.0
contiguous sites	140.8	—	—	—	—	—
with oral cavity or pharynx	149.8	—	—	—	—	—
frenulum-*see* Neoplasm, lip, internal						
inner aspect-*see* Neoplasm, lip, internal						
internal (buccal) (frenulum) (mucosa) (oral)	140.5	198.89	230.0	210.0	235.1	239.0
lower	140.4	198.89	230.0	210.0	235.1	239.0
upper	140.3	198.89	230.0	210.0	235.1	239.0
lower	140.1	198.89	230.0	210.0	235.1	239.0
internal (buccal) (frenulum) (mucosa) (oral)	140.4	198.89	230.0	210.0	235.1	239.0
mucosa-*see* Neoplasm, lip, internal						
oral aspect-*see* Neoplasm, lip, internal						
skin (commissure) (lower) (upper)	173.0	198.2	232.0	216.0	238.2	239.2
upper	140.0	198.89	230.0	210.0	235.1	239.0
internal (buccal) (frenulum) (mucosa) (oral)	140.3	198.89	230.0	210.0	235.1	239.0
liver	155.2	197.7	230.8	211.5	235.3	239.0
primary	155.0	—	—	—	—	—
lobe						
azygos	162.3	197.0	231.2	212.3	235.7	239.1
frontal	191.1	198.3	—	225.0	237.5	239.6
lower	162.5	197.0	231.2	212.3	235.7	239.1
middle	162.4	197.0	231.2	212.3	235.7	239.1
occipital	191.4	198.3	—	225.0	237.5	239.6
parietal	191.3	198.3	—	225.0	237.5	239.6
temporal	191.2	198.3	—	225.0	237.5	239.6
upper	162.3	197.0	231.2	212.3	235.7	239.1
lumbosacral plexus	171.6	198.4	—	215.6	238.1	239.2
lung	162.9	197.0	231.2	212.3	235.7	239.1
azygos lobe	162.3	197.0	231.2	212.3	235.7	239.1
carina	162.2	197.0	231.2	212.3	235.7	239.1
contiguous sites with bronchus or trachea	162.8	—	—	—	—	—
hilus	162.2	197.0	231.2	212.3	235.7	239.1
lingula	162.3	197.0	231.2	212.3	235.7	239.1
lobe NEC	162.9	197.0	231.2	212.3	235.7	239.1

	Malignant					
	Primary	Secondary	Ca in situ	Benign	Uncertain Behavior	Unspecified
Neoplasm *(Continued)*						
lung *(Continued)*						
lower lobe	162.5	197.0	231.2	212.3	235.7	239.1
main bronchus	162.2	197.0	231.2	212.3	235.7	239.1
middle lobe	162.4	197.0	231.2	212.3	235.7	239.1
upper lobe	162.3	197.0	231.2	212.3	235.7	239.1
lymph, lymphatic channel NEC *(see also* Neoplasm, connective tissue)	171.9	198.89	—	215.9	238.1	239.2
gland (secondary)	—	196.9	—	229.0	238.8	239.8
abdominal	—	196.2	—	229.0	238.8	239.8
aortic	—	196.2	—	229.0	238.8	239.8
arm	—	196.3	—	229.0	238.8	239.8
auricular (anterior) (posterior)	—	196.0	—	229.0	238.8	239.8
axilla, axillary	—	196.3	—	229.0	238.8	239.8
brachial	—	196.3	—	229.0	238.8	239.8
bronchial	—	196.1	—	229.0	238.8	239.8
bronchopulmonary	—	196.1	—	229.0	238.8	239.8
celiac	—	196.2	—	229.0	238.8	239.8
cervical	—	196.0	—	229.0	238.8	239.8
cervicofacial	—	196.0	—	229.0	238.8	239.8
Cloquet	—	196.5	—	229.0	238.8	239.8
colic	—	196.2	—	229.0	238.8	239.8
common duct	—	196.2	—	229.0	238.8	239.8
cubital	—	196.3	—	229.0	238.8	239.8
diaphragmatic	—	196.1	—	229.0	238.8	239.8
epigastric, inferior	—	196.6	—	229.0	238.8	239.8
epitrochlear	—	196.3	—	229.0	238.8	239.8
esophageal	—	196.1	—	229.0	238.8	239.8
face	—	196.0	—	229.0	238.8	239.8
femoral	—	196.5	—	229.0	238.8	239.8
gastric	—	196.2	—	229.0	238.8	239.8
groin	—	196.5	—	229.0	238.8	239.8
head	—	196.0	—	229.0	238.8	239.8
hepatic	—	196.2	—	229.0	238.8	239.8
hilar (pulmonary)	—	196.1	—	229.0	238.8	239.8
splenic	—	196.2	—	229.0	238.8	239.8
hypogastric	—	196.6	—	229.0	238.8	239.8
ileocolic	—	196.2	—	229.0	238.8	239.8
iliac	—	196.6	—	229.0	238.8	239.8
infraclavicular	—	196.3	—	229.0	238.8	239.8
inguina, inguinal	—	196.5	—	229.0	238.8	239.8
innominate	—	196.1	—	229.0	238.8	239.8
intercostal	—	196.1	—	229.0	238.8	239.8
intestinal	—	196.2	—	229.0	238.8	239.8
intrabdominal	—	196.2	—	229.0	238.8	239.8
intrapelvic	—	196.6	—	229.0	238.8	239.8
intrathoracic	—	196.1	—	229.0	238.8	239.9
jugular	—	196.0	—	229.0	238.8	239.8
leg	—	196.5	—	229.0	238.8	239.8
limb						
lower	—	196.5	—	229.0	238.8	239.8
upper	—	196.3	—	229.0	238.8	239.8
lower limb	—	196.5	—	229.0	238.8	238.9
lumbar	—	196.2	—	229.0	238.8	239.8
mandibular	—	196.0	—	229.0	238.8	239.8
mediastinal	—	196.1	—	229.0	238.8	239.8
mesenteric (inferior) (superior)	—	196.2	—	229.0	238.8	239.8
midcolic	—	196.2	—	229.0	238.8	239.8
multiple sites in categories 196.0-196.6	—	196.8	—	229.0	238.8	239.8
neck	—	196.0	—	229.0	238.8	239.8
obturator	—	196.6	—	229.0	238.8	239.8
occipital	—	196.0	—	229.0	238.8	239.8
pancreatic	—	196.2	—	229.0	238.8	239.8
para-aortic	—	196.2	—	229.0	238.8	239.8

	Malignant					
	Primary	Secondary	Ca in situ	Benign	Uncertain Behavior	Unspecified
Neoplasm *(Continued)*						
lymph, lymphatic channel NEC *(Continued)*						
gland *(Continued)*						
paracervical	—	196.6	—	229.0	238.8	239.8
parametrial	—	196.6	—	229.0	238.8	239.8
parasternal	—	196.1	—	229.0	238.8	239.8
parotid	—	196.0	—	229.0	238.8	239.8
pectoral	—	196.3	—	229.0	238.8	239.8
pelvic	—	196.6	—	229.0	238.8	239.8
peri-aortic	—	196.2	—	229.0	238.8	239.8
peripancreatic	—	196.2	—	229.0	238.8	239.8
popliteal	—	196.5	—	229.0	238.8	239.8
porta hepatis	—	196.2	—	229.0	238.8	239.8
portal	—	196.2	—	229.0	238.8	239.8
preauricular	—	196.0	—	229.0	238.8	239.8
prelaryngeal	—	196.0	—	229.0	238.8	239.8
presymphysial	—	196.6	—	229.0	238.8	239.8
pretracheal	—	196.0	—	229.0	238.8	239.8
primary (any site) NEC	202.9	—	—	—	—	—
pulmonary (hiler)	—	196.1	—	229.0	238.8	239.8
pyloric	—	196.2	—	229.0	238.8	239.8
retroperitoneal	—	196.2	—	229.0	238.8	239.8
retropharyngeal	—	196.0	—	229.0	238.8	239.8
Rosenmüller's	—	196.5	—	229.0	238.8	239.8
sacral	—	196.6	—	229.0	238.8	239.8
scalene	—	196.0	—	229.0	238.8	239.8
site NEC	—	196.9	—	229.0	238.8	239.8
splenic (hilar)	—	196.2	—	229.0	238.8	239.8
subclavicular	—	196.3	—	229.0	238.8	239.8
subinguinal	—	196.5	—	229.0	238.8	239.8
sublingual	—	196.0	—	229.0	238.8	239.8
submandibular	—	196.0	—	229.0	238.8	239.8
submaxillary	—	196.0	—	229.0	238.8	239.8
submental	—	196.0	—	229.0	238.8	239.8
subscapular	—	196.3	—	229.0	238.8	239.8
supraclavicular	—	196.0	—	229.0	238.8	239.8
thoracic	—	196.1	—	229.0	238.8	239.8
tibial	—	196.5	—	229.0	238.8	239.8
tracheal		196.1	—	229.0	238.8	239.8
tracheobronchial	—	196.1	—	229.0	238.8	239.8
upper limb	—	196.3	—	229.0	238.8	239.8
Virchow's	—	196.0	—	229.0	238.8	239.8
node-*see also* Neoplasm, lymph gland primary NEC	202.9					
vessel (*see also* Neoplasm, connective tissue)	171.9	198.89	—	215.9	238.1	239.2
Mackenrodt's ligament	183.8	198.82	233.3	221.8	236.3	239.5
malar region-*see* Neoplasm, cheek	170.0	198.5	—	213.0	238.0	239.2
mammary gland-*see* Neoplasm, breast						
mandible	170.1	198.5	—	213.1	238.0	239.2
alveolar						
mucosa	143.1	198.89	230.0	210.4	235.1	239.0
ridge or process	170.1	198.5	—	213.1	238.0	239.2
carcinoma	143.1	—	—	—	—	—
carcinoma	143.1	—	—	—	—	—
marrow (bone) NEC	202.9	198.5	—	—	—	238.7
mastectomy site (skin)	173.5	198.2	—	—	—	—
specified as breast tissue	174.8	198.81	—	—	—	—
mastoid (air cells) (antrum) (cavity)	160.1	197.3	231.8	212.0	235.9	239.1
bone or process	170.0	198.5	—	213.0	238.0	239.2
maxilla, maxillary (superior)	170.0	198.5	—	213.0	238.0	239.2
alveolar						
mucosa	143.0	198.89	230.0	210.4	235.1	239.0
ridge or process	170.0	198.5	—	213.0	238.0	239.2
carcinoma	143.0	—	—	—	—	—

	Malignant					
	Primary	Secondary	Ca in stiu	Benign	Uncertain Behavior	Unspecified
Neoplasm *(Continued)*						
maxilla, maxillary *(Continued)*						
antrum	160.2	197.3	231.8	212.0	235.9	239.1
carcinoma	143.0	—	—	—	—	—
inferior-*see* Neoplasm, mandible						
sinus	160.2	197.3	231.8	212.0	235.9	239.1
meatus						
external (ear)	173.2	198.2	232.2	216.2	238.2	239.2
Meckel's diverticulum	152.3	197.4	230.7	211.2	235.2	239.0
mediastinum, mediastinal	164.9	197.1	—	212.5	235.8	239.8
anterior	164.2	197.1	—	212.5	235.8	239.8
contiguous sites with heart and thymus	164.8	—	—	—	—	—
posterior	164.3	197.1	—	212.5	235.8	239.8
medulla						
adrenal	194.0	198.7	234.8	227.0	237.2	239.7
oblongata	191.7	198.3	—	225.0	237.5	239.6
meibomian gland	173.1	198.2	232.1	216.1	238.2	239.2
melanoma-*see* Melanoma						
meninges (brain) (cerebral) (cranial) (intracranial)	192.1	198.4	—	225.2	237.6	239.7
spinal (cord)	192.3	198.4	—	225.4	237.6	239.7
meniscus, knee joint (lateral) (medial)	170.7	198.5	—	213.7	238.0	239.2
mesentery, mesenteric	158.8	197.6	—	211.8	235.4	239.0
mesoappendix	158.8	197.6	—	211.8	235.4	239.0
mesocolon	158.8	197.6	—	211.8	235.4	239.0
mesopharynx-*see* Neoplasm, oropharynx						
mesosalpinx	183.3	198.82	233.3	221.0	236.3	239.5
mesovarium	183.3	198.82	233.3	221.0	236.3	239.5
metacarpus (any bone)	170.5	198.5	—	213.5	238.0	239.2
metastatic NEC-*see also* Neoplasm, by site, secondary	—	199.1	—	—	—	—
metatarsus (any bone)	170.8	198.5	—	213.8	238.0	239.2
midbrain	191.7	198.3	—	225.0	237.5	239.6
milk duct-*see* Neoplasm, breast						
mons						
pubis	184.4	198.82	233.3	221.2	236.3	239.5
veneris	184.4	198.82	233.3	221.2	236.3	239.5
motor tract	192.9	198.4	—	225.9	237.9	239.7
brain	191.9	198.3	—	225.0	237.5	239.6
spinal	192.2	198.3	—	225.3	237.5	239.7
mouth	145.9	198.89	230.0	210.4	235.1	239.0
contiguous sites	145.8	—	—	—	—	—
floor	144.9	198.89	230.0	210.3	235.1	239.0
anterior portion	144.0	198.89	230.0	210.3	235.1	239.0
contiguous sites	144.8	—	—	—	—	—
lateral portion	144.1	198.89	230.0	210.3	235.1	239.0
roof	145.5	198.89	230.0	210.4	235.1	239.0
specified part NEC	145.8	198.89	230.0	210.4	235.1	239.0
vestibule	145.1	198.89	230.0	210.4	235.1	239.0
mucosa						
alveolar (ridge or process)	143.9	198.89	230.0	210.4	235.1	239.0
lower	143.1	198.89	230.0	210.4	235.1	239.0
upper	143.0	198.89	230.0	210.4	235.1	239.0
buccal	145.0	198.89	230.0	210.4	235.1	239.0
cheek	145.0	198.89	230.0	210.4	235.1	239.0
lip-*see* Neoplasm, lip, internal						
nasal	160.0	197.3	231.8	212.0	235.9	239.1
oral	145.0	198.89	230.0	210.4	235.1	239.0
Müllerian duct						
female	184.8	198.82	233.3	221.8	236.3	239.5
male	187.8	198.82	233.6	222.8	236.6	239.5
multiple sites NEC	199.0	199.0	234.9	229.9	238.9	199.0
muscle-*see also* Neoplasm, connective tissue extraocular	190.1	198.4	234.0	224.1	238.8	239.8
myocardium	164.1	198.89	—	212.7	238.8	239.8
myometrium	182.0	198.82	233.2	219.1	236.0	239.5

	Malignant					
	Primary	Secondary	Ca in stiu	Benign	Uncertain Behavior	Unspecified
Neoplasm *(Continued)*						
myopericardium	164.1	198.89	—	212.7	238.8	239.8
nabothian gland (follicle)	180.0	198.82	233.1	219.0	236.0	239.5
nail	173.9	198.2	232.9	216.9	238.2	239.2
finger	173.6	198.2	232.6	216.6	238.2	239.2
toe	173.7	198.2	232.7	216.7	238.2	239.2
nares, naris (anterior) (posterior)	160.0	197.3	231.8	212.0	235.9	239.1
nasal-*see* Neoplasm, nose						
nasolabial groove	173.3	198.2	232.3	216.3	238.2	239.2
nasolacrimal duct	190.7	198.4	234.0	224.7	238.8	239.8
nasopharynx, nasopharyngeal	147.9	198.89	230.0	210.7	235.1	239.0
contiguous sites	147.8	—	—	—	—	—
floor	147.3	198.89	230.0	210.7	235.1	239.0
roof	147.0	198.89	230.0	210.7	235.1	239.0
specified site NEC	147.8	198.89	230.0	210.7	235.1	239.0
wall	147.9	198.89	230.0	210.7	235.1	239.0
anterior	147.3	198.89	230.0	210.7	235.1	239.0
lateral	147.2	198.89	230.0	210.7	235.1	239.0
posterior	147.1	198.89	230.0	210.7	235.1	239.0
superior	147.0	198.89	230.0	210.7	235.1	239.0
nates	173.5	198.2	232.5	216.5	238.2	239.2
neck NEC*	195.0	198.89	234.8	229.8	238.8	239.8
nerve (autonomic) (parasympathetic) (peripheral) (sympathetic) - *see also* Neoplasm, connective tissue						
abducens	192.0	198.4	—	225.1	237.9	239.7
accessory (spinal)	192.0	198.4	—	225.1	237.9	239.7
acoustic	192.0	198.4	—	225.1	237.9	239.7
auditory	192.0	198.4	—	225.1	237.9	239.7
brachial	171.2	198.89	—	215.2	238.1	239.2
cranial (any)	192.0	198.4	—	225.1	237.9	239.7
facial	192.0	198.4	—	225.1	237.9	239.7
femoral	171.3	198.89	—	215.3	238.1	239.2
glossopharyngeal	192.0	198.4	—	225.1	237.9	239.7
hypoglossal	192.0	198.4	—	225.1	237.9	239.7
intercostal	171.4	198.89	—	215.4	238.1	239.2
lumbar	171.7	198.89	—	215.7	238.1	239.2
median	171.2	198.89	—	215.2	238.1	239.2
obturator	171.3	198.89	—	215.3	238.1	239.2
oculomotor	192.0	198.4	—	225.1	237.9	239.7
olfactory	192.0	198.4	—	225.1	237.9	239.7
optic	192.0	198.4	—	225.1	237.9	239.7
peripheral NEC	171.9	198.89	—	215.9	238.1	239.2
radial	171.2	198.89	—	215.2	238.1	239.2
sacral	171.6	198.89	—	215.6	238.1	239.2
sciatic	171.3	198.89	—	215.3	238.1	239.2
spinal NEC	171.9	198.89	—	215.9	238.1	239.2
trigeminal	192.0	198.4	—	225.1	237.9	239.7
trochlear	192.0	198.4	—	225.1	237.9	239.7
ulnar	171.2	198.89	—	215.2	238.1	239.2
vagus	192.0	198.4	—	225.1	237.9	239.7
nervous system (central) NEC	192.9	198.4	—	225.9	237.9	239.7
autonomic NEC	171.9	198.89	—	215.9	238.1	239.2
brain-*see also* Neoplasm, brain membrane or meninges	192.1	198.4	—	225.2	237.6	239.7
contiguous sites	192.8	—	—	—	—	—
parasympathetic NEC	171.9	198.89	—	215.9	238.1	239.2
sympathetic NEC	171.9	198.89	—	215.9	238.1	239.2
nipple (female)	174.0	198.81	233.0	217	238.3	239.3
male	175.0	198.81	233.0	217	238.3	239.3
nose, nasal	195.0	198.89	234.8	229.8	238.8	239.8
ala (external)	173.3	198.2	232.3	216.3	238.2	239.2
bone	170.0	198.5	—	213.0	238.0	239.2
cartilage	160.0	197.3	231.8	212.0	235.9	239.1
cavity	160.0	197.3	231.8	212.0	235.9	239.1
contiguous sites with accessory sinuses or middle ear	160.8	—	—	—	—	—

◄▶ **New Code**　　◀▦▦▷ **Revised Code**

| | Malignant | | | | | |
	Primary	Secondary	Ca in situ	Benign	Uncertain Behavior	Unspecified
Neoplasm *(Continued)*						
nose, nasal *(Continued)*						
choana	147.3	198.89	230.0	210.7	235.1	239.0
external (skin)	173.3	198.2	232.3	216.3	238.2	239.2
fossa	160.0	197.3	231.8	212.0	235.9	239.1
internal	160.0	197.3	231.8	212.0	235.9	239.1
mucosa	160.0	197.3	231.8	212.0	235.9	239.1
septum	160.0	197.3	231.8	212.0	235.9	239.1
posterior margin	147.3	198.89	230.0	210.7	235.1	239.0
sinus-*see* Neoplasm, sinus						
skin	173.3	198.2	232.3	216.3	238.2	239.2
turbinate (mucosa)	160.0	197.3	231.8	212.0	235.9	239.1
bone	170.0	198.5	—	2130	238.0	239.2
vestibule	160.0	197.3	231.8	212.0	235.9	239.1
nostril	160.0	197.3	231.8	212.0	235.9	239.1
nucleus pulposus	170.2	198.5	—	213.2	238.0	230.2
occipital						
bone	170.0	198.5	—	213.0	238.0	239.2
lobe or pole, brain	191.4	198.3	—	225.0	237.5	239.6
odontogenic-*see* Neoplasm, jaw bone						
oesophagus-*see* Neoplasm, esophagus						
olfactory nerve or bulb	192.0	198.4	—	225.1	237.9	239.7
olive (brain)	191.7	198.3	—	225.0	237.5	239.6
omentum	158.8	197.6	—	211.8	235.4	239.0
operculum (brain)	191.0	198.3	—	225.0	237.5	239.6
optic nerve, chiasm, or tract	192.0	198.4	—	225.1	237.9	239.7
oral (cavity)	145.9	198.89	230.0	210.4	235.1	239.0
contiguous sites with lip or pharynx	149.8	—	—	—	—	—
ill-defined	149.9	198.89	230.0	210.4	235.1	239.0
mucosa	145.9	198.89	230.0	210.4	235.1	239.0
orbit	190.1	198.4	234.0	224.1	238.8	239.8
bone	170.0	198.5	—	213.0	238.0	239.2
eye	190.1	198.4	234.0	224.1	238.8	239.8
soft parts	190.1	198.4	234.0	224.1	238.8	239.8
organ of Zuckerkandl	194.6	198.89	—	227.6	237.3	239.7
oropharynx	146.9	198.89	230.0	210.6	235.1	239.0
branchial cleft (vestige)	146.8	198.89	230.0	210.6	235.1	239.0
contiguous sites	146.8	—	—	—	—	—
junctional region	146.5	198.89	230.0	210.6	235.1	239.0
lateral wall	146.6	198.89	230.0	210.6	235.1	239.0
pillars of fauces	146.2	198.89	230.0	210.6	235.1	239.0
posterior wall	146.7	198.89	230.0	210.6	235.1	239.0
specified part NEC	146.8	198.89	230.0	210.6	235.1	239.0
vallecula	146.3	198.89	230.0	210.6	235.1	239.0
os						
external	180.1	198.82	233.1	219.0	236.0	239.5
internal	180.0	198.82	233.1	219.0	236.0	239.5
ovary	183.0	198.6	233.3	220	236.2	239.5
oviduct	183.2	198.82	233.3	221.0	236.3	239.5
palate	145.5	198.89	230.0	210.4	235.1	239.0
hard	145.2	198.89	230.0	210.4	235.1	239.0
junction of hard and soft palate	145.5	198.89	230.0	210.4	235.1	239.0
soft	145.3	198.89	230.0	210.4	235.1	239.0
nasopharyngeal surface	147.3	198.89	230.0	210.7	235.1	239.0
posterior surface	147.3	198.89	230.0	210.7	235.1	239.0
superior surface	147.3	198.89	230.0	210.7	235.1	239.0
palatoglossal arch	146.2	198.89	230.0	210.6	235.1	239.0
palatopharyngeal arch	146.2	198.89	230.0	210.6	235.1	239.0
pallium	191.0	198.3	—	225.0	237.5	239.6
palpebra	173.1	198.2	232.1	216.1	238.2	239.2
pancreas	157.9	197.8	230.9	211.6	235.5	239.0
body	157.1	197.8	230.9	211.6	235.5	239.0
contiguous sites	157.8	—	—	—	—	—

	Malignant					
	Primary	Secondary	Ca in stiu	Benign	Uncertain Behavior	Unspecified
Neoplasm *(Continued)*						
pancreas *(Continued)*						
duct (of Santorini) (of Wirsung)	157.3	197.8	230.9	211.6	235.5	239.0
ectopic tissue	157.8	197.8				
head	157.0	197.8	230.9	211.6	235.5	239.0
islet cells	157.4	197.8	230.9	211.7	235.5	239.0
neck	157.8	197.8	230.9	211.6	235.5	239.0
tail	157.2	197.8	230.9	211.6	235.5	239.0
para-aortic body	194.6	198.89	—	227.6	237.3	239.7
paraganglion NEC	194.6	198.89	—	227.6	237.3	239.7
parametrium	183.4	198.82	—	221.0	236.3	239.5
paranephric	158.0	197.6	—	211.8	235.4	239.0
pararectal	195.3	198.89	—	229.8	238.8	239.8
parasagittal (region)	195.0	198.89	234.8	229.8	238.8	239.8
parasellar	192.9	198.4	—	225.9	237.9	239.7
parathyroid (gland)	194.1	198.89	234.8	227.1	237.4	239.7
paraurethral	195.3	198.89	—	229.8	238.8	239.8
gland	189.4	198.1	233.9	223.89	236.99	239.5
paravaginal	195.3	198.89	—	229.8	238.8	239.8
parenchyma, kidney	189.0	198.0	233.9	223.0	236.91	239.5
parietal						
bone	170.0	198.5	—	213.0	238.0	239.2
lobe, brain	191.3	198.3	—	225.0	237.5	239.6
paroophoron	183.3	198.82	233.3	221.0	236.3	239.5
parotid (duct) (gland)	142.0	198.89	230.0	210.2	235.0	239.0
parovarium	183.3	198.82	233.3	221.0	236.3	239.5
patella	170.8	198.5	—	213.8	238.0	239.2
peduncle, cerebral	191.7	198.3	—	225.0	237.5	239.6
pelvirectal junction	154.0	197.5	230.4	211.4	235.2	239.0
pelvis, pelvic	195.3	198.89	234.8	229.8	238.8	239.8
bone	170.6	198.5	—	213.6	238.0	239.2
floor	195.3	198.89	234.8	229.8	238.8	239.8
renal	189.1	198.0	233.9	223.1	236.91	239.5
viscera	195.3	198.89	234.8	229.8	238.8	239.8
wall	195.3	198.89	234.8	229.8	238.8	239.8
pelvo-abdominal	195.8	198.89	234.8	229.8	238.8	239.8
penis	187.4	198.82	233.5	222.1	236.6	239.5
body	187.3	198.82	233.5	222.1	236.6	239.5
corpus (cavernosum)	187.3	198.82	233.5	222.1	236.6	239.5
glans	187.2	198.82	233.5	222.1	236.6	239.5
skin NEC	187.4	198.82	233.5	222.1	236.6	239.5
periadrenal (tissue)	158.0	197.6	—	211.8	235.4	239.0
perianal (skin)	173.5	198.2	232.5	216.5	238.2	239.2
pericardium	164.1	198.89	—	212.7	238.8	239.8
perinephric	158.0	197.6	—	211.8	235.4	239.0
perineum	195.3	198.89	234.8	229.8	238.8	239.8
periodontal tissue NEC	143.9	198.89	230.0	210.4	235.1	239.0
periosteum-*see* Neoplasm, bone						
peripancreatic	158.0	197.6	—	211.8	235.4	239.0
peripheral nerve NEC	171.9	198.89	—	215.9	238.1	239.2
perirectal (tissue)	195.3	198.89	—	229.8	238.8	239.8
perirenal (tissue)	158.0	197.6	—	211.8	235.4	239.0
peritoneum, peritoneal (cavity)	158.9	197.6	—	211.8	235.4	239.0
contiguous sites	158.8	—	—	—	—	—
with digestive organs	159.8	—	—	—	—	—
parietal	158.8	197.6	—	211.8	235.4	239.0
pelvic	158.8	197.6	—	211.8	235.4	239.0
specified part NEC	158.8	197.6	—	211.8	235.4	239.0
peritonsillar (tissue)	195.0	198.89	234.8	229.8	238.8	239.8
periurethral tissue	195.3	198.89	—	229.8	238.8	239.8
phalanges	170.9	198.5	—	213.9	238.0	239.2
foot	170.8	198.5	—	213.8	238.0	239.2
hand	170.5	198.5	—	213.5	238.0	239.2

◄▶ **New Code**   ◄▦ ▦► **Revised Code**

| | Malignant | | | | | |
	Primary	Secondary	Ca in stiu	Benign	Uncertain Behavior	Unspecified
Neoplasm *(Continued)*						
pharynx, pharyngeal	149.0	198.89	230.0	210.9	235.1	239.0
bursa	147.1	198.89	230.0	210.7	235.1	239.0
fornix	147.3	198.89	230.0	210.7	235.1	239.0
recess	147.2	198.89	230.0	210.7	235.1	239.0
region	149.0	198.89	230.0	210.9	235.1	239.0
tonsil	147.1	198.89	230.0	210.7	235.1	239.0
wall (lateral) (posterior)	149.0	198.89	230.0	210.9	235.1	239.0
pia mater (cerebral) (cranial)	192.1	198.4	—	225.2	237.6	239.7
spinal	192.3	198.4	—	225.4	237.6	239.7
pillars of fauces	146.2	198.89	230.0	210.6	235.1	239.0
pineal (body) (gland)	194.4	198.89	234.8	227.4	237.1	239.7
pinna (ear) NEC	173.2	198.2	232.2	216.2	238.2	239.2
cartilage	171.0	198.89	—	215.0	238.1	239.2
piriform fossa or sinus	148.1	198.89	230.0	210.8	235.1	239.0
pituitary (body) (fossa) (gland) (lobe)	194.3	198.89	234.8	227.3	237.0	239.7
placenta	181	198.82	233.2	219.8	236.1	239.5
pleura, pleural (cavity)	163.9	197.2	—	212.4	235.8	239.1
contiguous sites	163.8	—	—	—	—	—
parietal	163.0	197.2	—	212.4	235.8	239.1
visceral	163.1	197.2	—	212.4	235.8	239.1
plexus						
brachial	171.2	198.89	—	215.2	238.1	239.2
cervical	171.0	198.89	—	215.0	238.1	239.2
choroid	191.5	198.3	—	225.0	237.5	239.6
lumbosacral	171.6	198.89	—	215.6	238.1	239.2
sacral	171.6	198.89	—	215.6	238.1	239.2
pluri-endocrine	194.8	198.89	234.8	227.8	237.4	239.7
pole						
frontal	191.1	198.3	—	225.0	237.5	239.6
occipital	191.4	198.3	—	225.0	237.5	239.6
pons (varolii)	191.7	198.3	—	225.0	237.5	239.6
popliteal fossa or space*	195.5	198.89	234.8	229.8	238.8	239.8
postcricoid (region)	148.0	198.89	230.0	210.8	235.1	239.0
posterior fossa (cranial)	191.6	198.3	—	225.0	237.5	239.6
postnasal space	147.9	198.89	230.0	210.7	235.1	239.0
prepuce	187.1	198.82	233.5	222.1	236.6	239.5
prepylorus	151.1	197.8	230.2	211.1	235.2	239.0
presacral (region)	195.3	198.89	—	229.8	238.8	239.8
prostate (gland)	185	198.82	233.4	222.2	236.5	239.5
utricle	189.3	198.1	233.9	223.81	236.99	239.5
pterygoid fossa	171.0	198.89	—	215.0	238.1	239.2
pubic bone	170.6	198.5	—	213.6	238.0	239.2
pudenda, pudendum (female)	184.4	198.82	233.3	221.2	236.3	239.5
pulmonary	162.9	197.0	231.2	212.3	235.7	239.1
putamen	191.0	198.3	—	225.0	237.5	239.6
pyloric						
antrum	151.2	197.8	230.2	211.1	235.2	239.0
canal	151.1	197.8	230.2	211.1	235.2	239.0
pylorus	151.1	197.8	230.2	211.1	235.2	239.0
pyramid (brain)	191.7	198.3	—	225.0	237.5	239.6
pyriform fossa or sinus	148.1	198.89	230.0	210.8	235.1	239.0
radius (any part)	170.4	198.5	—	213.4	238.0	239.2
Rathke's pouch	194.3	198.89	234.8	227.3	237.0	239.7
rectosigmoid (colon) (junction)	154.0	197.5	230.4	211.4	235.2	239.0
contiguous sites with anus or rectum	154.8	—	—	—	—	—
rectouterine pouch	158.8	197.6	—	211.8	235.4	239.0
rectovaginal septum or wall	195.3	198.89	234.8	229.8	238.8	239.8
rectovesical septum	195.3	198.89	234.8	229.8	238.8	239.8
rectum (ampulla)	154.1	197.5	230.4	211.4	235.2	239.0
and colon	154.0	197.5	230.4	211.4	235.2	239.0
contiguous sites with anus or rectosigmoid junction	154.8	—	—	—	—	—
renal	189.0	198.0	233.9	223.0	236.91	239.5

	Malignant					
	Primary	Secondary	Ca in situ	Benign	Uncertain Behavior	Unspecified
Neoplasm *(Continued)*						
renal *(Continued)*						
calyx	189.1	198.0	233.9	223.1	236.91	239.5
hilus	189.1	198.0	233.9	223.1	236.91	239.5
parenchyma	189.0	198.0	233.9	223.0	236.91	239.5
pelvis	189.1	198.0	233.9	223.1	236.91	239.5
respiratory						
organs or system NEC	165.9	197.3	231.9	212.9	235.9	239.1
contiguous sites with intrathoracic organs	165.8					
specified sites NEC	165.8	197.3	231.8	212.8	235.9	239.1
tract NEC	165.9	197.3	231.9	212.9	235.9	239.1
upper	165.0	197.3	231.9	212.9	235.9	239.1
retina	190.5	198.4	234.0	224.5	238.8	239.8
retrobulbar	190.1	198.4	—	224.1	238.8	239.8
retrocecal	158.0	197.6	—	211.8	235.4	239.0
retromolar (area) (triangle) (trigone)	145.6	198.89	230.0	210.4	235.1	239.0
retro-orbital	195.0	198.89	234.8	229.8	238.8	239.8
retroperitoneal (space) (tissue)	158.0	197.6	—	211.8	235.4	239.0
contiguous sites	158.8	—	—	—	—	—
retroperitoneum	158.0	197.6	—	211.8	235.4	239.0
contiguous sites	158.8	—	—	—	—	—
retropharyngeal	149.0	198.89	230.0	210.9	235.1	239.0
retrovesical (septum)	195.3	198.89	234.8	229.8	238.8	239.8
rhinencephalon	191.0	198.3	—	225.0	237.5	239.6
rib	170.3	198.5	—	213.3	238.0	239.2
Rosenmüller's fossa	147.2	198.89	230.0	210.7	235.1	239.0
round ligament	183.5	198.82	—	221.0	236.3	239.5
sacrococcyx, sacrococcygeal	170.6	198.5	—	213.6	238.0	239.2
region	195.3	198.89	234.8	229.8	238.8	239.8
sacrouterine ligament	183.4	198.82	—	221.0	236.3	239.5
sacrum, sacral (vertebra)	170.6	198.5	—	213.6	238.0	239.2
salivary gland or duct (major)	142.9	198.89	230.0	210.2	235.0	239.0
contiguous sites	142.8	—	—	—	—	—
minor NEC	145.9	198.89	230.0	210.4	235.1	239.0
parotid	142.0	198.89	230.0	210.2	235.0	239.0
pluriglandular	142.8	198.89	230.0	210.2	235.0	239.0
sublingual	142.2	198.89	230.0	210.2	235.0	239.0
submandibular	142.1	198.89	230.0	210.2	235.0	239.0
submaxillary	142.1	198.89	230.0	210.2	235.0	239.0
salpinx (uterine)	183.2	198.82	233.3	221.0	236.3	239.5
Santorini's duct	157.3	197.8	230.9	211.6	235.5	239.0
scalp	173.4	198.2	232.4	216.4	238.2	239.2
scapula (any part)	170.4	198.5	—	213.4	238.0	239.2
scapular region	195.1	198.89	234.8	229.8	238.8	239.8
scar NEC (*see also* Neoplasm, skin)	173.9	198.2	232.9	216.9	238.2	239.2
sciatic nerve	171.3	198.89	—	215.3	238.1	239.2
sclera	190.0	198.4	234.0	224.0	238.8	239.8
scrotum (skin)	187.7	198.82	233.6	222.4	236.6	239.5
sebaceous gland-*see* Neoplasm, skin						
sella turcica	194.3	198.89	234.8	227.3	237.0	239.7
bone	170.0	198.5	—	213.0	238.0	239.2
semilunar cartilage (knee)	170.7	198.5	—	213.7	238.0	239.2
seminal vesicle	187.8	198.82	233.6	222.8	236.6	239.5
septum						
nasal	160.0	197.3	231.8	212.0	235.9	239.1
posterior margin	147.3	198.89	230.0	210.7	235.1	239.0
rectovaginal	195.3	198.89	234.8	229.8	238.8	239.8
rectovesical	195.3	198.89	234.8	229.8	238.8	239.8
urethrovaginal	184.9	198.82	233.3	221.9	236.3	239.5
vesicovaginal	184.9	198.82	233.3	221.9	236.3	239.5
shoulder NEC*	195.4	198.89	232.6	229.8	238.8	239.8
sigmoid flexure (lower) (upper)	153.3	197.5	230.3	211.3	235.2	239.0
sinus (accessory)	160.9	197.3	231.8	212.0	235.9	239.1
bone (any)	170.0	198.5	—	213.0	238.0	239.2

◀ ▶ **New Code**   ◀▥▥ ▥▥▶ **Revised Code**

	Malignant					
	Primary	**Secondary**	**Ca in situ**	**Benign**	**Uncertain Behavior**	**Unspecified**
Neoplasm *(Continued)*						
sinus *(Continued)*						
contiguous sites with middle ear or nasal cavities	160.8	—	—	—	—	—
ethmoidal	160.3	197.3	231.8	212.0	235.9	239.1
frontal	160.4	197.3	231.8	212.0	235.9	239.1
maxillary	160.2	197.3	231.8	212.0	235.9	239.1
nasal, paranasal NEC	160.9	197.3	231.8	212.0	235.9	239.1
pyriform	148.1	198.89	230.0	210.8	235.1	239.0
sphenoidal	160.5	197.3	231.8	212.0	235.9	239.1
skeleton, skeletal NEC	170.9	198.5	—	213.9	238.0	239.2
Skene's gland	189.4	198.1	233.9	223.89	236.99	239.5
skin NEC	173.9	198.2	232.9	216.9	238.2	239.2
abdominal wall	173.5	198.2	232.5	216.5	238.2	239.2
ala nasi	173.3	198.2	232.3	216.3	238.2	239.2
ankle	173.7	198.2	232.7	216.7	238.2	239.2
antecubital space	173.6	198.2	232.6	216.6	238.2	239.2
anus	173.5	198.2	232.5	216.5	238.2	239.2
arm	173.6	198.2	232.6	216.6	238.2	239.2
auditory canal (external)	173.2	198.2	232.2	216.2	238.2	239.2
auricle (ear)	173.2	198.2	232.2	216.2	238.2	239.2
auricular canal (external)	173.2	198.2	232.2	216.2	238.2	239.2
axilla, axillary fold	173.5	198.2	232.5	216.5	238.2	239.2
back	173.5	198.2	232.5	216.5	238.2	239.2
breast	173.5	198.2	232.5	216.5	238.2	239.2
brow	173.3	198.2	232.3	216.3	238.2	239.2
buttock	173.5	198.2	232.5	216.5	238.2	239.2
calf	173.7	198.2	232.7	216.7	238.2	239.2
canthus (eye) (inner) (outer)	173.1	198.2	232.1	216.1	238.2	239.2
cervical region	173.4	198.2	232.4	216.4	238.2	239.2
cheek (external)	173.3	198.2	232.3	216.3	238.2	239.2
chest (wall)	173.5	198.2	232.5	216.5	238.2	239.2
chin	173.3	198.2	232.3	216.3	238.2	239.2
clavicular area	173.5	198.2	232.5	216.5	238.2	239.2
clitoris	184.3	198.82	233.3	221.2	236.3	239.5
columnella	173.3	198.2	232.3	216.3	238.2	239.2
concha	173.2	198.2	232.2	216.2	238.2	239.2
contiguous sites	173.8	—	—	—	—	—
ear (external)	173.2	198.2	232.2	216.2	238.2	239.2
elbow	173.6	198.2	232.6	216.6	238.2	239.2
eyebrow	173.3	198.2	232.3	216.3	238.2	239.2
eyelid	173.1	198.2	232.1	216.1	238.2	239.2
face NEC	173.3	198.2	232.3	216.3	238.2	239.2
female genital organs (external)	184.4	198.82	233.3	221.2	236.3	239.5
clitoris	184.3	198.82	233.3	221.2	236.3	239.5
labium NEC	184.4	198.82	233.3	221.2	236.3	239.5
majus	184.1	198.82	233.3	221.2	236.3	239.5
minus	184.2	198.82	233.3	221.2	236.3	239.5
pudendum	184.4	198.82	233.3	221.2	236.3	239.5
vulva	184.4	198.82	233.3	221.2	236.3	239.5
finger	173.6	198.2	232.6	216.6	238.2	239.2
flank	173.5	198.2	232.5	216.5	238.2	239.2
foot	173.7	198.2	232.7	216.7	238.2	239.2
forearm	173.6	198.2	232.6	216.6	238.2	239.2
forehead	173.3	198.2	232.3	216.3	238.2	239.2
glabella	173.3	198.2	232.3	216.3	238.2	239.2
gluteal region	173.5	198.2	232.5	216.5	238.2	239.2
groin	173.5	198.2	232.5	216.5	238.2	239.2
hand	173.6	198.2	232.6	216.6	238.2	239.2
head NEC	173.4	198.2	232.4	216.4	238.2	239.2
heel	173.7	198.2	232.7	216.7	238.2	239.2
helix	173.2	198.2	232.2	216.2	238.2	239.2
hip	173.7	198.2	232.7	216.7	238.2	239.2
infraclavicular region	173.5	198.2	232.5	216.5	238.2	239.2

ICD-9-CM

N

Vol. 2

	Malignant			Benign	Uncertain Behavior	Unspecified
	Primary	Secondary	Ca in situ			
Neoplasm *(Continued)*						
skin NEC *(Continued)*						
inguinal region	173.5	198.2	232.5	216.5	238.2	239.2
jaw	173.3	198.2	232.3	216.3	238.2	239.2
knee	173.7	198.2	232.7	216.7	238.2	239.2
labia						
majora	184.1	198.82	233.3	221.2	236.3	239.5
minora	184.2	198.82	233.3	221.2	236.3	239.5
leg	173.7	198.2	232.7	216.7	238.2	239.2
lid (lower) (upper)	173.1	198.2	232.1	216.1	238.2	239.2
limb NEC	173.9	198.2	232.9	216.9	238.2	239.5
lower	173.7	198.2	232.7	216.7	238.2	239.2
upper	173.6	198.2	232.6	216.6	238.2	239.2
lip (lower) (upper)	173.0	198.2	232.0	216.0	238.2	239.2
male genital organs	187.9	198.82	233.6	222.9	236.6	239.5
penis	187.4	198.82	233.5	222.1	236.6	239.5
prepuce	187.1	198.82	233.5	222.1	236.6	239.5
scrotum	187.7	198.82	233.6	222.4	236.6	239.5
mastectomy site	173.5	198.2	—	—	—	—
specified as breast tissue	174.8	198.81	—	—	—	—
meatus, acoustic (external)	173.2	198.2	232.2	216.2	238.2	239.2
nates	173.5	198.2	232.5	216.5	238.2	239.2
neck	173.4	198.2	232.4	216.4	238.2	239.2
nose (external)	173.3	198.2	232.3	216.3	238.2	239.2
palm	173.6	198.2	232.6	216.6	238.2	239.2
palpebra	173.1	198.2	232.1	216.1	238.2	239.2
penis NEC	187.4	198.82	233.5	222.1	236.6	239.5
perianal	173.5	198.2	232.5	216.5	238.2	239.2
perineum	173.5	198.2	232.5	216.5	238.2	239.2
pinna	173.2	198.2	232.2	216.2	238.2	239.2
plantar	173.7	198.2	232.7	216.7	238.2	239.2
popliteal fossa or space	173.7	198.2	232.7	216.7	238.2	239.2
prepuce	187.1	198.82	233.5	222.1	236.6	239.5
pubes	173.5	198.2	232.5	216.5	238.2	239.2
sacrococcygeal region	173.5	198.2	232.5	216.5	238.2	239.2
scalp	173.4	198.2	232.4	216.4	238.2	239.2
scapular region	173.5	198.2	232.5	216.5	238.2	239.2
scrotum	187.7	198.82	233.6	222.4	236.6	239.5
shoulder	173.6	198.2	232.6	216.6	238.2	239.2
sole (foot)	173.7	198.2	232.7	216.7	238.2	239.2
specified sites NEC	173.8	198.2	232.8	216.8	232.8	239.2
submammary fold	173.5	198.2	232.5	216.5	238.2	239.2
supraclavicular region	173.4	198.2	232.4	216.4	238.2	239.2
temple	173.3	198.2	232.3	216.3	238.2	239.2
thigh	173.7	198.2	232.7	216.7	238.2	239.2
thoracic wall	173.5	198.2	232.5	216.5	238.2	239.2
thumb	173.6	198.2	232.6	216.6	238.2	239.2
toe	173.7	198.2	232.7	216.7	238.2	239.2
tragus	173.2	198.2	232.2	216.2	238.2	239.2
trunk	173.5	198.2	232.5	216.5	238.2	239.2
umbilicus	173.5	198.2	232.5	216.5	238.2	239.2
vulva	184.4	198.82	233.3	221.2	236.3	239.5
wrist	173.6	198.2	232.6	216.6	238.2	239.2
skull	170.0	198.5	—	213.0	238.0	239.2
soft parts or tissues-*see* Neoplasm, connective tissue						
specified site NEC	195.8	198.89	234.8	229.8	238.8	239.8
spermatic cord	187.6	198.82	233.6	222.8	236.6	239.5
sphenoid	160.5	197.3	231.8	212.0	235.9	239.1
bone	170.0	198.5	—	213.0	238.0	239.2
sinus	160.5	197.3	231.8	212.0	235.9	239.1
sphincter						
anal	154.2	197.5	230.5	211.4	235.5	239.0
of Oddi	156.1	197.8	230.8	211.5	235.3	239.0

◀▶　**New Code**　　⬅▥▥ ▥▥➡　**Revised Code**

	Malignant					
	Primary	Secondary	Ca in situ	Benign	Uncertain Behavior	Unspecified
Neoplasm (*Continued*)						
spine, spinal (column)	170.2	198.5	—	213.2	238.0	239.2
bulb	191.7	198.3	—	225.0	237.5	239.6
coccyx	170.6	198.5	—	213.6	238.0	239.2
cord (cervical) (lumbar) (sacral) (thoracic)	192.2	198.3	—	225.3	237.5	239.7
dura mater	192.3	198.4	—	225.4	237.6	239.7
lumbosacral	170.2	198.5	—	213.2	238.0	239.2
membrane	192.3	198.4	—	225.4	237.6	239.7
meninges	192.3	198.4	—	225.4	237.6	239.7
nerve (root)	171.9	198.89	—	215.9	238.1	239.2
pia mater	192.3	198.4	—	225.4	237.6	239.7
root	171.9	198.89	—	215.9	238.1	239.2
sacrum	170.6	198.5	—	213.6	238.0	239.2
spleen, splenic NEC	159.1	197.8	230.9	211.9	235.5	239.0
flexure (colon)	153.7	197.5	230.3	211.3	235.2	239.0
stem, brain	191.7	198.3	—	225.0	237.5	239.6
Stensen's duct	142.0	198.89	230.0	210.2	235.0	239.0
sternum	170.3	198.5	—	213.3	238.0	239.2
stomach	151.9	197.8	230.2	211.1	235.2	239.0
antrum (pyloric)	151.2	197.8	230.2	211.1	235.2	239.0
body	151.4	197.8	230.2	211.1	235.2	239.0
cardia	151.0	197.8	230.2	211.1	235.2	239.0
cardiac orifice	151.0	197.8	230.2	211.1	235.2	239.0
contiguous sites	151.8	—	—	—	—	—
corpus	151.4	197.8	230.2	211.1	235.2	239.0
fundus	151.3	197.8	230.2	211.1	235.2	239.0
greater curvature NEC	151.6	197.8	230.2	211.1	235.2	239.0
lesser curvature NEC	151.5	197.8	230.2	211.1	235.2	239.0
prepylorus	151.1	197.8	230.2	211.1	235.2	239.0
pylorus	151.1	197.8	230.2	211.1	235.2	239.0
wall NEC	151.9	197.8	230.2	211.1	235.2	239.0
anterior NEC	151.8	197.8	230.2	211.1	235.2	239.0
posterior NEC	151.8	197.8	230.2	211.1	235.2	239.0
stroma, endometrial	182.0	198.82	233.2	219.1	236.0	239.5
stump, cervical	180.8	198.82	233.1	219.0	236.0	239.5
subcutaneous (nodule) (tissue) NEC-*see* Neoplasm, connective tissue						
subdural	192.1	198.4	—	225.2	237.6	239.7
subglottis, subglottic	161.2	197.3	231.0	212.1	235.6	239.1
sublingual	144.9	198.89	230.0	210.3	235.1	239.0
gland or duct	142.2	198.89	230.0	210.2	235.0	239.0
submandibular gland	142.1	198.89	230.0	210.2	235.0	239.0
submaxillary gland or duct	142.1	198.89	230.0	210.2	235.0	239.0
submental	195.0	198.89	234.8	229.8	238.8	239.8
subpleural	162.9	197.0	—	212.3	235.7	239.1
substernal	164.2	197.1	—	212.5	235.8	239.8
sudoriferous, sudoriparous gland, site unspecified	173.9	198.2	232.9	216.9	238.2	239.2
specified site-*see* Neoplasm, skin						
supraclavicular region	195.0	198.89	234.8	229.8	238.8	239.8
supraglottis	161.1	197.3	231.0	212.1	235.6	239.1
suprarenal (capsule) (cortex) (gland) (medulla)	194.0	198.7	234.8	227.0	237.2	239.7
suprasellar (region)	191.9	198.3	—	225.0	237.5	239.6
sweat gland (apocrine) (eccrine), site unspecified	173.9	198.2	232.9	216.9	238.2	239.2
specified site-*see* Neoplasm, skin						
sympathetic nerve or nervous system NEC	171.9	198.89	—	215.9	238.1	239.2
symphysis pubis	170.6	198.5	—	213.6	238.0	239.2
synovial membrane-*see* Neoplasm, connective tissue						
tapetum, brain	191.8	198.3	—	225.0	237.5	239.6
tarsus (any bone)	170.8	198.5	—	213.8	238.0	239.2
temple (skin)	173.3	198.2	232.3	216.3	238.2	239.2
temporal						
bone	170.0	198.5	—	213.0	238.0	239.2
lobe or pole	191.2	198.3	—	225.0	237.5	239.6
region	195.0	198.89	234.8	229.8	238.8	239.8
skin	173.3	198.2	232.3	216.3	238.2	239.2

◄ ▶ **New Code**　　　⬅▮▮▮ ▮▮▮➡ **Revised Code**

	Malignant					
	Primary	Secondary	Ca in stiu	Benign	Uncertain Behavior	Unspecified
Neoplasm *(Continued)*						
tendon (sheath)-*see* Neoplasm, connective tissue						
tentorium (cerebelli)	192.1	198.4	—	225.2	237.6	239.7
testis, testes (descended) (scrotal)	186.9	198.82	233.6	222.0	236.4	239.5
ectopic	186.0	198.82	233.6	222.0	236.4	239.5
retained	186.0	198.82	233.6	222.0	236.4	239.5
undescended	186.0	198.82	233.6	222.0	236.4	239.5
thalamus	191.0	198.3	—	225.0	237.5	239.6
thigh NEC*	195.5	198.89	234.8	229.8	238.8	239.8
thorax, thoracic (cavity) (organs NEC)	195.1	198.89	234.8	229.8	238.8	239.8
duct	171.4	198.89	—	215.4	238.1	239.2
wall NEC	195.1	198.89	234.8	229.8	238.8	239.8
throat	149.0	198.89	230.0	210.9	235.1	239.0
thumb NEC*	195.4	198.89	232.6	229.8	238.8	239.8
thymus (gland)	164.0	198.89	—	212.6	235.8	239.8
contiguous sites with heart and mediastinum	164.8	—	—	—	—	—
thyroglossal duct	193	198.89	234.8	226	237.4	239.7
thyroid (gland)	193	198.89	234.8	226	237.4	239.7
cartilage	161.3	197.3	231.0	212.1	235.6	239.1
tibia (any part)	170.7	198.5	—	213.7	238.0	239.2
toe NEC*	195.5	198.89	232.7	229.8	238.8	239.8
tongue	141.9	198.89	230.0	210.1	235.1	239.0
anterior (two-thirds) NEC	141.4	198.89	230.0	210.1	235.1	239.0
dorsal surface	141.1	198.89	230.0	210.1	235.1	239.0
ventral surface	141.3	198.89	230.0	210.1	235.1	239.0
base (dorsal surface)	141.0	198.89	230.0	210.1	235.1	239.0
border (lateral)	141.2	198.89	230.0	210.1	235.1	239.0
contiguous sites	141.8	—	—	—	—	—
dorsal surface NEC	141.1	198.89	230.0	210.1	235.1	239.0
fixed part NEC	141.0	198.89	230.0	210.1	235.1	239.0
foramen cecum	141.1	198.89	230.0	210.1	235.1	239.0
frenulum linguae	141.3	198.89	230.0	210.1	235.1	239.0
junctional zone	141.5	198.89	230.0	210.1	235.1	239.0
margin (lateral)	141.2	198.89	230.0	210.1	235.1	239.0
midline NEC	141.1	198.89	230.0	210.1	235.1	239.0
mobile part NEC	141.4	198.89	230.0	210.1	235.1	239.0
posterior (third)	141.0	198.89	230.0	210.1	235.1	239.0
root	141.0	198.89	230.0	210.1	235.1	239.0
surface (dorsal)	141.1	198.89	230.0	210.1	235.1	239.0
base	141.0	198.89	230.0	210.1	235.1	239.0
ventral	141.3	198.89	230.0	210.1	235.1	239.0
tip	141.2	198.89	230.0	210.1	235.1	239.0
tonsil	141.6	198.89	230.0	210.1	235.1	239.0
tonsil	146.0	198.89	230.0	210.5	235.1	239.0
fauces, faucial	146.0	198.89	230.0	210.5	235.1	239.0
lingual	141.6	198.89	230.0	210.1	235.1	239.0
palatine	146.0	198.89	230.0	210.5	235.1	239.0
pharyngeal	147.1	198.89	230.0	210.7	235.1	239.0
pillar (anterior) (posterior)	146.2	198.89	230.0	210.6	235.1	239.0
tonsillar fossa	146.1	198.89	230.0	210.6	235.1	239.0
tooth socket NEC	143.9	198.89	230.0	210.4	235.1	239.0
trachea (cartilage) (mucosa)	162.0	197.3	231.1	212.2	235.7	239.1
contiguous sites with bronchus or lung	162.8	—	—	—	—	—
tracheobronchial	162.8	197.3	231.1	212.2	235.7	239.1
contiguous sites with lung	162.8	—	—	—	—	—
tragus	173.2	198.2	232.2	216.2	238.2	239.2
trunk NEC*	195.8	198.89	232.5	229.8	238.8	239.8
tubo-ovarian	183.8	198.82	233.3	221.8	236.3	239.5
tunica vaginalis	187.8	198.82	233.6	222.8	236.6	239.5
turbinate (bone)	170.0	198.5	—	213.0	238.0	239.2
nasal	160.0	197.3	231.8	212.0	235.9	239.1
tympanic cavity	160.1	197.3	231.8	212.0	235.9	239.1
ulna (any part)	170.4	198.5	—	213.4	238.0	239.2

◀▶ **New Code**   ◀▥▥▶ **Revised Code**

	Malignant					
	Primary	Secondary	Ca in situ	Benign	Uncertain Behavior	Unspecified
Neoplasm *(Continued)*						
umbilicus, umbilical	173.5	198.2	232.5	216.5	238.2	239.2
uncus, brain	191.2	198.3	—	225.0	237.5	239.6
unknown site or unspecified	199.1	199.1	234.9	229.9	238.9	239.9
urachus	188.7	198.1	233.7	223.3	236.7	239.4
ureter, ureteral	189.2	198.1	233.9	223.2	236.91	239.5
orifice (bladder)	188.6	198.1	233.7	223.3	236.7	239.4
ureter-bladder (junction)	188.6	198.1	233.7	223.3	236.7	239.4
urethra, urethral (gland)	189.3	198.1	233.9	223.81	236.99	239.5
orifice, internal	188.5	198.1	233.7	223.3	236.7	239.4
urethrovaginal (septum)	184.9	198.82	233.3	221.9	236.3	239.5
urinary organ or system NEC	189.9	198.1	233.9	223.9	236.99	239.5
bladder-*see* Neoplasm, bladder						
contiguous sites	189.8	—	—	—	—	—
specified sites NEC	189.8	198.1	233.9	223.89	236.99	239.5
utero-ovarian	183.8	198.82	233.3	221.8	236.3	239.5
ligament	183.3	198.82	—	221.0	236.3	239.5
uterosacral ligament	183.4	198.82	—	221.0	236.3	239.5
uterus, uteri, uterine	179	198.82	233.2	219.9	236.0	239.5
adnexa NEC	183.9	198.82	233.3	221.8	236.3	239.5
contiguous sites	183.8	—	—	—	—	—
body	182.0	198.82	233.2	219.1	236.0	239.5
contiguous sites	182.8	—	—	—	—	—
cervix	180.9	198.82	233.1	219.0	236.0	239.5
cornu	182.0	198.82	233.2	219.1	236.0	239.5
corpus	182.0	198.82	233.2	219.1	236.0	239.5
endocervix (canal) (gland)	180.0	198.82	233.1	219.0	236.0	239.5
endometrium	182.0	198.82	233.2	219.1	236.0	239.5
exocervix	180.1	198.82	233.1	219.0	236.0	239.5
external os	180.1	198.82	233.1	219.0	236.0	239.5
fundus	182.0	198.82	233.2	219.1	236.0	239.5
internal os	180.0	198.82	233.1	219.0	236.0	239.5
isthmus	182.1	198.82	233.2	219.1	236.0	239.5
ligament	183.4	198.82	—	221.0	236.3	239.5
broad	183.3	198.82	233.3	221.0	236.3	239.5
round	183.5	198.82	—	221.0	236.3	239.5
lower segment	182.1	198.82	233.2	219.1	236.0	239.5
myometrium	182.0	198.82	233.2	219.1	236.0	239.5
squamocolumnar junction	180.8	198.82	233.1	219.0	236.0	239.5
tube	183.2	198.82	233.3	221.0	236.3	239.5
utricle, prostatic	189.3	198.1	233.9	223.81	236.99	239.5
uveal tract	190.0	198.4	234.0	224.0	238.8	239.8
uvula	145.4	198.89	230.0	210.4	235.1	239.0
vagina, vaginal (fornix) (vault) (wall)	184.0	198.82	233.3	221.1	236.3	239.5
vaginovesical	184.9	198.82	233.3	221.9	236.3	239.5
septum	194.9	198.82	233.3	221.9	236.3	239.5
vallecula (epiglottis)	146.3	198.89	230.0	210.6	235.1	239.0
vascular-*see* Neoplasm, connective tissue						
vas deferens	187.6	198.82	233.6	222.8	236.6	239.5
Vater's ampulla	156.2	197.8	230.8	211.5	235.3	239.0
vein, venous-*see* Neoplasm, connective tissue						
vena cava (abdominal) (inferior)	171.5	198.89	—	215.5	238.1	239.2
superior	171.4	198.89	—	215.4	238.1	239.2
ventricle (cerebral) (floor) (fourth) (lateral) (third)	191.5	198.3	—	225.0	237.5	239.6
cardiac (left) (right)	164.1	198.89	—	212.7	238.8	239.8
ventricular band of larynx	161.1	197.3	231.0	212.1	235.6	239.1
ventriculus-*see* Neoplasm, stomach						
vermillion border-*see* Neoplasm, lip						
vermis, cerebellum	191.6	198.3	—	225.0	237.5	239.6
vertebra (column)	170.2	198.5	—	213.2	238.0	239.2
coccyx	170.6	198.5	—	213.6	238.0	239.2
sacrum	170.6	198.5	—	213.6	238.0	239.2
vesical-*see* Neoplasm, bladder						

	Malignant					
	Primary	Secondary	Ca in stiu	Benign	Uncertain Behavior	Unspecified
Neoplasm *(Continued)*						
vesicle, seminal	187.8	198.82	233.6	222.8	236.6	239.5
vesicocervical tissue	184.9	198.82	233.3	221.9	236.3	239.5
vesicorectal	195.3	198.89	234.8	229.8	238.8	239.8
vesicovaginal	184.9	198.82	233.3	221.9	236.3	239.5
septum	184.9	198.82	233.3	221.9	236.3	239.5
vessel (blood)-*see* Neoplasm, connective tissue						
vestibular gland, greater	184.1	198.82	233.3	221.2	236.3	239.5
vestibule						
mouth	145.1	198.89	230.0	210.4	235.1	239.0
nose	160.0	197.3	231.8	212.0	235.9	239.1
Virchow's gland	—	196.0	—	229.0	238.8	239.8
viscera NEC	195.8	198.89	234.8	229.8	238.8	239.8
vocal cords (true)	161.0	197.3	231.0	212.1	235.6	239.1
false	161.1	197.3	231.0	212.1	235.6	239.1
vomer	170.0	198.5	—	213.0	238.0	239.2
vulva	184.4	198.82	233.3	221.2	236.3	239.5
vulvovaginal gland	184.4	198.82	233.3	221.2	236.3	239.5
Waldeyer's ring	149.1	198.89	230.0	210.9	235.1	239.0
Wharton's duct	142.1	198.89	230.0	210.2	235.0	239.0
white matter (central) (cerebral)	191.0	198.3	—	225.0	237.5	239.6
windpipe	162.0	197.3	231.1	212.2	235.7	239.1
Wirsung's duct	157.3	197.8	230.9	211.6	235.5	239.0
wolffian (body) (duct)						
female	184.8	198.82	233.3	221.8	236.3	239.5
male	187.8	198.82	233.6	222.8	236.6	239.5
womb-*see* Neoplasm, uterus						
wrist NEC*	195.4	198.89	232.6	229.8	238.8	239.8
xiphoid process	170.3	198.5	—	213.3	238.0	239.2
Zuckerkandl's organ	194.6	198.89	—	227.6	237.3	239.7

Neovascularization
  choroid 362.16
  ciliary body 364.42
  cornea 370.60
    deep 370.63
    localized 370.61
  iris 364.42
  retina 362.16
  subretinal 362.16
Nephralgia 788.0
Nephritis, nephritic (albuminuric) (azotemic) (congenital) (degenerative)
  (diffuse) (disseminated) (epithelial)
  (familial) (focal) (granulomatous)
  (hemorrhagic) (infantile) (nonsuppurative, excretory) (uremic)
  583.9
  with
    edema - *see* Nephrosis
    lesion of
      glomerulonephritis
        hypocomplementemic persistent
          583.2
          with nephrotic syndrome
            581.2
          chronic 582.2
        lobular 583.2
          with nephrotic syndrome
            581.2
          chronic 582.2
        membranoproliferative 583.2
          with nephrotic syndrome
            581.2
          chronic 582.2
        membranous 583.1
          with nephrotic syndrome
            581.1
          chronic 582.1
        mesangiocapillary 583.2
          with nephrotic syndrome
            581.2
          chronic 582.2
        mixed membranous and prolif-
          erative 583.2
          with nephrotic syndrome
            581.2
          chronic 582.2
        proliferative (diffuse) 583.0
          with nephrotic syndrome
            581.0
          acute 580.0
          chronic 582.0
        rapidly progressive 583.4
          acute 580.4
          chronic 582.4
      interstitial nephritis (diffuse) (fo-
        cal) 583.89
        with nephrotic syndrome
          581.89
        acute 580.89
        chronic 582.89
      necrotizing glomerulitis 583.4
        acute 580.4
        chronic 582.4
      renal necrosis 583.9
        cortical 583.6
        medullary 583.7
      specified pathology NEC 583.89
        with nephrotic syndrome 581.89
        acute 580.89
        chronic 582.89
    necrosis, renal 583.9
      cortical 583.6
      medullary (papillary) 583.7

Nephritis, nephritic (*Continued*)
  with (*Continued*)
    nephrotic syndrome (*see also* Ne-
      phrosis) 581.9
    papillary necrosis 583.7
    specified pathology NEC 583.89
  acute 580.9
    extracapillary with epithelial cres-
      cents 580.4
    hypertensive (*see also* Hypertension,
      kidney) 403.90
    necrotizing 580.4
    poststreptococcal 580.0
    proliferative (diffuse) 580.0
    rapidly progressive 580.4
    specified pathology NEC 580.89
  amyloid 277.3 *[583.81]*
    chronic 277.3 *[582.81]*
  arteriolar (*see also* Hypertension, kid-
    ney) 403.90
  arteriosclerotic (*see also* Hypertension,
    kidney) 403.90
  ascending (*see also* Pyelitis) 590.80
  atrophic 582.9
  basement membrane NEC 583.89
    with pulmonary hemorrhage (Good-
      pasture's syndrome) 446.21
      [583.81]
  calculous, calculus 592.0
  cardiac (*see also* Hypertension, kidney)
    403.90
  cardiovascular (*see also* Hypertension,
    kidney) 403.90
  chronic 582.9
    arteriosclerotic (*see also* Hyperten-
      sion, kidney) 403.90
    hypertensive (*see also* Hypertension,
      kidney) 403.90
  cirrhotic (*see also* Sclerosis, renal) 587
  complicating pregnancy, childbirth, or
    puerperium 646.2
    with hypertension 642.1
      affecting fetus or newborn 760.0
    affecting fetus or newborn 760.1
  croupous 580.9
  desquamative - *see* Nephrosis
  due to
    amyloidosis 277.3 *[583.81]*
      chronic 277.3 *[582.81]*
    arteriosclerosis (*see also* Hyperten-
      sion, kidney) 403.90
    diabetes mellitus 250.4 *[583.81]*
      with nephrotic syndrome 250.4
        [581.81]
    diphtheria 032.89 *[580.81]*
    gonococcal infection (acute) 098.19
      [583.81]
      chronic or duration of 2 months
        or over 098.39 *[583.81]*
    gout 274.10
    infectious hepatitis 070.9 *[580.81]*
    mumps 072.79 *[580.81]*
    specified kidney pathology NEC
      583.89
      acute 580.89
      chronic 582.89
    streptotrichosis 039.8 *[583.81]*
    subacute bacterial endocarditis 421.0
      [580.81]
    systemic lupus erythematosus 710.0
      [583.81]
      chronic 710.0 *[582.81]*
    typhoid fever 002.0 *[580.81]*
  endothelial 582.2

Nephritis, nephritic (*Continued*)
  end state (chronic) (terminal) NEC 585
  epimembranous 581.1
  exudative 583.89
    with nephrotic syndrome 581.89
    acute 580.89
    chronic 582.89
  gonococcal (acute) 098.19 *[583.81]*
    chronic or duration of 2 months or
      over 098.39 *[583.81]*
  gouty 274.10
  hereditary (Alport's syndrome) 759.89
  hydremic - *see* Nephrosis
  hypertensive (*see also* Hypertension,
    kidney) 403.90
  hypocomplementemic persistent 583.2
    with nephrotic syndrome 581.2
    chronic 582.2
  immune complex NEC 583.89
  infective (*see also* Pyelitis) 590.80
  interstitial (diffuse) (focal) 583.89
    with nephrotic syndrome 581.89
    acute 580.89
    chronic 582.89
  latent or quiescent - *see* Nephritis,
    chronic
  lead 984.9
    specified type of lead - *see* Table of
      Drugs and Chemicals
  lobular 583.2
    with nephrotic syndrome 581.2
    chronic 582.2
  lupus 710.0 *[583.81]*
    acute 710.0 *[580.81]*
    chronic 710.0 *[582.81]*
  membranoproliferative 583.2
    with nephrotic syndrome 581.2
    chronic 582.2
  membranous 583.1
    with nephrotic syndrome 581.1
    chronic 582.1
  mesangiocapillary 583.2
    with nephrotic syndrome 581.2
    chronic 582.2
  minimal change 581.3
  mixed membranous and proliferative
    583.2
    with nephrotic syndrome 581.2
    chronic 582.2
  necrotic, necrotizing 583.4
    acute 580.4
    chronic 582.4
  nephrotic - *see* Nephrosis
  old - *see* Nephritis, chronic
  parenchymatous 581.89
  polycystic 753.12
    adult type (APKD) 753.13
    autosomal dominant 753.13
    autosomal recessive 753.14
    childhood type (CPKD) 753.14
    infantile type 753.14
  poststreptococcal 580.0
  pregnancy - *see* Nephritis, complicating
    pregnancy
  proliferative 583.0
    with nephrotic syndrome 581.0
    acute 580.0
    chronic 582.0
  purulent (*see also* Pyelitis) 590.80
  rapidly progressive 583.4
    acute 580.4
    chronic 582.4
  salt-losing or salt-wasting (*see also* Dis-
    ease, renal) 593.9

Nephritis, nephritic (*Continued*)
saturnine 584.9
  specified type of lead - *see* Table of
      Drugs and Chemicals
septic (*see also* Pyelitis) 590.80
specified pathology NEC 583.89
  acute 580.89
  chronic 582.89
staphylococcal (*see also* Pyelitis) 590.80
streptotrichosis 039.8 [583.81]
subacute (*see also* Nephrosis) 581.9
suppurative (*see also* Pyelitis) 590.80
syphilitic (late) 095.4
  congenital 090.5 [583.81]
  early 091.69 [583.81]
terminal (chronic) (end-stage) NEC 585
toxic - *see* Nephritis, acute
tubal, tubular - *see* Nephrosis, tubular
tuberculous (*see also* Tuberculosis)
      016.0 [583.81]
type II (Ellis) - *see* Nephrosis
vascular - *see also* Hypertension, kidney
war 580.9
Nephroblastoma (M8960/3) 189.0
epithelial (M8961/3) 189.0
mesenchymal (M8962/3) 189.0
Nephrocalcinosis 275.49
Nephrocystitis, pustular (*see also* Pyelitis) 590.80
Nephrolithiasis (congenital) (pelvis) (recurrent) 592.0
uric acid 274.11
Nephroma (M8960/3) 189.0
mesoblastic (M8960/1) 236.9
Nephronephritis (*see also* Nephrosis)
      581.9
Nephronopthisis 753.16
Nephropathy (*see also* Nephritis) 583.9
with
  exudative nephritis 583.89
  interstitial nephritis (diffuse) (focal)
      583.89
  medullary necrosis 583.7
  necrosis 583.9
    cortical 583.6
    medullary or papillary 583.7
  papillary necrosis 583.7
  specified lesion or cause NEC 583.89
analgesic 583.89
  with medullary necrosis, acute 584.7
arteriolar (*see also* Hypertension, kidney) 403.90
arteriosclerotic (*see also* Hypertension, kidney) 403.90
complicating pregnancy 646.2
diabetic 250.4 [583.81]
gouty 274.10
  specified type NEC 274.19
hypercalcemic 588.8
hypertensive (*see also* Hypertension, kidney) 403.90
hypokalemic (vacuolar) 588.8
obstructive 593.89
  congenital 753.20
phenacetin 584.7
phosphate-losing 588.0
potassium depletion 588.8
proliferative (*see also* Nephritis, proliferative) 583.0
protein-losing 588.8
salt-losing or salt-wasting (*see also* Disease, renal) 593.9
sickle-cell (*see also* Disease, sickle-cell)
      282.60 [583.81]

Nephropathy (*Continued*)
toxic 584.5
vasomotor 584.5
water-losing 588.8
Nephroptosis (*see also* Disease, renal)
      593.0
congenital (displaced) 753.3
Nephropyosis (*see also* Abscess, kidney)
      590.2
Nephrorrhagia 593.81
Nephrosclerosis (arteriolar) (arteriosclerotic) (chronic) (hyaline) (*see also* Hypertension, kidney) 403.90
gouty 274.10
hyperplastic (arteriolar) (*see also* Hypertension, kidney) 403.90
senile (*see also* Sclerosis, renal) 587
Nephrosis, nephrotic (Epstein's) (syndrome) 581.9
with
  lesion of
    focal glomerulosclerosis 581.1
    glomerulonephritis
      endothelial 581.2
        hypocomplementemic persistent
            581.2
      lobular 581.2
      membranoproliferative 581.2
      membranous 581.1
      mesangiocapillary 581.2
      minimal change 581.3
      mixed membranous and proliferative 581.2
      proliferative 581.0
    segmental hyalinosis 581.1
    specified pathology NEC
        581.89
acute - *see* Nephrosis, tubular
anoxic - *see* Nephrosis, tubular
arteriosclerotic (*see also* Hypertension, kidney) 403.90
chemical - *see* Nephrosis, tubular
cholemic 572.4
complicating pregnancy, childbirth, or
    puerperium - *see* Nephritis, complicating pregnancy
diabetic 250.4 [581.81]
hemoglobinuric - *see* Nephrosis, tubular
in
  amyloidosis 277.3 [581.81]
  diabetes mellitus 250.4 [581.81]
  epidemic hemorrhagic fever 078.6
  malaria 084.9 [581.81]
  polyarteritis 446.0 [581.81]
  systemic lupus erythematosus 710.0
      [581.81]
ischemic - *see* Nephrosis, tubular
lipoid 581.3
lower nephron - *see* Nephrosis, tubular
lupoid 710.0 [581.81]
lupus 710.0 [581.81]
malarial 084.9 [581.81]
minimal change 581.3
necrotizing - *see* Nephrosis, tubular
osmotic (sucrose) 588.8
polyarteritic 446.0 [581.81]
radiation 581.9
specified lesion or cause NEC
      581.89
syphilitic 095.4
toxic - *see* Nephrosis, tubular
tubular (acute) 584.5

Nephrosis, nephrotic (*Continued*)
tubular (*Continued*)
  due to a procedure 997.5
  radiation 581.9
Nephrosonephritis hemorrhagic (endemic) 078.6
Nephrostomy status V44.6
with complication 997.5
Nerve - *see* condition
Nerves 799.2
Nervous (*see also* condition) 799.2
breakdown 300.9
heart 306.2
stomach 306.4
tension 799.2
Nervousness 799.2
Nesidioblastoma (M8150/0)
pancreas 211.7
specified site NEC - *see* Neoplasm, by
    site, benign
unspecified site 211.7
Netherton's syndrome (ichthyosiform erythroderma) 757.1
Nettle rash 708.8
Nettleship's disease (urticaria pigmentosa) 757.33
Neumann's disease (pemphigus vegetans) 694.4
Neuralgia, neuralgic (acute) (*see also* Neuritis) 729.2
accessory (nerve) 352.4
acoustic (nerve) 388.5
ankle 355.8
anterior crural 355.8
anus 787.99
arm 723.4
auditory (nerve) 388.5
axilla 353.0
bladder 788.1
brachial 723.4
brain - *see* Disorder, nerve, cranial
broad ligament 625.9
cerebral - *see* Disorder, nerve, cranial
ciliary 346.2
cranial nerve - *see also* Disorder, nerve, cranial
    fifth or trigeminal (*see also* Neuralgia, trigeminal) 350.1
ear 388.71
  middle 352.1
facial 351.8
finger 354.9
flank 355.8
foot 355.8
forearm 354.9
Fothergill's (*see also* Neuralgia, trigeminal) 350.1
  postherpetic 053.12
glossopharyngeal (nerve) 352.1
groin 355.8
hand 354.9
heel 355.8
Horton's 346.2
Hunt's 053.11
hypoglossal (nerve) 352.5
iliac region 355.8
infraorbital (*see also* Neuralgia, trigeminal) 350.1
inguinal 355.8
intercostal (nerve) 353.8
  postherpetic 053.19
jaw 352.1
kidney 788.0
knee 355.8

◄▶   New Code   ⬅▦ ▦➡   Revised Code

Neurofibroma *(Continued)*
　multiple (M9540/1) 237.70
　　type 1 237.71
　　type 2 237.72
　plexiform (M9550/0) - *see* Neoplasm,
　　connective tissue, benign
Neurofibromatosis (multiple) (M9540/1)
　237.70
　acoustic 237.72
　malignant (M9540/3) - *see* Neoplasm,
　　connective tissue, malignant
　type 1 237.71
　type 2 237.72
　von Recklinghausen's 237.71
Neurofibrosarcoma (M9540/3) - *see* Neo-
　plasm, connective tissue, malignant
Neurogenic - *see also* condition
　bladder (atonic) (automatic) (auto-
　　nomic) (flaccid) (hypertonic) (hy-
　　potonic) (inertia) (infranuclear) (ir-
　　ritable) (motor) (nonreflex)
　　(nuclear) (paralysis) (reflex) (sen-
　　sory) (spastic) (supranuclear) (un-
　　inhibited) 596.54
　　with cauda equina syndrome 344.61
　bowel 564.81　◄
　heart 306.2
Neuroglioma (M9505/1) - *see* Neoplasm,
　by site, uncertain behavior
Neurolabyrinthitis (of Dix and Hallpike)
　386.12
Neurolathyrism 988.2
Neuroleprosy 030.1
Neuroleptic malignant syndrome 333.92
Neurolipomatosis 272.8
Neuroma (M9570/0) - *see also* Neoplasm,
　connective tissue, benign
　acoustic (nerve) (M9560/0) 225.1
　amputation (traumatic) - *see also* In-
　　jury, nerve, by site
　　surgical complication (late) 997.61
　appendix 211.3
　auditory nerve 225.1
　digital 355.6
　　toe 355.6
　interdigital (toe) 355.6
　intermetatarsal 355.6
　Morton's 355.6
　multiple 237.70
　　type 1 237.71
　　type 2 237.72
　nonneoplastic 355.9
　　arm NEC 354.9
　　leg NEC 355.8
　　lower extremity NEC 355.8
　　specified site NEC - *see* Mononeuri-
　　　tis, by site
　　upper extremity NEC 354.9
　optic (nerve) 225.1
　plantar 355.6
　plexiform (M9550/0) - *see* Neoplasm,
　　connective tissue, benign
　surgical (nonneoplastic) 355.9
　　arm NEC 354.9
　　leg NEC 355.8
　　lower extremity NEC 355.8
　　upper extremity NEC 354.9
　traumatic - *see also* Injury, nerve, by site
　　old-see Neuroma, nonneoplastic
Neuromyalgia 729.1
Neuromyasthenia (epidemic) 049.8
Neuromyelitis 341.8
　ascending 357.0
　optica 341.0

Neuromyopathy NEC 358.9
Neuromyositis 729.1
Neuronevus (M8725/0) - *see* Neoplasm,
　skin, benign
Neuronitis 357.0
　ascending (acute) 355.2
　vestibular 386.12
Neuroparalytic - *see* condition
Neuropathy, neuropathic (*see also* Disor-
　der, nerve) 355.9
　alcoholic 357.5
　　with psychosis 291.1
　arm NEC 354.9
　autonomic (peripheral) - *see* Neuropa-
　　thy, peripheral, autonomic
　axillary nerve 353.0
　brachial plexus 353.0
　cervical plexus 353.2
　chronic
　　progressive segmentally demyelinat-
　　　ing 357.8
　　relapsing demyelinating 357.8
　congenital sensory 356.2
　Déjérine-Sottas 356.0
　diabetic 250.6 [357.2]
　entrapment 355.9
　　iliohypogastric nerve 355.79
　　ilioinguinal nerve 355.79
　　lateral cutaneous nerve of thigh
　　　355.1
　　median nerve 354.0
　　obturator nerve 355.79
　　peroneal nerve 355.3
　　posterior tibial nerve 355.5
　　saphenous nerve 355.79
　　ulnar nerve 354.2
　facial nerve 351.9
　hereditary 356.9
　　peripheral 356.0
　　sensory (radicular) 356.2
　hypertrophic
　　Charcôt-Marie-Tooth 356.1
　　Déjérine-Sottas 356.0
　　interstitial 356.9
　　Refsum 356.3
　intercostal nerve 354.8
　ischemic - *see* Disorder, nerve
　Jamaican (ginger) 357.7
　leg NEC 355.8
　lower extremity NEC 355.8
　lumbar plexus 353.1
　median nerve 354.1
　multiple (acute) (chronic) (*see also*
　　Polyneuropathy) 356.9
　optic 377.39
　　ischemic 377.41
　　nutritional 377.33
　　toxic 377.34
　peripheral (nerve) (*see also* Polyneurop-
　　athy) 356.9
　　arm NEC 354.9
　　autonomic 337.9
　　　amyloid 277.3 [337.1]
　　　idiopathic 337.0
　　　in
　　　　amyloidosis 277.3 [337.1]
　　　　diabetes (mellitus) 250.6
　　　　　[337.1]
　　　　diseases classified elsewhere
　　　　　337.1
　　　　gout 274.89 [337.1]
　　　　hyperthyroidism 242.9 [337.1]
　　　due to
　　　　antitetanus serum 357.6

Neuropathy, neuropathic *(Continued)*
　peripheral *(Continued)*
　　due to *(Continued)*
　　　arsenic 357.7
　　　drugs 357.6
　　　lead 357.7
　　　organophosphate compounds
　　　　357.7
　　　toxic agent NEC 357.7
　　hereditary 356.0
　　idiopathic 356.9
　　　progressive 356.4
　　　specified type NEC 356.8
　　in diseases classified elsewhere - *see*
　　　Polyneuropathy, in
　　leg NEC 355.8
　　lower extremity NEC 355.8
　　upper extremity NEC 354.9
　plantar nerves 355.6
　progressive hypertrophic interstitial
　　356.9
　radicular NEC 729.2
　　brachial 723.4
　　cervical NEC 723.4
　　hereditary sensory 356.2
　　lumbar 724.4
　　lumbosacral 724.4
　　thoracic NEC 724.4
　sacral plexus 353.1
　sciatic 355.0
　spinal nerve NEC 355.9
　　root (*see also* Radiculitis) 729.2
　toxic 357.7
　trigeminal sensory 350.8
　ulnar nerve 354.2
　upper extremity NEC 354.9
　uremic 585 [357.4]
　vitamin B$_{12}$ 266.2 [357.4]
　　with anemia (pernicious) 281.0 [357.4]
　　　due to dietary deficiency 281.1
　　　　[357.4]
Neurophthisis - *see also* Disorder, nerve
　peripheral 356.9
　diabetic 250.6 [357.2]
Neuropraxia - *see* Injury, nerve
Neuroretinitis 363.05
　syphilitic 094.85
Neurosarcoma (M9540/3) - *see* Neo-
　plasm, connective tissue, malignant
Neurosclerosis - *see* Disorder, nerve
Neurosis, neurotic 300.9
　accident 300.16
　anancastic, anankastic 300.3
　anxiety (state) 300.00
　　generalized 300.02
　　panic type 300.01
　asthenic 300.5
　bladder 306.53
　cardiac (reflex) 306.2
　cardiovascular 306.2
　climacteric, unspecified type 627.2
　colon 306.4
　compensation 300.16
　compulsive, compulsion 300.3
　conversion 300.11
　craft 300.89
　cutaneous 306.3
　depersonalization 300.6
　depressive (reaction) (type) 300.4
　endocrine 306.6
　environmental 300.89
　fatigue 300.5
　functional (*see also* Disorder, psychoso-
　　matic) 306.9

ICD-9-CM

N

Vol. 2

Newborn *(Continued)*
  multiple NEC *(Continued)*
    mates all stillborn
      born in hospital (without mention
        of cesarean delivery or sec-
        tion) V35.00
        with cesarean delivery or sec-
          tion V35.01
      born outside hospital
        hospitalized V35.1
        not hospitalized V35.2
    mates liveborn and stillborn
      born in hospital (without mention
        of cesarean delivery or sec-
        tion) V36.00
        with cesarean delivery or sec-
          tion V36.01
      born outside hospital
        hospitalized V36.1
        not hospitalized V36.2
  single
    born in hospital (without mention of
      cesarean delivery or section)
      V30.00
      with cesarean delivery or section
        V30.01
    born outside hospital
      hospitalized V30.1
      not hospitalized V30.2
  twin NEC
    born in hospital (without mention of
      cesarean delivery or section)
      V33.00
      with cesarean delivery or section
        V33.01
    born outside hospital
      hospitalized V33.1
      not hospitalized V33.2
    mate liveborn
      born in hospital V31.0
      born outside hospital
        hospitalized V31.1
        not hospitalized V31.2
    mate stillborn
      born in hospital V32.0
      born outside hospital
        hospitalized V32.1
        not hospitalized V32.2
  unspecified as to single or multiple
    birth
    born in hospital (without mention of
      cesarean delivery or section)
      V39.00
      with cesarean delivery or section
        V39.01
    born outside hospital
      hospitalized V39.1
      not hospitalized V39.2
Newcastle's conjunctivitis or disease
  077.8
Nezelof's syndrome (pure alymphocytosis) 279.13
Niacin (amide) deficiency 265.2
Nicolas-Durand-Favre disease (climatic
  bubo) 099.1
Nicolas-Favre disease (climatic bubo)
  099.1
Nicotinic acid (amide) deficiency
  265.2
Niemann-Pick disease (lipid histiocyto-
  sis) (splenomegaly) 272.7
Night
  blindness (*see also* Blindness, night)
    368.60

Night *(Continued)*
  blindness *(Continued)*
    congenital 368.61
      vitamin A deficiency 264.5
    cramps 729.82
    sweats 780.8
    terrors, child 307.46
Nightmare 307.47
  REM-sleep type 307.47
Nipple - *see* condition
Nisbet's chancre 099.0
Nishimoto (-Takeuchi) disease 437.5
Nitritoid crisis or reaction - *see* Crisis,
  nitritoid
Nitrogen retention, extrarenal 788.9
Nitrosohemoglobinemia 289.8
Njovera 104.0
No
  diagnosis 799.9
  disease (found) V71.9
  room at the inn V65.0
Nocardiasis - *see* Nocardiosis
Nocardiosis 039.9
  with pneumonia 039.1
  lung 039.1
  specified type NEC 039.8
Nocturia 788.43
  psychogenic 306.53
Nocturnal - *see also* condition
  dyspnea (paroxysmal) 786.09
  emissions 608.89
  enuresis 788.36
    psychogenic 307.6
  frequency (micturition) 788.43
    psychogenic 306.53
Nodal rhythm disorder 427.89
Nodding of head 781.0
Node(s) - *see also* Nodules
  Heberden's 715.04
  larynx 478.79
  lymph - *see* condition
  milkers' 051.1
  Osler's 421.0
  rheumatic 729.89
  Schmorl's 722.30
    lumbar, lumbosacral 722.32
    specified region NEC 722.39
    thoracic, thoracolumbar 722.31
  singers' 478.5
  skin NEC 782.2
  tuberculous - *see* Tuberculosis, lymph
    gland
  vocal cords 478.5
Nodosities, Haygarth's 715.04
Nodule(s), nodular
  actinomycotic (*see also* Actinomycosis)
    039.9
  arthritic - *see* Arthritis, nodosa
  cutaneous 782.2
  Haygarth's 715.04
  inflammatory - *see* Inflammation
  juxta-articular 102.7
    syphilitic 095.7
    yaws 102.7
  larynx 478.79
  lung, solitary 518.89
    emphysematous 492.8
  milkers' 051.1
  prostate 600
  rheumatic 729.89
  rheumatoid - *see* Arthritis rheumatoid
  scrotum (inflammatory) 608.4
  singers' 478.5
  skin NEC 782.2

Nodule(s) *(Continued)*
  solitary, lung 518.89
    emphysematous 492.8
  subcutaneous 782.2
  thyroid (gland) (nontoxic) (uninodular)
    241.0
    with
      hyperthyroidism 242.1
      thyrotoxicosis 242.1
    toxic or with hyperthyroidism 242.1
  vocal cords 478.5
Noma (gangrenous) (hospital) (infective)
  528.1
  auricle (*see also* Gangrene) 785.4
  mouth 528.1
  pudendi (*see also* Vulvitis) 616.10
  vulvae (*see also* Vulvitis) 616.10
Nomadism V60.0
Non-adherence ◄
  artificial skin graft 996.55 ◄
  decellularized allodermis graft
    996.55 ◄
Non-autoimmune hemolytic anemia
  NEC 283.10
Nonclosure - *see also* Imperfect, closure
  ductus
    arteriosus 747.0
    Botalli 747.0
  Eustachian valve 746.89
  foramen
    Botalli 745.5
    ovale 745.5
Noncompliance with medical treatment
  V15.81
Nondescent (congenital) - *see also* Malposition, congenital
  cecum 751.4
  colon 751.4
  testis 752.51
Nondevelopment
  brain 742.1
    specified part 742.2
  heart 746.89
  organ or site, congenital NEC - *see* Hy-
    poplasia
Nonengagement
  head NEC 652.5
  in labor 660.1
    affecting fetus or newborn 763.1
Nonexanthematous tick fever 066.1
Nonexpansion, lung (newborn) NEC
  770.4
Nonfunctioning
  cystic duct (*see also* Disease, gallblad-
    der) 575.8
  gallbladder (*see also* Disease, gallblad-
    der) 575.8
  kidney (*see also* Disease, renal) 593.9
  labyrinth 386.58
Nonhealing
  stump (surgical) 997.69
  wound, surgical 998.83
**Nonimplantation of ovum, causing in-
  fertility** 628.3
Noninsufflation, fallopian tube 628.2
Nonne-Milroy-Meige syndrome (chronic
  hereditary edema) 757.0
Nonovulation 628.0
Nonpatent fallopian tube 628.2
Nonpneumatization, lung NEC 770.4
Nonreflex bladder 596.54
  with cauda equina 344.61
Nonretention of food - *see* Vomiting
Nonrotation - *see* Malrotation

Nonsecretion, urine (*see also* Anuria) 788.5
 newborn 753.3
Nonunion
 fracture 733.82
 organ or site, congenital NEC - *see* Imperfect, closure
 symphysis pubis, congenital 755.69
 top sacrum, congenital 756.19
Nonviability 765.0
Nonvisualization, gallbladder 793.3
Nonvitalized tooth 522.9
Normal
 delivery - *see* category 650
 menses V65.5
 state (feared complaint unfounded) V65.5
Normoblastosis 289.8
Normocytic anemia (infectional) 285.9
 due to blood loss (chronic) 280.0
  acute 285.1
Norrie's disease (congenital) (progressive oculoacousticocerebral degeneration) 743.8
North American blastomycosis 116.0
Norwegian itch 133.0
Nose, nasal - *see* condition
Nosebleed 784.7
Nosomania 298.9
Nosophobia 300.29
Nostalgia 309.89
Notch of iris 743.46
Notched lip, congenital (*see also* Cleft, lip) 749.10
Notching nose, congenital (tip) 748.1

Nothnagel's
 syndrome 378.52
 vasomotor acroparesthesia 443.89
Novy's relapsing fever (American) 087.1
Noxious
 foodstuffs, poisoning by
  fish 988.0
  fungi 988.1
  mushrooms 988.1
  plants (food) 988.2
  shellfish 988.0
  specified type NEC 988.8
  toadstool 988.1
 substances transmitted through placenta or breast milk 760.70
  alcohol 760.71
  anti-infective agents 760.74
  cocaine 760.75
  "crack" 760.75
  diethylstilbestrol (DES) 760.76
  hallucinogenic agents NEC 760.73
  medicinal agents NEC 760.79
  narcotics 760.72
  obstetric anesthetic or analgesic 763.5
  specified agent NEC 760.79
  suspected, affecting management of pregnancy 655.5
Nuchal hitch (arm) 652.8
Nucleus pulposus - *see* condition
Numbness 782.0
Nuns' knee 727.2

Nursemaid's
 elbow 832.0
 shoulder 831.0
Nutmeg liver 573.8
Nutrition, deficient or insufficient (particular kind of food) 269.9
 due to
  insufficient food 994.2
  lack of
   care (child) (infant) 995.52
    adult 995.84
   food 994.2
Nyctalopia (*see also* Blindness, night) 368.60
 vitamin A deficiency 264.5
Nycturia 788.43
 psychogenic 306.53
Nymphomania 302.89
Nystagmus 379.50
 associated with vestibular system disorders 379.54
 benign paroxysmal positional 386.11
 central positional 386.2
 congenital 379.51
 deprivation 379.53
 dissociated 379.55
 latent 379.52
 miners' 300.89
 positional
  benign paroxysmal 386.11
  central 386.2
 specified NEC 379.56
 vestibular 379.54
 visual deprivation 379.53

O

Oasthouse urine disease 270.2
Obermeyer's relapsing fever (European)
 087.0
Obesity (constitutional) (exogenous) (familial) (nutritional) (simple) 278.00
 adrenal 255.8
 due to hyperalimentation 278.00
 endocrine NEC 259.9
 endogenous 259.9
 Fröhlich's (adiposogenital dystrophy)
  253.8
 glandular NEC 259.9
 hypothyroid (see also Hypothyroidism)
  244.9
 morbid 278.01
 of pregnancy 646.1
 pituitary 253.8
 thyroid (see also Hypothyroidism)
  244.9
Oblique - see also condition
 lie before labor, affecting fetus or newborn 761.7
Obliquity, pelvis 738.6
Obliteration
 abdominal aorta 446.7
 appendix (lumen) 543.9
 artery 447.1
 ascending aorta 446.7
 bile ducts 576.8
  with calculus, choledocholithiasis, or
   stones - see Choledocholithiasis
  congenital 751.61
   jaundice from 751.61 [774.5]
 common duct 576.8
  with calculus, choledocholithiasis, or
   stones - see Choledocholithiasis
  congenital 751.61
 cystic duct 575.8
  with calculus, choledocholithiasis, or
   stones - see Choledocholithiasis
 disease, arteriolar 447.1
 endometrium 621.8
 eye, anterior chamber 360.34
 fallopian tube 628.2
 lymphatic vessel 457.1
  postmastectomy 457.0
 organ or site, congenital NEC - see
  Atresia
 placental blood vessels - see Placenta,
  abnormal
 supra-aortic branches 446.7
 ureter 593.89
 urethra 599.84
 vein 459.9
 vestibule (oral) 525.8
Observation (for) V71.9
 without need for further medical care
  V71.9
 accident NEC V71.4
  at work V71.3
 criminal assault V71.6
 deleterious agent ingestion V71.8
 disease V71.9
  cardiovascular V71.7
  heart V71.7
  mental V71.09
  specified condition NEC V71.8
 foreign body ingestion V71.8
 growth and development variations
  V21.8
 injuries (accidental) V71.4
  inflicted NEC V71.6

Observation (Continued)
 injuries (Continued)
  inflicted NEC (Continued)
   during alleged rape or seduction
    V71.5
 malignant neoplasm, suspected V71.1
 postpartum
  immediately after delivery V24.0
  routine follow-up V24.2
 pregnancy
  high-risk V23.9
   specified problem NEC V23.8
  normal (without complication) V22.1
   with nonobstetric complication
    V22.2
   first V22.0
 rape or seduction, alleged V71.5
  injury during V71.5
 suicide attempt, alleged V71.8
 suspected (undiagnosed) (unproven)
  cardiovascular disease V71.7
  child or wife battering victim V71.6
  concussion (cerebral) V71.6
  condition NEC V71.8
   infant - see Observation, suspected, condition, newborn
   newborn V29.9
    cardiovascular disease V29.8
    congenital anomaly V29.8
    genetic V29.3 ◄
    infectious V29.0
    ingestion foreign object V29.8
    injury V29.8
    metabolic V29.3 ◄
    neoplasm V29.8
    neurological V29.1
    poison, poisoning V29.8
    respiratory V29.2
    specified NEC V29.8
  infectious disease not requiring isolation V71.8
  malignant neoplasm V71.1
  mental disorder V71.09
  neoplasm
   benign V71.8
   malignant V71.1
  specified condition NEC V71.8
  tuberculosis V71.2
 tuberculosis, suspected V71.2
Obsession, obsessional 300.3
 ideas and mental images 300.3
 impulses 300.3
 neurosis 300.3
 phobia 300.3
 psychasthenia 300.3
 ruminations 300.3
 state 300.3
 syndrome 300.3
Obsessive-compulsive 300.3
 neurosis 300.3
 reaction 300.3
Obstetrical trauma NEC (complicating
 delivery) 665.9
 with
  abortion - see Abortion, by type,
   with damage to pelvic organs
  ectopic pregnancy (see also categories
   633.0-633.9) 639.2
  molar pregnancy (see also categories
   630-632) 639.2
 affecting fetus or newborn 763.89 ⬅
 following
  abortion 639.2
  ectopic or molar pregnancy 639.2

Obstipation (see also Constipation) 564.0
 psychogenic 306.4
Obstruction, obstructed, obstructive
 airway NEC 519.8
  with
   allergic alveolitis NEC 495.9
   asthma NEC (see also Asthma)
    493.9
   bronchiectasis 494
   bronchitis (see also Bronchitis,
    chronic, obstructive) 491.20
   emphysema NEC 492.8
  chronic 496
   with
    allergic alveolitis NEC 495.5
    asthma NEC (see also Asthma)
     493.9
    bronchiectasis 494
    bronchitis (chronic) (see also
     Bronchitis, chronic, obstructive) 491.20
    emphysema NEC 492.8
  due to
   bronchospasm 519.1
   foreign body 934.9
   inhalation of fumes or vapors
    506.9
   laryngospasm 478.75
 alimentary canal (see also Obstruction,
  intestine) 560.9
 ampulla of Vater 576.2
  with calculus, cholelithiasis, or
   stones - see Choledocholithiasis
 aortic (heart) (valve) (see also Stenosis,
  aortic) 424.1
  rheumatic (see also Stenosis, aortic,
   rheumatic) 395.0
 aortoiliac 444.0
 aqueduct of Sylvius 331.4
  congenital 742.3
   with spina bifida (see also Spina
    bifida) 741.0
 Arnold-Chiari (see also Spina bifida)
  741.0
 artery (see also Embolism, artery) 444.9
  basilar (complete) (partial) (see also
   Occlusion, artery, basilar) 433.0
  carotid (complete) (partial) (see also
   Occlusion, artery, carotid) 433.1
  precerebral - see Occlusion, artery,
   precerebral NEC
  retinal (central) (see also Occlusion,
   retina) 362.30
  vertebral (complete) (partial) (see also
   Occlusion, artery, vertebral)
   433.2
 asthma (chronic) (with obstructive pulmonary disease) 493.2
 band (intestinal) 560.81
 bile duct or passage (see also Obstruction, biliary) 576.2
  congenital 751.61
   jaundice from 751.61 [774.5]
 biliary (duct) (tract) 576.2
  with calculus 574.51
   with cholecystitis (chronic) 574.41
    acute 574.31
  congenital 751.61
   jaundice from 751.61 [774.5]
  gallbladder 575.2
   with calculus 574.21
    with cholecystitis (chronic)
     574.11
     acute 574.01

Obstruction, obstructed, obstructive
  (Continued)
  bladder neck (acquired) 596.0
    congenital 753.6
  bowel (*see also* Obstruction, intestine)
    560.9
  bronchus 519.1
  canal, ear (*see also* Stricture, ear canal,
    acquired) 380.50
  cardia 537.89
  caval veins (inferior) (superior) 459.2
  cecum (*see also* Obstruction, intestine)
    560.9
  circulatory 459.9
  colon (*see also* Obstruction, intestine)
    560.9
    sympathicotonic 560.89
  common duct (*see also* Obstruction, bil-
    iary) 576.2
    congenital 751.61
  coronary (artery) (heart) - *see* Arterio-
    sclerosis, coronary
  cystic duct (*see also* Obstruction, gall-
    bladder) 575.2
    congenital 751.61
  device, implant, or graft - *see* Compli-
    cations, due to (presence of) any
    device, implant, or graft classified
    to 996.0-996.5 NEC
  due to foreign body accidentally left in
    operation wound 998.4
  duodenum 537.3
    congenital 751.1
    due to
      compression NEC 537.3
      cyst 537.3
      intrinsic lesion or disease NEC 537.3
      scarring 537.3
      torsion 537.3
      ulcer 532.91
      volvulus 537.3
  ejaculatory duct 608.89
  endocardium 424.90
    arteriosclerotic 424.99
    specified cause, except rheumatic
      424.99
  esophagus 530.3
  Eustachian tube (complete) (partial)
    381.60
    cartilaginous
      extrinsic 381.63
      intrinsic 381.62
    due to
      cholesteatoma 381.61
      osseous lesion NEC 381.61
      polyp 381.61
    osseous 381.61
  fallopian tube (bilateral) 628.2
  fecal 560.39
    with hernia - *see also* Hernia, by site,
      with obstruction
      gangrenous - *see* Hernia, by site,
        with gangrene
  foramen of Monro (congenital) 742.3
    with spina bifida (*see also* Spina bi-
      fida) 741.0
  foreign body - *see* Foreign body
  gallbladder 575.2
    with calculus, cholelithiasis, or
      stones 574.21
      with cholecystitis (chronic) 574.11
        acute 574.01
    congenital 751.69
      jaundice from 751.69 *[774.5]*

Obstruction, obstructed, obstructive
  (Continued)
  gastric outlet 537.0
  gastrointestinal (*see also* Obstruction,
    intestine) 560.9
  glottis 478.79
  hepatic 573.8
    duct (*see also* Obstruction, biliary)
      576.2
      congenital 751.61
  icterus (*see also* Obstruction, biliary)
    576.8
    congenital 751.61
  ileocecal coil (*see also* Obstruction, in-
    testine) 560.9
  ileum (*see also* Obstruction, intestine)
    560.9
  iliofemoral (artery) 444.81
  internal anastomosis - *see* Complica-
    tions, mechanical, graft
  intestine (mechanical) (neurogenic)
    (paroxysmal) (postinfectional) (re-
    flex) 560.9
    with
      adhesions (intestinal) (peritoneal)
        560.81
      hernia - *see also* Hernia, by site,
        with obstruction
        gangrenous - *see* Hernia, by site,
          with gangrene
    adynamic (*see also* Ileus) 560.1
    by gallstone 560.31
    congenital or infantile (small) 751.1
      large 751.2
    due to
      Ascaris lumbricoides 127.0
      mural thickening 560.89
      procedure 997.4
        involving urinary tract 997.5
    impaction 560.39
    infantile - *see* Obstruction, intestine,
      congenital
    newborn
      due to
        fecaliths 777.1
        inspissated milk 777.2
        meconium (plug) 777.1
          in mucoviscidosis 277.01
      transitory 777.4
    specified cause NEC 560.89
    transitory, newborn 777.4
    volvulus 560.2
  intracardiac ball valve prosthesis 996.02
  jaundice (*see also* Obstruction, biliary)
    576.8
    congenital 751.61
  jejunum (*see also* Obstruction, intestine)
    560.9
  kidney 593.89
  labor 660.9
    affecting fetus or newborn 763.1
    by
      bony pelvis (conditions classifiable
        to 653.0-653.9) 660.1
      deep transverse arrest 660.3
      impacted shoulder 660.4
      locked twins 660.5
      malposition (fetus) (conditions clas-
        sifiable to 652.0-652.9) 660.0
        head during labor 660.3
      persistent occipitoposterior posi-
        tion 660.3
      soft tissue, pelvic (conditions clas-
        sifiable to 654.0-654.9) 660.2

Obstruction, obstructed, obstructive
  (Continued)
  lacrimal
    canaliculi 375.53
      congenital 743.65
      punctum 375.52
      sac 375.54
  lacrimonasal duct 375.56
    congenital 743.65
    neonatal 375.55
  lacteal, with steatorrhea 579.2
  laryngitis (*see also* Laryngitis) 464.0
  larynx 478.79
    congenital 748.3
  liver 573.8
    cirrhotic (*see also* Cirrhosis, liver)
      571.5
  lung 518.89
    with
      asthma - *see* Asthma
      bronchitis (chronic) 491.2
      emphysema NEC 492.8
    airway, chronic 496
    chronic NEC 496
      with
        asthma (chronic) (obstructive)
          493.2
    disease, chronic 496
      with
        asthma (chronic) (obstructive)
          493.2
    emphysematous 492.8
  lymphatic 457.1
  meconium
    fetus or newborn 777.1
      in mucoviscidosis 277.01
    newborn due to fecaliths 777.1
  mediastinum 519.3
  mitral (rheumatic) - *see* Stenosis, mitral
  nasal 478.1
    duct 375.56
      neonatal 375.55
    sinus - *see* Sinusitis
  nasolacrimal duct 375.56
    congenital 743.65
    neonatal 375.55
  nasopharynx 478.29
  nose 478.1
  organ or site, congenital NEC - *see*
    Atresia
  pancreatic duct 577.8
  parotid gland 527.8
  pelviureteral junction (*see also* Obstruc-
    tion, ureter) 593.4
  pharynx 478.29
  portal (circulation) (vein) 452
  prostate 600
    valve (urinary) 596.0
  pulmonary
    valve (heart) (*see also* Endocarditis,
      pulmonary) 424.3
    vein, isolated 747.49
  pyemic - *see* Septicemia
  pylorus (acquired) 537.0
    congenital 750.5
    infantile 750.5
  rectosigmoid (*see also* Obstruction, in-
    testine) 560.9
  rectum 569.49
  renal 593.89
  respiratory 519.8
    chronic 496
  retinal (artery) (vein) (central) (*see also*
    Occlusion, retina) 362.30

Obstruction, obstructed, obstructive
(Continued)
  ureter *(Continued)*
    congenital 753.29
  urethra *(see also* Stricture, urethra) 598.9
    congenital 753.6
  uterus 621.8
  vagina 623.2
  vascular NEC 459.9
  vein - *see* Thrombosis
  vena cava (inferior) (superior) 453.2
  ventricle (brain) NEC 331.4
  vertebral (artery) - *see* Occlusion, artery, vertebral
  vessel (blood) NEC 459.9
  vulva 624.8
Occlusio pupillae 364.74
Occupational
  problems NEC V62.2
  therapy V57.21
Ochlophobia 300.29
Ochronosis (alkaptonuric) (congenital) (endogenous) 270.2
  with chloasma of eyelid 270.2
Ocular muscle - *see also* condition
  myopathy 359.1
Oculoauriculovertebral dysplasia 756.0
Oculogyric
  crisis or disturbance 378.87
    psychogenic 306.7
Oculomotor syndrome 378.81
Oddi's sphincter spasm 576.5
Odelberg's disease (juvenile osteochondrosis) 732.1
Odontalgia 525.9
Odontoameloblastoma (M9311/0) 213.1
  upper jaw (bone) 213.0
Odontoclasia 521.0
Odontoclasis 873.63
  complicated 873.73
Odontodysplasia, regional 520.4
Odontogenesis imperfecta 520.5
Odontoma (M9280/0) 213.1
  ameloblastic (M9311/0) 213.1
    upper jaw (bone) 213.0
  calcified (M9280/0) 213.1
    upper jaw (bone) 213.0
  complex (M9282/0) 213.1
    upper jaw (bone) 213.0
  compound (M9281/0) 213.1
    upper jaw (bone) 213.0
  fibroameloblastic (M9290/0) 213.1
    upper jaw (bone) 213.0
  follicular 526.0
    upper jaw (bone) 213.0
Odontomyelitis (closed) (open) 522.0
Odontonecrosis 521.0
Odontorrhagia 525.8
Odontosarcoma, ameloblastic (M9290/3) 170.1
  upper jaw (bone) 170.0
Odynophagia 787.2
Oesophagostomiasis 127.7
Oesophagostomum infestation 127.7
Oestriasis 134.0
Ogilvie's syndrome (sympathicotonic colon obstruction) 560.89
Oguchi's disease (retina) 368.61
Ohara's disease (*see also* Tularemia) 021.9
Oidiomycosis (*see also* Candidiasis) 112.9
Oidiomycotic meningitis 112.83
Oidium albicans infection (*see also* Candidiasis) 112.9

Old age 797
  dementia (of) 290.0
Olfactory - *see* condition
Oligemia 285.9
Oligergasia (*see also* Retardation, mental) 319
Oligoamnios 658.0
  affecting fetus or newborn 761.2
Oligoastrocytoma, mixed (M9382/3)
  specified site - *see* Neoplasm, by site, malignant
  unspecified site 191.9
Oligocythemia 285.9
Oligodendroblastoma (M9460/3)
  specified site - *see* Neoplasm, by site, malignant
  unspecified site 191.9
Oligodendroglioma (M9450/3)
  anaplastic type (M9451/3)
    specified site - *see* Neoplasm, by site, malignant
    unspecified site 191.9
  specified site - *see* Neoplasm, by site, malignant
  unspecified site 191.9
Oligodendroma - *see* Oligodendroglioma
Oligodontia (*see also* Anodontia) 520.0
Oligoencephalon 742.1
Oligohydramnios 658.0
  affecting fetus or newborn 761.2
  due to premature rupture of membranes 658.1
    affecting fetus or newborn 761.2
Oligohydrosis 705.0
Oligomenorrhea 626.1
Oligophrenia (*see also* Retardation, mental) 319
  phenylpyruvic 270.1
Oligospermia 606.1
Oligotrichia 704.09
  congenita 757.4
Oliguria 788.5
  with
    abortion - *see* Abortion, by type, with renal failure
    ectopic pregnancy (*see also* categories 633.0-633.9) 639.3
    molar pregnancy (*see also* categories 630-632) 639.3
  complicating
    abortion 639.3
    ectopic or molar pregnancy 639.3
    pregnancy 646.2
      with hypertension - *see* Toxemia, of pregnancy
  due to a procedure 997.5
  following labor and delivery 669.3
  heart or cardiac - *see* Failure, heart, congestive
  puerperal, postpartum 669.3
  specified due to a procedure 997.5
Ollier's disease (chondrodysplasia) 756.4
Omentitis (*see also* Peritonitis) 567.9
Omentocele (*see also* Hernia, omental) 553.8
Omentum, omental - *see* condition
Omphalitis (congenital) (newborn) 771.4
  not of newborn 686.9
  tetanus 771.3
Omphalocele 756.79
Omphalomesenteric duct, persistent 751.0
Omphalorrhagia, newborn 772.3
Omsk hemorrhagic fever 065.1

Onanism 307.9
Onchocerciasis 125.3
  eye 125.3 *[360.13]*
Onchocercosis 125.3
Oncocytoma (M8290/0) - *see* Neoplasm, by site, benign
Ondine's curse 348.8
Oneirophrenia (*see also* Schizophrenia) 295.4
Onychauxis 703.8
  congenital 757.5
Onychia (with lymphangitis) 681.9
  dermatophytic 110.1
  finger 681.02
  toe 681.11
Onychitis (with lymphangitis) 681.9
  finger 681.02
  toe 681.11
Onychocryptosis 703.0
Onychodystrophy 703.8
  congenital 757.5
Onychogryphosis 703.8
Onychogryposis 703.8
Onycholysis 703.8
Onychomadesis 703.8
Onychomalacia 703.8
Onychomycosis 110.1
  finger 110.1
  toe 110.1
Onycho-osteodysplasia 756.89
Onychophagy 307.9
Onychoptosis 703.8
Onychorrhexis 703.8
  congenital 757.5
Onychoschizia 703.8
Onychotrophia (*see also* Atrophy, nail) 703.8
O'Nyong Nyong fever 066.3
Onyxis (finger) (toe) 703.0
Onyxitis (with lymphangitis) 681.9
  finger 681.02
  toe 681.11
Oophoritis (cystic) (infectional) (interstitial) (*see also* Salpingo-oophoritis) 614.2
  complicating pregnancy 646.6
  fetal (acute) 752.0
  gonococcal (acute) 098.19
    chronic or duration of 2 months or over 098.39
  tuberculous (*see also* Tuberculosis) 016.6
Opacity, opacities
  cornea 371.00
    central 371.03
    congenital 743.43
      interfering with vision 743.42
    degenerative (*see also* Degeneration, cornea) 371.40
    hereditary (*see also* Dystrophy, cornea) 371.50
    inflammatory (*see also* Keratitis) 370.9
    late effect of trachoma (healed) 139.1
    minor 371.01
    peripheral 371.02
  enamel (fluoride) (nonfluoride) (teeth) 520.3
  lens (*see also* Cataract) 366.9
  snowball 379.22
  vitreous (humor) 379.24
    congenital 743.51
Opalescent dentin (hereditary) 520.5

Open, opening
abnormal, organ or site, congenital -
    see Imperfect, closure
angle with
    borderline intraocular pressure
        365.01
    cupping of discs 365.01
bite (anterior) (posterior) 524.2
false - *see* Imperfect, closure
wound - *see* Wound, open, by site
Operation
causing mutilation of fetus 763.89
destructive, on live fetus, to facilitate
    birth 763.89
for delivery, fetus or newborn
    763.89
maternal, unrelated to current delivery,
    affecting fetus or newborn 760.6
Operational fatigue 300.89
Operative - *see* condition
Operculitis (chronic) 523.4
acute 523.3
Operculum, retina 361.32
with detachment 361.01
Ophiasis 704.01
Ophthalmia (*see also* Conjunctivitis)
    372.30
actinic rays 370.24
allergic (acute) 372.05
    chronic 372.14
blennorrhagic (neonatorum) 098.40
catarrhal 372.03
diphtheritic 032.81
Egyptian 076.1
electric, electrica 370.24
gonococcal (neonatorum) 098.40
metastatic 360.11
migraine 346.8
neonatorum, newborn 771.6
    gonococcal 098.40
nodosa 360.14
phlyctenular 370.31
    with ulcer (*see also* Ulcer, cornea)
        370.00
sympathetic 360.11
Ophthalmitis - *see* Ophthalmia
Ophthalmocele (congenital) 743.66
Ophthalmoneuromyelitis 341.0
**Ophthalmopathy, infiltrative with thy-
    rotoxicosis** 242.0
Ophthalmoplegia (*see also* Strabismus)
    378.9
anterior internuclear 378.86
ataxia-areflexia syndrome 357.0
bilateral 378.9
diabetic 250.5 [*378.86*]
exophthalmic 242.0 [*376.22*]
external 378.55
    progressive 378.72
    total 378.56
internal (complete) (total) 367.52
internuclear 378.86
migraine 346.8
painful 378.55
Parinaud's 378.81
progressive external 378.72
supranuclear, progressive 333.0
total (external) 378.56
    internal 367.52
unilateral 378.9
Opisthognathism 524.00
Opisthorchiasis (felineus) (tenuicollis)
    (viverrini) 121.0
Opisthotonos, opisthotonus 781.0

Opitz's disease (congestive splenomeg-
    aly) 289.51
Opiumism (*see also* Dependence) 304.0
Oppenheim's disease 358.8
**Oppenheim-Urbach disease or syn-
    drome** (necrobiosis lipoidica diabeti-
    corum) 250.8 [*709.3*]
Opsoclonia 379.59
Optic nerve - *see* condition
Orbit - *see* condition
Orchioblastoma (M9071/3) 186.9
Orchitis (nonspecific) (septic) 604.90
with abscess 604.0
blennorrhagic (acute) 098.13
    chronic or duration of 2 months or
        over 098.33
diphtheritic 032.89 [*604.91*]
filarial 125.9 [*604.91*]
gangrenous 604.99
gonococcal (acute) 098.13
    chronic or duration of 2 months or
        over 098.33
mumps 072.0
parotidea 072.0
suppurative 604.99
syphilitic 095.8 [*604.91*]
tuberculous (*see also* Tuberculosis)
    016.5 [*608.81*]
Orf 051.2
Organic - *see also* condition
heart - *see* Disease, heart
insufficiency 799.8
Oriental
bilharziasis 120.2
schistosomiasis 120.2
sore 085.1
Orifice - *see* condition
**Origin, both great vessels from right
    ventricle** 745.11
Ormond's disease or syndrome 593.4
Ornithosis 073.9
with
    complication 073.8
        specified NEC 073.7
    pneumonia 073.0
    pneumonitis (lobular) 073.0
Orodigitofacial dysostosis 759.89
Oropouche fever 066.3
Orotaciduria, oroticaciduria (congenital)
    (hereditary) (pyrimidine deficiency)
    281.4
Oroya fever 088.0
Orthodontics V58.5
adjustment V53.4
aftercare V58.5
fitting V53.4
Orthopnea 786.02
Os, uterus - *see* condition
Osgood-Schlatter
disease 732.4
osteochondrosis 732.4
Osler's
disease (M9950/1) (polycythemia vera)
    238.4
nodes 421.0
Osler-Rendu disease (familial hemor-
    rhagic telangiectasia) 448.0
Osler-Vaquez disease (M9950/1) (poly-
    cythemia vera) 238.4
Osler-Weber-Rendu syndrome (famil-
    ial hemorrhagic telangiectasia)
    448.0
Osmidrosis 705.89
Osseous - *see* condition

Ossification
artery - *see* Arteriosclerosis
auricle (ear) 380.39
bronchus 519.1
cardiac (*see also* Degeneration, myocar-
    dial) 429.1
cartilage (senile) 733.99
coronary - *see* Arteriosclerosis, coronary
diaphragm 728.10
ear 380.39
    middle (*see also* Otosclerosis) 387.9
falx cerebri 349.2
fascia 728.10
fontanel
    defective or delayed 756.0
    premature 756.0
heart (*see also* Degeneration, myocar-
    dial) 429.1
    valve - *see* Endocarditis
larynx 478.79
ligament
    posterior longitudinal 724.8
        cervical 723.7
meninges (cerebral) 349.2
    spinal 336.8
multiple, eccentric centers 733.99
muscle 728.10
    heterotopic, postoperative 728.13
myocardium, myocardial (*see also* De-
    generation, myocardial) 429.1
penis 607.81
periarticular 728.89
sclera 379.16
tendon 727.82
trachea 519.1
tympanic membrane (*see also* Tympa-
    nosclerosis) 385.00
vitreous (humor) 360.44
Osteitis (*see also* Osteomyelitis) 730.2
acute 730.0
alveolar 526.5
chronic 730.1
condensans (ilii) 733.5
deformans (Paget's) 731.0
    due to or associated with malignant
        neoplasm (*see also* Neoplasm,
        bone, malignant) 170.9 [*731.1*]
due to yaws 102.6
fibrosa NEC 733.29
    cystica (generalisata) 252.0
    disseminata 756.59
    osteoplastica 252.0
fragilitans 756.51
Garré's (sclerosing) 730.1
infectious (acute) (subacute) 730.0
    chronic or old 730.1
jaw (acute) (chronic) (lower) (neonatal)
    (suppurative) (upper) 526.4
parathyroid 252.0
petrous bone (*see also* Petrositis) 383.20
pubis 733.5
sclerotic, nonsuppurative 730.1
syphilitic 095.5
tuberculosa
    cystica (of Jüngling) 135
    multiplex cystoides 135
Osteoarthritica spondylitis (spine) (*see
    also* Spondylosis) 721.90
Osteoarthritis (*see also* Osteoarthrosis)
    715.9
distal interphalangeal 715.9
hyperplastic 731.2
interspinalis (*see also* Spondylosis)
    721.90

> Note   Use the following fifth-digit subclassification with category 715:
>
> 0   site unspecified
> 1   shoulder region
> 2   upper arm
> 3   forearm
> 4   hand
> 5   pelvic region and thigh
> 6   lower leg
> 7   ankle and foot
> 8   other specified sites except spine
> 9   multiple sites

ICD-9-CM

Vol. 2

Osteomyelitis *(Continued)*

> Note   Use the following fifth-digit
> subclassification with category 730:
>
> 0   site unspecified
> 1   shoulder region
> 2   upper arm
> 3   forearm
> 4   hand
> 5   pelvic region and thigh
> 6   lower leg
> 7   ankle and foot
> 8   other specified sites
> 9   multiple sites

acute or subacute 730.0
chronic or old 730.1
due to or associated with
    diabetes mellitus 250.8 *[731.8]*
    tuberculosis (*see also* Tuberculosis,
        bone) 015.9 *[730.8]*
        limb bones 015.5 *[730.8]*
        specified bones NEC 015.7 *[730.8]*
        spine 015.0 *[730.8]*
        typhoid 002.0 *[730.8]*
Garré's 730.1
jaw (acute) (chronic) (lower) (neonatal)
    (suppurative) (upper) 526.4
nonsuppurating 730.1
orbital 376.03
petrous bone (*see also* Petrositis) 383.20
Salmonella 003.24
sclerosing, nonsuppurative 730.1
sicca 730.1
syphilitic 095.5
    congenital 090.0 *[730.8]*
tuberculous - *see* Tuberculosis, bone
typhoid 002.0 *[730.8]*
Osteomyelofibrosis 289.8
Osteomyelosclerosis 289.8
Osteonecrosis (*see also* Osteomyelitis)
    730.1
Osteo-onycho-arthro dysplasia 756.89
Osteo-onychodysplasia, hereditary
    756.89
Osteopathia
    condensans disseminata 756.53
    hyperostotica multiplex infantilis 756.59
    hypertrophica toxica 731.2
    striata 756.4
Osteopathy resulting from poliomyelitis
    (*see also* Poliomyelitis) 045.9 *[730.7]*
    familial dysplastic 731.2
Osteopecilia 756.53
Osteopenia 733.90
Osteoperiostitis (*see also* Osteomyelitis)
    730.2
    ossificans toxica 731.2
    toxica ossificans 731.2
Osteopetrosis (familial) 756.52
Osteophyte - *see* Exostosis
Osteophytosis - *see* Exostosis
Osteopoikilosis 756.53
Osteoporosis (generalized) 733.00
    circumscripta 731.0
    disuse 733.03
    drug-induced 733.09
    idiopathic 733.02
    postmenopausal 733.01
    posttraumatic 733.7
    senile 733.01
    specified type NEC 733.09
Osteoporosis-osteomalacia syndrome
    268.2

Osteopsathyrosis 756.51
Osteoradionecrosis, jaw 526.89
Osteosarcoma (M9180/3) - *see also* Neo-
    plasm, bone, malignant
    chondroblastic (M9181/3) - *see* Neo-
        plasm, bone, malignant
    fibroblastic (M9182/3) - *see* Neoplasm,
        bone, malignant
    in Paget's disease of bone (M9184/3) -
        see Neoplasm, bone, malignant
    juxtacortical (M9190/3) - *see* Neo-
        plasm, bone malignant
    parosteal (M9190/3) - *see* Neoplasm,
        bone, malignant
    telangiectatic (M9183/3) - *see* Neo-
        plasm, bone, malignant
Osteosclerosis 756.52
    fragilis (generalisata) 756.52
    myelofibrosis 289.8
Osteosclerotic anemia 289.8
Osteosis
    acromegaloid 757.39
    cutis 709.3
    parathyroid 252.0
    renal fibrocystic 588.0
Österreicher-Turner syndrome 756.89
Ostium
    atrioventriculare commune 745.69
    primum (arteriosum) (defect) (persist-
        ent) 745.61
    secundum (arteriosum) (defect) (pat-
        ent) (persistent) 745.5
Ostrum-Furst syndrome 756.59
Otalgia 388.70
    otogenic 388.71
    referred 388.72
Othematoma 380.31
Otitic hydrocephalus 348.2
Otitis 382.9
    with effusion 381.4
        purulent 382.4
        secretory 381.4
        serous 381.4
        suppurative 382.4
    acute 382.9
    adhesive (*see also* Adhesions, middle
        ear) 385.10
    chronic 382.9
        with effusion 381.3
        mucoid, mucous (simple) 381.20
        purulent 382.3
        secretory 381.3
        serous 381.10
        suppurative 382.3
    diffuse parasitic 136.8
    externa (acute) (diffuse) (hemorrhag-
        ica) 380.10
        actinic 380.22
        candidal 112.82
            chemical 380.22
            chronic 380.23
            mycotic - *see* Otitis, externa, mycotic
                specified type NEC 380.23
        circumscribed 380.10
        contact 380.22
        due to
            erysipelas 035 *[380.13]*
            impetigo 684 *[380.13]*
            seborrheic dermatitis 690.10
                [380.13]
        eczematoid 380.22
        furuncular 680.0 *[380.13]*
        infective 380.10
            chronic 380.16

Otitis *(Continued)*
    externa *(Continued)*
        malignant 380.14
        mycotic (chronic) 380.15
            due to
                aspergillosis 117.3 *[380.15]*
                moniliasis 112.82
                otomycosis 111.8 *[380.15]*
        reactive 380.22
        specified type NEC 380.22
        tropical 111.8 *[380.15]*
    insidiosa (*see also* Otosclerosis) 387.9
    interna (*see also* Labyrinthitis) 386.30
    media (hemorrhagic) (staphylococcal)
        (streptococcal) 382.9
        acute 382.9
            with effusion 381.00
                allergic 381.04
                    mucoid 381.05
                    sanguineous 381.06
                    serous 381.04
                catarrhal 381.00
                exudative 381.00
                mucoid 381.02
                    allergic 381.05
                necrotizing 382.00
                    with spontaneous rupture of ear
                        drum 382.01
                    in
                        influenza 487.8 *[382.02]*
                        measles 055.2
                        scarlet fever 034.1 *[382.02]*
                nonsuppurative 381.00
                purulent 382.00
                    with spontaneous rupture of ear
                        drum 382.01
                sanguineous 381.03
                    allergic 381.06
                secretory 381.01
                seromucinous 381.02
                serous 381.01
                    allergic 381.04
                suppurative 382.00
                    with spontaneous rupture of ear
                        drum 382.01
                    due to
                        influenza 487.8 *[382.02]*
                        scarlet fever 034.1 *[382.02]*
                transudative 381.00
        adhesive (*see also* Adhesions, middle
            ear) 385.10
        allergic 381.4
            acute 381.04
                mucoid 381.05
                sanguineous 381.06
                serous 381.04
            chronic 381.3
        catarrhal 381.4
            acute 381.00
            chronic (simple) 381.10
        chronic 382.9
            with effusion 381.3
            adhesive (*see also* Adhesions, mid-
                dle ear) 385.10
            allergic 381.3
            atticoantral, suppurative (with
                posterior or superior margin-
                al perforation of ear drum)
                382.2
            benign suppurative (with anterior
                perforation of ear drum) 382.1
            catarrhal 381.10
            exudative 381.3
            mucinous 381.20

Otitis *(Continued)*
  media *(Continued)*
    chronic *(Continued)*
      mucoid, mucous (simple) 381.20
      mucosanguineous 381.29
      nonsuppurative 381.3
      purulent 382.3
      secretory 381.3
      seromucinous 381.3
      serosanguineous 381.19
      serous (simple) 381.10
      suppurative 382.3
        atticoantral (with posterior or
          superior marginal perfora-
          tion of ear drum) 382.2
        benign (with anterior perfora-
          tion of ear drum) 382.1
        tuberculous *(see also* Tuberculo-
          sis) 017.4
        tubotympanic 382.1
      transudative 381.3
    exudative 381.4
      acute 381.00
      chronic 381.3
    fibrotic *(see also* Adhesions, middle
      ear) 385.10
    mucoid, mucous 381.4
      acute 381.02
      chronic (simple) 381.20
    mucosanguineous, chronic 381.29
    nonsuppurative 381.4
      acute 381.00
      chronic 381.3
    postmeasles 055.2
    purulent 382.4
      acute 382.00
        with spontaneous rupture of ear
          drum 382.01
      chronic 382.3
    sanguineous, acute 381.03
      allergic 381.06
    secretory 381.4
      acute or subacute 381.01
      chronic 381.3
    seromucinous 381.4
      acute or subacute 381.02
      chronic 381.3
    serosanguineous, chronic 381.19
    serous 381.4
      acute or subacute 381.01
      chronic (simple) 381.10
    subacute - *see* Otitis, media, acute
    suppurative 382.4
      acute 382.00
        with spontaneous rupture of ear
          drum 382.01
      chronic 382.3
        atticoantral 382.2
        benign 382.1
        tuberculous *(see also* Tuberculo-
          sis) 017.4
        tubotympanic 382.1
    transudative 381.4
      acute 381.00
      chronic 381.3
    tuberculous *(see also* Tuberculosis)
      017.4
  postmeasles 055.2
Otoconia 386.8

Otolith syndrome 386.19
Otomycosis 111.8 *[380.15]*
  in
    aspergillosis 117.3 *[380.15]*
    moniliasis 112.82
Otopathy 388.9
Otoporosis *(see also* Otosclerosis) 387.9
Otorrhagia 388.69
  traumatic - *see* nature of injury
Otorrhea 388.60
  blood 388.69
  cerebrospinal (fluid) 388.61
Otosclerosis (general) 387.9
  cochlear (endosteal) 387.2
  involving
    otic capsule 387.2
    oval window
      nonobliterative 387.0
      obliterative 387.1
    round window 387.2
  nonobliterative 387.0
  obliterative 387.1
  specified type NEC 387.8
Otospongiosis *(see also* Otosclerosis)
  387.9
Otto's disease or pelvis 715.35
Outburst, aggressive *(see also* Disturbance, conduct) 312.0
  in children and adolescents 313.9
Outcome of delivery
  multiple birth NEC V27.9
    all liveborn V27.5
    all stillborn V27.7
    some liveborn V27.6
    unspecified V27.9
  single V27.9
    liveborn V27.0
    stillborn V27.1
  twins V27.9
    both liveborn V27.2
    both stillborn V27.4
    one liveborn, one stillborn V27.3
Outlet - *see also* condition
  syndrome (thoracic) 353.0
Outstanding ears (bilateral) 744.29
Ovalocytosis (congenital) (hereditary)
  (see also Elliptocytosis) 282.1
Ovarian - *see also* condition
  pregnancy - *see* Pregnancy, ovarian
  vein syndrome 593.4
Ovaritis (cystic) *(see also* Salpingo-oophoritis) 614.2
Ovary, ovarian - *see* condition
Overactive - *see also* Hyperfunction
  eye muscle *(see also* Strabismus) 378.9
  hypothalamus 253.8
  thyroid *(see also* Thyrotoxicosis) 242.9
Overactivity, child 314.01
Overbite (deep) (excessive) (horizontal)
  (vertical) 524.2
Overbreathing *(see also* Hyperventilation)
  786.01
Overconscientious personality 301.4
Overdevelopment - *see also* Hypertrophy
  breast (female) (male) 611.1
  nasal bones 738.0
  prostate, congenital 752.8
Overdistention - *see* Distention

Overdose overdosage (drug) 977.9
  specified drug or substance - *see* Table
    of Drugs and Chemicals
Overeating 783.6
  with obesity 278.0
  nonorganic origin 307.51
Overexertion (effects) (exhaustion) 994.5
Overexposure (effects) 994.9
  exhaustion 994.4
Overfeeding *(see also* Overeating) 783.6
Overgrowth, bone NEC 733.99
Overheated (effects) (places) - *see* Heat
Overinhibited child 313.0
Overjet 524.2
Overlaid, overlying (suffocation) 994.7
Overlapping toe (acquired) 735.8
  congenital (fifth toe) 755.66
Overload
  fluid 276.6
  potassium (K) 276.7
  sodium (Na) 276.0
Overnutrition *(see also* Hyperalimenta-
  tion) 783.6
Overproduction - *see also* Hypersecretion
  ACTH 255.3
  cortisol 255.0
  growth hormone 253.0
  thyroid-stimulating hormone (TSH)
    242.8
Overriding
  aorta 747.21
  finger (acquired) 736.29
    congenital 755.59
  toe (acquired) 735.8
    congenital 755.66
Oversize
  fetus (weight of 4500 grams or more)
    766.0
    affecting management of pregnancy
      656.6
    causing disproportion 653.5
      with obstructed labor 660.1
      affecting fetus or newborn 763.1
Overstimulation, ovarian 256.1
Overstrained 780.79
  heart - *see* Hypertrophy, cardiac
Overweight *(see also* Obesity) 278.00
Overwork 780.79
Oviduct - *see* condition
Ovotestis 752.7
Ovulation (cycle)
  failure or lack of 628.0
  pain 625.2
Ovum
  blighted 631
  dropsical 631
  pathologic 631
Owren's disease or syndrome (parahem-
  ophilia) *(see also* Defect, coagulation)
  286.3
Oxalosis 271.8
Oxaluria 271.8
Ox heart - *see* Hypertrophy, cardiac
OX syndrome 758.6
Oxycephaly, oxycephalic 756.0
  syphilitic, congenital 090.0
Oxyuriasis 127.4
Oxyuris vermicularis (infestation) 127.4
Ozena 472.0

P

Pacemaker syndrome 429.4
Pachyderma, pachydermia 701.8
  laryngis 478.5
  laryngitis 478.79
  larynx (verrucosa) 478.79
Pachydermatitis 701.8
Pachydermatocele (congenital) 757.39
  acquired 701.8
Pachydermatosis 701.8
Pachydermoperiostitis
  secondary 731.2
Pachydermoperiostosis
  primary idiopathic 757.39
  secondary 731.2
Pachymeningitis (adhesive) (basal)
    (brain) (cerebral) (cervical) (chronic)
    (circumscribed) (external) (fibrous)
    (hemorrhagic) (hypertrophic) (inter-
    nal) (purulent) (spinal) (suppurative)
    (*see also* Meningitis) 322.9
  gonococcal 098.82
Pachyonychia (congenital) 757.5
  acquired 703.8
Pachyperiosteodermia
  primary or idiopathic 757.39
  secondary 731.2
Pachyperiostosis
  primary or idiopathic 757.39
  secondary 731.2
Pacinian tumor (M9507/0) - *see* Neo-
    plasm, skin, benign
Pads, knuckle or Garrod's 728.79
Paget's disease (osteitis deformans)
    731.0
  with infiltrating duct carcinoma of the
      breast (M8541/3) - *see* Neoplasm,
      breast, malignant
  bone 731.0
    osteosarcoma in (M9184/3) - *see* Ne-
      oplasm, bone, malignant
  breast (M8540/3) 174.0
  extramammary (M8542/3) - *see also*
    Neoplasm, skin, malignant
    anus 154.3
      skin 173.5
  malignant (M8540/3)
    breast 174.0
    specified site NEC (M8542/3) - *see*
      Neoplasm, skin, malignant
    unspecified site 174.0
  mammary (M8540/3) 174.0
  necrosis of bone 731.0
  nipple (M8540/3) 174.0
  osteitis deformans 731.0
Paget-Schroeter syndrome (intermittent
    venous claudication) 453.8
Pain(s)
  abdominal 789.0
  adnexa (uteri) 625.9
  alimentary, due to vascular insuffi-
    ciency 557.9
  anginoid (*see also* Pain, precordial)
    786.51
  anus 569.42
  arch 729.5
  arm 729.5
  back (postural) 724.5
    low 724.2
    psychogenic 307.89
  bile duct 576.9
  bladder 788.9
  bone 733.90

Pain(s) *(Continued)*
  breast 611.71
    psychogenic 307.89
  broad ligament 625.9
  cartilage NEC 733.90
  cecum 789.0
  cervicobrachial 723.3
  chest (central) 786.50
    atypical 786.59
    midsternal 786.51
    musculoskeletal 786.59
    noncardiac 786.59
    substernal 786.51
    wall (anterior) 786.52·
  coccyx 724.79
  colon 789.0
  common duct 576.9
  coronary - *see* Angina
  costochondral 786.52
  diaphragm 786.52
  due to (presence of) any device, im-
    plant, or graft classifiable to 996.0-
    996.5 - *see* Complications, due to
    (presence of) any device, implant,
    or graft classified to 996.0-996.5
    NEC
  ear (*see also* Otalgia) 388.70
  epigastric, epigastrium 789.06
  extremity (lower) (upper) 729.5
  eye 379.91
  face, facial 784.0
    atypical 350.2
    nerve 351.8
  false (labor) 644.1
  female genital organ NEC 625.9
    psychogenic 307.89
  finger 729.5
  flank 789.0
  foot 729.5
  gallbladder 575.9
  gas (intestinal) 787.3
  gastric 536.8
  generalized 780.9
  genital organ
    female 625.9
    male 608.9
    psychogenic 307.89
  groin 789.0
  growing 781.9
  hand 729.5
  head (*see also* Headache) 784.0
  heart (*see also* Pain, precordial) 786.51
  infraorbital (*see also* Neuralgia, trigemi-
    nal) 350.1
  intermenstrual 625.2
  jaw 526.9
  joint 719.40
    ankle 719.47
    elbow 719.42
    foot 719.47
    hand 719.44
    hip 719.45
    knee 719.46
    multiple sites 719.49
    pelvic region 719.45
    psychogenic 307.89
    shoulder (region) 719.41
    specified site NEC 719.48
    wrist 719.43
  kidney 788.0
  labor, false or spurious 644.1
  laryngeal 784.1
  leg 729.5
  limb 729.5

Pain(s) *(Continued)*
  low back 724.2
  lumbar region 724.2
  mastoid (*see also* Otalgia) 388.70
  maxilla 526.9
  metacarpophalangeal (joint) 719.44
  metatarsophalangeal (joint) 719.47
  mouth 528.9
  muscle 729.1
    intercostal 786.59
  nasal 478.1
  nasopharynx 478.29
  neck NEC 723.1
    psychogenic 307.89
  nerve NEC 729.2
  neuromuscular 729.1
  nose 478.1
  ocular 379.91
  ophthalmic 379.91
  orbital region 379.91
  osteocopic 733.90
  ovary 625.9
    psychogenic 307.89
  over heart (*see also* Pain, precordial)
    786.51
  ovulation 625.2
  pelvic (female) 625.9
    male NEC 789.0
      psychogenic 307.89
    psychogenic 307.89
  penis 607.9
    psychogenic 307.89
  pericardial (*see also* Pain, precordial)
    786.51
  perineum
    female 625.9
    male 608.9
  pharynx 478.29
  pleura, pleural, pleuritic 786.52
  postoperative - *see* Pain, by site
  preauricular 388.70
  precordial (region) 786.51
    psychogenic 307.89
  psychogenic 307.80
    cardiovascular system 307.89
    gastrointestinal system 307.89
    genitourinary system 307.89
    heart 307.89
    musculoskeletal system 307.89
    respiratory system 307.89
    skin 306.3
  radicular (spinal) (*see also* Radiculitis)
    729.2
  rectum 569.42
  respiration 786.52
  retrosternal 786.51
  rheumatic NEC 729.0
    muscular 729.1
  rib 786.50
  root (spinal) (*see also* Radiculitis) 729.2
  round ligament (stretch) 625.9
  sacroiliac 724.6
  sciatic 724.3
  scrotum 608.9
    psychogenic 307.89
  seminal vesicle 608.9
  sinus 478.1
  skin 782.0
  spermatic cord 608.9
  spinal root (*see also* Radiculitis) 729.2
  stomach 536.8
    psychogenic 307.89
  substernal 786.51
  temporomandibular (joint) 524.62

◀▶ **New Code**　　◀▥▥▷ **Revised Code**

Pain(s) *(Continued)*
   temporomaxillary joint 524.62
   testis 608.9
      psychogenic 307.89
   thoracic spine 724.1
      with radicular and visceral pain 724.4
   throat 784.1
   tibia 733.90
   toe 729.5
   tongue 529.6
   tooth 525.9
   trigeminal *(see also* Neuralgia, trigeminal) 350.1
   umbilicus 789.05
   ureter 788.0
   urinary (organ) (system) 788.0
   uterus 625.9
      psychogenic 307.89
   vagina 625.9
   vertebrogenic (syndrome) 724.5
   vesical 788.9
   vulva 625.9
   xiphoid 733.90
Painful - *see also* Pain
   arc syndrome 726.19
   coitus
      female 625.0
      male 608.89
         psychogenic 302.76
   ejaculation (semen) 608.89
      psychogenic 302.79
   erection 607.3
   feet syndrome 266.2
   menstruation 625.3
      psychogenic 306.52
   micturition 788.1
   ophthalmoplegia 378.55
   respiration 786.52
   scar NEC 709.2
   urination 788.1
   wire sutures 998.89
Painters' colic 984.9
   specified type of lead - *see* Table of Drugs and Chemicals
Palate - *see* condition
Palatoplegia 528.9
Palatoschisis *(see also* Cleft, palate) 749.00
Palilalia 784.69
Palindromic arthritis *(see also* Rheumatism, palindromic) 719.3
Palliative care V66.7
Pallor 782.61
   temporal, optic disc 377.15
Palmar - *see also* condition
   fascia - *see* condition
Palpable
   cecum 569.89
   kidney 593.89
   liver 573.9
   lymph nodes 785.6
   ovary 620.8
   prostate 602.9
   spleen *(see also* Splenomegaly) 789.2
   uterus 625.8
Palpitation (heart) 785.1
   psychogenic 306.52
Palsy *(see also* Paralysis) 344.9
   atrophic diffuse 335.20
   Bell's 351.0
      newborn 767.5
   birth 767.7
   brachial plexus 353.0
      fetus or newborn 767.6

Palsy *(Continued)*
   brain - *see also* Palsy, cerebral
      noncongenital or noninfantile 344.89
      due to vascular lesion - *see* Late effect(s) (of) cerebrovascular disease
      syphilitic 094.89
         congenital 090.49
   bulbar (chronic) (progressive) 335.22
      pseudo NEC 335.23
      supranuclear NEC 344.89
   cerebral (congenital) (infantile) (spastic) 343.9
      athetoid 333.7
      diplegic 343.0
      due to previous lesion - *see* Late effect(s) (of) cerebrovascular disease
      hemiplegic 343.1
      monoplegic 343.3
      noncongenital or noninfantile 437.8
      due to previous lesion - *see* Late effect(s) (of) cerebrovascular disease
      paraplegic 343.0
      quadriplegic 343.2
      spastic, not congenital or infantile 344.89
      syphilitic 094.89
         congenital 090.49
      tetraplegic 343.2
   cranial nerve - *see also* Disorder, nerve, cranial
      multiple 352.6
   creeping 335.21
   divers' 993.3
   erb's (birth injury) 767.6
   facial 351.0
      newborn 767.5
   glossopharyngeal 352.2
   Klumpke (-Déjérine) 767.6
   lead 984.9
      specified type of lead - *see* Table of Drugs and Chemicals
   median nerve (tardy) 354.0
   peroneal nerve (acute) (tardy) 355.3
   progressive supranuclear 333.0 ◄▥▥
   pseudobulbar NEC 335.23
   radial nerve (acute) 354.3
   seventh nerve 351.0
      newborn 767.5
   shaking *(see also* Parkinsonism) 332.0
   spastic (cerebral) (spinal) 343.9
      hemiplegic 343.1
   specified nerve NEC - *see* Disorder, nerve
   supranuclear NEC 356.8
      progressive 333.0 ◄▥▥
   ulnar nerve (tardy) 354.2
   wasting 335.21
Paltauf-Sternberg disease 201.9
Paludism - *see* Malaria
Panama fever 084.0
Panaris (with lymphangitis) 681.9
   finger 681.02
   toe 681.11
Panaritium (with lymphangitis) 681.9
   finger 681.02
   toe 681.11
Panarteritis (nodosa) 446.0
   brain or cerebral 437.4
Pancake heart 793.2
   with cor pulmonale (chronic) 416.9

Pancarditis (acute) (chronic) 429.89
   with
      rheumatic
         fever (active) (acute) (chronic) (subacute) 391.8
            inactive or quiescent 398.99
      rheumatic, acute 391.8
      chronic or inactive 398.99
Pancoast's syndrome or tumor (carcinoma, pulmonary apex) (M8010/3) 162.3
Pancoast-Tobias syndrome (M8010/3) (carcinoma, pulmonary apex) 162.3
Pancolitis 556.6
Pancreas, pancreatic - *see* condition
Pancreatitis 577.0
   acute (edematous) (hemorrhagic) (recurrent) 577.0
   annular 577.0
   apoplectic 577.0
   calcereous 577.0
   chronic (infectious) 577.1
      recurrent 577.1
   cystic 577.2
   fibrous 577.8
   gangrenous 577.0
   hemorrhagic (acute) 577.0
   interstitial (chronic) 577.1
      acute 577.0
   malignant 577.0
   mumps 072.3
   painless 577.1
   recurrent 577.1
   relapsing 577.1
   subacute 577.0
   suppurative 577.0
   syphilitic 095.8
Pancreatolithiasis 577.8
Pancytolysis 289.9
Pancytopenia (acquired) 284.8
   with malformations 284.0
   congenital 284.0
Panencephalitis - *see also* Encephalitis
   subacute, sclerosing 046.2
Panhematopenia 284.8
   congenital 284.0
   constitutional 284.0
   splenic, primary 289.4
Panhemocytopenia 284.8
   congenital 284.0
   constitutional 284.0
Panhypogonadism 257.2
Panhypopituitarism 253.2
   prepubertal 253.3
Panic (attack) (state) 300.01
   reaction to exceptional stress (transient) 308.0
Panmyelopathy, familial constitutional 284.0
Panmyelophthisis 284.9
   acquired (secondary) 284.8
   congenital 284.0
   idiopathic 284.9
Panmyelosis (acute) (M9951/1) 238.7
Panner's disease 732.3
   capitellum humeri 732.3
   head of humerus 732.3
   tarsal navicular (bone) (osteochondrosis) 732.5
Panneuritis endemica 265.0 *[357.4]*
Panniculitis 729.30
   back 724.8
   knee 729.31
   neck 723.6

Panniculitis (*Continued*)
nodular, nonsuppurative 729.30
sacral 724.8
specified site NEC 729.39
Panniculus adiposus (abdominal) 278.1
Pannus 370.62
allergic eczematous 370.62
degenerativus 370.62
keratic 370.62
rheumatoid - *see* Arthritis, rheumatoid
trachomatosus, trachomatous (active)
076.1 [370.62]
late effect 139.1
Panophthalmitis 360.02
Panotitis - *see* Otitis media
Pansinusitis (chronic) (hyperplastic)
(nonpurulent) (purulent) 473.8
acute 461.8
due to fungus NEC 117.9
tuberculous (*see also* Tuberculosis)
012.8
Panuveitis 360.12
sympathetic 360.11
Panvalvular disease - *see* Endocarditis,
mitral
Papageienkrankheit 073.9
Papanicolaou smear
cervix (screening test) V76.2
as part of gynecological examination
V72.3
for suspected malignant neoplasm
V76.2
no disease found V71.1
nonspecific abnormal finding 795.0
specified site, except cervix - *see also*
Screening, malignant neoplasm
for suspected malignant neoplasm -
see also Screening, malignant neoplasm
no disease found V71.1
nonspecific abnormal finding 795.1
Papilledema 377.00
associated with
decreased ocular pressure 377.02
increased intracranial pressure
377.01
retinal disorder 377.03
choked disc 377.00
infectional 377.00
Papillitis 377.31
anus 569.49
chronic lingual 529.4
necrotizing, kidney 584.7
optic 377.31
rectum 569.49
renal, necrotizing 584.7
tongue 529.0
Papilloma (M8050/0) - *see also* Neoplasm, by site, benign

Note   Except where otherwise indicated, the morphological varieties of
papilloma in the list below should be
coded by site as for "Neoplasm, benign".

Acuminatum (female) (male) 078.11
bladder (urinary) (transitional cell)
(M8120/1) 236.7
benign (M8120/0) 223.3
choroid plexus (M9390/0) 225.0
anaplastic type (M9390/3) 191.5
malignant (M9390/3) 191.5
ductal (M8503/0)

Papilloma (*Continued*)
dyskeratotic (M8052/0)
epidermoid (M8052/0)
hyperkeratotic (M8052/0)
intracystic (M8504/0)
intraductal (M8503/0)
inverted (M8053/0)
keratotic (M8052/0)
parakeratotic (M8052/0)
pinta (primary) 103.0
renal pelvis (transitional cell) (M8120/
1) 236.99
benign (M8120/0) 223.1
Schneiderian (M8121/0)
specified site - *see* Neoplasm, by site,
benign
unspecified site 212.0
serous surface (M8461/0)
borderline malignancy (M8461/1)
specified site - *see* Neoplasm, by
site, uncertain behavior
unspecified site 236.2
specified site - *see* Neoplasm, by site,
benign
unspecified site 220
squamous (cell) (M8052/0)
transitional (cell) (M8120/0)
bladder (urinary) (M8120/1) 236.7
inverted type (M8121/1) - *see* Neoplasm, by site, uncertain behavior
renal pelvis (M8120/1) 236.91
ureter (M8120/1) 236.91
ureter (transitional cell) (M8120/1)
236.91
benign (M8120/0) 223.2
urothelial (M8120/1) - *see* Neoplasm,
by site, uncertain behavior
verrucous (M8051/0)
villous (M8261/1) - *see* Neoplasm, by
site, uncertain behavior
yaws, plantar or palmar 102.1
Papillomata, multiple, of yaws 102.1
Papillomatosis (M8060/0) - *see also* Neoplasm, by site, benign
confluent and reticulate 701.8
cutaneous 701.8
ductal, breast 610.1
Gougerot-Carteaud (confluent reticulate) 701.8
intraductal (diffuse) (M8505/0) - *see*
Neoplasm, by site, benign
subareolar duct (M8506/0) 217
Papillon-Léage and Psaume syndrome
(orodigitofacial dysostosis) 759.89
Papule 709.8
carate (primary) 103.0
fibrous, of nose (M8724/0) 216.3
pinta (primary) 103.0
Papulosis, malignant 447.8
Papyraceous fetus 779.8
complicating pregnancy 646.0
Paracephalus 759.7
Parachute mitral valve 746.5
Paracoccidioidomycosis 116.1
mucocutaneous-lymphangitic 116.1
pulmonary 116.1
visceral 116.1
Paracoccidiomycosis - *see* Paracoccidioi-
domycosis
Paracusis 388.40
Paradentosis 523.5
Paradoxical facial movements 374.43
Paraffinoma 999.9

Paraganglioma (M8680/1)
adrenal (M8700/0) 227.0
malignant (M8700/3) 194.0
aortic body (M8691/1) 237.3
malignant (M8691/3) 194.6
carotid body (M8692/1) 237.3
malignant (M8692/3) 194.5
chromaffin (M8700/0) - *see also* Neoplasm, by site, benign
malignant (M8700/3) - *see* Neoplasm, by site, malignant
extra-adrenal (M8693/1)
malignant (M8693/3)
specified site - *see* Neoplasm, by
site, malignant
unspecified site 194.6
specified site - *see* Neoplasm, by site,
uncertain behavior
unspecified site 237.3
glomus jugulare (M8690/1) 237.3
malignant (M8690/3) 194.6
jugular (M8690/1) 237.3
malignant (M8680/3)
specified site - *see* Neoplasm, by site,
malignant
unspecified site 194.6
nonchromaffin (M8693/1)
malignant (M8693/3)
specified site - *see* Neoplasm, by
site, malignant
unspecified site 194.6
specified site - *see* Neoplasm, by site,
uncertain behavior
unspecified site 237.3
parasympathetic (M8682/1)
specified site - *see* Neoplasm, by site,
uncertain behavior
unspecified site 237.3
specified site - *see* Neoplasm, by site,
uncertain behavior
sympathetic (M8681/1)
specified site - *see* Neoplasm, by site,
uncertain behavior
unspecified site 237.3
unspecified site 237.3
Parageusia 781.1
psychogenic 306.7
Paragonimiasis 121.2
Paragranuloma, Hodgkin's (M9660/3)
201.0
Parahemophilia (*see also* Defect, coagulation) 286.3
Parakeratosis 690.8
psoriasiformis 696.2
variegata 696.2
Paralysis, paralytic (complete) (incomplete) 344.9
with
broken
back - *see* Fracture, vertebra, by
site, with spinal cord injury
neck - *see* Fracture, vertebra, cervical, with spinal cord injury
fracture, vertebra - *see* Fracture, vertebra, by site, with spinal cord
injury
syphilis 094.89
abdomen and back muscles 355.9
abdominal muscles 355.9
abducens (nerve) 378.54
abductor 355.9
lower extremity 355.8
upper extremity 354.9
accessory nerve 352.4

Paralysis, paralytic *(Continued)*
accommodation 367.51
  hysterical 300.11
acoustic nerve 388.5
agitans 332.0
  arteriosclerotic 332.0
alternating 344.89
  oculomotor 344.89
amyotrophic 335.20
ankle 355.8
anterior serratus 355.9
anus (sphincter) 569.49
apoplectic (current episode) *(see also* Disease, cerebrovascular, acute) 436
  late effect - *see* Late effect(s) (of) cerebrovascular disease
arm 344.40
  affecting
    dominant side 344.41
    nondominant side 344.42
  both 344.2
  hysterical 300.11
  late effect - *see* Late effect(s) (of) cerebrovascular disease
  psychogenic 306.0
  transient 781.4
    traumatic NEC *(see also* Injury, nerve, upper limb) 955.9
arteriosclerotic (current episode) 437.0
  late effect - *see* Late effect(s) (of) cerebrovascular disease
ascending (spinal), acute 357.0
associated, nuclear 344.89
asthenic bulbar 358.0
ataxic NEC 334.9
  general 094.1
athetoid 333.7
atrophic 356.9
  infantile, acute *(see also* Poliomyelitis, with paralysis) 045.1
  muscle NEC 355.9
  progressive 335.21
  spinal (acute) *(see also* Poliomyelitis, with paralysis) 045.1
attack *(see also* Disease, cerebrovascular, acute) 436
axillary 353.0
Babinski-Nageotte's 344.89
Bell's 351.0
  newborn 767.5
Benedikt's 344.89
birth (injury) 767.7
  brain 767.0
  intracranial 767.0
  spinal cord 767.4
bladder (sphincter) 596.53
  neurogenic 596.54
    with cauda equina syndrome 344.61
  puerperal, postpartum, childbirth 665.5
  sensory 596.54
    with cauda equina 344.61
  spastic 596.54
    with cauda equina 344.61
bowel, colon, or intestine *(see also* Ileus) 560.1
brachial plexus 353.0
  due to birth injury 767.6
  newborn 767.6
brain
  congenital - *see* Palsy, cerebral
  current episode 437.8

Paralysis, paralytic *(Continued)*
brain *(Continued)*
  diplegia 344.2
  due to previous vascular lesion - *see* Late effect(s) (of) cerebrovascular disease
  hemiplegia 342.9
    due to previous vascular lesion - *see* Late effect(s) (of) cerebrovascular disease
  infantile - *see* Palsy, cerebral
  monoplegia - *see also* Monoplegia
    due to previous vascular lesion - *see* Late effect(s) (of) cerebrovascular disease
  paraplegia 344.1
  quadriplegia - *see* Quadriplegia
  syphilitic, congenital 090.49
  triplegia 344.89
bronchi 519.1
Brown-Séquard's 344.89
bulbar (chronic) (progressive) 335.22
  infantile *(see also* Poliomyelitis, bulbar) 045.0
  poliomyelitic *(see also* Poliomyelitis, bulbar) 045.0
  pseudo 335.23
  supranuclear 344.89
bulbospinal 358.0
cardiac *(see also* Failure, heart) 428.9
cerebral
  current episode 437.8
  spastic, infantile - *see* Palsy, cerebral
cerebrocerebellar 437.8
  diplegic infantile 343.0
cervical
  plexus 353.2
  sympathetic NEC 337.0
Céstan-Chenais 344.89
Charcôt-Marie-Tooth type 356.1
childhood - *see* Palsy, cerebral
Clark's 343.9
colon *(see also* Ileus) 560.1
compressed air 993.3
compression
  arm NEC 354.9
  cerebral - *see* Paralysis, brain
  leg NEC 355.8
  lower extremity NEC 355.8
  upper extremity NEC 354.9
congenital (cerebral) (spastic) (spinal) - *see* Palsy, cerebral
conjugate movement (of eye) 378.81
  cortical (nuclear) (supranuclear) 378.81
convergence 378.83
cordis *(see also* Failure, heart) 428.9
cortical *(see also* Paralysis, brain) 437.8
cranial or cerebral nerve *(see also* Disorder, nerve, cranial) 352.9
creeping 335.21
crossed leg 344.89
crutch 953.4
deglutition 784.9
  hysterical 300.11
dementia 094.1
descending (spinal) NEC 335.9
diaphragm (flaccid) 519.4
  due to accidental section of phrenic nerve during procedure 998.2
digestive organs NEC 564.89
diplegic - *see* Diplegia
divergence (nuclear) 378.85
divers' 993.3
Duchenne's 335.22

Paralysis, paralytic *(Continued)*
due to intracranial or spinal birth injury - *see* Palsy, cerebral
embolic (current episode) *(see also* Embolism, brain) 434.1
  late effect - *see* Late effect(s) (of) cerebrovascular disease
enteric *(see also* Ileus) 560.1
  with hernia - *see* Hernia, by site, with obstruction
Erb's syphilitic spastic spinal 094.89
Erb (-Duchenne) (birth) (newborn) 767.6
esophagus 530.89
essential, infancy *(see also* Poliomyelitis) 045.9
extremity
  lower - *see* Paralysis, leg
  spastic (hereditary) 343.3
    noncongenital or noninfantile 344.1
  transient (cause unknown) 781.4
  upper - *see* Paralysis, arm
eye muscle (extrinsic) 378.55
  intrinsic 367.51
facial (nerve) 351.0
  birth injury 767.5
  congenital 767.5
  following operation NEC 998.2
  newborn 767.5
familial 359.3
  periodic 359.3
  spastic 334.1
fauces 478.29
finger NEC 354.9
foot NEC 355.8
gait 781.2
gastric nerve 352.3
gaze 378.81
general 094.1
  ataxic 094.1
  insane 094.1
  juvenile 090.40
  progressive 094.1
  tabetic 094.1
glossopharyngeal (nerve) 352.2
glottis *(see also* Paralysis, vocal cord) 478.30
gluteal 353.4
Gubler (-Millard) 344.89
hand 354.9
  hysterical 300.11
  psychogenic 306.0
heart *(see also* Failure, heart) 428.9
hemifacial, progressive 349.89
hemiplegic - *see* Hemiplegia
hyperkalemic periodic (familial) 359.3
hypertensive (current episode) 437.8
hypoglossal (nerve) 352.5
hypokalemic periodic 359.3
Hyrtl's sphincter (rectum) 569.49
hysterical 300.11
ileus *(see also* Ileus) 560.1
infantile *(see also* Poliomyelitis) 045.9
  atrophic acute 045.1
  bulbar 045.0
  cerebral - *see* Palsy, cerebral
  paralytic 045.1
  progressive acute 045.9
  spastic - *see* Palsy, cerebral
  spinal 045.9
infective *(see also* Poliomyelitis) 045.9
inferior nuclear 344.9
insane, general or progressive 094.1

Paralysis, paralytic *(Continued)*
spinal (cord) NEC *(Continued)*
atrophic (acute) *(see also* Poliomyelitis, with paralysis) 045.1
spastic, syphilitic 094.89
congenital NEC 343.9
hemiplegic - *see* Hemiplegia
hereditary 336.8
infantile *(see also* Poliomyelitis) 045.9
late effect NEC 344.89
monoplegic - *see* Monoplegia
nerve 355.9
progressive 335.10
quadriplegic - *see* Quadriplegia
spastic NEC 343.9
traumatic - *see* Injury, spinal, by site
sternomastoid 352.4
stomach 536.3
diabetic 250.6 *[536.3]*
nerve 352.3
stroke (current episode) *(see also* Disease, cerebrovascular, acute) 436
late effect - *see* Late effect(s) (of)
cerebrovascular disease
subscapularis 354.8
superior nuclear NEC 334.9
supranuclear 356.8
sympathetic
cervical NEC 337.0
nerve NEC *(see also* Neuropathy, peripheral, autonomic) 337.9
nervous system - *see* Neuropathy,
peripheral, autonomic
syndrome 344.9
specified NEC 344.89
syphilitic spastic spinal (Erb's) 094.89
tabetic general 094.1
thigh 355.8
throat 478.29
diphtheritic 032.0
muscle 478.29
thrombotic (current episode) *(see also*
Thrombosis, brain) 434.0
old - *see* Late effect(s) (of) cerebrovascular disease
thumb NEC 354.9
tick (-bite) 989.5
Todd's (postepileptic transitory paralysis) 344.89
toe 355.6
tongue 529.8
transient
arm or leg NEC 781.4
traumatic NEC *(see also* Injury,
nerve, by site) 957.9
trapezius 352.4
traumatic, transient NEC *(see also* Injury, nerve, by site) 957.9
trembling *(see also* Parkinsonism) 332.0
triceps brachii 354.9
trigeminal nerve 350.9
trochlear nerve 378.53
ulnar nerve 354.2
upper limb - *see also* Paralysis, arm
both *(see also* Diplegia) 344.2
uremic - *see* Uremia
uveoparotitic 135
uvula 528.9
hysterical 300.11
postdiphtheritic 032.0
vagus nerve 352.3
vasomotor NEC 337.9
velum palati 528.9
vesical *(see also* Paralysis, bladder) 596.53

Paralysis, paralytic *(Continued)*
vestibular nerve 388.5
visual field, psychic 368.16
vocal cord 478.30
bilateral (partial) 478.33
complete 478.34
complete (bilateral) 478.34
unilateral (partial) 478.31
complete 478.32
Volkmann's (complicating trauma)
958.6
wasting 335.21
Weber's 344.89
wrist NEC 354.9
Paramedial orifice, urethrovesical 753.8
Paramenia 626.9
Parametritis (chronic) *(see also* Disease,
pelvis, inflammatory) 614.4
acute 614.3
puerperal, postpartum, childbirth 670
Parametrium, parametric - *see* condition
Paramnesia *(see also* Amnesia) 780.9
Paramolar 520.1
causing crowding 524.3
Paramyloidosis 277.3
Paramyoclonus multiplex 333.2
Paramyotonia 359.2
congenita 359.2
Paraneoplastic syndrome - *see* condition
Parangi *(see also* Yaws) 102.9
Paranoia 297.1
alcoholic 291.5
querulans 297.8
senile 290.20
Paranoid
dementia *(see also* Schizophrenia)
295.3
praecox (acute) 295.3
senile 290.20
personality 301.0
psychosis 297.9
alcoholic 291.5
climacteric 297.2
drug-induced 292.11
involutional 297.2
menopausal 297.2
protracted reactive 298.4
psychogenic 298.4
acute 298.3
senile 290.20
reaction (chronic) 297.9
acute 298.3
schizophrenia (acute) *(see also* Schizophrenia) 295.3
state 297.9
alcohol-induced 291.5
climacteric 297.2
drug-induced 292.11
due to or associated with
arteriosclerosis (cerebrovascular)
290.42
presenile brain disease 290.12
senile brain disease 290.20
involutional 297.2
menopausal 297.2
senile 290.20
simple 297.0
specified type NEC 297.8
tendencies 301.0
traits 301.0
trends 301.0
type, psychopathic personality 301.0
Paraparesis *(see also* Paralysis) 344.9
Paraphasia 784.3

Paraphilia *(see also* Deviation, sexual)
302.9
Paraphimosis (congenital) 605
chancroidal 099.0
Paraphrenia, paraphrenic (late) 297.2
climacteric 297.2
dementia *(see also* Schizophrenia) 295.3
involutional 297.2
menopausal 297.2
schizophrenia (acute) *(see also* Schizophrenia) 295.3
Paraplegia 344.1
with
broken back - *see* Fracture, vertebra,
by site, with spinal cord injury
fracture, vertebra - *see* Fracture, vertebra, by site, with spinal cord
injury
ataxic - *see* Degeneration, combined,
spinal cord
brain (current episode) *(see also* Paralysis, brain) 437.8
cerebral (current episode) *(see also* Paralysis, brain) 437.8
congenital or infantile (cerebral) (spastic) (spinal) 343.0
cortical - *see* Paralysis, brain
familial spastic 334.1
functional (hysterical) 300.11
hysterical 300.11
infantile 343.0
late effect 344.1
Pott's *(see also* Tuberculosis) 015.0
[730.88]
psychogenic 306.0
spastic
Erb's spinal 094.89
hereditary 334.1
not infantile or congenital 344.1
spinal (cord)
traumatic NEC - *see* Injury, spinal,
by site
syphilitic (spastic) 094.89
traumatic NEC - *see* Injury, spinal, by
site
Paraproteinemia 273.2
benign (familial) 273.1
monoclonal 273.1
secondary to malignant or inflammatory disease 273.1
Parapsoriasis 696.2
en plaques 696.2
guttata 696.2
lichenoides chronica 696.2
retiformis 696.2
varioliformis (acuta) 696.2
Parascarlatina 057.8
Parasitic - *see also* condition
disease NEC *(see also* Infestation, parasitic) 136.9
contact V01.8
exposure to V01.8
intestinal NEC 129
skin NEC 134.9
stomatitis 112.0
sycosis 110.0
beard 110.0
scalp 110.0
twin 759.4
Parasitism NEC 136.9
intestinal NEC 129
skin NEC 134.9
specified - *see* Infestation
Parasitophobia 300.29

Parasomnia 780.59
 nonorganic origin 307.47
Paraspadias 752.69
Paraspasm facialis 351.8
Parathyroid gland - *see* condition
Parathyroiditis (autoimmune) 252.1
Parathyroprival tetany 252.1
Paratrachoma 077.0
Paratyphilitis (*see also* Appendicitis)
 541
Paratyphoid (fever) - *see* Fever, paraty-
 phoid
Paratyphus - *see* Fever, paratyphoid
Paraurethral duct 753.8
Para-urethritis 597.89
 gonococcal (acute) 098.0
 chronic or duration of 2 months or
 over 098.2
Paravaccinia NEC 051.9
 milkers' node 051.1
Paravaginitis (*see also* Vaginitis) 616.10
Parencephalitis (*see also* Encephalitis)
 323.9
 late effect - *see* category 326
Parergasia 298.9
Paresis (*see also* Paralysis) 344.9
 accommodation 367.51
 bladder (spastic) (sphincter) (*see also*
 Paralysis, bladder) 596.53
 tabetic 094.0
 bowel, colon, or intestine (*see also* Ileus) 560.1
 brain or cerebral - *see* Paralysis, brain
 extrinsic muscle, eye 378.55
 general 094.1
 arrested 094.1
 brain 094.1
 cerebral 094.1
 insane 094.1
 juvenile 090.40
 remission 090.49
 progressive 094.1
 remission (sustained) 094.1
 tabetic 094.1
 heart (*see also* Failure, heart) 428.9
 infantile (*see also* Poliomyelitis) 045.9
 insane 094.1
 juvenile 090.40
 late effect - *see* Paralysis, late effect
 luetic (general) 094.1
 peripheral progressive 356.9
 pseudohypertrophic 359.1
 senile NEC 344.9
 stomach 536.3
 syphilitic (general) 094.1
 congenital 090.40
 transient, limb 781.4
 vesical (sphincter) NEC 596.53
Paresthesia (*see also* Disturbance, sensation) 782.0
 Berger's (paresthesia of lower limb)
 782.0
 Bernhardt 355.1
 Magnan's 782.0
Paretic - *see* condition
Parinaud's
 conjunctivitis 372.02
 oculoglandular syndrome 372.02
 ophthalmoplegia 378.81
 syndrome (paralysis of conjugate upward gaze) 378.81
Parkes Weber and Dimitri syndrome
 (encephalocutaneous angiomatosis)
 759.6

Parkinson's disease, syndrome, or
 tremor - *see* Parkinsonism
Parkinsonism (arteriosclerotic) (idiopathic) (primary) 332.0
 associated with orthostatic hypotension (idiopathic) (symptomatic)
 333.0
 due to drugs 332.1
 secondary 332.1
 syphilitic 094.82
Parodontitis 523.4
Parodontosis 523.5
Paronychia (with lymphangitis) 681.9
 candidal (chronic) 112.3
 chronic 681.9
 candidal 112.3
 finger 681.02
 toe 681.11
 finger 681.02
 toe 681.11
 tuberculous (primary) (*see also* Tuberculosis) 017.0
Parorexia NEC 307.52
 hysterical 300.11
Parosmia 781.1
 psychogenic 306.7
Parotid gland - *see* condition
Parotiditis (*see also* Parotitis) 527.2
 epidemic 072.9
 infectious 072.9
Parotitis 527.2
 allergic 527.2
 chronic 527.2
 epidemic (*see also* Mumps) 072.9
 infectious (*see also* Mumps) 072.9
 noninfectious 527.2
 nonspecific toxic 527.2
 not mumps 527.2
 postoperative 527.2
 purulent 527.2
 septic 527.2
 suppurative (acute) 527.2
 surgical 527.2
 toxic 527.2
Paroxysmal - *see also* condition
 dyspnea (nocturnal) 786.09
Parrot's disease (syphilitic osteochondritis) 090.0
Parrot fever 073.9
Parry's disease or syndrome (exophthalmic goiter) 242.0
Parry-Romberg syndrome 349.89
Parson's disease (exophthalmic goiter)
 242.0
Parsonage-Aldren-Turner syndrome
 353.5
Parsonage-Turner syndrome 353.5
Pars planitis 363.21
Particolored infant 757.39
Parturition - *see* Delivery
Passage
 false, urethra 599.4
 of sounds or bougies (*see also*
 Attention to artificial opening)
 V55.9
Passive - *see* condition
Pasteurella septica 027.2
Pasteurellosis (*see also* Infection, Pasteu-
 rella) 027.2
PAT (paroxysmal atrial tachycardia)
 427.0
Patau's syndrome (trisomy D₁) 758.1
Patch
 herald 696.3

Patches
 mucous (syphilitic) 091.3
 congenital 090.0
 smokers' (mouth) 528.6
Patellar - *see* condition
Patent - *see also* Imperfect closure
 atrioventricular ostium 745.69
 canal of Nuck 752.41
 cervix 622.5
 complicating pregnancy 654.5
 affecting fetus or newborn 761.0
 ductus arteriosus or Botalli 747.0
 Eustachian
 tube 381.7
 valve 746.89
 foramen
 Botalli 745.5
 ovale 745.5
 interauricular septum 745.5
 interventricular septum 745.4
 omphalomesenteric duct 751.0
 os (uteri) - *see* Patent, cervix
 ostium secundum 745.5
 urachus 753.7
 vitelline duct 751.0
Paternity testing V70.4
Paterson's syndrome (sideropenic dysphagia) 280.8
Paterson (-Brown) (-Kelly) syndrome
 (sideropenic dysphagia) 280.8
Paterson-Kelly syndrome or web (sideropenic dysphagia) 280.8
Pathologic, pathological - *see also* condition
 asphyxia 799.0
 drunkenness 291.4
 emotionality 301.3
 fracture - *see* Fracture, pathologic
 liar 301.7
 personality 301.9
 resorption, tooth 521.4
 sexuality (*see also* Deviation, sexual)
 302.9
Pathology (of) - *see* Disease
Patterned motor discharge, idiopathic
 (*see also* Epilepsy) 345.5
Patulous - *see also* Patent
 anus 569.49
 Eustachian tube 381.7
Pause, sinoatrial 427.81
Pavor nocturnus 307.46
Pavy's disease 593.6
Paxton's disease (white piedra) 111.2
Payr's disease or syndrome (splenic flexure syndrome) 569.89
Pearls
 Elschnig 366.51
 enamel 520.2
Pearl-workers' disease (chronic osteo-
 myelitis) (*see also* Osteomyelitis)
 730.1
Pectenitis 569.49
Pectenosis 569.49
Pectoral - *see* condition
Pectus
 carinatum (congenital) 754.82
 acquired 738.3
 rachitic (*see also* Rickets) 268.0
 excavatum (congenital) 754.81
 acquired 738.3
 rachitic (*see also* Rickets) 268.0
 recurvatum (congenital) 754.81
 acquired 738.3
Pedatrophia 261

Pederosis 302.2
Pediculosis (infestation) 132.9
  capitis (head louse) (any site) 132.0
  corporis (body louse) (any site) 132.1
  eyelid 132.0 *[373.6]*
  mixed (classifiable to more than one
    category in 132.0-132.2) 132.3
  pubis (pubic louse) (any site) 132.2
  vestimenti 132.1
  vulvae 132.2
Pediculus (infestation) - *see* Pediculosis
Pedophilia 302.2
Peg-shaped teeth 520.2
Pel's crisis 094.0
Pel-Ebstein disease - *see* Disease, Hodgkin's
Pelade 704.01
Pelger-Huët anomaly or syndrome (hereditary hyposegmentation) 288.2
Peliosis (rheumatica) 287.0
Pelizaeus-Merzbacher
  disease 330.0
  sclerosis, diffuse cerebral 330.0
Pellagra (alcoholic or with alcoholism)
  265.2
  with polyneuropathy 265.2 *[357.4]*
**Pellagra-cerebellar-ataxia-renal aminoac-
  iduria syndrome** 270.0
Pellegrini's disease (calcification, knee
  joint) 726.62
Pellegrini (-Stieda) disease or syndrome
  (calcification, knee joint) 726.62
Pellizzi's syndrome (pineal) 259.8
Pelvic - *see also* condition
  congestion-fibrosis syndrome 625.5
  kidney 753.3
Pelvioectasis 591
Pelviolithiasis 592.0
Pelviperitonitis
  female (*see also* Peritonitis, pelvic, fe-
    male) 614.5
  male (*see also* Peritonitis) 567.2
Pelvis, pelvic - *see also* condition or
  type
  infantile 738.6
  Nägele's 738.6
  obliquity 738.6
  Robert's 755.69
Pemphigoid 694.5
  benign, mucous membrane 694.60
    with ocular involvement 694.61
  bullous 694.5
  cicatricial 694.60
    with ocular involvement 694.61
  juvenile 694.2
Pemphigus 694.4
  benign 694.5
    chronic familial 757.39
  Brazilian 694.4
  circinatus 694.0
  congenital, traumatic 757.39
  conjunctiva 694.61
  contagiosus 684
  erythematodes 694.4
  erythematosus 694.4
  foliaceus 694.4
  frambesiodes 694.4
  gangrenous (*see also* Gangrene) 785.4
  malignant 694.4
  neonatorum, newborn 684
  ocular 694.61
  papillaris 694.4
  seborrheic 694.4
  South American 694.4

Pemphigus (*Continued*)
  syphilitic (congenital) 090.0
  vegetans 694.4
  vulgaris 694.4
  wildfire 694.4
Pendred's syndrome (familial goiter
  with deaf-mutism) 243
Pendulous
  abdomen 701.9
    in pregnancy or childbirth 654.4
      affecting fetus or newborn
        763.89   ◀▥
  breast 611.8
Penetrating wound - *see also* Wound,
  open, by site
  with internal injury - *see* Injury, inter-
    nal, by site, with open wound
  eyeball 871.7
    with foreign body (nonmagnetic)
      871.6
      magnetic 871.5
  ocular (*see also* Penetrating wound,
    eyeball) 871.7
    adnexa 870.3
      with foreign body 870.4
    orbit 870.3
      with foreign body 870.4
**Penetration, pregnant uterus by instru-
  ment**
  with
    abortion - *see* Abortion, by type,
      with damage to pelvic organs
    ectopic pregnancy (*see also* categories
      633.0-633.9) 639.2
    molar pregnancy (*see also* categories
      630-632) 639.2
  complication of delivery 665.1
    affecting fetus or newborn
      763.89   ◀▥
  following
    abortion 639.2
    ectopic or molar pregnancy 639.2
Penfield's syndrome (*see also* Epilepsy)
  345.5
Penicilliosis of lung 117.3
Penis - *see* condition
Penitis 607.2
Penta X syndrome 758.81
Pentalogy (of Fallot) 745.2
Pentosuria (benign) (essential) 271.8
Peptic acid disease 536.8
Peregrinating patient V65.2
Perforated - *see* Perforation
Perforation, perforative (nontraumatic)
  antrum (*see also* Sinusitis, maxillary)
    473.0
  appendix 540.0
    with peritoneal abscess 540.1
  atrial septum, multiple 745.5
  attic, ear 384.22
    healed 384.81
  bile duct, except cystic (*see also* Dis-
    ease, biliary) 576.3
    cystic 575.4
  bladder (urinary) 596.6
    with
      abortion - *see* Abortion, by type,
        with damage to pelvic organs
      ectopic pregnancy (*see also* catego-
        ries 633.0-633.9) 639.2
      molar pregnancy (*see also* catego-
        ries 630-632) 639.2
    following
      abortion 639.2

Perforation, perforative (*Continued*)
  bladder (*Continued*)
    following (*Continued*)
      ectopic or molar pregnancy 639.2
      obstetrical trauma 665.5
  bowel 569.83
    with
      abortion - *see* Abortion, by type,
        with damage to pelvic organs
      ectopic pregnancy (*see also* catego-
        ries 633.0-633.9) 639.2
      molar pregnancy (*see also* catego-
        ries 630-632) 639.2
    fetus or newborn 777.6
    following
      abortion 639.2
      ectopic or molar pregnancy 639.2
    obstetrical trauma 665.5
  broad ligament
    with
      abortion - *see* Abortion, by type,
        with damage to pelvic organs
      ectopic pregnancy (*see also* catego-
        ries 633.0-633.9) 639.2
      molar pregnancy (*see also* catego-
        ries 630-632) 639.2
    following
      abortion 639.2
      ectopic or molar pregnancy 639.2
    obstetrical trauma 665.6
  by
    device, implant, or graft - *see* Com-
      plications, mechanical
    foreign body left accidentally in op-
      eration wound 998.4
    instrument (any) during a proce-
      dure, accidental 998.2
  cecum 540.0
    with peritoneal abscess 540.1
  cervix (uteri) - *see also* Injury, internal,
    cervix
    with
      abortion - *see* Abortion, by type,
        with damage to pelvic organs
      ectopic pregnancy (*see also* catego-
        ries 633.0-633.9) 639.2
      molar pregnancy (*see also* catego-
        ries 630-632) 639.2
    following
      abortion 639.2
      ectopic or molar pregnancy 639.2
    obstetrical trauma 665.3
  colon 569.83
  common duct (bile) 576.3
  cornea (*see also* Ulcer, cornea) 370.00
    due to ulceration 370.06
  cystic duct 575.4
  diverticulum (*see also* Diverticula) 562.10
    small intestine 562.00
  duodenum, duodenal (ulcer) - *see* Ul-
    cer, duodenum, with perforation
  ear drum - *see* Perforation, tympanum
  enteritis - *see* Enteritis
  esophagus 530.4
  ethmoidal sinus (*see also* Sinusitis, eth-
    moidal) 473.2
  foreign body (external site) - *see also*
    Wound, open, by site, complicated
    internal site, by ingested object - *see*
      Foreign body
  frontal sinus (*see also* Sinusitis, frontal)
    473.1
  gallbladder or duct (*see also* Disease,
    gallbladder) 575.4

Perforation, perforative *(Continued)*
gastric (ulcer) - *see* Ulcer, stomach,
      with perforation
   heart valve - *see* Endocarditis
   ileum (*see also* Perforation, intestine)
      569.83
   instrumental
      external - *see* Wound, open, by site
      pregnant uterus, complicating deliv-
         ery 665.9
      surgical (accidental) (blood vessel)
         (nerve) (organ) 998.2
   intestine 569.83
      with
         abortion - *see* Abortion, by type,
            with damage to pelvic
            organs
         ectopic pregnancy (*see also* catego-
            ries 633.0-633.9) 639.2
         molar pregnancy (*see also* catego-
            ries 630-632) 639.2
      fetus or newborn 777.6
      obstetrical trauma 665.5
      ulcerative NEC 569.83
   jejunum, jejunal 569.83
      ulcer - *see* Ulcer, gastrojejunal, with
         perforation
   mastoid (antrum) (cell) 383.89
   maxillary sinus (*see also* Sinusitis, max-
      illary) 473.0
   membrana tympani - *see* Perforation,
      tympanum
   nasal
      septum 478.1
         congenital 748.1
         syphilitic 095.8
      sinus (*see also* Sinusitis) 473.9
         congenital 748.1
   palate (hard) 526.89
      soft 528.9
         syphilitic 095.8
      syphilitic 095.8
   palatine vault 526.89
      syphilitic 095.8
         congenital 090.5
   pelvic
      floor
         with
            abortion - *see* Abortion, by type,
               with damage to pelvic or-
               gans
            ectopic pregnancy (*see also* cate-
               gories 633.0-633.9) 639.2
            molar pregnancy (*see also* cate-
               gories 630-632) 639.2
         obstetrical trauma 664.1
      organ
         with
            abortion - *see* Abortion, by type,
               with damage to pelvic or-
               gans
            ectopic pregnancy (*see also* cate-
               gories 633.0-633.9) 639.2
            molar pregnancy (*see also* cate-
               gories 630-632) 639.2
         following
            abortion 639.2
            ectopic or molar pregnancy 639.2
         obstetrical trauma 665.5
   perineum - *see* Laceration, perineum
   periurethral tissue
      with
         abortion - *see* Abortion, by type,
            with damage to pelvic organs

Perforation, perforative *(Continued)*
   periurethral tissue *(Continued)*
      with *(Continued)*
         ectopic pregnancy (*see also* catego-
            ries 630-632) 639.2
         molar pregnancy (*see also* catego-
            ries 630-632) 639.2
   pharynx 478.29
   pylorus, pyloric (ulcer) - *see* Ulcer,
      stomach, with perforation
   rectum 569.49
   sigmoid 569.83
   sinus (accessory) (chronic) (nasal) (*see
      also* Sinusitis) 473.9
   sphenoidal sinus (*see also* Sinusitis,
      sphenoidal) 473.3
   stomach (due to ulcer) - *see* Ulcer,
      stomach, with perforation
   surgical (accidental) (by instrument)
      (blood vessel) (nerve) (organ)
      998.2
   traumatic
      external - *see* Wound, open, by site
      eye (*see also* Penetrating wound, ocu-
         lar) 871.7
      internal organ - *see* Injury, internal,
         by site
   tympanum (membrane) (persistent
      posttraumatic) (postinflammatory)
      384.20
      with
      attic 384.22
      central 384.21
      healed 384.81
      marginal NEC 384.23
      multiple 384.24
      otitis media - *see* Otitis media   ◄
      pars flaccida 384.22
      total 384.25
      traumatic - *see* Wound, open, ear,
         drum
   typhoid, gastrointestinal 002.0
   ulcer - *see* Ulcer, by site, with perfora-
      tion
   ureter 593.89
   urethra
      with
         abortion - *see* Abortion, by type,
            with damage to pelvic organs
         ectopic pregnancy (*see also* catego-
            ries 633.0-633.9) 639.2
         molar pregnancy (*see also* catego-
            ries 630-632) 639.2
      following
         abortion 639.2
         ectopic or molar pregnancy 639.2
      obstetrical trauma 665.5
   uterus - *see also* Injury, internal, uterus
      with
         abortion - *see* Abortion, by type,
            with damage to pelvic organs
         ectopic pregnancy (*see also* catego-
            ries 633.0-633.9) 639.2
         molar pregnancy (*see also* catego-
            ries 630-632) 639.2
      by intrauterine contraceptive device
         996.32
      following
         abortion 639.2
         ectopic or molar pregnancy 639.2
      obstetrical trauma - *see* Injury, inter-
         nal, uterus, obstetrical trauma
   uvula 528.9
      syphilitic 095.8

Perforation, perforative *(Continued)*
   vagina - *see* Laceration, vagina
   viscus NEC 799.8
      traumatic 868.00
         with open wound into cavity 868.10
Periadenitis mucosa necrotica recurrens
   528.2
Periangiitis 446.0
Periantritis 535.4
Periappendicitis (acute) (*see also* Appendicitis) 541
Periarteritis (disseminated) (infectious)
   (necrotizing) (nodosa) 446.0
Periarthritis (joint) 726.90
   Duplay's 726.2
   gonococcal 098.50
   humeroscapularis 726.2
   scapulohumeral 726.2
   shoulder 726.2
   wrist 726.4
Periarthrosis (angioneural) - *see* Periarthritis
Peribronchitis 491.9
   tuberculous (*see also* Tuberculosis) 011.3
Pericapsulitis, adhesive (shoulder) 726.0
Pericarditis (granular) (with decompensation) (with effusion) 423.9
   with
      rheumatic fever (conditions classifia-
         ble to 390)
         active (*see also* Pericarditis, rheu-
            matic) 391.0
         inactive or quiescent 393
   actinomycotic 039.8 *[420.0]*
   acute (nonrheumatic) 420.90
      with chorea (acute) (rheumatic) (Sy-
         denham's) 392.0
      bacterial 420.99
      benign 420.91
      hemorrhagic 420.90
      idiopathic 420.91
      infective 420.90
      nonspecific 420.91
      rheumatic 391.0
         with chorea (acute) (rheumatic)
            (Sydenham's) 392.0
      sicca 420.90
      viral 420.91
   adhesive or adherent (external) (inter-
      nal) 423.1
   acute - *see* Pericarditis, acute
   rheumatic (external) (internal) 393
   amebic 006.8 *[420.0]*
   bacterial (acute) (subacute) (with serous
      or seropurulent effusion) 420.99
   calcareous 423.2
   cholesterol (chronic) 423.8
      acute 420.90
   chronic (nonrheumatic) 423.8
      rheumatic 393
   constrictive 423.2
   Coxsackie 074.21
   due to
      actinomycosis 039.8 *[420.0]*
      amebiasis 006.8 *[420.0]*
      Coxsackie (virus) 074.21
      histoplasmosis (*see also* Histoplasmo-
         sis) 115.93
      nocardiosis 039.8 *[420.0]*
      tuberculosis (*see also* Tuberculosis)
         017.9 *[420.0]*
   fibrinocaseous (*see also* Tuberculosis)
      017.9 *[420.0]*
   fibrinopurulent 420.99

Pericarditis (*Continued*)
fibrinous - *see* Pericarditis, rheumatic
fibropurulent 420.99
fibrous 423.1
gonococcal 098.83
hemorrhagic 423.0
idiopathic (acute) 420.91
infective (acute) 420.90
meningococcal 036.41
neoplastic (chronic) 423.8
    acute 420.90
nonspecific 420.91
obliterans, obliterating 423.1
plastic 423.1
pneumococcal (acute) 420.99
postinfarction 411.0
purulent (acute) 420.99
rheumatic (active) (acute) (with effu-
    sion) (with pneumonia) 391.0
    with chorea (acute) (rheumatic) (Sy-
        denham's) 392.0
    chronic or inactive (with chorea) 393
septic (acute) 420.99
serofibrinous - *see* Pericarditis, rheumatic
staphylococcal (acute) 420.99
streptococcal (acute) 420.99
suppurative (acute) 420.99
syphilitic 093.81
tuberculous (acute) (chronic) (*see also*
    Tuberculosis) 017.9 *[420.0]*
uremic 585 *[420.0]*
viral (acute) 420.91
Pericardium, pericardial - *see* condition
Pericellulitis (*see also* Cellulitis) 682.9
Pericementitis 523.4
acute 523.3
chronic (suppurative) 523.4
Pericholecystitis (*see also* Cholecystitis)
    575.10
Perichondritis
auricle 380.00
    acute 380.01
    chronic 380.02
bronchus 491.9
ear (external) 380.00
    acute 380.01
    chronic 380.02
larynx 478.71
    syphilitic 095.8
    typhoid 002.0 *[478.71]*
nose 478.1
pinna 380.00
    acute 380.01
    chronic 380.02
trachea 478.9
Periclasia 523.5
Pericolitis 569.89
Pericoronitis (chronic) 523.4
acute 523.3
Pericystitis (*see also* Cystitis) 595.9
Pericytoma (M9150/1) - *see also* Neo-
    plasm, connective tissue, uncertain
    behavior
benign (M9150/0) - *see* Neoplasm, con-
    nective tissue, benign
malignant (M9150/3) - *see* Neoplasm,
    connective tissue, malignant
Peridacryocystitis, acute 375.32
Peridiverticulitis (*see also* Diverticulitis)
    562.11
Periduodenitis 535.6
Periendocarditis (*see also* Endocarditis)
    424.90
acute or subacute 421.9

Periepididymitis (*see also* Epididymitis)
    604.90
Perifolliculitis (abscedens) 704.8
capitis, abscedens et suffodiens 704.8
dissecting, scalp 704.8
scalp 704.8
superficial pustular 704.8
Perigastritis (acute) 535.0
Perigastrojejunitis (acute) 535.0
Perihepatitis (acute) 573.3
chlamydial 099.56
gonococcal 098.86
Peri-ileitis (subacute) 569.89
Perilabyrinthitis (acute) - *see* Labyrinthitis
Perimeningitis - *see* Meningitis
Perimetritis (*see also* Endometritis) 615.9
Perimetrosalpingitis (*see also* Salpingo-
    oophoritis) 614.2
Perinephric - *see* condition
Perinephritic - *see* condition
Perinephritis (*see also* Infection, kidney)
    590.9
purulent (*see also* Abscess, kidney)
    590.2
Perineum, perineal - *see* condition
Perineuritis NEC 729.2
Periodic - *see also* condition
disease (familial) 277.3
edema 995.1
    hereditary 277.6
fever 277.3
paralysis (familial) 359.3
peritonitis 277.3
polyserositis 277.3
somnolence 347
Periodontal
cyst 522.8
pocket 523.8
Periodontitis (chronic) (complex) (com-
    pound) (local) (simplex) 523.4
acute 523.3
apical 522.6
    acute (pulpal origin) 522.4
Periodontoclasia 523.5
Periodontosis 523.5
Periods - *see also* Menstruation
heavy 626.2
irregular 626.4
Perionychia (with lymphangitis) 681.9
finger 681.02
toe 681.11
Perioophoritis (*see also* Salpingo-oophori-
    tis) 614.2
Periorchitis (*see also* Orchitis) 604.90
Periosteum, periosteal - *see* condition
Periostitis (circumscribed) (diffuse) (in-
    fective) 730.3

Note Use the following fifth-digit
subclassification with category 730:

    0   site unspecified
    1   shoulder region
    2   upper arm
    3   forearm
    4   hand
    5   pelvic region and thigh
    6   lower leg
    7   ankle and foot
    8   other specified sites
    9   multiple sites

with osteomyelitis (*see also* Osteomyeli-
    tis) 730.2
    acute or subacute 730.0

Periostitis (*Continued*)
with osteomyelitis (*Continued*)
    chronic or old 730.1
albuminosa, albuminosus 730.3
alveolar 526.5
alveolodental 526.5
dental 526.5
gonorrheal 098.89
hyperplastica, generalized 731.2
jaw (lower) (upper) 526.4
monomelic 733.99
orbital 376.02
syphilitic 095.5
    congenital 090.0 *[730.8]*
    secondary 091.61
tuberculous (*see also* Tuberculosis,
    bone) 015.9 *[730.8]*
yaws (early) (hypertrophic) (late) 102.6
Periostosis (*see also* Periostitis) 730.3
with osteomyelitis (*see also* Osteomyeli-
    tis) 730.2
    acute or subacute 730.0
    chronic or old 730.1
hyperplastic 756.59
Periphlebitis (*see also* Phlebitis) 451.9
lower extremity 451.2
    deep (vessels) 451.19
    superficial (vessels) 451.0
portal 572.1
retina 362.18
superficial (vessels) 451.0
tuberculous (*see also* Tuberculosis)
    017.9
    retina 017.3 *[362.18]*
Peripneumonia - *see* Pneumonia
Periproctitis 569.49
Periprostatitis (*see also* Prostatitis) 601.9
Perirectal - *see* condition
Perirenal - *see* condition
Perisalpingitis (*see also* Salpingo-oopho-
    ritis) 614.2
Perisigmoiditis 569.89
Perisplenitis (infectional) 289.59
Perispondylitis - *see* Spondylitis
Peristalsis reversed or visible 787.4
Peritendinitis (*see also* Tenosynovitis)
    726.90
adhesive (shoulder) 726.0
Perithelioma (M9150/1) - *see* Pericytoma
Peritoneum, peritoneal - *see* condition
Peritonitis (acute) (adhesive) (fibrinous)
    (hemorrhagic) (idiopathic) (localized)
    (perforative) (primary) (with adhe-
    sions) (with effusion) 567.9
with or following
    abortion - *see* Abortion, by type,
        with sepsis
    abscess 567.2
    appendicitis 540.0
        with peritoneal abscess 540.1
    ectopic pregnancy (*see also* categories
        633.0-633.9) 639.0
    molar pregnancy (*see also* categories
        630-632) 639.0
aseptic 998.7
bacterial 567.2
bile, biliary 567.8
chemical 998.7
chlamydial 099.56
chronic proliferative 567.8
congenital NEC 777.6
diaphragmatic 567.2
diffuse NEC 567.2
diphtheritic 032.83

Peritonitis *(Continued)*
  disseminated NEC 567.2
  due to
    bile 567.8
    foreign
      body or object accidentally left
        during a procedure (instru-
        ment) (sponge) (swab) 998.4
      substance accidentally left during
        a procedure (chemical) (pow-
        der) (talc) 998.7
    talc 998.7
    urine 567.8
  fibrinopurulent 567.2
  fibrinous 567.2
  fibrocaseous *(see also* Tuberculosis) 014.0
  fibropurulent 567.2
  general, generalized (acute) 567.2
  gonococcal 098.86
  in infective disease NEC 136.9 *[567.0]*
  meconium (newborn) 777.6
  pancreatic 577.8
  paroxysmal, benign 277.3
  pelvic
    female (acute) 614.5
      chronic NEC 614.7
        with adhesions 614.6
        puerperal, postpartum, childbirth
          670
    male (acute) 567.2
  periodic (familial) 277.3
  phlegmonous 567.2
  pneumococcal 567.1
  postabortal 639.0
  proliferative, chronic 567.8
  puerperal, postpartum, childbirth 670
  purulent 567.2
  septic 567.2
  staphylococcal 567.2
  streptococcal 567.2
  subdiaphragmatic 567.2
  subphrenic 567.2
  suppurative 567.2
  syphilitic 095.2
    congenital 090.0 *[567.0]*
  talc 998.7
  tuberculous *(see also* Tuberculosis) 014.0
  urine 567.8
Peritonsillar - *see* condition
Peritonsillitis 475
Perityphlitis *(see also* Appendicitis) 541
Periureteritis 593.89
Periurethral - *see* condition
Periurethritis (gangrenous) 597.89
Periuterine - *see* condition
Perivaginitis *(see also* Vaginitis) 616.10
Perivasculitis, retinal 362.18
Perivasitis (chronic) 608.4
Perivesiculitis (seminal) *(see also* Vesicu-
  litis) 608.0
Perlèche 686.8
  due to
    moniliasis 112.0
    riboflavin deficiency 266.0
Pernicious - *see* condition
Pernio, perniosis 991.5
Persecution
  delusion 297.9
  social V62.4
Perseveration (tonic) 784.69
Persistence, persistent (congenital)
  759.89
  anal membrane 751.2
  arteria stapedia 744.04

Persistence, persistent *(Continued)*
  atrioventricular canal 745.69
  bloody ejaculate 792.2
  branchial cleft 744.41
  bulbus cordis in left ventricle 745.8
  canal of Cloquet 743.51
  capsule (opaque) 743.51
  cilioretinal artery or vein 743.51
  cloaca 751.5
  communication - *see* Fistula, congenital
  convolutions
    aortic arch 747.21
    fallopian tube 752.19
    oviduct 752.19
    uterine tube 752.19
  double aortic arch 747.21
  ductus
    arteriosus 747.0
    Botalli 747.0
  fetal
    circulation 747.89
    form of cervix (uteri) 752.49
    hemoglobin (hereditary) ("Swiss va-
      riety") 282.7
    pulmonary hypertension 747.89
  foramen
    Botalli 745.5
    ovale 745.5
  Gartner's duct 752.11
  hemoglobin, fetal (hereditary) (HPFH)
    282.7
  hyaloid
    artery (generally incomplete) 743.51
    system 743.51
  hymen (tag)
    in pregnancy or childbirth 654.8
      causing obstructed labor 660.2
  lanugo 757.4
  left
    posterior cardinal vein 747.49
    root with right arch of aorta 747.21
    superior vena cava 747.49
  Meckel's diverticulum 751.0
  mesonephric duct 752.8
    fallopian tube 752.11
  mucosal disease (middle ear) (with
    posterior or superior marginal
    perforation of ear drum) 382.2
  nail(s), anomalous 757.5
  occiput, anterior or posterior 660.3
    fetus or newborn 763.1
  omphalomesenteric duct 751.0
  organ or site NEC - *see* Anomaly, spec-
    ified type NEC
  ostium
    atrioventriculare commune 745.69
    primum 745.61
    secundum 745.5
  ovarian rests in fallopian tube
    752.19
  pancreatic tissue in intestinal tract
    751.5
  primary (deciduous)
    teeth 520.6
    vitreous hyperplasia 743.51
  pulmonary hypertension 747.89
  pupillary membrane 743.46
    iris 743.46
    Rhesus (Rh) titer 999.7
  right aortic arch 747.21
  sinus
    urogenitalis 752.8
    venosus with imperfect incorpora-
      tion in right auricle 747.49

Persistence, persistent *(Continued)*
  thymus (gland) 254.8
    hyperplasia 254.0
  thyroglossal duct 759.2
  thyrolingual duct 759.2
  truncus arteriosus or communis 745.0
  tunica vasculosa lentis 743.39
  umbilical sinus 753.7
  urachus 753.7
  vegetative state 780.03
  vitelline duct 751.0
  wolffian duct 752.8
Person (with)
  admitted for clinical research, as con-
    trol subject V70.7
  awaiting admission to adequate facility
    elsewhere V63.2
    undergoing social agency investiga-
      tion V63.8
  concern (normal) about sick person in
    family V61.49
  consulting on behalf of another V65.1
  feared
    complaint in whom no diagnosis
      was made V65.5
    condition not demonstrated V65.5
  feigning illness V65.2
  healthy, accompanying sick person
    V65.0
  living (in)
    alone V60.3
    boarding school V60.6
    residence remote from hospital or
      medical care facility V63.0
    residential institution V60.6
    without
      adequate
        financial resources V60.2
        housing (heating) (space) V60.1
      housing (permanent) (temporary)
        V60.0
      material resources V60.2
      person able to render necessary
        care V60.4
      shelter V60.0
  medical services in home not available
    V63.1
  on waiting list V63.2
    undergoing social agency investiga-
      tion V63.8
  sick or handicapped in family V61.49
  "worried well" V65.5
Personality
  affective 301.10
  aggressive 301.3
  amoral 301.7
  anancastic, anankastic 301.4
  antisocial 301.7
  asocial 301.7
  asthenic 301.6
  avoidant 301.82
  borderline 301.83
  change 310.1
  compulsive 301.4
  cycloid 301.13
  cyclothymic 301.13
  dependent 301.6
  depressive (chronic) 301.12
  disorder, disturbance NEC 301.9
    with
      antisocial disturbance 301.7
      pattern disturbance NEC 301.9
      sociopathic disturbance 301.7
      trait disturbance 301.9

Personality *(Continued)*
  dual 300.14
  dyssocial 301.7
  eccentric 301.89
    "haltlose" type 301.89
  emotionally unstable 301.59
  epileptoid 301.3
  explosive 301.3
  fanatic 301.0
  histrionic 301.50
  hyperthymic 301.11
  hypomanic 301.11
  hypothymic 301.12
  hysterical 301.50
  immature 301.89
  inadequate 301.6
  labile 301.59
  masochistic 301.89
  morally defective 301.7
  multiple 300.14
  narcissistic 301.81
  obsessional 301.4
  obsessive (-compulsive) 301.4
  overconscientious 301.4
  paranoid 301.0
  passive (-dependent) 301.6
  passive-aggressive 301.84
  pathologic NEC 301.9
  pattern defect or disturbance 301.9
  pseudosocial 301.7
  psychoinfantile 301.59
  psychoneurotic NEC 301.89
  psychopathic 301.9
    with
      amoral trend 301.7
      antisocial trend 301.7
      asocial trend 301.7
      pathologic sexuality (*see also* Deviation, sexual) 302.9
    mixed types 301.9
  schizoid 301.20
    introverted 301.21
    schizotypal 301.22
    with sexual deviation (*see also* Deviation, sexual) 302.9
    antisocial 301.7
    dyssocial 301.7
  type A 301.4
  unstable (emotional) 301.59
Perthes' disease (capital femoral osteochondrosis) 732.1
Pertussis (*see also* Whooping cough) 033.9
  vaccination, prophylactic (against) V03.6
Peruvian wart 088.0
Perversion, perverted
  appetite 307.52
    hysterical 300.11
  function
    pineal gland 259.8
    pituitary gland 253.9
      anterior lobe
        deficient 253.2
        excessive 253.1
      posterior lobe 253.6
    placenta - *see* Placenta, abnormal
  sense of smell or taste 781.1
    psychogenic 306.7
  sexual (*see also* Deviation, sexual) 302.9
Pervious, congenital - *see also* Imperfect, closure
  ductus arteriosus 747.0

Pes (congenital) (*see also* Talipes) 754.70
  abductus (congenital) 754.60
    acquired 736.79
  acquired NEC 736.79
    planus 734
  adductus (congenital) 754.79
    acquired 736.79
  cavus 754.71
    acquired 736.73
  planovalgus (congenital) 754.69
    acquired 736.79
  planus (acquired) (any degree) 734
    congenital 754.61
    rachitic 268.1
  valgus (congenital) 754.61
    acquired 736.79
  varus (congenital) 754.50
    acquired 736.79
Pest (*see also* Plague) 020.9
Pestis (*see also* Plague) 020.9
  bubonica 020.0
  fulminans 020.0
  minor 020.8
  pneumonica - *see* Plague, pneumonic
Petechia, petechiae 782.7
  fetus or newborn 772.6
Petechial
  fever 036.0
  typhus 081.9
Petges-Cléjat or Petges-Clégat syndrome (poikilodermatomyositis) 710.3
Petit's
  disease (*see also* Hernia, lumbar) 553.8
Petit mal (idiopathic) (*see also* Epilepsy) 345.0
  status 345.2
Petrellidosis 117.6
Petrositis 383.20
  acute 383.21
  chronic 383.22
Peutz-Jeghers disease or syndrome 759.6
Peyronie's disease 607.89
Pfeiffer's disease 075
Phacentocele 379.32
  traumatic 921.3
Phacoanaphylaxis 360.19
Phacocele (old) 379.32
  traumatic 921.3
Phaehyphomycosis 117.8
Phagedena (dry) (moist) (*see also* Gangrene) 785.4
  arteriosclerotic 440.24
  geometric 686.09
  penis 607.89
  senile 440.24
  sloughing 785.4
  tropical (*see also* Ulcer, skin) 707.9
  vulva 616.50
Phagedenic - *see also* condition
  abscess - *see also* Abscess
  chancroid 099.0
  bubo NEC 099.8
  chancre 099.0
  ulcer (tropical) (*see also* Ulcer, skin) 707.9
Phagomania 307.52
Phakoma 362.89
Phantom limb (syndrome) 353.6
Pharyngeal - *see also* condition
  arch remnant 744.41
  pouch syndrome 279.11

Pharyngitis (acute) (catarrhal) (gangrenous) (infective) (malignant) (membranous) (phlegmonous) (pneumococcal) (pseudomembranous) (simple) (staphylococcal) (subacute) (suppurative) (ulcerative) (viral) 462
  with influenza, flu, or grippe 487.1
  aphthous 074.0
  atrophic 472.1
  chlamydial 099.51
  chronic 472.1
  Coxsackie virus 074.0
  diphtheritic (membranous) 032.0
  follicular 472.1
  fusospirochetal 101
  gonococcal 098.6
  granular (chronic) 472.1
  herpetic 054.79
  hypertrophic 472.1
  infectional, chronic 472.1
  influenzal 487.1
  lymphonodular, acute 074.8
  septic 034.0
  streptococcal 034.0
  tuberculous (*see also* Tuberculosis) 012.8
  vesicular 074.0
Pharyngoconjunctival fever 077.2
Pharyngoconjunctivitis, viral 077.2
Pharyngolaryngitis (acute) 465.0
  chronic 478.9
  septic 034.0
Pharyngoplegia 478.29
Pharyngotonsillitis 465.8
  tuberculous 012.8
Pharyngotracheitis (acute) 465.8
  chronic 478.9
Pharynx, pharyngeal - *see* condition
Phase of life problem NEC V62.89
Phenomenon
  Arthus' - *see* Arthus' phenomenon
  flashback (drug) 292.89
  jaw-winking 742.8
  Jod-Basedow 242.8
  L. E. cell 710.0
  lupus erythematosus cell 710.0
  Pelger-Huët (hereditary hyposegmentation) 288.2
  Raynaud's (paroxysmal digital cyanosis) (secondary) 443.0
  Reilly's (*see also* Neuropathy, peripheral, autonomic) 337.9
  vasomotor 780.2
  vasospastic 443.9
  vasovagal 780.2
  Wenckebach's, heart block (second degree) 426.13
Phenylketonuria (PKU) 270.1
Phenylpyruvicaciduria 270.1
Pheochromoblastoma (M8700/3)
  specified site - *see* Neoplasm, by site, malignant
  unspecified site 194.0
Pheochromocytoma (M8700/0)
  malignant (M8700/3)
    specified site - *see* Neoplasm, by site, malignant
    unspecified site 194.0
  specified site - *see* Neoplasm, by site, benign
  unspecified site 227.0
Phimosis (congenital) 605
  chancroidal 099.0
  due to infection 605

Phlebectasia (*see also* Varicose, vein) 454.9
  congenital NEC 747.60
  esophagus (*see also* Varix, esophagus)
    456.1
    with hemorrhage (*see also* Varix,
      esophagus, bleeding) 456.0
Phlebitis (infective) (pyemic) (septic)
  (suppurative) 451.9
  antecubital vein 451.82
  arm NEC 451.84
    axillary vein 451.89
    basilic vein 451.82
    deep 451.83
    superficial 451.82
  basilic vein 451.82
  blue 451.9
  brachial vein 451.83
  breast, superficial 451.89
  cavernous (venous) sinus - *see* Phlebi-
    tis, intracranial sinus
  cephalic vein 451.82
  cerebral (venous) sinus - *see* Phlebitis,
    intracranial sinus
  chest wall, superficial 451.89
  complicating pregnancy or puerperium
    671.9
    affecting fetus or newborn 760.3
  cranial (venous) sinus - *see* Phlebitis,
    intracranial sinus
  deep (vessels) 451.19
    femoral vein 451.11
    specified vessel NEC 451.19
  due to implanted device - *see* Compli-
    cations, due to (presence of) any
    device, implant, or graft classified
    to 996.0-996.5 NEC
  during or resulting from a procedure
    997.2
  femoral vein (deep) (superficial) 451.11
  femoropopliteal 451.19
  following infusion, perfusion, or trans-
    fusion 999.2
  gouty 274.89 [451.9]
  hepatic veins 451.89
  iliac vein 451.81
  iliofemoral 451.11
  intracranial sinus (any) (venous) 325
    late effect - *see* category 326
    nonpyogenic 437.6
      in pregnancy or puerperium 671.5
  jugular vein 451.89
  lateral (venous) sinus - *see* Phlebitis,
    intracranial sinus
  leg 451.2
    deep (vessels) 451.19
      specified vessel NEC 451.19
    superficial (vessels) 451.0
      femoral vein 451.11
  longitudinal sinus - *see* Phlebitis, intra-
    cranial sinus
  lower extremity 451.2
    deep (vessels) 451.19
      femoral vein 451.11
      specified vessel NEC 451.19
    superficial (vessels) 451.0
      femoral vein 451.11
  migrans, migrating (superficial) 453.1
  pelvic
    with
      abortion - *see* Abortion, by type,
        with sepsis
      ectopic pregnancy (*see also* catego-
        ries 633.0-633.9) 639.0
      molar pregnancy (*see also* catego-
        ries 630-632) 639.0

Phlebitis (*Continued*)
  pelvic (*Continued*)
    following
      abortion 639.0
      ectopic or molar pregnancy 639.0
    puerperal, postpartum 671.4
  popliteal vein 451.19
  portal (vein) 572.1
  postoperative 997.2
  pregnancy 671.9
    deep 671.3
    specified type NEC 671.5
  superficial 671.2
  puerperal, postpartum, childbirth 671.9
    deep 671.4
    lower extremities 671.2
    pelvis 671.4
    specified site NEC 671.5
      superficial 671.2
  radial vein 451.83
  retina 362.18
  saphenous (great) (long) 451.0
    accessory or small 451.0
  sinus (meninges) - *see* Phlebitis, intra-
    cranial sinus
  specified site NEC 451.89
  subclavian vein 451.89
  syphilitic 093.89
  tibial vein 451.19
  ulcer, ulcerative 451.9
    leg 451.2
      deep (vessels) 451.19
        femoral vein 451.11
        specified vessel NEC 451.19
      superficial (vessels) 451.0
        femoral vein 451.11
    lower extremity 451.2
      deep (vessels) 451.19
        femoral vein 451.11
        specified vessel NEC 451.19
      superficial (vessels) 451.0
  ulnar vein 451.83
  umbilicus 451.89
  upper extremity - *see* Phlebitis, arm
    deep (veins) 451.83
      brachial vein 451.83
      radial vein 451.83
      ulnar vein 451.83
    superficial (veins) 451.82
      antecubital vein 451.82
      basilic vein 451.82
      cephalic vein 451.82
  uterus (septic) (*see also* Endometritis)
    615.9
  varicose (leg) (lower extremity) (*see
    also* Varicose, vein) 454.1
Phlebofibrosis 459.89
Phleboliths 459.89
Phlebosclerosis 459.89
Phlebothrombosis - *see* Thrombosis
Phlebotomus fever 066.0
Phlegm, choked on 933.1
Phlegmasia
  alba dolens (deep vessels) 451.19
    complicating pregnancy 671.3
    nonpuerperal 451.19
    puerperal, postpartum, childbirth
      671.4
  cerulea dolens 451.19
Phlegmon (*see also* Abscess) 682.9
  erysipelatous (*see also* Erysipelas) 035
  iliac 682.2
    fossa 540.1
  throat 478.29

Phlegmonous - *see* condition
Phlyctenulosis (allergic) (keratoconjunctivitis) (nontuberculous) 370.31
  cornea 370.31
    with ulcer (*see also* Ulcer, cornea)
      370.00
  tuberculous (*see also* Tuberculosis)
    017.3 [370.31]
Phobia, phobic (reaction) 300.20
  animal 300.29
  isolated NEC 300.29
  obsessional 300.3
  simple NEC 300.29
  social 300.23
  specified NEC 300.29
  state 300.20
Phocas' disease 610.1
Phocomelia 755.4
  lower limb 755.32
    complete 755.33
    distal 755.35
    proximal 755.34
  upper limb 755.22
    complete 755.23
    distal 755.25
    proximal 755.24
Phoria (*see also* Heterophoria) 378.40
Phosphate-losing tubular disorder 588.0
Phosphatemia 275.3
Phosphaturia 275.3
Photoallergic response 692.72
Photocoproporphyria 277.1
Photodermatitis (sun) 692.72
  light other than sun 692.82
Photokeratitis 370.24
Photo-ophthalmia 370.24
Photophobia 368.13
Photopsia 368.15
Photoretinitis 363.31
Photoretinopathy 363.31
Photosensitiveness (sun) 692.72
  light other than sun 692.82
Photosensitization skin (sun) 692.72
  light other than sun 692.82
Phototoxic response 692.72
Phrenitis 323.9
Phrynoderma 264.8
Phthiriasis (pubis) (any site) 132.2
  with any infestation classifiable to
    132.0 and 132.1 132.3
Phthirus infestation - *see* Phthiriasis
Phthisis (*see also* Tuberculosis) 011.9
  bulbi (infectional) 360.41
  colliers' 011.4
  cornea 371.05
  eyeball (due to infection) 360.41
  millstone makers' 011.4
  miners' 011.4
  potters' 011.4
  sandblasters' 011.4
  stonemasons' 011.4
Phycomycosis 117.7
Physalopteriasis 127.7
Physical therapy NEC V57.1
  breathing exercises V57.0
Physiological cup, optic papilla
  borderline, glaucoma suspect 365.00
  enlarged 377.14
  glaucomatous 377.14
Phytobezoar 938
  intestine 936
  stomach 935.2
Pian (*see also* Yaws) 102.9
Pianoma 102.1

ICD-9-CM

Vol. 2

Placenta, placental (*Continued*)
  infarction 656.7
    affecting fetus or newborn 762.2
  insertion, vicious - *see* Placenta, previa
  insufficiency
    affecting
      fetus or newborn 762.2
      management of pregnancy
        656.5
  lateral - *see* Placenta, previa
  low implantation or insertion - *see* Placenta, previa
  low-lying - *see* Placenta, previa
  malformation - *see* Placenta, abnormal
  malposition - *see* Placenta, previa
  marginalis, marginata - *see* Placenta, previa
  marginal sinus (hemorrhage) (rupture) 641.2
    affecting fetus or newborn 762.1
  membranacea - *see* Placenta, abnormal
  multilobed - *see* Placenta, abnormal
  multipartita - *see* Placenta, abnormal
  necrosis - *see* Placenta, abnormal
  percreta (without hemorrhage) 667.0
    with hemorrhage 666.0
  polyp 674.4
  previa (central) (centralis) (complete) (lateral) (marginal) (marginalis) (partial) (partialis) (total) (with hemorrhage) 641.1
    affecting fetus or newborn 762.0
    noted
      before labor, without hemorrhage (with cesarean delivery) 641.0
      during pregnancy (without hemorrhage) 641.0
    without hemorrhage (before labor and delivery) (during pregnancy) 641.0
  retention (with hemorrhage) 666.0
    fragments, complicating puerperium (delayed hemorrhage) 666.2
      without hemorrhage 667.1
    postpartum, puerperal 666.2
    without hemorrhage 667.0
  separation (normally implanted) (partial) (premature) (with hemorrhage) 641.2
    affecting fetus or newborn 762.1
  septuplex - *see* Placenta, abnormal
  small - *see* Placenta, insufficiency
  softening (premature) - *see* Placenta, abnormal
  spuria - *see* Placenta, abnormal
  succenturiata - *see* Placenta, abnormal
  syphilitic 095.8
  transfusion syndromes 762.3
  transmission of chemical substance - *see* Absorption, chemical, through placenta
  trapped (with hemorrhage) 666.0
    without hemorrhage 667.0
  trilobate - *see* Placenta, abnormal
  tripartita - *see* Placenta, abnormal
  triplex - *see* Placenta, abnormal
  varicose vessel - *see* Placenta, abnormal
  vicious insertion - *see* Placenta, previa
Placentitis
  affecting fetus or newborn 762.7
  complicating pregnancy 658.4
Plagiocephaly (skull) 754.0

Plague 020.9
  abortive 020.8
  ambulatory 020.8
  bubonic 020.0
  cellulocutaneous 020.1
  lymphatic gland 020.0
  pneumonic 020.5
    primary 020.3
    secondary 020.4
  pulmonary - *see* Plague, pneumonic
  pulmonic - *see* Plague, pneumonic
  septicemic 020.2
  tonsillar 020.9
    septicemic 020.2
  vaccination, prophylactic (against) V03.3
Planning, family V25.09
  contraception V25.9
  procreation V26.4
Plaque
  artery, arterial - *see* Arteriosclerosis
  calcareous - *see* Calcification
  Hollenhorst's (retinal) 362.33
  tongue 528.6
Plasma cell myeloma 203.0
Plasmacytoma, plasmocytoma (solitary) (M9731/1) 238.6
  benign (M9731/0) - *see* Neoplasm, by site, benign
  malignant (M9731/3) 203.8
Plasmacytosis 288.8
Plaster ulcer (*see also* Decubitus) 707.0
Platybasia 756.0
Platyonychia (congenital) 757.5
  acquired 703.8
Platypelloid pelvis 738.6
  with disproportion (fetopelvic) 653.2
    affecting fetus or newborn 763.1
    causing obstructed labor 660.1
      affecting fetus or newborn 763.1
  congenital 755.69
Platyspondylia 756.19
Plethora 782.62
  newborn 776.4
Pleura, pleural - *see* condition
Pleuralgia 786.52
Pleurisy (acute) (adhesive) (chronic) (costal) (diaphragmatic) (double) (dry) (fetid) (fibrinous) (fibrous) (interlobar) (latent) (lung) (old) (plastic) (primary) (residual) (sicca) (sterile) (subacute) (unresolved) (with adherent pleura) 511.0
  with
    effusion (without mention of cause) 511.9
      bacterial, nontuberculous 511.1
      nontuberculous NEC 511.9
        bacterial 511.1
      pneumococcal 511.1
      specified type NEC 511.8
      staphylococcal 511.1
      streptococcal 511.1
      tuberculous (*see also* Tuberculosis, pleura) 012.0
        primary, progressive 010.1
    influenza, flu, or grippe 487.1
    tuberculosis - *see* Pleurisy, tuberculous
  encysted 511.8
  exudative (*see also* Pleurisy, with effusion) 511.9
    bacterial, nontuberculous 511.1
  fibrinopurulent 510.9
    with fistula 510.0

Pleurisy (*Continued*)
  fibropurulent 510.9
    with fistula 510.0
  hemorrhagic 511.8
  influenzal 487.1
  pneumococcal 511.0
    with effusion 511.1
  purulent 510.9
    with fistula 510.0
  septic 510.9
    with fistula 510.0
  serofibrinous (*see also* Pleurisy, with effusion) 511.9
    bacterial, nontuberculous 511.1
  seropurulent 510.9
    with fistula 510.0
  serous (*see also* Pleurisy, with effusion) 511.9
    bacterial, nontuberculous 511.1
  staphylococcal 511.0
    with effusion 511.1
  streptococcal 511.0
    with effusion 511.1
  suppurative 510.9
    with fistula 510.0
  traumatic (post) (current) 862.29
    with open wound into cavity 862.39
  tuberculous (with effusion) (*see also* Tuberculosis, pleura) 012.0
    primary, progressive 010.1
Pleuritis sicca - *see* Pleurisy
Pleurobronchopneumonia (*see also* Pneumonia, broncho-) 485
Pleurodynia 786.52
  epidemic 074.1
  viral 074.1
Pleurohepatitis 573.8
Pleuropericarditis (*see also* Pericarditis) 423.9
  acute 420.90
Pleuropneumonia (acute) (bilateral) (double) (septic) (*see also* Pneumonia) 486
  chronic (*see also* Fibrosis, lung) 515
Pleurorrhea (*see also* Hydrothorax) 511.8
Plexitis, brachial 353.0
Plica
  polonica 132.0
  tonsil 474.8
Plicae dysphonia ventricularis 784.49
Plicated tongue 529.5
  congenital 750.13
Plug
  bronchus NEC 519.1
  meconium (newborn) NEC 777.1
  mucus - *see* Mucus, plug
Plumbism 984.9
  specified type of lead - *see* Table of Drugs and Chemicals
Plummer's disease (toxic nodular goiter) 242.3
Plummer-Vinson syndrome (sideropenic dysphagia) 280.8
Pluricarential syndrome of infancy 260
Plurideficiency syndrome of infancy 260
Plus (and minus) hand (intrinsic) 736.09
PMS 625.4
Pneumathemia - *see* Air, embolism, by type
Pneumatic drill or hammer disease 994.9
Pneumatocele (lung) 518.89
  intracranial 348.8
  tension 492.0

Pneumatosis
  cystoides intestinalis 569.89
  peritonei 568.89
  pulmonum 492.8
Pneumaturia 599.84
Pneumoblastoma (M8981/3) - *see* Neoplasm, lung, malignant
Pneumocephalus 348.8
Pneumococcemia 038.2
Pneumococcus, pneumococcal - *see* condition
Pneumoconiosis (due to) (inhalation of) 505
  aluminum 503
  asbestos 501
  bagasse 495.1
  bauxite 503
  beryllium 503
  carbon electrode makers' 503
  coal
    miners' (simple) 500
    workers' (simple) 500
  cotton dust 504
  diatomite fibrosis 502
  dust NEC 504
    inorganic 503
    lime 502
    marble 502
    organic NEC 504
  fumes or vapors (from silo) 506.9
  graphite 503
  hard metal 503
  mica 502
  moldy hay 495.0
  rheumatoid 714.81
  silica NEC 502
    and carbon 500
  silicate NEC 502
  talc 502
Pneumocystis carinii pneumonia 136.3
Pneumocystosis 136.3
  with pneumonia 136.3
Pneumoenteritis 025
Pneumohemopericardium (*see also* Pericarditis) 423.9
Pneumohemothorax (*see also* Hemothorax) 511.8
  traumatic 860.4
    with open wound into thorax 860.5
Pneumohydropericardium (*see also* Pericarditis) 423.9
Pneumohydrothorax (*see also* Hydrothorax) 511.8
Pneumomediastinum 518.1
  congenital 770.2
  fetus or newborn 770.2
Pneumomycosis 117.9
Pneumonia (acute) (Alpenstich) (benign) (bilateral) (brain) (cerebral) (circumscribed) (congestive) (creeping) (delayed resolution) (double) (epidemic) (fever) (flash) (fulminant) (fungoid) (granulomatous) (hemorrhagic) (incipient) (infantile) (infectious) (infiltration) (insular) (intermittent) (latent) (lobe) (migratory) (newborn) (organized) (overwhelming) (primary) (progressive) (pseudolobar) (purulent) (resolved) (secondary) (senile) (septic) (suppurative) (terminal) (true) (unresolved) (vesicular) 486
  with influenza, flu, or grippe 487.0
  adenoviral 480.0
  adynamic 514

Pneumonia (*Continued*)
  alba 090.0
  allergic 518.3
  alveolar - *see* Pneumonia, lobar
  anaerobes 482.81
  anthrax 022.1 *[484.5]*
  apex, apical - *see* Pneumonia, lobar
  ascaris 127.0 *[484.8]*
  aspiration 507.0
    due to
      aspiration of microorganisms
        bacterial 482.9
          specified type NEC 482.89
        specified organism NEC 483.8
          bacterial NEC 482.89
        viral 480.9
          specified type NEC 480.8
      food (regurgitated) 507.0
      gastric secretions 507.0
      milk 507.0
      oils, essences 507.1
      solids, liquids NEC 507.8
      vomitus 507.0
    newborn 770.1
  asthenic 514
  atypical (disseminated) (focal) (primary) 486
    with influenza 487.0
  bacillus 482.9
    specified type NEC 482.89
  bacterial 482.9
    specified type NEC 482.89
  Bacteroides (fragilis) (oralis) (melaninogenicus) 482.81
  basal, basic, basilar - *see* Pneumonia, lobar
  broncho-, bronchial (confluent) (croupous) (diffuse) (disseminated) (hemorrhagic) (involving lobes) (lobar) (terminal) 485
    with influenza 487.0
    allergic 518.3
    aspiration (*see also* Pneumonia, aspiration) 507.0
    bacterial 482.9
      specified type NEC 482.89
    capillary 466.19
      with bronchospasm or obstruction 466.19
    chronic (*see also* Fibrosis, lung) 515
    congenital (infective) 770.0
    diplococcal 481
    Eaton's agent 483.0
    Escherichia coli (E. coli) 482.82
    Friedlander's bacillus 482.0
    Hemophilus influenzae 482.2
    hiberno-vernal 083.0 *[484.8]*
    hypostatic 514
    influenzal 487.0
    inhalation (*see also* Pneumonia, aspiration) 507.0
      due to fumes or vapors (chemical) 506.0
    Klebsiella 482.0
    lipid 507.1
      endogenous 516.8
    Mycoplasma (pneumoniae) 483.0
    ornithosis 073.0
    pleuropneumonia-like organisms (PPLO) 483.0
    pneumococcal 481
    Proteus 482.83
    Pseudomonas 482.1

Pneumonia (*Continued*)
  broncho-, bronchial (*Continued*)
    specified organism NEC 483.8
      bacterial NEC 482.89
    staphylococcal 482.40 ◀▥▥
      aureus 482.41 ◀
      specified type NEC 482.49 ◀
    streptococcal - *see* Pneumonia, streptococcal
    typhoid 002.0 *[484.8]*
    viral, virus (*see also* Pneumonia, viral) 480.9
  butyrivibirio (fibriosolvens) 482.81
  candida 112.4
  capillary 466.19
    with bronchospasm or obstruction 466.19
  caseous (*see also* Tuberculosis) 011.6
  catarrhal - *see* Pneumonia, broncho-
  central - *see* Pneumonia, lobar
  chlamydia, chlamydial 483.1
    pneumoniae 483.1
    psittaci 073.0
    specified type NEC 483.1
    trachomatis 483.1
  cholesterol 516.8
  chronic (*see also* Fibrosis, lung) 515
  cirrhotic (chronic) (*see also* Fibrosis, lung) 515
  clostridium (haemolyticum) (novyi) NEC 482.81
  confluent - *see* Pneumonia, broncho-
  congenital (infective) 770.0
    aspiration 770.1
  croupous - *see* Pneumonia, lobar
  cytomegalic inclusion 078.5 *[484.1]*
  deglutition (*see also* Pneumonia, aspiration) 507.0
  desquamative interstitial 516.8
  diffuse - *see* Pneumonia, broncho-
  diplococcal, diplococcus (broncho-) (lobar) 481
  disseminated (focal) - *see* Pneumonia, broncho-
  due to
    adenovirus 480.0
    anaerobes 482.81
    Bacterium anitratum 482.83
    Chlamydia, chlamydial 483.1
      pneumoniae 483.1
      psittaci 073.0
      specified type NEC 483.1
      trachomatis 483.1
    coccidioidomycosis 114.0
    Diplococcus (pneumoniae) 481
    Eaton's agent 483.0
    Escherichia coli (E. coli) 482.82
    Friedlander's bacillus 482.0
    fumes or vapors (chemical) (inhalation) 506.0
    fungus NEC 117.9 *[484.7]*
      coccidioidomycosis 114.0
    Hemophilus influenzae (H. influenzae) 482.2
    Herellea 482.83
    influenza 487.0
    Klebsiella pneumoniae 482.0
    Mycoplasma (pneumoniae) 483.0
    parainfluenza virus 480.2
    pleuropneumonia-like organism (PPLO) 483.0
    Pneumococcus 481
    Pneumocystis carinii 136.3
    Proteus 482.83

ICD-9-CM

P

Vol. 2

◄▶ **New Code**   ⬅⏵ **Revised Code**

Pneumonitis (*Continued*)
  postanesthetic (*Continued*)
    obstetric 668.0
    overdose or wrong substance given
      968.4
      specified anesthetic - *see* Table of
        Drugs and Chemicals
  postoperative 997.3
    obstetric 668.0
  radiation 508.0
  rubella, congenital 771.0
  "ventilation" 495.7
  wood-dust 495.8
Pneumonoconiosis - *see* Pneumoconiosis
Pneumoparotid 527.8
Pneumopathy NEC 518.89
  alveolar 516.9
    specified NEC 516.8
  due to dust NEC 504
  parietoalveolar 516.9
    specified condition NEC 516.8
Pneumopericarditis (*see also* Pericarditis)
  423.9
  acute 420.90
Pneumopericardium - *see also* Pericarditis
  congenital 770.2
  fetus or newborn 770.2
  traumatic (post) (*see also* Pneumo-
    thorax, traumatic) 860.0
    with open wound into thorax 860.1
Pneumoperitoneum 568.89
  fetus or newborn 770.2
Pneumophagia (psychogenic) 306.4
Pneumopleurisy, pneumopleuritis (*see*
  also Pneumonia) 486
Pneumopyopericardium 420.99
Pneumopyothorax (*see also* Pyopneumothorax) 510.9
  with fistula 510.0
Pneumorrhagia 786.3
  newborn 770.3
  tuberculous (*see also* Tuberculosis, pul-
    monary) 011.9
Pneumosiderosis (occupational) 503
Pneumothorax (acute) (chronic) 512.8
  congenital 770.2
  due to operative injury of chest wall
    or lung 512.1
    accidental puncture or laceration 512.1
  fetus or newborn 770.2
  iatrogenic 512.1
  postoperative 512.1
  spontaneous 512.8
    fetus or newborn 770.2
    tension 512.0
  sucking 512.8
    iatrogenic 512.1
    postoperative 512.1
  tense valvular, infectional 512.0
  tension 512.0
    iatrogenic 512.1
    postoperative 512.1
    spontaneous 512.0
  traumatic 860.0
    with
      hemothorax 860.4
        with open wound into thorax
          860.5
      open wound into thorax 860.1
  tuberculous (*see also* Tuberculosis) 011.7
Pocket(s)
  endocardial (*see also* Endocarditis) 424.90
  periodontal 523.8

Podagra 274.9
Podencephalus 759.89
Poikilocytosis 790.0
Poikiloderma 709.09
  Civatte's 709.09
  congenital 757.33
  vasculare atrophicans 696.2
Poikilodermatomyositis 710.3
Pointed ear 744.29
Poise imperfect 729.9
Poisoned - *see* Poisoning
Poisoning (acute) - *see also* Table of
  Drugs and Chemicals
  Bacillus, B.
    aertrycke (*see also* Infection, Salmo-
      nella) 003.9
    botulinus 005.1
    cholerae (suis) (*see also* Infection, Sal-
      monella) 003.9
    paratyphosus (*see also* Infection, Sal-
      monella) 003.9
    suipestifer (*see also* Infection, Salmo-
      nella) 003.9
  bacterial toxins NEC 005.9
  berries, noxious 988.2
  blood (general) - *see* Septicemia
  botulism 005.1
  bread, moldy, mouldy - *see* Poisoning,
    food
  damaged meat - *see* Poisoning, food
  death-cap (Amanita phalloides) (Ama-
    nita verna) 988.1
  decomposed food - *see* Poisoning, food
  diseased food - *see* Poisoning, food
  drug - *see* Table of Drugs and Chemi-
    cals
  epidemic, fish, meat, or other food -
    see Poisoning, food
  fava bean 282.2
  fish (bacterial) - *see also* Poisoning,
    food
    noxious 988.0
  food (acute) (bacterial) (diseased) (in-
    fected) NEC 005.9
    due to
      bacillus
        aertrycke (*see also* Poisoning, food,
          due to Salmonella) 003.9
        botulinus 005.1
        cereus 005.89
        choleraesuis (*see also* Poisoning,
          food, due to Salmonella)
          003.9
        paratyphosus (*see also* Poison-
          ing, food, due to Salmo-
          nella) 003.9
        suipestifer (*see also* Poisoning,
          food, due to Salmonella)
          003.9
      Clostridium 005.3
        botulinum 005.1
        perfringens 005.2
        welchii 005.2
      Salmonella (aertrycke) (callinarum)
        (choleraesuis) (enteritidis) (para-
        typhi) (suipestifer) 003.9with
        gastroenteritis 003.0
        localized infection(s) (*see also*
          Infection, Salmonella)
          003.20
        septicemia 003.1
        specified manifestation NEC
          003.8
      specified bacterium NEC 005.89

Poisoning (*Continued*)
  food (*Continued*)
    due to (*Continued*)
      Staphylococcus 005.0
      Streptococcus 005.89
      Vibrio parahaemolyticus 005.4
      Vibrio vulnificus 005.81
    noxious or naturally toxic 988.0
      berries 988.2
      fish 988.0
      mushroom 988.1
      plants NEC 988.2
  ice cream - *see* Poisoning, food
  ichthyotoxism (bacterial) 005.9
  kreotoxism, food 005.9
  malarial - *see* Malaria
  meat - *see* Poisoning, food
  mushroom (noxious) 988.1
  mussel - *see also* Poisoning, food
    noxious 988.0
  noxious foodstuffs (*see also* Poisoning,
    food, noxious) 988.9
    specified type NEC 988.8
  plants, noxious 988.2
  pork - *see also* Poisoning, food
    specified NEC 988.8
    Trichinosis 124
  ptomaine - *see* Poisoning, food
  putrefaction, food - *see* Poisoning, food
  radiation 508.0
  Salmonella (*see also* Infection, Salmo-
    nella) 003.9
  sausage - *see also* Poisoning, food
    Trichinosis 124
  saxitoxin 988.0
  shellfish - *see also* Poisoning, food
    noxious 988.0
  Staphylococcus, food 005.0
  toxic, from disease NEC 799.8
  truffles - *see* Poisoning, food
  uremic - *see* Uremia
  uric acid 274.9
Poison ivy, oak, sumac or other plant
  dermatitis 692.6
Poker spine 720.0
Policeman's disease 729.2
Polioencephalitis (acute) (bulbar) (*see*
  also Poliomyelitis, bulbar) 045.0
  inferior 335.22
  influenzal 487.8
  superior hemorrhagic (acute) (Werni-
    cke's) 265.1
  Wernicke's (superior hemorrhagic)
    265.1
Polioencephalomyelitis (acute) (anterior)
  (bulbar) (*see also* Polioencephalitis)
  045.0
Polioencephalopathy, superior hemor-
  rhagic 265.1
  with
    beriberi 265.0
    pellagra 265.2
Poliomeningoencephalitis - *see* Meningoencephalitis
Poliomyelitis (acute) (anterior) (epidemic) 045.9

> Note   Use the following fifth-digit
> subclassification with category 045:
>
> 0   poliovirus, unspecified type
> 1   poliovirus, type I
> 2   poliovirus, type II
> 3   poliovirus, type III

ICD-9-CM

P

Vol. 2

Poliomyelitis (*Continued*)
  with
    paralysis 045.1
      bulbar 045.0
  abortive 045.2
  ascending 045.9
    progressive 045.9
  bulbar 045.0
  cerebral 045.0
  chronic 335.21
  congenital 771.2
  contact V01.2
  deformities 138
  exposure to V01.2
  late effect 138
  nonepidemic 045.9
  nonparalytic 045.2
  old with deformity 138
  posterior, acute 053.19
  residual 138
  sequelae 138
  spinal, acute 045.9
  syphilitic (chronic) 094.89
  vaccination, prophylactic (against) V04.0
Poliosis (eyebrow) (eyelashes) 704.3
  circumscripta (congenital) 757.4
    acquired 704.3
  congenital 757.4
Pollakiuria 788.41
  psychogenic 306.53
Pollinosis 477.0
Pollitzer's disease (hidradenitis suppurativa) 705.83
Polyadenitis (*see also* Adenitis) 289.3
  malignant 020.0
Polyalgia 729.9
Polyangiitis (essential) 446.0
Polyarteritis (nodosa) (renal) 446.0
Polyarthralgia 719.49
  psychogenic 306.0
Polyarthritis, polyarthropathy NEC 716.59
  due to or associated with other specified conditions - *see* Arthritis, due to or associated with
  endemic (*see also* Disease, Kaschin-Beck) 716.0
  inflammatory 714.9
    specified type NEC 714.89
  juvenile (chronic) 714.30
    acute 714.31
  migratory - *see* Fever, rheumatic
  rheumatic 714.0
    fever (acute) - *see* Fever, rheumatic
Polycarential syndrome of infancy 260
Polychondritis (atrophic) (chronic) (relapsing) 733.99
Polycoria 743.46
Polycystic (congenital) (disease) 759.89
  degeneration, kidney - *see* Polycystic, kidney
  kidney (congenital) 753.12
    adult type (APKD) 753.13
    autosomal dominant 753.13
    autosomal recessive 753.14
    childhood type (CPKD) 753.14
    infantile type 753.14
  liver 751.62
  lung 518.89
    congenital 748.4
  ovary, ovaries 256.4
  spleen 759.0
Polycythemia (primary) (rubra) (vera) (M9950/1) 238.4
  acquired 289.0

Polycythemia (*Continued*)
  benign 289.0
    familial 289.6
  due to
    donor twin 776.4
    fall in plasma volume 289.0
    high altitude 289.0
    maternal-fetal transfusion 776.4
    stress 289.0
  emotional 289.0
  erythropoietin 289.0
  familial (benign) 289.6
  Gaisböck's (hypertonica) 289.0
  high altitude 289.0
  hypertonica 289.0
  hypoxemic 289.0
  neonatorum 776.4
  nephrogenous 289.0
  relative 289.0
  secondary 289.0
  spurious 289.0
  stress 289.0
Polycytosis cryptogenica 289.0
Polydactylism, polydactyly 755.00
  fingers 755.01
  toes 755.02
Polydipsia 783.5
Polydystrophic oligophrenia 277.5
Polyembryoma (M9072/3) - *see* Neoplasm, by site, malignant
Polygalactia 676.6
Polyglandular
  deficiency 258.9
  dyscrasia 258.9
  dysfunction 258.9
  syndrome 258.8
Polyhydramnios (*see also* Hydramnios) 657
Polymastia 757.6
Polymenorrhea 626.2
Polymicrogyria 742.2
Polymyalgia 725
  arteritica 446.5
  rheumatica 725
Polymyositis (acute) (chronic) (hemorrhagic) 710.4
  with involvement of
    lung 710.4 [517.8]
    skin 710.3
  ossificans (generalisata) (progressiva) 728.19
  Wagner's (dermatomyositis) 710.3
Polyneuritis, polyneuritic (*see also* Polyneuropathy) 356.9
  alcoholic 357.5
    with psychosis 291.1
  cranialis 352.6
  demyelinating, chronic inflammatory 357.8 ◄
  diabetic 250.6 [357.2]
  due to lack of vitamin NEC 269.2 [357.4]
  endemic 265.0 [357.4]
  erythredema 985.0
  febrile 357.0
  hereditary ataxic 356.3
  idiopathic, acute 357.0
  infective (acute) 357.0
  nutritional 269.9 [357.4]
  postinfectious 357.0
Polyneuropathy (peripheral) 356.9
  alcoholic 357.5
  amyloid 277.3 [357.4]
  arsenical 357.7

Polyneuropathy (*Continued*)
  diabetic 250.6 [357.2]
  due to
    antitetanus serum 357.6
    arsenic 357.7
    drug or medicinal substance 357.6
      correct substance properly administered 357.6
      overdose or wrong substance given or taken 977.9
        specified drug - *see* Table of Drugs and Chemicals
    lack of vitamin NEC 269.2 [357.4]
    lead 357.7
    organophosphate compounds 357.7
    pellagra 265.2 [357.4]
    porphyria 277.1 [357.4]
    serum 357.6
    toxic agent NEC 357.7
  hereditary 356.0
  idiopathic 356.9
    progressive 356.4
  in
    amyloidosis 277.3 [357.4]
    avitaminosis 269.2 [357.4]
      specified NEC 269.1 [357.4]
    beriberi 265.0 [357.4]
    collagen vascular disease NEC 710.9 [357.1]
    deficiency
      B-complex NEC 266.2 [357.4]
      vitamin B 266.9 [357.4]
      vitamin B_6 266.1 [357.4]
    diabetes 250.6 [357.2]
    diphtheria (*see also* Diphtheria) 032.89 [357.4]
    disseminated lupus erythematosus 710.0 [357.1]
    herpes zoster 053.13
    hypoglycemia 251.2 [357.4]
    malignant neoplasm (M8000/3) NEC 199.1 [357.3]
    mumps 072.72
    pellagra 265.2 [357.4]
    polyarteritis nodosa 446.0 [357.1]
    porphyria 277.1 [357.4]
    rheumatoid arthritis 714.0 [357.1]
    sarcoidosis 135 [357.4]
    uremia 585 [357.4]
  lead 357.7
  nutritional 269.9 [357.4]
    specified NEC 269.8 [357.4]
  postherpetic 053.13
  progressive 356.4
  sensory (hereditary) 356.2
Polyonychia 757.5
Polyopia 368.2
  refractive 368.15
Polyorchism, polyorchidism (three testes) 752.8
Polyorrhymenitis (peritoneal) (*see also* Polyserositis) 568.82
  pericardial 423.2
Polyostotic fibrous dysplasia 756.54
Polyotia 744.1
Polyp, polypus

> Note   Polyps of organs or sites that do not appear in the list below should be coded to the residual category for diseases of the organ or site concerned.

Polyp, polypus (*Continued*)
accessory sinus 471.8
adenoid tissue 471.0
adenomatous (M8210/0) - *see also* Neoplasm, by site, benign
   adenocarcinoma in (M8210/3) - *see* Neoplasm, by site, malignant
   carcinoma in (M8210/3) - *see* Neoplasm, by site, malignant
   multiple (M8221/0) - *see* Neoplasm, by site, benign
antrum 471.8
anus, anal (canal) (nonadenomatous) 569.0
   adenomatous 211.4
Bartholin's gland 624.6
bladder (M8120/1) 236.7
broad ligament 620.8
cervix (uteri) 622.7
   adenomatous 219.0
   in pregnancy or childbirth 654.6
      affecting fetus or newborn 763.89
         causing obstructed labor 660.2
   mucous 622.7
   nonneoplastic 622.7
choanal 471.0
cholesterol 575.6
clitoris 624.6
colon (M8210/0) (*see also* Polyp, adenomatous) 211.3
corpus uteri 621.0
dental 522.0
ear (middle) 385.30
endometrium 621.0
ethmoidal (sinus) 471.8
fallopian tube 620.8
female genital organs NEC 624.8
frontal (sinus) 471.8
gallbladder 575.6
gingiva 523.8
gum 523.8
labia 624.6
larynx (mucous) 478.4
malignant (M8000/3) - *see* Neoplasm, by site, malignant
maxillary (sinus) 471.8
middle ear 385.30
myometrium 621.0
nares
   anterior 471.9
   posterior 471.0
nasal (mucous) 471.9
   cavity 471.0
   septum 471.9
nasopharyngeal 471.0
neoplastic (M8210/0) - *see* Neoplasm, by site, benign
nose (mucous) 471.9
oviduct 620.8
paratubal 620.8
pharynx 478.29
   congenital 750.29
placenta, placental 674.4
prostate 600
pudenda 624.6
pulp (dental) 522.0
rectosigmoid 211.4
rectum (nonadenomatous) 569.0
   adenomatous 211.4
septum (nasal) 471.9
sinus (accessory) (ethmoidal) (frontal) (maxillary) (sphenoidal) 471.8
sphenoidal (sinus) 471.8
stomach (M8210/0) 211.1

Polyp, polypus (*Continued*)
tube, fallopian 620.8
turbinate, mucous membrane 471.8
ureter 593.89
urethra 599.3
uterine
   ligament 620.8
   tube 620.8
uterus (body) (corpus) (mucous) 621.0
   in pregnancy or childbirth 654.1
      affecting fetus or newborn 763.89 ◀
         causing obstructed labor 660.2
vagina 623.7
vocal cord (mucous) 478.4
vulva 624.6
Polyphagia 783.6
Polypoid - *see* condition
Polyposis - *see also* Polyp
coli (adenomatous) (M8220/0) 211.3
   adenocarcinoma in (M8220/3) 153.9
   carcinoma in (M8220/3) 153.9
familial (M8220/0) 211.3
intestinal (adenomatous) (M8220/0) 211.3
multiple (M8221/0) - *see* Neoplasm, by site, benign
Polyradiculitis (acute) 357.0
Polyradiculoneuropathy (acute) (segmentally demyelinating) 357.0
Polysarcia 278.00
Polyserositis (peritoneal) 568.82
due to pericarditis 423.2
paroxysmal (familial) 277.3
pericardial 423.2
periodic 277.3
pleural - *see* Pleurisy
recurrent 277.3
tuberculous (*see also* Tuberculosis, polyserositis) 018.9
Polysialia 527.7
Polysplenia syndrome 759.0
Polythelia 757.6
Polytrichia (*see also* Hypertrichosis) 704.1
Polyunguia (congenital) 757.5
acquired 703.8
Polyuria 788.42
Pompe's disease (glycogenosis II) 271.0
Pompholyx 705.81
Poncet's disease (tuberculous rheumatism) (*see also* Tuberculosis) 015.9
Pond fracture - *see* Fracture, skull, vault
Ponos 085.0
Pons, pontine - *see* condition
Poor
contractions, labor 661.2
   affecting fetus or newborn 763.7
fetal growth NEC 764.9
   affecting management of pregnancy 656.5
incorporation ◀
   artificial skin graft 996.55 ◀
   decellularized allodermis graft 996.55 ◀
obstetrical history V23.4
sucking reflex (newborn) 796.1
vision NEC 369.9
Poradenitis, nostras 099.1
Porencephaly (congenital) (developmental) (true) 742.4
acquired 348.0
nondevelopmental 348.0
traumatic (post) 310.2
Porocephaliasis 134.1

Porokeratosis 757.39
Poroma, eccrine (M8402/0) - *see* Neoplasm, skin, benign
Porphyria (acute) (congenital) (constitutional) (erythropoietic) (familial) (hepatica) (idiopathic) (idiosyncratic) (intermittent) (latent) (mixed hepatic) (photosensitive) (South African genetic) (Swedish) 277.1
acquired 277.1
cutaneatarda
   hereditaria 277.1
   symptomatica 277.1
due to drugs
   correct substance properly administered 277.1
   overdose or wrong substance given or taken 977.9
      specified drug - *see* Table of Drugs and Chemicals
secondary 277.1
toxic NEC 277.1
variegata 277.1
Porphyrinuria (acquired) (congenital) (secondary) 277.1
Porphyruria (acquired) (congenital) 277.1
Portal - *see* condition
Port wine nevus or mark 757.32
Posadas-Wernicke disease 114.9
Position
fetus, abnormal (*see also* Presentation, fetal) 652.9
teeth, faulty 524.3
Positive
culture (nonspecific) 795.3
   AIDS virus V08
   blood 790.7
   HIV V08
   human immunodeficiency virus V08
   nose 795.3
   skin lesion NEC 795.3
   spinal fluid 792.0
   sputum 795.3
   stool 792.1
   throat 795.3
   urine 599.0
   wound 795.3
HIV V08
human immunodeficiency virus (HIV) V08
PPD 795.5
serology
   AIDS virus V08
      inconclusive 795.71
   HIV V08
      inconclusive 795.71
   human immunodeficiency virus V08
      inconclusive 795.71
   syphilis 097.1
      with signs or symptoms - *see* Syphilis, by site and stage
      false 795.6
skin test 795.7
   tuberculin (without active tuberculosis) 795.5
VDRL 097.1
   with signs or symptoms - *see* Syphilis, by site and stage
   false 795.6
Wassermann reaction 097.1
   false 795.6
Postcardiotomy syndrome 429.4
Postcaval ureter 753.4
Postcholecystectomy syndrome 576.0

Postclimacteric bleeding 627.1
Postcommissurotomy syndrome 429.4
Postconcussional syndrome 310.2
Postcontusional syndrome 310.2
Postcricoid region - *see* condition
Post-dates (pregnancy) 645
Postencephalitic - *see also* condition
   syndrome 310.8
Posterior - *see* condition
Posterolateral sclerosis (spinal cord) - *see*
   Degeneration, combined
Postexanthematous - *see* condition
Postfebrile - *see* condition
Postgastrectomy dumping syndrome
   564.2
Posthemiplegic chorea 344.89
Posthemorrhagic anemia (chronic) 280.0
   acute 285.1
   newborn 776.5
Posthepatitis syndrome 780.79
Postherpetic neuralgia (intercostal) (syn-
   drome) (zoster) 053.19
   geniculate ganglion 053.11
   ophthalmica 053.19
   trigeminal 053.12
Posthitis 607.1
**Postimmunization complication or reac-
   tion** - *see* Complications, vaccination
Postinfectious - *see* condition
Postinfluenzal syndrome 780.79
Postlaminectomy syndrome 722.80
   cervical, cervicothoracic 722.81
   kyphosis 737.12
   lumbar, lumbosacral 722.83
   thoracic, thoracolumbar 722.82
Postleukotomy syndrome 310.0
Postlobectomy syndrome 310.0
Postmastectomy lymphedema (syndrome) 457.0
Postmaturity, postmature (fetus or newborn) 766.2
   affecting management of pregnancy 645
   syndrome 766.2
Postmeasles - *see also* condition
   complication 055.8
   specified NEC 055.79
Postmenopausal
   endometrium (atrophic) 627.8
      suppurative (*see also* Endometritis)
         615.9
   hormone replacement V07.4
Postnasal drip - *see* Sinusitis
Postnatal - *see* condition
Postoperative - *see also* condition
   confusion state 293.9
   psychosis 293.9
   status NEC (*see also* Status (post))
      V45.89
Postpancreatectomy hyperglycemia 251.3
Postpartum - *see also* condition
   observation
      immediately after delivery V24.0
      routine follow-up V24.2
Postperfusion syndrome NEC 999.8
   bone marrow 996.85
Postpoliomyelitic - *see* condition
Postsurgery status NEC (*see also* Status
   (post)) V45.89
Post-term (pregnancy) 645
   infant (294 days or more gestation)
      766.2
Posttraumatic - *see* condition
**Posttraumatic brain syndrome, nonpsy-
   chotic** 310.2

Post-typhoid abscess 002.0
Postures, hysterical 300.11
Postvaccinal reaction or complication -
   see Complications, vaccination
Postvagotomy syndrome 564.2
Postvalvulotomy syndrome 429.4
Postvasectomy sperm count V25.8
Potain's disease (pulmonary edema) 514
Potain's syndrome (gastrectasis with
   dyspepsia) 536.1
Pott's
   curvature (spinal) (*see also* Tuberculo-
      sis) 015.0 *[737.43]*
   disease or paraplegia (*see also* Tubercu-
      losis) 015.0 *[730.88]*
   fracture (closed) 824.4
      open 824.5
   gangrene 440.24
   osteomyelitis (*see also* Tuberculosis)
      015.0 *[730.88]*
   spinal curvature (*see also* Tuberculosis)
      015.0 *[737.43]*
   tumor, puffy (*see also* Osteomyelitis)
      730.2
Potter's
   asthma 502
   disease 753.0
   facies 754.0
   lung 502
   syndrome (with renal agenesis) 753.0
Pouch
   bronchus 748.3
   Douglas' - *see* condition
   esophagus, esophageal (congenital)
      750.4
      acquired 530.6
   gastric 537.1
   Hartmann's (abnormal sacculation of
      gallbladder neck) 575.8
   pharynx, pharyngeal (congenital) 750.27
Poulet's disease 714.2
Poultrymen's itch 133.8
Poverty V60.2
Prader-Labhart-Willi-Fanconi syndrome
   (hypogenital dystrophy with diabetic
   tendency) 759.81
Prader-Willi syndrome (hypogenital dystrophy with diabetic tendency)
   759.81
Preachers' voice 784.49
Pre-AIDS - *see* Human immunodeficiency virus (disease) (illness) (infection)
Preauricular appendage 744.1
Prebetalipoproteinemia (acquired) (essential) (familial) (hereditary) (primary) (secondary) 272.1
   with chylomicronemia 272.3
Precipitate labor 661.3
   affecting fetus or newborn 763.6
Preclimacteric bleeding 627.0
   menorrhagia 627.0
Precocious
   adrenarche 259.1
   menarche 259.1
   menstruation 626.8
   pubarche 259.1
   puberty NEC 259.1
   sexual development NEC 259.1
   thelarche 259.1
Precocity, sexual (constitutional) (cryptogenic) (female) (idiopathic) (male)
   NEC 259.1
   with adrenal hyperplasia 255.2

Precordial pain 786.51
   psychogenic 307.89
Predeciduous teeth 520.2
Prediabetes, prediabetic 790.2
   complicating pregnancy, childbirth, or
      puerperium 648.8
   fetus or newborn 775.8
Predislocation status of hip, at birth (*see
   also* Subluxation, congenital, hip)
   754.32
Pre-eclampsia (mild) 642.4
   with pre-existing hypertension 642.7
   affecting fetus or newborn 760.0
   severe 642.5
   superimposed on pre-existing hyper-
      tensive disease 642.7
Preeruptive color change, teeth, tooth
   520.8
Preexcitation 426.7
   atrioventricular conduction 426.7
   ventricular 426.7
Preglaucoma 365.00
Pregnancy (single) (uterine) (without
   sickness) V22.2

Note   Use the following fifth-digit
subclassification with categories 640-
648, 651-676:

0   unspecified as to episode of
     care
1   delivered, with or without
     mention of antepartum condi-
     tion
2   delivered, with mention of
     postpartum complication
3   antepartum condition or com-
     plication
4   postpartum condition or com-
     plication

---

   abdominal (ectopic) 633.0
      affecting fetus or newborn 761.4
   abnormal NEC 646.9
   ampullar - *see* Pregnancy, tubal
   broad ligament - *see* Pregnancy, cornual
   cervical - *see* Pregnancy, cornual
   combined (extrauterine and intrauter-
      ine) - *see* Pregnancy, cornual
   complicated (by)
      abnormal, abnormality NEC 646.9
         cervix 654.6
         cord (umbilical) 663.9
         glucose tolerance (conditions clas-
            sifiable to 790.2) 648.8
         pelvic organs or tissues NEC 654.9
         pelvis (bony) 653.0
         perineum or vulva 654.8
         placenta, placental (vessel) 656.7
         position
            cervix 654.4
            placenta 641.1
               without hemorrhage 641.0
            uterus 654.4
         size, fetus 653.5
         uterus (congenital) 654.0
      abscess or cellulitis
         bladder 646.6
         genitourinary tract (conditions
            classifiable to 590, 595, 597,
            599.0, 614-616) 646.6
         kidney 646.6
         urinary tract NEC 646.6
      air embolism 673.0

◄► **New Code**   ◄▬ ▬► **Revised Code**

Pregnancy (*Continued*)
  complicated (*Continued*)
    menstruation 640.8
    mental disorders (conditions classifiable to 290-303, 305-316, 317-319) 648.4
    mentum presentation 652.4
    missed
      abortion 632
      delivery (at or near term) 656.4
      labor (at or near term) 656.4
    necrosis
      genital organ or tract (conditions classifiable to 614-616) 646.6
      liver (conditions classifiable to 570) 646.7
      renal, cortical 646.2
    nephritis or nephrosis (conditions classifiable to 580-589) 646.2
      with hypertension 642.1
    nephropathy NEC 646.2
    neuritis (peripheral) 646.4
    nutritional deficiency (conditions classifiable to 260-269) 648.9
    oblique lie or presentation 652.3
      with successful version 652.1
    oligohydramnios NEC 658.0
    onset of contractions before 37 weeks 644.0
    oversize fetus 653.5
    papyraceous fetus 646.0
    patent cervix 654.5
    pelvic inflammatory disease (conditions classifiable to 614-616) 646.6
    placenta, placental
      abnormality 656.7
      abruptio or ablatio 641.2
      detachment 641.2
      disease 656.7
      infarct 656.7
      low implantation 641.1
        without hemorrhage 641.0
      malformation 656.7
      malposition 641.1
        without hemorrhage 641.0
      marginal sinus hemorrhage 641.2
      previa 641.1
        without hemorrhage 641.0
      separation (premature) (undelivered) 641.2
    placentitis 658.4
    polyhydramnios 657
    postmaturity 645
    prediabetes 648.8
    pre-eclampsia (mild) 642.4
      severe 642.5
      superimposed on pre-existing hypertensive disease 642.7
    premature rupture of membranes 658.1
      with delayed delivery 658.2
    previous
      infertility V23.0
      nonobstetric condition V23.8
      poor obstetrical history V23.4
      premature delivery V23.4
      trophoblastic disease (conditions classifiable to 630) V23.1
    prolapse, uterus 654.4
    proteinuria (gestational) 646.2
      with hypertension - *see* Toxemia, of pregnancy

Pregnancy (*Continued*)
  complicated (*Continued*)
    pruritus (neurogenic) 646.8
    psychosis or psychoneurosis 648.4
    ptyalism 646.8
    pyelitis (conditions classifiable to 590.0-590.9) 646.6
    renal disease or failure NEC 646.2
      with secondary hypertension 642.1
      hypertensive 642.2
    retention, retained dead ovum 631
    retroversion, uterus 654.3
    Rh immunization, incompatibility, or sensitization 656.1
    rubella (conditions classifiable to 056) 647.5
    rupture
      amnion (premature) 658.1
        with delayed delivery 658.2
      marginal sinus (hemorrhage) 641.2
      membranes (premature) 658.1
        with delayed delivery 658.2
      uterus (before onset of labor) 665.0
    salivation (excessive) 646.8
    salpingo-oophoritis (conditions classifiable to 614.0-614.2) 646.6
    septicemia (conditions classifiable to 038.0-038.9) 647.8
      postpartum 670 ◄
      puerperal 670 ◄
    spasms, uterus (abnormal) 646.8
    specified condition NEC 646.8
    spurious labor pains 644.1
    superfecundation 651.9
    superfetation 651.9
    syphilis (conditions classifiable to 090-097) 647.0
    threatened
      abortion 640.0
      premature delivery 644.2
      premature labor 644.0
    thrombophlebitis (superficial) 671.2
      deep 671.3
    thrombosis 671.9
      venous (superficial) 671.2
        deep 671.3
    thyroid dysfunction (conditions classifiable to 240-246) 648.1
    thyroiditis 648.1
    thyrotoxicosis 648.1
    torsion of uterus 654.4
    toxemia - *see* Toxemia, of pregnancy
    transverse lie or presentation 652.3
      with successful version 652.1
    trauma 648.9
      obstetrical 665.9
    tuberculosis (conditions classifiable to 010-018) 647.3
    tumor
      cervix 654.6
      ovary 654.4
      pelvic organs or tissue NEC 654.4
      uterus (body) 654.1
        cervix 654.6
      vagina 654.7
      vulva 654.8
    unstable lie 652.0
    uremia - *see* Pregnancy, complicated, renal disease
    urethritis 646.6
    vaginitis or vulvitis (conditions classifiable to 616.1) 646.6

Pregnancy (*Continued*)
  complicated (*Continued*)
    varicose
      placental vessels 656.7
      veins (legs) 671.0
        perineum 671.1
        vulva 671.1
    varicosity, labia or vulva 671.1
    venereal disease NEC (conditions classifiable to 099) 647.2
    viral disease NEC (conditions classifiable to 042, 050-055, 057-079) 647.6
    vomiting (incoercible) (pernicious) (persistent) (uncontrollable) (vicious) 643.9
      due to organic disease or other cause 643.8
      early - *see* Hyperemesis, gravidarum
      late (after 22 completed weeks gestation) 643.2
    young maternal age 659.8 ◄
  complications NEC 646.9
  cornual 633.8
    affecting fetus or newborn 761.4
  death, maternal NEC 646.9
  delivered - *see* Delivery
  ectopic (ruptured) NEC 633.9
    abdominal - *see* Pregnancy, abdominal
    affecting fetus or newborn 761.4
    combined (extrauterine and intrauterine) - *see* Pregnancy, cornual
    ovarian - *see* Pregnancy, ovarian
    specified type NEC 633.8
      affecting fetus or newborn 761.4
    tubal - *see* Pregnancy, tubal
  examination, pregnancy not confirmed V72.4
  extrauterine - *see* Pregnancy, ectopic
  fallopian - *see* Pregnancy, tubal
  false 300.11
    labor (pains) 644.1
  fatigue 646.8
  illegitimate V61.6
  incidental finding V22.2
  in double uterus 654.0
  interstitial - *see* Pregnancy, cornual
  intraligamentous - *see* Pregnancy, cornual
  intramural - *see* Pregnancy, cornual
  intraperitoneal - *see* Pregnancy, abdominal
  isthmian - *see* Pregnancy, tubal
  management affected by
    abnormal, abnormality
      fetus (suspected) 655.9
        specified NEC 655.8
      placenta 656.7
    advanced maternal age NEC 659.6
      multigravida 659.6 ◄
      primigravida 659.5
    antibodies (maternal)
      anti-c 656.1
      anti-d 656.1
      anti-e 656.1
      blood group (ABO) 656.2
        rh(esus) 656.1
    elderly multigravida 659.6 ◄
    elderly primigravida 659.5

Pregnancy (*Continued*)
  management affected by (*Continued*)
    fetal (suspected)
      abnormality 655.9
        acid-base balance 656.8 ◀▥▥
        heart rate or rhythm 659.7 ◀▥▥
        specified NEC 655.8
      acidemia 656.3
      anencephaly 655.0
      bradycardia 659.7 ◀▥▥
      central nervous system malformation 655.0
      chromosomal abnormalities (conditions classifiable to 758.0-758.9) 655.1
      damage from
        drugs 655.5
          obstetric, anesthetic, or sedative 655.5
        environmental toxins 655.8
        intrauterine contraceptive device 655.8
        maternal
          alcohol addiction 655.4
          disease NEC 655.4
          drug use 655.5
          listeriosis 655.4
          rubella 655.3
          toxoplasmosis 655.4
          viral infection 655.3
        radiation 655.6
      death (near term) 656.4
        early (before 22 completed weeks' gestation) 632
      distress 656.8 ◀▥▥
      excessive growth 656.6
      growth retardation 656.5
      hereditary disease 655.2
      hydrocephalus 655.0
      intrauterine death 656.4
      poor growth 656.5
      spina bifida (with myelomeningocele) 655.0
    fetal-maternal hemorrhage 656.0
    hereditary disease in family (possibly) affecting fetus 655.2
    incompatibility, blood groups (ABO) 656.2
      rh(esus) 656.1
    insufficient prenatal care V23.7
    intrauterine death 656.4
    isoimmunization (ABO) 656.2
      rh(esus) 656.1
    large-for-dates fetus 656.6
    light-for-dates fetus 656.5
    meconium in liquor 656.8 ◀▥▥
    mental disorder (conditions classifiable to 290-303, 305-316, 317-319) 648.4
    multiparity (grand) 659.4
    poor obstetric history V23.4
    postmaturity 645
    previous
      abortion V23.2
        habitual 646.3
      cesarean delivery 654.2
      difficult delivery V23.4
      forceps delivery V23.4
      habitual abortions 646.3
      hemorrhage, antepartum or postpartum V23.4
      hydatidiform mole V23.1
      infertility V23.0

Pregnancy (*Continued*)
  management affected by (*Continued*)
    previous (*Continued*)
      malignancy NEC V23.8
      nonobstetrical conditions V23.8
      premature delivery V23.4
      trophoblastic disease (conditions in 630) V23.1
      vesicular mole V23.1
    prolonged pregnancy 645
    small-for-dates fetus 656.5
    young maternal age 659.8 ◀
    maternal death NEC 646.9
    mesometric (mural) - *see* Pregnancy, cornual
    molar 631
      hydatidiform (*see also* Hydatidiform mole) 630
        previous, affecting management of pregnancy V23.1
      previous, affecting management of pregnancy V23.4
    multiple NEC 651.9
      with fetal loss and retention of one or more fetus(es) 651.6
      affecting fetus or newborn 761.5
      specified type NEC 651.8
        with fetal loss and retention of one or more fetus(es) 651.6
    mural - *see* Pregnancy, cornual
    observation NEC V22.1
      first pregnancy V22.0
      high-risk V23.9
        specified problem NEC V23.8
    ovarian 633.2
      affecting fetus or newborn 761.4
    postmature 645
    post-term 645
    prenatal care only V22.1
      first pregnancy V22.0
      high-risk V23.9
        specified problem NEC V23.8
    prolonged 645
    quadruplet NEC 651.2
      with fetal loss and retention of one or more fetus(es) 651.5
      affecting fetus or newborn 761.5
    quintuplet NEC 651.8
      with fetal loss and retention of one or more fetus(es) 651.6
      affecting fetus or newborn 761.5
    sextuplet NEC 651.8
      with fetal loss and retention of one or more fetus(es) 651.6
      affecting fetus or newborn 761.5
    spurious 300.11
    superfecundation NEC 651.9
      with fetal loss and retention of one or more fetus(es) 651.6
    superfetation NEC 651.9
      with fetal loss and retention of one or more fetus(es) 651.6
    supervision (of) (for) - *see also* Pregnancy, management affected by
      elderly ◀
        multigravida V23.82 ◀
        primigravida V23.81 ◀
      high-risk V23.9
        insufficient prenatal care V23.7
        specified problem NEC V23.8
      multiparity V23.3
      normal NEC V22.1
        first V22.0

Pregnancy (*Continued*)
  management affected by (*Continued*)
    poor
      obstetric history V23.4
      reproductive history V23.5
    previous
      abortion V23.2
      hydatidiform mole V23.1
      infertility V23.0
      neonatal death V23.5
      stillbirth V23.5
      trophoblastic disease V23.1
      vesicular mole V23.1
    specified problem NEC V23.8
    young ◀
      multigravida V23.84 ◀
      primigravida V23.83 ◀
    triplet NEC 651.1
      with fetal loss and retention of one or more fetus(es) 651.4
      affecting fetus or newborn 761.5
    tubal (with rupture) 633.1
      affecting fetus or newborn 761.4
    twin NEC 651.0
      with fetal loss and retention of one fetus 651.3
      affecting fetus or newborn 761.5
    unconfirmed V72.4
    undelivered (no other diagnosis) V22.2
      with false labor 644.1
      high-risk V23.9
        specified problem NEC V23.8
    unwanted NEC V61.7
    young ◀
      multigravida V23.84 ◀
      primigravida V23.83 ◀
Pregnant uterus - *see* condition
Preiser's disease (osteoporosis) 733.09
Prekwashiorkor 260
Preleukemia 238.7
Preluxation of hip, congenital (*see also* Subluxation, congenital, hip) 754.32
Premature - *see also* condition
  beats (nodal) 427.60
    atrial 427.61
    auricular 427.61
    postoperative 997.1
    specified type NEC 427.69
    supraventricular 427.61
    ventricular 427.69
  birth NEC 765.1
  closure
    cranial suture 756.0
    fontanel 756.0
    foramen ovale 745.8
  contractions 427.60
    atrial 427.61
    auricular 427.61
    auriculoventricular 427.61
    heart (extrasystole) 427.60
    junctional 427.60
    nodal 427.60
    postoperative 997.1
    ventricular 427.69
  ejaculation 302.75
  infant NEC 765.1
    excessive 765.0
    light-for-dates - *see* Light-for-dates
  labor 644.2
    threatened 644.0
  lungs 770.4
  menopause 256.3
  puberty 259.1

Problem *(Continued)*
life circumstance NEC V62.89
lifestyle V69.9
  specified NEC V69.8
limb V49.9
  deficiency V49.0
  disfigurement V49.4
  mechanical V49.1
  motor V49.2
  movement, involving
    musculoskeletal system V49.1
    nervous system V49.2
  sensory V49.3
  specified condition NEC V49.5
litigation V62.5
living alone V60.3
loneliness NEC V62.89
marital V61.10
  involving
    divorce V61.0
    estrangement V61.0
    psychosexual disorder 302.9
    sexual function V41.7
mastication V41.6
medical care, within family V61.49
mental V40.9
  specified NEC V40.2
mental hygiene, adult V40.9
multiparity V61.5
nail biting, child 307.9
neck V48.9
  deficiency V48.1
  disfigurement V48.7
  mechanical V48.3
  motor V48.3
  movement V48.3
  sensory V48.5
  specified condition NEC V48.8
neurological NEC 781.9
none (feared complaint unfounded) V65.5
occupational V62.2
parent-child V61.20
partner V61.10
personal NEC V62.89
  interpersonal conflict NEC V62.81
personality *(see also* Disorder, personality) 301.9
phase of life V62.89
placenta, affecting management of pregnancy 656.9
  specified type NEC 656.8
poverty V60.2
presence of sick or handicapped person in family or household V61.49
psychiatric 300.9
psychosocial V62.9
  specified type NEC V62.89
relational NEC V62.81
relationship, childhood 313.3
religious or spiritual belief
  other than medical care V62.89
  regarding medical care V62.6
self-damaging behavior V69.8
sexual
  behavior, high-risk V69.2
function NEC V41.7
sibling relational V61.8
sight V41.0
sleep disorder, child 307.40
smell V41.5
speech V40.1
spite reaction, child *(see also* Disturbance, conduct) 312.0

Problem *(Continued)*
spoiled child reaction *(see also* Disturbance, conduct) 312.1
swallowing V41.6
tantrum, child *(see also* Disturbance, conduct) 312.1
taste V41.5
thumb sucking, child 307.9
tic, child 307.21
trunk V48.9
  deficiency V48.1
  disfigurement V48.7
  mechanical V48.3
  motor V48.3
  movement V48.3
  sensory V48.5
  specified condition NEC V48.8
unemployment V62.0
urinary NEC V47.4
voice production V41.4
Procedure (surgical) not done NEC V64.3
  because of
    contraindication V64.1
    patient's decision V64.2
      for reasons of conscience or religion V62.6
    specified reason NEC V64.3
Procidentia
anus (sphincter) 569.1
rectum (sphincter) 569.1
stomach 537.89
uteri 618.1
Proctalgia 569.42
fugax 564.6
spasmodic 564.6
  psychogenic 307.89
Proctitis 569.49
amebic 006.8
chlamydial 099.52
gonococcal 098.7
granulomatous 555.1
idiopathic 556.2
  with ulcerative sigmoiditis 556.3
tuberculous *(see also* Tuberculosis) 014.8
ulcerative (chronic) (nonspecific) 556.2
  with ulcerative sigmoiditis 556.3
Proctocele
female (without uterine prolapse) 618.0
  with uterine prolapse 618.4
    complete 618.3
    incomplete 618.2
male 569.49
Proctocolitis, idiopathic 556.2
with ulcerative sigmoiditis 556.3
Proctoptosis 569.1
Proctosigmoiditis 569.89
ulcerative (chronic) 556.3
Proctospasm 564.6
psychogenic 306.4
Prodromal-AIDS - *see* Human immunodeficiency virus (disease) (illness) (infection)
Profichet's disease or syndrome 729.9
Progeria (adultorum) (syndrome) 259.8
Prognathism (mandibular) (maxillary) 524.00
Progonoma (melanotic) (M9363/0) - *see* Neoplasm, by site, benign
Progressive - *see* condition

Prolapse, prolapsed
anus, anal (canal) (sphincter) 569.1
arm or hand, complicating delivery 652.7
  causing obstructed labor 660.0
    affecting fetus or newborn 763.1
  fetus or newborn 763.1
bladder (acquired) (mucosa) (sphincter)
  congenital (female) (male) 756.71
  female 618.0
  male 596.8
breast implant (prosthetic) 996.54
cecostomy 569.69
cecum 569.89
cervix, cervical (stump) (hypertrophied) 618.1
  anterior lip, obstructing labor 660.2
    affecting fetus or newborn 763.1
  congenital 752.49
  postpartal (old) 618.1
ciliary body 871.1
colon (pedunculated) 569.89
colostomy 569.69
conjunctiva 372.73
cord - *see* Prolapse, umbilical cord
disc (intervertebral) - *see* Displacement, intervertebral disc
duodenum 537.89
eye implant (orbital) 996.59
  lens (ocular) 996.53
fallopian tube 620.4
fetal extremity, complicating delivery 652.8
  causing obstructed labor 660.0
  fetus or newborn 763.1
funis - *see* Prolapse, umbilical cord
gastric (mucosa) 537.89
genital, female 618.9
  specified NEC 618.8
globe 360.81
ileostomy bud 569.69
intervertebral disc - *see* Displacement, intervertebral disc
intestine (small) 569.89
iris 364.8
  traumatic 871.1
kidney *(see also* Disease, renal) 593.0
  congenital 753.3
laryngeal muscles or ventricle 478.79
leg, complicating delivery 652.8
  causing obstructed labor 660.0
  fetus or newborn 763.1
liver 573.8
meatus urinarius 599.5
mitral valve 424.0
ocular lens implant 996.53
organ or site, congenital NEC - *see* Malposition, congenital
ovary 620.4
pelvic (floor), female 618.8
perineum, female 618.8
pregnant uterus 654.4
rectum (mucosa) (sphincter) 569.1
  due to Trichuris trichiuria 127.3
spleen 289.59
stomach 537.89
umbilical cord
  affecting fetus or newborn 762.4
  complicating delivery 663.0
ureter 593.89
  with obstruction 593.4
ureterovesical orifice 593.89

Prolapse, prolapsed *(Continued)*
  urethra (acquired) (infected) (mucosa)
    599.5
    congenital 753.8
  uterovaginal 618.4
    complete 618.3
    incomplete 618.2
    specified NEC 618.8
  uterus (first degree) (second degree)
    (third degree) (complete) (without
    vaginal wall prolapse) 618.1
    with mention of vaginal wall pro-
      lapse - *see* Prolapse, uterovagi-
      nal
    congenital 752.3
    in pregnancy or childbirth 654.4
      affecting fetus or newborn 763.1
      causing obstructed labor 660.2
        affecting fetus or newborn 763.1
    postpartal (old) 618.1
  uveal 871.1
  vagina (anterior) (posterior) (vault)
    (wall) (without uterine prolapse)
    618.0
    with uterine prolapse 618.4
      complete 618.3
      incomplete 618.2
    posthysterectomy 618.5
  vitreous (humor) 379.26
    traumatic 871.1
  womb - *see* Prolapse, uterus
Prolapsus, female 618.9
Proliferative - *see* condition
Prolinemia 270.8
Prolinuria 270.8
Prolonged, prolongation
  bleeding time (*see also* Defect, coagula-
    tion) 790.92
  "idiopathic" (in von Willebrand's dis-
    ease) 286.4
  coagulation time (*see also* Defect, coag-
    ulation) 790.92
  gestation syndrome 766.2
  labor 662.1
    affecting fetus or newborn 763.89
    first stage 662.0
    second stage 662.2
  PR interval 426.11
  prothrombin time (*see also* Defect, co-
    agulation) 790.92
  rupture of membranes (24 hours or
    more prior to onset of labor) 658.2
  uterine contractions in labor 661.4
    affecting fetus or newborn 763.7
Prominauris 744.29
Prominence
  auricle (ear) (congenital) 744.29
    acquired 380.32
  ischial spine or sacral promontory
    with disproportion (fetopelvic) 653.3
      affecting fetus or newborn 763.1
      causing obstructed labor 660.1
        affecting fetus or newborn 763.1
  nose (congenital) 748.1
    acquired 738.0
Pronation
  ankle 736.79
  foot 736.79
    congenital 755.67
Prophylactic
  administration of
    antibiotics V07.39
    antitoxin, any V07.2
    antivenin V07.2

Prophylactic *(Continued)*
  administration of *(Continued)*
    chemotherapeutic agent NEC V07.39
      fluoride V07.31
    diphtheria antitoxin V07.2
    gamma globulin V07.2
    immune sera (gamma globulin)
      V07.2
    RhoGAM V07.2
    tetanus antitoxin V07.2
    chemotherapy NEC V07.39
      fluoride V07.31
    immunotherapy V07.2
    measure V07.9
      specified type NEC V07.8
    postmenopausal hormone replacement
      V07.4
    sterilization V25.2
Proptosis (ocular) (*see also* Exophthal-
    mos) 376.30
  thyroid 242.0
Propulsion
  eyeball 360.81
Prosecution, anxiety concerning V62.5
Prostate, prostatic - *see* condition
Prostatism 600
Prostatitis (congestive) (suppurative)
    601.9
  acute 601.0
  cavitary 601.8
  chlamydial 099.54
  chronic 601.1
  diverticular 601.8
  due to Trichomonas (vaginalis) 131.03
  fibrous 600
  gonococcal (acute) 098.12
    chronic or duration of 2 months or
      over 098.32
  granulomatous 601.8
  hypertrophic 600
  specified type NEC 601.8
  subacute 601.1
  trichomonal 131.03
  tuberculous (*see also* Tuberculosis)
    016.5 *[601.4]*
Prostatocystitis 601.3
Prostatorrhea 602.8
Prostatoseminovesiculitis, trichomonal
    131.03
Prostration 780.79
  heat 992.5
    anhydrotic 992.3
    due to
      salt (and water) depletion 992.4
      water depletion 992.3
  nervous 300.5
  newborn 779.8
  senile 797
Protanomaly 368.51
Protanopia (anomalous trichromat) (com-
    plete) (incomplete) 368.51
Protein
  deficiency 260
  malnutrition 260
  sickness (prophylactic) (therapeutic)
    999.5
Proteinemia 790.99
Proteinosis
  alveolar, lung or pulmonary 516.0
  lipid 272.8
  lipoid (of Urbach) 272.8
Proteinuria (*see also* Albuminuria)
    791.0
  Bence-Jones NEC 791.0

Proteinuria *(Continued)*
  gestational 646.2
    with hypertension - *see* Toxemia, of
      pregnancy
  orthostatic 593.6
  postural 593.6
Proteolysis, pathologic 286.6
Protocoproporphyria 277.1
Protoporphyria (erythrohepatic) (erythro-
    poietic) 277.1
Protrusio acetabuli 718.65
Protrusion
  acetabulum (into pelvis) 718.65
  device, implant, or graft - *see* Compli-
    cations, mechanical
  ear, congenital 744.29
  intervertebral disc - *see* Displacement,
    intervertebral disc
  nucleus pulposus - *see* Displacement,
    intervertebral disc
Proud flesh 701.5
Prune belly (syndrome) 756.71
Prurigo (ferox) (gravis) (Hebra's) (he-
    brae) (mitis) (simplex) 698.2
  agria 698.3
  asthma syndrome 691.8
  Besnier's (atopic dermatitis) (infantile
    eczema) 691.8
  eczematodes allergicum 691.8
  estivalis (Hutchinson's) 692.72
  Hutchinson's 692.72
  nodularis 698.3
  psychogenic 306.3
Pruritus, pruritic 698.9
  ani 698.0
    psychogenic 306.3
  conditions NEC 698.9
    psychogenic 306.3
  due to Onchocerca volvulus 125.3
  ear 698.9
  essential 698.9
  genital organ(s) 698.1
    psychogenic 306.3
  gravidarum 646.8
  hiemalis 698.8
  neurogenic (any site) 306.3
  perianal 698.0
  psychogenic (any site) 306.3
  scrotum 698.1
    psychogenic 306.3
  senile, senilis 698.8
  trichomonas 131.9
  vulva, vulvae 698.1
    psychogenic 306.3
Psammocarcinoma (M8140/3) - *see* Neo-
    plasm, by site, malignant
Pseudarthrosis, pseudoarthrosis (bone)
    733.82
  joint following fusion V45.4
Pseudoacanthosis
  nigricans 701.8
Pseudoaneurysm - *see* Aneurysm
Pseudoangina (pectoris) - *see* Angina
Pseudoangioma 452
Pseudo-Argyll-Robertson pupil 379.45
Pseudoarteriosus 747.89
Pseudoarthrosis - *see* Pseudarthrosis
Pseudoataxia 799.8
Pseudobursa 727.89
Pseudocholera 025
Pseudochromidrosis 705.89
Pseudocirrhosis, liver, pericardial 423.2
Pseudocoarctation 747.21
Pseudocowpox 051.1

Pseudocoxalgia 732.1
Pseudocroup 478.75
Pseudocyesis 300.11
Pseudocyst
lung 518.89
pancreas 577.2
retina 361.19
Pseudodementia 300.16
Pseudoelephantiasis neuroarthritica 757.0
Pseudoemphysema 518.89
Pseudoencephalitis
superior (acute) hemorrhagic 265.1
Pseudoerosion cervix, congenital 752.49
Pseudoexfoliation, lens capsule 366.11
Pseudofracture (idiopathic) (multiple) (spontaneous) (symmetrical) 268.2
Pseudoglanders 025
Pseudoglioma 360.44
Pseudogout - *see* Chondrocalcinosis
Pseudohallucination 780.1
Pseudohemianesthesia 782.0
Pseudohemophilia (Bernuth's) (hereditary) (type B) 286.4
type A 287.8
vascular 287.8
Pseudohermaphroditism 752.7
with chromosomal anomaly - *see* Anomaly, chromosomal
adrenal 255.2
female (without adrenocortical disorder) 752.7
with adrenocortical disorder 255.2
adrenal 255.2
male (without gonadal disorder) 752.7
with
adrenocortical disorder 255.2
cleft scrotum 752.7
feminizing testis 257.8
gonadal disorder 257.9
adrenal 255.2
Pseudohole, macula 362.54
Pseudo-Hurler's disease (mucolipidosis III) 272.7
Pseudohydrocephalus 348.2
Pseudohypertrophic muscular dystrophy (Erb's) 359.1
Pseudohypertrophy, muscle 359.1
Pseudohypoparathyroidism 275.49
Pseudoinfluenza 487.1
Pseudoinsomnia 307.49
Pseudoleukemia 288.8
infantile 285.8
Pseudomembranous - *see* condition
Pseudomeningocele (cerebral) (infective) (surgical) 349.2
spinal 349.2
Pseudomenstruation 626.8
Pseudomucinous
cyst (ovary) (M8470/0) 220
peritoneum 568.89
Pseudomyeloma 273.1
Pseudomyxoma peritonei (M8480/6) 197.6
Pseudoneuritis optic (nerve) 377.24
papilla 377.24
congenital 743.57
Pseudoneuroma - *see* Injury, nerve, by site
Pseudo-obstruction
intestine 564.89
Pseudopapilledema 377.24
Pseudoparalysis
arm or leg 781.4
atonic, congenital 358.8

Pseudopelade 704.09
Pseudophakia V43.1
Pseudopolycythemia 289.0
Pseudopolyposis, colon 556.4
Pseudoporencephaly 348.0
Pseudopseudohypoparathyroidism 275.49
Pseudopsychosis 300.16
Pseudopterygium 372.52
Pseudoptosis (eyelid) 374.34
Pseudorabies 078.89
Pseudoretinitis, pigmentosa 362.65
Pseudorickets 588.0
senile (Pozzi's) 731.0
Pseudorubella 057.8
Pseudoscarlatina 057.8
Pseudosclerema 778.1
Pseudosclerosis (brain)
Jakob's 046.1
of Westphal (-Strümpell) (hepatolenticular degeneration) 275.1
spastic 046.1
with dementia 046.1 [294.1]
Pseudotabes 799.8
diabetic 250.6 [337.1]
Pseudotetanus (*see also* Convulsions) 780.39
Pseudotetany 781.7
hysterical 300.11
Pseudothalassemia 285.0
Pseudotrichinosis 710.3
Pseudotruncus arteriosus 747.29
Pseudotuberculosis, pasteurella (infection) 027.2
Pseudotumor
cerebri 348.2
orbit (inflammatory) 376.11
Pseudo-Turner's syndrome 759.89
Pseudoxanthoma elasticum 757.39
Psilosis (sprue) (tropical) 579.1
Monilia 112.89
nontropical 579.0
not sprue 704.00
Psittacosis 073.9
Psoitis 728.89
Psora NEC 696.1
Psoriasis 696.1
any type, except arthropathic 696.1
arthritic, arthropathic 696.0
buccal 528.6
flexural 696.1
follicularis 696.1
guttate 696.1
inverse 696.1
mouth 528.6
nummularis 696.1
psychogenic 316 [696.1]
punctata 696.1
pustular 696.1
rupioides 696.1
vulgaris 696.1
Psorospermiasis 136.4
Psorospermosis 136.4
follicularis (vegetans) 757.39
Psychalgia 307.80
Psychasthenia 300.89
compulsive 300.3
mixed compulsive states 300.3
obsession 300.3
Psychiatric disorder or problem NEC 300.9
Psychogenic - *see also* condition
factors associated with physical conditions 316

Psychoneurosis, psychoneurotic (*see also* Neurosis) 300.9
anxiety (state) 300.00
climacteric 627.2
compensation 300.16
compulsion 300.3
conversion hysteria 300.11
depersonalization 300.6
depressive type 300.4
dissociative hysteria 300.15
hypochondriacal 300.7
hysteria 300.10
conversion type 300.11
dissociative type 300.15
mixed NEC 300.89
neurasthenic 300.5
obsessional 300.3
obsessive-compulsive 300.3
occupational 300.89
personality NEC 301.89
phobia 300.20
senile NEC 300.89
Psychopathic - *see also* condition
constitution, posttraumatic 310.2
with psychosis 293.9
personality 301.9
amoral trends 301.7
antisocial trends 301.7
asocial trends 301.7
mixed types 301.7
state 301.9
Psychopathy, sexual (*see also* Deviation, sexual) 302.9
Psychophysiologic, psychophysiological condition - *see* Reaction, psychophysiologic
Psychose passionelle 297.8
Psychosexual identity disorder 302.6
adult-life 302.85
childhood 302.6
Psychosis 298.9
acute hysterical 298.1
affecting management of pregnancy, childbirth, or puerperium 648.4
affective NEC 296.90
drug-induced 292.84 ◄
due to or associated with physical condition 293.83 ◄

> Note Use the following fifth-digit subclassification with categories 296.0-296.6:
>
> 0   unspecified
> 1   mild
> 2   moderate
> 3   severe, without mention of psychotic behavior
> 4   severe, specified as with psychotic behavior
> 5   in partial or unspecified remission
> 6   in full remission

involutional 296.2
recurrent episode 296.3
single episode 296.2
manic-depressive 296.80
circular (alternating) 296.7
currently depressed 296.5
currently manic 296.4
depressed type 296.2
atypical 296.82
recurrent episode 296.3
single episode 296.2

ICD-9-CM

P

Vol. 2

Puberty V21.1
  abnormal 259.9
  bleeding 626.3
  delayed 259.0
  precocious (constitutional) (crypto-
    genic) (idiopathic) NEC 259.1
    due to
      adrenal
        cortical hyperfunction 255.2
          hyperplasia 255.2
      cortical hyperfunction 255.2
      ovarian hyperfunction 256.1
        estrogen 256.0
      pineal tumor 259.8
      testicular hyperfunction 257.0
  premature 259.1
    due to
      adrenal cortical hyperfunction
        255.2
      pineal tumor 259.8
      pituitary (anterior) hyperfunction
        253.1
Puckering, macula 362.56
Pudenda, pudendum - *see* condition
Puente's disease (simple glandular cheil-
  itis) 528.5
Puerperal
  abscess
    areola 675.1
    Bartholin's gland 646.6
    breast 675.1
    cervix (uteri) 670
    fallopian tube 670
    genital organ 670
    kidney 646.6
    mammary 675.1
    mesosalpinx 670
    nabothian 646.6
    nipple 675.0
    ovary, ovarian 670
    oviduct 670
    parametric 670
    para-uterine 670
    pelvic 670
    perimetric 670
    periuterine 670
    retro-uterine 670
    subareolar 675.1
    suprapelvic 670
    tubal (ruptured) 670
    tubo-ovarian 670
    urinary tract NEC 646.6
    uterine, uterus 670
    vagina (wall) 646.6
    vaginorectal 646.6
    vulvovaginal gland 646.6
  accident 674.9
  adnexitis 670
  afibrinogenemia, or other coagulation
    defect 666.3
  albuminuria (acute) (subacute) 646.2
    pre-eclamptic 642.4
  anemia (conditions classifiable to 280-
    285) 648.2
  anuria 669.3
  apoplexy 674.0
  asymptomatic bacteriuria 646.5
  atrophy, breast 676.3
  blood dyscrasia 666.3
  caked breast 676.2
  cardiomyopathy 674.8
  cellulitis - *see* Puerperal, abscess
  cerebrovascular disorder (conditions clas-
    sifiable to 430-434, 436-437) 674.0

Puerperal (*Continued*)
  cervicitis (conditions classifiable to
    616.0) 646.6
  coagulopathy (any) 666.3
  complications 674.9
    specified type NEC 674.8
  convulsions (eclamptic) (uremic) 642.6
    with pre-existing hypertension 642.7
  cracked nipple 676.1
  cystitis 646.6
  cystopyelitis 646.6
  deciduitis (acute) 670
  delirium NEC 293.9
  diabetes (mellitus) (conditions classifia-
    ble to 250) 648.0
  disease 674.9
    breast NEC 676.3
    cerebrovascular (acute) 674.0
    nonobstetric NEC (*see also* Preg-
      nancy, complicated, current dis-
      ease or condition) 648.9
    pelvis inflammatory 670
    renal NEC 646.2
    tubo-ovarian 670
    Valsuani's (progressive pernicious
      anemia) 648.2
  disorder
    lactation 676.9
      specified type NEC 676.8
    nonobstetric NEC (*see also* Preg-
      nancy, complicated, current dis-
      ease or condition) 648.9
  disruption
    cesarean wound 674.1
    episiotomy wound 674.2
    perineal laceration wound 674.2
  drug dependence (conditions classifia-
    ble to 304) 648.3
  eclampsia 642.6
    with pre-existing hypertension 642.7
  embolism (pulmonary) 673.2
    air 673.0
    amniotic fluid 673.1
    blood clot 673.2
    brain or cerebral 674.0
    cardiac 674.8
    fat 673.8
    intracranial sinus (venous) 671.5
    pyemic 673.3
    septic 673.3
    spinal cord 671.5
  endometritis (conditions classifiable to
    615.0-615.9) 670
  endophlebitis - *see* Puerperal, phlebitis
  endotrachelitis 646.6
  engorgement, breasts 676.2
  erysipelas 670
  failure
    lactation 676.4
    renal, acute 669.3
  fever 670 ⬅
    meaning pyrexia (of unknown ori-
      gin) 672
    meaning sepsis 670 ◀
  fissure, nipple 676.1
  fistula
    breast 675.1
    mammary gland 675.1
    nipple 675.0
  galactophoritis 675.2
  galactorrhea 676.6
  gangrene
    gas 670
    uterus 670

Puerperal (*Continued*)
  gonorrhea (conditions classifiable to
    098) 647.1
  hematoma, subdural 674.0
  hematosalpinx, infectional 670
  hemiplegia, cerebral 674.0
  hemorrhage 666.1
    brain 674.0
    bulbar 674.0
    cerebellar 674.0
    cerebral 674.0
    cortical 674.0
    delayed (after 24 hours) (uterine) 666.2
    extradural 674.0
    internal capsule 674.0
    intracranial 674.0
    intrapontine 674.0
    meningeal 674.0
    pontine 674.0
    subarachnoid 674.0
    subcortical 674.0
    subdural 674.0
    uterine, delayed 666.2
    ventricular 674.0
  hemorrhoids 671.8
  hepatorenal syndrome 674.8
  hypertrophy
    breast 676.3
    mammary gland 676.3
  induration breast (fibrous) 676.3
  infarction
    lung - *see* Puerperal, embolism
    pulmonary - *see* Puerperal, embolism
  infection
    Bartholin's gland 646.6
    breast 675.2
      with nipple 675.9
        specified type NEC 675.8
    cervix 646.6
    endocervix 646.6
    fallopian tube 670
    generalized 670
    genital tract (major) 670
      minor or localized 646.6
    kidney (bacillus coli) 646.6
    mammary gland 675.2
      with nipple 675.9
        specified type NEC 675.8
    nipple 675.0
      with breast 675.9
        specified type NEC 675.8
    ovary 670
    pelvic 670
    peritoneum 670
    renal 646.6
    tubo-ovarian 670
    urinary (tract) NEC 646.6
      asymptomatic 646.5
    uterus, uterine 670
    vagina 646.6
  inflammation - *see also* Puerperal, in-
    fection
    areola 675.1
    Bartholin's gland 646.6
    breast 675.2
    broad ligament 670
    cervix (uteri) 646.6
    fallopian tube 670
    genital organs 670
      localized 646.6
    mammary gland 675.2
    nipple 675.0
    ovary 670
    oviduct 670

Puerperal *(Continued)*
  inflammation *(Continued)*
    pelvis 670
    periuterine 670
    tubal 670
    vagina 646.6
    vein - *see* Puerperal, phlebitis
  inversion, nipple 676.3
  ischemia, cerebral 674.0
  lymphangitis 670
    breast 675.2
  malaria (conditions classifiable to 084) 647.4
  malnutrition 648.9
  mammillitis 675.0
  mammitis 675.2
  mania 296.0
    recurrent episode 296.1
    single episode 296.0
  mastitis 675.2
    purulent 675.1
    retromammary 675.1
    submammary 675.1
  melancholia 296.2
    recurrent episode 296.3
    single episode 296.2
  mental disorder (conditions classifiable to 290-303, 305-316, 317-319) 648.4
  metritis (septic) (suppurative) 670
  metroperitonitis 670
  metrorrhagia 666.2
  metrosalpingitis 670
  metrovaginitis 670
  milk leg 671.4
  monoplegia, cerebral 674.0
  necrosis
    kidney, tubular 669.3
    liver (acute) (subacute) (conditions classifiable to 570) 674.8
    ovary 670
    renal cortex 669.3
  nephritis or nephrosis (conditions classifiable to 580-589) 646.2
    with hypertension 642.1
  nutritional deficiency (conditions classifiable to 260-269) 648.9
  occlusion, precerebral artery 674.0
  oliguria 669.3
  oophoritis 670
  ovaritis 670
  paralysis
    bladder (sphincter) 665.5
    cerebral 674.0
  paralytic stroke 674.0
  parametritis 670
  paravaginitis 646.6
  pelviperitonitis 670
  perimetritis 670
  perimetrosalpingitis 670
  perinephritis 646.6
  perioophoritis 670
  periphlebitis - *see* Puerperal, phlebitis
  perisalpingitis 670
  peritoneal infection 670
  peritonitis (pelvic) 670
  perivaginitis 646.6
  phlebitis 671.9
    deep 671.4
    intracranial sinus (venous) 671.5
    pelvic 671.4
    specified site NEC 671.5
    superficial 671.2
  phlegmasia alba dolens 671.4
  placental polyp 674.4

Puerperal *(Continued)*
  pneumonia, embolic - *see* Puerperal, embolism
  prediabetes 648.8
  pre-eclampsia (mild) 642.4
    with pre-existing hypertension 642.7
    severe 642.5
  psychosis, unspecified (*see also* Psychosis, puerperal) 293.89
  pyelitis 646.6
  pyelocystitis 646.6
  pyelohydronephrosis 646.6
  pyelonephritis 646.6
  pyelonephrosis 646.6
  pyemia 670
  pyocystitis 646.6
  pyohemia 670
  pyometra 670
  pyonephritis 646.6
  pyonephrosis 646.6
  pyo-oophoritis 670
  pyosalpingitis 670
  pyosalpinx 670
  pyrexia (of unknown origin) 672
  renal
    disease NEC 646.2
    failure, acute 669.3
  retention
    decidua (fragments) (with delayed hemorrhage) 666.2
      without hemorrhage 667.1
    placenta (fragments) (with delayed hemorrhage) 666.2
      without hemorrhage 667.1
    secundines (fragments) (with delayed hemorrhage) 666.2
      without hemorrhage 667.1
  retracted nipple 676.0
  rubella (conditions classifiable to 056) 647.5
  salpingitis 670
  salpingo-oophoritis 670
  salpingo-ovaritis 670
  salpingoperitonitis 670
  sapremia 670
  secondary perineal tear 674.2
  sepsis (pelvic) 670
  septicemia 670
  subinvolution (uterus) 674.8
  sudden death (cause unknown) 674.9
  suppuration - *see* Puerperal, abscess
  syphilis (conditions classifiable to 090-097) 647.0
  tetanus 670
  thelitis 675.0
  thrombocytopenia 666.3
  thrombophlebitis (superficial) 671.2
    deep 671.4
    pelvic 671.4
    specified site NEC 671.5
  thrombosis (venous) - *see* Thrombosis, puerperal
  thyroid dysfunction (conditions classifiable to 240-246) 648.1
  toxemia (*see also* Toxemia, of pregnancy) 642.4
    eclamptic 642.6
      with pre-existing hypertension 642.7
    pre-eclamptic (mild) 642.4
      with
        convulsions 642.6
        pre-existing hypertension 642.7
      severe 642.5

Puerperal *(Continued)*
  tuberculosis (conditions classifiable to 010-018) 647.3
  uremia 669.3
  vaginitis (conditions classifiable to 616.1) 646.6
  varicose veins (legs) 671.0
    vulva or perineum 671.1
  vulvitis (conditions classifiable to 616.1) 646.6
  vulvovaginitis (conditions classifiable to 616.1) 646.6
  white leg 671.4
Pulled muscle - *see* Sprain, by site
Pulmolithiasis 518.89
Pulmonary - *see* condition
Pulmonitis (unknown etiology) 486
Pulpitis (acute) (anachoretic) (chronic) (hyperplastic) (putrescent) (suppurative) (ulcerative) 522.0
Pulpless tooth 522.9
Pulse
  alternating 427.89
    psychogenic 306.2
  bigeminal 427.89
  fast 785.0
  feeble, rapid, due to shock following injury 958.4
  rapid 785.0
  slow 427.89
  strong 785.9
  trigeminal 427.89
  water-hammer (*see also* Insufficiency, aortic) 424.1
  weak 785.9
Pulseless disease 446.7
Pulsus
  alternans or trigeminy 427.89
    psychogenic 306.2
Punch drunk 310.2
Puncta lacrimalia occlusion 375.52
Punctiform hymen 752.49
Puncture (traumatic) - *see also* Wound, open, by site
  accidental, complicating surgery 998.2
  bladder, nontraumatic 596.6
  by
    device, implant, or graft - *see* Complications, mechanical
    foreign body
      internal organs - *see also* Injury, internal, by site
      by ingested object - *see* Foreign body
      left accidentally in operation wound 998.4
    instrument (any) during a procedure, accidental 998.2
  internal organs, abdomen, chest, or pelvis - *see* Injury, internal, by site
  kidney, nontraumatic 593.89
Pupil - *see* condition
Pupillary membrane 364.74
  persistent 743.46
Pupillotonia 379.46
  pseudotabetic 379.46
Purpura 287.2
  abdominal 287.0
  allergic 287.0
  anaphylactoid 287.0
  annularis telangiectodes 709.1
  arthritic 287.0
  autoerythrocyte sensitization 287.2
  autoimmune 287.0

ICD-9-CM

P

Vol. 2

Purpura *(Continued)*
  bacterial 287.0
  Bateman's (senile) 287.2
  capillary fragility (hereditary) (idio-
      pathic) 287.8
  cryoglobulinemic 273.2
  devil's pinches 287.2
  fibrinolytic *(see also* Fibrinolysis) 286.6
  fulminans, fulminous 286.6
  gangrenous 287.0
  hemorrhagic *(see also* Purpura, throm-
      bocytopenic) 287.3
    nodular 272.7
    nonthrombocytopenic 287.0
    thrombocytopenic 287.3
  Henoch's (purpura nervosa) 287.0
  Henoch-Schönlein (allergic) 287.0
  hypergammaglobulinemic (benign pri-
      mary) (Waldenström's) 273.0
  idiopathic 287.3
    nonthrombocytopenic 287.0
    thrombocytopenic 287.3
  infectious 287.0
  malignant 287.0
  neonatorum 772.6
  nervosa 287.0
  newborn NEC 772.6
  nonthrombocytopenic 287.2
    hemorrhagic 287.0
    idiopathic 287.0
  nonthrombopenic 287.2
  peliosis rheumatica 287.0
  pigmentaria, progressiva 709.09
  posttransfusion 287.4
  primary 287.0
  primitive 287.0
  red cell membrane sensitivity 287.2
  rheumatica 287.0
  Schönlein (-Henoch) (allergic) 287.0
  scorbutic 267
  senile 287.2
  simplex 287.2
  symptomatica 287.0
  telangiectasia annularis 709.1
  thrombocytopenic (congenital) (essential)
      (hereditary) (idiopathic) (primary)
      (see also Thrombocytopenia) 287.3
    neonatal, transitory *(see also* Throm-
        bocytopenia, neonatal transi-
        tory) 776.1
    puerperal, postpartum 666.3
    thrombotic 446.6
  thrombohemolytic *(see also* Fibrinoly-
      sis) 286.6
  thrombopenic (congenital) (essential)
      (see also Thrombocytopenia) 287.3
  thrombotic 446.6
    thrombocytic 446.6
    thrombocytopenic 446.6
  toxic 287.0
  variolosa 050.0
  vascular 287.0
  visceral symptoms 287.0
  Werlhof's *(see also* Purpura, thrombo-
      cytopenic) 287.3
Purpuric spots 782.7
Purulent - *see* condition
Pus
  absorption, general - *see* Septicemia
  in
    stool 792.1
    urine 599.0
  tube (rupture) *(see also* Salpingo-
      oophoritis) 614.2

Pustular rash 782.1
Pustule 686.9
  malignant 022.0
  nonmalignant 686.9
Putnam's disease (subacute combined
    sclerosis with pernicious anemia)
    281.0 *[336.2]*
Putnam-Dana syndrome (subacute com-
    bined sclerosis with pernicious ane-
    mia) 281.0 *[336.2]*
Putrefaction, intestinal 569.89
Putrescent pulp (dental) 522.1
Pyarthritis - *see* Pyarthrosis
Pyarthrosis *(see also* Arthritis, pyogenic)
    711.0
  tuberculous - *see* Tuberculosis, joint
Pycnoepilepsy, pycnolepsy (idiopathic)
    (see also Epilepsy) 345.0
Pyelectasia 593.89
Pyelectasis 593.89
Pyelitis (congenital) (uremic) 590.80
  with
    abortion - *see* Abortion, by type,
        with specified complication
        NEC
    contracted kidney 590.00
    ectopic pregnancy *(see also* categories
        633.0-633.9) 639.8
    molar pregnancy *(see also* categories
        630-632) 639.8
  acute 590.10
    with renal medullary necrosis 590.11
  chronic 590.00
    with
      renal medullary necrosis 590.01
  complicating pregnancy, childbirth, or
      puerperium 646.6
    affecting fetus or newborn 760.1
  cystica 590.3
  following
    abortion 639.8
    ectopic or molar pregnancy 639.8
  gonococcal 098.19
    chronic or duration of 2 months or
        over 098.39
  tuberculous *(see also* Tuberculosis)
      016.0 *[590.81]*
Pyelocaliectasis 593.89
Pyelocystitis *(see also* Pyelitis) 590.80
Pyelohydronephrosis 591
Pyelonephritis *(see also* Pyelitis) 590.80
  acute 590.10
    with renal medullary necrosis 590.11
  chronic 590.00
  syphilitic (late) 095.4
  tuberculous *(see also* Tuberculosis)
      016.0 *[590.81]*
Pyelonephrosis *(see also* Pyelitis) 590.80
  chronic 590.00
Pyelophlebitis 451.89
Pyelo-ureteritis cystica 590.3
Pyemia, pyemic (purulent) *(see also* Sep-
    ticemia) 038.9
  abscess - *see* Abscess
  arthritis *(see also* Arthritis, pyogenic)
      711.0
  Bacillus coli 038.42
  embolism - *see* Embolism, pyemic
  fever 038.9
  infection 038.9
  joint *(see also* Arthritis, pyogenic)
      711.0
  liver 572.1
  meningococcal 036.2

Pyemia, pyemic *(Continued)*
  newborn 771.8
  phlebitis - *see* Phlebitis
  pneumococcal 038.2
  portal 572.1
  postvaccinal 999.3
  specified organism NEC 038.8
  staphylococcal 038.10
    aureus 038.11
    specified organism NEC 038.19
  streptococcal 038.0
  tuberculous - *see* Tuberculosis, miliary
Pygopagus 759.4
Pykno-epilepsy, pyknolepsy (idiopathic)
    (see also Epilepsy) 345.0
Pyle (-Cohn) disease (craniometaphyseal
    dysplasia) 756.89
Pylephlebitis (suppurative) 572.1
Pylethrombophlebitis 572.1
Pylethrombosis 572.1
Pyloritis *(see also* Gastritis) 535.5
Pylorospasm (reflex) 537.81
  congenital or infantile 750.5
  neurotic 306.4
  newborn 750.5
  psychogenic 306.4
Pylorus, pyloric - *see* condition
Pyoarthrosis - *see* Pyarthrosis
Pyocele
  mastoid 383.00
  sinus (accessory) (nasal) *(see also* Sinus-
      itis) 473.9
  turbinate (bone) 473.9
  urethra *(see also* Urethritis) 597.0
Pyococcal dermatitis 686.00
Pyococcide, skin 686.00
Pyocolpos *(see also* Vaginitis) 616.10
Pyocyaneus dermatitis 686.09
Pyocystitis *(see also* Cystitis) 595.9
Pyoderma, pyodermia 686.00
  gangrenosum 686.01
  specified type NEC 686.09
  vegetans 686.8
Pyodermatitis 686.00
  vegetans 686.8
Pyogenic - *see* condition
Pyohemia - *see* Septicemia
Pyohydronephrosis *(see also* Pyelitis)
    590.80
Pyometra 615.9
Pyometritis *(see also* Endometritis) 615.9
Pyometrium *(see also* Endometritis)
    615.9
Pyomyositis 728.0
  ossificans 728.19
  tropical (bungpagga) 040.81
Pyonephritis *(see also* Pyelitis) 590.80
  chronic 590.00
Pyonephrosis (congenital) *(see also* Pyeli-
    tis) 590.80
  acute 590.10
Pyo-oophoritis *(see also* Salpingo-oopho-
    ritis) 614.2
Pyo-ovarium *(see also* Salpingo-oophori-
    tis) 614.2
Pyopericarditis 420.99
Pyopericardium 420.99
Pyophlebitis - *see* Phlebitis
Pyopneumopericardium 420.99
Pyopneumothorax (infectional) 510.9
  with fistula 510.0
  subdiaphragmatic *(see also* Peritonitis)
      567.2
  subphrenic *(see also* Peritonitis) 567.2

◄ ▶ **New Code**   ◀▥▥ ▥▥▶ **Revised Code**

Q

Q fever 083.0
 with pneumonia 083.0 *[484.8]*
Quadricuspid aortic valve 746.89
Quadrilateral fever 083.0
Quadriparesis - *see* Quadriplegia
Quadriplegia 344.00
 with fracture, vertebra (process) - *see*
  Fracture, vertebra, cervical, with
  spinal cord injury
 brain (current episode) 437.8
 C_1-C_4
  complete 344.01
  incomplete 344.02
 C_5-C_7
  complete 344.03
  incomplete 344.04
 cerebral (current episode) 437.8
 congenital or infantile (cerebral) (spastic) (spinal) 343.2
 cortical 437.8
 embolic (current episode) (*see also* Embolism, brain) 434.1
 infantile (cerebral) (spastic) (spinal) 343.2

Quadriplegia *(Continued)*
 newborn NEC 767.0
 specified NEC 344.09
 thrombotic (current episode) (*see also*
  Thrombosis, brain) 434.0
 traumatic - *see* Injury, spinal, cervical
Quadruplet
 affected by maternal complications of
  pregnancy 761.5
 healthy liveborn - *see* Newborn, multiple
 pregnancy (complicating delivery)
  NEC 651.8
  with fetal loss and retention of one
   or more fetus(es) 651.5
Quarrelsomeness 301.3
Quartan
 fever 084.2
 malaria (fever) 084.2
Queensland fever 083.0
 coastal 083.0
 seven-day 100.89
Quervain's disease 727.04
 thyroid (subacute granulomatous thyroiditis) 245.1

Queyrat's erythroplasia (M8080/2)
 specified site - *see* Neoplasm, skin, in
  situ
 unspecified site 233.5
Quincke's disease or edema - *see*
  Edema, angioneurotic
Quinquaud's disease (acne decalvans)
  704.09
Quinsy (gangrenous) 475
Quintan fever 083.1
Quintuplet
 affected by maternal complications of
  pregnancy 761.5
 healthy liveborn - *see* Newborn, multiple
 pregnancy (complicating delivery)
  NEC 651.2
  with fetal loss and retention of one
   or more fetus(es) 651.6
Quotidian
 fever 084.0
 malaria (fever) 084.0

R

Rabbia 071
Rabbit fever (*see also* Tularemia) 021.9
Rabies 071
  contact V01.5
  exposure to V01.5
  inoculation V04.5
    reaction - *see* Complications, vacci-
      nation
  vaccination, prophylactic (against)
    V04.5
Rachischisis (*see also* Spina bifida) 741.9
Rachitic - *see also* condition
  deformities of spine 268.1
  pelvis 268.1
    with disproportion (fetopelvic) 653.2
      affecting fetus or newborn 763.1
      causing obstructed labor 660.1
        affecting fetus or newborn 763.1
Rachitis, rachitism - *see also* Rickets
  acute 268.0
  fetalis 756.4
  renalis 588.0
  tarda 268.0
Racket nail 757.5
Radial nerve - *see* condition
Radiation effects or sickness - *see also*
  Effect, adverse, radiation
  cataract 366.46
  dermatitis 692.82
    sunburn 692.71
Radiculitis (pressure) (vertebrogenic)
  729.2
  accessory nerve 723.4
  anterior crural 724.4
  arm 723.4
  brachial 723.4
  cervical NEC 723.4
  due to displacement of intervertebral
    disc - *see* Neuritis, due to, dis-
    placement intervertebral disc
  leg 724.4
  lumbar NEC 724.4
  lumbosacral 724.4
  rheumatic 729.2
  syphilitic 094.89
  thoracic (with visceral pain) 724.4
Radiculomyelitis 357.0
  toxic, due to
    Clostridium tetani 037
    Corynebacterium diphtheriae 032.89
Radiculopathy (*see also* Radiculitis) 729.2
Radioactive substances, adverse effect -
  see Effect, adverse, radioactive substance
Radiodermal burns (acute) (chronic) (occupational) - *see* Burn, by site
Radiodermatitis 692.82
Radionecrosis - *see* Effect, adverse, radia-
  tion
Radiotherapy session V58.0
Radium, adverse effect - *see* Effect, ad-
  verse, radioactive substance
Raeder-Harbitz syndrome (pulseless dis-
  ease) 446.7
Rage (*see also* Disturbance, conduct)
  312.0
  meaning rabies 071
Rag sorters' disease 022.1
Raillietiniasis 123.8
Railroad neurosis 300.16
Railway spine 300.16
Raised - *see* Elevation

Raiva 071
Rake teeth, tooth 524.3
Rales 786.7
Ramifying renal pelvis 753.3
Ramsay Hunt syndrome (herpetic geniculate ganglionitis) 053.11
  meaning dyssynergia cerebellaris
    myoclonica 334.2
Ranke's primary infiltration (*see also* Tuberculosis) 010.0
Ranula 527.6
  congenital 750.26
Rape - *see* Injury, by site 959.9
  alleged, observation or examination
    V71.5
Rapid
  feeble pulse, due to shock, following
    injury 958.4
  heart (beat) 785.0
    psychogenic 306.2
  respiration 786.06
    psychogenic 306.1
  second stage (delivery) 661.3
    affecting fetus or newborn 763.6
  time-zone change syndrome 307.45
Rarefaction, bone 733.99
Rash 782.1
  canker 034.1
  diaper 691.0
  drug (internal use) 693.0
    contact 692.3
  ECHO 9 virus 078.89
  enema 692.89
  food (*see also* Allergy, food) 693.1
  heat 705.1
  napkin 691.0
  nettle 708.8
  pustular 782.1
  rose 782.1
    epidemic 056.9
    of infants 057.8
  scarlet 034.1
  serum (prophylactic) (therapeutic)
    999.5
  toxic 782.1
  wandering tongue 529.1
Rasmussen's aneurysm (*see also* Tuberculosis) 011.2
Rat-bite fever 026.9
  due to Streptobacillus moniliformis
    026.1
  spirochetal (morsus muris) 026.0
Rathke's pouch tumor (M9350/1)
  237.0
Raymond (-Céstan) syndrome 433.8
Raynaud's
  disease or syndrome (paroxysmal digi-
    tal cyanosis) 443.0
  gangrene (symmetric) 443.0 *[785.4]*
  phenomenon (paroxysmal digital cya-
    nosis) (secondary) 443.0
RDS 769
Reaction
  acute situational maladjustment (*see*
    also Reaction, adjustment) 309.9
  adaptation (*see also* Reaction, adjust-
    ment) 309.9
  adjustment 309.9
    with
      anxious mood 309.24
        with depressed mood 309.28
      conduct disturbance 309.3
        combined with disturbance of
        emotions 309.4

Reaction (*Continued*)
  adjustment (*Continued*)
    with (*Continued*)
      depressed mood 309.0
        brief 309.0
          with anxious mood 309.28
        prolonged 309.1
      elective mutism 309.83
      mixed emotions and conduct
        309.4
      mutism, elective 309.83
      physical symptoms 309.82
      predominant disturbance (of)
        conduct 309.3
        emotions NEC 309.29
          mixed 309.28
        mixed, emotions and conduct
          309.4
        specified type NEC 309.89
      specific academic or work inhibi-
        tion 309.23
      withdrawal 309.83
    depressive 309.0
      with conduct disturbance 309.4
      brief 309.0
      prolonged 309.1
    specified type NEC 309.89
  affective (*see also* Psychosis, affective)
    296.90
    specified type NEC 296.99
  aggressive 301.3
    unsocialized (*see also* Disturbance,
      conduct) 312.0
  allergic (*see also* Allergy) 995.3
    drug, medicinal substance, and bio-
      logical - *see* Allergy, drug
    food - *see* Allergy, food
    serum 999.5
  anaphylactic - *see* Shock, anaphylactic
  anesthesia - *see* Anesthesia, complica-
    tion
  anger 312.0
  antisocial 301.7
  antitoxin (prophylactic) (therapeutic) -
    see Complications, vaccination
  anxiety 300.00
  asthenic 300.5
  compulsive 300.3
  conversion (anesthetic) (autonomic)
    (hyperkinetic) (mixed paralytic)
    (paresthetic) 300.11
  deoxyribonuclease (DNA) (DNase) hy-
    persensitivity NEC 287.2
  depressive 300.4
    acute 309.0
    affective (*see also* Psychosis, affective)
      296.2
      recurrent episode 296.3
      single episode 296.2
    brief 309.0
    manic (*see also* Psychosis, affective)
      296.80
    neurotic 300.4
    psychoneurotic 300.4
    psychotic 298.0
  dissociative 300.15
  drug NEC (*see also* Table of Drugs and
    Chemicals) 995.2
    allergic - *see* Allergy, drug
    correct substance properly adminis-
      tered 995.2
    obstetric anesthetic or analgesic NEC
      668.9
      affecting fetus or newborn 763.5

Reaction *(Continued)*
  drug NEC *(Continued)*
    obstetric anesthetic or analgesic NEC *(Continued)*
      specified drug - *see* Table of Drugs and Chemicals
      overdose or poisoning 977.9
        specified drug - *see* Table of Drugs and Chemicals
      specific to newborn 779.4
      transmitted via placenta or breast milk - *see* Absorption, drug, through placenta
      withdrawal NEC 292.0
        infant of dependent mother 779.5
      wrong substance given or taken in error 977.9
        specified drug - *see* Table of Drugs and Chemicals
  dyssocial 301.7
  erysipeloid 027.1
  fear 300.20
    child 313.0
  fluid loss, cerebrospinal 349.0
  food - *see also* Allergy, food
    anaphylactic shock - *see* Anaphylactic shock, due to, food
  foreign
    body NEC 728.82
      in operative wound (inadvertently left) 998.4
        due to surgical material intentionally left - *see* Complications, due to (presence of) any device, implant, or graft classified to 996.0-996.5 NEC
    substance accidentally left during a procedure (chemical) (powder) (talc) 998.7
      body or object (instrument) (sponge) (swab) 998.4
  graft-versus-host (GVH) 996.85
  grief (acute) (brief) 309.0
    prolonged 309.1
  gross stress (*see also* Reaction, stress, acute) 308.9
  group delinquent (*see also* Disturbance, conduct) 312.2
  Herxheimer's 995.0
  hyperkinetic (*see also* Hyperkinesia) 314.9
  hypochondriacal 300.7
  hypoglycemic, due to insulin 251.0
    therapeutic misadventure 962.3
  hypomanic (*see also* Psychosis, affective) 296.0
    recurrent episode 296.1
    single episode 296.0
  hysterical 300.10
    conversion type 300.11
    dissociative 300.15
  id (bacterial cause) 692.89
  immaturity NEC 301.89
    aggressive 301.3
    emotional instability 301.59
  immunization - *see* Complications, vaccination
  incompatibility
    blood group (ABO) (infusion) (transfusion) 999.6
    Rh (factor) (infusion) (transfusion) 999.7
  inflammatory - *see* Infection

Reaction *(Continued)*
  infusion - *see* Complications, infusion
  inoculation (immune serum) - *see* Complications, vaccination
  insulin 995.2
  involutional
    paranoid 297.2
    psychotic (*see also* Psychosis, affective, depressive) 296.2
  leukemoid (lymphocytic) (monocytic) (myelocytic) 288.8
  LSD (*see also* Abuse, drugs, nondependent) 305.3
  lumbar puncture 349.0
  manic-depressive (*see also* Psychosis, affective) 296.80
    depressed 296.2
      recurrent episode 296.3
      single episode 296.2
    hypomanic 296.0
  neurasthenic 300.5
  neurogenic (*see also* Neurosis) 300.9
  neurotic NEC 300.9
  neurotic-depressive 300.4
  nitritoid - *see* Crisis, nitritoid
  obsessive (-compulsive) 300.3
  organic 293.9
    acute 293.0
    subacute 293.1
  overanxious, child or adolescent 313.0
  paranoid (chronic) 297.9
    acute 298.3
    climacteric 297.2
    involutional 297.2
    menopausal 297.2
    senile 290.20
    simple 297.0
  passive
    aggressive 301.84
    dependency 301.6
  personality (*see also* Disorder, personality) 301.9
  phobic 300.20
  postradiation - *see* Effect, adverse, radiation
  psychogenic NEC 300.9
  psychoneurotic (*see also* Neurosis) 300.9
    anxiety 300.00
    compulsive 300.3
    conversion 300.11
    depersonalization 300.6
    depressive 300.4
    dissociative 300.15
    hypochondriacal 300.7
    hysterical 300.10
      conversion type 300.11
      dissociative type 300.15
    neurasthenic 300.5
    obsessive 300.3
    obsessive-compulsive 300.3
    phobic 300.20
    tension state 300.9
  psychophysiologic NEC (*see also* Disorder, psychosomatic) 306.9
    cardiovascular 306.2
    digestive 306.4
    endocrine 306.6
    gastrointestinal 306.4
    genitourinary 306.50
    heart 306.2
    hemic 306.8
    intestinal (large) (small) 306.4

Reaction *(Continued)*
  psychophysiologic NEC *(Continued)*
    laryngeal 306.1
    lymphatic 306.8
    musculoskeletal 306.0
    pharyngeal 306.1
    respiratory 306.1
    skin 306.3
    special sense organs 306.7
  psychosomatic (*see also* Disorder, psychosomatic) 306.9
  psychotic (*see also* Psychosis) 298.9
    depressive 298.0
    due to or associated with physical condition (*see also* Psychosis, organic) 293.9
    involutional (*see also* Psychosis, affective) 296.2
      recurrent episode 296.3
      single episode 296.2
  pupillary (myotonic) (tonic) 379.46
  radiation - *see* Effect, adverse, radiation
  runaway - *see also* Disturbance, conduct
    socialized 312.2
    undersocialized, unsocialized 312.1
  scarlet fever toxin - *see* Complications, vaccination
  schizophrenic (*see also* Schizophrenia) 295.9
    latent 295.5
  serological for syphilis - *see* Serology for syphilis
  serum (prophylactic) (therapeutic) 999.5
    immediate 999.4
  situational (*see also* Reaction, adjustment) 309.9
    acute, to stress 308.3
    adjustment (*see also* Reaction, adjustment) 309.9
  somatization (*see also* Disorder, psychosomatic) 306.9
  spinal puncture 349.0
  spite, child (*see also* Disturbance, conduct) 312.0
  stress, acute 308.9
    with predominant disturbance (of)
      consciousness 308.1
      emotions 308.0
      mixed 308.4
      psychomotor 308.2
      specified type NEC 308.3
  surgical procedure - *see* Complications, surgical procedure
  tetanus antitoxin - *see* Complications, vaccination
  toxin-antitoxin - *see* Complications, vaccination
  transfusion (blood) (bone marrow) (lymphocytes) (allergic) - *see* Complications, transfusion
  tuberculin skin test, nonspecific (without active tuberculosis) 795.5
    positive (without active tuberculosis) 795.5
  ultraviolet - *see* Effect, adverse, ultraviolet
  undersocialized, unsocialized - *see also* Disturbance, conduct
    aggressive (type) 312.0
    unaggressive (type) 312.1

Reaction (*Continued*)
  vaccination (any) - *see* Complications, vaccination
  white graft (skin) 996.52
  withdrawing, child or adolescent 313.22
  x-ray - *see* Effect, adverse, x-rays
Reactive depression (*see also* Reaction, depressive) 300.4
  neurotic 300.4
  psychoneurotic 300.4
  psychotic 298.0
Rebound tenderness 789.6
Recalcitrant patient V15.81
Recanalization, thrombus - *see* Thrombosis
Recession, receding
  chamber angle (eye) 364.77
  chin 524.06
  gingival (generalized) (localized) (postinfective) (postoperative) 523.2
Recklinghausen's disease (M9540/1) 237.71
  bones (osteitis fibrosa cystica) 252.0
Recklinghausen-Applebaum disease (hemochromatosis) 275.0
Reclus' disease (cystic) 610.1
Recrudescent typhus (fever) 081.1
Recruitment, auditory 388.44
Rectalgia 569.42
Rectitis 569.49
Rectocele
  female (without uterine prolapse) 618.0
    with uterine prolapse 618.4
      complete 618.3
      incomplete 618.2
  in pregnancy or childbirth 654.4
    causing obstructed labor 660.2
      affecting fetus or newborn 763.1
  male 569.49
  vagina, vaginal (outlet) 618.0
Rectosigmoiditis 569.89
  ulcerative (chronic) 556.3
Rectosigmoid junction - *see* condition
Rectourethral - *see* condition
Rectovaginal - *see* condition
Rectovesical - *see* condition
Rectum, rectal - *see* condition
Recurrent - *see* condition
Red bugs 133.8
Red cedar asthma 495.8
Redness
  conjunctiva 379.93
  eye 379.93
  nose 478.1
Reduced ventilatory or vital capacity 794.2
Reduction
  function
    kidney (*see also* Disease, renal) 593.9
    liver 573.8
  ventilatory capacity 794.2
  vital capacity 794.2
Redundant, redundancy
  abdomen 701.9
  anus 751.5
  cardia 537.89
  clitoris 624.2
  colon (congenital) 751.5
  foreskin (congenital) 605
  intestine 751.5
  labia 624.3
  organ or site, congenital NEC - *see* Accessory

Redundant, redundancy (*Continued*)
  panniculus (abdominal) 278.1
  prepuce (congenital) 605
  pylorus 537.89
  rectum 751.5
  scrotum 608.89
  sigmoid 751.5
  skin (of face) 701.9
    eyelids 374.30
  stomach 537.89
  uvula 528.9
  vagina 623.8
Reduplication - *see* Duplication
Referral
  adoption (agency) V68.89
  nursing care V63.8
  patient without examination or treatment V68.81
  social services V63.8
Reflex - *see also* condition
  blink, deficient 374.45
  hyperactive gag 478.29
  neurogenic bladder NEC 596.54
    atonic 596.54
      with cauda equina syndrome 344.61
  vasoconstriction 443.9
  vasovagal 780.2
Reflux
  esophageal 530.81
    with esophagitis 530.11
  esophagitis 530.11
  gastroesophageal 530.81
  mitral - *see* Insufficiency, mitral
  ureteral - *see* Reflux, vesicoureteral
  vesicoureteral 593.70
    with
      reflux nephropathy 593.73
        bilateral 593.72
        unilateral 593.71
Reformed gallbladder 576.0
Reforming, artificial openings (*see also* Attention to, artificial, opening) V55.9
Refractive error (*see also* Error, refractive) 367.9
Refsum's disease or syndrome (heredopathia atactica polyneuritiformis) 356.3
Refusal of
  food 307.59
    hysterical 300.11
  treatment because of, due to
    patient's decision NEC V64.2
    reason of conscience or religion V62.6
Regaud
  tumor (M8082/3) - *see* Neoplasm, nasopharynx, malignant
  type carcinoma (M8082/3) - *see* Neoplasm, nasopharynx, malignant
Regional - *see* condition
Regulation feeding (elderly) (infant) 783.3
  newborn 779.3
Regurgitated
  food, choked on 933.1
  stomach contents, choked on 933.1
Regurgitation
  aortic (valve) (*see also* Insufficiency, aortic) 424.1
    congenital 746.4
    syphilitic 093.22

Regurgitation (*Continued*)
  food - *see also* Vomiting
    with reswallowing - *see* Rumination
    newborn 779.3
  gastric contents - *see* Vomiting
  heart - *see* Endocarditis
  mitral (valve) - *see also* Insufficiency, mitral
    congenital 746.6
  myocardial - *see* Endocarditis
  pulmonary (heart) (valve) (*see also* Endocarditis, pulmonary) 424.3
  stomach - *see* Vomiting
  tricuspid - *see* Endocarditis, tricuspid
  valve, valvular - *see* Endocarditis
  vesicoureteral - *see* Reflux, vesicoureteral
Rehabilitation V57.9
  multiple types V57.89
  occupational V57.21
  specified type NEC V57.89
  speech V57.3
  vocational V57.22
Reichmann's disease or syndrome (gastrosuccorrhea) 536.8
Reifenstein's syndrome (hereditary familial hypogonadism, male) 257.2
Reilly's syndrome or phenomenon (*see also* Neuropathy, peripheral, autonomic) 337.9
Reimann's periodic disease 277.3
Reinsertion, contraceptive device V25.42
Reiter's disease, syndrome, or urethritis 099.3 [711.1]
Rejection
  food, hysterical 300.11
  transplant 996.80
    bone marrow 996.85
    corneal 996.51
    organ (immune or nonimmune cause) 996.80
      bone marrow 996.85
      heart 996.83
      intestines 996.89
      kidney 996.81
      liver 996.82
      lung 996.84
      pancreas 996.86
      specified NEC 996.89
    skin 996.52
      artificial 996.55
      decellularized allodermis 996.55
Relapsing fever 087.9
  Carter's (Asiatic) 087.0
  Dutton's (West African) 087.1
  Koch's 087.9
  louse-borne (epidemic) 087.0
  Novy's (American) 087.1
  Obermeyer's (European) 087.0
  Spirillum 087.9
  tick-borne (endemic) 087.1
Relaxation
  anus (sphincter) 569.49
    due to hysteria 300.11
  arch (foot) 734
    congenital 754.61
  back ligaments 728.4
  bladder (sphincter) 596.59
  cardio-esophageal 530.89
  cervix (*see also* Incompetency, cervix) 622.5
  diaphragm 519.4
  inguinal rings - *see* Hernia, inguinal

ICD-9-CM

R

Vol. 2

Relaxation (*Continued*)
  joint (capsule) (ligament) (paralytic)
    (*see also* Derangement, joint) 718.90
    congenital 755.8
  lumbosacral joint 724.6
  pelvic floor 618.8
  pelvis 618.8
  perineum 618.8
  posture 729.9
  rectum (sphincter) 569.49
  sacroiliac (joint) 724.6
  scrotum 608.89
  urethra (sphincter) 599.84
  uterus (outlet) 618.8
  vagina (outlet) 618.8
  vesical 596.59
Remains
  canal of Cloquet 743.51
  capsule (opaque) 743.51
Remittent fever (malarial) 084.6
Remnant
  canal of Cloquet 743.51
  capsule (opaque) 743.51
  cervix, cervical stump (acquired) (post-
    operative) 622.8
  cystic duct, postcholecystectomy
    576.0
  fingernail 703.8
    congenital 757.5
  meniscus, knee 717.5
  thyroglossal duct 759.2
  tonsil 474.8
    infected 474.00
  urachus 753.7
Remote effect of cancer - *see* condition
Removal (of)
  catheter (urinary) (indwelling)
    V53.6
    from artificial opening - *see* Atten-
      tion to, artificial, opening
    non-vascular V58.82
    vascular V58.81
  cerebral ventricle (communicating)
    shunt V53.01
  device - *see also* Fitting (of)
    contraceptive V25.42
    fixation
      external V54.8
      internal V54.0
      traction V54.8
  dressing V58.3
  ileostomy V55.2
  Kirschner wire V54.8
  non-vascular catheter V58.82
  pin V54.0
  plaster cast V54.8
  plate (fracture) V54.0
  rod V54.0
  screw V54.0
  splint, external V54.8
  subdermal implantable contraceptive
    V25.43
  suture V58.3
  traction device, external V54.8
  vascular catheter V58.81
Ren
  arcuatus 753.3
  mobile, mobilis (*see also* Disease, renal)
    593.0
    congenital 753.3
    unguliformis 753.3
Renal - *see also* condition
  glomerulohyalinosis-diabetic syndrome
    250.4 *[581.81]*

Rendu-Osler-Weber disease or syn-
drome (familial hemorrhagic telangiectasia) 448.0
Reninoma (M8361/1) 236.91
Rénon-Delille syndrome 253.8
Repair
  pelvic floor, previous, in pregnancy or
    childbirth 654.4
    affecting fetus or newborn
      763.89
  scarred tissue V51
Replacement by artificial or mechanical
device or prosthesis of (*see also* Fitting (of))
  artificial skin V43.83
  bladder V43.5
  blood vessel V43.4
  breast V43.82
  eye globe V43.0
  heart V43.2
    valve V43.3
  intestine V43.89
  joint V43.60
    ankle V43.66
    elbow V43.62
    finger V43.69
    hip (partial) (total) V43.64
    knee V43.65
    shoulder V43.61
    specified NEC V43.69
    wrist V43.63
  kidney V43.89
  larynx V43.81
  lens V43.1
  limb(s) V43.7
  liver V43.89
  lung V43.89
  organ NEC V43.89
  pancreas V43.89
  skin (artificial) V43.83
  tissue NEC V43.89
Reprogramming
  cardiac pacemaker V53.31
Request for expert evidence V68.2
Reserve, decreased or low
  cardiac - *see* Disease, heart
    kidney (*see also* Disease, renal) 593.9
Residual - *see also* condition
  bladder 596.8
  foreign body - *see* Retention, foreign body
  state, schizophrenic (*see also* Schizo-
    phrenia) 295.6
  urine 788.69
Resistance, resistant (to)

> Note Use the following subclassifi-
> cation for categories V09.5, V09.7,
> V09.8, V09.9:
>
> 0   without mention of resistance
>   to multiple drugs
> 1   with resistance to multiple drugs
>   V09.5 quinolones and fluoro-
>   quinolones
>   V09.7 antimycobacterial agents
>   V09.8 specified drugs NEC
>   V09.9 unspecified drugs
> 9   multiple sites

  drugs by microorganisms V09.90
    amikacin V09.4
    aminoglycosides V09.4
    amodiaquine V09.5
    amoxicillin V09.0
    ampicillin V09.0

Resistance, resistant (*Continued*)
  drugs by microorganisms (*Continued*)
    antimycobacterial agents V09.7
    azithromycin V09.2
    azlocillin V09.0
    aztreonam V09.1
    B-lactam antibiotics V09.1
    bacampicillin V09.0
    bacitracin V09.8
    benznidazole V09.8
    capreomycin V09.7
    carbenicillin V09.0
    cefaclor V09.1
    cefadroxil V09.1
    cefamandole V09.1
    cefatetan V09.1
    cefazolin V09.1
    cefixime V09.1
    cefonicid V09.1
    cefoperazone V09.1
    ceforanide V09.1
    cefotaxime V09.1
    cefoxitin V09.1
    ceftazidine V09.1
    ceftizoxime V09.1
    ceftriaxone V09.1
    cefuroxime V09.1
    cephalexin V09.1
    cephaloglycin V09.1
    cephaloridine V09.1
    cephalosporins V09.1
    cephalothin V09.1
    cephapirin V09.1
    cephradine V09.1
    chloramphenicol V09.8
    chloraquine V09.5
    chlorguanide V09.8
    chlorproguanil V09.8
    chlortetracycline V09.3
    cinoxacin V09.5
    ciprofloxacin V09.5
    clarithromycin V09.2
    clindamycin V09.8
    clioquinol V09.5
    clofazimine V09.7
    cloxacillin V09.0
    cyclacillin V09.0
    cycloserine V09.7
    dapsone [Dz] V09.7
    demeclocycline V09.3
    dicloxacillin V09.0
    doxycycline V09.3
    enoxacin V09.5
    erythromycin V09.2
    ethambutol [Emb] V09.7
    ethionamide [Eta] V09.7
    fluoroquinolones NEC V09.5
    gentamicin V09.4
    halofantrine V09.8
    imipenem V09.1
    iodoquinol V09.5
    isoniazid [INH] V09.7
    kanamycin V09.4
    macrolides V09.2
    mafenide V09.6
    mefloquine V09.8
    melarsoprol V09.7
    methacillin V09.0
    methacycline V09.3
    methenamine V09.8
    metronidazole V09.8
    mezlocillin V09.0
    minocycline V09.3
    nafcillin V09.0

Resistance, resistant (*Continued*)
 drugs by microorganisms (*Continued*)
  nalidixic acid V09.5
  natamycin V09.2
  neomycin V09.4
  netilmicin V09.4
  nimorazole V09.8
  nitrofurantoin V09.8
  norfloxacin V09.5
  nystatin V09.2
  ofloxacin V09.5
  oleandomycin V09.2
  oxacillin V09.0
  oxytetracycline V09.3
  para-amino salicyclic acid [PAS]
   V09.7
  paromomycin V09.4
  penicillin (G) (V) (Vk) V09.0
  penicillins V09.0
  pentamidine V09.8
  piperacillin V09.0
  primaquine V09.5
  proguanil V09.8
  pyrazinamide [Pza] V09.7
  pyrimethamine/sulfalene V09.8
  pyrimethamine/sulfodoxine V09.8
  quinacrine V09.5
  quinidine V09.8
  quinine V09.8
  quinolones V09.5
  rifabutin V09.7
  rifampin [Rif] V09.7
  rifamycin V09.7
  rolitetracycline V09.3
  specified drugs NEC
   V09.8
  spectinomycin V09.8
  spiramycin V09.2
  streptomycin [Sm] V09.4
  sulfacetamide V09.6
  sulfacytine V09.6
  sulfadiazine V09.6
  sulfadoxine V09.6
  sulfamethoxazole V09.6
  sulfapyridine V09.6
  sulfasalizine V09.6
  sulfasoxazone V09.6
  sulfonamides V09.6
  sulfoxone V09.7
  tetracycline V09.3
  tetracyclines V09.3
  thiamphenicol V09.8
  ticarcillin V09.0
  tinidazole V09.8
  tobramycin V09.4
  triamphenicol V09.8
  trimethoprim V09.8
  vancomycin V09.8
Resorption
 biliary 576.8
  purulent or putrid (*see also* Cholecystitis) 576.8
 dental (roots) 521.4
  alveoli 525.8
 septic - *see* Septicemia
 teeth (external) (internal) (pathological)
  (roots) 521.4
Respiration
 asymmetrical 786.09
 bronchial 786.09
 Cheyne-Stokes (periodic respiration)
  786.04
 decreased, due to shock following injury 958.4

Respiration (*Continued*)
 disorder of 786.00
  psychogenic 306.1
  specified NEC 786.09
 failure 518.81
  acute 518.81
  acute and chronic 518.84
  chronic 518.83
  newborn 770.8
 insufficiency 786.09
  acute 518.82
  newborn NEC 770.8
 Kussmaul (air hunger) 786.09
 painful 786.52
 periodic 786.09
 poor 786.09
  newborn NEC 770.8
 sighing 786.7
  psychogenic 306.1
 wheezing 786.07
Respiratory - *see also* condition
 distress 786.09
  acute 518.82
  fetus or newborn NEC 770.8
  syndrome (newborn) 769
   adult (following shock, surgery, or
    trauma) 518.5
   specified NEC 518.82
 failure 518.81
  acute 518.81
  acute and chronic 518.84
  chronic 518.83
Respiratory syncytial virus (RSV)
 079.6
 bronchiolitis 466.11
 pneumonia 480.1
Response
 photoallergic 692.72
 phototoxic 692.72
Rest, rests
 mesonephric duct 752.8
  fallopian tube 752.11
 ovarian, in fallopian tubes 752.19
 wolffian duct 752.8
Restless leg (syndrome) 333.99
Restlessness 799.2
Restoration of organ continuity from
 previous sterilization (tuboplasty)
 (vasoplasty) V26.0
Restriction of housing space V60.1
Restzustand, schizophrenic (*see also*
 Schizophrenia) 295.6
Retained - *see* Retention
Retardation
 development, developmental, specific
  (*see also* Disorder, development,
  specific) 315.9
 learning, specific 315.2
  arithmetical 315.1
  language (skills) 315.31
   expressive 315.31
   mixed receptive-expressive
    315.32
  mathematics 315.1
  reading 315.00
   phonological 315.39
  written expression 315.2
 motor 315.4
 endochondral bone growth 733.91
 growth (physical) 783.4
  due to malnutrition 263.2
  fetal (intrauterine) 764.9
   affecting management of preg-
    nancy 656.5

Retardation (*Continued*)
 intrauterine growth 764.9
  affecting management of pregnancy
   656.5
 mental 319
  borderline V62.89
  mild, IQ 50-70 317
  moderate, IQ 35-49 318.0
  profound, IQ under 20 318.2
  severe, IQ 20-34 318.1
 motor, specific 315.4
 physical 783.4
  child 783.4
  due to malnutrition 263.2
  fetus (intrauterine) 764.9
   affecting management of preg-
    nancy 656.5
 psychomotor NEC 307.9
 reading 315.00
Retching - *see* Vomiting
Retention, retained
 bladder (*see also* Retention, urine)
  788.20
  psychogenic 306.53
 carbon dioxide 276.2
 cyst - *see* Cyst
 dead
  fetus (after 22 completed weeks' gestation) 656.4
   early fetal death (before 22 com-
    pleted weeks' gestation) 632
  ovum 631
 decidua (following delivery) (fragments) (with hemorrhage) 666.2
  without hemorrhage 667.1
 deciduous tooth 520.6
 dental root 525.3
 fecal (*see also* Constipation) 564.0
 fluid 276.6
 foreign body - *see also* Foreign body,
  retained
  bone 733.99
  current trauma - *see* Foreign body,
   by site or type
  middle ear 385.83
  muscle 729.6
  soft tissue NEC 729.6
 gastric 536.8
 membranes (following delivery) (with
  hemorrhage) 666.2
  with abortion - *see* Abortion, by type
  without hemorrhage 667.1
 menses 626.8
 milk (puerperal) 676.2
 nitrogen, extrarenal 788.9
 placenta (total) (with hemorrhage)
  666.0
  with abortion - *see* Abortion, by type
  portions or fragments 666.2
   without hemorrhage 667.1
  without hemorrhage 667.0
 products of conception
  early pregnancy (fetal death before
   22 completed weeks' gestation)
   632
  following
   abortion - *see* Abortion, by type
   delivery 666.2
    with hemorrhage 666.2
    without hemorrhage 667.1
 secundines (following delivery) (with
  hemorrhage) 666.2
  with abortion - *see* Abortion, by
   type

◀ ▶ **New Code**   ◀▥ ▥▶ **Revised Code**

ICD-9-CM

R

Vol. 2

Rubella *(Continued)*
  maternal
    with suspected fetal damage affecting management of pregnancy 655.3
    affecting fetus or newborn 760.2
      manifest rubella in infant 771.0
    specified complications NEC 056.79
    vaccination, prophylactic (against) V04.3
Rubeola (measles) *(see also* Measles) 055.9
  complicated 055.8
  meaning rubella *(see also* Rubella) 056.9
  scarlatinosis 057.8
Rubeosis iridis 364.42
  diabetica 250.5 [364.42]
Rubinstein-Taybi's syndrome (brachydactylia, short stature and mental retardation) 759.89
Rud's syndrome (mental deficiency, epilepsy, and infantilism) 759.89
Rudimentary (congenital) - *see also* Agenesis
  arm 755.22
  bone 756.9
  cervix uteri 752.49
  eye *(see also* Microphthalmos) 743.10
  fallopian tube 752.19
  leg 755.32
  lobule of ear 744.21
  patella 755.64
  respiratory organs in thoracopagus 759.4
  tracheal bronchus 748.3
  uterine horn 752.3
  uterus 752.3
    in male 752.7
    solid or with cavity 752.3
  vagina 752.49
Ruiter-Pompen (-Wyers) syndrome (angiokeratoma corporis diffusum) 272.7
Ruled out condition *(see also* Observation, suspected) V71.9
Rumination - *see also* Vomiting
  neurotic 300.3
  obsessional 300.3
  psychogenic 307.53
Runaway reaction - *see also* Disturbance, conduct
  socialized 312.2
  undersocialized, unsocialized 312.1
Runeberg's disease (progressive pernicious anemia) 281.0
Runge's syndrome (postmaturity) 766.2
Rupia 091.3
  congenital 090.0
  tertiary 095.9
Rupture, ruptured 553.9
  abdominal viscera NEC 799.8
    obstetrical trauma 665.5
  abscess (spontaneous) - *see* Abscess, by site
  amnion - *see* Rupture, membranes
  aneurysm - *see* Aneurysm
  anus (sphincter) - *see* Laceration, anus
  aorta, aortic 441.5
    abdominal 441.3
    arch 441.1
    ascending 441.1

Rupture, ruptured *(Continued)*
  aorta, aortic *(Continued)*
    descending 441.5
      abdominal 441.3
      thoracic 441.1
    syphilitic 093.0
    thoracoabdominal 441.6
    thorax, thoracic 441.1
    transverse 441.1
    traumatic (thoracic) 901.0
      abdominal 902.0
    valve or cusp *(see also* Endocarditis, aortic) 424.1
  appendix (with peritonitis) 540.0
    with peritoneal abscess 540.1
    traumatic - *see* Injury, internal, gastrointestinal tract
  arteriovenous fistula, brain (congenital) 430
  artery 447.2
    brain *(see also* Hemorrhage, brain) 431
    coronary *(see also* Infarct, myocardium) 410.9
    heart *(see also* Infarct, myocardium) 410.9
    pulmonary 417.8
    traumatic (complication) *(see also* Injury, blood vessel, by site) 904.9
  bile duct, except cystic *(see also* Disease, biliary) 576.3
    cystic 575.4
    traumatic - *see* Injury, internal, intraabdominal
  bladder (sphincter) 596.6
    with
      abortion - *see* Abortion, by type, with damage to pelvic organs
      ectopic pregnancy *(see also* categories 633.0-633.9) 639.2
      molar pregnancy *(see also* categories 630-632) 639.2
    following
      abortion 639.2
      ectopic or molar pregnancy 639.2
    nontraumatic 596.6
    obstetrical trauma 665.5
    spontaneous 596.6
    traumatic - *see* Injury, internal, bladder
  blood vessel *(see also* Hemorrhage) 459.0
    brain *(see also* Hemorrhage, brain) 431
    heart *(see also* Infarct, myocardium) 410.9
    traumatic (complication) *(see also* Injury, blood vessel, by site) 904.9
  bone - *see* Fracture, by site
  bowel 569.89
    traumatic - *see* Injury, internal, intestine
  Bowman's membrane 371.31
  brain
    aneurysm (congenital) *(see also* Hemorrhage, subarachnoid) 430
      late effect - *see* Late effect(s) (of) cerebrovascular disease
    syphilitic 094.87
    hemorrhagic *(see also* Hemorrhage, brain) 431
    injury at birth 767.0
    syphilitic 094.89

Rupture, ruptured *(Continued)*
  capillaries 448.9
  cardiac *(see also* Infarct, myocardium) 410.9
  cartilage (articular) (current) - *see also* Sprain, by site
    knee - *see* Tear, meniscus
    semilunar - *see* Tear, meniscus
  cecum (with peritonitis) 540.0
    with peritoneal abscess 540.1
    traumatic 863.89
      with open wound into cavity 863.99
  cerebral aneurysm (congenital) *(see also* Hemorrhage, subarachnoid) 430
    late effect - *see* Late effect(s) (of) cerebrovascular disease
  cervix (uteri)
    with
      abortion - *see* Abortion, by type, with damage to pelvic organs
      ectopic pregnancy *(see also* categories 633.0-633.9) 639.2
      molar pregnancy *(see also* categories 630-632) 639.2
    following
      abortion 639.2
      ectopic or molar pregnancy 639.2
    obstetrical trauma 665.3
    traumatic - *see* Injury, internal, cervix
  chordae tendineae 429.5
  choroid (direct) (indirect) (traumatic) 363.63
  circle of Willis *(see also* Hemorrhage, subarachnoid) 430
    late effect - *see* Late effect(s) (of) cerebrovascular disease
  colon 569.89
    traumatic - *see* Injury, internal, colon
  cornea (traumatic) - *see also* Rupture, eye
    due to ulcer 370.00
  coronary (artery) (thrombotic) *(see also* Infarct, myocardium) 410.9
  corpus luteum (infected) (ovary) 620.1
  cyst - *see* Cyst
  cystic duct *(see also* Disease, gallbladder) 575.4
  Descemet's membrane 371.33
    traumatic - *see* Rupture, eye
  diaphragm - *see also* Hernia, diaphragm
    traumatic - *see* Injury, internal, diaphragm
  diverticulum
    bladder 596.3
    intestine (large) *(see also* Diverticula) 562.10
      small 562.00
  duodenal stump 537.89
  duodenum (ulcer) - *see* Ulcer, duodenum, with perforation
  ear drum *(see also* Perforation, tympanum) 384.20
    with otitis media - *see* Otitis media
    traumatic - *see* Wound, open, ear
  esophagus 530.4
    traumatic 862.22
      with open wound into cavity 862.32
      cervical region - *see* Wound, open, esophagus

Rupture, ruptured (*Continued*)
eye (without prolapse of intraocular
   tissue) 871.0
   with
      exposure of intraocular tissue
         871.1
      partial loss of intraocular tissue
         871.2
      prolapse of intraocular tissue
         871.1
   due to burn 940.5
fallopian tube 620.8
   due to pregnancy - *see* Pregnancy,
      tubal
   traumatic - *see* Injury, internal, fallo-
      pian tube
fontanel 767.3
free wall (ventricle) (*see also* Infarct,
   myocardium) 410.9
gallbladder or duct (*see also* Disease,
   gallbladder) 575.4
   traumatic - *see* Injury, internal, gall-
      bladder
gastric (*see also* Rupture, stomach)
   537.89
   vessel 459.0
globe (eye) (traumatic) - *see* Rupture,
   eye
graafian follicle (hematoma) 620.0
heart (auricle) (ventricle) (*see also* Infarct, myocardium) 410.9
   infectional 422.90
   traumatic - *see* Rupture, myocar-
      dium, traumatic
hymen 623.8
internal
   organ, traumatic - *see also* Injury, in-
      ternal, by site
      heart - *see* Rupture, myocardium,
         traumatic
      kidney - *see* Rupture, kidney
      liver - *see* Rupture, liver
      spleen - *see* Rupture, spleen, trau-
         matic
      semilunar cartilage - *see* Tear, menis-
         cus
intervertebral disc - *see* Displacement,
   intervertebral disc
   traumatic (current) - *see* Dislocation,
      vertebra
intestine 569.89
   traumatic - *see* Injury, internal, intes-
      tine
intracranial, birth injury 767.0
iris 364.76
   traumatic - *see* Rupture, eye
joint capsule - *see* Sprain, by site
kidney (traumatic) 866.03
   with open wound into cavity 866.13
   due to birth injury 767.8
   nontraumatic 593.89
lacrimal apparatus (traumatic) 870.2
lens (traumatic) 366.20
ligament - *see also* Sprain, by site
   with open wound - *see* Wound,
      open, by site
   old (*see also* Disorder, cartilage, artic-
      ular) 718.0
liver (traumatic) 864.04
   with open wound into cavity
      864.14
   due to birth injury 767.8
   nontraumatic 573.8
lymphatic (node) (vessel) 457.8

Rupture, ruptured (*Continued*)
marginal sinus (placental) (with hemorrhage) 641.2
   affecting fetus or newborn 762.1
meaning hernia - *see* Hernia
membrana tympani (*see also* Perforation, tympanum) 384.20
   with otitis media - *see* Otitis media
   traumatic - *see* Wound, open, ear
membranes (spontaneous)
   artificial
      delayed delivery following 658.3
         affecting fetus or newborn 761.1
         fetus or newborn 761.1
   delayed delivery following 658.2
      affecting fetus or newborn 761.1
   premature (less than 24 hours prior
      to onset of labor) 658.1
      affecting fetus or newborn 761.1
      delayed delivery following 658.2
         affecting fetus or newborn 761.1
meningeal artery (*see also* Hemorrhage,
   subarachnoid) 430
   late effect - *see* Late effect(s) (of)
      cerebrovascular disease
meniscus (knee) - *see also* Tear, meniscus
   old (*see also* Derangement, meniscus)
      717.5
      site other than knee - *see* Disorder,
         cartilage, articular
   site other than knee - *see* Sprain, by
      site
mesentery 568.89
   traumatic - *see* Injury, internal, mes-
      entery
mitral - *see* Insufficiency, mitral
muscle (traumatic) NEC - *see also*
   Sprain, by site
   with open wound - *see* Wound,
      open, by site
   nontraumatic 728.83
musculotendinous cuff (nontraumatic)
   (shoulder) 840.4
mycotic aneurysm, causing cerebral
   hemorrhage (*see also* Hemorrhage,
   subarachnoid) 430
   late effect - *see* Late effect(s) (of)
      cerebrovascular disease
myocardium, myocardial (*see also* Infarct, myocardium) 410.9
   traumatic 861.03
      with open wound into thorax 861.13
   nontraumatic (meaning hernia) (*see also*
      Hernia, by site) 553.9
   obstructed (*see also* Hernia, by site,
      with obstruction) 552.9
   gangrenous (*see also* Hernia, by site,
      with gangrene) 551.9
operation wound 998.3
ovary, ovarian 620.8
   corpus luteum 620.1
   follicle (graafian) 620.0
oviduct 620.8
   due to pregnancy - *see* Pregnancy,
      tubal
pancreas 577.8
   traumatic - *see* Injury, internal, pan-
      creas
papillary muscle (ventricular) 429.6
pelvic
   floor, complicating delivery 664.1
   organ NEC - *see* Injury, pelvic, or-
      gans

Rupture, ruptured (*Continued*)
penis (traumatic) - *see* Wound, open,
   penis
perineum 624.8
   during delivery (*see also* Laceration,
      perineum, complicating deliv-
      ery) 664.4
pharynx (nontraumatic) (spontaneous)
   478.29
pregnant uterus (before onset of labor)
   665.0
prostate (traumatic) - *see* Injury, internal, prostate
pulmonary
   artery 417.8
   valve (heart) (*see also* Endocarditis,
      pulmonary) 424.3
   vein 417.8
   vessel 417.8
pupil, sphincter 364.75
pus tube (*see also* Salpingo-oophoritis)
   614.2
pyosalpinx (*see also* Salpingo-oophoritis) 614.2
rectum 569.49
   traumatic - *see* Injury, internal, rec-
      tum
retina, retinal (traumatic) (without detachment) 361.30
   with detachment (*see also* Detach-
      ment, retina, with retinal defect)
      361.00
rotator cuff (capsule) (traumatic) 840.4
   nontraumatic, complete 727.61
sclera 871.0
semilunar cartilage, knee (*see also* Tear,
   meniscus) 836.2
   old (*see also* Derangement, meniscus)
      717.5
septum (cardiac) 410.8
sigmoid 569.89
   traumatic - *see* Injury, internal, co-
      lon, sigmoid
sinus of Valsalva 747.29
spinal cord - *see also* Injury, spinal, by
   site
   due to injury at birth 767.4
   fetus or newborn 767.4
   syphilitic 094.89
   traumatic - *see also* Injury, spinal, by
      site
      with fracture - *see* Fracture, verte-
         bra, by site, with spinal cord
         injury
spleen 289.59
   congenital 767.8
   due to injury at birth 767.8
   malarial 084.9
   nontraumatic 289.59
   spontaneous 289.59
   traumatic 865.04
      with open wound into cavity
         865.14
splenic vein 459.0
stomach 537.89
   due to injury at birth 767.8
   traumatic - *see* Injury, internal, stom-
      ach
   ulcer - *see* Ulcer, stomach, with per-
      foration
synovium 727.50
   specified site NEC 727.59
tendon (traumatic) - *see also* Sprain, by
   site

Rupture, ruptured *(Continued)*
  tendon *(Continued)*
    with open wound - *see* Wound, open, by site
    Achilles 845.09
      nontraumatic 727.67
    ankle 845.09
      nontraumatic 727.68
    biceps (long bead) 840.8
      nontraumatic 727.62
    foot 845.10
      interphalangeal (joint) 845.13
      metatarsophalangeal (joint) 845.12
      nontraumatic 727.68
      specified site NEC 845.19
      tarsometatarsal (joint) 845.11
    hand 842.10
      carpometacarpal (joint) 842.11
      interphalangeal (joint) 842.13
      metacarpophalangeal (joint) 842.12
      nontraumatic 727.63
        extensors 727.63
        flexors 727.64
      specified site NEC 842.19
    nontraumatic 727.60
      specified site NEC 727.69
    patellar 844.8
      nontraumatic 727.66
    quadriceps 844.8
      nontraumatic 727.65
    rotator cuff (capsule) 840.4
      nontraumatic, complete 727.61
    wrist 842.00
      carpal (joint) 842.01
      nontraumatic 727.63
        extensors 727.63
        flexors 727.64
      radiocarpal (joint) (ligament) 842.02
      radioulnar (joint), distal 842.09
      specified site NEC 842.09
  testis (traumatic) 878.2
    complicated 878.3
    due to syphilis 095.8
  thoracic duct 457.8
  tonsil 474.8
  traumatic
    with open wound - *see* Wound, open, by site

Rupture, ruptured *(Continued)*
  traumatic *(Continued)*
    aorta - *see* Rupture, aorta, traumatic
    ear drum - *see* Wound, open, ear, drum
    external site - *see* Wound, open, by site
    eye 871.2
    globe (eye) - *see* Wound, open, eyeball
    internal organ (abdomen, chest, or pelvis) - *see also* Injury, internal, by site
      heart - *see* Rupture, myocardium, traumatic
      kidney - *see* Rupture, kidney
      liver - *see* Rupture, liver
      spleen - *see* Rupture, spleen, traumatic
    ligament, muscle, or tendon - *see also* Sprain, by site
      with open wound - *see* Wound, open, by site
    meaning hernia - *see* Hernia
  tricuspid (heart) (valve) - *see* Endocarditis, tricuspid
  tube, tubal 620.8
    abscess (*see also* Salpingo-oophoritis) 614.2
    due to pregnancy - *see* Pregnancy, tubal
  tympanum, tympanic (membrane) (*see also* Perforation, tympanum) 384.20
    with otitis media - *see* Otitis media
    traumatic - *see* Wound, open, ear, drum
  umbilical cord 663.8
    fetus or newborn 772.0
  ureter (traumatic) (*see also* Injury, internal, ureter) 867.2
    nontraumatic 593.89
  urethra 599.84
    with
      abortion - *see* Abortion, by type, with damage to pelvic organs
      ectopic pregnancy (*see also* categories 633.0-633.9) 639.2
      molar pregnancy (*see also* categories 630-632) 639.2
    following
      abortion 639.2
      ectopic or molar pregnancy 639.2

Rupture, ruptured *(Continued)*
  urethra *(Continued)*
    obstetrical trauma 665.5
    traumatic - *see* Injury, internal urethra
  uterosacral ligament 620.8
  uterus (traumatic) - *see also* Injury, internal, uterus
    affecting fetus or newborn 763.89
    during labor 665.1
    nonpuerperal, nontraumatic 621.8
    nontraumatic 621.8
    pregnant (during labor) 665.1
      before labor 665.0
  vagina 878.6
    complicated 878.7
    complicating delivery - *see* Laceration, vagina, complicating delivery
  valve, valvular (heart) - *see* Endocarditis
  varicose vein - *see* Varicose, vein
  varix - *see* Varix
  vena cava 459.0
  ventricle (free wall) (left) (*see also* Infarct, myocardium) 410.9
  vesical (urinary) 596.6
    traumatic - *see* Injury, internal, bladder
  vessel (blood) 459.0
    pulmonary 417.8
  viscus 799.8
  vulva 878.4
    complicated 878.5
    complicating delivery 664.0
Russell's dwarf (uterine dwarfism and craniofacial dysostosis) 759.89
Russell's dysentery 004.8
Russell (-Silver) syndrome (congenital hemihypertrophy and short stature) 759.89
Russian spring-summer type encephalitis 063.0
Rust's disease (tuberculous spondylitis) 015.0 *[720.81]*
Rustitskii's disease (multiple myeloma) (M9730/3) 203.0
Ruysch's disease (Hirschsprung's disease) 751.3
Rytand-Lipsitch syndrome (complete atrioventricular block) 426.0

S

Saber
 shin 090.5
 tibia 090.5
Sac, lacrimal - *see* condition
Saccharomyces infection (*see also* Candidiasis) 112.9
Saccharopinuria 270.7
Saccular - *see* condition
Sacculation
 aorta (nonsyphilitic) (*see also* Aneurysm, aorta) 441.9
  ruptured 441.5
  syphilitic 093.0
 bladder 596.3
 colon 569.89
 intralaryngeal (congenital) (ventricular) 748.3
 larynx (congenital) (ventricular) 748.3
 organ or site, congenital - *see* Distortion
 pregnant uterus, complicating delivery 654.4
  affecting fetus or newborn 763.1
   causing obstructed labor 660.2
    affecting fetus or newborn 763.1
 rectosigmoid 569.89
 sigmoid 569.89
 ureter 593.89
 urethra 599.2
 vesical 596.3
Sachs (-Tay) disease (amaurotic familial idiocy) 330.1
Sacks-Libman disease 710.0 [424.91]
Sacralgia 724.6
Sacralization
 fifth lumbar vertebra 756.15
 incomplete (vertebra) 756.15
Sacrodynia 724.6
Sacroiliac joint - *see* condition
Sacroiliitis NEC 720.2
Sacrum - *see* condition
Saddle
 back 737.8
 embolus, aorta 444.0
 nose 738.0
  congenital 754.0
  due to syphilis 090.5
Sadism (sexual) 302.84
Saemisch's ulcer 370.04
Saenger's syndrome 379.46
Sago spleen 277.3
Sailors' skin 692.74
Saint
 Anthony's fire (*see also* Erysipelas) 035
 Guy's dance - *see* Chorea
 Louis-type encephalitis 062.3
 triad (*see also* Hernia, diaphragm) 553.3
 Vitus' dance - *see* Chorea
Salicylism
 correct substance properly administered 535.4
 overdose or wrong substance given or taken 965.1
Salivary duct or gland - *see also* condition
 virus disease 078.5
Salivation (excessive) (*see also* Ptyalism) 527.7
Salmonella (aertrycke) (choleraesuis) (enteritidis) (gallinarum) (suipestifer) (typhimurium) (*see also* Infection, Salmonella) 003.9

Salmonella (*Continued*)
 arthritis 003.23
 carrier (suspected) of V02.3
 meningitis 003.21
 osteomyelitis 003.24
 pneumonia 003.22
 septicemia 003.1
 typhosa 002.0
  carrier (suspected) of V02.1
Salmonellosis 003.0
 with pneumonia 003.22
Salpingitis (catarrhal) (fallopian tube) (nodular) (pseudofollicular) (purulent) (septic) (*see also* Salpingo-oophoritis) 614.2
 ear 381.50
  acute 381.51
  chronic 381.52
 Eustachian (tube) 381.50
  acute 381.51
  chronic 381.52
 follicularis 614.1
 gonococcal (chronic) 098.37
  acute 098.17
 interstitial, chronic 614.1
 isthmica nodosa 614.1
 old - *see* Salpingo-oophoritis, chronic
 puerperal, postpartum, childbirth 670
 specific (chronic) 098.37
  acute 098.17
 tuberculous (acute) (chronic) (*see also* Tuberculosis) 016.6
 venereal (chronic) 098.37
  acute 098.17
Salpingocele 620.4
Salpingo-oophoritis (catarrhal) (purulent) (ruptured) (septic) (suppurative) 614.2
 acute 614.0
  with
   abortion - *see* Abortion, by type, with sepsis
   ectopic pregnancy (*see also* categories 633.0-633.9) 639.0
   molar pregnancy (*see also* categories 630-632) 639.0
  following
   abortion 639.0
   ectopic or molar pregnancy 639.0
  gonococcal 098.17
  puerperal, postpartum, childbirth 670
  tuberculous (*see also* Tuberculosis) 016.6
 chronic 614.1
  gonococcal 098.37
  tuberculous (*see also* Tuberculosis) 016.6
 complicating pregnancy 646.6
  affecting fetus or newborn 760.8
 gonococcal (chronic) 098.37
  acute 098.17
 old - *see* Salpingo-oophoritis, chronic
 puerperal 670
 specific - *see* Salpingo-oophoritis, gonococcal
 subacute (*see also* Salpingo-oophoritis, acute) 614.0
 tuberculous (acute) (chronic) (*see also* Tuberculosis) 016.6
 venereal - *see* Salpingo-oophoritis, gonococcal

Salpingo-ovaritis (*see also* Salpingo-oophoritis) 614.2
Salpingoperitonitis (*see also* Salpingo-oophoritis) 614.2
Salt-losing
 nephritis (*see also* Disease, renal) 593.9
 syndrome (*see also* Disease, renal) 593.9
Salt-rheum (*see also* Eczema) 692.9
Salzmann's nodular dystrophy 371.46
Sampson's cyst or tumor 617.1
Sandblasters'
 asthma 502
 lung 502
Sander's disease (paranoia) 297.1
Sandfly fever 066.0
Sandhoff's disease 330.1
Sanfilippo's syndrome (mucopolysaccharidosis III) 277.5
Sanger-Brown's ataxia 334.2
San Joaquin Valley fever 114.0
São Paulo fever or typhus 082.0
Saponification, mesenteric 567.8
Sapremia - *see* Septicemia
Sarcocele (benign)
 syphilitic 095.8
  congenital 090.5
Sarcoepiplocele (*see also* Hernia) 553.9
Sarcoepiplomphalocele (*see also* Hernia, umbilicus) 553.1
Sarcoid (any site) 135
 with lung involvement 135 [517.8]
 Boeck's 135
 Darier-Roussy 135
 Spiegler-Fendt 686.8
Sarcoidosis 135
 cardiac 135 [425.8]
 lung 135 [517.8]
Sarcoma (M8800/3) - *see also* Neoplasm, connective tissue, malignant
 alveolar soft part (M9581/3) - *see* Neoplasm, connective tissue, malignant
 ameloblastic (M9330/3) 170.1
  upper jaw (bone) 170.0
 botryoid (M8910/3) - *see* Neoplasm, connective tissue, malignant
 botryoides (M8910/3) - *see* Neoplasm, connective tissue, malignant
 cerebellar (M9480/3) 191.6
  circumscribed (arachnoidal) (M9471/3) 191.6
 circumscribed (arachnoidal) cerebellar (M9471/3) 191.6
 clear cell, of tendons and aponeuroses (M9044/3) - *see* Neoplasm, connective tissue, malignant
 embryonal (M8991/3) - *see* Neoplasm, connective tissue, malignant
 endometrial (stromal) (M8930/3) 182.0
  isthmus 182.1
 endothelial (M9130/3) - *see also* Neoplasm, connective tissue, malignant
  bone (M9260/3) - *see* Neoplasm, bone, malignant
 epithelioid cell (M8804/3) - *see* Neoplasm, connective tissue, malignant
 Ewing's (M9260/3) - *see* Neoplasm, bone, malignant
 germinoblastic (diffuse) (M9632/3) 202.8
  follicular (M9697/3) 202.0

Sarcoma *(Continued)*
  giant cell (M8802/3) - *see also* Neoplasm, connective tissue, malignant
    bone (M9250/3) - *see* Neoplasm, bone, malignant
  glomoid (M8710/3) - *see* Neoplasm, connective tissue, malignant
  granulocytic (M9930/3) 205.3
  hemangioendothelial (M9130/3) - *see* Neoplasm, connective tissue, malignant
  hemorrhagic, multiple (M9140/3) - *see* Kaposi's, sarcoma
  Hodgkin's (M9662/3) 201.2
  immunoblastic (M9612/3) 200.8
  Kaposi's (M9140/3) - *see* Kaposi's, sarcoma
  Kupffer cell (M9124/3) 155.0
  leptomeningeal (M9530/3) - *see* Neoplasm, meninges, malignant
  lymphangioendothelial (M9170/3) - *see* Neoplasm, connective tissue, malignant
  lymphoblastic (M9630/3) 200.1
  lymphocytic (M9620/3) 200.1
  mast cell (M9740/3) 202.6
  melanotic (M8720/3) - *see* Melanoma
  meningeal (M9530/3) - *see* Neoplasm, meninges, malignant
  meningothelial (M9530/3) - *see* Neoplasm, meninges, malignant
  mesenchymal (M8800/3) - *see also* Neoplasm, connective tissue, malignant
    mixed (M8990/3) - *see* Neoplasm, connective tissue, malignant
  mesothelial (M9050/3) - *see* Neoplasm, by site, malignant
  monstrocellular (M9481/3)
    specified site - *see* Neoplasm, by site, malignant
    unspecified site 191.9
  myeloid (M9930/3) 205.3
  neurogenic (M9540/3) - *see* Neoplasm, connective tissue, malignant
  odontogenic (M9270/3) 170.1
    upper jaw (bone) 170.0
  osteoblastic (M9180/3) - *see* Neoplasm, bone, malignant
  osteogenic (M9180/3) - *see also* Neoplasm, bone, malignant
    juxtacortical (M9190/3) - *see* Neoplasm, bone, malignant
    periosteal (M9190/3) - *see* Neoplasm, bone, malignant
  periosteal (M8812/3) - *see also* Neoplasm, bone, malignant
    osteogenic (M9190/3) - *see* Neoplasm, bone, malignant
  plasma cell (M9731/3) 203.8
  pleomorphic cell (M8802/3) - *see* Neoplasm, connective tissue, malignant
  reticuloendothelial (M9720/3) 202.3
  reticulum cell (M9640/3) 200.0
    nodular (M9642/3) 200.0
    pleomorphic cell type (M9641/3) 200.0
  round cell (M8803/3) - *see* Neoplasm, connective tissue, malignant
  small cell (M8803/3) - *see* Neoplasm, connective tissue, malignant

Sarcoma *(Continued)*
  spindle cell (M8801/3) - *see* Neoplasm, connective tissue, malignant
  stromal (endometrial) (M8930/3) 182.0
    isthmus 182.1
  synovial (M9040/3) - *see also* Neoplasm, connective tissue, malignant
    biphasic type (M9043/3) - *see* Neoplasm, connective tissue, malignant
    epithelioid cell type (M9042/3) - *see* Neoplasm, connective tissue, malignant
    spindle cell type (M9041/3) - *see* Neoplasm, connective tissue, malignant
Sarcomatosis
  meningeal (M9539/3) - *see* Neoplasm, meninges, malignant
  specified site NEC (M8800/3) - *see* Neoplasm, connective tissue, malignant
  unspecified site (M8800/6) 171.9
Sarcosinemia 270.8
Sarcosporidiosis 136.5
Saturnine - *see* condition
Saturnism 984.9
  specified type of lead - *see* Table of Drugs and Chemicals
Satyriasis 302.89
Sauriasis - *see* Ichthyosis
Sauriderma 757.39
Sauriosis - *see* Ichthyosis
Savill's disease (epidemic exfoliative dermatitis) 695.89
SBE (subacute bacterial endocarditis) 421.0
Scabies (any site) 133.0
Scabs 782.8
Scaglietti-Dagnini syndrome (acromegalic macrospondylitis) 253.0
Scald, scalded - *see also* Burn, by site
  skin syndrome 695.1
Scalenus anticus (anterior) syndrome 353.0
Scales 782.8
Scalp - *see* condition
Scaphocephaly 756.0
Scaphoiditis, tarsal 732.5
Scapulalgia 733.90
Scapulohumeral myopathy 359.1
Scar, scarring (*see also* Cicatrix) 709.2
  adherent 709.2
  atrophic 709.2
  cervix
    in pregnancy or childbirth 654.6
      affecting fetus or newborn 763.89
      causing obstructed labor 660.2
        affecting fetus or newborn 763.1
  cheloid 701.4
  chorioretinal 363.30
    disseminated 363.35
    macular 363.32
    peripheral 363.34
    posterior pole NEC 363.33
  choroid (*see also* Scar, chorioretinal) 363.30
  compression, pericardial 423.9
  congenital 757.39
  conjunctiva 372.64
  cornea 371.00
  xerophthalmic 264.6

Scar, scarring *(Continued)*
  due to previous cesarean delivery, complicating pregnancy or childbirth 654.2
    affecting fetus or newborn 763.89
  duodenal (bulb) (cap) 537.3
  hypertrophic 701.4
  keloid 701.4
  labia 624.4
  lung (base) 518.89
  macula 363.32
    disseminated 363.35
    peripheral 363.34
  muscle 728.89
  myocardium, myocardial 412
  painful 709.2
  papillary muscle 429.81
  posterior pole NEC 363.33
    macular - *see* Scar, macula
  postnecrotic (hepatic) (liver) 571.9
  psychic V15.49
  retina (*see also* Scar, chorioretinal) 363.30
  trachea 478.9
  uterus 621.8
    in pregnancy or childbirth NEC 654.9
      affecting fetus or newborn 763.89
      from previous cesarean delivery 654.2
  vulva 624.4
Scarabiasis 134.1
Scarlatina 034.1
  anginosa 034.1
  maligna 034.1
  myocarditis, acute 034.1 *[422.0]*
  old (*see also* Myocarditis) 429.0
  otitis media 034.1 *[382.02]*
  ulcerosa 034.1
Scarlatinella 057.8
Scarlet fever (albuminuria) (angina) (convulsions) (lesions of lid) (rash) 034.1
Schamberg's disease, dermatitis, or dermatosis (progressive pigmentary dermatosis) 709.09
Schatzki's ring (esophagus) (lower) (congenital) 750.3
  acquired 530.3
Schaufenster krankheit 413.9
Schaumann's
  benign lymphogranulomatosis 135
  disease (sarcoidosis) 135
  syndrome (sarcoidosis) 135
Scheie's syndrome (mucopolysaccharidosis IS) 277.5
Schenck's disease (sporotrichosis) 117.1
Scheuermann's disease or osteochondrosis 732.0
Scheuthauer-Marie-Sainton syndrome (cleidocranialis dysostosis) 755.59
Schilder (-Flatau) disease 341.1
Schilling-type monocytic leukemia (M9890/3) 206.9
Schimmelbusch's disease, cystic mastitis, or hyperplasia 610.1
Schirmer's syndrome (encephalocutaneous angiomatosis) 759.6
Schistocelia 756.79
Schistoglossia 750.13
Schistosoma infestation - *see* Infestation, Schistosoma

Schistosomiasis 120.9
Asiatic 120.2
bladder 120.0
chestermani 120.8
colon 120.1
cutaneous 120.3
due to
S. hematobium 120.0
S. japonicum 120.2
S. mansoni 120.1
S. mattheii 120.8
eastern 120.2
genitourinary tract 120.0
intestinal 120.1
lung 120.2
Manson's (intestinal) 120.1
Oriental 120.2
pulmonary 120.2
specified type NEC 120.8
vesical 120.0
Schizencephaly 742.4
Schizo-affective psychosis (*see also*
Schizophrenia) 295.7
Schizodontia 520.2
Schizoid personality 301.20
introverted 301.21
schizotypal 301.22
Schizophrenia, schizophrenic (reaction)
295.9

Note   Use the following fifth-digit
subclassification with category 295:

0	unspecified
1	subchronic
2	chronic
3	subchronic with acute exacer- bation
4	chronic with acute exacerba- tion
5	in remission

---

acute (attack) NEC 295.8
episode 295.4
atypical form 295.8
borderline 295.5
catalepsy 295.2
catatonic (type) (acute) (excited) (withdrawn) 295.2
childhood (type) (*see also* Psychosis,
childhood) 299.9
chronic NEC 295.6
coenesthesiopathic 295.8
cyclic (type) 295.7
disorganized (type) 295.1
flexibilitas cerea 295.2
hebephrenic (type) (acute) 295.1
incipient 295.5
latent 295.5
paranoid (type) (acute) 295.3
paraphrenic (acute) 295.3
prepsychotic 295.5
primary (acute) 295.0
prodromal 295.5
pseudoneurotic 295.5
pseudopsychopathic 295.5
reaction 295.9
residual (state) (type) 295.6
restzustand 295.6
schizo-affective (type) (depressed) (excited) 295.7
schizophreniform type 295.4
simple (type) (acute) 295.0
simplex (acute) 295.0
specified type NEC 295.8

Schizophrenia, schizophrenic (*Continued*)
syndrome of childhood NEC (*see also*
Psychosis, childhood) 299.9
undifferentiated 295.9
acute 295.8
chronic 295.6
Schizothymia 301.20
introverted 301.21
schizotypal 301.22
Schlafkrankheit 086.5
Schlatter's tibia (osteochondrosis) 732.4
Schlatter-Osgood disease (osteochondrosis, tibial tubercle) 732.4
Schloffer's tumor (*see also* Peritonitis)
567.2
Schmidt's syndrome
sphallo-pharyngo-laryngeal hemiplegia
352.6
thyroid-adrenocortical insufficiency
258.1
vagoaccessory 352.6
Schmincke
carcinoma (M8082/3) - *see* Neoplasm,
nasopharynx, malignant
tumor (M8082/3) - *see* Neoplasm, nasopharynx, malignant
Schmitz (-Stutzer) dysentery 004.0
Schmorl's disease or nodes 722.30
lumbar, lumbosacral 722.32
specified region NEC 722.39
thoracic, thoracolumbar 722.31
Schneider's syndrome 047.9
Schneiderian
carcinoma (M8121/3)
specified site - *see* Neoplasm, by site,
malignant
unspecified site 160.0
papilloma (M8121/0)
specified site - *see* Neoplasm, by site,
benign
unspecified site 212.0
Schoffer's tumor (*see also* Peritonitis)
567.2
Scholte's syndrome (malignant carcinoid) 259.2
Scholz's disease 330.0
Scholz (-Bielschowsky-Henneberg) syndrome 330.0
Schönlein (-Henoch) disease (primary)
(purpura) (rheumatic) 287.0
School examination V70.3
Schottmüller's disease (*see also* Fever,
paratyphoid) 002.9
Schroeder's syndrome (endocrine-hypertensive) 255.3
Schüller-Christian disease or syndrome
(chronic histiocytosis X) 277.8
Schultz's disease or syndrome (agranu-
locytosis) 288.0
Schultze's acroparesthesia, simple 443.89
Schwalbe-Ziehen-Oppenheimer disease
333.6
Schwannoma (M9560/0) - *see also* Neo-
plasm, connective tissue, benign
malignant (M9560/3) - *see* Neoplasm,
connective tissue, malignant
Schwartz (-Jampel) syndrome 756.89
Schwartz-Bartter syndrome (inappropriate secretion of antidiuretic hormone) 253.6
Schweninger-Buzzi disease (macular atrophy) 701.3
Sciatic - *see* condition

Sciatica (infectional) 724.3
due to
displacement of intervertebral disc
722.10
herniation, nucleus pulposus
722.10
Scimitar syndrome (anomalous venous
drainage, right lung to inferior vena
cava) 747.49
Sclera - *see* condition
Sclerectasia 379.11
Scleredema
adultorum 710.1
Buschke's 710.1
newborn 778.1
Sclerema
adiposum (newborn) 778.1
adultorum 710.1
edematosum (newborn) 778.1
neonatorum 778.1
newborn 778.1
Scleriasis - *see* Scleroderma
Scleritis 379.00
with corneal involvement 379.05
anterior (annular) (localized)
379.03
brawny 379.06
granulomatous 379.09
posterior 379.07
specified NEC 379.09
suppurative 379.09
syphilitic 095.0
tuberculous (nodular) (*see also* Tuberculosis) 017.3 [379.09]
Sclerochoroiditis (*see also* Scleritis) 379.00
Scleroconjunctivitis (*see also* Scleritis)
379.00
Sclerocystic ovary (syndrome) 256.4
Sclerodactylia 701.0
Scleroderma, sclerodermia (acrosclerotic)
(diffuse) (generalized) (progressive)
(pulmonary) 710.1
circumscribed 701.0
linear 701.0
localized (linear) 701.0
newborn 778.1
Sclerokeratitis 379.05
meaning sclerosing keratitis 370.54
tuberculous (*see also* Tuberculosis)
017.3 [379.09]
Scleroma, trachea 040.1
Scleromalacia
multiple 731.0
perforans 379.04
Scleromyxedema 701.8
Scleroperikeratitis 379.05
Sclerose en plaques 340
Sclerosis, sclerotic
adrenal (gland) 255.8
Alzheimer's 331.0
with dementia - *see* Alzheimer's, dementia
amyotrophic (lateral) 335.20
annularis fibrosi
aortic 424.1
mitral 424.0
aorta, aortic 440.0
valve (*see also* Endocarditis, aortic)
424.1
artery, arterial, arteriolar, arteriovascu-
lar - *see* Arteriosclerosis
ascending multiple 340
Baló's (concentric) 341.1
basilar - *see* Sclerosis, brain

Sclerosis, sclerotic *(Continued)*
 bone (localized) NEC 733.99
 brain (general) (lobular) 341.9
  Alzheimer's - *see* Alzheimer's, dementia
  artery, arterial 437.0
  atrophic lobar 331.0
   with dementia 331.0 *[294.1]*
  diffuse 341.1
   familial (chronic) (infantile) 330.0
   infantile (chronic) (familial) 330.0
   Pelizaeus-Merzbacher type 330.0
  disseminated 340
  hereditary 334.2
  infantile (degenerative) (diffuse) 330.0
  insular 340
  Krabbe's 330.0
  miliary 340
  multiple 340
  Pelizaeus-Merzbacher 330.0
  progressive familial 330.0
  senile 437.0
  tuberous 759.5
 bulbar, progressive 340
 bundle of His 426.50
  left 426.3
  right 426.4
 cardiac - *see* Arteriosclerosis, coronary
 cardiorenal (*see also* Hypertension, cardiorenal) 404.90
 cardiovascular (*see also* Disease, cardiovascular) 429.2
  renal (*see also* Hypertension, cardiorenal) 404.90
 centrolobar, familial 330.0
 cerebellar - *see* Sclerosis, brain
 cerebral - *see* Sclerosis, brain
 cerebrospinal 340
  disseminated 340
  multiple 340
 cerebrovascular 437.0
 choroid 363.40
  diffuse 363.56
 combined (spinal cord) - *see also* Degeneration, combined
  multiple 340
 concentric, Baló's 341.1
 cornea 370.54
 coronary (artery) - *see* Arteriosclerosis, coronary
 corpus cavernosum
  female 624.8
  male 607.89
 Dewitzky's
  aortic 424.1
  mitral 424.0
 diffuse NEC 341.1
 disease, heart - *see* Arteriosclerosis, coronary
 disseminated 340
 dorsal 340
 dorsolateral (spinal cord) - *see* Degeneration, combined
 endometrium 621.8
 extrapyramidal 333.90
 eye, nuclear (senile) 366.16
 Friedreich's (spinal cord) 334.0
 funicular (spermatic cord) 608.89
 gastritis 535.4
 general (vascular) - *see* Arteriosclerosis
 gland (lymphatic) 457.8
 hepatic 571.9

Sclerosis, sclerotic *(Continued)*
 hereditary
  cerebellar 334.2
  spinal 334.0
 idiopathic cortical (Garré's) (*see also* Osteomyelitis) 730.1
 ilium, piriform 733.5
 insular 340
  pancreas 251.8
 Islands of Langerhans 251.8
 kidney - *see* Sclerosis, renal
 larynx 478.79
 lateral 335.24
  amyotrophic 335.20
  descending 335.24
  primary 335.24
  spinal 335.24
 liver 571.9
 lobar, atrophic (of brain) 331.0
  with dementia 331.0 *[294.1]*
 lung (*see also* Fibrosis, lung) 515
 mastoid 383.1
 mitral - *see* Endocarditis, mitral
 Mönckeberg's (medial) (*see also* Arteriosclerosis, extremities) 440.20
 multiple (brain stem) (cerebral) (generalized) (spinal cord) 340
 myocardium, myocardial - *see* Arteriosclerosis, coronary
 nuclear (senile), eye 366.16
 ovary 620.8
 pancreas 577.8
 penis 607.89
 peripheral arteries (*see also* Arteriosclerosis, extremities) 440.20
 plaques 340
 pluriglandular 258.8
 polyglandular 258.8
 posterior (spinal cord) (syphilitic) 094.0
 posterolateral (spinal cord) - *see* Degeneration, combined
 prepuce 607.89
 primary lateral 335.24
 progressive systemic 710.1
 pulmonary (*see also* Fibrosis, lung) 515
  artery 416.0
  valve (heart) (*see also* Endocarditis, pulmonary) 424.3
 renal 587
  with
   cystine storage disease 270.0
   hypertension (*see also* Hypertension, kidney) 403.90
   hypertensive heart disease (conditions classifiable to 402) (*see also* Hypertension, cardiorenal) 404.90
   arteriolar (hyaline) (*see also* Hypertension, kidney) 403.90
   hyperplastic (*see also* Hypertension, kidney) 403.90
 retina (senile) (vascular) 362.17
 rheumatic
  aortic valve 395.9
  mitral valve 394.9
 Schilder's 341.1
 senile - *see* Arteriosclerosis
 spinal (cord) (general) (progressive) (transverse) 336.8
  ascending 357.0
  combined - *see also* Degeneration, combined
   multiple 340

Sclerosis, sclerotic *(Continued)*
 spinal *(Continued)*
  combined *(Continued)*
   syphilitic 094.89
  disseminated 340
  dorsolateral - *see* Degeneration, combined
  hereditary (Friedreich's) (mixed form) 334.0
  lateral (amyotrophic) 335.24
  multiple 340
  posterior (syphilitic) 094.0
 stomach 537.89
 subendocardial, congenital 425.3
 systemic (progressive) 710.1
  with lung involvement 710.1 *[517.2]*
 tricuspid (heart) (valve) - *see* Endocarditis, tricuspid
 tuberous (brain) 759.5
 tympanic membrane (*see also* Tympanosclerosis) 385.00
 valve, valvular (heart) - *see* Endocarditis
 vascular - *see* Arteriosclerosis
 vein 459.89
Sclerotenonitis 379.07
Sclerotitis (*see also* Scleritis) 379.00
 syphilitic 095.0
 tuberculous (*see also* Tuberculosis) 017.3 *[379.09]*
Scoliosis (acquired) (postural) 737.30
 congenital 754.2
 due to or associated with
  Charcôt-Marie-Tooth disease 356.1 *[737.43]*
  mucopolysaccharidosis 277.5 *[737.43]*
  neurofibromatosis 237.71 *[737.43]*
  osteitis
   deformans 731.0 *[737.43]*
   fibrosa cystica 252.0 *[737.43]*
  osteoporosis (*see also* Osteoporosis) 733.00 *[737.43]*
  poliomyelitis 138 *[737.43]*
  radiation 737.33
  tuberculosis (*see also* Tuberculosis) 015.0 *[737.43]*
 idiopathic 737.30
  infantile
   progressive 737.32
   resolving 737.31
 paralytic 737.39
 rachitic 268.1
 sciatic 724.3
 specified NEC 737.39
 thoracogenic 737.34
 tuberculous (*see also* Tuberculosis) 015.0 *[737.43]*
Scoliotic pelvis 738.6
 with disproportion (fetopelvic) 653.0
  affecting fetus or newborn 763.1
  causing obstructed labor 660.1
   affecting fetus or newborn 763.1
Scorbutus, scorbutic 267
 anemia 281.8
Scotoma (ring) 368.44
 arcuate 368.43
 Bjerrum 368.43
 blind spot area 368.42
 central 368.41
 centrocecal 368.41
 paracecal 368.42
 paracentral 368.41
 scintillating 368.12
 Seidel 368.43

ICD-9-CM
S
Vol. 2

◀▶ **New Code**   ◀▥ ▥▶ **Revised Code**

Screening *(Continued)*
  rickettsial disease V75.0
  rubella V73.3
  schistosomiasis V75.5
  senile macular lesions of eye V80.2
  sickle-cell anemia, disease, or trait
      V78.2
  skin condition V82.0
  sleeping sickness V75.3
  smallpox V73.1
  special V82.9
      specified condition NEC V82.8
  specified type NEC V82.8
  spirochetal disease V74.9
      specified type NEC V74.8
  stimulants in athletes V70.3
  syphilis V74.5
  tetanus V74.8
  thyroid disorder V77.0
  trachoma V73.6
  trypanosomiasis V75.3
  tuberculosis, pulmonary V74.1
  venereal disease V74.5
  viral encephalitis
      mosquito-borne V73.5
      tick-borne V73.5
  whooping cough V74.8
  worms, intestinal V75.7
  yaws V74.6
  yellow fever V73.4
Scrofula *(see also* Tuberculosis) 017.2
Scrofulide (primary) *(see also* Tuberculo-
    sis) 017.0
Scrofuloderma, scrofulodermia (any
    site) (primary) *(see also* Tuberculosis)
    017.0
Scrofulosis (universal) *(see also* Tubercu-
    losis) 017.2
Scrofulosis lichen (primary) *(see also* Tu-
    berculosis) 017.0
Scrofulous - *see* condition
Scrotal tongue 529.5
  congenital 750.13
Scrotum - *see* condition
Scurvy (gum) (infantile) (rickets) (scorbu-
    tic) 267
Sea-blue histiocyte syndrome 272.7
Seabright-Bantam syndrome (pseudohy-
    poparathyroidism) 275.49
Seasickness 994.6
Seatworm 127.4
Sebaceous
  cyst *(see also* Cyst, sebaceous)
      706.2
  gland disease NEC 706.9
Sebocystomatosis 706.2
Seborrhea, seborrheic 706.3
  adiposa 706.3
  capitis 690.11
  congestiva 695.4
  corporis 706.3
  dermatitis 690.10
      infantile 690.12
  diathesis in infants 695.89
  eczema 690.18
      infantile 690.12
  keratosis 702.19
      inflamed 702.11
  nigricans 759.89
  sicca 690.18
  wart 702.19
      inflamed 702.11
Seckel's syndrome 759.89
Seclusion pupil 364.74

Seclusiveness, child 313.22
Secondary - *see also* condition
  neoplasm - *see* Neoplasm, by site, ma-
      lignant, secondary
Secretan's disease or syndrome (post-
    traumatic edema) 782.3
Secretion
  antidiuretic hormone, inappropriate
      (syndrome) 253.6
  catecholamine, by pheochromocytoma
      255.6
  hormone
      antidiuretic, inappropriate (syn-
          drome) 253.6
      by
          carcinoid tumor 259.2
          pheochromocytoma 255.6
      ectopic NEC 259.3
  urinary
      excessive 788.42
      suppression 788.5
Section
  cesarean
      affecting fetus or newborn 763.4
      post mortem, affecting fetus or new-
          born 761.6
      previous, in pregnancy or childbirth
          654.2
          affecting fetus or newborn
              763.89   ◀▥
  nerve, traumatic - *see* Injury, nerve, by
      site
Seeligmann's syndrome (ichthyosis con-
    genita) 757.1
Segmentation, incomplete (congenital) -
    see also Fusion
  bone NEC 756.9
  lumbosacral (joint) 756.15
  vertebra 756.15
      lumbosacral 756.15
Seizure 780.39
  akinetic (idiopathic) *(see also* Epilepsy)
      345.0
      psychomotor 345.4
  apoplexy, apoplectic *(see also* Disease,
      cerebrovascular, acute) 436
  atonic *(see also* Epilepsy) 345.0
  autonomic 300.11
  brain or cerebral *(see also* Disease, cere-
      brovascular, acute) 436
  convulsive *(see also* Convulsions)
      780.39
  cortical (focal) (motor) *(see also* Epi-
      lepsy) 345.5
  epilepsy, epileptic (cryptogenic) *(see
      also* Epilepsy) 345.9
  epileptiform, epileptoid 780.39
      focal *(see also* Epilepsy) 345.5
  febrile 780.31
  heart - *see* Disease, heart
  hysterical 300.11
  Jacksonian (focal) *(see also* Epilepsy)
      345.5
      motor type 345.5
      sensory type 345.5
  newborn 779.0
  paralysis *(see also* Disease, cerebrovas-
      cular, acute) 436
  recurrent 780.39
      epileptic - *see* Epilepsy
  repetitive 780.39
      epileptic - *see* Epilepsy
  salaam *(see also* Epilepsy) 345.6
  uncinate *(see also* Epilepsy) 345.4

Self-mutilation 300.9
Semicoma 780.09
Semiconsciousness 780.09
Seminal
  vesicle - *see* condition
  vesiculitis *(see also* Vesiculitis) 608.0
Seminoma (M9061/3)
  anaplastic type (M9062/3)
      specified site - *see* Neoplasm, by site,
          malignant
      unspecified site 186.9
  specified site - *see* Neoplasm, by site,
      malignant
  spermatocytic (M9063/3)
      specified site - *see* Neoplasm, by site,
          malignant
      unspecified site 186.9
  unspecified site 186.9
Semliki Forest encephalitis 062.8
Senear-Usher disease or syndrome
    (pemphigus erythematosus)
    694.4
Senecio jacobae dermatitis 692.6
Senectus 797
Senescence 797
Senile *(see also* condition) 797
  cervix (atrophic) 622.8
  degenerative atrophy, skin 701.3
  endometrium (atrophic) 621.8
  fallopian tube (atrophic) 620.3
  heart (failure) 797
  lung 492.8
  ovary (atrophic) 620.3
  syndrome 259.8
  vagina, vaginitis (atrophic) 627.3
  wart 702.0
Senility 797
  with
      acute confusional state 290.3
      delirium 290.3
      mental changes 290.9
      psychosis NEC *(see also* Psychosis,
          senile) 290.20
  premature (syndrome) 259.8
Sensation
  burning *(see also* Disturbance, sensa-
      tion) 782.0
      tongue 529.6
  choking 784.9
  loss of *(see also* Disturbance, sensation)
      782.0
  prickling *(see also* Disturbance, sensa-
      tion) 782.0
  tingling *(see also* Disturbance, sensa-
      tion) 782.0
Sense loss (touch) *(see also* Disturbance,
    sensation) 782.0
  smell 781.1
  taste 781.1
Sensibility disturbance NEC (cortical)
    (deep) (vibratory) *(see also* Distur-
    bance, sensation) 782.0
Sensitive dentine 521.8
Sensitiver Beziehungswahn 297.8
Sensitivity, sensitization - *see also* Al-
    lergy
  autoerythrocyte 287.2
  carotid sinus 337.0
  child (excessive) 313.21
  cold, autoimmune 283.0
  methemoglobin 289.7
  suxamethonium 289.8
  tuberculin, without clinical or radio-
      logical symptoms 795.5

◀ ▶ **New Code**　　⬅ ⇦ ⇨ **Revised Code**

Sickness *(Continued)*
  sleeping *(Continued)*
    Gambian 086.3
    late effect 139.8
    Rhodesian 086.4
  sweating 078.2
  swing (motion) 994.6
  train (railway) (travel) 994.6
  travel (any vehicle) 994.6
Sick sinus syndrome 427.81
Sideropenia *(see also* Anemia, iron defi-
    ciency) 280.9
Siderosis (lung) (occupational) 503
  cornea 371.15
  eye (bulbi) (vitreous) 360.23
  lens 360.23
Siegal-Cattan-Mamou disease (periodic)
    277.3
Siemens' syndrome
  ectodermal dysplasia 757.31
  keratosis follicularis spinulosa (decal-
    vans) 757.39
Sighing respiration 786.7
Sigmoid
  flexure - *see* condition
  kidney 753.3
Sigmoiditis - *see* Enteritis
Silfverskiöld's syndrome 756.50
Silicosis, silicotic (complicated) (occupa-
    tional) (simple) 502
  fibrosis, lung (confluent) (massive) (oc-
    cupational) 502
  non-nodular 503
  pulmonum 502
Silicotuberculosis *(see also* Tuberculosis)
    011.4
Silo fillers' disease 506.9
Silver's syndrome (congenital hemihy-
    pertrophy and short stature) 759.89
Silver wire arteries, retina 362.13
Silvestroni-Bianco syndrome (thalasse-
    mia minima) 282.4
Simian crease 757.2
Simmonds' cachexia or disease (pitui-
    tary cachexia) 253.2
Simons' disease or syndrome (progres-
    sive lipodystrophy) 272.6
Simple, simplex - *see* condition
Sinding-Larsen disease (juvenile osteo-
    pathia patellae) 732.4
Singapore hemorrhagic fever 065.4
Singers' node or nodule 478.5
Single
  atrium 745.69
  coronary artery 746.85
  umbilical artery 747.5
  ventricle 745.3
Singultus 786.8
  epidemicus 078.89
Sinus - *see also* Fistula
  abdominal 569.81
  arrest 426.6
  arrhythmia 427.89
  bradycardia 427.89
    chronic 427.81
  branchial cleft (external) (internal)
    744.41
  coccygeal (infected) 685.1
    with abscess 685.0
  dental 522.7
  dermal (congenital) 685.1
    with abscess 685.0
  draining - *see* Fistula
  infected, skin NEC 686.9

Sinus *(Continued)*
  marginal, rupture or bleeding 641.2
    affecting fetus or newborn 762.1
  pause 426.6
  pericranii 742.0
  pilonidal (infected) (rectum) 685.1
    with abscess 685.0
  preauricular 744.46
  rectovaginal 619.1
  sacrococcygeal (dermoid) (infected)
    685.1
    with abscess 685.0
  skin
    infected NEC 686.9
    noninfected- *see* Ulcer, skin
  tachycardia 427.89
  tarsi syndrome 355.5
  testis 608.89
  tract (postinfectional) - *see* Fistula
  urachus 753.7
Sinuses, Rokitansky-Aschoff *(see also*
    Disease, gallbladder) 575.8
Sinusitis (accessory) (chronic) (hyper-
    plastic) (nasal) (nonpurulent) (puru-
    lent) 473.9
  with influenza, flu, or grippe 487.1
  acute 461.9
    ethmoidal 461.2
    frontal 461.1
    maxillary 461.0
    specified type NEC 461.8
    sphenoidal 461.3
  allergic *(see also* Fever, hay) 477.9
  antrum - *see* Sinusitis, maxillary
  due to
    fungus, any sinus 117.9
    high altitude 993.1
  ethmoidal 473.2
    acute 461.2
  frontal 473.1
    acute 461.1
  influenzal 478.1
  maxillary 473.0
    acute 461.0
  specified site NEC 473.8
  sphenoidal 473.3
    acute 461.3
  syphilitic, any sinus 095.8
  tuberculous, any sinus *(see also* Tuber-
    culosis) 012.8
Sinusitis-bronchiectasis-situs inversus
    (syndrome) (triad) 759.3
Sipple's syndrome (medullary thyroid
    carcinoma-pheochromocytoma)
    193
Sirenomelia 759.89
Siriasis 992.0
Sirkari's disease 085.0
Siti 104.0
Sitophobia 300.29
Situation, psychiatric 300.9
Situational
  disturbance (transient) *(see also* Reac-
    tion, adjustment) 309.9
    acute 308.3
  maladjustment, acute *(see also* Reaction,
    adjustment) 309.9
  reaction *(see also* Reaction, adjustment)
    309.9
    acute 308.3
Situs inversus or transversus 759.3
  abdominalis 759.3
  thoracis 759.3
Sixth disease 057.8

Sjögren (-Gougerot) syndrome or disease
    (keratoconjunctivitis sicca) 710.2
  with lung involvement 710.2 *[517.8]*
Sjögren-Larsson syndrome (ichthyosis
    congenita) 757.1
Skeletal - *see* condition
Skene's gland - *see* condition
Skenitis *(see also* Urethritis) 597.89
  gonorrheal (acute) 098.0
    chronic or duration of 2 months or
      over 098.2
Skerljevo 104.0
Skevas-Zerfus disease 989.5
Skin - *see also* condition
  donor V59.1
  hidebound 710.9
Slate-dressers' lung 502
Slate-miners' lung 502
Sleep
  disorder 780.50
    with apnea - *see* Apnea, sleep
    child 307.40
    nonorganic origin 307.40
      specified type NEC 307.49
  disturbance 780.50
    with apnea - *see* Apnea, sleep
    nonorganic origin 307.40
      specified type NEC 307.49
  drunkenness 307.47
  paroxysmal 347
  rhythm inversion 780.55
    nonorganic origin 307.45
  walking 307.46
    hysterical 300.13
Sleeping sickness 086.5
  late effect 139.8
Sleeplessness *(see also* Insomnia) 780.52
  menopausal 627.2
  nonorganic origin 307.41
Slipped, slipping
  epiphysis (postinfectional) 732.9
    traumatic (old) 732.9
      current - *see* Fracture, by site
      upper femoral (nontraumatic) 732.2
  intervertebral disc - *see* Displacement,
    intervertebral disc
  ligature, umbilical 772.3
  patella 717.89
  rib 733.99
  sacroiliac joint 724.6
  tendon 727.9
  ulnar nerve, nontraumatic 354.2
  vertebra NEC *(see also* Spondylolisthe-
    sis) 756.12
Slocumb's syndrome 255.3
Sloughing (multiple) (skin) 686.9
  abscess - *see* Abscess, by site
  appendix 543.9
  bladder 596.8
  fascia 728.9
  graft - *see* Complications, graft
  phagedena *(see also* Gangrene) 785.4
  reattached extremity *(see also* Compli-
    cations, reattached extremity)
    996.90
  rectum 569.49
  scrotum 608.89
  tendon 727.9
  transplanted organ *(see also* Rejection,
    transplant, organ, by site) 996.80
  ulcer *(see also* Ulcer, skin) 707.9
Slow
  feeding newborn 779.3
  fetal, growth NEC 764.9

ICD-9-CM

S

Vol. 2

Slow (*Continued*)
   fetal, growth NEC (*Continued*)
      affecting management of pregnancy
         656.5
Slowing
   heart 427.89
   urinary stream 788.62
Sluder's neuralgia or syndrome 337.0
Slurred, slurring, speech 784.5
Small, smallness
   cardia reserve - *see* Disease, heart
   for dates
      fetus or newborn 764.0
         with malnutrition 764.1
            affecting management of preg-
               nancy 656.5
      infant, term 764.0
         with malnutrition 764.1
            affecting management of pregnancy
               656.5
   introitus, vagina 623.3
   kidney, unknown cause 589.9
      bilateral 589.1
      unilateral 589.0
   ovary 620.8
   pelvis
      with disproportion (fetopelvic) 653.1
         affecting fetus or newborn 763.1
      causing obstructed labor 660.1
         affecting fetus or newborn 763.1
   placenta - *see* Placenta, insufficiency
   uterus 621.8
   white kidney 582.9
Small-for-dates (*see also* Light-for-dates)
      764.0
   affecting management of pregnancy
      656.5
Smallpox 050.9
   contact V01.3
   exposure to V01.3
   hemorrhagic (pustular) 050.0
   malignant 050.0
   modified 050.2
   vaccination
      complications - *see* Complications,
         vaccination
      prophylactic (against) V04.1
Smith's fracture (separation) (closed)
      813.41
   open 813.51
Smith-Lemli-Opitz syndrome (cerebro-
      hepatorenal syndrome) 759.89
Smith-Strang disease (oasthouse urine)
      270.2
Smokers'
   bronchitis 491.0
   cough 491.0
   syndrome (*see also* Abuse, drugs, non-
      dependent) 305.1
   throat 472.1
   tongue 528.6
Smothering spells 786.09
Snaggle teeth, tooth 524.3
Snapping
   finger 727.05
   hip 719.65
   jaw 524.69
   knee 717.9
   thumb 727.05
**Sneddon-Wilkinson disease or syn-
      drome** (subcorneal pustular derma-
      tosis) 694.1
Sneezing 784.9
   intractable 478.1

Sniffing
   cocaine (*see also* Dependence) 304.2
   ether (*see also* Dependence) 304.6
   glue (airplane) (*see also* Dependence)
      304.6
Snoring 786.09
Snow blindness 370.24
Snuffles (nonsyphilitic) 460
   syphilitic (infant) 090.0
Social migrant V60.0
Sodoku 026.0
Soemmering's ring 366.51
Soft - *see also* condition
   nails 703.8
Softening
   bone 268.2
   brain (necrotic) (progressive) 434.9
      arteriosclerotic 437.0
      congenital 742.4
      embolic (*see also* Embolism, brain)
         434.1
      hemorrhagic (*see also* Hemorrhage,
         brain) 431
      occlusive 434.9
      thrombotic (*see also* Thrombosis,
         brain) 434.0
   cartilage 733.92
   cerebellar - *see* Softening, brain
   cerebral - *see* Softening, brain
   cerebrospinal - *see* Softening, brain
   myocardial, heart (*see also* Degenera-
      tion, myocardial) 429.1
   nails 703.8
   spinal cord 336.8
   stomach 537.89
Solar fever 061
Soldier's
   heart 306.2
   patches 423.1
Solitary
   cyst
      bone 733.21
      kidney 593.2
   kidney (congenital) 753.0
   tubercle, brain (*see also* Tuberculosis,
      brain) 013.2
   ulcer, bladder 596.8
Somatization reaction, somatic reaction
      (*see also* Disorder, psychosomatic)
      306.9
   disorder 300.81
Somatoform disorder 300.82
   atypical 300.82
   severe 300.81
   undifferentiated 300.82
Somnambulism 307.46
   hysterical 300.13
Somnolence 780.09
   nonorganic origin 307.43
   periodic 349.89
Sonne dysentery 004.3
Soor 112.0
Sore
   Delhi 085.1
   desert (*see also* Ulcer, skin) 707.9
   eye 379.99
   Lahore 085.1
   mouth 528.9
      canker 528.2
      due to dentures 528.9
   muscle 729.1
   Naga (*see also* Ulcer, skin) 707.9
   oriental 085.1
   pressure 707.0

Sore (*Continued*)
   pressure (*Continued*)
      with gangrene 707.0 [785.4]
   skin NEC 709.9
   soft 099.0
   throat 462
      with influenza, flu, or grippe 487.1
      acute 462
      chronic 472.1
      clergyman's 784.49
      Coxsackie (virus) 074.0
      diphtheritic 032.0
      epidemic 034.0
      gangrenous 462
      herpetic 054.79
      influenzal 487.1
      malignant 462
      purulent 462
      putrid 462
      septic 034.0
      streptococcal (ulcerative) 034.0
      ulcerated 462
      viral NEC 462
         Coxsackie 074.0
   tropical (*see also* Ulcer, skin) 707.9
   veldt (*see also* Ulcer, skin) 707.9
Sotos' syndrome (cerebral gigantism)
      253.0
Sounds
   friction, pleural 786.7
   succussion, chest 786.7
**South African cardiomyopathy syn-
      drome** 425.2
South American
   blastomycosis 116.1
   trypanosomiasis - *see* Trypanosomiasis
Southeast Asian hemorrhagic fever
      065.4
Spacing, teeth, abnormal 524.3
Spade-like hand (congenital) 754.89
Spading nail 703.8
   congenital 757.5
Spanemia 285.9
Spanish collar 605
Sparganosis 123.5
Spasm, spastic, spasticity (*see also* condi-
      tion) 781.0
   accommodation 367.53
   ampulla of Vater (*see also* Disease, gall-
      bladder) 576.8
   anus, ani (sphincter) (reflex) 564.6
      psychogenic 306.4
   artery NEC 443.9
      basilar 435.0
      carotid 435.8
      cerebral 435.9
         specified artery NEC 435.8
      retinal (*see also* Occlusion, retinal, ar-
         tery) 362.30
      vertebral 435.1
      vertebrobasilar 435.3
   Bell's 351.1
   bladder (sphincter, external or inter-
      nal) 596.8
   bowel 564.1
      psychogenic 306.4
   bronchus, bronchiole 519.1
   cardia 530.0
   cardiac - *see* Angina
   carpopedal (*see also* Tetany) 781.7
   cecum 564.1
      psychogenic 306.4
   cerebral (arteries) (vascular) 435.9
      specified artery NEC 435.8

Spasm, spastic, spasticity (*Continued*)
cerebrovascular 435.9
cervix, complicating delivery 661.4
  affecting fetus or newborn 763.7
ciliary body (of accommodation) 367.53
colon 564.1
  psychogenic 306.4
common duct (*see also* Disease, biliary)
  576.8
compulsive 307.22
conjugate 378.82
convergence 378.84
coronary (artery) - *see* Angina
diaphragm (reflex) 786.8
  psychogenic 306.1
duodenum, duodenal (bulb)
  564.89
esophagus (diffuse) 530.5
  psychogenic 306.4
facial 351.8
fallopian tube 620.8
gait 781.2
gastrointestinal (tract) 536.8
  psychogenic 306.4
glottis 478.75
  hysterical 300.11
  psychogenic 306.1
    specified as conversion reaction
      300.11
  reflex through recurrent laryngeal
    nerve 478.75
habit 307.20
  chronic 307.22
  transient of childhood 307.21
heart - *see* Angina
hourglass - *see* Contraction, hourglass
hysterical 300.11
infantile (*see also* Epilepsy) 345.6
internal oblique, eye 378.51
intestinal 564.1
  psychogenic 306.4
larynx, laryngeal 478.75
  hysterical 300.11
  psychogenic 306.1
    specified as conversion reaction
      300.11
levator palpebrae superioris 333.81
lightning (*see also* Epilepsy) 345.6
mobile 781.0
muscle 728.85
  back 724.8
  psychogenic 306.0
nerve, trigeminal 350.1
nervous 306.0
nodding 307.3
  infantile (*see also* Epilepsy) 345.6
occupational 300.89
oculogyric 378.87
ophthalmic artery 362.30
orbicularis 781.0
perineal 625.8
peroneo-extensor (*see also* Flat, foot) 734
pharynx (reflex) 478.29
  hysterical 300.11
  psychogenic 306.1
    specified as conversion reaction
      300.11
pregnant uterus, complicating delivery
  661.4
psychogenic 306.0
pylorus 537.81
  adult hypertrophic 537.0
  congenital or infantile 750.5
  psychogenic 306.4

Spasm, spastic, spasticity (*Continued*)
rectum (sphincter) 564.6
  psychogenic 306.4
retinal artery NEC (*see also* Occlusion,
  retina, artery) 362.30
sacroiliac 724.6
salaam (infantile) (*see also* Epilepsy)
  345.6
saltatory 781.0
sigmoid 564.1
  psychogenic 306.4
sphincter of Oddi (*see also* Disease,
  gallbladder) 576.5
stomach 536.8
  neurotic 306.4
throat 478.29
  hysterical 300.11
  psychogenic 306.1
    specified as conversion reaction
      300.11
tic 307.20
  chronic 307.22
  transient of childhood 307.21
tongue 529.8
torsion 333.6
trigeminal nerve 350.1
  postherpetic 053.12
ureter 593.89
urethra (sphincter) 599.84
uterus 625.8
  complicating labor 661.4
    affecting fetus or newborn
      763.7
vagina 625.1
  psychogenic 306.51
vascular NEC 443.9
vasomotor NEC 443.9
vein NEC 459.89
vesical (sphincter, external or internal)
  596.8
viscera 789.0
Spasmodic - *see* condition
Spasmophilia (*see also* Tetany) 781.7
Spasmus nutans 307.3
Spastic - *see also* Spasm
  child 343.9
Spasticity - *see also* Spasm
  cerebral, child 343.9
Speakers' throat 784.49
Specific, specified - *see* condition
Speech
  defect, disorder, disturbance, impedi-
    ment NEC 784.5
  psychogenic 307.9
  therapy V57.3
Spells 780.39
  breath-holding 786.9
Spencer's disease (epidemic vomiting)
  078.82
Spens' syndrome (syncope with heart
  block) 426.9
Spermatic cord - *see* condition
Spermatocele 608.1
  congenital 752.8
Spermatocystitis 608.4
Spermatocytoma (M9063/3)
  specified site - *see* Neoplasm, by site,
    malignant
  unspecified site 186.9
Spermatorrhea 608.89
Sperm counts V26.2
  postvasectomy V25.8
Sphacelus (*see also* Gangrene) 785.4
Sphenoidal - *see* condition

Sphenoiditis (chronic) (*see also* Sinusitis,
  sphenoidal) 473.3
Sphenopalatine ganglion neuralgia 337.0
Sphericity, increased, lens 743.36
Spherocytosis (congenital) (familial) (he-
  reditary) 282.0
  hemoglobin disease 282.7
  sickle-cell (disease) 282.60
Spherophakia 743.36
Sphincter - *see* condition
Sphincteritis, sphincter of Oddi (*see also*
  Cholecystitis) 576.8
Sphingolipidosis 272.7
Sphingolipodystrophy 272.7
Sphingomyelinosis 272.7
Spicule tooth 520.2
Spider
  finger 755.59
  nevus 448.1
  vascular 448.1
Spiegler-Fendt sarcoid 686.8
Spielmeyer-Stock disease 330.1
Spielmeyer-Vogt disease 330.1
Spina bifida (aperta) 741.9

> Note   Use the following fifth-digit
> subclassification with category 741:
>
> 0   unspecified region
> 1   cervical region
> 2   dorsal [thoracic] region
> 3   lumbar region

  with hydrocephalus 741.0
    fetal (suspected), affecting manage-
      ment of pregnancy 655.0
  occulta 756.17
Spindle, Krukenberg's 371.13
Spine, spinal - *see* condition
Spiradenoma (eccrine) (M8403/0) - *see*
  Neoplasm, skin, benign
Spirillosis NEC (*see also* Fever, relaps-
  ing) 087.9
Spirillum minus 026.0
Spirillum obermeieri infection 087.0
Spirochetal - *see* condition
Spirochetosis 104.9
  arthritic, arthritica 104.9 [711.8]
  bronchopulmonary 104.8
  icterohemorrhagica 100.0
  lung 104.8
Spitting blood (*see also* Hemoptysis)
  786.3
Splanchnomegaly 569.89
Splanchnoptosis 569.89
Spleen, splenic - *see also* condition
  agenesis 759.0
  flexure syndrome 569.89
  neutropenia syndrome 288.0
  sequestration syndrome 282.60
Splenectasis (*see also* Splenomegaly)
  789.2
Splenitis (interstitial) (malignant) (nonspecific) 289.59
  malarial (*see also* Malaria) 084.6
  tuberculous (*see also* Tuberculosis)
    017.7
Splenocele 289.59
Splenomegalia - *see* Splenomegaly
Splenomegalic - *see* condition
Splenomegaly 789.2
  Bengal 789.2
  cirrhotic 289.51
  congenital 759.0
  congestive, chronic 289.51

ICD-9-CM

S

Vol. 2

Spur *(Continued)*
  nose (septum) 478.1
    bone 726.91
    septal 478.1
Spuria placenta - *see* Placenta, abnormal
Spurway's syndrome (brittle bones and
  blue sclera) 756.51
Sputum, abnormal (amount) (color) (excessive) (odor) (purulent) 786.4
  bloody 786.3
Squamous - *see also* condition
  cell metaplasia
    bladder 596.8
    cervix - *see* condition
  epithelium in
    cervical canal (congenital) 752.49
    uterine mucosa (congenital) 752.3
  metaplasia
    bladder 596.8
    cervix - *see* condition
Squashed nose 738.0
  congenital 754.0
Squeeze, divers' 993.3
Squint (*see also* Strabismus) 378.9
  accommodative (*see also* Esotropia)
    378.00
  concomitant (*see also* Heterotropia)
    378.30
Stab - *see also* Wound, open, by site
  internal organs - *see* Injury, internal, by
    site, with open wound
Staggering gait 781.2
  hysterical 300.11
Staghorn calculus 592.0
Stähl's
  ear 744.29
  pigment line (cornea) 371.11
Stähli's pigment lines (cornea) 371.11
Stain
  port wine 757.32
  tooth, teeth (hard tissues) 521.7
    due to
      accretions 523.6
      deposits (betel) (black) (green)
        (materia alba) (orange) (tobacco) 523.6
      metals (copper) (silver) 521.7
      nicotine 523.6
      pulpal bleeding 521.7
      tobacco 523.6
Stammering 307.0
Standstill
  atrial 426.6
  auricular 426.6
  cardiac (*see also* Arrest, cardiac) 427.5
  sinoatrial 426.6
  sinus 426.6
  ventricular (*see also* Arrest, cardiac)
    427.5
Stannosis 503
Stanton's disease (melioidosis) 025
Staphylitis (acute) (catarrhal) (chronic)
  (gangrenous) (membranous) (suppurative) (ulcerative) 528.3
Staphylococcemia 038.10
  aureus 038.11
  specified organism NEC 038.19
Staphylococcus, staphylococcal - *see* condition
Staphyloderma (skin) 686.00
Staphyloma 379.11
  anterior, localized 379.14
  ciliary 379.11
  cornea 371.73

Staphyloma *(Continued)*
  equatorial 379.13
  posterior 379.12
  posticum 379.12
  ring 379.15
  sclera NEC 379.11
Starch eating 307.52
Stargardt's disease 362.75
Starvation (inanition) (due to lack of
  food) 994.2
  edema 262
  voluntary NEC 307.1
Stasis
  bile (duct) (*see also* Disease, biliary)
    576.8
  bronchus (*see also* Bronchitis) 490
  cardiac (*see also* Failure, heart, congestive) 428.0
  cecum 564.89
  colon 564.89
  dermatitis (*see also* Varix, with stasis
    dermatitis) 454.1
  duodenal 536.8
  eczema (*see also* Varix, with stasis dermatitis) 454.1
  foot 991.4
  gastric 536.3
  ileocecal coil 564.89
  ileum 564.89
  intestinal 564.89
  jejunum 564.89
  kidney 586
  liver 571.9
    cirrhotic - *see* Cirrhosis, liver
  lymphatic 457.8
  pneumonia 514
  portal 571.9
  pulmonary 514
  rectal 564.89
  renal 586
    tubular 584.5
  stomach 536.3
  ulcer
    with varicose veins 454.0
    without varicose veins 459.81
  urine NEC (*see also* Retention, urine)
    788.20
  venous 459.81
State
  affective and paranoid, mixed, organic
    psychotic 294.8
  agitated 307.9
    acute reaction to stress 308.2
  anxiety (neurotic) (*see also* Anxiety)
    300.00
    specified type NEC 300.09
  apprehension (*see also* Anxiety) 300.00
    specified type NEC 300.09
  climacteric, female 627.2
    following induced menopause 627.4
  clouded
    epileptic (*see also* Epilepsy) 345.9
    paroxysmal (idiopathic) (*see also* Epilepsy) 345.9
  compulsive (mixed) (with obsession)
    300.3
  confusional 298.9
    acute 293.0
      with
        arteriosclerotic dementia 290.41
        presenile brain disease 290.11
        senility 290.3
      alcoholic 291.0
      drug-induced 292.81

State *(Continued)*
  epileptic 293.0
    postoperative 293.9
    reactive (emotional stress) (psychological trauma) 298.2
    subacute 293.1
  constitutional psychopathic 301.9
  convulsive (*see also* Convulsions)
    780.39
  depressive NEC 311
    induced by drug 292.84
    neurotic 300.4
  dissociative 300.15
  hallucinatory 780.1
    induced by drug 292.12
  hyperdynamic beta-adrenergic circulatory 429.82
  locked-in 344.81
  menopausal 627.2
    artificial 627.4
    following induced menopause 627.4
  neurotic NEC 300.9
    with depersonalization episode 300.6
  obsessional 300.3
  oneiroid (*see also* Schizophrenia) 295.4
  panic 300.01
  paranoid 297.9
    alcohol-induced 291.5
    arteriosclerotic 290.42
    climacteric 297.2
    drug-induced 292.11
    in
      presenile brain disease 290.12
      senile brain disease 290.20
    involutional 297.2
    menopausal 297.2
    senile 290.20
    simple 297.0
  postleukotomy 310.0
  pregnant (*see also* Pregnancy) V22.2
  psychogenic, twilight 298.2
  psychotic, organic (*see also* Psychosis,
    organic) 294.9
    mixed paranoid and affective 294.8
    senile or presenile NEC 290.9
    transient NEC 293.9
      with
        anxiety 293.84
        delusions 293.81
        depression 293.83
        hallucinations 293.82
  residual schizophrenic (*see also* Schizophrenia) 295.6
  tension (*see also* Anxiety) 300.9
  transient organic psychotic 293.9
    anxiety type 293.84
    depressive type 293.83
    hallucinatory type 293.83
    paranoid type 293.81
    specified type NEC 293.89
  twilight
    epileptic 293.0
    psychogenic 298.2
  vegetative (persistent) 780.03
Status (post)
  absence
    epileptic (*see also* Epilepsy) 345.2
    of organ, acquired (postsurgical) -
      see Absence, by site, acquired
  anastomosis of intestine (for bypass)
    V45.3
  angioplasty, percutaneous transluminal
    coronary V45.82
  anginosus 413.9

◀▶ **New Code**   ◀▥▥ ▥▥▶ **Revised Code**

Status (*Continued*)
ankle prosthesis V43.66
aortocoronary bypass or shunt V45.81
arthrodesis V45.4
artificially induced condition NEC
    V45.89
artificial opening (of) V44.9
    gastrointestinal tract NEC V44.4
    specified site NEC V44.8
    urinary tract NEC V44.6
    vagina V44.7
asthmaticus (*see also* Asthma) 493.9
breast implant removal V45.83
cardiac
    device (in situ) V45.00
        carotid sinus V45.09
            fitting or adjustment V53.39
        defibrillator, automatic implanta-
            ble V45.02
        pacemaker V45.01
            fitting or adjustment V53.31
carotid sinus stimulator V45.09
cataract extraction V45.61
chemotherapy V66.2
colostomy V44.3
contraceptive device V45.59
    intrauterine V45.51
    subdermal V45.52
convulsivus idiopathicus (*see also* Epi-
    lepsy) 345.3
coronary artery bypass or shunt
    V45.81
cystostomy V44.50
    appendico-vesicostomy V44.52
    cutaneous-vesicostomy V44.51
    specified type NEC V44.59
defibrillator, automatic implantable
    cardiac V45.02
dialysis V45.1
donor V59.9
drug therapy or regimen V67.59
    high-risk medication NEC V67.51
elbow prosthesis V43.62
enterostomy V44.4
epileptic, epilepticus (absence) (grand
    mal) (*see also* Epilepsy) 345.3
    focal motor 345.7
    partial 345.7
    petit mal 345.2
    psychomotor 345.7
    temporal lobe 345.7
eye (adnexa) surgery V45.69
filtering bleb (eye) (postglaucoma)
    V45.69
    with rupture or complication 997.99
    postcataract extraction (complica-
        tion) 997.99
finger joint prosthesis V43.69
gastrostomy V44.1
grand mal 345.3
heart valve prosthesis V43.3
hip prosthesis (joint) (partial) (total)
    V43.64
ileostomy V44.2
intestinal bypass V45.3
intrauterine contraceptive device V45.51
jejunostomy V44.4
knee joint prosthesis V43.65
lacunaris 437.8
lacunosis 437.8
lymphaticus 254.8
malignant neoplasm, ablated or ex-
    cised - *see* History, malignant neo-
    plasm

Status (*Continued*)
marmoratus 333.7
nephrostomy V44.6
neuropacemaker NEC V45.89
    brain V45.89
    carotid sinus V45.09
    neurologic NEC V45.89
organ replacement
    by artificial or mechanical device or
        prosthesis of
        artery V43.4
        artificial skin V43.83 ◄
        bladder V43.5
        blood vessel V43.4
        breast V43.82
        eye globe V43.0
        heart V43.2
            valve V43.3
        intestine V43.89
        joint V43.60
            ankle V43.66
            elbow V43.62
            finger V43.69
            hip (partial) (total) V43.64
            knee V43.65
            shoulder V43.61
            specified NEC V43.69
            wrist V43.63
        kidney V43.89
        larynx V43.81
        lens V43.1
        limb(s) V43.7
        liver V43.89
        lung V43.89
        organ NEC V43.89
        pancreas V43.89
        skin (artificial) V43.83 ◄
        tissue NEC V43.89
        vein V43.4
    by organ transplant (heterologous)
        (homologous) - *see* Status, trans-
        plant
pacemaker
    brain V45.89
    cardiac V45.01
    carotid sinus V45.09
    neurologic NEC V45.89
    specified site NEC V45.89
percutaneous transluminal coronary
    angioplasty V45.82
petit mal 345.2
postcommotio cerebri 310.2
postoperative NEC V45.89
postpartum NEC V24.2
    care immediately following delivery
        V24.0
    routine follow-up V24.2
postsurgical NEC V45.89
renal dialysis V45.1
reversed jejunal transposition (for by-
    pass) V45.3
shoulder prosthesis V43.61
shunt
    aortocoronary bypass V45.81
    arteriovenous (for dialysis) V45.1
    cerebrospinal fluid V45.2
    vascular NEC V45.89
        aortocoronary (bypass) V45.81
    ventricular (communicating) (for
        drainage) V45.2
sterilization ◄
    tubal ligation V26.51 ◄
    vasectomy V26.52 ◄
subdermal contraceptive device V45.52

Status (*Continued*)
thymicolymphaticus 254.8
thymicus 254.8
thymolymphaticus 254.8
tracheostomy V44.0
transplant
    blood vessel V42.89
    bone V42.4
        marrow V42.81
    cornea V42.5
    heart V42.1
        valve V42.2
    intestine V42.89
    kidney V42.0
    liver V42.7
    lung V42.6
    organ V42.9
        specified site NEC V42.89
    pancreas V42.83
    peripheral stem cells V42.82
    skin V42.3
    stem cells, peripheral V42.82
    tissue V42.9
        specified type NEC V42.89
    vessel, blood V42.89
tubal ligation V26.51 ◄
ureterostomy V44.6
urethrostomy V44.6
vagina, artificial V44.7
vascular shunt NEC V45.89
    aortocoronary (bypass) V45.81 ◄
vasectomy V26.52 ◄
wrist prosthesis V43.63
Stave fracture - *see* Fracture, metacarpus,
    metacarpal bone(s)
Steal
subclavian artery 435.2
vertebral artery 435.1
Stealing, solitary, child problem (*see also*
    Disturbance, conduct) 312.1
Steam burn - *see* Burn, by site
Steatocystoma multiplex 706.2
Steatoma (infected) 706.2
eyelid (cystic) 374.84
    infected 373.13
Steatorrhea (chronic) 579.8
with lacteal obstruction 579.2
idiopathic 579.0
    adult 579.0
    infantile 579.0
pancreatic 579.4
primary 579.0
secondary 579.8
specified cause NEC 579.8
tropical 579.1
Steatosis 272.8
heart (*see also* Degeneration, myocar-
    dial) 429.1
kidney 593.89
liver 571.8
Steele-Richardson (-Olszewski) syn-
    drome 333.0
Stein's syndrome (polycystic ovary)
    256.4
Stein-Leventhal syndrome (polycystic
    ovary) 256.4
Steinbrocker's syndrome (*see also* Neu-
    ropathy, peripheral, autonomic)
    337.9
Steinert's disease 359.2
Stenocardia (*see also* Angina) 413.9
Stenocephaly 756.0
Stenosis (cicatricial) - *see also* Stricture
ampulla of Vater 576.2

Stenosis *(Continued)*
  ampulla of Vater *(Continued)*
    with calculus, cholelithiasis, or
      stones - *see* Choledocholithiasis
  anus, anal (canal) (sphincter) 569.2
    congenital 751.2
  aorta (ascending) 747.22
    arch 747.10
    arteriosclerotic 440.0
    calcified 440.0
  aortic (valve) 424.1
    with
      mitral (valve)
        insufficiency or incompetence
          396.2
        stenosis or obstruction 396.0
    atypical 396.0
    congenital 746.3
    rheumatic 395.0
      with
        insufficiency, incompetency or
          regurgitation 395.2
          with mitral (valve) disease
            396.8
        mitral (valve)
          disease (stenosis) 396.0
          insufficiency or incompetence
            396.2
          stenosis or obstruction 396.0
    specified cause, except rheumatic
      424.1
    syphilitic 093.22
  aqueduct of Sylvius (congenital) 742.3
    with spina bifida (*see also* Spina
      bifida) 741.0
    acquired 331.4
  artery NEC 447.1
    basilar - *see* Narrowing, artery, basi-
      lar
    carotid (common) (internal) - *see*
      Narrowing, artery, carotid
    celiac 447.4
    cerebral 437.0
      due to
        embolism (*see also* Embolism,
          brain) 434.1
        thrombus (*see also* Thrombosis,
          brain) 434.0
    precerebral - *see* Narrowing, artery,
      precerebral
    pulmonary (congenital) 747.3
      acquired 417.8
    renal 440.1
    vertebral - *see* Narrowing, artery,
      vertebral
  bile duct or biliary passage (*see also*
    Obstruction, biliary) 576.2
    congenital 751.61
  bladder neck (acquired) 596.0
    congenital 753.6
  brain 348.8
  bronchus 519.1
    syphilitic 095.8
  cardia (stomach) 537.89
    congenital 750.7
  cardiovascular (*see also* Disease, cardio-
    vascular) 429.2
  carotid artery - *see* Narrowing, artery,
    carotid
  cervix, cervical (canal) 622.4
    congenital 752.49
    in pregnancy or childbirth 654.6
      affecting fetus or newborn
        763.89

Stenosis *(Continued)*
  cervix, cervical *(Continued)*
    in pregnancy or childbirth *(Contin-*
      ued)
      causing obstructed labor 660.2
        affecting fetus or newborn
          763.1
  colon (*see also* Obstruction, intestine)
    560.9
    congenital 751.2
  colostomy 569.62
  common bile duct (*see also* Obstruction,
    biliary) 576.2
    congenital 751.61
  coronary (artery) - *see* Arteriosclerosis,
    coronary
  cystic duct (*see also* Obstruction, gall-
    bladder) 575.2
    congenital 751.61
  due to (presence of) any device, im-
    plant, or graft classifiable to 996.0-
    996.5 - *see* Complications, due to
    (presence of) any device, implant,
    or graft classified to 996.0-996.5
    NEC
  duodenum 537.3
    congenital 751.1
  ejaculatory duct NEC 608.89
  endocervical os - *see* Stenosis, cervix
  enterostomy 569.62
  esophagus 530.3
    congenital 750.3
    syphilitic 095.8
      congenital 090.5
  external ear canal 380.50
    secondary to
      inflammation 380.53
      surgery 380.52
      trauma 380.51
  gallbladder (*see also* Obstruction, gall-
    bladder) 575.2
  glottis 478.74
  heart valve (acquired) - *see also* Endo-
    carditis
    congenital NEC 746.89
      aortic 746.3
      mitral 746.5
      pulmonary 746.02
      tricuspid 746.1
  hepatic duct (*see also* Obstruction, bili-
    ary) 576.2
  hymen 623.3
  hypertrophic subaortic (idiopathic)
    425.1
  infundibulum cardiac 746.83
  intestine (*see also* Obstruction, intes-
    tine) 560.9
    congenital (small) 751.1
    large 751.2
  lacrimal
    canaliculi 375.53
    duct 375.56
      congenital 743.65
    punctum 375.52
      congenital 743.65
    sac 375.54
      congenital 743.65
  lacrimonasal duct 375.56
    congenital 743.65
    neonatal 375.55
  larynx 478.74
    congenital 748.3
    syphilitic 095.8
      congenital 090.5

Stenosis *(Continued)*
  mitral (valve) (chronic) (inactive)
    394.0
    with
      aortic (valve)
        disease (insufficiency) 396.1
        insufficiency or incompetence
          396.1
        stenosis or obstruction 396.0
      incompetency, insufficiency or re-
        gurgitation 394.2
        with aortic valve disease 396.8
    active or acute 391.1
      with chorea (acute) (rheumatic)
        (Sydenham's) 392.0
    congenital 746.5
    specified cause, except rheumatic
      424.0
    syphilitic 093.21
  myocardium, myocardial (*see also* De-
    generation, myocardial) 429.1
    hypertrophic subaortic (idiopathic)
      425.1
  nares (anterior) (posterior) 478.1
    congenital 748.0
  nasal duct 375.56
    congenital 743.65
  nasolacrimal duct 375.56
    congenital 743.65
    neonatal 375.55
  organ or site, congenital NEC - *see*
    Atresia
  papilla of Vater 576.2
    with calculus, cholelithiasis, or
      stones - *see* Choledocholithiasis
  pulmonary (artery) (congenital) 747.3
    with ventricular septal defect, dex-
      traposition of aorta and hyper-
      trophy of right ventricle 745.2
    acquired 417.8
    infundibular 746.83
    in tetralogy of Fallot 745.2
    subvalvular 746.83
    valve (*see also* Endocarditis, pulmo-
      nary) 424.3
      congenital 746.02
    vein 747.49
      acquired 417.8
    vessel NEC 417.8
  pulmonic (congenital) 746.02
    infundibular 746.83
    subvalvular 746.83
  pylorus (hypertrophic) 537.0
    adult 537.0
    congenital 750.5
    infantile 750.5
  rectum (sphincter) (*see also* Stricture,
    rectum) 569.2
  renal artery 440.1
  salivary duct (any) 527.8
  sphincter of Oddi (*see also* Obstruction,
    biliary) 576.2
  spinal 724.00
    cervical 723.0
    lumbar, lumbosacral 724.02
    nerve (root) NEC 724.9
    specified region NEC 724.09
    thoracic, thoracolumbar 724.01
  stomach, hourglass 537.6
  subaortic 746.81
    hypertrophic (idiopathic) 425.1
  supra (valvular)-aortic 747.22
  trachea 519.1
    congenital 748.3

Stenosis *(Continued)*
  trachea *(Continued)*
    syphilitic 095.8
    tuberculous *(see also* Tuberculosis)
      012.8
  tracheostomy 519.02
  tricuspid (valve) *(see also* Endocarditis,
    tricuspid) 397.0
    congenital 746.1
    nonrheumatic 424.2
  tubal 628.2
  ureter *(see also* Stricture, ureter)
    593.3
    congenital 753.29
  urethra *(see also* Stricture, urethra)
    598.9
  vagina 623.2
    congenital 752.49
    in pregnancy or childbirth 654.7
      affecting fetus or newborn
        763.89
      causing obstructed labor 660.2
        affecting fetus or newborn 763.1
  valve (cardiac) (heart) *(see also* Endo-
    carditis) 424.90
    congenital NEC 746.89
      aortic 746.3
      mitral 746.5
      pulmonary 746.02
      tricuspid 746.1
      urethra 753.6
  valvular *(see also* Endocarditis) 424.90
    congenital NEC 746.89
      urethra 753.6
  vascular graft or shunt 996.1
    atherosclerosis - *see* Arteriosclerosis,
      extremities
    embolism 996.74
    occlusion NEC 996.74
    thrombus 996.74
  vena cava (inferior) (superior) 459.2
    congenital 747.49
  ventricular shunt 996.2
  vulva 624.8
Stercolith *(see also* Fecalith) 560.39
  appendix 543.9
Stercoraceous, stercoral ulcer 569.82
  anus or rectum 569.41
Stereopsis, defective
  with fusion 368.33
  without fusion 368.32
Stereotypies NEC 307.3
Sterility
  female - *see* Infertility, female
  male *(see also* Infertility, male)
    606.9
Sterilization, admission for V25.2
  status
    tubal ligation V26.51
    vasectomy V26.52
Sternalgia *(see also* Angina) 413.9
Sternopagus 759.4
Sternum bifidum 756.3
Sternutation 784.9
Steroid
  effects (adverse) (iatrogenic)
    cushingoid
      correct substance properly admin-
        istered 255.0
      overdose or wrong substance
        given or taken 962.0
    diabetes
      correct substance properly admin-
        istered 251.8

Steroid *(Continued)*
  effects *(Continued)*
    diabetes *(Continued)*
      overdose or wrong substance
        given or taken 962.0
      due to
        correct substance properly admin-
          istered 255.8
        overdose or wrong substance
          given or taken 962.0
    fever
      correct substance properly admin-
        istered 780.6
      overdose or wrong substance
        given or taken 962.0
    withdrawal
      correct substance properly admin-
        istered 255.4
      overdose or wrong substance
        given or taken 962.0
  responder 365.03
Stevens-Johnson disease or syndrome
  (erythema multiforme exudativum)
  695.1
Stewart-Morel syndrome (hyperostosis
  frontalis interna) 733.3
Sticker's disease (erythema infectiosum)
  057.0
Sticky eye 372.03
Stieda's disease (calcification, knee joint)
  726.62
Stiff
  back 724.8
  neck *(see also* Torticollis) 723.5
Stiff-man syndrome 333.91
Stiffness, joint NEC 719.50
  ankle 719.57
  back 724.8
  elbow 719.52
  finger 719.54
  hip 719.55
  knee 719.56
  multiple sites 719.59
  sacroiliac 724.6
  shoulder 719.51
  specified site NEC 719.58
  spine 724.9
  surgical fusion V45.4
  wrist 719.53
Stigmata, congenital syphilis 090.5
Still's disease or syndrome 714.30
Still-Felty syndrome (rheumatoid arthritis with splenomegaly and leukopenia) 714.1
Stillbirth, stillborn NEC 779.9
Stiller's disease (asthenia) 780.79
Stilling-Türk-Duane syndrome (ocular
  retraction syndrome) 378.71
Stimulation, ovary 256.1
Sting (animal) (bee) (fish) (insect) (jelly-
  fish) (Portuguese man-o-war) (wasp)
  (venomous) 989.5
  anaphylactic shock or reaction 989.5
  plant 692.6
Stippled epiphyses 756.59
Stitch
  abscess 998.59
  burst (in operation wound) 998.3
  in back 724.5
Stojano's (subcostal) syndrome 098.86
Stokes' disease (exophthalmic goiter)
  242.0
Stokes-Adams syndrome (syncope with
  heart block) 426.9

Stokvis' (-Talma) disease (enterogenous
  cyanosis) 289.7
Stomach - *see* condition
Stoma malfunction
  colostomy 569.62
  cystostomy 997.5
  enterostomy 569.62
  gastrostomy 536.42
  ileostomy 569.62
  nephrostomy 997.5
  tracheostomy 519.02
  ureterostomy 997.5
Stomatitis 528.0
  angular 528.5
    due to dietary or vitamin deficiency
      266.0
  aphthous 528.2
  candidal 112.0
  catarrhal 528.0
  denture 528.9
  diphtheritic (membranous) 032.0
  due to
    dietary deficiency 266.0
    thrush 112.0
    vitamin deficiency 266.0
  epidemic 078.4
  epizootic 078.4
  follicular 528.0
  gangrenous 528.1
  herpetic 054.2
  herpetiformis 528.2
  malignant 528.0
  membranous acute 528.0
  monilial 112.0
  mycotic 112.0
  necrotic 528.1
    ulcerative 101
  necrotizing ulcerative 101
  parasitic 112.0
  septic 528.0
  spirochetal 101
  suppurative (acute) 528.0
  ulcerative 528.0
    necrotizing 101
  ulceromembranous 101
  vesicular 528.0
    with exanthem 074.3
  Vincent's 101
Stomatocytosis 282.8
Stomatomycosis 112.0
Stomatorrhagia 528.9
Stone(s) - *see also* Calculus
  bladder 594.1
    diverticulum 594.0
  cystine 270.0
  heart syndrome *(see also* Failure, ven-
    tricular, left) 428.1
  kidney 592.0
  prostate 602.0
  pulp (dental) 522.2
  renal 592.0
  salivary duct or gland (any) 527.5
  ureter 592.1
  urethra (impacted) 594.2
  urinary (duct) (impacted) (passage)
    592.9
    bladder 594.1
      diverticulum 594.0
    lower tract NEC 594.9
    specified site 594.8
  xanthine 277.2
Stonecutters' lung 502
  tuberculous *(see also* Tuberculosis)
    011.4

Stonemasons'
  asthma, disease, or lung 502
    tuberculous (*see also* Tuberculosis)
      011.4
    phthisis (*see also* Tuberculosis) 011.4
Stoppage
  bowel (*see also* Obstruction, intestine)
    560.9
  heart (*see also* Arrest, cardiac) 427.5
  intestine (*see also* Obstruction, intes-
    tine) 560.9
  urine NEC (*see also* Retention, urine)
    788.20
Storm, thyroid (apathetic) (*see also* Thyrotoxicosis) 242.9
Strabismus (alternating) (congenital)
  (nonparalytic) 378.9
  concomitant (*see also* Heterotropia)
    378.30
    convergent (*see also* Esotropia) 378.00
    divergent (*see also* Exotropia) 378.10
  convergent (*see also* Esotropia) 378.00
  divergent (*see also* Exotropia) 378.10
  due to adhesions, scars - *see* Strabis-
    mus, mechanical
  in neuromuscular disorder NEC 378.73
    intermittent 378.20
      vertical 378.31
    latent 378.40
      convergent (esophoria) 378.41
      divergent (exophoria) 378.42
      vertical 378.43
  mechanical 378.60
    due to
      Brown's tendon sheath syndrome
        378.61
      specified musculofascial disorder
        NEC 378.62
  paralytic 378.50
    third or oculomotor nerve (partial)
      378.51
      total 378.52
    fourth or trochlear nerve 378.53
    sixth or abducens nerve 378.54
  specified type NEC 378.73
  vertical (hypertropia) 378.31
Strain - *see also* Sprain, by site
  eye NEC 368.13
  heart - *see* Disease, heart
  meaning gonorrhea - *see* Gonorrhea
  physical NEC V62.89
  postural 729.9
  psychological NEC V62.89
Strands
  conjunctiva 372.62
  vitreous humor 379.25
Strangulation, strangulated 994.7
  appendix 543.9
  asphyxiation or suffocation by 994.7
  bladder neck 596.0
  bowel - *see* Strangulation, intestine
  colon - *see* Strangulation, intestine
  cord (umbilical) - *see* Compression,
    umbilical cord
  due to birth injury 767.8
  food or foreign body (*see also* As-
    phyxia, food) 933.1
  hemorrhoids 455.8
    external 455.5
    internal 455.2
  hernia - *see also* Hernia, by site, with
    obstruction
    gangrenous - *see* Hernia, by site,
      with gangrene

Strangulation, strangulated (*Continued*)
  intestine (large) (small) 560.2
    with hernia - *see also* Hernia, by site,
      with obstruction
      gangrenous - *see* Hernia, by site,
        with gangrene
    congenital (small) 751.1
      large 751.2
  mesentery 560.2
  mucus (*see also* Asphyxia, mucus)
    933.1
    newborn 770.1
  omentum 560.2
  organ or site, congenital NEC - *see*
    Atresia
  ovary 620.8
    due to hernia 620.4
  penis 607.89
    foreign body 939.3
  rupture (*see also* Hernia, by site, with
    obstruction) 552.9
    gangrenous (*see also* Hernia, by site,
      with gangrene) 551.9
  stomach, due to hernia (*see also* Her-
    nia, by site, with obstruction)
    552.9
    with gangrene (*see also* Hernia, by
      site, with gangrene) 551.9
  umbilical cord - *see* Compression, um-
    bilical cord
  vesicourethral orifice 596.0
Strangury 788.1
Strawberry
  gallbladder (*see also* Disease, gallblad-
    der) 575.6
  mark 757.32
  tongue (red) (white) 529.3
Straw itch 133.8
Streak, ovarian 752.0
Strephosymbolia 315.01
  secondary to organic lesion 784.69
Streptobacillary fever 026.1
Streptobacillus moniliformis 026.1
Streptococcemia 038.0
Streptococcicosis - *see* Infection, strepto-
  coccal
Streptococcus, streptococcal - *see* condi-
  tion
Streptoderma 686.00
Streptomycosis - *see* Actinomycosis
Streptothricosis - *see* Actinomycosis
Streptothrix - *see* Actinomycosis
Streptotrichosis - *see* Actinomycosis
Stress
  fracture - *see* Fracture, pathologic
  polycythemia 289.0
  reaction (gross) (*see also* Reaction,
    stress, acute) 308.9
Stretching, nerve - *see* Injury, nerve, by
  site
Striae (albicantes) (atrophicae) (cutis dis-
  tensae) (distensae) 701.3
Striations of nails 703.8
Stricture (*see also* Stenosis) 799.8
  ampulla of Vater 576.2
    with calculus, cholelithiasis, or
      stones - *see* Choledocholithiasis
  anus (sphincter) 569.2
    congenital 751.2
    infantile 751.2
  aorta (ascending) 747.22
    arch 747.10
    arteriosclerotic 440.0
    calcified 440.0

Stricture (*Continued*)
  aortic (valve) (*see also* Stenosis, aortic)
    424.1
    congenital 746.3
  aqueduct of Sylvius (congenital) 742.3
    with spina bifida (*see also* Spina bi-
      fida) 741.0
    acquired 331.4
  artery 447.1
    basilar - *see* Narrowing, artery, basi-
      lar
    carotid (common) (internal) - *see*
      Narrowing, artery, carotid
    celiac 447.4
    cerebral 437.0
      congenital 747.81
      due to
        embolism (*see also* Embolism,
          brain) 434.1
        thrombus (*see also* Thrombosis,
          brain) 434.0
    congenital (peripheral) 747.60
      cerebral 747.81
      coronary 746.85
      gastrointestinal 747.61
      lower limb 747.64
      renal 747.62
      retinal 743.58
      specified NEC 747.69
      spinal 747.82
      umbilical 747.5
      upper limb 747.63
    coronary - *see* Arteriosclerosis, coro-
      nary
      congenital 746.85
    precerebral - *see* Narrowing, artery,
      precerebral NEC
    pulmonary (congenital) 747.3
      acquired 417.8
    renal 440.1
    vertebral - *see* Narrowing, artery,
      vertebral
  auditory canal (congenital) (external)
    744.02
    acquired (*see also* Stricture, ear canal,
      acquired) 380.50
  bile duct or passage (any) (postopera-
    tive) (*see also* Obstruction, biliary)
    576.2
    congenital 751.61
  bladder 596.8
    congenital 753.6
    neck 596.0
      congenital 753.6
  bowel (*see also* Obstruction, intestine)
    560.9
  brain 348.8
  bronchus 519.1
    syphilitic 095.8
  cardia (stomach) 537.89
    congenital 750.7
  cardiac - *see also* Disease, heart orifice
    (stomach) 537.89
  cardiovascular (*see also* Disease, cardio-
    vascular) 429.2
  carotid artery - *see* Narrowing, artery,
    carotid
  cecum (*see also* Obstruction, intestine)
    560.9
  cervix, cervical (canal) 622.4
    congenital 752.49
    in pregnancy or childbirth 654.6
      affecting fetus or newborn
        763.89

Stricture *(Continued)*
  cervix, cervical *(Continued)*
    in pregnancy or childbirth *(Continued)*
      causing obstructed labor 660.2
        affecting fetus or newborn 763.1
  colon *(see also* Obstruction, intestine) 560.9
    congenital 751.2
  colostomy 569.62
  common bile duct *(see also* Obstruction, biliary) 576.2
    congenital 751.61
  coronary (artery) - *see* Arteriosclerosis, coronary
    congenital 746.85
  cystic duct *(see also* Obstruction, gallbladder) 575.2
    congenital 751.61
  cystostomy 997.5
  digestive organs NEC, congenital 751.8
  duodenum 537.3
    congenital 751.1
  ear canal (external) (congenital) 744.02
    acquired 380.50
      secondary to
        inflammation 380.53
        surgery 380.52
        trauma 380.51
  ejaculatory duct 608.85
  enterostomy 569.62
  esophagus (corrosive) (peptic) 530.3
    congenital 750.3
    syphilitic 095.8
      congenital 090.5
  Eustachian tube *(see also* Obstruction, Eustachian tube) 381.60
    congenital 744.24
  fallopian tube 628.2
    gonococcal (chronic) 098.37
      acute 098.17
    tuberculous *(see also* Tuberculosis) 016.6
  gallbladder *(see also* Obstruction, gallbladder) 575.2
    congenital 751.69
  glottis 478.74
  heart - *see also* Disease, heart
    congenital NEC 746.89
    valve - *see also* Endocarditis
      congenital NEC 746.89
        aortic 746.3
        mitral 746.5
        pulmonary 746.02
        tricuspid 746.1
  hepatic duct *(see also* Obstruction, biliary) 576.2
  hourglass, of stomach 537.6
  hymen 623.3
  hypopharynx 478.29
  intestine *(see also* Obstruction, intestine) 560.9
    congenital (small) 751.1
      large 751.2
    ischemic 557.1
  lacrimal
    canaliculi 375.53
      congenital 743.65
    punctum 375.52
      congenital 743.65
    sac 375.54
      congenital 743.65

Stricture *(Continued)*
  lacrimonasal duct 375.56
    congenital 743.65
    neonatal 375.55
  larynx 478.79
    congenital 748.3
    syphilitic 095.8
      congenital 090.5
  lung 518.89
  meatus
    ear (congenital) 744.02
      acquired *(see also* Stricture, ear canal, acquired) 380.50
    osseous (congenital) (ear) 744.03
      acquired *(see also* Stricture, ear canal, acquired) 380.50
    urinarius *(see also* Stricture, urethra) 598.9
      congenital 753.6
  mitral (valve) *(see also* Stenosis, mitral) 394.0
    congenital 746.5
    specified cause, except rheumatic 424.0
  myocardium, myocardial *(see also* Degeneration, myocardial) 429.1
    hypertrophic subaortic (idiopathic) 425.1
  nares (anterior) (posterior) 478.1
    congenital 748.0
  nasal duct 375.56
    congenital 743.65
    neonatal 375.55
  nasolacrimal duct 375.56
    congenital 743.65
    neonatal 375.55
  nasopharynx 478.29
    syphilitic 095.8
  nephrostomy 997.5
  nose 478.1
    congenital 748.0
  nostril (anterior) (posterior) 478.1
    congenital 748.0
  organ or site, congenital NEC - *see* Atresia
  osseous meatus (congenital) (ear) 744.03
    acquired *(see also* Stricture, ear canal, acquired) 380.50
  os uteri *(see also* Stricture, cervix) 622.4
  oviduct - *see* Stricture, fallopian tube
  pelviureteric junction 593.3
  pharynx (dilation) 478.29
  prostate 602.8
  pulmonary, pulmonic
    artery (congenital) 747.3
      acquired 417.8
      noncongenital 417.8
    infundibulum (congenital) 746.83
    valve *(see also* Endocarditis, pulmonary) 424.3
      congenital 746.02
    vein (congenital) 747.49
      acquired 417.8
    vessel NEC 417.8
  punctum lacrimale 375.52
    congenital 743.65
  pylorus (hypertrophic) 537.0
    adult 537.0
    congenital 750.5
    infantile 750.5
  rectosigmoid 569.89
  rectum (sphincter) 569.2
    congenital 751.2

Stricture *(Continued)*
  rectum *(Continued)*
    due to
      chemical burn 947.3
      irradiation 569.2
      lymphogranuloma venereum 099.1
    gonococcal 098.7
    inflammatory 099.1
    syphilitic 095.8
    tuberculous *(see also* Tuberculosis) 014.8
  renal artery 440.1
  salivary duct or gland (any) 527.8
  sigmoid (flexure) *(see also* Obstruction, intestine) 560.9
  spermatic cord 608.85
  stoma (following) (of)
    colostomy 569.62
    cystostomy 997.5
    enterostomy 569.62
    gastrostomy 536.42
    ileostomy 569.62
    nephrostomy 997.5
    tracheostomy 519.02
    ureterostomy 997.5
  stomach 537.89
    congenital 750.7
    hourglass 537.6
  subaortic 746.81
    hypertrophic (acquired) (idiopathic) 425.1
  subglottic 478.74
  syphilitic NEC 095.8
  tendon (sheath) 727.81
  trachea 519.1
    congenital 748.3
    syphilitic 095.8
    tuberculous *(see also* Tuberculosis) 012.8
  tracheostomy 519.02
  tricuspid (valve) *(see also* Endocarditis, tricuspid) 397.0
    congenital 746.1
    nonrheumatic 424.2
  tunica vaginalis 608.85
  ureter (postoperative) 593.3
    congenital 753.29
    tuberculous *(see also* Tuberculosis) 016.2
  ureteropelvic junction 593.3
    congenital 753.21
  ureterovesical orifice 593.3
    congenital 753.22
  urethra (anterior) (meatal) (organic) (posterior) (spasmodic) 598.9
    associated with schistosomiasis *(see also* Schistosomiasis) 120.9 [598.01]
    congenital (valvular) 753.6
    due to
      infection 598.00
        syphilis 095.8 [598.01]
        trauma 598.1
    gonococcal 098.2 [598.01]
    gonorrheal 098.2 [598.01]
    infective 598.00
    late effect of injury 598.1
    postcatheterization 598.2
    postobstetric 598.1
    postoperative 598.2
    specified cause NEC 598.8
    syphilitic 095.8 [598.01]
    traumatic 598.1
    valvular, congenital 753.6

Stricture *(Continued)*
  urinary meatus *(see also* Stricture, urethra) 598.9
    congenital 753.6
  uterus, uterine 621.5
    os (external) (internal) - *see* Stricture, cervix
  vagina (outlet) 623.2
    congenital 752.49
  valve (cardiac) (heart) *(see also* Endocarditis) 424.90
    congenital (cardiac) (heart) NEC 746.89
      aortic 746.3
      mitral 746.5
      pulmonary 746.02
      tricuspid 746.1
      urethra 753.6
  valvular *(see also* Endocarditis) 424.90
  vascular graft or shunt 996.1
    vascular or shunt
      atherosclerosis - *see* Arteriosclerosis, extremities
      embolism 996.74
      occlusion NEC 996.74
      thrombus 996.74
  vas deferens 608.85
    congenital 752.8
  vein 459.2
  vena cava (inferior) (superior) NEC 459.2
    congenital 747.49
  ventricular shunt 996.2
  vesicourethral orifice 596.0
    congenital 753.6
  vulva (acquired) 624.8
Stridor 786.1
  congenital (larynx) 748.3
Stridulous - *see* condition
Strippling of nails 703.8
Stroke *(see also* Disease, cerebrovascular, acute) 436
  apoplectic *(see also* Disease, cerebrovascular, acute) 436
  brain *(see also* Disease, cerebrovascular, acute) 436
  epileptic - *see* Epilepsy
  healed or old V12.59
  heart - *see* Disease, heart
  heat 992.0
  iatrogenic 997.02
  in evolution 435.9
  late effect - *see* Late effect(s) (of) cerebrovascular disease
  lightning 994.0
  paralytic *(see also* Disease, cerebrovascular, acute) 436
  postoperative 997.02
  progressive 435.9
Stromatosis, endometrial (M8931/1) 236.0
Strong pulse 785.9
Strongyloides stercoralis infestation 127.2
Strongyloidiasis 127.2
Strongyloidosis 127.2
Strongylus (gibsoni) infestation 127.7
Strophulus (newborn) 779.8
  pruriginosus 698.2
Struck by lightning 994.0
Struma *(see also* Goiter) 240.9
  fibrosa 245.3
  Hashimoto (struma lymphomatosa) 245.2

Struma *(Continued)*
  lymphomatosa 245.2
  nodosa (simplex) 241.9
    endemic 241.9
    multinodular 241.1
    sporadic 241.9
    toxic or with hyperthyroidism 242.3
      multinodular 242.2
      uninodular 242.1
    toxicosa 242.3
      multinodular 242.2
      uninodular 242.1
    uninodular 241.0
  ovarii (M9090/0) 220
    and carcinoid (M9091/1) 236.2
    malignant (M9090/3) 183.0
  Riedel's (ligneous thyroiditis) 245.3
  scrofulous *(see also* Tuberculosis) 017.2
  tuberculous *(see also* Tuberculosis) 017.2
    abscess 017.2
    adenitis 017.2
    lymphangitis 017.2
    ulcer 017.2
Strumipriva cachexia *(see also* Hypothyroidism) 244.9
Strümpell-Marie disease or spine (ankylosing spondylitis) 720.0
Strümpell-Westphal pseudosclerosis (hepatolenticular degeneration) 275.1
Stuart's disease (congenital factor X deficiency) *(see also* Defect, coagulation) 286.3
Stuart-Prower factor deficiency (congenital factor X deficiency) *(see also* Defect, coagulation) 286.3
Students' elbow 727.2
Stuffy nose 478.1
Stump - *see also* Amputation
  cervix, cervical (healed) 622.8
Stupor 780.09
  catatonic *(see also* Schizophrenia) 295.2
  circular *(see also* Psychosis, manic-depressive, circular) 296.7
  manic 296.89
  manic-depressive *(see also* Psychosis, affective) 296.89
  mental (anergic) (delusional) 298.9
  psychogenic 298.8
  reaction to exceptional stress (transient) 308.2
  traumatic NEC - *see also* Injury, intracranial
    with spinal (cord)
      lesion - *see* Injury, spinal, by site
      shock - *see* Injury, spinal, by site
Sturge (-Weber) (-Dimitri) disease or syndrome (encephalocutaneous angiomatosis) 759.6
Sturge-Kalischer-Weber syndrome (encephalocutaneous angiomatosis) 759.6
Stuttering 307.0
Sty, stye 373.11
  external 373.11
  internal 373.12
  meibomian 373.12
Subacidity, gastric 536.8
  psychogenic 306.4
Subacute - *see* condition
Subarachnoid - *see* condition
Subclavian steal syndrome 435.2

Subcortical - *see* condition
Subcostal syndrome 098.86
  nerve compression 354.8
Subcutaneous, subcuticular - *see* condition
Subdelirium 293.1
Subdural - *see* condition
Subendocardium - *see* condition
Subependymoma (M9383/1) 237.5
Suberosis 495.3
Subglossitis - *see* Glossitis
Subhemophilia 286.0
Subinvolution (uterus) 621.1
  breast (postlactational) (postpartum) 611.8
  chronic 621.1
  puerperal, postpartum 674.8
Sublingual - *see* condition
Sublinguitis 527.2
Subluxation - *see also* Dislocation, by site
  congenital NEC - *see also* Malposition, congenital
    hip (unilateral) 754.32
      with dislocation of other hip 754.35
      bilateral 754.33
    joint
      lower limb 755.69
      shoulder 755.59
      upper limb 755.59
    lower limb (joint) 755.69
    shoulder (joint) 755.59
    upper limb (joint) 755.59
  lens 379.32
    anterior 379.33
    posterior 379.34
  rotary, cervical region of spine - *see* Fracture, vertebra, cervical
Submaxillary - *see* condition
Submersion (fatal) (nonfatal) 994.1
Submissiveness (undue), in child 313.0
Submucous - *see* condition
Subnormal, subnormality
  accommodation *(see also* Disorder, accommodation) 367.9
  mental *(see also* Retardation, mental) 319
    mild 317
    moderate 318.0
    profound 318.2
    severe 318.1
  temperature (accidental) 991.6
    not associated with low environmental temperature 780.9
Subphrenic - *see* condition
Subscapular nerve - *see* condition
Subseptus uterus 752.3
Subsiding appendicitis 542
Substernal thyroid *(see also* Goiter) 240.9
  congenital 759.2
Substitution disorder 300.11
Subtentorial - *see* condition
Subtertian
  fever 084.0
  malaria (fever) 084.0
Subthyroidism (acquired) *(see also* Hypothyroidism) 244.9
  congenital 243
Succenturiata placenta - *see* Placenta, abnormal
Succussion sounds, chest 786.7
Sucking thumb, child 307.9
Sudamen 705.1
Sudamina 705.1

◀▶   **New Code**   ⬅▥▶   **Revised Code**

Sudanese kala-azar 085.0
Sudden
death, cause unknown (less than 24
hours) 798.1
during childbirth 669.9
infant 798.0
puerperal, postpartum 674.9
hearing loss NEC 388.2
heart failure (*see also* Failure, heart)
428.9
infant death syndrome 798.0
Sudeck's atrophy, disease, or syndrome
733.7
SUDS (Sudden unexplained death)
798.2
Suffocation (*see also* Asphyxia) 799.0
by
bed clothes 994.7
bunny bag 994.7
cave-in 994.7
constriction 994.7
drowning 994.1
inhalation
food or foreign body (*see also* Asphyxia, food or foreign body)
933.1
oil or gasoline (*see also* Asphyxia,
food or foreign body) 933.1
overlying 994.7
plastic bag 994.7
pressure 994.7
strangulation 994.7
during birth 768.1
mechanical 994.7
Sugar
blood
high 790.6
low 251.2
in urine 791.5
Suicide, suicidal (attempted)
by poisoning - *see* Table of Drugs and
Chemicals
risk 300.9
tendencies 300.9
trauma NEC (*see also* nature and site
of injury) 959.9
Suipestifer infection (*see also* Infection,
Salmonella) 003.9
Sulfatidosis 330.0
**Sulfhemoglobinemia, sulphemoglobine-
mia** (acquired) (congenital) 289.7
Sumatran mite fever 081.2
Summer - *see* condition
Sunburn 692.71
dermatitis 692.71
Sunken
acetabulum 718.85
fontanels 756.0
Sunstroke 992.0
Superfecundation
with fetal loss and retention of one or
more fetus(es) 651.6
Superfetation 651.9
with fetal loss and retention of one or
more fetus(es) 651.6
Superinvolution uterus 621.8
Supernumerary (congenital)
aortic cusps 746.89
auditory ossicles 744.04
bone 756.9
breast 757.6
carpal bones 755.56
cusps, heart valve NEC 746.89
mitral 746.5

Supernumerary (*Continued*)
cusps, heart valve NEC (*Continued*)
pulmonary 746.09
digit(s) 755.00
finger 755.01
toe 755.02
ear (lobule) 744.1
fallopian tube 752.19
finger 755.01
hymen 752.49
kidney 753.3
lacrimal glands 743.64
lacrimonasal duct 743.65
lobule (ear) 744.1
mitral cusps 746.5
muscle 756.82
nipples 757.6
organ or site NEC - *see* Accessory
ossicles, auditory 744.04
ovary 752.0
oviduct 752.19
pulmonic cusps 746.09
rib 756.3
cervical or first 756.2
syndrome 756.2
roots (of teeth) 520.2
spinal vertebra 756.19
spleen 759.0
tarsal bones 755.67
teeth 520.1
causing crowding 524.3
testis 752.8
thumb 755.01
toe 755.02
uterus 752.2
vagina 752.49
vertebra 756.19
Supervision (of)
contraceptive method previously prescribed V25.40
intrauterine device V25.42
oral contraceptive (pill) V25.41
specified type NEC V25.49
subdermal implantable contraceptive
V25.43
dietary (for) V65.3
allergy (food) V65.3
colitis V65.3
diabetes mellitus V65.3
food allergy intolerance V65.3
gastritis V65.3
hypercholesterolemia V65.3
hypoglycemia V65.3
intolerance (food) V65.3
obesity V65.3
specified NEC V65.3
lactation V24.1
pregnancy - *see* Pregnancy, supervision
of
Supplemental teeth 520.1
causing crowding 524.3
Suppression
binocular vision 368.31
lactation 676.5
menstruation 626.8
ovarian secretion 256.3
renal 586
urinary secretion 788.5
urine 788.5
Suppuration, suppurative - *see also* condition
accessory sinus (chronic) (*see also* Sinusitis) 473.9
adrenal gland 255.8

Suppuration, suppurative (*Continued*)
antrum (chronic) (*see also* Sinusitis,
maxillary) 473.0
bladder (*see also* Cystitis) 595.89
bowel 569.89
brain 324.0
late effect 326
breast 611.0
puerperal, postpartum 675.1
dental periosteum 526.5
diffuse (skin) 686.00
ear (middle) (*see also* Otitis media)
382.4
external (*see also* Otitis, externa)
380.10
internal 386.33
ethmoidal (sinus) (chronic) (*see also* Sinusitis, ethmoidal) 473.2
fallopian tube (*see also* Salpingo-
oophoritis) 614.2
frontal (sinus) (chronic) (*see also* Sinusitis, frontal) 473.1
gallbladder (*see also* Cholecystitis,
acute) 575.0
gum 523.3
hernial sac - *see* Hernia, by site
intestine 569.89
joint (*see also* Arthritis, suppurative)
711.0
labyrinthine 386.33
lung 513.0
mammary gland 611.0
puerperal, postpartum 675.1
maxilla, maxillary 526.4
sinus (chronic) (*see also* Sinusitis,
maxillary) 473.0
muscle 728.0
nasal sinus (chronic) (*see also* Sinusitis)
473.9
pancreas 577.0
parotid gland 527.2
pelvis, pelvic
female (*see also* Disease, pelvis, inflammatory) 614.4
acute 614.3
male (*see also* Peritonitis) 567.2
pericranial (*see also* Osteomyelitis)
730.2
salivary duct or gland (any) 527.2
sinus (nasal) (*see also* Sinusitis) 473.9
sphenoidal (sinus) (chronic) (*see also* Sinusitis, sphenoidal) 473.3
thymus (gland) 254.1
thyroid (gland) 245.0
tonsil 474.8
uterus (*see also* Endometritis) 615.9
vagina 616.10
wound - *see also* Wound, open, by site,
complicated
dislocation - *see* Dislocation, by site,
compound
fracture - *see* Fracture, by site,
open
scratch or other superficial injury -
see Injury, superficial, by site
Suprapubic drainage 596.8
Suprarenal (gland) - *see* condition
Suprascapular nerve - *see* condition
Suprasellar - *see* condition
Supraspinatus syndrome 726.10
Surfer knots 919.8
infected 919.9
Surgery
cosmetic NEC V50.1

Surgery (*Continued*)
　cosmetic NEC (*Continued*)
　　following healed injury or operation
　　　V51
　　hair transplant V50.0
　　elective V50.9
　　　breast augmentation or reduction
　　　　V50.1
　　　circumcision, ritual or routine (in absence of medical indication)
　　　　V50.2
　　　cosmetic NEC V50.1
　　　ear piercing V50.3
　　　face-lift V50.1
　　　following healed injury or operation
　　　　V51
　　　hair transplant V50.0
　　not done because of
　　　contraindication V64.1
　　　patient's decision V64.2
　　　specified reason NEC V64.3
　　plastic
　　　breast augmentation or reduction
　　　　V50.1
　　　cosmetic V50.1
　　　face-lift V50.1
　　　following healed injury or operation
　　　　V51
　　　repair of scarred tissue (following
　　　　healed injury or operation) V51
　　　specified type NEC V50.8
　　previous, in pregnancy or childbirth
　　　cervix 654.6
　　　　affecting fetus or newborn
　　　　　763.89　　　　　　　⬅▥
　　　　causing obstructed labor 660.2
　　　　　affecting fetus or newborn 763.1
　　　pelvic soft tissues NEC 654.9
　　　　affecting fetus or newborn
　　　　　763.89　　　　　　　⬅▥
　　　　causing obstructed labor 660.2
　　　　　affecting fetus or newborn
　　　　　　763.1
　　　perineum or vulva 654.8
　　　uterus NEC 654.9
　　　　affecting fetus or newborn
　　　　　763.89　　　　　　　⬅▥
　　　　causing obstructed labor 660.2
　　　　　affecting fetus or newborn
　　　　　　763.1
　　　　from previous cesarean delivery
　　　　　654.2
　　　vagina 654.7
Surgical
　abortion - *see* Abortion, legal
　emphysema 998.81
　kidney (*see also* Pyelitis) 590.80
　operation NEC 799.9
　procedures, complication or misadventure - *see* Complications, surgical
　　procedure
　shock 998.0
Suspected condition, ruled out (*see also*
　Observation, suspected) V71.9
　specified condition NEC V71.8
**Suspended uterus, in pregnancy or
　childbirth** 654.4
　affecting fetus or newborn 763.89　⬅▥
　causing obstructed labor 660.2
　　affecting fetus or newborn 763.1
Sutton's disease 709.09
Sutton and Gull's disease (arteriolar
　nephrosclerosis) (*see also* Hypertension, kidney) 403.90

Suture
　burst (in operation wound) 998.3
　inadvertently left in operation wound
　　998.4
　removal V58.3
　shirodkar, in pregnancy (with or without cervical incompetence) 654.5
**Swab inadvertently left in operation
　wound** 998.4
Swallowed, swallowing
　difficulty (*see also* Dysphagia) 787.2
　foreign body NEC (*see also* Foreign
　　body) 938
Swamp fever 100.89
Swan neck hand (intrinsic) 736.09
Sweat(s), sweating
　disease or sickness 078.2
　excessive 780.8
　fetid 705.89
　fever 078.2
　gland disease 705.9
　　specified type NEC 705.89
　miliary 078.2
　night 780.8
Sweeley-Klionsky disease (angiokeratoma corporis diffusum) 272.7
Sweet's syndrome (acute febrile neutrophilic dermatosis) 695.89
Swelling
　abdominal (not referable to specific organ) 789.3
　adrenal gland, cloudy 255.8
　ankle 719.07
　anus 787.99
　arm 729.81
　breast 611.72
　Calabar 125.2
　cervical gland 785.6
　cheek 784.2
　chest 786.6
　ear 388.8
　epigastric 789.3
　extremity (lower) (upper) 729.81
　eye 379.92
　female genital organ 625.8
　finger 729.81
　foot 729.81
　glands 785.6
　gum 784.2
　hand 729.81
　head 784.2
　inflammatory - *see* Inflammation
　joint (*see also* Effusion, joint) 719.0
　　tuberculous - *see* Tuberculosis, joint
　kidney, cloudy 593.89
　leg 729.81
　limb 729.81
　liver 573.8
　lung 786.6
　lymph nodes 785.6
　mediastinal 786.6
　mouth 784.2
　muscle (limb) 729.81
　neck 784.2
　nose or sinus 784.2
　palate 784.2
　pelvis 789.3
　penis 607.83
　perineum 625.8
　rectum 787.99
　scrotum 608.86
　skin 782.2
　splenic (*see also* Splenomegaly)
　　789.2

Swelling (*Continued*)
　substernal 786.6
　superficial, localized (skin) 782.2
　testicle 608.86
　throat 784.2
　toe 729.81
　tongue 784.2
　tubular (*see also* Disease, renal)
　　593.9
　umbilicus 789.3
　uterus 625.8
　vagina 625.8
　vulva 625.8
　wandering, due to Gnathostoma (spinigerum) 128.1
　white - *see* Tuberculosis, arthritis
Swift's disease 985.0
Swimmers'
　ear (acute) 380.12
　itch 120.3
Swimming in the head 780.4
Swollen - *see also* Swelling
　glands 785.6
Swyer-James syndrome (unilateral hyperlucent lung) 492.8
Swyer's syndrome (XY pure gonadal
　dysgenesis) 752.7
Sycosis 704.8
　barbae (not parasitic) 704.8
　contagiosa 110.0
　lupoid 704.8
　mycotic 110.0
　parasitic 110.0
　vulgaris 704.8
Sydenham's chorea - *see* Chorea, Sydenham's
Sylvatic yellow fever 060.0
Sylvest's disease (epidemic pleurodynia)
　074.1
Symblepharon 372.63
　congenital 743.62
Symonds' syndrome 348.2
Sympathetic - *see* condition
Sympatheticotonia (*see also* Neuropathy,
　peripheral, autonomic) 337.9
Sympathicoblastoma (M9500/3)
　specified site - *see* Neoplasm, by site,
　　malignant
　unspecified site 194.0
Sympathicogonioma (M9500/3) - *see*
　Sympathicoblastoma
Sympathoblastoma (M9500/3) - *see* Sympathicoblastoma
Sympathogonioma (M9500/3) - *see* Sympathicoblastoma
Symphalangy (*see also* Syndactylism)
　755.10
Symptoms, specified (general) NEC
　780.9
　abdomen NEC 789.9
　bone NEC 733.90
　breast NEC 611.79
　cardiac NEC 785.9
　cardiovascular NEC 785.9
　chest NEC 786.9
　development NEC 783.9
　digestive system NEC 787.99
　eye NEC 379.99
　gastrointestinal tract NEC 787.99
　genital organs NEC
　　female 625.9
　　male 608.9
　head and neck NEC 784.9
　heart NEC 785.9

Symptoms, specified (*Continued*)
  joint NEC 719.60
    ankle 719.67
    elbow 719.62
    foot 719.67
    hand 719.64
    hip 719.65
    knee 719.66
    multiple sites 719.69
    pelvic region 719.65
    shoulder (region) 719.61
    specified site NEC 719.68
    wrist 719.63
  larynx NEC 784.9
  limbs NEC 729.89
  lymphatic system NEC 785.9
  menopausal 627.2
  metabolism NEC 783.9
  mouth NEC 528.9
  muscle NEC 728.9
  musculoskeletal NEC 781.9
    limbs NEC 729.89
  nervous system NEC 781.9
  neurotic NEC 300.9
  nutrition, metabolism, and develop-
      ment NEC 783.9
  pelvis NEC 789.9
    female 625.9
  peritoneum NEC 789.9
  respiratory system NEC 786.9
  skin and integument NEC 782.9
  subcutaneous tissue NEC 782.9
  throat NEC 784.9
  tonsil NEC 784.9
  urinary system NEC 788.9
  vascular NEC 785.9
Sympus 759.89
Synarthrosis 719.80
  ankle 719.87
  elbow 719.82
  foot 719.87
  hand 719.84
  hip 719.85
  knee 719.86
  multiple sites 719.89
  pelvic region 719.85
  shoulder (region) 719.81
  specified site NEC 719.88
  wrist 719.83
Syncephalus 759.4
Synchondrosis 756.9
  abnormal (congenital) 756.9
  ischiopubic (van Neck's) 732.1
Synchysis (senile) (vitreous humor)
    379.21
  scintillans 379.22
Syncope (near) (pre-) 780.2
  anginosa 413.9
  bradycardia 427.89
  cardiac 780.2
  carotid sinus 337.0
  complicating delivery 669.2
  due to lumbar puncture 349.0
  fatal 798.1
  heart 780.2
  heat 992.1
  laryngeal 786.2
  tussive 786.2
  vasoconstriction 780.2
  vasodepressor 780.2
  vasomotor 780.2
  vasovagal 780.2
Syncytial infarct - *see* Placenta, abnor-
    mal

Syndactylism, syndactyly (multiple sites)
    755.10
  fingers (without fusion of bone) 755.11
    with fusion of bone 755.12
  toes (without fusion of bone) 755.13
    with fusion of bone 755.14
Syndrome - *see also* Disease
  abdominal
    acute 789.0
    migraine 346.2
    muscle deficiency 756.79
  Abercrombie's (amyloid degeneration)
      277.3
  abnormal innervation 374.43
  abstinence
    alcohol 291.81
    drug 292.0
  Abt-Letterer-Siwe (acute histiocytosis
      X) (M9722/3) 202.5
  Achard-Thiers (adrenogenital) 255.2
  acid pulmonary aspiration 997.3
    obstetric (Mendelson's) 668.0
  acquired immune deficiency 042
  acquired immunodeficiency 042
  acrocephalosyndactylism 755.55
  acute abdominal 789.0
  Adair-Dighton (brittle bones and blue
      sclera, deafness) 756.51
  Adams-Stokes (-Morgagni) (syncope
      with heart block) 426.9
  Addisonian 255.4
  Adie (-Holmes) (pupil) 379.46
  adiposogenital 253.8
  adrenal
    hemorrhage 036.3
    meningococcic 036.3
  adrenocortical 255.3
  adrenogenital (acquired) (congenital)
      255.2
    feminizing 255.2
    iatrogenic 760.79
    virilism (acquired) (congenital) 255.2
  affective organic NEC 293.89
    drug-induced 292.84
  afferent loop NEC 537.89
  African macroglobulinemia 273.3
  Ahumada-Del Castillo (nonpuerperal
      galactorrhea and amenorrhea)
      253.1
  air blast concussion - *see* Injury, inter-
      nal, by site
  Albright (-Martin) (pseudohypopara-
      thyroidism) 275.49
  Albright-McCune-Sternberg (osteitis fi-
      brosa disseminata) 756.59
  alcohol withdrawal 291.81
  Alder's (leukocyte granulation anom-
      aly) 288.2
  Aldrich (-Wiskott) (eczema-thrombocy-
      topenia) 279.12
  Alibert-Bazin (mycosis fungoides)
      (M9700/3) 202.1
  Alice in Wonderland 293.89
  Allen-Masters 620.6
  Alligator baby (ichthyosis congenita)
      757.1
  Alport's (hereditary hematuria-ne-
      phropathy-deafness) 759.89
  Alvarez (transient cerebral ischemia)
      435.9
  alveolar capillary block 516.3
  Alzheimer's 331.0
    with dementia - *see* Alzheimer's, de-
      mentia

Syndrome (*Continued*)
  amnestic (confabulatory) 294.0
    alcoholic 291.1
    drug-induced 292.83
    posttraumatic 294.0
  amotivational 292.89
  amyostatic 275.1
  amyotrophic lateral sclerosis 335.20
  angina (*see also* Angina) 413.9
  ankyloglossia superior 750.0
  anterior
    chest wall 786.52
    compartment (tibial) 958.8
    spinal artery 433.8
      compression 721.1
    tibial (compartment) 958.8
  antibody deficiency 279.00
    agammaglobulinemic 279.00
    congenital 279.04
    hypogammaglobulinemic 279.00
  anticardiolipin antibody 795.79
  antimongolism 758.3
  antiphospholipid antibody 795.79
  Anton (-Babinski) (hemiasomatogno-
      sia) 307.9
  anxiety (*see also* Anxiety) 300.00
    organic 293.84
  aortic
    arch 446.7
    bifurcation (occlusion) 444.0
    ring 747.21
  Apert's (acrocephalosyndactyly) 755.55
  Apert-Gallais (adrenogenital) 255.2
  aphasia-apraxia-alexia 784.69
  "approximate answers" 300.16
  arcuate ligament (-celiac axis) 447.4
  arcus aortae 446.7
  arc welders' 370.24
  argentaffin, argentaffinoma 259.2
  Argonz-Del Castillo (nonpuerperal
      galactorrhea and amenorrhea)
      253.1
  Argyll Robertson's (syphilitic) 094.89
    nonsyphilitic 379.45
  arm-shoulder (*see also* Neuropathy, pe-
      ripheral, autonomic) 337.9
  Arnold-Chiari (*see also* Spina bifida)
      741.0
    type I 348.4
    type II 741.0
    type III 742.0
    type IV 742.2
  Arrillaga-Ayerza (pulmonary artery
      sclerosis with pulmonary hyper-
      tension) 416.0
  arteriomesenteric duodenum occlusion
      537.89
  arteriovenous steal 996.73
  arteritis, young female (obliterative
      brachiocephalic) 446.7
  aseptic meningitis - *see* Meningitis,
      aseptic
  Asherman's 621.5
  asphyctic (*see also* Anxiety) 300.00
  aspiration, of newborn, massive or me-
      conium 770.1
  ataxia-telangiectasia 334.8
  Audry's (acropachyderma) 757.39
  auriculotemporal 350.8
  autosomal - *see also* Abnormal, auto-
      somes NEC
    deletion 758.3
  Avellis' 344.89
  Axenfeld's 743.44

Syndrome (*Continued*)

Ayerza (-Arrillaga) (pulmonary artery sclerosis with pulmonary hypertension) 416.0

Baader's (erythema multiforme exudativum) 695.1

Baastrup's 721.5

Babinski (-Vaquez) (cardiovascular syphilis) 093.89

Babinski-Fröhlich (adiposogenital dystrophy) 253.8

Babinski-Nageotte 344.89

Bagratuni's (temporal arteritis) 446.5

Bakwin-Krida (craniometaphyseal dysplasia) 756.89

Balint's (psychic paralysis of visual disorientation) 368.16

Ballantyne (-Runge) (postmaturity) 766.2

ballooning posterior leaflet 424.0

Banti's - *see* Cirrhosis, liver

Bard-Pic's (carcinoma, head of pancreas) 157.0

Bardet-Biedl (obesity, polydactyly, and mental retardation) 759.89

Barlow's (mitral valve prolapse) 424.0

Barlow (-Möller) (infantile scurvy) 267

Baron Munchausen's 301.51

Barré-Guillain 357.0

Barré-Liéou (posterior cervical sympathetic) 723.2

Barrett's (chronic peptic ulcer of esophagus) 530.2

Bársony-Pólgar (corkscrew esophagus) 530.5

Bársony-Teschendorf (corkscrew esophagus) 530.5

Bartter's (secondary hyperaldosteronism with juxtaglomerular hyperplasia) 255.1

Basedow's (exophthalmic goiter) 242.0

basilar artery 435.0

basofrontal 377.04

Bassen-Kornzweig (abetalipoproteinemia) 272.5

Batten-Steinert 359.2

battered

  adult 995.81

  baby or child 995.54

  spouse 995.81

Baumgarten-Cruveilhier (cirrhosis of liver) 571.5

Bearn-Kunkel (-Slater) (lupoid hepatitis) 571.49

Beau's (*see also* Degeneration, myocardial) 429.1

Bechterew-Strümpell-Marie (ankylosing spondylitis) 720.0

Beck's (anterior spinal artery occlusion) 433.8

Beckwith (-Wiedemann) 759.89

Behçet's 136.1

Bekhterev-Strümpell-Marie (ankylosing spondylitis) 720.0

Benedikt's 344.89

Béquez César (-Steinbrinck-Chédiak-Higashi) (congenital gigantism of peroxidase granules) 288.2

Bernard-Horner (*see also* Neuropathy, peripheral, autonomic) 337.9

Bernard-Sergent (acute adrenocortical insufficiency) 255.4

Bernhardt-Roth 355.1

Syndrome (*Continued*)

Bernheim's (*see also* Failure, heart, congestive) 428.0

Bertolotti's (sacralization of fifth lumbar vertebra) 756.15

Besnier-Boeck-Schaumann (sarcoidosis) 135

Bianchi's (aphasia-apraxia-alexia syndrome) 784.69

Biedl-Bardet (obesity, polydactyly, and mental retardation) 759.89

Biemond's (obesity, polydactyly, and mental retardation) 759.89

big spleen 289.4

bilateral polycystic ovarian 256.4

Bing-Horton's 346.2

Biörck (-Thorson) (malignant carcinoid) 259.2

Blackfan-Diamond (congenital hypoplastic anemia) 284.0

black lung 500

black widow spider bite 989.5

bladder neck (*see also* Incontinence, urine) 788.30

blast (concussion) - *see* Blast, injury

blind loop (postoperative) 579.2

Block-Siemens (incontinentia pigmenti) 757.33

Bloch-Sulzberger (incontinentia pigmenti) 757.33

Bloom (-Machacek) (-Torre) 757.39

Blount-Barber (tibia vara) 732.4

blue

  bloater 491.2

  diaper 270.0

  drum 381.02

  sclera 756.51

  toe - *see* Atherosclerosis

Boder-Sedgwick (ataxia-telangiectasia) 334.8

Boerhaave's (spontaneous esophageal rupture) 530.4

Bonnevie-Ullrich 758.6

Bonnier's 386.19

Bouillaud's (rheumatic heart disease) 391.9

Bourneville (-Pringle) (tuberous sclerosis) 759.5

Bouveret (-Hoffmann) (paroxysmal tachycardia) 427.2

brachial plexus 353.0

Brachman-de Lange (Amsterdam dwarf, mental retardation, and brachycephaly) 759.89

bradycardia-tachycardia 427.81

Brailsford-Morquio (dystrophy) (mucopolysaccharidosis IV) 277.5

brain (acute) (chronic) (nonpsychotic) (organic) (with behavioral reaction) (with neurotic reaction) 310.9

  with

    presenile brain disease (*see also* Dementia, presenile) 290.10

    psychosis, psychotic reaction (*see also* Psychosis, organic) 294.9

  chronic alcoholic 291.2

  congenital (*see also* Retardation, mental) 319

  postcontusional 310.2

  posttraumatic

    nonpsychotic 310.2

    psychotic 293.9

     acute 293.0

Syndrome (*Continued*)

brain (*Continued*)

  posttraumatic (*Continued*)

    psychotic (*Continued*)

     chronic (*see also* Psychosis, organic) 294.8

     subacute 293.1

  psycho-organic (*see also* Syndrome, psycho-organic) 310.9

  psychotic (*see also* Psychosis, organic) 294.9

  senile (*see also* Dementia, senile) 290.0

branchial arch 744.41

Brandt's (acrodermatitis enteropathica) 686.8

Brennemann's 289.2

Briquet's 300.81

Brissaud-Meige (infantile myxedema) 244.9

broad ligament laceration 620.6

Brock's (atelectasis due to enlarged lymph nodes) 518.0

Brown's tendon sheath 378.61

Brown-Séquard 344.89

brown spot 756.59

Brugsch's (acropachyderma) 757.39

bubbly lung 770.7

Buchem's (hyperostosis corticalis) 733.3

Budd-Chiari (hepatic vein thrombosis) 453.0

Büdinger-Ludloff-Läwen 717.89

bulbar 335.22

  lateral (*see also* Disease, cerebrovascular, acute) 436

Bullis fever 082.8

bundle of Kent (anomalous atrioventricular excitation) 426.7

Burger-Grutz (essential familial hyperlipemia) 272.3

Burke's (pancreatic insufficiency and chronic neutropenia) 577.8

Burnett's (milk-alkali) 999.9

Burnier's (hypophyseal dwarfism) 253.3

burning feet 266.2

Bywaters' 958.5

Caffey's (infantile cortical hyperostosis) 756.59

Calvé-Legg-Perthes (osteochrondrosis, femoral capital) 732.1

Caplan (-Colinet) syndrome 714.81

capsular thrombosis (*see also* Thrombosis, brain) 434.0

carcinogenic thrombophlebitis 453.1

carcinoid 259.2

cardiac asthma (*see also* Failure, ventricular, left) 428.1

cardiacos negros 416.0

cardiopulmonary obesity 278.8

cardiorenal (*see also* Hypertension, cardiorenal) 404.90

cardiorespiratory distress (idiopathic), newborn 769

cardiovascular renal (*see also* Hypertension, cardiorenal) 404.90

cardiovasorenal 272.7

Carini's (ichthyosis congenita) 757.1

carotid

  artery (internal) 435.8

  body or sinus 337.0

carpal tunnel 354.0

Carpenter's 759.89

Cassidy (-Scholte) (malignant carcinoid) 259.2

Syndrome *(Continued)*
  cat-cry 758.3
  cauda equina 344.60
  causalgia 355.9
    lower limb 355.71
    upper limb 354.4
  cavernous sinus 437.6
  celiac 579.0
    artery compression 447.4
    axis 447.4
  cerebellomedullary malformation (*see*
      also Spina bifida) 741.0
  cerebral gigantism 253.0
  cerebrohepatorenal 759.89
  cervical (root) (spine) NEC 723.8
    disc 722.71
      posterior, sympathetic 723.2
      rib 353.0
      sympathetic paralysis 337.0
      traumatic (acute) NEC 847.0
  cervicobrachial (diffuse) 723.3
  cervicocranial 723.2
  cervicodorsal outlet 353.2
  Céstan's 344.89
  Céstan (-Raymond) 433.8
  Céstan-Chenais 344.89
  chancriform 114.1
  Charcôt's (intermittent claudication)
      443.9
    angina cruris 443.9
    due to atherosclerosis 440.21
  Charcôt-Marie-Tooth 356.1
  Charcôt-Weiss-Baker 337.0
  Cheadle (-Möller) (-Barlow) (infantile
      scurvy) 267
  Chédiak-Higashi (-Steinbrinck) (con-
      genital gigantism of peroxidase
      granules) 288.2
  chest wall 786.52
  Chiari's (hepatic vein thrombosis)
      453.0
  Chiari-Frommel 676.6
  chiasmatic 368.41
  Chilaiditi's (subphrenic displacement,
      colon) 751.4
  chondroectodermal dysplasia 756.55
  chorea-athetosis-agitans 275.1
  Christian's (chronic histiocytosis X)
      277.8
  chromosome 4 short arm deletion
      758.3
  Clarke-Hadfield (pancreatic infantil-
      ism) 577.8
  Claude's 352.6
  Claude Bernard-Horner (*see also* Neu-
      ropathy, peripheral, autonomic)
      337.9
  Clérambault's
    automatism 348.8
    erotomania 297.8
  Clifford's (postmaturity) 766.2
  climacteric 627.2
  Clouston's (hidrotic ectodermal dys-
      plasia) 757.31
  clumsiness 315.4
  Cockayne's (microencephaly and
      dwarfism) 759.89
  Cockayne-Weber (epidermolysis bul-
      losa) 757.39
  Cogan's (nonsyphilitic interstitial kera-
      titis) 370.52
  cold injury (newborn) 778.2
  Collet (-Sicard) 352.6
  combined immunity deficiency 279.2

Syndrome *(Continued)*
  compartment(al) (anterior) (deep) (pos-
      terior) (tibial) 958.8
  compression 958.5
    cauda equina 344.60
      with neurogenic bladder 344.61
  concussion 310.2
  congenital
    affecting more than one system
        759.7
      specified type NEC 759.89
    facial diplegia 352.6
    muscular hypertrophy-cerebral
        759.89
  congestion-fibrosis (pelvic) 625.5
  conjunctivourethrosynovial 099.3
  Conn (-Louis) (primary aldosteronism)
      255.1
  Conradi (-Hünermann) (chondrodys-
      plasia calcificans congenita)
      756.59
  conus medullaris 336.8
  Cooke-Apert-Gallais (adrenogenital)
      255.2
  Cornelia de Lange's (Amsterdam
      dwarf, mental retardation, and
      brachycephaly) 759.8
  coronary insufficiency or intermediate
      411.1
  cor pulmonale 416.9
  corticosexual 255.2
  Costen's (complex) 524.60
  costochondral junction 733.6
  costoclavicular 353.0
  costovertebral 253.0
  Cotard's (paranoia) 297.1
  craniovertebral 723.2
  Creutzfeldt-Jakob 046.1
    with dementia 046.1 *[294.1]*
  crib death 798.0
  cricopharyngeal 787.2
  cri-du-chat 758.3
  Crigler-Najjar (congenital hyperbiliru-
      binemia) 277.4
  crocodile tears 351.8
  Cronkhite-Canada 211.3
  croup 464.4
  CRST (cutaneous systemic sclerosis)
      710.1
  crush 958.5
  crushed lung (*see also* Injury, internal,
      lung) 861.20
  Cruveilhier-Baumgarten (cirrhosis of
      liver) 571.5
  cubital tunnel 354.2
  Cuiffini-Pancoast (M8010/3) (carci-
      noma, pulmonary apex) 162.3
  Curschmann (-Batten) (-Steinert) 359.2
  Cushing's (iatrogenic) (idiopathic) (pi-
      tuitary basophilism) (pituitary-de-
      pendent) 255.0
    overdose or wrong substance given
        or taken 962.0
  Cyriax's (slipping rib) 733.99
  cystic duct stump 576.0
  Da Costa's (neurocirculatory asthenia)
      306.2
  Dameshek's (erythroblastic anemia)
      282.4
  Dana-Putnam (subacute combined
      sclerosis with pernicious anemia)
      281.0 *[336.2]*
  Danbolt (-Closs) (acrodermatitis enter-
      opathica) 686.8

Syndrome *(Continued)*
  Dandy-Walker (atresia, foramen of
      Magendie) 742.3
    with spina bifida (*see also* Spina bi-
        fida) 741.0
  Danlos' 756.83
  Davies-Colley (slipping rib) 733.99
  dead fetus 641.3
  defeminization 255.2
  defibrination (*see also* Fibrinolysis) 286.6
  Degos' 447.8
  Deiters' nucleus 386.19
  Déjérine-Roussy 348.8
  Déjérine-Thomas 333.0
  de Lange's (Amsterdam dwarf, mental
      retardation, and brachycephaly)
      (Cornelia) 759.89
  Del Castillo's (germinal aplasia) 606.0
  deletion chromosomes 758.3
  delusional
    induced by drug 292.11
  dementia-aphonia, of childhood (*see
      also* Psychosis, childhood) 299.1
  demyelinating NEC 341.9
  denial visual hallucination 307.9
  depersonalization 300.6
  Dercum's (adiposis dolorosa) 272.8
  de Toni-Fanconi (-Debré) (cystinosis)
      270.0
  diabetes-dwarfism-obesity (juvenile)
      258.1
  diabetes mellitus-hypertension-nephro-
      sis 250.4 *[581.81]*
  diabetes mellitus in newborn infant
      775.1
  diabetes-nephrosis 250.4 *[581.81]*
  diabetic amyotrophy 250.6 *[358.1]*
  Diamond-Blackfan (congenital hypo-
      plastic anemia) 284.0
  Diamond-Gardner (autoerythrocyte
      sensitization) 287.2
  DIC (diffuse or disseminated intravas-
      cular coagulopathy) (*see also* Fibri-
      nolysis) 286.6
  diencephalohypophyseal NEC 253.8
  diffuse cervicobrachial 723.3
  diffuse obstructive pulmonary 496
  DiGeorge's (thymic hypoplasia) 279.11
  Dighton's 756.51
  Di Guglielmo's (erythremic myelosis)
      (M9841/3) 207.0
  disc - *see* Displacement, intervertebral
      disc
  discogenic - *see* Displacement, interver-
      tebral disc
  disequilibrium 276.9
  disseminated platelet thrombosis 446.6
  Ditthomska 307.81
  Doan-Wiseman (primary splenic neu-
      tropenia) 288.0
  Döhle body-panmyelopathic 288.2
  Donohue's (leprechaunism) 259.8
  dorsolateral medullary (*see also* Dis-
      ease, cerebrovascular, acute) 436
  double whammy 360.81
  Down's (mongolism) 758.0
  Dresbach's (elliptocytosis) 282.1
  Dressler's (postmyocardial infarction)
      411.0
    hemoglobinuria 283.2
  drug withdrawal, infant, of dependent
      mother 779.5
  dry skin 701.1
    eye 375.15

ICD-9-CM

S

Vol. 2

Syndrome *(Continued)*
  hairless women 257.8
  Hallermann-Strieff 756.0
  Hallervorden-Spatz 333.0
  Hamman's (spontaneous mediastinal emphysema) 518.1
  Hamman-Rich (diffuse interstitial pulmonary fibrosis) 516.3
  Hand-Schüller-Christian (chronic histiocytosis X) 277.8
  hand-foot 282.61
  Hanot-Chauffard (-Troisier) (bronze diabetes) 275.0
  Harada's 363.22
  Hare's (M8010/3) (carcinoma, pulmonary apex) 162.3
  Harkavy's 446.0
  harlequin color change 779.8
  Harris' (organic hyperinsulinism) 251.1
  Hart's (pellagra-cerebellar ataxia-renal aminoaciduria) 270.0
  Hayem-Faber (achlorhydric anemia) 280.9
  Hayem-Widal (acquired hemolytic jaundice) 283.9
  Heberden's (angina pectoris) 413.9
  Hedinger's (malignant carcinoid) 259.2
  Hegglin's 288.2
  Heller's (infantile psychosis) *(see also* Psychosis, childhood) 299.1
  H.E.L.L.P 642.5
  hemolytic-uremic (adult) (child) 283.11
  Hench-Rosenberg (palindromic arthritis) *(see also* Rheumatism, palindromic) 719.3
  Henoch-Schönlein (allergic purpura) 287.0
  hepatic flexure 569.89
  hepatorenal 572.4
    due to a procedure 997.4
    following delivery 674.8
  hepatourologic 572.4
  Herrick's (hemoglobin S disease) 282.61
  Herter (-Gee) (nontropical sprue) 579.0
  Heubner-Herter (nontropical sprue) 579.0
  Heyd's (hepatorenal) 572.4
  HHHO 759.81
  Hilger's 337.0
  Hoffa (-Kastert) (liposynovitis prepatellaris) 272.8
  Hoffmann's 244.9 *[359.5]*
  Hoffmann-Bouveret (paroxysmal tachycardia) 427.2
  Hoffmann-Werdnig 335.0
  Holländer-Simons (progressive lipodystrophy) 272.6
  Holmes' (visual disorientation) 368.16
  Holmes-Adie 379.46
  Hoppe-Goldflam 358.0
  Horner's *(see also* Neuropathy, peripheral, autonomic) 337.9
    traumatic - *see* Injury, nerve, cervical sympathetic
  hospital addiction 301.51
  Hunt's (herpetic geniculate ganglionitis) 053.11
    dyssynergia cerebellaris myoclonica 334.2
  Hunter (-Hurler) (mucopolysaccharidosis II) 277.5
  hunterian glossitis 529.4
  Hurler (-Hunter) (mucopolysaccharidosis II) 277.5

Syndrome *(Continued)*
  Hutchinson's incisors or teeth 090.5
  Hutchinson-Boeck (sarcoidosis) 135
  Hutchinson-Gilford (progeria) 259.8
  hydralazine
    correct substance properly administered 695.4
    overdose or wrong substance given or taken 972.6
  hydraulic concussion (abdomen) *(see also* Injury, internal, abdomen) 868.00
  hyperabduction 447.8
  hyperactive bowel 564.1
  hyperaldosteronism with hypokalemic alkalosis (Bartter's) 255.1
  hypercalcemic 275.42
  hypercoagulation NEC 289.8
  hypereosinophilic (idiopathic) 288.3
  hyperkalemic 276.7
  hyperkinetic - *see also* Hyperkinesia, heart 429.82
  hyperlipemia-hemolytic anemia-icterus 571.1
  hypermobility 728.5
  hypernatremia 276.0
  hyperosmolarity 276.0
  hypersomnia-bulimia 349.89
  hypersplenic 289.4
  hypersympathetic *(see also* Neuropathy, peripheral, autonomic) 337.9
  hypertransfusion, newborn 776.4
  hyperventilation, psychogenic 306.1
  hyperviscosity (of serum) NEC 273.3
    polycythemic 289.0
    sclerothymic 282.8
  hypoglycemic (familial) (neonatal) 251.2
    functional 251.1
  hypokalemic 276.8
  hypophyseal 253.8
  hypophyseothalamic 253.8
  hypopituitarism 253.2
  hypoplastic left heart 746.7
  hypopotassemia 276.8
  hyposmolality 276.1
  hypotension, maternal 669.2
  hypotonia-hypomentia-hypogonadism-obesity 759.81
  ICF (intravascular coagulation-fibrinolysis) *(see also* Fibrinolysis) 286.6
  idiopathic cardiorespiratory distress, newborn 769
  idiopathic nephrotic (infantile) 581.9
  Imerslund (-Gräsbeck) (anemia due to familial selective vitamin B_{12} malabsorption) 281.1
  immobility (paraplegic) 728.3
  immunity deficiency, combined 279.2
  impending coronary 411.1
  impingement
    shoulder 726.2
    vertebral bodies 724.4
  inappropriate secretion of antidiuretic hormone (ADH) 253.6
  incomplete
    mandibulofacial 756.0
  infant
    death, sudden (SIDS) 798.0
    Hercules 255.2
    of diabetic mother 775.0
    shaken 995.55
  infantilism 253.3

Syndrome *(Continued)*
  inferior vena cava 459.2
  influenza-like 487.1
  inspissated bile, newborn 774.4
  intermediate coronary (artery) 411.1
  internal carotid artery *(see also* Occlusion, artery, carotid) 433.1
  interspinous ligament 724.8
  intestinal
    carcinoid 259.2
    gas 787.3
    knot 560.2
  intravascular
    coagulation-fibrinolysis (ICF) *(see also* Fibrinolysis) 286.6
    coagulopathy *(see also* Fibrinolysis) 286.6
  inverted Marfan's 759.89
  IRDS (idiopathic respiratory distress, newborn) 769
  irritable
    bowel 564.1
    heart 306.2
    weakness 300.5
  ischemic bowel (transient) 557.9
    chronic 557.1
    due to mesenteric artery insufficiency 557.1
  Itsenko-Cushing (pituitary basophilism) 255.0
  IVC (intravascular coagulopathy) *(see also* Fibrinolysis) 286.6
  Ivemark's (asplenia with congenital heart disease) 759.0
  Jaccoud's 714.4
  Jackson's 344.89
  Jadassohn-Lewandowski (pachyonychia congenita) 757.5
  Jaffe-Lichtenstein (-Uehlinger) 252.0
  Jahnke's (encephalocutaneous angiomatosis) 759.6
  Jakob-Creutzfeldt 046.1
    with dementia 046.1 *[294.1]*
  Jaksch's (pseudoleukemia infantum) 285.8
  Jaksch-Hayem (-Luzet) (pseudoleukemia infantum) 285.8
  jaw-winking 742.8
  jejunal 564.2
  jet lag 307.45
  Jeune's (asphyxiating thoracic dystrophy of newborn) 756.4
  Job's (chronic granulomatous disease) 288.1
  Jordan's 288.2
  Joseph-Diamond-Blackfan (congenital hypoplastic anemia) 284.0
  jugular foramen 352.6
  Kahler's (multiple myeloma) (M9730/3) 203.0
  Kalischer's (encephalocutaneous angiomatosis) 759.6
  Kallmann's (hypogonadotropic hypogonadism with anosmia) 253.4
  Kanner's (autism) *(see also* Psychosis, childhood) 299.0
  Kartagener's (sinusitis, bronchiectasis, situs inversus) 759.3
  Kasabach-Merritt (capillary hemangioma associated with thrombocytopenic purpura) 287.3
  Kast's (dyschondroplasia with hemangiomas) 756.4

Syndrome *(Continued)*
Kaznelson's (congenital hypoplastic anemia) 284.0
Kelly's (sideropenic dysphagia) 280.8
Kimmelstiel-Wilson (intercapillary glomerulosclerosis) 250.4 *[581.81]*
Klauder's (erythema multiforme exudativum) 695.1
Klein-Waardenburg (ptosis-epicanthus) 270.2
Kleine-Levin 349.89
Klinefelter's 758.7
Klippel-Feil (brevicollis) 756.16
Klippel-Trenaunay 759.89
Klumpke (-Déjérine) (injury to brachial plexus at birth) 767.6
Klüver-Bucy (-Terzian) 310.0
Köhler-Pelligrini-Stieda (calcification, knee joint) 726.62
König's 564.89
Korsakoff's (nonalcoholic) 294.0
    alcoholic 291.1
Korsakoff (-Wernicke) (nonalcoholic) 294.0
    alcoholic 291.1
Kostmann's (infantile genetic agranulocytosis) 288.0
Krabbe's
    congenital muscle hypoplasia 756.89
    cutaneocerebral angioma 759.6
Kunkel (lupoid hepatitis) 571.49
labyrinthine 386.50
laceration, broad ligament 620.6
Langdon Down (mongolism) 758.0
Larsen's (flattened facies and multiple congenital dislocations) 755.8
lateral
    cutaneous nerve of thigh 355.1
    medullary (*see also* Disease, cerebrovascular, acute) 436
Launois' (pituitary gigantism) 253.0
Launois-Cléret (adiposogenital dystrophy) 253.8
Laurence-Moon (-Bardet)-Biedl (obesity, polydactyly, and mental retardation) 759.89
Lawford's (encephalocutaneous angiomatosis) 759.6
lazy
    leukocyte 288.0
    posture 728.3
Lederer-Brill (acquired infectious hemolytic anemia) 283.19
Legg-Calvé-Perthes (osteochondrosis capital femoral) 732.1
Lennox's (*see also* Epilepsy) 345.0
lenticular 275.1
Leopold-Levi's (paroxysmal thyroid instability) 242.9
Lepore hemoglobin 282.4
Léri-Weill 756.59
Leriche's (aortic bifurcation occlusion) 444.0
Lermoyez's (*see also* Disease, Meniere's) 386.00
Lesch-Nyhan (hypoxanthine-guanine-phosphoribosyltransferase deficiency) 277.2
Lev's (acquired complete heart block) 426.0
Levi's (pituitary dwarfism) 253.3
Lévy-Roussy 334.3

Syndrome *(Continued)*
Lichtheim's (subacute combined sclerosis with pernicious anemia) 281.0 *[336.2]*
Li-Fraumeni 758.3
Lightwood's (renal tubular acidosis) 588.8
Lignac (-de Toni) (-Fanconi) (-Debré) (cystinosis) 270.0
Likoff's (angina in menopausal women) 413.9
liver-kidney 572.4
Lloyd's 258.1
lobotomy 310.0
Löffler's (eosinophilic pneumonitis) 518.3
Löfgren's (sarcoidosis) 135
long arm 18 or 21 deletion 758.3
Looser (-Debray)-Milkman (osteomalacia with pseudofractures) 268.2
Lorain-Levi (pituitary dwarfism) 253.3
Louis-Bar (ataxia-telangiectasia) 334.8
low
    atmospheric pressure 993.2
    back 724.2
        psychogenic 306.0
    output (cardiac) (*see also* Failure, heart) 428.9
Lowe's (oculocerebrorenal dystrophy) 270.8
Lowe-Terrey-MacLachlan (oculocerebrorenal dystrophy) 270.8
lower radicular, newborn 767.4
Lown (-Ganong)-Levine (short P-R internal, normal QRS complex, and supraventricular tachycardia) 426.81
Lucey-Driscoll (jaundice due to delayed conjugation) 774.30
Luetscher's (dehydration) 276.5
lumbar vertebral 724.4
Lutembacher's (atrial septal defect with mitral stenosis) 745.5
Lyell's (toxic epidermal necrolysis) 695.1
    due to drug
        correct substance properly administered 695.1
        overdose or wrong substance given or taken 977.9
            specified drug - *see* Table of Drugs and Chemicals
MacLeod's 492.8
macrogenitosomia praecox 259.8
macroglobulinemia 273.3
Maffucci's (dyschondroplasia with hemangiomas) 756.4
Magenblase 306.4
magnesium-deficiency 781.7
malabsorption 579.9
    postsurgical 579.3
    spinal fluid 331.3
malignant carcinoid 259.2
Mallory-Weiss 530.7
mandibulofacial dysostosis 756.0
manic-depressive (*see also* Psychosis, affective) 296.80
Mankowsky's (familial dysplastic osteopathy) 731.2
maple syrup (urine) 270.3
Marable's (celiac artery compression) 447.4
Marchesani (-Weill) (brachymorphism and ectopia lentis) 759.89

Syndrome *(Continued)*
Marchiafava-Bignami 341.8
Marchiafava-Micheli (paroxysmal nocturnal hemoglobinuria) 283.2
Marcus Gunn's (jaw-winking syndrome) 742.8
Marfan's (arachnodactyly) 759.82
    meaning congenital syphilis 090.49
    with luxation of lens 090.49 *[379.32]*
Marie's (acromegaly) 253.0
    primary or idiopathic (acropachyderma) 757.39
    secondary (hypertrophic pulmonary osteoarthropathy) 731.2
Markus-Adie 379.46
Maroteaux-Lamy (mucopolysaccharidosis VI) 277.5
Martin's 715.27
Martin-Albright (pseudohypoparathyroidism) 275.49
Martorell-Fabré (pulseless disease) 446.7
massive aspiration of newborn 770.1
Masters-Allen 620.6
mastocytosis 757.33
maternal hypotension 669.2
maternal obesity 646.1
May (-Hegglin) 288.2
McArdle (-Schmid) (-Pearson) (glycogenosis V) 271.0
McCune-Albright (osteitis fibrosa disseminata) 756.59
McQuarrie's (idiopathic familial hypoglycemia) 251.2
meconium
    aspiration 770.1
    plug (newborn) NEC 777.1
median arcuate ligament 447.4
mediastinal fibrosis 519.3
Meekeren-Ehlers-Danlos 756.83
Meige (blepharospasm-oromandibular dystonia) 333.82
    -Milroy (chronic hereditary edema) 757.0
MELAS 758.89
Melkersson (-Rosenthal) 351.8
Mende's (ptosis-epicanthus) 270.2
Mendelson's (resulting from a procedure) 997.3
    during labor 668.0
    obstetric 668.0
Ménétrier's (hypertrophic gastritis) 535.2
Méniére's (*see also* Disease, Meniere's) 386.00
meningo-eruptive 047.1
Menkes' 759.89
    glutamic acid 759.89
    maple syrup (urine) disease 270.3
menopause 627.2
    postartificial 627.4
menstruation 625.4
MERFF 758.89
mesenteric
    artery, superior 557.1
    vascular insufficiency (with gangrene) 557.1
metastatic carcinoid 259.2
Meyenburg-Altherr-Uehlinger 733.99
Meyer-Schwickerath and Weyers (dysplasia oculodentodigitalis) 759.89
Micheli-Rietti (thalassemia minor) 282.4

Syndrome *(Continued)*
Michotte's 721.5
micrognathia-glossoptosis 756.0
microphthalmos (congenital) 759.89
midbrain 348.8
middle
    lobe (lung) (right) 518.0
    radicular 353.0
Miescher's
    familial acanthosis nigricans 701.2
    granulomatosis disciformis 709.3
Mieten's 759.89
migraine 346.0
Mikity-Wilson (pulmonary dysmaturity) 770.7
Mikulicz's (dryness of mouth, absent or decreased lacrimation) 527.1
milk alkali (milk drinkers') 999.9
Milkman (-Looser) (osteomalacia with pseudofractures) 268.2
Millard-Gubler 344.89
Miller Fisher's 357.0
Milles' (encephalocutaneous angiomatosis) 759.6
Minkowski-Chauffard (*see also* Spherocytosis) 282.0
Mirizzi's (hepatic duct stenosis) 576.2
    with calculus, cholelithiasis, or stones - *see* Choledocholithiasis
mitral
    click (-murmur) 785.2
    valve prolapse 424.0
Möbius'
    congenital oculofacial paralysis 352.6
    ophthalmoplegic migraine 346.8
Mohr's (types I and II) 759.89
monofixation 378.34
Moore's (*see also* Epilepsy) 345.5
Morel-Moore (hyperostosis frontalis interna) 733.3
Morel-Morgagni (hyperostosis frontalis interna) 733.3
Morgagni (-Stewart-Morel) (hyperostosis frontalis interna) 733.3
Morgagni-Adams-Stokes (syncope with heart block) 426.9
Morquio (-Brailsford) (-Ullrich) (mucopolysaccharidosis IV) 277.5
Morris (testicular feminization) 257.8
Morton's (foot) (metatarsalgia) (metatarsal neuralgia) (neuralgia) (neuroma) (toe) 355.6
Moschcowitz (-Singer-Symmers) (thrombotic thrombocytopenic purpura) 446.6
Mounier-Kuhn 494
Mucha-Haberman (acute parapsoriasis varioliformis) 696.2
mucocutaneous lymph node (acute) (febrile) (infantile) (MCLS) 446.1
multiple
    deficiency 260
    operations 301.51
Munchausen's 301.51
Munchmeyer's (exostosis luxurians) 728.11
Murchison-Sanderson - *see* Disease, Hodgkin's
myasthenic - *see* Myasthenia, syndrome
myelodysplastic 238.7
myeloproliferative (chronic) (M9960/1) 238.7
myofascial pain NEC 729.1

Syndrome *(Continued)*
Naffziger's 353.0
Nager-de Reynier (dysostosis mandibularis) 756.0
nail-patella (hereditary osteo-onychodysplasia) 756.89
Nebécourt's 253.3
Neill Dingwall (microencephaly and dwarfism) 759.89
nephrotic (*see also* Nephrosis) 581.9
    diabetic 250.4 *[581.81]*
Netherton's (ichthyosiform erythroderma) 757.1
neurocutaneous 759.6
neuroleptic malignant 333.92
Nezelof's (pure alymphocytosis) 279.13
Niemann-Pick (lipid histiocytosis) 272.7
Nonne-Milroy-Meige (chronic hereditary edema) 757.0
nonsense 300.16
Noonan's 759.89
Nothnagel's
    ophthalmoplegia-cerebellar ataxia 378.52
    vasomotor acroparesthesia 443.89
nucleus ambiguous-hypoglossal 352.6
OAV (oculoauriculovertebral dysplasia) 756.0
obsessional 300.3
oculocutaneous 364.24
oculomotor 378.81
oculourethroarticular 099.3
Ogilvie's (sympathicotonic colon obstruction) 560.89
ophthalmoplegia-cerebellar ataxia 378.52
Oppenheim-Urbach (necrobiosis lipoidica diabeticorum) 250.8 *[709.3]*
oral-facial-digital 759.89
organic
    affective NEC 293.83
        drug-induced 292.84
    anxiety 293.84
    delusional 293.81
        alcohol-induced 291.5
        drug-induced 292.11
        due to or associated with arteriosclerosis 290.42
            presenile brain disease 290.12
            senility 290.20
    depressive 293.83
        drug-induced 292.84
        due to or associated with arteriosclerosis 290.43
            presenile brain disease 290.13
            senile brain disease 290.21
    hallucinosis 293.82
        drug-induced 292.84
organic affective 293.83
    induced by drug 292.84
organic personality 310.1
    induced by drug 292.89
Ormond's 593.4
orodigitofacial 759.89
orthostatic hypotensive-dysautonomic-dyskinetic 333.0
Osler-Weber-Rendu (familial hemorrhagic telangiectasia) 448.0
osteodermopathic hyperostosis 757.39
osteoporosis-osteomalacia 268.2
Österreicher-Turner (hereditary osteo-onychodysplasia) 756.89
Ostrum-Furst 756.59

Syndrome *(Continued)*
otolith 386.19
otopalatodigital 759.89
outlet (thoracic) 353.0
ovarian vein 593.4
Owren's (*see also* Defect, coagulation) 286.3
OX 758.6
pacemaker 429.4
Paget-Schroetter (intermittent venous claudication) 453.8
pain - *see* Pain
painful
    apicocostal vertebral (M8010/3) 162.3
    arc 726.19
    bruising 287.2
    feet 266.2
Pancoast's (carcinoma, pulmonary apex) (M8010/3) 162.3
panhypopituitary (postpartum) 253.2
papillary muscle 429.81
    with myocardial infarction 410.8
Papillon-Léage and Psaume (orodigitofacial dysostosis) 759.89
paraneoplastic- see condition
parobiotic (transfusion)
    donor (twin) 772.0
    recipient (twin) 776.4
paralysis agitans 332.0
paralytic 344.9
    specified type NEC 344.89
paraneoplastic - *see* Condition
Parinaud's (paralysis of conjugate upward gaze) 378.81
    oculoglandular 372.02
Parkes Weber and Dimitri (encephalocutaneous angiomatosis) 759.6
Parkinson's (*see also* Parkinsonism) 332.0
parkinsonian (*see also* Parkinsonism) 332.0
Parry's (exophthalmic goiter) 242.0
Parry-Romberg 349.89
Parsonage-Aldren-Turner 353.5
Parsonage-Turner 353.5
Patau's (trisomy D_1) 758.1
Paterson (-Brown) (-Kelly) (sideropenic dysphagia) 280.8
Payr's (splenic flexure syndrome) 569.89
pectoral girdle 447.8
pectoralis minor 447.8
Pelger-Huët (hereditary hyposegmentation) 288.2
Pellagra-cerebellar ataxia-renal aminoaciduria 270.0
Pellegrini-Stieda 726.62
pellagroid 265.2
Pellizzi's (pineal) 259.8
pelvic congestion (-fibrosis) 625.5
Pendred's (familial goiter with deafmutism) 243
Penfield's (*see also* Epilepsy) 345.5
Penta X 758.81
peptic ulcer - *see* Ulcer, peptic 533.9
perabduction 447.8
periodic 277.3
periurethral fibrosis 593.4
persistent fetal circulation 747.9
Petges-Cléjat (poikilodermatomyositis) 710.3
Peutz-Jeghers 759.6
Pfeiffer (acrocephalosyndactyly) 755.55

ICD-9-CM

S

Vol. 2

Syndrome (*Continued*)
Rytand-Lipsitch (complete atrioventric-
    ular block) 426.0
sacralization-scoliosis-sciatica 756.15
sacroiliac 724.6
Saenger's 379.46
salt
    depletion (*see also* Disease, renal)
        593.9
        due to heat NEC 992.8
            causing heat exhaustion or pros-
                tration 992.4
    low (*see also* Disease, renal) 593.9
salt-losing (*see also* Disease, renal) 593.9
Sanfilippo's (mucopolysaccharidosis
    III) 277.5
Scaglietti-Dagnini (acromegalic macro-
    spondylitis) 253.0
scalded skin 695.1
scalenus anticus (anterior) 353.0
scapulocostal 354.8
scapuloperoneal 359.1
scapulovertebral 723.4
Schaumann's (sarcoidosis) 135
Scheie's (mucopolysaccharidosis IS)
    277.5
Scheuthauer-Marie-Sainton (cleidocra-
    nialis dysostosis) 755.59
Schirmer's (encephalocutaneous an-
    giomatosis) 759.6
schizophrenic, of childhood NEC (*see
    also* Psychosis, childhood) 299.9
Schmidt's
    sphallo-pharyngo-laryngeal hemiple-
        gia 352.6
    thyroid-adrenocortical insufficiency
        258.1
    vagoaccessory 352.6
Schneider's 047.9
Scholte's (malignant carcinoid) 259.2
Scholz (-Bielschowsky-Henneberg)
    330.0
Schroeder's (endocrine-hypertensive)
    255.3
Schüller-Christian (chronic histiocytosis
    X) 277.8
Schultz's (agranulocytosis) 288.0
Schwachman's 288.0
Schwartz (-Jampel) 756.89
Schwartz-Bartter (inappropriate secre-
    tion of antidiuretic hormone)
    253.6
scimitar (anomalous venous drainage,
    right lung to inferior vena cava)
    747.49
sclerocystic ovary 256.4
sea-blue histiocyte 272.7
Seabright-Bantam (pseudohypopara-
    thyroidism) 275.49
Seckel's 759.89
Secretan's (posttraumatic edema) 782.3
secretoinhibitor (keratoconjunctivitis
    sicca) 710.2
Seeligmann's (ichthyosis congenita)
    757.1
Senear-Usher (pemphigus erythemato-
    sus) 694.4
senilism 259.8
serotonin 333.99
serous meningitis 348.2
Sertoli cell (germinal aplasia) 606.0
sex chromosome mosaic 758.81
Sézary's (reticulosis) (M9701/3) 202.2
shaken infant 995.55

Syndrome (*Continued*)
Shaver's (bauxite pneumoconiosis) 503
Sheehan's (postpartum pituitary necro-
    sis) 253.2
shock (traumatic) 958.4
    kidney 584.5
        following crush injury 958.5
    lung 518.5
    neurogenic 308.9
    psychic 308.9
short
    bowel 579.3
    P-R interval 426.81
shoulder-arm (*see also* Neuropathy, pe-
    ripheral, autonomic) 337.9
shoulder-girdle 723.4
shoulder-hand (*see also* Neuropathy,
    peripheral, autonomic) 337.9
Shwachman's 288.0
Shy-Drager (orthostatic hypotension
    with multisystem degeneration)
    333.0
Sicard's 352.6
sicca (keratoconjunctivitis) 710.2
sick
    cell 276.1
    cilia 759.89
    sinus 427.81
sideropenic 280.8
Siemens'
    ectodermal dysplasia 757.31
    keratosis follicularis spinulosa (de-
        calvans) 757.39
Silfverskiöld's (osteochondrodystrophy,
    extremities) 756.50
Silver's (congenital hemihypertrophy
    and short stature) 759.89
Silvestroni-Bianco (thalassemia min-
    ima) 282.4
Simons' (progressive lipodystrophy)
    272.6
sinus tarsi 355.5
sinusitis-bronchiectasis-situs inversus
    759.3
Sipple's (medullary thyroid carcinoma-
    pheochromocytoma) 193
Sjögren (-Gougerot) (keratoconjunctivi-
    tis sicca) 710.2
    with lung involvement 710.2 *[517.8]*
Sjögren-Larsson (ichthyosis congenita)
    757.1
Slocumb's 255.3
Sluder's 337.0
Smith-Lemli-Opitz (cerebrohepatorenal
    syndrome) 759.89
smokers' 305.1
Sneddon-Wilkinson (subcorneal pustu-
    lar dermatosis) 694.1
Sotos' (cerebral gigantism) 253.0
South African cardiomyopathy 425.2
spasmodic
    upward movement, eye(s) 378.82
    winking 307.20
Spens' (syncope with heart block) 426.9
spherophakia-brachymorphia 759.89
spinal cord injury - *see also* Injury, spi-
    nal, by site
    with fracture, vertebra - *see* Fracture,
        vertebra, by site, with spinal
        cord injury
    cervical - *see* Injury, spinal, cervical
    fluid malabsorption (acquired) 331.3
splenic
    agenesis 759.0

Syndrome (*Continued*)
splenic (*Continued*)
    flexure 569.89
    neutropenia 288.0
    sequestration 282.60
Spurway's (brittle bones and blue
    sclera) 756.51
staphylococcal scalded skin 695.1
Stein's (polycystic ovary) 256.4
Stein-Leventhal (polycystic ovary)
    256.4
Steinbrocker's (*see also* Neuropathy, pe-
    ripheral, autonomic) 337.9
Stevens-Johnson (erythema multiforme
    exudativum) 695.1
Stewart-Morel (hyperostosis frontalis
    interna) 733.3
stiff-man 333.91
Still's (juvenile rheumatoid arthritis)
    714.30
Still-Felty (rheumatoid arthritis with
    splenomegaly and leukopenia)
    714.1
Stilling-Türk-Duane (ocular retraction
    syndrome) 378.71
Stojano's (subcostal) 098.86
Stokes (-Adams) (syncope with heart
    block) 426.9
Stokvis-Talma (enterogenous cyanosis)
    289.7
stone heart (*see also* Failure, ventricu-
    lar, left) 428.1
straight-back 756.19
stroke (*see also* Disease, cerebrovascu-
    lar, acute) 436
    little 435.9
Sturge-Kalischer-Weber (encephalotri-
    geminal angiomatosis) 759.6
Sturge-Weber (-Dimitri) (encephalocu-
    taneous angiomatosis) 759.6
subclavian-carotid obstruction
    (chronic) 446.7
subclavian steal 435.2
subcoracoid-pectoralis minor 447.8
subcostal 098.86
    nerve compression 354.8
subperiosteal hematoma 267
subphrenic interposition 751.4
sudden infant death (SIDS) 798.0
Sudeck's 733.7
Sudeck-Leriche 733.7
superior
    cerebellar artery (*see also* Disease,
        cerebrovascular, acute) 436
    mesenteric artery 557.1
    pulmonary sulcus (tumor) (M8010/
        3) 162.3
    vena cava 459.2
suprarenal cortical 255.3
supraspinatus 726.10
swallowed blood 777.3
sweat retention 705.1
Sweet's (acute febrile neutrophilic der-
    matosis) 695.89
Swyer-James (unilateral hyperlucent
    lung) 492.8
Swyer's (XY pure gonadal dysgenesis)
    752.7
Symonds' 348.2
sympathetic
    cervical paralysis 337.0
    pelvic 625.5
syndactylic oxycephaly 755.55
syphilitic-cardiovascular 093.89

Syndrome *(Continued)*
  systemic fibrosclerosing 710.8
  systolic click (-murmur) 785.2
  Tabagism 305.1
  tachycardia-bradycardia 427.81
  Takayasu (-Onishi) (pulseless disease)
      446.7
  Tapia's 352.6
  tarsal tunnel 355.5
  Taussig-Bing (transposition, aorta and
      overriding pulmonary artery)
      745.11
  Taybi's (otopalatodigital) 759.89
  Taylor's 625.5
  teething 520.7
  tegmental 344.89
  telangiectasis-pigmentation-cataract
      757.33
  temporal 383.02
    lobectomy behavior 310.0
  temporomandibular joint-pain-dys-
      function [TMJ] NEC 524.60
    specified NEC 524.69
  Terry's 362.21
  testicular feminization 257.8
  testis, nonvirilizing 257.8
  tethered (spinal) cord 742.59
  thalamic 348.8
  Thibierge-Weissenbach (cutaneous sys-
      temic sclerosis) 710.1
  Thiele 724.6
  thoracic outlet (compression) 353.0
  thoracogenous rheumatic (hyper-
      trophic pulmonary osteoarthropa-
      thy) 731.2
  Thorn's *(see also* Disease, renal) 593.9
  Thorson-Biörck (malignant carcinoid)
      259.2
  thrombopenia-hemangioma 287.3
  thyroid-adrenocortical insufficiency
      258.1
  Tietze's 733.6
  time-zone change (rapid) 307.45
  Tobias' (carcinoma, pulmonary apex)
      (M8010/3) 162.3
  toilet seat 926.0
  Tolosa-Hunt 378.55
  Toni-Fanconi (cystinosis) 270.0
  Touraine's (hereditary osteo-onycho-
      dysplasia) 756.89
  Touraine-Solente-Golé (acropachy-
      derma) 757.39
  toxic
    oil 710.5
    shock 040.89
  transfusion
    fetal-maternal 772.0
    twin
      donor (infant) 772.0
      recipient (infant) 776.4
  Treacher Collins' (incomplete mandib-
      ulofacial dysostosis) 756.0
  trigeminal plate 259.8
  triplex X female 758.81
  trisomy NEC 758.5
    13 or D₁ 758.1
    16-18 or E 758.2
    18 or E₃ 758.2
    20 758.5
    21 or G (mongolism) 758.0
    22 or G (mongolism) 758.0
    G 758.0
  Troisier-Hanot-Chauffard (bronze dia-
      betes) 275.0

Syndrome *(Continued)*
  tropical wet feet 991.4
  Trousseau's (thrombophlebitis migrans
      visceral cancer) 453.1
  Türk's (ocular retraction syndrome)
      378.71
  Turner's 758.6
  Turner-Varny 758.6
  twin-to-twin transfusion 762.3
    recipient twin 776.4
  Uehlinger's (acropachyderma) 757.39
  Ullrich (-Bonnevie) (-Turner) 758.6
  Ullrich-Feichtiger 759.89
  underwater blast injury (abdominal)
      (see also Injury, internal, abdomen)
      868.00
  universal joint, cervix 620.6
  Unverricht (-Lundborg) 333.2
  Unverricht-Wagner (dermatomyositis)
      710.3
  upward gaze 378.81
  Urbach-Oppenheim (necrobiosis li-
      poidica diabeticorum) 250.8
      [709.3]
  Urbach-Wiethe (lipoid proteinosis)
      272.8
  uremia, chronic 585
  urethral 597.81
  urethro-oculoarticular 099.3
  urethro-oculosynovial 099.3
  urohepatic 572.4
  uveocutaneous 364.24
  uveomeningeal, uveomeningitis 363.22
  vagohypoglossal 352.6
  vagovagal 780.2
  van Buchem's (hyperostosis corticalis)
      733.3
  van der Hoeve's (brittle bones and
      blue sclera, deafness) 756.51
  van der Hoeve-Halbertsma-Waarden-
      burg (ptosis-epicanthus) 270.2
  van der Hoeve-Waardenburg-Gualdi
      (ptosis-epicanthus) 270.2
  vanishing twin 651.33
  van Neck-Odelberg (juvenile osteo-
      chondrosis) 732.1
  vascular splanchnic 557.0
  vasomotor 443.9
  vasovagal 780.2
  VATER 759.89
  vena cava (inferior) (superior) (ob-
      struction) 459.2
  Verbiest's (claudicatio intermittens
      spinalis) 435.1
  Vernet's 352.6
  vertebral
    artery 435.1
      compression 721.1
    lumbar 724.4
    steal 435.1
  vertebrogenic (pain) 724.5
  vertiginous NEC 386.9
  video display tube 723.8
  Villaret's 352.6
  Vinson-Plummer (sideropenic dyspha-
      gia) 280.8
  virilizing adrenocortical hyperplasia,
      congenital 255.2
  virus, viral 079.99
  visceral larval migrans 128.0
  visual disorientation 368.16
  vitamin B₆ deficiency 266.1
  vitreous touch 997.99
  Vogt's (corpus striatum) 333.7

Syndrome *(Continued)*
  Vogt-Koyanagi 364.24
  Volkmann's 958.6
  von Bechterew-Strümpell (ankylosing
      spondylitis) 720.0
  von Graefe's 378.72
  von Hippel-Lindau (angiomatosis
      retinocerebellosa) 759.6
  von Schroetter's (intermittent venous
      claudication) 453.8
  von Willebrand (-Jürgens) (angiohemo-
      philia) 286.4
  Waardenburg-Klein (ptosis epicanthus)
      270.2
  Wagner (-Unverricht) (dermatomyosi-
      tis) 710.3
  Waldenström's (macroglobulinemia)
      273.3
  Waldenström-Kjellberg (sideropenic
      dysphagia) 280.8
  Wallenberg's (posterior inferior cere-
      bellar artery) *(see also* Disease,
      cerebrovascular, acute) 436
  Waterhouse (-Friderichsen) 036.3
  water retention 276.6
  Weber's 344.89
  Weber-Christian (nodular nonsuppura-
      tive panniculitis) 729.30
  Weber-Cockayne (epidermolysis bul-
      losa) 757.39
  Weber-Dimitri (encephalocutaneous
      angiomatosis) 759.6
  Weber-Gubler 344.89
  Weber-Leyden 344.89
  Weber-Osler (familial hemorrhagic tel-
      angiectasia) 448.0
  Wegener's (necrotizing respiratory
      granulomatosis) 446.4
  Weill-Marchesani (brachymorphism
      and ectopia lentis) 759.89
  Weingarten's (tropical eosinophilia)
      518.3
  Weiss-Baker (carotid sinus syncope)
      337.0
  Weissenbach-Thibierge (cutaneous sys-
      temic sclerosis) 710.1
  Werdnig-Hoffmann 335.0
  Werlhof-Wichmann *(see also* Purpura,
      thrombocytopenic) 287.3
  Wermer's (polyendocrine adenomato-
      sis) 258.0
  Werner's (progeria adultorum) 259.8
  Wernicke's (nonalcoholic) (superior
      hemorrhagic polioencephalitis)
      265.1
  Wernicke-Korsakoff (nonalcoholic)
      294.0
    alcoholic 291.1
  Westphal-Strümpell (hepatolenticular
      degeneration) 275.1
  wet
    brain (alcoholic) 303.9
    feet (maceration) (tropical) 991.4
    lung
      adult 518.5
      newborn 770.6
  whiplash 847.0
  Whipple's (intestinal lipodystrophy)
      040.2
  "whistling face" (craniocarpotarsal
      dystrophy) 759.89
  Widal (-Abrami) (acquired hemolytic
      jaundice) 283.9
  Wilkie's 557.1

Syndrome *(Continued)*
    Wilkinson-Sneddon (subcorneal pustular dermatosis) 694.1
    Willan-Plumbe (psoriasis) 696.1
    Willebrand (-Jürgens) (angiohemophilia) 286.4
    Willi-Prader (hypogenital dystrophy with diabetic tendency) 759.81
    Wilson's (hepatolenticular degeneration) 275.1
    Wilson-Mikity 770.7
    Wiskott-Aldrich (eczema-thrombocytopenia) 279.12
    withdrawal
        alcohol 291.81
        drug 292.0
            infant of dependent mother 779.5
    Woakes' (ethmoiditis) 471.1
    Wolff-Parkinson-White (anomalous atrioventricular excitation) 426.7
    Wright's (hyperabduction) 447.8
    X 413.9
    xiphoidalgia 733.99
    XO 758.6
    XXX 758.81
    XXXXY 758.81
    XXY 758.7
    yellow vernix (placental dysfunction) 762.2
    Zahorsky's 074.0
    Zieve's (jaundice, hyperlipemia and hemolytic anemia) 571.1
    Zollinger-Ellison (gastric hypersecretion with pancreatic islet cell tumor) 251.5
    Zuelzer-Ogden (nutritional megaloblastic anemia) 281.2
Synechia (iris) (pupil) 364.70
    anterior 364.72
        peripheral 364.73
    intrauterine (traumatic) 621.5
    posterior 364.71
    vulvae, congenital 752.49
Synesthesia *(see also* Disturbance, sensation) 782.0
Synodontia 520.2
Synophthalmus 759.89
Synorchidism 752.8
Synorchism 752.8
Synostosis (congenital) 756.59
    astragaloscaphoid 755.67
    radioulnar 755.53
    talonavicular (bar) 755.67
    tarsal 755.67
Synovial - *see* condition
Synovioma (M9040/3) - *see also* Neoplasm, connective tissue, malignant
    benign (M9040/0) - *see* Neoplasm, connective tissue, benign
Synoviosarcoma (M9040/3) - *see* Neoplasm, connective tissue, malignant
Synovitis 727.00
    chronic crepitant, wrist 727.2
    due to crystals - *see* Arthritis, due to crystals
    gonococcal 098.51
    gouty 274.0
    syphilitic 095.7
        congenital 090.0
    traumatic, current - *see* Sprain, by site
    tuberculous - *see* Tuberculosis, synovitis

Synovitis *(Continued)*
    villonodular 719.20
        ankle 719.27
        elbow 719.22
        foot 719.27
        hand 719.24
        hip 719.25
        knee 719.26
        multiple sites 719.29
        pelvic region 719.25
        shoulder (region) 719.21
        specified site NEC 719.28
        wrist 719.23
Syphilide 091.3
    congenital 090.0
    newborn 090.0
    tubercular 095.8
        congenital 090.0
Syphilis, syphilitic (acquired) 097.9
    with lung involvement 095.1
    abdomen (late) 095.2
    acoustic nerve 094.86
    adenopathy (secondary) 091.4
    adrenal (gland) 095.8
        with cortical hypofunction 095.8
    age under 2 years NEC *(see also* Syphilis, congenital) 090.9
        acquired 097.9
    alopecia (secondary) 091.82
    anemia 095.8
    aneurysm (artery) (ruptured) 093.89
        aorta 093.0
        central nervous system 094.89
        congenital 090.5
    anus 095.8
        primary 091.1
        secondary 091.3
    aorta, aortic (arch) (abdominal) (insufficiency) (pulmonary) (regurgitation) (stenosis) (thoracic) 093.89
        aneurysm 093.0
    arachnoid (adhesive) 094.2
    artery 093.89
        cerebral 094.89
        spinal 094.89
    arthropathy (neurogenic) (tabetic) 094.0 *[713.5]*
    asymptomatic - *see* Syphilis, latent
    ataxia, locomotor (progressive) 094.0
    atrophoderma maculatum 091.3
    auricular fibrillation 093.89
    Bell's palsy 094.89
    bladder 095.8
    bone 095.5
        secondary 091.61
    brain 094.89
    breast 095.8
    bronchus 095.8
    bubo 091.0
    bulbar palsy 094.89
    bursa (late) 095.7
    cardiac decompensation 093.89
    cardiovascular (early) (late) (primary) (secondary) (tertiary) 093.9
        specified type and site NEC 093.89
    causing death under 2 years of age *(see also* Syphilis, congenital) 090.9
        stated to be acquired NEC 097.9
    central nervous system (any site) (early) (late) (latent) (primary) (recurrent) (relapse) (secondary) (tertiary) 094.9

Syphilis, syphilitic *(Continued)*
    central nervous system *(Continued)*
        with
            ataxia 094.0
            paralysis, general 094.1
                juvenile 090.40
            paresis (general) 094.1
                juvenile 090.40
            tabes (dorsalis) 094.0
                juvenile 090.40
            taboparesis 094.1
                juvenile 090.40
        aneurysm (ruptured) 094.87
        congenital 090.40
        juvenile 090.40
        remission in (sustained) 094.9
        serology doubtful, negative, or positive 094.9
        specified nature or site NEC 094.89
        vascular 094.89
    cerebral 094.89
        meningovascular 094.2
        nerves 094.89
        sclerosis 094.89
        thrombosis 094.89
    cerebrospinal 094.89
        tabetic 094.0
    cerebrovascular 094.89
    cervix 095.8
    chancre (multiple) 091.0
        extragenital 091.2
        Rollet's 091.2
    Charcôt's joint 094.0 *[713.5]*
    choked disc 094.89 *[377.00]*
    chorioretinitis 091.51
        congenital 090.0 *[363.13]*
        late 094.83
    choroiditis 091.51†
        congenital 090.0 *[363.13]*
        late 094.83
        prenatal 090.0 *[363.13]*
    choroidoretinitis (secondary) 091.51
        congenital 090.0 *[363.13]*
        late 094.83
    ciliary body (secondary) 091.52
        late 095.8 *[364.11]*
    colon (late) 095.8
    combined sclerosis 094.89
    complicating pregnancy, childbirth, or puerperium 647.0
        affecting fetus or newborn 760.2
    condyloma (latum) 091.3
    congenital 090.9
        with
            encephalitis 090.41
            paresis (general) 090.40
            tabes (dorsalis) 090.40
            taboparesis 090.40
            chorioretinitis, choroiditis 090.0 *[363.13]*
        early or less than 2 years after birth NEC 090.2
            with manifestations 090.0
            latent (without manifestations) 090.1
                negative spinal fluid test 090.1
                serology, positive 090.1
            symptomatic 090.0
        interstitial keratitis 090.3
        juvenile neurosyphilis 090.40
        late or 2 years or more after birth NEC 090.7
            chorioretinitis, choroiditis 090.5 *[363.13]*

Syphilis, syphilitic (Continued)
  myocardium 093.82
  myositis 095.6
  nasal sinus 095.8
  neonatorum NEC (*see also* Syphilis, congenital) 090.9
  nerve palsy (any cranial nerve) 094.89
  nervous system, central 094.9
  neuritis 095.8
    acoustic nerve 094.86
  neurorecidive of retina 094.83
  neuroretinitis 094.85
  newborn (*see also* Syphilis, congenital) 090.9
  nodular superficial 095.8
  nonvenereal, endemic 104.0
  nose 095.8
    saddle back deformity 090.5
    septum 095.8
      perforated 095.8
  occlusive arterial disease 093.89
  ophthalmic 095.8 [363.13]
  ophthalmoplegia 094.89
  optic nerve (atrophy) (neuritis) (papilla) 094.84
  orbit (late) 095.8
  orchitis 095.8
  organic 097.9
  osseous (late) 095.5
  osteochondritis (congenital) 090.0
  osteoporosis 095.5
  ovary 095.8
  oviduct 095.8
  palate 095.8
    gumma 095.8
    perforated 090.5
  pancreas (late) 095.8
  pancreatitis 095.8
  paralysis 094.89
    general 094.1
    juvenile 090.40
  paraplegia 094.89
  paresis (general) 094.1
    juvenile 090.40
  paresthesia 094.89
  Parkinson's disease or syndrome 094.82
  paroxysmal tachycardia 093.89
  pemphigus (congenital) 090.0
  penis 091.0
    chancre 091.0
    late 095.8
  pericardium 093.81
  perichondritis, larynx 095.8
  periosteum 095.5
    congenital 090.0
    early 091.61
    secondary 091.61
  peripheral nerve 095.8
  petrous bone (late) 095.5
  pharynx 095.8
    secondary 091.3
  pituitary (gland) 095.8
  placenta 095.8
  pleura (late) 095.8
  pneumonia, white 090.0
  pontine (lesion) 094.89
  portal vein 093.89
  primary NEC 091.2
    anal 091.1
    and secondary (*see also* Syphilis, secondary) 091.9
    cardiovascular 093.9
    central nervous system 094.9

Syphilis, syphilitic (Continued)
  primary NEC (*Continued*)
    extragenital chancre NEC 091.2
    fingers 091.2
    genital 091.0
    lip 091.2
    specified site NEC 091.2
    tonsils 091.2
  prostate 095.8
  psychosis (intracranial gumma) 094.89
  ptosis (eyelid) 094.89
  pulmonary (late) 095.1
    artery 093.89
  pulmonum 095.1
  pyelonephritis 095.4
  recently acquired, symptomatic NEC 091.89
  rectum 095.8
  respiratory tract 095.8
  retina
    late 094.83
    neurorecidive 094.83
  retrobulbar neuritis 094.85
  salpingitis 095.8
  sclera (late) 095.0
  sclerosis
    cerebral 094.89
    coronary 093.89
    multiple 094.89
    subacute 094.89
  scotoma (central) 095.8
  scrotum 095.8
  secondary (and primary) 091.9
    adenopathy 091.4
    anus 091.3
    bone 091.61
    cardiovascular 093.9
    central nervous system 094.9
    chorioretinitis, choroiditis 091.51
    hepatitis 091.62
    liver 091.62
    lymphadenitis 091.4
    meningitis, acute 091.81
    mouth 091.3
    mucous membranes 091.3
    periosteum 091.61
    periostitis 091.61
    pharynx 091.3
    relapse (treated) (untreated) 091.7
    skin 091.3
    specified form NEC 091.89
    tonsil 091.3
    ulcer 091.3
    viscera 091.69
    vulva 091.3
  seminal vesicle (late) 095.8
  seronegative
    with signs or symptoms - *see* Syphilis, by site and stage
  seropositive
    with signs or symptoms - *see* syphilis, by site and stage
    follow-up of latent syphilis - *see* Syphilis, latent
    only finding - *see* Syphilis, latent
  seventh nerve (paralysis) 094.89
  sinus 095.8
  sinusitis 095.8
  skeletal system 095.5
  skin (early) (secondary) (with ulceration) 091.3
    late or tertiary 095.8
  small intestine 095.8
  spastic spinal paralysis 094.0

Syphilis, syphilitic (Continued)
  spermatic cord (late) 095.8
  spinal (cord) 094.89
    with
      paresis 094.1
      tabes 094.0
  spleen 095.8
  splenomegaly 095.8
  spondylitis 095.5
  staphyloma 095.8
  stigmata (congenital) 090.5
  stomach 095.8
  synovium (late) 095.7
  tabes dorsalis (early) (late) 094.0
    juvenile 090.40
  tabetic type 094.0
    juvenile 090.40
  taboparesis 094.1
    juvenile 090.40
  tachycardia 093.89
  tendon (late) 095.7
  tertiary 097.0
    with symptoms 095.8
    cardiovascular 093.9
    central nervous system 094.9
    multiple NEC 095.8
    specified site NEC 095.8
  testis 095.8
  thorax 095.8
  throat 095.8
  thymus (gland) 095.8
  thyroid (late) 095.8
  tongue 095.8
  tonsil (lingual) 095.8
    primary 091.2
    secondary 091.3
  trachea 095.8
  tricuspid valve 093.23
  tumor, brain 094.89
  tunica vaginalis (late) 095.8
  ulcer (any site) (early) (secondary) 091.3
    late 095.9
    perforating 095.9
      foot 094.0
  urethra (stricture) 095.8
  urogenital 095.8
  uterus 095.8
  uveal tract (secondary) 091.50
    late 095.8 [363.13]
  uveitis (secondary) 091.50
    late 095.8 [363.13]
  uvula (late) 095.8
    perforated 095.8
  vagina 091.0
    late 095.8
  valvulitis NEC 093.20
  vascular 093.89
    brain or cerebral 094.89
  vein 093.89
    cerebral 094.89
  ventriculi 095.8
  vesicae urinariae 095.8
  viscera (abdominal) 095.2
    secondary 091.69
  vitreous (hemorrhage) (opacities) 095.8
  vulva 091.0
    late 095.8
    secondary 091.3
Syphiloma 095.9
  cardiovascular system 093.9
  central nervous system 094.9
  circulatory system 093.9
  congenital 090.5

ICD-9-CM

S

Vol. 2

Syphilophobia 300.29
Syringadenoma (M8400/0) - *see also*
  Neoplasm, skin, benign
  papillary (M8406/0) - *see* Neoplasm,
    skin, benign
Syringobulbia 336.0
Syringocarcinoma (M8400/3) - *see Neo-
  plasm, skin, malignant*
Syringocystadenoma (M8400/0) - *see
  also* Neoplasm, skin,
  benign

Syringocystadenoma (*Continued*)
  papillary (M8406/0) - *see* Neoplasm,
    skin, benign
Syringocystoma (M8407/0) - *see*
  Neoplasm, skin,
  benign
Syringoma (M8407/0) - *see also* Neoplasm, skin, benign
  chondroid (M8940/0) - *see* Neoplasm,
    by site, benign
Syringomyelia 336.0

Syringomyelitis 323.9
  late effect - *see* category 326
Syringomyelocele (*see also* Spina bifida)
  741.9
Syringopontia 336.0
System, systemic - *see also condition*
  disease, combined - *see* Degeneration,
    combined
  fibrosclerosing syndrome 710.8
  lupus erythematosus 710.0
    inhibitor 286.5

T

Tab - *see* Tag
Tabacism 989.84
Tabacosis 989.84
Tabardillo 080
  flea-borne 081.0
  louse-borne 080
Tabes, tabetic
  with
    central nervous system syphilis 094.0
    Charcôt's joint 094.0 [713.5]
    cord bladder 094.0
    crisis, viscera (any) 094.0
    paralysis, general 094.1
    paresis (general) 094.1
    perforating ulcer 094.0
  arthropathy 094.0 [713.5]
  bladder 094.0
  bone 094.0
  cerebrospinal 094.0
  congenital 090.40
  conjugal 094.0
  dorsalis 094.0
    neurosyphilis 094.0
  early 094.0
  juvenile 090.40
  latent 094.0
  mesenterica (*see also* Tuberculosis) 014.8
  paralysis insane, general 094.1
  peripheral (nonsyphilitic) 799.8
  spasmodic 094.0
    not dorsal or dorsalis 343.9
  syphilis (cerebrospinal) 094.0
Taboparalysis 094.1
Taboparesis (remission) 094.1
  with
    Charcôt's joint 094.1 [713.5]
    cord bladder 094.1
    perforating ulcer 094.1
  juvenile 090.40
Tachyalimentation 579.3
Tachyarrhythmia, tachyrhythmia - *see*
  also Tachycardia
  paroxysmal with sinus bradycardia 427.81
Tachycardia 785.0
  atrial 427.89
  auricular 427.89
  nodal 427.89
    nonparoxysmal atrioventricular 426.89
  nonparoxysmal atrioventricular (nodal) 426.89
  paroxysmal 427.2
    with sinus bradycardia 427.81
    atrial (PAT) 427.0
      psychogenic 316 [427.0]
    atrioventricular (AV) 427.0
      psychogenic 316 [427.0]
    essential 427.2
    junctional 427.0
    nodal 427.0
    psychogenic 316 [427.2]
      atrial 316 [427.0]
      supraventricular 316 [427.0]
      ventricular 316 [427.1]
    supraventricular 427.0
      psychogenic 316 [427.0]
    ventricular 427.1
      psychogenic 316 [427.1]
  postoperative 997.1

Tachycardia (*Continued*)
  psychogenic 306.2
  sick sinus 427.81
  sinoauricular 427.89
  sinus 427.89
  supraventricular 427.89
  ventricular (paroxysmal) 427.1
    psychogenic 316 [427.1]
Tachypnea 786.06
  hysterical 300.11
  newborn (idiopathic) (transitory) 770.6
  psychogenic 306.1
  transitory, of newborn 770.6
Taenia (infection) (infestation) (*see also*
  Infestation, taenia) 123.3
  diminuta 123.6
  echinococcal infestation (*see also* Echinococcus) 122.9
  nana 123.6
  saginata infestation 123.2
  solium (intestinal form) 123.0
    larval form 123.1
Taeniasis (intestine) (*see also* Infestation,
  taenia) 123.3
  saginata 123.2
  solium 123.0
Taenzer's disease 757.4
Tag (hypertrophied skin) (infected) 701.9
  adenoid 474.8
  anus 455.9
  endocardial (*see also* Endocarditis) 424.90
  hemorrhoidal 455.9
  hymen 623.8
  perineal 624.8
  preauricular 744.1
  rectum 455.9
  sentinel 455.9
  skin 701.9
    accessory 757.39
    anus 455.9
    congenital 757.39
    preauricular 744.1
    rectum 455.9
  tonsil 474.8
  urethra, urethral 599.84
  vulva 624.8
Tahyna fever 062.5
Takayasu (-Onishi) disease or syndrome (pulseless disease) 446.7
Talc granuloma 728.82
Talcosis 502
Talipes (congenital) 754.70
  acquired NEC 736.79
    planus 734
  asymmetric 754.79
    acquired 736.79
  calcaneovalgus 754.62
    acquired 736.76
  calcaneovarus 754.59
    acquired 736.76
  calcaneus 754.79
    acquired 736.76
  cavovarus 754.59
    acquired 736.75
  cavus 754.71
    acquired 736.73
  equinovalgus 754.69
    acquired 736.72
  equinovarus 754.51
    acquired 736.71
  equinus 754.79
    acquired, NEC 736.72

Talipes (*Continued*)
  percavus 754.71
    acquired 736.73
  planovalgus 754.69
    acquired 736.79
  planus (acquired) (any degree) 734
    congenital 754.61
    due to rickets 268.1
  valgus 754.60
    acquired 736.79
  varus 754.50
    acquired 736.79
Talma's disease 728.85
Tamponade heart (Rose's) (*see also* Pericarditis) 423.9
Tanapox 078.89
Tangier disease (familial high-density lipoprotein deficiency) 272.5
Tank ear 380.12
Tantrum (childhood) (*see also* Disturbance, conduct) 312.1
Tapeworm (infection) (infestation) (*see also* Infestation, tapeworm) 123.9
Tapia's syndrome 352.6
Tarantism 297.8
Target-oval cell anemia 282.4
Tarlov's cyst 355.9
Tarral-Besnier disease (pityriasis rubra pilaris) 696.4
Tarsalgia 729.2
Tarsal tunnel syndrome 355.5
Tarsitis (eyelid) 373.00
  syphilitic 095.8 [373.00]
  tuberculous (*see also* Tuberculosis) 017.0 [373.4]
Tartar (teeth) 523.6
Tattoo (mark) 709.09
Taurodontism 520.2
Taussig-Bing defect, heart, or syndrome (transposition, aorta and overriding pulmonary artery) 745.11
Tay's choroiditis 363.41
Tay-Sachs
  amaurotic familial idiocy 330.1
  disease 330.1
Taybi's syndrome (otopalatodigital) 759.89
Taylor's
  disease (diffuse idiopathic cutaneous atrophy) 701.8
  syndrome 625.5
Tear, torn (traumatic) - *see also* Wound, open, by site
  anus, anal (sphincter) 863.89
    with open wound in cavity 863.99
    complicating delivery 664.2
      with mucosa 664.3
    nontraumatic, nonpuerperal 565.0
  articular cartilage, old (*see also* Disorder, cartilage, articular) 718.0
  bladder
    with
      abortion - *see* Abortion, by type, with damage to pelvic organs
      ectopic pregnancy (*see also* categories 633.0-633.9) 639.2
      molar pregnancy (*see also* categories 630-632) 639.2
    following
      abortion 639.2
      ectopic or molar pregnancy 639.2
    obstetrical trauma 665.5

ICD-9-CM

T

Vol. 2

◀▮▶   **New Code**   ◀▯▮▯ ▮▯▶   **Revised Code**

Tenderness *(Continued)*
rebound 789.6
skin 782.0
Tendinitis, tendonitis *(see also* Tenosynovitis) 726.90
Achilles 726.71
adhesive 726.90
shoulder 726.0
calcific 727.82
shoulder 726.11
gluteal 726.5
patellar 726.64
peroneal 726.79
pes anserinus 726.61
psoas 726.5
tibialis (anterior) (posterior) 726.72
trochanteric 726.5
Tendon - *see* condition
Tendosynovitis - *see* Tenosynovitis
Tendovaginitis - *see* Tenosynovitis
Tenesmus 787.99
rectal 787.99
vesical 788.9
Tenia - *see* Taenia
Teniasis - *see* Taeniasis
Tennis elbow 726.32
Tenonitis - *see also* Tenosynovitis
eye (capsule) 376.04
Tenontosynovitis - *see* Tenosynovitis
Tenontothecitis - *see* Tenosynovitis
Tenophyte 727.9
Tenosynovitis 727.00
adhesive 726.90
shoulder 726.0
ankle 727.06
bicipital (calcifying) 726.12
buttock 727.09
due to crystals - *see* Arthritis, due to crystals
elbow 727.09
finger 727.05
foot 727.06
gonococcal 098.51
hand 727.05
hip 727.09
knee 727.09
radial styloid 727.04
shoulder 726.10
adhesive 726.0
spine 720.1
supraspinatus 726.10
toe 727.06
tuberculous - *see* Tuberculosis, tenosynovitis
wrist 727.05
Tenovaginitis - *see* Tenosynovitis
Tension
arterial, high *(see also* Hypertension) 401.9
without diagnosis of hypertension 796.2
headache 307.81
intraocular (elevated) 365.00
nervous 799.2
ocular (elevated) 365.00
pneumothorax 512.0
iatrogenic 512.1
postoperative 512.1
spontaneous 512.0
premenstrual 625.4
state 300.9
Tentorium - *see* condition
Teratencephalus 759.89
Teratism 759.7

Teratoblastoma (malignant) (M9080/3) - *see* Neoplasm, by site, malignant
Teratocarcinoma (M9081/3) - *see also* Neoplasm, by site, malignant
liver 155.0
Teratoma (solid) (M9080/1) - *see also* Neoplasm, by site, uncertain behavior
adult (cystic) (M9080/0) - *see* Neoplasm, by site, benign
and embryonal carcinoma, mixed (M9081/3) - *see* Neoplasm, by site, malignant
benign (M9080/0) - *see* Neoplasm, by site, benign
combined with choriocarcinoma (M9101/3) - *see* Neoplasm, by site, malignant
cystic (adult) (M9080/0) - *see* Neoplasm, by site, benign
differentiated type (M9080/0) - *see* Neoplasm, by site, benign
embryonal (M9080/3) - *see also* Neoplasm, by site, malignant
liver 155.0
fetal
sacral, causing fetopelvic disproportion 653.7
immature (M9080/3) - *see* Neoplasm, by site, malignant
liver (M9080/3) 155.0
adult, benign, cystic, differentiated type, or mature (M9080/0) 211.5
malignant (M9080/3) - *see also* Neoplasm, by site, malignant
anaplastic type (M9082/3) - *see* Neoplasm, by site, malignant
intermediate type (M9083/3) - *see* Neoplasm, by site, malignant
liver (M9080/3) 155.0
trophoblastic (M9102/3)
specified site - *see* Neoplasm, by site, malignant
unspecified site 186.9
undifferentiated type (M9082/3) - *see* Neoplasm, by site, malignant
mature (M9080/0) - *see* Neoplasm, by site, benign
ovary (M9080/0) 220
embryonal, immature, or malignant (M9080/3) 183.0
suprasellar (M9080/3) - *see* Neoplasm, by site, malignant
testis (M9080/3) 186.9
adult, benign, cystic, differentiated type or mature (M9080/0) 222.0
undescended 186.0
Terminal care V66.7
Termination
anomalous - *see also* Malposition, congenital
portal vein 747.49
right pulmonary vein 747.42
pregnancy (legal) (therapeutic) *(see* Abortion, legal) 635.9
fetus NEC 779.6
illegal *(see also* Abortion, illegal) 636.9
Ternidens diminutus infestation 127.7
Terrors, night (child) 307.46
Terry's syndrome 362.21
Tertiary - *see* condition
Tessellated fundus, retina (tigroid) 362.89

Test(s)
AIDS virus V72.6
allergen V72.7
bacterial disease NEC *(see also* Screening, by name of disease) V74.9
basal metabolic rate V72.6
blood-alcohol V70.4
blood-drug V70.4
developmental, infant or child V20.2
Dick V74.8
fertility V26.2
hearing V72.1
HIV V72.6
human immunodeficiency virus V72.6
Kveim V82.8
laboratory V72.6
for medicolegal reason V70.4
Mantoux (for tuberculosis) V74.1
mycotic organism V75.4
parasitic agent NEC V75.8
paternity V70.4
pregnancy
positive V22.1
first pregnancy V22.0
unconfirmed V72.4
preoperative V72.84
cardiovascular V72.81
respiratory V72.82
specified NEC V72.83
sarcoidosis V82.8
Schick V74.3
Schultz-Charlton V74.8
skin, diagnostic
allergy V72.7
bacterial agent NEC *(see also* Screening, by name of disease) V74.9
Dick V74.8
hypersensitivity V72.7
Kveim V82.8
Mantoux V74.1
mycotic organism V75.4
parasitic agent NEC V75.8
sarcoidosis V82.8
Schick V74.3
Schultz-Charlton V74.8
tuberculin V74.1
specified type NEC V72.85
tuberculin V74.1
vision V72.0
Wassermann
positive *(see also* Serology for syphilis, positive) 097.1
false 795.6
Testicle, testicular, testis - *see also* condition
feminization (syndrome) 257.8
Tetanus, tetanic (cephalic) (convulsions) 037
with
abortion - *see* Abortion, by type, with sepsis
ectopic pregnancy *(see also* categories 633.0-633.9) 639.0
molar pregnancy *(see* categories 630-632) 639.0
following
abortion 639.0
ectopic or molar pregnancy 639.0
inoculation V03.7
reaction (due to serum) - *see* Complications, vaccination
neonatorum 771.3
puerperal, postpartum, childbirth 670

Tetany, tetanic 781.7
  alkalosis 276.3
  associated with rickets 268.0
  convulsions 781.7
    hysterical 300.11
  functional (hysterical) 300.11
  hyperkinetic 781.7
    hysterical 300.11
  hyperpnea 786.01
    hysterical 300.11
    psychogenic 306.1
  hyperventilation 786.01
    hysterical 300.11
    psychogenic 306.1
  hypocalcemic, neonatal 775.4
  hysterical 300.11
  neonatal 775.4
  parathyroid (gland) 252.1
  parathyroprival 252.1
  postoperative 252.1
  postthyroidectomy 252.1
  pseudotetany 781.7
    hysterical 300.11
  psychogenic 306.1
    specified as conversion reaction
      300.11
Tetralogy of Fallot 745.2
Tetraplegia - *see* Quadriplegia
Thailand hemorrhagic fever 065.4
Thalassanemia 282.4
Thalassemia (alpha) (beta) (disease) (Hb-
  C) (Hb-D) (Hb-E) (Hb-H) (Hb-I)
  (Hb-S) (high fetal gene) (high fetal
  hemoglobin) (intermedia) (major)
  (minima) (minor) (mixed) (sickle-
  cell) (trait) (with other hemoglobinopathy) 282.4
Thalassemic variants 282.4
Thaysen-Gee disease (nontropical sprue)
  579.0
Thecoma (M8600/0) 220
  malignant (M8600/3) 183.0
Thelarche, precocious 259.1
Thelitis 611.0
  puerperal, postpartum 675.0
Therapeutic - *see* condition
Therapy V57.9
  blood transfusion, without reported di-
    agnosis V58.2
  breathing V57.0
  chemotherapy V58.1
    fluoride V07.31
    prophylactic NEC V07.39
  dialysis (intermittent) (treatment)
    extracorporeal V56.0
    peritoneal V56.8
    renal V56.0
    specified type NEC V56.8
  exercise NEC V57.1
    breathing V57.0
  extracorporeal dialysis (renal)
    V56.0
  fluoride prophylaxis V07.31
  hemodialysis V56.0
  occupational V57.21
  orthoptic V57.4
  orthotic V57.81
  peritoneal dialysis V56.8
  physical NEC V57.1
  postmenopausal hormone replacement
    V07.4
  radiation V58.0
  speech V57.3
  vocational V57.22

Thermalgesia 782.0
Thermalgia 782.0
Thermanalgesia 782.0
Thermanesthesia 782.0
Thermic - *see* condition
Thermography (abnormal) 793.9
  breast 793.8
Thermoplegia 992.0
Thesaurismosis
  amyloid 277.3
  bilirubin 277.4
  calcium 275.40
  cystine 270.0
  glycogen (*see also* Disease, glycogen
    storage) 271.0
  kerasin 272.7
  lipoid 272.7
  melanin 255.4
  phosphatide 272.7
  urate 274.9
Thiaminic deficiency 265.1
  with beriberi 265.0
Thibierge-Weissenbach syndrome (cutaneous systemic sclerosis) 710.1
Thickening
  bone 733.99
    extremity 733.99
  breast 611.79
  hymen 623.3
  larynx 478.79
  nail 703.8
    congenital 757.5
  periosteal 733.99
  pleura (*see also* Pleurisy) 511.0
  skin 782.8
  subepiglottic 478.79
  tongue 529.8
  valve, heart - *see* Endocarditis
Thiele syndrome 724.6
Thigh - *see* condition
Thinning vertebra (*see also* Osteoporosis)
  733.00
Thirst, excessive 783.5
  due to deprivation of water 994.3
Thomsen's disease 359.2
Thomson's disease (congenital poikiloderma) 757.33
Thoracic - *see also* condition
  kidney 753.3
  outlet syndrome 353.0
  stomach - *see* Hernia, diaphragm
Thoracogastroschisis (congenital)
  759.89
Thoracopagus 759.4
Thoracoschisis 756.3
Thorax - *see* condition
Thorn's syndrome (*see also* Disease, renal) 593.9
Thornwaldt's, Tornwaldt's
  bursitis (pharyngeal) 478.29
  cyst 478.26
  disease (pharyngeal bursitis) 478.29
Thorson-Biörck syndrome (malignant
  carcinoid) 259.2
Threadworm (infection) (infestation)
  127.4
Threatened
  abortion or miscarriage 640.0
    with subsequent abortion (*see also*
      Abortion, spontaneous) 634.9
    affecting fetus 762.1
  labor 644.1
    affecting fetus or newborn 761.8
    premature 644.0

Threatened (*Continued*)
  miscarriage 640.0
    affecting fetus 762.1
  premature
    delivery 644.2
      affecting fetus or newborn 761.8
    labor 644.0
      before 22 completed weeks of ges-
        tation 640.0
Three-day fever 066.0
Threshers' lung 495.0
Thrix annulata (congenital) 757.4
Throat - *see* condition
Thrombasthenia (Glanzmann's) (hemor-
  rhagic) (hereditary) 287.1
Thromboangiitis 443.1
  obliterans (general) 443.1
    cerebral 437.1
    vessels
      brain 437.1
      spinal cord 437.1
Thromboarteritis - *see* Arteritis
Thromboasthenia (Glanzmann's) (hemorrhagic) (hereditary) 287.1
Thrombocytasthenia (Glanzmann's)
  287.1
Thrombocythemia (essential) (hemorrhagic) (primary) (M9962/1)
  238.7
  idiopathic (M9962/1) 238.7
Thrombocytopathy (dystrophic) (granu-
  lopenic) 287.1
Thrombocytopenia, thrombocytopenic
  287.5
  with giant hemangioma 287.3
  amegakaryocytic, congenital 287.3
  congenital 287.3
  cyclic 287.3
  dilutional 287.4
  due to
    drugs 287.4
    extracorporeal circulation of blood
      287.4
    massive blood transfusion 287.4
    platelet alloimmunization 287.4
  essential 287.3
  hereditary 287.3
  Kasabach-Merritt 287.3
  neonatal, transitory 776.1
    due to
      exchange transfusion 776.1
      idiopathic maternal thrombocyto-
        penia 776.1
      isoimmunization 776.1
  primary 287.3
  puerperal, postpartum 666.3
  purpura (*see also* Purpura, thrombocy-
    topenic) 287.3
    thrombotic 446.6
  secondary 287.4
  sex-linked 287.3
Thrombocytosis, essential 289.9
Thromboembolism - *see* Embolism
Thrombopathy (Bernard-Soulier) 287.1
  constitutional 286.4
  Willebrand-Jürgens (angiohemophilia)
    286.4
Thrombopenia (*see also* Thrombocytopenia) 287.5
Thrombophlebitis 451.9
  antecubital vein 451.82
  antepartum (superficial) 671.2
    affecting fetus or newborn 760.3
  deep 671.3

◀▶ New Code　　◀▬ ▬▶ Revised Code

Thrombophlebitis *(Continued)*
arm 451.89
deep 451.83
superficial 451.82
breast, superficial 451.89
cavernous (venous) sinus - *see* Thrombophlebitis, intracranial venous sinus
cephalic vein 451.82
cerebral (sinus) (vein) 325
late effect - *see* category 326
nonpyogenic 437.6
in pregnancy or puerperium 671.5
late effect - *see* Late effect(s) (of) cerebrovascular disease
due to implanted device - *see* Complications, due to (presence of) any device, implant, or graft classified to 996.0-996.5 NEC
during or resulting from a procedure NEC 997.2
femoral 451.11
femoropopliteal 451.19
following infusion, perfusion, or transfusion 999.2
hepatic (vein) 451.89
idiopathic, recurrent 453.1
iliac vein 451.81
iliofemoral 451.11
intracranial venous sinus (any) 325
late effect - *see* category 326
nonpyogenic 437.6
in pregnancy or puerperium 671.5
late effect - *see* Late effect(s) (of) cerebrovascular disease
jugular vein 451.89
lateral (venous) sinus - *see* Thrombophlebitis, intracranial venous sinus
leg 451.2
deep (vessels) 451.19
femoral vein 451.11
specified vessel NEC 451.19
superficial (vessels) 451.0
femoral vein 451.11
longitudinal (venous) sinus - *see* Thrombophlebitis, intracranial venous sinus
lower extremity 451.2
deep (vessels) 451.19
femoral vein 451.11
specified vessel NEC 451.19
superficial (vessels) 451.0
migrans, migrating 453.1
pelvic
with
abortion - *see* Abortion, by type, with sepsis
ectopic pregnancy (*see also* categories 633.0-633.9) 639.0
molar pregnancy (*see also* categories 630-632) 639.0
following
abortion 639.0
ectopic or molar pregnancy 639.0
puerperal 671.4
popliteal vein 451.19
portal (vein) 572.1
postoperative 997.2
pregnancy (superficial) 671.2
affecting fetus or newborn 760.3
deep 671.3
puerperal, postpartum, childbirth (extremities) (superficial) 671.2
deep 671.4

Thrombophlebitis *(Continued)*
puerperal, postpartum, childbirth *(Continued)*
pelvic 671.4
specified site NEC 671.5
radial vein 451.82
saphenous (greater) (lesser) 451.0
sinus (intracranial) - *see* Thrombophlebitis, intracranial venous sinus
specified site NEC 451.89
tibial vein 451.19
Thrombosis, thrombotic (marantic) (multiple) (progressive) (septic) (vein) (vessel) 453.9
with childbirth or during the puerperium - *see* Thrombosis, puerperal, postpartum
antepartum - *see* Thrombosis, pregnancy
aorta, aortic 444.1
abdominal 444.0
bifurcation 444.0
saddle 444.0
terminal 444.0
thoracic 444.1
valve - *see* Endocarditis, aortic
apoplexy (*see also* Thrombosis, brain) 434.0
late effect - *see* Late effect(s) (of) cerebrovascular disease
appendix, septic - *see* Appendicitis, acute
arteriolar-capillary platelet, disseminated 446.6
artery, arteries (postinfectional) 444.9
auditory, internal 433.8
basilar (*see also* Occlusion, artery, basilar) 433.0
carotid (common) (internal) (*see also* Occlusion, artery, carotid) 433.1
with other precerebral artery 433.3
cerebellar (anterior inferior) (posterior inferior) (superior) 433.8
cerebral (*see also* Thrombosis, brain) 434.0
choroidal (anterior) 433.8
communicating posterior 433.8
coronary (*see also* Infarct, myocardium) 410.9
without myocardial infarction 411.81
due to syphilis 093.89
healed or specified as old 412
extremities 444.22
lower 444.22
upper 444.21
femoral 444.22
hepatic 444.89
hypophyseal 433.8
meningeal, anterior or posterior 433.8
mesenteric (with gangrene) 557.0
ophthalmic (*see also* Occlusion, retina) 362.30
pontine 433.8
popliteal 444.22
precerebral - *see* Occlusion, artery, precerebral NEC
pulmonary 415.19
iatrogenic 415.11
postoperative 415.11
renal 593.81
retinal (*see also* Occlusion, retina) 362.30

Thrombosis, thrombotic *(Continued)*
artery, arteries *(Continued)*
specified site NEC 444.89
spinal, anterior or posterior 433.8
traumatic (complication) (early) (*see also* Injury, blood vessel, by site) 904.9
vertebral (*see also* Occlusion, artery, vertebral) 433.2
with other precerebral artery 433.3
atrial (endocardial) 424.90
due to syphilis 093.89
auricular (*see also* Infarct, myocardium) 410.9
axillary (vein) 453.8
basilar (artery) (*see also* Occlusion, artery, basilar) 433.0
bland NEC 453.9
brain (artery) (stem) 434.0
due to syphilis 094.89
iatrogenic 997.02
late effect - *see* Late effect(s) (of) cerebrovascular disease
postoperative 997.02
puerperal, postpartum, childbirth 674.0
sinus (*see also* Thrombosis, intracranial venous sinus) 325
capillary 448.9
arteriolar, generalized 446.6
cardiac (*see also* Infarct, myocardium) 410.9
due to syphilis 093.89
healed or specified as old 412
valve - *see* Endocarditis
carotid (artery) (common) (internal) (*see also* Occlusion, artery, carotid) 433.1
with other precerebral artery 433.3
cavernous sinus (venous) - *see* Thrombosis, intracranial venous sinus
cerebellar artery (anterior inferior) (posterior inferior) (superior) 433.8
late effect - *see* Late effect(s) (of) cerebrovascular disease
cerebral (arteries) (*see also* Thrombosis, brain) 434.0
late effect - *see* Late effect(s) (of) cerebrovascular disease
coronary (artery) (*see also* Infarct, myocardium) 410.9
without myocardial infarction 411.81
due to syphilis 093.89
healed or specified as old 412
corpus cavernosum 607.82
cortical (*see also* Thrombosis, brain) 434.0
due to (presence of) any device, implant, or graft classifiable to 996.0-996.5 - *see* Complications, due to (presence of) any device, implant, or graft classified to 996.0-996.5 NEC
effort 453.8
endocardial - *see* Infarct, myocardium
eye (*see also* Occlusion, retina) 362.30
femoral (vein) (deep) 453.8
with inflammation or phlebitis 451.11
artery 444.22
genital organ, male 608.83

Note   Use the following fifth-digit
subclassification with category 242:

0   without mention of thyrotoxic
crisis or storm
1   with mention of thyrotoxic crisis or storm

Thyrotoxicosis *(Continued)*
  with
    goiter (diffuse) 242.0
      adenomatous 242.3
        multinodular 242.2
        uninodular 242.1
      nodular 242.3
        multinodular 242.2
        uninodular 242.1
    infiltrative
      dermopathy 242.0
      ophthalmopathy 242.0
    thyroid acropachy 242.0
  complicating pregnancy, childbirth, or
    puerperium 648.1
  due to
    ectopic thyroid nodule 242.4
    ingestion of (excessive) thyroid ma-
      terial 242.8
    specified cause NEC 242.8
  factitia 242.8
  heart 242.9 *[425.7]*
  neonatal (transient) 775.3
TIA (transient ischemic attack) 435.9
  with transient neurologic deficit 435.9
  late effect - *see* Late effect(s) (of) cere-
    brovascular disease
Tibia vara 732.4
Tic 307.20
  breathing 307.20
  child problem 307.21
  compulsive 307.22
  convulsive 307.20
  degenerative (generalized) (localized)
    333.3
    facial 351.8
  douloureux (*see also* Neuralgia, trigem-
    inal) 350.1
    atypical 350.2
  habit 307.20
    chronic (motor or vocal) 307.22
    transient of childhood 307.21
  lid 307.20
    transient of childhood 307.21
  motor-verbal 307.23
  occupational 300.89
  orbicularis 307.20
    transient of childhood 307.21
  organic origin 333.3
  postchoreic - *see* Chorea
  psychogenic 307.20
    compulsive 307.22
  salaam 781.0
  spasm 307.20
    chronic (motor or vocal) 307.22
    transient of childhood 307.21
Tick (-borne) fever NEC 066.1
  American mountain 066.1
  Colorado 066.1
  hemorrhagic NEC 065.3
    Crimean 065.0
    Kyasanur Forest 065.2
    Omsk 065.1
  mountain 066.1
  nonexanthematous 066.1
Tick-bite fever NEC 066.1
  African 087.1
  Colorado (virus) 066.1
  Rocky Mountain 082.0
Tick paralysis 989.5
Tics and spasms, compulsive 307.22
Tietze's disease or syndrome 733.6
Tight, tightness
  anus 564.89

Tight, tightness *(Continued)*
  chest 786.59
  fascia (lata) 728.9
  foreskin (congenital) 605
  hymen 623.3
  introitus (acquired) (congenital) 623.3
  rectal sphincter 564.89
  tendon 727.81
    Achilles (heel) 727.81
  urethral sphincter 598.9
Tilting vertebra 737.9
Timidity, child 313.21
Tinea (intersecta) (tarsi) 110.9
  amiantacea 110.0
  asbestina 110.0
  barbae 110.0
  beard 110.0
  black dot 110.0
  blanca 111.2
  capitis 110.0
  corporis 110.5
  cruris 110.3
  decalvans 704.09
  flava 111.0
  foot 110.4
  furfuracea 111.0
  imbricata (Tokelau) 110.5
  lepothrix 039.0
  manuum 110.2
  microsporic (*see also* Dermatophytosis)
    110.9
  nigra 111.1
  nodosa 111.2
  pedis 110.4
  scalp 110.0
  specified site NEC 110.8
  sycosis 110.0
  tonsurans 110.0
  trichophytic (*see also* Dermatophytosis)
    110.9
  unguium 110.1
  versicolor 111.0
Tingling sensation (*see also* Disturbance,
  sensation) 782.0
Tin-miners' lung 503
Tinnitus (aurium) 388.30
  audible 388.32
  objective 388.32
  subjective 388.31
Tipping pelvis 738.6
  with disproportion (fetopelvic) 653.0
    affecting fetus or newborn 763.1
    causing obstructed labor 660.1
      affecting fetus or newborn 763.1
Tiredness 780.79
Tissue - *see* condition
Tobacco
  abuse (affecting health) NEC (*see also*
    Abuse, drugs, nondependent)
    305.1
  heart 989.84
Tobias' syndrome (carcinoma, pulmo-
  nary apex) (M8010/3) 162.3
Tocopherol deficiency 269.1
Todd's
  cirrhosis - *see* Cirrhosis, biliary
  paralysis (postepileptic transitory pa-
    ralysis) 344.89
Toe - *see* condition
Toilet, artificial opening (*see also* Atten-
  tion to, artificial, opening) V55.9
Tokelau ringworm 110.5
Tollwut 071
Tolosa-Hunt syndrome 378.55

Tommaselli's disease
  correct substance properly adminis-
    tered 599.7
  overdose or wrong substance given or
    taken 961.4
Tongue - *see also* condition
  worms 134.1
Tongue tie 750.0
Toni-Fanconi syndrome (cystinosis)
  270.0
Tonic pupil 379.46
Tonsil - *see* condition
Tonsillitis (acute) (catarrhal) (croupous)
  (follicular) (gangrenous) (infective)
  (lacunar) (lingual) (malignant)
  (membranous) (phlegmonous)
  (pneumococcal) (pseudomembranous) (purulent) (septic) (staphylococcal) (subacute) (suppurative) (toxic)
  (ulcerative) (vesicular) (viral) 463
  with influenza, flu, or grippe 487.1
  chronic 474.00
  diphtheritic (membranous) 032.0
  hypertrophic 474.00
  influenzal 487.1
  parenchymatous 475
  streptococcal 034.0
  tuberculous (*see also* Tuberculosis)
    012.8
  Vincent's 101
Tonsillopharyngitis 465.8
Tooth, teeth - *see* condition
Toothache 525.9
Topagnosis 782.0
Tophi (gouty) 274.0
  ear 274.81
  heart 274.82
  specified site NEC 274.82
Torn - *see* Tear, torn
Tornwaldt's bursitis (disease) (pharyngeal bursitis) 478.29
  cyst 478.26
Torpid liver 573.9
Torsion
  accessory tube 620.5
  adnexa (female) 620.5
  aorta (congenital) 747.29
    acquired 447.1
  appendix epididymis 608.2
  bile duct 576.8
    with calculus, choledocholithiasis or
      stones - *see* Choledocholithiasis
    congenital 751.69
  bowel, colon, or intestine 560.2
  cervix (*see also* Malposition, uterus)
    621.6
  duodenum 537.3
  dystonia - *see* Dystonia, torsion
  epididymis 608.2
    appendix 608.2
  fallopian tube 620.5
  gallbladder (*see also* Disease, gallblad-
    der) 575.8
    congenital 751.69
  gastric 537.89
  hydatid of Morgagni (female) 620.5
  kidney (pedicle) 593.89
  Meckel's diverticulum (congenital) 751.0
  mesentery 560.2
  omentum 560.2
  organ or site, congenital NEC - *see*
    Anomaly, specified type NEC
  ovary (pedicle) 620.5
    congenital 752.0

ICD-9-CM

T

Vol. 2

Torsion (Continued)
oviduct 620.5
penis 607.89
congenital 752.69
renal 593.89
spasm - *see* Dystonia, torsion
spermatic cord 608.2
spleen 289.59
testicle, testis 608.2
tibia 736.89
umbilical cord - *see* Compression, umbilical cord
uterus (*see also* Malposition, uterus) 621.6
Torticollis (intermittent) (spastic) 723.5
congenital 754.1
sternomastoid 754.1
due to birth injury 767.8
hysterical 300.11
psychogenic 306.0
specified as conversion reaction 300.11
rheumatic 723.5
rheumatoid 714.0
spasmodic 333.83
traumatic, current NEC 847.0
Tortuous
artery 447.1
fallopian tube 752.19
organ or site, congenital NEC - *see* Distortion
renal vessel (congenital) 747.62
retina vessel (congenital) 743.58
acquired 362.17
ureter 593.4
urethra 599.84
vein - *see* Varicose, vein
Torula, torular (infection) 117.5
histolytica 117.5
lung 117.5
Torulosis 117.5
Torus
mandibularis 526.81
palatinus 526.81
Touch, vitreous 997.99
Touraine's syndrome (hereditary osteo-onychodysplasia) 756.89
Touraine-Solente-Golé syndrome (acropachyderma) 757.39
Tourette's disease (motor-verbal tic) 307.23
Tower skull 756.0
with exophthalmos 756.0
Toxemia 799.8
with
abortion - *see* Abortion, by type, with toxemia
bacterial - *see* Septicemia
biliary (*see also* Disease, biliary) 576.8
burn - *see* Burn, by site
congenital NEC 779.8
eclamptic 642.6
with pre-existing hypertension 642.7
erysipelatous (*see also* Erysipelas) 035
fatigue 799.8
fetus or newborn NEC 779.8
food (*see also* Poisoning, food) 005.9
gastric 537.89
gastrointestinal 558.2
intestinal 558.2
kidney (*see also* Disease, renal) 593.9
lung 518.89

Toxemia (Continued)
malarial NEC (*see also* Malaria) 084.6
maternal (of pregnancy), affecting fetus or newborn 760.0
myocardial - *see* Myocarditis, toxic
of pregnancy (mild) (pre-eclamptic) 642.4
with
convulsions 642.6
pre-existing hypertension 642.7
affecting fetus or newborn 760.0
severe 642.5
pre-eclamptic - *see* Toxemia, of pregnancy
puerperal, postpartum - *see* Toxemia, of pregnancy
pulmonary 518.89
renal (*see also* Disease, renal) 593.9
septic (*see also* Septicemia) 038.9
small intestine 558.2
staphylococcal 038.10
aureus 038.11
due to food 005.0
specified organism NEC 038.19
stasis 799.8
stomach 537.89
uremic (*see also* Uremia) 586
urinary 586
Toxemica cerebropathia psychica (non-alcoholic) 294.0
alcoholic 291.1
Toxic (poisoning) - *see also* condition
from drug or poison - *see* Table of Drugs and Chemicals
oil syndrome 710.5
shock syndrome 040.89
thyroid (gland) (*see also* Thyrotoxicosis) 242.9
Toxicemia - *see* Toxemia
Toxicity
dilantin
asymptomatic 796.0
symptomatic -*see* Table of Drugs and Chemicals
drug ◀▥
asymptomatic 796.0 ◀
symptomatic - *see* Table of Drugs and Chemicals ◀
fava bean 282.2
from drug or poison ◀▥
asymptomatic 796.0 ◀
symptomatic - *see* Table of Drugs and Chemicals ◀
Toxicosis (*see also* Toxemia) 799.8
capillary, hemorrhagic 287.0
Toxinfection 799.8
gastrointestinal 558.2
Toxocariasis 128.0
Toxoplasma infection, generalized 130.9
Toxoplasmosis (acquired) 130.9
with pneumonia 130.4
congenital, active 771.2
disseminated (multisystemic) 130.8
maternal
with suspected damage to fetus affecting management of pregnancy 655.4
affecting fetus or newborn 760.2
manifest toxoplasmosis in fetus or newborn 771.2
multiple sites 130.8
multisystemic disseminated 130.8
specified site NEC 130.7

Trabeculation, bladder 596.8
Trachea - *see* condition
Tracheitis (acute) (catarrhal) (infantile) (membranous) (plastic) (pneumococcal) (septic) (suppurative) (viral) 464.10
with
bronchitis 490
acute or subacute 466.0
chronic 491.8
tuberculosis - *see* Tuberculosis, pulmonary
laryngitis (acute) 464.20
with obstruction 464.21
chronic 476.1
tuberculous (*see also* Tuberculosis, larynx) 012.3
obstruction 464.11
chronic 491.8
with
bronchitis (chronic) 491.8
laryngitis (chronic) 476.1
due to external agent - *see* Condition, respiratory, chronic, due to
diphtheritic (membranous) 032.3
due to external agent - *see* Inflammation, respiratory, upper, due to
edematous 464.11
influenzal 487.1
streptococcal 034.0
syphilitic 095.8
tuberculous (*see also* Tuberculosis) 012.8
Trachelitis (nonvenereal) (*see also* Cervicitis) 616.0
trichomonal 131.09
Tracheobronchial - *see* condition
Tracheobronchitis (*see also* Bronchitis) 490
acute or subacute 466.0
with bronchospasm or obstruction 466.0
chronic 491.8
influenzal 487.1
senile 491.8
Tracheobronchomegaly (congenital) 748.3
Tracheobronchopneumonitis - *see* Pneumonia, broncho
Tracheocele (external) (internal) 519.1
congenital 748.3
Tracheomalacia 519.1
congenital 748.3
Tracheopharyngitis (acute) 465.8
chronic 478.9
due to external agent - *see* Condition, respiratory, chronic, due to
due to external agent - *see* Inflammation, respiratory, upper, due to
Tracheostenosis 519.1
congenital 748.3
Tracheostomy
attention to V55.0
complication 519.02 ◀▥
hemorrhage 519.09 ◀▥
infection 519.01 ◀
malfunctioning 519.02 ◀▥
obstruction 519.09 ◀▥
sepsis 519.01 ◀▥
status V44.0
stenosis 519.02 ◀▥
Trachoma, trachomatous 076.9
active (stage) 076.1
contraction of conjunctiva 076.1

Trypanosomiasis *(Continued)*
due to Trypanosoma
  cruzi - *see* Trypanosomiasis, American
  gambiense 086.3
  rhodesiense 086.4
gambiensis, Gambian 086.3
North American - *see* Trypanosomiasis, American
rhodesiensis, Rhodesian 086.4
South American - *see* Trypanosomiasis, American

T-shaped incisors 520.2
Tsutsugamushi fever 081.2
Tube, tubal, tubular - *see also* condition
ligation, admission for V25.2
Tubercle - *see also* Tuberculosis
brain, solitary 013.2
Darwin's 744.29
epithelioid noncaseating 135
Ghon, primary infection 010.0
Tuberculid, tuberculide (indurating)
(lichenoid) (miliary) (papulonecrotic)
(primary) (skin) (subcutaneous) (*see also* Tuberculosis) 017.0
Tuberculoma - *see also* Tuberculosis
brain (any part) 013.2
meninges (cerebral) (spinal) 013.1
spinal cord 013.4
Tuberculosis, tubercular, tuberculous
(calcification) (calcified) (caseous)
(chromogenic acid-fast bacilli) (congenital) (degeneration) (disease) (fibrocaseous) (fistula) (gangrene) (interstitial) (isolated circumscribed
lesions) (necrosis) (parenchymatous)
(ulcerative) 011.9

> Note   Use the following fifth-digit
> subclassification with categories 010-018:
>
> 0   unspecified
> 1   bacteriological or histological
>   examination not done
> 2   bacteriological or histological
>   examination unknown (at
>   present)
> 3   tubercle bacilli found (in sputum) by microscopy
> 4   tubercle bacilli not found (in
>   sputum) by microscopy, but
>   found by bacterial culture
> 5   tubercle bacilli not found by
>   bacteriological examination,
>   but tuberculosis confirmed histologically
> 6   tubercle bacilli not found by
>   bacteriological or histological
>   examination, but tuberculosis
>   confirmed by other methods
>   [inoculation of animals]
>
> For tuberculous conditions specified
> as late effects or sequelae, *see* category 137.

abdomen 014.8
  lymph gland 014.8
abscess 011.9
  arm 017.9
  bone (*see also* Osteomyelitis, due to, tuberculosis) 015.9 *[730.8]*
    hip 015.1 *[730.85]*
    knee 015.2 *[730.86]*
    sacrum 015.0 *[730.88]*

Tuberculosis, tubercular, tuberculous
(Continued)
specified site NEC 015.7 *[730.88]*
spinal 015.0 *[730.88]*
vertebra 015.0 *[730.88]*
brain 013.3
breast 017.9
Cowper's gland 016.5
dura (mater) 013.8
  brain 013.3
  spinal cord 013.5
epidural 013.8
  brain 013.3
  spinal cord 013.5
frontal sinus - *see* Tuberculosis, sinus
genital organs NEC 016.9
  female 016.7
  male 016.5
genitourinary NEC 016.9
gland (lymphatic) - *see* Tuberculosis, lymph gland
hip 015.1
iliopsoas 015.0 *[730.88]*
intestine 014.8
ischiorectal 014.8
joint 015.9
  hip 015.1
  knee 015.2
  specified joint NEC 015.8
  vertebral 015.0 *[730.88]*
kidney 016.0 *[590.81]*
knee 015.2
lumbar 015.0 *[730.88]*
lung 011.2
  primary, progressive 010.8
meninges (cerebral) (spinal) 013.0
pelvic 016.9
  female 016.7
  male 016.5
perianal 014.8
  fistula 014.8
perinephritic 016.0 *[590.81]*
perineum 017.9
perirectal 014.8
psoas 015.0 *[730.88]*
rectum 014.8
retropharyngeal 012.8
sacrum 015.0 *[730.88]*
scrofulous 017.2
scrotum 016.5
skin 017.0
  primary 017.0
spinal cord 013.5
spine or vertebra (column) 015.0 *[730.88]*
strumous 017.2
subdiaphragmatic 014.8
testis 016.5
thigh 017.9
urinary 016.3
  kidney 016.0 *[590.81]*
uterus 016.7
accessory sinus - *see* Tuberculosis, sinus
Addison's disease 017.6
adenitis (*see also* Tuberculosis, lymph gland) 017.2
adenoids 012.8
adenopathy (*see also* Tuberculosis, lymph gland) 017.2
  tracheobronchial 012.1
    primary progressive 010.8
adherent pericardium 017.9 *[420.0]*

Tuberculosis, tubercular, tuberculous
(Continued)
adnexa (uteri) 016.7
adrenal (capsule) (gland) 017.6
air passage NEC 012.8
alimentary canal 014.8
anemia 017.9
ankle (joint) 015.8
  bone 015.5 *[730.87]*
anus 014.8
apex (*see also* Tuberculosis, pulmonary) 011.9
apical (*see also* Tuberculosis, pulmonary) 011.9
appendicitis 014.8
appendix 014.8
arachnoid 013.0
artery 017.9
arthritis (chronic) (synovial) 015.9 *[711.40]*
  ankle 015.8 *[730.87]*
  hip 015.1 *[711.45]*
  knee 015.2 *[711.46]*
  specified site NEC 015.8 *[711.48]*
  spine or vertebra (column) 015.0 *[720.81]*
  wrist 015.8 *[730.83]*
articular - *see* Tuberculosis, joint
ascites 014.0
asthma (*see also* Tuberculosis, pulmonary) 011.9
axilla, axillary 017.2
  gland 017.2
bilateral (*see also* Tuberculosis, pulmonary) 011.9
bladder 016.1
bone (*see also* Osteomyelitis, due to, tuberculosis) 015.9 *[730.8]*
  hip 015.1 *[730.85]*
  knee 015.2 *[730.86]*
  limb NEC 015.5 *[730.88]*
  sacrum 015.0 *[730.88]*
  specified site NEC 015.7 *[730.88]*
  spinal or vertebral column 015.0 *[730.88]*
bowel 014.8
  miliary 018.9
brain 013.2
breast 017.9
broad ligament 016.7
bronchi, bronchial, bronchus 011.3
  ectasia, ectasis 011.5
  fistula 011.3
    primary, progressive 010.8
  gland 012.1
    primary, progressive 010.8
  isolated 012.2
  lymph gland or node 012.1
    primary, progressive 010.8
bronchiectasis 011.5
bronchitis 011.3
bronchopleural 012.0
bronchopneumonia, bronchopneumonic 011.6
bronchorrhagia 011.3
bronchotracheal 011.3
  isolated 012.2
bronchus - *see* Tuberculosis, bronchi
bronze disease (Addison's) 017.6
buccal cavity 017.9
bulbourethral gland 016.5
bursa (*see also* Tuberculosis, joint) 015.9
cachexia NEC (*see also* Tuberculosis, pulmonary) 011.9

ICD-9-CM

Vol. 2

Tuberculosis, tubercular, tuberculous
(Continued)
  cardiomyopathy 017.9 *[425.8]*
  caries (*see also* Tuberculosis, bone)
    015.9 *[730.8]*
  cartilage (*see also* Tuberculosis, bone)
    015.9 *[730.8]*
    intervertebral 015.0 *[730.88]*
  catarrhal (*see also* Tuberculosis, pulmo-
    nary) 011.9
  cecum 014.8
  cellular tissue (primary) 017.0
  cellulitis (primary) 017.0
  central nervous system 013.9
    specified site NEC 013.8
  cerebellum (current) 013.2
  cerebral (current) 013.2
    meninges 013.0
  cerebrospinal 013.6
    meninges 013.0
  cerebrum (current) 013.2
  cervical 017.2
    gland 017.2
    lymph nodes 017.2
  cervicitis (uteri) 016.7
  cervix 016.7
  chest (*see also* Tuberculosis, pulmo-
    nary) 011.9
  childhood type or first infection
    010.0
  choroid 017.3 *[363.13]*
  choroiditis 017.3 *[363.13]*
  ciliary body 017.3 *[364.11]*
  colitis 014.8
  colliers' 011.4
  colliquativa (primary) 017.0
  colon 014.8
    ulceration 014.8
  complex, primary 010.0
  complicating pregnancy, childbirth, or
    puerperium 647.3
    affecting fetus or newborn 760.2
  congenital 771.2
  conjunctiva 017.3 *[370.31]*
  connective tissue 017.9
    bone - *see* Tuberculosis, bone
  contact V01.1
  converter (tuberculin skin test) (with-
    out disease) 795.5
  cornea (ulcer) 017.3 *[370.31]*
  Cowper's gland 016.5
  coxae 015.1 *[730.85]*
  coxalgia 015.1 *[730.85]*
  cul-de-sac of Douglas 014.8
  curvature, spine 015.0 *[737.40]*
  cutis (colliquativa) (primary) 017.0
  cyst, ovary 016.6
  cystitis 016.1
  dacryocystitis 017.3 *[375.32]*
  dactylitis 015.5
  diarrhea 014.8
  diffuse (*see also* Tuberculosis, miliary)
    018.9
    lung - *see* Tuberculosis, pulmonary
    meninges 013.0
  digestive tract 014.8
  disseminated (*see also* Tuberculosis,
    miliary) 018.9
    meninges 013.0
  duodenum 014.8
  dura (mater) 013.9
    abscess 013.8
      cerebral 013.3
      spinal 013.5

Tuberculosis, tubercular, tuberculous
(Continued)
  dysentery 014.8
  ear (inner) (middle) 017.4
    bone 015.6
    external (primary) 017.0
    skin (primary) 017.0
  elbow 015.8
  emphysema - *see* Tuberculosis, pulmo-
    nary
  empyema 012.0
  encephalitis 013.6
  endarteritis 017.9
  endocarditis (any valve) 017.9 *[424.91]*
  endocardium (any valve) 017.9
    [424.91]
  endocrine glands NEC 017.9
  endometrium 016.7
  enteric, enterica 014.8
  enteritis 014.8
  enterocolitis 014.8
  epididymis 016.4
  epididymitis 016.4
  epidural abscess 013.8
    brain 013.3
    spinal cord 013.5
  epiglottis 012.3
  episcleritis 017.3 *[379.00]*
  erythema (induratum) (nodosum) (pri-
    mary) 017.1
  esophagus 017.8
  Eustachian tube 017.4
  exposure to V01.1
  exudative 012.0
    primary, progressive 010.1
  eye 017.3
    glaucoma 017.3 *[365.62]*
  eyelid (primary) 017.0
    lupus 017.0 *[373.4]*
  fallopian tube 016.6
  fascia 017.9
  fauces 012.8
  finger 017.9
  first infection 010.0
  fistula, perirectal 014.8
  Florida 011.6
  foot 017.9
  funnel pelvis 137.3
  gallbladder 017.9
  galloping (*see also* Tuberculosis, pul-
    monary) 011.9
  ganglionic 015.9
  gastritis 017.9
  gastrocolic fistula 014.8
  gastroenteritis 014.8
  gastrointestinal tract 014.8
  general, generalized 018.9
    acute 018.0
    chronic 018.8
  genital organs NEC 016.9
    female 016.7
    male 016.5
  genitourinary NEC 016.9
  genu 015.2
  glandulae suprarenalis 017.6
  glandular, general 017.2
  glottis 012.3
  grinders' 011.4
  groin 017.2
  gum 017.9
  hand 017.9
  heart 017.9 *[425.8]*
  hematogenous - *see* Tuberculosis, mili-
    ary

Tuberculosis, tubercular, tuberculous
(Continued)
  hemoptysis (*see also* Tuberculosis, pul-
    monary) 011.9
  hemorrhage NEC (*see also* Tuberculo-
    sis, pulmonary) 011.9
  hemothorax 012.0
  hepatitis 017.9
  hilar lymph nodes 012.1
    primary, progressive 010.8
  hip (disease) (joint) 015.1
    bone 015.1 *[730.85]*
  hydrocephalus 013.8
  hydropneumothorax 012.0
  hydrothorax 012.0
  hypoadrenalism 017.6
  hypopharynx 012.8
  ileocecal (hyperplastic) 014.8
  ileocolitis 014.8
  ileum 014.8
  iliac spine (superior) 015.0 *[730.88]*
  incipient NEC (*see also* Tuberculosis,
    pulmonary) 011.9
  indurativa (primary) 017.1
  infantile 010.0
  infection NEC 011.9
    without clinical manifestation 010.0
  infraclavicular gland 017.2
  inguinal gland 017.2
  inguinalis 017.2
  intestine (any part) 014.8
  iris 017.3 *[364.11]*
  iritis 017.3 *[364.11]*
  ischiorectal 014.8
  jaw 015.7 *[730.88]*
  jejunum 014.8
  joint 015.9
    hip 015.1
    knee 015.2
    specified site NEC 015.8
    vertebral 015.0 *[730.88]*
  keratitis 017.3 *[370.31]*
    interstitial 017.3 *[370.59]*
  keratoconjunctivitis 017.3 *[370.31]*
  kidney 016.0
  knee (joint) 015.2
  kyphoscoliosis 015.0 *[737.43]*
  kyphosis 015.0 *[737.41]*
  lacrimal apparatus, gland 017.3
  laryngitis 012.3
  larynx 012.3
  leptomeninges, leptomeningitis (cere-
    bral) (spinal) 013.0
  lichenoides (primary) 017.0
  linguae 017.9
  lip 017.9
  liver 017.9
  lordosis 015.0 *[737.42]*
  lung - *see* Tuberculosis, pulmonary
  luposa 017.0
    eyelid 017.0 *[373.4]*
  lymphadenitis - *see* Tuberculosis,
    lymph gland
  lymphangitis - *see* Tuberculosis, lymph
    gland
  lymphatic (gland) (vessel) - *see* Tuber-
    culosis, lymph gland
  lymph gland or node (peripheral) 017.2
    abdomen 014.8
    bronchial 012.1
      primary, progressive 010.8
    cervical 017.2
    hilar 012.1
      primary, progressive 010.8

◀ ▶   **New Code**   ◀▥ ▥▶   **Revised Code**

Tuberculosis, tubercular, tuberculous
(Continued)
  lymph gland or node *(Continued)*
    intrathoracic 012.1
      primary, progressive 010.8
    mediastinal 012.1
      primary, progressive 010.8
    mesenteric 014.8
    peripheral 017.2
    retroperitoneal 014.8
    tracheobronchial 012.1
      primary, progressive 010.8
  malignant NEC (*see also* Tuberculosis,
    pulmonary) 011.9
  mammary gland 017.9
  marasmus NEC (*see also* Tuberculosis,
    pulmonary) 011.9
  mastoiditis 015.6
  maternal, affecting fetus or newborn
    760.2
  mediastinal (lymph) gland or node
    012.1
    primary, progressive 010.8
  mediastinitis 012.8
    primary, progressive 010.8
  mediastinopericarditis 017.9 *[420.0]*
  mediastinum 012.8
    primary, progressive 010.8
  medulla 013.9
    brain 013.2
    spinal cord 013.4
  melanosis, Addisonian 017.6
  membrane, brain 013.0
  meninges (cerebral) (spinal) 013.0
  meningitis (basilar) (brain) (cerebral)
    (cerebrospinal) (spinal) 013.0
  meningoencephalitis 013.0
  mesentery, mesenteric 014.8
    lymph gland or node 014.8
  miliary (any site) 018.9
    acute 018.0
    chronic 018.8
    specified type NEC 018.8
  millstone makers' 011.4
  miners' 011.4
  moulders' 011.4
  mouth 017.9
  multiple 018.9
    acute 018.0
    chronic 018.8
  muscle 017.9
  myelitis 013.6
  myocarditis 017.9 *[422.0]*
  myocardium 017.9 *[422.0]*
  nasal (passage) (sinus) 012.8
  nasopharynx 012.8
  neck gland 017.2
  nephritis 016.0 *[583.81]*
  nerve 017.9
  nose (septum) 012.8
  ocular 017.3
  old NEC 137.0
    without residuals V12.01
  omentum 014.8
  oophoritis (acute) (chronic) 016.6
  optic 017.3 *[377.39]*
    nerve trunk 017.3 *[377.39]*
    papilla, papillae 017.3 *[377.39]*
  orbit 017.3
  orchitis 016.5 *[608.81]*
  organ, specified NEC 017.9
  orificialis (primary) 017.0
  osseous (*see also* Tuberculosis, bone)
    015.9 *[730.8]*

Tuberculosis, tubercular, tuberculous
(Continued)
  osteitis (*see also* Tuberculosis, bone)
    015.9 *[730.8]*
  osteomyelitis (*see also* Tuberculosis,
    bone) 015.9 *[730.8]*
  otitis (media) 017.4
  ovaritis (acute) (chronic) 016.6
  ovary (acute) (chronic) 016.6
  oviducts (acute) (chronic) 016.6
  pachymeningitis 013.0
  palate (soft) 017.9
  pancreas 017.9
  papulonecrotic (primary) 017.0
  parathyroid glands 017.9
  paronychia (primary) 017.0
  parotid gland or region 017.9
  pelvic organ NEC 016.9
    female 016.7
    male 016.5
  pelvis (bony) 015.7 *[730.85]*
  penis 016.5
  peribronchitis 011.3
  pericarditis 017.9 *[420.0]*
  pericardium 017.9 *[420.0]*
  perichondritis, larynx 012.3
  perineum 017.9
  periostitis (*see also* Tuberculosis, bone)
    015.9 *[730.8]*
  periphlebitis 017.9
    eye vessel 017.3 *[362.18]*
    retina 017.3 *[362.18]*
  perirectal fistula 014.8
  peritoneal gland 014.8
  peritoneum 014.0
  peritonitis 014.0
  pernicious NEC (*see also* Tuberculosis,
    pulmonary) 011.9
  pharyngitis 012.8
  pharynx 012.8
  phlyctenulosis (conjunctiva) 017.3
    [370.31]
  phthisis NEC (*see also* Tuberculosis,
    pulmonary) 011.9
  pituitary gland 017.9
  placenta 016.7
  pleura, pleural, pleurisy, pleuritis (fibrin-
    ous) (obliterative) (purulent) (simple
    plastic) (with effusion) 012.0
    primary, progressive 010.1
  pneumonia, pneumonic 011.6
  pneumothorax 011.7
  polyserositis 018.9
    acute 018.0
    chronic 018.8
  potters' 011.4
  prepuce 016.5
  primary 010.9
    complex 010.0
    complicated 010.8
      with pleurisy or effusion 010.1
    progressive 010.8
      with pleurisy or effusion 010.1
    skin 017.0
  proctitis 014.8
  prostate 016.5 *[601.4]*
  prostatitis 016.5 *[601.4]*
  pulmonaris (*see also* Tuberculosis, pul-
    monary) 011.9
  pulmonary (artery) (incipient) (malig-
    nant) (multiple round foci) (perni-
    cious) (reinfection stage) 011.9
    cavitated or with cavitation 011.2
      primary, progressive 010.8

Tuberculosis, tubercular, tuberculous
(Continued)
  pulmonary *(Continued)*
    childhood type or first infection
      010.0
    chromogenic acid-fast bacilli
      795.3
    fibrosis or fibrotic 011.4
    infiltrative 011.0
      primary, progressive 010.9
    nodular 011.1
    specified NEC 011.8
    sputum positive only 795.3
    status following surgical collapse of
      lung NEC 011.9
  pyelitis 016.0 *[590.81]*
  pyelonephritis 016.0 *[590.81]*
  pyemia - *see* Tuberculosis, miliary
  pyonephrosis 016.0
  pyopneumothorax 012.0
  pyothorax 012.0
  rectum (with abscess) 014.8
    fistula 014.8
  reinfection stage (*see also* Tuberculosis,
    pulmonary) 011.9
  renal 016.0
  renes 016.0
  reproductive organ 016.7
  respiratory NEC (*see also* Tuberculosis,
    pulmonary) 011.9
    specified site NEC 012.8
  retina 017.3 *[363.13]*
  retroperitoneal (lymph gland or node)
    014.8
    gland 014.8
  retropharyngeal abscess 012.8
  rheumatism 015.9
  rhinitis 012.8
  sacroiliac (joint) 015.8
  sacrum 015.0 *[730.88]*
  salivary gland 017.9
  salpingitis (acute) (chronic) 016.6
  sandblasters' 011.4
  sclera 017.3 *[379.09]*
  scoliosis 015.0 *[737.43]*
  scrofulous 017.2
  scrotum 016.5
  seminal tract or vesicle 016.5 *[608.81]*
  senile NEC (*see also* Tuberculosis, pul-
    monary) 011.9
  septic NEC (*see also* Tuberculosis, mili-
    ary) 018.9
  shoulder 015.8
    blade 015.7 *[730.8]*
  sigmoid 014.8
  sinus (accessory) (nasal) 012.8
    bone 015.7 *[730.88]*
    epididymis 016.4
  skeletal NEC (*see also* Osteomyelitis,
    due to tuberculosis) 015.9 *[730.8]*
  skin (any site) (primary) 017.0
  small intestine 014.8
  soft palate 017.9
  spermatic cord 016.5
  spinal
    column 015.0 *[730.88]*
    cord 013.4
    disease 015.0 *[730.88]*
    medulla 013.4
    membrane 013.0
    meninges 013.0
  spine 015.0 *[730.88]*
  spleen 017.7
  splenitis 017.7

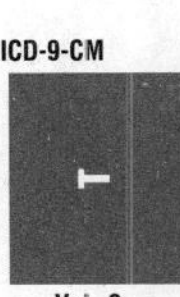

Tumor *(Continued)*
- desmoid (extra-abdominal) (M8821/1)
  - *see also* Neoplasm, connective tissue, uncertain behavior
  - abdominal (M8822/1) - *see* Neoplasm, connective tissue, uncertain behavior
- embryonal (mixed) (M9080/1) - *see also* Neoplasm, by site, uncertain behavior
  - liver (M9080/3) 155.0
- endodermal sinus (M9071/3)
  - specified site - *see* Neoplasm, by site, malignant
  - unspecified site
    - female 183.0
    - male 186.9
- epithelial
  - benign (M8010/0) - *see* Neoplasm, by site, benign
  - malignant (M8010/3) - *see* Neoplasm, by site, malignant
- Ewing's (M9260/3) - *see* Neoplasm, bone, malignant
- fatty - *see* Lipoma
- fetal, causing disproportion 653.7
  - causing obstructed labor 660.1
- fibroid (M8890/0) - *see* Leiomyoma
- G cell (M8153/1)
  - malignant (M8153/3)
    - pancreas 157.4
    - specified site NEC - *see* Neoplasm, by site, malignant
    - unspecified site 157.4
  - specified site - *see* Neoplasm, by site, uncertain behavior
  - unspecified site 235.5
- giant cell (type) (M8003/1) - *see also* Neoplasm, by site, unspecified nature
  - bone (M9250/1) 238.0
    - malignant (M9250/3) - *see* Neoplasm, bone, malignant
  - chondromatous (M9230/0) - *see* Neoplasm, bone, benign
  - malignant (M8003/3) - *see* Neoplasm, by site, malignant
  - peripheral (gingiva) 523.8
  - soft parts (M9251/1) - *see also* Neoplasm, connective tissue, uncertain behavior
    - malignant (M9251/3) - *see* Neoplasm, connective tissue, malignant
  - tendon sheath 727.02
- glomus (M8711/0) - *see also* Hemangioma, by site
  - jugulare (M8690/1) 237.3
    - malignant (M8690/3) 194.6
- gonadal stromal (M8590/1) - *see* Neoplasm, by site, uncertain behavior
- granular cell (M9580/0) - *see also* Neoplasm, connective tissue, benign
  - malignant (M9580/3) - *see* Neoplasm, connective tissue, malignant
- granulosa cell (M8620/1) 236.2
  - malignant (M8620/3) 183.0
- granulosa cell-theca cell (M8621/1) 236.2
  - malignant (M8621/3) 183.0
- Grawitz's (hypernephroma) (M8312/3) 189.0

Tumor *(Continued)*
- hazard-crile (M8350/3) 193
- hemorrhoidal - *see* Hemorrhoids
- hilar cell (M8660/0) 220
- Hürthle cell (benign) (M8290/0) 226
  - malignant (M8290/3) 193
- hydatid (*see also* Echinococcus) 122.9
- hypernephroid (M8311/1) - *see also* Neoplasm, by site, uncertain behavior
- interstitial cell (M8650/1) - *see also* Neoplasm, by site, uncertain behavior
  - benign (M8650/0) - *see* Neoplasm, by site, benign
  - malignant (M8650/3) - *see* Neoplasm, by site, malignant
- islet cell (M8150/0)
  - malignant (M8150/3)
    - pancreas 157.4
    - specified site - *see* Neoplasm, by site, malignant
    - unspecified site 157.4
  - pancreas 211.7
  - specified site NEC - *see* Neoplasm, by site, benign
  - unspecified site 211.7
- juxtaglomerular (M8361/1) 236.91
- Krukenberg's (M8490/6) 198.6
- Leydig cell (M8650/1)
  - benign (M8650/0)
    - specified site - *see* Neoplasm, by site, benign
    - unspecified site
      - female 220
      - male 222.0
  - malignant (M8650/3)
    - specified site - *see* Neoplasm, by site, malignant
    - unspecified site
      - female 183.0
      - male 186.9
  - specified site - *see* Neoplasm, by site, uncertain behavior
  - unspecified site
    - female 236.2
    - male 236.4
- lipid cell, ovary (M8670/0) 220
- lipoid cell, ovary (M8670/0) 220
- lymphomatous, benign (M9590/0) - *see also* Neoplasm, by site, benign
- Malherbe's (M8110/0) - *see* Neoplasm, skin, benign
- malignant (M8000/3) - *see also* Neoplasm, by site, malignant
  - fusiform cell (type) (M8004/3) - *see* Neoplasm, by site, malignant
  - giant cell (type) (M8003/3) - *see* Neoplasm, by site, malignant
  - mixed NEC (M8940/3) - *see* Neoplasm, by site, malignant
  - small cell (type) (M8002/3) - *see* Neoplasm, by site, malignant
  - spindle cell (type) (M8004/3) - *see* Neoplasm, by site, malignant
- mast cell (M9740/1) 238.5
  - malignant (M9740/3) 202.6
- melanotic, neuroectodermal (M9363/0) - *see* Neoplasm, by site, benign
- mesenchymal
  - malignant (M8800/3) - *see* Neoplasm, connective tissue, malignant

Tumor *(Continued)*
- mesenchymal *(Continued)*
  - mixed (M8990/1) - *see* Neoplasm, connective tissue, uncertain behavior
- mesodermal, mixed (M8951/3) - *see also* Neoplasm, by site, malignant
  - liver 155.0
- mesonephric (M9110/1) - *see also* Neoplasm, by site, uncertain behavior
  - malignant (M9110/3) - *see* Neoplasm, by site, malignant
- metastatic
  - from specified site (M8000/3) - *see* Neoplasm, by site, malignant
  - to specified site (M8000/6) - *see* Neoplasm, by site, malignant, secondary
- mixed NEC (M8940/0) - *see also* Neoplasm, by site, benign
  - malignant (M8940/3) - *see* Neoplasm, by site, malignant
- mucocarcinoid, malignant (M8243/3) - *see* Neoplasm, by site, malignant
- mucoepidermoid (M8430/1) - *see* Neoplasm, by site, uncertain behavior
- Mullerian, mixed (M8950/3) - *see* Neoplasm, by site, malignant
- myoepithelial (M8982/0) - *see* Neoplasm, by site, benign
- neurogenic olfactory (M9520/3) 160.0
- nonencapsulated sclerosing (M8350/3) 193
- odontogenic (M9270/1) 238.0
  - adenomatoid (M9300/0) 213.1
    - upper jaw (bone) 213.0
  - benign (M9270/0) 213.1
    - upper jaw (bone) 213.0
  - calcifying epithelial (M9340/0) 213.1
    - upper jaw (bone) 213.0
  - malignant (M9270/3) 170.1
    - upper jaw (bone) 170.0
  - squamous (M9312/0) 213.1
    - upper jaw (bone) 213.0
- ovarian stromal (M8590/1) 236.2
- ovary
  - in pregnancy or childbirth 654.4
    - affecting fetus or newborn 763.89
    - causing obstructed labor 660.2
      - affecting fetus or newborn 763.1
- pacinian (M9507/0) - *see* Neoplasm, skin, benign
- Pancoast's (M8010/3) 162.3
- papillary - *see* Papilloma
- pelvic, in pregnancy or childbirth 654.9
  - affecting fetus or newborn 763.89
  - causing obstructed labor 660.2
    - affecting fetus or newborn 763.1
- phantom 300.11
- plasma cell (M9731/1) 238.6
  - benign (M9731/0) - *see* Neoplasm, by site, benign
  - malignant (M9731/3) 203.8
- polyvesicular vitelline (M9071/3)
  - specified site - *see* Neoplasm, by site, malignant
  - unspecified site
    - female 183.0
    - male 186.9
- Pott's puffy (*see also* Osteomyelitis) 730.2
- Rathke's pouch (M9350/1) 237.0

Tumor *(Continued)*
  Regaud's (M8082/3) - *see* Neoplasm,
    nasopharynx, malignant
  rete cell (M8140/0) 222.0
  retinal anlage (M9363/0) - *see* Neo-
    plasm, by site, benign
  Rokitansky's 620.2
  salivary gland type, mixed (M8940/0)
    - *see also* Neoplasm, by site, be-
    nign
    malignant (M8940/3) - *see* Neo-
      plasm, by site, malignant
  Sampson's 617.1
  Schloffer's (*see also* Peritonitis) 567.2
  Schmincke's (M8082/3) - *see* Neo-
    plasm, nasopharynx, malignant
  sebaceous (*see also* Cyst, sebaceous)
    706.2
  secondary (M8000/6) - *see* Neoplasm,
    by site, secondary
  Sertoli cell (M8640/0)
    with lipid storage (M8641/0)
      specified site - *see* Neoplasm, by
        site, benign
      unspecified site
        female 220
        male 222.0
    specified site - *see* Neoplasm, by site,
      benign
    unspecified site
      female 220
      male 222.0
  Sertoli-Leydig cell (M8631/0)
    specified site - *see* Neoplasm, by site,
      benign
    unspecified site
      female 220
      male 222.0
  sex cord (-stromal) (M8590/1) - *see*
    Neoplasm, by site, uncertain be-
    havior
  skin appendage (M8390/0) - *see* Neo-
    plasm, skin, benign
  soft tissue
    benign (M8800/0) - *see* Neoplasm,
      connective tissue, benign
    malignant (M8800/3) - *see* Neo-
      plasm, connective tissue, malig-
      nant
  sternomastoid 754.1
  superior sulcus (lung) (pulmonary)
    (syndrome) (M8010/3) 162.3
  suprasulcus (M8010/3) 162.3
  sweat gland (M8400/1) - *see also* Neo-
    plasm, skin, uncertain behavior
    benign (M8400/0) - *see* Neoplasm,
      skin, benign
    malignant (M8400/3) - *see* Neo-
      plasm, skin, malignant
  syphilitic brain 094.89
    congenital 090.49
  testicular stromal (M8590/1) 236.4
  theca cell (M8600/0) 220
  theca cell-granulosa cell (M8621/1)
    236.2
  theca-lutein (M8610/0) 220
  turban (M8200/0) 216.4
  uterus
    in pregnancy or childbirth 654.1
      affecting fetus or newborn
        763.89
      causing obstructed labor 660.2
        affecting fetus or newborn
          763.1

Tumor *(Continued)*
  vagina
    in pregnancy or childbirth 654.7
      affecting fetus or newborn
        763.89
      causing obstructed labor 660.2
        affecting fetus or newborn 763.1
  varicose (*see also* Varicose, vein) 454.9
  von Recklinghausen's (M9540/1) 237.71
  vulva
    in pregnancy or childbirth 654.8
      affecting fetus or newborn
        763.89
      causing obstructed labor 660.2
        affecting fetus or newborn 763.1
  Warthin's (salivary gland) (M8561/0)
    210.2
  white - *see also* Tuberculosis, arthritis
  White-Darier 757.39
  Wilms' (nephroblastoma) (M8960/3)
    189.0
  yolk sac (M9071/3)
    specified site - *see* Neoplasm, by site,
      malignant
    unspecified site
      female 183.0
      male 186.9
Tumorlet (M8040/1) - *see* Neoplasm, by
  site, uncertain behavior
Tungiasis 134.1
Tunica vasculosa lentis 743.39
Tunnel vision 368.45
Turban tumor (M8200/0) 216.4
Türck's trachoma (chronic catarrhal lar-
  yngitis) 476.0
Türk's syndrome (ocular retraction syn-
  drome) 378.71
Turner's
  hypoplasia (tooth) 520.4
  syndrome 758.6
  tooth 520.4
Turner-Kieser syndrome (hereditary osteo-onychodysplasia) 756.89
Turner-Varny syndrome 758.6
Turricephaly 756.0
Tussis convulsiva (*see also* Whooping
  cough) 033.9
Twin
  affected by maternal complications of
    pregnancy 761.5
  conjoined 759.4
  healthy liveborn - *see* Newborn, twin
  pregnancy (complicating delivery)
    NEC 651.0
    with fetal loss and retention of one
      fetus 651.3
Twinning, teeth 520.2
Twist, twisted
  bowel, colon, or intestine 560.2
  hair (congenital) 757.4
  mesentery 560.2
  omentum 560.2
  organ or site, congenital NEC - *see*
    Anomaly, specified type NEC
  ovarian pedicle 620.5
    congenital 752.0
  umbilical cord - *see* Compression, um-
    bilical cord
Twitch 781.0
Tylosis 700
  buccalis 528.6
  gingiva 523.8
  linguae 528.6
  palmaris et plantaris 757.39

Tympanism 787.3
Tympanites (abdominal) (intestine)
  787.3
Tympanitis - *see* Myringitis
Tympanosclerosis 385.00
  involving
    combined sites NEC 385.09
      with tympanic membrane 385.03
    tympanic membrane 385.01
      with ossicles 385.02
        and middle ear 385.03
Tympanum - *see* condition
Tympany
  abdomen 787.3
  chest 786.7
Typhlitis (*see also* Appendicitis) 541
Typhoenteritis 002.0
Typhogastric fever 002.0
Typhoid (abortive) (ambulant) (any site)
  (fever) (hemorrhagic) (infection) (intermittent) (malignant) (rheumatic)
  002.0
  with pneumonia 002.0 [484.8]
  abdominal 002.0
  carrier (suspected) of V02.1
  cholecystitis (current) 002.0
  clinical (Widal and blood test negative)
    002.0
  endocarditis 002.0 [421.1]
  inoculation reaction - *see* Complica-
    tions, vaccination
  meningitis 002.0 [320.7]
  mesenteric lymph nodes 002.0
  myocarditis 002.0 [422.0]
  osteomyelitis (*see also* Osteomyelitis,
    due to, typhoid) 002.0 [730.8]
  perichondritis, larynx 002.0 [478.71]
  pneumonia 002.0 [484.8]
  spine 002.0 [720.81]
  ulcer (perforating) 002.0
  vaccination, prophylactic (against)
    V03.1
  Widal negative 002.0
Typhomalaria (fever) (*see also* Malaria)
  084.6
Typhomania 002.0
Typhoperitonitis 002.0
Typhus (fever) 081.9
  abdominal, abdominalis 002.0
  African tick 082.1
  amarillic (*see also* Fever, yellow)
    060.9
  brain 081.9
  cerebral 081.9
  classical 080
  endemic (flea-borne) 081.0
  epidemic (louse-borne) 080
  exanthematic NEC 080
  exanthematicus SAI 080
    brillii SAI 081.1
    mexicanus SAI 081.0
    pediculo vestimenti causa 080
    typhus murinus 081.0
  flea-borne 081.0
  Indian tick 082.1
  Kenya tick 082.1
  louse-borne 080
  Mexican 081.0
    flea-borne 081.0
    louse-borne 080
    tabardillo 080
  mite-borne 081.2
  murine 081.0
  North Asian tick-borne 082.2

Typhus *(Continued)*
  petechial 081.9
  Queensland tick 082.3
  rat 081.0
  recrudescent 081.1
  recurrent *(see also* Fever, relapsing)
      087.9

Typhus *(Continued)*
  São Paulo 082.0
  scrub (China) (India) (Malaya) (New
      Guinea) 081.2
  shop (of Malaya) 081.0
  Siberian tick 082.2
  tick-borne NEC 082.9

Typhus *(Continued)*
  tropical 081.2
  vaccination, prophylactic (against)
      V05.8
Tyrosinosis (Medes) (Sakai) 270.2
Tyrosinuria 270.2
Tyrosyluria 270.2

U

Uehlinger's syndrome (acropachyderma) 757.39
Uhl's anomaly or disease (hypoplasia of myocardium, right ventricle) 746.84
Ulcer, ulcerated, ulcerating, ulceration, ulcerative 707.9
with gangrene 707.9 [785.4]
abdomen (wall) (*see also* Ulcer, skin) 707.8
ala, nose 478.1
alveolar process 526.5
amebic (intestine) 006.9
skin 006.6
anastomotic - *see* Ulcer, gastrojejunal
anorectal 569.41
antral - *see* Ulcer, stomach
anus (sphincter) (solitary) 569.41
varicose - *see* Varicose, ulcer, anus
aphthous (oral) (recurrent) 528.2
genital organ(s)
female 616.8
male 608.89
mouth 528.2
arm (*see also* Ulcer, skin) 707.8
arteriosclerotic plaque - *see* Arteriosclerosis, by site
artery NEC 447.2
without rupture 447.8
atrophic NEC - *see* Ulcer, skin
Barrett's (chronic peptic ulcer of esophagus) 530.2
bile duct 576.8
bladder (solitary) (sphincter) 596.8
bilharzial (*see also* Schistosomiasis) 120.9 [595.4]
submucosal (*see also* Cystitis) 595.1
tuberculous (*see also* Tuberculosis) 016.1
bleeding NEC - *see* Ulcer, peptic, with hemorrhage
bone 730.9
bowel (*see also* Ulcer, intestine) 569.82
breast 611.0
bronchitis 491.8
bronchus 519.1
buccal (cavity) (traumatic) 528.9
burn (acute) - *see* Ulcer, duodenum
Buruli 031.1
buttock (*see also* Ulcer, skin) 707.8
decubitus (*see also* Ulcer, decubitus) 707.0
cancerous (M8000/3) - *see* Neoplasm, by site, malignant
cardia - *see* Ulcer, stomach
cardio-esophageal (peptic) 530.2
cecum (*see also* Ulcer, intestine) 569.82
cervix (uteri) (trophic) 622.0
with mention of cervicitis 616.0
chancroidal 099.0
chest (wall) (*see also* Ulcer, skin) 707.8
Chiclero 085.4
chin (pyogenic) (*see also* Ulcer, skin) 707.8
chronic (cause unknown) - *see also* Ulcer, skin
penis 607.89
Cochin-China 085.1
colitis - *see* Colitis, ulcerative
colon (*see also* Ulcer, intestine) 569.82
conjunctiva (acute) (postinfectional) 372.00

Ulcer, ulcerated, ulcerating, ulceration, ulcerative (*Continued*)
cornea (infectional) 370.00
with perforation 370.06
annular 370.02
catarrhal 370.01
central 370.03
dendritic 054.42
marginal 370.01
mycotic 370.05
phlyctenular, tuberculous (*see also* Tuberculosis) 017.3 [370.31]
ring 370.02
rodent 370.07
serpent, serpiginous 370.04
superficial marginal 370.01
tuberculous (*see also* Tuberculosis) 017.3 [370.31]
corpus cavernosum (chronic) 607.89
crural - *see* Ulcer, lower extremity
Curling's - *see* Ulcer, duodenum
Cushing's - *see* Ulcer, peptic
cystitis (interstitial) 595.1
decubitus (any site) 707.0
with gangrene 707.0 [785.4]
dendritic 054.42
diabetes, diabetic (mellitus) 250.8 [707.9]
lower limb 250.8 [707.1]
specified site NEC 250.8 [707.8]
Dieulafoy's - *see* Ulcer, stomach
due to
infection NEC - *see* Ulcer, skin
radiation, radium - *see* Ulcer, by site
trophic disturbance (any region) - *see* Ulcer, skin
x-ray - *see* Ulcer, by site
duodenum, duodenal (eroded) (peptic) 532.9

> Note   Use the following fifth-digit subclassification with categories 531-534:
>
> 0   without mention of obstruction
> 1   with obstruction

with
hemorrhage (chronic) 532.4
and perforation 532.6
perforation (chronic) 532.5
and hemorrhage 532.6
acute 532.3
with
hemorrhage 532.0
and perforation 532.2
perforation 532.1
and hemorrhage 532.2
bleeding (recurrent) - *see* Ulcer, duodenum, with hemorrhage
chronic 532.7
with
hemorrhage 532.4
and perforation 532.6
perforation 532.5
and hemorrhage 532.6
penetrating - *see* Ulcer, duodenum, with perforation
perforating - *see* Ulcer, duodenum, with perforation
dysenteric NEC 009.0
elusive 595.1
endocarditis (any valve) (acute) (chronic) (subacute) 421.0

Ulcer, ulcerated, ulcerating, ulceration, ulcerative (*Continued*)
enteritis - *see* Colitis, ulcerative
enterocolitis 556.0
epiglottis 478.79
esophagus (peptic) 530.2
due to ingestion
aspirin 530.2
chemicals 530.2
medicinal agents 530.2
fungal 530.2
infectional 530.2
varicose (*see also* Varix, esophagus) 456.1
bleeding (*see also* Varix, esophagus, bleeding) 456.0
eye NEC 360.00
dendritic 054.42
eyelid (region) 373.01
face (*see also* Ulcer, skin) 707.8
fauces 478.29
Fenwick (-Hunner) (solitary) (*see also* Cystitis) 595.1
fistulous NEC - *see* Ulcer, skin
foot (indolent) (*see also* Ulcer, lower extremity) 707.1
perforating 707.1
leprous 030.1
syphilitic 094.0
trophic 707.1
varicose 454.0
inflamed or infected 454.2
frambesial, initial or primary 102.0
gallbladder or duct 575.8
gall duct 576.8
gangrenous (*see also* Gangrene) 785.4
gastric - *see* Ulcer, stomach
gastrocolic - *see* Ulcer, gastrojejunal
gastroduodenal - *see* Ulcer, peptic
gastroesophageal - *see* Ulcer, stomach
gastrohepatic - *see* Ulcer, stomach
gastrointestinal - *see* Ulcer, gastrojejunal
gastrojejunal (eroded) (peptic) 534.9

> Note   Use the following fifth-digit subclassification with categories 531-534:
>
> 0   without mention of obstruction
> 1   with obstruction

with
hemorrhage (chronic) 534.4
and perforation 534.6
perforation 534.5
and hemorrhage 534.6
acute 534.3
with
hemorrhage 534.0
and perforation 534.2
perforation 534.1
and hemorrhage 534.2
bleeding (recurrent) - *see* Ulcer, gastrojejunal, with hemorrhage
chronic 534.7
with
hemorrhage 534.4
and perforation 534.6
perforation 534.5
and hemorrhage 534.6
penetrating - *see* Ulcer, gastrojejunal, with perforation
perforating - *see* Ulcer, gastrojejunal, with perforation

Ulcer, ulcerated, ulcerating, ulceration, ulcerative *(Continued)*
gastrojejunocolic - *see* Ulcer, gastrojejunal
genital organ
  female 629.8
  male 608.89
gingiva 523.8
gingivitis 523.1
glottis 478.79
granuloma of pudenda 099.2
groin *(see also* Ulcer, skin) 707.8
gum 523.8
gumma, due to yaws 102.4
hand *(see also* Ulcer, skin) 707.8
hard palate 528.9
heel *(see also* Ulcer, lower extremity) 707.1
  decubitus *(see also* Ulcer, decubitus) 707.0
hemorrhoids 455.8
  external 455.5
  internal 455.2
hip *(see also* Ulcer, skin) 707.8
  decubitus *(see also* Ulcer, decubitus) 707.0
Hunner's 595.1
hypopharynx 478.29
hypopyon (chronic) (subacute) 370.04
hypostaticum - *see* Ulcer, varicose
ileocolitis 556.1
ileum *(see also* Ulcer, intestine) 569.82
intestine, intestinal 569.82
  with perforation 569.83
  amebic 006.9
  duodenal - *see* Ulcer, duodenum
  granulocytopenic (with hemorrhage) 288.0
  marginal 569.82
  perforating 569.83
  small, primary 569.82
  stercoraceous 569.82
  stercoral 569.82
  tuberculous *(see also* Tuberculosis) 014.8
  typhoid (fever) 002.0
  varicose 456.8
ischemic 707.9
  lower extremity *(see also* Ulcer, lower extremity) 707.1
jejunum, jejunal - *see* Ulcer, gastrojejunal
keratitis *(see also* Ulcer, cornea) 370.00
knee - *see* Ulcer, lower extremity
labium (majus) (minus) 616.50
laryngitis *(see also* Laryngitis) 464.0
larynx (aphthous) (contact) 478.79
  diphtheritic 032.3
leg - *see* Ulcer, lower extremity
lip 528.5
Lipschütz's 616.50
lower extremity (atrophic) (chronic) (neurogenic) (perforating) (pyogenic) (trophic) (tropical) 707.1
  with gangrene 707.1 *[785.4]*
    arteriosclerotic 440.24
  arteriosclerotic 440.23
    with gangrene 440.24
  decubitus 707.0
    with gangrene 707.0 *[785.4]*
  varicose 454.0
    inflamed or infected 454.2
luetic - *see* Ulcer, syphilitic

Ulcer, ulcerated, ulcerating, ulceration, ulcerative *(Continued)*
lung 518.89
  tuberculous *(see also* Tuberculosis) 011.2
malignant (M8000/3) - *see* Neoplasm, by site, malignant
marginal NEC - *see* Ulcer, gastrojejunal
meatus (urinarius) 597.89
Meckel's diverticulum 751.0
Meleney's (chronic undermining) 686.09
Mooren's (cornea) 370.07
mouth (traumatic) 528.9
mycobacterial (skin) 031.1
nasopharynx 478.29
navel cord (newborn) 771.4
neck *(see also* Ulcer, skin) 707.8
  uterus 622.0
neurogenic NEC - *see* Ulcer, skin
nose, nasal (infectional) (passage) 478.1
  septum 478.1
    varicose 456.8
  skin - *see* Ulcer, skin
  spirochetal NEC 104.8
oral mucosa (traumatic) 528.9
palate (soft) 528.9
penetrating NEC - *see* Ulcer, peptic, with perforation
penis (chronic) 607.89
peptic (site unspecified) 533.9

> Note   Use the following fifth-digit subclassification with categories 531-534:
>
> 0   without mention of obstruction
> 1   with obstruction

  with
    hemorrhage 533.4
      and perforation 533.6
    perforation (chronic) 533.5
      and hemorrhage 533.6
  acute 533.3
    with
      hemorrhage 533.0
        and perforation 533.2
      perforation 533.1
        and hemorrhage 533.2
  bleeding (recurrent) - *see* Ulcer, peptic, with hemorrhage
  chronic 533.7
    with
      hemorrhage 533.4
        and perforation 533.6
      perforation 533.5
        and hemorrhage 533.6
  penetrating - *see* Ulcer, peptic, with perforation
  perforating NEC *(see also* Ulcer, peptic, with perforation) 533.5
  skin 707.9
perineum *(see also* Ulcer, skin) 707.8
peritonsillar 474.8
phagedenic (tropical) NEC - *see* Ulcer, skin
pharynx 478.29
phlebitis - *see* Phlebitis
plaster *(see also* Ulcer, decubitus) 707.0
popliteal space - *see* Ulcer, lower extremity
postpyloric - *see* Ulcer, duodenum
prepuce 607.89
prepyloric - *see* Ulcer, stomach
pressure *(see also* Ulcer, decubitus) 707.0

Ulcer, ulcerated, ulcerating, ulceration, ulcerative *(Continued)*
primary of intestine 569.82
  with perforation 569.83
proctitis 556.2
  with ulcerative sigmoiditis 556.3
prostate 601.8
pseudopeptic - *see* Ulcer, peptic
pyloric - *see* Ulcer, stomach
rectosigmoid 569.82
  with perforation 569.83
rectum (sphincter) (solitary) 569.41
  stercoraceous, stercoral 569.41
  varicose - *see* Varicose, ulcer, anus
retina *(see also* Chorioretinitis) 363.20
rodent (M8090/3) - *see also* Neoplasm, skin, malignant
  cornea 370.07
round - *see* Ulcer, stomach
sacrum (region) *(see also* Ulcer, skin) 707.8
Saemisch's 370.04
scalp *(see also* Ulcer, skin) 707.8
sclera 379.09
scrofulous *(see also* Tuberculosis) 017.2
scrotum 608.89
  tuberculous *(see also* Tuberculosis) 016.5
  varicose 456.4
seminal vesicle 608.89
sigmoid 569.82
  with perforation 569.83
skin (atrophic) (chronic) (neurogenic) (non-healing) (perforating) (pyogenic) (trophic) 707.9
  with gangrene 707.9 *[785.4]*
  amebic 006.6
  decubitus 707.0
    with gangrene 707.0 *[785.4]*
  in granulocytopenia 288.0
  lower extremity *(see also* Ulcer, lower extremity) 707.1
    with gangrene 707.1 *[785.4]*
      arteriosclerotic 440.24
    arteriosclerotic 440.23
      with gangrene 440.24
  mycobacterial 031.1
  syphilitic (early) (secondary) 091.3
  tuberculous (primary) *(see also* Tuberculosis) 017.0
  varicose - *see* Ulcer, varicose
sloughing NEC - *see* Ulcer, skin
soft palate 528.9
solitary, anus or rectum (sphincter) 569.41
sore throat 462
  streptococcal 034.0
spermatic cord 608.89
spine (tuberculous) 015.0 *[730.88]*
stasis (leg) (venous) 454.0
  inflamed or infected 454.2
stercoral, stercoraceous 569.82
  with perforation 569.83
  anus or rectum 569.41
stoma, stomal - *see* Ulcer, gastrojejunal
stomach (eroded) (peptic) (round) 531.9

> Note   Use the following fifth-digit subclassification with categories 531-534:
>
> 0   without mention of obstruction
> 1   with obstruction

ICD-9-CM

⊃

Vol. 2

Ulcer, ulcerated, ulcerating, ulceration, ulcerative *(Continued)*
stomach *(Continued)*
with
hemorrhage 531.4
and perforation 531.6
perforation (chronic) 531.5
and hemorrhage 531.6
acute 531.3
with
hemorrhage 531.0
and perforation 531.2
perforation 531.1
and hemorrhage 531.2
bleeding (recurrent) - *see* Ulcer,
stomach, with hemorrhage
chronic 531.7
with
hemorrhage 531.4
and perforation 531.6
perforation 531.5
and hemorrhage 531.6
penetrating - *see* Ulcer, stomach,
with perforation
perforating - *see* Ulcer, stomach,
with perforation
stomatitis 528.0
stress - *see* Ulcer, peptic
strumous (tuberculous) *(see also* Tuberculosis) 017.2
submental *(see also* Ulcer, skin) 707.8
submucosal, bladder 595.1
syphilitic (any site) (early) (secondary)
091.3
late 095.9
perforating 095.9
foot 094.0
testis 608.89
thigh - *see* Ulcer, lower extremity
throat 478.29
diphtheritic 032.0
toe - *see* Ulcer, lower extremity
tongue (traumatic) 529.0
tonsil 474.8
diphtheritic 032.0
trachea 519.1
trophic - *see* Ulcer, skin
tropical NEC *(see also* Ulcer, skin) 707.9
tuberculous - *see* Tuberculosis, ulcer
tunica vaginalis 608.89
turbinate 730.9
typhoid (fever) 002.0
perforating 002.0
umbilicus (newborn) 771.4
unspecified site NEC - *see* Ulcer, skin
urethra (meatus) *(see also* Urethritis)
597.89
uterus 621.8
cervix 622.0
with mention of cervicitis 616.0
neck 622.0
with mention of cervicitis 616.0
vagina 616.8
valve, heart 421.0
varicose (lower extremity, any part)
454.0
anus - *see* Varicose, ulcer, anus
broad ligament 456.5
esophagus *(see also* Varix, esophagus) 456.1
bleeding *(see also* Varix, esophagus, bleeding) 456.0
inflamed or infected 454.2
nasal septum 456.8

Ulcer, ulcerated, ulcerating, ulceration, ulcerative *(Continued)*
varicose *(Continued)*
perineum 456.6
rectum - *see* Varicose, ulcer, anus
scrotum 456.4
specified site NEC 456.8
sublingual 456.3
vulva 456.6
vas deferens 608.89
vesical *(see also* Ulcer, bladder) 596.8
vulva (acute) (infectional) 616.50
Behçet's syndrome 136.1 *[616.51]*
herpetic 054.12
tuberculous 016.7 *[616.51]*
vulvobuccal, recurring 616.50
x-ray - *see* Ulcer, by site
yaws 102.4
Ulcerosa scarlatina 034.1
Ulcus - *see also* Ulcer
cutis tuberculosum *(see also* Tuberculosis) 017.0
duodeni - *see* Ulcer, duodenum
durum 091.0
extragenital 091.2
gastrojejunale - *see* Ulcer, gastrojejunal
hypostaticum - *see* Ulcer, varicose
molle (cutis) (skin) 099.0
serpens corneae (pneumococcal) 370.04
ventriculi - *see* Ulcer, stomach
Ulegyria 742.4
Ulerythema
acneiforma 701.8
centrifugum 695.4
ophryogenes 757.4
Ullrich (-Bonnevie) (-Turner) syndrome
758.6
Ullrich-Feichtiger syndrome 759.89
Ulnar - *see* condition
Ulorrhagia 523.8
Ulorrhea 523.8
Umbilicus, umbilical - *see also* condition
cord necrosis, affecting fetus or newborn 762.6
Unavailability of medical facilities (at)
V63.9
due to
investigation by social service
agency V63.8
lack of services at home V63.1
remoteness from facility V63.0
waiting list V63.2
home V63.1
outpatient clinic V63.0
specified reason NEC V63.8
Uncinaria americana infestation 126.1
Uncinariasis *(see also* Ancylostomiasis)
126.9
Unconscious, unconsciousness 780.09
Underdevelopment - *see also* Undeveloped
sexual 259.0
Undernourishment 269.9
Undernutrition 269.9
Under observation - *see* Observation
Underweight 783.4
for gestational age - *see* Light-for-dates
Underwood's disease (sclerema neonatorum) 778.1
Undescended - *see also* Malposition, congenital
cecum 751.4
colon 751.4
testis 752.51

Undetermined diagnosis or cause 799.9
Undeveloped, undevelopment - *see also*
Hypoplasia
brain (congenital) 742.1
cerebral (congenital) 742.1
fetus or newborn 764.9
heart 746.89
lung 748.5
testis 257.2
uterus 259.0
Undiagnosed (disease) 799.9
Undulant fever *(see also* Brucellosis) 023.9
Unemployment, anxiety concerning V62.0
Unequal leg (acquired) (length) 736.81
congenital 755.30
Unerupted teeth, tooth 520.6
Unextracted dental root 525.3
Unguis incarnatus 703.0
Unicornis uterus 752.3
Unicorporeus uterus 752.3
Uniformis uterus 752.3
Unilateral - *see also* condition
development, breast 611.8
organ or site, congenital NEC - *see*
Agenesis
vagina 752.49
Unilateralis uterus 752.3
Unilocular heart 745.8
Uninhibited bladder 596.54
with cauda equina syndrome 344.61
neurogenic *(see also* Neurogenic, bladder) 596.54
Union, abnormal - *see also* Fusion
divided tendon 727.89
larynx and trachea 748.3
Universal
joint, cervix 620.6
mesentery 751.4
Unknown
cause of death 799.9
diagnosis 799.9
Unna's disease (seborrheic dermatitis)
690.10
Unresponsiveness, adrenocorticotropin
(ACTH) 255.4
Unsoundness of mind *(see also* Psychosis) 298.9
Unspecified cause of death 799.9
Unstable
back NEC 724.9
colon 569.89
joint - *see* Instability, joint
lie 652.0
affecting fetus or newborn (before
labor) 761.7
causing obstructed labor 660.0
affecting fetus or newborn 763.1
lumbosacral joint (congenital) 756.19
acquired 724.6
sacroiliac 724.6
spine NEC 724.9
Untruthfulness, child problem *(see also*
Disturbance, conduct) 312.0
Unverricht (-Lundborg) disease, syndrome, or epilepsy 333.2
Unverricht-Wagner syndrome (dermatomyositis) 710.3
Upper respiratory - *see* condition
Upset
gastric 536.8
psychogenic 306.4
gastrointestinal 536.8
psychogenic 306.4
virus *(see also* Enteritis, viral) 008.8

Upset (Continued)
  intestinal (large) (small) 564.9
    psychogenic 306.4
  menstruation 626.9
  mental 300.9
  stomach 536.8
    psychogenic 306.4
Urachus - see also condition
  patent 753.7
  persistent 753.7
Uratic arthritis 274.0
Urbach's lipoid proteinosis 272.8
Urbach-Oppenheim disease or syndrome (necrobiosis lipoidica diabeticorum) 250.8 [709.3]
Urbach-Wiethe disease or syndrome (lipoid proteinosis) 272.8
Urban yellow fever 060.1
Urea, blood, high - see Uremia
Uremia, uremic (absorption) (amaurosis) (amblyopia) (aphasia) (apoplexy) (coma) (delirium) (dementia) (dropsy) (dyspnea) (fever) (intoxication) (mania) (paralysis) (poisoning) (toxemia) (vomiting) 586
  with
    abortion - see Abortion, by type, with renal failure
    ectopic pregnancy (see also categories 633.0-633.9) 639.3
    hypertension (see also Hypertension, kidney) 403.91
    molar pregnancy (see also categories 630-632) 639.3
  chronic 585
  complicating
    abortion 639.3
    ectopic or molar pregnancy 639.3
    hypertension (see also Hypertension, kidney) 403.91
    labor and delivery 669.3
  congenital 779.8
  extrarenal 788.9
  hypertensive (chronic) (see also Hypertension, kidney) 403.91
  maternal NEC, affecting fetus or newborn 760.1
  neuropathy 585 [357.4]
  pericarditis 585 [420.0]
  prerenal 788.9
  pyelitic (see also Pyelitis) 590.80
Ureter, ureteral - see condition
Ureteralgia 788.0
Ureterectasis 593.89
Ureteritis 593.89
  cystica 590.3
  due to calculus 592.1
  gonococcal (acute) 098.19
    chronic or duration of 2 months or over 098.39
  nonspecific 593.89
Ureterocele (acquired) 593.89
  congenital 753.23
Ureterolith 592.1
Ureterolithiasis 592.1
Ureterostomy status V44.6
  with complication 997.5
Urethra, urethral - see condition
Urethralgia 788.9
Urethritis (abacterial) (acute) (allergic) (anterior) (chronic) (nonvenereal) (posterior) (recurrent) (simple) (subacute) (ulcerative) (undifferentiated) 597.80

Urethritis (Continued)
  diplococcal (acute) 098.0
    chronic or duration of 2 months or over 098.2
  due to Trichomonas (vaginalis) 131.02
  gonococcal (acute) 098.0
    chronic or duration of 2 months or over 098.2
  nongonococcal (sexually transmitted) 099.40
    Chlamydia trachomatis 099.41
    Reiter's 099.3
    specified organism NEC 099.49
  nonspecific (sexually transmitted) (see also Urethritis, nongonococcal) 099.40
  not sexually transmitted 597.80
  Reiter's 099.3
  trichomonal or due to Trichomonas (vaginalis) 131.02
  tuberculous (see also Tuberculosis) 016.3
  venereal NEC (see also Urethritis, nongonococcal) 099.40
Urethrocele
  female 618.0
    with uterine prolapse 618.4
      complete 618.3
      incomplete 618.2
  male 599.5
Urethrolithiasis 594.2
Urethro-oculoarticular syndrome 099.3
Urethro-oculosynovial syndrome 099.3
Urethrorectal - see condition
Urethrorrhagia 599.84
Urethrorrhea 788.7
Urethrostomy status V44.6
  with complication 997.5
Urethrotrigonitis 595.3
Urethrovaginal - see condition
Urhidrosis, uridrosis 705.89
Uric acid
  diathesis 274.9
  in blood 790.6
Uricacidemia 790.6
Uricemia 790.6
Uricosuria 791.9
Urination
  frequent 788.41
  painful 788.1
Urine, urinary - see also condition
  abnormality NEC 788.69
  blood in (see also Hematuria) 599.7
  discharge, excessive 788.42
  enuresis 788.30
    nonorganic origin 307.6
  extravasation 788.8
  frequency 788.41
  incontinence 788.30
    active 788.30
    female 788.30
      stress 625.6
        and urge 788.33
    male 788.30
      stress 788.32
        and urge 788.33
    mixed (stress and urge) 788.33
    neurogenic 788.39
    nonorganic origin 307.6
    stress (female) 625.6
      male NEC 788.32
  intermittent stream 788.61
  pus in 599.0

Urine, urinary (Continued)
  retention or stasis NEC 788.20
    bladder, incomplete emptying 788.21
    psychogenic 306.53
    specified NEC 788.29
  secretion
    deficient 788.5
    excessive 788.42
    frequency 788.41
  stream
    intermittent 788.61
    slowing 788.62
    splitting 788.61
    weak 788.62
Urinemia - see Uremia
Urinoma NEC 599.9
  bladder 596.8
  kidney 593.89
  renal 593.89
  ureter 593.89
  urethra 599.84
Uroarthritis, infectious 099.3
Urodialysis 788.5
Urolithiasis 592.9
Uronephrosis 593.89
Uropathy 599.9
  obstructive 599.6
Urosepsis 599.0
Urticaria 708.9
  with angioneurotic edema 995.1
    hereditary 277.6
  allergic 708.0
  cholinergic 708.5
  chronic 708.8
  cold, familial 708.2
  dermatographic 708.3
  due to
    cold or heat 708.2
    drugs 708.0
    food 708.0
    inhalants 708.0
    plants 708.8
    serum 999.5
  factitial 708.3
  giant 995.1
    hereditary 277.6
  gigantea 995.1
    hereditary 277.6
  idiopathic 708.1
  larynx 995.1
    hereditary 277.6
  neonatorum 778.8
  nonallergic 708.1
  papulosa (Hebra) 698.2
  perstans hemorrhagica 757.39
  pigmentosa 757.33
  recurrent periodic 708.8
  serum 999.5
  solare 692.72
  specified type NEC 708.8
  thermal (cold) (heat) 708.2
  vibratory 708.4
Urticarioides acarodermatitis 133.9
Use of
  nonprescribed drugs (see also Abuse, drugs, nondependent) 305.9
  patent medicines (see also Abuse, drugs, nondependent) 305.9
Usher-Senear disease (pemphigus erythematosus) 694.4
Uta 085.5
Uterine size-date discrepancy 655.8
Uteromegaly 621.2
Uterovaginal - see condition

ICD-9-CM

Vol. 2

Uterovesical - *see* condition
Uterus - *see* condition
Utriculitis (utriculus prostaticus) 597.89
Uveal - *see* condition
Uveitis (anterior) (*see also* Iridocyclitis)
   364.3
   acute or subacute 364.00
      due to or associated with
         gonococcal infection 098.41
         herpes (simplex) 054.44
            zoster 053.22
      primary 364.01
      recurrent 364.02
      secondary (noninfectious) 364.04
         infectious 364.03
   allergic 360.11
   chronic 364.10
      due to or associated with

Uveitis *(Continued)*
   chronic *(Continued)*
      due to or associated with *(Continued)*
         sarcoidosis 135 *[364.11]*
         tuberculosis (*see also* Tuberculosis)
            017.3 *[364.11]*
   due to
      operation 360.11
      toxoplasmosis (acquired) 130.2
         congenital (active) 771.2
   granulomatous 364.10
   heterochromic 364.21
   lens-induced 364.23
   nongranulomatous 364.00
   posterior 363.20
      disseminated - *see* Chorioretinitis,
         disseminated
      focal - *see* Chorioretinitis, focal

Uveitis *(Continued)*
   recurrent 364.02
   sympathetic 360.11
   syphilitic (secondary) 091.50
      congenital 090.0 *[363.13]*
      late 095.8 *[363.13]*
   tuberculous (*see also* Tuberculosis)
      017.3 *[364.11]*
Uveoencephalitis 363.22
Uveokeratitis (*see also* Iridocyclitis) 364.3
Uveoparotid fever 135
Uveoparotitis 135
Uvula - *see* condition
Uvulitis (acute) (catarrhal) (chronic)
      (gangrenous) (membranous) (suppu-
      rative) (ulcerative) 528.3

V

Vaccination
complication or reaction - *see* Complications, vaccination
not done (contraindicated) V64.0
 because of patient's decision V64.2
prophylactic (against) V05.9
 arthropod-borne viral
  disease NEC V05.1
  encephalitis V05.0
 chicken pox V05.4
 cholera (alone) V03.0
  with typhoid-paratyphoid (cholera TAB) V06.0
 common cold V04.7
 diphtheria (alone) V03.5
  with
   poliomyelitis (DTP polio) V06.3
   tetanus V06.5
    pertussis combined [DTP] V06.1
    typhoid-paratyphoid (DTP TAB) V06.2
 disease (single) NEC V05.9
  bacterial NEC V03.9
   specified type NEC V03.89
  combination NEC V06.9
   specified type NEC V06.8
  specified type NEC V05.8
 encephalitis, viral, arthropod-borne V05.0
 Haemophilus influenzae, type B [Hib] V03.81
 hepatitis, viral V05.3
 influenza V04.8
  with
   Streptococcus pneumoniae [pneumococcus] V06.6
 leishmaniasis V05.2
 measles (alone) V04.2
  with mumps-rubella (MMR) V06.4
 mumps (alone) V04.6
  with measles and rubella (MMR) V06.4
 pertussis alone V03.6
 plague V03.3
 poliomyelitis V04.0
  with diphtheria-tetanus-pertussis (DTP + polio) V06.3
 rabies V04.5
 rubella (alone) V04.3
  with measles and mumps (MMR) V06.4
 smallpox V04.1
 Streptococcus pneumoniae [pneumococcus] V03.82
  with
   influenza V06.6
 tetanus toxoid (alone) V03.7
  with diphtheria [Td] V06.5
   with
    pertussis (DTP) V06.1
     with poliomyelitis (DTP + polio) V06.3
 tuberculosis (BCG) V03.2
 tularemia V03.4
 typhoid-paratyphoid (TAB) (alone) V03.1
  with diphtheria-tetanus-pertussis (TAB DTP) V06.2
 varicella V05.4

Vaccination *(Continued)*
 prophylactic *(Continued)*
  viral
   encephalitis, arthropod-borne V05.0
   hepatitis V05.3
  yellow fever V04.4
Vaccinia (generalized) 999.0
 congenital 771.2
 conjunctiva 999.3
 eyelids 999.0 *[373.5]*
 localized 999.3
 nose 999.3
 not from vaccination 051.0
  eyelid 051.0 *[373.5]*
 sine vaccinatione 051.0
 without vaccination 051.0
Vacuum
 extraction of fetus or newborn 763.3
 in sinus (accessory) (nasal) (*see also* Sinusitis) 473.9
Vagabond V60.0
Vagabondage V60.0
Vagabonds' disease 132.1
Vagina, vaginal - *see* condition
Vaginalitis (tunica) 608.4
Vaginismus (reflex) 625.1
 functional 306.51
 hysterical 300.11
 psychogenic 306.51
Vaginitis (acute) (chronic) (circumscribed) (diffuse) (emphysematous) (Haemophilus vaginalis) (nonspecific) (nonvenereal) (ulcerative) 616.10
 with
  abortion - *see* Abortion, by type, with sepsis
  ectopic pregnancy (*see also* categories 633.0-633.9) 639.0
  molar pregnancy (*see also* categories 630-632) 639.0
 adhesive, congenital 752.49
 atrophic, postmenopausal 627.3
 bacterial 616.10
 blennorrhagic (acute) 098.0
  chronic or duration of 2 months or over 098.2
 candidal 112.1
 chlamydial 099.53
 complicating pregnancy or puerperium 646.6
  affecting fetus or newborn 760.8
 congenital (adhesive) 752.49
 due to
  C. albicans 112.1
  Trichomonas (vaginalis) 131.01
 following
  abortion 639.0
  ectopic or molar pregnancy 639.0
 gonococcal (acute) 098.0
  chronic or duration of 2 months or over 098.2
 granuloma 099.2
 Monilia 112.1
 mycotic 112.1
 pinworm 127.4 *[616.11]*
 postirradiation 616.10
 postmenopausal atrophic 627.3
 senile (atrophic) 627.3
 syphilitic (early) 091.0
  late 095.8
 trichomonal 131.01
 tuberculous (*see also* Tuberculosis) 016.7
 venereal NEC 099.8

Vaginosis - *see* Vaginitis
Vagotonia 352.3
Vagrancy V60.0
Vallecula - *see* condition
Valley fever 114.0
Valsuani's disease (progressive pernicious anemia, puerperal) 648.2
Valve, valvular (formation) - *see also* condition
 cerebral ventricle (communicating) in situ V45.2
 cervix, internal os 752.49
 colon 751.5
 congenital NEC - *see* Atresia
 formation, congenital, NEC - *see* Atresia
 heart defect - *see* Anomaly, heart, valve
 ureter 753.29
  pelvic junction 753.21
  vesical orifice 753.22
 urethra 753.6
Valvulitis (chronic) (*see also* Endocarditis) 424.90
 rheumatic (chronic) (inactive) (with chorea) 397.9
  active or acute (aortic) (mitral) (pulmonary) (tricuspid) 391.1
 syphilitic NEC 093.20
  aortic 093.22
  mitral 093.21
  pulmonary 093.24
  tricuspid 093.23
Valvulopathy - *see* Endocarditis
Van Bogaert's leukoencephalitis (sclerosing) (subacute) 046.2
Van Bogaert-Nijssen (-Peiffer) disease 330.0
Van Buchem's syndrome (hyperostosis corticalis) 733.3
Van Creveld-von Gierke disease (glycogenosis I) 271.0
Van den Bergh's disease (enterogenous cyanosis) 289.7
Van der Hoeve's syndrome (brittle bones and blue sclera, deafness) 756.51
Van der Hoeve-Halbertsma-Waardenburg syndrome (ptosis-epicanthus) 270.2
Van der Hoeve-Waardenburg-Gualdi syndrome (ptosis-epicanthus) 270.2
van Neck (-Odelberg) disease or syndrome (juvenile osteochondrosis) 732.1
Vanillism 692.89
Vanishing lung 492.0
Vanishing twin 651.33
Vapor asphyxia or suffocation NEC 987.9
 specified agent - *see* Table of Drugs and Chemicals
Vaquez's disease (M9950/1) 238.4
Vaquez-Osler disease (polycythemia vera) (M9950/1) 238.4
Variance, lethal ball, prosthetic heart valve 996.02
Variants, thalassemic 282.4
Variations in hair color 704.3
Varicella 052.9
 with
  complication 052.8
   specified NEC 052.7
  pneumonia 052.1
 vaccination and inoculation (against) (prophylactic) V05.4

◀ ▶   **New Code**   ⬅||||||⇒   **Revised Code**

Vegetation, vegetative
  adenoid (nasal fossa) 474.2
  consciousness (persistent) 780.03
  endocarditis (acute) (any valve)
    (chronic) (subacute) 421.0
  heart (mycotic) (valve) 421.0
  state (persistent) 780.03
Veil
  Jackson's 751.4
  over face (causing asphyxia) 768.9
Vein, venous - *see* condition
Veldt sore (*see also* Ulcer, skin) 707.9
Velpeau's hernia - *see* Hernia, femoral
Venereal
  balanitis NEC 099.8
  bubo 099.1
  disease 099.9
    specified nature or type NEC
      099.8
  granuloma inguinale 099.2
  lymphogranuloma (Durand-Nicolas-
    Favre), any site 099.1
  salpingitis 098.37
  urethritis (*see also* Urethritis, nongono-
    coccal) 099.40
  vaginitis NEC 099.8
  warts 078.19
Vengefulness, in child (*see also* Disturbance, conduct) 312.0
Venofibrosis 459.89
Venom, venomous
  bite or sting (animal or insect) 989.5
  poisoning 989.5
Venous - *see* condition
Ventouse delivery NEC 669.5
  affecting fetus or newborn 763.3
Ventral - *see* condition
Ventricle, ventricular - *see also* condition
  escape 427.69
  standstill (*see also* Arrest, cardiac)
    427.5
Ventriculitis, cerebral (*see also* Meningitis) 322.9
Ventriculostomy status V45.2
Verbiest's syndrome (claudicatio intermittens spinalis) 435.1
Vernet's syndrome 352.6
Verneuil's disease (syphilitic bursitis)
  095.7
Verruca (filiformis) 078.10
  acuminata (any site) 078.11
  necrogenica (primary) (*see also* Tuber-
    culosis) 017.0
  peruana 088.0
  peruviana 088.0
  plana (juvenilis) 078.19
  plantaris 078.19
  seborrheica 702.19
    inflamed 702.11
  senilis 702.0
  tuberculosa (primary) (*see also* Tuber-
    culosis) 017.0
  venereal 078.19
  viral NEC 078.10
Verrucosities (*see also* Verruca) 078.10
Verrucous endocarditis (acute) (any
  valve) (chronic) (subacute) 710.0
  [424.91]
  nonbacterial 710.0 *[424.91]*
Verruga
  peruana 088.0
  peruviana 088.0
Verse's disease (calcinosis intervertebralis) 275.49 *[722.90]*

Version
  before labor, affecting fetus or new-
    born 761.7
  cephalic (correcting previous malposi-
    tion) 652.1
    affecting fetus or newborn 763.1
  cervix (*see also* Malposition, uterus) 621.6
  uterus (postinfectional) (postpartal, old)
    (*see also* Malposition, uterus) 621.6
    forward - *see* Anteversion, uterus
    lateral - *see* Lateroversion, uterus
Vertebra, vertebral - *see* condition
Vertigo 780.4
  auditory 386.19
  aural 386.19
  benign paroxysmal positional 386.11
  central origin 386.2
  cerebral 386.2
  Dix and Hallpike (epidemic) 386.12
  endemic paralytic 078.81
  epidemic 078.81
    Dix and Hallpike 386.12
    Gerlier's 078.81
    Pedersen's 386.12
    vestibular neuronitis 386.12
  epileptic - *see* Epilepsy
  Gerlier's (epidemic) 078.81
  hysterical 300.11
  labyrinthine 386.10
  laryngeal 786.2
  malignant positional 386.2
  Ménière's (*see also* Disease, Meniere's)
    386.00
  menopausal 627.2
  otogenic 386.19
  paralytic 078.81
  paroxysmal positional, benign 386.11
  Pedersen's (epidemic) 386.12
  peripheral 386.10
    specified type NEC 386.19
  positional
    benign paroxysmal 386.11
    malignant 386.2
Verumontanitis (chronic) (*see also* Urethritis) 597.89
Vesania (*see also* Psychosis) 298.9
Vesical - *see* condition
Vesicle
  cutaneous 709.8
  seminal - *see* condition
  skin 709.8
Vesicocolic - *see* condition
Vesicoperineal - *see* condition
Vesicorectal - *see* condition
Vesicourethrorectal - *see* condition
Vesicovaginal - *see* condition
Vesicular - *see* condition
Vesiculitis (seminal) 608.0
  amebic 006.8
  gonorrheal (acute) 098.14
    chronic or duration of 2 months or
      over 098.34
  trichomonal 131.09
  tuberculous (*see also* Tuberculosis)
    016.5 *[608.81]*
Vestibulitis (ear) (*see also* Labyrinthitis)
  386.30
  nose (external) 478.1
  vulvar 616.10
Vestibulopathy, acute peripheral (recurrent) 386.12
Vestige, vestigial - *see also* Persistence
  branchial 744.41
  structures in vitreous 743.51

Vibriosis NEC 027.9
Vidal's disease (lichen simplex chronicus) 698.3
Video display tube syndrome 723.8
Vienna-type encephalitis 049.8
Villaret's syndrome 352.6
Villous - *see* condition
Vincent's
  angina 101
  bronchitis 101
  disease 101
  gingivitis 101
  infection (any site) 101
  laryngitis 101
  stomatitis 101
  tonsillitis 101
Vinson-Plummer syndrome (sideropenic
  dysphagia) 280.8
Viosterol deficiency (*see also* Deficiency,
  calciferol) 268.9
Virchow's disease 733.99
Viremia 790.8
Virilism (adrenal) (female) NEC 255.2
  with
    3-beta-hydroxysteroid dehydrogenase
      defect 255.2
    11-hydroxylase defect 255.2
    21-hydroxylase defect 255.2
  adrenal
    hyperplasia 255.2
    insufficiency (congenital) 255.2
  cortical hyperfunction 255.2
Virilization (female) (suprarenal) (*see
  also* Virilism) 255.2
  isosexual 256.4
Virulent bubo 099.0
Virus, viral - *see also* condition
  infection NEC (*see also* Infection, viral)
    079.99
  septicemia 079.99
Viscera, visceral - *see* condition
Visceroptosis 569.89
Visible peristalsis 787.4
Vision, visual
  binocular, suppression 368.31
  blurred, blurring 368.8
    hysterical 300.11
  defect, defective (*see also* Impaired, vi-
    sion) 369.9
  disorientation (syndrome) 368.16
  disturbance NEC (*see also* Disturbance,
    vision) 368.9
    hysterical 300.11
  examination V72.0
  field, limitation 368.40
  fusion, with defective stereopsis 368.33
  hallucinations 368.16
  halos 368.16
  loss 369.9
    both eyes (*see also* Blindness, both
      eyes) 369.3
    complete (*see also* Blindness, both
      eyes) 369.00
    one eye 369.8
    sudden 368.16
  low (both eyes) 369.20
    one eye (other eye normal) (*see also*
      Impaired, vision) 369.70
      blindness, other eye 369.10
  perception, simultaneous without fu-
    sion 368.32
  tunnel 368.45
Vitality, lack or want of 780.79 
  newborn 779.8

Vitamin deficiency NEC (*see also* Deficiency, vitamin) 269.2
Vitelline duct, persistent 751.0
Vitiligo 709.01
  due to pinta (carate) 103.2
  eyelid 374.53
  vulva 624.8
Vitium cordis - *see* Disease, heart
Vitreous - *see also* condition
  touch syndrome 997.99
Vocal cord - *see* condition
Vocational rehabilitation V57.22
Vogt's (Cecile) disease or syndrome 333.7
Vogt-Koyanagi syndrome 364.24
Vogt-Spielmeyer disease (amaurotic familial idiocy) 330.1
Voice
  change (*see also* Dysphonia) 784.49
  loss (*see also* Aphonia) 784.41
Volhard-Fahr disease (malignant nephrosclerosis) 403.00
Volhynian fever 083.1
Volkmann's ischemic contracture or paralysis (complicating trauma) 958.6
Voluntary starvation 307.1
Volvulus (bowel) (colon) (intestine) 560.2
  with
    hernia - *see also* Hernia, by site, with obstruction
      gangrenous - *see* Hernia, by site, with gangrene
    perforation 560.2
  congenital 751.5
  duodenum 537.3
  fallopian tube 620.5
  oviduct 620.5
  stomach (due to absence of gastrocolic ligament) 537.89
Vomiting 787.03
  with nausea 787.01
  allergic 535.4
  asphyxia 933.1
  bilious (cause unknown) 787.0
    following gastrointestinal surgery 564.3
  blood (*see also* Hematemesis) 578.0
  causing asphyxia, choking, or suffocation (*see also* Asphyxia, food) 933.1
  cyclical 536.2
    psychogenic 306.4
  epidemic 078.82
  fecal matter 569.89
  following gastrointestinal surgery 564.3
  functional 536.8
    psychogenic 306.4

Vomiting (*Continued*)
  habit 536.2
  hysterical 300.11
  nervous 306.4
  neurotic 306.4
  newborn 779.3
  of or complicating pregnancy 643.9
    due to
      organic disease 643.8
        specific cause NEC 643.8
    early - *see* Hyperemesis, gravidarum
    late (after 22 completed weeks of gestation) 643.2
  pernicious or persistent 536.2
    complicating pregnancy - *see* Hyperemesis, gravidarum
  psychogenic 306.4
  physiological 787.0
  psychic 306.4
  psychogenic 307.54
  stercoral 569.89
  uncontrollable 536.2
    psychogenic 306.4
  uremic - *see* Uremia
  winter 078.82
von Bechterew (-Strümpell) disease or syndrome (ankylosing spondylitis) 720.0
von Bezold's abscess 383.01
von Economo's disease (encephalitis lethargica) 049.8
von Eulenburg's disease (congenital paramyotonia) 359.2
von Gierke's disease (glycogenosis I) 271.0
von Gies' joint 095.8
von Graefe's disease or syndrome 378.72
von Hippel (-Lindau) disease or syndrome (retinocerebral angiomatosis) 759.6
von Jaksch's anemia or disease (pseudoleukemia infantum) 285.8
von Recklinghausen's
  disease or syndrome (nerves) (skin) (M9540/1) 237.71
    bones (osteitis fibrosa cystica) 252.0
  tumor (M9540/1) 237.71
von Recklinghausen-Applebaum disease (hemochromatosis) 275.0
von Schroetter's syndrome (intermittent venous claudication) 453.8
von Willebrand (-Jürgens) (-Minot) disease or syndrome (angiohemophilia) 286.4

von Zambusch's disease (lichen sclerosus et atrophicus) 701.0
Voorhoeve's disease or dyschondroplasia 756.4
Vossius' ring 921.3
  late effect 366.21
Voyeurism 302.82
Vrolik's disease (osteogenesis imperfecta) 756.51
Vulva - *see* condition
Vulvismus 625.1
Vulvitis (acute) (allergic) (aphthous) (chronic) (gangrenous) (hypertrophic) (intertriginous) 616.10
  with
    abortion - *see* Abortion, by type, with sepsis
    ectopic pregnancy (*see also* categories 633.0-633.9) 639.0
    molar pregnancy (*see also* categories 630-632) 639.0
  adhesive, congenital 752.49
  blennorrhagic (acute) 098.0
    chronic or duration of 2 months or over 098.2
  chlamydial 099.53
  complicating pregnancy or puerperium 646.6
  due to Ducrey's bacillus 099.0
  following
    abortion 639.0
    ectopic or molar pregnancy 639.0
  gonococcal (acute) 098.0
    chronic or duration of 2 months or over 098.2
  herpetic 054.11
  leukoplakic 624.0
  monilial 112.1
  puerperal, postpartum, childbirth 646.6
  syphilitic (early) 091.0
    late 095.8
  trichomonal 131.01
Vulvodynia 625.9
Vulvorectal - *see* condition
Vulvovaginitis (*see also* Vulvitis) 616.10
  amebic 006.8
  chlamydial 099.53
  gonococcal (acute) 098.0
    chronic or duration of 2 months or over 098.2
  herpetic 054.11
  monilial 112.1
  trichomonal (Trichomonas vaginalis) 131.01

W

Waardenburg's syndrome 756.89
  meaning ptosis-epicanthus 270.2
Waardenburg-Klein syndrome (ptosis-epicanthus) 270.2
Wagner's disease (colloid milium) 709.3
Wagner (-Unverricht) syndrome (dermatomyositis) 710.3
Waiting list, person on V63.2
  undergoing social agency investigation V63.8
Wakefulness disorder (see also Hypersomnia) 780.54
  nonorganic origin 307.43
Waldenström's
  disease (osteochondrosis, capital femoral) 732.1
  hepatitis (lupoid hepatitis) 571.49
  hypergammaglobulinemia 273.0
  macroglobulinemia 273.3
  purpura, hypergammaglobulinemic 273.0
  syndrome (macroglobulinemia) 273.3
Waldenström-Kjellberg syndrome (sideropenic dysphagia) 280.8
Walking
  difficulty 719.7
    psychogenic 307.9
  sleep 307.46
    hysterical 300.13
Wall, abdominal - see condition
Wallenberg's syndrome (posterior inferior cerebellar artery) (see also Disease, cerebrovascular, acute) 436
Wallgren's
  disease (obstruction of splenic vein with collateral circulation) 459.89
  meningitis (see also Meningitis, aseptic) 047.9
Wandering
  acetabulum 736.39
  gallbladder 751.69
  kidney, congenital 753.3
  organ or site, congenital NEC - see Malposition, congenital
  pacemaker (atrial) (heart) 427.89
  spleen 289.59
Wardrop's disease (with lymphangitis) 681.9
  finger 681.02
  toe 681.11
War neurosis 300.16
Wart (common) (digitate) (filiform) (infectious) (viral) 078.10
  external genital organs (venereal) 078.19
  fig 078.19
  Hassall-Henle's (of cornea) 371.41
  Henle's (of cornea) 371.41
  juvenile 078.19
  moist 078.10
  Peruvian 088.0
  plantar 078.19
  prosector (see also Tuberculosis) 017.0
  seborrheic 702.19
    inflamed 702.11
  senile 702.0
  specified NEC 078.19
  syphilitic 091.3
  tuberculous (see also Tuberculosis) 017.0
  venereal (female) (male) 078.19
Warthin's tumor (salivary gland) (M8561/0) 210.2
Washerwoman's itch 692.4

Wassilieff's disease (leptospiral jaundice) 100.0
Wasting
  disease 799.4
    due to malnutrition 261
  extreme (due to malnutrition) 261
  muscular NEC 728.2
  palsy, paralysis 335.21
Water
  clefts 366.12
  deprivation of 994.3
  in joint (see also Effusion, joint) 719.0
  intoxication 276.6
  itch 120.3
  lack of 994.3
  loading 276.6
  on
    brain - see Hydrocephalus
    chest 511.8
  poisoning 276.6
Waterbrash 787.1
Water-hammer pulse (see also Insufficiency, aortic) 424.1
Waterhouse (-Friderichsen) disease or syndrome 036.3
Water-losing nephritis 588.8
Wax in ear 380.4
Waxy
  degeneration, any site 277.3
  disease 277.3
  kidney 277.3 [583.81]
  liver (large) 277.3
  spleen 277.3
Weak, weakness (generalized) 780.79
  arches (acquired) 734
    congenital 754.61
  bladder sphincter 596.59
  congenital 779.8
  eye muscle - see Strabismus
  foot (double) - see Weak, arches
  heart, cardiac (see also Failure, heart) 428.9
    congenital 746.9
  mind 317
  muscle 728.9
  myocardium (see also Failure, heart) 428.9
  newborn 779.8
  pelvic fundus 618.8
  pulse 785.9
  senile 797
  urinary stream 788.62
  valvular - see Endocarditis
Wear, worn, tooth, teeth (approximal) (hard tissues) (interproximal) (occlusal) 521.1
Weather, weathered
  effects of
    cold NEC 991.9
      specified effect NEC 991.8
    hot (see also Heat) 992.9
  skin 692.74
Web, webbed (congenital) - see also Anomaly, specified type NEC
  canthus 743.63
  digits (see also Syndactylism) 755.10
  esophagus 750.3
  fingers (see also Syndactylism, fingers) 755.11
  larynx (glottic) (subglottic) 748.2
  neck (pterygium colli) 744.5
  Paterson-Kelly (sideropenic dysphagia) 280.8

Web, webbed (Continued)
  popliteal syndrome 756.89
  toes (see also Syndactylism, toes) 755.13
Weber's paralysis or syndrome 344.89
Weber-Christian disease or syndrome (nodular nonsuppurative panniculitis) 729.30
Weber-Cockayne syndrome (epidermolysis bullosa) 757.39
Weber-Dimitri syndrome 759.6
Weber-Gubler syndrome 344.89
Weber-Leyden syndrome 344.89
Weber-Osler syndrome (familial hemorrhagic telangiectasia) 448.0
Wedge-shaped or wedging vertebra (see also Osteoporosis) 733.00
Wegener's granulomatosis or syndrome 446.4
Wegner's disease (syphilitic osteochondritis) 090.0
Weight
  gain (abnormal) (excessive) 783.1
    during pregnancy 646.1
      insufficient 646.8
  less than 1000 grams at birth 765.0
  loss (cause unknown) 783.2
Weightlessness 994.9
Weil's disease (leptospiral jaundice) 100.0
Weill-Marchesani syndrome (brachymorphism and ectopia lentis) 759.89
Weingarten's syndrome (tropical eosinophilia) 518.3
Weir Mitchell's disease (erythromelalgia) 443.89
Weiss-Baker syndrome (carotid sinus syncope) 337.0
Weissenbach-Thibierge syndrome (cutaneous systemic sclerosis) 710.1
Wen (see also Cyst, sebaceous) 706.2
Wenckebach's phenomenon, heart block (second degree) 426.13
Werdnig-Hoffmann syndrome (muscular atrophy) 335.0
Werlhof's disease (see also Purpura, thrombocytopenic) 287.3
Werlhof-Wichmann syndrome (see also Purpura, thrombocytopenic) 287.3
Wermer's syndrome or disease (polyendocrine adenomatosis) 258.0
Werner's disease or syndrome (progeria adultorum) 259.8
Werner-His disease (trench fever) 083.1
Werner-Schultz disease (agranulocytosis) 288.0
Wernicke's encephalopathy, disease, or syndrome (superior hemorrhagic polioencephalitis) 265.1
Wernicke-Korsakoff syndrome or psychosis (nonalcoholic) 294.0
  alcoholic 291.1
Wernicke-Posadas disease (see also Coccidioidomycosis) 114.9
Wesselsbron fever 066.3
West African fever 084.8
West Nile fever 066.3
Westphal-Strümpell syndrome (hepatolenticular degeneration) 275.1
Wet
  brain (alcoholic) (see also Alcoholism) 303.9

Wet (*Continued*)
  feet, tropical (syndrome) (maceration) 991.4
  lung (syndrome)
    adult 518.5
    newborn 770.6
Wharton's duct - *see* condition
Wheal 709.8
Wheezing 786.07
Whiplash injury or syndrome 847.0
Whipple's disease or syndrome (intestinal lipodystrophy) 040.2
Whipworm 127.3
"Whistling face" syndrome (craniocarpotarsal dystrophy) 759.89
White - *see also* condition
  kidney
    large - *see* Nephrosis
    small 582.9
  leg, puerperal, postpartum, childbirth 671.4
    nonpuerperal 451.19
  mouth 112.0
  patches of mouth 528.6
  sponge nevus of oral mucosa 750.26
  spot lesions, teeth 521.0
White's disease (congenital) (keratosis follicularis) 757.39
Whitehead 706.2
Whitlow (with lymphangitis) 681.01
  herpetic 054.6
Whitmore's disease or fever (melioidosis) 025
Whooping cough 033.9
  with pneumonia 033.9 *[484.3]*
  due to
    Bordetella
      bronchoseptica 033.8
        with pneumonia 033.8 *[484.3]*
      parapertussis 033.1
        with pneumonia 033.1 *[484.3]*
      pertussis 033.0
        with pneumonia 033.0 *[484.3]*
    specified organism NEC 033.8
      with pneumonia 033.8 *[484.3]*
  vaccination, prophylactic (against) V03.6
Wichmann's asthma (laryngismus stridulus) 478.75
Widal (-Abrami) syndrome (acquired hemolytic jaundice) 283.9
Widening aorta (*see also* Aneurysm, aorta) 441.9
  ruptured 441.5
Wilkie's disease or syndrome 557.1
Wilkinson-Sneddon disease or syndrome (subcorneal pustular dermatosis) 694.1
Willan's lepra 696.1
Willan-Plumbe syndrome (psoriasis) 696.1
Willebrand (-Jürgens) syndrome or thrombopathy (angiohemophilia) 286.4
Willi-Prader syndrome (hypogenital dystrophy with diabetic tendency) 759.81
Willis' disease (diabetes mellitus) (*see also* Diabetes) 250.0
Wilms' tumor or neoplasm (nephroblastoma) (M8960/3) 189.0
Wilson's
  disease or syndrome (hepatolenticular degeneration) 275.1
  hepatolenticular degeneration 275.1
  lichen ruber 697.0

Wilson-Brocq disease (dermatitis exfoliativa) 695.89
Wilson-Mikity syndrome 770.7
Window - *see also* Imperfect, closure aorticopulmonary 745.0
Winged scapula 736.89
Winter - *see also* condition
  vomiting disease 078.82
Wise's disease 696.2
Wiskott-Aldrich syndrome (eczema-thrombocytopenia) 279.12
Withdrawal symptoms, syndrome
  alcohol 291.81
    delirium (acute) 291.0
      chronic 291.1
      newborn 760.71
  drug or narcotic 292.0
  newborn, infant of dependent mother 779.5
  steroid NEC
    correct substance properly administered 255.4
    overdose or wrong substance given or taken 962.0
Withdrawing reaction, child or adolescent 313.22
Witts' anemia (achlorhydric anemia) 280.9
Witzelsucht 301.9
Woakes' syndrome (ethmoiditis) 471.1
Wohlfart-Kugelberg-Welander disease 335.11
Woillez's disease (acute idiopathic pulmonary congestion) 518.5
Wolff-Parkinson-White syndrome (anomalous atrioventricular excitation) 426.7
Wolhynian fever 083.1
Wolman's disease (primary familial xanthomatosis) 272.7
Wood asthma 495.8
Woolly, wooly hair (congenital) (nevus) 757.4
Wool-sorters' disease 022.1
Word
  blindness (congenital) (developmental) 315.01
    secondary to organic lesion 784.61
  deafness (secondary to organic lesion) 784.69
  developmental 315.31
Worm(s) (colic) (fever) (infection) (infestation) (*see also* Infestation) 128.9
  guinea 125.7
  in intestine NEC 127.9
Worm-eaten soles 102.3
Worn out (*see also* Exhaustion) 780.79
"Worried well" V65.5
Wound, open (by cutting or piercing instrument) (by firearms) (cut) (dissection) (incised) (laceration) (penetration) (perforating) (puncture) (with initial hemorrhage, not internal) 879.8

Note For fracture with open wound, see Fracture.

For laceration, traumatic rupture, tear, or penetrating wound of internal organs, such as heart, lung, liver, kidney, pelvic organs, etc., whether or not accompanied by open wound or fracture in the same region, see Injury, internal.

Wound, open (*Continued*)

For contused wound, see Contusion. For crush injury, see Crush. For abrasion, insect bite (nonvenomous), blister, or scratch, see Injury, superficial.

Complicated includes wounds with:
  delayed healing
  delayed treatment
  foreign body
  primary infection

For late effect of open wound, see Late, effect, wound, open, by site.

---

  abdomen, abdominal (external) (muscle) 879.2
    complicated 879.3
    wall (anterior) 879.2
      complicated 879.3
      lateral 879.4
        complicated 879.5
  alveolar (process) 873.62
    complicated 873.72
  ankle 891.0
    with tendon involvement 891.2
    complicated 891.1
  anterior chamber, eye (*see also* Wound, open, intraocular) 871.9
  anus 879.6
    complicated 879.7
  arm 884.0
    with tendon involvement 884.2
    complicated 884.1
    forearm 881.00
      with tendon involvement 881.20
      complicated 881.10
    multiple sites - *see* Wound, open, multiple, upper limb
    upper 880.03
      with tendon involvement 880.23
      complicated 880.13
      multiple sites (with axillary or shoulder regions) 880.09
        with tendon involvement 880.29
        complicated 880.19
  artery - *see* Injury, blood vessel, by site
  auditory
    canal (external) (meatus) 872.02
      complicated 872.12
    ossicles (incus) (malleus) (stapes) 872.62
      complicated 872.72
  auricle, ear 872.01
    complicated 872.11
  axilla 880.02
    with tendon involvement 880.22
    complicated 880.12
      with tendon involvement 880.29
    involving other sites of upper arm 880.09
      complicated 880.19
  back 876.0
    complicated 876.1
  bladder - *see* Injury, internal, bladder
  blood vessel - *see* Injury, blood vessel, by site
  brain - *see* Injury, intracranial, with open intracranial wound
  breast 879.0
    complicated 879.1
  brow 873.42
    complicated 873.52
  buccal mucosa 873.61
    complicated 873.71

Wound, open (*Continued*)
- buttock 877.0
  - complicated 877.1
- calf 891.0
  - with tendon involvement 891.2
  - complicated 891.1
- canaliculus lacrimalis 870.8
  - with laceration of eyelid 870.2
- canthus, eye 870.8
  - laceration - *see* Laceration, eyelid
- cavernous sinus - *see* Injury, intracranial
- cerebellum - *see* Injury, intracranial
- cervical esophagus 874.4
  - complicated 874.5
- cervix - *see* Injury, internal, cervix
- cheek(s) (external) 873.41
  - complicated 873.51
  - internal 873.61
    - complicated 873.71
- chest (wall) (external) 875.0
  - complicated 875.1
- chin 873.44
  - complicated 873.54
- choroid 363.63
- ciliary body (eye) (*see also* Wound, open, intraocular) 871.9
- clitoris 878.8
  - complicated 878.9
- cochlea 872.64
  - complicated 872.74
- complicated 879.9
- conjunctiva - *see* Wound, open, intraocular
- cornea (nonpenetrating) (*see also* Wound, open, intraocular) 871.9
- costal region 875.0
  - complicated 875.1
- Descemet's membrane (*see also* Wound, open, intraocular) 871.9
- digit(s)
  - foot 893.0
    - with tendon involvement 893.2
    - complicated 893.1
  - hand 883.0
    - with tendon involvement 883.2
    - complicated 883.1
- drumhead, ear 872.61
  - complicated 872.71
- ear 872.8
  - canal 872.02
    - complicated 872.12
  - complicated 872.9
  - drum 872.61
    - complicated 872.71
  - external 872.00
    - complicated 872.10
  - multiple sites 872.69
    - complicated 872.79
  - ossicles (incus) (malleus) (stapes) 872.62
    - complicated 872.72
  - specified part NEC 872.69
    - complicated 872.79
- elbow 881.01
  - with tendon involvement 881.21
  - complicated 881.11
- epididymis 878.2
  - complicated 878.3
- epigastric region 879.2
  - complicated 879.3
- epiglottis 874.01
  - complicated 874.11

Wound, open (*Continued*)
- esophagus (cervical) 874.4
  - complicated 874.5
  - thoracic - *see* Injury, internal, esophagus
- Eustachian tube 872.63
  - complicated 872.73
- extremity
  - lower (multiple) NEC 894.0
    - with tendon involvement 894.2
    - complicated 894.1
  - upper (multiple) NEC 884.0
    - with tendon involvement 884.2
    - complicated 884.1
- eye(s) (globe) - *see* Wound, open, intraocular
- eyeball NEC 871.9
  - laceration (*see also* Laceration, eyeball) 871.4
  - penetrating (*see also* Penetrating wound, eyeball) 871.7
- eyebrow 873.42
  - complicated 873.52
- eyelid NEC 870.8
  - laceration - *see* Laceration, eyelid
- face 873.40
  - complicated 873.50
  - multiple sites 873.49
    - complicated 873.59
  - specified part NEC 873.49
    - complicated 873.59
- fallopian tube - *see* Injury, internal, fallopian tube
- finger(s) (nail) (subungual) 883.0
  - with tendon involvement 883.2
  - complicated 883.1
- flank 879.4
  - complicated 879.5
- foot (any part, except toe(s) alone) 892.0
  - with tendon involvement 892.2
  - complicated 892.1
- forearm 881.00
  - with tendon involvement 881.20
  - complicated 881.10
- forehead 873.42
  - complicated 873.52
- genital organs (external) NEC 878.8
  - complicated 878.9
  - internal - *see* Injury, internal, by site
- globe (eye) (*see also* Wound, open, eyeball) 871.9
- groin 879.4
  - complicated 879.5
- gum(s) 873.62
  - complicated 873.72
- hand (except finger(s) alone) 882.0
  - with tendon involvement 882.2
  - complicated 882.1
- head NEC 873.8
  - with intracranial injury - *see* Injury, intracranial
  - due to or associated with skull fracture - *see* Fracture, skull
  - complicated 873.9
  - scalp - *see* Wound, open, scalp
- heel 892.0
  - with tendon involvement 892.2
  - complicated 892.1
- high-velocity (grease gun) - *see* Wound, open, complicated, by site
- hip 890.0
  - with tendon involvement 890.2
  - complicated 890.1

Wound, open (*Continued*)
- hymen 878.6
  - complicated 878.7
- hypochondrium 879.4
  - complicated 879.5
- hypogastric region 879.2
  - complicated 879.3
- iliac (region) 879.4
  - complicated 879.5
- incidental to
  - dislocation - *see* Dislocation, open, by site
  - fracture - *see* Fracture, open, by site
  - intracranial injury - *see* Injury, intracranial, with open intracranial wound
  - nerve injury - *see* Injury, nerve, by site
- inguinal region 879.4
  - complicated 879.5
- instep 892.0
  - with tendon involvement 892.2
  - complicated 892.1
- interscapular region 876.0
  - complicated 876.1
- intracranial - *see* Injury, intracranial, with open intracranial wound
- intraocular 871.9
  - with
    - partial loss (of intraocular tissue) 871.2
    - prolapse or exposure (of intraocular tissue) 871.1
  - laceration (*see also* Laceration, eyeball) 871.4
  - penetrating 871.7
    - with foreign body (nonmagnetic) 871.6
    - magnetic 871.5
  - without prolapse (of intraocular tissue) 871.0
- iris (*see also* Wound, open, eyeball) 871.9
- jaw (fracture not involved) 873.44
  - with fracture - *see* Fracture, jaw
  - complicated 873.54
- knee 891.0
  - with tendon involvement 891.2
  - complicated 891.1
- labium (majus) (minus) 878.4
  - complicated 878.5
- lacrimal apparatus, gland, or sac 870.8
  - with laceration of eyelid 870.2
- larynx 874.01
  - with trachea 874.00
    - complicated 874.10
  - complicated 874.11
- leg (multiple) 891.0
  - with tendon involvement 891.2
  - complicated 891.1
  - lower 891.0
    - with tendon involvement 891.2
    - complicated 891.1
  - thigh 890.0
    - with tendon involvement 890.2
    - complicated 890.1
  - upper 890.0
    - with tendon involvement 890.2
    - complicated 890.1
- lens (eye) (alone) (*see also* Cataract, traumatic) 366.20
  - with involvement of other eye structures - *see* Wound, open, eyeball

Wound, open (*Continued*)
  limb
    lower (multiple) NEC 894.0
      with tendon involvement 894.2
      complicated 894.1
    upper (multiple) NEC 884.0
      with tendon involvement 884.2
      complicated 884.1
  lip 873.43
    complicated 873.53
  loin 876.0
    complicated 876.1
  lumbar region 876.0
    complicated 876.1
  malar region 873.41
    complicated 873.51
  mastoid region 873.49
    complicated 873.59
  mediastinum - *see* Injury, internal, mediastinum
  midthoracic region 875.0
    complicated 875.1
  mouth 873.60
    complicated 873.70
    floor 873.64
      complicated 873.74
    multiple sites 873.69
      complicated 873.79
    specified site NEC 873.69
      complicated 873.79
  multiple, unspecified site(s) 879.8

> Note   Multiple open wounds of sites classifiable to the same four-digit category should be classified to that category unless they are in different limbs.
>
> Multiple open wounds of sites classifiable to different four-digit categories, or to different limbs, should be coded separately.

    complicated 879.9
    lower limb(s) (one or both) (sites classifiable to more than one three-digit category in 890-893) 894.0
      with tendon involvement 894.2
      complicated 894.1
    upper limb(s) (one or both) (sites classifiable to more than one three-digit category in 880-883) 884.0
      with tendon involvement 884.2
      complicated 884.1
  muscle - *see* Sprain, by site
  nail
    finger(s) 883.0
      complicated 883.1
    thumb 883.0
      complicated 883.1
    toe(s) 893.0
      complicated 893.1
  nape (neck) 874.8
    complicated 874.9
    specified part NEC 874.8
      complicated 874.9
  nasal - *see also* Wound, open, nose
    cavity 873.22
      complicated 873.32
    septum 873.21
      complicated 873.31
    sinuses 873.23
      complicated 873.33

Wound, open (*Continued*)
  nasopharynx 873.22
    complicated 873.32
  neck 874.8
    complicated 874.9
    nape 874.8
      complicated 874.9
    specified part NEC 874.8
      complicated 874.9
  nerve - *see* Injury, nerve, by site
  non-healing surgical 998.83
  nose 873.20
    complicated 873.30
    multiple sites 873.29
      complicated 873.39
    septum 873.21
      complicated 873.31
    sinuses 873.23
      complicated 873.33
  occipital region - *see* Wound, open, scalp
  ocular NEC 871.9
    adnexa 870.9
      specified region NEC 870.8
    laceration (*see also* Laceration, ocular) 871.4
    muscle (extraocular) 870.3
      with foreign body 870.4
      eyelid 870.1
      intraocular - *see* Wound, open, eyeball
    penetrating (*see also* Penetrating wound, ocular) 871.7
  orbit 870.8
    penetrating 870.3
      with foreign body 870.4
  orbital region 870.9
  ovary - *see* Injury, internal, pelvic organs
  palate 873.65
    complicated 873.75
  palm 882.0
    with tendon involvement 882.2
    complicated 882.1
  parathyroid (gland) 874.2
    complicated 874.3
  parietal region - *see* Wound, open, scalp
  pelvic floor or region 879.6
    complicated 879.7
  penis 878.0
    complicated 878.1
  perineum 879.6
    complicated 879.7
  periocular area 870.8
    laceration of skin 870.0
  pharynx 874.4
    complicated 874.5
  pinna 872.01
    complicated 872.11
  popliteal space 891.0
    with tendon involvement 891.2
    complicated 891.1
  prepuce 878.0
    complicated 878.1
  pubic region 879.2
    complicated 879.3
  pudenda 878.8
    complicated 878.9
  rectovaginal septum 878.8
    complicated 878.9
  sacral region 877.0
    complicated 877.1
  sacroiliac region 877.0
    complicated 877.1

Wound, open (*Continued*)
  salivary (ducts) (glands) 873.69
    complicated 873.79
  scalp 873.0
    complicated 873.1
  scalpel, fetus or newborn 767.8
  scapular region 880.01
    with tendon involvement 880.21
    complicated 880.11
    involving other sites of upper arm 880.09
      with tendon involvement 880.29
      complicated 880.19
  sclera (*see also* Wound, open, intraocular) 871.9
  scrotum 878.2
    complicated 878.3
  seminal vesicle - *see* Injury, internal, pelvic organs
  shin 891.0
    with tendon involvement 891.2
    complicated 891.1
  shoulder 880.00
    with tendon involvement 880.20
    complicated 880.10
    involving other sites of upper arm 880.09
      with tendon involvement 880.29
      complicated 880.19
  skin NEC 879.8
    complicated 879.9
  skull - *see also* Injury, intracranial, with open intracranial wound
    with skull fracture - *see* Fracture, skull
  spermatic cord (scrotal) 878.2
    complicated 878.3
    pelvic region - *see* Injury, internal, spermatic cord
  spinal cord - *see* Injury, spinal
  sternal region 875.0
    complicated 875.1
  subconjunctival - *see* Wound, open, intraocular
  subcutaneous NEC 879.8
    complicated 879.9
  submaxillary region 873.44
    complicated 873.54
  submental region 873.44
    complicated 873.54
  subungual
    finger(s) (thumb) - *see* Wound, open, finger
    toe(s) - *see* Wound, open, toe
  supraclavicular region 874.8
    complicated 874.9
  supraorbital 873.42
    complicated 873.52
  surgical, non-healing 998.83
  temple 873.49
    complicated 873.59
  temporal region 873.49
    complicated 873.59
  testis 878.2
    complicated 878.3
  thigh 890.0
    with tendon involvement 890.2
    complicated 890.1
  thorax, thoracic (external) 875.0
    complicated 875.1
  throat 874.8
    complicated 874.9
  thumb (nail) (subungual) 883.0
    with tendon involvement 883.2
    complicated 883.1

◄ ▶   New Code   ⬅▦▶   Revised Code

◄ ▶ **New Code**   **◄▥ ▥▶ Revised Code**

X

Xanthelasma 272.2
eyelid 272.2 *[374.51]*
palpebrarum 272.2 *[374.51]*
Xanthelasmatosis (essential) 272.2
Xanthelasmoidea 757.33
Xanthine stones 277.2
Xanthinuria 277.2
Xanthofibroma (M8831/0) - *see* Neoplasm, connective tissue, benign
Xanthoma(s), xanthomatosis 272.2
with
hyperlipoproteinemia
type I 272.3
type III 272.2
type IV 272.1
type V 272.3
bone 272.7
craniohypophyseal 277.8
cutaneotendinous 272.7
diabeticorum 250.8 *[272.2]*
disseminatum 272.7
eruptive 272.2
eyelid 272.2 *[374.51]*
familial 272.7
hereditary 272.7
hypercholesterinemic 272.0
hypercholesterolemic 272.0

Xanthoma *(Continued)*
hyperlipemic 272.4
hyperlipidemic 272.4
infantile 272.7
joint 272.7
juvenile 272.7
multiple 272.7
multiplex 272.7
primary familial 272.7
tendon (sheath) 272.7
tuberosum 272.2
tuberous 272.2
tubo-eruptive 272.2
Xanthosis 709.09
surgical 998.81
Xenophobia 300.29
Xeroderma (congenital) 757.39
acquired 701.1
eyelid 373.33
eyelid 373.33
pigmentosum 757.33
vitamin A deficiency 264.8
Xerophthalmia 372.53
vitamin A deficiency 264.7
Xerosis
conjunctiva 372.53
with Bitôt's spot 372.53
vitamin A deficiency 264.1
vitamin A deficiency 264.0

Xerosis *(Continued)*
cornea 371.40
with corneal ulceration 370.00
vitamin A deficiency 264.3
vitamin A deficiency 264.2
cutis 706.8
skin 706.8
Xerostomia 527.7
Xiphodynia 733.90
Xiphoidalgia 733.90
Xiphoiditis 733.99
Xiphopagus 759.4
XO syndrome 758.6
X-ray
effects, adverse, NEC 990
of chest
for suspected tuberculosis V71.2
routine V72.5
XXX syndrome 758.81
XXXXY syndrome 758.81
XXY syndrome 758.7
Xyloketosuria 271.8
Xylosuria 271.8
Xylulosuria 271.8
XYY syndrome 758.81

Y

Yawning 786.09
  psychogenic 306.1
Yaws 102.9
  bone or joint lesions 102.6
  butter 102.1
  chancre 102.0
  cutaneous, less than five years after infection 102.2
  early (cutaneous) (macular) (maculopapular) (micropapular) (papular) 102.2
    frambeside 102.2
    skin lesions NEC 102.2
  eyelid 102.9 *[373.4]*
  ganglion 102.6
  gangosis, gangosa 102.5
  gumma, gummata 102.4
    bone 102.6
  gummatous
    frambeside 102.4
    osteitis 102.6
    periostitis 102.6
  hydrarthrosis 102.6
  hyperkeratosis (early) (late) (palmar) (plantar) 102.3
  initial lesions 102.0
  joint lesions 102.6
  juxta-articular nodules 102.7

Yaws *(Continued)*
  late nodular (ulcerated) 102.4
  latent (without clinical manifestations) (with positive serology) 102.8
  mother 102.0
  mucosal 102.7
  multiple papillomata 102.1
  nodular, late (ulcerated) 102.4
  osteitis 102.6
  papilloma, papillomata (palmar) (plantar) 102.1
  periostitis (hypertrophic) 102.6
  ulcers 102.4
  wet crab 102.1
Yeast infection *(see also* Candidiasis) 112.9
Yellow
  atrophy (liver) 570
    chronic 571.8
      resulting from administration of blood, plasma, serum, or other biological substance (within 8 months of administration) - *see* Hepatitis, viral
  fever - *see* Fever, yellow
  jack (*see also* Fever, yellow) 060.9
  jaundice (*see also* Jaundice) 782.4
Yersinia septica 027.8

Z

Zagari's disease (xerostomia) 527.7
Zahorsky's disease (exanthema subitum) 057.8
  syndrome (herpangina) 074.0
Zenker's diverticulum (esophagus) 530.6
Ziehen-Oppenheim disease 333.6
Zieve's syndrome (jaundice, hyperlipemia, and hemolytic anemia) 571.1
Zika fever 066.3
Zollinger-Ellison syndrome (gastric hypersecretion with pancreatic islet cell tumor) 251.5
Zona (*see also* Herpes, zoster) 053.9
Zoophilia (erotica) 302.1
Zoophobia 300.29
Zoster (herpes) (*see also* Herpes, zoster) 053.9
Zuelzer (-Ogden) anemia or syndrome (nutritional megaloblastic anemia) 281.2
Zygodactyly (*see also* Syndactylism) 755.10
Zygomycosis 117.7
Zymotic - *see* condition

SECTION II TABLE OF DRUGS AND CHEMICALS

ALPHABETIC INDEX TO POISONING AND EXTERNAL CAUSES OF ADVERSE EFFECTS OF DRUGS AND OTHER CHEMICAL SUBSTANCES

This table contains a classification of drugs and other chemical substances to identify poisoning states and external causes of adverse effects.

Each of the listed substances in the table is assigned a code according to the poisoning classification (960-989). These codes are used when there is a statement of poisoning, overdose, wrong substance given or taken, or intoxication.

The table also contains a listing of external causes of adverse effects. An adverse effect is a pathologic manifestation due to ingestion or exposure to drugs or other chemical substances (e.g., dermatitis, hypersensitivity reaction, aspirin gastritis). The adverse effect is to be identified by the appropriate code found in Section I, Index to Diseases and Injuries. An external cause code can then be used to identify the circumstances involved. The table headings pertaining to external causes are defined below:

Accidental poisoning (E850-E869)-accidental overdose of drug, wrong substance given or taken, drug taken inadvertently, accidents in the usage of drugs and biologicals in medical and surgical procedures, and to show external causes of poisonings classifiable to 980-989.

Therapeutic use (E930-E949)-a correct substance properly administered in therapeutic or prophylactic dosage as the external cause of adverse effects.

Suicide attempt (E950-E952)-instances in which self-inflicted injuries or poisonings are involved.

Assault (E961-E962)-injury or poisoning inflicted by another person with the intent to injure or kill.

Undetermined (E980-E982)-to be used when the intent of the poisoning or injury cannot be determined whether it was intentional or accidental.

The American Hospital Formulary Service (AHFS) list numbers are included in the table to help classify new drugs not identified in the table by name. The AHFS list numbers are keyed to the continually revised AHFS (American Hospital Formulary Service, 2 vol. Washington, D.C.: American Society of Hospital Pharmacists, 1959-). These listings are found in the table under the main term **Drug.**

Excluded from the table are radium and other radioactive substances. The classification of adverse effects and complications pertaining to these substances will be found in Index to Diseases and Injuries, and Index to External Causes of Injuries.

Although certain substances are indexed with one or more subentries, the majority are listed according to one use or state. It is recognized that many substances may be used in various ways, in medicine and in industry, and may cause adverse effects whatever the state of the agent (solid, liquid, or fumes arising from a liquid). In cases in which the reported data indicate a use or state not in the table, or which is clearly different from the one listed, an attempt should be made to classify the substance in the form which most nearly expresses the reported facts.

Substance	Poisoning	External Cause (E-Code)				
		Accident	Therapeutic Use	Suicide Attempt	Assault	Undetermined
1-propanol	980.3	E860.4	—	E950.9	E962.1	E980.9
2-propanol	980.2	E860.3	—	E950.9	E962.1	E980.9
2,4-D (dichlorophenoxyacetic acid)	989.4	E863.5	—	E950.6	E962.1	E980.7
2,4-toluene diisocyanate	983.0	E864.0	—	E950.7	E962.1	E980.6
2,4,5-T (trichlorophenoxyacetic acid)	989.2	E863.5	—	E950.6	E962.1	E980.7
14-hydroxydihydromorphinone	965.09	E850.2	E935.2	E950.0	E962.0	E980.0
ABOB	961.7	E857	E931.7	E950.4	E962.0	E980.4
Abrus (seed)	988.2	E865.3	—	E950.9	E962.1	E980.9
Absinthe	980.0	E860.1	—	E950.9	E962.1	E980.9
beverage	980.0	E860.0	—	E950.9	E962.1	E980.9
Acenocoumarin, acenocoumarol	964.2	E858.2	E934.2	E950.4	E962.0	E980.4
Acepromazine	969.1	E853.0	E939.1	E950.3	E962.0	E980.3
Acetal	982.8	E862.4	—	E950.9	E962.1	E980.9
Acetaldehyde (vapor)	987.8	E869.8	—	E952.8	E962.2	E982.8
liquid	989.89	E866.8	—	E950.9	E962.1	E980.9
Acetaminophen	965.4	E850.4	E935.4	E950.0	E962.0	E980.0
Acetaminosalol	965.1	E850.3	E935.3	E950.0	E962.0	E980.0
Acetanilid(e)	965.4	E850.4	E935.4	E950.0	E962.0	E980.0
Acetarsol, acetarsone	961.1	E857	E931.1	E950.4	E962.0	E980.4
Acetazolamide	974.2	E858.5	E944.2	E950.4	E962.0	E980.4
Acetic						
acid	983.1	E864.1	—	E950.7	E962.1	E980.6
with sodium acetate (ointment)	976.3	E858.7	E946.3	E950.4	E962.0	E980.4
irrigating solution	974.5	E858.5	E944.5	E950.4	E962.0	E980.4
lotion	976.2	E858.7	E946.2	E950.4	E962.0	E980.4
anhydride	983.1	E864.1	—	E950.7	E962.1	E980.6
ether (vapor)	982.8	E862.4	—	E950.9	E962.1	E980.9
Acetohexamide	962.3	E858.0	E932.3	E950.4	E962.0	E980.4
Acetomenaphthone	964.3	E858.2	E934.3	E950.4	E962.0	E980.4
Acetomorphine	965.01	E850.0	E935.0	E950.0	E962.0	E980.0
Acetone (oils) (vapor)	982.8	E862.4	—	E950.9	E962.1	E980.9
Acetophenazine (maleate)	969.1	E853.0	E939.1	E950.3	E962.0	E980.3
Acetophenetidin	965.4	E850.4	E935.4	E950.0	E962.0	E980.0
Acetophenone	982.0	E862.4	—	E950.9	E962.1	E980.9
Acetorphine	965.09	E850.2	E935.2	E950.0	E962.0	E980.0
Acetosulfone (sodium)	961.8	E857	E931.8	E950.4	E962.0	E980.4
Acetrizoate (sodium)	977.8	E858.8	E947.8	E950.4	E962.0	E980.4
Acetylcarbromal	967.3	E852.2	E937.3	E950.2	E962.0	E980.2
Acetylcholine (chloride)	971.0	E855.3	E941.0	E950.4	E962.0	E980.4
Acetylcysteine	975.5	E858.6	E945.5	E950.4	E962.0	E980.4
Acetyldigitoxin	972.1	E858.3	E942.1	E950.4	E962.0	E980.4
Acetyldihydrocodeine	965.09	E850.2	E935.2	E950.0	E962.0	E980.0
Acetyldihydrocodeinone	965.09	E850.2	E935.2	E950.0	E962.0	E980.0
Acetylene (gas) (industrial)	987.1	E868.1	—	E951.8	E962.2	E981.8
incomplete combustion of - *see* Carbon monoxide, fuel, utility						
tetrachloride (vapor)	982.3	E862.4	—	E950.9	E962.1	E980.9
Acetyliodosalicylic acid	965.1	E850.3	E935.3	E950.0	E962.0	E980.0
Acetylphenylhydrazine	965.8	E850.8	E935.8	E950.0	E962.0	E980.0
Acetylsalicylic acid	965.1	E850.3	E935.3	E950.0	E962.0	E980.0
Achromycin	960.4	E856	E930.4	E950.4	E962.0	E980.4
ophthalmic preparation	976.5	E858.7	E946.5	E950.4	E962.0	E980.4
topical NEC	976.0	E858.7	E946.0	E950.4	E962.0	E980.4
Acidifying agents	963.2	E858.1	E933.2	E950.4	E962.0	E980.4
Acids (corrosive) NEC	983.1	E864.1	—	E950.7	E962.1	E980.6
Aconite (wild)	988.2	E865.4	—	E950.9	E962.1	E980.9
Aconitine (liniment)	976.8	E858.7	E946.8	E950.4	E962.0	E980.4
Aconitum ferox	988.2	E865.4	—	E950.9	E962.1	E980.9
Acridine	983.0	E864.0	—	E950.7	E962.1	E980.6
vapor	987.8	E869.8	—	E952.8	E962.2	E982.8
Acriflavine	961.9	E857	E931.9	E950.4	E962.0	E980.4
Acrisorcin	976.0	E858.7	E946.0	E950.4	E962.0	E980.4

◄▶ **New Code**   ⬅▬▬➡ **Revised Code**

Substance	Poisoning	External Cause (E-Code)				
		Accident	Therapeutic Use	Suicide Attempt	Assault	Undetermined
Acrolein (gas)	987.8	E869.8	—	E952.8	E962.2	E982.8
liquid	989.89	E866.8	—	E950.9	E962.1	E980.9
Actaea spicata	988.2	E865.4	—	E950.9	E962.1	E980.9
Acterol	961.5	E857	E931.5	E950.4	E962.0	E980.4
ACTH	962.4	E858.0	E932.4	E950.4	E962.0	E980.4
Acthar	962.4	E858.0	E932.4	E950.4	E962.0	E980.4
Actinomycin (C) (D)	960.7	E856	E930.7	E950.4	E962.0	E980.4
Adalin (acetyl)	967.3	E852.2	E937.3	E950.2	E962.0	E980.2
Adenosine (phosphate)	977.8	E858.8	E947.8	E950.4	E962.0	E980.4
Adhesives	989.89	E866.6	—	E950.9	E962.1	E980.9
ADH	962.5	E858.0	E932.5	E950.4	E962.0	E980.4
Adicillin	960.0	E856	E930.0	E950.4	E962.0	E980.4
Adiphenine	975.1	E855.6	E945.1	E950.4	E962.0	E980.4
Adjunct, pharmaceutical	977.4	E858.8	E947.4	E950.4	E962.0	E980.4
Adrenal (extract, cortex or medulla) (glucocorticoids) (hormones)						
(mineralocorticoids)	962.0	E858.0	E932.0	E950.4	E962.0	E980.4
ENT agent	976.6	E858.7	E946.6	E950.4	E962.0	E980.4
ophthalmic preparation	976.5	E858.7	E946.5	E950.4	E962.0	E980.4
topical NEC	976.0	E858.7	E946.0	E950.4	E962.0	E980.4
Adrenalin	971.2	E855.5	E941.2	E950.4	E962.0	E980.4
Adrenergic blocking agents	971.3	E855.6	E941.3	E950.4	E962.0	E980.4
Adrenergics	971.2	E855.5	E941.2	E950.4	E962.0	E980.4
Adrenochrome (derivatives)	972.8	E858.3	E942.8	E950.4	E962.0	E980.4
Adrenocorticotropic hormone	962.4	E858.0	E932.4	E950.4	E962.0	E980.4
Adrenocorticotropin	962.4	E858.0	E932.4	E950.4	E962.0	E980.4
Adriamycin	960.7	E856	E930.7	E950.4	E962.0	E980.4
Aerosol spray - *see* Sprays						
Aerosporin	960.8	E856	E930.8	E950.4	E962.0	E980.4
ENT agent	976.6	E858.7	E946.6	E950.4	E962.0	E980.4
ophthalmic preparation	976.5	E858.7	E946.5	E950.4	E962.0	E980.4
topical NEC	976.0	E858.7	E946.0	E950.4	E962.0	E980.4
Aethusa cynapium	988.2	E865.4	—	E950.9	E962.1	E980.9
Afghanistan black	969.6	E854.1	E939.6	E950.3	E962.0	E980.3
Aflatoxin	989.7	E865.9	—	E950.9	E962.1	E980.9
African boxwood	988.2	E865.4	—	E950.9	E962.1	E980.9
Agar (-agar)	973.3	E858.4	E943.3	E950.4	E962.0	E980.4
Agricultural agent NEC	989.89	E863.9	—	E950.6	E962.1	E980.7
Agrypnal	967.0	E851	E937.0	E950.1	E962.0	E980.1
Air contaminant(s), source or type not specified						
specified type - *see* specific substance	987.9	E869.9	—	E952.9	E962.2	E982.9
Akee	988.2	E865.4	—	E950.9	E962.1	E980.9
Akrinol	976.0	E858.7	E946.0	E950.4	E962.0	E980.4
Alantolactone	961.6	E857	E931.6	E950.4	E962.0	E980.4
Albamycin	960.8	E856	E930.8	E950.4	E962.0	E980.4
Albumin (normal human serum)	964.7	E858.2	E934.7	E950.4	E962.0	E980.4
Alcohol	980.9	E860.9	—	E950.9	E962.1	E980.9
absolute	980.0	E860.1	—	E950.9	E962.1	E980.9
beverage	980.0	E860.0	E947.8	E950.9	E962.1	E980.9
amyl	980.3	E860.4	—	E950.9	E962.1	E980.9
antifreeze	980.1	E860.2	—	E950.9	E962.1	E980.9
butyl	980.3	E860.4	—	E950.9	E962.1	E980.9
dehydrated	980.0	E860.1	—	E950.9	E862.1	E980.9
beverage	980.0	E860.0	E947.8	E950.9	E962.1	E980.9
denatured	980.0	E860.1	—	E950.9	E962.1	E980.9
deterrents	977.3	E858.8	E947.3	E950.4	E962.0	E980.4
diagnostic (gastric function)	977.8	E858.8	E947.8	E950.4	E962.0	E980.4
ethyl	980.0	E860.1	—	E950.9	E962.1	E980.9
beverage	980.0	E860.0	E947.8	E950.9	E962.1	E980.9
grain	980.0	E860.1	—	E950.9	E962.1	E980.9
beverage	980.0	E860.0	E947.8	E950.9	E962.1	E980.9
industrial	980.9	E860.9	—	E950.9	E962.1	E980.9

◀ ▶ New Code   ⬅ ➡ Revised Code

ICD-9-CM

Drugs

Vol. 2

Substance	Poisoning	External Cause (E-Code)				
		Accident	Therapeutic Use	Suicide Attempt	Assault	Undetermined
Alcohol *(Continued)*						
isopropyl	980.2	E860.3	—	E950.9	E962.1	E980.9
methyl	980.1	E860.2	—	E950.9	E962.1	E980.9
preparation for consumption	980.0	E860.0	E947.8	E950.9	E962.1	E980.9
propyl	980.3	E860.4	—	E950.9	E962.1	E980.9
secondary	980.2	E860.3	—	E950.9	E962.1	E980.9
radiator	980.1	E860.2	—	E950.9	E962.1	E980.9
rubbing	980.2	E860.3	—	E950.9	E962.1	E980.9
specified type NEC	980.8	E860.8	—	E950.9	E962.1	E980.9
surgical	980.9	E860.9	—	E950.9	E962.1	E980.9
vapor (from any type of alcohol)	987.8	E869.8	—	E952.8	E962.2	E982.8
wood	980.1	E860.2	—	E950.9	E962.1	E980.9
Alcuronium chloride	975.2	E858.6	E945.2	E950.4	E962.0	E980.4
Aldactone	974.4	E858.5	E944.4	E950.4	E962.0	E980.4
Aldicarb	989.3	E863.2	—	E950.6	E962.1	E980.7
Aldomet	972.6	E858.3	E942.6	E950.4	E962.0	E980.4
Aldosterone	962.0	E858.0	E932.0	E950.4	E962.0	E980.4
Aldrin (dust)	989.2	E863.0	—	E950.6	E962.1	E980.7
Aleve - *see* Naproxen						
Algeldrate	973.0	E858.4	E943.0	E950.4	E962.0	E980.4
Alidase	963.4	E858.1	E933.4	E950.4	E962.0	E980.4
Aliphatic thiocyanates	989.0	E866.8	—	E950.9	E962.1	E980.9
Alkaline antiseptic solution (aromatic)	976.6	E858.7	E946.6	E950.4	E962.0	E980.4
Alkalinizing agents (medicinal)	963.3	E858.1	E933.3	E950.4	E962.0	E980.4
Alkalis, caustic	983.2	E864.2	—	E950.7	E962.1	E980.6
Alkalizing agents (medicinal)	963.3	E858.1	E933.3	E950.4	E962.0	E980.4
Alka-seltzer	965.1	E850.3	E935.3	E950.0	E962.0	E980.0
Alkavervir	972.6	E858.3	E942.6	E950.4	E962.0	E980.4
Allegron	969.0	E854.0	E939.0	E950.3	E962.0	E980.3
Allobarbital, allobarbitone	967.0	E851	E937.0	E950.1	E962.0	E980.1
Allopurinol	974.7	E858.5	E944.7	E950.4	E962.0	E980.4
Allylestrenol	962.2	E858.0	E932.2	E950.4	E962.0	E980.4
Allylisopropylacetylurea	967.8	E852.8	E937.8	E950.2	E962.0	E980.2
Allylisopropylmalonylurea	967.0	E851	E937.0	E950.1	E962.0	E980.1
Allyltribromide	967.3	E852.2	E937.3	E950.2	E962.0	E980.2
Aloe, aloes, aloin	973.1	E858.4	E943.1	E950.4	E962.0	E980.4
Aloxidone	966.0	E855.0	E936.0	E950.4	E962.0	E980.4
Aloxiprin	965.1	E850.3	E935.3	E950.0	E962.0	E980.0
Alpha amylase	963.4	E858.1	E933.4	E950.4	E962.0	E980.4
Alphaprodine (hydrochloride)	965.09	E850.2	E935.2	E950.0	E962.0	E980.0
Alpha tocopherol	963.5	E858.1	E933.5	E950.4	E962.0	E980.4
Alseroxylon	972.6	E858.3	E942.6	E950.4	E962.0	E980.4
Alum (ammonium) (potassium)	983.2	E864.2	—	E950.7	E962.1	E980.6
medicinal (astringent) NEC	976.2	E858.7	E946.2	E950.4	E962.0	E980.4
Aluminium, aluminum (gel) (hydroxide)	973.0	E858.4	E943.0	E950.4	E962.0	E980.4
acetate solution	976.2	E858.7	E946.2	E950.4	E962.0	E980.4
aspirin	965.1	E850.3	E935.3	E950.0	E962.0	E980.0
carbonate	973.0	E858.4	E943.0	E950.4	E962.0	E980.4
glycinate	973.0	E858.4	E943.0	E950.4	E962.0	E980.4
nicotinate	972.2	E858.3	E942.2	E950.4	E962.0	E980.4
ointment (surgical) (topical)	976.3	E858.7	E946.3	E950.4	E962.0	E980.4
phosphate	973.0	E858.4	E943.0	E950.4	E962.0	E980.4
subacetate	976.2	E858.7	E946.2	E950.4	E962.0	E980.4
topical NEC	976.3	E858.7	E946.3	E950.4	E962.0	E980.4
Alurate	967.0	E851	E937.0	E950.1	E962.0	E980.1
Alverine (citrate)	975.1	E858.6	E945.1	E950.4	E962.0	E980.4
Alvodine	965.09	E850.2	E935.2	E950.0	E962.0	E980.0
Amanita phalloides	988.1	E865.5	—	E950.9	E962.1	E980.9
Amantadine (hydrochloride)	966.4	E855.0	E936.4	E950.4	E962.0	E980.4
Ambazone	961.9	E857	E931.9	E950.4	E962.0	E980.4
Ambenonium	971.0	E855.3	E941.0	E950.4	E962.0	E980.4

◀ ▶   **New Code**   ⬅▦▦▶   **Revised Code**

Substance	Poisoning	External Cause (E-Code)				
		Accident	Therapeutic Use	Suicide Attempt	Assault	Undetermined
Ambutonium bromide	971.1	E855.4	E941.1	E950.4	E962.0	E990.4
Ametazole	977.8	E858.8	E947.8	E950.4	E962.0	E980.4
Amethocaine (infiltration) (topical)	968.5	E855.2	E938.5	E950.4	E962.0	E980.4
nerve block (peripheral) (plexus)	968.6	E855.2	E938.6	E950.4	E962.0	E980.4
spinal	968.7	E855.2	E938.7	E950.4	E962.0	E980.4
Amethopterin	963.1	E858.1	E933.1	E950.4	E962.0	E980.4
Amfepramone	977.0	E858.8	E947.0	E950.4	E962.0	E980.4
Amidone	965.02	E850.1	E935.1	E950.0	E962.0	E980.0
Amidopyrine	965.5	E850.5	E935.5	E950.0	E962.0	E980.0
Aminacrine	976.0	E858.7	E946.0	E950.4	E962.0	E980.4
Aminitrozole	961.5	E857	E931.5	E950.4	E962.0	E980.4
Aminoacetic acid	974.5	E858.5	E944.5	E950.4	E962.0	E980.4
Amino acids	974.5	E858.5	E944.5	E950.4	E962.0	E980.4
Aminocaproic acid	964.4	E858.2	E934.4	E950.4	E962.0	E980.4
Aminoethylisothiourium	963.8	E858.1	E933.8	E950.4	E962.0	E980.4
Aminoglutethimide	966.3	E855.0	E936.3	E950.4	E962.0	E980.4
Aminometradine	974.3	E858.5	E944.3	E950.4	E962.0	E980.4
Aminopentamide	971.1	E855.4	E941.1	E950.4	E962.0	E980.4
Aminophenazone	965.5	E850.5	E935.5	E950.0	E962.0	E980.0
Aminophenol	983.0	E864.0	—	E950.7	E962.1	E980.6
Aminophenylpyridone	969.5	E853.8	E939.5	E950.3	E962.0	E980.3
Aminophylline	975.7	E858.6	E945.7	E950.4	E962.0	E980.4
Aminopterin	963.1	E858.1	E933.1	E950.4	E962.0	E980.4
Aminopyrine	965.5	E850.5	E935.5	E950.0	E962.0	E980.0
Aminosalicylic acid	961.8	E857	E931.8	E950.4	E962.0	E980.4
Amiphenazole	970.1	E854.3	E940.1	E950.4	E962.0	E980.4
Amiquinsin	972.6	E858.3	E942.6	E950.4	E962.0	E980.4
Amisometradine	974.3	E858.5	E944.3	E950.4	E962.0	E980.4
Amitriptyline	969.0	E854.0	E939.0	E950.3	E962.0	E980.3
Ammonia (fumes) (gas) (vapor)	987.8	E869.8	—	E952.8	E962.2	E982.8
liquid (household) NEC	983.2	E861.4	—	E950.7	E962.1	E980.6
spirit, aromatic	970.8	E854.3	E940.8	E950.4	E962.0	E980.4
Ammoniated mercury	976.0	E858.7	E946.0	E950.4	E962.0	E980.4
Ammonium						
carbonate	983.2	E864.2	—	E950.7	E962.1	E980.6
chloride (acidifying agent)	963.2	E858.1	E933.2	E950.4	E962.0	E980.4
expectorant	975.5	E858.6	E945.5	E950.4	E962.0	E980.4
compounds (household) NEC	983.2	E861.4	—	E950.7	E962.1	E980.6
fumes (any usage)	987.8	E869.8	—	E952.8	E962.2	E982.8
industrial	983.2	E864.2	—	E950.7	E962.1	E980.6
ichthosulfonate	976.4	E858.7	E946.4	E950.4	E962.0	E980.4
mandelate	961.9	E857	E931.9	E950.4	E962.0	E980.4
Amobarbital	967.0	E851	E937.0	E950.1	E962.0	E980.1
Amodiaquin(e)	961.4	E857	E931.4	E950.4	E962.0	E980.4
Amopyroquin(e)	961.4	E857	E931.4	E950.4	E962.0	E980.4
Amphenidone	969.5	E853.8	E939.5	E950.3	E962.0	E980.3
Amphetamine	969.7	E854.2	E939.7	E950.3	E962.0	E980.3
Amphomycin	960.8	E856	E930.8	E950.4	E962.0	E980.4
Amphotericin B	960.1	E856	E930.1	E950.4	E962.0	E980.4
topical	976.0	E858.7	E946.0	E950.4	E962.0	E980.4
Ampicillin	960.0	E856	E930.0	E950.4	E962.0	E980.4
Amprotropine	971.1	E855.4	E941.1	E950.4	E962.0	E980.4
Amygdalin	977.8	E858.8	E947.8	E950.4	E962.0	E980.4
Amyl						
acetate (vapor)	982.8	E862.4	—	E950.9	E962.1	E980.9
alcohol	980.3	E860.4	—	E950.9	E962.1	E980.9
nitrite (medicinal)	972.4	E858.3	E942.4	E950.4	E962.0	E980.4
Amylase (alpha)	963.4	E858.1	E933.4	E950.4	E962.0	E980.4
Amylene hydrate	980.8	E860.8	—	E950.9	E962.1	E980.9
Amylobarbitone	967.0	E851	E937.0	E950.1	E962.0	E980.1
Amylocaine	968.9	E855.2	E938.9	E950.4	E962.0	E980.4

◄ ► **New Code**   ◄▥▥ ▥▥► **Revised Code**

ICD-9-CM

Drugs

Vol. 2

Substance	Poisoning	External Cause (E-Code)				
		Accident	Therapeutic Use	Suicide Attempt	Assault	Undetermined
Amylocaine *(Continued)*						
infiltration (subcutaneous)	968.5	E855.2	E938.5	E950.4	E962.0	E980.4
nerve block (peripheral) (plexus)	968.6	E855.2	E938.6	E950.4	E962.0	E980.4
spinal	968.7	E855.2	E938.7	E950.4	E962.0	E980.4
topical (surface)	968.5	E855.2	E938.5	E950.4	E962.0	E980.4
Amytal (sodium)	967.0	E851	E937.0	E950.1	E962.0	E980.1
Analeptics	970.0	E854.3	E940.0	E950.4	E962.0	E980.4
Analgesics	965.9	E850.9	E935.9	E950.0	E962.0	E980.0
aromatic NEC	965.4	E850.4	E935.4	E950.0	E962.0	E980.0
non-narcotic NEC	965.7	E850.7	E935.7	E950.0	E962.0	E980.0
specified NEC	965.8	E850.8	E935.8	E950.0	E962.0	E980.0
Anamirta cocculus	988.2	E865.3	—	E950.9	E962.1	E980.9
Ancillin	960.0	E856	E930.0	E950.4	E962.0	E980.4
Androgens (anabolic congeners)	962.1	E858.0	E932.1	E950.4	E962.0	E980.4
Androstalone	962.1	E858.0	E932.1	E950.4	E962.0	E980.4
Androsterone	962.1	E858.0	E932.1	E950.4	E962.0	E980.4
Anemone pulsatilia	988.2	E865.4	—	E950.9	E962.1	E980.9
Anesthesia, anesthetic (general) NEC	968.4	E855.1	E938.4	E950.4	E962.0	E980.4
block (nerve) (plexus)	968.6	E855.2	E938.6	E950.4	E962.0	E980.4
gaseous NEC	968.2	E855.1	E938.2	E950.4	E962.0	E980.4
halogenated hydrocarbon derivatives NEC	968.2	E855.1	E938.2	E950.4	E962.0	E980.4
infiltration (intradermal) (subcutaneous) (submucosal)	968.5	E855.2	E938.5	E950.4	E962.0	E980.4
intravenous	968.3	E855.1	E938.3	E950.4	E962.0	E980.4
local NEC	968.9	E855.2	E938.9	E950.4	E962.0	E980.4
nerve blocking (peripheral) (plexus)	968.6	E855.2	E938.6	E950.4	E962.0	E980.4
rectal NEC	968.3	E855.1	E938.3	E950.4	E962.0	E980.4
spinal	968.7	E855.2	E938.7	E950.4	E962.0	E980.4
surface	968.5	E855.2	E938.5	E950.4	E962.0	E980.4
topical	968.5	E855.2	E938.5	E950.4	E962.0	E980.4
Aneurine	963.5	E858.1	E933.5	E950.4	E962.0	E980.4
Angio-Conray	977.8	E858.8	E947.8	E950.4	E962.0	E980.4
Angiotensin	971.2	E855.5	E941.2	E950.4	E962.0	E980.4
Anhydrohydroxyprogesterone	962.2	E858.0	E932.2	E950.4	E962.0	E980.4
Anhydron	974.3	E858.5	E944.3	E950.4	E962.0	E980.4
Anileridine	965.09	E850.2	E935.2	E950.0	E962.0	E980.0
Aniline (dye) (liquid)	983.0	E864.0	—	E950.7	E962.1	E980.6
analgesic	965.4	E850.4	E935.4	E950.0	E962.0	E980.0
derivatives, therapeutic NEC	965.4	E850.4	E935.4	E950.0	E962.0	E980.0
vapor	987.8	E869.8	—	E952.8	E962.2	E982.8
Aniscoropine	971.1	E855.4	E941.1	E950.4	E962.0	E980.4
Anisindione	964.2	E858.2	E934.2	E950.4	E962.0	E980.4
Anorexic agents	977.0	E858.8	E947.0	E950.4	E962.0	E980.4
Ant (bite) (sting)	989.5	E905.5	—	E950.9	E962.1	E980.9
Antabuse	977.3	E858.8	E947.3	E950.4	E962.0	E980.4
Antacids	973.0	E858.4	E943.0	E950.4	E962.0	E980.4
Antazoline	963.0	E858.1	E933.0	E950.4	E962.0	E980.4
Anthelmintics	961.6	E857	E931.6	E950.4	E962.0	E980.4
Anthralin	976.4	E858.7	E946.4	E950.4	E962.0	E980.4
Anthramycin	960.7	E856	E930.7	E950.4	E962.0	E980.4
Antiadrenergics	971.3	E855.6	E941.3	E950.4	E962.0	E980.4
Antiallergic agents	963.0	E858.1	E933.0	E950.4	E962.0	E980.4
Antianemic agents NEC	964.1	E858.2	E934.1	E950.4	E962.0	E980.4
Antiaris toxicaria	988.2	E865.4	—	E950.9	E962.1	E980.9
Antiarteriosclerotic agents	972.2	E858.3	E942.2	E950.4	E962.0	E980.4
Antiasthmatics	975.7	E858.6	E945.7	E950.4	E962.0	E980.4
Antibiotics	960.9	E856	E930.9	E950.4	E962.0	E980.4
antifungal	960.1	E856	E930.1	E950.4	E962.0	E980.4
antimycobacterial	960.6	E856	E930.6	E950.4	E962.0	E980.4
antineoplastic	960.7	E856	E930.7	E950.4	E962.0	E980.4
cephalosporin (group)	960.5	E856	E930.5	E950.4	E962.0	E980.4
chloramphenicol (group)	960.2	E856	E930.2	E950.4	E962.0	E980.4
macrolides	960.3	E856	E930.3	E950.4	E962.0	E980.4

◄► New Code   ◄⫶⫶ ⫶⫶► Revised Code

		External Cause (E-Code)				
Substance	**Poisoning**	**Accident**	**Therapeutic Use**	**Suicide Attempt**	**Assault**	**Undetermined**
Antibiotics *(Continued)*						
specified NEC	960.8	E856	E930.8	E950.4	E962.0	E980.4
tetracycline (group)	960.4	E856	E930.4	E950.4	E962.0	E980.4
Anticancer agents NEC	963.1	E858.1	E933.1	E950.4	E962.0	E980.4
antibiotics	960.7	E856	E930.7	E950.4	E962.0	E980.4
Anticholinergics	971.1	E855.4	E941.1	E950.4	E962.0	E980.4
Anticholinesterase (organophosphorus) (reversible)	971.0	E855.3	E941.0	E950.4	E962.0	E980.4
Anticoagulants	964.2	E858.2	E934.2	E950.4	E962.0	E980.4
antagonists	964.5	E858.2	E934.5	E950.4	E962.0	E980.4
Anti-common cold agents NEC	975.6	E858.6	E945.6	E950.4	E962.0	E980.4
Anticonvulsants NEC	966.3	E855.0	E936.3	E950.4	E962.0	E980.4
Antidepressants	969.0	E854.0	E939.0	E950.3	E962.0	E980.3
Antidiabetic agents	962.3	E858.0	E932.3	E950.4	E962.0	E980.4
Antidiarrheal agents	973.5	E858.4	E943.5	E950.4	E962.0	E980.4
Antidiuretic hormone	962.5	E858.0	E932.5	E950.4	E962.0	E980.4
Antidotes NEC	977.2	E858.8	E947.2	E950.4	E962.0	E980.4
Antiemetic agents	963.0	E858.1	E933.0	E950.4	E962.0	E980.4
Antiepilepsy agent NEC	966.3	E855.0	E936.3	E950.4	E962.0	E980.4
Antifertility pills	962.2	E858.0	E932.2	E950.4	E962.0	E980.4
Antiflatulents	973.8	E858.4	E943.8	E950.4	E962.0	E980.4
Antifreeze	989.89	E866.8	—	E950.9	E962.1	E980.9
alcohol	980.1	E860.2	—	E950.9	E962.1	E980.9
ethylene glycol	982.8	E862.4	—	E950.9	E962.1	E980.9
Antifungals (nonmedicinal) (sprays)	989.4	E863.6	—	E950.6	E962.1	E980.7
medicinal NEC	961.9	E857	E931.9	E950.4	E962.0	E980.4
antibiotic	960.1	E856	E930.1	E950.4	E962.0	E980.4
topical	976.0	E858.7	E946.0	E950.4	E962.0	E980.4
Antigastric secretion agents	973.0	E858.4	E943.0	E950.4	E962.0	E980.4
Antihelmintics	961.6	E857	E931.6	E950.4	E962.0	E980.4
Antihemophilic factor (human)	964.7	E858.2	E934.7	E950.4	E962.0	E980.4
Antihistamine	963.0	E858.1	E933.0	E950.4	E962.0	E980.4
Antihypertensive agents NEC	972.6	E858.3	E942.6	E950.4	E962.0	E980.4
Anti-infectives NEC	961.9	E857	E931.9	E950.4	E962.0	E980.4
antibiotics	960.9	E856	E930.9	E950.4	E962.0	E980.4
specified NEC	960.8	E856	E930.8	E950.4	E962.0	E980.4
anthelmintic	961.6	E857	E931.6	E950.4	E962.0	E980.4
antimalarial	961.4	E857	E931.4	E950.4	E962.0	E980.4
antimycobacterial NEC	961.8	E857	E931.8	E950.4	E962.0	E980.4
antibiotics	960.6	E856	E930.6	E950.4	E962.0	E980.4
antiprotozoal NEC	961.5	E857	E931.5	E950.4	E962.0	E980.4
blood	961.4	E857	E931.4	E950.4	E962.0	E980.4
antiviral	961.7	E857	E931.7	E950.4	E962.0	E980.4
arsenical	961.1	E857	E931.1	E950.4	E962.0	E980.4
ENT agents	976.6	E858.7	E946.6	E950.4	E962.0	E980.4
heavy metals NEC	961.2	E857	E931.2	E950.4	E962.0	E980.4
local	976.0	E858.7	E946.0	E950.4	E962.0	E980.4
ophthalmic preparation	976.5	E858.7	E946.5	E950.4	E962.0	E980.4
topical NEC	976.0	E858.7	E946.0	E950.4	E962.0	E980.4
Anti-inflammatory agents (topical)	976.0	E858.7	E946.0	E950.4	E962.0	E980.4
Antiknock (tetraethyl lead)	984.1	E862.1	—	E950.9	E962.1	E980.9
Antilipemics	972.2	E858.3	E942.2	E950.4	E962.0	E980.4
Antimalarials	961.4	E857	E931.4	E950.4	E962.0	E980.4
Antimony (compounds) (vapor) NEC	985.4	E866.2	—	E950.9	E962.1	E980.9
anti-infectives	961.2	E857	E931.2	E950.4	E962.0	E980.4
pesticides (vapor)	985.4	E863.4	—	E950.6	E962.2	E980.7
potassium tartrate	961.2	E857	E931.2	E950.4	E962.0	E980.4
tartrated	961.2	E857	E931.2	E950.4	E962.0	E980.4
Antimuscarinic agents	971.1	E855.4	E941.1	E950.4	E962.0	E980.4
Antimycobacterials NEC	961.8	E857	E931.8	E950.4	E962.0	E980.4
antibiotics	960.6	E856	E930.6	E950.4	E962.0	E980.4
Antineoplastic agents	963.1	E858.1	E933.1	E950.4	E962.0	E980.4
antibiotics	960.7	E856	E930.7	E950.4	E962.0	E980.4

◀▶ **New Code**   ◀▥▥▶ **Revised Code**

Substance	Poisoning	External Cause (E-Code)				
		Accident	Therapeutic Use	Suicide Attempt	Assault	Undetermined
Anti-Parkinsonism agents	966.4	E855.0	E936.4	E950.4	E962.0	E980.4
Antiphlogistics	965.69	E850.6	E935.6	E950.0	E962.0	E980.0
Antiprotozoals NEC	961.5	E857	E931.5	E950.4	E962.0	E980.4
blood	961.4	E857	E931.4	E950.4	E962.0	E980.4
Antipruritics (local)	976.1	E858.7	E946.1	E950.4	E962.0	E980.4
Antipsychotic agents NEC	969.3	E853.8	E939.3	E950.3	E962.0	E980.3
Antipyretics	965.9	E850.9	E935.9	E950.0	E962.0	E980.0
specified NEC	965.8	E850.8	E935.8	E950.0	E962.0	E980.0
Antipyrine	965.5	E850.5	E935.5	E950.0	E962.0	E980.0
Antirabies serum (equine)	979.9	E858.8	E949.9	E950.4	E962.0	E980.4
Antirheumatics	965.69	E850.6	E935.6	E950.0	E962.0	E980.0
Antiseborrheics	976.4	E858.7	E946.4	E950.4	E962.0	E980.4
Antiseptics (external) (medicinal)	976.0	E858.7	E946.0	E950.4	E962.0	E980.4
Antistine	963.0	E858.1	E933.0	E950.4	E962.0	E980.4
Antithyroid agents	962.8	E858.0	E932.8	E950.4	E962.0	E980.4
Antitoxin, any	979.9	E858.8	E949.9	E950.4	E962.0	E980.4
Antituberculars	961.8	E857	E931.8	E950.4	E962.0	E980.4
antibiotics	960.6	E856	E930.6	E950.4	E962.0	E980.4
Antitussives	975.4	E858.6	E945.4	E950.4	E962.0	E980.4
Antivaricose agents (sclerosing)	972.7	E858.3	E942.7	E950.4	E962.0	E980.4
Antivenin (crotaline) (spider-bite)	979.9	E858.8	E949.9	E950.4	E962.0	E980.4
Antivert	963.0	E858.1	E933.0	E950.4	E962.0	E980.4
Antivirals NEC	961.7	E857	E931.7	E950.4	E962.0	E980.4
Ant poisons - *see* Pesticides						
Antrol	989.4	E863.4	—	E950.6	E962.1	E980.7
fungicide	989.4	E863.6	—	E950.6	E962.1	E980.7
Apomorphine hydrochloride (emetic)	973.6	E858.4	E943.6	E950.4	E962.0	E980.4
Appetite depressants, central	977.0	E858.8	E947.0	E950.4	E962.0	E980.4
Apresoline	972.6	E858.3	E942.6	E950.4	E962.0	E980.4
Aprobarbital, aprobarbitone	967.0	E851	E937.0	E950.1	E962.0	E980.1
Apronalide	967.8	E852.8	E937.8	E950.2	E962.0	E980.2
Aqua fortis	983.1	E864.1	—	E950.7	E962.1	E980.6
Arachis oil (topical)	976.3	E858.7	E946.3	E950.4	E962.0	E980.4
cathartic	973.2	E858.4	E943.2	E950.4	E962.0	E980.4
Aralen	961.4	E857	E931.4	E950.4	E962.0	E980.4
Arginine salts	974.5	E858.5	E944.5	E950.4	E962.0	E980.4
Argyrol	976.0	E858.7	E946.0	E950.4	E962.0	E980.4
ENT agent	976.6	E858.7	E946.6	E950.4	E962.0	E980.4
ophthalmic preparation	976.5	E858.7	E946.5	E950.4	E962.0	E980.4
Aristocort	962.0	E858.0	E932.0	E950.4	E962.0	E980.4
ENT agent	976.6	E858.7	E946.6	E950.4	E962.0	E980.4
ophthalmic preparation	976.5	E858.7	E946.5	E950.4	E962.0	E980.4
topical NEC	976.0	E858.7	E946.0	E950.4	E962.0	E980.4
Aromatics, corrosive	983.0	E864.0	—	E950.7	E962.1	E980.6
disinfectants	983.0	E861.4	—	E950.7	E962.1	E980.6
Arsenate of lead (insecticide)	985.1	E863.4	—	E950.8	E962.1	E980.8
herbicide	985.1	E863.5	—	E950.8	E962.1	E980.8
Arsenic, arsenicals (compounds) (dust) (fumes) (vapor) NEC	985.1	E866.3	—	E950.8	E962.1	E980.8
anti-infectives	961.1	E857	E931.1	E950.4	E962.0	E980.4
pesticide (dust) (fumes)	985.1	E863.4	—	E950.8	E962.1	E980.8
Arsine (gas)	985.1	E866.3	—	E950.8	E962.1	E980.8
Arsphenamine (silver)	961.1	E857	E931.1	E950.4	E962.0	E980.4
Arsthinol	961.1	E857	E931.1	E950.4	E962.0	E980.4
Artane	971.1	E855.4	E941.1	E950.4	E962.0	E980.4
Arthropod (venomous) NEC	989.5	E905.5	—	E950.9	E962.1	E980.9
Asbestos	989.81	E866.8	—	E950.9	E962.1	E980.9
Ascaridole	961.6	E857	E931.6	E950.4	E962.0	E980.4
Ascorbic acid	963.5	E858.1	E933.5	E950.4	E962.0	E980.4
Asiaticoside	976.0	E858.7	E946.0	E950.4	E962.0	E980.4
Aspidium (oleoresin)	961.6	E857	E931.6	E950.4	E962.0	E980.4
Aspirin	965.1	E850.3	E935.3	E950.0	E962.0	E980.0

◄ ▶ **New Code** ◄▌▐ ▐▌▶ **Revised Code**

Substance	Poisoning	External Cause (E-Code)				
		Accident	Therapeutic Use	Suicide Attempt	Assault	Undetermined
Astringents (local)	976.2	E858.7	E946.2	E950.4	E962.0	E980.4
Atabrine	961.3	E857	E931.3	E950.4	E962.0	E980.4
Ataractics	969.5	E853.8	E939.5	E950.3	E962.0	E980.3
Atonia drug, intestinal	973.3	E858.4	E943.3	E950.4	E962.0	E980.4
Atophan	974.7	E858.5	E944.7	E950.4	E962.0	E980.4
Atropine	971.1	E855.4	E941.1	E950.4	E962.0	E980.4
Attapulgite	973.5	E858.4	E943.5	E950.4	E962.0	E980.4
Attenuvax	979.4	E858.8	E949.4	E950.4	E962.0	E980.4
Aureomycin	960.4	E856	E930.4	E950.4	E962.0	E980.4
ophthalmic preparation	976.5	E858.7	E946.5	E950.4	E962.0	E980.4
topical NEC	976.0	E858.7	E946.0	E950.4	E962.0	E980.4
Aurothioglucose	965.69	E850.6	E935.6	E950.0	E962.0	E980.0
Aurothioglycanide	965.69	E850.6	E935.6	E950.0	E962.0	E980.0
Aurothiomalate	965.69	E850.6	E935.6	E950.0	E962.0	E980.0
Automobile fuel	981	E862.1	—	E950.9	E962.1	E980.9
Autonomic nervous system agents NEC	971.9	E855.9	E941.9	E950.4	E962.0	E980.4
Avlosulfon	961.8	E857	E931.8	E950.4	E962.0	E980.4
Avomine	967.8	E852.8	E937.8	E950.2	E962.0	E980.2
Azacyclonol	969.5	E853.8	E939.5	E950.3	E962.0	E980.3
Azapetine	971.3	E855.6	E941.3	E950.4	E962.0	E980.4
Azaribine	963.1	E858.1	E933.1	E950.4	E962.0	E980.4
Azaserine	960.7	E856	E930.7	E950.4	E962.0	E980.4
Azathioprine	963.1	E858.1	E933.1	E950.4	E962.0	E980.4
Azosulfamide	961.0	E857	E931.0	E950.4	E962.0	E980.4
Azulfidine	961.0	E857	E931.0	E950.4	E962.0	E980.4
Azuresin	977.8	E858.8	E947.8	E950.4	E962.0	E980.4
Bacimycin	976.0	E858.7	E946.0	E950.4	E962.0	E980.4
ophthalmic preparation	976.5	E858.7	E946.5	E950.4	E962.0	E980.4
Bacitracin	960.8	E856	E930.8	E950.4	E962.0	E980.4
ENT agent	976.6	E858.7	E946.6	E950.4	E962.0	E980.4
ophthalmic preparation	976.5	E858.7	E946.5	E950.4	E962.0	E980.4
topical NEC	976.0	E858.7	E946.0	E950.4	E962.0	E980.4
Baking soda	963.3	E858.1	E933.3	E950.4	E962.0	E980.4
BAL	963.8	E858.1	E933.8	E950.4	E962.0	E980.4
Bamethan (sulfate)	972.5	E858.3	E942.5	E950.4	E962.0	E980.4
Bamipine	963.0	E858.1	E933.0	E950.4	E962.0	E980.4
Baneberry	988.2	E865.4	—	E950.9	E962.1	E980.9
Banewort	988.2	E865.4	—	E950.9	E962.1	E980.9
Barbenyl	967.0	E851	E937.0	E950.1	E962.0	E980.1
Barbital, barbitone	967.0	E851	E937.0	E950.1	E962.0	E980.1
Barbiturates, barbituric acid	967.0	E851	E937.0	E950.1	E962.0	E980.1
anesthetic (intravenous)	968.3	E855.1	E938.3	E950.4	E962.0	E980.4
Barium (carbonate) (chloride) (sulfate)	985.8	E866.4	—	E950.9	E962.1	E980.9
diagnostic agent	977.8	E858.8	E947.8	E950.4	E962.0	E980.4
pesticide	985.8	E863.4	—	E950.6	E962.1	E980.7
rodenticide	985.8	E863.7	—	E950.6	E962.1	E980.7
Barrier cream	976.3	E858.7	E946.3	E950.4	E962.0	E980.4
Battery acid or fluid	983.1	E864.1	—	E950.7	E962.1	E980.6
Bay rum	980.8	E860.8	—	E950.9	E962.1	E980.9
BCG vaccine	978.0	E858.8	E948.0	E950.4	E962.0	E980.4
Bearsfoot	988.2	E865.4	—	E950.9	E962.1	E980.9
Beclamide	966.3	E855.0	E936.3	E950.4	E962.0	E980.4
Bee (sting) (venom)	989.5	E905.3	—	E950.9	E962.1	E980.9
Belladonna (alkaloids)	971.1	E855.4	E941.1	E950.4	E962.0	E980.4
Bemegride	970.0	E854.3	E940.0	E950.4	E962.0	E980.4
Benactyzine	969.8	E855.8	E939.8	E950.3	E962.0	E980.3
Benadryl	963.0	E858.1	E933.0	E950.4	E962.0	E980.4
Bendrofluazide	974.3	E858.5	E944.3	E950.4	E962.0	E980.4
Bendroflumethiazide	974.3	E858.5	E944.3	E950.4	E962.0	E980.4
Benemid	974.7	E858.5	E944.7	E950.4	E962.0	E980.4
Benethamine penicillin G	960.0	E856	E930.0	E950.4	E962.0	E980.4

◀▶ **New Code**　　◀▥▥▥▶ **Revised Code**

Substance	Poisoning	External Cause (E-Code)				
		Accident	Therapeutic Use	Suicide Attempt	Assault	Undetermined
Benisone	976.0	E858.7	E946.0	E950.4	E962.0	E980.4
Benoquin	976.8	E858.7	E946.8	E950.4	E962.0	E980.4
Benoxinate	968.5	E855.2	E938.5	E950.4	E962.0	E980.4
Bentonite	976.3	E858.7	E946.3	E950.4	E962.0	E980.4
Benzalkonium (chloride)	976.0	E858.7	E946.0	E950.4	E962.0	E980.4
ophthalmic preparation	976.5	E858.7	E946.5	E950.4	E962.0	E980.4
Benzamidosalicylate (calcium)	961.8	E857	E931.8	E950.4	E962.0	E980.4
Benzathine penicillin	960.0	E856	E930.0	E950.4	E962.0	E980.4
Benzcarbimine	963.1	E858.1	E933.1	E950.4	E962.0	E980.4
Benzedrex	971.2	E855.5	E941.2	E950.4	E962.0	E980.4
Benzedrine (amphetamine)	969.7	E854.2	E939.7	E950.3	E962.0	E980.3
Benzene (acetyl) (dimethyl) (methyl) (solvent) (vapor)	982.0	E862.4	—	E950.9	E962.1	E980.9
hexachloride (gamma) (insecticide) (vapor)	989.2	E863.0	—	E950.6	E962.1	E980.7
Benzethonium	976.0	E858.7	E946.0	E950.4	E962.0	E980.4
Benzhexol (chloride)	966.4	E855.0	E936.4	E950.4	E962.0	E980.4
Benzilonium	971.1	E855.4	E941.1	E950.4	E962.0	E980.4
Benzin(e) - *see* Ligroin						
Benziodarone	972.4	E858.3	E942.4	E950.4	E962.0	E980.4
Benzocaine	968.5	E855.2	E938.5	E950.4	E962.0	E980.4
Benzodiapin	969.4	E853.2	E939.4	E950.3	E962.0	E980.3
Benzodiazepines (tranquilizers) NEC	969.4	E853.2	E939.4	E950.3	E962.0	E980.3
Benzoic acid (with salicylic acid) (anti-infective)	976.0	E858.7	E946.0	E950.4	E962.0	E980.4
Benzoin	976.3	E858.7	E946.3	E950.4	E962.0	E980.4
Benzol (vapor)	982.0	E862.4	—	E950.9	E962.1	E980.9
Benzomorphan	965.09	E850.2	E935.2	E950.0	E962.0	E980.0
Benzonatate	975.4	E858.6	E945.4	E950.4	E962.0	E980.4
Benzothiadiazides	974.3	E858.5	E944.3	E950.4	E962.0	E980.4
Benzoylpas	961.8	E857	E931.8	E950.4	E962.0	E980.4
Benzperidol	969.5	E853.8	E939.5	E950.3	E962.0	E980.3
Benzphetamine	977.0	E858.8	E947.0	E950.4	E962.0	E980.4
Benzpyrinium	971.0	E855.3	E941.0	E950.4	E962.0	E980.4
Benzquinamide	963.0	E858.1	E933.0	E950.4	E962.0	E980.4
Benzthiazide	974.3	E858.5	E944.3	E950.4	E962.0	E980.4
Benztropine	971.1	E855.4	E941.1	E950.4	E962.0	E980.4
Benzyl						
acetate	982.8	E862.4	—	E950.9	E962.1	E980.9
benzoate (anti-infective)	976.0	E858.7	E946.0	E950.4	E962.0	E980.4
morphine	965.09	E850.2	E935.2	E950.0	E962.0	E980.0
penicillin	960.0	E856	E930.0	E950.4	E962.0	E980.4
Bephenium						
hydroxynapthoate	961.6	E857	E931.6	E950.4	E962.0	E980.4
Bergamot oil	989.89	E866.8	—	E950.9	E962.1	E980.9
Berries, poisonous	988.2	E865.3	—	E950.9	E962.1	E980.9
Beryllium (compounds) (fumes)	985.3	E866.4	—	E950.9	E962.1	E980.9
Beta-carotene	976.3	E858.7	E946.3	E950.4	E962.0	E980.4
Beta-Chlor	967.1	E852.0	E937.1	E950.2	E962.0	E980.2
Betamethasone	962.0	E858.0	E932.0	E950.4	E962.0	E980.4
topical	976.0	E858.7	E946.0	E950.4	E962.0	E980.4
Betazole	977.8	E858.8	E947.8	E950.4	E962.0	E980.4
Bethanechol	971.0	E855.3	E941.0	E950.4	E962.0	E980.4
Bethanidine	972.6	E858.3	E942.6	E950.4	E962.0	E980.4
Betula oil	976.3	E858.7	E946.3	E950.4	E962.0	E980.4
Bhang	969.6	E854.1	E939.6	E950.3	E962.0	E980.3
Bialamicol	961.5	E857	E931.5	E950.4	E962.0	E980.4
Bichloride of mercury - *see* Mercury, chloride						
Bichromates (calcium) (crystals) (potassium) (sodium)	983.9	E864.3	—	E950.7	E962.1	E980.6
fumes	987.8	E869.8	—	E952.8	E962.2	E982.8
Biguanide derivatives, oral	962.3	E858.0	E932.3	E950.4	E962.0	E980.4
Biligrafin	977.8	E858.8	E947.8	E950.4	E962.0	E980.4
Bilopaque	977.8	E858.8	E947.8	E950.4	E962.0	E980.4
Bioflavonoids	972.8	E858.3	E942.8	E950.4	E962.0	E980.4

◄ ► **New Code**   ◄▥▥ ▥▥► **Revised Code**

Substance	Poisoning	External Cause (E-Code)				
		Accident	Therapeutic Use	Suicide Attempt	Assault	Undetermined
Biological substance NEC	979.9	E858.8	E949.9	E950.4	E962.0	E980.4
Biperiden	966.4	E855.0	E936.4	E950.4	E962.0	E980.4
Bisacodyl	973.1	E858.4	E943.1	E950.4	E962.0	E980.4
Bishydroxycoumarin	964.2	E858.2	E934.2	E950.4	E962.0	E980.4
Bismarsen	961.1	E857	E931.1	E950.4	E962.0	E980.4
Bismuth (compounds) NEC	985.8	E866.4	—	E950.9	E962.1	E980.9
anti-infectives	961.2	E857	E931.2	E950.4	E962.0	E980.4
subcarbonate	973.5	E858.4	E943.5	E950.4	E962.0	E980.4
sulfarsphenamine	961.1	E857	E931.1	E950.4	E962.0	E980.4
Bithionol	961.6	E857	E931.6	E950.4	E962.0	E980.4
Bitter almond oil	989.0	E866.8	—	E950.9	E962.1	E980.9
Bittersweet	988.2	E865.4	—	E950.9	E962.1	E930.9
Black						
flag	989.4	E863.4	—	E950.6	E962.1	E980.7
henbane	988.2	E865.4	—	E950.9	E962.1	E980.9
leaf (40)	989.4	E863.4	—	E950.6	E962.1	E980.7
widow spider (bite)	989.5	E905.1	—	E950.9	E962.1	E980.9
antivenin	979.9	E858.8	E949.9	E950.4	E962.0	E980.4
Blast furnace gas (carbon monoxide from)	986	E868.8	—	E952.1	E962.2	E982.1
Bleach NEC	983.9	E864.3	—	E950.7	E962.1	E980.6
Bleaching solutions	983.9	E864.3	—	E950.7	E962.1	E980.6
Bleomycin (sulfate)	960.7	E856	E930.7	E950.4	E962.0	E980.4
Blockain	968.9	E855.2	E938.9	E950.4	E962.0	E980.4
infiltration (subcutaneous)	968.5	E855.2	E938.5	E950.4	E962.0	E980.4
nerve block (peripheral) (plexus)	968.6	E855.2	E938.6	E950.4	E962.0	E980.4
topical (surface)	968.5	E855.2	E938.5	E950.4	E962.0	E980.4
Blood (derivatives) (natural) (plasma) (whole)	964.7	E858.2	E934.7	E950.4	E962.0	E980.4
affecting agent	964.9	E858.2	E934.9	E950.4	E962.0	E980.4
specified NEC	964.8	E858.2	E934.8	E950.4	E962.0	E980.4
substitute (macromolecular)	964.8	E858.2	E934.8	E950.4	E962.0	E980.4
Blue velvet	965.09	E850.2	E935.2	E950.0	E962.0	E980.0
Bone meal	989.89	E866.5	—	E950.9	E962.1	E980.9
Bonine	963.0	E858.1	E933.0	E950.4	E962.0	E980.4
Boracic acid	976.0	E858.7	E946.0	E950.4	E962.0	E980.4
ENT agent	976.6	E858.7	E946.6	E950.4	E962.0	E980.4
ophthalmic preparation	976.5	E858.7	E946.5	E950.4	E962.0	E980.4
Borate (cleanser) (sodium)	989.6	E861.3	—	E950.9	E962.1	E980.9
Borax (cleanser)	989.6	E861.3	—	E950.9	E962.1	E980.9
Boric acid	976.0	E858.7	E946.0	E950.4	E962.0	E980.4
ENT agent	976.6	E858.7	E946.6	E950.4	E962.0	E980.4
ophthalmic preparation	976.5	E858.7	E946.5	E950.4	E962.0	E980.4
Boron hydride NEC	989.89	E866.8	—	E950.9	E962.1	E980.9
fumes or gas	987.8	E869.8	—	E952.8	E962.2	E982.8
Brake fluid vapor	987.8	E869.8	—	E952.8	E962.2	E982.8
Brass (compounds) (fumes)	985.8	E866.4	—	E950.9	E962.1	E980.9
Brasso	981	E861.3	—	E950.9	E962.1	E980.9
Bretylium (tosylate)	972.6	E858.3	E942.6	E950.4	E962.0	E980.4
Brevital (sodium)	968.3	E855.1	E938.3	E950.4	E962.0	E980.4
British antilewisite	963.8	E858.1	E933.8	E950.4	E962.0	E980.4
Bromal (hydrate)	967.3	E852.2	E937.3	E950.2	E962.0	E980.2
Bromelains	963.4	E858.1	E933.4	E950.4	E962.0	E980.4
Bromides NEC	967.3	E852.2	E937.3	E950.2	E962.0	E980.2
Bromine (vapor)	987.8	E869.8	—	E952.8	E962.2	E982.8
compounds (medicinal)	967.3	E852.2	E937.3	E950.2	E962.0	E980.2
Bromisovalum	967.3	E852.2	E937.3	E950.2	E962.0	E980.2
Bromobenzyl cyanide	987.5	E869.3	—	E952.8	E962.2	E982.8
Bromodiphenhydramine	963.0	E858.1	E933.0	E950.4	E962.0	E980.4
Bromoform	967.3	E852.2	E937.3	E950.2	E962.0	E980.2
Bromophenol blue reagent	977.8	E858.8	E947.8	E950.4	E962.0	E980.4
Bromosalicylhydroxamic acid	961.8	E857	E931.8	E950.4	E962.0	E980.4
Bromo-seltzer	965.4	E850.4	E935.4	E950.0	E962.0	E980.0

◄ ▶   **New Code**   ◄▦ ▦▶   **Revised Code**

Substance	Poisoning	External Cause (E-Code)				
		Accident	Therapeutic Use	Suicide Attempt	Assault	Undetermined
Brompheniramine	963.0	E858.1	E933.0	E950.4	E962.0	E980.4
Bromural	967.3	E852.2	E937.3	E950.2	E962.0	E980.2
Brown spider (bite) (venom)	989.5	E905.1	—	E950.9	E962.1	E980.9
Brucia	988.2	E865.3	—	E950.9	E962.1	E980.9
Brucine	989.1	E863.7	—	E950.6	E962.1	E980.7
Brunswick green - *see* Copper						
Bruten - *see* Ibuprofen						
Bryonia (alba) (dioica)	988.2	E865.4	—	E950.9	E962.1	E980.9
Buclizine	969.5	E853.8	E939.5	E950.3	E962.0	E980.3
Bufferin	965.1	E850.3	E935.3	E950.0	E962.0	E980.0
Bufotenine	969.6	E854.1	E939.6	E950.3	E962.0	E980.3
Buphenine	971.2	E855.5	E941.2	E950.4	E962.0	E980.4
Bupivacaine	968.9	E855.2	E938.9	E950.4	E962.0	E980.4
infiltration (subcutaneous)	968.5	E855.2	E938.5	E950.4	E962.0	E980.4
nerve block (peripheral) (plexus)	968.6	E855.2	E938.6	E950.4	E962.0	E980.4
Busulfan	963.1	E858.1	E933.1	E950.4	E962.0	E980.4
Butabarbital (sodium)	967.0	E851	E937.0	E950.1	E962.0	E980.1
Butabarbitone	967.0	E851	E937.0	E950.1	E962.0	E980.1
Butabarpal	967.0	E851	E937.0	E950.1	E962.0	E980.1
Butacaine	968.5	E855.2	E938.5	E950.4	E962.0	E980.4
Butallylonal	967.0	E851	E937.0	E950.1	E962.0	E980.1
Butane (distributed in mobile container)	987.0	E868.0	—	E951.1	E962.2	E981.1
distributed through pipes	987.0	E867	—	E951.0	E962.2	E981.0
incomplete combustion of - *see* Carbon monoxide, butane						
Butanol	980.3	E860.4	—	E950.9	E962.1	E980.9
Butanone	982.8	E862.4	—	E950.9	E962.1	E980.9
Butaperazine	969.1	E853.0	E939.1	E950.3	E962.0	E980.3
Butazolidin	965.5	E850.5	E935.5	E950.0	E962.0	E980.0
Butethal	967.0	E851	E937.0	E950.1	E962.0	E980.1
Butethamate	971.1	E855.4	E941.1	E950.4	E962.0	E980.4
Buthalitone (sodium)	968.3	E855.1	E938.3	E950.4	E962.0	E980.4
Butisol (sodium)	967.0	E851	E937.0	E950.1	E962.0	E980.1
Butobarbital, butobarbitone	967.0	E851	E937.0	E950.1	E962.0	E980.1
Butriptyline	969.0	E854.0	E939.0	E950.3	E962.0	E980.3
Buttercups	988.2	E865.4	—	E950.9	E962.1	E980.9
Butter of antimony - *see* Antimony						
Butyl						
acetate (secondary)	982.8	E862.4	—	E950.9	E962.1	E980.9
alcohol	980.3	E860.4	—	E950.9	E962.1	E980.9
carbinol	980.8	E860.8	—	E950.9	E962.1	E980.9
carbitol	982.8	E862.4	—	E950.9	E962.1	E980.9
cellosolve	982.8	E862.4	—	E950.9	E962.1	E980.9
chloral (hydrate)	967.1	E852.0	E937.1	E950.2	E962.0	E980.2
formate	982.8	E862.4	—	E950.9	E962.1	E980.9
scopolammonium bromide	971.1	E855.4	E941.1	E950.4	E962.0	E980.4
Butyn	968.5	E855.2	E938.5	E950.4	E962.0	E980.4
Butyrophenone (-based tranquilizers)	969.2	E853.1	E939.2	E950.3	E962.0	E980.3
Cacodyl, cacodylic acid - *see* Arsenic						
Cactinomycin	960.7	E856	E930.7	E950.4	E962.0	E980.4
Cade oil	976.4	E858.7	E946.4	E950.4	E962.0	E980.4
Cadmium (chloride) (compounds) (dust) (fumes) (oxide)	985.5	E866.4	—	E950.9	E962.1	E980.9
sulfide (medicinal) NEC	976.4	E858.7	E946.4	E950.4	E962.0	E980.4
Caffeine	969.7	E854.2	E939.7	E950.3	E962.0	E980.3
Calabar bean	988.2	E865.4	—	E950.9	E962.1	E980.9
Caladium seguinium	988.2	E865.4	—	E950.9	E962.1	E980.9
Calamine (liniment) (lotion)	976.3	E858.7	E946.3	E950.4	E962.0	E980.4
Calciferol	963.5	E858.1	E933.5	E950.4	E962.0	E980.4
Calcium (salts) NEC	974.5	E858.5	E944.5	E950.4	E962.0	E980.4
acetylsalicylate	965.1	E850.3	E935.3	E950.0	E962.0	E980.0
benzamidosalicylate	961.8	E857	E931.8	E950.4	E962.0	E980.4
carbaspirin	965.1	E850.3	E935.3	E950.0	E962.0	E980.0
carbimide (citrated)	977.3	E858.8	E947.3	E950.4	E962.0	E980.4

Substance	Poisoning	External Cause (E-Code)				
		Accident	Therapeutic Use	Suicide Attempt	Assault	Undetermined
Calcium *(Continued)*						
carbonate (antacid)	973.0	E858.4	E943.0	E950.4	E962.0	E980.4
cyanide (citrated)	977.3	E858.8	E947.3	E950.4	E962.0	E980.4
dioctyl sulfosuccinate	973.2	E858.4	E943.2	E950.4	E962.0	E980.4
disodium edathamil	963.8	E858.1	E933.8	E950.4	E962.0	E980.4
disodium edetate	963.8	E858.1	E933.8	E950.4	E962.0	E980.4
EDTA	963.8	E858.1	E933.8	E950.4	E962.0	E980.4
hydrate, hydroxide	983.2	E864.2	—	E950.7	E962.1	E980.6
mandelate	961.9	E857	E931.9	E950.4	E962.0	E980.4
oxide	983.2	E864.2	—	E950.7	E962.1	E980.6
Calomel - *see* Mercury, chloride						
Caloric agents NEC	974.5	E858.5	E944.5	E950.4	E962.0	E980.4
Calusterone	963.1	E858.1	E933.1	E950.4	E962.0	E980.4
Camoquin	961.4	E857	E931.4	E950.4	E962.0	E980.4
Camphor (oil)	976.1	E858.7	E946.1	E950.4	E962.0	E980.4
Candeptin	976.0	E858.7	E946.0	E950.4	E962.0	E980.4
Candicidin	976.0	E858.7	E946.0	E950.4	E962.0	E980.4
Cannabinols	969.6	E854.1	E939.6	E950.3	E962.0	E980.3
Cannabis (derivatives) (indica) (sativa)	969.6	E854.1	E939.6	E950.3	E962.0	E980.3
Canned heat	980.1	E860.2	—	E950.9	E962.1	E980.9
Cantharides, cantharidin, cantharis	976.8	E858.7	E946.8	E950.4	E962.0	E980.4
Capillary agents	972.8	E858.3	E942.8	E950.4	E962.0	E980.4
Capreomycin	960.6	E856	E930.6	E950.4	E962.0	E980.4
Captodiame, captodiamine	969.5	E853.8	E939.5	E950.3	E962.0	E980.3
Caramiphen (hydrochloride)	971.1	E855.4	E941.1	E950.4	E962.0	E980.4
Carbachol	971.0	E855.3	E941.0	E950.4	E962.0	E980.4
Carbacrylamine resins	974.5	E858.5	E944.5	E950.4	E962.0	E980.4
Carbamate (sedative)	967.8	E852.8	E937.8	E950.2	E962.0	E980.2
herbicide	989.3	E863.5	—	E950.6	E962.1	E980.7
insecticide	989.3	E863.2	—	E950.6	E962.1	E980.7
Carbamazepine	966.3	E855.0	E936.3	E950.4	E962.0	E980.4
Carbamic esters	967.8	E852.8	E937.8	E950.2	E962.0	E980.2
Carbamide	974.4	E858.5	E944.4	E950.4	E962.0	E980.4
topical	976.8	E858.7	E946.8	E950.4	E962.0	E980.4
Carbamylcholine chloride	971.0	E855.3	E941.0	E950.4	E962.0	E980.4
Carbarsone	961.1	E857	E931.1	E950.4	E962.0	E980.4
Carbaryl	989.3	E863.2	—	E950.6	E962.1	E980.7
Carbaspirin	965.1	E850.3	E935.3	E950.0	E962.0	E980.0
Carbazochrome	972.8	E858.3	E942.8	E950.4	E962.0	E980.4
Carbenicillin	960.0	E856	E930.0	E950.4	E962.0	E980.4
Carbenoxolone	973.8	E858.4	E943.8	E950.4	E962.0	E980.4
Carbetapentane	975.4	E858.6	E945.4	E950.4	E962.0	E980.4
Carbimazole	962.8	E858.0	E932.8	E950.4	E962.0	E980.4
Carbinol	980.1	E860.2	—	E950.9	E962.1	E980.9
Carbinoxamine	963.0	E858.1	E933.0	E950.4	E962.0	E980.4
Carbitol	982.8	E862.4	—	E950.9	E962.1	E980.9
Carbocaine	968.9	E855.2	E938.9	E950.4	E962.0	E980.4
infiltration (subcutaneous)	968.5	E855.2	E938.5	E950.4	E962.0	E980.4
nerve block (peripheral) (plexus)	968.6	E855.2	E938.6	E950.4	E962.0	E980.4
topical (surface)	968.5	E855.2	E938.5	E950.4	E962.0	E980.4
Carbol-fuchsin solution	976.0	E858.7	E946.0	E950.4	E962.0	E980.4
Carbolic acid (*see also* Phenol)	983.0	E864.0	—	E950.7	E962.1	E980.6
Carbomycin	960.8	E856	E930.8	E950.4	E962.0	E980.4
Carbon						
bisulfide (liquid) (vapor)	982.2	E862.4	—	E950.9	E962.1	E980.9
dioxide (gas)	987.8	E869.8	—	E952.8	E962.2	E982.8
disulfide (liquid) (vapor)	982.2	E862.4	—	E950.9	E962.1	E980.9
monoxide (from incomplete combustion of) (in) NEC	986	E868.9	—	E952.1	E962.2	E982.1
blast furnace gas	986	E868.8	—	E952.1	E962.2	E982.1
butane (distributed in mobile container)	986	E868.0	—	E951.1	E962.2	E981.1
distributed through pipes	986	E867	—	E951.0	E962.2	E981.0
charcoal fumes	986	E868.3	—	E952.1	E962.2	E982.1

◀▶   New Code   ⬅▦▦➡   Revised Code

Substance	Poisoning	External Cause (E-Code)				
		Accident	Therapeutic Use	Suicide Attempt	Assault	Undetermined
Carbon *(Continued)*						
coal						
gas (piped)	986	E867	—	E951.0	E962.2	E981.0
solid (in domestic stoves, fireplaces)	986	E868.3	—	E952.1	E962.2	E982.1
coke (in domestic stoves, fireplaces)	986	E868.3	—	E952.1	E962.2	E982.1
exhaust gas (motor) not in transit	986	E868.2	—	E952.0	E962.2	E982.0
combustion engine, any not in watercraft	986	E868.2	—	E952.0	E962.2	E982.0
farm tractor, not in transit	986	E868.2	—	E952.0	E962.2	E982.0
gas engine	986	E868.2	—	E952.0	E962.2	E982.0
motor pump	986	E868.2	—	E952.0	E962.2	E982.0
motor vehicle, not in transit	986	E868.2	—	E952.0	E962.2	E982.0
fuel (in domestic use)	986	E868.3	—	E952.1	E962.2	E982.1
gas (piped)	986	E867	—	E951.0	E962.2	E981.0
in mobile container	986	E868.0	—	E951.1	E962.2	E981.1
utility	986	E868.1	—	E951.8	E962.2	E981.1
in mobile container	986	E868.0	—	E951.1	E962.2	E981.1
piped (natural)	986	E867	—	E951.0	E962.2	E981.0
illuminating gas	986	E868.1	—	E951.8	E962.2	E981.8
industrial fuels or gases, any	986	E868.8	—	E952.1	E962.2	E982.1
kerosene (in domestic stoves, fireplaces)	986	E868.3	—	E952.1	E962.2	E982.1
kiln gas or vapor	986	E868.8	—	E952.1	E962.2	E982.1
motor exhaust gas, not in transit	986	E868.2	—	E952.0	E962.2	E982.0
piped gas (manufactured) (natural)	986	E867	—	E951.0	E962.2	E981.0
producer gas	986	E868.8	—	E952.1	E962.2	E982.1
propane (distributed in mobile container)	986	E868.0	—	E951.1	E962.2	E981.1
distributed through pipes	986	E867	—	E951.0	E962.2	E981.0
specified source NEC	986	E868.8	—	E952.1	E962.2	E982.1
stove gas	986	E868.1	—	E951.8	E962.2	E981.8
piped	986	E867	—	E951.0	E962.2	E981.0
utility gas	986	E868.1	—	E951.8	E962.2	E981.8
piped	986	E867	—	E951.0	E962.2	E981.0
water gas	986	E868.1	—	E951.8	E962.2	E981.8
wood (in domestic stoves, fireplaces)	986	E868.3	—	E952.1	E962.2	E982.1
tetrachloride (vapor) NEC	987.8	E869.8	—	E952.8	E962.2	E982.8
liquid (cleansing agent) NEC	982.1	E861.3	—	E950.9	E962.1	E980.9
solvent	982.1	E862.4	—	E950.9	E962.1	E980.9
Carbonic acid (gas)	987.8	E869.8	—	E952.8	E962.2	E982.8
anhydrase inhibitors	974.2	E858.5	E944.2	E950.4	E962.0	E980.4
Carbowax	976.3	E858.7	E946.3	E950.4	E962.0	E980.4
Carbrital	967.0	E851	E937.0	E950.1	E962.0	E980.1
Carbromal (derivatives)	967.3	E852.2	E937.3	E950.2	E962.0	E980.2
Cardiac						
depressants	972.0	E858.3	E942.0	E950.4	E962.0	E980.4
rhythm regulators	972.0	E858.3	E942.0	E950.4	E962.0	E980.4
Cardiografin	977.8	E858.8	E947.8	E950.4	E962.0	E980.4
Cardio-green	977.8	E858.8	E947.8	E950.4	E962.0	E980.4
Cardiotonic glycosides	972.1	E858.3	E942.1	E950.4	E962.0	E980.4
Cardiovascular agents NEC	972.9	E858.3	E942.9	E950.4	E962.0	E980.4
Cardrase	974.2	E858.5	E944.2	E950.4	E962.0	E980.4
Carfusin	976.0	E858.7	E946.0	E950.4	E962.0	E980.4
Carisoprodol	968.0	E855.1	E938.0	E950.4	E962.0	E980.4
Carmustine	963.1	E858.1	E933.1	E950.4	E962.0	E980.4
Carotene	963.5	E858.1	E933.5	E950.4	E962.0	E980.4
Carphenazine (maleate)	969.1	E853.0	E939.1	E950.3	E962.0	E980.3
Carter's Little Pills	973.1	E858.4	E943.1	E950.4	E962.0	E980.4
Cascara (sagrada)	973.1	E858.4	E943.1	E950.4	E962.0	E980.4
Cassava	988.2	E865.4	—	E950.9	E962.1	E980.9
Castellani's paint	976.0	E858.7	E946.0	E950.4	E962.0	E980.4
Castor						
bean	988.2	E865.3	—	E950.9	E962.1	E980.9
oil	973.1	E858.4	E943.1	E950.4	E962.0	E980.4
Caterpillar (sting)	989.5	E905.5	—	E950.9	E962.1	E980.9
Catha (edulis)	970.8	E854.3	E940.8	E950.4	E962.0	E980.4

◀ ▶ **New Code** ⬅ ➡ **Revised Code**

Substance	Poisoning	External Cause (E-Code)				
		Accident	Therapeutic Use	Suicide Attempt	Assault	Undetermined
Cathartics NEC	973.3	E858.4	E943.3	E950.4	E962.0	E980.4
contact	973.1	E858.4	E943.1	E950.4	E962.0	E980.4
emollient	973.2	E858.4	E943.2	E950.4	E962.0	E980.4
intestinal irritants	973.1	E858.4	E943.1	E950.4	E962.0	E980.4
saline	973.3	E858.4	E943.3	E950.4	E962.0	E980.4
Cathomycin	960.8	E856	E930.8	E950.4	E962.0	E980.4
Caustic(s)	983.9	E864.4	—	E950.7	E962.1	E980.6
alkali	983.2	E864.2	—	E950.7	E962.1	E980.6
hydroxide	983.2	E864.2	—	E950.7	E962.1	E980.6
potash	983.2	E864.2	—	E950.7	E962.1	E980.6
soda	983.2	E864.2	—	E950.7	E962.1	E980.6
specified NEC	983.9	E864.3	—	E950.7	E962.1	E980.6
Ceepryn	976.0	E858.7	E946.0	E950.4	E962.0	E980.4
ENT agent	976.6	E858.7	E946.6	E950.4	E962.0	E980.4
lozenges	976.6	E858.7	E946.6	E950.4	E962.0	E980.4
Celestone	962.0	E858.0	E932.0	E950.4	E962.0	E980.4
topical	976.0	E858.7	E946.0	E950.4	E962.0	E980.4
Cellosolve	982.8	E862.4	—	E950.9	E962.1	E980.9
Cell stimulants and proliferants	976.8	E858.7	E946.8	E950.4	E962.0	E980.4
Cellulose derivatives, cathartic	973.3	E858.4	E943.3	E950.4	E962.0	E980.4
nitrates (topical)	976.3	E858.7	E946.3	E950.4	E962.0	E980.4
Centipede (bite)	989.5	E905.4	—	E950.9	E962.1	E980.9
Central nervous system						
depressants	968.4	E855.1	E938.4	E950.4	E962.0	E980.4
anesthetic (general) NEC	968.4	E855.1	E938.4	E950.4	E962.0	E980.4
gases NEC	968.2	E855.1	E938.2	E950.4	E962.0	E980.4
intravenous	968.3	E855.1	E938.3	E950.4	E962.0	E980.4
barbiturates	967.0	E851	E937.0	E950.1	E962.0	E980.1
bromides	967.3	E852.2	E937.3	E950.2	E962.0	E980.2
cannabis sativa	969.6	E854.1	E939.6	E950.3	E962.0	E980.3
chloral hydrate	967.1	E852.0	E937.1	E950.2	E962.0	E980.2
hallucinogenics	969.6	E854.1	E939.6	E950.3	E962.0	E980.3
hypnotics	967.9	E852.9	E937.9	E950.2	E962.0	E980.2
specified NEC	967.8	E852.8	E937.8	E950.2	E962.0	E980.2
muscle relaxants	968.0	E855.1	E938.0	E950.4	E962.0	E980.4
paraldehyde	967.2	E852.1	E937.2	E950.2	E962.0	E980.2
sedatives	967.9	E852.9	E937.9	E950.2	E962.0	E980.2
mixed NEC	967.6	E852.5	E937.6	E950.2	E962.0	E980.2
specified NEC	967.8	E852.8	E937.8	E950.2	E962.0	E980.2
muscle-tone depressants	968.0	E855.1	E938.0	E950.4	E962.0	E980.4
stimulants	970.9	E854.3	E940.9	E950.4	E962.0	E980.4
amphetamines	969.7	E854.2	E939.7	E950.3	E962.0	E980.3
analeptics	970.0	E854.3	E940.0	E950.4	E962.0	E980.4
antidepressants	969.0	E854.0	E939.0	E950.3	E962.0	E980.3
opiate antagonists	970.1	E854.3	E940.0	E950.4	E962.0	E980.4
specified NEC	970.8	E854.3	E940.8	E950.4	E962.0	E980.4
Cephalexin	960.5	E856	E930.5	E950.4	E962.0	E980.4
Cephaloglycin	960.5	E856	E930.5	E950.4	E962.0	E980.4
Cephaloridine	960.5	E856	E930.5	E950.4	E962.0	E980.4
Cephalosporins NEC	960.5	E856	E930.5	E950.4	E962.0	E980.4
N (adicillin)	960.0	E856	E930.0	E950.4	E962.0	E980.4
Cephalothin (sodium)	960.5	E856	E930.5	E950.4	E962.0	E980.4
Cerbera (odallam)	988.2	E865.4	—	E950.9	E962.1	E980.9
Cerberin	972.1	E858.3	E942.1	E950.4	E962.0	E980.4
Cerebral stimulants	970.9	E854.3	E940.9	E950.4	E962.0	E980.4
psychotherapeutic	969.7	E854.2	E939.7	E950.3	E962.0	E980.3
specified NEC	970.8	E854.3	E940.8	E950.4	E962.0	E980.4
Cetalkonium (chloride)	976.0	E858.7	E946.0	E950.4	E962.0	E980.4
Cetoxime	963.0	E858.1	E933.0	E950.4	E962.0	E980.4
Cetrimide	976.2	E858.7	E946.2	E950.4	E962.0	E980.4

◄▶ **New Code**　　　⬅▥▥➡ **Revised Code**

Substance	Poisoning	External Cause (E-Code)				
		Accident	Therapeutic Use	Suicide Attempt	Assault	Undetermined
Cetylpyridinium	976.0	E858.7	E946.0	E950.4	E962.0	E980.4
ENT agent	976.6	E858.7	E946.6	E950.4	E962.0	E980.4
lozenges	976.6	E858.7	E946.6	E950.4	E962.0	E980.4
Cevadilla - *see* Sabadilla						
Cevitamic acid	963.5	E858.1	E933.5	E950.4	E962.0	E980.4
Chalk, precipitated	973.0	E858.4	E943.0	E950.4	E962.0	E980.4
Charcoal						
fumes (carbon monoxide)	986	E868.3	—	E952.1	E962.2	E982.1
industrial	986	E868.8	—	E952.1	E962.2	E982.1
medicinal (activated)	973.0	E858.4	E943.0	E950.4	E962.0	E980.4
Chelating agents NEC	977.2	E858.8	E947.2	E950.4	E962.0	E980.4
Chelidonium majus	988.2	E865.4	—	E950.9	E962.1	E980.9
Chemical substance	989.9	E866.9	—	E950.9	E962.1	E980.9
specified NEC	989.89	E866.8	—	E950.9	E962.1	E980.9
Chenopodium (oil)	961.6	E857	E931.6	E950.4	E962.0	E980.4
Cherry laurel	988.2	E865.4	—	E950.9	E962.1	E980.9
Chiniofon	961.3	E857	E931.3	E950.4	E962.0	E980.4
Chlophedianol	975.4	E858.6	E945.4	E950.4	E962.0	E980.4
Chloral (betaine) (formamide) (hydrate)	967.1	E852.0	E937.1	E950.2	E962.0	E980.2
Chloralamide	967.1	E852.0	E937.1	E950.2	E962.0	E980.2
Chlorambucil	963.1	E858.1	E933.1	E950.4	E962.0	E980.4
Chloramphenicol	960.2	E856	E930.2	E950.4	E962.0	E980.4
ENT agent	976.6	E858.7	E946.6	E950.4	E962.0	E980.4
ophthalmic preparation	976.5	E858.7	E946.5	E950.4	E962.0	E980.4
topical NEC	976.0	E858.7	E946.0	E950.4	E962.0	E980.4
Chlorate(s) (potassium) (sodium) NEC	983.9	E864.3	—	E950.7	E962.1	E980.6
herbicides	989.4	E863.5	—	E950.6	E962.1	E980.7
Chlorcyclizine	963.0	E858.1	E933.0	E950.4	E962.0	E980.4
Chlordan(e) (dust)	989.2	E863.0	—	E950.6	E962.1	E980.7
Chlordantoin	976.0	E858.7	E946.0	E950.4	E962.0	E980.4
Chlordiazepoxide	969.4	E853.2	E939.4	E950.3	E962.0	E980.3
Chloresium	976.8	E858.7	E946.8	E950.4	E962.0	E980.4
Chlorethiazol	967.1	E852.0	E937.1	E950.2	E962.0	E980.2
Chlorethyl - *see* Ethyl, chloride						
Chloretone	967.1	E852.0	E937.1	E950.2	E962.0	E980.2
Chlorex	982.3	E862.4	—	E950.9	E962.1	E980.9
Chlorhexadol	967.1	E852.0	E937.1	E950.2	E962.0	E980.2
Chlorhexidine (hydrochloride)	976.0	E858.7	E946.0	E950.4	E962.0	E980.4
Chlorhydroxyquinolin	976.0	E858.7	E946.0	E950.4	E962.0	E980.4
Chloride of lime (bleach)	983.9	E864.3	—	E950.7	E962.1	E980.6
Chlorinated						
camphene	989.2	E863.0	—	E950.6	E962.1	E980.7
diphenyl	989.89	E866.8	—	E950.9	E962.1	E980.9
hydrocarbons NEC	989.2	E863.0	—	E950.6	E962.1	E980.7
solvent	982.3	E862.4	—	E950.9	E962.1	E980.9
lime (bleach)	983.9	E864.3	—	E950.7	E962.1	E980.6
naphthalene - *see* Naphthalene						
pesticides NEC	989.2	E863.0	—	E950.6	E962.1	E980.7
soda - *see* Sodium, hypochlorite						
Chlorine (fumes) (gas)	987.6	E869.8	—	E952.8	E962.2	E982.8
bleach	983.9	E864.3	—	E950.7	E962.1	E980.6
compounds NEC	983.9	E864.3	—	E950.7	E962.1	E980.6
disinfectant	983.9	E861.4	—	E950.7	E962.1	E980.6
releasing agents NEC	983.9	E864.3	—	E950.7	E962.1	E980.6
Chlorisondamine	972.3	E858.3	E942.3	E950.4	E962.0	E980.4
Chlormadinone	962.2	E858.0	E932.2	E950.4	E962.0	E980.4
Chlormerodrin	974.0	E858.5	E944.0	E950.4	E962.0	E980.4
Chlormethiazole	967.1	E852.0	E937.1	E950.2	E962.0	E980.2
Chlormethylenecycline	960.4	E856	E930.4	E950.4	E962.0	E980.4
Chlormezanone	969.5	E853.8	E939.5	E950.3	E962.0	E980.3
Chloroacetophenone	987.5	E869.3	—	E952.8	E962.2	E982.8

Substance	Poisoning	External Cause (E-Code)				
		Accident	Therapeutic Use	Suicide Attempt	Assault	Undetermined
Chloroaniline	983.0	E864.0	—	E950.7	E962.1	E980.6
Chlorobenzene, chlorobenzol	982.0	E862.4	—	E950.9	E962.1	E980.9
Chlorobutanol	967.1	E852.0	E937.1	E950.2	E962.0	E980.2
Chlorodinitrobenzene	983.0	E864.0	—	E950.7	E962.1	E980.6
dust or vapor	987.8	E869.8	—	E952.8	E962.2	E982.8
Chloroethane - *see* Ethyl, chloride						
Chloroform (fumes) (vapor)	987.8	E869.8	—	E952.8	E962.2	E982.8
anesthetic (gas)	968.2	E855.1	E938.2	E950.4	E962.0	E980.4
liquid NEC	968.4	E855.1	E938.4	E950.4	E962.0	E980.4
solvent	982.3	E862.4	—	E950.9	E962.1	E980.9
Chloroguanide	961.4	E857	E931.4	E950.4	E962.0	E980.4
Chloromycetin	960.2	E856	E930.2	E950.4	E962.0	E980.4
ENT agent	976.6	E858.7	E946.6	E950.4	E962.0	E980.4
ophthalmic preparation	976.5	E858.7	E946.5	E950.4	E962.0	E980.4
otic solution	976.6	E858.7	E946.6	E950.4	E962.0	E980.4
topical NEC	976.0	E858.7	E946.0	E950.4	E962.0	E980.4
Chloronitrobenzene	983.0	E864.0	—	E950.7	E962.1	E980.6
dust or vapor	987.8	E869.8	—	E952.8	E962.2	E982.8
Chlorophenol	983.0	E864.0	—	E950.7	E962.1	E980.6
Chlorophenothane	989.2	E863.0	—	E950.6	E962.1	E980.7
Chlorophyll (derivatives)	976.8	E858.7	E946.8	E950.4	E962.0	E980.4
Chloropicrin (fumes)	987.8	E869.8	—	E952.8	E962.2	E982.8
fumigant	989.4	E863.8	—	E950.6	E962.1	E980.7
fungicide	989.4	E863.6	—	E950.6	E962.1	E980.7
pesticide (fumes)	989.4	E863.4	—	E950.6	E962.1	E980.7
Chloroprocaine	968.9	E855.2	E938.9	E950.4	E962.0	E980.4
infiltration (subcutaneous)	968.5	E855.2	E938.5	E950.4	E962.0	E980.4
nerve block (peripheral) (plexus)	968.6	E855.2	E938.6	E950.4	E962.0	E980.4
Chloroptic	976.5	E858.7	E946.5	E950.4	E962.0	E980.4
Chloropurine	963.1	E858.1	E933.1	E950.4	E962.0	E980.4
Chloroquine (hydrochloride) (phosphate)	961.4	E857	E931.4	E950.4	E962.0	E980.4
Chlorothen	963.0	E858.1	E933.0	E950.4	E962.0	E980.4
Chlorothiazide	974.3	E858.5	E944.3	E950.4	E962.0	E980.4
Chlorotrianisene	962.2	E858.0	E932.2	E950.4	E962.0	E980.4
Chlorovinyldichloroarsine	985.1	E866.3	—	E950.8	E962.1	E980.8
Chloroxylenol	976.0	E858.7	E946.0	E950.4	E962.0	E980.4
Chlorphenesin (carbamate)	968.0	E855.1	E938.0	E950.4	E962.0	E980.4
topical (antifungal)	976.0	E858.7	E946.0	E950.4	E962.0	E980.4
Chlorpheniramine	963.0	E858.1	E933.0	E950.4	E962.0	E980.4
Chlorphenoxamine	966.4	E855.0	E936.4	E950.4	E962.0	E980.4
Chlorphentermine	977.0	E858.8	E947.0	E950.4	E962.0	E980.4
Chlorproguanil	961.4	E857	E931.4	E950.4	E962.0	E980.4
Chlorpromazine	969.1	E853.0	E939.1	E950.3	E962.0	E980.3
Chlorpropamide	962.3	E858.0	E932.3	E950.4	E962.0	E980.4
Chlorprothixene	969.3	E853.8	E939.3	E950.3	E962.0	E980.3
Chlorquinaldol	976.0	E858.7	E946.0	E950.4	E962.0	E980.4
Chlortetracycline	960.4	E856	E930.4	E950.4	E962.0	E980.4
Chlorthalidone	974.4	E858.5	E944.4	E950.4	E962.0	E980.4
Chlortrianisene	962.2	E858.0	E932.2	E950.4	E962.0	E980.4
Chlor-Trimeton	963.0	E858.1	E933.0	E950.4	E962.0	E980.4
Chlorzoxazone	968.0	E855.1	E938.0	E950.4	E962.0	E980.4
Choke damp	987.8	E869.8	—	E952.8	E962.2	E982.8
Cholebrine	977.8	E858.8	E947.8	E950.4	E962.0	E980.4
Cholera vaccine	978.2	E858.8	E948.2	E950.4	E962.0	E980.4
Cholesterol-lowering agents	972.2	E858.3	E942.2	E950.4	E962.0	E980.4
Cholestyramine (resin)	972.2	E858.3	E942.2	E950.4	E962.0	E980.4
Cholic acid	973.4	E858.4	E943.4	E950.4	E962.0	E980.4
Choline						
dihydrogen citrate	977.1	E858.8	E947.1	E950.4	E962.0	E980.4
salicylate	965.1	E850.3	E935.3	E950.0	E962.0	E980.0
theophyllinate	974.1	E858.5	E944.1	E950.4	E962.0	E980.4

◄ ▶ **New Code**   ◄▥ ▥▶ **Revised Code**

Substance	Poisoning	External Cause (E-Code)				
		Accident	Therapeutic Use	Suicide Attempt	Assault	Undetermined
Cholinergics	971.0	E855.3	E941.0	E950.4	E962.0	E980.4
Cholografin	977.8	E858.8	E947.8	E950.4	E962.0	E980.4
Chorionic gonadotropin	962.4	E858.0	E932.4	E950.4	E962.0	E980.4
Chromates	983.9	E864.3	—	E950.7	E962.1	E980.6
dust or mist	987.8	E869.8	—	E952.8	E962.2	E982.8
lead	984.0	E866.0	—	E950.9	E962.1	E980.9
paint	984.0	E861.5	—	E950.9	E962.1	E980.9
Chromic acid	983.9	E864.3	—	E950.7	E962.1	E980.6
dust or mist	987.8	E869.8	—	E952.8	E962.2	E982.8
Chromium	985.6	E866.4	—	E950.9	E962.1	E980.9
compounds - *see* Chromates						
Chromonar	972.4	E858.3	E942.4	E950.4	E962.0	E980.4
Chromyl chloride	983.9	E864.3	—	E950.7	E962.1	E980.6
Chrysarobin (ointment)	976.4	E858.7	E946.4	E950.4	E962.0	E980.4
Chrysazin	973.1	E858.4	E943.1	E950.4	E962.0	E980.4
Chymar	963.4	E858.1	E933.4	E950.4	E962.0	E980.4
ophthalmic preparation	976.5	E858.7	E946.5	E950.4	E962.0	E980.4
Chymotrypsin	963.4	E858.1	E933.4	E950.4	E962.0	E980.4
ophthalmic preparation	976.5	E858.7	E946.5	E950.4	E962.0	E980.4
Cicuta maculata or virosa	988.2	E865.4	—	E950.9	E962.1	E980.9
Cigarette lighter fluid	981	E862.1	—	E950.9	E962.1	E980.9
Cinchocaine (spinal)	968.7	E855.2	E938.7	E950.4	E962.0	E980.4
topical (surface)	968.5	E855.2	E938.5	E950.4	E962.0	E980.4
Cinchona	961.4	E857	E931.4	E950.4	E962.0	E980.4
Cinchonine alkaloids	961.4	E857	E931.4	E950.4	E962.0	E980.4
Cinchophen	974.7	E858.5	E944.7	E950.4	E962.0	E980.4
Cinnarizine	963.0	E858.1	E933.0	E950.4	E962.0	E980.4
Citanest	968.9	E855.2	E938.9	E950.4	E962.0	E980.4
infiltration (subcutaneous)	968.5	E855.2	E938.5	E950.4	E962.0	E980.4
nerve block (peripheral) (plexus)	968.6	E855.2	E938.6	E950.4	E962.0	E980.4
Citric acid	989.89	E866.8	—	E950.9	E962.1	E980.9
Citrovorum factor	964.1	E858.2	E934.1	E950.4	E962.0	E980.4
Claviceps purpurea	988.2	E865.4	—	E950.9	E962.1	E980.9
Cleaner, cleansing agent NEC	989.89	E861.3	—	E950.9	E962.1	E980.9
of paint or varnish	982.8	E862.9	—	E950.9	E962.1	E980.9
Clematis vitalba	988.2	E865.4	—	E950.9	E962.1	E980.9
Clemizole	963.0	E858.1	E933.0	E950.4	E962.0	E980.4
penicillin	960.0	E856	E930.0	E950.4	E962.0	E980.4
Clidinium	971.1	E855.4	E941.1	E950.4	E962.0	E980.4
Clindamycin	960.8	E856	E930.8	E950.4	E962.0	E980.4
Cliradon	965.09	E850.2	E935.2	E950.0	E962.0	E980.0
Clocortolone	962.0	E858.0	E932.0	E950.4	E962.0	E980.4
Clofedanol	975.4	E858.6	E945.4	E950.4	E962.0	E980.4
Clofibrate	972.2	E858.3	E942.2	E950.4	E962.0	E980.4
Clomethiazole	967.1	E852.0	E937.1	E950.2	E962.0	E980.2
Clomiphene	977.8	E858.8	E947.8	E950.4	E962.0	E980.4
Clonazepam	969.4	E853.2	E939.4	E950.3	E962.0	E980.3
Clonidine	972.6	E858.3	E942.6	E950.4	E962.0	E980.4
Clopamide	974.3	E858.5	E944.3	E950.4	E962.0	E980.4
Clorazepate	969.4	E853.2	E939.4	E950.3	E962.0	E980.3
Clorexolone	974.4	E858.5	E944.4	E950.4	E962.0	E980.4
Clorox (bleach)	983.9	E864.3	—	E950.7	E962.1	E980.6
Clortermine	977.0	E858.8	E947.0	E950.4	E962.0	E980.4
Clotrimazole	976.0	E858.7	E946.0	E950.4	E962.0	E980.4
Cloxacillin	960.0	E856	E930.0	E950.4	E962.0	E980.4
Coagulants NEC	964.5	E858.2	E934.5	E950.4	E962.0	E980.4
Coal (carbon monoxide from) - *see also* Carbon, monoxide, coal						
oil - *see* Kerosene						
tar NEC	983.0	E864.0		E950.7	E962.1	E980.6
fumes	987.8	E869.8	—	E952.8	E962.2	E982.8
medicinal (ointment)	976.4	E858.7	E946.4	E950.4	E962.0	E980.4

◀▶ **New Code**   ◀|||| ||||▶ **Revised Code**

Substance	Poisoning	External Cause (E-Code)				
		Accident	Therapeutic Use	Suicide Attempt	Assault	Undetermined
Coal *(Continued)*						
analgesics NEC	965.5	E850.5	E935.5	E950.0	E962.0	E980.0
naphtha (solvent)	981	E862.0	—	E950.9	E962.1	E980.9
Cobalt (fumes) (industrial)	985.8	E866.4	—	E950.9	E962.1	E980.9
Cobra (venom)	989.5	E905.0	—	E950.9	E962.1	E980.9
Coca (leaf)	970.8	E854.3	E940.8	E950.4	E962.0	E980.4
Cocaine (hydrochloride) (salt)	968.5	E855.2	E938.5	E950.4	E962.0	E980.4
Coccidioidin	977.8	E858.8	E947.8	E950.4	E962.0	E980.4
Cocculus indicus	988.2	E865.3	—	E950.9	E962.1	E980.9
Cochineal	989.89	E866.8	—	E950.9	E962.1	E980.9
medicinal products	977.4	E858.8	E947.4	E950.4	E962.0	E980.4
Codeine	965.09	E850.2	E935.2	E950.0	E962.0	E980.0
Coffee	989.89	E866.8	—	E950.9	E962.1	E980.9
Cogentin	971.1	E855.4	E941.1	E950.4	E962.0	E980.4
Coke fumes or gas (carbon monoxide)	986	E868.3	—	E952.1	E962.2	E982.1
industrial use	986	E868.8	—	E952.1	E962.2	E982.1
Colace	973.2	E858.4	E943.2	E950.4	E962.0	E980.4
Colchicine	974.7	E858.5	E944.7	E950.4	E962.0	E980.4
Colchicum	988.2	E865.3	—	E950.9	E962.1	E980.9
Cold cream	976.3	E858.7	E946.3	E950.4	E962.0	E980.4
Colestipol	972.2	E858.3	E942.2	E950.4	E962.0	E980.4
Colistimethate	960.8	E856	E930.8	E950.4	E962.0	E980.4
Colistin	960.8	E856	E930.8	E950.4	E962.0	E980.4
Collagen	977.8	E866.8	E947.8	E950.9	E962.1	E980.9
Collagenase	976.8	E858.7	E946.8	E950.4	E962.0	E980.4
Collodion (flexible)	976.3	E858.7	E946.3	E950.4	E962.0	E980.4
Colocynth	973.1	E858.4	E943.1	E950.4	E962.0	E980.4
Coloring matter - *see* Dye(s)						
Combustion gas - *see* Carbon, monoxide						
Compazine	969.1	E853.0	E939.1	E950.3	E962.0	E980.3
Compound						
42 (warfarin)	989.4	E863.7	—	E950.6	E962.1	E980.7
269 (endrin)	989.2	E863.0	—	E950.6	E962.1	E980.7
497 (dieldrin)	989.2	E863.0	—	E950.6	E962.1	E980.7
1080 (sodium fluoroacetate)	989.4	E863.7	—	E950.6	E962.1	E980.7
3422 (parathion)	989.3	E863.1	—	E950.6	E962.1	E980.7
3911 (phorate)	989.3	E863.1	—	E950.6	E962.1	E980.7
3956 (toxaphene)	989.2	E863.0	—	E950.6	E962.1	E980.7
4049 (malathion)	989.3	E863.1	—	E950.6	E962.1	E980.7
4124 (dicapthon)	989.4	E863.4	—	E950.6	E962.1	E980.7
E (cortisone)	962.0	E858.0	E932.0	E950.4	E962.0	E980.4
F (hydrocortisone)	962.0	E858.0	E932.0	E950.4	E962.0	E980.4
Congo red	977.8	E858.8	E947.8	E950.4	E962.0	E980.4
Coniine, conine	965.7	E850.7	E935.7	E950.0	E962.0	E980.0
Conium (maculatum)	988.2	E865.4	—	E950.9	E962.1	E980.9
Conjugated estrogens (equine)	962.2	E858.0	E932.2	E950.4	E962.0	E980.4
Contac	975.6	E858.6	E945.6	E950.4	E962.0	E980.4
Contact lens solution	976.5	E858.7	E946.5	E950.4	E962.0	E980.4
Contraceptives (oral)	962.2	E858.0	E932.2	E950.4	E962.0	E980.4
vaginal	976.8	E858.7	E946.8	E950.4	E962.0	E980.4
Contrast media (roentgenographic)	977.8	E858.8	E947.8	E950.4	E962.0	E980.4
Convallaria majalis	988.2	E865.4	—	E950.9	E962.1	E980.9
Copper (dust) (fumes) (salts) NEC	985.8	E866.4	—	E950.9	E962.1	E980.9
arsenate, arsenite	985.1	E866.3	—	E950.8	E962.1	E980.8
insecticide	985.1	E863.4	—	E950.8	E962.1	E980.8
emetic	973.6	E858.4	E943.6	E950.4	E962.0	E980.4
fungicide	985.8	E863.6	—	E950.6	E962.1	E980.7
insecticide	985.8	E863.4	—	E950.6	E962.1	E980.7
oleate	976.0	E858.7	E946.0	E950.4	E962.0	E980.4
sulfate	983.9	E864.3	—	E950.7	E962.1	E980.6
fungicide	983.9	E863.6	—	E950.7	E962.1	E980.6

Substance	Poisoning	External Cause (E-Code)				
		Accident	Therapeutic Use	Suicide Attempt	Assault	Undetermined
Copper *(Continued)*						
cupric	973.6	E858.4	E943.6	E950.4	E962.0	E980.4
cuprous	983.9	E864.3	—	E950.7	E962.1	E980.6
Copperhead snake (bite) (venom)	989.5	E905.0	—	E950.9	E962.1	E980.9
Coral (sting)	989.5	E905.6	—	E950.9	E962.1	E980.9
snake (bite) (venom)	989.5	E905.0	—	E950.9	E962.1	E980.9
Cordran	976.0	E858.7	E946.0	E950.4	E962.0	E980.4
Corn cures	976.4	E858.7	E946.4	E950.4	E962.0	E980.4
Cornhusker's lotion	976.3	E858.7	E946.3	E950.4	E962.0	E980.4
Corn starch	976.3	E858.7	E946.3	E950.4	E962.0	E980.4
Corrosive	983.9	E864.4	—	E950.7	E962.1	E980.6
acids NEC	983.1	E864.1	—	E950.7	E962.1	E980.6
aromatics	983.0	E864.0	—	E950.7	E962.1	E980.6
disinfectant	983.0	E861.4	—	E950.7	E962.1	E980.6
fumes NEC	987.9	E869.9	—	E952.9	E962.2	E982.9
specified NEC	983.9	E864.3	—	E950.7	E962.1	E980.6
sublimate - *see* Mercury, chloride						
Cortate	962.0	E858.0	E932.0	E950.4	E962.0	E980.4
Cort-Dome	962.0	E858.0	E932.0	E950.4	E962.0	E980.4
ENT agent	976.6	E858.7	E946.6	E950.4	E962.0	E980.4
ophthalmic preparation	976.5	E858.7	E946.5	E950.4	E962.0	E980.4
topical NEC	976.0	E858.7	E946.0	E950.4	E962.0	E980.4
Cortef	962.0	E858.0	E932.0	E950.4	E962.0	E980.4
ENT agent	976.6	E858.7	E946.6	E950.4	E962.0	E980.4
ophthalmic preparation	976.5	E858.7	E946.5	E950.4	E962.0	E980.4
topical NEC	976.0	E858.7	E946.0	E950.4	E962.0	E980.4
Corticosteroids (fluorinated)	962.0	E858.0	E932.0	E950.4	E962.0	E980.4
ENT agent	976.6	E858.7	E946.6	E950.4	E962.0	E980.4
ophthalmic preparation	976.5	E858.7	E946.5	E950.4	E962.0	E980.4
topical NEC	976.0	E858.7	E946.0	E950.4	E962.0	E980.4
Corticotropin	962.4	E858.0	E932.4	E950.4	E962.0	E980.4
Cortisol	962.0	E858.0	E932.0	E950.4	E962.0	E980.4
ENT agent	976.6	E858.7	E946.6	E950.4	E962.0	E980.4
ophthalmic preparation	976.5	E858.7	E946.5	E950.4	E962.0	E980.4
topical NEC	976.0	E858.7	E946.0	E950.4	E962.0	E980.4
Cortisone derivatives (acetate)	962.0	E858.0	E932.0	E950.4	E962.0	E980.4
ENT agent	976.6	E858.7	E946.6	E950.4	E962.0	E980.4
ophthalmic preparation	976.5	E858.7	E946.5	E950.4	E962.0	E980.4
topical NEC	976.0	E858.7	E946.0	E950.4	E962.0	E980.4
Cortogen	962.0	E858.0	E932.0	E950.4	E962.0	E980.4
ENT agent	976.6	E858.7	E946.6	E950.4	E962.0	E980.4
ophthalmic preparation	976.5	E858.7	E946.5	E950.4	E962.0	E980.4
Cortone	962.0	E858.0	E932.0	E950.4	E962.0	E980.4
ENT agent	976.6	E858.7	E946.6	E950.4	E962.0	E980.4
ophthalmic preparation	976.5	E858.7	E946.5	E950.4	E962.0	E980.4
Cortril	962.0	E858.0	E932.0	E950.4	E962.0	E980.4
ENT agent	976.6	E858.7	E946.6	E950.4	E962.0	E980.4
ophthalmic preparation	976.5	E858.7	E946.5	E950.4	E962.0	E980.4
topical NEC	976.0	E858.7	E946.0	E950.4	E962.0	E980.4
Cosmetics	989.89	E866.7	—	E950.9	E962.1	E980.9
Cosyntropin	977.8	E858.8	E947.8	E950.4	E962.0	E980.4
Cotarnine	964.5	E858.2	E934.5	E950.4	E962.0	E980.4
Cottonseed oil	976.3	E858.7	E946.3	E950.4	E962.0	E980.4
Cough mixtures (antitussives)	975.4	E858.6	E945.4	E950.4	E962.0	E980.4
containing opiates	965.09	E850.2	E935.2	E950.0	E962.0	E980.0
expectorants	975.5	E858.6	E945.5	E950.4	E962.0	E980.4
Coumadin	964.2	E858.2	E934.2	E950.4	E962.0	E980.4
rodenticide	989.4	E863.7	—	E950.6	E962.1	E980.7
Coumarin	964.2	E858.2	E934.2	E950.4	E962.0	E980.43
Coumetarol	964.2	E858.2	E934.2	E950.4	E962.0	E980.4
Cowbane	988.2	E865.4	—	E950.9	E962.1	E980.9
Cozyme	963.5	E858.1	E933.5	E950.4	E962.0	E980.4

◀▶ **New Code**   ◀▥ ▥▶ **Revised Code**

Substance	Poisoning	External Cause (E-Code)				
		Accident	Therapeutic Use	Suicide Attempt	Assault	Undetermined
Creolin	983.0	E864.0	—	E950.7	E962.1	E980.6
disinfectant	983.0	E861.4	—	E950.7	E962.1	E980.6
Creosol (compound)	983.0	E864.0	—	E950.7	E962.1	E980.6
Creosote (beechwood) (coal tar)	983.0	E864.0	—	E950.7	E962.1	E980.6
medicinal (expectorant)	975.5	E858.6	E945.5	E950.4	E962.0	E980.4
syrup	975.5	E858.6	E945.5	E950.4	E962.0	E980.4
Cresol	983.0	E864.0	—	E950.7	E962.1	E980.6
disinfectant	983.0	E861.4	—	E950.7	E962.1	E980.6
Cresylic acid	983.0	E864.0	—	E950.7	E962.1	E980.6
Cropropamide	965.7	E850.7	E935.7	E950.0	E962.0	E980.0
with crotethamide	970.0	E854.3	E940.0	E950.4	E962.0	E980.4
Crotamiton	976.0	E858.7	E946.0	E950.4	E962.0	E980.4
Crotethamide	965.7	E850.7	E935.7	E950.0	E962.0	E980.0
with cropropamide	970.0	E854.3	E940.0	E950.4	E962.0	E980.4
Croton (oil)	973.1	E858.4	E943.1	E950.4	E962.0	E980.4
chloral	967.1	E852.0	E937.1	E950.2	E962.0	E980.2
Crude oil	981	E862.1	—	E950.9	E962.1	E980.9
Cryogenine	965.8	E850.8	E935.8	E950.0	E962.0	E980.0
Cryolite (pesticide)	989.4	E863.4	—	E950.6	E962.1	E980.7
Cryptenamine	972.6	E858.3	E942.6	E950.4	E962.0	E980.4
Crystal violet	976.0	E858.7	E946.0	E950.4	E962.0	E980.4
Cuckoopint	988.2	E865.4	—	E950.9	E962.1	E980.9
Cumetharol	964.2	E858.2	E934.2	E950.4	E962.0	E980.4
Cupric sulfate	973.6	E858.4	E943.6	E950.4	E962.0	E980.4
Cuprous sulfate	983.9	E864.3	—	E950.7	E962.1	E980.6
Curare, curarine	975.2	E858.6	E945.2	E950.4	E962.0	E980.4
Cyanic acid - *see* Cyanide(s)						
Cyanide(s) (compounds) (hydrogen) (potassium) (sodium) NEC	989.0	E866.8	—	E950.9	E962.1	E980.9
dust or gas (inhalation) NEC	987.7	E869.8	—	E952.8	E962.2	E982.8
fumigant	989.0	E863.8	—	E950.6	E962.1	E980.7
mercuric - *see* Mercury						
pesticide (dust) (fumes)	989.0	E863.4	—	E950.6	E962.1	E980.7
Cyanocobalamin	964.1	E858.2	E934.1	E950.4	E962.0	E980.4
Cyanogen (chloride) (gas)						
NEC	987.8	E869.8	—	E952.8	E962.2	E982.8
Cyclaine	968.5	E855.2	E938.5	E950.4	E962.0	E980.4
Cyclamen europaeum	988.2	E865.4	—	E950.9	E962.1	E980.9
Cyclandelate	972.5	E858.3	E942.5	E950.4	E962.0	E980.4
Cyclazocine	965.09	E850.2	E935.2	E950.0	E962.0	E980.0
Cyclizine	963.0	E858.1	E933.0	E950.4	E962.0	E980.4
Cyclobarbital, cyclobarbitone	967.0	E851	E937.0	E950.1	E962.0	E980.1
Cycloguanil	961.4	E857	E931.4	E950.4	E962.0	E980.4
Cyclohexane	982.0	E862.4	—	E950.9	E962.1	E980.9
Cyclohexanol	980.8	E860.8	—	E950.9	E962.1	E980.9
Cyclohexanone	982.8	E862.4	—	E950.9	E962.1	E980.9
Cyclomethycaine	968.5	E855.2	E938.5	E950.4	E962.0	E980.4
Cyclopentamine	971.2	E855.5	E941.2	E950.4	E962.0	E980.4
Cyclopenthiazide	974.3	E858.5	E944.3	E950.4	E962.0	E980.4
Cyclopentolate	971.1	E855.4	E941.1	E950.4	E962.0	E980.4
Cyclophosphamide	963.1	E858.1	E933.1	E950.4	E962.0	E980.4
Cyclopropane	968.2	E855.1	E938.2	E950.4	E962.0	E980.4
Cycloserine	960.6	E856	E930.6	E950.4	E962.0	E980.4
Cyclothiazide	974.3	E858.5	E944.3	E950.4	E962.0	E980.4
Cycrimine	966.4	E855.0	E936.4	E950.4	E962.0	E980.4
Cymarin	972.1	E858.3	E942.1	E950.4	E962.0	E980.4
Cyproheptadine	963.0	E858.1	E933.0	E950.4	E962.0	E980.4
Cyprolidol	969.0	E854.0	E939.0	E950.3	E962.0	E980.3
Cytarabine	963.1	E858.1	E933.1	E950.4	E962.0	E980.4
Cytisus						
laburnum	988.2	E865.4	—	E950.9	E962.1	E980.9
scoparius	988.2	E865.4	—	E950.9	E962.1	E980.9

Substance	Poisoning	External Cause (E-Code)				
		Accident	Therapeutic Use	Suicide Attempt	Assault	Undetermined
Cytomel	962.7	E858.0	E932.7	E950.4	E962.0	E980.4
Cytosine (antineoplastic)	963.1	E858.1	E933.1	E950.4	E962.0	E980.4
Cytoxan	963.1	E858.1	E933.1	E950.4	E962.0	E980.4
Dacarbazine	963.1	E858.1	E933.1	E950.4	E962.0	E980.4
Dactinomycin	960.7	E856	E930.7	E950.4	E962.0	E980.4
DADPS	961.8	E857	E931.8	E950.4	E962.0	E980.4
Dakin's solution (external)	976.0	E858.7	E946.0	E950.4	E962.0	E980.4
Dalmane	969.4	E853.2	E939.4	E950.3	E962.0	E980.3
DAM	977.2	E858.8	E947.2	E950.4	E962.0	E980.4
Danilone	964.2	E858.2	E934.2	E950.4	E962.0	E980.4
Danthron	973.1	E858.4	E943.1	E950.4	E962.0	E980.4
Dantrolene	975.2	E858.6	E945.2	E950.4	E962.0	E980.4
Daphne (gnidium) (mezereum)	988.2	E865.4	—	E950.9	E962.1	E980.9
berry	988.2	E865.3	—	E950.9	E962.1	E980.9
Dapsone	961.8	E857	E931.8	E950.4	E962.0	E980.4
Daraprim	961.4	E857	E931.4	E950.4	E962.0	E980.4
Darnel	988.2	E865.3	—	E950.9	E962.1	E980.9
Darvon	965.8	E850.8	E935.8	E950.0	E962.0	E980.0
Daunorubicin	960.7	E856	E930.7	E950.4	E962.0	E980.4
DBI	962.3	E858.0	E932.3	E950.4	E962.0	E980.4
D-Con (rodenticide)	989.4	E863.7	—	E950.6	E962.1	E980.7
DDS	961.8	E857	E931.8	E950.4	E962.0	E980.4
DDT	989.2	E863.0	—	E950.6	E962.1	E980.7
Deadly nightshade	988.2	E865.4	—	E950.9	E962.1	E980.9
berry	988.2	E865.3	—	E950.9	E962.1	E980.9
Deanol	969.7	E854.2	E939.7	E950.3	E962.0	E980.3
Debrisoquine	972.6	E858.3	E942.6	E950.4	E962.0	E980.4
Decaborane	989.89	E866.8	—	E950.9	E962.1	E980.9
fumes	987.8	E869.8	—	E952.8	E962.2	E982.8
Decadron	962.0	E858.0	E932.0	E950.4	E962.0	E980.4
ENT agent	976.6	E858.7	E946.6	E950.4	E962.0	E980.4
ophthalmic preparation	976.5	E858.7	E946.5	E950.4	E962.0	E980.4
topical NEC	976.0	E858.7	E946.0	E950.4	E962.0	E980.4
Decahydronaphthalene	982.0	E862.4	—	E950.9	E962.1	E980.9
Decalin	982.0	E862.4	—	E950.9	E962.1	E980.9
Decamethonium	975.2	E858.6	E945.2	E950.4	E962.0	E980.4
Decholin	973.4	E858.4	E943.4	E950.4	E962.0	E980.4
sodium (diagnostic)	977.8	E858.8	E947.8	E950.4	E962.0	E980.4
Declomycin	960.4	E856	E930.4	E950.4	E962.0	E980.4
Deferoxamine	963.8	E858.1	E933.8	E950.4	E962.0	E980.4
Dehydrocholic acid	973.4	E858.4	E943.4	E950.4	E962.0	E980.4
DeKalin	982.0	E862.4	—	E950.9	E962.1	E980.9
Delalutin	962.2	E858.0	E932.2	E950.4	E962.0	E980.4
Delphinium	988.2	E865.3	—	E950.9	E962.1	E980.9
Deltasone	962.0	E858.0	E932.0	E950.4	E962.0	E980.4
Deltra	962.0	E858.0	E932.0	E950.4	E962.0	E980.4
Delvinal	967.0	E851	E937.0	E950.1	E962.0	E980.1
Demecarium (bromide)	971.0	E855.3	E941.0	E950.4	E962.0	E980.4
Demeclocycline	960.4	E856	E930.4	E950.4	E962.0	E980.4
Demecolcine	963.1	E858.1	E933.1	E950.4	E962.0	E980.4
Demelanizing agents	976.8	E858.7	E946.8	E950.4	E962.0	E980.4
Demerol	965.09	E850.2	E935.2	E950.0	E962.0	E980.0
Demethylchlortetracycline	960.4	E856	E930.4	E950.4	E962.0	E980.4
Demethyltetracycline	960.4	E856	E930.4	E950.4	E962.0	E980.4
Demeton	989.3	E863.1	—	E950.6	E962.1	E980.7
Demulcents	976.3	E858.7	E946.3	E950.4	E962.0	E980.4
Demulen	962.2	E858.0	E932.2	E950.4	E962.0	E980.4
Denatured alcohol	980.0	E860.1	—	E950.9	E962.1	E980.9
Dendrid	976.5	E858.7	E946.5	E950.4	E962.0	E980.4
Dental agents, topical	976.7	E858.7	E946.7	E950.4	E962.0	E980.4
Deodorant spray (feminine hygiene)	976.8	E858.7	E946.8	E950.4	E962.0	E980.4

◀▶ **New Code**   ◀▥▥▶ **Revised Code**

Substance	Poisoning	External Cause (E-Code)				
		Accident	Therapeutic Use	Suicide Attempt	Assault	Undetermined
Deoxyribonuclease	963.4	E858.1	E933.4	E950.4	E962.0	E980.4
Depressants						
appetite, central	977.0	E858.8	E947.0	E950.4	E962.0	E980.4
cardiac	972.0	E858.3	E942.0	E950.4	E962.0	E980.4
central nervous system (anesthetic)	968.4	E855.1	E938.4	E950.4	E962.0	E980.4
psychotherapeutic	969.5	E853.9	E939.5	E950.3	E962.0	E980.3
Dequalinium	976.0	E858.7	E946.0	E950.4	E962.0	E980.4
Dermolate	976.2	E858.7	E946.2	E950.4	E962.0	E980.4
DES	962.2	E858.0	E932.2	E950.4	E962.0	E980.4
Desenex	976.0	E858.7	E946.0	E950.4	E962.0	E980.4
Deserpidine	972.6	E858.3	E942.6	E950.4	E962.0	E980.4
Desipramine	969.0	E854.0	E939.0	E950.3	E962.0	E980.3
Deslanocide	972.1	E858.3	E942.1	E950.4	E962.0	E980.4
Desocodeine	965.09	E850.2	E935.2	E950.0	E962.0	E980.0
Desomorphine	965.09	E850.2	E935.2	E950.0	E962.0	E980.0
Desonide	976.0	E858.7	E946.0	E950.4	E962.0	E980.4
Desoxycorticosterone derivatives	962.0	E858.0	E932.0	E950.4	E962.0	E980.4
Desoxyephedrine	969.7	E854.2	E939.7	E950.3	E962.0	E980.3
DET	969.6	E854.1	E939.6	E950.3	E962.0	E980.3
Detergents (ingested) (synthetic)	989.6	E861.0	—	E950.9	E962.1	E980.9
external medication	976.2	E858.7	E946.2	E950.4	E962.0	E980.4
Deterrent, alcohol	977.3	E858.8	E947.3	E950.4	E962.0	E980.4
Detrothyronine	962.7	E858.0	E932.7	E950.4	E962.0	E980.4
Dettol (external medication)	976.0	E858.7	E946.0	E950.4	E962.0	E980.4
Dexamethasone	962.0	E858.0	E932.0	E950.4	E962.0	E980.4
ENT agent	976.6	E858.7	E946.6	E950.4	E962.0	E980.4
ophthalmic preparation	976.5	E858.7	E946.5	E950.4	E962.0	E980.4
topical NEC	976.0	E858.7	E946.0	E950.4	E962.0	E980.4
Dexamphetamine	969.7	E854.2	E939.7	E950.3	E962.0	E980.3
Dexedrine	969.7	E854.2	E939.7	E950.3	E962.0	E980.3
Dexpanthenol	963.5	E858.1	E933.5	E950.4	E962.0	E980.4
Dextran	964.8	E858.2	E934.8	E950.4	E962.0	E980.4
Dextriferron	964.0	E858.2	E934.0	E950.4	E962.0	E980.4
Dextroamphetamine	969.7	E854.2	E939.7	E950.3	E962.0	E980.3
Dextro calcium pantothenate	963.5	E858.1	E933.5	E950.4	E962.0	E980.4
Dextromethorphan	975.4	E858.6	E945.4	E950.4	E962.0	E980.4
Dextromoramide	965.09	E850.2	E935.2	E950.0	E962.0	E980.0
Dextro pantothenyl alcohol	963.5	E858.1	E933.5	E950.4	E962.0	E980.4
topical	976.8	E858.7	E946.8	E950.4	E962.0	E980.4
Dextropropoxyphene (hydrochloride)	965.8	E850.8	E935.8	E950.0	E962.0	E980.0
Dextrorphan	965.09	E850.2	E935.2	E950.0	E962.0	E980.0
Dextrose NEC	974.5	E858.5	E944.5	E950.4	E962.0	E980.4
Dextrothyroxine	962.7	E858.0	E932.7	E950.4	E962.0	E980.4
DFP	971.0	E855.3	E941.0	E950.4	E962.0	E980.4
DHE-45	972.9	E858.3	E942.9	E950.4	E962.0	E980.4
Diabinese	962.3	E858.0	E932.3	E950.4	E962.0	E980.4
Diacetyl monoxime	977.2	E858.8	E947.2	E950.4	E962.0	E980.4
Diacetylmorphine	965.01	E850.0	E935.0	E950.0	E962.0	E980.0
Diagnostic agents	977.8	E858.8	E947.8	E950.4	E962.0	E980.4
Dial (soap)	976.2	E858.7	E946.2	E950.4	E962.0	E980.4
sedative	967.0	E851	E937.0	E950.1	E962.0	E980.1
Diallylbarbituric acid	967.0	E851	E937.0	E950.1	E962.0	E980.1
Diaminodiphenyisulfone	961.8	E857	E931.8	E950.4	E962.0	E980.4
Diamorphine	965.01	E850.0	E935.0	E950.0	E962.0	E980.0
Diamox	974.2	E858.5	E944.2	E950.4	E962.0	E980.4
Diamthazole	976.0	E858.7	E946.0	E950.4	E962.0	E980.4
Diaphenyisulfone	961.8	E857	E931.8	E950.4	E962.0	E980.4
Diasone (sodium)	961.8	E857	E931.8	E950.4	E962.0	E980.4
Diazepam	969.4	E853.2	E939.4	E950.3	E962.0	E980.3
Diazinon	989.3	E863.1	—	E950.6	E962.1	E980.7
Diazomethane (gas)	987.8	E869.8	—	E952.8	E962.2	E982.8

◀▶　**New Code**　　◀▥▥▶　**Revised Code**

Substance	Poisoning	External Cause (E-Code)				
		Accident	Therapeutic Use	Suicide Attempt	Assault	Undetermined
Diazoxide	972.5	E858.3	E942.5	E950.4	E962.0	E980.4
Dibenamine	971.3	E855.6	E941.3	E950.4	E962.0	E980.4
Dibenzheptropine	963.0	E858.1	E933.0	E950.4	E962.0	E980.4
Dibenzyline	971.3	E855.6	E941.3	E950.4	E962.0	E980.4
Diborane (gas)	987.8	E869.8	—	E952.8	E962.2	E982.8
Dibromomannitol	963.1	E858.1	E933.1	E950.4	E962.0	E980.4
Dibucaine (spinal)	968.7	E855.2	E938.7	E950.4	E962.0	E980.4
topical (surface)	968.5	E855.2	E938.5	E950.4	E962.0	E980.4
Dibunate sodium	975.4	E858.6	E945.4	E950.4	E962.0	E980.4
Dibutoline	971.1	E855.4	E941.1	E950.4	E962.0	E980.4
Dicapthon	989.4	E863.4	—	E950.6	E962.1	E980.7
Dichloralphenazone	967.1	E852.0	E937.1	E950.2	E962.0	E980.2
Dichlorodifluoromethane	987.4	E869.2	—	E952.8	E962.2	E982.8
Dichloroethane	982.3	E862.4	—	E950.9	E962.1	E980.9
Dichloroethylene	982.3	E862.4	—	E950.9	E962.1	E980.9
Dichloroethyl sulfide	987.8	E869.8	—	E952.8	E962.2	E982.8
Dichlorohydrin	982.3	E862.4	—	E950.9	E962.1	E980.9
Dichloromethane (solvent) (vapor)	982.3	E862.4	—	E950.9	E962.1	E980.9
Dichlorophen(e)	961.6	E857	E931.6	E950.4	E962.0	E980.4
Dichlorphenamide	974.2	E858.5	E944.2	E950.4	E962.0	E980.4
Dichlorvos	989.3	E863.1	—	E950.6	E962.1	E980.7
Diclofenac sodium	956.69	E850.6	E935.6	E950.0	E962.0	E980.0
Dicoumarin, dicumarol	964.2	E858.2	E934.2	E950.4	E962.0	E980.4
Dicyanogen (gas)	987.8	E869.8	—	E952.8	E962.2	E982.8
Dicyclomine	971.1	E855.4	E941.1	E950.4	E962.0	E980.4
Dieldrin (vapor)	989.2	E863.0	—	E950.6	E962.1	E980.7
Dienestrol	962.2	E858.0	E932.2	E950.4	E962.0	E980.4
Dietetics	977.0	E858.8	E947.0	E950.4	E962.0	E980.4
Diethazine	966.4	E855.0	E936.4	E950.4	E962.0	E980.4
Diethyl						
barbituric acid	967.0	E851	E937.0	E950.1	E962.0	E980.1
carbamazine	961.6	E857	E931.6	E950.4	E962.0	E980.4
carbinol	980.8	E860.8	—	E950.9	E962.1	E980.9
carbonate	982.8	E862.4	—	E950.9	E962.1	E980.9
ether (vapor) - *see* Ether(s)						
propion	977.0	E858.8	E947.0	E950.4	E962.0	E980.4
stilbestrol	962.2	E858.0	E932.2	E950.4	E962.0	E980.4
Diethylene						
dioxide	982.8	E862.4	—	E950.9	E962.1	E980.9
glycol (monoacetate) (monoethyl ether)	982.8	E862.4	—	E950.9	E962.1	E980.9
Diethylsulfone-diethylmethane	967.8	E852.8	E937.8	E950.2	E962.0	E980.2
Difencloxazine	965.09	E850.2	E935.2	E950.0	E962.0	E980.0
Diffusin	963.4	E858.1	E933.4	E950.4	E962.0	E980.4
Diflos	971.0	E855.3	E941.0	E950.4	E962.0	E980.4
Digestants	973.4	E858.4	E943.4	E950.4	E962.0	E980.4
Digitalin(e)	972.1	E858.3	E942.1	E950.4	E962.0	E980.4
Digitalis glycosides	972.1	E858.3	E942.1	E950.4	E962.0	E980.4
Digitoxin	972.1	E858.3	E942.1	E950.4	E962.0	E980.4
Digoxin	972.1	E858.3	E942.1	E950.4	E962.0	E980.4
Dihydrocodeine	965.09	E850.2	E935.2	E950.0	E962.0	E980.0
Dihydrocodeinone	965.09	E850.2	E935.2	E950.0	E962.0	E980.0
Dihydroergocristine	972.9	E858.3	E942.9	E950.4	E962.0	E980.4
Dihydroergotamine	972.9	E858.3	E942.9	E950.4	E962.0	E980.4
Dihydroergotoxine	972.9	E858.3	E942.9	E950.4	E962.0	E980.4
Dihydrohydroxycodeinone	965.09	E850.2	E935.2	E950.0	E962.0	E980.0
Dihydrohydroxymorphinone	965.09	E850.2	E935.2	E950.0	E962.0	E980.0
Dihydroisocodeine	965.09	E850.2	E935.2	E950.0	E962.0	E980.0
Dihydromorphine	965.09	E850.2	E935.2	E950.0	E962.0	E980.0
Dihydromorphinone	965.09	E850.2	E935.2	E950.0	E962.0	E980.0
Dihydrostreptomycin	960.6	E856	E930.6	E950.4	E962.0	E980.4
Dihydrotachysterol	962.6	E858.0	E932.6	E950.4	E962.0	E980.4

Substance	Poisoning	External Cause (E-Code)				
		Accident	Therapeutic Use	Suicide Attempt	Assault	Undetermined
Dihydroxyanthraquinone	973.1	E858.4	E943.1	E950.4	E962.0	E980.4
Dihydroxycodeinone	965.09	E850.2	E935.2	E950.0	E962.0	E980.0
Diiodohydroxyquin	961.3	E857	E931.3	E950.4	E962.0	E980.4
topical	976.0	E858.7	E946.0	E950.4	E962.0	E980.4
Diiodohydroxyquinoline	961.3	E857	E931.3	E950.4	E962.0	E980.4
Dilantin	966.1	E855.0	E936.1	E950.4	E962.0	E980.4
Dilaudid	965.09	E850.2	E935.2	E950.0	E962.0	E980.0
Diloxanide	961.5	E857	E931.5	E950.4	E962.0	E980.4
Dimefline	970.0	E854.3	E940.0	E950.4	E962.0	E980.4
Dimenhydrinate	963.0	E858.1	E933.0	E950.4	E962.0	E980.4
Dimercaprol	963.8	E858.1	E933.8	E950.4	E962.0	E980.4
Dimercaptopropanol	963.8	E858.1	E933.8	E950.4	E962.0	E980.4
Dimetane	963.0	E858.1	E933.0	E950.4	E962.0	E980.4
Dimethicone	976.3	E858.7	E946.3	E950.4	E962.0	E980.4
Dimethindene	963.0	E858.1	E933.0	E950.4	E962.0	E980.4
Dimethisoquin	968.5	E855.2	E938.5	E950.4	E962.0	E980.4
Dimethisterone	962.2	E858.0	E932.2	E950.4	E962.0	E980.4
Dimethoxanate	975.4	E858.6	E945.4	E950.4	E962.0	E980.4
Dimethyl						
arsine, arsinic acid - *see* Arsenic						
carbinol	980.2	E860.3	—	E950.9	E962.1	E980.9
diguanide	962.3	E858.0	E932.3	E950.4	E962.0	E980.4
ketone	982.8	E862.4	—	E950.9	E962.1	E980.9
vapor	987.8	E869.8	—	E952.8	E962.2	E982.8
meperidine	965.09	E850.2	E935.2	E950.0	E962.0	E980.0
parathion	989.3	E863.1	—	E950.6	E962.1	E980.7
polysiloxane	973.8	E858.4	E943.8	E950.4	E962.0	E980.4
sulfate (fumes)	987.8	E869.8	—	E952.8	E962.2	E982.8
liquid	983.9	E864.3	—	E950.7	E962.1	E980.6
sulfoxide NEC	982.8	E862.4	—	E950.9	E962.1	E980.9
medicinal	976.4	E858.7	E946.4	E950.4	E962.0	E980.4
triptamine	969.6	E854.1	E939.6	E950.3	E962.0	E980.3
tubocurarine	975.2	E858.6	E945.2	E950.4	E962.0	E980.4
Dindevan	964.2	E858.2	E934.2	E950.4	E962.0	E980.4
Dinitro (-ortho-) cresol (herbicide) (spray)	989.4	E863.5	—	E950.6	E962.1	E980.7
insecticide	989.4	E863.4	—	E950.6	E962.1	E980.7
Dinitrobenzene	983.0	E864.0	—	E950.7	E962.1	E980.6
vapor	987.8	E869.8	—	E952.8	E962.2	E982.8
Dinitro-orthocresol (herbicide)	989.4	E863.5	—	E950.6	E962.1	E980.7
insecticide	989.4	E863.4	—	E950.6	E962.1	E980.7
Dinitrophenol (herbicide) (spray)	989.4	E863.5	—	E950.6	E962.1	E980.7
insecticide	989.4	E863.4	—	E950.6	E962.1	E980.7
Dinoprost	975.0	E858.6	E945.0	E950.4	E962.0	E980.4
Dioctyl sulfosuccinate (calcium) (sodium)	973.2	E858.4	E943.2	E950.4	E962.0	E980.4
Diodoquin	961.3	E857	E931.3	E950.4	E962.0	E980.4
Dione derivatives NEC	966.3	E855.0	E936.3	E950.4	E962.0	E980.4
Dionin	965.09	E850.2	E935.2	E950.0	E962.0	E980.0
Dioxane	982.8	E862.4	—	E950.9	E962.1	E980.9
Dioxin - *see* herbicide						
Dioxyline	972.5	E858.3	E942.5	E950.4	E962.0	E980.4
Dipentene	982.8	E862.4	—	E950.9	E962.1	E980.9
Diphemanil	971.1	E855.4	E941.1	E950.4	E962.0	E980.4
Diphenadione	964.2	E858.2	E934.2	E950.4	E962.0	E980.4
Diphenhydramine	963.0	E858.1	E933.0	E950.4	E962.0	E980.4
Diphenidol	963.0	E858.1	E933.0	E950.4	E962.0	E980.4
Diphenoxylate	973.5	E858.4	E943.5	E950.4	E962.0	E980.4
Diphenylchlorarsine	985.1	E866.3	—	E950.8	E962.1	E980.8
Diphenylhydantoin (sodium)	966.1	E855.0	E936.1	E950.4	E962.0	E980.4
Diphenylpyraline	963.0	E858.1	E933.0	E950.4	E962.0	E980.4
Diphtheria						
antitoxin	979.9	E858.8	E949.9	E950.4	E962.0	E980.4

◄▶ **New Code**　　◄▦ ▦▶ **Revised Code**

	External Cause (E-Code)					
Substance	**Poisoning**	**Accident**	**Therapeutic Use**	**Suicide Attempt**	**Assault**	**Undetermined**
Diphtheria *(Continued)*						
toxoid	978.5	E858.8	E948.5	E950.4	E962.0	E980.4
with tetanus toxoid	978.9	E858.8	E948.9	E950.4	E962.0	E980.4
with pertussis component	978.6	E858.8	E948.6	E950.4	E962.0	E980.4
vaccine	978.5	E858.8	E948.5	E950.4	E962.0	E980.4
Dipipanone	965.09	E850.2	E935.2	E950.0	E962.0	E980.0
Diplovax	979.5	E858.8	E949.5	E950.4	E962.0	E980.4
Diprophylline	975.1	E858.6	E945.1	E950.4	E962.0	E980.4
Dipyridamole	972.4	E858.3	E942.4	E950.4	E962.0	E980.4
Dipyrone	965.5	E850.5	E935.5	E950.0	E962.0	E980.0
Diquat	989.4	E863.5	—	E950.6	E962.1	E980.7
Disinfectant NEC	983.9	E861.4	—	E950.7	E962.1	E980.6
alkaline	983.2	E861.4	—	E950.7	E962.1	E980.6
aromatic	983.0	E861.4	—	E950.7	E962.1	E980.6
Disipal	966.4	E855.0	E936.4	E950.4	E962.0	E980.4
Disodium edetate	963.8	E858.1	E933.8	E950.4	E962.0	E980.4
Disulfamide	974.4	E858.5	E944.4	E950.4	E962.0	E980.4
Disulfanilamide	961.0	E857	E931.0	E950.4	E962.0	E980.4
Disulfiram	977.3	E858.8	E947.3	E950.4	E962.0	E980.4
Dithiazanine	961.6	E857	E931.6	E950.4	E962.0	E980.4
Dithioglycerol	963.8	E858.1	E933.8	E950.4	E962.0	E980.4
Dithranol	976.4	E858.7	E946.4	E950.4	E962.0	E980.4
Diucardin	974.3	E858.5	E944.3	E950.4	E962.0	E980.4
Diupres	974.3	E858.5	E944.3	E950.4	E962.0	E980.4
Diuretics NEC	974.4	E858.5	E944.4	E950.4	E962.0	E980.4
carbonic acid anhydrase inhibitors	974.2	E858.5	E944.2	E950.4	E962.0	E980.4
mercurial	974.0	E858.5	E944.0	E950.4	E962.0	E980.4
osmotic	974.4	E858.5	E944.4	E950.4	E962.0	E980.4
purine derivatives	974.1	E858.5	E944.1	E950.4	E962.0	E980.4
saluretic	974.3	E858.5	E944.3	E950.4	E962.0	E980.4
Diuril	974.3	E858.5	E944.3	E950.4	E962.0	E980.4
Divinyl ether	968.2	E855.1	E938.2	E950.4	E962.0	E980.4
D-lysergic acid diethylamide	969.6	E854.1	E939.6	E950.3	E962.0	E980.3
DMCT	960.4	E856	E930.4	E950.4	E962.0	E980.4
DMSO	982.8	E862.4	—	E950.9	E962.1	E980.9
DMT	969.6	E854.1	E939.6	E950.3	E962.0	E980.3
DNOC	989.4	E863.5	—	E950.6	E962.1	E980.7
DOCA	962.0	E858.0	E932.0	E950.4	E962.0	E980.4
Dolophine	965.02	E850.1	E935.1	E950.0	E962.0	E980.0
Doloxene	965.8	E850.8	E935.8	E950.0	E962.0	E980.0
DOM	969.6	E854.1	E939.6	E950.3	E962.0	E980.3
Domestic gas - *see* Gas, utility						
Domiphen (bromide) (lozenges)	976.6	E858.7	E946.6	E950.4	E962.0	E980.4
Dopa (levo)	966.4	E855.0	E936.4	E950.4	E962.0	E980.4
Dopamine	971.2	E855.5	E941.2	E950.4	E962.0	E980.4
Doriden	967.5	E852.4	E937.5	E950.2	E962.0	E980.2
Dormiral	967.0	E851	E937.0	E950.1	E962.0	E980.1
Dormison	967.8	E852.8	E937.8	E950.2	E962.0	E980.2
Dornase	963.4	E858.1	E933.4	E950.4	E962.0	E980.4
Dorsacaine	968.5	E855.2	E938.5	E950.4	E962.0	E980.4
Dothiepin hydrochloride	969.0	E854.0	E939.0	E950.3	E962.0	E980.3
Doxapram	970.0	E854.3	E940.0	E950.4	E962.0	E980.4
Doxepin	969.0	E854.0	E939.0	E950.3	E962.0	E980.3
Doxorubicin	960.7	E856	E930.7	E950.4	E962.0	E980.4
Doxycycline	960.4	E856	E930.4	E950.4	E962.0	E980.4
Doxylamine	963.0	E858.1	E933.0	E950.4	E962.0	E980.4
Dramamine	963.0	E858.1	E933.0	E950.4	E962.0	E980.4
Drano (drain cleaner)	983.2	E864.2	—	E950.7	E962.1	E980.6
Dromoran	965.09	E850.2	E935.2	E950.0	E962.0	E980.0
Dromostanolone	962.1	E858.0	E932.1	E950.4	E962.0	E980.4
Droperidol	969.2	E853.1	E939.2	E950.3	E962.0	E980.3

Substance	Poisoning	External Cause (E-Code)				
		Accident	Therapeutic Use	Suicide Attempt	Assault	Undetermined
Drug	977.9	E858.9	E947.9	E950.5	E962.0	E980.5
specified NEC	977.8	E858.8	E947.8	E950.4	E962.0	E980.4
AHFS List						
4:00 antihistamine drugs	963.0	E858.1	E933.0	E950.4	E962.0	E980.4
8:04 amebacides	961.5	E857	E931.5	E950.4	E962.0	E980.4
arsenical anti-infectives	961.1	E857	E931.1	E950.4	E962.0	E980.4
quinoline derivatives	961.3	E857	E931.3	E950.4	E962.0	E980.4
8:08 anthelmintics	961.6	E857	E931.6	E950.4	E962.0	E980.4
quinoline derivatives	961.3	E857	E931.3	E950.4	E962.0	E980.4
8:12.04 antifungal antibiotics	960.1	E856	E930.1	E950.4	E962.0	E980.4
8:12.06 cephalosporins	960.5	E856	E930.5	E950.4	E962.0	E980.4
8:12.08 chloramphenicol	960.2	E856	E930.2	E950.4	E962.0	E980.4
8:12.12 erythromycins	960.3	E856	E930.3	E950.4	E962.0	E980.4
8:12.16 penicillins	960.0	E856	E930.0	E950.4	E962.0	E980.4
8:12.20 streptomycins	960.6	E856	E930.6	E950.4	E962.0	E980.4
8:12.24 tetracyclines	960.4	E856	E930.4	E950.4	E962.0	E980.4
8:12.28 other antibiotics	960.8	E856	E930.8	E950.4	E962.0	E980.4
antimycobacterial	960.6	E856	E930.6	E950.4	E962.0	E980.4
macrolides	960.3	E856	E930.3	E950.4	E962.0	E980.4
8:16 antituberculars	961.8	E857	E931.8	E950.4	E962.0	E980.4
antibiotics	960.6	E856	E930.6	E950.4	E962.0	E980.4
8:18 antivirals	961.7	E857	E931.7	E950.4	E962.0	E980.4
8:20 plasmodicides (antimalarials)	961.4	E857	E931.4	E950.4	E962.0	E980.4
8:24 sulfonamides	961.0	E857	E931.0	E950.4	E962.0	E980.4
8:26 sulfones	961.8	E857	E931.8	E950.4	E962.0	E980.4
8:28 treponemicides	961.2	E857	E931.2	E950.4	E962.0	E980.4
8:32 trichomonacides	961.5	E857	E931.5	E950.4	E962.0	E980.4
quinoline derivatives	961.3	E857	E931.3	E950.4	E962.0	E980.4
nitrofuran derivatives	961.9	E857	E931.9	E950.4	E962.0	E980.4
8:36 urinary germicides	961.9	E857	E931.9	E950.4	E962.0	E980.4
quinoline derivatives	961.3	E857	E931.3	E950.4	E962.0	E980.4
8:40 other anti-infectives	961.9	E857	E931.9	E950.4	E962.0	E980.4
10:00 antineoplastic agents	963.1	E858.1	E933.1	E950.4	E962.0	E980.4
antibiotics	960.7	E856	E930.7	E950.4	E962.0	E980.4
progestogens	962.2	E858.0	E932.2	E950.4	E962.0	E980.4
12:04 parasympathomimetic (cholinergic) agents	971.0	E855.3	E941.0	E950.4	E962.0	E980.4
12:08 parasympatholytic (cholinergic-blocking) agents	971.1	E855.4	E941.1	E950.4	E962.0	E980.4
12:12 sympathomimetic (adrenergic) agents	971.2	E855.5	E941.2	E950.4	E962.0	E980.4
12:16 sympatholytic (adrenergic-blocking) agents	971.3	E855.6	E941.3	E950.4	E962.0	E980.4
12:20 skeletal muscle relaxants						
central nervous system muscle-tone depressants	968.0	E855.1	E938.0	E950.4	E962.0	E980.4
myoneural blocking agents	975.2	E858.6	E945.2	E950.4	E962.0	E980.4
16:00 blood derivatives	964.7	E858.2	E934.7	E950.4	E962.0	E980.4
20:04 antianemia drugs	964.1	E858.2	E934.1	E950.4	E962.0	E980.4
20:04.04 iron preparations	964.0	E858.2	E934.0	E950.4	E962.0	E980.4
20:04.08 liver and stomach preparations	964.1	E858.2	E934.1	E950.4	E962.0	E980.4
20:12.04 anticoagulants	964.2	E858.2	E934.2	E950.4	E962.0	E980.4
20:12.08 antiheparin agents	964.5	E858.2	E934.5	E950.4	E962.0	E980.4
20:12.12 coagulants	964.5	E858.2	E934.5	E950.4	E962.0	E980.4
20:12.16 hemostatics NEC	964.5	E858.2	E934.5	E950.4	E962.0	E980.4
capillary active drugs	972.8	E858.3	E942.8	E950.4	E962.0	E980.4
24:04 cardiac drugs	972.9	E858.3	E942.9	E950.4	E962.0	E980.4
cardiotonic agents	972.1	E858.3	E942.1	E950.4	E962.0	E980.4
rhythm regulators	972.0	E858.3	E942.0	E950.4	E962.0	E980.4
24:06 antilipemic agents	972.2	E858.3	E942.2	E950.4	E962.0	E980.4
thyroid derivatives	962.7	E858.0	E932.7	E950.4	E962.0	E980.4
24:08 hypotensive agents	972.6	E858.3	E942.6	E950.4	E962.0	E980.4
adrenergic blocking agents	971.3	E855.6	E941.3	E950.4	E962.0	E980.4
ganglion blocking agents	972.3	E858.3	E942.3	E950.4	E962.0	E980.4
vasodilators	972.5	E858.3	E942.5	E950.4	E962.0	E980.4

◀ ▶ **New Code**   ◀▥ ▥▶ **Revised Code**

Substance	Poisoning	External Cause (E-Code)				
		Accident	Therapeutic Use	Suicide Attempt	Assault	Undetermined
Drug *(Continued)*						
24:12 vasodilating agents NEC	972.5	E858.3	E942.5	E950.4	E962.0	E980.4
coronary	972.4	E858.3	E942.4	E950.4	E962.0	E980.4
nicotinic acid derivatives	972.2	E858.3	E942.2	E950.4	E962.0	E980.4
24:16 sclerosing agents	972.7	E858.3	E942.7	E950.4	E962.0	E980.4
28:04 general anesthetics	968.4	E855.1	E938.4	E950.4	E962.0	E980.4
gaseous anesthetics	968.2	E855.1	E938.2	E950.4	E962.0	E980.4
halothane	968.1	E855.1	E938.1	E950.4	E962.0	E980.4
intravenous anesthetics	968.3	E855.1	E938.3	E950.4	E962.0	E980.4
28:08 analgesics and antipyretics	965.9	E850.9	E935.9	E950.0	E962.0	E980.0
antirheumatics	965.69	E850.6	E935.6	E950.0	E962.0	E980.0
aromatic analgesics	965.4	E850.4	E935.4	E950.0	E962.0	E980.0
non-narcotic NEC	965.7	E850.7	E935.7	E950.0	E962.0	E980.0
opium alkaloids	965.00	E850.2	E935.2	E950.0	E962.0	E980.0
heroin	965.01	E850.0	E935.0	E950.0	E962.0	E980.0
methadone	965.02	E850.1	E935.1	E950.0	E962.0	E980.0
specified type NEC	965.09	E850.2	E935.2	E950.0	E962.0	E980.0
pyrazole derivatives	965.5	E850.5	E935.5	E950.0	E962.0	E980.0
salicylates	965.1	E850.3	E935.3	E950.0	E962.0	E980.0
specified NEC	965.8	E850.8	E935.8	E950.0	E962.0	E980.0
28:10 narcotic antagonists	970.1	E854.3	E940.1	E950.4	E962.0	E980.4
28:12 anticonvulsants	966.3	E855.0	E936.3	E950.4	E962.0	E980.4
barbiturates	967.0	E851	E937.0	E950.1	E962.0	E980.1
benzodiazepine-based tranquilizers	969.4	E853.4	E939.4	E950.3	E962.0	E980.3
bromides	967.3	E852.2	E937.3	E950.2	E962.0	E980.2
hydantoin derivatives	966.1	E855.0	E936.1	E950.4	E962.0	E980.4
oxazolidine (derivatives)	966.0	E855.0	E936.0	E950.4	E962.0	E980.4
succinimides	966.2	E855.0	E936.2	E950.4	E962.0	E980.4
28:16.04 antidepressants	969.0	E854.0	E939.0	E950.3	E962.0	E980.3
28:16.08 tranquilizers	969.5	E853.9	E939.5	E950.3	E962.0	E980.3
benzodiazepine-based	969.4	E853.2	E939.4	E950.3	E962.0	E980.3
butyrophenone-based	969.2	E853.1	E939.2	E950.3	E962.0	E980.3
major NEC	969.3	E853.8	E939.3	E950.3	E962.0	E980.3
phenothiazine-based	969.1	E853.0	E939.1	E950.3	E962.0	E980.3
28:16.12 other psychotherapeutic agents	969.8	E855.8	E939.8	E950.3	E962.0	E980.3
28:20 respiratory and cerebral stimulants	970.9	E854.3	E940.9	E950.4	E962.0	E980.4
analeptics	970.0	E854.3	E940.0	E950.4	E962.0	E980.4
anorexigenic agents	977.0	E858.8	E947.0	E950.4	E962.0	E980.4
psychostimulants	969.7	E854.2	E939.7	E950.3	E962.0	E980.3
specified NEC	970.8	E854.3	E940.8	E950.4	E962.0	E980.4
28:24 sedatives and hypnotics	967.9	E852.9	E937.9	E950.2	E962.0	E980.2
barbiturates	967.0	E851	E937.0	E950.1	E962.0	E980.1
benzodiazepine-based tranquilizers	969.4	E853.2	E939.4	E950.3	E962.0	E980.3
chloral hydrate (group)	967.1	E852.0	E937.1	E950.2	E962.0	E980.2
glutethimide group	967.5	E852.4	E937.5	E950.2	E962.0	E980.2
intravenous anesthetics	968.3	E855.1	E938.3	E950.4	E962.0	E980.4
methaqualone (compounds)	967.4	E852.3	E937.4	E950.2	E962.0	E980.2
paraldehyde	967.2	E852.1	E937.2	E950.2	E962.0	E980.2
phenothiazine-based tranquilizers	969.1	E853.0	E939.1	E950.3	E962.0	E980.3
specified NEC	967.8	E852.8	E937.8	E950.2	E962.0	E980.2
thiobarbiturates	968.3	E855.1	E938.3	E950.4	E962.0	E980.4
tranquilizer NEC	969.5	E853.9	E939.5	E950.3	E962.0	E980.3
36:04 to 36:88 diagnostic agents	977.8	E858.8	E947.8	E950.4	E962.0	E980.4
40:00 electrolyte, caloric, and water balance agents NEC	974.5	E858.5	E944.5	E950.4	E962.0	E980.4
40:04 acidifying agents	963.2	E858.1	E933.2	E950.4	E962.0	E980.4
40:08 alkalinizing agents	963.3	E858.1	E933.3	E950.4	E962.0	E980.4
40:10 ammonia detoxicants	974.5	E858.5	E944.5	E950.4	E962.0	E980.4
40:12 replacement solutions	974.5	E858.5	E944.5	E950.4	E962.0	E980.4
plasma expanders	964.8	E858.2	E934.8	E950.4	E962.0	E980.4
40:16 sodium-removing resins	974.5	E858.5	E944.5	E950.4	E962.0	E980.4
40:18 potassium-removing resins	974.5	E858.5	E944.5	E950.4	E962.0	E980.4
40:20 caloric agents	974.5	E858.5	E944.5	E950.4	E962.0	E980.4

◀ ▶ **New Code**   ◀▦ ▦▶ **Revised Code**

Substance	Poisoning	External Cause (E-Code)				
		Accident	Therapeutic Use	Suicide Attempt	Assault	Undetermined
Drug *(Continued)*						
40:24 salt and sugar substitutes	974.5	E858.5	E944.5	E950.4	E962.0	E980.4
40:28 diuretics NEC	974.4	E858.5	E944.4	E950.4	E962.0	E980.4
carbonic acid anhydrase inhibitors	974.2	E858.5	E944.2	E950.4	E962.0	E980.4
mercurials	974.0	E858.5	E944.0	E950.4	E962.0	E980.4
purine derivatives	974.1	E858.5	E944.1	E950.4	E962.0	E980.4
saluretics	974.3	E858.5	E944.3	E950.4	E962.0	E980.4
thiazides	974.3	E858.5	E944.3	E950.4	E962.0	E980.4
40:36 irrigating solutions	974.5	E858.5	E944.5	E950.4	E962.0	E980.4
40:40 uricosuric agents	974.7	E858.5	E944.7	E950.4	E962.0	E980.4
44:00 enzymes	963.4	E858.1	E933.4	E950.4	E962.0	E980.4
fibrinolysis-affecting agents	964.4	E858.2	E934.4	E950.4	E962.0	E980.4
gastric agents	973.4	E858.4	E943.4	E950.4	E962.0	E980.4
48:00 expectorants and cough preparations						
antihistamine agents	963.0	E858.1	E933.0	E950.4	E962.0	E980.4
antitussives	975.4	E858.6	E945.4	E950.4	E962.0	E980.4
codeine derivatives	965.09	E850.2	E935.2	E950.0	E962.0	E980.0
expectorants	975.5	E858.6	E945.5	E950.4	E962.0	E980.4
narcotic agents NEC	965.09	E850.2	E935.2	E950.0	E962.0	E980.0
52:04 anti-infectives (EENT)						
ENT agent	976.6	E858.7	E946.6	E950.4	E962.0	E980.4
ophthalmic preparation	976.5	E858.7	E946.5	E950.4	E962.0	E980.4
52:04.04 antibiotics (EENT)						
ENT agent	976.6	E858.7	E946.6	E950.4	E962.0	E980.4
ophthalmic preparation	976.5	E858.7	E946.5	E950.4	E962.0	E980.4
52:04.06 antivirals (EENT)						
ENT agent	976.6	E858.7	E946.6	E950.4	E962.0	E980.4
ophthalmic preparation	976.5	E858.7	E946.5	E950.4	E962.0	E980.4
52:04.08 sulfonamides (EENT)						
ENT agent	976.6	E858.7	E946.6	E950.4	E962.0	E980.4
ophthalmic preparation	976.5	E858.7	E946.5	E950.4	E962.0	E980.4
52:04.12 miscellaneous anti-infectives (EENT)						
ENT agent	976.6	E858.7	E946.6	E950.4	E962.0	E980.4
ophthalmic preparation	976.5	E858.7	E946.5	E950.4	E962.0	E980.4
52:08 anti-inflammatory agents (EENT)						
ENT agent	976.6	E858.7	E946.6	E950.4	E962.0	E980.4
ophthalmic preparation	976.5	E858.7	E946.5	E950.4	E962.0	E980.4
52:10 carbonic anhydrase inhibitors	974.2	E858.5	E944.2	E950.4	E962.0	E980.4
52:12 contact lens solutions	976.5	E858.7	E946.5	E950.4	E962.0	E980.4
52:16 local anesthetics (EENT)	968.5	E855.2	E938.5	E950.4	E962.0	E980.4
52:20 miotics	971.0	E855.3	E941.0	E950.4	E962.0	E980.4
52:24 mydriatics						
adrenergics	971.2	E855.5	E941.2	E950.4	E962.0	E980.4
anticholinergics	971.1	E855.4	E941.1	E950.4	E962.0	E980.4
antimuscarinics	971.1	E855.4	E941.1	E950.4	E962.0	E980.4
parasympatholytics	971.1	E855.4	E941.1	E950.4	E962.0	E980.4
spasmolytics	971.1	E855.4	E941.1	E950.4	E962.0	E980.4
sympathomimetics	971.2	E855.5	E941.2	E950.4	E962.0	E980.4
52:28 mouth washes and gargles	976.6	E858.7	E946.6	E950.4	E962.0	E980.4
52:32 vasoconstrictors (EENT)	971.2	E855.5	E941.2	E950.4	E962.0	E980.4
52:36 unclassified agents (EENT)						
ENT agent	976.6	E858.7	E946.6	E950.4	E962.0	E980.4
ophthalmic preparation	976.5	E858.7	E946.5	E950.4	E962.0	E980.4
56:04 antacids and adsorbents	973.0	E858.4	E943.0	E950.4	E962.0	E980.4
56:08 antidiarrhea agents	973.5	E858.4	E943.5	E950.4	E962.0	E980.4
56:10 antiflatulents	973.8	E858.4	E943.8	E950.4	E962.0	E980.4
56:12 cathartics NEC	973.3	E858.4	E943.3	E950.4	E962.0	E980.4
emollients	973.2	E858.4	E943.2	E950.4	E962.0	E980.4
irritants	973.1	E858.4	E943.1	E950.4	E962.0	E980.4
56:16 digestants	973.4	E858.4	E943.4	E950.4	E962.0	E980.4
56:20 emetics and antiemetics						
antiemetics	963.0	E858.1	E933.0	E950.4	E962.0	E980.4
emetics	973.6	E858.4	E943.6	E950.4	E962.0	E980.4

◄▶ **New Code**   ◄▥▥ ▥▥▶ **Revised Code**

		External Cause (E-Code)				
Substance	**Poisoning**	**Accident**	**Therapeutic Use**	**Suicide Attempt**	**Assault**	**Undetermined**
Drug *(Continued)*						
56:24 lipotropic agents	977.1	E858.8	E947.1	E950.4	E962.0	E980.4
56:40 miscellaneous G.I. drugs	973.8	E858.4	E943.8	E950.4	E962.0	E980.4
60:00 gold compounds	965.69	E850.6	E935.6	E950.0	E962.0	E980.0
64:00 heavy metal antagonists	963.8	E858.1	E933.8	E950.4	E962.0	E980.4
68:04 adrenals	962.0	E858.0	E932.0	E950.4	E962.0	E980.4
68:08 androgens	962.1	E858.0	E932.1	E950.4	E962.0	E980.4
68:12 contraceptives, oral	962.2	E858.0	E932.2	E950.4	E962.0	E980.4
68:16 estrogens	962.2	E858.0	E932.2	E950.4	E962.0	E980.4
68:18 gonadotropins	962.4	E858.0	E932.4	E950.4	E962.0	E980.4
68:20 insulins and antidiabetic agents	962.3	E858.0	E932.3	E950.4	E962.0	E980.4
68:20.08 insulins	962.3	E858.0	E932.3	E950.4	E962.0	E980.4
68:24 parathyroid	962.6	E858.0	E932.6	E950.4	E962.0	E980.4
68:28 pituitary (posterior)	962.5	E858.0	E932.5	E950.4	E962.0	E980.4
anterior	962.4	E858.0	E932.4	E950.4	E962.0	E980.4
68:32 progestogens	962.2	E858.0	E932.2	E950.4	E962.0	E980.4
68:34 other corpus luteum hormones NEC	962.2	E858.0	E932.2	E950.4	E962.0	E980.4
68:36 thyroid and antithyroid						
antithyroid	962.8	E858.0	E932.8	E950.4	E962.0	E980.4
thyroid (derivatives)	962.7	E858.0	E932.7	E950.4	E962.0	E980.4
72:00 local anesthetics NEC	968.9	E855.2	E938.9	E950.4	E962.0	E980.4
topical (surface)	968.5	E855.2	E938.5	E950.4	E962.0	E980.4
infiltration (intradermal) (subcutaneous) (submucosal)	968.5	E855.2	E938.5	E950.4	E962.0	E980.4
nerve blocking (peripheral) (plexus) (regional)	968.6	E855.2	E938.6	E950.4	E962.0	E980.4
spinal	968.7	E855.2	E938.7	E950.4	E962.0	E980.4
76:00 oxytocics	975.0	E858.6	E945.0	E950.4	E962.0	E980.4
78:00 radioactive agents	990	—	—	—	—	—
80:04 serums NEC	979.9	E858.8	E949.9	E950.4	E962.0	E980.4
immune gamma globulin (human)	964.6	E858.2	E934.6	E950.4	E962.0	E980.4
80:08 toxoids NEC	978.8	E858.8	E948.8	E950.4	E962.0	E980.4
diphtheria	978.5	E858.8	E948.5	E950.4	E962.0	E980.4
and tetanus	978.9	E858.8	E948.9	E950.4	E962.0	E980.4
with pertussis component	978.6	E858.8	E948.6	E950.4	E962.0	E980.4
tetanus	978.4	E858.8	E948.4	E950.4	E962.0	E980.4
and diphtheria	978.9	E858.8	E948.9	E950.4	E962.0	E980.4
with pertussis component	978.6	E858.8	E948.6	E950.4	E962.0	E980.4
80:12 vaccines	979.9	E858.8	E949.9	E950.4	E962.0	E980.4
bacterial NEC	978.8	E858.8	E948.8	E950.4	E962.0	E980.4
with						
other bacterial components	978.9	E858.8	E948.9	E950.4	E962.0	E980.4
pertussis component	978.6	E858.8	E948.6	E950.4	E962.0	E980.4
viral and rickettsial components	979.7	E858.8	E949.7	E950.4	E962.0	E980.4
rickettsial NEC	979.6	E858.8	E949.6	E950.4	E962.0	E980.4
with						
bacterial component	979.7	E858.8	E949.7	E950.4	E962.0	E980.4
pertussis component	978.6	E858.8	E948.6	E950.4	E962.0	E980.4
viral component	979.7	E858.8	E949.7	E950.4	E962.0	E980.4
viral NEC	979.6	E858.8	E949.6	E950.4	E962.0	E980.4
with						
bacterial component	979.7	E858.8	E949.7	E950.4	E962.0	E980.4
pertussis component	978.6	E858.8	E948.6	E950.4	E962.0	E980.4
rickettsial component	979.7	E858.8	E949.7	E950.4	E962.0	E980.4
84:04.04 antibiotics (skin and mucous membrane)	976.0	E858.7	E946.0	E950.4	E962.0	E980.4
84:04.08 fungicides (skin and mucous membrane)	976.0	E858.7	E946.0	E950.4	E962.0	E980.4
84:04.12 scabicides and pediculicides (skin and mucous membrane)	976.0	E858.7	E946.0	E950.4	E962.0	E980.4
84:04.16 miscellaneous local anti-infectives (skin and mucous membrane)	976.0	E858.7	E946.0	E950.4	E962.0	E980.4
84:06 anti-inflammatory agents (skin and mucous membrane)	976.0	E858.7	E946.0	E950.4	E962.0	E980.4
84:08 antipruritics and local anesthetics						
antipruritics	976.1	E858.7	E946.1	E950.4	E962.0	E980.4
local anesthetics	968.5	E855.2	E938.5	E950.4	E962.0	E980.4
84:12 astringents	976.2	E858.7	E946.2	E950.4	E962.0	E980.4
84:16 cell stimulants and proliferants	976.8	E858.7	E946.8	E950.4	E962.0	E980.4
84:20 detergents	976.2	E858.7	E946.2	E950.4	E962.0	E980.4

◀▶ **New Code** ◀▥ ▥▶ **Revised Code**

Substance	Poisoning	External Cause (E-Code)				
		Accident	Therapeutic Use	Suicide Attempt	Assault	Undetermined
Drug *(Continued)*						
84:24 emollients, demulcents, and protectants	976.3	E858.7	E946.3	E950.4	E962.0	E980.4
84:28 keratolytic agents	976.4	E858.7	E946.4	E950.4	E962.0	E980.4
84:32 keratoplastic agents	976.4	E858.7	E946.4	E950.4	E962.0	E980.4
84:36 miscellaneous agents (skin and mucous membrane)	976.8	E858.7	E946.8	E950.4	E962.0	E980.4
86:00 spasmolytic agents	975.1	E858.6	E945.1	E950.4	E962.0	E980.4
antiasthmatics	975.7	E858.6	E945.7	E950.4	E962.0	E980.4
papaverine	972.5	E858.3	E942.5	E950.4	E962.0	E980.4
theophylline	974.1	E858.5	E944.1	E950.4	E962.0	E980.4
88:04 vitamin A	963.5	E858.1	E933.5	E950.4	E962.0	E980.4
88:08 vitamin B complex	963.5	E858.1	E933.5	E950.4	E962.0	E980.4
hematopoietic vitamin	964.1	E858.2	E934.1	E950.4	E962.0	E980.4
nicotinic acid derivatives	972.2	E858.3	E942.2	E950.4	E962.0	E980.4
88:12 vitamin C	963.5	E858.1	E933.5	E950.4	E962.0	E980.4
88:16 vitamin D	963.5	E858.1	E933.5	E950.4	E962.0	E980.4
88:20 vitamin E	963.5	E858.1	E933.5	E950.4	E962.0	E980.4
88:24 vitamin K activity	964.3	E858.2	E934.3	E950.4	E962.0	E980.4
88:28 multivitamin preparations	963.5	E858.1	E933.5	E950.4	E962.0	E980.4
92:00 unclassified therapeutic agents	977.8	E858.8	E947.8	E950.4	E962.0	E980.4
Duboisine	971.1	E855.4	E941.1	E950.4	E962.0	E980.4
Dulcolax	973.1	E858.4	E943.1	E950.4	E962.0	E980.4
Duponol (C) (EP)	976.2	E858.7	E946.2	E950.4	E962.0	E980.4
Durabolin	962.1	E858.0	E932.1	E950.4	E962.0	E980.4
Dyclone	968.5	E855.2	E938.5	E950.4	E962.0	E980.4
Dyclonine	968.5	E855.2	E938.5	E950.4	E962.0	E980.4
Dydrogesterone	962.2	E858.0	E932.2	E950.4	E962.0	E980.4
Dyes NEC	989.89	E866.8	—	E950.9	E962.1	E980.9
diagnostic agents	977.8	E858.8	E947.8	E950.4	E962.0	E980.4
pharmaceutical NEC	977.4	E858.8	E947.4	E950.4	E962.0	E980.4
Dyflos	971.0	E855.3	E941.0	E950.4	E962.0	E980.4
Dymelor	962.3	E858.0	E932.3	E950.4	E962.0	E980.4
Dynamite	989.89	E866.8	—	E950.9	E962.1	E980.9
fumes	987.8	E869.8	—	E952.8	E962.2	E982.8
Dyphylline	975.1	E858.6	E945.1	E950.4	E962.0	E980.4
Ear preparations	976.6	E858.7	E946.6	E950.4	E962.0	E980.4
Echothiopate, ecothiopate	971.0	E855.3	E941.0	E950.4	E962.0	E980.4
Ectylurea	967.8	E852.8	E937.8	E950.2	E962.0	E980.2
Edathamil disodium	963.8	E858.1	E933.8	E950.4	E962.0	E980.4
Edecrin	974.4	E858.5	E944.4	E950.4	E962.0	E980.4
Edetate, disodium (calcium)	963.8	E858.1	E933.8	E950.4	E962.0	E980.4
Edrophonium	971.0	E855.3	E941.0	E950.4	E962.0	E980.4
Elase	976.8	E858.7	E946.8	E950.4	E962.0	E980.4
Elaterium	973.1	E858.4	E943.1	E950.4	E962.0	E980.4
Elder	988.2	E865.4	—	E950.9	E962.1	E980.9
berry (unripe)	988.2	E865.3	—	E950.9	E962.1	E980.9
Electrolytes NEC	974.5	E858.5	E944.5	E950.4	E962.0	E980.4
Electrolytic agent NEC	974.5	E858.5	E944.5	E950.4	E962.0	E980.4
Embramine	963.0	E858.1	E933.0	E950.4	E962.0	E980.4
Emetics	973.6	E858.4	E943.6	E950.4	E962.0	E980.4
Emetine (hydrochloride)	961.5	E857	E931.5	E950.4	E962.0	E980.4
Emollients	976.3	E858.7	E946.3	E950.4	E962.0	E980.4
Emylcamate	969.5	E853.8	E939.5	E950.3	E962.0	E980.3
Encyprate	969.0	E854.0	E939.0	E950.3	E962.0	E980.3
Endocaine	968.5	E855.2	E938.5	E950.4	E962.0	E980.4
Endrin	989.2	E863.0	—	E950.6	E962.1	E980.7
Enflurane	968.2	E855.1	E938.2	E950.4	E962.0	E980.4
Enovid	962.2	E858.0	E932.2	E950.4	E962.0	E980.4
ENT preparations (anti-infectives)	976.6	E858.7	E946.6	E950.4	E962.0	E980.4
Enzodase	963.4	E858.1	E933.4	E950.4	E962.0	E980.4
Enzymes NEC	963.4	E858.1	E933.4	E950.4	E962.0	E980.4
Epanutin	966.1	E855.0	E936.1	E950.4	E962.0	E980.4
Ephedra (tincture)	971.2	E855.5	E941.2	E950.4	E962.0	E980.4

◄▶ **New Code**   ◄▥▥▥▥▶ **Revised Code**

Substance	Poisoning	External Cause (E-Code)				
		Accident	Therapeutic Use	Suicide Attempt	Assault	Undetermined
Ephedrine	971.2	E855.5	E941.2	E950.4	E962.0	E980.4
Epiestriol	962.2	E858.0	E932.2	E950.4	E962.0	E980.4
Epilim - see Sodium valproate						
Epinephrine	971.2	E855.5	E941.2	E950.4	E962.0	E980.4
Epsom salt	973.3	E858.4	E943.3	E950.4	E962.0	E980.4
Equanil	969.5	E853.8	E939.5	E950.3	E962.0	E980.3
Equisetum (diuretic)	974.4	E858.5	E944.4	E950.4	E962.0	E980.4
Ergometrine	975.0	E858.6	E945.0	E950.4	E962.0	E980.4
Ergonovine	975.0	E858.6	E945.0	E950.4	E962.0	E980.4
Ergot NEC	988.2	E865.4	—	E950.9	E962.1	E980.9
medicinal (alkaloids)	975.0	E858.6	E945.0	E950.4	E962.0	E980.4
Ergotamine (tartrate) (for migraine) NEC	972.9	E858.3	E942.9	E950.4	E962.0	E980.4
Ergotrate	975.0	E858.6	E945.0	E950.4	E962.0	E980.4
Erythrityl tetranitrate	972.4	E858.3	E942.4	E950.4	E962.0	E980.4
Erythrol tetranitrate	972.4	E858.3	E942.4	E950.4	E962.0	E980.4
Erythromycin	960.3	E856	E930.3	E950.4	E962.0	E980.4
ophthalmic preparation	976.5	E858.7	E946.5	E950.4	E962.0	E980.4
topical NEC	976.0	E858.7	E946.0	E950.4	E962.0	E980.4
Eserine	971.0	E855.3	E941.0	E950.4	E962.0	E980.4
Eskabarb	967.0	E851	E937.0	E950.1	E962.0	E980.1
Eskalith	969.8	E855.8	E939.8	E950.3	E962.0	E980.3
Estradiol (cypionate) (dipropionate) (valerate)	962.2	E858.0	E932.2	E950.4	E962.0	E980.4
Estriol	962.2	E858.0	E932.2	E950.4	E962.0	E980.4
Estrogens (with progestogens)	962.2	E858.0	E932.2	E950.4	E962.0	E980.4
Estrone	962.2	E858.0	E932.2	E950.4	E962.0	E980.4
Etafedrine	971.2	E855.5	E941.2	E950.4	E962.0	E980.4
Ethacrynate sodium	974.4	E858.5	E944.4	E950.4	E962.0	E980.4
Ethacrynic acid	974.4	E858.5	E944.4	E950.4	E962.0	E980.4
Ethambutol	961.8	E857	E931.8	E950.4	E962.0	E980.4
Ethamide	974.2	E858.5	E944.2	E950.4	E962.0	E980.4
Ethamivan	970.0	E854.3	E940.0	E950.4	E962.0	E980.4
Ethamsylate	964.5	E858.2	E934.5	E950.4	E962.0	E980.4
Ethanol	980.0	E860.1	—	E950.9	E962.1	E980.9
beverage	980.0	E860.0	—	E950.9	E962.1	E980.9
Ethchlorvynol	967.8	E852.8	E937.8	E950.2	E962.0	E980.2
Ethebenecid	974.7	E858.5	E944.7	E950.4	E962.0	E980.4
Ether(s) (diethyl) (ethyl) (vapor)	987.8	E869.8	—	E952.8	E962.2	E982.8
anesthetic	968.2	E855.1	E938.2	E950.4	E962.0	E980.4
petroleum - see Ligroin solvent	982.8	E862.4	—	E950.9	E962.1	E980.9
Ethidine chloride (vapor)	987.8	E869.8	—	E952.8	E962.2	E982.8
liquid (solvent)	982.3	E862.4	—	E950.9	E962.1	E980.9
Ethinamate	967.8	E852.8	E937.8	E950.2	E962.0	E980.2
Ethinylestradiol	962.2	E858.0	E932.2	E950.4	E962.0	E980.4
Ethionamide	961.8	E857	E931.8	E950.4	E962.0	E980.4
Ethisterone	962.2	E858.0	E932.2	E950.4	E962.0	E980.4
Ethobral	967.0	E851	E937.0	E950.1	E962.0	E980.1
Ethocaine (infiltration) (topical)	968.5	E855.2	E938.5	E950.4	E962.0	E980.4
nerve block (peripheral) (plexus)	968.6	E855.2	E938.6	E950.4	E962.0	E980.4
spinal	968.7	E855.2	E938.7	E950.4	E962.0	E980.4
Ethoheptazine (citrate)	965.7	E850.7	E935.7	E950.0	E962.0	E980.0
Ethopropazine	966.4	E855.0	E936.4	E950.4	E962.0	E980.4
Ethosuximide	966.2	E855.0	E936.2	E950.4	E962.0	E980.4
Ethotoin	966.1	E855.0	E936.1	E950.4	E962.0	E980.4
Ethoxazene	961.9	E857	E931.9	E950.4	E962.0	E980.4
Ethoxzolamide	974.2	E858.5	E944.2	E950.4	E962.0	E980.4
Ethyl						
acetate (vapor)	982.8	E862.4	—	E950.9	E962.1	E980.9
alcohol	980.0	E860.1	—	E950.9	E962.1	E980.9
beverage	980.0	E860.0	—	E950.9	E962.1	E980.9
aldehyde (vapor)	987.8	E869.8	—	E952.8	E962.2	E982.8
liquid	989.89	E866.8	—	E950.9	E962.1	E980.9
aminobenzoate	968.5	E855.2	E938.5	E950.4	E962.0	E980.4

Substance	Poisoning	External Cause (E-Code)				
		Accident	Therapeutic Use	Suicide Attempt	Assault	Undetermined
Ethyl *(Continued)*						
biscoumacetate	964.2	E858.2	E934.2	E950.4	E962.0	E980.4
bromide (anesthetic)	968.2	E855.1	E938.2	E950.4	E962.0	E980.4
carbamate (antineoplastic)	963.1	E858.1	E933.1	E950.4	E962.0	E980.4
carbinol	980.3	E860.4	—	E950.9	E962.1	E980.9
chaulmoograte	961.8	E857	E931.8	E950.4	E962.0	E980.4
chloride (vapor)	987.8	E869.8	—	E952.8	E962.2	E982.8
anesthetic (local)	968.5	E855.2	E938.5	E950.4	E962.0	E980.4
inhaled	968.2	E855.1	E938.2	E950.4	E962.0	E980.4
solvent	982.3	E862.4	—	E950.9	E962.1	E980.9
estranol	962.1	E858.0	E932.1	E950.4	E962.0	E980.4
ether - *see* Ether(s)						
formate (solvent) NEC	982.8	E862.4	—	E950.9	E962.1	E980.9
iodoacetate	987.5	E869.3	—	E952.8	E962.2	E982.8
lactate (solvent) NEC	982.8	E862.4	—	E950.9	E962.1	E980.9
methylcarbinol	980.8	E860.8	—	E950.9	E962.1	E980.9
morphine	965.09	E850.2	E935.2	E950.0	E962.0	E980.0
Ethylene (gas)	987.1	E869.8	—	E952.8	E962.2	E982.8
anesthetic (general)	968.2	E855.1	E938.2	E950.4	E962.0	E980.4
chlorohydrin (vapor)	982.3	E862.4	—	E950.9	E962.1	E980.9
dichloride (vapor)	982.3	E862.4	—	E950.9	E962.1	E980.9
glycol(s) (any) (vapor)	982.8	E862.4	—	E950.9	E962.1	E980.9
Ethylidene						
chloride NEC	982.3	E862.4	—	E950.9	E962.1	E980.9
diethyl ether	982.8	E862.4	—	E950.9	E962.1	E980.9
Ethynodiol	962.2	E858.0	E932.2	E950.4	E962.0	E980.4
Etidocaine	968.9	E855.2	E938.9	E950.4	E962.0	E980.4
infiltration (subcutaneous)	968.5	E855.2	E938.5	E950.4	E962.0	E980.4
nerve (peripheral) (plexus)	968.6	E855.2	E938.6	E950.4	E962.0	E980.4
Etilfen	967.0	E851	E937.0	E950.1	E962.0	E980.1
Etomide	965.7	E850.7	E935.7	E950.0	E962.0	E980.0
Etorphine	965.09	E850.2	E935.2	E950.0	E962.0	E980.0
Etoval	967.0	E851	E937.0	E950.1	E962.0	E980.1
Etryptamine	969.0	E854.0	E939.0	E950.3	E962.0	E980.3
Eucaine	968.5	E855.2	E938.5	E950.4	E962.0	E980.4
Eucalyptus (oil) NEC	975.5	E858.6	E945.5	E950.4	E962.0	E980.4
Eucatropine	971.1	E855.4	E941.1	E950.4	E962.0	E980.4
Eucodal	965.09	E850.2	E935.2	E950.0	E962.0	E980.0
Euneryl	967.0	E851	E937.0	E950.1	E962.0	E980.1
Euphthalmine	971.1	E855.4	E941.1	E950.4	E962.0	E980.4
Eurax	976.0	E858.7	E946.0	E950.4	E962.0	E980.4
Euresol	976.4	E858.7	E946.4	E950.4	E962.0	E980.4
Euthroid	962.7	E858.0	E932.7	E950.4	E962.0	E980.4
Evans blue	977.8	E858.8	E947.8	E950.4	E962.0	E980.4
Evipal	967.0	E851	E937.0	E950.1	E962.0	E980.1
sodium	968.3	E855.1	E938.3	E950.4	E962.0	E980.4
Evipan	967.0	E851	E937.0	E950.1	E962.0	E980.1
sodium	968.3	E855.1	E938.3	E950.4	E962.0	E980.4
Exalgin	965.4	E850.4	E935.4	E950.0	E962.0	E980.0
Excipients, pharmaceutical	977.4	E858.8	E947.4	E950.4	E962.0	E980.4
Exhaust gas - *see* Carbon, monoxide						
Ex-Lax (phenolphthalein)	973.1	E858.4	E943.1	E950.4	E962.0	E980.4
Expectorants	975.5	E858.6	E945.5	E950.4	E962.0	E980.4
External medications (skin) (mucous membrane)	976.9	E858.7	E946.9	E950.4	E962.0	E980.4
dental agent	976.7	E858.7	E946.7	E950.4	E962.0	E980.4
ENT agent	976.6	E858.7	E946.6	E950.4	E962.0	E980.4
ophthalmic preparation	976.5	E858.7	E946.5	E950.4	E962.0	E980.4
specified NEC	976.8	E858.7	E946.8	E950.4	E962.0	E980.4
Eye agents (anti-infective)	976.5	E858.7	E946.5	E950.4	E962.0	E980.4
Factor IX complex (human)	964.5	E858.2	E934.5	E950.4	E962.0	E980.4
Fecal softeners	973.2	E858.4	E943.2	E950.4	E962.0	E980.4
Fenbutrazate	977.0	E858.8	E947.0	E950.4	E962.0	E980.4

◀▶ **New Code**   ◀▦ ▦▶ **Revised Code**

Substance	External Cause (E-Code)					
	Poisoning	Accident	Therapeutic Use	Suicide Attempt	Assault	Undetermined
Fencamfamin	970.8	E854.3	E940.8	E950.4	E962.0	E980.4
Fenfluramine	977.0	E858.8	E947.0	E950.4	E962.0	E980.4
Fenoprofen	965.6	E850.6	E935.6	E950.0	E962.0	E980.0
Fentanyl	965.01	E850.2	E935.2	E950.0	E962.0	E980.0
Fentazin	969.1	E853.0	E939.1	E950.3	E962.0	E980.3
Fenticlor, fentichlor	976.0	E858.7	E946.0	E950.4	E962.0	E980.4
Fer de lance (bite) (venom)	989.5	E905.0	—	E950.9	E962.1	E980.9
Ferric - *see* Iron						
Ferrocholinate	964.0	E858.2	E934.0	E950.4	E962.0	E980.4
Ferrous fumerate, gluconate, lactate, salt NEC, sulfate (medicinal)	964.0	E858.2	E934.0	E950.4	E962.0	E980.4
Ferrum - *see* Iron						
Fertilizers NEC	989.89	E866.5	—	E950.9	E962.1	E980.4
with herbicide mixture	989.4	E863.5	—	E950.6	E962.1	E980.7
Fibrinogen (human)	964.7	E858.2	E934.7	E950.4	E962.0	E980.4
Fibrinolysin	964.4	E858.2	E934.4	E950.4	E962.0	E980.4
Fibrinolysis-affecting agents	964.4	E858.2	E934.4	E950.4	E962.0	E980.4
Filix mas	961.6	E857	E931.6	E950.4	E962.0	E980.4
Fiorinal	965.1	E850.3	E935.3	E950.0	E962.0	E980.0
Fire damp	987.1	E869.8	—	E952.8	E962.2	E982.8
Fish, nonbacterial or noxious	988.0	E865.2	—	E950.9	E962.1	E980.9
shell	988.0	E865.1	—	E950.9	E962.1	E980.9
Flagyl	961.5	E857	E931.5	E950.4	E962.0	E980.4
Flavoxate	975.1	E858.6	E945.1	E950.4	E962.0	E980.4
Flaxedil	975.2	E858.6	E945.2	E950.4	E962.0	E980.4
Flaxseed (medicinal)	976.3	E858.7	E946.3	E950.4	E962.0	E980.4
Florantyrone	973.4	E858.4	E943.4	E950.4	E962.0	E980.4
Floraquin	961.3	E857	E931.3	E950.4	E962.0	E980.4
Florinef	962.0	E858.0	E932.0	E950.4	E962.0	E980.4
ENT agent	976.6	E858.7	E946.6	E950.4	E962.0	E980.4
ophthalmic preparation	976.5	E858.7	E946.5	E950.4	E962.0	E980.4
topical NEC	976.0	E858.7	E946.0	E950.4	E962.0	E980.4
Flowers of sulfur	976.4	E858.7	E946.4	E950.4	E962.0	E980.4
Floxuridine	963.1	E858.1	E933.1	E950.4	E962.0	E980.4
Flucytosine	961.9	E857	E931.9	E950.4	E962.0	E980.4
Fludrocortisone	962.0	E858.0	E932.0	E950.4	E962.0	E980.4
ENT agent	976.6	E858.7	E946.6	E950.4	E962.0	E980.4
ophthalmic preparation	976.5	E858.7	E946.5	E950.4	E962.0	E980.4
topical NEC	976.0	E858.7	E946.0	E950.4	E962.0	E980.4
Flumethasone	976.0	E858.7	E946.0	E950.4	E962.0	E980.4
Flumethiazide	974.3	E858.5	E944.3	E950.4	E962.0	E980.4
Flumidin	961.7	E857	E931.7	E950.4	E962.0	E980.4
Fluocinolone	976.0	E858.7	E946.0	E950.4	E962.0	E980.4
Fluocortolone	962.0	E858.0	E932.0	E950.4	E962.0	E980.4
Fluohydrocortisone	962.0	E858.0	E932.0	E950.4	E962.0	E980.4
ENT agent	976.6	E858.7	E946.6	E950.4	E962.0	E980.4
ophthalmic preparation	976.5	E858.7	E946.5	E950.4	E962.0	E980.4
topical NEC	976.0	E858.7	E946.0	E950.4	E962.0	E980.4
Fluonid	976.0	E858.7	E946.0	E950.4	E962.0	E980.4
Fluopromazine	969.1	E853.0	E939.1	E950.3	E962.0	E980.3
Fluoracetate	989.4	E863.7	—	E950.6	E962.1	E980.7
Fluorescein (sodium)	977.8	E858.8	E947.8	E950.4	E962.0	E980.4
Fluoride(s) (pesticides) (sodium) NEC	989.4	E863.4	—	E950.6	E962.1	E980.7
hydrogen - *see* Hydrofluoric acid						
medicinal	976.7	E858.7	E946.7	E950.4	E962.0	E980.4
not pesticide NEC	983.9	E864.4	—	E950.7	E962.1	E980.6
stannous	976.7	E858.7	E946.7	E950.4	E962.0	E980.4
Fluorinated corticosteroids	962.0	E858.0	E932.0	E950.4	E962.0	E980.4
Fluorine (compounds) (gas)	987.8	E869.8	—	E952.8	E962.2	E982.8
salt - *see* Fluoride(s)						
Fluoristan	976.7	E858.7	E946.7	E950.4	E962.0	E980.4
Fluoroacetate	989.4	E863.7	—	E950.6	E962.1	E980.7
Fluorodeoxyuridine	963.1	E858.1	E933.1	E950.4	E962.0	E980.4

◄ ▶ New Code   ◄▦▦▶ Revised Code

		External Cause (E-Code)				
Substance	Poisoning	Accident	Therapeutic Use	Suicide Attempt	Assault	Undetermined
Fluorometholone (topical) NEC	976.0	E858.7	E946.0	E950.4	E962.0	E980.4
ophthalmic preparation	976.5	E858.7	E946.5	E950.4	E962.0	E980.4
Fluorouracil	963.1	E858.1	E933.1	E950.4	E962.0	E980.4
Fluothane	968.1	E855.1	E938.1	E950.4	E962.0	E980.4
Fluoxetine hydrochloride	969.0	E854.0	E939.0	E950.3	E962.0	E980.3
Fluoxymesterone	962.1	E858.0	E932.1	E950.4	E962.0	E980.4
Fluphenazine	969.1	E853.0	E939.1	E950.3	E962.0	E980.3
Fluprednisolone	962.0	E858.0	E932.0	E950.4	E962.0	E980.4
Flurandrenolide	976.0	E858.7	E946.0	E950.4	E962.0	E980.4
Flurazepam (hydrochloride)	969.4	E853.2	E939.4	E950.3	E962.0	E980.3
Flurbiprofen	965.61	E850.6	E935.6	E950.0	E962.0	E980.0
Flurobate	976.0	E858.7	E946.0	E950.4	E962.0	E980.4
Flurothyl	969.8	E855.8	E939.8	E950.3	E962.0	E980.3
Fluroxene	968.2	E855.1	E938.2	E950.4	E962.0	E980.4
Folacin	964.1	E858.2	E934.1	E950.4	E962.0	E980.4
Folic acid	964.1	E858.2	E934.1	E950.4	E962.0	E980.4
Follicle stimulating hormone	962.4	E858.0	E932.4	E950.4	E962.0	E980.4
Food, foodstuffs, nonbacterial or noxious	988.9	E865.9	—	E950.9	E962.1	E980.9
berries, seeds	988.2	E865.3	—	E950.9	E962.1	E980.9
fish	988.0	E865.2	—	E950.9	E962.1	E980.9
mushrooms	988.1	E865.5	—	E950.9	E962.1	E980.9
plants	988.2	E865.9	—	E950.9	E962.1	E980.9
specified type NEC	988.2	E865.4	—	E950.9	E962.1	E980.9
shellfish	988.0	E865.1	—	E950.9	E962.1	E980.9
specified NEC	988.8	E865.8	—	E950.9	E962.1	E980.9
Fool's parsley	988.2	E865.4	—	E950.9	E962.1	E980.9
Formaldehyde (solution)	989.89	E861.4	—	E950.9	E962.1	E980.9
fungicide	989.4	E863.6	—	E950.6	E962.1	E980.7
gas or vapor	987.8	E869.8	—	E952.8	E962.2	E982.8
Formalin	989.89	E861.4	—	E950.9	E962.1	E980.9
fungicide	989.4	E863.6	—	E950.6	E962.1	E980.7
vapor	987.8	E869.8	—	E952.8	E962.2	E982.8
Formic acid	983.1	E864.1	—	E950.7	E962.1	E980.6
vapor	987.8	E869.8	—	E952.8	E962.2	E982.8
Fowler's solution	985.1	E866.3	—	E950.8	E962.1	E980.8
Foxglove	988.2	E865.4	—	E950.9	E962.1	E980.9
Fox green	977.8	E858.8	E947.8	E950.4	E962.0	E980.4
Framycetin	960.8	E856	E930.8	E950.4	E962.0	E980.4
Frangula (extract)	973.1	E858.4	E943.1	E950.4	E962.0	E980.4
Frei antigen	977.8	E858.8	E947.8	E950.4	E962.0	E980.4
Freons	987.4	E869.2	—	E952.8	E962.2	E982.8
Fructose	974.5	E858.5	E944.5	E950.4	E962.0	E980.4
Frusemide	974.4	E858.5	E944.4	E950.4	E962.0	E980.4
FSH	962.4	E858.0	E932.4	E950.4	E962.0	E980.4
Fuel						
automobile	981	E862.1	—	E950.9	E962.1	E980.9
exhaust gas, not in transit	986	E868.2	—	E952.0	E962.2	E982.0
vapor NEC	987.1	E869.8	—	E952.8	E962.2	E982.8
gas (domestic use) - see also Carbon, monoxide, fuel						
utility	987.1	E868.1	—	E951.8	E962.2	E981.8
incomplete combustion of - see Carbon, monoxide, fuel, utility						
in mobile container	987.0	E868.0	—	E951.1	E962.2	E981.1
piped (natural)	987.1	E867	—	E951.0	E962.2	E981.0
industrial, incomplete combustion	986	E868.3	—	E952.1	E962.2	E982.1
Fugillin	960.8	E856	E930.8	E950.4	E962.0	E980.4
Fulminate of mercury	985.0	E866.1	—	E950.9	E962.1	E980.9
Fulvicin	960.1	E856	E930.1	E950.4	E962.0	E980.4
Fumadil	960.8	E856	E930.8	E950.4	E962.0	E980.4
Fumagillin	960.8	E856	E930.8	E950.4	E962.0	E980.4
Fumes (from)	987.9	E869.9	—	E952.9	E962.2	E982.9
carbon monoxide - see Carbon, monoxide						
charcoal (domestic use)	986	E868.3	—	E952.1	E962.2	E982.1

◄ ▶ **New Code**　　　⬅▥▥▥ ▥▥▥➡ **Revised Code**

Substance	Poisoning	External Cause (E-Code)				
		Accident	Therapeutic Use	Suicide Attempt	Assault	Undetermined
Fumes *(Continued)*						
chloroform - *see* Chloroform						
coke (in domestic stoves, fireplaces)	986	E868.3	—	E952.1	E962.2	E982.1
corrosive NEC	987.8	E869.8	—	E952.8	E962.2	E982.8
ether - *see* Ether(s)						
freons	987.4	E869.2	—	E952.8	E962.2	E982.8
hydrocarbons	987.1	E869.8	—	E952.8	E962.2	E982.8
petroleum (liquefied)	987.0	E868.0	—	E951.1	E962.2	E981.1
distributed through pipes (pure or mixed with air)	987.0	E867	—	E951.0	E962.2	E981.0
lead - *see* Lead						
metals - *see* specified metal						
nitrogen dioxide	987.2	E869.0	—	E952.8	E962.2	E982.8
pesticides - *see* Pesticides						
petroleum (liquefied)	987.0	E868.0	—	E951.1	E962.2	E981.1
distributed through pipes (pure or mixed with air)	987.0	E867	—	E951.0	E962.2	E981.0
polyester	987.8	E869.8	—	E952.8	E962.2	E982.8
specified source, other (*see also* substance specified)	987.8	E869.8	—	E952.8	E962.2	E982.8
sulfur dioxide	987.3	E869.1	—	E952.8	E962.2	E982.8
Fumigants	989.4	E863.8	—	E950.6	E962.1	E980.7
Fungi, noxious, used as food	988.1	E865.5	—	E950.9	E962.1	E980.9
Fungicides (*see also* Antifungals)	989.4	E863.6	—	E950.6	E962.1	E980.7
Fungizone	960.1	E856	E930.1	E950.4	E962.0	E980.4
topical	976.0	E858.7	E946.0	E950.4	E962.0	E980.4
Furacin	976.0	E858.7	E946.0	E950.4	E962.0	E980.4
Furadantin	961.9	E857	E931.9	E950.4	E962.0	E980.4
Furazolidone	961.9	E857	E931.9	E950.4	E962.0	E980.4
Furnace (coal burning) (domestic), gas from	986	E868.3	—	E952.1	E962.2	E982.1
industrial	986	E868.8	—	E952.1	E962.2	E982.1
Furniture polish	989.89	E861.2	—	E950.9	E962.1	E980.9
Furosemide	974.4	E858.5	E944.4	E950.4	E962.0	E980.4
Furoxone	961.9	E857	E931.9	E950.4	E962.0	E980.4
Fusel oil (amyl) (butyl) (propyl)	980.3	E860.4	—	E950.9	E962.1	E980.9
Fusidic acid	960.8	E856	E930.8	E950.4	E962.0	E980.4
Gallamine	975.2	E858.6	E945.2	E950.4	E962.0	E980.4
Gallotannic acid	976.2	E858.7	E946.2	E950.4	E962.0	E980.4
Gamboge	973.1	E858.4	E943.1	E950.4	E962.0	E980.4
Gamimune	964.6	E858.2	E934.6	E950.4	E962.0	E980.4
Gamma-benzene hexachloride (vapor)	989.2	E863.0	—	E950.6	E962.1	E980.7
Gamma globulin	964.6	E858.2	E934.6	E950.4	E962.0	E980.4
Gamulin	964.6	E858.2	E934.6	E950.4	E962.0	E980.4
Ganglionic blocking agents	972.3	E858.3	E942.3	E950.4	E962.0	E980.4
Ganja	969.6	E854.1	E939.6	E950.3	E962.0	E980.3
Garamycin	960.8	E856	E930.8	E950.4	E962.0	E980.4
ophthalmic preparation	976.5	E858.7	E946.5	E950.4	E962.0	E980.4
topical NEC	976.0	E858.7	E946.0	E950.4	E962.0	E980.4
Gardenal	967.0	E851	E937.0	E950.1	E962.0	E980.1
Gardepanyl	967.0	E851	E937.0	E950.1	E962.0	E980.1
Gas	987.9	E869.9	—	E952.9	E962.2	E982.9
acetylene	987.1	E868.1	—	E951.8	E962.2	E981.8
incomplete combustion of - *see* Carbon, monoxide, fuel, utility						
air contaminants, source or type not specified	987.9	E869.9	—	E952.9	E962.2	E982.9
anesthetic (general) NEC	968.2	E855.1	E938.2	E950.4	E962.0	E980.4
blast furnace	986	E868.8	—	E952.1	E962.2	E982.1
butane - *see* Butane						
carbon monoxide - *see* Carbon, monoxide, chlorine	987.6	E869.8	—	E952.8	E962.2	E982.8
coal - *see* Carbon, monoxide, coal						
cyanide	987.7	E869.8	—	E952.8	E962.2	E982.8
dicyanogen	987.8	E869.8	—	E952.8	E962.2	E982.8
domestic - *see* Gas, utility						
exhaust - *see* Carbon, monoxide, exhaust gas						
from wood- or coal-burning stove or fireplace	986	E868.3	—	E952.1	E962.2	E982.1
fuel (domestic use) - *see also* Carbon, monoxide, fuel						
industrial use	986	E868.8	—	E952.1	E962.2	E982.1

Substance	Poisoning	External Cause (E-Code)				
		Accident	Therapeutic Use	Suicide Attempt	Assault	Undetermined
Gas *(Continued)*						
fuel *(Continued)*						
utility	987.1	E868.1	—	E951.8	E962.2	E981.8
incomplete combustion of - *see* Carbon, monoxide, fuel, utility						
in mobile container	987.0	E868.0	—	E951.1	E962.2	E981.1
piped (natural)	987.1	E867	—	E951.0	E962.2	E981.0
garage	986	E868.2	—	E952.0	E962.2	E982.0
hydrocarbon NEC	987.1	E869.8	—	E952.8	E962.2	E982.8
incomplete combustion of - *see* Carbon, monoxide, fuel, utility						
liquefied (mobile container)	987.0	E868.0	—	E951.1	E962.2	E981.1
piped	987.0	E867	—	E951.0	E962.2	E981.0
hydrocyanic acid	987.7	E869.8	—	E952.8	E962.2	E982.8
illuminating - *see* Gas, utility						
incomplete combustion, any - *see* Carbon, monoxide						
kiln	986	E868.8	—	E952.1	E962.2	E982.1
lacrimogenic	987.5	E869.3	—	E952.8	E962.2	E982.8
marsh	987.1	E869.8	—	E952.8	E962.2	E982.8
motor exhaust, not in transit	986	E868.8	—	E952.1	E962.2	E982.1
mustard - *see* Mustard, gas						
natural	987.1	E867	—	E951.0	E962.2	E981.0
nerve (war)	987.9	E869.9	—	E952.9	E962.2	E982.9
oils	981	E862.1	—	E950.9	E962.1	E980.9
petroleum (liquefied) (distributed in mobile containers)	987.0	E868.0	—	E951.1	E962.2	E981.1
piped (pure or mixed with air)	987.0	E867	—	E951.1	E962.2	E981.1
piped (manufactured) (natural) NEC	987.1	E867	—	E951.0	E962.2	E981.0
producer	986	E868.8	—	E952.1	E962.2	E982.1
propane - *see* Propane						
refrigerant (freon)	987.4	E869.2	—	E952.8	E962.2	E982.8
not freon	987.9	E869.9	—	E952.9	E962.2	E982.9
sewer	987.8	E869.8	—	E952.8	E962.2	E982.8
specified source NEC (*see also* substance specified)	987.8	E869.8	—	E952.8	E962.2	E982.8
stove - *see* Gas, utility						
tear	987.5	E869.3	—	E952.8	E962.2	E982.8
utility (for cooking, heating, or lighting) (piped) NEC	987.1	E868.1	—	E951.8	E962.2	E981.8
incomplete combustion of - *see* Carbon, monoxide, fuel, utilty						
in mobile container	987.0	E868.0	—	E951.1	E962.2	E981.1
piped (natural)	987.1	E867	—	E951.0	E962.2	E981.0
water	987.1	E868.1	—	E951.8	E962.2	E981.8
incomplete combustion of - *see* Carbon, monoxide, fuel, utility						
Gaseous substance - *see* Gas						
Gasoline, gasolene	981	E862.1	—	E950.9	E962.1	E980.9
vapor	987.1	E869.8	—	E952.8	E962.2	E982.8
Gastric enzymes	973.4	E858.4	E943.4	E950.4	E962.0	E980.4
Gastrografin	977.8	E858.8	E947.8	E950.4	E962.0	E980.4
Gastrointestinal agents	973.9	E858.4	E943.9	E950.4	E962.0	E980.4
specified NEC	973.8	E858.4	E943.8	E950.4	E962.0	E980.4
Gaultheria procumbens	988.2	E865.4	—	E950.9	E961.1	E980.9
Gelatin (intravenous)	964.8	E858.2	E934.8	E950.4	E962.0	E980.4
absorbable (sponge)	964.5	E858.2	E934.5	E950.4	E962.0	E980.4
Gelfilm	976.8	E858.7	E946.8	E950.4	E962.0	E980.4
Gelfoam	964.5	E858.2	E934.5	E950.4	E962.0	E980.4
Gelsemine	970.8	E854.3	E940.8	E950.4	E962.0	E980.4
Gelsemium (sempervirens)	988.2	E865.4	—	E950.9	E961.1	E980.9
Gemonil	967.0	E851	E937.0	E950.1	E962.0	E980.1
Gentamicin	960.8	E856	E930.8	E950.4	E962.0	E980.4
ophthalmic preparation	976.5	E858.7	E946.5	E950.4	E962.0	E980.4
topical NEC	976.0	E858.7	E946.0	E950.4	E962.0	E980.4
Gentian violet	976.0	E858.7	E946.0	E950.4	E962.0	E980.4
Gexane	976.0	E858.7	E946.0	E950.4	E962.0	E980.4
Gila monster (venom)	989.5	E905.0	—	E950.9	E961.1	E980.9
Ginger, Jamaica	989.89	E866.8	—	E950.9	E961.1	E980.9
Gitalin	972.1	E858.3	E942.1	E950.4	E962.0	E980.4

◀▶ **New Code**   ◀▥ ▥▶ **Revised Code**

Substance	Poisoning	External Cause (E-Code)				
		Accident	Therapeutic Use	Suicide Attempt	Assault	Undetermined
Gitoxin	972.1	E858.3	E942.1	E950.4	E962.0	E980.4
Glandular extract (medicinal) NEC	977.9	E858.9	E947.9	E950.5	E962.0	E980.5
Glaucarubin	961.5	E857	E931.5	E950.4	E962.0	E980.4
Globin zinc insulin	962.3	E858.0	E932.3	E950.4	E962.0	E980.4
Glucagon	962.3	E858.0	E932.3	E950.4	E962.0	E980.4
Glucochloral	967.1	E852.0	E937.1	E950.2	E962.0	E980.2
Glucocorticoids	962.0	E858.0	E932.0	E950.4	E962.0	E980.4
Glucose	974.5	E858.5	E944.5	E950.4	E962.0	E980.4
oxidase reagent	977.8	E858.8	E947.8	E950.4	E962.0	E980.4
Glucosulfone sodium	961.8	E857	E931.8	E950.4	E962.0	E980.4
Glue(s)	989.89	E866.6	—	E950.9	E962.1	E980.9
Glutamic acid (hydrochloride)	973.4	E858.4	E943.4	E950.4	E962.0	E980.4
Glutathione	963.8	E858.1	E933.8	E950.4	E962.0	E980.4
Glutethimide (group)	967.5	E852.4	E937.5	E950.2	E962.0	E980.2
Glycerin (lotion)	976.3	E858.7	E946.3	E950.4	E962.0	E980.4
Glycerol (topical)	976.3	E858.7	E946.3	E950.4	E962.0	E980.4
Glyceryl						
gualacolate	975.5	E858.6	E945.5	E950.4	E962.0	E980.4
triacetate (topical)	976.0	E858.7	E946.0	E950.4	E962.0	E980.4
trinitrate	972.4	E858.3	E942.4	E950.4	E962.0	E980.4
Glycine	974.5	E858.5	E944.5	E950.4	E962.0	E980.4
Glycobiarsol	961.1	E857	E931.1	E950.4	E962.0	E980.4
Glycols (ether)	982.8	E862.4	—	E950.9	E962.1	E980.9
Glycopyrrolate	971.1	E855.4	E941.1	E950.4	E962.0	E980.4
Glymidine	962.3	E858.0	E932.3	E950.4	E962.0	E980.4
Gold (compounds) (salts)	965.69	E850.6	E935.6	E950.0	E962.0	E980.0
Golden sulfide of antimony	985.4	E866.2	—	E950.9	E962.1	E980.9
Goldylocks	988.2	E865.4	—	E950.9	E962.1	E980.9
Gonadal tissue extract	962.9	E858.0	E932.9	E950.4	E962.0	E980.4
female	962.2	E858.0	E932.2	E950.4	E962.0	E980.4
male	962.1	E858.0	E932.1	E950.4	E962.0	E980.4
Gonadotropin	962.4	E858.0	E932.4	E950.4	E962.0	E980.4
Grain alcohol	980.0	E860.1	—	E950.9	E962.1	E980.9
beverage	980.0	E860.0	—	E950.9	E962.1	E980.9
Gramicidin	960.8	E856	E930.8	E950.4	E962.0	E980.4
Gratiola officinalis	988.2	E865.4	—	E950.9	E962.1	E980.9
Grease	989.89	E866.8	—	E950.9	E962.1	E980.9
Green hellebore	988.2	E865.4	—	E950.9	E962.1	E980.9
Green soap	976.2	E858.7	E946.2	E950.4	E962.0	E980.4
Grifulvin	960.1	E856	E930.1	E950.4	E962.0	E980.4
Griseofulvin	960.1	E856	E930.1	E950.4	E962.0	E980.4
Growth hormone	962.4	E858.0	E932.4	E950.4	E962.0	E980.4
Guaiacol	975.5	E858.6	E945.5	E950.4	E962.0	E980.4
Giuaiac reagent	977.8	E858.8	E947.8	E950.4	E962.0	E980.4
Guaifenesin	975.5	E858.6	E945.5	E950.4	E962.0	E980.4
Guaiphenesin	975.5	E858.6	E945.5	E950.4	E962.0	E980.4
Guanatol	961.4	E857	E931.4	E950.4	E962.0	E980.4
Guanethidine	972.6	E858.3	E942.6	E950.4	E962.0	E980.4
Guano	989.89	E866.5	—	E950.9	E962.1	E980.9
Guanochlor	972.6	E858.3	E942.6	E950.4	E962.0	E980.4
Guanoctine	972.6	E858.3	E942.6	E950.4	E962.0	E980.4
Guanoxan	972.6	E858.3	E942.6	E950.4	E962.0	E980.4
Hair treatment agent NEC	976.4	E858.7	E946.4	E950.4	E962.0	E980.4
Halcinonide	976.0	E858.7	E946.0	E950.4	E962.0	E980.4
Halethazole	976.0	E858.7	E946.0	E950.4	E962.0	E980.4
Hallucinogens	969.6	E854.1	E939.6	E950.3	E962.0	E980.3
Haloperidol	969.2	E853.1	E939.2	E950.3	E962.0	E980.3
Haloprogin	976.0	E858.7	E946.0	E950.4	E962.0	E980.4
Halotex	976.0	E858.7	E946.0	E950.4	E962.0	E980.4
Halothane	968.1	E855.1	E938.1	E950.4	E962.0	E980.4
Halquinols	976.0	E858.7	E946.0	E950.4	E962.0	E980.4
Harmonyl	972.6	E858.3	E942.6	E950.4	E962.0	E980.4

◀▶ **New Code**　　　⬅▥▥▷ **Revised Code**

Substance	Poisoning	External Cause (E-Code)				
		Accident	Therapeutic Use	Suicide Attempt	Assault	Undetermined
Hartmann's solution	974.5	E858.5	E944.5	E950.4	E962.0	E980.4
Hashish	969.6	E854.1	E939.6	E950.3	E962.0	E980.3
Hawaiian wood rose seeds	969.6	E854.1	E939.6	E950.3	E962.0	E980.3
Headache cures, drugs, powders NEC	977.9	E858.9	E947.9	E950.5	E962.0	E980.9
Heavenly Blue (morning glory)	969.6	E854.1	E939.6	E950.3	E962.0	E980.3
Heavy metal antagonists	963.8	E858.1	E933.8	E950.4	E962.0	E980.4
anti-infectives	961.2	E857	E931.2	E950.4	E962.0	E980.4
Hedaquinium	976.0	E858.7	E946.0	E950.4	E962.0	E980.4
Hedge hyssop	988.2	E865.4	—	E950.9	E962.1	E980.9
Heet	976.8	E858.7	E946.8	E950.4	E962.0	E980.4
Helenin	961.6	E857	E931.6	E950.4	E962.0	E980.4
Hellebore (black) (green) (white)	988.2	E865.4	—	E950.9	E962.1	E980.9
Hemlock	988.2	E865.4	—	E950.9	E962.1	E980.9
Hemostatics	964.5	E858.2	E934.5	E950.4	E962.0	E980.4
capillary active drugs	972.8	E858.3	E942.8	E950.4	E962.0	E980.4
Henbane	988.2	E865.4	—	E950.9	E962.1	E980.9
Heparin (sodium)	964.2	E858.2	E934.2	E950.4	E962.0	E980.4
Heptabarbital, heptabarbitone	967.0	E851	E937.0	E950.1	E962.0	E980.1
Heptachlor	989.2	E863.0	—	E950.6	E962.1	E980.7
Heptalgin	965.09	E850.2	E935.2	E950.0	E962.0	E980.0
Herbicides	989.4	E863.5	—	E950.6	E962.1	E980.7
Heroin	965.01	E850.0	E935.0	E950.0	E962.0	E980.0
Herplex	976.5	E858.7	E946.5	E950.4	E962.0	E980.4
HES	964.8	E858.2	E934.8	E950.4	E962.0	E980.4
Hetastarch	964.8	E858.2	E934.8	E950.4	E962.0	E980.7
Hexachlorocyclohexane	989.2	E863.0	—	E950.6	E962.1	E980.7
Hexachlorophene	976.2	E858.7	E946.2	E950.4	E962.0	E980.4
Hexadimethrine (bromide)	964.5	E858.2	E934.5	E950.4	E962.0	E980.4
Hexafluorenium	975.2	E858.6	E945.2	E950.4	E962.0	E980.4
Hexa-germ	976.2	E858.7	E946.2	E950.4	E962.0	E980.4
Hexahydrophenol	980.8	E860.8	—	E950.9	E962.1	E980.9
Hexalen	980.8	E860.8	—	E950.9	E962.1	E980.9
Hexamethonium	972.3	E858.3	E942.3	E950.4	E962.0	E980.4
Hexamethylenamine	961.9	E857	E931.9	E950.4	E962.0	E980.4
Hexamine	961.9	E857	E931.9	E950.4	E962.0	E980.4
Hexanone	982.8	E862.4	—	E950.9	E962.1	E980.9
Hexapropymate	967.8	E852.8	E937.8	E950.2	E962.0	E980.2
Hexestrol	962.2	E858.0	E932.2	E950.4	E962.0	E980.4
Hexethal (sodium)	967.0	E851	E937.0	E950.1	E962.0	E980.1
Hexetidine	976.0	E858.7	E946.0	E950.4	E962.0	E980.4
Hexobarbital, hexobarbitone	967.0	E851	E937.0	E950.1	E962.0	E980.1
sodium (anesthetic)	968.3	E855.1	E938.3	E950.4	E962.0	E980.4
soluble	968.3	E855.1	E938.3	E950.4	E962.0	E980.4
Hexocyclium	971.1	E855.4	E941.1	E950.4	E962.0	E980.4
Hexoestrol	962.2	E858.0	E932.2	E950.4	E962.0	E980.4
Hexone	982.8	E862.4	—	E950.9	E962.1	E980.9
Hexylcaine	968.5	E855.2	E938.5	E950.4	E962.0	E980.4
Hexylresorcinol	961.6	E857	E931.6	E950.4	E962.0	E980.4
Hinkle's pills	973.1	E858.4	E943.1	E950.4	E962.0	E980.4
Histalog	977.8	E858.8	E947.8	E950.4	E962.0	E980.4
Histamine (phosphate)	972.5	E858.3	E942.5	E950.4	E962.0	E980.4
Histoplasmin	977.8	E858.8	E947.8	E950.4	E962.0	E980.4
Holly berries	988.2	E865.3	—	E950.9	E962.1	E980.9
Homatropine	971.1	E855.4	E941.1	E950.4	E962.0	E980.4
Homo-tet	964.6	E858.2	E934.6	E950.4	E962.0	E980.4
Hormones (synthetic substitute) NEC	962.9	E858.0	E932.9	E950.4	E962.0	E980.4
adrenal cortical steroids	962.0	E858.0	E932.0	E950.4	E962.0	E980.4
antidiabetic agents	962.3	E858.0	E932.3	E950.4	E962.0	E980.4
follicle stimulating	962.4	E858.0	E932.4	E950.4	E962.0	E980.4
gonadotropic	962.4	E858.0	E932.4	E950.4	E962.0	E980.4
growth	962.4	E858.0	E932.4	E950.4	E962.0	E980.4

◄ ▶ **New Code**   ◄▒ ▒▶ **Revised Code**

Substance	Poisoning	External Cause (E-Code)				
		Accident	Therapeutic Use	Suicide Attempt	Assault	Undetermined
Hormones *(Continued)*						
ovarian (substitutes)	962.2	E858.0	E932.2	E950.4	E962.0	E980.4
parathyroid (derivatives)	962.6	E858.0	E932.6	E950.4	E962.0	E980.4
pituitary (posterior)	962.5	E858.0	E932.5	E950.4	E962.0	E980.4
anterior	962.4	E858.0	E932.4	E950.4	E962.0	E980.4
thyroid (derivative)	962.7	E858.0	E932.7	E950.4	E962.0	E980.4
Hornet (sting)	989.5	E905.3	—	E950.9	E962.1	E980.9
Horticulture agent NEC	989.4	E863.9	—	E950.6	E962.1	E980.7
Hyaluronidase	963.4	E858.1	E933.4	E950.4	E962.0	E980.4
Hyazyme	963.4	E858.1	E933.4	E950.4	E962.0	E980.4
Hycodan	965.09	E850.2	E935.2	E950.0	E962.0	E980.0
Hydantoin derivatives	966.1	E855.0	E936.1	E950.4	E962.0	E980.4
Hydeltra	962.0	E858.0	E932.0	E950.4	E962.0	E980.4
Hydergine	971.3	E855.6	E941.3	E950.4	E962.0	E980.4
Hydrabamine penicillin	960.0	E856	E930.0	E950.4	E962.0	E980.4
Hydralazine, hydrallazine	972.6	E858.3	E942.6	E950.4	E962.0	E980.4
Hydrargaphen	976.0	E858.7	E946.0	E950.4	E962.0	E980.4
Hydrazine	983.9	E864.3	—	E950.7	E962.1	E980.6
Hydriodic acid	975.5	E858.6	E945.5	E950.4	E962.0	E980.4
Hydrocarbon gas	987.1	E869.8	—	E952.8	E962.2	E982.8
incomplete combustion of - *see* Carbon, monoxide, fuel, utility						
liquefied (mobile container)	987.0	E868.0	—	E951.1	E962.2	E981.1
piped (natural)	987.0	E867	—	E951.0	E962.2	E981.0
Hydrochloric acid (liquid)	983.1	E864.1	—	E950.7	E962.1	E980.6
medicinal	973.4	E858.4	E943.4	E950.4	E962.0	E980.4
vapor	987.8	E869.8	—	E952.8	E962.2	E982.8
Hydrochlorothiazide	974.3	E858.5	E944.3	E950.4	E962.0	E980.4
Hydrocodone	965.09	E850.2	E935.2	E950.0	E962.0	E980.0
Hydrocortisone	962.0	E858.0	E932.0	E950.4	E962.0	E980.4
ENT agent	976.6	E858.7	E946.6	E950.4	E962.0	E980.4
ophthalmic preparation	976.5	E858.7	E946.5	E950.4	E962.0	E980.4
topical NEC	976.0	E858.7	E946.0	E950.4	E962.0	E980.4
Hydrocortone	962.0	E858.0	E932.0	E950.4	E962.0	E980.4
ENT agent	976.6	E858.7	E946.6	E950.4	E962.0	E980.4
ophthalmic preparation	976.5	E858.7	E946.5	E950.4	E962.0	E980.4
topical NEC	976.0	E858.7	E946.0	E950.4	E962.0	E980.4
Hydrocyanic acid - *see* Cyanide(s)						
Hydroflumethiazide	974.3	E858.5	E944.3	E950.4	E962.0	E980.4
Hydrofluoric acid (liquid)	983.1	E864.1	—	E950.7	E962.1	E980.6
vapor	987.8	E869.8	—	E952.8	E962.2	E982.8
Hydrogen	987.8	E869.8	—	E952.8	E962.2	E982.8
arsenide	985.1	E866.3	—	E950.8	E962.1	E980.8
arseniurated	985.1	E866.3	—	E950.8	E962.1	E980.8
cyanide (salts)	989.0	E866.8	—	E950.9	E962.1	E980.9
gas	987.7	E869.8	—	E952.8	E962.2	E982.8
fluoride (liquid)	983.1	E864.1	—	E950.7	E962.1	E980.6
vapor	987.8	E869.8	—	E952.8	E962.2	E982.8
peroxide (solution)	976.6	E858.7	E946.6	E950.4	E962.0	E980.4
phosphorated	987.8	E869.8	—	E952.8	E962.2	E982.8
sulfide (gas)	987.8	E869.8	—	E952.8	E962.2	E982.8
arseniurated	985.1	E866.3	—	E950.8	E962.1	E980.8
sulfureted	987.8	E869.8	—	E952.8	E962.2	E982.8
Hydromorphinol	965.09	E850.2	E935.2	E950.0	E962.0	E980.0
Hydromorphinone	965.09	E850.2	E935.2	E950.0	E962.0	E980.0
Hydromorphone	965.09	E850.2	E935.2	E950.0	E962.0	E980.0
Hydromox	974.3	E858.5	E944.3	E950.4	E962.0	E980.4
Hydrophilic lotion	976.3	E858.7	E946.3	E950.4	E962.0	E980.4
Hydroquinone	983.0	E864.0	—	E950.7	E962.1	E980.6
vapor	987.8	E869.8	—	E952.8	E962.2	E982.8
Hydrosulfuric acid (gas)	987.8	E869.8	—	E952.8	E962.2	E982.8
Hydrous wool fat (lotion)	976.3	E858.7	E946.3	E950.4	E962.0	E980.4
Hydroxide, caustic	983.2	E864.2	—	E950.7	E962.1	E980.6

◀▶ **New Code**   ◀▥▥▶ **Revised Code**

Substance	Poisoning	External Cause (E-Code)				
		Accident	Therapeutic Use	Suicide Attempt	Assault	Undetermined
Hydroxocobalamin	964.1	E858.2	E934.1	E950.4	E962.0	E980.4
Hydroxyamphetamine	971.2	E855.5	E941.2	E950.4	E962.0	E980.4
Hydroxychloroquine	961.4	E857	E931.4	E950.4	E962.0	E980.4
Hydroxydihydrocodeinone	965.09	E850.2	E935.2	E950.0	E962.0	E980.0
Hydroxyethyl starch	964.8	E858.2	E934.8	E950.4	E962.0	E980.4
Hydroxyphenamate	969.5	E853.8	E939.5	E950.3	E962.0	E980.3
Hydroxyphenylbutazone	965.5	E850.5	E935.5	E950.0	E962.0	E980.0
Hydroxyprogesterone	962.2	E858.0	E932.2	E950.4	E962.0	E980.4
Hydroxyquinoline derivatives	961.3	E857	E931.3	E950.4	E962.0	E980.4
Hydroxystilbamidine	961.5	E857	E931.5	E950.4	E962.0	E980.4
Hydroxyurea	963.1	E858.1	E933.1	E950.4	E962.0	E980.4
Hydroxyzine	969.5	E853.8	E939.5	E950.3	E962.0	E980.3
Hyoscine (hydrobromide)	971.1	E855.4	E941.1	E950.4	E962.0	E980.4
Hyoscyamine	971.1	E855.4	E941.1	E950.4	E962.0	E980.4
Hyoscyamus (albus) (niger)	988.2	E865.4	—	E950.9	E962.1	E980.9
Hypaque	977.8	E858.8	E947.8	E950.4	E962.0	E980.4
Hypertussis	964.6	E858.2	E934.6	E950.4	E962.0	E980.4
Hypnotics NEC	967.9	E852.9	E937.9	E950.2	E962.0	E980.2
Hypochlorites - *see* Sodium, hypochlorite						
Hypotensive agents NEC	972.6	E858.3	E942.6	E950.4	E962.0	E980.4
Ibufenac	965.69	E850.6	E935.6	E950.0	E962.0	E980.0
Ibuprofen	965.61	E850.6	E935.6	E950.0	E962.0	E980.0
ICG	977.8	E858.8	E947.8	E950.4	E962.0	E980.4
Ichthammol	976.4	E858.7	E946.4	E950.4	E962.0	E980.4
Ichthyol	976.4	E858.7	E946.4	E950.4	E962.0	E980.4
Idoxuridine	976.5	E858.7	E946.5	E950.4	E962.0	E980.4
IDU	976.5	E858.7	E946.5	E950.4	E962.0	E980.4
Iletin	962.3	E858.0	E932.3	E950.4	E962.0	E980.4
Ilex	988.2	E865.4	—	E950.9	E962.1	E980.9
Illuminating gas - *see* Gas, utility						
Ilopan	963.5	E858.1	E933.5	E950.4	E962.0	E980.4
Ilotycin	960.3	E856	E930.3	E950.4	E962.0	E980.4
ophthalmic preparation	976.5	E858.7	E946.5	E950.4	E962.0	E980.4
topical NEC	976.0	E858.7	E946.0	E950.4	E962.0	E980.4
Imipramine	969.0	E854.0	E939.0	E950.3	E962.0	E980.3
Immu-G	964.6	E858.2	E934.6	E950.4	E962.0	E980.4
Immuglobin	964.6	E858.2	E934.6	E950.4	E962.0	E980.4
Immune serum globulin	964.6	E858.2	E934.6	E950.4	E962.0	E980.4
Immunosuppressive agents	963.1	E858.1	E933.1	E950.4	E962.0	E980.4
Immu-tetanus	964.6	E858.2	E934.6	E950.4	E962.0	E980.4
Indandione (derivatives)	964.2	E858.2	E934.2	E950.4	E962.0	E980.4
Inderal	972.0	E858.3	E942.0	E950.4	E962.0	E980.4
Indian						
hemp	969.6	E854.1	E939.6	E950.3	E962.0	E980.3
tobacco	988.2	E865.4	—	E950.9	E962.1	E980.9
Indigo carmine	977.8	E858.8	E947.8	E950.4	E962.0	E980.4
Indocin	965.69	E850.6	E935.6	E950.0	E962.0	E980.0
Indocyanine green	977.8	E858.8	E947.8	E950.4	E962.0	E980.4
Indomethacin	965.69	E850.6	E935.6	E950.0	E962.0	E980.0
Industrial						
alcohol	980.9	E860.9	—	E950.9	E962.1	E980.9
fumes	987.8	E869.8	—	E952.8	E962.2	E982.8
solvents (fumes) (vapors)	982.8	E862.9	—	E950.9	E962.1	E980.9
Influenza vaccine	979.6	E858.8	E949.6	E950.4	E962.0	E982.8
Ingested substances NEC	989.9	E866.9	—	E950.9	E962.1	E980.9
INH (isoniazid)	961.8	E857	E931.8	E950.4	E962.0	E980.4
Inhalation, gas (noxious) - *see* Gas						
Ink	989.89	E866.8	—	E950.9	E962.1	E980.9
Innovar	967.6	E852.5	E937.6	E950.2	E962.0	E982.2
Inositol niacinate	972.2	E858.3	E942.2	E950.4	E962.0	E980.4
Inproquone	963.1	E858.1	E933.1	E950.4	E962.0	E980.4

◀▶ **New Code**   ⬅▓▓▓▶ **Revised Code**

Substance	Poisoning	External Cause (E-Code)				
		Accident	Therapeutic Use	Suicide Attempt	Assault	Undetermined
Insect (sting), venomous	989.5	E905.5	—	E950.9	E962.1	E980.9
Insecticides (*see also* Pesticides)	989.4	E863.4	—	E950.6	E962.1	E980.7
chlorinated	989.2	E863.0	—	E950.6	E962.1	E980.7
mixtures	989.4	E863.3	—	E950.6	E962.1	E980.7
organochlorine (compounds)	989.2	E863.0	—	E950.6	E962.1	E980.7
organophosphorus (compounds)	989.3	E863.1	—	E950.6	E962.1	E980.7
Insular tissue extract	962.3	E858.0	E932.3	E950.4	E962.0	E980.4
Insulin (amorphous) (globin) (isophane) (Lente) (NPH) (Protamine) (Semilente) (Ultralente) (zinc)	962.3	E858.0	E932.3	E950.4	E962.0	E980.4
Intranarcon	968.3	E855.1	E938.3	E950.4	E962.0	E980.4
Inulin	977.8	E858.8	E947.8	E950.4	E962.0	E980.4
Invert sugar	974.5	E858.5	E944.5	E950.4	E962.0	E980.4
Inza - see Naproxen						
Iodide NEC (*see also* Iodine)	976.0	E858.7	E946.0	E950.4	E962.0	E980.4
mercury (ointment)	976.0	E858.7	E946.0	E950.4	E962.0	E980.4
methylate	976.0	E858.7	E946.0	E950.4	E962.0	E980.4
potassium (expectorant) NEC	975.5	E858.6	E945.5	E950.4	E962.0	E980.4
Iodinated glycerol	975.5	E858.6	E945.5	E950.4	E962.0	E980.4
Iodine (antiseptic, external) (tincture) NEC	976.0	E858.7	E946.0	E950.4	E962.0	E980.4
diagnostic	977.8	E858.8	E947.8	E950.4	E962.0	E980.4
for thyroid conditions (antithyroid)	962.8	E858.0	E932.8	E950.4	E962.0	E980.4
vapor	987.8	E869.8	—	E952.8	E962.2	E982.8
Iodized oil	977.8	E858.8	E947.8	E950.4	E962.0	E980.4
Iodobismitol	961.2	E857	E931.2	E950.4	E962.0	E980.4
Iodochlorhydroxyquin	961.3	E857	E931.3	E950.4	E962.0	E980.4
topical	976.0	E858.7	E946.0	E950.4	E962.0	E980.4
Iodoform	976.0	E858.7	E946.0	E950.4	E962.0	E980.4
Iodopanoic acid	977.8	E858.8	E947.8	E950.4	E962.0	E980.4
Iodophthalein	977.8	E858.8	E947.8	E950.4	E962.0	E980.4
Ion exchange resins	974.5	E858.5	E944.5	E950.4	E962.0	E980.4
Iopanoic acid	977.8	E858.8	E947.8	E950.4	E962.0	E980.4
Iophendylate	977.8	E858.8	E947.8	E950.4	E962.0	E980.4
Iothiouracil	962.8	E858.0	E932.8	E950.4	E962.0	E980.4
Ipecac	973.6	E858.4	E943.6	E950.4	E962.0	E980.4
Ipecacuanha	973.6	E858.4	E943.6	E950.4	E962.0	E980.4
Ipodate	977.8	E858.8	E947.8	E950.4	E962.0	E980.4
Ipral	967.0	E851	E937.0	E950.1	E962.0	E980.1
Iproniazid	969.0	E854.0	E939.0	E950.3	E962.0	E980.3
Iron (compounds) (medicinal) (preparations)	964.0	E858.2	E934.0	E950.4	E962.0	E980.4
dextran	964.0	E858.2	E934.0	E950.4	E962.0	E980.4
nonmedicinal (dust) (fumes) NEC	985.8	E866.4	—	E950.9	E962.1	E980.9
Irritant drug	977.9	E858.9	E947.9	E950.5	E962.0	E980.5
Ismelin	972.6	E858.3	E942.6	E950.4	E962.0	E980.4
Isoamyl nitrite	972.4	E858.3	E942.4	E950.4	E962.0	E980.4
Isobutyl acetate	982.8	E862.4	—	E950.9	E962.1	E980.9
Isocarboxazid	969.0	E854.0	E939.0	E950.3	E962.0	E980.3
Isoephedrine	971.2	E855.5	E941.2	E950.4	E962.0	E980.4
Isoetharine	971.2	E855.5	E941.2	E950.4	E962.0	E980.4
Isofluorophate	971.0	E855.3	E941.0	E950.4	E962.0	E980.4
Isoniazid (INH)	961.8	E857	E931.8	E950.4	E962.0	E980.4
Isopentaquine	961.4	E857	E931.4	E950.4	E962.0	E980.4
Isophane insulin	962.3	E858.0	E932.3	E950.4	E962.0	E980.4
Isopregnenone	962.2	E858.0	E932.2	E950.4	E962.0	E980.4
Isoprenaline	971.2	E855.5	E941.2	E950.4	E962.0	E980.4
Isopropamide	971.1	E855.4	E941.1	E950.4	E962.0	E980.4
Isopropanol	980.2	E860.3	—	E950.9	E962.1	E980.9
topical (germicide)	976.0	E858.7	E946.0	E950.4	E962.0	E980.4
Isopropyl						
acetate	982.8	E862.4	—	E950.9	E962.1	E980.9
alcohol	980.2	E860.3	—	E950.9	E962.1	E980.9
topical (germicide)	976.0	E858.7	E946.0	E950.4	E962.0	E980.4
ether	982.8	E862.4		E950.9	E962.1	E980.9

◄ ▶ **New Code**   ◄▥ ▥► **Revised Code**

Substance	Poisoning	External Cause (E-Code)				
		Accident	Therapeutic Use	Suicide Attempt	Assault	Undetermined
Isoproterenol	971.2	E855.5	E941.2	E950.4	E962.0	E980.4
Isosorbide dinitrate	972.4	E858.3	E942.4	E950.4	E962.0	E980.4
Isothipendyl	963.0	E858.1	E933.0	E950.4	E962.0	E980.4
Isoxazolyl penicillin	960.0	E856	E930.0	E950.4	E962.0	E980.4
Isoxsuprine hydrochloride	972.5	E858.3	E942.5	E950.4	E962.0	E980.4
l-thyroxine sodium	962.7	E858.0	E932.7	E950.4	E962.0	E980.4
Jaborandi (pilocarpus) (extract)	971.0	E855.3	E941.0	E950.4	E962.0	E980.4
Jalap	973.1	E858.4	E943.1	E950.4	E962.0	E980.4
Jamaica						
dogwood (bark)	965.7	E850.7	E935.7	E950.0	E962.0	E980.0
ginger	989.89	E866.8	—	E950.9	E962.1	E980.9
Jatropha	988.2	E865.4	—	E950.9	E962.1	E980.9
curcas	988.2	E865.3	—	E950.9	E962.1	E980.9
Jectofer	964.0	E858.2	E934.0	E950.4	E962.0	E980.4
Jellyfish (sting)	989.5	E905.6	—	E950.9	E962.1	E980.9
Jequirity (bean)	988.2	E865.3	—	E950.9	E962.1	E980.9
Jimson weed	988.2	E865.4	—	E950.9	E962.1	E980.9
seeds	988.2	E865.3	—	E950.9	E962.1	E980.9
Juniper tar (oil) (ointment)	976.4	E858.7	E946.4	E950.4	E962.0	E980.4
Kallikrein	972.5	E858.3	E942.5	E950.4	E962.0	E980.4
Kanamycin	960.6	E856	E930.6	E950.4	E962.0	E980.4
Kantrex	960.6	E856	E930.6	E950.4	E962.0	E980.4
Kaolin	973.5	E858.4	E943.5	E950.4	E962.0	E980.4
Karaya (gum)	973.3	E858.4	E943.3	E950.4	E962.0	E980.4
Kemithal	968.3	E855.1	E938.3	E950.4	E962.0	E980.4
Kenacort	962.0	E858.0	E932.0	E950.4	E962.0	E980.4
Keratolytics	976.4	E858.7	E946.4	E950.4	E962.0	E980.4
Keratoplastics	976.4	E858.7	E946.4	E950.4	E962.0	E980.4
Kerosene, kerosine (fuel) (solvent) NEC	981	E862.1	—	E950.9	E962.1	E980.9
insecticide	981	E863.4	—	E950.6	E962.1	E980.7
vapor	987.1	E869.8	—	E952.8	E962.2	E982.8
Ketamine	968.3	E855.1	E938.3	E950.4	E962.0	E980.4
Ketobemidone	965.09	E850.2	E935.2	E950.0	E962.0	E980.0
Ketols	982.8	E862.4	—	E950.9	E962.1	E980.9
Ketone oils	982.8	E862.4	—	E950.9	E962.1	E980.9
Ketoprofen	965.61	E850.6	E935.6	E950.0	E962.0	E980.0
Kiln gas or vapor (carbon monoxide)	986	E868.8	—	E952.1	E962.2	E982.1
Konsyl	973.3	E858.4	E943.3	E950.4	E962.0	E980.4
Kosam seed	988.2	E865.3	—	E950.9	E962.1	E980.9
Krait (venom)	989.5	E905.0	—	E950.9	E962.1	E980.9
Kwell (insecticide)	989.2	E863.0	—	E950.6	E962.1	E980.7
anti-infective (topical)	976.0	E858.7	E946.0	E950.4	E962.0	E980.4
Laburnum (flowers) (seeds)	988.2	E865.3	—	E950.9	E962.1	E980.9
leaves	988.2	E865.4	—	E950.9	E962.1	E980.9
Lacquers	989.89	E861.6	—	E950.9	E962.1	E980.9
Lacrimogenic gas	987.5	E869.3	—	E952.8	E962.2	E982.8
Lactic acid	983.1	E864.1	—	E950.7	E962.1	E980.6
Lactobacillus acidophilus	973.5	E858.4	E943.5	E950.4	E962.0	E980.4
Lactoflavin	963.5	E858.1	E933.5	E950.4	E962.0	E980.4
Lactuca (virosa) (extract)	967.8	E852.8	E937.8	E950.2	E962.0	E980.2
Lactucarium	967.8	E852.8	E937.8	E950.2	E962.0	E980.2
Laevulose	974.5	E858.5	E944.5	E950.4	E962.0	E980.4
Lanatoside (C)	972.1	E858.3	E942.1	E950.4	E962.0	E980.4
Lanolin (lotion)	976.3	E858.7	E946.3	E950.4	E962.0	E980.4
Largactil	969.1	E853.0	E939.1	E950.3	E962.0	E980.3
Larkspur	988.2	E865.3	—	E950.9	E962.1	E980.9
Laroxyl	969.0	E854.0	E939.0	E950.3	E962.0	E980.3
Lasix	974.4	E858.5	E944.4	E950.4	E962.0	E980.4
Latex	989.82	E866.8	—	E950.9	E962.1	E980.9
Lathyrus (seed)	988.2	E865.3	—	E950.9	E962.1	E980.9
Laudanum	965.09	E850.2	E935.2	E950.0	E962.0	E980.0
Laudexium	975.2	E858.6	E945.2	E950.4	E962.0	E980.4

◀▶ **New Code**   ⬅▥▥▥▷ **Revised Code**

Substance	Poisoning	External Cause (E-Code)				
		Accident	Therapeutic Use	Suicide Attempt	Assault	Undetermined
Laurel, black or cherry	988.2	E865.4	—	E950.9	E962.1	E980.9
Laurolinium	976.0	E858.7	E946.0	E950.4	E962.0	E980.4
Lauryl sulfoacetate	976.2	E858.7	E946.2	E950.4	E962.0	E980.4
Laxatives NEC	973.3	E858.4	E943.3	E950.4	E962.0	E980.4
emollient	973.2	E858.4	E943.2	E950.4	E962.0	E980.4
L-dopa	966.4	E855.0	E936.4	E950.4	E962.0	E980.4
L-Tryptophan - *see* amino acid						
Lead (dust) (fumes) (vapor) NEC	984.9	E866.0	—	E950.9	E962.1	E980.9
acetate (dust)	984.1	E866.0	—	E950.9	E962.1	E980.9
anti-infectives	961.2	E857	E931.2	E950.4	E962.0	E980.4
antiknock compound (tetra-ethyl)	984.1	E862.1	—	E950.9	E962.1	E980.9
arsenate, arsenite (dust) (insecticide) (vapor)	985.1	E863.4	—	E950.8	E962.1	E980.8
herbicide	985.1	E863.5	—	E950.8	E962.1	E980.8
carbonate	984.0	E866.0	—	E950.9	E962.1	E980.9
paint	984.0	E861.5	—	E950.9	E962.1	E980.9
chromate	984.0	E866.0	—	E950.9	E962.1	E980.9
paint	984.0	E861.5	—	E950.9	E962.1	E980.9
dioxide	984.0	E866.0	—	E950.9	E962.1	E980.9
inorganic (compound)	984.0	E866.0	—	E950.9	E962.1	E980.9
paint	984.0	E861.5	—	E950.9	E962.1	E980.9
iodide	984.0	E866.0	—	E950.9	E962.1	E980.9
pigment (paint)	984.0	E861.5	—	E950.9	E962.1	E980.9
monoxide (dust)	984.0	E866.0	—	E950.9	E962.1	E980.9
paint	984.0	E861.5	—	E950.9	E962.1	E980.9
organic	984.1	E866.0	—	E950.9	E962.1	E980.9
oxide	984.0	E866.0	—	E950.9	E962.1	E980.9
paint	984.0	E861.5	—	E950.9	E962.1	E980.9
paint	984.0	E861.5	—	E950.9	E962.1	E980.9
salts	984.0	E866.0	—	E950.9	E962.1	E980.9
specified compound NEC	984.8	E866.0	—	E950.9	E962.1	E980.9
tetra-ethyl	984.1	E862.1	—	E950.9	E962.1	E980.9
Lebanese red	969.6	E854.1	E939.6	E950.3	E962.0	E980.3
Lente Iletin (insulin)	962.3	E858.0	E932.3	E950.4	E962.0	E980.4
Leptazol	970.0	E854.3	E940.0	E950.4	E962.0	E980.4
Leritine	965.09	E850.2	E935.2	E950.0	E962.0	E980.0
Letter	962.7	E858.0	E932.7	E950.4	E962.0	E980.4
Lettuce opium	967.8	E852.8	E937.8	E950.2	E962.0	E980.2
Leucovorin (factor)	964.1	E858.2	E934.1	E950.4	E962.0	E980.4
Leukeran	963.1	E858.1	E933.1	E950.4	E962.0	E980.4
Levallorphan	970.1	E854.3	E940.1	E950.4	E962.0	E980.4
Levanil	967.8	E852.8	E937.8	E950.2	E962.0	E980.2
Levarterenol	971.2	E855.5	E941.2	E950.4	E962.0	E980.4
Levodopa	966.4	E855.0	E936.4	E950.4	E962.0	E980.4
Levo-dromoran	965.09	E850.2	E935.2	E950.0	E962.0	E980.0
Levoid	962.7	E858.0	E932.7	E950.4	E962.0	E980.4
Levo-iso-methadone	965.02	E850.1	E935.1	E950.0	E962.0	E980.0
Levomepromazine	967.8	E852.8	E937.8	E950.2	E962.0	E980.2
Levoprome	967.8	E852.8	E937.8	E950.2	E962.0	E980.2
Levopropoxyphene	975.4	E858.6	E945.4	E950.4	E962.0	E980.4
Levorphan, levophanol	965.09	E850.2	E935.2	E950.0	E962.0	E980.0
Levothyroxine (sodium)	962.7	E858.0	E932.7	E950.4	E962.0	E980.4
Levsin	971.1	E855.4	E941.1	E950.4	E962.0	E980.4
Levulose	974.5	E858.5	E944.5	E950.4	E962.0	E980.4
Lewisite (gas)	985.1	E866.3	—	E950.8	E962.1	E980.8
Librium	969.4	E853.2	E939.4	E950.3	E962.0	E980.3
Lidex	976.0	E858.7	E946.0	E950.4	E962.0	E980.4
Lidocaine (infiltration) (topical)	968.5	E855.2	E938.5	E950.4	E962.0	E980.4
nerve block (peripheral) (plexus)	968.6	E855.2	E938.6	E950.4	E962.0	E980.4
spinal	968.7	E855.2	E938.7	E950.4	E962.0	E980.4
Lighter fluid	981	E862.1	—	E950.9	E962.1	E980.9

◄▶ **New Code**   ◄▥▥▷ **Revised Code**

Substance	Poisoning	External Cause (E-Code)				
		Accident	Therapeutic Use	Suicide Attempt	Assault	Undetermined
Lignocaine (infiltration) (topical)	968.5	E855.2	E938.5	E950.4	E962.0	E980.4
nerve block (peripheral) (plexus)	968.6	E855.2	E938.6	E950.4	E962.0	E980.4
spinal	968.7	E855.2	E938.7	E950.4	E962.0	E980.4
Ligroin(e) (solvent)	981	E862.0	—	E950.9	E962.1	E980.9
vapor	987.1	E869.8	—	E952.8	E962.2	E982.8
Ligustrum vulgare	988.2	E865.3	—	E950.9	E962.1	E980.9
Lily of the valley	988.2	E865.4	—	E950.9	E962.1	E980.9
Lime (chloride)	983.2	E864.2	—	E950.7	E962.1	E980.6
solution, sulferated	976.4	E858.7	E946.4	E950.4	E962.0	E980.4
Limonene	982.8	E862.4	—	E950.9	E962.1	E980.9
Lincomycin	960.8	E856	E930.8	E950.4	E962.0	E980.4
Lindane (insecticide) (vapor)	989.2	E863.0	—	E950.6	E962.1	E980.7
anti-infective (topical)	976.0	E858.7	E946.0	E950.4	E962.0	E980.4
Liniments NEC	976.9	E858.7	E946.9	E950.4	E962.0	E980.4
Linoleic acid	972.2	E858.3	E942.2	E950.4	E962.0	E980.4
Liothyronine	962.7	E858.0	E932.7	E950.4	E962.0	E980.4
Liotrix	962.7	E858.0	E932.7	E950.4	E962.0	E980.4
Lipancreatin	973.4	E858.4	E943.4	E950.4	E962.0	E980.4
Lipo-Lutin	962.2	E858.0	E932.2	E950.4	E962.0	E980.4
Lipotropic agents	977.1	E858.8	E947.1	E950.4	E962.0	E980.4
Liquefied petroleum gases	987.0	E868.0	—	E951.1	E962.2	E981.1
piped (pure or mixed with air)	987.0	E867	—	E951.0	E962.2	E981.0
Liquid petrolatum	973.2	E858.4	E943.2	E950.4	E962.0	E980.4
substance	989.9	E866.9	—	E950.9	E962.1	E980.9
specified NEC	989.89	E866.8	—	E950.9	E962.1	E980.9
Lirugen	979.4	E858.8	E949.4	E950.4	E962.0	E980.4
Lithane	969.8	E855.8	E939.8	E950.3	E962.0	E980.3
Lithium	985.8	E866.4	—	E950.9	E962.1	E980.9
carbonate	969.8	E855.8	E939.8	E950.3	E962.0	E980.3
Lithonate	969.8	E855.8	E939.8	E950.3	E962.0	E980.3
Liver (extract) (injection) (preparations)	964.1	E858.2	E934.1	E950.4	E962.0	E980.4
Lizard (bite) (venom)	989.5	E905.0	—	E950.9	E962.1	E980.9
LMD	964.8	E858.2	E934.8	E950.4	E962.0	E980.4
Lobelia	988.2	E865.4	—	E950.9	E962.1	E980.9
Lobeline	970.0	E854.3	E940.0	E950.4	E962.0	E980.4
Locorten	976.0	E858.7	E946.0	E950.4	E962.0	E980.4
Lolium temulentum	988.2	E865.3	—	E950.9	E962.1	E980.9
Lomotil	973.5	E858.4	E943.5	E950.4	E962.0	E980.4
Lomustine	963.1	E858.1	E933.1	E950.4	E962.0	E980.4
Lophophora williamsii	969.6	E854.1	E939.6	E950.3	E962.0	E980.3
Lorazepam	969.4	E853.2	E939.4	E950.3	E962.0	E980.3
Lotions NEC	976.9	E858.7	E946.9	E950.4	E962.0	E980.4
Lotusate	967.0	E851	E937.0	E950.1	E962.0	E980.1
Lowila	976.2	E858.7	E946.2	E950.4	E962.0	E980.4
Loxapine	969.3	E853.8	E939.3	E950.3	E962.0	E980.3
Lozenges (throat)	976.6	E858.7	E946.6	E950.4	E962.0	E980.4
LSD (25)	969.6	E854.1	E939.6	E950.3	E962.0	E980.3
Lubricating oil NEC	981	E862.2	—	E950.9	E962.1	E980.9
Lucanthone	961.6	E857	E931.6	E950.4	E962.0	E980.4
Luminal	967.0	E851	E937.0	E950.1	E962.0	E980.1
Lung irritant (gas) NEC	987.9	E869.9	—	E952.9	E962.2	E982.9
Lutocylol	962.2	E858.0	E932.2	E950.4	E962.0	E980.4
Lutromone	962.2	E858.0	E932.2	E950.4	E962.0	E980.4
Lututrin	975.0	E858.6	E945.0	E950.4	E962.0	E980.4
Lye (concentrated)	983.2	E864.2	—	E950.7	E962.1	E980.6
Lygranum (skin test)	977.8	E858.8	E947.8	E950.4	E962.0	E980.4
Lymecycline	960.4	E856	E930.4	E950.4	E962.0	E980.4
Lymphogranuloma venereum antigen	977.8	E858.8	E947.8	E950.4	E962.0	E980.4
Lynestrenol	962.2	E858.0	E932.2	E950.4	E962.0	E980.4
Lyovac Sodium Edecrin	974.4	E858.5	E944.4	E950.4	E962.0	E980.4
Lypressin	962.5	E858.0	E932.5	E950.4	E962.0	E980.4

◀▶ **New Code**   ◀▥▥▶ **Revised Code**

Substance	Poisoning	External Cause (E-Code)				
		Accident	Therapeutic Use	Suicide Attempt	Assault	Undetermined
Lysergic acid (amide) (diethylamide)	969.6	E854.1	E939.6	E950.3	E962.0	E980.3
Lysergide	969.6	E854.1	E939.6	E950.3	E962.0	E980.3
Lysine vasopressin	962.5	E858.0	E932.5	E950.4	E962.0	E980.4
Lysol	983.0	E864.0	—	E950.7	E962.1	E980.6
Lytta (vitatta)	976.8	E858.7	E946.8	E950.4	E962.0	E980.4
Mace	987.5	E869.3	—	E952.8	E962.2	E982.8
Macrolides (antibiotics)	960.3	E856	E930.3	E950.4	E962.0	E980.4
Mafenide	976.0	E858.7	E946.0	E950.4	E962.0	E980.4
Magaldrate	973.0	E858.4	E943.0	E950.4	E962.0	E980.4
Magic mushroom	969.6	E854.1	E939.6	E950.3	E962.0	E980.3
Magnamycin	960.8	E856	E930.8	E950.4	E962.0	E980.4
Magnesia magma	973.0	E858.4	E943.0	E950.4	E962.0	E980.4
Magnesium (compounds) (fumes) NEC	985.8	E866.4	—	E950.9	E962.1	E980.9
antacid	973.0	E858.4	E943.0	E950.4	E962.0	E980.4
carbonate	973.0	E858.4	E943.0	E950.4	E962.0	E980.4
cathartic	973.3	E858.4	E943.3	E950.4	E962.0	E980.4
citrate	973.3	E858.4	E943.3	E950.4	E962.0	E980.4
hydroxide	973.0	E858.4	E943.0	E950.4	E962.0	E980.4
oxide	973.0	E858.4	E943.0	E950.4	E962.0	E980.4
sulfate (oral)	973.3	E858.4	E943.3	E950.4	E962.0	E980.4
intravenous	966.3	E855.0	E936.3	E950.4	E962.0	E980.4
trisilicate	973.0	E858.4	E943.0	E950.4	E962.0	E980.4
Malathion (insecticide)	989.3	E863.1	—	E950.6	E962.1	E980.7
Male fern (oleoresin)	961.6	E857	E931.6	E950.4	E962.0	E980.4
Mandelic acid	961.9	E857	E931.9	E950.4	E962.0	E980.4
Manganese compounds (fumes) NEC	985.2	E866.4	—	E950.9	E962.1	E980.9
Mannitol (diuretic) (medicinal) NEC	974.4	E858.5	E944.4	E950.4	E962.0	E980.4
hexanitrate	972.4	E858.3	E942.4	E950.4	E962.0	E980.4
mustard	963.1	E858.1	E933.1	E950.4	E962.0	E980.4
Mannomustine	963.1	E858.1	E933.1	E950.4	E962.0	E980.4
MAO inhibitors	969.0	E854.0	E939.0	E950.3	E962.0	E980.3
Mapharsen	961.1	E857	E931.1	E950.4	E962.0	E980.4
Marcaine	968.9	E855.2	E938.9	E950.4	E962.0	E980.4
infiltration (subcutaneous)	968.5	E855.2	E938.5	E950.4	E962.0	E980.4
nerve block (peripheral) (plexus)	968.6	E855.2	E938.6	E950.4	E962.0	E980.4
Marezine	963.0	E858.1	E933.0	E950.4	E962.0	E980.4
Marihuana, marijuana (derivatives)	969.6	E854.1	E939.6	E950.3	E962.0	E980.3
Marine animals or plants (sting)	989.5	E905.6	—	E950.9	E962.1	E980.9
Marplan	969.0	E854.0	E939.0	E950.3	E962.0	E980.3
Marsh gas	987.1	E869.8	—	E952.8	E962.2	E982.8
Marsilid	969.0	E854.0	E939.0	E950.3	E962.0	E980.3
Matulane	963.1	E858.1	E933.1	E950.4	E962.0	E980.4
Mazindol	977.0	E858.8	E947.0	E950.4	E962.0	E980.4
Meadow saffron	988.2	E865.3	—	E950.9	E962.1	E980.9
Measles vaccine	979.4	E858.8	E949.4	E950.4	E962.0	E980.4
Meat, noxious or nonbacterial	988.8	E865.0	—	E950.9	E962.1	E980.9
Mebanazine	969.0	E854.0	E939.0	E950.3	E962.0	E980.3
Mebaral	967.0	E851	E937.0	E950.1	E962.0	E980.1
Mebendazole	961.6	E857	E931.6	E950.4	E962.0	E980.4
Mebeverine	975.1	E858.6	E945.1	E950.4	E962.0	E980.4
Mebhydroline	963.0	E858.1	E933.0	E950.4	E962.0	E980.4
Mebrophenhydramine	963.0	E858.1	E933.0	E950.4	E962.0	E980.4
Mebutamate	969.5	E853.8	E939.5	E950.3	E962.0	E980.3
Mecamylamine (chloride)	972.3	E858.3	E942.3	E950.4	E962.0	E980.4
Mechlorethamine hydrochloride	963.1	E858.1	E933.1	E950.4	E962.0	E980.4
Meclizene (hydrochloride)	963.0	E858.1	E933.0	E950.4	E962.0	E980.4
Meclofenoxate	970.0	E854.3	E940.0	E950.4	E962.0	E980.4
Meclozine (hydrochloride)	963.0	E858.1	E933.0	E950.4	E962.0	E980.4
Medazepam	969.4	E853.2	E939.4	E950.3	E962.0	E980.3
Medicine, medicinal substance	977.9	E858.9	E947.9	E950.5	E962.0	E980.5
specified NEC	977.8	E858.8	E947.8	E950.4	E962.0	E980.4

Substance	Poisoning	External Cause (E-Code)				
		Accident	Therapeutic Use	Suicide Attempt	Assault	Undetermined
Medinal	967.0	E851	E937.0	E950.1	E962.0	E980.1
Medomin	967.0	E851	E937.0	E950.1	E962.0	E980.1
Medroxyprogesterone	962.2	E858.0	E932.2	E950.4	E962.0	E980.4
Medrysone	976.5	E858.7	E946.5	E950.4	E962.0	E980.4
Mefenamic acid	965.7	E850.7	E935.7	E950.0	E962.0	E980.0
Megahallucinogen	969.6	E854.1	E939.6	E950.3	E962.0	E980.3
Megestrol	962.2	E858.0	E932.2	E950.4	E962.0	E980.4
Meglumine	977.8	E858.8	E947.8	E950.4	E962.0	E980.4
Meladinin	976.3	E858.7	E946.3	E950.4	E962.0	E980.4
Melanizing agents	976.3	E858.7	E946.3	E950.4	E962.0	E980.4
Melarsoprol	961.1	E857	E931.1	E950.4	E962.0	E980.4
Melia azedarach	988.2	E865.3	—	E950.9	E962.1	E980.9
Mellaril	969.1	E853.0	E939.1	E950.3	E962.0	E980.3
Meloxine	976.3	E858.7	E946.3	E950.4	E962.0	E980.4
Melphalan	963.1	E858.1	E933.1	E950.4	E962.0	E980.4
Menadiol sodium diphosphate	964.3	E858.2	E934.3	E950.4	E962.0	E980.4
Menadione (sodium bisulfite)	964.3	E858.2	E934.3	E950.4	E962.0	E980.4
Menaphthone	964.3	E858.2	E934.3	E950.4	E962.0	E980.4
Meningococcal vaccine	978.8	E858.8	E948.8	E950.4	E962.0	E980.4
Menningovax-C	978.8	E858.8	E948.8	E950.4	E962.0	E980.4
Menotropins	962.4	E858.0	E932.4	E950.4	E962.0	E980.4
Menthol NEC	976.1	E858.7	E946.1	E950.4	E962.0	E980.4
Mepacrine	961.3	E857	E931.3	E950.4	E962.0	E980.4
Meparfynol	967.8	E852.8	E937.8	E950.2	E962.0	E980.2
Mepazine	969.1	E853.0	E939.1	E950.3	E962.0	E980.3
Mepenzolate	971.1	E855.4	E941.1	E950.4	E962.0	E980.4
Meperidine	965.09	E850.2	E935.2	E950.0	E962.0	E980.0
Mephenamin(e)	966.4	E855.0	E936.4	E950.4	E962.0	E980.4
Mephenesin (carbamate)	968.0	E855.1	E938.0	E950.4	E962.0	E980.4
Mephenoxalone	969.5	E853.8	E939.5	E950.3	E962.0	E980.3
Mephentermine	971.2	E855.5	E941.2	E950.4	E962.0	E980.4
Mephenytoin	966.1	E855.0	E936.1	E950.4	E962.0	E980.4
Mephobarbital	967.0	E851	E937.0	E950.1	E962.0	E980.1
Mepiperphenidol	971.1	E855.4	E941.1	E950.4	E962.0	E980.4
Mepivacaine	968.9	E855.2	E938.9	E950.4	E962.0	E980.4
infiltration (subcutaneous)	968.5	E855.2	E938.5	E950.4	E962.0	E980.4
nerve block (peripheral) (plexus)	968.6	E855.2	E938.6	E950.4	E962.0	E980.4
topical (surface)	968.5	E855.2	E938.5	E950.4	E962.0	E980.4
Meprednisone	962.0	E858.0	E932.0	E950.4	E962.0	E980.4
Meprobam	969.5	E853.8	E939.5	E950.3	E962.0	E980.3
Meprobamate	969.5	E853.8	E939.5	E950.3	E962.0	E980.3
Mepyramine (maleate)	963.0	E858.1	E933.0	E950.4	E962.0	E980.4
Meralluride	974.0	E858.5	E944.0	E950.4	E962.0	E980.4
Merbaphen	974.0	E858.5	E944.0	E950.4	E962.0	E980.4
Merbromin	976.0	E858.7	E946.0	E950.4	E962.0	E980.4
Mercaptomerin	974.0	E858.5	E944.0	E950.4	E962.0	E980.4
Mercaptopurine	963.1	E858.1	E933.1	E950.4	E962.0	E980.4
Mercumatilin	974.0	E858.5	E944.0	E950.4	E962.0	E980.4
Mercuramide	974.0	E858.5	E944.0	E950.4	E962.0	E980.4
Mercuranin	976.0	E858.7	E946.0	E950.4	E962.0	E980.4
Mercurochrome	976.0	E858.7	E946.0	E950.4	E962.0	E980.4
Mercury, mercuric, mercurous (compounds) (cyanide) (fumes) (nonmedicinal) (vapor) NEC	985.0	E866.1	—	E950.9	E962.1	E980.9
ammoniated	976.0	E858.7	E946.0	E950.4	E962.0	E980.4
anti-infective	961.2	E857	E931.2	E950.4	E962.0	E980.4
topical	976.0	E858.7	E946.0	E950.4	E962.0	E980.4
chloride (antiseptic) NEC	976.0	E858.7	E946.0	E950.4	E962.0	E980.4
fungicide	985.0	E863.6	—	E950.6	E962.1	E980.7
diuretic compounds	974.0	E858.5	E944.0	E950.4	E962.0	E980.4
fungicide	985.0	E863.6	—	E950.6	E962.1	E980.7
organic (fungicide)	985.0	E863.6	—	E950.6	E962.1	E980.7
Merethoxylline	974.0	E858.5	E944.0	E950.4	E962.0	E980.4

◀▶ **New Code**   ◀▬▬▶ **Revised Code**

Substance	Poisoning	External Cause (E-Code)				
		Accident	Therapeutic Use	Suicide Attempt	Assault	Undetermined
Mersalyl	974.0	E858.5	E944.0	E950.4	E962.0	E980.4
Merthiolate (topical)	976.0	E858.7	E946.0	E950.4	E962.0	E980.4
ophthalmic preparation	976.5	E858.7	E946.5	E950.4	E962.0	E980.4
Meruvax	979.4	E858.8	E949.4	E950.4	E962.0	E980.4
Mescal buttons	969.6	E854.1	E939.6	E950.3	E962.0	E980.3
Mescaline (salts)	969.6	E854.1	E939.6	E950.3	E962.0	E980.3
Mesoridazine besylate	969.1	E853.0	E939.1	E950.3	E962.0	E980.3
Mestanolone	962.1	E858.0	E932.1	E950.4	E962.0	E980.4
Mestranol	962.2	E858.0	E932.2	E950.4	E962.0	E980.4
Metactesylacetate	976.0	E858.7	E946.0	E950.4	E962.0	E980.4
Metaldehyde (snail killer) NEC	989.4	E863.4	—	E950.6	E962.1	E980.7
Metals (heavy) (nonmedicinal) NEC	985.9	E866.4	—	E950.9	E962.1	E980.9
dust, fumes, or vapor NEC	985.9	E866.4	—	E950.9	E962.1	E980.9
light NEC	985.9	E866.4	—	E950.9	E962.1	E980.9
dust, fumes, or vapor NEC	985.9	E866.4	—	E950.9	E962.1	E980.9
pesticides (dust) (vapor)	985.9	E863.4	—	E950.6	E962.1	E980.7
Metamucil	973.3	E858.4	E943.3	E950.4	E962.0	E980.4
Metaphen	976.0	E858.7	E946.0	E950.4	E962.0	E980.4
Metaproterenol	975.1	E858.6	E945.1	E950.4	E962.0	E980.4
Metaraminol	972.8	E858.3	E942.8	E950.4	E962.0	E980.4
Metaxalone	968.0	E855.1	E938.0	E950.4	E962.0	E980.4
Metformin	962.3	E858.0	E932.3	E950.4	E962.0	E980.4
Methacycline	960.4	E856	E930.4	E950.4	E962.0	E980.4
Methadone	965.02	E850.1	E935.1	E950.0	E962.0	E980.0
Methallenestril	962.2	E858.0	E932.2	E950.4	E962.0	E980.4
Methamphetamine	969.7	E854.2	E939.7	E950.3	E962.0	E980.3
Methandienone	962.1	E858.0	E932.1	E950.4	E962.0	E980.4
Methandriol	962.1	E858.0	E932.1	E950.4	E962.0	E980.4
Methandrostenolone	962.1	E858.0	E932.1	E950.4	E962.0	E980.4
Methane gas	987.1	E869.8	—	E952.8	E962.2	E982.8
Methanol	980.1	E860.2	—	E950.9	E962.1	E980.9
vapor	987.8	E869.8	—	E952.8	E962.2	E982.8
Methantheline	971.1	E855.4	E941.1	E950.4	E962.0	E980.4
Methaphenilene	963.0	E858.1	E933.0	E950.4	E962.0	E980.4
Methapyrilene	963.0	E858.1	E933.0	E950.4	E962.0	E980.4
Methaqualone (compounds)	967.4	E852.3	E937.4	E950.2	E962.0	E980.2
Metharbital, metharbitone	967.0	E851	E937.0	E950.1	E962.0	E980.1
Methazolamide	974.2	E858.5	E944.2	E950.4	E962.0	E980.4
Methdilazine	963.0	E858.1	E933.0	E950.4	E962.0	E980.4
Methedrine	969.7	E854.2	E939.7	E950.3	E962.0	E980.3
Methenamine (mandelate)	961.9	E857	E931.9	E950.4	E962.0	E980.4
Methenolone	962.1	E858.0	E932.1	E950.4	E962.0	E980.4
Methergine	975.0	E858.6	E945.0	E950.4	E962.0	E980.4
Methiacil	962.8	E858.0	E932.8	E950.4	E962.0	E980.4
Methicillin (sodium)	960.0	E856	E930.0	E950.4	E962.0	E980.4
Methimazole	962.8	E858.0	E932.8	E950.4	E962.0	E980.4
Methionine	977.1	E858.8	E947.1	E950.4	E962.0	E980.4
Methisazone	961.7	E857	E931.7	E950.4	E962.0	E980.4
Methitural	967.0	E851	E937.0	E950.1	E962.0	E980.1
Methixene	971.1	E855.4	E941.1	E950.4	E962.0	E980.4
Methobarbital, methobarbitone	967.0	E851	E937.0	E950.1	E962.0	E980.1
Methocarbamol	968.0	E855.1	E938.0	E950.4	E962.0	E980.4
Methohexital, methohexitone (sodium)	968.3	E855.1	E938.3	E950.4	E962.0	E980.4
Methoin	966.1	E855.0	E936.1	E950.4	E962.0	E980.4
Methopholine	965.7	E850.7	E935.7	E950.0	E962.0	E980.0
Methorate	975.4	E858.6	E945.4	E950.4	E962.0	E980.4
Methoserpidine	972.6	E858.3	E942.6	E950.4	E962.0	E980.4
Methotrexate	963.1	E858.1	E933.1	E950.4	E962.0	E980.4
Methotrimeprazine	967.8	E852.8	E937.8	E950.2	E962.0	E980.2
Methoxa-Dome	976.3	E858.7	E946.3	E950.4	E962.0	E980.4
Methoxamine	971.2	E855.5	E941.2	E950.4	E962.0	E980.4

◄▶ **New Code**   ◄▥▥▷ **Revised Code**

Substance	Poisoning	External Cause (E-Code)				
		Accident	Therapeutic Use	Suicide Attempt	Assault	Undetermined
Methoxsalen	976.3	E858.7	E946.3	E950.4	E962.0	E980.4
Methoxybenzyl penicillin	960.0	E856	E930.0	E950.4	E962.0	E980.4
Methoxychlor	989.2	E863.0	—	E950.6	E962.1	E980.7
Methoxyflurane	968.2	E855.1	E938.2	E950.4	E962.0	E980.4
Methoxyphenamine	971.2	E855.5	E941.2	E950.4	E962.0	E980.4
Methoxypromazine	969.1	E853.0	E939.1	E950.3	E962.0	E980.3
Methoxypsoralen	976.3	E858.7	E946.3	E950.4	E962.0	E980.4
Methscopolamine (bromide)	971.1	E855.4	E941.1	E950.4	E962.0	E980.4
Methsuximide	966.2	E855.0	E936.2	E950.4	E962.0	E980.4
Methyclothiazide	974.3	E858.5	E944.3	E950.4	E962.0	E980.4
Methyl						
acetate	982.8	E862.4	—	E950.9	E962.1	E980.9
acetone II	982.8	E862.4	—	E950.9	E962.1	E980.9
alcohol	980.1	E860.2	—	E950.9	E962.1	E980.9
amphetamine	969.7	E854.2	E939.7	E950.3	E962.0	E980.3
androstanolone	962.1	E858.0	E932.1	E950.4	E962.0	E980.4
atropine	971.1	E855.4	E941.1	E950.4	E962.0	E980.4
benzene	982.0	E862.4	—	E950.9	E962.1	E980.9
bromide (gas)	987.8	E869.8	—	E952.8	E962.2	E982.8
fumigant	987.8	E863.8	—	E950.6	E962.2	E980.7
butanol	980.8	E860.8	—	E950.9	E962.1	E980.9
carbinol	980.1	E860.2	—	E950.9	E962.1	E980.9
cellosolve	982.8	E862.4	—	E950.9	E962.1	E980.9
cellulose	973.3	E858.4	E943.3	E950.4	E961.0	E980.4
chloride (gas)	987.8	E869.8	—	E952.8	E962.2	E982.8
cyclohexane	982.8	E862.4	—	E950.9	E962.1	E980.9
cyclohexanone	982.8	E862.4	—	E950.9	E962.1	E980.9
dihydromorphinone	965.09	E850.2	E935.2	E950.0	E962.0	E980.0
ergometrine	975.0	E858.6	E945.0	E950.4	E962.0	E980.4
ergonovine	975.0	E858.6	E945.0	E950.4	E962.0	E980.4
ethyl ketone	982.8	E862.4	—	E950.9	E962.1	E980.9
hydrazine	983.9	E864.3	—	E950.7	E962.1	E980.6
isobutyl ketone	982.8	E862.4	—	E950.9	E962.1	E980.9
morphine NEC	965.09	E850.2	E935.2	E950.0	E962.0	E980.0
parafynol	967.8	E852.8	E937.8	E950.2	E962.0	E980.2
parathion	989.3	E863.1	—	E950.6	E962.1	E980.7
pentynol NEC	967.8	E852.8	E937.8	E950.2	E962.0	E980.2
peridol	969.2	E853.1	E939.2	E950.3	E962.0	E980.3
phenidate	969.7	E854.2	E939.7	E950.3	E962.0	E980.3
prednisolone	962.0	E858.0	E932.0	E950.4	E962.0	E980.4
ENT agent	976.6	E858.7	E946.6	E950.4	E962.0	E980.4
ophthalmic preparation	976.5	E858.7	E946.5	E950.4	E962.0	E980.4
topical NEC	976.0	E858.7	E946.0	E950.4	E962.0	E980.4
propylcarbinol	980.8	E860.8	—	E950.9	E962.1	E980.9
rosaniline NEC	976.0	E858.7	E946.0	E950.4	E962.0	E980.4
salicylate NEC	976.3	E858.7	E946.3	E950.4	E962.0	E980.4
sulfate (fumes)	987.8	E869.8	—	E952.8	E962.2	E982.8
liquid	983.9	E864.3	—	E950.7	E962.1	E980.6
sulfonal	967.8	E852.8	E937.8	E950.2	E962.0	E980.2
testosterone	962.1	E858.0	E932.1	E950.4	E962.0	E980.4
thiouracil	962.8	E858.0	E932.8	E950.4	E962.0	E980.4
Methylated spirit	980.0	E860.1	—	E950.9	E962.1	E980.9
Methyldopa	972.6	E858.3	E942.6	E950.4	E962.0	E980.4
Methylene blue	961.9	E857	E931.9	E950.4	E962.0	E980.4
chloride or dichloride (solvent) NEC	982.3	E862.4	—	E950.9	E962.1	E980.9
Methylhexabital	967.0	E851	E937.0	E950.1	E962.0	E980.1
Methylparaben (ophthalmic)	976.5	E858.7	E946.5	E950.4	E962.0	E980.4
Methyprylon	967.5	E852.4	E937.5	E950.2	E962.0	E980.2
Methysergide	971.3	E855.6	E941.3	E950.4	E962.0	E980.4
Metoclopramide	963.0	E858.1	E933.0	E950.4	E962.0	E980.4
Metofoline	965.7	E850.7	E935.7	E950.0	E962.0	E980.0

◀▶ **New Code**   ◀▦▦▶ **Revised Code**

Substance	Poisoning	External Cause (E-Code)				
		Accident	Therapeutic Use	Suicide Attempt	Assault	Undetermined
Metopon	965.09	E850.2	E935.2	E950.0	E962.0	E980.0
Metronidazole	961.5	E857	E931.5	E950.4	E962.0	E980.4
Metycaine	968.9	E855.2	E938.9	E950.4	E962.0	E980.4
infiltration (subcutaneous)	968.5	E855.2	E938.5	E950.4	E962.0	E980.4
nerve block (peripheral) (plexus)	968.6	E855.2	E938.6	E950.4	E962.0	E980.4
topical (surface)	968.5	E855.2	E938.5	E950.4	E962.0	E980.4
Metyrapone	977.8	E858.8	E947.8	E950.4	E962.0	E980.4
Mevinphos	989.3	E863.1	—	E950.6	E962.1	E980.7
Mezereon (berries)	988.2	E865.3	—	E950.9	E962.1	E980.9
Micatin	976.0	E858.7	E946.0	E950.4	E962.0	E980.4
Miconazole	976.0	E858.7	E946.0	E950.4	E962.0	E980.4
Midol	965.1	E850.3	E935.3	E950.0	E962.0	E980.0
Milk of magnesia	973.0	E858.4	E943.0	E950.4	E962.0	E980.4
Millipede (tropical) (venomous)	989.5	E905.4	—	E950.9	E962.1	E980.9
Miltown	969.5	E853.8	E939.5	E950.3	E962.0	E980.3
Mineral						
oil (medicinal)	973.2	E858.4	E943.2	E950.4	E962.0	E980.4
nonmedicinal	981	E862.1	—	E950.9	E962.1	E980.9
topical	976.3	E858.7	E946.3	E950.4	E962.0	E980.4
salts NEC	974.6	E858.5	E944.6	E950.4	E962.0	E980.4
spirits	981	E862.0	—	E950.9	E962.1	E980.9
Minocycline	960.4	E856	E930.4	E950.4	E962.0	E980.4
Mithramycin (antineoplastic)	960.7	E856	E930.7	E950.4	E962.0	E980.4
Mitobronitol	963.1	E858.1	E933.1	E950.4	E962.0	E980.4
Mitomycin (antineoplastic)	960.7	E856	E930.7	E950.4	E962.0	E980.4
Mitotane	963.1	E858.1	E933.1	E950.4	E962.0	E980.4
Moderil	972.6	E858.3	E942.6	E950.4	E962.0	E980.4
Mogadon - *see* Nitrazepam						
Molindone	969.3	E853.8	E939.3	E950.3	E962.0	E980.3
Monistat	976.0	E858.7	E946.0	E950.4	E962.0	E980.4
Monkshood	988.2	E865.4	—	E950.9	E962.1	E980.9
Monoamine oxidase inhibitors	969.0	E854.0	E939.0	E950.3	E962.0	E980.3
Monochlorobenzene	982.0	E862.4	—	E950.9	E962.1	E980.9
Monosodium glutamate	989.89	E866.8	—	E950.9	E962.1	E980.9
Monoxide, carbon - *see* Carbon, monoxide						
Moperone	969.2	E853.1	E939.2	E950.3	E962.0	E980.3
Morning glory seeds	969.6	E854.1	E939.6	E950.3	E962.0	E980.3
Moroxydine (hydrochloride)	961.7	E857	E931.7	E950.4	E962.0	E980.4
Morphazinamide	961.8	E857	E931.8	E950.4	E962.0	E980.4
Morphinans	965.09	E850.2	E935.2	E950.0	E962.0	E980.0
Morphine NEC	965.09	E850.2	E935.2	E950.0	E962.0	E980.0
antagonists	970.1	E854.3	E940.1	E950.4	E962.0	E980.4
Morpholinylethyl morphine	965.09	E850.2	E935.2	E950.0	E962.0	E980.0
Morrhuate sodium	972.7	E858.3	E942.7	E950.4	E962.0	E980.4
Moth balls (*see also* Pesticides)	989.4	E863.4	—	E950.6	E962.1	E980.7
naphthalene	983.0	E863.4	—	E950.7	E962.1	E980.6
Motor exhaust gas - *see* Carbon, monoxide, exhaust gas						
Mouth wash	976.6	E858.7	E946.6	E950.4	E962.0	E980.4
Mucolytic agent	975.5	E858.6	E945.5	E950.4	E962.0	E980.4
Mucomyst	975.5	E858.6	E945.5	E950.4	E962.0	E980.4
Mucous membrane agents (external)	976.9	E858.7	E946.9	E950.4	E962.0	E980.4
specified NEC	976.8	E858.7	E946.8	E950.4	E962.0	E980.4
Mumps						
immune globulin (human)	964.6	E858.2	E934.6	E950.4	E962.0	E980.4
skin test antigen	977.8	E858.8	E947.8	E950.4	E962.0	E980.4
vaccine	979.6	E858.8	E949.6	E950.4	E962.0	E980.4
Mumpsvax	979.6	E858.8	E949.6	E950.4	E962.0	E980.4
Muriatic acid - *see* Hydrochloric acid						
Muscarine	971.0	E855.3	E941.0	E950.4	E962.0	E980.4
Muscle affecting agents NEC	975.3	E858.6	E945.3	E950.4	E962.0	E980.4
oxytocic	975.0	E858.6	E945.0	E950.4	E962.0	E980.4

◀ ▶ **New Code**   ◀▥ ▥▶ **Revised Code**

Substance	Poisoning	External Cause (E-Code)				
		Accident	Therapeutic Use	Suicide Attempt	Assault	Undetermined
Muscle affecting agents NEC *(Continued)*						
relaxants	975.3	E858.6	E945.3	E950.4	E962.0	E980.4
central nervous system	968.0	E855.1	E938.0	E950.4	E962.0	E980.4
skeletal	975.2	E858.6	E945.2	E950.4	E962.0	E980.4
smooth	975.1	E858.6	E945.1	E950.4	E962.0	E980.4
Mushrooms, noxious	988.1	E865.5	—	E950.9	E962.1	E980.9
Mussel, noxious	988.0	E865.1	—	E950.9	E962.1	E980.9
Mustard (emetic)	973.6	E858.4	E943.6	E950.4	E962.0	E980.4
gas	987.8	E869.8	—	E952.8	E962.2	E982.8
nitrogen	963.1	E858.1	E933.1	E950.4	E962.0	E980.4
Mustine	963.1	E858.1	E933.1	E950.4	E962.0	E980.4
M-vac	979.4	E858.8	E949.4	E950.4	E962.0	E980.4
Mycifradin	960.8	E856	E930.8	E950.4	E962.0	E980.4
topical	976.0	E858.7	E946.0	E950.4	E962.0	E980.4
Mycitracin	960.8	E856	E930.8	E950.4	E962.0	E980.4
ophthalmic preparation	976.5	E858.7	E946.5	E950.4	E962.0	E980.4
Mycostatin	960.1	E856	E930.1	E950.4	E962.0	E980.4
topical	976.0	E858.7	E946.0	E950.4	E962.0	E980.4
Mydriacyl	971.1	E855.4	E941.1	E950.4	E962.0	E980.4
Myelobromal	963.1	E858.1	E933.1	E950.4	E962.0	E980.4
Myleran	963.1	E858.1	E933.1	E950.4	E962.0	E980.4
Myochrysin(e)	965.69	E850.6	E935.6	E950.0	E962.0	E980.0
Myoneural blocking agents	975.2	E858.6	E945.2	E950.4	E962.0	E980.4
Myristica fragrans	988.2	E865.3	—	E950.9	E962.1	E980.9
Myristicin	988.2	E865.3	—	E950.9	E962.1	E980.9
Mysoline	966.3	E855.0	E936.3	E950.4	E962.0	E980.4
Nafcillin (sodium)	960.0	E856	E930.0	E950.4	E962.0	E980.4
Nail polish remover	982.8	E862.4	—	E950.9	E962.1	E980.9
Nalidixic acid	961.9	E857	E931.9	E950.4	E962.0	E980.4
Nalorphine	970.1	E854.3	E940.1	E950.4	E962.0	E980.4
Naloxone	970.1	E854.3	E940.1	E950.4	E962.0	E980.4
Nandrolone (decanoate) (phenpropionate)	962.1	E858.0	E932.1	E950.4	E962.0	E980.4
Naphazoline	971.2	E855.5	E941.2	E950.4	E962.0	E980.4
Naphtha (painter's) (petroleum)	981	E862.0	—	E950.9	E962.1	E980.9
solvent	981	E862.0	—	E950.9	E962.1	E980.9
vapor	987.1	E869.8	—	E952.8	E962.2	E982.8
Naphthalene (chlorinated)	983.0	E864.0	—	E950.7	E962.1	E980.6
insecticide or moth repellent	983.0	E863.4	—	E950.7	E962.1	E980.6
vapor	987.8	E869.8	—	E952.8	E962.2	E982.8
Naphthol	983.0	E864.0	—	E950.7	E962.1	E980.6
Naphthylamine	983.0	E864.0	—	E950.7	E962.1	E980.6
Naprosyn - *see* Naproxen						
Naproxen	965.61	E850.6	E935.6	E950.0	E962.0	E980.0
Narcotic (drug)	967.9	E852.9	E937.9	E950.2	E962.0	E980.2
analgesic NEC	965.8	E850.8	E935.8	E950.0	E962.0	E980.0
antagonist	970.1	E854.3	E940.1	E950.4	E962.0	E980.4
specified NEC	967.8	E852.8	E937.8	E950.2	E962.0	E980.2
Narcotine	975.4	E858.6	E945.4	E950.4	E962.0	E980.4
Nardil	969.0	E854.0	E939.0	E950.3	E962.0	E980.3
Natrium cyanide - *see* Cyanide(s)						
Natural						
blood (product)	964.7	E858.2	E934.7	E950.4	E962.0	E980.4
gas (piped)	987.1	E867	—	E951.0	E962.2	E981.0
incomplete combustion	986	E867	—	E951.0	E962.2	E981.0
Nealbarbital, nealbarbitone	967.0	E851	E937.0	E950.1	E962.0	E980.1
Nectadon	975.4	E858.6	E945.4	E950.4	E962.0	E980.4
Nematocyst (sting)	989.5	E905.6	—	E950.9	E962.1	E980.9
Nembutal	967.0	E851	E937.0	E950.1	E962.0	E980.1
Neoarsphenamine	961.1	E857	E931.1	E950.4	E962.0	E980.4
Neocinchophen	974.7	E858.5	E944.7	E950.4	E962.0	E980.4
Neomycin	960.8	E856	E930.8	E950.4	E962.0	E980.4
ENT agent	976.6	E858.7	E946.6	E950.4	E962.0	E980.4

Substance	Poisoning	External Cause (E-Code)				
		Accident	Therapeutic Use	Suicide Attempt	Assault	Undetermined
Neomycin *(Continued)*						
ophthalmic preparation	976.5	E858.7	E946.5	E950.4	E962.0	E980.4
topical NEC	976.0	E858.7	E946.0	E950.4	E962.0	E980.4
Neonal	967.0	E851	E937.0	E950.1	E962.0	E980.1
Neoprontosil	961.0	E857	E931.0	E950.4	E962.0	E980.4
Neosalvarsan	961.1	E857	E931.1	E950.4	E962.0	E980.4
Neosilversalvarsan	961.1	E857	E931.1	E950.4	E962.0	E980.4
Neosporin	960.8	E856	E930.8	E950.4	E962.0	E980.4
ENT agent	976.6	E858.7	E946.6	E950.4	E962.0	E980.4
ophthalmic preparation	976.5	E858.7	E946.5	E950.4	E962.0	E980.4
topical NEC	976.0	E858.7	E946.0	E950.4	E962.0	E980.4
Neostigmine	971.0	E855.3	E941.0	E950.4	E962.0	E980.4
Neraval	967.0	E851	E937.0	E950.1	E962.0	E980.1
Neravan	967.0	E851	E937.0	E950.1	E962.0	E980.1
Nerium oleander	988.2	E865.4	—	E950.9	E962.1	E980.9
Nerve gases (war)	987.9	E869.9	—	E952.9	E962.2	E982.9
Nesacaine	968.9	E855.2	E938.9	E950.4	E962.0	E980.4
infiltration (subcutaneous)	968.5	E855.2	E938.5	E950.4	E962.0	E980.4
nerve block (peripheral) (plexus)	968.6	E855.2	E938.6	E950.4	E962.0	E980.4
Neurobarb	967.0	E851	E937.0	E950.1	E962.0	E980.1
Neuroleptics NEC	969.3	E853.8	E939.3	E950.3	E962.0	E980.3
Neutral spirits	980.0	E860.1	—	E950.9	E962.1	E980.9
beverage	980.0	E860.0	—	E950.9	E962.1	E980.9
Niacin, niacinamide	972.2	E858.3	E942.2	E950.4	E962.0	E980.4
Nialamide	969.0	E854.0	E939.0	E950.3	E962.0	E980.3
Nickle (carbonyl) (compounds) (fumes) (tetracarbonyl) (vapor)	985.8	E866.4	—	E950.9	E962.1	E980.9
Niclosamide	961.6	E857	E931.6	E950.4	E962.0	E980.4
Nicomorphine	965.09	E850.2	E935.2	E950.0	E962.0	E980.0
Nicotinamide	972.2	E858.3	E942.2	E950.4	E962.0	E980.4
Nicotine (insecticide) (spray) (sulfate) NEC	989.4	E863.4	—	E950.6	E962.1	E980.7
not insecticide	989.89	E866.8	—	E950.9	E962.1	E980.9
Nicotinic acid (derivatives)	972.2	E858.3	E942.2	E950.4	E962.0	E980.4
Nicotinyl alcohol	972.2	E858.3	E942.2	E950.4	E962.0	E980.4
Nicoumalone	964.2	E858.2	E934.2	E950.4	E962.0	E980.4
Nifenazone	965.5	E850.5	E935.5	E950.0	E962.0	E980.0
Nifuraldezone	961.9	E857	E931.9	E950.4	E962.0	E980.4
Nightshade (deadly)	988.2	E865.4	—	E950.9	E962.1	E980.9
Nikethamide	970.0	E854.3	E940.0	E950.4	E962.0	E980.4
Nilstat	960.1	E856	E930.1	E950.4	E962.0	E980.4
topical	976.0	E858.7	E946.0	E950.4	E962.0	E980.4
Niridazole	961.6	E857	E931.6	E950.4	E962.0	E980.4
Nisentil	965.09	E850.2	E935.2	E950.0	E962.0	E980.0
Nitrates	972.4	E858.3	E942.4	E950.4	E962.0	E980.4
Nitrazepam	969.4	E853.2	E939.4	E950.3	E962.0	E980.3
Nitric						
acid (liquid)	983.1	E864.1	—	E950.7	E962.1	E980.6
vapor	987.8	E869.8	—	E952.8	E962.2	E982.8
oxide (gas)	987.2	E869.0	—	E952.8	E962.2	E982.8
Nitrite, amyl (medicinal) (vapor)	972.4	E858.3	E942.4	E950.4	E962.0	E980.4
Nitroaniline	983.0	E864.0	—	E950.7	E962.1	E980.6
vapor	987.8	E869.8	—	E952.8	E962.2	E982.8
Nitrobenzene, nitrobenzol	983.0	E864.0	—	E950.7	E962.1	E980.6
vapor	987.8	E869.8	—	E952.8	E962.2	E982.8
Nitrocellulose	976.3	E858.7	E946.3	E950.4	E962.0	E980.4
Nitrofuran derivatives	961.9	E857	E931.9	E950.4	E962.0	E980.4
Nitrofurantoin	961.9	E857	E931.9	E950.4	E962.0	E980.4
Nitrofurazone	976.0	E858.7	E946.0	E950.4	E962.0	E980.4
Nitrogen (dioxide) (gas) (oxide)	987.2	E869.0	—	E952.8	E962.2	E982.8
mustard (antineoplastic)	963.1	E858.1	E933.1	E950.4	E962.0	E980.4
Nitroglycerin, nitroglycerol (medicinal)	972.4	E858.3	E942.4	E950.4	E962.0	E980.4
nonmedicinal	989.89	E866.8	—	E950.9	E962.1	E980.9
fumes	987.8	E869.8	—	E952.8	E962.2	E982.8

ICD-9-CM
Drugs
Vol. 2

Substance	Poisoning	External Cause (E-Code)				
		Accident	Therapeutic Use	Suicide Attempt	Assault	Undetermined
Nitrohydrochloric acid	983.1	E864.1	—	E950.7	E962.1	E980.6
Nitromersol	976.0	E858.7	E946.0	E950.4	E962.0	E980.4
Nitronaphthalene	983.0	E864.0	—	E950.7	E962.2	E980.6
Nitrophenol	983.0	E864.0	—	E950.7	E962.2	E980.6
Nitrothiazol	961.6	E857	E931.6	E950.4	E962.0	E980.4
Nitrotoluene, nitrotoluol	983.0	E864.0	—	E950.7	E962.1	E980.6
vapor	987.8	E869.8	—	E952.8	E962.2	E982.8
Nitrous	968.2	E855.1	E938.2	E950.4	E962.0	E980.4
acid (liquid)	983.1	E864.1	—	E950.7	E962.1	E980.6
fumes	987.2	E869.0	—	E952.8	E962.2	E982.8
oxide (anesthetic) NEC	968.2	E855.1	E938.2	E950.4	E962.0	E980.4
Nitrozone	976.0	E858.7	E946.0	E950.4	E962.0	E980.4
Noctec	967.1	E852.0	E937.1	E950.2	E962.0	E980.2
Noludar	967.5	E852.4	E937.5	E950.2	E962.0	E980.2
Noptil	967.0	E851	E937.0	E950.1	E962.0	E980.1
Noradrenalin	971.2	E855.5	E941.2	E950.4	E962.0	E980.4
Noramidopyrine	965.5	E850.5	E935.5	E950.0	E962.0	E980.0
Norepinephrine	971.2	E855.5	E941.2	E950.4	E962.0	E980.4
Norethandrolone	962.1	E858.0	E932.1	E950.4	E962.0	E980.4
Norethindrone	962.2	E858.0	E932.2	E950.4	E962.0	E980.4
Norethisterone	962.2	E858.0	E932.2	E950.4	E962.0	E980.4
Norethynodrel	962.2	E858.0	E932.2	E950.4	E962.0	E980.4
Norlestrin	962.2	E858.0	E932.2	E950.4	E962.0	E980.4
Norlutin	962.2	E858.0	E932.2	E950.4	E962.0	E980.4
Normison - *see* Benzodiazepines						
Normorphine	965.09	E850.2	E935.2	E950.0	E962.0	E980.0
Nortriptyline	969.0	E854.0	E939.0	E950.3	E962.0	E980.3
Noscapine	975.4	E858.6	E945.4	E950.4	E962.0	E980.4
Nose preparations	976.6	E858.7	E946.6	E950.4	E962.0	E980.4
Novobiocin	960.8	E856	E930.8	E950.4	E962.0	E980.4
Novocain (infiltration) (topical)	968.5	E855.2	E938.5	E950.4	E962.0	E980.4
nerve block (peripheral) (plexus)	968.6	E855.2	E938.6	E950.4	E962.0	E980.4
spinal	968.7	E855.2	E938.7	E950.4	E962.0	E980.4
Noxythiolin	961.9	E857	E931.9	E950.4	E962.0	E980.4
NPH Iletin (insulin)	962.3	E858.0	E932.3	E950.4	E962.0	E980.4
Numorphan	965.09	E850.2	E935.2	E950.0	E962.0	E980.0
Nunol	967.0	E851	E937.0	E950.1	E962.0	E980.1
Nupercaine (spinal anesthetic)	968.7	E855.2	E938.7	E950.4	E962.0	E980.4
topical (surface)	968.5	E855.2	E938.5	E950.4	E962.0	E980.4
Nutmeg oil (liniment)	976.3	E858.7	E946.3	E950.4	E962.0	E980.4
Nux vomica	989.1	E863.7	—	E950.6	E962.1	E980.7
Nydrazid	961.8	E857	E931.8	E950.4	E962.0	E980.4
Nylidrin	971.2	E855.5	E941.2	E950.4	E962.0	E980.4
Nystatin	960.1	E856	E930.1	E950.4	E962.0	E980.4
topical	976.0	E858.7	E946.0	E950.4	E962.0	E980.4
Nytol	963.0	E858.1	E933.0	E950.4	E962.0	E980.4
Oblivion	967.8	E852.8	E937.8	E950.2	E962.0	E980.2
Octyl nitrite	972.4	E858.3	E942.4	E950.4	E962.0	E980.4
Oestradiol (cypionate) (dipropionate) (valerate)	962.2	E858.0	E932.2	E950.4	E962.0	E980.4
Oestriol	962.2	E858.0	E932.2	E950.4	E962.0	E980.4
Oestrone	962.2	E858.0	E932.2	E950.4	E962.0	E980.4
Oil (of) NEC	989.89	E866.8	—	E950.9	E962.1	E980.9
bitter almond	989.0	E866.8	—	E950.9	E962.1	E980.9
camphor	976.1	E858.7	E946.1	E950.4	E962.0	E980.4
colors	989.89	E861.6	—	E950.9	E962.1	E980.9
fumes	987.8	E869.8	—	E952.8	E962.2	E982.8
lubricating	981	E862.2	—	E950.9	E962.1	E980.9
specified source, other - *see* substance specified						
vitriol (liquid)	983.1	E864.1	—	E950.7	E962.1	E980.6
fumes	987.8	E869.8	—	E952.8	E962.2	E982.8
wintergreen (bitter) NEC	976.3	E858.7	E946.3	E950.4	E962.0	E980.4

Substance	Poisoning	External Cause (E-Code)				
		Accident	Therapeutic Use	Suicide Attempt	Assault	Undetermined
Ointments NEC	976.9	E858.7	E946.9	E950.4	E962.0	E980.4
Oleander	988.2	E865.4	—	E950.9	E962.1	E980.9
Oleandomycin	960.3	E856	E930.3	E950.4	E962.0	E980.4
Oleovitamin A	963.5	E858.1	E933.5	E950.4	E962.0	E980.4
Oleum ricini	973.1	E858.4	E943.1	E950.4	E962.0	E980.4
Olive oil (medicinal) NEC	973.2	E858.4	E943.2	E950.4	E962.0	E980.4
OMPA	989.3	E863.1	—	E950.6	E962.1	E980.7
Oncovin	963.1	E858.1	E933.1	E950.4	E962.0	E980.4
Ophthaine	968.5	E855.2	E938.5	E950.4	E962.0	E980.4
Ophthetic	968.5	E855.2	E938.5	E950.4	E962.0	E980.4
Opiates, opioids, opium NEC	965.00	E850.2	E935.2	E950.0	E962.0	E980.0
antagonists	970.1	E854.3	E940.1	E950.4	E962.0	E980.4
Oracon	962.2	E858.0	E932.2	E950.4	E962.0	E980.4
Oragrafin	977.8	E858.8	E947.8	E950.4	E962.0	E980.4
Oral contraceptives	962.2	E858.0	E932.2	E950.4	E962.0	E980.4
Orciprenaline	975.1	E858.6	E945.1	E950.4	E962.0	E980.4
Organidin	975.5	E858.6	E945.5	E950.4	E962.0	E980.4
Organophosphates	989.3	E863.1	—	E950.6	E962.1	E980.7
Orimune	979.5	E858.8	E949.5	E950.4	E962.0	E980.4
Orinase	962.3	E858.0	E932.3	E950.4	E962.0	E980.4
Orphenadrine	966.4	E855.0	E936.4	E950.4	E962.0	E980.4
Ortal (sodium)	967.0	E851	E937.0	E950.1	E962.0	E980.1
Orthoboric acid	976.0	E858.7	E946.0	E950.4	E962.0	E980.4
ENT agent	976.6	E858.7	E946.6	E950.4	E962.0	E980.4
ophthalmic preparation	976.5	E858.7	E946.5	E950.4	E962.0	E980.4
Orthocaine	968.5	E855.2	E938.5	E950.4	E962.0	E980.4
Ortho-Novum	962.2	E858.0	E932.2	E950.4	E962.0	E980.4
Orthotolidine (reagent)	977.8	E858.8	E947.8	E950.4	E962.0	E980.4
Osmic acid (liquid)	983.1	E864.1	—	E950.7	E962.1	E980.6
fumes	987.8	E869.8	—	E952.8	E962.2	E982.8
Osmotic diuretics	974.4	E858.5	E944.4	E950.4	E962.0	E980.4
Ouabain	972.1	E858.3	E942.1	E950.4	E962.0	E980.4
Ovarian hormones (synthetic substitutes)	962.2	E858.0	E932.2	E950.4	E962.0	E980.4
Ovral	962.2	E858.0	E932.2	E950.4	E962.0	E980.4
Ovulation suppressants	962.2	E858.0	E932.2	E950.4	E962.0	E980.4
Ovulen	962.2	E858.0	E932.2	E950.4	E962.0	E980.4
Oxacillin (sodium)	960.0	E856	E930.0	E950.4	E962.0	E980.4
Oxalic acid	983.1	E864.1	—	E950.7	E962.1	E980.6
Oxanamide	969.5	E853.8	E939.5	E950.3	E962.0	E980.3
Oxandrolone	962.1	E858.0	E932.1	E950.4	E962.0	E980.4
Oxaprozin	965.61	E850.6	E935.6	E950.0	E962.0	E980.0
Oxazepam	969.4	E853.2	E939.4	E950.3	E962.0	E980.3
Oxazolidine derivatives	966.0	E855.0	E936.0	E950.4	E962.0	E980.4
Ox bile extract	973.4	E858.4	E943.4	E950.4	E962.0	E980.4
Oxedrine	971.2	E855.5	E941.2	E950.4	E962.0	E980.4
Oxeladin	975.4	E858.6	E945.4	E950.4	E962.0	E980.4
Oxethazaine NEC	968.5	E855.2	E938.5	E950.4	E962.0	E980.4
Oxidizing agents NEC	983.9	E864.3	—	E950.7	E962.1	E980.6
Oxolinic acid	961.3	E857	E931.3	E950.4	E962.0	E980.4
Oxophenarsine	961.1	E857	E931.1	E950.4	E962.0	E980.4
Oxsoralen	976.3	E858.7	E946.3	E950.4	E962.0	E980.4
Oxtriphylline	976.7	E858.6	E945.7	E950.4	E962.0	E980.4
Oxybuprocaine	968.5	E855.2	E938.5	E950.4	E962.0	E980.4
Oxybutynin	975.1	E858.6	E945.1	E950.4	E962.0	E980.4
Oxycodone	965.09	E850.2	E935.2	E950.0	E962.0	E980.0
Oxygen	987.8	E869.8	—	E952.8	E962.2	E982.8
Oxylone	976.0	E858.7	E946.0	E950.4	E962.0	E980.4
ophthalmic preparation	976.5	E858.7	E946.5	E950.4	E962.0	E980.4
Oxymesterone	962.1	E858.0	E932.1	E950.4	E962.0	E980.4
Oxymetazoline	971.2	E855.5	E941.2	E950.4	E962.0	E980.4
Oxymetholone	962.1	E858.0	E932.1	E950.4	E962.0	E980.4
Oxymorphone	965.09	E850.2	E935.2	E950.0	E962.0	E980.0

◄▶ **New Code**　　◀▦▦▶ **Revised Code**

Substance	Poisoning	External Cause (E-Code)				
		Accident	Therapeutic Use	Suicide Attempt	Assault	Undetermined
Oxypertine	969.0	E854.0	E939.0	E950.3	E962.0	E980.3
Oxyphenbutazone	965.5	E850.5	E935.5	E950.0	E962.0	E980.0
Oxyphencyclimine	971.1	E855.4	E941.1	E950.4	E962.0	E980.4
Oxyphenisatin	973.1	E858.4	E943.1	E950.4	E962.0	E980.4
Oxyphenonium	971.1	E855.4	E941.1	E950.4	E962.0	E980.4
Oxyquinoline	961.3	E857	E931.3	E950.4	E962.0	E980.4
Oxytetracycline	960.4	E856	E930.4	E950.4	E962.0	E980.4
Oxytocics	975.0	E858.6	E945.0	E950.4	E962.0	E980.4
Oxytocin	975.0	E858.6	E945.0	E950.4	E962.0	E980.4
Ozone	987.8	E869.8	—	E952.8	E962.2	E982.8
PABA	976.3	E858.7	E946.3	E950.4	E962.0	E980.4
Packed red cells	964.7	E858.2	E934.7	E950.4	E962.0	E980.4
Paint NEC	989.89	E861.6	—	E950.9	E962.1	E980.9
cleaner	982.8	E862.9	—	E950.9	E962.1	E980.9
fumes NEC	987.8	E869.8	—	E952.8	E962.1	E982.8
lead (fumes)	984.0	E861.5	—	E950.9	E962.1	E980.9
solvent NEC	982.8	E862.9	—	E950.9	E962.1	E980.9
stripper	982.8	E862.9	—	E950.9	E962.1	E980.9
Palfium	965.09	E850.2	E935.2	E950.0	E962.0	E980.0
Paludrine	961.4	E857	E931.4	E950.4	E962.0	E980.4
PAM	977.2	E855.8	E947.2	E950.4	E962.0	E980.4
Pamaquine (napthoate)	961.4	E857	E931.4	E950.4	E962.0	E980.4
Pamprin	965.1	E850.3	E935.3	E950.0	E962.0	E980.0
Panadol	965.4	E850.4	E935.4	E950.0	E962.0	E980.0
Pancreatic dornase (mucolytic)	963.4	E858.1	E933.4	E950.4	E962.0	E980.4
Pancreatin	973.4	E858.4	E943.4	E950.4	E962.0	E980.4
Pancrelipase	973.4	E858.4	E943.4	E950.4	E962.0	E980.4
Pangamic acid	963.5	E858.1	E933.5	E950.4	E962.0	E980.4
Panthenol	963.5	E858.1	E933.5	E950.4	E962.0	E980.4
topical	976.8	E858.7	E946.8	E950.4	E962.0	E980.4
Pantopaque	977.8	E858.8	E947.8	E950.4	E962.0	E980.4
Pantopon	965.00	E850.2	E935.2	E950.0	E962.0	E980.0
Pantothenic acid	963.5	E858.1	E933.5	E950.4	E962.0	E980.4
Panwarfin	964.2	E858.2	E934.2	E950.4	E962.0	E980.4
Papain	973.4	E858.4	E943.4	E950.4	E962.0	E980.4
Papaverine	972.5	E858.3	E942.5	E950.4	E962.0	E980.4
Para-aminobenzoic acid	976.3	E858.7	E946.3	E950.4	E962.0	E980.4
Para-aminophenol derivatives	965.4	E850.4	E935.4	E950.0	E962.0	E980.0
Para-aminosalicylic acid (derivatives)	961.8	E857	E931.8	E950.4	E962.0	E980.4
Paracetaldehyde (medicinal)	967.2	E852.1	E937.2	E950.2	E962.0	E980.2
Paracetamol	965.4	E850.4	E935.4	E950.0	E962.0	E980.0
Paracodin	965.09	E850.2	E935.2	E950.0	E962.0	E980.0
Paradione	966.0	E855.0	E936.0	E950.4	E962.0	E980.4
Paraffin(s) (wax)	981	E862	—	E950.9	E962.1	E980.9
liquid (medicinal)	973.2	E858.4	E943.2	E950.4	E962.0	E980.4
nonmedicinal (oil)	981	E962.1	—	E950.9	E962.1	E980.9
Paraldehyde (medicinal)	967.2	E852.1	E937.2	E950.2	E962.0	E980.2
Paramethadione	966.0	E855.0	E936.0	E950.4	E962.0	E980.4
Paramethasone	962.0	E858.0	E932.0	E950.4	E962.0	E980.4
Paraquat	989.4	E863.5	—	E950.6	E962.1	E980.7
Parasympatholytics	971.1	E855.4	E941.1	E950.4	E962.0	E980.4
Parasympathomimetics	971.0	E855.3	E941.0	E950.4	E962.0	E980.4
Parathion	989.3	E863.1	—	E950.6	E962.1	E980.7
Parathormone	962.6	E858.0	E932.6	E950.4	E962.0	E980.4
Parathyroid (derivatives)	962.6	E858.0	E932.6	E950.4	E962.0	E980.4
Paratyphoid vaccine	978.1	E858.8	E948.1	E950.4	E962.0	E980.4
Paredrine	971.2	E855.5	E941.2	E950.4	E962.0	E980.4
Paregoric	965.00	E850.2	E935.2	E950.0	E962.0	E980.0
Pargyline	972.3	E858.3	E942.3	E950.4	E962.0	E980.4
Paris green	985.1	E866.3	—	E950.8	E962.1	E980.8
insecticide	985.1	E863.4	—	E950.8	E962.1	E980.8

ICD-9-CM

Drugs

Vol. 2

Substance	Poisoning	External Cause (E-Code)				
		Accident	Therapeutic Use	Suicide Attempt	Assault	Undetermined
Parnate	969.0	E854.0	E939.0	E950.3	E962.0	E980.3
Paromomycin	960.8	E856	E930.8	E950.4	E962.0	E980.4
Paroxypropione	963.1	E858.1	E933.1	E950.4	E962.0	E980.4
Parzone	965.09	E850.2	E935.2	E950.0	E962.0	E980.0
PAS	961.8	E857	E931.8	E950.4	E962.0	E980.4
PCBs	981	E862.3	—	E950.9	E962.1	E980.9
PCP (pentachlorophenol)	989.4	E863.6	—	E950.6	E962.1	E980.7
herbicide	989.4	E863.5	—	E950.6	E962.1	E980.7
insecticide	989.4	E863.4	—	E950.6	E962.1	E980.7
phencyclidine	968.3	E855.1	E938.3	E950.4	E962.0	E980.4
Peach kernel oil (emulsion)	973.2	E858.4	E943.2	E950.4	E962.0	E980.4
Peanut oil (emulsion) NEC	973.2	E858.4	E943.2	E950.4	E962.0	E980.4
topical	976.3	E858.7	E946.3	E950.4	E962.0	E980.4
Pearly Gates (morning glory seeds)	969.6	E854.1	E939.6	E950.3	E962.0	E980.3
Pecazine	969.1	E853.0	E939.1	E950.3	E962.0	E980.3
Pecilocin	960.1	E856	E930.1	E950.4	E962.0	E980.4
Pectin (with kaolin) NEC	973.5	E858.4	E943.5	E950.4	E962.0	E980.4
Pelletierine tannate	961.6	E857	E931.6	E950.4	E962.0	E980.4
Pemoline	969.7	E854.2	E939.7	E950.3	E962.0	E980.3
Pempidine	972.3	E858.3	E942.3	E950.4	E962.0	E980.4
Penamecillin	960.0	E856	E930.0	E950.4	E962.0	E980.4
Penethamate hydriodide	960.0	E856	E930.0	E950.4	E962.0	E980.4
Penicillamine	963.8	E858.1	E933.8	E950.4	E962.0	E980.4
Penicillin (any type)	960.0	E856	E930.0	E950.4	E962.0	E980.4
Penicillinase	963.4	E858.1	E933.4	E950.4	E962.0	E980.4
Pentachlorophenol (fungicide)	989.4	E863.6	—	E950.6	E962.1	E980.7
herbicide	989.4	E863.5	—	E950.6	E962.1	E980.7
insecticide	989.4	E863.4	—	E950.6	E962.1	E980.7
Pentaerythritol	972.4	E858.3	E942.4	E950.4	E962.0	E980.4
chloral	967.1	E852.0	E937.1	E950.2	E962.0	E980.2
tetranitrate NEC	972.4	E858.3	E942.4	E950.4	E962.0	E980.4
Pentagastrin	977.8	E858.8	E947.8	E950.4	E962.0	E980.4
Pentalin	982.3	E862.4	—	E950.9	E962.1	E980.9
Pentamethonium (bromide)	972.3	E858.3	E942.3	E950.4	E962.0	E980.4
Pentamidine	961.5	E857	E931.5	E950.4	E962.0	E980.4
Pentanol	980.8	E860.8	—	E950.9	E962.1	E980.9
Pentaquine	961.4	E857	E931.4	E950.4	E962.0	E980.4
Pentazocine	965.8	E850.8	E935.8	E950.0	E962.0	E980.0
Penthienate	971.1	E855.4	E941.1	E950.4	E962.0	E980.4
Pentobarbital, pentobarbitone (sodium)	967.0	E851	E937.0	E950.1	E962.0	E980.1
Pentolinium (tartrate)	972.3	E858.3	E942.3	E950.4	E962.0	E980.4
Pentothal	968.3	E855.1	E938.3	E950.4	E962.0	E980.4
Pentylenetetrazol	970.0	E854.3	E940.0	E950.4	E962.0	E980.4
Pentylsalicylamide	961.8	E857	E931.8	E950.4	E962.0	E980.4
Pepsin	973.4	E858.4	E943.4	E950.4	E962.0	E980.4
Peptavlon	977.8	E858.8	E947.8	E950.4	E962.0	E980.4
Percaine (spinal)	968.7	E855.2	E938.7	E950.4	E962.0	E980.4
topical (surface)	968.5	E855.2	E938.5	E950.4	E962.0	E980.4
Perchloroethylene (vapor)	982.3	E862.4	—	E950.9	E962.1	E980.9
medicinal	961.6	E857	E931.6	E950.4	E962.0	E980.4
Percodan	965.09	E850.2	E935.2	E950.0	E962.0	E980.0
Percogesic	965.09	E850.2	E935.2	E950.0	E962.0	E980.0
Percorten	962.0	E858.0	E932.0	E950.4	E962.0	E980.4
Pergonal	962.4	E858.0	E932.4	E950.4	E962.0	E980.4
Perhexiline	972.4	E858.3	E942.4	E950.4	E962.0	E980.4
Periactin	963.0	E858.1	E933.0	E950.4	E962.0	E980.4
Periclor	967.1	E852.0	E937.1	E950.2	E962.0	E980.2
Pericyazine	969.1	E853.0	E939.1	E950.3	E962.0	E980.3
Peritrate	972.4	E858.3	E942.4	E950.4	E962.0	E980.4
Permanganates NEC	983.9	E864.3	—	E950.7	E962.1	E980.6
potassium (topical)	976.0	E858.7	E946.0	E950.4	E962.0	E980.4

◀▶ **New Code**　　⬅▦▦➡ **Revised Code**

Substance	Poisoning	External Cause (E-Code)				
		Accident	Therapeutic Use	Suicide Attempt	Assault	Undetermined
Pernocton	967.0	E851	E937.0	E950.1	E962.0	E980.1
Pernoston	967.0	E851	E937.0	E950.1	E962.0	E980.1
Peronin(e)	965.09	E850.2	E935.2	E950.0	E962.0	E980.0
Perphenazine	969.1	E853.0	E939.1	E950.3	E962.0	E980.3
Pertofrane	969.0	E854	E939.0	E950.3	E962.0	E980.3
Pertussis						
immune serum (human)	964.6	E858.2	E934.6	E950.4	E962.0	E980.4
vaccine (with diphtheria toxoid) (with tetanus toxoid)	978.6	E858.8	E948.6	E950.4	E962.0	E980.4
Peruvian balsam	976.8	E858.7	E946.8	E950.4	E962.0	E980.4
Pesticides (dust) (fumes) (vapor)	989.4	E863.4	—	E950.6	E962.1	E980.7
arsenic	985.1	E863.4	—	E950.8	E962.1	E980.8
chlorinated	989.2	E863.0	—	E950.6	E962.1	E980.7
cyanide	989.0	E863.4	—	E950.6	E962.1	E980.7
kerosene	981	E863.4	—	E950.6	E962.1	E980.7
mixture (of compounds)	989.4	E863.3	—	E950.6	E962.1	E980.7
naphthalene	983.0	E863.4	—	E950.7	E962.1	E980.6
organochlorine (compounds)	989.2	E863.0	—	E950.6	E962.1	E980.7
petroleum (distillate) (products) NEC	981	E863.4	—	E950.6	E962.1	E980.7
specified ingredient NEC	989.4	E863.4	—	E950.6	E962.1	E980.7
strychnine	989.1	E863.4	—	E950.6	E962.1	E980.7
thallium	985.8	E863.7	—	E950.6	E962.1	E980.7
Pethidine (hydrochloride)	965.09	E850.2	E935.2	E950.0	E962.0	E980.0
Petrichloral	967.1	E852.0	E937.1	E950.2	E962.0	E980.2
Petrol	981	E862.1	—	E950.9	E962.1	E980.9
vapor	987.1	E869.8	—	E952.8	E962.2	E982.8
Petrolatum (jelly) (ointment)	976.3	E858.7	E946.3	E950.4	E962.0	E980.4
hydrophilic	976.3	E858.7	E946.3	E950.4	E962.0	E980.4
liquid	973.2	E858.4	E943.2	E950.4	E962.0	E980.4
topical	976.3	E858.7	E946.3	E950.4	E962.0	E980.4
nonmedicinal	981	E862.1	—	E950.9	E962.1	E980.9
Petroleum (cleaners) (fuels) (products) NEC	981	E862.1	—	E950.9	E962.1	E980.9
benzin(e) - *see* Ligroin						
ether - *see* Ligroin						
jelly - *see* Petrolatum						
naphtha - *see* Ligroin						
pesticide	981	E863.4	—	E950.6	E962.1	E980.7
solids	981	E862.3	—	E950.9	E962.1	E980.9
solvents	981	E862.0	—	E950.9	E962.1	E980.9
vapor	987.1	E869.8	—	E952.8	E962.2	E982.8
Peyote	969.6	E854.1	E939.6	E950.3	E962.0	E980.3
Phanodorm, phanodorn	967.0	E851	E937.0	E950.1	E962.0	E980.1
Phanquinone, phanquone	961.5	E857	E931.5	E950.4	E962.0	E980.4
Pharmaceutical excipient or adjunct	977.4	E858.8	E947.4	E950.4	E962.0	E980.4
Phenacemide	966.3	E855.0	E936.3	E950.4	E962.0	E980.4
Phenacetin	965.4	E850.4	E935.4	E950.0	E962.0	E980.0
Phenadoxone	965.09	E850.2	E935.2	E950.0	E962.0	E980.0
Phenaglycodol	969.5	E853.8	E939.5	E950.3	E962.0	E980.3
Phenantoin	966.1	E855.0	E936.1	E950.4	E962.0	E980.4
Phenaphthazine reagent	977.8	E858.8	E947.8	E950.4	E962.0	E980.4
Phenazocine	965.09	E850.2	E935.2	E950.0	E962.0	E980.0
Phenazone	965.5	E850.5	E935.5	E950.0	E962.0	E980.0
Phenazopyridine	976.1	E858.7	E946.1	E950.4	E962.0	E980.4
Phenbenicillin	960.0	E856	E930.0	E950.4	E962.0	E980.4
Phenbutrazate	977.0	E858.8	E947.0	E950.4	E962.0	E980.4
Phencyclidine	968.3	E855.1	E938.3	E950.4	E962.0	E980.4
Phendimetrazine	977.0	E858.8	E947.0	E950.4	E962.0	E980.4
Phenelzine	969.0	E854.0	E939.0	E950.3	E962.0	E980.3
Phenergan	967.8	E852.8	E937.8	E950.2	E962.0	E980.2
Phenethicillin (potassium)	960.0	E856	E930.0	E950.4	E962.0	E980.4
Phenetsal	965.1	E850.3	E935.3	E950.0	E962.0	E980.0
Pheneturide	966.3	E855.0	E936.3	E950.4	E962.0	E980.4

◀▶ **New Code** ◀▥▥▶ **Revised Code**

Substance	Poisoning	External Cause (E-Code)				
		Accident	Therapeutic Use	Suicide Attempt	Assault	Undetermined
Phenformin	962.3	E858.0	E932.3	E950.4	E962.0	E980.4
Phenglutarimide	971.1	E855.4	E941.1	E950.4	E962.0	E980.4
Phenicarbazide	965.8	E850.8	E935.8	E950.0	E962.0	E980.0
Phenindamine (tartrate)	963.0	E858.1	E933.0	E950.4	E962.0	E980.4
Phenindione	964.2	E858.2	E934.2	E950.4	E962.0	E980.4
Pheniprazine	969.0	E854.0	E939.0	E950.3	E962.0	E980.3
Pheniramine (maleate)	963.0	E858.1	E933.0	E950.4	E962.0	E980.4
Phenmetrazine	977.0	E858.8	E947.0	E950.4	E962.0	E980.4
Phenobal	967.0	E851	E937.0	E950.1	E962.0	E980.1
Phenobarbital	967.0	E851	E937.0	E950.1	E962.0	E980.1
Phenobarbitone	967.0	E851	E937.0	E950.1	E962.0	E980.1
Phenoctide	976.0	E858.7	E946.0	E950.4	E962.0	E980.4
Phenol (derivatives) NEC	983.0	E864.0	—	E950.7	E962.1	E980.6
disinfectant	983.0	E864.0	—	E950.7	E962.1	E980.6
pesticide	989.4	E863.4	—	E950.6	E962.1	E980.7
red	977.8	E858.8	E947.8	E950.4	E962.0	E980.4
Phenolphthalein	973.1	E858.4	E943.1	E950.4	E962.0	E980.4
Phenolsulfonphthalein	977.8	E858.8	E947.8	E950.4	E962.0	E980.4
Phenomorphan	965.09	E850.2	E935.2	E950.0	E962.0	E980.0
Phenonyl	967.0	E851	E937.0	E950.1	E962.0	E980.1
Phenoperidine	965.09	E850.2	E935.2	E950.0	E962.0	E980.0
Phenoquin	974.7	E858.5	E944.7	E950.4	E962.0	E980.4
Phenothiazines (tranquilizers) NEC	969.1	E853.0	E939.1	E950.3	E962.0	E980.3
insecticide	989.3	E863.4	—	E950.6	E962.1	E980.7
Phenoxybenzamine	971.3	E855.6	E941.3	E950.4	E962.0	E980.4
Phenoxymethyl penicillin	960.0	E856	E930.0	E950.4	E962.0	E980.4
Phenprocoumon	964.2	E858.2	E934.2	E950.4	E962.0	E980.4
Phensuximide	966.2	E855.0	E936.2	E950.4	E962.0	E980.4
Phentermine	977.0	E858.8	E947.0	E950.4	E962.0	E980.4
Phentolamine	971.3	E855.6	E941.3	E950.4	E962.0	E980.4
Phenyl						
butazone	965.5	E850.5	E935.5	E950.0	E962.0	E980.0
enediamine	983.0	E864.0	—	E950.7	E962.1	E980.6
hydrazine	983.0	E864.0	—	E950.7	E962.1	E980.6
antineoplastic	963.1	E858.1	E933.1	E950.4	E962.0	E980.4
mercuric compounds - *see* Mercury						
salicylate	976.3	E858.7	E946.3	E950.4	E962.0	E980.4
Phenylephrine	971.2	E855.5	E941.2	E950.4	E962.0	E980.4
Phenylethylbiguanide	962.3	E858.0	E932.3	E950.4	E962.0	E980.4
Phenylpropanolamine	971.2	E855.5	E941.2	E950.4	E962.0	E980.4
Phenylsulfthion	989.3	E863.1	—	E950.6	E962.1	E980.7
Phenyramidol, phenyramidon	965.7	E850.7	E935.7	E950.0	E962.0	E980.0
Phenytoin	966.1	E855.0	E936.1	E950.4	E962.0	E980.4
pHisoHex	976.2	E858.7	E946.2	E950.4	E962.0	E980.4
Pholcodine	965.09	E850.2	E935.2	E950.0	E962.0	E980.0
Phorate	989.3	E863.1	—	E950.6	E962.1	E980.7
Phosdrin	989.3	E863.1	—	E950.6	E962.1	E980.7
Phosgene (gas)	987.8	E869.8	—	E952.8	E962.2	E982.8
Phosphate (tricresyl)	989.89	E866.8	—	E950.9	E962.1	E980.9
organic	989.3	E863.1	—	E950.6	E962.1	E980.7
solvent	982.8	E862.4	—	E950.9	E962.1	E980.9
Phosphine	987.8	E869.8	—	E952.8	E962.2	E982.8
fumigant	987.8	E863.8	—	E950.6	E962.2	E980.7
Phospholine	971.0	E855.3	E941.0	E950.4	E962.0	E980.4
Phosphoric acid	983.1	E864.1	—	E950.7	E962.1	E980.6
Phosphorus (compounds) NEC	983.9	E864.3	—	E950.7	E962.1	E980.6
rodenticide	983.9	E863.7	—	E950.7	E962.1	E980.6
Phthalimidoglutarimide	967.8	E852.8	E937.8	E950.2	E962.0	E980.2
Phthalylsulfathiazole	961.0	E857	E931.0	E950.4	E962.0	E980.4
Phylloquinone	964.3	E858.2	E934.3	E950.4	E962.0	E980.4
Physeptone	965.02	E850.1	E935.1	E950.0	E962.0	E980.0

◀ ▶   **New Code**   ◀▥ ▥▶   **Revised Code**

| | | External Cause (E-Code) | | | | |
Substance	Poisoning	Accident	Therapeutic Use	Suicide Attempt	Assault	Undetermined
Physostigma venenosum	988.2	E865.4	—	E950.9	E962.1	E980.9
Physostigmine	971.0	E855.3	E941.0	E950.4	E962.0	E980.4
Phytolacca decandra	988.2	E865.4	—	E950.9	E962.1	E980.9
Phytomenadione	964.3	E858.2	E934.3	E950.4	E962.0	E980.4
Phytonadione	964.3	E858.2	E934.3	E950.4	E962.0	E980.4
Picric (acid)	983.0	E864.0	—	E950.7	E962.1	E980.6
Picrotoxin	970.0	E854.3	E940.0	E950.4	E962.0	E980.4
Pilocarpine	971.0	E855.3	E941.0	E950.4	E962.0	E980.4
Pilocarpus (jaborandi) extract	971.0	E855.3	E941.0	E950.4	E962.0	E980.4
Pimaricin	960.1	E856	E930.1	E950.4	E962.0	E980.4
Piminodine	965.09	E850.2	E935.2	E950.0	E962.0	E980.0
Pine oil, pinesol (disinfectant)	983.9	E861.4	—	E950.7	E962.1	E980.6
Pinkroot	961.6	E857	E931.6	E950.4	E962.0	E980.4
Pipadone	965.09	E850.2	E935.2	E950.0	E962.0	E980.0
Pipamazine	963.0	E858.1	E933.0	E950.4	E962.0	E980.4
Pipazethate	975.4	E858.6	E945.4	E950.4	E962.0	E980.4
Pipenzolate	971.1	E855.4	E941.1	E950.4	E962.0	E980.4
Piperacetazine	969.1	E853.0	E939.1	E950.3	E962.0	E980.3
Piperazine NEC	961.6	E857	E931.6	E950.4	E962.0	E980.4
estrone sulfate	962.2	E858.0	E932.2	E950.4	E962.0	E980.4
Piper cubeba	988.2	E865.4	—	E950.9	E962.1	E980.9
Piperidione	975.4	E858.6	E945.4	E950.4	E962.0	E980.4
Piperidolate	971.1	E855.4	E941.1	E950.4	E962.0	E980.4
Piperocaine	968.9	E855.2	E938.9	E950.4	E962.0	E980.4
infiltration (subcutaneous)	968.5	E855.2	E938.5	E950.4	E962.0	E980.4
nerve block (peripheral) (plexus)	968.6	E855.2	E938.6	E950.4	E962.0	E980.4
topical (surface)	968.5	E855.2	E938.5	E950.4	E962.0	E980.4
Pipobroman	963.1	E858.1	E933.1	E950.4	E962.0	E980.4
Pipradrol	970.8	E854.3	E940.8	E950.4	E962.0	E980.4
Piscidia (bark) (erythrina)	965.7	E850.7	E935.7	E950.0	E962.0	E980.0
Pitch	983.0	E864.0	—	E950.7	E962.1	E980.6
Pitkin's solution	968.7	E855.2	E938.7	E950.4	E962.0	E980.4
Pitocin	975.0	E858.6	E945.0	E950.4	E962.0	E980.4
Pitressin (tannate)	962.5	E858.0	E932.5	E950.4	E962.0	E980.4
Pituitary extracts (posterior)	962.5	E858.0	E932.5	E950.4	E962.0	E980.4
anterior	962.4	E858.0	E932.4	E950.4	E962.0	E980.4
Pituitrin	962.5	E858.0	E932.5	E950.4	E962.0	E980.4
Placental extract	962.9	E858.0	E932.9	E950.4	E962.0	E980.4
Placidyl	967.8	E852.8	E937.8	E950.2	E962.0	E980.2
Plague vaccine	978.3	E858.8	E948.3	E950.4	E962.0	E980.4
Plant foods or fertilizers NEC	989.89	E866.5	—	E950.9	E962.1	E980.9
mixed with herbicides	989.4	E863.5	—	E950.6	E962.1	E930.7
Plants, noxious, used as food	988.2	E865.9	—	E950.9	E962.1	E980.9
berries and seeds	988.2	E865.3	—	E950.9	E962.1	E980.9
specified type NEC	988.2	E865.4	—	E950.9	E962.1	E980.9
Plasma (blood)	964.7	E858.2	E934.7	E950.4	E962.0	E980.4
expanders	964.8	E858.2	E934.8	E950.4	E962.0	E980.4
Plasmanate	964.7	E858.2	E934.7	E950.4	E962.0	E980.4
Plegicil	969.1	E853.0	E939.1	E950.3	E962.0	E980.3
Podophyllin	976.4	E858.7	E946.4	E950.4	E962.0	E980.4
Podophyllum resin	976.4	E858.7	E946.4	E950.4	E962.0	E980.4
Poison NEC	989.9	E866.9	—	E950.9	E962.1	E980.9
Poisonous berries	988.2	E865.3	—	E950.9	E962.1	E980.9
Pokeweed (any part)	988.2	E865.4	—	E950.9	E962.1	E980.9
Poldine	971.1	E855.4	E941.1	E950.4	E962.0	E980.4
Poliomyelitis vaccine	979.5	E858.8	E949.5	E950.4	E962.0	E980.4
Poliovirus vaccine	979.5	E858.8	E949.5	E950.4	E962.0	E980.4
Polish (car) (floor) (furniture) (metal) (silver)	989.89	E861.2	—	E950.9	E962.1	E980.9
abrasive	989.89	E861.3	—	E950.9	E962.1	E980.9
porcelain	989.89	E861.3	—	E950.9	E962.1	E980.9
Poloxalkol	973.2	E858.4	E943.2	E950.4	E962.0	E980.4

◄ ▶ **New Code**   ⬅▥ ▥➡ **Revised Code**

Substance	Poisoning	Accident	Therapeutic Use	Suicide Attempt	Assault	Undetermined
			External Cause (E-Code)			
Polyaminostyrene resins	974.5	E858.5	E944.5	E950.4	E962.0	E980.4
Polychlorinated biphenyl - *see* PCBs						
Polycycline	960.4	E856	E930.4	E950.4	E962.0	E980.4
Polyester resin hardener	982.8	E862.4	—	E950.9	E962.1	E980.9
fumes	987.8	E869.8	—	E952.8	E962.2	E982.8
Polyestradiol (phosphate)	962.2	E858.0	E932.2	E950.4	E962.0	E980.4
Polyethanolamine alkyl sulfate	976.2	E858.7	E946.2	E950.4	E962.0	E980.4
Polyethylene glycol	976.3	E858.7	E946.3	E950.4	E962.0	E980.4
Polyferose	964.0	E858.2	E934.0	E950.4	E962.0	E980.4
Polymyxin B	960.8	E856	E930.8	E950.4	E962.0	E980.4
ENT agent	976.6	E858.7	E946.6	E950.4	E962.0	E980.4
ophthalmic preparation	976.5	E858.7	E946.5	E950.4	E962.0	E980.4
topical NEC	976.0	E858.7	E946.0	E950.4	E962.0	E980.4
Polynoxylin(e)	976.0	E858.7	E946.0	E950.4	E962.0	E980.4
Polyoxymethyleneurea	976.0	E858.7	E946.0	E950.4	E962.0	E980.4
Polytetrafluoroethylene (inhaled)	987.8	E869.8	—	E952.8	E962.2	E982.8
Polythiazide	974.3	E858.5	E944.3	E950.4	E962.0	E980.4
Polyvinylpyrrolidone	964.8	E858.2	E934.8	E950.4	E962.0	E980.4
Pontocaine (hydrochloride) (infiltration) (topical)	968.5	E855.2	E938.5	E950.4	E962.0	E980.4
nerve block (peripheral) (plexus)	968.6	E855.2	E938.6	E950.4	E962.0	E980.4
spinal	968.7	E855.2	E938.7	E950.4	E962.0	E980.4
Pot	969.6	E854.1	E939.6	E950.3	E962.0	E980.3
Potash (caustic)	983.2	E864.2	—	E950.7	E962.1	E980.6
Potassic saline injection (lactated)	974.5	E858.5	E944.5	E950.4	E962.0	E980.4
Potassium (salts) NEC	974.5	E858.5	E944.5	E950.4	E962.0	E980.4
aminosalicylate	961.8	E857	E931.8	E950.4	E962.0	E980.4
arsenite (solution)	985.1	E866.3	—	E950.8	E962.1	E980.8
bichromate	983.9	E864.3	—	E950.7	E962.1	E980.6
bisulfate	983.9	E864.3	—	E950.7	E962.1	E980.6
bromide (medicinal) NEC	967.3	E852.2	E937.3	E950.2	E962.0	E980.2
carbonate	983.2	E864.2	—	E950.7	E962.1	E980.6
chlorate NEC	983.9	E864.3	—	E950.7	E962.1	E980.6
cyanide - *see* Cyanide						
hydroxide	983.2	E864.2	—	E950.7	E962.1	E980.6
iodide (expectorant) NEC	975.5	E858.6	E945.5	E950.4	E962.0	E980.4
nitrate	989.89	E866.8	—	E950.9	E962.1	E980.9
oxalate	983.9	E864.3	—	E950.7	E962.1	E980.6
perchlorate NEC	977.8	E858.8	E947.8	E950.4	E962.0	E980.4
antithyroid	962.8	E858.0	E932.8	E950.4	E962.0	E980.4
permanganate	976.0	E858.7	E946.0	E950.4	E962.0	E980.4
nonmedicinal	983.9	E864.3	—	E950.7	E962.1	E980.6
Povidone-iodine (anti-infective) NEC	976.0	E858.7	E946.0	E950.4	E962.0	E980.4
Practolol	972.0	E858.3	E942.0	E950.4	E962.0	E980.4
Pralidoxime (chloride)	977.2	E858.8	E947.2	E950.4	E962.0	E980.4
Pramoxine	968.5	E855.2	E938.5	E950.4	E962.0	E980.4
Prazosin	972.6	E858.3	E942.6	E950.4	E962.0	E980.4
Prednisolone	962.0	E858.0	E932.0	E950.4	E962.0	E980.4
ENT agent	976.6	E858.7	E946.6	E950.4	E962.0	E980.4
ophthalmic preparation	976.5	E858.7	E946.5	E950.4	E962.0	E980.4
topical NEC	976.0	E858.7	E946.0	E950.4	E962.0	E980.4
Prednisone	962.0	E858.0	E932.0	E950.4	E962.0	E980.4
Pregnanediol	962.2	E858.0	E932.2	E950.4	E962.0	E990.4
Pregneninolone	962.2	E858.0	E932.2	E950.4	E962.0	E980.4
Preludin	977.0	E858.8	E947.0	E950.4	E962.0	E980.4
Premarin	962.2	E858.0	E932.2	E950.4	E962.0	E980.4
Prenylamine	972.4	E858.3	E942.4	E950.4	E962.0	E980.4
Preparation H	976.8	E858.7	E946.8	E950.4	E962.0	E980.4
Preservatives	989.89	E866.8	—	E950.9	E962.1	E980.9
Pride of China	988.2	E865.3	—	E950.9	E962.1	E980.9
Prilocaine	968.9	E855.2	E938.9	E950.4	E962.0	E980.4
infiltration (subcutaneous)	968.5	E855.2	E938.5	E950.4	E962.0	E980.4
nerve block (peripheral) (plexus)	968.6	E855.2	E938.6	E950.4	E962.0	E980.4

Substance	Poisoning	External Cause (E-Code)				
		Accident	Therapeutic Use	Suicide Attempt	Assault	Undetermined
Primaquine	961.4	E857	E931.4	E950.4	E962.0	E980.4
Primidone	966.3	E855.0	E936.3	E950.4	E962.0	E980.4
Primula (veris)	988.2	E865.4	—	E950.9	E962.1	E980.9
Prinodol	965.09	E850.2	E935.2	E950.0	E962.0	E980.0
Priscol, Priscoline	971.3	E855.6	E941.3	E950.4	E962.0	E980.4
Privet	988.2	E865.4	—	E950.9	E962.1	E980.9
Privine	971.2	E855.5	E941.2	E950.4	E962.0	E980.4
Pro-Banthine	971.1	E855.4	E941.1	E950.4	E962.0	E980.4
Probarbital	967.0	E851	E937.0	E950.1	E962.0	E980.1
Probenecid	974.7	E858.5	E944.7	E950.4	E962.0	E990.4
Procainamide (hydrochloride)	972.0	E858.3	E942.0	E950.4	E962.0	E980.4
Procaine (hydrochloride) (infiltration) (topical)	968.5	E855.2	E938.5	E950.4	E962.0	E980.4
nerve block (periphreal) (plexus)	968.6	E855.2	E938.6	E950.4	E962.0	E980.4
penicillin G	960.0	E856	E930.0	E950.4	E962.0	E980.4
spinal	968.7	E855.2	E938.7	E950.4	E962.0	E980.4
Procalmidol	969.5	E853.8	E939.5	E950.3	E962.0	E980.3
Procarbazine	963.1	E858.1	E933.1	E950.4	E962.0	E980.4
Prochlorperazine	969.1	E853.0	E939.1	E950.3	E962.0	E980.3
Procyclidine	966.4	E855.0	E936.4	E950.4	E962.0	E980.4
Producer gas	986	E868.8	—	E952.1	E962.2	E982.1
Profenamine	966.4	E855.0	E936.4	E950.4	E962.0	E980.4
Profenil	975.1	E858.6	E945.1	E950.4	E962.0	E980.4
Progesterones	962.2	E858.0	E932.2	E950.4	E962.0	E980.4
Progestin	962.2	E858.0	E932.2	E950.4	E962.0	E980.4
Progestogens (with estrogens)	962.2	E858.0	E932.2	E950.4	E962.0	E980.4
Progestone	962.2	E858.0	E932.2	E950.4	E962.0	E980.4
Proguanil	961.4	E857	E931.4	E950.4	E962.0	E980.4
Prolactin	962.4	E858.0	E932.4	E950.4	E962.0	E980.4
Proloid	962.7	E858.0	E932.7	E950.4	E962.0	E980.4
Proluton	962.2	E858.0	E932.2	E950.4	E962.0	E980.4
Promacetin	961.8	E857	E931.8	E950.4	E962.0	E980.4
Promazine	969.1	E853.0	E939.1	E950.3	E962.0	E980.3
Promedrol	965.09	E850.2	E935.2	E950.0	E962.0	E980.0
Promethazine	967.8	E852.8	E937.8	E950.2	E962.0	E980.2
Promine	961.8	E857	E931.8	E950.4	E962.0	E980.4
Pronestyl (hydrochloride)	972.0	E858.3	E942.0	E950.4	E962.0	E980.4
Pronetalol, pronethalol	972.0	E858.3	E942.0	E950.4	E962.0	E980.4
Prontosil	961.0	E857	E931.0	E950.4	E962.0	E980.4
Propamidine isethionate	961.5	E857	E931.5	E950.4	E962.0	E980.4
Propanal (medicinal)	967.8	E852.8	E937.8	E950.2	E962.0	E980.2
Propane (gas) (distributed in mobile container)	987.0	E868.0	—	E951.1	E962.2	E981.1
distributed through pipes	987.0	E867	—	E951.0	E962.2	E981.0
incomplete combustion of - *see* Carbon monoxide, Propane						
Propanidid	968.3	E855.1	E938.3	E950.4	E962.0	E980.4
Propanol	980.3	E860.4	—	E950.9	E962.1	E980.9
Propantheline	971.1	E855.4	E941.1	E950.4	E962.0	E980.4
Proparacaine	968.5	E855.2	E938.5	E950.4	E962.0	E980.4
Propatyl nitrate	972.4	E858.3	E942.4	E950.4	E962.0	E980.4
Propicillin	960.0	E856	E930.0	E950.4	E962.0	E980.4
Propiolactone (vapor)	987.8	E869.8	—	E952.8	E962.2	E982.8
Propiomazine	967.8	E852.8	E937.8	E950.2	E962.0	E980.2
Propionaldehyde (medicinal)	967.8	E852.8	E937.8	E950.2	E962.0	E980.2
Propionate compound	976.0	E858.7	E946.0	E950.4	E962.0	E980.4
Propion gel	976.0	E858.7	E946.0	E950.4	E962.0	E980.4
Propitocaine	968.9	E855.2	E938.9	E950.4	E962.0	E980.4
infiltration (subcutaneous)	968.5	E855.2	E938.5	E950.4	E962.0	E980.4
nerve block (peripheral) (plexus)	968.6	E855.2	E938.6	E950.4	E962.0	E980.4
Propoxur	989.3	E863.2	—	E950.6	E962.1	E980.7
Propoxycaine	968.9	E855.2	E938.9	E950.4	E962.0	E980.4
infiltration (subcutaneous)	968.5	E855.2	E938.5	E950.4	E962.0	E980.4
nerve block (peripheral) (plexus)	968.6	E855.2	E938.6	E950.4	E962.0	E980.4
topical (surface)	968.5	E855.2	E938.5	E950.4	E962.0	E980.4

◄▶ **New Code**   ◄▥▥▥▶ **Revised Code**

Substance	Poisoning	External Cause (E-Code)				
		Accident	Therapeutic Use	Suicide Attempt	Assault	Undetermined
Propoxyphene (hydrochloride)	965.8	E850.8	E935.8	E950.0	E962.0	E980.0
Propranolol	972.0	E858.3	E942.0	E950.4	E962.0	E980.4
Propyl						
alcohol	980.3	E860.4	—	E950.9	E962.1	E980.9
carbinol	980.3	E860.4	—	E950.9	E962.1	E980.9
hexadrine	971.2	E855.5	E941.2	E950.4	E962.0	E980.4
iodone	977.8	E858.8	E947.8	E950.4	E962.0	E980.4
thiouracil	962.8	E858.0	E932.8	E950.4	E962.0	E980.4
Propylene	987.1	E869.8	—	E952.8	E962.2	E982.8
Propylparaben (ophthalmic)	976.5	E858.7	E946.5	E950.4	E962.0	E980.4
Proscillaridin	972.1	E858.3	E942.1	E950.4	E962.0	E980.4
Prostaglandins	975.0	E858.6	E945.0	E950.4	E962.0	E980.4
Prostigmin	971.0	E855.3	E941.0	E950.4	E962.0	E980.4
Protamine (sulfate)	964.5	E858.2	E934.5	E950.4	E962.0	E980.4
zinc insulin	962.3	E858.0	E932.3	E950.4	E962.0	E980.4
Protectants (topical)	976.3	E858.7	E946.3	E950.4	E962.0	E980.4
Protein hydrolysate	974.5	E858.5	E944.5	E950.4	E962.0	E980.4
Prothiaden - *see* Dothiepin hydrochloride						
Prothionamide	961.8	E857	E931.8	E950.4	E962.0	E980.4
Prothipendyl	969.5	E853.8	E939.5	E950.3	E962.0	E980.3
Protokylol	971.2	E855.5	E941.2	E950.4	E962.0	E980.4
Protopam	977.2	E858.8	E947.2	E950.4	E962.0	E980.4
Protoveratrine(s) (A) (B)	972.6	E858.3	E942.6	E950.4	E962.0	E980.4
Protriptyline	969.0	E854.0	E939.0	E950.3	E962.0	E980.3
Provera	962.2	E858.0	E932.2	E950.4	E962.0	E980.4
Provitamin A	963.5	E858.1	E933.5	E950.4	E962.0	E980.4
Proxymetacaine	968.5	E855.2	E938.5	E950.4	E962.0	E980.4
Proxyphylline	975.1	E858.6	E945.1	E950.4	E962.0	E980.4
Prozac - *see* Fluoxetine hydrochloride						
Prunus						
laurocerasus	988.2	E865.4	—	E950.9	E962.1	E980.9
virginiana	988.2	E865.4	—	E950.9	E962.1	E980.9
Prussic acid	989.0	E866.8	—	E950.9	E962.1	E980.9
vapor	987.7	E869.8	—	E952.8	E962.2	E982.8
Pseudoephedrine	971.2	E855.5	E941.2	E950.4	E962.0	E980.4
Psilocin	969.6	E854.1	E939.6	E950.3	E962.0	E980.3
Psilocybin	969.6	E854.1	E939.6	E950.3	E962.0	E980.3
PSP	977.8	E858.8	E947.8	E950.4	E962.0	E980.4
Psychedelic agents	969.6	E854.1	E939.6	E950.3	E962.0	E980.3
Psychodysleptics	969.6	E854.1	E939.6	E950.3	E962.0	E980.3
Psychostimulants	969.7	E854.2	E939.7	E950.3	E962.0	E980.3
Psychotherapeutic agents	969.9	E855.9	E939.9	E950.3	E962.0	E980.3
antidepressants	969.0	E854.0	E939.0	E950.3	E962.0	E980.3
specified NEC	969.8	E855.8	E939.8	E950.3	E962.0	E980.3
tranquilizers NEC	969.5	E853.9	E939.5	E950.3	E962.0	E980.3
Psychotomimetic agents	969.6	E854.1	E939.6	E950.3	E962.0	E980.3
Psychotropic agents	969.9	E854.8	E939.9	E950.3	E962.0	E980.3
specified NEC	969.8	E854.8	E939.8	E950.3	E962.0	E980.3
Psyllium	973.3	E858.4	E943.3	E950.4	E962.0	E980.4
Pteroylglutamic acid	964.1	E858.2	E934.1	E950.4	E962.0	E980.4
Pteroyltriglutamate	963.1	E858.1	E933.1	E950.4	E962.0	E980.4
PTFE	987.8	E869.8	—	E952.8	E962.2	E982.8
Pulsatilla	988.2	E865.4	—	E950.9	E962.1	E980.9
Purex (bleach)	983.9	E864.3	—	E950.7	E962.1	E980.6
Purine diuretics	974.1	E858.5	E944.1	E950.4	E962.0	E980.4
Purinethol	963.1	E858.1	E933.1	E950.4	E962.0	E980.4
PVP	964.8	E858.2	E934.8	E950.4	E962.0	E980.4
Pyrabital	965.7	E850.7	E935.7	E950.0	E962.0	E980.0
Pyramidon	965.5	E850.5	E935.5	E950.0	E962.0	E980.0
Pyrantel (pamoate)	961.6	E857	E931.6	E950.4	E962.0	E980.4
Pyrathiazine	963.0	E858.1	E933.0	E950.4	E962.0	E980.4

◀▶ **New Code**   ⬅▥▥➡ **Revised Code**

Substance	Poisoning	External Cause (E-Code)				
		Accident	Therapeutic Use	Suicide Attempt	Assault	Undetermined
Pyrazinamide	961.8	E857	E931.8	E950.4	E962.0	E980.4
Pyrazinoic acid (amide)	961.8	E857	E931.8	E950.4	E962.0	E980.4
Pyrazole (derivatives)	965.5	E850.5	E935.5	E950.0	E962.0	E980.0
Pyrazolone (analgesics)	965.5	E850.5	E935.5	E950.0	E962.0	E980.0
Pyrethrins, pyrethrum	989.4	E863.4	—	E950.6	E962.1	E980.7
Pyribenzamine	963.0	E858.1	E933.0	E950.4	E962.0	E980.4
Pyridine (liquid) (vapor)	982.0	E862.4	—	E950.9	E962.1	E980.9
aldoxime chloride	977.2	E858.8	E947.2	E950.4	E962.0	E980.4
Pyridium	976.1	E858.7	E946.1	E950.4	E962.0	E980.4
Pyridostigmine	971.0	E855.3	E941.0	E950.4	E962.0	E980.4
Pyridoxine	963.5	E858.1	E933.5	E950.4	E962.0	E980.4
Pyrilamine	963.0	E858.1	E933.0	E950.4	E962.0	E980.4
Pyrimethamine	961.4	E857	E931.4	E950.4	E962.0	E980.4
Pyrogallic acid	983.0	E864.0	—	E950.7	E962.1	E980.6
Pyroxylin	976.3	E858.7	E946.3	E950.4	E962.0	E980.4
Pyrrobutamine	963.0	E858.1	E933.0	E950.4	E962.0	E980.4
Pyrrocitine	968.5	E855.2	E938.5	E950.4	E962.0	E980.4
Pyrvinium (pamoate)	961.6	E857	E931.6	E950.4	E962.0	E980.4
PZI	962.3	E858.0	E932.3	E950.4	E962.0	E980.4
Quaalude	967.4	E852.3	E937.4	E950.2	E962.0	E980.2
Quaternary ammonium derivatives	971.1	E855.4	E941.1	E950.4	E962.0	E980.4
Quicklime	983.2	E864.2	—	E950.7	E962.1	E980.6
Quinacrine	961.3	E857	E931.3	E950.4	E962.0	E980.4
Quinaglute	972.0	E858.3	E942.0	E950.4	E962.0	E980.4
Quinalbarbitone	967.0	E851	E937.0	E950.1	E962.0	E980.1
Quinestradiol	962.2	E858.0	E932.2	E950.4	E962.0	E980.4
Quinethazone	974.3	E858.5	E944.3	E950.4	E962.0	E980.4
Quinidine (gluconate) (polygalacturonate) (salts) (sulfate)	972.0	E858.3	E942.0	E950.4	E962.0	E980.4
Quinine	961.4	E857	E931.4	E950.4	E962.0	E980.4
Quiniobine	961.3	E857	E931.3	E950.4	E962.0	E980.4
Quinolines	961.3	E857	E931.3	E950.4	E962.0	E980.4
Quotane	968.5	E855.2	E938.5	E950.4	E962.0	E980.4
Rabies						
immune globulin (human)	964.6	E858.2	E934.6	E950.4	E962.0	E980.4
vaccine	979.1	E858.8	E949.1	E950.4	E962.0	E980.4
Racemoramide	965.09	E850.2	E935.2	E950.0	E962.0	E980.0
Racemorphan	965.09	E850.2	E935.2	E950.0	E962.0	E980.0
Radiator alcohol	980.1	E860.2	—	E950.9	E962.1	E980.9
Radio-opaque (drugs) (materials)	977.8	E858.8	E947.8	E950.4	E962.0	E980.4
Ranunculus	988.2	E865.4	—	E950.9	E962.1	E980.9
Rat poison	989.4	E863.7	—	E950.6	E962.1	E980.7
Rattlesnake (venom)	989.5	E905.0	—	E950.9	E962.1	E980.9
Raudixin	972.6	E858.3	E942.6	E950.4	E962.0	E980.4
Rautensin	972.6	E858.3	E942.6	E950.4	E962.0	E980.4
Rautina	972.6	E858.3	E942.6	E950.4	E962.0	E980.4
Rautotal	972.6	E858.3	E942.6	E950.4	E962.0	E980.4
Rauwiloid	972.6	E858.3	E942.6	E950.4	E962.0	E980.4
Rauwoldin	972.6	E858.3	E942.6	E950.4	E962.0	E980.4
Rauwolfia (alkaloids)	972.6	E858.3	E942.6	E950.4	E962.0	E980.4
Realgar	985.1	E866.3	—	E950.8	E962.1	E980.8
Red cells, packed	964.7	E858.2	E934.7	E950.4	E962.0	E980.4
Reducing agents, industrial NEC	983.9	E864.3	—	E950.7	E962.1	E980.6
Refrigerant gas (freon)	987.4	E869.2	—	E952.8	E962.2	E982.8
not freon	987.9	E869.9	—	E952.9	E962.2	E982.9
Regroton	974.4	E858.5	E944.4	E950.4	E962.0	E980.4
Rela	968.0	E855.1	E938.0	E950.4	E962.0	E980.4
Relaxants, skeletal muscle (autonomic)	975.2	E858.6	E945.2	E950.4	E962.0	E980.4
central nervous system	968.0	E855.1	E938.0	E950.4	E962.0	E980.4
Renese	974.3	E858.5	E944.3	E950.4	E962.0	E980.4
Renografin	977.8	E858.8	E947.8	E950.4	E962.0	E980.4
Replacement solutions	974.5	E858.5	E944.5	E950.4	E962.0	E980.4

◀▶ **New Code**　　⬅▉▉▶ **Revised Code**

Substance	Poisoning	External Cause (E-Code)				
		Accident	Therapeutic Use	Suicide Attempt	Assault	Undetermined
Rescinnamine	972.6	E858.3	E942.6	E950.4	E962.0	E980.4
Reserpine	972.6	E858.3	E942.6	E950.4	E962.0	E980.4
Resorcin, resorcinol	976.4	E858.7	E946.4	E950.4	E962.0	E980.4
Respaire	975.5	E858.6	E945.5	E950.4	E962.0	E980.4
Respiratory agents NEC	975.8	E858.6	E945.8	E950.4	E962.0	E980.4
Retinoic acid	976.8	E858.7	E946.8	E950.4	E962.0	E980.4
Retinol	963.5	E858.1	E933.5	E950.4	E962.0	E980.4
Rh (D) immune globulin (human)	964.6	E858.2	E934.6	E950.4	E962.0	E980.4
Rhodine	965.1	E850.3	E935.3	E950.0	E962.0	E980.0
RhoGAM	964.6	E858.2	E934.6	E950.4	E962.0	E980.4
Riboflavin	963.5	E858.1	E933.5	E950.4	E962.0	E980.4
Ricin	989.89	E866.8	—	E950.9	E962.1	E980.9
Ricinus communis	988.2	E865.3	—	E950.9	E962.1	E980.9
Rickettsial vaccine NEC	979.6	E858.8	E949.6	E950.4	E962.0	E980.4
with viral and bacterial vaccine	979.7	E858.8	E949.7	E950.4	E962.0	E980.4
Rifampin	960.6	E856	E930.6	E950.4	E962.0	E980.4
Rimifon	961.8	E857	E931.8	E950.4	E962.0	E980.4
Ringer's injection (lactated)	974.5	E858.5	E944.5	E950.4	E962.0	E980.4
Ristocetin	960.8	E856	E930.8	E950.4	E962.0	E980.4
Ritalin	969.7	E854.2	E939.7	E950.3	E962.0	E980.3
Roach killers - *see* Pesticides						
Rocky Mountain spotted fever vaccine	979.6	E858.8	E949.6	E950.4	E962.0	E980.4
Rodenticides	989.4	E863.7	—	E950.6	E962.1	E980.7
Rolaids	973.0	E858.4	E943.0	E950.4	E962.0	E980.4
Rolitetracycline	960.4	E856	E930.4	E950.4	E962.0	E980.4
Romilar	975.4	E858.6	E945.4	E950.4	E962.0	E980.4
Rose water ointment	976.3	E858.7	E946.3	E950.4	E962.0	E980.4
Rotenone	989.4	E863.7	—	E950.6	E962.1	E980.7
Rotoxamine	963.0	E858.1	E933.0	E950.4	E962.0	E980.4
Rough-on-rats	989.4	E863.7	—	E950.6	E962.1	E980.7
Rubbing alcohol	980.2	E860.3	—	E950.9	E962.1	E980.9
Rubella virus vaccine	979.4	E858.8	E949.4	E950.4	E962.0	E980.4
Rubelogen	979.4	E858.8	E949.4	E950.4	E962.0	E980.4
Rubeovax	979.4	E858.8	E949.4	E950.4	E962.0	E980.4
Rubidomycin	960.7	E856	E930.7	E950.4	E962.0	E980.4
Rue	988.2	E865.4	—	E950.9	E962.1	E980.9
Ruta	988.2	E865.4	—	E950.9	E962.1	E980.9
Sabadilla (medicinal)	976.0	E858.7	E946.0	E950.4	E962.0	E980.4
pesticide	989.4	E863.4	—	E950.6	E962.1	E980.7
Sabin oral vaccine	979.5	E858.8	E949.5	E950.4	E962.0	E980.4
Saccharated iron oxide	964.0	E858.2	E934.0	E950.4	E962.0	E980.4
Saccharin	974.5	E858.5	E944.5	E950.4	E962.0	E980.4
Safflower oil	972.2	E858.3	E942.2	E950.4	E962.0	E980.4
Salbutamol sulfate	975.7	E858.6	E945.7	E950.4	E962.0	E980.4
Salicylamide	965.1	E850.3	E935.3	E950.0	E962.0	E980.0
Salicylate(s)	965.1	E850.3	E935.3	E950.0	E962.0	E980.0
methyl	976.3	E858.7	E946.3	E950.4	E962.0	E980.4
theobromine calcium	974.1	E858.5	E944.1	E950.4	E962.0	E980.4
Salicylazosulfapyridine	961.0	E857	E931.0	E950.4	E962.0	E980.4
Salicylhydroxamic acid	976.0	E858.7	E946.0	E950.4	E962.0	E980.4
Salicylic acid (keratolytic) NEC	976.4	E858.7	E946.4	E950.4	E962.0	E980.4
congeners	965.1	E850.3	E935.3	E950.0	E962.0	E980.0
salts	965.1	E850.3	E935.3	E950.0	E962.0	E980.0
Saliniazid	961.8	E857	E931.8	E950.4	E962.0	E980.4
Salol	976.3	E858.7	E946.3	E950.4	E962.0	E980.4
Salt (substitute) NEC	974.5	E858.5	E944.5	E950.4	E962.0	E980.4
Saluretics	974.3	E858.5	E944.3	E950.4	E962.0	E980.4
Saluron	974.3	E858.5	E944.3	E950.4	E962.0	E980.4
Salvarsan 606 (neosilver) (silver)	961.1	E857	E931.1	E950.4	E962.0	E980.4
Sambucus canadensis	988.2	E865.4	—	E950.9	E962.1	E980.9
berry	988.2	E865.3	—	E950.9	E962.1	E980.9

◄► **New Code**   ◄▥ ▥► **Revised Code**

Substance	Poisoning	External Cause (E-Code)				
		Accident	Therapeutic Use	Suicide Attempt	Assault	Undetermined
Sandril	972.6	E858.3	E942.6	E950.4	E962.0	E980.4
Sanguinaria canadensis	988.2	E865.4	—	E950.9	E962.1	E980.9
Saniflush (cleaner)	983.9	E861.3	—	E950.7	E962.1	E980.6
Santonin	961.6	E857	E931.6	E950.4	E962.0	E980.4
Santyl	976.8	E858.7	E946.8	E950.4	E962.0	E980.4
Sarkomycin	960.7	E856	E930.7	E950.4	E962.0	E980.4
Saroten	969.0	E854.0	E939.0	E950.3	E962.0	E980.3
Saturnine - *see* Lead						
Savin (oil)	976.4	E858.7	E946.4	E950.4	E962.0	E980.4
Scammony	973.1	E858.4	E943.1	E950.4	E962.0	E980.4
Scarlet red	976.8	E858.7	E946.8	E950.4	E962.0	E980.4
Scheele's green	985.1	E866.3	—	E950.8	E962.1	E980.8
insecticide	985.1	E863.4	—	E950.8	E962.1	E980.8
Schradan	989.3	E863.1	—	E950.6	E962.1	E980.7
Schweinfurt(h) green	985.1	E866.3	—	E950.8	E962.1	E980.8
insecticide	985.1	E863.4	—	E950.8	E962.1	E980.8
Scilla - *see* Squill						
Sclerosing agents	972.7	E858.3	E942.7	E950.4	E962.0	E980.4
Scopolamine	971.1	E855.4	E941.1	E950.4	E962.0	E980.4
Scouring powder	989.89	E861.3	—	E950.9	E962.1	E980.9
Sea						
anemone (sting)	989.5	E905.6	—	E950.9	E962.1	E980.9
cucumber (sting)	989.5	E905.6	—	E950.9	E962.1	E980.9
snake (bite) (venom)	989.5	E905.0	—	E950.9	E962.1	E980.9
urchin spine (puncture)	989.5	E905.6	—	E950.9	E962.1	E980.9
Secbutabarbital	967.0	E851	E937.0	E950.1	E962.0	E980.1
Secbutabarbitone	967.0	E851	E937.0	E950.1	E962.0	E980.1
Secobarbital	967.0	E851	E937.0	E950.1	E962.0	E980.1
Seconal	967.0	E851	E937.0	E950.1	E962.0	E980.1
Secretin	977.8	E858.8	E947.8	E950.4	E962.0	E980.4
Sedatives, nonbarbiturate	967.9	E852.9	E937.9	E950.2	E962.0	E980.2
specified NEC	967.8	E852.8	E937.8	E950.2	E962.0	E980.2
Sedormid	967.8	E852.8	E937.8	E950.2	E962.0	E980.2
Seed (plant)	988.2	E865.3	—	E950.9	E962.1	E980.9
disinfectant or dressing	989.89	E866.5	—	E950.9	E962.1	E980.9
Selenium (fumes) NEC	985.8	E866.4	—	E950.9	E962.1	E980.9
disulfide or sulfide	976.4	E858.7	E946.4	E950.4	E962.0	E980.4
Selsun	976.4	E858.7	E946.4	E950.4	E962.0	E980.4
Senna	973.1	E858.4	E943.1	E950.4	E962.0	E980.4
Septisol	976.2	E858.7	E946.2	E950.4	E962.0	E980.4
Serax	969.4	E853.2	E939.4	E950.3	E962.0	E980.3
Serenesil	967.8	E852.8	E937.8	E950.2	E962.0	E980.2
Serenium (hydrochloride)	961.9	E857	E931.9	E950.4	E962.0	E980.4
Serepax - *see* Oxazepam						
Sernyl	968.3	E855.1	E938.3	E950.4	E962.0	E980.4
Serotonin	977.8	E858.8	E947.8	E950.4	E962.0	E980.4
Serpasil	972.6	E858.3	E942.6	E950.4	E962.0	E980.4
Sewer gas	987.8	E869.8	—	E952.8	E962.2	E982.8
Shampoo	989.6	E861.0	—	E950.9	E962.1	E980.9
Shellfish, nonbacterial or noxious	988.0	E865.1	—	E950.9	E962.1	E980.9
Silicones NEC	989.83	E866.8	E947.8	E950.9	E962.1	E980.9
Silvadene	976.0	E858.7	E946.0	E950.4	E962.0	E980.4
Silver (compound) (medicinal) NEC	976.0	E858.7	E946.0	E950.4	E962.0	E980.4
anti-infectives	976.0	E858.7	E946.0	E950.4	E962.0	E980.4
arsphenamine	961.1	E857	E931.1	E950.4	E962.0	E980.4
nitrate	976.0	E858.7	E946.0	E950.4	E962.0	E980.4
ophthalmic preparation	976.5	E858.7	E946.5	E950.4	E962.0	E980.4
toughened (keratolytic)	976.4	E858.7	E946.4	E950.4	E962.0	E980.4
nonmedicinal (dust)	985.8	E866.4	—	E950.9	E962.1	E980.9
protein (mild) (strong)	976.0	E858.7	E946.0	E950.4	E962.0	E980.4
salvarsan	961.1	E857	E931.1	E950.4	E962.0	E980.4

◄▶ **New Code**   ◄▥ ▥► **Revised Code**

Substance	Poisoning	External Cause (E-Code)				
		Accident	Therapeutic Use	Suicide Attempt	Assault	Undetermined
Simethicone	973.8	E858.4	E943.8	E950.4	E962.0	E980.4
Sinequan	969.0	E854.0	E939.0	E950.3	E962.0	E980.3
Singoserp	972.6	E858.3	E942.6	E950.4	E962.0	E980.4
Sintrom	964.2	E858.2	E934.2	E950.4	E962.0	E980.4
Sitosterols	972.2	E858.3	E942.2	E950.4	E962.0	E980.4
Skeletal muscle relaxants	975.2	E858.6	E945.2	E950.4	E962.0	E980.4
Skin						
agents (external)	976.9	E858.7	E946.9	E950.4	E962.0	E980.4
specified NEC	976.8	E858.7	E946.8	E950.4	E962.0	E980.4
test antigen	977.8	E858.8	E947.8	E950.4	E962.0	E980.4
Sleep-eze	963.0	E858.1	E933.0	E950.4	E962.0	E980.4
Sleeping draught (drug) (pill) (tablet)	967.9	E852.9	E937.9	E950.2	E962.0	E980.2
Smallpox vaccine	979.0	E858.8	E949.0	E950.4	E962.0	E980.4
Smelter fumes NEC	985.9	E866.4	—	E950.9	E962.1	E980.9
Smog	987.3	E869.1	—	E952.8	E962.2	E982.8
Smoke NEC	987.9	E869.9	—	E952.9	E962.2	E982.9
Smooth muscle relaxant	975.1	E858.6	E945.1	E950.4	E962.0	E980.4
Snail killer	989.4	E863.4	—	E950.6	E962.1	E980.7
Snake (bite) (venom)	989.5	E905.0	—	E950.9	E962.1	E980.9
Snuff	989.89	E866.8	—	E950.9	E962.1	E980.9
Soap (powder) (product)	989.6	E861.1	—	E950.9	E962.1	E980.9
medicinal, soft	976.2	E858.7	E946.2	E950.4	E962.0	E980.4
Soda (caustic)	983.2	E864.2	—	E950.7	E962.1	E980.6
bicarb	963.3	E858.1	E933.3	E950.4	E962.0	E980.4
chlorinated - *see* Sodium, hypochlorite						
Sodium						
acetosulfone	961.8	E857	E931.8	E950.4	E962.0	E980.4
acetrizoate	977.8	E858.8	E947.8	E950.4	E962.0	E980.4
amytal	967.0	E851	E937.0	E950.1	E962.0	E980.1
arsenate - *see* Arsenic						
bicarbonate	963.3	E858.1	E933.3	E950.4	E962.0	E980.4
bichromate	983.9	E864.3	—	E950.7	E962.1	E980.6
biphosphate	963.2	E858.1	E933.2	E950.4	E962.0	E980.4
bisulfate	983.9	E864.3	—	E950.7	E962.1	E980.6
borate (cleanser)	989.6	E861.3	—	E950.9	E962.1	E980.9
bromide NEC	967.3	E852.2	E937.3	E950.2	E962.0	E980.2
cacodylate (nonmedicinal) NEC	978.8	E858.8	E948.8	E950.4	E962.0	E980.4
anti-infective	961.1	E857	E931.1	E950.4	E962.0	E980.4
herbicide	989.4	E863.5	—	E950.6	E962.1	E980.7
calcium edetate	963.8	E858.1	E933.8	E950.4	E962.0	E980.4
carbonate NEC	983.2	E864.2	—	E950.7	E962.1	E980.6
chlorate NEC	983.9	E864.3	—	E950.7	E962.1	E980.6
herbicide	983.9	E863.5	—	E950.7	E962.1	E980.6
chloride NEC	974.5	E858.5	E944.5	E950.4	E962.0	E980.4
chromate	983.9	E864.3	—	E950.7	E962.1	E980.6
citrate	963.3	E858.1	E933.3	E950.4	E962.0	E980.4
cyanide - *see* Cyanide(s)						
cyclamate	974.5	E858.5	E944.5	E950.4	E962.0	E980.4
diatrizoate	977.8	E858.8	E947.8	E950.4	E962.0	E980.4
dibunate	975.4	E858.6	E945.4	E950.4	E962.0	E980.4
dioctyl sulfosuccinate	973.2	E858.4	E943.2	E950.4	E962.0	E980.4
edetate	963.8	E858.1	E933.8	E950.4	E962.0	E980.4
ethacrynate	974.4	E858.5	E944.4	E950.4	E962.0	E980.4
fluoracetate (dust) (rodenticide)	989.4	E863.7	—	E950.6	E962.1	E980.7
fluoride - *see* Fluoride(s)						
free salt	974.5	E858.5	E944.5	E950.4	E962.0	E980.4
glucosulfone	961.8	E857	E931.8	E950.4	E962.0	E980.4
hydroxide	983.2	E864.2	—	E950.7	E962.1	E980.6
hypochlorite (bleach) NEC	983.9	E864.3	—	E950.7	E962.1	E980.6
disinfectant	983.9	E861.4	—	E950.7	E962.1	E980.6
medicinal (anti-infective) (external)	976.0	E858.7	E946.0	E950.4	E962.0	E980.4
vapor	987.8	E869.8	—	E952.8	E962.2	E982.8

◀▶ **New Code**   ◀▥▥▶ **Revised Code**

Substance	Poisoning	External Cause (E-Code)				
		Accident	Therapeutic Use	Suicide Attempt	Assault	Undetermined
Sodium *(Continued)*						
hyposulfite	976.0	E858.7	E946.0	E950.4	E962.0	E980.4
indigotindisulfonate	977.8	E858.8	E947.8	E950.4	E962.0	E980.4
iodide	977.8	E858.8	E947.8	E950.4	E962.0	E980.4
iothalamate	977.8	E858.8	E947.8	E950.4	E962.0	E980.4
iron edetate	964.0	E858.2	E934.0	E950.4	E962.0	E980.4
lactate	963.3	E858.1	E933.3	E950.4	E962.0	E980.4
lauryl sulfate	976.2	E858.7	E946.2	E950.4	E962.0	E980.4
L-triiodothyronine	962.7	E858.0	E932.7	E950.4	E962.0	E980.4
metrizoate	977.8	E858.8	E947.8	E950.4	E962.0	E980.4
monofluoracetate (dust) (rodenticide)	989.4	E863.7	—	E950.6	E962.1	E980.7
morrhuate	972.7	E858.3	E942.7	E950.4	E962.0	E980.4
nafcillin	960.0	E856	E930.0	E950.4	E962.0	E980.4
nitrate (oxidizing agent)	983.9	E864.3	—	E950.7	E962.1	E980.6
nitrite (medicinal)	972.4	E858.3	E942.4	E950.4	E962.0	E980.4
nitroferricyanide	972.6	E858.3	E942.6	E950.4	E962.0	E980.4
nitroprusside	972.6	E858.3	E942.6	E950.4	E962.0	E980.4
para-aminohippurate	977.8	E858.8	E947.8	E950.4	E962.0	E980.4
perborate (nonmedicinal) NEC	989.89	E866.8	—	E950.9	E962.1	E980.9
medicinal	976.6	E858.7	E946.6	E950.4	E962.0	E980.4
soap	989.6	E861.1	—	E950.9	E962.1	E980.9
percarbonate - *see* Sodium, perborate						
phosphate	973.3	E858.4	E943.3	E950.4	E962.0	E980.4
polystyrene sulfonate	974.5	E858.5	E944.5	E950.4	E962.0	E980.4
propionate	976.0	E858.7	E946.0	E950.4	E962.0	E980.4
psylliate	972.7	E858.3	E942.7	E950.4	E962.0	E980.4
removing resins	974.5	E858.5	E944.5	E950.4	E962.0	E980.4
salicylate	965.1	E850.3	E935.3	E950.0	E962.0	E980.0
sulfate	973.3	E858.4	E943.3	E950.4	E962.0	E980.4
sulfoxone	961.8	E857	E931.8	E950.4	E962.0	E980.4
tetradecyl sulfate	972.7	E858.3	E942.7	E950.4	E962.0	E980.4
thiopental	968.3	E855.1	E938.3	E950.4	E962.0	E980.4
thiosalicylate	965.1	E850.3	E935.3	E950.0	E962.0	E980.0
thiosulfate	976.0	E858.7	E946.0	E950.4	E962.0	E980.4
tolbutamide	977.8	E858.8	E947.8	E950.4	E962.0	E980.4
tyropanoate	977.8	E858.8	E947.8	E950.4	E962.0	E980.4
valproate	966.3	E855.0	E936.3	E950.4	E962.0	E980.4
Solanine	977.8	E858.8	E947.8	E950.4	E962.0	E980.4
Solanum dulcamara	988.2	E865.4	—	E950.9	E962.1	E980.9
Solapsone	961.8	E857	E931.8	E950.4	E962.0	E980.4
Solasulfone	961.8	E857	E931.8	E950.4	E962.0	E980.4
Soldering fluid	983.1	E864.1	—	E950.7	E962.1	E980.6
Solid substance	989.9	E866.9	—	E950.9	E962.1	E980.9
specified NEC	989.9	E866.8	—	E950.9	E962.1	E980.9
Solvents, industrial	982.8	E862.9	—	E950.9	E962.1	E980.9
naphtha	981	E862.0	—	E950.9	E962.1	E980.9
petroleum	981	E862.0	—	E950.9	E962.1	E980.9
specified NEC	982.8	E862.4	—	E950.9	E962.1	E980.9
Soma	968.0	E855.1	E938.0	E950.4	E962.0	E980.4
Somatotropin	962.4	E858.0	E932.4	E950.4	E962.0	E980.4
Sominex	963.0	E858.1	E933.0	E950.4	E962.0	E980.4
Somnos	967.1	E852.0	E937.1	E950.2	E962.0	E980.2
Somonal	967.0	E851	E937.0	E950.1	E962.0	E980.1
Soneryl	967.0	E851	E937.0	E950.1	E962.0	E980.1
Soothing syrup	977.9	E858.9	E947.9	E950.5	E962.0	E980.5
Sopor	967.4	E852.3	E937.4	E950.2	E962.0	E980.2
Soporific drug	967.9	E852.9	E937.9	E950.2	E962.0	E980.2
specified type NEC	967.8	E852.8	E937.8	E950.2	E962.0	E980.2
Sorbitol NEC	977.4	E858.8	E947.4	E950.4	E962.0	E980.4
Sotradecol	972.7	E858.3	E942.7	E950.4	E962.0	E980.4
Spacoline	975.1	E858.6	E945.1	E950.4	E962.0	E980.4
Spanish fly	976.8	E858.7	E946.8	E950.4	E962.0	E980.4

◀▶ **New Code**   ◀▥▥▶ **Revised Code**

Substance	Poisoning	External Cause (E-Code)				
		Accident	Therapeutic Use	Suicide Attempt	Assault	Undetermined
Sparine	969.1	E853.0	E939.1	E950.3	E962.0	E980.3
Sparteine	975.0	E858.6	E945.0	E950.4	E962.0	E980.4
Spasmolytics	975.1	E858.6	E945.1	E950.4	E962.0	E980.4
anticholinergics	971.1	E855.4	E941.1	E950.4	E962.0	E980.4
Spectinomycin	960.8	E856	E930.8	E950.4	E962.0	E980.4
Speed	969.7	E854.2	E939.7	E950.3	E962.0	E980.3
Spermicides	976.8	E858.7	E946.8	E950.4	E962.0	E980.4
Spider (bite) (venom)	989.5	E905.1	—	E950.9	E962.1	E980.9
antivenin	979.9	E858.8	E949.9	E950.4	E962.0	E980.4
Spigelia (root)	961.6	E857	E931.6	E950.4	E962.0	E980.4
Spiperone	969.2	E853.1	E939.2	E950.3	E962.0	E980.3
Spiramycin	960.3	E856	E930.3	E950.4	E962.0	E980.4
Spirilene	969.5	E853.8	E939.5	E950.3	E962.0	E980.3
Spirit(s) (neutral) NEC	980.0	E860.1	—	E950.9	E962.1	E980.9
beverage	980.0	E860.0	—	E950.9	E962.1	E980.9
industrial	980.9	E860.9	—	E950.9	E962.1	E980.9
mineral	981	E862.0	—	E950.9	E962.1	E980.9
of salt - *see* Hydrochloric acid						
surgical	980.9	E860.9	—	E950.9	E962.1	E980.9
Spironolactone	974.4	E858.5	E944.4	E950.4	E962.0	E980.4
Sponge, absorbable (gelatin)	964.5	E858.2	E934.5	E950.4	E962.0	E980.4
Sporostacin	976.0	E858.7	E946.0	E950.4	E962.0	E980.4
Sprays (aerosol)	989.89	E866.8	—	E950.9	E962.1	E980.9
cosmetic	989.89	E866.7	—	E950.9	E962.1	E980.9
medicinal NEC	977.9	E858.9	E947.9	E950.5	E962.0	E980.5
pesticides - *see* Pesticides						
specified content - *see* substance specified						
Spurge flax	988.2	E865.4	—	E950.9	E962.1	E980.9
Spurges	988.2	E865.4	—	E950.9	E962.1	E980.9
Squill (expectorant) NEC	975.5	E858.6	E945.5	E950.4	E962.0	E980.4
rat poison	989.4	E863.7	—	E950.6	E962.1	E980.7
Squirting cucumber (cathartic)	973.1	E858.4	E943.1	E950.4	E962.0	E980.4
Stains	989.89	E866.8	—	E950.9	E962.1	E980.9
Stannous - *see also* Tin fluoride	976.7	E858.7	E946.7	E950.4	E962.0	E980.4
Stanolone	962.1	E858.0	E932.1	E950.4	E962.0	E980.4
Stanozolol	962.1	E858.0	E932.1	E950.4	E962.0	E980.4
Staphisagria or stavesacre (pediculicide)	976.0	E858.7	E946.0	E950.4	E962.0	E980.4
Stelazine	969.1	E853.0	E939.1	E950.3	E962.0	E980.3
Stemetil	969.1	E853.0	E939.1	E950.3	E962.0	E980.3
Sterculia (cathartic) (gum)	973.3	E858.4	E943.3	E950.4	E962.0	E980.4
Sternutator gas	987.8	E869.8	—	E952.8	E962.2	E982.8
Steroids NEC	962.0	E858.0	E932.0	E950.4	E962.0	E980.4
ENT agent	976.6	E858.7	E946.6	E950.4	E962.0	E980.4
ophthalmic preparation	976.5	E858.7	E946.5	E950.4	E962.0	E980.4
topical NEC	976.0	E858.7	E946.0	E950.4	E962.0	E980.4
Stibine	985.8	E866.4	—	E950.9	E962.1	E980.9
Stibophen	961.2	E857	E931.2	E950.4	E962.0	E980.4
Stilbamide, stilbamidine	961.5	E857	E931.5	E950.4	E962.0	E980.4
Stilbestrol	962.2	E858.0	E932.2	E950.4	E962.0	E980.4
Stimulants (central nervous system)	970.9	E854.3	E940.9	E950.4	E962.0	E980.4
analeptics	970.0	E854.3	E940.0	E950.4	E962.0	E980.4
opiate antagonist	970.1	E854.3	E940.1	E950.4	E962.0	E980.4
psychotherapeutic NEC	969.0	E854.0	E939.0	E950.3	E962.0	E980.3
specified NEC	970.8	E854.3	E940.8	E950.4	E962.0	E980.4
Storage batteries (acid) (cells)	983.1	E864.1	—	E950.7	E962.1	E980.6
Stovaine	968.9	E855.2	E938.9	E950.4	E962.0	E980.4
infiltration (subcutaneous)	968.5	E855.2	E938.5	E950.4	E962.0	E980.4
nerve block (peripheral) (plexus)	968.6	E855.2	E938.6	E950.4	E962.0	E980.4
spinal	968.7	E855.2	E938.7	E950.4	E962.0	E980.4
topical (surface)	968.5	E855.2	E938.5	E950.4	E962.0	E980.4
Stovarsal	961.1	E857	E931.1	E950.4	E962.0	E980.4

Substance	Poisoning	External Cause (E-Code)				
		Accident	Therapeutic Use	Suicide Attempt	Assault	Undetermined
Stove gas - *see* Gas, utility						
Stoxil	976.5	E858.7	E946.5	E950.4	E962.0	E980.4
STP	969.6	E854.1	E939.6	E950.3	E962.0	E980.3
Stramonium (medicinal) NEC	971.1	E855.4	E941.1	E950.4	E962.0	E980.4
natural state	988.2	E865.4	—	E950.9	E962.1	E980.9
Streptodornase	964.4	E858.2	E934.4	E950.4	E962.0	E980.4
Streptoduocin	960.6	E856	E930.6	E950.4	E962.0	E980.4
Streptokinase	964.4	E858.2	E934.4	E950.4	E962.0	E980.4
Streptomycin	960.6	E856	E930.6	E950.4	E962.0	E980.4
Streptozocin	960.7	E856	E930.7	E950.4	E962.0	E980.4
Stripper (paint) (solvent)	982.8	E862.9	—	E950.9	E962.1	E980.9
Strobane	989.2	E863.0	—	E950.6	E962.1	E980.7
Strophanthin	972.1	E858.3	E942.1	E950.4	E962.0	E980.4
Strophanthus hispidus or kombe	988.2	E865.4	—	E950.9	E962.1	E980.9
Strychnine (rodenticide) (salts)	989.1	E863.7	—	E950.6	E962.1	E980.7
medicinal NEC	970.8	E854.3	E940.8	E950.4	E962.0	E980.4
Strychnos (ignatii) - *see* Strychnine						
Styramate	968.0	E855.1	E938.0	E950.4	E962.0	E980.4
Styrene	983.0	E864.0	—	E950.7	E962.1	E980.6
Succinimide (anticonvulsant)	966.2	E855.0	E936.2	E950.4	E962.0	E980.4
mercuric - *see* Mercury						
Succinylcholine	975.2	E858.6	E945.2	E950.4	E962.0	E980.4
Succinylsulfathiazole	961.0	E857	E931.0	E950.4	E962.0	E980.4
Sucrose	974.5	E858.5	E944.5	E950.4	E962.0	E980.4
Sulfacetamide	961.0	E857	E931.0	E950.4	E962.0	E980.4
ophthalmic preparation	976.5	E858.7	E946.5	E950.4	E962.0	E980.4
Sulfachlorpyridazine	961.0	E857	E931.0	E950.4	E962.0	E980.4
Sulfacytine	961.0	E857	E931.0	E950.4	E962.0	E980.4
Sulfadiazine	961.0	E857	E931.0	E950.4	E962.0	E980.4
silver (topical)	976.0	E858.7	E946.0	E950.4	E962.0	E980.4
Sulfadimethoxine	961.0	E857	E931.0	E950.4	E962.0	E980.4
Sulfadimidine	961.0	E857	E931.0	E950.4	E962.0	E980.4
Sulfaethidole	961.0	E857	E931.0	E950.4	E962.0	E980.4
Sulfafurazole	961.0	E857	E931.0	E950.4	E962.0	E980.4
Sulfaguanidine	961.0	E857	E931.0	E950.4	E962.0	E980.4
Sulfamerazine	961.0	E857	E931.0	E950.4	E962.0	E980.4
Sulfameter	961.0	E857	E931.0	E950.4	E962.0	E980.4
Sulfamethizole	961.0	E857	E931.0	E950.4	E962.0	E980.4
Sulfamethoxazole	961.0	E857	E931.0	E950.4	E962.0	E980.4
Sulfamethoxydiazine	961.0	E857	E931.0	E950.4	E962.0	E980.4
Sulfamethoxypyridazine	961.0	E857	E931.0	E950.4	E962.0	E980.4
Sulfamethylthiazole	961.0	E857	E931.0	E950.4	E962.0	E980.4
Sulfamylon	976.0	E858.7	E946.0	E950.4	E962.0	E980.4
Sulfan blue (diagnostic dye)	977.8	E858.8	E947.8	E950.4	E962.0	E980.4
Sulfanilamide	961.0	E857	E931.0	E950.4	E962.0	E980.4
Sulfanilylguanidine	961.0	E857	E931.0	E950.4	E962.0	E980.4
Sulfaphenazole	961.0	E857	E931.0	E950.4	E962.0	E980.4
Sulfaphenylthiazole	961.0	E857	E931.0	E950.4	E962.0	E980.4
Sulfaproxyline	961.0	E857	E931.0	E950.4	E962.0	E980.4
Sulfapyridine	961.0	E857	E931.0	E950.4	E962.0	E980.4
Sulfapyrimidine	961.0	E857	E931.0	E950.4	E962.0	E980.4
Sulfarsphenamine	961.1	E857	E931.1	E950.4	E962.0	E980.4
Sulfasalazine	961.0	E857	E931.0	E950.4	E962.0	E980.4
Sulfasomizole	961.0	E857	E931.0	E950.4	E962.0	E980.4
Sulfasuxidine	961.0	E857	E931.0	E950.4	E962.0	E980.4
Sulfinpyrazone	974.7	E858.5	E944.7	E950.4	E962.0	E980.4
Sulfisoxazole	961.0	E857	E931.0	E950.4	E962.0	E980.4
ophthalmic preparation	976.5	E858.7	E946.5	E950.4	E962.0	E980.4
Sulfomyxin	960.8	E856	E930.8	E950.4	E962.0	E980.4
Sulfonal	967.8	E852.8	E937.8	E950.2	E962.0	E980.2
Sulfonamides (mixtures)	961.0	E857	E931.0	E950.4	E962.0	E980.4

◀▶ **New Code**　　　◀▦▦▶ **Revised Code**

Substance	Poisoning	External Cause (E-Code)				
		Accident	Therapeutic Use	Suicide Attempt	Assault	Undetermined
Sulfones	961.8	E857	E931.8	E950.4	E962.0	E980.4
Sulfonethylmethane	967.8	E852.8	E937.8	E950.2	E962.0	E980.2
Sulfonmethane	967.8	E852.8	E937.8	E950.2	E962.0	E980.2
Sulfonphthal, sulfonphthol	977.8	E858.8	E947.8	E950.4	E962.0	E980.4
Sulfonylurea derivatives, oral	962.3	E858.0	E932.3	E950.4	E962.0	E980.4
Sulfoxone	961.8	E857	E931.8	E950.4	E962.0	E980.4
Sulfur, sulfureted, sulfuric, sulfurous, sulfuryl (compounds) NEC	989.89	E866.8	—	E950.9	E962.1	E980.9
acid	983.1	E864.1	—	E950.7	E962.1	E980.6
dioxide	987.3	E869.1	—	E952.8	E962.2	E982.8
ether - *see* Ether(s)						
hydrogen	987.8	E869.8	—	E952.8	E962.2	E982.8
medicinal (keratolytic) (ointment) NEC	976.4	E858.7	E946.4	E950.4	E962.0	E980.4
pesticide (vapor)	989.4	E863.4	—	E950.6	E962.1	E980.7
vapor NEC	987.8	E869.8	—	E952.8	E962.2	E982.8
Sulkowitch's reagent	977.8	E858.8	E947.8	E950.4	E962.0	E980.4
Sulph - *see also* Sulf-						
Sulphadione	961.8	E857	E931.8	E950.4	E962.0	E980.4
Sulthiame, sultiame	966.3	E855.0	E936.3	E950.4	E962.0	E980.4
Superinone	975.5	E858.6	E945.5	E950.4	E962.0	E980.4
Suramin	961.5	E857	E931.5	E950.4	E962.0	E980.4
Surfacaine	968.5	E855.2	E938.5	E950.4	E962.0	E980.4
Surital	968.3	E855.1	E938.3	E950.4	E962.0	E980.4
Sutilains	976.8	E858.7	E946.8	E950.4	E962.0	E980.4
Suxamethonium (bromide) (chloride) (iodide)	975.2	E858.6	E945.2	E950.4	E962.0	E980.4
Suxethonium (bromide)	975.2	E858.6	E945.2	E950.4	E962.0	E980.4
Sweet oil (birch)	976.3	E858.7	E946.3	E950.4	E962.0	E980.4
Sym-dichloroethyl ether	982.3	E862.4	—	E950.9	E962.1	E980.9
Sympatholytics	971.3	E855.6	E941.3	E950.4	E962.0	E980.4
Sympathomimetics	971.2	E855.5	E941.2	E950.4	E962.0	E980.4
Synalar	976.0	E858.7	E946.0	E950.4	E962.0	E980.4
Synthroid	962.7	E858.0	E932.7	E950.4	E962.0	E980.4
Syntocinon	975.0	E858.6	E945.0	E950.4	E962.0	E950.4
Syrosingopine	972.6	E858.3	E942.6	E950.4	E962.0	E980.4
Systemic agents (primarily)	963.9	E858.1	E933.9	E950.4	E962.0	E980.4
specified NEC	963.8	E858.1	E933.8	E950.4	E962.0	E980.4
Tablets (*see also* specified substance)	977.9	E858.9	E947.9	E950.5	E962.0	E980.5
Tace	962.2	E858.0	E932.2	E950.4	E962.0	E980.4
Tacrine	971.0	E855.3	E941.0	E950.4	E962.0	E980.4
Talbutal	967.0	E851	E937.0	E950.1	E962.0	E980.1
Talc	976.3	E858.7	E946.3	E950.4	E962.0	E980.4
Talcum	976.3	E858.7	E946.3	E950.4	E962.0	E980.4
Tandearil, tanderil	965.5	E850.5	E935.5	E950.0	E962.0	E980.0
Tannic acid	983.1	E864.1	—	E950.7	E962.1	E980.6
medicinal (astringent)	976.2	E858.7	E946.2	E950.4	E962.0	E980.4
Tannin - *see* Tannic acid						
Tansy	988.2	E865.4	—	E950.9	E962.1	E980.9
TAO	960.3	E856	E930.3	E950.4	E962.0	E980.4
Tapazole	962.8	E858.0	E932.8	E950.4	E962.0	E980.4
Tar NEC	983.0	E864.0	—	E950.7	E962.1	E980.6
camphor - *see* Naphthalene						
fumes	987.8	E869.8	—	E952.8	E962.2	E982.8
Taractan	969.3	E853.8	E939.3	E950.3	E962.0	E980.3
Tarantula (venomous)	989.5	E905.1	—	E950.9	E962.1	E980.9
Tartar emetic (anti-infective)	961.2	E857	E931.2	E950.4	E962.0	E980.4
Tartaric acid	983.1	E864.1	—	E950.7	E962.1	E980.6
Tartrated antimony (anti-infective)	961.2	E857	E931.2	E950.4	E962.0	E980.4
TCA - *see* Trichloroacetic acid						
TDI	983.0	E864.0	—	E950.7	E962.1	E980.6
vapor	987.8	E869.8	—	E952.8	E962.2	E982.8
Tear gas	987.5	E869.3	—	E952.8	E962.2	E982.8
Teclothiazide	974.3	E858.5	E944.3	E950.4	E962.0	E980.4

◄▶ **New Code**   ⬅▦▦➡ **Revised Code**

Substance	Poisoning	External Cause (E-Code)				
		Accident	Therapeutic Use	Suicide Attempt	Assault	Undetermined
Tegretol	966.3	E855.0	E936.3	E950.4	E962.0	E980.4
Telepaque	977.8	E858.8	E947.8	E950.4	E962.0	E980.4
Tellurium	985.8	E866.4	—	E950.9	E962.1	E980.9
fumes	985.8	E866.4	—	E950.9	E962.1	E980.9
TEM	963.1	E858.1	E933.1	E950.4	E962.0	E980.4
Temazepam - *see* Benzodiazepines						
TEPA	963.1	E858.1	E933.1	E950.4	E962.0	E980.4
TEPP	989.3	E863.1	—	E950.6	E962.1	E980.7
Terbutaline	971.2	E855.5	E941.2	E950.4	E962.0	E980.4
Teroxalene	961.6	E857	E931.6	E950.4	E962.0	E980.4
Terpin hydrate	975.5	E858.6	E945.5	E950.4	E962.0	E980.4
Terramycin	960.4	E856	E930.4	E950.4	E962.0	E980.4
Tessalon	975.4	E858.6	E945.4	E950.4	E962.0	E980.4
Testosterone	962.1	E858.0	E932.1	E950.4	E962.0	E980.4
Tetanus (vaccine)	978.4	E858.8	E948.4	E950.4	E962.0	E980.4
antitoxin	979.9	E858.8	E949.9	E950.4	E962.0	E980.4
immune globulin (human)	964.6	E858.2	E934.6	E950.4	E962.0	E980.4
toxoid	978.4	E858.8	E948.4	E950.4	E962.0	E980.4
with diphtheria toxoid	978.9	E858.8	E948.9	E950.4	E962.0	E980.4
with pertussis	978.6	E858.8	E948.6	E950.4	E962.0	E980.4
Tetrabenazine	969.5	E853.8	E939.5	E950.3	E962.0	E980.3
Tetracaine (infiltration) (topical)	968.5	E855.2	E938.5	E950.4	E962.0	E980.4
nerve block (peripheral) (plexus)	968.6	E855.2	E938.6	E950.4	E962.0	E980.4
spinal	968.7	E855.2	E938.7	E950.4	E962.0	E980.4
Tetrachlorethylene - *see* Tetrachloroethylene						
Tetrachlormethiazide	974.3	E858.5	E944.3	E950.4	E962.0	E980.4
Tetrachloroethane (liquid) (vapor)	982.3	E862.4	—	E950.9	E962.1	E980.9
paint or varnish	982.3	E861.6	—	E950.9	E962.1	E980.9
Tetrachloroethylene (liquid) (vapor)	982.3	E862.4	—	E950.9	E962.1	E980.9
medicinal	961.6	E857	E931.6	E950.4	E962.0	E980.4
Tetrachloromethane - *see* Carbon, tetrachloride						
Tetracycline	960.4	E856	E930.4	E950.4	E962.0	E980.4
ophthalmic preparation	976.5	E858.7	E946.5	E950.4	E962.0	E980.4
topical NEC	976.0	E858.7	E946.0	E950.4	E962.0	E980.4
Tetraethylammonium chloride	972.3	E858.3	E942.3	E950.4	E962.0	E980.4
Tetraethyl lead (antiknock compound)	984.1	E862.1	—	E950.9	E962.1	E980.9
Tetraethyl pyrophosphate	989.3	E863.1	—	E950.6	E962.1	E980.7
Tetraethylthiuram disulfide	977.3	E858.8	E947.3	E950.4	E962.0	E980.4
Tetrahydroaminoacridine	971.0	E855.3	E941.0	E950.4	E962.0	E980.4
Tetrahydrocannabinol	969.6	E854.1	E939.6	E950.3	E962.0	E980.3
Tetrahydronaphthalene	982.0	E862.4	—	E950.9	E962.1	E980.9
Tetrahydrozoline	971.2	E855.5	E941.2	E950.4	E962.0	E980.4
Tetralin	982.0	E862.4	—	E950.9	E962.1	E980.9
Tetramethylthiuram (disulfide) NEC	989.4	E863.6	—	E950.6	E962.1	E980.7
medicinal	976.2	E858.7	E946.2	E950.4	E962.0	E980.4
Tetronal	967.8	E852.8	E937.8	E950.2	E962.0	E980.2
Tetryl	983.0	E864.0	—	E950.7	E962.1	E980.6
Thalidomide	967.8	E852.8	E937.8	E950.2	E962.0	E980.2
Thallium (compounds) (dust) NEC	985.8	E866.4	—	E950.9	E962.1	E980.9
pesticide (rodenticide)	985.8	E863.7	—	E950.6	E962.1	E980.7
THC	969.6	E854.1	E939.6	E950.3	E962.0	E980.3
Thebacon	965.09	E850.2	E935.2	E950.0	E962.0	E980.0
Thebaine	965.09	E850.2	E935.2	E950.0	E962.0	E980.0
Theobromine (calcium salicylate)	974.1	E858.5	E944.1	E950.4	E962.0	E980.4
Theophylline (diuretic)	974.1	E858.5	E944.1	E950.4	E962.0	E980.4
ethylenediamine	975.7	E858.6	E945.7	E950.4	E962.0	E980.4
Thiabendazole	961.6	E857	E931.6	E950.4	E962.0	E980.4
Thialbarbital, thialbarbitone	968.3	E855.1	E938.3	E950.4	E962.0	E980.4
Thiamine	963.5	E858.1	E933.5	E950.4	E962.0	E980.4
Thiamylal (sodium)	968.3	E855.1	E938.3	E950.4	E962.0	E980.4
Thiazesim	969.0	E854.0	E939.0	E950.3	E962.0	E980.3

◄► New Code   ◄▥▥▥▷ Revised Code

Substance	Poisoning	External Cause (E-Code)				
		Accident	Therapeutic Use	Suicide Attempt	Assault	Undetermined
Thiazides (diuretics)	974.3	E858.5	E944.3	E950.4	E962.0	E980.4
Thiethylperazine	963.0	E858.1	E933.0	E950.4	E962.0	E980.4
Thimerosal (topical)	976.0	E858.7	E946.0	E950.4	E962.0	E980.4
ophthalmic preparation	976.5	E858.7	E946.5	E950.4	E962.0	E980.4
Thioacetazone	961.8	E857	E931.8	E950.4	E962.0	E980.4
Thiobarbiturates	968.3	E855.1	E938.3	E950.4	E962.0	E980.4
Thiobismol	961.2	E857	E931.2	E950.4	E962.0	E980.4
Thiocarbamide	962.8	E858.0	E932.8	E950.4	E962.0	E980.4
Thiocarbarsone	961.1	E857	E931.1	E950.4	E962.0	E980.4
Thiocarlide	961.8	E857	E931.8	E950.4	E962.0	E980.4
Thioguanine	963.1	E858.1	E933.1	E950.4	E962.0	E980.4
Thiomercaptomerin	974.0	E858.5	E944.0	E950.4	E962.0	E980.4
Thiomerin	974.0	E858.5	E944.0	E950.4	E962.0	E980.4
Thiopental, thiopentone (sodium)	968.3	E855.1	E938.3	E950.4	E962.0	E980.4
Thiopropazate	969.1	E853.0	E939.1	E950.3	E962.0	E980.3
Thioproperazine	969.1	E853.0	E939.1	E950.3	E962.0	E980.3
Thioridazine	969.1	E853.0	E939.1	E950.3	E962.0	E980.3
Thio-TEPA, thiotepa	963.1	E858.1	E933.1	E950.4	E962.0	E980.4
Thiothixene	969.3	E853.8	E939.3	E950.3	E962.0	E980.3
Thiouracil	962.8	E858.0	E932.8	E950.4	E962.0	E980.4
Thiourea	962.8	E858.0	E932.8	E950.4	E962.0	E980.4
Thiphenamil	971.1	E855.4	E941.1	E950.4	E962.0	E980.4
Thiram NEC	989.4	E863.	—	E950.6	E962.1	E980.7
medicinal	976.2	E858.7	E946.2	E950.4	E962.0	E980.4
Thonzylamine	963.0	E858.1	E933.0	E950.4	E962.0	E980.4
Thorazine	969.1	E853.0	E939.1	E950.3	E962.0	E980.3
Thornapple	988.2	E865.4	—	E950.9	E962.1	E980.9
Throat preparation (lozenges) NEC	976.6	E858.7	E946.6	E950.4	E962.0	E980.4
Thrombin	964.5	E858.2	E934.5	E950.4	E962.0	E980.4
Thrombolysin	964.4	E858.2	E934.4	E950.4	E962.0	E980.4
Thymol	983.0	E864.0	—	E950.7	E962.1	E980.6
Thymus extract	962.9	E858.0	E932.9	E950.4	E962.0	E980.4
Thyroglobulin	962.7	E858.0	E932.7	E950.4	E962.0	E980.4
Thyroid (derivatives) (extract)	962.7	E858.0	E932.7	E950.4	E962.0	E980.4
Thyrolar	962.7	E858.0	E932.7	E950.4	E962.0	E980.4
Thyrotrophin, thyrotropin	977.8	E858.8	E947.8	E950.4	E962.0	E980.4
Thyroxin(e)	962.7	E858.0	E932.7	E950.4	E962.0	E980.4
Tigan	963.0	E858.1	E933.0	E950.4	E962.0	E980.4
Tigloidine	968.0	E855.1	E938.0	E950.4	E962.0	E980.4
Tin (chloride) (dust) (oxide) NEC	985.8	E866.4	—	E950.9	E962.1	E980.9
anti-infectives	961.2	E857	E931.2	E950.4	E962.0	E980.4
Tinactin	976.0	E858.7	E946.0	E950.4	E962.0	E980.4
Tincture, iodine - *see* Iodine						
Tindal	969.1	E853.0	E939.1	E950.3	E962.0	E980.3
Titanium (compounds) (vapor)	985.8	E866.4	—	E950.9	E962.1	E980.9
ointment	976.3	E858.7	E946.3	E950.4	E962.0	E980.4
Titroid	962.7	E858.0	E932.7	E950.4	E962.0	E980.4
TMTD - *see* Tetramethylthiuram disulfide						
TNT	989.89	E866.8	—	E950.9	E962.1	E980.9
fumes	987.8	E869.8	—	E952.8	E962.2	E982.8
Toadstool	988.1	E865.5	—	E950.9	E962.1	E980.9
Tobacco NEC	989.84	E866.8	—	E950.9	E962.1	E980.9
Indian	988.2	E865.4	—	E950.9	E962.1	E980.9
smoke, second-hand	987.8	E869.4	—	—	—	—
Tocopherol	963.5	E858.1	E933.5	E950.4	E962.0	E980.4
Tocosamine	975.0	E858.6	E945.0	E950.4	E962.0	E980.4
Tofranil	969.0	E854.0	E939.0	E950.3	E962.0	E980.3
Toilet deodorizer	989.89	E866.8	—	E950.9	E962.1	E980.9
Tolazamide	962.3	E858.0	E932.3	E950.4	E962.0	E980.4
Tolazoline	971.3	E855.6	E941.3	E950.4	E962.0	E980.4
Tolbutamide	962.3	E858.0	E932.3	E950.4	E962.0	E980.4
sodium	977.8	E858.8	E947.8	E950.4	E962.0	E980.4

◀▶ **New Code**   ◀┅ ┅▶ **Revised Code**

Substance	Poisoning	External Cause (E-Code)				
		Accident	Therapeutic Use	Suicide Attempt	Assault	Undetermined
Tolmetin	965.6	E856.0	E935.6	E950.0	E962.0	E980.0
Tolnaftate	976.0	E858.7	E946.0	E950.4	E962.0	E980.4
Tolpropamine	976.1	E858.7	E946.1	E950.4	E962.0	E980.4
Tolserol	968.0	E855.1	E938.0	E950.4	E962.0	E980.4
Toluene (liquid) (vapor)	982.0	E862.4	—	E950.9	E962.1	E980.9
diisocyanate	983.0	E864.0	—	E950.7	E962.1	E980.6
Toluidine	983.0	E864.0	—	E950.7	E962.1	E980.6
vapor	987.8	E869.8	—	E952.8	E962.2	E982.8
Toluol (liquid) (vapor)	982.0	E862.4	—	E950.9	E962.1	E980.9
Tolylene-2,4-diisocyanate	983.0	E864.0	—	E950.7	E962.1	E980.6
Tonics, cardiac	972.1	E858.3	E942.1	E950.4	E962.0	E980.4
Toxaphene (dust) (spray)	989.2	E863.0	—	E950.6	E962.1	E980.7
Toxoids NEC	978.8	E858.8	E948.8	E950.4	E962.0	E980.4
Tractor fuel NEC	981	E862.1	—	E950.9	E962.1	E980.9
Tragacanth	973.3	E858.4	E943.3	E950.4	E962.0	E980.4
Tramazoline	971.2	E855.5	E941.2	E950.4	E962.0	E980.4
Tranquilizers	969.5	E853.9	E939.5	E950.3	E962.0	E980.3
benzodiazepine-based	969.4	E853.2	E939.4	E950.3	E962.0	E980.3
butyrophenone-based	969.2	E853.1	E939.2	E950.3	E962.0	E980.3
major NEC	969.3	E853.8	E939.3	E950.3	E962.0	E980.3
phenothiazine-based	969.1	E853.0	E939.1	E950.3	E962.0	E980.3
specified NEC	969.5	E853.8	E939.5	E950.3	E962.0	E980.3
Trantoin	961.9	E857	E931.9	E950.4	E962.0	E980.4
Tranxene	969.4	E853.2	E939.4	E950.3	E962.0	E980.3
Tranylcypromine (sulfate)	969.0	E854.0	E939.0	E950.3	E962.0	E980.3
Trasentine	975.1	E858.6	E945.1	E950.4	E962.0	E980.4
Travert	974.5	E858.5	E944.5	E950.4	E962.0	E980.4
Trecator	961.8	E857	E931.8	E950.4	E962.0	E980.4
Tretinoin	976.8	E858.7	E946.8	E950.4	E962.0	E980.4
Triacetin	976.0	E858.7	E946.0	E950.4	E962.0	E980.4
Triacetyloleandomycin	960.3	E856	E930.3	E950.4	E962.0	E980.4
Triamcinolone	962.0	E858.0	E932.0	E950.4	E962.0	E980.4
ENT agent	976.6	E858.7	E946.6	E950.4	E962.0	E980.4
ophthalmic preparation	976.5	E858.7	E946.5	E950.4	E962.0	E980.4
topical NEC	976.0	E858.7	E946.0	E950.4	E962.0	E980.4
Triamterene	974.4	E858.5	E944.4	E950.4	E962.0	E980.4
Triaziquone	963.1	E858.1	E933.1	E950.4	E962.0	E980.4
Tribromacetaldehyde	967.3	E852.2	E937.3	E950.2	E962.0	E980.2
Tribromoethanol	968.2	E855.1	E938.2	E950.4	E962.0	E980.4
Tribromomethane	967.3	E852.2	E937.3	E950.2	E962.0	E980.2
Trichlorethane	982.3	E862.4	—	E950.9	E962.1	E980.9
Trichlormethiazide	974.3	E858.5	E944.3	E950.4	E962.0	E980.4
Trichloroacetic acid	983.1	E864.1	—	E950.7	E962.1	E980.6
medicinal (keratolytic)	976.4	E858.7	E946.4	E950.4	E962.0	E980.4
Trichloroethanol	967.1	E852.0	E937.1	E950.2	E962.0	E980.2
Trichloroethylene (liquid) (vapor)	982.3	E862.4	—	E950.9	E962.1	E980.9
anesthetic (gas)	968.2	E855.1	E938.2	E950.4	E962.0	E980.4
Trichloroethyl phosphate	967.1	E852.0	E937.1	E950.2	E962.0	E980.2
Trichlorofluoromethane NEC	987.4	E869.2	—	E952.8	E962.2	E982.8
Trichlorotriethylamine	963.1	E858.1	E933.1	E950.4	E962.0	E980.4
Trichomonacides NEC	961.5	E857	E931.5	E950.4	E962.0	E980.4
Trichomycin	960.1	E856	E930.1	E950.4	E962.0	E980.4
Triclofos	967.1	E852.0	E937.1	E950.2	E962.0	E980.2
Tricresyl phosphate	989.89	E866.8	—	E950.9	E962.1	E980.9
solvent	982.8	E862.4	—	E950.9	E962.1	E980.9
Tricyclamol	966.4	E855.0	E936.4	E950.4	E962.0	E980.4
Tridesilon	976.0	E858.7	E946.0	E950.4	E962.0	E980.4
Tridihexethyl	971.1	E855.4	E941.1	E950.4	E962.0	E980.4
Tridione	966.0	E855.0	E936.0	E950.4	E962.0	E980.4

◄▶ **New Code**   ⬅▦▦▶ **Revised Code**

Substance	Poisoning	External Cause (E-Code)				
		Accident	Therapeutic Use	Suicide Attempt	Assault	Undetermined
Triethanolamine NEC	983.2	E864.2	—	E950.7	E962.1	E980.6
detergent	983.2	E861.0	—	E950.7	E962.1	E980.6
trinitrate	972.4	E858.3	E942.4	E950.4	E962.0	E980.4
Triethanomelamine	963.1	E858.1	E933.1	E950.4	E962.0	E980.4
Triethylene melamine	963.1	E858.1	E933.1	E950.4	E962.0	E980.4
Triethylenephosphoramide	963.1	E858.1	E933.1	E950.4	E962.0	E980.4
Triethylenethiophosphoramide	963.1	E858.1	E933.1	E950.4	E962.0	E980.4
Trifluoperazine	969.1	E853.0	E939.1	E950.3	E962.0	E980.3
Trifluperidol	969.2	E853.1	E939.2	E950.3	E962.0	E980.3
Triflupromazine	969.1	E853.0	E939.1	E950.3	E962.0	E980.3
Trihexyphenidyl	971.1	E855.4	E941.1	E950.4	E962.0	E980.4
Triiodothyronine	962.7	E858.0	E932.7	E950.4	E962.0	E980.4
Trilene	968.2	E855.1	E938.2	E950.4	E962.0	E980.4
Trimeprazine	963.0	E858.1	E933.0	E950.4	E962.0	E980.4
Trimetazidine	972.4	E858.3	E942.4	E950.4	E962.0	E980.4
Trimethadione	966.0	E855.0	E936.0	E950.4	E962.0	E980.4
Trimethaphan	972.3	E858.3	E942.3	E950.4	E962.0	E980.4
Trimethidinium	972.3	E858.3	E942.3	E950.4	E962.0	E980.4
Trimethobenzamide	963.0	E858.1	E933.0	E950.4	E962.0	E980.4
Trimethylcarbinol	980.8	E860.8	—	E950.9	E962.1	E980.9
Trimethylpsoralen	976.3	E858.7	E946.3	E950.4	E962.0	E980.4
Trimeton	963.0	E858.1	E933.0	E950.4	E962.0	E980.4
Trimipramine	969.0	E854.0	E939.0	E950.3	E962.0	E980.3
Trimustine	963.1	E858.1	E933.1	E950.4	E962.0	E980.4
Trinitrin	972.4	E858.3	E942.4	E950.4	E962.0	E980.4
Trinitrophenol	983.0	E864.0	—	E950.7	E962.1	E980.6
Trinitrotoluene	989.89	E866.8	—	E950.9	E962.1	E980.9
fumes	987.8	E869.8	—	E952.8	E962.2	E982.8
Trional	967.8	E852.8	E937.8	E950.2	E962.0	E980.2
Trioxide of arsenic - *see* Arsenic						
Trioxsalen	976.3	E858.7	E946.3	E950.4	E962.0	E980.4
Tripelennamine	963.0	E858.1	E933.0	E950.4	E962.0	E980.4
Triperidol	969.2	E853.1	E939.2	E950.3	E962.0	E980.3
Triprolidine	963.0	E858.1	E933.0	E950.4	E962.0	E980.4
Trisoralen	976.3	E858.7	E946.3	E950.4	E962.0	E980.4
Troleandomycin	960.3	E856	E930.3	E950.4	E962.0	E980.4
Trolnitrate (phosphate)	972.4	E858.3	E942.4	E950.4	E962.0	E980.4
Trometamol	963.3	E858.1	E933.3	E950.4	E962.0	E980.4
Tromethamine	963.3	E858.1	E933.3	E950.4	E962.0	E980.4
Tronothane	968.5	E855.2	E938.5	E950.4	E962.0	E980.4
Tropicamide	971.1	E855.4	E941.1	E950.4	E962.0	E980.4
Troxidone	966.0	E855.0	E936.0	E950.4	E962.0	E980.4
Tryparsamide	961.1	E857	E931.1	E950.4	E962.0	E980.4
Trypsin	963.4	E858.1	E933.4	E950.4	E962.0	E980.4
Tryptizol	969.0	E854.0	E939.0	E950.3	E962.0	E980.3
Tuaminoheptane	971.2	E855.5	E941.2	E950.4	E962.0	E980.4
Tuberculin (old)	977.8	E858.8	E947.8	E950.4	E962.0	E980.4
Tubocurare	975.2	E858.6	E945.2	E950.4	E962.0	E980.4
Tubocurarine	975.2	E858.6	E945.2	E950.4	E962.0	E980.4
Turkish green	969.6	E854.1	E939.6	E950.3	E962.0	E980.3
Turpentine (spirits of) (liquid) (vapor)	982.8	E862.4	—	E950.9	E962.1	E980.9
Tybamate	969.5	E853.8	E939.5	E950.3	E962.0	E980.3
Tyloxapol	975.5	E858.6	E945.5	E950.4	E962.0	E980.4
Tymazoline	971.2	E855.5	E941.2	E950.4	E962.0	E980.4
Typhoid vaccine	978.1	E858.8	E948.1	E950.4	E962.0	E980.4
Typhus vaccine	979.2	E858.8	E949.2	E950.4	E962.0	E980.4
Tyrothricin	976.0	E858.7	E946.0	E950.4	E962.0	E980.4
ENT agent	976.6	E858.7	E946.6	E950.4	E962.0	E980.4
ophthalmic preparation	976.5	E858.7	E946.5	E950.4	E962.0	E980.4
Undecenoic acid	976.0	E858.7	E946.0	E950.4	E962.0	E980.4
Undecylenic acid	976.0	E858.7	E946.0	E950.4	E962.0	E980.4

◄▶ **New Code**　　◀▥▥▶ **Revised Code**

Substance	Poisoning	External Cause (E-Code) Accident	Therapeutic Use	Suicide Attempt	Assault	Undetermined
Unna's boot	976.3	E858.7	E946.3	E950.4	E962.0	E980.4
Uracil mustard	963.1	E858.1	E933.1	E950.4	E962.0	E980.4
Uramustine	963.1	E858.1	E933.1	E950.4	E962.0	E980.4
Urari	975.2	E858.6	E945.2	E950.4	E962.0	E980.4
Urea	974.4	E858.5	E944.4	E950.4	E962.0	E980.4
topical	976.8	E858.7	E946.8	E950.4	E962.0	E980.4
Urethan(e) (antineoplastic)	963.1	E858.1	E933.1	E950.4	E962.0	E980.4
Urginea (maritima) (scilla) - *see* Squill						
Uric acid metabolism agents NEC	974.7	E858.5	E944.7	E950.4	E962.0	E980.4
Urokinase	964.4	E858.2	E934.4	E950.4	E962.0	E980.4
Urokon	977.8	E858.8	E947.8	E950.4	E962.0	E980.4
Urotropin	961.9	E857	E931.9	E950.4	E962.0	E980.4
Urtica	988.2	E865.4	—	E950.9	E962.1	E980.9
Utility gas - *see* Gas, utility						
Vaccine NEC	979.9	E858.8	E949.9	E950.4	E962.0	E980.4
bacterial NEC	978.8	E858.8	E948.8	E950.4	E962.0	E980.4
with						
other bacterial component	978.9	E858.8	E948.9	E950.4	E962.0	E980.4
pertussis component	978.6	E858.8	E948.6	E950.4	E962.0	E980.4
viral-rickettsial component	979.7	E858.8	E949.7	E950.4	E962.0	E980.4
mixed NEC	978.9	E858.8	E948.9	E950.4	E962.0	E980.4
BCG	978.0	E858.8	E948.0	E950.4	E962.0	E980.4
cholera	978.2	E858.8	E948.2	E950.4	E962.0	E980.4
diphtheria	978.5	E858.8	E948.5	E950.4	E962.0	E980.4
influenza	979.6	E858.8	E949.6	E950.4	E962.0	E980.4
measles	979.4	E858.8	E949.4	E950.4	E962.0	E980.4
meningococcal	978.8	E858.8	E948.8	E950.4	E962.0	E980.4
mumps	979.6	E858.8	E949.6	E950.4	E962.0	E980.4
paratyphoid	978.1	E858.8	E948.1	E950.4	E962.0	E980.4
pertussis (with diphtheria toxoid) (with tetanus toxoid)	978.6	E858.8	E948.6	E950.4	E962.0	E980.4
plague	978.3	E858.8	E948.3	E950.4	E962.0	E980.4
poliomyelitis	979.5	E858.8	E949.5	E950.4	E962.0	E980.4
poliovirus	979.5	E858.8	E949.5	E950.4	E962.0	E980.4
rabies	979.1	E858.8	E949.1	E950.4	E962.0	E980.4
rickettsial NEC	979.6	E858.8	E949.6	E950.4	E962.0	E980.4
with						
bacterial component	979.7	E858.8	E949.7	E950.4	E962.0	E980.4
pertussis component	978.6	E858.8	E948.6	E950.4	E962.0	E980.4
viral component	979.7	E858.8	E949.7	E950.4	E962.0	E980.4
Rocky Mountain spotted fever	979.6	E858.8	E949.6	E950.4	E962.0	E980.4
rubella virus	979.4	E858.8	E949.4	E950.4	E962.0	E980.4
sabin oral	979.5	E858.8	E949.5	E950.4	E962.0	E980.4
smallpox	979.0	E858.8	E949.0	E950.4	E962.0	E980.4
tetanus	978.4	E858.8	E948.4	E950.4	E962.0	E980.4
typhoid	978.1	E858.8	E948.1	E950.4	E962.0	E980.4
typhus	979.2	E858.8	E949.2	E950.4	E962.0	E980.4
viral NEC	979.6	E858.8	E949.6	E950.4	E962.0	E980.4
with						
bacterial component	979.7	E858.8	E949.7	E950.4	E962.0	E980.4
pertussis component	978.6	E858.8	E948.6	E950.4	E962.0	E980.4
rickettsial component	979.7	E858.8	E949.7	E950.4	E962.0	E980.4
yellow fever	979.3	E858.8	E949.3	E950.4	E962.0	E980.4
Vaccinia immune globulin (human)	964.6	E858.2	E934.6	E950.4	E962.0	E980.4
Vaginal contraceptives	976.8	E858.7	E946.8	E950.4	E962.0	E980.4
Valethamate	971.1	E855.4	E941.1	E950.4	E962.0	E980.4
Valisone	976.0	E858.7	E946.0	E950.4	E962.0	E980.4
Valium	969.4	E853.2	E939.4	E950.3	E962.0	E980.3
Valmid	967.8	E852.8	E937.8	E950.2	E962.0	E980.2
Vanadium	985.8	E866.4	—	E950.9	E962.1	E980.9
Vancomycin	960.8	E856	E930.8	E950.4	E962.0	E980.4

◀▶ New Code   ⬅▦➡ Revised Code

Substance	Poisoning	External Cause (E-Code)				
		Accident	Therapeutic Use	Suicide Attempt	Assault	Undetermined
Vapor (*see also* Gas)	987.9	E869.9	—	E952.9	E962.2	E982.9
kiln (carbon monoxide)	986	E868.8	—	E952.1	E962.2	E982.1
lead - *see* Lead						
specified source NEC - (*see also* specific substance)	987.8	E869.8	—	E952.8	E962.2	E982.8
Varidase	964.4	E858.2	E934.4	E950.4	E962.0	E980.4
Varnish	989.89	E861.6	—	E950.9	E962.1	E980.9
cleaner	982.8	E862.9	—	E950.9	E962.1	E980.9
Vaseline	976.3	E858.7	E946.3	E950.4	E962.0	E980.4
Vasodilan	972.5	E858.3	E942.5	E950.4	E962.0	E980.4
Vasodilators NEC	972.5	E858.3	E942.5	E950.4	E962.0	E980.4
coronary	972.4	E858.3	E942.4	E950.4	E962.0	E980.4
Vasopressin	962.5	E858.0	E932.5	E950.4	E962.0	E980.4
Vasopressor drugs	962.5	E858.0	E932.5	E950.4	E962.0	E980.4
Venom, venomous (bite) (sting)	989.5	E905.9	—	E950.9	E962.1	E980.9
arthropod NEC	989.5	E905.5	—	E950.9	E962.1	E980.9
bee	989.5	E905.3	—	E950.9	E962.1	E980.9
centipede	989.5	E905.4	—	E950.9	E962.1	E980.9
hornet	989.5	E905.3	—	E950.9	E962.1	E980.9
lizard	989.5	E905.0	—	E950.9	E962.1	E980.9
marine animals or plants	989.5	E905.6	—	E950.9	E962.1	E980.9
millipede (tropical)	989.5	E905.4	—	E950.9	E962.1	E980.9
plant NEC	989.5	E905.7	—	E950.9	E962.1	E980.9
marine	989.5	E905.6	—	E950.9	E962.1	E980.9
scorpion	989.5	E905.2	—	E950.9	E962.1	E980.9
snake	989.5	E905.0	—	E950.9	E962.1	E980.9
specified NEC	989.5	E905.8	—	E950.9	E962.1	E980.9
spider	989.5	E905.1	—	E950.9	E962.1	E980.9
wasp	989.5	E905.3	—	E950.9	E962.1	E980.9
Ventolin - *see* Salbutamol sulfate						
Veramon	967.0	E851	E937.0	E950.1	E962.0	E980.1
Veratrum						
album	988.2	E865.4	—	E950.9	E962.1	E980.9
alkaloids	972.6	E858.3	E942.6	E950.4	E962.0	E980.4
viride	988.2	E865.4	—	E950.9	E962.1	E980.9
Verdigris (*see also* Copper)	985.8	E866.4	—	E950.9	E962.1	E980.9
Veronal	967.0	E851	E937.0	E950.1	E962.0	E980.1
Veroxil	961.6	E857	E931.6	E950.4	E962.0	E980.4
Versidyne	965.7	E850.7	E935.7	E950.0	E962.0	E980.0
Vienna						
green	985.1	E866.3	—	E950.8	E962.1	E980.8
insecticide	985.1	E863.4	—	E950.6	E962.1	E980.7
red	989.89	E866.8	—	E950.9	E962.1	E980.9
pharmaceutical dye	977.4	E858.8	E947.4	E950.4	E962.0	E980.4
Vinbarbital, vinbarbitone	967.0	E851	E937.0	E950.1	E962.0	E980.1
Vinblastine	963.1	E858.1	E933.1	E950.4	E962.0	E980.4
Vincristine	963.1	E858.1	E933.1	E950.4	E962.0	E980.4
Vinesthene, vinethene	968.2	E855.1	E938.2	E950.4	E962.0	E980.4
Vinyl						
bital	967.0	E851	E937.0	E950.1	E962.0	E980.1
ether	968.2	E855.1	E938.2	E950.4	E962.0	E980.4
Vioform	961.3	E857	E931.3	E950.4	E962.0	E980.4
topical	976.0	E858.7	E946.0	E950.4	E962.0	E980.4
Viomycin	960.6	E856	E930.6	E950.4	E962.0	E980.4
Viosterol	963.5	E858.1	E933.5	E950.4	E962.0	E980.4
Viper (venom)	989.5	E905.0	—	E950.9	E962.1	E980.9
Viprynium (embonate)	961.6	E857	E931.6	E950.4	E962.0	E980.4
Virugon	961.7	E857	E931.7	E950.4	E962.0	E980.4
Visine	976.5	E858.7	E946.5	E950.4	E962.0	E980.4
Vitamins NEC	963.5	E858.1	E933.5	E950.4	E962.0	E980.4
B_{12}	964.1	E858.2	E934.1	E950.4	E962.0	E980.4

Substance	Poisoning	External Cause (E-Code)				
		Accident	Therapeutic Use	Suicide Attempt	Assault	Undetermined
Vitamins NEC *(Continued)*						
hematopoietic	964.1	E858.2	E934.1	E950.4	E962.0	E980.4
K	964.3	E858.2	E934.3	E950.4	E962.0	E980.4
Vleminckx's solution	976.4	E858.7	E946.4	E950.4	E962.0	E980.4
Voltaren - *see* Diclofenac sodium						
Warfarin (potassium) (sodium)	964.2	E858.2	E934.2	E950.4	E962.0	E980.4
rodenticide	989.4	E863.7	—	E950.6	E962.1	E980.7
Wasp (sting)	989.5	E905.3	—	E950.9	E962.1	E980.9
Water						
balance agents NEC	974.5	E858.5	E944.5	E950.4	E962.0	E980.4
gas	987.1	E868.1	—	E951.8	E962.2	E981.8
incomplete combustion of - *see* Carbon, monoxide, fuel, utility						
hemlock	988.2	E865.4	—	E950.9	E962.1	E980.9
moccasin (venom)	989.5	E905.0	—	E950.9	E962.1	E980.9
Wax (paraffin) (petroleum)	981	E862.3	—	E950.9	E962.1	E980.9
automobile	989.89	E861.2	—	E950.9	E962.1	E980.9
floor	981	E862.0	—	E950.9	E962.1	E980.9
Weed killers NEC	989.4	E863.5	—	E950.6	E962.1	E980.7
Welldorm	967.1	E852.0	E937.1	E950.2	E962.0	E980.2
White						
arsenic - *see* Arsenic						
hellebore	988.2	E865.4	—	E950.9	E962.1	E980.9
lotion (keratolytic)	976.4	E858.7	E946.4	E950.4	E962.0	E980.4
spirit	981	E862.0	—	E950.9	E962.1	E980.9
Whitewashes	989.89	E861.6	—	E950.9	E962.1	E980.9
Whole blood	964.7	E858.2	E934.7	E950.4	E962.0	E980.4
Wild						
black cherry	988.2	E865.4	—	E950.9	E962.1	E980.9
poisonous plants NEC	988.2	E865.4	—	E950.9	E962.1	E980.9
Window cleaning fluid	989.89	E861.3	—	E950.9	E962.1	E980.9
Wintergreen (oil)	976.3	E858.7	E946.3	E950.4	E962.0	E980.4
Witch hazel	976.2	E858.7	E946.2	E950.4	E962.0	E980.4
Wood						
alcohol	980.1	E860.2	—	E950.9	E962.1	E980.9
spirit	980.1	E860.2	—	E950.9	E962.1	E980.9
Woorali	975.2	E858.6	E945.2	E950.4	E962.0	E980.4
Wormseed, American	961.6	E857	E931.6	E950.4	E962.0	E980.4
Xanthine diuretics	974.1	E858.5	E944.1	E950.4	E962.0	E980.4
Xanthocillin	960.0	E856	E930.0	E950.4	E962.0	E980.4
Xanthotoxin	976.3	E858.7	E946.3	E950.4	E962.0	E980.4
Xylene (liquid) (vapor)	982.0	E862.4	—	E950.9	E962.1	E980.9
Xylocaine (infiltration) (topical)	968.5	E855.2	E938.5	E950.4	E962.0	E980.4
nerve block (peripheral) (plexus)	968.6	E855.2	E938.6	E950.4	E962.0	E980.4
spinal	968.7	E855.2	E938.7	E950.4	E962.0	E980.4
Xylol (liquid) (vapor)	982.0	E862.4	—	E950.9	E962.1	E980.9
Xylometazoline	971.2	E855.5	E941.2	E950.4	E962.0	E980.4
Yellow						
fever vaccine	979.3	E858.8	E949.3	E950.4	E962.0	E980.4
jasmine	988.2	E865.4	—	E950.9	E962.1	E980.9
Yew	988.2	E865.4	—	E950.9	E962.1	E980.9
Zactane	965.7	E850.7	E935.7	E950.0	E962.0	E980.0
Zaroxolyn	974.3	E858.5	E944.3	E950.4	E962.0	E980.4
Zephiran (topical)	976.0	E858.7	E946.0	E950.4	E962.0	E980.4
ophthalmic preparation	976.5	E858.7	E946.5	E950.4	E962.0	E980.4
Zerone	980.1	E860.2	—	E950.9	E962.1	E980.9
Zinc (compounds) (fumes) (salts) (vapor) NEC	985.8	E866.4	—	E950.9	E962.1	E980.9
anti-infectives	976.0	E858.7	E946.0	E950.4	E962.0	E980.4
antivaricose	972.7	E858.3	E942.7	E950.4	E962.0	E980.4
bacitracin	976.0	E858.7	E946.0	E950.4	E962.0	E980.4
chloride	976.2	E858.7	E946.2	E950.4	E962.0	E980.4
gelatin	976.3	E858.7	E946.3	E950.4	E962.0	E980.4
oxide	976.3	E858.7	E946.3	E950.4	E962.0	E980.4

◄▶ **New Code** ◄▦ ▦▶ **Revised Code**

	External Cause (E-Code)					
Substance	**Poisoning**	**Accident**	**Therapeutic Use**	**Suicide Attempt**	**Assault**	**Undetermined**
Zinc *(Continued)*						
peroxide	976.0	E858.7	E946.0	E950.4	E962.0	E980.4
pesticides	985.8	E863.4	—	E950.6	E962.1	E980.7
phosphide (rodenticide)	985.8	E863.7	—	E950.6	E962.1	E980.7
stearate	976.3	E858.7	E946.3	E950.4	E962.0	E980.4
sulfate (antivaricose)	972.7	E858.3	E942.7	E950.4	E962.0	E980.4
ENT agent	976.6	E858.7	E946.6	E950.4	E962.0	E980.4
ophthalmic solution	976.5	E858.7	E946.5	E950.4	E962.0	E980.4
topical NEC	976.0	E858.7	E946.0	E950.4	E962.0	E980.4
undecylenate	976.0	E858.7	E946.0	E950.4	E962.0	E980.4
Zoxazolamine	968.0	E855.1	E938.0	E950.4	E962.0	E980.4
Zygadenus (venenosus)	988.2	E865.4	—	E950.9	E962.1	E980.9

ICD-9-CM

Drugs

Vol. 2

SECTION III

INDEX TO EXTERNAL CAUSES OF INJURY (E CODE)

This section contains the index to the codes which classify environmental events, circumstances, and other conditions as the cause of injury and other adverse effects. Where a code from the section Supplementary Classification of External Causes of Injury and Poisoning (E800-E998) is applicable, it is intended that the E code shall be used in addition to a code from the main body of the classification, Chapters 1 to 17.

The alphabetic index to the E codes is organized by main terms which describe the accident, circumstance, event, or specific agent which caused the injury or other adverse effect.

Note   Transport accidents (E800-E848) include accidents involving:

   aircraft and spacecraft (E840-E845)
   watercraft (E830-E838)
   motor vehicle (E810-E825)
   railway (E800-E807)
   other road vehicles (E826-E829)

For definitions and examples related to transport accidents - see Supplementary Classification of External Causes of Injury and Poisoning (E800-E999).

The fourth-digit subdivisions for use with categories E800-E848 to identify the injured person are found at the end of this section.

For identifying the place in which an accident or poisoning occurred (circumstances classifiable to categories E850-E869 and E880-E928) - see the listing in this section under "Accident, occurring."

See the Table of Drugs and Chemicals (Section 2 of this volume) for identifying the specific agent involved in drug overdose or a wrong substance given or taken in error, and for intoxication or poisoning by a drug or other chemical substance.

The specific adverse effect, reaction, or localized toxic effect of a correct drug or substance properly administered in therapeutic or prophylactic dosage should be classified according to the nature of the adverse effect (e.g., allergy, dermatitis, tachycardia) listed in Section I of this volume.

A

Abandonment
causing exposure to weather conditions - *see* Exposure
child, with intent to injure or kill E968.4
helpless person, infant, newborn E904.0
with intent to injure or kill E968.4
Abortion, criminal, injury to child E968.8
Abuse (alleged) (suspected)
adult
by
child E967.4
ex-partner E967.3
ex-spouse E967.3
father E967.0
grandchild E967.7
grandparent E967.6
mother E967.2
non-related caregiver E967.8
other relative E967.7
other specified person E967.1
partner E967.3
sibling E967.5
spouse E967.3
stepfather E967.0
stepmother E967.2
unspecified person E967.9
child
by
child E967.4
ex-partner E967.3
ex-spouse E967.3
father E967.0
grandchild E967.7
grandparent E967.6
mother E967.2
non-related caregiver E967.8
other relative E967.7
other specified person(s) E967.1
partner E967.3
sibling E967.5
spouse E967.3
stepfather E967.0
stepmother E967.2
unspecified person E967.9
Accident (to) E928.9
aircraft (in transit) (powered) E841
at landing, take-off E840
due to, caused by cataclysm - *see* categories E908, E909
late effect of E929.1
unpowered (*see also* Collision, aircraft, unpowered) E842
while alighting, boarding E843
amphibious vehicle
on
land - *see* Accident, motor vehicle
water - *see* Accident, watercraft
animal, ridden NEC E828
animal-drawn vehicle NEC E827
balloon (*see also* Collision, aircraft, unpowered) E842
caused by, due to
abrasive wheel (metalworking) E919.3
animal NEC E906.9
being ridden (in sport or transport) E828
avalanche NEC E909.2
band saw E919.4

Accident (Continued)
caused by, due to (Continued)
bench saw E919.4
bore, earth-drilling or mining (land) (seabed) E919.1
bulldozer E919.7
cataclysmic
earth surface movement or eruption E909.9
storm E908.9
chain
hoist E919.2
agricultural operations E919.0
mining operations E919.1
saw E920.1
circular saw E919.4
cold (excessive) (*see also* Cold, exposure to) E901.9
combine E919.0
conflagration - *see* Conflagration
corrosive liquid, substance NEC E924.1
cotton gin E919.8
crane E919.2
agricultural operations E919.0
mining operations E919.1
cutting or piercing instrument (*see also* Cut) E920.9
dairy equipment E919.8
derrick E919.2
agricultural operations E919.0
mining operations E919.1
drill E920.1
earth (land) (seabed) E919.1
hand (powered) E920.1
not powered E920.4
metalworking E919.3
woodworking E919.4
earth(-)
drilling machine E919.1
moving machine E919.7
scraping machine E919.7
electric
current (*see also* Electric shock) E925.9
motor - *see also* Accident, machine, by type of machine
current (of) - *see* Electric shock
elevator (building) (grain) E919.2
agricultural operations E919.0
mining operations E919.1
environmental factors NEC E928.9
excavating machine E919.7
explosive material (*see also* Explosion) E923.9
farm machine E919.0
fire, flames - *see also* Fire
conflagration - *see* Conflagration
firearm missile - *see* Shooting
forging (metalworking) machine E919.3
forklift (truck) E919.2
agricultural operations E919.0
mining operations E919.1
gas turbine E919.5
harvester E919.0
hay derrick, mower, or rake E919.0
heat (excessive) (*see also* Heat) E900.9
hoist (*see also* Accident, caused by, due to, lift) E919.2
chain - *see* Accident, caused by, due to, chain
shaft E919.1

Accident (Continued)
caused by, due to (Continued)
hot
liquid E924.0
caustic or corrosive E924.1
object (not producing fire or flames) E924.8
substance E924.9
caustic or corrosive E924.1
liquid (metal) NEC E924.0
specified type NEC E924.8
ignition - *see* Ignition E919.4
internal combustion engine E919.5
landslide NEC E909.2
lathe (metalworking) E919.3
turnings E920.8
woodworking E919.4
lift, lifting (appliances) E919.2
agricultural operations E919.0
mining operations E919.1
shaft E919.1
lightning NEC E907
machine, machinery - *see also* Accident, machine
drilling, metal E919.3
manufacturing, for manufacture of steam
beverages E919.8
clothing E919.8
foodstuffs E919.8
paper E919.8
textiles E919.8
milling, metal E919.3
moulding E919.4
power press, metal E919.3
printing E919.8
rolling mill, metal E919.3
sawing, metal E919.3
specified type NEC E919.8
spinning E919.8
weaving E919.8
natural factor NEC E928.9
overhead plane E919.4
plane E920.4
overhead E919.4
powered
hand tool NEC E920.1
saw E919.4
hand E920.1
printing machine E919.8
pulley (block) E919.2
agricultural operations E919.0
mining operations E919.1
transmission E919.6
radial saw E919.4
radiation - *see* Radiation
reaper E919.0
road scraper E919.7 when in transport under its own power - *see* categories E810-E825
roller coaster E919.8
sander E919.4
saw E920.4
band E919.4
bench E919.4
chain E920.1
circular E919.4
hand E920.4
powered E920.1
powered, except hand E919.4
radial E919.4
sawing machine, metal E919.3
shaft
hoist E919.1

B

Barotitis, barodontalgia, barosinusitis, barotrauma (otitic) (sinus) - *see* Effects of, air pressure
Battered
  baby or child (syndrome) - *see* Abuse, child
  person other than baby or child - *see* Assault
Bayonet wound (*see also* Cut, by bayonet) E920.3
  in
    legal intervention E974
    war operations E995
Bean in nose E912
Bed set on fire NEC E898.0
Beheading (by guillotine)
  homicide E966
  legal execution E978
Bending, injury in E927
Bends E902.0
Bite
  animal (nonvenomous) NEC E906.5
    other specified (except arthropod) E906.3
      venomous NEC E905.9
  arthropod (nonvenomous) NEC E906.4
    venomous - *see* Sting
  black widow spider E905.1
  cat E906.3
  centipede E905.4
  cobra E905.0
  copperhead snake E905.0
  coral snake E905.0
  dog E906.0
  fer de lance E905.0
  gila monster E905.0
  human being E968.8
  insect (nonvenomous) E906.4
    venomous - *see* Sting
  krait E905.0
  late effect of - *see* Late effect
  lizard E906.2
    venomous E905.0
  mamba E905.0
  marine animal
    nonvenomous E906.3
      snake E906.2
    venomous E905.6
      snake E905.0
  millipede E906.4
    venomous E905.4
  moray eel E906.3
  rat E906.1
  rattlesnake E905.0
  rodent, except rat E906.3
  serpent - *see* Bite, snake
  shark E906.3
  snake (venomous) E905.0
    nonvenomous E906.2
    sea E905.0
  spider E905.1
    nonvenomous E906.4
  tarantula (venomous) E905.1
  venomous NEC E905.9
    by specific animal - *see* category E905
  viper E905.0
  water moccasin E905.0
Blast (air) in war operations E993
  from nuclear explosion E996
  underwater E992

Blizzard E908.3
Blow E928.9
  by law-enforcing agent, police (on duty) E975
    with blunt object (baton) (nightstick) (stave) (truncheon) E973
Blowing up (*see also* Explosion) E923.9
Brawl (hand) (fists) (foot) E960.0
Breakage (accidental)
  cable of cable car not on rails E847
  ladder (causing fall) E881.0
  part (any) of
    animal-drawn vehicle E827
    ladder (causing fall) E881.0
    motor vehicle
      in motion (on public highway) E818
        not on public highway E825
    nonmotor road vehicle, except animal-drawn vehicle or pedal cycle E829
    off-road type motor vehicle (not on public highway) NEC E821
    on public highway E818
    pedal cycle E826
    scaffolding (causing fall) E881.1
    snow vehicle, motor-driven (not on public highway) E820
    on public highway E818
    vehicle NEC - *see* Accident, vehicle
Broken
  glass, injury by E920.8
  power line (causing electric shock) E925.1
Bumping against, into (accidentally)
  object (moving) (projected) (stationary) E917.9
    with fall E888
    caused by crowd (with fall) E917.1
    in
      running water E917.2
      sports E917.0
  person(s) E917.9
    with fall E886.9
      in sports E886.0
    as, or caused by, a crowd (with fall) E917.1
    in sports E917.0
      with fall E886.0
Burning, burns (accidental) (by) (from) (on) E899
  acid (any kind) E924.1
    swallowed - *see* Table of Drugs and Chemicals
  bedclothes (*see also* Fire, specified NEC) E898.0
  blowlamp (*see also* Fire, specified NEC) E898.1
  blowtorch (*see also* Fire, specified NEC) E898.1
  boat, ship, watercraft - *see* categories E830, E831, E837
  bonfire (controlled) E897
    uncontrolled E892
  candle (*see also* Fire, specified NEC) E898.1
  caustic liquid, substance E924.1
    swallowed - *see* Table of Drugs and Chemicals
  chemical E924.1
    from swallowing caustic, corrosive substance - *see* Table of Drugs and Chemicals
    in war operations E997.2

Burning, burns (*Continued*)
  cigar(s) or cigarette(s) (*see also* Fire, specified NEC) E898.1
  clothes, clothing, nightdress - *see* Ignition, clothes
    with conflagration - *see* Conflagration
  conflagration - *see* Conflagration
  corrosive liquid, substance E924.1
    swallowed - *see* Table of Drugs and Chemicals
  electric current (*see also* Electric shock) E925.9
  fire, flames (*see also* Fire) E899
  flare, Verey pistol E922.8
  heat
    from appliance (electrical) E924.8
    in local application, or packing during medical or surgical procedure E873.5
  homicide (attempt) (*see also* Assault, burning) E968.0
  hot
    liquid E924.0
      caustic or corrosive E924.1
    object (not producing fire or flames) E924.8
    substance E924.9
      caustic or corrosive E924.1
      liquid (metal) NEC E924.0
      specified type NEC E924.8
    tap water E924.2
  ignition - *see also* Ignition
    clothes, clothing, nightdress - *see also* Ignition, clothes
    with conflagration - *see* Conflagration
    highly inflammable material (benzine) (fat) (gasoline) (kerosene) (paraffin) (petrol) E894
  inflicted by other person
    stated as
      homicidal, intentional (*see also* Assault, burning) E968.0
      undetermined whether accidental or intentional (*see also* Burn, stated as undetermined whether accidental or intentional) E988.1
  internal, from swallowed caustic, corrosive liquid, substance - *see* Table of Drugs and Chemicals
  in war operations (from fire-producing device or conventional weapon) E990.9
    from nuclear explosion E996
    petrol bomb E990.0
  lamp (*see also* Fire, specified NEC) E898.1
  late effect of NEC E929.4
  lighter (cigar) (cigarette) (*see also* Fire, specified NEC) E898.1
  lightning E907
  liquid (boiling) (hot) (molten) E924.0
    caustic, corrosive (external) E924.1
      swallowed - *see* Table of Drugs and Chemicals
  local application of externally applied substance in medical or surgical care E873.5
  machinery - *see* Accident, machine
  matches (*see also* Fire, specified NEC) E898.1
  medicament, externally applied E873.5

Burning, burns *(Continued)*
  metal, molten E924.0
  object (hot) E924.8
    producing fire or flames - *see* Fire
  oven (electric) (gas) E924.8
  pipe (smoking) *(see also* Fire, specified
    NEC) E898.1
  radiation - *see* Radiation
  railway engine, locomotive, train *(see
    also* Explosion, railway engine)
    E803
  self-inflicted (unspecified whether acci-
    dental or intentional) E988.1
    caustic or corrosive substance NEC
      E988.7
    stated as intentional, purposeful
      E958.1
    caustic or corrosive substance
      NEC E958.7
  stated as undetermined whether acci-
    dental or intentional E988.1
    caustic or corrosive substance NEC
      E988.7
  steam E924.0
    pipe E924.8
  substance (hot) E924.9
    boiling or molten E924.0
    caustic, corrosive (external) E924.1
      swallowed - *see* Table of Drugs
        and Chemicals
  suicidal (attempt) NEC E958.1
    caustic substance E958.7
    late effect of E959 (descent)
  therapeutic misadventure
    overdose of radiation E873.2
  torch, welding *(see also* Fire, specified
    NEC) E898.1
  trash fire *(see also* Burning, bonfire)
    E897
  vapor E924.0
  vitriol E924.1
  x-rays E926.3
    in medical, surgical procedure - *see*
      Misadventure, failure, in dos-
      age, radiation operations
Butted by animal E906.8

C

Cachexia, lead or saturnine E866.0
  from pesticide NEC *(see also* Table of
    Drugs and Chemicals) E863.4
Caisson disease E902.2
Capital punishment (any means) E978
Car sickness E903
Casualty (not due to war) NEC
  E928.9
  war *(see also* War operations) E995
Cat
  bite E906.3
  scratch E906.8
Cataclysmic (any injury)
  earth surface movement or eruption
    E909.9
    specified type NEC E909.8
  storm or flood resulting from storm
    E908.9
    specified type NEC E909.8
Catching fire - *see* Ignition
Caught
  between
    objects (moving) (stationary and
      moving) E918
    and machinery - *see* Accident, ma-
      chine
  by cable car, not on rails E847
  in
    machinery (moving parts of) - *see*
      Accident, machine
    object E918
Cave-in (causing asphyxia, suffocation
  (by pressure)) *(see also* Suffocation,
  due to, cave-in) E913.3
  with injury other than asphyxia or suf-
    focation E916
    with asphyxia or suffocation *(see also*
      Suffocation, due to, cave-in)
      E913.3
  struck or crushed by E916
    with asphyxia or suffocation *(see also*
      Suffocation, due to, cave-in)
      E913.3
Change(s) in air pressure - *see also* Effects of, air pressure
  sudden, in aircraft (ascent) (descent)
    (causing aeroneurosis or aviators'
    disease) E902.1
Chilblains E901.0
  due to manmade conditions E901.1
Choking (on) (any object except food or
  vomitus) E912
  apple E911
  bone E911
  food, any type (regurgitated) E911
  mucus or phlegm E912
  seed E911
Civil insurrection - *see* War operations
Cloudburst E908.8
Cold, exposure to (accidental) (excessive)
  (extreme) (place) E901.9
  causing chilblains or immersion foot
    E901.0
  due to
    manmade conditions E901.1
    specified cause NEC E901.8
    weather (conditions) E901.0
  late effect of NEC E929.5
  self-inflicted (undetermined whether
    accidental or intentional) E988.3
    suicidal E958.3 (herded)
  suicide E958.3

Colic, lead, painters', or saturnine - *see*
  category E866
Collapse
  building E916 (movable)
    burning E891.8
      private E890.8 higher
  dam E909.3
  due to heat - *see* Heat
  machinery - *see* Accident, machine or
    vehicle
  man-made structure E909.3
  postoperative NEC E878.9
  structure, burning NEC E891.8
Collision (accidental)

> Note   In the case of collisions be-
> tween different types of vehicles, per-
> sons and objects, priority in classifica-
> tion is in the following order:
>
>   Aircraft
>   Watercraft
>   Motor vehicle
>   Railway vehicle
>   Pedal Cycle
>   Animal-drawn vehicle
>   Animal being ridden
>   Streetcar or other
>   nonmotor road vehicle
>   Other vehicle
>   Pedestrian or person using pe-
>   destrian conveyance
>   Object (except where falling
>   from or set in motion by vehi-
>   cle etc. listed above)
>
> In the listing below, the combinations
> are listed only under the vehicle, etc.,
> having priority. For definitions, *see*
> Supplementary Classification of Ex-
> ternal Causes of Injury and Poisoning
> (E800-E999).

  aircraft (with object or vehicle) (fixed)-
    entrance (on (movable) (moving))
    E841
    with
      person (while landing, taking off)
        vehicle off the (without acci-
        dent to aircraft) E844
      powered (in transit) (with unpow-
        ered aircraft) E841
      while landing, taking off E840
      unpowered E842
      while landing, taking off E840
  animal being ridden (in sport or trans-
    port) E828
    and
      animal (being ridden) (herded)
        (unattended) E828
      nonmotor road vehicle, except
        pedal cycle or animal-drawn
        vehicle E828
      object (fallen) (fixed) (movable)
        (moving) not falling from or
        set in motion by vehicle of
        higher priority E828
      pedestrian (conveyance or vehicle)
        E828
  animal-drawn vehicle E827
    and
      animal (being ridden) (herded)
        (unattended) E827
      nonmotor road vehicle, except
        pedal cycle E827
      object (fallen) (fixed) (movable)

Collision *(Continued)*
snow vehicle, motor-driven *(Continued)*
and *(Continued)*
by aircraft or motor vehicle
on highway E820
pedal cycle E820
pedestrian (conveyance) E820
railway train E820
on public highway - *see* Collision,
motor vehicle
street car(s) E829
and
animal, herded, not being ridden,
unattended E829
nonmotor road vehicle NEC E829
object (fallen) (fixed) (movable)
(moving) not falling from or
set in motion by aircraft, animal-drawn vehicle, animal being ridden, motor vehicle,
pedal cycle, or railway train
E829
pedestrian (conveyance) E829
person (using pedestrian conveyance) E829
vehicle
animal-drawn - *see* Collision, animal-
drawn vehicle
motor - *see* Collision, motor vehicle
nonmotor
nonroad E848
and
another nonmotor, nonroad
vehicle E848
object (fallen) (fixed) (movable) (moving) not falling
from or set in motion by
aircraft, animal-drawn
vehicle, animal being ridden, motor vehicle, non-
motor road vehicle, pedal
cycle, railway train, or
streetcar E848
road, except animal being ridden,
animal-drawn vehicle, or
pedal cycle E829
and
animal, herded, not being ridden, unattended E829
another nonmotor road vehicle, except animal being
ridden, animal-drawn
vehicle, or pedal cycle
E829
object (fallen) (fixed) (movable)
(moving) not falling from
or set in motion by, air-
craft, animal-drawn vehi-
cle, animal being ridden,
motor vehicle, pedal cycle,
or railway train E829
pedestrian (conveyance) E829
person (using pedestrian conveyance) E829
vehicle, nonmotor, nonroad
E829
watercraft E838
and
person swimming or water skiing
E838
causing
drowning, submersion E830
injury except drowning, submersion E831

Combustion, spontaneous - *see* Ignition
Complication of medical or surgical
procedure or treatment
as an abnormal reaction - *see* Reaction,
abnormal
delayed, without mention of misadventure - *see* Reaction,
abnormal
due to misadventure - *see* Misadventure
Compression
divers' squeeze E902.2 or
trachea by
food E911
foreign body, except food E912
Conflagration
building or structure, except private
dwelling (barn) (church) (convalescent or residential home) (factory) (farm outbuilding) (hospital)
(hotel) or (institution (educational)
(dormitory) (residential)) (school)
(shop) (store) (theatre) E891.9
with or causing (injury due to)
accident or injury NEC E891.9
specified circumstance NEC
E891.8
burns, burning E891.3
carbon monoxide E891.2
fumes E891.2
polyvinylchloride (PVC) or similar
material E891.1
smoke E891.2
causing explosion E891.0
not in building or structure E892
private dwelling (apartment) (boarding
house) (camping place) (caravan)
(farmhouse) (home (private))
(house) (lodging house) (private
garage) (rooming house) (tenement) E890.9
with or causing (injury due to) accident or injury NEC E890.9
specified circumstance NEC
E890.8
burns, burning E890.3
carbon monoxide E890.2
fumes E890.2
polyvinylchloride (PVC) or similar material E890.1
smoke E890.2
causing explosion E890.0
Contact with
dry ice E901.1
liquid air, hydrogen, nitrogen E901.1
Cramp(s)
Heat - *see* Heat
swimmers (*see also* category E910)
E910.2
not in recreation or sport E910.3
Cranking (car) (truck) (bus) (engine) injury by E917.9
Crash
aircraft (in transit) (powered) E841
at landing, take-off E840
in war operations E994
on runway NEC E840
stated as
homicidal E968.8
suicidal E958.6
undetermined whether accidental
or intentional E988.6
unpowered E842
glider E842

Crash *(Continued)*
motor vehicle - *see also* Accident, motor vehicle
homicidal E968.5
suicidal E958.5
undetermined whether accidental or
intentional E988.5
Crushed (accidentally) E928.9
between
boat(s), ship(s), watercraft (and dock
or pier) (without accident to
watercraft) E838
after accident to, or collision, watercraft E831
objects (moving) (stationary and
moving) E918
by
avalanche NEC E909.2
boat, ship, watercraft after accident
to, collision, watercraft E831
cave-in E916
with asphyxiation or suffocation
(*see also* Suffocation, due to,
cave-in) E913.3
crowd, human stampede E917.1
falling
aircraft (*see also* Accident, aircraft)
E841
in war operations E994
earth, material E916
with asphyxiation or suffocation
(*see also* Suffocation, due to,
cave-in) E913.3
object E916
on ship, watercraft E838
while loading, unloading watercraft E838
landslide NEC E909.2
lifeboat after abandoning ship
E831
machinery - *see* Accident, machine
railway rolling stock, train, vehicle
(part of) E805
street car E829
vehicle NEC - *see* Accident, vehicle
NEC
in
machinery - *see* Accident, machine
object E918
transport accident - *see* categories
E800-E848
late effect of NEC E929.9
Cut, cutting (any part of body) (accidental) E920.9
by
arrow E920.8
axe E920.4
bayonet (*see also* Bayonet wound)
E920.3
blender E920.2
broken glass E920.8
can opener E920.4
powered E920.2
chisel E920.4
circular saw E919.4
cutting or piercing instrument - *see*
also category E920
late effect of E929.8
dagger E920.3
dart E920.8
drill - *see* Accident, caused by drill
edge of stiff paper E920.8
electric
beater E920.2

Electric shock, electrocution *(Continued)*
machinery *(Continued)*
factory E925.2
farm E925.8
home E925.0
misadventure in medical or surgical procedure
in electroshock therapy E873.4
self-inflicted (undetermined whether accidental or intentional) E988.4
stated as intentional E958.4
stated as undetermined whether accidental or intentional E988.4
suicidal (attempt) E958.4
transmission line E925.1
Electrocution - *see* Electric shock
Embolism
air (traumatic) NEC - *see* Air, embolism
Encephalitis
lead or saturnine E866.0
from pesticide NEC E863.4
Entanglement
in
bedclothes, causing suffocation E913.0
wheel of pedal cycle E826
Entry of foreign body, material, any - *see* Foreign body
Execution, legal (any method) E978
Exhaustion
cold - *see* Cold, exposure to
due to excessive exertion E927
heat - *see* Heat
Explosion (accidental) (in) (of) (on) E923.9
acetylene E923.2
aerosol can E921.8
aircraft (in transit) (powered) E841
at landing, take-off E840
in war operations E994
unpowered E842
air tank (compressed) (in machinery) E921.1
anesthetic gas in operating theatre E923.2
automobile tire NEC E921.8
causing transport accident - *see* categories E810-E825
blasting (cap) (materials) E923.1
boiler (machinery), not on transport vehicle E921.0
steamship - *see* Explosion, watercraft
bomb E923.8
in war operations E993
after cessation of hostilities E998
atom, hydrogen or nuclear E996
injury by fragments from E991.9
antipersonnel bomb E991.3
butane E923.2
caused by
other person
stated as
intentional, homicidal - *see* Assault, explosive
undetermined whether accidental or homicidal E985.5
coal gas E923.2
detonator E923.1
dynamite E923.1
explosive (material) NEC E923.9
gas(es) E923.2
missile E923.8
in war operations E993
injury by fragments from E991.9
antipersonnel bomb E991.3

Explosion *(Continued)*
explosive *(Continued)*
used in blasting operations E923.1
fire-damp E923.2
fireworks E923.0
gas E923.2
cylinder (in machinery) E921.1
pressure tank (in machinery) E921.1
gasoline (fumes) (tank) not in moving motor vehicle E923.2
grain store (military) (munitions) E923.8
grenade E923.8
in war operations E993
injury by fragments from E991.9
homicide (attempt) - *see* Assault, explosive
hot water heater, tank (in machinery) E921.0
in mine (of explosive gases) NEC E923.2
late effect of NEC E929.8
machinery - *see also* Accident, machine
pressure vessel - *see* Explosion, pressure vessel
methane E923.2
missile E923.8
in war operations E993
injury by fragments from E991.9
motor vehicle (part of)
in motion (on public highway) E818
not on public highway E825
munitions (dump) (factory) E923.8
in war operations E993
of mine E923.8
in war operations
after cessation of hostilities E998
at sea or in harbor E992
land E993
after cessation of hostilities E998
injury by fragments from E991.9
marine E992
own weapons in war operations E993
injury by fragments from E991.9
antipersonnel bomb E991.3
pressure
cooker E921.8
gas tank (in machinery) E921.1
vessel (in machinery) E921.9
on transport vehicle - *see* categories E800-E848
specified type NEC E921.8
propane E923.2
railway engine, locomotive, train (boiler) (with subsequent collision, derailment, fall) E803
with
collision (antecedent) (*see also* Collision, railway) E800
derailment (antecedent) E802
fire (without antecedent collision or derailment) E803
secondary fire resulting from - *see* Fire
self-inflicted (unspecified whether accidental or intentional) E985.5
stated as intentional, purposeful E955.5
shell (artillery) E923.8
in war operations E993
injury by fragments from E991.9
stated as undetermined whether caused accidentally or purposely inflicted E985.5

Explosion *(Continued)*
steam or water lines (in machinery) E921.0
suicide (attempted) E955.5
torpedo E923.8
in war operations E992
transport accident - *see* categories E800-E848
war operations - *see* War operations, explosion
watercraft (boiler) E837
causing drowning, submersion (after jumping from watercraft) E830
Exposure (weather) (conditions) (rain) (wind) E904.3
with homicidal intent E968.4
excessive E904.3
cold (*see also* Cold, exposure to) E901.9
self-inflicted - *see* Cold, exposure to, self-inflicted
heat (*see also* Heat) E900.9
helpless person, infant, newborn due to abandonment or neglect E904.0
noise E928.1
prolonged in deep-freeze unit or refrigerator E901.1
radiation - *see* Radiation
resulting from transport accident - *see* categories E800-E848
smoke from, due to
fire - *see* Fire
tobacco, second-hand E869.4
vibration E928.2

F

Fall, falling (accidental) E888
building E916
burning E891.8
private E890.8
down
escalator E880.0
ladder E881.0
in boat, ship, watercraft E833
staircase E880.9
stairs, steps - *see* Fall, from, stairs
earth (with asphyxia or suffocation (by pressure)) (*see also* Earth, falling) E913.3
from, off
aircraft (at landing, take-off) (in transit) (while alighting, boarding) E843
resulting from accident to aircraft - *see* categories E840-E842
animal (in sport or transport) E828
animal-drawn vehicle E827
balcony E882
bed E884.4
bicycle E826
boat, ship, watercraft (into water) E832
after accident to, collision, fire on E830
and subsequently struck by (part of) boat E831
and subsequently struck by (part of) while alighting, boat E838
burning, crushed, sinking E830
and subsequently struck by (part of) boat E831
bridge E882

Fall, falling (*Continued*)
through (*Continued*)
roof E882
window E882
timber E916
while alighting from, boarding, entering, leaving
aircraft (any kind) E843
motor bus, motor vehicle - *see* Fall, from, motor vehicle, while alighting, boarding
nonmotor road vehicle NEC E829
railway train E804
street car E829
Fallen on by
animal (horse) (not being ridden) E906.8
being ridden (in sport or transport) E828
Fell or jumped from high place, so stated - *see* Jumping, from, high place
Felo-de-se (*see also* Suicide) E958.9
Fever
heat - *see* Heat
thermic - *see* Heat
Fight (hand) (fist) (foot) (*see also* Assault, fight) E960.0
Fire (accidental) (caused by great heat from appliance (electrical), hot object or hot substance) (secondary, resulting from explosion) E899
conflagration - *see* Conflagration
controlled, normal (in brazier, fireplace, furnace, or stove) (charcoal) (coal) (coke) (electric) (gas) (wood) E897
bonfire E897
brazier, not in building or structure E897
in building or structure, except private dwelling (barn) (church) (convalescent or residential home) (factory) (farm outbuilding) (hospital) (hotel) (institution (educational) (dormitory) (residential)) (private garage) (school) (shop) (store) (theatre) E896
in private dwelling (apartment) (boarding house) (camping place) (caravan) (farmhouse) (home (private)) (house) (lodging house) (rooming house) (tenement) E895
not in building or structure E897
trash E897
forest (uncontrolled) E892
grass (uncontrolled) E892
hay (uncontrolled) E892
homicide (attempt) E968.0
late effect of E969
in, of, on, starting in
aircraft (in transit) (powered) E841
at landing, take-off E840
stationary E892
unpowered (balloon) (glider) E842
balloon E842
boat, ship, watercraft - *see* categories E830, E831, E837
building or structure, except private dwelling (barn) (church) (convalescent or residential home) (factory) (farm outbuilding) (hospital) (hotel) (institution

Fire (*Continued*)
in, of, on, starting in (*Continued*)
(educational) (dormitory) (residential)) (school) (shop) (store) (theatre) (*see also* Conflagration, building or structure, except private dwelling) E891.9
forest (uncontrolled) E892
glider E842
grass (uncontrolled) E892
hay (uncontrolled) E892
lumber (uncontrolled) E892
machinery - *see* Accident, machine
mine (uncontrolled) E892
motor vehicle (in motion) (on public highway) E818
not on public highway E825
stationary E892
prairie (uncontrolled) E892
private dwelling (apartment) (boarding house) (camping place) (caravan) (farmhouse) (home (private)) (house) (lodging house) (private garage) (rooming house) (tenement) (*see also* Conflagration, private dwelling) E890.9
railway rolling stock, train, vehicle (*see also* Explosion, railway engine) E803
stationary E892
room NEC E898.1
street car (in motion) E829
stationary E892
transport vehicle, stationary NEC E892
tunnel (uncontrolled) E892
war operations (by fire-producing device or conventional weapon) E990.9
from nuclear explosion E996
petrol bomb E990.0
late effect of NEC E929.4
lumber (uncontrolled) E892
mine (uncontrolled) E892
prairie (uncontrolled) E892
self-inflicted (unspecified whether accidental or intentional) E988.1
stated as intentional, purposeful E958.1
specified NEC E898.1
with
conflagration - *see* Conflagration
ignition (of)
clothing - *see* Ignition, clothes
highly inflammable material (benzine) (fat) (gasoline) (kerosene) (paraffin) (petrol) E894
started by other person
stated as
with intent to injure or kill E968.0
undetermined whether or not with intent to injure or kill E988.1
suicide (attempted) E958.1
late effect of E959
tunnel (uncontrolled) E892
Fireball effects from nuclear explosion in war operations E996
Fireworks (explosion) E923.0
Flash burns from explosion (*see also* Explosion) E923.9

Flood (any injury) (resulting from storm) E908.2
caused by collapse of dam or manmade structure E909.3
Forced landing (aircraft) E840
Foreign body, object or material (entrance into (accidental))
air passage (causing injury) E915
with asphyxia, obstruction, suffocation E912
food or vomitus E911
nose (with asphyxia, obstruction, suffocation) E912
causing injury without asphyxia, obstruction, suffocation E915
alimentary canal (causing injury) (with obstruction) E915
with asphyxia, obstruction respiratory passage, suffocation E912
food E911
mouth E915
with asphyxia, obstruction, suffocation E912
food E911
pharynx E915
with asphyxia, obstruction, suffocation E912
food E911
aspiration (with asphyxia, obstruction respiratory passage, suffocation) E912
causing injury without asphyxia, obstruction respiratory passage, suffocation E915
food (regurgitated) (vomited) E911
causing injury without asphyxia, obstruction respiratory passage, suffocation E915
mucus (not of newborn) E912
phlegm E912
bladder (causing injury or obstruction) E915
bronchus, bronchi - *see* Foreign body, air passages
conjunctival sac E914
digestive system - *see* Foreign body, alimentary canal
ear (causing injury or obstruction) E915
esophagus (causing injury or obstruction) (*see also* Foreign body, alimentary canal) E915
eye (any part) E914
eyelid E914
hairball (stomach) (with obstruction) E915
ingestion - *see* Foreign body, alimentary canal
inhalation - *see* Foreign body, aspiration
intestine (causing injury or obstruction) E915
iris E914
lacrimal apparatus E914
larynx - *see* Foreign body, air passage
late effect of NEC E929.8
lung - *see* Foreign body, air passage
mouth - *see* Foreign body, alimentary canal, mouth
nasal passage - *see* Foreign body, air passage, nose
nose - *see* Foreign body, air passage, nose
ocular muscle E914

Homicide, homicidal (attempt) (justifiable) (*see also* Assault) E968.9
Hot
  liquid, object, substance, accident caused by - *see also* Accident, caused by, hot, by type of substance
  late effect of E929.8
  place, effects - *see* Heat
  weather, effects E900.0
Humidity, causing problem E904.3
Hunger E904.1
  resulting from
    abandonment or neglect E904.0
    transport accident - *see* categories E800-E848
Hurricane (any injury) E908.0
Hypobarism, hypobaropathy - *see* Effects of, air pressure
Hypothermia - *see* Cold, exposure to

I

Ictus
  caloris - *see* Heat
  solaris E900.0
Ignition (accidental)
  anesthetic gas in operating theatre E923.2
  bedclothes
    with
      conflagration - *see* Conflagration
      ignition (of)
        clothing - *see* Ignition, clothes
        highly inflammable material obstruction (benzine) (fat) (gasoline) (kerosene) (paraffin) (petrol) E894
  benzine E894
  clothes, clothing (from controlled fire) (in building) E893.9
    with conflagration - *see* Conflagration
    from
      bonfire E893.2
      highly inflammable material E894
      sources or material as listed in E893.8
      trash fire E893.2
      uncontrolled fire - *see* Conflagration
    in
      private dwelling E893.0
      specified building or structure, except of private dwelling E893.1
    not in building or structure E893.2
  explosive material - *see* Explosion
  fat E894
  gasoline E894
  kerosene E894
  material
    explosive - *see* Explosion
    highly inflammable E894
      with conflagration - *see* Conflagration
      with explosion E923.2
  nightdress - *see* Ignition, clothes
  paraffin E894
  petrol E894
Immersion - *see* Submersion
Implantation of quills of porcupine E906.8

Inanition (from) E904.9
  hunger - *see* Lack of, food
  resulting from homicidal intent E968.4
  thirst - *see* Lack of, water
Inattention after, at birth E904.0
  homicidal, infanticidal intent E968.4
Infanticide (*see also* Assault)
Ingestion
  foreign body (causing injury) (with obstruction) - *see* Foreign body, alimentary canal
  poisonous substance NEC - *see* Table of Drugs and Chemicals
Inhalation
  excessively cold substance, manmade E901.1
  foreign body - *see* Foreign body, aspiration
  liquid air, hydrogen, nitrogen E901.1
  mucus, not of newborn (with asphyxia, obstruction respiratory passage, suffocation) E912
  phlegm (with asphyxia, obstruction respiratory passage, suffocation) E912
  poisonous gas - *see* Table of Drugs and Chemicals
  smoke from, due to
    fire - *see* Fire
    tobacco, second-hand E869.4
  vomitus (with asphyxia, obstruction respiratory passage, suffocation) E911
Injury, injured (accidental(ly)) NEC E928.9
  by, caused by, from
    air rifle (B-B gun) E922.4
    animal (not being ridden) NEC E906.9
      being ridden (in sport or transport) E828
    assault (*see also* Assault) E968.9
    avalanche E909.2
    bayonet (*see also* Bayonet wound) E920.3
    being thrown against some part of, or object in
      motor vehicle (in motion) (on public highway) E818
        not on public highway E825
      nonmotor road vehicle NEC E829
      off-road motor vehicle NEC E821
      railway train E806
      snow vehicle, motor-driven E820
      street car E829
    bending E927
    broken glass E920.8
    bullet - *see* Shooting
    cave-in (*see also* Suffocation, due to, cave-in) E913.3
      earth surface movement or eruption E909.9
      storm E908.9
      without asphyxiation or suffocation E916
    cloudburst E908.8
    cutting or piercing instrument (*see also* Cut) E920.9
    cyclone E908.1
    earthquake E909.0
    electric current (*see also* Electric shock) E925.9
    explosion (*see also* Explosion) E923.9
    fire - *see* Fire

Injury, injured (*Continued*)
  by, caused by, from (*Continued*)
    flare, Verey pistol E922.8
    flood E908.2
    foreign body - *see* Foreign body
    hailstones E904.3
    hurricane E908.0
    landslide E909.2
    law-enforcing agent, police, in course of legal intervention - *see* Legal intervention
    lightning E907
    live rail or live wire - *see* Electric shock
    machinery - *see also* Accident, machine aircraft, without accident to aircraft E844
      boat, ship, watercraft (deck) (engine room) (galley) (laundry) (loading) E836
    missile
      explosive E923.8
      firearm - *see* Shooting
      in war operations - *see* War operations, missile
    moving part of motor vehicle (in motion) (on public highway) E818
      not on public highway, nontraffic accident E825
      while alighting, boarding, entering, leaving - *see* Fall, from, motor vehicle, while alighting, boarding
    nail E920.8
    needle (sewing) E920.4
      hypodermic E920.5
    noise E928.1
    object
      fallen on
        motor vehicle (in motion) (on public highway) E818
        not on public highway E825
      falling - *see* Hit by, object, failing
    radiation - *see* Radiation
    railway rolling stock, train, vehicle (part of) E805
      door or window E806
    rotating propeller, aircraft E844
    rough landing of off-road type motor vehicle (after leaving ground or rough terrain) E821
      snow vehicle E820
    saber (*see also* Wound, saber) E920.3
    shot - *see* Shooting
    sound waves E928.1
    splinter or sliver, wood E920.8
    straining E927
    street car (door) E829
    suicide (attempt) E958.9
    sword E920.3
    third rail - *see* Electric shock
    thunderbolt E907
    tidal wave E909.4
      caused by storm E908.0
    tornado E908.1
    torrential rain E908.2
    twisting E927
    vehicle NEC - *see* Accident, vehicle NEC
    vibration E928.2
    volcanic eruption E909.1
    weapon burst, in war operations E993

Obstruction
air passages, larynx, respiratory passages
by
external means NEC - *see* Suffocation
food, any type (regurgitated) (vomited) E911
material or object, except food E912
mucus E912
phlegm E912
vomitus E911
digestive tract, except mouth or pharynx
by
food, any type E915
foreign body (any) E915
esophagus
food E911
foreign body, except food E912
without asphyxia or obstruction of respiratory passage E915
mouth or pharynx
by
food, any type E911
material or object, except food E912
respiration - *see* Obstruction, air passages
Oil in eye E914
Overdose
anesthetic (drug) - *see* Table of Drugs and Chemicals
drug - *see* Table of Drugs and Chemicals
Overexertion (lifting) (pulling) (pushing) E927
Overexposure (accidental) (to)
cold (*see also* Cold, exposure to) E901.9
due to manmade conditions E901.1
heat (*see also* Heat) E900.9
radiation - *see* Radiation
radioactivity - *see* Radiation
sun, except sunburn E900.0
weather - *see* Exposure
wind - *see* Exposure
Overheated (*see also* Heat) E900.9
Overlaid E913.0
Overturning (accidental)
animal-drawn vehicle E827
boat, ship, watercraft
causing
drowning, submersion E830
injury except drowning, submersion E831
machinery - *see* Accident, machine
motor vehicle (*see also* Loss of control, motor vehicle) E816
with antecedent collision on public highway - *see* Collision, motor vehicle
not on public highway, nontraffic accident E825
with antecedent collision - *see* Collision, motor vehicle, not on public highway
nonmotor road vehicle NEC E829
off-road type motor vehicle - *see* Loss of control, off-road type motor vehicle
pedal cycle E826
railway rolling stock, train, vehicle (*see also* Derailment, railway) E802
street car E829
vehicle NEC - *see* Accident, vehicle NEC

P

Palsy, divers' E902.2
Parachuting (voluntary) (without accident to aircraft) E844
due to accident to aircraft - *see* categories E840-E842
Paralysis
divers' E902.2
lead or saturnine E866.0
from pesticide NEC E863.4
Pecked by bird E906.8
Phlegm aspiration or inhalation (with asphyxia, obstruction respiratory passage, suffocation) E912
Piercing (*see also* Cut) E920.9
Pinched
between objects (moving) (stationary and moving) E918
in object E918
Pinned under
machine(ry) - *see* Accident, machine
Place of occurrence of accident - *see* Accident (to), occurring (at) (in)
Plumbism E866.0
from insecticide NEC E863.4
Poisoning (accidental) (by) - *see also* Table of Drugs and Chemicals
carbon monoxide
generated by
aircraft in transit E844
motor vehicle
in motion (on public highway) E818
not on public highway E825
watercraft (in transit) (not in transit) E838
caused by injection of poisons or toxins into or through skin by plant thorns, spines, or other mechanism E905.7
marine or sea plants E905.6
fumes or smoke due to
conflagration - *see* Conflagration
explosion or fire - *see* Fire
ignition - *see* Ignition
gas
in legal intervention E972
legal execution, by E978
on watercraft E838
used as anesthetic - *see* Table of Drugs and Chemicals
in war operations E997.2
late effect of - *see* Late effect
legal
execution E978
intervention
by gas E972
Pressure, external, causing asphyxia, suffocation (*see also* Suffocation) E913.9
Privation E904.9
food (*see also* Lack of, food) E904.1
helpless person, infant, newborn due to abandonment or neglect E904.0
late effect of NEC E929.5
resulting from transport accident - *see* categories E800-E848
water (*see also* Lack of, water) E904.2
Projected objects, striking against or struck by - *see* Striking against, object
Prolonged stay in
high altitude (causing conditions as listed in E902.0) E902.0
weightless environment E928.0

Prostration
heat - *see* Heat
Pulling, injury in E927
Puncture, puncturing (*see also* Cut) E920.9
by
plant thorns or spines E920.8
toxic reaction E905.7
marine or sea plants E905.6
sea-urchin spine E905.6
Pushing (injury in) (overexertion) E927
by other person(s) (accidental) E917.9
as, or caused by, a crowd, human stampede (with fall) E917.1
before moving vehicle or object
stated as
intentional, homicidal E968.8
undetermined whether accidental or intentional E988.8
from
high place
in accidental circumstances - *see* categories E880-E884
stated as
intentional, homicidal E968.1
undetermined whether accidental or intentional E987.9
man-made structure, except residential E987.1
natural site E987.2
residential E987.0
motor vehicle (*see also* Fall, from, motor vehicle) E818
stated as
intentional, homicidal E968.5
undetermined whether accidental or intentional E988.8
in sports E917.0
with fall E886.0
with fall E886.9
in sports E886.0

R

Radiation (exposure to) E926.9
abnormal reaction to medical test or therapy E879.2
arc lamps E926.2
atomic power plant (malfunction) NEC E926.9
in water transport E838
electromagnetic, ionizing E926.3
gamma rays E926.3
in
war operations (from or following nuclear explosion) (direct) (secondary) E996
laser(s) E997.0
water transport E838
inadvertent exposure of patient (receiving test or therapy) E873.3
infrared (heaters and lamps) E926.1
excessive heat E900.1
ionized, ionizing (particles, artificially accelerated) E926.8
electromagnetic E926.3
isotopes, radioactive - *see* Radiation, radioactive isotopes
laser(s) E926.4
in war operations E997.0
misadventure in medical care - *see* Misadventure, failure, in dosage, radiation

S

Scald, scalding *(Continued)*
  self-inflicted *(Continued)*
    stated as intentional, purposeful
      E958.2
    stated as undetermined whether acci-
      dental or intentional E988.2
    steam E924.0
    tap water (boiling) E924.2
    transport accident - *see* categories
      E800-E848
    vapor E924.0
Scratch, cat E906.8
Sea
  sickness E903
Self-mutilation - *see* Suicide
Shock
  anaphylactic (*see also* Table of Drugs
    and Chemicals) E947.9
    due to
      bite (venomous) - *see* Bite, venom-
        ous NEC
      sting - *see* Sting
  electric (*see also* Electric shock) E925.9
  from electric appliance or current (*see
    also* Electric shock) E925.9
Shooting, shot (accidental(ly)) E922.9
  air gun E922.4
  BB gun E922.4
  hand gun (pistol) (revolver) E922.0
  himself (*see also* Shooting, self-inflicted)
    E985.4
    hand gun (pistol) (revolver) E985.0
    military firearm, except hand gun
      E985.3
      hand gun (pistol) (revolver) E985.0
    rifle (hunting) E985.2
      military E985.3
    shotgun (automatic) E985.1
    specified firearm NEC E985.4
    Verey pistol E985.4
  homicide (attempt) E965.4
    air gun E968.6
    BB gun E968.6
    hand gun (pistol) (revolver) E965.0
    military firearm, except hand gun
      E965.3
      hand gun (pistol) (revolver) E965.0
    rifle (hunting) E965.2
      military E965.3
    shotgun (automatic) E965.1
    specified firearm NEC E965.4
    Verey pistol E965.4
  inflicted by other person
    in accidental circumstances E922.9
      hand gun (pistol) (revolver) E922.0
      military firearm, except hand gun
        E922.3
        hand gun (pistol) (revolver)
          E922.0
      rifle (hunting) E922.2
        military E922.3
      shotgun (automatic) E922.1
      specified firearm NEC E922.8
      Verey pistol E922.8
    stated as E922.8
      intentional, homicidal E965.4
        hand gun (pistol) (revolver)
          E965
        military firearm, except hand
          gun E965.3
          hand gun (pistol) (revolver)
            E965.0
        rifle (hunting) E965.2
          military E965.3

Shooting, shot *(Continued)*
  inflicted by other person *(Continued)*
    stated as *(Continued)*
      intentional, homicidal *(Continued)*
        shotgun (automatic) E965.1
        specified firearm E965.4
        Verey pistol E965.4
      undetermined whether accidental
        or intentional E985.4
        air gun E985.6
        BB gun E985.6
        hand gun (pistol) (revolver)
          E985.0
        military firearm, except hand
          gun E985.3
          hand gun (pistol) (revolver)
            E985.0
        rifle (hunting) E985.2
        shotgun (automatic) E985.1
        specified firearm NEC E985.4
        Verey pistol E985.4
    in war operations - *see* War operations,
      shooting
    legal
      execution E978
      intervention E970
    military firearm, except hand gun
      E922.3
      hand gun (pistol) (revolver) E922.0
    rifle (hunting) E922.2
      military E922.3
    self-inflicted (unspecified whether acci-
      dental or intentional) E985.4
      air gun E985.6
      BB gun E985.6
      hand gun (pistol) (revolver) E985.0
      military firearm, except hand gun
        E985.3
        hand gun (pistol) (revolver)
          E985.0
      rifle (hunting) E985.2
        military E985.3
      shotgun (automatic) E985.1
      specified firearm NEC E985.4
      stated as
        accidental E922.9
          hand gun (pistol) (revolver)
            E922.0
          military firearm, except hand
            gun E922.3
            hand gun (pistol) (revolver)
              E922.0
          rifle (hunting) E922.2
            military E922.3
          shotgun (automatic) E922.1
          specified firearm NEC E922.8
          Verey pistol E922.8
        intentional, purposeful E955.4
          hand gun (pistol) (revolver)
            E955.0
          military firearm, except hand
            gun E955.3
            hand gun (pistol) (revolver)
              E955.0
          rifle (hunting) E955.2
            military E955.3
          shotgun (automatic) E955.1
          specified firearm NEC E955.4
          Verey pistol E955.4
    shotgun (automatic) E922.1
    specified firearm NEC E922.8
    stated as undetermined whether acci-
      dental or intentional E985.4
      hand gun (pistol) (revolver) E985.0

Shooting, shot *(Continued)*
  stated as undetermined whether acci-
    dental or intentional *(Continued)*
    military firearm, except hand gun
      E985.3
      hand gun (pistol) (revolver) E985.0
    rifle (hunting) E985.2
      military E985.3
    shotgun (automatic) E985.1
    specified firearm NEC E985.4
    Verey pistol E985.4
  suicidal (attempt) E955.4
    air gun E985.6
    BB gun E985.6
    hand gun (pistol) (revolver) E955.0
    military firearm, except hand gun
      E955.3
    hand gun (pistol) (revolver) E955.0
    rifle (hunting) E955.2
      military E955.3
    shotgun (automatic) E955.1
    specified firearm NEC E955.4
    Verey pistol E955.4
  Verey pistol E922.8
Shoving (accidentally) by other person
  (*see also* Pushing by other person)
  E917.9
Sickness
  air E903
  alpine E902.0
  car E903
  motion E903
  mountain E902.0
  sea E903
  travel E903
Sinking (accidental)
  boat, ship, watercraft (causing drown-
    ing, submersion) E830
  causing injury except drowning,
    submersion E831
Siriasis E900.0
Skydiving E844
Slashed wrists (*see also* Cut, self-inflicted) E986
Slipping (accidental)
  on
    deck (of boat, ship, watercraft) (icy)
      (oily) (wet) E835
    ice E885
    ladder of ship E833
      due to accident to watercraft E831
    mud E885
    oil E885
    snow E885
    stairs of ship E833
      due to accident to watercraft E831
    surface
      slippery E885
      wet E885
Sliver, wood, injury by E920.8
Smothering, smothered (*see also* Suffoca-
  tion) E913.9
Sodomy (assault) E960.1
Solid substance in eye (any part) or ad-
  nexa E914
Sound waves (causing injury) E928.1
Splinter, injury by E920.8
Stab, stabbing E966
  accidental - *see* Cut
Starvation E904.1
  helpless person, infant, newborn - *see*
    Lack of food
  homicidal intent E968.4
  late effect of NEC E929.5

Suffocation *(Continued)*
  due to, by *(Continued)*
    phlegm (aspiration) (inhalation) E912
    pillow E913.0
    plastic bag - *see* Suffocation, in, plastic bag
    sheet (plastic) E913.0
    specified means NEC E913.8
    vomitus (aspiration) (inhalation) E911
  homicidal (attempt) E963
  in
    airtight enclosed place E913.2
    baby carriage E913.0
    bed E913.0
    closed place E913.2
    cot, cradle E913.0
    perambulator E913.0
    plastic bag (in accidental circumstances) E913.1
      homicidal, purposely inflicted by other person E963
      self-inflicted (unspecified whether accidental or intentional) E983.1
        in accidental circumstances E913.1
        intentional, suicidal E953.1
      stated as undetermined whether accidentally or purposely inflicted E983.1
      suicidal, purposely self-inflicted E953.1
    refrigerator E913.2
  self-inflicted - *see also* Suffocation, stated as undetermined whether accidental or intentional E953.9
    in accidental circumstances - *see* category E913
    stated as intentional, purposeful - *see* Suicide, suffocation
  stated as undetermined whether accidental or intentional E983.9
    by, in
      hanging E983.0
      plastic bag E983.1
      specified means NEC E983.8
  suicidal - *see* Suicide, suffocation

Suicide, suicidal (attempted) (by) E958.9
  burning, burns E958.1
  caustic substance E958.7
    poisoning E950.7
    swallowed E950.7
  cold, extreme E958.3
  cut (any part of body) E956
  cutting or piercing instrument (classifiable to E920) E956
  drowning E954
  electrocution E958.4
  explosive(s) (classifiable to E923) E955.5
  fire E958.1
  firearm (classifiable to E922) - *see* Shooting, suicidal
  hanging E953.0
  jumping
    before moving object, train, vehicle E958.0
    from high place - *see* Jumping, from, high place, stated as, suicidal
  knife E956
  late effect of E959
  motor vehicle, crashing of E958.5

Suicide, suicidal *(Continued)*
  poisoning - *see* Table of Drugs and Chemicals
  puncture (any part of body) E956
  scald E958.2
  shooting - *see* Shooting, suicidal
  specified means NEC E958.8
  stab (any part of body) E956
  strangulation - *see* Suicide, suffocation
  submersion E954
  suffocation E953.9
    by, in
      hanging E953.0
      plastic bag E953.1
      specified means NEC E953.8
  wound NEC E958.9
Sunburn E926.2
Sunstroke E900.0
Supersonic waves (causing injury) E928.1
Surgical procedure, complication of
  delayed or as an abnormal reaction without mention of misadventure, *see* Reaction, abnormal
  due to or as a result of misadventure - *see* Misadventure
Swallowed, swallowing
  foreign body - *see* Foreign body, alimentary canal
  poison - *see* Table of Drugs and Chemicals
  substance
    caustic - *see* Table of Drugs and Chemicals
    corrosive - *see* Table of Drugs and Chemicals
    poisonous - *see* Table of Drugs and Chemicals
Swimmers' cramp (*see also* category E910) E910.2
  not in recreation or sport E910.3
Syndrome, battered
  baby or child - *see* Abuse, child
  wife - *see* Assault

T

Tackle in sport E886.0
Thermic fever E900.9
Thermoplegia E900.9
Thirst - *see also* Lack of water
  resulting from accident connected with transport - *see* categories E800-E848
Thrown (accidentally)
  against object in or part of vehicle
    by motion of vehicle
      aircraft E844
      boat, ship, watercraft E838
      motor vehicle (on public highway) E818
        not on public highway E825
        off-road type (not on public highway) E821
          on public highway E818
        snow vehicle E820
          on public highway E818
      nonmotor road vehicle NEC E829
      railway rolling stock, train, vehicle E806
      street car E829
  from
    animal (being ridden) (in sport or transport) E828

Thrown *(Continued)*
  from *(Continued)*
    high place, homicide (attempt) E968.1
    machinery - *see* Accident, machine
    vehicle NEC - *see* Accident, vehicle NEC
  off - *see* Thrown, from
  overboard (by motion of boat, ship, watercraft) E832
    by accident to boat, ship, watercraft E830
Thunderbolt NEC E907
Tidal wave (any injury) E909.4
  caused by storm E908.0
Took
  overdose of drug - *see* Table of Drugs and Chemicals
  poison - *see* Table of Drugs and Chemicals
Tornado (any injury) E908.1
Torrential rain (any injury) E908.2
Traffic accident NEC E819
Trampled by animal E906.8
  being ridden (in sport or transport) E828
Trapped (accidentally)
  between
    objects (moving) (stationary and moving) E918
  by
    door of
      elevator E918
      motor vehicle (on public highway) (while alighting, boarding) - *see* Fall, from, motor vehicle, while alighting
      railway train (underground) E806
      street car E829
      subway train E806
  in object E918
Travel (effects) E903
  sickness E903
Tree
  falling on or hitting E916
    motor vehicle (in motion) (on public highway) E818
      not on public highway E825
    nonmotor road vehicle NEC E829
    pedal cycle E826
    person E916
    railway rolling stock, train, vehicle E806
    street car E829
Trench foot E901.0
Tripping over animal, carpet, curb, rug, or small object (with fall) E885
  without fall - *see* Striking against, object
Tsunami E909.4
Twisting, Injury in E927

V

Violence, nonaccidental (*see also* Assault) E968.9
Volcanic eruption (any injury) E909.1
Vomitus in air passages (with asphyxia, obstruction or suffocation) E911

W

War operations (during hostilities) (injury) (by) (in) E995

PART III

Diseases: Tabular List Volume 1

1. INFECTIOUS AND PARASITIC DISEASES (001–139)

Note: Categories for "late effects" of infectious and parasitic diseases are to be found at 137–139.

> **Includes:** diseases generally recognized as communicable or transmissible as well as a few diseases of unknown but possibly infectious origin

> **Excludes** *acute respiratory infections (460–466)*
> *carrier or suspected carrier of infectious organism (V02.0–V02.9)*
> *certain localized infections*
> *influenza (487.0–487.8)*

INTESTINAL INFECTIOUS DISEASES (001–009)

> **Excludes** *helminthiases (120.0–129)*

● **001 Cholera**

    001.0 Due to Vibrio cholerae

    001.1 Due to Vibrio cholerae el tor

    □ **001.9 Cholera, unspecified**

● **002 Typhoid and paratyphoid fevers**

    002.0 Typhoid fever
        Typhoid (fever) (infection) [any site]

    002.1 Paratyphoid fever A

    002.2 Paratyphoid fever B

    002.3 Paratyphoid fever C

    □ **002.9 Paratyphoid fever, unspecified**

● **003 Other salmonella infections**

> **Includes:** infection or food poisoning by Salmonella [any serotype]

    003.0 Salmonella gastroenteritis
        Salmonellosis

    003.1 Salmonella septicemia

● **003.2 Localized salmonella infections**

    □ **003.20 Localized salmonella infection, unspecified**

    003.21 Salmonella meningitis

    003.22 Salmonella pneumonia

    003.23 Salmonella arthritis

    003.24 Salmonella osteomyelitis

    □ **003.29 Other**

□ **003.8 Other specified salmonella infections**

□ **003.9 Salmonella infection, unspecified**

● **004 Shigellosis**

> **Includes:** bacillary dysentery

    004.0 Shigella dysenteriae
        Infection by group A Shigella (Schmitz) (Shiga)

    004.1 Shigella flexneri
        Infection by group B Shigella

    004.2 Shigella boydii
        Infection by group C Shigella

    004.3 Shigella sonnei
        Infection by group D Shigella

□ **004.8 Other specified shigella infections**

□ **004.9 Shigellosis, unspecified**

● **005 Other food poisoning (bacterial)**

> **Excludes** *salmonella infections (003.0–003.9)*
> *toxic effect of:*
>   *food contaminants (989.7)*
>   *noxious foodstuffs (988.0–988.9)*

    005.0 Staphylococcal food poisoning
        Staphylococcal toxemia specified as due to food

    005.1 Botulism
        Food poisoning due to Clostridium botulinum

    005.2 Food poisoning due to Clostridium perfringens [C. welchii]
        Enteritis necroticans

005.3 **Food poisoning due to other Clostridia**

005.4 **Food poisoning due to Vibrio parahaemolyticus**

● 005.8 **Other bacterial food poisoning**
　　Excludes *salmonella food poisoning (003.0–003.9)*

　　005.81 **Food poisoning due to Vibrio vulnificus**

　　□ 005.89 **Other bacterial food poisoning**
　　　　　Food poisoning due to Bacillus cereus

□ 005.9 **Food poisoning, unspecified**

● 006 **Amebiasis**

　　Includes: infection due to Entamoeba histolytica
　　Excludes *amebiasis due to organisms other than Ent-
　　　amoeba histolytica (007.8)*

006.0 **Acute amebic dysentery without mention of ab-
　　scess**
　　　Acute amebiasis

006.1 **Chronic intestinal amebiasis without mention of
　　abscess**
　　　Chronic:
　　　　amebiasis
　　　　amebic dysentery

006.2 **Amebic nondysenteric colitis**

006.3 **Amebic liver abscess**
　　　Hepatic amebiasis

006.4 **Amebic lung abscess**
　　　Amebic abscess of lung (and liver)

006.5 **Amebic brain abscess**
　　　Amebic abscess of brain (and liver) (and lung)

006.6 **Amebic skin ulceration**
　　　Cutaneous amebiasis

□ 006.8 **Amebic infection of other sites**
　　　Amebic:
　　　　appendicitis
　　　　balanitis
　　　Ameboma
　　Excludes *specific infections by free-living amebae (136.2)*

□ 006.9 **Amebiasis, unspecified**
　　　Amebiasis NOS

● 007 **Other protozoal intestinal diseases**

　　Includes: protozoal:
　　　　　colitis
　　　　　diarrhea
　　　　　dysentery

007.0 **Balantidiasis**
　　　Infection by Balantidium coli

007.1 **Giardiasis**
　　　Infection by Giardia lamblia
　　　Lambliasis

007.2 **Coccidiosis**
　　　Infection by Isospora belli and Isospora hominis
　　　Isosporiasis

007.3 **Intestinal trichomoniasis**

007.4 **Cryptosporidiosis**

□ 007.8 **Other specified protozoal intestinal diseases**
　　　Amebiasis due to organisms other than Ent-
　　　amoeba histolytica

□ 007.9 **Unspecified protozoal intestinal disease**
　　　Flagellate diarrhea
　　　Protozoal dysentery NOS

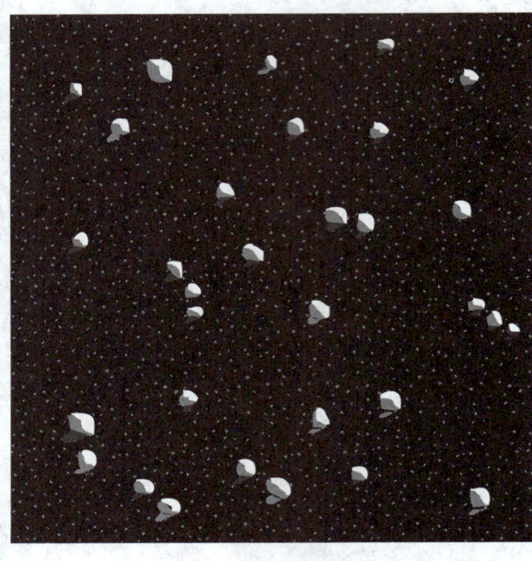

Figure 1–1 *E. coli* particles.

Item 1–1 ***Escherichia coli [E. coli]*** **is a gram-negative
bacterium found in the intestinal tracts of humans and
animals and is usually nonpathogenic. Pathogenic
strains can cause diarrhea or pyogenic (pus-producing)
infections.**

● 008 **Intestinal infections due to other organisms**

　　Includes: any condition classifiable to 009.0–009.3 with
　　　　　mention of the responsible organisms
　　Excludes *food poisoning by these organisms (005.0–005.9)*

● 008.0 **Escherichia coli [E. coli]**

　　□ 008.00 **E. coli, unspecified**
　　　　　E. coli enteritis NOS

　　008.01 **Enteropathogenic E. coli**

　　008.02 **Enterotoxigenic E. coli**

　　008.03 **Enteroinvasive E. coli**

　　008.04 **Enterohemorrhagic E. coli**

　　□ 008.09 **Other intestinal E. coli infections**

008.1 **Arizona group of paracolon bacilli**

008.2 **Aerobacter aerogenes**
　　　Enterobacter aerogenes

008.3 **Proteus (mirabilis) (morganii)**

● 008.4 **Other specified bacteria**

　　008.41 **Staphylococcus**
　　　　　Staphylococcal enterocolitis

　　008.42 **Pseudomonas**

　　008.43 **Campylobacter**

　　008.44 **Yersinia enterocolitica**

　　008.45 **Clostridium difficile**
　　　　　Pseudomembranous colitis

　　□ 008.46 **Other anaerobes**
　　　　　Anaerobic enteritis NOS
　　　　　Gram-negative anaerobes
　　　　　　Bacteroides (fragilis)

　　□ 008.47 **Other gram-negative bacteria**
　　　　　Gram-negative enteritis NOS
　　　Excludes *gram-negative anaerobes (008.46)*

　　□ 008.49 **Other**

□ 008.5 **Bacterial enteritis, unspecified**

　　◄► **New Code**　　⬅▮▮ ▮▮➡ **Revised Code**　　● **Not a Principal Diagnosis**　　● **Use Additional Digit(s)**　　□ **Nonspecific Code**

● **008.6 Enteritis due to specified virus**

    008.61 Rotavirus

    008.62 Adenovirus

    008.63 Norwalk virus
        Norwalk-like agent

    ☐ **008.64 Other small round viruses [SRVs]**
        Small round virus NOS

    008.65 Calcivirus

    008.66 Astrovirus

    008.67 Enterovirus NEC
        Coxsackie virus
        Echovirus

    | Excludes | *poliovirus (045.0–045.9)* |

    ☐ **008.69 Other viral enteritis**
        Torovirus

☐ **008.8 Other organism, not elsewhere classified**
    Viral:
        enteritis NOS
        gastroenteritis

    | Excludes | *influenza with involvement of gastrointestinal tract (487.8)* |

● **009 Ill-defined intestinal infections**

    | Excludes | *diarrheal disease or intestinal infection due to specified organism (001.0–008.8)* |
    diarrhea following gastrointestinal surgery (564.4)
    intestinal malabsorption (579.0–579.9)
    ischemic enteritis (557.0–557.9)
    other noninfectious gastroenteritis and colitis (558.1–558.9)
    regional enteritis (555.0–555.9)
    ulcerative colitis (556)

    009.0 Infectious colitis, enteritis, and gastroenteritis
        Colitis (septic)
        Dysentery:
          NOS
          catarrhal
          hemorrhagic
        Enteritis (septic)
        Gastroenteritis (septic)

009.1 Colitis, enteritis, and gastroenteritis of presumed infectious origin

    | Excludes | *colitis NOS (558.9)* |
    enteritis NOS (558.9)
    gastroenteritis NOS (558.9)

009.2 Infectious diarrhea
    Diarrhea:
        dysenteric
        epidemic
    Infectious diarrheal disease NOS

009.3 Diarrhea of presumed infectious origin

    | Excludes | *diarrhea NOS (787.91)* |

TUBERCULOSIS (010–018)

Includes: infection by Mycobacterium tuberculosis (human) (bovine)

| Excludes | *congenital tuberculosis (771.2)* |
late effects of tuberculosis (137.0–137.4)

The following fifth-digit subclassification is for use with categories 010–018:

  ☐ 0 unspecified
    1 bacteriological or histological examination not done
    2 bacteriological or histological examination unknown (at present)
    3 tubercle bacilli found (in sputum) by microscopy
    4 tubercle bacilli not found (in sputum) by microscopy, but found by bacterial culture
    5 tubercle bacilli not found by bacteriological examination, but tuberculosis confirmed histologically
    6 tubercle bacilli not found by bacteriological or histological examination, but tuberculosis confirmed by other methods [inoculation of animals]

Item 1–2 Tuberculosis is caused by the *Mycobacterium tuberculosis* organism. The first tuberculosis infection is called the **primary infection.** A Ghon lesion is the **initial lesion.** A **secondary lesion** occurs when the tubercle bacilli are carried to other areas.

● **010 Primary tuberculous infection**

    Requires fifth digit. See beginning of section 010–018 for codes and definitions.

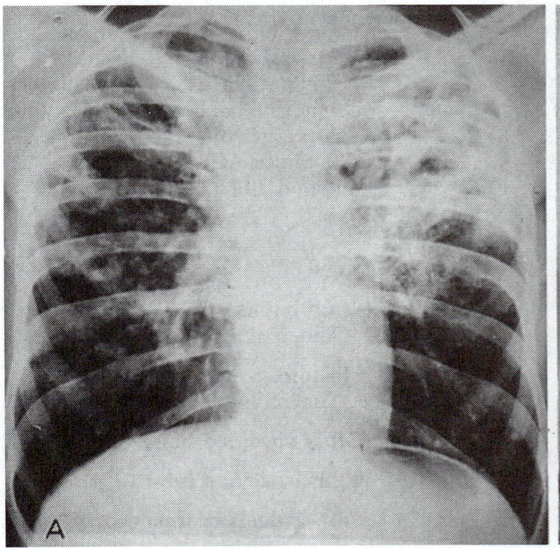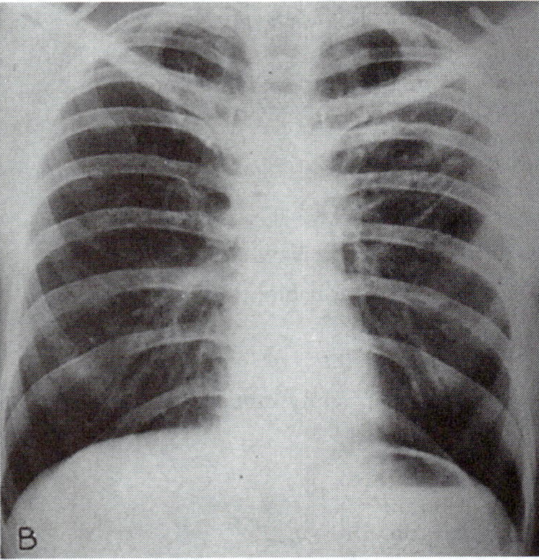

Figure 1–2   Far advanced bilateral pulmonary tuberculosis before and after 8 months of treatment with streptomycin, PAS, and isoniazid. (From Hinshaw HC, Garland LH: Diseases of the Chest, 2nd ed. Philadelphia, WB Saunders, 1963, p. 538.)

◄▶ **New Code**   ◄▦▶ **Revised Code**   ● **Not a Principal Diagnosis**   ● **Use Additional Digit(s)**   ☐ **Nonspecific Code**

● **010.0 Primary tuberculous infection**
Excludes *nonspecific reaction to tuberculin skin test without active tuberculosis (795.5)*
positive PPD (795.5)
positive tuberculin skin test without active tuberculosis (795.5)

● **010.1 Tuberculous pleurisy in primary progressive tuberculosis**

□● **010.8 Other primary progressive tuberculosis**
Excludes *tuberculous erythema nodosum (017.1)*

□● **010.9 Primary tuberculous infection, unspecified**

● **011 Pulmonary tuberculosis**

Requires fifth digit. See beginning of section 010–018 for codes and definitions.

Use additional code to identify any associated silicosis (502)

● **011.0 Tuberculosis of lung, infiltrative**

● **011.1 Tuberculosis of lung, nodular**

● **011.2 Tuberculosis of lung with cavitation**

● **011.3 Tuberculosis of bronchus**
Excludes *isolated bronchial tuberculosis (012.2)*

● **011.4 Tuberculous fibrosis of lung**

● **011.5 Tuberculous bronchiectasis**

● **011.6 Tuberculous pneumonia [any form]**

● **011.7 Tuberculous pneumothorax**

□● **011.8 Other specified pulmonary tuberculosis**

□● **011.9 Pulmonary tuberculosis, unspecified**
Respiratory tuberculosis NOS
Tuberculosis of lung NOS

● **012 Other respiratory tuberculosis**

Requires fifth digit. See beginning of section 010–018 for codes and definitions.
Excludes *respiratory tuberculosis, unspecified (011.9)*

● **012.0 Tuberculous pleurisy**
Tuberculosis of pleura
Tuberculous empyema
Tuberculous hydrothorax
Excludes *pleurisy with effusion without mention of cause (511.9)*
tuberculous pleurisy in primary progressive tuberculosis (010.1)

● **012.1 Tuberculosis of intrathoracic lymph nodes**
Tuberculosis of lymph nodes:
hilar
mediastinal
tracheobronchial
Tuberculous tracheobronchial adenopathy
Excludes *that specified as primary (010.0–010.9)*

● **012.2 Isolated tracheal or bronchial tuberculosis**

● **012.3 Tuberculous laryngitis**
Tuberculosis of glottis

□● **012.8 Other specified respiratory tuberculosis**
Tuberculosis of:
mediastinum
nasopharynx
nose (septum)
sinus [any nasal]

● **013 Tuberculosis of meninges and central nervous system**

Requires fifth digit. See beginning of section 010–018 for codes and definitions.

● **013.0 Tuberculous meningitis**
Tuberculosis of meninges (cerebral) (spinal)
Tuberculous:
leptomeningitis
meningoencephalitis
Excludes *tuberculoma of meninges (013.1)*

● **013.1 Tuberculoma of meninges**

● **013.2 Tuberculoma of brain**
Tuberculosis of brain (current disease)

● **013.3 Tuberculous abscess of brain**

● **013.4 Tuberculoma of spinal cord**

● **013.5 Tuberculous abscess of spinal cord**

● **013.6 Tuberculous encephalitis or myelitis**

□● **013.8 Other specified tuberculosis of central nervous system**

□● **013.9 Unspecified tuberculosis of central nervous system**
Tuberculosis of central nervous system NOS

● **014 Tuberculosis of intestines, peritoneum, and mesenteric glands**

Requires fifth digit. See beginning of section 010–018 for codes and definitions.

● **014.0 Tuberculous peritonitis**
Tuberculous ascites

□● **014.8 Other**
Tuberculosis (of):
anus
intestine (large) (small)
mesenteric glands
rectum
retroperitoneal (lymph nodes)
Tuberculous enteritis

● **015 Tuberculosis of bones and joints**

Requires fifth digit. See beginning of section 010–018 for codes and definitions.

Use additional code to identify manifestation, as:
tuberculous:
arthropathy (711.4)
necrosis of bone (730.8)
osteitis (730.8)
osteomyelitis (730.8)
synovitis (727.01)
tenosynovitis (727.01)

● **015.0 Vertebral column**
Pott's disease
Use additional code to identify manifestation, as:
curvature of spine [Pott's] (737.4)
kyphosis (737.4)
spondylitis (720.81)

● **015.1 Hip**

● **015.2 Knee**

● **015.5 Limb bones**
Tuberculous dactylitis

● **015.6 Mastoid**
Tuberculous mastoiditis

□● **015.7 Other specified bone**

□● **015.8 Other specified joint**

□● **015.9 Tuberculosis of unspecified bones and joints**

● **016 Tuberculosis of genitourinary system**

Requires fifth digit. See beginning of section 010–018 for codes and definitions.

 ◄► **New Code**   ⬅⬛ ⬛➡ **Revised Code**   ● **Not a Principal Diagnosis**   ● **Use Additional Digit(s)**   □ **Nonspecific Code**

● **016.0 Kidney**
Renal tuberculosis

Use additional code to identify manifestation, as:
tuberculous:
nephropathy (583.81)
pyelitis (590.81)
pyelonephritis (590.81)

● **016.1 Bladder**

● **016.2 Ureter**

☐● **016.3 Other urinary organs**

● **016.4 Epididymis**

☐● **016.5 Other male genital organs**
Use additional code to identify manifestation, as:
tuberculosis of:
prostate (601.4)
seminal vesicle (608.81)
testis (608.81)

● **016.6 Tuberculous oophoritis and salpingitis**

☐● **016.7 Other female genital organs**
Tuberculous:
cervicitis
endometritis

☐● **016.9 Genitourinary tuberculosis, unspecified**

● **017 Tuberculosis of other organs**

Requires fifth digit. See beginning of section 010–018 for codes and definitions.

● **017.0 Skin and subcutaneous cellular tissue**

Lupus:	Tuberculosis:
exedens	colliquativa
vulgaris	cutis
Scrofuloderma	lichenoides
	papulonecrotica
	verrucosa cutis

Excludes *lupus erythematosus (695.4)*
disseminated (710.0)
lupus NOS (710.0)
nonspecific reaction to tuberculin skin test without active tuberculosis (795.5)
positive PPD (795.5)
positive tuberculin skin test without active tuberculosis (795.5)

● **017.1 Erythema nodosum with hypersensitivity reaction in tuberculosis**
Bazin's disease
Erythema:
induratum
nodosum, tuberculous
Tuberculosis indurativa

Excludes *erythema nodosum NOS (695.2)*

● **017.2 Peripheral lymph nodes**
Scrofula
Scrofulous abscess
Tuberculous adenitis

Excludes *tuberculosis of lymph nodes:*
bronchial and mediastinal (012.1)
mesenteric and retroperitoneal (014.8)
tuberculous tracheobronchial adenopathy (012.1)

● **017.3 Eye**
Use additional code to identify manifestation, as:
tuberculous:
chorioretinitis, disseminated (363.13)
episcleritis (379.09)
interstitial keratitis (370.59)
iridocyclitis, chronic (364.11)
keratoconjunctivitis (phlyctenular) (370.31)

● **017.4 Ear**
Tuberculosis of ear
Tuberculous otitis media

Excludes *tuberculous mastoiditis (015.6)*

● **017.5 Thyroid gland**

● **017.6 Adrenal glands**
Addison's disease, tuberculous

● **017.7 Spleen**

● **017.8 Esophagus**

☐● **017.9 Other specified organs**
Use additional code to identify manifestation, as:
tuberculosis of:
endocardium [any valve] (424.91)
myocardium (422.0)
pericardium (420.0)

● **018 Miliary tuberculosis**

Requires fifth digit. See beginning of section 010–018 for codes and definitions.

Includes: tuberculosis:
disseminated
generalized
miliary, whether of a single specified site, multiple sites, or unspecified site
polyserositis

● **018.0 Acute miliary tuberculosis**

☐● **018.8 Other specified miliary tuberculosis**

☐● **018.9 Miliary tuberculosis, unspecified**

ZOONOTIC BACTERIAL DISEASES (020–027)

● **020 Plague**

Includes: infection by Yersinia [Pasteurella] pestis

020.0 Bubonic

020.1 Cellulocutaneous

020.2 Septicemic

020.3 Primary pneumonic

020.4 Secondary pneumonic

☐ **020.5 Pneumonic, unspecified**

☐ **020.8 Other specified types of plague**
Abortive plague
Ambulatory plague
Pestis minor

☐ **020.9 Plague, unspecified**

● **021 Tularemia**

Includes: deerfly fever
infection by Francisella [Pasteurella] tularensis
rabbit fever

021.0 Ulceroglandular tularemia

021.1 Enteric tularemia
Tularemia:
cryptogenic
intestinal
typhoidal

021.2 Pulmonary tularemia
Bronchopneumonic tularemia

021.3 Oculoglandular tularemia

☐ **021.8 Other specified tularemia**
Tularemia:
generalized or disseminated
glandular

☐ **021.9 Unspecified tularemia**

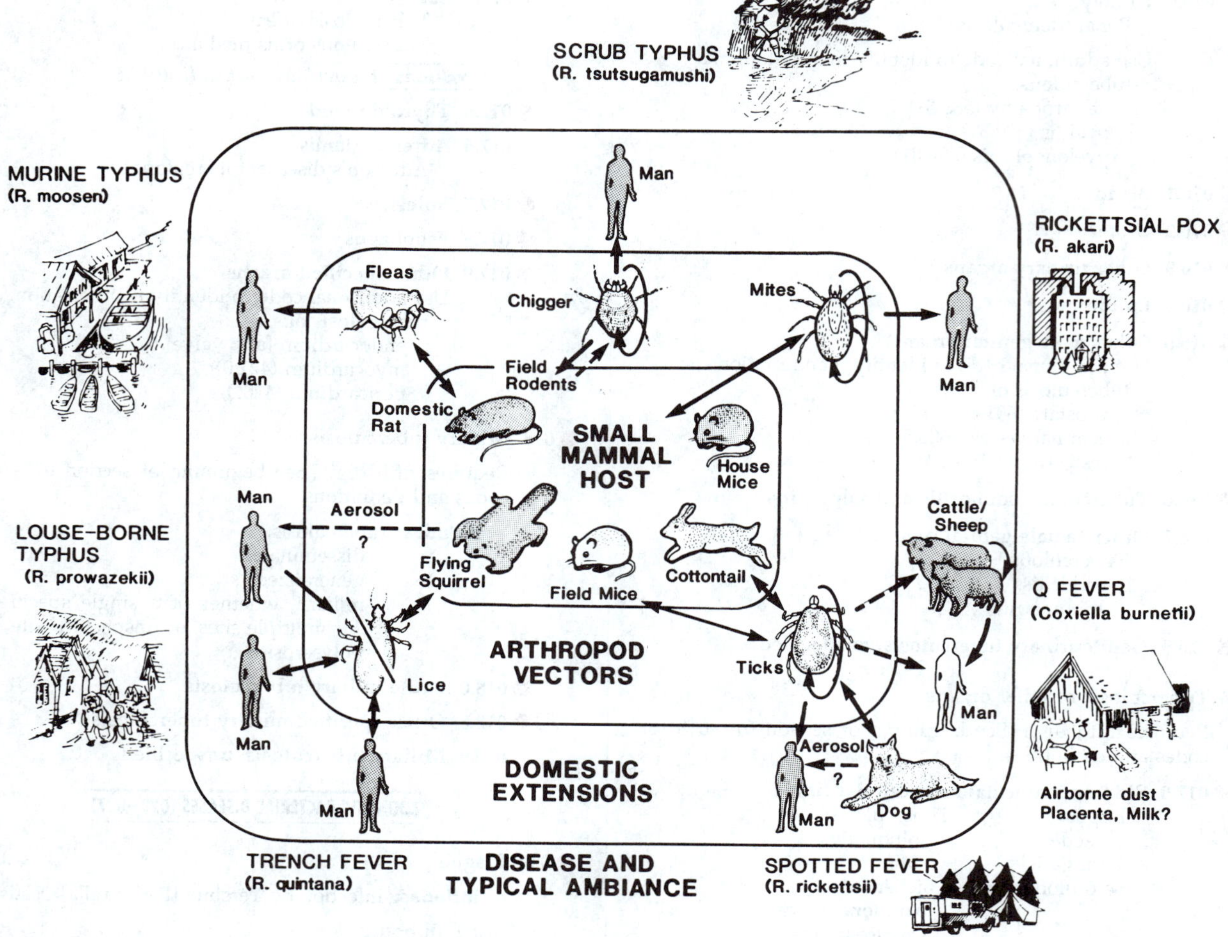

Figure 1–3 Schematic summary of some major interactions between rickettsial organisms and their small animal hosts and arthropod vectors, the participation of domestic animals, and examples of the typical ambiance under which each rickettsial infection is contacted by humans. (From Strickland GT: Hunter's Tropical Medicine, 7th ed. Philadelphia, WB Saunders, 1991, p. 261. Courtesy of Dr. J. K. Frenkel, University of Kansas Medical Center, Kansas City, KS.)

● **022 Anthrax**

  022.0 Cutaneous anthrax
    Malignant pustule

  022.1 Pulmonary anthrax
    Respiratory anthrax
    Wool-sorters' disease

  022.2 Gastrointestinal anthrax

  022.3 Anthrax septicemia

  □ **022.8 Other specified manifestations of anthrax**

  □ **022.9 Anthrax, unspecified**

● **023 Brucellosis**

  Includes: fever:
    Malta
    Mediterranean
    undulant

  023.0 Brucella melitensis

  023.1 Brucella abortus

  023.2 Brucella suis

  023.3 Brucella canis

  □ **023.8 Other brucellosis**
    Infection by more than one organism

  □ **023.9 Brucellosis, unspecified**

  024 Glanders
    Infection by:
     Actinobacillus mallei
     Malleomyces mallei
     Pseudomonas mallei
     Farcy
     Malleus

  025 Melioidosis
    Infection by:
     Malleomyces pseudomallei
     Pseudomonas pseudomallei
     Whitmore's bacillus
     Pseudoglanders

● **026 Rat-bite fever**

  026.0 Spirillary fever
    Rat-bite fever due to Spirillum minor [S. minus]
    Sodoku

  026.1 Streptobacillary fever
    Epidemic arthritic erythema
    Haverhill fever
    Rat-bite fever due to Streptobacillus moniliformis

  □ **026.9 Unspecified rat-bite fever**

  ◀▶ **New Code** ⬅▦▶ **Revised Code** ● **Not a Principal Diagnosis** ● **Use Additional Digit(s)** □ **Nonspecific Code**

● **027   Other zoonotic bacterial diseases**

027.0   Listeriosis
Infection by Listeria monocytogenes
Septicemia by Listeria monocytogenes

Use additional code to identify manifestations, as meningitis (320.7)

Excludes   *congenital listeriosis (771.2)*

027.1   Erysipelothrix infection
Erysipeloid (of Rosenbach)
Infection by Erysipelothrix insidiosa [E. rhusio-pathiae]
Septicemia by Erysipelothrix insidiosa [E. rhusio-pathiae]

027.2   Pasteurellosis
Pasteurella pseudotuberculosis infection by Pasteurella multocida [P. septica]
Mesenteric adenitis by Pasteurella multocida [P. septica]
Septic infection (cat bite) (dog bite) by Pasteurella multocida [P. septica]

Excludes   *infection by:*
Francisella [Pasteurella] tularensis (021.0–021.9)
Yersinia [Pasteurella] pestis (020.0–020.9)

☐ **027.8   Other specified zoonotic bacterial diseases**

☐ **027.9   Unspecified zoonotic bacterial disease**

OTHER BACTERIAL DISEASES (030–041)

Excludes   *bacterial venereal diseases (098.0–099.9)*
bartonellosis (088.0)

● **030   Leprosy**

Includes: Hansen's disease
infection by Mycobacterium leprae

030.0   Lepromatous [type L]
Lepromatous leprosy (macular) (diffuse) (infiltrated) (nodular) (neuritic)

030.1   Tuberculoid [type T]
Tuberculoid leprosy (macular) (maculoanesthetic) (major) (minor) (neuritic)

030.2   Indeterminate [group I]
Indeterminate [uncharacteristic] leprosy (macular) (neuritic)

030.3   Borderline [group B]
Borderline or dimorphous leprosy (infiltrated) (neuritic)

☐ **030.8   Other specified leprosy**

☐ **030.9   Leprosy, unspecified**

● **031   Diseases due to other mycobacteria**

031.0   Pulmonary
Battey disease
Infection by Mycobacterium:
avium
intracellulare [Battey bacillus]
kansasii

031.1   Cutaneous
Buruli ulcer
Infection by Mycobacterium:
marinum [M. balnei]
ulcerans

031.2   Disseminated
Disseminated mycobacterium avium-intracellulare complex (DMAC)
Mycobacterium avium-intracellulare complex (MAC) bacteremia

☐ **031.8   Other specified mycobacterial diseases**

☐ **031.9   Unspecified diseases due to mycobacteria**
Atypical mycobacterium infection NOS

● **032   Diphtheria**

Includes: infection by Corynebacterium diphtheriae

032.0   Faucial diphtheria
Membranous angina, diphtheritic

032.1   Nasopharyngeal diphtheria

032.2   Anterior nasal diphtheria

032.3   Laryngeal diphtheria
Laryngotracheitis, diphtheritic

● **032.8   Other specified diphtheria**

032.81   Conjunctival diphtheria
Pseudomembranous diphtheritic conjunctivitis

032.82   Diphtheritic myocarditis

032.83   Diphtheritic peritonitis

032.84   Diphtheritic cystitis

032.85   Cutaneous diphtheria

☐ **032.89   Other**

☐ **032.9   Diphtheria, unspecified**

● **033   Whooping cough**

Includes: pertussis
Use additional code to identify any associated pneumonia (484.3)

033.0   Bordetella pertussis [B. pertussis]

033.1   Bordetella parapertussis [B. parapertussis]

☐ **033.8   Whooping cough due to other specified organism**
Bordetella bronchiseptica [B. bronchiseptica]

☐ **033.9   Whooping cough, unspecified organism**

● **034   Streptococcal sore throat and scarlet fever**

034.0   Streptococcal sore throat
Septic:
angina
sore throat
Streptococcal:
angina
laryngitis
pharyngitis
tonsillitis

034.1   Scarlet fever
Scarlatina

Excludes   *parascarlatina (057.8)*

035   Erysipelas

Excludes   *postpartum or puerperal erysipelas (670)*

● **036   Meningococcal infection**

036.0   Meningococcal meningitis
Cerebrospinal fever (meningococcal)
Meningitis:
cerebrospinal
epidemic

036.1   Meningococcal encephalitis

036.2   Meningococcemia
Meningococcal septicemia

036.3   Waterhouse-Friderichsen syndrome, meningococcal
Meningococcal hemorrhagic adrenalitis
Meningococcic adrenal syndrome
Waterhouse-Friderichsen syndrome NOS

ICD-9-CM

001–099

Vol. 1

● 036.4 **Meningococcal carditis**

☐ 036.40 **Meningococcal carditis, unspecified**

036.41 **Meningococcal pericarditis**

036.42 **Meningococcal endocarditis**

036.43 **Meningococcal myocarditis**

● 036.8 **Other specified meningococcal infections**

036.81 **Meningococcal optic neuritis**

036.82 **Meningococcal arthropathy**

☐ 036.89 **Other**

☐ 036.9 **Meningococcal infection, unspecified**
Meningococcal infection NOS

037 **Tetanus**

| **Excludes** | *tetanus:* |
complicating:
abortion (634–638 with .0, 639.0)
ectopic or molar pregnancy (639.0)
neonatorum (771.3)
puerperal (670)

● 038 **Septicemia**

| **Excludes** | *bacteremia (790.7)* |

038.0 **Streptococcal septicemia**

● 038.1 **Staphylococcal septicemia**

☐ 038.10 **Staphylococcal septicemia, unspecified**

038.11 **Staphylococcus aureus septicemia**

☐ 038.19 **Other staphylococcal septicemia**

038.2 **Pneumococcal septicemia [Streptococcus pneumo-niae septicemia]**

038.3 **Septicemia due to anaerobes**
Septicemia due to Bacteroides

| **Excludes** | *gas gangrene (040.0)* |
that due to anaerobic streptococci (038.0)

● 038.4 **Septicemia due to other gram-negative organisms**

☐ 038.40 **Gram-negative organism, unspecified**
Gram-negative septicemia NOS

038.41 **Hemophilus influenzae [H. influenzae]**

038.42 **Escherichia coli [E. coli]**

038.43 **Pseudomonas**

038.44 **Serratia**

☐ 038.49 **Other**

☐ 038.8 **Other specified septicemias**

| **Excludes** | *septicemia (due to):* |
anthrax (022.3)
gonococcal (098.89)
herpetic (054.5)
meningococcal (036.2)
septicemic plague (020.2)

☐ 038.9 **Unspecified septicemia**
Septicemia NOS

| **Excludes** | *bacteremia NOS (790.7)* |

● 039 **Actinomycotic infections**

Includes: actinomycotic mycetoma
infection by Actinomycetales, such as species
of Actinomyces, Actinomadura, Nocardia,
Streptomyces
maduromycosis (actinomycotic)
schizomycetoma (actinomycotic)

039.0 **Cutaneous**
Erythrasma
Trichomycosis axillaris

039.1 **Pulmonary**
Thoracic actinomycosis

039.2 **Abdominal**

039.3 **Cervicofacial**

039.4 **Madura foot**

| **Excludes** | *madura foot due to mycotic infection (117.4)* |

☐ 039.8 **Of other specified sites**

☐ 039.9 **Of unspecified site**
Actinomycosis NOS
Maduromycosis NOS
Nocardiosis NOS

● 040 **Other bacterial diseases**

| **Excludes** | *bacteremia NOS (790.7)* |
bacterial infection NOS (041.9)

040.0 **Gas gangrene**
Gas bacillus infection or gangrene
Infection by Clostridium:
histolyticum
oedematiens
perfringens [welchii]
septicum
sordellii
Malignant edema
Myonecrosis, clostridial
Myositis, clostridial

040.1 **Rhinoscleroma**

040.2 **Whipple's disease**
Intestinal lipodystrophy

040.3 **Necrobacillosis**

● 040.8 **Other specified bacterial diseases**

040.81 **Tropical pyomyositis**

☐ 040.89 **Other**

● 041 **Bacterial infection in conditions classified elsewhere and of unspecified site**

Note: This category is provided to be used as an additional code to identify the bacterial agent in diseases classified elsewhere. This category will also be used to classify bacterial infections of unspecified nature or site.

| **Excludes** | *bacteremia NOS (790.7)* |
septicemia (038.0–038.9)

● 041.0 **Streptococcus**

☐ 041.00 **Streptococcus, unspecified**

041.01 **Group A**

041.02 **Group B**

041.03 **Group C**

041.04 **Group D [Enterococcus]**

041.05 **Group G**

☐ 041.09 **Other Streptococcus**

● 041.1 **Staphylococcus**

☐ 041.10 **Staphylococcus, unspecified**

041.11 **Staphylococcus aureus**

☐ 041.19 **Other Staphylococcus**

041.2 **Pneumococcus**

041.3 **Friedländer's bacillus**
Infection by Klebsiella pneumoniae

041.4 **Escherichia coli [E. coli]**

041.5 **Hemophilus influenzae [H. influenzae]**

041.6 **Proteus (mirabilis) (morganii)**

    ◀▶ **New Code**   ◀▥▥▷ **Revised Code**   ● **Not a Principal Diagnosis**   ● **Use Additional Digit(s)**   ☐ **Nonspecific Code**

041.7 **Pseudomonas**

● 041.8 **Other specified bacterial infections**

041.81 **Mycoplasma**
Eaton's agent
Pleuropneumonia-like organisms [PPLO]

041.82 **Bacillus fragilis**

041.83 **Clostridium perfringens**

□ 041.84 **Other anaerobes**
Gram-negative anaerobes
Bacteroides (fragilis)

Excludes *Helicobacter pylori (041.86)*

041.85 **Other gram-negative organisms**
Aerobacter aerogenes
Gram-negative bacteria NOS
Mima polymorpha
Serratia

Excludes *gram-negative anaerobes (041.84)*

041.86 **Helicobacter pylori (H. pylori)**

□ 041.89 **Other specified bacteria**

□ 041.9 **Bacterial infection, unspecified**

HUMAN IMMUNODEFICIENCY VIRUS (HIV) INFECTION (042)

Item 1–3 AIDS (acquired immune deficiency syndrome) is caused by HIV (human immunodeficiency virus). HIV affects certain white blood cells (T-4 lymphocytes) and destroys the ability of the cells to fight infections, making patients susceptible to a host of infectious diseases, e.g., *Pneumocystis carinii* pneumonia (PCP), Kaposi's sarcoma, and lymphoma. AIDS-related complex (ARC) is an early stage of AIDS in which tests for HIV are positive but the symptoms are mild.

042 **Human immunodeficiency virus [HIV] disease**
Acquired immune deficiency syndrome
Acquired immunodeficiency syndrome
AIDS
AIDS-like syndrome
AIDS-related complex
ARC
HIV infection, symptomatic

Use additional code(s) to identify all manifestations of HIV

Use additional code to identify HIV-2 infection (079.53)

Excludes *asymptomatic HIV infection status (V08)*
exposure to HIV virus (V01.7)
nonspecific serologic evidence of HIV (795.71)

POLIOMYELITIS AND OTHER NON-ARTHROPOD-BORNE VIRAL DISEASES OF CENTRAL NERVOUS SYSTEM (045–049)

● 045 **Acute poliomyelitis**

Excludes *late effects of acute poliomyelitis (138)*

The following fifth-digit subclassification is for use with category 045:
□ 0 poliovirus, unspecified type
1 poliovirus type I
2 poliovirus type II
3 poliovirus type III

● 045.0 **Acute paralytic poliomyelitis specified as bulbar**
Infantile paralysis (acute) specified as bulbar
Poliomyelitis (acute) (anterior) specified as bulbar
Polioencephalitis (acute) (bulbar)
Polioencephalomyelitis (acute) (anterior) (bulbar)

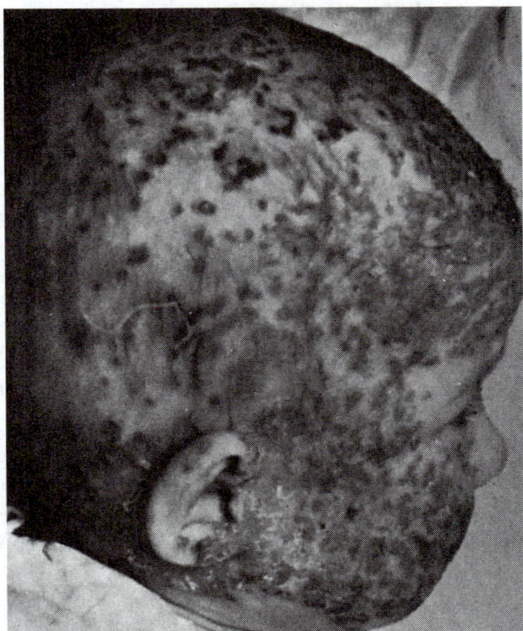

Figure 1–4 Vesicular, pustular, scabby, and necrotic lesions in Kaposi's sarcoma. (From Debre R, Celers J: Clinical Virology—The Evaluation and Management of Human Viral Infections. Philadelphia, WB Saunders, 1970, p. 460.)

□ ● 045.1 **Acute poliomyelitis with other paralysis**
Paralysis:
acute atrophic, spinal
infantile, paralytic
Poliomyelitis (acute) with paralysis except bulbar
anterior with paralysis except bulbar
epidemic with paralysis except bulbar

● 045.2 **Acute nonparalytic poliomyelitis**
Poliomyelitis (acute) specified as nonparalytic
anterior specified as nonparalytic
epidemic specified as nonparalytic

□ ● 045.9 **Acute poliomyelitis, unspecified**
Infantile paralysis unspecified whether paralytic or nonparalytic
Poliomyelitis (acute) unspecified whether paralytic or nonparalytic
anterior unspecified whether paralytic or nonparalytic
epidemic unspecified whether paralytic or nonparalytic

● 046 **Slow virus infection of central nervous system**

046.0 **Kuru**

046.1 **Jakob-Creutzfeldt disease**
Subacute spongiform encephalopathy

046.2 **Subacute sclerosing panencephalitis**
Dawson's inclusion body encephalitis
Van Bogaert's sclerosing leukoencephalitis

046.3 **Progressive multifocal leukoencephalopathy**
Multifocal leukoencephalopathy NOS

□ 046.8 **Other specified slow virus infection of central nervous system**

□ 046.9 **Unspecified slow virus infection of central nervous system**

● **047　Meningitis due to enterovirus**

  Includes: meningitis:
    abacterial
    aseptic
    viral

  | Excludes | *meningitis due to:*
    adenovirus (049.1)
    arthropod-borne virus (060.0–066.9)
    leptospira (100.81)
    virus of:
     herpes simplex (054.72)
     herpes zoster (053.0)
     lymphocytic choriomeningitis (049.0)
     mumps (072.1)
     poliomyelitis (045.0–045.9)
    any other infection specifically classified elsewhere

  047.0　Coxsackie virus

  047.1　ECHO virus
    Meningo-eruptive syndrome

 □ **047.8　Other specified viral meningitis**

 □ **047.9　Unspecified viral meningitis**
    Viral meningitis NOS

□ **048　Other enterovirus diseases of central nervous system**
  Boston exanthem

● **049　Other non-arthropod-borne viral diseases of central nervous system**

  | Excludes | *late effects of viral encephalitis (139.0)*

  049.0　Lymphocytic choriomeningitis
    Lymphocytic:
     meningitis (serous) (benign)
     meningoencephalitis (serous) (benign)

  049.1　Meningitis due to adenovirus

 □ **049.8　Other specified non-arthropod-borne viral diseases of central nervous system**
    Encephalitis:
     acute:
      inclusion body
      necrotizing
     epidemic
     lethargica
     Rio Bravo
    von Economo's disease

 □ **049.9　Unspecified non-arthropod-borne viral diseases of central nervous system**
    Viral encephalitis NOS

VIRAL DISEASES ACCOMPANIED BY EXANTHEM (050–057)

  | Excludes | *arthropod-borne viral diseases (060.0–066.9)*
    Boston exanthem (048)

● **050　Smallpox**

  050.0　Variola major
    Hemorrhagic (pustular) smallpox
    Malignant smallpox
    Purpura variolosa

  050.1　Alastrim
    Variola minor

  050.2　Modified smallpox
    Varioloid

 □ **050.9　Smallpox, unspecified**

● **051　Cowpox and paravaccinia**

  051.0　Cowpox
    Vaccinia not from vaccination
  | Excludes | *vaccinia (generalized) (from vaccination) (999.0)*

  051.1　Pseudocowpox
    Milkers' node

  051.2　Contagious pustular dermatitis
    Ecthyma contagiosum
    Orf

 □ **051.9　Paravaccinia, unspecified**

● **052　Chickenpox**

  052.0　Postvaricella encephalitis
    Postchickenpox encephalitis

  052.1　Varicella (hemorrhagic) pneumonitis

 □ **052.7　With other specified complications**

 □ **052.8　With unspecified complication**

  052.9　Varicella without mention of complication
    Chickenpox NOS
    Varicella NOS

● **053　Herpes zoster**

  Includes: shingles
    zona

  053.0　With meningitis

● **053.1　With other nervous system complications**

 □ **053.10　With unspecified nervous system complication**

  053.11　Geniculate herpes zoster
    Herpetic geniculate ganglionitis

  053.12　Postherpetic trigeminal neuralgia

  053.13　Postherpetic polyneuropathy

 □ **053.19　Other**

● **053.2　With ophthalmic complications**

  053.20　Herpes zoster dermatitis of eyelid
    Herpes zoster ophthalmicus

  053.21　Herpes zoster keratoconjunctivitis

  053.22　Herpes zoster iridocyclitis

 □ **053.29　Other**

● **053.7　With other specified complications**

  053.71　Otitis externa due to herpes zoster

 □ **053.79　Other**

 □ **053.8　With unspecified complication**

  053.9　Herpes zoster without mention of complication
    Herpes zoster NOS

Item 1–4　Herpes is a viral disease for which there is no cure. There are two types of the herpes simplex virus: Type I causes cold sores or fever blisters and Type II causes genital herpes. The virus can be spread from a sore on the lips to the genitals or from the genitals to the lips.

● **054　Herpes simplex**

  | Excludes | *congenital herpes simplex (771.2)*

  054.0　Eczema herpeticum
    Kaposi's varicelliform eruption

● **054.1　Genital herpes**

 □ **054.10　Genital herpes, unspecified**
    Herpes progenitalis

  054.11　Herpetic vulvovaginitis

  054.12　Herpetic ulceration of vulva

  054.13　Herpetic infection of penis

　◀▶ **New Code**　　◀▥▥▶ **Revised Code**　　● **Not a Principal Diagnosis**　　● **Use Additional Digit(s)**　　□ **Nonspecific Code**

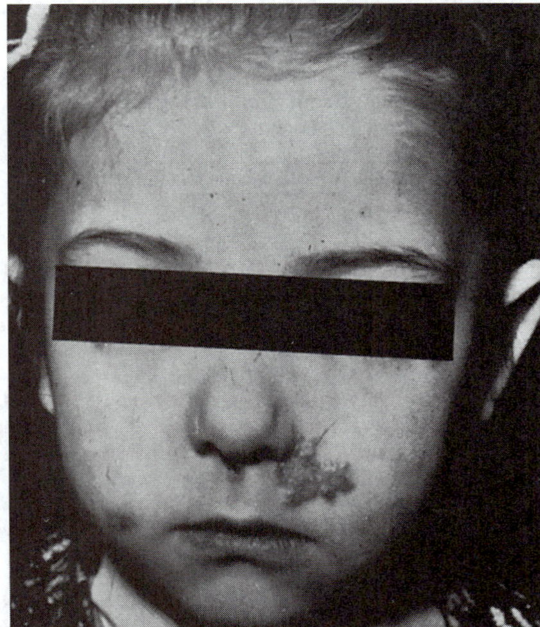

Figure 1–5   Grouped outbursts of herpes vesicles on the face. (From Debre R, Celers J: Clinical Virology—The Evaluation and Management of Human Viral Infections. Philadelphia, WB Saunders, 1970, p. 460.)

☐ **054.19 Other**

054.2 Herpetic gingivostomatitis

054.3 Herpetic meningoencephalitis
     Herpes encephalitis
     Simian B disease

● **054.4 With ophthalmic complications**

☐ **054.40 With unspecified ophthalmic complication**

054.41 Herpes simplex dermatitis of eyelid

054.42 Dendritic keratitis

054.43 Herpes simplex disciform keratitis

054.44 Herpes simplex iridocyclitis

☐ **054.49 Other**

054.5 Herpetic septicemia

054.6 Herpetic whitlow
     Herpetic felon

● **054.7 With other specified complications**

054.71 Visceral herpes simplex

054.72 Herpes simplex meningitis

054.73 Herpes simplex otitis externa

☐ **054.79 Other**

☐ **054.8 With unspecified complication**

054.9 Herpes simplex without mention of complication

● **055 Measles**

     Includes: morbilli
                 rubeola

055.0 Postmeasles encephalitis

055.1 Postmeasles pneumonia

055.2 Postmeasles otitis media

● **055.7 With other specified complications**

055.71 Measles keratoconjunctivitis
     Measles keratitis

☐ **055.79 Other**

☐ **055.8 With unspecified complication**

055.9 Measles without mention of complication

● **056 Rubella**

     Includes: German measles
     Excludes *congenital rubella (771.0)*

● **056.0 With neurological complications**

☐ **056.00 With unspecified neurological complication**

056.01 Encephalomyelitis due to rubella
     Encephalitis due to rubella
     Meningoencephalitis due to rubella

☐ **056.09 Other**

● **056.7 With other specified complications**

056.71 Arthritis due to rubella

☐ **056.79 Other**

☐ **056.8 With unspecified complications**

056.9 Rubella without mention of complication

● **057 Other viral exanthemata**

057.0 Erythema infectiosum [fifth disease]

☐ **057.8 Other specified viral exanthemata**
     Dukes (-Filatow) disease
     Exanthema subitum [sixth disease]
     Fourth disease
     Parascarlatina
     Pseudoscarlatina
     Roseola infantum

☐ **057.9 Viral exanthem, unspecified**

ARTHROPOD-BORNE VIRAL DISEASES (060–066)

Use additional code to identify any associated meningitis (321.2)

     Excludes *late effects of viral encephalitis (139.0)*

● **060 Yellow fever**

060.0 Sylvatic
     Yellow fever:
         jungle
         sylvan

060.1 Urban

☐ **060.9 Yellow fever, unspecified**

061 Dengue
     Breakbone fever
     Excludes *hemorrhagic fever caused by dengue virus (065.4)*

● **062 Mosquito-borne viral encephalitis**

062.0 Japanese encephalitis
     Japanese B encephalitis

062.1 Western equine encephalitis

062.2 Eastern equine encephalitis
     Excludes *Venezuelan equine encephalitis (066.2)*

062.3 St. Louis encephalitis

062.4 Australian encephalitis
     Australian arboencephalitis
     Australian X disease
     Murray Valley encephalitis

ICD-9-CM

001-099 Vol. 1

062.5   California virus encephalitis
Encephalitis:
California
La Crosse
Tahyna fever

062.8   Other specified mosquito-borne viral encephalitis
Encephalitis by Ilheus virus

062.9   Mosquito-borne viral encephalitis, unspecified

● **063   Tick-borne viral encephalitis**

     Includes: diphasic meningoencephalitis

063.0   Russian spring-summer [taiga] encephalitis

063.1   Louping ill

063.2   Central European encephalitis

063.8   Other specified tick-borne viral encephalitis
Langat encephalitis
Powassan encephalitis

063.9   Tick-borne viral encephalitis, unspecified

064   Viral encephalitis transmitted by other and unspecified arthropods
Arthropod-borne viral encephalitis, vector unknown
Negishi virus encephalitis
     Excludes   *viral encephalitis NOS (049.9)*

● **065   Arthropod-borne hemorrhagic fever**

065.0   Crimean hemorrhagic fever [CHF Congo virus]
Central Asian hemorrhagic fever

065.1   Omsk hemorrhagic fever

065.2   Kyasanur Forest disease

065.3   Other tick-borne hemorrhagic fever

065.4   Mosquito-borne hemorrhagic fever
Chikungunya hemorrhagic fever
Dengue hemorrhagic fever
     Excludes   *Chikungunya fever (066.3)*
                 dengue (061)
                 yellow fever (060.0–060.9)

065.8   Other specified arthropod-borne hemorrhagic fever
Mite-borne hemorrhagic fever

065.9   Arthropod-borne hemorrhagic fever, unspecified
Arbovirus hemorrhagic fever NOS

● **066   Other arthropod-borne viral diseases**

066.0   Phlebotomus fever
Changuinola fever
Sandfly fever

066.1   Tick-borne fever
Nairobi sheep disease
Tick fever:
American mountain
Colorado
Kemerovo
Quaranfil

066.2   Venezuelan equine fever
Venezuelan equine encephalitis

066.3   Other mosquito-borne fever

Fever (viral):	Fever (viral):
Bunyamwera	Oropouche
Bwamba	Pixuna
Chikungunya	Rift valley
Guama	Ross river
Mayaro	Wesselsbron
Mucambo	West Nile
O' Nyong-Nyong	Zika

     Excludes   *dengue (061)*
                 yellow fever (060.0–060.9)

066.8   Other specified arthropod-borne viral diseases
Chandipura fever
Piry fever

066.9   Arthropod-borne viral disease, unspecified
Arbovirus infection NOS

OTHER DISEASES DUE TO VIRUSES AND CHLAMYDIAE (070–079)

Item 1–5   Hepatitis A (HAV) was formerly called epidemic, infectious, short-incubation, or acute catarrhal jaundice hepatitis. The primary transmission mode is the oral–fecal route.

Item 1–6   Hepatitis B (HBV) was formerly called long-incubation period, serum, or homologous serum hepatitis. Transmission modes are through body fluids and from mother to neonate.

Item 1–7   Hepatitis C, caused by the hepatitis C virus, is primarily transfusion associated.

Item 1–8   Hepatitis D, also called delta hepatitis, is caused by the hepatitis D virus in patients formerly or currently infected with hepatitis B.

Item 1–9   Hepatitis E is also called enterically transmitted non-A, non-B hepatitis. The primary transmission mode is the oral–fecal route, usually through contaminated water.

● **070   Viral hepatitis**

     Includes: viral hepatitis (acute) (chronic)

     Excludes   *cytomegalic inclusion virus hepatitis (078.5)*

The following fifth-digit subclassification is for use with categories 070.2 and 070.3:
0 acute or unspecified, without mention of hepatitis delta
1 acute or unspecified, with hepatitis delta
   2 chronic, without mention of hepatitis delta
   3 chronic, with hepatitis delta

070.0   Viral hepatitis A with hepatic coma

070.1   Viral hepatitis A without mention of hepatic coma
Infectious hepatitis

● **070.2   Viral hepatitis B with hepatic coma**

● **070.3   Viral hepatitis B without mention of hepatic coma**
Serum hepatitis

● **070.4   Other specified viral hepatitis with hepatic coma**

070.41   Acute or unspecified hepatitis C with hepatic coma

070.42   Hepatitis delta without mention of active hepatitis B disease with hepatic coma
Hepatitis delta with hepatitis B carrier state

070.43   Hepatitis E with hepatic coma

070.44   Chronic hepatitis C with hepatic coma

070.49   Other specified viral hepatitis with hepatic coma

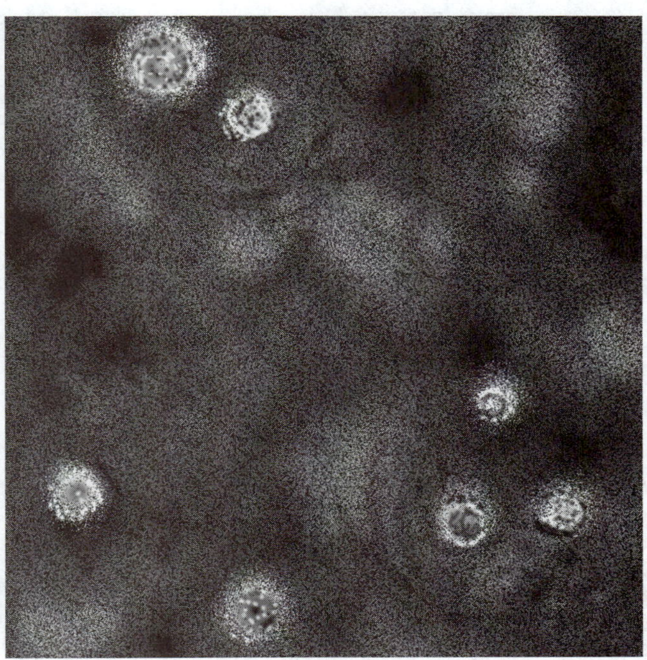

Figure 1-6   Hepatitis B virions (Dane particles).

● **070.5 Other specified viral hepatitis without mention of hepatic coma**

   ☐ **070.51 Acute or unspecified hepatitis C without mention of hepatic coma**

   070.52 Hepatitis delta without mention of active hepatitis B disease or hepatic coma

   070.53 Hepatitis E without mention of hepatic coma

   070.54 Chronic hepatitis C without mention of hepatic coma

   ☐ **070.59 Other specified viral hepatitis without mention of hepatic coma**

☐ **070.6 Unspecified viral hepatitis with hepatic coma**

☐ **070.9 Unspecified viral hepatitis without mention of hepatic coma**
    Viral hepatitis NOS

071 Rabies
    Hydrophobia
    Lyssa

● **072 Mumps**

   072.0 Mumps orchitis

   072.1 Mumps meningitis

   072.2 Mumps encephalitis
      Mumps meningoencephalitis

   072.3 Mumps pancreatitis

   ● **072.7 Mumps with other specified complications**

     072.71 Mumps hepatitis

     072.72 Mumps polyneuropathy

     ☐ **072.79 Other**

   ☐ **072.8 Mumps with unspecified complication**

   ☐ **072.9 Mumps without mention of complication**
      Epidemic parotitis
      Infectious parotitis

● **073 Ornithosis**

   Includes: parrot fever
          psittacosis

   073.0 With pneumonia
      Lobular pneumonitis due to ornithosis

   ☐ **073.7 With other specified complications**

   ☐ **073.8 With unspecified complication**

   ☐ **073.9 Ornithosis, unspecified**

● **074 Specific diseases due to Coxsackie virus**

   Excludes *Coxsackie virus:*
        infection NOS (079.2)
        meningitis (047.0)

   074.0 Herpangina
      Vesicular pharyngitis

   074.1 Epidemic pleurodynia
      Bornholm disease
      Devil's grip
      Epidemic:
        myalgia
        myositis

   ● **074.2 Coxsackie carditis**

     ☐ **074.20 Coxsackie carditis, unspecified**

     074.21 Coxsackie pericarditis

     074.22 Coxsackie endocarditis

     074.23 Coxsackie myocarditis
        Aseptic myocarditis of newborn

   074.3 Hand, foot, and mouth disease
      Vesicular stomatitis and exanthem

   ☐ **074.8 Other specified diseases due to Coxsackie virus**
      Acute lymphonodular pharyngitis

075 Infectious mononucleosis
    Glandular fever
    Monocytic angina
    Pfeiffer's disease

● **076 Trachoma**

   Excludes *late effect of trachoma (139.1)*

   076.0 Initial stage
      Trachoma dubium

   076.1 Active stage
      Granular conjunctivitis (trachomatous)
      Trachomatous:
        follicular conjunctivitis
        pannus

   ☐ **076.9 Trachoma, unspecified**
      Trachoma NOS

● **077 Other diseases of conjunctiva due to viruses and Chlamydiae**

   Excludes *ophthalmic complications of viral diseases classified elsewhere*

   077.0 Inclusion conjunctivitis
      Paratrachoma
      Swimming pool conjunctivitis

   Excludes *inclusion blennorrhea (neonatal) (771.6)*

   077.1 Epidemic keratoconjunctivitis
      Shipyard eye

   077.2 Pharyngoconjunctival fever
      Viral pharyngoconjunctivitis

   ☐ **077.3 Other adenoviral conjunctivitis**
      Acute adenoviral follicular conjunctivitis

077.4   Epidemic hemorrhagic conjunctivitis
Apollo:
    conjunctivitis
    disease
Conjunctivitis due to enterovirus type 70
Hemorrhagic conjunctivitis (acute) (epidemic)

❏ **077.8   Other viral conjunctivitis**
Newcastle conjunctivitis

● **077.9   Unspecified diseases of conjunctiva due to viruses and Chlamydiae**

    ❏ **077.98   Due to Chlamydiae**

    ❏ **077.99   Due to viruses**
       Viral conjunctivitis NOS

● **078   Other diseases due to viruses and Chlamydiae**

    Excludes   *viral infection NOS (079.0–079.9)*
                   viremia NOS (790.8)

078.0   Molluscum contagiosum

● **078.1   Viral warts**
Viral warts due to human papillomavirus

    ❏ **078.10   Viral warts, unspecified**
       Condyloma NOS
       Verruca NOS:
         NOS
         Vulgaris
       Warts (infectious)

    078.11   Condyloma acuminatum

    ❏ **078.19   Other specified viral warts**
       Genital warts NOS
       Verruca
         plana
         plantaris

078.2   Sweating fever
Miliary fever
Sweating disease

078.3   Cat-scratch disease
Benign lymphoreticulosis (of inoculation)
Cat-scratch fever

078.4   Foot and mouth disease
Aphthous fever
Epizootic:
    aphthae
    stomatitis

078.5   Cytomegaloviral disease
Cytomegalic inclusion disease
Salivary gland virus disease

Use additional code to identify manifestation, as:
cytomegalic inclusion virus:
    hepatitis (573.1)
    pneumonia (484.1)

    Excludes   *congenital cytomegalovirus infection (771.1)*

078.6   Hemorrhagic nephrosonephritis
Hemorrhagic fever:
    epidemic
    Korean
    Russian with renal syndrome

078.7   Arenaviral hemorrhagic fever
Hemorrhagic fever:
    Argentine
    Bolivian
    Junin virus
    Machupo virus

● **078.8   Other specified diseases due to viruses and Chlamydiae**

    Excludes   *epidemic diarrhea (009.2)*
                   lymphogranuloma venereum (099.1)

078.81   Epidemic vertigo

078.82   Epidemic vomiting syndrome
Winter vomiting disease

❏ **078.88   Other specified diseases due to Chlamydiae**

❏ **078.89   Other specified diseases due to viruses**
    Epidemic cervical myalgia
    Marburg disease
    Tanapox

● **079   Viral and chlamydial infection in conditions classified elsewhere and of unspecified site**

Note: This category is provided to be used as an additional code to identify the viral agent in diseases classifiable elsewhere. This category will also be used to classify virus infection of unspecified nature or site.

Item 1–10   Retrovirus develops by copying its RNA, genetic materials, into the DNA, which then produces new virus particles. It is from the Retroviridae virus family.
Human T-cell lymphotropic virus, Type I (HTLV-I) is also called human T-cell leukemia virus, Type I, and is a retrovirus thought to cause T-cell leukemia/lymphoma.
Human T-cell lymphotropic virus, Type II (HTLV-II), is also called human T-cell leukemia virus, Type II, and is a retrovirus associated with hematologic disorders.
HIV-2 is one of the serotypes of HIV and is usually confined to West Africa, whereas HIV-1 is found worldwide.

079.0   Adenovirus

079.1   ECHO virus

079.2   Coxsackie virus

079.3   Rhinovirus

079.4   Human papilloma virus

● **079.5   Retrovirus**

    Excludes   *human immunodeficiency virus, type 1 [HIV-1] (042)*
                  human T-cell lymphotropic virus, type III [HTLV-III] (042)
                  lymphadenopathy-associated virus [LAV] (042)

    ❏ **079.50   Retrovirus, unspecified**

    079.51   Human T-cell lymphotropic virus, type I [HTLV-I]

    079.52   Human T-cell lymphotropic virus, type II [HTLV-II]

    079.53   Human immunodeficiency virus, type 2 [HIV-2]

    ❏ **079.59   Other specified retrovirus**

079.6   Respiratory syncytial virus (RSV)

● **079.8   Other specified viral and chlamydial infections**

    079.81   Hantavirus

    ❏ **079.88   Other specified chlamydial infection**

    ❏ **079.89   Other specified viral infection**

● **079.9   Unspecified viral and chlamydial infections**

    Excludes   *viremia NOS (790.8)*

    ❏ **079.98   Unspecified chlamydial infection**
       Chlamydial infection NOS

    ❏ **079.99   Unspecified viral infection**
       Viral infection NOS

    ◀▶ **New Code**   ⬅▦ **Revised Code**   ● **Not a Principal Diagnosis**   ● **Use Additional Digit(s)**   ❏ **Nonspecific Code**

RICKETTSIOSES AND OTHER ARTHROPOD-BORNE DISEASES (080–088)

Excludes *arthropod-borne viral diseases (060.0–066.9)*

Item 1–11 Rickettsioses are diseases spread from ticks, lice, fleas, or mites to humans. See Figure 1–3. **Typhus** is spread to humans chiefly by the fleas of rats. **Endemic** identifies a disease as being present in low numbers of humans at all times, whereas, **epidemic** identifies a disease as being present in high numbers of humans at a specific time. Morbidity (death) is higher in epidemic diseases.
Brill's disease, also known as **Brill-Zinsser disease,** is spread from human to human by body lice and also from the lice of flying squirrels. **Scrub typhus** is spread in the same ways as Brill's disease.
Malaria is spread to humans by mosquitos.

080   Louse-borne [epidemic] typhus
     Typhus (fever):
        classical
        epidemic
        exanthematic NOS
        louse-borne

● **081   Other typhus**

     081.0   Murine [endemic] typhus
        Typhus (fever):
           endemic
           flea-borne

     081.1   Brill's disease
        Brill-Zinsser disease
        Recrudescent typhus (fever)

     081.2   Scrub typhus
        Japanese river fever
        Kedani fever
        Mite-borne typhus
        Tsutsugamushi

     □ **081.9   Typhus, unspecified**
        Typhus (fever) NOS

● **082   Tick-borne rickettsioses**

     082.0   Spotted fevers
        Rocky mountain spotted fever
        São Paulo fever

     082.1   Boutonneuse fever
        African tick typhus
        India tick typhus
        Kenya tick typhus
        Marseilles fever
        Mediterranean tick fever

     082.2   North Asian tick fever
        Siberian tick typhus

     082.3   Queensland tick typhus

     □ **082.8   Other specified tick-borne rickettsioses**
        Lone star fever

     □ **082.9   Tick-borne rickettsiosis, unspecified**
        Tick-borne typhus NOS

● **083   Other rickettsioses**

     083.0   Q fever

     083.1   Trench fever
        Quintan fever
        Wolhynian fever

     083.2   Rickettsialpox
        Vesicular rickettsiosis

□ **083.8   Other specified rickettsioses**

□ **083.9   Rickettsiosis, unspecified**

● **084   Malaria**
     Note: Subcategories 084.0–084.6 exclude the listed conditions with mention of pernicious complications (084.8–084.9).

     Excludes *congenital malaria (771.2)*

     084.0   Falciparum malaria [malignant tertian]
        Malaria (fever):
           by Plasmodium falciparum
           subtertian

     084.1   Vivax malaria [benign tertian]
        Malaria (fever) by Plasmodium vivax

     084.2   Quartan malaria
        Malaria (fever) by Plasmodium malariae
        Malariae malaria

     084.3   Ovale malaria
        Malaria (fever) by Plasmodium ovale

     □ **084.4   Other malaria**
        Monkey malaria

     084.5   Mixed malaria
        Malaria (fever) by more than one parasite

     □ **084.6   Malaria, unspecified**
        Malaria (fever) NOS

     084.7   Induced malaria
        Therapeutically induced malaria

     Excludes *accidental infection from syringe, blood transfusion, etc. (084.0–084.6, above, according to parasite species)*
        transmission from mother to child during delivery (771.2)

     084.8   Blackwater fever
        Hemoglobinuric:
           fever (bilious)
           malaria
        Malarial hemoglobinuria

     □ **084.9   Other pernicious complications of malaria**
        Algid malaria
        Cerebral malaria

     Use additional code to identify complication, as:
     malarial:
        hepatitis (573.2)
        nephrosis (581.81)

● **085   Leishmaniasis**

     085.0   Visceral [kala-azar]
        Dumdum fever
        Infection by Leishmania:
           donovani
           infantum
        Leishmaniasis:
           dermal, post-kala-azar
           Mediterranean
           visceral (Indian)

     085.1   Cutaneous, urban
        Aleppo boil
        Baghdad boil
        Delhi boil
        Infection by Leishmania tropica (minor)
        Leishmaniasis, cutaneous:
           dry form
           late
           recurrent
           ulcerating
        Oriental sore

ICD-9-CM

001-099

Vol. 1

085.2 Cutaneous, Asian desert
Infection by Leishmania tropica major
Leishmaniasis, cutaneous:
  acute necrotizing
  rural
  wet form
  zoonotic form

085.3 Cutaneous, Ethiopian
Infection by Leishmania ethiopica
Leishmaniasis, cutaneous:
  diffuse
  lepromatous

085.4 Cutaneous, American
Chiclero ulcer
Infection by Leishmania mexicana
Leishmaniasis tegumentaria diffusa

085.5 Mucocutaneous (American)
Espundia
Infection by Leishmania braziliensis
Uta

❑ **085.9 Leishmaniasis, unspecified**

● **086 Trypanosomiasis**

Use additional code to identify manifestations, as:
  trypanosomiasis:
    encephalitis (323.2)
    meningitis (321.3)

086.0 Chagas' disease with heart involvement
American trypanosomiasis with heart involvement
Infection by Trypanosoma cruzi with heart involvement
Any condition classifiable to 086.2 with heart involvement

086.1 Chagas' disease with other organ involvement
American trypanosomiasis with involvement of organ other than heart
Infection by Trypanosoma cruzi with involvement of organ other than heart
Any condition classifiable to 086.2 with involvement of organ other than heart

086.2 Chagas' disease without mention of organ involvement
American trypanosomiasis
Infection by Trypanosoma cruzi

086.3 Gambian trypanosomiasis
Gambian sleeping sickness
Infection by Trypanosoma gambiense

086.4 Rhodesian trypanosomiasis
Infection by Trypanosoma rhodesiense
Rhodesian sleeping sickness

❑ **086.5 African trypanosomiasis, unspecified**
Sleeping sickness NOS

❑ **086.9 Trypanosomiasis, unspecified**

● **087 Relapsing fever**

Includes: recurrent fever

087.0 Louse-borne

087.1 Tick-borne

❑ **087.9 Relapsing fever, unspecified**

● **088 Other arthropod-borne diseases**

088.0 Bartonellosis
Carrión's disease
Oroya fever
Verruga peruana

❑ **088.8 Other specified arthropod-borne diseases**

088.81 Lyme disease
Erythema chronicum migrans

088.82 Babesiosis
Babesiasis

❑ **088.89 Other**

❑ **088.9 Arthropod-borne disease, unspecified**

SYPHILIS AND OTHER VENEREAL DISEASES (090–099)

Excludes *nonvenereal endemic syphilis (104.0)*
urogenital trichomoniasis (131.0)

Item 1–12 Syphilis, also known as lues, is the most serious of the venereal diseases caused by *Treponema pallidum*. The **primary** stage is characterized by an ulceration known as **chancre**, which usually appears on the genitals but can also develop on the anus, lips, tonsils, breasts, or fingers.

The **secondary** stage is characterized by a rash that can affect any area of the body. **Latent** syphilis is divided into **early**, which is diagnosed within two years of infection, and **late**, which is diagnosed two years or more after infection. **Congenital** syphilis is also labeled **early** or **late** based on the time of diagnosis.

● **090 Congenital syphilis**

090.0 Early congenital syphilis, symptomatic
Congenital syphilitic:
  choroiditis
  coryza (chronic)
  hepatomegaly
  mucous patches
  periostitis
  splenomegaly
Syphilitic (congenital):
  epiphysitis
  osteochondritis
  pemphigus
Any congenital syphilitic condition specified as early or manifesting less than two years after birth

090.1 Early congenital syphilis, latent
Congenital syphilis without clinical manifestations, with positive serological reaction and negative spinal fluid test, less than two years after birth

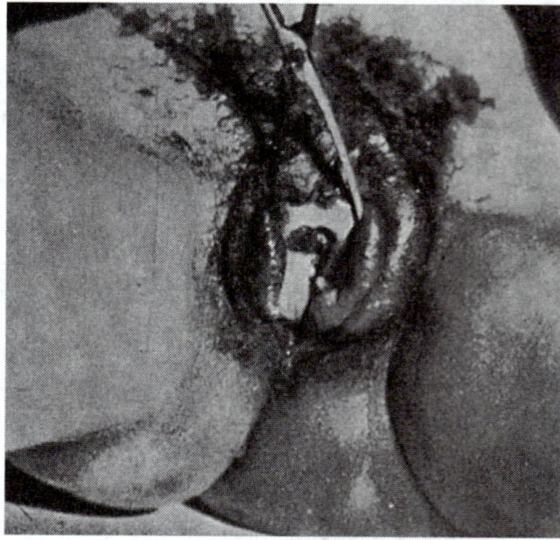

Figure 1–7 Chancre. (From Delp MH, Manning RT: Major Physical Diagnosis, 8th ed. Philadelphia, WB Saunders, 1975, p. 613.)

◀▶ **New Code**   ⬅➡ **Revised Code**   ● **Not a Principal Diagnosis**   ● **Use Additional Digit(s)**   ❑ **Nonspecific Code**

☐ **090.2 Early congenital syphilis, unspecified**
Congenital syphilis NOS, less than two years after birth

090.3 Syphilitic interstitial keratitis
Syphilitic keratitis:
   parenchymatous
   punctata profunda
Excludes *interstitial keratitis NOS (370.50)*

● **090.4 Juvenile neurosyphilis**

Use additional code to identify any associated mental disorder

☐ **090.40 Juvenile neurosyphilis, unspecified**
Congenital neurosyphilis
Dementia paralytica juvenilis
Juvenile:
   general paresis
   tabes
   taboparesis

090.41 Congenital syphilitic encephalitis

090.42 Congenital syphilitic meningitis

☐ **090.49 Other**

☐ **090.5 Other late congenital syphilis, symptomatic**
Gumma due to congenital syphilis
Hutchinson's teeth
Syphilitic saddle nose
Any congenital syphilitic condition specified as late or manifesting two years or more after birth

090.6 Late congenital syphilis, latent
Congenital syphilis without clinical manifestations, with positive serological reaction and negative spinal fluid test, two years or more after birth

☐ **090.7 Late congenital syphilis, unspecified**
Congenital syphilis NOS, two years or more after birth

☐ **090.9 Congenital syphilis, unspecified**

● **091 Early syphilis, symptomatic**
Excludes *early cardiovascular syphilis (093.0–093.9)*
early neurosyphilis (094.0–094.9)

091.0 Genital syphilis (primary)
Genital chancre

091.1 Primary anal syphilis

☐ **091.2 Other primary syphilis**
Primary syphilis of:
   breast
   fingers
   lip
   tonsils

091.3 Secondary syphilis of skin or mucous membranes
Condyloma latum
Secondary syphilis of:
   anus
   mouth
   pharynx
   skin
   tonsils
   vulva

091.4 Adenopathy due to secondary syphilis
Syphilitic adenopathy (secondary)
Syphilitic lymphadenitis (secondary)

● **091.5 Uveitis due to secondary syphilis**

☐ **091.50 Syphilitic uveitis, unspecified**

091.51 Syphilitic chorioretinitis (secondary)

091.52 Syphilitic iridocyclitis (secondary)

● **091.6 Secondary syphilis of viscera and bone**

091.61 Secondary syphilitic periostitis

091.62 Secondary syphilitic hepatitis
Secondary syphilis of liver

☐ **091.69 Other viscera**

091.7 Secondary syphilis, relapse
Secondary syphilis, relapse (treated) (untreated)

● **091.8 Other forms of secondary syphilis**

091.81 Acute syphilitic meningitis (secondary)

091.82 Syphilitic alopecia

☐ **091.89 Other**

☐ **091.9 Unspecified secondary syphilis**

● **092 Early syphilis, latent**

Includes: syphilis (acquired) without clinical manifestations, with positive serological reaction and negative spinal fluid test, less than two years after infection

092.0 Early syphilis, latent, serological relapse after treatment

☐ **092.9 Early syphilis, latent, unspecified**

● **093 Cardiovascular syphilis**

093.0 Aneurysm of aorta, specified as syphilitic
Dilatation of aorta, specified as syphilitic

093.1 Syphilitic aortitis

● **093.2 Syphilitic endocarditis**

☐ **093.20 Valve, unspecified**
Syphilitic ostial coronary disease

093.21 Mitral valve

093.22 Aortic valve
Syphilitic aortic incompetence or stenosis

093.23 Tricuspid valve

093.24 Pulmonary valve

● **093.8 Other specified cardiovascular syphilis**

093.81 Syphilitic pericarditis

093.82 Syphilitic myocarditis

☐ **093.89 Other**

☐ **093.9 Cardiovascular syphilis, unspecified**

● **094 Neurosyphilis**

Use additional code to identify any associated mental disorder

094.0 Tabes dorsalis
Locomotor ataxia (progressive)
Posterior spinal sclerosis (syphilitic)
Tabetic neurosyphilis

Use additional code to identify manifestation, as:
neurogenic arthropathy [Charcot's joint disease] (713.5)

094.1 General paresis
Dementia paralytica
General paralysis (of the insane) (progressive)
Paretic neurosyphilis
Taboparesis

094.2 Syphilitic meningitis
Meningovascular syphilis
Excludes *acute syphilitic meningitis (secondary) (091.81)*

094.3 Asymptomatic neurosyphilis

● **094.8 Other specified neurosyphilis**

094.81 Syphilitic encephalitis

094.82   Syphilitic Parkinsonism

094.83   Syphilitic disseminated retinochoroiditis

094.84   Syphilitic optic atrophy

094.85   Syphilitic retrobulbar neuritis

094.86   Syphilitic acoustic neuritis

094.87   Syphilitic ruptured cerebral aneurysm

❏ **094.89   Other**

❏ **094.9   Neurosyphilis, unspecified**
Gumma (syphilitic) of central nervous system NOS
Syphilis (early) (late) of central nervous system NOS
Syphiloma of central nervous system NOS

● **095   Other forms of late syphilis, with symptoms**

     Includes: gumma (syphilitic)
tertiary, or unspecified stage

095.0   Syphilitic episcleritis

095.1   Syphilis of lung

095.2   Syphilitic peritonitis

095.3   Syphilis of liver

095.4   Syphilis of kidney

095.5   Syphilis of bone

095.6   Syphilis of muscle
Syphilitic myositis

095.7   Syphilis of synovium, tendon, and bursa
Syphilitic:
bursitis
synovitis

❏ **095.8   Other specified forms of late symptomatic syphilis**
    | **Excludes** | *cardiovascular syphilis (093.0–093.9)*
neurosyphilis (094.0–094.9)

❏ **095.9   Late symptomatic syphilis, unspecified**

096   Late syphilis, latent
Syphilis (acquired) without clinical manifestations, with positive serological reaction and negative spinal fluid test, two years or more after infection

● **097   Other and unspecified syphilis**

❏ **097.0   Late syphilis, unspecified**

❏ **097.1   Latent syphilis, unspecified**
Positive serological reaction for syphilis

❏ **097.9   Syphilis, unspecified**
Syphilis (acquired) NOS
    | **Excludes** | *syphilis NOS causing death under two years of age (090.9)*

● **098   Gonococcal infections**

098.0   Acute, of lower genitourinary tract
Gonococcal:
Bartholinitis (acute)
urethritis (acute)
vulvovaginitis (acute)
Gonorrhea (acute):
NOS
genitourinary (tract) NOS

● **098.1   Acute, of upper genitourinary tract**

❏ **098.10   Gonococcal infection (acute) of upper genitourinary tract, site unspecified**

098.11   Gonococcal cystitis (acute)
Gonorrhea (acute) of bladder

098.12   Gonococcal prostatitis (acute)

098.13   Gonococcal epididymo-orchitis (acute)
Gonococcal orchitis (acute)

098.14   Gonococcal seminal vesiculitis (acute)
Gonorrhea (acute) of seminal vesicle

098.15   Gonococcal cervicitis (acute)
Gonorrhea (acute) of cervix

098.16   Gonococcal endometritis (acute)
Gonorrhea (acute) of uterus

098.17   Gonococcal salpingitis, specified as acute

❏ **098.19   Other**

098.2   Chronic, of lower genitourinary tract
Gonococcal specified as chronic or with duration of two months or more:
Bartholinitis specified as chronic or with duration of two months or more
urethritis specified as chronic or with duration of two months or more
vulvovaginitis specified as chronic or with duration of two months or more
Gonorrhea specified as chronic or with duration of two months or more:
NOS specified as chronic or with duration of two months or more
genitourinary (tract) specified as chronic or with duration of two months or more
Any condition classifiable to 098.0 specified as chronic or with duration of two months or more

● **098.3   Chronic, of upper genitourinary tract**
Includes: any condition classifiable to 098.1 stated as chronic or with a duration of two months or more

❏ **098.30   Chronic gonococcal infection of upper genitourinary tract, site unspecified**

098.31   Gonococcal cystitis, chronic
Any condition classifiable to 098.11, specified as chronic
Gonorrhea of bladder, chronic

098.32   Gonococcal prostatitis, chronic
Any condition classifiable to 098.12, specified as chronic

098.33   Gonococcal epididymo-orchitis, chronic
Any condition classifiable to 098.13, specified as chronic
Chronic gonococcal orchitis

098.34   Gonococcal seminal vesiculitis, chronic
Any condition classifiable to 098.14, specified as chronic
Gonorrhea of seminal vesicle, chronic

098.35   Gonococcal cervicitis, chronic
Any condition classifiable to 098.15, specified as chronic
Gonorrhea of cervix, chronic

098.36   Gonococcal endometritis, chronic
Any condition classifiable to 098.16, specified as chronic

098.37   Gonococcal salpingitis (chronic)

❏ **098.39   Other**

● **098.4   Gonococcal infection of eye**

098.40   Gonococcal conjunctivitis (neonatorum)
Gonococcal ophthalmia (neonatorum)

098.41   Gonococcal iridocyclitis

098.42   Gonococcal endophthalmia

098.43   Gonococcal keratitis

❏ **098.49   Other**

● **098.5 Gonococcal infection of joint**

098.50 Gonococcal arthritis
Gonococcal infection of joint NOS

098.51 Gonococcal synovitis and tenosynovitis

098.52 Gonococcal bursitis

098.53 Gonococcal spondylitis

❏ **098.59 Other**
Gonococcal rheumatism

098.6 Gonococcal infection of pharynx

098.7 Gonococcal infection of anus and rectum
Gonococcal proctitis

● **098.8 Gonococcal infection of other specified sites**

098.81 Gonococcal keratosis (blennorrhagica)

098.82 Gonococcal meningitis

098.83 Gonococcal pericarditis

098.84 Gonococcal endocarditis

❏ **098.85 Other gonococcal heart disease**

098.86 Gonococcal peritonitis

❏ **098.89 Other**
Gonococcemia

● **099 Other venereal diseases**

099.0 Chancroid
Bubo (inguinal):
  chancroidal
  due to Hemophilus ducreyi
Chancre:
  Ducrey's simple soft
Ulcus molle (cutis) (skin)

099.1 Lymphogranuloma venereum
Climatic or tropical bubo
(Durand-) Nicolas-Favre disease
Esthiomene
Lymphogranuloma inguinale

099.2 Granuloma inguinale
Donovanosis
Granuloma pudendi (ulcerating)
Granuloma venereum
Pudendal ulcer

099.3 Reiter's disease
Reiter's syndrome

◀ Use additional code for associated:
  arthropathy (711.1) ◀
  conjunctivitis (372.33) ◀

● **099.4 Other nongonococcal urethritis [NGU]**

❏ **099.40 Unspecified**
Nonspecific urethritis

099.41 Chlamydia trachomatis

❏ **099.49 Other specified organism**

● **099.5 Other venereal diseases due to Chlamydia trachomatis**

Excludes	Chlamydia trachomatis infection of conjunctiva (076.0–076.9, 077.0, 077.9) Lymphogranuloma venereum (099.1)

❏ **099.50 Unspecified site**

099.51 Pharynx

099.52 Anus and rectum

099.53 Lower genitourinary sites

Excludes	urethra (099.41)

Use additional code to specify site of infection, such as:
  bladder (595.4)
  cervix (616.0)
  vagina and vulva (616.11)

❏ **099.54 Other genitourinary sites**

Use additional code to specify site of infection, such as:
  pelvic inflammatory disease NOS (614.9)
  testis and epididymis (604.91)

❏ **099.55 Unspecified genitourinary site**

099.56 Peritoneum
Perihepatitis

❏ **099.59 Other specified site**

❏ **099.8 Other specified venereal diseases**

❏ **099.9 Venereal disease, unspecified**

OTHER SPIROCHETAL DISEASES (100–104)

● **100 Leptospirosis**

100.0 Leptospirosis icterohemorrhagica
Leptospiral or spirochetal jaundice (hemorrhagic)
Weil's disease

● **100.8 Other specified leptospiral infections**

100.81 Leptospiral meningitis (aseptic)

❏ **100.89 Other**
Fever:
  Fort Bragg
  pretibial
  swamp
Infection by Leptospira:
  australis
  bataviae
  pyrogenes

❏ **100.9 Leptospirosis, unspecified**

101 Vincent's angina
Acute necrotizing ulcerative:
  gingivitis
  stomatitis
Fusospirochetal pharyngitis
Spirochetal stomatitis
Trench mouth
Vincent's:
  gingivitis
  infection [any site]

● **102 Yaws**

Includes: frambesia
         pian

102.0 Initial lesions
Chancre of yaws
Frambesia, initial or primary
Initial frambesial ulcer
Mother yaw

102.1 Multiple papillomata and wet crab yaws
Butter yaws
Frambesioma
Pianoma
Plantar or palmar papilloma of yaws

❏ **102.2 Other early skin lesions**
Cutaneous yaws, less than five years after infection
Early yaws (cutaneous) (macular) (papular) (maculopapular) (micropapular)
Frambeside of early yaws

102.3 Hyperkeratosis
Ghoul hand
Hyperkeratosis, palmar or plantar (early) (late) due to yaws
Worm-eaten soles

ICD-9-CM
100–199
Vol. 1

102.4 Gummata and ulcers
Nodular late yaws (ulcerated)
Gummatous frambeside

102.5 Gangosa
Rhinopharyngitis mutilans

102.6 Bone and joint lesions
Goundou of yaws (late)
Gumma, bone of yaws (late)
Gummatous osteitis or periostitis of yaws (late)
Hydrarthrosis of yaws (early) (late)
Osteitis of yaws (early) (late)
Periostitis (hypertrophic) of yaws (early) (late)

☐**102.7 Other manifestations**
Juxta-articular nodules of yaws
Mucosal yaws

102.8 Latent yaws
Yaws without clinical manifestations, with positive serology

☐**102.9 Yaws, unspecified**

● **103 Pinta**

103.0 Primary lesions
Chancre (primary) of pinta [carate]
Papule (primary) of pinta [carate]
Pintid of pinta [carate]

103.1 Intermediate lesions
Erythematous plaques of pinta [carate]
Hyperchromic lesions of pinta [carate]
Hyperkeratosis of pinta [carate]

103.2 Late lesions
Cardiovascular lesions of pinta [carate]
Skin lesions of pinta [carate]:
achromic of pinta [carate]
cicatricial of pinta [carate]
dyschromic of pinta [carate]
Vitiligo of pinta [carate]

103.3 Mixed lesions
Achromic and hyperchromic skin lesions of pinta [carate]

☐**103.9 Pinta, unspecified**

● **104 Other spirochetal infection**

104.0 Nonvenereal endemic syphilis
Bejel
Njovera

☐**104.8 Other specified spirochetal infections**
> **Excludes** | *relapsing fever (087.0–087.9)*
> *syphilis (090.0–097.9)*

☐**104.9 Spirochetal infection, unspecified**

MYCOSES (110–118)

Use additional code to identify manifestation, as:
arthropathy (711.6)
meningitis (321.0–321.1)
otitis externa (380.15)
> **Excludes** | *infection by Actinomycetales, such as species of Actinomyces, Actinomadura, Nocardia, Streptomyces (039.0–039.9)*

● **110 Dermatophytosis**
Includes: infection by species of Epidermophyton, Microsporum, and Trichophyton
tinea, any type except those in 111

110.0 Of scalp and beard
Kerion
Sycosis, mycotic
Trichophytic tinea [black dot tinea], scalp

110.1 Of nail
Dermatophytic onychia
Onychomycosis
Tinea unguium

110.2 Of hand
Tinea manuum

110.3 Of groin and perianal area
Dhobie itch
Eczema marginatum
Tinea cruris

110.4 Of foot
Athlete's foot
Tinea pedis

110.5 Of the body
Herpes circinatus
Tinea imbricata [Tokelau]

110.6 Deep seated dermatophytosis
Granuloma trichophyticum
Majocchi's granuloma

☐**110.8 Of other specified sites**

☐**110.9 Of unspecified site**
Favus NOS
Microsporic tinea NOS
Ringworm NOS

● **111 Dermatomycosis, other and unspecified**

111.0 Pityriasis versicolor
Infection by Malassezia [Pityrosporum] furfur
Tinea flava
Tinea versicolor

111.1 Tinea nigra
Infection by Cladosporium species
Keratomycosis nigricans
Microsporosis nigra
Pityriasis nigra
Tinea palmaris nigra

111.2 Tinea blanca
Infection by Trichosporon (beigelii) cutaneum
White piedra

111.3 Black piedra
Infection by Piedraia hortai

☐**111.8 Other specified dermatomycoses**

☐**111.9 Dermatomycosis, unspecified**

● **112 Candidiasis**
Includes: infection by Candida species
moniliasis
> **Excludes** | *neonatal monilial infection (771.7)*

Item 1–13 Candidiasis, also called oidiomycosis or moniliasis, is a fungal infection. It most often appears on moist cutaneous areas of the body, but can also be responsible for a variety of systemic infections such as endocarditis, meningitis, arthritis, and myositis.

112.0 Of mouth
Thrush (oral)

112.1 Of vulva and vagina
Candidal vulvovaginitis
Monilial vulvovaginitis

☐**112.2 Of other urogenital sites**
Candidal balanitis

112.3 Of skin and nails
Candidal intertrigo
Candidal onychia
Candidal perionyxis [paronychia]

    ◄► **New Code**   ⬅ ➡ **Revised Code**   ● **Not a Principal Diagnosis**   ● **Use Additional Digit(s)**   ☐ **Nonspecific Code**

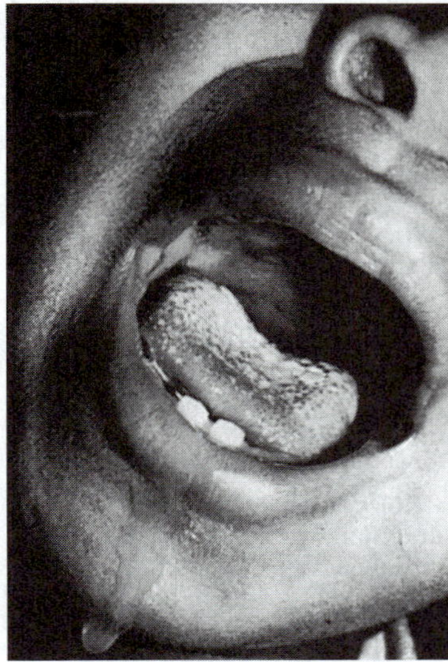

Figure 1–8   Oral candidiasis, also called thrush. (From Rippon JW: Medical Mycology, 3rd ed. Philadelphia, WB Saunders, 1988, p. 542.)

112.4 Of lung
Candidal pneumonia

112.5 Disseminated
Systemic candidiasis

● **112.8 Of other specified sites**

   112.81 Candidal endocarditis

   112.82 Candidal otitis externa
      Otomycosis in moniliasis

   112.83 Candidal meningitis

   112.84 Candidal esophagitis

   112.85 Candidal enteritis

   □ **112.89 Other**

□ **112.9 Of unspecified site**

● **114 Coccidioidomycosis**

   Includes: infection by Coccidioides (immitis)
          Posada-Wernicke disease

114.0 Primary coccidioidomycosis (pulmonary)
Acute pulmonary coccidioidomycosis
Coccidioidomycotic pneumonitis
Desert rheumatism
Pulmonary coccidioidomycosis
San Joaquin Valley fever

114.1 Primary extrapulmonary coccidioidomycosis
Chancriform syndrome
Primary cutaneous coccidioidomycosis

114.2 Coccidioidal meningitis

□ **114.3 Other forms of progressive coccidioidomycosis**
Coccidioidal granuloma
Disseminated coccidioidomycosis

114.4 Chronic pulmonary coccidioidomycosis

□ **114.5 Pulmonary coccidioidomycosis, unspecified**

□ **114.9 Coccidioidomycosis, unspecified**

● **115 Histoplasmosis**

The following fifth-digit subclassification is for use with category 115:
   0 without mention of manifestation
   1 meningitis
   2 retinitis
   3 pericarditis
   4 endocarditis
   5 pneumonia
  □ **9 other**

● **115.0 Infection by Histoplasma capsulatum**
American histoplasmosis
Darling's disease
Reticuloendothelial cytomycosis
Small form histoplasmosis

● **115.1 Infection by Histoplasma duboisii**
African histoplasmosis
Large form histoplasmosis

□● **115.9 Histoplasmosis, unspecified**
Histoplasmosis NOS

● **116 Blastomycotic infection**

116.0 Blastomycosis
Blastomycotic dermatitis
Chicago disease
Cutaneous blastomycosis
Disseminated blastomycosis
Gilchrist's disease
Infection by Blastomyces [Ajellomyces] dermatitidis
North American blastomycosis
Primary pulmonary blastomycosis

116.1 Paracoccidioidomycosis
Brazilian blastomycosis
Infection by Paracoccidioides [Blastomyces] brasi-
   liensis
Lutz-Splendore-Almeida disease
Mucocutaneous-lymphangitic paracoccidioidomy-
   cosis
Pulmonary paracoccidioidomycosis
South American blastomycosis
Visceral paracoccidioidomycosis

116.2 Lobomycosis
Infections by Loboa [Blastomyces] loboi
Keloidal blastomycosis
Lobo's disease

● **117 Other mycoses**

117.0 Rhinosporidiosis
Infection by Rhinosporidium seeberi

117.1 Sporotrichosis
Cutaneous sporotrichosis
Disseminated sporotrichosis
Infection by Sporothrix [Sporotrichum] schenckii
Lymphocutaneous sporotrichosis
Pulmonary sporotrichosis
Sporotrichosis of the bones

117.2 Chromoblastomycosis
Chromomycosis
Infection by Cladosporidium carrionii, Fonsecaea
   compactum, Fonsecaea pedrosoi, Phialophora
   verrucosa

117.3 Aspergillosis
Infection by Aspergillus species, mainly A. fumigatus, A. flavus group, A. terreus group

ICD-9-CM

100-199

Vol. 1

117.4 Mycotic mycetomas
Infection by various genera and species of Ascomycetes and Deuteromycetes, such as Acremonium [Cephalosporium] falciforme, Neotestudina rosatii, Madurella grisea, Madurella mycetomii, Pyrenochaeta romeroi, Zopfia [Leptosphaeria] senegalensis
Madura foot, mycotic
Maduromycosis, mycotic

Excludes *actinomycotic mycetomas (039.0–039.9)*

117.5 Cryptococcosis
Busse-Buschke's disease
European cryptococcosis
Infection by Cryptococcus neoformans
Pulmonary cryptococcosis
Systemic cryptococcosis
Torula

117.6 Allescheriosis [Petriellidosis]
Infections by Allescheria [Petriellidium] boydii [Monosporium apiospermum]

Excludes *mycotic mycetoma (117.4)*

117.7 Zygomycosis [Phycomycosis or Mucormycosis]
Infection by species of Absidia, Basidiobolus, Conidiobolus, Cunninghamella, Entomophthora, Mucor, Rhizopus, Saksenaea

117.8 Infection by dematiacious fungi [Phaehyphomycosis]
Infection by dematiacious fungi, such as Cladosporium trichoides [bantianum], Dreschlera hawaiiensis, Phialophora gougerotii, Phialophora jeanselmi

❑**117.9 Other and unspecified mycoses**

118 Opportunistic mycoses
Infection of skin, subcutaneous tissues, and/or organs by a wide variety of fungi generally considered to be pathogenic to compromised hosts only (e.g., infection by species of Alternaria, Dreschlera, Fusarium)

HELMINTHIASES (120–129)

● **120 Schistosomiasis [bilharziasis]**

120.0 Schistosoma haematobium
Vesical schistosomiasis NOS

120.1 Schistosoma mansoni
Intestinal schistosomiasis NOS

120.2 Schistosoma japonicum
Asiatic schistosomiasis NOS
Katayama disease or fever

120.3 Cutaneous
Cercarial dermatitis
Infection by cercariae of Schistosoma
Schistosome dermatitis
Swimmers' itch

❑**120.8 Other specified schistosomiasis**
Infection by Schistosoma:
bovis
intercalatum
mattheii
spindale
Schistosomiasis chestermani

❑**120.9 Schistosomiasis, unspecified**
Blood flukes NOS
Hemic distomiasis

● **121 Other trematode infections**

121.0 Opisthorchiasis
Infection by:
cat liver fluke
Opisthorchis (felineus) (tenuicollis) (viverrini)

121.1 Clonorchiasis
Biliary cirrhosis due to clonorchiasis
Chinese liver fluke disease
Hepatic distomiasis due to Clonorchis sinensis
Oriental liver fluke disease

121.2 Paragonimiasis
Infection by Paragonimus
Lung fluke disease (oriental)
Pulmonary distomiasis

121.3 Fascioliasis
Infection by Fasciola:
gigantica
hepatica
Liver flukes NOS
Sheep liver fluke infection

121.4 Fasciolopsiasis
Infection by Fasciolopsis (buski)
Intestinal distomiasis

121.5 Metagonimiasis
Infection by Metagonimus yokogawai

121.6 Heterophyiasis
Infection by:
Heterophyes heterophyes
Stellantchasmus falcatus

❑**121.8 Other specified trematode infections**
Infection by:
Dicrocoelium dendriticum
Echinostoma ilocanum
Gastrodiscoides hominis

❑**121.9 Trematode infection, unspecified**
Distomiasis NOS
Fluke disease NOS

● **122 Echinococcosis**

Includes: echinococciasis
hydatid disease
hydatidosis

122.0 Echinococcus granulosus infection of liver

122.1 Echinococcus granulosus infection of lung

122.2 Echinococcus granulosus infection of thyroid

❑**122.3 Echinococcus granulosus infection, other**

❑**122.4 Echinococcus granulosus infection, unspecified**

122.5 Echinococcus multilocularis infection of liver

❑**122.6 Echinococcus multilocularis infection, other**

❑**122.7 Echinococcus multilocularis infection, unspecified**

❑**122.8 Echinococcosis, unspecified, of liver**

❑**122.9 Echinococcosis, other and unspecified**

● **123 Other cestode infection**

123.0 Taenia solium infection, intestinal form
Pork tapeworm (adult) (infection)

123.1 Cysticercosis
Cysticerciasis
Infection by Cysticercus cellulosae [larval form of Taenia solium]

123.2 Taenia saginata infection
Beef tapeworm (infection)
Infection by Taeniarhynchus saginatus

❑**123.3 Taeniasis, unspecified**

123.4 Diphyllobothriasis, intestinal
Diphyllobothrium (adult) (latum) (pacificum) infection
Fish tapeworm (infection)

   ◀▶ **New Code**   ⬅▬▬➡ **Revised Code**   ● **Not a Principal Diagnosis**   ● **Use Additional Digit(s)**   ❑ **Nonspecific Code**

123.5 Sparganosis [larval diphyllobothriasis]
Infection by:
Diphyllobothrium larvae
Sparganum (mansoni) (proliferum)
Spirometra larvae

123.6 Hymenolepiasis
Dwarf tapeworm (infection)
Hymenolepis (diminuta) (nana) infection
Rat tapeworm (infection)

123.8 Other specified cestode infection
Diplogonoporus (grandis) infection
Dipylidium (caninum) infection
Dog tapeworm (infection)

123.9 Cestode infection, unspecified
Tapeworm (infection) NOS

124 Trichinosis
Trichinella spiralis infection
Trichinellosis
Trichiniasis

● **125 Filarial infection and dracontiasis**

125.0 Bancroftian filariasis
Chyluria due to Wuchereria bancrofti
Elephantiasis due to Wuchereria bancrofti
Infection due to Wuchereria bancrofti
Lymphadenitis due to Wuchereria bancrofti
Lymphangitis due to Wuchereria bancrofti
Wuchereriasis

125.1 Malayan filariasis
Brugia filariasis due to Brugia [Wuchereria] malayi
Chyluria due to Brugia [Wuchereria] malayi
Elephantiasis due to Brugia [Wuchereria] malayi
Infection due to Brugia [Wuchereria] malayi
Lymphadenitis due to Brugia [Wuchereria] malayi
Lymphangitis due to Brugia [Wuchereria] malayi

125.2 Loiasis
Eyeworm disease of Africa
Loa loa infection

125.3 Onchocerciasis
Onchocerca volvulus infection
Onchocercosis

125.4 Dipetalonemiasis
Infection by:
Acanthocheilonema perstans
Dipetalonema perstans

125.5 Mansonella ozzardi infection
Filariasis ozzardi

125.6 Other specified filariasis
Dirofilaria infection
Infection by:
Acanthocheilonema streptocerca
Dipetalonema streptocerca

125.7 Dracontiasis
Guinea-worm infection
Infection by Dracunculus medinensis

125.9 Unspecified filariasis

● **126 Ancylostomiasis and necatoriasis**

Includes: cutaneous larva migrans due to Ancylostoma
hookworm (disease) (infection)
uncinariasis

126.0 Ancylostoma duodenale

126.1 Necator americanus

126.2 Ancylostoma braziliense

126.3 Ancylostoma ceylanicum

126.8 Other specified Ancylostoma

126.9 Ancylostomiasis and necatoriasis, unspecified
Creeping eruption NOS
Cutaneous larva migrans NOS

● **127 Other intestinal helminthiases**

127.0 Ascariasis
Ascaridiasis
Infection by Ascaris lumbricoides
Roundworm infection

127.1 Anisakiasis
Infection by Anisakis larva

127.2 Strongyloidiasis
Infection by Strongyloides stercoralis

   Excludes   *trichostrongyliasis (127.6)*

127.3 Trichuriasis
Infection by Trichuris trichiuria
Trichocephaliasis
Whipworm (disease) (infection)

127.4 Enterobiasis
Infection by Enterobius vermicularis
Oxyuriasis
Oxyuris vermicularis infection
Pinworm (disease) (infection)
Threadworm infection

127.5 Capillariasis
Infection by Capillaria philippinensis

   Excludes   *infection by Capillaria hepatica (128.8)*

127.6 Trichostrongyliasis
Infection by Trichostrongylus species

127.7 Other specified intestinal helminthiasis
Infection by:
Oesophagostomum apiostomum and related
species
Ternidens diminutus
Other specified intestinal helminth
Physalopteriasis

127.8 Mixed intestinal helminthiasis
Infection by intestinal helminths classified to more
than one of the categories 120.0–127.7
Mixed helminthiasis NOS

127.9 Intestinal helminthiasis, unspecified

● **128 Other and unspecified helminthiases**

128.0 Toxocariasis
Larva migrans visceralis
Toxocara (canis) (cati) infection
Visceral larva migrans syndrome

128.1 Gnathostomiasis
Infection by Gnathostoma spinigerum and related
species

128.8 Other specified helminthiasis
Infection by:
Angiostrongylus cantonensis
Capillaria hepatica
Other specified helminth

128.9 Helminth infection, unspecified
Helminthiasis NOS
Worms NOS

129 Intestinal parasitism, unspecified

OTHER INFECTIOUS AND PARASITIC DISEASES (130–136)

Item 1-14   Toxoplasmosis is caused by the protozoa **Toxoplasma gondii,** of which the house cat can be a host. Human infection occurs when contact is made with materials containing the pathogen, such as feces or contaminated soil.
Infection can also occur with ingestion of lamb, goat, and pork meat, especially when the meat contains infected cysts.

● 130   Toxoplasmosis

   Includes: infection by toxoplasma gondii
   toxoplasmosis (acquired)

   Excludes   *congenital toxoplasmosis (771.2)*

   130.0   **Meningoencephalitis due to toxoplasmosis**
   Encephalitis due to acquired toxoplasmosis

   130.1   **Conjunctivitis due to toxoplasmosis**

   130.2   **Chorioretinitis due to toxoplasmosis**
   Focal retinochoroiditis due to acquired toxoplasmosis

   130.3   **Myocarditis due to toxoplasmosis**

   130.4   **Pneumonitis due to toxoplasmosis**

   130.5   **Hepatitis due to toxoplasmosis**

   □ 130.7   **Toxoplasmosis of other specified sites**

   130.8   **Multisystemic disseminated toxoplasmosis**
   Toxoplasmosis of multiple sites

   □ 130.9   **Toxoplasmosis, unspecified**

● 131   Trichomoniasis

   Includes: infection due to Trichomonas (vaginalis)

   ● 131.0   **Urogenital trichomoniasis**

      □ 131.00   **Urogenital trichomoniasis, unspecified**
      Fluor (vaginalis) trichomonal or due to Trichomonas (vaginalis)
      Leukorrhea (vaginalis) trichomonal or due to Trichomonas (vaginalis)

      131.01   **Trichomonal vulvovaginitis**
      Vaginitis, trichomonal or due to Trichomonas (vaginalis)

      131.02   **Trichomonal urethritis**

      131.03   **Trichomonal prostatitis**

      □ 131.09   **Other**

   □ 131.8   **Other specified sites**
      Excludes   *intestinal (007.3)*

   □ 131.9   **Trichomoniasis, unspecified**

● 132   Pediculosis and Phthirus infestation

   132.0   **Pediculus capitis [head louse]**

   132.1   **Pediculus corporis [body louse]**

   132.2   **Phthirus pubis [pubic louse]**
   Pediculus pubis

   132.3   **Mixed infestation**
   Infestation classifiable to more than one of the categories 132.0–132.2

   □ 132.9   **Pediculosis, unspecified**

● 133   Acariasis

   133.0   **Scabies**
   Infestation by Sarcoptes scabiei
   Norwegian scabies
   Sarcoptic itch

   □ 133.8   **Other acariasis**
   Chiggers
   Infestation by:
      Demodex folliculorum
      Trombicula

   □ 133.9   **Acariasis, unspecified**
   Infestation by mites NOS

● 134   Other infestation

   134.0   **Myiasis**
   Infestation by:
      Dermatobia (hominis)
      fly larvae
      Gasterophilus (intestinalis)
      maggots
      Oestrus ovis

   □ 134.1   **Other arthropod infestation**
   Infestation by:
      chigoe
      sand flea
      Tunga penetrans
      Jigger disease
      Scarabiasis
      Tungiasis

   134.2   **Hirudiniasis**
   Hirudiniasis (external) (internal)
   Leeches (aquatic) (land)

   □ 134.8   **Other specified infestations**

   □ 134.9   **Infestation, unspecified**
   Infestation (skin) NOS
   Skin parasites NOS

135   Sarcoidosis
   Besnier-Boeck-Schaumann disease
   Lupoid (miliary) of Boeck
   Lupus pernio (Besnier)
   Lymphogranulomatosis, benign (Schaumann's)
   Sarcoid (any site):
      NOS
      Boeck
      Darier-Roussy
   Uveoparotid fever

● 136   Other and unspecified infectious and parasitic diseases

   136.0   **Ainhum**
   Dactylolysis spontanea

   136.1   **Behçet's syndrome**

   136.2   **Specific infections by free-living amebae**
   Meningoencephalitis due to Naegleria

   136.3   **Pneumocystosis**
   Pneumonia due to Pneumocystis carinii

   136.4   **Psorospermiasis**

   136.5   **Sarcosporidiosis**
   Infection by Sarcocystis lindemanni

   □ 136.8   **Other specified infectious and parasitic diseases**
   Candiru infestation

   □ 136.9   **Unspecified infectious and parasitic diseases**
   Infectious disease NOS
   Parasitic disease NOS

LATE EFFECTS OF INFECTIOUS AND PARASITIC DISEASES (137–139)

● 137   Late effects of tuberculosis

   Note: This category is to be used to indicate conditions classifiable to 010–018 as the cause of late effects, which are themselves classified elsewhere. The "late effects" include those specified as such, as sequelae, or as due to old or inactive tuberculosis, without evidence of active disease.

☐ **137.0 Late effects of respiratory or unspecified tuberculosis**

137.1 Late effects of central nervous system tuberculosis

137.2 Late effects of genitourinary tuberculosis

137.3 Late effects of tuberculosis of bones and joints

☐ **137.4 Late effects of tuberculosis of other specified organs**

138 Late effects of acute poliomyelitis

Note: This category is to be used to indicate conditions classifiable to 045 as the cause of late effects, which are themselves classified elsewhere. The "late effects" include conditions specified as such, or as sequelae, or as due to old or inactive poliomyelitis, without evidence of active disease.

● **139 Late effects of other infectious and parasitic diseases**

Note: This category is to be used to indicate conditions classifiable to categories 001–009, 020–041, 046–136 as the cause of late effects, which are themselves classified elsewhere. The "late effects" include conditions specified as such; they also include sequelae of diseases classifiable to the above categories if there is evidence that the disease itself is no longer present.

139.0 Late effects of viral encephalitis
Late effects of conditions classifiable to 049.8–049.9, 062–064

139.1 Late effects of trachoma
Late effects of conditions classifiable to 076

☐ **139.8 Late effects of other and unspecified infectious and parasitic diseases**

2. NEOPLASMS (140–239)

1. Content:
   This chapter contains the following broad groups:
   140–195 Malignant neoplasms, stated or presumed to be primary, of specified sites, except of lymphatic and hematopoietic tissue
   196–198 Malignant neoplasms, stated or presumed to be secondary, of specified sites
   199   Malignant neoplasms, without specification of site
   200–208 Malignant neoplasms, stated or presumed to be primary, of lymphatic and hematopoietic tissue
   210–229 Benign neoplasms
   230–234 Carcinoma in situ
   235–238 Neoplasms of uncertain behavior [see Note, at beginning of section 235–238]
   239   Neoplasms of unspecified nature

2. Functional activity
   All neoplasms are classified in this chapter, whether or not functionally active. An additional code from Chapter 3 may be used to identify such functional activity associated with any neoplasm, e.g.:
   catecholamine-producing malignant pheochromocytoma of adrenal:
   code 194.0, additional code 255.6
   basophil adenoma of pituitary with Cushing's syndrome:
   code 227.3, additional code 255.0

3. Morphology [Histology]
   For those wishing to identify the histological type of neoplasms, a comprehensive coded nomenclature, which comprises the morphology rubrics of the ICD-Oncology, is given after the E-code chapter.

4. Malignant neoplasms overlapping site boundaries
   Categories 140–195 are for the classification of primary malignant neoplasms according to their point of origin. A malignant neoplasm that overlaps two or more subcategories within a three-digit rubric and whose point of origin cannot be determined should be classified to the subcategory .8 "Other." For example, "carcinoma involving tip and ventral surface of tongue" should be assigned to 141.8. On the other hand, "carcinoma of tip of tongue, extending to involve the ventral surface" should be coded to 141.2, as the point of origin, the tip, is known. Three subcategories (149.8, 159.8, 165.8) have been provided for malignant neoplasms that overlap the boundaries of three-digit rubrics within certain systems. Overlapping malignant neoplasms that cannot be classi-

ICD-9-CM

100-199

Vol. 1

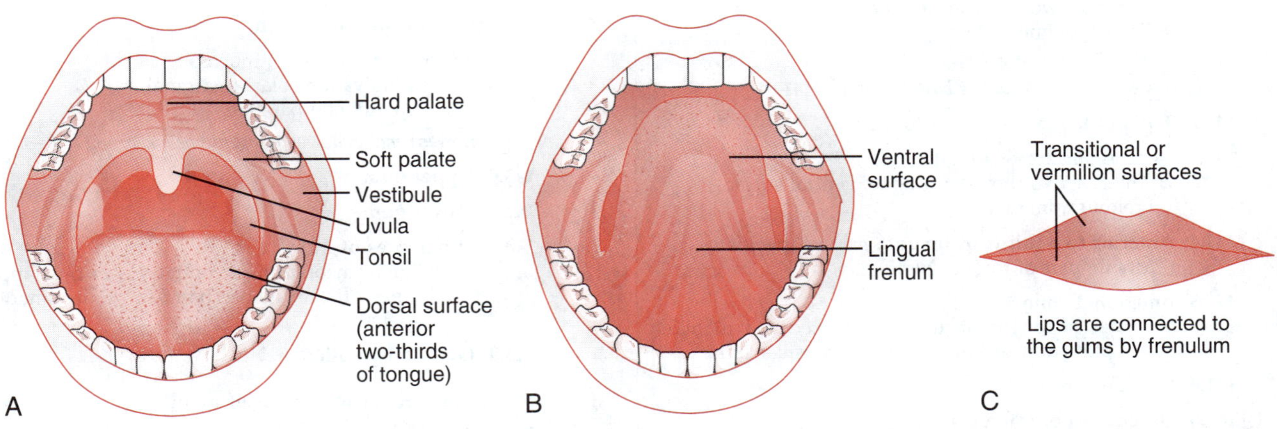

Figure 2–1 Anatomical structures of the mouth and lips. **A.** Dorsal surface. **B.** Ventral surface. **C.** Transitional or vermilion borders. Lips are connected to the gums by frenulum.

◀▶ **New Code**　　⬅▦▦➡ **Revised Code**　　● **Not a Principal Diagnosis**　　● **Use Additional Digit(s)**　　☐ **Nonspecific Code**

fied as indicated above should be assigned to the appropriate subdivision of category 195 (Malignant neoplasm of other and ill-defined sites).

MALIGNANT NEOPLASM OF LIP, ORAL CAVITY, AND PHARYNX (140–149)

Excludes *carcinoma in situ (230.0)*

● **140 Malignant neoplasm of lip**

Excludes *skin of lip (173.0)*

140.0 Upper lip, vermilion border
Upper lip: Upper lip:
  NOS   lipstick area
  external

140.1 Lower lip, vermilion border
Lower lip: Lower lip:
  NOS   lipstick area
  external

140.3 Upper lip, inner aspect
Upper lip: Upper lip:
  buccal aspect   mucosa
  frenulum   oral aspect

140.4 Lower lip, inner aspect
Lower lip: Lower lip:
  buccal aspect   mucosa
  frenulum   oral aspect

☐ **140.5 Lip, unspecified, inner aspect**
Lip, not specified whether upper or lower:
  buccal aspect
  frenulum
  mucosa
  oral aspect

140.6 Commissure of lip
Labial commissure

☐ **140.8 Other sites of lip**
Malignant neoplasm of contiguous or overlapping sites of lip whose point of origin cannot be determined

☐ **140.9 Lip, unspecified, vermilion border**
Lip, not specified as upper or lower:
  NOS
  external
  lipstick area

● **141 Malignant neoplasm of tongue**

141.0 Base of tongue
Dorsal surface of base of tongue
Fixed part of tongue NOS

141.1 Dorsal surface of tongue
Anterior two-thirds of tongue, dorsal surface
Dorsal tongue NOS
Midline of tongue

Excludes *dorsal surface of base of tongue (141.0)*

141.2 Tip and lateral border of tongue

141.3 Ventral surface of tongue
Anterior two-thirds of tongue, ventral surface
Frenulum linguae

☐ **141.4 Anterior two-thirds of tongue, part unspecified**
Mobile part of tongue NOS

141.5 Junctional zone
Border of tongue at junction of fixed and mobile parts at insertion of anterior tonsillar pillar

141.6 Lingual tonsil

☐ **141.8 Other sites of tongue**
Malignant neoplasm of contiguous or overlapping sites of tongue whose point of origin cannot be determined

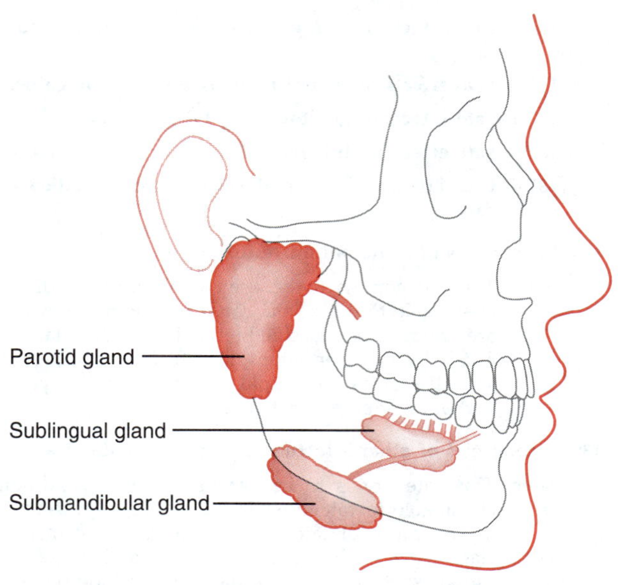

Figure 2–2 Major salivary glands.

☐ **141.9 Tongue, unspecified**
Tongue NOS

● **142 Malignant neoplasm of major salivary glands**

Includes: salivary ducts

Excludes *malignant neoplasm of minor salivary glands:*
  NOS (145.9)
  buccal mucosa (145.0)
  soft palate (145.3)
  tongue (141.0–141.9)
  tonsil, palatine (146.0)

142.0 Parotid gland

142.1 Submandibular gland
Submaxillary gland

142.2 Sublingual gland

☐ **142.8 Other major salivary glands**
Malignant neoplasm of contiguous or overlapping sites of salivary glands and ducts whose point of origin cannot be determined

☐ **142.9 Salivary gland, unspecified**
Salivary gland (major) NOS

● **143 Malignant neoplasm of gum**

Includes: alveolar (ridge) mucosa
  gingiva (alveolar) (marginal)
  interdental papillae

Excludes *malignant odontogenic neoplasms (170.0–170.1)*

143.0 Upper gum

143.1 Lower gum

☐ **143.8 Other sites of gum**
Malignant neoplasm of contiguous or overlapping sites of gum whose point of origin cannot be determined

☐ **143.9 Gum, unspecified**

● **144 Malignant neoplasm of floor of mouth**

144.0 Anterior portion
Anterior to the premolar-canine junction

144.1 Lateral portion

☐ **144.8   Other sites of floor of mouth**
Malignant neoplasm of contiguous or overlapping sites of floor of mouth whose point of origin cannot be determined

☐ **144.9   Floor of mouth, part unspecified**

● **145   Malignant neoplasm of other and unspecified parts of mouth**

> **Excludes**   *mucosa of lips (140.0–140.9)*

145.0   Cheek mucosa
Buccal mucosa
Cheek, inner aspect

145.1   Vestibule of mouth
Buccal sulcus (upper) (lower)
Labial sulcus (upper) (lower)

145.2   Hard palate

145.3   Soft palate

> **Excludes**   *nasopharyngeal [posterior] [superior] surface of soft palate (147.3)*

145.4   Uvula

☐ **145.5   Palate, unspecified**
Junction of hard and soft palate
Roof of mouth

145.6   Retromolar area

☐ **145.8   Other specified parts of mouth**
Malignant neoplasm of contiguous or overlapping sites of mouth whose point of origin cannot be determined

☐ **145.9   Mouth, unspecified**
Buccal cavity NOS
Minor salivary gland, unspecified site
Oral cavity NOS

● **146   Malignant neoplasm of oropharynx**

146.0   Tonsil
Tonsil: Tonsil:
   NOS   palatine
   faucial

> **Excludes**   *lingual tonsil (141.6)*
> *pharyngeal tonsil (147.1)*

146.1   Tonsillar fossa

146.2   Tonsillar pillars (anterior) (posterior)
Faucial pillar
Glossopalatine fold
Palatoglossal arch
Palatopharyngeal arch

146.3   Vallecula
Anterior and medial surface of the pharyngoepiglottic fold

146.4   Anterior aspect of epiglottis
Epiglottis, free border [margin]
Glossoepiglottic fold(s)

> **Excludes**   *epiglottis:*
> *NOS (161.1)*
> *suprahyoid portion (161.1)*

146.5   Junctional region
Junction of the free margin of the epiglottis, the aryepiglottic fold, and the pharyngoepiglottic fold

146.6   Lateral wall of oropharynx

146.7   Posterior wall of oropharynx

☐ **146.8   Other specified sites of oropharynx**
Branchial cleft
Malignant neoplasm of contiguous or overlapping sites of oropharynx whose point of origin cannot be determined

☐ **146.9   Oropharynx, unspecified**

● **147   Malignant neoplasm of nasopharynx**

147.0   Superior wall
Roof of nasopharynx

147.1   Posterior wall
Adenoid
Pharyngeal tonsil

147.2   Lateral wall
Fossa of Rosenmüller
Opening of auditory tube
Pharyngeal recess

147.3   Anterior wall
Floor of nasopharynx
Nasopharyngeal [posterior] [superior] surface of soft palate
Posterior margin of nasal septum and choanae

☐ **147.8   Other specified sites of nasopharynx**
Malignant neoplasm of contiguous or overlapping sites of nasopharynx whose point of origin cannot be determined

☐ **147.9   Nasopharynx, unspecified**
Nasopharyngeal wall NOS

● **148   Malignant neoplasm of hypopharynx**

148.0   Postcricoid region

148.1   Pyriform sinus
Pyriform fossa

148.2   Aryepiglottic fold, hypopharyngeal aspect
Aryepiglottic fold or interarytenoid fold:
   NOS
   marginal zone

> **Excludes**   *aryepiglottic fold or interarytenoid fold, laryngeal aspect (161.1)*

148.3   Posterior hypopharyngeal wall

☐ **148.8   Other specified sites of hypopharynx**
Malignant neoplasm of contiguous or overlapping sites of hypopharynx whose point of origin cannot be determined

☐ **148.9   Hypopharynx, unspecified**
Hypopharyngeal wall NOS
Hypopharynx NOS

● **149   Malignant neoplasm of other and ill-defined sites within the lip, oral cavity, and pharynx**

☐ **149.0   Pharynx, unspecified**

149.1   Waldeyer's ring

☐ **149.8   Other**
Malignant neoplasms of lip, oral cavity, and pharynx whose point of origin cannot be assigned to any one of the categories 140–148

> **Excludes**   *"book leaf" neoplasm [ventral surface of tongue and floor of mouth] (145.8)*

☐ **149.9   Ill-defined**

MALIGNANT NEOPLASM OF DIGESTIVE ORGANS AND PERITONEUM (150–159)

> **Excludes**   *carcinoma in situ (230.1–230.9)*

● **150   Malignant neoplasm of esophagus**

Item 2-1   The esophagus enters the stomach through the **cardiac orifice**, also called the **cardioesophageal junction**. The **cardia** is adjacent to the cardiac orifice. The stomach widens into the **greater** and **lesser curvatures**. The **pyloric antrum** precedes the **pylorus**, which connects to the duodenum.

ICD-9-CM
100-199
Vol. 1

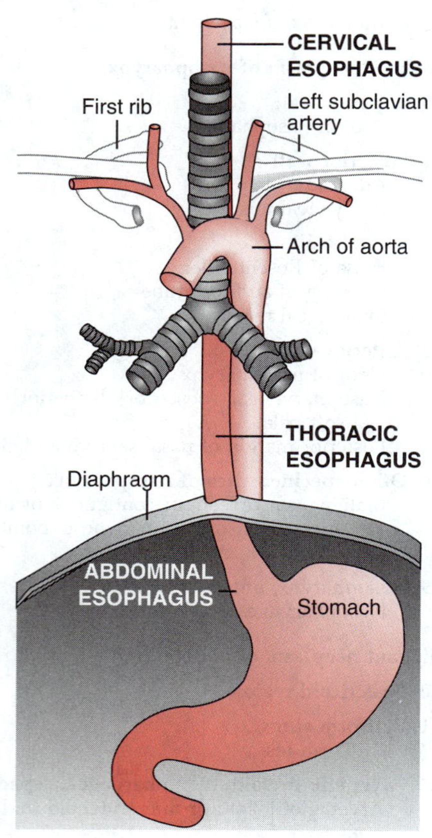

Figure 2–3   The esophagus is the muscular tube that connects the pharynx and the stomach. The 10 inch (25 cm) long esophagus is divided into three parts: **cervical, thoracic,** and **abdominal.**

150.0   **Cervical esophagus**

150.1   **Thoracic esophagus**

150.2   **Abdominal esophagus**

> **Excludes**   *adenocarcinoma (151.0)*
> *cardioesophageal junction (151.0)*

150.3   **Upper third of esophagus**
Proximal third of esophagus

150.4   **Middle third of esophagus**

150.5   **Lower third of esophagus**
Distal third of esophagus

> **Excludes**   *adenocarcinoma (151.0)*
> *cardioesophageal junction (151.0)*

150.8   **Other specified part**
Malignant neoplasm of contiguous or overlapping sites of esophagus whose point of origin cannot be determined

150.9   **Esophagus, unspecified**

● **151**   **Malignant neoplasm of stomach**

151.0   **Cardia**
Cardiac orifice
Cardioesophageal junction

> **Excludes**   *squamous cell carcinoma (150.2, 150.5)*

151.1   **Pylorus**
Prepylorus
Pyloric canal

151.2   **Pyloric antrum**
Antrum of stomach NOS

151.3   **Fundus of stomach**

151.4   **Body of stomach**

151.5   **Lesser curvature, unspecified**
Lesser curvature, not classifiable to 151.1–151.4

151.6   **Greater curvature, unspecified**
Greater curvature, not classifiable to 151.0–151.4

151.8   **Other specified sites of stomach**
Anterior wall, not classifiable to 151.0–151.4
Posterior wall, not classifiable to 151.0–151.4
Malignant neoplasm of contiguous or overlapping sites of stomach whose point of origin cannot be determined

151.9   **Stomach, unspecified**
Carcinoma ventriculi
Gastric cancer

● **152**   **Malignant neoplasm of small intestine, including duodenum**

152.0   **Duodenum**

152.1   **Jejunum**

152.2   **Ileum**

> **Excludes**   *ileocecal valve (153.4)*

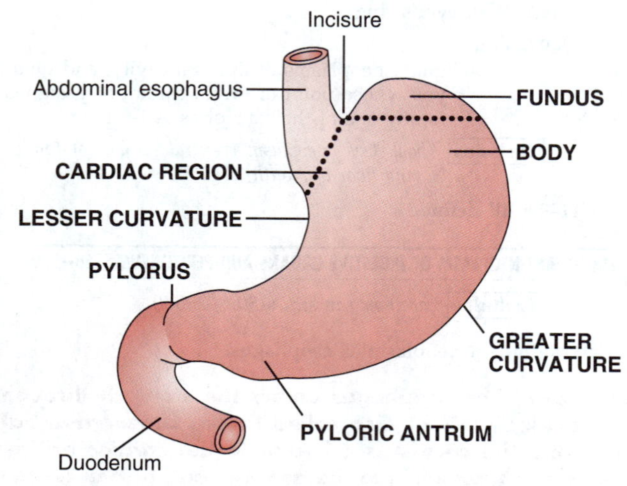

Figure 2–4   Parts of the stomach.

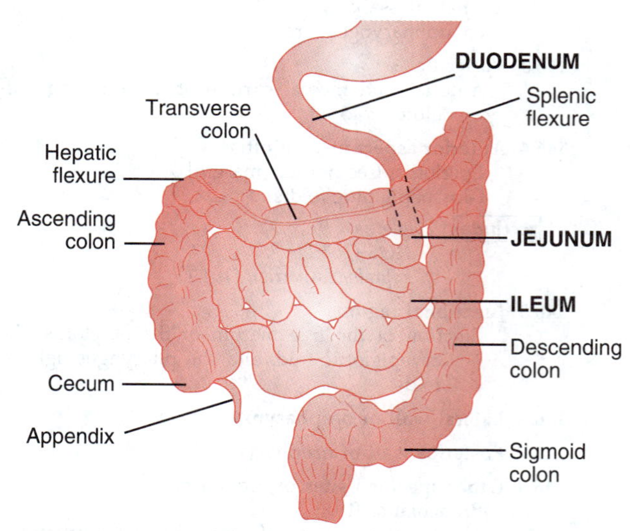

Figure 2–5   Small intestine and colon.

    ◀▶ **New Code**   ⬅▶ **Revised Code**   ● **Not a Principal Diagnosis**   ● **Use Additional Digit(s)**   ❑ **Nonspecific Code**

152.3 **Meckel's diverticulum**

☐ 152.8 **Other specified sites of small intestine**
Duodenojejunal junction
Malignant neoplasm of contiguous or overlapping
sites of small intestine whose point of origin
cannot be determined

☐ 152.9 **Small intestine, unspecified**

● **153** **Malignant neoplasm of colon**

153.0 **Hepatic flexure**

153.1 **Transverse colon**

153.2 **Descending colon**
Left colon

153.3 **Sigmoid colon**
Sigmoid (flexure)
Excludes *rectosigmoid junction (154.0)*

153.4 **Cecum**
Ileocecal valve

153.5 **Appendix**

153.6 **Ascending colon**
Right colon

153.7 **Splenic flexure**

☐ 153.8 **Other specified sites of large intestine**
Malignant neoplasm of contiguous or overlapping
sites of colon whose point of origin cannot be
determined
Excludes *ileocecal valve (153.4)*
rectosigmoid junction (154.0)

☐ 153.9 **Colon, unspecified**
Large intestine NOS

● **154** **Malignant neoplasm of rectum, rectosigmoid junction, and anus**

154.0 **Rectosigmoid junction**
Colon with rectum
Rectosigmoid (colon)

154.1 **Rectum**
Rectal ampulla

154.2 **Anal canal**
Anal sphincter
Excludes *skin of anus (172.5, 173.5)*

☐ 154.3 **Anus, unspecified**
Excludes *anus:*
margin (172.5, 173.5)
skin (172.5, 173.5)
perianal skin (172.5, 173.5)

☐ 154.8 **Other**
Anorectum
Cloacogenic zone
Malignant neoplasm of contiguous or overlapping
sites of rectum, rectosigmoid junction, and
anus whose point of origin cannot be determined

● **155** **Malignant neoplasm of liver and intrahepatic bile ducts**

155.0 **Liver, primary**
Carcinoma:
liver, specified as primary
hepatocellular
liver cell
Hepatoblastoma

155.1 **Intrahepatic bile ducts**
Canaliculi biliferi
Interlobular:
bile ducts
biliary canals
Intrahepatic:
biliary passages
canaliculi
gall duct
Excludes *hepatic duct (156.1)*

☐ 155.2 **Liver, not specified as primary or secondary**

● **156** **Malignant neoplasm of gallbladder and extrahepatic bile ducts**

156.0 **Gallbladder**

156.1 **Extrahepatic bile ducts**
Biliary duct or passage Cystic duct
NOS Hepatic duct
Common bile duct Sphincter of Oddi

156.2 **Ampulla of Vater**

☐ 156.8 **Other specified sites of gallbladder and extrahe-patic bile ducts**
Malignant neoplasm of contiguous or overlapping
sites of gallbladder and extrahepatic bile ducts
whose point of origin cannot be determined

☐ 156.9 **Biliary tract, part unspecified**
Malignant neoplasm involving both intrahepatic
and extrahepatic bile ducts

● **157** **Malignant neoplasm of pancreas**

157.0 **Head of pancreas**

157.1 **Body of pancreas**

157.2 **Tail of pancreas**

157.3 **Pancreatic duct**
Duct of:
Santorini
Wirsung

157.4 **Islets of Langerhans**
Islets of Langerhans, any part of pancreas
Use additional code to identify any functional activity

☐ 157.8 **Other specified sites of pancreas**
Ectopic pancreatic tissue
Malignant neoplasm of contiguous or overlapping
sites of pancreas whose point of origin cannot
be determined

☐ 157.9 **Pancreas, part unspecified**

● **158** **Malignant neoplasm of retroperitoneum and peritoneum**

158.0 **Retroperitoneum**
Periadrenal tissue
Perinephric tissue
Perirenal tissue
Retrocecal tissue

☐ 158.8 **Specified parts of peritoneum**
Cul-de-sac (of Douglas)
Mesentery
Mesocolon
Omentum
Peritoneum:
parietal
pelvic
Rectouterine pouch
Malignant neoplasm of contiguous or overlapping
sites of retroperitoneum and peritoneum
whose point of origin cannot be determined

☐ 158.9 **Peritoneum, unspecified**

● **159** **Malignant neoplasm of other and ill-defined sites within the digestive organs and peritoneum**

ICD-9-CM

100-199

Vol. 1

◀ ▶ **New Code** ⬅▦ ▦➡ **Revised Code** ● **Not a Principal Diagnosis** ● **Use Additional Digit(s)** ☐ **Nonspecific Code**

❏ **159.0 Intestinal tract, part unspecified**
Intestine NOS

❏ **159.1 Spleen, not elsewhere classified**
Angiosarcoma of spleen
Fibrosarcoma of spleen
> **Excludes** *Hodgkin's disease (201.0–201.9)*
> *lymphosarcoma (200.1)*
> *reticulosarcoma (200.0)*

❏ **159.8 Other sites of digestive system and intra-abdominal organs**
Malignant neoplasm of digestive organs and peritoneum whose point of origin cannot be assigned to any one of the categories 150–158
> **Excludes** *anus and rectum (154.8)*
> *cardioesophageal junction (151.0)*
> *colon and rectum (154.0)*

❏ **159.9 Ill-defined**
Alimentary canal or tract NOS
Gastrointestinal tract NOS
> **Excludes** *abdominal NOS (195.2)*
> *intra-abdominal NOS (195.2)*

MALIGNANT NEOPLASM OF RESPIRATORY AND INTRATHORACIC ORGANS (160–165)

> **Excludes** *carcinoma in situ (231.0–231.9)*

● **160 Malignant neoplasm of nasal cavities, middle ear, and accessory sinuses**

160.0 Nasal cavities
Cartilage of nose
Conchae, nasal
Internal nose
Septum of nose
Vestibule of nose
> **Excludes** *nasal bone (170.0)*
> *nose NOS (195.0)*
> *olfactory bulb (192.0)*
> *posterior margin of septum and choanae (147.3)*
> *skin of nose (172.3, 173.3)*
> *turbinates (170.0)*

160.1 Auditory tube, middle ear, and mastoid air cells
Antrum tympanicum
Eustachian tube
Tympanic cavity
> **Excludes** *auditory canal (external) (172.2, 173.2)*
> *bone of ear (meatus) (170.0)*
> *cartilage of ear (171.0)*
> *ear (external) (skin) (172.2, 173.2)*

160.2 Maxillary sinus
Antrum (Highmore) (maxillary)

160.3 Ethmoidal sinus

160.4 Frontal sinus

160.5 Sphenoidal sinus

❏ **160.8 Other**
Malignant neoplasm of contiguous or overlapping sites of nasal cavities, middle ear, and accessory sinuses whose point of origin cannot be determined

❏ **160.9 Accessory sinus, unspecified**

● **161 Malignant neoplasm of larynx**

161.0 Glottis
Intrinsic larynx
Laryngeal commissure (anterior) (posterior)
True vocal cord
Vocal cord NOS

161.1 Supraglottis
Aryepiglottic fold or interarytenoid fold, laryngeal aspect
Epiglottis (suprahyoid portion) NOS
Extrinsic larynx
False vocal cords
Posterior (laryngeal) surface of epiglottis
Ventricular bands
> **Excludes** *anterior aspect of epiglottis (146.4)*
> *aryepiglottic fold or interarytenoid fold:*
> *NOS (148.2)*
> *hypopharyngeal aspect (148.2)*
> *marginal zone (148.2)*

161.2 Subglottis

161.3 Laryngeal cartilages
Cartilage: Cartilage:
arytenoid   cuneiform
cricoid   thyroid

❏ **161.8 Other specified sites of larynx**
Malignant neoplasm of contiguous or overlapping sites of larynx whose point of origin cannot be determined

❏ **161.9 Larynx, unspecified**

● **162 Malignant neoplasm of trachea, bronchus, and lung**

162.0 Trachea
Cartilage of trachea
Mucosa of trachea

162.2 Main bronchus
Carina
Hilus of lung

162.3 Upper lobe, bronchus or lung

162.4 Middle lobe, bronchus or lung

162.5 Lower lobe, bronchus or lung

❏ **162.8 Other parts of bronchus or lung**
Malignant neoplasm of contiguous or overlapping sites of bronchus or lung whose point of origin cannot be determined

❏ **162.9 Bronchus and lung, unspecified**

● **163 Malignant neoplasm of pleura**

163.0 Parietal pleura

163.1 Visceral pleura

❏ **163.8 Other specified sites of pleura**
Malignant neoplasm of contiguous or overlapping sites of pleura whose point of origin cannot be determined

❏ **163.9 Pleura, unspecified**

● **164 Malignant neoplasm of thymus, heart, and mediastinum**

164.0 Thymus

164.1 Heart
Endocardium
Epicardium
Myocardium
Pericardium
> **Excludes** *great vessels (171.4)*

164.2 Anterior mediastinum

164.3 Posterior mediastinum

❏ **164.8 Other**
Malignant neoplasm of contiguous or overlapping sites of thymus, heart, and mediastinum whose point of origin cannot be determined

❏ **164.9 Mediastinum, part unspecified**

● **165 Malignant neoplasm of other and ill-defined sites within the respiratory system and intrathoracic organs**

❑ **165.0 Upper respiratory tract, part unspecified**

❑ **165.8 Other**
Malignant neoplasm of respiratory and intrathoracic organs whose point of origin cannot be assigned to any one of the categories 160–164

❑ **165.9 Ill-defined sites within the respiratory system**
Respiratory tract NOS

Excludes *intrathoracic NOS (195.1)*
thoracic NOS (195.1)

MALIGNANT NEOPLASM OF BONE, CONNECTIVE TISSUE, SKIN, AND BREAST (170–176)

Excludes *carcinoma in situ:*
breast (233.0)
skin (232.0–232.9)

● **170 Malignant neoplasm of bone and articular cartilage**

Includes: cartilage (articular) (joint)
periosteum

Excludes *bone marrow NOS (202.9)*
cartilage:
ear (171.0)
eyelid (171.0)
larynx (161.3)
nose (160.0)
synovia (171.0–171.9)

170.0 Bones of skull and face, except mandible

Bone:	Bone:
ethmoid	sphenoid
frontal	temporal
malar	zygomatic
nasal	Maxilla (superior)
occipital	Turbinate
orbital	Upper jaw bone
parietal	Vomer

Excludes *carcinoma, any type except intraosseous or odontogenic:*
maxilla, maxillary (sinus) (160.2)
upper jaw bone (143.0)
jaw bone (lower) (170.1)

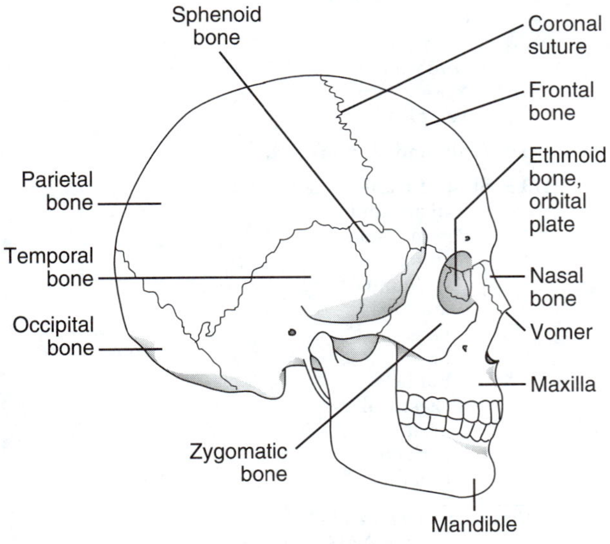

Figure 2–6 Bones of the skull and face.

170.1 Mandible
Inferior maxilla
Jaw bone NOS
Lower jaw bone

Excludes *carcinoma, any type except intraosseous or odontogenic:*
jaw bone NOS (143.9)
lower (143.1)
upper jaw bone (170.0)

170.2 Vertebral column, excluding sacrum and coccyx
Spinal column
Spine
Vertebra

Excludes *sacrum and coccyx (170.6)*

170.3 Ribs, sternum, and clavicle
Costal cartilage
Costovertebral joint
Xiphoid process

170.4 Scapula and long bones of upper limb

Acromion	Radius
Bones NOS of upper limb	Ulna
Humerus	

170.5 Short bones of upper limb

Carpal	Scaphoid (of hand)
Cuneiform, wrist	Semilunar or lunate
Metacarpal	Trapezium
Navicular, of hand	Trapezoid
Phalanges of hand	Unciform
Pisiform	

170.6 Pelvic bones, sacrum, and coccyx
Coccygeal vertebra
Ilium
Ischium
Pubic bone
Sacral vertebra

170.7 Long bones of lower limb
Bones NOS of lower limb
Femur
Fibula
Tibia

170.8 Short bones of lower limb

Astragalus [talus]	Navicular (of ankle)
Calcaneus	Patella
Cuboid	Phalanges of foot
Cuneiform, ankle	Tarsal
Metatarsal	

❑ **170.9 Bone and articular cartilage, site unspecified**

● **171 Malignant neoplasm of connective and other soft tissue**

Includes: blood vessel
bursa
fascia
fat
ligament, except uterine
muscle
peripheral, sympathetic, and parasympathetic nerves and ganglia
synovia
tendon (sheath)

Excludes *cartilage (of):*
articular (170.0–170.9)
larynx (161.3)
nose (160.0)
connective tissue:
breast (174.0–175.9)
internal organs - code to malignant neoplasm of the site [e.g., leiomyosarcoma of stomach, 151.9]
heart (164.1)
uterine ligament (183.4)

ICD-9-CM
100-199
Vol. 1

171.0   **Head, face, and neck**
Cartilage of:
    ear
    eyelid

171.2   **Upper limb, including shoulder**
Arm
Finger
Forearm
Hand

171.3   **Lower limb, including hip**
Foot
Leg
Popliteal space
Thigh
Toe

171.4   **Thorax**
Axilla
Diaphragm
Great vessels

> **Excludes**   *heart (164.1)*
> *mediastinum (164.2–164.9)*
> *thymus (164.0)*

171.5   **Abdomen**
Abdominal wall
Hypochondrium

> **Excludes**   *peritoneum (158.8)*
> *retroperitoneum (158.0)*

171.6   **Pelvis**
Buttock
Groin
Inguinal region
Perineum

> **Excludes**   *pelvic peritoneum (158.8)*
> *retroperitoneum (158.0)*
> *uterine ligament, any (183.3–183.5)*

❑ **171.7**   **Trunk, unspecified**
Back NOS
Flank NOS

❑ **171.8**   **Other specified sites of connective and other soft tissue**
Malignant neoplasm of contiguous or overlapping sites of connective tissue whose point of origin cannot be determined

❑ **171.9**   **Connective and other soft tissue, site unspecified**

● **172**   **Malignant melanoma of skin**

    Includes: melanocarcinoma
            melanoma (skin) NOS

> **Excludes**   *skin of genital organs (184.0–184.9, 187.1–187.9)*
> *sites other than skin - code to malignant neoplasm of the site*

172.0   **Lip**

> **Excludes**   *vermilion border of lip (140.0–140.1, 140.9)*

172.1   **Eyelid, including canthus**

172.2   **Ear and external auditory canal**
Auricle (ear)
Auricular canal, external
External [acoustic] meatus
Pinna

❑ **172.3**   **Other and unspecified parts of face**
Cheek (external)
Chin
Eyebrow
Forehead
Nose, external
Temple

172.4   **Scalp and neck**

172.5   **Trunk, except scrotum**
Axilla   Perianal skin
Breast   Perineum
Buttock   Umbilicus
Groin

> **Excludes**   *anal canal (154.2)*
> *anus NOS (154.3)*
> *scrotum (187.7)*

172.6   **Upper limb, including shoulder**
Arm   Forearm
Finger   Hand

172.7   **Lower limb, including hip**
Ankle   Leg
Foot   Popliteal area
Heel   Thigh
Knee   Toe

❑ **172.8**   **Other specified sites of skin**
Malignant melanoma of contiguous or overlapping sites of skin whose point of origin cannot be determined

❑ **172.9**   **Melanoma of skin, site unspecified**

● **173**   **Other malignant neoplasm of skin**

    Includes: malignant neoplasm of:
            sebaceous glands
            sudoriferous, sudoriparous glands
            sweat glands

> **Excludes**   *Kaposi's sarcoma (176.0–176.9)*
> *malignant melanoma of skin (172.0–172.9)*
> *skin of genital organs (184.0–184.9, 187.1–187.9)*

173.0   **Skin of lip**

> **Excludes**   *vermilion border of lip (140.0–140.1, 140.9)*

173.1   **Eyelid, including canthus**

> **Excludes**   *cartilage of eyelid (171.0)*

173.2   **Skin of ear and external auditory canal**
Auricle (ear)
Auricular canal, external
External meatus
Pinna

> **Excludes**   *cartilage of ear (171.0)*

❑ **173.3**   **Skin of other and unspecified parts of face**
Cheek, external
Chin
Eyebrow
Forehead
Nose, external
Temple

173.4   **Scalp and skin of neck**

173.5   **Skin of trunk, except scrotum**
Axillary fold
Perianal skin
Skin of:
    abdominal wall
    anus
    back
    breast
    buttock
    chest wall
    groin
    perineum
    umbilicus

> **Excludes**   *anal canal (154.2)*
> *anus NOS (154.3)*
> *skin of scrotum (187.7)*

◄► **New Code**   ⬅️➡️ **Revised Code**   ● **Not a Principal Diagnosis**   ● **Use Additional Digit(s)**   ❑ **Nonspecific Code**

173.6 Skin of upper limb, including shoulder
Arm
Finger
Forearm
Hand

173.7 Skin of lower limb, including hip
Ankle
Foot
Heel
Knee
Leg
Popliteal area
Thigh
Toe

☐ 173.8 Other specified sites of skin
Malignant neoplasm of contiguous or overlapping sites of skin whose point of origin cannot be determined

☐ 173.9 Skin, site unspecified

● 174 Malignant neoplasm of female breast

> **Includes:** breast (female)
> connective tissue
> soft parts
> Paget's disease of:
> breast
> nipple

> **Excludes** *skin of breast (172.5, 173.5)*

174.0 Nipple and areola

174.1 Central portion

174.2 Upper-inner quadrant

174.3 Lower-inner quadrant

174.4 Upper-outer quadrant

174.5 Lower-outer quadrant

174.6 Axillary tail

☐ 174.8 Other specified sites of female breast
Ectopic sites
Inner breast
Lower breast
Malignant neoplasm of contiguous or overlapping sites of breast whose point of origin cannot be determined
Midline of breast
Outer breast
Upper breast

☐ 174.9 Breast (female), unspecified

● 175 Malignant neoplasm of male breast

> **Excludes** *skin of breast (172.5, 173.5)*

175.0 Nipple and areola

☐ 175.9 Other and unspecified sites of male breast
Ectopic breast tissue, male

● 176 Kaposi's sarcoma

176.0 Skin

176.1 Soft tissue

> **Includes:** blood vessel
> connective tissue
> fascia
> ligament
> lymphatic(s) NEC
> muscle

> **Excludes** *lymph glands and nodes (176.5)*

176.2 Palate

176.3 Gastrointestinal sites

176.4 Lung

176.5 Lymph nodes

☐ 176.8 Other specified sites

> **Includes:** oral cavity NEC

☐ 176.9 Unspecified
Viscera NOS

MALIGNANT NEOPLASM OF GENITOURINARY ORGANS (179–189)

> **Excludes** *carcinoma in situ (233.1–233.9)*

☐ 179 Malignant neoplasm of uterus, part unspecified

● 180 Malignant neoplasm of cervix uteri

> **Includes:** invasive malignancy [carcinoma]

> **Excludes** *carcinoma in situ (233.1)*

180.0 Endocervix
Cervical canal NOS
Endocervical canal
Endocervical gland

180.1 Exocervix

☐ 180.8 Other specified sites of cervix
Cervical stump
Squamocolumnar junction of cervix
Malignant neoplasm of contiguous or overlapping sites of cervix uteri whose point of origin cannot be determined

☐ 180.9 Cervix uteri, unspecified

181 Malignant neoplasm of placenta
Choriocarcinoma NOS
Chorioepithelioma NOS

> **Excludes** *chorioadenoma (destruens) (236.1)*
> *hydatidiform mole (630)*
> *malignant (236.1)*
> *invasive mole (236.1)*
> *male choriocarcinoma NOS (186.0–186.9)*

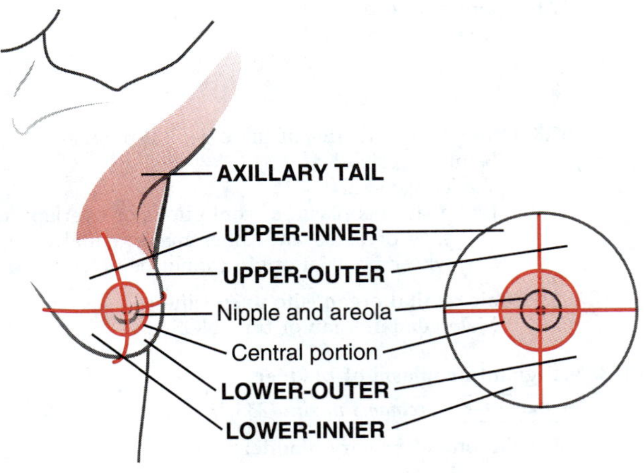

Figure 2–7 Female breast quadrants and axillary tail.

ICD-9-CM
100–199
Vol. 1

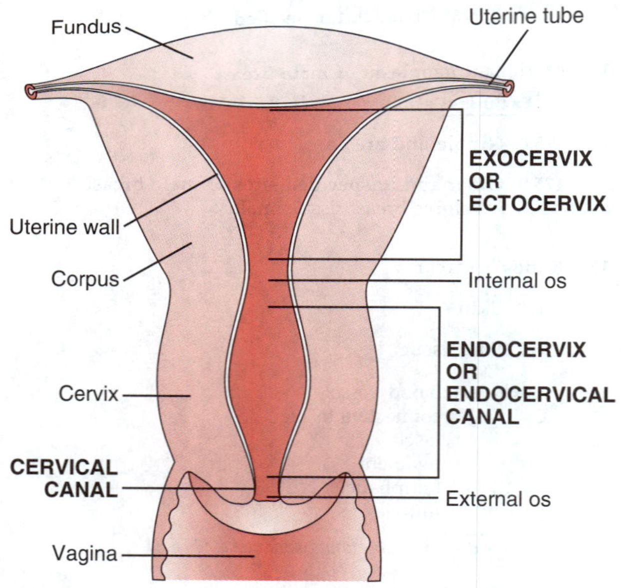

Figure 2–8   Cervix uteri.

● **182   Malignant neoplasm of body of uterus**

> **Excludes**   *carcinoma in situ (233.2)*

    182.0   Corpus uteri, except isthmus
      Cornu
      Endometrium
      Fundus
      Myometrium

    182.1   Isthmus
      Lower uterine segment

□ **182.8   Other specified sites of body of uterus**
      Malignant neoplasm of contiguous or overlapping
        sites of body of uterus whose point of origin
        cannot be determined

> **Excludes**   *uterus NOS (179)*

● **183   Malignant neoplasm of ovary and other uterine adnexa**

> **Excludes**   *Douglas' cul-de-sac (158.8)*

    183.0   Ovary

      Use additional code to identify any functional activity

    183.2   Fallopian tube
      Oviduct
      Uterine tube

    183.3   Broad ligament
      Mesovarium
      Parovarian region

    183.4   Parametrium
      Uterine ligament NOS
      Uterosacral ligament

    183.5   Round ligament

□ **183.8   Other specified sites of uterine adnexa**
      Tubo-ovarian
      Utero-ovarian
      Malignant neoplasm of contiguous or overlapping
        sites of ovary and other uterine adnexa
        whose point of origin cannot be determined

□ **183.9   Uterine adnexa, unspecified**

● **184   Malignant neoplasm of other and unspecified female genital organs**

> **Excludes**   *carcinoma in situ (233.3)*

    184.0   Vagina
      Gartner's duct
      Vaginal vault

    184.1   Labia majora
      Greater vestibular [Bartholin's] gland

    184.2   Labia minora

    184.3   Clitoris

□ **184.4   Vulva, unspecified**
      External female genitalia NOS
      Pudendum

□ **184.8   Other specified sites of female genital organs**
      Malignant neoplasm of contiguous or overlapping
        sites of female genital organs whose point of
        origin cannot be determined

□ **184.9   Female genital organ, site unspecified**
      Female genitourinary tract NOS

    185   Malignant neoplasm of prostate

> **Excludes**   *seminal vesicles (187.8)*

● **186   Malignant neoplasm of testis**

    Use additional code to identify any functional activity

    186.0   Undescended testis
      Ectopic testis
      Retained testis

□ **186.9   Other and unspecified testis**
      Testis:
        NOS
        descended
        scrotal

● **187   Malignant neoplasm of penis and other male genital organs**

    187.1   Prepuce
      Foreskin

    187.2   Glans penis

    187.3   Body of penis
      Corpus cavernosum

□ **187.4   Penis, part unspecified**
      Skin of penis NOS

    187.5   Epididymis

    187.6   Spermatic cord
      Vas deferens

    187.7   Scrotum
      Skin of scrotum

□ **187.8   Other specified sites of male genital organs**
      Seminal vesicle
      Tunica vaginalis
      Malignant neoplasm of contiguous or overlapping
        sites of penis and other male genital organs
        whose point of origin cannot be determined

□ **187.9   Male genital organ, site unspecified**
      Male genital organ or tract NOS

● **188   Malignant neoplasm of bladder**

> **Excludes**   *carcinoma in situ (233.7)*

    188.0   Trigone of urinary bladder

    188.1   Dome of urinary bladder

    188.2   Lateral wall of urinary bladder

◄► **New Code**   ◄■■ ■■► **Revised Code**   ● **Not a Principal Diagnosis**   ● **Use Additional Digit(s)**   □ **Nonspecific Code**

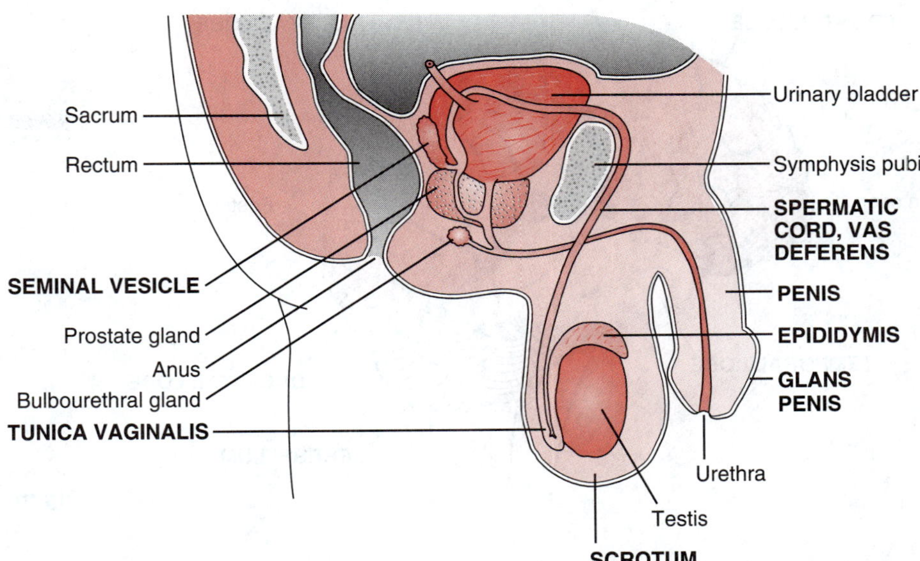

Figure 2–9 Penis and other male genital organs.

ICD-9-CM
100-199
Vol. 1

188.3 Anterior wall of urinary bladder

188.4 Posterior wall of urinary bladder

188.5 Bladder neck
Internal urethral orifice

188.6 Ureteric orifice

188.7 Urachus

☐ **188.8 Other specified sites of bladder**
Malignant neoplasm of contiguous or overlapping sites of bladder whose point of origin cannot be determined

☐ **188.9 Bladder, part unspecified**
Bladder wall NOS

● **189 Malignant neoplasm of kidney and other and unspecified urinary organs**

189.0 Kidney, except pelvis
Kidney NOS   Kidney parenchyma

189.1 Renal pelvis
Renal calyces   Ureteropelvic junction

189.2 Ureter
Excludes *ureteric orifice of bladder (188.6)*

189.3 Urethra
Excludes *urethral orifice of bladder (188.5)*

189.4 Paraurethral glands

☐ **189.8 Other specified sites of urinary organs**
Malignant neoplasm of contiguous or overlapping sites of kidney and other urinary organs whose point of origin cannot be determined

☐ **189.9 Urinary organ, site unspecified**
Urinary system NOS

MALIGNANT NEOPLASM OF OTHER AND UNSPECIFIED SITES (190–199)

Excludes *carcinoma in situ (234.0–234.9)*

● **190 Malignant neoplasm of eye**
Excludes *carcinoma in situ (234.0)*
eyelid (skin) (172.1, 173.1)
cartilage (171.0)
optic nerve (192.0)
orbital bone (170.0)

190.0 Eyeball, except conjunctiva, cornea, retina, and choroid
Ciliary body
Crystalline lens
Iris
Sclera
Uveal tract

190.1 Orbit
Connective tissue of orbit
Extraocular muscle
Retrobulbar
Excludes *bone of orbit (170.0)*

190.2 Lacrimal gland

190.3 Conjunctiva

190.4 Cornea

190.5 Retina

190.6 Choroid

190.7 Lacrimal duct
Lacrimal sac
Nasolacrimal duct

☐ **190.8 Other specified sites of eye**
Malignant neoplasm of contiguous or overlapping sites of eye whose point of origin cannot be determined

☐ **190.9 Eye, part unspecified**

● **191 Malignant neoplasm of brain**
Excludes *cranial nerves (192.0)*
retrobulbar area (190.1)

191.0 Cerebrum, except lobes and ventricles
Basal ganglia
Cerebral cortex
Corpus striatum
Globus pallidus
Hypothalamus
Thalamus

191.1 Frontal lobe

191.2 Temporal lobe
Hippocampus
Uncus

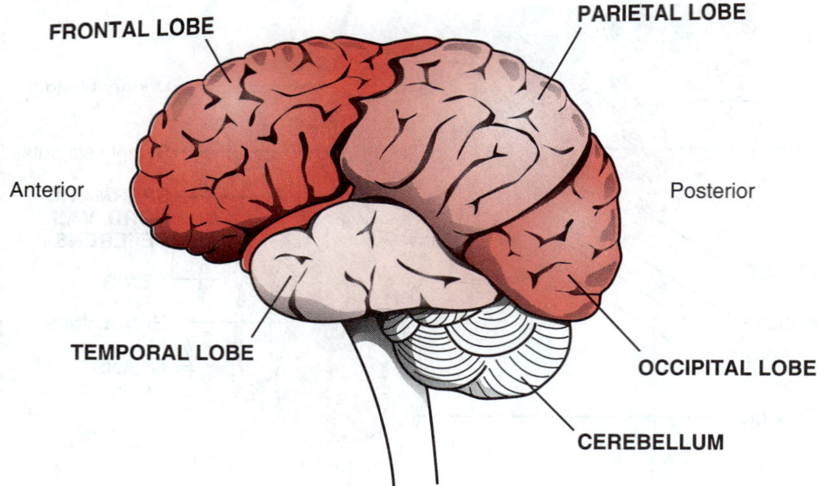

Figure 2–10 The brain.

191.3 Parietal lobe

191.4 Occipital lobe

191.5 Ventricles
Choroid plexus
Floor of ventricle

191.6 Cerebellum NOS
Cerebellopontine angle

191.7 Brain stem
Cerebral peduncle
Medulla oblongata
Midbrain
Pons

❑ **191.8 Other parts of brain**
Corpus callosum
Tapetum
Malignant neoplasm of contiguous or overlapping
sites of brain whose point of origin cannot be
determined

❑ **191.9 Brain, unspecified**
Cranial fossa NOS

● **192 Malignant neoplasm of other and unspecified parts of nervous system**

> **Excludes** *peripheral, sympathetic, and parasympathetic nerves and ganglia (171.0–171.9)*

192.0 Cranial nerves
Olfactory bulb

192.1 Cerebral meninges
Dura (mater)
Falx (cerebelli) (cerebri)
Meninges NOS
Tentorium

192.2 Spinal cord
Cauda equina

192.3 Spinal meninges

❑ **192.8 Other specified sites of nervous system**
Malignant neoplasm of contiguous or overlapping
sites of other parts of nervous system whose
point of origin cannot be determined

❑ **192.9 Nervous system, part unspecified**
Nervous system (central) NOS

> **Excludes** *meninges NOS (192.1)*

193 Malignant neoplasm of thyroid gland
Sipple's syndrome
Thyroglossal duct

Use additional code to identify any functional activity

● **194 Malignant neoplasm of other endocrine glands and related structures**

Use additional code to identify any functional activity

> **Excludes** *islets of Langerhans (157.4)*
> *ovary (183.0)*
> *testis (186.0–186.9)*
> *thymus (164.0)*

194.0 Adrenal gland
Adrenal cortex
Adrenal medulla
Suprarenal gland

194.1 Parathyroid gland

194.3 Pituitary gland and craniopharyngeal duct
Craniobuccal pouch
Hypophysis
Rathke's pouch
Sella turcica

194.4 Pineal gland

194.5 Carotid body

194.6 Aortic body and other paraganglia
Coccygeal body
Glomus jugulare
Para-aortic body

❑ **194.8 Other**
Pluriglandular involvement NOS

Note: If the sites of multiple involvements are
known, they should be coded separately.

❑ **194.9 Endocrine gland, site unspecified**

● **195 Malignant neoplasm of other and ill-defined sites**

Includes: malignant neoplasms of contiguous sites, not
elsewhere classified, whose point of origin
cannot be determined

> **Excludes** *malignant neoplasm:*
> *lymphatic and hematopoietic tissue (200.0–208.9)*
> *secondary sites (196.0–198.8)*
> *unspecified site (199.0–199.1)*

195.0 Head, face, and neck
    Cheek NOS
    Jaw NOS
    Nose NOS
    Supraclavicular region NOS

195.1 Thorax
    Axilla
    Chest (wall) NOS
    Intrathoracic NOS

195.2 Abdomen
    Intra-abdominal NOS

195.3 Pelvis
    Groin
    Inguinal region NOS
    Presacral region
    Sacrococcygeal region
    Sites overlapping systems within pelvis, as:
        rectovaginal (septum)
        rectovesical (septum)

195.4 Upper limb

195.5 Lower limb

☐ **195.8 Other specified sites**
    Back NOS
    Flank NOS
    Trunk NOS

● **196 Secondary and unspecified malignant neoplasm of lymph nodes**

> **Excludes** *any malignant neoplasm of lymph nodes, specified as primary (200.0–202.9)*
> *Hodgkin's disease (201.0–201.9)*
> *lymphosarcoma (200.1)*
> *reticulosarcoma (200.0)*
> *other forms of lymphoma (202.0–202.9)*

196.0 Lymph nodes of head, face, and neck
    Cervical   Scalene
    Cervicofacial   Supraclavicular

196.1 Intrathoracic lymph nodes
    Bronchopulmonary   Mediastinal
    Intercostal   Tracheobronchial

196.2 Intra-abdominal lymph nodes
    Intestinal   Retroperitoneal
    Mesenteric

196.3 Lymph nodes of axilla and upper limb
    Brachial   Infraclavicular
    Epitrochlear   Pectoral

196.5 Lymph nodes of inguinal region and lower limb
    Femoral   Popliteal
    Groin   Tibial

196.6 Intrapelvic lymph nodes
    Hypogastric   Obturator
    Iliac   Parametrial

☐ **196.8 Lymph nodes of multiple sites**

☐ **196.9 Site unspecified**
    Lymph nodes NOS

● **197 Secondary malignant neoplasm of respiratory and digestive systems**

> **Excludes** *lymph node metastasis (196.0–196.9)*

197.0 Lung
    Bronchus

197.1 Mediastinum

197.2 Pleura

☐ **197.3 Other respiratory organs**
    Trachea

197.4 Small intestine, including duodenum

197.5 Large intestine and rectum

197.6 Retroperitoneum and peritoneum

197.7 Liver, specified as secondary

☐ **197.8 Other digestive organs and spleen**

● **198 Secondary malignant neoplasm of other specified sites**

> **Excludes** *lymph node metastasis (196.0–196.9)*

198.0 Kidney

☐ **198.1 Other urinary organs**

198.2 Skin
    Skin of breast

198.3 Brain and spinal cord

☐ **198.4 Other parts of nervous system**
    Meninges (cerebral) (spinal)

198.5 Bone and bone marrow

198.6 Ovary

198.7 Adrenal gland
    Suprarenal gland

● **198.8 Other specified sites**

198.81 Breast

> **Excludes** *skin of breast (198.2)*

198.82 Genital organs

☐ **198.89 Other**

> **Excludes** *retroperitoneal lymph nodes (196.2)*

● **199 Malignant neoplasm without specification of site**

199.0 Disseminated
    Carcinomatosis unspecified site (primary) (secondary)
    Generalized:
        cancer unspecified site (primary) (secondary)
        malignancy unspecified site (primary) (secondary)
    Multiple cancer unspecified site (primary) (secondary)

☐ **199.1 Other**
    Cancer unspecified site (primary) (secondary)
    Carcinoma unspecified site (primary) (secondary)
    Malignancy unspecified site (primary) (secondary)

MALIGNANT NEOPLASM OF LYMPHATIC AND HEMATOPOIETIC TISSUE (200–208)

> **Excludes** *secondary neoplasm of:*
> *bone marrow (198.5)*
> *spleen (197.8)*
> *secondary and unspecified neoplasm of lymph nodes (196.0–196.9)*

The following fifth-digit subclassification is for use with categories 200–202:

☐ 0 unspecified site, extranodal and solid organ sites
  1 lymph nodes of head, face, and neck
  2 intrathoracic lymph nodes
  3 intra-abdominal lymph nodes
  4 lymph nodes of axilla and upper limb
  5 lymph nodes of inguinal region and lower limb
  6 intrapelvic lymph nodes
  7 spleen
  8 lymph nodes of multiple sites

● **200 Lymphosarcoma and reticulosarcoma**

Requires fifth digit. See note before section 200 for codes and definitions.

● **200.0 Reticulosarcoma**
Lymphoma (malignant):
  histiocytic (diffuse):
    nodular
    pleomorphic cell type
  reticulum cell type
Reticulum cell sarcoma:
  NOS
  pleomorphic cell type

● **200.1 Lymphosarcoma**
Lymphoblastoma (diffuse)
Lymphoma (malignant):
  lymphoblastic (diffuse)
  lymphocytic (cell type) (diffuse)
  lymphosarcoma type
Lymphosarcoma:
  NOS
  diffuse NOS
  lymphoblastic (diffuse)
  lymphocytic (diffuse)
  prolymphocytic

Excludes *lymphosarcoma:*
  follicular or nodular (202.0)
  mixed cell type (200.8)
  lymphosarcoma cell leukemia (207.8)

● **200.2 Burkitt's tumor or lymphoma**
Malignant lymphoma, Burkitt's type

□ ● **200.8 Other named variants**
Lymphoma (malignant):
  lymphoplasmacytoid type
  mixed lymphocytic-histiocytic (diffuse)
Lymphosarcoma, mixed cell type (diffuse)
Reticulolymphosarcoma (diffuse)

● **201 Hodgkin's disease**

Requires fifth digit. See note before section 200 for codes and definitions.

● **201.0 Hodgkin's paragranuloma**

● **201.1 Hodgkin's granuloma**

● **201.2 Hodgkin's sarcoma**

● **201.4 Lymphocytic-histiocytic predominance**

● **201.5 Nodular sclerosis**
Hodgkin's disease, nodular sclerosis:
  NOS
  cellular phase

● **201.6 Mixed cellularity**

● **201.7 Lymphocytic depletion**
Hodgkin's disease, lymphocytic depletion:
  NOS
  diffuse fibrosis
  reticular type

□ ● **201.9 Hodgkin's disease, unspecified**
Hodgkin's:
  disease NOS
  lymphoma NOS
Malignant:
  lymphogranuloma
  lymphogranulomatosis

● **202 Other malignant neoplasms of lymphoid and histiocytic tissue**

Requires fifth digit. See note before section 200 for codes and definitions.

● **202.0 Nodular lymphoma**
Brill-Symmers disease
Lymphoma:
  follicular (giant)
  lymphocytic, nodular
Lymphosarcoma:
  follicular (giant)
  nodular
Reticulosarcoma, follicular or nodular

● **202.1 Mycosis fungoides**

● **202.2 Sézary's disease**

● **202.3 Malignant histiocytosis**
Histiocytic medullary reticulosis
Malignant:
  reticuloendotheliosis
  reticulosis

● **202.4 Leukemic reticuloendotheliosis**
Hairy-cell leukemia

● **202.5 Letterer-Siwe disease**
Acute:
  differentiated progressive histiocytosis
  histiocytosis X (progressive)
  infantile reticuloendotheliosis
  reticulosis of infancy

Excludes *Hand-Schüller-Christian disease (277.8)*
  histiocytosis (acute) (chronic) (277.8)
  histiocytosis X (chronic) (277.8)

● **202.6 Malignant mast cell tumors**
Malignant:
  mastocytoma
  mastocytosis
Mast cell sarcoma
Systemic tissue mast cell disease

Excludes *mast cell leukemia (207.8)*

□ ● **202.8 Other lymphomas**
Lymphoma (malignant):
  NOS
  diffuse

Excludes *benign lymphoma (229.0)*

□ ● **202.9 Other and unspecified malignant neoplasms of lymphoid and histiocytic tissue**
Malignant neoplasm of bone marrow NOS

● **203 Multiple myeloma and immunoproliferative neoplasms**

The following fifth-digit subclassification is for use with category 203:
  0 without mention of remission
  1 in remission

● **203.0 Multiple myeloma**
Kahler's disease   Myelomatosis

Excludes *solitary myeloma (238.6)*

● **203.1 Plasma cell leukemia**
Plasmacytic leukemia

□ ● **203.8 Other immunoproliferative neoplasms**

● **204 Lymphoid leukemia**

Includes: leukemia:
  lymphatic   lymphocytic
  lymphoblastic   lymphogenous

The following fifth-digit subclassification is for use with category 204:
  0 without mention of remission
  1 in remission

● **204.0 Acute**

Excludes *acute exacerbation of chronic lymphoid leukemia (204.1)*

    ◀▶ **New Code**   ⬅➡ **Revised Code**   ● **Not a Principal Diagnosis**   ● **Use Additional Digit(s)**   □ **Nonspecific Code**

204.1 Chronic

204.2 Subacute

204.8 Other lymphoid leukemia
Aleukemic leukemia:
  lymphatic
  lymphocytic
  lymphoid

204.9 Unspecified lymphoid leukemia

205 Myeloid leukemia

Includes: leukemia:
  granulocytic
  myeloblastic
  myelocytic
  myelogenous
  myelomonocytic
  myelosclerotic
  myelosis

The following fifth-digit subclassification is for use with category 205:
  0 without mention of remission
  1 in remission

205.0 Acute
Acute promyelocytic leukemia

> **Excludes** *acute exacerbation of chronic myeloid leukemia (205.1)*

205.1 Chronic
Eosinophilic leukemia
Neutrophilic leukemia

205.2 Subacute

205.3 Myeloid sarcoma
Chloroma
Granulocytic sarcoma

205.8 Other myeloid leukemia
Aleukemic leukemia:
  granulocytic
  myelogenous
  myeloid
Aleukemic myelosis

205.9 Unspecified myeloid leukemia

206 Monocytic leukemia

Includes: leukemia:
  histiocytic
  monoblastic
  monocytoid

The following fifth-digit subclassification is for use with category 206:
  0 without mention of remission
  1 in remission

206.0 Acute

> **Excludes** *acute exacerbation of chronic monocytic leukemia (206.1)*

206.1 Chronic

206.2 Subacute

206.8 Other monocytic leukemia
Aleukemic:
  monocytic leukemia
  monocytoid leukemia

206.9 Unspecified monocytic leukemia

207 Other specified leukemia

> **Excludes** *leukemic reticuloendotheliosis (202.4)*
> *plasma cell leukemia (203.1)*

The following fifth-digit subclassification is for use with category 207:
  0 without mention of remission
  1 in remission

207.0 Acute erythremia and erythroleukemia
Acute erythremic myelosis
Di Guglielmo's disease
Erythremic myelosis

207.1 Chronic erythremia
Heilmeyer-Schöner disease

207.2 Megakaryocytic leukemia
Megakaryocytic myelosis
Thrombocytic leukemia

207.8 Other specified leukemia
Lymphosarcoma cell leukemia

208 Leukemia of unspecified cell type

The following fifth-digit subclassification is for use with category 208:
  0 without mention of remission
  1 in remission

208.0 Acute
Acute leukemia NOS
Blast cell leukemia
Stem cell leukemia

> **Excludes** *acute exacerbation of chronic unspecified leukemia (208.1)*

208.1 Chronic
Chronic leukemia NOS

208.2 Subacute
Subacute leukemia NOS

208.8 Other leukemia of unspecified cell type

208.9 Unspecified leukemia
Leukemia NOS

BENIGN NEOPLASMS (210–229)

210 Benign neoplasm of lip, oral cavity, and pharynx

> **Excludes** *cyst (of):*
> *jaw (526.0–526.2, 526.89)*
> *oral soft tissue (528.4)*
> *radicular (522.8)*

210.0 Lip
Frenulum labii
Lip (inner aspect) (mucosa) (vermilion border)

> **Excludes** *labial commissure (210.4)*
> *skin of lip (216.0)*

210.1 Tongue
Lingual tonsil

210.2 Major salivary glands
Gland:
  parotid
  sublingual
  submandibular

> **Excludes** *benign neoplasms of minor salivary glands:*
> *NOS (210.4)*
> *buccal mucosa (210.4)*
> *lips (210.0)*
> *palate (hard) (soft) (210.4)*
> *tongue (210.1)*
> *tonsil, palatine (210.5)*

210.3 Floor of mouth

ICD-9-CM

200-299

Vol. 1

❑ **210.4 Other and unspecified parts of mouth**
Gingiva
Gum (upper) (lower)
Labial commissure
Oral cavity NOS
Oral mucosa
Palate (hard) (soft)
Uvula

Excludes	*benign odontogenic neoplasms of bone (213.0–213.1)*

developmental odontogenic cysts (526.0)
mucosa of lips (210.0)
nasopharyngeal [posterior] [superior] surface of soft palate (210.7)

210.5 Tonsil
Tonsil (faucial) (palatine)

Excludes	*lingual tonsil (210.1)*

pharyngeal tonsil (210.7)
tonsillar:
  fossa (210.6)
  pillars (210.6)

❑ **210.6 Other parts of oropharynx**
Branchial cleft or vestiges
Epiglottis, anterior aspect
Fauces NOS
Mesopharynx NOS
Tonsillar:
  fossa
  pillars
Vallecula

Excludes	*epiglottis:*

  NOS (212.1)
  suprahyoid portion (212.1)

210.7 Nasopharynx
Adenoid tissue   Pharyngeal tonsil
Lymphadenoid tissue   Posterior nasal septum

210.8 Hypopharynx
Arytenoid fold   Postcricoid region
Laryngopharynx   Pyriform fossa

❑ **210.9 Pharynx, unspecified**
Throat NOS

● **211 Benign neoplasm of other parts of digestive system**

211.0 Esophagus

211.1 Stomach
Body of stomach
Cardia of stomach
Fundus of stomach
Cardiac orifice
Pylorus

211.2 Duodenum, jejunum, and ileum
Small intestine NOS

Excludes	*ampulla of Vater (211.5)*

ileocecal valve (211.3)

211.3 Colon
Appendix
Cecum
Ileocecal valve
Large intestine NOS

Excludes	*rectosigmoid junction (211.4)*

211.4 Rectum and anal canal
Anal canal or sphincter
Anus NOS
Rectosigmoid junction

Excludes	*anus:*

  margin (216.5)
  skin (216.5)
perianal skin (216.5)

211.5 Liver and biliary passages
Ampulla of Vater
Common bile duct
Cystic duct
Gallbladder
Hepatic duct
Sphincter of Oddi

211.6 Pancreas, except islets of Langerhans

211.7 Islets of Langerhans
Islet cell tumor

Use additional code to identify any functional activity

211.8 Retroperitoneum and peritoneum
Mesentery
Mesocolon
Omentum
Retroperitoneal tissue

❑ **211.9 Other and unspecified site**
Alimentary tract NOS
Digestive system NOS
Gastrointestinal tract NOS
Intestinal tract NOS
Intestine NOS
Spleen, not elsewhere classified

● **212 Benign neoplasm of respiratory and intrathoracic organs**

212.0 Nasal cavities, middle ear, and accessory sinuses
Cartilage of nose
Eustachian tube
Nares
Septum of nose
Sinus:
  ethmoidal
  frontal
  maxillary
  sphenoidal

Excludes	*auditory canal (external) (216.2)*

bone of:
  ear (213.0)
  nose [turbinates] (213.0)
cartilage of ear (215.0)
ear (external) (skin) (216.2)
nose NOS (229.8)
  skin (216.3)
olfactory bulb (225.1)
polyp of:
  accessory sinus (471.8)
  ear (385.30–385.35)
  nasal cavity (471.0)
posterior margin of septum and choanae (210.7)

212.1 Larynx
Cartilage:
  arytenoid
  cricoid
  cuneiform
  thyroid
Epiglottis (suprahyoid portion) NOS
Glottis
Vocal cords (false) (true)

Excludes	*epiglottis, anterior aspect (210.6)*

polyp of vocal cord or larynx (478.4)

212.2 Trachea

212.3 Bronchus and lung
Carina
Hilus of lung

212.4 Pleura

212.5 Mediastinum

212.6 Thymus

◀▶ **New Code**   ⬅▮▮ ▮▮➡ **Revised Code**   ● **Not a Principal Diagnosis**   ● **Use Additional Digit(s)**   ❑ **Nonspecific Code**

212.7 Heart

> **Excludes** *great vessels (215.4)*

☐ **212.8 Other specified sites**

☐ **212.9 Site unspecified**
Respiratory organ NOS
Upper respiratory tract NOS

> **Excludes** *intrathoracic NOS (229.8)*
> *thoracic NOS (229.8)*

● **213 Benign neoplasm of bone and articular cartilage**

> **Includes:** cartilage (articular) (joint)
> periosteum

> **Excludes** *cartilage of:*   *cartilage of:*
> *ear (215.0)*   *nose (212.0)*
> *eyelid (215.0)*   *exostosis NOS (726.91)*
> *larynx (212.1)*   *synovia (215.0–215.9)*

213.0 Bones of skull and face

> **Excludes** *lower jaw bone (213.1)*

213.1 Lower jaw bone

213.2 Vertebral column, excluding sacrum and coccyx

213.3 Ribs, sternum, and clavicle

213.4 Scapula and long bones of upper limb

213.5 Short bones of upper limb

213.6 Pelvic bones, sacrum, and coccyx

213.7 Long bones of lower limb

213.8 Short bones of lower limb

☐ **213.9 Bone and articular cartilage, site unspecified**

● **214 Lipoma**

> **Includes:** angiolipoma
> fibrolipoma
> hibernoma
> lipoma (fetal) (infiltrating) (intramuscular)
> myelolipoma
> myxolipoma

214.0 Skin and subcutaneous tissue of face

☐ **214.1 Other skin and subcutaneous tissue**

214.2 Intrathoracic organs

214.3 Intra-abdominal organs

214.4 Spermatic cord

☐ **214.8 Other specified sites**

☐ **214.9 Lipoma, unspecified site**

● **215 Other benign neoplasm of connective and other soft tissue**

> **Includes:** blood vessel
> bursa
> fascia
> ligament
> muscle
> peripheral, sympathetic, and parasympathetic
> nerves and ganglia
> synovia
> tendon (sheath)

> **Excludes** *cartilage:*
> *articular (213.0–213.9)*
> *larynx (212.1)*
> *nose (212.0)*
> *connective tissue of:*
> *breast (217)*
> *internal organ, except lipoma and hemangioma*
> *- code to benign neoplasm of the site*
> *lipoma (214.0–214.9)*

215.0 Head, face, and neck

215.2 Upper limb, including shoulder

215.3 Lower limb, including hip

215.4 Thorax

> **Excludes** *heart (212.7)*
> *mediastinum (212.5)*
> *thymus (212.6)*

215.5 Abdomen
Abdominal wall
Hypochondrium

215.6 Pelvis
Buttock
Groin
Inguinal region
Perineum

> **Excludes** *uterine:*
> *leiomyoma (218.0–218.9)*
> *ligament, any (221.0)*

☐ **215.7 Trunk, unspecified**
Back NOS
Flank NOS

☐ **215.8 Other specified sites**

☐ **215.9 Site unspecified**

● **216 Benign neoplasm of skin**

> **Includes:** blue nevus
> dermatofibroma
> hydrocystoma
> pigmented nevus
> syringoadenoma
> syringoma

> **Excludes** *skin of genital organs (221.0–222.9)*

216.0 Skin of lip

> **Excludes** *vermilion border of lip (210.0)*

216.1 Eyelid, including canthus

> **Excludes** *cartilage of eyelid (215.0)*

216.2 Ear and external auditory canal
Auricle (ear)
Auricular canal, external
External meatus
Pinna

> **Excludes** *cartilage of ear (215.0)*

☐ **216.3 Skin of other and unspecified parts of face**
Cheek, external
Eyebrow
Nose, external
Temple

216.4 Scalp and skin of neck

216.5 Skin of trunk, except scrotum
Axillary fold
Perianal skin
Skin of:
abdominal wall
anus
back
breast
buttock
chest wall
groin
perineum
Umbilicus

> **Excludes** *anal canal (211.4)*
> *anus NOS (211.4)*
> *skin of scrotum (222.4)*

ICD-9-CM

200-299

Vol. 1

216.6 Skin of upper limb, including shoulder

216.7 Skin of lower limb, including hip

☐ **216.8 Other specified sites of skin**

☐ **216.9 Skin, site unspecified**

217 Benign neoplasm of breast
Breast (male) (female)
  connective tissue
  glandular tissue
  soft parts

   | Excludes | *adenofibrosis (610.2)*
       benign cyst of breast (610.0)
       fibrocystic disease (610.1)
       skin of breast (216.5)

● **218 Uterine leiomyoma**

   Includes: fibroid (bleeding) (uterine)
      uterine:
        fibromyoma
        myoma

218.0 Submucous leiomyoma of uterus

218.1 Intramural leiomyoma of uterus
   Interstitial leiomyoma of uterus

218.2 Subserous leiomyoma of uterus
   Subperitoneal leiomyoma of uterus

☐ **218.9 Leiomyoma of uterus, unspecified**

● **219 Other benign neoplasm of uterus**

219.0 Cervix uteri

219.1 Corpus uteri
   Endometrium
   Fundus
   Myometrium

☐ **219.8 Other specified parts of uterus**

☐ **219.9 Uterus, part unspecified**

220 Benign neoplasm of ovary
Use additional code to identify any functional activity
(256.0–256.1)

   | Excludes | *cyst:*
       corpus albicans (620.2)
       corpus luteum (620.1)
       endometrial (617.1)
       follicular (atretic) (620.0)
       graafian follicle (620.0)
       ovarian NOS (620.2)
       retention (620.2)

● **221 Benign neoplasm of other female genital organs**

   Includes: adenomatous polyp
      benign teratoma

   | Excludes | *cyst:*
       epoophoron (752.11)
       fimbrial (752.11)
       Gartner's duct (752.11)
       parovarian (752.11)

221.0 Fallopian tube and uterine ligaments
   Oviduct
   Parametrium
   Uterine ligament (broad) (round) (uterosacral)
   Uterine tube

221.1 Vagina

221.2 Vulva
   Clitoris
   External female genitalia NOS
   Greater vestibular [Bartholin's] gland
   Labia (majora) (minora)
   Pudendum

   | Excludes | *Bartholin's (duct) (gland) cyst (616.2)*

☐ **221.8 Other specified sites of female genital organs**

☐ **221.9 Female genital organ, site unspecified**
   Female genitourinary tract NOS

● **222 Benign neoplasm of male genital organs**

222.0 Testis
   Use additional code to identify any functional activity

222.1 Penis
   Corpus cavernosum
   Glans penis
   Prepuce

222.2 Prostate

   | Excludes | *adenomatous hyperplasia of prostate (600)*
       prostatic:
        adenoma (600)
        enlargement (600)
        hypertrophy (600)

222.3 Epididymis

222.4 Scrotum
   Skin of scrotum

☐ **222.8 Other specified sites of male genital organs**
   Seminal vesicle
   Spermatic cord

☐ **222.9 Male genital organ, site unspecified**
   Male genitourinary tract NOS

● **223 Benign neoplasm of kidney and other urinary organs**

223.0 Kidney, except pelvis
   Kidney NOS

   | Excludes | *renal:*
       calyces (223.1)
       pelvis (223.1)

223.1 Renal pelvis

223.2 Ureter

   | Excludes | *ureteric orifice of bladder (223.3)*

223.3 Bladder

● **223.8 Other specified sites of urinary organs**

   223.81 Urethra

   | Excludes | *urethral orifice of bladder (223.3)*

   ☐ **223.89 Other**
      Paraurethral glands

☐ **223.9 Urinary organ, site unspecified**
   Urinary system NOS

● **224 Benign neoplasm of eye**

   | Excludes | *cartilage of eyelid (215.0)*
       eyelid (skin) (216.1)
       optic nerve (225.1)
       orbital bone (213.0)

224.0 Eyeball, except conjunctiva, cornea, retina, and choroid
   Ciliary body
   Iris
   Sclera
   Uveal tract

224.1 Orbit

> **Excludes** *bone of orbit (213.0)*

224.2 Lacrimal gland

224.3 Conjunctiva

224.4 Cornea

224.5 Retina

> **Excludes** *hemangioma of retina (228.03)*

224.6 Choroid

224.7 Lacrimal duct
    Lacrimal sac
    Nasolacrimal duct

☐ **224.8 Other specified parts of eye**

☐ **224.9 Eye, part unspecified**

● **225 Benign neoplasm of brain and other parts of nervous system**

> **Excludes** *hemangioma (228.02)*
> *neurofibromatosis (237.7)*
> *peripheral, sympathetic, and parasympathetic nerves and ganglia (215.0–215.9)*
> *retrobulbar (224.1)*

225.0 Brain

225.1 Cranial nerves

225.2 Cerebral meninges
    Meninges NOS
    Meningioma (cerebral)

225.3 Spinal cord
    Cauda equina

225.4 Spinal meninges
    Spinal meningioma

☐ **225.8 Other specified sites of nervous system**

☐ **225.9 Nervous system, part unspecified**
    Nervous system (central) NOS

> **Excludes** *meninges NOS (225.2)*

226 Benign neoplasm of thyroid glands

Use additional code to identify any functional activity

● **227 Benign neoplasm of other endocrine glands and related structures**

Use additional code to identify any functional activity

> **Excludes** *ovary (220)*
> *pancreas (211.6)*
> *testis (222.0)*

227.0 Adrenal gland
    Suprarenal gland

227.1 Parathyroid gland

227.3 Pituitary gland and craniopharyngeal duct (pouch)
    Craniobuccal pouch
    Hypophysis
    Rathke's pouch
    Sella turcica

227.4 Pineal gland
    Pineal body

227.5 Carotid body

227.6 Aortic body and other paraganglia
    Coccygeal body
    Glomus jugulare
    Para-aortic body

☐ **227.8 Other**

☐ **227.9 Endocrine gland, site unspecified**

● **228 Hemangioma and lymphangioma, any site**

> **Includes:** angioma (benign) (cavernous) (congenital) NOS
> cavernous nevus
> glomus tumor
> hemangioma (benign) (congenital)

> **Excludes** *benign neoplasm of spleen, except hemangioma and lymphangioma (211.9)*
> *glomus jugulare (227.6)*
> *nevus:*
>   *NOS (216.0–216.9)*
>   *blue or pigmented (216.0–216.9)*
>   *vascular (757.32)*

● **228.0 Hemangioma, any site**

☐ **228.00 Of unspecified site**

228.01 Of skin and subcutaneous tissue

228.02 Of intracranial structures

228.03 Of retina

228.04 Of intra-abdominal structures
    Peritoneum
    Retroperitoneal tissue

☐ **228.09 Of other sites**
    Systemic angiomatosis

228.1 Lymphangioma, any site
    Congenital lymphangioma
    Lymphatic nevus

● **229 Benign neoplasm of other and unspecified sites**

229.0 Lymph nodes

> **Excludes** *lymphangioma (228.1)*

☐ **229.8 Other specified sites**
    Intrathoracic NOS
    Thoracic NOS

☐ **229.9 Site unspecified**

CARCINOMA IN SITU (230–234)

> **Includes:** Bowen's disease
> erythroplasia
> Queyrat's erythroplasia

> **Excludes** *leukoplakia - see Alphabetic Index*

● **230 Carcinoma in situ of digestive organs**

230.0 Lip, oral cavity, and pharynx
    Gingiva
    Hypopharynx
    Mouth [any part]
    Nasopharynx
    Oropharynx
    Salivary gland or duct
    Tongue

> **Excludes** *aryepiglottic fold or interarytenoid fold, laryngeal aspect (231.0)*
> *epiglottis:*
>   *NOS (231.0)*
>   *suprahyoid portion (231.0)*
> *skin of lip (232.0)*

230.1 Esophagus

230.2 Stomach
    Body of stomach
    Cardia of stomach
    Fundus of stomach
    Cardiac orifice
    Pylorus

ICD-9-CM

200-299

Vol. 1

230.3 Colon
Appendix
Cecum
Ileocecal valve
Large intestine NOS
Excludes | *rectosigmoid junction (230.4)*

230.4 Rectum
Rectosigmoid junction

230.5 Anal canal
Anal sphincter

☐ **230.6 Anus, unspecified**
Excludes | *anus:*
margin (232.5)
skin (232.5)
perianal skin (232.5)

☐ **230.7 Other and unspecified parts of intestine**
Duodenum
Ileum
Jejunum
Small intestine NOS
Excludes | *ampulla of Vater (230.8)*

230.8 Liver and biliary system
Ampulla of Vater
Common bile duct
Cystic duct
Gallbladder
Hepatic duct
Sphincter of Oddi

☐ **230.9 Other and unspecified digestive organs**
Digestive organ NOS
Gastrointestinal tract NOS
Pancreas
Spleen

● **231 Carcinoma in situ of respiratory system**

231.0 Larynx
Cartilage:
arytenoid
cricoid
cuneiform
thyroid
Epiglottis:
NOS
posterior surface
suprahyoid portion
Vocal cords (false) (true)
Excludes | *aryepiglottic fold or interarytenoid fold:*
NOS (230.0)
hypopharyngeal aspect (230.0)
marginal zone (230.0)

231.1 Trachea

231.2 Bronchus and lung
Carina
Hilus of lung

☐ **231.8 Other specified parts of respiratory system**
Accessory sinuses
Middle ear
Nasal cavities
Pleura
Excludes | *ear (external) (skin) (232.2)*
nose NOS (234.8)
skin (232.3)

☐ **231.9 Respiratory system, part unspecified**
Respiratory organ NOS

● **232 Carcinoma in situ of skin**

Includes: pigment cells

232.0 Skin of lip
Excludes | *vermilion border of lip (230.0)*

232.1 Eyelid, including canthus

232.2 Ear and external auditory canal

☐ **232.3 Skin of other and unspecified parts of face**

232.4 Scalp and skin of neck

232.5 Skin of trunk, except scrotum

Anus, margin	Skin of:
Axillary fold	breast
Perianal skin	buttock
Skin of:	chest wall
abdominal wall	groin
anus	perineum
back	Umbilicus

Excludes | *anal canal (230.5)*
anus NOS (230.6)
skin of genital organs (233.3, 233.5–233.6)

232.6 Skin of upper limb, including shoulder

232.7 Skin of lower limb, including hip

☐ **232.8 Other specified sites of skin**

☐ **232.9 Skin, site unspecified**

● **233 Carcinoma in situ of breast and genitourinary system**

233.0 Breast
Excludes | *Paget's disease (174.0–174.9)*
skin of breast (232.5)

233.1 Cervix uteri

☐ **233.2 Other and unspecified parts of uterus**

☐ **233.3 Other and unspecified female genital organs**

233.4 Prostate

233.5 Penis

☐ **233.6 Other and unspecified male genital organs**

233.7 Bladder

☐ **233.9 Other and unspecified urinary organs**

● **234 Carcinoma in situ of other and unspecified sites**

234.0 Eye
Excludes | *cartilage of eyelid (234.8)*
eyelid (skin) (232.1)
optic nerve (234.8)
orbital bone (234.8)

☐ **234.8 Other specified sites**
Endocrine gland [any]

☐ **234.9 Site unspecified**
Carcinoma in situ NOS

NEOPLASMS OF UNCERTAIN BEHAVIOR (235–238)

Note: Categories 235–238 classify by site certain histo-morphologically well-defined neoplasms, the subsequent behavior of which cannot be predicted from the present appearance.

● **235 Neoplasm of uncertain behavior of digestive and respiratory systems**

235.0 Major salivary glands
Gland:
parotid
sublingual
submandibular
Excludes | *minor salivary glands (235.1)*

    ◄► **New Code**   ◄▦ ▦► **Revised Code**   ● **Not a Principal Diagnosis**   ● **Use Additional Digit(s)**   ☐ **Nonspecific Code**

235.1 Lip, oral cavity, and pharynx
Gingiva
Hypopharynx
Minor salivary glands
Mouth
Nasopharynx
Oropharynx
Tongue

> **Excludes** | *aryepiglottic fold or interarytenoid fold, laryngeal*
> *aspect (235.6)*
> *epiglottis:*
> *NOS (235.6)*
> *suprahyoid portion (235.6)*
> *skin of lip (238.2)*

235.2 Stomach, intestines, and rectum

235.3 Liver and biliary passages
Ampulla of Vater
Bile ducts [any]
Gallbladder
Liver

235.4 Retroperitoneum and peritoneum

☐ **235.5 Other and unspecified digestive organs**
Anal:
   canal
   sphincter
Anus NOS
Esophagus
Pancreas
Spleen

> **Excludes** | *anus:*
> *margin (238.2)*
> *skin (238.2)*
> *perianal skin (238.2)*

235.6 Larynx

> **Excludes** | *aryepiglottic fold or interarytenoid fold:*
> *NOS (235.1)*
> *hypopharyngeal aspect (235.1)*
> *marginal zone (235.1)*

235.7 Trachea, bronchus, and lung

235.8 Pleura, thymus, and mediastinum

☐ **235.9 Other and unspecified respiratory organs**
Accessory sinuses
Middle ear
Nasal cavities
Respiratory organ NOS

> **Excludes** | *ear (external) (skin) (238.2)*
> *nose (238.8)*
> *skin (238.2)*

● **236 Neoplasm of uncertain behavior of genitourinary organs**

236.0 Uterus

236.1 Placenta
Chorioadenoma (destruens)
Invasive mole
Malignant hydatid(iform) mole

236.2 Ovary

Use additional code to identify any functional activity

☐ **236.3 Other and unspecified female genital organs**

236.4 Testis

Use additional code to identify any functional activity

236.5 Prostate

☐ **236.6 Other and unspecified male genital organs**

236.7 Bladder

● **236.9 Other and unspecified urinary organs**

☐ **236.90 Urinary organ, unspecified**

236.91 Kidney and ureter

☐ **236.99 Other**

● **237 Neoplasm of uncertain behavior of endocrine glands and nervous system**

237.0 Pituitary gland and craniopharyngeal duct

Use additional code to identify any functional activity

237.1 Pineal gland

237.2 Adrenal gland
Suprarenal gland

Use additional code to identify any functional activity

237.3 Paraganglia
Aortic body
Carotid body
Coccygeal body
Glomus jugulare

☐ **237.4 Other and unspecified endocrine glands**
Parathyroid gland
Thyroid gland

237.5 Brain and spinal cord

237.6 Meninges
Meninges:
   NOS
   cerebral
   spinal

● **237.7 Neurofibromatosis**
von Recklinghausen's disease

☐ **237.70 Neurofibromatosis, unspecified**

237.71 Neurofibromatosis, type 1 [von Recklinghausen's disease]

237.72 Neurofibromatosis, type 2 [acoustic neurofibromatosis]

☐ **237.9 Other and unspecified parts of nervous system**
Cranial nerves

> **Excludes** | *peripheral, sympathetic, and parasympathetic*
> *nerves and ganglia (238.1)*

● **238 Neoplasm of uncertain behavior of other and unspecified sites and tissues**

238.0 Bone and articular cartilage

> **Excludes** | *cartilage:*
> *ear (238.1)*
> *eyelid (238.1)*
> *larynx (235.6)*
> *nose (235.9)*
> *synovia (238.1)*

☐ **238.1 Connective and other soft tissue**
Peripheral, sympathetic, and parasympathetic nerves and ganglia

> **Excludes** | *cartilage (of):*
> *articular (238.0)*
> *larynx (235.6)*
> *nose (235.9)*
> *connective tissue of breast (238.3)*

238.2 Skin

> **Excludes** | *anus NOS (235.5)*
> *skin of genital organs (236.3, 236.6)*
> *vermilion border of lip (235.1)*

ICD-9-CM

200-299

Vol. 1

238.3 Breast

> **Excludes** *skin of breast (238.2)*

238.4 Polycythemia vera

238.5 Histiocytic and mast cells
Mast cell tumor NOS
Mastocytoma NOS

238.6 Plasma cells
Plasmacytoma NOS
Solitary myeloma

☐ **238.7 Other lymphatic and hematopoietic tissues**
Disease:
lymphoproliferative (chronic) NOS
myeloproliferative (chronic) NOS
Idiopathic thrombocythemia
Megakaryocytic myelosclerosis
Myelodysplastic syndrome
Myelosclerosis with myeloid metaplasia
Panmyelosis (acute)

> **Excludes** *myelofibrosis (289.8)*
> *myelosclerosis NOS (289.8)*
> *myelosis:*
> *NOS (205.9)*
> *megakaryocytic (207.2)*

☐ **238.8 Other specified sites**
Eye
Heart

> **Excludes** *eyelid (skin) (238.2)*
> *cartilage (238.1)*

☐ **238.9 Site unspecified**

NEOPLASMS OF UNSPECIFIED NATURE (239)

● **239 Neoplasms of unspecified nature**

Note: Category 239 classifies by site neoplasms of unspecified morphology and behavior. The term "mass," unless otherwise stated, is not to be regarded as a neoplastic growth.

Includes: "growth" NOS
neoplasm NOS
new growth NOS
tumor NOS

239.0 Digestive system

> **Excludes** *anus:*
> *margin (239.2)*
> *skin (239.2)*
> *perianal skin (239.2)*

239.1 Respiratory system

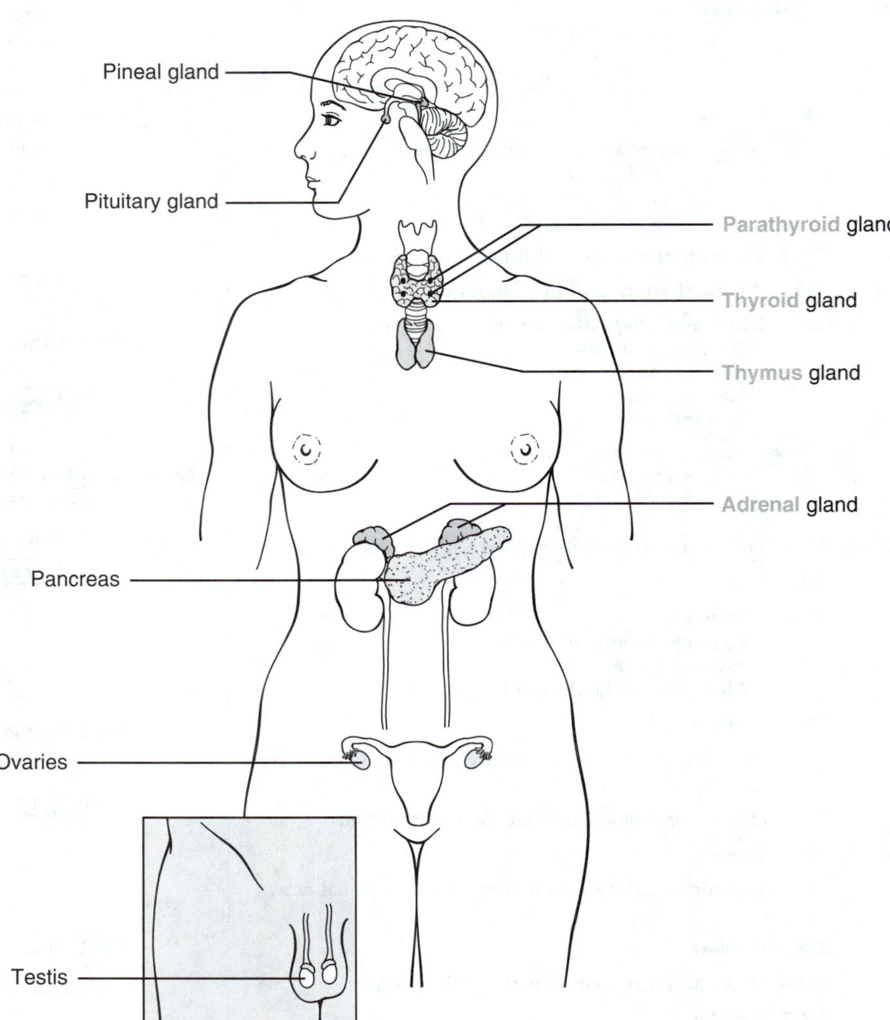

Figure 3–1 The endocrine system. (From Buck CJ: Step-by-Step Medical Coding, 2nd ed. Philadelphia, WB Saunders, 1998.)

   ◀▶ **New Code**   ⬅▥ ▥➡ **Revised Code**   ● **Not a Principal Diagnosis**   ● **Use Additional Digit(s)**   ☐ **Nonspecific Code**

239.2 Bone, soft tissue, and skin

| Excludes | anal canal (239.0)
anus NOS (239.0)
bone marrow (202.9)
cartilage:
  larynx (239.1)
  nose (239.1)
connective tissue of breast (239.3)
skin of genital organs (239.5)
vermilion border of lip (239.0)

239.3 Breast

| Excludes | skin of breast (239.2)

239.4 Bladder

239.5 Other genitourinary organs

239.6 Brain

| Excludes | cerebral meninges (239.7)
cranial nerves (239.7)

239.7 Endocrine glands and other parts of nervous system

| Excludes | peripheral, sympathetic, and parasympathetic nerves and ganglia (239.2)

239.8 Other specified sites

| Excludes | eyelid (skin) (239.2)
cartilage (239.2)
great vessels (239.2)
optic nerve (239.7)

239.9 Site unspecified

---

3. ENDOCRINE, NUTRITIONAL AND METABOLIC DISEASES, AND IMMUNITY DISORDERS (240–279)

| Excludes | endocrine and metabolic disturbances specific to the fetus and newborn (775.0–775.9)

Note: All neoplasms, whether functionally active or not, are classified in Chapter 2. Codes in Chapter 3 (i.e., 242.8, 246.0, 251–253, 255–259) may be used to identify such functional activity associated with any neoplasm, or by ectopic endocrine tissue.

DISORDERS OF THYROID GLAND (240–246)

Item 3–1 Simple indicates no nodules are present. The most common type of goiter is a diffuse colloidal, also called a nontoxic or endemic goiter. Goiters classifiable to 240.0 or 240.9 are those goiters without mention of nodules.

● **240 Simple and unspecified goiter**

    240.0 Goiter, specified as simple
        Any condition classifiable to 240.9, specified as simple

    240.9 Goiter, unspecified

Enlargement of thyroid	Goiter or struma:
Goiter or struma:	hyperplastic
NOS	nontoxic (diffuse)
diffuse colloid	parenchymatous
endemic	sporadic

| Excludes | congenital (dyshormonogenic) goiter (246.1)

● **241 Nontoxic nodular goiter**

| Excludes | adenoma of thyroid (226)
cystadenoma of thyroid (226)

    241.0 Nontoxic uninodular goiter
        Thyroid nodule
        Uninodular goiter (nontoxic)

    241.1 Nontoxic multinodular goiter
        Multinodular goiter (nontoxic)

    241.9 Unspecified nontoxic nodular goiter
        Adenomatous goiter
        Nodular goiter (nontoxic) NOS
        Struma nodosa (simplex)

ICD-9-CM

200-299

Vol. 1

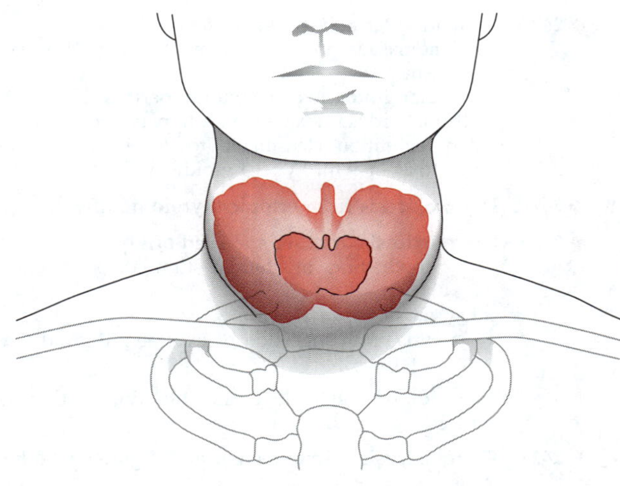

Figure 3–2 Goiter is an enlargement of the thyroid gland.

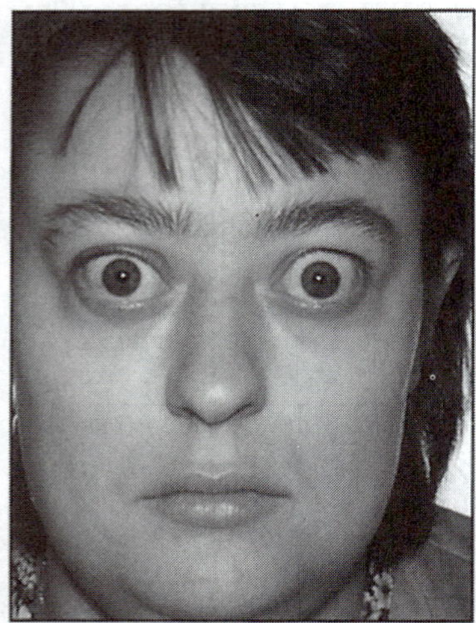

Figure 3–3   The characteristic protruding eyeballs **(exophthalmos)** of the patient with **Graves' disease.** (From Mir MA: Atlas of Clinical Diagnosis. Philadelphia, WB Saunders, 1995, p. 14.)

Item 3–2   Thyrotoxicosis is a condition caused by excessive amounts of the thyroid hormone thyroxine. The condition is also called hyperthyroidism. Graves' disease is associated with hyperthyroidism (known as Basedow's disease in Europe).

● **242   Thyrotoxicosis with or without goiter**

> **Excludes**   *neonatal thyrotoxicosis (775.3)*

The following fifth-digit subclassification is for use with category 242:

  0 without mention of thyrotoxic crisis or storm
  1 with mention of thyrotoxic crisis or storm

● **242.0   Toxic diffuse goiter**
Basedow's disease
Exophthalmic or toxic goiter NOS
Graves'disease
Primary thyroid hyperplasia

● **242.1   Toxic uninodular goiter**
Thyroid nodule, toxic or with hyperthyroidism
Uninodular goiter, toxic or with hyperthyroidism

● **242.2   Toxic multinodular goiter**
Secondary thyroid hyperplasia

☐ ● **242.3   Toxic nodular goiter, unspecified**
Adenomatous goiter, toxic or with hyperthyroidism
Nodular goiter, toxic or with hyperthyroidism
Struma nodosa, toxic or with hyperthyroidism
Any condition classifiable to 241.9 specified as toxic or with hyperthyroidism

● **242.4   Thyrotoxicosis from ectopic thyroid nodule**

☐ ● **242.8   Thyrotoxicosis of other specified origin**
Overproduction of thyroid-stimulating hormone [TSH]
Thyrotoxicosis:
  factitia from ingestion of excessive thyroid material

Use additional E code to identify cause, if drug-induced

☐ ● **242.9   Thyrotoxicosis without mention of goiter or other cause**
Hyperthyroidism NOS
Thyrotoxicosis NOS

243   Congenital hypothyroidism
Congenital thyroid insufficiency
Cretinism (athyrotic) (endemic)

Use additional code to identify associated mental retardation

> **Excludes**   *congenital (dyshormonogenic) goiter (246.1)*

Item 3–3   Hypothyroidism is a condition in which there are insufficient levels of thyroxine.
Cretinism is congenital hypothyroidism, which can result in mental and physical retardation.

● **244   Acquired hypothyroidism**

Includes: athyroidism (acquired)
            hypothyroidism (acquired)
            myxedema (adult) (juvenile)
            thyroid (gland) insufficiency (acquired)

244.0   Postsurgical hypothyroidism

☐ **244.1   Other postablative hypothyroidism**
Hypothyroidism following therapy, such as irradiation

244.2   Iodine hypothyroidism
Hypothyroidism resulting from administration or ingestion of iodide

Use additional E to identify drug

☐ **244.3   Other iatrogenic hypothyroidism**
Hypothyroidism resulting from:
  P-aminosalicylic acid [PAS]
  Phenylbutazone
  Resorcinol
Iatrogenic hypothyroidism NOS

Use additional E to identify drug

☐ **244.8   Other specified acquired hypothyroidism**
Secondary hypothyroidism NEC

☐ **244.9   Unspecified hypothyroidism**
Hypothyroidism, primary or NOS
Myxedema, primary or NOS

Figure 3–4   Myxedema is severe hypothyroidism.

● **245 Thyroiditis**

245.0 Acute thyroiditis
Abscess of thyroid
Thyroiditis:
   nonsuppurative, acute
   pyogenic
   suppurative

Use additional code to identify organism

245.1 Subacute thyroiditis
Thyroiditis:
   de Quervain's
   giant cell
   granulomatous
   viral

245.2 Chronic lymphocytic thyroiditis
Hashimoto's disease
Struma lymphomatosa
Thyroiditis:
   autoimmune
   lymphocytic (chronic)

245.3 Chronic fibrous thyroiditis
Struma fibrosa
Thyroiditis:
   invasive (fibrous)
   ligneous
   Riedel's

245.4 Iatrogenic thyroiditis

Use additional E to identify cause

☐ **245.8 Other and unspecified chronic thyroiditis**
Chronic thyroiditis:
   NOS
   nonspecific

☐ **245.9 Thyroiditis, unspecified**
Thyroiditis NOS

● **246 Other disorders of thyroid**

246.0 Disorders of thyrocalcitonin secretion
Hypersecretion of calcitonin or thyrocalcitonin

246.1 Dyshormonogenic goiter
Congenital (dyshormonogenic) goiter
Goiter due to enzyme defect in synthesis of thy-
   roid hormone
Goitrous cretinism (sporadic)

246.2 Cyst of thyroid

   Excludes   *cystadenoma of thyroid (226)*

246.3 Hemorrhage and infarction of thyroid

☐ **246.8 Other specified disorders of thyroid**
Abnormality of thyroid-binding globulin
Atrophy of thyroid
Hyper-TBG-nemia
Hypo-TBG-nemia

☐ **246.9 Unspecified disorder of thyroid**

DISEASES OF OTHER ENDOCRINE GLANDS (250–259)

● **250 Diabetes mellitus**

   Excludes   *gestational diabetes (648.8)*
                 hyperglycemia NOS (790.6)
                 neonatal diabetes mellitus (775.1)
                 nonclinical diabetes (790.2)

The following fifth-digit subclassification is for use with
category 250:
   0 type II [non-insulin dependent type] [NIDDM
   type] [adult-onset type] or unspecified type, not
   stated as uncontrolled

Fifth-digit 0 is for use for type II, adult-onset,
diabetic patients, even if the patient requires insulin
   1 type I [insulin dependent type] [IDDM] [juvenile
   type], not stated as uncontrolled
   2 type II [non-insulin dependent type] [NIDDM
   type] [adult-onset type] or unspecified type, uncontrolled

Fifth-digit 2 is for use for type II, adult-onset,
diabetic patients, even if the patient requires insulin
   3 type I [insulin dependent type] [IDDM] [juvenile
   type], uncontrolled

● **250.0 Diabetes mellitus without mention of complication**
Diabetes mellitus without mention of complication or manifestation classifiable to 250.1–
   250.9
Diabetes (mellitus) NOS

● **250.1 Diabetes with ketoacidosis**
Diabetic:
   acidosis without mention of coma
   ketosis without mention of coma

● **250.2 Diabetes with hyperosmolarity**
Hyperosmolar (nonketotic) coma

● **250.3 Diabetes with other coma**
Diabetic coma (with ketoacidosis)
Diabetic hypoglycemic coma
Insulin coma NOS

   Excludes   *diabetes with hyperosmolar coma (250.2)*

● **250.4 Diabetes with renal manifestations**

Use additional code to identify manifestation, as:
   diabetic:
      nephropathy NOS (583.81)
      nephrosis (581.81)
      intercapillary glomerulosclerosis (581.81)
      Kimmelstiel-Wilson syndrome (581.81)

● **250.5 Diabetes with ophthalmic manifestations**

Use additional code to identify manifestation, as:
   diabetic:
      blindness (369.00–369.9)
      cataract (366.41)
      glaucoma (365.44)
      retinal edema (362.83)
      retinopathy (362.01–362.02)

● **250.6 Diabetes with neurological manifestations**

Use additional code to identify manifestation, as:
   diabetic:
      amyotrophy (358.1)
      mononeuropathy (354.0–355.9)
      neurogenic arthropathy (713.5)
      peripheral autonomic neuropathy (337.1)
      polyneuropathy (357.2)

● **250.7 Diabetes with peripheral circulatory disorders**

Use additional code to identify manifestation, as:
   diabetic:
      gangrene (785.4)
      peripheral angiopathy (443.81)

☐ ● **250.8 Diabetes with other specified manifestations**
Diabetic hypoglycemia
Hypoglycemic shock

Use additional code to identify manifestation, as:
   diabetic bone changes (731.8)

Use additional E code to identify cause, if drug-
induced

☐ ● **250.9 Diabetes with unspecified complication**

● **251 Other disorders of pancreatic internal secretion**

ICD-9-CM
100-199
Vol. 1

251.0 Hypoglycemic coma
  Iatrogenic hyperinsulinism
  Non-diabetic insulin coma

  Use additional E code to identify cause, if drug-induced

  Excludes *hypoglycemic coma in diabetes mellitus (250.3)*

251.1 Other specified hypoglycemia
  Hyperinsulinism:
    NOS
    ectopic
    functional
  Hyperplasia of pancreatic islet beta cells NOS

  Excludes *hypoglycemia in diabetes mellitus (250.8)*
  hypoglycemia in infant of diabetic mother (775.0)
  hypoglycemic coma (251.0)
  neonatal hypoglycemia (775.6)

  Use additional E code to identify cause, if drug-induced

251.2 Hypoglycemia, unspecified
  Hypoglycemia:
    NOS
    reactive
    spontaneous

  Excludes *hypoglycemia:*
    with coma (251.0)
    in diabetes mellitus (250.8)
    leucine-induced (270.3)

251.3 Postsurgical hypoinsulinemia
  Hypoinsulinemia following complete or partial pancreatectomy
  Postpancreatectomy hyperglycemia

251.4 Abnormality of secretion of glucagon
  Hyperplasia of pancreatic islet alpha cells with glucagon excess

251.5 Abnormality of secretion of gastrin
  Hyperplasia of pancreatic alpha cells with gastrin excess
  Zollinger-Ellison syndrome

251.8 Other specified disorders of pancreatic internal secretion

251.9 Unspecified disorder of pancreatic internal secretion
  Islet cell hyperplasia NOS

Item 3-4 Hyperparathyroidism is an overactive parathyroid gland that secretes excessive parathormone, causing increased levels of circulating calcium. This results in a loss of calcium in the bone.
Hypoparathyroidism is an underactive parathyroid gland that results in decreased levels of circulating calcium. The primary manifestation is **tetany,** a continuous muscle spasm.

● **252 Disorders of parathyroid gland**

  252.0 Hyperparathyroidism
  Hyperplasia of parathyroid
  Osteitis fibrosa cystica generalisata
  von Recklinghausen's disease of bone

  Excludes *ectopic hyperparathyroidism (259.3)*
  secondary hyperparathyroidism (of renal origin) (588.8)

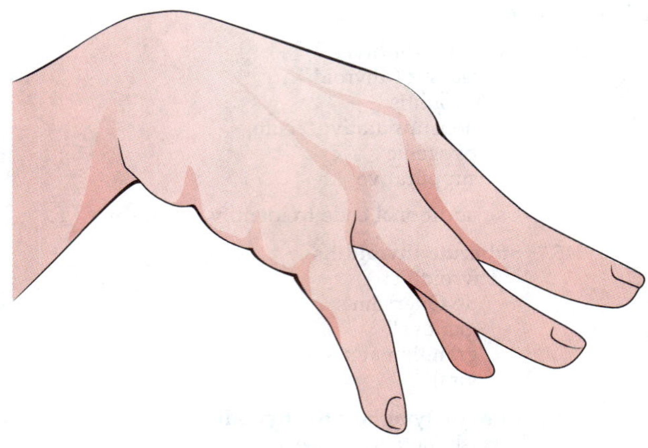

Figure 3–5 Tetany caused by hypoparathyroidism.

  252.1 Hypoparathyroidism
  Parathyroiditis (autoimmune)
  Tetany:
    parathyroid
    parathyroprival

  Excludes *pseudohypoparathyroidism (275.4)*
  pseudopseudohypoparathyroidism (275.4)
  tetany NOS (781.7)
  transitory neonatal hypoparathyroidism (775.4)

252.8 Other specified disorders of parathyroid gland
  Cyst of parathyroid gland
  Hemorrhage of parathyroid gland

252.9 Unspecified disorder of parathyroid gland

● **253 Disorders of the pituitary gland and its hypothalamic control**

  Includes: the listed conditions whether the disorder is in the pituitary or the hypothalamus

  Excludes *Cushing's syndrome (255.0)*

  253.0 Acromegaly and gigantism
  Overproduction of growth hormone

253.1 Other and unspecified anterior pituitary hyperfunction
  Forbes-Albright syndrome

  Excludes *overproduction of:*
    ACTH (255.3)
    thyroid-stimulating hormone [TSH] (242.8)

  253.2 Panhypopituitarism
  Cachexia, pituitary
  Necrosis of pituitary (postpartum)
  Pituitary insufficiency NOS
  Sheehan's syndrome
  Simmonds' disease

  Excludes *iatrogenic hypopituitarism (253.7)*

  253.3 Pituitary dwarfism
  Isolated deficiency of (human) growth hormone [HGH]
  Lorain-Levi dwarfism

253.4 Other anterior pituitary disorders
  Isolated or partial deficiency of an anterior pituitary hormone, other than growth hormone
  Prolactin deficiency

  253.5 Diabetes insipidus
  Vasopressin deficiency

  Excludes *nephrogenic diabetes insipidus (588.1)*

      ◄► **New Code**   ←▬ ▬→ **Revised Code**   ● **Not a Principal Diagnosis**   ● **Use Additional Digit(s)**   ❑ **Nonspecific Code**

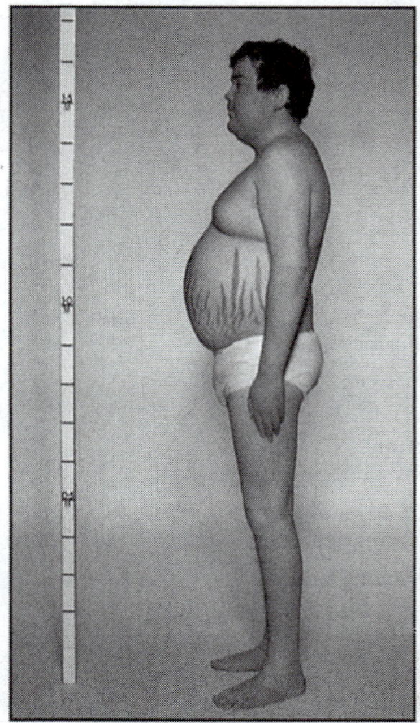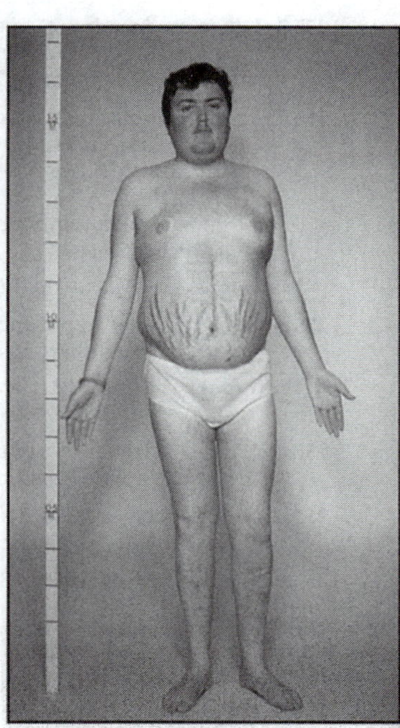

Figure 3–6 Cushing's syndrome, showing characteristic purple striae and abdominal obesity. (From Mir MA: Atlas of Clinical Diagnosis. Philadelphia, WB Saunders, 1995, p. 10.)

ICD-9-CM

200-299

Vol. 1

☐ **253.6 Other disorders of neurohypophysis**
Syndrome of inappropriate secretion of antidiuretic hormone [ADH]

Excludes *ectopic antidiuretic hormone secretion (259.3)*

253.7 Iatrogenic pituitary disorders
Hypopituitarism:
hormone-induced
hypophysectomy-induced
postablative
radiotherapy-induced

Use additional E code to identify cause

☐ **253.8 Other disorders of the pituitary and other syndromes of diencephalohypophyseal origin**
Abscess of pituitary
Adiposogenital dystrophy
Cyst of Rathke's pouch
Fröhlich's syndrome

Excludes *craniopharyngioma (237.0)*

☐ **253.9 Unspecified**
Dyspituitarism

● **254 Diseases of thymus gland**

Excludes *aplasia or dysplasia with immunodeficiency (279.2)*
hypoplasia with immunodeficiency (279.2)
myasthenia gravis (358.0)

254.0 Persistent hyperplasia of thymus
Hypertrophy of thymus

254.1 Abscess of thymus

☐ **254.8 Other specified diseases of thymus gland**
Atrophy of thymus
Cyst of thymus

Excludes *thymoma (212.6)*

☐ **254.9 Unspecified disease of thymus gland**

● **255 Disorders of adrenal glands**

Includes: the listed conditions whether the basic disorder is in the adrenals or is pituitary-induced

Item 3–5 Hyperadrenalism is overactivity of the adrenal cortex, which secretes a variety of hormones. Excessive glucocorticoid hormone results in hyperglycemia **(Cushing's syndrome),** and excessive aldosterone results in **Conn's syndrome. Adrenogenital syndrome** is the result of excessive secretion of androgens, male hormones, which stimulates premature sexual development. **Hypoadrenalism, Addison's disease,** is a condition in which the adrenal glands atrophy.

255.0 Cushing's syndrome
Adrenal hyperplasia due to excess ACTH
Cushing's syndrome:
NOS
iatrogenic
idiopathic
pituitary-dependent
Ectopic ACTH syndrome
Iatrogenic syndrome of excess cortisol
Overproduction of cortisol

Use additional E code to identify cause, if drug-induced

Excludes *congenital adrenal hyperplasia (255.2)*

255.1 Hyperaldosteronism
Aldosteronism (primary) (secondary)
Bartter's syndrome
Conn's syndrome

255.2 Adrenogenital disorders
Achard-Thiers syndrome
Adrenogenital syndromes, virilizing or feminizing, whether acquired or associated with congenital adrenal hyperplasia consequent on inborn enzyme defects in hormone synthesis
Congenital adrenal hyperplasia
Female adrenal pseudohermaphroditism
Male:
macrogenitosomia praecox
sexual precocity with adrenal hyperplasia
Virilization (female) (suprarenal)

Excludes *adrenal hyperplasia due to excess ACTH (255.0)*
isosexual virilization (256.4)

❑ **255.3 Other corticoadrenal overactivity**
Acquired benign adrenal androgenic overactivity
Overproduction of ACTH

255.4 Corticoadrenal insufficiency
Addisonian crisis   Adrenal:
Addison's disease NOS   crisis
Adrenal: hemorrhage
  atrophy (autoimmune)   infarction
  calcification   insufficiency NOS

Excludes *tuberculous Addison's disease (017.6)*

❑ **255.5 Other adrenal hypofunction**
Adrenal medullary insufficiency

Excludes *Waterhouse-Friderichsen syndrome (meningococ-cal) (036.3)*

255.6 Medulloadrenal hyperfunction
Catecholamine secretion by pheochromocytoma

❑ **255.8 Other specified disorders of adrenal glands**
Abnormality of cortisol-binding globulin

❑ **255.9 Unspecified disorder of adrenal glands**

● **256 Ovarian dysfunction**

256.0 Hyperestrogenism

❑ **256.1 Other ovarian hyperfunction**
Hypersecretion of ovarian androgens

256.2 Postablative ovarian failure
Ovarian failure:
  iatrogenic
  postirradiation
  postsurgical

❑ **256.3 Other ovarian failure**
Premature menopause NOS
Primary ovarian failure

256.4 Polycystic ovaries
Isosexual virilization Stein-Leventhal syndrome

❑ **256.8 Other ovarian dysfunction**

❑ **256.9 Unspecified ovarian dysfunction**

● **257 Testicular dysfunction**

257.0 Testicular hyperfunction
Hypersecretion of testicular hormones

257.1 Postablative testicular hypofunction
Testicular hypofunction:
  iatrogenic
  postirradiation
  postsurgical

❑ **257.2 Other testicular hypofunction**
Defective biosynthesis of testicular androgen
Eunuchoidism:
  NOS
  hypogonadotropic
Failure:
  Leydig's cell, adult
  seminiferous tubule, adult
Testicular hypogonadism

Excludes *azoospermia (606.0)*

❑ **257.8 Other testicular dysfunction**
Goldberg-Maxwell syndrome
Male pseudohermaphroditism with testicular feminization
Testicular feminization

❑ **257.9 Unspecified testicular dysfunction**

● **258 Polyglandular dysfunction and related disorders**

258.0 Polyglandular activity in multiple endocrine adenomatosis
Wermer's syndrome

❑ **258.1 Other combinations of endocrine dysfunction**
Lloyd's syndrome
Schmidt's syndrome

❑ **258.8 Other specified polyglandular dysfunction**

❑ **258.9 Polyglandular dysfunction, unspecified**

● **259 Other endocrine disorders**

259.0 Delay in sexual development and puberty, not elsewhere classified
Delayed puberty

259.1 Precocious sexual development and puberty, not elsewhere classified
Sexual precocity:
  NOS
  constitutional
  cryptogenic
  idiopathic

259.2 Carcinoid syndrome
Hormone secretion by carcinoid tumors

259.3 Ectopic hormone secretion, not elsewhere classified
Ectopic:
  antidiuretic hormone secretion [ADH]
  hyperparathyroidism

Excludes *ectopic ACTH syndrome (255.0)*

259.4 Dwarfism, not elsewhere classified
Dwarfism:
  NOS
  constitutional

Excludes *dwarfism:*
  achondroplastic (756.4)
  intrauterine (759.7)
  nutritional (263.2)
  pituitary (253.3)
  renal (588.0)
progeria (259.8)

❑ **259.8 Other specified endocrine disorders**
Pineal gland dysfunction
Progeria
Werner's syndrome

❑ **259.9 Unspecified endocrine disorder**
Disturbance:
  endocrine NOS
  hormone NOS
Infantilism NOS

NUTRITIONAL DEFICIENCIES (260–269)

Excludes *deficiency anemias (280.0–281.9)*

260 Kwashiorkor
Nutritional edema with dyspigmentation of skin and hair

261 Nutritional marasmus
Nutritional atrophy
Severe calorie deficiency
Severe malnutrition NOS

❑ **262 Other severe protein-calorie malnutrition**
Nutritional edema without mention of dyspigmentation of skin and hair

● **263 Other and unspecified protein-calorie malnutrition**

263.0 Malnutrition of moderate degree

263.1 Malnutrition of mild degree

263.2 Arrested development following protein-calorie malnutrition
Nutritional dwarfism
Physical retardation due to malnutrition

   ◀▶ **New Code**   ⬅▦⇒ **Revised Code**   ● **Not a Principal Diagnosis**   ● **Use Additional Digit(s)**   ❑ **Nonspecific Code**

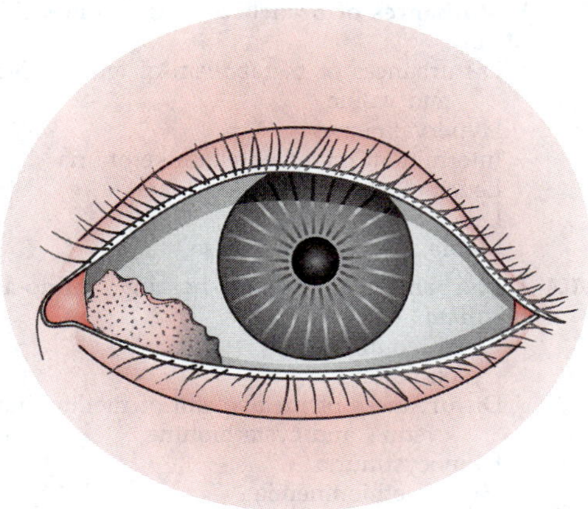

Figure 3–7   Bitot's spot on the conjunctiva.

❑ **263.8 Other protein-calorie malnutrition**

❑ **263.9 Unspecified protein-calorie malnutrition**
Dystrophy due to malnutrition
Malnutrition (calorie) NOS
Excludes *nutritional deficiency NOS (269.9)*

● **264 Vitamin A deficiency**

264.0 With conjunctival xerosis

264.1 With conjunctival xerosis and Bitot's spot
Bitot's spot in the young child

Item 3–6   **Bitot's spot** **is a gray, foamy erosion on the conjunctiva, usually associated with vitamin A deficiency. The disease may progress to** **keratomalacia,** **which can result in eventual prolapse of the iris and loss of the lens.**

264.2 With corneal xerosis

264.3 With corneal ulceration and xerosis

264.4 With keratomalacia

264.5 With night blindness

264.6 With xerophthalmic scars of cornea

❑ **264.7 Other ocular manifestations of vitamin A deficiency**
Xerophthalmia due to vitamin A deficiency

❑ **264.8 Other manifestations of vitamin A deficiency**
Follicular keratosis due to vitamin A deficiency
Xeroderma due to vitamin A deficiency

❑ **264.9 Unspecified vitamin A deficiency**
Hypovitaminosis A NOS

● **265 Thiamine and niacin deficiency states**

265.0 Beriberi

❑ **265.1 Other and unspecified manifestations of thiamine deficiency**
Other vitamin B₁ deficiency states

265.2 Pellagra
Deficiency:
niacin (-tryptophan)
nicotinamide
nicotinic acid
vitamin PP
Pellagra (alcoholic)

● **266 Deficiency of B-complex components**

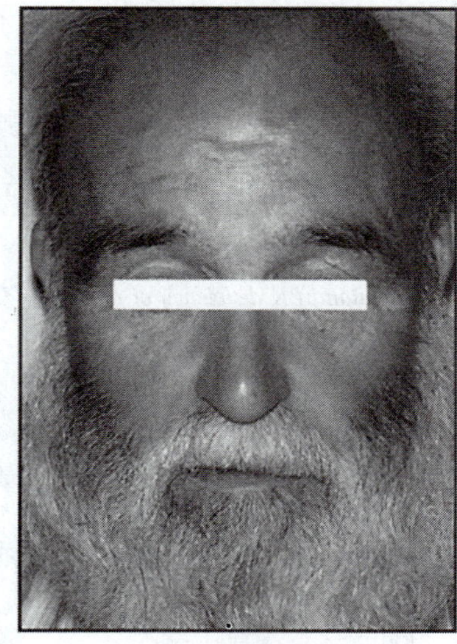

Figure 3–8   In chronic **pellagra,** the skin changes include thickening, scaling, pigmentation, and hyperkeratinization. (From Mir MA: Atlas of Clinical Diagnosis. Philadelphia, WB Saunders, 1995, p. 57.)

Item 3–7   **Pellagra is associated with a deficiency of niacin and its precursor,** **tryptophan. Characteristics of the condition include dermatitis on exposed skin surfaces. Beriberi is associated with thiamin deficiency.**

266.0 Ariboflavinosis
Riboflavin [vitamin B₂] deficiency

266.1 Vitamin B₆ deficiency
Deficiency:
pyridoxal
pyridoxamine
pyridoxine
Vitamin B₆ deficiency syndrome
Excludes *vitamin B₆-responsive sideroblastic anemia (285.0)*

❑ **266.2 Other B-complex deficiencies**
Deficiency:
cyanocobalamin
folic acid
vitamin B₁₂
Excludes *combined system disease with anemia (281.0–281.1)*
deficiency anemias (281.0–281.9)
subacute degeneration of spinal cord with anemia (281.0–281.1)

❑ **266.9 Unspecified vitamin B deficiency**

● **267 Ascorbic acid deficiency**
Deficiency of vitamin C
Scurvy
Excludes *scorbutic anemia (281.8)*

● **268 Vitamin D deficiency**
Excludes *vitamin D-resistant:*
osteomalacia (275.3)
rickets (275.3)

268.0 Rickets, active
Excludes *celiac rickets (579.0)*
renal rickets (588.0)

268.1 Rickets, late effect
Any condition specified as due to rickets and stated to be a late effect or sequela of rickets

Use additional code to identify the nature of late effect

ICD-9-CM

200-299

Vol. 1

❑ **268.2 Osteomalacia, unspecified**

❑ **268.9 Unspecified vitamin D deficiency**
    Avitaminosis D

● **269 Other nutritional deficiencies**

    269.0 Deficiency of vitamin K

        | Excludes | *deficiency of coagulation factor due to vitamin K deficiency (286.7)*
        vitamin K deficiency of newborn (776.0)

❑ **269.1 Deficiency of other vitamins**
    Deficiency:
        vitamin E
        vitamin P

❑ **269.2 Unspecified vitamin deficiency**
    Multiple vitamin deficiency NOS

    269.3 Mineral deficiency, not elsewhere classified
    Deficiency:
        calcium, dietary
        iodine

        | Excludes | *deficiency:*
        calcium NOS (275.4)
        potassium (276.8)
        sodium (276.1)

❑ **269.8 Other nutritional deficiency**

        | Excludes | *failure to thrive (783.4)*
        feeding problems (783.3)
        newborn (779.3)

❑ **269.9 Unspecified nutritional deficiency**

OTHER METABOLIC AND IMMUNITY DISORDERS (270–279)

Use additional code to identify any associated mental retardation

● **270 Disorders of amino-acid transport and metabolism**

    | Excludes | *abnormal findings without manifest disease (790.0–796.9)*
    disorders of purine and pyrimidine metabolism (277.1–277.2)
    gout (274.0–274.9)

    270.0 Disturbances of amino-acid transport
        Cystinosis
        Cystinuria
        Fanconi (-de Toni) (-Debré) syndrome
        Glycinuria (renal)
        Hartnup disease

    270.1 Phenylketonuria [PKU]
        Hyperphenylalaninemia

❑ **270.2 Other disturbances of aromatic amino-acid metabolism**
        Albinism
        Alkaptonuria
        Alkaptonuric ochronosis
        Disturbances of metabolism of tyrosine and tryptophan
        Homogentisic acid defects
        Hydroxykynureninuria
        Hypertyrosinemia
        Indicanuria
        Kynureninase defects
        Oasthouse urine disease
        Ochronosis
        Tyrosinosis
        Tyrosinuria
        Waardenburg syndrome

        | Excludes | *vitamin B_6-deficiency syndrome (266.1)*

270.3 Disturbances of branched-chain amino-acid metabolism
    Disturbances of metabolism of leucine, isoleucine, and valine
    Hypervalinemia
    Intermittent branched-chain ketonuria
    Leucine-induced hypoglycemia
    Leucinosis
    Maple syrup urine disease

270.4 Disturbances of sulphur-bearing amino-acid metabolism
    Cystathioninemia
    Cystathioninuria
    Disturbances of metabolism of methionine, homocystine, and cystathionine
    Homocystinuria
    Hypermethioninemia
    Methioninemia

270.5 Disturbances of histidine metabolism
    Carnosinemia
    Histidinemia
    Hyperhistidinemia
    Imidazole aminoaciduria

270.6 Disorders of urea cycle metabolism
    Argininosuccinic aciduria
    Citrullinemia
    Disorders of metabolism of ornithine, citrulline, argininosuccinic acid, arginine, and ammonia
    Hyperammonemia
    Hyperornithinemia

❑ **270.7 Other disturbances of straight-chain amino-acid metabolism**
    Glucoglycinuria
    Glycinemia (with methylmalonic acidemia)
    Hyperglycinemia
    Hyperlysinemia
    Pipecolic acidemia
    Saccharopinuria
    Other disturbances of metabolism of glycine, threonine, serine, glutamine, and lysine

❑ **270.8 Other specified disorders of amino-acid metabolism**
    Alaninemia
    Ethanolaminuria
    Glycoprolinuria
    Hydroxyprolinemia
    Hyperprolinemia
    Iminoacidopathy
    Prolinemia
    Prolinuria
    Sarcosinemia

❑ **270.9 Unspecified disorder of amino-acid metabolism**

● **271 Disorders of carbohydrate transport and metabolism**

    | Excludes | *abnormality of secretion of glucagon (251.4)*
    diabetes mellitus (250.0–250.9)
    hypoglycemia NOS (251.2)
    mucopolysaccharidosis (277.5)

    271.0 Glycogenosis
        Amylopectinosis
        Glucose-6-phosphatase deficiency
        Glycogen storage disease
        McArdle's disease
        Pompe's disease
        von Gierke's disease

    271.1 Galactosemia
        Galactose-1-phosphate uridyl transferase deficiency
        Galactosuria

    271.2 Hereditary fructose intolerance
        Essential benign fructosuria
        Fructosemia

    ◀▶ **New Code**   ⬅▐ ▐➡ **Revised Code**   ● **Not a Principal Diagnosis**   ● **Use Additional Digit(s)**   ❑ **Nonspecific Code**

271.3 Intestinal disaccharidase deficiencies and disaccharide malabsorption
    Intolerance or malabsorption (congenital) (of):
        glucose-galactose
        lactose
        sucrose-isomaltose

271.4 Renal glycosuria
    Renal diabetes

271.8 Other specified disorders of carbohydrate transport and metabolism
    Essential benign pentosuria
    Fucosidosis
    Glycolic aciduria
    Hyperoxaluria (primary)
    Mannosidosis
    Oxalosis
    Xylosuria
    Xylulosuria

271.9 Unspecified disorder of carbohydrate transport and metabolism

● **272 Disorders of lipoid metabolism**

    Excludes *localized cerebral lipidoses (330.1)*

272.0 Pure hypercholesterolemia
    Familial hypercholesterolemia
    Fredrickson Type IIa hyperlipoproteinemia
    Hyperbetalipoproteinemia
    Hyperlipidemia, Group A
    Low-density-lipoid-type [LDL] hyperlipoproteinemia

272.1 Pure hyperglyceridemia
    Endogenous hyperglyceridemia
    Fredrickson Type IV hyperlipoproteinemia
    Hyperlipidemia, Group B
    Hyperprebetalipoproteinemia
    Hypertriglyceridemia, essential
    Very-low-density-lipoid-type [VLDL] hyperlipoproteinemia

272.2 Mixed hyperlipidemia
    Broad- or floating-betalipoproteinemia
    Fredrickson Type IIb or III hyperlipoproteinemia
    Hypercholesterolemia with endogenous hyperglyceridemia
    Hyperbetalipoproteinemia with prebetalipoproteinemia
    Tubo-eruptive xanthoma
    Xanthoma tuberosum

272.3 Hyperchylomicronemia
    Bürger-Grütz syndrome
    Fredrickson type I or V hyperlipoproteinemia
    Hyperlipidemia, Group D
    Mixed hyperglyceridemia

272.4 Other and unspecified hyperlipidemia
    Alpha-lipoproteinemia
    Combined hyperlipidemia
    Hyperlipidemia NOS
    Hyperlipoproteinemia NOS

272.5 Lipoprotein deficiencies
    Abetalipoproteinemia
    Bassen-Kornzweig syndrome
    High-density lipoid deficiency
    Hypoalphalipoproteinemia
    Hypobetalipoproteinemia (familial)

272.6 Lipodystrophy
    Barraquer-Simons disease
    Progressive lipodystrophy

    Use additional E code to identify cause, if iatrogenic
    Excludes *intestinal lipodystrophy (040.2)*

272.7 Lipidoses
    Chemically induced lipidosis
    Disease:
        Anderson's
        Fabry's
        Gaucher's
        I cell [mucolipidosis I]
        lipoid storage NOS
        Niemann-Pick
        pseudo-Hurler's or mucolipidosis III
        triglyceride storage, Type I or II
        Wolman's or triglyceride storage, Type III
    Mucolipidosis II
    Primary familial xanthomatosis

    Excludes *cerebral lipidoses (330.1)*
           Tay-Sachs disease (330.1)

272.8 Other disorders of lipoid metabolism
    Hoffa's disease or liposynovitis prepatellaris
    Launois-Bensaude's lipomatosis
    Lipoid dermatoarthritis

272.9 Unspecified disorder of lipoid metabolism

● **273 Disorders of plasma protein metabolism**

    Excludes *agammaglobulinemia and hypogammaglobulinemia (279.0–279.2)*
           coagulation defects (286.0–286.9)
           hereditary hemolytic anemias (282.0–282.9)

273.0 Polyclonal hypergammaglobulinemia
    Hypergammaglobulinemic purpura:
        benign primary
        Waldenström's

273.1 Monoclonal paraproteinemia
    Benign monoclonal hypergammaglobulinemia [BMH]
    Monoclonal gammopathy:
        NOS
        associated with lymphoplasmacytic dyscrasias
        benign
    Paraproteinemia:
        benign (familial)
        secondary to malignant or inflammatory disease

273.2 Other paraproteinemias
    Cryoglobulinemic:
        purpura
        vasculitis
    Mixed cryoglobulinemia

273.3 Macroglobulinemia
    Macroglobulinemia (idiopathic) (primary)
    Waldenström's macroglobulinemia

273.8 Other disorders of plasma protein metabolism
    Abnormality of transport protein
    Bisalbuminemia

273.9 Unspecified disorder of plasma protein metabolism

● **274 Gout**

    Excludes *lead gout (984.0–984.9)*

274.0 Gouty arthropathy

● **274.1 Gouty nephropathy**

    274.10 Gouty nephropathy, unspecified

    274.11 Uric acid nephrolithiasis

    274.19 Other

● **274.8 Gout with other specified manifestations**

    274.81 Gouty tophi of ear

    274.82 Gouty tophi of other sites
        Gouty tophi of heart

ICD-9-CM

200-299

Vol. 1

☐ **274.89 Other**

Use additional code to identify manifestations, as:
  gouty:
    iritis (364.11)
    neuritis (357.4)

☐ **274.9 Gout, unspecified**

● **275 Disorders of mineral metabolism**

  | **Excludes** | *abnormal findings without manifest disease (790.0–796.9)*

275.0 Disorders of iron metabolism
  Bronzed diabetes
  Hemochromatosis
  Pigmentary cirrhosis (of liver)

  | **Excludes** | *anemia:*
    iron deficiency (280.0–280.9)
    sideroblastic (285.0)

275.1 Disorders of copper metabolism
  Hepatolenticular degeneration
  Wilson's disease

275.2 Disorders of magnesium metabolism
  Hypermagnesemia
  Hypomagnesemia

275.3 Disorders of phosphorus metabolism
  Familial hypophosphatemia
  Hypophosphatasia
  Vitamin D-resistant:
    osteomalacia
    rickets

● **275.4 Disorders of calcium metabolism**

  | **Excludes** | *parathyroid disorders (252.0–252.9)*
    vitamin D deficiency (268.0–268.9)

  ☐ **275.40 Unspecified disorder of calcium metabolism**

  275.41 Hypocalcemia

  275.42 Hypercalcemia

  ☐ **275.49 Other disorders of calcium metabolism**
    Nephrocalcinosis
    Pseudohypoparathyroidism
    Pseudopseudohypoparathyroidism

☐ **275.8 Other specified disorders of mineral metabolism**

☐ **275.9 Unspecified disorder of mineral metabolism**

● **276 Disorders of fluid, electrolyte, and acid-base balance**

  | **Excludes** | *diabetes insipidus (253.5)*
    familial periodic paralysis (359.3)

276.0 Hyperosmolality and/or hypernatremia
  Sodium [Na] excess
  Sodium [Na] overload

276.1 Hyposmolality and/or hyponatremia
  Sodium [Na] deficiency

276.2 Acidosis
  Acidosis:
    NOS   metabolic
    lactic   respiratory

  | **Excludes** | *diabetic acidosis (250.1)*

276.3 Alkalosis
  Alkalosis:
    NOS
    metabolic
    respiratory

276.4 Mixed acid-base balance disorder
  Hypercapnia with mixed acid-base disorder

276.5 Volume depletion
  Dehydration
  Depletion of volume of plasma or extracellular fluid
  Hypovolemia

  | **Excludes** | *hypovolemic shock:*
    postoperative (998.0)
    traumatic (958.4)

276.6 Fluid overload
  Fluid retention

  | **Excludes** | *ascites (789.5)*
    localized edema (782.3)

276.7 Hyperpotassemia
  Hyperkalemia
  Potassium [K]:
    excess   overload
    intoxication

276.8 Hypopotassemia
  Hypokalemia
  Potassium [K] deficiency

☐ **276.9 Electrolyte and fluid disorders not elsewhere classified**
  Electrolyte imbalance
  Hyperchloremia
  Hypochloremia

  | **Excludes** | *electrolyte imbalance:*
    associated with hyperemesis gravidarum (643.1)
    complicating labor and delivery (669.0)
    following abortion and ectopic or molar pregnancy (634–638 with .4, 639.4)

● **277 Other and unspecified disorders of metabolism**

● **277.0 Cystic fibrosis**
  Fibrocystic disease of the pancreas
  Mucoviscidosis

  277.00 Without mention of meconium ileus

  277.01 With meconium ileus
    Meconium:
      ileus (of newborn)
      obstruction of intestine in mucoviscidosis

277.1 Disorders of porphyrin metabolism
  Hematoporphyria
  Hematoporphyrinuria
  Hereditary coproporphyria
  Porphyria
  Porphyrinuria
  Protocoproporphyria
  Protoporphyria
  Pyrroloporphyria

☐ **277.2 Other disorders of purine and pyrimidine metabolism**
  Hypoxanthine-guanine-phosphoribosyltransferase deficiency [HG-PRT deficiency]
  Lesch-Nyhan syndrome
  Xanthinuria

  | **Excludes** | *gout (274.0–274.9)*
    orotic aciduric anemia (281.4)

277.3 Amyloidosis
  Amyloidosis:
    NOS
    inherited systemic
    nephropathic
    neuropathic (Portuguese) (Swiss)
    secondary
  Benign paroxysmal peritonitis
  Familial Mediterranean fever
  Hereditary cardiac amyloidosis

277.4 Disorders of bilirubin excretion
Hyperbilirubinemia: Syndrome:
    congenital   Crigler-Najjar
    constitutional   Dubin-Johnson
                     Gilbert's
                     Rotor's

> **Excludes** *hyperbilirubinemias specific to the perinatal period (774.0–774.7)*

277.5 Mucopolysaccharidosis
Gargoylism
Hunter's syndrome
Hurler's syndrome
Lipochondrodystrophy
Maroteaux-Lamy syndrome
Morquio-Brailsford disease
Osteochondrodystrophy
Sanfilippo's syndrome
Scheie's syndrome

☐277.6 Other deficiencies of circulating enzymes
Alpha 1-antitrypsin deficiency
Hereditary angioedema

☐277.8 Other specified disorders of metabolism
Hand-Schüller-Christian disease
Histiocytosis (acute) (chronic)
Histiocytosis X (chronic)

> **Excludes** *histiocytosis:*
> *acute differentiated progressive (202.5)*
> *X, acute (progressive) (202.5)*

☐277.9 Unspecified disorder of metabolism
Enzymopathy NOS

● 278 Obesity and other hyperalimentation

> **Excludes** *hyperalimentation NOS (783.6)*
> *poisoning by vitamins NOS (963.5)*
> *polyphagia (783.6)*

● 278.0 Obesity

> **Excludes** *adiposogenital dystrophy (253.8)*
> *obesity of endocrine origin NOS (259.9)*

☐278.00 Obesity, unspecified
Obesity NOS

278.01 Morbid obesity

278.1 Localized adiposity
Fat pad

278.2 Hypervitaminosis A

278.3 Hypercarotinemia

278.4 Hypervitaminosis D

☐278.8 Other hyperalimentation

● 279 Disorders involving the immune mechanism

● 279.0 Deficiency of humoral immunity

☐279.00 Hypogammaglobulinemia, unspecified
Agammaglobulinemia NOS

279.01 Selective IgA immunodeficiency

279.02 Selective IgM immunodeficiency

☐279.03 Other selective immunoglobulin deficiencies
Selective deficiency of IgG

279.04 Congenital hypogammaglobulinemia
Agammaglobulinemia:
    Bruton's type
    X-linked

279.05 Immunodeficiency with increased IgM
Immunodeficiency with hyper-IgM:
    autosomal recessive
    X-linked

279.06 Common variable immunodeficiency
Dysgammaglobulinemia (acquired) (congenital) (primary)
Hypogammaglobulinemia:
    acquired primary
    congenital non-sex-linked
    sporadic

☐279.09 Other
Transient hypogammaglobulinemia of infancy

● 279.1 Deficiency of cell-mediated immunity

☐279.10 Immunodeficiency with predominant T-cell defect, unspecified

279.11 DiGeorge's syndrome
Pharyngeal pouch syndrome
Thymic hypoplasia

279.12 Wiskott-Aldrich syndrome

279.13 Nezelof's syndrome
Cellular immunodeficiency with abnormal immunoglobulin deficiency

☐279.19 Other

> **Excludes** *ataxia-telangiectasia (334.8)*

279.2 Combined immunity deficiency
Agammaglobulinemia:
    autosomal recessive
    Swiss-type
    X-linked recessive
Severe combined immunodeficiency [SCID]
Thymic:
    alymphoplasia
    aplasia or dysplasia with immunodeficiency

> **Excludes** *thymic hypoplasia (279.11)*

☐279.3 Unspecified immunity deficiency

☐279.4 Autoimmune disease, not elsewhere classified
Autoimmune disease NOS

> **Excludes** *transplant failure or rejection (996.80–996.89)*

☐279.8 Other specified disorders involving the immune mechanism
Single complement [C_1-C_9] deficiency or dysfunction

☐279.9 Unspecified disorder of immune mechanism

ICD-9-CM

200-299

Vol. 1

4.   DISEASES OF THE BLOOD AND BLOOD-FORMING ORGANS (280–289)

> **Excludes** *anemia complicating pregnancy or the puerperium (648.2)*

● **280 Iron deficiency anemias**

> **Includes:** anemia:
>   asiderotic
>   hypochromic-microcytic
>   sideropenic

> **Excludes** *familial microcytic anemia (282.4)*

280.0 Secondary to blood loss (chronic)
    Normocytic anemia due to blood loss

> **Excludes** *acute posthemorrhagic anemia (285.1)*

280.1 Secondary to inadequate dietary iron intake

□ **280.8 Other specified iron deficiency anemias**
    Paterson-Kelly syndrome
    Plummer-Vinson syndrome
    Sideropenic dysphagia

□ **280.9 Iron deficiency anemia, unspecified**
    Anemia:
        achlorhydric
        chlorotic
        idiopathic hypochromic
        iron [Fe] deficiency NOS

● **281 Other deficiency anemias**

281.0 Pernicious anemia
    Anemia:
        Addison's
        Biermer's
        congenital pernicious
    Congenital intrinsic factor [Castle's] deficiency

> **Excludes** *combined system disease without mention of anemia (266.2)*
> *subacute degeneration of spinal cord without mention of anemia (266.2)*

□ **281.1 Other vitamin B_{12} deficiency anemia**
    Anemia:
        vegan's
        vitamin B_{12} deficiency (dietary)
        due to selective vitamin B_{12} malabsorption with proteinuria
    Syndrome:
        Imerslund's
        Imerslund-Gräsbeck

> **Excludes** *combined system disease without mention of anemia (266.2)*
> *subacute degeneration of spinal cord without mention of anemia (266.2)*

281.2 Folate-deficiency anemia
    Congenital folate malabsorption
    Folate or folic acid deficiency anemia:
        NOS
        dietary
        drug-induced
    Goat's milk anemia
    Nutritional megaloblastic anemia (of infancy)

    Use additional E code to identify drug

□ **281.3 Other specified megaloblastic anemias, not elsewhere classified**
    Combined B_{12} and folate-deficiency anemia
    Refractory megaloblastic anemia

281.4 Protein-deficiency anemia
    Amino-acid-deficiency anemia

□ **281.8 Anemia associated with other specified nutritional deficiency**
    Scorbutic anemia

□ **281.9 Unspecified deficiency anemia**
    Anemia:
        dimorphic
        macrocytic
        megaloblastic NOS
        nutritional NOS
        simple chronic

● **282 Hereditary hemolytic anemias**

282.0 Hereditary spherocytosis
    Acholuric (familial) jaundice
    Congenital hemolytic anemia (spherocytic)
    Congenital spherocytosis
    Minkowski-Chauffard syndrome
    Spherocytosis (familial)

> **Excludes** *hemolytic anemia of newborn (773.0–773.5)*

282.1 Hereditary elliptocytosis
    Elliptocytosis (congenital)
    Ovalocytosis (congenital) (hereditary)

282.2 Anemias due to disorders of glutathione metabolism
    Anemia:
        6-phosphogluconic dehydrogenase deficiency
        enzyme deficiency, drug-induced
        erythrocytic glutathione deficiency
        glucose-6-phosphate dehydrogenase [G-6-PD] deficiency
        glutathione-reductase deficiency
        hemolytic nonspherocytic (hereditary), type I
    Disorder of pentose phosphate pathway
    Favism

□ **282.3 Other hemolytic anemias due to enzyme deficiency**
    Anemia:
        hemolytic nonspherocytic (hereditary), type II
        hexokinase deficiency
        pyruvate kinase [PK] deficiency
        triosephosphate isomerase deficiency

282.4 Thalassemias
    Cooley's anemia
    Hereditary leptocytosis
    Mediterranean anemia (with other hemoglobinopathy)
    Microdrepanocytosis
    Sickle-cell thalassemia
    Thalassemia (alpha) (beta) (intermedia) (major) (minima) (minor) (mixed) (trait) (with other hemoglobinopathy)
    Thalassemia-Hb-S disease

> **Excludes** *sickle-cell:*
> *anemia (282.60–282.69)*
> *trait (282.5)*

282.5 Sickle-cell trait
    Hb-AS genotype
    Hemoglobin S [Hb-S] trait
    Heterozygous:
        hemoglobin S
        Hb-S

> **Excludes** *that with other hemoglobinopathy (282.60–282.69)*
> *that with thalassemia (282.4)*

● **282.6 Sickle-cell anemia**

> **Excludes** *sickle-cell thalassemia (282.4)*
> *sickle-cell trait (282.5)*

□ **282.60 Sickle-cell anemia, unspecified**

282.61 Hb-S disease without mention of crisis

282.62 Hb-S disease with mention of crisis
    Sickle-cell crisis NOS

   ◀▶ **New Code**   ⬅➡ **Revised Code**   ● **Not a Principal Diagnosis**   ● **Use Additional Digit(s)**   □ **Nonspecific Code**

282.63 Sickle-cell/Hb-C disease
Hb-S/Hb-C disease

☐ **282.69 Other**
Disease:
Hb-S/Hb-D
Hb-S/Hb-E
sickle-cell/Hb-D
sickle-cell/Hb-E

☐ **282.7 Other hemoglobinopathies**
Abnormal hemoglobin NOS
Congenital Heinz-body anemia
Disease:
Hb-Bart's
hemoglobin C [Hb-C]
hemoglobin D [Hb-D]
hemoglobin E [Hb-E]
hemoglobin Zurich [Hb-Zurich]
Hemoglobinopathy NOS
Hereditary persistence of fetal hemoglobin [HPFH]
Unstable hemoglobin hemolytic disease

> **Excludes** *familial polycythemia (289.6)*
> *hemoglobin M [Hb-M] disease (289.7)*
> *high-oxygen-affinity hemoglobin (289.0)*

☐ **282.8 Other specified hereditary hemolytic anemias**
Stomatocytosis

☐ **282.9 Hereditary hemolytic anemia, unspecified**
Hereditary hemolytic anemia NOS

● **283 Acquired hemolytic anemias**

283.0 Autoimmune hemolytic anemias
Autoimmune hemolytic disease (cold type) (warm type)
Chronic cold hemagglutinin disease
Cold agglutinin disease or hemoglobinuria
Hemolytic anemia:
cold type (secondary) (symptomatic)
drug-induced
warm type (secondary) (symptomatic)

Use additional E code to identify cause, if drug-induced

> **Excludes** *Evans'syndrome (287.3)*
> *hemolytic disease of newborn (773.0–773.5)*

● **283.1 Non-autoimmune hemolytic anemias**

☐ **283.10 Non-autoimmune hemolytic anemia, unspecified**

283.11 Hemolytic-uremic syndrome

☐ **283.19 Other non-autoimmune hemolytic anemias**
Hemolytic anemia:
mechanical
microangiopathic
toxic

Use additional E code to identify cause

283.2 Hemoglobinuria due to hemolysis from external causes
Acute intravascular hemolysis
Hemoglobinuria:
from exertion
march
paroxysmal (cold) (nocturnal)
due to other hemolysis
Marchiafava-Micheli syndrome

Use additional E code to identify cause

☐ **283.9 Acquired hemolytic anemia, unspecified**
Acquired hemolytic anemia NOS
Chronic idiopathic hemolytic anemia

● **284 Aplastic anemia**

☐ **284.0 Constitutional aplastic anemia**
Aplasia, (pure) red cell:
congenital
of infants
primary
Blackfan-Diamond syndrome
Familial hypoplastic anemia
Fanconi's anemia
Pancytopenia with malformations

☐ **284.8 Other specified aplastic anemias**
Aplastic anemia (due to):
chronic systemic disease
drugs
infection
radiation
toxic (paralytic)
Pancytopenia (acquired)
Red cell aplasia (acquired) (adult) (pure) (with thymoma)

Use additional E code to identify cause

☐ **284.9 Aplastic anemia, unspecified**
Anemia:
aplastic (idiopathic) NOS
aregenerative
hypoplastic NOS
nonregenerative
refractory
Medullary hypoplasia

● **285 Other and unspecified anemias**

285.0 Sideroblastic anemia
Anemia:
hypochromic with iron loading
sideroachrestic
sideroblastic
acquired
congenital
hereditary
primary
refractory
secondary (drug-induced) (due to disease)
sex-linked hypochromic
vitamin B_6-responsive
Pyridoxine-responsive (hypochromic) anemia

Use additional E code to identify cause, if drug-induced

285.1 Acute posthemorrhagic anemia
Anemia due to acute blood loss

> **Excludes** *anemia due to chronic blood loss (280.0)*
> *blood loss anemia NOS (280.0)*

☐ **285.8 Other specified anemias**
Anemia:
dyserythropoietic (congenital)
dyshematopoietic (congenital)
leukoerythroblastic
von Jaksch's
Infantile pseudoleukemia

☐ **285.9 Anemia, unspecified**
Anemia:
NOS
essential
normocytic, not due to blood loss
profound
progressive
secondary
Oligocythemia

> **Excludes** *anemia (due to):*
> *blood loss:*
> *acute (285.1)*
> *chronic or unspecified (280.0)*
> *iron deficiency (280.0–280.9)*

ICD-9-CM

200-299

Vol. 1

● **286 Coagulation defects**

286.0 Congenital factor VIII disorder
Antihemophilic globulin [AHG] deficiency
Factor VIII (functional) deficiency
Hemophilia:
  NOS
  A
  classical
  familial
  hereditary
Subhemophilia

Excludes *factor VIII deficiency with vascular defect (286.4)*

286.1 Congenital factor IX disorder
Christmas disease
Deficiency:
  factor IX (functional)
  plasma thromboplastin component [PTC]
Hemophilia B

286.2 Congenital factor XI deficiency
Hemophilia C
Plasma thromboplastin antecedent [PTA] deficiency
Rosenthal's disease

□ **286.3 Congenital deficiency of other clotting factors**
Congenital afibrinogenemia
Deficiency:
  AC globulin factor:
    I [fibrinogen]
    II [prothrombin]
    V [labile]
    VII [stable]
    X [Stuart-Prower]
    XII [Hageman]
    XIII [fibrin stabilizing]
  Laki-Lorand factor
  proaccelerin
Disease:
  Owren's
  Stuart-Prower
Dysfibrinogenemia (congenital)
Dysprothrombinemia (constitutional)
Hypoproconvertinemia
Hypoprothrombinemia (hereditary)
Parahemophilia

286.4 von Willebrand's disease
Angiohemophilia (A) (B)
Constitutional thrombopathy
Factor VIII deficiency with vascular defect
Pseudohemophilia type B
Vascular hemophilia
von Willebrand's (-Jürgens') disease

Excludes *factor VIII deficiency:*
    NOS (286.0)
    with functional defect (286.0)
  hereditary capillary fragility (287.8)

286.5 Hemorrhagic disorder due to circulating anticoagulants
Antithrombinemia
Antithromboplastinemia
Antithromboplastinogenemia
Hyperheparinemia
Increase in:
  anti-VIIIa
  anti-IXa
  anti-Xa
  anti-XIa
  antithrombin
Systemic lupus erythematosus [SLE] inhibitor

Use additional E code to identify cause, if drug-induced

286.6 Defibrination syndrome
Afibrinogenemia, acquired
Consumption coagulopathy
Diffuse or disseminated intravascular coagulation [DIC syndrome]
Fibrinolytic hemorrhage, acquired
Hemorrhagic fibrinogenolysis
Pathologic fibrinolysis
Purpura:
  fibrinolytic
  fulminans

Excludes *that complicating:*
    abortion (634–638 with .1, 639.1)
    pregnancy or the puerperium (641.3, 666.3)
  disseminated intravascular coagulation in newborn (776.2)

286.7 Acquired coagulation factor deficiency
Deficiency of coagulation factor due to:
  liver disease
  vitamin K deficiency
Hypoprothrombinemia, acquired

Excludes *vitamin K deficiency of newborn (776.0)*

Use additional E code to identify cause, if drug-induced

□ **286.9 Other and unspecified coagulation defects**
Defective coagulation NOS
Deficiency, coagulation factor NOS
Delay, coagulation
Disorder:
  coagulation
  hemostasis

Excludes *abnormal coagulation profile (790.92)*
  hemorrhagic disease of newborn (776.0)
  that complicating:
    abortion (634–638 with .1, 639.1)
    pregnancy or the puerperium (641.3, 666.3)

● **287 Purpura and other hemorrhagic conditions**

Excludes *hemorrhagic thrombocythemia (238.7)*
  purpura fulminans (286.6)

287.0 Allergic purpura
Peliosis rheumatica
Purpura:
  anaphylactoid
  autoimmune
  Henoch's
  nonthrombocytopenic:
    hemorrhagic
    idiopathic
  rheumatica
  Schönlein-Henoch
  vascular
Vasculitis, allergic

Excludes *hemorrhagic purpura (287.3)*
  purpura annularis telangiectodes (709.1)

287.1 Qualitative platelet defects
Thrombasthenia (hemorrhagic) (hereditary)
Thrombocytasthenia
Thrombocytopathy (dystrophic)
Thrombopathy (Bernard-Soulier)

Excludes *von Willebrand's disease (286.4)*

□ **287.2 Other nonthrombocytopenic purpuras**
Purpura:
  NOS
  senile
  simplex

◀▶ **New Code**   ⇐▬▬⇒ **Revised Code**   ● **Not a Principal Diagnosis**   ● **Use Additional Digit(s)**   □ **Nonspecific Code**

287.3 Primary thrombocytopenia
Evans'syndrome
Megakaryocytic hypoplasia
Purpura, thrombocytopenic
   congenital
   hereditary
   idiopathic
Thrombocytopenia:
   congenital
   hereditary
   primary
Tidal platelet dysgenesis

Excludes *thrombotic thrombocytopenic purpura (446.6)*
transient thrombocytopenia of newborn (776.1)

287.4 Secondary thrombocytopenia
Posttransfusion purpura
Thrombocytopenia (due to):
   dilutional
   drugs
   extracorporeal circulation of blood
   massive blood transfusion
   platelet alloimmunization

Use additional E code to identify cause

Excludes *transient thrombocytopenia of newborn (776.1)*

❑ **287.5 Thrombocytopenia, unspecified**

❑ **287.8 Other specified hemorrhagic conditions**
Capillary fragility (hereditary)
Vascular pseudohemophilia

❑ **287.9 Unspecified hemorrhagic conditions**
Hemorrhagic diathesis (familial)

● **288 Diseases of white blood cells**
Excludes *leukemia (204.0–208.9)*

288.0 Agranulocytosis
Infantile genetic agranulocytosis
Kostmann's syndrome
Neutropenia:
   NOS   immune
   cyclic   periodic
   drug-induced toxic
Neutropenic splenomegaly

Use additional E code to identify drug or other cause

Excludes *transitory neonatal neutropenia (776.7)*

288.1 Functional disorders of polymorphonuclear neutro-phils
Chronic (childhood) granulomatous disease
Congenital dysphagocytosis
Job's syndrome
Lipochrome histiocytosis (familial)
Progressive septic granulomatosis

288.2 Genetic anomalies of leukocytes
Anomaly (granulation) (granulocyte) or syndrome:
   Alder's (-Reilly)
   Chédiak-Steinbrinck (-Higashi)
   Jordan's
   May-Hegglin
   Pelger-Huet
Hereditary:
   hypersegmentation
   hyposegmentation
   leukomelanopathy

288.3 Eosinophilia
Eosinophilia
   allergic   idiopathic
   hereditary   secondary
Eosinophilic leukocytosis

Excludes *Löffler's syndrome (518.3)*
pulmonary eosinophilia (518.3)

❑ **288.8 Other specified disease of white blood cells**
Leukemoid reaction
   lymphocytic
   monocytic
   myelocytic
Leukocytosis
Lymphocytopenia
Lymphocytosis (symptomatic)
Lymphopenia
Monocytosis (symptomatic)
Plasmacytosis

Excludes *immunity disorders (279.0–279.9)*

❑ **288.9 Unspecified disease of white blood cells**

● **289 Other diseases of blood and blood-forming organs**

289.0 Polycythemia, secondary
High-oxygen-affinity hemoglobin
Polycythemia:
   acquired
   benign
   due to:
      fall in plasma volume
      high altitude
   emotional
   erythropoietin
   hypoxemic
   nephrogenous
   relative
   spurious
   stress

Excludes *polycythemia:*
neonatal (776.4)
primary (238.4)
vera (238.4)

289.1 Chronic lymphadenitis
Chronic:
   adenitis any lymph node, except mesenteric
   lymphadenitis any lymph node, except mesen-teric

Excludes *acute lymphadenitis (683)*
mesenteric (289.2)
enlarged glands NOS (785.6)

❑ **289.2 Nonspecific mesenteric lymphadenitis**
Mesenteric lymphadenitis (acute) (chronic)

❑ **289.3 Lymphadenitis, unspecified, except mesenteric**

289.4 Hypersplenism
"Big spleen" syndrome
Dyssplenism
Hypersplenia

Excludes *primary splenic neutropenia (288.0)*

● **289.5 Other diseases of spleen**

❑ **289.50 Disease of spleen, unspecified**

289.51 Chronic congestive splenomegaly

❑ **289.59 Other**
Lien migrans
Perisplenitis
Splenic:
   abscess
   atrophy
   cyst
   fibrosis
   infarction
   rupture, nontraumatic
Splenitis
Wandering spleen

Excludes *bilharzial splenic fibrosis (120.0–120.9)*
hepatolienal fibrosis (571.5)
splenomegaly NOS (789.2)

ICD-9-CM
200-299
Vol. 1

289.6 Familial polycythemia
Familial:
  benign polycythemia
  erythrocytosis

289.7 Methemoglobinemia
Congenital NADH [DPNH]-methemoglobin-reductase deficiency
Hemoglobin M [Hb-M] disease
Methemoglobinemia:
  NOS
  acquired (with sulfhemoglobinemia)
  hereditary
  toxic
Stokvis' disease
Sulfhemoglobinemia

Use additional E code to identify cause

☐ 289.8 Other specified diseases of blood and blood-forming organs
Hypergammaglobulinemia
Myelofibrosis
Pseudocholinesterase deficiency

☐ 289.9 Unspecified diseases of blood and blood-forming organs
Blood dyscrasia NOS
Erythroid hyperplasia

5. MENTAL DISORDERS (290–319)

In the International Classification of Diseases, 9th Revision (ICD-9), the corresponding Chapter V, "Mental Disorders," includes a glossary which defines the contents of each category. The introduction to Chapter V in ICD-9 indicates that the glossary is intended so that psychiatrists can make the diagnosis based on the descriptions provided rather than from the category titles. Lay coders are instructed to code whatever diagnosis the physician records.

Chapter 5, "Mental Disorders," in ICD-9-CM uses the standard classification format with inclusion and exclusion terms, omitting the glossary as part of the main text.

The mental disorders section of ICD-9-CM has been expanded to incorporate additional psychiatric disorders not listed in ICD-9. The glossary from ICD-9 does not contain all these terms. It now appears in Appendix B, which also contains descriptions and definitions for the terms added in ICD-9-CM. Some of these were provided by the American Psychiatric Association's Task Force on Nomenclature and Statistics who are preparing the Diagnostic and Statistical Manual, Third Edition (DSM-III), and others from A Psychiatric Glossary.

The American Psychiatric Association provided invaluable assistance in modifying Chapter 5 of ICD-9-CM to incorporate detail useful to American clinicians and gave permission to use material from the aforementioned sources.

1. Manual of the International Statistical Classification of Diseases, Injuries, and Causes of Death, 9th Revision, World Health Organization, Geneva, Switzerland, 1975.

2. American Psychiatric Association, Task Force on Nomenclature and Statistics, Robert L. Spitzer, M.D., Chairman.

3. A Psychiatric Glossary, Fourth Edition, American Psychiatric Association, Washington, D.C., 1975.

PSYCHOSES (290–299)

| Excludes | *mental retardation (317–319)* |

ORGANIC PSYCHOTIC CONDITIONS (290–294)

Includes: psychotic organic brain syndrome

| Excludes | *nonpsychotic syndromes of organic etiology (310.0–310.9)* |

psychoses classifiable to 295–298 and without impairment of orientation, comprehension, calculation, learning capacity, and judgment, but associated with physical disease, injury, or condition affecting the brain [e.g., following childbirth] (295.0–298.8)

● 290 Senile and presenile organic psychotic conditions

Code first the associated neurological condition

| Excludes | *dementia not classified as senile, presenile, or arteriosclerotic (294.1)* |

psychoses classifiable to 295–298 occurring in the senium without dementia or delirium (295.0–298.8)

senility with mental changes of nonpsychotic severity (310.1)

transient organic psychotic conditions (293.0–293.9)

    ◀▶ **New Code**   ⬅▮▮▮ ▮▮▮➡ **Revised Code**   ● **Not a Principal Diagnosis**   ● **Use Additional Digit(s)**   ☐ **Nonspecific Code**

290.0 Senile dementia, uncomplicated
Senile dementia:
   NOS   simple type

> **Excludes** *mild memory disturbances, not amounting to de-*
> *mentia, associated with senile brain disease*
> *(310.1)*
> *senile dementia with:*
> *delirium or confusion (290.3)*
> *delusional [paranoid] features (290.20)*
> *depressive features (290.21)*

● **290.1 Presenile dementia**
Brain syndrome with presenile brain disease

> **Excludes** *arteriosclerotic dementia (290.40–290.43)*
> *dementia associated with other cerebral condi-*
> *tions (294.1)*

    290.10 Presenile dementia, uncomplicated
    Presenile dementia:
       NOS
       simple type

    290.11 Presenile dementia with delirium
    Presenile dementia with acute confusional
    state

    290.12 Presenile dementia with delusional features
    Presenile dementia, paranoid type

    290.13 Presenile dementia with depressive features
    Presenile dementia, depressed type

● **290.2 Senile dementia with delusional or depressive features**

> **Excludes** *senile dementia:*
> *NOS (290.0)*
> *with delirium and/or confusion (290.3)*

    290.20 Senile dementia with delusional features
    Senile dementia, paranoid type
    Senile psychosis NOS

    290.21 Senile dementia with depressive features

290.3 Senile dementia with delirium
Senile dementia with acute confusional state

> **Excludes** *senile:*
> *dementia NOS (290.0)*
> *psychosis NOS (290.20)*

● **290.4 Arteriosclerotic dementia**
Multi-infarct dementia or psychosis

Use additional code to identify cerebral atherosclerosis (437.0)

> **Excludes** *suspected cases with no clear evidence of arterio-*
> *sclerosis (290.9)*

    290.40 Arteriosclerotic dementia, uncomplicated
    Arteriosclerotic dementia:
       NOS
       simple type

    290.41 Arteriosclerotic dementia with delirium
    Arteriosclerotic dementia with acute con-
    fusional state

    290.42 Arteriosclerotic dementia with delusional features
    Arteriosclerotic dementia, paranoid type

    290.43 Arteriosclerotic dementia with depressive features
    Arteriosclerotic dementia, depressed type

□ **290.8 Other specified senile psychotic conditions**
Presbyophrenic psychosis

□ **290.9 Unspecified senile psychotic condition**

● **291 Alcoholic psychoses**
> **Excludes** *alcoholism without psychosis (303.0–303.9)*

291.0 Alcohol withdrawal delirium
Alcoholic delirium
Delirium tremens

> **Excludes** *alcohol withdrawal (291.81)*

291.1 Alcoholic amnestic syndrome
Alcoholic polyneuritic psychosis
Korsakoff's psychosis, alcoholic
Wernicke-Korsakoff syndrome (alcoholic)

□ **291.2 Other alcoholic dementia**
Alcoholic dementia NOS
Alcoholism associated with dementia NOS
Chronic alcoholic brain syndrome

291.3 Alcohol withdrawal hallucinosis
Alcoholic:
   hallucinosis (acute)
   psychosis with hallucinosis

> **Excludes** *alcohol withdrawal with delirium (291.0)*
> *schizophrenia (295.0–295.9) and paranoid states*
> *(297.0–297.9) taking the form of chronic hal-*
> *lucinosis with clear consciousness in an alco-*
> *holic*

291.4 Idiosyncratic alcohol intoxication
Pathologic:
   alcohol intoxication
   drunkenness

> **Excludes** *acute alcohol intoxication (305.0)*
> *in alcoholism (303.0)*
> *simple drunkenness (305.0)*

291.5 Alcoholic jealousy
Alcoholic:
   paranoia
   psychosis, paranoid type

> **Excludes** *nonalcoholic paranoid states (297.0–297.9)*
> *schizophrenia, paranoid type (295.3)*

● **291.8 Other specified alcoholic psychosis**

    291.81 Alcohol withdrawal
    Alcohol:
       abstinence syndrome or symptoms
       withdrawal syndrome or symptoms

> **Excludes** *alcohol withdrawal:*
> *delirium (291.0)*
> *hallucinosis (291.3)*
> *delirium tremens (291.0)*

  □ **291.89 Other**

□ **291.9 Unspecified alcoholic psychosis**
Alcoholic:
   mania NOS
   psychosis NOS
Alcoholism (chronic) with psychosis

● **292 Drug psychoses**

> **Includes:** drug-induced mental disorders
> organic brain syndrome associated with con-
> sumption of drugs

Use additional code for any associated drug dependence
(304.0–304.9)

Use additional E code to identify drug

292.0 Drug withdrawal syndrome
Drug:
   abstinence syndrome or symptoms
   withdrawal syndrome or symptoms

● **292.1 Paranoid and/or hallucinatory states induced by drugs**

    292.11 Drug-induced organic delusional syndrome
    Paranoid state induced by drugs

ICD-9-CM

200-299

Vol. 1

292.12 Drug-induced hallucinosis
Hallucinatory state induced by drugs

Excludes *states following LSD or other hallucinogens, lasting only a few days or less ["bad trips"] (305.3)*

292.2 Pathological drug intoxication
Drug reaction: resulting in brief psychotic states
NOS
idiosyncratic
pathologic

Excludes *expected brief psychotic reactions to hallucinogens ["bad trips"] (305.3)*
physiological side-effects of drugs (e.g., dystonias)

● **292.8 Other specified drug-induced mental disorders**

292.81 Drug-induced delirium

292.82 Drug-induced dementia

292.83 Drug-induced amnestic syndrome

292.84 Drug-induced organic affective syndrome
Depressive state induced by drugs

❑ **292.89 Other**
Drug-induced organic personality syndrome

❑ **292.9 Unspecified drug-induced mental disorder**
Organic psychosis NOS due to or associated with drugs

● **293 Transient organic psychotic conditions**

Includes: transient organic mental disorders not associated with alcohol or drugs

Code first the associated physical or neurological condition

Excludes *confusional state or delirium superimposed on senile dementia (290.3)*
dementia due to:
alcohol (291.0–291.9)
arteriosclerosis (290.40–290.43)
drugs (292.82)
senility (290.0)

293.0 Acute delirium
Acute:
confusional state
infective psychosis
organic reaction
posttraumatic organic psychosis
psycho-organic syndrome
Acute psychosis associated with endocrine, metabolic, or cerebrovascular disorder
Epileptic:
confusional state
twilight state

293.1 Subacute delirium
Subacute:
confusional state
infective psychosis
organic reaction
posttraumatic organic psychosis
psycho-organic syndrome
psychosis associated with endocrine or metabolic disorder

● **293.8 Other specified transient organic mental disorders**

293.81 Organic delusional syndrome
Transient organic psychotic condition, paranoid type

293.82 Organic hallucinosis syndrome
Transient organic psychotic condition, hallucinatory type

293.83 Organic affective syndrome
Transient organic psychotic condition, depressive type

293.84 Organic anxiety syndrome

❑ **293.89 Other**

❑ **293.9 Unspecified transient organic mental disorder**
Organic psychosis:
infective NOS
posttraumatic NOS
transient NOS
Psycho-organic syndrome

● **294 Other organic psychotic conditions (chronic)**

Includes: organic psychotic brain syndromes (chronic), not elsewhere classified

294.0 Amnestic syndrome
Korsakoff's psychosis or syndrome (nonalcoholic)

Excludes *alcoholic:*
amnestic syndrome (291.1)
Korsakoff's psychosis (291.1)

294.1 Dementia in conditions classified elsewhere
Code first any underlying physical condition as:
dementia in:
Alzheimer's disease (331.0)
cerebral lipidoses (330.1)
epilepsy (345.0–345.9)
general paresis [syphilis] (094.1)
hepatolenticular degeneration (275.1)
Huntington's chorea (333.4)
Jakob-Creutzfeldt disease (046.1)
multiple sclerosis (340)
Pick's disease of the brain (331.1)
polyarteritis nodosa (446.0)
syphilis (094.1)

Excludes *dementia:*
arteriosclerotic (290.40–290.43)
presenile (290.10–290.13)
senile (290.0)
epileptic psychosis NOS (294.8)

❑ **294.8 Other specified organic brain syndromes (chronic)**
Epileptic psychosis NOS
Mixed paranoid and affective organic psychotic states

Use additional code for associated epilepsy (345.0–345.9)

Excludes *mild memory disturbances, not amounting to dementia (310.1)*

❑ **294.9 Unspecified organic brain syndrome (chronic)**
Organic psychosis (chronic)

OTHER PSYCHOSES (295–299)

Use additional code to identify any associated physical disease, injury, or condition affecting the brain with psychoses classifiable to 295–298

● **295 Schizophrenic disorders**

Includes: schizophrenia of the types described in 295.0–295.9 occurring in children

Excludes *childhood type schizophrenia (299.9)*
infantile autism (299.0)

The following fifth-digit subclassification is for use with category 295:
❑ **0 unspecified**
1 subchronic
2 chronic
3 subchronic with acute exacerbation
4 chronic with acute exacerbation
5 in remission

 ◀▶ **New Code** ◀▬ ▬▶ **Revised Code** ● **Not a Principal Diagnosis** ● **Use Additional Digit(s)** ❑ **Nonspecific Code**

● **295.0 Simple type**
Schizophrenia simplex

> **Excludes** *latent schizophrenia (295.5)*

● **295.1 Disorganized type**
Hebephrenia
Hebephrenic type schizophrenia

● **295.2 Catatonic type**

Catatonic (schizophrenia):	Schizophrenic:
agitation	catalepsy
excitation	catatonia
excited type	flexibilitas cerea
stupor	
withdrawn type	

● **295.3 Paranoid type**
Paraphrenic schizophrenia

> **Excludes** *involutional paranoid state (297.2)*
> *paranoia (297.1)*
> *paraphrenia (297.2)*

● **295.4 Acute schizophrenic episode**
Oneirophrenia
Schizophreniform:
  attack
  disorder
  psychosis, confusional type

> **Excludes** *acute forms of schizophrenia of:*
> *catatonic type (295.2)*
> *hebephrenic type (295.1)*
> *paranoid type (295.3)*
> *simple type (295.0)*
> *undifferentiated type (295.8)*

● **295.5 Latent schizophrenia**
Latent schizophrenic reaction
Schizophrenia:
  borderline
  incipient
  prepsychotic
  prodromal
  pseudoneurotic
  pseudopsychopathic

> **Excludes** *schizoid personality (301.20–301.22)*

● **295.6 Residual schizophrenia**
Chronic undifferentiated schizophrenia
Restzustand (schizophrenic)
Schizophrenic residual state

● **295.7 Schizo-affective type**
Cyclic schizophrenia
Mixed schizophrenic and affective psychosis
Schizo-affective psychosis
Schizophreniform psychosis, affective type

□ ● **295.8 Other specified types of schizophrenia**
Acute (undifferentiated) schizophrenia
Atypical schizophrenia
Cenesthopathic schizophrenia

> **Excludes** *infantile autism (299.0)*

□ ● **295.9 Unspecified schizophrenia**
Schizophrenia:
  NOS
  mixed NOS
  undifferentiated NOS
Schizophrenic reaction NOS
Schizophreniform psychosis NOS

● **296 Affective psychoses**

Includes: episodic affective disorders

> **Excludes** *neurotic depression (300.4)*
> *reactive depressive psychosis (298.0)*
> *reactive excitation (298.1)*

The following fifth-digit subclassification is for use with categories 296.0–296.6:

□ **0 unspecified**
1 mild
2 moderate
3 severe, without mention of psychotic behavior
4 severe, specified as with psychotic behavior
5 in partial or unspecified remission
6 in full remission

● **296.0 Manic disorder, single episode**
Hypomania (mild) NOS single episode or unspecified
Hypomanic psychosis single episode or unspecified
Mania (monopolar) NOS single episode or unspecified
Manic-depressive psychosis or reaction, single episode or unspecified:
  hypomanic, single episode or unspecified
  manic, single episode or unspecified

> **Excludes** *circular type, if there was a previous attack of depression (296.4)*

● **296.1 Manic disorder, recurrent episode**
Any condition classifiable to 296.0, stated to be recurrent

> **Excludes** *circular type, if there was a previous attack of depression (296.4)*

● **296.2 Major depressive disorder, single episode**
Depressive psychosis, single episode or unspecified
Endogenous depression, single episode or unspecified
Involutional melancholia, single episode or unspecified
Manic-depressive psychosis or reaction, depressed type, single episode or unspecified
Monopolar depression, single episode or unspecified
Psychotic depression, single episode or unspecified

> **Excludes** *circular type, if previous attack was of manic type (296.5)*
> *depression NOS (311)*
> *reactive depression (neurotic) (300.4)*
> *psychotic (298.0)*

● **296.3 Major depressive disorder, recurrent episode**
Any condition classifiable to 296.2, stated to be recurrent

> **Excludes** *circular type, if previous attack was of manic type (296.5)*
> *depression NOS (311)*
> *reactive depression (neurotic) (300.4)*
> *psychotic (298.0)*

● **296.4 Bipolar affective disorder, manic**
Bipolar disorder, now manic
Manic-depressive psychosis, circular type but currently manic

> **Excludes** *brief compensatory or rebound mood swings (296.99)*

● **296.5 Bipolar affective disorder, depressed**
Bipolar disorder, now depressed
Manic-depressive psychosis, circular type but currently depressed

> **Excludes** *brief compensatory or rebound mood swings (296.99)*

● **296.6 Bipolar affective disorder, mixed**
Manic-depressive psychosis, circular type, mixed

ICD-9-CM
200-299
Vol. 1

☐ **296.7 Bipolar affective disorder, unspecified**
Atypical bipolar affective disorder NOS
Manic-depressive psychosis, circular type, current condition not specified as either manic or depressive

● **296.8 Manic-depressive psychosis, other and unspecified**

☐ **296.80 Manic-depressive psychosis, unspecified**
Manic-depressive:
reaction NOS
syndrome NOS

296.81 Atypical manic disorder

296.82 Atypical depressive disorder

☐ **296.89 Other**
Manic-depressive psychosis, mixed type

● **296.9 Other and unspecified affective psychoses**
Excludes *psychogenic affective psychoses (298.0–298.8)*

☐ **296.90 Unspecified affective psychosis**
Affective psychosis NOS
Melancholia NOS

☐ **296.99 Other specified affective psychoses**
Mood swings:
brief compensatory
rebound

● **297 Paranoid states (Delusional disorders)** ◄▦

Includes: paranoid disorders
Excludes *acute paranoid reaction (298.3)*
alcoholic jealousy or paranoid state (291.5)
paranoid schizophrenia (295.3)

297.0 Paranoid state, simple

297.1 Paranoia
Chronic paranoid psychosis
Sander's disease
Systematized delusions
Excludes *paranoid personality disorder (301.0)*

297.2 Paraphrenia
Involutional paranoid state
Late paraphrenia
Paraphrenia (involutional)

297.3 Shared paranoid disorder
Folie à deux
Induced psychosis or paranoid disorder

☐ **297.8 Other specified paranoid states**
Paranoia querulans
Sensitiver Beziehungswahn
Excludes *acute paranoid reaction or state (298.3)*
senile paranoid state (290.20)

☐ **297.9 Unspecified paranoid state**
Paranoid:
disorder NOS   reaction NOS
psychosis NOS   state NOS

● **298 Other nonorganic psychoses**

Includes: psychotic conditions due to or provoked by:
emotional stress
environmental factors as major part of etiology

298.0 Depressive type psychosis
Psychogenic depressive psychosis
Psychotic reactive depression
Reactive depressive psychosis
Excludes *manic-depressive psychosis, depressed type (296.2–296.3)*
neurotic depression (300.4)
reactive depression NOS (300.4)

298.1 Excitative type psychosis
Acute hysterical psychosis
Psychogenic excitation
Reactive excitation
Excludes *manic-depressive psychosis, manic type (296.0–296.1)*

298.2 Reactive confusion
Psychogenic confusion
Psychogenic twilight state
Excludes *acute confusional state (293.0)*

298.3 Acute paranoid reaction
Acute psychogenic paranoid psychosis
Bouffée délirante
Excludes *paranoid states (297.0–297.9)*

298.4 Psychogenic paranoid psychosis
Protracted reactive paranoid psychosis

☐ **298.8 Other and unspecified reactive psychosis**
Brief reactive psychosis NOS
Hysterical psychosis
Psychogenic psychosis NOS
Psychogenic stupor
Excludes *acute hysterical psychosis (298.1)*

☐ **298.9 Unspecified psychosis**
Atypical psychosis
Psychosis NOS

● **299 Psychoses with origin specific to childhood**

Includes: pervasive developmental disorders
Excludes *adult type psychoses occurring in childhood, as:*
affective disorders (296.0–296.9)
manic-depressive disorders (296.0–296.9)
schizophrenia (295.0–295.9)

The following fifth-digit subclassification is for use with category 299:
0 current or active state
1 residual state

● **299.0 Infantile autism**
Childhood autism
Infantile psychosis
Kanner's syndrome
Excludes *disintegrative psychosis (299.1)*
Heller's syndrome (299.1)
schizophrenic syndrome of childhood (299.9)

● **299.1 Disintegrative psychosis**
Heller's syndrome

Use additional code to identify any associated neurological disorder

Excludes *infantile autism (299.0)*
schizophrenic syndrome of childhood (299.9)

☐● **299.8 Other specified early childhood psychoses**
Atypical childhood psychosis
Borderline psychosis of childhood
Excludes *simple stereotypes without psychotic disturbance (307.3)*

☐● **299.9 Unspecified**
Child psychosis NOS
Schizophrenia, childhood type NOS
Schizophrenic syndrome of childhood NOS
Excludes *schizophrenia of adult type occurring in childhood (295.0–295.9)*

    ◄▶ **New Code**   ◄▦ ▦▶ **Revised Code**   ● **Not a Principal Diagnosis**   ● **Use Additional Digit(s)**   ☐ **Nonspecific Code**

NEUROTIC DISORDERS, PERSONALITY DISORDERS, AND OTHER NONPSYCHOTIC MENTAL DISORDERS (300–316)

● **300 Neurotic disorders**

● **300.0 Anxiety states**

Excludes *anxiety in:*
acute stress reaction (308.0)
transient adjustment reaction (309.24)
neurasthenia (300.5)
psychophysiological disorders (306.0–306.9)
separation anxiety (309.21)

☐ **300.00 Anxiety state, unspecified**
Anxiety:
neurosis
reaction
state (neurotic)
Atypical anxiety disorder

300.01 Panic disorder
Panic:
attack
state

300.02 Generalized anxiety disorder

☐ **300.09 Other**

● **300.1 Hysteria**

Excludes *adjustment reaction (309.0–309.9)*
anorexia nervosa (307.1)
gross stress reaction (308.0–308.9)
hysterical personality (301.50–301.59)
psychophysiologic disorders (306.0–306.9)

☐ **300.10 Hysteria, unspecified**

300.11 Conversion disorder
Astasia-abasia, hysterical
Conversion hysteria or reaction
Hysterical:
blindness
deafness
paralysis

300.12 Psychogenic amnesia
Hysterical amnesia

300.13 Psychogenic fugue
Hysterical fugue

300.14 Multiple personality
Dissociative identity disorder

☐ **300.15 Dissociative disorder or reaction, unspecified**

300.16 Factitious illness with psychological symptoms
Compensation neurosis
Ganser's syndrome, hysterical

☐ **300.19 Other and unspecified factitious illness**
Factitious illness (with physical symptoms) NOS

Excludes *multiple operations or hospital addiction syndrome (301.51)*

● **300.2 Phobic disorders**

Excludes *anxiety state not associated with a specific situation or object (300.00–300.09)*
obsessional phobias (300.3)

☐ **300.20 Phobia, unspecified**
Anxiety-hysteria NOS   Phobia NOS

300.21 Agoraphobia with panic attacks
Fear of:
open spaces with panic attacks
streets with panic attacks
travel with panic attacks

300.22 Agoraphobia without mention of panic attacks
Any condition classifiable to 300.21 without mention of panic attacks

300.23 Social phobia
Fear of:
eating in public   washing in public
public speaking

☐ **300.29 Other isolated or simple phobias**
Acrophobia   Claustrophobia
Animal phobias   Fear of crowds

300.3 Obsessive-compulsive disorders
Anancastic neurosis
Compulsive neurosis
Obsessional phobia [any]

Excludes *obsessive-compulsive symptoms occurring in:*
endogenous depression (296.2–296.3)
organic states (e.g., encephalitis)
schizophrenia (295.0–295.9)

300.4 Neurotic depression
Anxiety depression   Dysthymic disorder
Depression with anxiety   Neurotic depressive state
Depressive reaction   Reactive depression

Excludes *adjustment reaction with depressive symptoms (309.0–309.1)*
depression NOS (311)
manic-depressive psychosis, depressed type (296.2–296.3)
reactive depressive psychosis (298.0)

300.5 Neurasthenia
Fatigue neurosis
Nervous debility
Psychogenic:
asthenia
general fatigue

Use additional code to identify any associated physical disorder

Excludes *anxiety state (300.00–300.09)*
neurotic depression (300.4)
psychophysiological disorders (306.0–306.9)
specific nonpsychotic mental disorders following organic brain damage (310.0–310.9)

300.6 Depersonalization syndrome
Depersonalization disorder
Derealization (neurotic)
Neurotic state with depersonalization episode

Excludes *depersonalization associated with:*
anxiety (300.00–300.09)
depression (300.4)
manic-depressive disorder or psychosis (296.0–296.9)
schizophrenia (295.0–295.9)

300.7 Hypochondriasis
Body dysmorphic disorder

Excludes *hypochondriasis in:*
hysteria (300.10–300.19)
manic-depressive psychosis, depressed type (296.2–296.3)
neurasthenia (300.5)
obsessional disorder (300.3)
schizophrenia (295.0–295.9)

● **300.8 Other neurotic disorders**

300.81 Somatization disorder
Briquet's disorder
Severe somatoform disorder

300.82 Undifferentiated somatoform disorder
Atypical somatoform disorder
Somatoform disorder NOS

ICD-9-CM

300–399

Vol. 1

❑ **300.89 Other**
  Occupational neurosis, including writers'
    cramp
  Psychasthenia
  Psychasthenic neurosis

❑ **300.9 Unspecified neurotic disorder**
  Neurosis NOS
  Psychoneurosis NOS

● **301 Personality disorders**

Includes: character neurosis

Use additional code to identify any associated neurosis or psychosis, or physical condition

Excludes *nonpsychotic personality disorder associated with organic brain syndromes (310.0–310.9)*

301.0 Paranoid personality disorder
  Fanatic personality
  Paranoid personality (disorder)
  Paranoid traits

Excludes *acute paranoid reaction (298.3)*
  alcoholic paranoia (291.5)
  paranoid schizophrenia (295.3)
  paranoid states (297.0–297.9)

● **301.1 Affective personality disorder**

Excludes *affective psychotic disorders (296.0–296.9)*
  neurasthenia (300.5)
  neurotic depression (300.4)

301.10 Affective personality disorder, unspecified

301.11 Chronic hypomanic personality disorder
  Chronic hypomanic disorder
  Hypomanic personality

301.12 Chronic depressive personality disorder
  Chronic depressive disorder
  Depressive character or personality

301.13 Cyclothymic disorder
  Cycloid personality
  Cyclothymia
  Cyclothymic personality

● **301.2 Schizoid personality disorder**

Excludes *schizophrenia (295.0–295.9)*

❑ **301.20 Schizoid personality disorder, unspecified**

301.21 Introverted personality

301.22 Schizotypal personality

301.3 Explosive personality disorder
  Aggressive:
    personality
    reaction
  Aggressiveness
  Emotional instability (excessive)
  Pathological emotionality
  Quarrelsomeness

Excludes *dyssocial personality (301.7)*
  hysterical neurosis (300.10–300.19)

301.4 Compulsive personality disorder
  Anancastic personality
  Obsessional personality

Excludes *obsessive-compulsive disorder (300.3)*
  phobic state (300.20–300.29)

● **301.5 Histrionic personality disorder**

Excludes *hysterical neurosis (300.10–300.19)*

❑ **301.50 Histrionic personality disorder, unspecified**
  Hysterical personality NOS

301.51 Chronic factitious illness with physical symptoms
  Hospital addiction syndrome
  Multiple operations syndrome
  Munchausen syndrome

❑ **301.59 Other histrionic personality disorder**
  Personality:
    emotionally unstable
    labile
    psychoinfantile

301.6 Dependent personality disorder
  Asthenic personality
  Inadequate personality
  Passive personality

Excludes *neurasthenia (300.5)*
  passive-aggressive personality (301.84)

301.7 Antisocial personality disorder
  Amoral personality
  Asocial personality
  Dyssocial personality
  Personality disorder with predominantly sociopathic or asocial manifestation

Excludes *disturbance of conduct without specifiable personality disorder (312.0–312.9)*
  explosive personality (301.3)

● **301.8 Other personality disorders**

301.81 Narcissistic personality

301.82 Avoidant personality

301.83 Borderline personality

301.84 Passive-aggressive personality

❑ **301.89 Other**
  Personality:
    eccentric   masochistic
    "haltlose" type   psychoneurotic
    immature

Excludes *psychoinfantile personality (301.59)*

❑ **301.9 Unspecified personality disorder**
  Pathological personality NOS
  Personality disorder NOS
  Psychopathic:
    constitutional state
    personality (disorder)

● **302 Sexual deviations and disorders**

Excludes *sexual disorder manifest in:*
  organic brain syndrome (290.0–294.9, 310.0–310.9)
  psychosis (295.0–298.9)

302.0 Ego-dystonic homosexuality
  Ego-dystonic lesbianism
  Homosexual conflict disorder

Excludes *homosexual pedophilia (302.2)*

302.1 Zoophilia
  Bestiality

302.2 Pedophilia

302.3 Transvestism

Excludes *trans-sexualism (302.5)*

302.4 Exhibitionism

● **302.5 Trans-sexualism**

Excludes *transvestism (302.3)*

❑ **302.50 With unspecified sexual history**

302.51 With asexual history

302.52 With homosexual history

302.53 With heterosexual history

302.6   Disorders of psychosexual identity
    Feminism in boys
    Gender identity disorder of childhood

    Excludes   *gender identity disorder in adult (302.85)*
       homosexuality (302.0)
       trans-sexualism (302.50–302.53)
       transvestism (302.3)

● **302.7   Psychosexual dysfunction**

    Excludes   *impotence of organic origin (607.84)*
       normal transient symptoms from ruptured hymen
       transient or occasional failures of erection due to fatigue, anxiety, alcohol, or drugs

   ☐ **302.70   Psychosexual dysfunction, unspecified**

    302.71   With inhibited sexual desire

    302.72   With inhibited sexual excitement
       Frigidity
       Impotence

    302.73   With inhibited female orgasm

    302.74   With inhibited male orgasm

    302.75   With premature ejaculation

    302.76   With functional dyspareunia
       Dyspareunia, psychogenic

   ☐ **302.79   With other specified psychosexual dysfunctions**

● **302.8   Other specified psychosexual disorders**

    302.81   Fetishism

    302.82   Voyeurism

    302.83   Sexual masochism

    302.84   Sexual sadism

    302.85   Gender identity disorder of adolescent or adult life

   ☐ **302.89   Other**
       Nymphomania
       Satyriasis

☐ **302.9   Unspecified psychosexual disorder**
    Pathologic sexuality NOS
    Sexual deviation NOS

● **303   Alcohol dependence syndrome**

    Use additional code to identify any associated condition, as:
       alcoholic psychoses (291.0–291.9)
       drug dependence (304.0–304.9)
       physical complications of alcohol, such as:
         cerebral degeneration (331.7)
         cirrhosis of liver (571.2)
         epilepsy (345.0–345.9)
         gastritis (535.3)
         hepatitis (571.1)
         liver damage NOS (571.3)

    Excludes   *drunkenness NOS (305.0)*

    The following fifth-digit subclassification is for use with category 303:
   ☐ **0   unspecified**
    1   continuous
    2   episodic
    3   in remission

● **303.0   Acute alcoholic intoxication**
    Acute drunkenness in alcoholism

☐● **303.9   Other and unspecified alcohol dependence**
    Chronic alcoholism
    Dipsomania

● **304   Drug dependence**

    Excludes   *nondependent abuse of drugs (305.1–305.9)*

    The following fifth-digit subclassification is for use with category 304:
   ☐ **0   unspecified**
    1   continuous
    2   episodic
    3   in remission

● **304.0   Opioid type dependence**
    Heroin
    Meperidine
    Methadone
    Morphine
    Opium
    Opium alkaloids and their derivatives
    Synthetics with morphine-like effects

● **304.1   Barbiturate and similarly acting sedative or hypnotic dependence**
    Barbiturates
    Nonbarbiturate sedatives and tranquilizers with a similar effect:
       chlordiazepoxide
       diazepam
       glutethimide
       meprobamate
       methaqualone

● **304.2   Cocaine dependence**
    Coca leaves and derivatives

● **304.3   Cannabis dependence**
    Hashish
    Hemp
    Marihuana

● **304.4   Amphetamine and other psychostimulant dependence**
    Methylphenidate
    Phenmetrazine

● **304.5   Hallucinogen dependence**
    Dimethyltryptamine [DMT]
    Lysergic acid diethylamide [LSD] and derivatives
    Mescaline
    Psilocybin

☐● **304.6   Other specified drug dependence**
    Absinthe addiction
    Glue sniffing

    Excludes   *tobacco dependence (305.1)*

● **304.7   Combinations of opioid type drug with any other**

● **304.8   Combinations of drug dependence excluding opioid type drug**

☐● **304.9   Unspecified drug dependence**
    Drug addiction NOS
    Drug dependence NOS

● **305   Nondependent abuse of drugs**

    Note: Includes cases where a person, for whom no other diagnosis is possible, has come under medical care because of the maladaptive effect of a drug on which he is not dependent and that he has taken on his own initiative to the detriment of his health or social functioning.

    Excludes   *alcohol dependence syndrome (303.0–303.9)*
       drug dependence (304.0–304.9)
       drug withdrawal syndrome (292.0)
       poisoning by drugs or medicinal substances (960.0–979.9)

ICD-9-CM

300-399

Vol. 1

◄► **New Code**   ⬅▮➡ **Revised Code**   ● **Not a Principal Diagnosis**   ● **Use Additional Digit(s)**   ☐ **Nonspecific Code**

The following fifth-digit subclassification is for use with codes 305.0, 305.2–305.9:

☐ **0 unspecified**
   1 continuous
   2 episodic
   3 in remission

●**305.0 Alcohol abuse**
Drunkenness NOS
Excessive drinking of alcohol NOS
"Hangover" (alcohol)
Inebriety NOS

> **Excludes** *acute alcohol intoxication in alcoholism (303.0)*
> *alcoholic psychoses (291.0–291.9)*

305.1 Tobacco use disorder
Tobacco dependence

> **Excludes** *history of tobacco use (V15.82)*

●**305.2 Cannabis abuse**

●**305.3 Hallucinogen abuse**
Acute intoxication from hallucinogens ["bad trips"]
LSD reaction

●**305.4 Barbiturate and similarly acting sedative or hypnotic abuse**

●**305.5 Opioid abuse**

●**305.6 Cocaine abuse**

●**305.7 Amphetamine or related acting sympathomimetic abuse**

●**305.8 Antidepressant type abuse**

☐●**305.9 Other, mixed, or unspecified drug abuse**
"Laxative habit"
Misuse of drugs NOS
Nonprescribed use of drugs or patent medicinals

●**306 Physiological malfunction arising from mental factors**

   Includes: psychogenic:
      physical symptoms not involving tissue damage
      physiological manifestations not involving tissue damage

> **Excludes** *hysteria (300.11–300.19)*
> *physical symptoms secondary to a psychiatric disorder classified elsewhere*
> *psychic factors associated with physical conditions involving tissue damage classified elsewhere (316)*
> *specific nonpsychotic mental disorders following organic brain damage (310.0–310.9)*

306.0 Musculoskeletal
Psychogenic paralysis
Psychogenic torticollis

> **Excludes** *Gilles de la Tourette's syndrome (307.23)*
> *paralysis as hysterical or conversion reaction (300.11)*
> *tics (307.20–307.22)*

306.1 Respiratory
Psychogenic:
  air hunger   hyperventilation
  cough   yawning
  hiccough

> **Excludes** *psychogenic asthma (316 and 493.9)*

306.2 Cardiovascular
Cardiac neurosis
Cardiovascular neurosis
Neurocirculatory asthenia
Psychogenic cardiovascular disorder

> **Excludes** *psychogenic paroxysmal tachycardia (316 and 427.2)*

306.3 Skin
Psychogenic pruritus

> **Excludes** *psychogenic:*
> *alopecia (316 and 704.00)*
> *dermatitis (316 and 692.9)*
> *eczema (316 and 691.8 or 692.9)*
> *urticaria (316 and 708.0–708.9)*

306.4 Gastrointestinal
Aerophagy
Cyclical vomiting, psychogenic
Diarrhea, psychogenic
Nervous gastritis
Psychogenic dyspepsia

> **Excludes** *cyclical vomiting NOS (536.2)*
> *globus hystericus (300.11)*
> *mucous colitis (316 and 564.1)*
> *psychogenic:*
> *cardiospasm (316 and 530.0)*
> *duodenal ulcer (316 and 532.0–532.9)*
> *gastric ulcer (316 and 531.0–531.9)*
> *peptic ulcer NOS (316 and 533.0–533.9)*
> *vomiting NOS (307.54)*

●**306.5 Genitourinary**

> **Excludes** *enuresis, psychogenic (307.6)*
> *frigidity (302.72)*
> *impotence (302.72)*
> *psychogenic dyspareunia (302.76)*

 ☐**306.50 Psychogenic genitourinary malfunction, unspecified**

   306.51 Psychogenic vaginismus
Functional vaginismus

   306.52 Psychogenic dysmenorrhea

   306.53 Psychogenic dysuria

 ☐**306.59 Other**

306.6 Endocrine

306.7 Organs of special sense

> **Excludes** *hysterical blindness or deafness (300.11)*
> *psychophysical visual disturbances (368.16)*

☐**306.8 Other specified psychophysiological malfunction**
Bruxism
Teeth grinding

☐**306.9 Unspecified psychophysiological malfunction**
Psychophysiologic disorder NOS
Psychosomatic disorder NOS

●**307 Special symptoms or syndromes, not elsewhere classified**

Note: This category is intended for use if the psychopathology is manifested by a single specific symptom or group of symptoms which are not part of an organic illness or other mental disorder classifiable elsewhere.

> **Excludes** *those due to mental disorders classified elsewhere*
> *those of organic origin*

307.0 Stammering and stuttering

> **Excludes** *dysphasia (784.5)*
> *lisping or lalling (307.9)*
> *retarded development of speech (315.31–315.39)*

307.1 Anorexia nervosa

> **Excludes** *eating disturbance NOS (307.50)*
> *feeding problem (783.3)*
> *of nonorganic origin (307.59)*
> *loss of appetite (783.0)*
> *of nonorganic origin (307.59)*

    ◀▶ **New Code**   ➤ **Revised Code**   ● **Not a Principal Diagnosis**   ● **Use Additional Digit(s)**   ☐ **Nonspecific Code**

● **307.2 Tics**

> **Excludes**   *nail-biting or thumb-sucking (307.9)*
> *stereotypes occurring in isolation (307.3)*
> *tics of organic origin (333.3)*

□ **307.20 Tic disorder, unspecified**

307.21 Transient tic disorder of childhood

307.22 Chronic motor tic disorder

307.23 Gilles de la Tourette's disorder
Motor-verbal tic disorder

307.3 Stereotyped repetitive movements
Body-rocking
Head banging
Spasmus nutans
Stereotypes NOS

> **Excludes**   *tics (307.20–307.23)*
> *of organic origin (333.3)*

● **307.4 Specific disorders of sleep of nonorganic origin**

> **Excludes**   *narcolepsy (347)*
> *those of unspecified cause (780.50–780.59)*

□ **307.40 Nonorganic sleep disorder, unspecified**

307.41 Transient disorder of initiating or maintaining sleep
Hyposomnia associated with acute or intermittent emotional reactions or conflicts
Insomnia associated with acute or intermittent emotional reactions or conflicts
Sleeplessness associated with acute or intermittent emotional reactions or conflicts

307.42 Persistent disorder of initiating or maintaining sleep
Hyposomnia, insomnia, or sleeplessness associated with:
anxiety
conditioned arousal
depression (major) (minor)
psychosis

307.43 Transient disorder of initiating or maintaining wakefulness
Hypersomnia associated with acute or intermittent emotional reactions or conflicts

307.44 Persistent disorder of initiating or maintaining wakefulness
Hypersomnia associated with depression (major) (minor)

307.45 Phase-shift disruption of 24-hour sleep-wake cycle
Irregular sleep-wake rhythm, nonorganic origin
Jet lag syndrome
Rapid time-zone change
Shifting sleep-work schedule

307.46 Somnambulism or night terrors

□ **307.47 Other dysfunctions of sleep stages or arousal from sleep**
Nightmares:
NOS
REM-sleep type
Sleep drunkenness

307.48 Repetitive intrusions of sleep
Repetitive intrusions of sleep with:
atypical polysomnographic features
environmental disturbances
repeated REM-sleep interruptions

□ **307.49 Other**
"Short-sleeper"
Subjective insomnia complaint

● **307.5 Other and unspecified disorders of eating**

> **Excludes**   *anorexia:*
> *nervosa (307.1)*
> *of unspecified cause (783.0)*
> *overeating, of unspecified cause (783.6)*
> *vomiting:*
> *NOS (787.0)*
> *cyclical (536.2)*
> *psychogenic (306.4)*

□ **307.50 Eating disorder, unspecified**

307.51 Bulimia
Overeating of nonorganic origin

307.52 Pica
Perverted appetite of nonorganic origin

307.53 Psychogenic rumination
Regurgitation, of nonorganic origin, of food with reswallowing

> **Excludes**   *obsessional rumination (300.3)*

307.54 Psychogenic vomiting

□ **307.59 Other**
Infantile feeding disturbances of nonorganic origin
Loss of appetite of nonorganic origin

307.6 Enuresis
Enuresis (primary) (secondary) of nonorganic origin

> **Excludes**   *enuresis of unspecified cause (788.3)*

307.7 Encopresis
Encopresis (continuous) (discontinuous) of nonorganic origin

> **Excludes**   *encopresis of unspecified cause (787.6)*

● **307.8 Psychalgia**

□ **307.80 Psychogenic pain, site unspecified**

307.81 Tension headache

> **Excludes**   *headache:*
> *NOS (784.0)*
> *migraine (346.0–346.9)*

□ **307.89 Other**
Psychogenic backache

> **Excludes**   *pains not specifically attributable to a psychological cause (in):*
> *back (724.5)*
> *joint (719.4)*
> *limb (729.5)*
> *lumbago (724.2)*
> *rheumatic (729.0)*

□ **307.9 Other and unspecified special symptoms or syndromes, not elsewhere classified**
Hair plucking   Masturbation
Lalling   Nail-biting
Lisping   Thumb-sucking

● **308 Acute reaction to stress**

Includes: catastrophic stress
combat fatigue
gross stress reaction (acute)
transient disorders in response to exceptional physical or mental stress which usually subside within hours or days

> **Excludes**   *adjustment reaction or disorder (309.0–309.9)*
> *chronic stress reaction (309.1–309.9)*

ICD-9-CM

300-399

Vol. 1

◀▶ **New Code**   ⬅▦▶ **Revised Code**   ● **Not a Principal Diagnosis**   ● **Use Additional Digit(s)**   □ **Nonspecific Code**

308.0 Predominant disturbance of emotions
Anxiety as acute reaction to exceptional [gross] stress
Emotional crisis as acute reaction to exceptional [gross] stress
Panic state as acute reaction to exceptional [gross] stress

308.1 Predominant disturbance of consciousness
Fugues as acute reaction to exceptional [gross] stress

308.2 Predominant psychomotor disturbance
Agitation states as acute reaction to exceptional [gross] stress
Stupor as acute reaction to exceptional [gross] stress

☐ 308.3 Other acute reactions to stress
Acute situational disturbance
Brief or acute posttraumatic stress disorder
> **Excludes** *prolonged posttraumatic emotional disturbance (309.81)*

308.4 Mixed disorders as reaction to stress

☐ 308.9 Unspecified acute reaction to stress

● 309 Adjustment reaction

Includes: adjustment disorders
reaction (adjustment) to chronic stress
> **Excludes** *acute reaction to major stress (308.0–308.9)*
> *neurotic disorders (300.0–300.9)*

309.0 Brief depressive reaction
Adjustment disorder with depressed mood
Grief reaction
> **Excludes** *affective psychoses (296.0–296.9)*
> *neurotic depression (300.4)*
> *prolonged depressive reaction (309.1)*
> *psychogenic depressive psychosis (298.0)*

309.1 Prolonged depressive reaction
> **Excludes** *affective psychoses (296.0–296.9)*
> *brief depressive reaction (309.0)*
> *neurotic depression (300.4)*
> *psychogenic depressive psychosis (298.0)*

● 309.2 With predominant disturbance of other emotions

309.21 Separation anxiety disorder

309.22 Emancipation disorder of adolescence and early adult life

309.23 Specific academic or work inhibition

309.24 Adjustment reaction with anxious mood

309.28 Adjustment reaction with mixed emotional features
Adjustment reaction with anxiety and depression

☐ 309.29 Other
Culture shock

309.3 With predominant disturbance of conduct
Conduct disturbance as adjustment reaction
Destructiveness as adjustment reaction
> **Excludes** *destructiveness in child (312.9)*
> *disturbance of conduct NOS (312.9)*
> *dyssocial behavior without manifest psychiatric disorder (V71.01–V71.02)*
> *personality disorder with predominantly sociopathic or asocial manifestations (301.7)*

309.4 With mixed disturbance of emotions and conduct

● 309.8 Other specified adjustment reactions

309.81 Prolonged posttraumatic stress disorder
Chronic posttraumatic stress disorder
Concentration camp syndrome
> **Excludes** *posttraumatic brain syndrome:*
> *nonpsychotic (310.2)*
> *psychotic (293.0–293.9)*

309.82 Adjustment reaction with physical symptoms

309.83 Adjustment reaction with withdrawal
Elective mutism as adjustment reaction
Hospitalism (in children) NOS

☐ 309.89 Other

☐ 309.9 Unspecified adjustment reaction
Adaptation reaction NOS
Adjustment reaction NOS

● 310 Specific nonpsychotic mental disorders due to organic brain damage
> **Excludes** *neuroses, personality disorders, or other nonpsychotic conditions occurring in a form similar to that seen with functional disorders but in association with a physical condition (300.0–300.9, 301.0–301.9)*

310.0 Frontal lobe syndrome
Lobotomy syndrome
Postleucotomy syndrome [state]
> **Excludes** *postcontusion syndrome (310.2)*

310.1 Organic personality syndrome
Cognitive or personality change of other type, of nonpsychotic severity
Mild memory disturbance
Organic psychosyndrome of nonpsychotic severity
Presbyophrenia NOS
Senility with mental changes of nonpsychotic severity

310.2 Postconcussion syndrome
Postcontusion syndrome or encephalopathy
Posttraumatic brain syndrome, nonpsychotic
Status postcommotio cerebri
> **Excludes** *any organic psychotic conditions following head injury (293.0–294.0)*
> *frontal lobe syndrome (310.0)*
> *postencephalitic syndrome (310.8)*

☐ 310.8 Other specified nonpsychotic mental disorders following organic brain damage
Postencephalitic syndrome
Other focal (partial) organic psychosyndromes

☐ 310.9 Unspecified nonpsychotic mental disorder following organic brain damage

311 Depressive disorder, not elsewhere classified
Depressive disorder NOS   Depression NOS
Depressive state NOS
> **Excludes** *acute reaction to major stress with depressive symptoms (308.0)*
> *affective personality disorder (301.10–301.13)*
> *affective psychoses (296.0–296.9)*
> *brief depressive reaction (309.0)*
> *depressive states associated with stressful events (309.0–309.1)*
> *disturbance of emotions specific to childhood and adolescence, with misery and unhappiness (313.1)*
> *mixed adjustment reaction with depressive symptoms (309.4)*
> *neurotic depression (300.4)*
> *prolonged depressive adjustment reaction (309.1)*
> *psychogenic depressive psychosis (298.0)*

   ◄► **New Code**   ⬅■➡ **Revised Code**   ● **Not a Principal Diagnosis**   ● **Use Additional Digit(s)**   ☐ **Nonspecific Code**

● **312 Disturbance of conduct, not elsewhere classified**

> **Excludes** *adjustment reaction with disturbance of conduct (309.3)*
> *drug dependence (304.0–304.9)*
> *dyssocial behavior without manifest psychiatric disorder (V71.01–V71.02)*
> *personality disorder with predominantly sociopathic or asocial manifestations (301.7)*
> *sexual deviations (302.0–302.9)*

The following fifth-digit subclassification is for use with categories 312.0–312.2:

□ **0** unspecified
   1 mild
   2 moderate
   3 severe

● **312.0 Undersocialized conduct disorder, aggressive type**
   Aggressive outburst
   Anger reaction
   Unsocialized aggressive disorder

● **312.1 Undersocialized conduct disorder, unaggressive type**
   Childhood truancy, unsocialized
   Solitary stealing
   Tantrums

● **312.2 Socialized conduct disorder**
   Childhood truancy, socialized
   Group delinquency

> **Excludes** *gang activity without manifest psychiatric disorder (V71.01)*

● **312.3 Disorders of impulse control, not elsewhere classified**

□ **312.30 Impulse control disorder, unspecified**

312.31 Pathological gambling

312.32 Kleptomania

312.33 Pyromania

312.34 Intermittent explosive disorder

312.35 Isolated explosive disorder

□ **312.39 Other**

312.4 Mixed disturbance of conduct and emotions
   Neurotic delinquency

> **Excludes** *compulsive conduct disorder (312.3)*

● **312.8 Other specified disturbances of conduct, not elsewhere classified**

312.81 Conduct disorder, childhood onset type

312.82 Conduct disorder, adolescent onset type

□ **312.89 Other conduct disorder**

□ **312.9 Unspecified disturbance of conduct**
   Delinquency (juvenile)

● **313 Disturbance of emotions specific to childhood and adolescence**

> **Excludes** *adjustment reaction (309.0–309.9)*
> *emotional disorder of neurotic type (300.0–300.9)*
> *masturbation, nail-biting, thumb-sucking, and other isolated symptoms (307.0–307.9)*

313.0 Overanxious disorder
   Anxiety and fearfulness of childhood and adolescence
   Overanxious disorder of childhood and adolescence

> **Excludes** *abnormal separation anxiety (309.21)*
> *anxiety states (300.00–300.09)*
> *hospitalism in children (309.83)*
> *phobic state (300.20–300.29)*

313.1 Misery and unhappiness disorder

> **Excludes** *depressive neurosis (300.4)*

● **313.2 Sensitivity, shyness, and social withdrawal disorder**

> **Excludes** *infantile autism (299.0)*
> *schizoid personality (301.20–301.22)*
> *schizophrenia (295.0–295.9)*

313.21 Shyness disorder of childhood
   Sensitivity reaction of childhood or adolescence

313.22 Introverted disorder of childhood
   Social withdrawal of childhood or adolescence
   Withdrawal reaction of childhood or adolescence

313.23 Elective mutism

> **Excludes** *elective mutism as adjustment reaction (309.83)*

313.3 Relationship problems
   Sibling jealousy

> **Excludes** *relationship problems associated with aggression, destruction, or other forms of conduct disturbance (312.0–312.9)*

● **313.8 Other or mixed emotional disturbances of childhood or adolescence**

313.81 Oppositional disorder

313.82 Identity disorder

313.83 Academic underachievement disorder

□ **313.89 Other**

□ **313.9 Unspecified emotional disturbance of childhood or adolescense**

● **314 Hyperkinetic syndrome of childhood**

> **Excludes** *hyperkinesis as symptom of underlying disorder—code the underlying disorder*

● **314.0 Attention deficit disorder**
   Adult
   Child

314.00 Without mention of hyperactivity
   Predominantly inattentive type

314.01 With hyperactivity
   Combined type
   Overactivity NOS
   Predominantly hyperactive/impulsive type
   Simple disturbance of attention with overactivity

314.1 Hyperkinesis with developmental delay
   Developmental disorder of hyperkinesis

Use additional code to identify any associated neurological disorder

314.2 Hyperkinetic conduct disorder
   Hyperkinetic conduct disorder without developmental delay

> **Excludes** *hyperkinesis with significant delays in specific skills (314.1)*

□ **314.8 Other specified manifestations of hyperkinetic syndrome**

□ **314.9 Unspecified hyperkinetic syndrome**
   Hyperkinetic reaction of childhood or adolescence NOS
   Hyperkinetic syndrome NOS

● **315 Specific delays in development**

> **Excludes** *that due to a neurological disorder (320.0–389.9)*

● **315.0 Specific reading disorder**

☐ **315.00 Reading disorder, unspecified**

315.01 Alexia

315.02 Developmental dyslexia

☐ **315.09 Other**
Specific spelling difficulty

315.1 Specific arithmetical disorder
Dyscalculia

☐ **315.2 Other specific learning difficulties**

| Excludes | specific arithmetical disorder (315.1) |
specific reading disorder (315.00–315.09)

● **315.3 Developmental speech or language disorder**

315.31 Developmental language disorder
Developmental aphasia
Expressive language disorder
Word deafness

| Excludes | acquired aphasia (784.3)
elective mutism (309.83, 313.0, 313.23)

315.32 Receptive language disorder (mixed)
Receptive expressive language disorder

☐ **315.39 Other**
Developmental articulation disorder
Dyslalia

| Excludes | lisping and lalling (307.9)
stammering and stuttering (307.0)

315.4 Coordination disorder
Clumsiness syndrome
Dyspraxia syndrome
Specific motor development disorder

315.5 Mixed development disorder

☐ **315.8 Other specified delays in development**

☐ **315.9 Unspecified delay in development**
Developmental disorder NOS

316 Psychic factors associated with diseases classified elsewhere
Psychologic factors in physical conditions classified elsewhere

Use additional code to identify the associated physical condition, as:
psychogenic:
asthma (493.9)
dermatitis (692.9)
duodenal ulcer (532.0–532.9)
eczema (691.8, 692.9)
gastric ulcer (531.0–531.9)
mucous colitis (564.1)
paroxysmal tachycardia (427.2)
ulcerative colitis (556)
urticaria (708.0–708.9)
psychosocial dwarfism (259.4)

| Excludes | physical symptoms and physiological malfunctions, not involving tissue damage, of mental origin (306.0–306.9)

MENTAL RETARDATION (317–319)

Use additional code (s) to identify any associated psychiatric or physical condition(s)

317 Mild mental retardation
High-grade defect
IQ 50–70
Mild mental subnormality

● **318 Other specified mental retardation**

318.0 Moderate mental retardation
IQ 35–49
Moderate mental subnormality

318.1 Severe mental retardation
IQ 20–34
Severe mental subnormality

318.2 Profound mental retardation
IQ under 20
Profound mental subnormality

☐ **319 Unspecified mental retardation**
Mental deficiency NOS
Mental subnormality NOS

   ◀▶ **New Code**   ◀▦ ▦▶ **Revised Code**   ● **Not a Principal Diagnosis**   ● **Use Additional Digit(s)**   ☐ **Nonspecific Code**

6. DISEASES OF THE NERVOUS SYSTEM AND SENSE ORGANS (320–389)

INFLAMMATORY DISEASES OF THE CENTRAL NERVOUS SYSTEM (320–326)

Item 6-1 The two major classifications of the nervous system are the peripheral nervous system and the central nervous system (CNS). The central nervous system contains the brain and the spinal cord. **Encephalitis** is the swelling of the brain. **Meningitis** is swelling of the covering of the brain, the meninges. Types and causes of brain infections are:

Type	Cause
purulent	bacterial
aseptic/abacterial	viral
chronic meningitis	mycobacterial and fungal

● **320 Bacterial meningitis**

    Includes: arachnoiditis bacterial
               leptomeningitis bacterial
               meningitis bacterial
               meningoencephalitis bacterial
               meningomyelitis bacterial
               pachymeningitis bacterial

    320.0 Haemophilus meningitis
         Meningitis due to Haemophilus influenzae [H. influenzae]

    320.1 Pneumococcal meningitis

    320.2 Streptococcal meningitis

    320.3 Staphylococcal meningitis

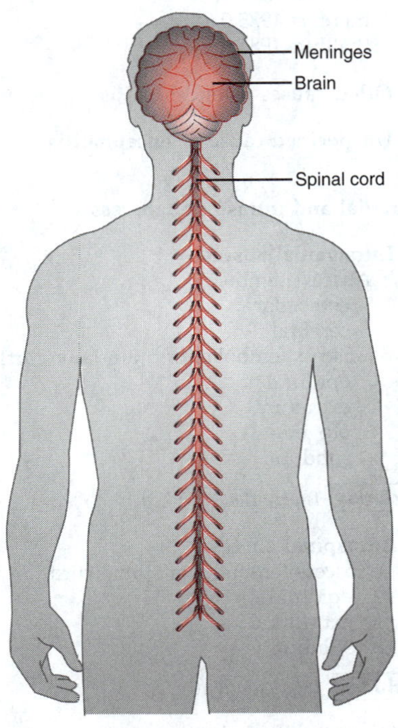

Figure 6-1 The brain and spinal cord make up the central nervous system.

● **320.7** *Meningitis in other bacterial diseases classified elsewhere*

    Code first underlying disease as:
        actinomycosis (039.8)
        listeriosis (027.0)
        typhoid fever (002.0)
        whooping cough (033.0–033.9)

    Excludes *meningitis (in):*
        epidemic (036.0)
        gonococcal (098.82)
        meningococcal (036.0)
        salmonellosis (003.21)
        syphilis:
           NOS (094.2)
           congenital (090.42)
           meningovascular (094.2)
           secondary (091.81)
        tuberculosis (013.0)

● **320.8 Meningitis due to other specified bacteria**

    320.81 Anaerobic meningitis
         Gram-negative anaerobes
         Bacteroides (fragilis)

    320.82 Meningitis due to gram-negative bacteria, not elsewhere classified
         Aerobacter aerogenes
         Escherichia coli [E. coli]
         Friedlander bacillus
         Klebsiella pneumoniae
         Proteus morganii
         Pseudomonas

    Excludes *gram-negative anaerobes (320.81)*

    ☐**320.89 Meningitis due to other specified bacteria**
         Bacillus pyocyaneus

    ☐**320.9 Meningitis due to unspecified bacterium**
         Meningitis:
           bacterial NOS
           purulent NOS
           pyogenic NOS
           suppurative NOS

● **321 Meningitis due to other organisms**

    Includes: arachnoiditis due to organisms other than bacteria
               leptomeningitis due to organisms other than bacteria
               meningitis due to organisms other than bacteria
               pachymeningitis due to organisms other than bacteria

● **321.0** *Cryptococcal meningitis*

    Code first underlying disease (117.5)

●☐ **321.1** *Meningitis in other fungal diseases*

    Code first underlying disease (110.0–118)

    Excludes *meningitis in:*
        candidiasis (112.83)
        coccidioidomycosis (114.2)
        histoplasmosis (115.01, 115.11, 115.91)

ICD-9-CM

300-399

Vol. 1

● **321.2 *Meningitis due to viruses not elsewhere classified***

Code first underlying disease, as:
    meningitis due to arbovirus (060.0–066.9)

> **Excludes** *meningitis (due to):*
>   *abacterial (047.0–047.9)*
>   *adenovirus (049.1)*
>   *aseptic NOS (047.9)*
>   *Coxsackie (virus) (047.0)*
>   *ECHO virus (047.1)*
>   *enterovirus (047.0–047.9)*
>   *herpes simplex virus (054.72)*
>   *herpes zoster virus (053.0)*
>   *lymphocytic choriomeningitis virus (049.0)*
>   *mumps (072.1)*
>   *viral NOS (047.9)*
>   *meningo-eruptive syndrome (047.1)*

● **321.3 *Meningitis due to trypanosomiasis***

Code first underlying disease (086.0–086.9)

● **321.4 *Meningitis in sarcoidosis***

Code first underlying disease (135)

●❑ **321.8 *Meningitis due to other nonbacterial organisms classified elsewhere***

Code first underlying disease

> **Excludes** *leptospiral meningitis (100.81)*

● **322 Meningitis of unspecified cause**

Includes: arachnoiditis with no organism specified as cause
leptomeningitis with no organism specified as cause
meningitis with no organism specified as cause
pachymeningitis with no organism specified as cause

322.0 Nonpyogenic meningitis
    Meningitis with clear cerebrospinal fluid

322.1 Eosinophilic meningitis

322.2 Chronic meningitis

❑ **322.9 Meningitis, unspecified**

● **323 Encephalitis, myelitis, and encephalomyelitis**

Includes: acute disseminated encephalomyelitis
meningoencephalitis, except bacterial
meningomyelitis, except bacterial
myelitis (acute):
    ascending
    transverse

> **Excludes** *bacterial:*
>   *meningoencephalitis (320.0–320.9)*
>   *meningomyelitis (320.0–320.9)*

● **323.0 *Encephalitis in viral diseases classified elsewhere***

Code first underlying disease, as:
    cat-scratch disease (078.3)
    infectious mononucleosis (075)
    ornithosis (073.7)

> **Excludes** *encephalitis (in):*
>   *arthropod-borne viral (062.0–064)*
>   *herpes simplex (054.3)*
>   *mumps (072.2)*
>   *poliomyelitis (045.0–045.9)*
>   *rubella (056.01)*
>   *slow virus infections of central nervous system (046.0–046.9)*
>   *other viral diseases of central nervous system (049.8–049.9)*
>   *viral NOS (049.9)*

● **323.1 *Encephalitis in rickettsial diseases classified elsewhere***

Code first underlying disease (080–083.9)

● **323.2 *Encephalitis in protozoal diseases classified elsewhere***

Code first underlying disease, as:
    malaria (084.0–084.9)
    trypanosomiasis (086.0–086.9)

●❑ **323.4 *Other encephalitis due to infection classified elsewhere***

Code first underlying disease

> **Excludes** *encephalitis (in):*
>   *meningococcal (036.1)*
>   *syphilis:*
>   *NOS (094.81)*
>   *congenital (090.41)*
>   *toxoplasmosis (130.0)*
>   *tuberculosis (013.6)*
>   *meningoencephalitis due to free-living ameba [Naegleria] (136.2)*

323.5 Encephalitis following immunization procedures
    Encephalitis postimmunization or postvaccinal
    Encephalomyelitis postimmunization or postvaccinal

Use additional E code to identify vaccine

● **323.6 *Postinfectious encephalitis***

Code first underlying disease

> **Excludes** *encephalitis:*
>   *postchickenpox (052.0)*
>   *postmeasles (055.0)*

● **323.7 *Toxic encephalitis***

Code first underlying cause, as:
    carbon tetrachloride (982.1)
    hydroxyquinoline derivatives (961.3)
    lead (984.0–984.9)
    mercury (985.0)
    thallium (985.8)

❑ **323.8 Other causes of encephalitis**

❑ **323.9 Unspecified cause of encephalitis**

● **324 Intracranial and intraspinal abscess**

324.0 Intracranial abscess
    Abscess (embolic):
      cerebellar
      cerebral
    Abscess (embolic) of brain [any part]:
      epidural
      extradural
      otogenic
      subdural

> **Excludes** *tuberculous (013.3)*

324.1 Intraspinal abscess
    Abscess (embolic) of spinal cord [any part]:
      epidural
      extradural
      subdural

> **Excludes** *tuberculous (013.5)*

❑ **324.9 Of unspecified site**
    Extradural or subdural abscess NOS

 ◄► **New Code**   ⟵⟶ **Revised Code**   ● **Not a Principal Diagnosis**   ● **Use Additional Digit(s)**   ❑ **Nonspecific Code**

325 Phlebitis and thrombophlebitis of intracranial venous sinuses

Embolism of cavernous, lateral, or other intracranial or unspecified intracranial venous sinus

Endophlebitis of cavernous, lateral, or other intracranial or unspecified intracranial venous sinus

Phlebitis, septic or suppurative of cavernous, lateral, or other intracranial or unspecified intracranial venous sinus

Thrombophlebitis of cavernous, lateral, or other intracranial or unspecified intracranial venous sinus

Thrombosis of cavernous, lateral, or other intracranial or unspecified intracranial venous sinus

> **Excludes** *that specified as:*
> *complicating pregnancy, childbirth, or the puerperium (671.5)*
> *of nonpyogenic origin (437.6)*

326 Late effects of intracranial abscess or pyogenic infection

Note: This category is to be used to indicate conditions whose primary classification is to 320–325 [excluding 320.7, 321.0–321.8, 323.0–323.4, 323.6–323.7] as the cause of late effects, themselves classifiable elsewhere. The "late effects" include conditions specified as such, or as sequelae, which may occur at any time after the resolution of the causal condition.

Use additional code to identify condition, as:
hydrocephalus (331.4)
paralysis (342.0–342.9, 344.0–344.9)

HEREDITARY AND DEGENERATIVE DISEASES OF THE CENTRAL NERVOUS SYSTEM (330–337)

> **Excludes** *hepatolenticular degeneration (275.1)*
> *multiple sclerosis (340)*
> *other demyelinating diseases of central nervous system (341.0–341.9)*

Item 6–2 Leukodystrophy is characterized by degeneration and/or failure of the myelin formation of the central nervous system and sometimes of the peripheral nervous system. The disease is inherited and progressive.

● **330 Cerebral degenerations usually manifest in childhood**

Use additional code to identify associated mental retardation

330.0 Leukodystrophy
Krabbe's disease
Leukodystrophy:
  NOS
  globoid cell
  metachromatic
  sudanophilic
Pelizaeus-Merzbacher disease
Sulfatide lipidosis

330.1 Cerebral lipidoses
Amaurotic (familial) idiocy
Disease:
  Batten
  Jansky-Bielschowsky
  Kufs'
  Spielmeyer-Vogt
  Tay-Sachs
Gangliosidosis

● ***330.2 Cerebral degeneration in generalized lipidoses***

Code first underlying disease, as:
Fabry's disease (272.7)
Gaucher's disease (272.7)
Niemann-Pick disease (272.7)
sphingolipidosis (272.7)

●☐ ***330.3 Cerebral degeneration of childhood in other diseases classified elsewhere***

Code first underlying disease, as:
Hunter's disease (277.5)
mucopolysaccharidosis (277.5)

☐ **330.8 Other specified cerebral degenerations in childhood**
Alpers' disease or gray-matter degeneration
Infantile necrotizing encephalomyelopathy
Leigh's disease
Subacute necrotizing encephalopathy or encephalomyelopathy

☐ **330.9 Unspecified cerebral degeneration in childhood**

Item 6–3 Pick's disease is the atrophy of the frontal and temporal lobes, causing dementia; Alzheimer's is characterized by a more diffuse cerebral atrophy.

● **331 Other cerebral degenerations**

331.0 Alzheimer's disease

331.1 Pick's disease

331.2 Senile degeneration of brain
> **Excludes** *senility NOS (797)*

331.3 Communicating hydrocephalus
> **Excludes** *congenital hydrocephalus (741.0, 742.3)*

331.4 Obstructive hydrocephalus
Acquired hydrocephalus NOS
> **Excludes** *congenital hydrocephalus (741.0, 742.3)*

● ***331.7 Cerebral degeneration in diseases classified elsewhere***

Code first underlying disease, as:
alcoholism (303.0–303.9)
beriberi (265.0)
cerebrovascular disease (430–438)
congenital hydrocephalus (741.0, 742.3)
neoplastic disease (140.0–239.9)
myxedema (244.0–244.9)
vitamin B_{12} deficiency (266.2)

> **Excludes** *cerebral degeneration in:*
> *Jakob-Creutzfeldt disease (046.1)*
> *progressive multifocal leukoencephalopathy (046.3)*
> *subacute spongiform encephalopathy (046.1)*

● **331.8 Other cerebral degeneration**

331.81 Reye's syndrome

☐ **331.89 Other**
Cerebral ataxia

☐ **331.9 Cerebral degeneration, unspecified**

● **332 Parkinson's disease**

332.0 Paralysis agitans
Parkinsonism or Parkinson's disease:
  NOS
  idiopathic
  primary

332.1 Secondary Parkinsonism
Parkinsonism due to drugs

Use additional E code to identify drug, if drug-induced

> **Excludes** *Parkinsonism (in):*
> *Huntington's disease (333.4)*
> *progressive supranuclear palsy (333.0)*
> *Shy-Drager syndrome (333.0)*
> *syphilitic (094.82)*

ICD-9-CM

300–399

Vol. 1

● **333 Other extrapyramidal disease and abnormal movement disorders**

> **Includes:** other forms of extrapyramidal, basal ganglia, or striatopallidal disease

> **Excludes** *abnormal movements of head NOS (781.0)*

□ **333.0 Other degenerative diseases of the basal ganglia**
Atrophy or degeneration:
   olivopontocerebellar [Déjérine-Thomas syndrome]
   pigmentary pallidal [Hallervorden-Spatz disease] striatonigral
Parkinsonian syndrome associated with:
   idiopathic orthostatic hypotension
   symptomatic orthostatic hypotension
Progressive supranuclear ophthalmoplegia
Shy-Drager syndrome

□ **333.1 Essential and other specified forms of tremor**
Benign essential tremor
Familial tremor

Use additional E code to identify drug, if drug-induced

> **Excludes** *tremor NOS (781.0)*

333.2 Myoclonus
Familial essential myoclonus
Progressive myoclonic epilepsy
Unverricht-Lundborg disease

Use additional E code to identify drug, if drug-induced

333.3 Tics of organic origin

> **Excludes** *Gilles de la Tourette's syndrome (307.23)*
> *habit spasm (307.22)*
> *tic NOS (307.20)*

Use additional E code to identify drug, if drug-induced

Item 6–4   Huntington's disease is characterized by ceaseless, jerky movements and progressive cognitive and behavioral deterioration.

333.4 Huntington's chorea

□ **333.5 Other choreas**
Hemiballism(us)
Paroxysmal choreo-athetosis

> **Excludes** *Sydenham's or rheumatic chorea (392.0–392.9)*

Use additional E code to identify drug, if drug-induced

333.6 Idiopathic torsion dystonia
Dystonia:
   deformans progressiva
   musculorum deformans
(Schwalbe-) Ziehen-Oppenheim disease

333.7 Symptomatic torsion dystonia
Athetoid cerebral palsy [Vogt's disease]
Double athetosis (syndrome)

Use additional E code to identify drug, if drug-induced

● **333.8 Fragments of torsion dystonia**

Use additional E code to identify drug, if drug-induced

333.81 Blepharospasm

333.82 Orofacial dyskinesia

333.83 Spasmodic torticollis

> **Excludes** *torticollis:*
> *NOS (723.5)*
> *hysterical (300.11)*
> *psychogenic (306.0)*

333.84 Organic writers' cramp

> **Excludes** *psychogenic (300.89)*

□ **333.89 Other**

● **333.9 Other and unspecified extrapyramidal diseases and abnormal movement disorders**

□ **333.90 Unspecified extrapyramidal disease and abnormal movement disorder**

333.91 Stiff-man syndrome

333.92 Neuroleptic malignant syndrome
Use additional E to identify drug

333.93 Benign shuddering attacks

□ **333.99 Other**
Restless legs

● **334 Spinocerebellar disease**

> **Excludes** *olivopontocerebellar degeneration (333.0)*
> *peroneal muscular atrophy (356.1)*

334.0 Friedreich's ataxia

334.1 Hereditary spastic paraplegia

334.2 Primary cerebellar degeneration
Cerebellar ataxia:
   Marie's
   Sanger-Brown
Dyssynergia cerebellaris myoclonica
Primary cerebellar degeneration:
   NOS
   hereditary
   sporadic

□ **334.3 Other cerebellar ataxia**
Cerebellar ataxia NOS

Use additional E code to identify drug, if drug-induced

● **334.4 *Cerebellar ataxia in diseases classified elsewhere***
Code first underlying disease, as:
   alcoholism (303.0–303.9)
   myxedema (244.0–244.9)
   neoplastic disease (140.0–239.9)

□ **334.8 Other spinocerebellar diseases**
Ataxia-telangiectasia [Louis-Bar syndrome]
Corticostriatal-spinal degeneration

□ **334.9 Spinocerebellar disease, unspecified**

● **335 Anterior horn cell disease**

335.0 Werdnig-Hoffmann disease
Infantile spinal muscular atrophy
Progressive muscular atrophy of infancy

● **335.1 Spinal muscular atrophy**

□ **335.10 Spinal muscular atrophy, unspecified**

335.11 Kugelberg-Welander disease
Spinal muscular atrophy:
   familial
   juvenile

□ **335.19 Other**
Adult spinal muscular atrophy

● **335.2 Motor neuron disease**

335.20 Amyotrophic lateral sclerosis
Motor neuron disease (bulbar) (mixed type)

335.21 Progressive muscular atrophy
Duchenne-Aran muscular atrophy
Progressive muscular atrophy (pure)

335.22 Progressive bulbar palsy

    ◄► **New Code**   ◄━ ━► **Revised Code**   ● **Not a Principal Diagnosis**   ● **Use Additional Digit(s)**   □ **Nonspecific Code**

335.23 **Pseudobulbar palsy**

335.24 **Primary lateral sclerosis**

☐335.29 **Other**

☐**335.8 Other anterior horn cell diseases**

☐**335.9 Anterior horn cell disease, unspecified**

● **336 Other diseases of spinal cord**

336.0 **Syringomyelia and syringobulbia**

336.1 **Vascular myelopathies**
Acute infarction of spinal cord (embolic) (nonembolic)
Arterial thrombosis of spinal cord
Edema of spinal cord
Hematomyelia
Subacute necrotic myelopathy

● 336.2 *Subacute combined degeneration of spinal cord in diseases classified elsewhere*

Code first underlying disease, as:
pernicious anemia (281.0)
other vitamin B$_{12}$ deficiency anemia (281.1)
vitamin B$_{12}$ deficiency (266.2)

● 336.3 *Myelopathy in other diseases classified elsewhere*

Code first underlying disease, as:
myelopathy in neoplastic disease (140.0–239.9)

| **Excludes** | *myelopathy in:* |
intervertebral disc disorder (722.70–722.73)
spondylosis (721.1, 721.41–721.42, 721.91)

☐336.8 **Other myelopathy**
Myelopathy:
drug-induced   radiation-induced

Use additional E code to identify cause

☐336.9 **Unspecified disease of spinal cord**
Cord compression NOS
Myelopathy NOS

| **Excludes** | *myelitis (323.0–323.9)* |
spinal (canal) stenosis (723.0, 724.00–724.09)

● **337 Disorders of the autonomic nervous system**

Includes: disorders of peripheral autonomic, sympathetic, parasympathetic, or vegetative system

| **Excludes** | *familial dysautonomia [Riley-Day syndrome]* |
(742.8)

337.0 **Idiopathic peripheral autonomic neuropathy**
Carotid sinus syncope or syndrome
Cervical sympathetic dystrophy or paralysis

● 337.1 *Peripheral autonomic neuropathy in disorders classified elsewhere*

Code first underlying disease, as:
amyloidosis (277.3)
diabetes (250.6)

● 337.2 **Reflex sympathetic dystrophy**

☐337.20 **Reflex sympathetic dystrophy, unspecified**

337.21 **Reflex sympathetic dystrophy of the upper limb**

337.22 **Reflex sympathetic dystrophy of the lower limb**

☐337.29 **Reflex sympathetic dystrophy of other specified site**

337.3 **Autonomic dysreflexia** ◄

Use additional code to identify the underlying cause, such as: ◄
decubitus ulcer (707.0) ◄
fecal impaction (560.39) ◄
urinary tract infection (599.0) ◄

☐**337.9 Unspecified disorder of autonomic nervous system**

OTHER DISORDERS OF THE CENTRAL NERVOUS SYSTEM (340–349)

340 Multiple sclerosis
Disseminated or multiple sclerosis:
NOS   cord
brain stem   generalized

● **341 Other demyelinating diseases of central nervous system**

341.0 **Neuromyelitis optica**

341.1 **Schilder's disease**
Balo's concentric sclerosis
Encephalitis periaxialis:
concentrica [Balo's]
diffusa [Schilder's]

☐341.8 **Other demyelinating diseases of central nervous system**
Central demyelination of corpus callosum
Central pontine myelinosis
Marchiafava (-Bignami) disease

☐341.9 **Demyelinating disease of central nervous system, unspecified**

● **342 Hemiplegia and hemiparesis**

Note: This category is to be used when hemiplegia (complete) (incomplete) is reported without further specification, or is stated to be old or long-standing but of unspecified cause. The category is also for use in multiple coding to identify these types of hemiplegia resulting from any cause.

| **Excludes** | *congenital (343.1)* |
hemiplegia due to late effect of cerebrovascular ◄
accident (438.20–438.22)
infantile NOS (343.4)

The following fifth digits are for use with codes 342.0–342.9
☐ **0 affecting unspecified side**
1 affecting dominant side
2 affecting nondominant side

● 342.0 **Flaccid hemiplegia**

● 342.1 **Spastic hemiplegia**

☐● 342.8 **Other specified hemiplegia**

☐● 342.9 **Hemiplegia, unspecified**

● **343 Infantile cerebral palsy**

Includes: cerebral:
palsy NOS
spastic infantile paralysis
congenital spastic paralysis (cerebral)
Little's disease
paralysis (spastic) due to birth injury:
intracranial
spinal

| **Excludes** | *hereditary cerebral paralysis, such as:* |
hereditary spastic paraplegia (334.1)
Vogt's disease (333.7)
spastic paralysis specified as noncongenital or noninfantile (344.0–344.9)

343.0 **Diplegic**
Congenital diplegia
Congenital paraplegia

343.1 **Hemiplegic**
Congenital hemiplegia

| **Excludes** | *infantile hemiplegia NOS (343.4)* |

ICD-9-CM

300-399

Vol. 1

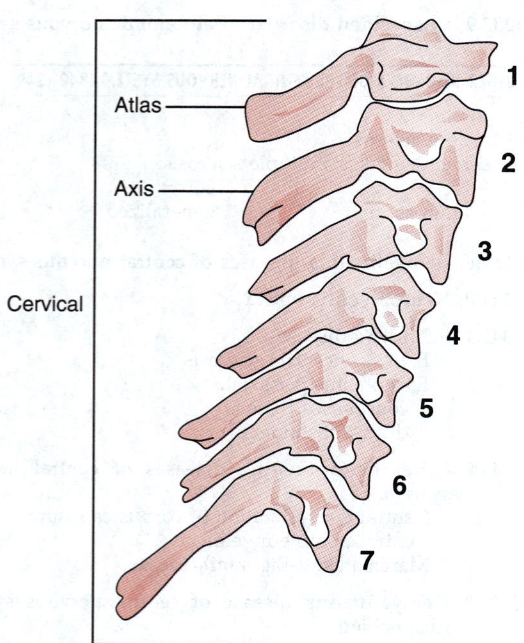

Figure 6–2 Cervical vertebrae.

343.2 Quadriplegic
Tetraplegic

343.3 Monoplegic

343.4 Infantile hemiplegia
Infantile hemiplegia (postnatal) NOS

343.8 Other specified infantile cerebral palsy

343.9 Infantile cerebral palsy, unspecified
Cerebral palsy NOS

Item 6–5 Quadriplegia, also called tetraplegia, is the paralysis of all four limbs. Quadriparesis is the incomplete paralysis of all four limbs. Nerve damage in C1–C4 is associated with lower limb paralysis and C5–C7 damage is associated with upper limb paralysis. Diplegia is the paralysis of the upper limbs. Monoplegia is the paralysis of the lower limbs.
Cauda equina syndrome is due to pressure on the roots of the spinal nerves and causes paresthesia (abnormal sensations).

344 Other paralytic syndromes

Note: This category is to be used when the listed conditions are reported without further specification or are stated to be old or long-standing but of unspecified cause. The category is also for use in multiple coding to identify these conditions resulting from any cause.

Includes: paralysis (complete) (incomplete), except as classifiable to 342 and 343

Excludes *congenital or infantile cerebral palsy (343.0–343.9)*
hemiplegia (342.0–342.9)
congenital or infantile (343.1, 343.4)

344.0 Quadriplegia and quadriparesis

344.00 Quadriplegia, unspecified

344.01 C_1-C_4, complete

344.02 C_1-C_4, incomplete

344.03 C_5-C_7, complete

344.04 C_5-C_7, incomplete

344.09 Other

344.1 Paraplegia
Paralysis of both lower limbs
Paraplegia (lower)

344.2 Diplegia of upper limbs
Diplegia (upper)
Paralysis of both upper limbs

344.3 Monoplegia of lower limb
Paralysis of lower limb

Excludes *Monoplegia of lower limb due to late effect of cerebrovascular accident (438.40–438.42)* ◄

344.30 Affecting unspecified side

344.31 Affecting dominant side

344.32 Affecting nondominant side

344.4 Monoplegia of upper limb
Paralysis of upper limb

Excludes *monoplegia of upper limb due to late effect of cerebrovascular accident (438.30–438.32)* ◄

344.40 Affecting unspecified side

344.41 Affecting dominant side

344.42 Affecting nondominant side

344.5 Unspecified monoplegia

344.6 Cauda equina syndrome

344.60 Without mention of neurogenic bladder

344.61 With neurogenic bladder
Acontractile bladder
Autonomic hyperreflexia of bladder
Cord bladder
Detrusor hyperreflexia

344.8 Other specified paralytic syndromes

344.81 Locked-in state

344.89 Other specified paralytic syndrome

344.9 Paralysis, unspecified

345 Epilepsy
The following fifth-digit subclassification is for use with categories 345.0, .1, .4-.9:
　0 without mention of intractable epilepsy
　1 with intractable epilepsy

Excludes *progressive myoclonic epilepsy (333.2)*

345.0 Generalized nonconvulsive epilepsy
Absences:　　　　　　Petit mal
　atonic　　　　　　　Pykno-epilepsy
　typical　　　　　　　Seizures:
Minor epilepsy　　　　　akinetic
　　　　　　　　　　　　atonic

345.1 Generalized convulsive epilepsy
Epileptic seizures:　　　Epileptic seizures:
　clonic　　　　　　　　tonic-clonic
　myoclonic　　　　　Grand mal
　tonic　　　　　　　　Major epilepsy

Excludes *convulsions:*
　　NOS (780.3)
　　infantile (780.3)
　　newborn (779.0)
　infantile spasms (345.6)

345.2 Petit mal status
Epileptic absence status

345.3 Grand mal status
Status epilepticus NOS

Excludes *epilepsia partialis continua (345.7) status:*
　　psychomotor (345.7)
　　temporal lobe (345.7)

◄▶ **New Code**　　⬅▬▬➡ **Revised Code**　　● **Not a Principal Diagnosis**　　● **Use Additional Digit(s)**　　☐ **Nonspecific Code**

345.4 Partial epilepsy, with impairment of consciousness
Epilepsy:
  limbic system
  partial:
    secondarily generalized
    with memory and ideational disturbances
  psychomotor
  psychosensory
  temporal lobe
  Epileptic automatism

345.5 Partial epilepsy, without mention of impairment of consciousness
Epilepsy: Epilepsy:
  Bravais-Jacksonian NOS   sensory-induced
  focal (motor) NOS   somatomotor
  Jacksonian NOS   somatosensory
  motor partial   visceral
  partial NOS   visual

345.6 Infantile spasms
Hypsarrhythmia   Salaam attacks
Lightning spasms
Excludes *salaam tic (781.0)*

345.7 Epilepsia partialis continua
Kojevnikov's epilepsy

345.8 Other forms of epilepsy
Epilepsy: Epilepsy:
  cursive [running]   gelastic

345.9 Epilepsy, unspecified
Epileptic convulsions, fits, or seizures NOS
Excludes *convulsive seizure or fit NOS (780.3)*

346 Migraine
The following fifth-digit subclassification is for use with category 346:
  0 without mention of intractable migraine
  1 with intractable migraine, so stated

346.0 Classical migraine
Migraine preceded or accompanied by transient focal neurological phenomena
Migraine with aura

346.1 Common migraine
Atypical migraine   Sick headache

346.2 Variants of migraine
Cluster headache   Migraine:
Histamine cephalgia   lower half
Horton's neuralgia   retinal
Migraine: Neuralgia:
  abdominal   ciliary
  basilar   migrainous

346.8 Other forms of migraine
Migraine: Migraine:
  hemiplegic   ophthalmoplegic

346.9 Migraine, unspecified

347 Cataplexy and narcolepsy

348 Other conditions of brain

348.0 Cerebral cysts
Arachnoid cyst   Porencephaly, acquired
Porencephalic cyst   Pseudoporencephaly
Excludes *porencephaly (congenital) (724.4)*

348.1 Anoxic brain damage
Excludes *that occurring in:*
  abortion (634–638 with .7, 639.8)
  ectopic or molar pregnancy (639.8)
  labor or delivery (668.2, 669.4)
  that of newborn (767.0, 768.0–768.9, 772.1–772.2)

Use additional E code to identify cause

348.2 Benign intracranial hypertension
Pseudotumor cerebri
Excludes *hypertensive encephalopathy (437.2)*

348.3 Encephalopathy, unspecified

348.4 Compression of brain
Compression brain (stem)
Herniation brain (stem)
Posterior fossa compression syndrome

348.5 Cerebral edema

348.8 Other conditions of brain
Cerebral: Cerebral:
  calcification   fungus

348.9 Unspecified condition of brain

349 Other and unspecified disorders of the nervous system

349.0 Reaction to spinal or lumbar puncture
Headache following lumbar puncture

349.1 Nervous system complications from surgically implanted device
Excludes *immediate postoperative complications (997.00–997.09)*
  mechanical complications of nervous system device (996.2)

349.2 Disorders of meninges, not elsewhere classified
Adhesions, meningeal (cerebral) (spinal)
Cyst, spinal meninges
Meningocele, acquired
Pseudomeningocele, acquired

349.8 Other specified disorders of nervous system

349.81 Cerebrospinal fluid rhinorrhea
Excludes *cerebrospinal fluid otorrhea (388.61)*

349.82 Toxic encephalopathy
Use additional E code to identify cause

349.89 Other

349.9 Unspecified disorders of nervous system
Disorder of nervous system (central) NOS

Item 6–6 The peripheral nervous system consists of 31 pairs of spinal nerves, 12 pairs of cranial nerves, and the autonomic nerves, which are divided into the parasympathetic and sympathetic nerves. The cranial nerves are: olfactory (I), optic (II), oculomotor (III), trochlear (IV), trigeminal (V), abducens (VI), facial (VII), vestibulocochlear (VIII), glossopharyngeal (IX), vagus (X), accessory (XI), and hypoglossal (XII).

DISORDERS OF THE PERIPHERAL NERVOUS SYSTEM (350–359)

Excludes *diseases of:*
  acoustic [8th] nerve (388.5)
  oculomotor [3rd, 4th, 6th] nerves (378.0–378.9)
  optic [2nd] nerve (377.0–377.9)
  peripheral autonomic nerves (337.0–337.9)
  neuralgia NOS or "rheumatic" (729.2)
  neuritis NOS or "rheumatic" (729.2)
  radiculitis NOS or "rheumatic" (729.2)
  peripheral neuritis in pregnancy (646.4)

350 Trigeminal nerve disorders
Includes: disorders of 5th cranial nerve

350.1 Trigeminal neuralgia
Tic douloureux
Trifacial neuralgia
Trigeminal neuralgia NOS
Excludes *postherpetic (053.12)*

ICD-9-CM

300–399

Vol. 1

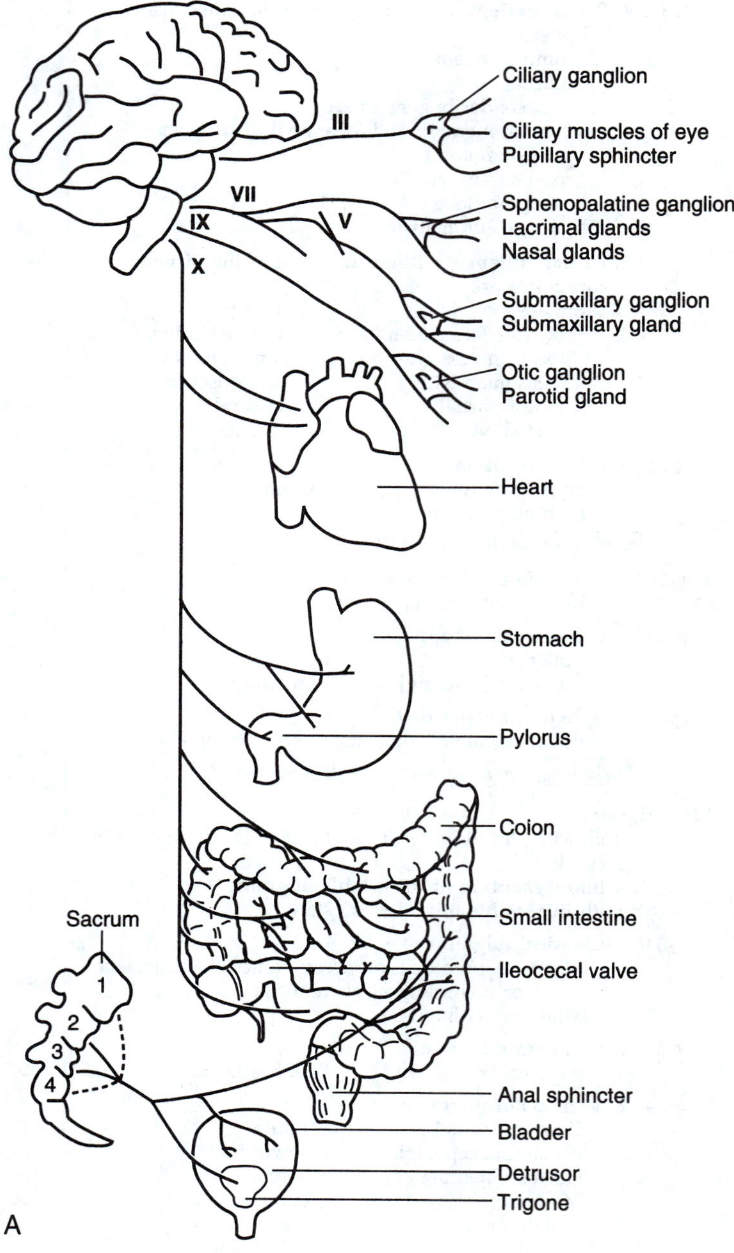

Figure 6-3   A. Parasympathetic nervous system.

350.2   **Atypical face pain**

❑ 350.8   **Other specified trigeminal nerve disorders**

❑ 350.9   **Trigeminal nerve disorder, unspecified**

● 351   **Facial nerve disorders**

> **Includes:** disorders of 7th cranial nerve
> **Excludes** *that in newborn (767.5)*

351.0   **Bell's palsy**
Facial palsy

351.1   **Geniculate ganglionitis**
Geniculate ganglionitis NOS
> **Excludes** *herpetic (053.11)*

❑ 351.8   **Other facial nerve disorders**
Facial myokymia
Melkersson's syndrome

❑ 351.9   **Facial nerve disorder, unspecified**

● 352   **Disorders of other cranial nerves**

352.0   **Disorders of olfactory [1st] nerve**

352.1   **Glossopharyngeal neuralgia**

❑ 352.2   **Other disorders of glossopharyngeal [9th] nerve**

352.3   **Disorders of pneumogastric [10th] nerve**
Disorders of vagal nerve
> **Excludes** *paralysis of vocal cords or larynx (478.30–478.34)*

352.4   **Disorders of accessory [11th] nerve**

352.5   **Disorders of hypoglossal [12th] nerve**

352.6   **Multiple cranial nerve palsies**
Collet-Sicard syndrome
Polyneuritis cranialis

❑ 352.9   **Unspecified disorder of cranial nerves**

◀▶ **New Code**   ⬅▌▐➡ **Revised Code**   ● **Not a Principal Diagnosis**   ● **Use Additional Digit(s)**   ❑ **Nonspecific Code**

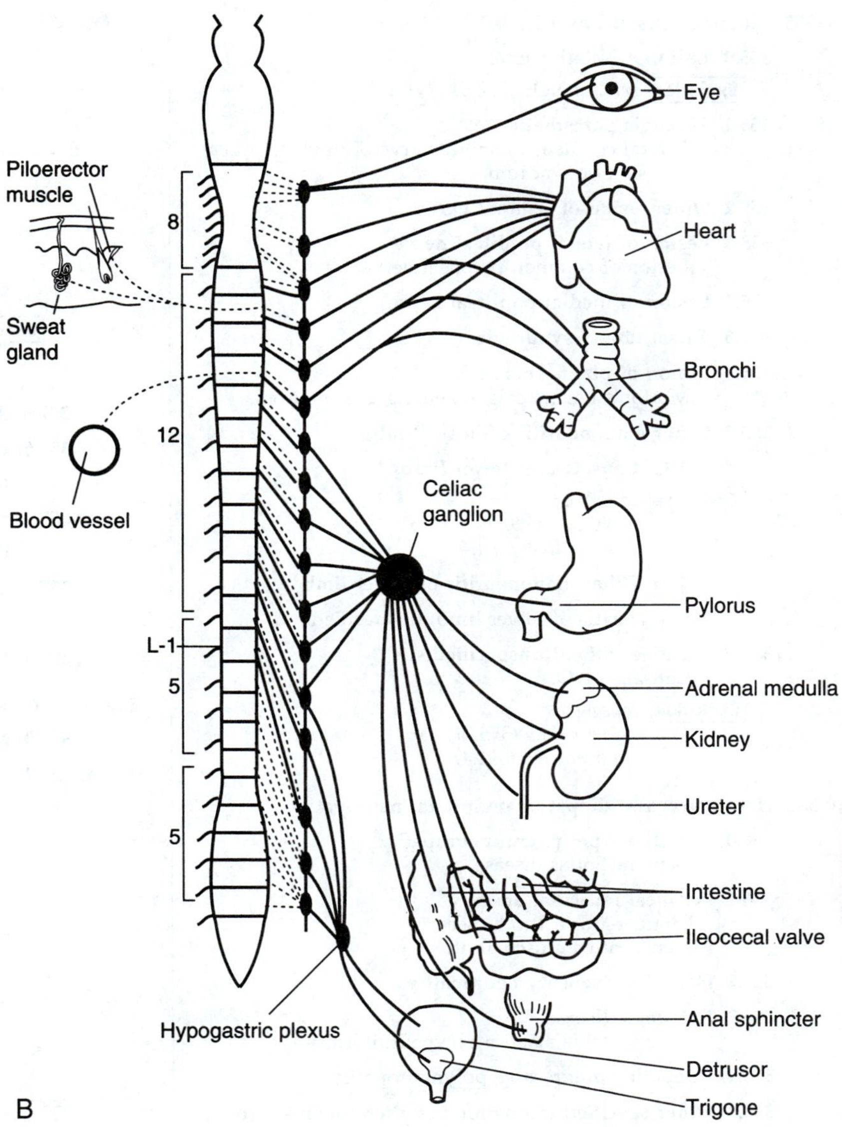

Figure 6–3 B. Sympathetic nervous system. (From Buck CJ: Step-by-Step Medical Coding, 2nd ed. Philadelphia, WB Saunders, 1998, pp 186 and 187.)

B

● 353 **Nerve root and plexus disorders**

> **Excludes** *conditions due to:*
> *intervertebral disc disorders (722.0–722.9)*
> *spondylosis (720.0–721.9)*
> *vertebrogenic disorders (723.0–724.9)*

353.0 **Brachial plexus lesions**
Cervical rib syndrome
Costoclavicular syndrome
Scalenus anticus syndrome
Thoracic outlet syndrome

> **Excludes** *brachial neuritis or radiculitis NOS (723.4)*
> *that in newborn (767.6)*

353.1 **Lumbosacral plexus lesions**

353.2 **Cervical root lesions, not elsewhere classified**

353.3 **Thoracic root lesions, not elsewhere classified**

353.4 **Lumbosacral root lesions, not elsewhere classified**

353.5 **Neuralgic amyotrophy**
Parsonage-Aldren-Turner syndrome

353.6 **Phantom limb (syndrome)**

☐ 353.8 **Other nerve root and plexus disorders**

☐ 353.9 **Unspecified nerve root and plexus disorder**

● 354 **Mononeuritis of upper limb and mononeuritis multiplex**

354.0 **Carpal tunnel syndrome**
Median nerve entrapment
Partial thenar atrophy

☐ 354.1 **Other lesion of median nerve**
Median nerve neuritis

354.2 **Lesion of ulnar nerve**
Cubital tunnel syndrome
Tardy ulnar nerve palsy

354.3 **Lesion of radial nerve**
Acute radial nerve palsy

354.4 **Causalgia of upper limb**

> **Excludes** *causalgia:*
> *NOS (355.9)*
> *lower limb (355.71)*

354.5 **Mononeuritis multiplex**
Combinations of single conditions classifiable to 354 or 355

☐ 354.8 **Other mononeuritis of upper limb**

☐ 354.9 **Mononeuritis of upper limb, unspecified**

◀▶ **New Code**   ⬅▪▪▪ ▪▪▪➡ **Revised Code**   ● **Not a Principal Diagnosis**   ● **Use Additional Digit(s)**   ☐ **Nonspecific Code**

● 355 **Mononeuritis of lower limb**

355.0 **Lesion of sciatic nerve**
Excludes *sciatica NOS (724.3)*

355.1 **Meralgia paresthetica**
Lateral cutaneous femoral nerve of thigh compression or syndrome

❏ 355.2 **Other lesion of femoral nerve**

355.3 **Lesion of lateral popliteal nerve**
Lesion of common peroneal nerve

355.4 **Lesion of medial popliteal nerve**

355.5 **Tarsal tunnel syndrome**

355.6 **Lesion of plantar nerve**
Morton's metatarsalgia, neuralgia, or neuroma

● 355.7 **Other mononeuritis of lower limb**

355.71 **Causalgia of lower limb**
Excludes *causalgia:*
NOS (355.9)
upper limb (354.4)

❏ 355.79 **Other mononeuritis of lower limb**

❏ 355.8 **Mononeuritis of lower limb, unspecified**

❏ 355.9 **Mononeuritis of unspecified site**
Causalgia NOS
Excludes *causalgia:*
lower limb (355.71)
upper limb (354.4)

● 356 **Hereditary and idiopathic peripheral neuropathy**

356.0 **Hereditary peripheral neuropathy**
Déjérine-Sottas disease

356.1 **Peroneal muscular atrophy**
Charcot-Marie-Tooth disease
Neuropathic muscular atrophy

356.2 **Hereditary sensory neuropathy**

356.3 **Refsum's disease**
Heredopathia atactica polyneuritiformis

356.4 **Idiopathic progressive polyneuropathy**

❏ 356.8 **Other specified idiopathic peripheral neuropathy**
Supranuclear paralysis

❏ 356.9 **Unspecified**

● 357 **Inflammatory and toxic neuropathy**

357.0 **Acute infective polyneuritis**
Guillain-Barre syndrome
Postinfectious polyneuritis

● 357.1 *Polyneuropathy in collagen vascular disease*

Code first underlying disease, as:
disseminated lupus erythematosus (710.0)
polyarteritis nodosa (446.0)
rheumatoid arthritis (714.0)

● 357.2 *Polyneuropathy in diabetes*

Code first underlying disease (250.6)

● 357.3 *Polyneuropathy in malignant disease*

Code first underlying disease (140.0–208.9)

●❏ 357.4 *Polyneuropathy in other diseases classified elsewhere*

Code first underlying disease, as:
amyloidosis (277.3)
beriberi (265.0)
deficiency of B vitamins (266.0–266.9)
diphtheria (032.0–032.9)
hypoglycemia (251.2)
pellagra (265.2)
porphyria (277.1)
sarcoidosis (135)
uremia (585)
Excludes *polyneuropathy in:*
herpes zoster (053.13)
mumps (072.72)

357.5 **Alcoholic polyneuropathy**

357.6 **Polyneuropathy due to drugs**
Use additional E code to identify drug

❏ 357.7 **Polyneuropathy due to other toxic agents**
Use additional E code to identify toxic agent

❏ 357.8 **Other**
Chronic inflammatory demyelinating polyneuritis ◀

❏ 357.9 **Unspecified**

● 358 **Myoneural disorders**

358.0 **Myasthenia gravis**

● 358.1 *Myasthenic syndromes in diseases classified elsewhere*
Amyotrophy from stated cause classified elsewhere
Eaton-Lambert syndrome from stated cause classified elsewhere

Code first underlying disease, as:
botulism (005.1)
diabetes mellitus (250.6)
hypothyroidism (244.0–244.9)
malignant neoplasm (140.0–208.9)
pernicious anemia (281.0)
thyrotoxicosis (242.0–242.9)

358.2 **Toxic myoneural disorders**
Use additional E code to identify toxic agent

❏ 358.8 **Other specified myoneural disorders**

❏ 358.9 **Myoneural disorders, unspecified**

● 359 **Muscular dystrophies and other myopathies**
Excludes *idiopathic polymyositis (710.4)*

359.0 **Congenital hereditary muscular dystrophy**
Benign congenital myopathy
Central core disease
Centronuclear myopathy
Myotubular myopathy
Nemaline body disease
Excludes *arthrogryposis multiplex congenita (754.89)*

359.1 **Hereditary progressive muscular dystrophy**
Muscular dystrophy:
NOS
distal
Duchenne
Erb's
fascioscapulohumeral
Gower's
Landouzy-Déjérine
limb-girdle
ocular
oculopharyngeal

   ◀▶ **New Code**   ⬅▦▦▶ **Revised Code**   ● **Not a Principal Diagnosis**   ● **Use Additional Digit(s)**   ❏ **Nonspecific Code**

359.2 Myotonic disorders
Dystrophia myotonica   Paramyotonia congenita
Eulenburg's disease   Steinert's disease
Myotonia congenita   Thomsen's disease

359.3 Familial periodic paralysis
Hypokalemic familial periodic paralysis

359.4 Toxic myopathy
Use additional E code to identify toxic agent

● *359.5 Myopathy in endocrine diseases classified elsewhere*
Code first underlying disease, as:
Addison's disease (255.4)
Cushing's syndrome (255.0)
hypopituitarism (253.2)
myxedema (244.0–244.9)
thyrotoxicosis (242.0–242.9)

● *359.6 Symptomatic inflammatory myopathy in diseases classified elsewhere*
Code first underlying disease, as:
amyloidosis (277.3)
disseminated lupus erythematosus (710.0)
malignant neoplasm (140.0–208.9)
polyarteritis nodosa (446.0)
rheumatoid arthritis (714.0)
sarcoidosis (135)
scleroderma (710.1)
Sjögren's disease (710.2)

□ **359.8 Other myopathies**

□ **359.9 Myopathy, unspecified**

DISORDERS OF THE EYE AND ADNEXA (360–379)

● **360 Disorders of the globe**
Includes: disorders affecting multiple structures of eye

● **360.0 Purulent endophthalmitis**
□ **360.00 Purulent endophthalmitis, unspecified**
360.01 Acute endophthalmitis
360.02 Panophthalmitis
360.03 Chronic endophthalmitis
360.04 Vitreous abscess

● **360.1 Other endophthalmitis**
360.11 Sympathetic uveitis
360.12 Panuveitis
360.13 Parasitic endophthalmitis NOS
360.14 Ophthalmia nodosa
□ **360.19 Other**
Phacoanaphylactic endophthalmitis

● **360.2 Degenerative disorders of globe**
□ **360.20 Degenerative disorder of globe, unspecified**
360.21 Progressive high (degenerative) myopia
Malignant myopia
360.23 Siderosis
□ **360.24 Other metallosis**
Chalcosis
□ **360.29 Other**
Excludes xerophthalmia (264.7)

● **360.3 Hypotony of eye**
□ **360.30 Hypotony, unspecified**
360.31 Primary hypotony
360.32 Ocular fistula causing hypotony
□ **360.33 Hypotony associated with other ocular disorders**

ICD-9-CM

300–399

Vol. 1

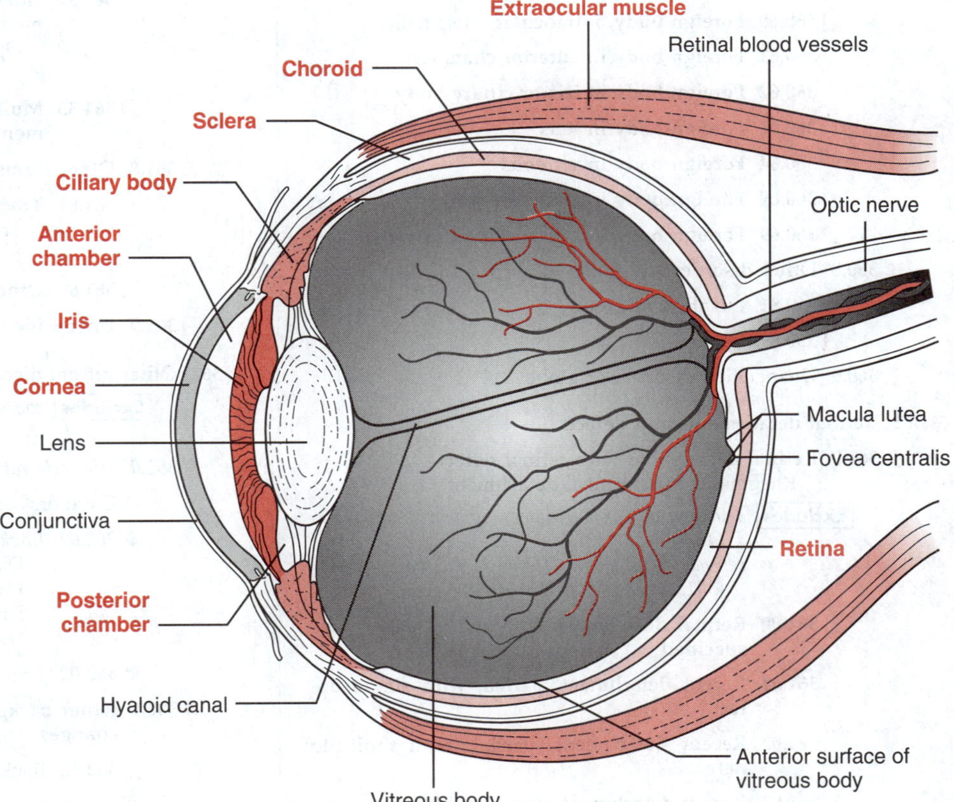

Figure 6–4 Eye and ocular adnexa. (From Buck CJ: Step-by-Step Medical Coding, 2nd ed. Philadelphia, WB Saunders, 1998, p 178.)

360.34   Flat anterior chamber

● 360.4   **Degenerated conditions of globe**

❑ 360.40   **Degenerated globe or eye, unspecified**

360.41   **Blind hypotensive eye**
Atrophy of globe   Phthisis bulbi

360.42   **Blind hypertensive eye**
Absolute glaucoma

360.43   **Hemophthalmos, except current injury**
Excludes *traumatic (871.0–871.9, 921.0–921.9)*

360.44   **Leucocoria**

● 360.5   **Retained (old) intraocular foreign body, magnetic**
Excludes *current penetrating injury with magnetic foreign body (871.5)*
retained (old) foreign body of orbit (376.6)

❑ 360.50   **Foreign body, magnetic, intraocular, unspecified**

360.51   **Foreign body, magnetic, in anterior chamber**

360.52   **Foreign body, magnetic, in iris or ciliary body**

360.53   **Foreign body, magnetic, in lens**

360.54   **Foreign body, magnetic, in vitreous**

360.55   **Foreign body, magnetic, in posterior wall**

❑ 360.59   **Foreign body, magnetic, in other or multiple sites**

● 360.6   **Retained (old) intraocular foreign body, nonmagnetic**
Retained (old) foreign body:
NOS
nonmagnetic
Excludes *current penetrating injury with (nonmagnetic) foreign body (871.6)*
retained (old) foreign body in orbit (376.6)

❑ 360.60   **Foreign body, intraocular, unspecified**

360.61   **Foreign body in anterior chamber**

360.62   **Foreign body in iris or ciliary body**

360.63   **Foreign body in lens**

360.64   **Foreign body in vitreous**

360.65   **Foreign body in posterior wall**

❑ 360.69   **Foreign body in other or multiple sites**

● 360.8   **Other disorders of globe**

360.81   **Luxation of globe**

❑ 360.89   **Other**

❑ 360.9   **Unspecified disorder of globe**

● 361   **Retinal detachments and defects**

● 361.0   **Retinal detachment with retinal defect**
Rhegmatogenous retinal detachment
Excludes *detachment of retinal pigment epithelium (362.42–362.43)*
retinal detachment (serous) (without defect) (361.2)

❑ 361.00   **Retinal detachment with retinal defect, unspecified**

361.01   **Recent detachment, partial, with single defect**

361.02   **Recent detachment, partial, with multiple defects**

361.03   **Recent detachment, partial, with giant tear**

361.04   **Recent detachment, partial, with retinal dialysis**
Dialysis (juvenile) of retina (with detachment)

361.05   **Recent detachment, total or subtotal**

361.06   **Old detachment, partial**
Delimited old retinal detachment

361.07   **Old detachment, total or subtotal**

● 361.1   **Retinoschisis and retinal cysts**
Excludes *juvenile retinoschisis (362.73)*
microcystoid degeneration of retina (362.62)
parasitic cyst of retina (360.13)

❑ 361.10   **Retinoschisis, unspecified**

361.11   **Flat retinoschisis**

361.12   **Bullous retinoschisis**

361.13   **Primary retinal cysts**

361.14   **Secondary retinal cysts**

❑ 361.19   **Other**
Pseudocyst of retina

361.2   **Serous retinal detachment**
Retinal detachment without retinal defect
Excludes *central serous retinopathy (362.41)*
retinal pigment epithelium detachment (362.42–362.43)

● 361.3   **Retinal defects without detachment**
Excludes *chorioretinal scars after surgery for detachment (363.30–363.35)*
peripheral retinal degeneration without defect (362.60–362.66)

❑ 361.30   **Retinal defect, unspecified**
Retinal break(s) NOS

361.31   **Round hole of retina without detachment**

361.32   **Horseshoe tear of retina without detachment**
Operculum of retina without mention of detachment

❑ 361.33   **Multiple defects of retina without detachment**

● 361.8   **Other forms of retinal detachment**

361.81   **Traction detachment of retina**
Traction detachment with vitreoretinal organization

❑ 361.89   **Other**

❑ 361.9   **Unspecified retinal detachment**

● 362   **Other retinal disorders**
Excludes *chorioretinal scars (363.30–363.35)*
chorioretinitis (363.0–363.2)

● 362.0   *Diabetic retinopathy*

Code first diabetes (250.5)

● 362.01   *Background diabetic retinopathy*
Diabetic macular edema
Diabetic retinal edema
Diabetic retinal microaneurysms
Diabetic retinopathy NOS

● 362.02   *Proliferative diabetic retinopathy*

● 362.1   **Other background retinopathy and retinal vascular changes**

❑ 362.10   **Background retinopathy, unspecified**

362.11   **Hypertensive retinopathy**

◀▶   **New Code**   ⬅▥▥▥➡   **Revised Code**   ●   **Not a Principal Diagnosis**   ●   **Use Additional Digit(s)**   ❑   **Nonspecific Code**

362.12 Exudative retinopathy
Coats'syndrome

362.13 Changes in vascular appearance
Vascular sheathing of retina

Use additional code for any associated atherosclerosis (440.8)

362.14 Retinal microaneurysms NOS

362.15 Retinal telangiectasia

362.16 Retinal neovascularization NOS
Neovascularization:
  choroidal
  subretinal

☐ **362.17 Other intraretinal microvascular abnormalities**
Retinal varices

362.18 Retinal vasculitis
Eales' disease
Retinal:
  arteritis
  endarteritis
  perivasculitis
  phlebitis

● **362.2 Other proliferative retinopathy**

362.21 Retrolental fibroplasia

☐ **362.29 Other nondiabetic proliferative retinopathy**

● **362.3 Retinal vascular occlusion**

☐ **362.30 Retinal vascular occlusion, unspecified**

362.31 Central retinal artery occlusion

362.32 Arterial branch occlusion

362.33 Partial arterial occlusion
Hollenhorst plaque
Retinal microembolism

362.34 Transient arterial occlusion
Amaurosis fugax

362.35 Central retinal vein occlusion

362.36 Venous tributary (branch) occlusion

362.37 Venous engorgement
Occlusion:
  of retinal vein
  incipient of retinal vein
  partial of retinal vein

● **362.4 Separation of retinal layers**
Excludes *retinal detachment (serous) (361.2)*
rhegmatogenous (361.00–361.07)

☐ **362.40 Retinal layer separation, unspecified**

362.41 Central serous retinopathy

362.42 Serous detachment of retinal pigment epithelium
Exudative detachment of retinal pigment epithelium

362.43 Hemorrhagic detachment of retinal pigment epithelium

● **362.5 Degeneration of macula and posterior pole**
Excludes *degeneration of optic disc (377.21–377.24)*
hereditary retinal degeneration [dystrophy] (362.70–362.77)

☐ **362.50 Macular degeneration (senile), unspecified**

362.51 Nonexudative senile macular degeneration
Senile macular degeneration:
  atrophic
  dry

362.52 Exudative senile macular degeneration
Kuhnt-Junius degeneration
Senile macular degeneration:
  disciform
  wet

362.53 Cystoid macular degeneration
Cystoid macular edema

362.54 Macular cyst, hole, or pseudohole

362.55 Toxic maculopathy

Use additional E code to identify drug, if drug induced

362.56 Macular puckering
Preretinal fibrosis

362.57 Drusen (degenerative)

● **362.6 Peripheral retinal degenerations**
Excludes *hereditary retinal degeneration [dystrophy] (362.70–362.77)*
retinal degeneration with retinal defect (361.00–361.07)

☐ **362.60 Peripheral retinal degeneration, unspecified**

362.61 Paving stone degeneration

362.62 Microcystoid degeneration
Blessig's cysts
Iwanoff's cysts

362.63 Lattice degeneration
Palisade degeneration of retina

362.64 Senile reticular degeneration

362.65 Secondary pigmentary degeneration
Pseudoretinitis pigmentosa

362.66 Secondary vitreoretinal degenerations

● **362.7 Hereditary retinal dystrophies**

☐ **362.70 Hereditary retinal dystrophy, unspecified**

● **362.71 *Retinal dystrophy in systemic or cerebro-retinal lipidoses***

Code first underlying disease, as:
  cerebroretinal lipidoses (330.1)
  systemic lipidoses (272.7)

●☐ **362.72 *Retinal dystrophy in other systemic disorders and syndromes***

Code first underlying disease, as:
  Bassen-Kornzweig syndrome (272.5)
  Refsum's disease (356.3)

362.73 Vitreoretinal dystrophies
Juvenile retinoschisis

362.74 Pigmentary retinal dystrophy
Retinal dystrophy, albipunctate
Retinitis pigmentosa

☐ **362.75 Other dystrophies primarily involving the sensory retina**
Progressive cone (-rod) dystrophy
Stargardt's disease

362.76 Dystrophies primarily involving the retinal pigment epithelium
Fundus flavimaculatus
Vitelliform dystrophy

362.77 Dystrophies primarily involving Bruch's membrane
Dystrophy:
  hyaline
  pseudoinflammatory foveal
Hereditary drusen

ICD-9-CM

300-399

Vol. 1

● **362.8 Other retinal disorders**

     Excludes *chorioretinal inflammations (363.0–363.2)*
                     chorioretinal scars (363.30–363.35)

     362.81 Retinal hemorrhage
         Hemorrhage:
            preretinal
            retinal (deep) (superficial)
            subretinal

     362.82 Retinal exudates and deposits

     362.83 Retinal edema
         Retinal:
            cotton wool spots
            edema (localized) (macular) (peripheral)

     362.84 Retinal ischemia

     362.85 Retinal nerve fiber bundle defects

     ❑ **362.89 Other retinal disorders**

❑ **362.9 Unspecified retinal disorder**

● **363 Chorioretinal inflammations, scars, and other disorders of choroid**

   ● **363.0 Focal chorioretinitis and focal retinochoroiditis**

     Excludes *focal chorioretinitis or retinochoroiditis in:*
        histoplasmosis (115.02, 115.12, 115.92)
        toxoplasmosis (130.2)
            congenital infection (771.2)

     ❑ **363.00 Focal chorioretinitis, unspecified**
         Focal:
            choroiditis or chorioretinitis NOS
            retinitis or retinochoroiditis NOS

     363.01 Focal choroiditis and chorioretinitis, juxtapapillary

     ❑ **363.03 Focal choroiditis and chorioretinitis of other posterior pole**

     363.04 Focal choroiditis and chorioretinitis, peripheral

     363.05 Focal retinitis and retinochoroiditis, juxtapapillary
         Neuroretinitis

     363.06 Focal retinitis and retinochoroiditis, macular or paramacular

     ❑ **363.07 Focal retinitis and retinochoroiditis of other posterior pole**

     363.08 Focal retinitis and retinochoroiditis, peripheral

   ● **363.1 Disseminated chorioretinitis and disseminated retinochoroiditis**

     Excludes *disseminated choroiditis or chorioretinitis in secondary syphilis (091.51)*
        neurosyphilitic disseminated retinitis or retinochoroiditis (094.83)
        retinal (peri)vasculitis (362.18)

     ❑ **363.10 Disseminated chorioretinitis, unspecified**
         Disseminated:
            choroiditis or chorioretinitis NOS
            retinitis or retinochoroiditis NOS

     363.11 Disseminated choroiditis and chorioretinitis, posterior pole

     363.12 Disseminated choroiditis and chorioretinitis, peripheral

     363.13 Disseminated choroiditis and chorioretinitis, generalized

         Code first any underlying disease, as:
            tuberculosis (017.3)

     363.14 Disseminated retinitis and retinochoroiditis, metastatic

     363.15 Disseminated retinitis and retinochoroiditis, pigment epitheliopathy
         Acute posterior multifocal placoid pigment epitheliopathy

   ● **363.2 Other and unspecified forms of chorioretinitis and retinochoroiditis**

     Excludes *panophthalmitis (360.02)*
        sympathetic uveitis (360.11)
        uveitis NOS (364.3)

     ❑ **363.20 Chorioretinitis, unspecified**
         Choroiditis NOS
         Retinitis NOS
         Uveitis, posterior NOS

     363.21 Pars planitis
         Posterior cyclitis

     363.22 Harada's disease

   ● **363.3 Chorioretinal scars**
         Scar (postinflammatory) (postsurgical) (posttraumatic):
         choroid
         retina

     ❑ **363.30 Chorioretinal scar, unspecified**

     363.31 Solar retinopathy

     ❑ **363.32 Other macular scars**

     ❑ **363.33 Other scars of posterior pole**

     363.34 Peripheral scars

     363.35 Disseminated scars

   ● **363.4 Choroidal degenerations**

     ❑ **363.40 Choroidal degeneration, unspecified**
         Choroidal sclerosis NOS

     363.41 Senile atrophy of choroid

     363.42 Diffuse secondary atrophy of choroid

     363.43 Angioid streaks of choroid

   ● **363.5 Hereditary choroidal dystrophies**
         Hereditary choroidal atrophy:
         partial [choriocapillaris]
         total [all vessels]

     ❑ **363.50 Hereditary choroidal dystrophy or atrophy, unspecified**

     363.51 Circumpapillary dystrophy of choroid, partial

     363.52 Circumpapillary dystrophy of choroid, total
         Helicoid dystrophy of choroid

     363.53 Central dystrophy of choroid, partial
         Dystrophy, choroidal:
            central areolar
            circinate

     363.54 Central choroidal atrophy, total
         Dystrophy, choroidal:
            central gyrate
            serpiginous

     363.55 Choroideremia

     ❑ **363.56 Other diffuse or generalized dystrophy, partial**
         Diffuse choroidal sclerosis

     ❑ **363.57 Other diffuse or generalized dystrophy, total**
         Generalized gyrate atrophy, choroid

   ● **363.6 Choroidal hemorrhage and rupture**

    ◀▶ **New Code**   ◀▥▥▶ **Revised Code**   ● **Not a Principal Diagnosis**   ● **Use Additional Digit(s)**   ❑ **Nonspecific Code**

❑ **363.61 Choroidal hemorrhage, unspecified**

363.62 Expulsive choroidal hemorrhage

363.63 Choroidal rupture

● **363.7 Choroidal detachment**

❑ **363.70 Choroidal detachment, unspecified**

363.71 Serous choroidal detachment

363.72 Hemorrhagic choroidal detachment

❑ **363.8 Other disorders of choroid**

❑ **363.9 Unspecified disorder of choroid**

● **364 Disorders of iris and ciliary body**

● **364.0 Acute and subacute iridocyclitis**
Anterior uveitis, acute, subacute
Cyclitis, acute, subacute
Iridocyclitis, acute, subacute
Iritis, acute, subacute

| **Excludes** | *gonococcal (098.41)*
herpes simplex (054.44)
herpes zoster (053.22)

❑ **364.00 Acute and subacute iridocyclitis, unspecified**

364.01 Primary iridocyclitis

364.02 Recurrent iridocyclitis

364.03 Secondary iridocyclitis, infectious

364.04 Secondary iridocyclitis, noninfectious
Aqueous:
    cells   flare
    fibrin

364.05 Hypopyon

● **364.1 Chronic iridocyclitis**

| **Excludes** | *posterior cyclitis (363.21)*

❑ **364.10 Chronic iridocyclitis, unspecified**

● *364.11 Chronic iridocyclitis in diseases classified elsewhere*

Code first underlying disease, as:
    sarcoidosis (135)
    tuberculosis (017.3)

| **Excludes** | *syphilitic iridocyclitis (091.52)*

● **364.2 Certain types of iridocyclitis**

| **Excludes** | *posterior cyclitis (363.21)*
sympathetic uveitis (360.11)

364.21 Fuchs' heterochromic cyclitis

364.22 Glaucomatocyclitic crises

364.23 Lens-induced iridocyclitis

364.24 Vogt-Koyanagi syndrome

❑ **364.3 Unspecified iridocyclitis**
Uveitis NOS

● **364.4 Vascular disorders of iris and ciliary body**

364.41 Hyphema
Hemorrhage of iris or ciliary body

364.42 Rubeosis iridis
Neovascularization of iris or ciliary body

● **364.5 Degenerations of iris and ciliary body**

364.51 Essential or progressive iris atrophy

364.52 Iridoschisis

364.53 Pigmentary iris degeneration
Acquired heterochromia of iris
Pigment dispersion syndrome of iris
Translucency of iris

364.54 Degeneration of pupillary margin
Atrophy of sphincter of iris
Ectropion of pigment epithelium of iris

364.55 Miotic cysts of pupillary margin

364.56 Degenerative changes of chamber angle

364.57 Degenerative changes of ciliary body

❑ **364.59 Other iris atrophy**
Iris atrophy (generalized) (sector shaped)

● **364.6 Cysts of iris, ciliary body, and anterior chamber**

| **Excludes** | *miotic pupillary cyst (364.55)*
parasitic cyst (360.13)

364.60 Idiopathic cysts

364.61 Implantation cysts
Epithelial down-growth, anterior chamber
Implantation cysts (surgical) (traumatic)

364.62 Exudative cysts of iris or anterior chamber

364.63 Primary cyst of pars plana

364.64 Exudative cyst of pars plana

● **364.7 Adhesions and disruptions of iris and ciliary body**

| **Excludes** | *flat anterior chamber (360.34)*

❑ **364.70 Adhesions of iris, unspecified**
Synechiae (iris) NOS

364.71 Posterior synechiae

364.72 Anterior synechiae

364.73 Goniosynechiae
Peripheral anterior synechiae

364.74 Pupillary membranes
Iris bombé
Pupillary:
    occlusion
    seclusion

364.75 Pupillary abnormalities
Deformed pupil
Ectopic pupil
Rupture of sphincter, pupil

364.76 Iridodialysis

364.77 Recession of chamber angle

❑ **364.8 Other disorders of iris and ciliary body**
Prolapse of iris NOS

| **Excludes** | *prolapse of iris in recent wound (871.1)*

❑ **364.9 Unspecified disorder of iris and ciliary body**

● **365 Glaucoma**

| **Excludes** | *hypertensive eye [absolute glaucoma] (360.42)*
congenital glaucoma (743.20–743.22)

● **365.0 Borderline glaucoma [glaucoma suspect]**

❑ **365.00 Preglaucoma, unspecified**

365.01 Open angle with borderline findings
Open angle with:
    borderline intraocular pressure
    cupping of optic discs

365.02 Anatomical narrow angle

365.03 Steroid responders

❑ **365.04 Ocular hypertension**

● **365.1 Open-angle glaucoma**

❑ **365.10 Open-angle glaucoma, unspecified**
Wide-angle glaucoma NOS

365.11 Primary open angle glaucoma
Chronic simple glaucoma

ICD-9-CM

300-399

Vol. 1

365.12   Low tension glaucoma

365.13   Pigmentary glaucoma

365.14   Glaucoma of childhood
Infantile or juvenile glaucoma

365.15   Residual stage of open angle glaucoma

● **365.2   Primary angle-closure glaucoma**

❏ **365.20   Primary angle-closure glaucoma, unspecified**

365.21   Intermittent angle-closure glaucoma
Angle-closure glaucoma:
    interval
    subacute

365.22   Acute angle-closure glaucoma

365.23   Chronic angle-closure glaucoma

365.24   Residual stage of angle-closure glaucoma

● **365.3   Corticosteroid-induced glaucoma**

365.31   Glaucomatous stage

365.32   Residual stage

● **365.4   Glaucoma associated with congenital anomalies, dystrophies, and systemic syndromes**

● *365.41   Glaucoma associated with chamber angle anomalies*

Code first associated disorder, as:
    Axenfeld's anomaly (743.44)
    Rieger's anomaly or syndrome (743.44)

● *365.42   Glaucoma associated with anomalies of iris*

Code first associated disorder, as:
    aniridia (743.45)
    essential iris atrophy (364.51)

●❏ *365.43   Glaucoma associated with other anterior segment anomalies*

Code first associated disorder, as:
    microcornea (743.41)

● *365.44   Glaucoma associated with systemic syndromes*

Code first associated disease, as:
    neurofibromatosis (237.7)
    Sturge-Weber (-Dimitri) syndrome (759.6)

● **365.5   Glaucoma associated with disorders of the lens**

365.51   Phacolytic glaucoma

Use additional code for associated hypermature cataract (366.18)

365.52   Pseudoexfoliation glaucoma

Use additional code for associated pseudoexfoliation of capsule (366.11)

❏ **365.59   Glaucoma associated with other lens disorders**

Use additional code for associated disorder, as:
    dislocation of lens (379.33–379.34)
    spherophakia (743.36)

● **365.6   Glaucoma associated with other ocular disorders**

❏ **365.60   Glaucoma associated with unspecified ocular disorder**

365.61   Glaucoma associated with pupillary block

Use additional code for associated disorder, as:
    seclusion of pupil [iris bombé] (364.74)

365.62   Glaucoma associated with ocular inflammations

Use additional code for associated disorder, as:
    glaucomatocyclitic crises (364.22)
    iridocyclitis (364.0–364.3)

365.63   Glaucoma associated with vascular disorders

Use additional code for associated disorder, as:
    central retinal vein occlusion (362.35)
    hyphema (364.41)

365.64   Glaucoma associated with tumors or cysts

Use additional code for associated disorder, as:
    benign neoplasm (224.0–224.9)
    epithelial down-growth (364.61)
    malignant neoplasm (190.0–190.9)

365.65   Glaucoma associated with ocular trauma

Use additional code for associated condition, as:
    contusion of globe (921.3)
    recession of chamber angle (364.77)

● **365.8   Other specified forms of glaucoma**

365.81   Hypersecretion glaucoma

365.82   Glaucoma with increased episcleral venous pressure

❏ **365.89   Other specified glaucoma**

❏ **365.9   Unspecified glaucoma**

● **366   Cataract**

Excludes   *congenital cataract (743.30–743.34)*

● **366.0   Infantile, juvenile, and presenile cataract**

❏ **366.00   Nonsenile cataract, unspecified**

366.01   Anterior subcapsular polar cataract

366.02   Posterior subcapsular polar cataract

366.03   Cortical, lamellar, or zonular cataract

366.04   Nuclear cataract

❏ **366.09   Other and combined forms of nonsenile cataract**

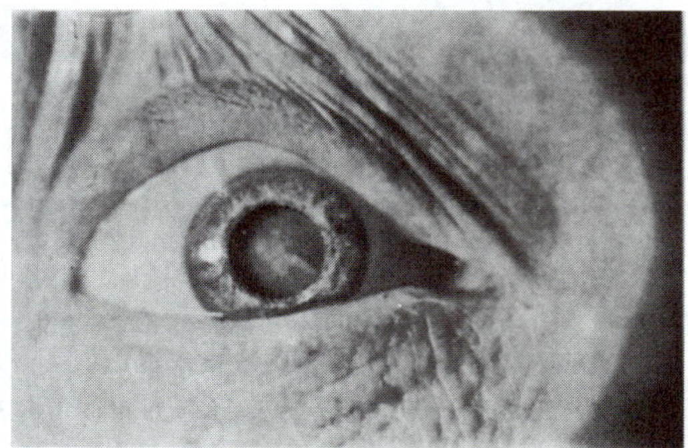

Figure 6–5   Mature cataract with gray fissures. (From Pau H: Differential Diagnosis of Eye Diseases. Philadelphia, WB Saunders, 1978, p 240.)

◀▶ **New Code**   ⬅▬ ▬➡ **Revised Code**   ● **Not a Principal Diagnosis**   ● **Use Additional Digit(s)**   ❏ **Nonspecific Code**

Item 6–7 Senile cataracts are linked to the aging process. The most common area for the formation of a cataract is the cortical area of the lens. **Polar cataracts** can be either anterior or posterior. **Anterior polar cataracts** are more common and are small, white, capsular cataracts located on the anterior portion of the lens.
Total cataracts, also called **complete** or **mature,** cause an opacity of all fibers of the lens.
Hypermature describes a mature cataract with a swollen, milky cortex that covers the entire lens.
Immature, also called **incipient,** cataracts have a clear cortex and are only slightly opaque.

● 366.1 Senile cataract

☐ 366.10 Senile cataract, unspecified

366.11 Pseudoexfoliation of lens capsule

366.12 Incipient cataract
Cataract:
coronary
immature NOS
punctate
Water clefts

366.13 Anterior subcapsular polar senile cataract

366.14 Posterior subcapsular polar senile cataract

366.15 Cortical senile cataract

366.16 Nuclear sclerosis
Cataracta brunescens
Nuclear cataract

366.17 Total or mature cataract

366.18 Hypermature cataract
Morgagni cataract

☐ 366.19 Other and combined forms of senile cataract

Item 6–8 Vossius' ring is the result of contusion-type traumatic injury and results in a ring of iris pigment pressed onto the anterior lens capsule.

● 366.2 Traumatic cataract

☐ 366.20 Traumatic cataract, unspecified

366.21 Localized traumatic opacities
Vossius' ring

366.22 Total traumatic cataract

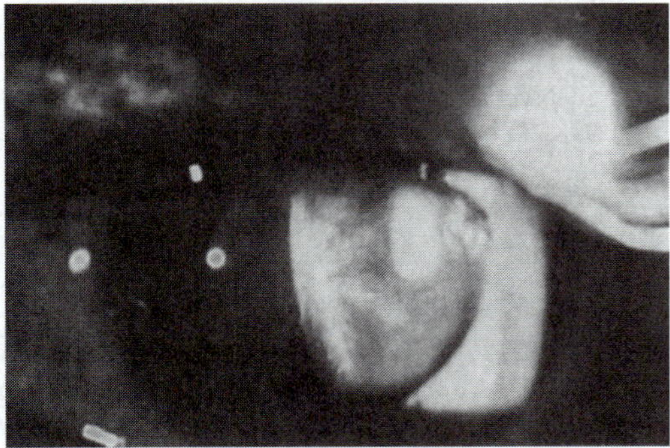

Figure 6–6 Perforation rosette of the lens; feathery opacities along suture lines beneath the posterior capsule. (From Pau H: Differential Diagnosis of Eye Diseases. Philadelphia, WB Saunders, 1978, p 250.)

366.23 Partially resolved traumatic cataract

● 366.3 Cataract secondary to ocular disorders

☐ 366.30 Cataracta complicata, unspecified

366.31 Glaucomatous flecks (subcapsular)
Code first underlying glaucoma (365.0–365.9)

366.32 Cataract in inflammatory disorders
Code first underlying condition, as:
chronic choroiditis (363.0–363.2)

366.33 Cataract with neovascularization
Code first underlying condition, as:
chronic iridocyclitis (364.10)

366.34 Cataract in degenerative disorders
Sunflower cataract
Code first underlying condition, as:
chalcosis (360.24)
degenerative myopia (360.21)
pigmentary retinal dystrophy (362.74)

● 366.4 Cataract associated with other disorders

● *366.41 Diabetic cataract*
Code first diabetes (250.5)

● *366.42 Tetanic cataract*
Code first underlying disease, as:
calcinosis (275.4)
hypoparathyroidism (252.1)

● *366.43 Myotonic cataract*
Code first underlying disorder (359.2)

●☐ *366.44 Cataract associated with other syndromes*
Code first underlying condition, as:
craniofacial dysostosis (756.0)
galactosemia (271.1)

366.45 Toxic cataract
Drug-induced cataract
Use additional E code to identify drug or other toxic substance

☐ 366.46 Cataract associated with radiation and other physical influences
Use additional E code to identify cause

● 366.5 After-cataract

☐ 366.50 After-cataract, unspecified
Secondary cataract NOS

366.51 Soemmering's ring

☐ 366.52 Other after-cataract, not obscuring vision

366.53 After-cataract, obscuring vision

☐ 366.8 Other cataract
Calcification of lens

☐ 366.9 Unspecified cataract

● 367 Disorders of refraction and accommodation

367.0 Hypermetropia
Far-sightedness
Hyperopia

367.1 Myopia
Near-sightedness

● 367.2 Astigmatism

☐ 367.20 Astigmatism, unspecified

367.21 Regular astigmatism

367.22 Irregular astigmatism

ICD-9-CM
300–399
Vol. 1

367.3 **Anisometropia and aniseikonia**

367.31 **Anisometropia**

367.32 **Aniseikonia**

367.4 **Presbyopia**

367.5 **Disorders of accommodation**

367.51 **Paresis of accommodation**
Cycloplegia

367.52 **Total or complete internal ophthalmoplegia**

367.53 **Spasm of accommodation**

367.8 **Other disorders of refraction and accommodation**

367.81 **Transient refractive change**

367.89 **Other**
Drug-induced disorders of refraction and accommodation
Toxic disorders of refraction and accommodation

367.9 **Unspecified disorder of refraction and accommodation**

368 **Visual disturbances**
Excludes *electrophysiological disturbances (794.11–794.14)*

368.0 **Amblyopia ex anopsia**

368.00 **Amblyopia, unspecified**

368.01 **Strabismic amblyopia**
Suppression amblyopia

368.02 **Deprivation amblyopia**

368.03 **Refractive amblyopia**

368.1 **Subjective visual disturbances**

368.10 **Subjective visual disturbance, unspecified**

368.11 **Sudden visual loss**

368.12 **Transient visual loss**
Concentric fading
Scintillating scotoma

368.13 **Visual discomfort**
Asthenopia
Eye strain
Photophobia

368.14 **Visual distortions of shape and size**
Macropsia
Metamorphopsia
Micropsia

368.15 **Other visual distortions and entoptic phenomena**
Photopsia
Refractive:
diplopia
polyopia
Visual halos

368.16 **Psychophysical visual disturbances**
Visual:
agnosia
disorientation syndrome
hallucinations

368.2 **Diplopia**
Double vision

368.3 **Other disorders of binocular vision**

368.30 **Binocular vision disorder, unspecified**

368.31 **Suppression of binocular vision**

368.32 **Simultaneous visual perception without fusion**

368.33 **Fusion with defective stereopsis**

368.34 **Abnormal retinal correspondence**

368.4 **Visual field defects**

368.40 **Visual field defect, unspecified**

368.41 **Scotoma involving central area**
Scotoma:
central
centrocecal
paracentral

368.42 **Scotoma of blind spot area**
Enlarged:
angioscotoma
blind spot
Paracecal scotoma

368.43 **Sector or arcuate defects**
Scotoma:
arcuate
Bjerrum
Seidel

368.44 **Other localized visual field defect**
Scotoma:
NOS
ring
Visual field defect:
nasal step
peripheral

368.45 **Generalized contraction or constriction**

368.46 **Homonymous bilateral field defects**
Hemianopsia (altitudinal) (homonymous)
Quadrant anopia

368.47 **Heteronymous bilateral field defects**
Hemianopsia:
binasal
bitemporal

368.5 **Color vision deficiencies**
Color blindness

368.51 **Protan defect**
Protanomaly
Protanopia

368.52 **Deutan defect**
Deuteranomaly
Deuteranopia

368.53 **Tritan defect**
Tritanomaly
Tritanopia

368.54 **Achromatopsia**
Monochromatism (cone) (rod)

368.55 **Acquired color vision deficiencies**

368.59 **Other color vision deficiencies**

368.6 **Night blindness**
Hemeralopia
Nyctalopia

368.60 **Night blindness, unspecified**

368.61 **Congenital night blindness**
Hereditary night blindness
Oguchi's disease

368.62 **Acquired night blindness**
Excludes *that due to vitamin A deficiency (264.5)*

368.63 **Abnormal dark adaptation curve**
Abnormal threshold of cones or rods
Delayed adaptation of cones or rods

368.69 **Other night blindness**

368.8 **Other specified visual disturbances**
Blurred vision NOS

368.9 **Unspecified visual disturbance**

      ◀▶ **New Code**   ⬅▦ ▦➡ **Revised Code**   ● **Not a Principal Diagnosis**   ⬤ **Use Additional Digit(s)**   ❑ **Nonspecific Code**

● **369 Blindness and low vision**

Excludes *correctable impaired vision due to refractive errors (367.0–367.9)*

Note: Visual impairment refers to a functional limitation of the eye (e.g., limited visual acuity or visual field). It should be distinguished from visual disability, indicating a limitation of the abilities of the individual (e.g., limited reading skills, vocational skills), and from visual handicap, indicating a limitation of personal and socioeconomic independence (e.g., limited mobility, limited employability).

The levels of impairment defined in the table after 369.9 are based on the recommendations of the WHO Study Group on Prevention of Blindness (Geneva, November 6–10, 1972; WHO Technical Report Series 518), and of the International Council of Ophthalmology (1976).

Note that definitions of blindness vary in different settings.

For international reporting, WHO defines blindness as profound impairment. This definition can be applied to blindness of one eye (369.1, 369.6) and to blindness of the individual (369.0).

For determination of benefits in the U.S.A., the definition of legal blindness as severe impairment is often used. This definition applies to blindness of the individual only.

● **369.0 Profound impairment, both eyes**

☐ **369.00 Impairment level not further specified**
Blindness:
    NOS according to WHO definition
    both eyes

369.01 Better eye: total impairment; lesser eye: total impairment

☐ **369.02 Better eye: near-total impairment; lesser eye: not further specified**

369.03 Better eye: near-total impairment; lesser eye: total impairment

369.04 Better eye: near-total impairment; lesser eye: near-total impairment

☐ **369.05 Better eye: profound impairment; lesser eye: not further specified**

369.06 Better eye: profound impairment; lesser eye: total impairment

369.07 Better eye: profound impairment; lesser eye: near-total impairment

369.08 Better eye: profound impairment; lesser eye: profound impairment

● **369.1 Moderate or severe impairment, better eye, profound impairment, lesser eye**

☐ **369.10 Impairment level not further specified**
Blindness, one eye, low vision, other eye

☐ **369.11 Better eye: severe impairment; lesser eye: blind, not further specified**

369.12 Better eye: severe impairment; lesser eye: total impairment

369.13 Better eye: severe impairment; lesser eye: near-total impairment

369.14 Better eye: severe impairment; lesser eye: profound impairment

☐ **369.15 Better eye: moderate impairment; lesser eye: blind, not further specified**

369.16 Better eye: moderate impairment; lesser eye: total impairment

369.17 Better eye: moderate impairment; lesser eye: near-total impairment

369.18 Better eye: moderate impairment; lesser eye: profound impairment

● **369.2 Moderate or severe impairment, both eyes**

☐ **369.20 Impairment level not further specified**
Low vision, both eyes NOS

☐ **369.21 Better eye: severe impairment; lesser eye: not further specified**

369.22 Better eye: severe impairment; lesser eye: severe impairment

☐ **369.23 Better eye: moderate impairment; lesser eye: not further specified**

369.24 Better eye: moderate impairment; lesser eye: severe impairment

369.25 Better eye: moderate impairment; lesser eye: moderate impairment

369.3 Unqualified visual loss, both eyes

Excludes *blindness NOS:*
legal [U.S.A. definition] (369.4)
WHO definition (369.00)

369.4 Legal blindness, as defined in U.S.A.
Blindness NOS according to U.S.A. definition

Excludes *legal blindness with specification of impairment level (369.01–369.08, 369.11–369.14, 369.21–369.22)*

● **369.6 Profound impairment, one eye**

☐ **369.60 Impairment level not further specified**
Blindness, one eye

☐ **369.61 One eye: total impairment; other eye: not specified**

369.62 One eye: total impairment; other eye: near-normal vision

369.63 One eye: total impairment; other eye: normal vision

☐ **369.64 One eye: near-total impairment; other eye: not specified**

369.65 One eye: near-total impairment; other eye: near-normal vision

369.66 One eye: near-total impairment; other eye: normal vision

☐ **369.67 One eye: profound impairment; other eye: not specified**

369.68 One eye: profound impairment; other eye: near-normal vision

369.69 One eye: profound impairment; other eye: normal vision

● **369.7 Moderate or severe impairment, one eye**

☐ **369.70 Impairment level not further specified**
Low vision, one eye

☐ **369.71 One eye: severe impairment; other eye: not specified**

369.72 One eye: severe impairment; other eye: near-normal vision

369.73 One eye: severe impairment; other eye: normal vision

☐ **369.74 One eye: moderate impairment; other eye: not specified**

369.75 One eye: moderate impairment; other eye: near-normal vision

ICD-9-CM

300-399

Vol. 1

369.76 One eye: moderate impairment; other eye: normal vision

369.8 Unqualified visual loss, one eye

☐ 369.9 Unspecified visual loss

Classification		Levels of Visual Impairment	Additional Descriptors Which May Be Encountered
"Legal"	WHO	Visual Acuity and/or Visual Field Limitation (Whichever Is Worse)	
	(Near-) normal vision	Range of Normal Vision 20/10 20/13 20/16 20/20 20/25 2.0 1.6 1.25 1.0 0.8	
		Near-Normal Vision 20/30 20/40 20/50 20/60 0.7 0.6 0.5 0.4 0.3	
	Low vision	Moderate Visual Impairment 20/70 20/80 20/100 20/125 20/160 0.25 0.20 0.16 0.12	Moderate low vision
Legal Blindness (U.S.A.) both eyes	Blindness (WHO) one or both eyes	Severe Visual Impairment 20/200 20/250 20/320 20/400 0.10 0.08 0.06 0.05 Visual field: 20 degrees or less	Severe low vision, "Legal" blindness
		Profound Visual Impairment 20/500 20/630 20/800 20/1000 0.04 0.03 0.025 0.02 Count fingers at: less than 3 m (10 ft) Visual field: 10 degrees or less	Profound low vision, Moderate blindness
		Near-Total Visual Impairment Visual acuity: less than 0.02 (20/1000) Count fingers: 1 m (3 ft) or less Hand movements: 5 m (15 ft) or less Light projection, light perception Visual field: 5 degrees or less	Severe blindness, Near-total blindness
		Total Visual Impairment No light perception (NLP)	Total blindness

Visual acuity refers to best achievable acuity with correction.
Non-listed Snellen fractions may be classified by converting to the nearest
  decimal equivalent, e.g., 10/200 = 0.05, 6/30 = 0.20.
CF (count fingers) without designation of distance, may be classified to
  profound impairment.
HM (hand motion) without designation of distance, may be classified to near-
  total impairment.
Visual field measurements refer to the largest field diameter for a 1/100
  white test object.

Item 6–9 An infected ulcer is usually called a **serpiginous** or **hypopyon** ulcer which is a pus sac in the anterior chamber of the eye.
Marginal ulcers are usually asymptomatic, not primary, and are often superficial and simple. More severe marginal ulcers spread to form a ring ulcer. **Ring** ulcers can extend around the entire corneal periphery.
Central corneal ulcers develop when there is an abrasion to the epithelium and an infection develops in the eroded area.
The **pyocyaneal** ulcer is the most serious corneal infection, which, if left untreated, can lead to loss of the eye.

● **370 Keratitis**

● **370.0 Corneal ulcer**

  Excludes *that due to vitamin A deficiency (264.3)*

  ☐ **370.00 Corneal ulcer, unspecified**

  370.01 Marginal corneal ulcer

  370.02 Ring corneal ulcer

  370.03 Central corneal ulcer

  370.04 Hypopyon ulcer
       Serpiginous ulcer

  370.05 Mycotic corneal ulcer

  370.06 Perforated corneal ulcer

  370.07 Mooren's ulcer

● **370.2 Superficial keratitis without conjunctivitis**

  Excludes *dendritic [herpes simplex] keratitis (054.42)*

  ☐ **370.20 Superficial keratitis, unspecified**

  370.21 Punctate keratitis
       Thygeson's superficial punctate keratitis

  370.22 Macular keratitis
       Keratitis:
          areolar
          nummular
          stellate
          striate

  370.23 Filamentary keratitis

  370.24 Photokeratitis
       Snow blindness
       Welders' keratitis

● **370.3 Certain types of keratoconjunctivitis**

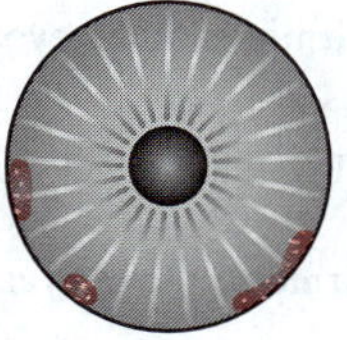
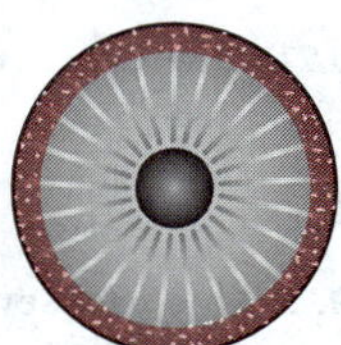
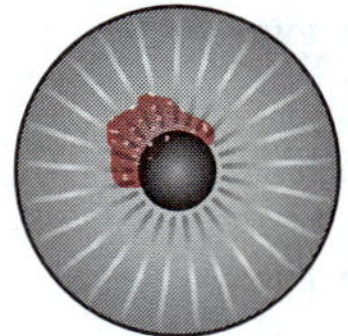
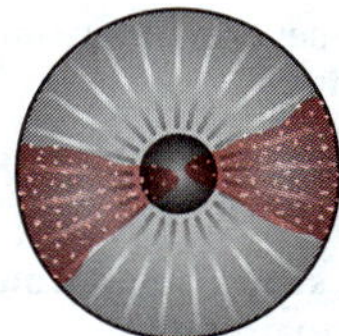
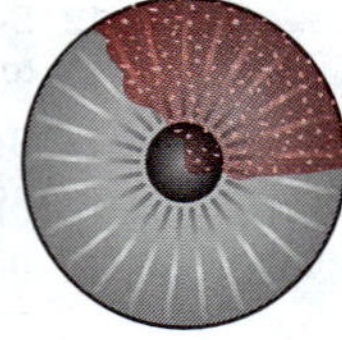

Figure 6–7 Corneal ulcers: marginal, ring, central corneal, rosacea, and Mooren's.

370.31   Phlyctenular keratoconjunctivitis
Phlyctenulosis

Use additional code for any associated tuberculosis (017.3)

370.32   Limbal and corneal involvement in vernal conjunctivitis

Use additional code for vernal conjunctivitis (372.13)

370.33   Keratoconjunctivitis sicca, not specified as Sjögren's
Excludes   *Sjögren's syndrome (710.2)*

370.34   Exposure keratoconjunctivitis

370.35   Neurotrophic keratoconjunctivitis

370.4   Other and unspecified keratoconjunctivitis

370.40   Keratoconjunctivitis, unspecified
Superficial keratitis with conjunctivitis NOS

370.44   *Keratitis or keratoconjunctivitis in exanthema*

Code first underlying condition (050.0–052.9)
Excludes   *herpes simplex (054.43)*
herpes zoster (053.21)
measles (055.71)

370.49   Other
Excludes   *epidemic keratoconjunctivitis (077.1)*

370.5   Interstitial and deep keratitis

370.50   Interstitial keratitis, unspecified

370.52   Diffuse interstitial keratitis
Cogan's syndrome

370.54   Sclerosing keratitis

370.55   Corneal abscess

370.59   Other
Excludes   *disciform herpes simplex keratitis (054.43)*
syphilitic keratitis (090.3)

370.6   Corneal neovascularization

370.60   Corneal neovascularization, unspecified

370.61   Localized vascularization of cornea

370.62   Pannus (corneal)

370.63   Deep vascularization of cornea

370.64   Ghost vessels (corneal)

370.8   Other forms of keratitis

370.9   Unspecified keratitis

371   Corneal opacity and other disorders of cornea

371.0   Corneal scars and opacities
Excludes   *that due to vitamin A deficiency (264.6)*

371.00   Corneal opacity, unspecified
Corneal scar NOS

371.01   Minor opacity of cornea
Corneal nebula

371.02   Peripheral opacity of cornea
Corneal macula not interfering with central vision

371.03   Central opacity of cornea
Corneal:
leucoma interfering with central vision
macula interfering with central vision

371.04   Adherent leucoma

371.05   *Phthisical cornea*

Code first underlying tuberculosis (017.3)

371.1   Corneal pigmentations and deposits

371.10   Corneal deposit, unspecified

371.11   Anterior pigmentations
Stähli's lines

371.12   Stromal pigmentations
Hematocornea

371.13   Posterior pigmentations
Krukenberg spindle

371.14   Kayser-Fleischer ring

371.15   Other deposits associated with metabolic disorders

371.16   Argentous deposits

371.2   Corneal edema

371.20   Corneal edema, unspecified

371.21   Idiopathic corneal edema

371.22   Secondary corneal edema

371.23   Bullous keratopathy

371.24   Corneal edema due to wearing of contact lenses

371.3   Changes of corneal membranes

371.30   Corneal membrane change, unspecified

371.31   Folds and rupture of Bowman's membrane

371.32   Folds in Descemet's membrane

371.33   Rupture in Descemet's membrane

371.4   Corneal degenerations

371.40   Corneal degeneration, unspecified

371.41   Senile corneal changes
Arcus senilis   Hassall-Henle bodies

371.42   Recurrent erosion of cornea
Excludes   *Mooren's ulcer (370.07)*

371.43   Band-shaped keratopathy

371.44   Other calcerous degenerations of cornea

371.45   Keratomalacia NOS
Excludes   *that due to vitamin A deficiency (264.4)*

371.46   Nodular degeneration of cornea
Salzmann's nodular dystrophy

371.48   Peripheral degenerations of cornea
Marginal degeneration of cornea [Terrien's]

371.49   Other
Discrete colliquative keratopathy

371.5   Hereditary corneal dystrophies

371.50   Corneal dystrophy, unspecified

371.51   Juvenile epithelial corneal dystrophy

371.52   Other anterior corneal dystrophies
Corneal dystrophy:
microscopic cystic
ring-like

371.53   Granular corneal dystrophy

371.54   Lattice corneal dystrophy

371.55   Macular corneal dystrophy

371.56   Other stromal corneal dystrophies
Crystalline corneal dystrophy

371.57   Endothelial corneal dystrophy
Combined corneal dystrophy
Cornea guttata
Fuchs' endothelial dystrophy

ICD-9-CM
300-399
Vol. 1

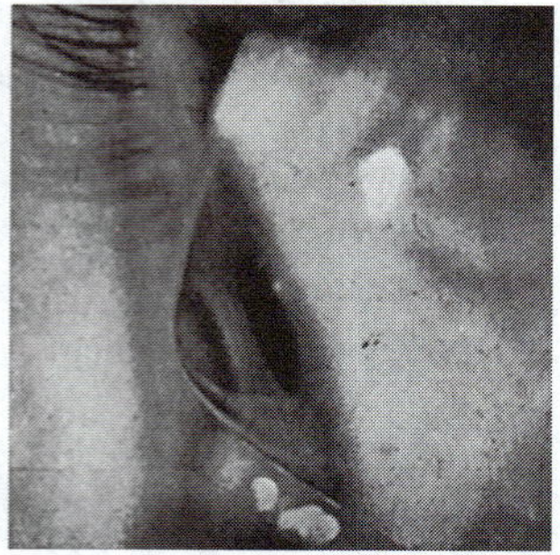

Figure 6–8   Keratoconus. (From Adler FH: Textbook of Ophthalmology, 7th ed. Philadelphia, WB Saunders, 1962, p 223.)

Item 6–10   Keratoconus is corneal degeneration that begins in childhood and gradually forms a cone at the apex of the eye even though the intraocular pressure is normal. The apex of the cornea becomes increasingly thin and can rupture, resulting in scarring.

☐ **371.58**   **Other posterior corneal dystrophies**
Polymorphous corneal dystrophy

● **371.6**   **Keratoconus**

☐ **371.60**   **Keratoconus, unspecified**

    371.61   **Keratoconus, stable condition**

    371.62   **Keratoconus, acute hydrops**

● **371.7**   **Other corneal deformities**

☐ **371.70**   **Corneal deformity, unspecified**

    371.71   **Corneal ectasia**

    371.72   **Descemetocele**

    371.73   **Corneal staphyloma**

☐ ● **371.8**   **Other corneal disorders**

    371.81   **Corneal anesthesia and hypoesthesia**

    371.82   **Corneal disorder due to contact lens**

    Excludes   *corneal edema due to contact lens (371.24)*

☐ **371.89**   **Other**

☐ **371.9**   **Unspecified corneal disorder**

● **372**   **Disorders of conjunctiva**

    Excludes   *keratoconjunctivitis (370.3–370.4)*

● **372.0**   **Acute conjunctivitis**

☐ **372.00**   **Acute conjunctivitis, unspecified**

    372.01   **Serous conjunctivitis, except viral**

    Excludes   *viral conjunctivitis NOS (077.9)*

    372.02   **Acute follicular conjunctivitis**
Conjunctival folliculosis NOS

    Excludes   *conjunctivitis:*
adenoviral (acute follicular) (077.3)
epidemic hemorrhagic (077.4)
inclusion (077.0)
Newcastle (077.8)
epidemic keratoconjunctivitis (077.1)
pharyngoconjunctival fever (077.2)

☐ **372.03**   **Other mucopurulent conjunctivitis**
Catarrhal conjunctivitis

    Excludes   *blennorrhea neonatorum (gonococcal) (098.40)*
neonatal conjunctivitis (771.6)
ophthalmia neonatorum NOS (771.6)

    372.04   **Pseudomembranous conjunctivitis**
Membranous conjunctivitis

    Excludes   *diphtheritic conjunctivitis (032.81)*

    372.05   **Acute atopic conjunctivitis**

● **372.1**   **Chronic conjunctivitis**

☐ **372.10**   **Chronic conjunctivitis, unspecified**

    372.11   **Simple chronic conjunctivitis**

    372.12   **Chronic follicular conjunctivitis**

    372.13   **Vernal conjunctivitis**

☐ **372.14**   **Other chronic allergic conjunctivitis**

● **372.15**   *Parasitic conjunctivitis*

    Code first underlying disease, as:
filariasis (125.0–125.9)
mucocutaneous leishmaniasis (085.5)

● **372.2**   **Blepharoconjunctivitis**

☐ **372.20**   **Blepharoconjunctivitis, unspecified**

    372.21   **Angular blepharoconjunctivitis**

    372.22   **Contact blepharoconjunctivitis**

● **372.3**   **Other and unspecified conjunctivitis**

☐ **372.30**   **Conjunctivitis, unspecified**

● **372.31**   *Rosacea conjunctivitis*

    Code first underlying rosacea dermatitis (695.3)

● **372.33**   *Conjunctivitis in mucocutaneous disease*

    Code first underlying disease, as:
erythema multiforme (695.1)
Reiter's disease (099.3)

    Excludes   *ocular pemphigoid (694.61)*

☐ **372.39**   **Other**

● **372.4**   **Pterygium**

    Excludes   *pseudopterygium (372.52)*

☐ **372.40**   **Pterygium, unspecified**

    372.41   **Peripheral pterygium, stationary**

    372.42   **Peripheral pterygium, progressive**

    372.43   **Central pterygium**

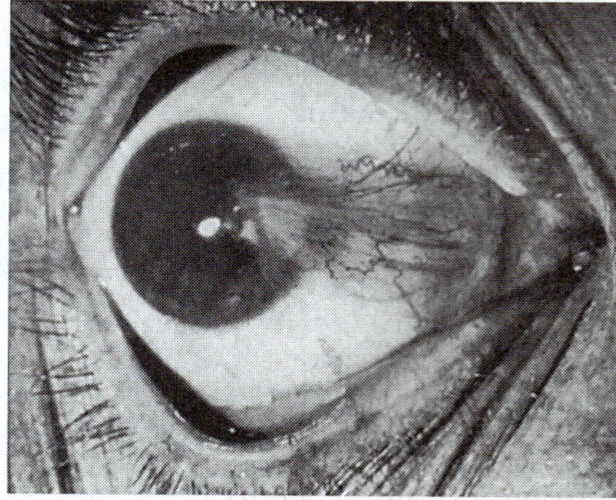

Figure 6–9   Pterygium. (From Adler FH: Textbook of Ophthalmology, 7th ed. Philadelphia, WB Saunders, 1962, p 194.)

Item 6–11   Pterygium is Greek for batlike. The condition is characterized by a membrane that extends from the limbus to the center of the cornea and resembles a wing.

    ◀▶ **New Code**   ⬅▭➡ **Revised Code**   ● **Not a Principal Diagnosis**   ● **Use Additional Digit(s)**   ☐ **Nonspecific Code**

372.44   Double pterygium

372.45   Recurrent pterygium

● **372.5**   Conjunctival degenerations and deposits

☐ **372.50**   Conjunctival degeneration, unspecified

372.51   Pinguecula

372.52   Pseudopterygium

372.53   Conjunctival xerosis

> **Excludes** *conjunctival xerosis due to vitamin A deficiency (264.0, 264.1, 264.7)*

372.54   Conjunctival concretions

372.55   Conjunctival pigmentations
Conjunctival argyrosis

372.56   Conjunctival deposits

● **372.6**   Conjunctival scars

372.61   Granuloma of conjunctiva

372.62   Localized adhesions and strands of conjunctiva

372.63   Symblepharon
Extensive adhesions of conjunctiva

372.64   Scarring of conjunctiva
Contraction of eye socket (after enucleation)

● **372.7**   Conjunctival vascular disorders and cysts

372.71   Hyperemia of conjunctiva

372.72   Conjunctival hemorrhage
Hyposphagma
Subconjunctival hemorrhage

372.73   Conjunctival edema
Chemosis of conjunctiva
Subconjunctival edema

372.74   Vascular abnormalities of conjunctiva
Aneurysm(ata) of conjunctiva

372.75   Conjunctival cysts

☐ **372.8**   Other disorders of conjunctiva

☐ **372.9**   Unspecified disorder of conjunctiva

Item 6-12 Blepharitis is a common condition in which the lid is swollen and yellow scaling and conjunctivitis develop. Usually the hair on the scalp and brow is involved.

● **373**   Inflammation of eyelids

● **373.0**   Blepharitis

> **Excludes** *blepharoconjunctivitis (372.20–372.22)*

☐ **373.00**   Blepharitis, unspecified

373.01   Ulcerative blepharitis

373.02   Squamous blepharitis

● **373.1**   Hordeolum and other deep inflammation of eyelid

373.11   Hordeolum externum
Hordeolum NOS
Stye

373.12   Hordeolum internum
Infection of meibomian gland

373.13   Abscess of eyelid
Furuncle of eyelid

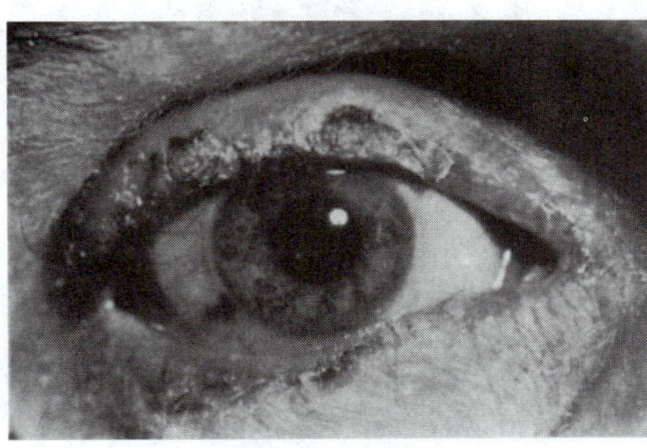

Figure 6–10   Ulcerating blepharitis caused by a staphylococcal infection. (From Pau H: Differential Diagnosis of Eye Diseases. Philadelphia, WB Saunders, 1978, p 106.)

Item 6-13 Hordeolum is the inflammation of the sebaceous gland of the eyelid.

373.2   Chalazion
Meibomian (gland) cyst

> **Excludes** *infected meibomian gland (373.12)*

● **373.3**   Noninfectious dermatoses of eyelid

373.31   Eczematous dermatitis of eyelid

373.32   Contact and allergic dermatitis of eyelid

373.33   Xeroderma of eyelid

373.34   Discoid lupus erythematosus of eyelid

● **373.4**   *Infective dermatitis of eyelid of types resulting in deformity*

Code first underlying disease, as:
leprosy (030.0–030.9)
lupus vulgaris (tuberculous) (017.0)
yaws (102.0–102.9)

●☐ **373.5**   *Other infective dermatitis of eyelid*

Code first underlying disease, as:
actinomycosis (039.3)
impetigo (684)
mycotic dermatitis (110.0–111.9)
vaccinia (051.0)
postvaccination (999.0)

> **Excludes** *herpes:*
> *simplex (054.41)*
> *zoster (053.20)*

● **373.6**   *Parasitic infestation of eyelid*

Code first underlying disease, as:
leishmaniasis (085.0–085.9)
loiasis (125.2)
onchocerciasis (125.3)
pediculosis (132.0)

☐ **373.8**   Other inflammations of eyelids

☐ **373.9**   Unspecified inflammation of eyelid

● **374**   Other disorders of eyelids

● **374.0**   Entropion and trichiasis of eyelid

☐ **374.00**   Entropion, unspecified

374.01   Senile entropion

374.02   Mechanical entropion

374.03   Spastic entropion

374.04   Cicatricial entropion

374.05   Trichiasis without entropion

ICD-9-CM

300-399

Vol. 1

● **374.1 Ectropion**

  ☐ **374.10 Ectropion, unspecified**

  374.11 Senile ectropion

  374.12 Mechanical ectropion

  374.13 Spastic ectropion

  374.14 Cicatricial ectropion

● **374.2 Lagophthalmos**

  ☐ **374.20 Lagophthalmos, unspecified**

  374.21 Paralytic lagophthalmos

  374.22 Mechanical lagophthalmos

  374.23 Cicatricial lagophthalmos

● **374.3 Ptosis of eyelid**

  ☐ **374.30 Ptosis of eyelid, unspecified**

  374.31 Paralytic ptosis

  374.32 Myogenic ptosis

  374.33 Mechanical ptosis

  374.34 Blepharochalasis
      Pseudoptosis

● **374.4 Other disorders affecting eyelid function**

  | Excludes | *blepharoclonus (333.81)* |
  blepharospasm (333.81)
  facial nerve palsy (351.0)
  third nerve palsy or paralysis (378.51–378.52)
  tic (psychogenic) (307.20–307.23)
    organic (333.3)

  374.41 Lid retraction or lag

  374.43 Abnormal innervation syndrome
      Jaw-blinking
      Paradoxical facial movements

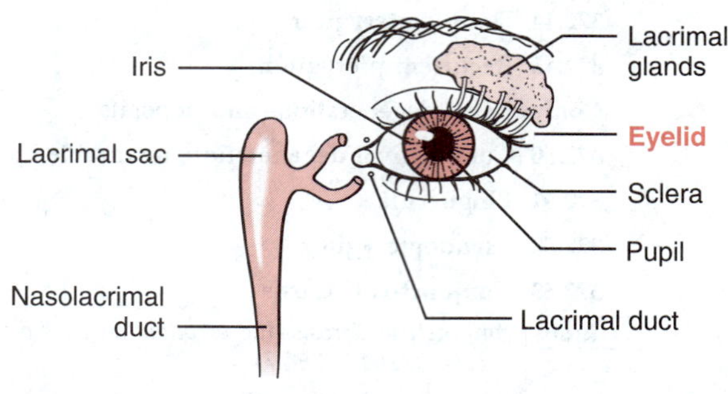

Figure 6–12   Lacrimal apparatus. (From Buck CJ: Step-by-Step Medical Coding, 2nd ed. Philadelphia, WB Saunders, 1998, p 179.)

  374.44 Sensory disorders

  ☐ **374.45 Other sensorimotor disorders**
      Deficient blink reflex

  374.46 Blepharophimosis
      Ankyloblepharon

● **374.5 Degenerative disorders of eyelid and periocular area**

  ☐ **374.50 Degenerative disorder of eyelid, unspecified**

  374.51 Xanthelasma
      Xanthoma (planum) (tuberosum) of eyelid

      Code first underlying condition (272.0–272.9)

  374.52 Hyperpigmentation of eyelid
      Chloasma
      Dyspigmentation

  374.53 Hypopigmentation of eyelid
      Vitiligo of eyelid

  374.54 Hypertrichosis of eyelid

  374.55 Hypotrichosis of eyelid
      Madarosis of eyelid

  ☐ **374.56 Other degenerative disorders of skin affecting eyelid**

● **374.8 Other disorders of eyelid**

  374.81 Hemorrhage of eyelid

  | Excludes | *black eye (921.0)* |

  374.82 Edema of eyelid
      Hyperemia of eyelid

  374.83 Elephantiasis of eyelid

  374.84 Cysts of eyelids
      Sebaceous cyst of eyelid

  374.85 Vascular anomalies of eyelid

  374.86 Retained foreign body of eyelid

  374.87 Dermatochalasis

  ☐ **374.89 Other disorders of eyelid**

☐ **374.9 Unspecified disorder of eyelid**

● **375 Disorders of lacrimal system**

● **375.0 Dacryoadenitis**

  ☐ **375.00 Dacryoadenitis, unspecified**

  375.01 Acute dacryoadenitis

  375.02 Chronic dacryoadenitis

  375.03 Chronic enlargement of lacrimal gland

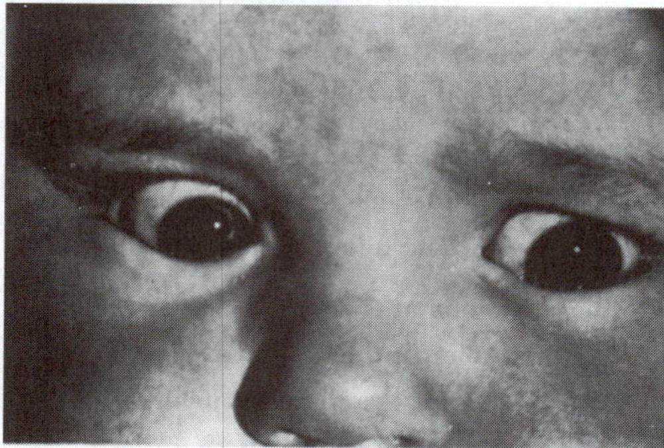

Figure 6–11   **A.** A 72-year-old male with senile ectropion on the left and postsurgical correction on the right. **B.** Entropion in a 6-month-old male infant. (From Pau H: Differential Diagnosis of Eye Diseases. Philadelphia, WB Saunders, 1978, p 90.)

    ◄► **New Code**   ◄▬▬▶ **Revised Code**   ● **Not a Principal Diagnosis**   ● **Use Additional Digit(s)**   ☐ **Nonspecific Code**

● **375.1 Other disorders of lacrimal gland**

   ☐ **375.11 Dacryops**

   ☐ **375.12 Other lacrimal cysts and cystic degeneration**

   375.13 Primary lacrimal atrophy

   375.14 Secondary lacrimal atrophy

   ☐ **375.15 Tear film insufficiency, unspecified**
       Dry eye syndrome

   375.16 Dislocation of lacrimal gland

● **375.2 Epiphora**

   ☐ **375.20 Epiphora, unspecified as to cause**

   375.21 Epiphora due to excess lacrimation

   375.22 Epiphora due to insufficient drainage

● **375.3 Acute and unspecified inflammation of lacrimal passages**

    Excludes *neonatal dacryocystitis (771.6)*

   ☐ **375.30 Dacryocystitis, unspecified**

   375.31 Acute canaliculitis, lacrimal

   375.32 Acute dacryocystitis
       Acute peridacryocystitis

   375.33 Phlegmonous dacryocystitis

● **375.4 Chronic inflammation of lacrimal passages**

   375.41 Chronic canaliculitis

   375.42 Chronic dacryocystitis

   375.43 Lacrimal mucocele

● **375.5 Stenosis and insufficiency of lacrimal passages**

   375.51 Eversion of lacrimal punctum

   375.52 Stenosis of lacrimal punctum

   375.53 Stenosis of lacrimal canaliculi

   375.54 Stenosis of lacrimal sac

   375.55 Obstruction of nasolacrimal duct, neonatal

    Excludes *congenital anomaly of nasolacrimal duct (743.65)*

   375.56 Stenosis of nasolacrimal duct, acquired

   375.57 Dacryolith

● **375.6 Other changes of lacrimal passages**

   375.61 Lacrimal fistula

   ☐ **375.69 Other**

● **375.8 Other disorders of lacrimal system**

   375.81 Granuloma of lacrimal passages

   ☐ **375.89 Other**

☐ **375.9 Unspecified disorder of lacrimal system**

● **376 Disorders of the orbit**

● **376.0 Acute inflammation of orbit**

   ☐ **376.00 Acute inflammation of orbit, unspecified**

   376.01 Orbital cellulitis
       Abscess of orbit

   376.02 Orbital periostitis

   376.03 Orbital osteomyelitis

   376.04 Tenonitis

● **376.1 Chronic inflammatory disorders of orbit**

   ☐ **376.10 Chronic inflammation of orbit, unspecified**

   376.11 Orbital granuloma
       Pseudotumor (inflammatory) of orbit

376.12 Orbital myositis

● **376.13 *Parasitic infestation of orbit***

    Code first underlying disease, as:
       hydatid infestation of orbit (122.3, 122.6, 122.9)
       myiasis of orbit (134.0)

● **376.2 *Endocrine exophthalmos***

    Code first underlying thyroid disorder (242.0–242.9)

   ● **376.21 *Thyrotoxic exophthalmos***

   ● **376.22 *Exophthalmic ophthalmoplegia***

● **376.3 Other exophthalmic conditions**

   ☐ **376.30 Exophthalmos, unspecified**

   376.31 Constant exophthalmos

   376.32 Orbital hemorrhage

   376.33 Orbital edema or congestion

   376.34 Intermittent exophthalmos

   376.35 Pulsating exophthalmos

   376.36 Lateral displacement of globe

● **376.4 Deformity of orbit**

   ☐ **376.40 Deformity of orbit, unspecified**

   376.41 Hypertelorism of orbit

   376.42 Exostosis of orbit

   376.43 Local deformities due to bone disease

   376.44 Orbital deformities associated with craniofacial deformities

   376.45 Atrophy of orbit

   376.46 Enlargement of orbit

   376.47 Deformity due to trauma or surgery

● **376.5 Enophthalmos**

   ☐ **376.50 Enophthalmos, unspecified as to cause**

   376.51 Enophthalmos due to atrophy of orbital tissue

   376.52 Enophthalmos due to trauma or surgery

376.6 Retained (old) foreign body following penetrating wound of orbit
       Retrobulbar foreign body

● **376.8 Other orbital disorders**

   376.81 Orbital cysts
       Encephalocele of orbit

   376.82 Myopathy of extraocular muscles

   ☐ **376.89 Other**

☐ **376.9 Unspecified disorder of orbit**

● **377 Disorders of optic nerve and visual pathways**

● **377.0 Papilledema**

   ☐ **377.00 Papilledema, unspecified**

   377.01 Papilledema associated with increased intracranial pressure

   377.02 Papilledema associated with decreased ocular pressure

   377.03 Papilledema associated with retinal disorder

   377.04 Foster-Kennedy syndrome

● **377.1 Optic atrophy**

   ☐ **377.10 Optic atrophy, unspecified**

   377.11 Primary optic atrophy

    Excludes *neurosyphilitic optic atrophy (094.84)*

ICD-9-CM

300-399

Vol. 1

377.12 **Postinflammatory optic atrophy**

377.13 **Optic atrophy associated with retinal dystrophies**

377.14 **Glaucomatous atrophy [cupping] of optic disc**

377.15 **Partial optic atrophy**
Temporal pallor of optic disc

377.16 **Hereditary optic atrophy**
Optic atrophy:
    dominant hereditary
    Leber's

● 377.2 **Other disorders of optic disc**

377.21 **Drusen of optic disc**

377.22 **Crater-like holes of optic disc**

377.23 **Coloboma of optic disc**

377.24 **Pseudopapilledema**

● 377.3 **Optic neuritis**

| **Excludes** | *meningococcal optic neuritis (036.81)* |

❑ 377.30 **Optic neuritis, unspecified**

377.31 **Optic papillitis**

377.32 **Retrobulbar neuritis (acute)**

| **Excludes** | *syphilitic retrobulbar neuritis (094.85)* |

377.33 **Nutritional optic neuropathy**

377.34 **Toxic optic neuropathy**
Toxic amblyopia

❑ 377.39 **Other**

| **Excludes** | *ischemic optic neuropathy (377.41)* |

● 377.4 **Other disorders of optic nerve**

377.41 **Ischemic optic neuropathy**

377.42 **Hemorrhage in optic nerve sheaths**

❑ 377.49 **Other**
Compression of optic nerve

● 377.5 **Disorders of optic chiasm**

377.51 **Associated with pituitary neoplasms and disorders**

❑ 377.52 **Associated with other neoplasms**

377.53 **Associated with vascular disorders**

377.54 **Associated with inflammatory disorders**

● 377.6 **Disorders of other visual pathways**

377.61 **Associated with neoplasms**

377.62 **Associated with vascular disorders**

377.63 **Associated with inflammatory disorders**

● 377.7 **Disorders of visual cortex**

Excludes	*visual:*
	agnosia (368.16)
	hallucinations (368.16)
	halos (368.15)

377.71 **Associated with neoplasms**

377.72 **Associated with vascular disorders**

377.73 **Associated with inflammatory disorders**

377.75 **Cortical blindness**

❑ 377.9 **Unspecified disorder of optic nerve and visual pathways**

● 378 **Strabismus and other disorders of binocular eye movements**

| **Excludes** | *nystagmus and other irregular eye movements (379.50–379.59)* |

● 378.0 **Esotropia**
Convergent concomitant strabismus

| **Excludes** | *intermittent esotropia (378.20–378.22)* |

❑ 378.00 **Esotropia, unspecified**

378.01 **Monocular esotropia**

378.02 **Monocular esotropia with A pattern**

378.03 **Monocular esotropia with V pattern**

❑ 378.04 **Monocular esotropia with other noncomitancies**
Monocular esotropia with X or Y pattern

378.05 **Alternating esotropia**

378.06 **Alternating esotropia with A pattern**

378.07 **Alternating esotropia with V pattern**

❑ 378.08 **Alternating esotropia with other noncomitancies**
Alternating esotropia with X or Y pattern

● 378.1 **Exotropia**
Divergent concomitant strabismus

| **Excludes** | *intermittent exotropia (378.20, 378.23–378.24)* |

❑ 378.10 **Exotropia, unspecified**

378.11 **Monocular exotropia**

378.12 **Monocular exotropia with A pattern**

378.13 **Monocular exotropia with V pattern**

❑ 378.14 **Monocular exotropia with other noncomitancies**
Monocular exotropia with X or Y pattern

378.15 **Alternating exotropia**

378.16 **Alternating exotropia with A pattern**

378.17 **Alternating exotropia with V pattern**

❑ 378.18 **Alternating exotropia with other noncomitancies**
Alternating exotropia with X or Y pattern

● 378.2 **Intermittent heterotropia**

| **Excludes** | *vertical heterotropia (intermittent) (378.31)* |

❑ 378.20 **Intermittent heterotropia, unspecified**
Intermittent:
    esotropia NOS
    exotropia NOS

378.21 **Intermittent esotropia, monocular**

378.22 **Intermittent esotropia, alternating**

378.23 **Intermittent exotropia, monocular**

378.24 **Intermittent exotropia, alternating**

● 378.3 **Other and unspecified heterotropia**

❑ 378.30 **Heterotropia, unspecified**

378.31 **Hypertropia**
Vertical heterotropia (constant) (intermittent)

378.32 **Hypotropia**

378.33 **Cyclotropia**

378.34 **Monofixation syndrome**
Microtropia

378.35 **Accommodative component in esotropia**

● 378.4 **Heterophoria**

❑ 378.40 **Heterophoria, unspecified**

378.41 **Esophoria**

378.42 **Exophoria**

378.43 **Vertical heterophoria**

◆▶ **New Code**   ◀▥ ▥▶ **Revised Code**   ● **Not a Principal Diagnosis**   ● **Use Additional Digit(s)**   ❑ **Nonspecific Code**

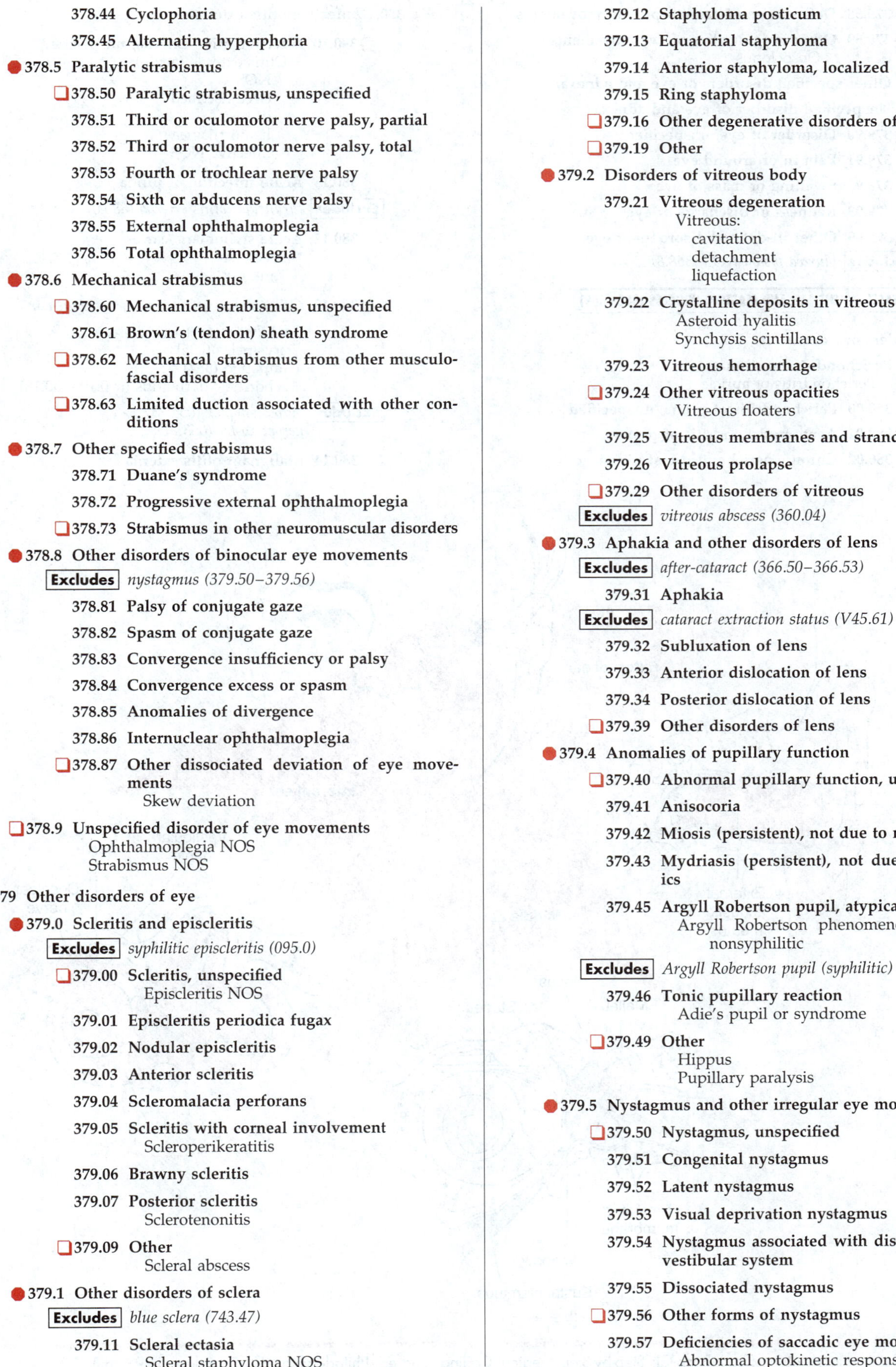

378.44   **Cyclophoria**

378.45   **Alternating hyperphoria**

● 378.5   **Paralytic strabismus**

☐ 378.50   **Paralytic strabismus, unspecified**

378.51   **Third or oculomotor nerve palsy, partial**

378.52   **Third or oculomotor nerve palsy, total**

378.53   **Fourth or trochlear nerve palsy**

378.54   **Sixth or abducens nerve palsy**

378.55   **External ophthalmoplegia**

378.56   **Total ophthalmoplegia**

● 378.6   **Mechanical strabismus**

☐ 378.60   **Mechanical strabismus, unspecified**

378.61   **Brown's (tendon) sheath syndrome**

☐ 378.62   **Mechanical strabismus from other musculo-fascial disorders**

☐ 378.63   **Limited duction associated with other conditions**

● 378.7   **Other specified strabismus**

378.71   **Duane's syndrome**

378.72   **Progressive external ophthalmoplegia**

☐ 378.73   **Strabismus in other neuromuscular disorders**

● 378.8   **Other disorders of binocular eye movements**

Excludes   *nystagmus (379.50–379.56)*

378.81   **Palsy of conjugate gaze**

378.82   **Spasm of conjugate gaze**

378.83   **Convergence insufficiency or palsy**

378.84   **Convergence excess or spasm**

378.85   **Anomalies of divergence**

378.86   **Internuclear ophthalmoplegia**

☐ 378.87   **Other dissociated deviation of eye movements**
Skew deviation

☐ 378.9   **Unspecified disorder of eye movements**
Ophthalmoplegia NOS
Strabismus NOS

● 379   **Other disorders of eye**

● 379.0   **Scleritis and episcleritis**

Excludes   *syphilitic episcleritis (095.0)*

☐ 379.00   **Scleritis, unspecified**
Episcleritis NOS

379.01   **Episcleritis periodica fugax**

379.02   **Nodular episcleritis**

379.03   **Anterior scleritis**

379.04   **Scleromalacia perforans**

379.05   **Scleritis with corneal involvement**
Scleroperikeratitis

379.06   **Brawny scleritis**

379.07   **Posterior scleritis**
Sclerotenonitis

☐ 379.09   **Other**
Scleral abscess

● 379.1   **Other disorders of sclera**

Excludes   *blue sclera (743.47)*

379.11   **Scleral ectasia**
Scleral staphyloma NOS

379.12   **Staphyloma posticum**

379.13   **Equatorial staphyloma**

379.14   **Anterior staphyloma, localized**

379.15   **Ring staphyloma**

☐ 379.16   **Other degenerative disorders of sclera**

☐ 379.19   **Other**

● 379.2   **Disorders of vitreous body**

379.21   **Vitreous degeneration**
Vitreous:
  cavitation
  detachment
  liquefaction

379.22   **Crystalline deposits in vitreous**
Asteroid hyalitis
Synchysis scintillans

379.23   **Vitreous hemorrhage**

☐ 379.24   **Other vitreous opacities**
Vitreous floaters

379.25   **Vitreous membranes and strands**

379.26   **Vitreous prolapse**

☐ 379.29   **Other disorders of vitreous**

Excludes   *vitreous abscess (360.04)*

● 379.3   **Aphakia and other disorders of lens**

Excludes   *after-cataract (366.50–366.53)*

379.31   **Aphakia**

Excludes   *cataract extraction status (V45.61)*

379.32   **Subluxation of lens**

379.33   **Anterior dislocation of lens**

379.34   **Posterior dislocation of lens**

☐ 379.39   **Other disorders of lens**

● 379.4   **Anomalies of pupillary function**

☐ 379.40   **Abnormal pupillary function, unspecified**

379.41   **Anisocoria**

379.42   **Miosis (persistent), not due to miotics**

379.43   **Mydriasis (persistent), not due to mydriatics**

379.45   **Argyll Robertson pupil, atypical**
Argyll Robertson phenomenon or pupil, nonsyphilitic

Excludes   *Argyll Robertson pupil (syphilitic) (094.89)*

379.46   **Tonic pupillary reaction**
Adie's pupil or syndrome

☐ 379.49   **Other**
Hippus
Pupillary paralysis

● 379.5   **Nystagmus and other irregular eye movements**

☐ 379.50   **Nystagmus, unspecified**

379.51   **Congenital nystagmus**

379.52   **Latent nystagmus**

379.53   **Visual deprivation nystagmus**

379.54   **Nystagmus associated with disorders of the vestibular system**

379.55   **Dissociated nystagmus**

☐ 379.56   **Other forms of nystagmus**

379.57   **Deficiencies of saccadic eye movements**
Abnormal optokinetic response

379.58   Deficiencies of smooth pursuit movements

379.59   Other irregularities of eye movements
Opsoclonus

379.8   Other specified disorders of eye and adnexa

379.9   Unspecified disorder of eye and adnexa

379.90   Disorder of eye, unspecified

379.91   Pain in or around eye

379.92   Swelling or mass of eye

379.93   Redness or discharge of eye

379.99   Other ill-defined disorders of eye

Excludes   *blurred vision NOS (368.8)*

DISEASES OF THE EAR AND MASTOID PROCESS (380–389)

380   Disorders of external ear

380.0   Perichondritis of pinna
Perichondritis of auricle

380.00   Perichondritis of pinna, unspecified

380.01   Acute perichondritis of pinna

380.02   Chronic perichondritis of pinna

380.1   Infective otitis externa

380.10   Infective otitis externa, unspecified
Otitis externa (acute):
   NOS
   circumscribed
   diffuse
   hemorrhagica
   infective NOS

380.11   Acute infection of pinna

Excludes   *furuncular otitis externa (680.0)*

380.12   Acute swimmers' ear
Beach ear
Tank ear

380.13   *Other acute infections of external ear*

Code first underlying disease, as:
   erysipelas (035)
   impetigo (684)
   seborrheic dermatitis (690.10–690.18)

Excludes   *herpes simplex (054.73)*
herpes zoster (053.71)

380.14   Malignant otitis externa

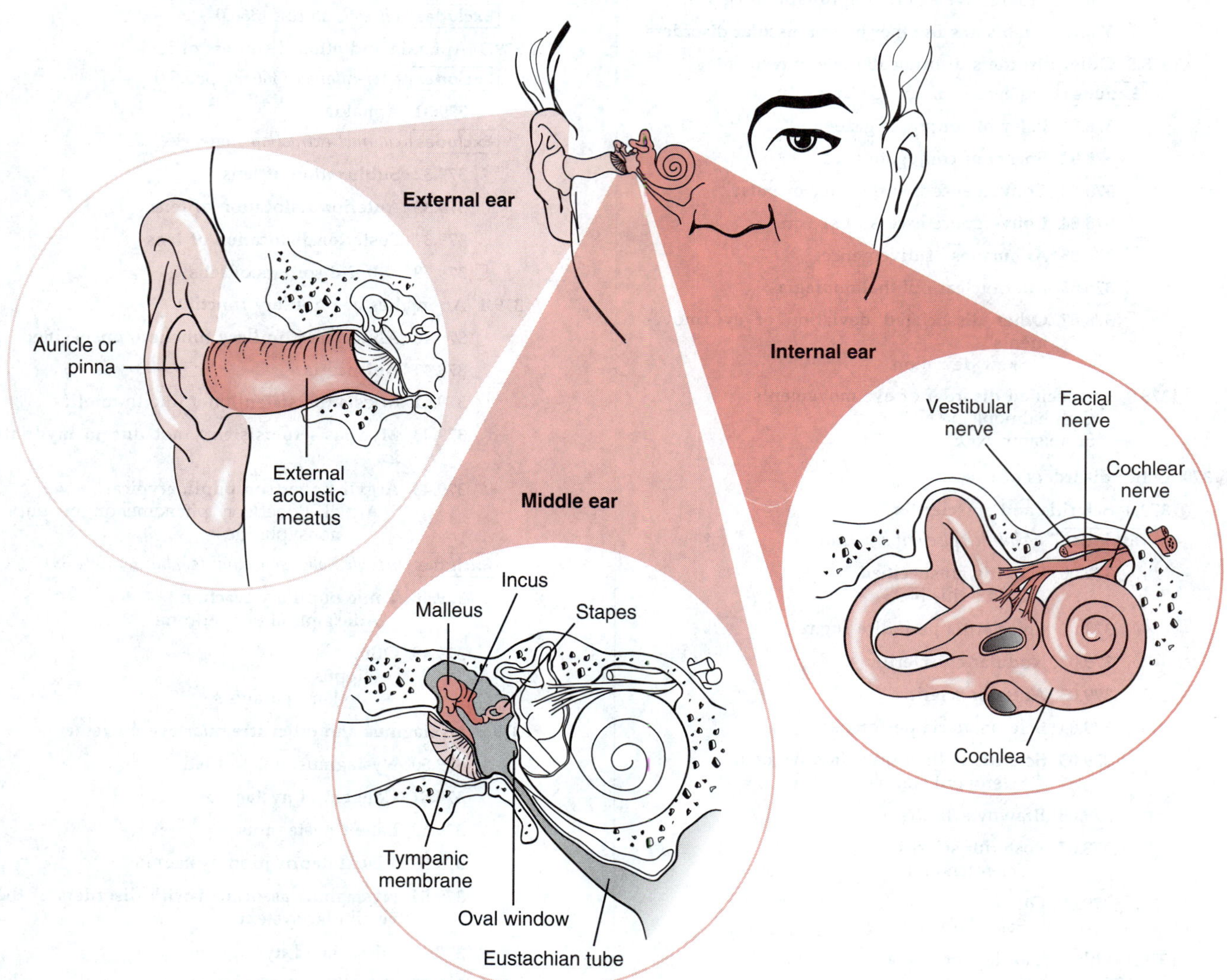

Figure 6–13   Auditory system. (From Buck CJ: Step-by-Step Medical Coding, 2nd ed. Philadelphia, WB Saunders, 1998, p 182.)

● **380.15 *Chronic mycotic otitis externa***

Code first underlying disease, as:
  aspergillosis (117.3)
  otomycosis NOS (111.9)

| Excludes | *candidal otitis externa (112.82)*

☐ **380.16 Other chronic infective otitis externa**
  Chronic infective otitis externa NOS

● **380.2 Other otitis externa**

380.21 Cholesteatoma of external ear
  Keratosis obturans of external ear (canal)

| Excludes | *cholesteatoma NOS (385.30–385.35)*
  postmastoidectomy (383.32)

☐ **380.22 Other acute otitis externa**
  Acute otitis externa:
    actinic
    chemical
    contact
    eczematoid
    reactive

☐ **380.23 Other chronic otitis externa**
  Chronic otitis externa NOS

● **380.3 Noninfectious disorders of pinna**

☐ **380.30 Disorder of pinna, unspecified**

380.31 Hematoma of auricle or pinna

380.32 Acquired deformities of auricle or pinna

| Excludes | *cauliflower ear (738.7)*

☐ **380.39 Other**

| Excludes | *gouty tophi of ear (274.81)*

380.4 Impacted cerumen
  Wax in ear

● **380.5 Acquired stenosis of external ear canal**
  Collapse of external ear canal

☐ **380.50 Acquired stenosis of external ear canal, unspecified as to cause**

380.51 Secondary to trauma

380.52 Secondary to surgery

380.53 Secondary to inflammation

● **380.8 Other disorders of external ear**

380.81 Exostosis of external ear canal

☐ **380.89 Other**

☐ **380.9 Unspecified disorder of external ear**

● **381 Nonsuppurative otitis media and Eustachian tube disorders**

● **381.0 Acute nonsuppurative otitis media**
  Acute tubotympanic catarrh
  Otitis media, acute or subacute:
    catarrhal
    exudative
    transudative
    with effusion

| Excludes | *otitic barotrauma (993.0)*

☐ **381.00 Acute nonsuppurative otitis media, unspecified**

381.01 Acute serous otitis media
  Acute or subacute secretory otitis media

381.02 Acute mucoid otitis media
  Acute or subacute seromucinous otitis media
  Blue drum syndrome

381.03 Acute sanguinous otitis media

381.04 Acute allergic serous otitis media

381.05 Acute allergic mucoid otitis media

381.06 Acute allergic sanguinous otitis media

● **381.1 Chronic serous otitis media**
  Chronic tubotympanic catarrh

381.10 Chronic serous otitis media, simple or unspecified

☐ **381.19 Other**
  Serosanguinous chronic otitis media

● **381.2 Chronic mucoid otitis media**
  Glue ear

| Excludes | *adhesive middle ear disease (385.10–385.19)*

381.20 Chronic mucoid otitis media, simple or unspecified

☐ **381.29 Other**
  Mucosanguinous chronic otitis media

☐ **381.3 Other and unspecified chronic nonsuppurative otitis media**
  Otitis media, chronic:
    allergic   seromucinous
    exudative   transudative
    secretory   with effusion

☐ **381.4 Nonsuppurative otitis media, not specified as acute or chronic**
  Otitis media:
    allergic   seromucinous
    catarrhal   serous
    exudative   transudative
    mucoid   with effusion
    secretory

● **381.5 Eustachian salpingitis**

☐ **381.50 Eustachian salpingitis, unspecified**

381.51 Acute Eustachian salpingitis

381.52 Chronic Eustachian salpingitis

● **381.6 Obstruction of Eustachian tube**
  Stenosis of Eustachian tube
  Stricture of Eustachian tube

☐ **381.60 Obstruction of Eustachian tube, unspecified**

381.61 Osseous obstruction of Eustachian tube
  Obstruction of Eustachian tube from cholesteatoma, polyp, or other osseous lesion

381.62 Intrinsic cartilaginous obstruction of Eustachian tube

381.63 Extrinsic cartilaginous obstruction of Eustachian tube
  Compression of Eustachian tube

381.7 Patulous Eustachian tube

● **381.8 Other disorders of Eustachian tube**

381.81 Dysfunction of Eustachian tube

☐ **381.89 Other**

☐ **381.9 Unspecified Eustachian tube disorder**

● **382 Suppurative and unspecified otitis media**

● **382.0 Acute suppurative otitis media**
  Otitis media, acute:
    necrotizing NOS
    purulent

382.00 Acute suppurative otitis media without spontaneous rupture of ear drum

382.01 Acute suppurative otitis media with spontaneous rupture of ear drum

ICD-9-CM

300-399

Vol. 1

●□ **382.02** *Acute suppurative otitis media in diseases classified elsewhere*

Code first underlying disease, as:
influenza (487.8)
scarlet fever (034.1)

Excludes *postmeasles otitis (055.2)*

382.1 Chronic tubotympanic suppurative otitis media
Benign chronic suppurative otitis media (with anterior perforation of ear drum)
Chronic tubotympanic disease (with anterior perforation of ear drum)

382.2 Chronic atticoantral suppurative otitis media
Chronic atticoantral disease (with posterior or superior marginal perforation of ear drum)
Persistent mucosal disease (with posterior or superior marginal perforation of ear drum)

□ **382.3 Unspecified chronic suppurative otitis media**
Chronic purulent otitis media

Excludes *tuberculous otitis media (017.4)*

□ **382.4 Unspecified suppurative otitis media**
Purulent otitis media NOS

□ **382.9 Unspecified otitis media**
Otitis media:
NOS
acute NOS
chronic NOS

● **383 Mastoiditis and related conditions**

● **383.0 Acute mastoiditis**
Abscess of mastoid
Empyema of mastoid

383.00 Acute mastoiditis without complications

383.01 Subperiosteal abscess of mastoid

□ **383.02 Acute mastoiditis with other complications**
Gradenigo's syndrome

383.1 Chronic mastoiditis
Caries of mastoid
Fistula of mastoid

Excludes *tuberculous mastoiditis (015.6)*

● **383.2 Petrositis**
Coalescing osteitis of petrous bone
Inflammation of petrous bone
Osteomyelitis of petrous bone

□ **383.20 Petrositis, unspecified**

383.21 Acute petrositis

383.22 Chronic petrositis

● **383.3 Complications following mastoidectomy**

□ **383.30 Postmastoidectomy complication, unspecified**

383.31 Mucosal cyst of postmastoidectomy cavity

383.32 Recurrent cholesteatoma of postmastoidectomy cavity

383.33 Granulations of postmastoidectomy cavity
Chronic inflammation of postmastoidectomy cavity

● **383.8 Other disorders of mastoid**

383.81 Postauricular fistula

□ **383.89 Other**

□ **383.9 Unspecified mastoiditis**

● **384 Other disorders of tympanic membrane**

● **384.0 Acute myringitis without mention of otitis media**

□ **384.00 Acute myringitis, unspecified**
Acute tympanitis NOS

384.01 Bullous myringitis
Myringitis bullosa hemorrhagica

□ **384.09 Other**

384.1 Chronic myringitis without mention of otitis media
Chronic tympanitis

● **384.2 Perforation of tympanic membrane**
Perforation of ear drum:
NOS
persistent posttraumatic
postinflammatory

Excludes *traumatic perforation [current injury] (872.61)*
otitis media with perforation of tympanic membrane (382.00–382.9) ◀

□ **384.20 Perforation of tympanic membrane, unspecified**

384.21 Central perforation of tympanic membrane

384.22 Attic perforation of tympanic membrane
Pars flaccida

□ **384.23 Other marginal perforation of tympanic membrane**

384.24 Multiple perforations of tympanic membrane

384.25 Total perforation of tympanic membrane

● **384.8 Other specified disorders of tympanic membrane**

384.81 Atrophic flaccid tympanic membrane
Healed perforation of ear drum

384.82 Atrophic nonflaccid tympanic membrane

□ **384.9 Unspecified disorder of tympanic membrane**

● **385 Other disorders of middle ear and mastoid**

Excludes *mastoiditis (383.0–383.9)*

● **385.0 Tympanosclerosis**

□ **385.00 Tympanosclerosis, unspecified as to involvement**

385.01 Tympanosclerosis involving tympanic membrane only

385.02 Tympanosclerosis involving tympanic membrane and ear ossicles

385.03 Tympanosclerosis involving tympanic membrane, ear ossicles, and middle ear

□ **385.09 Tympanosclerosis involving other combination of structures**

● **385.1 Adhesive middle ear disease**
Adhesive otitis
Otitis media:
chronic adhesive
fibrotic

Excludes *glue ear (381.20–381.29)*

□ **385.10 Adhesive middle ear disease, unspecified as to involvement**

385.11 Adhesions of drum head to incus

385.12 Adhesions of drum head to stapes

385.13 Adhesions of drum head to promontorium

□ **385.19 Other adhesions and combinations**

● **385.2 Other acquired abnormality of ear ossicles**

385.21 Impaired mobility of malleus
Ankylosis of malleus

 ◀▶ **New Code** ⬅▪▪▪ ▪▪▪➡ **Revised Code** ● **Not a Principal Diagnosis** ● **Use Additional Digit(s)** □ **Nonspecific Code**

□ **385.22 Impaired mobility of other ear ossicles**
 Ankylosis of ear ossicles, except malleus

385.23 Discontinuity or dislocation of ear ossicles

385.24 Partial loss or necrosis of ear ossicles

● **385.3 Cholesteatoma of middle ear and mastoid**
 Cholesterosis of (middle) ear
 Epidermosis of (middle) ear
 Keratosis of (middle) ear
 Polyp of (middle) ear

 Excludes *cholesteatoma:*
   external ear canal (380.21)
   recurrent of postmastoidectomy cavity (383.32)

□ **385.30 Cholesteatoma, unspecified**

385.31 Cholesteatoma of attic

385.32 Cholesteatoma of middle ear

385.33 Cholesteatoma of middle ear and mastoid

385.35 Diffuse cholesteatosis

● **385.8 Other disorders of middle ear and mastoid**

385.82 Cholesterin granuloma

385.83 Retained foreign body of middle ear

□ **385.89 Other**

□ **385.9 Unspecified disorder of middle ear and mastoid**

● **386 Vertiginous syndromes and other disorders of vestibular system**

 Excludes *vertigo NOS (780.4)*

● **386.0 Ménière's disease**
 Endolymphatic hydrops
 Lermoyez's syndrome
 Ménière's syndrome or vertigo

□ **386.00 Ménière's disease, unspecified**
 Ménière's disease (active)

386.01 Active Ménière's disease, cochleovestibular

386.02 Active Ménière's disease, cochlear

386.03 Active Ménière's disease, vestibular

386.04 Inactive Ménière's disease
 Ménière's disease in remission

● **386.1 Other and unspecified peripheral vertigo**

 Excludes *epidemic vertigo (078.81)*

□ **386.10 Peripheral vertigo, unspecified**

386.11 Benign paroxysmal positional vertigo
 Benign paroxysmal positional nystagmus

386.12 Vestibular neuronitis
 Acute (and recurrent) peripheral vestibulopathy

□ **386.19 Other**
 Aural vertigo
 Otogenic vertigo

386.2 Vertigo of central origin
 Central positional nystagmus
 Malignant positional vertigo

● **386.3 Labyrinthitis**

□ **386.30 Labyrinthitis, unspecified**

386.31 Serous labyrinthitis
 Diffuse labyrinthitis

386.32 Circumscribed labyrinthitis
 Focal labyrinthitis

386.33 Suppurative labyrinthitis
 Purulent labyrinthitis

386.34 Toxic labyrinthitis

386.35 Viral labyrinthitis

● **386.4 Labyrinthine fistula**

□ **386.40 Labyrinthine fistula, unspecified**

386.41 Round window fistula

386.42 Oval window fistula

386.43 Semicircular canal fistula

386.48 Labyrinthine fistula of combined sites

● **386.5 Labyrinthine dysfunction**

□ **386.50 Labyrinthine dysfunction, unspecified**

386.51 Hyperactive labyrinth, unilateral

386.52 Hyperactive labyrinth, bilateral

386.53 Hypoactive labyrinth, unilateral

386.54 Hypoactive labyrinth, bilateral

386.55 Loss of labyrinthine reactivity, unilateral

386.56 Loss of labyrinthine reactivity, bilateral

□ **386.58 Other forms and combinations**

□ **386.8 Other disorders of labyrinth**

□ **386.9 Unspecified vertiginous syndromes and labyrinthine disorders**

● **387 Otosclerosis**

 Includes: otospongiosis

387.0 Otosclerosis involving oval window, nonobliterative

387.1 Otosclerosis involving oval window, obliterative

387.2 Cochlear otosclerosis
 Otosclerosis involving:
  otic capsule
  round window

□ **387.8 Other otosclerosis**

□ **387.9 Otosclerosis, unspecified**

● **388 Other disorders of ear**

● **388.0 Degenerative and vascular disorders of ear**

□ **388.00 Degenerative and vascular disorders, unspecified**

388.01 Presbyacusis

388.02 Transient ischemic deafness

● **388.1 Noise effects on inner ear**

□ **388.10 Noise effects on inner ear, unspecified**

388.11 Acoustic trauma (explosive) to ear
 Otitic blast injury

388.12 Noise-induced hearing loss

□ **388.2 Sudden hearing loss, unspecified**

● **388.3 Tinnitus**

□ **388.30 Tinnitus, unspecified**

388.31 Subjective tinnitus

388.32 Objective tinnitus

● **388.4 Other abnormal auditory perception**

□ **388.40 Abnormal auditory perception, unspecified**

388.41 Diplacusis

388.42 Hyperacusis

388.43 Impairment of auditory discrimination

388.44 Recruitment

ICD-9-CM

300-399

Vol. 1

388.5 Disorders of acoustic nerve
Acoustic neuritis
Degeneration of acoustic or eighth nerve
Disorder of acoustic or eighth nerve

> **Excludes** *acoustic neuroma (225.1)*
> *syphilitic acoustic neuritis (094.86)*

● **388.6 Otorrhea**

☐ **388.60 Otorrhea, unspecified**
Discharging ear NOS

388.61 Cerebrospinal fluid otorrhea

> **Excludes** *cerebrospinal fluid rhinorrhea (349.81)*

☐ **388.69 Other**
Otorrhagia

● **388.7 Otalgia**

☐ **388.70 Otalgia, unspecified**
Earache NOS

388.71 Otogenic pain

388.72 Referred pain

☐ **388.8 Other disorders of ear**

☐ **388.9 Unspecified disorder of ear**

● **389 Hearing loss**

● **389.0 Conductive hearing loss**
Conductive deafness

☐ **389.00 Conductive hearing loss, unspecified**

389.01 Conductive hearing loss, external ear

389.02 Conductive hearing loss, tympanic membrane

389.03 Conductive hearing loss, middle ear

389.04 Conductive hearing loss, inner ear

389.08 Conductive hearing loss of combined types

● **389.1 Sensorineural hearing loss**
Perceptive hearing loss or deafness

> **Excludes** *abnormal auditory perception (388.40–388.44)*
> *psychogenic deafness (306.7)*

☐ **389.10 Sensorineural hearing loss, unspecified**

389.11 Sensory hearing loss

389.12 Neural hearing loss

389.14 Central hearing loss

389.18 Sensorineural hearing loss of combined types

389.2 Mixed conductive and sensorineural hearing loss
Deafness or hearing loss of type classifiable to 389.0 with type classifiable to 389.1

389.7 Deaf mutism, not elsewhere classifiable
Deaf, nonspeaking

☐ **389.8 Other specified forms of hearing loss**

☐ **389.9 Unspecified hearing loss**
Deafness NOS

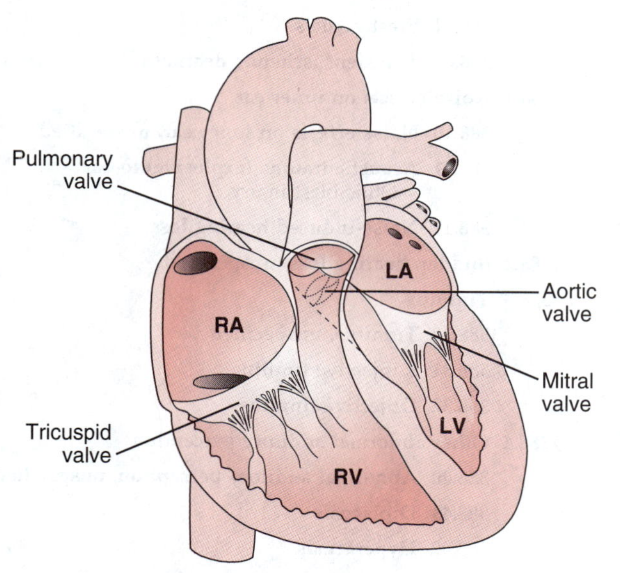

Figure 7–1 Cardiovascular valves.

   ◀▶ **New Code**   ⬌ **Revised Code**   ● **Not a Principal Diagnosis**   ● **Use Additional Digit(s)**   ☐ **Nonspecific Code**

7. DISEASES OF THE CIRCULATORY SYSTEM (390–459)

ACUTE RHEUMATIC FEVER (390–392)

Item 7–1 Rheumatic fever is the inflammation of the valve(s) of the heart, usually the mitral or aortic, which leads to valve damage. Rheumatic heart inflammations are usually pericarditis (heart), endocarditis (heart cavity), or myocarditis (heart muscle).

390 Rheumatic fever without mention of heart involvement
Arthritis, rheumatic, acute or subacute
Rheumatic fever (active) (acute)
Rheumatism, articular, acute or subacute

> **Excludes** *that with heart involvement (391.0–391.9)*

● **391 Rheumatic fever with heart involvement**

> **Excludes** *chronic heart diseases of rheumatic origin (393.0–398.9) unless rheumatic fever is also present or there is evidence of recrudescence or activity of the rheumatic process*

391.0 Acute rheumatic pericarditis
Rheumatic:
fever (active) (acute) with pericarditis
pericarditis (acute)
Any condition classifiable to 390 with pericarditis

> **Excludes** *that not specified as rheumatic (420.0–420.9)*

391.1 Acute rheumatic endocarditis
Rheumatic:
endocarditis, acute
fever (active) (acute) with endocarditis or valvulitis
valvulitis, acute
Any condition classifiable to 390 with endocarditis or valvulitis

391.2 Acute rheumatic myocarditis
Rheumatic fever (active) (acute) with myocarditis
Any condition classifiable to 390 with myocarditis

☐ **391.8 Other acute rheumatic heart disease**
Rheumatic:
fever (active) (acute) with other or multiple types of heart involvement
pancarditis, acute
Any condition classifiable to 390 with other or multiple types of heart involvement

☐ **391.9 Acute rheumatic heart disease, unspecified**
Rheumatic:
carditis, acute
fever (active) (acute) with unspecified type of heart involvement
heart disease, active or acute
Any condition classifiable to 390 with unspecified type of heart involvement

Item 7–2 Rheumatic chorea, also called Sydenham's, juvenile, minor, simple, or St. Vitus' dance, is a condition linked with rheumatic fever and is characterized by ceaseless, jerky movements.

● **392 Rheumatic chorea**

Includes: Sydenham's chorea

> **Excludes** *chorea:*
> *NOS (333.5)*
> *Huntington's (333.4)*

392.0 With heart involvement
Rheumatic chorea with heart involvement of any type classifiable to 391

392.9 Without mention of heart involvement

CHRONIC RHEUMATIC HEART DISEASE (393–398)

393 Chronic rheumatic pericarditis
Adherent pericardium, rheumatic
Chronic rheumatic:
mediastinopericarditis
myopericarditis

> **Excludes** *pericarditis NOS or not specified as rheumatic (423.0–423.9)*

Item 7–3 Mitral stenosis is the narrowing of the mitral valve. Mitral insufficiency is the improper closure of the mitral valve. These conditions lead to enlargement (hypertrophy) of the left atrium.

● **394 Diseases of mitral valve**

> **Excludes** *that with aortic valve involvement (396.0–396.9)*

394.0 Mitral stenosis
Mitral (valve):
obstruction (rheumatic)
stenosis NOS

394.1 Rheumatic mitral insufficiency
Rheumatic mitral:
incompetence
regurgitation

> **Excludes** *that not specified as rheumatic (424.0)*

394.2 Mitral stenosis with insufficiency
Mitral stenosis with incompetence or regurgitation

☐ **394.9 Other and unspecified mitral valve diseases**
Mitral (valve):
disease (chronic)
failure

Item 7–4 Aortic stenosis is the narrowing of the aortic valve. Aortic insufficiency is the improper closure of the aortic valve. These conditions lead to enlargement (hypertrophy) of the left ventricle.

● **395 Diseases of aortic valve**

> **Excludes** *that not specified as rheumatic (424.1)*
> *that with mitral valve involvement (396.0–396.9)*

395.0 Rheumatic aortic stenosis
Rheumatic aortic (valve) obstruction

395.1 Rheumatic aortic insufficiency
Rheumatic aortic:
incompetence
regurgitation

395.2 Rheumatic aortic stenosis with insufficiency
Rheumatic aortic stenosis with incompetence or regurgitation

☐ **395.9 Other and unspecified rheumatic aortic diseases**
Rheumatic aortic (valve) disease

Item 7–5 Mitral and aortic valve stenosis is the narrowing of these valves, which leads to enlargement (hypertrophy) of the left atrium and left ventricle.
Mitral and aortic insufficiency is the improper closure of the mitral and aortic valves, which leads to enlargement (hypertrophy) of the left atrium and left ventricle.

● **396 Diseases of mitral and aortic valves**

Includes: involvement of both mitral and aortic valves, whether specified as rheumatic or not

ICD-9-CM

300-399

Vol. 1

396.0 Mitral valve stenosis and aortic valve stenosis
Atypical aortic (valve) stenosis
Mitral and aortic (valve) obstruction (rheumatic)

396.1 Mitral valve stenosis and aortic valve insufficiency

396.2 Mitral valve insufficiency and aortic valve stenosis

396.3 Mitral valve insufficiency and aortic valve insufficiency
Mitral and aortic (valve):
incompetence
regurgitation

396.8 Multiple involvement of mitral and aortic valves
Stenosis and insufficiency of mitral or aortic valve
with stenosis or insufficiency, or both, of the
other valve

❑ **396.9 Mitral and aortic valve diseases, unspecified**

● **397 Diseases of other endocardial structures**

397.0 Diseases of tricuspid valve
Tricuspid (valve) (rheumatic):
disease
insufficiency
obstruction
regurgitation
stenosis

397.1 Rheumatic diseases of pulmonary valve
| **Excludes** | *that not specified as rheumatic (424.3)* |

❑ **397.9 Rheumatic diseases of endocardium, valve unspecified**
Rheumatic:
endocarditis (chronic)
valvulitis (chronic)
| **Excludes** | *that not specified as rheumatic (424.90–424.99)* |

● **398 Other rheumatic heart disease**

398.0 Rheumatic myocarditis
Rheumatic degeneration of myocardium
| **Excludes** | *myocarditis not specified as rheumatic (429.0)* |

● **398.9 Other and unspecified rheumatic heart diseases**

❑ **398.90 Rheumatic heart disease, unspecified**
Rheumatic:
carditis
heart disease NOS
| **Excludes** | *carditis not specified as rheumatic (429.89)* |
| | *heart disease NOS not specified as rheumatic (429.9)* |

398.91 Rheumatic heart failure (congestive)
Rheumatic left ventricular failure

❑ **398.99 Other**

HYPERTENSIVE DISEASE (401–405)

| **Excludes** | *that complicating pregnancy, childbirth, or the puerperium (642.0–642.9)* |
| | *that involving coronary vessels (410.00–414.9)* |

Item 7-6 Hypertension is caused by high arterial blood pressure in the arteries. **Essential, primary,** or **idiopathic** hypertension occurs without identifiable organic cause.
Secondary hypertension is that which has an organic cause. **Malignant** hypertension is severely elevated blood pressure. **Benign** hypertension is mildly elevated blood pressure.

● **401 Essential hypertension**

Includes: high blood pressure
hyperpiesia
hyperpiesis
hypertension (arterial) (essential) (primary) (systemic)
hypertensive vascular:
degeneration
disease
Excludes	*elevated blood pressure without diagnosis of hypertension (796.2)*
	pulmonary hypertension (416.0–416.9)
	that involving vessels of:
	brain (430–438)
	eye (362.11)

401.0 Malignant

401.1 Benign

❑ **401.9 Unspecified**

● **402 Hypertensive heart disease**

Includes: hypertensive:
cardiomegaly
cardiopathy
cardiovascular disease
heart (disease) (failure)
any condition classifiable to 428, 429.0–429.3, 429.8, 429.9 due to hypertension

● **402.0 Malignant**

402.00 Without congestive heart failure

402.01 With congestive heart failure

● **402.1 Benign**

402.10 Without congestive heart failure

402.11 With congestive heart failure

● **402.9 Unspecified**

❑ **402.90 Without congestive heart failure**

❑ **402.91 With congestive heart failure**

● **403 Hypertensive renal disease**

Includes: arteriolar nephritis
arteriosclerosis of:
kidney
renal arterioles
arteriosclerotic nephritis (chronic) (interstitial)
hypertensive:
nephropathy
renal failure
uremia (chronic)
nephrosclerosis
renal sclerosis with hypertension
any condition classifiable to 585, 586, or 587 with any condition classifiable to 401
Excludes	*acute renal failure (584.5–584.9)*
	renal disease stated as not due to hypertension
	renovascular hypertension (405.0–405.9 with fifth-digit 1)

The following fifth-digit subclassification is for use with category 403:
  0 **without mention of renal failure**
  1 **with renal failure**

● **403.0 Malignant**

● **403.1 Benign**

❑ ● **403.9 Unspecified**

● **404 Hypertensive heart and renal disease**

   Includes: disease:
   cardiorenal
   cardiovascular renal
   any condition classifiable to 402 with any condition classifiable to 403

The following fifth-digit subclassification is for use with category 404:
   0 without mention of congestive heart failure or renal failure
   1 with congestive heart failure
   2 with renal failure
   3 with congestive heart failure and renal failure

   ● **404.0 Malignant**

   ● **404.1 Benign**

   □ ● **404.9 Unspecified**

● **405 Secondary hypertension**

   ● **405.0 Malignant**

      405.01 Renovascular

      □ **405.09 Other**

   ● **405.1 Benign**

      405.11 Renovascular

      □ **405.19 Other**

   ● **405.9 Unspecified**

      □ **405.91 Renovascular**

      □ **405.99 Other**

ISCHEMIC HEART DISEASE (410–414)

   Includes: that with mention of hypertension

   Use additional code to identify presence of hypertension
   (401.0–405.9)

Item 7–7 Myocardial infarction is a sudden decrease in the coronary artery blood flow that results in death of the heart muscle. Classifications are based on the affected heart tissue.

● **410 Acute myocardial infarction**

   Includes: cardiac infarction
   coronary (artery):
      embolism
      occlusion
      rupture
      thrombosis
   infarction of heart, myocardium, or ventricle
   rupture of heart, myocardium, or ventricle
   any condition classifiable to 414.1–414.9 speci-
      fied as acute or with a stated duration of
      8 weeks or less

The following fifth-digit subclassification is for use with category 410:
   □ **0 episode of care unspecified**
      Use when the source document does not contain
      sufficient information for the assignment of fifth-
      digit 1 or 2.
   1 initial episode of care
      Use fifth-digit 1 to designate the first episode of
      care (regardless of facility site) for a newly diag-
      nosed myocardial infarction. The fifth-digit 1 is
      assigned regardless of the number of times a pa-
      tient may be transferred during the initial episode
      of care.
   2 subsequent episode of care
      Use fifth-digit 2 to designate an episode of care
      following the initial episode when the patient is
      admitted for further observation, evaluation or
      treatment for a myocardial infarction that has re-
      ceived initial treatment, but is still less than 8
      weeks old.

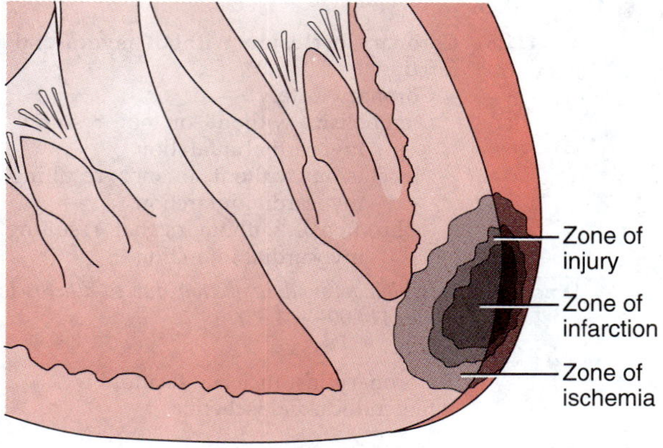

Figure 7–2 Myocardial infarction.

   ● **410.0 Of anterolateral wall**

   □ ● **410.1 Of other anterior wall**
      Infarction:
         anterior (wall) NOS (with contiguous portion of
            intraventricular septum)
         anteroapical (with contiguous portion of intra-
            ventricular septum)
         anteroseptal (with contiguous portion of intra-
            ventricular septum)

   ● **410.2 Of inferolateral wall**

   ● **410.3 Of inferoposterior wall**

   □ ● **410.4 Of other inferior wall**
      Infarction:
         diaphragmatic wall NOS (with contiguous por-
            tion of intraventricular septum)
         inferior (wall) NOS (with contiguous portion of
            intraventricular septum)

   □ ● **410.5 Of other lateral wall**
      Infarction:
         apical-lateral
         basal-lateral
         high lateral
         posterolateral

   ● **410.6 True posterior wall infarction**
      Infarction:
         posterobasal
         strictly posterior

   ● **410.7 Subendocardial infarction**
      Nontransmural infarction

   □ ● **410.8 Of other specified sites**
      Infarction of:
         atrium
         papillary muscle
         septum alone

   □ ● **410.9 Unspecified site**
      Acute myocardial infarction NOS
      Coronary occlusion NOS

● **411 Other acute and subacute forms of ischemic heart disease**

   411.0 Postmyocardial infarction syndrome
      Dressler's syndrome

   411.1 Intermediate coronary syndrome
      Impending infarction
      Preinfarction angina
      Preinfarction syndrome
      Unstable angina

      Excludes *angina (pectoris) (413.9)*
      decubitus (413.0)

ICD-9-CM

400–499

Vol. 1

◄ ► **New Code**   ◄▥ ▥► **Revised Code**   ● **Not a Principal Diagnosis**   ● **Use Additional Digit(s)**   □ **Nonspecific Code**   673

● **411.8 Other**

    411.81 Coronary occlusion without myocardial infarction
        Coronary (artery):
           embolism without or not resulting in myocardial infarction
           occlusion without or not resulting in myocardial infarction
           thrombosis without or not resulting in myocardial infarction

        Excludes *occlusion without infarction due to atherosclerosis (414.00–414.05)*

    ☐ **411.89 Other**
        Coronary insufficiency (acute)
        Subendocardial ischemia

412 Old myocardial infarction
    Healed myocardial infarction
    Past myocardial infarction diagnosed on ECG [EKG] or other special investigation, but currently presenting no symptoms

● **413 Angina pectoris**

    413.0 Angina decubitus
        Nocturnal angina

    413.1 Prinzmetal angina
        Variant angina pectoris

    ☐ **413.9 Other and unspecified angina pectoris**
        Angina:
          NOS
          cardiac
          of effort
        Anginal syndrome
        Status anginosus
        Stenocardia
        Syncope anginosa

        Excludes *preinfarction angina (411.1)*

● **414 Other forms of chronic ischemic heart disease**

    Excludes *arteriosclerotic cardiovascular disease [ASCVD] (429.2)*
        cardiovascular:
          arteriosclerosis or sclerosis (429.2)
          degeneration or disease (429.2)

● **414.0 Coronary atherosclerosis**
    Arteriosclerotic heart disease [ASHD]
    Atherosclerotic heart disease
    Coronary (artery):
        arteriosclerosis
        arteritis or endarteritis
        atheroma
        sclerosis
        stricture

    Excludes *embolism of graft (996.72)*
        occlusion NOS of graft (996.72)
        thrombus of graft (996.72)

    ☐ **414.00 Of unspecified type of vessel, native or graft**

    414.01 Of native coronary artery

    414.02 Of autologous biological bypass graft

    414.03 Of nonautologous biological bypass graft

    414.04 Of artery bypass graft
        Internal mammary artery

    414.05 Of unspecified type of bypass graft
        Bypass graft NOS

● **414.1 Aneurysm of heart**

    414.10 Of heart (wall)
        Aneurysm (arteriovenous):
          mural
          ventricular

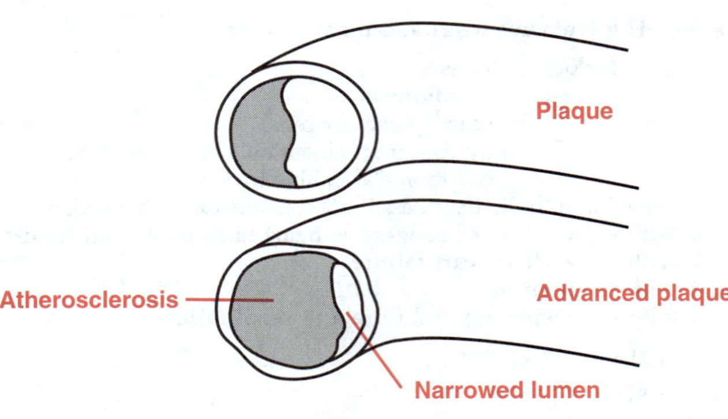

Figure 7–3 Atherosclerosis. (From Buck CJ: Step-by-Step Medical Coding. Philadelphia, WB Saunders, 1996, p 166.)

Item 7–8 Classification is based on the location of the atherosclerosis. "Of native coronary artery" indicates the atherosclerosis is within an original heart artery. "Of autologous vein bypass graft" indicates that the atherosclerosis is within a vein graft that was taken from within the patient. "Of nonautologous biological bypass graft" indicates the atherosclerosis is within a vessel grafted from other than the patient. "Of artery bypass graft" indicates the atherosclerosis is within an artery that was grafted from within the patient.

    414.11 Of coronary vessels
        Aneurysm (arteriovenous) of coronary vessels

    ☐ **414.19 Other**
        Arteriovenous fistula, acquired, of heart

☐ **414.8 Other specified forms of chronic ischemic heart disease**
    Chronic coronary insufficiency
    Ischemia, myocardial (chronic)
    Any condition classifiable to 410 specified as chronic, or presenting with symptoms after 8 weeks from date of infarction

    Excludes *coronary insufficiency (acute) (411.89)*

☐ **414.9 Chronic ischemic heart disease, unspecified**
    Ischemic heart disease NOS

DISEASES OF PULMONARY CIRCULATION (415–417)

● **415 Acute pulmonary heart disease**

    415.0 Acute cor pulmonale
        Excludes *cor pulmonale NOS (416.9)*

● **415.1 Pulmonary embolism and infarction**
    Pulmonary (artery) (vein):
        apoplexy
        embolism
        infarction (hemorrhagic)
        thrombosis

    Excludes *that complicating:*
        abortion (634–638 with .6, 639.6)
        ectopic or molar pregnancy (639.6)
        pregnancy, childbirth, or the puerperium (673.0–673.8)

    415.11 Iatrogenic pulmonary embolism and infarction

    ☐ **415.19 Other**

● **416 Chronic pulmonary heart disease**

     ◀▶ **New Code**   ⬅▦ ▦➡ **Revised Code**   ● **Not a Principal Diagnosis**   ● **Use Additional Digit(s)**   ☐ **Nonspecific Code**

416.0 Primary pulmonary hypertension
Idiopathic pulmonary arteriosclerosis
Pulmonary hypertension (essential) (idiopathic) (primary)

416.1 Kyphoscoliotic heart disease

416.8 Other chronic pulmonary heart diseases
Pulmonary hypertension, secondary

416.9 Chronic pulmonary heart disease, unspecified
Chronic cardiopulmonary disease
Cor pulmonale (chronic) NOS

417 Other diseases of pulmonary circulation

417.0 Arteriovenous fistula of pulmonary vessels
| Excludes | congenital arteriovenous fistula (747.3) |

417.1 Aneurysm of pulmonary artery
| Excludes | congenital aneurysm (747.3) |

417.8 Other specified diseases of pulmonary circulation
Pulmonary:
  arteritis
  endarteritis
Rupture of pulmonary vessel
Stricture of pulmonary vessel

417.9 Unspecified disease of pulmonary circulation

OTHER FORMS OF HEART DISEASE (420–429)

420 Acute pericarditis

Includes: acute:
  mediastinopericarditis
  myopericarditis
  pericardial effusion
  pleuropericarditis
  pneumopericarditis
| Excludes | acute rheumatic pericarditis (391.0) |
| | postmyocardial infarction syndrome [Dressler's] (411.0) |

420.0 Acute pericarditis in diseases classified elsewhere

Code first underlying disease, as:
  actinomycosis (039.8)
  amebiasis (006.8)
  nocardiosis (039.8)
  tuberculosis (017.9)
  uremia (585)
Excludes	pericarditis (acute) (in):
	Coxsackie (virus) (074.21)
	gonococcal (098.83)
	histoplasmosis (115.0–115.9 with fifth-digit 3)
	meningococcal infection (036.41)
	syphilitic (093.81)

420.9 Other and unspecified acute pericarditis

420.90 Acute pericarditis, unspecified
Pericarditis (acute):
  NOS   sicca
  infective NOS

420.91 Acute idiopathic pericarditis
Pericarditis, acute:
  benign   viral
  nonspecific

420.99 Other
Pericarditis (acute):
  pneumococcal
  purulent
  staphylococcal
  streptococcal
  suppurative
Pneumopyopericardium
Pyopericardium
| Excludes | pericarditis in diseases classified elsewhere (420.0) |

421 Acute and subacute endocarditis

421.0 Acute and subacute bacterial endocarditis
Endocarditis (acute) (chronic) (subacute):
  bacterial
  infective NOS
  lenta
  malignant
  purulent
  septic
  ulcerative
  vegetative
Infective aneurysm
Subacute bacterial endocarditis [SBE]

Use additional code, if desired, to identify infectious organism [e.g., Streptococcus 041.0, Staphylococcus 041.1]

421.1 Acute and subacute infective endocarditis in diseases classified elsewhere

Code first underlying disease, as:
  blastomycosis (116.0)
  Q fever (083.0)
  typhoid (fever) (002.0)
Excludes	endocarditis (in):
	Coxsackie (virus) (074.22)
	gonococcal (098.84)
	histoplasmosis (115.0–115.9 with fifth-digit 4)
	meningococcal infection (036.42)
	monilial (112.81)

421.9 Acute endocarditis, unspecified
Endocarditis, acute or subacute
Myoendocarditis, acute or subacute
Periendocarditis, acute or subacute
| Excludes | acute rheumatic endocarditis (391.1) |

422 Acute myocarditis
| Excludes | acute rheumatic myocarditis (391.2) |

422.0 Acute myocarditis in diseases classified elsewhere

Code first underlying disease, as:
  myocarditis (acute):
    influenzal (487.8)
    tuberculous (017.9)
Excludes	myocarditis (acute) (due to):
	aseptic, of newborn (074.23)
	Coxsackie (virus) (074.23)
	diphtheritic (032.82)
	meningococcal infection (036.43)
	syphilitic (093.82)
	toxoplasmosis (130.3)

422.9 Other and unspecified acute myocarditis

422.90 Acute myocarditis, unspecified
Acute or subacute (interstitial) myocarditis

422.91 Idiopathic myocarditis
Myocarditis (acute or subacute):
  Fiedler's
  giant cell
  isolated (diffuse) (granulomatous)
  nonspecific granulomatous

422.92 Septic myocarditis
Myocarditis, acute or subacute:
  pneumococcal
  staphylococcal

Use additional code to identify infectious organism [e.g., Staphylococcus 041.1]
Excludes	myocarditis, acute or subacute:
	in bacterial diseases classified elsewhere (422.0)
	streptococcal (391.2)

422.93 Toxic myocarditis

422.99 Other

ICD-9-CM

400-499

Vol. 1

● **423 Other diseases of pericardium**

> **Excludes**   *that specified as rheumatic (393)*

423.0 Hemopericardium

423.1 Adhesive pericarditis
Adherent pericardium
Fibrosis of pericardium
Milk spots
Pericarditis:
   adhesive
   obliterative
Soldiers' patches

423.2 Constrictive pericarditis
Concato's disease
Pick's disease of heart (and liver)

□ **423.8 Other specified diseases of pericardium**
Calcification of pericardium
Fistula of pericardium

□ **423.9 Unspecified disease of pericardium**

● **424 Other diseases of endocardium**

> **Excludes**   *bacterial endocarditis (421.0–421.9)*
> *rheumatic endocarditis (391.1, 394.0–397.9)*
> *syphilitic endocarditis (093.20–093.24)*

424.0 Mitral valve disorders
Mitral (valve):
   incompetence NOS of specified cause, except
      rheumatic
   insufficiency NOS of specified cause, except
      rheumatic
   regurgitation NOS of specified cause, except
      rheumatic

> **Excludes**   *mitral (valve):*
> *disease (394.9)*
> *failure (394.9)*
> *stenosis (394.0)*
> *the listed conditions:*
> *specified as rheumatic (394.1)*
> *unspecified as to cause but with mention of:*
> *diseases of aortic valve (396.0–396.9)*
> *mitral stenosis or obstruction (394.2)*

424.1 Aortic valve disorders
Aortic (valve):
   incompetence NOS of specified cause, except
      rheumatic
   insufficiency NOS of specified cause, except
      rheumatic
   regurgitation NOS of specified cause, except
      rheumatic
   stenosis NOS of specified cause, except rheu-
      matic

> **Excludes**   *hypertrophic subaortic stenosis (425.1)*
> *that specified as rheumatic (395.0–395.9)*
> *that of unspecified cause but with mention of*
> *diseases of mitral valve (396.0–396.9)*

424.2 Tricuspid valve disorders, specified as nonrheumatic
Tricuspid valve:
   incompetence of specified cause, except rheumatic
   insufficiency of specified cause, except rheumatic
   regurgitation of specified cause, except rheumatic
   stenosis of specified cause, except rheumatic

> **Excludes**   *rheumatic or of unspecified cause (397.0)*

424.3 Pulmonary valve disorders
Pulmonic:
   incompetence NOS
   insufficiency NOS
   regurgitation NOS
   stenosis NOS

> **Excludes**   *that specified as rheumatic (397.1)*

● **424.9 Endocarditis, valve unspecified**

□ **424.90 Endocarditis, valve unspecified, unspecified cause**
Endocarditis (chronic):
   NOS
   nonbacterial thrombotic
Valvular:
   incompetence of unspecified valve, un-
      specified cause
   insufficiency of unspecified valve, un-
      specified cause
   regurgitation of unspecified valve, un-
      specified cause
   stenosis of unspecified valve, unspeci-
      fied cause
Valvulitis (chronic)

●□ **424.91 *Endocarditis in diseases classified elsewhere***

> *Code first underlying disease, as:*
> atypical verrucous endocarditis [Lib-
>   man-Sacks] (710.0)
> disseminated lupus erythematosus (710.0)
> tuberculosis (017.9)

> **Excludes**   *syphilitic (093.20–093.24)*

□ **424.99 Other**
Any condition classifiable to 424.90 with
   specified cause, except rheumatic

> **Excludes**   *endocardial fibroelastosis (425.3)*
> *that specified as rheumatic (397.9)*

● **425 Cardiomyopathy**

Includes: myocardiopathy

425.0 Endomyocardial fibrosis

425.1 Hypertrophic obstructive cardiomyopathy
Hypertrophic subaortic stenosis (idiopathic)

425.2 Obscure cardiomyopathy of Africa
Becker's disease
Idiopathic mural endomyocardial disease

425.3 Endocardial fibroelastosis
Elastomyofibrosis

□ **425.4 Other primary cardiomyopathies**
Cardiomyopathy:
   NOS
   congestive
   constrictive
   familial
   hypertrophic
   idiopathic
   nonobstructive
   obstructive
   restrictive
Cardiovascular collagenosis

425.5 Alcoholic cardiomyopathy

● **425.7 *Nutritional and metabolic cardiomyopathy***

> *Code first underlying disease, as:*
> amyloidosis (277.3)
> beriberi (265.0)
> cardiac glycogenosis (271.0)
> mucopolysaccharidosis (277.5)
> thyrotoxicosis (242.0–242.9)

> **Excludes**   *gouty tophi of heart (274.82)*

●□ **425.8 *Cardiomyopathy in other diseases classified elsewhere***

> *Code first underlying disease, as:*
> Friedreich's ataxia (334.0)
> myotonia atrophica (359.2)
> progressive muscular dystrophy (359.1)
> sarcoidosis (135)

> **Excludes**   *cardiomyopathy in Chagas' disease (086.0)*

    ◀▶ **New Code**   ⬅▦➡ **Revised Code**   ● **Not a Principal Diagnosis**   ● **Use Additional Digit(s)**   □ **Nonspecific Code**

☐ **425.9 Secondary cardiomyopathy, unspecified**

● **426 Conduction disorders**

426.0 Atrioventricular block, complete
Third degree atrioventricular block

● **426.1 Atrioventricular block, other and unspecified**

☐ **426.10 Atrioventricular block, unspecified**
Atrioventricular [AV] block (incomplete) (partial)

426.11 First degree atrioventricular block
Incomplete atrioventricular block, first degree
Prolonged P-R interval NOS

426.12 Mobitz (type) II atrioventricular block
Incomplete atrioventricular block:
Mobitz (type) II
second degree, Mobitz (type) II

☐ **426.13 Other second degree atrioventricular block**
Incomplete atrioventricular block:
Mobitz (type) I [Wenckebach's]
second degree:
NOS
Mobitz (type) I
with 2:1 atrioventricular response [block]
Wenckebach's phenomenon

426.2 Left bundle branch hemiblock
Block:
left anterior fascicular
left posterior fascicular

☐ **426.3 Other left bundle branch block**
Left bundle branch block:
NOS
anterior fascicular with posterior fascicular
complete
main stem

426.4 Right bundle branch block

● **426.5 Bundle branch block, other and unspecified**

☐ **426.50 Bundle branch block, unspecified**

426.51 Right bundle branch block and left posterior fascicular block

426.52 Right bundle branch block and left anterior fascicular block

☐ **426.53 Other bilateral bundle branch block**
Bifascicular block NOS
Bilateral bundle branch block NOS
Right bundle branch with left bundle branch block (incomplete) (main stem)

426.54 Trifascicular block

☐ **426.6 Other heart block**
Intraventricular block:
NOS
diffuse
myofibrillar
Sinoatrial block
Sinoauricular block

426.7 Anomalous atrioventricular excitation
Atrioventricular conduction:
accelerated
accessory
pre-excitation
Ventricular pre-excitation
Wolff-Parkinson-White syndrome

● **426.8 Other specified conduction disorders**

426.81 Lown-Ganong-Levine syndrome
Syndrome of short P-R interval, normal QRS complexes, and supraventricular tachycardias

☐ **426.89 Other**
Dissociation:
atrioventricular [AV]
interference
isorhythmic
Nonparoxysmal AV nodal tachycardia

☐ **426.9 Conduction disorder, unspecified**
Heart block NOS
Stokes-Adams syndrome

● **427 Cardiac dysrhythmias**

Excludes *that complicating:*
abortion (634–638 with .7, 639.8)
ectopic or molar pregnancy (639.8)
labor or delivery (668.1, 669.4)

427.0 Paroxysmal supraventricular tachycardia
Paroxysmal tachycardia:
atrial [PAT]
atrioventricular [AV]
junctional
nodal

427.1 Paroxysmal ventricular tachycardia
Ventricular tachycardia (paroxysmal)

☐ **427.2 Paroxysmal tachycardia, unspecified**
Bouveret-Hoffmann syndrome
Paroxysmal tachycardia:
NOS
essential

● **427.3 Atrial fibrillation and flutter**

427.31 Atrial fibrillation

427.32 Atrial flutter

● **427.4 Ventricular fibrillation and flutter**

427.41 Ventricular fibrillation

427.42 Ventricular flutter

427.5 Cardiac arrest
Cardiorespiratory arrest

● **427.6 Premature beats**

☐ **427.60 Premature beats, unspecified**
Ectopic beats
Extrasystoles
Extrasystolic arrhythmia
Premature contractions or systoles NOS

427.61 Supraventricular premature beats
Atrial premature beats, contractions, or systoles

☐ **427.69 Other**
Ventricular premature beats, contractions, or systoles

● **427.8 Other specified cardiac dysrhythmias**

427.81 Sinoatrial node dysfunction
Sinus bradycardia:
persistent
severe
Syndrome:
sick sinus
tachycardia-bradycardia

Excludes *sinus bradycardia NOS (427.89)*

☐ **427.89 Other**
Rhythm disorder:
coronary sinus
ectopic
nodal
Wandering (atrial) pacemaker

Excludes *carotid sinus syncope (337.0)*
reflex bradycardia (337.0)
tachycardia NOS (785.0)

ICD-9-CM

400-499

Vol. 1

❑ **427.9 Cardiac dysrhythmia, unspecified**
Arrhythmia (cardiac) NOS

● **428 Heart failure**

Excludes *rheumatic (398.91)*
that complicating:
   abortion (634–638 with .7, 639.8)
   ectopic or molar pregnancy (639.8)
   labor or delivery (668.1, 669.4)
that due to hypertension (402.0–402.9 with fifth-
   digit 1)

428.0 Congestive heart failure
Congestive heart disease
Right heart failure (secondary to left heart failure)

428.1 Left heart failure
Acute edema of lung with heart disease NOS or
   heart failure
Acute pulmonary edema with heart disease NOS
   or heart failure
Cardiac asthma
Left ventricular failure

❑ **428.9 Heart failure, unspecified**
Cardiac failure NOS
Heart failure NOS
Myocardial failure NOS
Weak heart

● **429 Ill-defined descriptions and complications of heart disease**

❑ **429.0 Myocarditis, unspecified**
Myocarditis (with mention of arteriosclerosis):
   NOS (with mention of arteriosclerosis)
   chronic (interstitial) (with mention of arterio-
      sclerosis)
   fibroid (with mention of arteriosclerosis)
   senile (with mention of arteriosclerosis)

Use additional code to identify presence of arteriosclerosis

Excludes *acute or subacute (422.0–422.9)*
rheumatic (398.0)
   acute (391.2)
that due to hypertension (402.0–402.9)

429.1 Myocardial degeneration
Degeneration of heart or myocardium (with mention of arteriosclerosis):
   fatty (with mention of arteriosclerosis)
   mural (with mention of arteriosclerosis)
   muscular (with mention of arteriosclerosis)
Myocardial (with mention of arteriosclerosis):
   degeneration (with mention of arteriosclerosis)
   disease (with mention of arteriosclerosis)

Use additional code to identify presence of arteriosclerosis

Excludes *that due to hypertension (402.0–402.9)*

❑ **429.2 Cardiovascular disease, unspecified**
Arteriosclerotic cardiovascular disease [ASCVD]
Cardiovascular arteriosclerosis
Cardiovascular:
   degeneration (with mention of arteriosclerosis)
   disease (with mention of arteriosclerosis)
   sclerosis (with mention of arteriosclerosis)

Use additional code to identify presence of arteriosclerosis

Excludes *that due to hypertension (402.0–402.9)*

429.3 Cardiomegaly
Cardiac:
   dilatation
   hypertrophy
Ventricular dilatation

Excludes *that due to hypertension (402.0–402.9)*

429.4 Functional disturbances following cardiac surgery
Cardiac insufficiency following cardiac surgery or
   due to prosthesis
Heart failure following cardiac surgery or due to
   prosthesis
Postcardiotomy syndrome
Postvalvulotomy syndrome

Excludes *cardiac failure in the immediate postoperative pe-*
riod (997.1)

429.5 Rupture of chordae tendineae

429.6 Rupture of papillary muscle

● **429.7 Certain sequelae of myocardial infarction, not elsewhere classified**

Use additional code to identify the associated myocardial infarction:
   with onset of 8 weeks or less (410.00–410.92)
   with onset of more than 8 weeks (414.8)

Excludes *congenital defects of heart (745, 746)*
coronary aneurysm (414.11)
disorders of papillary muscle (429.6, 429.81)
postmyocardial infarction syndrome (411.0)
rupture of chordae tendineae (429.5)

429.71 Acquired cardiac septal defect

Excludes *acute septal infarction (410.00–410.92)*

❑ **429.79 Other**
Mural thrombus (atrial) (ventricular) acquired, following myocardial infarction

● **429.8 Other ill-defined heart diseases**

❑ **429.81 Other disorders of papillary muscle**
Papillary muscle:
   atrophy   incompetence
   degeneration   incoordination
   dysfunction   scarring

429.82 Hyperkinetic heart disease

❑ **429.89 Other**
Carditis

Excludes *that due to hypertension (402.0–402.9)*

❑ **429.9 Heart disease, unspecified**
Heart disease (organic) NOS
Morbus cordis NOS

Excludes *that due to hypertension (402.0–402.9)*

CEREBROVASCULAR DISEASE (430–438)

Includes: with mention of hypertension (conditions
   classifiable to 401–405)

Use additional code to identify presence of hypertension

Excludes *any condition classifiable to 430–434, 436, 437*
occurring during pregnancy, childbirth, or the
puerperium, or specified as puerperal (674.0)

430 Subarachnoid hemorrhage
Meningeal hemorrhage
Ruptured:
   berry aneurysm
   (congenital) cerebral aneurysm NOS

Excludes *syphilitic ruptured cerebral aneurysm (094.87)*

431 Intracerebral hemorrhage
Hemorrhage (of):
   basilar   internal capsule
   bulbar   intrapontine
   cerebellar   pontine
   cerebral   subcortical
   cerebromeningeal   ventricular
   cortical
Rupture of blood vessel in brain

● **432 Other and unspecified intracranial hemorrhage**

432.0 Nontraumatic extradural hemorrhage
    Nontraumatic epidural hemorrhage

432.1 Subdural hemorrhage
    Subdural hematoma, nontraumatic

☐ **432.9 Unspecified intracranial hemorrhage**
    Intracranial hemorrhage NOS

● **433 Occlusion and stenosis of precerebral arteries**

The following fifth-digit subclassification is for use with category 433:
  0 without mention of cerebral infarction
  1 with cerebral infarction

  Includes: embolism of basilar, carotid, and vertebral arteries
      narrowing of basilar, carotid, and vertebral arteries
      obstruction of basilar, carotid, and vertebral arteries
      thrombosis of basilar, carotid, and vertebral arteries

  Excludes *insufficiency NOS of precerebral arteries (435.0–435.9)*

● **433.0 Basilar artery**

● **433.1 Carotid artery**

● **433.2 Vertebral artery**

● **433.3 Multiple and bilateral**

☐ ● **433.8 Other specified precerebral artery**

☐ ● **433.9 Unspecified precerebral artery**
    Precerebral artery NOS

● **434 Occlusion of cerebral arteries**

The following fifth-digit subclassification is for use with category 434:
  0 without mention of cerebral infarction
  1 with cerebral infarction

● **434.0 Cerebral thrombosis**
    Thrombosis of cerebral arteries

● **434.1 Cerebral embolism**

☐ ● **434.9 Cerebral artery occlusion, unspecified**

● **435 Transient cerebral ischemia**

  Includes: cerebrovascular insufficiency (acute) with transient focal neurological signs and symptoms
      insufficiency of basilar, carotid, and vertebral arteries
      spasm of cerebral arteries

  Excludes *acute cerebrovascular insufficiency NOS (437.1)*
    that due to any condition classifiable to 433 (433.0–433.9)

435.0 Basilar artery syndrome

435.1 Vertebral artery syndrome

435.2 Subclavian steal syndrome

435.3 Vertebrobasilar artery syndrome

☐ **435.8 Other specified transient cerebral ischemias**

☐ **435.9 Unspecified transient cerebral ischemia**
    Impending cerebrovascular accident
    Intermittent cerebral ischemia
    Transient ischemic attack [TIA]

436 Acute, but ill-defined, cerebrovascular disease
    Apoplexy, apoplectic:
      NOS   cerebral
      attack   seizure
    Cerebral seizure
    Cerebrovascular accident [CVA] NOS
    Stroke

  Excludes *any condition classifiable to categories 430–435*

● **437 Other and ill-defined cerebrovascular disease**

437.0 Cerebral atherosclerosis
    Atheroma of cerebral arteries
    Cerebral arteriosclerosis

☐ **437.1 Other generalized ischemic cerebrovascular disease**
    Acute cerebrovascular insufficiency NOS
    Cerebral ischemia (chronic)

437.2 Hypertensive encephalopathy

437.3 Cerebral aneurysm, nonruptured
    Internal carotid artery, intracranial portion
    Internal carotid artery NOS

  Excludes *congenital cerebral aneurysm, nonruptured (747.81)*
    internal carotid artery, extracranial portion (442.81)

437.4 Cerebral arteritis

437.5 Moyamoya disease

437.6 Nonpyogenic thrombosis of intracranial venous sinus

  Excludes *pyogenic (325)*

437.7 Transient global amnesia

☐ **437.8 Other**

☐ **437.9 Unspecified**
    Cerebrovascular disease or lesion NOS

● **438 Late effects of cerebrovascular disease**

Note: This category is to be used to indicate conditions in 430–437 as the cause of late effects. The "late effects" include conditions specified as such, or as sequelae, which may occur at any time after the onset of the causal condition.

438.0 Cognitive deficits

● **438.1 Speech and language deficits**

☐ **438.10 Speech and language deficit, unspecified**

438.11 Aphasia

438.12 Dysphasia

☐ **438.19 Other speech and language deficits**

● **438.2 Hemiplegia/hemiparesis**

☐ **438.20 Hemiplegia affecting unspecified side**

438.21 Hemiplegia affecting dominant side

438.22 Hemiplegia affecting nondominant side

● **438.3 Monoplegia of upper limb**

☐ **438.30 Monoplegia of upper limb affecting unspecified side**

438.31 Monoplegia of upper limb affecting dominant side

438.32 Monoplegia of upper limb affecting nondominant side

● **438.4 Monoplegia of lower limb**

☐ **438.40 Monoplegia of lower limb affecting unspecified side**

438.41 Monoplegia of lower limb affecting dominant side

438.42 Monoplegia of lower limb affecting nondominant side

ICD-9-CM

400-499

Vol. 1

● **438.5 Other paralytic syndrome**

Use additional code to identify type of paralytic syndrome, such as: ◀
    locked-in state (344.81) ◀
    quadriplegia (344.00–344.09) ◀

| **Excludes** | *late effects of cerebrovascular accident with:* ◀ |

    hemiplegia/hemiparesis (438.20–438.22) ◀
    monoplegia of lower limb (438.40–438.42) ◀
    monoplegia of upper limb (438.30–438.32) ◀

☐ **438.50 Other paralytic syndrome affecting unspecified side**

438.51 Other paralytic syndrome affecting dominant side

438.52 Other paralytic syndrome affecting nondominant side

438.53 Other paralytic syndrome, bilateral

● **438.8 Other late effects of cerebrovascular disease**

438.81 Apraxia

438.82 Dysphagia

☐ **438.89 Other late effects of cerebrovascular disease**

☐ **438.9 Unspecified late effects of cerebrovascular disease**
Use additional code to identify the late effect ◀

DISEASES OF ARTERIES, ARTERIOLES, AND CAPILLARIES (440–448)

● **440 Atherosclerosis**

Includes: arteriolosclerosis
arteriosclerosis (obliterans) (senile)
arteriosclerotic vascular disease
atheroma
degeneration:
    arterial
    arteriovascular
    vascular
endarteritis deformans or obliterans
senile:
    arteritis
    endarteritis

| **Excludes** | *atherosclerosis of bypass graft of the extremities (440.30–440.32)* |

440.0 Of aorta

440.1 Of renal artery

| **Excludes** | *atherosclerosis of renal arterioles (403.00–403.91)* |

● **440.2 Of native arteries of the extremities**

| **Excludes** | *atherosclerosis of bypass graft of the extremities (440.30–440.32)* |

☐ **440.20 Atherosclerosis of the extremities, unspecified**

440.21 Atherosclerosis of the extremities with intermittent claudication

440.22 Atherosclerosis of the extremities with rest pain
Any condition classifiable to 440.21

440.23 Atherosclerosis of the extremities with ulceration
Any condition classifiable to 440.21–440.22

440.24 Atherosclerosis of the extremities with gangrene
Any condition classifiable to 440.21, 440.22, and 440.23 with ischemic gangrene 785.4

| **Excludes** | *gas gangrene (040.0)* |

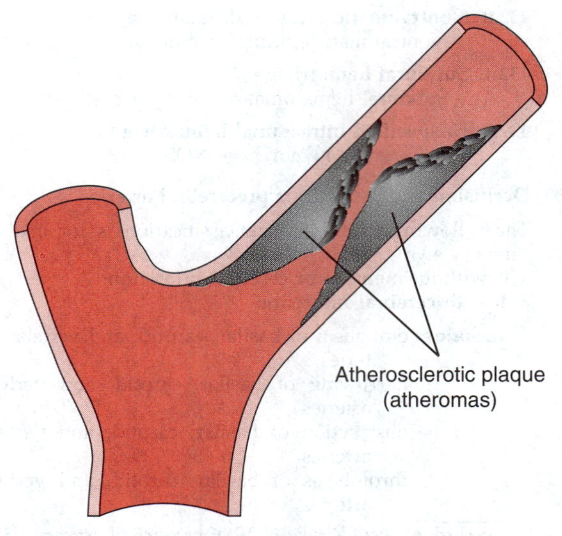

Figure 7–4   Atherosclerotic plaque.

Item 7–9   Classification is based on the location of the atherosclerosis.

☐ **440.29 Other**

● **440.3 Of bypass graft of the extremities**

| **Excludes** | *atherosclerosis of native artery of the extremity (440.21–440.24)* |
| | *embolism [occlusion NOS] [thrombus] of graft (996.74)* |

☐ **440.30 Of unspecified graft**

440.31 Of autologous vein bypass graft

440.32 Of nonautologous vein bypass graft

☐ **440.8 Of other specified arteries**

Excludes	*basilar (433.0)*
	carotid (433.1)
	cerebral (437.0)
	coronary (414.00–414.05)
	mesenteric (557.1)
	precerebral (433.0–433.9)
	pulmonary (416.0)
	vertebral (433.2)

☐ **440.9 Generalized and unspecified atherosclerosis**
Arteriosclerotic vascular disease NOS

| **Excludes** | *arteriosclerotic cardiovascular disease [ASCVD] (429.2)* |

● **441 Aortic aneurysm and dissection**

| **Excludes** | *syphilitic aortic aneurysm (093.0)* |
| | *traumatic aortic aneurysm (901.0, 902.0)* |

Item 7–10   Rupture is the tearing of the aneurysm.

● **441.0 Dissection of aorta**
Dissecting aneurysm of aorta (ruptured)

☐ **441.00 Unspecified site**

441.01 Thoracic

441.02 Abdominal

441.03 Thoracoabdominal

441.1 Thoracic aneurysm, ruptured

441.2 Thoracic aneurysm without mention of rupture

441.3 Abdominal aneurysm, ruptured

    ◀▶ **New Code**   ⬅▬▬➡ **Revised Code**   ● **Not a Principal Diagnosis**   ● **Use Additional Digit(s)**   ☐ **Nonspecific Code**

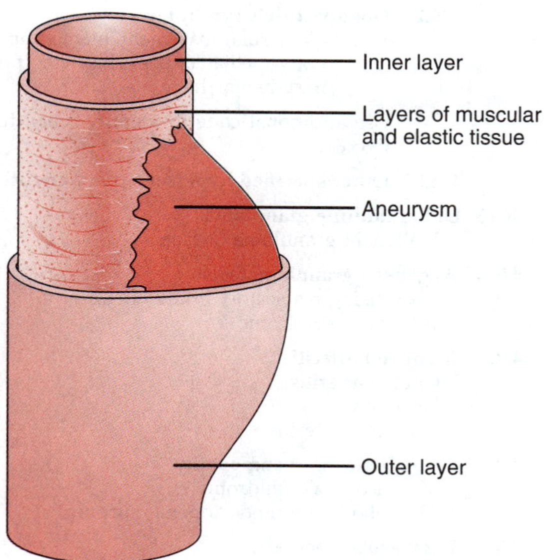

Figure 7–5   An aneurysm is an enclosed swelling on the wall of the vessel.

441.4 Abdominal aneurysm without mention of rupture

☐ **441.5 Aortic aneurysm of unspecified site, ruptured**
Rupture of aorta NOS

441.6 Thoracoabdominal aneurysm, ruptured

441.7 Thoracoabdominal aneurysm, without mention of rupture

☐ **441.9 Aortic aneurysm of unspecified site without mention of rupture**
Aneurysm
Dilatation of aorta
Hyaline necrosis of aorta

● **442 Other aneurysm**

Includes: aneurysm (ruptured) (cirsoid) (false) (varicose)
aneurysmal varix

Excludes   *arteriovenous aneurysm or fistula:*
acquired (447.0)
congenital (747.60–747.69)
traumatic (900.0–904.9)

442.0 Of artery of upper extremity

442.1 Of renal artery

442.2 Of iliac artery

442.3 Of artery of lower extremity
Aneurysm:
femoral artery
popliteal artery

● **442.8 Of other specified artery**

442.81 Artery of neck
Aneurysm of carotid artery (common) (external) (internal, extracranial portion)

Excludes   *internal carotid artery, intracranial portion (437.3)*

442.82 Subclavian artery

442.83 Splenic artery

☐ **442.84 Other visceral artery**
Aneurysm:
celiac artery
gastroduodenal artery
gastroepiploic artery
hepatic artery
pancreaticoduodenal artery
superior mesenteric artery

☐ **442.89 Other**
Aneurysm:
mediastinal artery   spinal artery

Excludes   *cerebral (nonruptured) (437.3)*
congenital (747.81)
ruptured (430)
coronary (414.11)
heart (414.10)
pulmonary (417.1)

☐ **442.9 Of unspecified site**

● **443 Other peripheral vascular disease**

443.0 Raynaud's syndrome
Raynaud's:
disease
phenomenon (secondary)

Use additional code to identify gangrene (785.4)

443.1 Thromboangiitis obliterans [Buerger's disease]
Presenile gangrene

● **443.8 Other specified peripheral vascular diseases**

● **443.81 Peripheral angiopathy in diseases classified elsewhere**

Code first underlying disease, as:
diabetes mellitus (250.7)

☐ **443.89 Other**
Acrocyanosis
Acroparesthesia:
simple [Schultze's type]
vasomotor [Nothnagel's type]
Erythrocyanosis
Erythromelalgia

Excludes   *chilblains (991.5)*
frostbite (991.0–991.3)
immersion foot (991.4)

☐ **443.9 Peripheral vascular disease, unspecified**
Intermittent claudication NOS
Peripheral:
angiopathy NOS
vascular disease NOS
Spasm of artery

Excludes   *atherosclerosis of the arteries of the extremities (440.20–440.22)*
spasm of cerebral artery (435.0–435.9)

Item 7–11 An embolus is a mass of undissolved matter present in the blood that is transported by the blood current. A thrombus is a blood clot that occludes or shuts off a vessel. When a thrombus is dislodged, it becomes an embolus.

● **444 Arterial embolism and thrombosis**

Includes: infarction:
embolic
thrombotic
occlusion

Excludes   *that complicating:*
abortion (634–638 with .6, 639.6)
ectopic or molar pregnancy (639.6)
pregnancy, childbirth, or the puerperium (673.0–673.8)

ICD-9-CM

400-499

Vol. 1

444.0 Of abdominal aorta
Aortic bifurcation syndrome
Aortoiliac obstruction
Leriche's syndrome
Saddle embolus

444.1 Of thoracic aorta
Embolism or thrombosis of aorta (thoracic)

● **444.2 Of arteries of the extremities**

   444.21 Upper extremity

   444.22 Lower extremity
Arterial embolism or thrombosis:
   femoral
   peripheral NOS
   popliteal

   Excludes *iliofemoral (444.81)*

● **444.8 Of other specified artery**

   444.81 Iliac artery

   ☐ **444.89 Other**

   Excludes *basilar (433.0)*
carotid (433.1)
cerebral (434.0–434.9)
coronary (410.00–410.92)
mesenteric (557.0)
ophthalmic (362.30–362.34)
precerebral (433.0–433.9)
pulmonary (415.19)
renal (593.81)
retinal (362.30–362.34)
vertebral (433.2)

☐ **444.9 Of unspecified artery**

● **446 Polyarteritis nodosa and allied conditions**

446.0 Polyarteritis nodosa
Disseminated necrotizing periarteritis
Necrotizing angiitis
Panarteritis (nodosa)
Periarteritis (nodosa)

446.1 Acute febrile mucocutaneous lymph node syndrome [MCLS]
Kawasaki disease

● **446.2 Hypersensitivity angiitis**

   Excludes *antiglomerular basement membrane disease without pulmonary hemorrhage (583.89)*

   ☐ **446.20 Hypersensitivity angiitis, unspecified**

446.21 Goodpasture's syndrome
Antiglomerular basement membrane antibody-mediated nephritis with pulmonary hemorrhage

Use additional code to identify renal disease (583.81)

☐ **446.29 Other specified hypersensitivity angiitis**

446.3 Lethal midline granuloma
Malignant granuloma of face

446.4 Wegener's granulomatosis
Necrotizing respiratory granulomatosis
Wegener's syndrome

446.5 Giant cell arteritis
Cranial arteritis
Horton's disease
Temporal arteritis

446.6 Thrombotic microangiopathy
Moschcowitz's syndrome
Thrombotic thrombocytopenic purpura

446.7 Takayasu's disease
Aortic arch arteritis
Pulseless disease

● **447 Other disorders of arteries and arterioles**

447.0 Arteriovenous fistula, acquired
Arteriovenous aneurysm, acquired

   Excludes *cerebrovascular (437.3)*
coronary (414.19)
pulmonary (417.0)
surgically created arteriovenous shunt or fistula:
   complication (996.1, 996.61–996.62)
   status or presence (V45.1)
traumatic (900.0–904.9)

447.1 Stricture of artery

447.2 Rupture of artery
Erosion of artery
Fistula, except arteriovenous, of artery
Ulcer of artery

   Excludes *traumatic rupture of artery (900.0–904.9)*

447.3 Hyperplasia of renal artery
Fibromuscular hyperplasia of renal artery

447.4 Celiac artery compression syndrome
Celiac axis syndrome
Marable's syndrome

447.5 Necrosis of artery

☐ **447.6 Arteritis, unspecified**
Aortitis NOS
Endarteritis NOS

   Excludes *arteritis, endarteritis:*
   aortic arch (446.7)
   cerebral (437.4)
   coronary (414.00–414.05)
   deformans (440.0–440.9)
   obliterans (440.0–440.9)
   pulmonary (417.8)
   senile (440.0–440.9)
polyarteritis NOS (446.0)
syphilitic aortitis (093.1)

☐ **447.8 Other specified disorders of arteries and arterioles**
Fibromuscular hyperplasia of arteries, except renal

☐ **447.9 Unspecified disorders of arteries and arterioles**

● **448 Disease of capillaries**

448.0 Hereditary hemorrhagic telangiectasia
Rendu-Osler-Weber disease

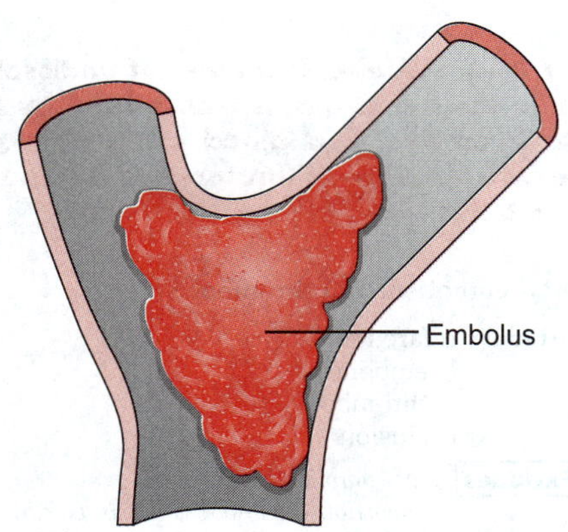

Figure 7–6 An arterial embolism.

448.1 Nevus, non-neoplastic
Nevus:

araneus	spider
senile	stellar

> **Excludes**   *neoplastic (216.0–216.9)*
> *port wine (757.32)*
> *strawberry (757.32)*

448.9 Other and unspecified capillary diseases
Capillary:
hemorrhage
hyperpermeability
thrombosis

> **Excludes**   *capillary fragility (hereditary) (287.8)*

DISEASES OF VEINS AND LYMPHATICS, AND OTHER DISEASES OF CIRCULATORY SYSTEM (451–459)

● **451 Phlebitis and thrombophlebitis**

Includes: endophlebitis
inflammation, vein
periphlebitis
suppurative phlebitis

Use additional E code to identify drug, if drug-induced

> **Excludes**   *that complicating:*
> *abortion (634–638 with .7, 639.8)*
> *ectopic or molar pregnancy (639.8)*
> *pregnancy, childbirth, or the puerperium (671.0–671.9)*
> *that due to or following:*
> *implant or catheter device (996.61–996.62)*
> *infusion, perfusion, or transfusion (999.2)*

451.0 Of superficial vessels of lower extremities
Saphenous vein (greater) (lesser)

● **451.1 Of deep vessels of lower extremities**

451.11 Femoral vein (deep) (superficial)

451.19 Other
Femoropopliteal vein
Popliteal vein
Tibial vein

451.2 Of lower extremities, unspecified

● **451.8 Of other sites**

> **Excludes**   *intracranial venous sinus (325)*
> *nonpyogenic (437.6)*
> *portal (vein) (572.1)*

451.81 Iliac vein

451.82 Of superficial veins of upper extremities

Antecubital vein	Cephalic vein
Basilic vein	

451.83 Of deep veins of upper extremities

Brachial vein	Ulnar vein
Radial vein	

451.84 Of upper extremities, unspecified

451.89 Other
Axillary vein
Jugular vein
Subclavian vein
Thrombophlebitis of breast (Mondor's disease)

451.9 Of unspecified site

452 Portal vein thrombosis
Portal (vein) obstruction

> **Excludes**   *hepatic vein thrombosis (453.0)*
> *phlebitis of portal vein (572.1)*

● **453 Other venous embolism and thrombosis**

> **Excludes**   *that complicating:*
> *abortion (634–638 with .7, 639.8)*
> *ectopic or molar pregnancy (639.8)*
> *pregnancy, childbirth, or the puerperium (671.0–671.9)*
> *that with inflammation, phlebitis, and thrombophlebitis (451.0–451.9)*

453.0 Budd-Chiari syndrome
Hepatic vein thrombosis

453.1 Thrombophlebitis migrans

453.2 Of vena cava

453.3 Of renal vein

453.8 Of other specified veins

> **Excludes**   *cerebral (434.0–434.9)*
> *coronary (410.00–410.92)*
> *intracranial venous sinus (325)*
> *nonpyogenic (437.6)*
> *mesenteric (557.0)*
> *portal (452)*
> *precerebral (433.0–433.9)*
> *pulmonary (415.19)*

453.9 Of unspecified site

Embolism of vein	Thrombosis (vein)

● **454 Varicose veins of lower extremities**

> **Excludes**   *that complicating pregnancy, childbirth, or the puerperium (671.0)*

454.0 With ulcer
Varicose ulcer (lower extremity, any part)
Varicose veins with ulcer of lower extremity [any part] or of unspecified site
Any condition classifiable to 454.9 with ulcer or specified as ulcerated

454.1 With inflammation
Stasis dermatitis
Varicose veins with inflammation of lower extremity [any part] or of unspecified site
Any condition classifiable to 454.9 with inflammation or specified as inflamed

454.2 With ulcer and inflammation
Varicose veins with ulcer and inflammation of lower extremity [any part] or of unspecified site
Any condition classifiable to 454.9 with ulcer and inflammation

454.9 Without mention of ulcer or inflammation
Phlebectasia of lower extremity [any part] or of unspecified site
Varicose veins of lower extremity [any part] or of unspecified site
Varix of lower extremity [any part] or of unspecified site

● **455 Hemorrhoids**

Includes: hemorrhoids (anus) (rectum)
piles
varicose veins, anus or rectum

> **Excludes**   *that complicating pregnancy, childbirth, or the puerperium (671.8)*

455.0 Internal hemorrhoids without mention of complication

455.1 Internal thrombosed hemorrhoids

455.2 Internal hemorrhoids with other complication
Internal hemorrhoids:

bleeding	strangulated
prolapsed	ulcerated

ICD-9-CM

400-499

Vol. 1

455.3   **External hemorrhoids without mention of complication**

455.4   **External thrombosed hemorrhoids**

☐ **455.5**   **External hemorrhoids with other complication**
External hemorrhoids:
bleeding
prolapsed
strangulated
ulcerated

☐ **455.6**   **Unspecified hemorrhoids without mention of complication**
Hemorrhoids NOS

☐ **455.7**   **Unspecified thrombosed hemorrhoids**
Thrombosed hemorrhoids, unspecified whether internal or external

☐ **455.8**   **Unspecified hemorrhoids with other complication**
Hemorrhoids, unspecified whether internal or external:
bleeding
prolapsed
strangulated
ulcerated

455.9   **Residual hemorrhoidal skin tags**
Skin tags, anus or rectum

● **456**   **Varicose veins of other sites**

456.0   **Esophageal varices with bleeding**

456.1   **Esophageal varices without mention of bleeding**

● **456.2**   *Esophageal varices in diseases classified elsewhere*

Code first underlying disease, as:
cirrhosis of liver (571.0–571.9)
portal hypertension (572.3)

    ● **456.20**   *With bleeding*

    ● **456.21**   *Without mention of bleeding*

456.3   **Sublingual varices**

456.4   **Scrotal varices**
Varicocele

456.5   **Pelvic varices**
Varices of broad ligament

456.6   **Vulval varices**
Varices of perineum

| **Excludes** | *that complicating pregnancy, childbirth, or the puerperium (671.1)* |

☐ **456.8**   **Varices of other sites**
Varicose veins of nasal septum (with ulcer)

Excludes	*placental varices (656.7)*
	retinal varices (362.17)
	varicose ulcer of unspecified site (454.0)
	varicose veins of unspecified site (454.9)

● **457**   **Noninfectious disorders of lymphatic channels**

457.0   **Postmastectomy lymphedema syndrome**
Elephantiasis due to mastectomy
Obliteration of lymphatic vessel due to mastectomy

☐ **457.1**   **Other lymphedema**
Elephantiasis (nonfilarial) NOS
Lymphangiectasis
Lymphedema:
acquired (chronic)   secondary
praecox
Obliteration, lymphatic vessel

Excludes	*elephantiasis (nonfilarial):*
	congenital (757.0)
	eyelid (374.83)
	vulva (624.8)

457.2   **Lymphangitis**
Lymphangitis:
NOS
chronic
subacute

| **Excludes** | *acute lymphangitis (682.0–682.9)* |

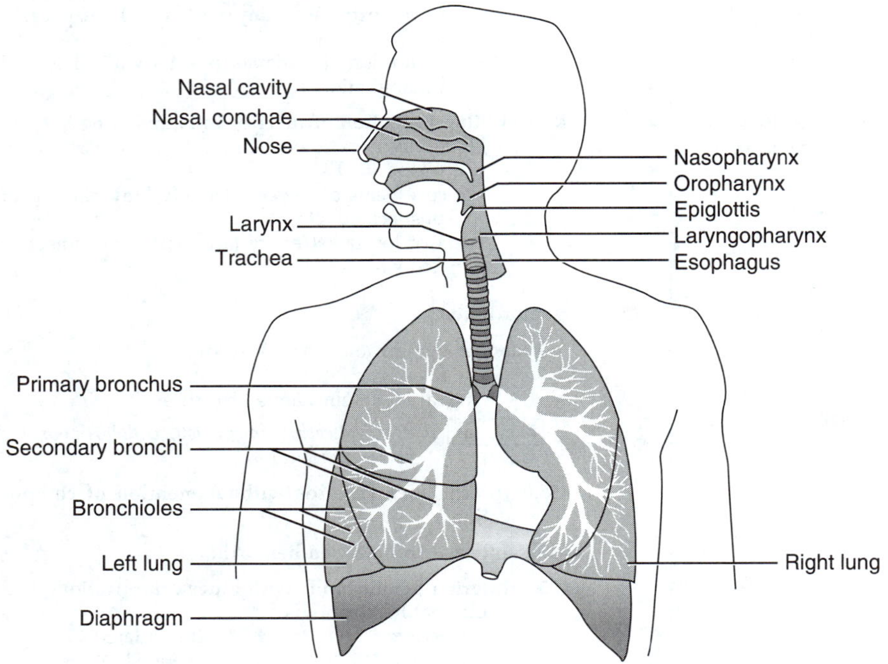

Figure 8–1   Respiratory system. (From Buck CJ: Step-by-Step Medical Coding, 2nd ed. Philadelphia, WB Saunders, 1998, p 134.)

❑ **457.8 Other noninfectious disorders of lymphatic channels**
Chylocele (nonfilarial)
Chylous:
   ascites
   cyst
Lymph node or vessel:
   fistula
   infarction
   rupture
> **Excludes** *chylocele:*
>   *filarial (125.0–125.9)*
>   *tunica vaginalis (nonfilarial) (608.84)*

❑ **457.9 Unspecified noninfectious disorder of lymphatic channels**

● **458 Hypotension**

Includes: hypopiesis
> **Excludes** *cardiovascular collapse (785.50)*
> *maternal hypotension syndrome (669.2)*
> *shock (785.50–785.59)*
> *Shy-Drager syndrome (333.0)*

458.0 Orthostatic hypotension
Hypotension:
   orthostatic (chronic)
   postural

458.1 Chronic hypotension
Permanent idiopathic hypotension

458.2 Iatrogenic hypotension
Postoperative hypotension

❑ **458.8 Other specified hypotension**

❑ **458.9 Hypotension, unspecified**
Hypotension (arterial) NOS

● **459 Other disorders of circulatory system**

❑ **459.0 Hemorrhage, unspecified**
Rupture of blood vessel NOS
Spontaneous hemorrhage NEC
> **Excludes** *hemorrhage:*
>   *gastrointestinal NOS (578.9)*
>   *in newborn NOS (772.9)*
>   *secondary or recurrent following trauma (958.2)*
>   *traumatic rupture of blood vessel (900.0–904.9)*

459.1 Postphlebitic syndrome

459.2 Compression of vein
Stricture of vein
Vena cava syndrome (inferior) (superior)

● **459.8 Other specified disorders of circulatory system**

❑ **459.81 Venous (peripheral) insufficiency, unspecified**
Chronic venous insufficiency NOS

Use additional code for any associated ulceration (707.1–707.9)

❑ **459.89 Other**
Collateral circulation (venous), any site
Phlebosclerosis
Venofibrosis

❑ **459.9 Unspecified circulatory system disorder**

8. DISEASES OF THE RESPIRATORY SYSTEM (460–519)

Use additional code to identify infectious organism

ACUTE RESPIRATORY INFECTIONS (460–466)

> **Excludes** *pneumonia and influenza (480.0–487.8)*

460 Acute nasopharyngitis [common cold]
Coryza (acute)
Nasal catarrh, acute
Nasopharyngitis:
   NOS
   acute
   infective NOS
Rhinitis:
   acute
   infective
> **Excludes** *nasopharyngitis, chronic (472.2)*
>   *pharyngitis:*
>   *acute or unspecified (462)*
>   *chronic (472.1)*
>   *rhinitis:*
>   *allergic (477.0–477.9)*
>   *chronic or unspecified (472.0)*
>   *sore throat:*
>   *acute or unspecified (462)*
>   *chronic (472.1)*

● **461 Acute sinusitis**

Includes: abscess, acute, of sinus (accessory) (nasal)
empyema, acute, of sinus (accessory) (nasal)
infection, acute, of sinus (accessory) (nasal)
inflammation, acute, of sinus (accessory) (nasal)
suppuration, acute, of sinus (accessory) (nasal)
> **Excludes** *chronic or unspecified sinusitis (473.0–473.9)*

461.0 Maxillary
Acute antritis

461.1 Frontal

461.2 Ethmoidal

461.3 Sphenoidal

❑ **461.8 Other acute sinusitis**
Acute pansinusitis

❑ **461.9 Acute sinusitis, unspecified**
Acute sinusitis NOS

462 Acute pharyngitis
Acute sore throat NOS
Pharyngitis (acute):
   NOS   pneumococcal
   gangrenous   staphylococcal
   infective   suppurative
   phlegmonous   ulcerative
Sore throat (viral) NOS
Viral pharyngitis
> **Excludes** *abscess:*
>   *peritonsillar [quinsy] (475)*
>   *pharyngeal NOS (478.29)*
>   *retropharyngeal (478.24)*
>   *chronic pharyngitis (472.1)*
>   *infectious mononucleosis (075)*
>   *that specified as (due to):*
>   *Coxsackie (virus) (074.0)*
>   *gonococcus (098.6)*
>   *herpes simplex (054.79)*
>   *influenza (487.1)*
>   *septic (034.0)*
>   *streptococcal (034.0)*

ICD-9-CM

400–499

Vol. 1

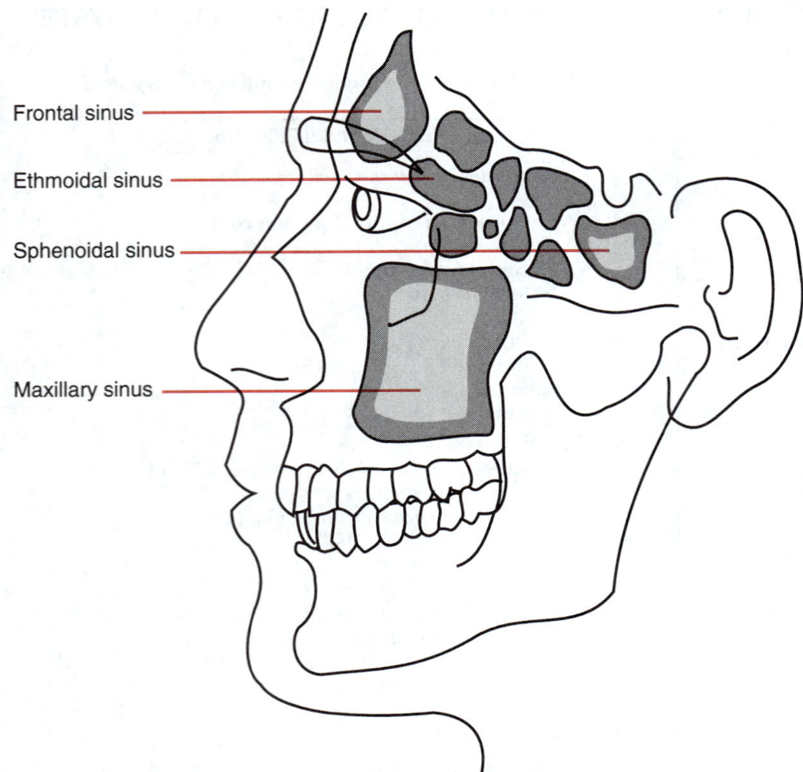

Figure 8–2 Paranasal sinuses. (From Buck CJ: Step-by-Step Medical Coding, 2nd ed. Philadelphia, WB Saunders, 1998, p 135.)

463 Acute tonsillitis
Tonsillitis (acute):

NOS	septic
follicular	staphylococcal
gangrenous	suppurative
infective	ulcerative
pneumococcal	viral

> **Excludes** *chronic tonsillitis (474.0)*
> *hypertrophy of tonsils (474.1)*
> *peritonsillar abscess [quinsy] (475)*
> *sore throat:*
>   *acute or NOS (462)*
>   *septic (034.0)*
> *streptococcal tonsillitis (034.0)*

● **464 Acute laryngitis and tracheitis**

> **Excludes** *that associated with influenza (487.1)*
> *that due to Streptococcus (034.0)*

464.0 Acute laryngitis
Laryngitis (acute):
NOS
edematous
Hemophilus influenzae [H. influenzae]
pneumococcal
septic
suppurative
ulcerative

> **Excludes** *chronic laryngitis (476.0–476.1)*
> *influenzal laryngitis (487.1)*

● **464.1 Acute tracheitis**
Tracheitis (acute):
NOS
catarrhal
viral

> **Excludes** *chronic tracheitis (491.8)*

464.10 Without mention of obstruction

464.11 With obstruction

● **464.2 Acute laryngotracheitis**
Laryngotracheitis (acute)
Tracheitis (acute) with laryngitis (acute)

> **Excludes** *chronic laryngotracheitis (476.1)*

464.20 Without mention of obstruction

464.21 With obstruction

● **464.3 Acute epiglottitis**
Viral epiglottitis

> **Excludes** *epiglottitis, chronic (476.1)*

464.30 Without mention of obstruction

464.31 With obstruction

464.4 Croup
Croup syndrome

● **465 Acute upper respiratory infections of multiple or unspecified sites**

> **Excludes** *upper respiratory infection due to:*
> *influenza (487.1)*
> *Streptococcus (034.0)*

465.0 Acute laryngopharyngitis

□ **465.8 Other multiple sites**
Multiple URI

□ **465.9 Unspecified site**
Acute URI NOS
Upper respiratory infection (acute)

● **466 Acute bronchitis and bronchiolitis**

> **Includes:** that with:
> bronchospasm
> obstruction

466.0 Acute bronchitis
Bronchitis, acute or subacute:

fibrinous	septic
membranous	viral
pneumococcal	with tracheitis
purulent	

Croupous bronchitis
Tracheobronchitis, acute

● 466.1 Acute bronchiolitis
Bronchiolitis (acute)
Capillary pneumonia

466.11 Acute bronchiolitis due to respiratory syncytial virus (RSV)

☐ 466.19 Acute bronchiolitis due to other infectious organisms
Use additional code to identify organism

OTHER DISEASES OF THE UPPER RESPIRATORY TRACT (470–478)

470 Deviated nasal septum
Deflected septum (nasal) (acquired)
Excludes *congenital (754.0)*

● 471 Nasal polyps
Excludes *adenomatous polyps (212.0)*

471.0 Polyp of nasal cavity
Polyp:
choanal
nasopharyngeal

471.1 Polypoid sinus degeneration
Woakes' syndrome or ethmoiditis

☐ 471.8 Other polyp of sinus
Polyp of sinus:
accessory
ethmoidal
maxillary
sphenoidal

☐ 471.9 Unspecified nasal polyp
Nasal polyp NOS

● 472 Chronic pharyngitis and nasopharyngitis

472.0 Chronic rhinitis
Ozena
Rhinitis:

NOS	obstructive
atrophic	purulent
granulomatous	ulcerative
hypertrophic	

Excludes *allergic rhinitis (477.0–477.9)*

472.1 Chronic pharyngitis
Chronic sore throat
Pharyngitis:
atrophic
granular (chronic)
hypertrophic

472.2 Chronic nasopharyngitis
Excludes *acute or unspecified nasopharyngitis (460)*

● 473 Chronic sinusitis
Includes: abscess (chronic) of sinus (accessory) (nasal)
empyema (chronic) of sinus (accessory) (nasal)
infection (chronic) of sinus (accessory) (nasal)
suppuration (chronic) of sinus (accessory) (nasal)

Excludes *acute sinusitis (461.0–461.9)*

473.0 Maxillary
Antritis (chronic)

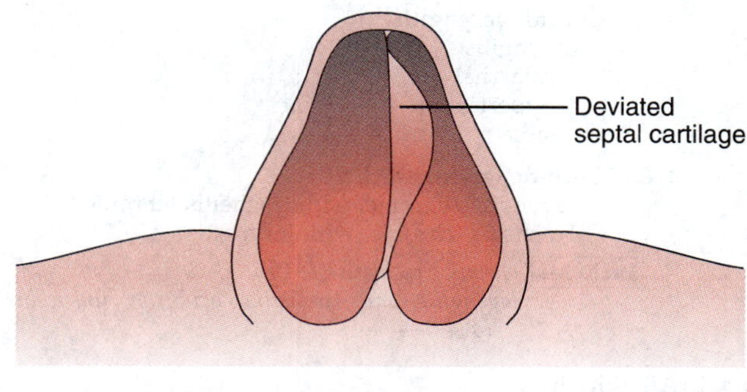

Figure 8–3　Deviated nasal septum.

Item 8–1　A deviated nasal septum is the displacement of the septal cartilage.

473.1 Frontal

473.2 Ethmoidal
Excludes *Woakes' ethmoiditis (471.1)*

473.3 Sphenoidal

☐ 473.8 Other chronic sinusitis
Pansinusitis (chronic)

☐ 473.9 Unspecified sinusitis (chronic)
Sinusitis (chronic) NOS

● 474 Chronic disease of tonsils and adenoids

● 474.0 Chronic tonsillitis and adenoiditis
Excludes *acute or unspecified tonsillitis (463)*

474.00 Chronic tonsillitis

474.01 Chronic adenoiditis

474.02 Chronic tonsillitis and adenoiditis

● 474.1 Hypertrophy of tonsils and adenoids
Enlargement of tonsils or adenoids
Hyperplasia of tonsils or adenoids
Hypertrophy of tonsils or adenoids

Excludes *that with:*
adenoiditis (474.01)
adenoiditis and tonsillitis (474.02)
tonsillitis (474.00)

474.10 Tonsils with adenoids

474.11 Tonsils alone

474.12 Adenoids alone

474.2 Adenoid vegetations

☐ 474.8 Other chronic disease of tonsils and adenoids
Amygdalolith
Calculus, tonsil
Cicatrix of tonsil (and adenoid)
Tonsillar tag
Ulcer, tonsil

☐ 474.9 Unspecified chronic disease of tonsils and adenoids
Disease (chronic) of tonsils (and adenoids)

475 Peritonsillar abscess
Abscess of tonsil
Peritonsillar cellulitis
Quinsy

Excludes *tonsillitis:*
acute or NOS (463)
chronic (474.0)

● 476 Chronic laryngitis and laryngotracheitis

ICD-9-CM

400-499

Vol. 1

476.0 Chronic laryngitis
  Laryngitis:
    catarrhal
    hypertrophic
    sicca

476.1 Chronic laryngotracheitis
  Laryngitis, chronic, with tracheitis (chronic)
  Tracheitis, chronic, with laryngitis

  Excludes *chronic tracheitis (491.8)*
              laryngitis and tracheitis, acute or unspecified
              (464.0–464.4)

● **477 Allergic rhinitis**

  Includes: allergic rhinitis (nonseasonal) (seasonal)
              hay fever
              spasmodic rhinorrhea

  Excludes *allergic rhinitis with asthma (bronchial) (493.0)*

  477.0 Due to pollen
    Pollinosis

  ☐ **477.8 Due to other allergen**

  ☐ **477.9 Cause unspecified**

● **478 Other diseases of upper respiratory tract**

  478.0 Hypertrophy of nasal turbinates

  ☐ **478.1 Other diseases of nasal cavity and sinuses**
    Abscess of nose (septum)
    Necrosis of nose (septum)
    Ulcer of nose (septum)
    Cyst or mucocele of sinus (nasal)
    Rhinolith

    Excludes *varicose ulcer of nasal septum (456.8)*

● **478.2 Other diseases of pharynx, not elsewhere classified**

  ☐ **478.20 Unspecified disease of pharynx**

  478.21 Cellulitis of pharynx or nasopharynx

  478.22 Parapharyngeal abscess

  478.24 Retropharyngeal abscess

  478.25 Edema of pharynx or nasopharynx

  478.26 Cyst of pharynx or nasopharynx

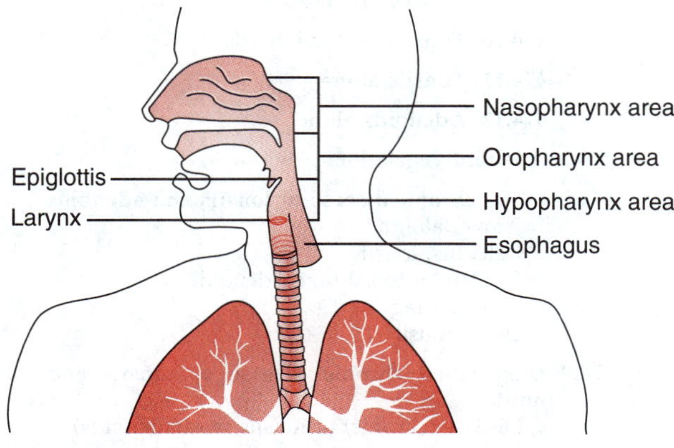

Figure 8–4 The pharynx.

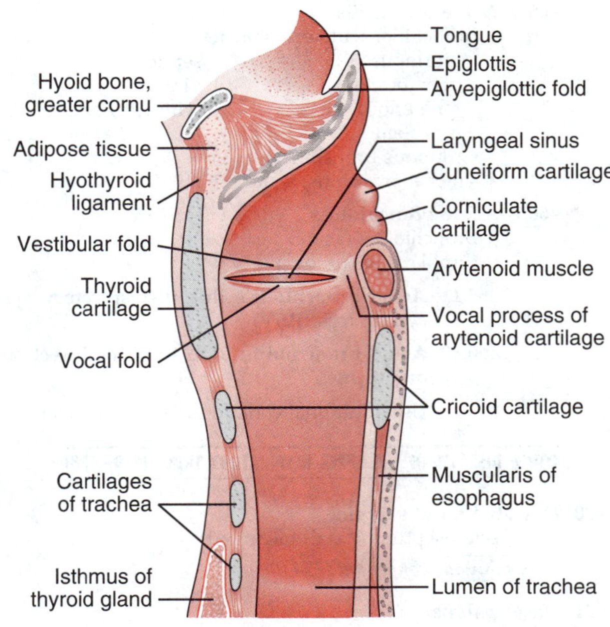

Figure 8–5 Coronal section of the larynx.

  ☐ **478.29 Other**
      Abscess of pharynx or nasopharynx

    Excludes *ulcerative pharyngitis (462)*

● **478.3 Paralysis of vocal cords or larynx**

  ☐ **478.30 Paralysis, unspecified**
      Laryngoplegia   Paralysis of glottis

  478.31 Unilateral, partial

  478.32 Unilateral, complete

  478.33 Bilateral, partial

  478.34 Bilateral, complete

  478.4 Polyp of vocal cord or larynx

    Excludes *adenomatous polyps (212.1)*

☐ **478.5 Other diseases of vocal cords**
    Abscess of vocal cords
    Cellulitis of vocal cords
    Granuloma of vocal cords
    Leukoplakia of vocal cords
    Chorditis (fibrinous) (nodosa) (tuberosa)
    Singers' nodes

  478.6 Edema of larynx
    Edema (of):
      glottis   supraglottic
      subglottic

● **478.7 Other diseases of larynx, not elsewhere classified**

  ☐ **478.70 Unspecified disease of larynx**

  478.71 Cellulitis and perichondritis of larynx

  478.74 Stenosis of larynx

  478.75 Laryngeal spasm
      Laryngismus (stridulus)

  ◀▶ **New Code**   ⬅▬▬➡ **Revised Code**   ● **Not a Principal Diagnosis**   ● **Use Additional Digit(s)**   ☐ **Nonspecific Code**

☐ **478.79 Other**
Abscess of larynx
Necrosis of larynx
Obstruction of larynx
Pachyderma of larynx
Ulcer of larynx

Excludes *ulcerative laryngitis (464.0)*

☐ **478.8 Upper respiratory tract hypersensitivity reaction, site unspecified**

Excludes *hypersensitivity reaction of lower respiratory tract, as:*
extrinsic allergic alveolitis (495.0–495.9)
pneumoconiosis (500–505)

☐ **478.9 Other and unspecified diseases of upper respiratory tract**
Abscess of trachea   Cicatrix of trachea

PNEUMONIA AND INFLUENZA (480–487)

Excludes *pneumonia:*
allergic or eosinophilic (518.3)
aspiration:
  NOS (507.0)
  newborn (770.1)
  solids and liquids (507.0–507.8)
congenital (770.0)
lipoid (507.1)
passive (514)
rheumatic (390)

● **480 Viral pneumonia**

480.0 Pneumonia due to adenovirus

480.1 Pneumonia due to respiratory syncytial virus

480.2 Pneumonia due to parainfluenza virus

☐ **480.8 Pneumonia due to other virus not elsewhere classified**

Excludes *congenital rubella pneumonitis (771.0)*
influenza with pneumonia, any form (487.0)
pneumonia complicating viral diseases classified elsewhere (484.1–484.8)

☐ **480.9 Viral pneumonia, unspecified**

481 Pneumococcal pneumonia [Streptococcus pneumoniae pneumonia]
Lobar pneumonia, organism unspecified

● **482 Other bacterial pneumonia**

482.0 Pneumonia due to Klebsiella pneumoniae

482.1 Pneumonia due to Pseudomonas

482.2 Pneumonia due to Haemophilus influenzae [H. influenzae]

● **482.3 Pneumonia due to Streptococcus**

Excludes *Streptococcus pneumoniae pneumonia (481)*

☐ **482.30 Streptococcus, unspecified**

482.31 Group A

482.32 Group B

☐ **482.39 Other Streptococcus**

● **482.4 Pneumonia due to Staphylococcus** ◄

☐ **482.40 Pneumonia due to *Staphylococcus,* unspecified** ◄

482.41 Pneumonia due to *Staphylococcus aureus* ◄

☐ **482.49 Other *Staphylococcus* pneumonia** ◄

● **482.8 Pneumonia due to other specified bacteria**

Excludes *pneumonia complicating infectious disease classified elsewhere (484.1–484.8)*

482.81 Anaerobes
Gram-negative anaerobes
Bacteroides (melaninogenicus)

482.82 Escherichia coli [E. coli]

☐ **482.83 Other gram-negative bacteria**
Gram-negative pneumonia NOS
Proteus
Serratia marcescens

Excludes *gram-negative anaerobes (482.81)*
Legionnaires' disease (482.84)

482.84 Legionnaires' disease

☐ **482.89 Other specified bacteria**

☐ **482.9 Bacterial pneumonia unspecified**

● **483 Pneumonia due to other specified organism**

483.0 Mycoplasma pneumoniae
Eaton's agent
Pleuropneumonia-like organisms [PPLO]

483.1 Chlamydia

☐ **483.8 Other specified organism**

● **484 Pneumonia in infectious diseases classified elsewhere**

Excludes *influenza with pneumonia, any form (487.0)*

● **484.1 Pneumonia in cytomegalic inclusion disease**

Code first underlying disease, as: (078.5)

● **484.3 Pneumonia in whooping cough**

Code first underlying disease, as: (033.0–033.9)

● **484.5 Pneumonia in anthrax**

Code first underlying disease (022.1)

● **484.6 Pneumonia in aspergillosis**

Code first underlying disease (117.3)

●☐ **484.7 Pneumonia in other systemic mycoses**

Code first underlying disease

Excludes *pneumonia in:*
candidiasis (112.4)
coccidioidomycosis (114.0)
histoplasmosis (115.0–115.9 with fifth-digit 5)

●☐ **484.8 Pneumonia in other infectious diseases classified elsewhere**

Code first underlying disease, as:
Q fever (083.0)
typhoid fever (002.0)

Excludes *pneumonia in:*
actinomycosis (039.1)
measles (055.1)
nocardiosis (039.1)
ornithosis (073.0)
Pneumocystis carinii (136.3)
salmonellosis (003.22)
toxoplasmosis (130.4)
tuberculosis (011.6)
tularemia (021.2)
varicella (052.1)

☐ **485 Bronchopneumonia, organism unspecified**
Bronchopneumonia:
hemorrhagic
terminal
Pleurobronchopneumonia
Pneumonia:
lobular
segmental

Excludes *bronchiolitis (acute) (466.11- 466.19)*
chronic (491.8)
lipoid pneumonia (507.1)

ICD-9-CM

400-499

Vol. 1

□ **486 Pneumonia, organism unspecified**

> **Excludes** *hypostatic or passive pneumonia (514)*
> *influenza with pneumonia, any form (487.0)*
> *inhalation or aspiration pneumonia due to for-*
> *eign materials (507.0–507.8)*
> *pneumonitis due to fumes and vapors (506.0)*

● **487 Influenza**

> **Excludes** *Hemophilus influenzae [H. influenzae]:*
> *infection NOS (041.5)*
> *laryngitis (464.0)*
> *meningitis (320.0)*
> *pneumonia (482.2)*

 487.0 With pneumonia
  Influenza with pneumonia, any form
  Influenzal:
   bronchopneumonia
   pneumonia

□ **487.1 With other respiratory manifestations**
  Influenza NOS
  Influenzal:
   laryngitis
   pharyngitis
   respiratory infection (upper) (acute)

□ **487.8 With other manifestations**
  Encephalopathy due to influenza
  Influenza with involvement of gastrointestinal tract

> **Excludes** *"intestinal flu" [viral gastroenteritis] (008.8)*

CHRONIC OBSTRUCTIVE PULMONARY DISEASE AND ALLIED CONDITIONS (490–496)

Item 8–4 Chronic bronchitis is usually defined as being present in any patient who has persistent cough with sputum production for at least three months in at least two consecutive years. Simple chronic bronchitis is marked by a productive cough but no pathological airflow obstruction. Chronic obstructive pulmonary disease (COPD) is a group of conditions—bronchitis, emphysema, asthma, bronchiectasis, allergic alveolitis—marked by dyspnea. Catarrhal bronchitis is an acute form of bronchitis marked by profuse mucus and pus production (mucopurulent discharge). Croupous bronchitis, also known as pseudomembranous, fibrinous, plastic, exudative, or membranous, is marked by a violent cough and dyspnea.

□ **490 Bronchitis, not specified as acute or chronic**
  Bronchitis NOS:
   catarrhal
   with tracheitis NOS
  Tracheobronchitis NOS

> **Excludes** *bronchitis:*
> *allergic NOS (493.9)*
> *asthmatic NOS (493.9)*
> *due to fumes and vapors (506.0)*

● **491 Chronic bronchitis**

> **Excludes** *chronic obstructive asthma (493.2)*

 491.0 Simple chronic bronchitis
  Catarrhal bronchitis, chronic
  Smokers' cough

 491.1 Mucopurulent chronic bronchitis
  Bronchitis (chronic) (recurrent):
   fetid
   mucopurulent
   purulent

● **491.2 Obstructive chronic bronchitis**
  Bronchitis:
   asthmatic, chronic
   emphysematous
   obstructive (chronic) (diffuse)
  Bronchitis with:
   chronic airway obstruction
   emphysema

> **Excludes** *asthmatic bronchitis (acute) (NOS) 493.9*
> *chronic obstructive asthma 493.2*

 491.20 Without mention of acute exacerbation
  Chronic asthmatic bronchitis
  Emphysema with chronic bronchitis

 491.21 With acute exacerbation
  Acute bronchitis with chronic obstructive
   pulmonary disease [COPD]
  Acute and chronic obstructive bronchitis
  Chronic asthmatic bronchitis with acute
   exacerbation
  Emphysema with acute and chronic bron-
   chitis

□ **491.8 Other chronic bronchitis**
  Chronic:
   tracheitis
   tracheobronchitis

□ **491.9 Unspecified chronic bronchitis**

● **492 Emphysema**

 492.0 Emphysematous bleb
  Giant bullous emphysema
  Ruptured emphysematous bleb
  Tension pneumatocele
  Vanishing lung

□ **492.8 Other emphysema**
  Emphysema (lung or pulmonary):
   NOS   panacinar
   centriacinar panlobular
   centrilobular unilateral
   obstructive vesicular
  MacLeod's syndrome
  Swyer-James syndrome
  Unilateral hyperlucent lung

> **Excludes** *emphysema:*
> *with both acute and chronic bronchitis*
> *(491.21)*
> *with chronic bronchitis (491.20)*
> *compensatory (518.2)*
> *due to fumes and vapors (506.4)*
> *interstitial (518.1)*
> *newborn (770.2)*
> *mediastinal (518.1)*
> *surgical (subcutaneous) (998.81)*
> *traumatic (958.7)*
> *with chronic bronchitis (491.20)*

Item 8–5 Asthma is a bronchial condition marked by airway obstruction, hyper-responsiveness, and inflammation. Extrinsic asthma, also known as allergic asthma, is characterized by the same symptoms that occur with exposure to allergens and is divided into the following types: atopic, occupational, and allergic bronchopulmonary aspergillosis. Intrinsic asthma occurs in patients who have no history of allergy or sensitivities to allergens and is divided into the following types: nonreaginic and pharmacologic. Status asthmaticus is the most severe form of asthma attack and can last for days or weeks.

◀▶ **New Code** ◀▦ ▦▶ **Revised Code** ● **Not a Principal Diagnosis** ● **Use Additional Digit(s)** □ **Nonspecific Code**

● **493 Asthma**

The following fifth-digit subclassification is for use with category 493:
    0 without mention of status asthmaticus
    1 with status asthmaticus

> **Excludes**   *wheezing NOS (786.07)* ◄

● **493.0 Extrinsic asthma**
Asthma:
    allergic with stated cause
    atopic
    childhood
    hay
    platinum
Hay fever with asthma

> **Excludes**   *asthma:*
>   *allergic NOS (493.9)*
>   *detergent (507.8)*
>   *miners' (500)*
>   *wood (495.8)*

● **493.1 Intrinsic asthma**
Late-onset asthma

● **493.2 Chronic obstructive asthma**
Asthma with chronic obstructive pulmonary disease (COPD)

> **Excludes**   *chronic asthmatic bronchitis (491.2)*
>   *chronic obstructive bronchitis (491.2)*

□ ● **493.9 Asthma, unspecified**
Asthma (bronchial) (allergic NOS)
Bronchitis:
    allergic   asthmatic

494 Bronchiectasis
Bronchiectasis (fusiform) (postinfectious) (recurrent)
Bronchiolectasis

> **Excludes**   *congenital (748.61)*
>   *tuberculous bronchiectasis (current disease) (011.5)*

● **495 Extrinsic allergic alveolitis**

> **Includes:** allergic alveolitis and pneumonitis due to inhaled organic dust particles of fungal, thermophilic actinomycete, or other origin

495.0 Farmers' lung

495.1 Bagassosis

495.2 Bird-fanciers' lung
Budgerigar-fanciers' disease or lung
Pigeon-fanciers' disease or lung

495.3 Suberosis
Cork-handlers' disease or lung

495.4 Malt workers' lung
Alveolitis due to Aspergillus clavatus

495.5 Mushroom workers' lung

495.6 Maple bark-strippers' lung
Alveolitis due to Cryptostroma corticale

495.7 "Ventilation" pneumonitis
Allergic alveolitis due to fungal, thermophilic actinomycete, and other organisms growing in ventilation [air conditioning] systems

□ **495.8 Other specified allergic alveolitis and pneumonitis**
Cheese-washers' lung
Coffee workers' lung
Fish-meal workers' lung
Furriers' lung
Grain-handlers' disease or lung
Pituitary snuff-takers' disease
Sequoiosis or red-cedar asthma
Wood asthma

□ **495.9 Unspecified allergic alveolitis and pneumonitis**
Alveolitis, allergic (extrinsic)
Hypersensitivity pneumonitis

□ **496 Chronic airway obstruction, not elsewhere classified**
Chronic:
    nonspecific lung disease
    obstructive lung disease
    obstructive pulmonary disease [COPD] NOS

Note: This code is not to be used with any code from categories 491–493

> **Excludes**   *chronic obstructive lung disease [COPD] specified (as) (with):*
>   *allergic alveolitis (495.0–495.9)*
>   *asthma (493.2)*
>   *bronchiectasis (494)*
>   *bronchitis (491.20–491.21) with emphysema (491.20–491.21)*
>   *emphysema (492.0–492.8)*

PNEUMOCONIOSES AND OTHER LUNG DISEASES DUE TO EXTERNAL AGENTS (500–508)

500 Coal workers' pneumoconiosis
Anthracosilicosis
Anthracosis
Black lung disease
Coal workers' lung
Miners' asthma

501 Asbestosis

□ **502 Pneumoconiosis due to other silica or silicates**
Pneumoconiosis due to talc
Silicotic fibrosis (massive) of lung
Silicosis (simple) (complicated)

□ **503 Pneumoconiosis due to other inorganic dust**
Aluminosis (of lung)
Bauxite fibrosis (of lung)
Berylliosis
Graphite fibrosis (of lung)
Siderosis
Stannosis

□ **504 Pneumonopathy due to inhalation of other dust**
Byssinosis
Cannabinosis
Flax-dressers' disease

> **Excludes**   *allergic alveolitis (495.0–495.9)*
>   *asbestosis (501)*
>   *bagassosis (495.1)*
>   *farmers' lung (495.0)*

□ **505 Pneumoconiosis, unspecified**

● **506 Respiratory conditions due to chemical fumes and vapors**

Use additional E code to identify cause

506.0 Bronchitis and pneumonitis due to fumes and vapors
Chemical bronchitis (acute)

506.1 Acute pulmonary edema due to fumes and vapors
Chemical pulmonary edema (acute)

> **Excludes**   *acute pulmonary edema NOS (518.4)*
>   *chronic or unspecified pulmonary edema (514)*

506.2 Upper respiratory inflammation due to fumes and vapors

□ **506.3 Other acute and subacute respiratory conditions due to fumes and vapors**

ICD-9-CM

500-599

Vol. 1

Figure 8–6 Progressive massive fibrosis superimposed on coalworkers' pneumoconiosis. The large, blackened scars are located principally in the upper lobe. Note extensions of scars into surrounding parenchyma and retraction of adjacent pleura. (From Cotran R, Kumar V, Robbins S: Robbins Pathologic Basis of Disease. Philadelphia, WB Saunders, 1994, p 708.)

Item 8–6 Pneumoconiosis refers to a lung condition resulting from exposure to inorganic or organic airborne particles, such as coal dust or moldy hay, as well as chemical fumes and vapors, such as insecticides. In this condition, the lungs retain the airborne particles.

506.4 Chronic respiratory conditions due to fumes and vapors
Emphysema (diffuse) (chronic) due to inhalation of chemical fumes and vapors
Obliterative bronchiolitis (chronic) (subacute) due to inhalation of chemical fumes and vapors
Pulmonary fibrosis (chronic) due to inhalation of chemical fumes and vapors

☐ **506.9 Unspecified respiratory conditions due to fumes and vapors**
Silo-fillers' disease

● **507 Pneumonitis due to solids and liquids**
Excludes *fetal aspiration pneumonitis (770.1)*

507.0 Due to inhalation of food or vomitus
Aspiration pneumonia (due to):
NOS   milk
food (regurgitated)   saliva
gastric secretions   vomitus

507.1 Due to inhalation of oils and essences
Lipoid pneumonia (exogenous)
Excludes *endogenous lipoid pneumonia (516.8)*

☐ **507.8 Due to other solids and liquids**
Detergent asthma

● **508 Respiratory conditions due to other and unspecified external agents**

Use additional E code to identify cause

508.0 Acute pulmonary manifestations due to radiation
Radiation pneumonitis

508.1 Chronic and other pulmonary manifestations due to radiation
Fibrosis of lung following radiation

☐ **508.8 Respiratory conditions due to other specified external agents**

☐ **508.9 Respiratory conditions due to unspecified external agent**

OTHER DISEASES OF RESPIRATORY SYSTEM (510–519)

● **510 Empyema**

Use additional code to identify infectious organism (041.0–041.9)
Excludes *abscess of lung (513.0)*

510.0 With fistula
Fistula:
bronchocutaneous   mediastinal
bronchopleural   pleural
hepatopleural   thoracic
Any condition classifiable to 510.9 with fistula

510.9 Without mention of fistula
Abscess:
pleura
thorax
Empyema (chest) (lung) (pleura)
Fibrinopurulent pleurisy
Pleurisy:
purulent
septic
seropurulent
suppurative
Pyopneumothorax
Pyothorax

● **511 Pleurisy**
Excludes *malignant pleural effusion (197.2)*
pleurisy with mention of tuberculosis, current disease (012.0)

511.0 Without mention of effusion or current tuberculosis
Adhesion, lung or pleura
Calcification of pleura
Pleurisy (acute) (sterile):
diaphragmatic
fibrinous
interlobar
Pleurisy:
NOS
pneumococcal
staphylococcal
streptococcal
Thickening of pleura

◀▶ **New Code**   ◀▬▬▶ **Revised Code**   ● **Not a Principal Diagnosis**   ● **Use Additional Digit(s)**   ☐ **Nonspecific Code**

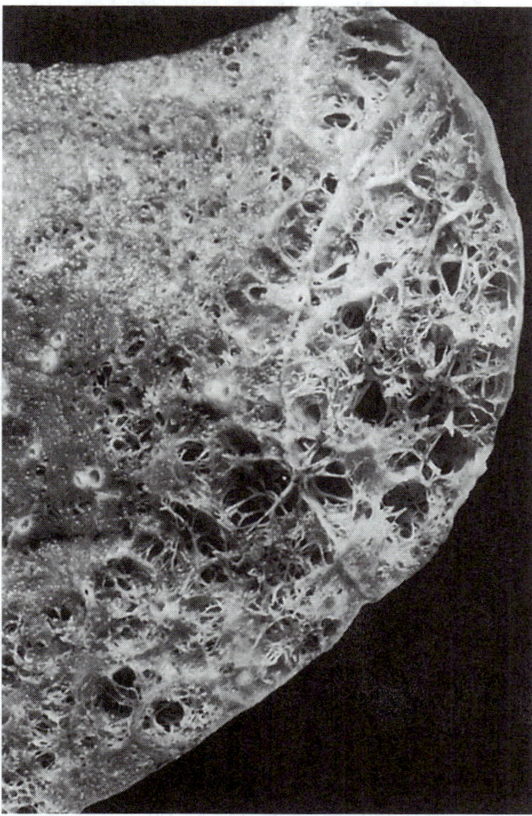

Figure 8–7   The apex of a lung (to the right) in a heavy cigarette smoker with severe emphysema (enlargement and distortion of the airspaces). (From Cotran R, Kumar V, Robbins S: Robbins Pathologic Basis of Disease. Philadelphia, WB Saunders, 1994, p 381.)

Item 8–7 Empyema is a condition in which pus accumulates in a body cavity. Empyema with fistula occurs when the pus passes from one cavity to another organ or structure.

511.1 With effusion, with mention of a bacterial cause other than tuberculosis
   Pleurisy with effusion (exudative) (serous):
      pneumococcal
      staphylococcal
      streptococcal
      other specified nontuberculous bacterial cause

511.8 Other specified forms of effusion, except tuberculous
   Encysted pleurisy
   Hemopneumothorax
   Hemothorax
   Hydropneumothorax
   Hydrothorax
   Excludes *traumatic (860.2–860.5)*

511.9 Unspecified pleural effusion
   Pleural effusion NOS
   Pleurisy:
      exudative
      serofibrinous
      serous
      with effusion NOS

● **512 Pneumothorax**

512.0 Spontaneous tension pneumothorax

512.1 Iatrogenic pneumothorax
   Postoperative pneumothorax

512.8 Other spontaneous pneumothorax
   Pneumothorax:
      NOS
      acute
      chronic
   Excludes *pneumothorax:*
      congenital (770.2)
      traumatic (860.0–860.1, 860.4–860.5)
      tuberculous, current disease (011.7)

● **513 Abscess of lung and mediastinum**

513.0 Abscess of lung
   Abscess (multiple) of lung
   Gangrenous or necrotic pneumonia
   Pulmonary gangrene or necrosis

513.1 Abscess of mediastinum

514 Pulmonary congestion and hypostasis
   Hypostatic:
      bronchopneumonia
      pneumonia
   Passive pneumonia
   Pulmonary congestion (chronic) (passive)
   Pulmonary edema:
      NOS
      chronic
   Excludes *acute pulmonary edema:*
      NOS (518.4)
      with mention of heart disease or failure (428.1)

515 Postinflammatory pulmonary fibrosis
   Cirrhosis of lung chronic or unspecified
   Fibrosis of lung (atrophic) (confluent) (massive) (perialveolar) (peribronchial) chronic or unspecified
   Induration of lung chronic or unspecified

● **516 Other alveolar and parietoalveolar pneumonopathy**

516.0 Pulmonary alveolar proteinosis

● **516.1 *Idiopathic pulmonary hemosiderosis***
   Essential brown induration of lung

   Code first underlying disease (275.0)

516.2 Pulmonary alveolar microlithiasis

516.3 Idiopathic fibrosing alveolitis
   Alveolar capillary block
   Diffuse (idiopathic) (interstitial) pulmonary fibrosis
   Hamman-Rich syndrome

516.8 Other specified alveolar and parietoalveolar pneumonopathies
   Endogenous lipoid pneumonia
   Interstitial pneumonia (desquamative) (lymphoid)
   Excludes *lipoid pneumonia, exogenous or unspecified (507.1)*

516.9 Unspecified alveolar and parietoalveolar pneumonopathy

● **517 Lung involvement in conditions classified elsewhere**
   Excludes *rheumatoid lung (714.81)*

● **517.1 *Rheumatic pneumonia***

   Code first underlying disease (390)

● **517.2 *Lung involvement in systemic sclerosis***

   Code first underlying disease (710.1)

ICD-9-CM

500-599

Vol. 1

● ☐ **517.8** *Lung involvement in other diseases classified else-where*

> *Code first underlying disease, as:*
> amyloidosis (277.3)
> polymyositis (710.4)
> sarcoidosis (135)
> Sjögren's disease (710.2)
> systemic lupus erythematosus (710.0)

> **Excludes** *syphilis (095.1)*

● **518 Other diseases of lung**

518.0 Pulmonary collapse
Atelectasis
Collapse of lung
Middle lobe syndrome

> **Excludes** *atelectasis:*
> *congenital (partial) (770.5)*
> *primary (770.4)*
> *tuberculous, current disease (011.8)*

518.1 Interstitial emphysema
Mediastinal emphysema

> **Excludes** *surgical (subcutaneous) emphysema (998.81)*
> *that in fetus or newborn (770.2)*
> *traumatic emphysema (958.7)*

518.2 Compensatory emphysema

518.3 Pulmonary eosinophilia
Eosinophilic asthma
Löffler's syndrome
Pneumonia:
  allergic
  eosinophilic
Tropical eosinophilia

☐ **518.4 Acute edema of lung, unspecified**
Acute pulmonary edema NOS
Pulmonary edema, postoperative

> **Excludes** *pulmonary edema:*
> *acute, with mention of heart disease or failure (428.1)*
> *chronic or unspecified (514)*
> *due to external agents (506.0–508.9)*

518.5 Pulmonary insufficiency following trauma and sur-gery
Adult respiratory distress syndrome
Pulmonary insufficiency following:
  shock
  surgery
  trauma
Shock lung

> **Excludes** *adult respiratory distress syndrome associated with other conditions (518.82)*
> *pneumonia:*
> *aspiration (507.0)*
> *hypostatic (514)*
> *respiratory failure in other conditions (518.81, 518.83–518.84)*

518.6 Allergic bronchopulmonary aspergillosis

● **518.8 Other diseases of lung**

518.81 Acute respiratory failure
Respiratory failure NOS

> **Excludes** *acute and chronic respiratory failure (518.84)*
> *acute respiratory distress (518.82)*
> *chronic respiratory failure (518.83)*
> *respiratory arrest (799.1)*
> *respiratory failure, newborn (770.8)*

☐ **518.82 Other pulmonary insufficiency, not else-where classified**
Acute respiratory distress
Acute respiratory insufficiency
Adult respiratory distress syndrome NEC

> **Excludes** *adult respiratory distress syndrome associated with trauma or surgery (518.5)*
> *pulmonary insufficiency following trauma or surgery (518.5)*
> *respiratory distress:*
> *NOS (786.09)*
> *newborn (770.8)*
> *syndrome, newborn (769)*
> *shock lung (518.5)*

518.83 Chronic respiratory failure

518.84 Acute and chronic respiratory failure
Acute on chronic respiratory failure

☐ **518.89 Other diseases of lung, not elsewhere clas-sified**
Broncholithiasis   Lung disease NOS
Calcification of lung   Pulmolithiasis

● **519 Other diseases of respiratory system**

● **519.0 Tracheostomy complications**

519.00 Tracheostomy complication, unspecified

519.01 Infection of tracheostomy

Use additional code to identify type of infection, such as:
  abscess or cellulitis of neck (682.1)
  septicemia (038.0–038.9)

Use additional code to identify organism (041.00–041.9)

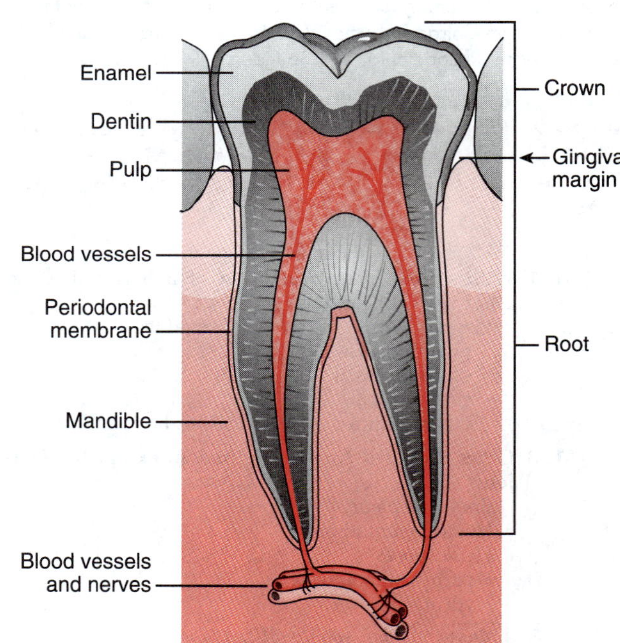

Figure 9–1   Anatomy of a tooth.

Item 9–1 Anodontia is the congenital absence of teeth. **Hypodontia** is partial anodontia. **Oligodontia** is the congenital absence of some teeth, whereas **super-numerary** is having more teeth than the normal num-ber. **Mesiodens** are small extra teeth that often appear in pairs, although single small teeth are not uncommon.

519.02 Mechanical complication of tracheostomy ◀
Tracheal stenosis due to tracheostomy ◀

519.09 Other tracheostomy complications ◀
Hemorrhage due to tracheostomy ◀
Tracheoesophageal fistula due to tracheostomy ◀

❏ **519.1 Other diseases of trachea and bronchus, not elsewhere classified**
Calcification of bronchus or trachea
Stenosis of bronchus or trachea
Ulcer of bronchus or trachea

519.2 Mediastinitis

❏ **519.3 Other diseases of mediastinum, not elsewhere classified**
Fibrosis of mediastinum
Hernia of mediastinum
Retraction of mediastinum

519.4 Disorders of diaphragm
Diaphragmitis
Paralysis of diaphragm
Relaxation of diaphragm

Excludes	*congenital defect of diaphragm (756.6)*

diaphragmatic hernia (551–553 with .3)
congenital (756.6)

❏ **519.8 Other diseases of respiratory system, not elsewhere classified**

❏ **519.9 Unspecified disease of respiratory system**
Respiratory disease (chronic) NOS

---

9. **DISEASES OF THE DIGESTIVE SYSTEM (520–579)**

DISEASES OF ORAL CAVITY, SALIVARY GLANDS, AND JAWS (520–529)

● **520 Disorders of tooth development and eruption**

520.0 Anodontia
Absence of teeth (complete) (congenital) (partial)
Hypodontia
Oligodontia

Excludes	*acquired absence of teeth (525.1)*

520.1 Supernumerary teeth
Distomolar
Fourth molar
Mesiodens
Paramolar
Supplemental teeth

Excludes	*supernumerary roots (520.2)*

520.2 Abnormalities of size and form
Concrescence of teeth
Fusion of teeth
Gemination of teeth
Dens evaginatus
Dens in dente
Dens invaginatus
Enamel pearls
Macrodontia
Microdontia
Peg-shaped [conical] teeth
Supernumerary roots
Taurodontism
Tuberculum paramolare

Excludes	*that due to congenital syphilis (090.5)*

tuberculum Carabelli, which is regarded as a normal variation

520.3 Mottled teeth
Dental fluorosis
Mottling of enamel
Nonfluoride enamel opacities

520.4 Disturbances of tooth formation
Aplasia and hypoplasia of cementum
Dilaceration of tooth
Enamel hypoplasia (neonatal) (postnatal) (prenatal)
Horner's teeth
Hypocalcification of teeth
Regional odontodysplasia
Turner's tooth

Excludes	*Hutchinson's teeth and mulberry molars in congenital syphilis (090.5)*

mottled teeth (520.3)

520.5 Hereditary disturbances in tooth structure, not elsewhere classified
Amelogenesis imperfecta
Dentinogenesis imperfecta
Odontogenesis imperfecta
Dentinal dysplasia
Shell teeth

ICD-9-CM

500-599

Vol. 1

520.6 Disturbances in tooth eruption
Teeth:
  embedded
  impacted
  natal
  neonatal
  primary [deciduous]:
    persistent
    shedding, premature
Tooth eruption:
  late
  obstructed
  premature

Excludes *exfoliation of teeth (attributable to disease of surrounding tissues) (525.0–525.1)*
impacted or embedded teeth with abnormal position of such teeth or adjacent teeth (524.3)

Item 9-2 **Each dental arch (jaw) normally contains 16 teeth. Tooth decay or dental caries is a disease of the enamel, dentin, and cementum of the tooth and can result in a cavity.**

520.7 Teething syndrome

520.8 Other specified disorders of tooth development and eruption
Color changes during tooth formation
Pre-eruptive color changes

Excludes *posteruptive color changes (521.7)*

520.9 Unspecified disorder of tooth development and eruption

● **521 Diseases of hard tissues of teeth**

521.0 Dental caries
Caries (of):
  arrested
  cementum
  dentin (acute) (chronic)
  enamel (acute) (chronic) (incipient)
Infantile melanodontia
Odontoclasia
White spot lesions of teeth

521.1 Excessive attrition
Approximal wear   Occlusal wear

521.2 Abrasion
Abrasion of teeth:
  dentifrice   ritual
  habitual   traditional
  occupational
Wedge defect NOS of teeth

521.3 Erosion
Erosion of teeth:
  NOS
  due to:
    medicine
    persistent vomiting
  idiopathic
  occupational

521.4 Pathological resorption
Internal granuloma of pulp
Resorption of tooth or root (external) (internal)

521.5 Hypercementosis
Cementation hyperplasia

521.6 Ankylosis of teeth

521.7 Posteruptive color changes
Staining [discoloration] of teeth:
  NOS
  due to:
    drugs   pulpal bleeding
    metals

Excludes *accretions [deposits] on teeth (523.6)*
pre-eruptive color changes (520.8)

521.8 Other specified diseases of hard tissues of teeth
Irradiated enamel   Sensitive dentin

521.9 Unspecified disease of hard tissues of teeth

● **522 Diseases of pulp and periapical tissues**

522.0 Pulpitis
Pulpal:
  abscess
  polyp
Pulpitis:
  acute
  chronic (hyperplastic) (ulcerative)
  suppurative

522.1 Necrosis of the pulp
Pulp gangrene

522.2 Pulp degeneration
Denticles   Pulp stones
Pulp calcifications

522.3 Abnormal hard tissue formation in pulp
Secondary or irregular dentin

522.4 Acute apical periodontitis of pulpal origin

522.5 Periapical abscess without sinus
Abscess:
  dental   dentoalveolar

Excludes *periapical abscess with sinus (522.7)*

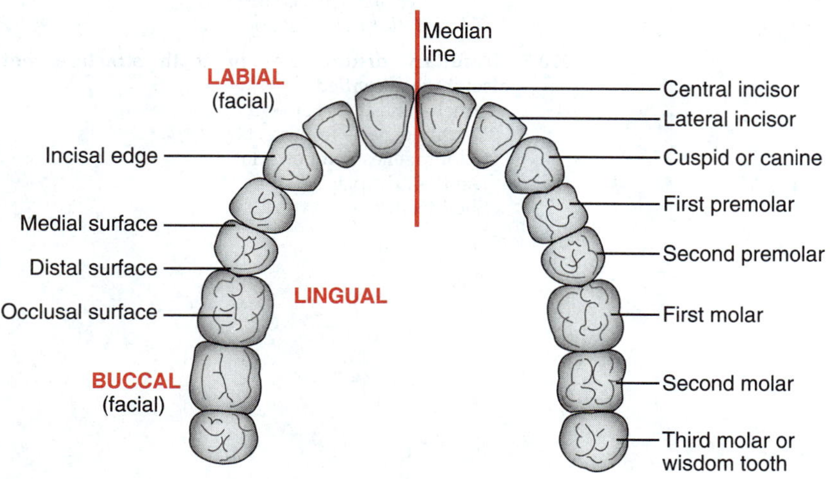

Figure 9-2   The permanent teeth within the dental arch.

◀ ▶ **New Code**   ⬤ ⬤ **Revised Code**   ● **Not a Principal Diagnosis**   ● **Use Additional Digit(s)**   ❑ **Nonspecific Code**

522.6 Chronic apical periodontitis
Apical or periapical granuloma
Apical periodontitis NOS

522.7 Periapical abscess with sinus
Fistula:
alveolar process
dental

522.8 Radicular cyst
Cyst:
apical (periodontal)
periapical
radiculodental
residual radicular

Excludes *lateral developmental or lateral periodontal cyst (526.0)*

522.9 Other and unspecified diseases of pulp and periapical tissues

Item 9–3 Acute gingivitis, also known as orilitis or ulitis, is the short-term, severe inflammation of the gums (gingiva) caused by bacteria. **Chronic gingivitis** is persistent inflammation of the gums. When the gingivitis moves into the periodontium it is called periodontitis, also known as paradentitis.

● **523 Gingival and periodontal diseases**

523.0 Acute gingivitis

Excludes *acute necrotizing ulcerative gingivitis (101) herpetic gingivostomatitis (054.2)*

523.1 Chronic gingivitis
Gingivitis (chronic):
NOS
desquamative
hyperplastic
simple marginal
ulcerative
Gingivostomatitis

Excludes *herpetic gingivostomatitis (054.2)*

523.2 Gingival recession
Gingival recession (generalized) (localized) (postinfective) (postoperative)

523.3 Acute periodontitis
Acute:
pericementitis
pericoronitis
Paradontal abscess
Periodontal abscess

Excludes *acute apical periodontitis (522.4) periapical abscess (522.5, 522.7)*

523.4 Chronic periodontitis
Alveolar pyorrhea
Chronic pericoronitis
Pericementitis (chronic)
Periodontitis:
NOS
complex
simplex

Excludes *chronic apical periodontitis (522.6)*

523.5 Periodontosis

523.6 Accretions on teeth
Dental calculus:
subgingival
supragingival
Deposits on teeth:
betel
materia alba
soft
tartar
tobacco

□ **523.8 Other specified periodontal diseases**
Giant cell:
epulis
peripheral granuloma
Gingival:
cysts
enlargement NOS
fibromatosis
Gingival polyp
Periodontal lesions due to traumatic occlusion
Peripheral giant cell granuloma

Excludes *leukoplakia of gingiva (528.6)*

□ **523.9 Unspecified gingival and periodontal disease**

Item 9–4 Hyperplasia is a condition of overdevelopment, whereas **hypoplasia** is a condition of underdevelopment. **Macrogenia** is overdevelopment of the chin, whereas microgenia is underdevelopment of the chin.

● **524 Dentofacial anomalies, including malocclusion**

● **524.0 Major anomalies of jaw size**

Excludes *hemifacial atrophy or hypertrophy (754.0) unilateral condylar hyperplasia or hypoplasia of mandible*

□ **524.00 Unspecified anomaly**

524.01 Maxillary hyperplasia

524.02 Mandibular hyperplasia

524.03 Maxillary hypoplasia

524.04 Mandibular hypoplasia

524.05 Macrogenia

524.06 Microgenia

□ **524.09 Other specified anomaly**

● **524.1 Anomalies of relationship of jaw to cranial base**

□ **524.10 Unspecified anomaly**
Prognathism
Retrognathism

524.11 Maxillary asymmetry

□ **524.12 Other jaw asymmetry**

□ **524.19 Other specified anomaly**

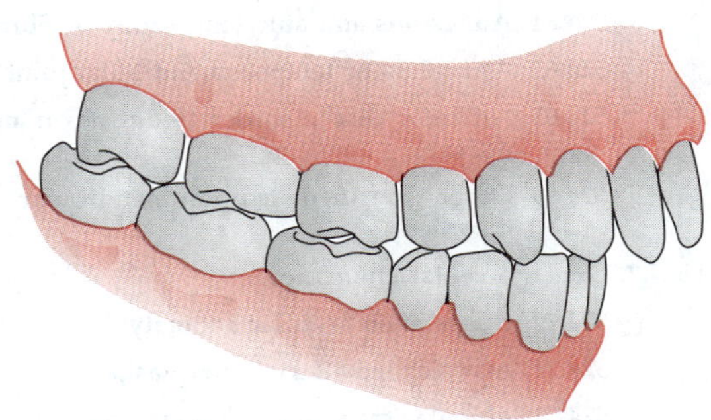

Figure 9–3 Dentofacial malocclusion.

524.2 Anomalies of dental arch relationship
Crossbite (anterior) (posterior)
Disto-occlusion
Mesio-occlusion
Midline deviation
Open bite (anterior) (posterior)
Overbite (excessive):
   deep
   horizontal
   vertical
Overjet
Posterior lingual occlusion of mandibular teeth
Soft tissue impingement

> **Excludes**   *hemifacial atrophy or hypertrophy (754.0)*
> *unilateral condylar hyperplasia or hypoplasia of*
> *mandible (526.89)*

524.3 Anomalies of tooth position
Crowding of tooth, teeth
Diastema of tooth, teeth
Displacement of tooth, teeth
Rotation of tooth, teeth
Spacing, abnormal, of tooth, teeth
Transposition of tooth, teeth
Impacted or embedded teeth with abnormal posi-
   tion of such teeth or adjacent teeth

☐ **524.4 Malocclusion, unspecified**

524.5 Dentofacial functional abnormalities
Abnormal jaw closure
Malocclusion due to:
   abnormal swallowing
   mouth breathing
   tongue, lip, or finger habits

Item 9-5   Dysfunction of the temporomandibular joint is termed temporomandibular joint (TMJ) syndrome and is characterized by pain and tenderness/spasm of the muscles of mastication, joint noise, and in the later stages, limited mandibular movement.

● **524.6 Temporomandibular joint disorders**

> **Excludes**   *current temporomandibular joint:*
> *dislocation (830.0–830.1)*
> *strain (848.1)*

☐ **524.60 Temporomandibular joint disorders, unspecified**
Temporomandibular joint-pain-dysfunction
   syndrome [TMJ]

524.61 Adhesions and ankylosis (bony or fibrous)

524.62 Arthralgia of temporomandibular joint

**524.63 Articular disc disorder (reducing or nonre-
ducing)**

☐ **524.69 Other specified temporomandibular joint
disorders**

● **524.7 Dental alveolar anomalies**

☐ **524.70 Unspecified alveolar anomaly**

524.71 Alveolar maxillary hyperplasia

524.72 Alveolar mandibular hyperplasia

524.73 Alveolar maxillary hypoplasia

524.74 Alveolar mandibular hypoplasia

☐ **524.79 Other specified alveolar anomaly**

☐ **524.8 Other specified dentofacial anomalies**

☐ **524.9 Unspecified dentofacial anomalies**

● **525 Other diseases and conditions of the teeth and supporting structures**

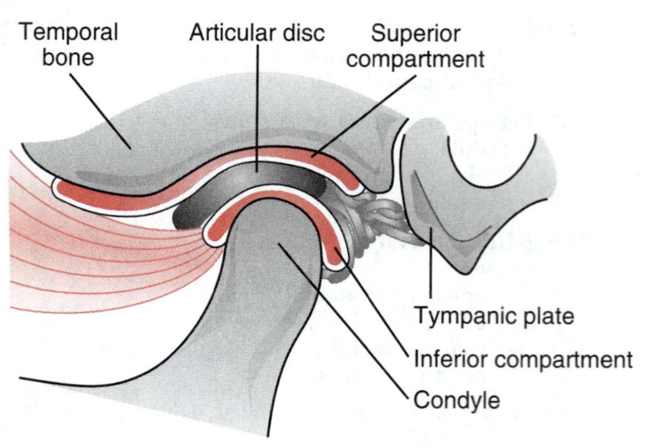

Figure 9-4   Temporomandibular joint.

525.0 Exfoliation of teeth due to systemic causes

**525.1 Loss of teeth due to accident, extraction, or local
periodontal disease**
Acquired absence of teeth

525.2 Atrophy of edentulous alveolar ridge

525.3 Retained dental root

☐ **525.8 Other specified disorders of the teeth and support-
ing structures**
Enlargement of alveolar ridge NOS
Irregular alveolar process

☐ **525.9 Unspecified disorder of the teeth and supporting
structures**

● **526 Diseases of the jaws**

526.0 Developmental odontogenic cysts
Cyst:
   dentigerous
   eruption
   follicular
   lateral developmental
   lateral periodontal
   primordial
Keratocyst

> **Excludes**   *radicular cyst (522.8)*

526.1 Fissural cysts of jaw
Cyst:
   globulomaxillary
   incisor canal
   median anterior maxillary
   median palatal
   nasopalatine
   palatine of papilla

> **Excludes**   *cysts of oral soft tissues (528.4)*

☐ **526.2 Other cysts of jaws**
Cyst of jaw:
   NOS   hemorrhagic
   aneurysmal   traumatic

526.3 Central giant cell (reparative) granuloma

> **Excludes**   *peripheral giant cell granuloma (523.8)*

526.4 Inflammatory conditions
Abscess of jaw (acute) (chronic) (suppurative)
Osteitis of jaw (acute) (chronic) (suppurative)
Osteomyelitis (neonatal) of jaw (acute) (chronic)
   (suppurative)
Periostitis of jaw (acute) (chronic) (suppurative)
Sequestrum of jaw bone

> **Excludes**   *alveolar osteitis (526.5)*

526.5 Alveolitis of jaw
Alveolar osteitis
Dry socket

● **526.8 Other specified diseases of the jaws**

526.81 Exostosis of jaw
Torus mandibularis
Torus palatinus

☐ **526.89 Other**
Cherubism
Fibrous dysplasia of jaw(s)
Latent bone cyst of jaw(s)
Osteoradionecrosis of jaw(s)
Unilateral condylar hyperplasia or hypoplasia of mandible

☐ **526.9 Unspecified disease of the jaws**

Item 9-6   Atrophy is wasting away of a tissue or organ, whereas hypertrophy is overdevelopment or enlargement of a tissue or organ. Sialoadenitis is salivary gland inflammation. Parotitis is the inflammation of the parotid gland. In the epidemic form, parotitis is also known as mumps.
Sialolithiasis is the formation of calculus within a salivary gland. Mucocele is a polyp composed of mucus.

● **527 Diseases of the salivary glands**

527.0 Atrophy

527.1 Hypertrophy

527.2 Sialoadenitis
Parotitis:
NOS
allergic
toxic
Sialoangitis
Sialodochitis
Excludes epidemic or infectious parotitis (072.0–072.9)
uveoparotid fever (135)

527.3 Abscess

527.4 Fistula
Excludes congenital fistula of salivary gland (750.24)

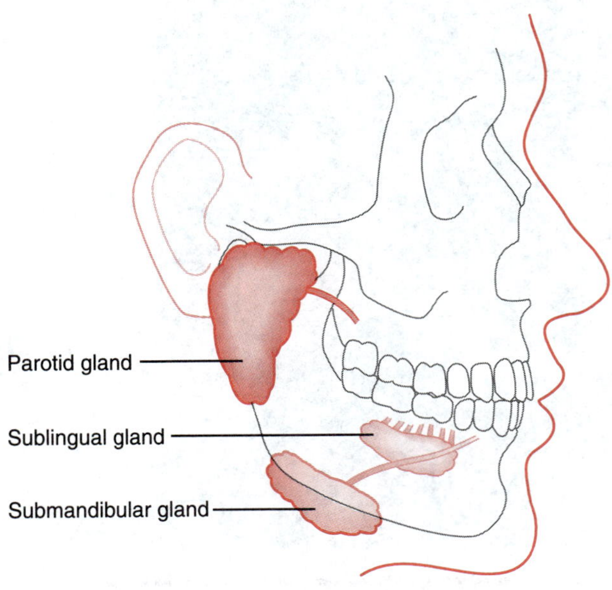

Figure 9-5 Major salivary glands.

527.5 Sialolithiasis
Calculus of salivary gland or duct
Stone of salivary gland or duct
Sialodocholithiasis

527.6 Mucocele
Mucous:
extravasation cyst of salivary gland
retention cyst of salivary gland
Ranula

527.7 Disturbance of salivary secretion
Hyposecretion
Ptyalism
Sialorrhea
Xerostomia

☐ **527.8 Other specified diseases of the salivary glands**
Benign lymphoepithelial lesion of salivary gland
Sialectasia
Sialosis
Stenosis of salivary duct
Stricture of salivary duct

☐ **527.9 Unspecified disease of the salivary glands**

Item 9-7   Stomatitis is the inflammation of the oral mucosa. Cancrum oris, also known as noma or gangrenous stomatitis, begins as an ulcer of the gingiva and results in a progressive gangrenous process.

● **528 Diseases of the oral soft tissues, excluding lesions specific for gingiva and tongue**

528.0 Stomatitis
Stomatitis:
NOS
ulcerative
Vesicular stomatitis
Excludes stomatitis:
acute necrotizing ulcerative (101)
aphthous (528.2)
gangrenous (528.1)
herpetic (054.2)
Vincent's (101)

528.1 Cancrum oris
Gangrenous stomatitis
Noma

528.2 Oral aphthae
Aphthous stomatitis
Canker sore
Periadenitis mucosa necrotica recurrens
Recurrent aphthous ulcer
Stomatitis herpetiformis
Excludes herpetic stomatitis (054.2)

528.3 Cellulitis and abscess
Cellulitis of mouth (floor)
Ludwig's angina
Oral fistula
Excludes abscess of tongue (529.0)
cellulitis or abscess of lip (528.5)
fistula (of):
dental (522.7)
lip (528.5)
gingivitis (523.0–523.1)

528.4 Cysts
Dermoid cyst of mouth
Epidermoid cyst of mouth
Epstein's pearl of mouth
Lymphoepithelial cyst of mouth
Nasoalveolar cyst of mouth
Nasolabial cyst of mouth
Excludes cyst:
gingiva (523.8)
tongue (529.8)

ICD-9-CM

500-599

Vol. 1

528.5   Diseases of lips
Abscess of lip(s)
Cellulitis of lip(s)
Fistula of lip(s)
Hypertrophy of lip(s)
Cheilitis:
    NOS
    angular
Cheilodynia
Cheilosis

Excludes	*actinic cheilitis (692.79)*
	congenital fistula of lip (750.25)
	leukoplakia of lips (528.6)

528.6   Leukoplakia of oral mucosa, including tongue
Leukokeratosis of oral mucosa
Leukoplakia of:
    gingiva
    lips
    tongue

Excludes	*carcinoma in situ (230.0, 232.0)*
	leukokeratosis nicotina palati (528.7)

528.7   Other disturbances of oral epithelium, including tongue
Erythroplakia of mouth or tongue
Focal epithelial hyperplasia of mouth or tongue
Leukoedema of mouth or tongue
Leukokeratosis nicotina palati

Excludes	*carcinoma in situ (230.0, 232.0)*
	leukokeratosis NOS (702)

528.8   Oral submucosal fibrosis, including of tongue

528.9   Other and unspecified diseases of the oral soft tissues
Cheek and lip biting
Denture sore mouth
Denture stomatitis
Melanoplakia
Papillary hyperplasia of palate
Eosinophilic granuloma of oral mucosa
Irritative hyperplasia of oral mucosa
Pyogenic granuloma of oral mucosa
Ulcer (traumatic) of oral mucosa

529   Diseases and other conditions of the tongue

529.0   Glossitis
Abscess of tongue
Ulceration (traumatic) of tongue

Excludes	*glossitis:*
	benign migratory (529.1)
	Hunter's (529.4)
	median rhomboid (529.2)
	Moeller's (529.4)

529.1   Geographic tongue
Benign migratory glossitis
Glossitis areata exfoliativa

529.2   Median rhomboid glossitis

529.3   Hypertrophy of tongue papillae
Black hairy tongue
Coated tongue
Hypertrophy of foliate papillae
Lingua villosa nigra

529.4   Atrophy of tongue papillae
Bald tongue
Glazed tongue
Glossitis:
    Hunter's
    Moeller's
Glossodynia exfoliativa
Smooth atrophic tongue

529.5   Plicated tongue
Fissured tongue
Furrowed tongue
Scrotal tongue

Excludes	*fissure of tongue, congenital (750.13)*

529.6   Glossodynia
Glossopyrosis
Painful tongue

Excludes	*glossodynia exfoliativa (529.4)*

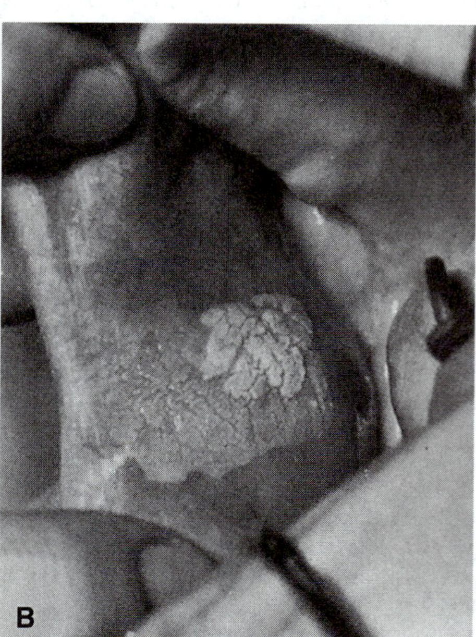

Figure 9–6   **A.** Lingual leukoplakia. **B.** Buccal leukoplakia. (From Pindborg JJ: In Jones JH, Mason DK (eds): Oral Manifestations of Systemic Disease. Philadelphia, WB Saunders, 1980, p 322.)

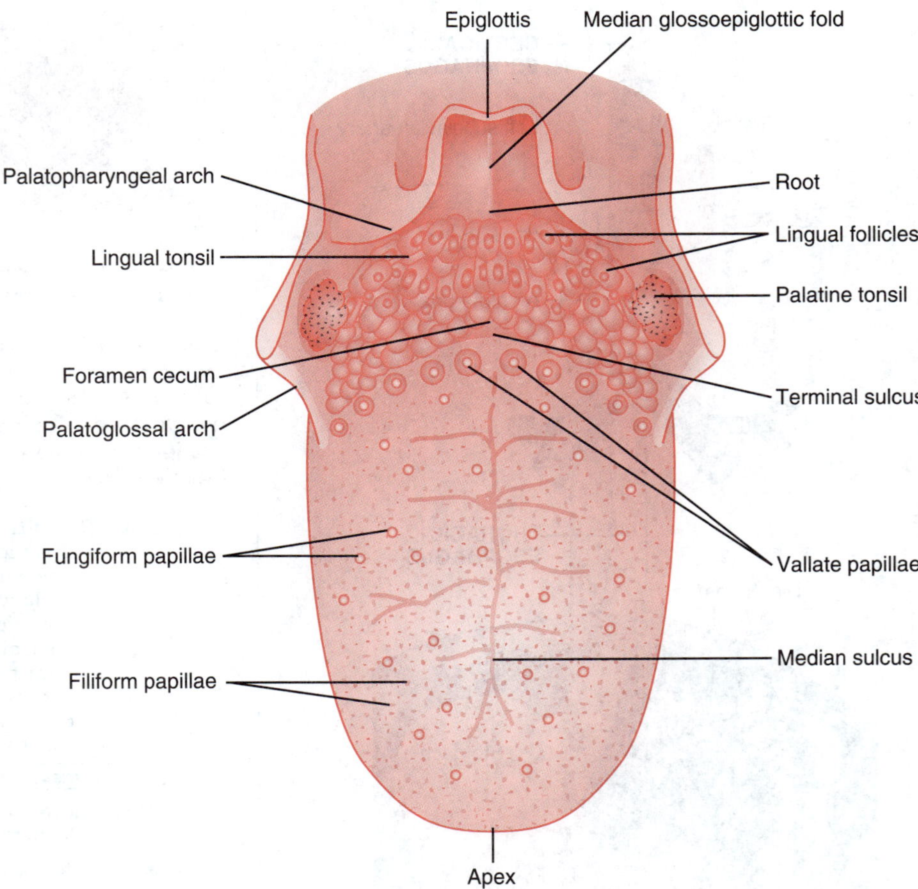

Figure 9-7   Structure of the tongue.

529.8 Other specified conditions of the tongue
Atrophy (of) tongue
Crenated (of) tongue
Enlargement (of) tongue
Hypertrophy (of) tongue
Glossocele
Glossoptosis

> **Excludes**   *erythroplasia of tongue (528.7)*
> *leukoplakia of tongue (528.6)*
> *macroglossia (congenital) (750.15)*
> *microglossia (congenital) (750.16)*
> *oral submucosal fibrosis (528.8)*

529.9 Unspecified condition of the tongue

DISEASES OF ESOPHAGUS, STOMACH, AND DUODENUM (530–537)

530 Diseases of esophagus

> **Excludes**   *esophageal varices (456.0–456.2)*

Item 9-8   **Achalasia** is a condition in which the smooth muscle fibers of the esophagus do not relax. Most frequently, this condition occurs at the esophagogastric sphincter. **Cardiospasm,** also known as **megaesophagus,** is achalasia of the thoracic esophagus.

530.0 Achalasia and cardiospasm
Achalasia (of cardia)
Aperistalsis of esophagus
Megaesophagus

> **Excludes**   *congenital cardiospasm (750.7)*

530.1 Esophagitis
Abscess of esophagus
Esophagitis:
NOS   postoperative
chemical   regurgitant
peptic

Use additional E code to identify cause, if induced by chemical

> **Excludes**   *tuberculous esophagitis (017.8)*

530.10 Esophagitis, unspecified

530.11 Reflux esophagitis

530.19 Other esophagitis

530.2 Ulcer of esophagus
Ulcer of esophagus
fungal   peptic
Ulcer of esophagus due to ingestion of:
aspirin   chemicals
medicines

Use additional E code to identify cause, if induced by chemical or drug

530.3 Stricture and stenosis of esophagus
Compression of esophagus
Obstruction of esophagus

> **Excludes**   *congenital stricture of esophagus (750.3)*

530.4 Perforation of esophagus
Rupture of esophagus

> **Excludes**   *traumatic perforation of esophagus (862.22, 862.32, 874.4–874.5)*

Item 9-9   **Dyskinesia** is difficulty in moving, and **diverticulum** is a sac or pouch.

ICD-9-CM

500–599

Vol. 1

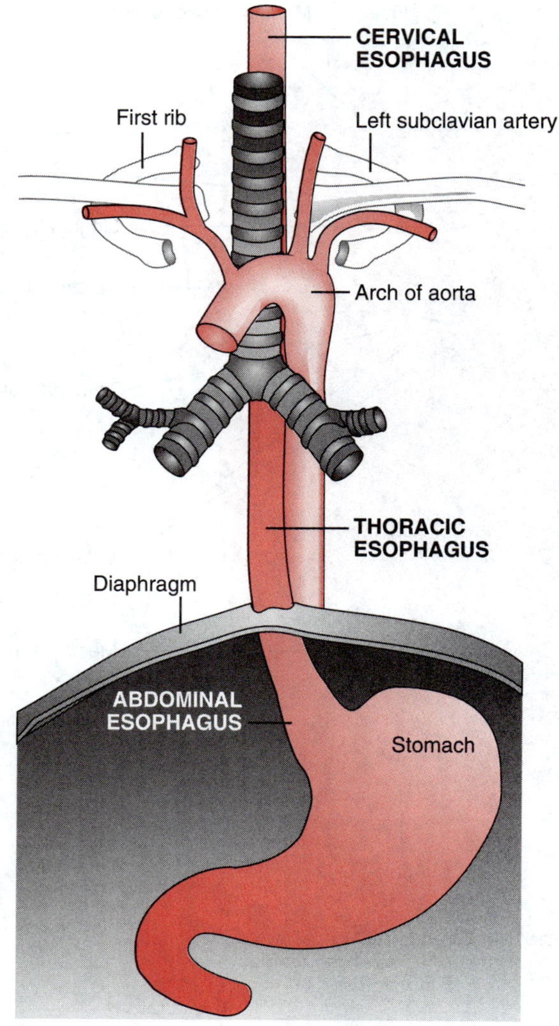

Figure 9–8   The esophagus is the muscular tube that connects the pharynx and the stomach. The 10 inch (25 cm) long esophagus is divided into three parts: **cervical, thoracic,** and **abdominal.**

Item 9–10   Esophageal reflux is the return flow of the contents of the stomach to the esophagus. Gastroesophageal reflux is the return flow of the contents of the stomach and duodenum to the esophagus. Esophageal leukoplakia are white areas on the mucous membrane of the esophagus for which no specific cause can be identified.

   530.5   Dyskinesia of esophagus
        Corkscrew esophagus
        Curling esophagus
        Esophagospasm
        Spasm of esophagus
     Excludes   *cardiospasm (530.0)*

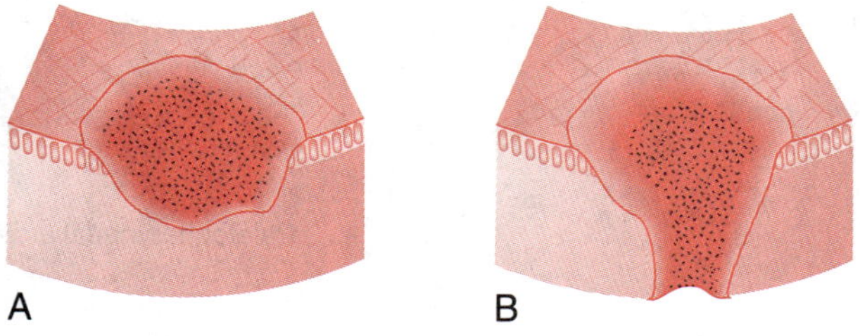

Figure 9–9   **A.** Ulcer. **B.** Perforated ulcer.

Item 9–11   Gastric ulcers are lesions of the stomach that result in the death of the tissue and a defect of the surface. Perforated ulcers are those in which the lesion penetrates the gastric wall, leaving a hole. Peptic ulcers are lesions of the stomach or the duodenum. Peptic refers to the gastric juice, pepsin.

   530.6   Diverticulum of esophagus, acquired
        Diverticulum, acquired:
           epiphrenic
           pharyngoesophageal
           pulsion
           subdiaphragmatic
           traction
           Zenker's (hypopharyngeal)
        Esophageal pouch, acquired
        Esophagocele, acquired
     Excludes   *congenital diverticulum of esophagus (750.4)*

   530.7   Gastroesophageal laceration-hemorrhage syndrome
        Mallory-Weiss syndrome

● **530.8   Other specified disorders of esophagus**

     530.81   Esophageal reflux
          Gastroesophageal reflux
     Excludes   *reflux esophagitis (530.11)*

     530.82   Esophageal hemorrhage
     Excludes   *hemorrhage due to esophageal varices (456.0– 456.2)*

     530.83   Esophageal leukoplakia

     530.84   Tracheoesophageal fistula
     Excludes   *congenital tracheoesophageal fistula (750.3)*

     □ **530.89   Other**
     Excludes   *Paterson-Kelly syndrome (280.8)*

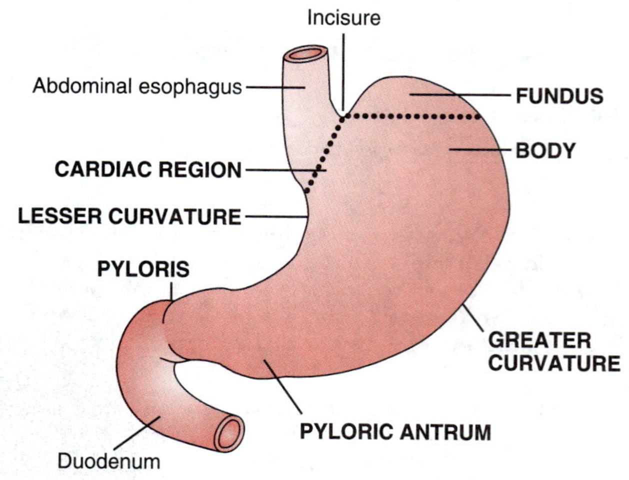

Figure 9–10   Parts of the stomach.

□ **530.9 Unspecified disorder of esophagus**

● **531 Gastric ulcer**

    Includes: ulcer (peptic):
            prepyloric
            pylorus
            stomach

    Use additional E code to identify drug, if drug-induced

        | **Excludes** | *peptic ulcer NOS (533.0–533.9)*

    The following fifth-digit subclassification is for use with category 531:
      0 without mention of obstruction
      1 with obstruction

● **531.0 Acute with hemorrhage**

● **531.1 Acute with perforation**

● **531.2 Acute with hemorrhage and perforation**

● **531.3 Acute without mention of hemorrhage or perforation**

● **531.4 Chronic or unspecified with hemorrhage**

● **531.5 Chronic or unspecified with perforation**

● **531.6 Chronic or unspecified with hemorrhage and perforation**

● **531.7 Chronic without mention of hemorrhage or perforation**

□● **531.9 Unspecified as acute or chronic, without mention of hemorrhage or perforation**

● **532 Duodenal ulcer**

    Includes: erosion (acute) of duodenum
           ulcer (peptic):
              duodenum
              postpyloric

    Use additional E code to identify drug, if drug-induced

        | **Excludes** | *peptic ulcer NOS (533.0–533.9)*

    The following fifth-digit subclassification is for use with category 532:
      0 without mention of obstruction
      1 with obstruction

● **532.0 Acute with hemorrhage**

● **532.1 Acute with perforation**

● **532.2 Acute with hemorrhage and perforation**

● **532.3 Acute without mention of hemorrhage or perforation**

● **532.4 Chronic or unspecified with hemorrhage**

● **532.5 Chronic or unspecified with perforation**

● **532.6 Chronic or unspecified with hemorrhage and perforation**

● **532.7 Chronic without mention of hemorrhage or perforation**

□● **532.9 Unspecified as acute or chronic, without mention of hemorrhage or perforation**

● **533 Peptic ulcer, site unspecified**

    Includes: gastroduodenal ulcer NOS
           peptic ulcer NOS
           stress ulcer NOS

    Use additional E code to identify drug, if drug-induced

        | **Excludes** | *peptic ulcer:*
            duodenal (532.0–532.9)
            gastric (531.0–531.9)

    The following fifth-digit subclassification is for use with category 533:
      0 without mention of obstruction
      1 with obstruction

● **533.0 Acute with hemorrhage**

● **533.1 Acute with perforation**

● **533.2 Acute with hemorrhage and perforation**

● **533.3 Acute without mention of hemorrhage and perforation**

● **533.4 Chronic or unspecified with hemorrhage**

● **533.5 Chronic or unspecified with perforation**

● **533.6 Chronic or unspecified with hemorrhage and perforation**

● **533.7 Chronic without mention of hemorrhage or perforation**

□● **533.9 Unspecified as acute or chronic, without mention of hemorrhage or perforation**

● **534 Gastrojejunal ulcer**

    Includes: ulcer (peptic) or erosion:
           anastomotic
           gastrocolic
           gastrointestinal
           gastrojejunal
           jejunal
           marginal
           stomal

        | **Excludes** | *primary ulcer of small intestine (569.82)*

    The following fifth-digit subclassification is for use with category 534:
      0 without mention of obstruction
      1 with obstruction

● **534.0 Acute with hemorrhage**

● **534.1 Acute with perforation**

● **534.2 Acute with hemorrhage and perforation**

● **534.3 Acute without mention of hemorrhage or perforation**

● **534.4 Chronic or unspecified with hemorrhage**

● **534.5 Chronic or unspecified with perforation**

● **534.6 Chronic or unspecified with hemorrhage and perforation**

● **534.7 Chronic without mention of hemorrhage or perforation**

□● **534.9 Unspecified as acute or chronic, without mention of hemorrhage or perforation**

Item 9–12 Gastritis is a severe inflammation of the stomach. Atrophic gastritis is a chronic inflammation of the stomach that results in destruction of the cells of the mucosa of the stomach.

● **535 Gastritis and duodenitis**

    The following fifth-digit subclassification is for use with category 535:
      0 without mention of hemorrhage
      1 with hemorrhage

● **535.0 Acute gastritis**

● **535.1 Atrophic gastritis**
      Gastritis:
        atrophic-hyperplastic
        chronic (atrophic)

● **535.2 Gastric mucosal hypertrophy**
      Hypertrophic gastritis

● **535.3 Alcoholic gastritis**

□● **535.4 Other specified gastritis**
      Gastritis:
        allergic
        bile induced
        irritant
        superficial
        toxic

□● **535.5 Unspecified gastritis and gastroduodenitis**

● **535.6 Duodenitis**

ICD-9-CM

500–599

Vol. 1

Item 9–13 Achlorhydria, also known as gastric anacidity, is the absence of gastric acid. **Gastroparesis** is
paralysis of the stomach.

● **536 Disorders of function of stomach**
  Excludes *functional disorders of stomach specified as psy-
    chogenic (306.4)*

  536.0 Achlorhydria

  536.1 Acute dilatation of stomach
    Acute distention of stomach

  536.2 Persistent vomiting
    Habit vomiting
    Persistent vomiting [not of pregnancy]
    Uncontrollable vomiting
    Excludes *excessive vomiting in pregnancy (643.0–643.9)
      vomiting NOS (787.0)*

  536.3 Gastroparesis

  ● **536.4 Gastrostomy complications** ◀▶

    □ **536.40 Gastrostomy complication, unspecified** ◀▶

    536.41 Infection of gastrostomy ◀▶

    Use additional code to specify type of infection,
    such as: ◀▶
      abscess or cellulitis of abdomen (682.2) ◀▶
      septicemia (038.0–038.9) ◀▶

    Use additional code to identify organism (041.00–
    041.9) ◀▶

    536.42 Mechanical complication of gastrostomy ◀▶

    □ **536.49 Other gastrostomy complications** ◀▶

  □ **536.8 Dyspepsia and other specified disorders of func-
    tion of stomach**
      Achylia gastrica
      Hourglass contraction of stomach
      Hyperacidity
      Hyperchlorhydria
      Hypochlorhydria
      Indigestion
    Excludes *achlorhydria (536.0)
      heartburn (787.1)*

  □ **536.9 Unspecified functional disorder of stomach**
      Functional gastrointestinal:
        disorder
        disturbance
        irritation

● **537 Other disorders of stomach and duodenum**

  537.0 Acquired hypertrophic pyloric stenosis
    Constriction of pylorus, acquired or adult
    Obstruction of pylorus, acquired or adult
    Stricture of pylorus, acquired or adult
    Excludes *congenital or infantile pyloric stenosis (750.5)*

  537.1 Gastric diverticulum
    Excludes *congenital diverticulum of stomach (750.7)*

  537.2 Chronic duodenal ileus

  □ **537.3 Other obstruction of duodenum**
    Cicatrix of duodenum
    Stenosis of duodenum
    Stricture of duodenum
    Volvulus of duodenum
    Excludes *congenital obstruction of duodenum (751.1)*

  537.4 Fistula of stomach or duodenum
    Gastrocolic fistula
    Gastrojejunocolic fistula

  537.5 Gastroptosis

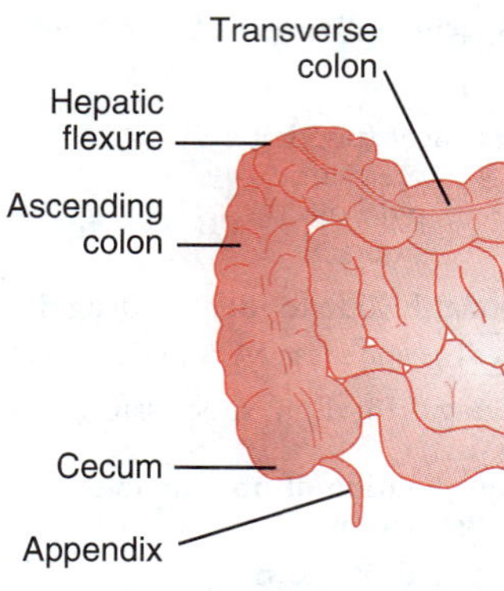

Figure 9–11 Acute appendicitis is the inflammation of the
appendix, usually associated with obstruction. Most often this is a
disease of adolescents and young adults.

  537.6 Hourglass stricture or stenosis of stomach
    Cascade stomach
    Excludes *congenital hourglass stomach (750.7)
      hourglass contraction of stomach (536.8)*

● **537.8 Other specified disorders of stomach and duodenum**

    537.81 Pylorospasm
    Excludes *congenital pylorospasm (750.5)*

    **537.82 Angiodysplasia of stomach and duodenum
      without mention of hemorrhage**

    **537.83 Angiodysplasia of stomach and duodenum
      with hemorrhage**

    □ **537.89 Other**
        Gastric or duodenal:
          prolapse   rupture
        Intestinal metaplasia of gastric mucosa
        Passive congestion of stomach
    Excludes *diverticula of duodenum (562.00–562.01)
      gastrointestinal hemorrhage (578.0–578.9)*

  □ **537.9 Unspecified disorder of stomach and duodenum**

APPENDICITIS (540–543)

● **540 Acute appendicitis**

  540.0 With generalized peritonitis
    Appendicitis (acute) with: perforation, peritonitis
      (generalized), rupture:
      fulminating   obstructive
      gangrenous
    Cecitis (acute) with: perforation, peritonitis (gener-
      alized), rupture
    Rupture of appendix
    Excludes *acute appendicitis with peritoneal abscess (540.1)*

  540.1 With peritoneal abscess
    Abscess of appendix
      With generalized peritonitis

  540.9 Without mention of peritonitis
    Acute:
      appendicitis without mention of perforation,
        peritonitis, or rupture:
        fulminating
        gangrenous
        inflamed
        obstructive
      cecitis without mention of perforation, peritoni-
        tis, or rupture

  ◀▶ **New Code**   ◀▦ ▦▶ **Revised Code**   ● **Not a Principal Diagnosis**   ● **Use Additional Digit(s)**   □ **Nonspecific Code**

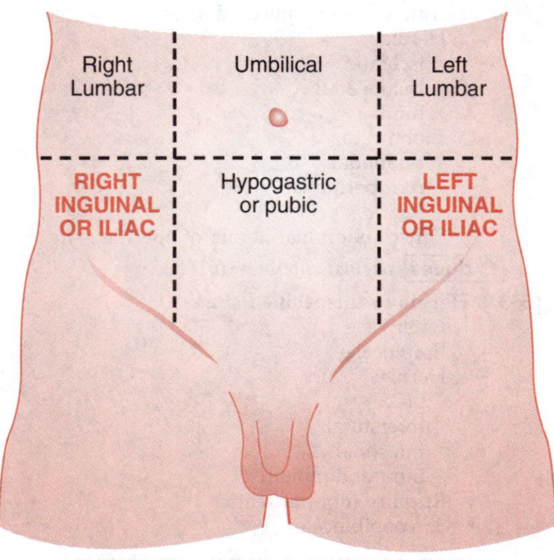

Figure 9–12 Inguinal hernias are those that are located in the inguinal or iliac areas of the abdomen.

Item 9–14 Hernias of the groin are the most common type, accounting for 80 percent of all hernias. There are two major types of inguinal hernias: indirect (oblique) and direct. Indirect inguinal hernias result when the intestines emerge through the abdominal wall in an indirect fashion through the inguinal canal. Direct inguinal hernias penetrate through the abdominal wall in a direct fashion.
Femoral hernias occur at the femoral ring where the femoral vessels enter the thigh.
Classification is based on location of the hernia and whether there is obstruction or gangrene.

☐ **541 Appendicitis, unqualified**

☐ **542 Other appendicitis**
Appendicitis:
    chronic   relapsing
    recurrent   subacute
    Excludes *hyperplasia (lymphoid) of appendix (543.0)*

● **543 Other diseases of appendix**
    543.0 Hyperplasia of appendix (lymphoid)
☐ **543.9 Other and unspecified diseases of appendix**
      Appendicular or appendiceal:
        colic
        concretion
        fistula
      Diverticulum of appendix
      Fecalith of appendix
      Intussusception of appendix
      Mucocele of appendix
      Stercolith of appendix

HERNIA OF ABDOMINAL CAVITY (550–553)

Includes: hernia:
    acquired
    congenital, except diaphragmatic or hiatal

● **550 Inguinal hernia**
Includes: bubonocele
    inguinal hernia (direct) (double) (indirect)
      (oblique) (sliding)
    scrotal hernia

The following fifth-digit subclassification is for use with category 550:
☐ **0 unilateral or unspecified (not specified as recurrent)**
    Unilateral NOS
    1 unilateral or unspecified, recurrent
    2 bilateral (not specified as recurrent)
      Bilateral NOS
    3 bilateral, recurrent

● **550.0 Inguinal hernia, with gangrene**
    Inguinal hernia with gangrene (and obstruction)

● **550.1 Inguinal hernia, with obstruction, without mention of gangrene**
    Inguinal hernia with mention of incarceration, irreducibility, or strangulation

● **550.9 Inguinal hernia, without mention of obstruction or gangrene**
    Inguinal hernia NOS

● **551 Other hernia of abdominal cavity, with gangrene**
    Includes: that with gangrene (and obstruction)

● **551.0 Femoral hernia with gangrene**
☐ **551.00 Unilateral or unspecified (not specified as recurrent)**
      Femoral hernia NOS with gangrene
    551.01 Unilateral or unspecified, recurrent
    551.02 Bilateral (not specified as recurrent)
    551.03 Bilateral, recurrent

551.1 Umbilical hernia with gangrene
    Parumbilical hernia specified as gangrenous

● **551.2 Ventral hernia with gangrene**
☐ **551.20 Ventral, unspecified, with gangrene**
    551.21 Incisional, with gangrene
      Hernia:
        postoperative specified as gangrenous
        recurrent, ventral specified as gangrenous
☐ **551.29 Other**
      Epigastric hernia specified as gangrenous

551.3 Diaphragmatic hernia with gangrene
    Hernia:
      hiatal (esophageal) (sliding) specified as gangrenous
      paraesophageal specified as gangrenous
    Thoracic stomach specified as gangrenous
    Excludes *congenital diaphragmatic hernia (756.6)*

☐ **551.8 Hernia of other specified sites, with gangrene**
    Any condition classifiable to 553.8 if specified as gangrenous

☐ **551.9 Hernia of unspecified site, with gangrene**
    Any condition classifiable to 553.9 if specified as gangrenous

● **552 Other hernia of abdominal cavity, with obstruction, but without mention of gangrene**
    Excludes *that with mention of gangrene (551.0–551.9)*

● **552.0 Femoral hernia with obstruction**
    Femoral hernia specified as incarcerated, irreducible, strangulated, or causing obstruction
☐ **552.00 Unilateral or unspecified (not specified as recurrent)**
    552.01 Unilateral or unspecified, recurrent
    552.02 Bilateral (not specified as recurrent)
    552.03 Bilateral, recurrent

552.1 Umbilical hernia with obstruction
    Parumbilical hernia specified as incarcerated, irreducible, strangulated, or causing obstruction

ICD-9-CM

500-599

Vol. 1

● **552.2 Ventral hernia with obstruction**
Ventral hernia specified as incarcerated, irreducible, strangulated, or causing obstruction

☐ **552.20 Ventral, unspecified, with obstruction**

552.21 Incisional, with obstruction
Hernia:
postoperative specified as incarcerated, irreducible, strangulated, or causing obstruction
recurrent, ventral specified as incarcerated, irreducible, strangulated, or causing obstruction

☐ **552.29 Other**
Epigastric hernia specified as incarcerated, irreducible, strangulated, or causing obstruction

552.3 Diaphragmatic hernia with obstruction
Hernia:
hiatal (esophageal) (sliding) specified as incarcerated, irreducible, strangulated, or causing obstruction
paraesophageal specified as incarcerated, irreducible, strangulated, or causing obstruction
Thoracic stomach specified as incarcerated, irreducible, strangulated, or causing obstruction
Excludes *congenital diaphragmatic hernia (756.6)*

☐ **552.8 Hernia of other specified sites, with obstruction**
Any condition classifiable to 553.8 if specified as incarcerated, irreducible, strangulated, or causing obstruction

☐ **552.9 Hernia of unspecified site, with obstruction**
Any condition classifiable to 553.9 if specified as incarcerated, irreducible, strangulated, or causing obstruction

● **553 Other hernia of abdominal cavity without mention of obstruction or gangrene**
Excludes *the listed conditions with mention of:*
gangrene (and obstruction) (551.0–551.9)
obstruction (552.0–552.9)

● **553.0 Femoral hernia**

☐ **553.00 Unilateral or unspecified (not specified as recurrent)**
Femoral hernia NOS

553.01 Unilateral or unspecified, recurrent

553.02 Bilateral (not specified as recurrent)

553.03 Bilateral, recurrent

553.1 Umbilical hernia
Parumbilical hernia

● **553.2 Ventral hernia**

☐ **553.20 Ventral, unspecified**

553.21 Incisional
Hernia:
postoperative
recurrent, ventral

☐ **553.29 Other**
Hernia:
epigastric
spigelian

553.3 Diaphragmatic hernia
Hernia:
hiatal (esophageal) (sliding)
paraesophageal
Thoracic stomach
Excludes *congenital:*
diaphragmatic hernia (756.6)
hiatal hernia (750.6)
esophagocele (530.6)

☐ **553.8 Hernia of other specified sites**
Hernia:
ischiatic
ischiorectal
lumbar
obturator
pudendal
retroperitoneal
sciatic
Other abdominal hernia of specified site
Excludes *vaginal enterocele (618.6)*

☐ **553.9 Hernia of unspecified site**
Enterocele
Epiplocele
Hernia:
NOS
interstitial
intestinal
intra-abdominal
Rupture (nontraumatic)
Sarcoepiplocele

NONINFECTIOUS ENTERITIS AND COLITIS (555–558)

● **555 Regional enteritis**
Includes: Crohn's disease
Granulomatous enteritis
Excludes *ulcerative colitis (556)*

555.0 Small intestine
Ileitis:
regional
segmental
terminal
Regional enteritis or Crohn's disease of:
duodenum
ileum
jejunum

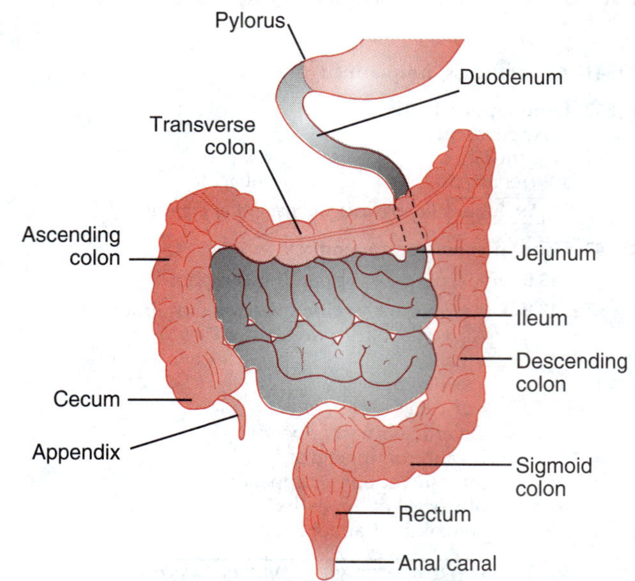

Figure 9-13 Small and large intestines.

Item 9-15 Crohn's disease, also known as **regional enteritis,** is a chronic inflammatory disease of the intestines. Classification is based on location in the small (duodenum, ileum, jejunum) or large (cecum, colon, rectum, anal canal) intestine.

  ◀▶ **New Code**   ⬅▮▮▮▮▮➡ **Revised Code**   ● **Not a Principal Diagnosis**   ● **Use Additional Digit(s)**   ☐ **Nonspecific Code**

555.1 Large intestine
    Colitis:
        granulomatous
        regional
        transmural
    Regional enteritis or Crohn's disease of:
        colon
        large bowel
        rectum

555.2 Small intestine with large intestine
    Regional ileocolitis

☐ **555.9 Unspecified site**
    Crohn's disease NOS
    Regional enteritis NOS

Item 9–16 Ulcerative colitis attacks the colonic mucosa and forms abscesses. The disease involves the intestines.
Classification is based on the location:
    enterocolitis: large and small intestine
    ileocolitis: ileum and colon
    proctitis: rectum
    proctosigmoiditis: sigmoid colon and rectum

● **556 Ulcerative colitis**

    556.0 Ulcerative (chronic) enterocolitis

    556.1 Ulcerative (chronic) ileocolitis

    556.2 Ulcerative (chronic) proctitis

    556.3 Ulcerative (chronic) proctosigmoiditis

    556.4 Pseudopolyposis of colon

    556.5 Left-sided ulcerative (chronic) colitis

    556.6 Universal ulcerative (chronic) colitis
        Pancolitis

    ☐ **556.8 Other ulcerative colitis**

    ☐ **556.9 Ulcerative colitis, unspecified**
        Ulcerative enteritis NOS

● **557 Vascular insufficiency of intestine**

    Excludes *necrotizing enterocolitis of the newborn (777.5)*

    557.0 Acute vascular insufficiency of intestine
        Acute:
            hemorrhagic enterocolitis
            ischemic colitis, enteritis, or enterocolitis
            massive necrosis of intestine
        Bowel infarction
        Embolism of mesenteric artery
        Fulminant enterocolitis
        Hemorrhagic necrosis of intestine
        Infarction of appendices epiploicae   ◄
        Intestinal gangrene
        Intestinal infarction (acute) (agnogenic) (hemorrhagic) (nonocclusive)
        Mesenteric infarction (embolic) (thrombotic)
        Necrosis of intestine   ◄
        Terminal hemorrhagic enteropathy
        Thrombosis of mesenteric artery

    557.1 Chronic vascular insufficiency of intestine
        Angina, abdominal
        Chronic ischemic colitis, enteritis, or enterocolitis
        Ischemic stricture of intestine
        Mesenteric:
            angina
            artery syndrome (superior)
            vascular insufficiency

    ☐ **557.9 Unspecified vascular insufficiency of intestine**
        Alimentary pain due to vascular insufficiency
        Ischemic colitis, enteritis, or enterocolitis NOS

● **558 Other noninfectious gastroenteritis and colitis**

    Excludes *infectious:*
        colitis, enteritis, or gastroenteritis (009.0–009.1)
        diarrhea (009.2–009.3)

    558.1 Gastroenteritis and colitis due to radiation
        Radiation enterocolitis

    558.2 Toxic gastroenteritis and colitis

        Use additional E code to identify cause

    ☐ **558.9 Other and unspecified noninfectious gastroenteritis and colitis**
        Colitis, NOS, allergic, dietetic, or noninfectious
        Diarrhea, allergic, dietetic, or noninfectious
        Enteritis, NOS, allergic, dietetic, or noninfectious
        Gastroenteritis, NOS, allergic, dietetic, or noninfectious
        Ileitis, NOS, allergic, dietetic, or noninfectious
        Jejunitis, NOS, allergic, dietetic, or noninfectious
        Sigmoiditis, NOS, allergic, dietetic, or noninfectious

OTHER DISEASES OF INTESTINES AND PERITONEUM (560–569)

● **560 Intestinal obstruction without mention of hernia**
    Excludes *duodenum (537.2–537.3)*
        inguinal hernia with obstruction (550.1)
        intestinal obstruction complicating hernia (552.0–552.9)
        mesenteric:
            embolism (557.0)
            infarction (557.0)
            thrombosis (557.0)
        neonatal intestinal obstruction (277.01, 777.1–777.2, 777.4)

Item 9–17 Intussusception is the prolapse of a part of the intestine into another adjacent part of the intestine. Intussusception may be enteric (ileoileal, jejunoileal, jejunojejunal), colic (colocolic), or intracolic (ileocecal, ileocolic).

    560.0 Intussusception
        Intussusception (colon) (intestine) (rectum)
        Invagination of intestine or colon
    Excludes *intussusception of appendix (543.9)*

    560.1 Paralytic ileus
        Adynamic ileus
        Ileus (of intestine) (of bowel) (of colon)
        Paralysis of intestine or colon
    Excludes *gallstone ileus (560.31)*

Item 9–18 Volvulus is the twisting of a segment of the intestine, resulting in obstruction.

    560.2 Volvulus
        Knotting of intestine, bowel, or colon
        Strangulation of intestine, bowel, or colon
        Torsion of intestine, bowel, or colon
        Twisting of intestine, bowel, or colon

● **560.3 Impaction of intestine**

    ☐ **560.30 Impaction of intestine, unspecified**
        Impaction of colon

    560.31 Gallstone ileus
        Obstruction of intestine by gallstone

    ☐ **560.39 Other**
        Concretion of intestine
        Enterolith
        Fecal impaction

ICD-9-CM

500-599

Vol. 1

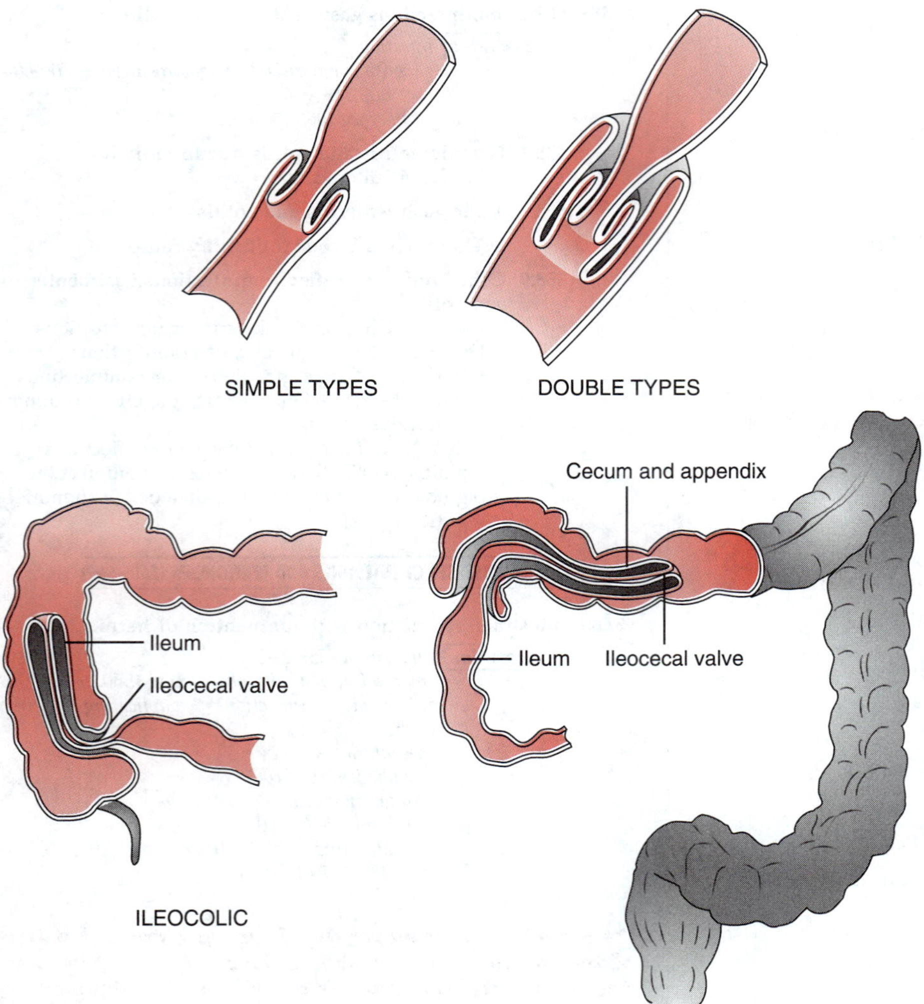

Figure 9–14   Types of intussusception.

● **560.8   Other specified intestinal obstruction**

     560.81   Intestinal or peritoneal adhesions with obstruction (postoperative) (postinfection)

     Excludes   *adhesions without obstruction (568.0)*

     ☐ **560.89   Other**
         Mural thickening causing obstruction

     Excludes   *ischemic stricture of intestine (557.1)*

☐ **560.9   Unspecified intestinal obstruction**
     Enterostenosis
     Obstruction of intestine or colon
     Occlusion of intestine or colon
     Stenosis of intestine or colon
     Stricture of intestine or colon

     Excludes   *congenital stricture or stenosis of intestine (751.1–751.2)*

Item 9–19   Diverticula of the intestines are acquired herniations of the mucosa.
Classification is based on location (small intestine or colon) and whether it occurs with or without hemorrhage.

● **562   Diverticula of intestine**

     Use additional code to identify any associated:
     peritonitis (567.0–567.9)

     Excludes   *congenital diverticulum of colon (751.5)*
         diverticulum of appendix (543.9)
         Meckel's diverticulum (751.0)

● **562.0   Small intestine**

     562.00   Diverticulosis of small intestine (without mention of hemorrhage)
         Diverticulosis:
             duodenum without mention of diverticulitis
             ileum without mention of diverticulitis
             jejunum without mention of diverticulitis

     562.01   Diverticulitis of small intestine (without mention of hemorrhage)
         Diverticulitis (with diverticulosis):
             duodenum
             ileum
             jejunum
             small intestine

     562.02   Diverticulosis of small intestine with hemorrhage

     562.03   Diverticulitis of small intestine with hemorrhage

    ◀▶ **New Code**   ⬅▮▮▶ **Revised Code**   ● **Not a Principal Diagnosis**   ● **Use Additional Digit(s)**   ☐ **Nonspecific Code**

● **562.1 Colon**

 562.10 Diverticulosis of colon (without mention of hemorrhage)
  Diverticulosis without mention of diverticulitis:
   NOS
   intestine (large) without mention of diverticulitis
  Diverticular disease (colon) without mention of diverticulitis

 562.11 Diverticulitis of colon without mention of hemorrhage
  Diverticulitis (with diverticulosis):
   NOS
   colon
   intestine (large)

 562.12 Diverticulosis of colon with hemorrhage

 562.13 Diverticulitis of colon with hemorrhage

● **564 Functional digestive disorders, not elsewhere classified**
 Excludes *functional disorders of stomach (536.0–536.9)*
   those specified as psychogenic (306.4)

 564.0 Constipation

 564.1 Irritable colon
  Colitis:
   adaptive
   membranous
   mucous
  Enterospasm
  Irritable bowel syndrome
  Spastic colon

 564.2 Postgastric surgery syndromes
  Dumping syndrome
  Jejunal syndrome
  Postgastrectomy syndrome
  Postvagotomy syndrome
  Excludes *malnutrition following gastrointestinal surgery (579.3)*
   postgastrojejunostomy ulcer (534.0–534.9)

 564.3 Vomiting following gastrointestinal surgery
  Vomiting (bilious) following gastrointestinal surgery

 □ **564.4 Other postoperative functional disorders**
  Diarrhea following gastrointestinal surgery
  Excludes *colostomy and enterostomy complications (569.60–569.69)*

 564.5 Functional diarrhea
  Excludes *diarrhea:*
   NOS (787.91)
   psychogenic (306.4)

 564.6 Anal spasm
  Proctalgia fugax

 564.7 Megacolon, other than Hirschsprung's
  Dilatation of colon
  Excludes *megacolon:*
   congenital [Hirschsprung's] (751.3)
   toxic (556)

 □ **564.8 Other specified functional disorders of intestine**
  Excludes *malabsorption (579.0–579.9)*

  564.81 Neurogenic bowel ◄

  □ **564.89 Other functional disorders of intestine** ◄
   Atony of colon ◄

 □ **564.9 Unspecified functional disorder of intestine**

Item 9-20 A fissure is a groove in the surface, whereas a fistula is an abnormal passage.

● **565 Anal fissure and fistula**

 565.0 Anal fissure
  Tear of anus, nontraumatic
  Excludes *traumatic (863.89, 863.99)*

 565.1 Anal fistula
  Fistula:
   anorectal
   rectal
   rectum to skin
  Excludes *fistula of rectum to internal organs-see Alphabetic Index*
   ischiorectal fistula (566)
   rectovaginal fistula (619.1)

● **566 Abscess of anal and rectal regions**
 Abscess: Cellulitis:
  ischiorectal   anal
  perianal   perirectal
  perirectal   rectal
 Ischiorectal fistula

● **567 Peritonitis**
 Excludes *peritonitis:*
  benign paroxysmal (277.3)
  pelvic, female (614.5, 614.7)
  periodic familial (277.3)
  puerperal (670)
  with or following:
   abortion (634–638 with .0, 639.0)
   appendicitis (540.0–540.1)
   ectopic or molar pregnancy (639.0)

 ● **567.0 Peritonitis in infectious diseases classified elsewhere**
  Code first underlying disease
  Excludes *peritonitis:*
   gonococcal (098.86)
   syphilitic (095.2)
   tuberculous (014.0)

 567.1 Pneumococcal peritonitis

 □ **567.2 Other suppurative peritonitis**
  Abscess (of):
   abdominopelvic retroperitoneal
   mesenteric   subdiaphragmatic
   omentum   subhepatic
   peritoneum   subphrenic
   retrocecal
  Peritonitis (acute):
   general   subphrenic
   pelvic, male   suppurative

 □ **567.8 Other specified peritonitis**
  Chronic proliferative peritonitis
  Fat necrosis of peritoneum
  Mesenteric saponification
  Peritonitis due to:
   bile   urine

 □ **567.9 Unspecified peritonitis**
  Peritonitis:
   NOS   of unspecified cause

● **568 Other disorders of peritoneum**

 568.0 Peritoneal adhesions (postoperative) (postinfection)
  Adhesions (of):
   abdominal (wall) mesenteric
   diaphragm   omentum
   intestine   stomach
   male pelvis
  Adhesive bands
  Excludes *adhesions:*
   pelvic, female (614.6)
   with obstruction:
    duodenum (537.3)
    intestine (560.81)

ICD-9-CM
500-599
Vol. 1

● **568.8   Other specified disorders of peritoneum**

    568.81   Hemoperitoneum (nontraumatic)

    568.82   Peritoneal effusion (chronic)

    Excludes   *ascites NOS (789.5)*

    ❑ **568.89   Other**
       Peritoneal:
         cyst
         granuloma

❑ **568.9   Unspecified disorder of peritoneum**

● **569   Other disorders of intestine**

    569.0   Anal and rectal polyp
       Anal and rectal polyp NOS

    Excludes   *adenomatous anal and rectal polyp (211.4)*

    569.1   Rectal prolapse
       Procidentia:
         anus (sphincter)
         rectum (sphincter)
       Proctoptosis
       Prolapse:
         anal canal
         rectal mucosa

    Excludes   *prolapsed hemorrhoids (455.2, 455.5)*

    569.2   Stenosis of rectum and anus
       Stricture of anus (sphincter)

    569.3   Hemorrhage of rectum and anus

    Excludes   *gastrointestinal bleeding NOS (578.9)*
           melena (578.1)

● **569.4   Other specified disorders of rectum and anus**

    569.41   Ulcer of anus and rectum
       Solitary ulcer of anus (sphincter) or rectum (sphincter)
       Stercoral ulcer of anus (sphincter) or rectum (sphincter)

    569.42   Anal or rectal pain

    ❑ **569.49   Other**
       Granuloma of rectum (sphincter)
       Rupture of rectum (sphincter)
       Hypertrophy of anal papillae
       Proctitis NOS

    Excludes   *fistula of rectum to:*
           internal organs - see Alphabetic Index
           skin (565.1)
         hemorrhoids (455.0–455.9)
         incontinence of sphincter ani (787.6)

    569.5   Abscess of intestine

    Excludes   *appendiceal abscess (540.1)*

● **569.6   Colostomy and enterostomy complications**

    ❑ **569.60   Colostomy and enterostomy complication, unspecified** ◀▥

    569.61   Infection of colostomy or enterostomy ◀▥

       Use additional code to identify organism (041.00–041.9)

       Use additional code to specify type of infection, such as:
         abscess or cellulitis of abdomen (682.2) ◀
         septicemia (038.0–038.9) ◀

    569.62   Mechanical complication of colostomy and enterostomy ◀
       Malfunction of colostomy and enterostomy ◀

    ❑ **569.69   Other complication**
       Fistula ◀
       Hernia ◀
       Prolapse ◀

● **569.8   Other specified disorders of intestine**

    569.81   Fistula of intestine, excluding rectum and anus
       Fistula:
         abdominal wall
         enterocolic
         enteroenteric
         ileorectal

    Excludes   *fistula of intestine to internal organs-see Alphabetic Index*
         persistent postoperative fistula (998.6)

    569.82   Ulceration of intestine
       Primary ulcer of intestine
       Ulceration of colon

    Excludes   *that with perforation (569.83)*

    569.83   Perforation of intestine

    569.84   Angiodysplasia of intestine (without mention of hemorrhage)

    569.85   Angiodysplasia of intestine with hemorrhage

    ❑ **569.89   Other**
       Enteroptosis
       Granuloma of intestine
       Prolapse of intestine
       Pericolitis
       Perisigmoiditis
       Visceroptosis

    Excludes   *gangrene of intestine, mesentery, or omentum (557.0)*
         hemorrhage of intestine NOS (578.9)
         obstruction of intestine (560.0–560.9)

❑ **569.9   Unspecified disorder of intestine**

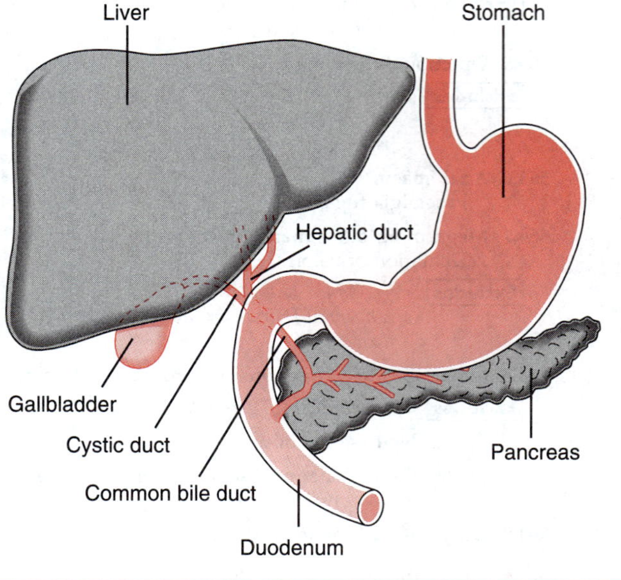

Figure 9–15   Liver and bile ducts.

    ◀▶ **New Code**   ◀▥ ▥▶ **Revised Code**   ● **Not a Principal Diagnosis**   ● **Use Additional Digit(s)**   ❑ **Nonspecific Code**

OTHER DISEASES OF DIGESTIVE SYSTEM (570–579)

570 Acute and subacute necrosis of liver
Acute hepatic failure
Acute or subacute hepatitis, not specified as infective
Necrosis of liver (acute) (diffuse) (massive) (subacute)
Parenchymatous degeneration of liver
Yellow atrophy (liver) (acute) (subacute)

> **Excludes** *icterus gravis of newborn (773.0–773.2)*
> *serum hepatitis (070.2–070.3)*
> *that with:*
> *abortion (634–638 with .7, 639.8)*
> *ectopic or molar pregnancy (639.8)*
> *pregnancy, childbirth, or the puerperium (646.7)*
> *viral hepatitis (070.0–070.9)*

Item 9–21 Cirrhosis is the progressive fibrosis of the liver resulting in loss of liver function. The main causes of cirrhosis of the liver are alcohol abuse, chronic hepatitis (inflammation of the liver), biliary disease, and excessive amounts of iron. Alcoholic cirrhosis of the liver is also called portal, Laënnec's, or fatty nutritional cirrhosis.

571 Chronic liver disease and cirrhosis

571.0 Alcoholic fatty liver

571.1 Acute alcoholic hepatitis
Acute alcoholic liver disease

571.2 Alcoholic cirrhosis of liver
Florid cirrhosis
Laënnec's cirrhosis (alcoholic)

571.3 Alcoholic liver damage, unspecified

571.4 Chronic hepatitis

> **Excludes** *viral hepatitis (acute) (chronic) (070.0–070.9)*

571.40 Chronic hepatitis, unspecified

571.41 Chronic persistent hepatitis

571.49 Other
Chronic hepatitis:
active
aggressive
Recurrent hepatitis

571.5 Cirrhosis of liver without mention of alcohol
Cirrhosis of liver:
NOS
cryptogenic
macronodular
micronodular
posthepatitic
postnecrotic
Healed yellow atrophy (liver)
Portal cirrhosis

571.6 Biliary cirrhosis
Chronic nonsuppurative destructive cholangitis
Cirrhosis:
cholangitic
cholestatic

571.8 Other chronic nonalcoholic liver disease
Chronic yellow atrophy (liver)
Fatty liver, without mention of alcohol

571.9 Unspecified chronic liver disease without mention of alcohol

572 Liver abscess and sequelae of chronic liver disease

572.0 Abscess of liver

> **Excludes** *amebic liver abscess (006.3)*

572.1 Portal pyemia
Phlebitis of portal vein
Portal thrombophlebitis
Pylephlebitis
Pylethrombophlebitis

572.2 Hepatic coma
Hepatic encephalopathy
Hepatocerebral intoxication
Portal-systemic encephalopathy

572.3 Portal hypertension

572.4 Hepatorenal syndrome

> **Excludes** *that following delivery (674.8)*

572.8 Other sequelae of chronic liver disease

573 Other disorders of liver

> **Excludes** *amyloid or lardaceous degeneration of liver (277.3)*
> *congenital cystic disease of liver (751.62)*
> *glycogen infiltration of liver (271.0)*
> *hepatomegaly NOS (789.1)*
> *portal vein obstruction (452)*

573.0 Chronic passive congestion of liver

573.1 Hepatitis in viral diseases classified elsewhere

Code first underlying disease, as:
Coxsackie virus disease (074.8)
cytomegalic inclusion virus disease (078.5)
infectious mononucleosis (075)

> **Excludes** *hepatitis (in):*
> *mumps (072.71)*
> *viral (070.0–070.9)*
> *yellow fever (060.0–060.9)*

573.2 Hepatitis in other infectious diseases classified elsewhere

Code first underlying disease, as:
malaria (084.9)

> **Excludes** *hepatitis in:*
> *late syphilis (095.3)*
> *secondary syphilis (091.62)*
> *toxoplasmosis (130.5)*

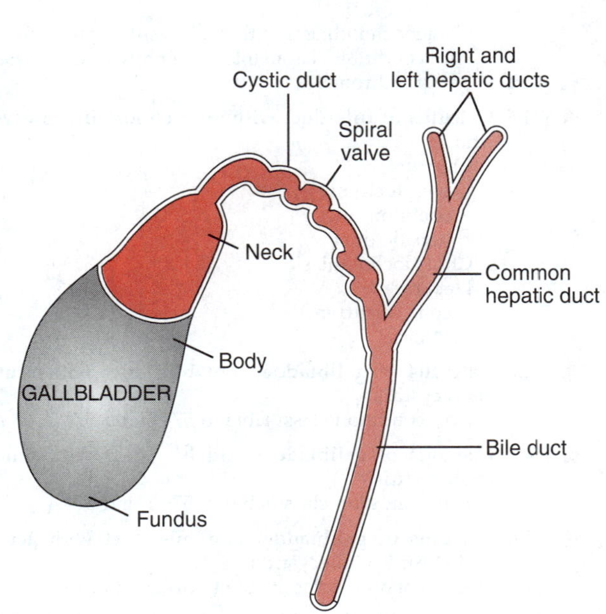

Figure 9–16 Gallbladder and bile ducts.

☐ **573.3 Hepatitis, unspecified**
Toxic (noninfectious) hepatitis

Use additional E code to identify cause

573.4 Hepatic infarction

☐ **573.8 Other specified disorders of liver**
Hepatoptosis

☐ **573.9 Unspecified disorder of liver**

● **574 Cholelithiasis**

The following fifth-digit subclassification is for use with category 574:

  0 without mention of obstruction
  1 with obstruction

● **574.0 Calculus of gallbladder with acute cholecystitis**
Biliary calculus with acute cholecystitis
Calculus of cystic duct with acute cholecystitis
Cholelithiasis with acute cholecystitis
Any condition classifiable to 574.2 with acute cholecystitis

☐● **574.1 Calculus of gallbladder with other cholecystitis**
Biliary calculus with cholecystitis
Calculus of cystic duct with cholecystitis
Cholelithiasis with cholecystitis
Cholecystitis with cholelithiasis NOS
Any condition classifiable to 574.2 with cholecystitis (chronic)

● **574.2 Calculus of gallbladder without mention of cholecystitis**
Biliary:
  calculus NOS
  colic NOS
Calculus of cystic duct
Cholelithiasis NOS
Colic (recurrent) of gallbladder
Gallstone (impacted)

● **574.3 Calculus of bile duct with acute cholecystitis**
Calculus of bile duct [any] with acute cholecystitis
Choledocholithiasis with acute cholecystitis
Any condition classifiable to 574.5 with acute cholecystitis

☐● **574.4 Calculus of bile duct with other cholecystitis**
Calculus of bile duct [any] with cholecystitis (chronic)
Choledocholithiasis with cholecystitis (chronic)
Any condition classifiable to 574.5 with cholecystitis (chronic)

● **574.5 Calculus of bile duct without mention of cholecystitis**
Calculus of:
  bile duct [any]
  common duct
  hepatic duct
Choledocholithiasis
Hepatic:
  colic (recurrent)
  lithiasis

● **574.6 Calculus of gallbladder and bile duct with acute cholecystitis**
Any condition classifiable to 574.0 and 574.3

● **574.7 Calculus of gallbladder and bile duct with other cholecystitis**
Any condition classifiable to 574.1 and 574.4

● **574.8 Calculus of gallbladder and bile duct with acute and chronic cholecystitis**
Any condition classifiable to 574.6 and 574.7

● **574.9 Calculus of gallbladder and bile duct without cholecystitis**
Any condition classifiable to 574.2 and 574.5

● **575 Other disorders of gallbladder**

575.0 Acute cholecystitis
Abscess of gallbladder without mention of calculus
Angiocholecystitis without mention of calculus
Cholecystitis without mention of calculus:
  emphysematous (acute)
  gangrenous
  suppurative
Empyema of gallbladder without mention of calculus
Gangrene of gallbladder without mention of calculus

> **Excludes** *that with:*
>   *acute and chronic cholecystitis (575.12)*
>   *choledocholithiasis (574.3)*
>   *choledocholithiasis and cholelithiasis (574.6)*
>   *cholelithiasis (574.0)*

● **575.1 Other cholecystitis**
Cholecystitis without mention of calculus:
  NOS without mention of calculus
  chronic without mention of calculus

> **Excludes** *that with:*
>   *choledocholithiasis (574.4)*
>   *choledocholithiasis and cholelithiasis (574.8)*
>   *cholelithiasis (574.1)*

☐ **575.10 Cholecystitis, unspecified**
Cholecystitis NOS

575.11 Chronic cholecystitis

575.12 Acute and chronic cholecystitis

575.2 Obstruction of gallbladder
Occlusion of cystic duct or gallbladder without mention of calculus
Stenosis of cystic duct or gallbladder without mention of calculus
Stricture of cystic duct or gallbladder without mention of calculus

> **Excludes** *that with calculus (574.0–574.2 with fifth digit 1)*

575.3 Hydrops of gallbladder
Mucocele of gallbladder

575.4 Perforation of gallbladder
Rupture of cystic duct or gallbladder

575.5 Fistula of gallbladder
Fistula:
  cholecystoduodenal
  cholecystoenteric

575.6 Cholesterolosis of gallbladder
Strawberry gallbladder

☐ **575.8 Other specified disorders of gallbladder**
Adhesions (of) cystic duct gallbladder
Atrophy (of) cystic duct gallbladder
Cyst (of) cystic duct gallbladder
Hypertrophy (of) cystic duct gallbladder
Nonfunctioning (of) cystic duct gallbladder
Ulcer (of) cystic duct gallbladder
Biliary dyskinesia

> **Excludes** *nonvisualization of gallbladder (793.3)*

☐ **575.9 Unspecified disorder of gallbladder**

● **576 Other disorders of biliary tract**

> **Excludes** *that involving the:*
>   *cystic duct (575.0–575.9)*
>   *gallbladder (575.0–575.9)*

576.0 Postcholecystectomy syndrome

    ◀▶ **New Code**   ⬅▸ **Revised Code**   ● **Not a Principal Diagnosis**   ● **Use Additional Digit(s)**   ☐ **Nonspecific Code**

576.1 Cholangitis

Cholangitis:

NOS	recurrent
acute	sclerosing
ascending	secondary
chronic	stenosing
primary	suppurative

576.2 Obstruction of bile duct

Occlusion of bile duct, except cystic duct, without mention of calculus

Stenosis of bile duct, except cystic duct, without mention of calculus

Stricture of bile duct, except cystic duct, without mention of calculus

> **Excludes** *congenital (751.61)*
> *that with calculus (574.3–574.5 with fifth-digit 1)*

576.3 Perforation of bile duct

Rupture of bile duct, except cystic duct

576.4 Fistula of bile duct

Choledochoduodenal fistula

576.5 Spasm of sphincter of Oddi

☐ **576.8 Other specified disorders of biliary tract**

Adhesions of bile duct [any]
Atrophy of bile duct [any]
Cyst of bile duct [any]
Hypertrophy of bile duct [any]
Stasis of bile duct [any]
Ulcer of bile duct [any]

> **Excludes** *congenital choledochal cyst (751.69)*

☐ **576.9 Unspecified disorder of biliary tract**

● **577 Diseases of pancreas**

577.0 Acute pancreatitis

Abscess of pancreas
Necrosis of pancreas:
  acute
  infective
Pancreatitis:

NOS	hemorrhagic
acute (recurrent)	subacute
apoplectic	suppurative

> **Excludes** *mumps pancreatitis (072.3)*

577.1 Chronic pancreatitis

Chronic pancreatitis:	Pancreatitis:
NOS	painless
infectious	recurrent
interstitial	relapsing

577.2 Cyst and pseudocyst of pancreas

☐ **577.8 Other specified diseases of pancreas**

Atrophy of pancreas
Calculus of pancreas
Cirrhosis of pancreas
Fibrosis of pancreas
Pancreatic:
  infantilism
  necrosis:
    NOS
    aseptic
    fat
Pancreatolithiasis

> **Excludes** *fibrocystic disease of pancreas (277.00–277.01)*
> *islet cell tumor of pancreas (211.7)*
> *pancreatic steatorrhea (579.4)*

☐ **577.9 Unspecified disease of pancreas**

● **578 Gastrointestinal hemorrhage**

> **Excludes** *that with mention of:*
> *angiodysplasia of stomach and duodenum (537.83)*
> *angiodysplasia of intestine (569.85)*
> *diverticulitis, intestine:*
> *large (562.13)*
> *small (562.03)*
> *diverticulosis, intestine:*
> *large (562.12)*
> *small (562.02)*
> *gastritis and duodenitis (535.0–535.6)*
> *ulcer:*
> *duodenal, gastric, gastrojejunal, or peptic (531.00–534.91)*

578.0 Hematemesis

Vomiting of blood

578.1 Blood in stool

Melena

> **Excludes** *melena of the newborn (772.4, 777.3)*
> *occult blood (792.1)*

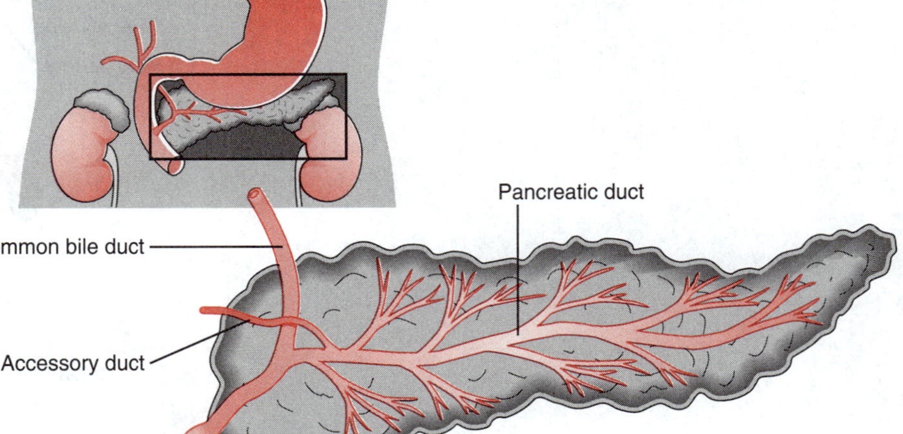

Figure 9–17   Pancreas.

☐ **578.9 Hemorrhage of gastrointestinal tract, unspecified**
    Gastric hemorrhage   Intestinal hemorrhage

● **579   Intestinal malabsorption**

579.0 Celiac disease
    Celiac: Gee (-Herter) disease
       crisis   Gluten enteropathy
       infantilism   Idiopathic steatorrhea
       rickets   Nontropical sprue

579.1 Tropical sprue
    Sprue:
       NOS
       tropical
    Tropical steatorrhea

579.2 Blind loop syndrome
    Postoperative blind loop syndrome

☐ **579.3 Other and unspecified postsurgical nonabsorption**
    Hypoglycemia following gastrointestinal surgery
    Malnutrition following gastrointestinal surgery

579.4 Pancreatic steatorrhea

☐ **579.8 Other specified intestinal malabsorption**
    Enteropathy:
       exudative   protein-losing
    Steatorrhea (chronic)

☐ **579.9 Unspecified intestinal malabsorption**
    Malabsorption syndrome NOS

10.   DISEASES OF THE GENITOURINARY SYSTEM (580–629)

NEPHRITIS, NEPHROTIC SYNDROME, AND NEPHROSIS (580–589)

Excludes *hypertensive renal disease (403.00–403.91)*

Item 10–1   Glomerulonephritis is nephritis accompanied by inflammation of the glomeruli of the kidney, resulting in the degeneration of the glomeruli and the nephrons.

Acute glomerulonephritis primarily affects children and young adults and is usually a result of a streptococcal infection.

Proliferative glomerulonephritis is the acute form of the disease resulting from a streptococcal infection.

Rapidly progressive glomerulonephritis, also known as **crescentic** or **malignant glomerulonephritis,** is the acute form of the disease, which leads quickly to rapid and progressive decline in renal function.

● **580   Acute glomerulonephritis**

    Includes: acute nephritis

    580.0 With lesion of proliferative glomerulonephritis
        Acute (diffuse) proliferative glomerulonephritis
        Acute poststreptococcal glomerulonephritis

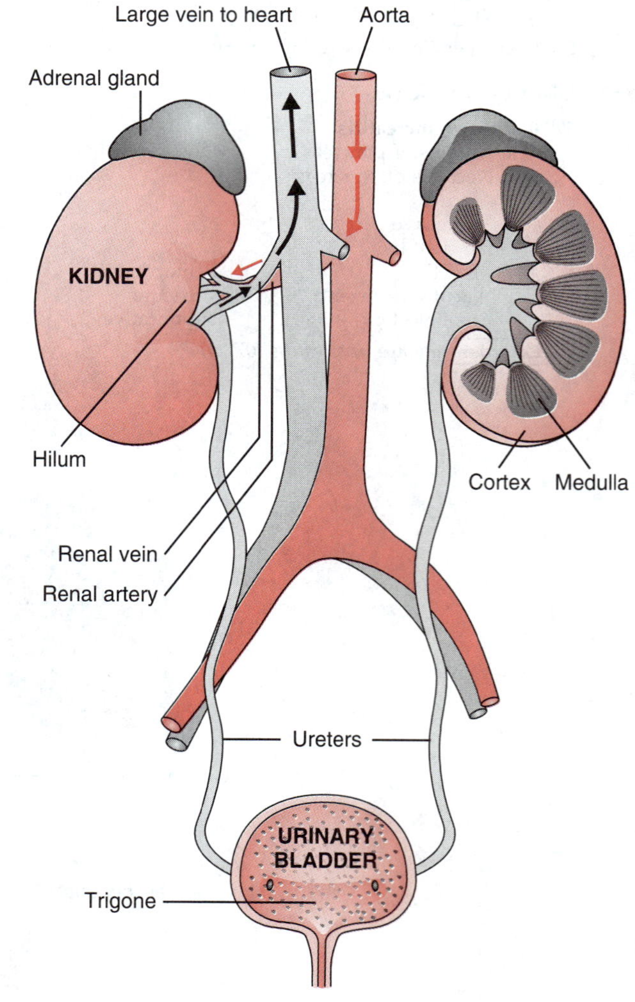

Figure 10–1   Kidneys within the urinary system.

◀▶ **New Code**   ◀▥ ▥▶ **Revised Code**   ● **Not a Principal Diagnosis**   ● **Use Additional Digit(s)**   ☐ **Nonspecific Code**

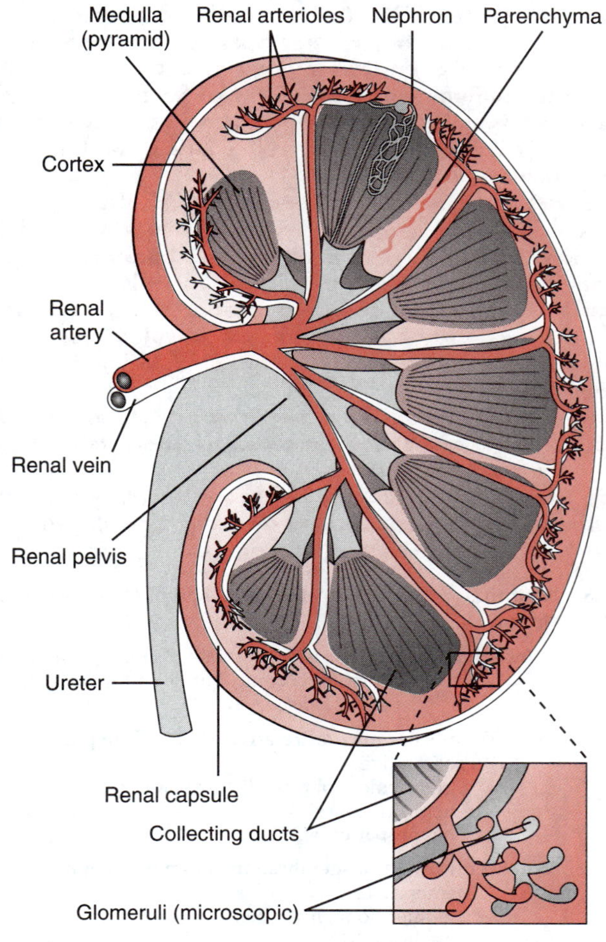

Figure 10–2 Kidney.

580.4 With lesion of rapidly progressive glomerulone-phritis
 Acute nephritis with lesion of necrotizing glomerulitis

● **580.8 With other specified pathological lesion in kidney**

● *580.81 Acute glomerulonephritis in diseases classified elsewhere*

 Code first underlying disease, as:
 infectious hepatitis (070.0–070.9)
 mumps (072.79)
 subacute bacterial endocarditis (421.0)
 typhoid fever (002.0)

☐ **580.89 Other**
 Glomerulonephritis, acute, with lesion of:
  exudative nephritis
  interstitial (diffuse) (focal) nephritis

☐ **580.9 Acute glomerulonephritis with unspecified pathological lesion in kidney**
 Glomerulonephritis: specified as acute
  NOS specified as acute
  hemorrhagic specified as acute
 Nephritis specified as acute
 Nephropathy specified as acute

● **581 Nephrotic syndrome**

581.0 With lesion of proliferative glomerulonephritis

581.1 With lesion of membranous glomerulonephritis
 Epimembranous nephritis
 Idiopathic membranous glomerular disease
 Nephrotic syndrome with lesion of:
  focal glomerulosclerosis
  sclerosing membranous glomerulonephritis
  segmental hyalinosis

581.2 With lesion of membranoproliferative glomerulonephritis
 Nephrotic syndrome with lesion (of):
  endothelial glomerulonephritis
  hypocomplementemic glomerulonephritis
   persistent glomerulonephritis
  lobular glomerulonephritis
  mesangiocapillary glomerulonephritis
  mixed membranous and proliferative glomerulonephritis

581.3 With lesion of minimal change glomerulonephritis
 Foot process disease
 Lipoid nephrosis
 Minimal change:
  glomerular disease
  glomerulitis
  nephrotic syndrome

● **581.8 With other specified pathological lesion in kidney**

● *581.81 Nephrotic syndrome in diseases classified elsewhere*

 Code first underlying disease, as:
 amyloidosis (277.3)
 diabetes mellitus (250.4)
 malaria (084.9)
 polyarteritis (446.0)
 systemic lupus erythematosus (710.0)

Excludes	nephrosis in epidemic hemorrhagic fever (078.6)

☐ **581.89 Other**
 Glomerulonephritis with edema and lesion of:
  exudative nephritis
  interstitial (diffuse) (focal) nephritis

☐ **581.9 Nephrotic syndrome with unspecified pathological lesion in kidney**
 Glomerulonephritis with edema NOS
 Nephritis:
  nephrotic NOS
  with edema NOS
 Nephrosis NOS
 Renal disease with edema NOS

ICD-9-CM

500-599

Vol. 1

Item 10-3 Chronic glomerulonephritis (GN) persists over a period of years, with remissions and exacerbation.
Chronic GN with lesion of proliferative glomerulonephritis results from a streptococcal infection.
Chronic GN with lesion of membranous glomerulonephritis, also known as membranous nephropathy, is characterized by deposits along the epithelial side of the basement membrane.
Chronic GN with lesion of membranoproliferative glomerulonephritis (MPGN) is a group of disorders characterized by alterations in the basement membranes of the kidney and the glomerular cells.
Chronic GN with lesion of rapidly progressive glomerulonephritis is characterized by necrosis, endothelial proliferation, and mesangial proliferation. The condition is marked by rapid and progressive decline in renal function.

● **582 Chronic glomerulonephritis**

> **Includes:** chronic nephritis

> **582.0 With lesion of proliferative glomerulonephritis**
> Chronic (diffuse) proliferative glomerulonephritis

> **582.1 With lesion of membranous glomerulonephritis**
> Chronic glomerulonephritis:
> > membranous
> > sclerosing
> Focal glomerulosclerosis
> Segmental hyalinosis

> **582.2 With lesion of membranoproliferative glomerulonephritis**
> Chronic glomerulonephritis:
> > endothelial
> > hypocomplementemic persistent
> > lobular
> > membranoproliferative
> > mesangiocapillary
> > mixed membranous and proliferative

> **582.4 With lesion of rapidly progressive glomerulonephritis**
> Chronic nephritis with lesion of necrotizing glomerulitis

● **582.8 With other specified pathological lesion in kidney**

> ● *582.81 Chronic glomerulonephritis in diseases classified elsewhere*
>
> > *Code first underlying disease, as:*
> > amyloidosis (277.3)
> > systemic lupus erythematosus (710.0)

> ☐ **582.89 Other**
> Chronic glomerulonephritis with lesion of:
> > exudative nephritis
> > interstitial (diffuse) (focal) nephritis

☐ **582.9 Chronic glomerulonephritis with unspecified pathological lesion in kidney**
> Glomerulonephritis: specified as chronic
> > NOS specified as chronic
> > hemorrhagic specified as chronic
> Nephritis specified as chronic
> Nephropathy specified as chronic

Item 10-4 Nephritis (inflammation) or nephropathy (disease) with lesion of proliferative glomerulonephritis results from a streptococcal infection.
Nephritis (inflammation) or nephropathy (disease) with lesion of membranous glomerulonephritis is characterized by deposits along the epithelial side of the basement membrane.
Nephritis (inflammation) or nephropathy (disease) with lesion of membranoproliferative glomerulonephritis is characterized by alterations in the basement membranes of the kidney and the glomerular cells.
Nephritis (inflammation) or nephropathy (disease) with lesion of rapidly progressive glomerulonephritis is characterized by rapid and progressive decline in renal function.
Nephritis (inflammation) or nephropathy (disease) with lesion of renal cortical necrosis is characterized by death of the cortical tissues.
Nephritis (inflammation) or nephropathy (disease) with lesion of renal medullary necrosis is characterized by death of the tissues that collect urine.

● **583 Nephritis and nephropathy, not specified as acute or chronic**

> **Includes:** "renal disease" so stated, not specified as acute or chronic but with stated pathology or cause

> **583.0 With lesion of proliferative glomerulonephritis**
> Proliferative:
> > glomerulonephritis (diffuse) NOS
> > nephritis NOS
> > nephropathy NOS

> **583.1 With lesion of membranous glomerulonephritis**
> Membranous:
> > glomerulonephritis NOS
> > nephritis NOS
> Membranous nephropathy NOS

> **583.2 With lesion of membranoproliferative glomerulonephritis**
> Membranoproliferative:
> > glomerulonephritis NOS
> > nephritis NOS
> > nephropathy NOS
> Nephritis NOS, with lesion of:
> > hypocomplementemic persistent glomerulonephritis
> > lobular glomerulonephritis
> > mesangiocapillary glomerulonephritis
> > mixed membranous and proliferative glomerulonephritis

> **583.4 With lesion of rapidly progressive glomerulonephritis**
> Necrotizing or rapidly progressive:
> > glomerulitis NOS
> > glomerulonephritis NOS
> > nephritis NOS
> > nephropathy NOS
> Nephritis, unspecified, with lesion of necrotizing glomerulitis

> **583.6 With lesion of renal cortical necrosis**
> Nephritis NOS with (renal) cortical necrosis
> Nephropathy NOS with (renal) cortical necrosis
> Renal cortical necrosis NOS

> **583.7 With lesion of renal medullary necrosis**
> Nephritis NOS with (renal) medullary [papillary] necrosis
> Nephropathy NOS with (renal) medullary [papillary] necrosis

● **583.8 With other specified pathological lesion in kidney**

● **583.81 Nephritis and nephropathy, not specified as acute or chronic, in diseases classified elsewhere**

Code first underlying disease, as:
    amyloidosis (277.3)
    diabetes mellitus (250.4)
    gonococcal infection (098.19)
    Goodpasture's syndrome (446.21)
    systemic lupus erythematosus (710.0)
    tuberculosis (016.0)

Excludes	*gouty nephropathy (274.10)*
	syphilitic nephritis (095.4)

□ **583.89 Other**
Glomerulitis with lesion of:
    exudative nephritis
    interstitial nephritis
Glomerulonephritis with lesion of:
    exudative nephritis
    interstitial nephritis
Nephritis with lesion of:
    exudative nephritis
    interstitial nephritis
Nephropathy with lesion of:
    exudative nephritis
    interstitial nephritis
Renal disease with lesion of:
    exudative nephritis
    interstitial nephritis

□ **583.9 With unspecified pathological lesion in kidney**
Glomerulitis NOS   Nephritis NOS
Glomerulonephritis NOS   Nephropathy NOS

Excludes	*nephropathy complicating pregnancy, labor, or the puerperium (642.0–642.9, 646.2)*
	renal disease NOS with no stated cause (593.9)

Item 10–5 Decreased blood flow is the usual cause of **acute renal failure** that offers a good prognosis for recovery. **Chronic renal failure** is usually the result of long-standing kidney disease and is a very serious condition that generally results in death.

● **584 Acute renal failure**

Excludes	*following labor and delivery (669.3)*
	posttraumatic (958.5)
	that complicating:
	abortion (634–638 with .3, 639.3)
	ectopic or molar pregnancy (639.3)

584.5 With lesion of tubular necrosis
Lower nephron nephrosis
Renal failure with (acute) tubular necrosis
Tubular necrosis:
    NOS
    acute

584.6 With lesion of renal cortical necrosis

584.7 With lesion of renal medullary [papillary] necrosis
Necrotizing renal papillitis

□ **584.8 With other specified pathological lesion in kidney**

□ **584.9 Acute renal failure, unspecified**

585 Chronic renal failure
Chronic uremia

Use additional code to identify manifestation as:
uremic:
    neuropathy (357.4)
    pericarditis (420.0)

Excludes	*that with any condition classifiable to 401 (403.0–403.9 with fifth-digit 1)*

□ **586 Renal failure, unspecified**
Uremia NOS

Excludes	*following labor and delivery (669.3)*
	posttraumatic renal failure (958.5)
	that complicating:
	abortion (634–638 with .3, 639.3)
	ectopic or molar pregnancy (639.3)
	uremia:
	extrarenal (788.9)
	prerenal (788.9)
	with any condition classifiable to 401 (403.0–403.9 with fifth-digit 1)

□ **587 Renal sclerosis, unspecified**
Atrophy of kidney
Contracted kidney
Renal:
    cirrhosis
    fibrosis

Excludes	*nephrosclerosis (arteriolar) (arteriosclerotic) (403.00–403.92)*
	with hypertension (403.00–403.92)

● **588 Disorders resulting from impaired renal function**

588.0 Renal osteodystrophy
Azotemic osteodystrophy
Phosphate-losing tubular disorders
Renal:
    dwarfism
    infantilism
    rickets

588.1 Nephrogenic diabetes insipidus

Excludes	*diabetes insipidus NOS (253.5)*

□ **588.8 Other specified disorders resulting from impaired renal function**
Hypokalemic nephropathy
Secondary hyperparathyroidism (of renal origin)

Excludes	*secondary hypertension (405.0–405.9)*

□ **588.9 Unspecified disorder resulting from impaired renal function**

● **589 Small kidney of unknown cause**

589.0 Unilateral small kidney

589.1 Bilateral small kidneys

□ **589.9 Small kidney, unspecified**

OTHER DISEASES OF URINARY SYSTEM (590–599)

● **590 Infections of kidney**

Use additional code to identify organism, such as Escherichia coli [E. coli] (041.4)

● **590.0 Chronic pyelonephritis**
Chronic pyelitis
Chronic pyonephrosis

Code first any associated vesicoureteral reflux (593.70–593.73)

590.00 Without lesion of renal medullary necrosis

590.01 With lesion of renal medullary necrosis

● **590.1 Acute pyelonephritis**
Acute pyelitis
Acute pyonephrosis

590.10 Without lesion of renal medullary necrosis

590.11 With lesion of renal medullary necrosis

ICD-9-CM

500–599

Vol. 1

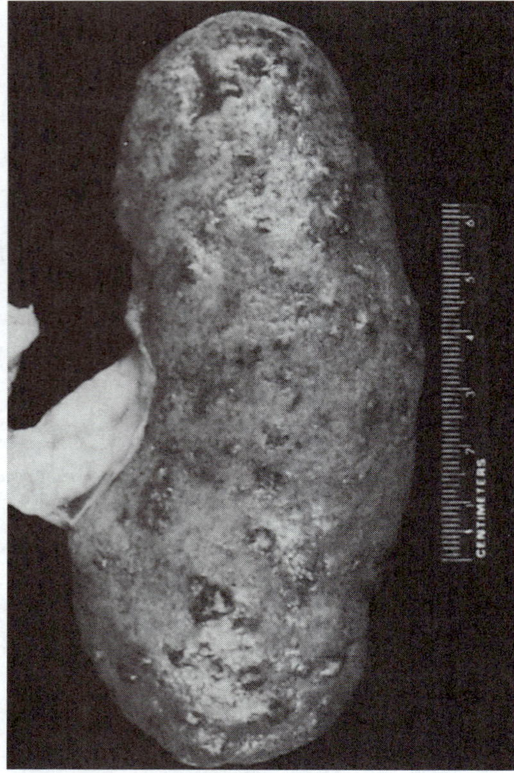

Figure 10–3   Acute pyelonephritis. Cortical surface is dotted with abscesses. (From Cotran R, Kumar V, Robbins S: Robbins Pathologic Basis of Disease. Philadelphia, WB Saunders, 1994, p 969.)

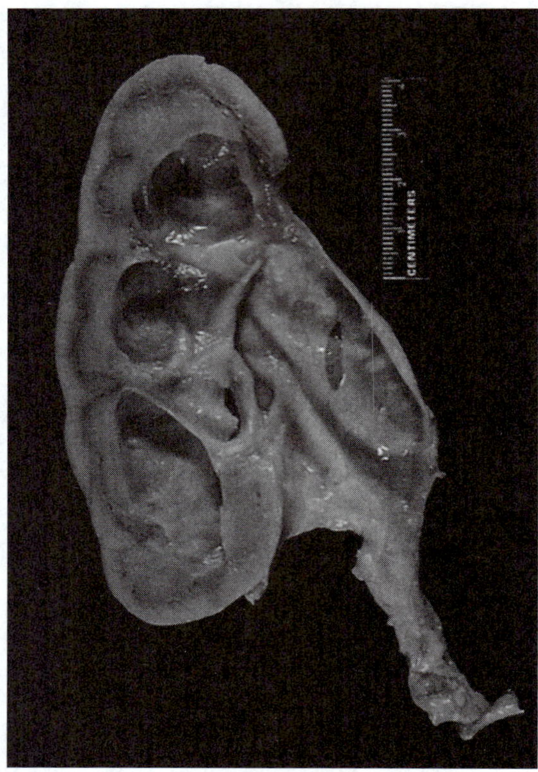

Figure 10–4   Hydronephrosis of the kidney, with marked dilatation of pelvis and calyces and thinning of renal parenchyma. (From Cotran R, Kumar V, Robbins S: Robbins Pathologic Basis of Disease. Philadelphia, WB Saunders, 1994, p 983.)

590.2   Renal and perinephric abscess
    Abscess:
      kidney
      nephritic
      perirenal
    Carbuncle of kidney

590.3   Pyeloureteritis cystica
    Infection of renal pelvis and ureter
    Ureteritis cystica

● **590.8   Other pyelonephritis or pyonephrosis, not specified as acute or chronic**

  ☐ **590.80   Pyelonephritis, unspecified**
      Pyelitis NOS
      Pyelonephritis NOS

  ● *590.81   Pyelitis or pyelonephritis in diseases classified elsewhere*

      Code first underlying disease, as:
      tuberculosis (016.0)

☐ **590.9   Infection of kidney, unspecified**
    Excludes   *urinary tract infection NOS (599.0)*

591   Hydronephrosis
    Hydrocalycosis
    Hydronephrosis
    Hydroureteronephrosis
    Excludes   *congenital hydronephrosis (753.29)*
                hydroureter (593.5)

● **592   Calculus of kidney and ureter**
    Excludes   *nephrocalcinosis (275.4)*

592.0   Calculus of kidney
    Nephrolithiasis NOS
    Renal calculus or stone
    Staghorn calculus
    Stone in kidney
    Excludes   *uric acid nephrolithiasis (274.11)*

592.1   Calculus of ureter
    Ureteric stone
    Ureterolithiasis

☐ **592.9   Urinary calculus, unspecified**

● **593   Other disorders of kidney and ureter**

593.0   Nephroptosis
    Floating kidney   Mobile kidney

593.1   Hypertrophy of kidney

593.2   Cyst of kidney, acquired
    Cyst (multiple) (solitary) of kidney, not congenital
    Peripelvic (lymphatic) cyst
    Excludes   *calyceal or pyelogenic cyst of kidney (591)*
                congenital cyst of kidney (753.1)
                polycystic (disease of) kidney (753.1)

593.3   Stricture or kinking of ureter
    Angulation of ureter (postoperative)
    Constriction of ureter (postoperative)
    Stricture of pelviureteric junction

☐ **593.4   Other ureteric obstruction**
    Idiopathic retroperitoneal fibrosis
    Occlusion NOS of ureter
    Excludes   *that due to calculus (592.1)*

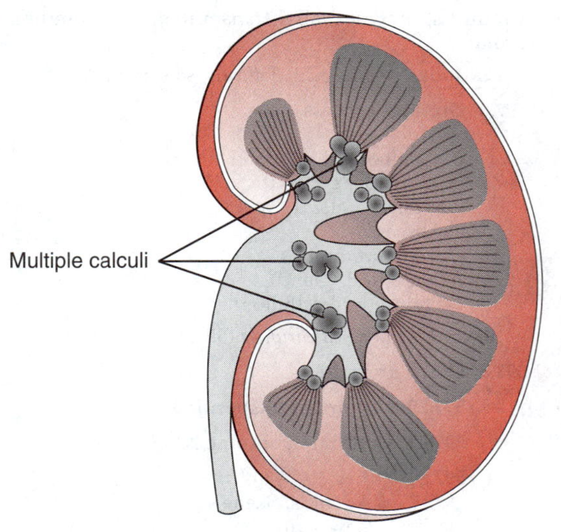

Figure 10–5   Multiple urinary calculi.

593.5 Hydroureter

> **Excludes** *congenital hydroureter (753.22)*
> *hydroureteronephrosis (591)*

593.6 Postural proteinuria
Benign postural proteinuria
Orthostatic proteinuria

> **Excludes** *proteinuria NOS (791.0)*

Item 10–6 Vesicoureteral reflux occurs when urine flows from the bladder back into the ureters, often resulting in urinary tract infection.

● **593.7 Vesicoureteral reflux**

Use additional code to identify:
chronic pyelonephritis (590.00–590.01)
renal agenesis (753.0)
renal dysplasia (753.15)

□ **593.70 Unspecified or without reflux nephropathy**

593.71 With reflux nephropathy, unilateral

593.72 With reflux nephropathy, bilateral

□ **593.73 With reflux nephropathy NOS**

● **593.8 Other specified disorders of kidney and ureter**

593.81 Vascular disorders of kidney
Renal (artery):
embolism
hemorrhage
thrombosis
Renal infarction

593.82 Ureteral fistula
Intestinoureteral fistula

> **Excludes** *fistula between ureter and female genital tract (619.0)*

□ **593.89 Other**
Adhesions, kidney or ureter
Periureteritis
Polyp of ureter
Pyelectasia
Ureterocele

> **Excludes** *tuberculosis of ureter (016.2)*
> *ureteritis cystica (590.3)*

□ **593.9 Unspecified disorder of kidney and ureter**
Renal disease NOS
Salt-losing nephritis or syndrome

> **Excludes** *cystic kidney disease (753.1)*
> *nephropathy, so stated (583.0–583.9)*
> *renal disease:*
> *acute (580.0–580.9)*
> *arising in pregnancy or the puerperium (642.1–642.2, 642.4–642.7, 646.2)*
> *chronic (582.0–582.9)*
> *not specified as acute or chronic, but with stated pathology or cause (583.0–583.9)*

● **594 Calculus of lower urinary tract**

594.0 Calculus in diverticulum of bladder

□ **594.1 Other calculus in bladder**
Urinary bladder stone

> **Excludes** *staghorn calculus (592.0)*

594.2 Calculus in urethra

□ **594.8 Other lower urinary tract calculus**

□ **594.9 Calculus of lower urinary tract, unspecified**

> **Excludes** *calculus of urinary tract NOS (592.9)*

● **595 Cystitis**

> **Excludes** *prostatocystitis (601.3)*

Use additional code to identify organism, such as Escherichia coli [E. coli] (041.4)

595.0 Acute cystitis

> **Excludes** *trigonitis (595.3)*

595.1 Chronic interstitial cystitis
Hunner's ulcer
Panmural fibrosis of bladder
Submucous cystitis

□ **595.2 Other chronic cystitis**
Chronic cystitis NOS
Subacute cystitis

> **Excludes** *trigonitis (595.3)*

595.3 Trigonitis
Follicular cystitis
Trigonitis (acute) (chronic)
Urethrotrigonitis

● **595.4 *Cystitis in diseases classified elsewhere***

Code first underlying disease, as:
actinomycosis (039.8)
amebiasis (006.8)
bilharziasis (120.0–120.9)
Echinococcus infestation (122.3, 122.6)

> **Excludes** *cystitis:*
> *diphtheritic (032.84)*
> *gonococcal (098.11, 098.31)*
> *monilial (112.2)*
> *trichomonal (131.09)*
> *tuberculous (016.1)*

● **595.8 Other specified types of cystitis**

595.81 Cystitis cystica

595.82 Irradiation cystitis

Use additional E code to identify cause

□ **595.89 Other**
Abscess of bladder
Cystitis:
bullous
emphysematous
glandularis

□ **595.9 Cystitis, unspecified**

● **596 Other disorders of bladder**

Use additional code to identify urinary incontinence (625.6, 788.30–788.39)

596.0 Bladder neck obstruction
Contracture (acquired) of bladder neck or vesico-urethral orifice
Obstruction (acquired) of bladder neck or vesico-urethral orifice
Stenosis (acquired) of bladder neck or vesicourethral orifice

Excludes *congenital (753.6)*

Item 10-7 Intestinovesical fistula is a passage between the bladder and the intestine. Diverticulum of the bladder is the formation of a sac from a herniation of the wall of the bladder through a deviation. Atony of the bladder is diminished tone of the bladder muscle.

596.1 Intestinovesical fistula
Fistula:
enterovesical   vesicoenteric
vesicocolic   vesicorectal

596.2 Vesical fistula, not elsewhere classified
Fistula:
bladder NOS   vesicocutaneous
urethrovesical   vesicoperineal

Excludes *fistula between bladder and female genital tract (619.0)*

596.3 Diverticulum of bladder
Diverticulitis of bladder
Diverticulum (acquired) (false) of bladder

Excludes *that with calculus in diverticulum of bladder (594.0)*

596.4 Atony of bladder
High compliance bladder
Hypotonicity of bladder
Inertia of bladder

Excludes *neurogenic bladder (596.54)*

● **596.5 Other functional disorders of bladder**

Excludes *cauda equina syndrome with neurogenic bladder (344.61)*

596.51 Hypertonicity of bladder
Hyperactivity

596.52 Low bladder compliance

596.53 Paralysis of bladder

596.54 Neurogenic bladder NOS

596.55 Detrusor sphincter dyssynergia

☐ **596.59 Other functional disorder of bladder**
Detrusor instability

596.6 Rupture of bladder, nontraumatic

596.7 Hemorrhage into bladder wall
Hyperemia of bladder

Excludes *acute hemorrhagic cystitis (595.0)*

☐ **596.8 Other specified disorders of bladder**
calcified
contracted
hemorrhage
hypertrophy

Excludes *cystocele, female (618.0, 618.2–618.4)*
hernia or prolapse of bladder, female (618.0, 618.2–618.4)

☐ **596.9 Unspecified disorder of bladder**

● **597 Urethritis, not sexually transmitted, and urethral syndrome**

Excludes *nonspecific urethritis, so stated (099.4)*

597.0 Urethral abscess
Abscess of:
bulbourethral gland
Cowper's gland
Littré's gland
Abscess:
periurethral
urethral (gland)
Periurethral cellulitis

Excludes *urethral caruncle (599.3)*

● **597.8 Other urethritis**

☐ **597.80 Urethritis, unspecified**

597.81 Urethral syndrome NOS

☐ **597.89 Other**
Adenitis, Skene's glands
Cowperitis
Meatitis, urethral
Ulcer, urethra (meatus)
Verumontanitis

Excludes *trichomonal (131.02)*

● **598 Urethral stricture**

Includes: pinhole meatus
stricture of urinary meatus

Use additional code to identify urinary incontinence (625.6, 788.30–788.39)

Excludes *congenital stricture of urethra and urinary meatus (753.6)*

● **598.0 Urethral stricture due to infection**

☐ **598.00 Due to unspecified infection**

● *598.01 Due to infective diseases classified elsewhere*

Code first underlying disease, as:
gonococcal infection (098.2)
schistosomiasis (120.0–120.9)
syphilis (095.8)

598.1 Traumatic urethral stricture
Stricture of urethra:
late effect of injury
postobstetric

Excludes *postoperative following surgery on genitourinary tract (598.2)*

598.2 Postoperative urethral stricture
Postcatheterization stricture of urethra

☐ **598.8 Other specified causes of urethral stricture**

☐ **598.9 Urethral stricture, unspecified**

● **599 Other disorders of urethra and urinary tract**

☐ **599.0 Urinary tract infection, site not specified**

Excludes *Candidiasis of urinary tract (112.2)*

Use additional code to identify organism, such as Escherichia coli [E. coli] (041.4)

599.1 Urethral fistula
Fistula:
urethroperineal
urethrorectal
Urinary fistula NOS

Excludes *fistula:*
urethroscrotal (608.89)
urethrovaginal (619.0)
urethrovesicovaginal (619.0)

599.2 Urethral diverticulum

    ◀▶ **New Code**   ⬅▦▶ **Revised Code**   ● **Not a Principal Diagnosis**   ● **Use Additional Digit(s)**   ☐ **Nonspecific Code**

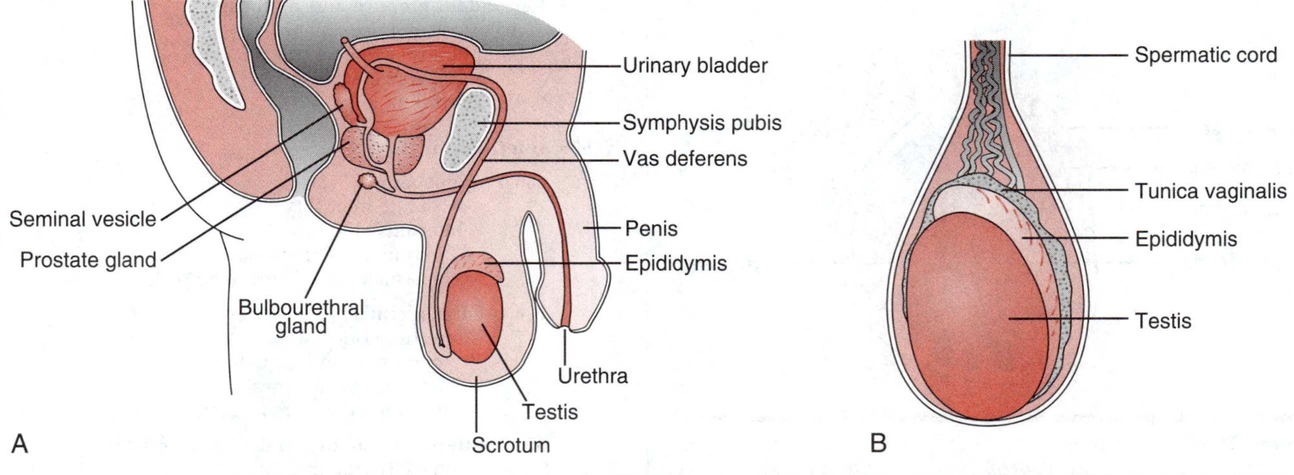

Figure 10–6 A. Male genital system. **B.** Testis.

599.3 Urethral caruncle
Polyp of urethra

599.4 Urethral false passage

599.5 Prolapsed urethral mucosa
Prolapse of urethra
Urethrocele

Excludes *urethrocele, female (618.0, 618.2–618.4)*

599.6 Urinary obstruction, unspecified
Obstructive uropathy NOS
Urinary (tract) obstruction NOS

Use additional code to identify urinary incontinence (625.6, 788.30–788.39)

Excludes *obstructive nephropathy NOS (593.89)*

599.7 Hematuria
Hematuria (benign) (essential)

Excludes *hemoglobinuria (791.2)*

599.8 Other specified disorders of urethra and urinary tract

Use additional code to identify urinary incontinence (625.6, 788.30–788.39)

Excludes *symptoms and other conditions classifiable to 788.0–788.2, 788.4–788.9, 791.0–791.9*

599.81 Urethral hypermobility

599.82 Intrinsic (urethral) sphincter deficiency [ISD]

599.83 Urethral instability

599.84 Other specified disorders of urethra
Rupture of urethra (nontraumatic)
Urethral:
cyst
granuloma

599.89 Other specified disorders of urinary tract

599.9 Unspecified disorder of urethra and urinary tract

DISEASES OF MALE GENITAL ORGANS (600–608)

600 Hyperplasia of prostate
Adenofibromatous hypertrophy of prostate
Adenoma (benign) of prostate
Enlargement (benign) of prostate
Fibroadenoma of prostate
Fibroma of prostate
Hypertrophy (benign) of prostate
Myoma of prostate
Median bar (prostate)
Prostatic obstruction NOS

Use additional code to identify urinary incontinence (788.30–788.39)

Excludes *benign neoplasms of prostate (222.2)*

601 Inflammatory diseases of prostate

Use additional code to identify organism, such as Staphylococcus (041.1), or Streptococcus (041.0)

601.0 Acute prostatitis

601.1 Chronic prostatitis

601.2 Abscess of prostate

601.3 Prostatocystitis

601.4 *Prostatitis in diseases classified elsewhere*

Code first underlying disease, as:
actinomycosis (039.8)
blastomycosis (116.0)
syphilis (095.8)
tuberculosis (016.5)

Excludes *prostatitis:*
gonococcal (098.12, 098.32)
monilial (112.2)
trichomonal (131.03)

601.8 Other specified inflammatory diseases of prostate
Prostatitis:
cavitary   granulomatous
diverticular

601.9 Prostatitis, unspecified
Prostatitis NOS

602 Other disorders of prostate

602.0 Calculus of prostate
Prostatic stone

602.1 Congestion or hemorrhage of prostate

ICD-9-CM

600–699

Vol. 1

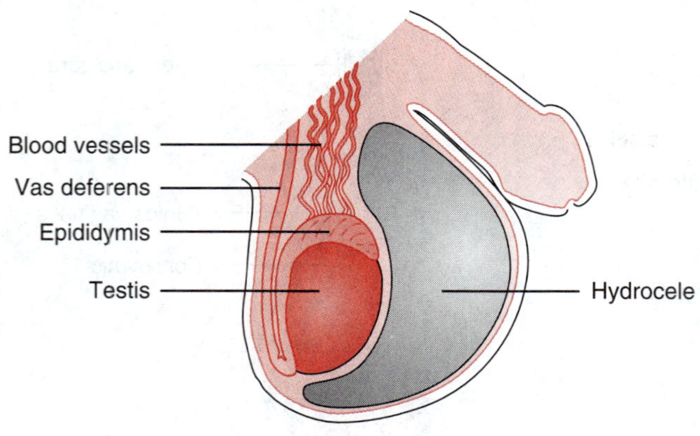

Figure 10–7　Hydrocele.

Item 10–8　Hydrocele is a sac of fluid in the testes membrane.

602.2　Atrophy of prostate

602.8　Other specified disorders of prostate
Fistula of prostate
Infarction of prostate
Stricture of prostate
Periprostatic adhesions

602.9　Unspecified disorder of prostate

603　Hydrocele

Includes: hydrocele of spermatic cord, testis, or tunica
vaginalis

Excludes　*congenital (778.6)*

603.0　Encysted hydrocele

603.1　Infected hydrocele

Use additional code to identify organism

603.8　Other specified types of hydrocele

603.9　Hydrocele, unspecified

604　Orchitis and epididymitis

Use additional code to identify organism, such as Escherichia coli [E. coli] (041.4), Staphylococcus (041.1), or Streptococcus (041.0)

604.0　Orchitis, epididymitis, and epididymo-orchitis, with abscess
Abscess of epididymis or testis

604.9　Other orchitis, epididymitis, and epididymo-orchitis, without mention of abscess

604.90　Orchitis and epididymitis, unspecified

604.91　*Orchitis and epididymitis in diseases classified elsewhere*

Code first underlying disease, as:
diphtheria (032.89)
filariasis (125.0–125.9)
syphilis (095.8)

Excludes　*orchitis:*
gonococcal (098.13, 098.33)
mumps (072.0)
tuberculous (016.5)
tuberculous epididymitis (016.4)

604.99　Other

605　Redundant prepuce and phimosis
Adherent prepuce
Paraphimosis
Phimosis (congenital)
Tight foreskin

606　Infertility, male

606.0　Azoospermia
Absolute infertility
Infertility due to:
germinal (cell) aplasia
spermatogenic arrest (complete)

606.1　Oligospermia
Infertility due to:
germinal cell desquamation
hypospermatogenesis
incomplete spermatogenic arrest

606.8　Infertility due to extratesticular causes
Infertility due to:
drug therapy
infection
obstruction of efferent ducts
radiation
systemic disease

606.9　Male infertility, unspecified

607　Disorders of penis
Excludes　*phimosis (605)*

607.0　Leukoplakia of penis
Kraurosis of penis

Excludes　*carcinoma in situ of penis (233.5)*
erythroplasia of Queyrat (233.5)

607.1　Balanoposthitis
Balanitis

Use additional code to identify organism

607.2　Other inflammatory disorders of penis
Abscess of corpus cavernosum or penis
Boil of corpus cavernosum or penis
Carbuncle of corpus cavernosum or penis
Cellulitis of corpus cavernosum or penis
Cavernitis (penis)

Use additional code to identify organism
Excludes　*herpetic infection (054.13)*

607.3　Priapism
Painful erection

607.8　Other specified disorders of penis

607.81　Balanitis xerotica obliterans
Induratio penis plastica

607.82　Vascular disorders of penis
Embolism of corpus cavernosum or penis
Hematoma (nontraumatic) of corpus cavernosum or penis
Hemorrhage of corpus cavernosum or penis
Thrombosis of corpus cavernosum or penis

607.83　Edema of penis

607.84　Impotence of organic origin
Excludes　*nonorganic or unspecified (302.72)*

607.89　Other
Atrophy of corpus cavernosum or penis
Fibrosis of corpus cavernosum or penis
Hypertrophy of corpus cavernosum or penis
Ulcer (chronic) of corpus cavernosum or penis

　◀▶ **New Code**　◀▥ ▥▶ **Revised Code**　● **Not a Principal Diagnosis**　● **Use Additional Digit(s)**　☐ **Nonspecific Code**

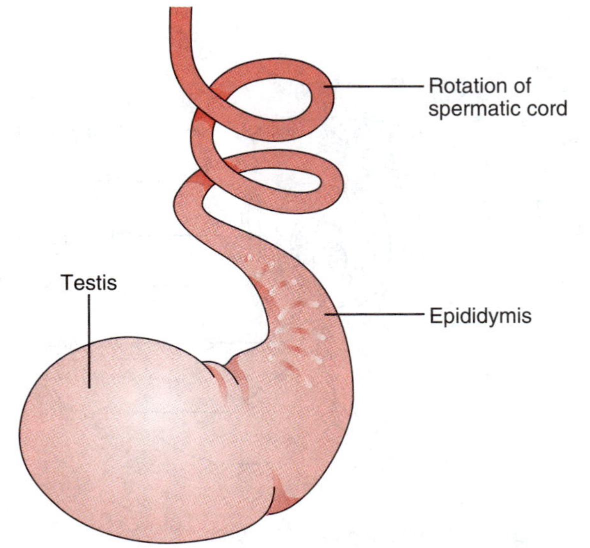

Figure 10-8 Torsion of testis.

Item 10-9 Rotation of the spermatic cord causes strangulation and infarction of the testis.

☐ **607.9 Unspecified disorder of penis**

● **608 Other disorders of male genital organs**

    608.0 Seminal vesiculitis
        Abscess of seminal vesicle
        Cellulitis of seminal vesicle
        Vesiculitis (seminal)

        Use additional code to identify organism
        Excludes *gonococcal infection (098.14, 098.34)*

    608.1 Spermatocele

    608.2 Torsion of testis
        Torsion of:
          epididymis
          spermatic cord
          testicle

    608.3 Atrophy of testis

☐ **608.4 Other inflammatory disorders of male genital organs**
        Abscess of scrotum, spermatic cord, testis [except abscess], tunica vaginalis, or vas deferens
        Boil of scrotum, spermatic cord, testis [except abscess], tunica vaginalis, or vas deferens
        Carbuncle of scrotum, spermatic cord, testis [except abscess], tunica vaginalis, or vas deferens
        Cellulitis of scrotum, spermatic cord, testis [except abscess], tunica vaginalis, or vas deferens
        Vasitis

        Use additional code to identify organism
        Excludes *abscess of testis (604.0)*

● **608.8 Other specified disorders of male genital organs**

    ● ***608.81 Disorders of male genital organs in diseases classified elsewhere***

        Code first underlying disease, as:
          filariasis (125.0–125.9)
          tuberculosis (016.5)

    608.83 Vascular disorders
        Hematoma (nontraumatic) of seminal vesicle, spermatic cord, testis, scrotum, tunica vaginalis, or vas deferens
        Hemorrhage of seminal vesicle, spermatic cord, testis, scrotum, tunica vaginalis, or vas deferens
        Thrombosis of seminal vesicle, spermatic cord, testis, scrotum, tunica vaginalis, or vas deferens
        Hematocele NOS, male

    608.84 Chylocele of tunica vaginalis

    608.85 Stricture
        Stricture of:
          spermatic cord
          tunica vaginalis
          vas deferens

    608.86 Edema

☐ **608.89 Other**
        Atrophy of seminal vesicle, spermatic cord, testis, scrotum, tunica vaginalis, or vas deferens
        Fibrosis of seminal vesicle, spermatic cord, testis, scrotum, tunica vaginalis, or vas deferens
        Hypertrophy of seminal vesicle, spermatic cord, testis, scrotum, tunica vaginalis, or vas deferens
        Ulcer of seminal vesicle, spermatic cord, testis, scrotum, tunica vaginalis, or vas deferens

    Excludes *atrophy of testis (608.3)*

☐ **608.9 Unspecified disorder of male genital organs**

DISORDERS OF BREAST (610–611)

● **610 Benign mammary dysplasias**

    610.0 Solitary cyst of breast
        Cyst (solitary) of breast

    610.1 Diffuse cystic mastopathy
        Chronic cystic mastitis
        Cystic breast
        Fibrocystic disease of breast

    610.2 Fibroadenosis of breast
        Fibroadenosis of breast:
          NOS   diffuse
          chronic   periodic
          cystic   segmental

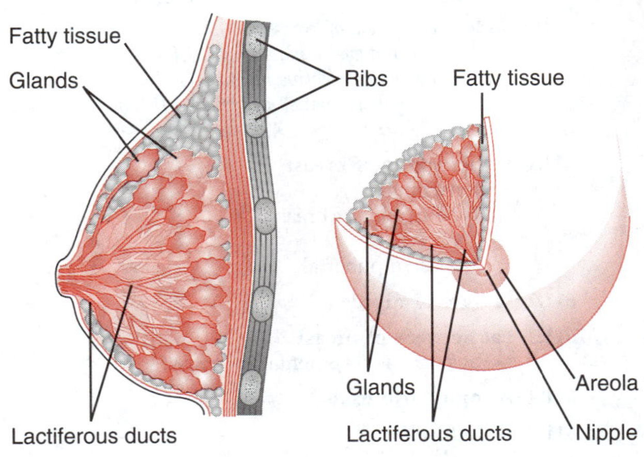

Figure 10-9 Breast.

ICD-9-CM

600–699

Vol. 1

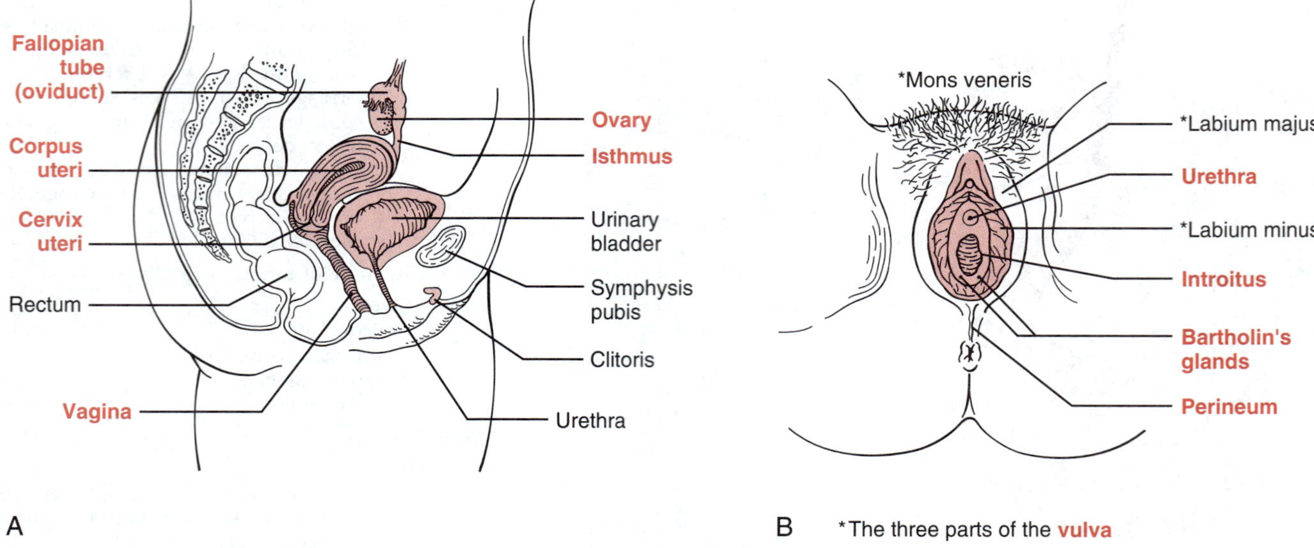

Figure 10–10 **A.** Female genital system. **B.** External female genital system. (From Buck CJ: Step-by-Step Medical Coding, 2nd ed. Philadelphia, WB Saunders, 1998, p 168.)

610.3 Fibrosclerosis of breast

610.4 Mammary duct ectasia
Comedomastitis
Duct ectasia
Mastitis:
  periductal
  plasma cell

❑**610.8 Other specified benign mammary dysplasias**
Mazoplasia
Sebaceous cyst of breast

❑**610.9 Benign mammary dysplasia, unspecified**

● **611 Other disorders of breast**
    | Excludes | *that associated with lactation or the puerperium (675.0–676.9)*

611.0 Inflammatory disease of breast
Abscess (acute) (chronic) (nonpuerperal) of:
  areola
  breast
Mammillary fistula
Mastitis (acute) (subacute) (nonpuerperal):
  NOS   retromammary
  infective   submammary
    | Excludes | *carbuncle of breast (680.2)*
    chronic cystic mastitis (610.1)
    neonatal infective mastitis (771.5)
    thrombophlebitis of breast [Mondor's disease] (451.89)

611.1 Hypertrophy of breast
Gynecomastia
Hypertrophy of breast:
  NOS
  massive pubertal

611.2 Fissure of nipple

611.3 Fat necrosis of breast
Fat necrosis (segmental) of breast

611.4 Atrophy of breast

611.5 Galactocele

611.6 Galactorrhea not associated with childbirth

● **611.7 Signs and symptoms in breast**

611.71 Mastodynia
Pain in breast

611.72 Lump or mass in breast

❑**611.79 Other**
Induration of breast
Inversion of nipple
Nipple discharge
Retraction of nipple

❑**611.8 Other specified disorders of breast**
Hematoma (nontraumatic) of breast
Infarction of breast
Occlusion of breast duct
Subinvolution of breast (postlactational) (postpartum)

❑**611.9 Unspecified breast disorder**

INFLAMMATORY DISEASE OF FEMALE PELVIC ORGANS (614–616)

Use additional code to identify organism, such as Staphylococcus (041.1), or Streptococcus (041.0)
    | Excludes | *that associated with pregnancy, abortion, childbirth, or the puerperium (630–676.9)*

● **614 Inflammatory disease of ovary, fallopian tube, pelvic cellular tissue, and peritoneum**
    | Excludes | *endometritis (615.0–615.9)*
    major infection following delivery (670)
    that complicating:
      abortion (634–638 with .0, 639.0)
      ectopic or molar pregnancy (639.0)
      pregnancy or labor (646.6)

614.0 Acute salpingitis and oophoritis
Any condition classifiable to 614.2, specified as acute or subacute

614.1 Chronic salpingitis and oophoritis
Hydrosalpinx
Salpingitis:
  follicularis
  isthmica nodosa
Any condition classifiable to 614.2, specified as chronic

◄▶ **New Code**   ⬅⮕ **Revised Code**   ● **Not a Principal Diagnosis**   ● **Use Additional Digit(s)**   ❑ **Nonspecific Code**

☐ **614.2 Salpingitis and oophoritis not specified as acute, subacute, or chronic**

Abscess (of):	Perioophoritis
fallopian tube	Perisalpingitis
ovary	Pyosalpinx
tubo-ovarian	Salpingitis
Oophoritis	Salpingo-oophoritis
Tubo-ovarian inflammatory disease	

> **Excludes** *gonococcal infection (chronic) (098.37)*
> *acute (098.17)*
> *tuberculous (016.6)*

614.3 Acute parametritis and pelvic cellulitis
Acute inflammatory pelvic disease
Any condition classifiable to 614.4, specified as acute

614.4 Chronic or unspecified parametritis and pelvic cellulitis
Abscess (of):
broad ligament chronic or NOS
parametrium chronic or NOS
pelvis, female chronic or NOS
pouch of Douglas chronic or NOS
Chronic inflammatory pelvic disease
Pelvic cellulitis, female

> **Excludes** *tuberculous (016.7)*

614.5 Acute or unspecified pelvic peritonitis, female

614.6 Pelvic peritoneal adhesions, female (postoperative) (postinfection)
Adhesions:
peritubal
tubo-ovarian

Use additional code to identify any associated infertility (628.2)

☐ **614.7 Other chronic pelvic peritonitis, female**

> **Excludes** *tuberculous (016.7)*

☐ **614.8 Other specified inflammatory disease of female pelvic organs and tissues**

☐ **614.9 Unspecified inflammatory disease of female pelvic organs and tissues**
Pelvic infection or inflammation, female NOS
Pelvic inflammatory disease [PID]

● **615 Inflammatory diseases of uterus, except cervix**

> **Excludes** *following delivery (670)*
> *hyperplastic endometritis (621.3)*
> *that complicating:*
> *abortion (634–638 with .0, 639.0)*
> *ectopic or molar pregnancy (639.0)*
> *pregnancy or labor (646.6)*

615.0 Acute
Any condition classifiable to 615.9, specified as acute or subacute

615.1 Chronic
Any condition classifiable to 615.9, specified as chronic

☐ **615.9 Unspecified inflammatory disease of uterus**

Endometritis	Perimetritis
Endomyometritis	Pyometra
Metritis	Uterine abscess
Myometritis	

● **616 Inflammatory disease of cervix, vagina, and vulva**

> **Excludes** *that complicating:*
> *abortion (634–638 with .0, 639.0)*
> *ectopic or molar pregnancy (639.0)*
> *pregnancy, childbirth, or the puerperium (646.6)*

616.0 Cervicitis and endocervicitis
Cervicitis with or without mention of erosion or ectropion
Endocervicitis with or without mention of erosion or ectropion
Nabothian (gland) cyst or follicle

> **Excludes** *erosion or ectropion without mention of cervicitis (622.0)*

● **616.1 Vaginitis and vulvovaginitis**

☐ **616.10 Vaginitis and vulvovaginitis, unspecified**
Vaginitis:
NOS
postirradiation
Vulvitis NOS
Vulvovaginitis NOS

Use additional code to identify organism, such as Escherichia coli [E. coli] (041.4), Staphylococcus (041.1), or Streptococcus (041.0)

> **Excludes** *noninfective leukorrhea (623.5)*
> *postmenopausal or senile vaginitis (627.3)*

● **616.11 Vaginitis and vulvovaginitis in diseases classified elsewhere**

Code first underlying disease, as:
pinworm vaginitis (127.4)

> **Excludes** *herpetic vulvovaginitis (054.11)*
> *monilial vulvovaginitis (112.1)*
> *trichomonal vaginitis or vulvovaginitis (131.01)*

616.2 Cyst of Bartholin's gland
Bartholin's duct cyst

616.3 Abscess of Bartholin's gland
Vulvovaginal gland abscess

☐ **616.4 Other abscess of vulva**

Abscess of vulva	Furuncle of vulva
Carbuncle of vulva	

● **616.5 Ulceration of vulva**

☐ **616.50 Ulceration of vulva, unspecified**
Ulcer NOS of vulva

● **616.51 Ulceration of vulva in diseases classified elsewhere**

Code first underlying disease, as:
Behçet's syndrome (136.1)
tuberculosis (016.7)

> **Excludes** *vulvar ulcer (in):*
> *gonococcal (098.0)*
> *herpes simplex (054.12)*
> *syphilitic (091.0)*

☐ **616.8 Other specified inflammatory diseases of cervix, vagina, and vulva**
Caruncle, vagina or labium
Ulcer, vagina

> **Excludes** *noninflammatory disorders of:*
> *cervix (622.0–622.9)*
> *vagina (623.0–623.9)*
> *vulva (624.0–624.9)*

☐ **616.9 Unspecified inflammatory disease of cervix, vagina, and vulva**

OTHER DISORDERS OF FEMALE GENITAL TRACT (617–629)

● **617 Endometriosis**

617.0 Endometriosis of uterus
Adenomyosis
Endometriosis:

cervix	myometrium
internal	

> **Excludes** *stromal endometriosis (236.0)*

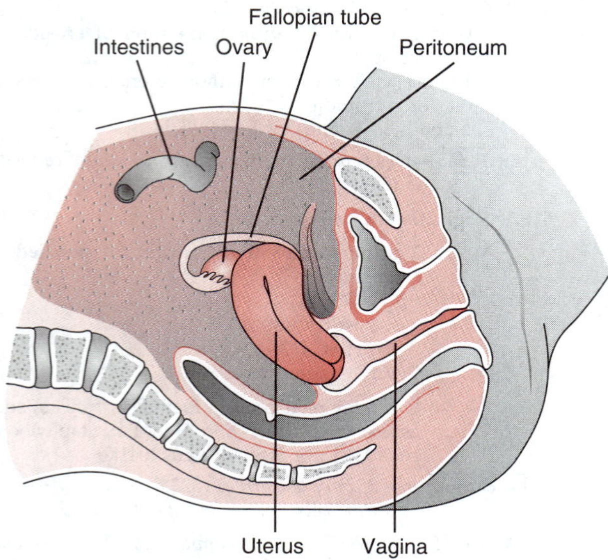

Figure 10–11   Sites of potential endometrial implants.

Item 10-10   **Endometriosis is a condition for which no clear cause has been identified. Endometrial tissue is expelled from the uterus into the body and can implant onto a variety of organs. Classification is based on the site of implant of the endometrial tissue.**

617.1   Endometriosis of ovary
     Chocolate cyst of ovary
     Endometrial cystoma of ovary

617.2   Endometriosis of fallopian tube

617.3   Endometriosis of pelvic peritoneum
     Endometriosis:
        broad ligament
        cul-de-sac (Douglas')
        parametrium
        round ligament

617.4   Endometriosis of rectovaginal septum and vagina

617.5   Endometriosis of intestine
     Endometriosis:
        appendix
        colon
        rectum

617.6   Endometriosis in scar of skin

☐ **617.8   Endometriosis of other specified sites**
     Endometriosis:
        bladder
        lung
        umbilicus
        vulva

☐ **617.9   Endometriosis, site unspecified**

● **618   Genital prolapse**

     Use additional code to identify urinary incontinence (625.6, 788.31, 788.33–788.39)

> **Excludes**   *that complicating pregnancy, labor, or delivery (654.4)*

618.0   Prolapse of vaginal walls without mention of uterine prolapse
     Cystocele
     Cystourethrocele
     Proctocele, female, without mention of uterine prolapse
     Rectocele, without mention of uterine prolapse
     Urethrocele, female, without mention of uterine prolapse
     Vaginal prolapse, without mention of uterine prolapse

> **Excludes**   *that with uterine prolapse (618.2–618.4)*
> *enterocele (618.6)*
> *vaginal vault prolapse following hysterectomy (618.5)*

618.1   Uterine prolapse without mention of vaginal wall prolapse
     Descensus uteri
     Uterine prolapse:
        NOS
        complete
        first degree
        second degree
        third degree

> **Excludes**   *that with mention of cystocele, urethrocele, or rectocele (618.2–618.4)*

618.2   Uterovaginal prolapse, incomplete

618.3   Uterovaginal prolapse, complete

☐ **618.4   Uterovaginal prolapse, unspecified**

618.5   Prolapse of vaginal vault after hysterectomy

618.6   Vaginal enterocele, congenital or acquired
     Pelvic enterocele, congenital or acquired

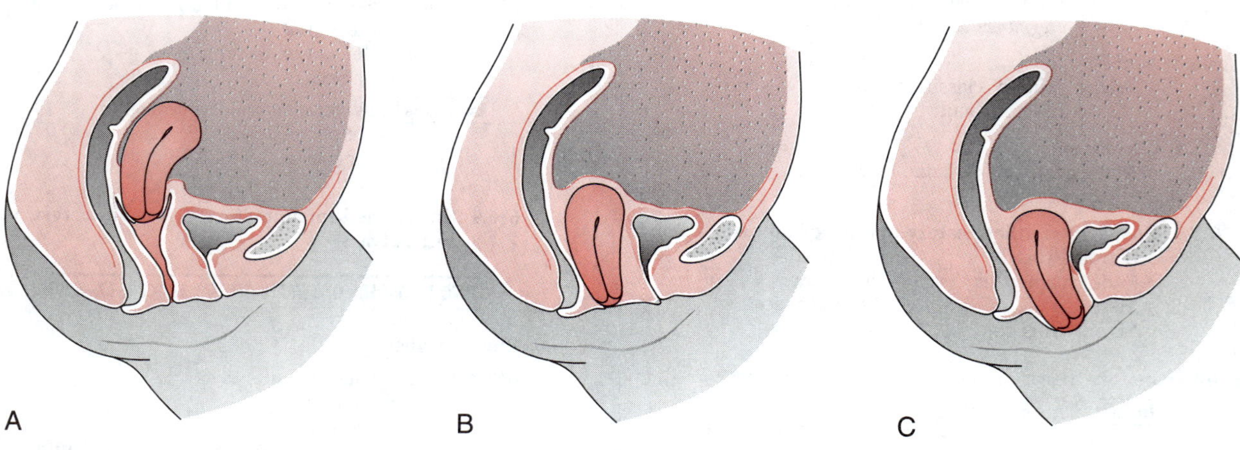

Figure 10–12   Three stages of uterine prolapse. **A.** Uterus is prolapsed. **B.** Vagina and uterus are prolapsed (incomplete uterovaginal prolapse). **C.** Vagina and uterus are completely prolapsed and are exposed through the external genitalia (complete uterovaginal prolapse).

    ◄▶ **New Code**   ⇐⇒ **Revised Code**   ● **Not a Principal Diagnosis**   ● **Use Additional Digit(s)**   ☐ **Nonspecific Code**

618.7 Old laceration of muscles of pelvic floor

❑ **618.8 Other specified genital prolapse**
Incompetence or weakening of pelvic fundus
Relaxation of vaginal outlet or pelvis

❑ **618.9 Unspecified genital prolapse**

● **619 Fistula involving female genital tract**
Excludes *vesicorectal and intestinovesical fistula (596.1)*

619.0 Urinary-genital tract fistula, female
Fistula:
cervicovesical
ureterovaginal
urethrovaginal
urethrovesicovaginal
uteroureteric
uterovesical
vesicocervicovaginal
vesicovaginal

619.1 Digestive-genital tract fistula, female
Fistula:
intestinouterine   rectovulval
intestinovaginal   sigmoidovaginal
rectovaginal   uterorectal

619.2 Genital tract-skin fistula, female
Fistula:
uterus to abdominal wall
vaginoperineal

❑ **619.8 Other specified fistulas involving female genital tract**
Fistula:
cervix
cul-de-sac (Douglas')
uterus
vagina

❑ **619.9 Unspecified fistula involving female genital tract**

● **620 Noninflammatory disorders of ovary, fallopian tube, and broad ligament**
Excludes *hydrosalpinx (614.1)*

620.0 Follicular cyst of ovary
Cyst of graafian follicle

620.1 Corpus luteum cyst or hematoma
Corpus luteum hemorrhage or rupture
Lutein cyst

❑ **620.2 Other and unspecified ovarian cyst**
Cyst of ovary:
NOS   serous
corpus albicans   theca-lutein
retention NOS
Simple cystoma of ovary

Excludes *cystadenoma (benign) (serous) (220)*
developmental cysts (752.0)
neoplastic cysts (220)
polycystic ovaries (256.4)
Stein-Leventhal syndrome (256.4)

620.3 Acquired atrophy of ovary and fallopian tube
Senile involution of ovary

620.4 Prolapse or hernia of ovary and fallopian tube
Displacement of ovary and fallopian tube
Salpingocele

620.5 Torsion of ovary, ovarian pedicle, or fallopian tube
Torsion:
accessory tube
hydatid of Morgagni

620.6 Broad ligament laceration syndrome
Masters-Allen syndrome

620.7 Hematoma of broad ligament
Hematocele, broad ligament

❑ **620.8 Other noninflammatory disorders of ovary, fallopian tube, and broad ligament**
Cyst of broad ligament or fallopian tube
Polyp of broad ligament or fallopian tube
Infarction of ovary or fallopian tube
Rupture of ovary or fallopian tube
Hematosalpinx of ovary or fallopian tube

Excludes *hematosalpinx in ectopic pregnancy (639.2)*
peritubal adhesions (614.6)
torsion of ovary, ovarian pedicle, or fallopian tube (620.5)

❑ **620.9 Unspecified noninflammatory disorder of ovary, fallopian tube, and broad ligament**

● **621 Disorders of uterus, not elsewhere classified**

621.0 Polyp of corpus uteri
Polyp:
endometrium
uterus NOS
Excludes *cervical polyp NOS (622.7)*

621.1 Chronic subinvolution of uterus
Excludes *puerperal (674.8)*

621.2 Hypertrophy of uterus
Bulky or enlarged uterus
Excludes *puerperal (674.8)*

621.3 Endometrial cystic hyperplasia
Hyperplasia (adenomatous) (cystic) (glandular) of endometrium
Hyperplastic endometritis

621.4 Hematometra
Hemometra
Excludes *that in congenital anomaly (752.2–752.3)*

621.5 Intrauterine synechiae
Adhesions of uterus   Band(s) of uterus

621.6 Malposition of uterus
Anteversion of uterus   Retroversion of uterus
Retroflexion of uterus
Excludes *malposition complicating pregnancy, labor, or delivery (654.3–654.4)*
prolapse of uterus (618.1–618.4)

621.7 Chronic inversion of uterus
Excludes *current obstetrical trauma (665.2)*
prolapse of uterus (618.1–618.4)

❑ **621.8 Other specified disorders of uterus, not elsewhere classified**
Atrophy, acquired of uterus
Cyst of uterus
Fibrosis NOS of uterus
Old laceration (postpartum) of uterus
Ulcer of uterus
Excludes *bilharzial fibrosis (120.0–120.9)*
endometriosis (617.0)
fistulas (619.0–619.8)
inflammatory diseases (615.0–615.9)

❑ **621.9 Unspecified disorder of uterus**

● **622 Noninflammatory disorders of cervix**
Excludes *abnormality of cervix complicating pregnancy, labor, or delivery (654.5–654.6)*
fistula (619.0–619.8)

622.0 Erosion and ectropion of cervix
Eversion of cervix
Ulcer of cervix
Excludes *that in chronic cervicitis (616.0)*

ICD-9-CM
600–699
Vol. 1

622.1　Dysplasia of cervix (uteri)
　　Anaplasia of cervix
　　Cervical atypism

　　Excludes *carcinoma in situ of cervix (233.1)*
　　　　　　　cervical intraepithelial neoplasia III [CIN III]
　　　　　　　(233.1)

622.2　Leukoplakia of cervix (uteri)

　　Excludes *carcinoma in situ of cervix (233.1)*

622.3　Old laceration of cervix
　　Adhesions of cervix
　　Band(s) of cervix
　　Cicatrix (postpartum) of cervix

　　Excludes *current obstetrical trauma (665.3)*

622.4　Stricture and stenosis of cervix
　　Atresia (acquired) of cervix
　　Contracture of cervix
　　Occlusion of cervix
　　Pinpoint os uteri

　　Excludes *congenital (752.49)*
　　　　　　　that complicating labor (654.6)

622.5　Incompetence of cervix

　　Excludes *complicating pregnancy (654.5)*
　　　　　　　that affecting fetus or newborn (761.0)

622.6　Hypertrophic elongation of cervix

622.7　Mucous polyp of cervix
　　Polyp NOS of cervix

　　Excludes *adenomatous polyp of cervix (219.0)*

☐**622.8　Other specified noninflammatory disorders of cervix**
　　Atrophy (senile) of cervix
　　Cyst of cervix
　　Fibrosis of cervix
　　Hemorrhage of cervix

　　Excludes *endometriosis (617.0)*
　　　　　　　fistula (619.0–619.8)
　　　　　　　inflammatory diseases (616.0)

☐**622.9　Unspecified noninflammatory disorder of cervix**

●**623　Noninflammatory disorders of vagina**

　　Excludes *abnormality of vagina complicating pregnancy,*
　　　　　　　labor, or delivery (654.7)
　　　　　　　congenital absence of vagina (752.49)
　　　　　　　congenital diaphragm or bands (752.49)
　　　　　　　fistulas involving vagina (619.0–619.8)

623.0　Dysplasia of vagina

　　Excludes *carcinoma in situ of vagina (233.3)*

623.1　Leukoplakia of vagina

623.2　Stricture or atresia of vagina
　　Adhesions (postoperative) (postradiation) of vagina
　　Occlusion of vagina
　　Stenosis, vagina

　　Use additional E code to identify any external cause

　　Excludes *congenital atresia or stricture (752.49)*

623.3　Tight hymenal ring
　　Rigid hymen acquired or congenital
　　Tight hymenal ring acquired or congenital
　　Tight introitus acquired or congenital

　　Excludes *imperforate hymen (752.42)*

623.4　Old vaginal laceration

　　Excludes *old laceration involving muscles of pelvic floor*
　　　　　　　(618.7)

623.5　Leukorrhea, not specified as infective
　　Leukorrhea NOS of vagina
　　Vaginal discharge NOS

　　Excludes *trichomonal (131.00)*

623.6　Vaginal hematoma

　　Excludes *current obstetrical trauma (665.7)*

623.7　Polyp of vagina

☐**623.8　Other specified noninflammatory disorders of vagina**
　　Cyst of vagina
　　Hemorrhage of vagina

☐**623.9　Unspecified noninflammatory disorder of vagina**

●**624　Noninflammatory disorders of vulva and perineum**

　　Excludes *abnormality of vulva and perineum complicating*
　　　　　　　pregnancy, labor, or delivery (654.8)
　　　　　　　condyloma acuminatum (078.1)
　　　　　　　fistulas involving:
　　　　　　　　perineum-see Alphabetic Index
　　　　　　　　vulva (619.0–619.8)
　　　　　　　vulval varices (456.6)
　　　　　　　vulvar involvement in skin conditions (690–
　　　　　　　709.9)

624.0　Dystrophy of vulva
　　Kraurosis of vulva
　　Leukoplakia of vulva

　　Excludes *carcinoma in situ of vulva (233.3)*

624.1　Atrophy of vulva

624.2　Hypertrophy of clitoris

　　Excludes *that in endocrine disorders (255.2, 256.1)*

624.3　Hypertrophy of labia
　　Hypertrophy of vulva NOS

624.4　Old laceration or scarring of vulva

624.5　Hematoma of vulva

　　Excludes *that complicating delivery (664.5)*

624.6　Polyp of labia and vulva

☐**624.8　Other specified noninflammatory disorders of vulva and perineum**
　　Cyst of vulva
　　Edema of vulva
　　Stricture of vulva

☐**624.9　Unspecified noninflammatory disorder of vulva and perineum**

●**625　Pain and other symptoms associated with female genital organs**

625.0　Dyspareunia

　　Excludes *psychogenic dyspareunia (302.76)*

625.1　Vaginismus
　　Colpospasm
　　Vulvismus

　　Excludes *psychogenic vaginismus (306.51)*

625.2　Mittelschmerz
　　Intermenstrual pain
　　Ovulation pain

625.3　Dysmenorrhea
　　Painful menstruation

　　Excludes *psychogenic dysmenorrhea (306.52)*

625.4　Premenstrual tension syndromes
　　Menstrual:
　　　migraine
　　　molimen
　　Premenstrual syndrome
　　Premenstrual tension NOS

　◀▶ **New Code**　　⬅▬ ▬➡ **Revised Code**　　● **Not a Principal Diagnosis**　　● **Use Additional Digit(s)**　　☐ **Nonspecific Code**

625.5 Pelvic congestion syndrome
Congestion-fibrosis syndrome
Taylor's syndrome

625.6 Stress incontinence, female
> **Excludes** *mixed incontinence (788.33)*
> *stress incontinence, male (788.32)*

☐**625.8 Other specified symptoms associated with female genital organs**

☐**625.9 Unspecified symptoms associated with female genital organs**

●**626 Disorders of menstruation and other abnormal bleeding from female genital tract**
> **Excludes** *menopausal and premenopausal bleeding (627.0)*
> *pain and other symptoms associated with menstrual cycle (625.2–625.4)*
> *postmenopausal bleeding (627.1)*

626.0 Absence of menstruation
Amenorrhea (primary) (secondary)

626.1 Scanty or infrequent menstruation
Hypomenorrhea
Oligomenorrhea

626.2 Excessive or frequent menstruation
Heavy periods
Menometrorrhagia
Menorrhagia
Polymenorrhea
> **Excludes** *premenopausal (627.0)*
> *that in puberty (626.3)*

626.3 Puberty bleeding
Excessive bleeding associated with onset of menstrual periods
Pubertal menorrhagia

626.4 Irregular menstrual cycle
Irregular:
bleeding NOS
menstruation
periods

626.5 Ovulation bleeding
Regular intermenstrual bleeding

626.6 Metrorrhagia
Bleeding unrelated to menstrual cycle
Irregular intermenstrual bleeding

626.7 Postcoital bleeding

☐**626.8 Other**
Dysfunctional or functional uterine hemorrhage NOS
Menstruation:
retained
suppression of

☐**626.9 Unspecified**

●**627 Menopausal and postmenopausal disorders**

627.0 Premenopausal menorrhagia
Excessive bleeding associated with onset of menopause
Menorrhagia:
climacteric
menopausal
preclimacteric

627.1 Postmenopausal bleeding

627.2 Menopausal or female climacteric states
Symptoms, such as flushing, sleeplessness, headache, lack of concentration, associated with the menopause

627.3 Postmenopausal atrophic vaginitis
Senile (atrophic) vaginitis

627.4 States associated with artificial menopause
Postartificial menopause syndromes
Any condition classifiable to 627.1, 627.2, or 627.3 which follows induced menopause

☐**627.8 Other specified menopausal and postmenopausal disorders**
> **Excludes** *premature menopause NOS (256.3)*

☐**627.9 Unspecified menopausal and postmenopausal disorder**

●**628 Infertility, female**
> **Includes:** primary and secondary sterility

628.0 Associated with anovulation
Anovulatory cycle

Use additional code for any associated Stein-Leventhal syndrome (256.4)

●**628.1 *Of pituitary-hypothalamic origin***
Code first underlying disease, as:
adiposogenital dystrophy (253.8)
anterior pituitary disorder (253.0–253.4)

628.2 Of tubal origin
Infertility associated with congenital anomaly of tube
Tubal:
block
occlusion
stenosis

Use additional code for any associated peritubal adhesions (614.6)

628.3 Of uterine origin
Infertility associated with congenital anomaly of uterus
Nonimplantation

Use additional code for any associated tuberculous endometritis (016.7)

628.4 Of cervical or vaginal origin
Infertility associated with:
anomaly or cervical mucus
congenital structural anomaly
dysmucorrhea

☐**628.8 Of other specified origin**

☐**628.9 Of unspecified origin**

●**629 Other disorders of female genital organs**

629.0 Hematocele, female, not elsewhere classified
> **Excludes** *hematocele or hematoma:*
> *broad ligament (620.7)*
> *fallopian tube (620.8)*
> *that associated with ectopic pregnancy (633.0–633.9)*
> *uterus (621.4)*
> *vagina (623.6)*
> *vulva (624.5)*

629.1 Hydrocele, canal of Nuck
Cyst of canal of Nuck (acquired)
> **Excludes** *congenital (752.41)*

☐**629.8 Other specified disorders of female genital organs**

☐**629.9 Unspecified disorder of female genital organs**
Habitual aborter without current pregnancy

ICD-9-CM

600–699

Vol. 1

11.   COMPLICATIONS OF PREGNANCY, CHILDBIRTH, AND THE PUERPERIUM (630–677)

ECTOPIC AND MOLAR PREGNANCY (630–633)

Use additional code from category 639 to identify any complications

Item 11–1   A hydatidiform mole is a benign tumor of the placenta. The tumor secretes a hormone, chorionic gonadotropic hormone (CGH), that indicates a positive pregnancy test.

630   Hydatidiform mole
Trophoblastic disease NOS
Vesicular mole
> **Excludes** *chorioadenoma (destruens) (236.1)*
> *chorioepithelioma (181)*
> *malignant hydatidiform mole (236.1)*

□ 631   Other abnormal product of conception
Blighted ovum
Mole:
NOS   fleshy
carneous   stone

632   Missed abortion
Early fetal death before completion of 22 weeks' gestation with retention of dead fetus
Retained products of conception, not following spontaneous or induced abortion or delivery
> **Excludes** *failed induced abortion (638.0–638.9)*
> *fetal death (intrauterine) (late) (656.4)*
> *missed delivery (656.4)*
> *that with abnormal product of conception (630, 631)*

Item 11–2   Ectopic pregnancy most often occurs in the fallopian tube. Pregnancy outside the uterus may end in a life-threatening rupture.

● 633   Ectopic pregnancy

Includes: ruptured ectopic pregnancy

633.0   Abdominal pregnancy
Intraperitoneal pregnancy

633.1   Tubal pregnancy
Fallopian pregnancy
Rupture of (fallopian) tube due to pregnancy
Tubal abortion

633.2   Ovarian pregnancy

□ 633.8   Other ectopic pregnancy
Pregnancy:
cervical   intraligamentous
combined   mesometric
cornual   mural

□ 633.9   Unspecified ectopic pregnancy

OTHER PREGNANCY WITH ABORTIVE OUTCOME (634–639)

The following fourth digit subdivisions are for use with categories 634–638:

.0   Complicated by genital tract and pelvic infection
Endometritis   Sepsis NOS
Salpingo-oophoritis   Septicemia NOS
Any condition classifiable to 639.0, with condition classifiable to 634–638

> **Excludes** *urinary tract infection (634–638 with .7)*

.1   Complicated by delayed or excessive hemorrhage
Afibrinogenemia   Intravascular hemolysis
Defibrination syndrome
Any condition classifiable to 639.1, with condition classifiable to 634–638

.2   Complicated by damage to pelvic organs and tissues
Laceration, perforation, or tear of:
bladder   uterus
Any condition classifiable to 639.2, with condition classifiable to 634–638

.3   Complicated by renal failure
Oliguria   Uremia
Any condition classifiable to 639.3, with condition classifiable to 634–638

.4   Complicated by metabolic disorder
Electrolyte imbalance with conditions classifiable to 634–638

.5   Complicated by shock
Circulatory collapse
Shock (postoperative) (septic)
Any condition classifiable to 639.5, with condition classifiable to 634–638

.6   Complicated by embolism
Embolism:
NOS   pulmonary
amniotic fluid
Any condition classifiable to 639.6, with condition classifiable to 634–638

□ .7   With other specified complications
Cardiac arrest or failure
Urinary tract infection
Any condition classifiable to 639.8, with condition classifiable to 634–638

□ .8   With unspecified complications
.9   Without mention of complication

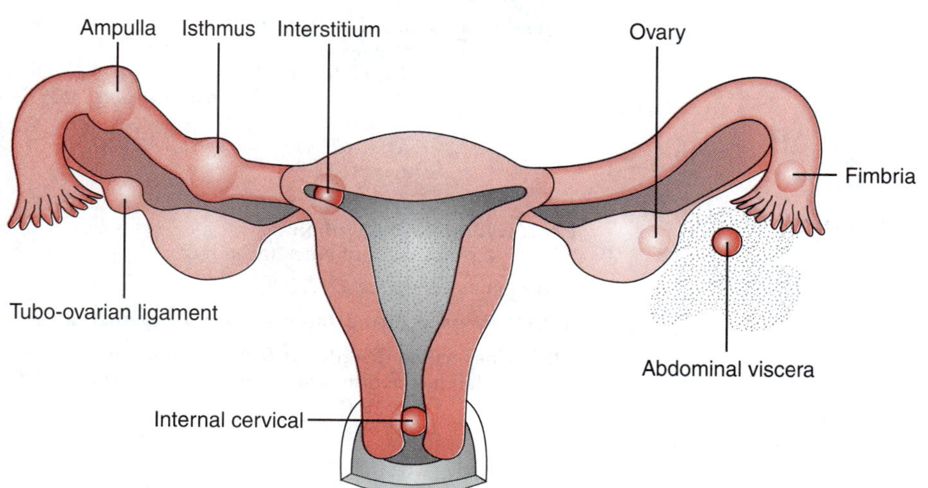

Figure 11–1   Implantation sites of ectopic pregnancy.

◀▶ **New Code**   ⬅▪▪▪▪▪➡ **Revised Code**   ● **Not a Principal Diagnosis**   ● **Use Additional Digit(s)**   □ **Nonspecific Code**

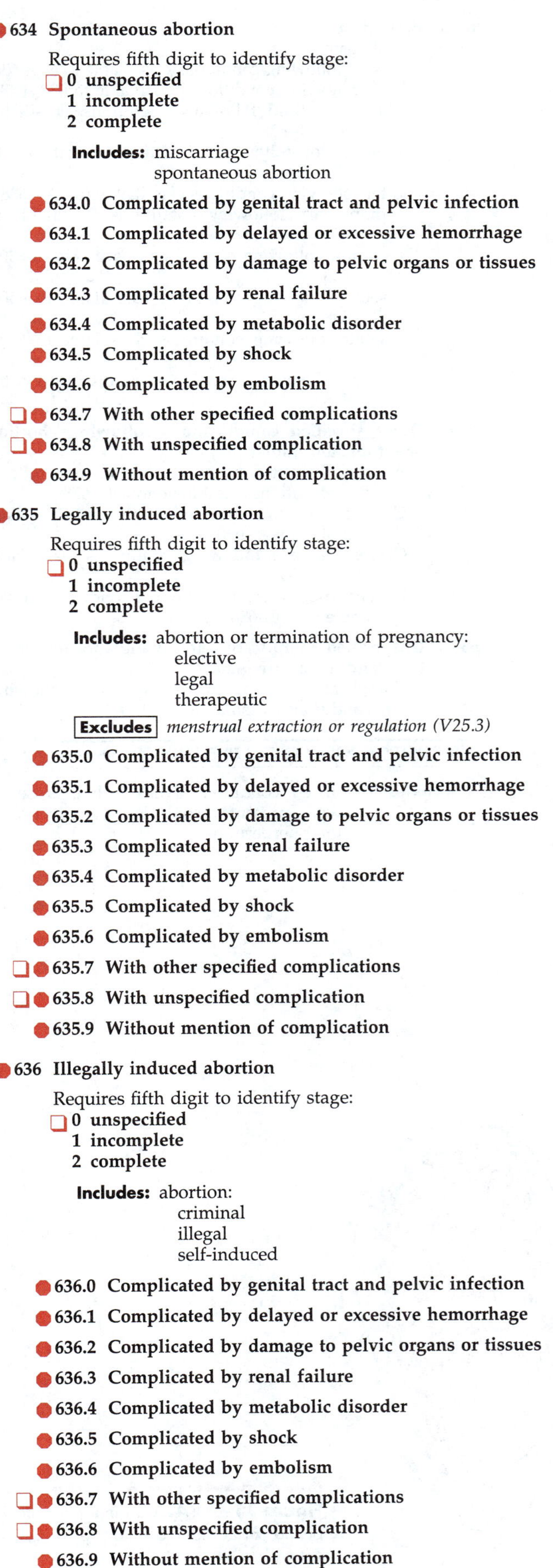

● **634 Spontaneous abortion**

Requires fifth digit to identify stage:
☐ 0 unspecified
   1 incomplete
   2 complete

Includes: miscarriage
              spontaneous abortion

● **634.0 Complicated by genital tract and pelvic infection**

● **634.1 Complicated by delayed or excessive hemorrhage**

● **634.2 Complicated by damage to pelvic organs or tissues**

● **634.3 Complicated by renal failure**

● **634.4 Complicated by metabolic disorder**

● **634.5 Complicated by shock**

● **634.6 Complicated by embolism**

☐● **634.7 With other specified complications**

☐● **634.8 With unspecified complication**

● **634.9 Without mention of complication**

● **635 Legally induced abortion**

Requires fifth digit to identify stage:
☐ 0 unspecified
   1 incomplete
   2 complete

Includes: abortion or termination of pregnancy:
              elective
              legal
              therapeutic

| **Excludes** | *menstrual extraction or regulation (V25.3)* |

● **635.0 Complicated by genital tract and pelvic infection**

● **635.1 Complicated by delayed or excessive hemorrhage**

● **635.2 Complicated by damage to pelvic organs or tissues**

● **635.3 Complicated by renal failure**

● **635.4 Complicated by metabolic disorder**

● **635.5 Complicated by shock**

● **635.6 Complicated by embolism**

☐● **635.7 With other specified complications**

☐● **635.8 With unspecified complication**

● **635.9 Without mention of complication**

● **636 Illegally induced abortion**

Requires fifth digit to identify stage:
☐ 0 unspecified
   1 incomplete
   2 complete

Includes: abortion:
              criminal
              illegal
              self-induced

● **636.0 Complicated by genital tract and pelvic infection**

● **636.1 Complicated by delayed or excessive hemorrhage**

● **636.2 Complicated by damage to pelvic organs or tissues**

● **636.3 Complicated by renal failure**

● **636.4 Complicated by metabolic disorder**

● **636.5 Complicated by shock**

● **636.6 Complicated by embolism**

☐● **636.7 With other specified complications**

☐● **636.8 With unspecified complication**

● **636.9 Without mention of complication**

● **637 Unspecified abortion**

Requires following fifth digit to identify stage:
☐ 0 unspecified
   1 incomplete
   2 complete

Includes: abortion NOS
              retained products of conception following
              abortion, not classifiable elsewhere

☐● **637.0 Complicated by genital tract and pelvic infection**

☐● **637.1 Complicated by delayed or excessive hemorrhage**

☐● **637.2 Complicated by damage to pelvic organs or tissues**

☐● **637.3 Complicated by renal failure**

☐● **637.4 Complicated by metabolic disorder**

☐● **637.5 Complicated by shock**

☐● **637.6 Complicated by embolism**

☐● **637.7 With other specified complications**

☐● **637.8 With unspecified complication**

☐● **637.9 Without mention of complication**

● **638 Failed attempted abortion**

Includes: failure of attempted induction of (legal) abortion

| **Excludes** | *incomplete abortion (634.0–637.9)* |

638.0 Complicated by genital tract and pelvic infection

638.1 Complicated by delayed or excessive hemorrhage

638.2 Complicated by damage to pelvic organs or tissues

638.3 Complicated by renal failure

638.4 Complicated by metabolic disorder

638.5 Complicated by shock

638.6 Complicated by embolism

☐ **638.7 With other specified complications**

☐ **638.8 With unspecified complication**

638.9 Without mention of complication

● **639 Complications following abortion and ectopic and molar pregnancies**

Note: This category is provided for use when it is required to classify separately the complications classifiable to the fourth digit level in categories 634–638; for example:
   a) when the complication itself was responsible for an episode of medical care, the abortion, ectopic or molar pregnancy itself having been dealt with at a previous episode
   b) when these conditions are immediate complications of ectopic or molar pregnancies classifiable to 630–633 where they cannot be identified at fourth digit level.

639.0 Genital tract and pelvic infection
Endometritis following conditions classifiable to 630–638
Parametritis following conditions classifiable to 630–638
Pelvic peritonitis following conditions classifiable to 630–638
Salpingitis following conditions classifiable to 630–638
Salpingo-oophoritis following conditions classifiable to 630–638
Sepsis NOS following conditions classifiable to 630–638
Septicemia NOS following conditions classifiable to 630–638

| **Excludes** | *urinary tract infection (639.8)* |

ICD-9-CM

630-639

Vol. 1

639.1 Delayed or excessive hemorrhage

Afibrinogenemia following conditions classifiable to 630–638

Defibrination syndrome following conditions classifiable to 630–638

Intravascular hemolysis following conditions classifiable to 630–638

639.2 Damage to pelvic organs and tissues

Laceration, perforation, or tear of:

bladder following conditions classifiable to 630–638

bowel following conditions classifiable to 630–638

broad ligament following conditions classifiable to 630–638

cervix following conditions classifiable to 630–638

periurethral tissue following conditions classifiable to 630–638

uterus following conditions classifiable to 630–638

vagina following conditions classifiable to 630–638

639.3 Renal failure

Oliguria following conditions classifiable to 630–638

Renal:

failure (acute) following conditions classifiable to 630–638

shutdown following conditions classifiable to 630–638

tubular necrosis following conditions classifiable to 630–638

Uremia following conditions classifiable to 630–638

639.4 Metabolic disorders

Electrolyte imbalance following conditions classifiable to 630–638

639.5 Shock

Circulatory collapse following conditions classifiable to 630–638

Shock (postoperative) (septic) following conditions classifiable to 630–638

639.6 Embolism

Embolism:

NOS following conditions classifiable to 630–638

air following conditions classifiable to 630–638

amniotic fluid following conditions classifiable to 630–638

blood-clot following conditions classifiable to 630–638

fat following conditions classifiable to 630–638

pulmonary following conditions classifiable to 630–638

pyemic following conditions classifiable to 630–638

septic following conditions classifiable to 630–638

septic following conditions classifiable to 630–638

soap following conditions classifiable to 630–638

☐ **639.8 Other specified complications following abortion or ectopic and molar pregnancy**

Acute yellow atrophy or necrosis of liver following conditions classifiable to 630–638

Cardiac arrest or failure following conditions classifiable to 630–638

Cerebral anoxia following conditions classifiable to 630–638

Urinary tract infection following conditions classifiable to 630–638

☐ **639.9 Unspecified complication following abortion or ectopic and molar pregnancy**

Complication(s) not further specified following conditions classifiable to 630–638

COMPLICATIONS MAINLY RELATED TO PREGNANCY (640–648)

Includes: the listed conditions even if they arose or were present during labor, delivery, or the puerperium

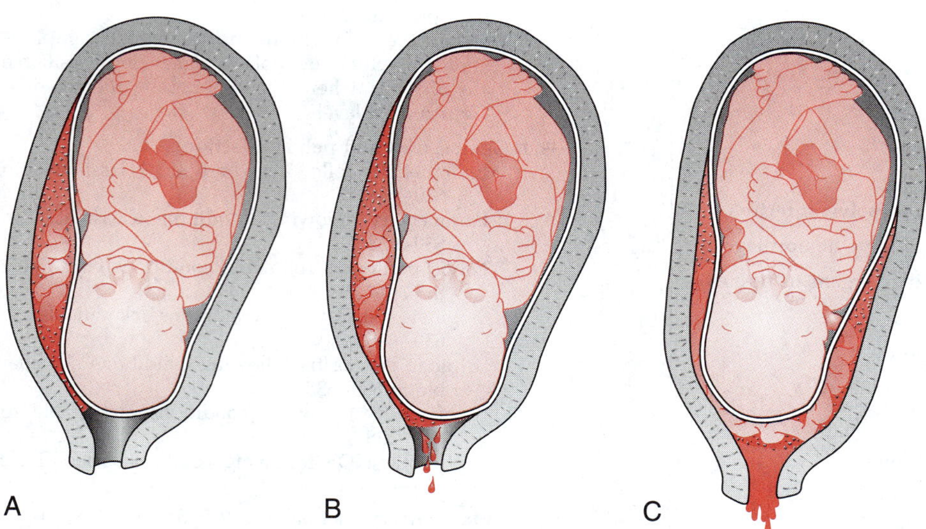

Figure 11–2 A. Marginal placenta previa. **B.** Partial placenta previa. **C.** Total placenta previa.

  ◄► **New Code**   **Revised Code**   ● **Not a Principal Diagnosis**   ● **Use Additional Digit(s)**   ☐ **Nonspecific Code**

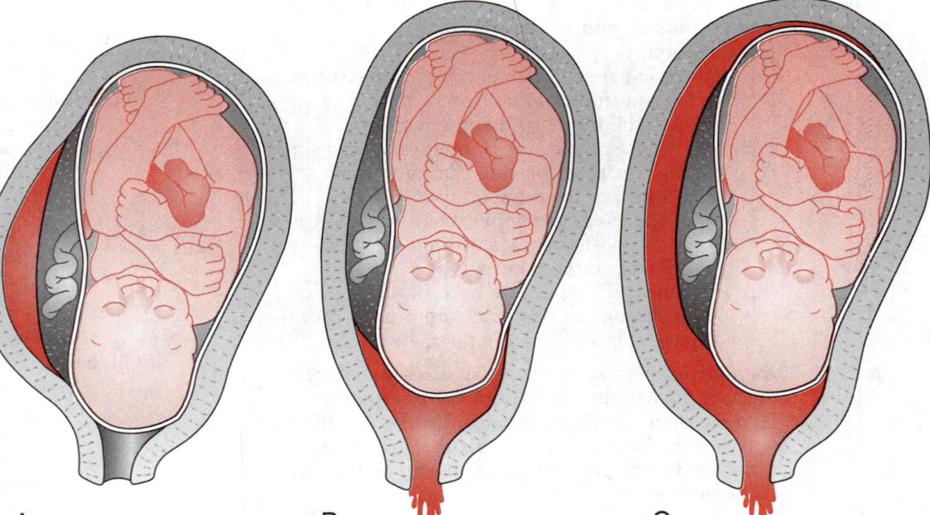

Figure 11–3 Abruptio placentae is classified according to the grade of separation of the placenta from the uterine wall. **A.** Mild separation in which hemorrhage is internal. **B.** Moderate separation in which there is external hemorrhage. **C.** Severe separation in which there is external hemorrhage and extreme separation.

The following fifth-digit subclassification is for use with categories 640–648 to denote the current episode of care:

☐ **0 unspecified as to episode of care or not applicable**
  1 delivered, with or without mention of antepartum condition
      Antepartum condition with delivery
      Delivery NOS (with mention of antepartum complication during current episode of care)
      Intrapartum
        obstetric condition (with mention of antepartum complication during current episode of care)
      Pregnancy, delivered (with mention of antepartum complication during current episode of care)
  2 delivered, with mention of postpartum complication
      Delivery with mention of puerperal complication during current episode of care
  3 antepartum condition or complication
      Antepartum obstetric condition, not delivered during the current episode of care
  4 postpartum condition or complication
      Postpartum or puerperal obstetric condition or complication following delivery that occurred:
        during previous episode of care
        outside hospital, with subsequent admission for observation or care

● **640 Hemorrhage in early pregnancy**

Requires fifth digit; valid digits are in [brackets] under each code. See beginning of section 640–648 for definitions.

  Includes: hemorrhage before completion of 22 weeks' gestation

  ● **640.0 Threatened abortion**
    [0,1,3]

☐ ● **640.8 Other specified hemorrhage in early pregnancy**
    [0,1,3]

☐ ● **640.9 Unspecified hemorrhage in early pregnancy**
    [0,1,3]

● **641 Antepartum hemorrhage, abruptio placentae, and placenta previa**

Requires fifth digit; valid digits are in [brackets] under each code. See beginning of section 640–648 for definitions.

● **641.0 Placenta previa without hemorrhage**
  [0,1,3] Low implantation of placenta without hemorrhage
      Placenta previa noted:
        during pregnancy without hemorrhage
        before labor (and delivered by cesarean delivery) without hemorrhage

● **641.1 Hemorrhage from placenta previa**
  [0,1,3] Low-lying placenta NOS or with hemorrhage (intrapartum)
      Placenta previa:
        incomplete NOS or with hemorrhage (intrapartum)
        marginal NOS or with hemorrhage (intrapartum)
        partial NOS or with hemorrhage (intrapartum)
        total NOS or with hemorrhage (intrapartum)

  Excludes *hemorrhage from vasa previa (663.5)*

● **641.2 Premature separation of placenta**
  [0,1,3] Ablatio placentae
      Abruptio placentae
      Accidental antepartum hemorrhage
      Couvelaire uterus
      Detachment of placenta (premature)
      Premature separation of normally implanted placenta

● **641.3 Antepartum hemorrhage associated with coagulation defects**
  [0,1,3]
      Antepartum or intrapartum hemorrhage associated with:
        afibrinogenemia
        hyperfibrinolysis
        hypofibrinogenemia

☐ ● **641.8 Other antepartum hemorrhage**
  [0,1,3] Antepartum or intrapartum hemorrhage associated with:
      trauma
      uterine leiomyoma

☐ ● **641.9 Unspecified antepartum hemorrhage**
  [0,1,3] Hemorrhage:
      antepartum NOS
      intrapartum NOS
      of pregnancy NOS

● **642 Hypertension complicating pregnancy, childbirth, and the puerperium**

Requires fifth digit; valid digits are in [brackets] under each code. See beginning of section 640–648 for definitions.

ICD-9-CM

600-699

Vol. 1

● **642.0 Benign essential hypertension complicating preg-**
[0–4] **nancy, childbirth, and the puerperium**
> Hypertension:
>> benign essential specified as complicating, or as a reason for obstetric care during pregnancy, childbirth, or the puerperium
>> chronic NOS specified as complicating, or as a reason for obstetric care during pregnancy, childbirth, or the puerperium
>> essential specified as complicating, or as a reason for obstetric care during pregnancy, childbirth, or the puerperium
>> pre-existing NOS specified as complicating, or as a reason for obstetric care during pregnancy, childbirth, or the puerperium

● **642.1 Hypertension secondary to renal disease, compli-**
[0–4] **cating pregnancy, childbirth, and the puerperium**
> Hypertension secondary to renal disease, specified as complicating, or as a reason for obstetric care during pregnancy, childbirth, or the puerperium

☐ ● **642.2 Other pre-existing hypertension complicating preg-**
[0–4] **nancy, childbirth, and the puerperium**
> Hypertensive:
>> heart and renal disease specified as complicating, or as a reason for obstetric care during pregnancy, childbirth, or the puerperium
>> heart disease specified as complicating, or as a reason for obstetric care during pregnancy, childbirth, or the puerperium
>> renal disease specified as complicating, or as a reason for obstetric care during pregnancy, childbirth, or the puerperium
> Malignant hypertension specified as complicating, or as a reason for obstetric care during pregnancy, childbirth, or the puerperium

● **642.3 Transient hypertension of pregnancy**
[0–4] Gestational hypertension
> Transient hypertension, so described, in pregnancy, childbirth, or the puerperium

● **642.4 Mild or unspecified pre-eclampsia**
[0–4] Hypertension in pregnancy, childbirth, or the puerperium, not specified as pre-existing, with either albuminuria or edema, or both; mild or unspecified

Pre-eclampsia:	Toxemia (pre-eclamptic):
NOS	NOS
mild	mild

> **Excludes** *albuminuria in pregnancy, without mention of hypertension (646.2)*
> *edema in pregnancy, without mention of hypertension (646.1)*

● **642.5 Severe pre-eclampsia**
[0–4] Hypertension in pregnancy, childbirth, or the puerperium, not specified as pre-existing, with either albuminuria or edema, or both; specified as severe
> Pre-eclampsia, severe
> Toxemia (pre-eclamptic), severe

● **642.6 Eclampsia**
[0–4] Toxemia:
>> eclamptic   with convulsions

● **642.7 Pre-eclampsia or eclampsia superimposed on pre-**
[0–4] **existing hypertension**
> Conditions classifiable to 642.4–642.6, with conditions classifiable to 642.0–642.2

☐ ● **642.9 Unspecified hypertension complicating pregnancy,**
[0–4] **childbirth, or the puerperium**
> Hypertension NOS, without mention of albuminuria or edema, complicating pregnancy, childbirth, or the puerperium

● **643 Excessive vomiting in pregnancy**
> Requires fifth digit; valid digits are in [brackets] under each code. See beginning of section 640–648 for definitions.

> **Includes:** hyperemesis arising during pregnancy
>> vomiting:
>>> persistent arising during pregnancy
>>> vicious arising during pregnancy
>> hyperemesis gravidarum

● **643.0 Mild hyperemesis gravidarum**
[0,1,3] Hyperemesis gravidarum, mild or unspecified, starting before the end of the 22nd week of gestation

● **643.1 Hyperemesis gravidarum with metabolic distur-**
[0,1,3] **bance**
> Hyperemesis gravidarum, starting before the end of the 22nd week of gestation, with metabolic disturbance, such as:
>> carbohydrate depletion
>> dehydration
>> electrolyte imbalance

● **643.2 Late vomiting of pregnancy**
[0,1,3] Excessive vomiting starting after 22 completed weeks of gestation

☐ ● **643.8 Other vomiting complicating pregnancy**
[0,1,3] Vomiting due to organic disease or other cause, specified as complicating pregnancy, or as a reason for obstetric care during pregnancy

> Use additional code to specify cause

☐ ● **643.9 Unspecified vomiting of pregnancy**
[0,1,3] Vomiting as a reason for care during pregnancy, length of gestation unspecified

● **644 Early or threatened labor**
> Requires fifth digit; valid digits are in [brackets] under each code. See beginning of section 640–648 for definitions.

● **644.0 Threatened premature labor**
[0,3] Premature labor after 22 weeks, but before 37 completed weeks of gestation without delivery

> **Excludes** *that occurring before 22 completed weeks of gestation (640.0)*

☐ ● **644.1 Other threatened labor**
[0,3] False labor:
>> NOS without delivery
>> after 37 completed weeks of gestation without delivery
> Threatened labor NOS without delivery

● **644.2 Early onset of delivery**
[0–1] Onset (spontaneous) of delivery before 37 completed weeks of gestation
> Premature labor with onset of delivery before 37 completed weeks of gestation

● **645 Prolonged pregnancy**
[0,1,3] Requires fifth digit; valid digits are in [brackets] under each code. See beginning of section 640–648 for definitions.

> Use 0 as fourth digit for category 645
>> Post term pregnancy
>> Pregnancy which has advanced beyond 42 weeks of gestation

● **646 Other complications of pregnancy, not elsewhere classified**

> Use additional code(s) to further specify complication

> Requires fifth digit; valid digits are in [brackets] under each code. See beginning of section 640–648 for definitions.

● **646.0 Papyraceous fetus**
[0,1,3]

● **646.1 Edema or excessive weight gain in pregnancy,**
[0–4] **without mention of hypertension**
     Gestational edema
     Maternal obesity syndrome

    Excludes   *that with mention of hypertension (642.0–642.9)*

□ ● **646.2 Unspecified renal disease in pregnancy, without**
[0–4] **mention of hypertension**
     Albuminuria in pregnancy or the puerperium,
       without mention of hypertension
     Nephropathy NOS in pregnancy or the puerpe-
       rium, without mention of hypertension
     Renal disease NOS in pregnancy or the puerpe-
       rium, without mention of hypertension
     Uremia in pregnancy or the puerperium, without
       mention of hypertension
     Gestational proteinuria in pregnancy or the puer-
       perium, without mention of hypertension

    Excludes   *that with mention of hypertension (642.0–642.9)*

● **646.3 Habitual aborter**
[0–1,3]

    Excludes   *with current abortion (634.0–634.9)*
               without current pregnancy (629.9)

● **646.4 Peripheral neuritis in pregnancy**
[0–4]

● **646.5 Asymptomatic bacteriuria in pregnancy**
[0–4]

● **646.6 Infections of genitourinary tract in pregnancy**
[0–4]   Conditions classifiable to 590, 595, 597, 599.0, 616
       complicating pregnancy, childbirth, or the pu-
       erperium
     Conditions classifiable to 614–615 complicating
       pregnancy or labor

    Excludes   *major puerperal infection (670)*

● **646.7 Liver disorders in pregnancy**
[0,1,3]   Acute yellow atrophy of liver (obstetric) (true) of
       pregnancy
     Icterus gravis of pregnancy
     Necrosis of liver of pregnancy

    Excludes   *hepatorenal syndrome following delivery (674.8)*
               viral hepatitis (647.6)

□ ● **646.8 Other specified complications of pregnancy**
[0–4]   Fatigue during pregnancy
     Herpes gestationis
     Insufficient weight gain of pregnancy

□ ● **646.9 Unspecified complication of pregnancy**
[0,1,3]

● **647 Infectious and parasitic conditions in the mother classifi-**
able elsewhere, but complicating pregnancy, childbirth,
or the puerperium

Use additional code(s) to further specify complication

Requires fifth digit; valid digits are in [brackets] under
each code. See beginning of section 640–648 for definitions.

    Includes: the listed conditions when complicating the
           pregnant state, aggravated by the preg-
           nancy, or when a main reason for obstet-
           ric care

    Excludes   *those conditions in the mother known or sus-*
              pected to have affected the fetus (655.0–655.9)

● **647.0 Syphilis**
[0–4]   Conditions classifiable to 090–097

● **647.1 Gonorrhea**
[0–4]   Conditions classifiable to 098

□ ● **647.2 Other venereal diseases**
[0–4]   Conditions classifiable to 099

● **647.3 Tuberculosis**
[0–4]   Conditions classifiable to 010–018

● **647.4 Malaria**
[0–4]   Conditions classifiable to 084

● **647.5 Rubella**
[0–4]   Conditions classifiable to 056

□ ● **647.6 Other viral diseases**
[0–4]   Conditions classifiable to 042 and 050–079, except
       056

□ ● **647.8 Other specified infectious and parasitic diseases**
[0–4]

□ ● **647.9 Unspecified infection or infestation**
[0–4]

● **648 Other current conditions in the mother classifiable else-**
where, but complicating pregnancy, childbirth, or the pu-
erperium

Use additional code(s) to identify the condition

Requires fifth digit; valid digits are in [brackets] under
each code. See beginning of section 640–648 for definitions.

    Includes: the listed conditions when complicating the
           pregnant state, aggravated by the preg-
           nancy, or when a main reason for obstet-
           ric care

    Excludes   *those conditions in the mother known or sus-*
              pected to have affected the fetus (655.0–665.9)

● **648.0 Diabetes mellitus**
[0–4]   Conditions classifiable to 250

    Excludes   *gestational diabetes (648.8)*

● **648.1 Thyroid dysfunction**
[0–4]   Conditions classifiable to 240–246

● **648.2 Anemia**
[0–4]   Conditions classifiable to 280–285

● **648.3 Drug dependence**
[0–4]   Conditions classifiable to 304

● **648.4 Mental disorders**
[0–4]   Conditions classifiable to 290–303, 305–316, 317–
       319

● **648.5 Congenital cardiovascular disorders**
[0–4]   Conditions classifiable to 745–747

□ ● **648.6 Other cardiovascular diseases**
[0–4]   Conditions classifiable to 390–398, 410–429

    Excludes   *cerebrovascular disorders in the puerperium*
              (674.0)
              venous complications (671.0–671.9)

● **648.7 Bone and joint disorders of back, pelvis, and**
[0–4] **lower limbs**
     Conditions classifiable to 720–724, and those clas-
       sifiable to 711–719 or 725–738, specified as
       affecting the lower limbs

● **648.8 Abnormal glucose tolerance**
[0–4]   Conditions classifiable to 790.2
     Gestational diabetes

□ ● **648.9 Other current conditions classifiable elsewhere**
[0–4]   Conditions classifiable to 440–459
     Nutritional deficiencies [conditions classifiable to
       260–269]

ICD-9-CM

600-699

Vol. 1

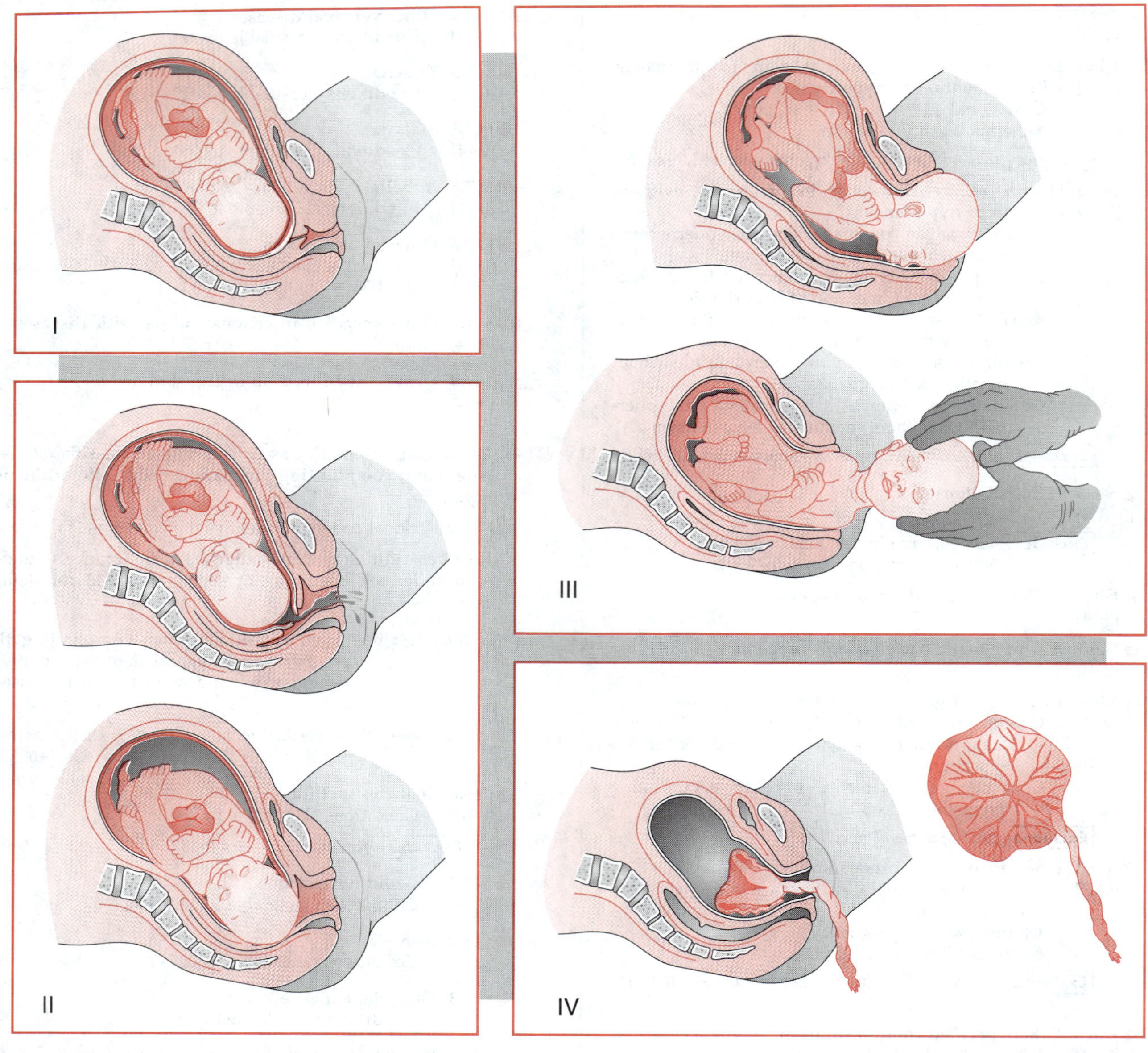

Figure 11-4   The four stages of normal delivery: **I.** Lightening, which occurs 2 to 4 weeks before birth, at which time the fetus turns with head toward the vagina. **II.** Regular contractions begin, the amniotic sac ruptures, and dilation is complete. **III.** Delivery of the head and rotation. **IV.** Recovery of the mother to full homeostasis.

NORMAL DELIVERY, AND OTHER INDICATIONS FOR CARE IN PREGNANCY, LABOR, AND DELIVERY (650–659)

The following fifth-digit subclassification is for use with categories 651–659 to denote the current episode of care:

- ☐ **0** unspecified as to episode of care or not applicable
- **1** delivered, with or without mention of antepartum condition
- **2** delivered, with mention of postpartum complication
- **3** antepartum condition or complication
- **4** postpartum condition or complication

650 Normal delivery

Delivery requiring minimal or no assistance, with or without episiotomy, without fetal manipulation [e.g., rotation version] or instrumentation [forceps] of a spontaneous, cephalic, vaginal, full-term, single, live-born infant. This code is for use as a single diagnosis code and is not to be used with any other code in the range 630–676.

Use additional code to indicate outcome of delivery (V27.0)

> **Excludes**   *breech delivery (assisted) (spontaneous) NOS (652.2)*
> *delivery by vacuum extractor, forceps, cesarean section, or breech extraction, without specified complication (669.5–669.7)*

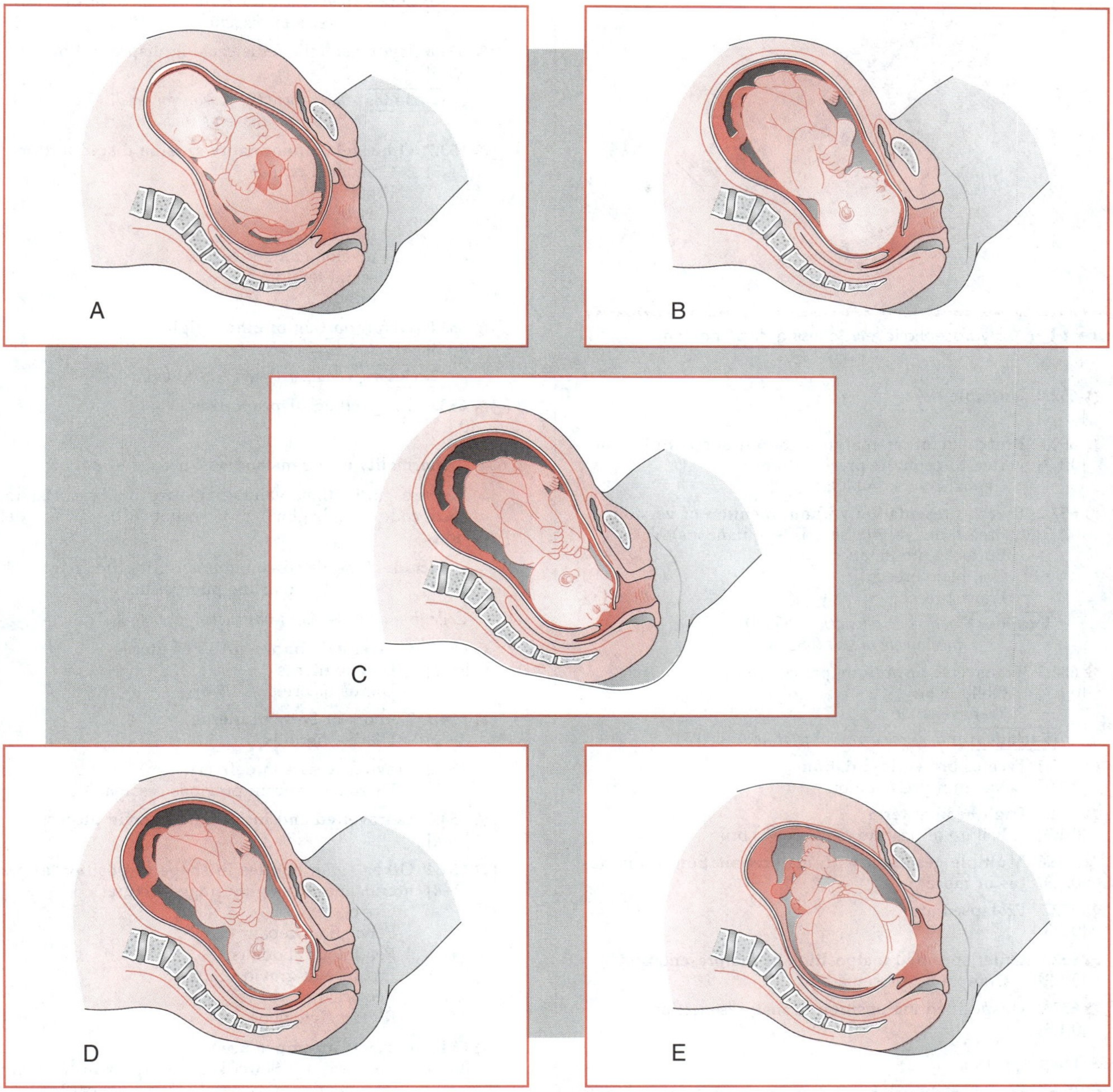

Figure 11–5   Five types of malposition and malpresentation of the fetus: **A.** Breech. **B.** Vertex. **C.** Face. **D.** Brow. **E.** Shoulder.

● **651 Multiple gestation**

Requires fifth digit; valid digits are in [brackets] under each code. See beginning of section 650–659 for definitions.

● **651.0 Twin pregnancy**
[0,1,3]

● **651.1 Triplet pregnancy**
[0,1,3]

● **651.2 Quadruplet pregnancy**
[0,1,3]

● **651.3 Twin pregnancy with fetal loss and retention of**
[0,1,3] **one fetus**

● **651.4 Triplet pregnancy with fetal loss and retention of**
[0,1,3] **one or more fetus(es)**

● **651.5 Quadruplet pregnancy with fetal loss and reten-**
[0,1,3] **tion of one or more fetus(es)**

☐ ● **651.6 Other multiple pregnancy with fetal loss and re-**
[0,1,3] **tention of one or more fetus(es)**

☐ ● **651.8 Other specified multiple gestation**
[0,1,3]

☐ ● **651.9 Unspecified multiple gestation**
[0,1,3]

● **652 Malposition and malpresentation of fetus**

Requires fifth digit; valid digits are in [brackets] under each code. See beginning of section 650–659 for definitions.

Code first any associated obstructed labor (660.0)

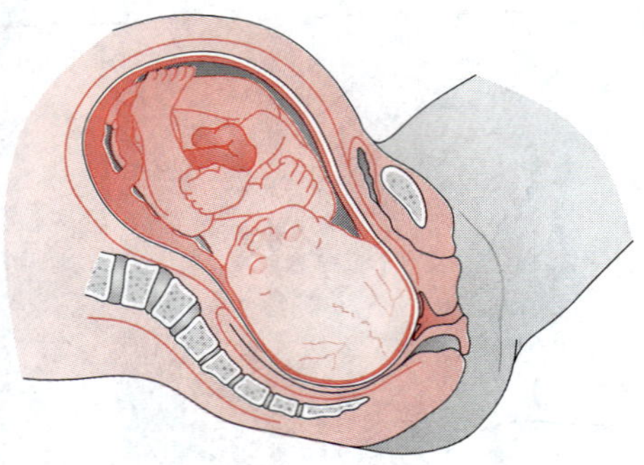

Figure 11–6   Hydrocephalic fetus causing disproportion.

● **652.0 Unstable lie**
[0,1,3]

● **652.1 Breech or other malpresentation successfully con-**
[0,1,3] **verted to cephalic presentation**
Cephalic version NOS

● **652.2 Breech presentation without mention of version**
[0,1,3] Breech delivery (assisted) (spontaneous) NOS
Buttocks presentation ◀
Complete breech ◀
Frank breech ◀
> **Excludes** *footling presentation (652.8)*
> *incomplete breech (652.8)*

● **652.3 Transverse or oblique presentation**
[0,1,3] Oblique lie
Transverse lie
> **Excludes** *transverse arrest of fetal head (660.3)*

● **652.4 Face or brow presentation**
[0,1,3] Mentum presentation

● **652.5 High head at term**
[0,1,3] Failure of head to enter pelvic brim

● **652.6 Multiple gestation with malpresentation of one fe-**
[0,1,3] **tus or more**

● **652.7 Prolapsed arm**
[0,1,3]

□ ● **652.8 Other specified malposition or malpresentation**
[0,1,3] Compound presentation

□ ● **652.9 Unspecified malposition or malpresentation**
[0,1,3]

● **653 Disproportion**

Requires fifth digit; valid digits are in [brackets] under each
code. See beginning of section 650–659 for definitions.

Code first any associated obstructed labor (660.1)

● **653.0 Major abnormality of bony pelvis, not further**
[0,1,3] **specified**
Pelvic deformity NOS

● **653.1 Generally contracted pelvis**
[0,1,3] Contracted pelvis NOS

● **653.2 Inlet contraction of pelvis**
[0,1,3] Inlet contraction (pelvis)

● **653.3 Outlet contraction of pelvis**
[0,1,3] Outlet contraction (pelvis)

● **653.4 Fetopelvic disproportion**
[0,1,3] Cephalopelvic disproportion NOS
Disproportion of mixed maternal and fetal origin,
with normally formed fetus

● **653.5 Unusually large fetus causing disproportion**
[0,1,3] Disproportion of fetal origin with normally
formed fetus
Fetal disproportion NOS

> **Excludes** *that when the reason for medical care was con-*
> *cern for the fetus (656.6)*

● **653.6 Hydrocephalic fetus causing disproportion**
[0,1,3]
> **Excludes** *that when the reason for medical care was con-*
> *cern for the fetus (655.0)*

□ ● **653.7 Other fetal abnormality causing disproportion**
[0,1,3] Conjoined twins
Fetal:
ascites
hydrops
myelomeningocele
sacral teratoma
tumor

□ ● **653.8 Disproportion of other origin**
[0,1,3]
> **Excludes** *shoulder (girdle) dystocia (660.4)*

□ ● **653.9 Unspecified disproportion**
[0,1,3]

● **654 Abnormality of organs and soft tissues of pelvis**

Requires fifth digit; valid digits are in [brackets] under
each code. See beginning of section 650–659 for definitions.

Includes: the listed conditions during pregnancy, childbirth, or the puerperium

Code first any associated obstructed labor (660.2)

● **654.0 Congenital abnormalities of uterus**
[0–4] Double uterus
Uterus bicornis

● **654.1 Tumors of body of uterus**
[0–4] Uterine fibroids

● **654.2 Previous cesarean delivery**
[0,1,3] Uterine scar from previous cesarean delivery

● **654.3 Retroverted and incarcerated gravid uterus**
[0–4]

□ ● **654.4 Other abnormalities in shape or position of gravid**
[0–4] **uterus and of neighboring structures**
Cystocele
Pelvic floor repair
Pendulous abdomen
Prolapse of gravid uterus
Rectocele
Rigid pelvic floor

● **654.5 Cervical incompetence**
[0–4] Presence of Shirodkar suture with or without
mention of cervical incompetence

□ ● **654.6 Other congenital or acquired abnormality of cervix**
[0–4] Cicatricial cervix
Polyp of cervix
Previous surgery to cervix
Rigid cervix (uteri)
Stenosis or stricture of cervix
Tumor of cervix

● **654.7 Congenital or acquired abnormality of vagina**
[0–4] Previous surgery to vagina
Septate vagina
Stenosis of vagina (acquired) (congenital)
Stricture of vagina
Tumor of vagina

● **654.8 Congenital or acquired abnormality of vulva**
[0–4] Fibrosis of perineum
Persistent hymen
Previous surgery to perineum or vulva
Rigid perineum
Tumor of vulva
> **Excludes** *varicose veins of vulva (671.1)*

    ◀▶ **New Code**   ◀▦▦▶ **Revised Code**   ● **Not a Principal Diagnosis**   ● **Use Additional Digit(s)**   □ **Nonspecific Code**

654.9 Other and unspecified
[0–4]   Uterine scar NEC

655 Known or suspected fetal abnormality affecting management of mother

Requires fifth digit; valid digits are in [brackets] under each code. See beginning of section 650–659 for definitions.

> **Includes:** the listed conditions in the fetus as a reason for observation or obstetrical care of the mother, or for termination of pregnancy

655.0 Central nervous system malformation in fetus
[0,1,3]   Fetal or suspected fetal:
    anencephaly
    hydrocephalus
    spina bifida (with myelomeningocele)

655.1 Chromosomal abnormality in fetus
[0,1,3]

655.2 Hereditary disease in family possibly affecting fetus
[0,1,3]

655.3 Suspected damage to fetus from viral disease in the mother
[0,1,3]
    Suspected damage to fetus from maternal rubella

655.4 Suspected damage to fetus from other disease in the mother
[0,1,3]
    Suspected damage to fetus from maternal:
      alcohol addiction
      listeriosis
      toxoplasmosis

655.5 Suspected damage to fetus from drugs
[0,1,3]

655.6 Suspected damage to fetus from radiation
[0,1,3]

655.7 Decreased fetal movements
[0,1,3]

655.8 Other known or suspected fetal abnormality, not elsewhere classified
[0,1,3]
    Suspected damage to fetus from:
      environmental toxins
      intrauterine contraceptive device

655.9 Unspecified
[0,1,3]

656 Other fetal and placental problems affecting management of mother

Requires fifth digit; valid digits are in [brackets] under each code. See beginning of section 650–659 for definitions.

656.0 Fetal-maternal hemorrhage
[0,1,3]   Leakage (microscopic) of fetal blood into maternal circulation

656.1 Rhesus isoimmunization
[0,1,3]   Anti-D [Rh] antibodies
    Rh incompatibility

656.2 Isoimmunization from other and unspecified blood-group incompatibility
[0,1,3]
    ABO isoimmunization

656.3 Fetal distress
[0,1,3]   Fetal metabolic acidemia

> **Excludes** abnormal fetal acid-base balance (656.8)
> abnormality in fetal heart rate or rhythm (659.7)
> fetal bradycardia (659.7)
> fetal distress NOS (656.8)
> fetal tachycardia (659.7)
> meconium in liquor (656.8)

656.4 Intrauterine death
[0,1,3]   Fetal death:
    NOS
    after completion of 22 weeks' gestation
    late
    Missed delivery

> **Excludes** missed abortion (632)

656.5 Poor fetal growth
[0,1,3]   "Light-for-dates"
    "Placental insufficiency"
    "Small-for-dates"

656.6 Excessive fetal growth
[0,1,3]   "Large-for-dates"

656.7 Other placental conditions
[0,1,3]   Abnormal placenta
    Placental infarct

> **Excludes** placental polyp (674.4)
> placentitis (658.4)

656.8 Other specified fetal and placental problems
[0,1,3]   Abnormal acid-base balance
    Intrauterine acidosis
    Lithopedian
    Meconium in liquor

656.9 Unspecified fetal and placental problem
[0,1,3]

657 Polyhydramnios
[0,1,3]   Hydramnios

Requires fifth digit; valid digits are in [brackets] under each code. See beginning of section 650–659 for definitions.

Use 0 as fourth digit for category 657

658 Other problems associated with amniotic cavity and membranes

Requires fifth digit; valid digits are in [brackets] under each code. See beginning of section 650–659 for definitions.

> **Excludes** amniotic fluid embolism (673.1)

658.0 Oligohydramnios
[0,1,3]   Oligohydramnios without mention of rupture of membranes

658.1 Premature rupture of membranes
[0,1,3]   Rupture of amniotic sac less than 24 hours prior to the onset of labor

658.2 Delayed delivery after spontaneous or unspecified rupture of membranes
[0,1,3]
    Prolonged rupture of membranes NOS
    Rupture of amniotic sac 24 hours or more prior to the onset of labor

658.3 Delayed delivery after artificial rupture of membranes
[0,1,3]

658.4 Infection of amniotic cavity
[0,1,3]   Amnionitis
    Chorioamnionitis
    Membranitis
    Placentitis

658.8 Other
[0,1,3]   Amnion nodosum
    Amniotic cyst

658.9 Unspecified
[0,1,3]

659 Other indications for care or intervention related to labor and delivery, not elsewhere classified

Requires fifth digit; valid digits are in [brackets] under each code. See beginning of section 650–659 for definitions.

659.0 Failed mechanical induction
[0,1,3]   Failure of induction of labor by surgical or other instrumental methods

ICD-9-CM

650–
659

Vol. 1

659.1 Failed medical or unspecified induction
[0,1,3]   Failed induction NOS
        Failure of induction of labor by medical methods, such as oxytocic drugs

659.2 Maternal pyrexia during labor, unspecified
[0,1,3]

659.3 Generalized infection during labor
[0,1,3]   Septicemia during labor

659.4 Grand multiparity
[0,1,3]

> | Excludes | supervision only, in pregnancy (V23.3)
> without current pregnancy (V61.5)

659.5 Elderly primigravida
[0,1,3]   First pregnancy in a woman who will be 35 years of age or older at expected date of delivery ◄

> | Excludes | supervision only, in pregnancy (V23.81)

659.6 Elderly multigravida
[0,1,3]   Second or more pregnancy in a woman who will be 35 years of age or older at expected date of delivery ◄

> | Excludes | elderly primigravida (659.5)

659.7 Abnormality in fetal heart rate or rhythm ◄
[0,1,3]   Depressed fetal heart tones ◄
        Fetal:
           bradycardia ◄
           tachycardia ◄
        Fetal heart rate decelerations ◄
        Non-reassuring fetal heart rate or rhythm ◄

659.8 Other specified indications for care or intervention
[0,1,3] **related to labor and delivery**
        Pregnancy in a female less than 16 years old at expected date of delivery ◄
        Very young maternal age ◄

659.9 Unspecified indication for care or intervention re-
[0,1,3] **lated to labor and delivery**

COMPLICATIONS OCCURRING MAINLY IN THE COURSE OF LABOR AND DELIVERY (660–669)

The following fifth-digit subclassification is for use with categories 660–669 to denote the current episode of care:
0 unspecified as to episode of care or not applicable
1 delivered, with or without mention of antepartum condition
2 delivered, with mention of postpartum complication
3 antepartum condition or complication
4 postpartum condition or complication

660 Obstructed labor

Requires fifth digit; valid digits are in [brackets] under each code. See beginning of section 660–669 for definitions.

660.0 Obstruction caused by malposition of fetus at on-
[0,1,3] **set of labor**
        Any condition classifiable to 652, causing obstruction during labor

        Use additional code from 652.0–652.9 to identify condition

660.1 Obstruction by bony pelvis
[0,1,3]   Any condition classifiable to 653, causing obstruction during labor

        Use additional code from 653.0–653.9 to identify condition

660.2 Obstruction by abnormal pelvic soft tissues
[0,1,3]   Prolapse of anterior lip of cervix
        Any condition classifiable to 654, causing obstruction during labor

        Use additional code from 654.0–654.9 to identify condition

660.3 Deep transverse arrest and persistent occipitopos-
[0,1,3] **terior position**

660.4 Shoulder (girdle) dystocia
[0,1,3]   Impacted shoulders

660.5 Locked twins
[0,1,3]

660.6 Failed trial of labor, unspecified
[0,1,3]   Failed trial of labor, without mention of condition or suspected condition

660.7 Failed forceps or vacuum extractor, unspecified
[0,1,3]   Application of ventouse or forceps, without mention of condition

660.8 Other causes of obstructed labor
[0,1,3]

660.9 Unspecified obstructed labor
[0,1,3]   Dystocia:
        NOS
        fetal NOS
        maternal NOS

661 Abnormality of forces of labor

Requires fifth digit; valid digits are in [brackets] under each code. See beginning of section 660–669 for definitions.

661.0 Primary uterine inertia
[0,1,3]   Failure of cervical dilation
        Hypotonic uterine dysfunction, primary
        Prolonged latent phase of labor

661.1 Secondary uterine inertia
[0,1,3]   Arrested active phase of labor
        Hypotonic uterine dysfunction, secondary

661.2 Other and unspecified uterine inertia
[0,1,3]   Desultory labor
        Irregular labor
        Poor contractions
        Slow slope active phase of labor

661.3 Precipitate labor
[0,1,3]

661.4 Hypertonic, incoordinate, or prolonged uterine
[0,1,3] **contractions**
        Cervical spasm
        Contraction ring (dystocia)
        Dyscoordinate labor
        Hourglass contraction of uterus
        Hypertonic uterine dysfunction
        Incoordinate uterine action
        Retraction ring (Bandl's) (pathological)
        Tetanic contractions
        Uterine dystocia NOS
        Uterine spasm

661.9 Unspecified abnormality of labor
[0,1,3]

662 Long labor

Requires fifth digit; valid digits are in [brackets] under each code. See beginning of section 660–669 for definitions.

662.0 Prolonged first stage
[0,1,3]

662.1 Prolonged labor, unspecified
[0,1,3]

662.2 Prolonged second stage
[0,1,3]

662.3 Delayed delivery of second twin, triplet, etc.
[0,1,3]

663 Umbilical cord complications

Requires fifth digit; valid digits are in [brackets] under each code. See beginning of section 660–669 for definitions.

663.0 Prolapse of cord
[0,1,3]   Presentation of cord

  ◄▶ **New Code** ◀▥▶ **Revised Code** ● **Not a Principal Diagnosis** ● **Use Additional Digit(s)** ❑ **Nonspecific Code**

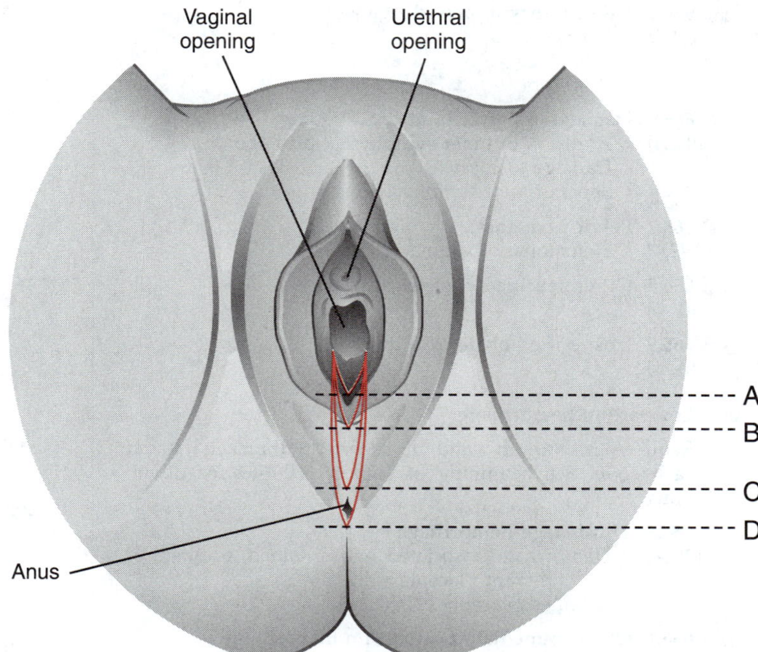

Figure 11–7 Perineal lacerations: **A.** First-degree is laceration of superficial tissues. **B.** Second-degree is limited to the pelvic floor and may involve the perineal or vaginal muscles. **C.** Third-degree involves the anal sphincter. **D.** Fourth-degree involves anal or rectal mucosa.

● **663.1 Cord around neck, with compression**
[0,1,3] Cord tightly around neck

□ ● **663.2 Other and unspecified cord entanglement, with**
[0,1,3] **compression**
  Entanglement of cords of twins in mono-amniotic sac
  Knot in cord (with compression)

□ ● **663.3 Other and unspecified cord entanglement, without**
[0,1,3] **mention of compression**

● **663.4 Short cord**
[0,1,3]

● **663.5 Vasa previa**
[0,1,3] Velamentous insertion of umbilical cord

● **663.6 Vascular lesions of cord**
[0,1,3] Bruising of cord
  Hematoma of cord
  Thrombosis of vessels of cord

□ ● **663.8 Other umbilical cord complications**
[0,1,3]

□ ● **663.9 Unspecified umbilical cord complication**
[0,1,3]

● **664 Trauma to perineum and vulva during delivery**

Requires fifth digit; valid digits are in [brackets] under each code. See beginning of section 660–669 for definitions.

  Includes: damage from instruments
    that from extension of episiotomy

● **664.0 First-degree perineal laceration**
[0,1,4] Perineal laceration, rupture, or tear involving:
  fourchette   skin
  hymen   vagina
  labia   vulva

● **664.1 Second-degree perineal laceration**
[0,1,4] Perineal laceration, rupture, or tear (following episiotomy) involving:
    pelvic floor
    perineal muscles
    vaginal muscles

  Excludes *that involving anal sphincter (664.2)*

● **664.2 Third-degree perineal laceration**
[0,1,4] Perineal laceration, rupture, or tear (following episiotomy) involving:
  anal sphincter
  rectovaginal septum
  sphincter NOS

  Excludes *that with anal or rectal mucosal laceration (664.3)*

● **664.3 Fourth-degree perineal laceration**
[0,1,4] Perineal laceration, rupture, or tear as classifiable to 664.2 and involving also:
  anal mucosa
  rectal mucosa

□ ● **664.4 Unspecified perineal laceration**
[0,1,4] Central laceration

● **664.5 Vulval and perineal hematoma**
[0,1,4]

□ ● **664.8 Other specified trauma to perineum and vulva**
[0,1,4]

□ ● **664.9 Unspecified trauma to perineum and vulva**
[0,1,4]

● **665 Other obstetrical trauma**

Requires fifth digit; valid digits are in [brackets] under each code. See beginning of section 660–669 for definitions.

  Includes: damage from instruments

● **665.0 Rupture of uterus before onset of labor**
[0,1,3]

● **665.1 Rupture of uterus during labor**
[0,1] Rupture of uterus NOS

● **665.2 Inversion of uterus**
[0,2,4]

● **665.3 Laceration of cervix**
[0,1,4]

● **665.4 High vaginal laceration**
[0,1,4] Laceration of vaginal wall or sulcus without mention of perineal laceration

ICD-9-CM
600–699
Vol. 1

❑ ● **665.5 Other injury to pelvic organs**
[0,1,4]   Injury to:
       bladder
       urethra

● **665.6 Damage to pelvic joints and ligaments**
[0,1,4]   Avulsion of inner symphyseal cartilage
     Damage to coccyx
     Separation of symphysis (pubis)

● **665.7 Pelvic hematoma**
[0–2,4]   Hematoma of vagina

❑ ● **665.8 Other specified obstetrical trauma**
[0–4]

❑ ● **665.9 Unspecified obstetrical trauma**
[0–4]

● **666 Postpartum hemorrhage**

Requires fifth digit; valid digits are in [brackets] under each code. See beginning of section 660–669 for definitions.

● **666.0 Third-stage hemorrhage**
[0,2,4]   Hemorrhage associated with retained, trapped, or
       adherent placenta
     Retained placenta NOS

❑ ● **666.1 Other immediate postpartum hemorrhage**
[0,2,4]   Atony of uterus
     Hemorrhage within the first 24 hours following
       delivery of placenta
     Postpartum hemorrhage (atonic) NOS

● **666.2 Delayed and secondary postpartum hemorrhage**
[0,2,4]   Hemorrhage:
       after the first 24 hours following delivery
       associated with retained portions of placenta or
         membranes
     Postpartum hemorrhage specified as delayed or
       secondary
     Retained products of conception NOS, following
       delivery

● **666.3 Postpartum coagulation defects**
[0,2,4]   Postpartum:
       afibrinogenemia
       fibrinolysis

● **667 Retained placenta without hemorrhage**

Requires fifth digit; valid digits are in [brackets] under each code. See beginning of section 660–669 for definitions.

● **667.0 Retained placenta without hemorrhage**
[0,2,4]   Placenta accreta without hemorrhage
     Retained placenta:
       NOS without hemorrhage
       total without hemorrhage

● **667.1 Retained portions of placenta or membranes, with-**
[0,2,4] **out hemorrhage**
     Retained products of conception following deliv-
       ery, without hemorrhage

● **668 Complications of the administration of anesthetic or other sedation in labor and delivery**

Use additional code(s) to further specify complication

Requires fifth digit; valid digits are in [brackets] under each code. See beginning of section 660–669 for definitions.

Includes: complications arising from the administration
       of a general or local anesthetic, analgesic,
       or other sedation in labor and delivery

   Excludes *reaction to spinal or lumbar puncture (349.0)*
       spinal headache (349.0)

● **668.0 Pulmonary complications**
[0–4]   Inhalation [aspiration] of stomach contents or se-
       cretions following anesthesia or other seda-
       tion in labor or delivery
     Mendelson's syndrome following anesthesia or
       other sedation in labor or delivery
     Pressure collapse of lung following anesthesia or
       other sedation in labor or delivery

● **668.1 Cardiac complications**
[0–4]   Cardiac arrest or failure following anesthesia or
       other sedation in labor and delivery

● **668.2 Central nervous system complications**
[0–4]   Cerebral anoxia following anesthesia or other se-
       dation in labor and delivery

❑ ● **668.8 Other complications of anesthesia or other seda-**
[0–4] **tion in labor and delivery**

❑ ● **668.9 Unspecified complication of anesthesia and other**
[0–4] **sedation**

● **669 Other complications of labor and delivery, not elsewhere classified**

Requires fifth digit; valid digits are in [brackets] under each code. See beginning of section 660–669 for definitions.

● **669.0 Maternal distress**
[0–4]   Metabolic disturbance in labor and delivery

● **669.1 Shock during or following labor and delivery**
[0–4]   Obstetric shock

● **669.2 Maternal hypotension syndrome**
[0–4]

● **669.3 Acute renal failure following labor and delivery**
[0,2,4]

❑ ● **669.4 Other complications of obstetrical surgery and pro-**
[0–4] **cedures**
     Cardiac:
       arrest following cesarean or other obstetrical
         surgery or procedure, including delivery
         NOS
       failure following cesarean or other obstetrical
         surgery or procedure, including delivery
         NOS
     Cerebral anoxia following cesarean or other ob-
       stetrical surgery or procedure, including de-
       livery NOS

   Excludes *complications of obstetrical surgical wounds*
       (674.1–674.3)

● **669.5 Forceps or vacuum extractor delivery without men-**
[0,1] **tion of indication**
     Delivery by ventouse, without mention of indica-
       tion

● **669.6 Breech extraction, without mention of indication**
[0,1]

   Excludes *breech delivery NOS (652.2)*

● **669.7 Cesarean delivery, without mention of indication**
[0,1]

❑ ● **669.8 Other complications of labor and delivery**
[0–4]

❑ ● **669.9 Unspecified complication of labor and delivery**
[0–4]

    ◀▶ **New Code**   ⬅▬▬➡ **Revised Code**   ● **Not a Principal Diagnosis**   ● **Use Additional Digit(s)**   ❑ **Nonspecific Code**

COMPLICATIONS OF THE PUERPERIUM (670–677)

Note: Categories 671 and 673–676 include the listed conditions even if they occur during pregnancy or childbirth.

The following fifth-digit subclassification is for use with categories 670–676 to denote the current episode of care:

□ **0 unspecified as to episode of care or not applicable**
 1 delivered, with or without mention of antepartum condition
 2 delivered, with mention of postpartum complication
 3 antepartum condition or complication
 4 postpartum condition or complication

● **670 Major puerperal infection**
[0,2,4]

Requires fifth digit; valid digits are in [brackets] under each code. See beginning of section 670–676 for definitions.

Use 0 as fourth digit for category 670
Puerperal:
 endometritis
 fever (septic)
 pelvic:
  cellulitis
  sepsis
 peritonitis
 pyemia
 salpingitis
 septicemia

 Excludes *infection following abortion (639.0)*
  minor genital tract infection following delivery (646.6)
  puerperal fever NOS (672)
  puerperal pyrexia NOS (672)
  puerperal pyrexia of unknown origin (672)
  urinary tract infection following delivery (646.6)

● **671 Venous complications in pregnancy and the puerperium**

Requires fifth digit; valid digits are in [brackets] under each code. See beginning of section 670–676 for definitions.

● **671.0 Varicose veins of legs**
[0–4] Varicose veins NOS

● **671.1 Varicose veins of vulva and perineum**
[0–4]

● **671.2 Superficial thrombophlebitis**
[0–4] Thrombophlebitis (superficial)

● **671.3 Deep phlebothrombosis, antepartum**
[0,1,3] Deep-vein thrombosis, antepartum

● **671.4 Deep phlebothrombosis, postpartum**
[0,2,4] Deep-vein thrombosis, postpartum
  Pelvic thrombophlebitis, postpartum
  Phlegmasia alba dolens (puerperal)

□ ● **671.5 Other phlebitis and thrombosis**
[0–4] Cerebral venous thrombosis
  Thrombosis of intracranial venous sinus

□ ● **671.8 Other venous complications**
[0–4] Hemorrhoids

□ ● **671.9 Unspecified venous complication**
[0–4] Phlebitis NOS
  Thrombosis NOS

● **672 Pyrexia of unknown origin during the puerperium**
[0,2,4] Postpartum fever NOS
  Puerperal fever NOS
  Puerperal pyrexia NOS

Requires fifth digit; valid digits are in [brackets] under each code. See beginning of section 670–676 for definitions.

Use 0 as fourth digit for category 672

● **673 Obstetrical pulmonary embolism**

Requires fifth digit; valid digits are in [brackets] under each code. See beginning of section 670–676 for definitions.

 Includes: pulmonary emboli in pregnancy, childbirth, or the puerperium, or specified as puerperal

 Excludes *embolism following abortion (639.6)*

● **673.0 Obstetrical air embolism**
[0–4]

● **673.1 Amniotic fluid embolism**
[0–4]

● **673.2 Obstetrical blood-clot embolism**
[0–4] Puerperal pulmonary embolism NOS

● **673.3 Obstetrical pyemic and septic embolism**
[0–4]

□ ● **673.8 Other pulmonary embolism**
[0–4] Fat embolism

● **674 Other and unspecified complications of the puerperium, not elsewhere classified**

Requires fifth digit; valid digits are in [brackets] under each code. See beginning of section 670–676 for definitions.

● **674.0 Cerebrovascular disorders in the puerperium**
[0–4] Any condition classifiable to 430–434, 436–437 occurring during pregnancy, childbirth, or the puerperium, or specified as puerperal

 Excludes *intracranial venous sinus thrombosis (671.5)*

● **674.1 Disruption of cesarean wound**
[0,2,4] Dehiscence or disruption of uterine wound

● **674.2 Disruption of perineal wound**
[0,2,4] Breakdown of perineum
  Disruption of wound of:
   episiotomy
   perineal laceration
  Secondary perineal tear

□ ● **674.3 Other complications of obstetrical surgical wounds**
[0,2,4] Hematoma of cesarean section or perineal wound
  Hemorrhage of cesarean section or perineal wound
  Infection of cesarean section or perineal wound

 Excludes *damage from instruments in delivery (664.0–665.9)*

● **674.4 Placental polyp**
[0,2,4]

□ ● **674.8 Other**
[0,2,4] Hepatorenal syndrome, following delivery
  Postpartum:
   cardiomyopathy
   subinvolution of uterus
   uterine hypertrophy

□ ● **674.9 Unspecified**
[0,2,4] Sudden death of unknown cause during the puerperium

● **675 Infections of the breast and nipple associated with childbirth**

Requires fifth digit; valid digits are in [brackets] under each code. See beginning of section 670–676 for definitions.

 Includes: the listed conditions during pregnancy, childbirth, or the puerperium

● **675.0 Infections of nipple**
[0–4] Abscess of nipple

ICD-9-CM

600–699

Vol. 1

675.1 Abscess of breast
[0–4]   Abscess:
        mammary
        subareolar
        submammary
    Mastitis:
        purulent
        retromammary
        submammary

675.2 Nonpurulent mastitis
[0–4]   Lymphangitis of breast
    Mastitis:
        NOS
        interstitial
        parenchymatous

675.8 Other specified infections of the breast and nipple
[0–4]

675.9 Unspecified infection of the breast and nipple
[0–4]

676 Other disorders of the breast associated with childbirth and disorders of lactation

Requires fifth digit; valid digits are in [brackets] under each code. See beginning of section 670–676 for definitions.

    Includes: the listed conditions during pregnancy, the puerperium, or lactation

676.0 Retracted nipple
[0–4]

676.1 Cracked nipple
[0–4]   Fissure of nipple

676.2 Engorgement of breasts
[0–4]

676.3 Other and unspecified disorder of breast
[0–4]

676.4 Failure of lactation
[0–4]   Agalactia

676.5 Suppressed lactation
[0–4]

676.6 Galactorrhea
[0–4]

    Excludes *galactorrhea not associated with childbirth (611.6)*

676.8 Other disorders of lactation
[0–4]   Galactocele

676.9 Unspecified disorder of lactation
[0–4]

677 Late effect of complication of pregnancy, childbirth, and the puerperium

Note: This category is to be used to indicate conditions in 632–648.9 and 651–676.9 as the cause of the late effect, themselves classifiable elsewhere. The "late effects" include conditions specified as such, or as sequelae, which may occur at any time after the puerperium.

Code first any sequelae

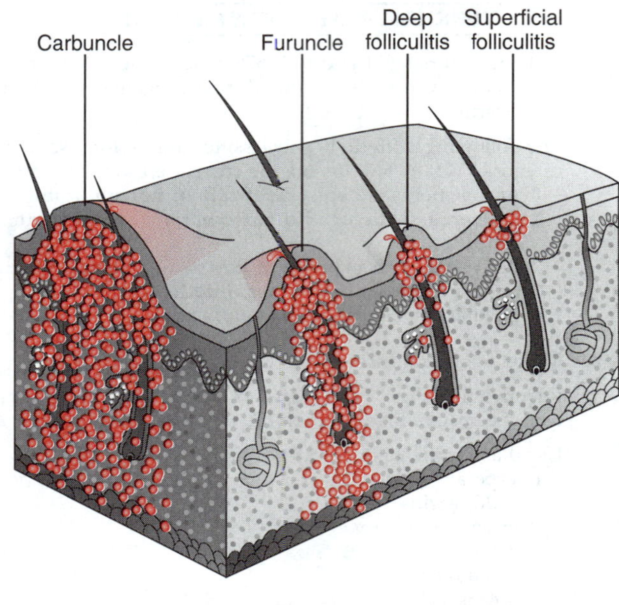

Figure 12-1 Furuncle, also known as a boil, is a staphylococcal infection. The organism enters the body through a hair follicle and so furuncles usually appear in hairy areas of the body. A cluster of furuncles is known as a carbuncle and involves infection into the deep subcutaneous fascia. These usually appear on the back and neck.

12. DISEASES OF THE SKIN AND SUBCUTANEOUS TISSUE (680–709)

INFECTIONS OF SKIN AND SUBCUTANEOUS TISSUE (680–686)

    Excludes *certain infections of skin classified under "Infectious and Parasitic Diseases," such as:*
        erysipelas (035)
        erysipeloid of Rosenbach (027.1)
        herpes:
            simplex (054.0–054.9)
            zoster (053.0–053.9)
        molluscum contagiosum (078.0)
        viral warts (078.1)

680 Carbuncle and furuncle

    Includes: boil
              furunculosis

680.0 Face
    Ear [any part]   Nose (septum)
    Face [any part, except eye] Temple (region)

    Excludes *eyelid (373.13)*
        lacrimal apparatus (375.31)
        orbit (376.01)

680.1 Neck

680.2 Trunk
    Abdominal wall
    Back [any part, except buttocks]
    Breast
    Chest wall
    Flank
    Groin
    Pectoral region
    Perineum
    Umbilicus

    Excludes *buttocks (680.5)*
        external genital organs:
            female (616.4)
            male (607.2, 608.4)

    ◀▶ **New Code**   ⬅➡ **Revised Code**   ● **Not a Principal Diagnosis**   ● **Use Additional Digit(s)**   ☐ **Nonspecific Code**

680.3   Upper arm and forearm
    Arm [any part, except hand]
    Axilla
    Shoulder

680.4   Hand
    Finger [any]   Wrist
    Thumb

680.5   Buttock
    Anus   Gluteal region

680.6   Leg, except foot
    Ankle   Knee
    Hip   Thigh

680.7   Foot
    Heel   Toe

☐ **680.8   Other specified sites**
    Head [any part, except face]
    Scalp

    Excludes   *external genital organs:*
        female (616.4)
        male (607.2, 608.4)

☐ **680.9   Unspecified site**
    Boil NOS   Furuncle NOS
    Carbuncle NOS

● **681   Cellulitis and abscess of finger and toe**

    Includes: that with lymphangitis

    Use additional code to identify organism, such as Staphylococcus (041.1)

● **681.0   Finger**

    681.00   Cellulitis and abscess, unspecified

    681.01   Felon
       Pulp abscess   Whitlow

    Excludes   *herpetic whitlow (054.6)*

    681.02   Onychia and paronychia of finger
       Panaritium of finger
       Perionychia of finger

● **681.1   Toe**

    ☐ **681.10   Cellulitis and abscess, unspecified**

    681.11   Onychia and paronychia of toe
       Panaritium of toe
       Perionychia of toe

☐ **681.9   Cellulitis and abscess of unspecified digit**
    Infection of nail NOS

● **682   Other cellulitis and abscess**

    Includes: abscess (acute) (with lymphangitis) except of finger or toe
       cellulitis (diffuse) (with lymphangitis) except of finger or toe
       lymphangitis, acute (with lymphangitis) except of finger or toe

    Use additional code to identify organism, such as Staphylococcus (041.1)

    Excludes   *lymphangitis (chronic) (subacute) (457.2)*

682.0   Face
    Cheek, external   Nose, external
    Chin   Submandibular
    Forehead   Temple (region)

    Excludes   *ear [any part] (380.10–380.16)*
       eyelid (373.13)
       lacrimal apparatus (375.31)
       lip (528.5)
       mouth (528.3)
       nose (internal) (478.1)
       orbit (376.01)

682.1   Neck

682.2   Trunk
    Abdominal wall
    Back [any part, except buttocks]
    Chest wall
    Flank
    Groin
    Pectoral region
    Perineum
    Umbilicus, except newborn

    Excludes   *anal and rectal regions (566)*
       breast:
         NOS (611.0)
         puerperal (675.1)
       external genital organs:
         female (616.3–616.4)
         male (604.0, 607.2, 608.4)
       umbilicus, newborn (771.4)

682.3   Upper arm and forearm
    Arm [any part, except hand]
    Axilla
    Shoulder

    Excludes   *hand (682.4)*

682.4   Hand, except fingers and thumb
    Wrist

    Excludes   *fingers and thumb (681.00–681.02)*

682.5   Buttocks
    Gluteal region

    Excludes   *anal and rectal regions (566)*

682.6   Leg, except foot
    Ankle
    Hip
    Knee
    Thigh

682.7   Foot, except toes
    Heel

    Excludes   *toe (681.10–681.11)*

☐ **682.8   Other specified sites**
    Head [except face]
    Scalp

    Excludes   *face (682.0)*

☐ **682.9   Unspecified site**
    Abscess NOS
    Cellulitis NOS
    Lymphangitis, acute NOS

    Excludes   *lymphangitis NOS (457.2)*

683   Acute lymphadenitis
    Abscess (acute) lymph gland or node, except mesenteric
    Adenitis, acute lymph gland or node, except mesenteric
    Lymphadenitis, acute lymph gland or node, except mesenteric

    Use additional code to identify organism such as Staphylococcus (041.1)

    Excludes   *enlarged glands NOS (785.6)*
       lymphadenitis:
         chronic or subacute, except mesenteric (289.1)
         mesenteric (acute) (chronic) (subacute) (289.2)
         unspecified (289.3)

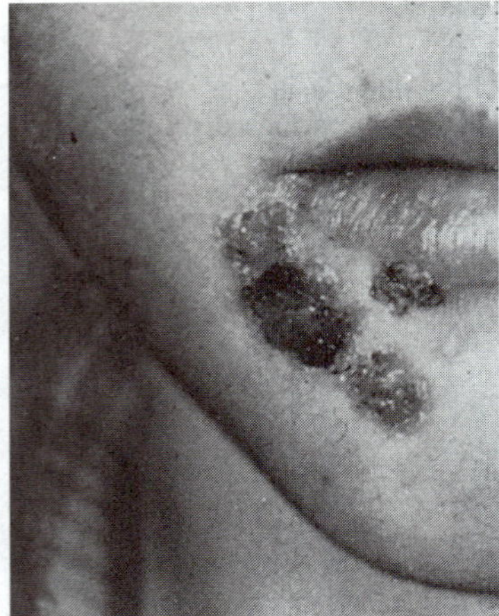

Figure 12–2 Impetigo is a contagious, superficial skin infection caused by *Staphylococcus aureus.* It appears most frequently in infants. (From Lewis GM, Wheeler CE, Jr: Practical Dermatology, 3rd ed. Philadelphia, WB Saunders, 1967, p 234, Plate 79B.)

684 Impetigo
Impetiginization of other dermatoses
Impetigo (contagiosa) [any site] [any organism]:
   bullous   neonatorum
   circinate   simplex
Pemphigus neonatorum

| **Excludes** | *impetigo herpetiformis (694.3)l* |

Item 12–1 Pilonidal cyst, also called a coccygeal cyst, is the result of a disorder called pilonidal disease. The cyst usually contains hair and pus.

● **685 Pilonidal cyst**

Includes: fistula, coccygeal or pilonidal
          sinus, coccygeal or pilonidal

685.0 With abscess

685.1 Without mention of abscess

● **686 Other local infections of skin and subcutaneous tissue**

Use additional code to identify any infectious organism (041.0–041.8)

● **686.0 Pyoderma**
Dermatitis:
   purulent
   septic
   suppurative

☐ **686.00 Pyoderma, unspecified**

686.01 Pyoderma gangrenosum

☐ **686.09 Other pyoderma**

686.1 Pyogenic granuloma
Granuloma:
   septic
   suppurative
   telangiectaticum

| **Excludes** | *pyogenic granuloma of oral mucosa (528.9)* |

☐ **686.8 Other specified local infections of skin and subcutaneous tissue**
   Bacterid (pustular)   Ecthyma
   Dermatitis vegetans   Perlèche

| **Excludes** | *dermatitis infectiosa eczematoides (690.8)* |
| | *panniculitis (729.30–729.39)* |

☐ **686.9 Unspecified local infection of skin and subcutaneous tissue**
   Fistula of skin NOS
   Skin infection NOS

| **Excludes** | *fistula to skin from internal organs—see Alphabetic Index* |

OTHER INFLAMMATORY CONDITIONS OF SKIN AND SUBCUTANEOUS TISSUE (690–698)

| **Excludes** | *panniculitis (729.30–729.39)* |

● **690 Erythematosquamous dermatosis**

Excludes	*eczematous dermatitis of eyelid (373.31)*
	parakeratosis variegata (696.2)
	psoriasis (696.0–696.1)
	seborrheic keratosis (702)

690.1 Seborrheic dermatitis

☐ **690.10 Seborrheic dermatitis, unspecified**
   Seborrheic dermatitis NOS

690.11 Seborrhea capitis
   Cradle cap

690.12 Seborrheic infantile dermatitis

☐ **690.18 Other seborrheic dermatitis**

☐ **690.8 Other erythematosquamous dermatosis**

● **691 Atopic dermatitis and related conditions**

691.0 Diaper or napkin rash
   Ammonia dermatitis
   Diaper or napkin:
      dermatitis
      erythema
      rash
   Psoriasiform napkin eruption

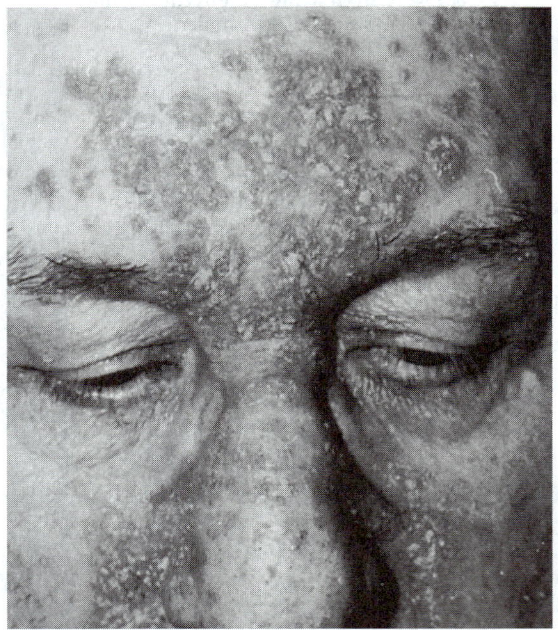

Figure 12–3 Severe seborrheic dermatitis. (From Arnold HL, Odom RB, James WD: Andrews' Diseases of the Skin, Clinical Dermatology, 8th ed. Philadelphia, WB Saunders, 1990, p 195.)

Item 12–2 Seborrheic dermatitis is characterized by greasy, scaly, red patches and is associated with oily skin and scalp.

☐ **691.8 Other atopic dermatitis and related conditions**
    Atopic dermatitis
    Besnier's prurigo
    Eczema:
      atopic
      flexural
      intrinsic (allergic)
    Neurodermatitis:
      atopic
      diffuse (of Brocq)

● **692 Contact dermatitis and other eczema**

    Includes: dermatitis:
      NOS
      contact
      occupational
      venenata
    eczema (acute) (chronic):
      NOS
      allergic
      erythematous
      occupational

    Excludes *allergy NOS (995.3)*
    contact dermatitis of eyelids (373.32)
    dermatitis due to substances taken internally
      (693.0–693.9)
    eczema of external ear (380.22)
    perioral dermatitis (695.3)
    urticarial reactions (708.0–708.9, 995.1)

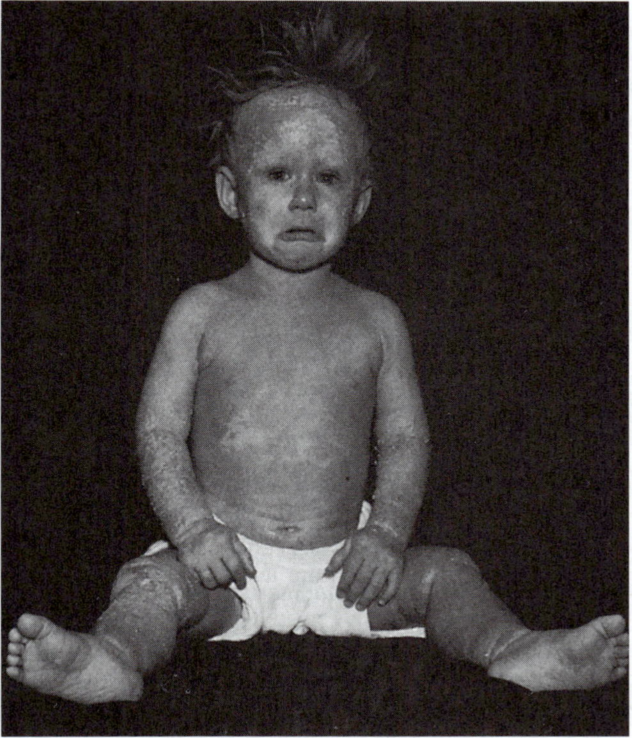

Figure 12–4 Atopic dermatitis. (From Moschella SL, Hurley HJ: Dermatology, 2nd ed. Philadelphia, WB Saunders, 1985, p 336.)

Item 12–3 Atopic dermatitis, also known as atopic eczema, infantile eczema, disseminated neurodermatitis, flexural eczema, and *prurigo diathesique* (Besnier), is characterized by intense itching and is often hereditary.

692.0 Due to detergents

692.1 Due to oils and greases

692.2 Due to solvents
    Dermatitis due to solvents of:
      chlorocompound group
      cyclohexane group
      ester group
      glycol group
      hydrocarbon group
      ketone group

692.3 Due to drugs and medicines in contact with skin
    Dermatitis (allergic) (contact) due to:
      arnica
      fungicides
      iodine
      keratolytics
      mercurials
      neomycin
      pediculocides
      phenols
      scabicides
      any drug applied to skin
    Dermatitis medicamentosa due to drug applied to
      skin

    Use additional E code to identify drug

    Excludes *allergy NOS due to drugs (995.2)*
    dermatitis due to ingested drugs (693.0)
    dermatitis medicamentosa NOS (693.0)

☐ **692.4 Due to other chemical products**

Dermatitis due to:	Dermatitis due to:
acids	insecticide
adhesive plaster	nylon
alkalis	plastic
caustics	rubber
dichromate	

692.5 Due to food in contact with skin
    Dermatitis, contact, due to:
      cereals
      fish
      flour
      fruit
      meat
      milk

    Excludes *dermatitis due to:*
      dyes (692.89)
      ingested foods (693.1)
      preservatives (692.89)

692.6 Due to plants [except food]
    Dermatitis due to:
      lacquer tree [Rhus verniciflua]
      poison:
        ivy [Rhus toxicodendron]
        oak [Rhus diversiloba]
        sumac [Rhus venenata]
        vine [Rhus radicans]
      primrose [Primula]
      ragweed [Senecio jacobae]
      other plants in contact with the skin

    Excludes *allergy NOS due to pollen (477.0)*
    nettle rash (708.8)

● **692.7 Due to solar radiation**

    ☐ **692.70 Unspecified dermatitis due to sun**

    692.71 Sunburn

692.72 Acute dermatitis due to solar radiation
Berloque dermatitis
Photoallergic response
Phototoxic response
Polymorphous light eruption
Acute solar skin damage NOS

| Excludes | *sunburn (692.71)* |

Use additional E code to identify drug, if drug induced

692.73 Actinic reticuloid and actinic granuloma

692.74 Other chronic dermatitis due to solar radiation
Chronic solar skin damage NOS
Solar elastosis

| Excludes | *actinic [solar] keratosis (702.0)* |

692.79 Other dermatitis due to solar radiation
Hydroa aestivale
Photodermatitis (due to sun)
Photosensitiveness (due to sun)
Solar skin damage NOS

● **692.8 Due to other specified agents**

692.81 Dermatitis due to cosmetics

692.82 Dermatitis due to other radiation
Infrared rays
Light, except from sun
Radiation NOS
Ultraviolet rays, except from sun
X-rays

| Excludes | *that due to solar radiation (692.70–692.79)* |

692.83 Dermatitis due to metals
Jewelry

692.89 Other
Dermatitis due to:
cold weather
dyes
furs
hot weather
preservatives

| Excludes | *allergy NOS due to animal hair, dander (animal), or dust (477.8)* |
| | *sunburn (692.71)* |

692.9 Unspecified cause
Dermatitis:
NOS
contact NOS
venenata NOS
Eczema NOS

● **693 Dermatitis due to substances taken internally**

Excludes	*adverse effect NOS of drugs and medicines (995.2)*
	allergy NOS (995.3)
	contact dermatitis (692.0–692.9)
	urticarial reactions (708.0–708.9, 995.1)

693.0 Due to drugs and medicines
Dermatitis medicamentosa NOS

Use additional E code to identify drug

| Excludes | *that due to drugs in contact with skin (692.3)* |

693.1 Due to food

693.8 Due to other specified substances taken internally

693.9 Due to unspecified substance taken internally

| Excludes | *dermatitis NOS (692.9)* |

● **694 Bullous dermatoses**

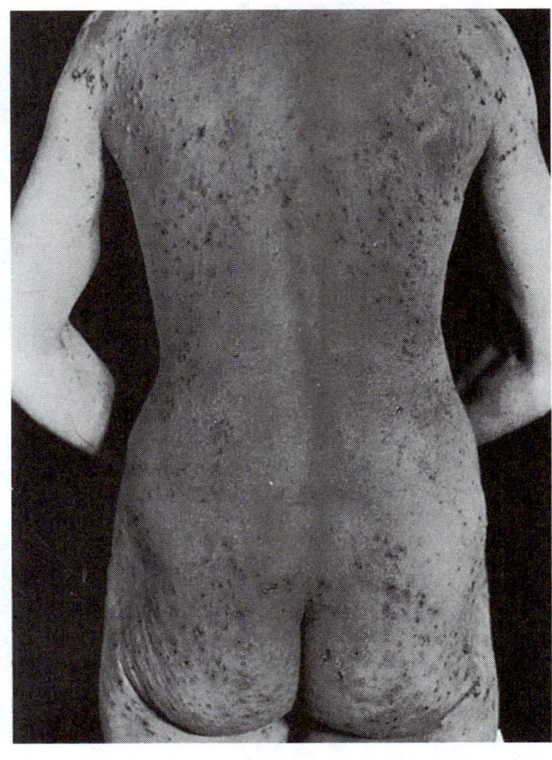

Figure 12–5 Dermatitis herpetiformis. (From Arnold HL, Odom RB, James WD: Andrews' Diseases of the Skin, Clinical Dermatology, 8th ed. Philadelphia, WB Saunders, 1990, p 553.)

Item 12-4 Dermatitis herpetiformis, also known as Duhring's disease, is a systemic disease characterized by small blisters (3 to 5 mm) and occasionally large bullae (+5 mm).

694.0 Dermatitis herpetiformis
Dermatosis herpetiformis
Duhring's disease
Hydroa herpetiformis

Excludes	*herpes gestationis (646.8)*
	dermatitis herpetiformis:
	juvenile (694.2)
	senile (694.5)

694.1 Subcorneal pustular dermatosis
Sneddon-Wilkinson disease or syndrome

694.2 Juvenile dermatitis herpetiformis
Juvenile pemphigoid

694.3 Impetigo herpetiformis

694.4 Pemphigus
Pemphigus:
NOS
erythematosus
foliaceus
malignant
vegetans
vulgaris

| Excludes | *pemphigus neonatorum (684)* |

694.5 Pemphigoid
Benign pemphigus NOS
Bullous pemphigoid
Herpes circinatus bullosus
Senile dermatitis herpetiformis

● **694.6 Benign mucous membrane pemphigoid**
Cicatricial pemphigoid
Mucosynechial atrophic bullous dermatitis

694.60 Without mention of ocular involvement

694.61 With ocular involvement
Ocular pemphigus

☐ **694.8 Other specified bullous dermatoses**
Excludes *herpes gestationis (646.8)*

☐ **694.9 Unspecified bullous dermatoses**

● **695 Erythematous conditions**

695.0 Toxic erythema
Erythema venenatum

695.1 Erythema multiforme
Erythema iris
Herpes iris
Lyell's syndrome
Scalded skin syndrome
Stevens-Johnson syndrome
Toxic epidermal necrolysis

695.2 Erythema nodosum
Excludes *tuberculous erythema nodosum (017.1)*

695.3 Rosacea
Acne: Perioral dermatitis
  erythematosa   Rhinophyma
  rosacea

695.4 Lupus erythematosus
Lupus:
  erythematodes (discoid)
  erythematosus (discoid), not disseminated
Excludes *lupus (vulgaris) NOS (017.0)*
systemic [disseminated] lupus erythematosus
(710.0)

● **695.8 Other specified erythematous conditions**

695.81 Ritter's disease
Dermatitis exfoliativa neonatorum

☐ **695.89 Other**
Erythema intertrigo
Intertrigo
Pityriasis rubra (Hebra)
Excludes *mycotic intertrigo (111.0–111.9)*

☐ **695.9 Unspecified erythematous condition**
Erythema NOS
Erythroderma (secondary)

● **696 Psoriasis and similar disorders**

696.0 Psoriatic arthropathy

☐ **696.1 Other psoriasis**
Acrodermatitis continua
Dermatitis repens
Psoriasis:
  NOS
  any type, except arthropathic
Excludes *psoriatic arthropathy (696.0)*

696.2 Parapsoriasis
Parakeratosis variegata
Parapsoriasis lichenoides chronica
Pityriasis lichenoides et varioliformis

696.3 Pityriasis rosea
Pityriasis circinata (et maculata)

696.4 Pityriasis rubra pilaris
Devergie's disease
Lichen ruber acuminatus
Excludes *pityriasis rubra (Hebra) (695.89)*

Figure 12–6 Psoriasis. (From Moschella SL, Hurley HJ: Dermatology, 2nd ed. Philadelphia, WB Saunders, 1985, p 512.)

Item 12–5 Psoriasis is a chronic, recurrent inflammatory skin disease characterized by small patches covered with thick silvery scales. Parapsoriasis is a treatment-resistant erythroderma. Pityriasis rosea is characterized by a herald patch that is a single large lesion and that usually appears on the trunk and is followed by scattered, smaller lesions.

☐ **696.5 Other and unspecified pityriasis**
Pityriasis:
  NOS
  alba
  streptogenes
Excludes *pityriasis:*
simplex (690.18)
versicolor (111.0)

☐ **696.8 Other**

● **697 Lichen**
Excludes *lichen:*
obtusus corneus (698.3)
pilaris (congenital) (757.39)
ruber acuminatus (696.4)
sclerosus et atrophicus (701.0)
scrofulosus (017.0)
simplex chronicus (698.3)
spinulosus (congenital) (757.39)
urticatus (698.2)

697.0 Lichen planus
Lichen:
  planopilaris
  ruber planus

697.1 Lichen nitidus
Pinkus' disease

☐ **697.8 Other lichen, not elsewhere classified**
Lichen:
  ruber moniliforme
  striata

☐ **697.9 Lichen, unspecified**

● **698 Pruritus and related conditions**
Excludes *pruritus specified as psychogenic (306.3)*

698.0 Pruritus ani
Perianal itch

698.1 Pruritus of genital organs

698.2 Prurigo
Lichen urticatus
Prurigo:
NOS
Hebra's
mitis
simplex
Urticaria papulosa (Hebra)

| Excludes | *prurigo nodularis (698.3)* |

698.3 Lichenification and lichen simplex chronicus
Hyde's disease
Neurodermatitis (circumscripta) (local)
Prurigo nodularis

| Excludes | *neurodermatitis, diffuse (of Brocq) (691.8)* |

698.4 Dermatitis factitia [artefacta]
Dermatitis ficta
Neurotic excoriation

Use additional code to identify any associated mental disorder

❑ **698.8 Other specified pruritic conditions**
Pruritus:
hiemalis
senilis
Winter itch

❑ **698.9 Unspecified pruritic disorder**
Itch NOS
Pruritus NOS

OTHER DISEASES OF SKIN AND SUBCUTANEOUS TISSUE (700–709)

| Excludes | *conditions confined to eyelids (373.0–374.9)* |
| | *congenital conditions of skin, hair, and nails (757.0–757.9)* |

700 Corns and callosities
Callus
Clavus

Item 12–6 Keratoderma is characterized by firm horny papules that have a cobblestone appearance. Keratoderma climactericum, also known as endocrine keratoderma, is hyperkeratosis located on the palms and soles.

● **701 Other hypertrophic and atrophic conditions of skin**

Excludes	*dermatomyositis (710.3)*
	hereditary edema of legs (757.0)
	scleroderma (generalized) (710.1)

701.0 Circumscribed scleroderma
Addison's keloid
Dermatosclerosis, localized
Lichen sclerosus et atrophicus
Morphea
Scleroderma, circumscribed or localized

701.1 Keratoderma, acquired
Acquired:
ichthyosis
keratoderma palmaris et plantaris
Elastosis perforans serpiginosa
Hyperkeratosis:
NOS
follicularis in cutem penetrans
palmoplantaris climacterica
Keratoderma:
climactericum
tylodes, progressive
Keratosis (blennorrhagica)

Excludes	*Darier's disease [keratosis follicularis] (congenital) (757.39)*
	keratosis:
	arsenical (692.4)
	gonococcal (098.81)

701.2 Acquired acanthosis nigricans
Keratosis nigricans

701.3 Striae atrophicae
Atrophic spots of skin
Atrophoderma maculatum
Atrophy blanche (of Milian)
Degenerative colloid atrophy
Senile degenerative atrophy
Striae distensae

701.4 Keloid scar
Cheloid
Hypertrophic scar
Keloid

❑ **701.5 Other abnormal granulation tissue**
Excessive granulation

❑ **701.8 Other specified hypertrophic and atrophic conditions of skin**
Acrodermatitis atrophicans chronica
Atrophia cutis senilis
Atrophoderma neuriticum
Confluent and reticulate papillomatosis
Cutis laxa senilis
Elastosis senilis
Folliculitis ulerythematosa reticulata
Gougerot-Carteaud syndrome or disease

❑ **701.9 Unspecified hypertrophic and atrophic conditions of skin**
Atrophoderma

● **702 Other dermatoses**

| Excludes | *carcinoma in situ (232.0–232.9)* |

702.0 Actinic keratosis

● **702.1 Seborrheic keratosis**

702.11 Inflamed seborrheic keratosis

❑ **702.19 Other seborrheic keratosis**
Seborrheic keratosis NOS

❑ **702.8 Other specified dermatoses**

● **703 Diseases of nail**

| Excludes | *congenital anomalies (757.5)* |
| | *onychia and paronychia (681.02, 681.11)* |

703.0 Ingrowing nail
Ingrowing nail with infection
Unguis incarnatus

| Excludes | *infection, nail NOS (681.9)* |

❑ **703.8 Other specified diseases of nail**
Dystrophia unguium
Hypertrophy of nail
Koilonychia
Leukonychia (punctata) (striata)
Onychauxis
Onychogryposis
Onycholysis

❑ **703.9 Unspecified disease of nail**

● **704 Diseases of hair and hair follicles**
Excludes *congenital anomalies (757.4)*

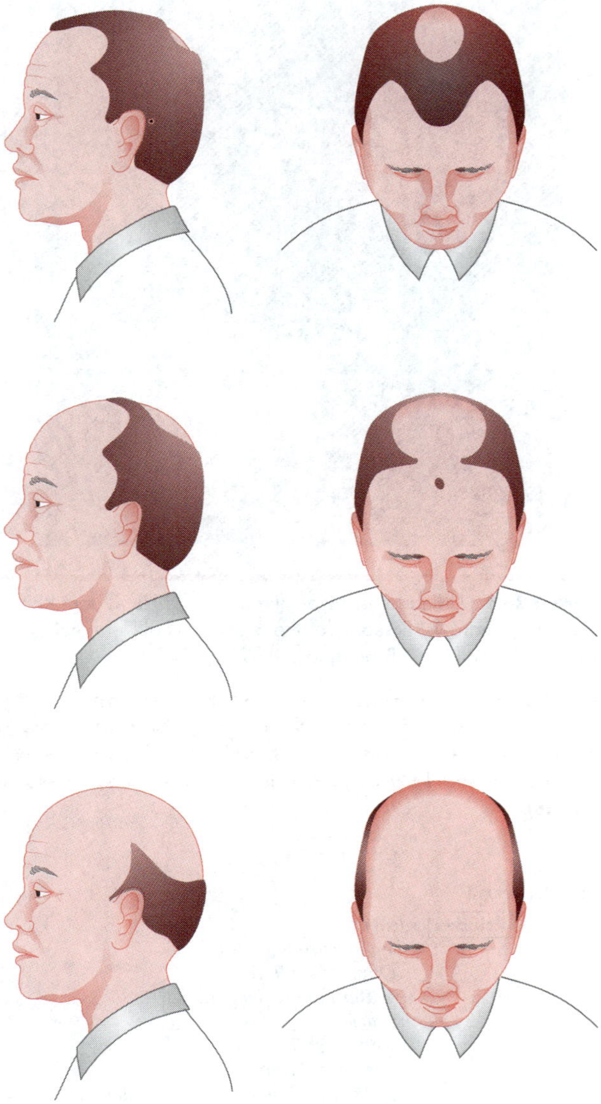

Figure 12-7 *Male pattern alopecia.*

Item 12-7 Alopecia is lack of hair and takes many forms. The most common is male pattern alopecia, also known as **androgenetic alopecia. Telogen** effluvium is early and excessive loss of hair resulting from a trauma to the hair (fever, drugs, surgery, etc.).

● **704.0 Alopecia**
Excludes *madarosis (374.55)*
syphilitic alopecia (091.82)

❑ **704.00 Alopecia, unspecified**
Baldness
Loss of hair

704.01 Alopecia areata
Ophiasis

704.02 Telogen effluvium

❑ **704.09 Other**
Folliculitis decalvans
Hypotrichosis:
NOS
postinfectional NOS
Pseudopelade

Item 12-8 Hirsutism is excessive growth of hair.

704.1 Hirsutism
Hypertrichosis:
NOS
lanuginosa, acquired
Polytrichia
Excludes *hypertrichosis of eyelid (374.54)*

704.2 Abnormalities of the hair
Atrophic hair
Clastothrix
Fragilitas crinium
Trichiasis:
NOS
cicatrical
Trichorrhexis (nodosa)
Excludes *trichiasis of eyelid (374.05)*

704.3 Variations in hair color
Canities (premature)
Grayness, hair (premature)
Heterochromia of hair
Poliosis:
NOS
circumscripta, acquired

❑ **704.8 Other specified diseases of hair and hair follicles**
Folliculitis:
NOS
abscedens et suffodiens
pustular
Perifolliculitis:
NOS
capitis abscedens et suffodiens
scalp
Sycosis:
NOS
barbae [not parasitic]
lupoid
vulgaris

❑ **704.9 Unspecified disease of hair and hair follicles**

● **705 Disorders of sweat glands**

705.0 Anhidrosis
Hypohidrosis
Oligohidrosis

705.1 Prickly heat
Heat rash
Miliaria rubra (tropicalis)
Sudamina

● **705.8 Other specified disorders of sweat glands**

705.81 Dyshidrosis
Cheiropompholyx
Pompholyx

ICD-9-CM
700-799
Vol. 1

705.82 Fox-Fordyce disease

705.83 Hidradenitis
    Hidradenitis suppurativa

❑**705.89 Other**
    Bromhidrosis
    Chromhidrosis
    Granulosis rubra nasi
    Urhidrosis
    Excludes *hidrocystoma (216.0–216.9)*
    hyperhidrosis (780.8)

❑**705.9 Unspecified disorder of sweat glands**
    Disorder of sweat glands NOS

● **706 Diseases of sebaceous glands**

706.0 Acne varioliformis
    Acne: Acne:
     frontalis   necrotica

❑**706.1 Other acne**
    Acne:
     NOS
     conglobata
     cystic
     pustular
     vulgaris
    Blackhead
    Comedo
    Excludes *acne rosacea (695.3)*

706.2 Sebaceous cyst
    Atheroma, skin   Wen
    Keratin cyst

706.3 Seborrhea
    Excludes *seborrhea:*
       capitis (704.8)
       sicca (690.18)
     seborrheic keratosis (702)

❑**706.8 Other specified diseases of sebaceous glands**
    Asteatosis (cutis)
    Xerosis cutis

❑**706.9 Unspecified disease of sebaceous glands**

● **707 Chronic ulcer of skin**

    Includes: non-infected sinus of skin
         non-healing ulcer
    Excludes *specific infections classified under "Infectious and*
       Parasitic Diseases" (001.0–136.9)
     varicose ulcer (454.0, 454.2)

707.0 Decubitus ulcer
    Bed sore
    Decubitus ulcer [any site]
    Plaster ulcer
    Pressure ulcer

707.1 Ulcer of lower limbs, except decubitus
    Ulcer, chronic, of lower limb:
     neurogenic of lower limb
     trophic of lower limb
    Excludes *that with atherosclerosis of the extremities*
      (440.23)

❑**707.8 Chronic ulcer of other specified sites**
    Ulcer, chronic, of other specified sites:
     neurogenic of other specified sites
     trophic of other specified sites

❑**707.9 Chronic ulcer of unspecified site**
    Chronic ulcer NOS
    Trophic ulcer NOS
    Tropical ulcer NOS
    Ulcer of skin NOS

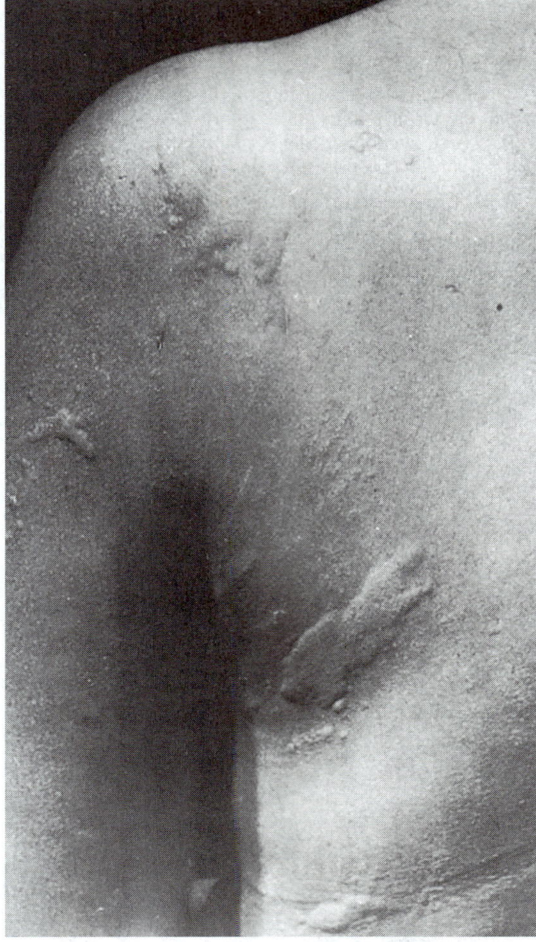

Figure 12–8   Urticaria, or hives. (From Arnold HL, Odom RB, James WD: Andrews' Diseases of the Skin, Clinical Dermatology, 8th ed. Philadelphia, WB Saunders, 1990, p 148.)

Item 12–9   Urticaria is a vascular reaction in which wheals surrounded by a red halo appear and cause severe itching. The causes of urticaria or hives are extensive and varied (e.g., food, heat, cold, drugs, stress, infections).

● **708 Urticaria**
    Excludes *edema:*
       angioneurotic (995.1)
       Quincke's (995.1)
     hereditary angioedema (277.6)
     urticaria:
       giant (995.1)
       papulosa (Hebra) (698.2)
       pigmentosa (juvenile) (congenital) (757.33)

708.0 Allergic urticaria

708.1 Idiopathic urticaria

708.2 Urticaria due to cold and heat
    Thermal urticaria

708.3 Dermatographic urticaria
    Dermatographia
    Factitial urticaria

708.4 Vibratory urticaria

708.5 Cholinergic urticaria

☐ **708.8   Other specified urticaria**
Nettle rash
Urticaria:
   chronic
   recurrent periodic

☐ **708.9   Urticaria, unspecified**
Hives NOS

● **709   Other disorders of skin and subcutaneous tissue**

  ● **709.0   Dyschromia**

    | Excludes | *albinism (270.2)*
        pigmented nevus (216.0–216.9)
        that of eyelid (374.52–374.53)

  ☐ **709.00   Dyschromia, unspecified**

    709.01   Vitiligo

  ☐ **709.09   Other**

  709.1   Vascular disorders of skin
    Angioma serpiginosum
    Purpura (primary) annularis telangiectodes

  709.2   Scar conditions and fibrosis of skin
    Adherent scar (skin)
    Cicatrix
    Disfigurement (due to scar)
    Fibrosis, skin NOS
    Scar NOS

    | Excludes | *keloid scar (701.4)*

  709.3   Degenerative skin disorders
    Calcinosis:
      circumscripta
      cutis
    Colloid milium
    Degeneration, skin
    Deposits, skin
    Senile dermatosis NOS
    Subcutaneous calcification

  709.4   Foreign body granuloma of skin and subcutaneous tissue

    | Excludes | *residual foreign body without granuloma of skin*
        and subcutaneous tissue (729.6)
        that of muscle (728.82)

  ☐ **709.8   Other specified disorders of skin**
    Epithelial hyperplasia
    Menstrual dermatosis
    Vesicular eruption

  ☐ **709.9   Unspecified disorder of skin and subcutaneous tissue**
    Dermatosis NOS

---

13.   DISEASES OF THE MUSCULOSKELETAL SYSTEM AND CONNECTIVE TISSUE (710–739)

The following fifth-digit subclassification is for use with categories 711–712, 715–716, 718–719, and 730:

☐ **0   site unspecified**
  1   shoulder region
    Acromioclavicular joint(s)
    Clavicle
    Glenohumeral joint(s)
    Scapula
    Sternoclavicular joint(s)
  2   upper arm
    Elbow joint
    Humerus
  3   forearm
    Radius
    Ulna
    Wrist joint
  4   hand
    Carpus
    Metacarpus
    Phalanges [fingers]
  5   pelvic region and thigh
    Buttock
    Femur
    Hip (joint)
  6   lower leg
    Fibula
    Knee joint
    Patella
    Tibia
  7   ankle and foot
    Ankle joint
    Digits [toes]
    Metatarsus
    Phalanges, foot
    Tarsus
    Other joints in foot
☐ **8   other specified sites**
    Head
    Neck
    Ribs
    Skull
    Trunk
    Vertebral column
☐ **9   multiple sites**

ARTHROPATHIES AND RELATED DISORDERS (710–719)

| Excludes | *disorders of spine (720.0–724.9)*

● **710   Diffuse diseases of connective tissue**

  Includes: all collagen diseases whose effects are not mainly confined to a single system

  Use additional code to identify manifestation, as:
    lung involvement (517.8)
    myopathy (359.6)

    | Excludes | *those affecting mainly the cardiovascular system, i.e., polyarteritis nodosa and allied conditions (446.0–446.7)*

  710.0   Systemic lupus erythematosus
    Disseminated lupus erythematosus
    Libman-Sacks disease

    Use additional code to identify manifestation, as:
      endocarditis (424.91)
      nephritis (583.81)
        chronic (582.81)
      nephrotic syndrome (581.81)

    | Excludes | *lupus erythematosus (discoid) NOS (695.4)*

ICD-9-CM

700–799

Vol. 1

710.1 Systemic sclerosis
    Acrosclerosis
    CRST syndrome
    Progressive systemic sclerosis
    Scleroderma

    Excludes   *circumscribed scleroderma (701.0)*

710.2 Sicca syndrome
    Keratoconjunctivitis sicca
    Sjögren's disease

710.3 Dermatomyositis
    Poikilodermatomyositis
    Polymyositis with skin involvement

710.4 Polymyositis

710.5 Eosinophilia myalgia syndrome
    Toxic oil syndrome

    Use additional E code to identify drug, if drug induced

710.8 Other specified diffuse diseases of connective tissue
    Multifocal fibrosclerosis (idiopathic) NEC
    Systemic fibrosclerosing syndrome

710.9 Unspecified diffuse connective tissue disease
    Collagen disease NOS

711 Arthropathy associated with infections

    Includes: arthritis associated with conditions classifiable below
        arthropathy associated with conditions classifiable below
        polyarthritis associated with conditions classifiable below
        polyarthropathy associated with conditions classifiable below

    Excludes   *rheumatic fever (390)*

The following fifth-digit subclassification is for use with category 711; valid digits are in [brackets] under each code. See list at beginning of chapter for definitions:

    0 site unspecified
    1 shoulder region
    2 upper arm
    3 forearm
    4 hand
    5 pelvic region and thigh
    6 lower leg
    7 ankle and foot
    8 other specified sites
    9 multiple sites

711.0 Pyogenic arthritis
[0–9]   Arthritis or polyarthritis (due to):
        coliform [*Escherichia coli*]
        Hemophilus influenzae [*H. influenzae*]
        pneumococcal
        Pseudomonas
        staphylococcal
        streptococcal
        Pyarthrosis

    Use additional code to identify infectious organism (041.0–041.8)

711.1 Arthropathy associated with Reiter's disease and nonspecific urethritis
[0–9]

    Code first underlying disease, as:
        nonspecific urethritis (099.4)
        Reiter's disease (099.3)

711.2 Arthropathy in Behçet's syndrome
[0–9]   *Code first underlying disease (136.1)*

711.3 Postdysentericarthropathy
[0–9]

    Code first underlying disease, as:
        dysentery (009.0)
        enteritis, infectious (008.0–009.3)
        paratyphoid fever (002.1–002.9)
        typhoid fever (002.0)

    Excludes   *salmonella arthritis (003.23)*

711.4 Arthropathy associated with other bacterial diseases
[0–9]

    Code first underlying disease, as:
        diseases classifiable to 010–040, 090–099, except as in 711.1, 711.3, and 713.5
        leprosy (030.0–030.9)
        tuberculosis (015.0–015.9)

    Excludes   *gonococcal arthritis (098.50)*
            meningococcal arthritis (036.82)

711.5 Arthropathy associated with other viral diseases
[0–9]

    Code first underlying disease, as:
        diseases classifiable to 045–049, 050–079, 480, 487
        O'nyong-nyong (066.3)

    Excludes   *that due to rubella (056.71)*

711.6 Arthropathy associated with mycoses
[0–9]   *Code first underlying disease (110.0–118)*

711.7 Arthropathy associated with helminthiasis
[0–9]   Code first underlying disease, as:
        filariasis (125.0–125.9)

711.8 Arthropathy associated with other infectious and parasitic diseases
[0–9]

    Code first underlying disease, as:
        diseases classifiable to 080–088, 100–104, 130–136

    Excludes   *arthropathy associated with sarcoidosis (713.7)*

711.9 Unspecified infective arthritis
[0–9]   Infective arthritis or polyarthritis (acute) (chronic) (subacute) NOS

712 Crystal arthropathies

    Includes: crystal-induced arthritis and synovitis
    Excludes   *gouty arthropathy (274.0)*

The following fifth-digit subclassification is for use with category 712; valid digits are in [brackets] under each code. See list at beginning of chapter for definitions:

    0 site unspecified
    1 shoulder region
    2 upper arm
    3 forearm
    4 hand
    5 pelvic region and thigh
    6 lower leg
    7 ankle and foot
    8 other specified sites
    9 multiple sites

712.1 Chondrocalcinosis due to dicalcium phosphate crystals
[0–9]
    Chondrocalcinosis due to dicalcium phosphate crystals (with other crystals)

    Code first underlying disease (275.4)

712.2 Chondrocalcinosis due to pyrophosphate crystals
[0–9]   *Code first underlying disease (275.4)*

712.3 Chondrocalcinosis, unspecified
[0–9]   *Code first underlying disease (275.4)*

712.8 Other specified crystal arthropathies
[0–9]

    ◀▶ **New Code**   ⬅▬ ▬➡ **Revised Code**   ● **Not a Principal Diagnosis**   ● **Use Additional Digit(s)**   ☐ **Nonspecific Code**

☐ ● **712.9 Unspecified crystal arthropathy**
[0–9]

● **713 Arthropathy associated with other disorders classified elsewhere**

Includes: arthritis associated with conditions classifiable below
arthropathy associated with conditions classifiable below
polyarthritis associated with conditions classifiable below
polyarthropathy associated with conditions classifiable below

● ☐ **713.0 Arthropathy associated with other endocrine and metabolic disorders**

Code first underlying disease, as:
acromegaly (253.0)
hemochromatosis (275.0)
hyperparathyroidism (252.0)
hypogammaglobulinemia (279.00–279.09)
hypothyroidism (243–244.9)
lipoid metabolism disorder (272.0–272.9)
ochronosis (270.2)

Excludes *arthropathy associated with:*
amyloidosis (713.7)
crystal deposition disorders, except gout (712.1–712.9)
diabetic neuropathy (713.5)
gouty arthropathy (274.0)

● **713.1 Arthropathy associated with gastrointestinal conditions other than infections**

Code first underlying disease, as:
regional enteritis (555.0–555.9)
ulcerative colitis (556)

● **713.2 Arthropathy associated with hematological disorders**

Code first underlying disease, as:
hemoglobinopathy (282.4–282.7)
hemophilia (286.0–286.2)
leukemia (204.0–208.9)
malignant reticulosis (202.3)
multiple myelomatosis (203.0)

Excludes *arthropathy associated with Henoch-Schönlein purpura (713.6)*

● **713.3 Arthropathy associated with dermatological disorders**

Code first underlying disease, as:
erythema multiforme (695.1)
erythema nodosum (695.2)

Excludes *psoriatic arthropathy (696.0)*

● **713.4 Arthropathy associated with respiratory disorders**

Code first underlying disease, as:
diseases classifiable to 490–519

Excludes *arthropathy associated with respiratory infections (711.0, 711.4–711.8)*

● **713.5 Arthropathy associated with neurological disorders**
Charcot's arthropathy associated with diseases classifiable elsewhere
Neuropathic arthritis associated with diseases classifiable elsewhere

Code first underlying disease, as:
neuropathic joint disease [Charcot's joints]:
NOS (094.0)
diabetic (250.6)
syringomyelic (336.0)
tabetic [syphilitic] (094.0)

● **713.6 Arthropathy associated with hypersensitivity reaction**

Code first underlying disease, as:
Henoch (-Schönlein) purpura (287.0)
serum sickness (999.5)

Excludes *allergic arthritis NOS (716.2)*

● ☐ **713.7 Other general diseases with articular involvement**

Code first underlying disease, as:
amyloidosis (277.3)
familial Mediterranean fever (277.3)
sarcoidosis (135)

● ☐ **713.8 Arthropathy associated with other conditions classifiable elsewhere**

Code first underlying disease, as:
conditions classifiable elsewhere except as in 711.1–711.8, 712, and 713.0–713.7

● **714 Rheumatoid arthritis and other inflammatory polyarthropathies**

Excludes *rheumatic fever (390)*
rheumatoid arthritis of spine NOS (720.0)

714.0 Rheumatoid arthritis
Arthritis or polyarthritis:
atrophic
rheumatic (chronic)

Use additional code to identify manifestation, as:
myopathy (359.6)
polyneuropathy (357.1)

Excludes *juvenile rheumatoid arthritis NOS (714.30)*

714.1 Felty's syndrome
Rheumatoid arthritis with splenoadenomegaly and leukopenia

☐ **714.2 Other rheumatoid arthritis with visceral or systemic involvement**
Rheumatoid carditis

● **714.3 Juvenile chronic polyarthritis**

☐ **714.30 Polyarticular juvenile rheumatoid arthritis, chronic or unspecified**
Juvenile rheumatoid arthritis NOS
Still's disease

714.31 Polyarticular juvenile rheumatoid arthritis, acute

714.32 Pauciarticular juvenile rheumatoid arthritis

714.33 Monoarticular juvenile rheumatoid arthritis

714.4 Chronic postrheumatic arthropathy
Chronic rheumatoid nodular fibrositis
Jaccoud's syndrome

● **714.8 Other specified inflammatory polyarthropathies**

714.81 Rheumatoid lung
Caplan's syndrome
Diffuse interstitial rheumatoid disease of lung
Fibrosing alveolitis, rheumatoid

☐ **714.89 Other**

☐ **714.9 Unspecified inflammatory polyarthropathy**
Inflammatory polyarthropathy or polyarthritis NOS

Excludes *polyarthropathy NOS (716.5)*

ICD-9-CM

700-
799

Vol. 1

● **715 Osteoarthrosis and allied disorders**

Note: Localized, in the subcategories below, includes bilateral involvement of the same site.

Includes: arthritis or polyarthritis:
 degenerative
 hypertrophic
 degenerative joint disease
 osteoarthritis

 Excludes *Marie-Strümpell spondylitis (720.0)*
  osteoarthrosis [osteoarthritis] of spine (721.0–721.9)

The following fifth-digit subclassification is for use with category 715; valid digits are in [brackets] under each code. See list at beginning of chapter for definitions:

❑ **0 site unspecified**
 1 shoulder region
 2 upper arm
 3 forearm
 4 hand
 5 pelvic region and thigh
 6 lower leg
 7 ankle and foot
❑ **8 other specified sites**
❑ **9 multiple sites**

● **715.0 Osteoarthrosis, generalized**
[0,4,9] Degenerative joint disease, involving multiple joints
  Primary generalized hypertrophic osteoarthrosis

● **715.1 Osteoarthrosis, localized, primary**
[0–8] Localized osteoarthropathy, idiopathic

● **715.2 Osteoarthrosis, localized, secondary**
[0–8] Coxae malum senilis

❑● **715.3 Osteoarthrosis, localized, not specified whether**
[0–8] **primary or secondary**
  Otto's pelvis

❑● **715.8 Osteoarthrosis involving, or with mention of more**
[0,9] **than one site, but not specified as generalized**

❑● **715.9 Osteoarthrosis, unspecified whether generalized or**
[0–8] **localized**

● **716 Other and unspecified arthropathies**

 Excludes *cricoarytenoid arthropathy (478.79)*

The following fifth-digit subclassification is for use with category 716; valid digits are in [brackets] under each code. See list at beginning of chapter for definitions:

❑ **0 site unspecified**
 1 shoulder region
 2 upper arm
 3 forearm
 4 hand
 5 pelvic region and thigh
 6 lower leg
 7 ankle and foot
❑ **8 other specified sites**
❑ **9 multiple sites**

● **716.0 Kaschin-Beck disease**
[0–9] Endemic polyarthritis

● **716.1 Traumatic arthropathy**
[0–9]

● **716.2 Allergic arthritis**
[0–9]

 Excludes *arthritis associated with Henoch-Schönlein purpura or serum sickness (713.6)*

● **716.3 Climacteric arthritis**
[0–9] Menopausal arthritis

● **716.4 Transient arthropathy**
[0–9]

 Excludes *palindromic rheumatism (719.3)*

❑● **716.5 Unspecified polyarthropathy or polyarthritis**
[0–9]

❑● **716.6 Unspecified monoarthritis**
[0–8] Coxitis

❑● **716.8 Other specified arthropathy**
[0–9]

❑● **716.9 Arthropathy, unspecified**
[0–9] Arthritis (acute) (chronic) (subacute)
  Arthropathy (acute) (chronic) (subacute)
  Articular rheumatism (chronic)
  Inflammation of joint NOS

● **717 Internal derangement of knee**

Includes: degeneration of articular cartilage or meniscus of knee
 rupture, old of articular cartilage or meniscus of knee
 tear, old of articular cartilage or meniscus of knee

 Excludes *acute derangement of knee (836.0–836.6)*
  ankylosis (718.5)
  contracture (718.4)
  current injury (836.0–836.6)
  deformity (736.4–736.6)
  recurrent dislocation (718.3)

717.0 Old bucket handle tear of medial meniscus
 Old bucket handle tear of unspecified cartilage

717.1 Derangement of anterior horn of medial meniscus

717.2 Derangement of posterior horn of medial meniscus

❑ **717.3 Other and unspecified derangement of medial meniscus**
 Degeneration of internal semilunar cartilage

● **717.4 Derangement of lateral meniscus**

❑ **717.40 Derangement of lateral meniscus, unspecified**

 717.41 Bucket handle tear of lateral meniscus

 717.42 Derangement of anterior horn of lateral meniscus

 717.43 Derangement of posterior horn of lateral meniscus

❑ **717.49 Other**

717.5 Derangement of meniscus, not elsewhere classified
 Congenital discoid meniscus
 Cyst of semilunar cartilage
 Derangement of semilunar cartilage NOS

717.6 Loose body in knee
 Joint mice, knee
 Rice bodies, knee (joint)

717.7 Chondromalacia of patella
 Chondromalacia patellae
 Degeneration [softening] of articular cartilage of patella

● **717.8 Other internal derangement of knee**

 717.81 Old disruption of lateral collateral ligament

 717.82 Old disruption of medial collateral ligament

 717.83 Old disruption of anterior cruciate ligament

 717.84 Old disruption of posterior cruciate ligament

❑ **717.85 Old disruption of other ligaments of knee**
 Capsular ligament of knee

 ◀▶ **New Code** ⬅▦➡ **Revised Code** ● **Not a Principal Diagnosis** ● **Use Additional Digit(s)** ❑ **Nonspecific Code**

❑ **717.89 Other**
Old disruption of ligaments of knee NOS

❑ **717.9 Unspecified internal derangement of knee**
Derangement NOS of knee

● **718 Other derangement of joint**

Excludes	current injury (830.0–848.9)
	jaw (524.6)

The following fifth-digit subclassification is for use with category 718; valid digits are in [brackets] under each code. See list at beginning of chapter for definitions:
❑ **0 site unspecified**
  1 shoulder region
  2 upper arm
  3 forearm
  4 hand
  5 pelvic region and thigh
  6 lower leg
  7 ankle and foot
❑ **8 other specified sites**
❑ **9 multiple sites**

● **718.0 Articular cartilage disorder**
[0–5,7–9]   Meniscus:
       disorder
       rupture, old
       tear, old
      Old rupture of ligament(s) of joint NOS

Excludes	articular cartilage disorder:
	in ochronosis (270.2)
	knee (717.0–717.9)
	chondrocalcinosis (275.4)
	metastatic calcification (275.4)

● **718.1 Loose body in joint**
[0–5,7–9]   Joint mice

Excludes	knee (717.6)

● **718.2 Pathological dislocation**
[0–9]   Dislocation or displacement of joint, not recurrent
      and not current

● **718.3 Recurrent dislocation of joint**
[0–9]

● **718.4 Contracture of joint**
[0–9]

● **718.5 Ankylosis of joint**
[0–9]   Ankylosis of joint (fibrous) (osseous)

Excludes	spine (724.9)
	stiffness of joint without mention of ankylosis
	(719.5)

❑● **718.6 Unspecified intrapelvic protrusion of acetabulum**
[0,5]   Protrusio acetabuli, unspecified

❑● **718.8 Other joint derangement, not elsewhere classified**
[0–9]   Flail joint (paralytic)
      Instability of joint

Excludes	deformities classifiable to 736 (736.0–736.9)

❑● **718.9 Unspecified derangement of joint**
[0–5,7–9]

Excludes	knee (717.9)

● **719 Other and unspecified disorders of joint**

Excludes	jaw (524.6)

The following fifth-digit subclassification is for use with category 719; valid digits are in [brackets] under each code. See list at beginning of chapter for definitions:
❑ **0 site unspecified**
  1 shoulder region
  2 upper arm
  3 forearm
  4 hand
  5 pelvic region and thigh
  6 lower leg
  7 ankle and foot
❑ **8 other specified sites**
❑ **9 multiple sites**

● **719.0 Effusion of joint**
[0–9]   Hydrarthrosis
      Swelling of joint, with or without pain

Excludes	intermittent hydrarthrosis (719.3)

● **719.1 Hemarthrosis**
[0–9]

Excludes	current injury (840.0–848.9)

● **719.2 Villonodular synovitis**
[0–9]

● **719.3 Palindromic rheumatism**
[0–9]   Hench-Rosenberg syndrome
      Intermittent hydrarthrosis

● **719.4 Pain in joint**
[0–9]   Arthralgia

● **719.5 Stiffness of joint, not elsewhere classified**
[0–9]

❑● **719.6 Other symptoms referable to joint**
[0–9]   Joint crepitus
      Snapping hip

● **719.7 Difficulty in walking**
[0,5–9]

Excludes	abnormality of gait (781.2)

❑● **719.8 Other specified disorders of joint**
[0–9]   Calcification of joint
      Fistula of joint

Excludes	temporomandibular joint-pain-dysfunction syndrome [Costen's syndrome] (524.6)

❑● **719.9 Unspecified disorder of joint**
[0–9]

DORSOPATHIES (720–724)

Excludes	curvature of spine (737.0–737.9)
	osteochondrosis of spine (juvenile) (732.0) adult
	(732.8)

● **720 Ankylosing spondylitis and other inflammatory spondylopathies**

720.0 Ankylosing spondylitis
   Rheumatoid arthritis of spine NOS
   Spondylitis: Spondylitis:
    Marie-Strümpell   rheumatoid

720.1 Spinal enthesopathy
   Disorder of peripheral ligamentous or muscular
      attachments of spine
   Romanus lesion

720.2 Sacroiliitis, not elsewhere classified
   Inflammation of sacroiliac joint NOS

● **720.8 Other inflammatory spondylopathies**

● **720.81 Inflammatory spondylopathies in diseases classified elsewhere**

   Code first underlying disease, as:
    tuberculosis (015.0)

ICD-9-CM

700-799

Vol. 1

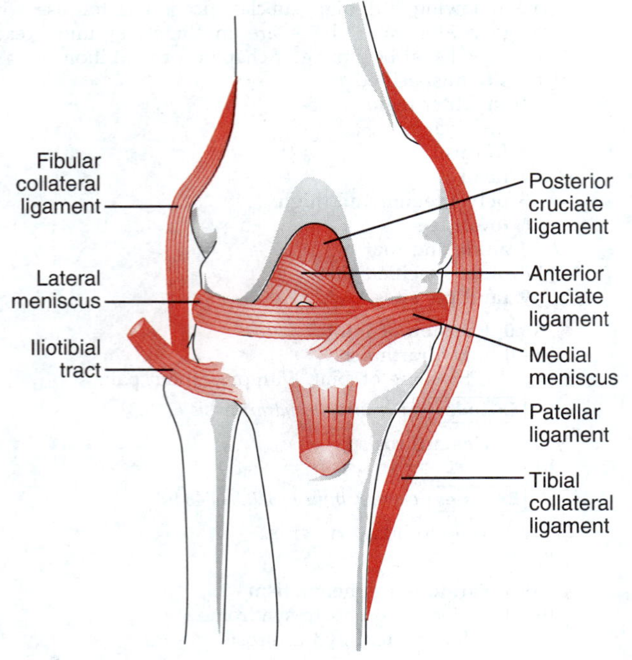

Figure 13–1   Anterior aspect of the right knee joint.

☐ **720.89 Other**

☐ **720.9 Unspecified inflammatory spondylopathy**
Spondylitis NOS

● **721 Spondylosis and allied disorders**

721.0 Cervical spondylosis without myelopathy
Cervical or cervicodorsal:
   arthritis
   osteoarthritis
   spondylarthritis

721.1 Cervical spondylosis with myelopathy
Anterior spinal artery compression syndrome
Spondylogenic compression of cervical spinal cord
Vertebral artery compression syndrome

721.2 Thoracic spondylosis without myelopathy
Thoracic:
   arthritis
   osteoarthritis
   spondylarthritis

721.3 Lumbosacral spondylosis without myelopathy
Lumbar or lumbosacral:
   arthritis
   osteoarthritis
   spondylarthritis

● **721.4 Thoracic or lumbar spondylosis with myelopathy**

721.41 Thoracic region
Spondylogenic compression of thoracic spinal cord

721.42 Lumbar region
Spondylogenic compression of lumbar spinal cord

721.5 Kissing spine
Baastrup's syndrome

721.6 Ankylosing vertebral hyperostosis

721.7 Traumatic spondylopathy
Kümmell's disease or spondylitis

☐ **721.8 Other allied disorders of spine**

● **721.9 Spondylosis of unspecified site**

721.90 Without mention of myelopathy
Spinal:
   arthritis (deformans) (degenerative) (hypertrophic)
   osteoarthritis NOS
Spondylarthrosis NOS

721.91 With myelopathy
Spondylogenic compression of spinal cord NOS

● **722 Intervertebral disc disorders**

722.0 Displacement of cervical intervertebral disc without myelopathy
Neuritis (brachial) or radiculitis due to displacement or rupture of cervical intervertebral disc
Any condition classifiable to 722.2 of the cervical or cervicothoracic intervertebral disc

● **722.1 Displacement of thoracic or lumbar intervertebral disc without myelopathy**

722.10 Lumbar intervertebral disc without myelopathy
Lumbago or sciatica due to displacement of intervertebral disc
Neuritis or radiculitis due to displacement or rupture of lumbar intervertebral disc
Any condition classifiable to 722.2 of the lumbar or lumbosacral intervertebral disc

722.11 Thoracic intervertebral disc without myelopathy
Any condition classifiable to 722.2 of thoracic intervertebral disc

☐ **722.2 Displacement of intervertebral disc, site unspecified, without myelopathy**
Discogenic syndrome NOS
Herniation of nucleus pulposus NOS
Intervertebral disc NOS:
   extrusion
   prolapse
   protrusion
   rupture
Neuritis or radiculitis due to displacement or rupture of intervertebral disc

● **722.3 Schmorl's nodes**

☐ **722.30 Unspecified region**

722.31 Thoracic region

722.32 Lumbar region

☐ **722.39 Other**

722.4 Degeneration of cervical intervertebral disc
Degeneration of cervicothoracic intervertebral disc

● **722.5 Degeneration of thoracic or lumbar intervertebral disc**

722.51 Thoracic or thoracolumbar intervertebral disc

722.52 Lumbar or lumbosacral intervertebral disc

☐ **722.6 Degeneration of intervertebral disc, site unspecified**
Degenerative disc disease NOS
Narrowing of intervertebral disc or space NOS

● **722.7 Intervertebral disc disorder with myelopathy**

☐ **722.70 Unspecified region**

722.71 Cervical region

◀▶ **New Code**   ⬅▮▮▮▮➡ **Revised Code**   ● **Not a Principal Diagnosis**   ● **Use Additional Digit(s)**   ☐ **Nonspecific Code**

722.72   **Thoracic region**

722.73   **Lumbar region**

● 722.8   **Postlaminectomy syndrome**

  ❑ 722.80   **Unspecified region**

  722.81   **Cervical region**

  722.82   **Thoracic region**

  722.83   **Lumbar region**

● 722.9   **Other and unspecified disc disorder**
    Calcification of intervertebral cartilage or disc Discitis

  ❑ 722.90   **Unspecified region**

  722.91   **Cervical region**

  722.92   **Thoracic region**

  722.93   **Lumbar region**

● 723   **Other disorders of cervical region**

   Excludes   *conditions due to:*
      intervertebral disc disorders (722.0–722.9)
      spondylosis (721.0–721.9)

723.0   **Spinal stenosis of cervical region**

723.1   **Cervicalgia**
    Pain in neck

723.2   **Cervicocranial syndrome**
    Barré-Liéou syndrome
    Posterior cervical sympathetic syndrome

723.3   **Cervicobrachial syndrome (diffuse)**

723.4   **Brachia neuritis or radiculitis NOS**
    Cervical radiculitis
    Radicular syndrome of upper limbs

❑ 723.5   **Torticollis, unspecified**
    Contracture of neck

   Excludes   *congenital (754.1)*
      due to birth injury (767.8)
      hysterical (300.11)
      psychogenic (306.0)
      spasmodic (333.83)
      traumatic, current (847.0)

723.6   **Panniculitis specified as affecting neck**

723.7   **Ossification of posterior longitudinal ligament in cervical region**

❑ 723.8   **Other syndromes affecting cervical region**
    Cervical syndrome NEC
    Klippel's disease

❑ 723.9   **Unspecified musculoskeletal disorders and symptoms referable to neck**
    Cervical (region) disorder NOS

● 724   **Other and unspecified disorders of back**

   Excludes   *collapsed vertebra (code to cause, e.g., osteoporosis, 733.00–733.09)*
      conditions due to:
       intervertebral disc disorders (722.0–722.9)
       spondylosis (721.0–721.9)

● 724.0   **Spinal stenosis, other than cervical**

  ❑ 724.00   **Spinal stenosis, unspecified region**

  724.01   **Thoracic region**

  724.02   **Lumbar region**

  ❑ 724.09   **Other**

724.1   **Pain in thoracic spine**

724.2   **Lumbago**
    Low back pain
    Low back syndrome
    Lumbalgia

724.3   **Sciatica**
    Neuralgia or neuritis of sciatic nerve

   Excludes   *specified lesion of sciatic nerve (355.0)*

❑ 724.4   **Thoracic or lumbosacral neuritis or radiculitis, unspecified**
    Radicular syndrome of lower limbs

❑ 724.5   **Backache, unspecified**
    Vertebrogenic (pain) syndrome NOS

724.6   **Disorders of sacrum**
    Ankylosis, lumbosacral or sacroiliac (joint)
    Instability, lumbosacral or sacroiliac (joint)

● 724.7   **Disorders of coccyx**

  ❑ 724.70   **Unspecified disorder of coccyx**

  724.71   **Hypermobility of coccyx**

  ❑ 724.79   **Other**
    Coccygodynia

❑ 724.8   **Other symptoms referable to back**
    Ossification of posterior longitudinal ligament NOS
    Panniculitis specified as sacral or affecting back

❑ 724.9   **Other unspecified back disorders**
    Ankylosis of spine NOS
    Compression of spinal nerve root NEC
    Spinal disorder NOS

   Excludes   *sacroiliitis (720.2)*

RHEUMATISM, EXCLUDING THE BACK (725–729)

Includes: disorders of muscles and tendons and their attachments, and of other soft tissues

Item 13-1 Polymyalgia rheumatica is a syndrome characterized by aching and morning stiffness and is related to aging and hereditary predisposition.

725   **Polymyalgia rheumatica**

● 726   **Peripheral enthesopathies and allied syndromes**

   Note: Enthesopathies are disorders of peripheral ligamentous or muscular attachments.

   Excludes   *spinal enthesopathy (720.1)*

726.0   **Adhesive capsulitis of shoulder**

● 726.1   **Rotator cuff syndrome of shoulder and allied disorders**

  ❑ 726.10   **Disorders of bursae and tendons in shoulder region, unspecified**
    Rotator cuff syndrome NOS
    Supraspinatus syndrome NOS

  726.11   **Calcifying tendinitis of shoulder**

  726.12   **Bicipital tenosynovitis**

  ❑ 726.19   **Other specified disorders**

   Excludes   *complete rupture of rotator cuff, nontraumatic (727.61)*

❑ 726.2   **Other affections of shoulder region, not elsewhere classified**
    Periarthritis of shoulder
    Scapulohumeral fibrositis

● 726.3   **Enthesopathy of elbow region**

  ❑ 726.30   **Enthesopathy of elbow, unspecified**

726.31 Medial epicondylitis

726.32 Lateral epicondylitis
Epicondylitis NOS   Tennis elbow
Golfers' elbow

726.33 Olecranon bursitis
Bursitis of elbow

❏ **726.39 Other**

726.4 Enthesopathy of wrist and carpus
Bursitis of hand or wrist
Periarthritis of wrist

726.5 Enthesopathy of hip region
Bursitis of hip
Gluteal tendinitis
Iliac crest spur
Psoas tendinitis
Trochanteric tendinitis

● **726.6 Enthesopathy of knee**

❏ **726.60 Enthesopathy of knee, unspecified**
Bursitis of knee NOS

726.61 Pes anserinus tendinitis or bursitis

726.62 Tibial collateral ligament bursitis
Pellegrini-Stieda syndrome

726.63 Fibular collateral ligament bursitis

726.64 Patellar tendinitis

726.65 Prepatellar bursitis

❏ **726.69 Other**
Bursitis:
infrapatellar
subpatellar

● **726.7 Enthesopathy of ankle and tarsus**

❏ **726.70 Enthesopathy of ankle and tarsus, unspecified**
Metatarsalgia NOS

Excludes   *Morton's metatarsalgia (355.6)*

726.71 Achilles bursitis or tendinitis

726.72 Tibialis tendinitis
Tibialis (anterior) (posterior) tendinitis

726.73 Calcaneal spur

❏ **726.79 Other**
Peroneal tendinitis

❏ **726.8 Other peripheral enthesopathies**

● **726.9 Unspecified enthesopathy**

❏ **726.90 Enthesopathy of unspecified site**
Capsulitis NOS
Periarthritis NOS
Tendinitis NOS

❏ **726.91 Exostosis of unspecified site**
Bone spur NOS

● **727 Other disorders of synovium, tendon, and bursa**

● **727.0 Synovitis and tenosynovitis**

❏ **727.00 Synovitis and tenosynovitis, unspecified**
Synovitis NOS
Tenosynovitis NOS

● **727.01 *Synovitis and tenosynovitis in diseases classified elsewhere***

Code first underlying disease, as:
tuberculosis (015.0–015.9)

Excludes   *crystal-induced (275.4)*
gonococcal (098.51)
gouty (274.0)
syphilitic (095.7)

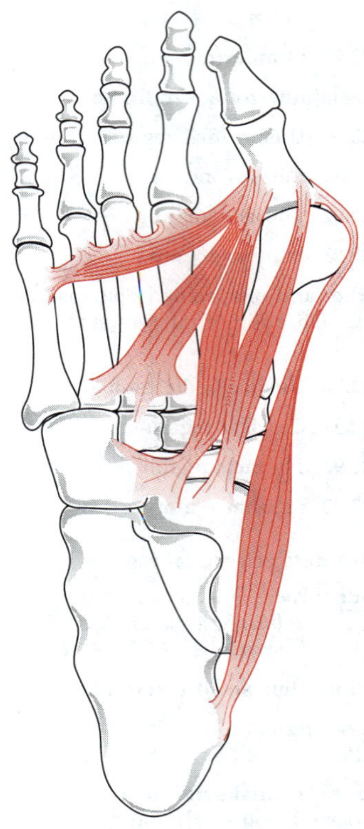

Figure 13–2   Hallux valgus or bunion.

Item 13-2   Hallux valgus, or bunion, is a bursa usually found along the medial aspect of the big toe. It is most often attributed to heredity or poorly fitted shoes.

727.02 Giant cell tumor of tendon sheath

727.03 Trigger finger (acquired)

727.04 Radial styloid tenosynovitis
de Quervain's disease

❏ **727.05 Other tenosynovitis of hand and wrist**

727.06 Tenosynovitis of foot and ankle

❏ **727.09 Other**

727.1 Bunion

❏ **727.2 Specific bursitides often of occupational origin**
Beat:
elbow
hand
knee
Chronic crepitant synovitis of wrist
Miners':
elbow
knee

❏ **727.3 Other bursitis**
Bursitis NOS

Excludes   *bursitis:*
gonococcal (098.52)
subacromial (726.19)
subcoracoid (726.19)
subdeltoid (726.19)
syphilitic (095.7)
"frozen shoulder" (726.0)

● **727.4 Ganglion and cyst of synovium, tendon, and bursa**

❏ **727.40 Synovial cyst, unspecified**

Excludes   *that of popliteal space (727.51)*

    ◀▶ **New Code**   ⬅▬⮞ **Revised Code**   ● **Not a Principal Diagnosis**   ● **Use Additional Digit(s)**   ❏ **Nonspecific Code**

727.41 Ganglion of joint

727.42 Ganglion of tendon sheath

☐ **727.43 Ganglion, unspecified**

☐ **727.49 Other**
Cyst of bursa

● **727.5 Rupture of synovium**

☐ **727.50 Rupture of synovium, unspecified**

727.51 Synovial cyst of popliteal space
Baker's cyst (knee)

☐ **727.59 Other**

● **727.6 Rupture of tendon, nontraumatic**

☐ **727.60 Nontraumatic rupture of unspecified tendon**

727.61 Complete rupture of rotator cuff

727.62 Tendons of biceps (long head)

727.63 Extensor tendons of hand and wrist

727.64 Flexor tendons of hand and wrist

727.65 Quadriceps tendon

727.66 Patellar tendon

727.67 Achilles tendon

☐ **727.68 Other tendons of foot and ankle**

☐ **727.69 Other**

● **727.8 Other disorders of synovium, tendon, and bursa**

727.81 Contracture of tendon (sheath)
Short Achilles tendon (acquired)

727.82 Calcium deposits in tendon and bursa
Calcification of tendon NOS
Calcific tendinitis NOS

| **Excludes** | peripheral ligamentous or muscular attachments (726.0–726.9) |

☐ **727.89 Other**
Abscess of bursa or tendon

| **Excludes** | xanthomatosis localized to tendons (272.7) |

☐ **727.9 Unspecified disorder of synovium, tendon, and bursa**

● **728 Disorders of muscle, ligament, and fascia**

| **Excludes** | enthesopathies (726.0–726.9)
muscular dystrophies (359.0–359.1)
myoneural disorders (358.0–358.9)
myopathies (359.2–359.9)
old disruption of ligaments of knee (717.81–717.89) |

728.0 Infective myositis
Myositis:
purulent
suppurative

| **Excludes** | myositis:
epidemic (074.1)
interstitial (728.81)
syphilitic (095.6)
tropical (040.81) |

● **728.1 Muscular calcification and ossification**

☐ **728.10 Calcification and ossification, unspecified**
Massive calcification (paraplegic)

728.11 Progressive myositis ossificans

728.12 Traumatic myositis ossificans
Myositis ossificans (circumscripta)

728.13 Postoperative heterotopic calcification

☐ **728.19 Other**
Polymyositis ossificans

728.2 Muscular wasting and disuse atrophy, not elsewhere classified
Amyotrophia NOS
Myofibrosis

| **Excludes** | neuralgic amyotrophy (353.5)
progressive muscular atrophy (335.0–335.9) |

☐ **728.3 Other specific muscle disorders**
Arthrogryposis
Immobility syndrome (paraplegic)

| **Excludes** | arthrogryposis multiplex congenita (754.89)
stiff-man syndrome (333.91) |

728.4 Laxity of ligament

728.5 Hypermobility syndrome

728.6 Contracture of palmar fascia
Dupuytren's contracture

● **728.7 Other fibromatoses**

728.71 Plantar fascial fibromatosis
Contracture of plantar fascia
Plantar fasciitis (traumatic)

☐ **728.79 Other**
Garrod's or knuckle pads
Nodular fasciitis
Pseudosarcomatous fibromatosis (proliferative) (subcutaneous)

● **728.8 Other disorders of muscle, ligament, and fascia**

728.81 Interstitial myositis

728.82 Foreign body granuloma of muscle
Talc granuloma of muscle

728.83 Rupture of muscle, nontraumatic

728.84 Diastasis of muscle
Diastasis recti (abdomen)

| **Excludes** | diastasis recti complicating pregnancy, labor, and delivery (665.8) |

728.85 Spasm of muscle

728.86 Necrotizing fasciitis

Use additional code to identify:
infectious organism (041.00–041.89)
gangrene (785.4), if applicable

☐ **728.89 Other**
Eosinophilic fasciitis

Use additional E code to identify drug, if drug induced

☐ **728.9 Unspecified disorder of muscle, ligament, and fascia**

● **729 Other disorders of soft tissues**

| **Excludes** | acroparesthesia (443.89)
carpal tunnel syndrome (354.0)
disorders of the back (720.0–724.9)
entrapment syndromes (354.0–355.9)
palindromic rheumatism (719.3)
periarthritis (726.0–726.9)
psychogenic rheumatism (306.0) |

☐ **729.0 Rheumatism, unspecified, and fibrositis**

☐ **729.1 Myalgia and myositis, unspecified**
Fibromyositis NOS

☐ **729.2 Neuralgia, neuritis, and radiculitis, unspecified**

| **Excludes** | brachia radiculitis (723.4)
cervical radiculitis (723.4)
lumbosacral radiculitis (724.4)
mononeuritis (354.0–355.9)
radiculitis due to intervertebral disc involvement (722.0–722.2,722.7)
sciatica (724.3) |

ICD-9-CM

700-799

Vol. 1

Item 13-3   Panniculitis is an inflammation of the adipose tissue of the heel pad.

- **729.3   Panniculitis, unspecified**
  - ☐ **729.30   Panniculitis, unspecified site**
    Weber-Christian disease
  - **729.31   Hypertrophy of fat pad, knee**
    Hypertrophy of infrapatellar fat pad
  - ☐ **729.39   Other site**
    | Excludes | *panniculitis specified as (affecting):*
    back (724.8)
    neck (723.6)
    sacral (724.8)

- ☐ **729.4   Fasciitis, unspecified**
  | Excludes | *necrotizing fasciitis (728.86)*
  nodular fasciitis (728.79)

729.5   Pain in limb

729.6   Residual foreign body in soft tissue
  | Excludes | *foreign body granuloma:*
  muscle (728.82)
  skin and subcutaneous tissue (709.4)

- **729.8   Other musculoskeletal symptoms referable to limbs**
  - **729.81   Swelling of limb**
  - **729.82   Cramp**
  - ☐ **729.89   Other**
    | Excludes | *abnormality of gait (781.2)*
    tetany (781.7)
    transient paralysis of limb (781.4)

- ☐ **729.9   Other and unspecified disorders of soft tissue**
  Polyalgia

Item 13-4   Osteomyelitis is an inflammation of the bone. **Acute osteomyelitis** is a rapidly destructive, pus-producing infection capable of causing severe bone destruction. **Chronic osteomyelitis** can remain long after the initial acute episode has passed and may lead to a recurrence of the acute phase. **Brodie's abscess** is an encapsulated focal abscess that must be surgically drained.

OSTEOPATHIES, CHONDROPATHIES, AND ACQUIRED MUSCULOSKELETAL DEFORMITIES (730–739)

- **730   Osteomyelitis, periostitis, and other infections involving bone**
  | Excludes | *jaw (526.4–526.5)*
  petrous bone (383.2)

  Use additional code to identify organism, such as Staphylococcus (041.1)

  The following fifth-digit subclassification is for use with category 730; valid digits are in [brackets] under each code. See list at beginning of chapter for definitions:
  - ☐ 0 site unspecified
  - 1 shoulder region
  - 2 upper arm
  - 3 forearm
  - 4 hand
  - 5 pelvic region and thigh
  - 6 lower leg
  - 7 ankle and foot
  - ☐ 8 other specified sites
  - ☐ 9 multiple sites

- **730.0   Acute osteomyelitis**
  [0–9]   Abscess of any bone except accessory sinus, jaw, or mastoid
  Acute or subacute osteomyelitis, with or without mention of periostitis

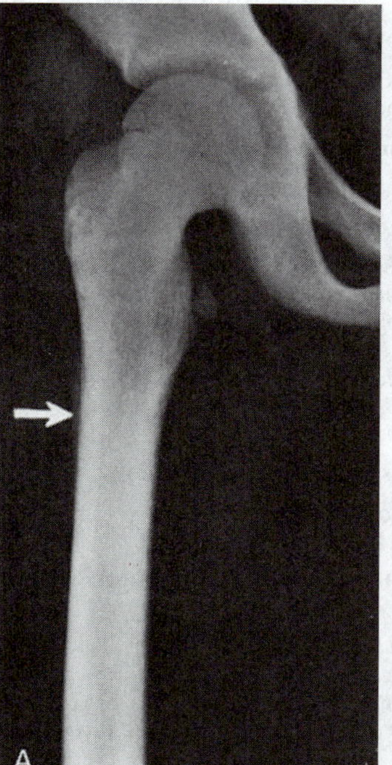
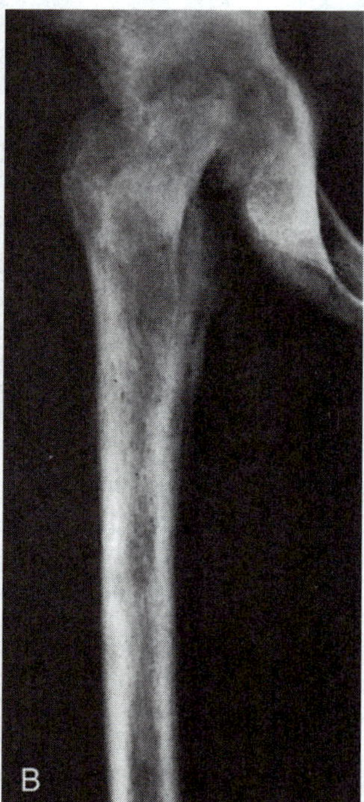

Figure 13-3   Suppurative osteomyelitis. The initial radiograph **(A)** shows only minimal periosteal reaction along the lateral aspect of the proximal femur *(arrow)*. Eight months after onset **(B)** there is gross destruction of the joint and the proximal femur. (From Aegerter E, Kirkpatrick J Jr: Orthopedic Diseases, 4th ed. Philadelphia, WB Saunders, 1975, p 257.)

    ◀▶ **New Code**   ◀▦ ▦▶ **Revised Code**   ● **Not a Principal Diagnosis**   ● **Use Additional Digit(s)**   ☐ **Nonspecific Code**

730.1 Chronic osteomyelitis
[0–9]   Brodie's abscess
Chronic or old osteomyelitis, with or without
mention of periostitis
Necrosis (acute) of bone
Sequestrum
Sclerosing osteomyelitis of Garré

Excludes *aseptic necrosis of bone (733.40–733.49)*

730.2 Unspecified osteomyelitis
[0–9]   Osteitis or osteomyelitis NOS, with or without
mention of periostitis

730.3 Periostitis without mention of osteomyelitis
[0–9]   Abscess of periosteum, without mention of osteomyelitis
Periostosis, without mention of osteomyelitis

Excludes *that in secondary syphilis (091.61)*

730.7 *Osteopathy resulting from poliomyelitis*
[0–9]   *Code first underlying disease (045.0–045.9)*

730.8 *Other infections involving bone in disease classified*
[0–9]   ***elsewhere***

Code first underlying disease, as:
tuberculosis (015.0–015.9)
typhoid fever (002.0)

Excludes *syphilitis of bone NOS (095.5)*

730.9 Unspecified infection of bone
[0–9]

**731 Osteitis deformans and osteopathies associated with
other disorders classified elsewhere**

731.0 Osteitis deformans without mention of bone tumor
Paget's disease of bone

731.1 *Osteitis deformans in diseases classified elsewhere*

Code first underlying disease, as:
malignant neoplasm of bone (170.0–170.9)

731.2 Hypertrophic pulmonary osteoarthropathy
Bamberger-Marie disease

**731.8 *Other bone involvement in diseases classified else-
where***

Code first underlying disease, as:
diabetes mellitus (250.8)

Use additional code to specify bone condition, such
as:
acute osteomyelitis (730.00–730.09)

732 Osteochondropathies

732.0 Juvenile osteochondrosis of spine
Juvenile osteochondrosis (of):
marginal or vertebral ephiphysis (of Scheuermann) spine NOS
Vertebral epiphysitis

Excludes *adolescent postural kyphosis (737.0)*

732.1 Juvenile osteochondrosis of hip and pelvis
Coxa plana
Ischiopubic synchondrosis (of van Neck)
Osteochondrosis (juvenile) of:
acetabulum
head of femur (of Legg-Calvé-Perthes)
iliac crest (of Buchanan)
symphysis pubis (of Pierson)
Pseudocoxalgia

732.2 Nontraumatic slipped upper femoral epiphysis
Slipped upper femoral epiphysis NOS

732.3 Juvenile osteochondrosis of upper extremity
Osteochondrosis (juvenile) of:
capitulum of humerus (of Panner)
carpal lunate (of Kienbock)
hand NOS
head of humerus (of Haas)
heads of metacarpals (of Mauclaire)
lower ulna (of Burns)
radial head (of Brailsford)
upper extremity NOS

**732.4 Juvenile osteochondrosis of lower extremity, ex-
cluding foot**
Osteochondrosis (juvenile) of:
lower extremity NOS
primary patellar center (of Köhler)
proximal tibia (of Blount)
secondary patellar center (of Sinding-Larsen)
tibial tubercle (of Osgood-Schlatter)
Tibia vara

732.5 Juvenile osteochondrosis of foot
Calcaneal apophysitis
Epiphysitis, os calcis
Osteochondrosis (juvenile) of:
astragalus (of Diaz)
calcaneum (of Sever)
foot NOS
metatarsal:
second (of Freiberg)
fifth (of Iselin)
os tibiale externum (of Haglund)
tarsal navicular (of Köhler)

732.6 Other juvenile osteochondrosis
Apophysitis specified as juvenile, of other site, or
site NOS
Epiphysitis specified as juvenile, of other site, or
site NOS
Osteochondritis specified as juvenile, of other site,
or site NOS
Osteochondrosis specified as juvenile, of other
site, or site NOS

732.7 Osteochondritis dissecans

732.8 Other specified forms of osteochondropathy
Adult osteochondrosis of spine

732.9 Unspecified osteochondropathy
Apophysitis
NOS
not specified as adult or juvenile, of unspecified
site
Epiphysitis
NOS
not specified as adult or juvenile, of unspecified
site
Osteochondritis
NOS
not specified as adult or juvenile, of unspecified
site
Osteochondrosis
NOS
not specified as adult or juvenile, of unspecified
site

733 Other disorders of bone and cartilage

Excludes *bone spur (726.91)*
*cartilage of, or loose body in, joint (717.0–717.9,
718.0–718.9)*
giant cell granuloma of jaw (526.3)
osteitis fibrosa cystica generalisata (252.0)
osteomalacia (268.2)
polyostotic fibrous dysplasia of bone (756.54)
prognathism, retrognathism (524.1)
xanthomatosis localized to bone (272.7)

ICD-9-CM

**700-
799**

Vol. 1

● **733.0 Osteoporosis**

❑ **733.00 Osteoporosis, unspecified**
Wedging of vertebra NOS

733.01 Senile osteoporosis
Postmenopausal osteoporosis

733.02 Idiopathic osteoporosis

733.03 Disuse osteoporosis

❑ **733.09 Other**
Drug-induced osteoporosis
Use additional E code to identify drug

● **733.1 Pathologic fracture**
Spontaneous fracture

| Excludes | traumatic fractures (800–829) |

❑ **733.10 Pathologic fracture, unspecified site**

733.11 Pathologic fracture of humerus

733.12 Pathologic fracture of distal radius and ulna
Wrist NOS

733.13 Pathologic fracture of vertebrae
Collapse of vertebra NOS

733.14 Pathologic fracture of neck of femur
Femur NOS
Hip NOS

❑ **733.15 Pathologic fracture of other specified part of femur**

733.16 Pathologic fracture of tibia and fibula
Ankle NOS

❑ **733.19 Pathologic fracture of other specified site**

● **733.2 Cyst of bone**

❑ **733.20 Cyst of bone (localized), unspecified**

733.21 Solitary bone cyst
Unicameral bone cyst

733.22 Aneurysmal bone cyst

❑ **733.29 Other**
Fibrous dysplasia (monostotic)

| Excludes | cyst of jaw (526.0–526.2, 526.89)
osteitis fibrosa cystica (252.0)
polyostotic fibrous dysplasia of bone (756.54) |

733.3 Hyperostosis of skull
Hyperostosis interna frontalis
Leontiasis ossium

● **733.4 Aseptic necrosis of bone**

| Excludes | necrosis of bone NOS (730.1)
osteochondropathies (732.0–732.9) |

❑ **733.40 Aseptic necrosis of bone, site unspecified**

733.41 Head of humerus

733.42 Head and neck of femur
Femur NOS

| Excludes | Legg-Calvé-Perthes disease (732.1) |

733.43 Medial femoral condyle

733.44 Talus

❑ **733.49 Other**

733.5 Osteitis condensans
Piriform sclerosis of ilium

733.6 Tietze's disease
Costochondral junction syndrome
Costochondritis

733.7 Algoneurodystrophy
Disuse atrophy of bone
Sudeck's atrophy

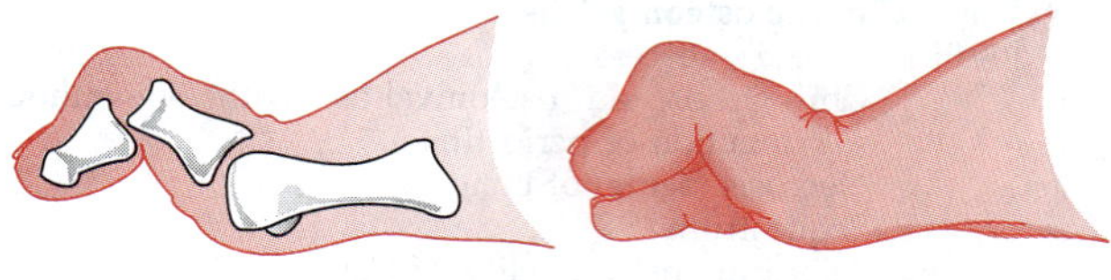

Figure 13–4 Claw toe.

Item 13–5 Claw toe is caused by a contraction of the flexor tendon producing a flexion deformity characterized by hyperextension of the big toe.

● **733.8 Malunion and nonunion of fracture**

733.81 Malunion of fracture

733.82 Nonunion of fracture
Pseudoarthrosis (bone)

● **733.9 Other and unspecified disorders of bone and cartilage**

❑ **733.90 Disorder of bone and cartilage, unspecified**

733.91 Arrest of bone development or growth
Epiphyseal arrest

733.92 Chondromalacia
Chondromalacia:
NOS
localized, except patella
systemic
tibial plateau

| Excludes | chondromalacia of patella (717.7) |

❑ **733.99 Other**
Diaphysitis
Hypertrophy of bone
Relapsing polychondritis

734 Flat foot
Pes planus (acquired)
Talipes planus (acquired)

| Excludes | congenital (754.61)
rigid flat foot (754.61)
spastic (everted) flat foot (754.61) |

● **735 Acquired deformities of toe**

| Excludes | congenital (754.60–754.69, 755.65–755.66) |

735.0 Hallux valgus (acquired)

735.1 Hallux varus (acquired)

735.2 Hallux rigidus

735.3 Hallux malleus

❑ **735.4 Other hammer toe (acquired)**

735.5 Claw toe (acquired)

❑ **735.8 Other acquired deformities of toe**

❑ **735.9 Unspecified acquired deformity of toe**

● **736 Other acquired deformities of limbs**

| Excludes | congenital (754.3–755.9) |

● **736.0 Acquired deformities of forearm, excluding fingers**

❑ **736.00 Unspecified deformity**
Deformity of elbow, forearm, hand, or wrist (acquired) NOS

736.01 Cubitus valgus (acquired)

736.02 Cubitus varus (acquired)

736.03 Valgus deformity of wrist (acquired)

736.04 Varus deformity of wrist (acquired)

   ◀▶ **New Code**   ⬅➡ **Revised Code**   ● **Not a Principal Diagnosis**   ● **Use Additional Digit(s)**   ❑ **Nonspecific Code**

736.05   **Wrist drop (acquired)**

736.06   **Claw hand (acquired)**

736.07   **Club hand (acquired)**

☐736.09   **Other**

736.1   **Mallet finger**

● 736.2   **Other acquired deformities of finger**

☐736.20   **Unspecified deformity**
Deformity of finger (acquired) NOS

736.21   **Boutonniere deformity**

736.22   **Swan-neck deformity**

☐736.29   **Other**

| **Excludes** | *trigger finger (727.03)* |

● 736.3   **Acquired deformities of hip**

☐736.30   **Unspecified deformity**
Deformity of hip (acquired) NOS

736.31   **Coxa valga (acquired)**

736.32   **Coxa vara (acquired)**

☐736.39   **Other**

● 736.4   **Genu valgum or varum (acquired)**

736.41   **Genu valgum (acquired)**

736.42   **Genu varum (acquired)**

736.5   **Genu recurvatum (acquired)**

☐736.6   **Other acquired deformities of knee**
Deformity of knee (acquired) NOS

● 736.7   **Other acquired deformities of ankle and foot**

| **Excludes** | *deformities of toe (acquired) (735.0–735.9)* |
| | *pes planus (acquired) (734)* |

☐736.70   **Unspecified deformity of ankle and foot, acquired**

736.71   **Acquired equinovarus deformity**
Clubfoot, acquired

| **Excludes** | *clubfoot not specified as acquired (754.5–754.7)* |

736.72   **Equinus deformity of foot, acquired**

736.73   **Cavus deformity of foot**

| **Excludes** | *that with claw foot (736.74)* |

Item 13-6   Equinus foot is a term referring to the hoof of a horse. The deformity is usually congenital or spastic.

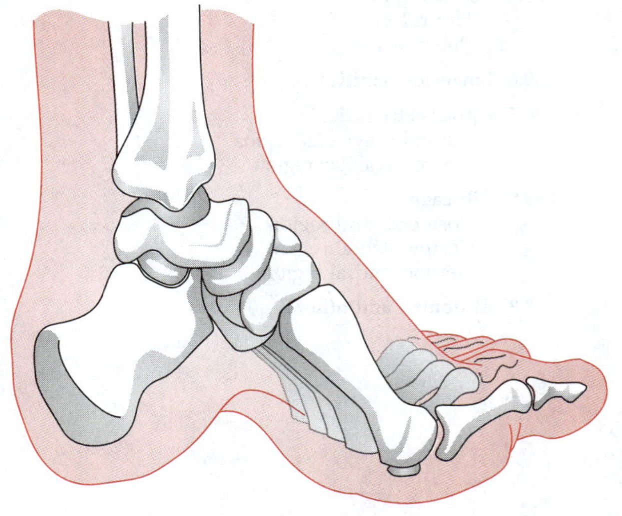

Figure 13-5   Pes cavovarus, meaning "foot with high arch."

736.74   **Claw foot, acquired**

736.75   **Cavovarus deformity of foot, acquired**

☐736.76   **Other calcaneus deformity**

☐736.79   **Other**
Acquired:
pes not elsewhere classified
talipes not elsewhere classified

● 736.8   **Acquired deformities of other parts of limbs**

736.81   **Unequal leg length (acquired)**

☐736.89   **Other**
Deformity (acquired):
arm or leg, not elsewhere classified
shoulder

☐736.9   **Acquired deformity of limb, site unspecified**

Item 13-7   Kyphosis is an abnormal curvature of the spine. Senile kyphosis is a result of disc degeneration causing ossification (turning to bone). Adolescent or juvenile kyphosis is also known as Scheuermann's disease, a condition in which the discs of the lower thoracic spine herniate, causing the disc space to narrow and the spine to tilt forward. This condition is attributed to poor posture.

Item 13-8   Spondylolisthesis is a condition caused by the slipping forward of one disc over another.

● 737   **Curvature of spine**

| **Excludes** | *congenital (754.2)* |

737.0   **Adolescent postural kyphosis**

| **Excludes** | *osteochondrosis of spine (juvenile) (732.0)* |
| | *adult (732.8)* |

☐737.1   **Kyphosis (acquired)**

737.10   **Kyphosis (acquired) (postural)**

737.11   **Kyphosis due to radiation**

737.12   **Kyphosis, postlaminectomy**

☐737.19   **Other**

| **Excludes** | *that associated with conditions classifiable elsewhere (737.41)* |

● 737.2   **Lordosis (acquired)**

737.20   **Lordosis (acquired) (postural)**

737.21   **Lordosis, postlaminectomy**

737.22   **Other postsurgical lordosis**

☐737.29   **Other**

| **Excludes** | *that associated with conditions classifiable elsewhere (737.42)* |

● 737.3   **Kyphoscoliosis and scoliosis**

737.30   **Scoliosis [and kyphoscoliosis], idiopathic**

737.31   **Resolving infantile idiopathic scoliosis**

737.32   **Progressive infantile idiopathic scoliosis**

737.33   **Scoliosis due to radiation**

737.34   **Thoracogenic scoliosis**

☐737.39   **Other**

| **Excludes** | *that associated with conditions classifiable elsewhere (737.43)* |
| | *that in kyphoscoliotic heart disease (416.1)* |

ICD-9-CM

700-799

Vol. 1

◄ ►   **New Code**   ◄▦▦►   **Revised Code**   ●   **Not a Principal Diagnosis**   ●   **Use Additional Digit(s)**   ☐   **Nonspecific Code**

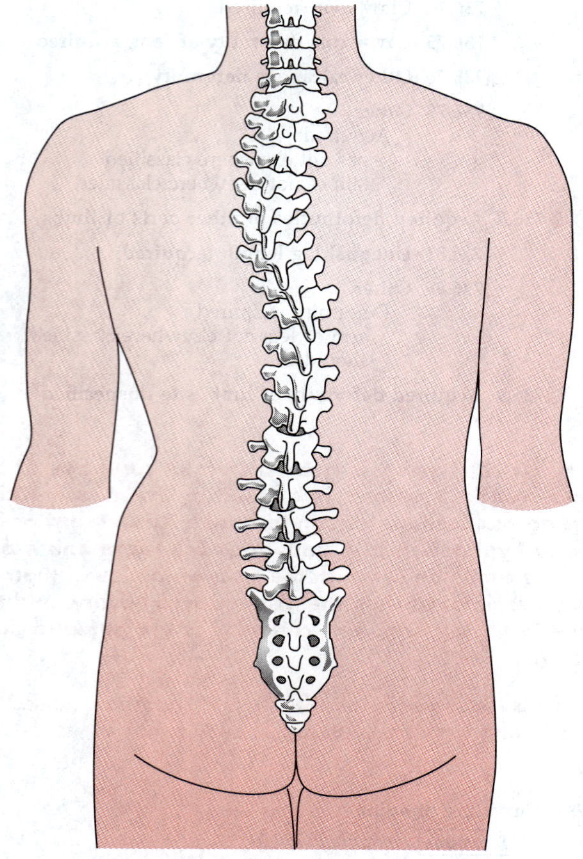

Figure 13–6 Scoliosis is a lateral curvature of the spine.

● **737.4 *Curvature of spine associated with other conditions***

> *Code first associated condition, as:*
> Charcot-Marie-Tooth disease (356.1)
> mucopolysaccharidosis (277.5)
> neurofibromatosis (237.7)
> osteitis deformans (731.0)
> osteitis fibrosa cystica (252.0)
> osteoporosis (733.00–733.09)
> poliomyelitis (138)
> tuberculosis [Pott's curvature] (015.0)

   ●❑ **737.40 *Curvature of spine, unspecified***

   ● **737.41 *Kyphosis***

   ● **737.42 *Lordosis***

   ● **737.43 *Scoliosis***

❑ **737.8 Other curvatures of spine**

❑ **737.9 Unspecified curvature of spine**
Curvature of spine (acquired) (idiopathic) NOS
Hunchback, acquired

> **Excludes** *deformity of spine NOS (738.5)*

● **738 Other acquired deformity**

> **Excludes** *congenital (754.0–756.9, 758.0–759.9)*
> *dentofacial anomalies (524.0–524.9)*

738.0 Acquired deformity of nose
Deformity of nose (acquired)
Overdevelopment of nasal bones

> **Excludes** *deflected or deviated nasal septum (470)*

● **738.1 Other acquired deformity of head**

   ❑ **738.10 Unspecified deformity**

   738.11 Zygomatic hyperplasia

   738.12 Zygomatic hypoplasia

   ❑ **738.19 Other specified deformity**

738.2 Acquired deformity of neck

738.3 Acquired deformity of chest and rib
Deformity:
   chest (acquired)
   rib (acquired)
Pectus:
   carinatum, acquired
   excavatum, acquired

738.4 Acquired spondylolisthesis
Degenerative spondylolisthesis
Spondylolysis, acquired

> **Excludes** *congenital (756.12)*

❑ **738.5 Other acquired deformity of back or spine**
Deformity of spine NOS

> **Excludes** *curvature of spine (737.0–737.9)*

738.6 Acquired deformity of pelvis
Pelvic obliquity

> **Excludes** *intrapelvic protrusion of acetabulum (718.6)*
> *that in relation to labor and delivery (653.0–*
> *653.4, 653.8–653.9)*

738.7 Cauliflower ear

❑ **738.8 Acquired deformity of other specified site**
Deformity of clavicle

❑ **738.9 Acquired deformity of unspecified site**

● **739 Nonallopathic lesions, not elsewhere classified**

> **Includes:** segmental dysfunction
> somatic dysfunction

739.0 Head region
Occipitocervical region

739.1 Cervical region
Cervicothoracic region

739.2 Thoracic region
Thoracolumbar region

739.3 Lumbar region
Lumbosacral region

739.4 Sacral region
Sacrococcygeal region
Sacroiliac region

739.5 Pelvic region
Hip region
Pubic region

739.6 Lower extremities

739.7 Upper extremities
Acromioclavicular region
Sternoclavicular region

739.8 Rib cage
Costochondral region
Costovertebral region
Sternochondral region

739.9 Abdomen and other

    ◀▶ **New Code**   ⬅▪▪▪▶ **Revised Code**   ● **Not a Principal Diagnosis**   ● **Use Additional Digit(s)**   ❑ **Nonspecific Code**

14. CONGENITAL ANOMALIES (740–759)

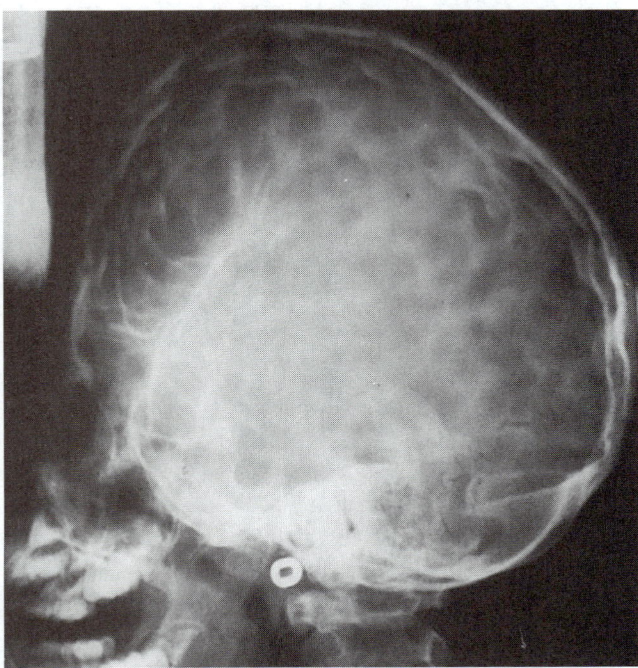

Figure 14–1 Generalized craniosynostosis in a 4-year-old girl without symptoms or signs of increased intracranial pressure. The child was referred for medical evaluation because of abnormal facial characteristics, features similar to those of her mother and aunt. Her fronto-occipital head circumference was found to be 47 cm. (From Bell WE, McCormick WF: Increased Intracranial Pressure in Children, 2nd ed. Philadelphia, WB Saunders, 1978, p 116.)

Item 14–1 Anencephalus is a congenital deformity of the cranial vault. Craniosynostosis, also known as craniostenosis and stenocephaly, signifies any form of congenital deformity of the skull that results from the premature closing of the sutures of the skull. Iniencephaly is a deformity in which the head and neck are flexed backward to a great extent and the head is very large in comparison to the shortened body.

● **740 Anencephalus and similar anomalies**

    740.0 Anencephalus
        Acrania
        Amyelencephalus
        Hemianencephaly
        Hemicephaly

    740.1 Craniorachischisis

    740.2 Iniencephaly

Item 14–2 Spina bifida is a midline spinal defect in which one or more vertebrae fail to fuse, leaving an opening in the vertebral canal. When the defect is not visible, it is called spina bifida occulta, and when it is visible, it is called spina bifida cystica.

● **741 Spina bifida**

    Excludes *spina bifida occulta (756.17)*

    The following fifth-digit subclassification is for use with category 741:
    ☐ **0 unspecified region**
      1 cervical region
      2 dorsal (thoracic) region
      3 lumbar region

● **741.0 With hydrocephalus**
    Arnold-Chiari syndrome, type II
    Chiari malformation, type II
    Any condition classifiable to 741.9 with any condition classifiable to 742.3

● **741.9 Without mention of hydrocephalus**
    Hydromeningocele (spinal)
    Hydromyelocele
    Meningocele (spinal)
    Meningomyelocele
    Myelocele
    Myelocystocele
    Rachischisis
    Spina bifida (aperta)
    Syringomyelocele

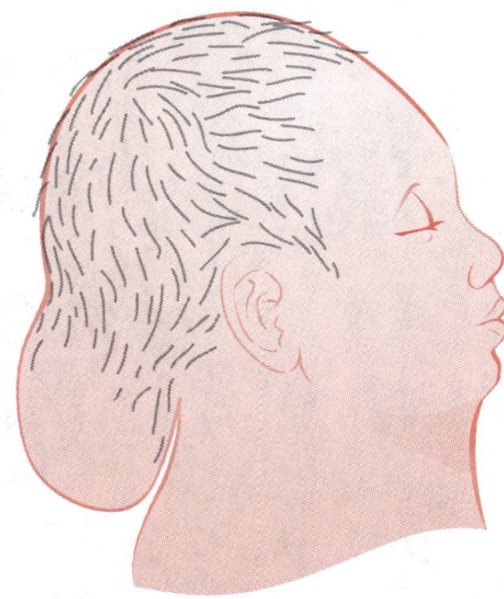

Figure 14–2 Encephalocele is a protrusion of the brain through an opening in the skull.

● **742 Other congenital anomalies of nervous system**

    742.0 Encephalocele
        Encephalocystocele
        Encephalomyelocele
        Hydroencephalocele
        Hydromeningocele, cranial
        Meningocele, cerebral
        Meningoencephalocele

    742.1 Microcephalus
        Hydromicrocephaly
        Micrencephaly

    742.2 Reduction deformities of brain
        Absence of part of brain
        Agenesis of part of brain
        Agyria
        Aplasia of part of brain
        Arhinencephaly
        Holoprosencephaly
        Hypoplasia of part of brain
        Microgyria

ICD-9-CM

700-799

Vol. 1

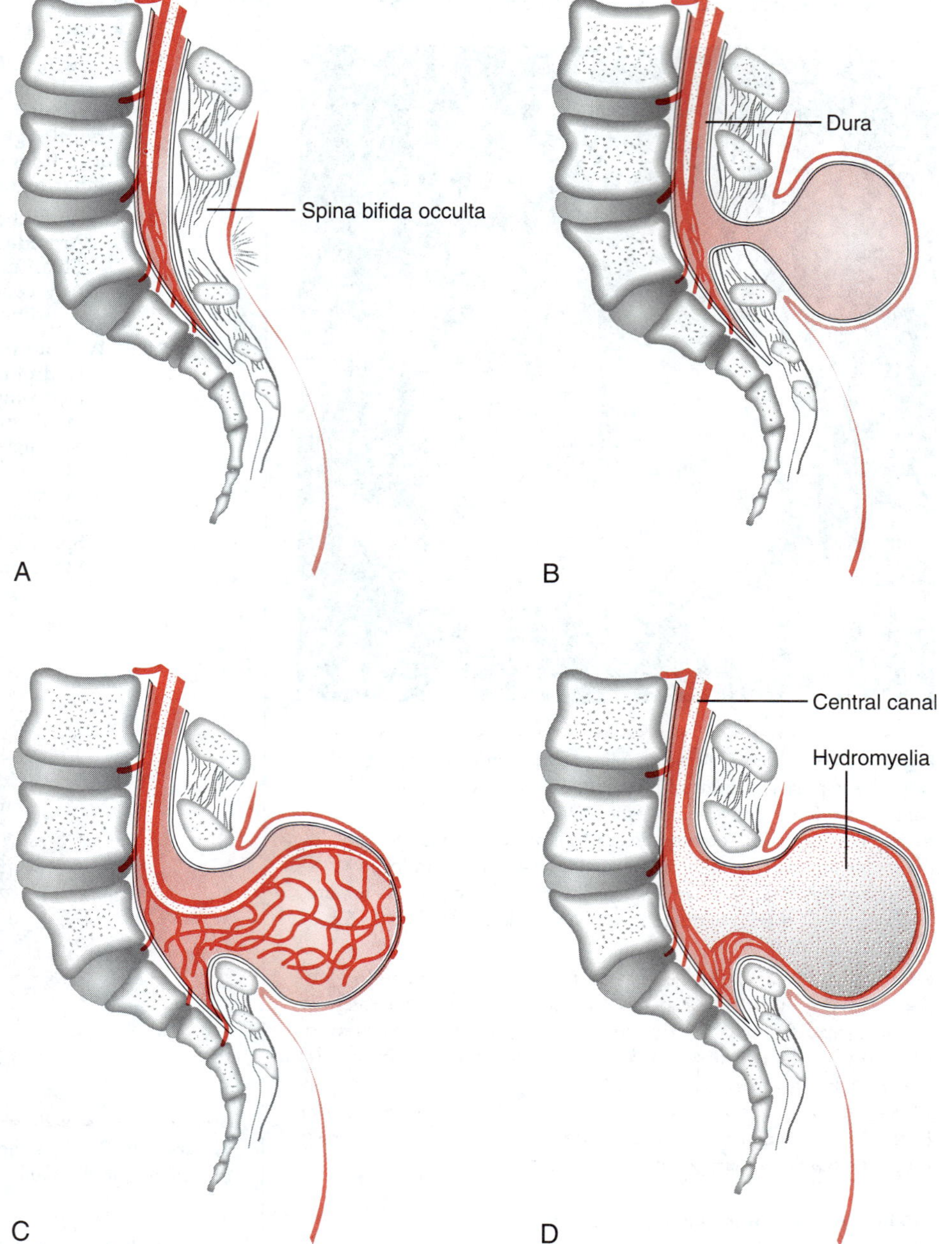

Figure 14–3 **A.** Spina bifida occulta. **B.** Meningocele. **C.** Myelomeningocele. **D.** Myelocystocele (syringomyelocele) or hydromyelia

742.3 Congenital hydrocephalus
    Aqueduct of Sylvius:
      anomaly
      obstruction, congenital
      stenosis
    Atresia of foramina of Magendie and Luschka
    Hydrocephalus in newborn

> **Excludes** *hydrocephalus:*
>   *acquired (331.3–331.4)*
>   *due to congenital toxoplasmosis (771.2)*
>   *with any condition classifiable to 741.9 (741.0)*

☐ 742.4 Other specified anomalies of brain
    Congenital cerebral cyst
    Macroencephaly
    Macrogyria
    Megalencephaly
    Multiple anomalies of brain NOS
    Porencephaly
    Ulegyria

● 742.5 Other specified anomalies of spinal cord

742.51 Diastematomyelia

742.53 Hydromyelia
    Hydrorhachis

☐ 742.59 Other
    Amyelia
    Atelomyelia
    Congenital anomaly of spinal meninges
    Defective development of cauda equina
    Hypoplasia of spinal cord
    Myelatelia
    Myelodysplasia

    ◄► **New Code**   ◄▌▌▌▌▶ **Revised Code**   ● **Not a Principal Diagnosis**   ● **Use Additional Digit(s)**   ☐ **Nonspecific Code**

❏**742.8 Other specified anomalies of nervous system**
Agenesis of nerve
Displacement of brachial plexus
Familial dysautonomia
Jaw-winking syndrome
Marcus-Gunn syndrome
Riley-Day syndrome

Excludes *neurofibromatosis (237.7)*

❏**742.9 Unspecified anomaly of brain, spinal cord, and nervous system**
Anomaly of brain, nervous system, and spinal cord
Congenital, of brain, nervous system, and spinal cord:
disease of brain, nervous system, and spinal cord
lesion of brain, nervous system, and spinal cord
Deformity of brain, nervous system, and spinal cord

Item 14–3 Anophthalmia is the absence of the eye and the optic pit. Microphthalmia is the partial absence of the eye and optic pit.

●**743 Congenital anomalies of eye**

●**743.0 Anophthalmos**

❏**743.00 Clinical anophthalmos, unspecified**
Agenesis
Congenital absence of eye
Anophthalmos NOS

743.03 Cystic eyeball, congenital

743.06 Cryptophthalmos

●**743.1 Microphthalmos**
Dysplasia of eye
Hypoplasia of eye
Rudimentary eye

❏**743.10 Microphthalmos, unspecified**

743.11 Simple microphthalmos

❏**743.12 Microphthalmos associated with other anomalies of eye and adnexa**

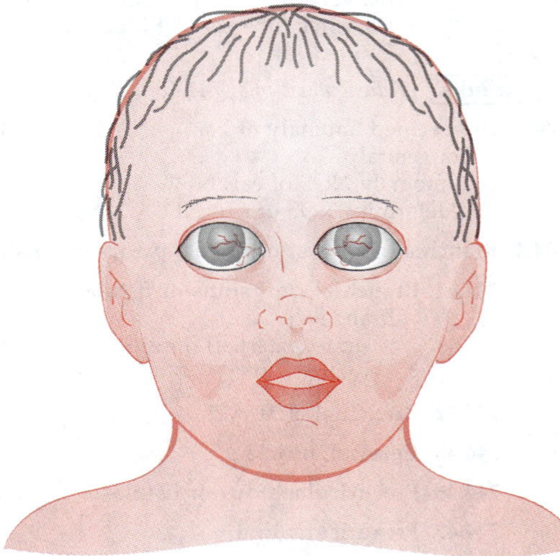

Figure 14–4 Bilateral congenital hydrophthalmia, in which the eyes are very large in comparison to the other facial features.

●**743.2 Buphthalmos**
Glaucoma:
congenital
newborn
Hydrophthalmos

Excludes *glaucoma of childhood (365.14)*
traumatic glaucoma due to birth injury (767.8)

❏**743.20 Buphthalmos, unspecified**

743.21 Simple buphthalmos

❏**743.22 Buphthalmos associated with other ocular anomalies**
Keratoglobus, congenital, associated with buphthalmos
Megalocornea associated with buphthalmos

●**743.3 Congenital cataract and lens anomalies**

Excludes *infantile cataract (366.00–366.09)*

❏**743.30 Congenital cataract, unspecified**

743.31 Capsular and subcapsular cataract

743.32 Cortical and zonular cataract

743.33 Nuclear cataract

743.34 Total and subtotal cataract, congenital

743.35 Congenital aphakia
Congenital absence of lens

743.36 Anomalies of lens shape
Microphakia
Spherophakia

743.37 Congenital ectopic lens

❏**743.39 Other**

●**743.4 Coloboma and other anomalies of anterior segment**

743.41 Anomalies of corneal size and shape
Microcornea

Excludes *that associated with buphthalmos (743.22)*

743.42 Corneal opacities, interfering with vision, congenital

❏**743.43 Other corneal opacities, congenital**

❏**743.44 Specified anomalies of anterior chamber, chamber angle, and related structures**
Anomaly:
Axenfeld's
Peters'
Rieger's

743.45 Aniridia

❏**743.46 Other specified anomalies of iris and ciliary body**
Anisocoria, congenital
Atresia of pupil
Coloboma of iris
Corectopia

❏**743.47 Specified anomalies of sclera**

❏**743.48 Multiple and combined anomalies of anterior segment**

❏**743.49 Other**

●**743.5 Congenital anomalies of posterior segment**

743.51 Vitreous anomalies
Congenital vitreous opacity

743.52 Fundus coloboma

743.53 Chorioretinal degeneration, congenital

743.54 Congenital folds and cysts of posterior segment

ICD-9-CM

700–799

Vol. 1

◀▶ **New Code**   ⬅▦ ▦➡ **Revised Code**   ● **Not a Principal Diagnosis**   ● **Use Additional Digit(s)**   ❏ **Nonspecific Code**   769

743.55 Congenital macular changes

☐ **743.56 Other retinal changes, congenital**

743.57 Specified anomalies of optic disc
Coloboma of optic disc (congenital)

743.58 Vascular anomalies
Congenital retinal aneurysm

☐ **743.59 Other**

● **743.6 Congenital anomalies of eyelids, lacrimal system, and orbit**

743.61 Congenital ptosis

743.62 Congenital deformities of eyelids
Ablepharon
Absence of eyelid
Accessory eyelid
Congenital:
ectropion
entropion

☐ **743.63 Other specified congenital anomalies of eyelid**
Absence, agenesis, of cilia

☐ **743.64 Specified congenital anomalies of lacrimal gland**

☐ **743.65 Specified congenital anomalies of lacrimal passages**
Absence, agenesis, of:
lacrimal apparatus
punctum lacrimale
Accessory lacrimal canal

☐ **743.66 Specified congenital anomalies of orbit**

☐ **743.69 Other**
Accessory eye muscles

☐ **743.8 Other specified anomalies of eye**

> **Excludes** *congenital nystagmus (379.51)*
> *ocular albinism (270.2)*
> *retinitis pigmentosa (362.74)*

☐ **743.9 Unspecified anomaly of eye**
Congenital:
anomaly NOS of eye [any part]
deformity NOS of eye [any part]

● **744 Congenital anomalies of ear, face, and neck**

> **Excludes** *anomaly of:*
> *cervical spine (754.2, 756.10–756.19)*
> *larynx (748.2–748.3)*
> *nose (748.0–748.1)*
> *parathyroid gland (759.2)*
> *thyroid gland (759.2)*
> *cleft lip (749.10–749.25)*

☐ **744.0 Anomalies of ear causing impairment of hearing**

> **Excludes** *congenital deafness without mention of cause (380.0–389.9)*

☐ **744.00 Unspecified anomaly of ear with impairment of hearing**

744.01 Absence of external ear
Absence of:
auditory canal (external)
auricle (ear) (with stenosis or atresia of auditory canal)

☐ **744.02 Other anomalies of external ear with impairment of hearing**
Atresia or stricture of auditory canal (external)

744.03 Anomaly of middle ear, except ossicles
Atresia or stricture of osseous meatus (ear)

744.04 Anomalies of ear ossicles
Fusion of ear ossicles

744.05 Anomalies of inner ear
Congenital anomaly of:
membranous labyrinth
organ of Corti

☐ **744.09 Other**
Absence of ear, congenital

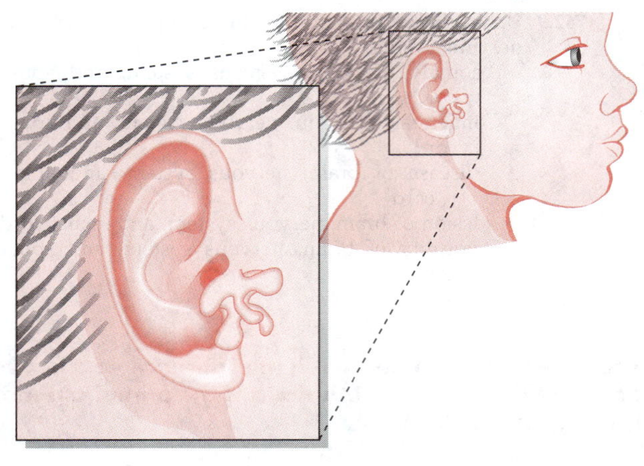

Figure 14–5   Multiple auricular appendage.

744.1 Accessory auricle
Accessory tragus
Polyotia
Preauricular appendage
Supernumerary:
ear
lobule

● **744.2 Other specified anomalies of ear**

> **Excludes** *that with impairment of hearing (744.00–744.09)*

744.21 Absence of ear lobe, congenital

744.22 Macrotia

744.23 Microtia

☐ **744.24 Specified anomalies of Eustachian tube**
Absence of Eustachian tube

☐ **744.29 Other**
Bat ear   Prominence of auricle
Darwin's tubercle   Ridge ear
Pointed ear

> **Excludes** *preauricular sinus (744.46)*

☐ **744.3 Unspecified anomaly of ear**
Congenital:
anomaly NOS of ear, NEC
deformity NOS of ear, NEC

● **744.4 Branchial cleft cyst or fistula; preauricular sinus**

744.41 Branchial cleft sinus or fistula
Branchial:
sinus (external) (internal)
vestige

744.42 Branchial cleft cyst

744.43 Cervical auricle

744.46 Preauricular sinus or fistula

744.47 Preauricular cyst

☐ **744.49 Other**
Fistula (of):
auricle, congenital
cervicoaural

   ◀▶ **New Code**   ⬅▮▮▮ ▮▮▮➡ **Revised Code**   ● **Not a Principal Diagnosis**   ● **Use Additional Digit(s)**   ☐ **Nonspecific Code**

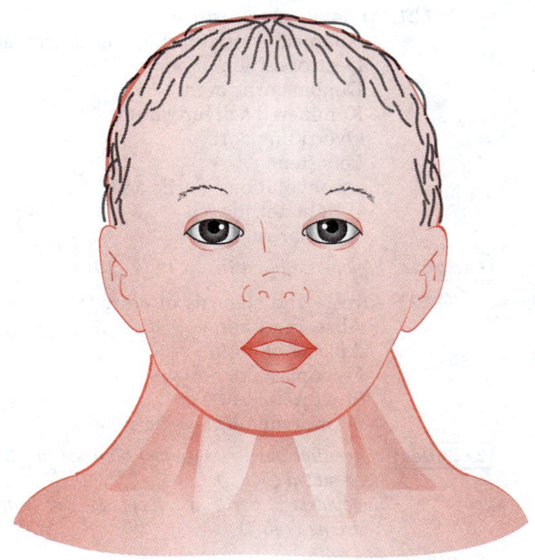

Figure 14-6 Webbing of the neck.

744.5 Webbing of neck
Pterygium colli

● **744.8 Other specified anomalies of face and neck**

744.81 Macrocheilia
Hypertrophy of lip, congenital

744.82 Microcheilia

744.83 Macrostomia

744.84 Microstomia

☐ **744.89 Other**

Excludes *congenital fistula of lip (750.25)*
musculoskeletal anomalies (754.0–754.1, 756.0)

☐ **744.9 Unspecified anomalies of face and neck**
Congenital:
anomaly NOS of face [any part] or neck [any part]
deformity NOS of face [any part] or neck [any part]

● **745 Bulbus cordis anomalies and anomalies of cardiac septal closure**

745.0 Common truncus
Absent septum between aorta and pulmonary artery
Communication (abnormal) between aorta and pulmonary artery
Aortic septal defect
Common aortopulmonary trunk
Persistent truncus arteriosus

● **745.1 Transposition of great vessels**

745.10 Complete transposition of great vessels
Transposition of great vessels:
NOS
classical

745.11 Double outlet right ventricle
Dextrotransposition of aorta
Incomplete transposition of great vessels
Origin of both great vessels from right ventricle
Taussig-Bing syndrome or defect

745.12 Corrected transposition of great vessels

☐ **745.19 Other**

745.2 Tetralogy of Fallot
Fallot's pentalogy
Ventricular septal defect with pulmonary stenosis or atresia, dextroposition of aorta, and hypertrophy of right ventricle

Excludes *Fallot's triad (746.09)*

745.3 Common ventricle
Cor triloculare biatriatum
Single ventricle

745.4 Ventricular septal defect
Eisenmenger's defect or complex
Gerbode defect
Interventricular septal defect
Left ventricular-right atrial communication
Roger's disease

Excludes *common atrioventricular canal type (745.69)*
single ventricle (745.3)

745.5 Ostium secundum type atrial septal defect
Defect:
atrium secundum
fossa ovalis
Lutembacher's syndrome
Patent or persistent:
foramen ovale
ostium secundum

● **745.6 Endocardial cushion defects**

☐ **745.60 Endocardial cushion defect, unspecified type**

745.61 Ostium primum defect
Persistent ostium primum

☐ **745.69 Other**
Absence of atrial septum
Atrioventricular canal type ventricular septal defect
Common atrioventricular canal
Common atrium

745.7 Cor biloculare
Absence of atrial and ventricular septa

☐ **745.8 Other**

☐ **745.9 Unspecified defect of septal closure**
Septal defect NOS

● **746 Other congenital anomalies of heart**

Excludes *endocardial fibroelastosis (425.3)*

● **746.0 Anomalies of pulmonary valve**

Excludes *infundibular or subvalvular pulmonic stenosis (746.83)*
tetralogy of Fallot (745.2)

☐ **746.00 Pulmonary valve anomaly, unspecified**

746.01 Atresia, congenital
Congenital absence of pulmonary valve

746.02 Stenosis, congenital

☐ **746.09 Other**
Congenital insufficiency of pulmonary valve
Fallot's triad or trilogy

746.1 Tricuspid atresia and stenosis, congenital
Absence of tricuspid valve

746.2 Ebstein's anomaly

746.3 Congenital stenosis of aortic valve
Congenital aortic stenosis

Excludes *congenital:*
subaortic stenosis (746.81)
supravalvular aortic stenosis (747.22)

ICD-9-CM

700-799

Vol. 1

746.4　Congenital insufficiency of aortic valve
　　Bicuspid aortic valve
　　Congenital aortic insufficiency

746.5　Congenital mitral stenosis
　　Fused commissure of mitral valve
　　Parachute deformity of mitral valve
　　Supernumerary cusps of mitral valve

746.6　Congenital mitral insufficiency

746.7　Hypoplastic left heart syndrome
　　Atresia, or marked hypoplasia, of aortic orifice or valve, with hypoplasia of ascending aorta and defective development of left ventricle (with mitral valve atresia)

● **746.8　Other specified anomalies of heart**

746.81　Subaortic stenosis

746.82　Cor triatriatum

746.83　Infundibular pulmonic stenosis
　　Subvalvular pulmonic stenosis

746.84　Obstructive anomalies of heart, NEC
　　Uhl's disease

746.85　Coronary artery anomaly
　　Anomalous origin or communication of coronary artery
　　Arteriovenous malformation of coronary artery
　　Coronary artery:
　　　absence
　　　arising from aorta or pulmonary trunk
　　　single

746.86　Congenital heart block
　　Complete or incomplete atrioventricular [AV] block

746.87　Malposition of heart and cardiac apex
　　Abdominal heart
　　Dextrocardia
　　Ectopia cordis
　　Levocardia (isolated)
　　Mesocardia

　Excludes *dextrocardia with complete transposition of viscera (759.3)*

☐ **746.89　Other**
　　Atresia of cardiac vein
　　Hypoplasia of cardiac vein
　　Congenital:
　　　cardiomegaly
　　　diverticulum, left ventricle
　　　pericardial defect

☐ **746.9　Unspecified anomaly of heart**
　　Congenital:
　　　anomaly of heart NOS
　　　heart disease NOS

● **747　Other congenital anomalies of circulatory system**

747.0　Patent ductus arteriosus
　　Patent ductus Botalli
　　Persistent ductus arteriosus

● **747.1　Coarctation of aorta**

747.10　Coarctation of aorta (preductal) (postductal)
　　Hypoplasia of aortic arch

747.11　Interruption of aortic arch

● **747.2　Other anomalies of aorta**

☐ **747.20　Anomaly of aorta, unspecified**

747.21　Anomalies of aortic arch
　　Anomalous origin, right subclavian artery
　　Dextroposition of aorta
　　Double aortic arch
　　Kommerell's diverticulum
　　Overriding aorta
　　Persistent:
　　　convolutions, aortic arch
　　　right aortic arch
　　Vascular ring

　Excludes *hypoplasia of aortic arch (747.10)*

747.22　Atresia and stenosis of aorta
　　Absence of aorta
　　Aplasia of aorta
　　Hypoplasia of aorta
　　Stricture of aorta
　　Supra (valvular)-aortic stenosis

　Excludes *congenital aortic (valvular) stenosis or stricture, so stated (746.3)*
　　　hypoplasia of aorta in hypoplastic left heart syndrome (746.7)

☐ **747.29　Other**
　　Aneurysm of sinus of Valsalva
　　Congenital:
　　　aneurysm of aorta
　　　dilation of aorta

747.3　Anomalies of pulmonary artery
　　Agenesis of pulmonary artery
　　Anomaly of pulmonary artery
　　Atresia of pulmonary artery
　　Coarctation of pulmonary artery
　　Hypoplasia of pulmonary artery
　　Stenosis of pulmonary artery
　　Pulmonary arteriovenous aneurysm

● **747.4　Anomalies of great veins**

☐ **747.40　Anomaly of great veins, unspecified**
　　Anomaly NOS of:
　　　pulmonary veins
　　　vena cava

747.41　Total anomalous pulmonary venous connection
　　Total anomalous pulmonary venous return [TAPVR]:
　　　subdiaphragmatic
　　　supradiaphragmatic

747.42　Partial anomalous pulmonary venous connection
　　Partial anomalous pulmonary venous return

☐ **747.49　Other anomalies of great veins**
　　Absence of vena cava (inferior) (superior)
　　Congenital stenosis of vena cava (inferior) (superior)
　　Persistent:
　　　left posterior cardinal vein
　　　left superior vena cava
　　Scimitar syndrome
　　Transposition of pulmonary veins NOS

747.5　Absence or hypoplasia of umbilical artery
　　Single umbilical artery

　◀▶ **New Code**　　⬅▥▥▥▥▶ **Revised Code**　　● **Not a Principal Diagnosis**　　● **Use Additional Digit(s)**　　☐ **Nonspecific Code**

● **747.6 Other anomalies of peripheral vascular system**
    Absence of artery or vein, NEC
    Anomaly of artery or vein, NEC
    Atresia of artery or vein, NEC
    Arteriovenous aneurysm (peripheral)
    Arteriovenous malformation of the peripheral vascular system
    Congenital:
      aneurysm (peripheral)
      phlebectasia
      stricture, artery
      varix
    Multiple renal arteries

    | **Excludes** | *anomalies of:* |

        cerebral vessels (747.81)
          pulmonary artery (747.3)
        congenital retinal aneurysm (743.58)
        hemangioma (228.00–228.09)
        lymphangioma (228.1)

□ **747.60 Anomaly of the peripheral vascular system, unspecified site**

747.61 Gastrointestinal vessel anomaly

747.62 Renal vessel anomaly

747.63 Upper limb vessel anomaly

747.64 Lower limb vessel anomaly

□ **747.69 Anomalies of other specified sites of peripheral vascular system**

● **747.8 Other specified anomalies of circulatory system**

747.81 Anomalies of cerebrovascular system
    Arteriovenous malformation of brain
    Cerebral arteriovenous aneurysm, congenital
    Congenital anomalies of cerebral vessels

| **Excludes** | *ruptured cerebral (arteriovenous) aneurysm (430)* |

747.82 Spinal vessel anomaly
    Arteriovenous malformation of spinal vessel

□ **747.89 Other**
    Aneurysm, congenital, specified site not elsewhere classified

| **Excludes** | *congenital aneurysm:* |

    coronary (746.85)
    peripheral (747.6)
    pulmonary (747.3)
    retinal (743.58)

□ **747.9 Unspecified anomaly of circulatory system**

● **748 Congenital anomalies of respiratory system**

| **Excludes** | *congenital defect of diaphragm (756.6)* |

748.0 Choanal atresia
    Atresia of nares (anterior) (posterior)
    Congenital stenosis of nares (anterior) (posterior)

□ **748.1 Other anomalies of nose**
    Absent nose
    Accessory nose
    Cleft nose
    Deformity of wall of nasal sinus
    Congenital:
      deformity of nose
      notching of tip of nose
      perforation of wall of nasal sinus

| **Excludes** | *congenital deviation of nasal septum (754.0)* |

748.2 Web of larynx
    Web of larynx:
      NOS
      glottic
      subglottic

□ **748.3 Other anomalies of larynx, trachea, and bronchus**
    Absence or agenesis of:
      bronchus
      larynx
      trachea
    Anomaly (of):
      cricoid cartilage
      epiglottis
      thyroid cartilage
      tracheal cartilage
    Atresia (of):
      epiglottis
      glottis
      larynx
      trachea
    Cleft thyroid, cartilage, congenital
    Congenital:
      dilation, trachea
      stenosis:
        larynx
        trachea
        tracheocele
    Diverticulum:
      bronchus
      trachea
    Fissure of epiglottis
    Laryngocele
    Posterior cleft of cricoid cartilage (congenital)
    Rudimentary tracheal bronchus
    Stridor, laryngeal, congenital

748.4 Congenital cystic lung
    Disease, lung:
      cystic, congenital
      polycystic, congenital
    Honeycomb lung, congenital

| **Excludes** | *acquired or unspecified cystic lung (518.89)* |

748.5 Agenesis, hypoplasia, and dysplasia of lung
    Absence of lung (fissures) (lobe)
    Aplasia of lung
    Hypoplasia of lung (lobe)
    Sequestration of lung

● **748.6 Other anomalies of lung**

□ **748.60 Anomaly of lung, unspecified**

748.61 Congenital bronchiectasis

□ **748.69 Other**
    Accessory lung (lobe)
    Azygos lobe (fissure), lung

□ **748.8 Other specified anomalies of respiratory system**
    Abnormal communication between pericardial and pleural sacs
    Anomaly, pleural folds
    Atresia of nasopharynx
    Congenital cyst of mediastinum

□ **748.9 Unspecified anomaly of respiratory system**
    Anomaly of respiratory system NOS

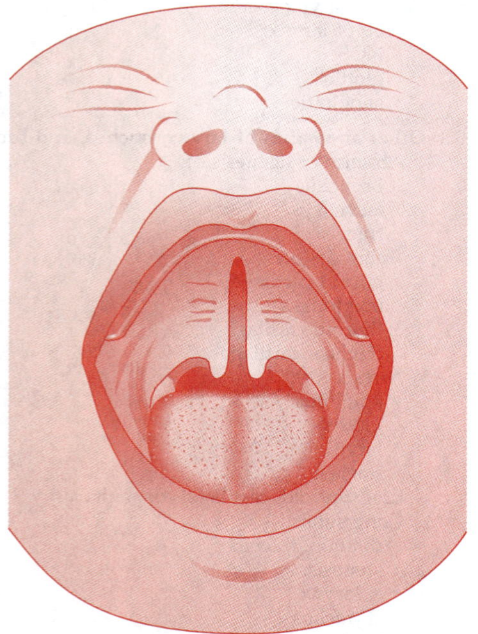

Figure 14–7   Cleft palate.

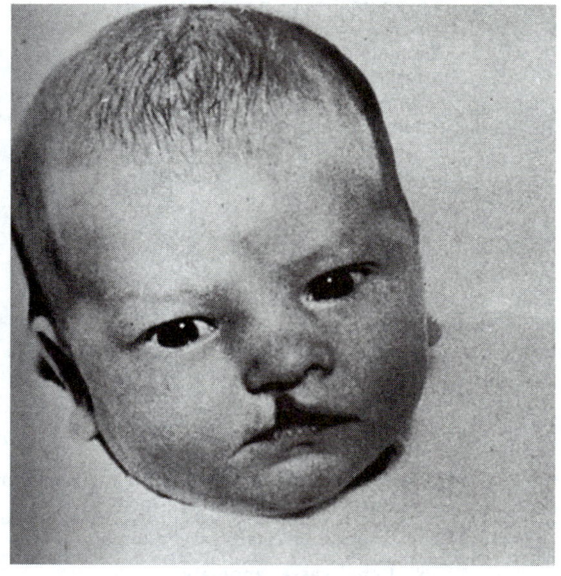

Figure 14–8   Cleft lip. (From Jones KL: Smith's Recognizable Patterns of Human Malformation, 4th ed. Philadelphia, WB Saunders, 1988, p 199.)

● **749 Cleft palate and cleft lip**

  ● **749.0 Cleft palate**

    ❑ **749.00 Cleft palate, unspecified**

    749.01 Unilateral, complete

    749.02 Unilateral, incomplete
        Cleft uvula

    749.03 Bilateral, complete

    749.04 Bilateral, incomplete

  ● **749.1 Cleft lip**
      Cheiloschisis
      Congenital fissure of lip
      Harelip
      Labium leporinum

    ❑ **749.10 Cleft lip, unspecified**

    749.11 Unilateral, complete

    749.12 Unilateral, incomplete

    749.13 Bilateral, complete

    749.14 Bilateral, incomplete

  ● **749.2 Cleft palate with cleft lip**
      Cheilopalatoschisis

    ❑ **749.20 Cleft palate with cleft lip, unspecified**

    749.21 Unilateral, complete

    749.22 Unilateral, incomplete

    749.23 Bilateral, complete

    749.24 Bilateral, incomplete

    ❑ **749.25 Other combinations**

● **750 Other congenital anomalies of upper alimentary tract**
    Excludes   *dentofacial anomalies (524.0–524.9)*

  750.0 Tongue tie
    Ankyloglossia

  ● **750.1 Other anomalies of tongue**

    ❑ **750.10 Anomaly of tongue, unspecified**

    750.11 Aglossia

    750.12 Congenital adhesions of tongue

    750.13 Fissure of tongue
        Bifid tongue
        Double tongue

    750.15 Macroglossia
        Congenital hypertrophy of tongue

    750.16 Microglossia
        Hypoplasia of tongue

  ❑ **750.19 Other**

  ● **750.2 Other specified anomalies of mouth and pharynx**

    750.21 Absence of salivary gland

    750.22 Accessory salivary gland

    750.23 Atresia, salivary gland
        Imperforate salivary duct

    750.24 Congenital fistula of salivary gland

    750.25 Congenital fistula of lip
        Congenital (mucus) lip pits

    ❑ **750.26 Other specified anomalies of mouth**
        Absence of uvula

    750.27 Diverticulum of pharynx
        Pharyngeal pouch

    ❑ **750.29 Other specified anomalies of pharynx**
        Imperforate pharynx

  750.3 Tracheoesophageal fistula, esophageal atresia and stenosis
    Absent esophagus
    Atresia of esophagus
    Congenital:
      esophageal ring
      stenosis of esophagus
      stricture of esophagus
    Congenital fistula:
      esophagobronchial
      esophagotracheal
    Imperforate esophagus
    Webbed esophagus

❑ **750.4 Other specified anomalies of esophagus**
Dilatation, congenital, of esophagus
Displacement, congenital, of esophagus
Diverticulum of esophagus
Duplication of esophagus
Esophageal pouch
Giant esophagus
> **Excludes** *congenital hiatus hernia (750.6)*

750.5 Congenital hypertrophic pyloric stenosis
Congenital or infantile:
constriction of pylorus
hypertrophy of pylorus
spasm of pylorus
stenosis of pylorus
stricture of pylorus

750.6 Congenital hiatus hernia
Displacement of cardia through esophageal hiatus
> **Excludes** *congenital diaphragmatic hernia (756.6)*

❑ **750.7 Other specified anomalies of stomach**
Congenital:
cardiospasm
hourglass stomach
Displacement of stomach
Diverticulum of stomach, congenital
Duplication of stomach
Megalogastria
Microgastria
Transposition of stomach

❑ **750.8 Other specified anomalies of upper alimentary tract**

❑ **750.9 Unspecified anomaly of upper alimentary tract**
Congenital:
anomaly NOS of upper alimentary tract [any part, except tongue]
deformity NOS of upper alimentary tract [any part, except tongue]

● **751 Other congenital anomalies of digestive system**

751.0 Meckel's diverticulum
Meckel's diverticulum (displaced) (hypertrophic)
Persistent:
omphalomesenteric duct
vitelline duct

751.1 Atresia and stenosis of small intestine
Atresia of: Atresia of:
duodenum   intestine NOS
ileum
Congenital:
absence of small intestine or intestine NOS
obstruction of small intestine or intestine NOS
stenosis of small intestine or intestine NOS
stricture of small intestine or intestine NOS
Imperforate jejunum

751.2 Atresia and stenosis of large intestine, rectum, and anal canal
Absence:
anus (congenital)
appendix, congenital
large instestine, congenital
rectum
Atresia of: Atresia of:
anus   rectum
colon
Congenital or infantile:
obstruction of large intestine
occlusion of anus
stricture of anus
Imperforate:
anus
rectum
Stricture of rectum, congenital

❑ **751.3 Hirschsprung's disease and other congenital functional disorders of colon**
Aganglionosis
Congenital dilation of colon
Congenital megacolon
Macrocolon

751.4 Anomalies of intestinal fixation
Congenital adhesions:
omental, anomalous
peritoneal
Jackson's membrane
Malrotation of colon
Rotation of cecum or colon:
failure of
incomplete
insufficient
Universal mesentery

❑ **751.5 Other anomalies of intestine**
Congenital diverticulum,   Megaloappendix
    colon   Megaloduodenum
Dolichocolon   Microcolon
Duplication of: Persistent cloaca
    anus   Transposition of:
    appendix   appendix
    cecum   colon
    intestine   intestine
Ectopic anus

● **751.6 Anomalies of gallbladder, bile ducts, and liver**

❑ **751.60 Unspecified anomaly of gallbladder, bile ducts, and liver**

751.61 Biliary atresia
Congenital:
absence of bile duct (common) or passage
hypoplasia of bile duct (common) or passage
obstruction of bile duct (common) or passage
stricture of bile duct (common) or passage

751.62 Congenital cystic disease of liver
Congenital polycystic disease of liver
Fibrocystic disease of liver

❑ **751.69 Other anomalies of gallbladder, bile ducts, and liver**
Absence of: Absence of:
    gallbladder, congenital   liver (lobe)
Accessory: Accessory:
    hepatic ducts   liver
Congenital: Congenital:
    choledochal cyst   hepatomegaly
Duplication of: Duplication of:
    biliary duct   gallbladder
    cystic duct   liver
Floating: Floating:
    gallbladder   liver
Intrahepatic gallbladder

751.7 Anomalies of pancreas
Absence of pancreas
Accessory pancreas
Agenesis of pancreas
Annular pancreas
Ectopic pancreatic tissue
Hypoplasia of pancreas
Pancreatic heterotopia
> **Excludes** *diabetes mellitus:*
>   *congenital (250.0–250.9)*
>   *neonatal (775.1)*
> *fibrocystic disease of pancreas (277.00–277.01)*

ICD-9-CM

700-799

Vol. 1

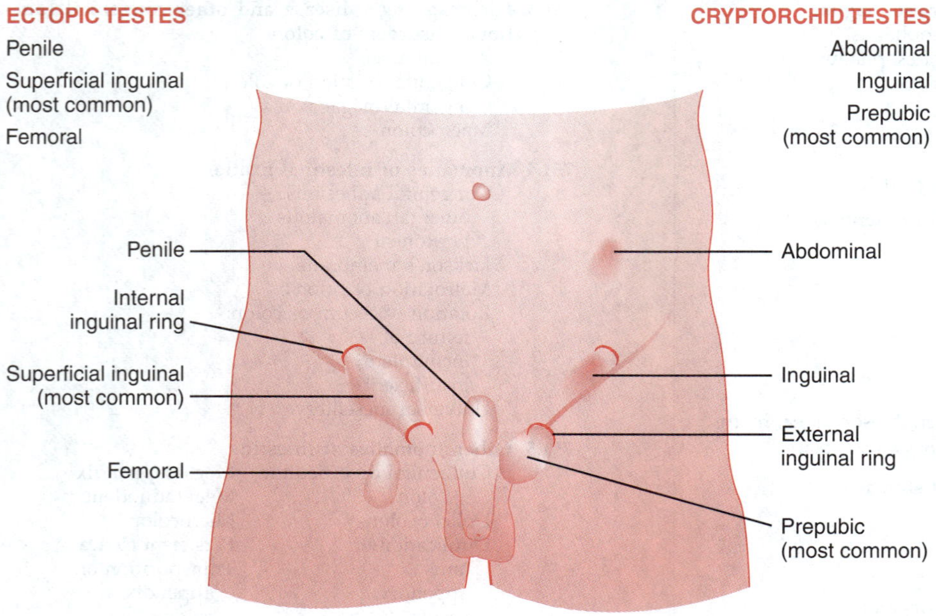

ECTOPIC TESTES

Penile

Superficial inguinal
(most common)

Femoral

CRYPTORCHID TESTES

Abdominal

Inguinal

Prepubic
(most common)

Penile

Internal
inguinal ring

Superficial inguinal
(most common)

Femoral

Abdominal

Inguinal

External
inguinal ring

Prepubic
(most common)

Figure 14–9 Undescended testes and the positions of the testes in various types of cryptorchidism or abnormal paths of descent.

☐ **751.8 Other specified anomalies of digestive system**
Absence (complete) (partial) of alimentary tract
NOS
Duplication of digestive organs NOS
Malposition, congenital, of digestive organs NOS

| Excludes | congenital diaphragmatic hernia (756.6) |
congenital hiatus hernia (750.6)

☐ **751.9 Unspecified anomaly of digestive system**
Congenital:
anomaly NOS of digestive system NOS
deformity NOS of digestive system NOS

● **752 Congenital anomalies of genital organs**

| Excludes | syndromes associated with anomalies in the
number and form of chromosomes (758.0–
758.9)
testicular feminization syndrome (257.8)

752.0 Anomalies of ovaries
Absence, congenital, of ovary
Accessory ovary
Ectopic ovary
Streak of ovary

● **752.1 Anomalies of fallopian tubes and broad ligaments**

☐ **752.10 Unspecified anomaly of fallopian tubes and broad ligaments**

752.11 Embryonic cyst of fallopian tubes and broad ligaments
Cyst:
epoöphoron
fimbrial
Gartner's duct
parovarian

☐ **752.19 Other**
Absence of fallopian tube or broad ligament
Accessory fallopian tube or broad ligament
Atresia of fallopian tube or broad ligament

752.2 Doubling of uterus
Didelphic uterus
Doubling of uterus [any degree] (associated with doubling of cervix and vagina)

☐ **752.3 Other anomalies of uterus**
Absence, congenital, of uterus
Agenesis of uterus
Aplasia of uterus
Bicornuate uterus
Uterus unicornis
Uterus with only one functioning horn

● **752.4 Anomalies of cervix, vagina, and external female genitalia**

☐ **752.40 Unspecified anomaly of cervix, vagina, and external female genitalia**

752.41 Embryonic cyst of cervix, vagina, and external female genitalia
Cyst of:
canal of Nuck, congenital
vagina, embryonal
vulva, congenital

752.42 Imperforate hymen

☐ **752.49 Other anomalies of cervix, vagina, and external female genitalia**
Absence of cervix, clitoris, vagina, or vulva
Agenesis of cervix, clitoris, vagina, or vulva
Congenital stenosis or stricture of:
cervical canal
vagina

| Excludes | double vagina associated with total duplication (752.2)

● **752.5 Undescended and retractile testicle**

752.51 Undescended testis
Cryptorchism
Ectopic testis

752.52 Retractile testis

● **752.6 Hypospadias and epispadias and other penile anomalies**

752.61 Hypospadias

752.62 Epispadias
Anaspadias

752.63   Congenital chordee

752.64   Micropenis

752.65   Hidden penis

❑ **752.69   Other penile anomalies**

752.7   Indeterminate sex and pseudohermaphroditism
Gynandrism
Hermaphroditism
Ovotestis
Pseudohermaphroditism (male) (female)
Pure gonadal dysgenesis

Excludes   *pseudohermaphroditism:*
female, with adrenocortical disorder (255.2)
male, with gonadal disorder (257.8)
with specified chromosomal anomaly (758.0–
758.9)
testicular feminization syndrome (257.8)

❑ **752.8   Other specified anomalies of genital organs**
Absence of:
prostate
spermatic cord
vas deferens
Anorchism
Aplasia (congenital) of:
prostate
round ligament
testicle
Atresia of:
ejaculatory duct
vas deferens
Fusion of testes
Hypoplasia of testis
Monorchism
Polyorchism

Excludes   *congenital hydrocele (778.6)*
penile anomalies (752.61–752.69)
phimosis or paraphimosis (605)

❑ **752.9   Unspecified anomaly of genital organs**
Congenital:
anomaly NOS of genital organ, NEC
deformity NOS of genital organ, NEC

● **753   Congenital anomalies of urinary system**

753.0   Renal agenesis and dysgenesis
Atrophy of kidney:
congenital
infantile
Congenital absence of kidney(s)
Hypoplasia of kidney(s)

Code first any associated vesicoureteral reflux (593.70–
593.73)

● **753.1   Cystic kidney disease**

Excludes   *acquired cyst of kidney (593.2)*

❑ **753.10   Cystic kidney disease, unspecified**

753.11   Congenital single renal cyst

❑ **753.12   Polycystic kidney, unspecified type**

753.13   Polycystic kidney, autosomal dominant

753.14   Polycystic kidney, autosomal recessive

753.15   Renal dysplasia

Code first any associated vesicoureteral reflux
(593.70–593.73)

753.16   Medullary cystic kidney
Nephronophthisis

753.17   Medullary sponge kidney

❑ **753.19   Other specified cystic kidney disease**
Multicystic kidney

● ❑ **753.2   Obstructive defects of renal pelvis and ureter**

❑ **753.20   Unspecified obstructive defect of renal pelvis and ureter**

753.21   Congenital obstruction of ureteropelvic junction

753.22   Congenital obstruction of ureterovesical junction
Adynamic ureter
Congenital hydroureter

753.23   Congenital ureterocele

❑ **753.29   Other**

❑ **753.3   Other specified anomalies of kidney**
Accessory kidney
Congenital:
calculus of kidney
displaced kidney
Discoid kidney
Double kidney with double pelvis
Ectopic kidney
Fusion of kidneys
Giant kidney
Horseshoe kidney
Hyperplasia of kidney
Lobulation of kidney
Malrotation of kidney
Trifid kidney (pelvis)

❑ **753.4   Other specified anomalies of ureter**
Absent ureter
Accessory ureter
Deviaton of ureter
Displaced ureteric orifice
Double ureter
Ectopic ureter
Implantation, anomalous, of ureter

753.5   Exstrophy of urinary bladder
Ectopia vesicae
Extroversion of bladder

753.6   Atresia and stenosis of urethra and bladder neck
Congenital obstruction:
bladder neck
urethra
Congenital stricture of:
urethra (valvular)
urinary meatus
vesicourethral orifice
Imperforate urinary meatus
Impervious urethra
Urethral valve formation

753.7   Anomalies of urachus
Cyst (of) urachus
Fistula (of) urachus
Patent (of) urachus
Persistent umbilical sinus

❑ **753.8   Other specified anomalies of bladder and urethra**
Absence, congenital, of:
bladder
urethra
Accessory:
bladder
urethra
Congenital:
diverticulum of bladder
hernia of bladder
Congenital urethrorectal fistula
Congenital prolapse of:
bladder (mucosa)
urethra
Double:
urethra
urinary meatus

☐ **753.9 Unspecified anomaly of urinary system**
Congenital:
  anomaly NOS of urinary system [any part, except urachus]
  deformity NOS of urinary system [any part, except urachus]

● **754 Certain congenital musculoskeletal deformities**

Includes: nonteratogenic deformities which are considered to be due to intrauterine malposition and pressure

754.0 Of skull, face, and jaw
Asymmetry of face
Compression facies
Depressions in skull
Deviation of nasal septum, congenital
Dolichocephaly
Plagiocephaly
Potter's facies
Squashed or bent nose, congenital

Excludes *dentofacial anomalies (524.0–524.9)*
syphilitic saddle nose (090.5)

754.1 Of sternocleidomastoid muscle
Congenital sternomastoid torticollis
Congenital wryneck
Contracture of sternocleidomastoid (muscle)
Sternomastoid tumor

754.2 Of spine
Congenital postural:
  lordosis
  scoliosis

● **754.3 Congenital dislocation of hip**

754.30 Congenital dislocation of hip, unilateral
Congenital dislocation of hip NOS

754.31 Congenital dislocation of hip, bilateral

754.32 Congenital subluxation of hip, unilateral
Congenital flexion deformity, hip or thigh
Predislocation status of hip at birth
Preluxation of hip, congenital

754.33 Congenital subluxation of hip, bilateral

754.35 Congenital dislocation of one hip with subluxation of other hip

● **754.4 Congenital genu recurvatum and bowing of long bones of leg**

754.40 Genu recurvatum

754.41 Congenital dislocation of knee (with genu recurvatum)

754.42 Congenital bowing of femur

754.43 Congenital bowing of tibia and fibula

☐ **754.44 Congenital bowing of unspecified long bones of leg**

● **754.5 Varus deformities of feet**
Excludes *acquired (736.71, 736.75, 736.79)*

754.50 Talipes varus
Congenital varus deformity of foot, unspecified
Pes varus

754.51 Talipes equinovarus
Equinovarus (congenital)

754.52 Metatarsus primus varus

754.53 Metatarsus varus

☐ **754.59 Other**
Talipes calcaneovarus

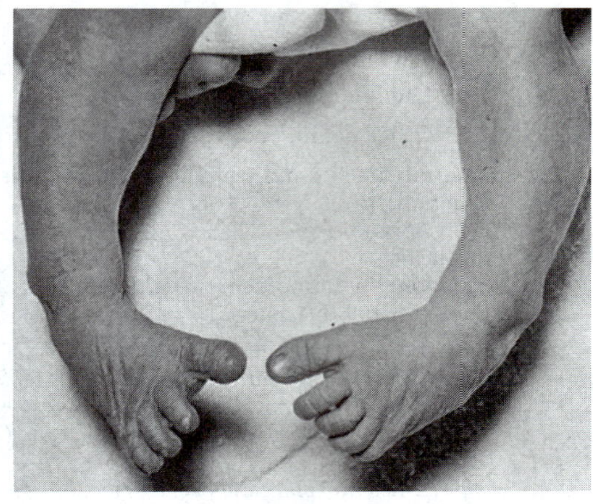

Figure 14–10 Mild to moderate inbowing of the lower leg. (From Jones KL: Smith's Recognizable Patterns of Human Malformation, 4th ed. Philadelphia, WB Saunders, 1988, p 671.)

● **754.6 Valgus deformities of feet**
Excludes *valgus deformity of foot (acquired) (736.79)*

754.60 Talipes valgus
Congenital valgus deformity of foot, unspecified

754.61 Congenital pes planus
Congenital rocker bottom flat foot
Flat foot, congenital

Excludes *pes planus (acquired) (734)*

754.62 Talipes calcaneovalgus

☐ **754.69 Other**
Talipes:
  equinovalgus
  planovalgus

● **754.7 Other deformities of feet**
Excludes *acquired (736.70–736.79)*

☐ **754.70 Talipes, unspecified**
Congenital deformity of foot NOS

754.71 Talipes cavus
Cavus foot (congenital)

☐ **754.79 Other**
Asymmetric talipes
Talipes:
  calcaneus
  equinus

● **754.8 Other specified nonteratogenic anomalies**

754.81 Pectus excavatum
Congenital funnel chest

754.82 Pectus carinatum
Congenital pigeon chest [breast]

☐ **754.89 Other**
Club hand (congenital)
Congenital:
  deformity of chest wall
  dislocation of elbow
Generalized flexion contractures of lower limb joints, congenital
Spade-like hand (congenital)

    ◀▶ **New Code**   ⬅▦➡ **Revised Code**   ● **Not a Principal Diagnosis**   ● **Use Additional Digit(s)**   ☐ **Nonspecific Code**

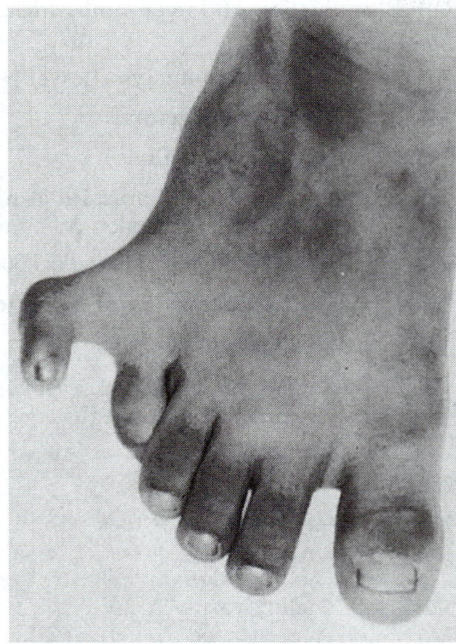

Figure 14–11 Polydactyly. (From Tachdjian MO: Pediatric Orthopedics, 2nd ed, Vol 4. Philadelphia, WB Saunders, 1990, p 2644.)

● **755 Other congenital anomalies of limbs**

  Excludes *those deformities classifiable to 754.0–754.8*

● **755.0 Polydactyly**

 □ **755.00 Polydactyly, unspecified digits**
   Supernumerary digits

  755.01 Of fingers
   Accessory fingers

  755.02 Of toes
   Accessory toes

● **755.1 Syndactyly**
  Symphalangy
  Webbing of digits

 □ **755.10 Of multiple and unspecified sites**

  755.11 Of fingers without fusion of bone

  755.12 Of fingers with fusion of bone

  755.13 Of toes without fusion of bone

  755.14 Of toes with fusion of bone

● **755.2 Reduction deformities of upper limb**

 □ **755.20 Unspecified reduction deformity of upper limb**
   Ectromelia NOS of upper limb
   Hemimelia NOS of upper limb
   Shortening of arm, congenital

  755.21 Transverse deficiency of upper limb
   Amelia of upper limb
   Congenital absence of:
    fingers, all (complete or partial)
    forearm, including hand and fingers
    upper limb, complete
   Congenital amputation of upper limb
   Transverse hemimelia of upper limb

  755.22 Longitudinal deficiency of upper limb, NEC
   Phocomelia NOS of upper limb
   Rudimentary arm

  755.23 Longitudinal deficiency, combined, involving humerus, radius, and ulna (complete or incomplete)
   Congenital absence of arm and forearm (complete or incomplete) with or without metacarpal deficiency and/or phalangeal deficiency, incomplete
   Phocomelia, complete, of upper limb

  755.24 Longitudinal deficiency, humeral, complete or partial (with or without distal deficiencies, incomplete)
   Congenital absence of humerus (with or without absence of some [but not all] distal elements)
   Proximal phocomelia of upper limb

  755.25 Longitudinal deficiency, radioulnar, complete or partial (with or without distal deficiencies, incomplete)
   Congenital absence of radius and ulna (with or without absence of some [but not all] distal elements)
   Distal phocomelia of upper limb

  755.26 Longitudinal deficiency, radial, complete or partial (with or without distal deficiencies, incomplete)
   Agenesis of radius
   Congenital absence of radius (with or without absence of some [but not all] distal elements)

  755.27 Longitudinal deficiency, ulnar, complete or partial (with or without distal deficiencies, incomplete)
   Agenesis of ulna
   Congenital absence of ulna (with or without absence of some [but not all] distal elements)

  755.28 Longitudinal deficiency, carpals or metacarpals, complete or partial (with or without incomplete phalangeal deficiency)

  755.29 Longitudinal deficiency, phalanges, complete or partial
   Absence of finger, congenital
   Aphalangia of upper limb, terminal, complete or partial

  Excludes *terminal deficiency of all five digits (755.21)*
   transverse deficiency of phalanges (755.21)

● **755.3 Reduction deformities of lower limb**

 □ **755.30 Unspecified reduction deformity of lower limb**
   Ectromelia NOS of lower limb
   Hemimelia NOS of lower limb
   Shortening of leg, congenital

  755.31 Transverse deficiency of lower limb
   Amelia of lower limb
   Congenital absence of:
    foot
    leg, including foot and toes
    lower limb, complete
    toes, all, complete
   Transverse hemimelia of lower limb

  755.32 Longitudinal deficiency of lower limb, NEC
   Phocomelia NOS of lower limb

  755.33 Longitudinal deficiency, combined, involving femur, tibia, and fibula (complete or incomplete)
   Congenital absence of thigh and (lower) leg (complete or incomplete) with or without metacarpal deficiency and/or phalangeal deficiency, incomplete
   Phocomelia, complete, of lower limb

ICD-9-CM

700-799

Vol. 1

755.34 Longitudinal deficiency, femoral, complete or partial (with or without distal deficiencies, incomplete)
Congenital absence of femur (with or without absence of some [but not all] distal elements)
Proximal phocomelia of lower limb

755.35 Longitudinal deficiency, tibiofibular, complete or partial (with or without distal deficiencies, incomplete)
Congenital absence of tibia and fibula (with or without absence of some [but not all] distal elements)
Distal phocomelia of lower limb

755.36 Longitudinal deficiency, tibia, complete or partial (with or without distal deficiencies, incomplete)
Agenesis of tibia
Congenital absence of tibia (with or without absence of some [but not all] distal elements)

755.37 Longitudinal deficiency, fibular, complete or partial (with or without distal deficiencies, incomplete)
Agenesis of fibula
Congenital absence of fibula (with or without absence of some [but not all] distal elements)

755.38 Longitudinal deficiency, tarsals or metatarsals, complete or partial (with or without incomplete phalangeal deficiency)

755.39 Longitudinal deficiency, phalanges, complete or partial
Absence of toe, congenital
Aphalangia of lower limb, terminal, complete or partial

Excludes	*terminal deficiency of all five digits (755.31)*
	transverse deficiency of phalanges (755.31)

☐ **755.4 Reduction deformities, unspecified limb**
Absence, congenital (complete or partial) of limb NOS
Amelia of unspecified limb
Ectromelia of unspecified limb
Hemimelia of unspecified limb
Phocomelia of unspecified limb

● **755.5 Other anomalies of upper limb, including shoulder girdle**

☐ **755.50 Unspecified anomaly of upper limb**

755.51 Congenital deformity of clavicle

755.52 Congenital elevation of scapula
Sprengel's deformity

755.53 Radioulnar synostosis

755.54 Madelung's deformity

755.55 Acrocephalosyndactyly
Apert's syndrome

755.56 Accessory carpal bones

755.57 Macrodactylia (fingers)

755.58 Cleft hand, congenital
Lobster-claw hand

☐ **755.59 Other**
Cleidocranial dysostosis
Cubitus:
   valgus, congenital
   varus, congenital

Excludes	*club hand (congenital) (754.89)*
	congenital dislocation of elbow (754.89)

● **755.6 Other anomalies of lower limb, including pelvic girdle**

☐ **755.60 Unspecified anomaly of lower limb**

755.61 Coxa valga, congenital

755.62 Coxa vara, congenital

☐ **755.63 Other congenital deformity of hip (joint)**
Congenital anteversion of femur (neck)

Excludes	*congenital dislocation of hip (754.30–754.35)*

755.64 Congenital deformity of knee (joint)
Congenital:
   absence of patella
   genu valgum [knock-knee]
   genu varum [bowleg]
Rudimentary patella

755.65 Macrodactylia of toes

☐ **755.66 Other anomalies of toes**
Congenital:
   hallux valgus
   hallux varus
   hammer toe

755.67 Anomalies of foot, NEC
Astragaloscaphoid synostosis
Calcaneonavicular bar
Coalition of calcaneus
Talonavicular synostosis
Tarsal coalitions

☐ **755.69 Other**
Congenital:
   angulation of tibia
   deformity (of):
      ankle (joint)
      sacroiliac (joint)
   fusion of sacroiliac joint

☐ **755.8 Other specified anomalies of unspecified limb**

☐ **755.9 Unspecified anomaly of unspecified limb**
Congenital:
   anomaly NOS of unspecified limb
   deformity NOS of unspecified limb

Excludes	*reduction deformity of unspecified limb (755.4)*

● **756 Other congenital musculoskeletal anomalies**

Excludes	*those deformities classifiable to 754.0–754.8*

756.0 Anomalies of skull and face bones
Absence of skull bones
Acrocephaly
Congenital deformity of forehead
Craniosynostosis
Crouzon's disease
Hypertelorism
Imperfect fusion of skull
Oxycephaly
Platybasia
Premature closure of cranial sutures
Tower skull
Trigonocephaly

Excludes	*acrocephalosyndactyly [Apert's syndrome] (755.55)*
	dentofacial anomalies (524.0–524.9)
	skull defects associated with brain anomalies, such as:
	anencephalus (740.0)
	encephalocele (742.0)
	hydrocephalus (742.3)
	microcephalus (742.1)

● **756.1 Anomalies of spine**

☐ **756.10 Anomaly of spine, unspecified**

◀▶ **New Code**   ⬤➡ **Revised Code**   ● **Not a Principal Diagnosis**   ● **Use Additional Digit(s)**   ☐ **Nonspecific Code**

756.11 Spondylolysis, lumbosacral region
Prespondylolisthesis (lumbosacral)

756.12 Spondylolisthesis

756.13 Absence of vertebra, congenital

756.14 Hemivertebra

756.15 Fusion of spine [vertebra], congenital

756.16 Klippel-Feil syndrome

756.17 Spina bifida occulta

Excludes *spina bifida (aperta) (741.0–741.9)*

☐ **756.19 Other**
Platyspondylia
Supernumerary vertebra

756.2 Cervical rib
Supernumerary rib in the cervical region

☐ **756.3 Other anomalies of ribs and sternum**
Congenital absence of:
rib
sternum
Congenital:
fissure of sternum
fusion of ribs
Sternum bifidum

Excludes *nonteratogenic deformity of chest wall (754.81–754.89)*

756.4 Chondrodystrophy
Achondroplasia
Chondrodystrophia (fetalis)
Dyschondroplasia
Enchondromatosis
Ollier's disease

Excludes *lipochondrodystrophy [Hurler's syndrome] (277.5)*
Morquio's disease (277.5)

● **756.5 Osteodystrophies**

☐ **756.50 Osteodystrophy, unspecified**

756.51 Osteogenesis imperfecta
Fragilitas ossium
Osteopsathyrosis

756.52 Osteopetrosis

756.53 Osteopoikilosis

756.54 Polyostotic fibrous dysplasia of bone

756.55 Chondroectodermal dysplasia
Ellis-van Creveld syndrome

756.56 Multiple epiphyseal dysplasia

☐ **756.59 Other**
Albright (-McCune)-Sternberg syndrome

756.6 Anomalies of diaphragm
Absence of diaphragm
Congenital hernia:
diaphragmatic
foramen of Morgagni
Eventration of diaphragm

Excludes *congenital hiatus hernia (750.6)*

● **756.7 Anomalies of abdominal wall**

☐ **756.70 Anomaly of abdominal wall, unspecified**

756.71 Prune belly syndrome
Eagle-Barrett syndrome
Prolapse of bladder mucosa

☐ **756.79 Other congenital anomalies of abdominal wall**
Exomphalos   Omphalocele
Gastroschisis

Excludes *umbilical hernia (551–553 with .1)*

● **756.8 Other specified anomalies of muscle, tendon, fascia, and connective tissue**

756.81 Absence of muscle and tendon
Absence of muscle (pectoral)

756.82 Accessory muscle

756.83 Ehlers-Danlos syndrome

☐ **756.89 Other**
Amyotrophia congenita
Congenital shortening of tendon

☐ **756.9 Other and unspecified anomalies of musculoskeletal system**
Congenital:
anomaly NOS of musculoskeletal system, NEC
deformity NOS of musculoskeletal system, NEC

● **757 Congenital anomalies of the integument**

Includes: anomalies of skin, subcutaneous tissue, hair, nails, and breast

Excludes *hemangioma (228.00–228.09)*
pigmented nevus (216.0–216.9)

757.0 Hereditary edema of legs
Congenital lymphedema
Hereditary trophedema
Milroy's disease

757.1 Ichthyosis congenita
Congenital ichthyosis
Harlequin fetus
Ichthyosiform erythroderma

757.2 Dermatoglyphic anomalies
Abnormal palmar creases

● **757.3 Other specified anomalies of skin**

757.31 Congenital ectodermal dysplasia

757.32 Vascular hamartomas
Birthmarks
Port-wine stain
Strawberry nevus

757.33 Congenital pigmentary anomalies of skin
Congenital poikiloderma
Urticaria pigmentosa
Xeroderma pigmentosum

Excludes *albinism (270.2)*

☐ **757.39 Other**
Accessory skin tags, congenital
Congenital scar
Epidermolysis bullosa
Keratoderma (congenital)

Excludes *pilonidal cyst (685.0–685.1)*

☐ **757.4 Specified anomalies of hair**
Congenital:
alopecia
atrichosis
beaded hair
hypertrichosis
monilethrix
Persistent lanugo

☐ **757.5 Specified anomalies of nails**
Anonychia
Congenital:
clubnail
koilonychia
leukonychia
onychauxis
pachyonychia

☐757.6 Specified anomalies of breast
Absent breast or nipple
Accessory breast or nipple
Supernumerary breast or nipple
Hypoplasia of breast
> **Excludes** *absence of pectoral muscle (756.81)*

☐757.8 Other specified anomalies of the integument

☐757.9 Unspecified anomaly of the integument
Congenital:
    anomaly NOS of integument
    deformity NOS of integument

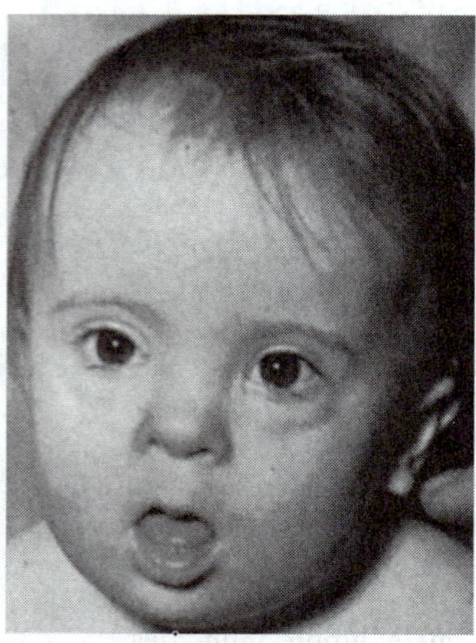

Figure 14–12 Down's syndrome with flat face, straight hair, and protrusion of tongue. (From Jones KL: Smith's Recognizable Patterns of Human Malformation, 4th ed. Philadelphia, WB Saunders, 1988, p 14.)

●758 Chromosomal anomalies

> **Includes:** syndromes associated with anomalies in the number and form of chromosomes

758.0 Down's syndrome
Mongolism
Translocation Down's syndrome
Trisomy:
    21 or 22
    G

758.1 Patau's syndrome
Trisomy:
    13
    D_1

758.2 Edwards's syndrome
Trisomy:
    18
    E_3

758.3 Autosomal deletion syndromes
Antimongolism syndrome
Cri-du-chat syndrome

758.4 Balanced autosomal translocation in normal individual

☐758.5 Other conditions due to autosomal anomalies
Accessory autosomes, NEC

758.6 Gonadal dysgenesis
Ovarian dysgenesis
Turner's syndrome
XO syndrome
> **Excludes** *pure gonadal dysgenesis (752.7)*

758.7 Klinefelter's syndrome
XXY syndrome

●758.8 Other conditions due to chromosome anomalies

☐758.81 Other conditions due to sex chromosome anomalies

☐758.89 Other

☐758.9 Conditions due to anomaly of unspecified chromosome

●759 Other and unspecified congenital anomalies

759.0 Anomalies of spleen
Aberrant spleen   Congenital splenomegaly
Absent spleen   Ectopic spleen
Accessory spleen   Lobulation of spleen

759.1 Anomalies of adrenal gland
Aberrant adrenal gland
Absent adrenal gland
Accessory adrenal gland
> **Excludes** *adrenogenital disorders (255.2)*
> *congenital disorders of steroid metabolism (255.2)*

☐759.2 Anomalies of other endocrine glands
Absent parathyroid gland
Accessory thyroid gland
Persistent thyroglossal or thyrolingual duct
Thyroglossal (duct) cyst
> **Excludes** *congenital:*
> *goiter (246.1)*
> *hypothyroidism (243)*

759.3 Situs inversus
Situs inversus or transversus:
    abdominalis
    thoracis
Transposition of viscera:
    abdominal
    thoracic
> **Excludes** *dextrocardia without mention of complete transposition (746.87)*

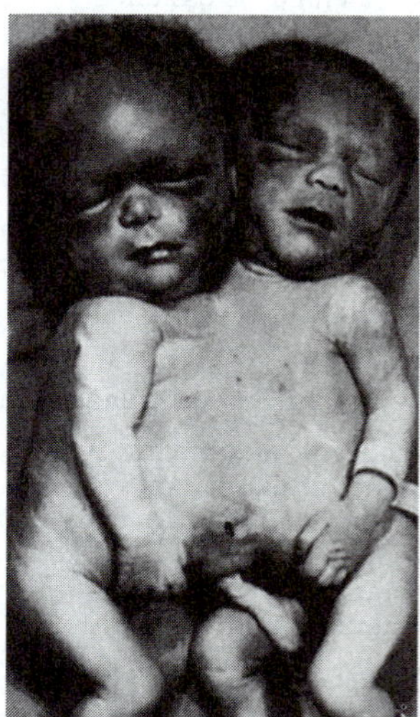

Figure 14–13 Conjoined twins in the most common type of chest attachment (thoracopagus). (From Jones KL: Smith's Recognizable Patterns of Human Malformation, 4th ed. Philadelphia, WB Saunders, 1988, p 595.)

759.4 Conjoined twins
Craniopagus   Thoracopagus
Dicephalus   Xiphopagus
Pygopagus

759.5 Tuberous sclerosis
Bourneville's disease
Epiloia

☐ **759.6 Other hamartoses, NEC**
Syndrome:
Peutz-Jeghers
Sturge-Weber (-Dimitri)
von Hippel-Lindau

Excludes neurofibromatosis (237.7)

759.7 Multiple congenital anomalies, so described
Congenital:
anomaly, multiple NOS
deformity, multiple NOS

● **759.8 Other specified anomalies**

759.81 Prader-Willi syndrome

759.82 Marfan syndrome

759.83 Fragile X syndrome

☐ **759.89 Other**
Congenital malformation syndromes affecting multiple systems, NEC
Laurence-Moon-Biedl syndrome

☐ **759.9 Congenital anomaly, unspecified**

15. CERTAIN CONDITIONS ORIGINATING IN THE PERINATAL PERIOD (760–779)

Includes: conditions which have their origin in the perinatal period even though death or morbidity occurs later

Use additional code(s) to further specify condition

MATERNAL CAUSES OF PERINATAL MORBIDITY AND MORTALITY (760–763)

● **760 Fetus or newborn affected by maternal conditions which may be unrelated to present pregnancy**

Includes: the listed maternal conditions only when specified as a cause of mortality or morbidity of the fetus or newborn

Excludes maternal endocrine and metabolic disorders affecting fetus or newborn (775.0–775.9)

760.0 Maternal hypertensive disorders
Fetus or newborn affected by maternal conditions classifiable to 642

760.1 Maternal renal and urinary tract diseases
Fetus or newborn affected by maternal conditions classifiable to 580–599

760.2 Maternal infections
Fetus or newborn affected by maternal infectious disease classifiable to 001–136 and 487, but fetus or newborn not manifesting that disease

Excludes congenital infectious diseases (771.0–771.8)
maternal genital tract and other localized infections (760.8)

☐ **760.3 Other chronic maternal circulatory and respiratory diseases**
Fetus or newborn affected by chronic maternal conditions classifiable to 390–459, 490–519, 745–748

760.4 Maternal nutritional disorders
Fetus or newborn affected by:
maternal disorders classifiable to 260–269
maternal malnutrition NOS

Excludes fetal malnutrition (764.10–764.29)

760.5 Maternal injury
Fetus or newborn affected by maternal conditions classifiable to 800–995

760.6 Surgical operation on mother

Excludes cesarean section for present delivery (763.4)
damage to placenta from amniocentesis, cesarean section, or surgical induction (762.1)
previous surgery to uterus or pelvic organs (763.89) ◀

● **760.7 Noxious influences affecting fetus via placenta or breast milk**
Fetus or newborn affected by noxious substance transmitted via placenta or breast milk

Excludes anesthetic and analgesic drugs administered during labor and delivery (763.5)
drug withdrawal syndrome in newborn (779.5)

☐ **760.70 Unspecified noxious substance**
Fetus or newborn affected by:
Drug, NEC

760.71 Alcohol
Fetal alcohol syndrome

760.72 Narcotics

760.73 Hallucinogenic agents

760.74 Anti-infectives
Antibiotics

760.75 Cocaine

ICD-9-CM

700-799

Vol. 1

760.76 Diethylstilbestrol [DES]

❏ 760.79 Other
Fetus or newborn affected by:
immune sera transmitted via placenta or breast milk
medicinal agents, NEC, transmitted via placenta or breast milk
toxic substance, NEC, transmitted via placenta or breast milk

❏ 760.8 Other specified maternal conditions affecting fetus or newborn
Maternal genital tract and other localized infection affecting fetus or newborn, but fetus or newborn not manifesting that disease

Excludes *maternal urinary tract infection affecting fetus or newborn (760.1)*

❏ 760.9 Unspecified maternal condition affecting fetus or newborn

● **761 Fetus or newborn affected by maternal complications of pregnancy**

Includes: the listed maternal conditions only when specified as a cause of mortality or morbidity of the fetus or newborn

761.0 Incompetent cervix

761.1 Premature rupture of membranes

761.2 Oligohydramnios

Excludes *that due to premature rupture of membranes (761.1)*

761.3 Polyhydramnios
Hydramnios (acute) (chronic)

761.4 Ectopic pregnancy
Pregnancy:
abdominal
intraperitoneal
tubal

761.5 Multiple pregnancy
Triplet (pregnancy)
Twin (pregnancy)

761.6 Maternal death

761.7 Malpresentation before labor
Breech presentation before labor
External version before labor
Oblique lie before labor
Transverse lie before labor
Unstable lie before labor

❏ 761.8 Other specified maternal complications of pregnancy affecting fetus or newborn
Spontaneous abortion, fetus

❏ 761.9 Unspecified maternal complication of pregnancy affecting fetus or newborn

● **762 Fetus or newborn affected by complications of placenta, cord, and membranes**

Includes: the listed maternal conditions only when specified as a cause of mortality or morbidity in the fetus or newborn

762.0 Placenta previa

❏ 762.1 Other forms of placental separation and hemorrhage
Abruptio placentae
Antepartum hemorrhage
Damage to placenta from amniocentesis, cesarean section, or surgical induction
Maternal blood loss
Premature separation of placenta
Rupture of marginal sinus

❏ 762.2 Other and unspecified morphological and functional abnormalities of placenta
Placental:
dysfunction
infarction
insufficiency

762.3 Placental transfusion syndromes
Placental and cord abnormality resulting in twin-to-twin or other transplacental transfusion

Use additional code to indicate resultant condition in fetus or newborn:
fetal blood loss (772.0)
polycythemia neonatorum (776.4)

762.4 Prolapsed cord
Cord presentation

❏ 762.5 Other compression of umbilical cord
Cord around neck
Entanglement of cord
Knot in cord
Torsion of cord

❏ 762.6 Other and unspecified conditions of umbilical cord
Short cord
Thrombosis of umbilical cord
Varices of umbilical cord
Velamentous insertion of umbilical cord
Vasa previa

Excludes *infection of umbilical cord (771.4)*
single umbilical artery (747.5)

762.7 Chorioamnionitis
Amnionitis
Membranitis
Placentitis

❏ 762.8 Other specified abnormalities of chorion and amnion

❏ 762.9 Unspecified abnormality of chorion and amnion

● **763 Fetus or newborn affected by other complications of labor and delivery**

Includes: the listed conditions only when specified as a cause of mortality or morbidity in the fetus or newborn

763.0 Breech delivery and extraction

❏ 763.1 Other malpresentation, malposition, and disproportion during labor and delivery
Fetus or newborn affected by:
abnormality of bony pelvis
contracted pelvis
persistent occipitoposterior position
shoulder presentation
transverse lie
conditions classifiable to 652, 653, and 660

763.2 Forceps delivery
Fetus or newborn affected by forceps extraction

763.3 Delivery by vacuum extractor

763.4 Cesarean delivery

Excludes *placental separation or hemorrhage from cesarean section (762.1)*

763.5 Maternal anesthesia and analgesia
Reactions and intoxications from maternal opiates and tranquilizers during labor and delivery

Excludes *drug withdrawal syndrome in newborn (779.5)*

763.6 Precipitate delivery
Rapid second stage

◀▶ **New Code**   ⬅▦➡ **Revised Code**   ● **Not a Principal Diagnosis**   ● **Use Additional Digit(s)**   ❏ **Nonspecific Code**

763.7 Abnormal uterine contractions
Fetus or newborn affected by:
contraction ring
hypertonic labor
hypotonic uterine dysfunction
uterine inertia or dysfunction
conditions classifiable to 661, except 661.3

● **763.8 Other specified complications of labor and delivery affecting fetus or newborn**

763.81 Abnormality in fetal heart rate or rhythm before the onset of labor ◀

763.82 Abnormality in fetal heart rate or rhythm during labor ◀

❑ **763.83 Abnormality in fetal heart rate or rhythm, unspecified as to time of onset** ◀

❑ **763.89 Other specified complications of labor and delivery affecting fetus or newborn** ◀
Fetus or newborn affected by: ◀
abnormality of maternal soft tissues ◀
destructive operation on live fetus to facilitate delivery ◀
induction of labor (medical) ◀
previous surgery to uterus or pelvic organs ◀
other conditions classifiable to 650–669 ◀
other procedures used in labor and delivery ◀

❑ **763.9 Unspecified complication of labor and delivery affecting fetus or newborn**

OTHER CONDITIONS ORIGINATING IN THE PERINATAL PERIOD (764–779)

The following fifth-digit subclassification is for use with categories 764–765 to denote birthweight:
❑ **0** unspecified [weight]
1 less than 500 grams
2 500–749 grams
3 750–999 grams
4 1,000–1,249 grams
5 1,250–1,499 grams
6 1,500–1,749 grams
7 1,750–1,999 grams
8 2,000–2,499 grams
9 2,500 grams and over

● **764 Slow fetal growth and fetal malnutrition**

Requires fifth digit. See beginning of section 764–779 for codes and definitions.

● **764.0 "Light-for-dates" without mention of fetal malnutrition**
Infants underweight for gestational age
"Small-for-dates"

● **764.1 "Light-for-dates" with signs of fetal malnutrition**
Infants "light-for-dates" classifiable to 764.0, who in addition show signs of fetal malnutrition, such as dry peeling skin and loss of subcutaneous tissue

● **764.2 Fetal malnutrition without mention of "light-for-dates"**
Infants, not underweight for gestational age, showing signs of fetal malnutrition, such as dry peeling skin and loss of subcutaneous tissue
Intrauterine malnutrition

❑● **764.9 Fetal growth retardation, unspecified**
Intrauterine growth retardation

● **765 Disorders relating to short gestation and unspecified low birthweight**

Requires fifth digit. See beginning of section 764–779 for codes and definitions.

Includes: the listed conditions, without further specification, as causes of mortality, morbidity, or additional care, in fetus or newborn

● **765.0 Extreme immaturity**

Note: Usually implies a birthweight of less than 1,000 grams and/or a gestation of less than 28 completed weeks.

❑● **765.1 Other preterm infants**

Note: Usually implies birthweight of 1,000–2,499 grams and/or a gestation of 28–37 completed weeks.
Prematurity NOS
Prematurity or small size, not classifiable to 765.0 or as "light-for-dates" in 764

● **766 Disorders relating to long gestation and high birthweight**

Includes: the listed conditions, without further specification, as causes of mortality, morbidity, or additional care, in fetus or newborn

766.0 Exceptionally large baby

Note: Usually implies a birthweight of 4,500 grams or more.

❑ **766.1 Other "heavy-for-dates" infants**
Other fetus or infant "heavy-" or "large-for-dates" regardless of period of gestation

766.2 Post-term infant, not "heavy-for-dates"
Fetus or infant with gestation period of 294 days or more [42 or more completed weeks], not "heavy-" or "large-for-dates"
Postmaturity NOS

● **767 Birth trauma**

767.0 Subdural and cerebral hemorrhage
Subdural and cerebral hemorrhage, whether described as due to birth trauma or to intrapartum anoxia or hypoxia
Subdural hematoma (localized)
Tentorial tear

Use additional code to identify cause

Excludes *intraventricular hemorrhage (772.1)*
subarachnoid hemorrhage (772.2)

767.1 Injuries to scalp
Caput succedaneum
Cephalhematoma
Chignon (from vacuum extraction)
Massive epicranial subaponeurotic hemorrhage

767.2 Fracture of clavicle

❑ **767.3 Other injuries to skeleton**
Fracture of:
long bones
skull

Excludes *congenital dislocation of hip (754.30–754.35)*
fracture of spine, congenital (767.4)

767.4 Injury to spine and spinal cord
Dislocation of spine or spinal cord due to birth trauma
Fracture of spine or spinal cord due to birth trauma
Laceration of spine or spinal cord due to birth trauma
Rupture of spine or spinal cord due to birth trauma

767.5 Facial nerve injury
Facial palsy

767.6 Injury to brachial plexus
Palsy or paralysis:
   brachial
   Erb (-Duchenne)
   Klumpke (-Déjérine)

❑ **767.7 Other cranial and peripheral nerve injuries**
Phrenic nerve paralysis

❑ **767.8 Other specified birth trauma**
Eye damage
Hematoma of:
   liver (subcapsular)
   testes
   vulva
Rupture of:
   liver
   spleen
Scalpel wound
Traumatic glaucoma

> **Excludes** *hemorrhage classifiable to 772.0–772.9*

❑ **767.9 Birth trauma, unspecified**
Birth injury NOS

● **768 Intrauterine hypoxia and birth asphyxia**

Use only when associated with newborn morbidity classifiable elsewhere

❑ **768.0 Fetal death from asphyxia or anoxia before onset of labor or at unspecified time**

768.1 Fetal death from asphyxia or anoxia during labor

768.2 Fetal distress before onset of labor, in liveborn infant
Fetal metabolic acidemia before onset of labor, in liveborn infant   ◄

768.3 Fetal distress first noted during labor, in liveborn infant
Fetal metabolic acidemia first noted during labor, in liveborn infant   ◄

❑ **768.4 Fetal distress, unspecified as to time of onset, in liveborn infant**
Fetal metabolic acidemia unspecified as to time of onset, in liveborn infant   ◄

768.5 Severe birth asphyxia
Birth asphyxia with neurologic involvement

768.6 Mild or moderate birth asphyxia
Other specified birth asphyxia (without mention of neurologic involvement)

❑ **768.9 Unspecified birth asphyxia in liveborn infant**
Anoxia NOS, in liveborn infant
Asphyxia NOS, in liveborn infant
Hypoxia NOS, in liveborn infant

769 Respiratory distress syndrome
Cardiorespiratory distress syndrome of newborn
Hyaline membrane disease (pulmonary)
Idiopathic respiratory distress syndrome [IRDS or RDS] of newborn
Pulmonary hypoperfusion syndrome

> **Excludes** *transient tachypnea of newborn (770.6)*

● **770 Other respiratory conditions of fetus and newborn**

770.0 Congenital pneumonia
Infective pneumonia acquired prenatally

> **Excludes** *pneumonia from infection acquired after birth (480.0–486)*

770.1 Meconium aspiration syndrome
Aspiration of contents of birth canal NOS
Meconium aspiration below vocal cords
Pneumonitis:
   fetal aspiration
   meconium

770.2 Interstitial emphysema and related conditions
Pneumomediastinum originating in the perinatal period
Pneumopericardium originating in the perinatal period
Pneumothorax originating in the perinatal period

770.3 Pulmonary hemorrhage
Hemorrhage:
   alveolar (lung) originating in the perinatal period
   intra-alveolar (lung) originating in the perinatal period
   massive pulmonary originating in the perinatal period

770.4 Primary atelectasis
Pulmonary immaturity NOS

❑ **770.5 Other and unspecified atelectasis**
Atelectasis:
   NOS originating in the perinatal period
   partial originating in the perinatal period
   secondary originating in the perinatal period
Pulmonary collapse originating in the perinatal period

770.6 Transitory tachypnea of newborn
Idiopathic tachypnea of newborn
Wet lung syndrome

> **Excludes** *respiratory distress syndrome (769)*

770.7 Chronic respiratory disease arising in the perinatal period
Bronchopulmonary dysplasia
Interstitial pulmonary fibrosis of prematurity
Wilson-Mikity syndrome

❑ **770.8 Other respiratory problems after birth**
Apneic spells NOS originating in the perinatal period
Cyanotic attacks NOS originating in the perinatal period
Fetal acidosis affecting newborn   ◄
Fetal anoxia affecting newborn   ◄
Fetal asphyxia affecting newborn   ◄
Fetal hypercapnia affecting newborn   ◄
Fetal hypoxia affecting newborn   ◄
Respiratory depression of newborn   ◄
Respiratory distress NOS originating in the perinatal period   ◄
Respiratory failure NOS originating in the perinatal period   ◄

❑ **770.9 Unspecified respiratory condition of fetus and newborn**

● **771 Infections specific to the perinatal period**

> **Includes:** infections acquired before or during birth or via the umbilicus

> **Excludes** *congenital pneumonia (770.0)*
> *congenital syphilis (090.0–090.9)*
> *maternal infectious disease as a cause of mortality or morbidity in fetus or newborn, but fetus or newborn not manifesting the disease (760.2)*
> *ophthalmia neonatorum due to gonococcus (098.40)*
> *other infections not specifically classified to this category*

771.0 Congenital rubella
Congenital rubella pneumonitis

◄► **New Code**   ⬅⬛⬛➡ **Revised Code**   ● **Not a Principal Diagnosis**   ● **Use Additional Digit(s)**   ❑ **Nonspecific Code**

771.1 Congenital cytomegalovirus infection
Congenital cytomegalic inclusion disease

☐ **771.2 Other congenital infections**
Congenital: Congenital:
herpes simplex toxoplasmosis
listeriosis tuberculosis
malaria

771.3 Tetanus neonatorum
Tetanus omphalitis
Excludes *hypocalcemic tetany (775.4)*

771.4 Omphalitis of the newborn
Infection: Infection:
navel cord umbilical stump
Excludes *tetanus omphalitis (771.3)*

771.5 Neonatal infective mastitis
Excludes *noninfective neonatal mastitis (778.7)*

771.6 Neonatal conjunctivitis and dacryocystitis
Ophthalmia neonatorum NOS
Excludes *ophthalmia neonatorum due to gonococcus (098.40)*

771.7 Neonatal Candida infection
Neonatal moniliasis
Thrush in newborn

☐ **771.8 Other infection specific to the perinatal period**
Intra-amniotic infection of fetus:
NOS
clostridial
Escherichia coli [E. coli]
Intrauterine sepsis of fetus
Neonatal urinary tract infection
Septicemia [sepsis] of newborn

● **772 Fetal and neonatal hemorrhage**
Excludes *hematological disorders of fetus and newborn (776.0–776.9)*

772.0 Fetal blood loss
Fetal blood loss from:
cut end of co-twin's cord
placenta
ruptured cord
vasa previa
Fetal exsanguination
Fetal hemorrhage into:
co-twin
mother's circulation

772.1 Intraventricular hemorrhage
Intraventricular hemorrhage from any perinatal cause

772.2 Subarachnoid hemorrhage
Subarachnoid hemorrhage from any perinatal cause
Excludes *subdural and cerebral hemorrhage (767.0)*

772.3 Umbilical hemorrhage after birth
Slipped umbilical ligature

772.4 Gastrointestinal hemorrhage
Excludes *swallowed maternal blood (777.3)*

772.5 Adrenal hemorrhage

772.6 Cutaneous hemorrhage
Bruising in fetus or newborn
Ecchymoses in fetus or newborn
Petechiae in fetus or newborn
Superficial hematoma in fetus or newborn

☐ **772.8 Other specified hemorrhage of fetus or newborn**
Excludes *hemorrhagic disease of newborn (776.0)*
pulmonary hemorrhage (770.3)

☐ **772.9 Unspecified hemorrhage of newborn**

● **773 Hemolytic disease of fetus or newborn, due to isoimmunization**

773.0 Hemolytic disease due to Rh isoimmunization
Anemia due to RH:
antibodies
isoimmunization
maternal/fetal incompatibility
Erythroblastosis (fetalis) due to RH:
antibodies
isoimmunization
maternal/fetal incompatibility
Hemolytic disease (fetus) (newborn) due to RH:
antibodies
isoimmunization
maternal/fetal incompatibility
Jaundice due to RH:
antibodies
isoimmunization
maternal/fetal incompatibility
Rh hemolytic disease
Rh isoimmunization

773.1 Hemolytic disease due to ABO isoimmunization
ABO hemolytic disease
ABO isoimmunization
Anemia due to ABO:
antibodies
isoimmunization
maternal/fetal incompatibility
Erythroblastosis (fetalis) due to ABO:
antibodies
isoimmunization
maternal/fetal incompatibility
Hemolytic disease (fetus) (newborn) due to ABO:
antibodies
isoimmunization
maternal/fetal incompatibility
Jaundice due to ABO:
antibodies
isoimmunization
maternal/fetal incompatibility

☐ **773.2 Hemolytic disease due to other and unspecified isoimmunization**
Erythroblastosis (fetalis) (neonatorum) NOS
Hemolytic disease (fetus) (newborn) NOS
Jaundice or anemia due to other and unspecified blood-group incompatibility

773.3 Hydrops fetalis due to isoimmunization
Use additional code , if desired, to identify type of isoimmunization (773.0–773.2)

773.4 Kernicterus due to isoimmunization
Use additional code , if desired, to identify type of isoimmunization (773.0–773.2)

773.5 Late anemia due to isoimmunization

● **774 Other perinatal jaundice**

● **774.0 *Perinatal jaundice from hereditary hemolytic anemias***
Code first underlying disease (282.0–282.9)

☐ **774.1 Perinatal jaundice from other excessive hemolysis**
Fetal or neonatal jaundice from:
bruising
drugs or toxins transmitted from mother
infection
polycythemia
swallowed maternal blood
Use additional code to identify cause
Excludes *jaundice due to isoimmunization (773.0–773.2)*

ICD-9-CM

700-799

Vol. 1

774.2 Neonatal jaundice associated with preterm delivery
Hyperbilirubinemia of prematurity
Jaundice due to delayed conjugation associated with preterm delivery

● **774.3 Neonatal jaundice due to delayed conjugation from other causes**

☐ **774.30 Neonatal jaundice due to delayed conjugation, cause unspecified**

● *774.31 Neonatal jaundice due to delayed conjugation in diseases classified elsewhere*

Code first underlying diseases, as:
congenital hypothyroidism (243)
Crigler-Najjar syndrome (277.4)
Gilbert's syndrome (277.4)

☐ **774.39 Other**
Jaundice due to delayed conjugation from causes, such as:
breast milk inhibitors
delayed development of conjugating system

774.4 Perinatal jaundice due to hepatocellular damage
Fetal or neonatal hepatitis
Giant cell hepatitis
Inspissated bile syndrome

●☐ **774.5 *Perinatal jaundice from other causes***

Code first underlying cause, as:
congenital obstruction of bile duct (751.61)
galactosemia (271.1)
mucoviscidosis (277.00–277.01)

☐ **774.6 Unspecified fetal and neonatal jaundice**
Icterus neonatorum
Neonatal hyperbilirubinemia (transient)
Physiologic jaundice NOS in newborn

Excludes *that in preterm infants (774.2)*

774.7 Kernicterus not due to isoimmunization
Bilirubin encephalopathy
Kernicterus of newborn NOS

Excludes *kernicterus due to isoimmunization (773.4)*

● **775 Endocrine and metabolic disturbances specific to the fetus and newborn**

Includes: transitory endocrine and metabolic disturbances caused by the infant's response to maternal endocrine and metabolic factors, its removal from them, or its adjustment to extrauterine existence

775.0 Syndrome of "infant of a diabetic mother"
Maternal diabetes mellitus affecting fetus or newborn (with hypoglycemia)

775.1 Neonatal diabetes mellitus
Diabetes mellitus syndrome in newborn infant

775.2 Neonatal myasthenia gravis

775.3 Neonatal thyrotoxicosis
Neonatal hyperthyroidism (transient)

775.4 Hypocalcemia and hypomagnesemia of newborn
Cow's milk hypocalcemia
Hypocalcemic tetany, neonatal
Neonatal hypoparathyroidism
Phosphate-loading hypocalcemia

☐ **775.5 Other transitory neonatal electrolyte disturbances**
Dehydration, neonatal

775.6 Neonatal hypoglycemia

Excludes *infant of mother with diabetes mellitus (775.0)*

775.7 Late metabolic acidosis of newborn

☐ **775.8 Other transitory neonatal endocrine and metabolic disturbances**
Amino-acid metabolic disorders described as transitory

☐ **775.9 Unspecified endocrine and metabolic disturbances specific to the fetus and newborn**

● **776 Hematological disorders of fetus and newborn**

Includes: disorders specific to the fetus or newborn

776.0 Hemorrhagic disease of newborn
Hemorrhagic diathesis of newborn
Vitamin K deficiency of newborn

Excludes *fetal or neonatal hemorrhage (772.0–772.9)*

776.1 Transient neonatal thrombocytopenia
Neonatal thrombocytopenia due to:
exchange transfusion
idiopathic maternal thrombocytopenia
isoimmunization

776.2 Disseminated intravascular coagulation in newborn

☐ **776.3 Other transient neonatal disorders of coagulation**
Transient coagulation defect, newborn

776.4 Polycythemia neonatorum
Plethora of newborn
Polycythemia due to:
donor twin transfusion
maternal-fetal transfusion

776.5 Congenital anemia
Anemia following fetal blood loss

Excludes *anemia due to isoimmunization (773.0–773.2, 773.5)*
hereditary hemolytic anemias (282.0–282.9)

776.6 Anemia of prematurity

776.7 Transient neonatal neutropenia
Isoimmune neutropenia
Maternal transfer neutropenia

Excludes *congenital neutropenia (nontransient) (288.0)*

☐ **776.8 Other specified transient hematological disorders**

☐ **776.9 Unspecified hematological disorder specific to fetus or newborn**

● **777 Perinatal disorders of digestive system**

Includes: disorders specific to the fetus and newborn
Excludes *intestinal obstruction classifiable to 560.0–560.9*

777.1 Meconium obstruction
Congenital fecaliths
Delayed passage of meconium
Meconium ileus NOS
Meconium plug syndrome

Excludes *meconium ileus in cystic fibrosis (277.01)*

777.2 Intestinal obstruction due to inspissated milk

777.3 Hematemesis and melena due to swallowed maternal blood
Swallowed blood syndrome in newborn

Excludes *that not due to swallowed maternal blood (772.4)*

777.4 Transitory ileus of newborn

Excludes *Hirschsprung's disease (751.3)*

777.5 Necrotizing enterocolitis in fetus or newborn
Pseudomembranous enterocolitis in newborn

777.6 Perinatal intestinal perforation
Meconium peritonitis

☐ **777.8 Other specified perinatal disorders of digestive system**

☐ **777.9 Unspecified perinatal disorder of digestive system**

    ◀▶ **New Code**   ⬅▦▦➡ **Revised Code**   ● **Not a Principal Diagnosis**   ● **Use Additional Digit(s)**   ☐ **Nonspecific Code**

● **778 Conditions involving the integument and temperature regulation of fetus and newborn**

778.0 Hydrops fetalis not due to isoimmunization
Idiopathic hydrops

> **Excludes** *hydrops fetalis due to isoimmunization (773.3)*

778.1 Sclerema neonatorum

778.2 Cold injury syndrome of newborn

☐ **778.3 Other hypothermia of newborn**

☐ **778.4 Other disturbances of temperature regulation of newborn**
Dehydration fever in newborn
Environmentally induced pyrexia
Hyperthermia in newborn
Transitory fever of newborn

☐ **778.5 Other and unspecified edema of newborn**
Edema neonatorum

778.6 Congenital hydrocele
Congenital hydrocele of tunica vaginalis

778.7 Breast engorgement in newborn
Noninfective mastitis of newborn

> **Excludes** *infective mastitis of newborn (771.5)*

☐ **778.8 Other specified conditions involving the integument of fetus and newborn**
Urticaria neonatorum

> **Excludes** *impetigo neonatorum (684)*
> *pemphigus neonatorum (684)*

☐ **778.9 Unspecified condition involving the integument and temperature regulation of fetus and newborn**

● **779 Other and ill-defined conditions originating in the perinatal period**

779.0 Convulsions in newborn
Fits in newborn
Seizures in newborn

☐ **779.1 Other and unspecified cerebral irritability in newborn**

779.2 Cerebral depression, coma, and other abnormal cerebral signs
CNS dysfunction in newborn NOS

779.3 Feeding problems in newborn
Regurgitation of food in newborn
Slow feeding in newborn
Vomiting in newborn

779.4 Drug reactions and intoxications specific to newborn
Gray syndrome from chloramphenicol administration in newborn

> **Excludes** *fetal alcohol syndrome (760.71)*
> *reactions and intoxications from maternal opiates and tranquilizers (763.5)*

779.5 Drug withdrawal syndrome in newborn
Drug withdrawal syndrome in infant of dependent mother

> **Excludes** *fetal alcohol syndrome (760.71)*

779.6 Termination of pregnancy (fetus)
Fetal death due to:
induced abortion
termination of pregnancy

> **Excludes** *spontaneous abortion (fetus) (761.8)*

☐ **779.8 Other specified conditions originating in the perinatal period**

☐ **779.9 Unspecified condition originating in the perinatal period**
Congenital debility NOS
Stillbirth, NEC

16. SYMPTOMS, SIGNS, AND ILL-DEFINED CONDITIONS (780–799)

This section includes symptoms, signs, abnormal results of laboratory or other investigative procedures, and ill-defined conditions regarding which no diagnosis classifiable elsewhere is recorded.

Signs and symptoms that point rather definitely to a given diagnosis are assigned to some category in the preceding part of the classification. In general, categories 780–796 include the more ill-defined conditions and symptoms that point with perhaps equal suspicion to two or more diseases or to two or more systems of the body, and without the necessary study of the case to make a final diagnosis. Practically all categories in this group could be designated as "not otherwise specified," or as "unknown etiology," or as "transient." The Alphabetic Index should be consulted to determine which symptoms and signs are to be allocated here and which to more specific sections of the classification; the residual subcategories numbered .9 are provided for other relevant symptoms which cannot be allocated elsewhere in the classification.

The conditions and signs or symptoms included in categories 780–796 consist of: (a) cases for which no more specific diagnosis can be made even after all facts bearing on the case have been investigated; (b) signs or symptoms existing at the time of initial encounter that proved to be transient and whose causes could not be determined; (c) provisional diagnoses in a patient who failed to return for further investigation or care; (d) cases referred elsewhere for investigation or treatment before the diagnosis was made; (e) cases in which a more precise diagnosis was not available for any other reason; (f) certain symptoms which represent important problems in medical care and which it might be desired to classify in addition to a known cause.

SYMPTOMS (780–789)

● **780 General symptoms**

● **780.0 Alteration of consciousness**

> **Excludes** *coma:*
> *diabetic (250.2–250.3)*
> *hepatic (572.2)*
> *originating in the perinatal period (779.2)*

780.01 Coma

780.02 Transient alteration of awareness

780.03 Persistent vegetative state

☐ **780.09 Other**
Drowsiness
Semicoma
Somnolence
Stupor
Unconsciousness

780.1 Hallucinations
Hallucinations:
NOS
auditory
gustatory
olfactory
tactile

> **Excludes** *those associated with mental disorders, as functional psychoses (295.0–298.9)*
> *organic brain syndromes (290.0–294.9, 310.0–310.9)*
> *visual hallucinations (368.16)*

780.2 Syncope and collapse
Blackout
Fainting
(Near) (Pre)syncope
Vasovagal attack

    Excludes *carotid sinus syncope (337.0)*
heat syncope (992.1)
neurocirculatory asthenia (306.2)
orthostatic hypotension (458.0)
shock NOS (785.50)

● **780.3 Convulsions**

    Excludes *convulsions:*
epileptic (345.10–345.91)
in newborn (779.0)

    780.31 Febrile convulsions
Febrile seizures

    ☐ **780.39 Other convulsions**
Convulsive disorder NOS
Fits NOS
Seizures NOS

780.4 Dizziness and giddiness
Light-headedness
Vertigo NOS

    Excludes *Ménière's disease and other specified vertiginous*
syndromes (386.0–386.9)

● **780.5 Sleep disturbances**

    Excludes *that of nonorganic origin (307.40–307.49)*

    ☐ **780.50 Sleep disturbance, unspecified**

    780.51 Insomnia with sleep apnea

    ☐ **780.52 Other insomnia**
Insomnia NOS

    780.53 Hypersomnia with sleep apnea

    ☐ **780.54 Other hypersomnia**
Hypersomnia NOS

    780.55 Disruptions of 24-hour sleep-wake cycle
Inversion of sleep rhythm
Irregular sleep-wake rhythm NOS
Non-24-hour sleep-wake rhythm

    780.56 Dysfunctions associated with sleep stages or arousal from sleep

    ☐ **780.57 Other and unspecified sleep apnea**

    ☐ **780.59 Other**

780.6 Fever
Chills with fever
Fever NOS
Fever of unknown origin (FUO)
Hyperpyrexia NOS
Pyrexia NOS
Pyrexia of unknown origin

    Excludes *pyrexia of unknown origin (during):*
in newborn (778.4)
labor (659.2)
the puerperium (672)

● **780.7 Malaise and fatigue**

    Excludes *debility, unspecified (799.3)*
fatigue (during):
combat (308.0–308.9)
heat (992.6)
pregnancy (646.8)
neurasthenia (300.5)
senile asthenia (797)

    780.71 Chronic fatigue syndrome ◀

    ☐ **780.79 Other malaise and fatigue** ◀
Asthenia NOS ◀
Lethargy ◀
Postviral (asthenic) syndrome ◀
Tiredness ◀

780.8 Hyperhidrosis
Diaphoresis
Excessive sweating

☐ **780.9 Other general symptoms**
Amnesia (retrograde)
Chill(s) NOS
Generalized pain
Hypothermia, not associated with low environ-
mental temperature

    Excludes *hypothermia:*
NOS (accidental) (991.6)
due to anesthesia (995.89)
memory disturbance as part of a pattern of
mental disorder
of newborn (778.2–778.3)

● **781 Symptoms involving nervous and musculoskeletal systems**

    Excludes *depression NOS (311)*
disorders specifically relating to:
back (724.0–724.9)
hearing (388.0–389.9)
joint (718.0–719.9)
limb (729.0–729.9)
neck (723.0–723.9)
vision (368.0–369.9)
pain in limb (729.5)

781.0 Abnormal involuntary movements
Abnormal head movements
Fasciculation
Spasms NOS
Tremor NOS

    Excludes *abnormal reflex (796.1)*
chorea NOS (333.5)
infantile spasms (345.60–345.61)
spastic paralysis (342.1, 343.0–344.9)
specified movement disorders classifiable to 333
(333.0–333.9)
that of nonorganic origin (307.2–307.3)

781.1 Disturbances of sensation of smell and taste
Anosmia
Parageusia
Parosmia

781.2 Abnormality of gait
Gait:
ataxic
paralytic
spastic
staggering

    Excludes *ataxia:*
NOS (781.3)
locomotor (progressive) (094.0)
difficulty in walking (719.7)

781.3 Lack of coordination
Ataxia NOS
Muscular incoordination

    Excludes *ataxic gait (781.2)*
cerebellar ataxia (334.0–334.9)
difficulty in walking (719.7)
vertigo NOS (780.4)

781.4 Transient paralysis of limb
Monoplegia, transient NOS

    Excludes *paralysis (342.0–344.9)*

781.5 Clubbing of fingers

◀▶ **New Code**   ⬅▦➡ **Revised Code**   ● **Not a Principal Diagnosis**   ● **Use Additional Digit(s)**   ☐ **Nonspecific Code**

781.6 Meningismus
Dupré's syndrome
Meningism

781.7 Tetany
Carpopedal spasm

> **Excludes** *tetanus neonatorum (771.3)*
> *tetany:*
> *hysterical (300.11)*
> *newborn (hypocalcemic) (775.4)*
> *parathyroid (252.1)*
> *psychogenic (306.0)*

781.8 Neurologic neglect syndrome

Asomatognosia	Left-sided neglect
Hemi-akinesia	Sensory extinction
Hemi-inattention	Sensory neglect
Hemispatial neglect	Visuospatial neglect

☐ **781.9 Other symptoms involving nervous and musculo-skeletal systems**
Abnormal posture

● **782 Symptoms involving skin and other integumentary tissue**

> **Excludes** *symptoms relating to breast (611.71–611.79)*

782.0 Disturbance of skin sensation
Anesthesia of skin
Burning or prickling sensation
Hyperesthesia
Hypoesthesia
Numbness
Paresthesia
Tingling

☐ **782.1 Rash and other nonspecific skin eruption**
Exanthem

> **Excludes** *vesicular eruption (709.8)*

782.2 Localized superficial swelling, mass, or lump
Subcutaneous nodules

> **Excludes** *localized adiposity (278.1)*

782.3 Edema
Anasarca
Dropsy
Localized edema NOS

> **Excludes** *ascites (789.5)*
> *edema of:*
> *newborn NOS (778.5)*
> *pregnancy (642.0–642.9, 646.1)*
> *fluid retention (276.6)*
> *hydrops fetalis (773.3, 778.0)*
> *hydrothorax (511.8)*
> *nutritional edema (260, 262)*

☐ **782.4 Jaundice, unspecified, not of newborn**
Cholemia NOS
Icterus NOS

> **Excludes** *due to isoimmunization (773.0–773.2, 773.4)*
> *jaundice in newborn (774.0–774.7)*

782.5 Cyanosis

> **Excludes** *newborn (770.8)*

● **782.6 Pallor and flushing**

782.61 Pallor

782.62 Flushing
Excessive blushing

782.7 Spontaneous ecchymoses
Petechiae

> **Excludes** *ecchymosis in fetus or newborn (772.6)*
> *purpura (287.0–287.9)*

782.8 Changes in skin texture
Induration of skin
Thickening of skin

☐ **782.9 Other symptoms involving skin and integumentary tissues**

● **783 Symptoms concerning nutrition, metabolism, and development**

783.0 Anorexia
Loss of appetite

> **Excludes** *anorexia nervosa (307.1)*
> *loss of appetite of nonorganic origin (307.59)*

783.1 Abnormal weight gain

> **Excludes** *excessive weight gain in pregnancy (646.1)*
> *obesity (278.00)*
> *morbid (278.01)*

783.2 Abnormal loss of weight

783.3 Feeding difficulties and mismanagement
Feeding problem (elderly) (infant)

> **Excludes** *feeding disturbance or problems:*
> *in newborn (779.3)*
> *of nonorganic origin (307.50–307.59)*

783.4 Lack of expected normal physiological development

Delayed milestone	Lack of growth
Failure to gain weight	Physical retardation
Failure to thrive	Short stature

> **Excludes** *delay in sexual development and puberty (259.0)*
> *specific delays in mental development (315.0–315.9)*

783.5 Polydipsia
Excessive thirst

783.6 Polyphagia
Excessive eating
Hyperalimentation NOS

> **Excludes** *disorders of eating of nonorganic origin (307.50–307.59)*

☐ **783.9 Other symptoms concerning nutrition, metabolism, and development**
Hypometabolism

> **Excludes** *abnormal basal metabolic rate (794.7)*
> *dehydration (276.5)*
> *other disorders of fluid, electrolyte, and acid-base balance (276.0–276.9)*

● **784 Symptoms involving head and neck**

> **Excludes** *encephalopathy NOS (348.3)*
> *specific symptoms involving neck classifiable to 723 (723.0–723.9)*

784.0 Headache
Facial pain
Pain in head NOS

> **Excludes** *atypical face pain (350.2)*
> *migraine (346.0–346.9)*
> *tension headache (307.81)*

784.1 Throat pain

> **Excludes** *dysphagia (787.2)*
> *neck pain (723.1)*
> *sore throat (462)*
> *chronic (472.1)*

784.2 Swelling, mass, or lump in head and neck
Space-occupying lesion, intracranial NOS

784.3 Aphasia

> **Excludes** *developmental aphasia (315.31)*

● **784.4 Voice disturbance**

☐ **784.40 Voice disturbance, unspecified**

784.41 Aphonia
Loss of voice

ICD-9-CM

700-799

Vol. 1

❑ **784.49 Other**
Change in voice
Dysphonia
Hoarseness
Hypernasality
Hyponasality

❑ **784.5 Other speech disturbance**
Dysarthria
Dysphasia
Slurred speech

Excludes *stammering and stuttering (307.0)*
that of nonorganic origin (307.0, 307.9)

● **784.6 Other symbolic dysfunction**

Excludes *developmental learning delays (315.0–315.9)*

❑ **784.60 Symbolic dysfunction, unspecified**

784.61 Alexia and dyslexia
Alexia (with agraphia)

❑ **784.69 Other**
Acalculia
Agnosia
Agraphia NOS
Apraxia

784.7 Epistaxis
Hemorrhage from nose
Nosebleed

784.8 Hemorrhage from throat

Excludes *hemoptysis (786.3)*

❑ **784.9 Other symptoms involving head and neck**
Choking sensation
Halitosis
Mouth breathing
Sneezing

● **785 Symptoms involving cardiovascular system**

Excludes *heart failure NOS (428.9)*

❑ **785.0 Tachycardia, unspecified**
Rapid heart beat

Excludes *paroxysmal tachycardia (427.0–427.2)*

785.1 Palpitations
Awareness of heart beat

Excludes *specified dysrhythmias (427.0–427.9)*

785.2 Undiagnosed cardiac murmurs
Heart murmur NOS

❑ **785.3 Other abnormal heart sounds**
Cardiac dullness, increased or decreased
Friction fremitus, cardiac
Precordial friction

785.4 Gangrene
Gangrene:
  NOS
  spreading cutaneous
Gangrenous cellulitis
Phagedena

Code first any associated underlying condition
diabetes (250.7)
Raynaud's syndrome (443.0)

Excludes *gangrene of certain sites—see Alphabetic Index*
gangrene with atherosclerosis of the extremities
(440.24)
gas gangrene (040.0)

● **785.5 Shock without mention of trauma**

❑ **785.50 Shock, unspecified**
Failure of peripheral circulation

785.51 Cardiogenic shock

❑ **785.59 Other**
Shock:
  endotoxic
  gram-negative
  hypovolemic
  septic

Excludes *shock (due to):*
anesthetic (995.4)
anaphylactic (995.0)
  due to serum (999.4)
electric (994.8)
following abortion (639.5)
lightning (994.0)
obstetrical (669.1)
postoperative (998.0)
traumatic (958.4)

785.6 Enlargement of lymph nodes
Lymphadenopathy
"Swollen glands"

Excludes *lymphadenitis (chronic) (289.1–289.3)*
acute (683)

❑ **785.9 Other symptoms involving cardiovascular system**
Bruit (arterial)
Weak pulse

● **786 Symptoms involving respiratory system and other chest symptoms**

● **786.0 Dyspnea and respiratory abnormalities**

❑ **786.00 Respiratory abnormality, unspecified**

786.01 Hyperventilation

Excludes *hyperventilation, psychogenic (306.1)*

786.02 Orthopnea

786.03 Apnea ◀

Excludes *sleep apnea (780.51, 780.53, 780.57)* ◀

786.04 Cheyne-Stokes respiration ◀

786.05 Shortness of breath ◀

786.06 Tachypnea ◀

Excludes *transitory tachypnea of newborn (770.6)* ◀

786.07 Wheezing ◀

Excludes *asthma (493.00–493.91)* ◀

❑ **786.09 Other**
Respiratory:
  distress
  insufficiency

Excludes *respiratory distress:*
following trauma and surgery (518.5)
newborn (770.8)
respiratory failure (518.81, 518.83–518.84) ◀▬
  newborn (770.8)
syndrome (newborn) (769)
  adult (518.5)

786.1 Stridor

Excludes *congenital laryngeal stridor (748.3)*

786.2 Cough

Excludes *cough:*
psychogenic (306.1)
smokers' (491.0)
with hemorrhage (786.3)

786.3 Hemoptysis
Cough with hemorrhage
Pulmonary hemorrhage NOS

Excludes *pulmonary hemorrhage of newborn (770.3)*

    ◀▶ **New Code**   ▬◀ ▬▶ **Revised Code**   ● **Not a Principal Diagnosis**   ● **Use Additional Digit(s)**   ❑ **Nonspecific Code**

786.4 Abnormal sputum
Abnormal:
    amount of sputum
    color of sputum
    odor of sputum
    Excessive sputum

● **786.5 Chest pain**

□ **786.50 Chest pain, unspecified**

786.51 Precordial pain

786.52 Painful respiration
Pain:
    anterior chest wall
    pleuritic
    pleurodynia
| Excludes | *epidemic pleurodynia (074.1)* |

□ **786.59 Other**
Discomfort in chest
Pressure in chest
Tightness in chest
| Excludes | *pain in breast (611.71)* |

786.6 Swelling, mass, or lump in chest
| Excludes | *lump in breast (611.72)* |

786.7 Abnormal chest sounds
Abnormal percussion, chest
Friction sounds, chest
Rales
Tympany, chest
| Excludes | *wheezing (786.07)* |

786.8 Hiccough
| Excludes | *psychogenic hiccough (306.1)* |

□ **786.9 Other symptoms involving respiratory system and chest**
Breath-holding spell

● **787 Symptoms involving digestive system**
Excludes	*constipation (564.0)*
	pylorospasm (537.81)
	congenital (750.5)

● **787.0 Nausea and vomiting**
Emesis
Excludes	*hematemesis NOS (578.0)*
	vomiting:
	bilious, following gastrointestinal surgery (564.3)
	cyclical (536.2)
	psychogenic (306.4)
	excessive, in pregnancy (643.0–643.9)
	habit (536.2)
	of newborn (779.3)
	psychogenic NOS (307.54)

787.01 Nausea with vomiting

787.02 Nausea alone

787.03 Vomiting alone

787.1 Heartburn
Pyrosis
Waterbrash
| Excludes | *dyspepsia or indigestion (536.8)* |

787.2 Dysphagia
Difficulty in swallowing

787.3 Flatulence, eructation, and gas pain
Abdominal distention (gaseous)
Bloating
Tympanites (abdominal) (intestinal)
| Excludes | *aerophagy (306.4)* |

787.4 Visible peristalsis
Hyperperistalsis

787.5 Abnormal bowel sounds
Absent bowel sounds
Hyperactive bowel sounds

787.6 Incontinence of feces
Encopresis NOS
Incontinence of sphincter ani
| Excludes | *that of nonorganic origin (307.7)* |

787.7 Abnormal feces
Bulky stools
Excludes	*abnormal stool content (792.1)*
	melena:
	NOS (578.1)
	newborn (772.4, 777.3)

● **787.9 Other symptoms involving digestive system**
Excludes	*gastrointestinal hemorrhage (578.0–578.9)*
	intestinal obstruction (560.0–560.9)
	specific functional digestive disorders:
	esophagus (530.0–530.9)
	stomach and duodenum (536.0–536.9)
	those not elsewhere classified (564.0–564.9)

787.91 Diarrhea
Diarrhea NOS

787.99 Other
Change in bowel habits
Tenesmus (rectal)

● **788 Symptoms involving urinary system**
Excludes	*hematuria (599.7)*
	nonspecific findings on examination of the urine (791.0–791.9)
	small kidney of unknown cause (589.0–589.9)
	uremia NOS (586)

788.0 Renal colic
Colic (recurrent) of:
    kidney
    ureter

788.1 Dysuria
Painful urination
Strangury

● **788.2 Retention of urine**

□ **788.20 Retention of urine, unspecified**

788.21 Incomplete bladder emptying

□ **788.29 Other specified retention of urine**

● **788.3 Urinary incontinence**
| Excludes | *that of nonorganic origin (307.6)* |

Code first any underlying condition, such as:
    congenital ureterocele (753.23)
    genital prolapse (618.0–618.9)

□ **788.30 Urinary incontinence, unspecified**
Enuresis NOS

788.31 Urge incontinence

788.32 Stress incontinence, male
| Excludes | *stress incontinence, female (625.6)* |

788.33 Mixed incontinence (female) (male)
Urge and stress

788.34 Incontinence without sensory awareness

788.35 Post-void dribbling

788.36 Nocturnal enuresis

788.37 Continuous leakage

□ **788.39 Other urinary incontinence**

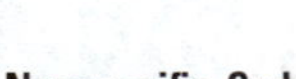

● **788.4 Frequency of urination and polyuria**

    788.41 Urinary frequency
         Frequency of micturition

    788.42 Polyuria

    788.43 Nocturia

788.5 Oliguria and anuria
     Deficient secretion of urine
     Suppression of urinary secretion

     | Excludes | *that complicating:*
         abortion (634–638 with .3, 639.3)
         ectopic or molar pregnancy (639.3)
         pregnancy, childbirth, or the puerperium
             (642.0–642.9, 646.2)

● **788.6 Other abnormality of urination**

    788.61 Splitting of urinary stream
         Intermittent urinary stream

    788.62 Slowing of urinary stream
         Weak stream

    ❑ **788.69 Other**

788.7 Urethral discharge
     Penile discharge   Urethrorrhea

788.8 Extravasation of urine

❑ **788.9 Other symptoms involving urinary system**
     Extrarenal uremia
     Vesical:
         pain
         tenesmus

● **789 Other symptoms involving abdomen and pelvis**

The following fifth-digit subclassification is to be used for codes 789.0, 789.3, 789.4, 789.6

  ❑ **0 unspecified site**
    1 right upper quadrant
    2 left upper quadrant
    3 right lower quadrant
    4 left lower quadrant
    5 periumbilic
    6 epigastric
  ❑ **7 generalized**
  ❑ **9 other specified site**
     multiple sites

     | Excludes | *symptoms referable to genital organs:*
         female (625.0–625.9)
         male (607.0–608.9)
         psychogenic (302.70–302.79)

● **789.0 Abdominal pain**
     Colic:
         NOS
         infantile
     Cramps, abdominal

     | Excludes | *renal colic (788.0)*

789.1 Hepatomegaly
     Enlargement of liver

789.2 Splenomegaly
     Enlargement of spleen

● **789.3 Abdominal or pelvic swelling, mass, or lump**
     Diffuse or generalized swelling or mass:
         abdominal NOS
         umbilical

     | Excludes | *abdominal distention (gaseous) (787.3)*
         ascites (789.5)

● **789.4 Abdominal rigidity**

789.5 Ascites
     Fluid in peritoneal cavity

● **789.6 Abdominal tenderness**
     Rebound tenderness

❑ **789.9 Other symptoms involving abdomen and pelvis**
     Umbilical:
         bleeding
         discharge

NONSPECIFIC ABNORMAL FINDINGS (790–796)

● **790 Nonspecific findings on examination of blood**

     | Excludes | *abnormality of:*
         platelets (287.0–287.9)
         thrombocytes (287.0–287.9)
         white blood cells (288.0–288.9)

    790.0 Abnormality of red blood cells
         Abnormal red cell:
             morphology NOS
             volume NOS
         Anisocytosis
         Poikilocytosis

         | Excludes | *anemia:*
             congenital (776.5)
             newborn, due to isoimmunization (773.0–
                 773.2, 773.5)
             of premature infant (776.6)
             other specified types (280.0–285.9)
         hemoglobin disorders (282.5–282.7)
         polycythemia:
             familial (289.6)
             neonatorum (776.4)
             secondary (289.0)
             vera (238.4)

    790.1 Elevated sedimentation rate

    790.2 Abnormal glucose tolerance test

         | Excludes | *that complicating pregnancy, childbirth, or the*
             puerperium (648.8)

    790.3 Excessive blood level of alcohol
         Elevated blood-alcohol

    ❑ **790.4 Nonspecific elevation of levels of transaminase or lactic acid dehydrogenase [LDH]**

    ❑ **790.5 Other nonspecific abnormal serum enzyme levels**
         Abnormal serum level of:
             acid phosphatase
             alkaline phosphatase
             amylase
             lipase

         | Excludes | *deficiency of circulating enzymes (277.6)*

    ❑ **790.6 Other abnormal blood chemistry**
         Abnormal blood levels of:
             cobalt
             copper
             iron
             lithium
             magnesium
             mineral
             zinc

         | Excludes | *abnormality of electrolyte or acid-base balance*
             (276.0–276.9)
         hypoglycemia NOS (251.2)
         specific finding indicating abnormality of:
             amino-acid transport and metabolism (270.0–
                 270.9)
             carbohydrate transport and metabolism
                 (271.0–271.9)
             lipid metabolism (272.0–272.9)
         uremia NOS (586)

    790.7 Bacteremia

         | Excludes | *septicemia (038)*

         Use additional code to identify organism (041)

◀▶ **New Code**   ⬅▣ ▣➡ **Revised Code**   ● **Not a Principal Diagnosis**   ● **Use Additional Digit(s)**   ❑ **Nonspecific Code**

❑ **790.8 Viremia, unspecified**

● **790.9 Other nonspecific findings on examination of blood**

790.91 Abnormal arterial blood gases

790.92 Abnormal coagulation profile
Abnormal or prolonged:
  bleeding time
  coagulation time
  partial thromboplastin time [PTT]
  prothrombin time [PT]

| Excludes | *coagulation (hemorrhagic) disorders (286.0–286.9)* |

790.93 Elevated prostate specific antigen [PSA]

790.94 Euthyroid sick syndrome

❑ **790.99 Other**

● **791 Nonspecific findings on examination of urine**

| Excludes | *hematuria NOS (599.7)* |
specific findings indicating abnormality of:
  amino-acid transport and metabolism (270.0–270.9)
  carbohydrate transport and metabolism (271.0–271.9)

791.0 Proteinuria
Albuminuria
Bence-Jones proteinuria

| Excludes | *postural proteinuria (593.6)* |
that arising during pregnancy or the puerperium (642.0–642.9, 646.2)

791.1 Chyluria

| Excludes | *filarial (125.0–125.9)* |

791.2 Hemoglobinuria

791.3 Myoglobinuria

791.4 Biliuria

791.5 Glycosuria

| Excludes | *renal glycosuria (271.4)* |

791.6 Acetonuria
Ketonuria

❑ **791.7 Other cells and casts in urine**

❑ **791.9 Other nonspecific findings on examination of urine**
Crystalluria
Elevated urine levels of:
  17-ketosteroids
  catecholamines
  indolacetic acid
  vanillylmandelic acid [VMA]
Melanuria

● **792 Nonspecific abnormal findings in other body substances**

| Excludes | *that in chromosomal analysis (795.2)* |

792.0 Cerebrospinal fluid

792.1 Stool contents
Abnormal stool color
Fat in stool
Mucus in stool
Occult blood
Pus in stool

| Excludes | *blood in stool [melena] (578.1)* |
newborn (772.4, 777.3)

792.2 Semen
Abnormal spermatozoa

| Excludes | *azoospermia (606.0)* |
oligospermia (606.1)

792.3 Amniotic fluid

792.4 Saliva

| Excludes | *that in chromosomal analysis (795.2)* |

❑ **792.9 Other nonspecific abnormal findings in body substances**
Peritoneal fluid
Pleural fluid
Synovial fluid
Vaginal fluids

● **793 Nonspecific abnormal findings on radiological and other examination of body structure**

Includes: nonspecific abnormal findings of:
  thermography
  ultrasound examination [echogram]
  x-ray examination

| Excludes | *abnormal results of function studies and radioisotope scans (794.0–794.9)* |

793.0 Skull and head

| Excludes | *nonspecific abnormal echoencephalogram (794.01)* |

793.1 Lung field
Coin lesion lung
Shadow, lung

❑ **793.2 Other intrathoracic organ**
Abnormal:
  echocardiogram
  heart shadow
  ultrasound cardiogram
Mediastinal shift

793.3 Biliary tract
Nonvisualization of gallbladder

793.4 Gastrointestinal tract

793.5 Genitourinary organs
Filling defect:
  bladder
  kidney
  ureter

793.6 Abdominal area, including retroperitoneum

793.7 Musculoskeletal system

793.8 Breast
Abnormal mammogram

❑ **793.9 Other**
Abnormal:
  placental finding by x-ray or ultrasound method
  radiological findings in skin and subcutaneous tissue

| Excludes | *abnormal finding by radioisotope localization of placenta (794.9)* |

● **794 Nonspecific abnormal results of function studies**

Includes: radioisotope:
  scans
  uptake studies
  scintiphotography

● **794.0 Brain and central nervous system**

❑ **794.00 Abnormal function study, unspecified**

794.01 Abnormal echoencephalogram

794.02 Abnormal electroencephalogram [EEG]

❑ **794.09 Other**
Abnormal brain scan

● **794.1 Peripheral nervous system and special senses**

❑ **794.10 Abnormal response to nerve stimulation, unspecified**

794.11 Abnormal retinal function studies
Abnormal electroretinogram [ERG]

794.12 Abnormal electro-oculogram [EOG]

794.13 Abnormal visually evoked potential

794.14 Abnormal oculomotor studies

794.15 Abnormal auditory function studies

794.16 Abnormal vestibular function studies

794.17 Abnormal electromyogram [EMG]

Excludes *that of eye (794.14)*

794.19 Other

794.2 Pulmonary
Abnormal lung scan
Reduced:
  ventilatory capacity
  vital capacity

● **794.3 Cardiovascular**

794.30 Abnormal function study, unspecified

794.31 Abnormal electrocardiogram [ECG] [EKG]

794.39 Other
Abnormal:
  ballistocardiogram
  phonocardiogram
  vectorcardiogram

794.4 Kidney
Abnormal renal function test

794.5 Thyroid
Abnormal thyroid:
  scan
  uptake

794.6 Other endocrine function study

794.7 Basal metabolism
Abnormal basal metabolic rate [BMR]

794.8 Liver
Abnormal liver scan

794.9 Other
Bladder
Pancreas
Placenta
Spleen

● **795 Nonspecific abnormal histological and immunological findings**

Excludes *nonspecific abnormalities of red blood cells (790.0)*

795.0 Nonspecific abnormal Papanicolaou smear of cervix
Dyskaryotic cervical smear

795.1 Nonspecific abnormal Papanicolaou smear of other site

795.2 Nonspecific abnormal findings on chromosomal analysis
Abnormal karyotype

795.3 Nonspecific positive culture findings
Positive culture findings in:
  nose
  sputum
  throat
  wound

Excludes *that of:*
  blood (790.7–790.8)
  urine (599.0)

795.4 Other nonspecific abnormal histological findings

795.5 Nonspecific reaction to tuberculin skin test without active tuberculosis
Abnormal result of Mantoux test
PPD positive
Tuberculin (skin test):
  positive
  reactor

795.6 False positive serological test for syphilis
False positive Wassermann reaction

● **795.7 Other nonspecific immunological findings**

Excludes *isoimmunization, in pregnancy (656.1–656.2)*
  affecting fetus or newborn (773.0–773.2)

795.71 Nonspecific serologic evidence of human immunodeficiency virus [HIV]
Inconclusive human immunodeficiency virus [HIV] test (adult) (infant)

Note: This code is ONLY to be used when a test finding is reported as nonspecific. Asymptomatic positive findings are coded to V08. If any HIV infection symptom or condition is present, see code 042. Negative findings are not coded.

Excludes *acquired immunodeficiency syndrome [AIDS] (042)*
  asymptomatic human immunodeficiency virus [HIV] infection status (V08)
  HIV infection, symptomatic (042)
  human immunodeficiency virus [HIV] disease (042)
  positive (status) NOS (V08)

795.79 Other and unspecified nonspecific immunological findings
Raised antibody titer
Raised level of immunoglobulins

● **796 Other nonspecific abnormal findings**

796.0 Nonspecific abnormal toxicological findings
Abnormal levels of heavy metals or drugs in blood, urine, or other tissue

Excludes *excessive blood level of alcohol (790.3)*

796.1 Abnormal reflex

796.2 Elevated blood pressure reading without diagnosis of hypertension

Note: This category is to be used to record an episode of elevated blood pressure in a patient in whom no formal diagnosis of hypertension has been made, or as an incidental finding.

796.3 Nonspecific low blood pressure reading

796.4 Other abnormal clinical findings

796.5 Abnormal finding on antenatal screening

796.9 Other

ILL-DEFINED AND UNKNOWN CAUSES OF MORBIDITY AND MORTALITY (797–799)

797 Senility without mention of psychosis
Old age   Senile:
Senescence   debility
Senile asthenia   exhaustion

Excludes *senile psychoses (290.0–290.9)*

● **798 Sudden death, cause unknown**

798.0 Sudden infant death syndrome
Cot death
Crib death
Sudden death of nonspecific cause in infancy

     ◄► **New Code**   ⬅▬ ▬➡ **Revised Code**   ● **Not a Principal Diagnosis**   ● **Use Additional Digit(s)**   ☐ **Nonspecific Code**

798.1 Instantaneous death

798.2 Death occurring in less than 24 hours from onset of symptoms, not otherwise explained
Death known not to be violent or instantaneous, for which no cause could be discovered
Died without sign of disease

798.9 Unattended death
Death in circumstances where the body of the deceased was found and no cause could be discovered
Found dead

● **799 Other ill-defined and unknown causes of morbidity and mortality**

799.0 Asphyxia
Excludes *asphyxia (due to):*
carbon monoxide (986)
inhalation of food or foreign body (932–934.9)
newborn (768.0–768.9)
traumatic (994.7)

799.1 Respiratory arrest
Cardiorespiratory failure
Excludes *cardiac arrest (427.5)*
failure of peripheral circulation (785.50)
respiratory distress:
NOS (786.09)
acute (518.82)
following trauma or surgery (518.5)
newborn (770.8)
syndrome (newborn) (769)
adult (following trauma or surgery) (518.5)
other (518.82)
respiratory failure (518.81, 518.83–518.84) ◀▦
newborn (770.8)
respiratory insufficiency (786.09)
acute (518.82)

799.2 Nervousness
"Nerves"

☐ **799.3 Debility, unspecified**
Excludes *asthenia (780.79)*   ◀▦
nervous debility (300.5)
neurasthenia (300.5)
senile asthenia (797)

799.4 Cachexia
Wasting disease
Excludes *nutritional marasmus (261)*

☐ **799.8 Other ill-defined conditions**

☐ **799.9 Other unknown and unspecified cause**
Undiagnosed disease, not specified as to site or system involved
Unknown cause of morbidity or mortality

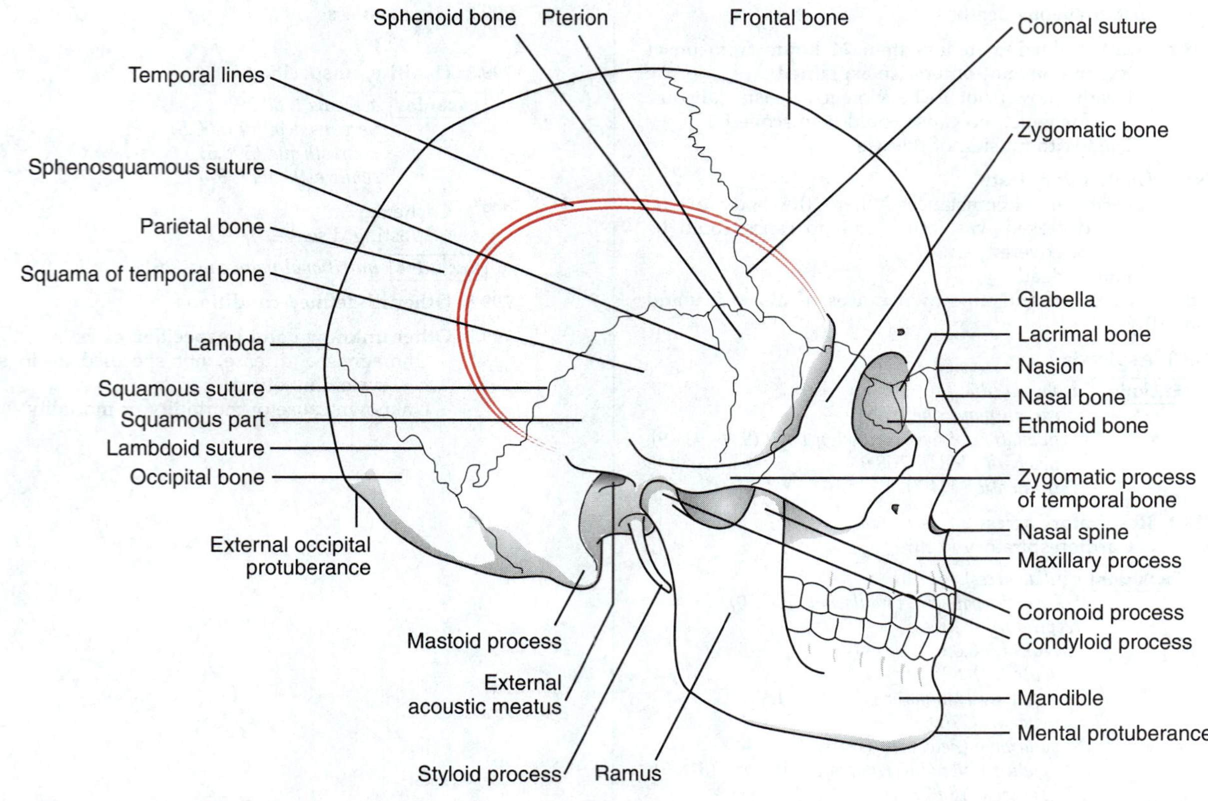

Figure 17–1 Lateral view of skull.

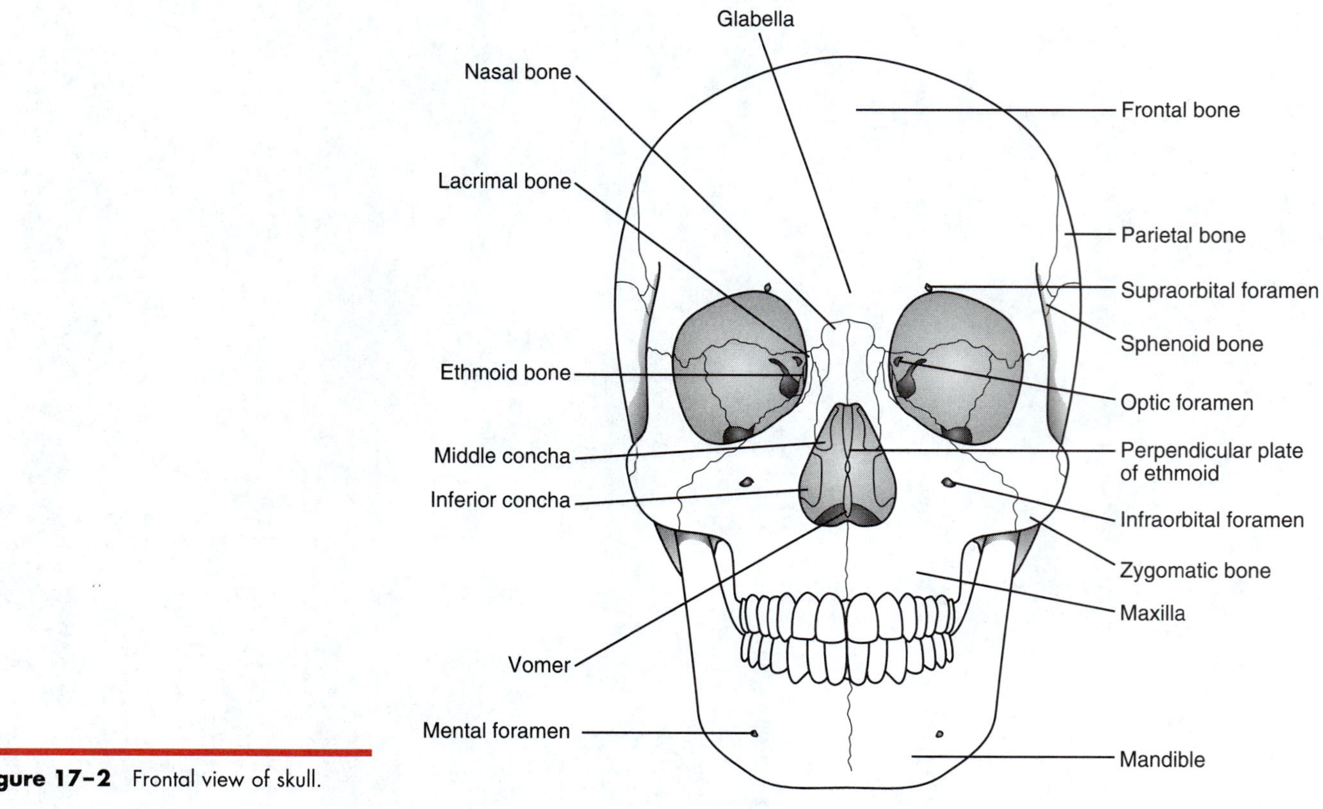

Figure 17–2 Frontal view of skull.

  ◀▶ **New Code**   ⬅ ➡ **Revised Code**   ● **Not a Principal Diagnosis**   ● **Use Additional Digit(s)**   ☐ **Nonspecific Code**

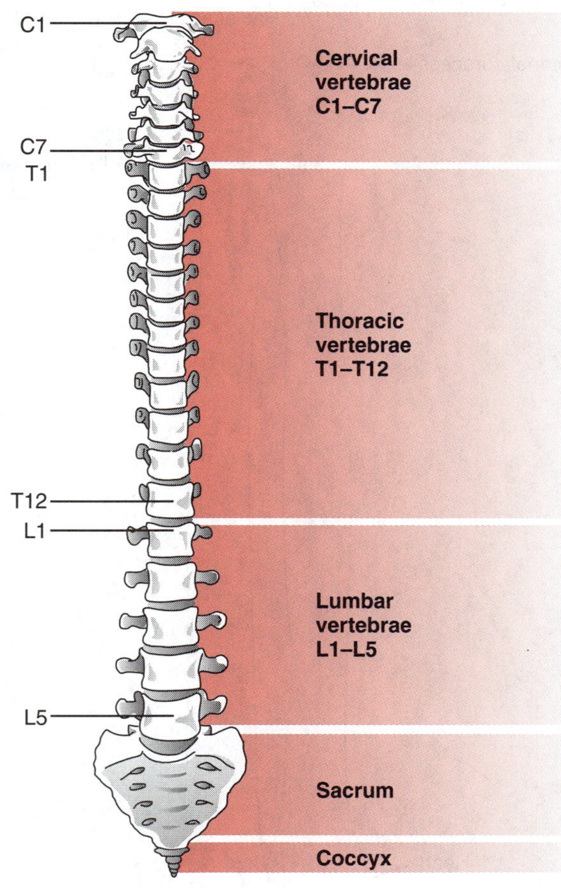

Figure 17–3 Anterior view of vertebral column.

Figure 17–4 Vertebra viewed from above.

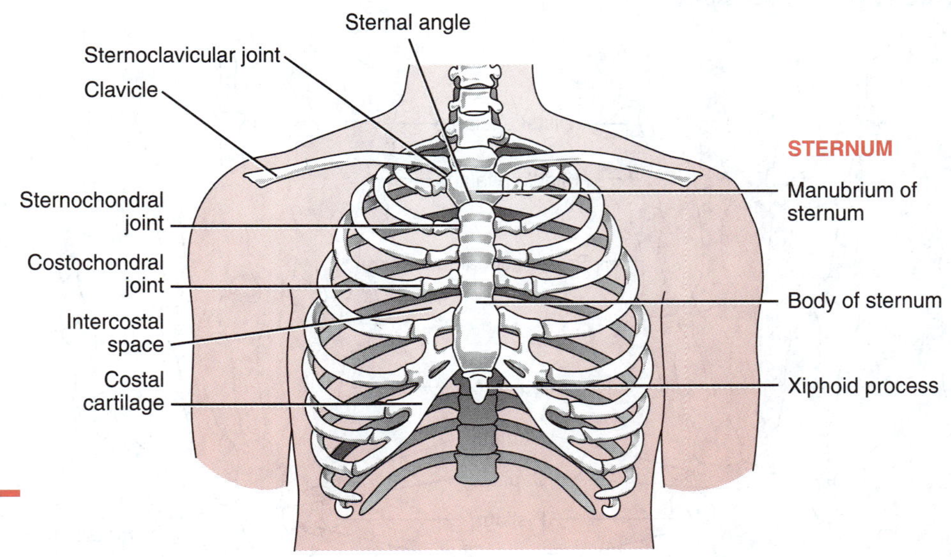

Figure 17–5 Anterior view of rib cage.

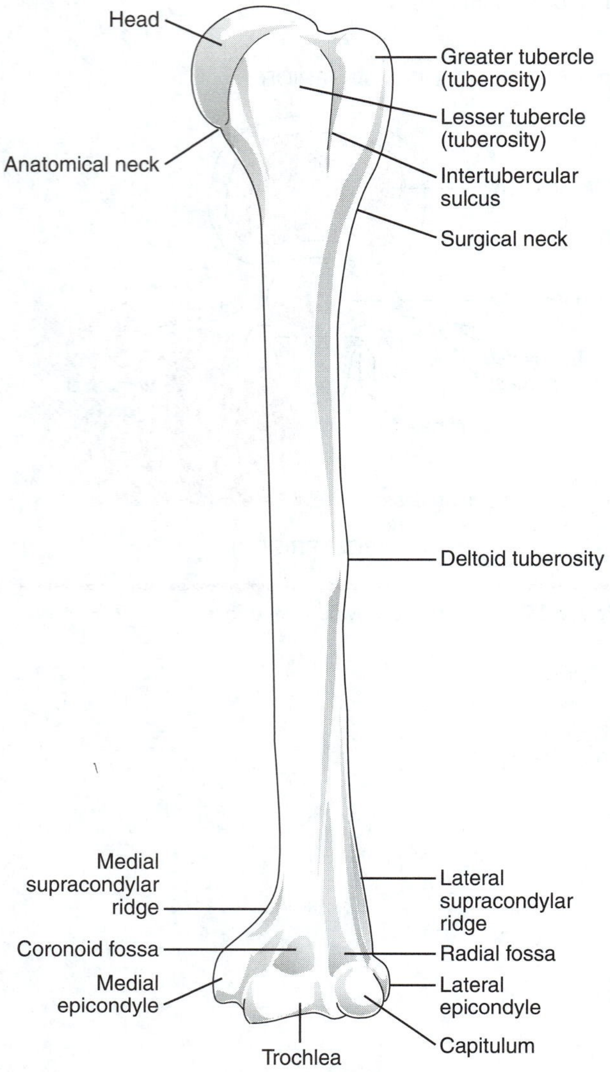

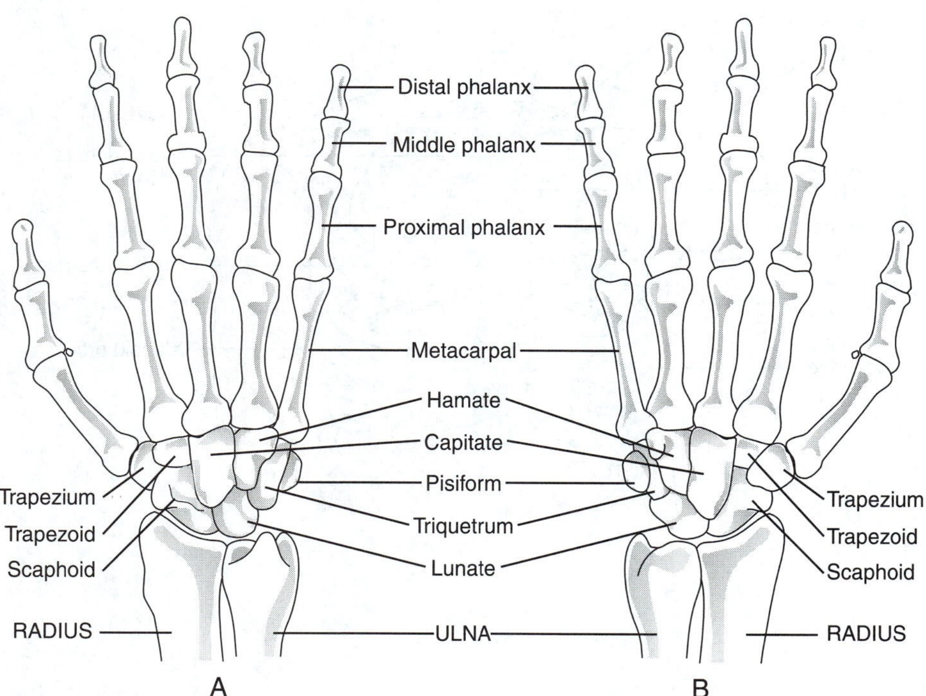

Figure 17-6 Anterior aspect of left humerus.

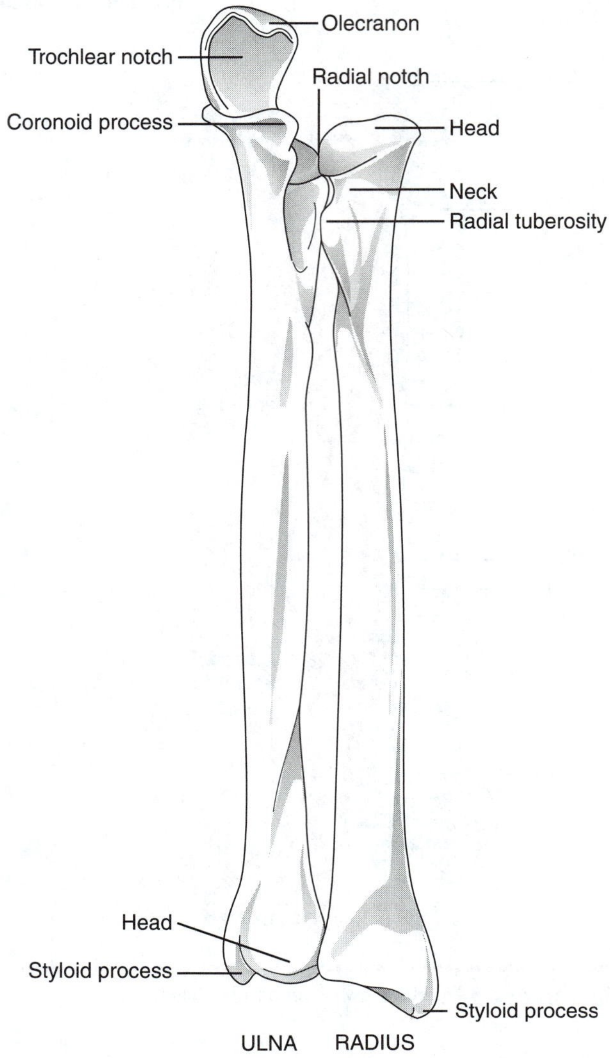

Figure 17-7 Anterior aspect of left radius and ulna.

Figure 17-8 Right hand and wrist: **A.** Dorsal surface. **B.** Palmar surface.

◀▶ **New Code**   ◀▥▥▶ **Revised Code**   ● **Not a Principal Diagnosis**   ● **Use Additional Digit(s)**   ❑ **Nonspecific Code**

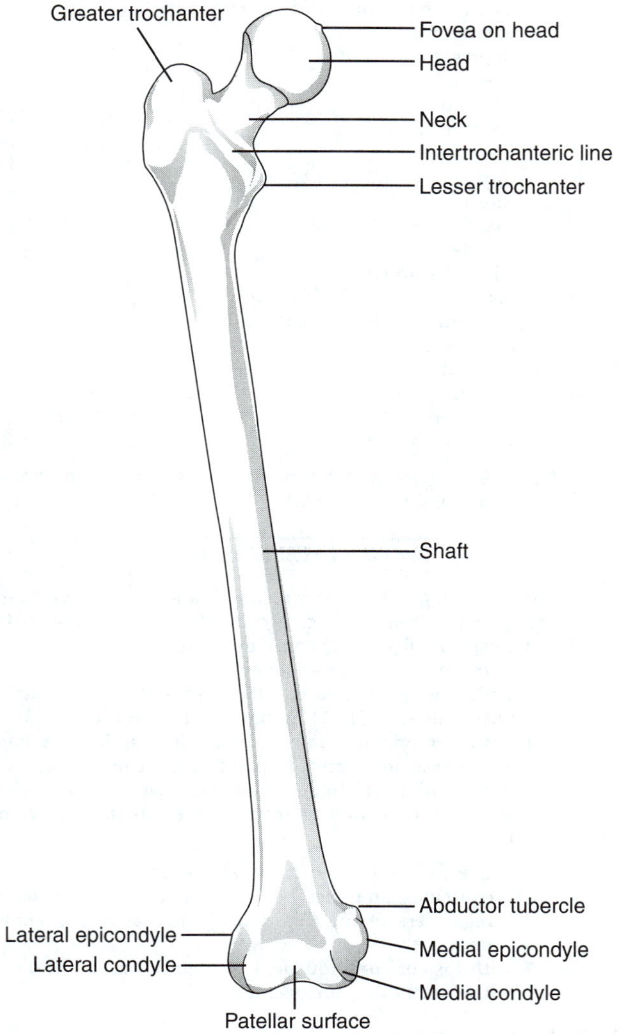

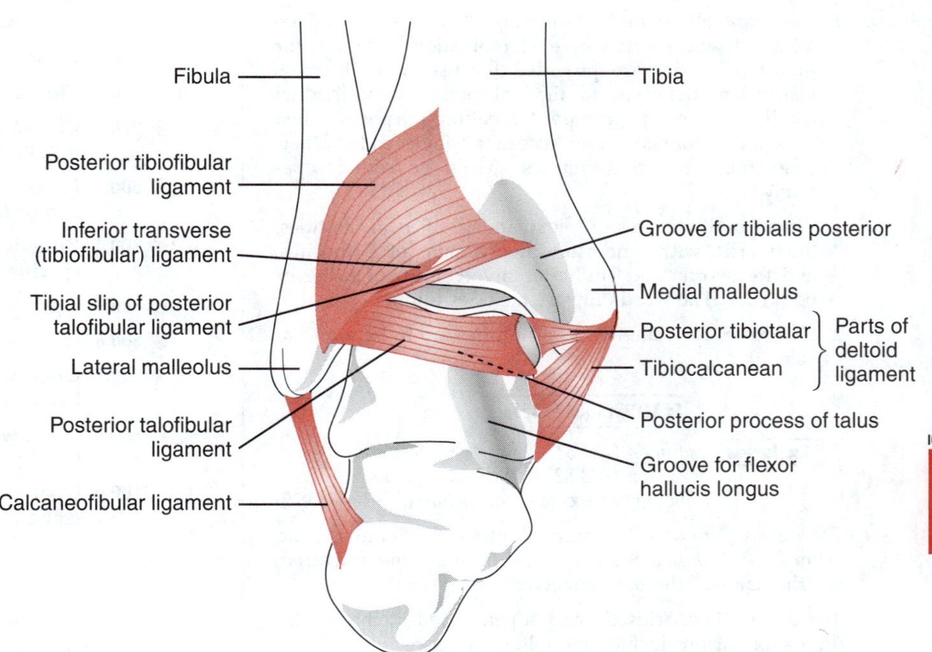

Figure 17–9 Anterior aspect of right femur.

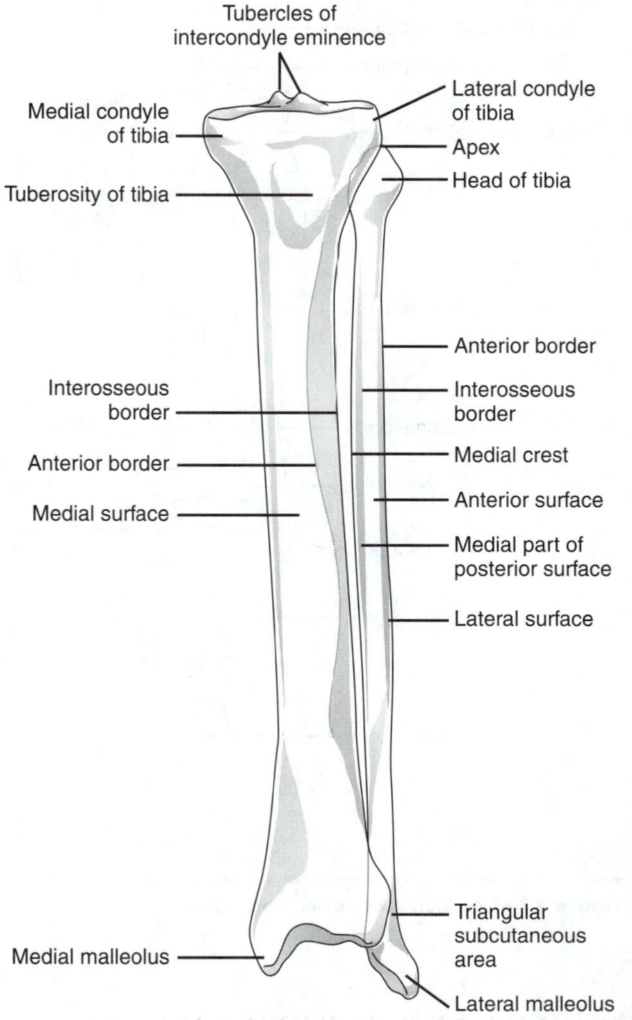

Figure 17–10 Anterior aspect of left tibia and fibula.

Figure 17–11 Posterior aspect of the left ankle joint.

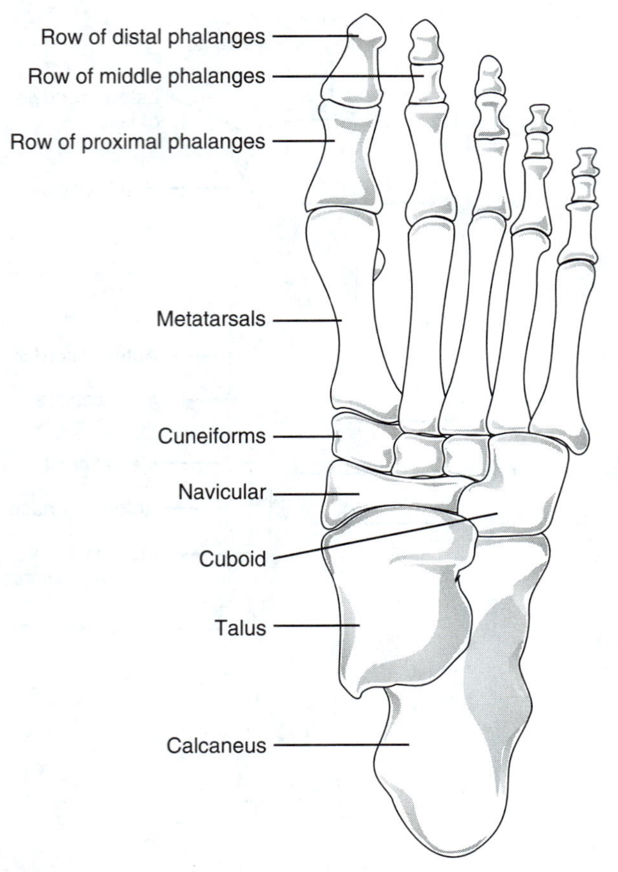

Figure 17-12　Right foot viewed from above.

17.　INJURY AND POISONING (800–999)

Use E code(s) to identify the cause and intent of the injury or poisoning (E800-E999)

Note:

1. The principle of multiple coding of injuries should be followed wherever possible. Combination categories for multiple injuries are provided for use when there is insufficient detail as to the nature of the individual conditions, or for primary tabulation purposes when it is more convenient to record a single code; otherwise, the component injuries should be coded separately.

   Where multiple sites of injury are specified in the titles, the word "with" indicates involvement of both sites, and the word "and" indicates involvement of either or both sites. The word "finger" includes thumb.

2. Categories for "late effect" of injuries are to be found at 905–909.

FRACTURES (800–829)

Excludes *malunion (733.81)*
nonunion (733.82)
pathologic or spontaneous fracture (733.10–733.19)

The terms "condyle," "coronoid process," "ramus," and "symphysis" indicate the portion of the bone fractured, not the name of the bone involved.

The descriptions "closed" and "open" used in the fourth-digit subdivisions include the following terms:

closed (with or without delayed healing):
  comminuted
  depressed
  elevated
  fissured
  fracture NOS
  greenstick
  impacted
  linear
  march
  simple
  slipped epiphysis
  spiral
open (with or without delayed healing):
  compound
  infected
  missile
  puncture
  with foreign body

Note: A fracture not indicated as closed or open should be classified as closed.

FRACTURE OF SKULL (800–804)

The following fifth-digit subclassification is for use with the appropriate codes in categories 800, 801, 803, and 804:

☐ **0** unspecified state of consciousness
  1 with no loss of consciousness
  2 with brief [less than one hour] loss of consciousness
  3 with moderate [1–24 hours] loss of consciousness
  4 with prolonged [more than 24 hours] loss of consciousness and return to pre-existing conscious level
  5 with prolonged [more than 24 hours] loss of consciousness, without return to pre-existing conscious level

    Use fifth-digit 5 to designate when a patient is unconscious and dies before regaining consciousness, regardless of the duration of the loss of consciousness

☐ **6** with loss of consciousness of unspecified duration
☐ **9** with concussion, unspecified

● **800**　**Fracture of vault of skull**

  Requires fifth digit. See beginning of section 800–804 for codes and definitions.

  Includes: frontal bone
          parietal bone

● **800.0**　**Closed without mention of intracranial injury**

● **800.1**　**Closed with cerebral laceration and contusion**

● **800.2**　**Closed wtih subarachnoid, subdural, and extradural hemorrhage**

☐● **800.3**　**Closed with other and unspecified intracranial hemorrhage**

☐● **800.4**　**Closed with intracranial injury of other and unspecified nature**

● **800.5**　**Open without mention of intracranial injury**

● **800.6**　**Open with cerebral laceration and contusion**

● **800.7**　**Open with subarachnoid, subdural, and extradural hemorrhage**

☐● **800.8**　**Open with other and unspecified intracranial hemorrhage**

☐● **800.9**　**Open with intracranial injury of other and unspecified nature**

　◄▶ **New Code**　⬅▮▮▮➡ **Revised Code**　● **Not a Principal Diagnosis**　● **Use Additional Digit(s)**　☐ **Nonspecific Code**

● **801 Fracture of base of skull**

Requires fifth digit. See beginning of section 800–804 for codes and definitions.

    Includes: fossa:
        anterior
        middle
        posterior
      occiput bone
      orbital roof
      sinus:
        ethmoid
        frontal
      sphenoid bone
      temporal bone

● **801.0 Closed without mention of intracranial injury**

● **801.1 Closed with cerebral laceration and contusion**

● **801.2 Closed with subarachnoid, subdural, and extra-dural hemorrhage**

□● **801.3 Closed with other and unspecified intracranial hemorrhage**

□● **801.4 Closed with intracranial injury of other and un-specified nature**

● **801.5 Open without mention of intracranial injury**

● **801.6 Open with cerebral laceration and contusion**

● **801.7 Open with subarachnoid, subdural, and extradural hemorrhage**

□● **801.8 Open with other and unspecified intracranial hemorrhage**

□● **801.9 Open with intracranial injury of other and unspecified nature**

● **802 Fracture of face bones**

   802.0 Nasal bones, closed

   802.1 Nasal bones, open

● **802.2 Mandible, closed**
      Inferior maxilla
      Lower jaw (bone)

   □ **802.20 Unspecified site**

    802.21 Condylar process

    802.22 Subcondylar

    802.23 Coronoid process

   □ **802.24 Ramus, unspecified**

    802.25 Angle of jaw

    802.26 Symphysis of body

    802.27 Alveolar border of body

   □ **802.28 Body, other and unspecified**

   □ **802.29 Multiple sites**

● **802.3 Mandible, open**

   □ **802.30 Unspecified site**

    802.31 Condylar process

    802.32 Subcondylar

    802.33 Coronoid process

   □ **802.34 Ramus, unspecified**

    802.35 Angle of jaw

    802.36 Symphysis of body

    802.37 Alveolar border of body

   □ **802.38 Body, other and unspecified**

   □ **802.39 Multiple sites**

   802.4 Malar and maxillary bones, closed
      Superior maxilla
      Upper jaw (bone)
      Zygoma
      Zygomatic arch

   802.5 Malar and maxillary bones, open

   802.6 Orbital floor (blow-out), closed

   802.7 Orbital floor (blow-out), open

□ **802.8 Other facial bones, closed**
      Alveolus
      Orbit:
        NOS
        part other than roof or floor
      Palate

   Excludes orbital:
      floor (802.6)
      roof (801.0–801.9)

□ **802.9 Other facial bones, open**

● **803 Other and unqualified skull fractures**

Requires fifth digit. See beginning of section 800–804 for codes and definitions.

    Includes: skull NOS
          skull multiple NOS

● **803.0 Closed without mention of intracranial injury**

● **803.1 Closed with cerebral laceration and contusion**

● **803.2 Closed with subarachnoid, subdural, and extra-dural hemorrhage**

□● **803.3 Closed with other and unspecified intracranial hemorrhage**

□● **803.4 Closed with intracranial injury of other and un-specified nature**

● **803.5 Open without mention of intracranial injury**

● **803.6 Open with cerebral laceration and contusion**

● **803.7 Open with subarachnoid, subdural, and extradural hemorrhage**

□● **803.8 Open with other and unspecified intracranial hemorrhage**

□● **803.9 Open with intracranial injury of other and unspecified nature**

● **804 Multiple fractures involving skull or face with other bones**

Requires fifth digit. See beginning of section 800–804 for codes and definitions.

● **804.0 Closed without mention of intracranial injury**

● **804.1 Closed with cerebral laceration and contusion**

● **804.2 Closed with subarachnoid, subdural, and extra-dural hemorrhage**

□● **804.3 Closed with other and unspecified intracranial hemorrhage**

□● **804.4 Closed with intracranial injury of other and un-specified nature**

● **804.5 Open without mention of intracranial injury**

● **804.6 Open with cerebral laceration and contusion**

● **804.7 Open with subarachnoid, subdural, and extradural hemorrhage**

□● **804.8 Open with other and unspecified intracranial hemorrhage**

□● **804.9 Open with intracranial injury of other and unspecified nature**

ICD-9-CM

800–899

Vol. 1

◀▶ **New Code**   ◀▮▮▮▶ **Revised Code**   ● **Not a Principal Diagnosis**   ● **Use Additional Digit(s)**   □ **Nonspecific Code**

FRACTURE OF NECK AND TRUNK (805–809)

● **805 Fracture of vertebral column without mention of spinal cord injury**

    Includes: neural arch
                spine
                spinous process
                transverse process
                vertebra

The following fifth-digit subclassification is for use with codes 805.0–805.1:

☐ 0 cervical vertebra, unspecified level
   1 first cervical vertebra
   2 second cervical vertebra
   3 third cervical vertebra
   4 fourth cervical vertebra
   5 fifth cervical vertebra
   6 sixth cervical vertebra
   7 seventh cervical vertebra
☐ 8 multiple cervical vertebrae

● **805.0 Cervical, closed**
      Atlas
      Axis

● **805.1 Cervical, open**

  805.2 Dorsal [thoracic], closed

  805.3 Dorsal [thoracic], open

  805.4 Lumbar, closed

  805.5 Lumbar, open

  805.6 Sacrum and coccyx, closed

  805.7 Sacrum and coccyx, open

☐ **805.8 Unspecified, closed**

☐ **805.9 Unspecified, open**

● **806 Fracture of vertebral column with spinal cord injury**

    Includes: any condition classifiable to 805 with:
            complete or incomplete transverse lesion (of cord)
            hematomyelia
            injury to:
                cauda equina
                nerve
            paralysis
            paraplegia
            quadriplegia
            spinal concussion

● **806.0 Cervical, closed**

☐ **806.00 C_1-C_4 level with unspecified spinal cord injury**
      Cervical region NOS with spinal cord injury NOS

  806.01 C_1-C_4 level with complete lesion of cord

  806.02 C_1-C_4 level with anterior cord syndrome

  806.03 C_1-C_4 level with central cord syndrome

☐ **806.04 C_1-C_4 level with other specified spinal cord injury**
      C_1-C_4 level with:
        incomplete spinal cord lesion NOS
        posterior cord syndrome

☐ **806.05 C_5-C_7 level with unspecified spinal cord injury**

  806.06 C_5-C_7 level with complete lesion of cord

  806.07 C_5-C_7 level with anterior cord syndrome

  806.08 C_5-C_7 level with central cord syndrome

☐ **806.09 C_5-C_7 level with other specified spinal cord injury**
      C_5-C_7 level with:
        incomplete spinal cord lesion NOS
        posterior cord syndrome

● **806.1 Cervical, open**

☐ **806.10 C_1-C_4 level with unspecified spinal cord injury**

  806.11 C_1-C_4 level with complete lesion of cord

  806.12 C_1-C_4 level with anterior cord syndrome

  806.13 C_1-C_4 level with central cord syndrome

☐ **806.14 C_1-C_4 level with other specified spinal cord injury**
      C_1-C_4 level with:
        incomplete spinal cord lesion NOS
        posterior cord syndrome

☐ **806.15 C_5-C_7 level with unspecified spinal cord injury**

  806.16 C_5-C_7 level with complete lesion of cord

  806.17 C_5-C_7 level with anterior cord syndrome

  806.18 C_5-C_7 level with central cord syndrome

☐ **806.19 C_5-C_7 level with other specified spinal cord injury**
      C_5-C_7 level with:
        incomplete spinal cord lesion NOS
        posterior cord syndrome

● **806.2 Dorsal [thoracic], closed**

☐ **806.20 T_1-T_6 level with unspecified spinal cord injury**
      Thoracic region NOS with spinal cord injury NOS

  806.21 T_1-T_6 level with complete lesion of cord

  806.22 T_1-T_6 level with anterior cord syndrome

  806.23 T_1-T_6 level with central cord syndrome

☐ **806.24 T_1-T_6 level with other specified spinal cord injury**
      T_1-T_6 level with:
        incomplete spinal cord lesion NOS
        posterior cord syndrome

☐ **806.25 T_7-T_{12} level with unspecified spinal cord injury**

  806.26 T_7-T_{12} level with complete lesion of cord

  806.27 T_7-T_{12} level with anterior cord syndrome

  806.28 T_7-T_{12} level with central cord syndrome

☐ **806.29 T_7-T_{12} level with other specified spinal cord injury**
      T_7-T_{12} level with:
        incomplete spinal cord lesion NOS
        posterior cord syndrome

● **806.3 Dorsal [thoracic], open**

☐ **806.30 T_1-T_6 level with unspecified spinal cord injury**

  806.31 T_1-T_6 level with complete lesion of cord

  806.32 T_1-T_6 level with anterior cord syndrome

  806.33 T_1-T_6 level with central cord syndrome

☐ **806.34 T_1-T_6 level with other specified spinal cord injury**
      T_1-T_6 level with:
        incomplete spinal cord lesion NOS
        posterior cord syndrome

☐ **806.35 T_7-T_{12} level with unspecified spinal cord injury**

806.36 T$_7$-T$_{12}$ level with complete lesion of cord

806.37 T$_7$-T$_{12}$ level with anterior cord syndrome

806.38 T$_7$-T$_{12}$ level with central cord syndrome

☐806.39 T$_7$-T$_{12}$ level with other specified spinal cord injury
  T$_7$-T$_{12}$ level with:
    incomplete spinal cord lesion NOS
    posterior cord syndrome

806.4 Lumbar, closed

806.5 Lumbar, open

●806.6 Sacrum and coccyx, closed

☐806.60 With unspecified spinal cord injury

806.61 With complete cauda equina lesion

☐806.62 With other cauda equina injury

☐806.69 With other spinal cord injury

●806.7 Sacrum and coccyx, open

☐806.70 With unspecified spinal cord injury

806.71 With complete cauda equina lesion

☐806.72 With other cauda equina injury

☐806.79 With other spinal cord injury

☐806.8 Unspecified, closed

☐806.9 Unspecified, open

●807 Fracture of rib(s), sternum, larynx, and trachea

The following fifth-digit subclassification is for use with codes 807.0–807.1:
☐ 0 rib(s), unspecified
  1 one rib
  2 two ribs
  3 three ribs
  4 four ribs
  5 five ribs
  6 six ribs
  7 seven ribs
  8 eight or more ribs
☐ 9 multiple ribs, unspecified

●807.0 Rib(s), closed

●807.1 Rib(s), open

807.2 Sternum, closed

807.3 Sternum, open

807.4 Flail chest

807.5 Larynx and trachea, closed
  Hyoid bone   Trachea
  Thyroid cartilage

807.6 Larynx and trachea, open

●808 Fracture of pelvis

808.0 Acetabulum, closed

808.1 Acetabulum, open

808.2 Pubis, closed

808.3 Pubis, open

●808.4 Other specified part, closed

808.41 Ilium

808.42 Ischium

☐808.43 Multiple pelvic fractures with disruption of pelvic circle

☐808.49 Other
  Innominate bone   Pelvic rim

●808.5 Other specified part, open

808.51 Ilium

808.52 Ischium

☐808.53 Multiple pelvic fractures with disruption of pelvic circle

☐808.59 Other

☐808.8 Unspecified, closed

☐808.9 Unspecified, open

●809 Ill-defined fractures of bones of trunk

Includes: bones of trunk with other bones except those of skull and face
multiple bones of trunk

Excludes *multiple fractures of:*
  pelvic bones alone (808.0–808.9)
  ribs alone (807.0–807.1, 807.4)
  ribs or sternum with limb bones (819.0–819.1, 828.0–828.1)
  skull or face with other bones (804.0–804.9)

809.0 Fracture of bones of trunk, closed

809.1 Fracture of bones of trunk, open

FRACTURE OF UPPER LIMB (810–819)

●810 Fracture of clavicle

Includes: collar bone
  interligamentous part of clavicle

The following fifth-digit subclassification is for use with category 810:
☐ 0 unspecified part
  clavicle NOS
  1 sternal end of clavicle
  2 shaft of clavicle
  3 acromial end of clavicle

●810.0 Closed

●810.1 Open

●811 Fracture of scapula

Includes: shoulder blade

The following fifth-digit subclassification is for use with category 811:
☐ 0 unspecified part
  1 acromial process
    acromion (process)
  2 coracoid process
  3 glenoid cavity and neck of scapula
☐ 9 other

●811.0 Closed

●811.1 Open

●812 Fracture of humerus

●812.0 Upper end, closed

☐812.00 Upper end, unspecified part
  Proximal end
  Shoulder

812.01 Surgical neck
  Neck of humerus NOS

812.02 Anatomical neck

812.03 Greater tuberosity

☐812.09 Other
  Head
  Upper epiphysis

●812.1 Upper end, open

☐812.10 Upper end, unspecified part

ICD-9-CM

800-899

Vol. 1

812.11 **Surgical neck**

812.12 **Anatomical neck**

812.13 **Greater tuberosity**

☐812.19 **Other**

● 812.2 **Shaft or unspecified part, closed**

☐812.20 **Unspecified part of humerus**
 Humerus NOS
 Upper arm NOS

812.21 **Shaft of humerus**

● 812.3 **Shaft or unspecified part, open**

☐812.30 **Unspecified part of humerus**

812.31 **Shaft of humerus**

● 812.4 **Lower end, closed**
 Distal end of humerus
 Elbow

☐812.40 **Lower end, unspecified part**

812.41 **Supracondylar fracture of humerus**

812.42 **Lateral condyle**
 External condyle

812.43 **Medial condyle**
 Internal epicondyle

☐812.44 **Condyle(s), unspecified**
 Articular process NOS
 Lower epiphysis

☐812.49 **Other**
 Multiple fractures of lower end
 Trochlea

● 812.5 **Lower end, open**

☐812.50 **Lower end, unspecified part**

812.51 **Supracondylar fracture of humerus**

812.52 **Lateral condyle**

812.53 **Medial condyle**

☐812.54 **Condyle(s), unspecified**

☐812.59 **Other**

● 813 **Fracture of radius and ulna**

● 813.0 **Upper end, closed**
 Proximal end

☐813.00 **Upper end of forearm, unspecified**

813.01 **Olecranon process of ulna**

813.02 **Coronoid process of ulna**

813.03 **Monteggia's fracture**

☐813.04 **Other and unspecified fractures of proximal end of ulna (alone)**
 Multiple fractures of ulna, upper end

813.05 **Head of radius**

813.06 **Neck of radius**

☐813.07 **Other and unspecified fractures of proximal end of radius (alone)**
 Multiple fractures of radius, upper end

813.08 **Radius with ulna, upper end [any part]**

● 813.1 **Upper end, open**

☐813.10 **Upper end of forearm, unspecified**

813.11 **Olecranon process of ulna**

813.12 **Coronoid process of ulna**

813.13 **Monteggia's fracture**

☐813.14 **Other and unspecified fractures of proximal end of ulna (alone)**

813.15 **Head of radius**

813.16 **Neck of radius**

☐813.17 **Other and unspecified fractures of proximal end of radius (alone)**

813.18 **Radius with ulna, upper end [any part]**

● 813.2 **Shaft, closed**

☐813.20 **Shaft, unspecified**

813.21 **Radius (alone)**

813.22 **Ulna (alone)**

813.23 **Radius with ulna**

● 813.3 **Shaft, open**

☐813.30 **Shaft, unspecified**

813.31 **Radius (alone)**

813.32 **Ulna (alone)**

813.33 **Radius with ulna**

● 813.4 **Lower end, closed**
 Distal end

☐813.40 **Lower end of forearm, unspecified**

813.41 **Colles' fracture**
 Smith's fracture

☐813.42 **Other fractures of distal end of radius (alone)**
 Dupuytren's fracture, radius
 Radius, lower end

813.43 **Distal end of ulna (alone)**
 Ulna:
  head
  lower end
  lower epiphysis
  styloid process

813.44 **Radius with ulna, lower end**

● 813.5 **Lower end, open**

☐813.50 **Lower end of forearm, unspecified**

813.51 **Colles' fracture**

☐813.52 **Other fractures of distal end of radius (alone)**

813.53 **Distal end of ulna (alone)**

813.54 **Radius with ulna, lower end**

● 813.8 **Unspecified part, closed**

☐813.80 **Forearm, unspecified**

☐813.81 **Radius (alone)**

☐813.82 **Ulna (alone)**

☐813.83 **Radius with ulna**

● 813.9 **Unspecified part, open**

☐813.90 **Forearm, unspecified**

☐813.91 **Radius (alone)**

☐813.92 **Ulna (alone)**

☐813.93 **Radius with ulna**

  ◀▶ **New Code** ⬅▮▮➡ **Revised Code** ● **Not a Principal Diagnosis** ● **Use Additional Digit(s)** ☐ **Nonspecific Code**

● **814 Fracture of carpal bone(s)**

The following fifth-digit subclassification is for use with category 814:

☐ **0 carpal bone, unspecified**
    Wrist NOS
    1 navicular [scaphoid] of wrist
    2 lunate [semilunar] bone of wrist
    3 triquetral [cuneiform] bone of wrist
    4 pisiform
    5 trapezium bone [larger multangular]
    6 trapezoid bone [smaller multangular]
    7 capitate bone [os magnum]
    8 hamate [unciform] bone
☐ **9 other**

 ● **814.0 Closed**

 ● **814.1 Open**

● **815 Fracture of metacarpal bone(s)**

    Includes: hand [except finger]
            metacarpus

The following fifth-digit subclassification is for use with category 815:

☐ **0 metacarpal bone(s), site unspecified**
    1 base of thumb [first] metacarpal
       Bennett's fracture
    2 base of other metacarpal bone(s)
    3 shaft of metacarpal bone(s)
    4 neck of metacarpal bone(s)
☐ **9 multiple sites of metacarpus**

 ● **815.0 Closed**

 ● **815.1 Open**

● **816 Fracture of one or more phalanges of hand**

    Includes: finger(s)
            thumb

The following fifth-digit subclassification is for use with category 816:

☐ **0 phalanx or phalanges, unspecified**
    1 middle or proximal phalanx or phalanges
    2 distal phalanx or phalanges
☐ **3 multiple sites**

 ● **816.0 Closed**

 ● **816.1 Open**

● **817 Multiple fractures of hand bones**

    Includes: metacarpal bone(s) with phalanx or phalanges
                  of same hand

    817.0 Closed

    817.1 Open

● **818 Ill-defined fractures of upper limb**

    Includes: arm NOS
            multiple bones of same upper limb

    Excludes *multiple fractures of:*
         metacarpal bone(s) with phalanx or phalanges
            (817.0–817.1)
         phalanges of hand alone (816.0–816.1)
         radius with ulna (813.0–813.9)

☐ **818.0 Closed**

☐ **818.1 Open**

● **819 Multiple fractures involving both upper limbs, and upper limb with rib(s) and sternum**

    Includes: arm(s) with rib(s) or sternum
            both arms [any bones]

    819.0 Closed

    819.1 Open

FRACTURE OF LOWER LIMB (820–829)

● **820 Fracture of neck of femur**

 ● **820.0 Transcervical fracture, closed**

   ☐ **820.00 Intracapsular section, unspecified**

       820.01 Epiphysis (separation) (upper)
          Transepiphyseal

       820.02 Midcervical section
          Transcervical NOS

       820.03 Base of neck
          Cervicotrochanteric section

   ☐ **820.09 Other**
          Head of femur
          Subcapital

 ● **820.1 Transcervical fracture, open**

   ☐ **820.10 Intracapsular section, unspecified**

       820.11 Epiphysis (separation) (upper)

       820.12 Midcervical section

       820.13 Base of neck

   ☐ **820.19 Other**

 ● **820.2 Pertrochanteric fracture, closed**

   ☐ **820.20 Trochanteric section, unspecified**
          Trochanter:
            NOS
            greater
            lesser

       820.21 Intertrochanteric section

       820.22 Subtrochanteric section

 ● **820.3 Pertrochanteric fracture, open**

   ☐ **820.30 Trochanteric section, unspecified**

       820.31 Intertrochanteric section

       820.32 Subtrochanteric section

 ☐ **820.8 Unspecified part of neck of femur, closed**
      Hip NOS
      Neck of femur NOS

 ☐ **820.9 Unspecified part of neck of femur, open**

● **821 Fracture of other and unspecified parts of femur**

 ● **821.0 Shaft or unspecified part, closed**

   ☐ **821.00 Unspecified part of femur**
          Thigh
          Upper leg

      Excludes *hip NOS (820.8)*

       821.01 Shaft

 ● **821.1 Shaft or unspecified part, open**

   ☐ **821.10 Unspecified part of femur**

       821.11 Shaft

 ● **821.2 Lower end, closed**
      Distal end

   ☐ **821.20 Lower end, unspecified part**

       821.21 Condyle, femoral

       821.22 Epiphysis, lower (separation)

       821.23 Supracondylar fracture of femur

   ☐ **821.29 Other**
          Multiple fractures of lower end

 ● **821.3 Lower end, open**

   ☐ **821.30 Lower end, unspecified part**

821.31   Condyle, femoral

821.32   Epiphysis, lower (separation)

821.33   Supracondylar fracture of femur

❑ 821.39   Other

● **822   Fracture of patella**

822.0   Closed

822.1   Open

● **823   Fracture of tibia and fibula**

> **Excludes**   *Dupuytren's fracture (824.4–824.5)*
>   *ankle (824.4–824.5)*
>   *radius (813.42, 813.52)*
>   *Pott's fracture (824.4–824.5)*
>   *that involving ankle (824.0–824.9)*

The following fifth-digit subclassification is for use with category 823:
   0   tibia alone
   1   fibula alone
   2   fibula with tibia

● 823.0   Upper end, closed
    Head
    Proximal end
    Tibia:
      condyles
      tuberosity

● 823.1   Upper end, open

● 823.2   Shaft, closed

● 823.3   Shaft, open

❑● 823.8   Unspecified part, closed
    Lower leg NOS

❑● 823.9   Unspecified part, open

● **824   Fracture of ankle**

824.0   Medial malleolus, closed
    Tibia involving:
      ankle
      malleolus

824.1   Medial malleolus, open

824.2   Lateral malleolus, closed
    Fibula involving:
      ankle
      malleolus

824.3   Lateral malleolus, open

824.4   Bimalleolar, closed
    Dupuytren's fracture, fibula
    Pott's fracture

824.5   Bimalleolar, open

824.6   Trimalleolar, closed
    Lateral and medial malleolus with anterior or posterior lip of tibia

824.7   Trimalleolar, open

❑ 824.8   Unspecified, closed
    Ankle NOS

❑ 824.9   Unspecified, open

● **825   Fracture of one or more tarsal and metatarsal bones**

❑ 825.0   Fracture of calcaneus, closed
    Heel bone
    Os calcis

825.1   Fracture of calcaneus, open

● 825.2   Fracture of other tarsal and metatarsal bones, closed

❑ 825.20   Unspecified bone(s) of foot [except toes]
    Instep

825.21   Astragalus
    Talus

825.22   Navicular [scaphoid], foot

825.23   Cuboid

825.24   Cuneiform, foot

825.25   Metatarsal bone(s)

❑ 825.29   Other
    Tarsal with metatarsal bone(s) only

> **Excludes**   *calcaneus (825.0)*

● 825.3   Fracture of other tarsal and metatarsal bones, open

❑ 825.30   Unspecified bone(s) of foot [except toes]

825.31   Astragalus

825.32   Navicular [scaphoid], foot

825.33   Cuboid

825.34   Cuneiform, foot

825.35   Metatarsal bone(s)

❑ 825.39   Other

● **826   Fracture of one or more phalanges of foot**

    Includes: toe(s)

826.0   Closed

826.1   Open

● **827   Other, multiple, and ill-defined fractures of lower limb**

    Includes: leg NOS
       multiple bones of same lower limb

> **Excludes**   *multiple fractures of:*
>   *ankle bones alone (824.4–824.9)*
>   *phalanges of foot alone (826.0–826.1)*
>   *tarsal with metatarsal bones (825.29, 825.39)*
>   *tibia with fibula (823.0–823.9 with fifth-digit 2)*

827.0   Closed

827.1   Open

● **828   Multiple fractures involving both lower limbs, lower with upper limb, and lower limb(s) with rib(s) and sternum**

    Includes: arm(s) with leg(s) [any bones]
       both legs [any bones]
       leg(s) with rib(s) or sternum

828.0   Closed

828.1   Open

● **829   Fracture of unspecified bones**

❑ 829.0   Unspecified bone, closed

❑ 829.1   Unspecified bone, open

DISLOCATION (830–839)

Includes: displacement
       subluxation

> **Excludes**   *congenital dislocation (754.0–755.8)*
>   *pathological dislocation (718.2)*
>   *recurrent dislocation (718.3)*

    ◀▶ **New Code**   ◀▥ ▥▶ **Revised Code**   ● **Not a Principal Diagnosis**   ● **Use Additional Digit(s)**   ❑ **Nonspecific Code**

The descriptions "closed" and "open," used in the fourth-digit subdivisions, include the following terms:

    closed:
        complete
        dislocation NOS
        partial
        simple
        uncomplicated
    open:
        compound
        infected
        with foreign body

Note: A dislocation not indicated as closed or open should be classified as closed.

● **830 Dislocation of jaw**

    Includes: jaw (cartilage) (meniscus)
        mandible
        maxilla (inferior)
        temporomandibular (joint)

  830.0 Closed dislocation

  830.1 Open dislocation

● **831 Dislocation of shoulder**

    Excludes *sternoclavicular joint (839.61, 839.71)*
                sternum (839.61, 839.71)

The following fifth-digit subclassification is for use with category 831:
  ☐ **0 shoulder, unspecified**
      humerus NOS
    1 anterior dislocation of humerus
    2 posterior dislocation of humerus
    3 inferior dislocation of humerus
    4 acromioclavicular (joint)
      clavicle
  ☐ **9 other**
      Scapula

  ● **831.0 Closed dislocation**

  ● **831.1 Open dislocation**

● **832 Dislocation of elbow**

The following fifth-digit subclassification is for use with category 832:
  ☐ **0 elbow unspecified**
    1 anterior dislocation of elbow
    2 posterior dislocation of elbow
    3 medial dislocation of elbow
    4 lateral dislocation of elbow
  ☐ **9 other**

  ● **832.0 Closed dislocation**

  ● **832.1 Open dislocation**

● **833 Dislocation of wrist**

The following fifth-digit subclassification is for use with category 833:
  ☐ **0 wrist, unspecified part**
      carpal (bone)
      radius, distal end
    1 radioulnar (joint), distal
    2 radiocarpal (joint)
    3 midcarpal (joint)
    4 carpometacarpal (joint)
    5 metacarpal (bone), proximal end
  ☐ **9 other**
      ulna, distal end

  ● **833.0 Closed dislocation**

  ● **833.1 Open dislocation**

● **834 Dislocation of finger**

    Includes: finger(s)
        phalanx of hand
        thumb

The following fifth-digit subclassification is for use with category 834:
  ☐ **0 finger, unspecified part**
    1 metacarpophalangeal (joint)
      metacarpal (bone), distal end
    2 interphalangeal (joint), hand

  ● **834.0 Closed dislocation**

  ● **834.1 Open dislocation**

● **835 Dislocation of hip**

The following fifth-digit subclassification is for use with category 835:
  ☐ **0 dislocation of hip, unspecified**
    1 posterior dislocation
    2 obturator dislocation
  ☐ **3 other anterior dislocation**

  ● **835.0 Closed dislocation**

  ● **835.1 Open dislocation**

● **836 Dislocation of knee**

    Excludes *dislocation of knee:*
        old or pathological (718.2)
        recurrent (718.3)
    internal derangement of knee joint (717.0–717.5, 717.8–717.9)
    old tear of cartilage or meniscus of knee (717.0–717.5, 717.8–717.9)

  836.0 Tear of medial cartilage or meniscus of knee, current
      Bucket handle tear:
        NOS current injury
        medial meniscus current injury

  836.1 Tear of lateral cartilage or meniscus of knee, current

  ☐ **836.2 Other tear of cartilage or meniscus of knee, current**
      Tear of:
        cartilage (semilunar) current injury, not specified as medial or lateral
        meniscus current injury, not specified as medial or lateral

  836.3 Dislocation of patella, closed

  836.4 Dislocation of patella, open

  ● **836.5 Other dislocation of knee, closed**

    ☐ **836.50 Dislocation of knee, unspecified**

    836.51 Anterior dislocation of tibia, proximal end
      Posterior dislocation of femur, distal end

    836.52 Posterior dislocation of tibia, proximal end
      Anterior dislocation of femur, distal end

    836.53 Medial dislocation of tibia, proximal end

    836.54 Lateral dislocation of tibia, proximal end

    ☐ **836.59 Other**

  ● **836.6 Other dislocation of knee, open**

    ☐ **836.60 Dislocation of knee, unspecified**

    836.61 Anterior dislocation of tibia, proximal end

    836.62 Posterior dislocation of tibia, proximal end

    836.63 Medial dislocation of tibia, proximal end

    836.64 Lateral dislocation of tibia, proximal end

    ☐ **836.69 Other**

ICD-9-CM

800-899

Vol. 1

● **837 Dislocation of ankle**

Includes: astragalus
fibula, distal end
navicular, foot
scaphoid, foot
tibia, distal end

837.0 Closed dislocation

837.1 Open dislocation

● **838 Dislocation of foot**

The following fifth-digit subclassification is for use with category 838:

❑ 0 **foot, unspecified**
1 **tarsal (bone), joint unspecified**
2 **midtarsal (joint)**
3 **tarsometatarsal (joint)**
4 **metatarsal (bone), joint unspecified**
5 **metatarsophalangeal (joint)**
6 **interphalangeal (joint), foot**
❑ 9 **other**
phalanx of foot
toe(s)

● **838.0 Closed dislocation**

● **838.1 Open dislocation**

● **839 Other, multiple, and ill-defined dislocations**

● **839.0 Cervical vertebra, closed**
Cervical spine
Neck

❑ **839.00 Cervical vertebra, unspecified**

839.01 First cervical vertebra

839.02 Second cervical vertebra

839.03 Third cervical vertebra

839.04 Fourth cervical vertebra

839.05 Fifth cervical vertebra

839.06 Sixth cervical vertebra

839.07 Seventh cervical vertebra

❑ **839.08 Multiple cervical vertebrae**

● **839.1 Cervical vertebra, open**

❑ **839.10 Cervical vertebra, unspecified**

839.11 First cervical vertebra

839.12 Second cervical vertebra

839.13 Third cervical vertebra

839.14 Fourth cervical vertebra

839.15 Fifth cervical vertebra

839.16 Sixth cervical vertebra

839.17 Seventh cervical vertebra

❑ **839.18 Multiple cervical vertebrae**

● **839.2 Thoracic and lumbar vertebra, closed**

839.20 Lumbar vertebra

839.21 Thoracic vertebra
Dorsal [thoracic] vertebra

● **839.3 Thoracic and lumbar vertebra, open**

839.30 Lumbar vertebra

839.31 Thoracic vertebra

● **839.4 Other vertebra, closed**

❑ **839.40 Vertebra, unspecified site**
Spine NOS

839.41 Coccyx

839.42 Sacrum
Sacroiliac (joint)

❑ **839.49 Other**

● **839.5 Other vertebra, open**

❑ **839.50 Vertebra, unspecified site**

839.51 Coccyx

839.52 Sacrum

❑ **839.59 Other**

● **839.6 Other location, closed**

839.61 Sternum
Sternoclavicular joint

❑ **839.69 Other**
Pelvis

● **839.7 Other location, open**

839.71 Sternum

❑ **839.79 Other**

❑ **839.8 Multiple and ill-defined, closed**
Arm
Back
Hand
Multiple locations, except fingers or toes alone
Other ill-defined locations
Unspecified location

❑ **839.9 Multiple and ill-defined, open**

SPRAINS AND STRAINS OF JOINTS AND ADJACENT MUSCLES (840–848)

Includes: avulsion of joint capsule, ligament, muscle, tendon
hemarthrosis of joint capsule, ligament, muscle, tendon
laceration of joint capsule, ligament, muscle, tendon
rupture of joint capsule, ligament, muscle, tendon
sprain of joint capsule, ligament, muscle, tendon
strain of joint capsule, ligament, muscle, tendon
tear of joint capsule, ligament, muscle, tendon

Excludes *laceration of tendon in open wounds (880–884 and 890–894 with .2)*

● **840 Sprains and strains of shoulder and upper arm**

840.0 Acromioclavicular (joint) (ligament)

840.1 Coracoclavicular (ligament)

840.2 Coracohumeral (ligament)

840.3 Infraspinatus (muscle) (tendon)

840.4 Rotator cuff (capsule)

840.5 Subscapularis (muscle)

840.6 Supraspinatus (muscle) (tendon)

❑ **840.8 Other specified sites of shoulder and upper arm**

❑ **840.9 Unspecified site of shoulder and upper arm**
Arm NOS
Shoulder NOS

● **841 Sprains and strains of elbow and forearm**

841.0 Radial collateral ligament

841.1 Ulnar collateral ligament

841.2 Radiohumeral (joint)

841.3 Ulnohumeral (joint)

❑ **841.8 Other specified sites of elbow and forearm**

   ◀▶ **New Code**   ⬅ ⠿ ➡ **Revised Code**   ● **Not a Principal Diagnosis**   ● **Use Additional Digit(s)**   ❑ **Nonspecific Code**

❑ **841.9 Unspecified site of elbow and forearm**
 Elbow NOS

● **842 Sprains and strains of wrist and hand**
 ● **842.0 Wrist**
  ❑ **842.00 Unspecified site**
  842.01 Carpal (joint)
  842.02 Radiocarpal (joint) (ligament)
  ❑ **842.09 Other**
   Radioulnar joint, distal
 ● **842.1 Hand**
  ❑ **842.10 Unspecified site**
  842.11 Carpometacarpal (joint)
  842.12 Metacarpophalangeal (joint)
  842.13 Interphalangeal (joint)
  ❑ **842.19 Other**
   Midcarpal (joint)

● **843 Sprains and strains of hip and thigh**
 843.0 Iliofemoral (ligament)
 843.1 Ischiocapsular (ligament)
 ❑ **843.8 Other specified sites of hip and thigh**
 ❑ **843.9 Unspecified site of hip and thigh**
  Hip NOS
  Thigh NOS

● **844 Sprains and strains of knee and leg**
 844.0 Lateral collateral ligament of knee
 844.1 Medial collateral ligament of knee
 844.2 Cruciate ligament of knee
 844.3 Tibiofibular (joint) (ligament), superior
 ❑ **844.8 Other specified sites of knee and leg**
 ❑ **844.9 Unspecified site of knee and leg**
  Knee NOS
  Leg NOS

● **845 Sprains and strains of ankle and foot**
 ● **845.0 Ankle**
  ❑ **845.00 Unspecified site**
  845.01 Deltoid (ligament), ankle
   Internal collateral (ligament), ankle
  845.02 Calcaneofibular (ligament)
  845.03 Tibiofibular (ligament), distal
  ❑ **845.09 Other**
   Achilles tendon
 ● **845.1 Foot**
  ❑ **845.10 Unspecified site**
  845.11 Tarsometatarsal (joint) (ligament)
  845.12 Metatarsophalangeal (joint)
  845.13 Interphalangeal (joint), toe
  ❑ **845.19 Other**

● **846 Sprains and strains of sacroiliac region**
 846.0 Lumbosacral (joint) (ligament)
 846.1 Sacroiliac ligament
 846.2 Sacrospinatus (ligament)
 846.3 Sacrotuberous (ligament)
 ❑ **846.8 Other specified sites of sacroiliac region**

❑ **846.9 Unspecified site of sacroiliac region**

● **847 Sprains and strains of other and unspecified parts of back**
 Excludes *lumbosacral (846.0)*
 847.0 Neck
  Anterior longitudinal (ligament), cervical
  Atlanto-axial (joints)
  Atlanto-occipital (joints)
  Whiplash injury
  Excludes *neck injury NOS (959.09)*
   thyroid region (848.2)
 847.1 Thoracic
 847.2 Lumbar
 847.3 Sacrum
  Sacrococcygeal (ligament)
 847.4 Coccyx
 ❑ **847.9 Unspecified site of back**
  Back NOS

● **848 Other and ill-defined sprains and strains**
 848.0 Septal cartilage of nose
 848.1 Jaw
  Temporomandibular (joint) (ligament)
 848.2 Thyroid region
  Cricoarytenoid (joint) (ligament)
  Cricothyroid (joint) (ligament)
  Thyroid cartilage
 848.3 Ribs
  Chondrocostal (joint) without mention of injury to sternum
  Costal cartilage without mention of injury to sternum
 ● **848.4 Sternum**
  ❑ **848.40 Unspecified site**
  848.41 Sternoclavicular (joint) (ligament)
  848.42 Chondrosternal (joint)
  ❑ **848.49 Other**
   Xiphoid cartilage
 848.5 Pelvis
  Symphysis pubis
  Excludes *that in childbirth (665.6)*
 ❑ **848.8 Other specified sites of sprains and strains**
 ❑ **848.9 Unspecified site of sprain and strain**

ICD-9-CM

800-899

Vol. 1

◀ ▶ **New Code** ⬅▮▮▮ ▮▮▮➡ **Revised Code** ● **Not a Principal Diagnosis** ● **Use Additional Digit(s)** ❑ **Nonspecific Code** 811

INTRACRANIAL INJURY, EXCLUDING THOSE WITH SKULL FRACTURE (850–854)

> **Excludes** *intracranial injury with skull fracture (800–801 and 803–804, except .0 and .5)*
> *open wound of head without intracranial injury (870.0–873.9)*
> *skull fracture alone (800–801 and 803–804 with .0, .5)*

Note: The description "with open intracranial wound," used in the fourth-digit subdivisions, includes those specified as open or with mention of infection or foreign body.

The following fifth-digit subclassification is for use with categories 851–854:

- ☐ **0** unspecified state of consciousness
- **1** with no loss of consciousness
- **2** with brief [less than one hour] loss of consciousness
- **3** with moderate [1–24 hours] loss of consciousness
- **4** with prolonged [more than 24 hours] loss of consciousness and return to pre-existing conscious level
- **5** with prolonged [more than 24 hours] loss of consciousness without return to pre-existing conscious level

  Use fifth-digit 5 to designate when a patient is unconscious and dies before regaining consciousness, regardless of the duration of the loss of consciousness

- ☐ **6** with loss of consciousness of unspecified duration
- ☐ **9** with concussion, unspecified

● **850 Concussion**

Includes: commotio cerebri

> **Excludes** *concussion with:* ◀▭▭
> *cerebral laceration or contusion (851.0–851.9)*
> *cerebral hemorrhage (852–853)*
> *head injury NOS (959.01)* ◀

850.0 With no loss of consciousness
Concussion with mental confusion or disorientation, without loss of consciousness

850.1 With brief loss of consciousness
Loss of consciousness for less than one hour

850.2 With moderate loss of consciousness
Loss of consciousness for 1–24 hours

850.3 With prolonged loss of consciousness and return to pre-existing conscious level
Loss of consciousness for more than 24 hours with complete recovery

850.4 With prolonged loss of consciousness, without return to pre-existing conscious level

☐ **850.5 With loss of consciousness of unspecified duration**

☐ **850.9 Concussion, unspecified**

● **851 Cerebral laceration and contusion**

Requires fifth digit. See beginning of section 850–854 for codes and definitions.

● **851.0 Cortex (cerebral) contusion without mention of open intracranial wound**

● **851.1 Cortex (cerebral) contusion with open intracranial wound**

● **851.2 Cortex (cerebral) laceration without mention of open intracranial wound**

● **851.3 Cortex (cerebral) laceration with open intracranial wound**

● **851.4 Cerebellar or brain stem contusion without mention of open intracranial wound**

● **851.5 Cerebellar or brain stem contusion with open intracranial wound**

● **851.6 Cerebellar or brain stem laceration without mention of open intracranial wound**

● **851.7 Cerebellar or brain stem laceration with open intracranial wound**

☐● **851.8 Other and unspecified cerebral laceration and contusion, without mention of open intracranial wound**
Brain (membrane) NOS

☐● **851.9 Other and unspecified cerebral laceration and contusion, with open intracranial wound**

● **852 Subarachnoid, subdural, and extradural hemorrhage, following injury**

Requires fifth digit. See beginning of section 850–854 for codes and definitions.

> **Excludes** *cerebral contusion or laceration (with hemorrhage) (851.0–851.9)*

● **852.0 Subarachnoid hemorrhage following injury without mention of open intracranial wound**
Middle meningeal hemorrhage following injury

● **852.1 Subarachnoid hemorrhage following injury with open intracranial wound**

● **852.2 Subdural hemorrhage following injury without mention of open intracranial wound**

● **852.3 Subdural hemorrhage following injury with open intracranial wound**

● **852.4 Extradural hemorrhage following injury without mention of open intracranial wound**
Epidural hematoma following injury

● **852.5 Extradural hemorrhage following injury with open intracranial wound**

● **853 Other and unspecified intracranial hemorrhage following injury**

Requires fifth digit. See beginning of section 850–854 for codes and definitions.

☐● **853.0 Without mention of open intracranial wound**
Cerebral compression due to injury
Intracranial hematoma following injury
Traumatic cerebral hemorrhage

☐● **853.1 With open intracranial wound**

● **854 Intracranial injury of other and unspecified nature**

Includes: injury:
    brain NOS
    cavernous sinus
    intracranial

> **Excludes** *any condition classifiable to 850–853*
> *head injury NOS (959.01)*

☐● **854.0 Without mention of open intracranial wound**

☐● **854.1 With open intracranial wound**

◀▶ **New Code**   ◀▭▭ ▭▭▶ **Revised Code**   ● **Not a Principal Diagnosis**   ● **Use Additional Digit(s)**   ☐ **Nonspecific Code**

INTERNAL INJURY OF THORAX, ABDOMEN, AND PELVIS (860–869)

Includes: blast injuries of internal organs
blunt trauma of internal organs
bruise of internal organs
concussion injuries (except cerebral) of internal organs
crushing of internal organs
hematoma of internal organs
laceration of internal organs
puncture of internal organs
tear of internal organs
traumatic rupture of internal organs

Excludes *concussion NOS (850.0–850.9)*
flail chest (807.4)
foreign body entering through orifice (930.0–939.9)
injury to blood vessels (901.0–902.9)

Note: The description "with open wound," used in the fourth-digit subdivisions, includes those with mention of infection or foreign body.

● 860   **Traumatic pneumothorax and hemothorax**

860.0   **Pneumothorax without mention of open wound into thorax**

860.1   **Pneumothorax with open wound into thorax**

860.2   **Hemothorax without mention of open wound into thorax**

860.3   **Hemothorax with open wound into thorax**

860.4   **Pneumohemothorax without mention of open wound into thorax**

860.5   **Pneumohemothorax with open wound into thorax**

● 861   **Injury to heart and lung**

Excludes *injury to blood vessels of thorax (901.0–901.9)*

● 861.0   **Heart, without mention of open wound into thorax**

□ 861.00   **Unspecified injury**

861.01   **Contusion**
Cardiac contusion
Myocardial contusion

861.02   **Laceration without penetration of heart chambers**

861.03   **Laceration with penetration of heart chambers**

● 861.1   **Heart, with open wound into thorax**

□ 861.10   **Unspecified injury**

861.11   **Contusion**

861.12   **Laceration without penetration of heart chambers**

861.13   **Laceration with penetration of heart chambers**

● 861.2   **Lung, without mention of open wound into thorax**

□ 861.20   **Unspecified injury**

861.21   **Contusion**

861.22   **Laceration**

● 861.3   **Lung, with open wound into thorax**

□ 861.30   **Unspecified injury**

861.31   **Contusion**

861.32   **Laceration**

● 862   **Injury to other and unspecified intrathoracic organs**

Excludes *injury to blood vessels of thorax (901.0–901.9)*

862.0   **Diaphragm, without mention of open wound into cavity**

862.1   **Diaphragm, with open wound into cavity**

● 862.2   **Other specified intrathoracic organs, without mention of open wound into cavity**

862.21   **Bronchus**

862.22   **Esophagus**

□ 862.29   **Other**
Pleura   Thymus gland

● 862.3   **Other specified intrathoracic organs, with open wound into cavity**

862.31   **Bronchus**

862.32   **Esophagus**

□ 862.39   **Other**

□ 862.8   **Multiple and unspecified intrathoracic organs, without mention of open wound into cavity**
Crushed chest
Multiple intrathoracic organs

□ 862.9   **Multiple and unspecified intrathoracic organs, with open wound into cavity**

● 863   **Injury to gastrointestinal tract**

Excludes *anal sphincter laceration during delivery (664.2)*
bile duct (868.0–868.1 with fifth-digit 2)
gallbladder (868.0–868.1 with fifth-digit 2)

863.0   **Stomach, without mention of open wound into cavity**

863.1   **Stomach, with open wound into cavity**

● 863.2   **Small intestine, without mention of open wound into cavity**

□ 863.20   **Small intestine, unspecified site**

863.21   **Duodenum**

□ 863.29   **Other**

● 863.3   **Small intestine, with open wound into cavity**

□ 863.30   **Small intestine, unspecified site**

863.31   **Duodenum**

□ 863.39   **Other**

● 863.4   **Colon or rectum, without mention of open wound into cavity**

□ 863.40   **Colon, unspecified site**

863.41   **Ascending [right] colon**

863.42   **Transverse colon**

863.43   **Descending [left] colon**

863.44   **Sigmoid colon**

863.45   **Rectum**

□ 863.46   **Multiple sites in colon and rectum**

□ 863.49   **Other**

● 863.5   **Colon or rectum, with open wound into cavity**

□ 863.50   **Colon, unspecified site**

863.51   **Ascending [right] colon**

863.52   **Transverse colon**

863.53   **Descending [left] colon**

863.54   **Sigmoid colon**

863.55   **Rectum**

□ 863.56   **Multiple sites in colon and rectum**

□ 863.59   **Other**

● 863.8   **Other and unspecified gastrointestinal sites, without mention of open wound into cavity**

ICD-9-CM
860–869
Vol. 1

□ 863.80 **Gastrointestinal tract, unspecified site**

863.81 **Pancreas, head**

863.82 **Pancreas, body**

863.83 **Pancreas, tail**

□ 863.84 **Pancreas, multiple and unspecified sites**

863.85 **Appendix**

□ 863.89 **Other**
     Intestine NOS

● 863.9 **Other and unspecified gastrointestinal sites, with open wound into cavity**

□ 863.90 **Gastrointestinal tract, unspecified site**

863.91 **Pancreas, head**

863.92 **Pancreas, body**

863.93 **Pancreas, tail**

□ 863.94 **Pancreas, multiple and unspecified sites**

863.95 **Appendix**

□ 863.99 **Other**

● 864 **Injury to liver**

The following fifth-digit subclassification is for use with category 864:

□ **0 unspecified injury**
1 hematoma and contusion
2 laceration, minor
     Laceration involving capsule only, or without significant involvement of hepatic parenchyma [i.e., less than 1 cm deep]
3 laceration, moderate
     Laceration involving parenchyma but without major disruption of parenchyma [i.e., less than 10 cm long and less than 3 cm deep]
4 laceration, major
     Laceration with significant disruption of hepatic parenchyma [i.e., 10 cm long and 3 cm deep]
     Multiple moderate lacerations, with or without hematoma
     Stellate lacerations of liver
□ **5 laceration, unspecified**
□ **9 other**

● 864.0 **Without mention of open wound into cavity**

● 864.1 **With open wound into cavity**

● 865 **Injury to spleen**

The following fifth-digit subclassification is for use with category 865:

□ **0 unspecified injury**
1 hematoma without rupture of capsule
2 capsular tears, without major disruption of parenchyma
3 laceration extending into parenchyma
4 massive parenchymal disruption
□ **9 other**

● 865.0 **Without mention of open wound into cavity**

● 865.1 **With open wound into cavity**

● 866 **Injury to kidney**

The following fifth-digit subclassification is for use with category 866:

□ **0 unspecified injury**
1 hematoma without rupture of capsule
2 laceration
3 complete disruption of kidney parenchyma

● 866.0 **Without mention of open wound into cavity**

● 866.1 **With open wound into cavity**

● 867 **Injury to pelvic organs**

> **Excludes** *injury during delivery (664.0–665.9)*

867.0 **Bladder and urethra, without mention of open wound into cavity**

867.1 **Bladder and urethra, with open wound into cavity**

867.2 **Ureter, without mention of open wound into cavity**

867.3 **Ureter, with open wound into cavity**

867.4 **Uterus, without mention of open wound into cavity**

867.5 **Uterus, with open wound into cavity**

□ 867.6 **Other specified pelvic organs, without mention of open wound into cavity**
     Fallopian tube
     Ovary
     Prostate
     Seminal vesicle
     Vas deferens

□ 867.7 **Other specified pelvic organs, with open wound into cavity**

□ 867.8 **Unspecified pelvic organ, without mention of open wound into cavity**

□ 867.9 **Unspecified pelvic organ, with open wound into cavity**

● 868 **Injury to other intra-abdominal organs**

The following fifth-digit subclassification is for use with category 868:

□ **0 unspecified intra-abdominal organ**
1 adrenal gland
2 bile duct and gallbladder
3 peritoneum
4 retroperitoneum
□ **9 other and multiple intra-abdominal organs**

● 868.0 **Without mention of open wound into cavity**

● 868.1 **With open wound into cavity**

● 869 **Internal injury to unspecified or ill-defined organs**

> **Includes:** internal injury NOS
>   multiple internal injury NOS

□ 869.0 **Without mention of open wound into cavity**

□ 869.1 **With open wound into cavity**

OPEN WOUND (870–897)

> **Includes:** animal bite
>   avulsion
>   cut
>   laceration
>   puncture wound
>   traumatic amputation

> **Excludes** *burn (940.0–949.5)*
> *crushing (925–929.9)*
> *puncture of internal organs (860.0–869.1)*
> *superficial injury (910.0–919.9)*
> *that incidental to:*
>   *dislocation (830.0–839.9)*
>   *fracture (800.0–829.1)*
>   *internal injury (860.0–869.1)*
>   *intracranial injury (851.0–854.1)*

Note: The description "complicated" used in the fourth-digit subdivisions includes those with mention of delayed healing, delayed treatment, foreign body, or major infection.

    ◀▶ **New Code**   ⬅▦➡ **Revised Code**   ● **Not a Principal Diagnosis**   ● **Use Additional Digit(s)**   □ **Nonspecific Code**

OPEN WOUND OF HEAD, NECK, AND TRUNK (870–879)

● 870 Open wound of ocular adnexa

 870.0 Laceration of skin of eyelid and periocular area

 870.1 Laceration of eyelid, full-thickness, not involving lacrimal passages

 870.2 Laceration of eyelid involving lacrimal passages

 870.3 Penetrating wound of orbit, without mention of foreign body

 870.4 Penetrating wound of orbit with foreign body

  Excludes *retained (old) foreign body in orbit (376.6)*

 □ 870.8 Other specified open wounds of ocular adnexa

 □ 870.9 Unspecified open wound of ocular adnexa

● 871 Open wound of eyeball

  Excludes *2nd cranial nerve [optic] injury (950.0–950.9)*
    3rd cranial nerve [oculomotor] injury (951.0)

 871.0 Ocular laceration without prolapse of intraocular tissue

 871.1 Ocular laceration with prolapse or exposure of intraocular tissue

 871.2 Rupture of eye with partial loss of intraocular tissue

 871.3 Avulsion of eye
   Traumatic enucleation

 □ 871.4 Unspecified laceration of eye

 871.5 Penetration of eyeball with magnetic foreign body

  Excludes *retained (old) magnetic foreign body in globe (360.50–360.59)*

 871.6 Penetration of eyeball with (nonmagnetic) foreign body

  Excludes *retained (old) (nonmagnetic) foreign body in globe (360.60–360.69)*

 □ 871.7 Unspecified ocular penetration

 □ 871.9 Unspecified open wound of eyeball

● 872 Open wound of ear

 ● 872.0 External ear, without mention of complication

  □ 872.00 External ear, unspecified site

  872.01 Auricle, ear
    Pinna

  872.02 Auditory canal

 ● 872.1 External ear, complicated

  □ 872.10 External ear, unspecified site

  872.11 Auricle, ear

  872.12 Auditory canal

 ● 872.6 Other specified parts of ear, without mention of complication

  872.61 Ear drum
    Drumhead
    Tympanic membrane

  872.62 Ossicles

  872.63 Eustachian tube

  872.64 Cochlea

  □ 872.69 Other and multiple sites

 ● 872.7 Other specified parts of ear, complicated

  872.71 Ear drum

  872.72 Ossicles

  872.73 Eustachian tube

  872.74 Cochlea

  □ 872.79 Other and multiple sites

 □ 872.8 Ear, part unspecified, without mention of complication
   Ear NOS

 □ 872.9 Ear, part unspecified, complicated

● 873 Other open wound of head

 873.0 Scalp, without mention of complication

 873.1 Scalp, complicated

 ● 873.2 Nose, without mention of complication

  □ 873.20 Nose, unspecified site

  873.21 Nasal septum

  873.22 Nasal cavity

  873.23 Nasal sinus

  □ 873.29 Multiple sites

 ● 873.3 Nose, complicated

  □ 873.30 Nose, unspecified site

  873.31 Nasal septum

  873.32 Nasal cavity

  873.33 Nasal sinus

  □ 873.39 Multiple sites

 ● 873.4 Face, without mention of complication

  □ 873.40 Face, unspecified site

  873.41 Cheek

  873.42 Forehead
    Eyebrow

  873.43 Lip

  873.44 Jaw

  □ 873.49 Other and multiple sites

 ● 873.5 Face, complicated

  □ 873.50 Face, unspecified site

  873.51 Cheek

  873.52 Forehead

  873.53 Lip

  873.54 Jaw

  □ 873.59 Other and multiple sites

 ● 873.6 Internal structures of mouth, without mention of complication

  □ 873.60 Mouth, unspecified site

  873.61 Buccal mucosa

  873.62 Gum (alveolar process)

  873.63 Tooth (broken)

  873.64 Tongue and floor of mouth

  873.65 Palate

  □ 873.69 Other and multiple sites

 ● 873.7 Internal structures of mouth, complicated

  □ 873.70 Mouth, unspecified site

  873.71 Buccal mucosa

  873.72 Gum (alveolar process)

  873.73 Tooth (broken)

  873.74 Tongue and floor of mouth

ICD-9-CM

800-899

Vol. 1

873.75   Palate

□ 873.79   Other and multiple sites

□ 873.8   Other and unspecified open wound of head without mention of complication
     Head NOS

□ 873.9   Other and unspecified open wound of head, complicated

● 874   Open wound of neck

   ● 874.0   Larynx and trachea, without mention of complication

      874.00   Larynx with trachea

      874.01   Larynx

      874.02   Trachea

   ● 874.1   Larynx and trachea, complicated

      874.10   Larynx with trachea

      874.11   Larynx

      874.12   Trachea

   874.2   Thyroid gland, without mention of complication

   874.3   Thyroid gland, complicated

   874.4   Pharynx, without mention of complication
     Cervical esophagus

   874.5   Pharynx, complicated

□ 874.8   Other and unspecified parts, without mention of complication
     Nape of neck
     Supraclavicular region
     Throat NOS

□ 874.9   Other and unspecified parts, complicated

● 875   Open wound of chest (wall)

   Excludes   *open wound into thoracic cavity (860.0–862.9)*
     traumatic pneumothorax and hemothorax (860.1, 860.3, 860.5)

   875.0   Without mention of complication

   875.1   Complicated

● 876   Open wound of back

   Includes: loin
     lumbar region

   Excludes   *open wound into thoracic cavity (860.0–862.9)*
     traumatic pneumothorax and hemothorax (860.1, 860.3, 860.5)

   876.0   Without mention of complication

   876.1   Complicated

● 877   Open wound of buttock

   Includes: sacroiliac region

   877.0   Without mention of complication

   877.1   Complicated

● 878   Open wound of genital organs (external), including traumatic amputation

   Excludes   *injury during delivery (664.0–665.9)*
     internal genital organs (867.0–867.9)

   878.0   Penis, without mention of complication

   878.1   Penis, complicated

   878.2   Scrotum and testes, without mention of complication

   878.3   Scrotum and testes, complicated

878.4   Vulva, without mention of complication
     Labium (majus) (minus)

878.5   Vulva, complicated

878.6   Vagina, without mention of complication

878.7   Vagina, complicated

□ 878.8   Other and unspecified parts, without mention of complication

□ 878.9   Other and unspecified parts, complicated

● 879   Open wound of other and unspecified sites, except limbs

879.0   Breast, without mention of complication

879.1   Breast, complicated

879.2   Abdominal wall, anterior, without mention of complication
     Abdominal wall NOS   Pubic region
     Epigastric region   Umbilical region
     Hypogastric region

879.3   Abdominal wall, anterior, complicated

879.4   Abdominal wall, lateral, without mention of complication
     Flank   Iliac (region)
     Groin   Inguinal region
     Hypochondrium

879.5   Abdominal wall, lateral, complicated

□ 879.6   Other and unspecified parts of trunk, without mention of complication
     Pelvic region   Trunk NOS
     Perineum

□ 879.7   Other and unspecified parts of trunk, complicated

□ 879.8   Open wound(s) (multiple) of unspecified site(s), without mention of complication
     Multiple open wounds NOS
     Open wound NOS

□ 879.9   Open wound(s) (multiple) of unspecified site(s), complicated

OPEN WOUND OF UPPER LIMB (880–887)

● 880   Open wound of shoulder and upper arm

The following fifth-digit subclassification is for use with category 880:
     0 shoulder region
     1 scapular region
     2 axillary region
     3 upper arm
   □ 9 multiple sites

   ● 880.0   Without mention of complication

   ● 880.1   Complicated

   ● 880.2   With tendon involvement

● 881   Open wound of elbow, forearm, and wrist

The following fifth-digit subclassification is for use with category 881:
     0 forearm
     1 elbow
     2 wrist

   ● 881.0   Without mention of complication

   ● 881.1   Complicated

   ● 881.2   With tendon involvement

● 882   Open wound of hand except finger(s) alone

882.0   Without mention of complication

882.1   Complicated

882.2   With tendon involvement

◀▶ **New Code**   ⬅▬▬➡ **Revised Code**   ● **Not a Principal Diagnosis**   ● **Use Additional Digit(s)**   □ **Nonspecific Code**

● 883 **Open wound of finger(s)**

   Includes: fingernail
              thumb (nail)

   883.0 **Without mention of complication**

   883.1 **Complicated**

   883.2 **With tendon involvement**

● 884 **Multiple and unspecified open wound of upper limb**

   Includes: arm NOS
              multiple sites of one upper limb
              upper limb NOS

   □ 884.0 **Without mention of complication**

   □ 884.1 **Complicated**

   □ 884.2 **With tendon involvement**

● 885 **Traumatic amputation of thumb (complete) (partial)**

   Includes: thumb(s) (with finger(s) of either hand)

   885.0 **Without mention of complication**

   885.1 **Complicated**

● 886 **Traumatic amputation of other finger(s) (complete) (partial)**

   Includes: finger(s) of one or both hands, without mention of thumb(s)

   886.0 **Without mention of complication**

   886.1 **Complicated**

● 887 **Traumatic amputation of arm and hand (complete) (partial)**

   887.0 **Unilateral, below elbow, without mention of complication**

   887.1 **Unilateral, below elbow, complicated**

   887.2 **Unilateral, at or above elbow, without mention of complication**

   887.3 **Unilateral, at or above elbow, complicated**

   □ 887.4 **Unilateral, level not specified, without mention of complication**

   □ 887.5 **Unilateral, level not specified, complicated**

   887.6 **Bilateral [any level], without mention of complication**
        One hand and other arm

   887.7 **Bilateral [any level], complicated**

OPEN WOUND OF LOWER LIMB (890–897)

● 890 **Open wound of hip and thigh**

   890.0 **Without mention of complication**

   890.1 **Complicated**

   890.2 **With tendon involvement**

● 891 **Open wound of knee, leg [except thigh], and ankle**

   Includes: leg NOS
              multiple sites of leg, except thigh

   Excludes *that of thigh (890.0–890.2)*
        with multiple sites of lower limb (894.0–894.2)

   891.0 **Without mention of complication**

   891.1 **Complicated**

   891.2 **With tendon involvement**

● 892 **Open wound of foot except toe(s) alone**

   Includes: heel

   892.0 **Without mention of complication**

   892.1 **Complicated**

   892.2 **With tendon involvement**

● 893 **Open wound of toe(s)**

   Includes: toenail

   893.0 **Without mention of complication**

   893.1 **Complicated**

   893.2 **With tendon involvement**

● 894 **Multiple and unspecified open wound of lower limb**

   Includes: lower limb NOS
              multiple sites of one lower limb, with thigh

   □ 894.0 **Without mention of complication**

   □ 894.1 **Complicated**

   □ 894.2 **With tendon involvement**

● 895 **Traumatic amputation of toe(s) (complete) (partial)**

   Includes: toe(s) of one or both feet

   895.0 **Without mention of complication**

   895.1 **Complicated**

● 896 **Traumatic amputation of foot (complete) (partial)**

   896.0 **Unilateral, without mention of complication**

   896.1 **Unilateral, complicated**

   896.2 **Bilateral, without mention of complication**
   Excludes *one foot and other leg (897.6–897.7)*

   896.3 **Bilateral, complicated**

● 897 **Traumatic amputation of leg(s) (complete) (partial)**

   897.0 **Unilateral, below knee, without mention of complication**

   897.1 **Unilateral, below knee, complicated**

   897.2 **Unilateral, at or above knee, without mention of complication**

   897.3 **Unilateral, at or above knee, complicated**

   □ 897.4 **Unilateral, level not specified, without mention of complication**

   □ 897.5 **Unilateral, level not specified, complicated**

   897.6 **Bilateral [any level], without mention of complication**
        One foot and other leg

   897.7 **Bilateral [any level], complicated**

INJURY TO BLOOD VESSELS (900–904)

   Includes: arterial hematoma of blood vessel, secondary to other injuries, e.g., fracture or open wound
        avulsion of blood vessel, secondary to other injuries, e.g., fracture or open wound
        cut of blood vessel, secondary to other injuries, e.g., fracture or open wound
        laceration of blood vessel, secondary to other injuries, e.g., fracture or open wound
        rupture of blood vessel, secondary to other injuries, e.g., fracture or open wound
        traumatic aneurysm or fistula (arteriovenous) of blood vessel, secondary to other injuries, e.g., fracture or open wound

   Excludes *accidental puncture or laceration during medical procedure (998.2)*
        intracranial hemorrhage following injury (851.0–854.1)

ICD-9-CM
800–999
Vol. 1

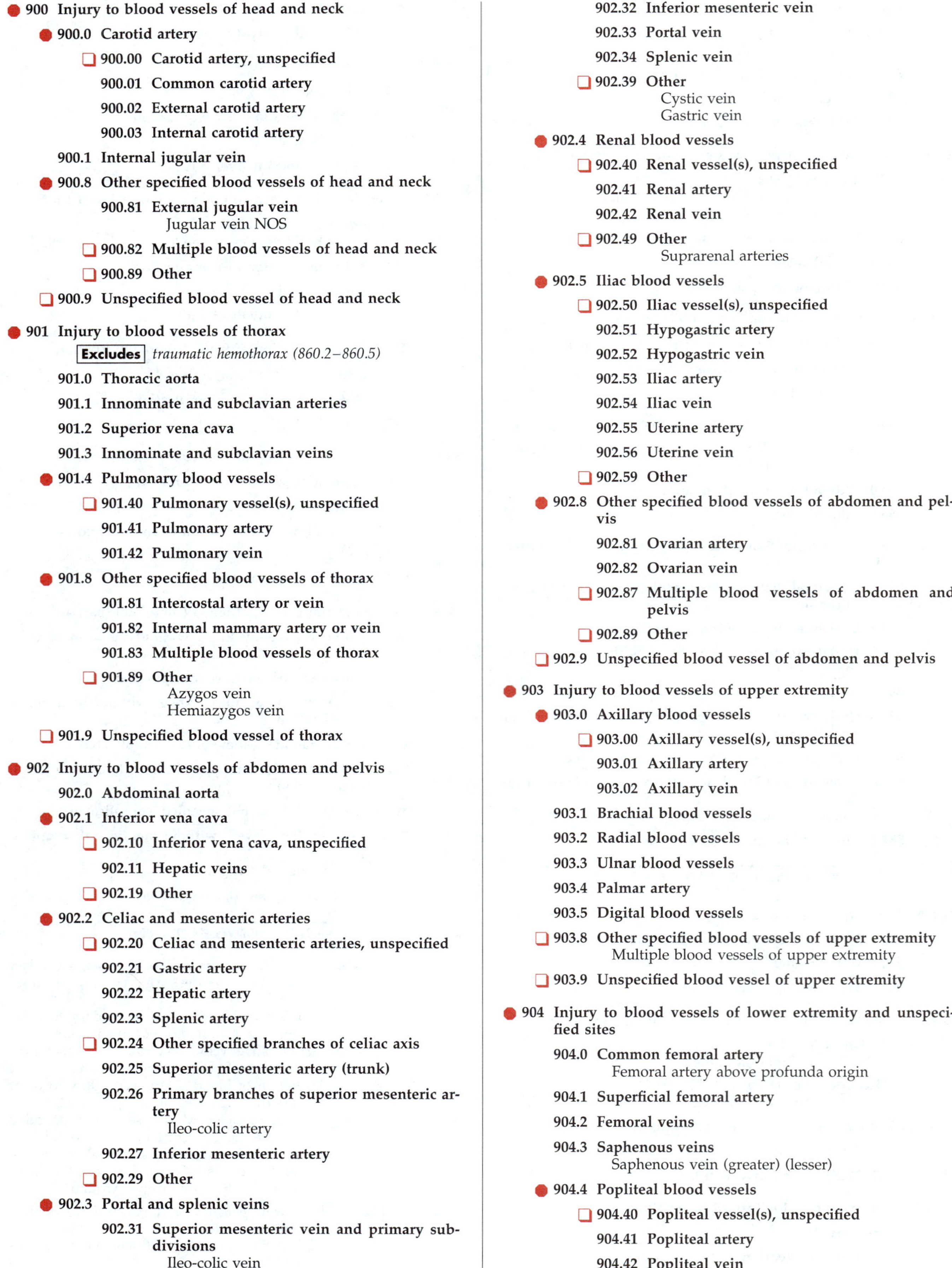

● **900 Injury to blood vessels of head and neck**
  ● **900.0 Carotid artery**
    ❑ **900.00 Carotid artery, unspecified**
    900.01 Common carotid artery
    900.02 External carotid artery
    900.03 Internal carotid artery
  900.1 Internal jugular vein
  ● **900.8 Other specified blood vessels of head and neck**
    900.81 External jugular vein
      Jugular vein NOS
    ❑ **900.82 Multiple blood vessels of head and neck**
    ❑ **900.89 Other**
  ❑ **900.9 Unspecified blood vessel of head and neck**

● **901 Injury to blood vessels of thorax**
  Excludes *traumatic hemothorax (860.2–860.5)*
  901.0 Thoracic aorta
  901.1 Innominate and subclavian arteries
  901.2 Superior vena cava
  901.3 Innominate and subclavian veins
  ● **901.4 Pulmonary blood vessels**
    ❑ **901.40 Pulmonary vessel(s), unspecified**
    901.41 Pulmonary artery
    901.42 Pulmonary vein
  ● **901.8 Other specified blood vessels of thorax**
    901.81 Intercostal artery or vein
    901.82 Internal mammary artery or vein
    901.83 Multiple blood vessels of thorax
    ❑ **901.89 Other**
      Azygos vein
      Hemiazygos vein
  ❑ **901.9 Unspecified blood vessel of thorax**

● **902 Injury to blood vessels of abdomen and pelvis**
  902.0 Abdominal aorta
  ● **902.1 Inferior vena cava**
    ❑ **902.10 Inferior vena cava, unspecified**
    902.11 Hepatic veins
    ❑ **902.19 Other**
  ● **902.2 Celiac and mesenteric arteries**
    ❑ **902.20 Celiac and mesenteric arteries, unspecified**
    902.21 Gastric artery
    902.22 Hepatic artery
    902.23 Splenic artery
    ❑ **902.24 Other specified branches of celiac axis**
    902.25 Superior mesenteric artery (trunk)
    902.26 Primary branches of superior mesenteric artery
      Ileo-colic artery
    902.27 Inferior mesenteric artery
    ❑ **902.29 Other**
  ● **902.3 Portal and splenic veins**
    902.31 Superior mesenteric vein and primary subdivisions
      Ileo-colic vein

    902.32 Inferior mesenteric vein
    902.33 Portal vein
    902.34 Splenic vein
    ❑ **902.39 Other**
      Cystic vein
      Gastric vein
  ● **902.4 Renal blood vessels**
    ❑ **902.40 Renal vessel(s), unspecified**
    902.41 Renal artery
    902.42 Renal vein
    ❑ **902.49 Other**
      Suprarenal arteries
  ● **902.5 Iliac blood vessels**
    ❑ **902.50 Iliac vessel(s), unspecified**
    902.51 Hypogastric artery
    902.52 Hypogastric vein
    902.53 Iliac artery
    902.54 Iliac vein
    902.55 Uterine artery
    902.56 Uterine vein
    ❑ **902.59 Other**
  ● **902.8 Other specified blood vessels of abdomen and pelvis**
    902.81 Ovarian artery
    902.82 Ovarian vein
    ❑ **902.87 Multiple blood vessels of abdomen and pelvis**
    ❑ **902.89 Other**
  ❑ **902.9 Unspecified blood vessel of abdomen and pelvis**

● **903 Injury to blood vessels of upper extremity**
  ● **903.0 Axillary blood vessels**
    ❑ **903.00 Axillary vessel(s), unspecified**
    903.01 Axillary artery
    903.02 Axillary vein
  903.1 Brachial blood vessels
  903.2 Radial blood vessels
  903.3 Ulnar blood vessels
  903.4 Palmar artery
  903.5 Digital blood vessels
  ❑ **903.8 Other specified blood vessels of upper extremity**
    Multiple blood vessels of upper extremity
  ❑ **903.9 Unspecified blood vessel of upper extremity**

● **904 Injury to blood vessels of lower extremity and unspecified sites**
  904.0 Common femoral artery
    Femoral artery above profunda origin
  904.1 Superficial femoral artery
  904.2 Femoral veins
  904.3 Saphenous veins
    Saphenous vein (greater) (lesser)
  ● **904.4 Popliteal blood vessels**
    ❑ **904.40 Popliteal vessel(s), unspecified**
    904.41 Popliteal artery
    904.42 Popliteal vein

  ◀▶ **New Code** ◀▥▥▶ **Revised Code** ● **Not a Principal Diagnosis** ● **Use Additional Digit(s)** ❑ **Nonspecific Code**

● **904.5 Tibial blood vessels**

    ☐ **904.50 Tibial vessel(s), unspecified**

    904.51 Anterior tibial artery

    904.52 Anterior tibial vein

    904.53 Posterior tibial artery

    904.54 Posterior tibial vein

904.6 Deep plantar blood vessels

☐ **904.7 Other specified blood vessels of lower extremity**
Multiple blood vessels of lower extremity

☐ **904.8 Unspecified blood vessel of lower extremity**

☐ **904.9 Unspecified site**
Injury to blood vessel NOS

LATE EFFECTS OF INJURIES, POISONINGS, TOXIC EFFECTS, AND OTHER EXTERNAL CAUSES (905–909)

Note: These categories are to be used to indicate conditions classifiable to 800–999 as the cause of late effects, which are themselves classified elsewhere. The "late effects" include those specified as such, or as sequelae, which may occur at any time after the acute injury.

● **905 Late effects of musculoskeletal and connective tissue injuries**

905.0 Late effect of fracture of skull and face bones
Late effect of injury classifiable to 800–804

905.1 Late effect of fracture of spine and trunk without mention of spinal cord lesion
Late effect of injury classifiable to 805, 807–809

905.2 Late effect of fracture of upper extremities
Late effect of injury classifiable to 810–819

905.3 Late effect of fracture of neck of femur
Late effect of injury classifiable to 820

905.4 Late effect of fracture of lower extremities
Late effect of injury classifiable to 821–827

☐ **905.5 Late effect of fracture of multiple and unspecified bones**
Late effect of injury classifiable to 828–829

905.6 Late effect of dislocation
Late effect of injury classifiable to 830–839

905.7 Late effect of sprain and strain without mention of tendon injury
Late effect of injury classifiable to 840–848, except tendon injury

905.8 Late effect of tendon injury
Late effect of tendon injury due to:
open wound [injury classifiable to 880–884 with .2, 890–894 with .2]
sprain and strain [injury classifiable to 840–848]

905.9 Late effect of traumatic amputation
Late effect of injury classifiable to 885–887, 895–897

    Excludes *late amputation stump complication (997.60–997.69)*

● **906 Late effects of injuries to skin and subcutaneous tissues**

906.0 Late effect of open wound of head, neck, and trunk
Late effect of injury classifiable to 870–879

906.1 Late effect of open wound of extremities without mention of tendon injury
Late effect of injury classifiable to 880–884, 890–894 except .2

906.2 Late effect of superficial injury
Late effect of injury classifiable to 910–919

906.3 Late effect of contusion
Late effect of injury classifiable to 920–924

906.4 Late effect of crushing
Late effect of injury classifiable to 925–929

906.5 Late effect of burn of eye, face, head, and neck
Late effect of injury classifiable to 940–941

906.6 Late effect of burn of wrist and hand
Late effect of injury classifiable to 944

☐ **906.7 Late effect of burn of other extremities**
Late effect of injury classifiable to 943 or 945

☐ **906.8 Late effect of burns of other specified sites**
Late effect of injury classifiable to 942, 946–947

☐ **906.9 Late effect of burn of unspecified site**
Late effect of injury classifiable to 948–949

● **907 Late effects of injuries to the nervous system**

907.0 Late effect of intracranial injury without mention of skull fracture
Late effect of injury classifiable to 850–854

907.1 Late effect of injury to cranial nerve
Late effect of injury classifiable to 950–951

907.2 Late effect of spinal cord injury
Late effect of injury classifiable to 806, 952

☐ **907.3 Late effect of injury to nerve root(s), spinal plexus(es), and other nerves of trunk**
Late effect of injury classifiable to 953–954

907.4 Late effect of injury to peripheral nerve of shoulder girdle and upper limb
Late effect of injury classifiable to 955

907.5 Late effect of injury to peripheral nerve of pelvic girdle and lower limb
Late effect of injury classifiable to 956

☐ **907.9 Late effect of injury to other and unspecified nerve**
Late effect of injury classifiable to 957

● **908 Late effects of other and unspecified injuries**

908.0 Late effect of internal injury to chest
Late effect of injury classifiable to 860–862

908.1 Late effect of internal injury to intra-abdominal organs
Late effect of injury classifiable to 863–866, 868

☐ **908.2 Late effect of internal injury to other internal organs**
Late effect of injury classifiable to 867 or 869

908.3 Late effect of injury to blood vessel of head, neck, and extremities
Late effect of injury classifiable to 900, 903–904

908.4 Late effect of injury to blood vessel of thorax, abdomen, and pelvis
Late effect of injury classifiable to 901–902

908.5 Late effect of foreign body in orifice
Late effect of injury classifiable to 930–939

☐ **908.6 Late effect of certain complications of trauma**
Late effect of complications classifiable to 958

☐ **908.9 Late effect of unspecified injury**
Late effect of injury classifiable to 959

● **909 Late effects of other and unspecified external causes**

909.0 Late effect of poisoning due to drug, medicinal or biological substance
Late effect of conditions classifiable to 960–979

    Excludes *Late effect of adverse effect of drug, medicinal or biological substance (909.5)*

909.1 Late effect of toxic effects of nonmedical substances
Late effect of conditions classifiable to 980–989

909.2 Late effect of radiation
Late effect of conditions classifiable to 990

909.3 Late effect of complications of surgical and medical care
Late effect of conditions classifiable to 996–999

☐ **909.4 Late effect of certain other external causes**
Late effect of conditions classifiable to 991–994

909.5 Late effect of adverse effect of drug, medicinal or biological substance
> **Excludes** late effect of poisoning due to drug, medicinal or biological substances (909.0)

☐ **909.9 Late effect of other and unspecified external causes**

SUPERFICIAL INJURY (910–919)

> **Excludes** burn (blisters) (940.0–949.5)
> contusion (920–924.9)
> foreign body:
>   granuloma (728.82)
>   inadvertently left in operative wound (998.4)
>   residual, in soft tissue (729.6)
>   insect bite, venomous (989.5)
>   open wound with incidental foreign body (870.0–897.7)

● **910 Superficial injury of face, neck, and scalp except eye**

> **Includes:** cheek   lip
> ear   nose
> gum   throat

> **Excludes** eye and adnexa (918.0–918.9)

910.0 Abrasion or friction burn without mention of infection

910.1 Abrasion or friction burn, infected

910.2 Blister without mention of infection

910.3 Blister, infected

910.4 Insect bite, nonvenomous, without mention of infection

910.5 Insect bite, nonvenomous, infected

910.6 Superficial foreign body (splinter) without major open wound and without mention of infection

910.7 Superficial foreign body (splinter) without major open wound, infected

☐ **910.8 Other and unspecified superficial injury of face, neck, and scalp without mention of infection**

☐ **910.9 Other and unspecified superficial injury of face, neck, and scalp, infected**

● **911 Superficial injury of trunk**

> **Includes:** abdominal wall
> anus
> back
> breast
> buttock
> chest wall
> flank
> groin
> interscapular region
> labium (majus) (minus)
> penis
> perineum
> scrotum
> testis
> vagina
> vulva

> **Excludes** hip (916.0–916.9)
> scapular region (912.0–912.9)

911.0 Abrasion or friction burn without mention of infection

911.1 Abrasion or friction burn, infected

911.2 Blister without mention of infection

911.3 Blister, infected

911.4 Insect bite, nonvenomous, without mention of infection

911.5 Insect bite, nonvenomous, infected

911.6 Superficial foreign body (splinter) without major open wound and without mention of infection

911.7 Superficial foreign body (splinter) without major open wound, infected

☐ **911.8 Other and unspecified superficial injury of trunk without mention of infection**

☐ **911.9 Other and unspecified superficial injury of trunk, infected**

● **912 Superficial injury of shoulder and upper arm**

> **Includes:** axilla
> scapular region

912.0 Abrasion or friction burn without mention of infection

912.1 Abrasion or friction burn, infected

912.2 Blister without mention of infection

912.3 Blister, infected

912.4 Insect bite, nonvenomous, without mention of infection

912.5 Insect bite, nonvenomous, infected

912.6 Superficial foreign body (splinter) without major open wound and without mention of infection

912.7 Superficial foreign body (splinter) without major open wound, infected

☐ **912.8 Other and unspecified superficial injury of shoulder and upper arm without mention of infection**

☐ **912.9 Other and unspecified superficial injury of shoulder and upper arm, infected**

● **913 Superficial injury of elbow, forearm, and wrist**

913.0 Abrasion or friction burn without mention of infection

913.1 Abrasion or friction burn, infected

913.2 Blister without mention of infection

913.3 Blister, infected

913.4 Insect bite, nonvenomous, without mention of infection

913.5 Insect bite, nonvenomous, infected

913.6 Superficial foreign body (splinter) without major open wound and without mention of infection

913.7 Superficial foreign body (splinter) without major open wound, infected

☐ **913.8 Other and unspecified superficial injury of elbow, forearm, and wrist without mention of infection**

☐ **913.9 Other and unspecified superficial injury of elbow, forearm, and wrist, infected**

● **914 Superficial injury of hand(s) except finger(s) alone**

914.0 Abrasion or friction burn without mention of infection

914.1 Abrasion or friction burn, infected

914.2 Blister without mention of infection

914.3 Blister, infected

    ◄▶ **New Code**   ⬅▪▶ **Revised Code**   ● **Not a Principal Diagnosis**   ● **Use Additional Digit(s)**   ☐ **Nonspecific Code**

914.4 **Insect bite, nonvenomous, without mention of infection**

914.5 **Insect bite, nonvenomous, infected**

914.6 **Superficial foreign body (splinter) without major open wound and without mention of infection**

914.7 **Superficial foreign body (splinter) without major open wound, infected**

☐ 914.8 **Other and unspecified superficial injury of hand without mention of infection**

☐ 914.9 **Other and unspecified superficial injury of hand, infected**

● 915 **Superficial injury of finger(s)**

Includes: fingernail
thumb (nail)

915.0 **Abrasion or friction burn without mention of infection**

915.1 **Abrasion or friction burn, infected**

915.2 **Blister without mention of infection**

915.3 **Blister, infected**

915.4 **Insect bite, nonvenomous, without mention of infection**

915.5 **Insect bite, nonvenomous, infected**

915.6 **Superficial foreign body (splinter) without major open wound and without mention of infection**

915.7 **Superficial foreign body (splinter) without major open wound, infected**

☐ 915.8 **Other and unspecified superficial injury of fingers without mention of infection**

☐ 915.9 **Other and unspecified superficial injury of fingers, infected**

● 916 **Superficial injury of hip, thigh, leg, and ankle**

916.0 **Abrasion or friction burn without mention of infection**

916.1 **Abrasion or friction burn, infected**

916.2 **Blister without mention of infection**

916.3 **Blister, infected**

916.4 **Insect bite, nonvenomous, without mention of infection**

916.5 **Insect bite, nonvenomous, infected**

916.6 **Superficial foreign body (splinter) without major open wound and without mention of infection**

916.7 **Superficial foreign body (splinter) without major open wound, infected**

☐ 916.8 **Other and unspecified superficial injury of hip, thigh, leg, and ankle without mention of infection**

☐ 916.9 **Other and unspecified superficial injury of hip, thigh, leg, and ankle, infected**

● 917 **Superficial injury of foot and toe(s)**

Includes: heel
toenail

917.0 **Abrasion or friction burn without mention of infection**

917.1 **Abrasion or friction burn, infected**

917.2 **Blister without mention of infection**

917.3 **Blister, infected**

917.4 **Insect bite, nonvenomous, without mention of infection**

917.5 **Insect bite, nonvenomous, infected**

917.6 **Superficial foreign body (splinter) without major open wound and without mention of infection**

917.7 **Superficial foreign body (splinter) without major open wound, infected**

☐ 917.8 **Other and unspecified superficial injury of foot and toes without mention of infection**

☐ 917.9 **Other and unspecified superficial injury of foot and toes, infected**

● 918 **Superficial injury of eye and adnexa**

Excludes	burn (940.0–940.9)
	foreign body on external eye (930.0–930.9)

918.0 **Eyelids and periocular area**
Abrasion
Insect bite
Superficial foreign body (splinter)

918.1 **Cornea**
Corneal abrasion
Superficial laceration

Excludes	corneal injury due to contact lens (371.82)

918.2 **Conjunctiva**

☐ 918.9 **Other and unspecified superficial injuries of eye**
Eye (ball) NOS

● 919 **Superficial injury of other, multiple, and unspecified sites**

Excludes	multiple sites classifiable to the same three-digit category (910.0–918.9)

☐ 919.0 **Abrasion or friction burn without mention of infection**

☐ 919.1 **Abrasion or friction burn, infected**

☐ 919.2 **Blister without mention of infection**

☐ 919.3 **Blister, infected**

☐ 919.4 **Insect bite, nonvenomous, without mention of infection**

☐ 919.5 **Insect bite, nonvenomous, infected**

☐ 919.6 **Superficial foreign body (splinter) without major open wound and without mention of infection**

☐ 919.7 **Superficial foreign body (splinter) without major open wound, infected**

☐ 919.8 **Other and unspecified superficial injury without mention of infection**

☐ 919.9 **Other and unspecified superficial injury, infected**

CONTUSION WITH INTACT SKIN SURFACE (920–924)

Includes: bruise without fracture or open wound
hematoma without fracture or open wound

Excludes	concussion (850.0–850.9)
	hemarthrosis (840.0–848.9)
	internal organs (860.0–869.1)
	that incidental to:
	crushing injury (925–929.9)
	dislocation (830.0–839.9)
	fracture (800.0–829.1)
	internal injury (860.0–869.1)
	intracranial injury (850.0–854.1)
	nerve injury (950.0–957.9)
	open wound (870.0–897.7)

920 **Contusion of face, scalp, and neck except eye(s)**

Cheek	Mandibular joint area
Ear (auricle)	Nose
Gum	Throat
Lip	

● **921 Contusion of eye and adnexa**

☐ **921.0 Black eye, NOS**

921.1 Contusion of eyelids and periocular area

921.2 Contusion of orbital tissues

921.3 Contusion of eyeball

☐ **921.9 Unspecified contusion of eye**
Injury of eye NOS

● **922 Contusion of trunk**

922.0 Breast

922.1 Chest wall

922.2 Abdominal wall
Flank
Groin

● **922.3 Back**

922.31 Back
Excludes *interscapular region (922.33)*

922.32 Buttock

922.33 Interscapular region
Excludes *scapular region (923.01)*

922.4 Genital organs
Labium (majus) (minus)
Penis
Perineum
Scrotum
Testis
Vagina
Vulva

☐ **922.8 Multiple sites of trunk**

☐ **922.9 Unspecified part**
Trunk NOS

● **923 Contusion of upper limb**

● **923.0 Shoulder and upper arm**

923.00 Shoulder region

923.01 Scapular region

923.02 Axillary region

923.03 Upper arm

☐ **923.09 Multiple sites**

● **923.1 Elbow and forearm**

923.10 Forearm

923.11 Elbow

● **923.2 Wrist and hand(s), except finger(s) alone**

923.20 Hand(s)

923.21 Wrist

923.3 Finger
Fingernail
Thumb (nail)

☐ **923.8 Multiple sites of upper limb**

☐ **923.9 Unspecified part of upper limb**
Arm NOS

● **924 Contusion of lower limb and of other and unspecified sites**

● **924.0 Hip and thigh**

924.00 Thigh

924.01 Hip

● **924.1 Knee and lower leg**

924.10 Lower leg

924.11 Knee

● **924.2 Ankle and foot, excluding toe(s)**

924.20 Foot
Heel

924.21 Ankle

924.3 Toe
Toenail

☐ **924.4 Multiple sites of lower limb**

☐ **924.5 Unspecified part of lower limb**
Leg NOS

☐ **924.8 Multiple sites, not elsewhere classified**

☐ **924.9 Unspecified site**

CRUSHING INJURY (925–929)

Excludes *concussion (850.0–850.9)*
fractures (800–829)
internal organs (860.0–869.1)
that incidental to:
   internal injury (860.0–869.1)
   intracranial injury (850.0–854.1)

● **925 Crushing injury of face, scalp, and neck**
Cheek
Ear
Larynx
Pharynx
Throat

925.1 Crushing injury of face and scalp
Cheek
Ear

925.2 Crushing injury of neck
Larynx
Throat
Pharynx

● **926 Crushing injury of trunk**
Excludes *crush injury of internal organs (860.0–869.1)*

926.0 External genitalia
Labium (majus) (minus)
Penis
Scrotum
Testis
Vulva

● **926.1 Other specified sites**

926.11 Back

926.12 Buttock

☐ **926.19 Other**
Breast
Excludes *crushing of chest (860.0–862.9)*

☐ **926.8 Multiple sites of trunk**

☐ **926.9 Unspecified site**
Trunk NOS

● **927 Crushing injury of upper limb**

● **927.0 Shoulder and upper arm**

927.00 Shoulder region

927.01 Scapular region

927.02 Axillary region

927.03 Upper arm

☐ **927.09 Multiple sites**

● **927.1 Elbow and forearm**

 ◀▶ **New Code**   ⬅▪▮ ▮▪➡ **Revised Code**   ● **Not a Principal Diagnosis**   ● **Use Additional Digit(s)**   ☐ **Nonspecific Code**

927.10   **Forearm**

927.11   **Elbow**

● 927.2   **Wrist and hand(s), except finger(s) alone**

927.20   **Hand(s)**

927.21   **Wrist**

927.3   **Finger(s)**

☐ 927.8   **Multiple sites of upper limb**

☐ 927.9   **Unspecified site**
Arm NOS

● 928   **Crushing injury of lower limb**

● 928.0   **Hip and thigh**

928.00   **Thigh**

928.01   **Hip**

● 928.1   **Knee and lower leg**

928.10   **Lower leg**

928.11   **Knee**

● 928.2   **Ankle and foot, excluding toe(s) alone**

928.20   **Foot**
Heel

928.21   **Ankle**

928.3   **Toe(s)**

☐ 928.8   **Multiple sites of lower limb**

☐ 928.9   **Unspecified site**
Leg NOS

● 929   **Crushing injury of multiple and unspecified sites**

> **Excludes**   *multiple internal injury NOS (869.0–869.1)*

☐ 929.0   **Multiple sites, not elsewhere classified**

☐ 929.9   **Unspecified site**

EFFECTS OF FOREIGN BODY ENTERING THROUGH ORIFICE (930–939)

> **Excludes**   *foreign body:*
> *granuloma (728.82)*
> *inadvertently left in operative wound (998.4, 998.7)*
> *in open wound (800–839, 851–897)*
> *residual, in soft tissues (729.6)*
> *superficial without major open wound (910– 919 with .6 or .7)*

● 930   **Foreign body on external eye**

> **Excludes**   *foreign body in penetrating wound of:*
> *eyeball (871.5–871.6)*
> *retained (old) (360.5–360.6)*
> *ocular adnexa (870.4)*
> *retained (old) (376.6)*

930.0   **Corneal foreign body**

930.1   **Foreign body in conjunctival sac**

930.2   **Foreign body in lacrimal punctum**

☐ 930.8   **Other and combined sites**

☐ 930.9   **Unspecified site**
External eye NOS

931   **Foreign body in ear**
Auditory canal
Auricle

932   **Foreign body in nose**
Nasal sinus
Nostril

● 933   **Foreign body in pharynx and larynx**

933.0   **Pharynx**
Nasopharynx
Throat NOS

933.1   **Larynx**
Asphyxia due to foreign body
Choking due to:
    food (regurgitated)
    phlegm

● 934   **Foreign body in trachea, bronchus, and lung**

934.0   **Trachea**

934.1   **Main bronchus**

☐ 934.8   **Other specified parts**
Bronchioles
Lung

☐ 934.9   **Respiratory tree, unspecified**
Inhalation of liquid or vomitus, lower respiratory tract NOS

● 935   **Foreign body in mouth, esophagus, and stomach**

935.0   **Mouth**

935.1   **Esophagus**

935.2   **Stomach**

936   **Foreign body in intestine and colon**

937   **Foreign body in anus and rectum**
Rectosigmoid (junction)

☐ 938   **Foreign body in digestive system, unspecified**
Alimentary tract NOS
Swallowed foreign body

● 939   **Foreign body in genitourinary tract**

939.0   **Bladder and urethra**

939.1   **Uterus, any part**

> **Excludes**   *intrauterine contraceptive device:*
> *complications from (996.32, 996.65)*
> *presence of (V45.51)*

939.2   **Vulva and vagina**

939.3   **Penis**

☐ 939.9   **Unspecified site**

BURNS (940–949)

Includes: burns from:
    electrical heating appliance
    electricity
    flame
    hot object
    lightning
    radiation
    chemical burns (external) (internal)
    scalds

> **Excludes**   *friction burns (910–919 with .0, .1)*
> *sunburn (692.71)*

● 940   **Burn confined to eye and adnexa**

940.0   **Chemical burn of eyelids and periocular area**

☐ 940.1   **Other burns of eyelids and periocular area**

940.2   **Alkaline chemical burn of cornea and conjunctival sac**

940.3   **Acid chemical burn of cornea and conjunctival sac**

☐ 940.4   **Other burn of cornea and conjunctival sac**

940.5 Burn with resulting rupture and destruction of eyeball

☐ **940.9 Unspecified burn of eye and adnexa**

● **941 Burn of face, head, and neck**

    Excludes *mouth (947.0)*

The following fifth-digit subclassification is for use with category 941:

☐ **0 face and head, unspecified site**
    1 ear [any part]
    2 eye (with other parts of face, head, and neck)
    3 lip(s)
    4 chin
    5 nose (septum)
    6 scalp [any part]
       temple (region)
    7 forehead and cheek
    8 neck
☐ **9 multiple sites [except with eye] of face, head, and neck**

☐● **941.0 Unspecified degree**

● **941.1 Erythema [first degree]**

● **941.2 Blisters, epidermal loss [second degree]**

● **941.3 Full-thickness skin loss [third degree NOS]**

● **941.4 Deep necrosis of underlying tissues [deep third degree] without mention of loss of a body part**

● **941.5 Deep necrosis of underlying tissues [deep third degree] with loss of a body part**

● **942 Burn of trunk**

    Excludes *scapular region (943.0–943.5 with fifth-digit 6)*

The following fifth-digit subclassification is for use with category 942:

☐ **0 trunk, unspecified site**
    1 breast
    2 chest wall, excluding breast and nipple
    3 abdominal wall
       flank
       groin
    4 back [any part]
       buttock
       interscapular region
    5 genitalia
       labium (majus) (minus)
       penis
       perineum
       scrotum
       testis
       vulva
☐ **9 other and multiple sites of trunk**

☐● **942.0 Unspecified degree**

● **942.1 Erythema [first degree]**

● **942.2 Blisters, epidermal loss [second degree]**

● **942.3 Full-thickness skin loss [third degree NOS]**

● **942.4 Deep necrosis of underlying tissues [deep third degree] without mention of loss of a body part**

● **942.5 Deep necrosis of underlying tissues [deep third degree] with loss of a body part**

● **943 Burn of upper limb, except wrist and hand**

The following fifth-digit subclassification is for use with category 943:

☐ **0 upper limb, unspecified site**
    1 forearm
    2 elbow
    3 upper arm
    4 axilla
    5 shoulder
    6 scapular region
☐ **9 multiple sites of upper limb, except wrist and hand**

☐● **943.0 Unspecified degree**

● **943.1 Erythema [first degree]**

● **943.2 Blisters, epidermal loss [second degree]**

● **943.3 Full-thickness skin loss [third degree NOS]**

● **943.4 Deep necrosis of underlying tissues [deep third degree] without mention of loss of a body part**

● **943.5 Deep necrosis of underlying tissues [deep third degree] with loss of a body part**

● **944 Burn of wrist(s) and hand(s)**

The following fifth-digit subclassification is for use with category 944:

☐ **0 hand, unspecified site**
    1 single digit [finger (nail)] other than thumb
    2 thumb (nail)
    3 two or more digits, not including thumb
    4 two or more digits including thumb
    5 palm
    6 back of hand
    7 wrist
☐ **8 multiple sites of wrist(s) and hand(s)**

☐● **944.0 Unspecified degree**

● **944.1 Erythema [first degree]**

● **944.2 Blisters, epidermal loss [second degree]**

● **944.3 Full-thickness skin loss [third degree NOS]**

● **944.4 Deep necrosis of underlying tissues [deep third degree] without mention of loss of a body part**

● **944.5 Deep necrosis of underlying tissues [deep third degree] with loss of a body part**

● **945 Burn of lower limb(s)**

The following fifth-digit subclassification is for use with category 945:

☐ **0 lower limb [leg], unspecified site**
    1 toe(s) (nail)
    2 foot
    3 ankle
    4 lower leg
    5 knee
    6 thigh [any part]
☐ **9 multiple sites of lower limb(s)**

☐● **945.0 Unspecified degree**

● **945.1 Erythema [first degree]**

● **945.2 Blisters, epidermal loss [second degree]**

● **945.3 Full-thickness skin loss [third degree NOS]**

● **945.4 Deep necrosis of underlying tissues [deep third degree] without mention of loss of a body part**

● **945.5 Deep necrosis of underlying tissues [deep third degree] with loss of a body part**

● **946 Burns of multiple specified sites**

    Includes: burns of sites classifiable to more than one three-digit category in 940–945

    Excludes *multiple burns NOS (949.0–949.5)*

    ◀▶ **New Code**   ⬅⬛⬛➡ **Revised Code**   ● **Not a Principal Diagnosis**   ● **Use Additional Digit(s)**   ☐ **Nonspecific Code**

☐ **946.0 Unspecified degree**

946.1 Erythema [first degree]

946.2 Blisters, epidermal loss [second degree]

946.3 Full-thickness skin loss [third degree NOS]

946.4 Deep necrosis of underlying tissues [deep third degree] without mention of loss of a body part

946.5 Deep necrosis of underlying tissues [deep third degree] with loss of a body part

● **947 Burn of internal organs**

> **Includes:** burns from chemical agents (ingested)

947.0 Mouth and pharynx
> Gum
> Tongue

947.1 Larynx, trachea, and lung

947.2 Esophagus

947.3 Gastrointestinal tract
> Colon
> Rectum
> Small intestine
> Stomach

947.4 Vagina and uterus

☐ **947.8 Other specified sites**

☐ **947.9 Unspecified site**

● **948 Burns classified according to extent of body surface involved**

> Note: This category is to be used when the site of the burn is unspecified, or with categories 940–947 when the site is specified.

> **Excludes**   *sunburn (692.71)* ◄

The following fifth-digit subclassification is for use with category 948 to indicate the percent of body surface with third degree burn; valid digits are in [brackets] under each code:
> 0 less than 10 percent or unspecified
> 1 10–19%
> 2 20–29%
> 3 30–39%
> 4 40–49%
> 5 50–59%
> 6 60–69%
> 7 70–79%
> 8 80–89%
> 9 90% or more of body surface

● **948.0 Burn [any degree] involving less than 10 percent**
[0] **of body surface**

● **948.1 10–19 percent of body surface**
[0–1]

● **948.2 20–29 percent of body surface**
[0–2]

● **948.3 30–39 percent of body surface**
[0–3]

● **948.4 40–49 percent of body surface**
[0–4]

● **948.5 50–59 percent of body surface**
[0–5]

● **948.6 60–69 percent of body surface**
[0–6]

● **948.7 70–79 percent of body surface**
[0–7]

● **948.8 80–89 percent of body surface**
[0–8]

● **948.9 90 percent or more of body surface**
[0–9]

● **949 Burn, unspecified**

> **Includes:** burn NOS
> multiple burns NOS

> **Excludes**   *burn of unspecified site but with statement of the extent of body surface involved (948.0–948.9)*

☐ **949.0 Unspecified degree**

☐ **949.1 Erythema [first degree]**

☐ **949.2 Blisters, epidermal loss [second degree]**

☐ **949.3 Full-thickness skin loss [third degree NOS]**

☐ **949.4 Deep necrosis of underlying tissues [deep third degree] without mention of loss of a body part**

☐ **949.5 Deep necrosis of underlying tissues [deep third degree] with loss of a body part**

INJURY TO NERVES AND SPINAL CORD (950–957)

> **Includes:** division of nerve
> lesion in continuity (with open wound)
> traumatic neuroma (with open wound)
> traumatic transient paralysis (with open wound)

> **Excludes**   *accidental puncture or laceration during medical procedure (998.2)*

● **950 Injury to optic nerve and pathways**

950.0 Optic nerve injury
> Second cranial nerve

950.1 Injury to optic chiasm

950.2 Injury to optic pathways

950.3 Injury to visual cortex

☐ **950.9 Unspecified**
> Traumatic blindness NOS

● **951 Injury to other cranial nerve(s)**

951.0 Injury to oculomotor nerve
> Third cranial nerve

951.1 Injury to trochlear nerve
> Fourth cranial nerve

951.2 Injury to trigeminal nerve
> Fifth cranial nerve

951.3 Injury to abducens nerve
> Sixth cranial nerve

951.4 Injury to facial nerve
> Seventh cranial nerve

951.5 Injury to acoustic nerve
> Auditory nerve
> Eighth cranial nerve
> Traumatic deafness NOS

951.6 Injury to accessory nerve
> Eleventh cranial nerve

951.7 Injury to hypoglossal nerve
> Twelfth cranial nerve

☐ **951.8 Injury to other specified cranial nerves**
> Glossopharyngeal [9th cranial] nerve
> Olfactory [1st cranial] nerve
> Pneumogastric [10th cranial] nerve
> Traumatic anosmia NOS
> Vagus [10th cranial] nerve

☐ **951.9 Injury to unspecified cranial nerve**

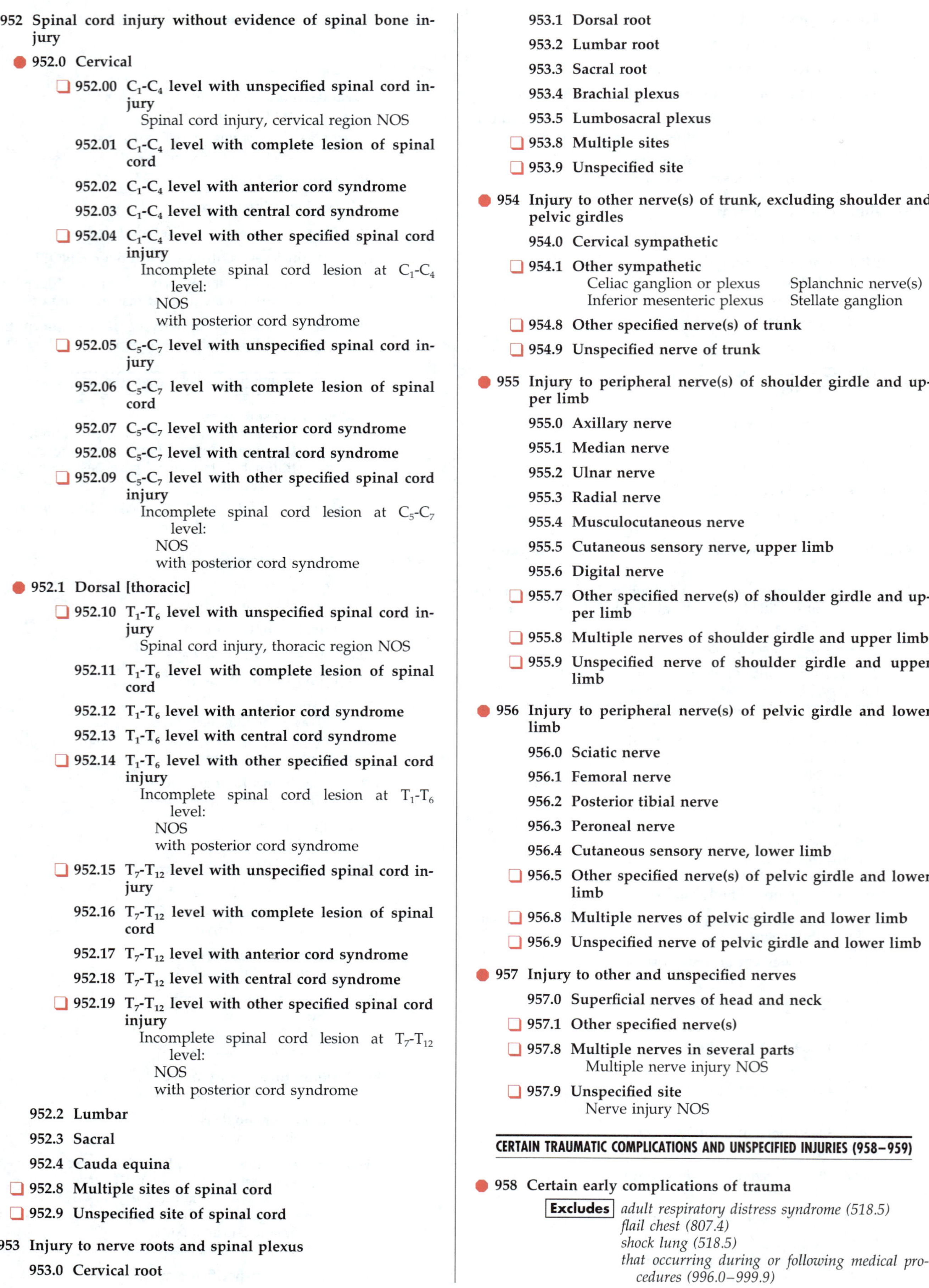

● **952 Spinal cord injury without evidence of spinal bone injury**

  ● **952.0 Cervical**

    ☐ 952.00 C₁-C₄ level with unspecified spinal cord injury
      Spinal cord injury, cervical region NOS

    952.01 C₁-C₄ level with complete lesion of spinal cord

    952.02 C₁-C₄ level with anterior cord syndrome

    952.03 C₁-C₄ level with central cord syndrome

    ☐ 952.04 C₁-C₄ level with other specified spinal cord injury
      Incomplete spinal cord lesion at C₁-C₄ level:
        NOS
        with posterior cord syndrome

    ☐ 952.05 C₅-C₇ level with unspecified spinal cord injury

    952.06 C₅-C₇ level with complete lesion of spinal cord

    952.07 C₅-C₇ level with anterior cord syndrome

    952.08 C₅-C₇ level with central cord syndrome

    ☐ 952.09 C₅-C₇ level with other specified spinal cord injury
      Incomplete spinal cord lesion at C₅-C₇ level:
        NOS
        with posterior cord syndrome

  ● **952.1 Dorsal [thoracic]**

    ☐ 952.10 T₁-T₆ level with unspecified spinal cord injury
      Spinal cord injury, thoracic region NOS

    952.11 T₁-T₆ level with complete lesion of spinal cord

    952.12 T₁-T₆ level with anterior cord syndrome

    952.13 T₁-T₆ level with central cord syndrome

    ☐ 952.14 T₁-T₆ level with other specified spinal cord injury
      Incomplete spinal cord lesion at T₁-T₆ level:
        NOS
        with posterior cord syndrome

    ☐ 952.15 T₇-T₁₂ level with unspecified spinal cord injury

    952.16 T₇-T₁₂ level with complete lesion of spinal cord

    952.17 T₇-T₁₂ level with anterior cord syndrome

    952.18 T₇-T₁₂ level with central cord syndrome

    ☐ 952.19 T₇-T₁₂ level with other specified spinal cord injury
      Incomplete spinal cord lesion at T₇-T₁₂ level:
        NOS
        with posterior cord syndrome

  952.2 Lumbar

  952.3 Sacral

  952.4 Cauda equina

  ☐ 952.8 Multiple sites of spinal cord

  ☐ 952.9 Unspecified site of spinal cord

● **953 Injury to nerve roots and spinal plexus**

  953.0 Cervical root

  953.1 Dorsal root

  953.2 Lumbar root

  953.3 Sacral root

  953.4 Brachial plexus

  953.5 Lumbosacral plexus

  ☐ 953.8 Multiple sites

  ☐ 953.9 Unspecified site

● **954 Injury to other nerve(s) of trunk, excluding shoulder and pelvic girdles**

  954.0 Cervical sympathetic

  ☐ 954.1 Other sympathetic
      Celiac ganglion or plexus   Splanchnic nerve(s)
      Inferior mesenteric plexus   Stellate ganglion

  ☐ 954.8 Other specified nerve(s) of trunk

  ☐ 954.9 Unspecified nerve of trunk

● **955 Injury to peripheral nerve(s) of shoulder girdle and upper limb**

  955.0 Axillary nerve

  955.1 Median nerve

  955.2 Ulnar nerve

  955.3 Radial nerve

  955.4 Musculocutaneous nerve

  955.5 Cutaneous sensory nerve, upper limb

  955.6 Digital nerve

  ☐ 955.7 Other specified nerve(s) of shoulder girdle and upper limb

  ☐ 955.8 Multiple nerves of shoulder girdle and upper limb

  ☐ 955.9 Unspecified nerve of shoulder girdle and upper limb

● **956 Injury to peripheral nerve(s) of pelvic girdle and lower limb**

  956.0 Sciatic nerve

  956.1 Femoral nerve

  956.2 Posterior tibial nerve

  956.3 Peroneal nerve

  956.4 Cutaneous sensory nerve, lower limb

  ☐ 956.5 Other specified nerve(s) of pelvic girdle and lower limb

  ☐ 956.8 Multiple nerves of pelvic girdle and lower limb

  ☐ 956.9 Unspecified nerve of pelvic girdle and lower limb

● **957 Injury to other and unspecified nerves**

  957.0 Superficial nerves of head and neck

  ☐ 957.1 Other specified nerve(s)

  ☐ 957.8 Multiple nerves in several parts
      Multiple nerve injury NOS

  ☐ 957.9 Unspecified site
      Nerve injury NOS

CERTAIN TRAUMATIC COMPLICATIONS AND UNSPECIFIED INJURIES (958–959)

● **958 Certain early complications of trauma**

  Excludes *adult respiratory distress syndrome (518.5)*
  flail chest (807.4)
  shock lung (518.5)
  that occurring during or following medical procedures (996.0–999.9)

◀▶ **New Code**   ⬅▦⬆ **Revised Code**   ● **Not a Principal Diagnosis**   ● **Use Additional Digit(s)**   ☐ **Nonspecific Code**

958.0 Air embolism
Pneumathemia

Excludes *that complicating:*
abortion (634–638 with .6, 639.6)
ectopic or molar pregnancy (639.6)
pregnancy, childbirth, or the puerperium (673.0)

958.1 Fat embolism

Excludes *that complicating:*
abortion (634–638 with .6, 639.6)
pregnancy, childbirth, or the puerperium (673.8)

958.2 Secondary and recurrent hemorrhage

958.3 Posttraumatic wound infection, not elsewhere classified

958.4 Traumatic shock
Shock (immediate) (delayed) following injury

Excludes *shock:*
anaphylactic (995.0)
due to serum (999.4)
anesthetic (995.4)
electric (994.8)
following abortion (639.5)
lightning (994.0)
nontraumatic NOS (785.50)
obstetric (669.1)
postoperative (998.0)

958.5 Traumatic anuria
Crush syndrome
Renal failure following crushing

Excludes *that due to a medical procedure (997.5)*

958.6 Volkmann's ischemic contracture
Posttraumatic muscle contracture

958.7 Traumatic subcutaneous emphysema

Excludes *subcutaneous emphysema resulting from a procedure (998.81)*

☐**958.8 Other early complications of trauma**

●**959 Injury, other and unspecified**

Includes: injury NOS

Excludes *injury NOS of:*
blood vessels (900.0–904.9)
eye (921.0–921.9)
internal organs (860.0–869.1)
intracranial sites (854.0–854.1)
nerves (950.0–951.9, 953.0–957.9)
spinal cord (952.0–952.9)

●**959.0 Head, face and neck**

☐**959.01 Head injury, unspecified**

Excludes *concussion (850.1–850.9)*
with head injury NOS (850.1–850.9)
specified intracranial injuries (850.0–854.1)

☐**959.09 Injury of face and neck**

☐**959.1 Trunk**
Abdominal wall
Back
Breast
Buttock
Chest wall
External genital organs
Flank
Groin
Interscapular region
Perineum

Excludes *scapular region (959.2)*

☐**959.2 Shoulder and upper arm**
Axilla
Scapular region

☐**959.3 Elbow, forearm, and wrist**

☐**959.4 Hand, except finger**

☐**959.5 Finger**
Fingernail
Thumb (nail)

☐**959.6 Hip and thigh**
Upper leg

☐**959.7 Knee, leg, ankle, and foot**

☐**959.8 Other specified sites, including multiple**

Excludes *multiple sites classifiable to the same four-digit category (959.0–959.7)*

☐**959.9 Unspecified site**

POISONING BY DRUGS, MEDICINAL AND BIOLOGICAL SUBSTANCES (960–979)

Includes: overdose of these substances
wrong substance given or taken in error

Excludes *adverse effects ["hypersensitivity," "reaction," etc.] of correct substance properly administered. Such cases are to be classified according to the nature of the adverse effect, such as:*
adverse effect NOS (995.2)
allergic lymphadenitis (289.3)
aspirin gastritis (535.4)
blood disorders (280.0–289.9)
dermatitis:
contact (692.0–692.9)
due to ingestion (693.0–693.9)
nephropathy (583.9)
[The drug giving rise to the adverse effect may be identified by use of categories E930–E949.]
drug dependence (304.0–304.9)
drug reaction and poisoning affecting the newborn (760.0–779.9)
nondependent abuse of drugs (305.0–305.9)
pathological drug intoxication (292.2)

Use additional code to specify the effects of the poisoning

●**960 Poisoning by antibiotics**

Excludes *antibiotics:*
ear, nose, and throat (976.6)
eye (976.5)
local (976.0)

960.0 Penicillins
Ampicillin
Carbenicillin
Cloxacillin
Penicillin G

960.1 Antifungal antibiotics
Amphotericin B
Griseofulvin
Nystatin
Trichomycin

Excludes *preparations intended for topical use (976.0–976.9)*

960.2 Chloramphenicol group
Chloramphenicol
Thiamphenicol

960.3 Erythromycin and other macrolides
Oleandomycin
Spiramycin

960.4 Tetracycline group
Doxycycline
Minocycline
Oxytetracycline

960.5 Cephalosporin group
Cephalexin
Cephaloglycin
Cephaloridine
Cephalothin

960.6 Antimycobacterial antibiotics
Cycloserine
Kanamycin
Rifampin
Streptomycin

960.7 Antineoplastic antibiotics
Actinomycin such as:
Bleomycin
Cactinomycin
Dactinomycin
Daunorubicin
Mitomycin

☐ **960.8 Other specified antibiotics**

☐ **960.9 Unspecified antibiotic**

● **961 Poisoning by other anti-infectives**
Excludes anti-infectives:
ear, nose, and throat (976.6)
eye (976.5)
local (976.0)

961.0 Sulfonamides
Sulfadiazine
Sulfafurazole
Sulfamethoxazole

961.1 Arsenical anti-infectives

961.2 Heavy metal anti-infectives
Compounds of: Compounds of:
antimony   lead
bismuth   mercury
Excludes mercurial diuretics (974.0)

961.3 Quinoline and hydroxyquinoline derivatives
Chiniofon
Diiodohydroxyquin
Excludes antimalarial drugs (961.4)

961.4 Antimalarials and drugs acting on other blood protozoa
Chloroquine
Cycloguanil
Primaquine
Proguanil [chloroguanide]
Pyrimethamine
Quinine

☐ **961.5 Other antiprotozoal drugs**
Emetine

961.6 Anthelmintics
Hexylresorcinol   Thiabendazole
Piperazine

961.7 Antiviral drugs
Methisazone
Excludes amantadine (966.4)
cytarabine (963.1)
idoxuridine (976.5)

☐ **961.8 Other antimycobacterial drugs**
Ethambutol
Ethionamide
Isoniazid
Para-aminosalicylic acid derivatives
Sulfones

☐ **961.9 Other and unspecified anti-infectives**
Flucytosine
Nitrofuran derivatives

● **962 Poisoning by hormones and synthetic substitutes**
Excludes oxytocic hormones (975.0)

962.0 Adrenal cortical steroids
Cortisone derivatives
Desoxycorticosterone derivatives
Fluorinated corticosteroids

962.1 Androgens and anabolic congeners
Methandriol
Nandrolone
Oxymetholone
Testosterone

962.2 Ovarian hormones and synthetic substitutes
Contraceptives, oral
Estrogens
Estrogens and progestogens, combined
Progestogens

962.3 Insulins and antidiabetic agents
Acetohexamide
Biguanide derivatives, oral
Chlorpropamide
Glucagon
Insulin
Phenformin
Sulfonylurea derivatives, oral
Tolbutamide

962.4 Anterior pituitary hormones
Corticotropin
Gonadotropin
Somatotropin [growth hormone]

962.5 Posterior pituitary hormones
Vasopressin
Excludes oxytocic hormones (975.0)

962.6 Parathyroid and parathyroid derivatives

962.7 Thyroid and thyroid derivatives
Dextrothyroxin
Levothyroxine sodium
Liothyronine
Thyroglobulin

962.8 Antithyroid agents
Iodides
Thiouracil
Thiourea

☐ **962.9 Other and unspecified hormones and synthetic substitutes**

● **963 Poisoning by primarily systemic agents**

963.0 Antiallergic and antiemetic drugs
Antihistamines   Diphenylpyraline
Chlorpheniramine   Thonzylamine
Diphenhydramine   Tripelennamine
Excludes phenothiazine-based tranquilizers (969.1)

963.1 Antineoplastic and immunosuppressive drugs
Azathioprine
Busulfan
Chlorambucil
Cyclophosphamide
Cytarabine
Fluorouracil
Mercaptopurine
thio-TEPA
Excludes antineoplastic antibiotics (960.7)

963.2 Acidifying agents

963.3 Alkalizing agents

    ◄► **New Code**   ⬅▦▦➡ **Revised Code**   ● **Not a Principal Diagnosis**   ● **Use Additional Digit(s)**   ☐ **Nonspecific Code**

963.4 Enzymes, not elsewhere classified
Penicillinase

963.5 Vitamins, not elsewhere classified
Vitamin A
Vitamin D
Excludes *nicotinic acid (972.2)*
vitamin K (964.3)

963.8 Other specified systemic agents
Heavy metal antagonists

963.9 Unspecified systemic agent

● **964 Poisoning by agents primarily affecting blood constituents**

964.0 Iron and its compounds
Ferric salts
Ferrous sulfate and other ferrous salts

964.1 Liver preparations and other antianemic agents
Folic acid

964.2 Anticoagulants
Coumarin
Heparin
Phenindione
Warfarin sodium

964.3 Vitamin K [phytonadione]

964.4 Fibrinolysis-affecting drugs
Aminocaproic acid
Streptodornase
Streptokinase
Urokinase

964.5 Anticoagulant antagonists and other coagulants
Hexadimethrine
Protamine sulfate

964.6 Gamma globulin

964.7 Natural blood and blood products
Blood plasma   Packed red cells
Human fibrinogen   Whole blood
Excludes *transfusion reactions (999.4–999.8)*

964.8 Other specified agents affecting blood constituents
Macromolecular blood substitutes
Plasma expanders

964.9 Unspecified agents affecting blood constituents

● **965 Poisoning by analgesics, antipyretics, and antirheumatics**
Excludes *drug dependence (304.0–304.9)*
nondependent abuse (305.0–305.9)

● **965.0 Opiates and related narcotics**

965.00 Opium (alkaloids), unspecified

965.01 Heroin
Diacetylmorphine

965.02 Methadone

965.09 Other
Codeine [methylmorphine]
Meperidine [pethidine]
Morphine

965.1 Salicylates
Acetylsalicylic acid [aspirin]
Salicylic acid salts

965.4 Aromatic analgesics, not elsewhere classified
Acetanilid
Paracetamol [acetaminophen]
Phenacetin [acetophenetidin]

965.5 Pyrazole derivatives
Aminophenazone [aminopyrine]
Phenylbutazone

● **965.6 Antirheumatics [antiphlogistics]**
Excludes *salicylates (965.1)*
steroids (962.0–962.9)

965.61 Propionic acid derivatives ◀
Fenoprofen ◀
Flurbiprofen ◀
Ibuprofen ◀
Ketoprofen ◀
Naproxen ◀
Oxaprozin ◀

965.69 Other antirheumatics ◀
Gold salts ◀
Indomethacin ◀

965.7 Other non-narcotic analgesics
Pyrabital

965.8 Other specified analgesics and antipyretics
Pentazocine

965.9 Unspecified analgesic and antipyretic

● **966 Poisoning by anticonvulsants and anti-Parkinsonism drugs**

966.0 Oxazolidine derivatives
Paramethadione
Trimethadione

966.1 Hydantoin derivatives
Phenytoin

966.2 Succinimides
Ethosuximide
Phensuximide

966.3 Other and unspecified anticonvulsants
Primidone
Excludes *barbiturates (967.0)*
sulfonamides (961.0)

966.4 Anti-Parkinsonism drugs
Amantadine
Ethopropazine [profenamine]
Levodopa [L-dopa]

● **967 Poisoning by sedatives and hypnotics**
Excludes *drug dependence (304.0–304.9)*
nondependent abuse (305.0–305.9)

967.0 Barbiturates
Amobarbital [amylobarbitone]
Barbital [barbitone]
Butabarbital [butabarbitone]
Pentobarbital [pentobarbitone]
Phenobarbital [phenobarbitone]
Secobarbital [quinalbarbitone]
Excludes *thiobarbiturate anesthetics (968.3)*

967.1 Chloral hydrate group

967.2 Paraldehyde

967.3 Bromine compounds
Bromide
Carbromal (derivatives)

967.4 Methaqualone compounds

967.5 Glutethimide group

967.6 Mixed sedatives, not elsewhere classified

967.8 Other sedatives and hypnotics

967.9 Unspecified sedative or hypnotic
Sleeping:
  drug NOS
  pill NOS
  tablet NOS

● **968 Poisoning by other central nervous system depressants and anesthetics**

> **Excludes**   *drug dependence (304.0–304.9)*
> *nondependent abuse (305.0–305.9)*

968.0 Central nervous system muscle-tone depressants
Chlorphenesin (carbamate)
Mephenesin
Methocarbamol

968.1 Halothane

☐ **968.2 Other gaseous anesthetics**
Ether
Halogenated hydrocarbon derivatives, except halothane
Nitrous oxide

968.3 Intravenous anesthetics
Ketamine
Methohexital [methohexitone]
Thiobarbiturates, such as thiopental sodium

☐ **968.4 Other and unspecified general anesthetics**

968.5 Surface [topical] and infiltration anesthetics
Cocaine
Lidocaine [lignocaine]
Procaine
Tetracaine

968.6 Peripheral nerve- and plexus-blocking anesthetics

968.7 Spinal anesthetics

☐ **968.9 Other and unspecified local anesthetics**

● **969 Poisoning by psychotropic agents**

> **Excludes**   *drug dependence (304.0–304.9)*
> *nondependent abuse (305.0–305.9)*

969.0 Antidepressants
Amitriptyline
Imipramine
Monoamine oxidase [MAO] inhibitors

969.1 Phenothiazine-based tranquilizers
Chlorpromazine
Fluphenazine
Prochlorperazine
Promazine

969.2 Butyrophenone-based tranquilizers
Haloperidol   Trifluperidol
Spiperone

☐ **969.3 Other antipsychotics, neuroleptics, and major tranquilizers**

969.4 Benzodiazepine-based tranquilizers
Chlordiazepoxide   Lorazepam
Diazepam   Medazepam
Flurazepam   Nitrazepam

☐ **969.5 Other tranquilizers**
Hydroxyzine
Meprobamate

969.6 Psychodysleptics [hallucinogens]
Cannabis (derivatives)
Lysergide [LSD]
Marijuana (derivatives)
Mescaline
Psilocin
Psilocybin

969.7 Psychostimulants
Amphetamine
Caffeine

> **Excludes**   *central appetite depressants (977.0)*

☐ **969.8 Other specified psychotropic agents**

☐ **969.9 Unspecified psychotropic agent**

● **970 Poisoning by central nervous system stimulants**

970.0 Analeptics
Lobeline
Nikethamide

970.1 Opiate antagonists
Levallorphan
Nalorphine
Naloxone

☐ **970.8 Other specified central nervous system stimulants**

☐ **970.9 Unspecified central nervous system stimulant**

● **971 Poisoning by drugs primarily affecting the autonomic nervous system**

971.0 Parasympathomimetics [cholinergics]
Acetylcholine
Anticholinesterase:
    organophosphorus
    reversible
Pilocarpine

971.1 Parasympatholytics [anticholinergics and antimuscarinics] and spasmolytics
Atropine
Homatropine
Hyoscine [scopolamine]
Quaternary ammonium derivatives

> **Excludes**   *papaverine (972.5)*

971.2 Sympathomimetics [adrenergics]
Epinephrine [adrenalin]
Levarterenol [noradrenalin]

971.3 Sympatholytics [antiadrenergics]
Phenoxybenzamine
Tolazoline hydrochloride

☐ **971.9 Unspecified drug primarily affecting autonomic nervous system**

● **972 Poisoning by agents primarily affecting the cardiovascular system**

972.0 Cardiac rhythm regulators
Practolol
Procainamide
Propranolol
Quinidine

> **Excludes**   *lidocaine (968.5)*

972.1 Cardiotonic glycosides and drugs of similar action
Digitalis glycosides
Digoxin
Strophanthins

972.2 Antilipemic and antiarteriosclerotic drugs
Clofibrate
Nicotinic acid derivatives

972.3 Ganglion-blocking agents
Pentamethonium bromide

972.4 Coronary vasodilators
Dipyridamole
Nitrates [nitroglycerin]
Nitrites

☐ **972.5 Other vasodilators**
Cyclandelate
Diazoxide
Papaverine

> **Excludes**   *nicotinic acid (972.2)*

☐ **972.6 Other antihypertensive agents**
Clonidine
Guanethidine
Rauwolfia alkaloids
Reserpine

    ◀ ▶ **New Code**   ⬅⬆➡ **Revised Code**   ● **Not a Principal Diagnosis**   ● **Use Additional Digit(s)**   ☐ **Nonspecific Code**

972.7 Antivaricose drugs, including sclerosing agents
Sodium morrhuate
Zinc salts

972.8 Capillary-active drugs
Adrenochrome derivatives
Metaraminol

972.9 Other and unspecified agents primarily affecting the cardiovascular system

● **973 Poisoning by agents primarily affecting the gastrointestinal system**

973.0 Antacids and antigastric secretion drugs
Aluminum hydroxide
Magnesium trisilicate

973.1 Irritant cathartics
Bisacodyl
Castor oil
Phenolphthalein

973.2 Emollient cathartics
Dioctyl sulfosuccinates

973.3 Other cathartics, including intestinal atonia drugs
Magnesium sulfate

973.4 Digestants
Pancreatin
Papain
Pepsin

973.5 Antidiarrheal drugs
Kaolin
Pectin

Excludes *anti-infectives (960.0–961.9)*

973.6 Emetics

973.8 Other specified agents primarily affecting the gastrointestinal system

973.9 Unspecified agent primarily affecting the gastrointestinal system

● **974 Poisoning by water, mineral, and uric acid metabolism drugs**

974.0 Mercurial diuretics
Chlormerodrin
Mercaptomerin
Mersalyl

974.1 Purine derivative diuretics
Theobromine
Theophylline

Excludes *aminophylline [theophylline ethylenediamine] (975.7)*
caffeine (969.7)

974.2 Carbonic acid anhydrase inhibitors
Acetazolamide

974.3 Saluretics
Benzothiadiazides
Chlorothiazide group

974.4 Other diuretics
Ethacrynic acid
Furosemide

974.5 Electrolytic, caloric, and water-balance agents

974.6 Other mineral salts, not elsewhere classified

974.7 Uric acid metabolism drugs
Allopurinol
Colchicine
Probenecid

● **975 Poisoning by agents primarily acting on the smooth and skeletal muscles and respiratory system**

975.0 Oxytocic agents
Ergot alkaloids
Oxytocin
Prostaglandins

975.1 Smooth muscle relaxants
Adiphenine
Metaproterenol [orciprenaline]

Excludes *papaverine (972.5)*

975.2 Skeletal muscle relaxants

975.3 Other and unspecified drugs acting on muscles

975.4 Antitussives
Dextromethorphan
Pipazethate

975.5 Expectorants
Acetylcysteine
Guaifenesin
Terpin hydrate

975.6 Anti-common cold drugs

975.7 Antiasthmatics
Aminophylline [theophylline ethylenediamine]

975.8 Other and unspecified respiratory drugs

● **976 Poisoning by agents primarily affecting skin and mucous membrane, ophthalmological, otorhinolaryngological, and dental drugs**

976.0 Local anti-infectives and anti-inflammatory drugs

976.1 Antipruritics

976.2 Local astringents and local detergents

976.3 Emollients, demulcents, and protectants

976.4 Keratolytics, keratoplastics, other hair treatment drugs and preparations

976.5 Eye anti-infectives and other eye drugs
Idoxuridine

976.6 Anti-infectives and other drugs and preparations for ear, nose, and throat

976.7 Dental drugs topically applied

Excludes *anti-infectives (976.0)*
local anesthetics (968.5)

976.8 Other agents primarily affecting skin and mucous membrane
Spermicides [vaginal contraceptives]

976.9 Unspecified agent primarily affecting skin and mucous membrane

● **977 Poisoning by other and unspecified drugs and medicinal substances**

977.0 Dietetics
Central appetite depressants

977.1 Lipotropic drugs

977.2 Antidotes and chelating agents, not elsewhere classified

977.3 Alcohol deterrents

977.4 Pharmaceutical excipients
Pharmaceutical adjuncts

977.8 Other specified drugs and medicinal substances
Contrast media used for diagnostic x-ray procedures
Diagnostic agents and kits

977.9 Unspecified drug or medicinal substance

● **978 Poisoning by bacterial vaccines**

978.0 BCG

978.1 **Typhoid and paratyphoid**

978.2 **Cholera**

978.3 **Plague**

978.4 **Tetanus**

978.5 **Diphtheria**

978.6 **Pertussis vaccine, including combinations with a pertussis component**

❏ 978.8 **Other and unspecified bacterial vaccines**

978.9 **Mixed bacterial vaccines, except combinations with a pertussis component**

● 979 **Poisoning by other vaccines and biological substances**

> **Excludes** *gamma globulin (964.6)*

979.0 **Smallpox vaccine**

979.1 **Rabies vaccine**

979.2 **Typhus vaccine**

979.3 **Yellow fever vaccine**

979.4 **Measles vaccine**

979.5 **Poliomyelitis vaccine**

❏ 979.6 **Other and unspecified viral and rickettsial vaccines**
Mumps vaccine

979.7 **Mixed viral-rickettsial and bacterial vaccines, except combinations with a pertussis component**

> **Excludes** *combinations with a pertussis component (978.6)*

❏ 979.9 **Other and unspecified vaccines and biological substances**

TOXIC EFFECTS OF SUBSTANCES CHIEFLY NONMEDICINAL AS TO SOURCE (980–989)

> **Excludes** *burns from chemical agents (ingested) (947.0–947.9)*
> *localized toxic effects indexed elsewhere (001.0–799.9)*
> *respiratory conditions due to external agents (506.0–508.9)*

Use additional code to specify the nature of the toxic effect

● 980 **Toxic effect of alcohol**

980.0 **Ethyl alcohol**
Denatured alcohol
Ethanol
Grain alcohol

Use additional code to identify any associated:
acute alcohol intoxication (305.0)
in alcoholism (303.0)
drunkenness (simple) (305.0)
pathological (291.4)

980.1 **Methyl alcohol**
Methanol
Wood alcohol

980.2 **Isopropyl alcohol**
Dimethyl carbinol
Isopropanol
Rubbing alcohol

980.3 **Fusel oil**
Alcohol:
amyl
butyl
propyl

❏ 980.8 **Other specified alcohols**

❏ 980.9 **Unspecified alcohol**

981 **Toxic effect of petroleum products**
Benzine   Petroleum:
Gasoline   ether
Kerosene   naphtha
Paraffin wax   spirit

● 982 **Toxic effect of solvents other than petroleum based**

982.0 **Benzene and homologues**

982.1 **Carbon tetrachloride**

982.2 **Carbon disulfide**
Carbon bisulfide

❏ 982.3 **Other chlorinated hydrocarbon solvents**
Tetrachloroethylene
Trichloroethylene

> **Excludes** *chlorinated hydrocarbon preparations other than solvents (989.2)*

982.4 **Nitroglycol**

❏ 982.8 **Other nonpetroleum-based solvents**
Acetone

● 983 **Toxic effect of corrosive aromatics, acids, and caustic alkalis**

983.0 **Corrosive aromatics**
Carbolic acid or phenol   Cresol

983.1 **Acids**
Acid:
hydrochloric
nitric
sulfuric

983.2 **Caustic alkalis**
Lye
Potassium hydroxide
Sodium hydroxide

❏ 983.9 **Caustic, unspecified**

● 984 **Toxic effect of lead and its compounds (including fumes)**

> **Includes:** that from all sources except medicinal substances

984.0 **Inorganic lead compounds**
Lead dioxide
Lead salts

984.1 **Organic lead compounds**
Lead acetate
Tetraethyl lead

❏ 984.8 **Other lead compounds**

❏ 984.9 **Unspecified lead compound**

● 985 **Toxic effect of other metals**

> **Includes:** that from all sources except medicinal substances

985.0 **Mercury and its compounds**
Minamata disease

985.1 **Arsenic and its compounds**

985.2 **Manganese and its compounds**

985.3 **Beryllium and its compounds**

985.4 **Antimony and its compounds**

985.5 **Cadmium and its compounds**

985.6 **Chromium**

❏ 985.8 **Other specified metals**
Brass fumes
Copper salts
Iron compounds
Nickel compounds

❏ 985.9 **Unspecified metal**

   ◀▶ **New Code**   ⬅⬅ ➡➡ **Revised Code**   ● **Not a Principal Diagnosis**   ● **Use Additional Digit(s)**   ❏ **Nonspecific Code**

986   Toxic effect of carbon monoxide

● **987   Toxic effect of other gases, fumes, or vapors**

     987.0   Liquefied petroleum gases
         Butane
         Propane

     ☐ **987.1   Other hydrocarbon gas**

     987.2   Nitrogen oxides
         Nitrogen dioxide
         Nitrous fumes

     987.3   Sulfur dioxide

     987.4   Freon
         Dichloromonofluoromethane

     987.5   Lacrimogenic gas
         Bromobenzyl cyanide
         Chloroacetophenone
         Ethyliodoacetate

     987.6   Chlorine gas

     987.7   Hydrocyanic acid gas

     ☐ **987.8   Other specified gases, fumes, or vapors**
         Phosgene
         Polyester fumes

     ☐ **987.9   Unspecified gas, fume, or vapor**

● **988   Toxic effect of noxious substances eaten as food**

     Excludes   *allergic reaction to food, such as:*
         gastroenteritis (558.9)
         rash (692.5, 693.1)
         food poisoning (bacterial) (005.0–005.9)
         toxic effects of food contaminants, such as:
         aflatoxin and other mycotoxin (989.7)
         mercury (985.0)

     988.0   Fish and shellfish

     988.1   Mushrooms

     988.2   Berries and other plants

     ☐ **988.8   Other specified noxious substances eaten as food**

     ☐ **988.9   Unspecified noxious substance eaten as food**

● **989   Toxic effect of other substances, chiefly nonmedicinal as to source**

     989.0   Hydrocyanic acid and cyanides
         Potassium cyanide
         Sodium cyanide

     Excludes   *gas and fumes (987.7)*

     989.1   Strychnine and salts

     989.2   Chlorinated hydrocarbons
         Aldrin
         Chlordane
         DDT
         Dieldrin

     Excludes   *chlorinated hydrocarbon solvents (982.0–982.3)*

     989.3   Organophosphate and carbamate
         Carbaryl   Parathion
         Dichlorvos   Phorate
         Malathion   Phosdrin

     ☐ **989.4   Other pesticides, not elsewhere classified**
         Mixtures of insecticides

     989.5   Venom
         Bites of venomous snakes, lizards, and spiders
         Tick paralysis

     989.6   Soaps and detergents

     989.7   Aflatoxin and other mycotoxin [food contaminants]

●   ☐ **989.8   Other substances, chiefly nonmedicinal as to source**

     989.81   Asbestos

     Excludes   *asbestosis (501)*
         exposure to asbestos (V15.84)

     989.82   Latex

     989.83   Silicone

     Excludes   *silicone used in medical devices, implants and grafts (996.00–996.79)*

     989.84   Tobacco

     ☐ **989.89   Other**

     ☐ **989.9   Unspecified substance, chiefly nonmedicinal as to source**

OTHER AND UNSPECIFIED EFFECTS OF EXTERNAL CAUSES (990–995)

☐ **990   Effects of radiation, unspecified**
     Complication of:
         phototherapy
         radiation therapy
     Radiation sickness

     Excludes   *specified adverse effects of radiation. Such conditions are to be classified according to the nature of the adverse effect, as:*
         burns (940.0–949.5)
         dermatitis (692.7–692.8)
         leukemia (204.0–208.9)
         pneumonia (508.0)
         sunburn (692.71)
         [The type of radiation giving rise to the adverse effect may be identified by use of the E codes.]

● **991   Effects of reduced temperature**

     991.0   Frostbite of face

     991.1   Frostbite of hand

     991.2   Frostbite of foot

     ☐ **991.3   Frostbite of other and unspecified sites**

     991.4   Immersion foot
         Trench foot

     991.5   Chilblains
         Erythema pernio
         Perniosis

     991.6   Hypothermia
         Hypothermia (accidental)

     Excludes   *hypothermia following anesthesia (995.89)*
         hypothermia not associated with low environmental temperature (780.9)

     ☐ **991.8   Other specified effects of reduced temperature**

     ☐ **991.9   Unspecified effect of reduced temperature**
         Effects of freezing or excessive cold NOS

● **992   Effects of heat and light**

     Excludes   *burns (940.0–949.5)*
         diseases of sweat glands due to heat (705.0–705.9)
         malignant hyperpyrexia following anesthesia (995.86)
         sunburn (692.71)

     992.0   Heat stroke and sunstroke
         Heat apoplexy
         Heat pyrexia
         Ictus solaris
         Siriasis
         Thermoplegia

     992.1   Heat syncope
         Heat collapse

992.2 Heat cramps

992.3 Heat exhaustion, anhydrotic
Heat prostration due to water depletion

Excludes *that associated with salt depletion (992.4)*

992.4 Heat exhaustion due to salt depletion
Heat prostration due to salt (and water) depletion

☐ **992.5 Heat exhaustion, unspecified**
Heat prostration NOS

992.6 Heat fatigue, transient

992.7 Heat edema

☐ **992.8 Other specified heat effects**

☐ **992.9 Unspecified**

● **993 Effects of air pressure**

993.0 Barotrauma, otitic
Aero-otitis media
Effects of high altitude on ears

993.1 Barotrauma, sinus
Aerosinusitis
Effects of high altitude on sinuses

☐ **993.2 Other and unspecified effects of high altitude**
Alpine sickness
Andes disease
Anoxia due to high altitude
Hypobaropathy
Mountain sickness

993.3 Caisson disease
Bends
Compressed-air disease
Decompression sickness
Divers' palsy or paralysis

993.4 Effects of air pressure caused by explosion

☐ **993.8 Other specified effects of air pressure**

☐ **993.9 Unspecified effect of air pressure**

● **994 Effects of other external causes**

Excludes *certain adverse effects not elsewhere classified (995.0–995.8)*

994.0 Effects of lightning
Shock from lightning
Struck by lightning NOS

Excludes *burns (940.0–949.5)*

994.1 Drowning and nonfatal submersion
Bathing cramp   Immersion

994.2 Effects of hunger
Deprivation of food   Starvation

994.3 Effects of thirst
Deprivation of water

994.4 Exhaustion due to exposure

994.5 Exhaustion due to excessive exertion
Overexertion

994.6 Motion sickness
Air sickness   Travel sickness
Seasickness

994.7 Asphyxiation and strangulation
Suffocation (by):   Suffocation (by):
  bedclothes   plastic bag
  cave-in   pressure
  constriction   strangulation
  mechanical

Excludes *asphyxia from:*
carbon monoxide (986)
inhalation of food or foreign body (932–934.9)
other gases, fumes, and vapors (987.0–987.9)

994.8 Electrocution and nonfatal effects of electric current
Shock from electric current

Excludes *electric burns (940.0–949.5)*

☐ **994.9 Other effects of external causes**
Effects of:
abnormal gravitational [G] forces or states
weightlessness

● **995 Certain adverse effects not elsewhere classified**

Excludes *complications of surgical and medical care (996.0–999.9)*

☐ **995.0 Other anaphylactic shock**
Allergic shock NOS or due to adverse effect of correct medicinal substance properly administered
Anaphylactic reaction NOS or due to adverse effect of correct medicinal substance properly administered
Anaphylaxis NOS or due to adverse effect of correct medicinal substance properly administered

Excludes *anaphylactic reaction to serum (999.4)*
anaphylactic shock due to adverse food reaction (995.60–995.69)

Code first any underlying condition such as:
poisoning by drugs, medicinals and biologic substances (960–979)
toxic effects of substances chiefly nonmedical as to source (980–989)

Use additional E code to identify external cause, such as:
adverse effects of correct medicinal substance properly administered [E930-E949]

995.1 Angioneurotic edema
Giant urticaria

Excludes *urticaria:*
due to serum (999.5)
other specified (698.2, 708.0–708.9, 757.33)

☐ **995.2 Unspecified adverse effect of drug, medicinal and biological substance (due) to correct medicinal substance properly administered**
Adverse effect to correct medicinal substance properly administered
Allergic reaction to correct medicinal substance properly administered
Hypersensitivity to correct medicinal substance properly administered
Idiosyncrasy due to correct medicinal substance properly administered
Drug:
hypersensitivity NOS
reaction NOS

Excludes *pathological drug intoxication (292.2)*

☐ **995.3 Allergy, unspecified**
Allergic reaction NOS
Hypersensitivity NOS
Idiosyncrasy NOS

Excludes *allergic reaction NOS to correct medicinal substance properly administered (995.2)*
specific types of allergic reaction, such as:
allergic diarrhea (558.9)
dermatitis (691.0–693.9)
hayfever (477.0–477.9)

  ◀▶ **New Code** ◀▦▦▶ **Revised Code** ● **Not a Principal Diagnosis** ● **Use Additional Digit(s)** ☐ **Nonspecific Code**

995.4 Shock due to anesthesia

Shock due to anesthesia in which the correct substance was properly administered

Excludes *complications of anesthesia in labor or delivery (668.0–668.9)*

overdose or wrong substance given (968.0–969.9)

postoperative shock NOS (998.0)

specified adverse effects of anesthesia classified elsewhere, such as:
    anoxic brain damage (348.1)
    hepatitis (070.0–070.9), etc.

unspecified adverse effect of anesthesia (995.2)

● **995.5 Child maltreatment syndrome**

Use additional code(s), if applicable, to identify any associated injuries

Use additional E code to identify:
    nature of abuse (E960-E968)
    perpetrator (E967.0-E967.9)

□ **995.50 Child abuse, unspecified**

995.51 Child emotional/psychological abuse

995.52 Child neglect (nutritional)

995.53 Child sexual abuse

995.54 Child physical abuse
Battered baby or child syndrome

Excludes *Shaken infant syndrome (995.55)*

995.55 Shaken infant syndrome

Use additional code(s) to identify any associated injuries

□ **995.59 Other child abuse and neglect**
Multiple forms of abuse

● **995.6 Anaphylactic shock due to adverse food reaction**
Anaphylactic shock due to nonpoisonous foods

□ **995.60 Due to unspecified food**

995.61 Due to peanuts

995.62 Due to crustaceans

995.63 Due to fruits and vegetables

995.64 Due to tree nuts and seeds

995.65 Due to fish

995.66 Due to food additives

995.67 Due to milk products

995.68 Due to eggs

□ **995.69 Due to other specified food**

● **995.8 Other specified adverse effects, not elsewhere classified**

□ **995.80 Adult maltreatment, unspecified**
Abused person NOS

Use additional code to identify:
    any associated injury
    perpetrator (E967.0-E967.9)

995.81 Adult physical abuse
Battered:
    person syndrome, NEC
    man
    spouse
    woman

Use additional code to identify:
    any associated injury
    nature of abuse (E960-E968)
    perpetrator (E967.0-E967.9)

995.82 Adult emotional/psychological abuse

Use additional E code to identify perpetrator (E967.0-E967.9)

995.83 Adult sexual abuse

Use additional code to identify:
    any associated injury
    perpetrator (E967.0-E967.9)

995.84 Adult neglect (nutritional)

Use additional code to identify:
    intent of neglect (E904.0-E968.4)
    perpetrator (E967.0-E967.9)

□ **995.85 Other adult abuse and neglect**
Multiple forms of abuse and neglect

Use additional code to identify any associated injury
    intent of neglect (E904.0, E968.4)
    nature of abuse (E960-E968)
    perpetrator (E967.0-E967.9)

995.86 Malignant hyperthermia ◄
Malignant hyperpyrexia due to ◄
    anesthesia

□ **995.89 Other**
Hypothermia due to anesthesia ◄

COMPLICATIONS OF SURGICAL AND MEDICAL CARE, NOT ELSEWHERE CLASSIFIED (996–999)

Excludes *adverse effects of medicinal agents (001.0–799.9, 995.0–995.8)*

burns from local applications and irradiation (940.0–949.5)

complications of:
    conditions for which the procedure was performed
    surgical procedures during abortion, labor, and delivery (630–676.9)

poisoning and toxic effects of drugs and chemicals (960.0–989.9)

postoperative conditions in which no complications are present, such as:
    artificial opening status (V44.0–V44.9)
    closure of external stoma (V55.0–V55.9)
    fitting of prosthetic device (V52.0–V52.9)

specified complications classified elsewhere
    anesthetic shock (995.4)
    electrolyte imbalance (276.0–276.9)
    postlaminectomy syndrome (722.80–722.83)
    postmastectomy lymphedema syndrome (457.0)
    postoperative psychosis (293.0–293.9)

any other condition classified elsewhere in the Alphabetic Index when described as due to a procedure

996 Complications peculiar to certain specified procedures

Includes: complications, not elsewhere classified, in the use of artificial substitutes [e.g., Dacron, metal, Silastic, Teflon] or natural sources [e.g., bone] involving:
anastomosis (internal)
graft (bypass) (patch)
implant
internal device:
   catheter
   electronic
   fixation
   prosthetic
reimplant
transplant

Excludes *accidental puncture or laceration during procedure (998.2)*
complications of internal anastomosis of:
   gastrointestinal tract (997.4)
   urinary tract (997.5)
other specified complications classified elsewhere, such as:
   hemolytic anemia (283.1)
   functional cardiac disturbances (429.4)
   serum hepatitis (070.2–070.3)

● 996.0 Mechanical complication of cardiac device, implant, and graft
Breakdown (mechanical)
Displacement
Leakage
Obstruction, mechanical
Perforation
Protrusion

□ 996.00 Unspecified device, implant, and graft

996.01 Due to cardiac pacemaker (electrode)

996.02 Due to heart valve prosthesis

996.03 Due to coronary bypass graft

Excludes *atherosclerosis of graft (414.02, 414.03)*
embolism [occlusion NOS] [thrombus] of graft (996.72)

996.04 Due to automatic implantable cardiac defibrillator

□ 996.09 Other

□ 996.1 Mechanical complication of other vascular device, implant, and graft
Mechanical complications involving:
aortic (bifurcation) graft (replacement)
arteriovenous:
   dialysis catheter　◀
   fistula surgically created
   shunt surgically created
balloon (counterpulsation) device, intra-aortic
carotid artery bypass graft
femoral-popliteal bypass graft
umbrella device, vena cava

Excludes *atherosclerosis of biological graft (440.30–440.32)*
embolism [occlusion NOS] [thrombus] of (biological) (synthetic) graft (996.74)
peritoneal dialysis catheter (996.56)　◀

996.2 Mechanical complication of nervous system device, implant, and graft
Mechanical complications involving:
dorsal column stimulator
electrodes implanted in brain [brain "pacemaker"]
peripheral nerve graft
ventricular (communicating) shunt

● 996.3 Mechanical complication of genitourinary device, implant, and graft

□ 996.30 Unspecified device, implant, and graft

996.31 Due to urethral [indwelling] catheter

996.32 Due to intrauterine contraceptive device

□ 996.39 Other
Cystostomy catheter
Prosthetic reconstruction of vas deferens
Repair (graft) of ureter without mention of resection

Excludes *complications due to:*
external stoma of urinary tract (997.5)
internal anastomosis of urinary tract (997.5)

996.4 Mechanical complication of internal orthopedic device, implant, and graft
Mechanical complications involving:
external (fixation) device utilizing internal screw(s), pin(s) or other methods of fixation
grafts of bone, cartilage, muscle, or tendon
internal (fixation) device such as nail, plate, rod, etc.

Excludes *complications of external orthopedic device, such as:*
pressure ulcer due to cast (707.0)

● 996.5 Mechanical complication of other specified prosthetic device, implant, and graft
Mechanical complications involving:
prosthetic implant in:
   bile duct
   breast
   chin
   orbit of eye
nonabsorbable surgical material NOS
other graft, implant, and internal device, not elsewhere classified

996.51 Due to corneal graft

□ 996.52 Due to graft of other tissue, not elsewhere classified
Skin graft failure or rejection

Excludes *failure of artificial skin graft (996.55)*　◀
failure of decellularized allodermis (996.55)　◀
sloughing of temporary skin allografts or xenografts (pigskin)-omit code

996.53 Due to ocular lens prosthesis

Excludes *contact lenses—code to condition*

996.54 Due to breast prosthesis
Breast capsule (prosthesis)
Mammary implant

996.55 Due to artificial skin graft and decellularized allodermis　◀
Dislodgement　◀
Displacement　◀
Failure　◀
Non-adherence　◀
Poor incorporation　◀
Shearing

996.56 Due to peritoneal dialysis catheter　◀

Excludes *mechanical complication of arteriovenous dialysis catheter (996.1)*　◀

□ 996.59 Due to other implant and internal device, not elsewhere classified
Nonabsorbable surgical material NOS
Prosthetic implant in:
   bile duct
   chin
   orbit of eye

◀▶ **New Code**　⇐⇒ **Revised Code**　● **Not a Principal Diagnosis**　● **Use Additional Digit(s)**　□ **Nonspecific Code**

● **996.6 Infection and inflammatory reaction due to internal prosthetic device, implant, and graft**
> Infection (causing obstruction) due to (presence of) any device, implant, and graft classifiable to 996.0–996.5
> Inflammation due to (presence of) any device, implant, and graft classifiable to 996.0–996.5

Use additional code to identify specified infections ◀

☐ **996.60 Due to unspecified device, implant and graft**

996.61 Due to cardiac device, implant and graft
> Cardiac pacemaker or defibrillator:
>   electrode(s), lead(s)
>   pulse generator
>   subcutaneous pocket
> Coronary artery bypass graft
> Heart valve prosthesis

☐ **996.62 Due to vascular device, implant and graft**
> Arterial graft
> Arteriovenous fistula or shunt
> Infusion pump
> Vascular catheter (arterial) (dialysis) (venous)

996.63 Due to nervous system device, implant and graft
> Electrodes implanted in brain
> Peripheral nerve graft
> Spinal canal catheter
> Ventricular (communicating) shunt (catheter)

996.64 Due to indwelling urinary catheter
> Use additional code to identify specified infections, such as: ◀
>   Cystitis (595.0–595.9) ◀
>   Sepsis (038.0–038.9) ◀

☐ **996.65 Due to other genitourinary device, implant and graft**
> Intrauterine contraceptive device

996.66 Due to internal joint prosthesis

☐ **996.67 Due to other internal orthopedic device, implant and graft**
> Bone growth stimulator (electrode)
> Internal fixation device (pin) (rod) (screw)

996.68 Due to peritoneal dialysis catheter ◀
> Exit-site infection or inflammation ◀

☐ **996.69 Due to other internal prosthetic device, implant, and graft**
> Breast prosthesis
> Ocular lens prosthesis
> Prosthetic orbital implant

● **996.7 Other complications of internal (biological) (synthetic) prosthetic device, implant, and graft**
> Complication NOS due to (presence of) any device, implant, and graft classifiable to 996.0–996.5
>   occlusion NOS
> Embolism due to (presence of) any device, implant, and graft classifiable to 996.0–996.5
> Fibrosis due to (presence of) any device, implant, and graft classifiable to 996.0–996.5
> Hemorrhage due to (presence of) any device, implant, and graft classifiable to 996.0–996.5
> Pain due to (presence of) any device, implant, and graft classifiable to 996.0–996.5
> Stenosis due to (presence of) any device, implant, and graft classifiable to 996.0–996.5
> Thrombus due to (presence of) any device, implant, and graft classifiable to 996.0–996.5

Excludes transplant rejection (996.8)

☐ **996.70 Due to unspecified device, implant, and graft**

996.71 Due to heart valve prosthesis

☐ **996.72 Due to other cardiac device, implant, and graft**
> Cardiac pacemaker or defibrillator:
>   electrode(s), lead(s)
>   subcutaneous pocket
> Coronary artery bypass (graft)

Excludes occlusion due to atherosclerosis (414.02–414.03)

996.73 Due to renal dialysis device, implant, and graft

☐ **996.74 Due to vascular device, implant, and graft**

Excludes occlusion of biological graft due to atherosclerosis (440.30–440.32)

996.75 Due to nervous system device, implant, and graft

996.76 Due to genitourinary device, implant, and graft

996.77 Due to internal joint prosthesis

☐ **996.78 Due to other internal orthopedic device, implant, and graft**

☐ **996.79 Due to other internal prosthetic device, implant, and graft**

● **996.8 Complications of transplanted organ**
> Transplant failure or rejection

Use additional code to identify nature of complication, such as:
> Cytomegalovirus [CMV] infection (078.5)

☐ **996.80 Transplanted organ, unspecified**

996.81 Kidney

996.82 Liver

996.83 Heart

996.84 Lung

996.85 Bone marrow
> Graft-versus-host disease (acute) (chronic)

996.86 Pancreas

☐ **996.89 Other specified transplanted organ**
> Intestines

● **996.9 Complications of reattached extremity or body part**

☐ **996.90 Unspecified extremity**

996.91 Forearm

996.92 Hand

996.93 Finger(s)

☐ **996.94 Upper extremity, other and unspecified**

996.95 Foot and toe(s)

☐ **996.96 Lower extremity, other and unspecified**

☐ **996.99 Other specified body part**

● **997 Complications affecting specified body systems, not elsewhere classified**

Use additional code to identify complication

Excludes the listed conditions when specified as:
> causing shock (998.0)
> complications of:
>   anesthesia:
>   adverse effect (001.0–799.9, 995.0–995.8)
>   in labor or delivery (668.0–668.9)
>   poisoning (968.0–969.9)
>   implanted device or graft (996.0–996.9)
>   obstetrical procedures (669.0–669.4)
>   reattached extremity (996.90–996.96)
>   transplanted organ (996.80–996.89)

● **997.0   Nervous system complications**

❏ **997.00   Nervous system complication, unspecified**

997.01   Central nervous system complication
Anoxic brain damage
Cerebral hypoxia

Excludes   *Cerebrovascular hemorrhage or infarction (997.02)*

997.02   Iatrogenic cerebrovascular infarction or hemorrhage
Postoperative stroke

❏ **997.09   Other nervous system complications**

997.1   Cardiac complications
Cardiac:
   arrest during or resulting from a procedure
   insufficiency during or resulting from a procedure
Cardiorespiratory failure during or resulting from a procedure
Heart failure during or resulting from a procedure

Excludes   *the listed conditions as long-term effects of cardiac surgery or due to the presence of cardiac prosthetic device (429.4)*

997.2   Peripheral vascular complications
Phlebitis or thrombophlebitis during or resulting from a procedure

Excludes   *the listed conditions due to:*
   implant or catheter device (996.62)
   infusion, perfusion, or transfusion (999.2)
   complications affecting internal blood vessels, such as:
     mesenteric artery (997.4)
     renal artery (997.5)

997.3   Respiratory complications
Mendelson's syndrome resulting from a procedure
Pneumonia (aspiration) resulting from a procedure

Excludes   *iatrogenic [postoperative] pneumothorax (512.1)*
iatrogenic pulmonary embolism (415.11)
Mendelson's syndrome in labor and delivery (668.0)
specified complications classified elsewhere, such as:
   adult respiratory distress syndrome (518.5)
   pulmonary edema, postoperative (518.4)
   respiratory insufficiency, acute, postoperative (518.5)
   shock lung (518.5)
   tracheostomy complication (519.00–519.09) ◀▥▶

997.4   Digestive system complications
Complications of:
   Intestinal (internal) anastomosis and bypass, not elsewhere classified, except that involving urinary tract
Hepatic failure specified as due to a procedure
Hepatorenal syndrome specified as due to a procedure
Intestinal obstruction NOS specified as due to a procedure

Excludes   *specified gastrointestinal complications classified elsewhere, such as:*
   blind loop syndrome (579.2)
   colostomy or enterostomy complications (569.60–569.69)
   gastrojejunal ulcer (534.0–534.9)
   gastrostomy complications (536.40–536.49) ◀
   infection of external stoma (569.61)
   pelvic peritoneal adhesions, female (614.6)
   peritoneal adhesions (568.0)
   peritoneal adhesions with obstruction (560.81)
   postcholecystectomy syndrome (576.0)
   postgastric surgery syndromes (564.2)

997.5   Urinary complications
Complications of:
   external stoma of urinary tract
   internal anastomosis and bypass of urinary tract, including that involving intestinal tract
Oliguria or anuria specified as due to procedure
Renal:
   failure (acute) specified as due to procedure
   insufficiency (acute) specified as due to procedure
Tubular necrosis (acute) specified as due to procedure

Excludes   *specified complications classified elsewhere, such as:*
   postoperative stricture of:
     ureter (593.3)
     urethra (598.2)

● **997.6   Amputation stump complication**

Excludes   *admission for treatment for a current traumatic amputation—code to complicated traumatic amptutation*
phantom limb (syndrome) (353.6)

❏ **997.60   Unspecified complication**

997.61   Neuroma of amputation stump

997.62   Infection (chronic)
Use additional code to identify the organism

❏ **997.69   Other**

● **997.9   Complications affecting other specified body systems, not elsewhere classified**

Excludes   *specified complications classified elsewhere, such as:*
   broad ligament laceration syndrome (620.6)
   postartificial menopause syndrome (627.4)
   postoperative stricture of vagina (623.2)

997.91   Hypertension

Excludes   *Essential hypertension (401.0–401.9)*

❏ **997.99   Other**
Vitreous touch syndrome

● **998   Other complications of procedures, NEC**

998.0   Postoperative shock
Collapse NOS during or resulting from a surgical procedure
Shock (endotoxic) (hypovolemic) (septic) during or resulting from a surgical procedure

Excludes   *shock:*
   anaphylactic due to serum (999.4)
   anesthetic (995.4)
   electric (994.8)
   following abortion (639.5)
   obstetric (669.1)
   traumatic (958.4)

● **998.1   Hemorrhage or hematoma or seroma complicating a procedure**

Excludes   *hemorrhage, hematoma or seroma:*
   complicating cesarean section or puerperal perineal wound (674.3)

998.11   Hemorrhage complicating a procedure

998.12   Hematoma complicating a procedure

998.13   Seroma complicating a procedure

998.2 Accidental puncture or laceration during a procedure
Accidental perforation by catheter or other instrument during a procedure on:
blood vessel
nerve
organ

Excludes *iatrogenic [postoperative] pneumothorax (512.1)*
puncture or laceration caused by implanted device intentionally left in operation wound (996.0–996.5)
specified complications classified elsewhere, such as:
broad ligament laceration syndrome (620.6)
trauma from instruments during delivery (664.0–665.9)

998.3 Disruption of operation wound
Dehiscence of operation wound
Rupture of operation wound

Excludes *disruption of:*
cesarean wound (674.1)
perineal wound, puerperal (674.2)

998.4 Foreign body accidentally left during a procedure
Adhesions due to foreign body accidentally left in operative wound or body cavity during a procedure
Obstruction due to foreign body accidentally left in operative wound or body cavity during a procedure
Perforation due to foreign body accidentally left in operative wound or body cavity during a procedure

Excludes *obstruction or perforation caused by implanted device intentionally left in body (996.0–996.5)*

● **998.5 Postoperative infection**

Excludes *infection due to:*
implanted device (996.60–996.69)
infusion, perfusion, or transfusion (999.3)
postoperative obstetrical wound infection (674.3)

998.51 Infected postoperative seroma

Use additional code to identify organism

☐ **998.59 Other postoperative infection**
Abscess: postoperative
intra-abdominal postoperative
stitch postoperative
subphrenic postoperative
wound postoperative
Septicemia postoperative

Use additional code to identify infection

998.6 Persistent postoperative fistula

998.7 Acute reaction to foreign substance accidentally left during a procedure
Peritonitis:
aseptic
chemical

● **998.8 Other specified complications of procedures, not elsewhere classified**

998.81 Emphysema (subcutaneous) (surgical) resulting from a procedure

998.82 Cataract fragments in eye following cataract surgery

998.83 Non-healing surgical wound

☐ **998.89 Other specified complications**

☐ **998.9 Unspecified complication of procedure, not elsewhere classified**
Postoperative complication NOS

Excludes *complication NOS of obstetrical surgery or procedure (669.4)*

● **999 Complications of medical care, not elsewhere classified**

Includes: complications, not elsewhere classified, of:
dialysis (hemodialysis) (peritoneal) (renal)
extracorporeal circulation
hyperalimentation therapy
immunization
infusion
inhalation therapy
injection
inoculation
perfusion
transfusion
vaccination
ventilation therapy

Excludes *specified complications classified elsewhere such as:*
complications of implanted device (996.0–996.9)
contact dermatitis due to drugs (692.3)
dementia dialysis (294.8)
transient (293.9)
dialysis disequilibrium syndrome (276.0–276.9)
poisoning and toxic effects of drugs and chemicals (960.0–989.9)
postvaccinal encephalitis (323.5)
water and electrolyte imbalance (276.0–276.9)

999.0 Generalized vaccinia

999.1 Air embolism
Air embolism to any site following infusion, perfusion, or transfusion

Excludes *embolism specified as:*
complicating:
abortion (634–638 with .6, 639.6)
ectopic or molar pregnancy (639.6)
pregnancy, childbirth, or the puerperium (673.0)
due to implanted device (996.7)
traumatic (958.0)

☐ **999.2 Other vascular complications**
Phlebitis following infusion, perfusion, or transfusion
Thromboembolism following infusion, perfusion, or transfusion
Thrombophlebitis following infusion, perfusion, or transfusion

Excludes *the listed conditions when specified as:*
due to implanted device (996.61–996.62, 996.72–996.74)
postoperative NOS (997.2)

☐ **999.3 Other infection**
Infection following infusion, injection, transfusion, or vaccination
Sepsis following infusion, injection, transfusion, or vaccination
Septicemia following infusion, injection, transfusion, or vaccination

Excludes *the listed conditions when specified as:*
due to implanted device (996.60–996.69)
postoperative NOS (998.51–998.59)

999.4   Anaphylactic shock due to serum

Excludes   *shock:*
    allergic NOS (995.0)
    anaphylactic:
      NOS (995.0)
      due to drugs and chemicals (995.0)

❏ **999.5   Other serum reaction**
    Intoxication by serum
    Protein sickness
    Serum rash
    Serum sickness
    Urticaria due to serum

Excludes   *serum hepatitis (070.2–070.3)*

999.6   ABO incompatibility reaction
    Incompatible blood transfusion
    Reaction to blood group incompatibility in infusion or transfusion

999.7   Rh incompatibility reaction
    Reactions due to Rh factor in infusion or transfusion

❏ **999.8   Other transfusion reaction**
    Septic shock due to transfusion
    Transfusion reaction NOS

Excludes   *postoperative shock (998.0)*

❏ **999.9   Other and unspecified complications of medical care, not elsewhere classified**
    Complications, not elsewhere classified, of:
      electroshock therapy
      inhalation therapy
      ultrasound therapy
      ventilation therapy
    Unspecified misadventure of medical care

Excludes   *unspecified complication of:*
    phototherapy (990)
    radiation therapy (990)

    ◀▶ **New Code**   ◀▥ ▥▶ **Revised Code**   ● **Not a Principal Diagnosis**   ● **Use Additional Digit(s)**   ❏ **Nonspecific Code**

V-Codes—SUPPLEMENTARY CLASSIFICATION OF FACTORS INFLUENCING HEALTH STATUS AND CONTACT WITH HEALTH SERVICES (V01–V82)

This classification is provided to deal with occasions when circumstances other than a disease or injury classifiable to categories 001–999 (the main part of ICD) are recorded as "diagnoses" or "problems." This can arise mainly in three ways:

a) When a person who is not currently sick encounters the health services for some specific purpose, such as to act as a donor of an organ or tissue, to receive prophylactic vaccination, or to discuss a problem which is in itself not a disease or injury. This will be a fairly rare occurrence among hospital inpatients, but will be relatively more common among hospital outpatients and patients of family practitioners, health clinics, etc.

b) When a person with a known disease or injury, whether it is current or resolving, encounters the health care system for a specific treatment of that disease or injury (e.g., dialysis for renal disease; chemotherapy for malignancy; cast change).

c) When some circumstance or problem is present which influences the person's health status but is not in itself a current illness or injury. Such factors may be elicited during population surveys, when the person may or may not be currently sick, or be recorded as an additional factor to be borne in mind when the person is receiving care for some current illness or injury classifiable to categories 001–999.

In the latter circumstances the V code should be used only as a supplementary code and should not be the one selected for use in primary, single cause tabulations. Examples of these circumstances are a personal history of certain diseases, or a person with an artificial heart valve in situ.

PERSONS WITH POTENTIAL HEALTH HAZARDS RELATED TO COMMUNICABLE DISEASES (V01–V06)

Excludes *family history of infectious and parasitic diseases (V18.8)*
personal history of infectious and parasitic diseases (V12.0)

● **V01 Contact with or exposure to communicable diseases**

    V01.0 Cholera
        Conditions classifiable to 001

    V01.1 Tuberculosis
        Conditions classifiable to 010–018

    V01.2 Poliomyelitis
        Conditions classifiable to 045

    V01.3 Smallpox
        Conditions classifiable to 050

    V01.4 Rubella
        Conditions classifiable to 056

    V01.5 Rabies
        Conditions classifiable to 071

    V01.6 Venereal diseases
        Conditions classifiable to 090–099

    □ **V01.7 Other viral diseases**
        Conditions classifiable to 042–078, and V08, except as above

    □ **V01.8 Other communicable diseases**
        Conditions classifiable to 001–136, except as above

    □ **V01.9 Unspecified communicable disease**

● **V02 Carrier or suspected carrier of infectious diseases**

    V02.0 Cholera

    V02.1 Typhoid

    V02.2 Amebiasis

    □ **V02.3 Other gastrointestinal pathogens**

    V02.4 Diphtheria

    ● **V02.5 Other specified bacterial diseases**

        V02.51 Group B streptococcus ◄

        □ **V02.52 Other streptococcus** ◄

        □ **V02.59 Other specified bacterial diseases** ◄
            Meningococcal ◄
            Staphylococcal ◄

    ● **V02.6 Viral hepatitis**

        □ **V02.60 Viral hepatitis carrier, unspecified**

        V02.61 Hepatitis B carrier

        V02.62 Hepatitis C carrier

        □ **V02.69 Other viral hepatitis carrier**

    V02.7 Gonorrhea

    □ **V02.8 Other venereal diseases**

    □ **V02.9 Other specified infectious organism**

● **V03 Need for prophylactic vaccination and inoculation against bacterial diseases**

    Excludes *vaccination not carried out because of contraindication (V64.0)*
    vaccines against combinations of diseases (V06.0–V06.9)

    V03.0 Cholera alone

    V03.1 Typhoid-paratyphoid alone [TAB]

    V03.2 Tuberculosis [BCG]

    V03.3 Plague

    V03.4 Tularemia

    V03.5 Diphtheria alone

    V03.6 Pertussis alone

    V03.7 Tetanus toxoid alone

    ● **V03.8 Other specified vaccinations against single bacterial diseases**

        V03.81 Haemophilus influenzae, type B [Hib]

        V03.82 Streptococcus pneumoniae [pneumococcus]

        □ **V03.89 Other specified vaccination**

    □ **V03.9 Unspecified single bacterial disease**

● **V04 Need for prophylactic vaccination and inoculation against certain diseases**

    Excludes *vaccines against combinations of diseases (V06.0–V06.9)*

    V04.0 Poliomyelitis

    V04.1 Smallpox

    V04.2 Measles alone

    V04.3 Rubella alone

    V04.4 Yellow fever

    V04.5 Rabies

    V04.6 Mumps alone

    V04.7 Common cold

    V04.8 Influenza

● **V05 Need for prophylactic vaccination and inoculation against single diseases**

    Excludes *vaccines against combinations of diseases (V06.0–V06.9)*

    V05.0 Arthropod-borne viral encephalitis

    □ **V05.1 Other arthropod-borne viral diseases**

V05.2 Leishmaniasis

V05.3 Viral hepatitis

V05.4 Varicella
    Chicken pox

❑ V05.8 Other specified disease

❑ V05.9 Unspecified single disease

● **V06 Need for prophylactic vaccination and inoculation against combinations of diseases**

    Note: Use additional single vaccination codes from categories V03–V05 to identify any vaccinations not included in a combination code.

V06.0 Cholera with typhoid-paratyphoid [cholera TAB]

V06.1 Diphtheria-tetanus-pertussis, combined [DTP]

V06.2 Diphtheria-tetanus-pertussis with typhoid-paratyphoid [DTP TAB]

V06.3 Diphtheria-tetanus-pertussis with poliomyelitis [DTP+polio]

V06.4 Measles-mumps-rubella [MMR]

V06.5 Tetanus-diphtheria [Td]

V06.6 Streptococcus pneumoniae [pneumococcus] and influenza

❑ V06.8 Other combinations
    Excludes *multiple single vaccination codes (V03.0–V05.9)*

❑ V06.9 Unspecified combined vaccine

PERSONS WITH NEED FOR ISOLATION, OTHER POTENTIAL HEALTH HAZARDS AND PROPHYLACTIC MEASURES (V07–V09)

● **V07 Need for isolation and other prophylactic measures**
    Excludes *prophylactic organ removal (V50.41–V50.49)*

V07.0 Isolation
    Admission to protect the individual from his surroundings or for isolation of individual after contact with infectious diseases

V07.1 Desensitization to allergens

V07.2 Prophylactic immunotherapy
    Administration of:
      antivenin
      immune sera [gamma globulin]
      RhoGAM
      tetanus antitoxin

● V07.3 Other prophylactic chemotherapy

    V07.31 Prophylactic fluoride administration

    ❑ V07.39 Other prophylactic chemotherapy
    Excludes *maintenance chemotherapy following disease (V58.1)*

V07.4 Postmenopausal hormone replacement therapy

❑ V07.8 Other specified prophylactic measure

❑ V07.9 Unspecified prophylactic measure

● **V08 Asymptomatic human immunodeficiency virus [HIV] infection status**
    HIV positive NOS

    Note: This code is ONLY to be used when NO HIV infection symptoms or conditions are present. If any HIV infection symptoms or conditions are present, see code 042.

    Excludes *AIDS (042)*
      human immunodeficiency virus [HIV] disease (042)
      exposure to HIV (V01.7)
      nonspecific serologic evidence of HIV (795.71)
      symptomatic human immunodeficiency virus [HIV] infection (042)

● **V09 Infection with drug-resistant microorganisms**

    Note: This category is intended for use as an additional code for infectious conditions classified elsewhere to indicate the presence of drug-resistance of the infectious organism.

● V09.0 Infection with microorganisms resistant to penicillins

● V09.1 Infection with microorganisms resistant to cephalosporins and other B-lactam antibiotics

● V09.2 Infection with microorganisms resistant to macrolides

● V09.3 Infection with microorganisms resistant to tetracyclines

● V09.4 Infection with microorganisms resistant to aminoglycosides

● V09.5 Infection with microorganisms resistant to quinolones and fluoroquinolones

    ● V09.50 Without mention of resistance to multiple quinolones and fluoroquinols

    ● V09.51 With resistance to multiple quinolones and fluoroquinols

● V09.6 Infection with microorganisms resistant to sulfonamides

● V09.7 Infection with microorganisms resistant to other specified antimycobacterial agents
    Excludes *amikacin (V09.4)*
      kanamycin (V09.4)
      streptomycin [SM] (V09.4)

    ●❑ V09.70 Without mention of resistance to multiple antimycobacterial agents

    ●❑ V09.71 With resistance to multiple antimycobacterial agents

● V09.8 Infection with microorganisms resistant to other specified drugs

    ●❑ V09.80 Without mention of resistance to multiple drugs

    ●❑ V09.81 With resistance to multiple drugs

● V09.9 Infection with drug-resistant microorganisms, unspecified
    Drug resistance NOS

    ●❑ V09.90 Without mention of multiple drug resistance

    ●❑ V09.91 With multiple drug resistance
      Multiple drug resistance NOS

PERSONS WITH POTENTIAL HEALTH HAZARDS RELATED TO PERSONAL AND FAMILY HISTORY (V10–V19)

Excludes *obstetric patients where the possibility that the fetus might be affected is the reason for observation or management during pregnancy (655.0–655.9)*

● **V10 Personal history of malignant neoplasm**

● **V10.0 Gastrointestinal tract**
History of conditions classifiable to 140–159

- ●□ V10.00 Gastrointestinal tract, unspecified
- ● V10.01 Tongue
- ●□ V10.02 Other and unspecified oral cavity and pharynx
- ● V10.03 Esophagus
- ● V10.04 Stomach
- ● V10.05 Large intestine
- ● V10.06 Rectum, rectosigmoid junction, and anus
- ● V10.07 Liver
- ●□ V10.09 Other

● **V10.1 Trachea, bronchus, and lung**
History of conditions classifiable to 162

- ● V10.11 Bronchus and lung
- ● V10.12 Trachea

● **V10.2 Other respiratory and intrathoracic organs**
History of conditions classifiable to 160, 161, 163–165

- ●□ V10.20 Respiratory organ, unspecified
- ● V10.21 Larynx
- ● V10.22 Nasal cavities, middle ear, and accessory sinuses
- ●□ V10.29 Other

● **V10.3 Breast**
History of conditions classifiable to 174 and 175

● **V10.4 Genital organs**
History of conditions classifiable to 179–187

- ●□ V10.40 Female genital organ, unspecified
- ● V10.41 Cervix uteri
- ●□ V10.42 Other parts of uterus
- ● V10.43 Ovary
- ●□ V10.44 Other female genital organs
- ●□ V10.45 Male genital organ, unspecified
- ● V10.46 Prostate
- ● V10.47 Testis
- ● V10.48 Epididymis ◄
- ●□ V10.49 Other male genital organs

● **V10.5 Urinary organs**
History of conditions classifiable to 188 and 189

- ●□ V10.50 Urinary organ, unspecified
- ● V10.51 Bladder
- ● V10.52 Kidney
- ●□ V10.59 Other

● **V10.6 Leukemia**
Conditions classifiable to 204–208

Excludes *leukemia in remission (204–208)*

- ●□ V10.60 Leukemia, unspecified
- ● V10.61 Lymphoid leukemia
- ● V10.62 Myeloid leukemia
- ● V10.63 Monocytic leukemia
- ●□ V10.69 Other

● **V10.7 Other lymphatic and hematopoietic neoplasms**
Conditions classifiable to 200–203

Excludes *listed conditions in 200–203 in remission*

- ● V10.71 Lymphosarcoma and reticulosarcoma
- ● V10.72 Hodgkin's disease
- ●□ V10.79 Other

● **V10.8 Personal history of malignant neoplasm of other sites**
History of conditions classifiable to 170–173, 190–195

- ● V10.81 Bone
- ● V10.82 Malignant melanoma of skin
- ●□ V10.83 Other malignant neoplasm of skin
- ● V10.84 Eye
- ● V10.85 Brain
- ●□ V10.86 Other parts of nervous system

Excludes *peripheral, sympathetic, and parasympathetic nerves (V10.89)*

- ● V10.87 Thyroid
- ●□ V10.88 Other endocrine glands and related structures
- ●□ V10.89 Other

●□ **V10.9 Unspecified personal history of malignant neoplasm**

● **V11 Personal history of mental disorder**

● V11.0 Schizophrenia

Excludes *that in remission (295.0–295.9 with fifth-digit 5)*

● V11.1 Affective disorders
Personal history of manic-depressive psychosis

Excludes *that in remission (296.0–296.6 with fifth-digit 5, 6)*

● V11.2 Neurosis

● V11.3 Alcoholism

●□ V11.8 Other mental disorders

●□ V11.9 Unspecified mental disorder

● **V12 Personal history of certain other diseases**

●● **V12.0 Infectious and parasitic diseases**

- ●□ V12.00 Unspecified infectious and parasitic disease
- ● V12.01 Tuberculosis
- ● V12.02 Poliomyelitis
- ● V12.03 Malaria
- ●□ V12.09 Other

● V12.1 Nutritional deficiency

● V12.2 Endocrine, metabolic, and immunity disorders

Excludes *history of allergy (V14.0–V14.9, V15.0)*

● V12.3 Diseases of blood and blood-forming organs

● **V12.4 Disorders of nervous system and sense organs**

  ● ☐ **V12.40 Unspecified disorder of nervous system and sense organs**

  ● **V12.41 Benign neoplasm of the brain**

  ● ☐ **V12.49 Other disorders of nervous system and sense organs**

● **V12.5 Diseases of circulatory system**

  Excludes: *old myocardial infarction (412)*
  postmyocardial infarction syndrome (411.0)

  ● ☐ **V12.50 Unspecified circulatory disease**

  ● **V12.51 Venous thrombosis and embolism**
    Pulmonary embolism

  ● **V12.52 Thrombophlebitis**

  ● ☐ **V12.59 Other**

● **V12.6 Diseases of respiratory system**

● **V12.7 Diseases of digestive system**

  ● ☐ **V12.70 Unspecified digestive disease**

  ● **V12.71 Peptic ulcer disease**

  ● **V12.72 Colonic polyps**

  ● ☐ **V12.79 Other**

● **V13 Personal history of other diseases**

● **V13.0 Disorders of urinary system**

  ● ☐ **V13.00 Unspecified urinary disorder**

  ● **V13.01 Urinary calculi**

  ● ☐ **V13.09 Other**

● **V13.1 Trophoblastic disease**

  Excludes: *supervision during a current pregnancy (V23.1)*

● ☐ **V13.2 Other genital system and obstetric disorders**

  Excludes: *supervision during a current pregnancy of a woman with poor obstetric history (V23.0–V23.9)*
  habitual aborter (646.3)
  without current pregnancy (629.9)

● **V13.3 Diseases of skin and subcutaneous tissue**

● ☐ **V13.4 Arthritis**

● ☐ **V13.5 Other musculoskeletal disorders**

● **V13.6 Congenital malformations**

  ● **V13.61 Hypospadias** ◄

  ● ☐ **V13.69 Other congenital malformations** ◄

● **V13.7 Perinatal problems**

● ☐ **V13.8 Other specified diseases**

● ☐ **V13.9 Unspecified disease**

● **V14 Personal history of allergy to medicinal agents**

● **V14.0 Penicillin**

● ☐ **V14.1 Other antibiotic agent**

● **V14.2 Sulfonamides**

● ☐ **V14.3 Other anti-infective agent**

● **V14.4 Anesthetic agent**

● **V14.5 Narcotic agent**

● **V14.6 Analgesic agent**

● **V14.7 Serum or vaccine**

● ☐ **V14.8 Other specified medicinal agents**

● ☐ **V14.9 Unspecified medicinal agent**

● **V15 Other personal history presenting hazards to health**

● ☐ **V15.0 Allergy, other than to medicinal agents**

● **V15.1 Surgery to heart and great vessels**

  Excludes: *replacement by transplant or other means (V42.1–V42.2, V43.2–V43.4)*

● ☐ **V15.2 Surgery to other major organs**

  Excludes: *replacement by transplant or other means (V42.0–V43.8)*

● **V15.3 Irradiation**
  Previous exposure to therapeutic or other ionizing radiation

● **V15.4 Psychological trauma**

  Excludes: *history of condition classifiable to 290–316 (V11.0–V11.9)*

  ● **V15.41 History of physical abuse**
    Rape

  ● **V15.42 History of emotional abuse**
    Neglect

  ● ☐ **V15.49 Other**

● **V15.5 Injury**

● **V15.6 Poisoning**

● **V15.7 Contraception**

  Excludes: *current contraceptive management (V25.0–V25.4)*
  presence of intrauterine contraceptive device as incidental finding (V45.5)

● **V15.8 Other specified personal history presenting hazards to health**

  ● **V15.81 Noncompliance with medical treatment**

  ● **V15.82 History of tobacco use**

  Excludes: *tobacco dependence (305.1)*

  ● **V15.84 Exposure to asbestos**

  ● **V15.85 Exposure to potentially hazardous body fluids**

  ● **V15.86 Exposure to lead**

  ● ☐ **V15.89 Other**

● ☐ **V15.9 Unspecified personal history presenting hazards to health**

● **V16 Family history of malignant neoplasm**

● **V16.0 Gastrointestinal tract**
  Family history of condition classifiable to 140–159

● **V16.1 Trachea, bronchus, and lung**
  Family history of condition classifiable to 162

● ☐ **V16.2 Other respiratory and intrathoracic organs**
  Family history of condition classifiable to 160–161, 163–165

● **V16.3 Breast**
  Family history of condition classifiable to 174

● **V16.4 Genital organs**
  Family history of condition classifiable to 179–187

  ● ☐ **V16.40 Genital organ, unspecified**

  ● **V16.41 Ovary**

  ● **V16.42 Prostate**

  ● **V16.43 Testis**

  ● ☐ **V16.49 Other**

◄▶ **New Code**   ⬅▪▪▪▶ **Revised Code**   ● **Not a Principal Diagnosis**   ● **Use Additional Digit(s)**   ☐ **Nonspecific Code**

● **V16.5 Urinary organs**
Family history of condition classifiable to 189

   ● **V16.51 Kidney** ◄

   ●❑ **V16.59 Other** ◄

● **V16.6 Leukemia**
Family history of condition classifiable to
204–208

●❑ **V16.7 Other lymphatic and hematopoietic neoplasms**
Family history of condition classifiable to
200–203

●❑ **V16.8 Other specified malignant neoplasm**
Family history of other condition classifiable
to 140–199

●❑ **V16.9 Unspecified malignant neoplasm**

● **V17 Family history of certain chronic disabling diseases**

   ● **V17.0 Psychiatric condition**
   Excludes *family history of mental retardation (V18.4)*

   ● **V17.1 Stroke (cerebrovascular)**

   ●❑ **V17.2 Other neurological diseases**
     Epilepsy
     Huntington's chorea

   ● **V17.3 Ischemic heart disease**

   ●❑ **V17.4 Other cardiovascular diseases**

   ● **V17.5 Asthma**

   ●❑ **V17.6 Other chronic respiratory conditions**

   ● **V17.7 Arthritis**

   ●❑ **V17.8 Other musculoskeletal diseases**

● **V18 Family history of certain other specific conditions**

   ● **V18.0 Diabetes mellitus**

   ●❑ **V18.1 Other endocrine and metabolic diseases**

   ● **V18.2 Anemia**

   ●❑ **V18.3 Other blood disorders**

   ● **V18.4 Mental retardation**

   ● **V18.5 Digestive disorders**

   ● **V18.6 Kidney diseases**

     ● **V18.61 Polycystic kidney** ◄

     ●❑ **V18.69 Other kidney diseases** ◄

   ●❑ **V18.7 Other genitourinary diseases**

   ● **V18.8 Infectious and parasitic diseases**

● **V19 Family history of other conditions**

   ● **V19.0 Blindness or visual loss**

   ●❑ **V19.1 Other eye disorders**

   ● **V19.2 Deafness or hearing loss**

   ●❑ **V19.3 Other ear disorders**

   ● **V19.4 Skin conditions**

   ● **V19.5 Congenital anomalies**

   ● **V19.6 Allergic disorders**

   ● **V19.7 Consanguinity**

   ●❑ **V19.8 Other condition**

PERSONS ENCOUNTERING HEALTH SERVICES IN CIRCUMSTANCES RELATED TO REPRODUCTION AND DEVELOPMENT (V20–V29)

● **V20 Health supervision of infant or child**

   V20.0 Foundling

   ❑ **V20.1 Other healthy infant or child receiving care**
   Medical or nursing care supervision of
     healthy infant in cases of:
     maternal illness, physical or psychiatric
     socioeconomic adverse condition at home
     too many children at home preventing or
     interfering with normal care

   V20.2 Routine infant or child health check
   Developmental testing of infant or child
   Immunizations appropriate for age
   Routine vision and hearing testing

   Excludes *special screening for developmental handicaps (V79.3)*

   Use additional code(s) to identify:
   Special screening examination(s) performed
   (V73.0–V82.9)

● **V21 Constitutional states in development**

   ● **V21.0 Period of rapid growth in childhood**

   ● **V21.1 Puberty**

   ●❑ **V21.2 Other adolescence**

   ●❑ **V21.8 Other specified constitutional states in development**

   ●❑ **V21.9 Unspecified constitutional state in development**

● **V22 Normal pregnancy**

   Excludes *pregnancy examination or test, pregnancy unconfirmed (V72.4)*

   V22.0 Supervision of normal first pregnancy

   V22.1 Supervision of other normal pregnancy

   V22.2 Pregnant state, incidental
   Pregnant state NOS

● **V23 Supervision of high-risk pregnancy**

   V23.0 Pregnancy with history of infertility

   V23.1 Pregnancy with history of trophoblastic disease
   Pregnancy with history of:
     hydatidiform mole
     vesicular mole

   Excludes *that without current pregnancy (V13.1)*

   V23.2 Pregnancy with history of abortion
   Pregnancy with history of conditions classifiable to 634–638

   Excludes *habitual aborter:*
     care during pregnancy (646.3)
     that without current pregnancy (629.9)

   V23.3 Grand multiparity

   Excludes *care in relation to labor and delivery (659.4)*
     that without current pregnancy (V61.5)

   ❑ **V23.4 Pregnancy with other poor obstetric history**
   Pregnancy with history of other conditions
     classifiable to 630–676

   ❑ **V23.5 Pregnancy with other poor reproductive history**
   Pregnancy with history of stillbirth or neonatal death

   V23.7 Insufficient prenatal care
   History of little or no prenatal care

● **V23.8 Other high-risk pregnancy**

ICD-9-CM
V01–V99
Vol. 1

V23.81 Elderly primigravida ◄
First pregnancy in a woman who will be 35 years of age or older at expected date of delivery ◄

Excludes *elderly primigravida complcating pregnancy (659.5)* ◄

V23.82 Elderly multigravida ◄
Second or more pregnancy in a woman who will be 35 years of age or older at expected date of delivery ◄

Excludes *elderly multigravida complicating pregnancy (659.6)* ◄

V23.83 Young primigravida ◄
First pregnancy in a female less than 16 years old at expected date of delivery ◄

Excludes *young primigravida complicating pregnancy (659.8)* ◄

V23.84 Young multigravida ◄
Second or more pregnancy in a female less than 16 years old at expected date of delivery ◄

Excludes *young multigravida complicating pregnancy (659.8)* ◄

☐ **V23.89 Other high-risk pregnancy** ◄

☐ **V23.9 Unspecified high-risk pregnancy**

● **V24 Postpartum care and examination**

V24.0 Immediately after delivery
Care and observation in uncomplicated cases

V24.1 Lactating mother
Supervision of lactation

V24.2 Routine postpartum follow-up

● **V25 Encounter for contraceptive management**

● **V25.0 General counseling and advice**

V25.01 Prescription of oral contraceptives

☐ **V25.02 Initiation of other contraceptive measures**
Fitting of diaphragm
Prescription of foams, creams, or other agents

☐ **V25.09 Other**
Family planning advice

V25.1 Insertion of intrauterine contraceptive device

V25.2 Sterilization
Admission for interruption of fallopian tubes or vas deferens

V25.3 Menstrual extraction
Menstrual regulation

● **V25.4 Surveillance of previously prescribed contraceptive methods**
Checking, reinsertion, or removal of contraceptive device
Repeat prescription for contraceptive method
Routine examination in connection with contraceptive maintenance

Excludes *presence of intrauterine contraceptive device as incidental finding (V45.5)*

☐ **V25.40 Contraceptive surveillance, unspecified**

V25.41 Contraceptive pill

V25.42 Intrauterine contraceptive device
Checking, reinsertion, or removal of intrauterine device

V25.43 Implantable subdermal contraceptive

☐ **V25.49 Other contraceptive method**

V25.5 Insertion of implantable subdermal contraceptive

☐ **V25.8 Other specified contraceptive management**
Postvasectomy sperm count

☐ **V25.9 Unspecified contraceptive management**

● **V26 Procreative management**

V26.0 Tuboplasty or vasoplasty after previous sterilization

V26.1 Artificial insemination

V26.2 Investigation and testing
Fallopian insufflation
Sperm counts

Excludes *postvasectomy sperm count (V25.8)*

V26.3 Genetic counseling

V26.4 General counseling and advice

● **V26.5 Sterilization status** ◄

V26.51 Tubal ligation status ◄

Excludes *infertility not due to previous tubal ligation (628.0–628.9)* ◄

V26.52 Vasectomy status ◄

☐ **V26.8 Other specified procreative management**

☐ **V26.9 Unspecified procreative management**

● **V27 Outcome of delivery**

Note: This category is intended for the coding of the outcome of delivery on the mother's record.

● **V27.0 Single liveborn**

● **V27.1 Single stillborn**

● **V27.2 Twins, both liveborn**

● **V27.3 Twins, one liveborn and one stillborn**

● **V27.4 Twins, both stillborn**

●☐ **V27.5 Other multiple birth, all liveborn**

●☐ **V27.6 Other multiple birth, some liveborn**

●☐ **V27.7 Other multiple birth, all stillborn**

●☐ **V27.9 Unspecified outcome of delivery**
single birth, outcome to infant unspecified
multiple birth, outcome to infant unspecified

● **V28 Antenatal screening**

Excludes *abnormal findings on screening—code to findings*
routine prenatal care (V22.0–V23.9)

V28.0 Screening for chromosomal anomalies by amniocentesis

V28.1 Screening for raised alpha-fetoprotein levels in amniotic fluid

☐ **V28.2 Other screening based on amniocentesis**

V28.3 Screening for malformation using ultrasonics

V28.4 Screening for fetal growth retardation using ultrasonics

V28.5 Screening for isoimmunization

V28.6 Screening for Streptococcus B

   ◄▶ **New Code**   ⬅▥▥▶ **Revised Code**   ● **Not a Principal Diagnosis**   ● **Use Additional Digit(s)**   ☐ **Nonspecific Code**

☐ **V28.8** Other specified antenatal screening

☐ **V28.9** Unspecified antenatal screening

● **V29** Observation and evaluation of newborns for suspected condition not found

    Note: This category is to be used for newborns, within the neonatal period (the first 28 days of life), who are suspected of having an abnormal condition resulting from exposure from the mother or the birth process, but without signs or symptoms, and which, after examination and observation, is found not to exist.

    V29.0 Observation for suspected infectious condition

    V29.1 Observation for suspected neurological condition

    V29.2 Observation for suspected respiratory condition

    V29.3 Observation for suspected genetic or metabolic condition ◀

☐ **V29.8** Observation for other specified suspected condition

☐ **V29.9** Observation for unspecified suspected condition

LIVEBORN INFANTS ACCORDING TO TYPE OF BIRTH (V30–V39)

    Note: These categories are intended for the coding of liveborn infants who are consuming health care [e.g., crib or bassinet occupancy].

The following fourth-digit subdivisions are for use with categories V30–V39:
    .0 **Born in hospital**
    .1 **Born before admission to hospital**
    .2 **Born outside hospital and not hospitalized**

The following two fifth-digits are for use with the fourth-digit .0, born in hospital:
    0 **delivered without mention of cesarean delivery**
    1 **delivered by cesarean delivery**

● **V30** Single liveborn

● **V31** Twin, mate liveborn

● **V32** Twin, mate stillborn

☐● **V33** Twin, unspecified

☐● **V34** Other multiple, mates all liveborn

☐● **V35** Other multiple, mates all stillborn

☐● **V36** Other multiple, mates live- and stillborn

☐● **V37** Other multiple, unspecified

☐● **V39** Unspecified

PERSONS WITH A CONDITION INFLUENCING THEIR HEALTH STATUS (V40–V49)

    Note: These categories are intended for use when these conditions are recorded as "diagnoses" or "problems."

● **V40** Mental and behavioral problems

    ● **V40.0** Problems with learning

    ● **V40.1** Problems with communication [including speech]

    ●☐ **V40.2** Other mental problems

    ●☐ **V40.3** Other behavioral problems

    ●☐ **V40.9** Unspecified mental or behavioral problem

● **V41** Problems with special senses and other special functions   ICD-9-CM

    ● **V41.0** Problems with sight

    ●☐ **V41.1** Other eye problems

    ● **V41.2** Problems with hearing

    ●☐ **V41.3** Other ear problems

    ● **V41.4** Problems with voice production

    ● **V41.5** Problems with smell and taste

    ● **V41.6** Problems with swallowing and mastication

    ● **V41.7** Problems with sexual function

        Excludes *marital problems (V61.10)*
        psychosexual disorders (302.0–302.9)

    ● **V41.8** Other problems with special functions

    ● **V41.9** Unspecified problem with special functions

● **V42** Organ or tissue replaced by transplant

    Includes: homologous or heterologous (animal) (human) transplant organ status

    ● **V42.0** Kidney

    ● **V42.1** Heart

    ● **V42.2** Heart valve

    ● **V42.3** Skin

    ● **V42.4** Bone

    ● **V42.5** Cornea

    ● **V42.6** Lung

    ● **V42.7** Liver

    ● **V42.8** Other specified organ or tissue

        ● **V42.81** Bone marrow

        ● **V42.82** Peripheral stem cells

        ● **V42.83** Pancreas

        ●☐ **V42.89** Other

    ●☐ **V42.9** Unspecified organ or tissue

● **V43** Organ or tissue replaced by other means

    Includes: replacement of organ by:
        artificial device
        mechanical device
        prosthesis

    Excludes *cardiac pacemaker in situ (V45.01)*
    fitting and adjustment of prosthetic device (V52.0–V52.9)
    renal dialysis status (V45.1)

    ● **V43.0** Eye globe

    ● **V43.1** Lens
        Pseudophakos

    ● **V43.2** Heart

    ● **V43.3** Heart valve

    ● **V43.4** Blood vessel

    ● **V43.5** Bladder

    ● **V43.6** Joint

        ☐ **V43.60** Unspecified joint

        ● **V43.61** Shoulder

        ● **V43.62** Elbow

        ● **V43.63** Wrist

V01-
V99

- V43.64 Hip
- V43.65 Knee
- V43.66 Ankle
- V43.69 Other
- V43.7 Limb
- V43.8 Other organ or tissue
  - V43.81 Larynx
  - V43.82 Breast
  - V43.83 Artificial skin   ◀
  - V43.89 Other

- **V44 Artificial opening status**
  Excludes *artificial openings requiring attention or management (V55.0–V55.9)*
  - V44.0 Tracheostomy
  - V44.1 Gastrostomy
  - V44.2 Ileostomy
  - V44.3 Colostomy
  - V44.4 Other artificial opening of gastrointestinal tract
  - V44.5 Cystostomy
    - V44.50 Cystostomy, unspecified   ◀
    - V44.51 Cutaneous-vesicostomy   ◀
    - V44.52 Appendico-vesicostomy   ◀
    - V44.59 Other cystostomy   ◀
  - V44.6 Other artificial opening of urinary tract
    Nephrostomy
    Ureterostomy
    Urethrostomy
  - V44.7 Artificial vagina
  - V44.8 Other artificial opening status
  - V44.9 Unspecified artificial opening status

- **V45 Other postsurgical states**
  Excludes *aftercare management (V51–V58.9)*
  malfunction or other complication—code to condition
  - V45.0 Cardiac device in situ
    - V45.00 Unspecified cardiac device
    - V45.01 Cardiac pacemaker
    - V45.02 Automatic implantable cardiac defibrillator
    - V45.09 Other specified cardiac device
      Carotid sinus pacemaker in situ
  - V45.1 Renal dialysis status
    Patient requiring intermittent renal dialysis
    Presence of arterial-venous shunt (for dialysis)
    Excludes *admission for dialysis treatment or session (V56.0)*
  - V45.2 Presence of cerebrospinal fluid drainage device
    Cerebral ventricle (communicating) shunt, valve, or device in situ
    Excludes *malfunction (996.2)*
  - V45.3 Intestinal bypass or anastomosis status
  - V45.4 Arthrodesis status

- V45.5 Presence of contraceptive device
  Excludes *checking, reinsertion, or removal of device (V25.42)*
  complication from device (996.32)
  insertion of device (V25.1)
  - V45.51 Intrauterine contraceptive device
  - V45.52 Subdermal contraceptive implant
  - V45.59 Other
- V45.6 States following surgery of eye and adnexa
  Excludes *aphakia (379.31)*
  artificial:
  eye globe (V43.0)
  - V45.61 Cataract extraction status
    Use additional code for associated artificial lens status (V43.1)   ◀
  - V45.69 Other states following surgery of eye and adnexa
- V45.7 Acquired absence of organ
  - V45.71 Acquired absence of breast
  - V45.72 Acquired absence of intestine (large) (small)
  - V45.73 Acquired absence of kidney
- V45.8 Other postsurgical status
  - V45.81 Aortocoronary bypass status
  - V45.82 Percutaneous transluminal coronary angioplasty status
  - V45.83 Breast implant removal status
  - V45.89 Other
    Presence of neuropacemaker or other electronic device
    Excludes *artificial heart valve in situ (V43.3)*
    vascular prosthesis in situ (V43.4)

- **V46 Other dependence on machines**
  - V46.0 Aspirator
  - V46.1 Respirator
    Iron lung
  - V46.8 Other enabling machines
    Hyperbaric chamber
    Possum [Patient-Operated-Selector-Mechanism]
    Excludes *cardiac pacemaker (V45.0)*
    kidney dialysis machine (V45.1)
  - V46.9 Unspecified machine dependence

- **V47 Other problems with internal organs**
  - V47.0 Deficiencies of internal organs
  - V47.1 Mechanical and motor problems with internal organs
  - V47.2 Other cardiorespiratory problems
    Cardiovascular exercise intolerance with pain (with):
    at rest
    less than ordinary activity
    ordinary activity
  - V47.3 Other digestive problems
  - V47.4 Other urinary problems
  - V47.5 Other genital problems
  - V47.9 Unspecified

- **V48 Problems with head, neck, and trunk**

   ◀▶ **New Code**   ⬅▦▦▶ **Revised Code**   ● **Not a Principal Diagnosis**   ● **Use Additional Digit(s)**   ☐ **Nonspecific Code**

● **V48.0 Deficiencies of head**

Excludes *deficiencies of ears, eyelids, and nose (V48.8)*

● **V48.1 Deficiencies of neck and trunk**

● **V48.2 Mechanical and motor problems with head**

● **V48.3 Mechanical and motor problems with neck and trunk**

● **V48.4 Sensory problem with head**

● **V48.5 Sensory problem with neck and trunk**

● **V48.6 Disfigurements of head**

● **V48.7 Disfigurements of neck and trunk**

●□ **V48.8 Other problems with head, neck, and trunk**

●□ **V48.9 Unspecified problem with head, neck, or trunk**

● **V49 Problems with limbs and other problems**

● **V49.0 Deficiencies of limbs**

● **V49.1 Mechanical problems with limbs**

● **V49.2 Motor problems with limbs**

● **V49.3 Sensory problems with limbs**

● **V49.4 Disfigurements of limbs**

□ **V49.5 Other problems of limbs**

● **V49.6 Upper limb amputation status**

   ●□ **V49.60 Unspecified level**

   ● **V49.61 Thumb**

   ●□ **V49.62 Other finger(s)**

   ● **V49.63 Hand**

   ● **V49.64 Wrist**
      Disarticulation of wrist

   ● **V49.65 Below elbow**

   ● **V49.66 Above elbow**
      Disarticulation of elbow

   ● **V49.67 Shoulder**
      Disarticulation of shoulder

● **V49.7 Lower limb amputation status**

   ●□ **V49.70 Unspecified level**

   ● **V49.71 Great toe**

   ●□ **V49.72 Other toe(s)**

   ● **V49.73 Foot**

   ● **V49.74 Ankle**
      Disarticulation of ankle

   ● **V49.75 Below knee**

   ● **V49.76 Above knee**
      Disarticulation of knee

   ● **V49.77 Hip**
      Disarticulation of hip

●□ **V49.8 Other specified problems influencing health status**

●□ **V49.9 Unspecified**

PERSONS ENCOUNTERING HEALTH SERVICES FOR SPECIFIC PROCEDURES AND AFTERCARE (V50–V59)

Note: Categories V51–V58 are intended for use to indicate a reason for care in patients who may have already been treated for some disease or injury not now present, or who are receiving care to consolidate the treatment, to deal with residual states, or to prevent recurrence.

Excludes *follow-up examination for medical surveillance following treatment (V67.0–V67.9)*

● **V50 Elective surgery for purposes other than remedying health states**

V50.0 Hair transplant

□ **V50.1 Other plastic surgery for unacceptable cosmetic appearance**
   Breast augmentation or reduction
   Face-lift

Excludes *plastic surgery following healed injury or operation (V51)*

V50.2 Routine or ritual circumcision
   Circumcision in the absence of significant medical indication

V50.3 Ear piercing

● **V50.4 Prophylactic organ removal**

Excludes *organ donations (V59.0–V59.9)*
   therapeutic organ removal—code to condition

   V50.41 Breast

   V50.42 Ovary

   □ **V50.49 Other**

□ **V50.8 Other**

□ **V50.9 Unspecified**

V51 Aftercare involving the use of plastic surgery
   Plastic surgery following healed injury or operation

Excludes *cosmetic plastic surgery (V50.1)*
   plastic surgery as treatment for current injury— code to condition
   repair of scar tissue—code to scar

● **V52 Fitting and adjustment of prosthetic device and implant**

Includes: removal of device

Excludes *malfunction or complication of prosthetic device (996.0–996.7)*
   status only, without need for care (V43.0– V43.8)

V52.0 Artificial arm (complete) (partial)

V52.1 Artificial leg (complete) (partial)

V52.2 Artificial eye

V52.3 Dental prosthetic device

V52.4 Breast prosthesis and implant

Excludes *admission for breast implant insertion (V50.1)*

□ **V52.8 Other specified prosthetic device**

□ **V52.9 Unspecified prosthetic device**

● **V53 Fitting and adjustment of other device**

Includes: removal of device
   replacement of device

Excludes *status only, without need for care (V45.0– V45.8)*

● **V53.0 Devices related to nervous system and special senses**

V53.01 Fitting and adjustment of cerebral ventricle (communicating) shunt

V53.02 Neuropacemaker (brain) (peripheral nerve) (spinal cord)

V53.09 Fitting and adjustment of other devices related to nervous system and special senses
Auditory substitution device
Visual substitution device

V53.1 Spectacles and contact lenses

V53.2 Hearing aid

● **V53.3 Cardiac device**
Reprogramming

V53.31 Cardiac pacemaker

Excludes *mechanical complication of cardiac pacemaker (996.01)*

V53.32 Automatic implantable cardiac defibrillator

❑ **V53.39 Other cardiac device**

V53.4 Orthodontic devices

V53.5 Other intestinal appliance

Excludes *colostomy (V55.3)*
ileostomy (V55.2)
other artifical opening of digestive tract (V55.4)

V53.6 Urinary devices
Urinary catheter

Excludes *cystostomy (V55.5)*
nephrostomy (V55.6)
ureterostomy (V55.6)
urethrostomy (V55.6)

V53.7 Orthopedic devices
Orthopedic:
brace
cast
corset
shoes

Excludes *other orthopedic aftercare (V54)*

V53.8 Wheelchair

❑ **V53.9 Other and unspecified device**

● **V54 Other orthopedic aftercare**

Excludes *fitting and adjustment of orthopedic devices (V53.7)*
malfunction of internal orthopedic device (996.4)
other complication of nonmechanical nature (996.60–996.79)

❑ **V54.0 Aftercare involving removal of fracture plate or other internal fixation device**
Removal of:
pins
plates
rods
screws

Excludes *removal of external fixation device (V54.8)*

❑ **V54.8 Other orthopedic aftercare**
Change, checking, or removal of:
Kirschner wire
plaster cast
splint, external
other external fixation or traction device

❑ **V54.9 Unspecified orthopedic aftercare**

● **V55 Attention to artificial openings**

Includes: adjustment or repositioning of catheter
closure
passage of sounds or bougies
reforming
removal or replacement of catheter
toilet or cleansing

Excludes *complications of external stoma (519.00–519.09, 569.60–569.69, 997.4, 997.5)*
status only, without need for care (V44.0–V44.9)

V55.0 Tracheostomy

V55.1 Gastrostomy

V55.2 Ileostomy

V55.3 Colostomy

❑ **V55.4 Other artificial opening of digestive tract**

V55.5 Cystostomy

❑ **V55.6 Other artificial opening of urinary tract**
Nephrostomy
Ureterostomy
Urethrostomy

V55.7 Artificial vagina

❑ **V55.8 Other specified artificial opening**

❑ **V55.9 Unspecified artificial opening**

● **V56 Encounter for dialysis and dialysis catheter care**

Use additional code to identify the associated condition

Excludes *dialysis preparation—code to condition*

V56.0 Extracorporeal dialysis
Dialysis (renal) NOS

Excludes *dialysis status (V45.1)*

V56.1 Fitting and adjustment of extracoporeal dialysis catheter
Removal or replacement of catheter
Toilet or cleansing

Use additional code for any concurrent extracorporeal dialysis (V56.0) ◄

V56.2 Fitting and adjustment of peritoneal dialysis catheter

Use additional code for any concurrent peritoneal dialysis (V56.8) ◄

❑ **V56.8 Other dialysis**
Peritoneal dialysis

● **V57 Care involving use of rehabilitation procedures**

Use additional code to identify underlying condition

V57.0 Breathing exercises

❑ **V57.1 Other physical therapy**
Therapeutic and remedial exercises, except breathing

● **V57.2 Occupational therapy and vocational rehabilitation**

V57.21 Encounter for occupational therapy

V57.22 Encounter for vocational therapy

V57.3 Speech therapy

V57.4 Orthoptic training

● **V57.8 Other specified rehabilitation procedure**

V57.81 Orthotic training
Gait training in the use of artificial limbs

 ◄▶ **New Code**   ⬅▦▦▶ **Revised Code**   ● **Not a Principal Diagnosis**   ● **Use Additional Digit(s)**   ❑ **Nonspecific Code**

ICD-9-CM

□ **V57.89 Other**
Multiple training or therapy

□ **V57.9 Unspecified rehabilitation procedure**

● **V58 Encounter for other and unspecified procedures and aftercare**

Excludes *convalescence and palliative care (V66.0–V66.9)*

V58.0 Radiotherapy
Encounter or admission for radiotherapy

Excludes *encounter for radioactive implant—code to condition*
radioactive iodine therapy—code to condition

V58.1 Chemotherapy
Encounter or admission for chemotherapy

Excludes *prophylactic chemotherapy against disease which has never been present (V03.0–V07.9)*

V58.2 Blood transfusion, without reported diagnosis

V58.3 Attention to surgical dressings and sutures
Change of dressings
Removal of sutures

● **V58.4 Other aftercare following surgery**

Excludes *attention to artificial openings (V55.0–V55.9)*
orthopedic aftercare (V54.0–V54.9)

V58.41 Encounter for planned post-operative wound closure

Excludes *disruption of operative wound (998.3)*

□ **V58.49 Other specified aftercare following surgery**

V58.5 Orthodontics

Excludes *fitting and adjustment of orthodontic device (V53.4)*

● **V58.6 Long-term (current) drug use**

Excludes *drug abuse (305.00–305.93)*
drug dependence (304.00–304.93)

V58.61 Long-term (current) use of anticoagulants

V58.62 Long-term (current) use of antibiotics ◄

□ **V58.69 Long-term (current) use of other medications**
High-risk medications

● **V58.8 Other specified procedures and aftercare**

V58.81 Fitting and adjustment of vascular catheter
Removal or replacement of catheter
Toilet or cleansing

Excludes *complications of renal dialysis (996.73)*
complications of vascular catheter (996.74)
dialysis preparation—code to condition
encounter for dialysis (V56.0–V56.8)
fitting and adjustment of dialysis catheter (V56.2) ◄■■

V58.82 Fitting and adjustment of non-vascular catheter, NEC
Removal or replacement of catheter
Toilet or cleansing

Excludes *fitting and adjustment of peritoneal dialysis catheter (V56.2)*
fitting and adjustment of urinary catheter (V53.6)

□ **V58.89 Other specified aftercare**

□ **V58.9 Unspecified aftercare**

● **V59 Donors**

Excludes *examination of potential donor (V70.8)*
self-donation of organ or tissue—code to condition

● **V59.0 Blood**

V59.01 Whole blood

V59.02 Stem cells

□ **V59.09 Other**

V59.1 Skin

V59.2 Bone

V59.3 Bone marrow

V59.4 Kidney

V59.5 Cornea

V59.6 Liver

V59.8 Other specified organ or tissue

V59.9 Unspecified organ or tissue

PERSONS ENCOUNTERING HEALTH SERVICES IN OTHER CIRCUMSTANCES (V60–V68)

● **V60 Housing, household, and economic circumstances**

V60.0 Lack of housing
Hobos
Social migrants
Tramps
Transients
Vagabonds

V60.1 Inadequate housing
Lack of heating
Restriction of space
Technical defects in home preventing adequate care

V60.2 Inadequate material resources
Economic problem
Poverty NOS

V60.3 Person living alone

V60.4 No other household member able to render care
Person requiring care (has) (is):
family member too handicapped, ill, or otherwise unsuited to render care
partner temporarily away from home
temporarily away from usual place of abode

Excludes *holiday relief care (V60.5)*

V60.5 Holiday relief care
Provision of health care facilities to a person normally cared for at home, to enable relatives to take a vacation

V60.6 Person living in residential institution
Boarding school resident

□ **V60.8 Other specified housing or economic circumstances**

□ **V60.9 Unspecified housing or economic circumstance**

● **V61 Other family circumstances**

Includes: when these circumstances or fear of them, affecting the person directly involved or others, are mentioned as the reason, justified or not, for seeking or receiving medical advice or care

V61.0 Family disruption
Divorce
Estrangement

● **V61.1 Counseling for marital and partner problems**

Excludes *problems related to:*
psychosexual disorders (302.0–302.9)
sexual function (V41.7)

V61.10 Counseling for marital and partner problems, unspecified
Marital conflict
Partner conflict

V61.11 Counseling for victim of spousal and partner abuse

Excludes *encounter for treatment of current injuries due to abuse (995.80–995.85)*

V61.12 Counseling for perpetrator of spousal and partner abuse

● **V61.2 Parent-child problems**

☐ **V61.20 Counseling for parent-child problem, unspecified**
Concern about behavior of child
Parent-child conflict

V61.21 Counseling for victim of child abuse
Child battering
Child neglect

Excludes *current injuries due to abuse (995.50–995.59)*

V61.22 Counseling for perpetrator of parental child abuse

Excludes *counseling for non-parental abuser (V62.83)*

☐ **V61.29 Other**
Problem concerning adopted or foster child

V61.3 Problems with aged parents or in-laws

● **V61.4 Health problems within family**

V61.41 Alcoholism in family

☐ **V61.49 Other**
Care of sick or handicapped person in family or household
Presence of sick or handicapped person in family or household

V61.5 Multiparity

V61.6 Illegitimacy or illegitimate pregnancy

☐ **V61.7 Other unwanted pregnancy**

☐ **V61.8 Other specified family circumstances**
Problems with family members, NEC

☐ **V61.9 Unspecified family circumstance**

● **V62 Other psychosocial circumstances**

Includes: those circumstances or fear of them, affecting the person directly involved or others, mentioned as the reason, justified or not, for seeking or receiving medical advice or care

Excludes *previous psychological trauma (V15.41–V15.49)*

V62.0 Unemployment

Excludes *circumstances when main problem is economic inadequacy or poverty (V60.2)*

V62.1 Adverse effects of work environment

☐ **V62.2 Other occupational circumstances or maladjustment**
Career choice problem
Dissatisfaction with employment

V62.3 Educational circumstances
Dissatisfaction with school environment
Educational handicap

V62.4 Social maladjustment
Cultural deprivation
Political, religious, or sex discrimination
Social:
isolation
persecution

V62.5 Legal circumstances
Imprisonment   Litigation
Legal investigation   Prosecution

V62.6 Refusal of treatment for reasons of religion or conscience

● **V62.8 Other psychological or physical stress, not elsewhere classified**

V62.81 Interpersonal problems, not elsewhere classified

V62.82 Bereavement, uncomplicated

Excludes *bereavement as adjustment reaction (309.0)*

V62.83 Counseling for perpetrator of physical/sexual abuse

Excludes *counseling for perpetrator of parental child abuse (V61.22)*
counseling for perpetrator of spousal and partner abuse (V61.12)

☐ **V62.89 Other**
Life circumstance problems
Phase of life problems

☐ **V62.9 Unspecified psychosocial circumstance**

● **V63 Unavailability of other medical facilities for care**

V63.0 Residence remote from hospital or other health care facility

V63.1 Medical services in home not available

Excludes *no other household member able to render care (V60.4)*

V63.2 Person awaiting admission to adequate facility elsewhere

☐ **V63.8 Other specified reasons for unavailability of medical facilities**
Person on waiting list undergoing social agency investigation

☐ **V63.9 Unspecified reason for unavailability of medical facilities**

● **V64 Persons encountering health services for specific procedures, not carried out**

V64.0 Vaccination not carried out because of contraindication

V64.1 Surgical or other procedure not carried out because of contraindication

V64.2 Surgical or other procedure not carried out because of patient's decision

☐ **V64.3 Procedure not carried out for other reasons**

V64.4 Laparoscopic surgical procedure converted to open procedure

● **V65 Other persons seeking consultation without complaint or sickness**

V65.0 Healthy person accompanying sick person
Boarder

V65.1 Person consulting on behalf of another person
Advice or treatment for nonattending third party

Excludes *concern (normal) about sick person in family (V61.41–V61.49)*

    ◀▶ **New Code**   ⬅━ ━➡ **Revised Code**   ● **Not a Principal Diagnosis**   ● **Use Additional Digit(s)**   ☐ **Nonspecific Code**

V65.2 Person feigning illness
Malingerer
Peregrinating patient

V65.3 Dietary surveillance and counseling
Dietary surveillance and counseling (in):
NOS
colitis
diabetes mellitus
food allergies or intolerance
gastritis
hypercholesterolemia
hypoglycemia
obesity

● **V65.4 Other counseling, not elsewhere classified**
Health:
advice
education
instruction

Excludes *counseling (for):*
contraception (V25.40–V25.49)
genetic (V26.3)
on behalf of third party (V65.1)
procreative management (V26.4)

V65.40 Counseling NOS

V65.41 Exercise counseling

V65.42 Counseling on substance use and abuse

V65.43 Counseling on injury prevention

V65.44 Human immunodeficiency virus [HIV] counseling

□ **V65.45 Counseling on other sexually transmitted diseases**

□ **V65.49 Other specified counseling**

V65.5 Person with feared complaint in whom no diagnosis was made
Feared condition not demonstrated
Problem was normal state
"Worried well"

□ **V65.8 Other reasons for seeking consultation**

Excludes *specified symptoms*

□ **V65.9 Unspecified reason for consultation**

● **V66 Convalescence and palliative care**

V66.0 Following surgery

V66.1 Following radiotherapy

V66.2 Following chemotherapy

V66.3 Following psychotherapy and other treatment for mental disorder

V66.4 Following treatment of fracture

□ **V66.5 Following other treatment**

□ **V66.6 Following combined treatment**

● **V66.7 Encounter for palliative care**
End-of-life care   Terminal care
Hospice care

Code first underlying disease

□ **V66.9 Unspecified convalescence**

● **V67 Follow-up examination**

Includes: surveillance only following completed treatment

Excludes *surveillance of contraception (V25.40–V25.49)*

V67.0 Following surgery

V67.1 Following radiotherapy

V67.2 Following chemotherapy
Cancer chemotherapy follow-up

V67.3 Following psychotherapy and other treatment for mental disorder

V67.4 Following treatment of healed fracture

Excludes *current (healing) fracture aftercare (V54.0–V54.9)*

● **V67.5 Following other treatment**

V67.51 Following completed treatment with high-risk medication, not elsewhere classified

Excludes *Long-term (current) drug use (V58.61–V58.69)*

□ **V67.59 Other**

□ **V67.6 Following combined treatment**

□ **V67.9 Unspecified follow-up examination**

● **V68 Encounters for administrative purposes**

V68.0 Issue of medical certificates
Issue of medical certificate of:
cause of death
fitness
incapacity

Excludes *encounter for general medical examination (V70.0–V70.9)*

V68.1 Issue of repeat prescriptions
Issue of repeat prescription for:
appliance
glasses
medications

Excludes *repeat prescription for contraceptives (V25.41–V25.49)*

V68.2 Request for expert evidence

● **V68.8 Other specified administrative purpose**

V68.81 Referral of patient without examination or treatment

□ **V68.89 Other**

□ **V68.9 Unspecified administrative purpose**

● **V69 Problems related to lifestyle**

V69.0 Lack of physical exercise

V69.1 Inappropriate diet and eating habits

Excludes *anorexia nervosa (307.1)*
bulimia (783.6)
malnutrition and other nutritional deficiencies (260–269.9)
other and unspecified eating disorders (307.50–307.59)

V69.2 High-risk sexual behavior

V69.3 Gambling and betting

Excludes *pathological gambling (312.31)*

□ **V69.8 Other problems related to lifestyle**
Self-damaging behavior

□ **V69.9 Problem related to lifestyle, unspecified**

PERSONS WITHOUT REPORTED DIAGNOSIS ENCOUNTERED DURING EXAMINATION AND INVESTIGATION OF INDIVIDUALS AND POPULATIONS (V70–V82)

Note: Nonspecific abnormal findings disclosed at the time of these examinations are classifiable to categories 790–796.

● **V70 General medical examination**

Use additional code(s) to identify any special screening examination(s) performed (V73.0–V82.9)

ICD-9-CM

V01–
V99

Vol. 1

V70.0 Routine general medical examination at a health care facility
     Health checkup

> **Excludes** *health checkup of infant or child (V20.2)*

V70.1 General psychiatric examination, requested by the authority

☐ **V70.2 General psychiatric examination, other and unspecified**

☐ **V70.3 Other medical examination for administrative purposes**
     General medical examination for:
         admission to old age home
         adoption
         camp
         driving license
         immigration and naturalization
         insurance certification
         marriage
         prison
         school admission
         sports competition

> **Excludes** *attendance for issue of medical certificates (V68.0)*
> *pre-employment screening (V70.5)*

V70.4 Examination for medicolegal reasons
     Blood-alcohol tests
     Blood-drug tests
     Paternity testing

> **Excludes** *examination and observation following:*
> *accidents (V71.3, V71.4)*
> *assault (V71.6)*
> *rape (V71.5)*

V70.5 Health examination of defined subpopulations
     Armed forces personnel
     Inhabitants of institutions
     Occupational health examinations
     Pre-employment screening
     Preschool children
     Prisoners
     Prostitutes
     Refugees
     School children
     Students

V70.6 Health examination in population surveys

> **Excludes** *special screening (V73.0–V82.9)*

V70.7 Examination for normal comparison or control in clinical research

☐ **V70.8 Other specified general medical examinations**
     Examination of potential donor of organ or tissue

☐ **V70.9 Unspecified general medical examination**

● **V71 Observation and evaluation for suspected conditions not found**

     Note: This category is to be used when persons without a diagnosis are suspected of having an abnormal condition, without signs or symptoms, which requires study, but after examination and observation, is found not to exist. This category is also for use for administrative and legal observation status.

● **V71.0 Observation for suspected mental condition**

     V71.01 Adult antisocial behavior
         Dyssocial behavior or gang activity in adult without manifest psychiatric disorder

     V71.02 Childhood or adolescent antisocial behavior
         Dyssocial behavior or gang activity in child or adolescent without manifest psychiatric disorder

     ☐ **V71.09 Other suspected mental condition**

V71.1 Observation for suspected malignant neoplasm

V71.2 Observation for suspected tuberculosis

V71.3 Observation following accident at work

☐ **V71.4 Observation following other accident**
     Examination of individual involved in motor vehicle traffic accident

V71.5 Observation following alleged rape or seduction
     Examination of victim or culprit

☐ **V71.6 Observation following other inflicted injury**
     Examination of victim or culprit

V71.7 Observation for suspected cardiovascular disease

☐ **V71.8 Observation for other specified suspected conditions**

☐ **V71.9 Observation for unspecified suspected condition**

● **V72 Special investigations and examinations**

     Includes: routine examination of specific system

> **Excludes** *general medical examination (V70.0–70.4)*
> *general screening examination of defined popula-iton groups (V70.5, V70.6, V70.7)*
> *routine examination of infant or child (V20.2)*

     Use additional code(s) to identify any special screening examination(s) performed (V73.0–V82.9)

V72.0 Examination of eyes and vision

V72.1 Examination of ears and hearing

V72.2 Dental examination

V72.3 Gynecological examination
     Papanicolaou smear as part of general gynecological examination
     Pelvic examination (annual) (periodic)

> **Excludes** *cervical Papanicolaou smear without general gynecological examination (V76.2)*
> *routine examination in contraceptive management (V25.40–V25.49)*

V72.4 Pregnancy examination or test, pregnancy unconfirmed
     Possible pregnancy, not (yet) confirmed

> **Excludes** *pregnancy examination with immediate confirmation (V22.0–V22.1)*

V72.5 Radiological examination, not elsewhere classified
     Routine chest x-ray

> **Excludes** *examination for suspected tuberculosis (V71.2)*

V72.6 Laboratory examination

> **Excludes** *that for suspected disorder (V71.0–V71.9)*

V72.7 Diagnostic skin and sensitization tests
     Allergy tests
     Skin tests for hypersensitivity

> **Excludes** *diagnostic skin tests for bacterial diseases (V74.0–V74.9)*

● **V72.8 Other specified examinations**

     V72.81 Preoperative cardiovascular examination

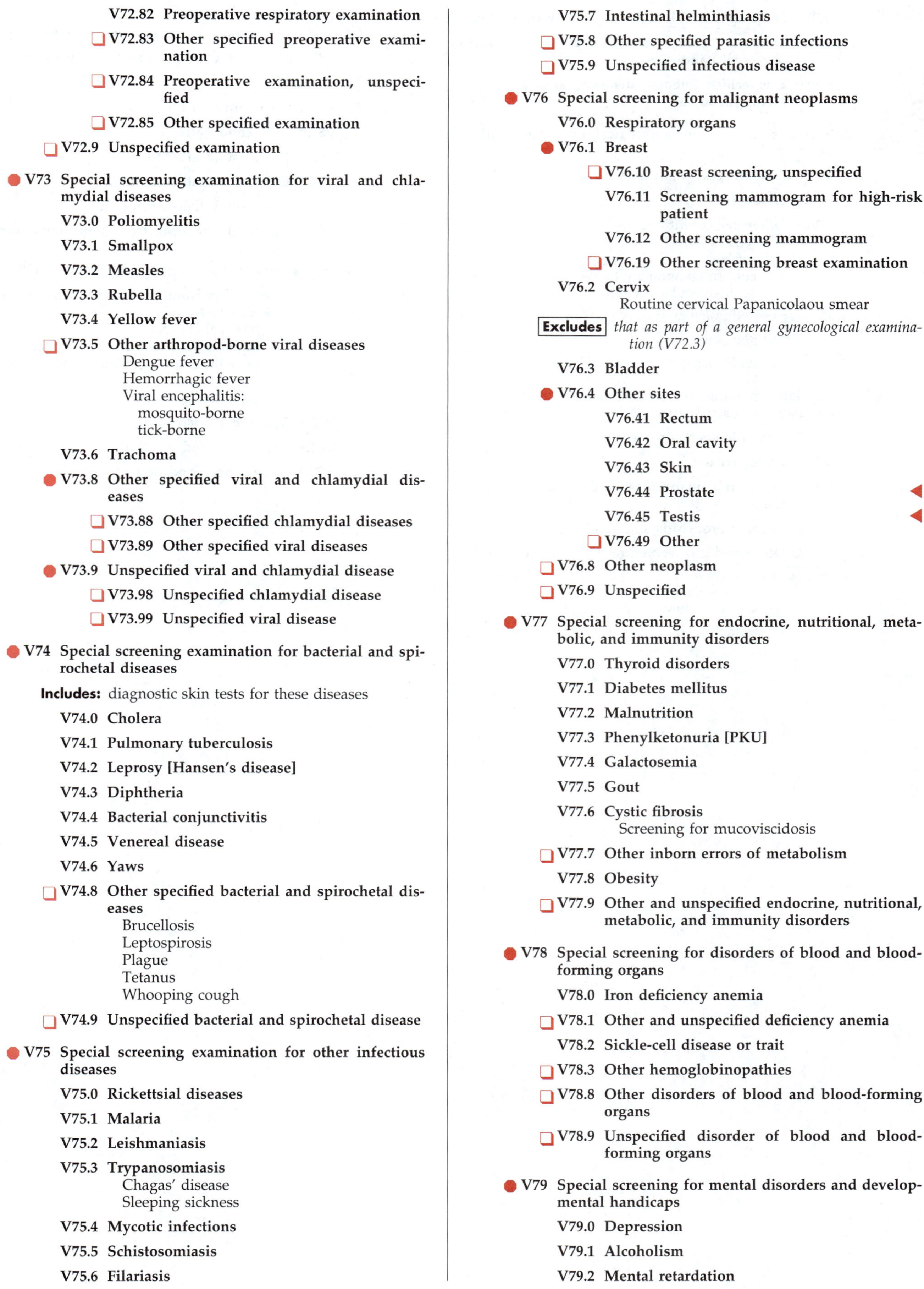

        V72.82 Preoperative respiratory examination

❑ V72.83 Other specified preoperative examination

❑ V72.84 Preoperative examination, unspecified

❑ V72.85 Other specified examination

❑ V72.9 Unspecified examination

● V73 Special screening examination for viral and chlamydial diseases

  V73.0 Poliomyelitis

  V73.1 Smallpox

  V73.2 Measles

  V73.3 Rubella

  V73.4 Yellow fever

❑ V73.5 Other arthropod-borne viral diseases
    Dengue fever
    Hemorrhagic fever
    Viral encephalitis:
      mosquito-borne
      tick-borne

  V73.6 Trachoma

● V73.8 Other specified viral and chlamydial diseases

❑ V73.88 Other specified chlamydial diseases

❑ V73.89 Other specified viral diseases

● V73.9 Unspecified viral and chlamydial disease

❑ V73.98 Unspecified chlamydial disease

❑ V73.99 Unspecified viral disease

● V74 Special screening examination for bacterial and spirochetal diseases

Includes: diagnostic skin tests for these diseases

  V74.0 Cholera

  V74.1 Pulmonary tuberculosis

  V74.2 Leprosy [Hansen's disease]

  V74.3 Diphtheria

  V74.4 Bacterial conjunctivitis

  V74.5 Venereal disease

  V74.6 Yaws

❑ V74.8 Other specified bacterial and spirochetal diseases
    Brucellosis
    Leptospirosis
    Plague
    Tetanus
    Whooping cough

❑ V74.9 Unspecified bacterial and spirochetal disease

● V75 Special screening examination for other infectious diseases

  V75.0 Rickettsial diseases

  V75.1 Malaria

  V75.2 Leishmaniasis

  V75.3 Trypanosomiasis
    Chagas' disease
    Sleeping sickness

  V75.4 Mycotic infections

  V75.5 Schistosomiasis

  V75.6 Filariasis

  V75.7 Intestinal helminthiasis

❑ V75.8 Other specified parasitic infections

❑ V75.9 Unspecified infectious disease

● V76 Special screening for malignant neoplasms

  V76.0 Respiratory organs

● V76.1 Breast

❑ V76.10 Breast screening, unspecified

  V76.11 Screening mammogram for high-risk patient

  V76.12 Other screening mammogram

❑ V76.19 Other screening breast examination

  V76.2 Cervix
    Routine cervical Papanicolaou smear

    Excludes *that as part of a general gynecological examination (V72.3)*

  V76.3 Bladder

● V76.4 Other sites

  V76.41 Rectum

  V76.42 Oral cavity

  V76.43 Skin

  V76.44 Prostate ◀

  V76.45 Testis ◀

❑ V76.49 Other

❑ V76.8 Other neoplasm

❑ V76.9 Unspecified

● V77 Special screening for endocrine, nutritional, metabolic, and immunity disorders

  V77.0 Thyroid disorders

  V77.1 Diabetes mellitus

  V77.2 Malnutrition

  V77.3 Phenylketonuria [PKU]

  V77.4 Galactosemia

  V77.5 Gout

  V77.6 Cystic fibrosis
    Screening for mucoviscidosis

❑ V77.7 Other inborn errors of metabolism

  V77.8 Obesity

❑ V77.9 Other and unspecified endocrine, nutritional, metabolic, and immunity disorders

● V78 Special screening for disorders of blood and blood-forming organs

  V78.0 Iron deficiency anemia

❑ V78.1 Other and unspecified deficiency anemia

  V78.2 Sickle-cell disease or trait

❑ V78.3 Other hemoglobinopathies

❑ V78.8 Other disorders of blood and blood-forming organs

❑ V78.9 Unspecified disorder of blood and blood-forming organs

● V79 Special screening for mental disorders and developmental handicaps

  V79.0 Depression

  V79.1 Alcoholism

  V79.2 Mental retardation

V79.3 Developmental handicaps in early childhood

❑ V79.8 Other specified mental disorders and developmental handicaps

❑ V79.9 Unspecified mental disorder and developmental handicap

● V80 Special screening for neurological, eye, and ear diseases

V80.0 Neurological conditions

V80.1 Glaucoma

❑ V80.2 Other eye conditions
Screening for:
cataract
congenital anomaly of eye
senile macular lesions

Excludes *general vision examination (V72.0)*

V80.3 Ear diseases

Excludes *general hearing examination (V72.1)*

● V81 Special screening for cardiovascular, respiratory, and genitourinary diseases

V81.0 Ischemic heart disease

V81.1 Hypertension

❑ V81.2 Other and unspecified cardiovascular conditions

V81.3 Chronic bronchitis and emphysema

❑ V81.4 Other and unspecified respiratory conditions

Excludes *screening for:*
lung neoplasm (V76.0)
pulmonary tuberculosis (V74.1)

V81.5 Nephropathy
Screening for asymptomatic bacteriuria

❑ V81.6 Other and unspecified genitourinary conditions

● V82 Special screening for other conditions

V82.0 Skin conditions

V82.1 Rheumatoid arthritis

❑ V82.2 Other rheumatic disorders

V82.3 Congenital dislocation of hip

V82.4 Maternal screening for chromosomal anomalies ◄▦

Excludes *antenatal screening by amniocentesis (V28.0)*

V82.5 Chemical poisoning and other contamination
Screening for:
heavy metal poisoning
ingestion of radioactive substance
poisoning from contaminated water supply
radiation exposure

V82.6 Multiphasic screening

❑ V82.8 Other specified conditions

❑ V82.9 Unspecified condition

E-Codes—SUPPLEMENTARY CLASSIFICATION OF EXTERNAL CAUSES OF INJURY AND POISONING (E800-E999)

This section is provided to permit the classification of environmental events, circumstances, and conditions as the cause of injury, poisoning, and other adverse effects. Where a code from this section is applicable, it is intended that it shall be used in addition to a code from one of the main chapters of ICD-9-CM, indicating the nature of the condition. Certain other conditions which may be stated to be due to external causes are classified in Chapters 1 to 16 of ICD-9-CM. For these, the "E" code classification should be used as an additional code for more detailed analysis.

Machinery accidents [other than those connected with transport] are classifiable to category E919, in which the fourth digit allows a broad classification of the type of machinery involved. If a more detailed classification of type of machinery is required, it is suggested that the "Classification of Industrial Accidents according to Agency," prepared by the International Labor Office, be used in addition; it is included in this publication.

Categories for "late effects" of accidents and other external causes are to be found at E929, E959, E969, E977, E989, and E999.

Definitions and examples related to transport accidents:

(a) A transport accident (E800-E848) is any accident involving a device designed primarily for, or being used at the time primarily for, conveying persons or goods from one place to another.

    Includes: accidents involving:
        aircraft and spacecraft (E840-E845)
        watercraft (E830-E838)
        motor vehicle (E810-E825)
        railway (E800-E807)
        other road vehicles (E826-E829)

In classifying accidents which involve more than one kind of transport, the above order of precedence of transport accidents should be used.

Accidents involving agricultural and construction machines, such as tractors, cranes, and bulldozers, are regarded as transport accidents only when these vehicles are under their own power on a highway [otherwise the vehicles are regarded as machinery]. Vehicles which can travel on land or water, such as hovercraft and other amphibious vehicles, are regarded as watercraft when on the water, as motor vehicles when on the highway, and as off-road motor vehicles when on land, but off the highway.

    Excludes *accidents:*
        in sports which involve the use of transport but where the transport vehicle itself was not involved in the accident
        involving vehicles which are part of industrial equipment used entirely on industrial premises
        occurring during transportation but unrelated to the hazards associated with the means of transportation [e.g., injuries received in a fight on board ship; transport vehicle involved in a cataclysm such as an earthquake]
        to persons engaged in the maintenance or repair of transport equipment or vehicle not in motion, unless injured by another vehicle in motion

(b) A railway accident is a transport accident involving a railway train or other railway vehicle operated on rails, whether in motion or not.

    Excludes *accidents:*
        in repair shops
        in roundhouse or on turntable
        on railway premises but not involving a train or other railway vehicle

(c) A railway train or railway vehicle is any device with or without cars coupled to it, designed for traffic on a railway.

    Includes: interurban:
        electric car (operated chiefly on its own right-of-way, not open to other traffic)
        streetcar (operated chiefly on its own right-of-way, not open to other traffic)
        railway train, any power [diesel] [electric] [steam]
        funicular
        monorail or two-rail
        subterranean or elevated
        other vehicle designed to run on a railway track

    Excludes *interurban electric cars [streetcars] specified to be operating on a right-of-way that forms part of the public street or highway [definition (n)]*

(d) A railway or railroad is a right-of-way designed for traffic on rails, which is used by carriages or wagons transporting passengers or freight, and by other rolling stock, and which is not open to other public vehicular traffic

(e) A motor vehicle accident is a transport accident involving a motor vehicle. It is defined as a motor vehicle traffic accident or as a motor vehicle nontraffic accident according to whether the accident occurs on a public highway or elsewhere.

    Excludes *injury or damage due to cataclysm*
        injury or damage while a motor vehicle, not under its own power, is being loaded on, or unloaded from, another conveyance

(f) A motor vehicle traffic accident is any motor vehicle accident occurring on a public highway [i.e., originating, terminating, or involving a vehicle partially on the highway]. A motor vehicle accident is assumed to have occurred on the highway unless another place is specified, except in the case of accidents involving only off-road motor vehicles which are classified as nontraffic accidents unless the contrary is stated.

(g) A motor vehicle nontraffic accident is any motor vehicle accident which occurs entirely in any place other than a public highway.

(h) A public highway [trafficway] or street is the entire width between property lines [or other boundary lines] of every way or place, of which any part is open to the use of the public for purposes of vehicular traffic as a matter of right or custom. A roadway is that part of the public highway designed, improved, and ordinarily used, for vehicular travel.

    Includes: approaches (public) to:
        docks
        public building
        station
    Excludes *driveway (private)*
        parking lot
        ramp
        roads in:
            airfield
            farm
            industrial premises
            mine
            private grounds
            quarry

ICD-9-CM

E800-E899

Vol. 1

(i) A motor vehicle is any mechanically or electrically powered device, not operated on rails, upon which any person or property may be transported or drawn upon a highway. Any object such as a trailer, coaster, sled, or wagon being towed by a motor vehicle is considered a part of the motor vehicle.

> **Includes:** automobile [any type]
> bus
> construction machinery, farm and industrial machinery, steam roller, tractor, army tank, highway grader, or similar vehicle on wheels or treads, while in transport under own power
> fire engine (motorized)
> motorcycle
> motorized bicycle [moped] or scooter
> trolley bus not operating on rails
> truck
> van
>
> **Excludes** *devices used solely to move persons or materials within the confines of a building and its premises, such as:*
> *building elevator*
> *coal car in mine*
> *electric baggage or mail truck used solely within a railroad station*
> *electric truck used solely within an industrial plant*
> *moving overhead crane*

(j) A motorcycle is a two-wheeled motor vehicle having one or two riding saddles and sometimes having a third wheel for the support of a sidecar. The sidecar is considered part of the motorcycle.

> **Includes:** motorized:
> bicycle [moped]
> scooter
> tricycle

(k) An off-road motor vehicle is a motor vehicle of special design, to enable it to negotiate rough or soft terrain or snow. Examples of special design are high construction, special wheels and tires, driven by treads, or support on a cushion of air.

> **Includes:** all terrain vehicle [ATV]
> army tank
> hovercraft, on land or swamp
> snowmobile

(l) A driver of a motor vehicle is the occupant of the motor vehicle operating it or intending to operate it. A motorcyclist is the driver of a motorcycle. Other authorized occupants of a motor vehicle are passengers.

(m) An other road vehicle is any device, except a motor vehicle, in, on, or by which any person or property may be transported on a highway.

> **Includes:** animal carrying a person or goods
> animal-drawn vehicle
> animal harnessed to conveyance
> bicycle [pedal cycle]
> streetcar
> tricycle (pedal)
>
> **Excludes** *pedestrian conveyance [definition (q)]*

(n) A streetcar is a device designed and used primarily for transporting persons within a municipality, running on rails, usually subject to normal traffic control signals, and operated principally on a right-of-way that forms part of the traffic way. A trailer being towed by a streetcar is considered a part of the streetcar.

> **Includes:** interurban or intraurban electric or streetcar, when specified to be operating on a street or public highway
> tram (car)
> trolley (car)

(o) A pedal cycle is any road transport vehicle operated solely by pedals.

> **Includes:** bicycle
> pedal cycle
> tricycle
>
> **Excludes** *motorized bicycle [definition (i)]*

(p) A pedal cyclist is any person riding on a pedal cycle or in a sidecar attached to such a vehicle.

(q) A pedestrian conveyance is any human powered device by which a pedestrian may move other than by walking or by which a walking person may move another pedestrian.

> **Includes:** baby carriage
> coaster wagon
> ice skates
> perambulator
> pushcart
> pushchair
> roller skates
> scooter
> skateboard
> skis
> sled
> wheelchair

(r) A pedestrian is any person involved in an accident who was not at the time of the accident riding in or on a motor vehicle, railroad train, streetcar, animal-drawn or other vehicle, or on a bicycle or animal.

> **Includes:** person:
> changing tire of vehicle
> in or operating a pedestrian conveyance
> making adjustment to motor of vehicle
> on foot

(s) A watercraft is any device for transporting passengers or goods on the water.

(t) A small boat is any watercraft propelled by paddle, oars, or small motor, with a passenger capacity of less than ten.

> **Includes:** boat NOS
> canoe
> coble
> dinghy
> punt
> raft
> rowboat
> rowing shell
> scull
> skiff
> small motorboat
>
> **Excludes** *barge*
> *lifeboat (used after abandoning ship)*
> *raft (anchored) being used as a diving platform*
> *yacht*

(u) An aircraft is any device for transporting passengers or goods in the air.

> **Includes:** airplane [any type]
> balloon
> bomber
> dirigible
> glider (hang)
> military aircraft
> parachute

(v) A commercial transport aircraft is any device for collective passenger or freight transportation by air, whether run on commercial lines for profit or by government authorities, with the exception of military craft.

RAILWAY ACCIDENTS (E800-E807)

Note: For definitions of railway accident and related terms see definitions (a) to (d).

Excludes *accidents involving railway train and:*
aircraft (E840.0-E845.9)
motor vehicle (E810.0-E825.9)
watercraft (E830.0-E838.9)

The following fourth-digit subdivisions are for use with categories E800-E807 to identify the injured person:

.0 Railway employee
Any person who by virtue of his employment in connection with a railway, whether by the railway company or not, is at increased risk of involvement in a railway accident, such as:
catering staff of train
driver
guard
porter
postal staff on train
railway fireman
shunter
sleeping car attendant

.1 Passenger on railway
Any authorized person traveling on a train, except a railway employee.

Excludes *intending passenger waiting at station (8)*
unauthorized rider on railway vehicle (8)

.2 Pedestrian
See definition (r)

.3 Pedal cyclist
See definition (p)

☐ **.8 Other specified person**
Intending passenger or bystander waiting at station
Unauthorized rider on railway vehicle

☐ **.9 Unspecified person**

●● **E800 Railway accident involving collision with rolling stock**

Requires fourth digit. See beginning of section E800-E845 for codes and definitions.

Includes: collision between railway trains or railway vehicles, any kind
collision NOS on railway
derailment with antecedent collision with rolling stock or NOS

●☐● **E801 Railway accident involving collision with other object**

Requires fourth digit. See beginning of section E800-E845 for codes and definitions.

Includes: collision of railway train with:
buffers
fallen tree on railway
gates
platform
rock on railway
streetcar
other nonmotor vehicle
other object

Excludes *collision with:*
aircraft (E840.0-E842.9)
motor vehicle (E810.0-E810.9, E820.0-E822.9)

●● **E802 Railway accident involving derailment without antecedent collision**

Requires fourth digit. See beginning of section E800-E845 for codes and definitions.

●● **E803 Railway accident involving explosion, fire, or burning**

Requires fourth digit. See beginning of section E800-E845 for codes and definitions.

Excludes *explosion or fire, with antecedent derailment (E802.0-E802.9)*
explosion or fire, with mention of antecedent collision (E800.0-E801.9)

●● **E804 Fall in, on, or from railway train**

Requires fourth digit. See beginning of section E800-E845 for codes and definitions.

Includes: fall while alighting from or boarding railway train

Excludes *fall related to collision, derailment, or explosion of railway train (E800.0-E803.9)*

●● **E805 Hit by rolling stock**

Requires fourth digit. See beginning of section E800-E845 for codes and definitions.

Includes: crushed by railway train or part
injured by railway train or part
killed by railway train or part
knocked down by railway train or part
run over by railway train or part

Excludes *pedestrian hit by object set in motion by railway train (E806.0-E806.9)*

●☐● **E806 Other specified railway accident**

Requires fourth digit. See beginning of section E800-E845 for codes and definitions.

Includes: hit by object falling in railway train
injured by door or window on railway train
nonmotor road vehicle or pedestrian hit by object set in motion by railway train
railway train hit by falling:
earth NOS
rock
tree
other object

Excludes *railway accident due to cataclysm (E908-E909)*

●☐● **E807 Railway accident of unspecified nature**

Requires fourth digit. See beginning of section E800-E845 for codes and definitions.

Includes: found dead on railway right-of-way NOS
injured on railway right-of-way NOS
railway accident NOS

MOTOR VEHICLE TRAFFIC ACCIDENTS (E810-E819)

Note: For definitions of motor vehicle traffic accident, and related terms, see definitions (e) to (k).

Excludes *accidents involving motor vehicle and aircraft (E840.0-E845.9)*

The following fourth-digit subdivisions are for use with categories E810-E819 to identify the injured person:

.0 Driver of motor vehicle other than motorcycle
See definition (l)

.1 Passenger in motor vehicle other than motorcycle
See definition (l)

.2 Motorcyclist
See definition (l)

.3 Passenger on motorcycle
See definition (l)

.4 Occupant of streetcar

.5 Rider of animal; occupant of animal-drawn vehicle

.6 Pedal cyclist
See definition (p)

.7 Pedestrian
See definition (r)

☐ **.8 Other specified person**
Occupant of vehicle other than above
Person in railway train involved in accident
Unauthorized rider of motor vehicle

☐ **.9 Unspecified person**

●● **E810 Motor vehicle traffic accident involving collision with train**

Requires fourth digit. See beginning of section E800-E845 for codes and definitions.

Excludes *motor vehicle collision with object set in motion by railway train (E815.0-E815.9)*
railway train hit by object set in motion by motor vehicle (E818.0-E818.9)

●● **E811 Motor vehicle traffic accident involving re-entrant collision with another motor vehicle**

Requires fourth digit. See beginning of section E800-E845 for codes and definitions.

Includes: collision between motor vehicle which accidentally leaves the roadway then re-enters the same roadway, or the opposite roadway on a divided highway, and another motor vehicle

Excludes *collision on the same roadway when none of the motor vehicles involved have left and re-entered the roadway (E812.0-E812.9)*

●☐● **E812 Other motor vehicle traffic accident involving collision with motor vehicle**

Requires fourth digit. See beginning of section E800-E845 for codes and definitions.

Includes: collision with another motor vehicle parked, stopped, stalled, disabled, or abandoned on the highway
motor vehicle collision NOS

Excludes *collision with object set in motion by another motor vehicle (E815.0-E815.9)*
re-entrant collision with another motor vehicle (E811.0-E811.9)

●☐☐ **E813 Motor vehicle traffic accident involving collision with other vehicle**

Requires fourth digit. See beginning of section E800-E845 for codes and definitions.

Includes: collision between motor vehicle, any kind, and:
other road (nonmotor transport) vehicle, such as:
animal carrying a person
animal-drawn vehicle
pedal cycle
streetcar

Excludes *collision with:*
object set in motion by nonmotor road vehicle (E815.0-E815.9)
pedestrian (E814.0-E814.9)
nonmotor road vehicle hit by object set in motion by motor vehicle (E818.0-E818.9)

●● **E814 Motor vehicle traffic accident involving collision with pedestrian**

Requires fourth digit. See beginning of section E800-E845 for codes and definitions.

Includes: collision between motor vehicle, any kind, and pedestrian
pedestrian dragged, hit, or run over by motor vehicle, any kind

Excludes *pedestrian hit by object set in motion by motor vehicle (E818.0-E818.9)*

●☐● **E815 Other motor vehicle traffic accident involving collision on the highway**

Requires fourth digit. See beginning of section E800-E845 for codes and definitions.

Includes: collision (due to loss of control) (on highway) between motor vehicle, any kind, and:
abutment (bridge) (overpass)
animal (herded) (unattended)
fallen stone, traffic sign, tree, utility pole
guard rail or boundary fence
interhighway divider
landslide (not moving)
object set in motion by railway train or road vehicle (motor) (nonmotor)
object thrown in front of motor vehicle
safety island
temporary traffic sign or marker
wall of cut made for road
other object, fixed, movable, or moving

Excludes *collision with:*
any object off the highway (resulting from loss of control) (E816.0-E816.9)
any object which normally would have been off the highway and is not stated to have been on it (E816.0-E816.9)
motor vehicle parked, stopped, stalled, disabled, or abandoned on highway (E812.0-E812.9)
moving landslide (E909.2)
motor vehicle hit by object:
set in motion by railway train or road vehicle (motor) (nonmotor) (E818.0-E818.9)
thrown into or on vehicle (E818.0-E818.9)

   ◀▶ **New Code**   ◀▦▶ **Revised Code**   ● **Not a Principal Diagnosis**   ● **Use Additional Digit(s)**   ☐ **Nonspecific Code**

●● **E816 Motor vehicle traffic accident due to loss of control, without collision on the highway**

Requires fourth digit. See beginning of section E800-E845 for codes and definitions.

Includes: motor vehicle:
　failing to make curve and:
　　colliding with object off the highway
　　overturning
　　stopping abruptly off the highway
　going out of control (due to)
　　blowout and:
　　　colliding with object off the highway
　　　overturning
　　　stopping abruptly off the highway
　　burst tire and:
　　　colliding with object off the highway
　　　overturning
　　　stopping abruptly off the highway
　　driver falling asleep and:
　　　colliding with object off the highway
　　　overturning
　　　stopping abruptly off the highway
　　driver inattention and:
　　　colliding with object off the highway
　　　overturning
　　　stopping abruptly off the highway
　　excessive speed and:
　　　colliding with object off the highway
　　　overturning
　　　stopping abruptly off the highway
　　failure of mechanical part and:
　　　colliding with object off the highway
　　　overturning
　　　stopping abruptly off the highway

Excludes *collision on highway following loss of control (E810.0-E815.9)*
loss of control of motor vehicle following collision on the highway (E810.0-E815.9)

●● **E817 Noncollision motor vehicle traffic accident while boarding or alighting**

Requires fourth digit. See beginning of section E800-E845 for codes and definitions.

Includes: fall down stairs of motor bus while boarding or alighting
　fall from car in street while boarding or alighting
　injured by moving part of the vehicle while boarding or alighting
　trapped by door of motor bus while boarding or alighting

●□● **E818 Other noncollision motor vehicle traffic accident**

Requires fourth digit. See beginning of section E800-E845 for codes and definitions.

Includes: accidental poisoning from exhaust gas generated by motor vehicle while in motion
　breakage of any part of motor vehicle while in motion
　explosion of any part of motor vehicle while in motion
　fall, jump, or being accidentally pushed from motor vehicle while in motion
　fire starting in motor vehicle while in motion
　hit by object thrown into or on motor vehicle while in motion
　injured by being thrown against some part of, or object in, motor vehicle while in motion
　injury from moving part of motor vehicle while in motion
　object falling in or on motor vehicle while in motion
　object thrown on motor vehicle while in motion
　collision of railway train or road vehicle except motor vehicle, with object set in motion by motor vehicle
　motor vehicle hit by object set in motion by railway train or road vehicle (motor) (nonmotor)
　pedestrian, railway train, or road vehicle (motor) (nonmotor) hit by object set in motion by motor vehicle

Excludes *collision between motor vehicle and:*
object set in motion by railway train or road vehicle (motor) (nonmotor) (E815.0-E815.9)
object thrown towards the motor vehicle (E815.0-E815.9)
person overcome by carbon monoxide generated by stationary motor vehicle off the roadway with motor running (E868.2)

●□● **E819 Motor vehicle traffic accident of unspecified nature**

Requires fourth digit. See beginning of section E800-E845 for codes and definitions.

Includes: motor vehicle traffic accident NOS
　traffic accident NOS

MOTOR VEHICLE NONTRAFFIC ACCIDENTS (E820-E825)

Note: For definitions of motor vehicle nontraffic accident and related terms see definitions (a) to (k).

Includes: accidents involving motor vehicles being used in recreational or sporting activities off the highway
collision and noncollision motor vehicle accidents occurring entirely off the highway

Excludes *accidents involving motor vehicle and:*
aircraft (E840.0-E845.9)
watercraft (E830.0-E838.9)
accidents, not on the public highway, involving agricultural and construction machinery but not involving another motor vehicle (E919.0, E919.2, E919.7)

The following fourth-digit subdivisions are for use with categories E820-E825 to identify the injured person:

.0 **Driver of motor vehicle other than motorcycle**
See definition (l)
.1 **Passenger in motor vehicle other than motorcycle**
See definition (l)
.2 **Motorcyclist**
See definition (l)
.3 **Passenger on motorcycle**
See definition (l)
.4 **Occupant of streetcar**
.5 **Rider of animal; occupant of animal-drawn vehicle**
.6 **Pedal cyclist**
See definition (p)
.7 **Pedestrian**
See definition (r)
☐ .8 **Other specified person**
Occupant of vehicle other than above
Person on railway train involved in accident
Unauthorized rider of motor vehicle
☐ .9 **Unspecified person**

●● **E820 Nontraffic accident involving motor-driven snow vehicle**

Requires fourth digit. See beginning of section E800-E845 for codes and definitions.

Includes: breakage of part of motor-driven snow vehicle (not on public highway)
fall from motor-driven snow vehicle (not on public highway)
hit by motor-driven snow vehicle (not on public highway)
overturning of motor-driven snow vehicle (not on public highway)
run over or dragged by motor-driven snow vehicle (not on public highway)
collision of motor-driven snow vehicle with:
animal (being ridden) (-drawn vehicle)
another off-road motor vehicle
other motor vehicle, not on public highway
railway train
other object, fixed or movable
injury caused by rough landing of motor-driven snow vehicle (after leaving ground on rough terrain)

Excludes *accident on the public highway involving motor driven snow vehicle (E810.0-E819.9)*

●☐● **E821 Nontraffic accident involving other off-road motor vehicle**

Requires fourth digit. See beginning of section E800-E845 for codes and definitions.

Includes: breakage of part of off-road motor vehicle, except snow vehicle (not on public highway)
fall from off-road motor vehicle, except snow vehicle (not on public highway)
hit by off-road motor vehicle, except snow vehicle (not on public highway)
overturning of off-road motor vehicle, except snow vehicle (not on public highway)
run over or dragged by off-road motor vehicle, except snow vehicle (not on public highway)
thrown against some part of or object in off-road motor vehicle, except snow vehicle (not on public highway)
collision with:
animal (being ridden) (-drawn vehicle)
another off-road motor vehicle, except snow vehicle
other motor vehicle, not on public highway
other object, fixed or movable

Excludes *accident on public highway involving off-road motor vehicle (E810.0-E819.9)*
collision between motor driven snow vehicle and other off-road motor vehicle (E820.0-E820.9)
hovercraft accident on water (E830.0-E838.9)

●☐● **E822 Other motor vehicle nontraffic accident involving collision with moving object**

Requires fourth digit. See beginning of section E800-E845 for codes and definitions.

Includes: collision, not on public highway, between motor vehicle, except off-road motor vehicle and:
animal
nonmotor vehicle
other motor vehicle, except off-road motor vehicle
pedestrian
railway train
other moving object

Excludes *collision with:*
motor-driven snow vehicle (E820.0-E820.9)
other off-road motor vehicle (E821.0-E821.9)

●☐● **E823 Other motor vehicle nontraffic accident involving collision with stationary object**

Requires fourth digit. See beginning of section E800-E845 for codes and definitions.

Includes: collision, not on public highway, between motor vehicle, except off-road motor vehicle, and any object, fixed or movable, but not in motion

●☐● **E824 Other motor vehicle nontraffic accident while boarding and alighting**

Requires fourth digit. See beginning of section E800-E845 for codes and definitions.

Includes: fall while boarding or alighting from motor vehicle except off-road motor vehicle, not on public highway
injury from moving part of motor vehicle while boarding or alighting from motor vehicle except off-road motor vehicle, not on public highway
trapped by door of motor vehicle while boarding or alighting from motor vehicle except off-road motor vehicle, not on public highway

◄▶ **New Code**   ◀▦ ▦▶ **Revised Code**   ● **Not a Principal Diagnosis**   ● **Use Additional Digit(s)**   ☐ **Nonspecific Code**

●□● **E825 Other motor vehicle nontraffic accident of other and unspecified nature**

Requires fourth digit. See beginning of section E800-E845 for codes and definitions.

Includes: accidental poisoning from carbon monoxide generated by motor vehicle while in motion, not on public highway

breakage of any part of motor vehicle while in motion, not on public highway

explosion of any part of motor vehicle while in motion, not on public highway

fall, jump, or being accidentally pushed from motor vehicle while in motion, not on public highway

fire starting in motor vehicle while in motion, not on public highway

hit by object thrown into, towards, or on motor vehicle while in motion, not on public highway

injured by being thrown against some part of, or object in, motor vehicle while in motion, not on public highway

injury from moving part of motor vehicle while in motion, not on public highway

object falling in or on motor vehicle while in motion, not on public highway

motor vehicle nontraffic accident NOS

Excludes *fall from or in stationary motor vehicle (E884.9, E885)*

overcome by carbon monoxide or exhaust gas generated by stationary motor vehicle off the roadway with motor running (E868.2)

struck by falling object from or in stationary motor vehicle (E916)

OTHER ROAD VEHICLE ACCIDENTS (E826-E829)

Note: Other road vehicle accidents are transport accidents involving road vehicles other than motor vehicles. For definitions of other road vehicle and related terms see definitions (m) to (o).

Includes: accidents involving other road vehicles being used in recreational or sporting activities

Excludes *collision of other road vehicle [any] with:*
aircraft (E840.0-E845.9)
motor vehicle (E813.0-E813.9, E820.0-E822.9)
railway train (E801.0-E801.9)

The following fourth-digit subdivisions are for use with categories E826-E829 to identify the injured person:

.0 **Pedestrian**
See definition (r)
.1 **Pedal cyclist**
See definition (p)
.2 **Rider of animal**
.3 **Occupant of animal-drawn vehicle**
.4 **Occupant of streetcar**
□ .8 **Other specified person**
□ .9 **Unspecified person**

●● **E826 Pedal cycle accident**
[0–9]

Requires fourth digit. See beginning of section E800-E845 for codes and definitions.

Includes: breakage of any part of pedal cycle
collision between pedal cycle and:
animal (being ridden) (herded) (unattended)
another pedal cycle
nonmotor road vehicle, any
pedestrian
other object, fixed, movable, or moving, not set in motion by motor vehicle, railway train, or aircraft
entanglement in wheel of pedal cycle
fall from pedal cycle
hit by object falling or thrown on the pedal cycle
pedal cycle accident NOS
pedal cycle overturned

●● **E827 Animal-drawn vehicle accident**
[0,2–4,8,9]

Requires fourth digit. See beginning of section E800-E845 for codes and definitions.

Includes: breakage of any part of vehicle
collision between animal-drawn vehicle and:
animal (being ridden) (herded) (unattended)
nonmotor road vehicle, except pedal cycle
pedestrian, pedestrian conveyance, or pedestrian vehicle
other object, fixed, movable, or moving, not set in motion by motor vehicle, railway train, or aircraft
fall from animal-drawn vehicle
knocked down by animal-drawn vehicle
overturning of animal-drawn vehicle
run over by animal-drawn vehicle
thrown from animal-drawn vehicle

Excludes *collision of animal-drawn vehicle with pedal cycle (E826.0-E826.9)*

●● **E828 Accident involving animal being ridden**
[0,2,4,8,9]

Requires fourth digit. See beginning of section E800-E845 for codes and definitions.

Includes: collision between animal being ridden and:
    another animal
    nonmotor road vehicle, except pedal cycle, and animal-drawn vehicle
    pedestrian, pedestrian conveyance, or pedestrian vehicle
    other object, fixed, movable, or moving, not set in motion by motor vehicle, railway train, or aircraft
    fall from animal being ridden
    knocked down by animal being ridden
    thrown from animal being ridden
    trampled by animal being ridden
    ridden animal stumbled and fell

Excludes *collision of animal being ridden with:*
    animal-drawn vehicle (E827.0-E827.9)
    pedal cycle (E826.0-E826.9)

●□● **E829 Other road vehicle accidents**
[0,4,8,9]

Requires fourth digit. See beginning of section E800-E845 for codes and definitions.

Includes: accident while boarding or alighting from
    streetcar
    nonmotor road vehicle not classifiable to E826-E828
    blow from object in
    streetcar
    nonmotor road vehicle not classifiable to E826-E828
    breakage of any part of
    streetcar
    nonmotor road vehicle not classifiable to E826-E828
    caught in door of
    streetcar
    nonmotor road vehicle not classifiable to E826-E828
    derailment of
    streetcar
    nonmotor road vehicle not classifiable to E826-E828
    fall in, on, or from
    streetcar
    nonmotor road vehicle not classifiable to E826-E828
    fire in
    streetcar
    nonmotor road vehicle not classifiable to E826-E828
    collision between streetcar or nonmotor road vehicle, except as in E826-E828, and:
    animal (not being ridden)
    another nonmotor road vehicle not classifiable to E826-E828
    pedestrian
    other object, fixed, movable, or moving, not set in motion by motor vehicle, railway train, or aircraft
    nonmotor road vehicle accident NOS
    streetcar accident NOS

Excludes *collision with:*
    animal being ridden (E828.0-E828.9)
    animal-drawn vehicle (E827.0-E827.9)
    pedal cycle (E826.0-E826.9)

WATER TRANSPORT ACCIDENTS (E830-E838)

Note: For definitions of water transport accident and related terms see definitions (a), (s), and (t).

Includes: watercraft accidents in the course of recreational activities

Excludes *accidents involving both aircraft, including objects set in motion by aircraft, and watercraft (E840.0-E845.9)*

The following fourth-digit subdivisions are for use with categories E830-E838 to identify the injured person:

.0 Occupant of small boat, unpowered
.1 Occupant of small boat, powered
    See definition (t)

Excludes *water skier (4)*

□ **.2 Occupant of other watercraft-crew**
    Persons:
    engaged in operation of watercraft
    providing passenger services [cabin attendants, ship's physician, catering personnel]
    working on ship during voyage in other capacity [musician in band, operators of shops and beauty parlors]

□ **.3 Occupant of other watercraft -- other than crew**
    Passenger
    Occupant of lifeboat, other than crew, after abandoning ship

.4 Water skier
.5 Swimmer
.6 Dockers, stevedores
    Longshoreman employed on the dock in loading and unloading ships

□ **.8 Other specified person**
    Immigration and customs officials on board ship
    Person:
    accompanying passenger or member of crew visiting boat
    Pilot (guiding ship into port)

□ **.9 Unspecified person**

●● **E830 Accident to watercraft causing submersion**

Requires fourth digit. See beginning of section E800-E845 for codes and definitions.

Includes: submersion and drowning due to:
    boat overturning
    boat submerging
    falling or jumping from burning ship
    falling or jumping from crushed watercraft
    ship sinking
    other accident to watercraft

●□● **E831 Accident to watercraft causing other injury**

Requires fourth digit. See beginning of section E800-E845 for codes and definitions.

Includes: any injury, except submersion and drowning, as a result of an accident to watercraft
    burned while ship on fire
    crushed between ships in collision
    crushed by lifeboat after abandoning ship
    fall due to collision or other accident to watercraft
    hit by falling object due to accident to watercraft
    injured in watercraft accident involving collision
    struck by boat or part thereof after fall or jump from damaged boat

Excludes *burns from localized fire or explosion on board ship (E837.0-E837.9)*

◀▶ **New Code**   ⬅▪ ▪➡ **Revised Code**   ● **Not a Principal Diagnosis**   ● **Use Additional Digit(s)**   □ **Nonspecific Code**

● ☐ ● **E832 Other accidental submersion or drowning in water transport accident**

Requires fourth digit. See beginning of section E800-E845 for codes and definitions.

Includes: submersion or drowning as a result of an accident other than accident to the watercraft, such as:
> fall:
>> from gangplank
>> from ship
>> overboard
> thrown overboard by motion of ship
> washed overboard

> **Excludes** *submersion or drowning of swimmer or diver who voluntarily jumps from boat not involved in an accident (E910.0-E910.9)*

● ● **E833 Fall on stairs or ladders in water transport**

Requires fourth digit. See beginning of section E800-E845 for codes and definitions.

> **Excludes** *fall due to accident to watercraft (E831.0-E831.9)*

● ☐ ● **E834 Other fall from one level to another in water transport**

Requires fourth digit. See beginning of section E800-E845 for codes and definitions.

> **Excludes** *fall due to accident to watercraft (E831.0-E831.9)*

● ☐ ● **E835 Other and unspecified fall in water transport**

Requires fourth digit. See beginning of section E800-E845 for codes and definitions.

> **Excludes** *fall due to accident to watercraft (E831.0-E831.9)*

● ● **E836 Machinery accident in water transport**

Requires fourth digit. See beginning of section E800-E845 for codes and definitions.

Includes: injuries in water transport caused by:
> deck machinery
> engine room machinery
> galley machinery
> laundry machinery
> loading machinery

● ● **E837 Explosion, fire, or burning in watercraft**

Requires fourth digit. See beginning of section E800-E845 for codes and definitions.

Includes: explosion of boiler on steamship
> localized fire on ship

> **Excludes** *burning ship (due to collision or explosion) resulting in:*
>> *submersion or drowning (E830.0-E830.9)*
>> *other injury (E831.0-E831.9)*

● ☐ ● **E838 Other and unspecified water transport accident**

Requires fourth digit. See beginning of section E800-E845 for codes and definitions.

Includes: accidental poisoning by gases or fumes on ship
> atomic power plant malfunction in watercraft
> crushed between ship and stationary object [wharf]
> crushed between ships without accident to watercraft
> crushed by falling object on ship or while loading or unloading
> hit by boat while water skiing
> struck by boat or part thereof (after fall from boat)
> watercraft accident NOS

AIR AND SPACE TRANSPORT ACCIDENTS (E840-E845)

Note: For definition of aircraft and related terms see definitions (u) and (v).

The following fourth-digit subdivisions are for use with categories E840-E845 to identify the injured person:

.0 Occupant of spacecraft

.1 Occupant of military aircraft, any
> Crew in military aircraft [air force] [army] [national guard] [navy]
> Passenger (civilian) (military) in military aircraft [air force] [army] [national guard] [navy]
> Troops in military aircraft [air force] [army] [national guard] [navy]

> **Excludes** *occupants of aircraft operated under jurisdiction of police departments (5)*
> *parachutist (7)*

.2 Crew of commercial aircraft (powered) in surface-to-surface transport

☐ **.3 Other occupant of commercial aircraft (powered) in surface-to-surface transport**
> Flight personnel:
>> not part of crew
>> on familiarization flight
> Passenger on aircraft (powered) NOS

.4 Occupant of commercial aircraft (powered) in surface-to-air transport
> Occupant [crew] [passenger] of aircraft (powered) engaged in activities, such as:
>> aerial spraying (crops) (fire retardants)
>> air drops of emergency supplies
>> air drops of parachutists, except from military craft
>> crop dusting
>> lowering of construction material [bridge or telephone pole]
>> sky writing

☐ **.5 Occupant of other powered aircraft**
> Occupant [crew] [passenger] of aircraft [powered] engaged in activities, such as:
>> aerobatic flying
>> aircraft racing
>> rescue operation
>> storm surveillance
>> traffic surveillance
> Occupant of private plane NOS

.6 Occupant of unpowered aircraft, except parachutist
> Occupant of aircraft classifiable to E842

.7 Parachutist (military) (other)
> Person making voluntary descent

> **Excludes** *person making descent after accident to aircraft (.1-.6)*

.8 Ground crew, airline employee
> Persons employed at airfields (civil) (military) or launching pads, not occupants of aircraft

☐ **.9 Other person**

● ● **E840 Accident to powered aircraft at takeoff or landing**

Requires fourth digit. See beginning of section E800-E845 for codes and definitions.

Includes: collision of aircraft with any object, fixed, movable, or moving while taking off or landing
> crash while taking off or landing
> explosion on aircraft while taking off or landing
> fire on aircraft while taking off or landing
> forced landing

◀▶ **New Code**   ◀▦▶ **Revised Code**   ● **Not a Principal Diagnosis**   ● **Use Additional Digit(s)**   ☐ **Nonspecific Code**

● □ ● **E841 Accident to powered aircraft, other and unspecified**

    Requires fourth digit. See beginning of section E800-E845 for codes and definitions.

    Includes: aircraft accident NOS
        aircraft crash or wreck NOS
        any accident to powered aircraft while in transit or when not specified whether in transit, taking off, or landing
        collision of aircraft with another aircraft, bird, or any object, while in transit
        explosion on aircraft while in transit
        fire on aircraft while in transit

● ● **E842 Accident to unpowered aircraft**
   [6–9]

    Requires fourth digit. See beginning of section E800-E845 for codes and definitions.

    Includes: any accident, except collision with powered aircraft, to:
        balloon
        glider
        hang glider
        kite carrying a person
        hit by object falling from unpowered aircraft

● ● **E843 Fall in, on, or from aircraft**
   [0–9]

    Requires fourth digit. See beginning of section E800-E845 for codes and definitions.

    Includes: accident in boarding or alighting from aircraft, any kind
        fall in, on, or from aircraft [any kind], while in transit, taking off, or landing, except when as a result of an accident to aircraft

● □ ● **E844 Other specified air transport accidents**
   [0–9]

    Requires fourth digit. See beginning of section E800-E845 for codes and definitions.

    Includes: hit by aircraft without accident to aircraft
        hit by object falling from aircraft without accident to aircraft
        injury by or from machinery on aircraft without accident to aircraft
        injury by or from rotating propeller without accident to aircraft
        injury by or from voluntary parachute descent without accident to aircraft
        poisoning by carbon monoxide from aircraft while in transit without accident to aircraft
        sucked into jet without accident to aircraft
        any accident involving other transport vehicle (motor) (nonmotor) due to being hit by object set in motion by aircraft (powered)

    Excludes *air sickness (E903)*
        effects of:
            high altitude (E902.0-E902.1)
            pressure change (E902.0-E902.1)
        injury in parachute descent due to accident to aircraft (E840.0-E842.9)

● ● **E845 Accident involving spacecraft**
   [0,8,9]

    Requires fourth digit. See beginning of section E800-E845 for codes and definitions.

    Includes: launching pad accident

    Excludes *effects of weightlessness in spacecraft (E928.0)*

VEHICLE ACCIDENTS NOT ELSEWHERE CLASSIFIABLE (E846-E848)

● **E846 Accidents involving powered vehicles used solely within the buildings and premises of industrial or commercial establishment**
    Accident to, on, or involving:
        battery-powered airport passenger vehicle
        battery-powered trucks (baggage) (mail)
        coal car in mine
        logging car
        self-propelled truck, industrial
        station baggage truck (powered)
        tram, truck, or tub (powered) in mine or quarry
    Breakage of any part of vehicle
    Collision with:
        pedestrian
        other vehicle or object within premises
    Explosion of powered vehicle, industrial or commercial
    Fall from powered vehicle, industrial or commercial
    Overturning of powered vehicle, industrial or commercial
    Struck by powered vehicle, industrial or commercial

    Excludes *accidental poisoning by exhaust gas from vehicle not elsewhere classifiable (E868.2)*
        injury by crane, lift (fork), or elevator (E919.2)

● **E847 Accidents involving cable cars not running on rails**
    Accident to, on, or involving:
        cable car, not on rails
        ski chair-lift
        ski-lift with gondola
        teleferique
    Breakage of cable
        Caught or dragged by cable car, not on rails
        Fall or jump from cable car, not on rails
        Object thrown from or in cable car not on rails

● □ **E848 Accidents involving other vehicles, not elsewhere classifiable**
    Accident to, on, or involving:
        ice yacht
        land yacht
        nonmotor, nonroad vehicle NOS

● **E849 *Place of occurrence***

    Note: The following category is for use to denote the place where the injury or poisoning occurred.

● **E849.0 Home**
        Apartment
        Boarding house
        Farm house
        Home premises
        House (residential)
        Noninstitutional place of residence
        Private:
            driveway
            garage
            garden
            home
            walk
        Swimming pool in private house or garden
        Yard of home

    Excludes *home under construction but not yet occupied (E849.3)*
        institutional place of residence (E849.7)

● **E849.1 Farm**
        buildings
        land under cultivation

    Excludes *farm house and home premises of farm (E849.0)*

● **E849.2 Mine and quarry**
    Gravel pit
    Sand pit
    Tunnel under construction

● **E849.3 Industrial place and premises**
    Building under construction
    Dockyard
    Dry dock
    Factory
      building
      premises
    Garage (place of work)
    Industrial yard
    Loading platform (factory) (store)
    Plant, industrial
    Railway yard
    Shop (place of work)
    Warehouse
    Workhouse

● **E849.4 Place for recreation and sport**

Amusement park	*Playground, including*
Baseball field	*school playground*
Basketball court	*Public park*
Beach resort	*Racecourse*
Cricket ground	*Resort NOS*
Fives court	*Riding school*
Football field	*Rifle range*
Golf course	*Seashore resort*
Gymnasium	*Skating rink*
Hockey field	*Sports palace*
Holiday camp	*Stadium*
Ice palace	*Swimming pool, public*
Lake resort	*Tennis court*
Mountain resort	*Vacation resort*

> **Excludes** *that in private house or garden (E849.0)*

● **E849.5 Street and highway**

● **E849.6 Public building**
    Building (including adjacent grounds) used by
      the general public or by a particular group
      of the public, such as:
      airport
      bank
      cafe
      casino
      church
      cinema
      clubhouse
      courthouse
      dance hall
      garage building (for car storage)
      hotel
      market (grocery or other commodity)
      movie house
      music hall
      nightclub
      office
      office building
      opera house
      post office
      public hall
      radio broadcasting station
      restaurant
      school (state) (public) (private)
      shop, commercial
      station (bus) (railway)
      store
      theater

> **Excludes** *home garage (E849.0)*
> *industrial building or workplace (E849.3)*

● **E849.7 Residential institution**
    Children's home
    Dormitory
    Hospital
    Jail
    Old people's home
    Orphanage
    Prison
    Reform school

● ☐ **E849.8 Other specified places**
    Beach NOS
    Canal
    Caravan site NOS
    Derelict house
    Desert
    Dock
    Forest
    Harbor
    Hill
    Lake NOS
    Mountain
    Parking lot
    Parking place
    Pond or pool (natural)
    Prairie
    Public place NOS
    Railway line
    Reservoir
    River
    Sea
    Seashore NOS
    Stream
    Swamp
    Trailer court
    Woods

● ☐ **E849.9 Unspecified place**

ACCIDENTAL POISONING BY DRUGS, MEDICINAL SUBSTANCES, AND BIOLOGICALS (E850-E858)

Includes: accidental overdose of drug, wrong drug given or taken in error, and drug taken inadvertently
accidents in the use of drugs and biologicals in medical and surgical procedures

> **Excludes** *administration with suicidal or homicidal intent or intent to harm, or in circumstances classifiable to E980-E989 (E950.0-E950.5, E962.0, E980.0-E980.5)*
> *correct drug properly administered in therapeutic or prophylactic dosage, as the cause of adverse effect (E930.0-E949.9)*

Note: See Alphabetic Index for more complete list of specific drugs to be classified under the fourth-digit subdivisions. The American Hospital Formulary numbers can be used to classify new drugs listed by the American Hospital Formulary Service (AHFS). See appendix C.

● **E850 Accidental poisoning by analgesics, antipyretics, and antirheumatics**

● **E850.0 Heroin**
    Diacetylmorphine

● **E850.1 Methadone**

● ☐ **E850.2 Other opiates and related narcotics**
    Codeine [methylmorphine]
    Meperidine [pethidine]
    Morphine
    Opium (alkaloids)

ICD-9-CM
E800-E899
Vol. 1

● **E850.3 Salicylates**
     Acetylsalicylic acid [aspirin]
     Amino derivatives of salicylic acid
     Salicylic acid salts

● **E850.4 Aromatic analgesics, not elsewhere classified**
     Acetanilid
     Paracetamol [acetaminophen]
     Phenacetin [acetophenetidin]

● **E850.5 Pyrazole derivatives**
     Aminophenazone [amidopyrine]
     Phenylbutazone

● **E850.6 Antirheumatics [antiphlogistics]**
     Gold salts
     Indomethacin
     Excludes   *salicylates (E850.3)*
                steroids (E858.0)

●□ **E850.7 Other non-narcotic analgesics**
     Pyrabital

●□ **E850.8 Other specified analgesics and antipyretics**
     Pentazocine

●□ **E850.9 Unspecified analgesic or antipyretic**

● **E851 Accidental poisoning by barbiturates**
     Amobarbital [amylobarbitone]
     Barbital [barbitone]
     Butabarbital [butabarbitone]
     Pentobarbital [pentobarbitone]
     Phenobarbital [phenobarbitone]
     Secobarbital [quinalbarbitone]
     Excludes   *thiobarbiturates (E855.1)*

● **E852 Accidental poisoning by other sedatives and hypnotics**

   ● **E852.0 Chloral hydrate group**

   ● **E852.1 Paraldehyde**

   ● **E852.2 Bromine compounds**
         Bromides
         Carbromal (derivatives)

   ● **E852.3 Methaqualone compounds**

   ● **E852.4 Glutethimide group**

   ● **E852.5 Mixed sedatives, not elsewhere classified**

   ●□ **E852.8 Other specified sedatives and hypnotics**

   ●□ **E852.9 Unspecified sedative or hypnotic**
         Sleeping:
            drug NOS
            pill NOS
            tablet NOS

● **E853 Accidental poisoning by tranquilizers**

   ● **E853.0 Phenothiazine-based tranquilizers**
         Chlorpromazine
         Fluphenazine
         Prochlorperazine
         Promazine

   ● **E853.1 Butyrophenone-based tranquilizers**
         Haloperidol
         Spiperone
         Trifluperidol

   ● **E853.2 Benzodiazepine-based tranquilizers**
         Chlordiazepoxide   Lorazepam
         Diazepam   Medazepam
         Flurazepam   Nitrazepam

   ●□ **E853.8 Other specified tranquilizers**
         Hydroxyzine
         Meprobamate

   ●□ **E853.9 Unspecified tranquilizer**

● **E854 Accidental poisoning by other psychotropic agents**

   ● **E854.0 Antidepressants**
         Amitriptyline
         Imipramine
         Monoamine oxidase [MAO] inhibitors

   ● **E854.1 Psychodysleptics [hallucinogens]**
         Cannabis derivatives
         Lysergide [LSD]
         Marihuana (derivatives)
         Mescaline
         Psilocin
         Psilocybin

   ● **E854.2 Psychostimulants**
         Amphetamine
         Caffeine
         Excludes   *central appetite depressants (E858.8)*

   ● **E854.3 Central nervous system stimulants**
         Analeptics
         Opiate antagonists

   ● **E854.8 Other psychotropic agents**

● **E855 Accidental poisoning by other drugs acting on central and autonomic nervous system**

   ● **E855.0 Anticonvulsant and anti-Parkinsonism drugs**
         Amantadine
         Hydantoin derivatives
         Levodopa [L-dopa]
         Oxazolidine derivatives [paramethadione]
            [trimethadione]
         Succinimides

   ●□ **E855.1 Other central nervous system depressants**
         Ether
         Gaseous anesthetics
         Halogenated hydrocarbon derivatives
         Intravenous anesthetics
         Thiobarbiturates, such as thiopental sodium

   ● **E855.2 Local anesthetics**
         Cocaine
         Lidocaine [lignocaine]
         Procaine
         Tetracaine

   ● **E855.3 Parasympathomimetics [cholinergics]**
         Acetylcholine
         Anticholinesterase:
            organophosphorus
            reversible
         Pilocarpine

   ● **E855.4 Parasympatholytics [anticholinergics and antimuscarinics] and spasmolytics**
         Atropine
         Homatropine
         Hyoscine [scopolamine]
         Quaternary ammonium derivatives

   ● **E855.5 Sympathomimetics [adrenergics]**
         Epinephrine [adrenalin]
         Levarterenol [noradrenalin]

   ● **E855.6 Sympatholytics [antiadrenergics]**
         Phenoxybenzamine
         Tolazoline hydrochloride

   ●□ **E855.8 Other specified drugs acting on central and autonomic nervous systems**

   ●□ **E855.9 Unspecified drug acting on central and autonomic nervous systems**

● **E856 Accidental poisoning by antibiotics**

●□ **E857 Accidental poisoning by other anti-infectives**

▲▶ **New Code**   ◀▦▦▶ **Revised Code**   ● **Not a Principal Diagnosis**   ● **Use Additional Digit(s)**   □ **Nonspecific Code**

● **E858 Accidental poisoning by other drugs**

● **E858.0 Hormones and synthetic substitutes**

● **E858.1 Primarily systemic agents**

● **E858.2 Agents primarily affecting blood constituents**

● **E858.3 Agents primarily affecting cardiovascular system**

● **E858.4 Agents primarily affecting gastrointestinal system**

E858.5 Water, mineral, and uric acid metabolism drugs

● **E858.6 Agents primarily acting on the smooth and skeletal muscles and respiratory system**

● **E858.7 Agents primarily affecting skin and mucous membrane, ophthalmological, otorhinolaryngological, and dental drugs**

● □ **E858.8 Other specified drugs**
　　Central appetite depressants

● □ **E858.9 Unspecified drug**

ACCIDENTAL POISONING BY OTHER SOLID AND LIQUID SUBSTANCES, GASES, AND VAPORS (E860-E869)

Note: Categories in this section are intended primarily to indicate the external cause of poisoning states classifiable to 980–989. They may also be used to indicate external causes of localized effects classifiable to 001–799.

● **E860 Accidental poisoning by alcohol, not elsewhere classified**

● **E860.0 Alcoholic beverages**
　　Alcohol in preparations intended for consumption

● □ **E860.1 Other and unspecified ethyl alcohol and its products**
　　Denatured alcohol
　　Ethanol NOS
　　Grain alcohol NOS
　　Methylated spirit

● **E860.2 Methyl alcohol**
　　Methanol
　　Wood alcohol

● **E860.3 Isopropyl alcohol**
　　Dimethyl carbinol
　　Isopropanol
　　Rubbing alcohol substitute
　　Secondary propyl alcohol

● **E860.4 Fusel oil**
　　Alcohol:
　　　amyl
　　　butyl
　　　propyl

● □ **E860.8 Other specified alcohols**

● □ **E860.9 Unspecified alcohol**

● **E861 Accidental poisoning by cleansing and polishing agents, disinfectants, paints, and varnishes**

● **E861.0 Synthetic detergents and shampoos**

● **E861.1 Soap products**

● **E861.2 Polishes**

● □ **E861.3 Other cleansing and polishing agents**
　　Scouring powders

● **E861.4 Disinfectants**
　　Household and other disinfectants not ordinarily used on the person

Excludes *carbolic acid or phenol (E864.0)*

● **E861.5 Lead paints**

● □ **E861.6 Other paints and varnishes**
　　Lacquers
　　Oil colors
　　Paints, other than lead
　　Whitewashes

● □ **E861.9 Unspecified**

● **E862 Accidental poisoning by petroleum products, other solvents and their vapors, not elsewhere classified**

● **E862.0 Petroleum solvents**
　　Petroleum:
　　　ether
　　　benzine
　　　naphtha

● **E862.1 Petroleum fuels and cleaners**
　　Antiknock additives to petroleum fuels
　　Gas oils
　　Gasoline or petrol
　　Kerosene

Excludes *kerosene insecticides (E863.4)*

● **E862.2 Lubricating oils**

● **E862.3 Petroleum solids**
　　Paraffin wax

● □ **E862.4 Other specified solvents**
　　Benzene

● □ **E862.9 Unspecified solvent**

● **E863 Accidental poisoning by agricultural and horticultural chemical and pharmaceutical preparations other than plant foods and fertilizers**

Excludes *plant foods and fertilizers (E866.5)*

● **E863.0 Insecticides of organochlorine compounds**
　　Benzene hexachloride　　Dieldrin
　　Chlordane　　Endrine
　　DDT　　Toxaphene

● **E863.1 Insecticides of organophosphorus compounds**
　　Demeton　　Parathion
　　Diazinon　　Phenylsulphthion
　　Dichlorvos　　Phorate
　　Malathion　　Phosdrin
　　Methyl parathion

● **E863.2 Carbamates**
　　Aldicarb
　　Carbaryl
　　Propoxur

● **E863.3 Mixtures of insecticides**

● □ **E863.4 Other and unspecified insecticides**
　　Kerosene insecticides

● **E863.5 Herbicides**
　　2,4-Dichlorophenoxyacetic acid [2, 4-D]
　　2,4,5-Trichlorophenoxyacetic acid [2, 4, 5-T]
　　Chlorates
　　Diquat
　　Mixtures of plant foods and fertilizers with herbicides
　　Paraquat

● **E863.6 Fungicides**
　　Organic mercurials (used in seed dressing)
　　Pentachlorophenols

ICD-9-CM

E800-E899

Vol. 1

- **E863.7 Rodenticides**
  Fluoroacetates   Warfarin
  Squill and derivatives   Zinc phosphide
  Thallium

- **E863.8 Fumigants**
  Cyanides   Phosphine
  Methyl bromide

- **E863.9 Other and unspecified**

- **E864 Accidental poisoning by corrosives and caustics, not elsewhere classified**

  Excludes *those as components of disinfectants (E861.4)*

  - **E864.0 Corrosive aromatics**
    Carbolic acid or phenol

  - **E864.1 Acids**
    Acid:
      hydrochloric
      nitric
      sulfuric

  - **E864.2 Caustic alkalis**
    Lye

  - **E864.3 Other specified corrosives and caustics**

  - **E864.4 Unspecified corrosives and caustics**

- **E865 Accidental poisoning from poisonous foodstuffs and poisonous plants**

  Includes: any meat, fish, or shellfish
      plants, berries, and fungi eaten as, or in mistake for food, or by a child

  Excludes *anaphlyactic shock due to adverse food reaction (995.60–995.69)*
    food poisoning (bacterial) (005.0–005.9)
    poisoning and toxic reactions to venomous plants (E905.6-E905.7)

  - **E865.0 Meat**

  - **E865.1 Shellfish**

  - **E865.2 Other fish**

  - **E865.3 Berries and seeds**

  - **E865.4 Other specified plants**

  - **E865.5 Mushrooms and other fungi**

  - **E865.8 Other specified foods**

  - **E865.9 Unspecified foodstuff or poisonous plant**

- **E866 Accidental poisoning by other and unspecified solid and liquid substances**

  Excludes *these substances as a component of:*
    medicines (E850.0-E858.9)
    paints (E861.5-E861.6)
    pesticides (E863.0-E863.9)
    petroleum fuels (E862.1)

  - **E866.0 Lead and its compounds and fumes**

  - **E866.1 Mercury and its compounds and fumes**

  - **E866.2 Antimony and its compounds and fumes**

  - **E866.3 Arsenic and its compounds and fumes**

  - **E866.4 Other metals and their compounds and fumes**
    Beryllium (compounds)
    Brass fumes
    Cadmium (compounds)
    Copper salts
    Iron (compounds)
    Manganese (compounds)
    Nickel (compounds)
    Thallium (compounds)

- **E866.5 Plant foods and fertilizers**

  Excludes *mixtures with herbicides (E863.5)*

- **E866.6 Glues and adhesives**

- **E866.7 Cosmetics**

- **E866.8 Other specified solid or liquid substances**

- **E866.9 Unspecified solid or liquid substance**

- **E867 Accidental poisoning by gas distributed by pipeline**
  Carbon monoxide from incomplete combustion of piped gas
  Coal gas NOS
  Liquefied petroleum gas distributed through pipes (pure or mixed with air)
  Piped gas (natural) (manufactured)

- **E868 Accidental poisoning by other utility gas and other carbon monoxide**

  - **E868.0 Liquefied petroleum gas distributed in mobile containers**
    Butane or carbon monoxide from incomplete combustion of these gases
    Liquefied hydrocarbon gas NOS or carbon monoxide from incomplete combustion of these gases
    Propane or carbon monoxide from incomplete combustion of these gases

  - **E868.1 Other and unspecified utility gas**
    Acetylene or carbon monoxide from incomplete combustion of these gases
    Gas NOS used for lighting, heating, or cooking or carbon monoxide from incomplete combustion of these gases
    Water gas or carbon monoxide from incomplete combustion of these gases

  - **E868.2 Motor vehicle exhaust gas**
    Exhaust gas from:
      farm tractor, not in transit
      gas engine
      motor pump
      motor vehicle, not in transit
      any type of combustion engine not in watercraft

    Excludes *poisoning by carbon monoxide from:*
      aircraft while in transit (E844.0-E844.9)
      motor vehicle while in transit (E818.0-E818.9)
      watercraft whether or not in transit (E838.0-E838.9)

  - **E868.3 Carbon monoxide from incomplete combustion of other domestic fuels**
    Carbon monoxide from incomplete combustion of:
      coal in domestic stove or fireplace
      coke in domestic stove or fireplace
      kerosene in domestic stove or fireplace
      wood in domestic stove or fireplace

    Excludes *carbon monoxide from smoke and fumes due to conflagration (E890.0-E893.9)*

  - **E868.8 Carbon monoxide from other sources**
    Carbon monoxide from:
      blast furnace gas
      incomplete combustion of fuels in industrial use
      kiln vapor

  - **E868.9 Unspecified carbon monoxide**

◀▶ **New Code**   ◀▦ ▦▶ **Revised Code**   ● **Not a Principal Diagnosis**   ● **Use Additional Digit(s)**   ☐ **Nonspecific Code**

● **E869 Accidental poisoning by other gases and vapors**

> **Excludes** *effects of gases used as anesthetics (E855.1, E938.2)*
> *fumes from heavy metals (E866.0-E866.4)*
> *smoke and fumes due to conflagration or explosion (E890.0-E899)*

● **E869.0 Nitrogen oxides**

● **E869.1 Sulfur dioxide**

● **E869.2 Freon**

● **E869.3 Lacrimogenic gas [tear gas]**
> Bromobenzyl cyanide
> Chloroacetophenone
> Ethyliodoacetate

● **E869.4 Second-hand tobacco smoke**

●☐ **E869.8 Other specified gases and vapors**
> Chlorine
> Hydrocyanic acid gas

●☐ **E869.9 Unspecified gases and vapors**

MISADVENTURES TO PATIENTS DURING SURGICAL AND MEDICAL CARE (E870-E876)

> **Excludes** *accidental overdose of drug and wrong drug given in error (E850.0-E858.9)*
> *surgical and medical procedures as the cause of abnormal reaction by the patient, without mention of misadventure at the time of procedure (E878.0-E879.9)*

● **E870 Accidental cut, puncture, perforation, or hemorrhage during medical care**

● **E870.0 Surgical operation**

● **E870.1 Infusion or transfusion**

● **E870.2 Kidney dialysis or other perfusion**

● **E870.3 Injection or vaccination**

● **E870.4 Endoscopic examination**

● **E870.5 Aspiration of fluid or tissue, puncture, and catheterization**
> Abdominal paracentesis
> Aspirating needle biopsy
> Blood sampling
> Lumbar puncture
> Thoracentesis

> **Excludes** *heart catheterization (E870.6)*

● **E870.6 Heart catheterization**

● **E870.7 Administration of enema**

●☐ **E870.8 Other specified medical care**

●☐ **E870.9 Unspecified medical care**

● **E871 Foreign object left in body during procedure**

● **E871.0 Surgical operation**

● **E871.1 Infusion or transfusion**

● **E871.2 Kidney dialysis or other perfusion**

● **E871.3 Injection or vaccination**

● **E871.4 Endoscopic examination**

● **E871.5 Aspiration of fluid or tissue, puncture, and catheterization**
> Abdominal paracentesis
> Aspiration needle biopsy
> Blood sampling
> Lumbar puncture
> Thoracentesis

> **Excludes** *heart catheterization (E871.6)*

● **E871.6 Heart catheterization**

● **E871.7 Removal of catheter or packing**

●☐ **E871.8 Other specified procedures**

●☐ **E871.9 Unspecified procedure**

● **E872 Failure of sterile precautions during procedure**

● **E872.0 Surgical operation**

● **E872.1 Infusion or transfusion**

● **E872.2 Kidney dialysis and other perfusion**

● **E872.3 Injection or vaccination**

● **E872.4 Endoscopic examination**

● **E872.5 Aspiration of fluid or tissue, puncture, and catheterization**
> Abdominal paracentesis
> Aspirating needle biopsy
> Blood sampling
> Lumbar puncture
> Thoracentesis

> **Excludes** *heart catheterization (E872.6)*

● **E872.6 Heart catheterization**

●☐ **E872.8 Other specified procedures**

●☐ **E872.9 Unspecified procedure**

● **E873 Failure in dosage**

> **Excludes** *accidental overdose of drug, medicinal or biological substance (E850.0-E858.9)*

●☐ **E873.0 Excessive amount of blood or other fluid during transfusion or infusion**

● **E873.1 Incorrect dilution of fluid during infusion**

● **E873.2 Overdose of radiation in therapy**

● **E873.3 Inadvertent exposure of patient to radiation during medical care**

● **E873.4 Failure in dosage in electroshock or insulin-shock therapy**

● **E873.5 Inappropriate [too hot or too cold] temperature in local application and packing**

● **E873.6 Nonadministration of necessary drug or medicinal substance**

●☐ **E873.8 Other specified failure in dosage**

●☐ **E873.9 Unspecified failure in dosage**

● **E874 Mechanical failure of instrument or apparatus during procedure**

● **E874.0 Surgical operation**

● **E874.1 Infusion and transfusion**
> Air in system

● **E874.2 Kidney dialysis and other perfusion**

● **E874.3 Endoscopic examination**

● **E874.4 Aspiration of fluid or tissue, puncture, and catheterization**
> Abdominal paracentesis
> Aspirating needle biopsy
> Blood sampling
> Lumbar puncture
> Thoracentesis

> **Excludes** *heart catheterization (E874.5)*

● **E874.5 Heart catheterization**

●☐ **E874.8 Other specified procedures**

●☐ **E874.9 Unspecified procedure**

ICD-9-CM

E800-E899

Vol. 1

◀▶ **New Code** ⬤▶ **Revised Code** ● **Not a Principal Diagnosis** ● **Use Additional Digit(s)** ☐ **Nonspecific Code**

● **E875 Contaminated or infected blood, other fluid, drug, or biological substance**

　Includes: presence of:
　　　bacterial pyrogens
　　　endotoxin-producing bacteria
　　　serum hepatitis-producing agent

● **E875.0 Contaminated substance transfused or infused**

● **E875.1 Contaminated substance injected or used for vaccination**

●❑ **E875.2 Contaminated drug or biological substance administered by other means**

●❑ **E875.8 Other**

●❑ **E875.9 Unspecified**

● **E876 Other and unspecified misadventures during medical care**

● **E876.0 Mismatched blood in transfusion**

● **E876.1 Wrong fluid in infusion**

● **E876.2 Failure in suture and ligature during surgical operation**

● **E876.3 Endotracheal tube wrongly placed during anesthetic procedure**

●❑ **E876.4 Failure to introduce or to remove other tube or instrument**

　Excludes *foreign object left in body during procedure (E871.0-E871.9)*

● **E876.5 Performance of inappropriate operation**

●❑ **E876.8 Other specified misadventures during medical care**
　　　Performance of inappropriate treatment, NEC

●❑ **E876.9 Unspecified misadventure during medical care**

SURGICAL AND MEDICAL PROCEDURES AS THE CAUSE OF ABNORMAL REACTION OF PATIENT OR LATER COMPLICATION, WITHOUT MENTION OF MISADVENTURE AT THE TIME OF PROCEDURE (E878-E879)

　Includes: procedures as the cause of abnormal reaction, such as:
　　　displacement or malfunction of prosthetic device
　　　hepatorenal failure, postoperative
　　　malfunction of external stoma
　　　postoperative intestinal obstruction
　　　rejection of transplanted organ

　Excludes *anesthetic management properly carried out as the cause of adverse effect (E937.0-E938.9)*
　　infusion and transfusion, without mention of misadventure in the technique of procedure (E930.0-E949.9)

● **E878 Surgical operation and other surgical procedures as the cause of abnormal reaction of patient, or of later complication, without mention of misadventure at the time of operation**

● **E878.0 Surgical operation with transplant of whole organ**
　　　Transplantation of:
　　　　heart
　　　　kidney
　　　　liver

● **E878.1 Surgical operation with implant of artificial internal device**
　　　Cardiac pacemaker
　　　Electrodes implanted in brain
　　　Heart valve prosthesis
　　　Internal orthopedic device

● **E878.2 Surgical operation with anastomosis, bypass, or graft, with natural or artificial tissues used as implant**
　　　Anastomosis:
　　　　arteriovenous
　　　　gastrojejunal
　　　Graft of blood vessel, tendon, or skin

　Excludes *external stoma (E878.3)*

● **E878.3 Surgical operation with formation of external stoma**
　　　Colostomy
　　　Cystostomy
　　　Duodenostomy
　　　Gastrostomy
　　　Ureterostomy

●❑ **E878.4 Other restorative surgery**

● **E878.5 Amputation of limb(s)**

●❑ **E878.6 Removal of other organ (partial) (total)**

●❑ **E878.8 Other specified surgical operations and procedures**

●❑ **E878.9 Unspecified surgical operations and procedures**

● **E879 Other procedures, without mention of misadventure at the time of procedure, as the cause of abnormal reaction of patient, or of later complication**

● **E879.0 Cardiac catheterization**

● **E879.1 Kidney dialysis**

● **E879.2 Radiological procedure and radiotherapy**

　Excludes *radio-opaque dyes for diagnostic x-ray procedures (E947.8)*

● **E879.3 Shock therapy**
　　　Electroshock therapy
　　　Insulin-shock therapy

● **E879.4 Aspiration of fluid**
　　　Lumbar puncture　　　　　　　Thoracentesis

● **E879.5 Insertion of gastric or duodenal sound**

● **E879.6 Urinary catheterization**

● **E879.7 Blood sampling**

●❑ **E879.8 Other specified procedures**
　　　Blood transfusion

●❑ **E879.9 Unspecified procedure**

ACCIDENTAL FALLS (E880-E888)

　Excludes *falls (in or from):*
　　burning building (E890.8, E891.8)
　　into fire (E890.0-E899)
　　into water (with submersion or drowning) (E910.0-E910.9)
　　machinery (in operation) (E919.0-E919.9)
　　on edged, pointed, or sharp object (E920.0-E920.9)
　　transport vehicle (E800.0-E845.9)
　　vehicle not elsewhere classifiable (E846-E848)

● **E880 Fall on or from stairs or steps**

● **E880.0 Escalator**

● **E880.1 Fall on or from sidewalk curb**

　Excludes *fall from moving sidewalk (E885)*

●❑ **E880.9 Other stairs or steps**

● **E881 Fall on or from ladders or scaffolding**

● **E881.0 Fall from ladder**

● **E881.1 Fall from scaffolding**

　◀▶ **New Code**　　⬅▥▥▥▶ **Revised Code**　　● **Not a Principal Diagnosis**　　● **Use Additional Digit(s)**　　❑ **Nonspecific Code**

●□ **E882 Fall from or out of building or other structure**
    Fall from:
        balcony
        bridge
        building
        flagpole
        tower
        turret
        viaduct
        wall
        window
    Fall through roof

    Excludes *collapse of a building or structure (E916)*
        fall or jump from burning building (E890.8, E891.8)

● **E883 Fall into hole or other opening in surface**

    Includes: fall into:
        cavity
        dock
        hole
        pit
        quarry
        shaft
        swimming pool
        tank
        well

    Excludes *fall into water NOS (E910.9)*
        that resulting in drowning or submersion without mention of injury (E910.0-E910.9)

● **E883.0 Accident from diving or jumping into water [swimming pool]**
    Strike or hit:
        against bottom when jumping or diving into water
        wall or board of swimming pool
        water surface

    Excludes *diving with insufficient air supply (E913.2)*
        effects of air pressure from diving (E902.2)

● **E883.1 Accidental fall into well**

● **E883.2 Accidental fall into storm drain or manhole**

●□ **E883.9 Fall into other hole or other opening in surface**

● **E884 Other fall from one level to another**

  ● **E884.0 Fall from playground equipment**

    Excludes *recreational machinery (E919.8)*

  ● **E884.1 Fall from cliff**

  ● **E884.2 Fall from chair**

  ● **E884.3 Fall from wheelchair**

  ● **E884.4 Fall from bed**

  ● **E884.5 Fall from other furniture**

  ● **E884.6 Fall from commode**
      Toilet

  ●□ **E884.9 Other fall from one level to another**
    Fall from:
        embankment
        haystack
        stationary vehicle
        tree

● **E885 Fall on same level from slipping, tripping, or stumbling**
    Fall on moving sidewalk

●○ **E886 Fall on same level from collision, pushing, or shoving, by or with other person**

    Excludes *crushed or pushed by a crowd or human stampede (E917.1)*

  ● **E886.0 In sports**
      Tackles in sports

    Excludes *kicked, stepped on, struck by object, in sports (E917.0)*

  ●□ **E886.9 Other and unspecified**
      Fall from collision of pedestrian (conveyance) with another pedestrian (conveyance)

●□ **E887 Fracture, cause unspecified**

●□ **E888 Other and unspecified fall**
    Accidental fall NOS
    Fall from bumping against object
    Fall on same level NOS

ACCIDENTS CAUSED BY FIRE AND FLAMES (E890-E899)

    Includes: asphyxia or poisoning due to conflagration or ignition
        burning by fire
        secondary fires resulting from explosion

    Excludes *arson (E968.0)*
        fire in or on:
          machinery (in operation) (E919.0-E919.9)
          transport vehicle other than stationary vehicle (E800.0-E845.9)
          vehicle not elsewhere classifiable (E846-E848)

● **E890 Conflagration in private dwelling**

    Includes: conflagration in:
        apartment
        boarding house
        camping place
        caravan
        farmhouse
        house
        lodging house
        mobile home
        private garage
        rooming house
        tenement
    conflagration originating from sources classifiable to E893-E898 in the above buildings

  ● **E890.0 Explosion caused by conflagration**

  ● **E890.1 Fumes from combustion of polyvinylchloride [PVC] and similar material in conflagration**

  ●□ **E890.2 Other smoke and fumes from conflagration**
      Carbon monoxide from conflagration in private building
      Fumes NOS from conflagration in private building
      Smoke NOS from conflagration in private building

  ● **E890.3 Burning caused by conflagration**

  ●□ **E890.8 Other accident resulting from conflagration**
      Collapse of burning private building
      Fall from burning private building
      Hit by object falling from burning private building
      Jump from burning private building

  ●□ **E890.9 Unspecified accident resulting from conflagration in private dwelling**

ICD-9-CM

E800–E899

Vol. 1

● **E891 Conflagration in other and unspecified building or structure**

Conflagration in:
   barn
   church
   convalescent and other residential home
   dormitory of educational institution
   factory
   farm outbuildings
   hospital
   hotel
   school
   store
   theater
Conflagration originating from sources classifiable to E893-E898, in the above buildings

● **E891.0 Explosion caused by conflagration**

● **E891.1 Fumes from combustion of polyvinylchloride [PVC] and similar material in conflagration**

●□ **E891.2 Other smoke and fumes from conflagration**
   Carbon monoxide from conflagration in building or structure
   Fumes NOS from conflagration in building or structure
   Smoke NOS from conflagration in building or structure

● **E891.3 Burning caused by conflagration**

●□ **E891.8 Other accident resulting from conflagration**
   Collapse of burning building or structure
   Fall from burning building or structure
   Hit by object falling from burning building or structure
   Jump from burning building or structure

●□ **E891.9 Unspecified accident resulting from conflagration of other and unspecified building or structure**

● **E892 Conflagration not in building or structure**
Fire (uncontrolled) (in) (of):
   forest
   grass
   hay
   lumber
   mine
   prairie
   transport vehicle [any], except while in transit
   tunnel

● **E893 Accident caused by ignition of clothing**

> **Excludes** *ignition of clothing:*
> *from highly inflammable material (E894)*
> *with conflagration (E890.0-E892)*

● **E893.0 From controlled fire in private dwelling**
Ignition of clothing from:
   normal fire (charcoal) (coal) (electric) (gas) (wood) in:
      brazier in private dwelling (as listed in E890)
      fireplace in private dwelling (as listed in E890)
      furnace in private dwelling (as listed in E890)
      stove in private dwelling (as listed in E890)

●□ **E893.1 From controlled fire in other building or structure**
Ignition of clothing from:
   normal fire (charcoal) (coal) (electric) (gas) (wood) in:
      brazier in other building or structure (as listed in E891)
      fireplace in other building or structure (as listed in E891)
      furnace in other building or structure (as listed in E891)
      stove in other building or structure (as listed in E891)

● **E893.2 From controlled fire not in building or structure**
Ignition of clothing from:
   bonfire (controlled)
   brazier fire (controlled), not in building or structure
   trash fire (controlled)

> **Excludes** *conflagration not in building (E892)*
> *trash fire out of control (E892)*

●□ **E893.8 From other specified sources**
Ignition of clothing from:
   blowlamp
   blowtorch
   burning bedspread
   candle
   cigar
   cigarette
   lighter
   matches
   pipe
   welding torch

●□ **E893.9 Unspecified source**
Ignition of clothing (from controlled fire NOS) (in building NOS) NOS

● **E894 Ignition of highly inflammable material**
Ignition of:
   benzine (with ignition of clothing)
   gasoline (with ignition of clothing)
   fat (with ignition of clothing)
   kerosene (with ignition of clothing)
   paraffin (with ignition of clothing)
   petrol (with ignition of clothing)

> **Excludes** *ignition of highly inflammable material with:*
> *conflagration (E890.0-E892)*
> *explosion (E923.0-E923.9)*

● **E895 Accident caused by controlled fire in private dwelling**
Burning by (flame of) normal fire (charcoal) (coal) (electric) (gas) (wood) in:
   brazier in private dwelling (as listed in E890)
   fireplace in private dwelling (as listed in E890)
   furnace in private dwelling (as listed in E890)
   stove in private dwelling (as listed in E890)

> **Excludes** *burning by hot objects not producing fire or flames (E924.0-E924.9)*
> *ignition of clothing from these sources (E893.0)*
> *poisoning by carbon monoxide from incomplete combustion of fuel (E867-E868.9)*
> *that with conflagration (E890.0-E890.9)*

◀▶ **New Code**   ⬅▦➡ **Revised Code**   ● **Not a Principal Diagnosis**   ● **Use Additional Digit(s)**   □ **Nonspecific Code**

● ☐ **E896 Accident caused by controlled fire in other and un-specified building or structure**
 Burning by (flame of) normal fire (charcoal) (coal) (electric) (gas) (wood) in:
  brazier in other building or structure (as listed in E891)
  fireplace in other building or structure (as listed in E891)
  furnace in other building or structure (as listed in E891)
  stove in other building or structure (as listed in E891)

 Excludes *burning by hot objects not producing fire or flames (E924.0-E924.9)*
  ignition of clothing from these sources (E893.1)
  poisoning by carbon monoxide from incomplete combustion of fuel (E867-E868.9)
  that with conflagration (E891.0-E891.9)

● **E897 Accident caused by controlled fire not in building or structure**
 Burns from flame of:
  bonfire (controlled)
  brazier fire (controlled), not in building or structure
  trash fire (controlled)

 Excludes *ignition of clothing from these sources (E893.2)*
  trash fire out of control (E892)
  that with conflagration (E892)

● **E898 Accident caused by other specified fire and flames**
 Excludes *conflagration (E890.0-E892)*
  that with ignition of:
   clothing (E893.0-E893.9)
   highly inflammable material (E894)

 ● **E898.0 Burning bedclothes**
  Bed set on fire NOS

 ● ☐ **E898.1 Other**
  Burning by: Burning by:
   blowlamp   lamp
   blowtorch   lighter
   candle   matches
   cigar   pipe
   cigarette   welding torch
   fire in room NOS

● ☐ **E899 Accident caused by unspecified fire**
 Burning NOS

ACCIDENTS DUE TO NATURAL AND ENVIRONMENTAL FACTORS (E900-E909)

● **E900 Excessive heat**

 ● **E900.0 Due to weather conditions**
  Excessive heat as the external cause of:
   ictus solaris
   siriasis
   sunstroke

 ● **E900.1 Of man-made origin**
  Heat (in):
   boiler room
   drying room
   factory
   furnace room
   generated in transport vehicle
   kitchen

 ● ☐ **E900.9 Of unspecified origin**

● **E901 Excessive cold**

 ● **E901.0 Due to weather conditions**
  Excessive cold as the cause of:
   chilblains NOS
   immersion foot

● **E901.1 Of man-made origin**
 Contact with or inhalation of:
  dry ice
  liquid air
  liquid hydrogen
  liquid nitrogen
 Prolonged exposure in:
  deep freeze unit
  refrigerator

● ☐ **E901.8 Other specified origin**

● ☐ **E901.9 Of unspecified origin**

● **E902 High and low air pressure and changes in air pressure**

 ● **E902.0 Residence or prolonged visit at high altitude**
  Residence or prolonged visit at high altitude as the cause of:
   Acosta syndrome
   Alpine sickness
   altitude sickness
   Andes disease
   anoxia, hypoxia
   barotitis, barodontalgia, barosinusitis, otitic barotrauma
   hypobarism, hypobaropathy
   mountain sickness
   range disease

 ● **E902.1 In aircraft**
  Sudden change in air pressure in aircraft during ascent or descent as the cause of:
   aeroneurosis
   aviators' disease

 ● **E902.2 Due to diving**
  High air pressure from rapid descent in water as the cause of:
   caisson disease
   divers' disease
   divers' palsy or paralysis
  Reduction in atmospheric pressure while surfacing from deep water diving as the cause of:
   caisson disease
   divers' disease
   divers' palsy or paralysis

 ● ☐ **E902.8 Due to other specified causes**
  Reduction in atmospheric pressure while surfacing from under ground

 ● ☐ **E902.9 Unspecified cause**

● **E903 Travel and motion**

● **E904 Hunger, thirst, exposure, and neglect**
 Excludes *any condition resulting from homicidal intent (E968.0-E968.9)*
  hunger, thirst, and exposure resulting from accidents connected with transport (E800.0-E848)

 ● **E904.0 Abandonment or neglect of infants and helpless persons**
  Exposure to weather conditions resulting from abandonment or neglect
  Hunger or thirst resulting from abandonment or neglect
  Desertion of newborn
  Inattention at or after birth
  Lack of care (helpless person) (infant)

 Excludes *criminal [purposeful] neglect (E968.4)*

ICD-9-CM

E800-E899

Vol. 1

● **E904.1 Lack of food**
  Lack of food as the cause of:
    inanition
    insufficient nourishment
    starvation

Excludes *hunger resulting from abandonment or neglect (E904.0)*

● **E904.2 Lack of water**
  Lack of water as the cause of:
    dehydration
    inanition

Excludes *dehydration due to acute fluid loss (276.5)*

● **E904.3 Exposure (to weather conditions), not elsewhere classifiable**
    Exposure NOS
    Humidity
    Struck by hailstones

Excludes *struck by lightning (E907)*

● **E904.9 Privation, unqualified**
    Destitution

● **E905 Venomous animals and plants as the cause of poisoning and toxic reactions**

Includes: chemical released by animal
    insects
    release of venom through fangs, hairs, spines,
      tentacles, and other venom apparatus

Excludes *eating of poisonous animals or plants (E865.0-E865.9)*

● **E905.0 Venomous snakes and lizards**
    Cobra   Mamba
    Copperhead snake   Rattlesnake
    Coral snake   Sea snake
    Fer de lance   Snake (venomous)
    Gila monster   Viper
    Krait   Water moccasin

Excludes *bites of snakes and lizards known to be nonvenomous (E906.2)*

● **E905.1 Venomous spiders**
    Black widow spider
    Brown recluse spider
    Tarantula (venomous)

● **E905.2 Scorpion**

● **E905.3 Hornets, wasps, and bees**
    Yellow jacket

● **E905.4 Centipede and venomous millipede (tropical)**

●□ **E905.5 Other venomous arthropods**
    Sting of:
      ant
      caterpillar

● **E905.6 Venomous marine animals and plants**
    Puncture by sea urchin spine
    Sting of:
      coral
      jelly fish
      nematocysts
      sea anemone
      sea cucumber
      other marine animal or plant

Excludes *bites and other injuries caused by nonvenomous marine animal (E906.2-E906.8)*
bite of sea snake (venomous) (E905.0)

●□ **E905.7 Poisoning and toxic reactions caused by other plants**
    Injection of poisons or toxins into or
      through skin by plant thorns, spines, or
      other mechanisms

Excludes *puncture wound NOS by plant thorns or spines (E920.8)*

●□ **E905.8 Other specified**

●□ **E905.9 Unspecified**
    Sting NOS
    Venomous bite NOS

● **E906 Other injury caused by animals**

Excludes *poisoning and toxic reactions caused by venomous animals and insects (E905.0-E905.9)*
road vehicle accident involving animals (E827.0-E828.9)
tripping or falling over an animal (E885)

● **E906.0 Dog bite**

● **E906.1 Rat bite**

● **E906.2 Bite of nonvenomous snakes and lizards**

●□ **E906.3 Bite of other animal except arthropod**
    Cats   Rodents, except rats
    Moray eel   Shark

● **E906.4 Bite of nonvenomous arthropod**
    Insect bite NOS

● **E906.5 Bite by unspecified animal**
    Animal bite NOS

●□ **E906.8 Other specified injury caused by animal**
    Butted by animal
    Fallen on by horse or other animal, not being ridden
    Gored by animal
    Implantation of quills of porcupine
    Pecked by bird
    Run over by animal, not being ridden
    Stepped on by animal, not being ridden

Excludes *injury by animal being ridden (E828.0-E828.9)*

●□ **E906.9 Unspecified injury caused by animal**

● **E907 Lightning**

Excludes *injury from:*
    fall of tree or other object caused by lightning (E916)
    fire caused by lightning (E890.0-E892)

● **E908 Cataclysmic storms, and floods resulting from storms**

Excludes *collapse of dam or man-made structure causing flood (E909.3)*

● **E908.0 Hurricane**
    Storm surge
    "Tidal wave" caused by storm action
    Typhoon

● **E908.1 Tornado**
    Cyclone
    Twisters

● **E908.2 Floods**
    Torrential rainfall
    Flash flood

Excludes *collapse of dam or man-made structure causing flood (E909.3)*

● **E908.3 Blizzard (snow) (ice)**

● **E908.4 Dust storm**

● **E908.8 Other cataclysmic storms**

   ◀▶ **New Code**   ⬅▪▪ ▪▪➡ **Revised Code**   ● **Not a Principal Diagnosis**   ● **Use Additional Digit(s)**   □ **Nonspecific Code**

● **E908.9 Unspecified cataclysmic storms, and floods resulting from storms**
    Storm NOS

● **E909 Cataclysmic earth surface movements and eruptions**

  ● **E909.0 Earthquakes**

  ● **E909.1 Volcanic eruptions**
      Burns from lava   Ash inhalation

  ● **E909.2 Avalanche, landslide, or mudslide**

  ● **E909.3 Collapse of dam or man-made structure**

  ● **E909.4 Tidal wave caused by earthquake**
      Tidal wave NOS   Tsunami

    Excludes *tidal wave caused by tropical storm (E908.0)*

  ● **E909.8 Other cataclysmic earth surface movements and eruptions**

  ● **E909.9 Unspecified cataclysmic earth surface movements and eruptions**

ACCIDENTS CAUSED BY SUBMERSION, SUFFOCATION, AND FOREIGN BODIES (E910-E915)

● **E910 Accidental drowning and submersion**

  Includes: immersion
        swimmers' cramp

    Excludes *diving accident (NOS) (resulting in injury except drowning) (E883.0)*
        diving with insufficient air supply (E913.2)
        drowning and submersion due to:
        cataclysm (E908-E909)
        machinery accident (E919.0-E919.9)
        transport accident (E800.0-E845.9)
        effect of high and low air pressure (E902.2)
        injury from striking against objects while in running water (E917.2)

  ● **E910.0 While water-skiing**
      Fall from water skis with submersion or drowning

    Excludes *accident to water-skier involving a watercraft and resulting in submersion or other injury (E830.4, E831.4)*

  ●□ **E910.1 While engaged in other sport or recreational activity with diving equipment**
      Scuba diving NOS
      Skin diving NOS
      Underwater spear fishing NOS

  ●□ **E910.2 While engaged in other sport or recreational activity without diving equipment**
      Fishing or hunting, except from boat or with diving equipment
      Ice skating
      Playing in water
      Surfboarding
      Swimming NOS
      Voluntarily jumping from boat, not involved in accident, for swim NOS
      Wading in water

    Excludes *jumping into water to rescue another person (E910.3)*

  ● **E910.3 While swimming or diving for purposes other than recreation or sport**
      Marine salvage (with diving equipment)
      Pearl diving (with diving equipment)
      Placement of fishing nets (with diving equipment)
      Rescue (attempt) of another person (with diving equipment)
      Underwater construction or repairs (with diving equipment)

  ● **E910.4 In bathtub**

  ●□ **E910.8 Other accidental drowning or submersion**
      Drowning in:
        quenching tank
        swimming pool

  ●□ **E910.9 Unspecified accidental drowning or submersion**
      Accidental fall into water NOS
      Drowning NOS

● **E911 Inhalation and ingestion of food causing obstruction of respiratory tract or suffocation**
      Aspiration and inhalation of food [any] (into respiratory tract) NOS
      Asphyxia by food [including bone, seed in food, regurgitated food]
      Choked on food [including bone, seed in food, regurgitated food]
      Suffocation by food [including bone, seed in food, regurgitated food]
      Compression of trachea by food lodged in esophagus
      Interruption of respiration by food lodged in esophagus
      Obstruction of respiration by food lodged in esophagus
      Obstruction of pharynx by food (bolus)

    Excludes *injury, except asphyxia and obstruction of respiratory passage, caused by food (E915)*
        obstruction of esophagus by food without mention of asphyxia or obstruction of respiratory passage (E915)

●□ **E912 Inhalation and ingestion of other object causing obstruction of respiratory tract or suffocation**
      Aspiration and inhalation of foreign body except food (into respiratory tract) NOS
      Foreign object [bean] [marble] in nose
      Obstruction of pharynx by foreign body
      Compression by foreign body in esophagus
      Interruption of respiration by foreign body in esophagus
      Obstruction of respiration by foreign body in esophagus

    Excludes *injury, except asphyxia and obstruction of respiratory passage, caused by foreign body (E915)*
        obstruction of esophagus by foreign body without mention of asphyxia or obstruction in respiratory passage (E915)

● **E913 Accidental mechanical suffocation**

    Excludes *mechanical suffocation from or by:*
        accidental inhalation or ingestion of:
        food (E911)
        foreign object (E912)
        cataclysm (E908-E909)
        explosion (E921.0-E921.9, E923.0-E923.9)
        machinery accident (E919.0-E919.9)

  ● **E913.0 In bed or cradle**

    Excludes *suffocation by plastic bag (E913.1)*

  ● **E913.1 By plastic bag**

  ● **E913.2 Due to lack of air (in closed place)**
      Accidentally closed up in refrigerator or other airtight enclosed space
      Diving with insufficient air supply

    Excludes *suffocation by plastic bag (E913.1)*

  ● **E913.3 By falling earth or other substance**
      Cave-in NOS

    Excludes *cave-in caused by cataclysmic earth surface movements and eruptions (E909.8)*
        struck by cave-in without asphyxiation or suffocation (E916)

ICD-9-CM

E900-E999

Vol. 1

● ☐ **E913.8　Other specified means**
　　Accidental hanging, except in bed or cradle

● ☐ **E913.9　Unspecified means**
　　Asphyxia, mechanical NOS
　　Strangulation NOS
　　Suffocation NOS

● **E914　Foreign body accidentally entering eye and adnexa**
　　| Excludes | *corrosive liquid (E924.1)*

● ☐ **E915　Foreign body accidentally entering other orifice**
　　| Excludes | *aspiration and inhalation of foreign body, any,*
　　　　(into respiratory tract) NOS (E911-E912)

OTHER ACCIDENTS (E916-E928)

● **E916　Struck accidentally by falling object**
　　Collapse of building, except on fire
　　Falling:　　　　　　　　Falling:
　　　rock　　　　　　　　　　stone
　　　snowslide NOS　　　　　tree
　　Object falling from:
　　　machine, not in operation
　　　stationary vehicle

　　Code first: collapse of building on fire (E890.0-E891.9)
　　　falling object in:
　　　　cataclysm (E908-E909)
　　　　machinery accidents (E919.0-E919.9)
　　　　transport accidents (E800.0-E845.9)
　　　　vehicle accidents not elsewhere classifiable (E846-
　　　　　E848)
　　　object set in motion by:
　　　　explosion (E921.0-E921.9, E923.0-E923.9)
　　　　firearm (E922.0-E922.9)
　　　　projected object (E917.0-E917.9)

● **E917　Striking against or struck accidentally by objects or persons**

　　Includes: bumping into or against
　　　　　object (moving) (projected) (stationary)
　　　　　pedestrian conveyance
　　　　　person
　　　　colliding with
　　　　　object (moving) (projected) (stationary)
　　　　　pedestrian conveyance
　　　　　person
　　　　kicking against
　　　　　object (moving) (projected) (stationary)
　　　　　pedestrian conveyance
　　　　　person
　　　　stepping on
　　　　　object (moving) (projected) (stationary)
　　　　　pedestrian conveyance
　　　　　person
　　　　struck by
　　　　　object (moving) (projected) (stationary)
　　　　　pedestrian conveyance
　　　　　person
　　| Excludes | *fall from:*
　　　　　bumping into or against object (E888)
　　　　　collision with another person, except when
　　　　　　caused by a crowd (E886.0-E886.9)
　　　　　stumbling over object (E885)
　　　　injury caused by:
　　　　　assault (E960.0-E960.1, E967.0-E967.9)
　　　　　cutting or piercing instrument (E920.0-
　　　　　　E920.9)
　　　　　explosion (E921.0-E921.9, E923.0-E923.9)
　　　　　firearm (E922.0-E922.9)
　　　　　machinery (E919.0-E919.9)
　　　　　transport vehicle (E800.0-E845.9)
　　　　　vehicle not elsewhere classifiable (E846-E848)

● **E917.0　In sports**
　　Kicked or stepped on during game (foot-
　　　ball) (rugby)
　　Knocked down while boxing
　　Struck by hit or thrown ball
　　Struck by hockey stick or puck

● **E917.1　Caused by a crowd, by collective fear or panic**
　　Crushed by crowd or human stampede
　　Pushed by crowd or human stampede
　　Stepped on by crowd or human stampede

● **E917.2　In running water**
　　| Excludes | *drowning or submersion (E910.0-E910.9) that in*
　　　　sports (E917.0)

● ☐ **E917.9　Other**

● **E918　Caught accidentally in or between objects**
　　Caught, crushed, jammed, or pinched in or be-
　　　tween moving or stationary objects, such as:
　　escalator
　　folding object
　　hand tools, appliances, or implements
　　sliding door and door frame
　　under packing crate
　　washing machine wringer
　　| Excludes | *injury caused by:*
　　　　cutting or piercing instrument (E920.0-E920.9)
　　　　machinery (E919.0-E919.9)
　　　　transport vehicle (E800.0-E845.9)
　　　　vehicle not elsewhere classifiable (E846-E848)
　　　　struck accidentally by:
　　　　falling object (E916)
　　　　object (moving) (projected) (E917.0-E917.9)

● **E919　Accidents caused by machinery**

　　Includes: burned by machinery (accident)
　　　　caught in (moving parts of) machinery (acci-
　　　　　dent)
　　　　collapse of machinery (accident)
　　　　crushed by machinery (accident)
　　　　cut or pierced by machinery (accident)
　　　　drowning or submersion caused by ma-
　　　　　chinery (accident)
　　　　explosion of, on, in machinery (accident)
　　　　fall from or into moving part of machinery
　　　　　(accident)
　　　　fire starting in or on machinery (accident)
　　　　mechanical suffocation caused by machinery
　　　　　(accident)
　　　　object falling from, on, in motion by ma-
　　　　　chinery (accident)
　　　　overturning of machinery (accident)
　　　　pinned under machinery (accident)
　　　　run over by machinery (accident)
　　　　struck by machinery (accident)
　　　　thrown from machinery (accident)
　　　　caught between machinery and other object
　　　　machinery accident NOS
　　| Excludes | *accidents involving machinery, not in operation*
　　　　(E884.9, E916-E918)
　　　　injury caused by:
　　　　　electric current in connection with machinery
　　　　　　(E925.0-E925.9)
　　　　　escalator (E880.0, E918)
　　　　　explosion of pressure vessel in connection with
　　　　　　machinery (E921.0-E921.9)
　　　　　moving sidewalk (E885)
　　　　　powered hand tools, appliances, and implements
　　　　　　(E916-E918, E920.0-E921.9, E923.0-E926.9)
　　　　　transport vehicle accidents involving ma-
　　　　　　chinery (E800.0-E848.9)
　　　　　poisoning by carbon monoxide generated by
　　　　　　machine (E868.8)

　◀▶ **New Code**　　⬅▬ ▬▶ **Revised Code**　　● **Not a Principal Diagnosis**　　● **Use Additional Digit(s)**　　☐ **Nonspecific Code**

● **E919.0 Agricultural machines**
    Animal-powered agricultural machine
    Combine
    Derrick, hay
    Farm machinery NOS
    Farm tractor
    Harvester
    Hay mower or rake
    Reaper
    Thresher

Excludes *that in transport under own power on the highway (E810.0-E819.9)*
that being towed by another vehicle on the highway (E810.0-E819.9, E827.0-E827.9, E829.0-E829.9)
that involved in accident classifiable to E820-E829 (E820.0-E829.9)

● **E919.1 Mining and earth-drilling machinery**
    Bore or drill (land) (seabed)
    Shaft hoist
    Shaft lift
    Under-cutter

Excludes *coal car, tram, truck, and tub in mine (E846)*

● **E919.2 Lifting machines and appliances**
    Chain hoist except in agricultural or mining operations
    Crane except in agricultural or mining operations
    Derrick except in agricultural or mining operations
    Elevator (building) (grain) except in agricultural or mining operations
    Forklift truck except in agricultural or mining operations
    Lift except in agricultural or mining operations
    Pulley block except in agricultural or mining operations
    Winch except in agricultural or mining operations

Excludes *that being towed by another vehicle on the highway (E810.0-E819.9, E827.0-E827.9, E829.0-E829.9)*
that in transport under own power on the highway (E810.0-E819.9)
that involved in accident classifiable to E820-E829 (E820.0-E829.9)

● **E919.3 Metalworking machines**
    Abrasive wheel
    Forging machine
    Lathe
    Mechanical shears
    Metal:
      drilling machine
    Metal:
      milling machine
      power press
      rolling-mill
      sawing machine

● **E919.4 Woodworking and forming machines**
    Band saw
    Bench saw
    Circular saw
    Molding machine
    Overhead plane
    Powered saw
    Radial saw
    Sander

Excludes *hand saw (E920.1)*

● **E919.5 Prime movers, except electrical motors**
    Gas turbine
    Internal combustion engine
    Steam engine
    Water driven turbine

Excludes *that being towed by other vehicle on the highway (E810.0-E819.9, E827.0-E827.9, E829.0-E829.9)*
that in transport under own power on the highway (E810.0-E819.9)

● **E919.6 Transmission machinery**
    Transmission:
      belt
      cable
      chain
      gear
    Transmission:
      pinion
      pulley
      shaft

● **E919.7 Earth moving, scraping, and other excavating machines**
    Bulldozer
    Road scraper
    Steam shovel

Excludes *that being towed by other vehicle on the highway (E810.0-E819.9)*
that in transport under own power on the highway (E810.0-E819.9)

●☐ **E919.8 Other specified machinery**
    Machines for manufacture of:
      clothing
      foodstuffs and beverages
      paper
    Printing machine
    Recreational machinery
    Spinning, weaving, and textile machines

●☐ **E919.9 Unspecified machinery**

● **E920 Accidents caused by cutting and piercing instruments or objects**

Includes: accidental injury or fall (on)(by) object:
    edged
    pointed
    sharp

● **E920.0 Powered lawn mower**

●☐ **E920.1 Other powered hand tools**
    Any powered hand tool [compressed air] [electric] [explosive cartridge] [hydraulic power], such as:
      drill
      hand saw
      hedge clipper
      rivet gun
      snow blower
      staple gun

Excludes *band saw (E919.4)*
bench saw (E919.4)

● **E920.2 Powered household appliances and implements**
    Blender
    Electric:
      beater or mixer
      can opener
      fan
      knife
      sewing machine
    Garbage disposal appliance

● **E920.3 Knives, swords, and daggers**

●☐ **E920.4 Other hand tools and implements**
    Axe
    Can opener NOS
    Chisel
    Fork
    Hand saw
    Hoe
    Ice pick
    Needle (sewing)
    Paper cutter
    Pitchfork
    Rake
    Scissors
    Screwdriver
    Sewing machine, not powered
    Shovel

ICD-9-CM
E900-E999
Vol. 1

● **E920.5 Hypodermic needle**
   Contaminated needle
   Needle stick

●❑ **E920.8 Other specified cutting and piercing instruments or objects**
   Arrow   Nail
   Broken glass   Plant thorn
   Dart   Splinter
   Edge of stiff paper   Tin can lid
   Lathe turnings

   Excludes *animal spines or quills (E906.8)*
   flying glass due to explosion (E921.0-E923.9)

●❑ **E920.9 Unspecified cutting and piercing instrument or object**

● **E921 Accident caused by explosion of pressure vessel**

   Includes: accidental explosion of pressure vessels, whether or not part of machinery

   Excludes *explosion of pressure vessel on transport vehicle (E800.0-E845.9)*

● **E921.0 Boilers**

● **E921.1 Gas cylinders**
   Air tank   Pressure gas tank

●❑ **E921.8 Other specified pressure vessels**
   Aerosol can
   Automobile tire
   Pressure cooker

●❑ **E921.9 Unspecified pressure vessel**

● **E922 Accident caused by firearm and air gun missile**

● **E922.0 Handgun**
   Pistol
   Revolver

   Excludes *Very pistol (E922.8)*

● **E922.1 Shotgun (automatic)**

● **E922.2 Hunting rifle**

● **E922.3 Military firearms**
   Army rifle
   Machine gun

   E922.4 Air gun
   BB gun
   Pellet gun

●❑ **E922.8 Other specified firearm missile**
   Very pistol [flare]

●❑ **E922.9 Unspecified firearm missile**
   Gunshot wound NOS
   Shot NOS

● **E923 Accident caused by explosive material**

   Includes: flash burns and other injuries resulting from explosion of explosive material
   ignition of highly explosive material with explosion

   Excludes *explosion:*
   in or on machinery (E919.0-E919.9)
   on any transport vehicle, except stationary motor vehicle (E800.0-E848)
   with conflagration (E890.0, E891.0, E892)
   secondary fires resulting from explosion (E890.0-E899)

● **E923.0 Fireworks**

● **E923.1 Blasting materials**
   Blasting cap
   Detonator
   Dynamite
   Explosive [any] used in blasting operations

● **E923.2 Explosive gases**
   Acetylene
   Butane
   Coal gas
   Explosion in mine NOS
   Fire damp
   Gasoline fumes
   Methane
   Propane

●❑ **E923.8 Other explosive materials**
   Bomb
   Explosive missile
   Grenade
   Mine
   Shell
   Torpedo
   Explosion in munitions:
      dump
      factory

●❑ **E923.9 Unspecified explosive material**
   Explosion NOS

● **E924 Accident caused by hot substance or object, caustic or corrosive material, and steam**

   Excludes *burning NOS (E899)*
   chemical burn resulting from swallowing a corrosive substance (E860.0-E864.4)
   fire caused by these substances and objects (E890.0-E894)
   radiation burns (E926.0-E926.9)
   therapeutic misadventures (E870.0-E876.9)

● **E924.0 Hot liquids and vapors, including steam**
   Burning or scalding by:
      boiling water
      hot or boiling liquids not primarily caustic or corrosive
      liquid metal
      steam
      other hot vapor

   Excludes *hot (boiling) tap water (E924.2)*

● **E924.1 Caustic and corrosive substances**
   Burning by:
      acid [any kind]
      ammonia
      caustic oven cleaner or other substance
      corrosive substance
      lye
      vitriol

● **E924.2 Hot (boiling) tap water**

●❑ **E924.8 Other**
   Burning by:
      heat from electric heating appliance
      hot object NOS
      light bulb
      steam pipe

●❑ **E924.9 Unspecified**

● **E925 Accident caused by electric current**

   Includes: electric current from exposed wire, faulty appliance, high voltage cable, live rail, or open electric socket as the cause of:
   burn
   cardiac fibrillation
   convulsion
   electric shock
   electrocution
   puncture wound
   respiratory paralysis

   Excludes *burn by heat from electrical appliance (E924.8)*
   lightning (E907)

   ◀▶ **New Code**   ⬅▪▪ ▪▪➡ **Revised Code**   ● **Not a Principal Diagnosis**   ● **Use Additional Digit(s)**   ❑ **Nonspecific Code**

- ● **E925.0 Domestic wiring and appliances**
- ● **E925.1 Electric power generating plants, distribution stations, transmission lines**
  - Broken power line
- ● **E925.2 Industrial wiring, appliances, and electrical machinery**
  - Conductors
  - Control apparatus
  - Electrical equipment and machinery
  - Transformers
- ● □ **E925.8 Other electric current**
  - Wiring and appliances in or on:
    - farm [not farmhouse]
    - outdoors
    - public building
    - residential institutions
    - schools
- ● □ **E925.9 Unspecified electric current**
  - Burns or other injury from electric current NOS
  - Electric shock NOS
  - Electrocution NOS

● **E926 Exposure to radiation**

> **Excludes** *abnormal reaction to or complication of treatment without mention of misadventure (E879.2)*
> *atomic power plant malfunction in water transport (E838.0-E838.9)*
> *misadventure to patient in surgical and medical procedures (E873.2-E873.3)*
> *use of radiation in war operations (E996-E997.9)*

- ● **E926.0 Radiofrequency radiation**
  - Overexposure to:
    - microwave radiation from:
      - high-powered radio and television transmitters
      - industrial radiofrequency induction heaters
      - radar installations
    - radar radiation from:
      - high-powered radio and television transmitters
      - industrial radiofrequency induction heaters
      - radar installations
    - radiofrequency from:
      - high-powered radio and television transmitters
      - industrial radiofrequency induction heaters
      - radar installations
    - radiofrequency radiation [any] from:
      - high-powered radio and television transmitters
      - industrial radiofrequency induction heaters
      - radar installations
- ● **E926.1 Infra-red heaters and lamps**
  - Exposure to infra-red radiation from heaters and lamps as the cause of:
    - blistering
    - burning
    - charring
    - inflammatory change

> **Excludes** *physical contact with heater or lamp (E924.8)*

- ● **E926.2 Visible and ultraviolet light sources**
  - Arc lamps
  - Black light sources
  - Electrical welding arc
  - Oxygas welding torch
  - Sun rays

> **Excludes** *excessive heat from these sources (E900.1-E900.9)*

- ● **E926.3 X-rays and other electromagnetic ionizing radiation**
  - Gamma rays
  - X-rays (hard) (soft)
- ● **E926.4 Lasers**
- ● **E926.5 Radioactive isotopes**
  - Radiobiologicals
  - Radiopharmaceuticals
- ● □ **E926.8 Other specified radiation**
  - Artificially accelerated beams of ionized particles generated by:
    - betatrons
    - synchrotrons
- ● □ **E926.9 Unspecified radiation**
  - Radiation NOS

- ● **E927 Overexertion and strenuous movements**
  - Excessive physical exercise
  - Overexertion (from):
    - lifting
    - pulling
    - pushing
  - Strenuous movements in:
    - recreational activities
    - other activities

● **E928 Other and unspecified environmental and accidental causes**

- ● **E928.0 Prolonged stay in weightless environment**
  - Weightlessness in spacecraft (simulator)
- ● **E928.1 Exposure to noise**
  - Noise (pollution)
  - Sound waves
  - Supersonic waves
- ● **E928.2 Vibration**
- ● □ **E928.8 Other**
- ● □ **E928.9 Unspecified accident**
  - Accident NOS stated as accidentally inflicted
  - Blow NOS stated as accidentally inflicted
  - Casualty (not due to war) stated as accidentally inflicted
  - Decapitation stated as accidentally inflicted
  - Injury [any part of body, or unspecified] stated as accidentally inflicted, but not otherwise specified
  - Killed stated as accidentally inflicted, but not otherwise specified
  - Knocked down stated as accidentally inflicted, but not otherwise specified
  - Mangled stated as accidentally inflicted, but not otherwise specified
  - Wound stated as accidentally inflicted, but not otherwise specified

> **Excludes** *fracture, cause unspecified (E887)*
> *injuries undetermined whether accidentally or purposely inflicted (E980.0-E989)*

LATE EFFECTS OF ACCIDENTAL INJURY (E929)

Note: This category is to be used to indicate accidental injury as the cause of death or disability from late effects, which are themselves classifiable elsewhere. The "late effects" include conditions reported as such or as sequelae, which may occur at any time after the acute accidental injury.

●● **E929 Late effects of accidental injury**

> **Excludes** *late effects of:*
> *surgical and medical procedures (E870.0-E879.9)*
> *therapeutic use of drugs and medicines (E930.0-E949.9)*

● **E929.0 Late effects of motor vehicle accident**
Late effects of accidents classifiable to E810-E825

●☐ **E929.1 Late effects of other transport accident**
Late effects of accidents classifiable to E800-E807, E826-E838, E840-E848

● **E929.2 Late effects of accidental poisoning**
Late effects of accidents classifiable to E850-E858, E860-E869

● **E929.3 Late effects of accidental fall**
Late effects of accidents classifiable to E880-E888

● **E929.4 Late effects of accident caused by fire**
Late effects of accidents classifiable to E890-E899

● **E929.5 Late effects of accident due to natural and environmental factors**
Late effects of accidents classifiable to E900-E909

●☐ **E929.8 Late effects of other accidents**
Late effects of accidents classifiable to E910-E928.8

●☐ **E929.9 Late effects of unspecified accident**
Late effects of accidents classifiable to E928.9

DRUGS, MEDICINAL AND BIOLOGICAL SUBSTANCES CAUSING ADVERSE EFFECTS IN THERAPEUTIC USE (E930-E949)

> **Includes:** correct drug properly administered in therapeutic or prophylactic dosage, as the cause of any adverse effect including allergic or hypersensitivity reactions

> **Excludes** *accidental overdose of drug and wrong drug given or taken in error (E850.0-E858.9)*
> *accidents in the technique of administration of drug or biological substance such as accidental puncture during injection, or contamination of drug (E870.0-E876.9)*
> *administration with suicidal or homicidal intent or intent to harm, or in circumstances classifiable to E980-E989 (E950.0-E950.5, E962.0, E980.0-E980.5)*
> *See Alphabetic Index for more complete list of specific drugs to be classified under the fourth-digit subdivisions. The American Hospital Formulary numbers can be used to classify new drugs listed by the American Hospital Formulary Service (AHFS). See appendix C.*

●● **E930 Antibiotics**

> **Excludes** *that used as eye, ear, nose, and throat [ENT], and local anti-infectives (E946.0-E946.9)*

● **E930.0 Penicillins**
Natural
Synthetic
Semisynthetic, such as:
  ampicillin
  cloxacillin
  nafcillin
  oxacillin

● **E930.1 Antifungal antibiotics**
Amphotericin B
Griseofulvin
Hachimycin [trichomycin]
Nystatin

● **E930.2 Chloramphenicol group**
Chloramphenicol   Thiamphenicol

● **E930.3 Erythromycin and other macrolides**
Oleandomycin   Spiramycin

● **E930.4 Tetracycline group**
Doxycycline   Oxytetracycline
Minocycline

● **E930.5 Cephalosporin group**
Cephalexin
Cephaloglycin
Cephaloridine
Cephalothin

● **E930.6 Antimycobacterial antibiotics**
Cycloserine
Kanamycin
Rifampin
Streptomycin

● **E930.7 Antineoplastic antibiotics**
Actinomycins, such as:
  Bleomycin
  Cactinomycin
  Dactinomycin
  Daunorubicin
  Mitomycin

> **Excludes** *other antineoplastic drugs (E933.1)*

     ◀▶ **New Code**   ⬅▥▶ **Revised Code**   ● **Not a Principal Diagnosis**   ● **Use Additional Digit(s)**   ☐ **Nonspecific Code**

● ☐ **E930.8 Other specified antibiotics**

● ☐ **E930.9 Unspecified antibiotic**

●● ● **E931 Other anti-infectives**

> **Excludes** *ENT, and local anti-infectives (E946.0-E946.9)*

● **E931.0 Sulfonamides**
    Sulfadiazine
    Sulfafurazole
    Sulfamethoxazole

● **E931.1 Arsenical anti-infectives**

● **E931.2 Heavy metal anti-infectives**
    Compounds of:
      antimony
      bismuth
      lead
      mercury

> **Excludes** *mercurial diuretics (E944.0)*

● **E931.3 Quinoline and hydroxyquinoline derivatives**
    Chiniofon
    Diiodohydroxyquin

> **Excludes** *antimalarial drugs (E931.4)*

● **E931.4 Antimalarials and drugs acting on other blood protozoa**
    Chloroquine phosphate
    Cycloguanil
    Primaquine
    Proguanil [chloroguanide]
    Pyrimethamine
    Quinine (sulphate)

● ☐ **E931.5 Other antiprotozoal drugs**
    Emetine

● **E931.6 Anthelmintics**
    Hexylresorcinol
    Male fern oleoresin
    Piperazine
    Thiabendazole

● **E931.7 Antiviral drugs**
    Methisazone

> **Excludes** *amantadine (E936.4)*
> *cytarabine (E933.1)*
> *idoxuridine (E946.5)*

● ☐ **E931.8 Other antimycobacterial drugs**
    Ethambutol
    Ethionamide
    Isoniazid
    Para-aminosalicylic acid derivatives
    Sulfones

● ☐ **E931.9 Other and unspecified anti-infectives**
    Flucytosine
    Nitrofuran derivatives

●● ● **E932 Hormones and synthetic substitutes**

● **E932.0 Adrenal cortical steroids**
    Cortisone derivatives
    Desoxycorticosterone derivatives
    Fluorinated corticosteroids

● **E932.1 Androgens and anabolic congeners**
    Nandrolone phenpropionate
    Oxymetholone
    Testosterone and preparations

● **E932.2 Ovarian hormones and synthetic substitutes**
    Contraceptives, oral
    Estrogens
    Estrogens and progestogens combined
    Progestogens

● **E932.3 Insulins and antidiabetic agents**
    Acetohexamide
    Biguanide derivatives, oral
    Chlorpropamide
    Glucagon
    Insulin
    Phenformin
    Sulfonylurea derivatives, oral
    Tolbutamide

> **Excludes** *adverse effect of insulin administered for shock therapy (E879.3)*

● **E932.4 Anterior pituitary hormones**
    Corticotropin
    Gonadotropin
    Somatotropin [growth hormone]

● **E932.5 Posterior pituitary hormones**
    Vasopressin

> **Excludes** *oxytocic agents (E945.0)*

● **E932.6 Parathyroid and parathyroid derivatives**

● **E932.7 Thyroid and thyroid derivatives**
    Dextrothyroxine
    Levothyroxine sodium
    Liothyronine
    Thyroglobulin

● **E932.8 Antithyroid agents**
    Iodides
    Thiouracil
    Thiourea

● ☐ **E932.9 Other and unspecified hormones and synthetic substitutes**

●● ● **E933 Primarily systemic agents**

● **E933.0 Antiallergic and antiemetic drugs**
    Antihistamines
    Chlorpheniramine
    Diphenhydramine
    Diphenylpyraline
    Thonzylamine
    Tripelennamine

> **Excludes** *phenothiazine-based tranquilizers (E939.1)*

● **E933.1 Antineoplastic and immunosuppressive drugs**
    Azathioprine
    Busulfan
    Chlorambucil
    Cyclophosphamide
    Cytarabine
    Fluorouracil
    Mechlorethamine hydrochloride
    Mercaptopurine
    Triethylenethiophosphoramide [thio-TEPA]

> **Excludes** *antineoplastic antibiotics (E930.7)*

● **E933.2 Acidifying agents**

● **E933.3 Alkalizing agents**

● **E933.4 Enzymes, not elsewhere classified**
    Penicillinase

● **E933.5 Vitamins, not elsewhere classified**
    Vitamin A
    Vitamin D

> **Excludes** *nicotinic acid (E942.2)*
> *vitamin K (E934.3)*

● ☐ **E933.8 Other systemic agents, not elsewhere classified**
    Heavy metal antagonists

● ☐ **E933.9 Unspecified systemic agent**

●● **E934 Agents primarily affecting blood constituents**

● **E934.0 Iron and its compounds**
　　Ferric salts
　　Ferrous sulphate and other ferrous salts

●☐ **E934.1 Liver preparations and other antianemic agents**
　　Folic acid

● **E934.2 Anticoagulants**
　　Coumarin
　　Heparin
　　Phenindione
　　Prothrombin synthesis inhibitor
　　Warfarin sodium

● **E934.3 Vitamin K [phytonadione]**

● **E934.4 Fibrinolysis-affecting drugs**
　　Aminocaproic acid
　　Streptodornase
　　Streptokinase
　　Urokinase

●☐ **E934.5 Anticoagulant antagonists and other coagulants**
　　Hexadimethrine bromide
　　Protamine sulfate

● **E934.6 Gamma globulin**

● **E934.7 Natural blood and blood products**
　　Blood plasma
　　Human fibrinogen
　　Packed red cells
　　Whole blood

●☐ **E934.8 Other agents affecting blood constituents**
　　Macromolecular blood substitutes

●☐ **E934.9 Unspecified agent affecting blood constituents**

●● **E935 Analgesics, antipyretics, and antirheumatics**

● **E935.0 Heroin**
　　Diacetylmorphine

● **E935.1 Methadone**

●☐ **E935.2 Other opiates and related narcotics**
　　Codeine [methylmorphine]
　　Morphine
　　Opium (alkaloids)
　　Meperidine [pethidine]

● **E935.3 Salicylates**
　　Acetylsalicylic acid [aspirin]
　　Amino derivatives of salicylic acid
　　Salicylic acid salts

● **E935.4 Aromatic analgesics, not elsewhere classified**
　　Acetanilid
　　Paracetamol [acetaminophen]
　　Phenacetin [acetophenetidin]

● **E935.5 Pyrazole derivatives**
　　Aminophenazone [aminopyrine]
　　Phenylbutazone

● **E935.6 Antirheumatics [antiphlogistics]**
　　Gold salts
　　Indomethacin

Excludes	salicylates (E935.3)
	steroids (E932.0)

●☐ **E935.7 Other non-narcotic analgesics**
　　Pyrabital

●☐ **E935.8 Other specified analgesics and antipyretics**
　　Pentazocine

●☐ **E935.9 Unspecified analgesic and antipyretic**

●● **E936 Anticonvulsants and anti-Parkinsonism drugs**

● **E936.0 Oxazolidine derivatives**
　　Paramethadione
　　Trimethadione

● **E936.1 Hydantoin derivatives**
　　Phenytoin

● **E936.2 Succinimides**
　　Ethosuximide
　　Phensuximide

●☐ **E936.3 Other and unspecified anticonvulsants**
　　Beclamide
　　Primidone

● **E936.4 Anti-Parkinsonism drugs**
　　Amantadine
　　Ethopropazine [profenamine]
　　Levodopa [L-dopa]

●● **E937 Sedatives and hypnotics**

● **E937.0 Barbiturates**
　　Amobarbital [amylobarbitone]
　　Barbital [barbitone]
　　Butabarbital [butabarbitone]
　　Pentobarbital [pentobarbitone]
　　Phenobarbital [phenobarbitone]
　　Secobarbital [quinalbarbitone]

Excludes	thiobarbiturates (E938.3)

● **E937.1 Chloral hydrate group**

● **E937.2 Paraldehyde**

● **E937.3 Bromine compounds**
　　Bromide
　　Carbromal (derivatives)

● **E937.4 Methaqualone compounds**

● **E937.5 Glutethimide group**

● **E937.6 Mixed sedatives, not elsewhere classified**

●☐ **E937.8 Other sedatives and hypnotics**

●☐ **E937.9 Unspecified**
　　Sleeping:
　　　　drug NOS
　　　　pill NOS
　　　　tablet NOS

●● **E938 Other central nervous system depressants and anesthetics**

● **E938.0 Central nervous system muscle-tone depressants**
　　Chlorphenesin (carbamate)
　　Mephenesin
　　Methocarbamol

● **E938.1 Halothane**

●☐ **E938.2 Other gaseous anesthetics**
　　Ether
　　Halogenated hydrocarbon derivatives, except halothane
　　Nitrous oxide

● **E938.3 Intravenous anesthetics**
　　Ketamine
　　Methohexital [methohexitone]
　　Thiobarbiturates, such as thiopental sodium

　◀▶ **New Code**　　⬅■➡ **Revised Code**　　● **Not a Principal Diagnosis**　　● **Use Additional Digit(s)**　　☐ **Nonspecific Code**

- ● ☐ **E938.4 Other and unspecified general anesthetics**

- ● **E938.5 Surface and infiltration anesthetics**
  Cocaine
  Lidocaine [lignocaine]
  Procaine
  Tetracaine

- ● **E938.6 Peripheral nerve- and plexus-blocking anesthetics**

- ● **E938.7 Spinal anesthetics**

- ● ☐ **E938.9 Other and unspecified local anesthetics**

● ● **E939 Psychotropic agents**

- ● **E939.0 Antidepressants**
  Amitriptyline
  Imipramine
  Monoamine oxidase [MAO] inhibitors

- ● **E939.1 Phenothiazine-based tranquilizers**
  Chlorpromazine
  Fluphenazine
  Phenothiazine
  Prochlorperazine
  Promazine

- ● **E939.2 Butyrophenone-based tranquilizers**
  Haloperidol
  Spiperone
  Trifluperidol

- ● ☐ **E939.3 Other antipsychotics, neuroleptics, and major tranquilizers**

- ● **E939.4 Benzodiazepine-based tranquilizers**
  Chlordiazepoxide
  Diazepam
  Flurazepam
  Lorazepam
  Medazepam
  Nitrazepam

- ● ☐ **E939.5 Other tranquilizers**
  Hydroxyzine
  Meprobamate

- ● **E939.6 Psychodysleptics [hallucinogens]**
  Cannabis (derivatives)
  Lysergide [LSD]
  Marihuana (derivatives)
  Mescaline
  Psilocin
  Psilocybin

- ● **E939.7 Psychostimulants**
  Amphetamine
  Caffeine
  Excludes *central appetite depressants (E947.0)*

- ● ☐ **E939.8 Other psychotropic agents**

- ● ☐ **E939.9 Unspecified psychotropic agent**

● ● **E940 Central nervous system stimulants**

- ● **E940.0 Analeptics**
  Lobeline
  Nikethamide

- ● **E940.1 Opiate antagonists**
  Levallorphan
  Nalorphine
  Naloxone

- ● ☐ **E940.8 Other specified central nervous system stimulants**

- ● ☐ **E940.9 Unspecified central nervous system stimulant**

● ● **E941 Drugs primarily affecting the autonomic nervous system**

- ● **E941.0 Parasympathomimetics [cholinergics]**
  Acetylcholine
  Anticholinesterase:
    organophosphorus
    reversible
  Pilocarpine

- ● **E941.1 Parasympatholytics [anticholinergics and antimuscarinics] and spasmolytics**
  Atropine
  Homatropine
  Hyoscine [scopolamine]
  Quaternary ammonium derivatives
  Excludes *papaverine (E942.5)*

- ● **E941.2 Sympathomimetics [adrenergics]**
  Epinephrine [adrenalin]
  Levarterenol [noradrenalin]

- ● **E941.3 Sympatholytics [antiadrenergics]**
  Phenoxybenzamine
  Tolazoline hydrochloride

- ● ☐ **E941.9 Unspecified drug primarily affecting the autonomic nervous system**

● ● **E942 Agents primarily affecting the cardiovascular system**

- ● **E942.0 Cardiac rhythm regulators**
  Practolol
  Procainamide
  Propranolol
  Quinidine

- ● **E942.1 Cardiotonic glycosides and drugs of similar action**
  Digitalis glycosides
  Digoxin
  Strophanthins

- ● **E942.2 Antilipemic and antiarteriosclerotic drugs**
  Cholestyramine
  Clofibrate
  Nicotinic acid derivatives
  Sitosterols
  Excludes *dextrothyroxine (E932.7)*

- ● **E942.3 Ganglion-blocking agents**
  Pentamethonium bromide

- ● **E942.4 Coronary vasodilators**
  Dipyridamole
  Nitrates [nitroglycerin]
  Nitrites
  Prenylamine

- ● ☐ **E942.5 Other vasodilators**
  Cyclandelate
  Diazoxide
  Hydralazine
  Papaverine

- ● ☐ **E942.6 Other antihypertensive agents**
  Clonidine
  Guanethidine
  Rauwolfia alkaloids
  Reserpine

- ● **E942.7 Antivaricose drugs, including sclerosing agents**
  Monoethanolamine
  Zinc salts

ICD-9-CM

E900–E999

Vol. 1

◄ ► **New Code**   ⬅▦➡ **Revised Code**   ● **Not a Principal Diagnosis**   ● **Use Additional Digit(s)**   ☐ **Nonspecific Code**

● E942.8 **Capillary-active drugs**
    Adrenochrome derivatives
    Bioflavonoids
    Metaraminol

●□ E942.9 **Other and unspecified agents primarily affecting the cardiovascular system**

●● E943 **Agents primarily affecting gastrointestinal system**

● E943.0 **Antacids and antigastric secretion drugs**
    Aluminum hydroxide
    Magnesium trisilicate

● E943.1 **Irritant cathartics**
    Bisacodyl
    Castor oil
    Phenolphthalein

● E943.2 **Emollient cathartics**
    Sodium dioctyl sulfosuccinate

●□ E943.3 **Other cathartics, including intestinal atonia drugs**
    Magnesium sulfate

● E943.4 **Digestants**
    Pancreatin
    Papain
    Pepsin

● E943.5 **Antidiarrheal drugs**
    Bismuth subcarbonate
    Kaolin
    Pectin

Excludes *anti-infectives (E930.0-E931.9)*

● E943.6 **Emetics**

●□ E943.8 **Other specified agents primarily affecting the gastrointestinal system**

●□ E943.9 **Unspecified agent primarily affecting the gastrointestinal system**

●● E944 **Water, mineral, and uric acid metabolism drugs**

● E944.0 **Mercurial diuretics**
    Chlormerodrin
    Mercaptomerin
    Mercurophylline
    Mersalyl

● E944.1 **Purine derivative diuretics**
    Theobromine
    Theophylline

Excludes *aminophylline [theophylline ethylenediamine] (E945.7)*

● E944.2 **Carbonic acid anhydrase inhibitors**
    Acetazolamide

● E944.3 **Saluretics**
    Benzothiadiazides
    Chlorothiazide group

●□ E944.4 **Other diuretics**
    Ethacrynic acid
    Furosemide

● E944.5 **Electrolytic, caloric, and water-balance agents**

●□ E944.6 **Other mineral salts, not elsewhere classified**

● E944.7 **Uric acid metabolism drugs**
    Cinchophen and congeners
    Colchicine
    Phenoquin
    Probenecid

●● E945 **Agents primarily acting on the smooth and skeletal muscles and respiratory system**

● E945.0 **Oxytocic agents**
    Ergot alkaloids
    Prostaglandins

● E945.1 **Smooth muscle relaxants**
    Adiphenine
    Metaproterenol [orciprenaline]

Excludes *papaverine (E942.5)*

● E945.2 **Skeletal muscle relaxants**
    Alcuronium chloride
    Suxamethonium chloride

●□ E945.3 **Other and unspecified drugs acting on muscles**

● E945.4 **Antitussives**
    Dextromethorphan
    Pipazethate hydrochloride

● E945.5 **Expectorants**
    Acetylcysteine
    Cocillana
    Guaifenesin [glyceryl guaiacolate]
    Ipecacuanha
    Terpin hydrate

● E945.6 **Anti-common cold drugs**

● E945.7 **Antiasthmatics**
    Aminophylline [theophylline ethylenediamine]

●□ E945.8 **Other and unspecified respiratory drugs**

●● E946 **Agents primarily affecting skin and mucous membrane, ophthalmological, otorhinolaryngological, and dental drugs**

● E946.0 **Local anti-infectives and anti-inflammatory drugs**

● E946.1 **Antipruritics**

● E946.2 **Local astringents and local detergents**

● E946.3 **Emollients, demulcents, and protectants**

● E946.4 **Keratolytics, keratoplastics, other hair treatment drugs and preparations**

● E946.5 **Eye anti-infectives and other eye drugs**
    Idoxuridine

● E946.6 **Anti-infectives and other drugs and preparations for ear, nose, and throat**

● E946.7 **Dental drugs topically applied**

●□ E946.8 **Other agents primarily affecting skin and mucous membrane**
    Spermicides

●□ E946.9 **Unspecified agent primarily affecting skin and mucous membrane**

●● E947 **Other and unspecified drugs and medicinal substances**

● E947.0 **Dietetics**

● E947.1 **Lipotropic drugs**

● E947.2 **Antidotes and chelating agents, not elsewhere classified**

● E947.3 **Alcohol deterrents**

● E947.4 **Pharmaceutical excipients**

   ◀▶ **New Code**   ⬅▬ ▬➡ **Revised Code**   ● **Not a Principal Diagnosis**   ● **Use Additional Digit(s)**   □ **Nonspecific Code**

● □ **E947.8 Other drugs and medicinal substances**
    Contrast media used for diagnostic x-ray procedures
    Diagnostic agents and kits

● □ **E947.9 Unspecified drug or medicinal substance**

●● **E948 Bacterial vaccines**

● **E948.0 BCG vaccine**

● **E948.1 Typhoid and paratyphoid**

● **E948.2 Cholera**

● **E948.3 Plague**

● **E948.4 Tetanus**

● **E948.5 Diphtheria**

● **E948.6 Pertussis vaccine, including combinations with a pertussis component**

● □ **E948.8 Other and unspecified bacterial vaccines**

● **E948.9 Mixed bacterial vaccines, except combinations with a pertussis component**

●● **E949 Other vaccines and biological substances**

> **Excludes** *gamma globulin (E934.6)*

● **E949.0 Smallpox vaccine**

● **E949.1 Rabies vaccine**

● **E949.2 Typhus vaccine**

● **E949.3 Yellow fever vaccine**

● **E949.4 Measles vaccine**

● **E949.5 Poliomyelitis vaccine**

● □ **E949.6 Other and unspecified viral and rickettsial vaccines**
    Mumps vaccine

● **E949.7 Mixed viral-rickettsial and bacterial vaccines, except combinations with a pertussis component**

> **Excludes** *combinations with a pertussis component (E948.6)*

● □ **E949.9 Other and unspecified vaccines and biological substances**

SUICIDE AND SELF-INFLICTED INJURY (E950-E959)

Includes: injuries in suicide and attempted suicide
self-inflicted injuries specified as intentional

●● **E950 Suicide and self-inflicted poisoning by solid or liquid substances**

● **E950.0 Analgesics, antipyretics, and antirheumatics**

● **E950.1 Barbiturates**

● □ **E950.2 Other sedatives and hypnotics**

● **E950.3 Tranquilizers and other psychotropic agents**

● □ **E950.4 Other specified drugs and medicinal substances**

● □ **E950.5 Unspecified drug or medicinal substance**

● **E950.6 Agricultural and horticultural chemical and pharmaceutical preparations other than plant foods and fertilizers**

● **E950.7 Corrosive and caustic substances**
    Suicide and self-inflicted poisoning by substances classifiable to E864

● □ **E950.8 Arsenic and its compounds**

● □ **E950.9 Other and unspecified solid and liquid substances**

●● **E951 Suicide and self-inflicted poisoning by gases in domestic use**

● **E951.0 Gas distributed by pipeline**

● **E951.1 Liquefied petroleum gas distributed in mobile containers**

● □ **E951.8 Other utility gas**

●● **E952 Suicide and self-inflicted poisoning by other gases and vapors**

● **E952.0 Motor vehicle exhaust gas**

● □ **E952.1 Other carbon monoxide**

● □ **E952.8 Other specified gases and vapors**

● □ **E952.9 Unspecified gases and vapors**

●● **E953 Suicide and self-inflicted injury by hanging, strangulation, and suffocation**

● **E953.0 Hanging**

● **E953.1 Suffocation by plastic bag**

● □ **E953.8 Other specified means**

● □ **E953.9 Unspecified means**

● **E954 Suicide and self-inflicted injury by submersion [drowning]**

●● **E955 Suicide and self-inflicted injury by firearms, air guns and explosives**

● **E955.0 Handgun**

● **E955.1 Shotgun**

● **E955.2 Hunting rifle**

● **E955.3 Military firearms**

● □ **E955.4 Other and unspecified firearm**
    Gunshot NOS
    Shot NOS

● **E955.5 Explosives**

● **E955.6 Air gun**
    BB gun
    Pellet gun

● □ **E955.9 Unspecified**

● **E956 Suicide and self-inflicted injury by cutting and piercing instrument**

●● **E957 Suicide and self-inflicted injuries by jumping from high place**

● **E957.0 Residential premises**

● □ **E957.1 Other man-made structures**

● **E957.2 Natural sites**

● □ **E957.9 Unspecified**

●● **E958 Suicide and self-inflicted injury by other and unspecified means**

● **E958.0 Jumping or lying before moving object**

● **E958.1 Burns, fire**

● **E958.2 Scald**

● **E958.3 Extremes of cold**

● **E958.4 Electrocution**

● **E958.5 Crashing of motor vehicle**

ICD-9-CM
**E900-
E999**
Vol. 1

● **E958.6**   **Crashing of aircraft**

● **E958.7**   **Caustic substances, except poisoning**

     Excludes   *poisoning by caustic substance (E950.7)*

●□ **E958.8**   **Other specified means**

●□ **E958.9**   **Unspecified means**

●● **E959**   **Late effects of self-inflicted injury**

     Note: This category is to be used to indicate circumstances classifiable to E950-E958 as the cause of death or disability from late effects, which are themselves classifiable elsewhere. The "late effects" include conditions reported as such or as sequelae which may occur at any time after the attempted suicide or self-inflicted injury.

HOMICIDE AND INJURY PURPOSELY INFLICTED BY OTHER PERSONS (E960-E969)

     Includes: injuries inflicted by another person with intent to injure or kill, by any means

     Excludes   *injuries due to:*
         legal intervention (E970-E978)
         operations of war (E990-E999)

●● **E960**   **Fight, brawl, rape**

● **E960.0**   **Unarmed fight or brawl**
     Beatings NOS
     Brawl or fight with hands, fists, feet
     Injured or killed in fight NOS

     Excludes   *homicidal:*
         injury by weapons (E965.0-E966, E969)
         strangulation (E963)
         submersion (E964)

● **E960.1**   **Rape**

● **E961**   **Assault by corrosive or caustic substance, except poisoning**
     Injury or death purposely caused by corrosive or caustic substance, such as:
     acid [any]
     corrosive substance
     vitriol

     Excludes   *burns from hot liquid (E968.3)*
         chemical burns from swallowing a corrosive substance (E962.0-E962.9)

●● **E962**   **Assault by poisoning**

● **E962.0**   **Drugs and medicinal substances**
     Homicidal poisoning by any drug or medicinal substance

●□ **E962.1**   **Other solid and liquid substances**

●□ **E962.2**   **Other gases and vapors**

●□ **E962.9**   **Unspecified poisoning**

● **E963**   **Assault by hanging and strangulation**
     Homicidal (attempt):
     garrotting or ligature
     hanging
     strangulation
     suffocation

● **E964**   **Assault by submersion [drowning]**

●● **E965**   **Assault by firearms and explosives**

● **E965.0**   **Handgun**
     Pistol
     Revolver

● **E965.1**   **Shotgun**

● **E965.2**   **Hunting rifle**

● **E965.3**   **Military firearms**

●□ **E965.4**   **Other and unspecified firearm**

● **E965.5**   **Antipersonnel bomb**

● **E965.6**   **Gasoline bomb**

● **E965.7**   **Letter bomb**

●□ **E965.8**   **Other specified explosive**
     Bomb NOS (placed in):
       car
       house
     Dynamite

●□ **E965.9**   **Unspecified explosive**

● **E966**   **Assault by cutting and piercing instrument**
     Assassination (attempt), homicide (attempt) by any instrument classifiable under E920
     Homicidal:
     cut any part of body
     puncture any part of body
     stab any part of body
     Stabbed any part of body

●● **E967**   **Child and adult battering and other maltreatment**

● **E967.0**   **By father or stepfather**

●□ **E967.1**   **By other specified person**

● **E967.2**   **By mother or stepmother**

● **E967.3**   **By spouse or partner**
     Ex-spouse
     Ex-partner

● **E967.4**   **By child**

● **E967.5**   **By sibling**

● **E967.6**   **By grandparent**

●□ **E967.7**   **By other relative**

●□ **E967.8**   **By non-related caregiver**

●□ **E967.9**   **By unspecified person**

●● **E968**   **Assault by other and unspecified means**

● **E968.0**   **Fire**
     Arson
     Homicidal burns NOS

     Excludes   *burns from hot liquid (E968.3)*

● **E968.1**   **Pushing from a high place**

● **E968.2**   **Striking by blunt or thrown object**

● **E968.3**   **Hot liquid**
     Homicidal burns by scalding

● **E968.4**   **Criminal neglect**
     Abandonment of child, infant, or other helpless person with intent to injure or kill

● **E968.5**   **Transport vehicle**
     Being struck by other vehicle or run down with intent to injure
     Pushed in front of, thrown from, or dragged by moving vehicle with intent to injure

● **E968.6**   **Air gun**
     BB gun
     Pellet gun

●□ **E968.8**   **Other specified means**
     Bite of human being

◀▶ **New Code**   ⬛➡ **Revised Code**   ● **Not a Principal Diagnosis**   ● **Use Additional Digit(s)**   □ **Nonspecific Code**

● ☐ **E968.9 Unspecified means**
Assassination (attempt) NOS
Homicidal (attempt):
  injury NOS
  wound NOS
Manslaughter (nonaccidental)
Murder (attempt) NOS
Violence, non-accidental

● **E969 Late effects of injury purposely inflicted by other person**

Note: This category is to be used to indicate circumstances classifiable to E960-E968 as the cause of death or disability from late effects, which are themselves classifiable elsewhere. The "late effects" include conditions reported as such, or as sequelae which may occur at any time after the injury purposely inflicted by another person.

LEGAL INTERVENTION (E970-E978)

Includes: injuries inflicted by the police or other law-enforcing agents, including military on duty, in the course of arresting or attempting to arrest lawbreakers, suppressing disturbances, maintaining order, and other legal action
legal execution

Excludes *injuries caused by civil insurrections (E990.0-E999)*

● **E970 Injury due to legal intervention by firearms**
Gunshot wound
Injury by:
  machine gun
  revolver
  rifle pellet or rubber bullet
  shot NOS

● **E971 Injury due to legal intervention by explosives**
Injury by:
  dynamite
  explosive shell
  grenade
  motor bomb

● **E972 Injury due to legal intervention by gas**
Asphyxiation by gas
Injury by tear gas
Poisoning by gas

● **E973 Injury due to legal intervention by blunt object**
Hit, struck by:
  baton (nightstick)
  blunt object
  stave

● **E974 Injury due to legal intervention by cutting and piercing instrument**
Cut
Incised wound
Injured by bayonet
Stab wound

● ☐ **E975 Injury due to legal intervention by other specified means**
Blow
Manhandling

● ☐ **E976 Injury due to legal intervention by unspecified means**

● **E977 Late effects of injuries due to legal intervention**

Note: This category is to be used to indicate circumstances classifiable to E970-E976 as the cause of death or disability from late effects, which are themselves classifiable elsewhere. The "late effects" include conditions reported as such, or as sequelae which may occur at any time after the injury due to legal intervention.

● **E978 Legal execution**
All executions performed at the behest of the judiciary or ruling authority [whether permanent or temporary] as:
asphyxiation by gas
beheading, decapitation (by guillotine)
capital punishment
electrocution
hanging
poisoning
shooting
other specified means

INJURY UNDETERMINED WHETHER ACCIDENTALLY OR PURPOSELY INFLICTED (E980-E989)

Note: Categories E980-E989 are for use when it is unspecified or it cannot be determined whether the injuries are accidental (unintentional), suicide (attempted), or assault.

● ● **E980 Poisoning by solid or liquid substances, undetermined whether accidentally or purposely inflicted**

● **E980.0 Analgesics, antipyretics, and antirheumatics**

● **E980.1 Barbiturates**

● ☐ **E980.2 Other sedatives and hypnotics**

● **E980.3 Tranquilizers and other psychotropic agents**

● ☐ **E980.4 Other specified drugs and medicinal substances**

● ☐ **E980.5 Unspecified drug or medicinal substance**

● **E980.6 Corrosive and caustic substances**
Poisoning, undetermined whether accidental or purposeful, by substances classifiable to E864

● **E980.7 Agricultural and horticultural chemical and pharmaceutical preparations other than plant foods and fertilizers**

● **E980.8 Arsenic and its compounds**

● ☐ **E980.9 Other and unspecified solid and liquid substances**

● ● **E981 Poisoning by gases in domestic use, undetermined whether accidentally or purposely inflicted**

● **E981.0 Gas distributed by pipeline**

● **E981.1 Liquefied petroleum gas distributed in mobile containers**

● ☐ **E981.8 Other utility gas**

● ● **E982 Poisoning by other gases, undetermined whether accidentally or purposely inflicted**

● **E982.0 Motor vehicle exhaust gas**

● ☐ **E982.1 Other carbon monoxide**

● ☐ **E982.8 Other specified gases and vapors**

● ☐ **E982.9 Unspecified gases and vapors**

● ● **E983 Hanging, strangulation, or suffocation, undetermined whether accidentally or purposely inflicted**

ICD-9-CM
E900-
E999
Vol. 1

- ● E983.0 Hanging
- ● E983.1 Suffocation by plastic bag
- ●☐ E983.8 Other specified means
- ●☐ E983.9 Unspecified means

- ● E984 Submersion [drowning], undetermined whether accidentally or purposely inflicted

- ● E985 Injury by firearms, air guns and explosives, undetermined whether accidentally or purposely inflicted

  - ● E985.0 Handgun
  - ● E985.1 Shotgun
  - ● E985.2 Hunting rifle
  - ● E985.3 Military firearms
  - ●☐ E985.4 Other and unspecified firearm
  - ● E985.5 Explosives
  - ● E985.6 Air gun
    BB gun
    Pellet gun

- ● E986 Injury by cutting and piercing instruments, undetermined whether accidentally or purposely inflicted

- ●● E987 Falling from high place, undetermined whether accidentally or purposely inflicted

  - ● E987.0 Residential premises
  - ●☐ E987.1 Other man-made structures
  - ● E987.2 Natural sites
  - ●☐ E987.9 Unspecified site

- ●● E988 Injury by other and unspecified means, undetermined whether accidentally or purposely inflicted

  - ● E988.0 Jumping or lying before moving object
  - ● E988.1 Burns, fire
  - ● E988.2 Scald
  - ● E988.3 Extremes of cold
  - ● E988.4 Electrocution
  - ● E988.5 Crashing of motor vehicle
  - ● E988.6 Crashing of aircraft
  - ● E988.7 Caustic substances, except poisoning
  - ●☐ E988.8 Other specified means
  - ●☐ E988.9 Unspecified means

- ● E989 Late effects of injury, undetermined whether accidentally or purposely inflicted

  Note: This category is to be used to indicate circumstances classifiable to E980-E988 as the cause of death or disability from late effects, which are themselves classifiable elsewhere. The "late effects" include conditions reported as such or as sequelae which may occur at any time after injury, undetermined whether accidentally or purposely inflicted.

INJURY RESULTING FROM OPERATIONS OF WAR (E990-E999)

Includes: injuries to military personnel and civilians caused by war and civil insurrections and occurring during the time of war and insurrection

Excludes *accidents during training of military personnel, manufacture of war material and transport, unless attributable to enemy action*

- ●● E990 Injury due to war operations by fires and conflagrations

  Includes: asphyxia, burns, or other injury originating from fire caused by a fire-producing device or indirectly by any conventional weapon

  - ● E990.0 From gasoline bomb
  - ●☐ E990.9 From other and unspecified source

- ●● E991 Injury due to war operations by bullets and fragments

  - ● E991.0 Rubber bullets (rifle)
  - ● E991.1 Pellets (rifle)
  - ●☐ E991.2 Other bullets
    Bullet [any, except rubber bullets and pellets]
    carbine
    machine gun
    pistol
    rifle
    shotgun
  - ● E991.3 Antipersonnel bomb (fragments)
  - ●☐ E991.9 Other and unspecified fragments
    Fragments from:
    artillery shell
    bombs, except antipersonnel
    grenade
    guided missile
    land mine
    rockets
    shell
    Shrapnel

- ● E992 Injury due to war operations by explosion of marine weapons
    Depth charge
    Marine mines
    Mine NOS, at sea or in harbor
    Sea-based artillery shell
    Torpedo
    Underwater blast

- ●☐ E993 Injury due to war operations by other explosion
    Accidental explosion of munitions being used in war
    Accidental explosion of own weapons
    Air blast NOS
    Blast NOS
    Explosion NOS
    Explosion of:
    artillery shell
    breech block
    cannon block
    mortar bomb
    Injury by weapon burst

- ● E994 Injury due to war operations by destruction of aircraft
    Airplane:
    burned
    exploded
    shot down
    Crushed by falling airplane

- ●☐ E995 Injury due to war operations by other and unspecified forms of conventional warfare
    Battle wounds
    Bayonet injury
    Drowned in war operations

   ◀▶ **New Code**   ⬅▥➡ **Revised Code**   ● **Not a Principal Diagnosis**   ● **Use Additional Digit(s)**   ☐ **Nonspecific Code**

● **E996 Injury due to war operations by nuclear weapons**
Blast effects
Exposure to ionizing radiation from nuclear weapons
Fireball effects
Heat
Other direct and secondary effects of nuclear weapons

●● **E997 Injury due to war operations by other forms of unconventional warfare**

  ● **E997.0 Lasers**

  ● **E997.1 Biological warfare**

  ● **E997.2 Gases, fumes, and chemicals**

  ●□ **E997.8 Other specified forms of unconventional warfare**

  ●□ **E997.9 Unspecified form of unconventional warfare**

● **E998 Injury due to war operations but occurring after cessation of hostilities**
Injuries due to operations of war but occurring after cessation of hostilities by any means classifiable under E990-E997
Injuries by explosion of bombs or mines placed in the course of operations of war, if the explosion occurred after cessation of hostilities

● **E999 Late effect of injury due to war operations**

Note: This category is to be used to indicate circumstances classifiable to E990-E998 as the cause of death or disability from late effects, which are themselves classifiable elsewhere. The "late effects" include conditions reported as such or as sequelae which may occur at any time after injury resulting from operations of war.

ICD-9-CM

**E900-
E999**

Vol. 1

MORPHOLOGY OF NEOPLASMS

The World Health Organization has published an adaptation of the International Classification of Diseases for Oncology (ICD-O). It contains a coded nomenclature for the morphology of neoplasms, which is reproduced here for those who wish to use it in conjunction with Chapter 2 of the International Classification of Diseases, 9th Revision, Clinical Modification.

The morphology code numbers consist of five digits; the first four identify the histological type of the neoplasm and the fifth indicates its behavior. The one-digit behavior code is as follows:

/0 Benign
/1 Uncertain whether benign or malignant
    Borderline malignancy
/2 Carcinoma in situ
    Intraepithelial
    Noninfiltrating
    Noninvasive
/3 Malignant, primary site
/6 Malignant, metastatic site
    Secondary site
/9 Malignant, uncertain whether primary or metastatic site

In the nomenclature below, the morphology code numbers include the behavior code appropriate to the histological type of neoplasm, but this behavior code should be changed if other reported information makes this necessary. For example, "chordoma (M9370/3)" is assumed to be malignant; the term "benign chordoma" should be coded M9370/0. Similarly, "superficial spreading adenocarcinoma (M8143/3)" described as "noninvasive" should be coded M8143/2 and "melanoma (M8720/3)" described as "secondary" should be coded M8720/6.

The following table shows the correspondence between the morphology code and the different sections of Chapter 2:

Morphology Code Histology/Behavior			ICD-9-CM Chapter 2
Any	0	210-229	Benign neoplasms
M800-M8004	1	239	Neoplasms of unspecified nature
M8010+	1	235-238	Neoplasms of uncertain behavior
Any	2	230-234	Carcinoma in situ
Any	3	140-195	Malignant neoplasms, stated or
		200-208	presumed to be primary
Any	6	196-198	Malignant neoplasms, stated or
			presumed to be secondary

The ICD-O behavior digit/9 is inapplicable in an ICD context, since all malignant neoplasms are presumed to be primary (/3) or secondary (/6) according to other information on the medical record.

Only the first-listed term of the full ICD-O morphology nomenclature appears against each code number in the list below. The ICD-9-CM Alphabetical Index (Volume 2), however, includes all the ICD-O synonyms as well as a number of other morphological names still likely to be encountered on medical records but omitted from ICD-O as outdated or otherwise undesirable.

A coding difficulty sometimes arises where a morphological diagnosis contains two qualifying adjectives that have different code numbers. An example is "transitional cell epidermoid carcinomas." "Transitional cell carcinoma NOS" is M8120/3 and "epidermoid carcinoma NOS" is M8070/3. In such circumstances, the higher number (M8120/3 in this example) should be used, as it is usually more specific.

CODED NOMENCLATURE FOR MORPHOLOGY OF NEOPLASMS

M800	**Neoplasms NOS**
M8000/0	*Neoplasm, benign*
M8000/1	*Neoplasm, uncertain whether benign or malignant*
M8000/3	*Neoplasm, malignant*
M8000/6	*Neoplasm, metastatic*
M8000/9	*Neoplasm, malignant, uncertain whether primary or metastatic*
M8001/0	*Tumor cells, benign*
M8001/1	*Tumor cells, uncertain whether benign or malignant*
M8001/3	*Tumor cells, malignant*
M8002/3	*Malignant tumor, small cell type*
M8003/3	*Malignant tumor, giant cell type*
M8004/3	*Malignant tumor, fusiform cell type*
M801-M804	**Epithelial neoplasms NOS**
M8010/0	*Epithelial tumor, benign*
M8010/2	*Carcinoma in situ NOS*
M8010/3	*Carcinoma NOS*
M8010/6	*Carcinoma, metastatic NOS*
M8010/9	*Carcinomatosis*
M8011/0	*Epithelioma, benign*
M8011/3	*Epithelioma, malignant*
M8012/3	*Large cell carcinoma NOS*
M8020/3	*Carcinoma, undifferentiated type NOS*
M8021/3	*Carcinoma, anaplastic type NOS*
M8022/3	*Pleomorphic carcinoma*
M8030/3	*Giant cell and spindle cell carcinoma*
M8031/3	*Giant cell carcinoma*
M8032/3	*Spindle cell carcinoma*
M8033/3	*Pseudosarcomatous carcinoma*
M8034/3	*Polygonal cell carcinoma*
M8035/3	*Spheroidal cell carcinoma*
M8040/1	*Tumorlet*
M8041/3	*Small cell carcinoma NOS*
M8042/3	*Oat cell carcinoma*
M8043/3	*Small cell carcinoma, fusiform cell type*
M805-M808	**Papillary and squamous cell neoplasms**
M8050/0	*Papilloma NOS (except Papilloma of urinary bladder M8120/1)*
M8050/2	*Papillary carcinoma in situ*
M8050/3	*Papillary carcinoma NOS*
M8051/0	*Verrucous papilloma*
M8051/3	*Verrucous carcinoma NOS*
M8052/0	*Squamous cell papilloma*
M8052/3	*Papillary squamous cell carcinoma*
M8053/0	*Inverted papilloma*
M8060/0	*Papillomatosis NOS*
M8070/2	*Squamous cell carcinoma in situ NOS*
M8070/3	*Squamous cell carcinoma NOS*
M8070/6	*Squamous cell carcinoma, metastatic NOS*
M8071/3	*Squamous cell carcinoma, keratinizing type NOS*
M8072/3	*Squamous cell carcinoma, large cell, nonkeratinizing type*
M8073/3	*Squamous cell carcinoma, small cell, nonkeratinizing type*
M8074/3	*Squamous cell carcinoma, spindle cell type*
M8075/3	*Adenoid squamous cell carcinoma*
M8076/2	*Squamous cell carcinoma in situ with questionable stromal invasion*
M8076/3	*Squamous cell carcinoma, microinvasive*
M8080/2	*Queyrat's erythroplasia*
M8081/2	*Bowen's disease*
M8082/3	*Lymphoepithelial carcinoma*
M809-M811	**Basal cell neoplasms**
M8090/1	*Basal cell tumor*
M8090/3	*Basal cell carcinoma NOS*
M8091/3	*Multicentric basal cell carcinoma*
M8092/3	*Basal cell carcinoma, morphea type*
M8093/3	*Basal cell carcinoma, fibroepithelial type*
M8094/3	*Basosquamous carcinoma*
M8095/3	*Metatypical carcinoma*
M8096/0	*Intraepidermal epithelioma of Jadassohn*
M8100/0	*Trichoepithelioma*
M8101/0	*Trichofolliculoma*
M8102/0	*Tricholemmoma*

M8110/0   Pilomatrixoma

M812-M813   Transitional cell papillomas and carcinomas
M8120/0   Transitional cell papilloma NOS
M8120/1   Urothelial papilloma
M8120/2   Transitional cell carcinoma in situ
M8120/3   Transitional cell carcinoma NOS
M8121/0   Schneiderian papilloma
M8121/1   Transitional cell papilloma, inverted type
M8121/3   Schneiderian carcinoma
M8122/3   Transitional cell carcinoma, spindle cell type
M8123/3   Basaloid carcinoma
M8124/3   Cloacogenic carcinoma
M8130/3   Papillary transitional cell carcinoma

M814-M838   Adenomas and adenocarcinomas
M8140/0   Adenoma NOS
M8140/1   Bronchial adenoma NOS
M8140/2   Adenocarcinoma in situ
M8140/3   Adenocarcinoma NOS
M8140/6   Adenocarcinoma, metastatic NOS
M8141/3   Scirrhous adenocarcinoma
M8142/3   Linitis plastica
M8143/3   Superficial spreading adenocarcinoma
M8144/3   Adenocarcinoma, intestinal type
M8145/3   Carcinoma, diffuse type
M8146/0   Monomorphic adenoma
M8147/0   Basal cell adenoma
M8150/0   Islet cell adenoma
M8150/3   Islet cell carcinoma
M8151/0   Insulinoma NOS
M8151/3   Insulinoma, malignant
M8152/0   Glucagonoma NOS
M8152/3   Glucagonoma, malignant
M8153/1   Gastrinoma NOS
M8153/3   Gastrinoma, malignant
M8154/3   Mixed islet cell and exocrine adenocarcinoma
M8160/0   Bile duct adenoma
M8160/3   Cholangiocarcinoma
M8161/0   Bile duct cystadenoma
M8161/3   Bile duct cystadenocarcinoma
M8170/0   Liver cell adenoma
M8170/3   Hepatocellular carcinoma NOS
M8180/0   Hepatocholangioma, benign
M8180/3   Combined hepatocellular carcinoma and cholangiocarci-
           noma
M8190/0   Trabecular adenoma
M8190/3   Trabecular adenocarcinoma
M8191/0   Embryonal adenoma
M8200/0   Eccrine dermal cylindroma
M8200/3   Adenoid cystic carcinoma
M8201/3   Cribriform carcinoma
M8210/0   Adenomatous polyp NOS
M8210/3   Adenocarcinoma in adenomatous polyp
M8211/0   Tubular adenoma NOS
M8211/3   Tubular adenocarcinoma
M8220/0   Adenomatous polyposis coli
M8220/3   Adenocarcinoma in adenomatous polyposis coli
M8221/0   Multiple adenomatous polyps
M8230/3   Solid carcinoma NOS
M8231/3   Carcinoma simplex
M8240/1   Carcinoid tumor NOS
M8240/3   Carcinoid tumor, malignant
M8241/1   Carcinoid tumor, argentaffin NOS
M8241/3   Carcinoid tumor, argentaffin, malignant
M8242/1   Carcinoid tumor, nonargentaffin NOS
M8242/3   Carcinoid tumor, nonargentaffin, malignant
M8243/3   Mucocarcinoid tumor, malignant
M8244/3   Composite carcinoid
M8250/1   Pulmonary adenomatosis
M8250/3   Bronchiolo-alveolar adenocarcinoma
M8251/0   Alveolar adenoma
M8251/3   Alveolar adenocarcinoma
M8260/0   Papillary adenoma NOS
M8260/3   Papillary adenocarcinoma NOS

M8261/1   Villous adenoma NOS
M8261/3   Adenocarcinoma in villous adenoma
M8262/3   Villous adenocarcinoma
M8263/0   Tubulovillous adenoma
M8270/0   Chromophobe adenoma
M8270/3   Chromophobe carcinoma
M8280/0   Acidophil adenoma
M8280/3   Acidophil carcinoma
M8281/0   Mixed acidophil-basophil adenoma
M8281/3   Mixed acidophil-basophil carcinoma
M8290/0   Oxyphilic adenoma
M8290/3   Oxyphilic adenocarcinoma
M8300/0   Basophil adenoma
M8300/3   Basophil carcinoma
M8310/0   Clear cell adenoma
M8310/3   Clear cell adenocarcinoma NOS
M8311/1   Hypernephroid tumor
M8312/3   Renal cell carcinoma
M8313/0   Clear cell adenofibroma
M8320/3   Granular cell carcinoma
M8321/0   Chief cell adenoma
M8322/0   Water-clear cell adenoma
M8322/3   Water-clear cell adenocarcinoma
M8323/0   Mixed cell adenoma
M8323/3   Mixed cell adenocarcinoma
M8324/0   Lipoadenoma
M8330/0   Follicular adenoma
M8330/3   Follicular adenocarcinoma NOS
M8331/3   Follicular adenocarcinoma, well differentiated type
M8332/3   Follicular adenocarcinoma, trabecular type
M8333/0   Microfollicular adenoma
M8334/0   Macrofollicular adenoma
M8340/0   Papillary and follicular adenocarcinoma
M8350/3   Nonencapsulated sclerosing carcinoma
M8360/1   Multiple endocrine adenomas
M8361/1   Juxtaglomerular tumor
M8370/0   Adrenal cortical adenoma NOS
M8370/3   Adrenal cortical carcinoma
M8371/0   Adrenal cortical adenoma, compact cell type
M8372/0   Adrenal cortical adenoma, heavily pigmented variant
M8373/0   Adrenal cortical adenoma, clear cell type
M8374/0   Adrenal cortical adenoma, glomerulosa cell type
M8375/0   Adrenal cortical adenoma, mixed cell type
M8380/0   Endometrioid adenoma NOS
M8380/1   Endometrioid adenoma, borderline malignancy
M8380/3   Endometrioid carcinoma
M8381/0   Endometrioid adenofibroma NOS
M8381/1   Endometrioid adenofibroma, borderline malignancy
M8381/3   Endometrioid adenofibroma, malignant

M839-M842   Adnexal and skin appendage neoplasms
M8390/0   Skin appendage adenoma
M8390/3   Skin appendage carcinoma
M8400/0   Sweat gland adenoma
M8400/1   Sweat gland tumor NOS
M8400/3   Sweat gland adenocarcinoma
M8401/0   Apocrine adenoma
M8401/3   Apocrine adenocarcinoma
M8402/0   Eccrine acrospiroma
M8403/0   Eccrine spiradenoma
M8404/0   Hidrocystoma
M8405/0   Papillary hydradenoma
M8406/0   Papillary syringadenoma
M8407/0   Syringoma NOS
M8410/0   Sebaceous adenoma
M8410/3   Sebaceous adenocarcinoma
M8420/0   Ceruminous adenoma
M8420/3   Ceruminous adenocarcinoma

M843   Mucoepidermoid neoplasms
M8430/1   Mucoepidermoid tumor
M8430/3   Mucoepidermoid carcinoma

M844-M849   Cystic, mucinous, and serous neoplasms
M8440/0   Cystadenoma NOS
M8440/3   Cystadenocarcinoma NOS

M8441/0	*Serous cystadenoma NOS*
M8441/1	*Serous cystadenoma, borderline malignancy*
M8441/3	*Serous cystadenocarcinoma NOS*
M8450/0	*Papillary cystadenoma NOS*
M8450/1	*Papillary cystadenoma, borderline malignancy*
M8450/3	*Papillary cystadenocarcinoma NOS*
M8460/0	*Papillary serous cystadenoma NOS*
M8460/1	*Papillary serous cystadenoma, borderline malignancy*
M8460/3	*Papillary serous cystadenocarcinoma*
M8461/0	*Serous surface papilloma NOS*
M8461/1	*Serous surface papilloma, borderline malignancy*
M8461/3	*Serous surface papillary carcinoma*
M8470/0	*Mucinous cystadenoma NOS*
M8470/1	*Mucinous cystadenoma, borderline malignancy*
M8470/3	*Mucinous cystadenocarcinoma NOS*
M8471/0	*Papillary mucinous cystadenoma NOS*
M8471/1	*Papillary mucinous cystadenoma, borderline malignancy*
M8471/3	*Papillary mucinous cystadenocarcinoma*
M8480/0	*Mucinous adenoma*
M8480/3	*Mucinous adenocarcinoma*
M8480/6	*Pseudomyxoma peritonei*
M8481/3	*Mucin-producing adenocarcinoma*
M8490/3	*Signet ring cell carcinoma*
M8490/6	*Metastatic signet ring cell carcinoma*

M850-M854	**Ductal, lobular, and medullary neoplasms**
M8500/2	*Intraductal carcinoma, noninfiltrating NOS*
M8500/3	*Infiltrating duct carcinoma*
M8501/2	*Comedocarcinoma, noninfiltrating*
M8501/3	*Comedocarcinoma NOS*
M8502/3	*Juvenile carcinoma of the breast*
M8503/0	*Intraductal papilloma*
M8503/2	*Noninfiltrating intraductal papillary adenocarcinoma*
M8504/0	*Intracystic papillary adenoma*
M8504/2	*Noninfiltrating intracystic carcinoma*
M8505/0	*Intraductal papillomatosis NOS*
M8506/0	*Subareolar duct papillomatosis*
M8510/3	*Medullary carcinoma NOS*
M8511/3	*Medullary carcinoma with amyloid stroma*
M8512/3	*Medullary carcinoma with lymphoid stroma*
M8520/2	*Lobular carcinoma in situ*
M8520/3	*Lobular carcinoma NOS*
M8521/3	*Infiltrating ductular carcinoma*
M8530/3	*Inflammatory carcinoma*
M8540/3	*Paget's disease, mammary*
M8541/3	*Paget's disease and infiltrating duct carcinoma of breast*
M8542/3	*Paget's disease, extramammary (except Paget's disease of bone)*

M855	**Acinar cell neoplasms**
M8550/0	*Acinar cell adenoma*
M8550/1	*Acinar cell tumor*
M8550/3	*Acinar cell carcinoma*

M856-M858	**Complex epithelial neoplasms**
M8560/3	*Adenosquamous carcinoma*
M8561/0	*Adenolymphoma*
M8570/3	*Adenocarcinoma with squamous metaplasia*
M8571/3	*Adenocarcinoma with cartilaginous and osseous metaplasia*
M8572/3	*Adenocarcinoma with spindle cell metaplasia*
M8573/3	*Adenocarcinoma with apocrine metaplasia*
M8580/0	*Thymoma, benign*
M8580/3	*Thymoma, malignant*

M859-M867	**Specialized gonadal neoplasms**
M8590/1	*Sex cord-stromal tumor*
M8600/0	*Thecoma NOS*
M8600/3	*Theca cell carcinoma*
M8610/0	*Luteoma NOS*
M8620/1	*Granulosa cell tumor NOS*
M8620/3	*Granulosa cell tumor, malignant*
M8621/1	*Granulosa cell-theca cell tumor*
M8630/0	*Androblastoma, benign*
M8630/1	*Androblastoma NOS*

M8630/3	*Androblastoma, malignant*
M8631/0	*Sertoli-Leydig cell tumor*
M8632/1	*Gynandroblastoma*
M8640/0	*Tubular androblastoma NOS*
M8640/3	*Sertoli cell carcinoma*
M8641/0	*Tubular androblastoma with lipid storage*
M8650/0	*Leydig cell tumor, benign*
M8650/1	*Leydig cell tumor NOS*
M8650/3	*Leydig cell tumor, malignant*
M8660/0	*Hilar cell tumor*
M8670/0	*Lipid cell tumor of ovary*
M8671/0	*Adrenal rest tumor*

M868-M871	**Paragangliomas and glomus tumors**
M8680/1	*Paraganglioma NOS*
M8680/3	*Paraganglioma, malignant*
M8681/1	*Sympathetic paraganglioma*
M8682/1	*Parasympathetic paraganglioma*
M8690/1	*Glomus jugulare tumor*
M8691/1	*Aortic body tumor*
M8692/1	*Carotid body tumor*
M8693/1	*Extra-adrenal paraganglioma NOS*
M8693/3	*Extra-adrenal paraganglioma, malignant*
M8700/0	*Pheochromocytoma NOS*
M8700/3	*Pheochromocytoma, malignant*
M8710/3	*Glomangiosarcoma*
M8711/0	*Glomus tumor*
M8712/0	*Glomangioma*

M872-M879	**Nevi and melanomas**
M8720/0	*Pigmented nevus NOS*
M8720/3	*Malignant melanoma NOS*
M8721/3	*Nodular melanoma*
M8722/0	*Balloon cell nevus*
M8722/3	*Balloon cell melanoma*
M8723/0	*Halo nevus*
M8724/0	*Fibrous papule of the nose*
M8725/0	*Neuronevus*
M8726/0	*Magnocellular nevus*
M8730/0	*Nonpigmented nevus*
M8730/3	*Amelanotic melanoma*
M8740/0	*Junctional nevus*
M8740/3	*Malignant melanoma in junctional nevus*
M8741/2	*Precancerous melanosis NOS*
M8741/3	*Malignant melanoma in precancerous melanosis*
M8742/2	*Hutchinson's melanotic freckle*
M8742/3	*Malignant melanoma in Hutchinson's melanotic freckle*
M8743/3	*Superficial spreading melanoma*
M8750/0	*Intradermal nevus*
M8760/0	*Compound nevus*
M8761/1	*Giant pigmented nevus*
M8761/3	*Malignant melanoma in giant pigmented nevus*
M8770/0	*Epithelioid and spindle cell nevus*
M8771/3	*Epithelioid cell melanoma*
M8772/3	*Spindle cell melanoma NOS*
M8773/3	*Spindle cell melanoma, type A*
M8774/3	*Spindle cell melanoma, type B*
M8775/3	*Mixed epithelioid and spindle cell melanoma*
M8780/0	*Blue nevus NOS*
M8780/3	*Blue nevus, malignant*
M8790/0	*Cellular blue nevus*

M880	**Soft tissue tumors and sarcomas NOS**
M8800/0	*Soft tissue tumor, benign*
M8800/3	*Sarcoma NOS*
M8800/9	*Sarcomatosis NOS*
M8801/3	*Spindle cell sarcoma*
M8802/3	*Giant cell sarcoma (except of bone M9250/3)*
M8803/3	*Small cell sarcoma*
M8804/3	*Epithelioid cell sarcoma*

M881-M883	**Fibromatous neoplasms**
M8810/0	*Fibroma NOS*
M8810/3	*Fibrosarcoma NOS*
M8811/0	*Fibromyxoma*
M8811/3	*Fibromyxosarcoma*

M8812/0	Periosteal fibroma
M8812/3	Periosteal fibrosarcoma
M8813/0	Fascial fibroma
M8813/3	Fascial fibrosarcoma
M8814/3	Infantile fibrosarcoma
M8820/0	Elastofibroma
M8821/1	Aggressive fibromatosis
M8822/1	Abdominal fibromatosis
M8823/1	Desmoplastic fibroma
M8830/0	Fibrous histiocytoma NOS
M8830/1	Atypical fibrous histiocytoma
M8830/3	Fibrous histiocytoma, malignant
M8831/0	Fibroxanthoma NOS
M8831/1	Atypical fibroxanthoma
M8831/3	Fibroxanthoma, malignant
M8832/0	Dermatofibroma NOS
M8832/1	Dermatofibroma protuberans
M8832/3	Dermatofibrosarcoma NOS

M884 **Myxomatous neoplasms**

M8840/0	Myxoma NOS
M8840/3	Myxosarcoma

M885-M888 **Lipomatous neoplasms**

M8850/0	Lipoma NOS
M8850/3	Liposarcoma NOS
M8851/0	Fibrolipoma
M8851/3	Liposarcoma, well differentiated type
M8852/0	Fibromyxolipoma
M8852/3	Myxoid liposarcoma
M8853/3	Round cell liposarcoma
M8854/3	Pleomorphic liposarcoma
M8855/3	Mixed type liposarcoma
M8856/0	Intramuscular lipoma
M8857/0	Spindle cell lipoma
M8860/0	Angiomyolipoma
M8860/3	Angiomyoliposarcoma
M8861/0	Angiolipoma NOS
M8861/1	Angiolipoma, infiltrating
M8870/0	Myelolipoma
M8880/0	Hibernoma
M8881/0	Lipoblastomatosis

M889-M892 **Myomatous neoplasms**

M8890/0	Leiomyoma NOS
M8890/1	Intravascular leiomyomatosis
M8890/3	Leiomyosarcoma NOS
M8891/1	Epithelioid leiomyoma
M8891/3	Epithelioid leiomyosarcoma
M8892/1	Cellular leiomyoma
M8893/0	Bizarre leiomyoma
M8894/0	Angiomyoma
M8894/3	Angiomyosarcoma
M8895/0	Myoma
M8895/3	Myosarcoma
M8900/0	Rhabdomyoma NOS
M8900/3	Rhabdomyosarcoma NOS
M8901/3	Pleomorphic rhabdomyosarcoma
M8902/3	Mixed type rhabdomyosarcoma
M8903/0	Fetal rhabdomyoma
M8904/0	Adult rhabdomyoma
M8910/3	Embryonal rhabdomyosarcoma
M8920/3	Alveolar rhabdomyosarcoma

M893-M899 **Complex mixed and stromal neoplasms**

M8930/3	Endometrial stromal sarcoma
M8931/1	Endolymphatic stromal myosis
M8932/0	Adenomyoma
M8940/0	Pleomorphic adenoma
M8940/3	Mixed tumor, malignant NOS
M8950/3	Mullerian mixed tumor
M8951/3	Mesodermal mixed tumor
M8960/1	Mesoblastic nephroma
M8960/3	Nephroblastoma NOS
M8961/3	Epithelial nephroblastoma
M8962/3	Mesenchymal nephroblastoma

M8970/3	Hepatoblastoma
M8980/3	Carcinosarcoma NOS
M8981/3	Carcinosarcoma, embryonal type
M8982/0	Myoepithelioma
M8990/0	Mesenchymoma, benign
M8990/1	Mesenchymoma NOS
M8990/3	Mesenchymoma, malignant
M8991/3	Embryonal sarcoma

M900-M903 **Fibroepithelial neoplasms**

M9000/0	Brenner tumor NOS
M9000/1	Brenner tumor, borderline malignancy
M9000/3	Brenner tumor, malignant
M9010/0	Fibroadenoma NOS
M9011/0	Intracanalicular fibroadenoma NOS
M9012/0	Pericanalicular fibroadenoma
M9013/0	Adenofibroma NOS
M9014/0	Serous adenofibroma
M9015/0	Mucinous adenofibroma
M9020/0	Cellular intracanalicular fibroadenoma
M9020/1	Cystosarcoma phyllodes NOS
M9020/3	Cystosarcoma phyllodes, malignant
M9030/0	Juvenile fibroadenoma

M904 **Synovial neoplasms**

M9040/0	Synovioma, benign
M9040/3	Synovial sarcoma NOS
M9041/3	Synovial sarcoma, spindle cell type
M9042/3	Synovial sarcoma, epithelioid cell type
M9043/3	Synovial sarcoma, biphasic type
M9044/3	Clear cell sarcoma of tendons and aponeuroses

M905 **Mesothelial neoplasms**

M9050/0	Mesothelioma, benign
M9050/3	Mesothelioma, malignant
M9051/0	Fibrous mesothelioma, benign
M9051/3	Fibrous mesothelioma, malignant
M9052/0	Epithelioid mesothelioma, benign
M9052/3	Epithelioid mesothelioma, malignant
M9053/0	Mesothelioma, biphasic type, benign
M9053/3	Mesothelioma, biphasic type, malignant
M9054/0	Adenomatoid tumor NOS

M906-M909 **Germ cell neoplasms**

M9060/3	Dysgerminoma
M9061/3	Seminoma NOS
M9062/3	Seminoma, anaplastic type
M9063/3	Spermatocytic seminoma
M9064/3	Germinoma
M9070/3	Embryonal carcinoma NOS
M9071/3	Endodermal sinus tumor
M9072/3	Polyembryoma
M9073/1	Gonadoblastoma
M9080/0	Teratoma, benign
M9080/1	Teratoma NOS
M9080/3	Teratoma, malignant NOS
M9081/3	Teratocarcinoma
M9082/3	Malignant teratoma, undifferentiated type
M9083/3	Malignant teratoma, intermediate type
M9084/0	Dermoid cyst
M9084/3	Dermoid cyst with malignant transformation
M9090/0	Struma ovarii NOS
M9090/3	Struma ovarii, malignant
M9091/1	Strumal carcinoid

M910 **Trophoblastic neoplasms**

M9100/0	Hydatidiform mole NOS
M9100/1	Invasive hydatidiform mole
M9100/3	Choriocarcinoma
M9101/3	Choriocarcinoma combined with teratoma
M9102/3	Malignant teratoma, trophoblastic

M911 **Mesonephromas**

M9110/0	Mesonephroma, benign
M9110/1	Mesonephric tumor
M9110/3	Mesonephroma, malignant
M9111/1	Endosalpingioma

M912-M916	**Blood vessel tumors**
M9120/0	*Hemangioma NOS*
M9120/3	*Hemangiosarcoma*
M9121/0	*Cavernous hemangioma*
M9122/0	*Venous hemangioma*
M9123/0	*Racemose hemangioma*
M9124/3	*Kupffer cell sarcoma*
M9130/0	*Hemangioendothelioma, benign*
M9130/1	*Hemangioendothelioma NOS*
M9130/3	*Hemangioendothelioma, malignant*
M9131/0	*Capillary hemangioma*
M9132/0	*Intramuscular hemangioma*
M9140/3	*Kaposi's sarcoma*
M9141/0	*Angiokeratoma*
M9142/0	*Verrucous keratotic hemangioma*
M9150/0	*Hemangiopericytoma, benign*
M9150/1	*Hemangiopericytoma NOS*
M9150/3	*Hemangiopericytoma, malignant*
M9160/0	*Angiofibroma NOS*
M9161/1	*Hemangioblastoma*

M917 **Lymphatic vessel tumors**
M9170/0 *Lymphangioma NOS*
M9170/3 *Lymphangiosarcoma*
M9171/0 *Capillary lymphangioma*
M9172/0 *Cavernous lymphangioma*
M9173/0 *Cystic lymphangioma*
M9174/0 *Lymphangiomyoma*
M9174/1 *Lymphangiomyomatosis*
M9175/0 *Hemolymphangioma*

M918-M920 **Osteomas and osteosarcomas**
M9180/0 *Osteoma NOS*
M9180/3 *Osteosarcoma NOS*
M9181/3 *Chondroblastic osteosarcoma*
M9182/3 *Fibroblastic osteosarcoma*
M9183/3 *Telangiectatic osteosarcoma*
M9184/3 *Osteosarcoma in Paget's disease of bone*
M9190/3 *Juxtacortical osteosarcoma*
M9191/0 *Osteoid osteoma NOS*
M9200/0 *Osteoblastoma*

M921-M924 **Chondromatous neoplasms**
M9210/0 *Osteochondroma*
M9210/1 *Osteochondromatosis NOS*
M9220/0 *Chondroma NOS*
M9220/1 *Chondromatosis NOS*
M9220/3 *Chondrosarcoma NOS*
M9221/0 *Juxtacortical chondroma*
M9221/3 *Juxtacortical chondrosarcoma*
M9230/0 *Chondroblastoma NOS*
M9230/3 *Chondroblastoma, malignant*
M9240/3 *Mesenchymal chondrosarcoma*
M9241/0 *Chondromyxoid fibroma*

M925 **Giant cell tumors**
M9250/1 *Giant cell tumor of bone NOS*
M9250/3 *Giant cell tumor of bone, malignant*
M9251/1 *Giant cell tumor of soft parts NOS*
M9251/3 *Malignant giant cell tumor of soft parts*

M926 **Miscellaneous bone tumors**
M9260/3 *Ewing's sarcoma*
M9261/3 *Adamantinoma of long bones*
M9262/0 *Ossifying fibroma*

M927-M934 **Odontogenic tumors**
M9270/0 *Odontogenic tumor, benign*
M9270/1 *Odontogenic tumor NOS*
M9270/3 *Odontogenic tumor, malignant*
M9271/0 *Dentinoma*
M9272/0 *Cementoma NOS*
M9273/0 *Cementoblastoma, benign*
M9274/0 *Cementifying fibroma*
M9275/0 *Gigantiform cementoma*
M9280/0 *Odontoma NOS*
M9281/0 *Compound odontoma*

M9282/0 *Complex odontoma*
M9290/0 *Ameloblastic fibro-odontoma*
M9290/3 *Ameloblastic odontosarcoma*
M9300/0 *Adenomatoid odontogenic tumor*
M9301/0 *Calcifying odontogenic cyst*
M9310/0 *Ameloblastoma NOS*
M9310/3 *Ameloblastoma, malignant*
M9311/0 *Odontoameloblastoma*
M9312/0 *Squamous odontogenic tumor*
M9320/0 *Odontogenic myxoma*
M9321/0 *Odontogenic fibroma NOS*
M9330/0 *Ameloblastic fibroma*
M9330/3 *Ameloblastic fibrosarcoma*
M9340/0 *Calcifying epithelial odontogenic tumor*

M935-M937 **Miscellaneous tumors**
M9350/1 *Craniopharyngioma*
M9360/1 *Pinealoma*
M9361/1 *Pineocytoma*
M9362/3 *Pineoblastoma*
M9363/0 *Melanotic neuroectodermal tumor*
M9370/3 *Chordoma*

M938-M948 **Gliomas**
M9380/3 *Glioma, malignant*
M9381/3 *Gliomatosis cerebri*
M9382/3 *Mixed glioma*
M9383/1 *Subependymal glioma*
M9384/1 *Subependymal giant cell astrocytoma*
M9390/0 *Choroid plexus papilloma NOS*
M9390/3 *Choroid plexus papilloma, malignant*
M9391/3 *Ependymoma NOS*
M9392/3 *Ependymoma, anaplastic type*
M9393/1 *Papillary ependymoma*
M9394/1 *Myxopapillary ependymoma*
M9400/3 *Astrocytoma NOS*
M9401/3 *Astrocytoma, anaplastic type*
M9410/3 *Protoplasmic astrocytoma*
M9411/3 *Gemistocytic astrocytoma*
M9420/3 *Fibrillary astrocytoma*
M9421/3 *Pilocytic astrocytoma*
M9422/3 *Spongioblastoma NOS*
M9423/3 *Spongioblastoma polare*
M9430/3 *Astroblastoma*
M9440/3 *Glioblastoma NOS*
M9441/3 *Giant cell glioblastoma*
M9442/3 *Glioblastoma with sarcomatous component*
M9443/3 *Primitive polar spongioblastoma*
M9450/3 *Oligodendroglioma NOS*
M9451/3 *Oligodendroglioma, anaplastic type*
M9460/3 *Oligodendroblastoma*
M9470/3 *Medulloblastoma NOS*
M9471/3 *Desmoplastic medulloblastoma*
M9472/3 *Medullomyoblastoma*
M9480/3 *Cerebellar sarcoma NOS*
M9481/3 *Monstrocellular sarcoma*

M949-M952 **Neuroepitheliomatous neoplasms**
M9490/0 *Ganglioneuroma*
M9490/3 *Ganglioneuroblastoma*
M9491/0 *Ganglioneuromatosis*
M9500/3 *Neuroblastoma NOS*
M9501/3 *Medulloepithelioma NOS*
M9502/3 *Teratoid medulloepithelioma*
M9503/3 *Neuroepithelioma NOS*
M9504/3 *Spongioneuroblastoma*
M9505/1 *Ganglioglioma*
M9506/0 *Neurocytoma*
M9507/0 *Pacinian tumor*
M9510/3 *Retinoblastoma NOS*
M9511/3 *Retinoblastoma, differentiated type*
M9512/3 *Retinoblastoma, undifferentiated type*
M9520/3 *Olfactory neurogenic tumor*
M9521/3 *Esthesioneurocytoma*
M9522/3 *Esthesioneuroblastoma*
M9523/3 *Esthesioneuroepithelioma*

M953	**Meningiomas**
M9530/0	*Meningioma NOS*
M9530/1	*Meningiomatosis NOS*
M9530/3	*Meningioma, malignant*
M9531/0	*Meningotheliomatous meningioma*
M9532/0	*Fibrous meningioma*
M9533/0	*Psammomatous meningioma*
M9534/0	*Angiomatous meningioma*
M9535/0	*Hemangioblastic meningioma*
M9536/0	*Hemangiopericytic meningioma*
M9537/0	*Transitional meningioma*
M9538/1	*Papillary meningioma*
M9539/3	*Meningeal sarcomatosis*

M954-M957	**Nerve sheath tumor**
M9540/0	*Neurofibroma NOS*
M9540/1	*Neurofibromatosis NOS*
M9540/3	*Neurofibrosarcoma*
M9541/0	*Melanotic neurofibroma*
M9550/0	*Plexiform neurofibroma*
M9560/0	*Neurilemmoma NOS*
M9560/1	*Neurinomatosis*
M9560/3	*Neurilemmoma, malignant*
M9570/0	*Neuroma NOS*

M958	**Granular cell tumors and alveolar soft part sarcoma**
M9580/0	*Granular cell tumor NOS*
M9580/3	*Granular cell tumor, malignant*
M9581/3	*Alveolar soft part sarcoma*

M959-M963	**Lymphomas, NOS or diffuse**
M9590/0	*Lymphomatous tumor, benign*
M9590/3	*Malignant lymphoma NOS*
M9591/3	*Malignant lymphoma, non Hodgkin's type*
M9600/3	*Malignant lymphoma, undifferentiated cell type NOS*
M9601/3	*Malignant lymphoma, stem cell type*
M9602/3	*Malignant lymphoma, convoluted cell type NOS*
M9610/3	*Lymphosarcoma NOS*
M9611/3	*Malignant lymphoma, lymphoplasmacytoid type*
M9612/3	*Malignant lymphoma, immunoblastic type*
M9613/3	*Malignant lymphoma, mixed lymphocytic-histiocytic NOS*
M9614/3	*Malignant lymphoma, centroblastic-centrocytic, diffuse*
M9615/3	*Malignant lymphoma, follicular center cell NOS*
M9620/3	*Malignant lymphoma, lymphocytic, well differentiated NOS*
M9621/3	*Malignant lymphoma, lymphocytic, intermediate differentiation NOS*
M9622/3	*Malignant lymphoma, centrocytic*
M9623/3	*Malignant lymphoma, follicular center cell, cleaved NOS*
M9630/3	*Malignant lymphoma, lymphocytic, poorly differentiated NOS*
M9631/3	*Prolymphocytic lymphosarcoma*
M9632/3	*Malignant lymphoma, centroblastic type NOS*
M9633/3	*Malignant lymphoma, follicular center cell, noncleaved NOS*

M964	**Reticulosarcomas**
M9640/3	*Reticulosarcoma NOS*
M9641/3	*Reticulosarcoma, pleomorphic cell type*
M9642/3	*Reticulosarcoma, nodular*

M965-M966	**Hodgkin's disease**
M9650/3	*Hodgkin's disease NOS*
M9651/3	*Hodgkin's disease, lymphocytic predominance*
M9652/3	*Hodgkin's disease, mixed cellularity*
M9653/3	*Hodgkin's disease, lymphocytic depletion NOS*
M9654/3	*Hodgkin's disease, lymphocytic depletion, diffuse fibrosis*
M9655/3	*Hodgkin's disease, lymphocytic depletion, reticular type*
M9656/3	*Hodgkin's disease, nodular sclerosis NOS*
M9657/3	*Hodgkin's disease, nodular sclerosis, cellular phase*
M9660/3	*Hodgkin's paragranuloma*
M9661/3	*Hodgkin's granuloma*

M9662/3	*Hodgkin's sarcoma*

M969	**Lymphomas, nodular or follicular**
M9690/3	*Malignant lymphoma, nodular NOS*
M9691/3	*Malignant lymphoma, mixed lymphocytic-histiocytic, nodular*
M9692/3	*Malignant lymphoma, centroblastic-centrocytic, follicular*
M9693/3	*Malignant lymphoma, lymphocytic, well differentiated, nodular*
M9694/3	*Malignant lymphoma, lymphocytic, intermediate differentiation, nodular*
M9695/3	*Malignant lymphoma, follicular center cell, cleaved, follicular*
M9696/3	*Malignant lymphoma, lymphocytic, poorly differentiated, nodular*
M9697/3	*Malignant lymphoma, centroblastic type, follicular*
M9698/3	*Malignant lymphoma, follicular center cell, noncleaved, follicular*

M970	**Mycosis fungoides**
M9700/3	*Mycosis fungoides*
M9701/3	*Sezary's disease*

M971-M972	**Miscellaneous reticuloendothelial neoplasms**
M9710/3	*Microglioma*
M9720/3	*Malignant histiocytosis*
M9721/3	*Histiocytic medullary reticulosis*
M9722/3	*Letterer-Siwe's disease*

M973	**Plasma cell tumors**
M9730/3	*Plasma cell myeloma*
M9731/0	*Plasma cell tumor, benign*
M9731/1	*Plasmacytoma NOS*
M9731/3	*Plasma cell tumor, malignant*

M974	**Mast cell tumors**
M9740/1	*Mastocytoma NOS*
M9740/3	*Mast cell sarcoma*
M9741/3	*Malignant mastocytosis*

M975	**Burkitt's tumor**
M9750/3	*Burkitt's tumor*

M980-M994	**Leukemias**

M980	**Leukemias NOS**
M9800/3	*Leukemia NOS*
M9801/3	*Acute leukemia NOS*
M9802/3	*Subacute leukemia NOS*
M9803/3	*Chronic leukemia NOS*
M9804/3	*Aleukemic leukemia NOS*

M981	**Compound leukemias**
M9810/3	*Compound leukemia*

M982	**Lymphoid leukemias**
M9820/3	*Lymphoid leukemia NOS*
M9821/3	*Acute lymphoid leukemia*
M9822/3	*Subacute lymphoid leukemia*
M9823/3	*Chronic lymphoid leukemia*
M9824/3	*Aleukemic lymphoid leukemia*
M9825/3	*Prolymphocytic leukemia*

M983	**Plasma cell leukemias**
M9830/3	*Plasma cell leukemia*

M984	**Erythroleukemias**
M9840/3	*Erythroleukemia*
M9841/3	*Acute erythremia*
M9842/3	*Chronic erythremia*

M985	**Lymphosarcoma cell leukemias**
M9850/3	*Lymphosarcoma cell leukemia*

M986	**Myeloid leukemias**
M9860/3	*Myeloid leukemia NOS*
M9861/3	*Acute myeloid leukemia*
M9862/3	*Subacute myeloid leukemia*

M9863/3	*Chronic myeloid leukemia*
M9864/3	*Aleukemic myeloid leukemia*
M9865/3	*Neutrophilic leukemia*
M9866/3	*Acute promyelocytic leukemia*

M987   **Basophilic leukemias**
M9870/3   *Basophilic leukemia*

M988   **Eosinophilic leukemias**
M9880/3   *Eosinophilic leukemia*

M989   **Monocytic leukemias**
M9890/3	*Monocytic leukemia NOS*
M9891/3	*Acute monocytic leukemia*
M9892/3	*Subacute monocytic leukemia*
M9893/3	*Chronic monocytic leukemia*
M9894/3	*Aleukemic monocytic leukemia*

M990-M994   **Miscellaneous leukemias**
M9900/3	*Mast cell leukemia*
M9910/3	*Megakaryocytic leukemia*
M9920/3	*Megakaryocytic myelosis*
M9930/3	*Myeloid sarcoma*
M9940/3	*Hairy cell leukemia*

M995-M997   **Miscellaneous myeloproliferative and lympho-proliferative disorders**
M9950/1	*Polycythemia vera*
M9951/1	*Acute panmyelosis*
M9960/1	*Chronic myeloproliferative disease*
M9961/1	*Myelosclerosis with myeloid metaplasia*
M9962/1	*Idiopathic thrombocythemia*
M9970/1	*Chronic lymphoproliferative disease*

APPENDIX B

GLOSSARY OF MENTAL DISORDERS

The psychiatric terms which appear in Chapter 5, "Mental Disorders," are listed here in alphabetic sequence. Many of the glossary descriptions originally appeared in the section on Mental Disorders in the International Classification of Diseases, 9th Revision,[1] and others are included to define the psychiatric conditions added to ICD-9-CM. The additional definitions are based on material furnished by the American Psychiatric Association's Task Force on Nomenclature and Statistics[2] and from A Psychiatric Glossary.[3] In a few instances definitions were obtained from Dorland's Illustrated Medical Dictionary[4] and from Stedman's Medical Dictionary, Illustrated.[5]

1. Manual of the International Classification of Diseases, Injuries, and Causes of Death, 9th Revision. World Health Organization, Geneva, Switzerland, 1975.
2. American Psychiatric Association, Task Force on Nomenclature and Statistics, Robert L. Spitzer, Chairman.
3. A Psychiatric Glossary. Fourth Edition, American Psychiatric Association, Washington, D.C., 1975.
4. Dorland's Illustrated Medical Dictionary. Twenty-fifth Edition, W. B. Saunders Company, Philadelphia, 1974.
5. Stedman's Medical Dictionary, Illustrated. Twenty-third Edition, the Williams and Wilkins Company, Baltimore, 1976.

Academic underachievement disorder: Failure to achieve in most school tasks despite adequate intellectual capacity, a supportive and encouraging social environment, and apparent effort. The failure occurs in the absence of a demonstrable specific learning disability and is caused by emotional conflict not clearly associated with any other mental disorder.[2]

Adaptation reaction—*see* Adjustment reaction

Adjustment reaction or disorder: Mild or transient disorders lasting longer than acute stress reactions which occur in individuals of any age without any apparent pre-existing mental disorder. Such disorders are often relatively circumscribed or situation-specific, are generally reversible, and usually last only a few months. They are usually closely related in time and content to stresses such as bereavement, migration, or other experiences. Reactions to major stress that last longer than a few days are also included. In children such disorders are associated with no significant distortion of development.[1]

  conduct disturbance: Mild or transient disorders in which the main disturbance predominantly involves a disturbance of conduct (e.g., an adolescent grief reaction resulting in aggressive or antisocial disorder).[1]

  depressive reaction: States of depression, not specifiable as manic-depressive, psychotic, or neurotic.[1]

    brief: Generally transient, in which the depressive symptoms are usually closely related in time and content to some stressful event.[1]

    prolonged: Generally long-lasting, usually developing in association with prolonged exposure to a stressful situation.[1]

  emotional disturbance: An adjustment disorder in which the main symptoms are emotional in type (e.g., anxiety, fear, worry) but not specifically depressive.[1]

  mixed conduct and emotional disturbance: An adjustment reaction in which both emotional disturbance and disturbance of conduct are prominent features.[1]

Affective psychoses: Mental disorders, usually recurrent, in which there is a severe disturbance of mood (mostly compounded of depression and anxiety but also manifested as elation, and excitement) which is accompanied by one or more of the following: delusions, perplexity, disturbed attitude to self, disorder of perception and behavior; these are all in keeping with the individual's prevailing mood (as are hallucinations when they occur). There is a strong tendency to suicide. For practical reasons, mild disorders of mood may also be included here if the symptoms match closely the descriptions given; this applies particularly to mild hypomania.[1]

  bipolar: A manic-depressive psychosis which has appeared in both the depressive and manic form, either alternating or separated by an interval of normality.[1]

  atypical: An episode of affective psychosis with some, but not all, of the features of the one form of the disorder in individuals who have had a previous episode of the other form of the disorder.[2]

  depressed: A manic-depressive psychosis, circular type, in which the depressive form is currently present.[1]

  manic: A manic-depressive psychosis, circular type, in which the manic form is currently present.[1]

  mixed: A manic-depressive psychosis, circular type, in which both manic and depressive symptoms are present at the same time.[1]

  depressed type: A manic-depressive psychosis in which there is a widespread depressed mood of gloom and wretchedness with some degree of anxiety. There is often reduced activity but there may be restlessness and agitation. There is marked tendency to recurrence; in a few cases this may be at regular intervals.[1]

    atypical: An affective depressive disorder that cannot be classified as a manic-depressive psychosis, depressed type, or chronic depressive personality disorder, or as an adjustment disorder.[2]

  manic type: A manic-depressive psychosis characterized by states of elation or excitement out of keeping with the individual's circumstances and varying from enhanced liveliness (hypomania) to violent, almost uncontrollable, excitement. Aggression and anger, flight of ideas, distractibility, impaired judgment, and grandiose ideas are common.[1]

  mixed type: Manic-depressive psychosis syndromes corresponding to both the manic and depressed types, but which for other reasons cannot be classified more specifically.[1]

Aggressive personality—*see* Personality disorder, explosive type

Agoraphobia—*see* agoraphobia under Phobia

Alcohol dependence syndrome: A state, psychic and usually also physical, resulting from taking alcohol, characterized by behavioral and other responses that always include a compulsion to take alcohol on a continuous or periodic basis in order to experience its psychic effects, and sometimes to avoid the discomfort of its absence; tolerance may or may not be present. A person may be dependent on alcohol and other drugs; if so, also record the diagnosis of drug dependence to identify the agent. If alcohol dependence is associated with alcoholic psychosis or with physical complications, both diagnoses should be recorded.[1]

Alcohol intoxication

  acute: A psychic and physical state resulting from alcohol ingestion characterized by slurred speech, unsteady gait, poor coordination, flushed facies, nystagmus, sluggish reflexes, fetor alcoholica, loud speech, emotional instability (e.g., jollity followed by lugubriousness), excessive conviviality, loquacity, and poorly inhibited sexual and aggressive behavior.[2]

  idiosyncratic: Acute psychotic episodes induced by relatively small amounts of alcohol. These are regarded as individual idiosyncratic reactions to alcohol, not due to excessive consumption and without conspicuous neurological signs of intoxication.[1]

  pathological—*see* Alcohol intoxication, idiosyncratic

Alcoholic psychoses: Organic psychotic states due mainly to excessive consumption of alcohol; defects of nutrition are thought to play an important role.[1]

  alcohol abstinence syndrome—*see* alcohol withdrawal syndrome below

  alcohol amnestic syndrome: A syndrome of prominent and lasting reduction of memory span, including striking loss of recent memory, disordered time appreciation and confabulation, occurring in alcoholics as the sequel to an acute alcoholic psychosis (especially delirium tremens) or, more rarely, in the course of chronic alcoholism. It is usually accompanied by peripheral neuritis and may be associated with Wernicke's encephalopathy.[1]

alcohol withdrawal delirium [delirium tremens]: Acute or subacute organic psychotic states in alcoholics, characterized by clouded consciousness, disorientation, fear, illusions, delusions, hallucinations of any kind, notably visual and tactile, and restlessness, tremor and sometimes fever.[1]

alcohol withdrawal hallucinosis: A psychosis usually of less than six months' duration, with slight or no clouding of consciousness and much anxious restlessness in which auditory hallucinations, mostly of voices uttering insults and threats, predominate.[1]

alcohol withdrawal syndrome: Tremor of hands, tongue, and eyelids following cessation of prolonged heavy drinking of alcohol. Nausea and vomiting, dry mouth, headache, heavy perspiration, fitful sleep, acute anxiety attacks, mood depression, feelings of guilt and remorse, and irritability are associated features.[2]

alcohol delirium—*see* alcohol withdrawal delirium above

alcoholic dementia: Nonhallucinatory dementias occurring in association with alcoholism, but not characterized by the features of either alcohol withdrawal delirium [delirium tremens] or alcohol amnestic syndrome [Korsakoff's alcoholic psychosis].[1]

alcoholic hallucinosis—*see* alcohol withdrawal hallucinosis above

alcoholic jealousy: Chronic paranoid psychosis characterized by delusional jealousy and associated with alcoholism.

alcoholic paranoia—*see* alcoholic jealousy

alcoholic polyneuritic psychosis—*see* alcohol amnestic syndrome above

Alcoholism

acute—*see* Alcohol intoxication, acute

chronic—*see* Alcohol dependence syndrome

Alexia: Loss of a previously possessed reading facility that cannot be explained by defective visual acuity.[3]

Amnesia, psychogenic: A form of dissociative hysteria in which there is a temporary disturbance in the ability to recall important personal information which has already been registered and stored in memory. The sudden onset of this disturbance in the absence of an underlying organic mental disorder, and the extent of the disturbance being too great to be explained by ordinary forgetfulness, are the essential features.[2]

Amnestic syndrome: A syndrome of prominent and lasting reduction of memory span, including striking loss of recent memory, disordered time appreciation, and confabulation. The commonest causes are chronic alcoholism [alcohol amnestic syndrome; Korsakoff's alcoholic psychosis], chronic barbiturate dependence, and malnutrition. An amnestic syndrome may be the predominating disturbance in the early states of presenile and senile dementia, arteriosclerotic dementia, and in encephalitis and other inflammatory and degenerative diseases in which there is particular bilateral involvement of the temporal lobes, and certain temporal lobe tumors.[2]

alcoholic—*see* alcohol amnestic syndrome under Alcoholic psychoses

Amoral personality—*see* Personality disorder, antisocial type

Anancastic [anankastic] neurosis—*see* Neurotic disorder, obsessive-compulsive

Anancastic [anankastic] personality—*see* Personality disorder, compulsive type

Anorexia nervosa: A disorder in which the main features are persistent active refusal to eat and marked loss of weight. The level of activity and alertness is characteristically high in relation to the degree of emaciation. Typically the disorder begins in teenage girls but it may sometimes begin before puberty and rarely it occurs in males. Amenorrhea is usual and there may be a variety of other physiological changes including slow pulse and respiration, low body temperature, and dependent edema. Unusual eating habits and attitudes toward food are typical and sometimes starvation follows or alternates with periods of overeating. The accompanying psychiatric symptoms are diverse.[1]

Anxiety hysteria—*see* phobia under Neurotic disorders

Anxiety state (neurotic): Apprehension, tension, or uneasiness that stems from the anticipation of danger, the source of which is largely unknown or unrecognized.[3]

atypical: An anxiety disorder that does not fulfill the criteria of generalized or panic attack anxiety. An example might be an individual with a single morbid fear.[2]

generalized: A disorder of at least six months' duration in which the predominant feature is limited to diffuse and persistent anxiety without the specific symptoms that characterize phobic disorders, panic disorder, or obsessive-compulsive disorder.[2]

panic attack: An episodic and often chronic, recurrent disorder in which the predominant features are anxiety attacks and nervousness. The anxiety attacks are manifested by discrete periods of sudden onset of intense apprehension, fearfulness, or terror often associated with feelings of impending doom.[2]

Aphasia, developmental: A delay in the production of spoken language. Rarely, there is also a developmental delay in the comprehension of speech sounds.[1]

Arteriosclerotic dementia: Dementia attributable, because of physical signs (on examination of the central nervous system), to degenerative arterial disease of the brain. Symptoms suggesting a focal lesion in the brain are common. There may be a fluctuating or patchy intellectual defect with insight, and an intermittent course is common. Clinical differentiation from senile or presenile dementia, which may coexist with it, may be very difficult or impossible. The diagnosis of cerebral atherosclerosis should also be recorded.[1]

Asocial personality—*see* Personality disorder, antisocial type

Astasia-abasia, hysterical: A form of conversion hysteria in which the individual is unable to stand or walk although the legs are otherwise under control.[4]

Asthenia, psychogenic—*see* neurasthenia under Neurotic disorders

Asthenic personality—*see* Personality disorder, dependent type

Attention deficit disorder—*see* attention deficit disorder under Hyperkinetic syndrome of childhood

Autism, infantile: A syndrome present from birth or beginning almost invariably in the first 30 months. Responses to auditory and sometimes to visual stimuli are abnormal, and there are usually severe problems in the understanding of spoken language. Speech is delayed and, if it develops, is characterized by echolalia, the reversal of pronouns, immature grammatical structure, and inability to use abstract terms. There is generally an impairment in the social use of both verbal and gestural language. Problems in social relationships are most severe before the age of five years and include an impairment in the development of eye-to-eye gaze, social attachments, and cooperative play. Ritualistic behavior is usual and may include abnormal routines, resistance to change, attachment to odd objects, and stereotyped patterns of play. The capacity for abstract or symbolic thought and for imaginative play is diminished. Intelligence ranges from severely subnormal to normal or above. Performance is usually better on tasks involving rote memory or visuospatial skills than on those requiring symbolic or linguistic skills.[1]

Avoidant personality—*see* Personality disorder, avoidant type

"Bad trips": Acute intoxication from hallucinogen abuse, manifested by hallucinatory states lasting only a few days or less.[1]

Barbiturate abuse: Cases where an individual has taken the drug to the detriment of his health or social functioning, in doses above or for periods beyond those normally regarded as therapeutic.[1]

Bestiality—*see* Zoophilia

Bipolar disorder—*see* Affective psychosis, bipolar

atypical—*see* Affective psychosis, bipolar, atypical

Body-rocking—*see* Stereotyped repetitive movements

Borderline personality—*see* Personality disorder, borderline type

Borderline psychosis of childhood—*see* Psychosis, atypical childhood

Borderline schizophrenia—*see* Schizophrenia, latent

Bouffée délirante—*see* Paranoid reaction, acute

Briquet's disorder—*see* somatization disorder under Neurotic disorders

Bulimia: An episodic pattern of overeating [binge eating] accompanied by an awareness of the disordered eating pattern with a fear of not being able to stop eating voluntarily. Depressive moods and self-deprecating thoughts follow the episodes of binge eating.[2]

Catalepsy schizophrenia—*see* Schizophrenia, catatonic type

Catastrophic stress—*see* Gross stress reaction

Catatonia (schizophrenic)—*see* Schizophrenia, catatonic type

Character neurosis—*see* Personality disorders

Childhood autism—*see* Autism, infantile

Childhood type schizophrenia—*see* Psychosis, child

Chronic alcoholic brain syndrome—*see* alcoholic dementia under Alcoholic psychoses

Clay-eating—*see* Pica

Clumsiness syndrome—*see* coordination disorder under Developmental delay disorders, specific

Combat fatigue—*see* Posttraumatic disorder, acute

Compensation neurosis—*see* compensation neurosis under Neurotic disorders

Compulsive conduct disorder—*see* impulse control disorders under Conduct disorders

Compulsive neurosis—*see* Neurotic disorder, obsessive-compulsive

Compulsive personality—*see* Personality disorder, compulsive type

Concentration camp syndrome—*see* Posttraumatic stress disorder, prolonged

Conduct disorders: Disorders mainly involving aggressive and destructive behavior and disorders involving delinquency. It should be used for abnormal behavior, in individuals of any age, which gives rise to social disapproval but which is not part of any other psychiatric condition. Minor emotional disturbances may also be present. To be included, the behavior, as judged by its frequency, severity, and type of associations with other symptoms, must be abnormal in its context. Disturbances of conduct are distinguished from an adjustment reaction by a longer duration and by a lack of close relationship in time and content to some stress. They differ from a personality disorder by the absence of deeply ingrained maladaptive patterns of behavior present from adolescence or earlier.[1]

  impulse control disorders: A failure to resist an impulse, drive, or temptation to perform some action which is harmful to the individual or to others. The impulse may or may not be consciously resisted, and the act may or may not be premeditated or planned. Prior to committing the act, there is an increasing sense of tension, and at the time of committing the act, there is an experience of either pleasure, gratification, or release. Immediately following the act, there may or may not be genuine regret, self-reproach, or guilt.[2] See also Intermittent explosive disorder, Isolated explosive disorder, Kleptomania, Pathological gambling, and Pyromania.

  mixed disturbance of conduct and emotions: A disorder characterized by features of undersocialized and socialized disturbance of conduct, but in which there is also considerable emotional disturbance as shown, for example, by anxiety, misery, or obsessive manifestations.[1]

  socialized conduct disorder: Conduct disorders in individuals who have acquired the values or behavior of a delinquent peer group to whom they are loyal and with whom they characteristically steal, play truant, and stay out late at night. There may also be sexual promiscuity.[1]

  undersocialized conduct disturbance

    aggressive type: A disorder characterized by a persistent pattern of disrespect for the feelings and well-being of others (bullying, physical aggression, cruel behavior, hostility, verbal abusiveness, impudence, defiance, negativism), aggressive antisocial behavior (destructiveness, stealing, persistent lying, frequent truancy, and vandalism), and failure to develop close and stable relationships with others.[2]

    unaggressive type: A disorder in which there is a lack of concern for the rights and feelings of others to a degree which indicates a failure to establish a normal degree of affection, empathy, or bond with others. There are two patterns of behavior found. In one, the child is fearful and timid, lacking self-assertiveness, resorts to self-protective and manipulative lying, indulges in whining demanding-

ness and temper tantrums, feels rejected and unfairly treated, and is mistrustful of others. In the other pattern of the disorder, the child approaches others strictly for his own gains and acts exclusively because of exploitative and extractive goals. The child lies brazenly and steals, appearing to feel no guilt, and forms no social bonds to other individuals.[2]

Confusion, psychogenic—*see* Psychosis, reactive confusion

Confusion, reactive—*see* Psychosis, reactive confusion

Confusional state

  acute—*see* Delirium, acute

  epileptic—*see* Delirium, acute

  subacute—*see* Delirium, subacute

Conversion hysteria—*see* hysteria, conversion type under Neurotic disorders

Coordination disorder—*see* coordination disorder under Developmental delay disorders, specific

Culture shock: A form of stress reaction associated with an individual's assimilation into a new culture which is vastly different from that in which he was raised.[5]

Cyclic schizophrenia—*see* Schizophrenia, schizo-affective type

Cyclothymic personality or disorder—*see* Personality disorder, cyclothymic type

Delirium: Transient organic psychotic conditions with a short course in which there is a rapidly developing onset of disorganization of higher mental processes manifested by some degree of impairment of information processing, impaired or abnormal attention, perception, memory, and thinking. Clouded consciousness, confusion, disorientation, delusions, illusions, and often vivid hallucinations predominate in the clinical picture.[1,2]

  acute: short-lived states, lasting hours or days, of the above type.[1]

  subacute: states of the above type in which the symptoms, usually less florid, last for several weeks or longer, during which they may show marked fluctuations in intensity.[1]

Delirium tremens—*see* alcohol withdrawal delirium under Alcoholic psychoses

Delusions, systematized—*see* Paranoia

Dementia: A decrement in intellectual functioning of sufficient severity to interfere with occupational or social performance, or both. There is impairment of memory and abstract thinking, the ability to learn new skills, problem solving, and judgment. There is often also personality change or impairment in impulse control. Dementia in organic psychoses may be of a chronic or progressive nature, which if untreated is usually irreversible and terminal.[1,2]

  alcoholic—*see* alcoholic dementia under Alcoholic psychoses

  arteriosclerotic—*see* Arteriosclerotic dementia

  multi-infarct—*see* Arteriosclerotic dementia

  presenile—*see* Presenile dementia

  repeated infarct—*see* Arteriosclerotic dementia

  senile—*see* Senile dementia

Depersonalization syndrome—*see* depersonalization syndrome under Neurotic disorders

Depression: States of depression, usually of moderate but occasionally of marked intensity, which have no specifically manic-depressive or other psychotic depressive features, and which do not appear to be associated with stressful events or other features specified under neurotic depressions.[1]

  anxiety—*see* depression under Neurotic disorders

  endogenous—*see* Affective psychosis, depressed type

  monopolar—*see* Affective psychosis, depressed type

  neurotic—*see* depression under Neurotic disorders

  psychotic—*see* Affective psychosis, depressed type

  psychotic reactive—*see* Psychosis, depressive

  reactive—*see* depression under Neurotic disorders

  reactive psychotic—*see* Psychosis, depressive

Depressive personality or character—*see* Personality disorder, chronic depressive type

Depressive reaction—*see* depressive reaction under Adjustment reaction

Depressive psychosis—*see* Affective psychosis, depressed type

Derealization (neurotic)—*see* depersonalization syndrome under Neurotic disorders

Developmental delay disorders, specific: A group of disorders in which a specific delay in development is the main feature. For many the delay is not explicable in terms of general intellectual retardation or of inadequate schooling. In each case development is related to biological maturation, but it is also influenced by nonbiological factors. A diagnosis of a specific developmental delay carries no etiological implications. A diagnosis of specific delay in development should not be made if it is due to a known neurological disorder.[1]

arithmetical disorder: Disorders in which the main feature is a serious impairment in the development of arithmetical skills.[1]

articulation disorder: A delay in the development of normal word-sound production resulting in defects of articulation. Omissions or substitutions of consonants are most frequent.[1]

coordination disorder: Disorders in which the main feature is a serious impairment in the development of motor coordination which is not explicable in terms of general intellectual retardation. The clumsiness is commonly associated with perceptual difficulties.[1]

mixed development disorder: A delay in the development of one specific skill (e.g., reading, arithmetic, speech, or coordination) is frequently associated with lesser delays in other skills. When this occurs the diagnosis should be made according to the skill most seriously impaired. The mixed category should be used only where the mixture of delayed skills is such that no one skill is preponderantly affected.[1]

motor retardation—*see* coordination disorder above

reading disorder or retardation: Disorders in which the main feature is a serious impairment in the development of reading or spelling skills which is not explicable in terms of general intellectual retardation or of inadequate schooling. Speech or language difficulties, impaired right-left differentiation, perceptuo-motor problems, and coding difficulties are frequently associated. Similar problems are often present in other members of the family. Adverse psychosocial factors may be present.[1]

speech or language disorder: Disorders in which the main feature is a serious impairment in the development of speech or language (syntax or semantic) which is not explicable in terms of general intellectual retardation. Most commonly there is a delay in the development of normal word-sound production resulting in defects of articulation. Omissions or substitutions of consonants are most frequent. There may also be a delay in the production of spoken language. Rarely, there is also a developmental delay in the comprehension of sounds. Includes cases in which delay is largely due to environmental privation.[1]

Dipsomania—*see* Alcohol dependence syndrome

Disorganized schizophrenia—*see* Schizophrenia, disorganized type

Dissociative hysteria—*see* hysteria, dissociative type under Neurotic disorders

Drug abuse: Includes cases where an individual, for whom no other diagnosis is possible, has come under medical care because of the maladaptive effect of a drug on which he is not dependent (*see* Drug dependence) and that he has taken on his own initiative to the detriment of his health or social functioning. When drug abuse is secondary to a psychiatric disorder, record the disorder as an additional diagnosis.[1]

Drug dependence: A state, psychic and sometimes also physical, resulting from taking a drug, characterized by behavioral and other responses that always include a compulsion to take a drug on a continuous or periodic basis in order to experience its psychic effects, and sometimes to avoid the discomfort of its absence. Tolerance may or may not be present. A person may be dependent on more than one drug.[1]

Drug psychoses: Organic mental syndromes which are due to consumption of drugs (notably amphetamines, barbiturates, and opiate and LSD groups) and solvents. Some of the syndromes in this group are not as severe as most conditions labeled "psychotic," but they are included here for practical reasons. The drug should be identified, and also a diagnosis of drug dependence should be recorded, if present.[1]

drug-induced hallucinosis: Hallucinatory states of more than a few days, but not more than a few months' duration, associated with large or prolonged intake of drugs, notably of the amphetamine and LSD groups. Auditory hallucinations usually predominate and there may be anxiety or restlessness. States following LSD or other hallucinogens lasting only a few days or less ["bad trips"] are not included.[1]

drug-induced organic delusional syndrome: Paranoid states of more than a few days, but not more than a few months' duration, associated with large or prolonged intake of drugs, notably of the amphetamine and LSD groups.[1]

drug withdrawal syndrome: States associated with drug withdrawal ranging from severe, as specified for alcohol withdrawal delirium [delirium tremens], to less severe states characterized by one or more symptoms such as convulsions, tremor, anxiety, restlessness, gastrointestinal and muscular complaints, and mild disorientation and memory disturbance.[1]

Drunkenness:

acute—*see* Alcohol intoxication, acute

pathologic—*see* Alcohol intoxication, idiosyncratic

simple: A state of inebriation due to alcohol consumption without conspicuous neurological signs of intoxications.[2]

sleep: An inability to fully arouse from the sleep state characterized by failure to attain full consciousness after arousal.[2]

Dyscalculia—*see* arithmetical disorder under Developmental delay disorders, specific

Dyslalia—*see* articulation disorder under Developmental delay disorders, specific

Dyslexia, developmental: A disorder in which the main feature is a serious impairment of reading skills which is not explicable in terms of general intellectual retardation or of inadequate schooling. Word-blindness and strephosymbolia (tendency to reverse letters and words in reading) are included.[1,3]

Dysmenorrhea, psychogenic: Painful menstruation due to disturbance of psychic control.[4]

Dyspareunia, functional—*see* functional dyspareunia under Psychosexual dysfunctions

Dyspraxia syndrome—*see* coordination disorder under Developmental delay disorders, specific

Dyssocial personality—*see* Personality disorder, antisocial type

Dysuria, psychogenic: Difficulty in passing urine due to psychic factors.[4]

Eating disorders: A group of disorders characterized by a conspicuous disturbance in eating behavior.[2] See also Bulimia, Pica, and Rumination, psychogenic.

Eccentric personality—*see* Personality disorder, eccentric type

Elective mutism: A pervasive and persistent refusal to speak in situations not attributable to a mental disorder. In some cases the behavior may manifest a form of withdrawal reaction to a specific stressful situation, or as a predominant feature in children exhibiting shyness or social withdrawal disorders.[2]

Emancipation disorder: An adjustment reaction in adolescents or young adults in which there is symptomatic expression (e.g., difficulty in making independent decisions, increased dependence on parental advice, adoption of values deliberately oppositional to parents) of a conflict over independence following the recent assumption of a status in which the individual is more independent of parental control or supervision.[2]

Emotional disturbances specific to childhood and adolescence: Less well-differentiated emotional disorders characteristic of the childhood period. When the emotional disorder takes the form of a neurosis, the appropriate diagnosis should be made. These disorders differ from adjustment reactions in terms of longer duration and by the lack of close relationship in time and content to some stress.[1] See also Academic underachievement disorder, Elective mutism, Identity disorder, Introverted disorder of childhood, Misery and unhappiness disorder, Oppositional disorder, Overanxious disorder, and Shyness disorder of childhood.

Encopresis: A disorder in which the main manifestation is the persistent voluntary or involuntary passage of formed stools of normal or near-normal consistency into places not intended for that purpose in the individual's own sociocultural setting. Sometimes the child has failed to gain bowel control, and sometimes he has gained control but then later again became encopretic. There may be a variety of associated psychiatric symptoms and there may be smearing of feces. The condition would not usually be diagnosed under the age of four years.[1]

Endogenous depression—*see* Affective psychosis, depressed type

Enuresis: A disorder in which the main manifestation is a persistent involuntary voiding of urine by day or night which is considered abnormal for the age of the individual. Sometimes the child will have failed to gain bladder control and in other cases he will have gained control and then lost it. Episodic or fluctuating enuresis should be included. The disorder would not usually be diagnosed under the age of four years.[1]

Epileptic confusional or twilight state—*see* Delirium, acute

Excitation

   catatonic—*see* Schizophrenia, catatonic type

   psychogenic—*see* Psychosis, excitative type

   reactive—*see* Psychosis, excitative type

Exhaustion delirium—*see* Stress reaction, acute

Exhibitionism: Sexual deviation in which the main sexual pleasure and gratification is derived from exposure of the genitals to a person of the opposite sex.[1]

Explosive personality disorder—*see* Personality disorder, explosive type

Factitious illness: A form of hysterical neurosis in which there are physical or psychological symptoms that are not real, genuine, or natural, which are produced by the individual and are under his voluntary control.[2]

   physical symptom type: The presentation of physical symptoms that may be total fabrication, self-inflicted, an exaggeration or exacerbation of a pre-existing physical condition, or any combination or variation of these.[2]

   psychological symptom type: The voluntary production of symptoms suggestive of a mental disorder. Behavior may mimic psychosis or, rather, the individual's idea of psychosis.[2]

Fanatic personality—*see* Personality disorder, paranoid type

Fatigue neurosis—*see* neurasthenia under Neurotic disorders

Feeble-minded—*see* Mental retardation, mild

Fetishism: A sexual deviation in which nonliving objects are utilized as a preferred or exclusive method of stimulating erotic arousal.[2]

Finger-flicking—*see* Stereotyped repetitive movements

Folie à deux—*see* Shared paranoid disorder

Frigidity: A psychosexual dysfunction in which there is partial or complete failure to attain or maintain the lubrication-swelling response of sexual excitement until completion of the sexual act.[2]

Frontal lobe syndrome: Changes in behavior following damage to the frontal areas of the brain or following interference with the connections of those areas. There is a general diminution of self-control, foresight, creativity, and spontaneity, which may be manifest as increased irritability, selfishness, restlessness and lack of concern for others. Conscientiousness and powers of concentration are often diminished, but measurable deterioration of intellect or memory is not necessarily present. The overall picture is often one of emotional dullness, lack of drive, and slowness; but, particularly in persons previously with energetic, restless, or aggressive characteristics, there may be a change towards impulsiveness, boastfulness, temper outbursts, silly fatuous humor, and the development of unrealistic ambitions; the direction of change usually depends upon the previous personality. A considerable degree of recovery is possible and may continue over the course of several years.[1]

Fugue, psychogenic: A form of dissociative hysteria characterized by an episode of wandering with inability to recall one's prior identity. Both onset and recovery are rapid. Following recovery there is no recollection of events which took place during the fugue state.[2]

Ganser's syndrome (hysterical): A form of factitious illness in which the patient voluntarily produces symptoms suggestive of a mental disorder.[2]

Gender identity disorder—*see* gender identity disorder under Psychosexual identity disorders

Gilles de la Tourette's disorder or syndrome—*see* Gilles de la Tourette's disorder under Tics

Grief reaction—*see* depressive reaction, brief under Adjustment reaction

Gross stress reaction—*see* Stress reaction, acute

Group delinquency—*see* socialized conduct disorder under Conduct disorders

Habit spasm—*see* chronic motor tic disorder under Tics

Hangover (alcohol)—*see* Drunkenness, simple

Head-banging—*see* Stereotyped repetitive movements

Hebephrenia—*see* Schizophrenia, disorganized type

Heller's syndrome—*see* Psychosis, disintegrative

High grade defect—*see* Mental retardation, mild

Homosexuality: Exclusive or predominant sexual attraction for persons of the same sex with or without physical relationship. Record homosexuality as a diagnosis whether or not it is considered as a mental disorder.[1]

Hospital addiction syndrome—*see* Munchausen syndrome

Hospital hoboes—*see* Munchausen syndrome

Hospitalism: A mild or transient adjustment reaction characterized by withdrawal seen in hospitalized patients. In young children this may be manifested by elective mutism.[1]

Hyperkinetic syndrome of childhood: Disorders in which the essential features are short attention span and distractibility. In early childhood the most striking symptom is disinhibited, poorly organized and poorly regulated extreme overactivity but in adolescence this may be replaced by underactivity. Impulsiveness, marked mood fluctuations, and aggression are also common symptoms. Delays in the development of specific skills are often present and disturbed, poor relationships are common. If the hyperkinesis is symptomatic of an underlying disorder, the diagnosis of the underlying disorder is recorded instead.[1]

   attention deficit disorder: Cases of hyperkinetic syndrome in which short attention span, distractibility, and overactivity are the main manifestations without significant disturbance of conduct or delay in specific skills.[1]

   hyperkinesis with developmental delay: Cases in which the hyperkinetic syndrome is associated with speech delay, clumsiness, reading difficulties, or other delays of specific skills.[1]

   hyperkinetic conduct disorder: Cases in which the hyperkinetic syndrome is associated with marked conduct disturbance but not developmental delay.[1]

Hypersomnia: A disorder of initiating arousal from sleep or maintaining wakefulness.[2]

   persistent: Chronic difficulty in initiating arousal from sleep or maintaining wakefulness associated with major or minor depressive mental disorders.[2]

   transient: Episodes of difficulty in arousal from sleep or maintaining wakefulness associated with acute or intermittent emotional reactions or conflicts.[2]

Hypochondriasis—*see* hypochondriasis under Neurotic disorders

Hypomania—*see* Affective psychosis, manic type

Hypomanic personality—*see* Personality disorder, chronic hypomanic type

Hyposomnia—*see* Insomnia

Hysteria—*see* hysteria under Neurotic disorders

   anxiety—*see* phobia under Neurotic disorders

   psychosis—*see* Psychosis, reactive

     acute—*see* Psychosis, excitative type

Hysterical personality—*see* Personality disorder, histrionic type

Identity disorder: An emotional disorder caused by distress over the inability to reconcile aspects of the self into a relatively coherent and acceptable sense of self, not secondary to another mental disorder. The disturbance is manifested by intense subjective distress regarding uncertainty about a variety of issues relating to identity, including long-term goals, career choice, friendship patterns, values, and loyalties.[2]

Idiocy—*see* Mental retardation, profound

Imbecile—*see* Mental retardation, moderate

Impotence: A psychosexual dysfunction in which there is partial or complete failure to attain or maintain erection until completion of the sexual act.[2]

Impulse control disorder—*see* impulse control disorders under Conduct disorders

Inadequate personality—*see* Personality disorder, dependent type

Induced paranoid disorder—*see* Shared paranoid disorder

Inebriety—*see* Drunkenness, simple

Infantile autism—*see* Autism, infantile

Insomnia: A disorder of initiating or maintaining sleep.[2]

> **persistent:** A chronic state of sleeplessness associated with chronic anxiety, major or minor depressive disorders, or psychoses.[2]

> **transient:** Episodes of sleeplessness associated with acute or intermittent emotional reactions or conflicts.[2]

Intermittent explosive disorder: Recurrent episodes of sudden and significant loss of control of aggressive impulses, not accounted for by any other mental disorder, which results in serious assault or destruction of property. The magnitude of the behavior during an episode is grossly out of proportion to any psychosocial stressors which may have played a role in eliciting the episode of lack of control. Following each episode there is genuine regret or self-reproach at the consequences of the action and the inability to control the aggressive impulse.[2]

Introverted disorder of childhood: An emotional disturbance in children chiefly manifested by a lack of interest in social relationships and indifference to social praise or criticism.[2]

Introverted personality—*see* Personality disorder, introverted type

Involutional melancholia—*see* Affective psychosis, depressed type

Involutional paranoid state—*see* Paraphrenia

Isolated explosive disorder: A disorder of impulse control in which there is a single discrete episode characterized by failure to resist an impulse which leads to a single, violent externally-directed act, which has a catastrophic impact on others, and for which the available information does not justify the diagnosis of another mental disorder.[2]

Isolated phobia—*see* simple phobia under Phobia

Jet lag syndrome: A phase-shift disruption of the 24-hour sleep-wake cycle due to rapid time-zone changes experienced in long-distance travel.[2]

Kanner's syndrome—*see* Autism, infantile

Kleptomania: A disorder of impulse control characterized by a recurrent failure to resist impulses to steal objects not for immediate use or their monetary value. An increasing sense of tension is experienced prior to committing the act, with an intense experience of gratification at the time of committing the theft.[2]

Korsakoff's psychosis:

> **alcoholic**—*see* alcohol amnestic syndrome under Alcoholic psychoses

> **nonalcoholic**—*see* Amnestic syndrome

Latent schizophrenia—*see* Schizophrenia, latent

Lesbianism—*see* Homosexuality

Lobotomy syndrome—*see* Frontal lobe syndrome

LSD reaction: Acute intoxication from hallucinogen abuse, manifested by hallucinatory states lasting only a few days or less.[1]

Major depressive disorder—*see* Affective psychosis, depressed type

Malingering: A clinical picture in which the predominant feature is the presentation of fake or grossly exaggerated physical or psychiatric illness apparently under voluntary control. In contrast to factitious illness, the symptoms produced in malingering are in pursuit of a goal which, when known, is recognizable and obviously understandable in light of knowledge of the individual's circumstances. Examples of understandable goals include, but are not limited to, becoming a "patient" in order to avoid conscription or military duty, avoid work, obtain financial compensation, evade criminal prosecution, and obtain drugs.[2]

Mania (monopolar)—*see* Affective psychosis, manic type

Manic-depressive psychosis

> **circular type**—*see* Affective psychosis, bipolar

> **depressed type**—*see* Affective psychosis, depressed type

> **manic type**—*see* Affective psychosis, manic type

> **mixed type**—*see* Affective psychosis, mixed type

Manic disorder—*see* Affective psychosis, manic type

> **atypical**—*see* Affective psychosis, manic type, atypical

Masochistic personality—*see* Personality disorder, masochistic type

Melancholia—*see* Affective psychoses

> **involutional**—*see* Affective psychosis, depressed type

Mental retardation: A condition of arrested or incomplete development of mind which is especially characterized by subnormality of intelligence. The coding should be made on the individual's current level of functioning without regard to its nature or causation, such as psychosis, cultural deprivation, Down's syndrome, etc. Where there is a specific cognitive handicap—such as in speech—the diagnosis of mental retardation should be based on assessments of cognition outside the area of specific handicap. The assessment of intellectual level should be based on whatever information is available, including clinical evidence, adaptive behavior, and psychometric findings. The IQ levels given are based on a test with a mean of 100 and a standard deviation of 15, such as the Wechsler scales. They are provided only as a guide and should not be applied rigidly. Mental retardation often involves psychiatric disturbances and may often develop as a result of some physical disease or injury. In these cases, an additional diagnosis should be recorded to identify any associated condition, psychiatric or physical.[1]

> **mild mental retardation:** IQ criteria 50–70. Individuals with this level of retardation are usually educable. During the preschool period they can develop social and communication skills, have minimal retardation in sensorimotor areas, and often are not distinguished from normal children until a later age. During the school age period they can learn academic skills up to approximately the sixth-grade level. During the adult years, they can usually achieve social and vocational skills adequate for minimum self-support, but may need guidance and assistance when under social or economic stress.[2]

> **moderate mental retardation:** IQ criteria 35–49. Individuals with this level of retardation are usually trainable. During the pre-school period they can talk or learn to communicate. They have poor social awareness and fair motor development. During the school age period they can profit from training in social and occupational skills, but they are unlikely to progress beyond the second-grade level in academic subjects. During their adult years they may achieve self-maintenance in unskilled or semi-skilled work under sheltered conditions. They need supervision and guidance when under mild social or economic stress.[2]

> **severe mental retardation:** IQ criteria 20–34. Individuals with this level of retardation evidence poor motor development, minimal speech, and are generally unable to profit from training and self-help during the pre-school period. During the school age period they can talk or learn to communicate, can be trained in elementary health habits, and may profit from systematic habit training. During the adult years they may contribute partially to self-maintenance under complete supervision.[2]

> **profound mental retardation:** IQ criteria under 20. Individuals with this level of retardation evidence minimal capacity for sensorimotor functioning and need nursing care during the pre-school period. During the school age period some further motor development may occur, and they may respond to minimal or limited training in self-help. During the adult years some motor and speech development may occur, and they may achieve very limited self-care and need nursing care.[2]

Merycism—*see* Rumination, psychogenic

Minimal brain dysfunction [MBD]—*see* Hyperkinetic syndrome of childhood

Misery and unhappiness disorder: An emotional disorder characteristic of childhood in which the main symptoms involve misery and unhappiness. There may also be eating and sleep disturbances.[1]

Mood swings (brief compensatory) (rebound): Mild disorders of mood (depression and anxiety or elation and excitement, occurring alternatingly or episodically) seen in affective psychosis.[1]

Motor tic disorders—*see* Tics

Motor-verbal tic disorder—*see* Gilles de la Tourette's disorder under Tics

Multi-infarct dementia or psychosis—*see* Arteriosclerotic dementia

Multiple operations syndrome—*see* Munchausen syndrome

Multiple personality: A form of dissociative hysteria in which there is the domination of the individual at any one time by one of two or more distinct personalities. Each personality is a fully-integrated and complex unit with memories, behavior patterns, and social friendships which determine the nature of the individual's acts when uppermost in consciousness.[2]

Munchausen syndrome: A chronic form of factitious illness in which the individual demonstrates a plausible presentation of voluntarily produced physical symptomatology of such a degree that he is able to obtain and sustain multiple hospitalizations.[2]

Narcissistic personality—*see* Personality disorder, narcissistic type

Nervous debility—*see* neurasthenia under Neurotic disorders

Neurasthenia—*see* neurasthenia under Neurotic disorders

Neurotic delinquency—*see* mixed disturbance of conduct and emotions under Conduct disorders

Neurotic disorders: Neurotic disorders are mental disorders without any demonstrable organic basis in which the individual may have considerable insight and has unimpaired reality testing, in that he usually does not confuse his morbid subjective experiences and fantasies with external reality. Behavior may be greatly affected although usually remaining within socially acceptable limits, but personality is not disorganized. The principal manifestations include excessive anxiety, hysterical symptoms, phobias, obsessional and compulsive symptoms, and depression.[1]

anxiety states: Various combinations of physical and mental manifestations of anxiety, not attributable to real danger and occurring either in attacks [*see* Anxiety state, panic attacks] or as a persisting state [*see* Anxiety state, generalized]. The anxiety is usually diffuse and may extend to panic. Other neurotic features such as obsessional or hysterical symptoms may be present but do not dominate the clinical picture.[1]

compensation neurosis: Certain unconscious neurotic reactions in which features of secondary gain, such as a situational or financial advantage, are prominent.[3]

depersonalization: A neurotic disorder with an unpleasant state of disturbed perception in which external objects or parts of one's own body are experienced as changed in their quality, unreal, remote, or automatized. The patient is aware of the subjective nature of the change he experiences. If depersonalization occurs as a feature of anxiety, schizophrenia, or other mental disorder, the condition is classified according to the major psychiatric disorder.[1]

depression: A neurotic disorder characterized by disproportionate depression which has usually recognizably ensued on a distressing experience; it does not include among its features delusions or hallucinations, and there is often preoccupation with the psychic trauma which preceded the illness, e.g., loss of a cherished person or possession. Anxiety is also frequently present and mixed states of anxiety and depression should be included here. The distinction between depressive neurosis and psychosis should be made not only upon the degree of depression but also on the presence or absence of other neurotic and psychotic characteristics, and upon the degree of disturbance of the individual's behavior.[1]

hypochondriasis: A neurotic disorder in which the conspicuous features are excessive concern with one's health in general or the integrity and functioning of some part of one's body, or less frequently, one's mind. It is usually associated with anxiety and depression. It may occur as a feature of some other severe mental disorder (e.g., manic-depressive psychosis, depressed type, schizophrenia, hysteria) and in that case should be classified according to the corresponding major disorder.[1]

hysteria: A neurotic mental disorder in which motives, of which the patient seems unaware, produce either a restriction of the field of consciousness or disturbances of motor or sensory function which may seem to have psychological advantage or symbolic value.[1] There are three subtypes:

conversion type: The chief or only symptoms of the hysterical neurosis consist of psychogenic disturbance of function in some part of the body, e.g., paralysis, tremor, blindness, deafness, seizures.[1]

dissociative type: The most prominent feature of the hysterical neurosis is a narrowing of the field of consciousness which seems to serve an unconscious purpose and is commonly accompanied or followed by a selective amnesia. There may be dramatic but essentially superficial changes of personality [multiple personality], or sometimes the patient enters into a wandering state [fugue].[1]

factitious illness: Physical or psychological symptoms that are not real, genuine, or natural, which are produced by the individual and are under his voluntary control.[2]

neurasthenia: A neurotic disorder characterized by fatigue, irritability, headache, depression, insomnia, difficulty in concentration, and lack of capacity for enjoyment [anhedonia]. It may follow or accompany an infection or exhaustion, or arise from continued emotional stress. If neurasthenia is associated with a physical disorder, the latter should also be recorded as a diagnosis.[1]

obsessive-compulsive: States in which the outstanding symptom is a feeling of subjective compulsion, which must be resisted, to carry out some action, to dwell on an idea, to recall an experience, or to ruminate on an abstract topic. Unwanted thoughts which intrude, the insistency of words or ideas, ruminations or trains of thought are perceived by the individual to be inappropriate or nonsensical. The obsessional urge or idea is recognized as alien to the personality but as coming from within the self. Obsessional actions may be quasi-ritual performances designed to relieve anxiety, e.g., washing the hands to cope with contamination. Attempts to dispel the unwelcome thoughts or urges may lead to a severe inner struggle, with intense anxiety.[1]

occupational: A neurosis characterized by a functional disorder of a group of muscles used chiefly in one's occupation, marked by the occurrence of spasm, paresis, or incoordination on attempt to repeat the habitual movements (e.g., writers' cramp).[5]

phobic disorders: Neurotic states with abnormally intense dread of certain objects or specific situations which would not normally have that effect. If the anxiety tends to spread from a specified situation or object to a wider range of circumstances, it becomes akin to or identical with anxiety state and should be classified as such.[1] See also Phobia.

somatization disorder: A chronic, but fluctuating, neurotic disorder which begins early in life and is characterized by recurrent and multiple somatic complaints for which medical attention is sought but which are not apparently due to any physical illness. Complaints are presented in a dramatic, vague, or exaggerated way, or are part of a complicated medical history in which often many specific diagnoses have allegedly been made by other physicians. Complaints invariably refer to many organ systems (headache, fatigue, palpitations, fainting, nausea and vomiting, abdominal pains, bowel trouble, allergies, menstrual and sexual difficulties), and the individual frequently receives medical care from a number of physicians, sometimes simultaneously.[2]

Neurosis—*see* Neurotic disorders

Nightmares: Anxiety attacks occurring in dreams during REM sleep.[2]

Night terrors: A pathology of arousal from stage 4 sleep in which the individual experiences excessive terror and extreme panic (screaming, verbalizations), symptoms of autonomic activity, confusion, and poor recall for event.[2]

Nymphomania: Abnormal and excessive need or desire in the woman for sexual intercourse.[3]

Obsessional personality—*see* Personality disorder, compulsive type

Occupational neurosis—*see* Neurotic disorder, occupational

Oneirophrenia—*see* Schizophrenia, acute episode

Oppositional disorder of childhood or adolescence: A disorder characterized by pervasive opposition to all in authority regardless of self-interest, a continuous argumentativeness, and an unwillingness to respond to reasonable persuasion, not accounted for by a conduct disorder, adjustment disorder, or a psychosis of childhood. The oppositional behavior in this disorder is evoked by any demand, rule, suggestion, request, or admonishment placed on the individual.[2]

Organic affective syndrome: A clinical picture in which the predominating symptoms closely resemble those seen in either the depressive or manic affective disorders, occurring in the presence of evidence or history of a specific organic factor which is etiologically related to the disturbance, such as head trauma, endocranial tumors, and exocranial tumors secreting neurotoxic diatheses (e.g., pancreatic carcinoma). Excessive use of steroids, Cushing's syndrome, and other endocrine disorders may lead to an organic affective syndrome.[2]

Organic personality syndrome: Chronic, mild states of memory disturbance and intellectual deterioration, of nonpsychotic nature, often accompanied by increased irritability, querulousness, lassitude, and complaints of physical weakness. These states are often associated with old age, and may precede more severe states due to brain damage classifiable under senile or presenile dementia, dementia associated with other chronic organic psychotic brain syndromes, or delirium, delusions, hallucinosis, and depression in transient organic psychotic conditions.[1]

Organic psychosyndrome, focal (partial): A nonpsychotic organic mental disorder resembling the postconcussion syndrome associated with localized diseases of the brain or surrounding tissues.[1]

Organic psychotic conditions: Syndromes in which there is impairment of orientation, memory, comprehension, calculation, learning capacity, and judgment. These are the essential features but there may also be shallowness or lability of affect, or a more persistent disturbance of mood, lowering of ethical standards and exaggeration or emergence of personality traits, and diminished capacity for independent decision.[1] See also Alcohol psychoses, Arteriosclerotic dementia, Drug psychoses, Presenile dementia, and Senile dementia.

   mixed paranoid and affective: Organic psychosis in which depressive and paranoid symptoms are the main features.[1]

   transient: States characterized by clouded consciousness, confusion, disorientation, illusions, and often vivid hallucinations. They are usually due to some intra- or extracerebral toxic, infectious, metabolic or other systemic disturbance and are generally reversible. Depressive and paranoid symptoms may also be present but are not the main feature. The diagnosis of the associated physical or neurological condition should also be recorded.[1]

     acute delirium: Short-lived states, lasting hours or days, of the above type.[1]

     subacute delirium: States of the above type in which the symptoms, usually less florid, last for several weeks or longer during which they may show marked fluctuations in intensity.[1]

Organic reaction—*see* Organic psychotic conditions, transient

Overanxious disorder: An ill-defined emotional disorder characteristic of childhood in which the main symptoms involve anxiety and fearfulness.[1]

Panic disorder—*see* panic attack under Anxiety state

Paranoia: A rare chronic psychosis in which logically constructed systematized delusions have developed gradually without concomitant hallucinations or the schizophrenic type of disordered thinking. The delusions are mostly of grandeur (the paranoiac prophet or inventor), persecution, or somatic abnormality.[1]

   alcoholic—*see* alcoholic jealousy under Alcoholic psychoses

   querulans: A paranoid state which, though in many ways akin to schizophrenic or affective states, differs from other paranoid states and psychogenic paranoid psychosis.[1]

   senile—*see* Paraphrenia

Paranoid personality—*see* Personality disorder, paranoid type

Paranoid reaction, acute: Paranoid states apparently provoked by some emotional stress. The stress is often misconstrued as an attack or threat. Such states are particularly prone to occur in prisoners or as acute reactions to a strange and threatening environment, e.g., in immigrants.[1]

Paranoid schizophrenia—*see* Schizophrenia, paranoid type

Paranoid state

involutional—*see* Paraphrenia

senile—*see* Paraphrenia

simple: A psychosis, acute or chronic, not classifiable as schizophrenia or affective psychosis, in which delusions, especially of being influenced, persecuted, or treated in some special way, are the main symptoms. The delusions are of a fairly fixed, elaborate, and systematized kind.[1]

Paranoid traits—*see* Personality disorder, paranoid type

Paraphilia—*see* Sexual deviations

Paraphrenia: Paranoid psychosis in which there are conspicuous hallucinations, often in several modalities. Affective symptoms and disordered thinking, if present, do not dominate the clinical picture, and the personality is well preserved.[1]

Paraphrenic schizophrenia—*see* Schizophrenia, paranoid type

Passive-aggressive personality—*see* Personality disorder, passive-aggressive type

Passive personality—*see* Personality disorder, dependent type

Pathological

   alcohol intoxication—*see* Alcohol intoxication, idiosyncratic

   drug intoxication: Individual idiosyncratic reactions to comparatively small quantities of a drug, which take the form of acute, brief psychotic states of any type.[1]

   drunkenness—*see* Alcohol intoxication, idiosyncratic

   gambling: A disorder of impulse control characterized by a chronic and progressive preoccupation with gambling and urge to gamble, with subsequent gambling behavior that compromises, disrupts, or damages personal, family, and vocational pursuits.[2]

   personality—*see* Personality disorder

Pedophilia: Sexual deviations in which an adult engages in sexual activity with a child of the same or opposite sex.[1]

Peregrinating patient—*see* Malingering

Personality disorders: Deeply ingrained maladaptive patterns of behavior generally recognizable by the time of adolescence or earlier and continuing throughout most of adult life, although often becoming less obvious in middle or old age. The personality is abnormal either in the balance of its components, their quality and expression, or in its total aspect. Because of this deviation or psychopathy the patient suffers or others have to suffer, and there is an adverse effect upon the individual or on society. It includes what is sometimes called psychopathic personality, but if this is determined primarily by malfunctioning of the brain, it should be classified as one of the nonpsychotic organic brain syndromes. When the patient exhibits an anomaly of personality directly related to his neurosis or psychosis, e.g., schizoid personality and schizophrenia or anancastic personality and obsessive compulsive neurosis, the relevant neurosis or psychosis which is in evidence should be diagnosed in addition.[1]

   affective type: A chronic personality disorder characterized by lifelong predominance of a pronounced mood. The illness does not have a clear onset, and there may be intermittent periods of disturbed mood separated by periods of normal mood.[1]

   anancastic [anankastic] type—*see* Personality disorder, compulsive type

   antisocial type: A personality disorder characterized by disregard for social obligations, lack of feeling for others, and impetuous violence or callous unconcern. There is a gross disparity between behavior and the prevailing social norms. Behavior is not readily modifiable by experience, including punishment. People with this personality are often affectively cold, and may be abnormally aggressive or irresponsible. Their tolerance to frustration is low; they blame others or offer plausible rationalizations for the behavior which brings them into conflict with society.[1]

   asthenic type—*see* Personality disorder, dependent type

   avoidant type: Individuals with this disorder exhibit excessive social inhibitions and shyness, a tendency to withdraw from opportunities for developing close relationships, and a fearful expectation that they will be belittled and humiliated. Desires for affection and acceptance are strong, but they are unwilling to enter relationships unless given unusually strong guarantees that they will be uncritically accepted. Therefore, they have few close relationships and suffer from feelings of lone-liness and isolation.[2]

borderline type: Individuals with this disorder are character-ized by instability in a variety of areas, including interper-sonal relationships, behavior, mood, and self image. Interper-sonal relationships are often intense and unstable with marked shifts of attitude over time. Frequently there is im-pulsive and unpredictable behavior which is potentially physically self-damaging. There may be problems tolerating being alone, and chronic feelings of emptiness or boredom.[2]

chronic depressive type: An affective personality disorder char-acterized by lifelong predominance of a chronic nonpsychotic disturbance involving either intermittent or sustained periods of depressed mood (marked by worry, pessimism, low out-put of energy, and a sense of futility).[2]

chronic hypomanic type: An affective personality disorder characterized by lifelong predominance of a chronic nonpsy-chotic disturbance involving either intermittent or sustained periods of abnormally elevated mood (unshakable optimism and an enhanced zest for life and activity).[2]

compulsive type: A personality disorder characterized by feel-ings of personal insecurity, doubt, and incompleteness lead-ing to excessive conscientiousness, checking, stubbornness, and caution. There may be insistent and unwelcome thoughts or impulses which do not attain the severity of an obses-sional neurosis. There is perfectionism and meticulous accu-racy and a need to check repeatedly in an attempt to ensure this. Rigidity and excessive doubt may be conspicuous.[1]

cyclothymic type: A chronic nonpsychotic disturbance involv-ing depressed and elevated mood, lasting at least two years, separated by periods of normal mood.[2]

dependent type: A personality disorder characterized by pas-sive compliance with the wishes of elders and others and a weak inadequate response to the demands of daily life. Lack of vigor may show itself in the intellectual or emotional spheres; there is little capacity for enjoyment.[1]

eccentric type: A personality disorder characterized by oddities of behavior which do not conform to the clinical syndromes of personality disorders described elsewhere.[2]

explosive type: A personality disorder characterized by insta-bility of mood with liability to intemperate outbursts of an-ger, hate, violence, or affection. Aggression may be expressed in words or in physical violence. The outbursts cannot read-ily be controlled by the affected persons, who are not other-wise prone to antisocial behavioral.[1]

histrionic type: A personality disorder characterized by shal-low, labile affectivity, dependence on others, craving for ap-preciation and attention, suggestibility, and theatricality. There is often sexual immaturity, e.g., frigidity and over-responsiveness to stimuli. Under stress hysterical symptoms [neurosis] may develop.[1]

hysterical type—*see* Personality disorder, histrionic type

inadequate type—*see* Personality disorder, dependent type

introverted type: A form of schizoid personality in which the essential features are a profound defect in the ability to form social relationships and to respond to the usual forms of social reinforcements. Such patients are characteristically "loners " who do not appear distressed by their social dis-tance and are not interested in greater social involvement.[2]

masochistic type: A personality disorder in which the individ-ual appears to arrange life situations so as to be defeated and humiliated.[2]

narcissistic type: A personality disorder in which interpersonal difficulties are caused by an inflated sense of self-worth, and indifference to the welfare of others. Achievement deficits and social irresponsibilities are justified and sustained by a boastful arrogance, expansive fantasies, facile rationalization, and frank prevarication.[2]

paranoid type: A personality disorder in which there is exces-sive sensitiveness to setbacks or to what are taken to be humiliations and rebuffs, a tendency to distort experience by misconstruing the neutral or friendly actions of others as hostile or contemptuous, and a combative and tenacious sense of personal rights. There may be a proneness to jeal-ousy or excessive self-importance. Such persons may feel helplessly humiliated and put upon; others, likewise exces-sively sensitive, are aggressive and insistent. In all cases there is excessive self-reference.[1]

passive-aggressive type: A personality disorder characterized by aggressive behavior manifested in passive ways, such as obstructionism, pouting, procrastination, intentional ineffi-ciency, or stubbornness. The aggression often arises from re-sentment at failing to find gratification in a relationship with an individual or institution upon which the individual is overdependent.[3]

passive type—*see* Personality disorder, dependent type

schizoid type: A personality disorder in which there is with-drawal from affectional, social, and other contacts with autis-tic preference for fantasy and introspective reserve. Behavior may be slightly eccentric or indicate avoidance of competitive situations. Apparent coolness and detachment may mask an incapacity to express feeling.[1]

schizotypal type: A form of schizoid personality in which indi-viduals with this disorder manifest various oddities of think-ing, perception, communication, and behavior. The distur-bance in thinking may be expressed as magical thinking, ideas of reference, or paranoid ideation. Perceptual distur-bances may include recurrent illusions and derealization [de-personalization]. Frequently, but not invariably, the behav-ioral manifestations include social isolation and constricted or inappropriate affect which interferes with rapport in face-to-face interaction without any of the frank psychotic features which characterize schizophrenia.[2]

Phobia: Neurotic states with abnormally intense dread of certain objects or specific situations which would not normally have that effect. If the anxiety tends to spread from a specified situa-tion or object to a wider range of circumstances, it becomes akin to or identical with anxiety state, and should be classified as such.[1]

acrophobia: Fear of heights[3]

agoraphobia: Fear of leaving the familiar setting of the home, and is almost always preceded by a phase during which there are recurrent panic attacks. Because of the anticipatory fear of helplessness when having a panic attack, the patient is reluctant or refuses to be alone, travel or walk alone, or to be in situations where there is no ready access to help, such as in crowds, closed or open spaces, or crowded stores.[2]

ailurophobia: Fear of cats[3]

algophobia: Fear of pain[3]

claustrophobia: Fear of closed spaces[3]

isolated phobia—*see* simple phobia below

mysophobia: Fear of dirt or germs[3]

obsessional—*see* Neurotic disorder, obsessive-compulsive

panphobia: Fear of everything

simple phobia: Fear of a discrete object or situation which is neither fear of leaving the familiar setting of the home [ago-raphobia], or of being observed by others in certain situations [social phobia]. Examples of simple phobia are fear of ani-mals, acrophobia, and claustrophobia.[2]

social phobia: Fear of situations in which the subject is exposed to possible scrutiny by others, and the possibility exists that he may act in a fashion that will be considered shameful. The most common social phobias are fears of public speaking, blushing, eating in public, writing in front of others, or using public lavatories.[2]

xenophobia: Fear of strangers[3]

Pica: Perverted appetite of nonorganic origin in which there is persistent eating of non-nutritional substances. Typically, in-fants ingest paint, plaster, string, hair, or cloth. Older children may have access to animal droppings, sand, bugs, leaves, or pebbles. In the adult, eating of starch or clay-earth has been observed.[2]

Postconcussion syndrome: States occurring after generalized con-tusion of the brain, in which the symptom picture may resem-ble that of the frontal lobe syndrome or that of any of the neurotic disorders, but in which in addition, headache, giddi-ness, fatigue, insomnia, and a subjective feeling of impaired intellectual ability are usually prominent. Mood may fluctuate, and quite ordinary stress may produce exaggerated fear and apprehension. There may be marked intolerance of mental and physical exertion, undue sensitivity to noise, and hypochondriacal preoccupation. The symptoms are more common in persons who have previously suffered from neurotic or personality disorders, or when there is a possibility of compensation. This syndrome is particularly associated with the closed type of head injury when signs of localized brain damage are slight or absent, but it may also occur in other conditions.[1]

Postcontusion syndrome or encephalopathy—*see* Postconcussion syndrome

Postencephalitic syndrome: A nonpsychotic organic mental disorder resembling the postconcussion syndrome associated with central nervous system infections.[1]

Postleucotomy syndrome—*see* Frontal lobe syndrome

Posttraumatic brain syndrome, nonpsychotic—*see* Postconcussion syndrome

Posttraumatic organic psychosis—*see* Organic psychotic conditions, transient

Posttraumatic stress disorder: The development of characteristic symptoms (re-experiencing the traumatic event, numbing of responsiveness to or involvement with the external world, and a variety of other autonomic, dysphoric, or cognitive symptoms) after experiencing a psychologically traumatic event or events outside the normal range of human experience (e.g., rape or assault, military combat, natural catastrophes such as flood or earthquake, or other disaster, such as airplane crash, fires, bombings).[2]

  acute: Brief, episodic, or recurrent disorders lasting less than six months' duration after the onset of trauma.[2]

  prolonged: Chronic disorders of the above type lasting six months or more following the trauma.[2]

Premature ejaculation—*see* premature ejaculation under Psychosexual dysfunctions

Prepsychotic schizophrenia—*see* Schizophrenia, latent

Presbyophrenia—*see* Organic personality syndrome

Presenile dementia: Dementia occurring usually before the age of 65 in patients with the relatively rare forms of diffuse or lobar cerebral atrophy. The associated neurological condition (e.g., Alzheimer's disease, Pick's disease, Jakob-Creutzfeldt disease) should also be recorded as a diagnosis.[1]

Prodromal schizophrenia—*see* Schizophrenia, latent

Pseudoneurotic schizophrenia—*see* Schizophrenia, latent

Psychalgia: Pains of mental origin, e.g., headache or backache, for which a more precise medical or psychiatric diagnosis cannot be made.[1]

Psychasthenia: A functional neurosis marked by stages of pathological fear or anxiety, obsessions, fixed ideas, tics, feelings of inadequacy, self-accusation, and peculiar feelings of strangeness, unreality, and depersonalization.[4]

Psychic shock: A sudden disturbance of mental equilibrium produced by strong emotion in response to physical or mental stress.[4]

Psychic factors associated with physical diseases: Mental disturbances or psychic factors of any type thought to have played a major part in the etiology of physical conditions, usually involving tissue damage, classified elsewhere. The mental disturbance is usually mild and nonspecific, and the psychic factors (worry, fear, conflict, etc.) may be present without any overt psychiatric disorder. Examples of these conditions are asthma, dermatitis, eczema, duodenal ulcer, ulcerative colitis, and urticaria, specified as due to psychogenic factors.

  Use an additional diagnosis to identify the physical condition. In the rare instance that an overt psychiatric disorder is thought to have caused the physical condition, the psychiatric diagnosis should be recorded in addition.[1]

Psychoneurosis—*see* Neurotic disorders

Psycho-organic syndrome—*see* Organic psychotic conditions, transient

Psychopathic constitutional state—*see* Personality disorders

Psychopathic personality—*see* Personality disorders

Psychophysiological disorders: A variety of physical symptoms or types of physiological malfunctions of mental origin, not involving tissue damage, and usually mediated through the autonomic nervous system. The disorders are classified according to the body system involved. If the physical symptom is secondary to a psychiatric disorder classifiable elsewhere, the physical symptom is not classified as a psychophysiological disorder. If tissue damage is involved, then the diagnosis is classified as a psychic factor associated with diseases classified elsewhere.[1]

Psychosexual dysfunctions: A group of disorders in which there is recurrent and persistent dysfunction encountered during sexual activity. The dysfunction may be lifelong or acquired, generalized or situational, and total or partial.[2]

  functional dyspareunia: Recurrent and persistent genital pain associated with coitus.[2]

  functional vaginismus: A history of recurrent and persistent involuntary spasm of the musculature of the outer one-third of the vagina that interferes with sexual activity.[2]

  inhibited female orgasm: Recurrent and persistent inhibition of the female orgasm as manifested by a delay or absence of orgasm following a normal sexual excitement phase during sexual activity.[2]

  inhibited male orgasm: Recurrent and persistent inhibition of the male orgasm as manifested by a delay or absence of either the emission or ejaculation phases, or more usually, both following an adequate phase of sexual excitement.[2]

  inhibited sexual desire: Persistent inhibition of desire for engaging in a particular form of sexual activity.[2]

  inhibited sexual excitement: Recurrent and persistent inhibition of sexual excitement during sexual activity, manifested either by partial or complete failure to attain or maintain erection until completion of the sexual act [impotence], or partial or complete failure to attain or maintain the lubrication-swelling response of sexual excitement until completion of the sexual act [frigidity].[2]

  premature ejaculation: Ejaculation occurs before the individual wishes it, because of recurrent and persistent absence of reasonable voluntary control of ejaculation and orgasm during sexual activity.[2]

Psychosexual gender identity disorders: Behavior occurring in preadolescents of immature psychosexuality, or in adults, in which there is an incongruence between the individual's anatomic sex and gender identity.[2]

  gender identity disorder: In children or in adults a condition in which the individual would prefer to be of the other sex, and strongly prefers the clothes, toys, activities, and companionship of the other sex. Cross-dressing is intermittent, although it may be frequent. In children the commonest form is feminism in boys.[2]

  trans-sexualism: A psychosexual identity disorder centered around fixed beliefs that the overt bodily sex is wrong. The resulting behavior is directed towards either changing the sexual organs by operation, or completely concealing the bodily sex by adopting both the dress and behavior of the opposite sex.[1]

Psychosomatic disorders—*see* Psychophysiological disorders

Psychosis: Mental disorders in which impairment of mental function has developed to a degree that interferes grossly with insight, ability to meet some ordinary demands of life or to maintain adequate contact with reality. It is not an exact or well defined term. Mental retardation is excluded.[1]

  affective—*see* Affective psychoses

  alcoholic—*see* Alcoholic psychoses

  atypical childhood: A variety of atypical infantile psychoses which may show some, but not all, of the features of infantile autism. Symptoms may include stereotyped repetitive movements, hyperkinesis, self-injury, retarded speech development, echolalia, and impaired social relationships. Such disorders may occur in children of any level of intelligence but are particularly common in those with mental retardation.[1]

  borderline, of childhood—*see* Psychosis, atypical childhood

  child: A group of disorders in children, characterized by distortions in the timing, rate, and sequence of many psychological functions involving language development and social relations in which the severe qualitative abnormalities are not normal for any stage of development.[2] See also Autism, infantile, Psychosis, disintegrative, Psychosis, atypical childhood.

depressive—*see* Affective psychosis, depressed type

depressive type: A depressive psychosis which can be similar in its symptoms to manic-depressive psychosis, depressed type but is apparently provoked by saddening stress such as a bereavement, or a severe disappointment or frustration. There may be less diurnal variation of symptoms than in manic-depressive psychosis, depressed type, and the delusions are more often understandable in the context of the life experiences. There is usually a serious disturbance of behavior, e.g., major suicidal attempt.[1]

disintegrative: A disorder in which normal or near-normal development for the first few years is followed by a loss of social skills and of speech, together with a severe disorder of emotions, behavior, and relationships. Usually this loss of speech and of social competence takes place over a period of a few months and is accompanied by the emergence of overactivity and of stereotypies. In most cases there is intellectual impairment, but this is not a necessary part of the disorder. The condition may follow overt brain disease, such as measles encephalitis, but it may also occur in the absence of any known organic brain disease or damage. Any associated neurological disorder should also be recorded.[1]

epileptic: An organic psychotic condition associated with epilepsy.[1]

excitative type: An affective psychosis similar in its symptoms to manic-depressive psychosis, manic type, but apparently provoked by emotional stress.[1]

hypomanic—*see* Affective psychosis, manic type

hysterical—*see* Psychosis, reactive

acute—*see* Psychosis, excitative type

induced—*see* Shared paranoid disorder

infantile—*see* Autism, infantile

infective—*see* Organic psychotic conditions, transient

Korsakoff's:

alcoholic—*see* alcohol amnestic syndrome under Alcoholic psychoses

nonalcoholic—*see* Amnestic syndrome

manic-depressive—*see* Affective psychoses

multi-infarct—*see* Arteriosclerotic dementia

paranoid

chronic—*see* Paranoia

protracted reactive—*see* Psychosis, paranoid, psychogenic

psychogenic: Psychogenic or reactive paranoid psychosis of any type which is more protracted than the reactions described under Paranoid reaction, acute.[1]

acute—*see* Paranoid reaction, acute

postpartum—*see* Psychosis, puerperal

psychogenic—*see* Psychosis, reactive

depressive—*see* Psychosis, depressive type

puerperal: Any psychosis occurring within a fixed period (approximately 90 days) after childbirth.[3] The diagnosis should be classified according to the predominant symptoms or characteristics, such as schizophrenia, affective psychosis, paranoid states, or other specified psychosis.

reactive: A psychotic condition which is largely or entirely attributable to a recent life experience. This diagnosis is not used for the wider range of psychoses in which environmental factors play some, but not the major, part in etiology.[1]

brief: A florid psychosis of at least a few hours' duration but lasting no more than two weeks, with sudden onset immediately following a severe environmental stress and eventually terminating in complete recovery to the pre-psychotic state.[2]

confusion: Mental disorders with clouded consciousness, disorientation (though less marked than in organic confusion), and diminished accessibility often accompanied by excessive activity and apparently provoked by emotional stress.[1]

depressive—*see* Psychosis, depressive type

schizo-affective—*see* Schizophrenia, schizo-affective type

schizophrenic—*see* Schizophrenia

schizophreniform—*see* Schizophrenia

affective type—*see* Schizophrenia, schizo-affective type

confusional type—*see* Schizophrenia, acute episode

senile—*see* Senile dementia, delusional type

Pyromania: A disorder of impulse control characterized by a recurrent failure to resist impulses to set fires without regard for the consequences, or with deliberate destructive intent. Invariably there is intense fascination with the setting of fires, seeing fires burn, and a satisfaction with the resultant destruction.[2]

Relationship problems of childhood: Emotional disorders characteristic of childhood in which the main symptoms involve relationship problems.[1]

Repeated infarct dementia—*see* Arteriosclerotic dementia

Residual schizophrenia—*see* Schizophrenia, residual type

Restzustand (schizophrenia)—*see* Schizophrenia, residual type

Rumination:

obsessional: The constant preoccupation with certain thoughts, with inability to dismiss them from the mind.[4] See Neurotic disorder, obsessive-compulsive.

psychogenic: In children the regurgitation of food, with failure to thrive or weight loss developing after a period of normal functioning. Food is brought up without nausea, retching, or disgust. The food is then ejected from the mouth, or chewed and reswallowed.[2]

Sander's disease—*see* Paranoia

Satyriasis: Pathologic or exaggerated sexual desire or excitement in the man.[3]

Schizoid personality disorder—*see* Personality disorder, schizoid type

Schizophrenia: A group of psychoses in which there is a fundamental disturbance of personality, a characteristic distortion of thinking, often a sense of being controlled by alien forces, delusions which may be bizarre, disturbed perception, abnormal affect out of keeping with the real situation, and autism. Nevertheless, clear consciousness and intellectual capacity are usually maintained. The disturbance of personality involves its most basic functions which give the normal person his feeling of individuality, uniqueness, and self-direction. The most intimate thoughts, feelings, and acts are often felt to be known to or shared by others and explanatory delusions may develop, to the effect that natural or supernatural forces are at work to influence the schizophrenic person's thoughts and actions in ways that are often bizarre. He may see himself as the pivot of all that happens. Hallucinations, especially of hearing, are common and may comment on the patient or address him. Perception is frequently disturbed in other ways; there may be perplexity, irrelevant features may become all-important and accompanied by passivity feelings, and may lead the patient to believe that everyday objects and situations possess a special, usually sinister, meaning intended for him. In the characteristic schizophrenic disturbance of thinking, peripheral and irrelevant features of a total concept, which are inhibited in normal directed mental activity, are brought to the forefront and utilized in place of the elements relevant and appropriate to the situation. Thus, thinking becomes vague, elliptical and obscure, and its expression in speech sometimes incomprehensible. Breaks and interpolations in the flow of consecutive thought are frequent, and the patient may be convinced that his thoughts are being withdrawn by some outside agency. Mood may be shallow, capricious, or incongruous. Ambivalence and disturbance of volition may appear as inertia, negativism, or stupor. Catatonia may be present. The diagnosis "schizophrenia " should not be made unless there is, or has been evident during the same illness, characteristic disturbance of thought, perception, mood, conduct, or personality—preferably in at least two of these areas. The diagnosis should not be restricted to conditions running a protracted, deteriorating, or chronic course. In addition to making the diagnosis on the criteria just given, effort should be made to specify one of the following subtypes of schizophrenia, according to the predominant symptoms.[1]

acute (undifferentiated): Schizophrenia of florid nature which cannot be classified as simple, catatonic, hebephrenic, paranoid, or any other types.[1]

acute episode: Schizophrenic disorders, other than simple, hebephrenic, catatonic, and paranoid, in which there is a dream-like state with slight clouding of consciousness and perplexity. External things, people, and events may become charged with personal significance for the patient. There may be ideas of reference and emotional turmoil. In many such cases remission occurs within a few weeks or months, even without treatment.[1]

atypical—*see* Schizophrenia, acute (undifferentiated)

borderline—*see* Schizophrenia, latent

catatonic type: Includes as an essential feature prominent psychomotor disturbances often alternating between extremes such as hyperkinesis and stupor, or automatic obedience and negativism. Constrained attitudes may be maintained for long periods: if the patient's limbs are put in some unnatural position they may be held there for some time after the external force has been removed. Severe excitement may be a striking feature of the condition. Depressive or hypomanic concomitants may be present.[1]

cenesthopathic—*see* Schizophrenia, acute (undifferentiated)

childhood type—*see* Psychosis, child

chronic undifferentiated—*see* Schizophrenia, residual

cyclic—*see* Schizophrenia, schizo-affective type

disorganized type: A form of schizophrenia in which affective changes are prominent, delusions and hallucinations fleeting and fragmentary, behavior irresponsible and unpredictable, and mannerisms common. The mood is shallow and inappropriate, accompanied by giggling or self-satisfied, self-absorbed smiling, or by a lofty manner, grimaces, mannerisms, pranks, hypochondriacal complaints, and reiterated phrases. Thought is disorganized. There is a tendency to remain solitary, and behavior seems empty of purpose and feeling. This form of schizophrenia usually starts between the ages of 15 and 25 years.[1]

hebephrenic type—*see* Schizophrenia, disorganized type

latent: It has not been possible to produce a generally acceptable description for this condition. It is not recommended for general use, but a description is provided for those who believe it to be useful: a condition of eccentric or inconsequent behavior and anomalies of affect which give the impression of schizophrenia though no definite and characteristic schizophrenic anomalies, present or past, have been manifest.[1]

paranoid type: The form of schizophrenia in which relatively stable delusions, which may be accompanied by hallucinations, dominate the clinical picture. The delusions are frequently of persecution, but may take other forms (for example, of jealousy, exalted birth, Messianic mission, or bodily change). Hallucinations and erratic behavior may occur; in some cases conduct is seriously disturbed from the outset, thought disorder may be gross, and affective flattening with fragmentary delusions and hallucinations may develop.[1]

prepsychotic—*see* Schizophrenia, latent

prodromal—*see* Schizophrenia, latent

pseudoneurotic—*see* Schizophrenia, latent

pseudopsychopathic—*see* Schizophrenia, latent

residual: A chronic form of schizophrenia in which the symptoms that persist from the acute phase have mostly lost their sharpness. Emotional response is blunted and thought disorder, even when gross, does not prevent the accomplishment of routine work.[1]

schizo-affective type: A psychosis in which pronounced manic or depressive features are intermingled with schizophrenic features and which tends towards remission without permanent defect, but which is prone to recur. The diagnosis should be made only when both the affective and schizophrenic symptoms are pronounced.[1]

simple type: A psychosis in which there is insidious development of oddities of conduct, inability to meet the demands of society, and decline in total performance. Delusions and hallucinations are not in evidence and the condition is less obviously psychotic than are the hebephrenic, catatonic, and paranoid types of schizophrenia. With increasing social impoverishment vagrancy may ensue and the patient becomes self-absorbed, idle, and aimless. Because the schizophrenic symptoms are not clear-cut, diagnosis of this form should be made sparingly, if at all.[1]

simplex—*see* Schizophrenia, simple type

Schizophrenic syndrome of childhood—*see* Psychosis, child

Schizophreniform

    attack—*see* Schizophrenia, acute episode

    disorder—*see* Schizophrenia, acute episode

    psychosis—*see* Schizophrenia

        affective type—*see* Schizophrenia, schizo-affective type

        confusional type—*see* Schizophrenia, acute episode

Schizotypal personality—*see* Personality disorder, schizotypal type

Senile dementia: Dementia occurring usually after the age of 65 in which any cerebral pathology other than that of senile atrophic change can be reasonably excluded.[1]

    delirium: Senile dementia with a superimposed reversible episode of acute confusional state.[1]

    delusional type: A type of senile dementia characterized by development in advanced old age, progressive in nature, in which delusions, varying from simple poorly formed paranoid delusions to highly formed paranoid delusional states, and hallucinations are also present.[1,2]

    depressed type: A type of senile dementia characterized by development in advanced old age, progressive in nature, in which depressive features, ranging from mild to severe forms of manic-depressive affective psychosis, are also present. Disturbance of the sleep-waking cycle and preoccupation with dead people are often particularly prominent.[1,2]

    paranoid type—*see* Senile dementia, delusional type

    simple type—*see* Senile dementia

Sensitiver Beziehungswahn: A paranoid state which, though in many ways akin to schizophrenic or affective states, differs from paranoia, simple paranoid state, shared paranoid disorder, or psychogenic psychosis.[1]

Sensitivity reaction of childhood or adolescence—*see* Shyness disorder of childhood

Separation anxiety disorder: A clinical disorder in children in which the predominant disturbance is exaggerated distress at separation from parents, home, or other familial surroundings. When separation is instituted, the child may experience anxiety to the point of panic. In adults a similar disorder is seen in agoraphobic reactions.[2]

Sexual deviations: Abnormal sexual inclinations or behavior which are part of a referral problem. The limits and features of normal sexual behavior have not been stated absolutely in different societies and cultures, but are broadly such as serve approved social and biological purposes. The sexual activity of affected persons is directed primarily either towards people not of the opposite sex, or towards sexual acts not associated with coitus normally, or towards coitus performed under abnormal circumstances. If the anomalous behavior becomes manifest only during psychosis or other mental illness the condition should be classified under the major illness. It is common for more than one anomaly to occur together in the same individual; in that case the predominant deviation is classified. It is preferable not to diagnose sexual deviation in individuals who perform deviant sexual acts when normal sexual outlets are not available to them.[1] See also Exhibitionism, Fetishism, Homosexuality, Nymphomania, Pedophilia, Satyriasis, Sexual masochism, Sexual sadism, Transvestism, Voyeurism, and Zoophilia.

Gender identity disorder and trans-sexualism are considered to be psychosexual gender identity disorders and are not included here.

Sexual masochism: A sexual deviation in which sexual arousal and pleasure is produced in an individual by his own physical or psychological suffering, and in which there are insistent and persistent fantasies wherein sexual excitement is produced as a result of suffering.[2]

Sexual sadism: A sexual deviation in which physical or psychological suffering inflicted on another person is utilized as a method of stimulating erotic excitement and orgasm, and in which there are insistent and persistent fantasies wherein sexual excitement is produced as a result of suffering inflicted on the partner.[2]

Shared paranoid disorder: Mainly delusional psychosis, usually chronic and often without florid features, which appears to have developed as a, result of a close, if not dependent, relationship with another person who already has an established similar psychosis. The delusions are at least partly shared. The rare cases in which several persons are affected should also be included here.[1]

Shifting sleep-work schedule: A sleep disorder in which the phase-shift disruption of the 24-hour sleep-wake cycle occurs due to rapid changes in the individual's work schedule.[2]

Short sleeper: Individuals who typically need only 4-6 hours of sleep within the 24-hour cycle.[2]

Shyness disorder of childhood: A persistent and excessive shrinking from familiarity or contact with all strangers of sufficient severity as to interfere with peer functioning, yet there are warm and satisfying relationships with family members. A critical feature of this disorder is that the avoidant behavior with strangers persists even after prolonged exposure or contact.[2]

Sibling jealousy or rivalry: An emotional disorder related to competition between siblings for the love of a parent or for other recognition or gain.[3]

Simple phobia—*see* simple phobia under Phobia

Situational disturbance, acute—*see* Stress reaction, acute

Social phobia—*see* social phobia under Phobia

Social withdrawal of childhood—*see* Introverted disorder of childhood

Socialized conduct disorder—*see* socialized conduct disorder under Conduct disorders

Somatization disorder—*see* somatization disorder under Neurotic disorders

Somatoform disorder, atypical—*see* hypochondriasis under Neurotic disorders

Spasmus nutans—*see* Stereotyped repetitive movements

Specific academic or work inhibition: An adjustment reaction in which a specific academic or work inhibition occurs in an individual whose intellectual capacity, skills, and previous academic or work performance have been at least adequate, and in which the inhibition occurs despite apparent effort and is not due to any other mental disorder.[2]

Stammering—*see* Stuttering

Starch-eating—*see* Pica

Status postcommotio cerebri—*see* Postconcussion syndrome

Stereotyped repetitive movements: Disorders in which voluntary repetitive stereotyped movements, which are not due to any psychiatric or neurological condition, constitute the main feature. Includes head-banging, spasmus nutans, rocking, twirling, finger-flicking mannerisms, and eye poking. Such movements are particularly common in cases of mental retardation with sensory impairment or with environmental monotony.[1]

Stereotypies—*see* Stereotyped repetitive movements

Stress reaction

  acute: Acute transient disorders of any severity and nature of emotions, consciousness, and psychomotor states (singly or in combination) which occur in individuals, without any apparent pre-existing mental disorder, in response to exceptional physical or mental stress, such as natural catastrophe or battle, and which usually subside within hours or days.[1]

  chronic—*see* Adjustment reaction

Stupor

  catatonic—*see* Schizophrenia, catatonic type

  psychogenic—*see* Psychosis, reactive

Stuttering: Disorders in the rhythm of speech, in which the individual knows precisely what he wishes to say, but at the time is unable to say it because of an involuntary, repetitive prolongation or cessation of a sound.[1]

Subjective insomnia complaint: A complaint of insomnia made by the individual, which has not been investigated or proven.[2]

Tension headache: Headache of mental origin for which a more precise medical or psychiatric diagnosis cannot be made.[1]

Systematized delusions—*see* Paranoia

Tics: Disorders of no known organic origin in which the outstanding feature consists of quick, involuntary, apparently purposeless, and frequently repeated movements which are not due to any neurological condition. Any part of the body may be involved but the face is most frequently affected. Only one form of tic may be present, or there may be a combination of tics which are carried out simultaneously, alternatively, or consecutively.[1]

  chronic motor tic disorder: A tic disorder starting in childhood and persisting into adult life. The tic is limited to no more than three motor areas, and rarely has a verbal component.[2]

  Gilles de la Tourette's disorder [motor-verbal tic disorder]: A rare disorder occurring in individuals of any level of intelligence in which facial tics and tic-like throat noises become more marked and more generalized, and in which later whole words or short sentences (often with obscene content) are ejaculated spasmodically and involuntarily. There is some overlap with other varieties of tic.[1]

  transient tic disorder of childhood: Facial or other tics beginning in childhood, but limited to one year in duration.[2]

Tobacco use disorder: Cases in which tobacco is used to the detriment of a person's health or social functioning or in which there is tobacco dependence. Dependence is included here rather than under drug dependence because tobacco differs from other drugs of dependence in its psychotoxic effects.[1]

Tranquilizer abuse: Cases where an individual has taken the drug to the detriment of his health or social functioning, in doses above or for periods beyond those normally regarded as therapeutic.[1]

Transient organic psychotic condition—*see* Organic psychotic conditions, transient

Trans-sexualism—*see* trans-sexualism under Psychosexual identity disorders

Transvestism: Sexual deviation in which there is recurrent and persistent dressing in clothes of the opposite sex, and initially in the early stage of the illness, for the purpose of sexual arousal.[2]

Twilight state

  confusional—*see* Delirium, acute

  psychogenic—*see* Psychosis, reactive confusion

Undersocialized conduct disorder—*see* undersocialized conduct disorder under Conduct disorders

Unsocialized aggressive disorder—*see* undersocialized conduct disorder, aggressive type under Conduct disorders

Vaginismus, functional—*see* functional vaginismus under Psychosexual dysfunctions

Vorbeireden: The symptom of the approximate answer or talking past the point, seen in the Ganser syndrome, a form of factitious illness.[2]

Voyeurism: A sexual deviation in which the individual repetitively seeks out situations in which he engages in looking at unsuspecting women who are either naked, in the act of disrobing, or engaging in sexual activity. The act of looking is accompanied by sexual excitement, frequently with orgasm. In its severe form, the act of peeping constitutes the preferred or exclusive sexual activity of the individual.[2]

Wernicke-Korsakoff syndrome—*see* alcohol amnestic syndrome under Alcoholic psychoses

Withdrawal reaction of childhood or adolescence—*see* Introverted disorder of childhood

Word-deafness: A developmental delay in the comprehension of speech sounds.[1]

Zoophilia: Sexual or anal intercourse with animals.[1]

APPENDIX C

CLASSIFICATION OF DRUGS BY AMERICAN HOSPITAL FORMULARY SERVICES LIST NUMBER AND THEIR ICD-9-CM EQUIVALENTS

The coding of adverse effects of drugs is keyed to the continually revised Hospital Formulary of the American Hospital Formulary Service (AHFS) published under the direction of the American Society of Hospital Pharmacists.

The following section gives the ICD-9-CM diagnosis code for each AHFS list.

AHFS List		ICD-9-CM Diagnosis Code
4:00	**ANTIHISTAMINE DRUGS**	**963.0**
8:00	**ANTI-INFECTIVE AGENTS**	
8:04	Amebicides	961.5
	hydroxyquinoline derivatives	961.3
	arsenical anti-infectives	961.1
8:08	Anthelmintics	961.6
	quinoline derivatives	961.3
8:12.04	Antifungal Antibiotics	960.1
	nonantibiotics	961.9
8:12.06	Cephalosporins	960.5
8:12.08	Chloramphenicol	960.2
8:12.12	The Erythromycins	960.3
8:12.16	The Penicillins	960.0
8:12.20	The Streptomycins	960.6
8:12.24	The Tetracyclines	960.4
8:12.28	Other Antibiotics	960.8
	antimycobacterial antibiotics	960.6
	macrolides	960.3
8:16	Antituberculars	961.8
	antibiotics	960.6
8:18	Antivirals	961.7
8:20	Plasmodicides (antimalarials)	961.4
8:24	Sulfonamides	961.0
8:26	The Sulfones	961.8
8:28	Treponemicides	961.2
8:32	Trichomonacides	961.5
	hydroxyquinoline derivatives	961.3
	nitrofuran derivatives	961.9
8:36	Urinary Germicides	961.9
	quinoline derivatives	961.3
8:40	Other Anti-Infectives	961.9
10:00	**ANTINEOPLASTIC AGENTS**	**963.1**
	antibiotics	960.7
	progestogens	962.2
12:00	**AUTONOMIC DRUGS**	
12:04	Parasympathomimetic (Cholinergic) Agents	971.0
12:08	Parasympatholytic (Cholinergic Blocking) Agents	971.1
12:12	Sympathomimetic (Adrenergic) Agents	971.2
12:16	Sympatholytic (Adrenergic Blocking) Agents	971.3
12:20	Skeletal Muscle Relaxants	975.2
	central nervous system muscle-tone depressants	968.0
16:00	**BLOOD DERIVATIVES**	**964.7**
20:00	**BLOOD FORMATION AND COAGULATION**	
20:04	Antianemia Drugs	964.1
20:04.04	Iron Preparations	964.0
20:04.08	Liver and Stomach Preparations	964.1
20:12.04	Anticoagulants	964.2
20:12.08	Antiheparin agents	964.5
20:12.12	Coagulants	964.5
20.12.16	Hemostatics	964.5
	capillary-active drugs	972.8
	fibrinolysis-affecting agents	964.4
	natural products	964.7

AHFS List		ICD-9-CM Diagnosis Code
24:00	**CARDIOVASCULAR DRUGS**	
24:04	Cardiac Drugs	972.9
	cardiotonic agents	972.1
	rhythm regulators	972.0
24:06	Antilipemic Agents	972.2
	thyroid derivatives	962.7
24:08	Hypotensive Agents	972.6
	adrenergic blocking agents	971.3
	ganglion-blocking agents	972.3
	vasodilators	972.5
24:12	Vasodilating Agents	972.5
	coronary	972.4
	nicotinic acid derivatives	972.2
24:16	Sclerosing Agents	972.7
28:00	**CENTRAL NERVOUS SYSTEM DRUGS**	
28:04	General Anesthetics	968.4
	gaseous anesthetics	968.2
	halothane	968.1
	intravenous anesthetics	968.3
28:08	Analgesics and Antipyretics	965.9
	antirheumatics	965.6
	aromatic analgesics	965.4
	non-narcotics NEC	965.7
	opium alkaloids	965.00
	heroin	965.01
	methadone	965.02
	specified type NEC	965.09
	pyrazole derivatives	965.5
	salicylates	965.1
	specified type NEC	965.8
28:10	Narcotic Antagonists	970.1
28:12	Anticonvulsants	966.3
	barbiturates	967.0
	benzodiazepine-based tranquilizers	969.4
	bromides	967.3
	hydantoin derivatives	966.1
	oxazolidine derivative	966.0
	succinamides	966.2
28:16.04	Antidepressants	969.0
28:16.08	Tranquilizers	969.5
	benzodiazepine-based	969.4
	butyrophenone-based	969.2
	major NEC	969.3
	phenothiazine-based	969.1
28:16.12	Other Psychotherapeutic Agents	969.8
28:20	Respiratory and Cerebral Stimulants	970.9
	analeptics	970.0
	anorexigenic agents	977.0
	psychostimulants	969.7
	specified type NEC	970.8
28:24	Sedatives and Hypnotics	967.9
	barbiturates	967.0
	benzodiazepine-based tranquilizers	969.4
	chloral hydrate group	967.1
	glutethimide group	967.5
	intravenous anesthetics	968.3
	methaqualone	967.4
	paraldehyde	967.2
	phenothiazine-based tranquilizers	969.1
	specified type NEC	967.8
	thiobarbiturates	968.3
	tranquilizer NEC	969.5
36:00	**DIAGNOSTIC AGENTS**	**977.8**
40:00	**ELECTROLYTE, CALORIC, AND WATER BALANCE AGENTS NEC**	**974.5**

APPENDIX D

CLASSIFICATION OF INDUSTRIAL ACCIDENTS
ACCORDING TO AGENCY

Annex B to the Resolution concerning Statistics of Employment Injuries adopted by the Tenth International Conference of Labor Statisticians on 12 October 1962

1 MACHINES

11 Prime-Movers, except Electrical Motors
111 *Steam engines*
112 *Internal combustion engines*
119 *Others*

12 Transmission Machinery
121 *Transmission shafts*
122 *Transmission belts, cables, pulleys, pinions, chains, gears*
129 *Others*

13 Metalworking Machines
131 *Power presses*
132 *Lathes*
133 *Milling machines*
134 *Abrasive wheels*
135 *Mechanical shears*
136 *Forging machines*
137 *Rolling-mills*
139 *Others*

14 Wood and Assimilated Machines
141 *Circular saws*
142 *Other saws*
143 *Molding machines*
144 *Overhand planes*
149 *Others*

15 Agricultural Machines
151 *Reapers (including combine reapers)*
152 *Threshers*
159 *Others*

16 Mining Machinery
161 *Under-cutters*
169 *Others*

19 Other Machines Not Elsewhere Classified
191 *Earth-moving machines, excavating and scraping machines, except means of transport*
192 *Spinning, weaving and other textile machines*
193 *Machines for the manufacture of foodstuffs and beverages*
194 *Machines for the manufacture of paper*
195 *Printing machines*
199 *Others*

2 MEANS OF TRANSPORT AND LIFTING EQUIPMENT

21 Lifting Machines and Appliances
211 *Cranes*
212 *Lifts and elevators*
213 *Winches*
214 *Pulley blocks*
219 *Others*

22 Means of Rail Transport
221 *Inter-urban railways*
222 *Rail transport in mines, tunnels, quarries, industrial establishments, docks, etc.*
229 *Others*

23 Other Wheeled Means of Transport, Excluding Rail Transport
231 *Tractors*
232 *Lorries*
233 *Trucks*
234 *Motor vehicles, not elsewhere classified*
235 *Animal-drawn vehicles*
236 *Hand-drawn vehicles*
239 *Others*

24 Means of Air Transport

25 Means of Water Transport
251 *Motorized means of water transport*
252 *Non-motorized means of water transport*

26 Other Means of Transport
261 *Cable-cars*
262 *Mechanical conveyors, except cable-cars*
269 *Others*

3 OTHER EQUIPMENT

31 Pressure Vessels
311 *Boilers*
312 *Pressurized containers*
313 *Pressurized piping and accessories*
314 *Gas cylinders*
315 *Caissons, diving equipment*
319 *Others*

32 Furnaces, Ovens, Kilns
321 *Blast furnaces*
322 *Refining furnaces*
323 *Other furnaces*
324 *Kilns*
325 *Ovens*

33 Refrigerating Plants

34 Electrical Installations, Including Electric Motors, but Excluding Electric Hand Tools
341 *Rotating machines*
342 *Conductors*
343 *Transformers*
344 *Control apparatus*
349 *Others*

35 Electric Hand Tools

36 Tools, Implements, and Appliances, Except Electric Hand Tools
361 *Power-driven hand tools, except electric hand tools*
362 *Hand tools, not power-driven*
369 *Others*

37 Ladders, Mobile Ramps

38 Scaffolding

39 Other Equipment, Not Elsewhere Classified

4 MATERIALS, SUBSTANCES, AND RADIATIONS

41 Explosives

42 Dusts, Gases, Liquids and Chemicals, Excluding Explosives
421 *Dusts*
422 *Gases, vapors, fumes*
423 *Liquids, not elsewhere classified*
424 *Chemicals, not elsewhere classified*

43 Flying Fragments

44 Radiations
441 *Ionizing radiations*
449 *Others*

49   Other Materials and Substances Not Elsewhere
      Classified

5 WORKING ENVIRONMENT

51   **Outdoor**
      511 *Weather*
      512 *Traffic and working surfaces*
      513 *Water*
      519 *Others*

52   **Indoor**
      521 *Floors*
      522 *Confined quarters*
      523 *Stairs*
      524 *Other traffic and working surfaces*
      525 *Floor openings and wall openings*
      526 *Environmental factors (lighting, ventilation,
          temperature, noise, etc.)*
      529 *Others*

53   **Underground**
      531 *Roofs and faces of mine roads and tunnels, etc.*
      532 *Floors of mine roads and tunnels, etc.*
      533 *Working-faces of mines, tunnels, etc.*
      534 *Mine shafts*
      535 *Fire*
      536 *Water*
      539 *Others*

6 OTHER AGENCIES, NOT ELSEWHERE CLASSIFIED

61   **Animals**
      611 *Live animals*
      612 *Animals products*

69   **Other Agencies, Not Elsewhere Classified**

7 AGENCIES NOT CLASSIFIED FOR LACK OF SUFFICIENT DATA

APPENDIX E

LIST OF THREE-DIGIT CATEGORIES

1. INFECTIOUS AND PARASITIC DISEASES

Intestinal infectious diseases (001–009)
001 Cholera
002 Typhoid and paratyphoid fevers
003 Other salmonella infections
004 Shigellosis
005 Other food poisoning (bacterial)
006 Amebiasis
007 Other protozoal intestinal diseases
008 Intestinal infections due to other organisms
009 Ill-defined intestinal infections

Tuberculosis (010–018)
010 Primary tuberculous infection
011 Pulmonary tuberculosis
012 Other respiratory tuberculosis
013 Tuberculosis of meninges and central nervous system
014 Tuberculosis of intestines, peritoneum, and mesenteric glands
015 Tuberculosis of bones and joints
016 Tuberculosis of genitourinary system
017 Tuberculosis of other organs
018 Miliary tuberculosis

Zoonotic bacterial diseases (020–027)
020 Plague
021 Tularemia
022 Anthrax
023 Brucellosis
024 Glanders
025 Melioidosis
026 Rat-bite fever
027 Other zoonotic bacterial diseases

Other bacterial diseases (030–041)
030 Leprosy
031 Diseases due to other mycobacteria
032 Diphtheria
033 Whooping cough
034 Streptococcal sore throat and scarlet fever
035 Erysipelas
036 Meningococcal infection
037 Tetanus
038 Septicemia
039 Actinomycotic infections
040 Other bacterial diseases
041 Bacterial infection in conditions classified elsewhere and of unspecified site

Human immunodeficiency virus (042)
042 Human immunodeficiency virus [HIV] disease

Poliomyelitis and other non-arthropod-borne viral diseases of central nervous system (045–049)
045 Acute poliomyelitis
046 Slow virus infection of central nervous system
047 Meningitis due to enterovirus
048 Other enterovirus diseases of central nervous system
049 Other non-arthropod-borne viral diseases of central nervous system

Viral diseases accompanied by exanthem (050–057)
050 Smallpox
051 Cowpox and paravaccinia
052 Chickenpox
053 Herpes zoster
054 Herpes simplex
055 Measles
056 Rubella
057 Other viral exanthemata

Arthropod-borne viral diseases (060–066)
060 Yellow fever
061 Dengue
062 Mosquito-borne viral encephalitis
063 Tick-borne viral encephalitis
064 Viral encephalitis transmitted by other and unspecified arthropods
065 Arthropod-borne hemorrhagic fever
066 Other arthropod-borne viral diseases

Other diseases due to viruses and Chlamydiae (070–079)
070 Viral hepatitis
071 Rabies
072 Mumps
073 Ornithosis
074 Specific diseases due to Coxsackie virus
075 Infectious mononucleosis
076 Trachoma
077 Other diseases of conjunctiva due to viruses and Chlamydiae
078 Other diseases due to viruses and Chlamydiae
079 Viral infection in conditions classified elsewhere and of unspecified site

Rickettsioses and other arthropod-borne diseases (080–088)
080 Louse-borne [epidemic] typhus
081 Other typhus
082 Tick-borne rickettsioses
083 Other rickettsioses
084 Malaria
085 Leishmaniasis
086 Trypanosomiasis
087 Relapsing fever
088 Other arthropod-borne diseases

Syphilis and other venereal diseases (090–099)
090 Congenital syphilis
091 Early syphilis, symptomatic
092 Early syphilis, latent
093 Cardiovascular syphilis
094 Neurosyphilis
095 Other forms of late syphilis, with symptoms
096 Late syphilis, latent
097 Other and unspecified syphilis
098 Gonococcal infections
099 Other venereal diseases

Other spirochetal diseases (100–104)
100 Leptospirosis
101 Vincent's angina
102 Yaws
103 Pinta
104 Other spirochetal infection

Mycoses (110–118)
110 Dermatophytosis
111 Dermatomycosis, other and unspecified
112 Candidiasis
114 Coccidioidomycosis
115 Histoplasmosis
116 Blastomycotic infection
117 Other mycoses
118 Opportunistic mycoses

Helminthiases (120–129)
120 Schistosomiasis [bilharziasis]
121 Other trematode infections
122 Echinococcosis
123 Other cestode infection
124 Trichinosis
125 Filarial infection and dracontiasis
126 Ancylostomiasis and necatoriasis
127 Other intestinal helminthiases
128 Other and unspecified helminthiases
129 Intestinal parasitism, unspecified

Other infectious and parasitic diseases (130–136)
130   Toxoplasmosis
131   Trichomoniasis
132   Pediculosis and phthirus infestation
133   Acariasis
134   Other infestation
135   Sarcoidosis
136   Other and unspecified infectious and parasitic diseases

Late effects of infectious and parasitic diseases (137–139)
137   Late effects of tuberculosis
138   Late effects of acute poliomyelitis
139   Late effects of other infectious and parasitic diseases

2. NEOPLASMS

Malignant neoplasm of lip, oral cavity, and pharynx (140–149)
140   Malignant neoplasm of lip
141   Malignant neoplasm of tongue
142   Malignant neoplasm of major salivary glands
143   Malignant neoplasm of gum
144   Malignant neoplasm of floor of mouth
145   Malignant neoplasm of other and unspecified parts of mouth
146   Malignant neoplasm of oropharynx
147   Malignant neoplasm of nasopharynx
148   Malignant neoplasm of hypopharynx
149   Malignant neoplasm of other and ill-defined sites within the lip, oral cavity, and pharynx

Malignant neoplasm of digestive organs and peritoneum (150–159)
150   Malignant neoplasm of esophagus
151   Malignant neoplasm of stomach
152   Malignant neoplasm of small intestine, including duodenum
153   Malignant neoplasm of colon
154   Malignant neoplasm of rectum, rectosigmoid junction, and anus
155   Malignant neoplasm of liver and intrahepatic bile ducts
156   Malignant neoplasm of gallbladder and extrahepatic bile ducts
157   Malignant neoplasm of pancreas
158   Malignant neoplasm of retroperitoneum and peritoneum
159   Malignant neoplasm of other and ill-defined sites within the digestive organs and peritoneum

Malignant neoplasm of respiratory and intrathoracic organs (160–165)
160   Malignant neoplasm of nasal cavities, middle ear, and accessory sinuses
161   Malignant neoplasm of larynx
162   Malignant neoplasm of trachea, bronchus, and lung
163   Malignant neoplasm of pleura
164   Malignant neoplasm of thymus, heart, and mediastinum
165   Malignant neoplasm of other and ill-defined sites within the respiratory system and intrathoracic organs

Malignant neoplasm of bone, connective tissue, skin, and breast (170–176)
170   Malignant neoplasm of bone and articular cartilage
171   Malignant neoplasm of connective and other soft tissue
172   Malignant melanoma of skin
173   Other malignant neoplasm of skin
174   Malignant neoplasm of female breast
175   Malignant neoplasm of male breast

Kaposi's sarcoma (176)
176   Kaposi's sarcoma

Malignant neoplasm of genitourinary organs (179–189)
179   Malignant neoplasm of uterus, part unspecified
180   Malignant neoplasm of cervix uteri
181   Malignant neoplasm of placenta
182   Malignant neoplasm of body of uterus
183   Malignant neoplasm of ovary and other uterine adnexa
184   Malignant neoplasm of other and unspecified female genital organs

185   Malignant neoplasm of prostate
186   Malignant neoplasm of testis
187   Malignant neoplasm of penis and other male genital organs
188   Malignant neoplasm of bladder
189   Malignant neoplasm of kidney and other and unspecified urinary organs

Malignant neoplasm of other and unspecified sites (190–199)
190   Malignant neoplasm of eye
191   Malignant neoplasm of brain
192   Malignant neoplasm of other and unspecified parts of nervous system
193   Malignant neoplasm of thyroid gland
194   Malignant neoplasm of other endocrine glands and related structures
195   Malignant neoplasm of other and ill-defined sites
196   Secondary and unspecified malignant neoplasm of lymph nodes
197   Secondary malignant neoplasm of respiratory and digestive systems
198   Secondary malignant neoplasm of other specified sites
199   Malignant neoplasm without specification of site

Malignant neoplasm of lymphatic and hematopoietic tissue (200–208)
200   Lymphosarcoma and reticulosarcoma
201   Hodgkin's disease
202   Other malignant neoplasm of lymphoid and histiocytic tissue
203   Multiple myeloma and immunoproliferative neoplasms
204   Lymphoid leukemia
205   Myeloid leukemia
206   Monocytic leukemia
207   Other specified leukemia
208   Leukemia of unspecified cell type

Benign neoplasms (210–229)
210   Benign neoplasm of lip, oral cavity, and pharynx
211   Benign neoplasm of other parts of digestive system
212   Benign neoplasm of respiratory and intrathoracic organs
213   Benign neoplasm of bone and articular cartilage
214   Lipoma
215   Other benign neoplasm of connective and other soft tissue
216   Benign neoplasm of skin
217   Benign neoplasm of breast
218   Uterine leiomyoma
219   Other benign neoplasm of uterus
220   Benign neoplasm of ovary
221   Benign neoplasm of other female genital organs
222   Benign neoplasm of male genital organs
223   Benign neoplasm of kidney and other urinary organs
224   Benign neoplasm of eye
225   Benign neoplasm of brain and other parts of nervous system
226   Benign neoplasm of thyroid gland
227   Benign neoplasm of other endocrine glands and related structures
228   Hemangioma and lymphangioma, any site
229   Benign neoplasm of other and unspecified sites

Carcinoma in situ (230–234)
230   Carcinoma in situ of digestive organs
231   Carcinoma in situ of respiratory system
232   Carcinoma in situ of skin
233   Carcinoma in situ of breast and genitourinary system
234   Carcinoma in situ of other and unspecified sites

Neoplasms of uncertain behavior (235–238)
235   Neoplasm of uncertain behavior of digestive and respiratory systems
236   Neoplasm of uncertain behavior of genitourinary organs
237   Neoplasm of uncertain behavior of endocrine glands and nervous system
238   Neoplasm of uncertain behavior of other and unspecified sites and tissues

Neoplasms of unspecified nature (239)
239   Neoplasm of unspecified nature

3. ENDOCRINE, NUTRITIONAL AND METABOLIC DISEASES, AND IMMUNITY DISORDERS

Disorders of thyroid gland (240–246)
240   Simple and unspecified goiter
241   Nontoxic nodular goiter
242   Thyrotoxicosis with or without goiter
243   Congenital hypothyroidism
244   Acquired hypothyroidism
245   Thyroiditis
246   Other disorders of thyroid

Diseases of other endocrine glands (250–259)
250   Diabetes mellitus
251   Other disorders of pancreatic internal secretion
252   Disorders of parathyroid gland
253   Disorders of the pituitary gland and its hypothalamic control
254   Diseases of thymus gland
255   Disorders of adrenal glands
256   Ovarian dysfunction
257   Testicular dysfunction
258   Polyglandular dysfunction and related disorders
259   Other endocrine disorders

Nutritional deficiencies (260–269)
260   Kwashiorkor
261   Nutritional marasmus
262   Other severe protein-calorie malnutrition
263   Other and unspecified protein-calorie malnutrition
264   Vitamin A deficiency
265   Thiamine and niacin deficiency states
266   Deficiency of B-complex components
267   Ascorbic acid deficiency
268   Vitamin D deficiency
269   Other nutritional deficiencies

Other metabolic disorders and immunity disorders (270–279)
270   Disorders of amino-acid transport and metabolism
271   Disorders of carbohydrate transport and metabolism
272   Disorders of lipid metabolism
273   Disorders of plasma protein metabolism
274   Gout
275   Disorders of mineral metabolism
276   Disorders of fluid, electrolyte, and acid-base balance
277   Other and unspecified disorders of metabolism
278   Obesity and other hyperalimentation
279   Disorders involving the immune mechanism

4. DISEASES OF BLOOD AND BLOOD-FORMING ORGANS

Diseases of the blood and blood-forming organs (280–289)
280   Iron deficiency anemias
281   Other deficiency anemias
282   Hereditary hemolytic anemias
283   Acquired hemolytic anemias
284   Aplastic anemia
285   Other and unspecified anemias
286   Coagulation defects
287   Purpura and other hemorrhagic conditions
288   Diseases of white blood cells
289   Other diseases of blood and blood-forming organs

5. MENTAL DISORDERS

Organic psychotic conditions (290–294)
290   Senile and presenile organic psychotic conditions
291   Alcoholic psychoses
292   Drug psychoses
293   Transient organic psychotic conditions
294   Other organic psychotic conditions (chronic)

Other psychoses (295–299)
295   Schizophrenic psychoses

296   Affective psychoses
297   Paranoid states
298   Other nonorganic psychoses
299   Psychoses with origin specific to childhood

Neurotic disorders, personality disorders, and other nonpsychotic mental disorders (300–316)
300   Neurotic disorders
301   Personality disorders
302   Sexual deviations and disorders
303   Alcohol dependence syndrome
304   Drug dependence
305   Nondependent abuse of drugs
306   Physiological malfunction arising from mental factors
307   Special symptoms or syndromes, not elsewhere classified
308   Acute reaction to stress
309   Adjustment reaction
310   Specific nonpsychotic mental disorders following organic brain damage
311   Depressive disorder, not elsewhere classified
312   Disturbance of conduct, not elsewhere classified
313   Disturbance of emotions specific to childhood and adolescence
314   Hyperkinetic syndrome of childhood
315   Specific delays in development
316   Psychic factors associated with diseases classified elsewhere

Mental retardation (317–319)
317   Mild mental retardation
318   Other specified mental retardation
319   Unspecified mental retardation

6. DISEASES OF THE NERVOUS SYSTEM AND SENSE ORGANS

Inflammatory diseases of the central nervous system (320–326)
320   Bacterial meningitis
321   Meningitis due to other organisms
322   Meningitis of unspecified cause
323   Encephalitis, myelitis, and encephalomyelitis
324   Intracranial and intraspinal abscess
325   Phlebitis and thrombophlebitis of intracranial venous sinuses
326   Late effects of intracranial abscess or pyogenic infection

Hereditary and degenerative diseases of the central nervous system (330–337)
330   Cerebral degenerations usually manifest in childhood
331   Other cerebral degenerations
332   Parkinson's disease
333   Other extrapyramidal disease and abnormal movement disorders
334   Spinocerebellar disease
335   Anterior horn cell disease
336   Other diseases of spinal cord
337   Disorders of the autonomic nervous system

Other disorders of the central nervous system (340–349)
340   Multiple sclerosis
341   Other demyelinating diseases of central nervous system
342   Hemiplegia and hemiparesis
343   Infantile cerebral palsy
344   Other paralytic syndromes
345   Epilepsy
346   Migraine
347   Cataplexy and narcolepsy
348   Other conditions of brain
349   Other and unspecified disorders of the nervous system

Disorders of the peripheral nervous system (350–359)
350   Trigeminal nerve disorders
351   Facial nerve disorders
352   Disorders of other cranial nerves
353   Nerve root and plexus disorders
354   Mononeuritis of upper limb and mononeuritis multiplex
355   Mononeuritis of lower limb

356	Hereditary and idiopathic peripheral neuropathy
357	Inflammatory and toxic neuropathy
358	Myoneural disorders
359	Muscular dystrophies and other myopathies

Disorders of the eye and adnexa (360–379)

360	Disorders of the globe
361	Retinal detachments and defects
362	Other retinal disorders
363	Chorioretinal inflammations and scars and other disorders of choroid
364	Disorders of iris and ciliary body
365	Glaucoma
366	Cataract
367	Disorders of refraction and accommodation
368	Visual disturbances
369	Blindness and low vision
370	Keratitis
371	Corneal opacity and other disorders of cornea
372	Disorders of conjunctiva
373	Inflammation of eyelids
374	Other disorders of eyelids
375	Disorders of lacrimal system
376	Disorders of the orbit
377	Disorders of optic nerve and visual pathways
378	Strabismus and other disorders of binocular eye movements
379	Other disorders of eye

Diseases of the ear and mastoid process (380–389)

380	Disorders of external ear
381	Nonsuppurative otitis media and eustachian tube disorders
382	Suppurative and unspecified otitis media
383	Mastoiditis and related conditions
384	Other disorders of tympanic membrane
385	Other disorders of middle ear and mastoid
386	Vertiginous syndromes and other disorders of vestibular system
387	Otosclerosis
388	Other disorders of ear
389	Hearing loss

7. DISEASES OF THE CIRCULATORY SYSTEM

Acute rheumatic fever (390–392)

390	Rheumatic fever without mention of heart involvement
391	Rheumatic fever with heart involvement
392	Rheumatic chorea

Chronic rheumatic heart disease (393–398)

393	Chronic rheumatic pericarditis
394	Diseases of mitral valve
395	Diseases of aortic valve
396	Diseases of mitral and aortic valves
397	Diseases of other endocardial structures
398	Other rheumatic heart disease

Hypertensive disease (401–405)

401	Essential hypertension
402	Hypertensive heart disease
403	Hypertensive renal disease
404	Hypertensive heart and renal disease
405	Secondary hypertension

Ischemic heart disease (410–414)

410	Acute myocardial infarction
411	Other acute and subacute form of ischemic heart disease
412	Old myocardial infarction
413	Angina pectoris
414	Other forms of chronic ischemic heart disease

Diseases of pulmonary circulation (415–417)

415	Acute pulmonary heart disease
416	Chronic pulmonary heart disease
417	Other diseases of pulmonary circulation

Other forms of heart disease (420–429)

420	Acute pericarditis
421	Acute and subacute endocarditis
422	Acute myocarditis
423	Other diseases of pericardium
424	Other diseases of endocardium
425	Cardiomyopathy
426	Conduction disorders
427	Cardiac dysrhythmias
428	Heart failure
429	Ill-defined descriptions and complications of heart disease

Cerebrovascular disease (430–438)

430	Subarachnoid hemorrhage
431	Intracerebral hemorrhage
432	Other and unspecified intracranial hemorrhage
433	Occlusion and stenosis of precerebral arteries
434	Occlusion of cerebral arteries
435	Transcient cerebral ischemia
436	Acute but ill-defined cerebrovascular disease
437	Other and ill-defined cerebrovascular disease
438	Late effects of cerebrovascular disease

Diseases of arteries, arterioles, and capillaries (440–448)

440	Atherosclerosis
441	Aortic aneurysm and dissection
442	Other aneurysm
443	Other peripheral vascular disease
444	Arterial embolism and thrombosis
446	Polyarteritis nodosa and allied conditions
447	Other disorders of arteries and arterioles
448	Diseases of capillaries

Diseases of veins and lymphatics, and other diseases of circulatory system (451–459)

451	Phlebitis and thrombophlebitis
452	Portal vein thrombosis
453	Other venous embolism and thrombosis
454	Varicose veins of lower extremities
455	Hemorrhoids
456	Varicose veins of other sites
457	Noninfective disorders of lymphatic channels
458	Hypotension
459	Other disorders of circulatory system

8. DISEASES OF THE RESPIRATORY SYSTEM

Acute respiratory infections (460–466)

460	Acute nasopharyngitis [common cold]
461	Acute sinusitis
462	Acute pharyngitis
463	Acute tonsillitis
464	Acute laryngitis and tracheitis
465	Acute upper respiratory infections of multiple or unspecified sites
466	Acute bronchitis and bronchiolitis

Other diseases of upper respiratory tract (470–478)

470	Deviated nasal septum
471	Nasal polyps
472	Chronic pharyngitis and nasopharyngitis
473	Chronic sinusitis
474	Chronic disease of tonsils and adenoids
475	Peritonsillar abscess
476	Chronic laryngitis and laryngotracheitis
477	Allergic rhinitis
478	Other diseases of upper respiratory tract

Pneumonia and influenza (480–487)

480	Viral pneumonia
481	Pneumococcal pneumonia [*Streptococcus pneumoniae* pneumonia]
482	Other bacterial pneumonia
483	Pneumonia due to other specified organism
484	Pneumonia in infectious diseases classified elsewhere
485	Bronchopneumonia, organism unspecified

486   Pneumonia, organism unspecified
487   Influenza

Chronic obstructive pulmonary disease and allied conditions (490–496)
490   Bronchitis, not specified as acute or chronic
491   Chronic bronchitis
492   Emphysema
493   Asthma
494   Bronchiectasis
495   Extrinsic allergic alveolitis
496   Chronic airways obstruction, not elsewhere classified

Pneumoconioses and other lung diseases due to external agents (500–508)
500   Coalworkers' pneumoconiosis
501   Asbestosis
502   Pneumoconiosis due to other silica or silicates
503   Pneumoconiosis due to other inorganic dust
504   Pneumopathy due to inhalation of other dust
505   Pneumoconiosis, unspecified
506   Respiratory conditions due to chemical fumes and vapors
507   Pneumonitis due to solids and liquids
508   Respiratory conditions due to other and unspecified external agents

Other diseases of respiratory system (510–519)
510   Empyema
511   Pleurisy
512   Pneumothorax
513   Abscess of lung and mediastinum
514   Pulmonary congestion and hypostasis
515   Postinflammatory pulmonary fibrosis
516   Other alveolar and parietoalveolar pneumopathy
517   Lung involvement in conditions classified elsewhere
518   Other diseases of lung
519   Other diseases of respiratory system

9. DISEASES OF THE DIGESTIVE SYSTEM

Diseases of oral cavity, salivary glands, and jaws (520–529)
520   Disorders of tooth development and eruption
521   Diseases of hard tissues of teeth
522   Diseases of pulp and periapical tissues
523   Gingival and periodontal diseases
524   Dentofacial anomalies, including malocclusion
525   Other diseases and conditions of the teeth and supporting structures
526   Diseases of the jaws
527   Diseases of the salivary glands
528   Diseases of the oral soft tissues, excluding lesions specific for gingiva and tongue
529   Diseases and other conditions of the tongue

Diseases of esophagus, stomach, and duodenum (530–537)
530   Diseases of esophagus
531   Gastric ulcer
532   Duodenal ulcer
533   Peptic ulcer, site unspecified
534   Gastrojejunal ulcer
535   Gastritis and duodenitis
536   Disorders of function of stomach
537   Other disorders of stomach and duodenum

Appendicitis (540–543)
540   Acute appendicitis
541   Appendicitis, unqualified
542   Other appendicitis
543   Other diseases of appendix

Hernia of abdominal cavity (550–553)
550   Inguinal hernia
551   Other hernia of abdominal cavity, with gangrene
552   Other hernia of abdominal cavity, with obstruction, but without mention of gangrene
553   Other hernia of abdominal cavity without mention of obstruction or gangrene

Noninfective enteritis and colitis (555–558)
555   Regional enteritis
556   Ulcerative colitis
557   Vascular insufficiency of intestine
558   Other noninfective gastroenteritis and colitis

Other diseases of intestines and peritoneum (560–569)
560   Intestinal obstruction without mention of hernia
562   Diverticula of intestine
564   Functional digestive disorders, not elsewhere classified
565   Anal fissure and fistula
566   Abscess of anal and rectal regions
567   Peritonitis
568   Other disorders of peritoneum
569   Other disorders of intestine

Other diseases of digestive system (570–579)
570   Acute and subacute necrosis of liver
571   Chronic liver disease and cirrhosis
572   Liver abscess and sequelae of chronic liver disease
573   Other disorders of liver
574   Cholelithiasis
575   Other disorders of gallbladder
576   Other disorders of biliary tract
577   Diseases of pancreas
578   Gastrointestinal hemorrhage
579   Intestinal malabsorption

10. DISEASES OF THE GENITOURINARY SYSTEM

Nephritis, nephrotic syndrome, and nephrosis (580–589)
580   Acute glomerulonephritis
581   Nephrotic syndrome
582   Chronic glomerulonephritis
583   Nephritis and nephropathy, not specified as acute or chronic
584   Acute renal failure
585   Chronic renal failure
586   Renal failure, unspecified
587   Renal sclerosis, unspecified
588   Disorders resulting from impaired renal function
589   Small kidney of unknown cause

Other diseases of urinary system (590–599)
590   Infections of kidney
591   Hydronephrosis
592   Calculus of kidney and ureter
593   Other disorders of kidney and ureter
594   Calculus of lower urinary tract
595   Cystitis
596   Other disorders of bladder
597   Urethritis, not sexually transmitted, and urethral syndrome
598   Urethral stricture
599   Other disorders of urethra and urinary tract

Diseases of male genital organs (600–608)
600   Hyperplasia of prostate
601   Inflammatory diseases of prostate
602   Other disorders of prostate
603   Hydrocele
604   Orchitis and epididymitis
605   Redundant prepuce and phimosis
606   Infertility, male
607   Disorders of penis
608   Other disorders of male genital organs

Disorders of breast (610–611)
610   Benign mammary dysplasias
611   Other disorders of breast

Inflammatory disease of female pelvic organs (614–616)
614   Inflammatory disease of ovary, fallopian tube, pelvic cellular tissue, and peritoneum
615   Inflammatory diseases of uterus, except cervix
616   Inflammatory disease of cervix, vagina, and vulva

ICD-9-CM

Appx E

Vol. 1

Other disorders of female genital tract (617–629)
617 Endometriosis
618 Genital prolapse
619 Fistula involving female genital tract
620 Noninflammatory disorders of ovary, fallopian tube, and broad ligament
621 Disorders of uterus, not elsewhere classified
622 Noninflammatory disorders of cervix
623 Noninflammatory disorders of vagina
624 Noninflammatory disorders of vulva and perineum
625 Pain and other symptoms associated with female genital organs
626 Disorders of menstruation and other abnormal bleeding from female genital tract
627 Menopausal and postmenopausal disorders
628 Infertility, female
629 Other disorders of female genital organs

11. COMPLICATIONS OF PREGNANCY, CHILDBIRTH, AND THE PUERPERIUM

Ectopic and molar pregnancy and other pregnancy with abortive outcome (630–639)
630 Hydatidiform mole
631 Other abnormal product of conception
632 Missed abortion
633 Ectopic pregnancy
634 Spontaneous abortion
635 Legally induced abortion
636 Illegally induced abortion
637 Unspecified abortion
638 Failed attempted abortion
639 Complications following abortion and ectopic and molar pregnancies

Complications mainly related to pregnancy (640–648)
640 Hemorrhage in early pregnancy
641 Antepartum hemorrhage, abruptio placentae, and placenta previa
642 Hypertension complicating pregnancy, childbirth, and the puerperium
643 Excessive vomiting in pregnancy
644 Early or threatened labor
645 Prolonged pregnancy
646 Other complications of pregnancy, not elsewhere classified
647 Infective and parasitic conditions in the mother classifiable elsewhere but complicating pregnancy, childbirth, and the puerperium
648 Other current conditions in the mother classifiable elsewhere but complicating pregnancy, childbirth, and the puerperium

Normal delivery, and other indications for care in pregnancy, labor, and delivery (650–659)
650 Normal delivery
651 Multiple gestation
652 Malposition and malpresentation of fetus
653 Disproportion
654 Abnormality of organs and soft tissues of pelvis
655 Known or suspected fetal abnormality affecting management of mother
656 Other fetal and placental problems affecting management of mother
657 Polyhydramnios
658 Other problems associated with amniotic cavity and membranes
659 Other indications for care or intervention related to labor and delivery and not elsewhere classified

Complications occurring mainly in the course of labor and delivery (660–669)
660 Obstructed labor
661 Abnormality of forces of labor
662 Long labor
663 Umbilical cord complications

664 Trauma to perineum and vulva during delivery
665 Other obstetrical trauma
666 Postpartum hemorrhage
667 Retained placenta or membranes, without hemorrhage
668 Complications of the administration of anesthetic or other sedation in labor and delivery
669 Other complications of labor and delivery, not elsewhere classified

Complications of the puerperium (670–677)
670 Major puerperal infection
671 Venous complications in pregnancy and the puerperium
672 Pyrexia of unknown origin during the puerperium
673 Obstetrical pulmonary embolism
674 Other and unspecified complications of the puerperium, not elsewhere classified
675 Infections of the breast and nipple associated with childbirth
676 Other disorders of the breast associated with childbirth, and disorders of lactation
677 Late effect of complication of pregnancy, childbirth, and the puerperium

12. DISEASES OF THE SKIN AND SUBCUTANEOUS TISSUE

Infections of skin and subcutaneous tissue (680–686)
680 Carbuncle and furuncle
681 Cellulitis and abscess of finger and toe
682 Other cellulitis and abscess
683 Acute lymphadenitis
684 Impetigo
685 Pilonidal cyst
686 Other local infections of skin and subcutaneous tissue

Other inflammatory conditions of skin and subcutaneous tissue (690–698)
690 Erythematosquamous dermatosis
691 Atopic dermatitis and related conditions
692 Contact dermatitis and other eczema
693 Dermatitis due to substances taken internally
694 Bullous dermatoses
695 Erythematous conditions
696 Psoriasis and similar disorders
697 Lichen
698 Pruritus and related conditions

Other diseases of skin and subcutaneous tissue (700–709)
700 Corns and callosities
701 Other hypertrophic and atrophic conditions of skin
702 Other dermatoses
703 Diseases of nail
704 Diseases of hair and hair follicles
705 Disorders of sweat glands
706 Diseases of sebaceous glands
707 Chronic ulcer of skin
708 Urticaria
709 Other disorders of skin and subcutaneous tissue

13. DISEASES OF THE MUSCULOSKELETAL SYSTEM AND CONNECTIVE TISSUE

Arthropathies and related disorders (710–719)
710 Diffuse diseases of connective tissue
711 Arthropathy associated with infections
712 Crystal arthropathies
713 Arthropathy associated with other disorders classified elsewhere
714 Rheumatoid arthritis and other inflammatory polyarthropathies
715 Osteoarthrosis and allied disorders
716 Other and unspecified arthropathies
717 Internal derangement of knee
718 Other derangement of joint
719 Other and unspecified disorder of joint

Dorsopathies (720–724)
720   Ankylosing spondylitis and other inflammatory spondylopathies
721   Spondylosis and allied disorders
722   Intervertebral disc disorders
723   Other disorders of cervical region
724   Other and unspecified disorders of back

Rheumatism, excluding the back (725–729)
725   Polymyalgia rheumatica
726   Peripheral enthesopathies and allied syndromes
727   Other disorders of synovium, tendon, and bursa
728   Disorders of muscle, ligament, and fascia
729   Other disorders of soft tissues

Osteopathies, chondropathies, and acquired musculoskeletal deformities (730–739)
730   Osteomyelitis, periostitis, and other infections involving bone
731   Osteitis deformans and osteopathies associated with other disorders classified elsewhere
732   Osteochondropathies
733   Other disorders of bone and cartilage
734   Flat foot
735   Acquired deformities of toe
736   Other acquired deformities of limbs
737   Curvature of spine
738   Other acquired deformity
739   Nonallopathic lesions, not elsewhere classified

14. CONGENITAL ANOMALIES

Congential anomalies (740–759)
740   Anencephalus and similar anomalies
741   Spina bifida
742   Other congenital anomalies of nervous system
743   Congenital anomalies of eye
744   Congenital anomalies of ear, face, and neck
745   Bulbus cordis anomalies and anomalies of cardiac septal closure
746   Other congenital anomalies of heart
747   Other congenital anomalies of circulatory system
748   Congenital anomalies of respiratory system
749   Cleft palate and cleft lip
750   Other congenital anomalies of upper alimentary tract
751   Other congenital anomalies of digestive system
752   Congenital anomalies of genital organs
753   Congenital anomalies of urinary system
754   Certain congenital musculoskeletal deformities
755   Other congenital anomalies of limbs
756   Other congenital musculoskeletal anomalies
757   Congenital anomalies of the integument
758   Chromosomal anomalies
759   Other and unspecified congenital anomalies

15. CERTAIN CONDITIONS ORIGINATING IN THE PERINATAL PERIOD

Maternal causes of perinatal morbidity and mortality (760–763)
760   Fetus or newborn affected by maternal conditions which may be unrelated to present pregnancy
761   Fetus or newborn affected by maternal complications of pregnancy
762   Fetus or newborn affected by complications of placenta, cord, and membranes
763   Fetus or newborn affected by other complications of labor and delivery

Other conditions originating in the perinatal period (764–779)
764   Slow fetal growth and fetal malnutrition
765   Disorders relating to short gestation and unspecified low birthweight
766   Disorders relating to long gestation and high birthweight
767   Birth trauma
768   Intrauterine hypoxia and birth asphyxia
769   Respiratory distress syndrome
770   Other respiratory conditions of fetus and newborn
771   Infections specific to the perinatal period
772   Fetal and neonatal hemorrhage
773   Hemolytic disease of fetus or newborn, due to isoimmunization
774   Other perinatal jaundice
775   Endocrine and metabolic disturbances specific to the fetus and newborn
776   Hematological disorders of fetus and newborn
777   Perinatal disorders of digestive system
778   Conditions involving the integument and temperature regulation of fetus and newborn
779   Other and ill-defined conditions originating in the perinatal period

16. SYMPTOMS, SIGNS, AND ILL-DEFINED CONDITIONS

Symptoms (780–789)
780   General symptoms
781   Symptoms involving nervous and musculoskeletal systems
782   Symptoms involving skin and other integumentary tissue
783   Symptoms concerning nutrition, metabolism, and development
784   Symptoms involving head and neck
785   Symptoms involving cardiovascular system
786   Symptoms involving respiratory system and other chest symptoms
787   Symptoms involving digestive system
788   Symptoms involving urinary system
789   Other symptoms involving abdomen and pelvis

Nonspecific abnormal findings (790–796)
790   Nonspecific findings on examination of blood
791   Nonspecific findings on examination of urine
792   Nonspecific abnormal findings in other body substances
793   Nonspecific abnormal findings on radiological and other examination of body structure
794   Nonspecific abnormal results of function studies
795   Nonspecific abnormal histological and immunological findings
796   Other nonspecific abnormal findings

Ill-defined and unknown causes of morbidity and mortality (797–799)
797   Senility without mention of psychosis
798   Sudden death, cause unknown
799   Other ill-defined and unknown causes of morbidity and mortality

17. INJURY AND POISONING

Fracture of skull (800–804)
800   Fracture of vault of skull
801   Fracture of base of skull
802   Fracture of face bones
803   Other and unqualified skull fractures
804   Multiple fractures involving skull or face with other bones

Fracture of spine and trunk (805–809)
805   Fracture of vertebral column without mention of spinal cord lesion
806   Fracture of vertebral column with spinal cord lesion
807   Fracture of rib(s), sternum, larynx, and trachea
808   Fracture of pelvis
809   Ill-defined fractures of bones of trunk

Fracture of upper limb (810–819)
810   Fracture of clavicle
811   Fracture of scapula
812   Fracture of humerus
813   Fracture of radius and ulna
814   Fracture of carpal bone(s)
815   Fracture of metacarpal bone(s)
816   Fracture of one or more phalanges of hand
817   Multiple fractures of hand bones

ICD-9-CM

Appx E

Vol. 1

818   Ill-defined fractures of upper limb
819   Multiple fractures involving both upper limbs, and upper limb with rib(s) and sternum

Fracture of lower limb (820–829)
820   Fracture of neck of femur
821   Fracture of other and unspecified parts of femur
822   Fracture of patella
823   Fracture of tibia and fibula
824   Fracture of ankle
825   Fracture of one or more tarsal and metatarsal bones
826   Fracture of one or more phalanges of foot
827   Other, multiple, and ill-defined fractures of lower limb
828   Multiple fractures involving both lower limbs, lower with upper limb, and lower limb(s) with rib(s) and sternum
829   Fracture of unspecified bones

Dislocation (830–839)
830   Dislocation of jaw
831   Dislocation of shoulder
832   Dislocation of elbow
833   Dislocation of wrist
834   Dislocation of finger
835   Dislocation of hip
836   Dislocation of knee
837   Dislocation of ankle
838   Dislocation of foot
839   Other, multiple, and ill-defined dislocations

Sprains and strains of joints and adjacent muscles (840–848)
840   Sprains and strains of shoulder and upper arm
841   Sprains and strains of elbow and forearm
842   Sprains and strains of wrist and hand
843   Sprains and strains of hip and thigh
844   Sprains and strains of knee and leg
845   Sprains and strains of ankle and foot
846   Sprains and strains of sacroiliac region
847   Sprains and strains of other and unspecified parts of back
848   Other and ill-defined sprains and strains

Intracranial injury, excluding those with skull fracture (850–854)
850   Concussion
851   Cerebral laceration and contusion
852   Subarachnoid, subdural, and extradural hemorrhage, following injury
853   Other and unspecified intracranial hemorrhage following injury
854   Intracranial injury of other and unspecified nature

Internal injury of chest, abdomen, and pelvis (860–869)
860   Traumatic pneumothorax and hemothorax
861   Injury to heart and lung
862   Injury to other and unspecified intrathoracic organs
863   Injury to gastrointestinal tract
864   Injury to liver
865   Injury to spleen
866   Injury to kidney
867   Injury to pelvic organs
868   Injury to other intra-abdominal organs
869   Internal injury to unspecified or ill-defined organs

Open wound of head, neck, and trunk (870–879)
870   Open wound of ocular adnexa
871   Open wound of eyeball
872   Open wound of ear
873   Other open wound of head
874   Open wound of neck
875   Open wound of chest (wall)
876   Open wound of back
877   Open wound of buttock
878   Open wound of genital organs (external), including traumatic amputation
879   Open wound of other and unspecified sites, except limbs

Open wound of upper limb (880–887)
880   Open wound of shoulder and upper arm
881   Open wound of elbow, forearm, and wrist
882   Open wound of hand except finger(s) alone
883   Open wound of finger(s)
884   Multiple and unspecified open wound of upper limb
885   Traumatic amputation of thumb (complete) (partial)
886   Traumatic amputation of other finger(s) (complete) (partial)
887   Traumatic amputation of arm and hand (complete) (partial)

Open wound of lower limb (890–897)
890   Open wound of hip and thigh
891   Open wound of knee, leg [except thigh], and ankle
892   Open wound of foot except toe(s) alone
893   Open wound of toe(s)
894   Multiple and unspecified open wound of lower limb
895   Traumatic amputation of toe(s) (complete) (partial)
896   Traumatic amputation of foot (complete) (partial)
897   Traumatic amputation of leg(s) (complete) (partial)

Injury to blood vessels (900–904)
900   Injury to blood vessels of head and neck
901   Injury to blood vessels of thorax
902   Injury to blood vessels of abdomen and pelvis
903   Injury to blood vessels of upper extremity
904   Injury to blood vessels of lower extremity and unspecified sites

Late effects of injuries, poisonings, toxic effects, and other external causes (905–909)
905   Late effects of musculoskeletal and connective tissue injuries
906   Late effects of injuries to skin and subcutaneous tissues
907   Late effects of injuries to the nervous system
908   Late effects of other and unspecified injuries
909   Late effects of other and unspecified external causes

Superficial injury (910–919)
910   Superficial injury of face, neck, and scalp except eye
911   Superficial injury of trunk
912   Superficial injury of shoulder and upper arm
913   Superficial injury of elbow, forearm, and wrist
914   Superficial injury of hand(s) except finger(s) alone
915   Superficial injury of finger(s)
916   Superficial injury of hip, thigh, leg, and ankle
917   Superficial injury of foot and toe(s)
918   Superficial injury of eye and adnexa
919   Superficial injury of other, multiple, and unspecified sites

Contusion with intact skin surface (920–924)
920   Contusion of face, scalp, and neck except eye(s)
921   Contusion of eye and adnexa
922   Contusion of trunk
923   Contusion of upper limb
924   Contusion of lower limb and of other and unspecified sites

Crushing injury (925–929)
925   Crushing injury of face, scalp, and neck
926   Crushing injury of trunk
927   Crushing injury of upper limb
928   Crushing injury of lower limb
929   Crushing injury of multiple and unspecified sites

Effects of foreign body entering through orifice (930–939)
930   Foreign body on external eye
931   Foreign body in ear
932   Foreign body in nose
933   Foreign body in pharynx and larynx
934   Foreign body in trachea, bronchus, and lung
935   Foreign body in mouth, esophagus, and stomach
936   Foreign body in intestine and colon
937   Foreign body in anus and rectum
938   Foreign body in digestive system, unspecified
939   Foreign body in genitourinary tract

Burns (940–949)
940   Burn confined to eye and adnexa
941   Burn of face, head, and neck

942 Burn of trunk
943 Burn of upper limb, except wrist and hand
944 Burn of wrist(s) and hand(s)
945 Burn of lower limb(s)
946 Burns of multiple specified sites
947 Burn of internal organs
948 Burns classified according to extent of body surface involved
949 Burn, unspecified

Injury to nerves and spinal cord (950–957)
950 Injury to optic nerve and pathways
951 Injury to other cranial nerve(s)
952 Spinal cord injury without evidence of spinal bone injury
953 Injury to nerve roots and spinal plexus
954 Injury to other nerve(s) of trunk excluding shoulder and pelvic girdles
955 Injury to peripheral nerve(s) of shoulder girdle and upper limb
956 Injury to peripheral nerve(s) of pelvic girdle and lower limb
957 Injury to other and unspecified nerves

Certain traumatic complications and unspecified injuries (958–959)
958 Certain early complications of trauma
959 Injury, other and unspecified

Poisoning by drugs, medicinals and biological substances (960–979)
960 Poisoning by antibiotics
961 Poisoning by other anti-infectives
962 Poisoning by hormones and synthetic substitutes
963 Poisoning by primarily systemic agents
964 Poisoning by agents primarily affecting blood constituents
965 Poisoning by analgesics, antipyretics, and antirheumatics
966 Poisoning by anticonvulsants and anti-parkinsonism drugs
967 Poisoning by sedatives and hypnotics
968 Poisoning by other central nervous system depressants and anesthetics
969 Poisoning by psychotropic agents
970 Poisoning by central nervous system stimulants
971 Poisoning by drugs primarily affecting the autonomic nervous system
972 Poisoning by agents primarily affecting the cardiovascular system
973 Poisoning by agents primarily affecting the gastrointestinal system
974 Poisoning by water, mineral, and uric acid metabolism drugs
975 Poisoning by agents primarily acting on the smooth and skeletal muscles and respiratory system
976 Poisoning by agents primarily affecting skin and mucous membrane, ophthalmological, otorhinolaryngological, and dental drugs
977 Poisoning by other and unspecified drugs and medicinals
978 Poisoning by bacterial vaccines
979 Poisoning by other vaccines and biological substances

Toxic effects of substances chiefly nonmedicinal as to source (980–989)
980 Toxic effect of alcohol
981 Toxic effect of petroleum products
982 Toxic effect of solvents other than petroleum-based
983 Toxic effect of corrosive aromatics, acids, and caustic alkalis
984 Toxic effect of lead and its compounds (including fumes)
985 Toxic effect of other metals
986 Toxic effect of carbon monoxide
987 Toxic effect of other gases, fumes, or vapors
988 Toxic effect of noxious substances eaten as food
989 Toxic effect of other substances, chiefly nonmedicinal as to source

Other and unspecified effects of external causes (990–995)
990 Effects of radiation, unspecified
991 Effects of reduced temperature
992 Effects of heat and light
993 Effects of air pressure
994 Effects of other external causes
995 Certain adverse effects, not elsewhere classified

Complications of surgical and medical care, not elsewhere classified (996–999)
996 Complications peculiar to certain specified procedures
997 Complications affecting specified body systems, not elsewhere classified
998 Other complications of procedures, not elsewhere classified
999 Complications of medical care, not elsewhere classified

SUPPLEMENTARY CLASSIFICATION OF FACTORS INFLUENCING HEALTH STATUS AND CONTACT WITH HEALTH SERVICES

Persons with potential health hazards related to communicable diseases (V01–V09)
V01 Contact with or exposure to communicable diseases
V02 Carrier or suspected carrier of infectious diseases
V03 Need for prophylactic vaccination and inoculation against bacterial diseases
V04 Need for prophylactic vaccination and inoculation against certain viral diseases
V05 Need for other prophylactic vaccination and inoculation against single diseases
V06 Need for prophylactic vaccination and inoculation against combinations of diseases
V07 Need for isolation and other prophylactic measures
V08 Asymptomatic human immunodeficiency virus [HIV] infection status
V09 Infection with drug-resistant microorganisms

Persons with potential health hazards related to personal and family history (V10–V19)
V10 Personal history of malignant neoplasm
V11 Personal history of mental disorder
V12 Personal history of certain other diseases
V13 Personal history of other diseases
V14 Personal history of allergy to medicinal agents
V15 Other personal history presenting hazards to health
V16 Family history of malignant neoplasm
V17 Family history of certain chronic disabling diseases
V18 Family history of certain other specific conditions
V19 Family history of other conditions

Persons encountering health services in circumstances related to reproduction and development (V20–V29)
V20 Health supervision of infant or child
V21 Constitutional states in development
V22 Normal pregnancy
V23 Supervision of high-risk pregnancy
V24 Postpartum care and examination
V25 Encounter for contraceptive management
V26 Procreative management
V27 Outcome of delivery
V28 Antenatal screening
V29 Observation and evaluation of newborns and infants for suspected condition not found

Liveborn infants according to type of birth (V30–V39)
V30 Single liveborn
V31 Twin, mate liveborn
V32 Twin, mate stillborn
V33 Twin, unspecified
V34 Other multiple, mates all liveborn
V35 Other multiple, mates all stillborn
V36 Other multiple, mates live- and stillborn
V37 Other multiple, unspecified
V39 Unspecified

Persons with a condition influencing their health status (V40–V49)
V40 Mental and behavioral problems

V41 Problems with special senses and other special functions
V42 Organ or tissue replaced by transplant
V43 Organ or tissue replaced by other means
V44 Artificial opening status
V45 Other postsurgical states
V46 Other dependence on machines
V47 Other problems with internal organs
V48 Problems with head, neck, and trunk
V49 Problems with limbs and other problems

Persons encountering health services for specific procedures and aftercare (V50–V59)

V50 Elective surgery for purposes other than remedying health states
V51 Aftercare involving the use of plastic surgery
V52 Fitting and adjustment of prosthetic device
V53 Fitting and adjustment of other device
V54 Other orthopedic aftercare
V55 Attention to artificial openings
V56 Encounter for dialysis and dialysis catheter care
V57 Care involving use of rehabilitation procedures
V58 Other and unspecified aftercare
V59 Donors

Persons encountering health services in other circumstances (V60–V69)

V60 Housing, household, and economic circumstances
V61 Other family circumstances
V62 Other psychosocial circumstances
V63 Unavailability of other medical facilities for care
V64 Persons encountering health services for specific procedures, not carried out
V65 Other persons seeking consultation without complaint or sickness
V66 Convalescence and palliative care
V67 Follow-up examination
V68 Encounters for administrative purposes
V69 Problems related to lifestyle

Persons without reported diagnosis encountered during examination and investigation of individuals and populations (V70–V82)

V70 General medical examination
V71 Observation and evaluation for suspected conditions
V72 Special investigations and examinations
V73 Special screening examination for viral and chlamydial diseases
V74 Special screening examination for bacterial and spirochetal diseases
V75 Special screening examination for other infectious diseases
V76 Special screening for malignant neoplasms
V77 Special screening for endocrine, nutritional, metabolic, and immunity disorders
V78 Special screening for disorders of blood and blood-forming organs
V79 Special screening for mental disorders and developmental handicaps
V80 Special screening for neurological, eye, and ear diseases
V81 Special screening for cardiovascular, respiratory, and genitourinary diseases
V82 Special screening for other conditions

SUPPLEMENTARY CLASSIFICATION OF EXTERNAL CAUSES OF INJURY AND POISONING

Railway accidents (E800–E807)

E800 Railway accident involving collision with rolling stock
E801 Railway accident involving collision with other object
E802 Railway accident involving derailment without antecedent collision
E803 Railway accident involving explosion, fire, or burning
E804 Fall in, on, or from railway train
E805 Hit by rolling stock
E806 Other specified railway accident
E807 Railway accident of unspecified nature

Motor vehicle traffic accidents (E810–E819)

E810 Motor vehicle traffic accident involving collision with train
E811 Motor vehicle traffic accident involving re-entrant collision with another motor vehicle
E812 Other motor vehicle traffic accident involving collision with another motor vehicle
E813 Motor vehicle traffic accident involving collision with other vehicle
E814 Motor vehicle traffic accident involving collision with pedestrian
E815 Other motor vehicle traffic accident involving collision on the highway
E816 Motor vehicle traffic accident due to loss of control, without collision on the highway
E817 Noncollision motor vehicle traffic accident while boarding or alighting
E818 Other noncollision motor vehicle traffic accident
E819 Motor vehicle traffic accident of unspecified nature

Motor vehicle nontraffic accidents (E820–E825)

E820 Nontraffic accident involving motor-driven snow vehicle
E821 Nontraffic accident involving other off-road motor vehicle
E822 Other motor vehicle nontraffic accident involving collision with moving object
E823 Other motor vehicle nontraffic accident involving collision with stationary object
E824 Other motor vehicle nontraffic accident while boarding and alighting
E825 Other motor vehicle nontraffic accident of other and unspecified nature

Other road vehicle accidents (E826–E829)

E826 Pedal cycle accident
E827 Animal-drawn vehicle accident
E828 Accident involving animal being ridden
E829 Other road vehicle accidents

Water transport accidents (E830–E838)

E830 Accident to watercraft causing submersion
E831 Accident to watercraft causing other injury
E832 Other accidental submersion or drowning in water transport accident
E833 Fall on stairs or ladders in water transport
E834 Other fall from one level to another in water transport
E835 Other and unspecified fall in water transport
E836 Machinery accident in water transport
E837 Explosion, fire, or burning in watercraft
E838 Other and unspecified water transport accident

Air and space transport accidents (E840–E845)

E840 Accident to powered aircraft at takeoff or landing
E841 Accident to powered aircraft, other and unspecified
E842 Accident to unpowered aircraft
E843 Fall in, on, or from aircraft
E844 Other specified air transport accidents
E845 Accident involving spacecraft

Vehicle accidents, not elsewhere classifiable (E846–E849)

E846 Accidents involving powered vehicles used solely within the buildings and premises of an industrial or commercial establishment
E847 Accidents involving cable cars not running on rails
E848 Accidents involving other vehicles, not elsewhere classifiable
E849 Place of occurrence

Accidental poisoning by drugs, medicinal substances, and biologicals (E850–E858)

E850 Accidental poisoning by analgesics, antipyretics, and antirheumatics
E851 Accidental poisoning by barbiturates
E852 Accidental poisoning by other sedatives and hypnotics
E853 Accidental poisoning by tranquilizers
E854 Accidental poisoning by other psychotropic agents

E855   Accidental poisoning by other drugs acting on central and autonomic nervous systems
E856   Accidental poisoning by antibiotics
E857   Accidental poisoning by anti-infectives
E858   Accidental poisoning by other drugs

Accidental poisoning by other solid and liquid substances, gases, and vapors (E860–E869)
E860   Accidental poisoning by alcohol, not elsewhere classified
E861   Accidental poisoning by cleansing and polishing agents, disinfectants, paints, and varnishes
E862   Accidental poisoning by petroleum products, other solvents and their vapors, not elsewhere classified
E863   Accidental poisoning by agricultural and horticultural chemical and pharmaceutical preparations other than plant foods and fertilizers
E864   Accidental poisoning by corrosives and caustics, not elsewhere classified
E865   Accidental poisoning from poisonous foodstuffs and poisonous plants
E866   Accidental poisoning by other and unspecified solid and liquid substances
E867   Accidental poisoning by gas distributed by pipeline
E868   Accidental poisoning by other utility gas and other carbon monoxide
E869   Accidental poisoning by other gases and vapors

Misadventures to patients during surgical and medical care (E870–E876)
E870   Accidental cut, puncture, perforation, or hemorrhage during medical care
E871   Foreign object left in body during procedure
E872   Failure of sterile precautions during procedure
E873   Failure in dosage
E874   Mechanical failure of instrument or apparatus during procedure
E875   Contaminated or infected blood, other fluid, drug, or biological substance
E876   Other and unspecified misadventures during medical care

Surgical and medical procedures as the cause of abnormal reaction of patient or later complication, without mention of misadventure at the time of procedure (E878–E879)
E878   Surgical operation and other surgical procedures as the cause of abnormal reaction of patient, or of later complication, without mention of misadventure at the time of operation
E879   Other procedures, without mention of misadventure at the time of procedure, as the cause of abnormal reaction of patient, or of later complication

Accidental falls (E880–E888)
E880   Fall on or from stairs or steps
E881   Fall on or from ladders or scaffolding
E882   Fall from or out of building or other structure
E883   Fall into hole or other opening in surface
E884   Other fall from one level to another
E885   Fall on same level from slipping, tripping, or stumbling
E886   Fall on same level from collision, pushing or shoving, by or with other person
E887   Fracture, cause unspecified
E888   Other and unspecified fall

Accidents caused by fire and flames (E890–E899)
E890   Conflagration in private dwelling
E891   Conflagration in other and unspecified building or structure
E892   Conflagration not in building or structure
E893   Accident caused by ignition of clothing
E894   Ignition of highly inflammable material
E895   Accident caused by controlled fire in private dwelling
E896   Accident caused by controlled fire in other and unspecified building or structure
E897   Accident caused by controlled fire not in building or structure

E898   Accident caused by other specified fire and flames
E899   Accident caused by unspecified fire

Accidents due to natural and environmental factors (E900–E909)
E900   Excessive heat
E901   Excessive cold
E902   High and low air pressure and changes in air pressure
E903   Travel and motion
E904   Hunger, thirst, exposure, and neglect
E905   Venomous animals and plants as the cause of poisoning and toxic reactions
E906   Other injury caused by animals
E907   Lightning
E908   Cataclysmic storms, and floods resulting from storms
E909   Cataclysmic earth surface movements and eruptions

Accidents caused by submersion, suffocation, and foreign bodies (E910–E915)
E910   Accidental drowning and submersion
E911   Inhalation and ingestion of food causing obstruction of respiratory tract or suffocation
E912   Inhalation and ingestion of other object causing obstruction of respiratory tract or suffocation
E913   Accidental mechanical suffocation
E914   Foreign body accidentally entering eye and adnexa
E915   Foreign body accidentally entering other orifice

Other accidents (E916–E928)
E916   Struck accidentally by falling object
E917   Striking against or struck accidentally by objects or persons
E918   Caught accidentally in or between objects
E919   Accidents caused by machinery
E920   Accidents caused by cutting and piercing instruments or objects
E921   Accident caused by explosion of pressure vessel
E922   Accident caused by firearm missile
E923   Accident caused by explosive material
E924   Accident caused by hot substance or object, caustic or corrosive material, and steam
E925   Accident caused by electric current
E926   Exposure to radiation
E927   Overexertion and strenuous movements
E928   Other and unspecified environmental and accidental causes

Late effects of accidental injury (E929)
E929   Late effects of accidental injury

Drugs, medicinal and biological substances causing adverse effects in therapeutic use (E930–E949)
E930   Antibiotics
E931   Other anti-infectives
E932   Hormones and synthetic substitutes
E933   Primarily systemic agents
E934   Agents primarily affecting blood constituents
E935   Analgesics, antipyretics, and antirheumatics
E936   Anticonvulsants and anti-parkinsonism drugs
E937   Sedatives and hypnotics
E938   Other central nervous system depressants and anesthetics
E939   Psychotropic agents
E940   Central nervous system stimulants
E941   Drugs primarily affecting the autonomic nervous system
E942   Agents primarily affecting the cardiovascular system
E943   Agents primarily affecting gastrointestinal system
E944   Water, mineral, and uric acid metabolism drugs
E945   Agents primarily acting on the smooth and skeletal muscles and respiratory system
E946   Agents primarily affecting skin and mucous membrane, ophthalmological, otorhinolaryngological, and dental drugs
E947   Other and unspecified drugs and medicinal substances
E948   Bacterial vaccines
E949   Other vaccines and biological substances

Suicide and self-inflicted injury (E950–E959)

E950   Suicide and self-inflicted poisoning by solid or liquid substances

E951   Suicide and self-inflicted poisoning by gases in domestic use

E952   Suicide and self-inflicted poisoning by other gases and vapors

E953   Suicide and self-inflicted injury by hanging, strangulation, and suffocation

E954   Suicide and self-inflicted injury by submersion [drowning]

E955   Suicide and self-inflicted injury by firearms and explosives

E956   Suicide and self-inflicted injury by cutting and piercing instruments

E957   Suicide and self-inflicted injuries by jumping from high place

E958   Suicide and self-inflicted injury by other and unspecified means

E959   Late effects of self-inflicted injury

Homicide and injury purposely inflicted by other persons (E960–E969)

E960   Fight, brawl, and rape

E961   Assault by corrosive or caustic substance, except poisoning

E962   Assault by poisoning

E963   Assault by hanging and strangulation

E964   Assault by submersion [drowning]

E965   Assault by firearms and explosives

E966   Assault by cutting and piercing instrument

E967   Child and adult battering and other maltreatment

E968   Assault by other and unspecified means

E969   Late effects of injury purposely inflicted by other person

Legal intervention (E970–E978)

E970   Injury due to legal intervention by firearms

E971   Injury due to legal intervention by explosives

E972   Injury due to legal intervention by gas

E973   Injury due to legal intervention by blunt object

E974   Injury due to legal intervention by cutting and piercing instruments

E975   Injury due to legal intervention by other specified means

E976   Injury due to legal intervention by unspecified means

E977   Late effects of injuries due to legal intervention

E978   Legal execution

Injury undetermined whether accidentally or purposely inflicted (E980–E989)

E980   Poisoning by solid or liquid substances, undetermined whether accidentally or purposely inflicted

E981   Poisoning by gases in domestic use, undetermined whether accidentally or purposely inflicted

E982   Poisoning by other gases, undetermined whether accidentally or purposely inflicted

E983   Hanging, strangulation, or suffocation, undetermined whether accidentally or purposely inflicted

E984   Submersion [drowning], undetermined whether accidentally or purposely inflicted

E985   Injury by firearms and explosives, undetermined whether accidentally or purposely inflicted

E986   Injury by cutting and piercing instruments, undetermined whether accidentally or purposely inflicted

E987   Falling from high place, undetermined whether accidentally or purposely inflicted

E988   Injury by other and unspecified means, undetermined whether accidentally or purposely inflicted

E989   Late effects of injury, undetermined whether accidentally or purposely inflicted

Injury resulting from operations of war (E990–E999)

E990   Injury due to war operations by fires and conflagrations

E991   Injury due to war operations by bullets and fragments

E992   Injury due to war operations by explosion of marine weapons

E993   Injury due to war operations by other explosion

E994   Injury due to war operations by destruction of aircraft

E995   Injury due to war operations by other and unspecified forms of conventional warfare

E996   Injury due to war operations by nuclear weapons

E997   Injury due to war operations by other forms of unconventional warfare

E998   Injury due to war operations but occurring after cessation of hostilities

E999   Late effects of injury due to war operations

DIAGNOSES DEFINED AS COMPLICATIONS OR COMORBIDITIES

Appendix F lists all the diagnosis codes considered as complications and comorbidities (CC) for the DRGs. These codes are shown in bold print. Following each CC code is a list of diagnosis codes that, when used as the principal diagnosis, will not consider the CC as a complication or comorbidity. For any CC allowed with all principal diagnoses, the phrase "No Exclusions" follows the CC code.

00841 Staphylococc enteritis
0011,0020,0029-0030,0049-0052,0060-0062,0069,0071-0090,
01480-01486,11285,129,4878,5363-5368,5550-5579,5582-5589,5641,
7750-7759,7775,7778

00842 Pseudomonas enteritis
0011,0020,0029-0030,0049-0052,0060-0062,0069,0071-0090,
01480-01486,11285,129,4878,5363-5368,5550-5579,5582-5589,5641,
7750-7759,7775,7778

00843 Int infec campylobacter
0011,0020,0029-0030,0049-0052,0060-0062,0069,0071-0090,
01480-01486,11285,129,4878,5363-5368,5550-5579,5582-5589,5641,
7750-7759,7775,7778

00844 Int inf yrsnia entrcltca
0011,0020,0029-0030,0049-0052,0060-0062,0069,0071-0090,
01480-01486,11285,129,4878,5363-5368,5550-5579,5582-5589,5641,
7750-7759,7775,7778

00845 Int inf clstrdium dfcile
0011,0020,0029-0030,0049-0052,0060-0062,0069,0071-0090,
01480-01486,11285,129,4878,5363-5368,5550-5579,5582-5589,5641,
7750-7759,7775,7778

00846 Intes infec oth anerobes
0011,0020,0029-0030,0049-0052,0060-0062,0069,0071-0090,
01480-01486,11285,129,4878,5363-5368,5550-5579,5582-5589,5641,
7750-7759,7775,7778

00847 Int inf oth grm neg bctr
0011,0020,0029-0030,0049-0052,0060-0062,0069,0071-0090,
01480-01486,11285,129,4878,5363-5368,5550-5579,5582-5589,5641,
7750-7759,7775,7778

00849 Bacterial enteritis NEC
0011,0020,0029-0030,0049-0052,0060-0062,0069,0071-0090,
01480-01486,11285,129,4878,5363-5368,5550-5579,5582-5589,5641,
7750-7759,7775,7778

01100 TB lung infiltr-unspec
01100-01286,01790-01896,0310,0312-0319,04181-0419,1370,1398,
4800-4871,494-5089,5171,51889

01101 TB lung infiltr-no exam
01100-01286,01790-01896,0310,0312-0319,04181-0419,1370,1398,
4800-4871,494-5089,5171,51889

01102 TB lung infiltr-exm unkn
01100-01286,01790-01896,0310,0312-0319,04181-0419,1370,1398,
4800-4871,494-5089,5171,51889

01103 TB lung infiltr-micro dx
01100-01286,01790-01896,0310,0312-0319,04181-0419,1370,1398,
4800-4871,494-5089,5171,51889

01104 TB lung infiltr-cult dx
01100-01286,01790-01896,0310,0312-0319,04181-0419,1370,1398,
4800-4871,494-5089,5171,51889

01105 TB lung infiltr-histo dx
01100-01286,01790-01896,0310,0312-0319,04181-0419,1370,1398,
4800-4871,494-5089,5171,51889

01106 TB lung infiltr-oth test
01100-01286,01790-01896,0310,0312-0319,04181-0419,1370,1398,
4800-4871,494-5089,5171,51889

01110 TB lung nodular-unspec
01100-01286,01790-01896,0310,0312-0319,04181-0419,1370,1398,
4800-4871,494-5089,5171,51889

01111 TB lung nodular-no exam
01100-01286,01790-01896,0310,0312-0319,04181-0419,1370,1398,
4800-4871,494-5089,5171,51889

01112 TB lung nodul-exam unkn
01100-01286,01790-01896,0310,0312-0319,04181-0419,1370,1398,
4800-4871,494-5089,5171,51889

01113 TB lung nodular-micro dx
01100-01286,01790-01896,0310,0312-0319,04181-0419,1370,1398,
4800-4871,494-5089,5171,51889

01114 TB lung nodular-cult dx
01100-01286,01790-01896,0310,0312-0319,04181-0419,1370,1398,
4800-4871,494-5089,5171,51889

01115 TB lung nodular-histo dx
01100-01286,01790-01896,0310,0312-0319,04181-0419,1370,1398,
4800-4871,494-5089,5171,51889

01116 TB lung nodular-oth test
01100-01286,01790-01896,0310,0312-0319,04181-0419,1370,1398,
4800-4871,494-5089,5171,51889

01120 TB lung w cavity-unspec
01100-01286,01790-01896,0310,0312-0319,04181-0419,1370,1398,
4800-4871,494-5089,5171,51889

01121 TB lung w cavity-no exam
01100-01286,01790-01896,0310,0312-0319,04181-0419,1370,1398,
4800-4871,494-5089,5171,51889

01122 TB lung cavity-exam unkn
01100-01286,01790-01896,0310,0312-0319,04181-0419,1370,1398,
4800-4871,494-5089,5171,51889

01123 TB lung w cavit-micro dx
01100-01286,01790-01896,0310,0312-0319,04181-0419,1370,1398,
4800-4871,494-5089,5171,51889

01124 TB lung w cavity-cult dx
01100-01286,01790-01896,0310,0312-0319,04181-0419,1370,1398,
4800-4871,494-5089,5171,51889

01125 TB lung w cavit-histo dx
01100-01286,01790-01896,0310,0312-0319,04181-0419,1370,1398,
4800-4871,494-5089,5171,51889

01126 TB lung w cavit-oth test
01100-01286,01790-01896,0310,0312-0319,04181-0419,1370,1398,
4800-4871,494-5089,5171,51889

01130 TB of bronchus-unspec
01100-01286,01790-01896,0310,0312-0319,04181-0419,1370,1398,
4800-4871,494-5089,5171,51889

01131 TB of bronchus-no exam
01100-01286,01790-01896,0310,0312-0319,04181-0419,1370,1398,
4800-4871,494-5089,5171,51889

01132 TB of bronchus-exam unkn
01100-01286,01790-01896,0310,0312-0319,04181-0419,1370,1398,
4800-4871,494-5089,5171,51889

01133 TB of bronchus-micro dx
01100-01286,01790-01896,0310,0312-0319,04181-0419,1370,1398,
4800-4871,494-5089,5171,51889

01134 TB of bronchus-cult dx
01100-01286,01790-01896,0310,0312-0319,04181-0419,1370,1398,
4800-4871,494-5089,5171,51889

01135 TB of bronchus-histo dx
01100-01286,01790-01896,0310,0312-0319,04181-0419,1370,1398,
4800-4871,494-5089,5171,51889

01136 TB of bronchus-oth test
01100-01286,01790-01896,0310,0312-0319,04181-0419,1370,1398,
4800-4871,494-5089,5171,51889

01140 TB lung fibrosis-unspec
01100-01286,01790-01896,0310,0312-0319,04181-0419,1370,1398,
4800-4871,494-5089,5171,51889

01141 TB lung fibrosis-no exam
01100-01286,01790-01896,0310,0312-0319,04181-0419,1370,1398,
4800-4871,494-5089,5171,51889

01142 TB lung fibros-exam unkn
01100-01286,01790-01896,0310,0312-0319,04181-0419,1370,1398,
4800-4871,494-5089,5171,51889

01143　TB lung fibros-micro dx
01100-01286,01790-01896,0310,0312-0319,04181-0419,1370,1398,
4800-4871,494-5089,5171,51889
01144　TB lung fibrosis-cult dx
01100-01286,01790-01896,0310,0312-0319,04181-0419,1370,1398,
4800-4871,494-5089,5171,51889
01145　TB lung fibros-histo dx
01100-01286,01790-01896,0310,0312-0319,04181-0419,1370,1398,
4800-4871,494-5089,5171,51889
01146　TB lung fibros-oth test
01100-01286,01790-01896,0310,0312-0319,04181-0419,1370,1398,
4800-4871,494-5089,5171,51889
01150　TB bronchiectasis-unspec
01100-01286,01790-01896,0310,0312-0319,04181-0419,1370,1398,
4800-4871,494-5089,5171,51889
01151　TB bronchiect-no exam
01100-01286,01790-01896,0310,0312-0319,04181-0419,1370,1398,
4800-4871,494-5089,5171,51889
01152　TB bronchiect-exam unkn
01100-01286,01790-01896,0310,0312-0319,04181-0419,1370,1398,
4800-4871,494-5089,5171,51889
01153　TB bronchiect-micro dx
01100-01286,01790-01896,0310,0312-0319,04181-0419,1370,1398,
4800-4871,494-5089,5171,51889
01154　TB bronchiect-cult dx
01100-01286,01790-01896,0310,0312-0319,04181-0419,1370,1398,
4800-4871,494-5089,5171,51889
01155　TB bronchiect-histo dx
01100-01286,01790-01896,0310,0312-0319,04181-0419,1370,1398,
4800-4871,494-5089,5171,51889
01156　TB bronchiect-oth test
01100-01286,01790-01896,0310,0312-0319,04181-0419,1370,1398,
4800-4871,494-5089,5171,51889
01160　TB pneumonia-unspec
01100-01286,01790-01896,0310,0312-0319,04181-0419,1370,1398,
4800-4871,494-5089,5171,51889
01161　TB pneumonia-no exam
01100-01286,01790-01896,0310,0312-0319,04181-0419,1370,1398,
4800-4871,494-5089,5171,51889
01162　TB pneumonia-exam unkn
01100-01286,01790-01896,0310,0312-0319,04181-0419,1370,1398,
4800-4871,494-5089,5171,51889
01163　TB pneumonia-micro dx
01100-01286,01790-01896,0310,0312-0319,04181-0419,1370,1398,
4800-4871,494-5089,5171,51889
01164　TB pneumonia-cult dx
01100-01286,01790-01896,0310,0312-0319,04181-0419,1370,1398,
4800-4871,494-5089,5171,51889
01165　TB pneumonia-histo dx
01100-01286,01790-01896,0310,0312-0319,04181-0419,1370,1398,
4800-4871,494-5089,5171,51889
01166　TB pneumonia-oth test
01166,1398,4800-4871,494-5089,5171,51889
01170　TB pneumothorax-unspec
01100-01286,01790-01896,0310,0312-0319,04181-0419,1370,1398,
4800-4871,494-5089,5171,51889
01171　TB pneumothorax-no exam
01100-01286,01790-01896,0310,0312-0319,04181-0419,1370,1398,
4800-4871,494-5089,5171,51889
01172　TB pneumothorx-exam unkn
01100-01286,01790-01896,0310,0312-0319,04181-0419,1370,1398,
4800-4871,494-5089,5171,51889
01173　TB pneumothorax-micro dx
01100-01286,01790-01896,0310,0312-0319,04181-0419,1370,1398,
4800-4871,494-5089,5171,51889
01174　TB pneumothorax-cult dx
01100-01286,01790-01896,0310,0312-0319,04181-0419,1370,1398,
4800-4871,494-5089,5171,51889
01175　TB pneumothorax-histo dx
01100-01286,01790-01896,0310,0312-0319,04181-0419,1370,1398,
4800-4871,494-5089,5171,51889
01176　TB pneumothorax-oth test
01100-01286,01790-01896,0310,0312-0319,04181-0419,1370,1398,
4800-4871,494-5089,5171,51889

01180　Pulmonary TB NEC-unspec
01100-01286,01790-01896,0310,0312-0319,04181-0419,1370,1398,
4800-4871,494-5089,5171,51889
01181　Pulmonary TB NEC-no exam
01100-01286,01790-01896,0310,0312-0319,04181-0419,1370,1398,
4800-4871,494-5089,5171,51889
01182　Pulmon TB NEC-exam unkn
01100-01286,01790-01896,0310,0312-0319,04181-0419,1370,1398,
4800-4871,494-5089,5171,51889
01183　Pulmon TB NEC-micro dx
01100-01286,01790-01896,0310,0312-0319,04181-0419,1370,1398,
4800-4871,494-5089,5171,51889
01184　Pulmon TB NEC-cult dx
01100-01286,01790-01896,0310,0312-0319,04181-0419,1370,1398,
4800-4871,494-5089,5171,51889
01185　Pulmon TB NEC-histo dx
01100-01286,01790-01896,0310,0312-0319,04181-0419,1370,1398,
4800-4871,494-5089,5171,51889
01186　Pulmon TB NEC-oth test
01100-01286,01790-01896,0310,0312-0319,04181-0419,1370,1398,
4800-4871,494-5089,5171,51889
01190　Pulmonary TB NOS-unspec
01100-01286,01790-01896,0310,0312-0319,04181-0419,1370,1398,
4800-4871,494-5089,5171,51889
01191　Pulmonary TB NOS-no exam
01100-01286,01790-01896,0310,0312-0319,04181-0419,1370,1398,
4800-4871,494-5089,5171,51889
01192　Pulmon TB NOS-exam unkn
01100-01286,01790-01896,0310,0312-0319,04181-0419,1370,1398,
4800-4871,494-5089,5171,51889
01193　Pulmon TB NOS-micro dx
01100-01286,01790-01896,0310,0312-0319,04181-0419,1370,1398,
4800-4871,494-5089,5171,51889
01194　Pulmon TB NOS-cult dx
01100-01286,01790-01896,0310,0312-0319,04181-0419,1370,1398,
4800-4871,494-5089,5171,51889
01195　Pulmon TB NOS-histo dx
01100-01286,01790-01896,0310,0312-0319,04181-0419,1370,1398,
4800-4871,494-5089,5171,51889
01196　Pulmon TB NOS-oth test
01100-01286,01790-01896,0310,0312-0319,04181-0419,1370,1398,
4800-4871,494-5089,5171,51889
01200　TB pleurisy-unspec
01100-01286,01790-01896,0310,0312-0319,04181-0419,1370,1398,
4800-4871,494-5089,5171,51889
01201　TB pleurisy-no exam
01100-01286,01790-01896,0310,0312-0319,04181-0419,1370,1398,
4800-4871,494-5089,5171,51889
01202　TB pleurisy-exam unkn
01100-01286,01790-01896,0310,0312-0319,04181-0419,1370,1398,
4800-4871,494-5089,5171,51889
01203　TB pleurisy-micro dx
01100-01286,01790-01896,0310,0312-0319,04181-0419,1370,1398,
4800-4871,494-5089,5171,51889
01204　TB pleurisy-cult dx
01100-01286,01790-01896,0310,0312-0319,04181-0419,1370,1398,
4800-4871,494-5089,5171,51889
01205　TB pleurisy-histolog dx
01100-01286,01790-01896,0310,0312-0319,04181-0419,1370,1398,
4800-4871,494-5089,5171,51889
01206　TB pleurisy-oth test
01100-01286,01790-01896,0310,0312-0319,04181-0419,1370,1398,
4800-4871,494-5089,5171,51889
01210　TB thoracic nodes-unspec
01100-01286,01790-01896,0310,0312-0319,04181-0419,1370,1398,
4800-4871,494-5089,5171,51889
01211　TB thorax node-no exam
01100-01286,01790-01896,0310,0312-0319,04181-0419,1370,1398,
4800-4871,494-5089,5171,51889
01212　TB thorax node-exam unkn
01100-01286,01790-01896,0310,0312-0319,04181-0419,1370,1398,
4800-4871,494-5089,5171,51889

01213 TB thorax node-micro dx
01100-01286,01790-01896,0310,0312-0319,04181-0419,1370,1398,
4800-4871,494-5089,5171,51889

01214 TB thorax node-cult dx
01100-01286,01790-01896,0310,0312-0319,04181-0419,1370,1398,
4800-4871,494-5089,5171,51889

01215 TB thorax node-histo dx
01100-01286,01790-01896,0310,0312-0319,04181-0419,1370,1398,
4800-4871,494-5089,5171,51889

01216 TB thorax node-oth test
01100-01286,01790-01896,0310,0312-0319,04181-0419,1370,1398,
4800-4871,494-5089,5171,51889

01300 TB meningitis-unspec
00321,01300-01316,01340-01356,01380-01396,01790-01796,
0312-0319,0360,04181-0419,0470-0479,0490-0491,0530,05472,0721,
09042,09181,0942,09889,10081,11283,1142,11501,11511,11591,1300,
1371,1398,3200-3229,34989-3499,3570

01301 TB meningitis-no exam
00321,01300-01316,01340-01356,01380-01396,01790-01796,
0312-0319,0360,04181-0419,0470-0479,0490-0491,0530,05472,0721,
09042,09181,0942,09889,10081,11283,1142,11501,11511,11591,1300,
1371,1398,3200-3229,34989-3499,3570

01302 TB meningitis-exam unkn
00321,01300-01316,01340-01356,01380-01396,01790-01796,
0312-0319,0360,04181-0419,0470-0479,0490-0491,0530,05472,0721,
09042,09181,0942,09889,10081,11283,1142,11501,11511,11591,1300,
1371,1398,3200-3229,34989-3499,3570

01303 TB meningitis-micro dx
00321,01300-01316,01340-01356,01380-01396,01790-01796,
0312-0319,0360,04181-0419,0470-0479,0490-0491,0530,05472,0721,
09042,09181,0942,09889,10081,11283,1142,11501,11511,11591,1300,
1371,1398,3200-3229,34989-3499,3570

01304 TB meningitis-cult dx
00321,01300-01316,01340-01356,01380-01396,01790-01796,
0312-0319,0360,04181-0419,0470-0479,0490-0491,0530,05472,0721,
09042,09181,0942,09889,10081,11283,1142,11501,11511,11591,1300,
1371,1398,3200-3229,34989-3499,3570

01305 TB meningitis-histo dx
00321,01300-01316,01340-01356,01380-01396,01790-01796,
0312-0319,0360,04181-0419,0470-0479,0490-0491,0530,05472,0721,
09042,09181,0942,09889,10081,11283,1142,11501,11511,11591,1300,
1371,1398,3200-3229,34989-3499,3570

01306 TB meningitis-oth test
00321,01300-01316,01340-01356,01380-01396,01790-01796,
0312-0319,0360,04181-0419,0470-0479,0490-0491,0530,05472,0721,
09042,09181,0942,09889,10081,11283,1142,11501,11511,11591,1300,
1371,1398,3200-3229,34989-3499,3570

01310 Tubrclma meninges-unspec
00321,01300-01316,01340-01356,01380-01396,01790-01796,
0312-0319,0360,04181-0419,0470-0479,0490-0491,0530,05472,0721,
09042,09181,0942,09889,10081,11283,1142,11501,11511,11591,1300,
1371,1398,3200-3229,34989-3499,3570

01311 Tubrclma mening-no exam
00321,01300-01316,01340-01356,01380-01396,01790-01796,
0312-0319,0360,04181-0419,0470-0479,0490-0491,0530,05472,0721,
09042,09181,0942,09889,10081,11283,1142,11501,11511,11591,1300,
1371,1398,3200-3229,34989-3499,3570

01312 Tubrclma menin-exam unkn
00321,01300-01316,01340-01356,01380-01396,01790-01796,
0312-0319,0360,04181-0419,0470-0479,0490-0491,0530,05472,0721,
09042,09181,0942,09889,10081,11283,1142,11501,11511,11591,1300,
1371,1398,3200-3229,34989-3499,3570

01313 Tubrclma mening-micro dx
00321,01300-01316,01340-01356,01380-01396,01790-01796,
0312-0319,0360,04181-0419,0470-0479,0490-0491,0530,05472,0721,
09042,09181,0942,09889,10081,11283,1142,11501,11511,11591,1300,
1371,1398,3200-3229,34989-3499,3570

01314 Tubrclma mening-cult dx
00321,01300-01316,01340-01356,01380-01396,01790-01796,
0312-0319,0360,04181-0419,0470-0479,0490-0491,0530,05472,0721,
09042,09181,0942,09889,10081,11283,1142,11501,11511,11591,1300,
1371,1398,3200-3229,34989-3499,3570

01315 Tubrclma mening-histo dx
00321,01300-01316,01340-01356,01380-01396,01790-01796,
0312-0319,0360,04181-0419,0470-0479,0490-0491,0530,05472,0721,
09042,09181,0942,09889,10081,11283,1142,11501,11511,11591,1300,
1371,1398,3200-3229,34989-3499,3570

01316 Tubrclma mening-oth test
00321,01300-01316,01340-01356,01380-01396,01790-01796,
0312-0319,0360,04181-0419,0470-0479,0490-0491,0530,05472,0721,
09042,09181,0942,09889,10081,11283,1142,11501,11511,11591,1300,
1371,1398,3200-3229,34989-3499,3570

01320 Tuberculoma brain-unspec
01320-01336,01360-01396,01790-01796,0312-0319,04181-0419,1371,
1398

01321 Tubrcloma brain-no exam
01320-01336,01360-01396,01790-01796,0312-0319,04181-0419,1371,
1398

01322 Tubrclma brain-exam unkn
01320-01336,01360-01396,01790-01796,0312-0319,04181-0419,1371,
1398

01323 Tubrcloma brain-micro dx
01320-01336,01360-01396,01790-01796,0312-0319,04181-0419,1371,
1398

01324 Tubrcloma brain-cult dx
01320-01336,01360-01396,01790-01796,0312-0319,04181-0419,1371,
1398

01325 Tubrcloma brain-histo dx
01320-01336,01360-01396,01790-01796,0312-0319,04181-0419,1371,
1398

01326 Tubrcloma brain-oth test
01320-01336,01360-01396,01790-01796,0312-0319,04181-0419,1371,
1398

01330 TB brain abscess-unspec
01320-01336,01360-01396,01790-01796,0312-0319,04181-0419,1371,
1398

01331 TB brain abscess-no exam
01320-01336,01360-01396,01790-01796,0312-0319,04181-0419,1371,
1398

01332 TB brain absc-exam unkn
01320-01336,01360-01396,01790-01796,0312-0319,04181-0419,1371,
1398

01333 TB brain absc-micro dx
01320-01336,01360-01396,01790-01796,0312-0319,04181-0419,1371,
1398

01334 TB brain abscess-cult dx
01320-01336,01360-01396,01790-01796,0312-0319,04181-0419,1371,
1398

01335 TB brain absc-histo dx
01320-01336,01360-01396,01790-01796,0312-0319,04181-0419,1371,
1398

01336 TB brain absc-oth test
01320-01336,01360-01396,01790-01796,0312-0319,04181-0419,1371,
1398

01340 Tubrclma sp cord-unspec
01300-01316,01340-01356,01380-01396,01790-01796,0312-0319,
04181-0419,1371,1398

01341 Tubrclma sp cord-no exam
01300-01316,01340-01356,01380-01396,01790-01796,0312-0319,
04181-0419,1371,1398

01342 Tubrclma sp cd-exam unkn
01300-01316,01340-01356,01380-01396,01790-01796,0312-0319,
04181-0419,1371,1398

01343 Tubrclma sp crd-micro dx
01300-01316,01340-01356,01380-01396,01790-01796,0312-0319,
04181-0419,1371,1398

01344 Tubrclma sp cord-cult dx
01300-01316,01340-01356,01380-01396,01790-01796,0312-0319,
04181-0419,1371,1398

01345 Tubrclma sp crd-histo dx
01300-01316,01340-01356,01380-01396,01790-01796,0312-0319,
04181-0419,1371,1398

01346 Tubrclma sp crd-oth test
01300-01316,01340-01356,01380-01396,01790-01796,0312-0319,
04181-0419,1371,1398

01350 TB sp crd abscess-unspec
01300-01316,01340-01356,01380-01396,01790-01796,0312-0319,
04181-0419,1371,1398
01351 TB sp crd absc-no exam
01300-01316,01340-01356,01380-01396,01790-01796,0312-0319,
04181-0419,1371,1398
01352 TB sp crd absc-exam unkn
01300-01316,01340-01356,01380-01396,01790-01796,0312-0319,
04181-0419,1371,1398
01353 TB sp crd absc-micro dx
01300-01316,01340-01356,01380-01396,01790-01796,0312-0319,
04181-0419,1371,1398
01354 TB sp crd absc-cult dx
01300-01316,01340-01356,01380-01396,01790-01796,0312-0319,
04181-0419,1371,1398
01355 TB sp crd absc-histo dx
01300-01316,01340-01356,01380-01396,01790-01796,0312-0319,
04181-0419,1371,1398
01356 TB sp crd absc-oth test
01300-01316,01340-01356,01380-01396,01790-01796,0312-0319,
04181-0419,1371,1398
01360 TB encephalitis-unspec
01320-01336,01360-01396,01790-01796,0312-0319,04181-0419,1371,
1398
01361 TB encephalitis-no exam
01320-01336,01360-01396,01790-01796,0312-0319,04181-0419,1371,
1398
01362 TB encephalit-exam unkn
01320-01336,01360-01396,01790-01796,0312-0319,04181-0419,1371,
1398
01363 TB encephalitis-micro dx
01320-01336,01360-01396,01790-01796,0312-0319,04181-0419,1371,
1398
01364 TB encephalitis-cult dx
01320-01336,01360-01396,01790-01796,0312-0319,04181-0419,1371,
1398
01365 TB encephalitis-histo dx
01320-01336,01360-01396,01790-01796,0312-0319,04181-0419,1371,
1398
01366 TB encephalitis-oth test
01320-01336,01360-01396,01790-01796,0312-0319,04181-0419,1371,
1398
01380 Cns TB NEC-unspec
01380-01396,01790-01796,0312-0319,04181-0419,1371,1398
01381 Cns TB NEC-no exam
01380-01396,01790-01796,0312-0319,04181-0419,1371,1398
01382 Cns TB NEC-exam unkn
01380-01396,01790-01796,0312-0319,04181-0419,1371,1398
01383 Cns TB NEC-micro dx
01380-01396,01790-01796,0312-0319,04181-0419,1371,1398
01384 Cns TB NEC-cult dx
01380-01396,01790-01796,0312-0319,04181-0419,1371,1398
01385 Cns TB NEC-histo dx
01380-01396,01790-01796,0312-0319,04181-0419,1371,1398
01386 Cns TB NEC-oth test
01380-01396,01790-01796,0312-0319,04181-0419,1371,1398
01390 Cns TB NOS-unspec
01380-01396,01790-01796,0312-0319,04181-0419,1371,1398
01391 Cns TB NOS-no exam
01380-01396,01790-01796,0312-0319,04181-0419,1371,1398
01392 Cns TB NOS-exam unkn
01380-01396,01790-01796,0312-0319,04181-0419,1371,1398
01393 Cns TB NOS-micro dx
01380-01396,01790-01796,0312-0319,04181-0419,1371,1398
01394 Cns TB NOS-cult dx
01380-01396,01790-01796,0312-0319,04181-0419,1371,1398
01395 Cns TB NOS-histo dx
01380-01396,01790-01796,0312-0319,04181-0419,1371,1398
01396 Cns TB NOS-oth test
01380-01396,01790-01796,0312-0319,04181-0419,1371,1398
01400 TB peritonitis-unspec
01400-01486,01790-01796,0312-0319,04181-0419,1398
01401 TB peritonitis-no exam
01400-01486,01790-01796,0312-0319,04181-0419,1398

01402 TB peritonitis-exam unkn
01400-01486,01790-01796,0312-0319,04181-0419,1398
01403 TB peritonitis-micro dx
01400-01486,01790-01796,0312-0319,04181-0419,1398
01404 TB peritonitis-cult dx
01400-01486,01790-01796,0312-0319,04181-0419,1398
01405 TB peritonitis-histo dx
01400-01486,01790-01796,0312-0319,04181-0419,1398
01406 TB peritonitis-oth test
01400-01486,01790-01796,0312-0319,04181-0419,1398
01480 Intestinal TB NEC-unspec
01400-01486,01790-01796,0312-0319,04181-0419,1398
01481 Intestin TB NEC-no exam
01481,1398
01482 Intest TB NEC-exam unkn
01400-01486,01790-01796,0312-0319,04181-0419,1398
01483 Intestin TB NEC-micro dx
01400-01486,01790-01796,0312-0319,04181-0419,1398
01484 Intestin TB NEC-cult dx
01400-01486,01790-01796,0312-0319,04181-0419,1398
01485 Intestin TB NEC-histo dx
01400-01486,01790-01796,0312-0319,04181-0419,1398
01486 Intestin TB NEC-oth test
01400-01486,01790-01796,0312-0319,04181-0419,1398
01600 TB of kidney-unspec
01600-01636,01690-01696,01790-01796,0312-0319,04181-0419,1372,
1398
01601 TB of kidney-no exam
01600-01636,01690-01696,01790-01796,0312-0319,04181-0419,1372,
1398
01602 TB of kidney-exam unkn
01600-01636,01690-01696,01790-01796,0312-0319,04181-0419,1372,
1398
01603 TB of kidney-micro dx
01600-01636,01690-01696,01790-01796,0312-0319,04181-0419,1372,
1398
01604 TB of kidney-cult dx
01600-01636,01690-01696,01790-01796,0312-0319,04181-0419,1372,
1398
01605 TB of kidney-histo dx
01600-01636,01690-01696,01790-01796,0312-0319,04181-0419,1372,
1398
01606 TB of kidney-oth test
01600-01636,01690-01696,01790-01796,0312-0319,04181-0419,1372,
1398
01610 TB of bladder-unspec
01600-01636,01690-01696,01790-01796,0312-0319,04181-0419,1372,
1398
01611 TB of bladder-no exam
01600-01636,01690-01696,01790-01796,0312-0319,04181-0419,1372,
1398
01612 TB of bladder-exam unkn
01600-01636,01690-01696,01790-01796,0312-0319,04181-0419,1372,
1398
01613 TB of bladder-micro dx
01600-01636,01690-01696,01790-01796,0312-0319,04181-0419,1372,
1398
01614 TB of bladder-cult dx
01600-01636,01690-01696,01790-01796,0312-0319,04181-0419,1372,
1398
01615 TB of bladder-histo dx
01600-01636,01690-01696,01790-01796,0312-0319,04181-0419,1372,
1398
01616 TB of bladder-oth test
01600-01636,01690-01696,01790-01796,0312-0319,04181-0419,1372,
1398
01620 TB of ureter-unspec
01600-01636,01690-01696,01790-01796,0312-0319,04181-0419,1372,
1398
01621 TB of ureter-no exam
01600-01636,01690-01696,01790-01796,0312-0319,04181-0419,1372,
1398
01622 TB of ureter-exam unkn
01600-01636,01690-01696,01790-01796,0312-0319,04181-0419,1372,
1398

01623   TB of ureter-micro dx
01600-01636,01690-01696,01790-01796,0312-0319,04181-0419,1372, 1398

01624   TB of ureter-cult dx
01600-01636,01690-01696,01790-01796,0312-0319,04181-0419,1372, 1398

01625   TB of ureter-histo dx
01600-01636,01690-01696,01790-01796,0312-0319,04181-0419,1372, 1398

01626   TB of ureter-oth test
01600-01636,01690-01696,01790-01796,0312-0319,04181-0419,1372, 1398

01630   TB urinary NEC-unspec
01600-01636,01690-01696,01790-01796,0312-0319,04181-0419,1372, 1398

01631   TB urinary NEC-no exam
01600-01636,01690-01696,01790-01796,0312-0319,04181-0419,1372, 1398

01632   TB urinary NEC-exam unkn
01600-01636,01690-01696,01790-01796,0312-0319,04181-0419,1372, 1398

01633   TB urinary NEC-micro dx
01600-01636,01690-01696,01790-01796,0312-0319,04181-0419,1372, 1398

01634   TB urinary NEC-cult dx
01600-01636,01690-01696,01790-01796,0312-0319,04181-0419,1372, 1398

01635   TB urinary NEC-histo dx
01600-01636,01690-01696,01790-01796,0312-0319,04181-0419,1372, 1398

01636   TB urinary NEC-oth test
01600-01636,01690-01696,01790-01796,0312-0319,04181-0419,1372, 1398

01640   TB epididymis-unspec
01640-01656,01690-01696,01790-01796,0312-0319,04181-0419,1372, 1398

01641   TB epididymis-no exam
01640-01656,01690-01696,01790-01796,0312-0319,04181-0419,1372, 1398

01642   TB epididymis-exam unkn
01640-01656,01690-01696,01790-01796,0312-0319,04181-0419,1372, 1398

01643   TB epididymis-micro dx
01640-01656,01690-01696,01790-01796,0312-0319,04181-0419,1372, 1398

01644   TB epididymis-cult dx
01640-01656,01690-01696,01790-01796,0312-0319,04181-0419,1372, 1398

01645   TB epididymis-histo dx
01640-01656,01690-01696,01790-01796,0312-0319,04181-0419,1372, 1398

01646   TB epididymis-oth test
01640-01656,01690-01696,01790-01796,0312-0319,04181-0419,1372, 1398

01650   TB male genit NEC-unspec
01640-01656,01690-01696,01790-01796,0312-0319,04181-0419,1372, 1398

01651   TB male gen NEC-no exam
01640-01656,01690-01696,01790-01796,0312-0319,04181-0419,1372, 1398

01652   TB male gen NEC-ex unkn
01640-01656,01690-01696,01790-01796,0312-0319,04181-0419,1372, 1398

01653   TB male gen NEC-micro dx
01640-01656,01690-01696,01790-01796,0312-0319,04181-0419,1372, 1398

01654   TB male gen NEC-cult dx
01640-01656,01690-01696,01790-01796,0312-0319,04181-0419,1372, 1398

01655   TB male gen NEC-histo dx
01640-01656,01690-01696,01790-01796,0312-0319,04181-0419,1372, 1398

01656   TB male gen NEC-oth test
01640-01656,01690-01696,01790-01796,0312-0319,04181-0419,1372, 1398

01660   TB ovary & tube-unspec
01660-01696,01790-01796,0312-0319,04181-0419,1372,1398

01661   TB ovary & tube-no exam
01660-01696,01790-01796,0312-0319,04181-0419,1372,1398

01662   TB ovary/tube-exam unkn
01660-01696,01790-01796,0312-0319,04181-0419,1372,1398

01663   TB ovary & tube-micro dx
01660-01696,01790-01796,0312-0319,04181-0419,1372,1398

01664   TB ovary & tube-cult dx
01660-01696,01790-01796,0312-0319,04181-0419,1372,1398

01665   TB ovary & tube-histo dx
01660-01696,01790-01796,0312-0319,04181-0419,1372,1398

01666   TB ovary & tube-oth test
01660-01696,01790-01796,0312-0319,04181-0419,1372,1398

01670   TB female gen NEC-unspec
01660-01696,01790-01796,0312-0319,04181-0419,1372,1398

01671   TB fem gen NEC-no exam
01660-01696,01790-01796,0312-0319,04181-0419,1372,1398

01672   TB fem gen NEC-exam unkn
01660-01696,01790-01796,0312-0319,04181-0419,1372,1398

01673   TB fem gen NEC-micro dx
01660-01696,01790-01796,0312-0319,04181-0419,1372,1398

01674   TB fem gen NEC-cult dx
01660-01696,01790-01796,0312-0319,04181-0419,1372,1398

01675   TB fem gen NEC-histo dx
01660-01696,01790-01796,0312-0319,04181-0419,1372,1398

01676   TB fem gen NEC-oth test
01660-01696,01790-01796,0312-0319,04181-0419,1372,1398

01690   Gu TB NOS-unspec
01690-01696,01790-01796,0312-0319,04181-0419,1372,1398

01691   Gu TB NOS-no exam
01690-01696,01790-01796,0312-0319,04181-0419,1372,1398

01692   Gu TB NOS-exam unkn
01690-01696,01790-01796,0312-0319,04181-0419,1372,1398

01693   Gu TB NOS-micro dx
01690-01696,01790-01796,0312-0319,04181-0419,1372,1398

01694   Gu TB NOS-cult dx
01690-01696,01790-01796,0312-0319,04181-0419,1372,1398

01695   Gu TB NOS-histo dx
01690-01696,01790-01796,0312-0319,04181-0419,1372,1398

01696   Gu TB NOS-oth test
01690-01696,01790-01796,0312-0319,04181-0419,1372,1398

01720   TB periph lymph-unspec
01720-01726,01790-01796,0312-0319,04181-0419,1398

01721   TB periph lymph-no exam
01720-01726,01790-01796,0312-0319,04181-0419,1398

01722   TB periph lymph-exam unkn
01720-01726,01790-01796,0312-0319,04181-0419,1398

01723   TB periph lymph-micro dx
01720-01726,01790-01796,0312-0319,04181-0419,1398

01724   TB periph lymph-cult dx
01720-01726,01790-01796,0312-0319,04181-0419,1398

01725   TB periph lymph-histo dx
01720-01726,01790-01796,0312-0319,04181-0419,1398

01726   TB periph lymph-oth test
01720-01726,01790-01796,0312-0319,04181-0419,1398

01730   TB of eye-unspec
01730-01736,01790-01796,0312-0319,04181-0419,1398

01731   TB of eye-no exam
01730-01736,01790-01796,0312-0319,04181-0419,1398

01732   TB of eye-exam unkn
01730-01736,01790-01796,0312-0319,04181-0419,1398

01733   TB of eye-micro dx
01730-01736,01790-01796,0312-0319,04181-0419,1398

01734   TB of eye-cult dx
01730-01736,01790-01796,0312-0319,04181-0419,1398

01735   TB of eye-histo dx
01730-01736,01790-01796,0312-0319,04181-0419,1398

01736   TB of eye-oth test
01730-01736,01790-01796,0312-0319,04181-0419,1398

01740   TB of ear-unspec
01740-01746,01790-01796,0312-0319,04181-0419,1398

01741   TB of ear-no exam
01740-01746,01790-01796,0312-0319,04181-0419,1398

01742   TB of ear-exam unkn
01740-01746,01790-01796,0312-0319,04181-0419,1398
01743   TB of ear-micro dx
01740-01746,01790-01796,0312-0319,04181-0419,1398
01744   TB of ear-cult dx
01740-01746,01790-01796,0312-0319,04181-0419,1398
01745   TB of ear-histo dx
01740-01746,01790-01796,0312-0319,04181-0419,1398
01746   TB of ear-oth test
01740-01746,01790-01796,0312-0319,04181-0419,1398
01750   TB of thyroid-unspec
01750-01756,01790-01796,0312-0319,04181-0419,1398
01751   TB of thyroid-no exam
01750-01756,01790-01796,0312-0319,04181-0419,1398
01752   TB of thyroid-exam unkn
01750-01756,01790-01796,0312-0319,04181-0419,1398
01753   TB of thyroid-micro dx
01750-01756,01790-01796,0312-0319,04181-0419,1398
01754   TB of thyroid-cult dx
01750-01756,01790-01796,0312-0319,04181-0419,1398
01755   TB of thyroid-histo dx
01750-01756,01790-01796,0312-0319,04181-0419,1398
01756   TB of thyroid-oth test
01750-01756,01790-01796,0312-0319,04181-0419,1398
01760   TB of adrenal-unspec
01760-01766,01790-01796,0312-0319,04181-0419,1398
01761   TB of adrenal-no exam
01760-01766,01790-01796,0312-0319,04181-0419,1398
01762   TB of adrenal-exam unkn
01760-01766,01790-01796,0312-0319,04181-0419,1398
01763   TB of adrenal-micro dx
01760-01766,01790-01796,0312-0319,04181-0419,1398
01764   TB of adrenal-cult dx
01760-01766,01790-01796,0312-0319,04181-0419,1398
01765   TB of adrenal-histo dx
01760-01766,01790-01796,0312-0319,04181-0419,1398
01766   TB of adrenal-oth test
01760-01766,01790-01796,0312-0319,04181-0419,1398
01770   TB of spleen-unspec
01770-01776,01790-01796,0312-0319,04181-0419,1398
01771   TB of spleen-no exam
01770-01776,01790-01796,0312-0319,04181-0419,1398
01772   TB of spleen-exam unkn
01770-01776,01790-01796,0312-0319,04181-0419,1398
01773   TB of spleen-micro dx
01770-01776,01790-01796,0312-0319,04181-0419,1398
01774   TB of spleen-cult dx
01770-01776,01790-01796,0312-0319,04181-0419,1398
01775   TB of spleen-histo dx
01770-01776,01790-01796,0312-0319,04181-0419,1398
01776   TB of spleen-oth test
01770-01776,01790-01796,0312-0319,04181-0419,1398
01780   TB esophagus-unspec
01780-01796,0312-0319,04181-0419,1398
01781   TB esophagus-no exam
01780-01796,0312-0319,04181-0419,1398
01782   TB esophagus-exam unkn
01780-01796,0312-0319,04181-0419,1398
01783   TB esophagus-micro dx
01780-01796,0312-0319,04181-0419,1398
01784   TB esophagus-cult dx
01780-01796,0312-0319,04181-0419,1398
01785   TB esophagus-histo dx
01780-01796,0312-0319,04181-0419,1398
01786   TB esophagus-oth test
01780-01796,0312-0319,04181-0419,1398
01790   TB of organ NEC-unspec
01790-01796,0312-0319,04181-0419,1398
01791   TB of organ NEC-no exam
01790-01796,0312-0319,04181-0419,1398
01792   TB organ NEC-exam unkn
01790-01796,0312-0319,04181-0419,1398

01793   TB of organ NEC-micro dx
01790-01796,0312-0319,04181-0419,1398
01794   TB of organ NEC-cult dx
01790-01796,0312-0319,04181-0419,1398
01795   TB of organ NEC-histo dx
01790-01796,0312-0319,04181-0419,1398
01796   TB of organ NEC-oth test
01790-01796,0312-0319,04181-0419,1398
01800   Acute miliary tb-unspec
01790-01896,0312-0319,04181-0419,1398
01801   Acute miliary tb-no exam
01790-01896,0312-0319,04181-0419,1398
01802   Ac miliary tb-exam unkn
01790-01896,0312-0319,04181-0419,1398
01803   Ac miliary tb-micro dx
01790-01896,0312-0319,04181-0419,1398
01804   Acute miliary tb-cult dx
01790-01896,0312-0319,04181-0419,1398
01805   Ac miliary tb-histo dx
01790-01896,0312-0319,04181-0419,1398
01806   Ac miliary tb-oth test
01790-01896,0312-0319,04181-0419,1398
01880   Miliary TB NEC-unspec
01790-01896,0312-0319,04181-0419,1398
01881   Miliary TB NEC-no exam
01790-01896,0312-0319,04181-0419,1398
01882   Miliary TB NEC-exam unkn
01790-01896,0312-0319,04181-0419,1398
01883   Miliary TB NEC-micro dx
01790-01896,0312-0319,04181-0419,1398
01884   Miliary TB NEC-cult dx
01790-01896,0312-0319,04181-0419,1398
01885   Miliary TB NEC-histo dx
01790-01896,0312-0319,04181-0419,1398
01886   Miliary TB NEC-oth test
01790-01896,0312-0319,04181-0419,1398
01890   Miliary TB NOS-unspec
01790-01896,0312-0319,04181-0419,1398
01891   Miliary TB NOS-no exam
01790-01896,0312-0319,04181-0419,1398
01892   Miliary TB NOS-exam unkn
01790-01896,0312-0319,04181-0419,1398
01893   Miliary TB NOS-micro dx
01790-01896,0312-0319,04181-0419,1398
01894   Miliary TB NOS-cult dx
01790-01896,0312-0319,04181-0419,1398
01895   Miliary TB NOS-histo dx
01790-01896,0312-0319,04181-0419,1398
01896   Miliary TB NOS-oth test
01790-01896,0312-0319,04181-0419,1398
0310   Pulmonary mycobacteria
01100-01286,01790-01796,0310,0312-0319,04181-0419,1370,1398,
4800-4871,494-5089,5171,51889
0360   Meningococcal meningitis
00321,01300-01316,0360,03689-0369,04181-0419,0470-0479,
0490-0491,0530,05472,0721,09042,09181,0942,09889,10081,11283,
1142,11501,11511,11591,1300,1398,3200-3229,34989-3499,3570
0361   Meningococc encephalitis
0361,03689-0369,04181-0419,1398
0362   Meningococcemia
0031,0202,0362,03689-0369,0380-0389,04181-0419,0545,1398
0363   Meningococc adrenal synd
0363,03689-0369,04181-0419,1398
03640   Meningococc carditis NOS
03640,03689-0369,04181-0419,1398
03641   Meningococc pericarditis
03641,03689-0369,04181-0419,1398
03642   Meningococc endocarditis
03642,03689-0369,04181-0419,1398
03643   Meningococc myocarditis
03643,04181-0419,1398
03681   Meningococc optic neurit
03681,03689-0369,04181-0419,1398

03682   Meningococc arthropathy
03682-0369,04181-0419,1398
03689   Meningococcal infect NEC
03689-0369,04181-0419,1398
0369   Meningococcal infect NOS
03689-0369,04181-0419,1398
037   Tetanus
037,1398
0380   Streptococcal septicemia
0031,0202,0362,0380-0389,04089-0419,0545,1398,V090-V0991
03810   Staphylcocc septicem NOS
0031,0202,0362,0380-0389,04089-0419,0545,1398,V090-V0991
03811   Staph aureus septicemia
0031,0202,0362,0380-0389,04089-0419,0545,1398,V090-V0991
03819   Staphylcocc septicem NEC
0031,0202,0362,0380-0389,04089-0419,0545,1398,V090-V0991
0382   Pneumococcal septicemia
0031,0202,0362,0380-0389,04089-0419,0545,1398,V090-V0991
0383   Anaerobic septicemia
0031,0202,0362,0380-0389,04089-0419,0545,1398,V090-V0991
03840   Gram-neg septicemia NOS
0031,0202,0362,0380-0389,04089-0419,0545,1398,V090-V0991
03841   H. influenae septicemia
0031,0202,0362,0380-0389,04089-0419,0545,1398,V090-V0991
03842   E. coli septicemia
0031,0202,0362,0380-0389,04089-0419,0545,1398,V090-V0991
03843   Pseudomonas septicemia
0031,0202,0362,0380-0389,04089-0419,0545,1398,V090-V0991
03844   Serratia septicemia
0031,0202,0362,0380-0389,04089-0419,0545,1398,V090-V0991
03849   Gram-neg septicemia NEC
0031,0202,0362,0380-0389,04089-0419,0545,1398,V090-V0991
0388   Septicemia NEC
0031,0202,0362,0380-0389,04089-0419,0545,1398,V090-V0991
0389   Septicemia NOS
0031,0202,0362,0380-0389,04089-0419,0545,1398,V090-V0991
0400   Gas gangrene
0400,1398
042   Human immuno virus dis
042,1398
0462   Subac scleros panenceph
0462,1398
0520   Postvaricella encephalit
0519-0520,0527-0529,07888-07889,07981-07999,1398
0521   Varicella pneumonitis
0519,0521-0529,07888-07889,07981-07999,1398
0527   Varicella complicat NEC
0519,0527-0529,07888-07889,07981-07999,1398
0528   Varicella complicat NOS
0519,0527-0529,07888-07889,07981-07999,1398
0529   Varicella uncomplicated
0519,0527-0529,07888-07889,07981-07999,1398
0530   Herpes zoster meningitis
00321,01300-01316,0360,0470-0479,0490-0491,0530-05319,
05379-0539,05472,05479-0549,0721,07888-07889,07981-07999,09042,
09181,0942,09889,10081,11283,1142,11501,11511,11591,1300,1398,
3200-3229,34989-3499,3570
05310   H zoster nerv syst NOS
0530-05319,05379-0539,05472,05479-0549,07888-07889,07981-07999,
1398
05311   Geniculate herpes zoster
0530-05319,05379-0539,05472,05479-0549,07888-07889,07981-07999,
1398
05312   Postherpes trigem neural
0530-05319,05379-0539,05472,05479-0549,07888-07889,07981-07999,
1398
05313   Postherpes polyneuropath
0530-05319,05379-0539,05472,05479-0549,07888-07889,07981-07999,
1398
05319   H zoster nerv syst NEC
0530-05319,05379-0539,05472,05479-0549,07888-07889,07981-07999,
1398
05379   H zoster complicated NEC
0530-05471,05473-0549,07888-07889,07981-07999,1398

0538   H zoster complicated NOS
0530-05471,05473-0549,07888-07889,07981-07999,1398
0543   Herpetic encephalitis
0543,05479-0549,1398
0545   Herpetic septicemia
0031,0202,0362,0380-0389,0545,05479-0549,1398
05471   Visceral herpes simplex
05471-05472,05479-0549,1398
05472   H simplex meningitis
00321,01300-01316,0360,0470-0479,0490-0491,0530,05472,
05479-0549,0721,09042,09181,0942,09889,10081,11283,1142,11501,
11511,11591,1300,1398,3200-3229,34989-3499,3570
05479   H simplex complicat NEC
05479-0549,07888-07889,07981-07999,1398
0548   H simplex complicat NOS
05479-0549,07888-07889,07981-07999,1398
0550   Postmeasles encephalitis
0550,05579-0559,07888-07889,07981-07999,1398
0551   Postmeasles pneumonia
0551,05579-0559,07888-07889,07981-07999,1398
0552   Postmeasles otitis media
0552,05579-0559,07888-07889,07981-07999,1398
05571   Measles keratitis
05571-0559,07888-07889,07981-07999,1398
05579   Measles complication NEC
05579-0559,07888-07889,07981-07999,1398
0558   Measles complication NOS
05579-0559,05609,07888-07889,07981-07999,1398
05600   Rubella nerve compl NOS
05600-05609,05679-0569,07888-07889,07981-07999,1398
05601   Rubella encephalitis
05600-05609,05679-0569,07888-07889,07981-07999,1398
05609   Rubella nerve compl NEC
05600-05609,05679-0569,07888-07889,07981-07999,1398
05671   Arthritis due to rubella
05671-0569,07888-07889,07981-07999,1398
05679   Rubella complication NEC
05600-05609,05679-0569,07888-07889,07981-07999,1398
0568   Rubella complication NOS
05600-05601,05679-0569,07888-07889,07981-07999,1398
07020   Hpt B acte coma wo dlta
0700-0709,07888-07889,07981-07999,1398
07021   Hpt B acte coma w dlta
0700-0709,07888-07889,07981-07999,1398
07022   Hpt B chrn coma wo dlta
0700-0709,07888-07889,07981-07999,1398
07023   Hpt B chrn coma w dlta
0700-0709,07888-07889,07981-07999,1398
07030   Hpt B acte wo cm wo dlta
0700-0709,07888-07889,07981-07999,1398
07031   Hpt B acte wo cm w dlta
0700-0709,07888-07889,07981-07999,1398
07032   Hpt B chrn wo cm wo dlta
0700-0709,07888-07889,07981-07999,1398
07033   Hpt B chrn wo cm w dlta
0700-0709,07888-07889,07981-07999,1398
07041   Hpt C acute w hepat Coma
0700-0709,07888-07889,07981-07999,1398
07042   Hpt dlt wo b w hpt coma
0700-0709,07888-07889,07981-07999,1398
07043   Hpt E w hepat Coma
0700-0709,07888-07889,07981-07999,1398
07044   Chrnc hpt C w hepat Coma
0700-0709,07888-07889,07981-07999,1398
07049   Oth vrl hepat w hpt coma
0700-0709,07888-07889,07981-07999,1398
07051   Hpt C acute wo hpat coma
0700-0709,07888-07889,07981-07999,1398
07052   Hpt dlt wo b wo hpt coma
0700-0709,07888-07889,07981-07999,1398
07053   Hpt E wo hepat Coma
0700-0709,07888-07889,07981-07999,1398
07054   Chrnc hpt C wo hpat coma
0700-0709,07888-07889,07981-07999,1398

07059 Oth vrl hpat wo hpt coma
0700-0709,07888-07889,07981-07999,1398
0706 Viral hepat NOS w coma
0700-0709,07888-07889,07981-07999,1398
0709 Viral hepat NOS w/o coma
0700-0709,07888-07889,07981-07999,1398
0720 Mumps orchitis
0720,07279-0729,07888-07889,07981-07999,1398
0721 Mumps meningitis
00321,01300-01316,0360,0470-0479,0490-0491,0530,05472,0721,
07279-0729,07888-07889,07981-07999,09042,09181,0942,09889,
10081,11283,1142,11501,11511,11591,1300,1398,3200-3229,
34989-3499,3570
0722 Mumps encephalitis
0722,07279-0729,07888-07889,07981-07999,1398
0723 Mumps pancreatitis
0723,07279-0729,07888-07889,07981-07999,1398
07271 Mumps hepatitis
07271,07279-0729,07888-07889,07981-07999,1398
07272 Mumps polyneuropathy
07272-0729,07888-07889,07981-07999,1398
07279 Mumps complication NEC
07279-0729,07888-07889,07981-07999,1398
0728 Mumps complication NOS
07279-0729,07888-07889,07981-07999
0860 Chagas disease of heart
0860,1398
09040 Juvenile neurosyph NOS
0900-0979,09940-0999,1398
09041 Congen syph encephalitis
0900-0979,09940-0999,1398
09042 Congen syph meningitis
00321,01300-01316,0360,0470-0479,0490-0491,0530,05472,0721,
0900-0979,09889,09940-0999,10081,11283,1142,11501,11511,11591,
1300,1398,3200-3229,34989-3499,3570
09049 Juvenile neurosyph NEC
0900-0979,09940-0999,1398
0930 Aortic aneurysm, syphil
0900-0979,09940-0999,1398
0931 Syphilitic aortitis
0900-0979,09940-0999,1398
09320 Syphil endocarditis NOS
0900-0979,09940-0999,1398
09321 Syphilitic mitral valve
0900-0979,09940-0999,1398
09322 Syphilitic aortic valve
0900-0979,09940-0999,1398
09323 Syphil tricuspid valve
0900-0979,09940-0999,1398
09324 Syphil pulmonary valve
0900-0979,09940-0999,1398
09381 Syphilitic pericarditis
0900-0979,09940-0999,1398
09382 Syphilitic myocarditis
0900-0979,09940-0999,1398
09389 Cardiovascular syph NEC
0900-0979,09940-0999,1398
0939 Cardiovascular syph NOS
0900-0979,09940-0999,1398
0940 Tabes dorsalis
0900-0979,09940-0999,1398
0941 General paresis
0900-0979,09940-0999,1398
0942 Syphilitic meningitis
00321,01300-01316,0360,0470-0479,0490-0491,0530,05472,0721,
0900-0979,09889,09940-0999,10081,11283,1142,11501,11511,11591,
1300,1398,3200-3229,34989-3499,3570
0943 Asymptomat neurosyphilis
0900-0979,09940-0999,1398
09481 Syphilitic encephalitis
0900-0979,09940-0999,1398
09487 Syph rupt cereb aneurysm
0900-0979,09940-0999,1398

09489 Neurosyphilis NEC
0900-0979,09940-0999,1398
0949 Neurosyphilis NOS
0900-0979,09940-0999,1398
0980 Acute gc infect lower gu
0980-09839,09889,09940-0999,1398
0980 Acute gc infect lower gu
0980-09839,09889,09940-0999,1398
09810 Gc (acute) upper gu NOS
0980-09839,09889,09940-0999,1398
09810 Gc (acute) upper gu NOS
0980-09839,09889,09940-0999,1398
09811 Gc cystitis (acute)
0980-09839,09889,09940-0999,1398
09812 Gc prostatitis (acute)
0980-09839,09889,09940-0999,1398
09813 Gc orchitis (acute)
0980-09839,09889,09940-0999,1398
09814 Gc sem vesiculit (acute)
0980-09839,09889,09940-0999,1398
09815 Gc cervicitis (acute)
0980-09839,09889,09940-0999,1398
09816 Gc endometritis (acute)
0980-09839,09889,09940-0999,1398
09817 Acute gc salpingitis
0980-09839,09889,09940-0999,1398
09819 Gc (acute) upper gu NEC
0980-09839,09889,09940-0999,1398
09819 Gc (acute) upper gu NEC
0980-09839,09889,09940-0999,1398
1120 Thrush
1120-1129,1179,1398
1124 Candidiasis of lung
1120-1129,1179,1398
1125 Disseminated candidiasis
1120-1129,1179,1398
11281 Candidal endocarditis
1120-1129,1179,1398
11282 Candidal otitis externa
1120-1129,1179,1398
11283 Candidal meningitis
00321,01300-01316,0360,0470-0479,0490-0491,0530,05472,0721,
09042,09181,0942,09889,10081,1120-1129,1142,11501,11511,11591,
1179,1300,1398,3200-3229,34989-3499,3570
11284 Candidal esophagitis
1120-1129,1179,1398
11285 Candidal enteritis
1120-1129,1179,1398
1140 Primary coccidioidomycos
1140,1143-1149,1179,1398
1142 Coccidioidal meningitis
00321,01300-01316,0360,0470-0479,0490-0491,0530,05472,0721,
09042,09181,0942,09889,10081,11283,1142-1143,1149,11501,11511,
11591,1179,1300,1398,3200-3229,34989-3499,3570
1143 Progress coccidioid NEC
1143,1149,1179,1398
1149 Coccidioidomycosis NOS
1143,1149,1179,1398
11500 Histoplasma capsulat NOS
11500,11509,11590,11599,1179,1398
11501 Histoplasm capsul mening
00321,01300-01316,0360,0470-0479,0490-0491,0530,05472,0721,
09042,09181,0942,09889,10081,11283,1142,11500-11501,11509,
11511,11590-11591,11599,1179,1300,1398,3200-3229,34989-3499,
3570
11502 Histoplasm capsul retina
11500,11502,11509,11590,11592,11599,1179,1398
11503 Histoplasm caps pericard
11500,11503,11509,11590,11593,11599,1179,1398
11504 Histoplasm caps endocard
11500,11504,11509,11590,11594,11599,1179,1398
11505 Histoplasm caps pneumon
11500,11505-11509,11590,11595-11599,1179,1398,4800-4871,
494-5089,5171,51889

11510   Histoplasma duboisii NOS
11510,11519-11590,11599,1179,1398
11511   Histoplasm dubois mening
00321,01300-01316,0360,0470-0479,0490-0491,0530,05472,0721,
09042,09181,0942,09889,10081,11283,1142,11501,11510-11511,
11519-11591,11599,1179,1300,1398,3200-3229,34989-3499,3570
11512   Histoplasm dubois retina
11510,11512,11519-11590,11592,11599,1179,1398
11513   Histoplasm dub pericard
11510,11513,11519-11590,11593,11599,1179,1398
11514   Histoplasm dub endocard
11510,11514,11519-11590,11594,11599,1179,1398
11515   Histoplasm dub pneumonia
11505,11510,11515-11590,11595-11599,1179,1398,4800-4871,
494-5089,5171,51889
11519   Histoplasma duboisii NEC
11510,11519-11590,11599,1179,1398
11590   Histoplasmosis NOS
11590,11599,1179,1398
11591   Histoplasmosis meningit
00321,01300-01316,0360,0470-0479,0490-0491,0530,05472,0721,
09042,09181,0942,09889,10081,11283,1142,11501,11511,11591,11599,
1179,1300,1398,3200-3229,34989-3499,3570
11592   Histoplasmosis retinitis
11592,11599,1179,1398
11593   Histoplasmosis pericard
11593,11599,1179,1398
11594   Histoplasmosis endocard
11594,11599,1179,1398
11595   Histoplasmosis pneumonia
11505,11515,11595-11599,1179,1398
11599   Histoplasmosis NEC
11599,1179,1398
1160   Blastomycosis
1160,1179,1398
1161   Paracoccidioidomycosis
1161,1179,1398
1173   Aspergillosis
1173,1179,1398
1174   Mycotic mycetomas
1174,1179,1398
1175   Cryptococcosis
1175,1179,1398
1176   Allescheriosis
1176,1179,1398
1177   Zygomycosis
1177,1179,1398
118   Opportunistic mycoses
1179-118,1398
1300   Toxoplasm meningoenceph
1300,1307-1309,1398
1301   Toxoplasm conjunctivitis
1301,1307-1309,1398
1302   Toxoplasm chorioretinit
1302,1307-1309,1398
1303   Toxoplasma myocarditis
1303,1307-1309,1398
1304   Toxoplasma pneumonitis
1304,1307-1309,1398,4800-4871,494-5089,5171,51889
1305   Toxoplasma hepatitis
1305-1309,1398
1307   Toxoplasmosis site NEC
1307-1309,1398
1308   Multisystem toxoplasmos
1307-1309,1398
135   Sarcoidosis
135,1398
1363   Pneumocystosis
1363,1398,4800-4871,494-5089,5171,51889
1370   Late effect tb, resp/NOS
1370,1398
1371   Late effect cns TB
1371,1398

1372   Late effect gu TB
1372,1398
138   Late effect acute polio
138,1398
1500   Mal neo cervical esophag
1500-1509,1590,1598-1599,1763,1958,1990-1991,2390,2398-2399
1501   Mal neo thoracic esophag
1500-1509,1590,1598-1599,1763,1958,1990-1991,2390,2398-2399
1502   Mal neo abdomin esophag
1500-1509,1590,1598-1599,1763,1958,1990-1991,2390,2398-2399
1503   Mal neo upper 3rd esoph
1500-1509,1590,1598-1599,1763,1958,1990-1991,2390,2398-2399
1504   Mal neo middle 3rd esoph
1500-1509,1590,1598-1599,1763,1958,1990-1991,2390,2398-2399
1505   Mal neo lower 3rd esoph
1500-1509,1590,1598-1599,1763,1958,1990-1991,2390,2398-2399
1508   Mal neo esophagus NEC
1500-1509,1590,1598-1599,1763,1958,1990-1991,2390,2398-2399
1509   Mal neo esophagus NOS
1500-1509,1590,1598-1599,1763,1958,1990-1991,2390,2398-2399
1510   Mal neo stomach cardia
1510-1519,1590,1598-1599,1763,1958,1990-1991,2390,2398-2399
1511   Malignant neo pylorus
1510-1519,1590,1598-1599,1763,1958,1990-1991,2390,2398-2399
1512   Mal neo pyloric antrum
1510-1519,1590,1598-1599,1763,1958,1990-1991,2390,2398-2399
1513   Mal neo stomach fundus
1510-1519,1590,1598-1599,1763,1958,1990-1991,2390,2398-2399
1514   Mal neo stomach body
1510-1519,1590,1598-1599,1763,1958,1990-1991,2390,2398-2399
1515   Mal neo stom lesser curv
1510-1519,1590,1598-1599,1763,1958,1990-1991,2390,2398-2399
1516   Mal neo stom great curv
1510-1519,1590,1598-1599,1763,1958,1990-1991,2390,2398-2399
1518   Malig neopl stomach NEC
1510-1519,1590,1598-1599,1763,1958,1990-1991,2390,2398-2399
1519   Malig neopl stomach NOS
1510-1519,1590,1598-1599,1763,1958,1990-1991,2390,2398-2399
1520   Malignant neopl duodenum
1520,1528-1529,1590,1598-1599,1763,1958,1990-1991,2390,
2398-2399
1521   Malignant neopl jejunum
1521,1528-1529,1590,1598-1599,1763,1958,1990-1991,2390,
2398-2399
1522   Malignant neoplasm ileum
1522,1528-1529,1590,1598-1599,1763,1958,1990-1991,2390,
2398-2399
1523   Mal neo meckel's divert
1523-1529,1590,1598-1599,1763,1958,1990-1991,2390,2398-2399
1528   Mal neo small bowel NEC
1528-1529,1590,1598-1599,1763,1958,1990-1991,2390,2398-2399
1529   Mal neo small bowel NOS
1528-1529,1590,1598-1599,1763,1958,1990-1991,2390,2398-2399
1530   Mal neo hepatic flexure
1530,1538-1539,1590,1598-1599,1763,1958,1990-1991,2390,
2398-2399
1531   Mal neo transverse colon
1531,1538-1539,1590,1598-1599,1763,1958,1990-1991,2390,
2398-2399
1532   Mal neo descend colon
1532,1538-1539,1590,1598-1599,1763,1958,1990-1991,2390,
2398-2399
1533   Mal neo sigmoid colon
1533,1538-1539,1590,1598-1599,1763,1958,1990-1991,2390,
2398-2399
1534   Malignant neoplasm cecum
1534,1538-1539,1590,1598-1599,1763,1958,1990-1991,2390,
2398-2399
1535   Malignant neo appendix
1535,1538-1539,1590,1598-1599,1763,1958,1990-1991,2390,
2398-2399

ICD-9-CM

Appx F

Vol. 1

1536   Malig neo ascend colon
  1536,1538-1539,1590,1598-1599,1763,1958,1990-1991,2390,
  2398-2399
1537   Mal neo splenic flexure
  1537-1539,1590,1598-1599,1763,1958,1990-1991,2390,2398-2399
1538   Malignant neo colon NEC
  1538-1539,1590,1598-1599,1763,1958,1990-1991,2390,2398-2399
1539   Malignant neo colon NOS
  1538-1539,1590,1598-1599,1763,1958,1990-1991,2390,2398-2399
1540   Mal neo rectosigmoid jct
  1540,1548,1590,1598-1599,1763,1958,1990-1991,2390,2398-2399
1541   Malignant neopl rectum
  1541,1548,1590,1598-1599,1763,1958,1990-1991,2390,2398-2399
1542   Malig neopl anal canal
  1542-1548,1590,1598-1599,1763,1958,1990-1991,2390,2398-2399
1543   Malignant neo anus NOS
  1542-1548,1590,1598-1599,1763,1958,1990-1991,2390,2398-2399
1548   Mal neo rectum/anus NEC
  1548,1590,1598-1599,1763,1958,1990-1991,2390,2398-2399
1550   Mal neo liver, primary
  1550-1552,1590,1598-1599,1763,1958,1990-1991,2390,2398-2399
1551   Mal neo intrahepat ducts
  1550-1552,1590,1598-1599,1763,1958,1990-1991,2390,2398-2399
1552   Malignant neo liver NOS
  1550-1552,1590,1598-1599,1763,1958,1990-1991,2390,2398-2399
1560   Malig neo gallbladder
  1560,1568-1569,1590,1598-1599,1763,1958,1990-1991,2390,
  2398-2399
1561   Mal neo extrahepat ducts
  1561,1568-1569,1590,1598-1599,1763,1958,1990-1991,2390,
  2398-2399
1562   Mal neo ampulla of vater
  1562-1569,1590,1598-1599,1763,1958,1990-1991,2390,2398-2399
1568   Malig neo biliary NEC
  1568-1569,1590,1598-1599,1763,1958,1990-1991,2390,2398-2399
1569   Malig neo biliary NOS
  1568-1569,1590,1598-1599,1763,1958,1990-1991,2390,2398-2399
1570   Mal neo pancreas head
  1570-1579,1590,1598-1599,1763,1958,1990-1991,2390,2398-2399
1571   Mal neo pancreas body
  1570-1579,1590,1598-1599,1763,1958,1990-1991,2390,2398-2399
1572   Mal neo pancreas tail
  1570-1579,1590,1598-1599,1763,1958,1990-1991,2390,2398-2399
1573   Mal neo pancreatic duct
  1570-1579,1590,1598-1599,1763,1958,1990-1991,2390,2398-2399
1574   Mal neo islet langerhans
  1570-1579,1590,1598-1599,1763,1958,1990-1991,2390,2398-2399
1578   Malig neo pancreas NEC
  1570-1579,1590,1598-1599,1763,1958,1990-1991,2390,2398-2399
1579   Malig neo pancreas NOS
  1570-1579,1590,1598-1599,1763,1958,1990-1991,2390,2398-2399
1622   Malig neo main bronchus
  1622,1628-1629,1658-1659,1764,1958,1990-1991,2391,2398-2399
1623   Mal neo upper lobe lung
  1623,1628-1629,1658-1659,1764,1958,1990-1991,2391,2398-2399
1624   Mal neo middle lobe lung
  1624,1628-1629,1658-1659,1764,1958,1990-1991,2391,2398-2399
1625   Mal neo lower lobe lung
  1625-1629,1658-1659,1764,1958,1990-1991,2391,2398-2399
1628   Mal neo bronch/lung NEC
  1628-1629,1658-1659,1764,1958,1990-1991,2391,2398-2399
1629   Mal neo bronch/lung NOS
  1628-1629,1658-1659,1764,1958,1990-1991,2391,2398-2399
1630   Mal neo parietal pleura
  1630-1639,1658-1659,1958,1990-1991,2391,2398-2399
1631   Mal neo visceral pleura
  1630-1639,1658-1659,1958,1990-1991,2391,2398-2399
1638   Malig neopl pleura NEC
  1630-1639,1658-1659,1958,1990-1991,2391,2398-2399
1639   Malig neopl pleura NOS
  1630-1639,1658-1659,1958,1990-1991,2391,2398-2399
1640   Malignant neopl thymus
  1640

1641   Malignant neopl heart
  1641
1642   Mal neo ant mediastinum
  1642-1649,1658-1659,1958,1990-1991,2391,2398-2399
1643   Mal neo post mediastinum
  1642-1649,1658-1659,1958,1990-1991,2391,2398-2399
1648   Mal neo mediastinum NEC
  1642-1649,1658-1659,1958,1990-1991,2391,2398-2399
1649   Mal neo mediastinum NOS
  1642-1649,1658-1659,1958,1990-1991,2391,2398-2399
1764   Lung - kaposi's sarcoma
  1628-1629,1658-1659,1764,1958,1990-1991,2391,2398-2399
1765   Lym nds - kpsi's sarcoma
  1765,1958-1969,1990-1991,2398-2399
1890   Malig neopl kidney
  1890-1891,1898-1899,1958,1990-1991,2395,2398-2399
1891   Malig neo renal pelvis
  1890-1891,1898-1899,1958,1990-1991,2395,2398-2399
1892   Malign neopl ureter
  1892,1898-1899,1958,1990-1991,2395,2398-2399
1910   Malign neopl cerebrum
  1910-1921,1928-1929,1958,1990-1991,2396-2399
1911   Malig neo frontal lobe
  1910-1921,1928-1929,1958,1990-1991,2396-2399
1912   Mal neo temporal lobe
  1910-1921,1928-1929,1958,1990-1991,2396-2399
1913   Mal neo parietal lobe
  1910-1921,1928-1929,1958,1990-1991,2396-2399
1914   Mal neo occipital lobe
  1910-1921,1928-1929,1958,1990-1991,2396-2399
1915   Mal neo cereb ventricle
  1910-1921,1928-1929,1958,1990-1991,2396-2399
1916   Mal neo cerebellum NOS
  1910-1921,1928-1929,1958,1990-1991,2396-2399
1917   Mal neo brain stem
  1910-1921,1928-1929,1958,1990-1991,2396-2399
1918   Malig neo brain NEC
  1910-1921,1928-1929,1958,1990-1991,2396-2399
1919   Malig neo brain NOS
  1910-1921,1928-1929,1958,1990-1991,2396-2399
1920   Mal neo cranial nerves
  1920,1928-1929,1958,1990-1991,2396-2399
1921   Mal neo cerebral mening
  1921,1928-1929,1958,1990-1991,2396-2399
1922   Mal neo spinal cord
  1922,1928-1929,1958,1990-1991,2396-2399
1923   Mal neo spinal meninges
  1923-1929,1958,1990-1991,2396-2399
1928   Mal neo nervous syst NEC
  1910-1929,1958,1990-1991,2396-2399
1960   Mal neo lymph-head/neck
  1765,1958-1969,1990-1991,2398-2399
1961   Mal neo lymph-intrathor
  1765,1958-1969,1990-1991,2398-2399
1962   Mal neo lymph intra-abd
  1765,1958-1969,1990-1991,2398-2399
1963   Mal neo lymph-axilla/arm
  1765,1958-1969,1990-1991,2398-2399
1965   Mal neo lymph-inguin/leg
  1765,1958-1969,1990-1991,2398-2399
1966   Mal neo lymph-intrapelv
  1765,1958-1969,1990-1991,2398-2399
1968   Mal neo lymph node-mult
  1765,1958-1969,1990-1991,2398-2399
1969   Mal neo lymph node NOS
  1765,1958-1969,1990-1991,2398-2399
1970   Secondary malig neo lung
  1958,1970,1973,19889-1991,2398-2399
1971   Sec mal neo mediastinum
  1958,1971,1973,19889-1991,2398-2399
1972   Second malig neo pleura
  1958,1972-1973,19889-1991,2398-2399
1973   Sec malig neo resp NEC
  1958,1970-1973,19889-1991,2398-2399

1974 Sec malig neo sm bowel
1958,1974,1978,19889-1991,2398-2399
1975 Sec malig neo lg bowel
1958,1975,1978,19889-1991,2398-2399
1976 Sec mal neo peritoneum
1958,1976,1978,19889-1991,2398-2399
1977 Second malig neo liver
1958,1977-1978,19889-1991,2398-2399
1978 Sec mal neo GI NEC
1958,1974-1978,19889-1991,2398-2399
1980 Second malig neo kidney
1958,1980-1981,19889-1991,2398-2399
1981 Sec malig neo urin NEC
1958,1980-1981,19889-1991,2398-2399
1982 Secondary malig neo skin
1958,1982,19889-1991,2398-2399
1983 Sec mal neo brain/spine
1958,1983,19889-1991,2398-2399
1984 Sec malig neo nerve NEC
1958,1984,19889-1991,2398-2399
1985 Secondary malig neo bone
1958,1985,19889-1991,2398-2399
1986 Second malig neo ovary
1958,1986,19889-1991,2398-2399
1987 Second malig neo adrenal
1958,1987,19889-1991,2398-2399
19881 Second malig neo breast
1958,19881,19889-1991,2398-2399
19882 Second malig neo genital
1958,19882-1991,2398-2399
19882 Second malig neo genital
1958,19882-1991,2398-2399
19889 Secondary malig neo NEC
1958,19889-1991,2398-2399
1990 Malig neo disseminated
1958,19889-1991,2398-2399
20000 Retclsrc unsp xtrndl org
20000-20008,2398-2399
20001 Reticulosarcoma head
20000-20001,20008,2398-2399
20002 Reticulosarcoma thorax
20000,20002,20008,2398-2399
20003 Reticulosarcoma abdom
20000,20003,20008,2398-2399
20004 Reticulosarcoma axilla
20000,20004,20008,2398-2399
20005 Reticulosarcoma inguin
20000,20005,20008,2398-2399
20006 Reticulosarcoma pelvic
20000,20006,20008,2398-2399
20007 Reticulosarcoma spleen
20000,20007-20008,2398-2399
20008 Reticulosarcoma mult
20000-20008,2398-2399
20010 Lymphsrc unsp xtrndl org
20010-20018,2398-2399
20011 Lymphosarcoma head
20010-20011,20018,2398-2399
20012 Lymphosarcoma thorax
20010,20012,20018,2398-2399
20013 Lymphosarcoma abdom
20010,20013,20018,2398-2399
20014 Lymphosarcoma axilla
20010,20014,20018,2398-2399
20015 Lymphosarcoma inguin
20010,20015,20018,2398-2399
20016 Lymphosarcoma pelvic
20010,20016,20018,2398-2399
20017 Lymphosarcoma spleen
20010,20017-20018,2398-2399
20018 Lymphosarcoma mult
20010-20018,2398-2399
20020 Brkt tmr unsp xtrndl org
20020-20028,2398-2399

20021 Burkitt's tumor head
20020-20021,20028,2398-2399
20022 Burkitt's tumor thorax
20020,20022,20028,2398-2399
20023 Burkitt's tumor abdom
20020,20023,20028,2398-2399
20024 Burkitt's tumor axilla
20020,20024,20028,2398-2399
20025 Burkitt's tumor inguin
20020,20025,20028,2398-2399
20026 Burkitt's tumor pelvic
20020,20026,20028,2398-2399
20027 Burkitt's tumor spleen
20020,20027-20028,2398-2399
20028 Burkitt's tumor mult
20020-20028,2398-2399
20080 Oth varn unsp xtrndl org
20080-20088,2398-2399
20081 Mixed lymphosarc head
20080-20081,20088,2398-2399
20082 Mixed lymphosarc thorax
20080,20082,20088,2398-2399
20083 Mixed lymphosarc abdom
20080,20083,20088,2398-2399
20084 Mixed lymphosarc axilla
20080,20084,20088,2398-2399
20085 Mixed lymphosarc inguin
20080,20085,20088,2398-2399
20086 Mixed lymphosarc pelvic
20080,20086,20088,2398-2399
20087 Mixed lymphosarc spleen
20080,20087-20088,2398-2399
20088 Mixed lymphosarc mult
20080-20088,2398-2399
20100 Hdgk prg unsp xtrndl org
20100-20108,20190,2398-2399
20101 Hodgkins paragran head
20100-20101,20108,20190-20191,2398-2399
20102 Hodgkins paragran thorax
20100,20102,20108,20190,20192,2398-2399
20103 Hodgkins paragran abdom
20100,20103,20108,20190,20193,2398-2399
20104 Hodgkins paragran axilla
20100,20104,20108,20190,20194,2398-2399
20105 Hodgkins paragran inguin
20100,20105,20108,20190,20195,2398-2399
20106 Hodgkins paragran pelvic
20100,20106,20108,20190,20196,2398-2399
20107 Hodgkins paragran spleen
20100,20107-20108,20190,20197,2398-2399
20108 Hodgkins paragran mult
20100-20108,20190,20198,2398-2399
20110 Hdgk grn unsp xtrndl org
20110-20118,20190,20198,2398-2399
20111 Hodgkins granulom head
20110-20111,20118,20190-20191,20198,2398-2399
20112 Hodgkins granulom thorax
20110,20112,20118,20190,20192,20198,2398-2399
20113 Hodgkins granulom abdom
20110,20113,20118,20190,20193,20198,2398-2399
20114 Hodgkins granulom axilla
20110,20114,20118,20190,20194,20198,2398-2399
20115 Hodgkins granulom inguin
20110,20115,20118,20190,20195,20198,2398-2399
20116 Hodgkins granulom pelvic
20110,20116,20118,20190,20196,20198,2398-2399
20117 Hodgkins granulom spleen
20110,20117-20118,20190,20197-20198,2398-2399
20118 Hodgkins granulom mult
20110-20118,20190,20198,2398-2399
20120 Hdgk src unsp xtrndl org
20120-20128,20190,20198,2398-2399
20121 Hodgkins sarcoma head
20120-20121,20128,20190-20191,20198,2398-2399

20122   Hodgkins sarcoma thorax
20120,20122,20128,20190,20192,20198,2398-2399
20123   Hodgkins sarcoma abdom
20120,20123,20128,20190,20193,20198,2398-2399
20124   Hodgkins sarcoma axilla
20120,20124,20128,20190,20194,20198,2398-2399
20125   Hodgkins sarcoma inguin
20120,20125,20128,20190,20195,20198,2398-2399
20126   Hodgkins sarcoma pelvic
20120,20126,20128,20190,20196,20198,2398-2399
20127   Hodgkins sarcoma spleen
20120,20127-20128,20190,20197-20198,2398-2399
20128   Hodgkins sarcoma mult
20120-20128,20190,20198,2398-2399
20140   Lym-hst unsp xtrndl orgn
20140-20148,20190,20198,2398-2399
20141   Hodg lymph-histio head
20140-20141,20148,20190-20191,20198,2398-2399
20142   Hodg lymph-histio thorax
20140,20142,20148,20190,20192,20198,2398-2399
20143   Hodg lymph-histio abdom
20140,20143,20148,20190,20193,20198,2398-2399
20144   Hodg lymph-histio axilla
20140,20144,20148,20190,20194,20198,2398-2399
20145   Hodg lymph-histio inguin
20140,20145,20148,20190,20195,20198,2398-2399
20146   Hodg lymph-histio pelvic
20140,20146,20148,20190,20196,20198,2398-2399
20147   Hodg lymph-histio spleen
20140,20147-20148,20190,20197-20198,2398-2399
20148   Hodg lymph-histio mult
20140-20148,20190,20198,2398-2399
20150   Ndr sclr unsp xtrndl org
20150-20158,20190,20198,2398-2399
20151   Hodg nodul sclero head
20150-20151,20158,20190-20191,20198,2398-2399
20152   Hodg nodul sclero thorax
20150,20152,20158,20190,20192,20198,2398-2399
20153   Hodg nodul sclero abdom
20150,20153,20158,20190,20193,20198,2398-2399
20154   Hodg nodul sclero axilla
20150,20154,20158,20190,20194,20198,2398-2399
20155   Hodg nodul sclero inguin
20150,20155,20158,20190,20195,20198,2398-2399
20156   Hodg nodul sclero pelvic
20150,20156,20158,20190,20196,20198,2398-2399
20157   Hodg nodul sclero spleen
20150,20157-20158,20190,20197-20198,2398-2399
20158   Hodg nodul sclero mult
20150-20158,20190,20198,2398-2399
20160   Mxd celr unsp xtrndl org
20160-20168,20190,20198,2398-2399
20161   Hodgkins mix cell head
20160-20161,20168,20190-20191,20198,2398-2399
20162   Hodgkins mix cell thorax
20160,20162,20168,20190,20192,20198,2398-2399
20163   Hodgkins mix cell abdom
20160,20163,20168,20190,20193,20198,2398-2399
20164   Hodgkins mix cell axilla
20160,20164,20168,20190,20194,20198,2398-2399
20165   Hodgkins mix cell inguin
20160,20165,20168,20190,20195,20198,2398-2399
20166   Hodgkins mix cell pelvic
20160,20166,20168,20190,20196,20198,2398-2399
20167   Hodgkins mix cell spleen
20160,20167-20168,20190,20197-20198,2398-2399
20168   Hodgkins mix cell mult
20160-20168,20190,20198,2398-2399
20170   Lym dplt unsp xtrndl org
20170-20190,20198,2398-2399
20171   Hodg lymph deplet head
20170-20171,20178,20191,20198,2398-2399

20172   Hodg lymph deplet thorax
20170,20172,20178,20192,20198,2398-2399
20173   Hodg lymph deplet abdom
20170,20173,20178,20193,20198,2398-2399
20174   Hodg lymph deplet axilla
20170,20174,20178,20194,20198,2398-2399
20175   Hodg lymph deplet inguin
20170,20175,20178,20195,20198,2398-2399
20176   Hodg lymph deplet pelvic
20170,20176,20178,20196,20198,2398-2399
20177   Hodg lymph deplet spleen
20170,20177-20178,20197-20198,2398-2399
20178   Hodg lymph deplet mult
20170-20178,20198,2398-2399
20190   Hdgk dis unsp xtrndl org
20190-20198,2398-2399
20191   Hodgkins dis NOS head
20190-20191,20198,2398-2399
20192   Hodgkins dis NOS thorax
20190,20192,20198,2398-2399
20193   Hodgkins dis NOS abdom
20190,20193,20198,2398-2399
20194   Hodgkins dis NOS axilla
20190,20194,20198,2398-2399
20195   Hodgkins dis NOS inguin
20190,20195,20198,2398-2399
20196   Hodgkins dis NOS pelvic
20190,20196,20198,2398-2399
20197   Hodgkins dis NOS spleen
20190,20197-20198,2398-2399
20198   Hodgkins dis NOS mult
20190-20198,2398-2399
20200   Ndlr lym unsp xtrndl org
20200-20208,20280,20290,2398-2399
20201   Nodular lymphoma head
20200-20201,20208,20281,20291,2398-2399
20202   Nodular lymphoma thorax
20200,20202,20208,20282,20292,2398-2399
20203   Nodular lymphoma abdom
20200,20203,20208,20283,20293,2398-2399
20204   Nodular lymphoma axilla
20200,20204,20208,20284,20294,2398-2399
20205   Nodular lymphoma inguin
20200,20205,20208,20285,20295,2398-2399
20206   Nodular lymphoma pelvic
20200,20206,20208,20286,20296,2398-2399
20207   Nodular lymphoma spleen
20200,20207-20208,20287,20297,2398-2399
20208   Nodular lymphoma mult
20200-20208,20288,20298,2398-2399
20210   Mycs fng unsp xtrndl org
20210-20218,20280,20290,2398-2399
20211   Mycosis fungoides head
20210-20211,20218,20281,20291,2398-2399
20212   Mycosis fungoides thorax
20210,20212,20218,20282,20292,2398-2399
20213   Mycosis fungoides abdom
20210,20213,20218,20283,20293,2398-2399
20214   Mycosis fungoides axilla
20210,20214,20218,20284,20294,2398-2399
20215   Mycosis fungoides inguin
20210,20215,20218,20285,20295,2398-2399
20216   Mycosis fungoides pelvic
20210,20216,20218,20286,20296,2398-2399
20217   Mycosis fungoides spleen
20210,20217-20218,20287,20297,2398-2399
20218   Mycosis fungoides mult
20210-20218,20288,20298,2398-2399
20220   Szry dis unsp xtrndl org
20220-20228,20280,20290,2398-2399
20221   Sezary's disease head
20220-20221,20228,20281,20291,2398-2399
20222   Sezary's disease thorax
20220,20222,20228,20282,20292,2398-2399

20223   Sezary's disease abdom
20220,20223,20228,20283,20293,2398-2399
20224   Sezary's disease axilla
20220,20224,20228,20284,20294,2398-2399
20225   Sezary's disease inguin
20220,20225,20228,20285,20295,2398-2399
20226   Sezary's disease pelvic
20220,20226,20228,20286,20296,2398-2399
20227   Sezary's disease spleen
20220,20227-20228,20287,20297,2398-2399
20228   Sezary's disease mult
20220-20228,20288,20298,2398-2399
20230   Mlg hist unsp xtrndl org
20230-20238,20280,20290,2398-2399
20231   Mal histiocytosis head
20230-20231,20238,20281,20291,2398-2399
20232   Mal histiocytosis thorax
20230,20232,20238,20282,20292,2398-2399
20233   Mal histiocytosis abdom
20230,20233,20238,20283,20293,2398-2399
20234   Mal histiocytosis axilla
20230,20234,20238,20284,20294,2398-2399
20235   Mal histiocytosis inguin
20230,20235,20238,20285,20295,2398-2399
20236   Mal histiocytosis pelvic
20230,20236,20238,20286,20296,2398-2399
20237   Mal histiocytosis spleen
20230,20237-20238,20287,20297,2398-2399
20238   Mal histiocytosis mult
20230-20238,20288,20298,2398-2399
20240   Lk rtctl unsp xtrndl org
20240-20248,20280,20290,2398-2399
20241   Hairy-cell leukem head
20240-20241,20248,20281,20291,2398-2399
20242   Hairy-cell leukem thorax
20240,20242,20248,20282,20292,2398-2399
20243   Hairy-cell leukem abdom
20240,20243,20248,20283,20293,2398-2399
20244   Hairy-cell leukem axilla
20240,20244,20248,20284,20294,2398-2399
20245   Hairy-cell leukem inguin
20240,20245,20248,20285,20295,2398-2399
20246   Hairy-cell leukem pelvic
20240,20246,20248,20286,20296,2398-2399
20247   Hairy-cell leukem spleen
20240,20247-20248,20287,20297,2398-2399
20248   Hairy-cell leukem mult
20240-20248,20288,20298,2398-2399
20250   Ltr-siwe unsp xtrndl org
20250-20258,20280,20290,2398-2399
20251   Letterer-siwe dis head
20250-20251,20258,20281,20291,2398-2399
20252   Letterer-siwe dis thorax
20250,20252,20258,20282,20292,2398-2399
20253   Letterer-siwe dis abdom
20250,20253,20258,20283,20293,2398-2399
20254   Letterer-siwe dis axilla
20250,20254,20258,20284,20294,2398-2399
20255   Letterer-siwe dis inguin
20250,20255,20258,20285,20295,2398-2399
20256   Letterer-siwe dis pelvic
20250,20256,20258,20286,20296,2398-2399
20257   Letterer-siwe dis spleen
20250,20257-20258,20287,20297,2398-2399
20258   Letterer-siwe dis mult
20250-20258,20288,20298,2398-2399
20260   Mlg mast unsp xtrndl org
20260-20280,20290,2398-2399
20261   Mal mastocytosis head
20260-20261,20268,20281,20291,2398-2399
20262   Mal mastocytosis thorax
20260,20262,20268,20282,20292,2398-2399
20263   Mal mastocytosis abdom
20260,20263,20268,20283,20293,2398-2399

20264   Mal mastocytosis axilla
20260,20264,20268,20284,20294,2398-2399
20265   Mal mastocytosis inguin
20260,20265,20268,20285,20295,2398-2399
20266   Mal mastocytosis pelvic
20260,20266,20268,20286,20296,2398-2399
20267   Mal mastocytosis spleen
20260,20267-20268,20287,20297,2398-2399
20268   Mal mastocytosis mult
20260-20268,20288,20298,2398-2399
20280   Oth lymp unsp xtrndl org
20280-20290,2398-2399
20281   Lymphomas NEC head
20280-20281,20288,20291,2398-2399
20282   Lymphomas NEC thorax
20280,20282,20288,20292,2398-2399
20283   Lymphomas NEC abdom
20280,20283,20288,20293,2398-2399
20284   Lymphomas NEC axilla
20280,20284,20288,20294,2398-2399
20285   Lymphomas NEC inguin
20280,20285,20288,20295,2398-2399
20286   Lymphomas NEC pelvic
20280,20286,20288,20296,2398-2399
20287   Lymphomas NEC spleen
20280,20287-20288,20297,2398-2399
20288   Lymphomas NEC mult
20280-20288,20298,2398-2399
20290   Unsp lym unsp xtrndl org
20290-20298,2398-2399
20291   Lymphoid mal NEC head
20290-20291,20298,2398-2399
20292   Lymphoid mal NEC thorax
20290,20292,20298,2398-2399
20293   Lymphoid mal NEC abdom
20290,20293,20298,2398-2399
20294   Lymphoid mal NEC axilla
20290,20294,20298,2398-2399
20295   Lymphoid mal NEC inguin
20290,20295,20298,2398-2399
20296   Lymphoid mal NEC pelvic
20290,20296,20298,2398-2399
20297   Lymphoid mal NEC spleen
20290,20297-20298,2398-2399
20298   Lymphoid mal NEC mult
20290-20298,2398-2399
20300   Mult myelm w/o remission
20300-20891,2398-2399
20301   Mult myelm w remission
20300-20891,2398-2399
20310   Plsm cell leuk w/o rmson
20300-20891,2398-2399
20311   Plsm cell leuk w rmson
20300-20891,2398-2399
20380   Oth imnprfl npl w/o rmsn
20300-20891,2398-2399
20381   Oth imnprfl npl w rmsn
20300-20891,2398-2399
20400   Act lym leuk w/o rmsion
20300-20891,2398-2399
20401   Act lym leuk w rmsion
20300-20891,2398-2399
20410   Chr lym leuk w/o rmsion
20300-20891,2398-2399
20411   Chr lym leuk w rmsion
20300-20891,2398-2399
20420   Sbac lym leuk w/o rmsion
20300-20891,2398-2399
20421   Sbac lym leuk w rmsion
20300-20891,2398-2399
20480   Oth lym leuk w/o rmsion
20300-20891,2398-2399
20481   Oth lym leuk w rmsion
20300-20891,2398-2399

20490 Uns lym leuk w/o rmsion
20300-20891,2398-2399
20491 Uns lym leuk w rmsion
20300-20891,2398-2399
20500 Act myl leuk w/o rmsion
20300-20891,2398-2399
20501 Act myl leuk w rmsion
20300-20891,2398-2399
20510 Chr myl leuk w/o rmsion
20300-20891,2398-2399
20511 Chr myl leuk w rmsion
20300-20891,2398-2399
20520 Sbac myl leuk w/o rmsion
20300-20891,2398-2399
20521 Sbac myl leuk w rmsion
20300-20891,2398-2399
20530 Myl srcoma w/o rmsion
20300-20891,2398-2399
20531 Myl srcoma w rmsion
20300-20891,2398-2399
20580 Oth myl leuk w/o rmsion
20300-20891,2398-2399
20581 Oth myl leuk w rmsion
20300-20891,2398-2399
20590 Uns myl leuk w/o rmsion
20300-20891,2398-2399
20591 Uns myl leuk w rmsion
20300-20891,2398-2399
20600 Act mono leuk w/o rmsion
20300-20891,2398-2399
20601 Act mono leuk w rmsion
20300-20891,2398-2399
20610 Chr mono leuk w/o rmsion
20300-20891,2398-2399
20611 Chr mono leuk w rmsion
20300-20891,2398-2399
20620 Sbac mono leuk w/o rmson
20300-20891,2398-2399
20621 Sbac mono leuk w rmsion
20300-20891,2398-2399
20680 Oth mono leuk w/o rmsion
20300-20891,2398-2399
20681 Oth mono leuk w rmsion
20300-20891,2398-2399
20690 Uns mono leuk w/o rmsion
20300-20891,2398-2399
20691 Uns mono leuk w rmsion
20300-20891,2398-2399
20700 Act erth/erylk w/o rmson
20300-20891,2398-2399
20701 Act erth/erylk w rmson
20300-20891,2398-2399
20710 Chr erythrm w/o remision
20300-20891,2398-2399
20711 Chr erythrm w remision
20300-20891,2398-2399
20720 Mgkrycyt leuk w/o rmsion
20300-20891,2398-2399
20721 Mgkrycyt leuk w rmsion
20300-20891,2398-2399
20780 Oth spf leuk w/o remsion
20300-20891,2398-2399
20781 Oth spf leuk w remsion
20300-20891,2398-2399
20800 Act leuk uns cl w/o rmsn
20300-20891,2398-2399
20801 Act leuk uns cl w rmson
20300-20891,2398-2399
20810 Chr leuk uns cl w/o rmsn
20300-20891,2398-2399
20811 Chr leuk uns cl w rmson
20300-20891,2398-2399
20820 Sbac leuk uns cl w/o rms
20300-20891,2398-2399

20821 Sbac leuk uns cl w rmson
20300-20891,2398-2399
20880 Oth leuk uns cl w/o rmsn
20300-20891,2398-2399
20881 Oth leuk uns cl w rmson
20300-20891,2398-2399
20890 Leukemia NOS w/o remsion
20300-20891,2398-2399
20891 Leukemia NOS w remission
20300-20891,2398-2399
24200 Tox dif goiter no crisis
01750-01756,01790-01796,2400-2469,2598-2599
24201 Tox dif goiter w crisis
01750-01756,01790-01796,2400-2469,2598-2599
24210 Tox uninod goit no cris
01750-01756,01790-01796,2400-2469,2598-2599
24211 Tox uninod goit w crisis
01750-01756,01790-01796,2400-2469,2598-2599
24220 Tox multnod goit no cris
01750-01756,01790-01796,2400-2469,2598-2599
24221 Tox multnod goit w cris
01750-01756,01790-01796,2400-2469,2598-2599
24230 Tox nod goiter no crisis
01750-01756,01790-01796,2400-2469,2598-2599
24231 Tox nod goiter w crisis
01750-01756,01790-01796,2400-2469,2598-2599
24240 Thyrotox-ect nod no cris
01750-01756,01790-01796,2400-2469,2598-2599
24241 Thyrotox-ect nod w cris
01750-01756,01790-01796,2400-2469,2598-2599
24280 Thyrtox orig NEC no cris
01750-01756,01790-01796,2400-2469,2598-2599
24281 Thyrotox orig NEC w cris
01750-01756,01790-01796,2400-2469,2598-2599
24290 Thyrotox NOS no crisis
01750-01756,01790-01796,2400-2469,2598-2599
24291 Thyrotox NOS w crisis
01750-01756,01790-01796,2400-2469,2598-2599
25001 DMI wo cmp nt st uncntrl
25000-2513,2598-2599
25002 DMII wo cmp uncntrld
25000-2513,2598-2599
25003 DMI wo cmp uncntrld
25000-2513,2598-2599
25011 DMI keto nt st uncntrld
25000-2513,2598-2599
25012 DMII ketoacd uncontrold
25000-2513,2598-2599
25013 DMI ketoacd uncontrold
25000-2513,2598-2599
25021 DMI hprsm nt st uncntrld
25000-2513,2598-2599
25022 DMII hprosmlr uncontrold
25000-2513,2598-2599
25023 DMI hprosmlr uncontrold
25000-2513,2598-2599
25031 DMI o cm nt st uncntrld
25000-2513,2598-2599
25032 DMII oth coma uncontrold
25000-2513,2598-2599
25033 DMI oth coma uncontrold
25000-2513,2598-2599
25041 DMI renl nt st uncntrld
25000-2513,2598-2599
25042 DMII renal uncntrld
25000-2513,2598-2599
25043 DMI renal uncntrld
25000-2513,2598-2599
25051 DMI ophth nt st uncntrld
25000-2513,2598-2599
25052 DMII ophth uncntrld
25000-2513,2598-2599
25053 DMI ophth uncntrld
25000-2513,2598-2599

25061 DMI neuro nt st uncntrld
25000-2513,2598-2599
25062 DMII neuro uncntrld
25000-2513,2598-2599
25063 DMI neuro uncntrld
25000-2513,2598-2599
25071 DMI circ nt st uncntrld
25000-2513,2598-2599
25072 DMII circ uncntrld
25000-2513,2598-2599
25073 DMI circ uncntrld
25000-2513,2598-2599
25081 DMI oth nt st uncntrld
25000-2513,2598-2599
25082 DMII oth uncntrld
25000-2513,2598-2599
25083 DMI oth uncntrld
25000-2513,2598-2599
25091 DMI unspf nt st uncntrld
25000-2513,2598-2599
25092 DMII unspf uncntrld
25000-2513,2598-2599
25093 DMI unspf uncntrld
25000-2513,2598-2599
2510 Hypoglycemic coma
25000-2513,2598-2599
2513 Postsurg hypoinsulinemia
25000-2513,2598-2599
2521 Hypoparathyroidism
2520-2529,2598-2599
2532 Panhypopituitarism
2530-2539,2598-2599
2535 Diabetes insipidus
2531-2532,2534-2539,2598-2599
2541 Abscess of thymus
2540-2549,2598-2599
2550 Cushing's syndrome
2550-2552,2598-2599
2553 Corticoadren overact NEC
01760-01766,01790-01796,2553-2559,2598-2599
2554 Corticoadrenal insuffic
01760-01766,01790-01796,2553-2559,2598-2599
2555 Adrenal hypofunction NEC
01760-01766,01790-01796,2553-2559,2598-2599
2556 Medulloadrenal hyperfunc
01760-01766,01790-01796,2553-2559,2598-2599
2580 Wermer's syndrome
2400-2599
2581 Comb endocr dysfunct NEC
2400-2599
2588 Polyglandul dysfunc NEC
2400-2599
2589 Polyglandul dysfunc NOS
2400-2599
2592 Carcinoid syndrome
2592-2593,2598-2599
260 Kwashiorkor
260-2639
261 Nutritional marasmus
260-2639
262 Oth severe malnutrition
260-2639
2630 Malnutrition mod degree
260-2639
2631 Malnutrition mild degree
260-2639
2632 Arrest devel d/t malnutr
260-2639
2638 Protein-cal malnutr NEC
260-2639
2639 Protein-cal malnutr NOS
260-2639
2690 Deficiency of vitamin k
2690

2733 Macroglobulinemia
2730-2739
2760 Hyperosmolality
2760-2769
2761 Hyposmolality
2760-2769
2762 Acidosis
2760-2769
2763 Alkalosis
2760-2769
2764 Mixed acid-base bal dis
2760-2769
2765 Hypovolemia
2760-2769
2766 Fluid overload
2760-2769
2767 Hyperpotassemia
2760-2769
2769 Electrolyt/fluid dis NEC
2760-2769
27700 Cystic fibros w/o ileus
27700-27701
27701 Cystic fibrosis w ileus
27700-27701
27902 Selective IgM immunodef
27902-2799
27903 Selective ig defic NEC
27902-2799
27904 Cong hypogammaglobulinem
27902-2799
27905 Immunodefic w hyper-igm
27902-2799
27906 Common variabl immunodef
27902-2799
27909 Humoral immunity def NEC
27902-2799
27910 Immundef t-cell def NOS
27902-2799
27911 Digeorge's syndrome
27902-2799
27912 Wiskott-aldrich syndrome
27902-2799
27913 Nezelof's syndrome
27902-2799
27919 Defic cell immunity NOS
27902-2799
2792 Combined immunity defic
27902-2799
2793 Immunity deficiency NOS
27902-2799
2794 Autoimmune disease NEC
27902-2799
2798 Immune mechanism dis NEC
27902-2799
2799 Immune mechanism dis NOS
27902-2799
2800 Chr blood loss anemia
2800-2859,2898-2899
2814 Protein defic anemia
2800-2859,2898-2899
2818 Nutritional anemia NEC
2800-2859,2898-2899
2824 Thalassemias
2800-2859,2898-2899
28260 Sickle-cell anemia NOS
2800-2859,2898-2899
28261 Hb-s disease w/o crisis
2800-2859,2898-2899
28262 Hb-s disease with crisis
2800-2859,2898-2899
28263 Sickle-cell/hb-c disease
2800-2859,2898-2899
28269 Sickle-cell anemia NEC
2800-2859,2898-2899

ICD-9-CM

Appx F

Vol. 1

2830   Autoimmun hemolytic anem
2800-2859,2898-2899

28310   Nonauto hem anemia NOS
2800-2859,2898-2899

28311   Hemolytic uremic synd
2800-2859,2898-2899

28319   Oth nonauto hem anemia
2800-2859,2898-2899

2832   Hemolytic hemoglobinuria
2800-2859,2898-2899

2839   Acq hemolytic anemia NOS
2800-2859,2898-2899

2840   Congen aplastic anemia
2800-2859,2898-2899

2848   Aplastic anemias NEC
2800-2859,2898-2899

2849   Aplastic anemia NOS
2800-2859,2898-2899

2850   Sideroblastic anemia
2800-2859,2898-2899

2851   Ac posthemorrhag anemia
2800-2859,2898-2899,9582

2860   Cong factor viii diord
2860-2879,2898-2899

2861   Cong factor ix disorder
2860-2879,2898-2899

2862   Cong factor xi disorder
2860-2879,2898-2899

2863   Cong def clot factor NEC
2860-2879,2898-2899

2864   Von willebrand's disease
2860-2879,2898-2899

2865   Circulating anticoag dis
2860-2879,2898-2899

2866   Defibrination syndrome
2860-2879,2898-2899

2867   Acq coagul factor defic
2860-2879,2898-2899

2869   Coagulat defect NEC/NOS
2860-2879,2898-2899

2870   Allergic purpura
2860-2879,2898-2899

2871   Thrombocytopathy
2860-2879,2898-2899

2872   Purpura NOS
2860-2879,2898-2899

2873   Primary thrombocytopenia
2860-2879,2898-2899

2874   Second thrombocytopenia
2860-2879,2898-2899

2875   Thrombocytopenia NOS
2860-2879,2898-2899

2878   Hemorrhagic cond NEC
2860-2879,2898-2899

2879   Hemorrhagic cond NOS
2860-2879,2898-2899

2880   Agranulocytosis
2880-2889,2898-2899

2881   Function dis neutrophils
2880-2889,2898-2899

2910   Delirium tremens
2910-2949,30300-30503,30520-30593,7903

2911   Alcohol amnestic synd
2910-2949,30300-30503,30520-30593,7903

2912   Alcoholic dementia NEC
2910-2949,30300-30503,30520-30593,7903

2913   Alcohol hallucinosis
2910-2949,30300-30503,30520-30593,7903

2914   Pathologic alcohol intox
2910-2949,30300-30503,30520-30593,7903

29181   Alcohol withdrawal
2910-2949,30300-30503,30520-30593,7903

29189   Alcoholic psychosis NEC
2910-2949,30300-30503,30520-30593,7903

2919   Alcoholic psychosis NOS
2910-2949,30300-30503,30520-30593,7903

2920   Drug withdrawal syndrome
2910-2949,30300-30503,30520-30593,7903

29211   Drug paranoid state
2910-2949,30300-30503,30520-30593,7903

29212   Drug hallucinosis
2910-2949,30300-30503,30520-30593,7903

2922   Pathologic drug intox
2910-2949,30300-30503,30520-30593,7903

29281   Drug-induced delirium
2910-2949,30300-30503,30520-30593,7903

29282   Drug-induced dementia
2910-2949,30300-30503,30520-30593,7903

29283   Drug amnestic syndrome
2910-2949,30300-30503,30520-30593,7903

29284   Drug depressive syndrome
2910-2949,30300-30503,30520-30593,7903

29289   Drug mental disorder NEC
2910-2949,30300-30503,30520-30593,7903

2929   Drug mental disorder NOS
2910-2949,30300-30503,30520-30593,7903

29381   Organic delusional synd
2910-2949,30300-30503,30520-30593,7903

29382   Organic hallucinosis syn
2910-2949,30300-30503,30520-30593,7903

29383   Organic affective synd
2910-2949,30300-30503,30520-30593,7903

29384   Organic anxiety syndrome
2910-2949,30300-30503,30520-30593,7903

29500   Simpl schizophren-unspec
29500-3019,3060-319

29501   Simpl schizophren-subchr
29500-3019,3060-319

29502   Simple schizophren-chr
29500-3019,3060-319

29503   Simp schiz-subchr/exacer
29500-3019,3060-319

29504   Simpl schizo-chr/exacerb
29500-3019,3060-319

29510   Hebephrenia-unspec
29500-3019,3060-319

29511   Hebephrenia-subchronic
29500-3019,3060-319

29512   Hebephrenia-chronic
29500-3019,3060-319

29513   Hebephren-subchr/exacerb
29500-3019,3060-319

29514   Hebephrenia-chr/exacerb
29500-3019,3060-319

29521   Catatonia-subchronic
29500-3019,3060-319

29522   Catatonia-chronic
29500-3019,3060-319

29523   Catatonia-subchr/exacerb
29500-3019,3060-319

29524   Catatonia-chr/exacerb
29500-3019,3060-319

29530   Paranoid schizo-unspec
29500-3019,3060-319

29531   Paranoid schizo-subchr
29500-3019,3060-319

29532   Paranoid schizo-chronic
29500-3019,3060-319

29533   Paran schizo-subchr/exac
29500-3019,3060-319

29534   Paran schizo-chr/exacerb
29500-3019,3060-319

29540   Ac schizophrenia-unspec
29500-3019,3060-319

29541   Ac schizophrenia-subchr
29500-3019,3060-319

29542 Ac schizophrenia-chr
29500-3019,3060-319
29543 Ac schizo-subchr/exacerb
29500-3019,3060-319
29544 Ac schizophr-chr/exacerb
29500-3019,3060-319
29560 Resid schizophren-unsp
29500-3019,3060-319
29561 Resid schizophren-subchr
29500-3019,3060-319
29562 Residual schizophren-chr
29500-3019,3060-319
29563 Resid schizo-subchr/exac
29500-3019,3060-319
29564 Resid schizo-chr/exacerb
29500-3019,3060-319
29570 Schizoaffective-unspec
29500-3019,3060-319
29571 Schizoaffective-subchr
29500-3019,3060-319
29572 Schizoaffective-chronic
29500-3019,3060-319
29573 Schizoaff-subchr/exacer
29500-3019,3060-319
29574 Schizoaffect-chr/exacer
29500-3019,3060-319
29580 Schizophrenia NEC-unspec
29500-3019,3060-319
29581 Schizophrenia NEC-subchr
29500-3019,3060-319
29582 Schizophrenia NEC-chr
29500-3019,3060-319
29583 Schizo NEC-subchr/exacer
29500-3019,3060-319
29584 Schizo NEC-chr/exacerb
29500-3019,3060-319
29590 Schizophrenia NOS-unspec
29500-3019,3060-319
29591 Schizophrenia NOS-subchr
29500-3019,3060-319
29592 Schizophrenia NOS-chr
29500-3019,3060-319
29593 Schizo NOS-subchr/exacer
29500-3019,3060-319
29594 Schizo NOS-chr/exacerb
29500-3019,3060-319
29604 Manic dis-severe w psych
29500-3019,3060-319
29614 Recur manic-sev w psycho
29500-3019,3060-319
29634 Rec depr psych-psychotic
29500-3019,3060-319
29644 Bipol manic-sev w psych
29500-3019,3060-319
29654 Bipol depr-sev w psych
29500-3019,3060-319
29664 Bipol mixed-sev w psych
29500-3019,3060-319
2980 React depress psychosis
29500-3019,3060-319
2983 Acute paranoid reaction
29500-3019,3060-319
2984 Psychogen paranoid psych
29500-3019,3060-319
29900 Infantile autism-active
29500-3019,3060-319
29910 Disintegr psych-active
29500-3019,3060-319
29980 Child psychos NEC-active
29500-3019,3060-319
29990 Child psychos NOS-active
29500-3019,3060-319
30300 Ac alcohol intox-unspec
2910-2929,30300-30503,30520-30593,7903

30301 Ac alcohol intox-contin
2910-2929,30300-30503,30520-30593,7903
30302 Ac alcohol intox-episod
2910-2929,30300-30503,30520-30593,7903
30390 Alcoh dep NEC/NOS-unspec
2910-2929,30300-30503,30520-30593,7903
30391 Alcoh dep NEC/NOS-contin
2910-2929,30300-30503,30520-30593,7903
30392 Alcoh dep NEC/NOS-episod
2910-2929,30300-30503,30520-30593,7903
30400 Opioid dependence-unspec
2910-2929,30300-30503,30520-30593,7903
30401 Opioid dependence-contin
2910-2929,30300-30503,30520-30593,7903
30402 Opioid dependence-episod
2910-2929,30300-30503,30520-30593,7903
30410 Barbiturat depend-unspec
2910-2929,30300-30503,30520-30593,7903
30411 Barbiturat depend-contin
2910-2929,30300-30503,30520-30593,7903
30412 Barbiturat depend-episod
2910-2929,30300-30503,30520-30593,7903
30420 Cocaine depend-unspec
2910-2929,30300-30503,30520-30593,7903
30421 Cocaine depend-contin
2910-2929,30300-30503,30520-30593,7903
30422 Cocaine depend-episodic
2910-2929,30300-30503,30520-30593,7903
30440 Amphetamin depend-unspec
2910-2929,30300-30503,30520-30593,7903
30441 Amphetamin depend-contin
2910-2929,30300-30503,30520-30593,7903
30442 Amphetamin depend-episod
2910-2929,30300-30503,30520-30593,7903
30450 Hallucinogen dep-unspec
2910-2929,30300-30503,30520-30593,7903
30451 Hallucinogen dep-contin
2910-2929,30300-30503,30520-30593,7903
30452 Hallucinogen dep-episod
2910-2929,30300-30503,30520-30593,7903
30460 Drug depend NEC-unspec
2910-2929,30300-30503,30520-30593,7903
30461 Drug depend NEC-contin
2910-2929,30300-30503,30520-30593,7903
30462 Drug depend NEC-episodic
2910-2929,30300-30503,30520-30593,7903
30470 Opioid/other dep-unspec
2910-2929,30300-30503,30520-30593,7903
30471 Opioid/other dep-contin
2910-2929,30300-30503,30520-30593,7903
30472 Opioid/other dep-episod
2910-2929,30300-30503,30520-30593,7903
30480 Comb drug dep NEC-unspec
2910-2929,30300-30503,30520-30593,7903
30481 Comb drug dep NEC-contin
2910-2929,30300-30503,30520-30593,7903
30482 Comb drug dep NEC-episode
2910-2929,30300-30503,30520-30593,7903
30490 Drug depend NOS-unspec
2910-2929,30300-30503,30520-30593,7903
30491 Drug depend NOS-contin
2910-2929,30300-30503,30520-30593,7903
30492 Drug depend NOS-episodic
2910-2929,30300-30503,30520-30593,7903
30500 Alcohol abuse-unspec
2910-2929,30300-30503,30520-30593,7903
30501 Alcohol abuse-continuous
2910-2929,30300-30503,30520-30593,7903
30502 Alcohol abuse-episodic
2910-2929,30300-30503,30520-30593,7903
30530 Hallucinog abuse-unspec
2910-2929,30300-30503,30520-30593,7903
30531 Hallucinog abuse-contin
2910-2929,30300-30503,30520-30593,7903

30532   Hallucinog abuse-episod
2910-2929,30300-30503,30520-30593,7903
30540   Barbiturate abuse-unspec
2910-2929,30300-30503,30520-30593,7903
30541   Barbiturate abuse-contin
2910-2929,30300-30503,30520-30593,7903
30542   Barbiturate abuse-episod
2910-2929,30300-30503,30520-30593,7903
30550   Opioid abuse-unspec
2910-2929,30300-30503,30520-30593,7903
30551   Opioid abuse-continuous
2910-2929,30300-30503,30520-30593,7903
30552   Opioid abuse-episodic
2910-2929,30300-30503,30520-30593,7903
30560   Cocaine abuse-unspec
2910-2929,30300-30503,30520-30593,7903
30561   Cocaine abuse-continuous
2910-2929,30300-30503,30520-30593,7903
30562   Cocaine abuse-episodic
2910-2929,30300-30503,30520-30593,7903
30570   Amphetamine abuse-unspec
2910-2929,30300-30503,30520-30593,7903
30571   Amphetamine abuse-contin
2910-2929,30300-30503,30520-30593,7903
30572   Amphetamine abuse-episod
2910-2929,30300-30503,30520-30593,7903
30590   Drug abuse NEC-unspec
2910-2929,30300-30503,30520-30593,7903
30591   Drug abuse NEC-contin
2910-2929,30300-30503,30520-30593,7903
30592   Drug abuse NEC-episodic
2910-2929,30300-30503,30520-30593,7903
3071   Anorexia nervosa
3064,3068-3069,3071,30750-30759,30922
3200   Hemophilus meningitis
00321,01300-01316,0360,0470-0479,0490-0491,0530,05472,0721,
09042,09181,0942,09889,10081,11283,1142,11501,11511,11591,1300,
25060-25063,25080-25093,3200-3229,34989-3499,3570
3201   Pneumococcal meningitis
00321,01300-01316,0360,0470-0479,0490-0491,0530,05472,0721,
09042,09181,0942,09889,10081,11283,1142,11501,11511,11591,1300,
25060-25063,25080-25093,3200-3229,34989-3499,3570
3202   Streptococcal meningitis
00321,01300-01316,0360,0470-0479,0490-0491,0530,05472,0721,
09042,09181,0942,09889,10081,11283,1142,11501,11511,11591,1300,
25060-25063,25080-25093,3200-3229,34989-3499,3570
3203   Staphylococc meningitis
00321,01300-01316,0360,0470-0479,0490-0491,0530,05472,0721,
09042,09181,0942,09889,10081,11283,1142,11501,11511,11591,1300,
25060-25063,25080-25093,3200-3229,34989-3499,3570
3207   Mening in oth bact dis
00321,01300-01316,0360,0470-0479,0490-0491,0530,05472,0721,
09042,09181,0942,09889,10081,11283,1142,11501,11511,11591,1300,
25060-25063,25080-25093,3200-3229,34989-3499,3570
32081   Anaerobic meningitis
00321,01300-01316,0360,0470-0479,0490-0491,0530,05472,0721,
09042,09181,0942,09889,10081,11263,1142,11501,11511,11591,1300,
25060-25063,25080-25093,3200-3229,34989-3499,3570
32082   Mningts gram-neg bct NEC
00321,01300-01316,0360,0470-0479,0490-0491,0530,05472,0721,
09042,09181,0942,09889,10081,11283,1142,11501,11511,11591,1300,
25060-25063,25080-25093,3200-3229,34989-3499,3570
32089   Meningitis oth spcf bact
00321,01300-01316,0360,0470-0479,0490-0491,0530,05472,0721,
09042,09181,0942,09889,10081,11283,1142,11501,11511,11591,1300,
25060-25063,25080-25093,3200-3229,34989-3499,3570
3209   Bacterial meningitis NOS
00321,01300-01316,0360,0470-0479,0490-0491,0530,05472,0721,
09042,09181,0942,09889,10081,11283,1142,11501,11511,11591,1300,
25060-25063,25080-25093,3200-3229,34989-3499,3570
3210   Cryptococcal meningitis
00321,01300-01316,0360,0470-0479,0490-0491,0530,05472,0721,
09042,09181,0942,09889,10081,11283,1142,11501,11511,11591,1300,
25060-25063,25080-25093,3200-3229,34989-3499,3570

3211   Mening in oth fungal dis
00321,01300-01316,0360,0470-0479,0490-0491,0530,05472,0721,
09042,09181,0942,09889,10081,11283,1142,11501,11511,11591,1300,
25060-25063,25080-25093,3200-3229,34989-3499,3570
3212   Mening in oth viral dis
00321,01300-01316,0360,0470-0479,0490-0491,0530,05472,0721,
09042,09181,0942,09889,10081,11283,1142,11501,11511,11591,1300,
3200-3229,34989-3499,3570
3213   Trypanosomiasis meningit
00321,01300-01316,0360,0470-0479,0490-0491,0530,05472,0721,
09042,09181,0942,09889,10081,11283,1142,11501,11511,11591,1300,
25060-25063,25080-25093,3200-3229,34989-3499,3570
3214   Meningit d/t sarcoidosis
00321,01300-01316,0360,0470-0479,0490-0491,0530,05472,0721,
09042,09181,0942,09889,10081,11283,1142,11501,11511,11591,1300,
25060-25063,25080-25093,3200-3229,34989-3499,3570
3218   Mening in oth nonbac dis
00321,01300-01316,0360,0470-0479,0490-0491,0530,05472,0721,
09042,09181,0942,09889,10081,11283,1142,11501,11511,11591,1300,
25060-25063,25080-25093,3200-3229,34989-3499,3570
3220   Nonpyogenic meningitis
00321,01300-01316,0360,0470-0479,0490-0491,0530,05472,0721,
09042,09181,0942,09889,10081,11283,1142,11501,11511,11591,1300,
25060-25063,25080-25093,3200-3229,34989-3499,3570
3221   Eosinophilic meningitis
00321,01300-01316,0360,0470-0479,0490-0491,0530,05472,0721,
09042,09181,0942,09889,10081,11283,1142,11501,11511,11591,1300,
25060-25063,25080-25093,3200-3229,34989-3499,3570
3222   Chronic meningitis
00321,01300-01316,0360,0470-0479,0490-0491,0530,05472,0721,
09042,09181,0942,09889,10081,11283,1142,11501,11511,11591,1300,
25060-25063,25080-25093,3200-3229,34989-3499,3570
3229   Meningitis NOS
00321,01300-01316,0360,0470-0479,0490-0491,0530,05472,0721,
09042,09181,0942,09889,10081,11283,1142,11501,11511,11591,1300,
25060-25063,25080-25093,3200-3229,34989-3499,3570
3240   Intracranial abscess
0065,01320-01336,25060-25063,25080-25093,3240-325,3488-3489
3241   Intraspinal abscess
0065,01320-01336,25060-25063,25080-25093,3241
3249   Cns abscess NOS
0065,01320-01336,25060-25063,25080-25093,3240-325
325   Phlebitis intrcran sinus
0065,01320-01336,25060-25063,25080-25093,3240-325
3314   Obstructiv hydrocephalus
25060-25063,25080-25093,3313-3317,33189-3319,3488-3489,
74100-74103,7423-7424,74259-7429
3350   Werdnig-hoffmann disease
25060-25063,25080-25093,3348-3379,34989-3499
33510   Spinal muscl atrophy NOS
25060-25063,25080-25093,3348-3379,34989-3499
33511   Kugelberg-welander dis
25060-25063,25080-25093,3348-3379,34989-3499
33519   Spinal muscl atrophy NEC
25060-25063,25080-25093,3348-3379,34989-3499
33520   Amyotrophic sclerosis
25060-25063,25080-25093,3348-3379,34989-3499
33521   Prog muscular atrophy
25060-25063,25080-25093,3348-3379,34989-3499
33522   Progressive bulbar palsy
25060-25063,25080-25093,3348-3379,34989-3499
33523   Pseudobulbar palsy
25060-25063,25080-25093,3348-3379,34989-3499
33524   Prim lateral sclerosis
25060-25063,25080-25093,3348-3379,34989-3499
33529   Motor neuron disease NEC
25060-25063,25080-25093,3348-3379,34989-3499
3358   Ant horn cell dis NEC
25060-25063,25080-25093,3348-3379,34989-3499
3359   Ant horn cell dis NOS
25060-25063,25080-25093,3348-3379,34989-3499

340 Multiple sclerosis
25060-25063,25080-25093,340,3418-3419

3432 Congenital quadriplegia
25060-25063,25080-25093,34200-3449,3488-3489,34989-3499,
74259-7429

34400 Quadriplegia, unspecifd
25060-25063,25080-25093,34200-3449,3488-3489,34989-3499,
74259-7429

34401 Quadrplg c1-c4, complete
25060-25063,25080-25093,34200-3449,3488-3489,34989-3499,
74259-7429

34402 Quadrplg c1-c4, incomplt
25060-25063,25080-25093,34200-3449,3488-3489,34989-3499,
74259-7429

34403 Quadrplg c5-c7, complete
25060-25063,25080-25093,34200-3449,3488-3489,34989-3499,
74259-7429

34404 Quadrplg c5-c7, incomplt
25060-25063,25080-25093,34200-3449,3488-3489,34989-3499,
74259-7429

34409 Other quadriplegia
25060-25063,25080-25093,34200-3449,3488-3489,34989-3499,
74259-7429

34501 Gen nonconv ep w intr ep
25060-25063,34500-34591,3488-3489,34989-3499

34510 Gen cnv epil w/o intr ep
25060-25063,34500-34591,3488-3489,34989-3499

34511 Gen cnv epil w intr epil
25060-25063,34500-34591,3488-3489,34989-3499

3452 Petit mal status
25060-25063,25080-25093,34500-34591,3488-3489,34989-3499

3453 Grand mal status
25060-25063,25080-25093,34500-34591,3488-3489,34989-3499

34541 Psymotr epil w intr epil
25060-25063,34500-34591,3488-3489,34989-3499

34551 Part epil w intr epil
25060-25063,34500-34591,3488-3489,34989-3499

34561 Inf spasm w intract epil
25060-25063,34500-34591,3488-3489,34989-3499

34571 Epil par cont w intr epi
25060-25063,34500-34591,3488-3489,34989-3499

34581 Epilepsy NEC w intr epil
25060-25063,34500-34591,3488-3489,34989-3499

34591 Epilepsy NOS w intr epil
25060-25063,34500-34591,3488-3489,34989-3499

3481 Anoxic brain damage
25060-25063,25080-25093,3481-3482,34989-3499

3491 Complication cns device
25060-25063,25080-25093,3491,34989-3499

34981 Cerebrospinal rhinorrhea
25060-25063,25080-25093,34981,34989-3499

34982 Toxic encephalopathy
01360-01366,01790-01796,0361,0498-0499,0520,0543,0620-0639,
0722,09041,09481,1300,25060-25063,25080-25093,3230-3239,3483,
3488-3489,34982-3499

3570 Ac infect polyneuritis
00321,01300-01316,0360,03689-0369,04181-0419,0470-0479,
0490-0491,0530,05472,0721,09042,09181,0942,09889,10081,11283,
1142,11501,11511,11591,1300,1398,3200-3229,34989-3499,3570

3580 Myasthenia gravis
25060-25063,25080-25093,34989-3499,3580-3581

3581 Myasthenia in oth dis
25060-25063,25080-25093,34989-3499,3580-3581

3590 Cong hered musc dystrphy
25060-25063,25080-25093,34989-3499,3590-3591

3591 Hered prog musc dystrphy
25060-25063,25080-25093,34989-3499,3590-3591

37700 Papilledema NOS
01730-01736,01790-01796,03681,25050-25053,25080-25093,
37700-37703,37714,37724,3798-37990,37999,7438-7439

37701 Papilledema w incr press
01730-01736,01790-01796,03681,25050-25053,25080-25093,
37700-37703,37714,37724,3798-37990,37999,7438-7439

37702 Papilledema w decr press
01730-01736,01790-01796,03681,25050-25053,25080-25093,
37700-37703,37714,37724,3798-37990,37999,7438-7439

38301 Subperi mastoid abscess
01560-01566,01740-01746,01790-01796,38300-3839,38871-3889,
74400,74402,74409,74429-7443

38330 Postmastoid compl NOS
01560-01566,01740-01746,01790-01796,38300-3839,38871-3889,
74400,74402,74409,74429-7443

38381 Postauricular fistula
01560-01566,01740-01746,01790-01796,38300-3839,38871-3889,
74400,74402,74409,74429-7443

3940 Mitral stenosis
390,3918-3919,3940-3949,3960-3969,3979,39890,39899,4240,
45989-4599

3941 Rheumatic mitral insuff
390,3918-3919,3940-3949,3960-3969,3979,39890,39899,4240,
45989-4599

3942 Mitral stenosis w insuff
390,3918-3919,3940-3949,3960-3969,3979,39890,39899,4240,
45989-4599

3949 Mitral valve dis NEC/NOS
390,3918-3919,3940-3949,3960-3969,3979,39890,39899,4240,
45989-4599

3950 Rheumat aortic stenosis
390,3918-3919,3950-3969,3979,39890,39899,4241,45989-4599

3951 Rheumatic aortic insuff
390,3918-3919,3950-3969,3979,39890,39899,4241,45989-4599

3952 Rheum aortic sten/insuff
390,3918-3919,3950-3969,3979,39890,39899,4241,45989-4599

3959 Rheum aortic dis NEC/NOS
390,3918-3919,3950-3969,3979,39890,39899,4241,45989-4599

3960 Mitral/aortic stenosis
390,3918-3919,3940-3969,3979,39890,39899,4240-4241,45989-4599

3961 Mitral stenos/aort insuf
390,3918-3919,3940-3969,3979,39890,39899,4240-4241,45989-4599

3962 Mitral insuf/aort stenos
390,3918-3919,3940-3969,3979,39890,39899,4240-4241,45989-4599

3963 Mitral/aortic val insuff
390,3918-3919,3940-3969,3979,39890,39899,4240-4241,45989-4599

3968 Mitr/aortic mult involv
390,3918-3919,3940-3969,3979,39890,39899,4240-4241,45989-4599

3969 Mitral/aortic v dis NOS
390,3918-3919,3940-3969,3979,39890,39899,4240-4241,45989-4599

3970 Tricuspid valve disease
3970,39890,39899,4242,45989-4599

3971 Rheum pulmon valve dis
3971,39890,39899,4243,45989-4599

3979 Rheum endocarditis NOS
390,3911,3918-3919,3940-3959,3971-3979,39890,39899,4210-4219,
4240-42499,45989-4599

3980 Rheumatic myocarditis
390,3912-3919,3980-39890,39899,4220-42299,4290,42971-42979,
45989-4599

39891 Rheumatic heart failure
39890-39899,40201,40211,40291,4280-4289,45989-4599

4010 Malignant hypertension
4010-40599,45989-4599

40200 Mal hyperten hrt dis NOS
4010-40599,45989-4599

40201 Mal hypert hrt dis w chf
39891,4010-40599,4280-4289,45989-4599

40211 Benign hyp hrt dis w chf
39891,4010-40599,4280-4289,45989-4599

40291 Hyperten heart dis w chf
39891,4010-40599,4280-4289,45989-4599

40300 Mal hyp ren w/o ren fail
4010-40599,45989-4599

40301 Mal hyp ren w renal fail
4010-40599,45989-4599

40311 Ben hyp renal w ren fail
4010-40599,45989-4599
40391 Hyp renal NOS w ren fail
4010-40599,45989-4599
40400 Mal hy ht/ren w/o chf/rf
4010-40599,45989-4599
40401 Mal hyper hrt/ren w chf
4010-40599,45989-4599
40402 Mal hy ht/ren w ren fail
4010-40599,45989-4599
40403 Mal hyp hrt/ren w chf&rf
4010-40599,45989-4599
40411 Ben hyper hrt/ren w chf
4010-40599,45989-4599
40412 Ben hy ht/ren w ren fail
4010-40599,45989-4599
40413 Ben hyp hrt/ren w chf&rf
4010-40599,45989-4599
40491 Hyper hrt/ren NOS w chf
4010-40599,45989-4599
40492 Hy ht/ren NOS w ren fail
4010-40599,45989-4599
40493 Hyp ht/ren NOS w chf&rf
4010-40599,45989-4599
40501 Mal renovasc hypertens
4010-40599,45989-4599
40509 Mal second hyperten NEC
4010-40599,45989-4599
41001 AMI anterolateral, init
41000-41092,45989-4599
41011 AMI anterior wall, init
41000-41092,45989-4599
41021 AMI inferolateral, init
41000-41092,45989-4599
41031 AMI inferopost, initial
41000-41092,45989-4599
41041 AMI inferior wall, init
41000-41092,45989-4599
41051 AMI lateral NEC, initial
41000-41092,45989-4599
41061 True post infarct, init
41000-41092,45989-4599
41071 Subendo infarct, initial
41000-41092,45989-4599
41081 AMI NEC, initial
41000-41092,45989-4599
41091 AMI NOS, initial
41000-41092,45989-4599
4110 Post MI syndrome
4110,41181-41189,45989-4599
4111 Intermed coronary synd
41000-41092,4111-41189,4130-4139,4148-4149,45989-4599
41181 Coronary occlsn w/o MI
41000-41189,4130-4139,4148-4149,45989-4599
41189 Ac ischemic hrt dis NEC
41000-41189,4130-4139,4148-4149,45989-4599
4130 Angina decubitus
41000-41092,4111-41189,4130-4139,4148-4149,45989-4599
4131 Prinzmetal angina
41000-41092,4111-41189,4130-4139,4148-4149,45989-4599
4139 Angina pectoris NEC/NOS
41000-41092,4111-41189,4130-4139,4148-4149,45989-4599
4150 Acute cor pulmonale
4150,4168-4169,45989-4599
41511 Iatrogen pulm emb/infarc
41511-41519,45989-4599
41519 Pulm embol/infarct NEC
41511-41519,45989-4599
4160 Prim pulm hypertension
4160,4168-4169,4178-4179,45989-4599
4200 Ac pericardit in oth dis
3910,393,4200-42099,4238-4239,45989-4599
42090 Acute pericarditis NOS
3910,393,4200-42099,4238-4239,45989-4599

42091 Ac idiopath pericarditis
3910,393,4200-42099,4238-4239,45989-4599
42099 Acute pericarditis NEC
3910,393,4200-42099,4238-4239,45989-4599
4210 Ac/subac bact endocard
3911,3979,4210-4219,42490-42499,45989-4599
4211 Ac endocardit in oth dis
3911,3979,4210-4219,42490-42499,45989-4599
4219 Ac/subac endocardit NOS
3911,3979,4210-4219,42490-42499,45989-4599
4220 Ac myocardit in oth dis
3912,3980,4220-42299,4290,42971-42979,45989-4599
42290 Acute myocarditis NOS
3912,3980,4220-42299,4290,42971-42979,45989-4599
42291 Idiopathic myocarditis
3912,3980,4220-42299,4290,42971-42979,45989-4599
42292 Septic myocarditis
3912,3980,4220-42299,4290,42971-42979,45989-4599
42293 Toxic myocarditis
3912,3980,4220-42299,4290,42971-42979,45989-4599
42299 Acute myocarditis NEC
3912,3980,4220-42299,4290,42971-42979,45989-4599
4230 Hemopericardium
4230-4239,45989-4599
4231 Adhesive pericarditis
4230-4239,45989-4599
4232 Constrictiv pericarditis
4230-4239,45989-4599
4240 Mitral valve disorder
3940-3949,3960-3969,4240,45989-4599
4241 Aortic valve disorder
3950-3969,4241,45989-4599
4242 Nonrheum tricusp val dis
3970,4242,45989-4599
4243 Pulmonary valve disorder
3971,4243,45989-4599
42490 Endocarditis NOS
42490-42499,45989-4599
42491 Endocarditis in oth dis
42490-42499,45989-4599
42499 Endocarditis NEC
42490-42499,45989-4599
4250 Endomyocardial fibrosis
4250-4259,45989-4599
4251 Hypertr obstr cardiomyop
4250-4259,45989-4599
4252 Obsc afric cardiomyopath
4250-4259,45989-4599
4253 Endocard fibroelastosis
4250-4259,45989-4599
4254 Prim cardiomyopathy NEC
4250-4259,45989-4599
4255 Alcoholic cardiomyopathy
4250-4259,45989-4599
4257 Metabolic cardiomyopathy
4250-4259,45989-4599
4258 Cardiomyopath in oth dis
4250-4259,45989-4599
4259 Second cardiomyopath NOS
4250-4259,45989-4599
4260 Atriovent block complete
4260-4275,42789,45989-4599
42612 Atrioven block-mobitz ii
4260-4275,42789,45989-4599
42613 Av block-2nd degree NEC
4260-4275,42789,45989-4599
42653 Bilat bb block NEC
4260-4275,42789,45989-4599
42654 Trifascicular block
4260-4275,42789,45989-4599
4266 Other heart block
4260-4275,42789,45989-4599

4267 Anomalous av excitation
4260-4275,42789,45989-4599

42681 Lown-ganong-levine synd
4260-4275,42789,45989-4599

42689 Conduction disorder NEC
4260-4275,42789,45989-4599

4269 Conduction disorder NOS
4260-4275,42789,45989-4599

4270 Parox atrial tachycardia
4260-4275,42789,45989-4599

4271 Parox ventric tachycard
4260-4275,42789,45989-4599

4272 Parox tachycardia NOS
4260-4275,42789,45989-4599

42731 Atrial fibrillation
4260-4275,42789,45989-4599

42732 Atrial flutter
4260-4275,42789,45989-4599

42741 Ventricular fibrillation
4260-4275,42789,45989-4599

42742 Ventricular flutter
4260-4275,42789,45989-4599

4275 Cardiac arrest
4270-4275,45989-4599

4280 Congestive heart failure
39891,40201,40211,40291,4280-4289,45989-4599,5184

4281 Left heart failure
39891,40201,40211,40291,4280-4289,45989-4599

4289 Heart failure NOS
39891,40201,40211,40291,4280-4289,45989-4599

4294 Hrt dis postcardiac surg
4294,42971-42979,45989-4599

4295 Chordae tendinae rupture
4295,42971-42979,45989-4599

4296 Papillary muscle rupture
4296-42981,45989-4599

42971 Acq cardiac septl defect
4220-42299,4290,4294-42982,45989-4599,7450-7459,74689-7469,
74789-7479,7597-75989

42979 Other sequelae of MI NEC
4220-42299,4290,4294-42982,45989-4599,7450-7459,74689-7469,
74789-7479,7597-75989

42981 Papillary muscle dis NEC
4296-42981,45989-4599

42982 Hyperkinetic heart dis
42971-42979,42982,45989-4599

430 Subarachnoid hemorrhage
430-4329,45989-4599,78001-78009,80000-80199,80300-80496,
8500-85219,85221-85419

431 Intracerebral hemorrhage
430-4329,45989-4599,78001-78009,80000-80199,80300-80496,
8500-85219,85221-85419

4320 Nontraum extradural hem
430-4329,45989-4599,78001-78009,80000-80199,80300-80496,
8500-85219,85221-85419

4321 Subdural hemorrhage
430-4329,45989-4599,78001-78009,80000-80199,80300-80496,
8500-85219,85221-85419

43301 Ocl bslr art w infrct
25070-25093,43300-43391,4350,45989-4599

43311 Ocl crtd art w infrct
25070-25093,43300-43391,45989-4599

43321 Ocl vrtb art w infrct
25070-25093,43300-43391,4351,45989-4599

43331 Ocl mlt bi art w infrct
25070-25093,43300-43391,45989-4599

43381 Ocl spcf art w infrct
25070-25093,43300-43391,4350,45989-4599

43391 Ocl art NOS w infrct
25070-25093,43300-43391,4350,45989-4599

43401 Crbl thrmbs w infrct
25070-25093,43400-43491,436,45989-4599

43411 Crbl emblsm w infrct
25070-25093,43400-43491,436,45989-4599

43491 Crbl art ocl NOS w infrc
25070-25093,43400-43491,436,45989-4599

436 Cva
25070-25093,430-4329,43400-43491,436,45989-4599,78001-78009,
80000-80199,80300-80496,8500-85219,85221-85419

4372 Hypertens encephalopathy
25070-25093,4372,45989-4599

4374 Cerebral arteritis
25070-25093,4374,45989-4599

4375 Moyamoya disease
25070-25093,4375,45989-4599

4376 Nonpyogen thrombos sinus
25070-25093,4376,45989-4599

44024 Ath ext ntv art gngrene
44024,7809,7854,7998

44100 Dsct of aorta unsp site
25070-25093,44100-4419,45989-4599

44101 Dsct of thoracic aorta
25070-25093,44100-4419,45989-4599

44102 Dsct of abdominal aorta
25070-25093,44100-4419,45989-4599

44103 Dsct of thoracoabd aorta
25070-25093,44100-4419,45989-4599

4411 Ruptur thoracic aneurysm
25070-25093,44100-4419,45989-4599

4413 Rupt abd aortic aneurysm
25070-25093,44100-4419,45989-4599

4415 Rupt aortic aneurysm NOS
25070-25093,44100-4419,45989-4599

4416 Thoracoabd aneurysm rupt
25070-25093,44100-4419,45989-4599

4440 Abd aortic embolism
25070-25093,4440,44489-4449,45989-4599

4441 Thoracic aortic embolism
25070-25093,4441,44489-4449,45989-4599

44421 Upper extremity embolism
25070-25093,44421,44489-4449,45989-4599

44422 Lower extremity embolism
25070-25093,44422,44489-4449,45989-4599

44481 Iliac artery embolism
25070-25093,44481-4449,45989-4599

44489 Arterial embolism NEC
25070-25093,44489-4449,45989-4599

4449 Arterial embolism NOS
25070-25093,44489-4449,45989-4599

4460 Polyarteritis nodosa
25070-25093,4460-4467,45989-4599

44620 Hypersensit angiitis NOS
25070-25093,4460-4467,45989-4599

44621 Goodpasture's syndrome
25070-25093,4460-4467,45989-4599

44629 Hypersensit angiitis NEC
25070-25093,4460-4467,45989-4599

4463 Lethal midline granuloma
25070-25093,4460-4467,45989-4599

4464 Wegener's granulomatosis
25070-25093,4460-4467,45989-4599

4465 Giant cell arteritis
25070-25093,4460-4467,45989-4599

4466 Thrombot microangiopathy
25070-25093,4460-4467,45989-4599

4467 Takayasu's disease
25070-25093,4460-4467,45989-4599

4510 Superfic phlebitis-leg
25070-25093,4510-4519,45989-4599

45111 Femoral vein phlebitis
25070-25093,4510-4519,45989-4599

45119 Deep phlebitis-leg NEC
25070-25093,4510-4519,45989-4599

4512 Thrombophlebitis leg NOS
25070-25093,4510-4519,45989-4599

45181   Iliac thrombophlebitis
25070-25093,4510-4519,45989-4599
452   Portal vein thrombosis
25070-25093,452,4538-4539,45989-4599
4530   Budd-chiari syndrome
25070-25093,4530,4538-4539,45989-4599
4531   Thrombophlebitis migrans
25070-25093,4531,4538-4539,45989-4599
4532   Vena cava thrombosis
25070-25093,4532,4538-4539,45989-4599
4533   Renal vein thrombosis
25070-25093,4533-4539,45989-4599
4538   Venous thrombosis NEC
25070-25093,4538-4539,45989-4599
4539   Venous thrombosis NOS
25070-25093,4538-4539,45989-4599
4560   Esophag varices w bleed
2515,4560,45620,45989-4599,5302,5307,53082,53100-53491,53501,
53511,53521,53531,53541,53551,53561,53783,56202-56203,
56212-56213,5693,56985,5780-5789
45620   Bleed esoph var oth dis
4560,45620,45989-4599,53082
4590   Hemorrhage NOS
4590,45989-4599
46411   Ac tracheitis w obstruct
01220-01286,01790-01796,46410-46431,5198-5199
46421   Ac laryngotrach w obstr
01220-01286,01790-01796,46410-46431,5198-5199
46431   Ac epiglottitis w obstr
01220-01286,01790-01796,46410-46431,5198-5199
475   Peritonsillar abscess
475,5198-5199
47821   Cellulitis of pharynx
47820-47824,5198-5199
47822   Parapharyngeal abscess
47820-47824,5198-5199
47824   Retropharyngeal abscess
47820-47824,5198-5199
47830   Vocal cord paralysis NOS
47830-47834,4785,47870,5198-5199
47831   Vocal paral unilat part
47830-47834,4785,47870,5198-5199
47832   Vocal paral unilat total
47830-47834,4785,47870,5198-5199
47833   Vocal paral bilat part
47830-47834,4785,47870,5198-5199
47834   Vocal paral bilat total
47830-47834,4785,47870,5198-5199
481   Pneumococcal pneumonia
01100-01216,01280-01286,01790-01796,0212,0310,0391,11505,11515,
11595,1221,1304,1363,4800-4871,494-5089,5171,5178,51889,
5198-5199,74861
4820   K. pneumoniae pneumonia
01100-01216,01280-01286,01790-01796,0212,0310,0391,11505,11515,
11595,1221,1304,1363,4800-4871,494-5089,5171,5178,51889,
5198-5199,74861
4821   Pseudomonal pneumonia
01100-01216,01280-01286,01790-01796,0212,0310,0391,11505,11515,
11595,1221,1304,1363,4800-4871,494-5089,5171,5178,51889,
5198-5199,74861
4822   H. influenzae pneumonia
01100-01216,01280-01286,01790-01796,0212,0310,0391,11505,11515,
11595,1221,1304,1363,4800-4871,494-5089,5171,5178,51889,
5198-5199,74861
48230   Streptococcal pneumn NOS
01100-01216,01280-01286,01790-01796,0212,0310,0391,11505,11515,
11595,1221,1304,1363,4800-4871,494-5089,5171,5178,51889,
5198-5199,74861
48231   Pneumonia strptococcus a
01100-01216,01280-01286,01790-01796,0212,0310,0391,11505,11515,
11595,1221,1304,1363,4800-4871,494-5089,5171,5178,51889,
5198-5199,74861

48232   Pneumonia strptococcus b
01100-01216,01280-01286,01790-01796,0212,0310,0391,11505,11515,
11595,1221,1304,1363,4800-4871,494-5089,5171,5178,51889,
5198-5199,74861
48239   Pneumonia oth strep
01100-01216,01280-01286,01790-01796,0212,0310,0391,11505,11515,
11595,1221,1304,1363,4800-4871,494-5089,5171,5178,51889,
5198-5199,74861
48240   Staphylococcal pneu NOS
01100-01216,01280-01286,01790-01796,0212,0310,0391,11505,11515,
11595,1221,1304,1363,4800-4871,494-5089,5171,5178,51889,
5198-5199,74861
48241   Staph aureus pneumonia
01100-01216,01280-01286,01790-01796,0212,0310,0391,11505,11515,
11595,1221,1304,1363,4800-4871,494-5089,5171,5178,51889,
5198-5199,74861
48249   Staph pneumonia NEC
01100-01216,01280-01286,01790-01796,0212,0310,0391,11505,11515,
11595,1221,1304,1363,4800-4871,494-5089,5171,5178,51889,
5198-5199,74861
48281   Pneumonia anaerobes
01100-01216,01280-01286,01790-01796,0212,0310,0391,11505,11515,
11595,1221,1304,1363,4800-4871,494-5089,5171,5178,51889,
5198-5199,74861
48282   Pneumonia e coli
01100-01216,01280-01286,01790-01796,0212,0310,0391,11505,11515,
11595,1221,1304,1363,4800-4871,494-5089,5171,5178,51889,
5198-5199,74861
48283   Pneumo oth grm-neg bact
01100-01216,01280-01286,01790-01796,0212,0310,0391,11505,11515,
11595,1221,1304,1363,4800-4871,494-5089,5171,5178,51889,
5198-5199,74861
48284   Legionnaires' disease
01100-01216,01280-01286,01790-01796,0212,0310,0391,11505,11515,
11595,1221,1304,1363,4800-4871,494-5089,5171,5178,51889,
5198-5199,74861
48289   Pneumonia oth spcf bact
01100-01216,01280-01286,01790-01796,0212,0310,0391,11505,11515,
11595,1221,1304,1363,4800-4871,494-5089,5171,5178,51889,
5198-5199,74861
4829   Bacterial pneumonia NOS
01100-01216,01280-01286,01790-01796,0212,0310,0391,11505,11515,
11595,1221,1304,1363,4800-4871,494-5089,5171,5178,51889,
5198-5199,74861
4830   Pneu mycplsm pneumoniae
01100-01216,01280-01286,01790-01796,0212,0310,0391,11505,11515,
11595,1221,1304,1363,4800-4871,494-5089,5171,5178,51889,
5198-5199,74861
4831   Pneumonia d/t chlamydia
01100-01216,01280-01286,01790-01796,0212,0310,0391,11505,11515,
11595,1221,1304,1363,4800-4871,494-5089,5171,5178,51889,
5198-5199,74861
4838   Pneumon oth spec orgnsm
01100-01216,01280-01286,01790-01796,0212,0310,0391,11505,11515,
11595,1221,1304,1363,4800-4871,494-5089,5171,5178,51889,
5198-5199,74861
4841   Pneum w cytomeg incl dis
01100-01216,01280-01286,01790-01796,0212,0310,0391,11505,11515,
11595,1221,1304,1363,4800-4871,494-5089,5171,5178,51889,
5198-5199,74861
4843   Pneumonia in whoop cough
01100-01216,01280-01286,01790-01796,0212,0310,0391,11505,11515,
11595,1221,1304,1363,4800-4871,494-5089,5171,5178,51889,
5198-5199,74861
4845   Pneumonia in anthrax
01100-01216,01280-01286,01790-01796,0212,0310,0391,11505,11515,
11595,1221,1304,1363,4800-4871,494-5089,5171,5178,51889,
5198-5199,74861
4846   Pneum in aspergillosis
01100-01216,01280-01286,01790-01796,0212,0310,0391,11505,11515,
11595,1221,1304,1363,4800-4871,494-5089,5171,5178,51889,
5198-5199,74861

4847　Pneum in oth sys mycoses
01100-01216,01280-01286,01790-01796,0212,0310,0391,11505,11515,
11595,1221,1304,1363,4800-4871,494-5089,5171,5178,51889,
5198-5199,74861

4848　Pneum in infect dis NEC
01100-01216,01280-01286,01790-01796,0212,0310,0391,11505,11515,
11595,1221,1304,1363,4800-4871,494-5089,5171,5178,51889,
5198-5199,74861

485　Bronchopneumonia org NOS
01100-01216,01280-01286,01790-01796,0212,0310,0391,11505,11515,
11595,1221,1304,1363,4800-4871,494-5089,5171,5178,51889,
5198-5199,74861

486　Pneumonia, organism NOS
01100-01216,01280-01286,01790-01796,0212,0310,0391,11505,11515,
11595,1221,1304,1363,4800-4871,494-5089,5171,5178,51889,
5198-5199,74861

4870　Influenza with pneumonia
01100-01216,01280-01286,01790-01796,0212,0310,0391,11505,11515,
11595,1221,1304,1363,4800-4871,494-5089,5171,5178,51889,
5198-5199,74861

4911　Mucopurul chr bronchitis
4911-4919,49320-49321

49120　Obs chr brnc w/o act exa
4911-4919,49320-49321

49121　Obs chr brnc w act exa
4911-4919,49320-49321

4918　Chronic bronchitis NEC
4911-4919,49320-49321

4919　Chronic bronchitis NOS
4911-4919,49320-49321

4928　Emphysema NEC
4920-4928,49320-49321

49301　Ext asthma w status asth
49300-49391,5178,51889,5198-5199

49311　Int asthma w status asth
49300-49391,5178,51889,5198-5199

49320　Ch ob asth w/o stat asth
4911-49391,5178,51889,5198-5199

49321　Ch ob asthma w stat asth
4911-49391,5178,51889,5198-5199

49391　Asthma w status asthmat
49300-49391,5178,51889,5198-5199

494　Bronchiectasis
01790-01796,4871,494,496,5061,5064-5069,74861

4950　Farmers' lung
01100-01216,01280-01286,01790-01796,0212,0310,0391,11505,11515,
11595,1221,1304,1363,4800-4871,494-5089,5171,5178,51889,
5198-5199,74861

4951　Bagassosis
01100-01216,01280-01286,01790-01796,0212,0310,0391,11505,11515,
11595,1221,1304,1363,4800-4871,494-5089,5171,5178,51889,
5198-5199,74861

4952　Bird-fanciers' lung
01100-01216,01280-01286,01790-01796,0212,0310,0391,11505,11515,
11595,1221,1304,1363,4800-4871,494-5089,5171,5178,51889,
5198-5199,74861

4953　Suberosis
01100-01216,01280-01286,01790-01796,0212,0310,0391,11505,11515,
11595,1221,1304,1363,4800-4871,494-5089,5171,5178,51889,
5198-5199,74861

4954　Malt workers' lung
01100-01216,01280-01286,01790-01796,0212,0310,0391,11505,11515,
11595,1221,1304,1363,4800-4871,494-5089,5171,5178,51889,
5198-5199,74861

4955　Mushroom workers' lung
01100-01216,01280-01286,01790-01796,0212,0310,0391,11505,11515,
11595,1221,1304,1363,4800-4871,494-5089,5171,5178,51889,
5198-5199,74861

4956　Mapl bark-stripprs' lung
01100-01216,01280-01286,01790-01796,0212,0310,0391,11505,11515,
11595,1221,1304,1363,4800-4871,494-5089,5171,5178,51889,
5198-5199,74861

4957　"ventilation" pneumonit
01100-01216,01280-01286,01790-01796,0212,0310,0391,11505,11515,
11595,1221,1304,1363,4800-4871,494-5089,5171,5178,51889,
5198-5199,74861

4958　Allerg alveol/pneum NEC
01100-01216,01280-01286,01790-01796,0212,0310,0391,11505,11515,
11595,1221,1304,1363,4800-4871,494-5089,5171,5178,51889,
5198-5199,74861

4959　Allerg alveol/pneum NOS
01100-01216,01280-01286,01790-01796,0212,0310,0391,11505,11515,
11595,1221,1304,1363,4800-4871,494-5089,5171,5178,51889,
5198-5199,74861

496　Chr airway obstruct NEC
01790-01796,4871,494,496,5061,5064-5069,74861

5060　Fum/vapor bronc/pneumon
01100-01216,01280-01286,01790-01796,0212,0310,0391,11505,11515,
11595,1221,1304,1363,4800-4871,494-5089,5171,5178,51889,
5198-5199,74861

5061　Fum/vapor ac pulm edema
01100-01216,01280-01286,01790-01796,0212,0310,0391,11505,11515,
11595,1221,1304,1363,4800-4871,494-5089,5171,5178,51889,
5198-5199,74861

5070　Food/vomit pneumonitis
01100-01216,01280-01286,01790-01796,0212,0310,0391,11505,11515,
11595,1221,1304,1363,4800-4871,494-5089,5171,5178,51889,
5198-5199,74861

5071　Oil/essence pneumonitis
01100-01216,01280-01286,01790-01796,0212,0310,0391,11505,11515,
11595,1221,1304,1363,4800-4871,494-5089,5171,5178,51889,
5198-5199,74861

5078　Solid/liq pneumonit NEC
01100-01216,01280-01286,01790-01796,0212,0310,0391,11505,11515,
11595,1221,1304,1363,4800-4871,494-5089,5171,5178,51889,
5198-5199,74861

5080　Ac pul manif d/t radiat
01100-01216,01280-01286,01790-01796,0212,0310,0391,11505,11515,
11595,1221,1304,1363,4800-4871,494-5089,5171,5178,51889,
5198-5199,74861

5081　Chr pul manif d/t radiat
01100-01216,01280-01286,01790-01796,0212,0310,0391,11505,11515,
11595,1221,1304,1363,4800-4871,494-5089,5171,5178,51889,
5198-5199,74861

5100　Empyema with fistula
5100-5109,5178,51889,5198-5199

5109　Empyema w/o fistula
5100-5109,5178,51889,5198-5199

5111　Bact pleur/effus not TB
01100-01216,01280-01286,01790-01796,5110-5119,5178,51889,
5198-5199

5118　Pleural effus NEC not TB
01100-01216,01280-01286,01790-01796,5110-5119,5178,51889,
5198-5199

5119　Pleural effusion NOS
01100-01216,01280-01286,01790-01796,5110-5119,5178,51889,
5198-5199

5120　Spont tens pneumothorax
5120-5128,5178,51889,5198-5199

5121　Iatrogenic pneumothorax
5120-5128,5178,51889,5198-5199

5128　Spont pneumothorax NEC
5120-5128,5178,51889,5198-5199

5130　Abscess of lung
0064,01100-01216,01280-01286,01790-01796,5130,5198-5199

5131　Abscess of mediastinum
5131,5198-5199

515　Postinflam pulm fibrosis
01100-01216,01280-01286,01790-01796,494-5089,515-5169,
5172-5178,51889,5198-5199,74861

5160　Pul alveolar proteinosis
01100-01216,01280-01286,01790-01796,494-5089,515-5169,
5172-5178,51889,5198-5199,74861

5161   Idio pulm hemosiderosis
01100-01216,01280-01286,01790-01796,494-5089,515-5169,
5172-5178,51889,5198-5199,74861
5162   Pulm alveolar microlith
01100-01216,01280-01286,01790-01796,494-5089,515-5169,
5172-5178,51889,5198-5199,74861
5163   Idio fibros alveolitis
01100-01216,01280-01286,01790-01796,494-5089,515-5169,
5172-5178,51889,5198-5199,74861
5168   Alveol pneumonopathy NEC
01100-01216,01280-01286,01790-01796,494-5089,515-5169,
5172-5178,51889,5198-5199,74861
5169   Alveol pneumonopathy NOS
01100-01216,01280-01286,01790-01796,494-5089,515-5169,
5172-5178,51889,5198-5199,74861
5171   Rheumatic pneumonia
01100-01216,01280-01286,01790-01796,4800-4871,494-5089,
515-5178,51889,5198-5199,74861
5172   Syst sclerosis lung dis
01100-01216,01280-01286,01790-01796,494-5089,515-5169,
5172-5178,51889,5198-5199,74861
5178   Lung involv in oth dis
01100-01216,01280-01286,01790-01796,494-5089,515-5169,
5172-5178,51889,5198-5199,74861
5180   Pulmonary collapse
5180,5198-5199
5181   Interstitial emphysema
5181,5198-5199
5184   Acute lung edema NOS
39891,4280-4289,5184,5198-5199
5185   Post traum pulm insuffic
5185,5198-5199
5186   Alrgc brncpul asprglosis
5186,5198-5199
51881   Respiratory failure
51881-51884,5198-5199,7991
51882   Other pulmonary insuff
51881-51884,5198-5199,7991
51883   Chr respi failure
51881-51884,5198-5199,7991
51884   Ac/chr respi failure
51881-51884,5198-5199,7991
51900   Tracheostomy comp NOS
51900-5191,5198-5199
51901   Tracheostomy infection
51900-5191,5198-5199
51902   Tracheostomy-mech comp
51900-5191,5198-5199
51909   Tracheostomy comp NEC
51900-5191,5198-5199
5192   Mediastinitis
5192-5193,5198-5199
5273   Salivary gland abscess
5270-5279,53789-5379
5274   Salivary gland fistula
5270-5279,53789-5379
5283   Cellulitis/abscess mouth
5280,5283,5290,5292
5304   Perforation of esophagus
5304,5307-53081,53083-5309
5307   Mallory-weiss syndrome
2515,4560,5302,5304,5307-53491,53501,53511,53521,53531,53541,
53551,53561,53783,56202-56203,56212-56213,5693,56985,5780-5789
53082   Esophageal hemorrhage
2515,4560,45620,45989-4599,5302,5307,53082,53100-53491,53501,
53511,53521,53531,53541,53551,53561,53783,56202-56203,
56212-56213,5693,56985,5780-5789
53084   Tracheoesophageal fstula
5304,5307-53081,53083-5309
53100   Ac stomach ulcer w hem
2515,4560,5302,5307,53082,53100-53491,53501,53511,53521,53531,
53541,53551,53561,53783-5379,56202-56203,56212-56213,5693,
56985,5780-5789

53101   Ac stomac ulc w hem-obst
2515,4560,5302,5307,53082,53100-53491,53501,53511,53521,53531,
53541,53551,53561,53783-5379,56202-56203,56212-56213,5693,
56985,5780-5789
53110   Ac stomach ulcer w perf
2515,4560,5302,5307,53082,53100-53491,53501,53511,53521,53531,
53541,53551,53561,53783-5379,56202-56203,56212-56213,5693,
56985,5780-5789
53111   Ac stom ulc w perf-obst
2515,4560,5302,5307,53082,53100-53491,53501,53511,53521,53531,
53541,53551,53561,53783-5379,56202-56203,56212-56213,5693,
56985,5780-5789
53120   Ac stomac ulc w hem/perf
2515,4560,5302,5307,53082,53100-53491,53501,53511,53521,53531,
53541,53551,53561,53783-5379,56202-56203,56212-56213,5693,
56985,5780-5789
53121   Ac stom ulc hem/perf-obs
2515,4560,5302,5307,53082,53100-53491,53501,53511,53521,53531,
53541,53551,53561,53783-5379,56202-56203,56212-56213,5693,
56985,5780-5789
53131   Ac stomach ulc NOS-obstr
2515,4560,5302,5307,53082,53100-53491,53501,53511,53521,53531,
53541,53551,53561,53783-5379,56202-56203,56212-56213,5693,
56985,5780-5789
53140   Chr stomach ulc w hem
2515,4560,5302,5307,53082,53100-53491,53501,53511,53521,53531,
53541,53551,53561,53783-5379,56202-56203,56212-56213,5693,
56985,5780-5789
53141   Chr stom ulc w hem-obstr
2515,4560,5302,5307,53082,53100-53491,53501,53511,53521,53531,
53541,53551,53561,53783-5379,56202-56203,56212-56213,5693,
56985,5780-5789
53150   Chr stomach ulcer w perf
2515,4560,5302,5307,53082,53100-53491,53501,53511,53521,53531,
53541,53551,53561,53783-5379,56202-56203,56212-56213,5693,
56985,5780-5789
53151   Chr stom ulc w perf-obst
2515,4560,5302,5307,53082,53100-53491,53501,53511,53521,53531,
53541,53551,53561,53783-5379,56202-56203,56212-56213,5693,
56985,5780-5789
53160   Chr stomach ulc hem/perf
2515,4560,5302,5307,53082,53100-53491,53501,53511,53521,53531,
53541,53551,53561,53783-5379,56202-56203,56212-56213,5693,
56985,5780-5789
53161   Chr stom ulc hem/perf-ob
2515,4560,5302,5307,53082,53100-53491,53501,53511,53521,53531,
53541,53551,53561,53783-5379,56202-56203,56212-56213,5693,
56985,5780-5789
53171   Chr stomach ulc NOS-obst
2515,4560,5302,5307,53082,53100-53491,53501,53511,53521,53531,
53541,53551,53561,53783-5379,56202-56203,56212-56213,5693,
56985,5780-5789
53191   Stomach ulcer NOS-obstr
2515,4560,5302,5307,53082,53100-53491,53501,53511,53521,53531,
53541,53551,53561,53783-5379,56202-56203,56212-56213,5693,
56985,5780-5789
53200   Ac duodenal ulcer w hem
2515,4560,5302,5307,53082,53100-53491,53501,53511,53521,53531,
53541,53551,53561,5373,53783-5379,56202-56203,56212-56213,5693,
56985,5780-5789
53201   Ac duoden ulc w hem-obst
2515,4560,5302,5307,53082,53100-53491,53501,53511,53521,53531,
53541,53551,53561,5373,53783-5379,56202-56203,56212-56213,5693,
56985,5780-5789
53210   Ac duodenal ulcer w perf
2515,4560,5302,5307,53082,53100-53491,53501,53511,53521,53531,
53541,53551,53561,5373,53783-5379,56202-56203,56212-56213,5693,
56985,5780-5789
53211   Ac duoden ulc perf-obstr
2515,4560,5302,5307,53082,53100-53491,53501,53511,53521,53531,
53541,53551,53561,5373,53783-5379,56202-56203,56212-56213,5693,
56985,5780-5789

53220 Ac duoden ulc w hem/perf
2515,4560,5302,5307,53082,53100-53491,53501,53511,53521,53531,
53541,53551,53561,5373,53783-5379,56202-56203,56212-56213,5693,
56985,5780-5789

53221 Ac duod ulc hem/perf-obs
2515,4560,5302,5307,53082,53100-53491,53501,53511,53521,53531,
53541,53551,53561,5373,53783-5379,56202-56203,56212-56213,5693,
56985,5780-5789

53231 Ac duodenal ulc NOS-obst
2515,4560,5302,5307,53082,53100-53491,53501,53511,53521,53531,
53541,53551,53561,5373,53783-5379,56202-56203,56212-56213,5693,
56985,5780-5789

53240 Chr duoden ulcer w hem
2515,4560,5302,5307,53082,53100-53491,53501,53511,53521,53531,
53541,53551,53561,5373,53783-5379,56202-56203,56212-56213,5693,
56985,5780-5789

53241 Chr duoden ulc hem-obstr
2515,4560,5302,5307,53082,53100-53491,53501,53511,53521,53531,
53541,53551,53561,5373,53783-5379,56202-56203,56212-56213,5693,
56985,5780-5789

53250 Chr duoden ulcer w perf
2515,4560,5302,5307,53082,53100-53491,53501,53511,53521,53531,
53541,53551,53561,5373,53783-5379,56202-56203,56212-56213,5693,
56985,5780-5789

53251 Chr duoden ulc perf-obst
2515,4560,5302,5307,53082,53100-53491,53501,53511,53521,53531,
53541,53551,53561,5373,53783-5379,56202-56203,56212-56213,5693,
56985,5780-5789

53260 Chr duoden ulc hem/perf
2515,4560,5302,5307,53082,53100-53491,53501,53511,53521,53531,
53541,53551,53561,5373,53783-5379,56202-56203,56212-56213,5693,
56985,5780-5789

53261 Chr duod ulc hem/perf-ob
2515,4560,5302,5307,53082,53100-53491,53501,53511,53521,53531,
53541,53551,53561,5373,53783-5379,56202-56203,56212-56213,5693,
56985,5780-5789

53271 Chr duoden ulc NOS-obstr
2515,4560,5302,5307,53082,53100-53491,53501,53511,53521,53531,
53541,53551,53561,5373,53783-5379,56202-56203,56212-56213,5693,
56985,5780-5789

53291 Duodenal ulcer NOS-obstr
2515,4560,5302,5307,53082,53100-53491,53501,53511,53521,53531,
53541,53551,53561,5373,53783-5379,56202-56203,56212-56213,5693,
56985,5780-5789

53300 Ac peptic ulcer w hemorr
2515,4560,5302,5307,53082,53100-53491,53501,53511,53521,53531,
53541,53551,53561,5373,53783-5379,56202-56203,56212-56213,5693,
56985,5780-5789

53301 Ac peptic ulc w hem-obst
2515,4560,5302,5307,53082,53100-53491,53501,53511,53521,53531,
53541,53551,53561,5373,53783-5379,56202-56203,56212-56213,5693,
56985,5780-5789

53310 Ac peptic ulcer w perfor
2515,4560,5302,5307,53082,53100-53491,53501,53511,53521,53531,
53541,53551,53561,5373,53783-5379,56202-56203,56212-56213,5693,
56985,5780-5789

53311 Ac peptic ulc w perf-obs
2515,4560,5302,5307,53082,53100-53491,53501,53511,53521,53531,
53541,53551,53561,5373,53783-5379,56202-56203,56212-56213,5693,
56985,5780-5789

53320 Ac peptic ulc w hem/perf
2515,4560,5302,5307,53082,53100-53491,53501,53511,53521,53531,
53541,53551,53561,5373,53783-5379,56202-56203,56212-56213,5693,
56985,5780-5789

53321 Ac pept ulc hem/perf-obs
2515,4560,5302,5307,53082,53100-53491,53501,53511,53521,53531,
53541,53551,53561,5373,53783-5379,56202-56203,56212-56213,5693,
56985,5780-5789

53331 Ac peptic ulcer NOS-obst
2515,4560,5302,5307,53082,53100-53491,53501,53511,53521,53531,
53541,53551,53561,5373,53783-5379,56202-56203,56212-56213,5693,
56985,5780-5789

53340 Chr peptic ulcer w hem
2515,4560,5302,5307,53082,53100-53491,53501,53511,53521,53531,
53541,53551,53561,5373,53783-5379,56202-56203,56212-56213,5693,
56985,5780-5789

53341 Chr peptic ulc w hem-obs
2515,4560,5302,5307,53082,53100-53491,53501,53511,53521,53531,
53541,53551,53561,5373,53783-5379,56202-56203,56212-56213,5693,
56985,5780-5789

53350 Chr peptic ulcer w perf
2515,4560,5302,5307,53082,53100-53491,53501,53511,53521,53531,
53541,53551,53561,5373,53783-5379,56202-56203,56212-56213,5693,
56985,5780-5789

53351 Chr peptic ulc perf-obst
2515,4560,5302,5307,53082,53100-53491,53501,53511,53521,53531,
53541,53551,53561,5373,53783-5379,56202-56203,56212-56213,5693,
56985,5780-5789

53360 Chr pept ulc w hem/perf
2515,4560,5302,5307,53082,53100-53491,53501,53511,53521,53531,
53541,53551,53561,5373,53783-5379,56202-56203,56212-56213,5693,
56985,5780-5789

53361 Chr pept ulc hem/perf-ob
2515,4560,5302,5307,53082,53100-53491,53501,53511,53521,53531,
53541,53551,53561,5373,53783-5379,56202-56203,56212-56213,5693,
56985,5780-5789

53371 Chr peptic ulcer NOS-obs
2515,4560,5302,5307,53082,53100-53491,53501,53511,53521,53531,
53541,53551,53561,5373,53783-5379,56202-56203,56212-56213,5693,
56985,5780-5789

53391 Peptic ulcer NOS-obstruc
2515,4560,5302,5307,53082,53100-53491,53501,53511,53521,53531,
53541,53551,53561,5373,53783-5379,56202-56203,56212-56213,5693,
56985,5780-5789

53400 Ac marginal ulcer w hem
2515,4560,5302,5307,53082,53100-53491,53501,53511,53521,53531,
53541,53551,53561,53783-5379,56202-56203,56212-56213,5693,
56985,5780-5789

53401 Ac margin ulc w hem-obst
2515,4560,5302,5307,53082,53100-53491,53501,53511,53521,53531,
53541,53551,53561,53783-5379,56202-56203,56212-56213,5693,
56985,5780-5789

53410 Ac marginal ulcer w perf
2515,4560,5302,5307,53082,53100-53491,53501,53511,53521,53531,
53541,53551,53561,53783-5379,56202-56203,56212-56213,5693,
56985,5780-5789

53411 Ac margin ulc w perf-obs
2515,4560,5302,5307,53082,53100-53491,53501,53511,53521,53531,
53541,53551,53561,53783-5379,56202-56203,56212-56213,5693,
56985,5780-5789

53420 Ac margin ulc w hem/perf
2515,4560,5302,5307,53082,53100-53491,53501,53511,53521,53531,
53541,53551,53561,53783-5379,56202-56203,56212-56213,5693,
56985,5780-5789

53421 Ac marg ulc hem/perf-obs
2515,4560,5302,5307,53082,53100-53491,53501,53511,53521,53531,
53541,53551,53561,53783-5379,56202-56203,56212-56213,5693,
56985,5780-5789

53431 Ac marginal ulc NOS-obst
2515,4560,5302,5307,53082,53100-53491,53501,53511,53521,53531,
53541,53551,53561,53783-5379,56202-56203,56212-56213,5693,
56985,5780-5789

53440 Chr marginal ulcer w hem
2515,4560,5302,5307,53082,53100-53491,53501,53511,53521,53531,
53541,53551,53561,53783-5379,56202-56203,56212-56213,5693,
56985,5780-5789

53441 Chr margin ulc w hem-obs
2515,4560,5302,5307,53082,53100-53491,53501,53511,53521,53531,
53541,53551,53561,53783-5379,56202-56203,56212-56213,5693,
56985,5780-5789

53450 Chr marginal ulc w perf
2515,4560,5302,5307,53082,53100-53491,53501,53511,53521,53531,
53541,53551,53561,53783-5379,56202-56203,56212-56213,5693,
56985,5780-5789

53451   Chr margin ulc perf-obst
2515,4560,5302,5307,53082,53100-53491,53501,53511,53521,53531,
53541,53551,53561,53783-5379,56202-56203,56212-56213,5693,
56985,5780-5789
53460   Chr margin ulc hem/perf
2515,4560,5302,5307,53082,53100-53491,53501,53511,53521,53531,
53541,53551,53561,53783-5379,56202-56203,56212-56213,5693,
56985,5780-5789
53461   Chr marg ulc hem/perf-ob
2515,4560,5302,5307,53082,53100-53491,53501,53511,53521,53531,
53541,53551,53561,53783-5379,56202-56203,56212-56213,5693,
56985,5780-5789
53471   Chr marginal ulc NOS-obs
2515,4560,5302,5307,53082,53100-53491,53501,53511,53521,53531,
53541,53551,53561,53783-5379,56202-56203,56212-56213,5693,
56985,5780-5789
53491   Gastrojejun ulc NOS-obst
2515,4560,5302,5307,53082,53100-53491,53501,53511,53521,53531,
53541,53551,53561,53783-5379,56202-56203,56212-56213,5693,
56985,5780-5789
53501   Acute gastritis w hmrhg
2515,4560,5302,5307,53082,53100-53491,53501,53511,53521,53531,
53541,53551,53561,53783,56202-56203,56212-56213,5693,56985,
5780-5789
53511   Atrph gastritis w hmrhg
2515,4560,5302,5307,53082,53100-53491,53501,53511,53521,53531,
53541,53551,53561,53783,56202-56203,56212-56213,5693,56985,
5780-5789
53521   Gstr mcsl hyprt w hmrg
2515,4560,5302,5307,53082,53100-53491,53501,53511,53521,53531,
53541,53551,53561,53783,56202-56203,56212-56213,5693,56985,
5780-5789
53531   Alchl gstritis w hmrhg
2515,4560,5302,5307,53082,53100-53491,53501,53511,53521,53531,
53541,53551,53561,53783,56202-56203,56212-56213,5693,56985,
5780-5789
53541   Oth spf gastrt w hmrhg
2515,4560,5302,5307,53082,53100-53491,53501,53511,53521,53531,
53541,53551,53561,53783,56202-56203,56212-56213,5693,56985,
5780-5789
53551   Gstr/ddnts NOS w hmrhg
2515,4560,5302,5307,53082,53100-53491,53501,53511,53521,53531,
53541,53551,53561,53783,56202-56203,56212-56213,5693,56985,
5780-5789
53561   Duodenitis w hmrhg
2515,4560,5302,5307,53082,53100-53491,53501,53511,53521,53531,
53541,53551,53561,53783,56202-56203,56212-56213,5693,56985,
5780-5789
5361   Ac dilation of stomach
5361
53640   Gastrostomy comp NOS
53640-53649,9974,99791-99799,99881,99883-9989
53641   Gastrostomy infection
53640-53649,9974,99791-99799,99881,99883-9989
53642   Gastrostomy comp-mech
53640-53649,9974,99791-99799,99881,99883-9989
53649   Gastrostomy comp NEC
53640-53649,9974,99791-99799,99881,99883-9989
5370   Acq pyloric stenosis
5363-5370,5373,7505,7508-7509,7511,7515
5373   Duodenal obstruction NEC
5373,7508-7509,7511,7515
5374   Gastric/duodenal fistula
5374,7508-7509,7515
53783   Angio stm/dudn w hmrhg
2515,4560,5302,5307,53082,53100-53491,53501,53511,53521,53531,
53541,53551,53561,53783,56202-56203,56212-56213,5693,56985,
5780-5789
5400   Ac append w peritonitis
53789-5439
5401   Abscess of appendix
53789-5439

5409   Acute appendicitis NOS
53789-5439
55000   Unilat ing hernia w gang
53789-5379,55000-55093,5528-5529,5538-5539
55001   Recur unil ing hern-gang
53789-5379,55000-55093,5528-5529,5538-5539
55002   Bilat ing hernia w gang
53789-5379,55000-55093,5528-5529,5538-5539
55003   Recur bil ing hern-gang
53789-5379,55000-55093,5528-5529,5538-5539
55010   Unilat ing hernia w obst
53789-5379,55000-55093,5528-5529,5538-5539
55011   Recur unil ing hern-obst
53789-5379,55000-55093,5528-5529,5538-5539
55012   Bilat ing hernia w obst
53789-5379,55000-55093,5528-5529,5538-5539
55013   Recur bil ing hern-obstr
53789-5379,55000-55093,5528-5529,5538-5539
55100   Unil femoral hern w gang
53789-5379,55100-55103,5528-55303,5538-5539
55101   Rec unil fem hern w gang
53789-5379,55100-55103,5528-55303,5538-5539
55102   Bilat fem hern w gang
53789-5379,55100-55103,5528-55303,5538-5539
55103   Recur bil fem hern-gang
53789-5379,55100-55103,5528-55303,5538-5539
5511   Umbilical hernia w gangr
53789-5379,5511-55129,5521-55229,5528-5529,5531-55329,5538-5539
55120   Gangr ventral hernia NOS
53789-5379,5511-55129,5521-55229,5528-5529,5531-55329,5538-5539
55121   Gangr incisional hernia
53789-5379,5511-55129,5521-55229,5528-5529,5531-55329,5538-5539
55129   Gang ventral hernia NEC
53789-5379,5511-55129,5521-55229,5528-5529,5531-55329,5538-5539
5513   Diaphragm hernia w gangr
5513,5523-5529,5533-5539
5518   Hernia, site NEC w gangr
53789-5379,55000-5539
5519   Hernia, site NOS w gangr
53789-5379,55000-5539
55200   Unil femoral hern w obst
53789-5379,55100-55103,55200-55203,5528-55303,5538-5539
55201   Rec unil fem hern w obst
53789-5379,55100-55103,55200-55203,5528-55303,5538-5539
55202   Bil femoral hern w obstr
53789-5379,55100-55103,55200-55203,5528-55303,5538-5539
55203   Rec bil fem hern w obstr
53789-5379,55100-55103,55200-55203,5528-55303,5538-5539
5521   Umbilical hernia w obstr
5511-55129,5521-55229,5528-5529,5538-5539
55220   Obstr ventral hernia NOS
5511-55129,5521-55229,5528-5529,5538-5539
55221   Obstr incisional hernia
5511-55129,5521-55229,5528-5529,5538-5539
55229   Obstr ventral hernia NEC
5511-55129,5521-55229,5528-5529,5538-5539
5523   Diaphragm hernia w obstr
5513,5523-5529,5533-5539
5528   Hernia, site NEC w obstr
55000-5539
5529   Hernia, site NOS w obstr
55000-5539
5570   Ac vasc insuff intestine
5570-5571
5581   Radiation gastroenterit
5581
5582   Toxic gastroenteritis
5582
5600   Intussusception
5600-5609,56989-5699
5601   Paralytic ileus
5600-5609,56989-5699

5602   Volvulus of intestine
5600-5609,56989-5699
56030   Impaction intestine NOS
5600-5609,56989-5699
56031   Gallstone ileus
5600-5609,56989-5699
56039   Impaction intestine NEC
5600-5609,56989-5699
56081   Intestinal adhes w obstr
5600-5609,56989-5699
56089   Intestinal obstruct NEC
5600-5609,56989-5699
5609   Intestinal obstruct NOS
5600-5609,56989-5699
56202   Dvrtclo sml int w hmrhg
2515,4560,5302,5307,53082,53100-53491,53501,53511,53521,53531,
53541,53551,53561,53783,56202-56203,56212-56213,5693,56985,
5780-5789
56203   Dvrtcli sml int w hmrhg
2515,4560,5302,5307,53082,53100-53491,53501,53511,53521,53531,
53541,53551,53561,53783,56202-56203,56212-56213,5693,56985,
5780-5789
56212   Dvrtclo colon w hmrhg
2515,4560,5302,5307,53082,53100-53491,53501,53511,53521,53531,
53541,53551,53561,53783,56202-56203,56212-56213,5693,56985,
5780-5789
56213   Dvrtcli colon w hmrhg
2515,4560,5302,5307,53082,53100-53491,53501,53511,53521,53531,
53541,53551,53561,53783,56202-56203,56212-56213,5693,56985,
5780-5789
566   Anal & rectal abscess
566
5670   Peritonitis in infec dis
5670-5679,56989-5699
5671   Pneumococcal peritonitis
5670-5679,56989-5699
5672   Suppurat peritonitis NEC
5670-5679,56989-5699
5678   Peritonitis NEC
5670-5679,56989-5699
5679   Peritonitis NOS
5670-5679,56989-5699
56881   Hemoperitoneum
56881
5693   Rectal & anal hemorrhage
2515,4560,5302,5307,53082,53100-53491,53501,53511,53521,53531,
53541,53551,53561,53783,56202-56203,56212-56213,5693,56985,
5780-5789
5695   Intestinal abscess
5695
56960   Colstomy/enter comp NOS
56960-56969
56961   Colosty/enterost infectn
56960-56969
56962   Colosty/enter comp-mech
53640-53649,56960-56969,9974,99791-99799,99881,99883-9989
56969   Colstmy/enteros comp NEC
56960-56969
56983   Perforation of intestine
56983
56985   Angio intes w hmrhg
2515,4560,5302,5307,53082,53100-53491,53501,53511,53521,53531,
53541,53551,53561,53783,56202-56203,56212-56213,5693,56985,
5780-5789
570   Acute necrosis of liver
570,5734-5739
5712   Alcohol cirrhosis liver
5712,5738-5739
57149   Chronic hepatitis NEC
57149-5719,5738-5739
5715   Cirrhosis of liver NOS
57149-5719,5738-5739

5716   Biliary cirrhosis
57149-5719,5738-5739
5720   Abscess of liver
0063,5720-5721,5738-5739
5721   Portal pyemia
0063,5720-5721,5738-5739
5722   Hepatic coma
5722,5738-5739
5724   Hepatorenal syndrome
5724,5738-5739
5731   Hepatitis in viral dis
5731-5733,5738-5739
5732   Hepatitis in oth inf dis
5731-5733,5738-5739
5733   Hepatitis NOS
5731-5733,5738-5739
5734   Hepatic infarction
570,5734-5739
57400   Cholelith w ac cholecyst
57400-57421,57440,57460-57461,57480-57481,5750-57512,5759,
5768-5769
57401   Cholelith/ac gb inf-obst
57400-57421,57460-57461,57480-57481,5750-57512,5759,5768-5769
57410   Cholelith w cholecys NEC
57400-57421,57460-57461,57480-57481,5750-57512,5759,5768-5769
57411   Cholelith/gb inf NEC-obs
57400-57421,57460-57461,57480-57481,5750-57512,5759,5768-5769
57421   Cholelithias NOS w obstr
57400-57421,57460-57461,57480-57481,5750-57512,5759,5768-5769
57430   Choledocholith/ac gb inf
57430-57512,5768-5769
57431   Choledochlith/ac gb-obst
57430-57512,5768-5769
57440   Choledochlith/gb inf NEC
57430-57512,5768-5769
57441   Choledochlith/gb NEC-obs
57430-57512,5768-5769
57450   Choledocholithiasis NOS
57430-57512,5768-5769
57451   Choledochlith NOS w obst
57430-57512,5768-5769
57460   Gall&bil cal w/ac w/o ob
57460-57461,5750-57512,5759,5768-5769
57461   Gall&bil cal w/ac w obs
57460-57461,5750-57512,5759,5768-5769
57470   Gal&bil cal w/oth w/o ob
57430-57512,5768-5769
57471   Gall&bil cal w/oth w obs
57430-57512,5768-5769
57480   Gal&bil cal w/ac&chr w/o
57480-57481,5750-57512,5759,5768-5769
57481   Gall&bil cal w/ac&ch w ob
57480-57481,5750-57512,5759,5768-5769
57490   Gall&bil cal w/o cho w/o
57430-57512,5768-5769
57491   Gall&bil cal w/o ch w ob
57430-57512,5768-5769
5750   Acute cholecystitis
57460-57461,57480-57481,5750-57512,5759,5768-5769
57512   Acte & chr cholecystitis
5750-57512,5759,5768-5769
5752   Obstruction gallbladder
5752-5759,5768-5769
5753   Hydrops of gallbladder
5752-5759,5768-5769
5754   Perforation gallbladder
5752-5759,5768-5769
5755   Fistula of gallbladder
5752-5759,5768-5769
5761   Cholangitis
5761,5768-5769
5763   Perforation of bile duct
5763-5764,5768-5769

5764   Fistula of bile duct
5763-5764,5768-5769
5770   Acute pancreatitis
5770-5771,5778-5779
5772   Pancreat cyst/pseudocyst
5772-5779
5780   Hematemesis
2515,4560,5302,5307,53082,53100-53491,53501,53511,53521,53531,
53541,53551,53561,53783,56202-56203,56212-56213,5693,56985,
5780-5789
5781   Blood in stool
2515,4560,5302,5307,53082,53100-53491,53501,53511,53521,53531,
53541,53551,53561,53783,56202-56203,56212-56213,5693,56985,
5780-5789
5789   Gastrointest hemorr NOS
2515,4560,5302,5307,53082,53100-53491,53501,53511,53521,53531,
53541,53551,53561,53783,56202-56203,56212-56213,5693,56985,
5780-5789
5793   Intest postop nonabsorb
5793-5799
5800   Ac proliferat nephritis
01600-01606,01630-01636,01690-01696,01790-01796,09810,09819,
09830-09831,09889,1122,13100,1318-1319,25040-25043,25080-25093,
27410,27419,5800-591,5930-5932,59389-5939,5997-5999
5804   Ac rapidly progr nephrit
01600-01606,01630-01636,01690-01696,01790-01796,09810,09819,
09830-09831,09889,1122,13100,1318-1319,25040-25043,25080-25093,
27410,27419,5800-591,5930-5932,59389-5939,5997-5999
58081   Ac nephritis in oth dis
01600-01606,01630-01636,01690-01696,01790-01796,09810,09819,
09830-09831,09889,1122,13100,1318-1319,25040-25043,25080-25093,
27410,27419,5800-591,5930-5932,59389-5939,5997-5999
58089   Acute nephritis NEC
01600-01606,01630-01636,01690-01696,01790-01796,09810,09819,
09830-09831,09889,1122,13100,1318-1319,27410,27419,5800-591,
5930-5932,59389-5939,5997-5999
5809   Acute nephritis NOS
01600-01606,01630-01636,01690-01696,01790-01796,09810,09819,
09830-09831,09889,1122,13100,1318-1319,25040-25043,25080-25093,
27410,27419,5800-591,5930-5932,59389-5939,5997-5999
5810   Nephrotic syn, prolifer
01600-01606,01630-01636,01690-01696,01790-01796,09810,09819,
09830-09831,09889,1122,13100,1318-1319,25040-25043,25080-25093,
27410,27419,5800-591,5930-5932,59389-5939,5997-5999
5811   Epimembranous nephritis
01600-01606,01630-01636,01690-01696,01790-01796,09810,09819,
09830-09831,09889,1122,13100,1318-1319,25040-25043,25080-25093,
27410,27419,5800-591,5930-5932,59389-5939,5997-5999
5812   Membranoprolif nephrosis
01600-01606,01630-01636,01690-01696,01790-01796,09810,09819,
09830-09831,09889,1122,13100,1318-1319,25040-25043,25080-25093,
27410,27419,5800-591,5930-5932,59389-5939,5997-5999
5813   Minimal change nephrosis
01600-01606,01630-01636,01690-01696,01790-01796,09810,09819,
09830-09831,09889,1122,13100,1318-1319,25040-25043,25080-25093,
27410,27419,5800-591,5930-5932,59389-5939,5997-5999
58181   Nephrotic syn in oth dis
01600-01606,01630-01636,01690-01696,01790-01796,09810,09819,
09830-09831,09889,1122,13100,1318-1319,25040-25043,25080-25093,
27410,27419,5800-591,5930-5932,59389-5939,5997-5999
58189   Nephrotic syndrome NEC
01600-01606,01630-01636,01690-01696,01790-01796,09810,09819,
09830-09831,09889,1122,13100,1318-1319,25040-25043,25080-25093,
27410,27419,5800-591,5930-5932,59389-5939,5997-5999
5819   Nephrotic syndrome NOS
01600-01606,01630-01636,01690-01696,01790-01796,09810,09819,
09830-09831,09889,1122,13100,1318-1319,25040-25043,25080-25093,
27410,27419,5800-591,5930-5932,59389-5939,5997-5999
5834   Rapidly prog nephrit NOS
01600-01606,01630-01636,01690-01696,01790-01796,09810,09819,
09830-09831,09889,1122,13100,1318-1319,25040-25043,25080-25093,
27410,27419,5800-591,5930-5932,59389-5939,5997-5999

5845   Lower nephron nephrosis
25040-25043,25080-25093,27410,27419,5800-591,5930-5932,
59389-5939,5997-5999,7530-7533,7539
5846   Ac renal fail, cort necr
25040-25043,25080-25093,27410,27419,5800-591,5930-5932,
59389-5939,5997-5999,7530-7533,7539
5847   Ac ren fail, medull necr
25040-25043,25080-25093,27410,27419,5800-591,5930-5932,
59389-5939,5997-5999,7530-7533,7539
5848   Ac renal failure NEC
25040-25043,25080-25093,27410,27419,5800-591,5930-5932,
59389-5939,5997-5999
5849   Acute renal failure NOS
25040-25043,25080-25093,27410,27419,5800-591,5930-5932,
59389-5939,5997-5999,7530-7533,7539
585   Chronic renal failure
25040-25043,25080-25093,27410,27419,5800-591,5930-5932,
59389-5939,5997-5999,7530-7533,7539
59010   Ac pyelonephritis NOS
01600-01606,01630-01636,01690-01696,01790-01796,09810,09819,
09830-09831,09889,1122,13100,1318-1319,25040-25043,25080-25093,
27410,27419,5800-591,5930-5932,59389-5939,5990,5997-5999
59011   Ac pyelonephr w med necr
01600-01606,01630-01636,01690-01696,01790-01796,09810,09819,
09830-09831,09889,1122,13100,1318-1319,25040-25043,25080-25093,
27410,27419,5800-591,5930-5932,59389-5939,5990,5997-5999
5902   Renal/perirenal abscess
01600-01606,01630-01636,01690-01696,01790-01796,09810,09819,
09830-09831,09889,1122,13100,1318-1319,25040-25043,25080-25093,
27410,27419,5800-591,5930-5932,59389-5939,5990,5997-5999
5903   Pyeloureteritis cystica
01600-01606,01630-01636,01690-01696,01790-01796,09810,09819,
09830-09831,09889,1122,13100,1318-1319,27410,27419,5800-591,
5930-5932,59389-5939,5990,5997-5999
59080   Pyelonephritis NOS
01600-01606,01630-01636,01690-01696,01790-01796,09810,09819,
09830-09831,09889,1122,13100,1318-1319,27410,27419,5800-591,
5930-5932,59389-5939,5990,5997-5999
59081   Pyelonephrit in oth dis
01600-01606,01630-01636,01690-01696,01790-01796,09810,09819,
09830-09831,09889,1122,13100,1318-1319,27410,27419,5800-591,
5930-5932,59389-5939,5990,5997-5999
5909   Infection of kidney NOS
01600-01606,01630-01636,01690-01696,01790-01796,09810,09819,
09830-09831,09889,1122,13100,1318-1319,27410,27419,5800-591,
5930-5932,59389-5939,5990,5997-5999
591   Hydronephrosis
01600-01606,01630-01636,01690-01696,01790-01796,09810,09819,
09830-09831,09889,1122,13100,1318-1319,27410,27419,5800-591,
5930-5932,59389-5939,5990,5997-5999
5921   Calculus of ureter
5920-5929,5933-5935,59389-5949,5996-5999
5935   Hydroureter
5933-5935,59389-5939,5950-5959,5968-5969,5990,5996-5999,
7534-7535,7539
5950   Acute cystitis
01610-01616,01630-01636,01690-01696,01790-01796,0980,09811,
0982,09839,09889,1122,13100,1318-1319,5933-5935,59389-5939,
5950-5959,5968-5969,5990,5996-5999
5951   Chr interstit cystitis
01610-01616,01630-01636,01690-01696,01790-01796,0980,09811,
0982,09839,09889,1122,13100,1318-1319,5933-5935,59389-5939,
5950-5959,5968-5969,5990,5996-5999
5952   Chronic cystitis NEC
01610-01616,01630-01636,01690-01696,01790-01796,0980,09811,
0982,09839,09889,1122,13100,1318-1319,5933-5935,59389-5939,
5950-5959,5968-5969,5990,5996-5999
5954   Cystitis in oth dis
01610-01616,01630-01636,01690-01696,01790-01796,0980,09811,
0982,09839,09889,1122,13100,1318-1319,5933-5935,59389-5939,
5950-5959,5968-5969,5990,5996-5999

59581   Cystitis cystica
01610-01616,01630-01636,01690-01696,01790-01796,0980,09811,
0982,09839,09889,1122,13100,1318-1319,5933-5935,59389-5939,
5950-5959,5968-5969,5990,5996-5999

59582   Irradiation cystitis
01610-01616,01630-01636,01690-01696,01790-01796,0980,09811,
0982,09839,09889,1122,13100,1318-1319,5933-5935,59389-5939,
5950-5959,5968-5969,5990,5996-5999

59589   Cystitis NEC
01610-01616,01630-01636,01690-01696,01790-01796,0980,09811,
0982,09839,09889,1122,13100,1318-1319,5933-5935,59389-5939,
5950-5959,5968-5969,5990,5996-5999

5959   Cystitis NOS
01610-01616,01630-01636,01690-01696,01790-01796,0980,09811,
0982,09839,09889,1122,13100,1318-1319,5933-5935,59389-5939,
5950-5959,5968-5969,5990,5996-5999

5960   Bladder neck obstruction
185,1880-1889,1893-1899,5960,5964-59659,5968-5969,600-6029

5961   Intestinovesical fistula
0980,0982,09839,09889,5961-5962,5968-5969,5997-5999,7881

5962   Vesical fistula NEC
0980,0982,09839,09889,5961-5962,5968-5969,5997-5999,7881

5964   Atony of bladder
5964-59659,5968-5969,5997-5999,7881

5966   Bladder rupt, nontraum
5966-5969,5997-5999,7881

5967   Bladder wall hemorrhage
5966-5969,5997-5999,7881

5970   Urethral abscess
0980,0982,09839,09889,09940-09949,1122,13100,13102,1318-1319,
5970-59801,5988-5990,5996-5999,6071-60783,60789-6079,
6084-60881,60885,60889,75261-75269,7528-7529,7536-7539,7881

5981   Traum urethral stricture
0980,0982,09839,09889,13102,5981-5989,5996-5999,75261-75269,
7536-7539,7881

5982   Postop urethral strictur
0980,0982,09839,09889,13102,5981-5989,5996-5999,75261-75269,
7536-7539,7881

5990   Urin tract infection NOS
0982,09839,09889,09940-09949,1122,13100,1318-1319,59010-591,
59389-5939,5950-5959,5990,5996-5999,7881,99664

5994   Urethral false passage
5970-5989,5991-5999,6071-60783,60789-6079,6084-60881,60885,
60889,75261-75269,7528-7529,7539,7881

5996   Urinary obstruction NOS
185,1880-1889,1892-1899,27411,34461,5921-5929,5933-5935,
59389-5960,59651-59659,5968-6029,7530-7539,7881

5997   Hematuria
5920-5929,59389-5949,5966-5967,5997-5999

6010   Acute prostatitis
09812,09832,09889,1122,13100,13103,1318-1319,600-6029

6012   Abscess of prostate
09812,09832,09889,1122,13100,13103,1318-1319,600-6029

6013   Prostatocystitis
09812,09832,09889,1122,13100,13103,1318-1319,600-6029

6021   Prostatic congest/hemorr
09812,09832,09889,1122,13100,13103,1318-1319,600-6029

6031   Infected hydrocele
1122,13100,1318-1319,6030-6039

6040   Orchitis with abscess
0720,09813-09814,09833-09834,09889,1122,13100,1318-1319,
6040-60499

61172   Lump or mass in breast
6100-6119

6140   Ac salpingo-oophoritis
01660-01696,01790-01796,09815-09817,09835-09837,09889,1122,
13100,1318-1319,6140-6159,6168-6169,6258-6259,6298-6299,
7528-7529

6143   Acute parametritis
01660-01696,01790-01796,09815-09817,09835-09837,09889,1122,
13100,1318-1319,6140-6159,6168-6169,6258-6259,6298-6299,
7528-7529

6145   Ac pelv peritonitis-fem
01660-01696,01790-01796,09815-09817,09835-09837,09889,1122,
13100,1318-1319,6140-6159,6168-6169,6258-6259,6298-6299,
7528-7529

6150   Ac uterine inflammation
01660-01696,01790-01796,09815-09817,09835-09837,09889,1122,
13100,1318-1319,6140-6160,6168-6169,6218-6219,6258-6259,
6298-6299,7528-7529

6163   Bartholin's glnd abscess
01670-01696,01790-01796,1121-1122,13100-13101,1318-1319,
61610-6169,6243-6249,6258-6259,6298-6299,7528-7529

6164   Abscess of vulva NEC
01670-01696,01790-01796,1121-1122,13100-13101,1318-1319,
61610-6169,6243-6249,6258-6259,6298-6299,7528-7529

6207   Broad ligament hematoma
6206-6209,6258-6259,6298-6299,7528-7529

63400   Spon abor w pel inf-unsp
63400-6389,64000-64123,64680-64693,64890-650,66940-66944,
66980-66994

63401   Spon abor w pelv inf-inc
63400-6389,64000-64123,64680-64693,64890-650,66940-66944,
66980-66994

63402   Spon abor w pel inf-comp
63400-6389,64000-64123,64680-64693,64890-650,66940-66944,
66980-66994

63410   Spon abor w hemorr-unsp
63400-6389,64000-64123,64680-64693,64890-650,66940-66944,
66980-66994

63411   Spon abort w hemorr-inc
63400-6389,64000-64123,64680-64693,64890-650,66940-66944,
66980-66994

63412   Spon abort w hemorr-comp
63400-6389,64000-64123,64680-64693,64890-650,66940-66944,
66980-66994

63420   Spon ab w pel damag-unsp
63400-6389,64000-64123,64680-64693,64890-650,66940-66944,
66980-66994

63421   Spon ab w pelv damag-inc
63400-6389,64000-64123,64680-64693,64890-650,66940-66944,
66980-66994

63422   Spon ab w pel damag-comp
63400-6389,64000-64123,64680-64693,64890-650,66940-66944,
66980-66994

63430   Spon ab w ren fail-unsp
63400-6389,64000-64123,64680-64693,64890-650,66940-66944,
66980-66994

63431   Spon ab w ren fail-inc
63400-6389,64000-64123,64680-64693,64890-650,66940-66944,
66980-66994

63432   Spon ab w ren fail-comp
63400-6389,64000-64123,64680-64693,64890-650,66940-66944,
66980-66994

63440   Spon ab w metab dis-unsp
63400-6389,64000-64123,64680-64693,64890-650,66940-66944,
66980-66994

63441   Spon ab w metab dis-inc
63400-6389,64000-64123,64680-64693,64890-650,66940-66944,
66980-66994

63442   Spon ab w metab dis-comp
63400-6389,64000-64123,64680-64693,64890-650,66940-66944,
66980-66994

63450   Spon abort w shock-unsp
63400-6389,64000-64123,64680-64693,64890-650,66940-66944,
66980-66994

63451   Spon abort w shock-inc
63400-6389,64000-64123,64680-64693,64890-650,66940-66944,
66980-66994

63452   Spon abort w shock-comp
63400-6389,64000-64123,64680-64693,64890-650,66940-66944,
66980-66994

63460   Spon abort w embol-unsp
63400-6389,64000-64123,64680-64693,64890-650,66940-66944,
66980-66994

63461   Spon abort w embol-inc
63400-6389,64000-64123,64680-64693,64890-650,66940-66944,
66980-66994
63462   Spon abort w embol-comp
63400-6389,64000-64123,64680-64693,64890-650,66940-66944,
66980-66994
63470   Spon ab w compl NEC-unsp
63400-6389,64000-64123,64680-64693,64890-650,66940-66944,
66980-66994
63471   Spon ab w compl NEC-inc
63400-6389,64000-64123,64680-64693,64890-650,66940-66944,
66980-66994
63472   Spon ab w compl NEC-comp
63400-6389,64000-64123,64680-64693,64890-650,66940-66944,
66980-66994
63480   Spon ab w compl NOS-unsp
63400-6389,64000-64123,64680-64693,64890-650,66940-66944,
66980-66994
63481   Spon ab w compl NOS-inc
63400-6389,64000-64123,64680-64693,64890-650,66940-66944,
66980-66994
63482   Spon ab w compl NOS-comp
63400-6389,64000-64123,64680-64693,64890-650,66940-66944,
66980-66994
63490   Spon abort uncompl-unsp
63400-6389,64000-64123,64680-64693,64890-650,66940-66944,
66980-66994
63491   Spon abort uncompl-inc
63400-6389,64000-64123,64680-64693,64890-650,66940-66944,
66980-66994
63492   Spon abort uncompl-comp
63400-6389,64000-64123,64680-64693,64890-650,66940-66944,
66980-66994
6390   Postabortion gu infect
6390,6392-64123,64680-64693,64890-650,66940-66944,66980-66994
6391   Postabortion hemorrhage
6391-64123,64680-64693,64890-650,66940-66944,66980-66994
6392   Postabort pelvic damage
6392-64123,64680-64693,64890-650,66940-66944,66980-66994
6393   Postabort renal failure
6392-64123,64680-64693,64890-650,66940-66944,66980-66994
6394   Postabort metabolic dis
6392-64123,64680-64693,64890-650,66940-66944,66980-66994
6395   Postabortion shock
6392-64123,64680-64693,64890-650,66940-66944,66980-66994
6396   Postabortion embolism
6392-64123,64680-64693,64890-650,66940-66944,66980-66994
6398   Postabortion compl NEC
6392-64123,64680-64693,64890-650,66940-66944,66980-66994
6399   Postabortion compl NOS
6392-64123,64680-64693,64890-650,66940-66944,66980-66994
64000   Threatened abort-unspec
64000-64113,64680-64693,64890-650,66940-66944,66980-66994
64001   Threatened abort-deliver
64000-64113,64680-64693,64890-650,66940-66944,66980-66994
64003   Threaten abort-antepart
64000-64113,64680-64693,64890-650,66940-66944,66980-66994
64080   Hem early preg NEC-unsp
64000-64113,64680-64693,64890-650,66940-66944,66980-66994
64081   Hem early preg NEC-deliv
64000-64113,64680-64693,64890-650,66940-66944,66980-66994
64083   Hem early pg NEC-antepar
64000-64113,64680-64693,64890-650,66940-66944,66980-66994
64090   Hemorr early preg-unspec
64000-64113,64680-64693,64890-650,66940-66944,66980-66994
64091   Hem early preg-delivered
64000-64113,64680-64693,64890-650,66940-66944,66980-66994
64093   Hem early preg-antepart
64000-64113,64680-64693,64890-650,66940-66944,66980-66994
64100   Placenta previa-unspec
64000-64113,64680-64693,64890-650,66940-66944,66980-66994
64101   Placenta previa-deliver
64000-64113,64680-64693,64890-650,66940-66944,66980-66994

64103   Placenta previa-antepart
64000-64113,64680-64693,64890-650,66940-66944,66980-66994
64110   Placenta prev hem-unspec
64000-64113,64680-64693,64890-650,66940-66944,66980-66994
64111   Placenta prev hem-deliv
64000-64113,64680-64693,64890-650,66940-66944,66980-66994
64113   Placen prev hem-antepart
64000-64113,64680-64693,64890-650,66940-66944,66980-66994
64130   Coag def hemorr-unspec
64130-64193,64680-64693,64890-650,66940-66944,66980-66994
64131   Coag def hemorr-deliver
64130-64193,64680-64693,64890-650,66940-66944,66980-66994
64133   Coag def hemorr-antepart
64130-64193,64680-64693,64890-650,66940-66944,66980-66994
64180   Antepart hem NEC-unspec
64130-64193,64680-64693,64890-650,66940-66944,66980-66994
64181   Antepartum hem NEC-deliv
64130-64193,64680-64693,64890-650,66940-66944,66980-66994
64183   Antepart hem NEC-antepar
64130-64193,64680-64693,64890-650,66940-66944,66980-66994
64190   Antepart hem NOS-unspec
64130-64193,64680-64693,64890-650,66940-66944,66980-66994
64191   Antepartum hem NOS-deliv
64130-64193,64680-64693,64890-650,66940-66944,66980-66994
64193   Antepart hem NOS-antepar
64130-64193,64680-64693,64890-650,66940-66944,66980-66994
64240   Mild/NOS preeclamp-unsp
64200-64294,64610-64614,64680-64693,64890-650,66940-66944,
66980-66994
64241   Mild/NOS preeclamp-deliv
64200-64294,64610-64614,64680-64693,64890-650,66940-66944,
66980-66994
64242   Mild preeclamp-del w p/p
64200-64294,64610-64614,64680-64693,64890-650,66940-66944,
66980-66994
64243   Mild/NOS preeclamp-antep
64200-64294,64610-64614,64680-64693,64890-650,66940-66944,
66980-66994
64244   Mild/NOS preeclamp-p/p
64200-64294,64610-64614,64680-64693,64890-650,66940-66944,
66980-66994
64250   Severe preeclamp-unspec
64200-64294,64610-64614,64680-64693,64890-650,66940-66944,
66980-66994
64251   Severe preeclamp-deliver
64200-64294,64610-64614,64680-64693,64890-650,66940-66944,
66980-66994
64252   Sev preeclamp-del w p/p
64200-64294,64610-64614,64680-64693,64890-650,66940-66944,
66980-66994
64253   Sev preeclamp-antepartum
64200-64294,64610-64614,64680-64693,64890-650,66940-66944,
66980-66994
64254   Sev preeclamp-postpartum
64200-64294,64610-64614,64680-64693,64890-650,66940-66944,
66980-66994
64260   Eclampsia-unspecified
64200-64294,64610-64614,64680-64693,64890-650,66940-66944,
66980-66994
64261   Eclampsia-delivered
64200-64294,64610-64614,64680-64693,64890-650,66940-66944,
66980-66994
64262   Eclampsia-deliv w p/p
64200-64294,64610-64614,64680-64693,64890-650,66940-66944,
66980-66994
64263   Eclampsia-antepartum
64200-64294,64610-64614,64680-64693,64890-650,66940-66944,
66980-66994
64264   Eclampsia-postpartum
64200-64294,64610-64614,64680-64693,64890-650,66940-66944,
66980-66994

64270 Tox w old hyperten-unsp
64200-64294,64610-64614,64680-64693,64890-650,66940-66944,
66980-66994
64271 Tox w old hyperten-deliv
64200-64294,64610-64614,64680-64693,64890-650,66940-66944,
66980-66994
64272 Tox w old hyp-del w p/p
64200-64294,64610-64614,64680-64693,64890-650,66940-66944,
66980-66994
64273 Tox w old hyper-antepart
64200-64294,64610-64614,64680-64693,64890-650,66940-66944,
66980-66994
64274 Tox w old hyper-postpart
64200-64294,64610-64614,64680-64693,64890-650,66940-66944,
66980-66994
64400 Threat prem labor-unspec
64400-64421,64680-64693,64890-650,66940-66944,66980-66994
64403 Thrt prem labor-antepart
64400-64421,64680-64693,64890-650,66940-66944,66980-66994
64410 Threat labor NEC-unspec
64400-64421,64680-64693,64890-650,66940-66944,66980-66994
64413 Threat labor NEC-antepar
64400-64421,64680-64693,64890-650,66940-66944,66980-66994
64660 Gu infect in preg-unspec
64660-64664,64680-64693,64890-650,66940-66944,66980-66994
64661 Gu infection-delivered
64660-64664,64680-64693,64890-650,66940-66944,66980-66994
64662 Gu infection-deliv w p/p
64660-64664,64680-64693,64890-650,66940-66944,66980-66994
64663 Gu infection-antepartum
64660-64664,64680-64693,64890-650,66940-66944,66980-66994
64664 Gu infection-postpartum
64660-64664,64680-64693,64890-650,66940-66944,66980-66994
64670 Liver dis in preg-unspec
64670-64693,64890-650,66940-66944,66980-66994
64671 Liver disorder-delivered
64670-64693,64890-650,66940-66944,66980-66994
64673 Liver disorder-antepart
64670-64693,64890-650,66940-66944,66980-66994
64730 TB in preg-unspecified
64680-64693,64730-64734,64890-650,66940-66944,66980-66994
64731 Tuberculosis-delivered
64680-64693,64730-64734,64890-650,66940-66944,66980-66994
64732 Tuberculosis-deliv w p/p
64680-64693,64730-64734,64890-650,66940-66944,66980-66994
64733 Tuberculosis-antepartum
64680-64693,64730-64734,64890-650,66940-66944,66980-66994
64734 Tuberculosis-postpartum
64680-64693,64730-64734,64890-650,66940-66944,66980-66994
64740 Malaria in preg-unspec
64680-64693,64740-64744,64890-650,66940-66944,66980-66994
64741 Malaria-delivered
64680-64693,64740-64744,64890-650,66940-66944,66980-66994
64742 Malaria-delivered w p/p
64680-64693,64740-64744,64890-650,66940-66944,66980-66994
64743 Malaria-antepartum
64680-64693,64740-64744,64890-650,66940-66944,66980-66994
64744 Malaria-postpartum
64680-64693,64740-64744,64890-650,66940-66944,66980-66994
64800 Diabetes in preg-unspec
64680-64693,64800-64804,64890-650,66940-66944,66980-66994
64801 Diabetes-delivered
64680-64693,64800-64804,64890-650,66940-66944,66980-66994
64802 Diabetes-delivered w p/p
64680-64693,64800-64804,64890-650,66940-66944,66980-66994
64803 Diabetes-antepartum
64680-64693,64800-64804,64890-650,66940-66944,66980-66994
64804 Diabetes-postpartum
64680-64693,64800-64804,64890-650,66940-66944,66980-66994
64820 Anemia in preg-unspec
64680-64693,64820-64824,64890-650,66940-66944,66980-66994
64821 Anemia-delivered
64680-64693,64820-64824,64890-650,66940-66944,66980-66994

64822 Anemia-delivered w p/p
64680-64693,64820-64824,64890-650,66940-66944,66980-66994
64823 Anemia-antepartum
64680-64693,64820-64824,64890-650,66940-66944,66980-66994
64824 Anemia-postpartum
64680-64693,64820-64824,64890-650,66940-66944,66980-66994
64830 Drug depend preg-unspec
64680-64693,64830-64834,64890-650,66940-66944,66980-66994
64831 Drug dependence-deliver
64680-64693,64830-64834,64890-650,66940-66944,66980-66994
64832 Drug dependen-del w p/p
64680-64693,64830-64834,64890-650,66940-66944,66980-66994
64833 Drug dependence-antepart
64680-64693,64830-64834,64890-650,66940-66944,66980-66994
64834 Drug dependence-postpart
64680-64693,64830-64834,64890-650,66940-66944,66980-66994
64850 Congen CV dis preg-unsp
64680-64693,64850-64864,64890-650,66940-66944,66980-66994
64851 Congen CV dis-delivered
64680-64693,64850-64864,64890-650,66940-66944,66980-66994
64852 Congen CV dis-del w p/p
64680-64693,64850-64864,64890-650,66940-66944,66980-66994
64853 Congen CV dis-antepartum
64680-64693,64850-64864,64890-650,66940-66944,66980-66994
64854 Congen CV dis-postpartum
64680-64693,64850-64864,64890-650,66940-66944,66980-66994
64860 CV dis NEC preg-unspec
64680-64693,64850-64864,64890-650,66940-66944,66980-66994
64861 CV dis NEC preg-deliver
64680-64693,64850-64864,64890-650,66940-66944,66980-66994
64862 CV dis NEC-deliver w p/p
64680-64693,64850-64864,64890-650,66940-66944,66980-66994
64863 CV dis NEC-antepartum
64680-64693,64850-64864,64890-650,66940-66944,66980-66994
64864 CV dis NEC-postpartum
64680-64693,64850-64864,64890-650,66940-66944,66980-66994
65930 Septicemia in labor-unsp
64680-64693,64890-650,65930-65933,66940-66944,66980-66994
65931 Septicem in labor-deliv
64680-64693,64890-650,65930-65933,66940-66944,66980-66994
65933 Septicem in labor-antepa
64680-64693,64890-650,65930-65933,66940-66944,66980-66994
66500 Prelabor rupt uter-unsp
64680-64693,64890-650,65570-65573,66500-66511,66550-66554,
66580-66594,66940-66944,66980-66994
66501 Prelabor rupt uterus-del
64680-64693,64890-650,65570-65573,66500-66511,66550-66554,
66580-66594,66940-66944,66980-66994
66503 Prelab rupt uter-antepar
64680-64693,64890-650,65570-65573,66500-66511,66550-66554,
66580-66594,66940-66944,66980-66994
66510 Rupture uterus NOS-unsp
64680-64693,64890-650,65570-65573,66500-66511,66550-66554,
66580-66594,66940-66944,66980-66994
66511 Rupture uterus NOS-deliv
64680-64693,64890-650,65570-65573,66500-66511,66550-66554,
66580-66594,66940-66944,66980-66994
66632 P/p coag def-del w p/p
64680-64693,64890-650,66600-66634,66940-66944,66980-66994
66634 Postpart coag def-postpa
64680-64693,64890-650,66600-66634,66940-66944,66980-66994
66800 Pulm compl in del-unspec
64680-64693,64890-650,66800-66804,66940-66944,66980-66994
66801 Pulm compl in del-deliv
64680-64693,64890-650,66800-66804,66940-66944,66980-66994
66802 Pulm complic-del w p/p
64680-64693,64890-650,66800-66804,66940-66944,66980-66994
66803 Pulm complicat-antepart
64680-64693,64890-650,66800-66804,66940-66944,66980-66994
66804 Pulm complicat-postpart
64680-64693,64890-650,66800-66804,66940-66944,66980-66994
66810 Heart compl in del-unsp
64680-64693,64890-650,66810-66814,66940-66944,66980-66994

66811 Heart compl in del-deliv
64680-64693,64890-650,66810-66814,66940-66944,66980-66994
66812 Heart compl-del w p/p
64680-64693,64890-650,66810-66814,66940-66944,66980-66994
66813 Heart complic-antepart
64680-64693,64890-650,66810-66814,66940-66944,66980-66994
66814 Heart complic-postpart
64680-64693,64890-650,66810-66814,66940-66944,66980-66994
66820 Cns compl labor/del-unsp
64680-64693,64890-650,66820-66824,66940-66944,66980-66994
66821 Cns compl lab/del-deliv
64680-64693,64890-650,66820-66824,66940-66944,66980-66994
66822 Cns complic-del w p/p
64680-64693,64890-650,66820-66824,66940-66944,66980-66994
66823 Cns compl in del-antepar
64680-64693,64890-650,66820-66824,66940-66944,66980-66994
66824 Cns compl in del-postpar
64680-64693,64890-650,66820-66824,66940-66944,66980-66994
66880 Anesth comp del NEC-unsp
64680-64693,64890-650,66880-66894,66940-66944,66980-66994
66881 Anesth compl NEC-deliver
64680-64693,64890-650,66880-66894,66940-66944,66980-66994
66882 Anesth compl NEC-del p/p
64680-64693,64890-650,66880-66894,66940-66944,66980-66994
66883 Anesth compl antepartum
64680-64693,64890-650,66880-66894,66940-66944,66980-66994
66884 Anesth compl-postpartum
64680-64693,64890-650,66880-66894,66940-66944,66980-66994
66890 Anesth comp del NOS-unsp
64680-64693,64890-650,66880-66894,66940-66944,66980-66994
66891 Anesth compl NOS-deliver
64680-64693,64890-650,66880-66894,66940-66944,66980-66994
66892 Anesth compl NOS-del p/p
64680-64693,64890-650,66880-66894,66940-66944,66980-66994
66893 Anesth compl-antepartum
64680-64693,64890-650,66880-66894,66940-66944,66980-66994
66894 Anesth compl-postpartum
64680-64693,64890-650,66880-66894,66940-66944,66980-66994
66910 Obstetric shock-unspec
64680-64693,64890-650,66910-66914,66940-66944,66980-66994
66911 Obstetric shock-deliver
64680-64693,64890-650,66910-66914,66940-66944,66980-66994
66912 Obstet shock-deliv w p/p
64680-64693,64890-650,66910-66914,66940-66944,66980-66994
66913 Obstetric shock-antepar
64680-64693,64890-650,66910-66914,66940-66944,66980-66994
66914 Obstetric shock-postpart
64680-64693,64890-650,66910-66914,66940-66944,66980-66994
66930 Ac ren fail w deliv-unsp
64680-64693,64890-650,66930-66944,66980-66994
66932 Ac ren fail-deliv w p/p
64680-64693,64890-650,66930-66944,66980-66994
66934 Ac renal failure-postpar
64680-64693,64890-650,66930-66944,66980-66994
67000 Major puerp infect-unsp
64680-64693,64890-650,66940-66944,66980-67004
67002 Major puerp inf-del p/p
64680-64693,64890-650,66940-66944,66980-67004
67004 Major puerp inf-postpart
64680-64693,64890-650,66940-66944,66980-67004
67120 Thrombophleb preg-unspec
64680-64693,64890-650,66940-66944,66980-66994,67120-67194
67121 Thrombophlebitis-deliver
64680-64693,64890-650,66940-66944,66980-66994,67120-67194
67122 Thrombophleb-deliv w p/p
64680-64693,64890-650,66940-66944,66980-66994,67120-67194
67123 Thrombophlebit-antepart
64680-64693,64890-650,66940-66944,66980-66994,67120-67194
67124 Thrombophlebit-postpart
64680-64693,64890-650,66940-66944,66980-66994,67120-67194
67130 Deep thromb antepar-unsp
64680-64693,64890-650,66940-66944,66980-66994,67120-67194
67131 Deep throm antepar-deliv
64680-64693,64890-650,66940-66944,66980-66994,67120-67194

67133 Deep vein thromb-antepar
64680-64693,64890-650,66940-66944,66980-66994,67120-67194
67140 Deep thromb postpar-unsp
64680-64693,64890-650,66940-66944,66980-66994,67120-67194
67142 Thromb postpar-del w p/p
64680-64693,64890-650,66940-66944,66980-66994,67120-67194
67144 Deep vein thromb-postpar
64680-64693,64890-650,66940-66944,66980-66994,67120-67194
67300 Ob air embolism-unspec
64680-64693,64890-650,66940-66944,66980-66994,67300-67384
67301 Ob air embolism-deliver
64680-64693,64890-650,66940-66944,66980-66994,67300-67384
67302 Ob air embol-deliv w p/p
64680-64693,64890-650,66940-66944,66980-66994,67300-67384
67303 Ob air embolism-antepart
64680-64693,64890-650,66940-66944,66980-66994,67300-67384
67304 Ob air embolism-postpart
64680-64693,64890-650,66940-66944,66980-66994,67300-67384
67310 Amniotic embolism-unspec
64680-64693,64890-650,66940-66944,66980-66994,67300-67384
67311 Amniotic embolism-deliv
64680-64693,64890-650,66940-66944,66980-66994,67300-67384
67312 Amniot embol-deliv w p/p
64680-64693,64890-650,66940-66944,66980-66994,67300-67384
67313 Amniotic embol-antepart
64680-64693,64890-650,66940-66944,66980-66994,67300-67384
67314 Amniotic embol-postpart
64680-64693,64890-650,66940-66944,66980-66994,67300-67384
67320 Ob pulm embol NOS-unspec
64680-64693,64890-650,66940-66944,66980-66994,67300-67384
67321 Pulm embol NOS-delivered
64680-64693,64890-650,66940-66944,66980-66994,67300-67384
67322 Pulm embol NOS-del w p/p
64680-64693,64890-650,66940-66944,66980-66994,67300-67384
67323 Pulm embol NOS-antepart
64680-64693,64890-650,66940-66944,66980-66994,67300-67384
67324 Pulm embol NOS-postpart
64680-64693,64890-650,66940-66944,66980-66994,67300-67384
67330 Ob pyemic embol-unspec
64680-64693,64890-650,66940-66944,66980-66994,67300-67384
67331 Ob pyemic embol-deliver
64680-64693,64890-650,66940-66944,66980-66994,67300-67384
67332 Ob pyem embol-del w p/p
64680-64693,64890-650,66940-66944,66980-66994,67300-67384
67333 Ob pyemic embol-antepart
64680-64693,64890-650,66940-66944,66980-66994,67300-67384
67334 Ob pyemic embol-postpart
64680-64693,64890-650,66940-66944,66980-66994,67300-67384
67380 Ob pulmon embol NEC-unsp
64680-64693,64890-650,66940-66944,66980-66994,67300-67384
67381 Pulmon embol NEC-deliver
64680-64693,64890-650,66940-66944,66980-66994,67300-67384
67382 Pulm embol NEC-del w p/p
64680-64693,64890-650,66940-66944,66980-66994,67300-67384
67383 Pulmon embol NEC-antepar
64680-64693,64890-650,66940-66944,66980-66994,67300-67384
67384 Pulmon embol NEC-postpar
64680-64693,64890-650,66940-66944,66980-66994,67300-67384
67400 Puerp cerebvasc dis-unsp
64680-64693,64890-650,66940-66944,66980-66994,67400-67404
67401 Puerp cerebvas dis-deliv
64680-64693,64890-650,66940-66944,66980-66994,67400-67404
67402 Cerebvas dis-deliv w p/p
64680-64693,64890-650,66940-66944,66980-66994,67400-67404
67403 Cerebrovasc dis-antepart
64680-64693,64890-650,66940-66944,66980-66994,67400-67404
67404 Cerebrovasc dis-postpart
64680-64693,64890-650,66940-66944,66980-66994,67400-67404
67410 Disrupt c-sect wnd-unsp
64680-64693,64890-650,66940-66944,66980-66994,67410-67434
67412 Disrupt c-sect-del w p/p
64680-64693,64890-650,66940-66944,66980-66994,67410-67434
67420 Disrupt perineum-unspec
64680-64693,64890-650,66940-66944,66980-66994,67410-67434

67422   Disrupt perin-del w p/p
64680-64693,64890-650,66940-66944,66980-66994,67410-67434
67424   Disrupt perineum-postpar
64680-64693,64890-650,66940-66944,66980-66994,67410-67434
67510   Breast abscess preg-unsp
64680-64693,64890-650,66940-66944,66980-66994,67500-67594
67511   Breast abscess-delivered
64680-64693,64890-650,66940-66944,66980-66994,67500-67594
67512   Breast abscess-del w p/p
64680-64693,64890-650,66940-66944,66980-66994,67500-67594
6800   Carbuncle of face
01700-01706,01790-01796,04089-0419,6800,6808-6809,68600-6869,
70583,7098,V090-V0991
6801   Carbuncle of neck
01700-01706,01790-01796,04089-0419,6801,6808-6809,68600-6869,
70583,7098,V090-V0991
6802   Carbuncle of trunk
01700-01706,01790-01796,04089-0419,6802,6808-6809,68600-6869,
70583,7098,V090-V0991
6803   Carbuncle of arm
01700-01706,01790-01796,04089-0419,6803,6808-6809,68600-6869,
70583,7098,V090-V0991
6804   Carbuncle of hand
01700-01706,01790-01796,04089-0419,6804,6808-6809,68600-6869,
70583,7098,V090-V0991
6805   Carbuncle of buttock
01700-01706,01790-01796,04089-0419,6805,6808-6809,68600-6869,
70583,7098,V090-V0991
6806   Carbuncle of leg
01700-01706,01790-01796,04089-0419,6806,6808-6809,68600-6869,
70583,7098,V090-V0991
6807   Carbuncle of foot
01700-01706,01790-01796,04089-0419,6807-6809,68600-6869,70583,
7098,V090-V0991
6808   Carbuncle, site NEC
01700-01706,01790-01796,04089-0419,6808-6809,68600-6869,70583,
7098,V090-V0991
6809   Carbuncle NOS
01700-01706,01790-01796,04089-0419,6808-6809,68600-6869,70583,
7098,V090-V0991
6820   Cellulitis of face
01700-01706,01790-01796,04089-0419,6820,6828-6829,68600-6869,
70583,7098,V090-V0991
6821   Cellulitis of neck
01700-01706,01790-01796,04089-0419,6821,6828-6829,68600-6869,
70583,7098,V090-V0991
6822   Cellulitis of trunk
01700-01706,01790-01796,04089-0419,6822,6828-6829,68600-6869,
70583,7098,V090-V0991
6823   Cellulitis of arm
01700-01706,01790-01796,04089-0419,6823,6828-6829,68600-6869,
70583,7098,V090-V0991
6825   Cellulitis of buttock
01700-01706,01790-01796,04089-0419,6825,6828-6829,68600-6869,
70583,7098,V090-V0991
6826   Cellulitis of leg
01700-01706,01790-01796,04089-0419,6826,6828-6829,68600-6869,
70583,7098,V090-V0991
6827   Cellulitis of foot
01700-01706,01790-01796,04089-0419,6827-6829,68600-6869,70583,
7098,V090-V0991
6828   Cellulitis, site NEC
01700-01706,01790-01796,04089-0419,6828-6829,68600-6869,70583,
7098,V090-V0991
6829   Cellulitis NOS
01700-01706,01790-01796,04089-0419,6828-6829,68600-6869,70583,
7098,V090-V0991
684   Impetigo
684,68600-6869,7098
6850   Pilonidal cyst w abscess
6850-6851,7098
6944   Pemphigus
6944-6949,7098

6945   Pemphigoid
6944-6949,7098
6950   Toxic erythema
6950-6954,7098
6960   Psoriatic arthropathy
01580-01596,01790-01796,03682,05671,09850-09851,09859,09889,
6960,71100-7140,71500,71509-71510,71518-71699,71800-71808,
71900-71910,71918-71999
7070   Decubitus ulcer
7070,7078-7079,7098
7071   Chronic ulcer of leg
44023,7071-7079,7098
7100   Syst lupus erythematosus
7100
7101   Systemic sclerosis
7101
7103   Dermatomyositis
7103
7104   Polymyositis
7104
7105   Eosinophilia myalgia snd
2920-2939,7105
7108   Diff connect tis dis NEC
7108
71100   Pyogen arthritis-unspec
01580-01596,01790-01796,03682,05671,09850-09851,09859,09889,
71100-7140,71500,71509-71510,71518-71699,71800-71808,
71900-71910,71918-71999
71101   Pyogen arthritis-shlder
01580-01596,01790-01796,03682,05671,09850-09851,09859,09889,
71100-71101,71108-71111,71118-71121,71128-71131,71138-71141,
71148-71151,71158-71161,71168-71171,71178-71181,71188-71191,
71198-71211,71218-71221,71228-71231,71238-71281,71288-71291,
71298-7140,71500,71509-71511,71518-71521,71528-71531,
71538-71591,71598-71601,71608-71611,71618-71621,71628-71631,
71638-71641,71648-71651,71658-71661,71668-71681,71688-71691,
71698-71699,71800-71801,71808,71900-71901,71908-71911,
71918-71921,71928-71931,71938-71941,71948-71951,71958-71961,
71968-71970,71978-71981,71988-71991,71998-71999
71102   Pyogen arthritis-up/arm
01580-01596,01790-01796,03682,05671,09850-09851,09859,09889,
71100,71102,71108-71110,71112,71118-71120,71122,71128-71130,
71132,71138-71140,71142,71148-71150,71152,71158-71160,71162,
71168-71170,71172,71178-71180,71182,71188-71190,71192,
71198-71210,71212,71218-71220,71222,71228-71230,71232,
71238-71280,71282,71288-71290,71292,71298-7140,71500,
71509-71510,71512,71518-71520,71522,71528-71530,71532,
71538-71590,71592,71598-71600,71602,71608-71610,71612,
71618-71620,71622,71628-71630,71632,71638-71640,71642,
71648-71650,71652,71658-71660,71662,71668-71680,71682,
71688-71690,71692,71698-71699,71800,71802,71808,71900,71902,
71908-71910,71912,71918-71920,71922,71928-71930,71932,
71938-71940,71942,71948-71950,71952,71958-71960,71962,
71968-71970,71978-71980,71982,71988-71990,71992,71998-71999
71103   Pyogen arthritis-forearm
01580-01596,01790-01796,03682,05671,09850-09851,09859,09889,
71100,71103,71108-71110,71113,71118-71120,71123,71128-71130,
71133,71138-71140,71143,71148-71150,71153,71158-71160,71163,
71168-71170,71173,71178-71180,71183,71188-71190,71193,
71198-71210,71213,71218-71220,71223,71228-71230,71233,
71238-71280,71283,71288-71290,71293,71298-7140,71500,
71509-71510,71513,71518-71520,71523,71528-71530,71533,
71538-71590,71593,71598-71600,71603,71608-71610,71613,
71618-71620,71623,71628-71630,71633,71638-71640,71643,
71648-71650,71653,71658-71660,71663,71668-71680,71683,
71688-71690,71693,71698-71699,71800,71803,71808,71900,71903,
71908-71910,71913,71918-71920,71923,71928-71930,71933,
71938-71940,71943,71948-71950,71953,71958-71960,71963,
71968-71970,71978-71980,71983,71988-71990,71993,71998-71999

71104   Pyogen arthritis-hand
01580-01596,01790-01796,03682,05671,09850-09851,09859,09889,
71100,71104,71108-71110,71114,71118-71120,71124,71128-71130,
71134,71138-71140,71144,71148-71150,71154,71158-71160,71164,
71168-71170,71174,71178-71180,71184,71188-71190,71194,
71198-71210,71214,71218-71220,71224,71228-71230,71234,
71238-71280,71284,71288-71290,71294,71298-7140,71500-71510,
71514,71518-71520,71524,71528-71530,71534,71538-71590,71594,
71598-71600,71604,71608-71610,71614,71618-71620,71624,
71628-71630,71634,71638-71640,71644,71648-71650,71654,
71658-71660,71664,71668-71680,71684,71688-71690,71694,
71698-71699,71800,71804,71808,71900,71904,71908-71910,71914,
71918-71920,71924,71928-71930,71934,71938-71940,71944,
71948-71950,71954,71958-71960,71964,71968-71970,71978-71980,
71984,71988-71990,71994,71998-71999

71105   Pyogen arthritis-pelvis
01580-01596,01790-01796,03682,05671,09850-09851,09859,09889,
71100,71105,71108-71110,71115,71118-71120,71125,71128-71130,
71135,71138-71140,71145,71148-71150,71155,71158-71160,71165,
71168-71170,71175,71178-71180,71185,71188-71190,71195,
71198-71210,71215,71218-71220,71225,71228-71230,71235,
71238-71280,71285,71288-71290,71295,71298-7140,71500,
71509-71510,71515,71518-71520,71525,71528-71530,71535,
71538-71590,71595,71598-71600,71605,71608-71610,71615,
71618-71620,71625,71628-71630,71635,71638-71640,71645,
71648-71650,71655,71658-71660,71665,71668-71680,71685,
71688-71690,71695,71698-71699,71800,71805,71808,71900,71905,
71908-71910,71915,71918-71920,71925,71928-71930,71935,
71938-71940,71945,71948-71950,71955,71958-71960,71965,
71968-71975,71978-71980,71985,71988-71990,71995,71998-71999

71106   Pyogen arthritis-l/leg
01580-01596,01790-01796,03682,05671,09850-09851,09859,09889,
71100,71106,71108-71110,71116,71118-71120,71126,71128-71130,
71136,71138-71140,71146,71148-71150,71156,71158-71160,71166,
71168-71170,71176,71178-71180,71186,71188-71190,71196,
71198-71210,71216,71218-71220,71226,71228-71230,71236,
71238-71280,71286,71288-71290,71296,71298-7140,71500,
71509-71510,71516,71518-71520,71526,71528-71530,71536,
71538-71590,71596,71598-71600,71606,71608-71610,71616,
71618-71620,71626,71628-71630,71636,71638-71640,71646,
71648-71650,71656,71658-71660,71666,71668-71680,71686,
71688-71690,71696,71698-71699,71800,71808,71900,71906,
71908-71910,71916,71918-71920,71926,71928-71930,71936,
71938-71940,71946,71948-71950,71956,71958-71960,71966,
71968-71970,71976,71978-71980,71986,71988-71990,71996,
71998-71999

71107   Pyogen arthritis-ankle
01580-01596,01790-01796,03682,05671,09850-09851,09859,09889,
71100,71107-71110,71117-71120,71127-71130,71137-71140,
71147-71150,71157-71160,71167-71170,71177-71180,71187-71190,
71197-71210,71217-71220,71227-71230,71237-71280,71287-71290,
71297-7140,71500,71509-71510,71517-71520,71527-71530,
71537-71590,71597-71600,71607-71610,71617-71620,71627-71630,
71637-71640,71647-71650,71657-71660,71667-71680,71687-71690,
71697-71699,71800,71807-71808,71900,71907-71910,71917-71920,
71927-71930,71937-71940,71947-71950,71957-71960,71967-71970,
71977-71980,71987-71990,71997-71999

71108   Pyogen arthritis NEC
01580-01596,01790-01796,03682,05671,09850-09851,09859,09889,
71100-7140,71500,71509-71510,71518-71699,71800-71808,
71900-71910,71918-71999

71109   Pyogen arthritis-mult
01580-01596,01790-01796,03682,05671,09850-09851,09859,09889,
71100-7140,71500,71509-71510,71518-71699,71800-71808,
71900-71910,71918-71999

71160   Mycotic arthritis-unspec
01580-01596,01790-01796,03682,05671,09850-09851,09859,09889,
71100-7140,71500,71509-71510,71518-71699,71800-71808,
71900-71910,71918-71999

71161   Mycotic arthritis-shlder
01580-01596,01790-01796,03682,05671,09850-09851,09859,09889,
71100-71101,71108-71111,71118-71121,71128-71131,71138-71141,
71148-71151,71158-71161,71168-71171,71178-71181,71188-71191,
71198-71211,71218-71221,71228-71231,71238-71281,71288-71291,
71298-7140,71500,71509-71511,71518-71521,71528-71531,
71538-71591,71598-71601,71608-71611,71618-71621,71628-71631,
71638-71641,71648-71651,71658-71661,71668-71681,71688-71691,
71698-71699,71800-71801,71808,71900-71901,71908-71911,
71918-71921,71928-71931,71938-71941,71948-71951,71958-71961,
71968-71970,71978-71981,71988-71991,71998-71999

71162   Mycotic arthritis-up/arm
01580-01596,01790-01796,03682,05671,09850-09851,09859,09889,
71100,71102,71108-71110,71112,71118-71120,71122,71128-71130,
71132,71138-71140,71142,71148-71150,71152,71158-71160,71162,
71168-71170,71172,71178-71180,71182,71188-71190,71192,
71198-71210,71212,71218-71220,71222,71228-71230,71232,
71238-71280,71282,71288-71290,71292,71298-7140,71500,
71509-71510,71512,71518-71520,71522,71528-71530,71532,
71538-71590,71592,71598-71600,71602,71608-71610,71612,
71618-71620,71622,71628-71630,71632,71638-71640,71642,
71648-71650,71652,71658-71660,71662,71668-71680,71682,
71688-71690,71692,71698-71699,71800,71802,71808,71900,71902,
71908-71910,71912,71918-71920,71922,71928-71930,71932,
71938-71940,71942,71948-71950,71952,71958-71960,71962,
71968-71970,71978-71980,71982,71988-71990,71992,71998-71999

71163   Mycotic arthrit-forearm
01580-01596,01790-01796,03682,05671,09850-09851,09859,09889,
71100,71103,71108-71110,71113,71118-71120,71123,71128-71130,
71133,71138-71140,71143,71148-71150,71153,71158-71160,71163,
71168-71170,71173,71178-71180,71183,71188-71190,71193,
71198-71210,71213,71218-71220,71223,71228-71230,71233,
71238-71280,71283,71288-71290,71293,71298-7140,71500,
71509-71510,71513,71518-71520,71523,71528-71530,71533,
71538-71590,71593,71598-71600,71603,71608-71610,71613,
71618-71620,71623,71628-71630,71633,71638-71640,71643,
71648-71650,71653,71658-71660,71663,71668-71680,71683,
71688-71690,71693,71698-71699,71800,71803,71808,71900,71903,
71908-71910,71913,71918-71920,71923,71928-71930,71933,
71938-71940,71943,71948-71950,71953,71958-71960,71963,
71968-71970,71978-71980,71983,71988-71990,71993,71998-71999

71164   Mycotic arthritis-hand
01580-01596,01790-01796,03682,05671,09850-09851,09859,09889,
71100,71104,71108-71110,71114,71118-71120,71124,71128-71130,
71134,71138-71140,71144,71148-71150,71154,71158-71160,71164,
71168-71170,71174,71178-71180,71184,71188-71190,71194,
71198-71210,71214,71218-71220,71224,71228-71230,71234,
71238-71280,71284,71288-71290,71294,71298-7140,71500-71510,
71514,71518-71520,71524,71528-71530,71534,71538-71590,71594,
71598-71600,71604,71608-71610,71614,71618-71620,71624,
71628-71630,71634,71638-71640,71644,71648-71650,71654,
71658-71660,71664,71668-71680,71684,71688-71690,71694,
71698-71699,71800,71804,71808,71900,71904,71908-71910,71914,
71918-71920,71924,71928-71930,71934,71938-71940,71944,
71948-71950,71954,71958-71960,71964,71968-71970,71978-71980,
71984,71988-71990,71994,71998-71999

71165   Mycotic arthritis-pelvis
01580-01596,01790-01796,03682,05671,09850-09851,09859,09889,
71100,71105,71108-71110,71115,71118-71120,71125,71128-71130,
71135,71138-71140,71145,71148-71150,71155,71158-71160,71165,
71168-71170,71175,71178-71180,71185,71188-71190,71195,
71198-71210,71215,71218-71220,71225,71228-71230,71235,
71238-71280,71285,71288-71290,71295,71298-7140,71500,
71509-71510,71515,71518-71520,71525,71528-71530,71535,
71538-71590,71595,71598-71600,71605,71608-71610,71615,
71618-71620,71625,71628-71630,71635,71638-71640,71645,
71648-71650,71655,71658-71660,71665,71668-71680,71685,
71688-71690,71695,71698-71699,71800,71805,71808,71900,71905,
71908-71910,71915,71918-71920,71925,71928-71930,71935,
71938-71940,71945,71948-71950,71955,71958-71960,71965,
71968-71975,71978-71980,71985,71988-71990,71995,71998-71999

71166   Mycotic arthritis-l/leg
01580-01596,01790-01796,03682,05671,09850-09851,09859,09889,
71100,71106,71108-71110,71116,71118-71120,71126,71128-71130,
71136,71138-71140,71146,71148-71150,71156,71158-71160,71166,
71168-71170,71176,71178-71180,71186,71188-71190,71196,
71198-71210,71216,71218-71220,71226,71228-71230,71236,
71238-71280,71286,71288-71290,71296,71298-7140,71500,
71509-71510,71516,71518-71520,71526,71528-71530,71536,
71538-71590,71596,71598-71600,71606,71608-71610,71616,
71618-71620,71626,71628-71630,71636,71638-71640,71646,
71648-71650,71656,71658-71660,71666,71668-71680,71686,
71688-71690,71696,71698-71699,71800,71808,71900,71906,
71908-71910,71916,71918-71920,71926,71928-71930,71936,
71938-71940,71946,71948-71950,71956,71958-71960,71966,
71968-71970,71976,71978-71980,71986,71988-71990,71996,
71998-71999

71167   Mycotic arthritis-ankle
01580-01596,01790-01796,03682,05671,09850-09851,09859,09889,
71100,71107-71110,71117-71120,71127-71130,71137-71140,
71147-71150,71157-71160,71167-71170,71177-71180,71187-71190,
71197-71210,71217-71220,71227-71230,71237-71280,71287-71290,
71297-7140,71500,71509-71510,71517-71520,71527-71530,
71537-71590,71597-71600,71607-71610,71617-71620,71627-71630,
71637-71640,71647-71650,71657-71660,71667-71680,71687-71690,
71697-71699,71800,71807-71808,71900,71907-71910,71917-71920,
71927-71930,71937-71940,71947-71950,71957-71960,71967-71970,
71977-71980,71987-71990,71997-71999

71168   Mycotic arthritis NEC
01580-01596,01790-01796,03682,05671,09850-09851,09859,09889,
71100-7140,71500,71509-71510,71518-71699,71800-71808,
71900-71910,71918-71999

71169   Mycotic arthritis-mult
01580-01596,01790-01796,03682,05671,09850-09851,09859,09889,
71100-7140,71500,71509-71510,71518-71699,71800-71808,
71900-71910,71918-71999

7141   Felty's syndrome
03682,05671,71100-7144,71500,71509-71510,71518-71699,
71800-71808,71900-71910,71918-71999

7142   Syst rheum arthritis NEC
03682,05671,71100-7144,71500,71509-71510,71518-71699,
71800-71808,71900-71910,71918-71999

71430   Juv rheum arthritis NOS
03682,05671,71100-7144,71500,71509-71510,71518-71699,
71800-71808,71900-71910,71918-71999

71431   Polyart juv rheum arthr
03682,05671,71100-7144,71500,71509-71510,71518-71699,
71800-71808,71900-71910,71918-71999

71432   Pauciart juv rheum arthr
03682,05671,71100-7144,71500,71509-71510,71518-71699,
71800-71808,71900-71910,71918-71999

71433   Monoart juv rheum arthr
03682,05671,71100-7144,71500,71509-71510,71518-71699,
71800-71808,71900-71910,71918-71999

72280   Postlaminectomy synd NOS
72251-72293

72281   Postlaminect synd-cerv
72251-72293

72282   Postlaminect synd-thorac
72251-72293

72283   Postlaminect synd-lumbar
72251-72293

7234   Brachial neuritis NOS
7226-72271,72280-72281,72290-72291,7230-7239

7235   Torticollis NOS
05371,7226-72271,72280-72281,72290-72291,7230-7239

7280   Infective myositis
7280,72811-7283,72881,72886

72886   Necrotizing fasciitis
7280,72811-7283,72881,72886

73000   Ac osteomyelitis-unspec
01550-01556,01570-01576,01590-01596,01790-01796,73000-73039,
73080-73099

73001   Ac osteomyelitis-shlder
01550-01556,01570-01576,01590-01596,01790-01796,73000,
73008-73011,73018-73021,73028-73031,73038-73039,73080-73081,
73088-73091,73098-73099

73002   Ac osteomyelitis-up/arm
01550-01556,01570-01576,01590-01596,01790-01796,73000,
73008-73010,73012,73018-73020,73022,73028-73030,73032,
73038-73039,73080,73082,73088-73090,73092,73098-73099

73003   Ac osteomyelitis-forearm
01550-01556,01570-01576,01590-01596,01790-01796,73000,
73008-73010,73013,73018-73020,73023,73028-73030,73033,
73038-73039,73080,73083,73088-73090,73093,73098-73099

73004   Ac osteomyelitis-hand
01550-01556,01570-01576,01590-01596,01790-01796,73000,
73008-73010,73014,73018-73020,73024,73028-73030,73034,
73038-73039,73080,73084,73088-73090,73094,73098-73099

73005   Ac osteomyelitis-pelvis
01510-01516,01550-01556,01570-01576,01590-01596,01790-01796,
73000,73008-73010,73015,73018-73020,73025,73028-73030,73035,
73038-73039,73080,73085,73088-73090,73095,73098-73099

73006   Ac osteomyelitis-l/leg
01520-01556,01570-01576,01590-01596,01790-01796,73000,
73008-73010,73016,73018-73020,73026,73028-73030,73036,
73038-73039,73080,73086,73088-73090,73096,73098-73099

73007   Ac osteomyelitis-ankle
01550-01556,01570-01576,01590-01596,01790-01796,73000,
73008-73010,73017-73020,73027-73030,73037-73039,73080,
73087-73090,73097-73099

73008   Ac osteomyelitis NEC
01500-01506,01550-01556,01570-01576,01590-01596,01790-01796,
73000-73039,73080-73099

73009   Ac osteomyelitis-mult
01550-01556,01570-01576,01590-01596,01790-01796,73000-73039,
73080-73099

73080   Bone infect NEC-unspec
01550-01556,01570-01576,01590-01596,01790-01796,73000-73039,
73080-73099

73081   Bone infect NEC-shlder
01550-01556,01570-01576,01590-01596,01790-01796,73000-73001,
73008-73011,73018-73021,73028-73031,73038-73039,73080,
73088-73091,73098-73099

73082   Bone infect NEC-up/arm
01550-01556,01570-01576,01590-01596,01790-01796,73000,73002,
73008-73010,73012,73018-73020,73022,73028-73030,73032,
73038-73039,73080,73088-73090,73092,73098-73099

73083   Bone infect NEC-forearm
01550-01556,01570-01576,01590-01596,01790-01796,73000,73003,
73008-73010,73013,73018-73020,73023,73028-73030,73033,
73038-73039,73080,73088-73090,73093,73098-73099

73084   Bone infect NEC-hand
01550-01556,01570-01576,01590-01596,01790-01796,73000,73004,
73008-73010,73014,73018-73020,73024,73028-73030,73034,
73038-73039,73080,73088-73090,73094,73098-73099

73085   Bone infect NEC-pelvis
01510-01516,01550-01556,01570-01576,01590-01596,01790-01796,
73000,73005,73008-73010,73015,73018-73020,73025,73028-73030,
73035,73038-73039,73080,73088-73090,73095,73098-73099

73086   Bone infect NEC-l/leg
01520-01556,01570-01576,01590-01596,01790-01796,73000,73006,
73008-73010,73016,73018-73020,73026,73028-73030,73036,
73038-73039,73080,73088-73090,73096,73098-73099

73087   Bone infect NEC-ankle
01550-01556,01570-01576,01590-01596,01790-01796,73000,
73007-73010,73017-73020,73027-73030,73037-73039,73080,
73088-73090,73097-73099

73088   Bone infect NEC-oth site
01500-01506,01550-01556,01570-01576,01590-01596,01790-01796,
73000-73039,73080-73099

73089   Bone infect NEC-mult
01550-01556,01570-01576,01590-01596,01790-01796,73000-73039,
73080-73099

73090   Bone infec NOS-unsp site
01550-01556,01570-01576,01590-01596,01790-01796,73000-73039,
73080-73099

73091   Bone infect NOS-shlder
01550-01556,01570-01576,01590-01596,01790-01796,73000-73001,
73008-73011,73018-73021,73028-73031,73038-73039,73080-73081,
73088-73090,73098-73099

73092   Bone infect NOS-up/arm
01550-01556,01570-01576,01590-01596,01790-01796,73000,73002,
73008-73010,73012,73018-73020,73022,73028-73030,73032,
73038-73039,73080,73082,73088-73090,73098-73099

73093   Bone infect NOS-forearm
01550-01556,01570-01576,01590-01596,01790-01796,73000,73003,
73008-73010,73013,73018-73020,73023,73028-73030,73033,
73038-73039,73080,73083,73088-73090,73098-73099

73094   Bone infect NOS-hand
01550-01556,01570-01576,01590-01596,01790-01796,73000,73004,
73008-73010,73014,73018-73020,73024,73028-73030,73034,
73038-73039,73080,73084,73088-73090,73098-73099

73095   Bone infect NOS-pelvis
01510-01516,01550-01556,01570-01576,01590-01596,01790-01796,
73000,73005,73008-73010,73015,73018-73020,73025,73028-73030,
73035,73038-73039,73080,73085,73088-73090,73098-73099

73096   Bone infect NOS-l/leg
01520-01556,01570-01576,01590-01596,01790-01796,73000,73006,
73008-73010,73016,73018-73020,73026,73028-73030,73036,
73038-73039,73080,73086,73088-73090,73098-73099

73097   Bone infect NOS-ankle
01550-01556,01570-01576,01590-01596,01790-01796,73000,
73007-73010,73017-73020,73027-73030,73037-73039,73080,
73087-73090,73098-73099

73098   Bone infect NOS-oth site
01500-01506,01550-01556,01570-01576,01590-01596,01790-01796,
73000-73039,73080-73099

73099   Bone infect NOS-mult
01550-01556,01570-01576,01590-01596,01790-01796,73000-73039,
73080-73099

73310   Path fx unspecified site
73310-73319

73311   Path fx humerus
73310-73319

73312   Path fx dstl radius ulna
73310-73319

73313   Path fx vertebrae
73310-73319

73314   Path fx neck of femur
73310-73319

73315   Path fx oth spcf prt fmr
73310-73319

73316   Path fx tibia fibula
73310-73319

73319   Path fx oth specif site
73310-73319

73381   Malunion of fracture
73381-73382

73382   Nonunion of fracture
73381-73382

74100   Spin bif w hydroceph NOS
74100-74193,74259-7429,7597-75989

74101   Spin bif w hydrceph-cerv
74100-74193,74259-7429,7597-75989

74102   Spin bif w hydrceph-dors
74100-74193,74259-7429,7597-75989

74103   Spin bif w hydrceph-lumb
74100-74193,74259-7429,7597-75989

74190   Spina bifida
74100-74193,74259-7429,7597-75989

74191   Spina bifida-cerv
74100-74193,74259-7429,7597-75989

74192   Spina bifida-dorsal
74100-74193,74259-7429,7597-75989

74193   Spina bifida-lumbar
74100-74193,74259-7429,7597-75989

7450   Common truncus
42971-42979,7450-7459,74689-7469,74789-7479,7597-75989

74510   Compl transpos great ves
42971-42979,7450-7459,74689-7469,74789-7479,7597-75989

74511   Double outlet rt ventric
42971-42979,7450-7459,74689-7469,74789-7479,7597-75989

74512   Correct transpos grt ves
42971-42979,7450-7459,74689-7469,74789-7479,7597-75989

74519   Transpos great vess NEC
42971-42979,7450-7459,74689-7469,74789-7479,7597-75989

7452   Tetralogy of fallot
42971-42979,7450-7459,74689-7469,74789-7479,7597-75989

7453   Common ventricle
42971-42979,7450-7459,74689-7469,74789-7479,7597-75989

7454   Ventricular sept defect
42971-42979,7450-7459,74689-7469,74789-7479,7597-75989

74560   Endocard cushion def NOS
42971-42979,7450-7459,74689-7469,74789-7479,7597-75989

74569   Endocard cushion def NEC
42971-42979,7450-7459,74689-7469,74789-7479,7597-75989

7457   Cor biloculare
42971-42979,7450-7459,74689-7469,74789-7479,7597-75989

74601   Cong pulmon valv atresia
74600-74609,74689-7469,74789-7479,7597-75989

74602   Cong pulmon valve stenos
74600-74609,74689-7469,74789-7479,7597-75989

7461   Cong tricusp atres/sten
7461-7467,74689-7469,74789-7479,7597-75989

7462   Ebstein's anomaly
7461-7467,74689-7469,74789-7479,7597-75989

7463   Cong aorta valv stenosis
7461-7467,74689-7469,74789-7479,7597-75989

7464   Cong aorta valv insuffic
7461-7467,74689-7469,74789-7479,7597-75989

7465   Congen mitral stenosis
7461-7467,74689-7469,74789-7479,7597-75989

7466   Cong mitral insufficienc
7461-7467,74689-7469,74789-7479,7597-75989

7467   Hypoplas left heart synd
7461-7467,74689-7469,74789-7479,7597-75989

74681   Cong subaortic stenosis
74681-74684,74689-7469,74789-7479,7597-75989

74682   Cor triatriatum
74681-74684,74689-7469,74789-7479,7597-75989

74683   Infundib pulmon stenosis
74681-74684,74689-7469,74789-7479,7597-75989

74684   Obstruct heart anom NEC
74681-74684,74689-7469,74789-7479,7597-75989

74686   Congenital heart block
74686,74689-7469,74789-7479,7597-75989

74710   Coarctation of aorta
No Exclusions

74711   Interrupt of aortic arch
74710-74722,74789-7479,7597-75989

74722   Aortic atresia/stenosis
74710-74722,74789-7479,7597-75989

7484   Congenital cystic lung
7484-7489

7485   Agenesis of lung
7484-7489

74861   Congen bronchiectasis
494,496,5061,5064-5069,74861

76501   Extreme immatur <500g
76400-76519,7678-7679,7798

76502   Extreme immatur 500-749g
76400-76519,7678-7679,7798

76503   Extreme immatur 750-999g
76400-76519,7678-7679,7798

76504   Extreme immat 1000-1249g
76400-76519,7678-7679,7798

76505   Extreme immat 1250-1499g
76400-76519,7678-7679,7798

76506   Extreme immat 1500-1749g
76400-76519,7678-7679,7798

76507   Extreme immat 1750-1999g
76400-76519,7678-7679,7798

76508   Extreme immat 2000-2499g
76400-76519,7678-7679,7798

7670   Cerebral hem at birth
7670,7678-7679,7798
7685   Severe birth asphyxia
7685-7709,7798
769   Respiratory distress syn
7685-7709,7798
7700   Congenital pneumonia
7685-7709,7798
7701   Meconium aspiratn syndrm
7685-7709,7798
7702   NB interstit emphysema
7685-7709,7798
7703   NB pulmonary hemorrhage
7685-7709,7798
7704   Primary atelectasis
7685-7709,7798
7705   NB atelectasis NEC/NOS
7685-7709,7798
7707   Perinatal chr resp dis
7685-7709,7798
7710   Congenital rubella
7710-7712,7798
7711   Cong cytomegalovirus inf
7710-7712,7798
7713   Tetanus neonatorum
7713,7798
7718   Perinatal infection NEC
7714-7718,7760-7769,7798
7721   NB intraventricular hem
7720-7722,7728-7729,7760-7769,7798
7722   NB subarachnoid hemorr
7720-7722,7728-7729,7760-7769,7798
7724   NB GI hemorrhage
7720,7724-7725,7728-7729,7760-7769,7798
7725   NB adrenal hemorrhage
7720,7724-7725,7728-7729,7760-7769,7798
7730   NB hemolyt dis:rh isoimm
7730-7735,7798
7731   NB hemolyt dis-abo isoim
7730-7735,7798
7732   NB hemolyt dis-isoim NEC
7730-7735,7798
7733   Hydrops fetalis:isoimm
7730-7735,7798
7734   NB kernicterus:isoimmun
7730-7735,7798
7740   Perinat jaund-hered anem
7740-7747,7798
7741   Perinat jaund:hemolysis
7740-7747,7798
7742   Neonat jaund preterm del
7740-7747,7798
77430   Delay conjugat jaund NOS
7740-7747,7798
77431   Neonat jaund in oth dis
7740-7747,7798
77439   Delay conjugat jaund NEC
7740-7747,7798
7744   Fetal/neonatal hepatitis
7740-7747,7798
7745   Perinatal jaundice NEC
7740-7747,7798
7747   NB kernicterus
7740-7747,7798
7751   Neonat diabetes mellitus
7750-7759,7798
7752   Neonat myasthenia gravis
7750-7759,7798
7753   Neonatal thyrotoxicosis
7750-7759,7798
7754   Hypocalcem/hypomagnes NB
7750-7759,7798
7755   Neonatal dehydration
7750-7759,7798

7756   Neonatal hypoglycemia
7750-7759,7798
7757   Late metab acidosis NB
7750-7759,7798
7760   NB hemorrhagic disease
7760-7769,7798
7761   Neonatal thrombocytopen
7760-7769,7798
7762   Dissem intravasc coag NB
7760-7769,7798
7763   Oth neonatal coag dis
7760-7769,7798
7771   Meconium obstruction
7771-7779,7798
7772   Intest obst-inspiss milk
7771-7779,7798
7775   Necrot enterocolitis NB
7771-7779,7798
7776   Perinatal intest perfor
7771-7779,7798
7780   Hydrops fetalis no isoim
7780,7798
7790   Convulsions in newborn
7790-7791,7798
7791   NB cereb irrit NEC/NOS
7790-7791,7798
7793   NB feeding problems
7793
7794   NB drug reaction/intoxic
7794-7795
78001   Coma
0700-0709,25000-2513,3488-3489,34989-3499,430-4329,5722,
78001-78009,7802,7804,7809,7998,80000-80199,80300-80496,
8500-85219,85221-85419
78003   Persistent vegtv state
0700-0709,25000-2513,3488-3489,34989-3499,430-4329,5722,
78001-78009,7802,7804,7809,7998,80000-80199,80300-80496,
8500-85219,85221-85419
7801   Hallucinations
7801,7804,7809,7998
78031   Febrile convulsions
34500-34591,3488-3489,34989-3499,7790-7791,78031-78039,7809,
7998
78039   Convulsions NEC
34500-34591,3488-3489,34989-3499,7790-7791,78031-78039,7809,
7998
7817   Tetany
037,3320-3344,34210-34212,7713,7809,7817,7998
7854   Gangrene
44024,7809,7854,7998
78550   Shock NOS
7809,78550-78559,7859,7998
78551   Cardiogenic shock
7809,78550-78559,7859,7998
78559   Shock w/o trauma NEC
7809,78550-78559,7859,7998
78603   Apnea
51881-51884,5198-5199,78603-78604,7991
78604   Cheyne-Stokes respir
51881-51884,5198-5199,78603-78604,7991
7863   Hemoptysis
7809,7863-7864,7869,7998
78820   Retention urine NOS
27411,34461,5933-5935,5960,5964-59659,5968-5969,5996,600-6029,
7530-7539,7809,78820-78829,78861-78869,7889,7998
78829   Oth spcf retention urine
27411,34461,5933-5935,5960,5964-59659,5968-5969,5996,600-6029,
7530-7539,7809,78820-78829,78861-78869,7889,7998
7895   Ascites
7809,78930-7895,7899,7998
7907   Bacteremia
7809,7907-79099,7998
7911   Chyluria
7809,7911,7919,7998

7913   Myoglobinuria
7809,7912-7913,7919,7998
7991   Respiratory arrest
51881-51884,7809,7980,7990-7991,7998
7994   Cachexia
7809,7993-7998
80000   Closed skull vault fx
80000-80199,80300-80499,8290-8291,8500-85219,85221-85419,
8738-8739,8798-8799,9050,9251-9252,9290-9299,9588-95909,
9598-9599
80001   Cl skull vlt fx w/o coma
80000-80199,80300-80499,8290-8291,8500-85219,85221-85419,
8738-8739,8798-8799,9050,9251-9252,9290-9299,9588-95909,
9598-9599
80002   Cl skull vlt fx-brf coma
80000-80199,80300-80499,8290-8291,8500-85219,85221-85419,
8738-8739,8798-8799,9050,9251-9252,9290-9299,9588-95909,
9598-9599
80003   Cl skull vlt fx-mod coma
80000-80199,80300-80499,8290-8291,8500-85219,85221-85419,
8738-8739,8798-8799,9050,9251-9252,9290-9299,9588-95909,
9598-9599
80004   Cl skl vlt fx-proln coma
80000-80199,80300-80499,8290-8291,8500-85219,85221-85419,
8738-8739,8798-8799,9050,9251-9252,9290-9299,9588-95909,
9598-9599
80005   Cl skul vlt fx-deep coma
80000-80199,80300-80499,8290-8291,8500-85219,85221-85419,
8738-8739,8798-8799,9050,9251-9252,9290-9299,9588-95909,
9598-9599
80006   Cl skull vlt fx-coma NOS
80000-80199,80300-80499,8290-8291,8500-85219,85221-85419,
8738-8739,8798-8799,9050,9251-9252,9290-9299,9588-95909,
9598-9599
80009   Cl skl vlt fx-concus NOS
80000-80199,80300-80499,8290-8291,8500-85219,85221-85419,
8738-8739,8798-8799,9050,9251-9252,9290-9299,9588-95909,
9598-9599
80010   Cl skl vlt fx/cerebr lac
80000-80199,80300-80499,8290-8291,8500-85219,85221-85419,
8738-8739,8798-8799,9050,9251-9252,9290-9299,9588-95909,
9598-9599
80011   Cl skull vlt fx w/o coma
80000-80199,80300-80499,8290-8291,8500-85219,85221-85419,
8738-8739,8798-8799,9050,9251-9252,9290-9299,9588-95909,
9598-9599
80012   Cl skull vlt fx-brf coma
80000-80199,80300-80499,8290-8291,8500-85219,85221-85419,
8738-8739,8798-8799,9050,9251-9252,9290-9299,9588-95909,
9598-9599
80013   Cl skull vlt fx-mod coma
80000-80199,80300-80499,8290-8291,8500-85219,85221-85419,
8738-8739,8798-8799,9050,9251-9252,9290-9299,9588-95909,
9598-9599
80014   Cl skl vlt fx-proln coma
80000-80199,80300-80499,8290-8291,8500-85219,85221-85419,
8738-8739,8798-8799,9050,9251-9252,9290-9299,9588-95909,
9598-9599
80015   Cl skul vlt fx-deep coma
80000-80199,80300-80499,8290-8291,8500-85219,85221-85419,
8738-8739,8798-8799,9050,9251-9252,9290-9299,9588-95909,
9598-9599
80016   Cl skull vlt fx-coma NOS
80000-80199,80300-80499,8290-8291,8500-85219,85221-85419,
8738-8739,8798-8799,9050,9251-9252,9290-9299,9588-95909,
9598-9599
80019   Cl skl vlt fx-concus NOS
80000-80199,80300-80499,8290-8291,8500-85219,85221-85419,
8738-8739,8798-8799,9050,9251-9252,9290-9299,9588-95909,
9598-9599
80020   Cl skl vlt fx/mening hem
80000-80199,80300-80499,8290-8291,8500-85219,85221-85419,
8738-8739,8798-8799,9050,9251-9252,9290-9299,9588-95909,
9598-9599

80021   Cl skull vlt fx w/o coma
80000-80199,80300-80499,8290-8291,8500-85219,85221-85419,
8738-8739,8798-8799,9050,9251-9252,9290-9299,9588-95909,
9598-9599
80022   Cl skull vlt fx-brf coma
80000-80199,80300-80499,8290-8291,8500-85219,85221-85419,
8738-8739,8798-8799,9050,9251-9252,9290-9299,9588-95909,
9598-9599
80023   Cl skull vlt fx-mod coma
80000-80199,80300-80499,8290-8291,8500-85219,85221-85419,
8738-8739,8798-8799,9050,9251-9252,9290-9299,9588-95909,
9598-9599
80024   Cl skl vlt fx-proln coma
80000-80199,80300-80499,8290-8291,8500-85219,85221-85419,
8738-8739,8798-8799,9050,9251-9252,9290-9299,9588-95909,
9598-9599
80025   Cl skul vlt fx-deep coma
80000-80199,80300-80499,8290-8291,8500-85219,85221-85419,
8738-8739,8798-8799,9050,9251-9252,9290-9299,9588-95909,
9598-9599
80026   Cl skull vlt fx-coma NOS
80000-80199,80300-80499,8290-8291,8500-85219,85221-85419,
8738-8739,8798-8799,9050,9251-9252,9290-9299,9588-95909,
9598-9599
80029   Cl skl vlt fx-concus NOS
80000-80199,80300-80499,8290-8291,8500-85219,85221-85419,
8738-8739,8798-8799,9050,9251-9252,9290-9299,9588-95909,
9598-9599
80030   Cl skull vlt fx/hem NEC
80000-80199,80300-80499,8290-8291,8500-85219,85221-85419,
8738-8739,8798-8799,9050,9251-9252,9290-9299,9588-95909,
9598-9599
80031   Cl skull vlt fx w/o coma
80000-80199,80300-80499,8290-8291,8500-85219,85221-85419,
8738-8739,8798-8799,9050,9251-9252,9290-9299,9588-95909,
9598-9599
80032   Cl skull vlt fx-brf coma
80000-80199,80300-80499,8290-8291,8500-85219,85221-85419,
8738-8739,8798-8799,9050,9251-9252,9290-9299,9588-95909,
9598-9599
80033   Cl skull vlt fx-mod coma
80000-80199,80300-80499,8290-8291,8500-85219,85221-85419,
8738-8739,8798-8799,9050,9251-9252,9290-9299,9588-95909,
9598-9599
80034   Cl skl vlt fx-proln coma
80000-80199,80300-80499,8290-8291,8500-85219,85221-85419,
8738-8739,8798-8799,9050,9251-9252,9290-9299,9588-95909,
9598-9599
80035   Cl skul vlt fx-deep coma
80000-80199,80300-80499,8290-8291,8500-85219,85221-85419,
8738-8739,8798-8799,9050,9251-9252,9290-9299,9588-95909,
9598-9599
80036   Cl skull vlt fx-coma NOS
80000-80199,80300-80499,8290-8291,8500-85219,85221-85419,
8738-8739,8798-8799,9050,9251-9252,9290-9299,9588-95909,
9598-9599
80039   Cl skl vlt fx-concus NOS
80000-80199,80300-80499,8290-8291,8500-85219,85221-85419,
8738-8739,8798-8799,9050,9251-9252,9290-9299,9588-95909,
9598-9599
80040   Cl skl vlt fx/br inj NEC
80000-80199,80300-80499,8290-8291,8500-85219,85221-85419,
8738-8739,8798-8799,9050,9251-9252,9290-9299,9588-95909,
9598-9599
80041   Cl skull vlt fx w/o coma
80000-80199,80300-80499,8290-8291,8500-85219,85221-85419,
8738-8739,8798-8799,9050,9251-9252,9290-9299,9588-95909,
9598-9599
80042   Cl skull vlt fx-brf coma
80000-80199,80300-80499,8290-8291,8500-85219,85221-85419,
8738-8739,8798-8799,9050,9251-9252,9290-9299,9588-95909,
9598-9599

80043   Cl skull vlt fx-mod coma
80000-80199,80300-80499,8290-8291,8500-85219,85221-85419,
8738-8739,8798-8799,9050,9251-9252,9290-9299,9588-95909,
9598-9599

80044   Cl skl vlt fx-proln coma
80000-80199,80300-80499,8290-8291,8500-85219,85221-85419,
8738-8739,8798-8799,9050,9251-9252,9290-9299,9588-95909,
9598-9599

80045   Cl skul vlt fx-deep coma
80000-80199,80300-80499,8290-8291,8500-85219,85221-85419,
8738-8739,8798-8799,9050,9251-9252,9290-9299,9588-95909,
9598-9599

80046   Cl skull vlt fx-coma NOS
80000-80199,80300-80499,8290-8291,8500-85219,85221-85419,
8738-8739,8798-8799,9050,9251-9252,9290-9299,9588-95909,
9598-9599

80049   Cl skl vlt fx-concus NOS
80000-80199,80300-80499,8290-8291,8500-85219,85221-85419,
8738-8739,8798-8799,9050,9251-9252,9290-9299,9588-95909,
9598-9599

80050   Opn skull vault fracture
80000-80199,80300-80499,8290-8291,8500-85219,85221-85419,
8738-8739,8798-8799,9050,9251-9252,9290-9299,9588-95909,
9598-9599

80051   Opn skul vlt fx w/o coma
80000-80199,80300-80499,8290-8291,8500-85219,85221-85419,
8738-8739,8798-8799,9050,9251-9252,9290-9299,9588-95909,
9598-9599

80052   Opn skul vlt fx-brf coma
80000-80199,80300-80499,8290-8291,8500-85219,85221-85419,
8738-8739,8798-8799,9050,9251-9252,9290-9299,9588-95909,
9598-9599

80053   Opn skul vlt fx-mod coma
80000-80199,80300-80499,8290-8291,8500-85219,85221-85419,
8738-8739,8798-8799,9050,9251-9252,9290-9299,9588-95909,
9598-9599

80054   Opn skl vlt fx-proln com
80000-80199,80300-80499,8290-8291,8500-85219,85221-85419,
8738-8739,8798-8799,9050,9251-9252,9290-9299,9588-95909,
9598-9599

80055   Opn skl vlt fx-deep coma
80000-80199,80300-80499,8290-8291,8500-85219,85221-85419,
8738-8739,8798-8799,9050,9251-9252,9290-9299,9588-95909,
9598-9599

80056   Opn skul vlt fx-coma NOS
80000-80199,80300-80499,8290-8291,8500-85219,85221-85419,
8738-8739,8798-8799,9050,9251-9252,9290-9299,9588-95909,
9598-9599

80059   Op skl vlt fx-concus NOS
80000-80199,80300-80499,8290-8291,8500-85219,85221-85419,
8738-8739,8798-8799,9050,9251-9252,9290-9299,9588-95909,
9598-9599

80060   Opn skl vlt fx/cereb lac
80000-80199,80300-80499,8290-8291,8500-85219,85221-85419,
8738-8739,8798-8799,9050,9251-9252,9290-9299,9588-95909,
9598-9599

80061   Opn skul vlt fx w/o coma
80000-80199,80300-80499,8290-8291,8500-85219,85221-85419,
8738-8739,8798-8799,9050,9251-9252,9290-9299,9588-95909,
9598-9599

80062   Opn skul vlt fx-brf coma
80000-80199,80300-80499,8290-8291,8500-85219,85221-85419,
8738-8739,8798-8799,9050,9251-9252,9290-9299,9588-95909,
9598-9599

80063   Opn skul vlt fx-mod coma
80000-80199,80300-80499,8290-8291,8500-85219,85221-85419,
8738-8739,8798-8799,9050,9251-9252,9290-9299,9588-95909,
9598-9599

80064   Opn skl vlt fx-proln com
80000-80199,80300-80499,8290-8291,8500-85219,85221-85419,
8738-8739,8798-8799,9050,9251-9252,9290-9299,9588-95909,
9598-9599

80065   Opn skl vlt fx-deep coma
80000-80199,80300-80499,8290-8291,8500-85219,85221-85419,
8738-8739,8798-8799,9050,9251-9252,9290-9299,9588-95909,
9598-9599

80066   Opn skul vlt fx-coma NOS
80000-80199,80300-80499,8290-8291,8500-85219,85221-85419,
8738-8739,8798-8799,9050,9251-9252,9290-9299,9588-95909,
9598-9599

80069   Op skl vlt fx-concus NOS
80000-80199,80300-80499,8290-8291,8500-85219,85221-85419,
8738-8739,8798-8799,9050,9251-9252,9290-9299,9588-95909,
9598-9599

80070   Opn skl vlt fx/menin hem
80000-80199,80300-80499,8290-8291,8500-85219,85221-85419,
8738-8739,8798-8799,9050,9251-9252,9290-9299,9588-95909,
9598-9599

80071   Opn skul vlt fx w/o coma
80000-80199,80300-80499,8290-8291,8500-85219,85221-85419,
8738-8739,8798-8799,9050,9251-9252,9290-9299,9588-95909,
9598-9599

80072   Opn skul vlt fx-brf coma
80000-80199,80300-80499,8290-8291,8500-85219,85221-85419,
8738-8739,8798-8799,9050,9251-9252,9290-9299,9588-95909,
9598-9599

80073   Opn skul vlt fx-mod coma
80000-80199,80300-80499,8290-8291,8500-85219,85221-85419,
8738-8739,8798-8799,9050,9251-9252,9290-9299,9588-95909,
9598-9599

80074   Opn skl vlt fx-proln com
80000-80199,80300-80499,8290-8291,8500-85219,85221-85419,
8738-8739,8798-8799,9050,9251-9252,9290-9299,9588-95909,
9598-9599

80075   Opn skul vlt fx-deep coma
80000-80199,80300-80499,8290-8291,8500-85219,85221-85419,
8738-8739,8798-8799,9050,9251-9252,9290-9299,9588-95909,
9598-9599

80076   Opn skul vlt fx-coma NOS
80000-80199,80300-80499,8290-8291,8500-85219,85221-85419,
8738-8739,8798-8799,9050,9251-9252,9290-9299,9588-95909,
9598-9599

80079   Op skl vlt fx-concus NOS
80000-80199,80300-80499,8290-8291,8500-85219,85221-85419,
8738-8739,8798-8799,9050,9251-9252,9290-9299,9588-95909,
9598-9599

80080   Opn skull vlt fx/hem NEC
80000-80199,80300-80499,8290-8291,8500-85219,85221-85419,
8738-8739,8798-8799,9050,9251-9252,9290-9299,9588-95909,
9598-9599

80081   Opn skul vlt fx w/o coma
80000-80199,80300-80499,8290-8291,8500-85219,85221-85419,
8738-8739,8798-8799,9050,9251-9252,9290-9299,9588-95909,
9598-9599

80082   Opn skul vlt fx-brf coma
80000-80199,80300-80499,8290-8291,8500-85219,85221-85419,
8738-8739,8798-8799,9050,9251-9252,9290-9299,9588-95909,
9598-9599

80083   Opn skul vlt fx-mod coma
80000-80199,80300-80499,8290-8291,8500-85219,85221-85419,
8738-8739,8798-8799,9050,9251-9252,9290-9299,9588-95909,
9598-9599

80084   Opn skl vlt fx-proln com
80000-80199,80300-80499,8290-8291,8500-85219,85221-85419,
8738-8739,8798-8799,9050,9251-9252,9290-9299,9588-95909,
9598-9599

80085   Opn skl vlt fx-deep coma
80000-80199,80300-80499,8290-8291,8500-85219,85221-85419,
8738-8739,8798-8799,9050,9251-9252,9290-9299,9588-95909,
9598-9599

80086   Opn skul vlt fx-coma NOS
80000-80199,80300-80499,8290-8291,8500-85219,85221-85419,
8738-8739,8798-8799,9050,9251-9252,9290-9299,9588-95909,
9598-9599

ICD-9-CM
Appx F
Vol. 1

80089 Op skl vlt fx-concus NOS
80000-80199,80300-80499,8290-8291,8500-85219,85221-85419,
8738-8739,8798-8799,9050,9251-9252,9290-9299,9588-95909,
9598-9599

80090 Op skl vlt fx/br inj NEC
80000-80199,80300-80499,8290-8291,8500-85219,85221-85419,
8738-8739,8798-8799,9050,9251-9252,9290-9299,9588-95909,
9598-9599

80091 Opn skul vlt fx w/o coma
80000-80199,80300-80499,8290-8291,8500-85219,85221-85419,
8738-8739,8798-8799,9050,9251-9252,9290-9299,9588-95909,
9598-9599

80092 Opn skul vlt fx-brf coma
80000-80199,80300-80499,8290-8291,8500-85219,85221-85419,
8738-8739,8798-8799,9050,9251-9252,9290-9299,9588-95909,
9598-9599

80093 Opn skul vlt fx-mod coma
80000-80199,80300-80499,8290-8291,8500-85219,85221-85419,
8738-8739,8798-8799,9050,9251-9252,9290-9299,9588-95909,
9598-9599

80094 Opn skul vlt fx-proln com
80000-80199,80300-80499,8290-8291,8500-85219,85221-85419,
8738-8739,8798-8799,9050,9251-9252,9290-9299,9588-95909,
9598-9599

80095 Op skul vlt fx-deep coma
80000-80199,80300-80499,8290-8291,8500-85219,85221-85419,
8738-8739,8798-8799,9050,9251-9252,9290-9299,9588-95909,
9598-9599

80096 Opn skul vlt fx-coma NOS
80000-80199,80300-80499,8290-8291,8500-85219,85221-85419,
8738-8739,8798-8799,9050,9251-9252,9290-9299,9588-95909,
9598-9599

80099 Op skl vlt fx-concus NOS
80000-80199,80300-80499,8290-8291,8500-85219,85221-85419,
8738-8739,8798-8799,9050,9251-9252,9290-9299,9588-95909,
9598-9599

80100 Clos skull base fracture
80000-80199,80300-80499,8290-8291,8500-85219,85221-85419,
8738-8739,8798-8799,9050,9251-9252,9290-9299,9588-95909,
9598-9599

80101 Cl skul base fx w/o coma
80000-80199,80300-80499,8290-8291,8500-85219,85221-85419,
8738-8739,8798-8799,9050,9251-9252,9290-9299,9588-95909,
9598-9599

80102 Cl skul base fx-brf coma
80000-80199,80300-80499,8290-8291,8500-85219,85221-85419,
8738-8739,8798-8799,9050,9251-9252,9290-9299,9588-95909,
9598-9599

80103 Cl skul base fx-mod coma
80000-80199,80300-80499,8290-8291,8500-85219,85221-85419,
8738-8739,8798-8799,9050,9251-9252,9290-9299,9588-95909,
9598-9599

80104 Cl skl base fx-prol coma
80000-80199,80300-80499,8290-8291,8500-85219,85221-85419,
8738-8739,8798-8799,9050,9251-9252,9290-9299,9588-95909,
9598-9599

80105 Cl skl base fx-deep coma
80000-80199,80300-80499,8290-8291,8500-85219,85221-85419,
8738-8739,8798-8799,9050,9251-9252,9290-9299,9588-95909,
9598-9599

80106 Cl skul base fx-coma NOS
80000-80199,80300-80499,8290-8291,8500-85219,85221-85419,
8738-8739,8798-8799,9050,9251-9252,9290-9299,9588-95909,
9598-9599

80109 Cl skull base fx-concuss
80000-80199,80300-80499,8290-8291,8500-85219,85221-85419,
8738-8739,8798-8799,9050,9251-9252,9290-9299,9588-95909,
9598-9599

80110 Cl skl base fx/cereb lac
80000-80199,80300-80499,8290-8291,8500-85219,85221-85419,
8738-8739,8798-8799,9050,9251-9252,9290-9299,9588-95909,
9598-9599

80111 Cl skul base fx w/o coma
80000-80199,80300-80499,8290-8291,8500-85219,85221-85419,
8738-8739,8798-8799,9050,9251-9252,9290-9299,9588-95909,
9598-9599

80112 Cl skul base fx-brf coma
80000-80199,80300-80499,8290-8291,8500-85219,85221-85419,
8738-8739,8798-8799,9050,9251-9252,9290-9299,9588-95909,
9598-9599

80113 Cl skul base fx-mod coma
80000-80199,80300-80499,8290-8291,8500-85219,85221-85419,
8738-8739,8798-8799,9050,9251-9252,9290-9299,9588-95909,
9598-9599

80114 Cl skl base fx-prol coma
80000-80199,80300-80499,8290-8291,8500-85219,85221-85419,
8738-8739,8798-8799,9050,9251-9252,9290-9299,9588-95909,
9598-9599

80115 Cl skl base fx-deep coma
80000-80199,80300-80499,8290-8291,8500-85219,85221-85419,
8738-8739,8798-8799,9050,9251-9252,9290-9299,9588-95909,
9598-9599

80116 Cl skul base fx-coma NOS
80000-80199,80300-80499,8290-8291,8500-85219,85221-85419,
8738-8739,8798-8799,9050,9251-9252,9290-9299,9588-95909,
9598-9599

80119 Cl skull base fx-concuss
80000-80199,80300-80499,8290-8291,8500-85219,85221-85419,
8738-8739,8798-8799,9050,9251-9252,9290-9299,9588-95909,
9598-9599

80120 Cl skl base fx/menin hem
80000-80199,80300-80499,8290-8291,8500-85219,85221-85419,
8738-8739,8798-8799,9050,9251-9252,9290-9299,9588-95909,
9598-9599

80121 Cl skul base fx w/o coma
80000-80199,80300-80499,8290-8291,8500-85219,85221-85419,
8738-8739,8798-8799,9050,9251-9252,9290-9299,9588-95909,
9598-9599

80122 Cl skul base fx/brf coma
80000-80199,80300-80499,8290-8291,8500-85219,85221-85419,
8738-8739,8798-8799,9050,9251-9252,9290-9299,9588-95909,
9598-9599

80123 Cl skul base fx-mod coma
80000-80199,80300-80499,8290-8291,8500-85219,85221-85419,
8738-8739,8798-8799,9050,9251-9252,9290-9299,9588-95909,
9598-9599

80124 Cl skl base fx-prol coma
80000-80199,80300-80499,8290-8291,8500-85219,85221-85419,
8738-8739,8798-8799,9050,9251-9252,9290-9299,9588-95909,
9598-9599

80125 Cl skl base fx-deep coma
80000-80199,80300-80499,8290-8291,8500-85219,85221-85419,
8738-8739,8798-8799,9050,9251-9252,9290-9299,9588-95909,
9598-9599

80126 Cl skul base fx-coma NOS
80000-80199,80300-80499,8290-8291,8500-85219,85221-85419,
8738-8739,8798-8799,9050,9251-9252,9290-9299,9588-95909,
9598-9599

80129 Cl skull base fx-concuss
80000-80199,80300-80499,8290-8291,8500-85219,85221-85419,
8738-8739,8798-8799,9050,9251-9252,9290-9299,9588-95909,
9598-9599

80130 Cl skull base fx/hem NEC
80000-80199,80300-80499,8290-8291,8500-85219,85221-85419,
8738-8739,8798-8799,9050,9251-9252,9290-9299,9588-95909,
9598-9599

80131 Cl skul base fx w/o coma
80000-80199,80300-80499,8290-8291,8500-85219,85221-85419,
8738-8739,8798-8799,9050,9251-9252,9290-9299,9588-95909,
9598-9599

80132 Cl skul base fx-brf coma
80000-80199,80300-80499,8290-8291,8500-85219,85221-85419,
8738-8739,8798-8799,9050,9251-9252,9290-9299,9588-95909,
9598-9599

80133 Cl skul base fx-mod coma
80000-80199,80300-80499,8290-8291,8500-85219,85221-85419,
8738-8739,8798-8799,9050,9251-9252,9290-9299,9588-95909,
9598-9599

80134 Cl skl base fx-prol coma
80000-80199,80300-80499,8290-8291,8500-85219,85221-85419,
8738-8739,8798-8799,9050,9251-9252,9290-9299,9588-95909,
9598-9599

80135 Cl skl base fx-deep coma
80000-80199,80300-80499,8290-8291,8500-85219,85221-85419,
8738-8739,8798-8799,9050,9251-9252,9290-9299,9588-95909,
9598-9599

80136 Cl skul base fx-coma NOS
80000-80199,80300-80499,8290-8291,8500-85219,85221-85419,
8738-8739,8798-8799,9050,9251-9252,9290-9299,9588-95909,
9598-9599

80139 Cl skull base fx-concuss
80000-80199,80300-80499,8290-8291,8500-85219,85221-85419,
8738-8739,8798-8799,9050,9251-9252,9290-9299,9588-95909,
9598-9599

80140 Cl sk base fx/br inj NEC
80000-80199,80300-80499,8290-8291,8500-85219,85221-85419,
8738-8739,8798-8799,9050,9251-9252,9290-9299,9588-95909,
9598-9599

80141 Cl skul base fx w/o coma
80000-80199,80300-80499,8290-8291,8500-85219,85221-85419,
8738-8739,8798-8799,9050,9251-9252,9290-9299,9588-95909,
9598-9599

80142 Cl skul base fx-brf coma
80000-80199,80300-80499,8290-8291,8500-85219,85221-85419,
8738-8739,8798-8799,9050,9251-9252,9290-9299,9588-95909,
9598-9599

80143 Cl skul base fx-mod coma
80000-80199,80300-80499,8290-8291,8500-85219,85221-85419,
8738-8739,8798-8799,9050,9251-9252,9290-9299,9588-95909,
9598-9599

80144 Cl skl base fx-prol coma
80000-80199,80300-80499,8290-8291,8500-85219,85221-85419,
8738-8739,8798-8799,9050,9251-9252,9290-9299,9588-95909,
9598-9599

80145 Cl skl base fx-deep coma
80000-80199,80300-80499,8290-8291,8500-85219,85221-85419,
8738-8739,8798-8799,9050,9251-9252,9290-9299,9588-95909,
9598-9599

80146 Cl skul base fx-coma NOS
80000-80199,80300-80499,8290-8291,8500-85219,85221-85419,
8738-8739,8798-8799,9050,9251-9252,9290-9299,9588-95909,
9598-9599

80149 Cl skull base fx-concuss
80000-80199,80300-80499,8290-8291,8500-85219,85221-85419,
8738-8739,8798-8799,9050,9251-9252,9290-9299,9588-95909,
9598-9599

80150 Open skull base fracture
80000-80199,80300-80499,8290-8291,8500-85219,85221-85419,
8738-8739,8798-8799,9050,9251-9252,9290-9299,9588-95909,
9598-9599

80151 Opn skl base fx w/o coma
80000-80199,80300-80499,8290-8291,8500-85219,85221-85419,
8738-8739,8798-8799,9050,9251-9252,9290-9299,9588-95909,
9598-9599

80152 Opn skl base fx-brf coma
80000-80199,80300-80499,8290-8291,8500-85219,85221-85419,
8738-8739,8798-8799,9050,9251-9252,9290-9299,9588-95909,
9598-9599

80153 Opn skl base fx-mod coma
80000-80199,80300-80499,8290-8291,8500-85219,85221-85419,
8738-8739,8798-8799,9050,9251-9252,9290-9299,9588-95909,
9598-9599

80154 Op skl base fx-prol coma
80000-80199,80300-80499,8290-8291,8500-85219,85221-85419,
8738-8739,8798-8799,9050,9251-9252,9290-9299,9588-95909,
9598-9599

80155 Op skl base fx-deep coma
80000-80199,80300-80499,8290-8291,8500-85219,85221-85419,
8738-8739,8798-8799,9050,9251-9252,9290-9299,9588-95909,
9598-9599

80156 Opn skl base fx-coma NOS
80000-80199,80300-80499,8290-8291,8500-85219,85221-85419,
8738-8739,8798-8799,9050,9251-9252,9290-9299,9588-95909,
9598-9599

80159 Opn skul base fx-concuss
80000-80199,80300-80499,8290-8291,8500-85219,85221-85419,
8738-8739,8798-8799,9050,9251-9252,9290-9299,9588-95909,
9598-9599

80160 Op skl base fx/cereb lac
80000-80199,80300-80499,8290-8291,8500-85219,85221-85419,
8738-8739,8798-8799,9050,9251-9252,9290-9299,9588-95909,
9598-9599

80161 Opn skl base fx w/o coma
80000-80199,80300-80499,8290-8291,8500-85219,85221-85419,
8738-8739,8798-8799,9050,9251-9252,9290-9299,9588-95909,
9598-9599

80162 Opn skl base fx-brf coma
80000-80199,80300-80499,8290-8291,8500-85219,85221-85419,
8738-8739,8798-8799,9050,9251-9252,9290-9299,9588-95909,
9598-9599

80163 Opn skl base fx-mod coma
80000-80199,80300-80499,8290-8291,8500-85219,85221-85419,
8738-8739,8798-8799,9050,9251-9252,9290-9299,9588-95909,
9598-9599

80164 Op skl base fx-prol coma
80000-80199,80300-80499,8290-8291,8500-85219,85221-85419,
8738-8739,8798-8799,9050,9251-9252,9290-9299,9588-95909,
9598-9599

80165 Op skl base fx-deep coma
80000-80199,80300-80499,8290-8291,8500-85219,85221-85419,
8738-8739,8798-8799,9050,9251-9252,9290-9299,9588-95909,
9598-9599

80166 Opn skl base fx-coma NOS
80000-80199,80300-80499,8290-8291,8500-85219,85221-85419,
8738-8739,8798-8799,9050,9251-9252,9290-9299,9588-95909,
9598-9599

80169 Opn skul base fx-concuss
80000-80199,80300-80499,8290-8291,8500-85219,85221-85419,
8738-8739,8798-8799,9050,9251-9252,9290-9299,9588-95909,
9598-9599

80170 Op skl base fx/menin hem
80000-80199,80300-80499,8290-8291,8500-85219,85221-85419,
8738-8739,8798-8799,9050,9251-9252,9290-9299,9588-95909,
9598-9599

80171 Opn skl base fx w/o coma
80000-80199,80300-80499,8290-8291,8500-85219,85221-85419,
8738-8739,8798-8799,9050,9251-9252,9290-9299,9588-95909,
9598-9599

80172 Opn skl base fx-brf coma
80000-80199,80300-80499,8290-8291,8500-85219,85221-85419,
8738-8739,8798-8799,9050,9251-9252,9290-9299,9588-95909,
9598-9599

80173 Opn skl base fx-mod coma
80000-80199,80300-80499,8290-8291,8500-85219,85221-85419,
8738-8739,8798-8799,9050,9251-9252,9290-9299,9588-95909,
9598-9599

80174 Op skl base fx-prol coma
80000-80199,80300-80499,8290-8291,8500-85219,85221-85419,
8738-8739,8798-8799,9050,9251-9252,9290-9299,9588-95909,
9598-9599

80175 Op skl base fx-deep coma
80000-80199,80300-80499,8290-8291,8500-85219,85221-85419,
8738-8739,8798-8799,9050,9251-9252,9290-9299,9588-95909,
9598-9599

80176 Opn skl base fx-coma NOS
80000-80199,80300-80499,8290-8291,8500-85219,85221-85419,
8738-8739,8798-8799,9050,9251-9252,9290-9299,9588-95909,
9598-9599

ICD-9-CM

Appx F

Vol. 1

80179   Opn skul base fx-concuss
80000-80199,80300-80499,8290-8291,8500-85219,85221-85419,
8738-8739,8798-8799,9050,9251-9252,9290-9299,9588-95909,
9598-9599

80180   Opn skul base fx/hem NEC
80000-80199,80300-80499,8290-8291,8500-85219,85221-85419,
8738-8739,8798-8799,9050,9251-9252,9290-9299,9588-95909,
9598-9599

80181   Opn skl base fx w/o coma
80000-80199,80300-80499,8290-8291,8500-85219,85221-85419,
8738-8739,8798-8799,9050,9251-9252,9290-9299,9588-95909,
9598-9599

80182   Opn skl base fx-brf coma
80000-80199,80300-80499,8290-8291,8500-85219,85221-85419,
8738-8739,8798-8799,9050,9251-9252,9290-9299,9588-95909,
9598-9599

80183   Opn skl base fx-mod coma
80000-80199,80300-80499,8290-8291,8500-85219,85221-85419,
8738-8739,8798-8799,9050,9251-9252,9290-9299,9588-95909,
9598-9599

80184   Op skl base fx-prol coma
80000-80199,80300-80499,8290-8291,8500-85219,85221-85419,
8738-8739,8798-8799,9050,9251-9252,9290-9299,9588-95909,
9598-9599

80185   Op skl base fx-deep coma
80000-80199,80300-80499,8290-8291,8500-85219,85221-85419,
8738-8739,8798-8799,9050,9251-9252,9290-9299,9588-95909,
9598-9599

80186   Opn skl base fx-coma NOS
80000-80199,80300-80499,8290-8291,8500-85219,85221-85419,
8738-8739,8798-8799,9050,9251-9252,9290-9299,9588-95909,
9598-9599

80189   Opn skul base fx-concuss
80000-80199,80300-80499,8290-8291,8500-85219,85221-85419,
8738-8739,8798-8799,9050,9251-9252,9290-9299,9588-95909,
9598-9599

80190   Op sk base fx/br inj NEC
80000-80199,80300-80499,8290-8291,8500-85219,85221-85419,
8738-8739,8798-8799,9050,9251-9252,9290-9299,9588-95909,
9598-9599

80191   Op skul base fx w/o coma
80000-80199,80300-80499,8290-8291,8500-85219,85221-85419,
8738-8739,8798-8799,9050,9251-9252,9290-9299,9588-95909,
9598-9599

80192   Opn skl base fx-brf coma
80000-80199,80300-80499,8290-8291,8500-85219,85221-85419,
8738-8739,8798-8799,9050,9251-9252,9290-9299,9588-95909,
9598-9599

80193   Opn skl base fx-mod coma
80000-80199,80300-80499,8290-8291,8500-85219,85221-85419,
8738-8739,8798-8799,9050,9251-9252,9290-9299,9588-95909,
9598-9599

80194   Op skl base fx-prol coma
80000-80199,80300-80499,8290-8291,8500-85219,85221-85419,
8738-8739,8798-8799,9050,9251-9252,9290-9299,9588-95909,
9598-9599

80195   Op skl base fx-deep coma
80000-80199,80300-80499,8290-8291,8500-85219,85221-85419,
8738-8739,8798-8799,9050,9251-9252,9290-9299,9588-95909,
9598-9599

80196   Opn skl base fx-coma NOS
80000-80199,80300-80499,8290-8291,8500-85219,85221-85419,
8738-8739,8798-8799,9050,9251-9252,9290-9299,9588-95909,
9598-9599

80199   Opn skul base fx-concuss
80000-80199,80300-80499,8290-8291,8500-85219,85221-85419,
8738-8739,8798-8799,9050,9251-9252,9290-9299,9588-95909,
9598-9599

8021   Nasal bone fx-open
80000-8021,80300-80499,8290-8291,8500-85219,85221-85419,
8738-8739,8798-8799,9050,9251-9252,9290-9299,9588-95909,
9598-9599

80220   Mandible fx NOS-closed
80000-80199,80220-8025,80300-80499,8290-8301,8500-85219,
85221-85419,8738-8739,8798-8799,9050,9251-9252,9290-9299,
9588-95909,9598-9599

80221   Fx condyl proc mandib-cl
80000-80199,80220-8025,80300-80499,8290-8301,8500-85219,
85221-85419,8738-8739,8798-8799,9050,9251-9252,9290-9299,
9588-95909,9598-9599

80222   Subcondylar fx mandib-cl
80000-80199,80220-8025,80300-80499,8290-8301,8500-85219,
85221-85419,8738-8739,8798-8799,9050,9251-9252,9290-9299,
9588-95909,9598-9599

80223   Fx coron proc mandib-cl
80000-80199,80220-8025,80300-80499,8290-8301,8500-85219,
85221-85419,8738-8739,8798-8799,9050,9251-9252,9290-9299,
9588-95909,9598-9599

80224   Fx ramus NOS-closed
80000-80199,80220-8025,80300-80499,8290-8301,8500-85219,
85221-85419,8738-8739,8798-8799,9050,9251-9252,9290-9299,
9588-95909,9598-9599

80225   Fx angle of jaw-closed
80000-80199,80220-8025,80300-80499,8290-8301,8500-85219,
85221-85419,8738-8739,8798-8799,9050,9251-9252,9290-9299,
9588-95909,9598-9599

80226   Fx symphy mandib body-cl
80000-80199,80220-8025,80300-80499,8290-8301,8500-85219,
85221-85419,8738-8739,8798-8799,9050,9251-9252,9290-9299,
9588-95909,9598-9599

80227   Fx alveolar bord mand-cl
80000-80199,80220-8025,80300-80499,8290-8301,8500-85219,
85221-85419,8738-8739,8798-8799,9050,9251-9252,9290-9299,
9588-95909,9598-9599

80228   Fx mandible body NEC-cl
80000-80199,80220-8025,80300-80499,8290-8301,8500-85219,
85221-85419,8738-8739,8798-8799,9050,9251-9252,9290-9299,
9588-95909,9598-9599

80229   Mult fx mandible-closed
80000-80199,80220-8025,80300-80499,8290-8301,8500-85219,
85221-85419,8738-8739,8798-8799,9050,9251-9252,9290-9299,
9588-95909,9598-9599

80230   Mandible fx NOS-open
80000-80199,80220-8025,80300-80499,8290-8301,8500-85219,
85221-85419,8738-8739,8798-8799,9050,9251-9252,9290-9299,
9588-95909,9598-9599

80231   Fx condyl proc mand-open
80000-80199,80220-8025,80300-80499,8290-8301,8500-85219,
85221-85419,8738-8739,8798-8799,9050,9251-9252,9290-9299,
9588-95909,9598-9599

80232   Subcondyl fx mandib-open
80000-80199,80220-8025,80300-80499,8290-8301,8500-85219,
85221-85419,8738-8739,8798-8799,9050,9251-9252,9290-9299,
9588-95909,9598-9599

80233   Fx coron proc mandib-opn
80000-80199,80220-8025,80300-80499,8290-8301,8500-85219,
85221-85419,8738-8739,8798-8799,9050,9251-9252,9290-9299,
9588-95909,9598-9599

80234   Fx ramus NOS-open
80000-80199,80220-8025,80300-80499,8290-8301,8500-85219,
85221-85419,8738-8739,8798-8799,9050,9251-9252,9290-9299,
9588-95909,9598-9599

80235   Fx angle of jaw-open
80000-80199,80220-8025,80300-80499,8290-8301,8500-85219,
85221-85419,8738-8739,8798-8799,9050,9251-9252,9290-9299,
9588-95909,9598-9599

80236   Fx symphy mandib bdy-opn
80000-80199,80220-8025,80300-80499,8290-8301,8500-85219,
85221-85419,8738-8739,8798-8799,9050,9251-9252,9290-9299,
9588-95909,9598-9599

80237   Fx alv bord mand bdy-opn
80000-80199,80220-8025,80300-80499,8290-8301,8500-85219,
85221-85419,8738-8739,8798-8799,9050,9251-9252,9290-9299,
9588-95909,9598-9599

80238   Fx mandible body NEC-opn
80000-80199,80220-8025,80300-80499,8290-8301,8500-85219,
85221-85419,8738-8739,8798-8799,9050,9251-9252,9290-9299,
9588-95909,9598-9599

80239   Mult fx mandible-open
80000-80199,80220-8025,80300-80499,8290-8301,8500-85219,
85221-85419,8738-8739,8798-8799,9050,9251-9252,9290-9299,
9588-95909,9598-9599

8024   Fx malar/maxillary-close
80000-80199,80220-8025,80300-80499,8290-8301,8500-85219,
85221-85419,8738-8739,8798-8799,9050,9251-9252,9290-9299,
9588-95909,9598-9599

8025   Fx malar/maxillary-open
80000-80199,80220-8025,80300-80499,8290-8301,8500-85219,
85221-85419,8738-8739,8798-8799,9050,9251-9252,9290-9299,
9588-95909,9598-9599

8026   Fx orbital floor-closed
80000-80199,8026-80499,8290-8291,8500-85219,85221-85419,
8738-8739,8798-8799,9050,9251-9252,9290-9299,9588-95909,
9598-9599

8027   Fx orbital floor-open
80000-80199,8026-80499,8290-8291,8500-85219,85221-85419,
8738-8739,8798-8799,9050,9251-9252,9290-9299,9588-95909,
9598-9599

8028   Fx facial bone NEC-close
80000-80199,8026-80499,8290-8291,8500-85219,85221-85419,
8738-8739,8798-8799,9050,9251-9252,9290-9299,9588-95909,
9598-9599

8029   Fx facial bone NEC-open
80000-80199,8026-80499,8290-8291,8500-85219,85221-85419,
8738-8739,8798-8799,9050,9251-9252,9290-9299,9588-95909,
9598-9599

80300   Close skull fracture NEC
80000-80199,80300-80499,8290-8291,8500-85219,85221-85419,
8738-8739,8798-8799,9050,9251-9252,9290-9299,9588-95909,
9598-9599

80301   Cl skull fx NEC w/o coma
80000-80199,80300-80499,8290-8291,8500-85219,85221-85419,
8738-8739,8798-8799,9050,9251-9252,9290-9299,9588-95909,
9598-9599

80302   Cl skull fx NEC-brf coma
80000-80199,80300-80499,8290-8291,8500-85219,85221-85419,
8738-8739,8798-8799,9050,9251-9252,9290-9299,9588-95909,
9598-9599

80303   Cl skull fx NEC-mod coma
80000-80199,80300-80499,8290-8291,8500-85219,85221-85419,
8738-8739,8798-8799,9050,9251-9252,9290-9299,9588-95909,
9598-9599

80304   Cl skl fx NEC-proln coma
80000-80199,80300-80499,8290-8291,8500-85219,85221-85419,
8738-8739,8798-8799,9050,9251-9252,9290-9299,9588-95909,
9598-9599

80305   Cl skul fx NEC-deep coma
80000-80199,80300-80499,8290-8291,8500-85219,85221-85419,
8738-8739,8798-8799,9050,9251-9252,9290-9299,9588-95909,
9598-9599

80306   Cl skull fx NEC-coma NOS
80000-80199,80300-80499,8290-8291,8500-85219,85221-85419,
8738-8739,8798-8799,9050,9251-9252,9290-9299,9588-95909,
9598-9599

80309   Cl skull fx NEC-concuss
80000-80199,80300-80499,8290-8291,8500-85219,85221-85419,
8738-8739,8798-8799,9050,9251-9252,9290-9299,9588-95909,
9598-9599

80310   Cl skl fx NEC/cerebr lac
80000-80199,80300-80499,8290-8291,8500-85219,85221-85419,
8738-8739,8798-8799,9050,9251-9252,9290-9299,9588-95909,
9598-9599

80311   Cl skull fx NEC w/o coma
80000-80199,80300-80499,8290-8291,8500-85219,85221-85419,
8738-8739,8798-8799,9050,9251-9252,9290-9299,9588-95909,
9598-9599

80312   Cl skull fx NEC-brf coma
80000-80199,80300-80499,8290-8291,8500-85219,85221-85419,
8738-8739,8798-8799,9050,9251-9252,9290-9299,9588-95909,
9598-9599

80313   Cl skull fx NEC-mod coma
80000-80199,80300-80499,8290-8291,8500-85219,85221-85419,
8738-8739,8798-8799,9050,9251-9252,9290-9299,9588-95909,
9598-9599

80314   Cl skl fx NEC-proln coma
80000-80199,80300-80499,8290-8291,8500-85219,85221-85419,
8738-8739,8798-8799,9050,9251-9252,9290-9299,9588-95909,
9598-9599

80315   Cl skul fx NEC-deep coma
80000-80199,80300-80499,8290-8291,8500-85219,85221-85419,
8738-8739,8798-8799,9050,9251-9252,9290-9299,9588-95909,
9598-9599

80316   Cl skull fx NEC-coma NOS
80000-80199,80300-80499,8290-8291,8500-85219,85221-85419,
8738-8739,8798-8799,9050,9251-9252,9290-9299,9588-95909,
9598-9599

80319   Cl skull fx NEC-concuss
80000-80199,80300-80499,8290-8291,8500-85219,85221-85419,
8738-8739,8798-8799,9050,9251-9252,9290-9299,9588-95909,
9598-9599

80320   Cl skl fx NEC/mening hem
80000-80199,80300-80499,8290-8291,8500-85219,85221-85419,
8738-8739,8798-8799,9050,9251-9252,9290-9299,9588-95909,
9598-9599

80321   Cl skull fx NEC w/o coma
80000-80199,80300-80499,8290-8291,8500-85219,85221-85419,
8738-8739,8798-8799,9050,9251-9252,9290-9299,9588-95909,
9598-9599

80322   Cl skull fx NEC-brf coma
80000-80199,80300-80499,8290-8291,8500-85219,85221-85419,
8738-8739,8798-8799,9050,9251-9252,9290-9299,9588-95909,
9598-9599

80323   Cl skull fx NEC-mod coma
80000-80199,80300-80499,8290-8291,8500-85219,85221-85419,
8738-8739,8798-8799,9050,9251-9252,9290-9299,9588-95909,
9598-9599

80324   Cl skl fx NEC-proln coma
80000-80199,80300-80499,8290-8291,8500-85219,85221-85419,
8738-8739,8798-8799,9050,9251-9252,9290-9299,9588-95909,
9598-9599

80325   Cl skul fx NEC-deep coma
80000-80199,80300-80499,8290-8291,8500-85219,85221-85419,
8738-8739,8798-8799,9050,9251-9252,9290-9299,9588-95909,
9598-9599

80326   Cl skull fx NEC-coma NOS
80000-80199,80300-80499,8290-8291,8500-85219,85221-85419,
8738-8739,8798-8799,9050,9251-9252,9290-9299,9588-95909,
9598-9599

80329   Cl skull fx NEC-concuss
80000-80199,80300-80499,8290-8291,8500-85219,85221-85419,
8738-8739,8798-8799,9050,9251-9252,9290-9299,9588-95909,
9598-9599

80330   Cl skull fx NEC/hem NEC
80000-80199,80300-80499,8290-8291,8500-85219,85221-85419,
8738-8739,8798-8799,9050,9251-9252,9290-9299,9588-95909,
9598-9599

80331   Cl skull fx NEC w/o coma
80000-80199,80300-80499,8290-8291,8500-85219,85221-85419,
8738-8739,8798-8799,9050,9251-9252,9290-9299,9588-95909,
9598-9599

80332   Cl skull fx NEC-brf coma
80000-80199,80300-80499,8290-8291,8500-85219,85221-85419,
8738-8739,8798-8799,9050,9251-9252,9290-9299,9588-95909,
9598-9599

80333   Cl skull fx NEC-mod coma
80000-80199,80300-80499,8290-8291,8500-85219,85221-85419,
8738-8739,8798-8799,9050,9251-9252,9290-9299,9588-95909,
9598-9599

80334   Cl skl fx NEC-proln coma
80000-80199,80300-80499,8290-8291,8500-85219,85221-85419,
8738-8739,8798-8799,9050,9251-9252,9290-9299,9588-95909,
9598-9599

80335   Cl skul fx NEC-deep coma
80000-80199,80300-80499,8290-8291,8500-85219,85221-85419,
8738-8739,8798-8799,9050,9251-9252,9290-9299,9588-95909,
9598-9599

80336   Cl skull fx NEC-coma NOS
80000-80199,80300-80499,8290-8291,8500-85219,85221-85419,
8738-8739,8798-8799,9050,9251-9252,9290-9299,9588-95909,
9598-9599

80339   Cl skull fx NEC-concuss
80000-80199,80300-80499,8290-8291,8500-85219,85221-85419,
8738-8739,8798-8799,9050,9251-9252,9290-9299,9588-95909,
9598-9599

80340   Cl skl fx NEC/br inj NEC
80000-80199,80300-80499,8290-8291,8500-85219,85221-85419,
8738-8739,8798-8799,9050,9251-9252,9290-9299,9588-95909,
9598-9599

80341   Cl skull fx NEC w/o coma
80000-80199,80300-80499,8290-8291,8500-85219,85221-85419,
8738-8739,8798-8799,9050,9251-9252,9290-9299,9588-95909,
9598-9599

80342   Cl skull fx NEC-brf coma
80000-80199,80300-80499,8290-8291,8500-85219,85221-85419,
8738-8739,8798-8799,9050,9251-9252,9290-9299,9588-95909,
9598-9599

80343   Cl skull fx NEC-mod coma
80000-80199,80300-80499,8290-8291,8500-85219,85221-85419,
8738-8739,8798-8799,9050,9251-9252,9290-9299,9588-95909,
9598-9599

80344   Cl skl fx NEC-proln coma
80000-80199,80300-80499,8290-8291,8500-85219,85221-85419,
8738-8739,8798-8799,9050,9251-9252,9290-9299,9588-95909,
9598-9599

80345   Cl skul fx NEC-deep coma
80000-80199,80300-80499,8290-8291,8500-85219,85221-85419,
8738-8739,8798-8799,9050,9251-9252,9290-9299,9588-95909,
9598-9599

80346   Cl skull fx NEC-coma NOS
80000-80199,80300-80499,8290-8291,8500-85219,85221-85419,
8738-8739,8798-8799,9050,9251-9252,9290-9299,9588-95909,
9598-9599

80349   Cl skull fx NEC-concuss
80000-80199,80300-80499,8290-8291,8500-85219,85221-85419,
8738-8739,8798-8799,9050,9251-9252,9290-9299,9588-95909,
9598-9599

80350   Open skull fracture NEC
80000-80199,80300-80499,8290-8291,8500-85219,85221-85419,
8738-8739,8798-8799,9050,9251-9252,9290-9299,9588-95909,
9598-9599

80351   Opn skul fx NEC w/o coma
80000-80199,80300-80499,8290-8291,8500-85219,85221-85419,
8738-8739,8798-8799,9050,9251-9252,9290-9299,9588-95909,
9598-9599

80352   Opn skul fx NEC-brf coma
80000-80199,80300-80499,8290-8291,8500-85219,85221-85419,
8738-8739,8798-8799,9050,9251-9252,9290-9299,9588-95909,
9598-9599

80353   Opn skul fx NEC-mod coma
80000-80199,80300-80499,8290-8291,8500-85219,85221-85419,
8738-8739,8798-8799,9050,9251-9252,9290-9299,9588-95909,
9598-9599

80354   Opn skl fx NEC-prol coma
80000-80199,80300-80499,8290-8291,8500-85219,85221-85419,
8738-8739,8798-8799,9050,9251-9252,9290-9299,9588-95909,
9598-9599

80355   Opn skl fx NEC-deep coma
80000-80199,80300-80499,8290-8291,8500-85219,85221-85419,
8738-8739,8798-8799,9050,9251-9252,9290-9299,9588-95909,
9598-9599

80356   Opn skul fx NEC-coma NOS
80000-80199,80300-80499,8290-8291,8500-85219,85221-85419,
8738-8739,8798-8799,9050,9251-9252,9290-9299,9588-95909,
9598-9599

80359   Opn skull fx NEC-concuss
80000-80199,80300-80499,8290-8291,8500-85219,85221-85419,
8738-8739,8798-8799,9050,9251-9252,9290-9299,9588-95909,
9598-9599

80360   Opn skl fx NEC/cereb lac
80000-80199,80300-80499,8290-8291,8500-85219,85221-85419,
8738-8739,8798-8799,9050,9251-9252,9290-9299,9588-95909,
9598-9599

80361   Opn skul fx NEC w/o coma
80000-80199,80300-80499,8290-8291,8500-85219,85221-85419,
8738-8739,8798-8799,9050,9251-9252,9290-9299,9588-95909,
9598-9599

80362   Opn skul fx NEC-brf coma
80000-80199,80300-80499,8290-8291,8500-85219,85221-85419,
8738-8739,8798-8799,9050,9251-9252,9290-9299,9588-95909,
9598-9599

80363   Opn skul fx NEC-mod coma
80000-80199,80300-80499,8290-8291,8500-85219,85221-85419,
8738-8739,8798-8799,9050,9251-9252,9290-9299,9588-95909,
9598-9599

80364   Opn skl fx NEC-proln com
80000-80199,80300-80499,8290-8291,8500-85219,85221-85419,
8738-8739,8798-8799,9050,9251-9252,9290-9299,9588-95909,
9598-9599

80365   Opn skl fx NEC-deep coma
80000-80199,80300-80499,8290-8291,8500-85219,85221-85419,
8738-8739,8798-8799,9050,9251-9252,9290-9299,9588-95909,
9598-9599

80366   Opn skul fx NEC-coma NOS
80000-80199,80300-80499,8290-8291,8500-85219,85221-85419,
8738-8739,8798-8799,9050,9251-9252,9290-9299,9588-95909,
9598-9599

80369   Opn skull fx NEC-concuss
80000-80199,80300-80499,8290-8291,8500-85219,85221-85419,
8738-8739,8798-8799,9050,9251-9252,9290-9299,9588-95909,
9598-9599

80370   Opn skl fx NEC/menin hem
80000-80199,80300-80499,8290-8291,8500-85219,85221-85419,
8738-8739,8798-8799,9050,9251-9252,9290-9299,9588-95909,
9598-9599

80371   Opn skul fx NEC w/o coma
80000-80199,80300-80499,8290-8291,8500-85219,85221-85419,
8738-8739,8798-8799,9050,9251-9252,9290-9299,9588-95909,
9598-9599

80372   Opn skul fx NEC-brf coma
80000-80199,80300-80499,8290-8291,8500-85219,85221-85419,
8738-8739,8798-8799,9050,9251-9252,9290-9299,9588-95909,
9598-9599

80373   Opn skul fx NEC-mod coma
80000-80199,80300-80499,8290-8291,8500-85219,85221-85419,
8738-8739,8798-8799,9050,9251-9252,9290-9299,9588-95909,
9598-9599

80374   Opn skl fx NEC-prol coma
80000-80199,80300-80499,8290-8291,8500-85219,85221-85419,
8738-8739,8798-8799,9050,9251-9252,9290-9299,9588-95909,
9598-9599

80375   Opn skl fx NEC-deep coma
80000-80199,80300-80499,8290-8291,8500-85219,85221-85419,
8738-8739,8798-8799,9050,9251-9252,9290-9299,9588-95909,
9598-9599

80376   Opn skul fx NEC-coma NOS
80000-80199,80300-80499,8290-8291,8500-85219,85221-85419,
8738-8739,8798-8799,9050,9251-9252,9290-9299,9588-95909,
9598-9599

80379   Opn skull fx NEC-concuss
80000-80199,80300-80499,8290-8291,8500-85219,85221-85419,
8738-8739,8798-8799,9050,9251-9252,9290-9299,9588-95909,
9598-9599

80380　Opn skull fx NEC/hem NEC
80000-80199,80300-80499,8290-8291,8500-85219,85221-85419,
8738-8739,8798-8799,9050,9251-9252,9290-9299,9588-95909,
9598-9599

80381　Opn skul fx NEC w/o coma
80000-80199,80300-80499,8290-8291,8500-85219,85221-85419,
8738-8739,8798-8799,9050,9251-9252,9290-9299,9588-95909,
9598-9599

80382　Opn skul fx NEC-brf coma
80000-80199,80300-80499,8290-8291,8500-85219,85221-85419,
8738-8739,8798-8799,9050,9251-9252,9290-9299,9588-95909,
9598-9599

80383　Opn skul fx NEC-mod coma
80000-80199,80300-80499,8290-8291,8500-85219,85221-85419,
8738-8739,8798-8799,9050,9251-9252,9290-9299,9588-95909,
9598-9599

80384　Opn skl fx NEC-prol coma
80000-80199,80300-80499,8290-8291,8500-85219,85221-85419,
8738-8739,8798-8799,9050,9251-9252,9290-9299,9588-95909,
9598-9599

80385　Opn skl fx NEC-deep coma
80000-80199,80300-80499,8290-8291,8500-85219,85221-85419,
8738-8739,8798-8799,9050,9251-9252,9290-9299,9588-95909,
9598-9599

80386　Opn skul fx NEC-coma NOS
80000-80199,80300-80499,8290-8291,8500-85219,85221-85419,
8738-8739,8798-8799,9050,9251-9252,9290-9299,9588-95909,
9598-9599

80389　Opn skull fx NEC-concuss
80000-80199,80300-80499,8290-8291,8500-85219,85221-85419,
8738-8739,8798-8799,9050,9251-9252,9290-9299,9588-95909,
9598-9599

80390　Op skl fx NEC/br inj NEC
80000-80199,80300-80499,8290-8291,8500-85219,85221-85419,
8738-8739,8798-8799,9050,9251-9252,9290-9299,9588-95909,
9598-9599

80391　Opn skul fx NEC w/o coma
80000-80199,80300-80499,8290-8291,8500-85219,85221-85419,
8738-8739,8798-8799,9050,9251-9252,9290-9299,9588-95909,
9598-9599

80392　Opn skul fx NEC-brf coma
80000-80199,80300-80499,8290-8291,8500-85219,85221-85419,
8738-8739,8798-8799,9050,9251-9252,9290-9299,9588-95909,
9598-9599

80393　Opn skul fx NEC-mod coma
80000-80199,80300-80499,8290-8291,8500-85219,85221-85419,
8738-8739,8798-8799,9050,9251-9252,9290-9299,9588-95909,
9598-9599

80394　Opn skl fx NEC-prol coma
80000-80199,80300-80499,8290-8291,8500-85219,85221-85419,
8738-8739,8798-8799,9050,9251-9252,9290-9299,9588-95909,
9598-9599

80395　Opn skl fx NEC-deep coma
80000-80199,80300-80499,8290-8291,8500-85219,85221-85419,
8738-8739,8798-8799,9050,9251-9252,9290-9299,9588-95909,
9598-9599

80396　Opn skul fx NEC-coma NOS
80000-80199,80300-80499,8290-8291,8500-85219,85221-85419,
8738-8739,8798-8799,9050,9251-9252,9290-9299,9588-95909,
9598-9599

80399　Opn skull fx NEC-concuss
80000-80199,80300-80499,8290-8291,8500-85219,85221-85419,
8738-8739,8798-8799,9050,9251-9252,9290-9299,9588-95909,
9598-9599

80400　Cl skul fx w oth bone fx
80000-80199,80300-80499,8290-8291,8500-85219,85221-85419,
8738-8739,8798-8799,9050,9251-9252,9290-9299,9588-95909,
9598-9599

80401　Cl skl w oth fx w/o coma
80000-80199,80300-80499,8290-8291,8500-85219,85221-85419,
8738-8739,8798-8799,9050,9251-9252,9290-9299,9588-95909,
9598-9599

80402　Cl skl w oth fx-brf coma
80000-80199,80300-80499,8290-8291,8500-85219,85221-85419,
8738-8739,8798-8799,9050,9251-9252,9290-9299,9588-95909,
9598-9599

80403　Cl skl w oth fx-mod coma
80000-80199,80300-80499,8290-8291,8500-85219,85221-85419,
8738-8739,8798-8799,9050,9251-9252,9290-9299,9588-95909,
9598-9599

80404　Cl skl/oth fx-proln coma
80000-80199,80300-80499,8290-8291,8500-85219,85221-85419,
8738-8739,8798-8799,9050,9251-9252,9290-9299,9588-95909,
9598-9599

80405　Cl skul/oth fx-deep coma
80000-80199,80300-80499,8290-8291,8500-85219,85221-85419,
8738-8739,8798-8799,9050,9251-9252,9290-9299,9588-95909,
9598-9599

80406　Cl skl w oth fx-coma NOS
80000-80199,80300-80499,8290-8291,8500-85219,85221-85419,
8738-8739,8798-8799,9050,9251-9252,9290-9299,9588-95909,
9598-9599

80409　Cl skul w oth fx-concuss
80000-80199,80300-80499,8290-8291,8500-85219,85221-85419,
8738-8739,8798-8799,9050,9251-9252,9290-9299,9588-95909,
9598-9599

80410　Cl sk w oth fx/cereb lac
80000-80199,80300-80499,8290-8291,8500-85219,85221-85419,
8738-8739,8798-8799,9050,9251-9252,9290-9299,9588-95909,
9598-9599

80411　Cl skl w oth fx w/o coma
80000-80199,80300-80499,8290-8291,8500-85219,85221-85419,
8738-8739,8798-8799,9050,9251-9252,9290-9299,9588-95909,
9598-9599

80412　Cl skl w oth fx-brf coma
80000-80199,80300-80499,8290-8291,8500-85219,85221-85419,
8738-8739,8798-8799,9050,9251-9252,9290-9299,9588-95909,
9598-9599

80413　Cl skl w oth fx-mod coma
80000-80199,80300-80499,8290-8291,8500-85219,85221-85419,
8738-8739,8798-8799,9050,9251-9252,9290-9299,9588-95909,
9598-9599

80414　Cl skl/oth fx-proln coma
80000-80199,80300-80499,8290-8291,8500-85219,85221-85419,
8738-8739,8798-8799,9050,9251-9252,9290-9299,9588-95909,
9598-9599

80415　Cl skul/oth fx-deep coma
80000-80199,80300-80499,8290-8291,8500-85219,85221-85419,
8738-8739,8798-8799,9050,9251-9252,9290-9299,9588-95909,
9598-9599

80416　Cl skl w oth fx-coma NOS
80000-80199,80300-80499,8290-8291,8500-85219,85221-85419,
8738-8739,8798-8799,9050,9251-9252,9290-9299,9588-95909,
9598-9599

80419　Cl skul w oth fx-concuss
80000-80199,80300-80499,8290-8291,8500-85219,85221-85419,
8738-8739,8798-8799,9050,9251-9252,9290-9299,9588-95909,
9598-9599

80420　Cl skl/oth fx/mening hem
80000-80199,80300-80499,8290-8291,8500-85219,85221-85419,
8738-8739,8798-8799,9050,9251-9252,9290-9299,9588-95909,
9598-9599

80421　Cl skl w oth fx w/o coma
80000-80199,80300-80499,8290-8291,8500-85219,85221-85419,
8738-8739,8798-8799,9050,9251-9252,9290-9299,9588-95909,
9598-9599

80422　Cl skl w oth fx-brf coma
80000-80199,80300-80499,8290-8291,8500-85219,85221-85419,
8738-8739,8798-8799,9050,9251-9252,9290-9299,9588-95909,
9598-9599

80423　Cl skl w oth fx-mod coma
80000-80199,80300-80499,8290-8291,8500-85219,85221-85419,
8738-8739,8798-8799,9050,9251-9252,9290-9299,9588-95909,
9598-9599

80424   Cl skl/oth fx-proln coma
80000-80199,80300-80499,8290-8291,8500-85219,85221-85419,
8738-8739,8798-8799,9050,9251-9252,9290-9299,9588-95909,
9598-9599

80425   Cl skul/oth fx-deep coma
80000-80199,80300-80499,8290-8291,8500-85219,85221-85419,
8738-8739,8798-8799,9050,9251-9252,9290-9299,9588-95909,
9598-9599

80426   Cl skl w oth fx-coma NOS
80000-80199,80300-80499,8290-8291,8500-85219,85221-85419,
8738-8739,8798-8799,9050,9251-9252,9290-9299,9588-95909,
9598-9599

80429   Cl skul w oth fx-concuss
80000-80199,80300-80499,8290-8291,8500-85219,85221-85419,
8738-8739,8798-8799,9050,9251-9252,9290-9299,9588-95909,
9598-9599

80430   Cl skul w oth fx/hem NEC
80000-80199,80300-80499,8290-8291,8500-85219,85221-85419,
8738-8739,8798-8799,9050,9251-9252,9290-9299,9588-95909,
9598-9599

80431   Cl skl w oth fx w/o coma
80000-80199,80300-80499,8290-8291,8500-85219,85221-85419,
8738-8739,8798-8799,9050,9251-9252,9290-9299,9588-95909,
9598-9599

80432   Cl skl w oth fx-brf coma
80000-80199,80300-80499,8290-8291,8500-85219,85221-85419,
8738-8739,8798-8799,9050,9251-9252,9290-9299,9588-95909,
9598-9599

80433   Cl skl w oth fx-mod coma
80000-80199,80300-80499,8290-8291,8500-85219,85221-85419,
8738-8739,8798-8799,9050,9251-9252,9290-9299,9588-95909,
9598-9599

80434   Cl skl/oth fx-proln coma
80000-80199,80300-80499,8290-8291,8500-85219,85221-85419,
8738-8739,8798-8799,9050,9251-9252,9290-9299,9588-95909,
9598-9599

80435   Cl skul/oth fx-deep coma
80000-80199,80300-80499,8290-8291,8500-85219,85221-85419,
8738-8739,8798-8799,9050,9251-9252,9290-9299,9588-95909,
9598-9599

80436   Cl skl w oth fx-coma NOS
80000-80199,80300-80499,8290-8291,8500-85219,85221-85419,
8738-8739,8798-8799,9050,9251-9252,9290-9299,9588-95909,
9598-9599

80439   Cl skul w oth fx-concuss
80000-80199,80300-80499,8290-8291,8500-85219,85221-85419,
8738-8739,8798-8799,9050,9251-9252,9290-9299,9588-95909,
9598-9599

80440   Cl skl/oth fx/br inj NEC
80000-80199,80300-80499,8290-8291,8500-85219,85221-85419,
8738-8739,8798-8799,9050,9251-9252,9290-9299,9588-95909,
9598-9599

80441   Cl skl w oth fx w/o coma
80000-80199,80300-80499,8290-8291,8500-85219,85221-85419,
8738-8739,8798-8799,9050,9251-9252,9290-9299,9588-95909,
9598-9599

80442   Cl skl w oth fx-brf coma
80000-80199,80300-80499,8290-8291,8500-85219,85221-85419,
8738-8739,8798-8799,9050,9251-9252,9290-9299,9588-95909,
9598-9599

80443   Cl skl w oth fx-mod coma
80000-80199,80300-80499,8290-8291,8500-85219,85221-85419,
8738-8739,8798-8799,9050,9251-9252,9290-9299,9588-95909,
9598-9599

80444   Cl skl/oth fx-proln coma
80000-80199,80300-80499,8290-8291,8500-85219,85221-85419,
8738-8739,8798-8799,9050,9251-9252,9290-9299,9588-95909,
9598-9599

80445   Cl skul/oth fx-deep coma
80000-80199,80300-80499,8290-8291,8500-85219,85221-85419,
8738-8739,8798-8799,9050,9251-9252,9290-9299,9588-95909,
9598-9599

80446   Cl skl w oth fx-coma NOS
80000-80199,80300-80499,8290-8291,8500-85219,85221-85419,
8738-8739,8798-8799,9050,9251-9252,9290-9299,9588-95909,
9598-9599

80449   Cl skul w oth fx-concuss
80000-80199,80300-80499,8290-8291,8500-85219,85221-85419,
8738-8739,8798-8799,9050,9251-9252,9290-9299,9588-95909,
9598-9599

80450   Opn skull fx/oth bone fx
80000-80199,80300-80499,8290-8291,8500-85219,85221-85419,
8738-8739,8798-8799,9050,9251-9252,9290-9299,9588-95909,
9598-9599

80451   Opn skul/oth fx w/o coma
80000-80199,80300-80499,8290-8291,8500-85219,85221-85419,
8738-8739,8798-8799,9050,9251-9252,9290-9299,9588-95909,
9598-9599

80452   Opn skul/oth fx-brf coma
80000-80199,80300-80499,8290-8291,8500-85219,85221-85419,
8738-8739,8798-8799,9050,9251-9252,9290-9299,9588-95909,
9598-9599

80453   Opn skul/oth fx-mod coma
80000-80199,80300-80499,8290-8291,8500-85219,85221-85419,
8738-8739,8798-8799,9050,9251-9252,9290-9299,9588-95909,
9598-9599

80454   Opn skl/oth fx-prol coma
80000-80199,80300-80499,8290-8291,8500-85219,85221-85419,
8738-8739,8798-8799,9050,9251-9252,9290-9299,9588-95909,
9598-9599

80455   Opn skl/oth fx-deep coma
80000-80199,80300-80499,8290-8291,8500-85219,85221-85419,
8738-8739,8798-8799,9050,9251-9252,9290-9299,9588-95909,
9598-9599

80456   Opn skul/oth fx-coma NOS
80000-80199,80300-80499,8290-8291,8500-85219,85221-85419,
8738-8739,8798-8799,9050,9251-9252,9290-9299,9588-95909,
9598-9599

80459   Opn skull/oth fx-concuss
80000-80199,80300-80499,8290-8291,8500-85219,85221-85419,
8738-8739,8798-8799,9050,9251-9252,9290-9299,9588-95909,
9598-9599

80460   Opn skl/oth fx/cereb lac
80000-80199,80300-80499,8290-8291,8500-85219,85221-85419,
8738-8739,8798-8799,9050,9251-9252,9290-9299,9588-95909,
9598-9599

80461   Opn skul/oth fx w/o coma
80000-80199,80300-80499,8290-8291,8500-85219,85221-85419,
8738-8739,8798-8799,9050,9251-9252,9290-9299,9588-95909,
9598-9599

80462   Opn skul/oth fx-brf coma
80000-80199,80300-80499,8290-8291,8500-85219,85221-85419,
8738-8739,8798-8799,9050,9251-9252,9290-9299,9588-95909,
9598-9599

80463   Opn skul/oth fx-mod coma
80000-80199,80300-80499,8290-8291,8500-85219,85221-85419,
8738-8739,8798-8799,9050,9251-9252,9290-9299,9588-95909,
9598-9599

80464   Opn skl/oth fx-prol coma
80000-80199,80300-80499,8290-8291,8500-85219,85221-85419,
8738-8739,8798-8799,9050,9251-9252,9290-9299,9588-95909,
9598-9599

80465   Opn skl/oth fx-deep coma
80000-80199,80300-80499,8290-8291,8500-85219,85221-85419,
8738-8739,8798-8799,9050,9251-9252,9290-9299,9588-95909,
9598-9599

80466   Opn skul/oth fx-coma NOS
80000-80199,80300-80499,8290-8291,8500-85219,85221-85419,
8738-8739,8798-8799,9050,9251-9252,9290-9299,9588-95909,
9598-9599

80469   Opn skull/oth fx-concuss
80000-80199,80300-80499,8290-8291,8500-85219,85221-85419,
8738-8739,8798-8799,9050,9251-9252,9290-9299,9588-95909,
9598-9599

80470   Opn skl/oth fx/menin hem
80000-80199,80300-80499,8290-8291,8500-85219,85221-85419,
8738-8739,8798-8799,9050,9251-9252,9290-9299,9588-95909,
9598-9599

80471   Opn skul/oth fx w/o coma
80000-80199,80300-80499,8290-8291,8500-85219,85221-85419,
8738-8739,8798-8799,9050,9251-9252,9290-9299,9588-95909,
9598-9599

80472   Opn skul/oth fx-brf coma
80000-80199,80300-80499,8290-8291,8500-85219,85221-85419,
8738-8739,8798-8799,9050,9251-9252,9290-9299,9588-95909,
9598-9599

80473   Opn skul/oth fx-mod coma
80000-80199,80300-80499,8290-8291,8500-85219,85221-85419,
8738-8739,8798-8799,9050,9251-9252,9290-9299,9588-95909,
9598-9599

80474   Opn skl/oth fx-prol coma
80000-80199,80300-80499,8290-8291,8500-85219,85221-85419,
8738-8739,8798-8799,9050,9251-9252,9290-9299,9588-95909,
9598-9599

80475   Opn skl/oth fx-deep coma
80000-80199,80300-80499,8290-8291,8500-85219,85221-85419,
8738-8739,8798-8799,9050,9251-9252,9290-9299,9588-95909,
9598-9599

80476   Opn skul/oth fx-coma NOS
80000-80199,80300-80499,8290-8291,8500-85219,85221-85419,
8738-8739,8798-8799,9050,9251-9252,9290-9299,9588-95909,
9598-9599

80479   Opn skull/oth fx-concuss
80000-80199,80300-80499,8290-8291,8500-85219,85221-85419,
8738-8739,8798-8799,9050,9251-9252,9290-9299,9588-95909,
9598-9599

80480   Opn skl w oth fx/hem NEC
80000-80199,80300-80499,8290-8291,8500-85219,85221-85419,
8738-8739,8798-8799,9050,9251-9252,9290-9299,9588-95909,
9598-9599

80481   Opn skul/oth fx w/o coma
80000-80199,80300-80499,8290-8291,8500-85219,85221-85419,
8738-8739,8798-8799,9050,9251-9252,9290-9299,9588-95909,
9598-9599

80482   Opn skul/oth fx-brf coma
80000-80199,80300-80499,8290-8291,8500-85219,85221-85419,
8738-8739,8798-8799,9050,9251-9252,9290-9299,9588-95909,
9598-9599

80483   Opn skul/oth fx-mod coma
80000-80199,80300-80499,8290-8291,8500-85219,85221-85419,
8738-8739,8798-8799,9050,9251-9252,9290-9299,9588-95909,
9598-9599

80484   Opn skl/oth fx-prol coma
80000-80199,80300-80499,8290-8291,8500-85219,85221-85419,
8738-8739,8798-8799,9050,9251-9252,9290-9299,9588-95909,
9598-9599

80485   Opn skl/oth fx-deep coma
80000-80199,80300-80499,8290-8291,8500-85219,85221-85419,
8738-8739,8798-8799,9050,9251-9252,9290-9299,9588-95909,
9598-9599

80486   Opn skul/oth fx-coma NOS
80000-80199,80300-80499,8290-8291,8500-85219,85221-85419,
8738-8739,8798-8799,9050,9251-9252,9290-9299,9588-95909,
9598-9599

80489   Opn skull/oth fx-concuss
80000-80199,80300-80499,8290-8291,8500-85219,85221-85419,
8738-8739,8798-8799,9050,9251-9252,9290-9299,9588-95909,
9598-9599

80490   Op skl/oth fx/br inj NEC
80000-80199,80300-80499,8290-8291,8500-85219,85221-85419,
8738-8739,8798-8799,9050,9251-9252,9290-9299,9588-95909,
9598-9599

80491   Opn skul/oth fx w/o coma
80000-80199,80300-80499,8290-8291,8500-85219,85221-85419,
8738-8739,8798-8799,9050,9251-9252,9290-9299,9588-95909,
9598-9599

80492   Opn skul/oth fx-brf coma
80000-80199,80300-80499,8290-8291,8500-85219,85221-85419,
8738-8739,8798-8799,9050,9251-9252,9290-9299,9588-95909,
9598-9599

80493   Opn skul/oth fx-mod coma
80000-80199,80300-80499,8290-8291,8500-85219,85221-85419,
8738-8739,8798-8799,9050,9251-9252,9290-9299,9588-95909,
9598-9599

80494   Opn skl/oth fx-prol coma
80000-80199,80300-80499,8290-8291,8500-85219,85221-85419,
8738-8739,8798-8799,9050,9251-9252,9290-9299,9588-95909,
9598-9599

80495   Opn skl/oth fx-deep coma
80000-80199,80300-80499,8290-8291,8500-85219,85221-85419,
8738-8739,8798-8799,9050,9251-9252,9290-9299,9588-95909,
9598-9599

80496   Opn skul/oth fx-coma NOS
80000-80199,80300-80499,8290-8291,8500-85219,85221-85419,
8738-8739,8798-8799,9050,9251-9252,9290-9299,9588-95909,
9598-9599

80499   Opn skull/oth fx-concuss
80000-80199,80300-80499,8290-8291,8500-85219,85221-85419,
8738-8739,8798-8799,9050,9251-9252,9290-9299,9588-95909,
9598-9599

80500   Fx cervical vert NOS-cl
80500-80518,8058-80619,8068-8069,8290-8291,83900-83918,83940,
83949-83950,83959,83969,83979-8399,8470,8479,8488-8489,
8798-8799,9051,92611,9290-9299,95200-95209,9528-9529,9588,9591,
9598-9599

80501   Fx c1 vertebra-closed
80500-80518,8058-80619,8068-8069,8290-8291,83900-83918,83940,
83949-83950,83959,83969,83979-8399,8470,8479,8488-8489,
8798-8799,9051,92611,9290-9299,95200-95209,9528-9529,9588,9591,
9598-9599

80502   Fx c2 vertebra-closed
80500-80518,8058-80619,8068-8069,8290-8291,83900-83918,83940,
83949-83950,83959,83969,83979-8399,8470,8479,8488-8489,
8798-8799,9051,92611,9290-9299,95200-95209,9528-9529,9588,9591,
9598-9599

80503   Fx c3 vertebra-closed
80500-80518,8058-80619,8068-8069,8290-8291,83900-83918,83940,
83949-83950,83959,83969,83979-8399,8470,8479,8488-8489,
8798-8799,9051,92611,9290-9299,95200-95209,9528-9529,9588,9591,
9598-9599

80504   Fx c4 vertebra-closed
80500-80518,8058-80619,8068-8069,8290-8291,83900-83918,83940,
83949-83950,83959,83969,83979-8399,8470,8479,8488-8489,
8798-8799,9051,92611,9290-9299,95200-95209,9528-9529,9588,9591,
9598-9599

80505   Fx c5 vertebra-closed
80500-80518,8058-80619,8068-8069,8290-8291,83900-83918,83940,
83949-83950,83959,83969,83979-8399,8470,8479,8488-8489,
8798-8799,9051,92611,9290-9299,95200-95209,9528-9529,9588,9591,
9598-9599

80506   Fx c6 vertebra-closed
80500-80518,8058-80619,8068-8069,8290-8291,83900-83918,83940,
83949-83950,83959,83969,83979-8399,8470,8479,8488-8489,
8798-8799,9051,92611,9290-9299,95200-95209,9528-9529,9588,9591,
9598-9599

80507   Fx c7 vertebra-closed
80500-80518,8058-80619,8068-8069,8290-8291,83900-83918,83940,
83949-83950,83959,83969,83979-8399,8470,8479,8488-8489,
8798-8799,9051,92611,9290-9299,95200-95209,9528-9529,9588,9591,
9598-9599

80508   Fx mult cervical vert-cl
80500-80518,8058-80619,8068-8069,8290-8291,83900-83918,83940,
83949-83950,83959,83969,83979-8399,8470,8479,8488-8489,
8798-8799,9051,92611,9290-9299,95200-95209,9528-9529,9588,9591,
9598-9599

80510   Fx cervical vert NOS-opn
80500-80518,8058-80619,8068-8069,8290-8291,83900-83918,83940,
83949-83950,83959,83969,83979-8399,8470,8479,8488-8489,
8798-8799,9051,92611,9290-9299,95200-95209,9528-9529,9588,9591,
9598-9599

80511   Fx c1 vertebra-open
80500-80518,8058-80619,8068-8069,8290-8291,83900-83918,83940,
83949-83950,83959,83969,83979-8399,8470,8479,8488-8489,
8798-8799,9051,92611,9290-9299,95200-95209,9528-9529,9588,9591,
9598-9599

80512   Fx c2 vertebra-open
80500-80518,8058-80619,8068-8069,8290-8291,83900-83918,83940,
83949-83950,83959,83969,83979-8399,8470,8479,8488-8489,
8798-8799,9051,92611,9290-9299,95200-95209,9528-9529,9588,9591,
9598-9599

80513   Fx c3 vertebra-open
80500-80518,8058-80619,8068-8069,8290-8291,83900-83918,83940,
83949-83950,83959,83969,83979-8399,8470,8479,8488-8489,
8798-8799,9051,92611,9290-9299,95200-95209,9528-9529,9588,9591,
9598-9599

80514   Fx c4 vertebra-open
80500-80518,8058-80619,8068-8069,8290-8291,83900-83918,83940,
83949-83950,83959,83969,83979-8399,8470,8479,8488-8489,
8798-8799,9051,92611,9290-9299,95200-95209,9528-9529,9588,9591,
9598-9599

80515   Fx c5 vertebra-open
80500-80518,8058-80619,8068-8069,8290-8291,83900-83918,83940,
83949-83950,83959,83969,83979-8399,8470,8479,8488-8489,
8798-8799,9051,92611,9290-9299,95200-95209,9528-9529,9588,9591,
9598-9599

80516   Fx c6 vertebra-open
80500-80518,8058-80619,8068-8069,8290-8291,83900-83918,83940,
83949-83950,83959,83969,83979-8399,8470,8479,8488-8489,
8798-8799,9051,92611,9290-9299,95200-95209,9528-9529,9588,9591,
9598-9599

80517   Fx c7 vertebra-open
80500-80518,8058-80619,8068-8069,8290-8291,83900-83918,83940,
83949-83950,83959,83969,83979-8399,8470,8479,8488-8489,
8798-8799,9051,92611,9290-9299,95200-95209,9528-9529,9588,9591,
9598-9599

80518   Fx mlt cervical vert-opn
80500-80518,8058-80619,8068-8069,8290-8291,83900-83918,83940,
83949-83950,83959,83969,83979-8399,8470,8479,8488-8489,
8798-8799,9051,92611,9290-9299,95200-95209,9528-9529,9588,9591,
9598-9599

8052   Fx dorsal vertebra-close
8052-8053,8058-8059,80620-80639,8068-8069,8290-8291,83921,
83931-83940,83949-83950,83959,83969,83979-8399,8471,8479,
8488-8489,8798-8799,9051,92611,9290-9299,95210-95219,9528-9529,
9588,9591,9598-9599

8053   Fx dorsal vertebra-open
8052-8053,8058-8059,80620-80639,8068-8069,8290-8291,83921,
83931-83940,83949-83950,83959,83969,83979-8399,8471,8479,
8488-8489,8798-8799,9051,92611,9290-9299,95210-95219,9528-9529,
9588,9591,9598-9599

8054   Fx lumbar vertebra-close
8054-8055,8058-8059,8064-8065,8068-8069,8290-8291,83920,83930,
83940,83949-83950,83959,83969,83979-8399,8472,8479,8488-8489,
8798-8799,9051,92611,9290-9299,9522,9528-9529,9588,9591,
9598-9599

8055   Fxlumbar vertebra-open
8054-8055,8058-8059,8064-8065,8068-8069,8290-8291,83920,83930,
83940,83949-83950,83959,83969,83979-8399,8472,8479,8488-8489,
8798-8799,9051,92611,9290-9299,9522,9528-9529,9588,9591,
9598-9599

8056   Fx sacrum/coccyx-closed
8056-8059,80660-8069,8290-8291,83940-83959,83969,83979-8399,
8460-8469,8473-8479,8485-8489,8798-8799,9051,92611,9290-9299,
9523-9529,9588,9591,9598-9599

8057   Fx sacrum/coccyx-open
8056-8059,80660-8069,8290-8291,83940-83959,83969,83979-8399,
8460-8469,8473-8479,8485-8489,8798-8799,9051,92611,9290-9299,
9523-9529,9588,9591,9598-9599

8058   Vertebral fx NOS-closed
73310-73319,80500-8069,8290-8291,83900-83959,83969,83979-8399,
8460-8479,8485-8489,8798-8799,9051,92611,9290-9299,95200-9529,
9588,9591,9598-9599

8059   Vertebral fx NOS-open
73310-73319,80500-8069,8290-8291,83900-83959,83969,83979-8399,
8460-8479,8485-8489,8798-8799,9051,92611,9290-9299,95200-9529,
9588,9591,9598-9599

80600   C1-c4 fx-cl/cord inj NOS
73310-73319,80500-80518,8058-80619,8068-8069,8290-8291,
83900-83918,83940,83949-83950,83959,83969,83979-8399,8479,
8488-8489,8798-8799,9051,92611,9290-9299,95200-95209,9528-9529,
9588,9591,9598-9599

80601   C1-c4 fx-cl/com cord les
73310-73319,80500-80518,8058-80619,8068-8069,8290-8291,
83900-83918,83940,83949-83950,83959,83969,83979-8399,8479,
8488-8489,8798-8799,9051,92611,9290-9299,95200-95209,9528-9529,
9588,9591,9598-9599

80602   C1-c4 fx-cl/ant cord syn
73310-73319,80500-80518,8058-80619,8068-8069,8290-8291,
83900-83918,83940,83949-83950,83959,83969,83979-8399,8479,
8488-8489,8798-8799,9051,92611,9290-9299,95200-95209,9528-9529,
9588,9591,9598-9599

80603   C1-c4 fx-cl/cen cord syn
73310-73319,80500-80518,8058-80619,8068-8069,8290-8291,
83900-83918,83940,83949-83950,83959,83969,83979-8399,8479,
8488-8489,8798-8799,9051,92611,9290-9299,95200-95209,9528-9529,
9588,9591,9598-9599

80604   C1-c4 fx-cl/cord inj NEC
73310-73319,80500-80518,8058-80619,8068-8069,8290-8291,
83900-83918,83940,83949-83950,83959,83969,83979-8399,8479,
8488-8489,8798-8799,9051,92611,9290-9299,95200-95209,9528-9529,
9588,9591,9598-9599

80605   C5-c7 fx-cl/cord inj NOS
73310-73319,80500-80518,8058-80619,8068-8069,8290-8291,
83900-83918,83940,83949-83950,83959,83969,83979-8399,8479,
8488-8489,8798-8799,9051,92611,9290-9299,95200-95209,9528-9529,
9588,9591,9598-9599

80606   C5-c7 fx-cl/com cord les
73310-73319,80500-80518,8058-80619,8068-8069,8290-8291,
83900-83918,83940,83949-83950,83959,83969,83979-8399,8479,
8488-8489,8798-8799,9051,92611,9290-9299,95200-95209,9528-9529,
9588,9591,9598-9599

80607   C5-c7 fx-cl/ant cord syn
73310-73319,80500-80518,8058-80619,8068-8069,8290-8291,
83900-83918,83940,83949-83950,83959,83969,83979-8399,8479,
8488-8489,8798-8799,9051,92611,9290-9299,95200-95209,9528-9529,
9588,9591,9598-9599

80608   C5-c7 fx-cl/cen cord syn
73310-73319,80500-80518,8058-80619,8068-8069,8290-8291,
83900-83918,83940,83949-83950,83959,83969,83979-8399,8479,
8488-8489,8798-8799,9051,92611,9290-9299,95200-95209,9528-9529,
9588,9591,9598-9599

80609   C5-c7 fx-cl/cord inj NEC
73310-73319,80500-80518,8058-80619,8068-8069,8290-8291,
83900-83918,83940,83949-83950,83959,83969,83979-8399,8479,
8488-8489,8798-8799,9051,92611,9290-9299,95200-95209,9528-9529,
9588,9591,9598-9599

80610   C1-c4 fx-op/cord inj NOS
73310-73319,80500-80518,8058-80619,8068-8069,8290-8291,
83900-83918,83940,83949-83950,83959,83969,83979-8399,8479,
8488-8489,8798-8799,9051,92611,9290-9299,95200-95209,9528-9529,
9588,9591,9598-9599

80611   C1-c4 fx-op/com cord les
73310-73319,80500-80518,8058-80619,8068-8069,8290-8291,
83900-83918,83940,83949-83950,83959,83969,83979-8399,8479,
8488-8489,8798-8799,9051,92611,9290-9299,95200-95209,9528-9529,
9588,9591,9598-9599

80612   C1-c4 fx-op/ant cord syn
73310-73319,80500-80518,8058-80619,8068-8069,8290-8291,
83900-83918,83940,83949-83950,83959,83969,83979-8399,8479,
8488-8489,8798-8799,9051,92611,9290-9299,95200-95209,9528-9529,
9588,9591,9598-9599

80613   C1-c4 fx-op/cen cord syn
73310-73319,80500-80518,8058-80619,8068-8069,8290-8291,
83900-83918,83940,83949-83950,83959,83969,83979-8399,8479,
8488-8489,8798-8799,9051,92611,9290-9299,95200-95209,9528-9529,
9588,9591,9598-9599

80614   C1-c4 fx-op/cord inj NEC
73310-73319,80500-80518,8058-80619,8068-8069,8290-8291,
83900-83918,83940,83949-83950,83959,83969,83979-8399,8479,
8488-8489,8798-8799,9051,92611,9290-9299,95200-95209,9528-9529,
9588,9591,9598-9599

80615   C5-c7 fx-op/cord inj NOS
73310-73319,80500-80518,8058-80619,8068-8069,8290-8291,
83900-83918,83940,83949-83950,83959,83969,83979-8399,8479,
8488-8489,8798-8799,9051,92611,9290-9299,95200-95209,9528-9529,
9588,9591,9598-9599

80616   C5-c7 fx-op/com cord les
73310-73319,80500-80518,8058-80619,8068-8069,8290-8291,
83900-83918,83940,83949-83950,83959,83969,83979-8399,8479,
8488-8489,8798-8799,9051,92611,9290-9299,95200-95209,9528-9529,
9588,9591,9598-9599

80617   C5-c7 fx-op/ant cord syn
73310-73319,80500-80518,8058-80619,8068-8069,8290-8291,
83900-83918,83940,83949-83950,83959,83969,83979-8399,8479,
8488-8489,8798-8799,9051,92611,9290-9299,95200-95209,9528-9529,
9588,9591,9598-9599

80618   C5-c7 fx-op/cen cord syn
73310-73319,80500-80518,8058-80619,8068-8069,8290-8291,
83900-83918,83940,83949-83950,83959,83969,83979-8399,8479,
8488-8489,8798-8799,9051,92611,9290-9299,95200-95209,9528-9529,
9588,9591,9598-9599

80619   C5-c7 fx-op/cord inj NEC
73310-73319,80500-80518,8058-80619,8068-8069,8290-8291,
83900-83918,83940,83949-83950,83959,83969,83979-8399,8479,
8488-8489,8798-8799,9051,92611,9290-9299,95200-95209,9528-9529,
9588,9591,9598-9599

80620   T1-t6 fx-cl/cord inj NOS
73310-73319,8052-8053,8058-8059,80620-80639,8068-8069,
8290-8291,83921,83931-83940,83949-83950,83959,83969,83979-8399,
8471,8479,8488-8489,8798-8799,9051,92611,9290-9299,95210-95219,
9528-9529,9588,9591,9598-9599

80621   T1-t6 fx-cl/com cord les
73310-73319,8052-8053,8058-8059,80620-80639,8068-8069,
8290-8291,83921,83931-83940,83949-83950,83959,83969,83979-8399,
8471,8479,8488-8489,8798-8799,9051,92611,9290-9299,95210-95219,
9528-9529,9588,9591,9598-9599

80622   T1-t6 fx-cl/ant cord syn
73310-73319,8052-8053,8058-8059,80620-80639,8068-8069,
8290-8291,83921,83931-83940,83949-83950,83959,83969,83979-8399,
8471,8479,8488-8489,8798-8799,9051,92611,9290-9299,95210-95219,
9528-9529,9588,9591,9598-9599

80623   T1-t6 fx-cl/cen cord syn
73310-73319,8052-8053,8058-8059,80620-80639,8068-8069,
8290-8291,83921,83931-83940,83949-83950,83959,83969,83979-8399,
8471,8479,8488-8489,8798-8799,9051,92611,9290-9299,95210-95219,
9528-9529,9588,9591,9598-9599

80624   T1-t6 fx-cl/cord inj NEC
73310-73319,8052-8053,8058-8059,80620-80639,8068-8069,
8290-8291,83921,83931-83940,83949-83950,83959,83969,83979-8399,
8471,8479,8488-8489,8798-8799,9051,92611,9290-9299,95210-95219,
9528-9529,9588,9591,9598-9599

80625   T7-t12 fx-cl/crd inj NOS
73310-73319,8052-8053,8058-8059,80620-80639,8068-8069,
8290-8291,83921,83931-83940,83949-83950,83959,83969,83979-8399,
8471,8479,8488-8489,8798-8799,9051,92611,9290-9299,95210-95219,
9528-9529,9588,9591,9598-9599

80626   T7-t12 fx-cl/com crd les
73310-73319,8052-8053,8058-8059,80620-80639,8068-8069,
8290-8291,83921,83931-83940,83949-83950,83959,83969,83979-8399,
8471,8479,8488-8489,8798-8799,9051,92611,9290-9299,95210-95219,
9528-9529,9588,9591,9598-9599

80627   T7-t12 fx-cl/ant crd syn
73310-73319,8052-8053,8058-8059,80620-80639,8068-8069,
8290-8291,83921,83931-83940,83949-83950,83959,83969,83979-8399,
8471,8479,8488-8489,8798-8799,9051,92611,9290-9299,95210-95219,
9528-9529,9588,9591,9598-9599

80628   T7-t12 fx-cl/cen crd syn
73310-73319,8052-8053,8058-8059,80620-80639,8068-8069,
8290-8291,83921,83931-83940,83949-83950,83959,83969,83979-8399,
8471,8479,8488-8489,8798-8799,9051,92611,9290-9299,95210-95219,
9528-9529,9588,9591,9598-9599

80629   T7-t12 fx-cl/crd inj NEC
73310-73319,8052-8053,8058-8059,80620-80639,8068-8069,
8290-8291,83931,83931-83940,83949-83950,83959,83969,83979-8399,
8471,8479,8488-8489,8798-8799,9051,92611,9290-9299,95210-95219,
9528-9529,9588,9591,9598-9599

80630   T1-t6 fx-op/cord inj NOS
73310-73319,8052-8053,8058-8059,80620-80639,8068-8069,
8290-8291,83921,83931-83940,83949-83950,83959,83969,83979-8399,
8471,8479,8488-8489,8798-8799,9051,92611,9290-9299,95210-95219,
9528-9529,9588,9591,9598-9599

80631   T1-t6 fx-op/com cord les
73310-73319,8052-8053,8058-8059,80620-80639,8068-8069,
8290-8291,83921,83931-83940,83949-83950,83959,83969,83979-8399,
8471,8479,8488-8489,8798-8799,9051,92611,9290-9299,95210-95219,
9528-9529,9588,9591,9598-9599

80632   T1-t6 fx-op/ant cord syn
73310-73319,8052-8053,8058-8059,80620-80639,8068-8069,
8290-8291,83921,83931-83940,83949-83950,83959,83969,83979-8399,
8471,8479,8488-8489,8798-8799,9051,92611,9290-9299,95210-95219,
9528-9529,9588,9591,9598-9599

80633   T1-t6 fx-op/cen cord syn
73310-73319,8052-8053,8058-8059,80620-80639,8068-8069,
8290-8291,83921,83931-83940,83949-83950,83959,83969,83979-8399,
8471,8479,8488-8489,8798-8799,9051,92611,9290-9299,95210-95219,
9528-9529,9588,9591,9598-9599

80634   T1-t6 fx-op/cord inj NEC
73310-73319,8052-8053,8058-8059,80620-80639,8068-8069,
8290-8291,83921,83931-83940,83949-83950,83959,83969,83979-8399,
8471,8479,8488-8489,8798-8799,9051,92611,9290-9299,95210-95219,
9528-9529,9588,9591,9598-9599

80635   T7-t12 fx-op/crd inj NOS
73310-73319,8052-8053,8058-8059,80620-80639,8068-8069,
8290-8291,83921,83931-83940,83949-83950,83959,83969,83979-8399,
8471,8479,8488-8489,8798-8799,9051,92611,9290-9299,95210-95219,
9528-9529,9588,9591,9598-9599

80636   T7-t12 fx-op/com crd les
73310-73319,8052-8053,8058-8059,80620-80639,8068-8069,
8290-8291,83921,83931-83940,83949-83950,83959,83969,83979-8399,
8471,8479,8488-8489,8798-8799,9051,92611,9290-9299,95210-95219,
9528-9529,9588,9591,9598-9599

80637   T7-t12 fx-op/ant crd syn
73310-73319,8052-8053,8058-8059,80620-80639,8068-8069,
8290-8291,83921,83931-83940,83949-83950,83959,83969,83979-8399,
8471,8479,8488-8489,8798-8799,9051,92611,9290-9299,95210-95219,
9528-9529,9588,9591,9598-9599

80638   T7-t12 fx-op/cen crd syn
73310-73319,8052-8053,8058-8059,80620-80639,8068-8069,
8290-8291,83921,83931-83940,83949-83950,83959,83969,83979-8399,
8471,8479,8488-8489,8798-8799,9051,92611,9290-9299,95210-95219,
9528-9529,9588,9591,9598-9599

80639   T7-t12 fx-op/crd inj NEC
73310-73319,8052-8053,8058-8059,80620-80639,8068-8069,
8290-8291,83921,83931-83940,83949-83950,83959,83969,83979-8399,
8471,8479,8488-8489,8798-8799,9051,92611,9290-9299,95210-95219,
9528-9529,9588,9591,9598-9599

8064   Cl lumbar fx w cord inj
73310-73319,8054-8055,8058-8059,8064-8065,8068-8069,8290-8291,
83920,83930,83940,83949-83950,83959,83969,83979-8399,8472,8479,
8488-8489,8798-8799,9051,92611,9290-9299,9522,9528-9529,9588,
9591,9598-9599

8065   Opn lumbar fx w cord inj
73310-73319,8054-8055,8058-8059,8064-8065,8068-8069,8290-8291,
83920,83930,83940,83949-83950,83959,83969,83979-8399,8472,8479,
8488-8489,8798-8799,9051,92611,9290-9299,9522,9528-9529,9588,
9591,9598-9599

80660   Fx sacrum-cl/crd inj NOS
73310-73319,8056-8059,80660-8069,8290-8291,83940-83959,83969,
83979-8399,8460-8470,8473-8479,8485-8489,8798-8799,9051,92611,
9290-9299,9523-9529,9588,9591,9598-9599

80661   Fx sacr-cl/cauda equ les
73310-73319,8056-8059,80660-8069,8290-8291,83940-83959,83969,
83979-8399,8460-8470,8473-8479,8485-8489,8798-8799,9051,92611,
9290-9299,9523-9529,9588,9591,9598-9599

80662   Fx sacr-cl/cauda inj NEC
73310-73319,8056-8059,80660-8069,8290-8291,83940-83959,83969,
83979-8399,8460-8470,8473-8479,8485-8489,8798-8799,9051,92611,
9290-9299,9523-9529,9588,9591,9598-9599

80669   Fx sacrum-cl/crd inj NEC
73310-73319,8056-8059,80660-8069,8290-8291,83940-83959,83969,
83979-8399,8460-8470,8473-8479,8485-8489,8798-8799,9051,92611,
9290-9299,9523-9529,9588,9591,9598-9599

80670   Fx sacrum-op/crd inj NOS
73310-73319,8056-8059,80660-8069,8290-8291,83940-83959,83969,
83979-8399,8460-8470,8473-8479,8485-8489,8798-8799,9051,92611,
9290-9299,9523-9529,9588,9591,9598-9599

80671   Fx sacr-op/cauda equ les
73310-73319,8056-8059,80660-8069,8290-8291,83940-83959,83969,
83979-8399,8460-8470,8473-8479,8485-8489,8798-8799,9051,92611,
9290-9299,9523-9529,9588,9591,9598-9599

80672   Fx sacr-op/cauda inj NEC
73310-73319,8056-8059,80660-8069,8290-8291,83940-83959,83969,
83979-8399,8460-8470,8473-8479,8485-8489,8798-8799,9051,92611,
9290-9299,9523-9529,9588,9591,9598-9599

80679   Fx sacrum-op/crd inj NEC
73310-73319,8056-8059,80660-8069,8290-8291,83940-83959,83969,
83979-8399,8460-8470,8473-8479,8485-8489,8798-8799,9051,92611,
9290-9299,9523-9529,9588,9591,9598-9599

8068   Vert fx NOS-cl w crd inj
73310-73319,80500-8069,8290-8291,83900-83959,83969,83979-8399,
8460-8479,8485-8489,8798-8799,9051,92611,9290-9299,95200-9529,
9588,9591,9598-9599

8069   Vert fx NOS-op w crd inj
73310-73319,80500-8069,8290-8291,83900-83959,83969,83979-8399,
8460-8479,8485-8489,8798-8799,9051,92611,9290-9299,95200-9529,
9588,9591,9598-9599

80704   Fracture four ribs-close
80700-80719,8074,8190-8191,8280-8291,8488-8489,8798-8799,
9290-9299,9588,9598-9599

80705   Fracture five ribs-close
80700-80719,8074,8190-8191,8280-8291,8488-8489,8798-8799,
9290-9299,9588,9598-9599

80706   Fracture six ribs-closed
80700-80719,8074,8190-8191,8280-8291,8488-8489,8798-8799,
9290-9299,9588,9598-9599

80707   Fracture seven ribs-clos
80700-80719,8074,8190-8191,8280-8291,8488-8489,8798-8799,
9290-9299,9588,9598-9599

80708   Fx eight/more rib-closed
80700-80719,8074,8190-8191,8280-8291,8488-8489,8798-8799,
9290-9299,9588,9598-9599

80709   Fx mult ribs NOS-closed
80700-80719,8074,8190-8191,8280-8291,8488-8489,8798-8799,
9290-9299,9588,9598-9599

80710   Fracture rib NOS-open
80700-80719,8074,8190-8191,8280-8291,8488-8489,8798-8799,
9290-9299,9588,9598-9599

80711   Fracture one rib-open
80700-80719,8074,8190-8191,8280-8291,8488-8489,8798-8799,
9290-9299,9588,9598-9599

80712   Fracture two ribs-open
80700-80719,8074,8190-8191,8280-8291,8488-8489,8798-8799,
9290-9299,9588,9598-9599

80713   Fracture three ribs-open
80700-80719,8074,8190-8191,8280-8291,8488-8489,8798-8799,
9290-9299,9588,9598-9599

80714   Fracture four ribs-open
80700-80719,8074,8190-8191,8280-8291,8488-8489,8798-8799,
9290-9299,9588,9598-9599

80715   Fracture five ribs-open
80700-80719,8074,8190-8191,8280-8291,8488-8489,8798-8799,
9290-9299,9588,9598-9599

80716   Fracture six ribs-open
80700-80719,8074,8190-8191,8280-8291,8488-8489,8798-8799,
9290-9299,9588,9598-9599

80717   Fracture seven ribs-open
80700-80719,8074,8190-8191,8280-8291,8488-8489,8798-8799,
9290-9299,9588,9598-9599

80718   Fx eight/more ribs-open
80700-80719,8074,8190-8191,8280-8291,8488-8489,8798-8799,
9290-9299,9588,9598-9599

80719   Fx mult ribs NOS-open
80700-80719,8074,8190-8191,8280-8291,8488-8489,8798-8799,
9290-9299,9588,9598-9599

8072   Fracture of sternum-clos
8072-8074,8290-8291,8488-8489,8798-8799,9290-9299,9588,
9598-9599

8073   Fracture of sternum-open
8072-8074,8290-8291,8488-8489,8798-8799,9290-9299,9588,
9598-9599

8074   Flail chest
80700-8074,8290-8291,8488-8489,8798-8799,9290-9299,9588,
9598-9599

8075   Fx larynx/trachea-closed
8075-8076,8290-8291,8488-8489,8798-8799,9290-9299,9588,
9598-9599

8076   Fx larynx/trachea-open
8075-8076,8290-8291,8488-8489,8798-8799,9290-9299,9588,
9598-9599

8080   Fracture acetabulum-clos
73310-73319,8080-8081,80843-80849,80853-8091,8290-8291,
83500-83513,8430-8439,8460-8469,8485-8489,8798-8799,9290-9299,
9588,9596,9598-9599

8081   Fracture acetabulum-open
8080-8081,80843-80849,80853-8091,8290-8291,83500-83513,
8430-8439,8460-8469,8485-8489,8798-8799,9290-9299,9588,9596,
9598-9599

8082   Fracture of pubis-closed
73310-73319,8082-8083,80843-80849,80853-8091,8290-8291,
83500-83513,8430-8439,8460-8469,8485-8489,8798-8799,9290-9299,
9588,9596,9598-9599

8083   Fracture of pubis-open
73310-73319,8082-8083,80843-80849,80853-8091,8290-8291,
83500-83513,8430-8439,8460-8469,8485-8489,8798-8799,9290-9299,
9588,9596,9598-9599

80843   Pelv fx-clos/pelv disrup
73310-73319,8080-8091,8290-8291,83500-83513,8430-8439,
8460-8469,8485-8489,8798-8799,9290-9299,9588,9596,9598-9599

80849   Pelvic fracture NEC-clos
73310-73319,8080-8091,8290-8291,83500-83513,8430-8439,
8460-8469,8485-8489,8798-8799,9290-9299,9588,9596,9598-9599

80851   Fracture of ilium-open
73310-73319,80841,80843-80851,80853-8091,8290-8291,83500-83513,
8430-8439,8460-8469,8485-8489,8798-8799,9290-9299,9588,9596,
9598-9599

80852   Fracture of ischium-open
73310-73319,80842-80849,80852-8091,8290-8291,83500-83513,
8430-8439,8460-8469,8485-8489,8798-8799,9290-9299,9588,9596,
9598-9599

80853   Pelv fx-open/pelv disrup
73310-73319,8080-8091,8290-8291,83500-83513,8430-8439,
8460-8469,8485-8489,8798-8799,9290-9299,9588,9596,9598-9599

80859   Pelvic fracture NEC-open
73310-73319,8080-8091,8290-8291,83500-83513,8430-8439,
8460-8469,8485-8489,8798-8799,9290-9299,9588,9596,9598-9599

8088   Pelvic fracture NOS-clos
73310-73319,8080-8091,8290-8291,83500-83513,8430-8439,
8460-8469,8485-8489,8798-8799,9290-9299,9588,9596,9598-9599

8089   Pelvic fracture NOS-open
73310-73319,8080-8091,8290-8291,83500-83513,8430-8439,
8460-8469,8485-8489,8798-8799,9290-9299,9588,9596,9598-9599

82000   Fx femur intrcaps NOS-cl
73310-73319,82000-82139,8270-8291,8430-8439,8488-8489,
8798-8799,9290-9299,9588,9596,9598-9599

82001   Fx up femur epiphy-clos
73310-73319,82000-82139,8270-8291,8430-8439,8488-8489,
8798-8799,9290-9299,9588,9596,9598-9599
82002   Fx femur, midcervic-clos
73310-73319,82000-82139,8270-8291,8430-8439,8488-8489,
8798-8799,9290-9299,9588,9596,9598-9599
82003   Fx base femoral nck-clos
73310-73319,82000-82139,8270-8291,8430-8439,8488-8489,
8798-8799,9290-9299,9588,9596,9598-9599
82009   Fx femur intrcaps NEC-cl
73310-73319,82000-82139,8270-8291,8430-8439,8488-8489,
8798-8799,9290-9299,9588,9596,9598-9599
82010   Fx femur intrcap NOS-opn
73310-73319,82000-82139,8270-8291,8430-8439,8488-8489,
8798-8799,9290-9299,9588,9596,9598-9599
82011   Fx up femur epiphy-open
73310-73319,82000-82139,8270-8291,8430-8439,8488-8489,
8798-8799,9290-9299,9588,9596,9598-9599
82012   Fx femur, midcervic-open
73310-73319,82000-82139,8270-8291,8430-8439,8488-8489,
8798-8799,9290-9299,9588,9596,9598-9599
82013   Fx base femoral nck-open
73310-73319,82000-82139,8270-8291,8430-8439,8488-8489,
8798-8799,9290-9299,9588,9596,9598-9599
82019   Fx femur intrcap NEC-opn
73310-73319,82000-82139,8270-8291,8430-8439,8488-8489,
8798-8799,9290-9299,9588,9596,9598-9599
82020   Trochanteric fx NOS-clos
73310-73319,82000-82139,8270-8291,8430-8439,8488-8489,
8798-8799,9290-9299,9588,9596,9598-9599
82021   Intertrochanteric fx-cl
73310-73319,82000-82139,8270-8291,8430-8439,8488-8489,
8798-8799,9290-9299,9588,9596,9598-9599
82022   Subtrochanteric fx-close
73310-73319,82000-82139,8270-8291,8430-8439,8488-8489,
8798-8799,9290-9299,9588,9596,9598-9599
82030   Trochanteric fx NOS-open
73310-73319,82000-82139,8270-8291,8430-8439,8488-8489,
8798-8799,9290-9299,9588,9596,9598-9599
82031   Intertrochanteric fx-opn
73310-73319,82000-82139,8270-8291,8430-8439,8488-8489,
8798-8799,9290-9299,9588,9596,9598-9599
82032   Subtrochanteric fx-open
73310-73319,82000-82139,8270-8291,8430-8439,8488-8489,
8798-8799,9290-9299,9588,9596,9598-9599
8208   Fx neck of femur NOS-cl
73310-73319,82000-82139,8270-8291,8430-8439,8488-8489,
8798-8799,9290-9299,9588,9596,9598-9599
8209   Fx neck of femur NOS-opn
73310-73319,82000-82139,8270-8291,8430-8439,8488-8489,
8798-8799,9290-9299,9588,9596,9598-9599
82100   Fx femur NOS-closed
73310-73319,82000-82139,8270-8291,8430-8439,8488-8489,
8798-8799,9290-9299,9588,9596,9598-9599
82101   Fx femur shaft-closed
73310-73319,82000-82139,8270-8291,8430-8439,8488-8489,
8798-8799,9290-9299,9588,9596,9598-9599
82110   Fx femur NOS-open
73310-73319,82000-82139,8270-8291,8430-8439,8488-8489,
8798-8799,9290-9299,9588,9596,9598-9599
82111   Fx femur shaft-open
73310-73319,82000-82139,8270-8291,8430-8439,8488-8489,
8798-8799,9290-9299,9588,9596,9598-9599
83819   Dislocat foot NEC-open
No Exclusions
83900   Disloc cerv vert NOS-cl
80500-80518,80600-80619,8068-8069,83900-83918,8470,8488-8489,
8798-8799,9290-9299,95200-95209,9588,9598-9599
83901   Disloc 1st cerv vert-cl
80500-80518,80600-80619,8068-8069,83900-83918,8470,8488-8489,
8798-8799,9290-9299,95200-95209,9588,9598-9599
83902   Disloc 2nd cerv vert-cl
80500-80518,80600-80619,8068-8069,83900-83918,8470,8488-8489,
8798-8799,9290-9299,95200-95209,9588,9598-9599

83903   Disloc 3rd cerv vert-cl
80500-80518,80600-80619,8068-8069,83900-83918,8470,8488-8489,
8798-8799,9290-9299,95200-95209,9588,9598-9599
83904   Disloc 4th cerv vert-cl
80500-80518,80600-80619,8068-8069,83900-83918,8470,8488-8489,
8798-8799,9290-9299,95200-95209,9588,9598-9599
83905   Disloc 5th cerv vert-cl
80500-80518,80600-80619,8068-8069,83900-83918,8470,8488-8489,
8798-8799,9290-9299,95200-95209,9588,9598-9599
83906   Disloc 6th cerv vert-cl
80500-80518,80600-80619,8068-8069,83900-83918,8470,8488-8489,
8798-8799,9290-9299,95200-95209,9588,9598-9599
83907   Disloc 7th cerv vert-cl
80500-80518,80600-80619,8068-8069,83900-83918,8470,8488-8489,
8798-8799,9290-9299,95200-95209,9588,9598-9599
83908   Disloc mult cerv vert-cl
80500-80518,80600-80619,8068-8069,83900-83918,8470,8488-8489,
8798-8799,9290-9299,95200-95209,9588,9598-9599
83910   Disloc cerv vert NOS-opn
80500-80518,80600-80619,8068-8069,83900-83918,8470,8488-8489,
8798-8799,9290-9299,95200-95209,9588,9598-9599
83911   Disloc 1st cerv vert-opn
80500-80518,80600-80619,8068-8069,83900-83918,8470,8488-8489,
8798-8799,9290-9299,95200-95209,9588,9598-9599
83912   Disloc 2nd cerv vert-opn
80500-80518,80600-80619,8068-8069,83900-83918,8470,8488-8489,
8798-8799,9290-9299,95200-95209,9588,9598-9599
83913   Disloc 3rd cerv vert-opn
80500-80518,80600-80619,8068-8069,83900-83918,8470,8488-8489,
8798-8799,9290-9299,95200-95209,9588,9598-9599
83914   Disloc 4th cerv vert-opn
80500-80518,80600-80619,8068-8069,83900-83918,8470,8488-8489,
8798-8799,9290-9299,95200-95209,9588,9598-9599
83915   Disloc 5th cerv vert-opn
80500-80518,80600-80619,8068-8069,83900-83918,8470,8488-8489,
8798-8799,9290-9299,95200-95209,9588,9598-9599
83916   Disloc 6th cerv vert-opn
80500-80518,80600-80619,8068-8069,83900-83918,8470,8488-8489,
8798-8799,9290-9299,95200-95209,9588,9598-9599
83917   Disloc 7th cerv vert-opn
80500-80518,80600-80619,8068-8069,83900-83918,8470,8488-8489,
8798-8799,9290-9299,95200-95209,9588,9598-9599
83918   Disloc mlt cerv vert-opn
80500-80518,80600-80619,8068-8069,83900-83918,8470,8488-8489,
8798-8799,9290-9299,95200-95209,9588,9598-9599
8500   Concussion w/o coma
80000-80199,80300-80499,8500-85219,85221-85419,8738-8739,
8798-8799,9050,9251-9252,9290-9299,9588-95909,9598-9599
8501   Concussion-brief coma
80000-80199,80300-80499,8500-85219,85221-85419,8738-8739,
8798-8799,9050,9251-9252,9290-9299,9588-95909,9598-9599
8502   Concussion-moderate coma
80000-80199,80300-80499,8500-85219,85221-85419,8738-8739,
8798-8799,9050,9251-9252,9290-9299,9588-95909,9598-9599
8503   Concussion-prolong coma
80000-80199,80300-80499,8500-85219,85221-85419,8738-8739,
8798-8799,9050,9251-9252,9290-9299,9588-95909,9598-9599
8504   Concussion-deep coma
80000-80199,80300-80499,8500-85219,85221-85419,8738-8739,
8798-8799,9050,9251-9252,9290-9299,9588-95909,9598-9599
8505   Concussion w coma NOS
80000-80199,80300-80499,8500-85219,85221-85419,8738-8739,
8798-8799,9050,9251-9252,9290-9299,9588-95909,9598-9599
8509   Concussion NOS
80000-80199,80300-80499,8500-85219,85221-85419,8738-8739,
8798-8799,9050,9251-9252,9290-9299,9588-95909,9598-9599
85100   Cerebral cortx contusion
80000-80199,80300-80499,8500-85219,85221-85419,8738-8739,
8798-8799,9050,9251-9252,9290-9299,9588-95909,9598-9599
85101   Cortex contusion-no coma
80000-80199,80300-80499,8500-85219,85221-85419,8738-8739,
8798-8799,9050,9251-9252,9290-9299,9588-95909,9598-9599

ICD-9-CM

Appx F

Vol. 1

85102   Cortex contus-brief coma
80000-80199,80300-80499,8500-85219,85221-85419,8738-8739,
8798-8799,9050,9251-9252,9290-9299,9588-95909,9598-9599
85103   Cortex contus-mod coma
80000-80199,80300-80499,8500-85219,85221-85419,8738-8739,
8798-8799,9050,9251-9252,9290-9299,9588-95909,9598-9599
85104   Cortx contus-prolng coma
80000-80199,80300-80499,8500-85219,85221-85419,8738-8739,
8798-8799,9050,9251-9252,9290-9299,9588-95909,9598-9599
85105   Cortex contus-deep coma
80000-80199,80300-80499,8500-85219,85221-85419,8738-8739,
8798-8799,9050,9251-9252,9290-9299,9588-95909,9598-9599
85106   Cortex contus-coma NOS
80000-80199,80300-80499,8500-85219,85221-85419,8738-8739,
8798-8799,9050,9251-9252,9290-9299,9588-95909,9598-9599
85109   Cortex contus-concus NOS
80000-80199,80300-80499,8500-85219,85221-85419,8738-8739,
8798-8799,9050,9251-9252,9290-9299,9588-95909,9598-9599
85110   Cortex contusion/opn wnd
80000-80199,80300-80499,8500-85219,85221-85419,8738-8739,
8798-8799,9050,9251-9252,9290-9299,9588-95909,9598-9599
85111   Opn cortx contus-no coma
80000-80199,80300-80499,8500-85219,85221-85419,8738-8739,
8798-8799,9050,9251-9252,9290-9299,9588-95909,9598-9599
85112   Opn cort contus-brf coma
80000-80199,80300-80499,8500-85219,85221-85419,8738-8739,
8798-8799,9050,9251-9252,9290-9299,9588-95909,9598-9599
85113   Opn cort contus-mod coma
80000-80199,80300-80499,8500-85219,85221-85419,8738-8739,
8798-8799,9050,9251-9252,9290-9299,9588-95909,9598-9599
85114   Opn cort contu-prol coma
80000-80199,80300-80499,8500-85219,85221-85419,8738-8739,
8798-8799,9050,9251-9252,9290-9299,9588-95909,9598-9599
85115   Opn cort contu-deep coma
80000-80199,80300-80499,8500-85219,85221-85419,8738-8739,
8798-8799,9050,9251-9252,9290-9299,9588-95909,9598-9599
85116   Opn cort contus-coma NOS
80000-80199,80300-80499,8500-85219,85221-85419,8738-8739,
8798-8799,9050,9251-9252,9290-9299,9588-95909,9598-9599
85119   Opn cortx contus-concuss
80000-80199,80300-80499,8500-85219,85221-85419,8738-8739,
8798-8799,9050,9251-9252,9290-9299,9588-95909,9598-9599
85120   Cerebral cortex lacerat
80000-80199,80300-80499,8500-85219,85221-85419,8738-8739,
8798-8799,9050,9251-9252,9290-9299,9588-95909,9598-9599
85121   Cortex lacerat w/o coma
80000-80199,80300-80499,8500-85219,85221-85419,8738-8739,
8798-8799,9050,9251-9252,9290-9299,9588-95909,9598-9599
85122   Cortex lacera-brief coma
80000-80199,80300-80499,8500-85219,85221-85419,8738-8739,
8798-8799,9050,9251-9252,9290-9299,9588-95909,9598-9599
85123   Cortex lacerat-mod coma
80000-80199,80300-80499,8500-85219,85221-85419,8738-8739,
8798-8799,9050,9251-9252,9290-9299,9588-95909,9598-9599
85124   Cortex lacerat-prol coma
80000-80199,80300-80499,8500-85219,85221-85419,8738-8739,
8798-8799,9050,9251-9252,9290-9299,9588-95909,9598-9599
85125   Cortex lacerat-deep coma
80000-80199,80300-80499,8500-85219,85221-85419,8738-8739,
8798-8799,9050,9251-9252,9290-9299,9588-95909,9598-9599
85126   Cortex lacerat-coma NOS
80000-80199,80300-80499,8500-85219,85221-85419,8738-8739,
8798-8799,9050,9251-9252,9290-9299,9588-95909,9598-9599
85129   Cortex lacerat-concuss
80000-80199,80300-80499,8500-85219,85221-85419,8738-8739,
8798-8799,9050,9251-9252,9290-9299,9588-95909,9598-9599
85130   Cortex lacer w opn wound
80000-80199,80300-80499,8500-85219,85221-85419,8738-8739,
8798-8799,9050,9251-9252,9290-9299,9588-95909,9598-9599
85131   Opn cortex lacer-no coma
80000-80199,80300-80499,8500-85219,85221-85419,8738-8739,
8798-8799,9050,9251-9252,9290-9299,9588-95909,9598-9599

85132   Opn cortx lac-brief coma
80000-80199,80300-80499,8500-85219,85221-85419,8738-8739,
8798-8799,9050,9251-9252,9290-9299,9588-95909,9598-9599
85133   Opn cortx lacer-mod coma
80000-80199,80300-80499,8500-85219,85221-85419,8738-8739,
8798-8799,9050,9251-9252,9290-9299,9588-95909,9598-9599
85134   Opn cortx lac-proln coma
80000-80199,80300-80499,8500-85219,85221-85419,8738-8739,
8798-8799,9050,9251-9252,9290-9299,9588-95909,9598-9599
85135   Opn cortex lac-deep coma
80000-80199,80300-80499,8500-85219,85221-85419,8738-8739,
8798-8799,9050,9251-9252,9290-9299,9588-95909,9598-9599
85136   Opn cortx lacer-coma NOS
80000-80199,80300-80499,8500-85219,85221-85419,8738-8739,
8798-8799,9050,9251-9252,9290-9299,9588-95909,9598-9599
85139   Opn cortx lacer-concuss
80000-80199,80300-80499,8500-85219,85221-85419,8738-8739,
8798-8799,9050,9251-9252,9290-9299,9588-95909,9598-9599
85140   Cerebel/brain stm contus
80000-80199,80300-80499,8500-85219,85221-85419,8738-8739,
8798-8799,9050,9251-9252,9290-9299,9588-95909,9598-9599
85141   Cerebell contus w/o coma
80000-80199,80300-80499,8500-85219,85221-85419,8738-8739,
8798-8799,9050,9251-9252,9290-9299,9588-95909,9598-9599
85142   Cerebell contus-brf coma
80000-80199,80300-80499,8500-85219,85221-85419,8738-8739,
8798-8799,9050,9251-9252,9290-9299,9588-95909,9598-9599
85143   Cerebell contus-mod coma
80000-80199,80300-80499,8500-85219,85221-85419,8738-8739,
8798-8799,9050,9251-9252,9290-9299,9588-95909,9598-9599
85144   Cerebel contus-prol coma
80000-80199,80300-80499,8500-85219,85221-85419,8738-8739,
8798-8799,9050,9251-9252,9290-9299,9588-95909,9598-9599
85145   Cerebel contus-deep coma
80000-80199,80300-80499,8500-85219,85221-85419,8738-8739,
8798-8799,9050,9251-9252,9290-9299,9588-95909,9598-9599
85146   Cerebell contus-coma NOS
80000-80199,80300-80499,8500-85219,85221-85419,8738-8739,
8798-8799,9050,9251-9252,9290-9299,9588-95909,9598-9599
85149   Cerebell contus-concuss
80000-80199,80300-80499,8500-85219,85221-85419,8738-8739,
8798-8799,9050,9251-9252,9290-9299,9588-95909,9598-9599
85150   Cerebel contus w opn wnd
80000-80199,80300-80499,8500-85219,85221-85419,8738-8739,
8798-8799,9050,9251-9252,9290-9299,9588-95909,9598-9599
85151   Opn cerebe cont w/o coma
80000-80199,80300-80499,8500-85219,85221-85419,8738-8739,
8798-8799,9050,9251-9252,9290-9299,9588-95909,9598-9599
85152   Opn cerebe cont-brf coma
80000-80199,80300-80499,8500-85219,85221-85419,8738-8739,
8798-8799,9050,9251-9252,9290-9299,9588-95909,9598-9599
85153   Opn cerebe cont-mod coma
80000-80199,80300-80499,8500-85219,85221-85419,8738-8739,
8798-8799,9050,9251-9252,9290-9299,9588-95909,9598-9599
85154   Opn cerebe cont-prol com
80000-80199,80300-80499,8500-85219,85221-85419,8738-8739,
8798-8799,9050,9251-9252,9290-9299,9588-95909,9598-9599
85155   Opn cerebe cont-deep com
80000-80199,80300-80499,8500-85219,85221-85419,8738-8739,
8798-8799,9050,9251-9252,9290-9299,9588-95909,9598-9599
85156   Opn cerebe cont-coma NOS
80000-80199,80300-80499,8500-85219,85221-85419,8738-8739,
8798-8799,9050,9251-9252,9290-9299,9588-95909,9598-9599
85159   Opn cerebel cont-concuss
80000-80199,80300-80499,8500-85219,85221-85419,8738-8739,
8798-8799,9050,9251-9252,9290-9299,9588-95909,9598-9599
85160   Cerebel/brain stem lacer
80000-80199,80300-80499,8500-85219,85221-85419,8738-8739,
8798-8799,9050,9251-9252,9290-9299,9588-95909,9598-9599
85161   Cerebel lacerat w/o coma
80000-80199,80300-80499,8500-85219,85221-85419,8738-8739,
8798-8799,9050,9251-9252,9290-9299,9588-95909,9598-9599

85162   Cerebel lacer-brief coma
80000-80199,80300-80499,8500-85219,85221-85419,8738-8739,
8798-8799,9050,9251-9252,9290-9299,9588-95909,9598-9599

85163   Cerebel lacerat-mod coma
80000-80199,80300-80499,8500-85219,85221-85419,8738-8739,
8798-8799,9050,9251-9252,9290-9299,9588-95909,9598-9599

85164   Cerebel lacer-proln coma
80000-80199,80300-80499,8500-85219,85221-85419,8738-8739,
8798-8799,9050,9251-9252,9290-9299,9588-95909,9598-9599

85165   Cerebell lacer-deep coma
80000-80199,80300-80499,8500-85219,85221-85419,8738-8739,
8798-8799,9050,9251-9252,9290-9299,9588-95909,9598-9599

85166   Cerebel lacerat-coma NOS
80000-80199,80300-80499,8500-85219,85221-85419,8738-8739,
8798-8799,9050,9251-9252,9290-9299,9588-95909,9598-9599

85169   Cerebel lacer-concussion
80000-80199,80300-80499,8500-85219,85221-85419,8738-8739,
8798-8799,9050,9251-9252,9290-9299,9588-95909,9598-9599

85170   Cerebel lacer w open wnd
80000-80199,80300-80499,8500-85219,85221-85419,8738-8739,
8798-8799,9050,9251-9252,9290-9299,9588-95909,9598-9599

85171   Opn cerebel lac w/o coma
80000-80199,80300-80499,8500-85219,85221-85419,8738-8739,
8798-8799,9050,9251-9252,9290-9299,9588-95909,9598-9599

85172   Opn cerebel lac-brf coma
80000-80199,80300-80499,8500-85219,85221-85419,8738-8739,
8798-8799,9050,9251-9252,9290-9299,9588-95909,9598-9599

85173   Opn cerebel lac-mod coma
80000-80199,80300-80499,8500-85219,85221-85419,8738-8739,
8798-8799,9050,9251-9252,9290-9299,9588-95909,9598-9599

85174   Opn cerebe lac-prol coma
80000-80199,80300-80499,8500-85219,85221-85419,8738-8739,
8798-8799,9050,9251-9252,9290-9299,9588-95909,9598-9599

85175   Opn cerebe lac-deep coma
80000-80199,80300-80499,8500-85219,85221-85419,8738-8739,
8798-8799,9050,9251-9252,9290-9299,9588-95909,9598-9599

85176   Opn cerebel lac-coma NOS
80000-80199,80300-80499,8500-85219,85221-85419,8738-8739,
8798-8799,9050,9251-9252,9290-9299,9588-95909,9598-9599

85179   Opn cerebell lac-concuss
80000-80199,80300-80499,8500-85219,85221-85419,8738-8739,
8798-8799,9050,9251-9252,9290-9299,9588-95909,9598-9599

85180   Brain laceration NEC
80000-80199,80300-80499,8500-85219,85221-85419,8738-8739,
8798-8799,9050,9251-9252,9290-9299,9588-95909,9598-9599

85181   Brain lacer NEC w/o coma
80000-80199,80300-80499,8500-85219,85221-85419,8738-8739,
8798-8799,9050,9251-9252,9290-9299,9588-95909,9598-9599

85182   Brain lac NEC-brief coma
80000-80199,80300-80499,8500-85219,85221-85419,8738-8739,
8798-8799,9050,9251-9252,9290-9299,9588-95909,9598-9599

85183   Brain lacer NEC-mod coma
80000-80199,80300-80499,8500-85219,85221-85419,8738-8739,
8798-8799,9050,9251-9252,9290-9299,9588-95909,9598-9599

85184   Brain lac NEC-proln coma
80000-80199,80300-80499,8500-85219,85221-85419,8738-8739,
8798-8799,9050,9251-9252,9290-9299,9588-95909,9598-9599

85185   Brain lac NEC-deep coma
80000-80199,80300-80499,8500-85219,85221-85419,8738-8739,
8798-8799,9050,9251-9252,9290-9299,9588-95909,9598-9599

85186   Brain lacer NEC-coma NOS
80000-80199,80300-80499,8500-85219,85221-85419,8738-8739,
8798-8799,9050,9251-9252,9290-9299,9588-95909,9598-9599

85189   Brain lacer NEC-concuss
80000-80199,80300-80499,8500-85219,85221-85419,8738-8739,
8798-8799,9050,9251-9252,9290-9299,9588-95909,9598-9599

85190   Brain lac NEC w open wnd
80000-80199,80300-80499,8500-85219,85221-85419,8738-8739,
8798-8799,9050,9251-9252,9290-9299,9588-95909,9598-9599

85191   Opn brain lacer w/o coma
80000-80199,80300-80499,8500-85219,85221-85419,8738-8739,
8798-8799,9050,9251-9252,9290-9299,9588-95909,9598-9599

85192   Opn brain lac-brief coma
80000-80199,80300-80499,8500-85219,85221-85419,8738-8739,
8798-8799,9050,9251-9252,9290-9299,9588-95909,9598-9599

85193   Opn brain lacer-mod coma
80000-80199,80300-80499,8500-85219,85221-85419,8738-8739,
8798-8799,9050,9251-9252,9290-9299,9588-95909,9598-9599

85194   Opn brain lac-proln coma
80000-80199,80300-80499,8500-85219,85221-85419,8738-8739,
8798-8799,9050,9251-9252,9290-9299,9588-95909,9598-9599

85195   Open brain lac-deep coma
80000-80199,80300-80499,8500-85219,85221-85419,8738-8739,
8798-8799,9050,9251-9252,9290-9299,9588-95909,9598-9599

85196   Opn brain lacer-coma NOS
80000-80199,80300-80499,8500-85219,85221-85419,8738-8739,
8798-8799,9050,9251-9252,9290-9299,9588-95909,9598-9599

85199   Open brain lacer-concuss
80000-80199,80300-80499,8500-85219,85221-85419,8738-8739,
8798-8799,9050,9251-9252,9290-9299,9588-95909,9598-9599

85200   Traum subarachnoid hem
80000-80199,80300-80499,8500-85219,85221-85419,8738-8739,
8798-8799,9050,9251-9252,9290-9299,9588-95909,9598-9599

85201   Subarachnoid hem-no coma
80000-80199,80300-80499,8500-85219,85221-85419,8738-8739,
8798-8799,9050,9251-9252,9290-9299,9588-95909,9598-9599

85202   Subarach hem-brief coma
80000-80199,80300-80499,8500-85219,85221-85419,8738-8739,
8798-8799,9050,9251-9252,9290-9299,9588-95909,9598-9599

85203   Subarach hem-mod coma
80000-80199,80300-80499,8500-85219,85221-85419,8738-8739,
8798-8799,9050,9251-9252,9290-9299,9588-95909,9598-9599

85204   Subarach hem-prolng coma
80000-80199,80300-80499,8500-85219,85221-85419,8738-8739,
8798-8799,9050,9251-9252,9290-9299,9588-95909,9598-9599

85205   Subarach hem-deep coma
80000-80199,80300-80499,8500-85219,85221-85419,8738-8739,
8798-8799,9050,9251-9252,9290-9299,9588-95909,9598-9599

85206   Subarach hem-coma NOS
80000-80199,80300-80499,8500-85219,85221-85419,8738-8739,
8798-8799,9050,9251-9252,9290-9299,9588-95909,9598-9599

85209   Subarach hem-concussion
80000-80199,80300-80499,8500-85219,85221-85419,8738-8739,
8798-8799,9050,9251-9252,9290-9299,9588-95909,9598-9599

85210   Subarach hem w opn wound
80000-80199,80300-80499,8500-85219,85221-85419,8738-8739,
8798-8799,9050,9251-9252,9290-9299,9588-95909,9598-9599

85211   Opn subarach hem-no coma
80000-80199,80300-80499,8500-85219,85221-85419,8738-8739,
8798-8799,9050,9251-9252,9290-9299,9588-95909,9598-9599

85212   Op subarach hem-brf coma
80000-80199,80300-80499,8500-85219,85221-85419,8738-8739,
8798-8799,9050,9251-9252,9290-9299,9588-95909,9598-9599

85213   Op subarach hem-mod coma
80000-80199,80300-80499,8500-85219,85221-85419,8738-8739,
8798-8799,9050,9251-9252,9290-9299,9588-95909,9598-9599

85214   Op subarach hem-prol com
80000-80199,80300-80499,8500-85219,85221-85419,8738-8739,
8798-8799,9050,9251-9252,9290-9299,9588-95909,9598-9599

85215   Op subarach hem-deep com
80000-80199,80300-80499,8500-85219,85221-85419,8738-8739,
8798-8799,9050,9251-9252,9290-9299,9588-95909,9598-9599

85216   Op subarach hem-coma NOS
80000-80199,80300-80499,8500-85219,85221-85419,8738-8739,
8798-8799,9050,9251-9252,9290-9299,9588-95909,9598-9599

85219   Opn subarach hem-concuss
80000-80199,80300-80499,8500-85219,85221-85419,8738-8739,
8798-8799,9050,9251-9252,9290-9299,9588-95909,9598-9599

85220   Traumatic subdural hem
80000-80199,80300-80499,8500-85419,8738-8739,8798-8799,9050,
9251-9252,9290-9299,9588-95909,9598-9599

85221   Subdural hem w/o coma
80000-80199,80300-80499,8500-85219,85221-85419,8738-8739,
8798-8799,9050,9251-9252,9290-9299,9588-95909,9598-9599

85222   Subdural hem-brief coma
80000-80199,80300-80499,8500-85219,85221-85419,8738-8739,
8798-8799,9050,9251-9252,9290-9299,9588-95909,9598-9599

85223   Subdural hemorr-mod coma
80000-80199,80300-80499,8500-85219,85221-85419,8738-8739,
8798-8799,9050,9251-9252,9290-9299,9588-95909,9598-9599

85224   Subdural hem-prolng coma
80000-80199,80300-80499,8500-85219,85221-85419,8738-8739,
8798-8799,9050,9251-9252,9290-9299,9588-95909,9598-9599

85225   Subdural hem-deep coma
80000-80199,80300-80499,8500-85219,85221-85419,8738-8739,
8798-8799,9050,9251-9252,9290-9299,9588-95909,9598-9599

85226   Subdural hemorr-coma NOS
80000-80199,80300-80499,8500-85219,85221-85419,8738-8739,
8798-8799,9050,9251-9252,9290-9299,9588-95909,9598-9599

85229   Subdural hem-concussion
80000-80199,80300-80499,8500-85219,85221-85419,8738-8739,
8798-8799,9050,9251-9252,9290-9299,9588-95909,9598-9599

85230   Subdural hem w opn wound
80000-80199,80300-80499,8500-85219,85221-85419,8738-8739,
8798-8799,9050,9251-9252,9290-9299,9588-95909,9598-9599

85231   Open subdur hem w/o coma
80000-80199,80300-80499,8500-85219,85221-85419,8738-8739,
8798-8799,9050,9251-9252,9290-9299,9588-95909,9598-9599

85232   Opn subdur hem-brf coma
80000-80199,80300-80499,8500-85219,85221-85419,8738-8739,
8798-8799,9050,9251-9252,9290-9299,9588-95909,9598-9599

85233   Opn subdur hem-mod coma
80000-80199,80300-80499,8500-85219,85221-85419,8738-8739,
8798-8799,9050,9251-9252,9290-9299,9588-95909,9598-9599

85234   Opn subdur hem-prol coma
80000-80199,80300-80499,8500-85219,85221-85419,8738-8739,
8798-8799,9050,9251-9252,9290-9299,9588-95909,9598-9599

85235   Opn subdur hem-deep coma
80000-80199,80300-80499,8500-85219,85221-85419,8738-8739,
8798-8799,9050,9251-9252,9290-9299,9588-95909,9598-9599

85236   Opn subdur hem-coma NOS
80000-80199,80300-80499,8500-85219,85221-85419,8738-8739,
8798-8799,9050,9251-9252,9290-9299,9588-95909,9598-9599

85239   Opn subdur hem-concuss
80000-80199,80300-80499,8500-85219,85221-85419,8738-8739,
8798-8799,9050,9251-9252,9290-9299,9588-95909,9598-9599

85240   Traumatic extradural hem
80000-80199,80300-80499,8500-85219,85221-85419,8738-8739,
8798-8799,9050,9251-9252,9290-9299,9588-95909,9598-9599

85241   Extradural hem w/o coma
80000-80199,80300-80499,8500-85219,85221-85419,8738-8739,
8798-8799,9050,9251-9252,9290-9299,9588-95909,9598-9599

85242   Extradur hem-brief coma
80000-80199,80300-80499,8500-85219,85221-85419,8738-8739,
8798-8799,9050,9251-9252,9290-9299,9588-95909,9598-9599

85243   Extradural hem-mod coma
80000-80199,80300-80499,8500-85219,85221-85419,8738-8739,
8798-8799,9050,9251-9252,9290-9299,9588-95909,9598-9599

85244   Extradur hem-proln coma
80000-80199,80300-80499,8500-85219,85221-85419,8738-8739,
8798-8799,9050,9251-9252,9290-9299,9588-95909,9598-9599

85245   Extradural hem-deep coma
80000-80199,80300-80499,8500-85219,85221-85419,8738-8739,
8798-8799,9050,9251-9252,9290-9299,9588-95909,9598-9599

85246   Extradural hem-coma NOS
80000-80199,80300-80499,8500-85219,85221-85419,8738-8739,
8798-8799,9050,9251-9252,9290-9299,9588-95909,9598-9599

85249   Extadural hem-concuss
80000-80199,80300-80499,8500-85219,85221-85419,8738-8739,
8798-8799,9050,9251-9252,9290-9299,9588-95909,9598-9599

85250   Extradural hem w opn wnd
80000-80199,80300-80499,8500-85219,85221-85419,8738-8739,
8798-8799,9050,9251-9252,9290-9299,9588-95909,9598-9599

85251   Extradural hemor-no coma
80000-80199,80300-80499,8500-85219,85221-85419,8738-8739,
8798-8799,9050,9251-9252,9290-9299,9588-95909,9598-9599

85252   Extradur hem-brief coma
80000-80199,80300-80499,8500-85219,85221-85419,8738-8739,
8798-8799,9050,9251-9252,9290-9299,9588-95909,9598-9599

85253   Extradural hem-mod coma
80000-80199,80300-80499,8500-85219,85221-85419,8738-8739,
8798-8799,9050,9251-9252,9290-9299,9588-95909,9598-9599

85254   Extradur hem-proln coma
80000-80199,80300-80499,8500-85219,85221-85419,8738-8739,
8798-8799,9050,9251-9252,9290-9299,9588-95909,9598-9599

85255   Extradur hem-deep coma
80000-80199,80300-80499,8500-85219,85221-85419,8738-8739,
8798-8799,9050,9251-9252,9290-9299,9588-95909,9598-9599

85256   Extradural hem-coma NOS
80000-80199,80300-80499,8500-85219,85221-85419,8738-8739,
8798-8799,9050,9251-9252,9290-9299,9588-95909,9598-9599

85259   Extradural hem-concuss
80000-80199,80300-80499,8500-85219,85221-85419,8738-8739,
8798-8799,9050,9251-9252,9290-9299,9588-95909,9598-9599

85300   Traumatic brain hem NEC
80000-80199,80300-80499,8500-85219,85221-85419,8738-8739,
8798-8799,9050,9251-9252,9290-9299,9588-95909,9598-9599

85301   Brain hem NEC w/o coma
80000-80199,80300-80499,8500-85219,85221-85419,8738-8739,
8798-8799,9050,9251-9252,9290-9299,9588-95909,9598-9599

85302   Brain hem NEC-brief coma
80000-80199,80300-80499,8500-85219,85221-85419,8738-8739,
8798-8799,9050,9251-9252,9290-9299,9588-95909,9598-9599

85303   Brain hem NEC-mod coma
80000-80199,80300-80499,8500-85219,85221-85419,8738-8739,
8798-8799,9050,9251-9252,9290-9299,9588-95909,9598-9599

85304   Brain hem NEC-proln coma
80000-80199,80300-80499,8500-85219,85221-85419,8738-8739,
8798-8799,9050,9251-9252,9290-9299,9588-95909,9598-9599

85305   Brain hem NEC-deep coma
80000-80199,80300-80499,8500-85219,85221-85419,8738-8739,
8798-8799,9050,9251-9252,9290-9299,9588-95909,9598-9599

85306   Brain hem NEC-coma NOS
80000-80199,80300-80499,8500-85219,85221-85419,8738-8739,
8798-8799,9050,9251-9252,9290-9299,9588-95909,9598-9599

85309   Brain hem NEC-concussion
80000-80199,80300-80499,8500-85219,85221-85419,8738-8739,
8798-8799,9050,9251-9252,9290-9299,9588-95909,9598-9599

85310   Brain hem NEC w opn wnd
80000-80199,80300-80499,8500-85219,85221-85419,8738-8739,
8798-8799,9050,9251-9252,9290-9299,9588-95909,9598-9599

85311   Brain hem opn w/o coma
80000-80199,80300-80499,8500-85219,85221-85419,8738-8739,
8798-8799,9050,9251-9252,9290-9299,9588-95909,9598-9599

85312   Brain hem opn-brf coma
80000-80199,80300-80499,8500-85219,85221-85419,8738-8739,
8798-8799,9050,9251-9252,9290-9299,9588-95909,9598-9599

85313   Brain hem open-mod coma
80000-80199,80300-80499,8500-85219,85221-85419,8738-8739,
8798-8799,9050,9251-9252,9290-9299,9588-95909,9598-9599

85314   Brain hem opn-proln coma
80000-80199,80300-80499,8500-85219,85221-85419,8738-8739,
8798-8799,9050,9251-9252,9290-9299,9588-95909,9598-9599

85315   Brain hem open-deep coma
80000-80199,80300-80499,8500-85219,85221-85419,8738-8739,
8798-8799,9050,9251-9252,9290-9299,9588-95909,9598-9599

85316   Brain hem open-coma NOS
80000-80199,80300-80499,8500-85219,85221-85419,8738-8739,
8798-8799,9050,9251-9252,9290-9299,9588-95909,9598-9599

85319   Brain hem opn-concussion
80000-80199,80300-80499,8500-85219,85221-85419,8738-8739,
8798-8799,9050,9251-9252,9290-9299,9588-95909,9598-9599

85400   Brain injury NEC
80000-80199,80300-80499,8500-85219,85221-85419,8738-8739,
8798-8799,9050,9251-9252,9290-9299,9588-95909,9598-9599

85401   Brain injury NEC-no coma
80000-80199,80300-80499,8500-85219,85221-85419,8738-8739,
8798-8799,9050,9251-9252,9290-9299,9588-95909,9598-9599

85402 Brain inj NEC-brief coma
80000-80199,80300-80499,8500-85219,85221-85419,8738-8739,
8798-8799,9050,9251-9252,9290-9299,9588-95909,9598-9599

85403 Brain inj NEC-mod coma
80000-80199,80300-80499,8500-85219,85221-85419,8738-8739,
8798-8799,9050,9251-9252,9290-9299,9588-95909,9598-9599

85404 Brain inj NEC-proln coma
80000-80199,80300-80499,8500-85219,85221-85419,8738-8739,
8798-8799,9050,9251-9252,9290-9299,9588-95909,9598-9599

85405 Brain inj NEC-deep coma
80000-80199,80300-80499,8500-85219,85221-85419,8738-8739,
8798-8799,9050,9251-9252,9290-9299,9588-95909,9598-9599

85406 Brain inj NEC-coma NOS
80000-80199,80300-80499,8500-85219,85221-85419,8738-8739,
8798-8799,9050,9251-9252,9290-9299,9588-95909,9598-9599

85409 Brain inj NEC-concussion
80000-80199,80300-80499,8500-85219,85221-85419,8738-8739,
8798-8799,9050,9251-9252,9290-9299,9588-95909,9598-9599

85410 Brain injury w opn wnd
80000-80199,80300-80499,8500-85219,85221-85419,8738-8739,
8798-8799,9050,9251-9252,9290-9299,9588-95909,9598-9599

85411 Opn brain inj w/o coma
80000-80199,80300-80499,8500-85219,85221-85419,8738-8739,
8798-8799,9050,9251-9252,9290-9299,9588-95909,9598-9599

85412 Opn brain inj-brief coma
80000-80199,80300-80499,8500-85219,85221-85419,8738-8739,
8798-8799,9050,9251-9252,9290-9299,9588-95909,9598-9599

85413 Opn brain inj-mod coma
80000-80199,80300-80499,8500-85219,85221-85419,8738-8739,
8798-8799,9050,9251-9252,9290-9299,9588-95909,9598-9599

85414 Opn brain inj-proln coma
80000-80199,80300-80499,8500-85219,85221-85419,8738-8739,
8798-8799,9050,9251-9252,9290-9299,9588-95909,9598-9599

85415 Opn brain inj-deep coma
80000-80199,80300-80499,8500-85219,85221-85419,8738-8739,
8798-8799,9050,9251-9252,9290-9299,9588-95909,9598-9599

85416 Open brain inj-coma NOS
80000-80199,80300-80499,8500-85219,85221-85419,8738-8739,
8798-8799,9050,9251-9252,9290-9299,9588-95909,9598-9599

85419 Opn brain inj-concussion
80000-80199,80300-80499,8500-85219,85221-85419,8738-8739,
8798-8799,9050,9251-9252,9290-9299,9588-95909,9598-9599

8600 Traum pneumothorax-close
8600-8605,86120-86132,86229,86239-8629,8750-8751,8798-8799,
9290-9299,9587-9588,9598-9599

8601 Traum pneumothorax-open
8600-8605,86120-86132,86229,86239-8629,8750-8751,8798-8799,
9290-9299,9587-9588,9598-9599

8602 Traum hemothorax-closed
8600-8605,86120-86132,86229,86239-8629,8750-8751,8798-8799,
9290-9299,9587-9588,9598-9599

8603 Traum hemothorax-open
8600-8605,86120-86132,86229,86239-8629,8750-8751,8798-8799,
9290-9299,9587-9588,9598-9599

8604 Traum pneumohemothor-cl
8600-8605,86120-86132,86229,86239-8629,8750-8751,8798-8799,
9290-9299,9587-9588,9598-9599

8605 Traum pneumohemothor-opn
8600-8605,86120-86132,86229,86239-8629,8750-8751,8798-8799,
9290-9299,9587-9588,9598-9599

86101 Heart contusion-closed
86100-86113,86229,86239-8629,8750-8751,8798-8799,9290-9299,
9587-9588,9598-9599

86102 Heart laceration-closed
86100-86113,86229,86239-8629,8750-8751,8798-8799,9290-9299,
9587-9588,9598-9599

86103 Heart chamber lacerat-cl
86100-86113,86229,86239-8629,8750-8751,8798-8799,9290-9299,
9587-9588,9598-9599

86110 Heart injury NOS-open
86100-86113,86229,86239-8629,8750-8751,8798-8799,9290-9299,
9587-9588,9598-9599

86111 Heart contusion-open
86100-86113,86229,86239-8629,8750-8751,8798-8799,9290-9299,
9587-9588,9598-9599

86112 Heart laceration-open
86100-86113,86229,86239-8629,8750-8751,8798-8799,9290-9299,
9587-9588,9598-9599

86113 Heart chamber lacer-opn
86100-86113,86229,86239-8629,8750-8751,8798-8799,9290-9299,
9587-9588,9598-9599

86122 Lung laceration-closed
86120-86132,86229,86239-8629,8750-8751,8798-8799,9290-9299,
9587-9588,9598-9599

86130 Lung injury NOS-open
86120-86132,86229,86239-8629,8750-8751,8798-8799,9290-9299,
9587-9588,9598-9599

86131 Lung contusion-open
86120-86132,86229,86239-8629,8750-8751,8798-8799,9290-9299,
9587-9588,9598-9599

86132 Lung laceration-open
86120-86132,86229,86239-8629,8750-8751,8798-8799,9290-9299,
9587-9588,9598-9599

8621 Diaphragm injury-open
8620-8621,86229,86239-8629,8750-8751,8798-8799,9290-9299,
9587-9588,9598-9599

86221 Bronchus injury-closed
86221,86229-86231,86239-8629,8750-8751,8798-8799,9290-9299,
9587-9588,9598-9599

86222 Esophagus injury-closed
86222-86229,86232-8629,8750-8751,8798-8799,9290-9299,9587-9588,
9598-9599

86229 Intrathoracic inj NEC-cl
86229,86239-8629,8750-8751,8798-8799,9290-9299,9587-9588,
9598-9599

86231 Bronchus injury-open
86221,86229-86231,86239-8629,8750-8751,8798-8799,9290-9299,
9587-9588,9598-9599

86232 Esophagus injury-open
86222-86229,86232-8629,8750-8751,8798-8799,9290-9299,9587-9588,
9598-9599

86239 Intrathorac inj NEC-open
86229,86239-8629,8750-8751,8798-8799,9290-9299,9587-9588,
9598-9599

8629 Intrathorac inj NOS-open
86229,86239-8629,8750-8751,8798-8799,9290-9299,9587-9588,
9598-9599

8631 Stomach injury-open
8630-8631,86380,86389-86390,86399,86800,86803-86810,86813-8691,
8792-8799,9290-9299,9588,9598-9599

86330 Small intest inj NOS-opn
86320-86339,86380,86389-86390,86399,86800,86803-86810,
86813-8691,8792-8799,9290-9299,9588,9598-9599

86331 Duodenum injury-open
86321,86331-86339,86380,86389-86390,86399,86800,86803-86810,
86813-8691,8792-8799,9290-9299,9588,9598-9599

86339 Small intest inj NEC-opn
86320-86339,86380,86389-86390,86399,86800,86803-86810,
86813-8691,8792-8799,9290-9299,9588,9598-9599

86350 Colon injury NOS-open
86340-86380,86389-86390,86399,86800,86803-86810,86813-8691,
8792-8799,9290-9299,9588,9598-9599

86351 Ascending colon inj-open
86340-86380,86389-86390,86800,86803-86810,86813-8691,
8792-8799,9290-9299,9588,9598-9599

86352 Transverse colon inj-opn
86340-86380,86389-86390,86399,86800,86803-86810,86813-8691,
8792-8799,9290-9299,9588,9598-9599

86353 Descending colon inj-opn
86340-86380,86389-86390,86399,86800,86803-86810,86813-8691,
8792-8799,9290-9299,9588,9598-9599

86354 Sigmoid colon inj-open
86340-86380,86389-86390,86399,86800,86803-86810,86813-8691,
8792-8799,9290-9299,9588,9598-9599

86355   Rectum injury-open
86340-86380,86389-86390,86399,86800,86803-86810,86813-8691,
8792-8799,9290-9299,9588,9598-9599
86356   Colon inj mult site-open
86340-86380,86389-86390,86399,86800,86803-86810,86813-8691,
8792-8799,9290-9299,9588,9598-9599
86359   Colon injury NEC-open
86340-86380,86389-86390,86399,86800,86803-86810,86813-8691,
8792-8799,9290-9299,9588,9598-9599
86390   GI injury NOS-open
86380-86384,86389-86394,86399,86800,86803-86810,86813-8691,
8792-8799,9290-9299,9588,9598-9599
86391   Pancreas, head inj-open
86380-86384,86391-86394,86399,86800,86803-86810,86813-8691,
8792-8799,9290-9299,9588,9598-9599
86392   Pancreas, body inj-open
86380-86384,86391-86394,86399,86800,86803-86810,86813-8691,
8792-8799,9290-9299,9588,9598-9599
86393   Pancreas, tail inj-open
86380-86384,86391-86394,86399,86800,86803-86810,86813-8691,
8792-8799,9290-9299,9588,9598-9599
86394   Pancreas injury NOS-open
86380-86384,86391-86394,86399,86800,86803-86810,86813-8691,
8792-8799,9290-9299,9588,9598-9599
86395   Appendix injury-open
86380,86385,86395-86399,86800,86803-86810,86813-8691,8792-8799,
9290-9299,9588,9598-9599
86399   GI injury NEC-open
86380,86399,86800,86803-86810,86813-8691,8792-8799,9290-9299,
9588,9598-9599
86400   Liver injury NOS-closed
86380,86399-86419,86800,86803-86810,86813-8691,8792-8799,
9290-9299,9588,9598-9599
86401   Liver hematoma/contusion
86380,86399-86419,86800,86803-86810,86813-8691,8792-8799,
9290-9299,9588,9598-9599
86402   Liver laceration, minor
86380,86399-86419,86800,86803-86810,86813-8691,8792-8799,
9290-9299,9588,9598-9599
86403   Liver laceration, mod
86380,86399-86419,86800,86803-86810,86813-8691,8792-8799,
9290-9299,9588,9598-9599
86404   Liver laceration, major
86380,86399-86419,86800,86803-86810,86813-8691,8792-8799,
9290-9299,9588,9598-9599
86405   Liver lacerat unspcf cls
86380,86399-86419,86800,86803-86810,86813-8691,8792-8799,
9290-9299,9588,9598-9599
86409   Liver injury NEC-closed
86380,86399-86419,86800,86803-86810,86813-8691,8792-8799,
9290-9299,9588,9598-9599
86410   Liver injury NOS-open
86380,86399-86419,86800,86803-86810,86813-8691,8792-8799,
9290-9299,9588,9598-9599
86411   Liver hematom/contus-opn
86380,86399-86419,86800,86803-86810,86813-8691,8792-8799,
9290-9299,9588,9598-9599
86412   Liver lacerat, minor-opn
86380,86399-86419,86800,86803-86810,86813-8691,8792-8799,
9290-9299,9588,9598-9599
86413   Liver lacerat, mod-open
86380,86399-86419,86800,86803-86810,86813-8691,8792-8799,
9290-9299,9588,9598-9599
86414   Liver lacerat, major-opn
86380,86399-86419,86800,86803-86810,86813-8691,8792-8799,
9290-9299,9588,9598-9599
86415   Liver lacerat unspcf opn
86380,86399-86419,86800,86803-86810,86813-8691,8792-8799,
9290-9299,9588,9598-9599
86419   Liver injury NEC-open
86380,86399-86419,86800,86803-86810,86813-8691,8792-8799,
9290-9299,9588,9598-9599

86500   Spleen injury NOS-closed
86500-86519,86800,86803-86810,86813-8691,8792-8799,9290-9299,
9588,9598-9599
86501   Spleen hematoma-closed
86500-86519,86800,86803-86810,86813-8691,8792-8799,9290-9299,
9588,9598-9599
86502   Spleen capsular tear
86500-86519,86800,86803-86810,86813-8691,8792-8799,9290-9299,
9588,9598-9599
86503   Spleen parenchyma lacer
86500-86519,86800,86803-86810,86813-8691,8792-8799,9290-9299,
9588,9598-9599
86504   Spleen disruption-clos
86500-86519,86800,86803-86810,86813-8691,8792-8799,9290-9299,
9588,9598-9599
86509   Spleen injury NEC-closed
86500-86519,86800,86803-86810,86813-8691,8792-8799,9290-9299,
9588,9598-9599
86510   Spleen injury NOS-open
86500-86519,86800,86803-86810,86813-8691,8792-8799,9290-9299,
9588,9598-9599
86511   Spleen hematoma-open
86500-86519,86800,86803-86810,86813-8691,8792-8799,9290-9299,
9588,9598-9599
86512   Spleen capsular tear-opn
86500-86519,86800,86803-86810,86813-8691,8792-8799,9290-9299,
9588,9598-9599
86513   Spleen parnchym lac-opn
86500-86519,86800,86803-86810,86813-8691,8792-8799,9290-9299,
9588,9598-9599
86514   Spleen disruption-open
86500-86519,86800,86803-86810,86813-8691,8792-8799,9290-9299,
9588,9598-9599
86519   Spleen injury NEC-open
86500-86519,86800,86803-86810,86813-8691,8792-8799,9290-9299,
9588,9598-9599
86600   Kidney injury NOS-closed
86600-86613,86800,86803-86810,86813-8691,8792-8799,9290-9299,
9588,9598-9599
86601   Kidney hematoma-closed
86600-86613,86800,86803-86810,86813-8691,8792-8799,9290-9299,
9588,9598-9599
86602   Kidney laceration-closed
86600-86613,86800,86803-86810,86813-8691,8792-8799,9290-9299,
9588,9598-9599
86603   Kidney disruption-closed
86600-86613,86800,86803-86810,86813-8691,8792-8799,9290-9299,
9588,9598-9599
86610   Kidney injury NOS-open
86600-86613,86800,86803-86810,86813-8691,8792-8799,9290-9299,
9588,9598-9599
86611   Kidney hematoma-open
86600-86613,86800,86803-86810,86813-8691,8792-8799,9290-9299,
9588,9598-9599
86612   Kidney laceration-open
86600-86613,86800,86803-86810,86813-8691,8792-8799,9290-9299,
9588,9598-9599
86613   Kidney disruption-open
86600-86613,86800,86803-86810,86813-8691,8792-8799,9290-9299,
9588,9598-9599
8670   Bladder/urethra inj-clos
8670-8671,8676-86800,86803-86810,86813-8691,8792-8799,
9290-9299,9588,9598-9599
8671   Bladder/urethra inj-open
8670-8671,8676-86800,86803-86810,86813-8691,8792-8799,
9290-9299,9588,9598-9599
8672   Ureter injury-closed
8672-8673,8676-86800,86803-86810,86813-8691,8792-8799,
9290-9299,9588,9598-9599
8673   Ureter injury-open
8672-8673,8676-86800,86803-86810,86813-8691,8792-8799,
9290-9299,9588,9598-9599

8674   Uterus injury-closed
8674-86800,86803-86810,86813-8691,8792-8799,9290-9299,9588,
9598-9599

8675   Uterus injury-open
8674-86800,86803-86810,86813-8691,8792-8799,9290-9299,9588,
9598-9599

8676   Pelvic organ inj NEC-cl
8676-86800,86803-86810,86813-8691,8792-8799,9290-9299,9588,
9598-9599

8677   Pelvic organ inj NEC-opn
8676-86800,86803-86810,86813-8691,8792-8799,9290-9299,9588,
9598-9599

8678   Pelvic organ inj NOS-cl
8676-86800,86803-86810,86813-8691,8792-8799,9290-9299,9588,
9598-9599

8679   Pelvic organ inj NOS-opn
8676-86800,86803-86810,86813-8691,8792-8799,9290-9299,9588,
9598-9599

86800   Intra-abdom inj NOS-clos
86800,86803-86810,86813-8691,8792-8799,9290-9299,9588,9598-9599

86801   Adrenal gland injury-cl
86800-86801,86803-86811,86813-8691,8792-8799,9290-9299,9588,
9598-9599

86802   Biliary tract injury-cl
86800,86802-86810,86813-8691,8792-8799,9290-9299,9588,9598-9599

86803   Peritoneum injury-closed
86800,86803-86810,86813-8691,8792-8799,9290-9299,9588,9598-9599

86804   Retroperitoneum inj-cl
86800,86803-86810,86813-8691,8792-8799,9290-9299,9588,9598-9599

86809   Intra-abdom inj NEC-clos
86800,86803-86810,86813-8691,8792-8799,9290-9299,9588,9598-9599

86810   Intra-abdom inj NOS-open
86800,86803-86810,86813-8691,8792-8799,9290-9299,9588,9598-9599

86811   Adrenal gland injury-opn
86800-86801,86803-86811,86813-8691,8792-8799,9290-9299,9588,
9598-9599

86812   Biliary tract injury-opn
86800,86803-86810,86812-8691,8792-8799,9290-9299,9588,9598-9599

86813   Peritoneum injury-open
86800,86803-86810,86813-8691,8792-8799,9290-9299,9588,9598-9599

86814   Retroperitoneum inj-open
86800,86803-86810,86813-8691,8792-8799,9290-9299,9588,9598-9599

86819   Intra-abdom inj NEC-open
86800,86803-86810,86813-8691,8792-8799,9290-9299,9588,9598-9599

8690   Internal inj NOS-closed
86800,86803-86810,86813-8691,8792-8799,9290-9299,9588,9598-9599

8691   Internal injury NOS-open
86800,86803-86810,86813-8691,8792-8799,9290-9299,9588,9598-9599

8703   Penetr wnd orbit w/o FB
8700-8719,8798-8799,9290-9299,9588,9598-9599

8704   Penetrat wnd orbit w FB
8700-8719,8798-8799,9290-9299,9588,9598-9599

8708   Opn wnd ocular adnex NEC
8700-8719,8798-8799,9290-9299,9588,9598-9599

8709   Opn wnd ocular adnex NOS
8700-8719,8798-8799,9290-9299,9588,9598-9599

8710   Ocular lac w/o prolapse
8700-8719,8798-8799,9290-9299,9588,9598-9599

8711   Ocular lacera w prolapse
8700-8719,8798-8799,9290-9299,9588,9598-9599

8712   Rupture eye w tissu loss
8700-8719,8798-8799,9290-9299,9588,9598-9599

8713   Avulsion of eye
8700-8719,8798-8799,9290-9299,9588,9598-9599

8714   Laceration of eye NOS
8700-8719,8798-8799,9290-9299,9588,9598-9599

8719   Opn wound of eyeball NOS
8700-8719,8798-8799,9290-9299,9588,9598-9599

87272   Open wnd ossicles-compl
87200-8729,8798-8799,9290-9299,9588,9598-9599

87273   Opn wnd eustach tb-compl
87200-8729,8798-8799,9290-9299,9588,9598-9599

87274   Open wound cochlea-compl
87200-8729,8798-8799,9290-9299,9588,9598-9599

87333   Open wnd nas sinus-compl
87320-87339,8798-8799,9290-9299,9588,9598-9599

8739   Open wnd head NEC-compl
8470,87340-87379,8739,8748-8749,8798-8799,9290-9299,9588,
9598-9599

87400   Opn wnd larynx w trachea
8470,87400-87412,8748-8749,8798-8799,9290-9299,9588,9598-9599

87401   Open wound of larynx
8470,87400-87412,8748-8749,8798-8799,9290-9299,9588,9598-9599

87402   Open wound of trachea
8470,87400-87412,8748-8749,8798-8799,9290-9299,9588,9598-9599

87410   Opn wnd lary w trac-comp
8470,87400-87412,8748-8749,8798-8799,9290-9299,9588,9598-9599

87411   Open wound larynx-compl
8470,87400-87412,8748-8749,8798-8799,9290-9299,9588,9598-9599

87412   Open wound trachea-compl
8470,87400-87412,8748-8749,8798-8799,9290-9299,9588,9598-9599

8743   Open wound thyroid-compl
8470,8742-8743,8748-8749,8798-8799,9290-9299,9588,9598-9599

8745   Open wound pharynx-compl
8470,8744-8749,8798-8799,9290-9299,9588,9598-9599

8750   Open wound of chest
8471,86229,86239-8629,8750-8751,8798-8799,9290-9299,9587-9588,
9598-9599

8751   Open wound chest-compl
8471,86229,86239-8629,8750-8751,8798-8799,9290-9299,9587-9588,
9598-9599

8870   Amput below elb, unilat
88000-8877,9290-9299,9588,9598-9599

8871   Amp below elb, unil-comp
88000-8877,9290-9299,9588,9598-9599

8872   Amput abv elbow, unilat
88000-8877,9290-9299,9588,9598-9599

8873   Amput abv elb, unil-comp
88000-8877,9290-9299,9588,9598-9599

8874   Amputat arm, unilat NOS
88000-8877,9290-9299,9588,9598-9599

8875   Amput arm, unil NOS-comp
88000-8877,9290-9299,9588,9598-9599

8876   Amputation arm, bilat
88000-8877,9290-9299,9588,9598-9599

8877   Amputat arm, bilat-compl
88000-8877,9290-9299,9588,9598-9599

8960   Amputation foot, unilat
8900-8977,9290-9299,9588,9598-9599

8961   Amput foot, unilat-compl
8900-8977,9290-9299,9588,9598-9599

8962   Amputation foot, bilat
8900-8977,9290-9299,9588,9598-9599

8963   Amputat foot, bilat-comp
8900-8977,9290-9299,9588,9598-9599

8970   Amput below knee, unilat
8900-8977,9290-9299,9588,9598-9599

8971   Amputat bk, unilat-compl
8900-8977,9290-9299,9588,9598-9599

8972   Amput above knee, unilat
8900-8977,9290-9299,9588,9598-9599

8973   Amput abv kn, unil-compl
8900-8977,9290-9299,9588,9598-9599

8974   Amputat leg, unilat NOS
8900-8977,9290-9299,9588,9598-9599

8975   Amput leg, unil NOS-comp
8900-8977,9290-9299,9588,9598-9599

8976   Amputation leg, bilat
8900-8977,9290-9299,9588,9598-9599

8977   Amputat leg, bilat-compl
8900-8977,9290-9299,9588,9598-9599

90000   Injur carotid artery NOS
90000,90082-9009,9049,9290-9299,9588,9598-9599

90001   Inj common carotid arter
90000,90082-9009,9049,9290-9299,9588,9598-9599

90002   Inj external carotid art
90000,90082-9009,9049,9290-9299,9588,9598-9599
90003   Inj internal carotid art
90000,90082-9009,9049,9290-9299,9588,9598-9599
9001   Inj internl jugular vein
90082-9009,9049,9290-9299,9588,9598-9599
90081   Inj extern jugular vein
90082-9009,9049,9290-9299,9588,9598-9599
90082   Inj mlt head/neck vessel
90082-9009,9049,9290-9299,9588,9598-9599
90089   Inj head/neck vessel NEC
90082-9009,9049,9290-9299,9588,9598-9599
9009   Inj head/neck vessel NOS
90082-9009,9049,9290-9299,9588,9598-9599
9010   Injury thoracic aorta
9010,9049,9290-9299,9588,9598-9599
9011   Inj innomin/subclav art
9011,9049,9290-9299,9588,9598-9599
9012   Inj superior vena cava
9012,9049,9290-9299,9588,9598-9599
9013   Inj innomin/subclav vein
9013,9049,9290-9299,9588,9598-9599
90141   Injury pulmonary artery
90140-90141,9049,9290-9299,9588,9598-9599
90142   Injury pulmonary vein
90140,90142,9049,9290-9299,9588,9598-9599
90183   Inj mult thoracic vessel
9049,9290-9299,9588,9598-9599
9020   Injury abdominal aorta
9020,90287-9029,9049,9290-9299,9588,9598-9599
90210   Inj infer vena cava NOS
90210,90287-9029,9049,9290-9299,9588,9598-9599
90211   Injury hepatic veins
90211,90287-9029,9049,9290-9299,9588,9598-9599
90219   Inj infer vena cava NEC
90219,90287-9029,9049,9290-9299,9588,9598-9599
90220   Inj celiac/mesen art NOS
90220,90287-9029,9049,9290-9299,9588,9598-9599
90222   Injury hepatic artery
90222,90287-9029,9049,9290-9299,9588,9598-9599
90223   Injury splenic artery
90223,90287-9029,9049,9290-9299,9588,9598-9599
90224   Injury celiac axis NEC
90224,90287-9029,9049,9290-9299,9588,9598-9599
90225   Inj super mesenteric art
90225,90287-9029,9049,9290-9299,9588,9598-9599
90226   Inj brnch sup mesent art
90226,90287-9029,9049,9290-9299,9588,9598-9599
90227   Inj infer mesenteric art
90227,90287-9029,9049,9290-9299,9588,9598-9599
90229   Inj mesenteric vess NEC
90229,90287-9029,9049,9290-9299,9588,9598-9599
90231   Inj superior mesent vein
90231,90287-9029,9049,9290-9299,9588,9598-9599
90232   Inj inferior mesent vein
90232,90287-9029,9049,9290-9299,9588,9598-9599
90233   Injury portal vein
90233,90287-9029,9049,9290-9299,9588,9598-9599
90234   Injury splenic vein
90234,90287-9029,9049,9290-9299,9588,9598-9599
90239   Inj port/splen vess NEC
90239,90287-9029,9049,9290-9299,9588,9598-9599
90240   Injury renal vessel NOS
90240,90287-9029,9049,9290-9299,9588,9598-9599
90241   Injury renal artery
90241,90287-9029,9049,9290-9299,9588,9598-9599
90242   Injury renal vein
90242,90287-9029,9049,9290-9299,9588,9598-9599
90249   Injury renal vessel NEC
90249,90287-9029,9049,9290-9299,9588,9598-9599
90250   Injury iliac vessel NOS
90250,90253-90254,90259,90287-9029,9049,9290-9299,9588,
9598-9599

90251   Inj hypogastric artery
90251,90287-9029,9049,9290-9299,9588,9598-9599
90252   Injury hypogastric vein
90252,90287-9029,9049,9290-9299,9588,9598-9599
90253   Injury iliac artery
90250,90253,90259,90287-9029,9049,9290-9299,9588,9598-9599
90254   Injury iliac vein
90250,90254,90259,90287-9029,9049,9290-9299,9588,9598-9599
90259   Injury iliac vessel NEC
90250,90253-90254,90259,90287-9029,9049,9290-9299,9588,
9598-9599
90287   Inj mult abd/pelv vessel
90287-9029,9049,9290-9299,9588,9598-9599
9040   Inj common femoral arter
No Exclusions
9251   Crush inj face scalp
8738-8739,9050,9251-9252,9290-9299,9588-95909,9598-9599
9252   Crush inj neck
8738-8739,9050,9251-9252,9290-9299,9588-95909,9598-9599
9290   Crush inj mult site NEC
9290-9299,9588,9598-9599
95200   C1-c4 spin cord inj NOS
80500-80518,8058-80619,8068-8069,83900-83918,83940,83949-83950,
83959,83969,83979-8399,8479,9051,92611,95200-95209,9528-9529,
9588,9591,9598-9599
95201   Complete les cord/c1-c4
80500-80518,8058-80619,8068-8069,83900-83918,83940,83949-83950,
83959,83969,83979-8399,8479,9051,92611,95200-95209,9528-9529,
9588,9591,9598-9599
95202   Anterior cord synd/c1-c4
80500-80518,8058-80619,8068-8069,83900-83918,83940,83949-83950,
83959,83969,83979-8399,8479,9051,92611,95200-95209,9528-9529,
9588,9591,9598-9599
95203   Central cord synd/c1-c4
80500-80518,8058-80619,8068-8069,83900-83918,83940,83949-83950,
83959,83969,83979-8399,8479,9051,92611,95200-95209,9528-9529,
9588,9591,9598-9599
95204   C1-c4 spin cord inj NEC
80500-80518,8058-80619,8068-8069,83900-83918,83940,83949-83950,
83959,83969,83979-8399,8479,9051,92611,95200-95209,9528-9529,
9588,9591,9598-9599
95205   C5-c7 spin cord inj NOS
80500-80518,8058-80619,8068-8069,83900-83918,83940,83949-83950,
83959,83969,83979-8399,8479,9051,92611,95200-95209,9528-9529,
9588,9591,9598-9599
95206   Complete les cord/c5-c7
80500-80518,8058-80619,8068-8069,83900-83918,83940,83949-83950,
83959,83969,83979-8399,8479,9051,92611,95200-95209,9528-9529,
9588,9591,9598-9599
95207   Anterior cord synd/c5-c7
80500-80518,8058-80619,8068-8069,83900-83918,83940,83949-83950,
83959,83969,83979-8399,8479,9051,92611,95200-95209,9528-9529,
9588,9591,9598-9599
95208   Central cord synd/c5-c7
80500-80518,8058-80619,8068-8069,83900-83918,83940,83949-83950,
83959,83969,83979-8399,8479,9051,92611,95200-95209,9528-9529,
9588,9591,9598-9599
95209   C5-c7 spin cord inj NEC
80500-80518,8058-80619,8068-8069,83900-83918,83940,83949-83950,
83959,83969,83979-8399,8479,9051,92611,95200-95209,9528-9529,
9588,9591,9598-9599
95210   T1-t6 spin cord inj NOS
8058-8059,80620-80639,83940,83949-83950,83959,83969,83979-8399,
8479,9051,92611,95210-95219,9528-9529,9588,9591,9598-9599
95211   Complete les cord/t1-t6
8058-8059,80620-80639,83940,83949-83950,83959,83969,83979-8399,
8479,9051,92611,95210-95219,9528-9529,9588,9591,9598-9599
95212   Anterior cord synd/t1-t6
8058-8059,80620-80639,83940,83949-83950,83959,83969,83979-8399,
8479,9051,92611,95210-95219,9528-9529,9588,9591,9598-9599
95213   Central cord synd/t1-t6
8058-8059,80620-80639,83940,83949-83950,83959,83969,83979-8399,
8479,9051,92611,95210-95219,9528-9529,9588,9591,9598-9599

95214   **T1-t6 spin cord inj NEC**
8058-8059,80620-80639,83940,83949-83950,83959,83969,83979-8399,
8479,9051,92611,95210-95219,9528-9529,9588,9591,9598-9599

95215   **T7-t12 spin cord inj NOS**
8058-8059,80620-80639,83940,83949-83950,83959,83969,83979-8399,
8479,9051,92611,95210-95219,9528-9529,9588,9591,9598-9599

95216   **Complete les cord/t7-t12**
8058-8059,80620-80639,83940,83949-83950,83959,83969,83979-8399,
8479,9051,92611,95210-95219,9528-9529,9588,9591,9598-9599

95217   **Anterior cord syn/t7-t12**
8058-8059,80620-80639,83940,83949-83950,83959,83969,83979-8399,
8479,9051,92611,95210-95219,9528-9529,9588,9591,9598-9599

95218   **Central cord syn/t7-t12**
8058-8059,80620-80639,83940,83949-83950,83959,83969,83979-8399,
8479,9051,92611,95210-95219,9528-9529,9588,9591,9598-9599

95219   **T7-t12 spin cord inj NEC**
8058-8059,80620-80639,83940,83949-83950,83959,83969,83979-8399,
8479,9051,92611,95210-95219,9528-9529,9588,9591,9598-9599

9522   **Lumbar spinal cord injur**
8058-8059,8064-8065,83940,83949-83950,83959,83969,83979-8399,
8479,9051,92611,9522,9528-9529,9588,9591,9598-9599

9523   **Sacral spinal cord injur**
8058-8059,80660-80679,83940,83949-83950,83959,83969,83979-8399,
8479,9051,92611,9523-9529,9588,9591,9598-9599

9524   **Cauda equina injury**
8058-8059,80660-80679,83940,83949-83950,83959,83969,83979-8399,
8479,9051,92611,9523-9529,9588,9591,9598-9599

9528   **Spin cord inj-mult site**
8058-8059,83940,83949-83950,83959,83969,83979-8399,8479,9051,
92611,9528-9529,9588,9591,9598-9599

9529   **Spinal cord injury NOS**
8058-8059,83940,83949-83950,83959,83969,83979-8399,8479,9051,
92611,9528-9529,9588,9591,9598-9599

9530   **Cervical root injury**
9538-9539,9588,9598-9599

9531   **Dorsal root injury**
9538-9539,9588,9598-9599

9532   **Lumbar root injury**
9538-9539,9588,9598-9599

9533   **Sacral root injury**
9538-9539,9588,9598-9599

9534   **Brachial plexus injury**
9538-9539,9588,9598-9599

9535   **Lumbosacral plex injury**
9538-9539,9588,9598-9599

9538   **Mult nerve root/plex inj**
9538-9539,9588,9598-9599

9539   **Inj nerve root/plex NOS**
9538-9539,9588,9598-9599

9580   **Air embolism**
9580,9588,9598-9599,99791-99799,99881,99883-9989,9991

9581   **Fat embolism**
9581,9588,9598-9599,99791-99799,99881,99883-9989

9582   **Secondary/recur hemorr**
9582,9588,9598-9599,99791-99799,99881,99883-9989

9583   **Posttraum wnd infec NEC**
9583,9588,9598-9599,99791-99799,99881,99883-9989

9584   **Traumatic shock**
9584,9588,9598-9599,99791-99799,99881,99883-9989

9585   **Traumatic anuria**
9585,9588,9598-9599,9954,99791-99813,99881,99883-9989

9587   **Traum subcutan emphysema**
8600-8605,86120-8621,86229-8629,8750-8751,9587-9588,9598-9599,
99791-99799,99881,99883-9989

9954   **Shock due to anesthesia**
9584,9954,99791-99813,99881,99883-9989

99586   **Malignant hyperthermia**
9584,9954,99586,99791-99813,99881,99883-9989

99600   **Malfunc card dev/grf NOS**
99600,99604,99661-99662,99670-99674,99791-99799,99881,
99883-9989

99601   **Malfunc cardiac pacemake**
99601,99791-99799,99881,99883-9989

99602   **Malfunc prosth hrt valve**
99602,99791-99799,99881,99883-9989

99603   **Malfunc coron bypass grf**
99603,99791-99799,99881,99883-9989

99604   **Mch cmp autm mplnt dfbrl**
99604,99791-99799,99881,99883-9989

99609   **Malfunc card dev/grf NEC**
99609,99791-99799,99881,99883-9989

9961   **Malfunc vasc device/graf**
9961,99791-99799,99881,99883-9989

9962   **Malfunc neuro device/graf**
9962,99663,99675,99791-99799,99881,99883-9989

99630   **Malfunc gu dev/graft NOS**
99630,99664-99665,99676,99791-99799,99881,99883-9989

99639   **Malfunc gu dev/graft NEC**
99639,99664-99665,99676,99791-99799,99881,99883-9989

9964   **Malf int orthped dev/grf**
9964,99666-99667,99677-99678,99791-99799,99881,99883-9989

99651   **Corneal grft malfunction**
99651,99791-99799

99652   **Oth tissue graft malfunc**
99652,99655,99791-99799

99653   **Lens prosthesis malfunc**
99653,99791-99799

99654   **Breast prosth malfunc**
99654,99791-99799

99655   **Comp-artificial skin grf**
99652,99655-99660,99668-99670,99679,99791-99799

99656   **Comp-periton dialys cath**
99656-99660,99668-99670,99679,99791-99799

99659   **Malfunc oth device/graft**
99656-99660,99668-99670,99679,99791-99799

99660   **Reaction-unsp devic/grft**
99600-99630,99639-99679,99791-99799,99881,99883-9989

99661   **React-cardiac dev/graft**
99600-9961,99652,99659-99662,99669-99674,99679,99791-99799,
99881,99883-9989

99662   **React-oth vasc dev/graft**
99600-9961,99652,99659-99662,99669-99674,99679,99791-99799,
99881,99883-9989

99663   **React-nerv sys dev/graft**
9962,99652,99659-99660,99663,99669-99670,99675,99679,
99791-99799,99881,99883-9989

99664   **React-indwell urin cath**
5990,99630,99639,99659-99660,99664-99665,99669-99670,99676,
99679,99791-99799,99881,99883-9989

99665   **React-oth genitourin dev**
99630,99639,99652,99659-99660,99664-99665,99669-99670,99676,
99679,99791-99799,99881,99883-9989

99666   **React-inter joint prost**
9964,99652,99659-99660,99666-99670,99677-99679,99791-99799,
99881,99883-9989

99667   **React-oth int ortho dev**
9964,99652,99659-99660,99666-99670,99677-99679,99791-99799,
99881,99883-9989

99668   **React-periton dialy cath**
99656-99660,99668-99670,99679,99791-99799

99669   **React-int pros devic NEC**
99600-99630,99639-99679,99791-99799,99881,99883-9989

99670   **Comp-unsp device/graft**
99600-99630,99639-99679,99791-99799,99881,99883-9989

99671   **Comp-heart valve prosth**
99600,99602,99609-9961,99652,99659-99662,99669-99674,99679,
99791-99799,99881,99883-9989

99672   **Comp-oth cardiac device**
99600-99602,99604-9961,99652,99659-99662,99669-99674,99679,
99791-99799,99881,99883-9989

99673   **Comp-ren dialys dev/grft**
9961,99652,99659-99660,99669-99670,99673,99679,99791-99799,
99881,99883-9989

99674   **Comp-oth vasc dev/graft**
99600-9961,99652,99659-99662,99669-99674,99679,99791-99799,
99881,99883-9989

99675   Comp-nerv sys dev/graft
9962,99652,99659-99660,99663,99669-99670,99675,99679,
99791-99799,99881,99883-9989
99676   Comp-genitourin dev/grft
99630,99639,99652,99659-99660,99664-99665,99669-99670,99676,
99679,99791-99799,99881,99883-9989
99677   Comp-internal joint pros
9964,99652,99659-99660,99666-99670,99677-99679,99791-99799,
99881,99883-9989
99678   Comp-oth int ortho devic
9964,99652,99659-99660,99666-99670,99677-99679,99791-99799,
99881,99883-9989
99679   Comp-int prost devic NEC
99600-99630,99639-99679,99791-99799,99881,99883-9989
99680   Comp organ transplnt NOS
99680,99791-99799
99681   Compl kidney transplant
99681,99791-99799
99682   Compl liver transplant
99682,99791-99799
99683   Compl heart transplant
99683,99791-99799
99684   Compl lung transplant
99684,99791-99799
99685   Compl marrow transplant
99685,99791-99799
99686   Compl pancreas transplnt
99686,99791-99799
99689   Comp oth organ transplnt
99689,99791-99799
99690   Comp reattach extrem NOS
99690,99791-99799,99881,99883-9989
99691   Compl reattached forearm
99691,99791-99799,99881,99883-9989
99692   Compl reattached hand
99692,99791-99799,99881,99883-9989
99693   Compl reattached finger
99693,99791-99799,99881,99883-9989
99694   Compl reattached arm NEC
99694,99791-99799,99881,99883-9989
99695   Compl reattached foot
99695,99791-99799,99881,99883-9989
99696   Compl reattached leg NEC
99696,99791-99799,99881,99883-9989
99699   Compl reattach part NEC
99699,99791-99799,99881,99883-9989
99700   Nervous syst complc NOS
99700-99709,99791-99799,99881,99883-9989
99701   Surg complication - cns
99700-99709,99791-99799,99881,99883-9989
99702   Iatrogen CV infarc/hmrhg
99700-99709,99791-99799,99881,99883-9989
99709   Surg comp nerv systm NEC
99700-99709,99791-99799,99881,99883-9989
9971   Surg compl-heart
9971,99791-99799,99881,99883-9989
9972   Surg comp-peri vasc syst
9972,99791-99799,99881,99883-9989
9973   Surg complic-respir syst
9973,99791-99799,99881,99883-9989
9974   Surg comp-digestv system
53640-53649,9974,99791-99799,99881,99883-9989
9975   Surg compl-urinary tract
9975,99791-99799,99881,99883-9989
99762   Infection amputat stump
99760,99762-99799,99881,99883-9989
99799   Surg compl-body syst NEC
99791-99799,99881,99883-9989
9980   Postoperative shock
9584,9954,99791-99813,99881,99883-9989

99811   Hemorrhage complic proc
4560,45620,53081-53083,53089,53100-53101,53120-53121,
53140-53141,53160-53161,53200-53201,53220-53221,53240-53241,
53260-53261,53300-53301,53320-53321,53340-53341,53360-53361,
53400-53401,53420-53421,53440-53441,53460-53461,53501,53511,
53521,53531,53541,53551,53561,53783,56202-56203,56212-56213,
5693,56985,5780-5789,7724,99791-99813,99881,99889-9989
99812   Hematoma complic proc
4560,45620,53081-53083,53089,53100-53101,53120-53121,
53140-53141,53160-53161,53200-53201,53220-53221,53240-53241,
53260-53261,53300-53301,53320-53321,53340-53341,53360-53361,
53400-53401,53420-53421,53440-53441,53460-53461,53501,53511,
53521,53531,53541,53551,53561,53783,56202-56203,56212-56213,
5693,56985,5780-5789,7724,99791-99813,99881,99889-9989
99813   Seroma complicting proc
4560,45620,53081-53083,53089,53100-53101,53120-53121,
53140-53141,53160-53161,53200-53201,53220-53221,53240-53241,
53260-53261,53300-53301,53320-53321,53340-53341,53360-53361,
53400-53401,53420-53421,53440-53441,53460-53461,53501,53511,
53521,53531,53541,53551,53561,53783,56202-56203,56212-56213,
5693,56985,5780-5789,7724,99791-99813,99881,99889-9989
9982   Accidental op laceration
99791-99799,9982,99881,99883-9989
9983   Postop wound disruption
99791-99799,9983,99881,99883-9989
9984   FB left during procedure
99791-99799,9984,99881,99883-9989
99851   Infected postop seroma
99791-99799,99851-99859,99881,99889-9989
99859   Other postop infection
99791-99799,99851-99859,99881,99889-9989
9986   Persist postop fistula
99791-99799,9986,99881,99883-9989
9987   Postop forgn subst react
99791-99799,9987-99881,99883-9989
99883   Non-healing surgcl wound
99791-99799,99881,99883-9989
99889   Oth spcf cmplc procd NEC
99791-99799,99881,99883-9989
9989   Surgical complicat NOS
99791-99799,99881,99883-9989
9991   Air embol comp med care
9580,9991
9992   Vasc comp med care NEC
9992
9993   Infec compl med care NEC
9993
9994   Anaphylactic shock-serum
9994
9995   Serum reaction NEC
9995
9996   Abo incompatibility reac
9996
9997   Rh incompatibility react
9997
9998   Transfusion reaction NEC
9998
V237   Insufficnt prenatal care
V220-V239
V2381   Suprv elderly primigrav
V220-V239
V2382   Suprv elderly multigrav
V220-V239
V2383   Suprv young primigrav
V220-V239
V2384   Suprv young multigrav
V220-V239
V2389   Suprv high-risk preg NEC
V220-V239
V239   Suprv high-risk preg NOS
V220-V239

V420   Kidney transplant status
99680-99681,V420,V4289-V429

V421   Heart transplant status
99680,99683,V421,V4289-V429

V422   Heart valve transplant
99671,V422,V4289-V429

V426   Lung transplant status
99680,99684,V426,V4289-V429

V427   Liver transplant status
99680,99682,V427,V4289-V429

V4281   Trnspl status-bne marrow
99680,99685,V429

V4282   Trspl sts-perip stm cell
99680,V429

V4283   Trnspl status-pancreas
99680,99686,V4283,V429

V4289   Trnspl status organ NEC
99680,99689,V4289-V429

V432   Heart replacement NEC
99680,99683,V421,V432

V451   Renal dialysis status
99673,V451

V461   Dependence on respirator
V460-V469

PART IV

Procedures
Volume 3

A

Abbe operation
  construction of vagina 70.61
  intestinal anastomosis - *see* Anastomosis, intestine
Abciximab, infusion 99.20
Abdominocentesis 54.91
Abdominohysterectomy 68.4
Abdominoplasty 86.83
Abdominoscopy 54.21
Abdominouterotomy 68.0
  obstetrical 74.99
Abduction, arytenoid 31.69
Ablation
  biliary tract (lesion) by ERCP 51.64
  endometrial (hysteroscopic) 68.23
  inner ear (cryosurgery) (ultrasound) 20.79
    by injection 20.72
  lesion
    esophagus 42.39
      endoscopic 42.33
    heart (ventricular) 37.33
      by cardiac catheter 37.34
    intestine
      large 45.49
        endoscopic 45.43
    large intestine 45.49
      endoscopic 45.43
  pituitary 07.69
    by
      Cobalt-60 92.32
      implantation (strontium-yttrium) (Y) NEC 07.68
        transfrontal approach 07.64
        transsphenoidal approach 07.65
      proton beam (Bragg peak) 92.33
  prostate
    by
      cryoablation 60.62
      radical cryosurgical ablation (RCSA) 60.62
Abortion, therapeutic 69.51
  by
    aspiration curettage 69.51
    dilation and curettage 69.01
    hysterectomy - *see* Hysterectomy
    hysterotomy 74.91
    insertion
      laminaria 69.93
      prostaglandin suppository 96.49
    intra-amniotic injection (saline) 75.0
Abrasion
  corneal epithelium 11.41
    for smear or culture 11.21
  epicardial surface 36.39
  pleural 34.6
  skin 86.25
Abscission, cornea 11.49
Absorptiometry
  photon (dual) (single) 88.98
Aburel operation (intra-amniotic injection for abortion) 75.0
Accouchement forcé 73.99
Acetabulectomy 77.85
Acetabuloplasty NEC 81.40
  with prosthetic implant 81.52
Achillorrhaphy 83.64
  delayed 83.62

Achillotenotomy 83.11
  plastic 83.85
Achillotomy 83.11
  plastic 83.85
Acid peel, skin 86.24
Acromionectomy 77.81
Acromioplasty 81.83
  for recurrent dislocation of shoulder 81.82
  partial replacement 81.81
  total replacement 81.80
Actinotherapy 99.82
Activities of daily living (ADL)
  therapy 93.83
  training for the blind 93.78
Acupuncture 99.92
  with smouldering moxa 93.35
  for anesthesia 99.91
Adams operation
  advancement of round ligament 69.22
  crushing of nasal septum 21.88
  excision of palmar fascia 82.35
Adenectomy - *see also* Excision, by site
  prostate NEC 60.69
  retropubic 60.4
Adenoidectomy (without tonsillectomy) 28.6
  with tonsillectomy 28.3
Adhesiolysis - *see also* Lysis, adhesions
  for collapse of lung 33.39
  middle ear 20.23
Adipectomy 86.83
Adjustment
  cardiac pacemaker program (reprogramming) - *omit code*
  cochlear prosthetic device (external components) 95.49
  dental 99.97
  occlusal 24.8
  spectacles 95.31
Administration (of) - *see also* Injection
  antitoxins NEC 99.58
    botulism 99.57
    diphtheria 99.58
    gas gangrene 99.58
    scarlet fever 99.58
    tetanus 99.56
  Bender Visual-Motor Gestalt test 94.02
  Benton Visual Retention test 94.02
  intelligence test or scale (Stanford-Binet) (Wechsler) (adult) (children) 94.01
    Minnesota Multiphasic Personality Inventory (MMPI) 94.02
    MMPI (Minnesota Multiphasic Personality Inventory) 94.02
  psychologic test 94.02
  Stanford-Binet test 94.01
  toxoid
    diphtheria 99.36
      with tetanus and pertussis, combined (DTP) 99.39
    tetanus 99.38
      with diphtheria and pertussis, combined (DTP) 99.39
  vaccine - *see also* Vaccination
    BCG 99.33
    measles-mumps-rubella (MMR) 99.48
    poliomyelitis 99.41
    TAB 99.32

Administration (*Continued*)
  Wechsler
    Intelligence Scale (adult) (children) 94.01
    Memory Scale 94.02
Adrenalectomy (unilateral) 07.22
  with partial removal of remaining gland 07.29
  bilateral 07.3
    partial 07.29
    subtotal 07.29
  complete 07.3
  partial NEC 07.29
  remaining gland 07.3
  subtotal NEC 07.29
  total 07.3
Adrenalorrhaphy 07.44
Adrenalotomy (with drainage) 07.41
Advancement
  extraocular muscle 15.12
    multiple (with resection or recession) 15.3
  eyelid muscle 08.59
  eye muscle 15.12
    multiple (with resection or recession) 15.3
  graft - *see* Graft
  leaflet (heart) 35.10
  pedicle (flap) 86.72
  profundus tendon (Wagner) 82.51
  round ligament 69.22
  tendon 83.71
    hand 82.51
    profundus (Wagner) 82.51
  Wagner (profundus tendon) 82.51
Albee operation
  bone peg, femoral neck 78.05
  graft for slipping patella 78.06
  sliding inlay graft, tibia 78.07
Albert operation (arthrodesis of knee) 81.22
Aldridge (-Studdiford) operation (urethral sling) 59.5
Alexander operation
  prostatectomy
    perineal 60.62
    suprapubic 60.3
  shortening of round ligaments 69.22
Alexander-Adams operation (shortening of round ligaments) 69.22
Alimentation, parenteral 99.29
Allograft - *see* Graft
Almoor operation (extrapetrosal drainage) 20.22
Altemeier operation (perineal rectal pull-through) 48.49
Alveolectomy (interradicular) (intraseptal) (radical) (simple) (with graft) (with implant) 24.5
Alveoloplasty (with graft or implant) 24.5
Alveolotomy (apical) 24.0
Ambulatory cardiac monitoring (ACM) 89.50
Ammon operation (dacryocystotomy) 09.53
Amniocentesis (transuterine) (diagnostic) 75.1
  with intra-amniotic injection of saline 75.0
Amniography 87.81
Amnioinfusion 75.37
Amnioscopy, internal 75.31

Angiectomy (Continued)
  with (Continued)
    anastomosis (Continued)
      abdominal
        artery 38.36
        vein 38.37
      aorta (arch) (ascending) (descending) 38.34
      head and neck NEC 38.32
      intracranial NEC 38.31
      lower limb
        artery 38.38
        vein 38.39
      thoracic vessel NEC 38.35
      upper limb (artery) (vein) 38.33
    graft replacement (interposition) 38.40
      abdominal
        aorta 38.44
        artery 38.46
        vein 38.47
      aorta (arch) (ascending) (descending thoracic)
        abdominal 38.44
        thoracic 38.45
        thoracoabdominal 38.45 [38.44]
      head and neck NEC 38.42
      intracranial NEC 38.41
      lower limb
        artery 38.48
        vein 38.49
      thoracic vessel NEC 38.45
      upper limb (artery) (vein) 38.43
Angiocardiography (selective) 88.50
  carbon dioxide (negative contrast) 88.58
  combined right and left heart 88.54
  left heart (aortic valve) (atrium) (ventricle) (ventricular outflow tract) 88.53
    combined with right heart 88.54
  right heart (atrium) (pulmonary valve) (ventricle) (ventricular outflow tract) 88.52
    combined with left heart 88.54
  vena cava (inferior) (superior) 88.51
Angiography (arterial) - *see also* Arteriography 88.40
  by radioisotope - *see* Scan, radioisotope, by site
  by ultrasound - *see* Ultrasonography, by site
  basilar 88.41
  brachial 88.49
  carotid (internal) 88.41
  celiac 88.47
  cerebral (posterior circulation) 88.41
  coronary NEC 88.57
  eye (fluorescein) 95.12
  femoral 88.48
  heart 88.50
  intra-abdominal NEC 88.47
  intracranial 88.41
  intrathoracic vessels NEC 88.44
  lower extremity NEC 88.48
  neck 88.41
  placenta 88.46
  pulmonary 88.43
  renal 88.45
  specified artery NEC 88.49
  transfemoral 88.48
  upper extremity NEC 88.49
  veins - *see* Phlebography
  vertebral 88.41

Angioplasty (laser) - *see also* Repair, blood vessel
  balloon (percutaneous transluminal) NEC 39.50
    coronary artery (single vessel) 36.01
      with thrombolytic agent infusion 36.02
      multiple vessels 36.05
    other sites (femoropopliteal) (iliac) (non-coronary) (renal) (vertebral) 39.50
  coronary 36.09
    open chest approach 36.03
    percutaneous transluminal (balloon) (single vessel) 36.01
      with thrombolytic agent infusion 36.02
      multiple vessels 36.05
  percutaneous transluminal (balloon) (single vessel) 39.50
    basilar 39.50
    carotid 39.50
    coronary (balloon) (single vessel) 36.01
      with thrombolytic agent infusion 36.02
      multiple vessels 36.05
    femoropopliteal 39.50
    head and neck 39.50
    iliac 39.50
    lower extremity NOS 39.50
    mesenteric 39.50
    renal 39.50
    upper extremity NOS 39.50
    vertebral 39.50
  specified site NEC 39.50
Angiorrhaphy 39.30
  artery 39.31
  vein 39.32
Angioscopy, percutaneous 38.22
  eye (fluorescein) 95.12
Angiotomy 38.00
  abdominal
    artery 38.06
    vein 38.07
  aorta (arch) (ascending) (descending) 38.04
  head and neck NEC 38.02
  intracranial NEC 38.01
  lower limb
    artery 38.08
    vein 38.09
  thoracic NEC 38.05
  upper limb (artery) (vein) 38.03
Angiotripsy 39.98
Ankylosis, production of - *see* Arthrodesis
Annuloplasty (heart) (posteromedial) 35.33
Anoplasty 49.79
  with hemorrhoidectomy 49.46
Anoscopy 49.21
Antibiogram - *see* Examination, microscopic
Antiembolic filter, vena cava 38.7
Antiphobic treatment 94.39
Antrectomy
  mastoid 20.49
  maxillary 22.39
    radical 22.31
  pyloric 43.6
Antrostomy - *see* Antrotomy
Antrotomy (exploratory) (nasal sinus) 22.2
  Caldwell-Luc (maxillary sinus) 22.39

Antrotomy (Continued)
  Caldwell-Luc (Continued)
    with removal of membrane lining 22.31
  intranasal 22.2
    with external approach (Caldwell-Luc) 22.39
    radical 22.31
  maxillary (simple) 22.2
    with Caldwell-Luc approach 22.39
      with removal of membrane lining 22.31
    external (Caldwell-Luc approach) 22.39
      with removal of membrane lining 22.31
    radical (with removal of membrane lining) 22.31
Antrum window operation - *see* Antrotomy, maxillary
Aorticopulmonary window operation 39.59
Aortogram, aortography (abdominal) (retrograde) (selective) (translumbar) 88.42
Aortoplasty (aortic valve) (gusset type) 35.11
Aortotomy 38.04
Apexcardiogram (with ECG lead) 89.57
Apheresis, therapeutic - *see* category 99.7
Apicectomy
  lung 32.3
  petrous pyramid 20.59
  tooth (root) 23.73
    with root canal therapy 23.72
Apicoectomy 23.73
  with root canal therapy 23.72
Apicolysis (lung) 33.39
Apicostomy, alveolar 24.0
Aponeurectomy 83.42
  hand 82.33
Aponeurorrhaphy - *see also* Suture, tendon 83.64
  hand - *see also* Suture, tendon, hand 82.45
Aponeurotomy 83.13
  hand 82.11
Appendectomy (with drainage) 47.09
  incidental 47.19
    laparoscopic 47.11
  laparoscopic 47.01
Appendicectomy (with drainage) 47.09
  incidental 47.19
    laparoscopic 47.11
  laparoscopic 47.01
Appendicocecostomy 47.91
Appendicoenterostomy 47.91
Appendicolysis 54.59
  with appendectomy 47.09
    laparoscopic 47.01
    other 47.09
  laparoscopic 54.51
Appendicostomy 47.91
  closure 47.92
Appendicotomy 47.2
Application
  anti-shock trousers 93.58
  arch bars (orthodontic) 24.7
    for immobilization (fracture) 93.55
  Barton's tongs (skull) (with synchronous skeletal traction) 02.94
  bone growth stimulator (surface) (transcutaneous) 99.86

B

Bacterial smear - *see* Examination, microscopic

Baffes operation (interatrial transposition of venous return) 35.91

Baffle, atrial or interatrial 35.91

Balanoplasty 64.69

Baldy-Webster operation (uterine suspension) 69.22

Ballistocardiography 89.59

Balloon
angioplasty - *see* Angioplasty, balloon
pump, intra-aortic 37.61
systostomy (atrial) 35.41

Ball operation
herniorrhaphy - *see* Repair, hernia, inguinal
undercutting 49.02

Bandage 93.37
elastic 93.56

Banding, pulmonary artery 38.85

Bankhart operation (capsular repair into glenoid, for shoulder dislocation) 81.82

Bardenheurer operation (ligation of innominate artery) 38.85

Barium swallow 87.61

Barkan operation (goniotomy) 12.52
with goniopuncture 12.53

Barr operation (transfer of tibialis posterior tendon) 83.75

Barsky operation (closure of cleft hand) 82.82

Basal metabolic rate 89.39

Basiotripsy 73.8

Bassett operation (vulvectomy with inguinal lymph node dissection) 71.5 [40.3]

Bassini operation - *see* Repair, hernia, inguinal

Batch-Spittler-McFaddin operation (knee disarticulation) 84.16

Batista operation (partial ventriculectomy) (ventricular reduction) (ventricular remodeling) 37.35

Beck operation
aorta-coronary sinus shunt 36.39 ◄▦
epicardial poudrage 36.39 ◄▦

Beck-Jianu operation (permanent gastrostomy) 43.19

Behavior modification 94.33

Bell-Beuttner operation (subtotal abdominal hysterectomy) 68.3

Belsey operation (esophagogastric sphincter) 44.65

Benenenti operation (rotation of bulbous urethra) 58.49

Berke operation (levator resection of eyelid) 08.33

Bicuspidization of heart valve 35.10
aortic 35.11
mitral 35.12

Bicycle dynamometer 93.01

Biesenberger operation (size reduction of breast, bilateral) 85.32
unilateral 85.31

Bifurcation, bone - *see also* Osteotomy 77.30

Bigelow operation (litholapaxy) 57.0

Bililite therapy (ultraviolet) 99.82

Billroth I operation (partial gastrectomy with gastroduodenostomy) 43.6

Billroth II operation (partial gastrectomy with gastrojejunostomy) 43.7

Binnie operation (hepatopexy) 50.69

Biofeedback, psychotherapy 94.39

Biopsy
abdominal wall 54.22
adenoid 28.11
adrenal gland NEC 07.11
   closed 07.11
   open 07.12
   percutaneous (aspiration) (needle) 07.11
alveolus 24.12
anus 49.23
appendix 45.26
artery (any site) 38.21
aspiration - *see* Biopsy, by site
bile ducts 51.14
   closed (endoscopic) 51.14
   open 51.13
   percutaneous (needle) 51.12
bladder 57.33
   closed 57.33
   open 57.34
   transurethral 57.33
blood vessel (any site) 38.21
bone 77.40
   carpal, metacarpal 77.44
   clavicle 77.41
   facial 76.11
   femur 77.45
   fibula 77.47
   humerus 77.42
   marrow 41.31
   patella 77.46
   pelvic 77.49
   phalanges (foot) (hand) 77.49
   radius 77.43
   scapula 77.41
   specified site NEC 77.49
   tarsal, metatarsal 77.48
   thorax (ribs) (sternum) 77.41
   tibia 77.47
   ulna 77.43
   vertebrae 77.49
bowel - *see* Biopsy, intestine
brain NEC 01.13
   closed 01.13
   open 01.14
   percutaneous (needle) 01.13
breast 85.11
   blind 85.11
   closed 85.11
   open 85.12
   percutaneous (needle) (Vimm-Silverman) 85.11
bronchus NEC 33.24
   brush 33.24
   closed (endoscopic) 33.24
   open 33.25
   washings 33.24
bursa 83.21
cardioesophageal (junction) 44.14
   closed (endoscopic) 44.14
   open 44.15
cecum 45.25
   brush 45.25
   closed (endoscopic) 45.25
   open 45.26
cerebral meninges NEC 01.11
   closed 01.11
   open 01.12
   percutaneous (needle) 01.11
cervix (punch) 67.12

Biopsy (*Continued*)
cervix (*Continued*)
   conization (sharp) 67.2
chest wall 34.23
clitoris 71.11
colon 45.25
   brush 45.25
   closed (endoscopic) 45.25
   open 45.26
conjunctiva 10.21
cornea 11.22
cul-de-sac 70.23
diaphragm 34.27
duodenum 45.14
   brush 45.14
   closed (endoscopic) 45.14
   open 45.15
ear (external) 18.12
   middle or inner 20.32
endocervix 67.11
endometrium NEC 68.16
   by
      aspiration curettage 69.59
      dilation and curettage 69.09
   closed (endoscopic) 68.16
   open 68.13
epididymis 63.01
esophagus 42.24
   closed (endoscopic) 42.24
   open 42.25
extraocular muscle or tendon 15.01
eye 16.23
   muscle (oblique) (rectus) 15.01
eyelid 08.11
fallopian tube 66.11
fascia 83.21
fetus 75.33
gallbladder 51.12
   closed (endoscopic) 51.14
   open 51.13
   percutaneous (needle) 51.12
ganglion (cranial) (peripheral) NEC 04.11
   closed 04.11
   open 04.12
   percutaneous (needle) 04.11
   sympathetic nerve 05.11
gum 24.11
heart 37.25
hypophysis - *see also* Biopsy, pituitary gland 07.15
ileum 45.14
   brush 45.14
   closed (endoscopic) 45.14
   open 45.15
intestine NEC 45.27
   large 45.25
      brush 45.25
      closed (endoscopic) 45.25
      open 45.26
   small 45.14
      brush 45.14
      closed (endoscopic) 45.14
      open 45.15
intra-abdominal mass 54.24
   closed 54.24
   percutaneous (needle) 54.24
iris 12.22
jejunum 45.14
   brush 45.14
   closed (endoscopic) 45.14
   open 45.15
joint structure (aspiration) 80.30
   ankle 80.37

ICD-9-CM
B
Vol. 3

◀ ▶ **New Code**   ◀▥ ▥▶ **Revised Code**

ICD-9-CM

B

Vol. 3

C

Caldwell operation (sulcus extension) 24.91
Caldwell-Luc operation (maxillary sinusotomy) 22.39
  with removal of membrane lining 22.31
Calibration, urethra 89.29
Calicectomy (renal) 55.4
Callander operation (knee disarticulation) 84.16
Caloric test, vestibular function 95.44
Calycectomy (renal) 55.4
Calyco-ileoneocystostomy 55.86
Calycotomy (renal) 55.11
Campbell operation
  bone block, ankle 81.11
  fasciotomy (iliac crest) 83.14
  reconstruction of anterior cruciate ligament 81.45
Campimetry 95.05
Canaliculodacryocystorhinostomy 09.81
Canaliculoplasty 09.73
Canaliculorhinostomy 09.81
Canaloplasty, external auditory meatus 18.6
Cannulation - *see also* Insertion, catheter
  ampulla of Vater 51.99
  antrum 22.01
  arteriovenous 39.93
  artery 38.91
  caval-mesenteric vein 39.1
  cisterna chyli 40.61
  Eustachian tube 20.8
  lacrimal apparatus 09.42
  lymphatic duct, left (thoracic) 40.61
  nasal sinus (by puncture) 22.01
    through natural ostium 22.02
  pancreatic duct 52.92
    by retrograde endoscopy (ERP) 52.93
  renoportal 39.1
  sinus (nasal) (by puncture) 22.01
    through natural ostium 22.02
  splenorenal (venous) 39.1
    arterial 39.26
  thoracic duct (cervical approach) (thoracic approach) 40.61
Cannulization - *see* Cannulation
Canthocystostomy 09.82
Canthoplasty 08.59
Canthorrhaphy 08.52
  division or severing 08.02
Canthotomy 08.51
Capsulectomy
  joint - *see also* Arthrectomy 80.90
  kidney 55.91
  lens 13.65
    with extraction of lens 13.51
  ovary 65.29
    laparoscopic 65.25
Capsulo-iridectomy 13.65
Capsuloplasty - *see* Arthroplasty
Capsulorrhaphy 81.96
  with arthroplasty - *see* Arthroplasty
  ankle 81.94
  foot 81.94
  lower extremity NEC 81.95
  upper extremity 81.93
Capsulotomy
  joint - *see also* Division, joint capsule 80.40
    for claw toe repair 77.57
  lens 13.64

Capsulotomy (Continued)
  lens (Continued)
    with
      discission of lens 13.2
      removal of foreign body 13.02
        by magnet extraction 13.01
Cardiac
  mapping 37.27
  massage (external) (closed chest) 99.63
    open chest 37.91
  retraining 93.36
Cardiectomy (stomach) 43.5
Cardiocentesis 37.0
Cardiography - *see also* Angiocardiography 88.50
Cardiolysis 37.10
Cardiomyopexy 36.39
Cardiomyotomy 42.7
Cardio-omentopexy 36.39
Cardiopericardiopexy 36.39
Cardioplasty (stomach and esophagus) 44.65
  stomach alone 44.66
Cardioplegia 39.63
Cardiopneumopexy 36.39
Cardiorrhaphy 37.4
Cardioschisis 37.12
Cardiosplenopexy 36.39
Cardiotomy (exploratory) 37.11
Cardiovalvulotomy - *see* Valvulotomy, heart
Cardioversion (external) 99.62
  atrial 99.61
Carotid pulse tracing with ECG lead 89.56
Carpectomy (partial) 77.84
  total 77.94
Carroll and Taber arthroplasty (proximal interphalangeal joint) 81.72
Casting (for immobilization) NEC 93.53
  with fracture-reduction - *see* Reduction, fracture
Castration
  female (oophorectomy, bilateral) 65.51
    laparoscopic 65.53
  male 62.41
C.A.T. (computerized axial tomography) - *see also* Scan, C.A.T. 88.38
Catheterization - *see also* Insertion, catheter
  arteriovenous 39.93
  artery 38.91
  bladder, indwelling 57.94
    percutaneous (cystostomy) 57.17
    suprapubic NEC 57.18
  bronchus 96.05
    with lavage 96.56
  cardiac (right) 37.21
    combined left and right 37.23
    left 37.22
      combined with right heart 37.23
    right 37.21
      combined with left heart 37.23
  central venous NEC 38.93
    peripherally inserted central catheter (PICC) 38.93
  chest 34.04
    revision (with lysis of adhesions) 34.04
  Eustachian tube 20.8
  heart (right) 37.21
    combined left and right 37.23
    left 37.22
      combined with right heart 37.23

Catheterization (Continued)
  heart (Continued)
    right 37.21
      combined with left heart 37.23
    hepatic vein 38.93
    inferior vena cava 38.93
    intercostal space (with water seal), for drainage 34.04
      revision (with lysis of adhesions) 34.04
    lacrimonasal duct 09.44
    laryngeal 96.05
    nasolacrimal duct 09.44
    pancreatic cyst 52.01
    renal vein 38.93
    Swan-Ganz (pulmonary) 89.64
    transtracheal for oxygenation 31.99
    umbilical vein 38.92
    ureter (to kidney) 59.8
      for retrograde pyelogram 87.74
    urethra, indwelling 57.94
    vein NEC 38.93
      for renal dialysis 38.95
Cattell operation (herniorrhaphy) 53.51
Cauterization - *see also* Destruction, lesion, by site
  anus NEC 49.39
    endoscopic 49.31
  Bartholin's gland 71.24
  broad ligament 69.19
  bronchus 32.09
    endoscopic 32.01
  canaliculi 09.73
  cervix 67.32
  chalazion 08.25
  choroid plexus 02.14
  conjunctiva 10.33
    lesion 10.32
  cornea (fistula) (ulcer) 11.42
  ear, external 18.29
  endometrial implant - *see* Excision, lesion, by site
  entropion 08.41
  esophagus 42.39
    endoscopic 42.33
  eyelid 08.25
    for entropion or ectropion 08.41
  fallopian tube 66.61
    by endoscopy (hysteroscopy) (laparoscopy) 66.29
  hemorrhoids 49.43
  iris 12.41
  lacrimal
    gland 09.21
    punctum 09.72
      for eversion 09.71
    sac 09.6
  larynx 30.09
  liver 50.29
  lung 32.29
    endoscopic 32.28
  meibomian gland 08.25
  nose, for epistaxis (with packing) 21.03
  ovary 65.29
    laparoscopic 65.25
  palate (bony) 27.31
  pannus (superficial) 11.42
  pharynx 29.39
  punctum, lacrimal 09.72
    for eversion 09.71
  rectum 48.32
    radical 48.31
  round ligament 69.19
  sclera 12.84

ICD-9-CM

C

Vol. 3

ICD-9-CM

3

Vol. 3

ICD-9-CM

C

Vol. 3

D

Dacryoadenectomy 09.20
  partial 09.22
  total 09.23
Dacryoadenotomy 09.0
Dacryocystectomy (complete) (partial)
  09.6
Dacryocystogram 87.05
Dacryocystorhinostomy (DCR) (by intubation) (external) (intranasal) 09.81
Dacryocystostomy 09.53
Dacryocystosyringotomy 09.53
Dacryocystotomy 09.53
Dahlman operation (excision of esophageal diverticulum) 42.31
Dana operation (posterior rhizotomy)
  03.1
Danforth operation (fetal) 73.8
Darrach operation (ulnar resection)
  77.83
Davis operation (intubated ureterotomy)
  56.2
Deaf training 95.49
Debridement
  abdominal wall 54.3
  bone - *see also* Excision, lesion, bone
    77.60
    fracture - *see* Debridement, open
      fracture
  brain 01.59
  burn (skin) 86.28
    excisional 86.22
    nonexcisional 86.28
  cerebral meninges 01.51
  dental 96.54
  flap graft 86.75
  graft (flap) (pedicle) 86.75
  heart valve (calcified) - *see* Valvuloplasty, heart
  infection (skin) 86.28
    excisional 86.22
    nail (bed) (fold) 86.27
    nonexcisional 86.28
  joint - *see* Excision, lesion, joint
  meninges (cerebral) 01.51
    spinal 03.4
  muscle 83.45
    hand 82.36
  nail (bed) (fold) 86.27
  nerve (peripheral) 04.07
  open fracture (compound) 79.60
    arm NEC 79.62
    carpal, metacarpal 79.63
    facial bone 76.2
    femur 79.65
    fibula 79.66
    foot NEC 79.67
    hand NEC 79.63
    humerus 79.61
    leg NEC 79.66
    phalanges
      foot 79.68
      hand 79.64
    radius 79.62
    specified site NEC 79.69
    tarsal, metatarsal 79.67
    tibia 79.66
    ulna 79.62
  patella 77.66
  pedicle graft 86.75
  skin or subcutaneous tissue (burn) (infection) (wound) 86.28

Debridement (*Continued*)
  skin or subcutaneous tissue (*Continued*)
    cardioverter/defibrillator (automatic)
      pocket 37.99
    excisional 86.22
    graft 86.75
    nail, nail bed, or nail fold 86.27
    nonexcisional 86.28
    pacemaker pocket 37.79
    pocket
      cardiac pacemaker 37.79
      cardioverter/defibrillator (automatic) 37.99
  skull 01.25
    compound fracture 02.02
  spinal cord (meninges) 03.4
  wound (skin) 86.28
    excisional 86.22
    nonexcisional 86.28
Decapitation, fetal 73.8
Decapsulation, kidney 55.91
Declotting - *see also* Removal, thrombus
  arteriovenous cannula or shunt
    39.49
Decompression
  anus (imperforate) 48.0
  biliary tract 51.49
    by intubation 51.43
      endoscopic 51.87
      percutaneous 51.98
  brain 01.24
  carpal tunnel 04.43
  cauda equina 03.09
  chamber 93.97
  colon 96.08
    by incision 45.03
    endoscopic (balloon) 46.85
  common bile duct 51.42
    by intubation 51.43
      endoscopic 51.87
      percutaneous 51.98
  cranial 01.24
    for skull fracture 02.02
  endolymphatic sac 20.79
  ganglion (peripheral) NEC 04.49
    cranial NEC 04.42
  gastric 96.07
  heart 37.0
  intestine 96.08
    by incision 45.00
    endoscopic (balloon) 46.85
  intracranial 01.24
  labyrinth 20.79
  laminectomy 03.09
  laminotomy 03.09
  median nerve 04.43
  muscle 83.02
    hand 82.02
  nerve (peripheral) NEC 04.49
    auditory 04.42
    cranial NEC 04.42
    median 04.43
    trigeminal (root) 04.41
  orbit - *see also* Orbitotomy 16.09
  pancreatic duct 52.92
    endoscopic 52.93
  pericardium 37.0
  rectum 48.0
  skull fracture 02.02
  spinal cord (canal) 03.09
  tarsal tunnel 04.44
  tendon (sheath) 83.01
    hand 82.01

Decompression (*Continued*)
  thoracic outlet
    by
      myotomy (division of scalenus anticus muscle) 83.19
      tenotomy 83.13
  trigeminal (nerve root) 04.41
Decortication
  arterial 05.25
  brain 01.51
  cerebral meninges 01.51
  heart 37.31
  kidney 55.91
  lung (partial) (total) 34.51
  nasal turbinates - *see* Turbinectomy
  nose 21.89
  ovary 65.29
    laparoscopic 65.25
  periarterial 05.25
  pericardium 37.31
  ventricle, heart (complete) 37.31
Deepening
  alveolar ridge 24.5
  buccolabial sulcus 24.91
  lingual sulcus 24.91
Defatting, flap or pedicle graft 86.75
Defibrillation, electric (external) (internal) 99.62
  automatic cardioverter/defibrillator - *see* category 37.9
de Grandmont operation (tarsectomy)
  08.35
Delaying of pedicle graft 86.71
Delivery (with)
  assisted spontaneous 73.59
  breech extraction (assisted) 72.52
    partial 72.52
      with forceps to aftercoming head 72.51
    total 72.54
      with forceps to aftercoming head 72.53
    unassisted (spontaneous delivery) -
      omit code
  cesarean section - *see* Cesarean section
  Credé maneuver 73.59
  De Lee maneuver 72.4
  forceps 72.9
    application to aftercoming head (Piper) 72.6
      with breech extraction
        partial 72.51
        total 72.53
    Barton's 72.4
    failed 73.3
    high 72.39
      with episiotomy 72.31
    low (outlet) 72.0
      with episiotomy 72.1
    mid- 72.29
      with episiotomy 72.21
    outlet (low) 72.0
      with episiotomy 72.1
    rotation of fetal head 72.4
    trial 73.3
  instrumental NEC 72.9
    specified NEC 72.8
  key-in-lock rotation 72.4
  Kielland rotation 72.4
  Malstrom's extraction 72.79
    with episiotomy 72.71
  manually assisted (spontaneous) 73.59
  spontaneous (unassisted) 73.59
    assisted 73.59

ICD-9-CM

D

Vol. 3

ICD-9-CM

Vol. 3

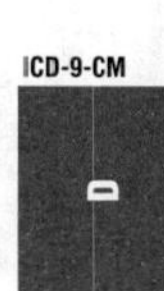
ICD-9-CM
Vol. 3

ICD-9-CM

Vol. 3

Note   Use the following fourth-digit subclassification with categories 90-91 to identify type of examination:

1	bacterial smear
2	culture
3	culture and sensitivity
4	parasitology
5	toxicology
6	cell block and Papanicolaou smear
9	other microscopic examination

ICD-9-CM

Vol. 3

Excision *(Continued)*
  lacrimal
    gland 09.20
      partial 09.22
      total 09.23
    passage 09.6
    sac 09.6
  lesion (local)
    abdominal wall 54.3
    accessory sinus - *see* Excision, lesion,
        nasal sinus
    adenoids 28.92
    adrenal gland(s) 07.21
    alveolus 24.4
    ampulla of Vater 51.62
    anterior chamber (eye) NEC 12.40
    anus 49.39
      endoscopic 49.31
    apocrine gland 86.3
    artery 38.60
      abdominal 38.66
      aorta (arch) (ascending) (descend-
          ing thoracic) 38.64
        with end-to-end anastomosis
            38.45
          abdominal 38.44
          thoracic 38.45
          thoracoabdominal 38.45
              [38.44]
        with graft interposition graft re-
            placement 38.45
          abdominal 38.44
          thoracic 38.45
          thoracoabdominal 38.45
              [38.44]
      head and neck NEC 38.62
      intracranial NEC 38.61
      lower limb 38.68
      thoracic NEC 38.65
      upper limb 38.63
    atrium 37.33
    auditory canal or meatus, external
        18.29
      radical 18.31
    auricle, ear 18.29
      radical 18.31
    biliary ducts 51.69
      endoscopic 51.64
    bladder (transurethral) 57.49
      open 57.59
      suprapubic 57.59
    blood vessel 38.60
      abdominal
        artery 38.66
        vein 38.67
      aorta (arch) (ascending) (descend-
          ing) 38.64
      head and neck NEC 38.62
      intracranial NEC 38.61
      lower limb
        artery 38.68
        vein 38.69
      thoracic NEC 38.65
      upper limb (artery) (vein) 38.63
    bone 77.60
      carpal, metacarpal 77.64
      clavicle 77.61
      facial 76.2
      femur 77.65
      fibula 77.67
      humerus 77.62
      jaw 76.2
        dental 24.4
      patella 77.66

Excision *(Continued)*
  lesion *(Continued)*
    bone *(Continued)*
      pelvic 77.69
      phalanges (foot) (hand) 77.69
      radius 77.63
      scapula 77.61
      skull 01.6
      specified site NEC 77.69
      tarsal, metatarsal 77.68
      thorax (ribs) (sternum) 77.61
      tibia 77.67
      ulna 77.63
      vertebrae 77.69
    brain (transtemporal approach) NEC
        01.59
      by stereotactic radiosurgery
          92.30
        cobalt 60 92.32
        linear accelerator (LINAC)
            92.31
        multi-source 92.32
        particle beam 92.33
        particulate 92.33
        radiosurgery NEC 92.39
        single source photon 92.31
    breast (segmental) (wedge)
        85.21
    broad ligament 69.19
    bronchus NEC 32.09
      endoscopic 32.01
    cerebral (cortex) NEC 01.59
      meninges 01.51
    cervix (myoma) 67.39
    chest wall 34.4
    choroid plexus 02.14
    ciliary body 12.44
    colon 45.41
      endoscopic NEC 45.43
        polypectomy 45.42
    conjunctiva 10.31
    cornea 11.49
    cranium 01.6
    cul-de-sac (Douglas') 70.32
    dental (jaw) 24.4
    diaphragm 34.81
    duodenum (local) 45.31
      endoscopic 45.30
    ear, external 18.29
      radical 18.31
    endometrium 68.29
    epicardium 37.31
    epididymis 63.3
    epiglottis 30.09
    esophagus NEC 42.32
      endoscopic 42.33
    eye, eyeball 16.93
      anterior segment NEC 12.40
    eyebrow (skin) 08.20
    eyelid 08.20
      by
        halving procedure 08.24
        wedge resection 08.24
      major
        full-thickness 08.24
        partial-thickness 08.23
      minor 08.22
    fallopian tube 66.61
    fascia 83.39
      hand 82.29
    groin region (abdominal wall) (in-
        guinal) 54.3
    skin 86.3
    subcutaneous tissue 86.3

Excision *(Continued)*
  lesion *(Continued)*
    gum 24.31
    heart 37.33
    hepatic duct 51.69
    inguinal canal 54.3
    intestine
      large 45.41
        endoscopic NEC 45.43
          polypectomy 45.42
      small NEC 45.33
    intracranial NEC 01.59
    intranasal 21.31
    intraspinal 03.4
    iris 12.42
    jaw 76.2
      dental 24.4
    joint 80.80
      ankle 80.87
      elbow 80.82
      foot and toe 80.88
      hand and finger 80.84
      hip 80.85
      knee 80.86
      shoulder 80.81
      specified site NEC 80.89
      spine 80.89
      wrist 80.83
    kidney 55.39
      with partial nephrectomy 55.4
    labia 71.3
    lacrimal
      gland (frontal approach) 09.21
      passage 09.6
      sac 09.6
    larynx 30.09
    ligament (joint) - *see also* Excision, le-
        sion, joint 80.80
      broad 69.19
      round 69.19
      uterosacral 69.19
    lip 27.43
      by wide excision 27.42
    liver 50.29
    lung NEC 32.29
      by lung volume reduction surgery
          32.22
      by wide excision 32.3
      endoscopic 32.28
    lymph structure(s) (channel) (vessel)
        NEC 40.29
      node - *see* Excision, lymph, node
    mammary duct 85.21
    mastoid (bone) 20.49
    mediastinum 34.3
    meninges (cerebral) 01.51
      spinal 03.4
    mesentery 54.4
    middle ear 20.51
    mouth NEC 27.49
    muscle 83.32
      hand 82.22
      ocular 15.13
    myocardium 37.33
    nail 86.23
    nasal sinus 22.60
      antrum 22.62
        with Caldwell-Luc approach
            22.61
        specified approach NEC
            22.62
      ethmoid 22.63
      frontal 22.42
      maxillary 22.62

ICD-9-CM

E

Vol. 3

Excision *(Continued)*
  lesion *(Continued)*
    nasal sinus *(Continued)*
      maxillary *(Continued)*
        with Caldwell-Luc approach 22.61
        specified approach NEC 22.62
      sphenoid 22.64
    nasopharynx 29.3
    nerve (cranial) (peripheral) 04.07
      sympathetic 05.29
    nonodontogenic 24.31
    nose 21.30
      intranasal 21.31
      polyp 21.31
      skin 21.32
      specified site NEC 21.32
    odontogenic 24.4
    omentum 54.4
    orbit 16.92
    ovary 65.29
      by wedge resection 65.22
        laparoscopic 65.24
      that by laparoscope 65.25
    palate (bony) 27.31
      by wide excision 27.32
      soft 27.49
    pancreas (local) 52.22
      endoscopic 52.21
    parathyroid 06.89
    parotid gland or duct NEC 26.29
    pelvic wall 54.3
    pelvirectal tissue 48.82
    penis 64.2
    pericardium 37.31
    perineum (female) 71.3
      male 86.3
    periprostatic tissue 60.82
    perirectal tissue 48.82
    perirenal tissue 59.91
    peritoneum 54.4
    perivesical tissue 59.91
    pharynx 29.3
      diverticulum 29.32
    pineal gland 07.53
    pinna 18.29
      radical 18.31
    pituitary (gland) - *see also* Hypophysectomy, partial 07.63
      by stereotactic radiosurgery 92.30 ⬅
        cobalt 60 92.32 ◄
        linear accelerator (LINAC) 92.31 ◄
        multi-source 92.32 ◄
        particle beam 92.33 ◄
        particulate 92.33 ◄
        radiosurgery NEC 92.39 ◄
        single source photon 92.31 ◄
    pleura 34.59
    pouch of Douglas 70.32
    preauricular (ear) 18.21
    presacral 54.4
    prostate (transurethral) 60.61
    pulmonary (fibrosis) 32.29
      endoscopic 32.28
    rectovaginal septum 48.82
    rectum 48.35
      polyp (endoscopic) 48.36
    retroperitoneum 54.4
    salivary gland or duct NEC 26.29
      en bloc 26.32
    sclera 12.84
    scrotum 61.3

Excision *(Continued)*
  lesion *(Continued)*
    sinus (nasal) - *see* Excision, lesion, nasal sinus
    Skene's gland 71.3
    skin 86.3
      breast 85.21
      nose 21.32
      radical (wide) (involving underlying or adjacent structure) (with flap closure) 86.4
      scrotum 61.3
    skull 01.6
    soft tissue NEC 83.39
      hand 82.29
    spermatic cord 63.3
    sphincter of Oddi 51.62
      endoscopic 51.64
    spinal cord (meninges) 03.4
    spleen (cyst) 41.42
    stomach NEC 43.42
      endoscopic 43.41
        polyp 43.41
      polyp (endoscopic) 43.41
    subcutaneous tissue 86.3
      breast 85.21
    subgingival 24.31
    sweat gland 86.3
    tendon 83.39
      hand 82.29
      ocular 15.13
      sheath 83.31
        hand 82.21
    testis 62.2
    thorax 34.4
    thymus 07.81
    thyroid 06.31
      substernal or transsternal route 06.51
    tongue 25.1
    tonsil 28.92
    trachea 31.5
    tunica vaginalis 61.92
    ureter 56.41
    urethra 58.39
      endoscopic 58.31
    uterine ligament 69.19
    uterosacral ligament 69.19
    uterus 68.29
    vagina 70.33
    vein 38.60
      abdominal 38.67
      head and neck NEC 38.62
      intracranial NEC 38.61
      lower limb 38.69
      thoracic NEC 38.65
      upper limb 38.63
    ventricle (heart) 37.33
    vocal cords 30.09
    vulva 71.3
  ligament - *see also* Arthrectomy 80.90
    broad 69.19
    round 69.19
    uterine 69.19
    uterosacral 69.19
  ligamentum flavum (spine) - *omit code*
  lingual tonsil 28.5
  lip 27.43
  liver (partial) 50.22
  loose body
    bone - *see* Sequestrectomy, bone
    joint 80.10
  lung (complete) (with mediastinal dissection) 32.5

Excision *(Continued)*
  lung *(Continued)*
    accessory or ectopic tissue 32.29
      endoscopic 32.28
    segmental 32.3
    specified type NEC 32.29
      endoscopic 32.28
    volume reduction surgery 32.22
    wedge 32.29
  lymph, lymphatic
    drainage area 40.29
      radical - *see* Excision, lymph, node, radical
      regional (with lymph node, skin, subcutaneous tissue, and fat) 40.3
    node (simple) NEC 40.29
      with
        lymphatic drainage area (including skin, subcutaneous tissue, and fat) 40.3
        mastectomy - *see* Mastectomy, radical
        muscle and deep fascia - *see* Excision, lymph, node, radical
      axillary 40.23
        radical 40.51
        regional (extended) 40.3
      cervical (deep) (with excision of scalene fat pad) 40.21
        with laryngectomy 30.4
        radical (including muscle and deep fascia) 40.40
          bilateral 40.42
          unilateral 40.41
        regional (extended) 40.3
        superficial 40.29
      groin 40.24
        radical 40.54
        regional (extended) 40.3
      iliac 40.29
        radical 40.53
        regional (extended) 40.3
      inguinal (deep) (superficial) 40.24
        radical 40.54
        regional (extended) 40.3
      jugular - *see* Excision, lymph, node, cervical
      mammary (internal) 40.22
        external 40.29
          radical 40.59
          regional (extended) 40.3
        radical 40.59
          regional (extended) 40.3
      paratracheal - *see* Excision, lymph, node, cervical
      periaortic 40.29
        radical 40.52
        regional (extended) 40.3
      radical 40.50
        with mastectomy - *see* Mastectomy, radical
        specified site NEC 40.59
      regional (extended) 40.3
      sternal - *see* Excision, lymph, node, mammary
    structure(s) (simple) NEC 40.29
      radical 40.59
      regional (extended) 40.3
  lymphangioma (simple) - *see also* Excision, lymph, lymphatic, node, 40.29
  lymphocele 40.29

ICD-9-CM

Vol. 3

F

Face lift 86.82
Facetectomy 77.89
Facilitation, intraocular circulation NEC
    12.59
Failed (trial) forceps 73.3
Family
    counselling (medical) (social) 94.49
    therapy 94.42
Farabeuf operation (ischiopubiotomy)
    77.39
Fasanella-Servatt operation (blepharop-
    tosis repair) 08.35
Fasciaplasty - *see* Fascioplasty
Fascia sling operation - *see* Operation,
    sling
Fasciectomy 83.44
    for graft 83.43
        hand 82.34
    hand 82.35
        for graft 82.34
    palmar (release of Dupuytren's con-
        tracture) 82.35
Fasciodesis 83.89
    hand 82.89
Fascioplasty - *see also* Repair, fascia 83.89
    hand - *see also* Repair, fascia, hand
        82.89
Fasciorrhaphy - *see* Suture, fascia
Fasciotomy 83.14
    Dupuytren's 82.12
        with excision 82.35
    Dwyer 83.14
    hand 82.12
    Ober-Yount 83.14
    orbital - *see also* Orbitotomy 16.09
    palmar (release of Dupuytren's con-
        tracture) 82.12
        with excision 82.35
Fenestration
    aneurysm (dissecting), thoracic aorta
        39.54
    aortic aneurysm 39.54
    cardiac valve 35.10
    chest wall 34.01
    ear
        inner (with graft) 20.61
            revision 20.62
        tympanic 19.55
    labyrinth (with graft) 20.61
    Lempert's (endaural) 19.9
    operation (aorta) 39.54
    oval window, ear canal 19.55
    palate 27.1
    pericardium 37.12
    semicircular canals (with graft) 20.61
    stapes foot plate (with vein graft)
        19.19
        with incus replacement 19.11
    tympanic membrane 19.55
    vestibule (with graft) 20.61
Ferguson operation (hernia repair) 53.00
Fetography 87.81
Fetoscopy 75.31
Fiberoscopy - *see* Endoscopy, by site
Fibroidectomy, uterine 68.29
Fick operation (perforation of foot plate)
    19.0
Filipuncture (aneurysm) (cerebral) 39.52
Filleting
    hammer toe 77.56
    pancreas 52.3

Filling, tooth (amalgam) (plastic) (sili-
    cate) 23.2
    root canal - *see also* Therapy, root canal
        23.70
Fimbriectomy - *see also* Salpingectomy,
    partial 66.69
    Uchida (with tubal ligation) 66.32
Finney operation (pyloroplasty) 44.29
Fissurectomy, anal 49.39
    endoscopic 49.31
    skin (subcutaneous tissue) 49.04
Fistulectomy - *see also* Closure, fistula,
    by site
    abdominothoracic 34.83
    abdominouterine 69.42
    anus 49.12
    appendix 47.92
    bile duct 51.79
    biliary tract NEC 51.79
    bladder (transurethral approach) 57.84
    bone - *see also* Excision, lesion, bone
        77.60
    branchial cleft 29.52
    bronchocutaneous 33.42
    bronchoesophageal 33.42
    bronchomediastinal 34.73
    bronchopleural 34.73
    bronchopleurocutaneous 34.73
    bronchopleuromediastinal 34.73
    bronchovisceral 33.42
    cervicosigmoidal 67.62
    cholecystogastroenteric 51.93
    cornea 11.49
    diaphragm 34.83
    enterouterine 69.42
    esophagopleurocutaneous 34.73
    esophagus NEC 42.84
    fallopian tube 66.73
    gallbladder 51.93
    gastric NEC 44.63
    hepatic duct 51.79
    hepatopleural 34.73
    hepatopulmonary 34.73
    intestine
        large 46.76
        small 46.74
    intestinouterine 69.42
    joint - *see also* Excision, lesion, joint
        80.80
    lacrimal
        gland 09.21
        sac 09.6
    laryngotracheal 31.62
    larynx 31.62
    mediastinocutaneous 34.73
    mouth NEC 27.53
    nasal 21.82
        sinus 22.71
    nasolabial 21.82
    nasopharyngeal 21.82
    oroantral 22.71
    oronasal 21.82
    pancreas 52.95
    perineorectal 71.72
    perineosigmoidal 71.72
    perirectal, not opening into rectum
        48.93
    pharyngoesophageal 29.53
    pharynx NEC 29.53
    pleura 34.73
    rectolabial 71.72
    rectourethral 58.43
    rectouterine 69.42
    rectovaginal 70.73

Fistulectomy (*Continued*)
    rectovesical 57.83
    rectovulvar 71.72
    rectum 48.73
    salivary (duct) (gland) 26.42
    scrotum 61.42
    skin 86.3
    stomach NEC 44.63
    subcutaneous tissue 86.3
    thoracoabdominal 34.83
    thoracogastric 34.83
    thoracointestinal 34.83
    thorax NEC 34.73
    trachea NEC 31.73
    tracheoesophageal 31.73
    ureter 56.84
    urethra 58.43
    uteroenteric 69.42
    uterointestinal 69.42
    uterorectal 69.42
    uterovaginal 69.42
    vagina 70.75
    vesicosigmoidovaginal 57.83
    vocal cords 31.62
    vulvorectal 71.72
Fistulization
    appendix 47.91
    arteriovenous 39.27
    cisterna chyli 40.62
    endolymphatic sac (for decompression)
        20.79
    esophagus, external 42.10
        cervical 42.11
        specified technique NEC 42.19
    interatrial 35.41
    labyrinth (for decompression) 20.79
    lacrimal sac into nasal cavity 09.81
    larynx 31.29
    lymphatic duct, left (thoracic) 40.62
    orbit 16.09
    peritoneal 54.93
    salivary gland 26.49
    sclera 12.69
        by trephination 12.61
        with iridectomy 12.65
    sinus, nasal NEC 22.9
    subarachnoid space 02.2
    thoracic duct 40.62
    trachea 31.29
    tracheoesophageal 31.95
    urethrovaginal 58.0
    ventricle, cerebral - *see also* Shunt, ven-
        tricular 02.2
Fistulogram
    abdominal wall 88.03
    chest wall 87.38
    retroperitoneum 88.14
Fistulotomy, anal 49.11
Fitting
    arch bars (orthodontic) 24.7
        for immobilization (fracture) 93.55
    artificial limb 84.40
    contact lens 95.32
    denture (total) 99.97
        bridge (fixed) 23.42
            removable 23.43
        partial (fixed) 23.42
            removable 23.43
    hearing aid 95.48
    obturator (orthodontic) 24.7
    ocular prosthetics 95.34
    orthodontic
        appliance 24.7
        obturator 24.7

ICD-9-CM

Vol. 3

Fusion *(Continued)*
  spinal *(Continued)*
    cervical *(Continued)*
      posterior (interbody), posterolateral technique 81.03
        for pseudarthrosis 81.09
      craniocervical (anterior transoral) (posterior) 81.01
        for pseudarthrosis NEC 81.09
    dorsal, dorsolumbar NEC 81.05
      anterior (interbody), anterolateral technique 81.04
        for pseudarthrosis 81.09

Fusion *(Continued)*
  spinal *(Continued)*
    dorsal *(Continued)*
      for pseudarthrosis 81.09
      posterior (interbody), posterolateral technique 81.05
        for pseudarthrosis 81.09
    lumbar, lumbosacral NEC 81.08
      anterior (interbody), anterolateral technique 81.06
        for pseudarthrosis 81.09
      for pseudarthrosis 81.09

Fusion *(Continued)*
  spinal *(Continued)*
    lumbar *(Continued)*
      lateral transverse process technique 81.07
        for pseudarthrosis 81.09
      posterior (interbody), posterolateral technique 81.08
        for pseudarthrosis 81.09
      occiput-C2 (anterior transoral) (posterior) 81.01
        for pseudarthrosis 81.09
  tongue (to lip) 25.59

G

Gait training 93.22
Galeaplasty 86.89
Galvanoionization 99.27
Games
competitive 94.39
organized 93.89
Gamma irradiation, stereotactic 92.32
Ganglionectomy
gasserian 04.05
lumbar sympathetic 05.23
nerve (cranial) (peripheral) NEC 04.06
sympathetic 05.29
sphenopalatine (Meckel's) 05.21
tendon sheath (wrist) 82.21
site other than hand 83.31
trigeminal 04.05
Ganglionotomy, trigeminal (radiofrequency) 04.02
Gant operation (wedge osteotomy of trochanter) 77.25
Garceau operation (tibial tendon transfer) 83.75
Gardner operation (spinal meningocele repair) 03.51
Gas endarterectomy 38.10
abdominal 38.16
aorta (arch) (ascending) (descending) 38.14
coronary artery 36.09
head and neck NEC 38.12
intracranial NEC 38.11
lower limb 38.18
thoracic NEC 38.15
upper limb 38.13
Gastrectomy (partial) (subtotal) NEC 43.89
with
anastomosis (to) NEC 43.89
duodenum 43.6
esophagus 43.5
gastrogastric 43.89
jejunum 43.7
esophagogastrostomy 43.5
gastroduodenostomy (bypass) 43.6
gastroenterostomy (bypass) 43.7
gastrogastrostomy (bypass) 43.89
gastrojejunostomy (bypass) 43.7
jejunal transposition 43.81
complete NEC 43.99
with intestinal interposition 43.91
distal 43.6
Hofmeister 43.7
Polya 43.7
proximal 43.5
radical NEC 43.99
with intestinal interposition 43.91
total NEC 43.99
with intestinal interposition 43.91
Gastrocamera 44.19
Gastroduodenectomy - see Gastrectomy
Gastroduodenoscopy 45.13
through stoma (artificial) 45.12
transabdominal (operative) 45.11
Gastroduodenostomy (bypass) (Jaboulay's) 44.39
with partial gastrectomy 43.6
Gastroenterostomy (bypass) NEC 44.39
with partial gastrectomy 43.7
Gastrogastrostomy (bypass) 44.39
with partial gastrectomy 43.89
Gastrojejunostomy (bypass) 44.39
with partial gastrectomy 43.7

Gastrolysis 54.59
laparoscopic 54.51
Gastropexy 44.64
Gastroplasty NEC 44.69
Gastroplication 44.69
Gastropylorectomy 43.6
Gastrorrhaphy 44.61
Gastroscopy NEC 44.13
through stoma (artificial) 44.12
transabdominal (operative) 44.11
Gastrostomy (Brunschwig's) (decompression) (fine caliber tube) (Kader) (permanent) (Stamm) (Stamm-Kader) (temporary) (tube) (Witzel) 43.19
Beck-Jianu 43.19
Frank's 43.19
Janeway 43.19
percutaneous (endoscopic) (PEG) 43.11
Spivack's 43.19
Ssabanejew-Frank 43.19
Gastrotomy 43.0
for control of hemorrhage 44.49
Gavage, gastric 96.35
Gelman operation (release of clubfoot) 83.84
Genioplasty (augmentation) (with graft) (with implant) 76.68
reduction 76.67
Ghormley operation (hip fusion) 81.21
Gifford operation
destruction of lacrimal sac 09.6
keratotomy (delimiting) 11.1
radial (refractive) 11.75
Gill operation
arthrodesis of shoulder 81.23
laminectomy 03.09
Gill-Stein operation (carporadial arthrodesis) 81.25
Gilliam operation (uterine suspension) 69.22
Gingivectomy 24.31
Gingivoplasty (with bone graft) (with soft tissue graft) 24.2
Girdlestone operation
laminectomy with spinal fusion 81.00
muscle transfer for claw toe repair 77.57
resection of femoral head and neck 77.85
Girdlestone-Taylor operation (muscle transfer for claw toe repair) 77.57
Glenn operation (anastomosis of superior vena cava to right pulmonary artery) 39.21
Glenoplasty, shoulder 81.83
with
partial replacement 81.81
total replacement 81.80
for recurrent dislocation 81.82
Glomectomy
carotid 39.8
jugulare 20.51
Glossectomy (complete) (total) 25.3
partial or subtotal 25.2
radical 25.4
Glossopexy 25.59
Glossoplasty NEC 25.59
Glossorrhaphy 25.51
Glossotomy NEC 25.94
for tongue tie 25.91
Glycoprotein IIB/IIIa inhibitor 99.20 ◀
Goebel-Frangenheim-Stoeckel operation (urethrovesical suspension) 59.4
Goldner operation (clubfoot release) 80.48

Goldthwaite operation
ankle stabilization 81.11
patellar stabilization 81.44
tendon transfer for stabilization of patella 81.44
Gonadectomy
ovary
bilateral 65.51
laparoscopic 65.53
unilateral 65.39
laparoscopic 65.31
testis
bilateral 62.41
unilateral 62.3
Goniopuncture 12.51
with goniotomy 12.53
Gonioscopy 12.29
Goniospasis 12.59
Goniotomy (Barkan's) 12.52
with goniopuncture 12.53
Goodal-Power operation (vagina) 70.8
Gordon-Taylor operation (hindquarter amputation) 84.19
GP IIB/IIIa inhibitor, infusion 99.20 ◀
Graber-Duvernay operation (drilling of femoral head) 77.15
Graft, grafting
aneurysm 39.52
artery, arterial (patch) 39.58
with
excision or resection of vessel - see Arteriectomy, with graft replacement
synthetic patch (Dacron) (Teflon) 39.57
tissue patch (vein) (autogenous) (homograft) 39.56
blood vessel (patch) 39.58
with
excision or resection of vessel - see Angiectomy, with graft replacement
synthetic patch (Dacron) (Teflon) 39.57
tissue patch (vein) (autogenous) (homograft) 39.56
bone (autogenous) (bone bank) (dual onlay) (heterogeneous) (inlay) (massive onlay) (multiple) (osteoperiosteal) (peg) (subperiosteal) (with metallic fixation) 78.00
with
arthrodesis - see Arthrodesis
arthroplasty - see Arthroplasty
gingivoplasty 24.2
lengthening - see Lengthening, bone
carpals, metacarpals 78.04
clavicle 78.01
facial NEC 76.91
with total ostectomy 76.44
femur 78.05
fibula 78.07
humerus 78.02
joint - see Arthroplasty
mandible 76.91
with total mandibulectomy 76.41
marrow - see Transplant, bone, marrow
nose - see Graft, nose
patella 78.06
pelvic 78.09
pericranial 02.04
phalanges (foot) (hand) 78.09

◀▶ **New Code**   ◀▌▌ ▌▌▶ **Revised Code**

H

Hagner operation (epididymotomy) 63.92
Halsted operation - *see* Repair, hernia, inguinal
Hampton operation (anastomosis small intestine to rectal stump) 45.92
Hanging hip operation (muscle release) 83.19
Harelip operation 27.54
Harrison-Richardson operation (vaginal suspension) 70.77
Hartmann resection (of intestine) (with pouch) - *see* Colectomy, by site
Harvesting
  bone marrow 41.91
  stem cells 99.79
Hauser operation
  achillotenotomy 83.11
  bunionectomy with adductor tendon transfer 77.53
  stabilization of patella 81.44
Heaney operation (vaginal hysterectomy) 68.59
  laparoscopically assisted (LAVH) 68.51
Hearing aid (with battery replacement) 95.49
Hearing test 95.47
Hegar operation (perineorrhaphy) 71.79
Heine operation (cyclodialysis) 12.55
Heineke-Mikulicz operation (pyloroplasty) 44.29
Heller operation (esophagomyotomy) 42.7
Hellström operation (transplantation of aberrant renal vessel) 39.55
Hemicolectomy
  left 45.75
  right (extended) 45.73
Hemicystectomy 57.6
Hemigastrectomy - *see* Gastrectomy
Hemiglossectomy 25.2
Hemilaminectomy (decompression) (exploration) 03.09
Hemilaryngectomy (anterior) (lateral) (vertical) 30.1
Hemimandibulectomy 76.31
Hemimastectomy (radical) 85.23
Hemimaxillectomy (with bone graft) (with prosthesis) 76.39
Heminephrectomy 55.4
Hemipelvectomy 84.19
Hemispherectomy (cerebral) 01.52
Hemithyroidectomy (with removal of isthmus) (with removal of portion of remaining lobe) 06.2
Hemodiafiltration (extracorporeal) 39.95
Hemodialysis (extracorporeal) 39.95
Hemodilution 99.03
Hemofiltration (extracorporeal) 39.95
Hemorrhage control - *see* Control, hemorrhage
Hemorrhoidectomy 49.46
  by
    cautery, cauterization 49.43
    crushing 49.45
    cryotherapy, cryosurgery 49.44
    excision 49.46
    injection 49.42
    ligation 49.45
Hemostasis - *see* Control, hemorrhage
Henley operation (jejunal transposition) 43.81
Hepatectomy (complete) (total) 50.4
  partial or subtotal 50.22

Hepatic assistance, extracorporeal 50.92
Hepaticocholangiojejunostomy 51.37
Hepaticocystoduodenostomy 51.37
Hepaticodochotomy 51.59
Hepaticoduodenostomy 51.37
Hepaticojejunostomy 51.37
Hepaticolithectomy 51.49
  endoscopic 51.88
Hepaticolithotomy 51.49
  endoscopic 51.88
Hepaticostomy 51.59
Hepaticotomy 51.59
Hepatocholangiocystoduodenostomy 51.37
Hepatocholedochostomy 51.43
  endoscopic 51.87
Hepatoduodenostomy 50.69
Hepatogastrostomy 50.69
Hepatojejunostomy 50.69
Hepatolithotomy
  hepatic duct 51.49
  liver 50.0
Hepatopexy 50.69
Hepatorrhaphy 50.61
Hepatostomy (external) (internal) 50.69
Hepatotomy (with packing) 50.0
Hernioplasty - *see* Repair, hernia
Herniorrhaphy - *see* Repair, hernia
Herniotomy - *see* Repair, hernia
Heterograft - *see* Graft
Heterotransplant, heterotransplantation - *see* Transplant
Hey operation (amputation of foot) 84.12
Hey-Groves operation (reconstruction of anterior cruciate ligament) 81.45
Heyman operation (soft tissue release for clubfoot) 83.84
Heyman-Herndon (-Strong) operation (correction of metatarsus varus) 80.48
Hibbs operation (lumbar spinal fusion) - *see* Fusion, lumbar
Higgins operation - *see* Repair, hernia, femoral
High forceps delivery 72.39
  with episiotomy 72.31
Hill-Allison operation (hiatal hernia repair, transpleural approach) 53.80
Hinging, mitral valve 35.12
His bundle recording 37.29
Hitchcock operation (anchoring tendon of biceps) 83.88
Hofmeister operation (gastrectomy) 43.7
Hoke operation
  midtarsal fusion 81.14
  triple arthrodesis 81.12
Holth operation
  iridencleisis 12.63
  sclerectomy 12.65
Homans operation (correction of lymphedema) 40.9
Homograft - *see* Graft
Homotransplant, homotransplantation - *see* Transplant
Hosiery, elastic 93.59
Hutch operation (ureteroneocystostomy) 56.74
Hybinette-Eden operation (glenoid bone block) 78.01
Hydrocelectomy
  canal of Nuck (female) 69.19
    male 63.1
  round ligament 69.19
  spermatic cord 63.1
  tunica vaginalis 61.2

Hydrotherapy 93.33
  assisted exercise in pool 93.31
  whirlpool 93.32
Hymenectomy 70.31
Hymenoplasty 70.76
Hymenorrhaphy 70.76
Hymenotomy 70.11
Hyperalimentation (parenteral) 99.15
Hyperbaric oxygenation 93.95
  wound 93.59
Hyperextension, joint 93.25
Hyperthermia NEC 93.35
  for cancer treatment (interstitial) (local) (radiofrequency) (regional) (ultrasound) (whole-body) 99.85
Hypnodrama, psychiatric 94.32
Hypnosis (psychotherapeutic) 94.32
  for anesthesia - *omit code*
Hypnotherapy 94.32
Hypophysectomy (complete) (total) 07.69
  partial or subtotal 07.63
    transfrontal approach 07.61
    transsphenoidal approach 07.62
  specified approach NEC 07.68
  transfrontal approach (complete) (total) 07.64
    partial 07.61
  transsphenoidal approach (complete) (total) 07.65
    partial 07.62
Hypothermia (central) (local) 99.81
  gastric (cooling) 96.31
    freezing 96.32
  systemic (in open heart surgery) 39.62
Hypotympanotomy 20.23
Hysterectomy 68.9
  abdominal 68.4
    partial or subtotal (supracervical) (supravaginal) 68.3
    radical (modified) (Wertheim's) 68.6
  vaginal (complete) (partial) (subtotal) (total) 68.59
    laparoscopically assisted (LAVH) 68.51
    radical (Schauta) 68.7
Hysterocolpectomy (radical) (vaginal) 68.7
  abdominal 68.6
Hysterogram NEC 87.85
  percutaneous 87.84
Hysterolysis 54.59
  laparoscopic 54.51
Hysteromyomectomy 68.29
Hysteropexy 69.22
Hysteroplasty 69.49
Hysterorrhaphy 69.41
Hysterosalpingography gas (contrast) 87.82
  opaque dye (contrast) 87.83
Hysterosalpingostomy 66.74
Hysteroscopy 68.12
  with
    ablation
      endometrial 68.23
    biopsy 68.16
Hysterotomy (with removal of foreign body) (with removal of hydatidiform mole) 68.0
  for intrauterine transfusion 75.2
  obstetrical 74.99
    for termination of pregnancy 74.91
Hysterotrachelectomy 67.4
Hysterotracheloplasty 69.49
Hysterotrachelorrhaphy 69.41
Hysterotrachelotomy 69.95

ICD-9-CM

Vol. 3

I

ICCE (intracapsular cataract extraction)
13.19
Ileal
  bladder
    closed 57.87 [45.51]
    open (ileoureterostomy) 56.51
  conduit (ileoureterostomy) 56.51
Ileocecostomy 45.93
Ileocolectomy 45.73
Ileocolostomy 45.93
Ileocolotomy 45.00
Ileocystoplasty (isolated segment anastomosis) (open loop) 57.87 [45.51]
Ileoduodenotomy 45.01
Ileoectomy (partial) 45.62
  with cecectomy 45.72
Ileoentectropy 46.99
Ileoesophagostomy 42.54
Ileoileostomy 45.91
  proximal to distal segment 45.62
Ileoloopogram 87.78
Ileopancreatostomy 52.96
Ileopexy 46.61
Ileoproctostomy 45.95
Ileorectostomy 45.93
Ileorrhaphy 46.73
Ileoscopy 45.13
  through stoma (artificial) 45.12
  transabdominal (operative) 45.11
Ileosigmoidostomy 45.93
Ileostomy 46.20
  continent (permanent) 46.22
    for urinary diversion 56.51
  delayed opening 46.24
  Hendon (temporary) 46.21
  loop 46.01
  Paul (temporary) 46.21
  permanent 46.23
    continent 46.22
  repair 46.41
  revision 46.41
  tangential (temporary) 46.21
  temporary 46.21
  transplantation to new site 46.23
  tube (temporary) 46.21
  ureteral
    external 56.51
    internal 56.71
Ileotomy 45.02
Ileotransversostomy 45.93
Ileoureterostomy (Bricker's) (ileal bladder) 56.51
Imaging (diagnostic)
  diagnostic, not elsewhere classified
    88.90
  magnetic resonance (nuclear) (proton)
    NEC 88.97
    abdomen 88.97
    bladder (urinary) 88.95
    bone marrow blood supply 88.94
    brain (brain stem) 88.91
    chest (hilar) (mediastinal) 88.92
    extremity (lower) (upper) 88.94
    eye orbit 88.97
    face 88.97
    head NEC 88.97
    musculoskeletal 88.94
    myocardium 88.92
    neck 88.97
    orbit of eye 88.97
    prostate 88.95
    specified site NEC 88.97

Imaging (Continued)
  magnetic resonance (Continued)
    spinal canal (cord) (spine) 88.93
Immobilization (by)
  with fracture-reduction - see Reduction,
    fracture
  bandage 93.59
  bone 93.53
  cast NEC 93.53
    with reduction of fracture or dislocation - see Reduction, fracture,
      and Reduction, dislocation
  device NEC 93.59
  pressure dressing 93.56
  splint (plaster) (tray) 93.54
    with reduction of fracture or dislocation - see Reduction, fracture,
      and Reduction, dislocation
  stereotactic head frame 93.59
Immunization - see also Vaccination
  allergy 99.12
  autoimmune disease 99.13
  BCG 99.33
  brucellosis 99.55
  cholera 99.31
  diphtheria 99.36
  DPT 99.39
  epidemic parotitis 99.46
  German measles 99.47
  Hemophilus influenzae 99.52
  influenza 99.52
  measles 99.45
  meningococcus 99.55
  mumps 99.46
  pertussis 99.37
  plague 99.34
  poliomyelitis 99.41
  rabies 99.44
  rubella 99.47
  salmonella 99.55
  smallpox 99.42
  staphylococcus 99.55
  TAB 99.32
  tetanus 99.38
  triple vaccine 99.48
  tuberculosis 99.33
  tularemia 99.35
  typhoid-paratyphoid 99.32
  typhus 99.55
  viral NEC 99.55
  whooping cough 99.37
  yellow fever 99.43
Immunotherapy, antineoplastic 99.28
  C-Parvum 99.28
  Interferon 99.28
  Interleukin-2 99.28
  Levamisole 99.28
  Thymosin 99.28
Implant, implantation
  abdominal artery to coronary artery
    36.17
  artery
    aortic branches to heart muscle
      36.2
    mammary to ventricular wall (Vineberg) 36.2
  baffle, atrial or interatrial 35.91
  biliary fistulous tract into stomach or
    intestine 51.39
  bipolar endoprosthesis (femoral head)
    81.52
  bladder sphincter, artificial (inflatable)
    58.93
  blood vessels to myocardium 36.2

Implant, implantation (Continued)
  bone growth stimulator (invasive)
    (percutaneous) (semi-invasive) -
    see category 78.9
  breast (for augmentation) (bilateral)
    85.54
    unilateral 85.53
  cardiomyostimulation system
    37.67
  cardioverter/defibrillator (automatic)
    37.94
    leads only (patch electrode) (pacing)
      (sensing) 37.95
    pulse generator only 37.96
    total system 37.94
  chest wall (mesh) (silastic) 34.79
  chin (polyethylene) (silastic) 76.68
  cochlear (electrode) 20.96
    prosthetic device (electrode and receiver) 20.96
      channel (single) 20.97
        multiple 20.98
      electrode only 20.99
      internal coil only 20.99
  cornea 11.73
  custodis eye 14.41
  dental (endosseous) (prosthetic) 23.6
  device, vascular access 86.07
  diaphragmatic pacemaker 34.85
  electrode(s)
    brain 02.93
      depth 02.93
      foramen ovale 02.93
      sphenoidal 02.96
    cardiac (initial) (transvenous) 37.70
      atrium (initial) 37.73
        replacement 37.76
      atrium and ventricle (initial) 37.72
        replacement 37.76
      epicardium (sternotomy or thoracotomy approach) 37.74
      temporary transvenous pacemaker
        system 37.78
        during and immediately following cardiac surgery 39.64
      ventricle (initial) 37.71
        replacement 37.76
    depth 02.93
    foramen ovale 02.93
    heart - see also Implant, electrode(s),
      cardiac 37.70
    intracranial 02.93
    osteogenic (invasive) for bone growth
      stimulation - see category 78.9
    peripheral nerve 04.92
    sphenoidal 02.96
    spine 03.93
  electroencephalographic receiver
    brain 02.93
    intracranial 02.93
  electronic stimulator
    anus (subcutaneous) 49.92
    bladder 57.96
    bone growth (invasive) (percutaneous) (semi-invasive) 78.9
    brain 02.93
    carotid sinus 39.8
    cochlear 20.96
      channel (single) 20.97
        multiple 20.98
    intracranial 02.93
    peripheral nerve 04.92
    phrenic nerve 34.85
    skeletal muscle 83.92

Implant, implantation (*Continued*)
  prosthesis (*Continued*)
    penis (internal) (non-inflatable) 64.95
    inflatable (internal) 64.97
    skin (dermal regenerative) (matrix)
      86.67
    testicular (bilateral) (unilateral) 62.7
  pulsation balloon (phase-shift) 37.61
  pump, infusion 86.06
  radial artery 36.19
  radioactive isotope 92.27
  radium (radon) 92.27
  retinal attachment 14.41
    with buckling 14.41
  Rickham reservoir 02.2
  silicone
    breast (bilateral) 85.54
    unilateral 85.53
    skin (for filling of defect) 86.02
    for augmentation NEC 86.89
  skin (dermal regenerative) (matrix)
    86.67 ◄
  stimoceiver
    brain 02.93
    intracranial 02.93
    peripheral nerve 04.92
    spine 03.93
  sudural
    grids 02.93
    strips 02.93
  Swanson prosthesis (joint) (silastic)
    NEC 81.96
    carpocarpal, carpometacarpal 81.74
    finger 81.71
    hand (interphalangeal) (metacarpo-
      phalangeal) 81.71
    interphalangeal 81.71
    knee (partial) (total) 81.54
      revision 81.55
    metacarpophalangeal 81.71
    toe 81.57
      for hallux valgus repair 77.59
    wrist (partial) 81.74
      total 81.73
  systemic arteries into myocardium
    (Vineberg type operation) 36.2
  testicular prosthesis (bilateral) (unilat-
    eral) 62.7
  tissue expander (skin) NEC 86.93
    breast 85.95
  tissue mandril (for vascular graft) 39.99
    with
      blood vessel repair 39.56
      vascular bypass or shunt - *see* By-
        pass, vascular
  tooth (bud) (germ) 23.5
    prosthetic 23.6
  umbrella, vena cava 38.7
  ureters into
    bladder 56.74
    intestine 56.71
      external diversion 56.51
    skin 56.61
  urethra
    for repair of urinary stress inconti-
      nence
      collagen 59.72
      fat 59.72
      polytef 59.72
  urethral sphincter, artificial (inflatable)
    58.93
  urinary sphincter, artificial (inflatable)
    58.93
  vascular access device 86.07

Implant, implantation (*Continued*)
  vitreous (silicone) 14.75
    for retinal reattachment 14.41
      with buckling 14.41
  vocal cord(s) (paraglottic) 31.98
Implosion (psychologic desensitization)
  94.33
Incision (and drainage)
  with
    exploration - *see* Exploration
    removal of foreign body - *see* Re-
      moval, foreign body
  abdominal wall 54.0
    as operative approach - *omit code*
  abscess - *see also* Incision, by site
    appendix 47.2
      with appendectomy 47.09
        laparoscopic 47.01
    extraperitoneal 54.0
    ischiorectal 49.01
    lip 27.0
    omental 54.19
    perianal 49.01
    perigastric 54.19
    perisplenic 54.19
    peritoneal NEC 54.19
      pelvic (female) 70.12
    retroperitoneal 54.0
    sclera 12.89
    skin 86.04
    subcutaneous tissue 86.04
    subdiaphragmatic 54.19
    subhepatic 54.19
    subphrenic 54.19
    vas deferens 63.6
  adrenal gland 07.41
  alveolus, alveolar bone 24.0
  antecubital fossa 86.09
  anus NEC 49.93
    fistula 49.11
    septum 49.91
  appendix 47.2
  artery 38.00
    abdominal 38.06
      aorta (arch) (ascending) (descend-
        ing) 38.04
    head and neck NEC 38.02
    intracranial NEC 38.01
    lower limb 38.08
    thoracic NEC 38.05
    upper limb 38.03
  atrium (heart) 37.11
  auditory canal or meatus, external
    18.02
  auricle 18.09
  axilla 86.09
  Bartholin's gland or cyst 71.22
  bile duct (with T or Y tube insertion)
    NEC 51.59
    common (exploratory) 51.51
      for
        relief of obstruction NEC 51.42
        removal of calculus 51.41
    for
      exploration 51.59
      relief of obstruction 51.49
  bladder 57.19
    neck (transurethral) 57.91
    percutaneous suprapubic (closed)
      57.17
    suprapubic NEC 57.18
  blood vessel - *see also* Angiotomy 38.00
  bone 77.10
    alveolus, alveolar 24.0

Incision (*Continued*)
  bone (*Continued*)
    carpals, metacarpals 77.14
    clavicle 77.11
    facial 76.09
    femur 77.15
    fibula 77.17
    humerus 77.12
    patella 77.16
    pelvic 77.19
    phalanges (foot) (hand) 77.19
    radius 77.13
    scapula 77.11
    skull 01.24
    specified site NEC 77.19
    tarsals, metatarsals 77.18
    thorax (ribs) (sternum) 77.11
    tibia 77.17
    ulna 77.13
    vertebrae 77.19
  brain 01.39
    cortical adhesions 02.91
  breast (skin) 85.0
    with removal of tissue expander
      85.96
  bronchus 33.0
  buccal space 27.0
  bulbourethral gland 58.91
  bursa 83.03
    hand 82.03
    pharynx 29.0
  carotid body 39.8
  cerebral (meninges) 01.39
    epidural or extradural space 01.24
    subarachnoid or subdural space
      01.31
  cerebrum 01.39
  cervix 69.95
    to
      assist delivery 73.93
      replace inverted uterus 75.93
  chalazion 08.09
    with removal of capsule 08.21
  cheek 86.09
  chest wall (for extrapleural drainage)
    (for removal of foreign body)
    34.01
    as operative approach - *omit code*
  common bile duct (for exploration)
    51.51
    for
      relief of obstruction 51.42
      removal of calculus 51.41
  common wall between posterior left
    atrium and coronary sinus (with
    roofing of resultant defect with
    patch graft) 35.82
  conjunctiva 10.1
  cornea 11.1
    radial (refractive) 11.75
  cranial sinus 01.21
  craniobuccal pouch 07.72
  cul-de-sac 70.12
  cyst
    dentigerous 24.0
    radicular (apical) (periapical) 24.0
  Duhrssen's (cervix, to assist delivery)
    73.93
  duodenum 45.01
  ear
    external 18.09
    inner 20.79
    middle 20.23
  endocardium 37.11

ICD-9-CM

Vol. 3

ICD-9-CM

Vol. 3

Insertion (*Continued*)
  pack (*Continued*)
    vagina (nonobstetrical) 96.14
      after delivery or abortion 75.8
  penile prosthesis (internal) (non-inflat-
    able) 64.95
    inflatable (internal) 64.97
  periodontal splint (orthodontic) 24.7
  peripheral blood vessel - *see* non-coro-
    nary
  pessary
    cervix 96.18
      to assist delivery or induce labor
        73.1
    vagina 96.18
  pharyngeal valve, artificial 31.75
  port, vascular access 86.07
  prostaglandin suppository (for abor-
    tion) 96.49
  prosthesis, prosthetic device
    acetabulum (partial) 81.52
      revision 81.53
    ankle (total) 81.56
    arm (bioelectric) (cineplastic) (kine-
      plastic) 84.44
    biliary tract 51.99
    breast (bilateral) 85.54
      unilateral 85.53
    chin (polyethylene) (silastic) 76.68
    elbow (total) 81.84
      revision 81.97
    extremity (bioelectric) (cineplastic)
      (kineplastic) 84.40
      lower 84.48
      upper 84.44
    fallopian tube 66.93
    femoral head (Austin-Moore) (bipo-
      lar) (Eicher) (Thompson) 81.52
    hip (partial) 81.52
      revision 81.53
      total 81.51
        revision 81.53
    joint - *see* Arthroplasty
    knee (partial) (total) 81.54
      revision 81.55
    leg (bioelectric) (cineplastic) (kine-
      plastic) 84.48
    ocular (secondary) 16.61
      with orbital exenteration 16.42
    outflow tract (heart) (gusset type)
      in
        pulmonary valvuloplasty 35.26
        total repair of tetralogy of Fallot
          35.81
    penis (internal) (noninflatable) 64.95
      with
        construction 64.43
        reconstruction 64.44
      inflatable (internal) 64.97
    Rosen (for urinary incontinence)
      59.79
    shoulder
      partial 81.81
      revision 81.97
      total 81.80
    testicular (bilateral) (unilateral) 62.7
    toe 81.57
      hallux valgus repair 77.59
  pseudophakos - *see also* Insertion, lens
    13.70
  pump, infusion 86.06
  radioactive isotope 92.27
  radium 92.27
  radon seeds 92.27

Insertion (*Continued*)
  Reuter bobbin (with intubation) 20.01
  Rickham reservoir 02.2
  Rosen prosthesis (for urinary inconti-
    nence) 59.79
  Scribner shunt 39.93
  Sengstaken-Blakemore tube 96.06
  sieve, vena cava 38.7
  skeletal muscle stimulator 83.92
  skull
    plate 02.05
    stereotactic frame 93.59
    tongs (Barton) (caliper) (Gardner
      Wells) (Vinke) (with synchro-
      nous skeletal traction) 02.94
  spacer (cement) in joint 80.00
  sphenoidal electrodes 02.96
  Spitz-Holter valve 02.2
  Steinmann pin 93.44
    with reduction of fracture or disloca-
      tion - *see* Reduction, fracture *and*
      Reduction, dislocation
  stent(s) (stent graft)
    bile duct 51.43
      endoscopic 51.87
      percutaneous transhepatic 51.98
    coronary (artery) 36.06
    esophagus (endoscopic) (fluoro-
      scopic) 42.81
    non-coronary vessel 39.90
      with angioplasty or atherectomy
        39.50
      with bypass - *omit code*
    pancreatic duct 52.92
      endoscopic 52.93
    peripheral vessel - *see* non-coronary
      vessel
    tracheobronchial 96.05
  stimoceiver - *see* Implant, stimoceiver,
    by site
  stimulator for bone growth - *see* cate-
    gory 78.9
  subdural
    grids 02.93
    strips 02.93
  suppository
    prostaglandin (for abortion) 96.49
    vagina 96.49
  Swan-Ganz catheter (pulmonary)
    89.64
  tampon
    esophagus 96.06
    uterus 69.91
    vagina 96.14
      after delivery or abortion 75.8
  testicular prosthesis (bilateral) (unilat-
    eral) 62.7
  tissue expander (skin) NEC 86.93
    breast 85.95
  tissue mandril (peripheral vessel) (Da-
    cron) (Spark's type) 39.99
    with
      blood vessel repair 39.56
      vascular bypass or shunt - *see* By-
        pass, vascular
  tongs, skull (with synchronous skeletal
    traction) 02.94
  totally implanted device for bone
    growth (invasive) - *see* category
    78.9
  tube - *see also* Catheterization and In-
    tubation
    bile duct 51.43
      endoscopic 51.87

Insertion (*Continued*)
  tube (*Continued*)
    chest 34.04
      revision (with lysis of adhesions)
        34.04
    endotracheal 96.04
    esophagus (nonoperative) (Sengs-
      taken) 96.06
      permanent (silicone) (Souttar)
        42.81
    feeding
      esophageal 42.81
      gastric 96.6
      nasogastric 96.6
    gastric
      by gastrostomy - *see* category 43.1
      for
        decompression, intestinal 96.07
        feeding 96.6
    intercostal (with water seal), for
      drainage 34.04
      revision (with lysis of adhesions)
        34.04
    Miller-Abbott (for intestinal decom-
      pression) 96.08
    nasobiliary (drainage) 51.86
    nasogastric (for intestinal decom-
      pression) NEC 96.07
    nasopancreatic drainage (endo-
      scopic) 52.97
    pancreatic duct 52.92
      endoscopic 52.93
    rectum 96.09
    stomach (nasogastric) (for intestinal
      decompression) NEC 96.07
      for feeding 96.6
    tracheobronchial 96.05
  umbrella device
    atrial septum (King-Mills) 35.52
    vena cava (Mobitz-Uddin) 38.7
  ureteral stent (transurethral) 59.8
    with ureterotomy 59.8 [56.2]
  urinary sphincter, artificial (AUS) (in-
    flatable) 58.93
  vaginal mold 96.15
  valve
    Holter 02.2
    Hufnagel - *see* Replacement, heart
      valve
    pharyngeal (artificial) 31.75
    Spitz-Holter 02.2
    vas deferens 63.95
  vascular access device, totally implant-
    able 86.07
  vena cava sieve or umbrella 38.7
  Vinke tongs (skull) (with synchronous
    skeletal traction) 02.94
Instillation
  bladder 96.49
  digestive tract, except gastric gavage
    96.43
  genitourinary NEC 96.49
  radioisotope (intracavitary) (intrave-
    nous) 92.28
Insufflation
  Eustachian tube 20.8
  fallopian tube (air) (dye) (gas) (saline)
    66.8
    for radiography - *see* Hysterosal-
      pingography
    therapeutic substance 66.95
  lumbar retroperitoneal, bilateral 88.15
Intercricothyroidotomy (for assistance in
  breathing) 31.1

ICD-9-CM

—

Vol. 3

J

Jaboulay operation (gastroduodenostomy) 44.39
Janeway operation (permanent gastrostomy) 43.19
Jatene operation (arterial switch) 35.84
Jejunectomy 45.62
Jejunocecostomy 45.93
Jejunocholecystostomy 51.32
Jejunocolostomy 45.93
Jejunoileostomy 45.91
Jejunojejunostomy 45.91
Jejunopexy 46.61
Jejunorrhaphy 46.73
Jejunostomy (feeding) 46.39
　delayed opening 46.31
　loop 46.01
　percutaneous (endoscopic) (PEJ) 46.32
　revision 46.41
Jejunotomy 45.02
Johanson operation (urethral reconstruction) 58.46
Jones operation
　claw toe (transfer of extensor hallucis
　　longus tendon) 77.57
　　modified (with arthrodesis) 77.57
　dacryocystorhinostomy 09.81
　hammer toe (interphalangeal fusion)
　　77.56
　modified (tendon transfer with arthrodesis) 77.57
　repair of peroneal tendon 83.88
Joplin operation (exostectomy with tendon transfer) 77.53

K

Kader operation (temporary gastrostomy) 43.19

Kaufman operation (for urinary stress
　incontinence) 59.79
Kazanjian operation (buccal vestibular
　sulcus extension) 24.91
Kehr operation (hepatopexy) 50.69
Keller operation (bunionectomy)
　77.59
Kelly (-Kennedy) operation (urethrovesical plication) 59.3
Kelly-Stoeckel operation (urethrovesical
　plication) 59.3
Kelotomy 53.9
Keratectomy (complete) (partial) (superficial) 11.49
　for pterygium 11.39
　with corneal graft 11.32
Keratocentesis (for hyphema) 12.91
Keratomileusis 11.71
Keratophakia 11.72
Keratoplasty (tectonic) (with autograft)
　(with homograft) 11.60
　lamellar (nonpenetrating) (with homograft) 11.62
　　with autograft 11.61
　penetrating (full-thickness) (with homograft) 11.64
　　with autograft 11.63
　perforating - *see* Keratoplasty, penetrating
　refractive 11.71
　specified type NEC 11.69
Keratoprosthesis 11.73
Keratotomy (delimiting) (posterior) 11.1
　radial (refractive) 11.75
Kerr operation (low cervical cesarean
　section) 74.1
Kessler operation (arthroplasty, carpometacarpal joint) 81.74

Kidner operation (excision of accessory
　navicular bone) (with tendon transfer) 77.98
Killian operation (frontal sinusotomy)
　22.41
Kineplasty - *see* Cineplasty
King-Steelquist operation (hindquarter
　amputation) 84.19
Kirk operation (amputation through
　thigh) 84.17
Kock pouch
　bowel anastomosis - *omit code*
　continent ileostomy 46.22
　cutaneous uretero-ileostomy 56.51
　ESWL (electrocorporeal shock wave
　　lithotripsy) 98.51
　removal, calculus 57.19
　revision, cutaneous uretero-ileostomy
　　56.52
　urinary diversion procedure 56.51
Kockogram (ileal conduitogram) 87.78
Kockoscopy 45.12
Kondoleon operation (correction of
　lymphedema) 40.9
Krause operation (sympathetic denervation) 05.29
Kroener operation (partial salpingectomy) 66.69
Kroenlein operation (lateral orbitotomy)
　16.01
Krönig operation (low cervical cesarean
　section) 74.1
Krunkenberg operation (reconstruction of below-elbow amputation)
　82.89
Kuhnt-Szymanowski operation (ectropion repair with lid reconstruction)
　08.44

ICD-9-CM

J, K

Vol. 3

L

Labbe operation (gastrotomy) 43.0
Labiectomy (bilateral) 71.62
unilateral 71.61
Labyrinthectomy (transtympanic) 20.79
Labyrinthotomy (transtympanic) 20.79
Ladd operation (mobilization of intestine) 54.95
Lagrange operation (iridosclerectomy) 12.65
Lambrinudi operation (triple arthrodesis) 81.12
Laminectomy (decompression) (for exploration) 03.09
as operative approach - *omit code*
with
excision of herniated intervertebral disc (nucleus pulposus) 80.51
excision of other intraspinal lesion (tumor) 03.4
reopening of site 03.02
Laminography - *see* Radiography
Laminotomy (decompression) (for exploration) 03.09
as operative approach - *omit code*
reopening of site 03.02
Langenbeck operation (cleft palate repair) 27.62
Laparoamnioscopy 75.31
Lapararorrhaphy 54.63
Laparoscopy 54.21
with
biopsy (intra-abdominal) 54.24
uterine ligaments 68.15
uterus 68.16
destruction of fallopian tubes - *see* Destruction, fallopian tube
Laparotomy NEC 54.19
as operative approach - *omit code*
exploratory (pelvic) 54.11
reopening of recent operative site (for control of hemorrhage) (for exploration) (for incision of hematoma) 54.12
Laparotrachelotomy 74.1
Lapidus operation (bunionectomy with metatarsal osteotomy) 77.51
Larry operation (shoulder disarticulation) 84.08
Laryngectomy
with radical neck dissection (with synchronous thyroidectomy) (with synchronous tracheostomy) 30.4
complete (with partial laryngectomy) (with synchronous tracheostomy) 30.3
with radical neck dissection (with synchronous thyroidectomy) (with synchronous tracheostomy) 30.4
frontolateral partial (extended) 30.29
glottosupraglottic partial 30.29
lateral partial 30.29
partial (frontolateral) (glottosupraglottic) (lateral) (submucous) (supraglottic) (vertical) 30.29
radical (with synchronous thyroidectomy) (with synchronous tracheostomy) 30.4
submucous (partial) 30.29
supraglottic partial 30.29
total (with partial pharyngectomy) (with synchronous tracheostomy) 30.3

Laryngectomy (*Continued*)
total (*Continued*)
with radical neck dissection (with synchronous thyroidectomy) (with synchronous tracheostomy) 30.4
vertical partial 30.29
wide field 30.3
Laryngocentesis 31.3
Laryngoesophagectomy 30.4
Laryngofissure 30.29
Laryngogram 87.09
contrast 87.07
Laryngopharyngectomy (with synchronous tracheostomy) 30.3
radical (with synchronous thyroidectomy) 30.4
Laryngopharyngoesophagectomy (with synchronous tracheostomy) 30.3
with radical neck dissection (with synchronous thyroidectomy) 30.4
Laryngoplasty 31.69
Laryngorrhaphy 31.61
Laryngoscopy (suspension) (through artificial stoma) 31.42
Laryngostomy (permanent) 31.29
revision 31.63
temporary (emergency) 31.1
Laryngotomy 31.3
Laryngotracheobronchoscopy 33.23
with biopsy 33.24
Laryngotracheoscopy 31.42
Laryngotracheostomy (permanent) 31.29
temporary (emergency) 31.1
Laryngotracheotomy (temporary) 31.1
permanent 31.29
Laser - *see also* Coagulation, Destruction, *and* Photocoagulation, by site
angioplasty, percutaneous transluminal 39.59
coronary - *see* Angioplasty, coronary
Lash operation (internal cervical os repair) 67.5
Latzko operation
cesarean section 74.2
colpocleisis 70.4
Lavage
antral 22.00
bronchus NEC 96.56
endotracheal 96.56
gastric 96.33
nasal sinus(es) 22.00
by puncture 22.01
through natural ostium 22.02
peritoneal (diagnostic) 54.25
trachea NEC 96.56
Leadbetter operation (urethral reconstruction) 58.46
Leadbetter-Politano operation (ureteroneocystostomy) 56.74
LEEP (loop electrosurgical excision procedure) of cervix 67.32 ◀
Le Fort operation (colpocleisis) 70.8
LeMesurier operation (cleft lip repair) 27.54
Lengthening
bone (with bone graft) 78.30
femur 78.35
for reconstruction of thumb 82.69
specified site NEC - *see also* category 78.3, 78.39
tibia 78.37
ulna 78.33

Lengthening (*Continued*)
extraocular muscle NEC 15.21
multiple (two or more muscles) 15.4
fascia 83.89
hand 82.89
hamstring NEC 83.85
heel cord 83.85
leg
femur 78.35
tibia 78.37
levator palpebrae muscle 08.38
muscle 83.85
extraocular 15.21
multiple (two or more muscles) 15.4
hand 82.55
palate 27.62
secondary or subsequent 27.63
tendon 83.85
for claw toe repair 77.57
hand 82.55
Leriche operation (periarterial sympathectomy) 05.25
Leucotomy, leukotomy 01.32
Leukopheresis, therapeutic 99.72
Lid suture operation (blepharoptosis) 08.31
Ligation
adrenal vessel (artery) (vein) 07.43
aneurysm 39.52
appendages, dermal 86.26
arteriovenous fistula 39.53
coronary artery 36.99
artery 38.80
abdominal 38.86
adrenal 07.43
aorta (arch) (ascending) (descending) 38.84
coronary (anomalous) 36.99
ethmoidal 21.04
external carotid 21.06
for control of epistaxis - *see* Control, epistaxis
head and neck NEC 38.82
intracranial NEC 38.81
lower limb 38.88
maxillary (transantral) 21.05
middle meningeal 02.13
thoracic NEC 38.85
thyroid 06.92
upper limb 38.83
atrium, heart 37.99
auricle, heart 37.99
bleeding vessel - *see* Control, hemorrhage
blood vessel 38.80
abdominal
artery 38.86
vein 38.87
adrenal 07.43
aorta (arch) (ascending) (descending) 38.84
esophagus 42.91
endoscopic 42.33
head and neck 38.82
intracranial NEC 38.81
lower limb
artery 38.88
vein 38.89
meningeal (artery) (longitudinal sinus) 02.13
thoracic NEC 38.85
thyroid 06.92
upper limb (artery) (vein) 38.83

ICD-9-CM

Vol. 3

M

Madlener operation (tubal ligation) 66.31
Magnet extraction
  foreign body
    anterior chamber, eye 12.01
    choroid 14.01
    ciliary body 12.01
    conjunctiva 98.22
    cornea 11.0
    eye, eyeball NEC 98.21
      anterior segment 12.01
      posterior segment 14.01
    intraocular (anterior segment) 12.01
    iris 12.01
    lens 13.01
    orbit 98.21
    retina 14.01
    sclera 12.01
    vitreous 14.01
Magnetic resonance imaging (nuclear) -
  see Imaging, magnetic resonance
Magnuson (-Stack) operation (arthro-
  plasty for recurrent shoulder dislo-
  cation) 81.82
Malleostapediopexy 19.19
  with incus replacement 19.11
Malström's vacuum extraction 72.79
  with episiotomy 72.71
Mammaplasty - *see* Mammoplasty
Mammectomy - *see also* Mastectomy
  subcutaneous (unilateral) 85.34
    with synchronous implant 85.33
    bilateral 85.36
      with synchronous implant 85.35
Mammilliplasty 85.87
Mammography NEC 87.37
Mammoplasty 85.89
  with
    full-thickness graft 85.83
    muscle flap 85.85
    pedicle graft 85.84
    split-thickness graft 85.82
  amputative (reduction) (bilateral) 85.32
    unilateral 85.31
  augmentation 85.50
    with
      breast implant (bilateral) 85.54
        unilateral 85.53
      injection into breast (bilateral)
        85.52
        unilateral 85.51
  reduction (bilateral) 85.32
    unilateral 85.31
  revision 85.89
  size reduction (gynecomastia) (bilat-
    eral) 85.32
    unilateral 85.31
Mammotomy 85.0
Manchester (-Donald) (-Fothergill) oper-
  ation (uterine suspension) 69.22
Mandibulectomy (partial) 76.31
  total 76.42
    with reconstruction 76.41
Maneuver (method)
  Bracht 72.52
  Credé 73.59
  De Lee (key-in-lock) 72.4
  Kristeller 72.54
  Loveset's (extraction of arms in breech
    birth) 72.52
  Mauriceau (-Smellie-Veit) 72.52
  Pinard (total breech extraction) 72.54

Maneuver (Continued)
  Prague 72.52
  Ritgen 73.59
  Scanzoni (rotation) 72.4
  Van Hoorn 72.52
  Wigand-Martin 72.52
Manipulation
  with reduction of fracture or disloca-
    tion - *see* Reduction, fracture *and*
    Reduction, dislocation
  enterostomy stoma (with dilation)
    96.24
  intestine (intra-abdominal) 46.80
    large 46.82
    small 46.81
  joint
    adhesions 93.26
      temporomandibular 76.95
    dislocation - *see* Reduction, disloca-
      tion
  lacrimal passage (tract) NEC 09.49
  muscle structures 93.27
  musculoskeletal (physical therapy)
    NEC 93.29
  nasal septum, displaced 21.88
  osteopathic NEC 93.67
    for general mobilization (general ar-
      ticulation) 93.61
    high-velocity, low-amplitude forces
      (thrusting) 93.62
    indirect forces 93.65
    isotonic, isometric forces 93.64
    low-velocity, high-amplitude forces
      (springing) 93.63
    to move tissue fluids 93.66
  rectum 96.22
  salivary duct 26.91
  stomach, intraoperative 44.92
  temporomandibular joint NEC 76.95
  ureteral calculus by catheter
    with removal 56.0
    without removal 59.8
  uterus NEC 69.98
    gravid 75.99
    inverted
      manual replacement (following
        delivery) 75.94
    surgical - *see* Repair, inverted uterus
Manometry
  esophageal 89.32
  spinal fluid 89.15
  urinary 89.21
Manual arts therapy 93.81
Mapping
  cardiac (electrophysiologic) 37.27
    doppler (flow) 88.72
  electrocardiogram only 89.52
Marckwald operation (cervical os repair)
  67.5
Marshall-Marchetti (-Krantz) operation
  (retropubic urethral suspension) 59.5
Marsupialization - *see also* Destruction,
  lesion, by site
  cyst
    Bartholin's 71.23
    brain 01.59
    cervical (nabothian) 67.31
    dental 24.4
    dentigerous 24.4
    kidney 55.31
    larynx 30.01
    liver 50.21
    ovary 65.21
      laparoscopic 65.23

Marsupialization (Continued)
  cyst (Continued)
    pancreas 52.3
    pilonidal (open excision) (with par-
      tial closure) 86.21
    salivary gland 26.21
    spinal (intraspinal) (meninges) 03.4
    spleen, splenic 41.41
  lesion
    brain 01.59
    cerebral 01.59
    liver 50.21
  pilonidal cyst or sinus (open excision)
    (with partial closure) 86.21
  pseudocyst, pancreas 52.3
  ranula, salivary gland 26.21
Massage
  cardiac (external) (manual) (closed)
    99.63
    open 37.91
  prostatic 99.94
  rectal (for levator spasm) 99.93
MAST (military anti-shock trousers)
  93.58
Mastectomy (complete) (prophylactic)
  (simple) (unilateral) 85.41
  with
    excision of regional lymph nodes
      85.43
      bilateral 85.44
    preservation of skin and nipple
      85.34
      with synchronous implant 85.33
      bilateral 85.36
        with synchronous implant
          85.35
  bilateral 85.42
  extended
    radical (Urban) (unilateral) 85.47
      bilateral 85.48
    simple (with regional lymphadenec-
      tomy) (unilateral) 85.43
      bilateral 85.44
  modified radical (unilateral) 85.43
    bilateral 85.44
  partial 85.23
  radical (Halsted) (Meyer) (unilateral)
    85.45
    bilateral 85.46
    extended (Urban) (unilateral) 85.47
      bilateral 85.48
    modified (unilateral) 85.43
      bilateral 85.44
  subcutaneous 85.34
    with synchronous implant 85.33
    bilateral 85.36
      with synchronous implant 85.35
  subtotal 85.23
Masters' stress test (two-step) 89.42
Mastoidectomy (cortical) (conservative)
  20.49
  complete (simple) 20.41
  modified radical 20.49
  radical 20.42
    modified 20.49
  simple (complete) 20.41
Mastoidotomy 20.21
Mastoidotympanectomy 20.42
Mastopexy 85.6
Mastoplasty - *see* Mammoplasty
Mastorrhaphy 85.81
Mastotomy 85.0
Matas operation (aneurysmorrhaphy)
  39.52

ICD-9-CM

M

Vol. 3

Myelogram, myelography (air) (gas) 87.21
  posterior fossa 87.02
Myelotomy
  spine, spinal (cord) (tract) (one-stage) (two-stage) 03.29
    percutaneous 03.21
Myocardiectomy (infarcted area) 37.33
Myocardiotomy 37.11
Myoclasis 83.99
  hand 82.99
Myomectomy (uterine) 68.29
  broad ligament 69.19
Myoplasty - *see also* Repair, muscle 83.87
  hand - *see also* Repair, muscle, hand 82.89
  mastoid 19.9
Myorrhaphy 83.65
  hand 82.46
Myosuture 83.65
  hand 82.46
Myotasis 93.27
Myotenontoplasty - *see also* Repair, tendon 83.88
  hand 82.86
Myotenoplasty - *see also* Repair, tendon 83.88
  hand 82.86
Myotenotomy 83.13
  hand 82.11
Myotomy 83.02
  with division 83.19
    hand 82.19
  colon NEC 46.92
    sigmoid 46.91
  cricopharyngeal 29.31
    that for pharyngeal (pharyngoesophageal) diverticulectomy 29.32
  esophagus 42.7
  eye (oblique) (rectus) 15.21
    multiple (two or more muscles) 15.4
  hand 82.02
    with division 82.19
  levator palpebrae 08.38
  sigmoid (colon) 46.91
Myringectomy 20.59
Myringodectomy 20.59
Myringomalleolabyrinthopexy 19.52
Myringoplasty (epitympanic, type I) (by cauterization) (by graft) 19.4
  revision 19.6
Myringostapediopexy 19.53
Myringostomy 20.01
Myringotomy (with aspiration) (with drainage) 20.09
  with insertion of tube or drainage device (button) (grommet) 20.01

N

Nailing, intramedullary 79.30
  femur 79.35
  fibula 79.36
  humerus 79.31
  radius 79.32
  tibia 79.36
  ulna 79.32
Narcoanalysis 94.21
Narcosynthesis 94.21
Narrowing, palpebral fissure 08.51
Nasopharyngogram 87.09
  contrast 87.06
Necropsy 89.8
Needleoscopy (fetus) 75.31
Needling
  Bartholin's gland (cyst) 71.21
  cataract (secondary) 13.64
  fallopian tube 66.91
  hydrocephalic head 73.8
  lens (capsule) 13.2
  pupillary membrane (iris) 12.35
Nephrectomy (complete) (total) (unilateral) 55.51
  bilateral 55.54
  partial (wedge) 55.4
  remaining or solitary kidney 55.52
  removal, transplanted kidney 55.53
Nephrocolopexy 55.7
Nephrocystanastomosis NEC 56.73
Nephrolithotomy 55.01
Nephrolysis 59.02
  laparoscopic 59.03
Nephropexy 55.7
Nephroplasty 55.89
Nephropyeloplasty 55.87
Nephropyeloureterostomy 55.86
Nephrorrhaphy 55.81
Nephroscopy 55.21
Nephrostolithotomy, percutaneous 55.03
Nephrostomy (with drainage tube) 55.02
  closure 55.82
  percutaneous 55.03
    with fragmentation (ultrasound) 55.04
Nephrotomogram, nephrotomography NEC 87.72
Nephrotomy 55.01
Nephroureterectomy (with bladder cuff) 55.51
Nephroureterocystectomy 55.51 [57.79]
Nerve block (cranial) (peripheral) NEC - *see also* Block, by site 04.81
Neurectasis (cranial) (peripheral) 04.91

Neurectomy (cranial) (infraorbital) (occipital) (peripheral) (spinal) NEC 04.07
  gastric (vagus) - *see also* Vagotomy 44.00
  opticociliary 12.79
  paracervical 05.22
  presacral 05.24
  retrogasserian 04.07
  sympathetic - *see* Sympathectomy
  trigeminal 04.07
  tympanic 20.91
Neurexeresis NEC 04.07
Neuroanastomosis (cranial) (peripheral) NEC 04.74
  accessory-facial 04.72
  accessory-hypoglossal 04.73
  hypoglossal-facial 04.71
Neurolysis (peripheral nerve) NEC 04.49
  carpal tunnel 04.43
  cranial nerve NEC 04.42
  spinal (cord) (nerve roots) 03.6
  tarsal tunnel 04.44
  trigeminal nerve 04.41
Neuroplasty (cranial) (peripheral) NEC 04.79
  of old injury (delayed repair) 04.76
  revision 04.75
Neurorrhaphy (cranial) (peripheral) 04.3
Neurotomy (cranial) (peripheral) (spinal) NEC 04.04
  acoustic 04.01
  glossopharyngeal 29.92
  lacrimal branch 05.0
  retrogasserian 04.02
  sympathetic 05.0
  vestibular 04.01
Neurotripsy (peripheral) NEC 04.03
  trigeminal 04.02
Nicola operation (tenodesis for recurrent dislocation of shoulder) 81.82
Nissen operation (fundoplication of stomach) 44.66
Noble operation (plication of small intestine) 46.62
Norman Miller operation (vaginopexy) 70.77
Norton operation (extraperitoneal cesarean section) 74.2
Nuclear magnetic resonance imaging - *see* Imaging, magnetic resonance
Nutrition, concentrated substances
  enteral infusion (of) 96.6
  parenteral (total) 99.15
    peripheral parenteral 99.15

O

Ober (-Yount) operation (gluteal-iliotib-
ial fasciotomy) 83.14
Obliteration
  bone cavity - *see also* Osteoplasty 78.40
  calyceal diverticulum 55.39
  canaliculi 09.6
  cerebrospinal fistula 02.12
  cul-de-sac 70.92
  frontal sinus (with fat) 22.42
  lacrimal punctum 09.91
  lumbar pseudomeningocele 03.51
  lymphatic structure(s) (peripheral) 40.9
  maxillary sinus 22.31
  meningocele (sacral) 03.51
  pelvic 68.8
  pleural cavity 34.6
  sacral meningocele 03.51
  Skene's gland 71.3
  tympanomastoid cavity 19.9
  vagina, vaginal (partial) (total) 70.4
    vault 70.8
Occlusal molds (dental) 89.31
Occlusion
  artery - *see* Ligation, artery
  fallopian tube - *see* Ligation, fallopian
    tube
  patent ductus arteriosus (PDA) 38.85
  vein - *see* Ligation, vein
  vena cava (surgical) 38.7
Occupational therapy 93.83
O'Donoghue operation (triad knee re-
  pair) 81.43
Odontectomy NEC - *see also* Removal,
  tooth, surgical 23.19
Oleothorax 33.39
Olshausen operation (uterine suspen-
  sion) 69.22
Omentectomy 54.4
Omentofixation 54.74
Omentopexy 54.74
Omentoplasty 54.74
Omentorrhaphy 54.74
Omentotomy 54.19
Omphalectomy 54.3
Onychectomy 86.23
Onychoplasty 86.86
Onychotomy 86.09
  with drainage 86.04
Oophorectomy (unilateral) 65.39
  with salpingectomy 65.49
    laparoscopic 65.41
  bilateral (same operative episode)
    65.51
    laparoscopic 65.53
    with salpingectomy 65.61
      laparoscopic 65.63
  laparoscopic 65.31
  partial 65.29
    laparoscopic 65.25
    wedge 65.22
      that by laparoscope 65.24
  remaining ovary 65.52
    laparoscopic 65.54
    with tube 65.62
      laparoscopic 65.64
Oophorocystectomy 65.29
  laparoscopic 65.25
Oophoropexy 65.79
Oophoroplasty 65.79
Oophororrhaphy 65.71
  laparoscopic 65.74

Oophorostomy 65.09
  laparoscopic 65.01
Oophorotomy 65.09
  laparoscopic 65.01
Opening
  bony labyrinth (ear) 20.79
  cranial suture 02.01
  heart valve
    closed heart technique - *see* Valvu-
      lotomy, by site
    open heart technique - *see* Valvulo-
      plasty, by site
  spinal dura 03.09
Operation
  Abbe
    construction of vagina 70.61
    intestinal anastomosis - *see* Anasto-
      mosis, intestine
  abdominal (region) NEC 54.99
  abdominoperineal NEC 48.5
  Aburel (intra-amniotic injection for
    abortion) 75.0
  Adams
    advancement of round ligament
      69.22
    crushing of nasal septum 21.88
    excision of palmar fascia 82.35
  adenoids NEC 28.99
  adrenal (gland) (nerve) (vessel) NEC
    07.49
  Albee
    bone peg, femoral neck 78.05
    graft for slipping patella 78.06
    sliding inlay graft, tibia 78.07
  Albert (arthrodesis, knee) 81.22
  Aldridge (-Studdiford) (urethral sling)
    59.5
  Alexander
    prostatectomy
      perineal 60.62
      suprapubic 60.3
    shortening of round ligaments of
      uterus 69.22
  Alexander-Adams (shortening of
    round ligaments of uterus) 69.22
  Almoor (extrapetrosal drainage) 20.22
  Altemeier (perineal rectal pull-
    through) 48.49
  Ammon (dacryocystotomy) 09.53
  Anderson (tibial lengthening) 78.37
  Anel (dilation of lacrimal duct) 09.42
  anterior chamber (eye) NEC 12.99
  anti-incontinence NEC 59.79
  antrum window (nasal sinus) 22.2
    with Caldwell-Luc approach 22.39
  anus NEC 49.99
  aortic body NEC 39.8
  aorticopulmonary window 39.59
  appendix NEC 47.99
  Arslan (fenestration of inner ear) 20.61
  artery NEC 39.99
  Asai (larynx) 31.75
  Baffes (interatrial transposition of ve-
    nous return) 35.91
  Baldy-Webster (uterine suspension)
    69.22
  Ball
    herniorrhaphy - *see* Repair, hernia,
      inguinal
    undercutting 49.02
  Bankhart (capsular repair into glenoid,
    for shoulder dislocation) 81.82
  Bardenheuer (ligation of innominate
    artery) 38.85

Operation (*Continued*)
  Barkan (goniotomy) 12.52
    with goniopuncture 12.53
  Barr (transfer of tibialis posterior ten-
    don) 83.75
  Barsky (closure of cleft hand) 82.82
  Bassett (vulvectomy with inguinal
    lymph node dissection) 71.5 [40.3]
  Bassini (herniorrhaphy) - *see* Repair,
    hernia, inguinal
  Batch-Spittler-McFaddin (knee disartic-
    ulation) 84.16
  Batista (partial ventriculectomy) (ven-
    tricular reduction) (ventricular re-
    modeling) 37.35
  Beck I (epicardial poudrage)
    36.39   ◄▥
  Beck II (aorta-coronary sinus shunt)
    36.39   ◄▥
  Beck-Jianu (permanent gastrostomy)
    43.19
  Bell-Beuttner (subtotal abdominal hys-
    terectomy) 68.3
  Belsey (esophagogastric sphincter) 44.65
  Benenenti (rotation of bulbous urethra)
    58.49
  Berke (levator resection, eyelid) 08.33
  Biesenberger (size reduction of breast,
    bilateral) 85.32
    unilateral 85.31
  Bigelow (litholapaxy) 57.0
  biliary (duct) (tract) NEC 51.99
  Billroth I (partial gastrectomy with
    gastroduodenostomy) 43.6
  Billroth II (partial gastrectomy with
    gastrojejunostomy) 43.7
  Binnie (hepatopexy) 50.69
  Bischoff (ureteroneocystostomy) 56.74
  bisection hysterectomy 68.3
  Bishoff (spinal myelotomy) 03.29
  bladder NEC 57.99
    flap 56.74
  Blalock (systemic-pulmonary anasto-
    mosis) 39.0
  Blalock-Hanlon (creation of atrial sep-
    tal defect) 35.42
  Blalock-Taussig (subclavian-pulmonary
    anastomosis) 39.0
  Blascovic (resection and advancement
    of levator palpebrae superioris)
    08.33
  blood vessel NEC 39.99
  Blount
    femoral shortening (with blade
      plate) 78.25
    by epiphyseal stapling 78.25
  Boari (bladder flap) 56.74
  Bobb (cholelithotomy) 51.04
  bone NEC - *see* category 78.4
    facial 76.99
    injury NEC - *see* category 79.9
    marrow NEC 41.98
    skull NEC 02.99
  Bonney (abdominal hysterectomy) 68.4
  Borthen (iridotasis) 12.63
  Bost
    plantar dissection 80.48
    radiocarpal fusion 81.26
  Bosworth
    arthroplasty for acromioclavicular
      separation 81.83
    fusion of posterior lumbar spine
      81.08
    for pseudarthrosis 81.09

Operation (*Continued*)
  Bosworth (*Continued*)
    resection of radial head ligaments (for tennis elbow) 80.92
    shelf procedure, hip 81.40
  Bottle (repair of hydrocele of tunica vaginalis) 61.2
  Boyd (hip disarticulation) 84.18
  brain NEC 02.99
  Brauer (cardiolysis) 37.10
  breast NEC 85.99
  Bricker (ileoureterostomy) 56.51
  Bristow (repair of shoulder dislocation) 81.82
  Brock (pulmonary valvulotomy) 35.03
  Brockman (soft tissue release for clubfoot) 83.84
  bronchus NEC 33.98
  Browne (-Denis) (hypospadias repair) 58.45
  Brunschwig (temporary gastrostomy) 43.19
  buccal cavity NEC 27.99
  Bunnell (tendon transfer) 82.56
  Burch procedure (retropubic urethral suspension for urinary stress incontinence) 59.5
  Burgess (amputation of ankle) 84.14
  bursa NEC 83.99
    hand 82.99
  bypass - *see* Bypass
  Caldwell (sulcus extension) 24.91
  Caldwell-Luc (maxillary sinusotomy) 22.39
    with removal of membrane lining 22.31
  Callander (knee disarticulation) 84.16
  Campbell
    bone block, ankle 81.11
    fasciotomy (iliac crest) 83.14
    reconstruction of anterior cruciate ligaments 81.45
  canthus NEC 08.99
  cardiac NEC 37.99
    septum NEC 35.98
    valve NEC 35.99
  carotid body or gland NEC 39.8
  Carroll and Taber (arthroplasty, proximal interphalangeal joint) 81.72
  Cattell (herniorrhaphy) 53.51
  Cecil (urethral reconstruction) 58.46
  cecum NEC 46.99
  cerebral (meninges) NEC 02.99
  cervix NEC 69.99
  Chandler (hip fusion) 81.21
  Charles (correction of lymphedema) 40.9
  Charnley (compression arthrodesis)
    ankle 81.11
    hip 81.21
    knee 81.22
  Cheatle-Henry - *see* Repair, hernia, femoral
  chest cavity NEC 34.99
  Chevalier-Jackson (partial laryngectomy) 30.29
  Child (radical subtotal pancreatectomy) 52.53
  Chopart (midtarsal amputation) 84.12
  chordae tendineae NEC 35.32
  choroid NEC 14.9
  ciliary body NEC 12.98
  cisterna chyli NEC 40.69

Operation (*Continued*)
  Clagett (closure of chest wall following open flap drainage) 34.72
  Clayton (resection of metatarsal heads and bases of phalanges) 77.88
  clitoris NEC 71.4
  cocked hat (metacarpal lengthening and transfer of local flap) 82.69
  Cockett (varicose vein)
    lower limb 38.59
    upper limb 38.53
  Cody tack (perforation of footplate) 19.0
  Coffey (uterine suspension) (Meig's modification) 69.22
  Cole (anterior tarsal wedge osteotomy) 77.28
  Collis-Nissen (hiatal hernia repair) 53.80
  colon NEC 46.99
  Colonna
    adductor tenotomy (first stage) 83.12
    hip arthroplasty (second stage) 81.40
    reconstruction of hip (second stage) 81.40
  commando (radical glossectomy) 25.4
  conjunctiva NEC 10.99
    destructive NEC 10.33
  cornea NEC 11.99
  Coventry (tibial wedge osteotomy) 77.27
  Crawford (tarso-frontalis sling of eyelid) 08.32
  cul-de-sac NEC 70.92
  Culp-Deweerd (spiral flap pyeloplasty) 55.87
  Culp-Scardino (ureteral flap pyeloplasty) 55.87
  Curtis (interphalangeal joint arthroplasty) 81.72
  cystocele NEC 70.51
  Dahlman (excision of esophageal diverticulum) 42.31
  Dana (posterior rhizotomy) 03.1
  Danforth (fetal) 73.8
  Darrach (ulnar resection) 77.83
  Davis (intubated ureterotomy) 56.2
  de Grandmont (tarsectomy) 08.35
  Delorme
    pericardiectomy 37.31
    proctopexy 48.76
    repair of prolapsed rectum 48.76
    thoracoplasty 33.34
  Denker (radical maxillary antrotomy) 22.31
  Dennis-Varco (herniorrhaphy) - *see* Repair, hernia, femoral
  Denonvilliers (limited rhinoplasty) 21.86
  dental NEC 24.99
    orthodontic NEC 24.8
  Derlacki (tympanoplasty) 19.4
  diaphragm NEC 34.89
  Dickson (fascial transplant) 83.82
  Dickson-Diveley (tendon transfer and arthrodesis to correct claw toe) 77.57
  Dieffenbach (hip disarticulation) 84.18
  digestive tract NEC 46.99
  Doléris (shortening of round ligaments) 69.22
  D'Ombrain (excision of pterygium with corneal graft) 11.32
  Dorrance (push-back operation for cleft palate) 27.62

Operation (*Continued*)
  Dotter (transluminal angioplasty) 39.59
  Douglas (suture of tongue to lip for micrognathia) 25.59
  Doyle (paracervical uterine denervation) 69.3
  Dühamel (abdominoperineal pull-through) 48.65
  Duhrssen's (vaginofixation of uterus) 69.22
  Dunn (triple arthrodesis) 81.12
  duodenum NEC 46.99
  Dupuytren
    fasciectomy 82.35
    fasciotomy 82.12
      with excision 82.35
    shoulder disarticulation 84.08
  Durham (-Caldwell) (transfer of biceps femoris tendon) 83.75
  DuToit and Roux (staple capsulorrhaphy of shoulder) 81.82
  DuVries (tenoplasty) 83.88
  Dwyer
    fasciotomy 83.14
    soft tissue release NEC 83.84
    wedge osteotomy, calcaneus 77.28
  Eagleton (extrapetrosal drainage) 20.22
  ear (external) NEC 18.9
    middle or inner NEC 20.99
  Eden-Hybinette (glenoid bone block) 78.01
  Effler (heart) 36.2
  Eggers
    tendon release (patellar retinacula) 83.13
    tendon transfer (biceps femoris tendon) (hamstring tendon) 83.75
  Elliot (scleral trephination with iridectomy) 12.61
  Ellis Jones (repair of peroneal tendon) 83.88
  Ellison (reinforcement of collateral ligament) 81.44
  Elmslie-Cholmeley (tarsal wedge osteotomy) 77.28
  Eloesser
    thoracoplasty 33.34 ◄
    thoracostomy 34.09 ◄
  Emmet (cervix) 67.61
  endorectal pull-through 48.41
  epididymis NEC 63.99
  esophagus NEC 42.99
  Estes (ovary) 65.72
    laparoscopic 65.75
  Estlander (thoracoplasty) 33.34
  Evans (release of clubfoot) 83.84
  extraocular muscle NEC 15.9
    multiple (two or more muscles) 15.4
      with temporary detachment from globe 15.3
    revision 15.6
    single 15.29
      with temporary detachment from globe 15.19
  eyeball NEC 16.99
  eyelid(s) NEC 08.99
  face NEC 27.99
  facial bone or joint NEC 76.99
  fallopian tube NEC 66.99
  Farabeuf (ischiopubiotomy) 77.39
  Fasanella-Servatt (blepharoptosis repair) 08.35

Operation (*Continued*)

pharynx, pharyngeal (pouch) NEC 29.99

pineal gland NEC 07.59

Pinsker (obliteration of nasoseptal telangiectasia) 21.07

Piper (forceps) 72.6

Pirogoff (ankle amputation through malleoli of tibia and fibula) 84.14

pituitary gland NEC 07.79

plastic - *see* Repair, by site

pleural cavity NEC 34.99

Politano-Leadbetter (ureteroneocystostomy) 56.74

pollicization (with nerves and blood supply) 82.61

Polya (gastrectomy) 43.7

Pomeroy (ligation and division of fallopian tubes) 66.32

Poncet
lengthening of Achilles tendon 83.85
urethrostomy, perineal 58.0

Porro (cesarean section) 74.99

posterior chamber (eye) NEC 14.9

Potts-Smith (descending aorta-left pulmonary artery anastomosis) 39.0

Printen and Mason (high gastric bypass) 44.31

prostate NEC - *see also* Prostatectomy 60.69
specified type 60.99

pterygium 11.39
with corneal graft 11.32

Puestow (pancreaticojejunostomy) 52.96

pull-through NEC 48.49

pulmonary NEC 33.99

push-back (cleft palate repair) 27.62

Putti-Platt (capsulorrhaphy of shoulder for recurrent dislocation) 81.82

pyloric exclusion 44.39

pyriform sinus NEC 29.99

"rabbit ear" (anterior urethropexy) (Tudor) 59.79

Ramadier (intrapetrosal drainage) 20.22

Ramstedt (pyloromyotomy) (with wedge resection) 43.3

Rankin
exteriorization of intestine 46.03
proctectomy (complete) 48.5

Rashkind (balloon septostomy) 35.41

Rastelli (creation of conduit between right ventricle and pulmonary artery) 35.92
in repair of
pulmonary artery atresia 35.92
transposition of great vessels 35.92
truncus arteriosus 35.83

Raz-Pereyra procedure (bladder neck suspension) 59.79

rectal NEC 48.99

rectocele NEC 70.52

re-entry (aorta) 39.54

renal NEC 55.99

respiratory (tract) NEC 33.99

retina NEC 14.9

Ripstein (repair of rectal prolapse) 48.75

Rodney Smith (radical subtotal pancreatectomy) 52.53

Roux-en-Y
bile duct 51.36
cholecystojejunostomy 51.32

Operation (*Continued*)

Roux-en-Y (*Continued*)
esophagus (intrathoracic) 42.54
pancreaticojejunostomy 52.96

Roux-Goldthwait (repair of patellar dislocation) 81.44

Roux-Herzen-Judine (jejunal loop interposition) 42.63

Ruiz-Mora (proximal phalangectomy for hammer toe) 77.99

Russe (bone graft of scaphoid) 78.04

Saemisch (corneal section) 11.1

salivary gland or duct NEC 26.99

Salter (innominate osteotomy) 77.39

Sauer-Bacon (abdominoperineal resection) 48.5

Schanz (femoral osteotomy) 77.35

Schauta (-Amreich) (radical vaginal hysterectomy) 68.7

Schede (thoracoplasty) 33.34

Scheie
cautery of sclera 12.62
sclerostomy 12.62

Schlatter (total gastrectomy) 43.99

Schroeder (endocervical excision) 67.39

Schuchardt (nonobstetrical episiotomy) 71.09

Schwartze (simple mastoidectomy) 20.41

sclera NEC 12.89

Scott
intestinal bypass for obesity 45.93
jejunocolostomy (bypass) 45.93

scrotum NEC 61.99

Seddon-Brooks (transfer of pectoralis major tendon) 83.75

Semb (apicolysis of lung) 33.39

seminal vesicle NEC 60.79

Senning (correction of transposition of great vessels) 35.91

Sever (division of soft tissue of arm) 83.19

Sewell (heart) 36.2

sex transformation NEC 64.5

Sharrard (iliopsoas muscle transfer) 83.77

shelf (hip arthroplasty) 81.40

Shirodkar (encirclement suture, cervix) 67.5

sigmoid NEC 46.99

Silver (bunionectomy) 77.59

Sistrunk (excision of thyroglossal cyst) 06.7

Skene's gland NEC 71.8

skin NEC 86.99

skull NEC 02.99

sling
eyelid
fascia lata, palpebral 08.36
frontalis fascial 08.32
levator muscle 08.33
orbicularis muscle 08.36
palpebrae ligament, fascia lata 08.36
tarsus muscle 08.35
fascial (fascia lata)
eye 08.32
for facial weakness (trigeminal nerve paralysis) 86.81
palpebral ligament 08.36
tongue 25.59
tongue (fascial) 25.59
urethra (suprapubic) 59.4
retropubic 59.5
urethrovesical 59.5

Operation (*Continued*)

Slocum (pes anserinus transfer) 81.47

Sluder (tonsillectomy) 28.2

Smith (open osteotomy of mandible) 76.62

Smith-Peterson (radiocarpal arthrodesis) 81.25

Smithwick (sympathectomy) 05.29

Soave (endorectal pull-through) 48.41

soft tissue NEC 83.99
hand 82.99

Sonneberg (inferior maxillary neurectomy) 04.07

Sorondo-Ferré (hindquarter amputation) 84.19

Soutter (iliac crest fasciotomy) 83.14

Spalding-Richardson (uterine suspension) 69.22

spermatic cord NEC 63.99

sphincter of Oddi NEC 51.89

spinal (canal) (cord) (structures) NEC 03.99

Spinelli (correction of inverted uterus) 75.93

Spivack (permanent gastrostomy) 43.19

spleen NEC 41.99

S.P. Rogers (knee disarticulation) 84.16

Ssabanejew-Frank (permanent gastrostomy) 43.19

Stacke (simple mastoidectomy) 20.41

Stallard (conjunctivocystorhinostomy) 09.82
with insertion of tube or stent 09.83

Stamm (-Kader) (temporary gastrostomy) 43.19

Steinberg 44.5

Steindler
fascia stripping (for cavus deformity) 83.14
flexorplasty (elbow) 83.77
muscle transfer 83.77

sterilization NEC
female - *see also* specific operation 66.39
male - *see also* Ligation, vas deferens 63.70

Stewart (renal plication with pyeloplasty) 55.87

stomach NEC 44.99

Stone (anoplasty) 49.79

Strassman (metroplasty) 69.49
metroplasty (Jones modification) 69.49
uterus 68.22

Strayer (gastrocnemius recession) 83.72

stress incontinence - *see* Repair, stress incontinence

Stromeyer-Little (hepatotomy) 50.0

Strong (unbridling of celiac artery axis) 39.91

Sturmdorf (conization of cervix) 67.2

subcutaneous tissue NEC 86.99

sublingual gland or duct NEC 26.99

submaxillary gland or duct NEC 26.99

Summerskill (dacryocystorhinostomy by intubation) 09.81

Surmay (jejunostomy) 46.39

Swenson
bladder reconstruction 57.87
proctectomy 48.49

Swinney (urethral reconstruction) 58.46

Vol. 3

Operation *(Continued)*
  Syme
    ankle amputation through malleoli of tibia and fibula 84.14
    urethrotomy, external 58.0
  sympathetic nerve NEC 05.89
  Taarnhoj (trigeminal nerve root decompression) 04.41
  Tack (sacculotomy) 20.79
  Talma-Morison (omentopexy) 54.74
  Tanner (devascularization of stomach) 44.99
  TAPVC NEC 35.82
  tarsus NEC 08.99
    muscle sling 08.35
  tendon NEC 83.99
    extraocular NEC 15.9
    hand NEC 82.99
  testis NEC 62.99
  tetralogy of Fallot
    partial repair - *see* specific procedure
    total (one-stage) 35.81
  Thal (repair of esophageal stricture) 42.85
  thalamus (stereotactic) 01.41
  Thiersch
    anus 49.79
    skin graft 86.69
      hand 86.62
  Thompson
    cleft lip repair 27.54
    correction of lymphedema 40.9
    quadricepsplasty 83.86
    thumb apposition with bone graft 82.69
  thoracic duct NEC 40.69
  thorax NEC 34.99
  Thorek (partial cholecystectomy) 51.21
  three-snip, punctum 09.51
  thymus NEC 07.99
  thyroid gland NEC 06.98
  TKP (thermokeratoplasty) 11.74
  Tomkins (metroplasty) 69.49
  tongue NEC 25.99
    flap, palate 27.62
    tie 25.91
  tonsil NEC 28.99
  Torek (-Bevan) (orchidopexy) (first stage) (second stage) 62.5
  Torkildsen (ventriculocisternal shunt) 02.2
  Torpin (cul-de-sac resection) 70.92
  Toti (dacryocystorhinostomy) 09.81
  Touchas 86.83
  Touroff (ligation of subclavian artery) 38.85
  trabeculae corneae cordis (heart) NEC 35.35
  trachea NEC 31.99
  Trauner (lingual sulcus extension) 24.91
  truncus arteriosus NEC 35.83
  Tsuge (macrodactyly repair) 82.83
  Tudor "rabbit ear" (anterior urethropexy) 59.79
  Tuffier
    apicolysis of lung 33.39
    vaginal hysterectomy 68.59
      laparoscopically assisted (LAVH) 68.51
  tunica vaginalis NEC 61.99
  Turco (release of joint capsules in clubfoot) 80.48
  Uchida (tubal ligation with or without fimbriectomy) 66.32

Operation *(Continued)*
  umbilicus NEC 54.99
  urachus NEC 57.51
  Urban (mastectomy) (unilateral) 85.47
    bilateral 85.48
  ureter NEC 56.99
  urethra NEC 58.99
  urinary system NEC 59.99
  uterus NEC 69.99
    supporting structures NEC 69.98
  uvula NEC 27.79
  vagina NEC 70.91
  vascular NEC 39.99
  vas deferens NEC 63.99
    ligation NEC 63.71
  vein NEC 39.99
  vena cava sieve 38.7
  vertebra NEC 78.49
  vesical (bladder) NEC 57.99
  vessel NEC 39.99
    cardiac NEC 36.99
  Vicq d'Azyr (larynx) 31.1
  Vidal (varicocele ligation) 63.1
  Vineberg (implantation of mammary artery into ventricle) 36.2
  vitreous NEC 14.79
  vocal cord NEC 31.98
  von Kraske (proctectomy) 48.64
  Voss (hanging hip operation) 83.19
  Vulpius (-Compere) (lengthening of gastrocnemius muscle) 83.85
  vulva NEC 71.8
  Ward-Mayo (vaginal hysterectomy) 68.59
    laparoscopically assisted (LAVH) 68.51
  Wardill (cleft palate) 27.62
  Waters (extraperitoneal cesarean section) 74.2
  Waterston (aorta-right pulmonary artery anastomosis) 39.0
  Watkins (-Wertheim) (uterus interposition) 69.21
  Watson-Jones
    hip arthrodesis 81.21
    reconstruction of lateral ligaments, ankle 81.49
    shoulder arthrodesis (extra-articular) 81.23
    tenoplasty 83.88
  Weir
    appendicostomy 47.91
    correction of nostrils 21.86
  Wertheim (radical hysterectomy) 68.6
  West (dacryocystorhinostomy) 09.81
  Wheeler
    entropion repair 08.44
    halving procedure (eyelid) 08.24
  Whipple (radical pancreaticoduodenectomy) 52.7
    Child modification (radical subtotal pancreatectomy) 52.53
    Rodney Smith modification (radical subtotal pancreatectomy) 52.53
  White (lengthening of tendo calcaneus by incomplete tenotomy) 83.11
  Whitehead
    glossectomy, radical 25.4
    hemorrhoidectomy 49.46
  Whitman
    foot stabilization (talectomy) 77.98
    hip reconstruction 81.40
    repair of serratus anterior muscle 83.87

Operation *(Continued)*
  Whitman *(Continued)*
    talectomy 77.98
    trochanter wedge osteotomy 77.25
  Wier (entropion repair) 08.44
  Williams-Richardson (vaginal construction) 70.61
  Wilms (thoracoplasty) 33.34
  Wilson (angulation osteotomy for hallux valgus) 77.51
  window
    antrum (nasal sinus) - *see* Antrotomy, maxillary
    aorticopulmonary 39.59
    bone cortex - *see also* Incision, bone 77.10
      facial 76.09
    nasoantral - *see* Antrotomy, maxillary
    pericardium 37.12
    pleural 34.09
  Winiwarter (cholecystoenterostomy) 51.32
  Witzel (temporary gastrostomy) 43.19
  Woodward (release of high riding scapula) 81.83
  Young
    epispadias repair 58.45
    tendon transfer (anterior tibialis) (repair of flat foot) 83.75
  Yount (division of iliotibial band) 83.14
  Zancolli
    capsuloplasty 81.72
    tendon transfer (biceps) 82.56
  Ziegler (iridectomy) 12.14
Operculectomy 24.6
Ophthalmectomy 16.49
  with implant (into Tenon's capsule) 16.42
  with attachment of muscles 16.41
Ophthalmoscopy 16.21
Opponensplasty (hand) 82.56
Orbitomaxillectomy, radical 16.51
Orbitotomy (anterior) (frontal) (temporofrontal) (transfrontal) NEC 16.09
  with
    bone flap 16.01
    insertion of implant 16.02
  Kroenlein (lateral) 16.01
  lateral 16.01
Orchidectomy (with epididymectomy) (unilateral) 62.3
  bilateral (radical) 62.41
  remaining or solitary testis 62.42
Orchidopexy 62.5
Orchidoplasty 62.69
Orchidorrhaphy 62.61
Orchidotomy 62.0
Orchiectomy (with epididymectomy) (unilateral) 62.3
  bilateral (radical) 62.41
  remaining or solitary testis 62.42
Orchiopexy 62.5
Orchioplasty 62.69
Orthoroentgenography - *see* Radiography
Oscar Miller operation (midtarsal arthrodesis) 81.14
Osmond-Clark operation (soft tissue release with peroneus brevis tendon transfer) 83.75
Ossiculectomy NEC 19.3
  with
    stapedectomy - *see also* Stapedectomy 19.19

P

Pacemaker
cardiac - *see also* Insertion, pacemaker, cardiac
intraoperative (temporary) 39.64
temporary (during and immediately following cardiac surgery) 39.64
Packing - *see also* Insertion, pack
auditory canal 96.11
nose, for epistaxis (anterior) 21.01
posterior (and anterior) 21.02
rectal 96.19
sella turcica 07.79
vaginal 96.14
Palatoplasty 27.69
for cleft palate 27.62
secondary or subsequent 27.63
Palatorrhaphy 27.61
for cleft palate 27.62
Pallidectomy 01.42
Pallidoansotomy 01.42
Pallidotomy 01.42
Panas operation (linear proctotomy) 48.0
Pancoast operation (division of trigeminal nerve at foramen ovale) 04.02
Pancreatectomy (total) (with synchronous duodenectomy) 52.6
partial NEC 52.59
distal (tail) (with part of body) 52.52
proximal (head) (with part of body) (with synchronous duodenectomy) 52.51
radical 52.53
subtotal 52.53
radical 52.7
subtotal 52.53
Pancreaticocystoduodenostomy 52.4
Pancreaticocystoenterostomy 52.4
Pancreaticocystogastrostomy 52.4
Pancreaticocystojejunostomy 52.4
Pancreaticoduodenectomy (total) 52.6
partial NEC 52.59
proximal 52.51
radical subtotal 52.53
radical (one-stage) (two-stage) 52.7
subtotal 52.53
Pancreaticoduodenostomy 52.96
Pancreaticoenterostomy 52.96
Pancreaticogastrostomy 52.96
Pancreaticoileostomy 52.96
Pancreaticojejunostomy 52.96
Pancreatoduodenectomy (total) 52.6
partial NEC 52.59
radical (one-stage) (two-stage) 52.7
subtotal 52.53
Pancreatogram 87.66
endoscopic retrograde (ERP) 52.13
Pancreatolithotomy 52.09
endoscopic 52.94
Pancreatotomy 52.09
Pancreolithotomy 52.09
endoscopic 52.94
Panendoscopy 57.32
specified site, other than bladder - *see* Endoscopy, by site
through artificial stoma 57.31
Panhysterectomy (abdominal) 68.4
vaginal 68.59
laparoscopically assisted (LAVH) 68.51
Panniculectomy 86.83
Panniculotomy 86.83

Pantaloon operation (revision of gastric anastomosis) 44.5
Papillectomy, anal 49.39
endoscopic 49.31
Papillotomy (pancreas) 51.82
endoscopic 51.85
Paquin operation (ureteroneocystostomy) 56.74
Paracentesis
abdominal (percutaneous) 54.91
anterior chamber, eye 12.91
bladder 57.11
cornea 12.91
eye (anterior chamber) 12.91
thoracic, thoracis 34.91
tympanum 20.09
with intubation 20.01
Parasitology - *see* Examination, microscopic
Parathyroidectomy (partial) (subtotal) NEC 06.89
complete 06.81
ectopic 06.89
global removal 06.81
mediastinal 06.89
total 06.81
Parenteral nutrition, total 99.15
peripheral 99.15
Parotidectomy 26.30
complete 26.32
partial 26.31
radical 26.32
Partsch operation (marsupialization of dental cyst) 24.4
Passage - *see* Insertion and Intubation
Passage of sounds, urethra 58.6
Patch
blood, spinal (epidural) 03.95
graft - *see* Graft
spinal, blood (epidural) 03.95
subdural, brain 02.12
Patellapexy 78.46
Patellaplasty NEC 78.46
Patellectomy 77.96
partial 77.86
Pattee operation (auditory canal) 18.6
Pectenotomy - *see also* Sphincterotomy, anal 49.59
Pedicle flap - *see* Graft, skin, pedicle
Peet operation (splanchnic resection) 05.29
PEG (percutaneous endoscopic gastrostomy) 43.11
PEJ (percutaneous endoscopic jejunostomy) 46.32
Pelvectomy, kidney (partial) 55.4
Pelvimetry 88.25
gynecological 89.26
Pelviolithotomy 55.11
Pelvioplasty, kidney 55.87
Pelviostomy 55.12
closure 55.82
Pelviotomy 77.39
to assist delivery 73.94
Pelvi-ureteroplasty 55.87
Pemberton operation
osteotomy of ilium 77.39
rectum (mobilization and fixation for prolapse repair) 48.76
Penectomy 64.3
Pereyra operation (paraurethral suspension) 59.6
Perforation
stapes footplate 19.0

Perfusion NEC 39.97
carotid artery 39.97
coronary artery 39.97
for
chemotherapy NEC 99.25
hormone therapy NEC 99.24
head 39.97
hyperthermic (lymphatic), localized region or site 93.35
intestine (large) (local) 46.96
small 46.95
kidney, local 55.95
limb (lower) (upper) 39.97
liver, localized 50.93
neck 39.97
subarachnoid (spinal cord) (refrigerated saline) 03.92
total body 39.96
Pericardiectomy 37.31
Pericardiocentesis 37.0
Pericardiolysis 37.12
Pericardioplasty 37.4
Pericardiorrhaphy 37.4
Pericardiostomy (tube) 37.12
Pericardiotomy 37.12
Peridectomy 10.31
Perilimbal suction 89.11
Perimetry 95.05
Perineoplasty 71.79
Perineorrhaphy 71.71
obstetrical laceration (current) 75.69
Perineotomy (nonobstetrical) 71.09
to assist delivery - *see* Episiotomy
Periosteotomy - *see also* Incision, bone 77.10
facial bone 76.09
Perirectofistulectomy 48.93
Peritectomy 10.31
Peritomy 10.1
Peritoneocentesis 54.91
Peritoneoscopy 54.21
Peritoneotomy 54.19
Peritoneumectomy 54.4
Phacoemulsification (ultrasonic) (with aspiration) 13.41
Phacofragmentation (mechanical) (with aspiration) 13.43
posterior route 13.42
ultrasonic 13.41
Phalangectomy (partial) 77.89
claw toe 77.57
cockup toe 77.58
hammer toe 77.56
overlapping toe 77.58
total 77.99
Phalangization (fifth metacarpal) 82.81
Pharyngeal flap operation (cleft palate repair) 27.62
secondary or subsequent 27.63
Pharyngectomy (partial) 29.33
with laryngectomy 30.3
Pharyngogram 87.09
contrast 87.06
Pharyngolaryngectomy 30.3
Pharyngoplasty (with silastic implant) 29.4
for cleft palate 27.62
secondary or subsequent 27.63
Pharyngorrhaphy 29.51
for cleft palate 27.62
Pharyngoscopy 29.11
Pharyngotomy 29.0
Phenopeel (skin) 86.24

ICD-9-CM

P, Q

Vol. 3

R

Rachicentesis 03.31
Rachitomy 03.09
Radiation therapy - *see also* Therapy, radiation
   teleradiotherapy - *see* Teleradiotherapy
Radical neck dissection - *see* Dissection, neck
Radicotomy 03.1
Radiculectomy 03.1
Radiculotomy 03.1
Radiography (diagnostic) NEC 88.39
   abdomen, abdominal (flat plate) NEC 88.19
     wall (soft tissue) NEC 88.09
   adenoid 87.09
   ankle (skeletal) 88.28
     soft tissue 88.37
   bone survey 88.31
   bronchus 87.49
   chest (routine) 87.44
     wall NEC 87.39
   clavicle 87.43
   contrast (air) (gas) (radio-opaque substance) NEC
     abdominal wall 88.03
     arteries (by fluoroscopy) - *see* Arteriography
     bile ducts NEC 87.54
     bladder NEC 87.77
     brain 87.02
     breast 87.35
     bronchus NEC (transcricoid) 87.32
       endotracheal 87.31
     epididymis 87.93
     esophagus 87.61
     fallopian tubes
       gas 87.82
       opaque dye 87.83
     fistula (sinus tract) - *see also* Radiography, contrast, by site
       abdominal wall 88.03
       chest wall 87.38
     gallbladder NEC 87.59
     intervertebral disc(s) 87.21
     joints 88.32
     larynx 87.07
     lymph - *see* Lymphangiogram
     mammary ducts 87.35
     mediastinum 87.33
     nasal sinuses 87.15
     nasolacrimal ducts 87.05
     nasopharynx 87.06
     orbit 87.14
     pancreas 87.66
     pelvis
       gas 88.12
       opaque dye 88.11
     peritoneum NEC 88.13
     retroperitoneum NEC 88.15
     seminal vesicles 87.91
     sinus tract - *see also* Radiography, contrast, by site
       abdominal wall 88.03
       chest wall 87.38
       nose 87.15
     skull 87.02
     spinal disc(s) 87.21
     trachea 87.32
     uterus
       gas 87.82
       opaque dye 87.83

Radiography *(Continued)*
   contrast *(Continued)*
     vas deferens 87.94
     veins (by fluoroscopy) - *see* Phlebography
     vena cava (inferior) (superior) 88.51
   dental NEC 87.12
   diaphragm 87.49
   digestive tract NEC 87.69
     barium swallow 87.61
     lower GI series 87.64
     small bowel series 87.63
     upper GI series 87.62
   elbow (skeletal) 88.22
     soft tissue 88.35
   epididymis NEC 87.95
   esophagus 87.69
     barium-swallow 87.61
   eye 95.14
   face, head, and neck 87.09
   facial bones 87.16
   fallopian tubes 87.85
   foot 88.28
   forearm (skeletal) 88.22
     soft tissue 88.35
   frontal area, facial 87.16
   genital organs
     female NEC 87.89
     male NEC 87.99
   hand (skeletal) 88.23
     soft tissue 88.35
   head NEC 87.09
   heart 87.49
   hip (skeletal) 88.26
     soft tissue 88.37
   intestine NEC 87.65
   kidney-ureter-bladder (KUB) 87.79
   knee (skeletal) 88.27
     soft tissue 88.37
   KUB (kidney-ureter-bladder) 87.79
   larynx 87.09
   lower leg (skeletal) 88.27
     soft tissue 88.37
   lower limb (skeletal) NEC 88.29
     soft tissue NEC 88.37
   lung 87.49
   mandible 87.16
   maxilla 87.16
   mediastinum 87.49
   nasal sinuses 87.16
   nasolacrimal duct 87.09
   nasopharynx 87.09
   neck NEC 87.09
   nose 87.16
   orbit 87.16
   pelvis (skeletal) 88.26
     pelvimetry 88.25
     soft tissue 88.19
   prostate NEC 87.92
   retroperitoneum NEC 88.16
   ribs 87.43
   root canal 87.12
   salivary gland 87.09
   seminal vesicles NEC 87.92
   shoulder (skeletal) 88.21
     soft tissue 88.35
   skeletal NEC 88.33
     series (whole or complete) 88.31
   skull (lateral, sagittal or tangential projection) NEC 87.17
   spine NEC 87.29
     cervical 87.22
     lumbosacral 87.24
     sacrococcygeal 87.24

Radiography *(Continued)*
   spine NEC *(Continued)*
     thoracic 87.23
   sternum 87.43
   supraorbital area 87.16
   symphysis menti 87.16
   teeth NEC 87.12
     full-mouth 87.11
   thigh (skeletal) 88.27
     soft tissue 88.37
   thyroid region 87.09
   tonsils and adenoids 87.09
   trachea 87.49
   ultrasonic - *see* Ultrasonography
   upper arm (skeletal) 88.21
     soft tissue 88.35
   upper limb (skeletal) NEC 88.24
     soft tissue NEC 88.35
   urinary system NEC 87.79
   uterus NEC 87.85
     gravid 87.81
   uvula 87.09
   vas deferens NEC 87.95
   wrist 88.23
   zygomaticomaxillary complex 87.16
Radioisotope
   scanning - *see* Scan, radioisotope
   therapy - *see* Therapy, radioisotope
Radiology
   diagnostic - *see* Radiography
   therapeutic - *see* Therapy, radiation
Radiosurgery, stereotactic 92.30 ◀◀
   cobalt 60 92.32 ◀
   linear accelerator (LINAC) 92.31 ◀
   multi-source 92.32 ◀
   particle beam 92.33 ◀
   particulate 92.33 ◀
   radiosurgery NEC 92.39 ◀
   single source photon 92.31 ◀
Raising, pedicle graft 86.71
Ramadier operation (intrapetrosal drainage) 20.22
Ramisection (sympathetic) 05.0
Ramstedt operation (pyloromyotomy) (with wedge resection) 43.3
Range of motion testing 93.05
Rankin operation
   exteriorization of intestine 46.03
   proctectomy (complete) 48.5
Rashkind operation (balloon septostomy) 35.41
Rastelli operation (creation of conduit between right ventricle and pulmonary artery) 35.92
   in repair of
     pulmonary artery atresia 35.92
     transposition of great vessels 35.92
     truncus arteriosus 35.83
Raz-Pereyra procedure (bladder neck suspension) 59.79
RCSA (radical cryosurgical ablation) of prostate 60.62
Readjustment - *see* Adjustment
Reamputation, stump 84.3
Reanastomosis - *see* Anastomosis
Reattachment
   amputated ear 18.72
   ankle 84.27
   arm (upper) NEC 84.24
   choroid and retina NEC 14.59
     by
       cryotherapy 14.52
       diathermy 14.51

Removal *(Continued)*
  calculus *(Continued)*
    prostate 60.0
    salivary gland (by incision) 26.0
      by probe 26.91
    ureter (by incision) 56.2
      without incision 56.0
    urethra (by incision) 58.0
      without incision 58.6
  caliper tongs (skull) 02.95
  cannula
    for extracorporeal membrane oxygenation (ECMO) - *omit code*
  cardiac pacemaker (device) (initial) (permanent) 37.89
    with replacement (by)
      dual chamber device 37.87
      single-chamber device 37.85
        rate responsive 37.86
  cardioverter/defibrillator pulse generator without replacement 37.99
  cast 97.88
    with reapplication 97.13
      lower limb 97.12
      upper limb 97.11
  catheter (indwelling) - *see also* Removal, tube
    bladder 97.64
    middle ear (tympanum) 20.1
    ureter 97.62
    urinary 97.64
    ventricular (cerebral) 02.43
      with synchronous replacement 02.42
  cerclage material, cervix 69.96
  cerumen, ear 96.52
  corneal epithelium 11.41
    for smear or culture 11.21
  coronary artery obstruction (thrombus) 36.09
    direct intracoronary artery infusion 36.04
    open chest approach 36.03
    percutaneous transluminal (balloon) (single vessel) 36.01
      with thrombolytic agent infusion 36.02
    multiple vessels 36.05
  Crutchfield tongs (skull) 02.95
    with synchronous replacement 02.94
  cyst - *see also* Excision, lesion, by site
    dental 24.4
    lung 32.29
      endoscopic 32.28
  cystic duct remnant 51.61
  decidua (by)
    aspiration curettage 69.52
    curettage (D and C) 69.02
    manual 75.4
  dental wiring (immobilization device) 97.33
    orthodontic 24.8
  device (therapeutic) NEC 97.89
    abdomen NEC 97.86
    digestive system NEC 97.59
    drainage - *see* Removal, tube
    external fixation device 97.88
      mandibular NEC 97.36
      minifixator (bone) - *see* category 78.6
    for musculoskeletal immobilization NEC 97.88
    genital tract NEC 97.79

Removal *(Continued)*
  device *(Continued)*
    head and neck NEC 97.39
    intrauterine contraceptive 97.71
    thorax NEC 97.49
    trunk NEC 97.87
    urinary system NEC 97.69
  diaphragm, vagina 97.73
  drainage device - *see* Removal, tube
  dye, spinal canal 03.31
  ectopic fetus (from) 66.02
    abdominal cavity 74.3
    extraperitoneal (intraligamentous) 74.3
    fallopian tube (by salpingostomy) 66.02
      by salpingotomy 66.01
      with salpingectomy 66.62
    intraligamentous 74.3
    ovarian 74.3
    peritoneal (following uterine or tubal rupture) 74.3
    site NEC 74.3
    tubal (by salpingostomy) 66.02
      by salpingotomy 66.01
      with salpingectomy 66.62
  electrodes
    bone growth stimulator - *see* category 78.6
    brain 01.22
      depth 01.22
        with synchronous replacement 02.93
      foramen ovale 01.22
        with synchronous replacement 02.93
      sphenoidal - *omit code*
      with synchronous replacement 02.96
    cardiac pacemaker (atrial) (transvenous) (ventricular) 37.77
      with replacement 37.76
    depth 01.22
      with synchronous replacement 02.93
    epicardial (myocardial) 37.77
      with replacement (by)
        atrial and/or ventricular lead(s) (electrode) 37.76
        epicardial lead 37.74
    epidural pegs 01.22
      with synchronous replacement 02.93
    foramen ovale 01.22
      with synchronous replacement 02.93
    intracranial 01.22
      with synchronous replacement 02.93
    peripheral nerve 04.93
      with synchronous replacement 04.92
    sphenoidal - *omit code*
      with synchronous replacement 02.96
    spinal 03.94
      with synchronous replacement 03.93
    temporary transvenous pacemaker system - *omit code*
  electroencephalographic receiver (brain) (intracranial) 01.22
    with synchronous replacement 02.93

Removal *(Continued)*
  electronic
    stimulator
      bladder 57.98
      bone 78.6
      brain 01.22
        with synchronous replacement 02.93
      intracranial 01.22
        with synchronous replacement 02.93
      peripheral nerve 04.93
        with synchronous replacement 04.92
      skeletal muscle 83.93
        with synchronous replacement 83.92
      spinal 03.94
        with synchronous replacement 03.93
      ureter 56.94
  electrostimulator - *see* Removal, electronic, stimulator, by site
  embolus 38.00
    with endarterectomy - *see* Endarterectomy
    abdominal
      artery 38.06
      vein 38.07
    aorta (arch) (ascending) (descending) 38.04
    arteriovenous shunt or cannula 39.49
    bovine graft 39.49
    head and neck vessel NEC 38.02
    intracranial vessel NEC 38.01
    lower limb
      artery 38.08
      vein 38.09
    pulmonary (artery) (vein) 38.05
    thoracic vessel NEC 38.05
    upper limb (artery) (vein) 38.03
  embryo - *see* Removal, ectopic fetus
  encircling tube, eye (episcleral) 14.6
  epithelial downgrowth, anterior chamber 12.93
  external fixation device 97.88
    mandibular NEC 97.36
    minifixator (bone) - *see* category 78.6
  extrauterine embryo - *see* Removal, ectopic fetus
  eyeball 16.49
    with implant 16.42
      with attachment of muscles 16.41
  fallopian tube - *see* Salpingectomy
  feces (impacted) (by flushing) (manual) 96.38
  fetus, ectopic - *see* Removal, ectopic fetus
  fingers, supernumerary 86.26
  fixation device
    external 97.88
      mandibular NEC 97.36
      minifixator (bone) - *see* category 78.6
    internal 78.60
      carpal, metacarpal 78.64
      clavicle 78.61
      facial (bone) 76.97
      femur 78.65
      fibula 78.67
      humerus 78.62
      patella 78.66
      pelvic 78.69
      phalanges (foot) (hand) 78.69

ICD-9-CM

R

Vol. 3

◀▶ **New Code**   ⬅▬▬▶ **Revised Code**

ICD-9-CM

Vol. 3

ICD-9-CM

R

Vol. 3

ICD-9-CM
Vol. 3

ICD-9-CM

R

Vol. 3

ICD-9-CM

R

Vol. 3

◀▶   **New Code**   ◀▥▥ ▥▥▶   **Revised Code**

ICD-9-CM

S

Vol. 3

T

Taarnhoj operation (trigeminal nerve root decompression) 04.41
Tack operation (sacculotomy) 20.79
Take-down
  anastomosis
    arterial 39.49
    blood vessel 39.49
    gastric, gastrointestinal 44.5
    intestine 46.93
    stomach 44.5
    vascular 39.49
    ventricular 02.43
  arterial bypass 39.49
  arteriovenous shunt 39.43
    with creation of new shunt 39.42
  cecostomy 46.52
  colostomy 46.52
  duodenostomy 46.51
  enterostomy 46.50
  esophagostomy 42.83
  gastroduodenostomy 44.5
  gastrojejunostomy 44.5
  ileostomy 46.51
  intestinal stoma 46.50
    large 46.52
    small 46.51
  jejunoileal bypass 46.93
  jejunostomy 46.51
  laryngostomy 31.62
  sigmoidostomy 46.52
  stoma
    bile duct 51.79
    bladder 57.82
    bronchus 33.42
    common duct 51.72
    esophagus 42.83
    gallbladder 51.92
    hepatic duct 51.79
    intestine 46.50
      large 46.52
      small 46.51
    kidney 55.82
    larynx 31.62
    rectum 48.72
    stomach 44.62
    thorax 34.72
    trachea 31.72
    ureter 56.83
    urethra 58.42
  systemic-pulmonary artery anastomosis 39.49
    in total repair of tetralogy of Fallot 35.81
  tracheostomy 31.72
  vascular anastomosis or bypass 39.49
  ventricular shunt (cerebral) 02.43
Talectomy 77.98
Talma-Morison operation (omentopexy) 54.74
Tamponade
  esophageal 96.06
  intrauterine (nonobstetric) 69.91
    after delivery or abortion 75.8
    antepartum 73.1
  vagina 96.14
    after delivery or abortion 75.8
    antepartum 73.1
Tanner operation (devascularization of stomach) 44.99
Tap
  abdomen 54.91

Tap (*Continued*)
  chest 34.91
  cisternal 01.01
  cranial 01.09
  joint 81.91
  lumbar (diagnostic) (removal of dye) 03.31
  perilymphatic 20.79
  spinal (diagnostic) 03.31
  subdural (through fontanel) 01.09
  thorax 34.91
Tarsectomy 08.20
  de Grandmont 08.35
Tarsoplasty - *see also* Reconstruction, eyelid 08.70
Tarsorrhaphy (lateral) 08.52
  division or severing 08.02
Tattooing
  cornea 11.91
  skin 86.02
Tautening, eyelid for entropion 08.42
Telemetry (cardiac) 89.54
Teleradiotherapy
  beta particles 92.25
  Betatron 92.24
  cobalt-60 92.23
  electrons 92.25
  iodine-125 92.23
  linear accelerator 92.24
  neutrons 92.26
  particulate radiation NEC 92.26
  photons 92.24
  protons 92.26
  radioactive cesium 92.23
  radioisotopes NEC 92.23
Temperament assessment 94.02
Temperature gradient study - *see also* Thermography 88.89
Tendinoplasty - *see* Repair, tendon
Tendinosuture (immediate) (primary) - *see also* Suture, tendon 83.64
  hand - *see also* Suture, tendon, hand 82.45
Tendolysis 83.91
  hand 82.91
Tendoplasty - *see* Repair, tendon
Tenectomy 83.39
  eye 15.13
    levator palpebrae 08.33
    multiple (two or more tendons) 15.3
  hand 82.29
  levator palpebrae 08.33
  tendon sheath 83.31
    hand 82.21
Tenodesis (tendon fixation to skeletal attachment) 83.88
  Fowler 82.85
  hand 82.85
Tenolysis 83.91
  hand 82.91
Tenomyoplasty - *see also* Repair, tendon 83.88
  hand - *see also* Repair, tendon, hand 82.86
Tenomyotomy - *see* Tenonectomy
Tenonectomy 83.42
  for graft 83.41
    hand 82.32
  hand 82.33
    for graft 82.32
Tenontomyoplasty - *see* Repair, tendon
Tenontoplasty - *see* Repair, tendon
Tenoplasty - *see also* Repair, tendon 83.88

Tenoplasty (*Continued*)
  hand - *see also* Repair, tendon, hand 82.86
Tenorrhaphy - *see also* Suture, tendon 83.64
  hand - *see also* Suture, tendon, hand 82.45
  to skeletal attachment 83.88
    hand 82.85
Tenosuspension 83.88
  hand 82.86
Tenosuture - *see also* Suture, tendon 83.64
  hand - *see also* Suture, tendon, hand 82.45
  to skeletal attachment 83.88
    hand 82.85
Tenosynovectomy 83.42
  hand 82.33
Tenotomy 83.13
  Achilles tendon 83.11
  adductor (hip) (subcutaneous) 83.12
  eye 15.12
    levator palpebrae 08.38
    multiple (two or more tendons) 15.4
  hand 82.11
  levator palpebrae 08.38
  pectoralis minor tendon (decompression, thoracic outlet) 83.13
  stapedius 19.0
  tensor tympani 19.0
Tenovaginotomy - *see* Tenotomy
Tensing, orbicularis oculi 08.59
Termination of pregnancy
  by
    aspiration curettage 69.51
    dilation and curettage 69.01
    hysterectomy - *see* Hysterectomy
    hysterotomy 74.91
    intra-amniotic injection (saline) 75.0
Test, testing (for)
  14 C-Urea breath 89.39
  auditory function NEC 95.46
  Bender Visual-Motor Gestalt 94.02
  Benton Visual Retention 94.02
  cardiac (vascular)
    function NEC 89.59
    stress 89.44
      bicycle ergometer 89.43
      Masters' two-step 89.42
      treadmill 89.41
  Denver developmental (screening) 94.02
  fetus, fetal
    nonstress (fetal activity acceleration determinations) 75.35
    oxytocin challenge (contraction stress) 75.35
    sensitivity (to oxytocin) - *omit code*
  function
    cardiac NEC 89.59
    hearing NEC 95.46
    muscle (by)
      electromyography 93.08
      manual 93.04
    neurologic NEC 89.15
    vestibular 95.46
      clinical 95.44
  glaucoma NEC 95.26
  hearing 95.47
    clinical NEC 95.42
  intelligence 94.01
  internal jugular-subclavian venous reflux 89.62

ICD-9-CM

T

Vol. 3

U

V

ICD-9-CM

V–Z

Vol. 3

◀▶ **New Code**   ◀▥ ▥▶ **Revised Code**

TABULAR LIST OF PROCEDURES

1. OPERATIONS ON THE NERVOUS SYSTEM (01–05)

● **01   Incision and excision of skull, brain, and cerebral meninges**

  ● **01.0   Cranial puncture**

    01.01   Cisternal puncture
       Cisternal tap

    Excludes   *pneumocisternogram (87.02)*

    01.02   Ventriculopuncture through previously implanted catheter
       Puncture of ventricular shunt tubing

    01.09   Other cranial puncture
       Aspiration of:
         subarachnoid space
         subdural space
       Cranial aspiration NOS
       Puncture of anterior fontanel
       Subdural tap (through fontanel)

  ● **01.1   Diagnostic procedures on skull, brain, and cerebral meninges**

    01.11   Closed [percutaneous] [needle] biopsy of cerebral meninges
       Burr hole approach

    ✖ **01.12   Open biopsy of cerebral meninges**

    01.13   Closed [percutaneous] [needle] biopsy of brain
       Burr hole approach
       Stereotactic method

    ✖ **01.14   Open biopsy of brain**

    ✖ **01.15   Biopsy of skull**

    ✖ **01.18   Other diagnostic procedures on brain and cerebral meninges**

    Excludes   *cerebral:*
         arteriography (88.41)
         thermography (88.81)
       contrast radiogram of brain (87.01–87.02)
       echoencephalogram (88.71)
       electroencephalogram (89.14)
       microscopic examination of specimen from nervous system and of spinal fluid (90.01–90.09)
       neurologic examination (89.13)
       phlebography of head and neck (88.61)
       pneumoencephalogram (87.01)
       radioisotope scan:
         cerebral (92.11)
         head NEC (92.12)
       tomography of head:
         C.A.T. scan (87.03)
         other (87.04)

    ✖ **01.19   Other diagnostic procedures on skull**

    Excludes   *transillumination of skull (89.16)*
       x-ray of skull (87.17)

  ● **01.2   Craniotomy and craniectomy**

    Excludes   *decompression of skull fracture (02.02)*
       exploration of orbit (16.01–16.09)
       that as operative approach—omit code

    ✖ **01.21   Incision and drainage of cranial sinus**

    ✖ **01.22   Removal of intracranial neurostimulator**

    Excludes   *removal with synchronous replacement (02.93)*

    ✖ **01.23   Reopening of craniotomy site**

    ✖ **01.24   Other craniotomy**
       Cranial:
         decompression
         exploration
         trephination
       Craniotomy NOS
       Craniotomy with removal of:
         epidural abscess
         extradural hematoma
         foreign body of skull

    Excludes   *removal of foreign body with incision into brain (01.39)*

    ✖ **01.25   Other craniectomy**
       Debridement of skull NOS
       Sequestrectomy of skull

    Excludes   *debridement of compound fracture of skull (02.02)*
       strip craniectomy (02.01)

  ● **01.3   Incision of brain and cerebral meninges**

    ✖ **01.31   Incision of cerebral meninges**
       Drainage of:
         intracranial hygroma
         subarachnoid abscess (cerebral)
         subdural empyema

    ✖ **01.32   Lobotomy and tractotomy**
       Division of:
         brain tissue
         cerebral tracts
       Percutaneous (radiofrequency) cingulotomy

    ✖ **01.39   Other incision of brain**
       Amygdalohippocampotomy
       Drainage of intracerebral hematoma
       Incision of brain NOS

    Excludes   *division of cortical adhesions (02.91)*

  ● **01.4   Operations on thalamus and globus pallidus**

    ✖ **01.41   Operations on thalamus**
       Chemothalamectomy
       Thalamotomy

    ✖ **01.42   Operations on globus pallidus**
       Pallidoansectomy
       Pallidotomy

  ● **01.5   Other excision or destruction of brain and meninges**

    ✖ **01.51   Excision of lesion or tissue of cerebral meninges**
       Decortication of (cerebral) meninges
       Resection of (cerebral) meninges
       Stripping of subdural membrane of (cerebral) meninges

    Excludes   *biopsy of cerebral meninges (01.11–01.12)*

    ✖ **01.52   Hemispherectomy**

    ✖ **01.53   Lobectomy of brain**

    ✖ **01.59   Other excision or destruction of lesion or tissue of brain**
       Curettage of brain
       Debridement of brain
       Marsupialization of brain cyst
       Transtemporal (mastoid) excision of brain tumor

    Excludes   *biopsy of brain (01.13–01.14)*
       that by stereotactic radiosurgery (92.3)

✖ **01.6 Excision of lesion of skull**
Removal of granulation tissue of cranium

> **Excludes** *biopsy of skull (01.15)*
> *sequestrectomy (01.25)*

● **02 Other operations on skull, brain, and cerebral meninges**

● **02.0 Cranioplasty**

> **Excludes** *that with synchronous repair of encephalocele (02.12)*

✖ **02.01 Opening of cranial suture**
Linear craniectomy
Strip craniectomy

✖ **02.02 Elevation of skull fracture fragments**
Debridement of compound fracture of skull
Decompression of skull fracture
Reduction of skull fracture

Code also any synchronous debridement of brain (01.59)

> **Excludes** *debridement of skull NOS (01.25)*
> *removal of granulation tissue of cranium (01.6)*

✖ **02.03 Formation of cranial bone flap**
Repair of skull with flap

✖ **02.04 Bone graft to skull**
Pericranial graft (autogenous) (heterogenous)

✖ **02.05 Insertion of skull plate**
Replacement of skull plate

✖ **02.06 Other cranial osteoplasty**
Repair of skull NOS
Revision of bone flap of skull

✖ **02.07 Removal of skull plate**

> **Excludes** *removal with synchronous replacement (02.05)*

● **02.1 Repair of cerebral meninges**

> **Excludes** *marsupialization of cerebral lesion (01.59)*

✖ **02.11 Simple suture of dura mater of brain**

✖ **02.12 Other repair of cerebral meninges**
Closure of fistula of cerebrospinal fluid
Dural graft
Repair of encephalocele including synchronous cranioplasty
Repair of meninges NOS
Subdural patch

✖ **02.13 Ligation of meningeal vessel**
Ligation of:
longitudinal sinus
middle meningeal artery

✖ **02.14 Choroid plexectomy**
Cauterization of choroid plexus

✖ **02.2 Ventriculostomy**
Anastomosis of ventricle to:
cervical subarachnoid space
cisterna magna
Insertion of Holter valve
Ventriculocisternal intubation

● **02.3 Extracranial ventricular shunt**

Includes: that with insertion of valve

✖ **02.31 Ventricular shunt to structure in head and neck**
Ventricle to nasopharynx shunt
Ventriculomastoid anastomosis

✖ **02.32 Ventricular shunt to circulatory system**
Ventriculoatrial anastomosis
Ventriculocaval shunt

✖ **02.33 Ventricular shunt to thoracic cavity**
Ventriculopleural anastomosis

✖ **02.34 Ventricular shunt to abdominal cavity and organs**
Ventriculocholecystostomy
Ventriculoperitoneostomy

✖ **02.35 Ventricular shunt to urinary system**
Ventricle to ureter shunt

✖ **02.39 Other operations to establish drainage of ventricle**
Ventricle to bone marrow shunt
Ventricular shunt to extracranial site NEC

● **02.4 Revision, removal, and irrigation of ventricular shunt**

> **Excludes** *revision of distal catheter of ventricular shunt (54.95)*

02.41 Irrigation of ventricular shunt

✖ **02.42 Replacement of ventricular shunt**
Reinsertion of Holter valve
Replacement of ventricular catheter
Revision of ventriculoperitoneal shunt at ventricular site

✖ **02.43 Removal of ventricular shunt**

● **02.9 Other operations on skull, brain, and cerebral meninges**

> **Excludes** *operations on:*
> *pineal gland (07.17, 07.51–07.59)*
> *pituitary gland [hypophysis] (07.13–07.15, 07.61–07.79)*

✖ **02.91 Lysis of cortical adhesions**

✖ **02.92 Repair of brain**

✖ **02.93 Implantation of intracranial neurostimulator**
Implantation, insertion, placement, or replacement of intracranial:
brain pacemaker [neuropacemaker]
depth electrodes
epidural pegs
electroencephalographic receiver
foramen ovale electrodes
intracranial electrostimulator
subdural grids
subdural strips

✖ **02.94 Insertion or replacement of skull tongs or halo traction device**

02.95 Removal of skull tongs or halo traction device

02.96 Insertion of sphenoidal electrodes

✖ **02.99 Other**

> **Excludes** *chemical shock therapy (94.24)*
> *electroshock therapy:*
> *subconvulsive (94.26)*
> *other (94.27)*

● **03 Operations on spinal cord and spinal canal structures**

● **03.0 Exploration and decompression of spinal canal structures**

✖ **03.01 Removal of foreign body from spinal canal**

✖ **03.02 Reopening of laminectomy site**

✖ **03.09 Other exploration and decompression of spinal canal**
Decompression:
laminectomy
laminotomy
Exploration of spinal nerve root
Foraminotomy

> **Excludes** *drainage of spinal fluid by anastomosis (03.71–03.79)*
> *laminectomy with excision of intervertebral disc (80.51)*
> *spinal tap (03.31)*
> *that as operative approach—omit code*

✖ **03.1　Division of intraspinal nerve root**
Rhizotomy

● **03.2　Chordotomy**

✖ **03.21　Percutaneous chordotomy**
Stereotactic chordotomy

✖ **03.29　Other chordotomy**
Chordotomy NOS
Tractotomy (one-stage) (two-stage) of spinal cord
Transection of spinal cord tracts

● **03.3　Diagnostic procedures on spinal cord and spinal canal structures**

03.31　Spinal tap
Lumbar puncture for removal of dye

| **Excludes** | *lumbar puncture for injection of dye [myelogram] (87.21)* |

✖ **03.32　Biopsy of spinal cord or spinal meninges**

✖ **03.39　Other diagnostic procedures on spinal cord and spinal canal structures**

| **Excludes** | *microscopic examination of specimen from nervous system or of spinal fluid (90.01–90.09)* |
| | *x-ray of spine (87.21–87.29)* |

✖ **03.4　Excision or destruction of lesion of spinal cord or spinal meninges**
Curettage of spinal cord or spinal meninges
Debridement of spinal cord or spinal meninges
Marsupialization of cyst of spinal cord or spinal meninges
Resection of spinal cord or spinal meninges

| **Excludes** | *biopsy of spinal cord or meninges (03.32)* |

● **03.5　Plastic operations on spinal cord structures**

✖ **03.51　Repair of spinal meningocele**
Repair of meningocele NOS

✖ **03.52　Repair of spinal myelomeningocele**

✖ **03.53　Repair of vertebral fracture**
Elevation of spinal bone fragments
Reduction of fracture of vertebrae
Removal of bony spicules from spinal canal

✖ **03.59　Other repair and plastic operations on spinal cord structures**
Repair of:
diastematomyelia
spina bifida NOS
spinal cord NOS
spinal meninges NOS
vertebral arch defect

✖ **03.6　Lysis of adhesions of spinal cord and nerve roots**

● **03.7　Shunt of spinal theca**

Includes: that with valve

✖ **03.71　Spinal subarachnoid-peritoneal shunt**

✖ **03.72　Spinal subarachnoid-ureteral shunt**

✖ **03.79　Other shunt of spinal theca**
Lumbar-subarachnoid shunt NOS
Pleurothecal anastomosis
Salpingothecal anastomosis

03.8　Injection of destructive agent into spinal canal

● **03.9　Other operations on spinal cord and spinal canal structures**

03.90　Insertion of catheter into spinal canal for infusion of therapeutic or palliative substances
Insertion of catheter into epidural, subarachnoid, or subdural space of spine with intermittent or continuous infusion of drug (with creation of any reservoir)

Code also any implantation of infusion pump (86.06)

03.91　Injection of anesthetic into spinal canal for analgesia

| **Excludes** | *that for operative anesthesia—omit code* |

03.92　Injection of other agent into spinal canal
Intrathecal injection of steroid
Subarachnoid perfusion of refrigerated saline

Excludes	*injection of:*
	contrast material for myelogram (87.21)
	destructive agent into spinal canal (03.8)

✖ **03.93　Insertion or replacement of spinal neurostimulator**

✖ **03.94　Removal of spinal neurostimulator**

03.95　Spinal blood patch

03.96　Percutaneous denervation of facet

✖ **03.97　Revision of spinal thecal shunt**

✖ **03.98　Removal of spinal thecal shunt**

✖ **03.99　Other**

● **04　Operations on cranial and peripheral nerves**

● **04.0　Incision, division, and excision of cranial and peripheral nerves**

| **Excludes** | *opticociliary neurectomy (12.79)* |
| | *sympathetic ganglionectomy (05.21–05.29)* |

✖ **04.01　Excision of acoustic neuroma**
That by craniotomy

| **Excludes** | *that by stereotactic radiosurgery (92.3)* |

✖ **04.02　Division of trigeminal nerve**
Retrogasserian neurotomy

✖ **04.03　Division or crushing of other cranial and peripheral nerves**

Excludes	*that of:*
	glossopharyngeal nerve (29.92)
	laryngeal nerve (31.91)
	nerves to adrenal glands (07.42)
	phrenic nerve for collapse of lung (33.31)
	vagus nerve (44.00–44.03)

✖ **04.04　Other incision of cranial and peripheral nerves**

✖ **04.05　Gasserian ganglionectomy**

✖ **04.06　Other cranial or peripheral ganglionectomy**

| **Excludes** | *sympathetic ganglionectomy (05.21–05.29)* |

✖ **04.07　Other excision or avulsion of cranial and peripheral nerves**
Curettage of peripheral nerve
Debridement of peripheral nerve
Resection of peripheral nerve
Excision of peripheral neuroma [Morton's]

| **Excludes** | *biopsy of cranial or peripheral nerve (04.11–04.12)* |

● **04.1　Diagnostic procedures on peripheral nervous system**

04.11　Closed [percutaneous] [needle] biopsy of cranial or peripheral nerve or ganglion

✖ **04.12　Open biopsy of cranial or peripheral nerve or ganglion**

✖ **04.19　Other diagnostic procedures on cranial and peripheral nerves and ganglia**

| **Excludes** | *microscopic examination of specimen from nervous system (90.01–90.09)* |
| | *neurologic examination (89.13)* |

04.2　Destruction of cranial and peripheral nerves
Destruction of cranial or peripheral nerves by:
cryoanalgesia
injection of neurolytic agent
radiofrequency

✖ **04.3   Suture of cranial and peripheral nerves**

● **04.4   Lysis of adhesions and decompression of cranial and peripheral nerves**

    ✖ **04.41   Decompression of trigeminal nerve root**

    ✖ **04.42   Other cranial nerve decompression**

    ✖ **04.43   Release of carpal tunnel**

    ✖ **04.44   Release of tarsal tunnel**

    ✖ **04.49   Other peripheral nerve or ganglion decompression or lysis of adhesions**
       Peripheral nerve neurolysis NOS

✖ **04.5   Cranial or peripheral nerve graft**

✖ **04.6   Transposition of cranial and peripheral nerves**
    Nerve transplantation

● **04.7   Other cranial or peripheral neuroplasty**

    ✖ **04.71   Hypoglossal-facial anastomosis**

    ✖ **04.72   Accessory-facial anastomosis**

    ✖ **04.73   Accessory-hypoglossal anastomosis**

    ✖ **04.74   Other anastomosis of cranial or peripheral nerve**

    ✖ **04.75   Revision of previous repair of cranial and peripheral nerves**

    ✖ **04.76   Repair of old traumatic injury of cranial and peripheral nerves**

    ✖ **04.79   Other neuroplasty**

● **04.8   Injection into peripheral nerve**

    Excludes   *destruction of nerve (by injection of neurolytic agent) (04.2)*

    04.80   Peripheral nerve injection, not otherwise specified

    04.81   Injection of anesthetic into peripheral nerve for analgesia

    Excludes   *that for operative anesthesia—omit code*

    04.89   Injection of other agent, except neurolytic

    Excludes   *injection of neurolytic agent (04.2)*

● **04.9   Other operations on cranial and peripheral nerves**

    ✖ **04.91   Neurectasis**

    ✖ **04.92   Implantation or replacement of peripheral neurostimulator**

    ✖ **04.93   Removal of peripheral neurostimulator**

    ✖ **04.99   Other**

● **05   Operations on sympathetic nerves or ganglia**

    Excludes   *paracervical uterine denervation (69.3)*

✖ **05.0   Division of sympathetic nerve or ganglion**

    Excludes   *that of nerves to adrenal glands (07.42)*

● **05.1   Diagnostic procedures on sympathetic nerves or ganglia**

    ✖ **05.11   Biopsy of sympathetic nerve or ganglion**

    ✖ **05.19   Other diagnostic procedures on sympathetic nerves or ganglia**

● **05.2   Sympathectomy**

    ✖ **05.21   Sphenopalatine ganglionectomy**

    ✖ **05.22   Cervical sympathectomy**

    ✖ **05.23   Lumbar sympathectomy**

    ✖ **05.24   Presacral sympathectomy**

    ✖ **05.25   Periarterial sympathectomy**

    ✖ **05.29   Other sympathectomy and ganglionectomy**
       Excision or avulsion of sympathetic nerve NOS
       Sympathetic ganglionectomy NOS

    Excludes   *biopsy of sympathetic nerve or ganglion (05.11)*
       opticociliary neurectomy (12.79)
       periarterial sympathectomy (05.25)
       tympanosympathectomy (20.91)

● **05.3   Injection into sympathetic nerve or ganglion**

    Excludes   *injection of ciliary sympathetic ganglion (12.79)*

    05.31   Injection of anesthetic into sympathetic nerve for analgesia

    05.32   Injection of neurolytic agent into sympathetic nerve

    05.39   Other injection into sympathetic nerve or ganglion

● **05.8   Other operations on sympathetic nerves or ganglia**

    ✖ **05.81   Repair of sympathetic nerve or ganglion**

    ✖ **05.89   Other**

✖ **05.9   Other operations on nervous system**

2. OPERATIONS ON THE ENDOCRINE SYSTEM (06–07)

● **06 Operations on thyroid and parathyroid glands**

    Includes: incidental resection of hyoid bone

    06.0 Incision of thyroid field

      Excludes *division of isthmus (06.91)*

      06.01 Aspiration of thyroid field
       Percutaneous or needle drainage of thyroid field

       Excludes *aspiration biopsy of thyroid (06.11)*
       drainage by incision (06.09)
       postoperative aspiration of field (06.02)

      ✖ **06.02 Reopening of wound of thyroid field**
       Reopening of wound of thyroid field for:
        control of (postoperative) hemorrhage
        examination
        exploration
        removal of hematoma

      ✖ **06.09 Other incision of thyroid field**
       Drainage of hematoma by incision
       Drainage of thyroglossal tract by incision
       Exploration:
        neck by incision
        thyroid (field) by incision
       Removal of foreign body by incision
       Thyroidotomy NOS by incision

       Excludes *postoperative exploration (06.02)*
       removal of hematoma by aspiration (06.01)

● **06.1 Diagnostic procedures on thyroid and parathyroid glands**

      06.11 Closed [percutaneous] [needle] biopsy of thyroid gland
       Aspiration biopsy of thyroid

      ✖ **06.12 Open biopsy of thyroid gland**

      ✖ **06.13 Biopsy of parathyroid gland**

      ✖ **06.19 Other diagnostic procedures on thyroid and parathyroid glands**

       Excludes *radioisotope scan of:*
        parathyroid (92.13)
        thyroid (92.01)
       soft tissue x-ray of thyroid field (87.09)

✖ **06.2 Unilateral thyroid lobectomy**
      Complete removal of one lobe of thyroid (with removal of isthmus or portion of other lobe)
      Hemithyroidectomy

      Excludes *partial substernal thyroidectomy (06.51)*

● **06.3 Other partial thyroidectomy**

      ✖ **06.31 Excision of lesion of thyroid**

       Excludes *biopsy of thyroid (06.11–06.12)*

      ✖ **06.39 Other**
       Isthmectomy
       Partial thyroidectomy NOS

       Excludes *partial substernal thyroidectomy (06.51)*

✖ **06.4 Complete thyroidectomy**

      Excludes *complete substernal thyroidectomy (06.52)*
      that with laryngectomy (30.3–30.4)

● **06.5 Substernal thyroidectomy**

      ✖ **06.50 Substernal thyroidectomy, not otherwise specified**

      ✖ **06.51 Partial substernal thyroidectomy**

      ✖ **06.52 Complete substernal thyroidectomy**

    ✖ **06.6 Excision of lingual thyroid**
      Excision of thyroid by:
       submental route
       transoral route

    ✖ **06.7 Excision of thyroglossal duct or tract**

● **06.8 Parathyroidectomy**

      ✖ **06.81 Complete parathyroidectomy**

      ✖ **06.89 Other parathyroidectomy**
       Parathyroidectomy NOS
       Partial parathyroidectomy

       Excludes *biopsy of parathyroid (06.13)*

● **06.9 Other operations on thyroid (region) and parathyroid**

      ✖ **06.91 Division of thyroid isthmus**
       Transection of thyroid isthmus

      ✖ **06.92 Ligation of thyroid vessels**

      ✖ **06.93 Suture of thyroid gland**

      ✖ **06.94 Thyroid tissue reimplantation**
       Autotransplantation of thyroid tissue

      ✖ **06.95 Parathyroid tissue reimplantation**
       Autotransplantation of parathyroid tissue

      ✖ **06.98 Other operations on thyroid glands**

      ✖ **06.99 Other operations on parathyroid glands**

● **07 Operations on other endocrine glands**

    Includes: operations on:
      adrenal glands
      pineal gland
      pituitary gland
      thymus

      Excludes *operations on:*
       aortic and carotid bodies (39.8)
       ovaries (65.0–65.99)
       pancreas (52.01–52.99)
       testes (62.0–62.99)

● **07.0 Exploration of adrenal field**

      Excludes *incision of adrenal (gland) (07.41)*

      ✖ **07.00 Exploration of adrenal field, not otherwise specified**

      ✖ **07.01 Unilateral exploration of adrenal field**

      ✖ **07.02 Bilateral exploration of adrenal field**

● **07.1 Diagnostic procedures on adrenal glands, pituitary gland, pineal gland, and thymus**

      07.11 Closed [percutaneous] [needle] biopsy of adrenal gland

      ✖ **07.12 Open biopsy of adrenal gland**

      ✖ **07.13 Biopsy of pituitary gland, transfrontal approach**

      ✖ **07.14 Biopsy of pituitary gland, transsphenoidal approach**

      ✖ **07.15 Biopsy of pituitary gland, unspecified approach**

      ✖ **07.16 Biopsy of thymus**

      ✖ **07.17 Biopsy of pineal gland**

      ✖ **07.19 Other diagnostic procedures on adrenal glands, pituitary gland, pineal gland, and thymus**

       Excludes *microscopic examination of specimen from endocrine gland (90.11–90.19)*
       radioisotope scan of pituitary gland (92.11)

● **07.2 Partial adrenalectomy**

      ✖ **07.21 Excision of lesion of adrenal gland**

       Excludes *biopsy of adrenal gland (07.11–07.12)*

✖ **07.22 Unilateral adrenalectomy**
Adrenalectomy NOS

| **Excludes** | *excision of remaining adrenal gland (07.3)* |

✖ **07.29 Other partial adrenalectomy**
Partial adrenalectomy NOS

● ✖ **07.3 Bilateral adrenalectomy**
Excision of remaining adrenal gland

| **Excludes** | *bilateral partial adrenalectomy (07.29)* |

● **07.4 Other operations on adrenal glands, nerves, and vessels**

✖ **07.41 Incision of adrenal gland**
Adrenalotomy (with drainage)

✖ **07.42 Division of nerves to adrenal glands**

✖ **07.43 Ligation of adrenal vessels**

✖ **07.44 Repair of adrenal gland**

✖ **07.45 Reimplantation of adrenal tissue**
Autotransplantation of adrenal tissue

✖ **07.49 Other**

● **07.5 Operations on pineal gland**

✖ **07.51 Exploration of pineal field**

| **Excludes** | *that with incision of pineal gland (07.52)* |

✖ **07.52 Incision of pineal gland**

✖ **07.53 Partial excision of pineal gland**

| **Excludes** | *biopsy of pineal gland (07.17)* |

✖ **07.54 Total excision of pineal gland**
Pinealectomy (complete) (total)

✖ **07.59 Other operations on pineal gland**

● **07.6 Hypophysectomy**

✖ **07.61 Partial excision of pituitary gland, transfrontal approach**
Cryohypophysectomy, partial transfrontal approach
Division of hypophyseal stalk transfrontal approach
Excision of lesion of pituitary [hypophysis] transfrontal approach
Hypophysectomy, subtotal transfrontal approach
Infundibulectomy, hypophyseal transfrontal approach

| **Excludes** | *biopsy of pituitary gland, transfrontal approach (07.13)* |

✖ **07.62 Partial excision of pituitary gland, transsphenoidal approach**

| **Excludes** | *biopsy of pituitary gland, transsphenoidal approach (07.14)* |

✖ **07.63 Partial excision of pituitary gland, unspecified approach**

| **Excludes** | *biopsy of pituitary gland NOS (07.15)* |

✖ **07.64 Total excision of pituitary gland, transfrontal approach**
Ablation of pituitary by implantation (strontium-yttrium) (Y) transfrontal approach
Cryohypophysectomy, complete transfrontal approach

✖ **07.65 Total excision of pituitary gland, transsphenoidal approach**

✖ **07.68 Total excision of pituitary gland, other specified approach**

✖ **07.69 Total excision of pituitary gland, unspecified approach**
Hypophysectomy NOS
Pituitectomy NOS

● **07.7 Other operations on hypophysis**

✖ **07.71 Exploration of pituitary fossa**

| **Excludes** | *exploration with incision of pituitary gland (07.72)* |

✖ **07.72 Incision of pituitary gland**
Aspiration of:
craniobuccal pouch
craniopharyngioma
hypophysis
pituitary gland
Rathke'spouch

✖ **07.79 Other**
Insertion of pack into sella turcica

● **07.8 Thymectomy**

✖ **07.80 Thymectomy, not otherwise specified**

✖ **07.81 Partial excision of thymus**

| **Excludes** | *biopsy of thymus (07.16)* |

✖ **07.82 Total excision of thymus**

● **07.9 Other operations on thymus**

✖ **07.91 Exploration of thymus field**

| **Excludes** | *exploration with incision of thymus (07.92)* |

✖ **07.92 Incision of thymus**

✖ **07.93 Repair of thymus**

✖ **07.94 Transplantation of thymus**

✖ **07.99 Other**
Thymopexy

3. OPERATIONS ON THE EYE (08–16)

● 08 Operations on eyelids

Includes: operations on the eyebrow

● 08.0 Incision of eyelid

08.01 Incision of lid margin

08.02 Severing of blepharorrhaphy

08.09 Other incision of eyelid

● 08.1 Diagnostic procedures on eyelid

✖ 08.11 Biopsy of eyelid

08.19 Other diagnostic procedures on eyelid

● 08.2 Excision or destruction of lesion or tissue of eyelid

Code also any synchronous reconstruction (08.61–08.74)

Excludes *biopsy of eyelid (08.11)*

✖ 08.20 Removal of lesion of eyelid, not otherwise specified

Removal of meibomian gland NOS

✖ 08.21 Excision of chalazion

✖ 08.22 Excision of other minor lesion of eyelid

Excision of:
verucca
wart

✖ 08.23 Excision of major lesion of eyelid, partial-thickness

Excision involving one-fourth or more of lid margin, partial-thickness

✖ 08.24 Excision of major lesion of eyelid, full-thickness

Excision involving one-fourth or more of lid margin, full-thickness
Wedge resection of eyelid

✖ 08.25 Destruction of lesion of eyelid

● 08.3 Repair of blepharoptosis and lid retraction

✖ 08.31 Repair of blepharoptosis by frontalis muscle technique with suture

✖ 08.32 Repair of blepharoptosis by frontalis muscle technique with fascial sling

✖ 08.33 Repair of blepharoptosis by resection or advancement of levator muscle or aponeurosis

✖ 08.34 Repair of blepharoptosis by other levator muscle techniques

✖ 08.35 Repair of blepharoptosis by tarsal technique

✖ 08.36 Repair of blepharoptosis by other techniques

Correction of eyelid ptosis NOS
Orbicularis oculi muscle sling for correction of blepharoptosis

✖ 08.37 Reduction of overcorrection of ptosis

✖ 08.38 Correction of lid retraction

● 08.4 Repair of entropion or ectropion

✖ 08.41 Repair of entropion or ectropion by thermocauterization

✖ 08.42 Repair of entropion or ectropion by suture technique

✖ 08.43 Repair of entropion or ectropion with wedge resection

✖ 08.44 Repair of entropion or ectropion with lid reconstruction

✖ 08.49 Other repair of entropion or ectropion

● 08.5 Other adjustment of lid position

✖ 08.51 Canthotomy

Enlargement of palpebral fissure

✖ 08.52 Blepharorrhaphy

Canthorrhaphy
Tarsorrhaphy

✖ 08.59 Other

Canthoplasty NOS
Repair of epicanthal fold

● 08.6 Reconstruction of eyelid with flaps or grafts

Excludes *that associated with repair of entropion and ectropion (08.44)*

✖ 08.61 Reconstruction of eyelid with skin flap or graft

✖ 08.62 Reconstruction of eyelid with mucous membrane flap or graft

✖ 08.63 Reconstruction of eyelid with hair follicle graft

✖ 08.64 Reconstruction of eyelid with tarsoconjunctival flap

Transfer of tarsoconjunctival flap from opposing lid

✖ 08.69 Other reconstruction of eyelid with flaps or grafts

● 08.7 Other reconstruction of eyelid

Excludes *that associated with repair of entropion and ectropion (08.44)*

✖ 08.70 Reconstruction of eyelid, not otherwise specified

✖ 08.71 Reconstruction of eyelid involving lid margin, partial-thickness

✖ 08.72 Other reconstruction of eyelid, partial-thickness

✖ 08.73 Reconstruction of eyelid involving lid margin, full-thickness

✖ 08.74 Other reconstruction of eyelid, full-thickness

● 08.8 Other repair of eyelid

08.81 Linear repair of laceration of eyelid or eyebrow

08.82 Repair of laceration involving lid margin, partial-thickness

08.83 Other repair of laceration of eyelid, partial-thickness

08.84 Repair of laceration involving lid margin, full-thickness

08.85 Other repair of laceration of eyelid, full-thickness

08.86 Lower eyelid rhytidectomy

08.87 Upper eyelid rhytidectomy

08.89 Other eyelid repair

● 08.9 Other operations on eyelids

✖ 08.91 Electrosurgical epilation of eyelid

✖ 08.92 Cryosurgical epilation of eyelid

✖ 08.93 Other epilation of eyelid

✖ 08.99 Other

● 09 Operations on lacrimal system

✖ 09.0 Incision of lacrimal gland

Incision of lacrimal cyst (with drainage)

● 09.1 Diagnostic procedures on lacrimal system

09.11 Biopsy of lacrimal gland

09.12 Biopsy of lacrimal sac

✖ 09.19 Other diagnostic procedures on lacrimal system

Excludes *contrast dacryocystogram (87.05)*
soft tissue x-ray of nasolacrimal duct (87.09)

● **Use Additional Digit(s)**   ✖ **Valid O.R. Procedure**   ◀▶ **New Code**   ⬅▦ ▦➡ **Revised Code**

● **09.2 Excision of lesion or tissue of lacrimal gland**

✖ **09.20 Excision of lacrimal gland, not otherwise specified**

✖ **09.21 Excision of lesion of lacrimal gland**

Excludes *biopsy of lacrimal gland (09.11)*

✖ **09.22 Other partial dacryoadenectomy**

Excludes *biopsy of lacrimal gland (09.11)*

✖ **09.23 Total dacryoadenectomy**

✖ **09.3 Other operations on lacrimal gland**

● **09.4 Manipulation of lacrimal passage**

Includes: removal of calculus
that with dilation

Excludes *contrast dacryocystogram (87.05)*

✖ **09.41 Probing of lacrimal punctum**

✖ **09.42 Probing of lacrimal canaliculi**

✖ **09.43 Probing of nasolacrimal duct**

Excludes *that with insertion of tube or stent (09.44)*

✖ **09.44 Intubation of nasolacrimal duct**
Insertion of stent into nasolacrimal duct

✖ **09.49 Other manipulation of lacrimal passage**

● **09.5 Incision of lacrimal sac and passages**

✖ **09.51 Incision of lacrimal punctum**

✖ **09.52 Incision of lacrimal canaliculi**

✖ **09.53 Incision of lacrimal sac**

✖ **09.59 Other incision of lacrimal passages**
Incision (and drainage) of nasolacrimal duct NOS

✖ **09.6 Excision of lacrimal sac and passage**

Excludes *biopsy of lacrimal sac (09.12)*

● **09.7 Repair of canaliculus and punctum**

Excludes *repair of eyelid (08.81–08.89)*

✖ **09.71 Correction of everted punctum**

✖ **09.72 Other repair of punctum**

✖ **09.73 Repair of canaliculus**

● **09.8 Fistulization of lacrimal tract to nasal cavity**

✖ **09.81 Dacryocystorhinostomy [DCR]**

✖ **09.82 Conjunctivocystorhinostomy**
Conjunctivodacryocystorhinostomy [CDCR]

Excludes *that with insertion of tube or stent (09.83)*

✖ **09.83 Conjunctivorhinostomy with insertion of tube or stent**

● **09.9 Other operations on lacrimal system**

✖ **09.91 Obliteration of lacrimal punctum**

✖ **09.99 Other**

● **10 Operations on conjunctiva**

✖ **10.0 Removal of embedded foreign body from conjunctiva by incision**

Excludes *removal of:*
embedded foreign body without incision (98.22)
superficial foreign body (98.21)

✖ **10.1 Other incision of conjunctiva**

● **10.2 Diagnostic procedures on conjunctiva**

✖ **10.21 Biopsy of conjunctiva**

✖ **10.29 Other diagnostic procedures on conjunctiva**

● **10.3 Excision or destruction of lesion or tissue of conjunctiva**

✖ **10.31 Excision of lesion or tissue of conjunctiva**
Excision of ring of conjunctiva around cornea

Excludes *biopsy of conjunctiva (10.21)*

✖ **10.32 Destruction of lesion of conjunctiva**

Excludes *excision of lesion (10.31)*
thermocauterization for entropion (08.41)

✖ **10.33 Other destructive procedures on conjunctiva**
Removal of trachoma follicles

● **10.4 Conjunctivoplasty**

✖ **10.41 Repair of symblepharon with free graft**

✖ **10.42 Reconstruction of conjunctival cul-de-sac with free graft**

Excludes *revision of enucleation socket with graft (16.63)*

✖ **10.43 Other reconstruction of conjunctival cul-de-sac**

Excludes *revision of enucleation socket (16.64)*

✖ **10.44 Other free graft to conjunctiva**

✖ **10.49 Other conjunctivoplasty**

Excludes *repair of cornea with conjunctival flap (11.53)*

✖ **10.5 Lysis of adhesions of conjunctiva and eyelid**
Division of symblepharon (with insertion of conformer)

✖ **10.6 Repair of laceration of conjunctiva**

Excludes *that with repair of sclera (12.81)*

● **10.9 Other operations on conjunctiva**

✖ **10.91 Subconjunctival injection**

✖ **10.99 Other**

● **11 Operations on cornea**

✖ **11.0 Magnetic removal of embedded foreign body from cornea**

Excludes *that with incision (11.1)*

✖ **11.1 Incision of cornea**
Incision of cornea for removal of foreign body

● **11.2 Diagnostic procedures on cornea**

✖ **11.21 Scraping of cornea for smear or culture**

✖ **11.22 Biopsy of cornea**

✖ **11.29 Other diagnostic procedures on cornea**

● **11.3 Excision of pterygium**

✖ **11.31 Transposition of pterygium**

✖ **11.32 Excision of pterygium with corneal graft**

✖ **11.39 Other excision of pterygium**

● **11.4 Excision or destruction of tissue or other lesion of cornea**

✖ **11.41 Mechanical removal of corneal epithelium**
That by chemocauterization

Excludes *that for smear or culture (11.21)*

✖ **11.42 Thermocauterization of corneal lesion**

✖ **11.43 Cryotherapy of corneal lesion**

✖ **11.49 Other removal or destruction of corneal lesion**
Excision of cornea NOS

Excludes *biopsy of cornea (11.22)*

● **11.5 Repair of cornea**

✖ **11.51 Suture of corneal laceration**

✖ **11.52 Repair of postoperative wound dehiscence of cornea**

✖ **11.53 Repair of corneal laceration or wound with conjunctival flap**

✖ **11.59 Other repair of cornea**

- ● 11.6 Corneal transplant
  - Excludes *excision of pterygium with corneal graft (11.32)*
  - ✖ 11.60 **Corneal transplant, not otherwise specified**
    Keratoplasty NOS
  - ✖ 11.61 **Lamellar keratoplasty with autograft**
  - ✖ 11.62 **Other lamellar keratoplasty**
  - ✖ 11.63 **Penetrating keratoplasty with autograft**
    Perforating keratoplasty with autograft
  - ✖ 11.64 **Other penetrating keratoplasty**
    Perforating keratoplasty (with homograft)
  - ✖ 11.69 **Other corneal transplant**
- ● 11.7 **Other reconstructive and refractive surgery on cornea**
  - ✖ 11.71 **Keratomileusis**
  - ✖ 11.72 **Keratophakia**
  - ✖ 11.73 **Keratoprosthesis**
  - ✖ 11.74 **Thermokeratoplasty**
  - ✖ 11.75 **Radial keratotomy**
  - ✖ 11.76 **Epikeratophakia**
  - ✖ 11.79 **Other**
- ● 11.9 **Other operations on cornea**
  - ✖ 11.91 **Tattooing of cornea**
  - ✖ 11.92 **Removal of artificial implant from cornea**
  - ✖ 11.99 **Other**
- ● 12 **Operations on iris, ciliary body, sclera, and anterior chamber**
  - Excludes *operations on cornea (11.0–11.99)*
- ● 12.0 **Removal of intraocular foreign body from anterior segment of eye**
  - ✖ 12.00 **Removal of intraocular foreign body from anterior segment of eye, not otherwise specified**
  - ✖ 12.01 **Removal of intraocular foreign body from anterior segment of eye with use of magnet**
  - ✖ 12.02 **Removal of intraocular foreign body from anterior segment of eye without use of magnet**
- ● 12.1 **Iridotomy and simple iridectomy**
  - Excludes *iridectomy associated with:*
    cataract extraction (13.11–13.69)
    removal of lesion (12.41–12.42)
    scleral fistulization (12.61–12.69)
  - ✖ 12.11 **Iridotomy with transfixion**
  - ✖ 12.12 **Other iridotomy**
    Corectomy
    Discission of iris
    Iridotomy NOS
  - ✖ 12.13 **Excision of prolapsed iris**
  - ✖ 12.14 **Other iridectomy**
    Iridectomy (basal) (peripheral) (total)
- ● 12.2 **Diagnostic procedures on iris, ciliary body, sclera, and anterior chamber**
  - ✖ 12.21 **Diagnostic aspiration of anterior chamber of eye**
  - ✖ 12.22 **Biopsy of iris**
  - ✖ 12.29 **Other diagnostic procedures on iris, ciliary body, sclera, and anterior chamber**
- ● 12.3 **Iridoplasty and coreoplasty**
  - ✖ 12.31 **Lysis of goniosynechiae**
    Lysis of goniosynechiae by injection of air or liquid

- ✖ 12.32 **Lysis of other anterior synechiae**
  Lysis of anterior synechiae:
  NOS
  by injection of air or liquid
- ✖ 12.33 **Lysis of posterior synechiae**
  Lysis of iris adhesions NOS
- ✖ 12.34 **Lysis of corneovitreal adhesions**
- ✖ 12.35 **Coreoplasty**
  Needling of pupillary membrane
- ✖ 12.39 **Other iridoplasty**
- ● 12.4 **Excision or destruction of lesion of iris and ciliary body**
  - ✖ 12.40 **Removal of lesion of anterior segment of eye, not otherwise specified**
  - ✖ 12.41 **Destruction of lesion of iris, nonexcisional**
    Destruction of lesion of iris by:
    cauterization
    cryotherapy
    photocoagulation
  - ✖ 12.42 **Excision of lesion of iris**
    Excludes *biopsy of iris (12.22)*
  - ✖ 12.43 **Destruction of lesion of ciliary body, nonexcisional**
  - ✖ 12.44 **Excision of lesion of ciliary body**
- ● 12.5 **Facilitation of intraocular circulation**
  - ✖ 12.51 **Goniopuncture without goniotomy**
  - ✖ 12.52 **Goniotomy without goniopuncture**
  - ✖ 12.53 **Goniotomy with goniopuncture**
  - ✖ 12.54 **Trabeculotomy ab externo**
  - ✖ 12.55 **Cyclodialysis**
  - ✖ 12.59 **Other facilitation of intraocular circulation**
- ● 12.6 **Scleral fistulization**
  - Excludes *exploratory sclerotomy (12.89)*
  - ✖ 12.61 **Trephination of sclera with iridectomy**
  - ✖ 12.62 **Thermocauterization of sclera with iridectomy**
  - ✖ 12.63 **Iridencleisis and iridotasis**
  - ✖ 12.64 **Trabeculectomy ab externo**
  - ✖ 12.65 **Other scleral fistulization with iridectomy**
  - ✖ 12.66 **Postoperative revision of scleral fistulization procedure**
    Revision of filtering bleb
    Excludes *repair of fistula (12.82)*
  - ✖ 12.69 **Other fistulizing procedure**
- ● 12.7 **Other procedures for relief of elevated intraocular pressure**
  - ✖ 12.71 **Cyclodiathermy**
  - ✖ 12.72 **Cyclocryotherapy**
  - ✖ 12.73 **Cyclophotocoagulation**
  - ✖ 12.74 **Diminution of ciliary body, not otherwise specified**
  - ✖ 12.79 **Other glaucoma procedures**
- ● 12.8 **Operations on sclera**
  - Excludes *those associated with:*
    retinal reattachment (14.41–14.59)
    scleral fistulization (12.61–12.69)
  - ✖ 12.81 **Suture of laceration of sclera**
    Suture of sclera with synchronous repair of conjunctiva

● **Use Additional Digit(s)**   ✖ **Valid O.R. Procedure**   ◀▶ **New Code**   ⬅▥ ▥➡ **Revised Code**

✖ **12.82 Repair of scleral fistula**

Excludes *postoperative revision of scleral fistulization procedure (12.66)*

✖ **12.83 Revision of operative wound of anterior segment, not elsewhere classified**

Excludes *postoperative revision of scleral fistulization procedure (12.66)*

✖ **12.84 Excision or destruction of lesion of sclera**

✖ **12.85 Repair of scleral staphyloma with graft**

✖ **12.86 Other repair of scleral staphyloma**

✖ **12.87 Scleral reinforcement with graft**

✖ **12.88 Other scleral reinforcement**

✖ **12.89 Other operations on sclera**
Exploratory sclerotomy

● **12.9 Other operations on iris, ciliary body, and anterior chamber**

✖ **12.91 Therapeutic evacuation of anterior chamber**
Paracentesis of anterior chamber

Excludes *diagnostic aspiration (12.21)*

✖ **12.92 Injection into anterior chamber**
Injection of:
air into anterior chamber
liquid into anterior chamber
medication into anterior chamber

✖ **12.93 Removal or destruction of epithelial downgrowth from anterior chamber**

Excludes *that with iridectomy (12.41–12.42)*

✖ **12.97 Other operations on iris**

✖ **12.98 Other operations on ciliary body**

✖ **12.99 Other operations on anterior chamber**

● **13 Operations on lens**

● **13.0 Removal of foreign body from lens**

Excludes *removal of pseudophakos (13.8)*

✖ **13.00 Removal of foreign body from lens, not otherwise specified**

✖ **13.01 Removal of foreign body from lens with use of magnet**

✖ **13.02 Removal of foreign body from lens without use of magnet**

● **13.1 Intracapsular extraction of lens**

Code also any synchronous insertion of pseudophakos (13.71)

✖ **13.11 Intracapsular extraction of lens by temporal inferior route**

✖ **13.19 Other intracapsular extraction of lens**
Cataract extraction NOS
Cryoextraction of lens
Erysiphake extraction of cataract
Extraction of lens NOS

✖ **13.2 Extracapsular extraction of lens by linear extraction technique**

✖ **13.3 Extracapsular extraction of lens by simple aspiration (and irrigation) technique**
Irrigation of traumatic cataract

● **13.4 Extracapsular extraction of lens by fragmentation and aspiration technique**

✖ **13.41 Phacoemulsification and aspiration of cataract**

✖ **13.42 Mechanical phacofragmentation and aspiration of cataract by posterior route**

Code also any synchronous vitrectomy (14.74)

✖ **13.43 Mechanical phacofragmentation and other aspiration of cataract**

● **13.5 Other extracapsular extraction of lens**

Code also any synchronous insertion of pseudophakos (13.71)

✖ **13.51 Extracapsular extraction of lens by temporal inferior route**

✖ **13.59 Other extracapsular extraction of lens**

● **13.6 Other cataract extraction**

Code also any synchronous insertion of pseudophakos (13.71)

✖ **13.64 Discission of secondary membrane [after cataract]**

✖ **13.65 Excision of secondary membrane [after cataract]**
Capsulectomy

✖ **13.66 Mechanical fragmentation of secondary membrane [after cataract]**

✖ **13.69 Other cataract extraction**

● **13.7 Insertion of prosthetic lens [pseudophakos]**

✖ **13.70 Insertion of pseudophakos, not otherwise specified**

✖ **13.71 Insertion of intraocular lens prosthesis at time of cataract extraction, one-stage**

Code also synchronous extraction of cataract (13.11–13.69)

✖ **13.72 Secondary insertion of intraocular lens prosthesis**

✖ **13.8 Removal of implanted lens**
Removal of pseudophakos

✖ **13.9 Other operations on lens**

● **14 Operations on retina, choroid, vitreous, and posterior chamber**

● **14.0 Removal of foreign body from posterior segment of eye**

Excludes *removal of surgically implanted material (14.6)*

✖ **14.00 Removal of foreign body from posterior segment of eye, not otherwise specified**

✖ **14.01 Removal of foreign body from posterior segment of eye with use of magnet**

✖ **14.02 Removal of foreign body from posterior segment of eye without use of magnet**

● **14.1 Diagnostic procedures on retina, choroid, vitreous, and posterior chamber**

✖ **14.11 Diagnostic aspiration of vitreous**

✖ **14.19 Other diagnostic procedures on retina, choroid, vitreous, and posterior chamber**

● **14.2 Destruction of lesion of retina and choroid**

Includes: destruction of chorioretinopathy or isolated chorioretinal lesion

Excludes *that for repair of retina (14.31–14.59)*

✖ **14.21 Destruction of chorioretinal lesion by diathermy**

✖ **14.22 Destruction of chorioretinal lesion by cryotherapy**

14.23 Destruction of chorioretinal lesion by xenon arc photocoagulation

14.24 Destruction of chorioretinal lesion by laser photocoagulation

14.25 Destruction of chorioretinal lesion by photocoagulation of unspecified type

✖ **14.26** Destruction of chorioretinal lesion by radiation therapy

✖ **14.27** Destruction of chorioretinal lesion by implantation of radiation source

✖ **14.29** Other destruction of chorioretinal lesion
Destruction of lesion of retina and choroid NOS

● **14.3** Repair of retinal tear

Includes: repair of retinal defect

Excludes | *repair of retinal detachment (14.41–14.59)*

✖ **14.31** Repair of retinal tear by diathermy

✖ **14.32** Repair of retinal tear by cryotherapy

14.33 Repair of retinal tear by xenon arc photocoagulation

14.34 Repair of retinal tear by laser photocoagulation

14.35 Repair of retinal tear by photocoagulation of unspecified type

✖ **14.39** Other repair of retinal tear

● **14.4** Repair of retinal detachment with scleral buckling and implant

✖ **14.41** Scleral buckling with implant

✖ **14.49** Other scleral buckling
Scleral buckling with:
air tamponade
resection of sclera
vitrectomy

● **14.5** Other repair of retinal detachment

Includes: that with drainage

✖ **14.51** Repair of retinal detachment with diathermy

✖ **14.52** Repair of retinal detachment with cryotherapy

✖ **14.53** Repair of retinal detachment with xenon arc photocoagulation

✖ **14.54** Repair of retinal detachment with laser photocoagulation

✖ **14.55** Repair of retinal detachment with photocoagulation of unspecified type

✖ **14.59** Other

✖ **14.6** Removal of surgically implanted material from posterior segment of eye

● **14.7** Operations on vitreous

✖ **14.71** Removal of vitreous, anterior approach
Open sky technique
Removal of vitreous, anterior approach (with replacement)

✖ **14.72** Other removal of vitreous
Aspiration of vitreous by posterior sclerotomy

✖ **14.73** Mechanical vitrectomy by anterior approach

✖ **14.74** Other mechanical vitrectomy

✖ **14.75** Injection of vitreous substitute

Excludes | *that associated with removal (14.71–14.72)*

✖ **14.79** Other operations on vitreous

✖ **14.9** Other operations on retina, choroid, and posterior chamber

● **15** Operations on extraocular muscles

● **15.0** Diagnostic procedures on extraocular muscles or tendons

✖ **15.01** Biopsy of extraocular muscle or tendon

✖ **15.09** Other diagnostic procedures on extraocular muscles and tendons

● **15.1** Operations on one extraocular muscle involving temporary detachment from globe

✖ **15.11** Recession of one extraocular muscle

✖ **15.12** Advancement of one extraocular muscle

✖ **15.13** Resection of one extraocular muscle

✖ **15.19** Other operations on one extraocular muscle involving temporary detachment from globe

Excludes | *transposition of muscle (15.5)*

● **15.2** Other operations on one extraocular muscle

✖ **15.21** Lengthening procedure on one extraocular muscle

✖ **15.22** Shortening procedure on one extraocular muscle

✖ **15.29** Other

✖ **15.3** Operations on two or more extraocular muscles involving temporary detachment from globe, one or both eyes

✖ **15.4** Other operations on two or more extraocular muscles, one or both eyes

✖ **15.5** Transposition of extraocular muscles

Excludes | *that for correction of ptosis (08.31–08.36)*

✖ **15.6** Revision of extraocular muscle surgery

✖ **15.7** Repair of injury of extraocular muscle
Freeing of entrapped extraocular muscle
Lysis of adhesions of extraocular muscle
Repair of laceration of extraocular muscle, tendon, or Tenon's capsule

✖ **15.9** Other operations on extraocular muscles and tendons

● **16** Operations on orbit and eyeball

Excludes | *reduction of fracture of orbit (76.78–76.79)*

● **16.0** Orbitotomy

✖ **16.01** Orbitotomy with bone flap
Orbitotomy with lateral approach

✖ **16.02** Orbitotomy with insertion of orbital implant

Excludes | *that with bone flap (16.01)*

✖ **16.09** Other orbitotomy

● **16.1** Removal of penetrating foreign body from eye, not otherwise specified

Excludes | *removal of nonpenetrating foreign body (98.21)*

● **16.2** Diagnostic procedures on orbit and eyeball

16.21 Ophthalmoscopy

✖ **16.22** Diagnostic aspiration of orbit

✖ **16.23** Biopsy of eyeball and orbit

✖ **16.29** Other diagnostic procedures on orbit and eyeball

Excludes | *examination of form and structure of eye (95.11–95.16)*
general and subjective eye examination (95.01–95.09)
microscopic examination of specimen from eye (90.21–90.29)
objective functional tests of eye (95.21–95.26)
ocular thermography (88.82)
tonometry (89.11)
x-ray of orbit (87.14, 87.16)

● **16.3** Evisceration of eyeball

✖ 16.31   Removal of ocular contents with synchronous implant into scleral shell

✖ 16.39   Other evisceration of eyeball

● 16.4   Enucleation of eyeball

✖ 16.41   Enucleation of eyeball with synchronous implant into Tenon's capsule with attachment of muscles
Integrated implant of eyeball

✖ 16.42   Enucleation of eyeball with other synchronous implant

✖ 16.49   Other enucleation of eyeball
Removal of eyeball NOS

● 16.5   Exenteration of orbital contents

✖ 16.51   Exenteration of orbit with removal of adjacent structures
Radical orbitomaxillectomy

✖ 16.52   Exenteration of orbit with therapeutic removal of orbital bone

✖ 16.59   Other exenteration of orbit
Evisceration of orbit NOS
Exenteration of orbit with temporalis muscle transplant

● 16.6   Secondary procedures after removal of eyeball

> **Excludes** *that with synchronous:*
> *enucleation of eyeball (16.41–16.42)*
> *evisceration of eyeball (16.31)*

✖ 16.61   Secondary insertion of ocular implant

✖ 16.62   Revision and reinsertion of ocular implant

✖ 16.63   Revision of enucleation socket with graft

✖ 16.64   Other revision of enucleation socket

✖ 16.65   Secondary graft to exenteration cavity

✖ 16.66   Other revision of exenteration cavity

✖ 16.69   Other secondary procedures after removal of eyeball

● 16.7   Removal of ocular or orbital implant

✖ 16.71   Removal of ocular implant

✖ 16.72   Removal of orbital implant

● 16.8   Repair of injury of eyeball and orbit

✖ 16.81   Repair of wound of orbit

> **Excludes** *reduction of orbital fracture (76.78–76.79)*
> *repair of extraocular muscles (15.7)*

✖ 16.82   Repair of rupture of eyeball
Repair of multiple structures of eye

> **Excludes** *repair of laceration of:*
> *cornea (11.51–11.59)*
> *sclera (12.81)*

✖ 16.89   Other repair of injury of eyeball or orbit

● 16.9   Other operations on orbit and eyeball

> **Excludes** *irrigation of eye (96.51)*
> *prescription and fitting of low vision aids (95.31–95.33)*
> *removal of:*
> *eye prosthesis NEC (97.31)*
> *nonpenetrating foreign body from eye without incision (98.21)*

16.91   Retrobulbar injection of therapeutic agent

> **Excludes** *injection of radiographic contrast material (87.14)*
> *opticociliary injection (12.79)*

✖ 16.92   Excision of lesion of orbit

> **Excludes** *biopsy of orbit (16.23)*

✖ 16.93   Excision of lesion of eye, unspecified structure

> **Excludes** *biopsy of eye NOS (16.23)*

✖ 16.98   Other operations on orbit

✖ 16.99   Other operations on eyeball

4. OPERATIONS ON THE EAR (18–20)

● **18 Operations on external ear**

Includes: operations on:
    external auditory canal
    skin and cartilage of:
      auricle
      meatus

● **18.0 Incision of external ear**
    Excludes *removal of intraluminal foreign body (98.11)*

    18.01 Piercing of ear lobe
      Piercing of pinna

    18.02 Incision of external auditory canal

    18.09 Other incision of external ear

● **18.1 Diagnostic procedures on external ear**

    18.11 Otoscopy

    18.12 Biopsy of external ear

    18.19 Other diagnostic procedures on external ear
    Excludes *microscopic examination of specimen from ear*
      (90.31–90.39)

● **18.2 Excision or destruction of lesion of external ear**

    ✖ **18.21 Excision of preauricular sinus**
      Radical excision of preauricular sinus or cyst
    Excludes *excision of preauricular remnant [appendage]*
      (18.29)

    **18.29 Excision or destruction of other lesion of exter-
    nal ear**
      Cauterization of external ear
      Coagulation of external ear
      Cryosurgery of external ear
      Curettage of external ear
      Electrocoagulation of external ear
      Enucleation of external ear
      Excision of:
        exostosis of external auditory canal
        preauricular remnant [appendage]
      Partial excision of ear
    Excludes *biopsy of external ear (18.12)*
      radical excision of lesion (18.31)
      removal of cerumen (96.52)

● **18.3 Other excision of external ear**
    Excludes *biopsy of external ear (18.12)*

    ✖ **18.31 Radical excision of lesion of external ear**
    Excludes *radical excision of preauricular sinus (18.21)*

    ✖ **18.39 Other**
      Amputation of external ear
    Excludes *excision of lesion (18.21–18.29, 18.31)*

    18.4 Suture of laceration of external ear

✖ **18.5 Surgical correction of prominent ear**
      Ear:
        pinning
        setback

✖ **18.6 Reconstruction of external auditory canal**
      Canaloplasty of external auditory meatus
      Construction [reconstruction] of external meatus
        of ear:
        osseous portion
        skin-lined portion (with skin graft)

● **18.7 Other plastic repair of external ear**

    ✖ **18.71 Construction of auricle of ear**
      Prosthetic appliance for absent ear
      Reconstruction:
        auricle
        ear

    ✖ **18.72 Reattachment of amputated ear**

    ✖ **18.79 Other plastic repair of external ear**
      Otoplasty NOS
      Postauricular skin graft
      Repair of lop ear

    ✖ **18.9 Other operations on external ear**
    Excludes *irrigation of ear (96.52)*
      packing of external auditory canal (96.11)
      removal of:
        cerumen (96.52)
        foreign body (without incision) (98.11)

● **19 Reconstructive operations on middle ear**

    ✖ **19.0 Stapes mobilization**
      Division, otosclerotic:
        material
        process
      Remobilization of stapes
      Stapediolysis
      Transcrural stapes mobilization
    Excludes *that with synchronous stapedectomy (19.11–*
      19.19)

● **19.1 Stapedectomy**
    Excludes *revision of previous stapedectomy (19.21–19.29)*
      stapes mobilization only (19.0)

    ✖ **19.11 Stapedectomy with incus replacement**
      Stapedectomy with incus:
        homograft
        prosthesis

    ✖ **19.19 Other stapedectomy**

● **19.2 Revision of stapedectomy**

    ✖ **19.21 Revision of stapedectomy with incus replace-
    ment**

    ✖ **19.29 Other revision of stapedectomy**

✖ **19.3 Other operations on ossicular chain**
      Incudectomy NOS
      Ossiculectomy NOS
      Reconstruction of ossicles, second stage

✖ **19.4 Myringoplasty**
      Epitympanic, type I
      Myringoplasty by:
        cauterization
        graft
      Tympanoplasty (type I)

● **19.5 Other tympanoplasty**

    ✖ **19.52 Type II tympanoplasty**
      Closure of perforation with graft against incus
        or malleus

    ✖ **19.53 Type III tympanoplasty**
      Graft placed in contact with mobile and intact
        stapes

    ✖ **19.54 Type IV tympanoplasty**
      Mobile footplate left exposed with air pocket
        between round window and graft

    ✖ **19.55 Type V tympanoplasty**
      Fenestra in horizontal semicircular canal cov-
        ered by graft

    ✖ **19.6 Revision of tympanoplasty**

    ✖ **19.9 Other repair of middle ear**
      Closure of mastoid fistula
      Mastoid myoplasty
      Obliteration of tympanomastoid cavity

● **20 Other operations on middle and inner ear**

● **20.0 Myringotomy**

✖ 20.01 Myringotomy with insertion of tube
Myringostomy

✖ 20.09 Other myringotomy
Aspiration of middle ear NOS

20.1 Removal of tympanostomy tube

● 20.2 Incision of mastoid and middle ear

✖ 20.21 Incision of mastoid

✖ 20.22 Incision of petrous pyramid air cells

✖ 20.23 Incision of middle ear
Atticotomy
Division of tympanum
Lysis of adhesions of middle ear

Excludes	*division of otosclerotic process (19.0)*

stapediolysis (19.0)
that with stapedectomy (19.11–19.19)

● 20.3 Diagnostic procedures on middle and inner ear

20.31 Electrocochleography

✖ 20.32 Biopsy of middle and inner ear

✖ 20.39 Other diagnostic procedures on middle and inner ear

Excludes	*auditory and vestibular function tests (89.13,*

95.41–95.49)
microscopic examination of specimen from ear (90.31–90.39)

● 20.4 Mastoidectomy
Code also any:
skin graft (18.79)
tympanoplasty (19.4–19.55)

Excludes	*that with implantation of cochlear prosthetic device (20.96–20.98)*

✖ 20.41 Simple mastoidectomy

✖ 20.42 Radical mastoidectomy

✖ 20.49 Other mastoidectomy
Atticoantrostomy
Mastoidectomy:
NOS
modified radical

● 20.5 Other excision of middle ear

Excludes	*that with synchronous mastoidectomy (20.41–20.49)*

✖ 20.51 Excision of lesion of middle ear

Excludes	*biopsy of middle ear (20.32)*

✖ 20.59 Other
Apicectomy of petrous pyramid
Tympanectomy

● 20.6 Fenestration of inner ear

✖ 20.61 Fenestration of inner ear (initial)
Fenestration of:
labyrinth with graft (skin) (vein)
semicircular canals with graft (skin) (vein)
vestibule with graft (skin) (vein)

Excludes	*that with tympanoplasty, type V (19.55)*

✖ 20.62 Revision of fenestration of inner ear

● 20.7 Incision, excision, and destruction of inner ear

✖ 20.71 Endolymphatic shunt

✖ 20.72 Injection into inner ear
Destruction by injection (alcohol):
inner ear
semicircular canals
vestibule

✖ 20.79 Other incision, excision, and destruction of inner ear
Decompression of labyrinth
Drainage of inner ear
Fistulization:
endolymphatic sac
labyrinth
Incision of endolymphatic sac
Labyrinthectomy (transtympanic)
Opening of bony labyrinth
Perilymphatic tap

Excludes	*biopsy of inner ear (20.32)*

20.8 Operations on Eustachian tube
Catheterization of eustachian tube
Inflation of eustachian tube
Injection (Teflon paste) of eustachian tube
Insufflation (boric acid-salicylic acid) intubation of eustachian tube
Politzerization of eustachian tube

● 20.9 Other operations on inner and middle ear

✖ 20.91 Tympanosympathectomy

✖ 20.92 Revision of mastoidectomy

✖ 20.93 Repair of oval and round windows
Closure of fistula:
oval window
perilymph
round window

20.94 Injection of tympanum

✖ 20.95 Implantation of electromagnetic hearing device
Bone conduction hearing device

Excludes	*cochlear prosthetic device (20.96–20.98)*

✖ 20.96 Implantation or replacement of cochlear prosthetic device, not otherwise specified
Implantation of receiver (within skull) and insertion of electrode(s) in the cochlea

Includes: mastoidectomy

Excludes	*electromagnetic hearing device (20.95)*

✖ 20.97 Implantation or replacement of cochlear prosthetic device, single channel
Implantation of receiver (within skull) and insertion of electrode in the cochlea

Includes: mastoidectomy

Excludes	*electromagnetic hearing device (20.95)*

✖ 20.98 Implantation or replacement of cochlear prosthetic device, multiple channel
Implantation of receiver (within skull) and insertion of electrodes in the cochlea

Includes: mastoidectomy

Excludes	*electromagnetic hearing device (20.95)*

✖ 20.99 Other operations on middle and inner ear
Repair or removal of cochlear prosthetic device (receiver) (electrode)

Excludes	*adjustment (external components) of cochlear prosthetic device (95.49)*

fitting of hearing aid (95.48)

5. OPERATIONS ON THE NOSE, MOUTH, AND PHARYNX (21–29)

● **21 Operations on nose**

Includes: operations on:
bone of nose
skin of nose

● **21.0 Control of epistaxis**

21.00 Control of epistaxis, not otherwise specified

21.01 Control of epistaxis by anterior nasal packing

21.02 Control of epistaxis by posterior (and anterior) packing

21.03 Control of epistaxis by cauterization (and packing)

✖ **21.04 Control of epistaxis by ligation of ethmoidal arteries**

✖ **21.05 Control of epistaxis by (transantral) ligation of the maxillary artery**

✖ **21.06 Control of epistaxis by ligation of the external carotid artery**

✖ **21.07 Control of epistaxis by excision of nasal mucosa and skin grafting of septum and lateral nasal wall**

✖ **21.09 Control of epistaxis by other means**

21.1 Incision of nose
Chondrotomy
Incision of skin of nose
Nasal septotomy

● **21.2 Diagnostic procedures on nose**

21.21 Rhinoscopy

21.22 Biopsy of nose

21.29 Other diagnostic procedures on nose

Excludes *microscopic examination of specimen from nose (90.31–90.39)*
nasal:
function study (89.12)
x-ray (87.16)
rhinomanometry (89.12)

● **21.3 Local excision or destruction of lesion of nose**

Excludes *biopsy of nose (21.22)*
nasal fistulectomy (21.82)

21.30 Excision or destruction of lesion of nose, not otherwise specified

21.31 Local excision or destruction of intranasal lesion
Nasal polypectomy

21.32 Local excision or destruction of other lesion of nose

✖ **21.4 Resection of nose**
Amputation of nose

✖ **21.5 Submucous resection of nasal septum**

● **21.6 Turbinectomy**

✖ **21.61 Turbinectomy by diathermy or cryosurgery**

✖ **21.62 Fracture of the turbinates**

✖ **21.69 Other turbinectomy**

Excludes *turbinectomy associated with sinusectomy (22.31–22.39, 22.42, 22.60–22.64)*

● **21.7 Reduction of nasal fracture**

21.71 Closed reduction of nasal fracture

✖ **21.72 Open reduction of nasal fracture**

● **21.8 Repair and plastic operations on the nose**

21.81 Suture of laceration of nose

✖ **21.82 Closure of nasal fistula**
Nasolabial fistulectomy
Nasopharyngeal fistulectomy
Oronasal fistulectomy

✖ **21.83 Total nasal reconstruction**
Reconstruction of nose with:
arm flap
forehead flap

✖ **21.84 Revision rhinoplasty**
Rhinoseptoplasty
Twisted nose rhinoplasty

✖ **21.85 Augmentation rhinoplasty**
Augmentation rhinoplasty with:
graft
synthetic implant

✖ **21.86 Limited rhinoplasty**
Plastic repair of nasolabial flaps
Tip rhinoplasty

✖ **21.87 Other rhinoplasty**
Rhinoplasty NOS

✖ **21.88 Other septoplasty**
Crushing of nasal septum
Repair of septal perforation

Excludes *septoplasty associated with submucous resection of septum (21.5)*

✖ **21.89 Other repair and plastic operations on nose**
Reattachment of amputated nose

● **21.9 Other operations on nose**

21.91 Lysis of adhesions of nose
Posterior nasal scrub

✖ **21.99 Other**

Excludes *dilation of frontonasal duct (96.21)*
irrigation of nasal passages (96.53)
removal of:
intraluminal foreign body without incision (98.12)
nasal packing (97.32)
replacement of nasal packing (97.21)

● **22 Operations on nasal sinuses**

● **22.0 Aspiration and lavage of nasal sinus**

22.00 Aspiration and lavage of nasal sinus, not otherwise specified

22.01 Puncture of nasal sinus for aspiration or lavage

22.02 Aspiration or lavage of nasal sinus through natural ostium

● **22.1 Diagnostic procedures on nasal sinus**

22.11 Closed [endoscopic] [needle] biopsy of nasal sinus

✖ **22.12 Open biopsy of nasal sinus**

22.19 Other diagnostic procedures on nasal sinuses
Endoscopy without biopsy

Excludes *transillumination of sinus (89.35)*
x-ray of sinus (87.15–87.16)

22.2 Intranasal antrotomy

Excludes *antrotomy with external approach (22.31–22.39)*

● **22.3 External maxillary antrotomy**

✖ **22.31 Radical maxillary antrotomy**
Removal of lining membrane of maxillary sinus using Caldwell-Luc approach

22.39 Other external maxillary antrotomy
Exploration of maxillary antrum with Caldwell-Luc approach

22.4 Frontal sinusotomy and sinusectomy

22.41 Frontal sinusotomy

22.42 Frontal sinusectomy
Excision of lesion of frontal sinus
Obliteration of frontal sinus (with fat)

Excludes *biopsy of nasal sinus (22.11–22.12)*

22.5 Other nasal sinusotomy

22.50 Sinusotomy, not otherwise specified

22.51 Ethmoidotomy

22.52 Sphenoidotomy

22.53 Incision of multiple nasal sinuses

22.6 Other nasal sinusectomy

Includes: that with incidental turbinectomy

Excludes *biopsy of nasal sinus (22.11–22.12)*

22.60 Sinusectomy, not otherwise specified

22.61 Excision of lesion of maxillary sinus with Caldwell-Luc approach

22.62 Excision of lesion of maxillary sinus with other approach

22.63 Ethmoidectomy

22.64 Sphenoidectomy

22.7 Repair of nasal sinus

22.71 Closure of nasal sinus fistula
Repair of oro-antral fistula

22.79 Other repair of nasal sinus
Reconstruction of frontonasal duct
Repair of bone of accessory sinus

22.9 Other operations on nasal sinuses
Exteriorization of maxillary sinus
Fistulization of sinus

Excludes *dilation of frontonasal duct (96.21)*

23 Removal and restoration of teeth

23.0 Forceps extraction of tooth

23.01 Extraction of deciduous tooth

23.09 Extraction of other tooth
Extraction of tooth NOS

23.1 Surgical removal of tooth

23.11 Removal of residual root

23.19 Other surgical extraction of tooth
Odontectomy NOS
Removal of impacted tooth
Tooth extraction with elevation of mucoperiosteal flap

23.2 Restoration of tooth by filling

23.3 Restoration of tooth by inlay

23.4 Other dental restoration

23.41 Application of crown

23.42 Insertion of fixed bridge

23.43 Insertion of removable bridge

23.49 Other

23.5 Implantation of tooth

23.6 Prosthetic dental implant
Endosseous dental implant

23.7 Apicoectomy and root canal therapy

23.70 Root canal, not otherwise specified

23.71 Root canal therapy with irrigation

23.72 Root canal therapy with apicoectomy

23.73 Apicoectomy

24 Other operations on teeth, gums, and alveoli

24.0 Incision of gum or alveolar bone
Apical alveolotomy

24.1 Diagnostic procedures on teeth, gums, and alveoli

24.11 Biopsy of gum

24.12 Biopsy of alveolus

24.19 Other diagnostic procedures on teeth, gums, and alveoli

Excludes *dental:*
examination (89.31)
x-ray:
full-mouth (87.11)
other (87.12)
microscopic examination of dental specimen (90.81–90.89)

24.2 Gingivoplasty
Gingivoplasty with bone or soft tissue graft

24.3 Other operations on gum

24.31 Excision of lesion or tissue of gum

Excludes *biopsy of gum (24.11)*
excision of odontogenic lesion (24.4)

24.32 Suture of laceration of gum

24.39 Other

24.4 Excision of dental lesion of jaw
Excision of odontogenic lesion

24.5 Alveoloplasty
Alveolectomy (interradicular) (intraseptal) (radical) (simple) (with graft or implant)

Excludes *biopsy of alveolus (24.12)*
en bloc resection of alveolar process and palate (27.32)

24.6 Exposure of tooth

24.7 Application of orthodontic appliance
Application, insertion, or fitting of:
arch bars
orthodontic obturator
orthodontic wiring
periodontal splint

Excludes *nonorthodontic dental wiring (93.55)*

24.8 Other orthodontic operation
Closure of diastema (alveolar) (dental)
Occlusal adjustment
Removal of arch bars
Repair of dental arch

Excludes *removal of nonorthodontic wiring (97.33)*

24.9 Other dental operations

24.91 Extension or deepening of buccolabial or lingual sulcus

24.99 Other

> **Excludes** *dental:*
> *debridement (96.54)*
> *examination (89.31)*
> *prophylaxis (96.54)*
> *scaling and polishing (96.54)*
> *wiring (93.55)*
> *fitting of dental appliance [denture] (99.97)*
> *microscopic examination of dental specimen (90.81–90.89)*
> *removal of dental:*
> *packing (97.34)*
> *prosthesis (97.35)*
> *wiring (97.33)*
> *replacement of dental packing (97.22)*

● **25 Operations on tongue**

● **25.0 Diagnostic procedures on tongue**

25.01 Closed [needle] biopsy of tongue

✖ **25.02 Open biopsy of tongue**
Wedge biopsy

25.09 Other diagnostic procedures on tongue

✖ **25.1 Excision or destruction of lesion or tissue of tongue**

> **Excludes** *biopsy of tongue (25.01–25.02)*
> *frenumectomy:*
> *labial (27.41)*
> *lingual (25.92)*

✖ **25.2 Partial glossectomy**

✖ **25.3 Complete glossectomy**
Glossectomy NOS

Code also any neck dissection (40.40–40.42)

✖ **25.4 Radical glossectomy**

Code also any:
neck dissection (40.40–40.42)
tracheostomy (31.1–31.29)

● **25.5 Repair of tongue and glossoplasty**

25.51 Suture of laceration of tongue

✖ **25.59 Other repair and plastic operations on tongue**
Fascial sling of tongue
Fusion of tongue (to lip)
Graft of mucosa or skin to tongue

> **Excludes** *lysis of adhesions of tongue (25.93)*

● **25.9 Other operations on tongue**

25.91 Lingual frenotomy

> **Excludes** *labial frenotomy (27.91)*

25.92 Lingual frenectomy

> **Excludes** *labial frenectomy (27.41)*

25.93 Lysis of adhesions of tongue

✖ **25.94 Other glossotomy**

✖ **25.99 Other**

● **26 Operations on salivary glands and ducts**

Includes: operations on:
lesser salivary gland and duct
parotid gland and duct
sublingual gland and duct
submaxillary gland and duct

Code also any neck dissection (40.40–40.42)

26.0 Incision of salivary gland or duct

● **26.1 Diagnostic procedures on salivary glands and ducts**

26.11 Closed [needle] biopsy of salivary gland or duct

✖ **26.12 Open biopsy of salivary gland or duct**

26.19 Other diagnostic procedures on salivary glands and ducts

> **Excludes** *x-ray of salivary gland (87.09)*

● **26.2 Excision of lesion of salivary gland**

✖ **26.21 Marsupialization of salivary gland cyst**

✖ **26.29 Other excision of salivary gland lesion**

> **Excludes** *biopsy of salivary gland (26.11–26.12)*
> *salivary fistulectomy (26.42)*

● **26.3 Sialoadenectomy**

✖ **26.30 Sialoadenectomy, not otherwise specified**

✖ **26.31 Partial sialoadenectomy**

✖ **26.32 Complete sialoadenectomy**
En bloc excision of salivary gland lesion
Radical sialoadenectomy

● **26.4 Repair of salivary gland or duct**

✖ **26.41 Suture of laceration of salivary gland**

✖ **26.42 Closure of salivary fistula**

✖ **26.49 Other repair and plastic operations on salivary gland or duct**
Fistulization of salivary gland
Plastic repair of salivary gland or duct NOS
Transplantation of salivary duct opening

● **26.9 Other operations on salivary gland or duct**

26.91 Probing of salivary duct

✖ **26.99 Other**

● **27 Other operations on mouth and face**

Includes: operations on:
lips
palate
soft tissue of face and mouth, except tongue and gingiva

> **Excludes** *operations on:*
> *gingiva (24.0–24.99)*
> *tongue (25.01–25.99)*

✖ **27.0 Drainage of face and floor of mouth**
Drainage of:
facial region (abscess)
fascial compartment of face
Ludwig's angina

> **Excludes** *drainage of thyroglossal tract (06.09)*

✖ **27.1 Incision of palate**

● **27.2 Diagnostic procedures on oral cavity**

✖ **27.21 Biopsy of bony palate**

✖ **27.22 Biopsy of uvula and soft palate**

27.23 Biopsy of lip

27.24 Biopsy of mouth, unspecified structure

27.29 Other diagnostic procedures on oral cavity

> **Excludes** *soft tissue x-ray (87.09)*

● **27.3 Excision of lesion or tissue of bony palate**

✖ **27.31 Local excision or destruction of lesion or tissue of bony palate**
Local excision or destruction of palate by:
cautery
chemotherapy
cryotherapy

> **Excludes** *biopsy of bony palate (27.21)*

✖ **27.32 Wide excision or destruction of lesion or tissue of bony palate**
En bloc resection of alveolar process and palate

● **Use Additional Digit(s)**   ✖ **Valid O.R. Procedure**   ◀▶ **New Code**   ⬅▶ **Revised Code**

● **27.4 Excision of other parts of mouth**

  27.41 Labial frenectomy

  Excludes *division of labial frenum (27.91)*

✖ **27.42 Wide excision of lesion of lip**

✖ **27.43 Other excision of lesion or tissue of lip**

✖ **27.49 Other excision of mouth**

  Excludes *biopsy of mouth NOS (27.24)*
  excision of lesion of:
  palate (27.31–27.32)
  tongue (25.1)
  uvula (27.72)
  fistulectomy of mouth (27.53)
  frenectomy of:
  lip (27.41)
  tongue (25.92)

● **27.5 Plastic repair of mouth**

  Excludes *palatoplasty (27.61–27.69)*

  27.51 Suture of laceration of lip

  27.52 Suture of laceration of other part of mouth

✖ **27.53 Closure of fistula of mouth**

  Excludes *fistulectomy:*
  nasolabial (21.82)
  oro-antral (22.71)
  oronasal (21.82)

✖ **27.54 Repair of cleft lip**

✖ **27.55 Full-thickness skin graft to lip and mouth**

✖ **27.56 Other skin graft to lip and mouth**

✖ **27.57 Attachment of pedicle or flap graft to lip and mouth**

✖ **27.59 Other plastic repair of mouth**

● **27.6 Palatoplasty**

✖ **27.61 Suture of laceration of palate**

✖ **27.62 Correction of cleft palate**
  Correction of cleft palate by push-back operation

  Excludes *revision of cleft palate repair (27.63)*

✖ **27.63 Revision of cleft palate repair**
  Secondary:
  attachment of pharyngeal flap
  lengthening of palate

✖ **27.69 Other plastic repair of palate**

  Excludes *fistulectomy of mouth (27.53)*

● **27.7 Operations on uvula**

✖ **27.71 Incision of uvula**

✖ **27.72 Excision of uvula**

  Excludes *biopsy of uvula (27.22)*

✖ **27.73 Repair of uvula**

  Excludes *that with synchronous cleft palate repair (27.62)*
  uranostaphylorrhaphy (27.62)

✖ **27.79 Other operations on uvula**

● **27.9 Other operations on mouth and face**

  27.91 Labial frenotomy
  Division of labial frenum

  Excludes *lingual frenotomy (25.91)*

✖ **27.92 Incision of mouth, unspecified structure**

  Excludes *incision of:*
  gum (24.0)
  palate (27.1)
  salivary gland or duct (26.0)
  tongue (25.94)
  uvula (27.71)

✖ **27.99 Other operations on oral cavity**
  Graft of buccal sulcus

  Excludes *removal of:*
  intraluminal foreign body (98.01)
  penetrating foreign body from mouth without incision (98.22)

● **28 Operations on tonsils and adenoids**

  28.0 Incision and drainage of tonsil and peritonsillar structures
  Drainage (oral) (transcervical) of:
  parapharyngeal abscess
  peritonsillar abscess
  retropharyngeal abscess
  tonsillar abscess

● **28.1 Diagnostic procedures on tonsils and adenoids**

✖ **28.11 Biopsy of tonsils and adenoids**

✖ **28.19 Other diagnostic procedures on tonsils and adenoids**

  Excludes *soft tissue x-ray (87.09)*

✖ **28.2 Tonsillectomy without adenoidectomy**

✖ **28.3 Tonsillectomy with adenoidectomy**

✖ **28.4 Excision of tonsil tag**

✖ **28.5 Excision of lingual tonsil**

✖ **28.6 Adenoidectomy without tonsillectomy**
  Excision of adenoid tag

✖ **28.7 Control of hemorrhage after tonsillectomy and adenoidectomy**

● **28.9 Other operations on tonsils and adenoids**

✖ **28.91 Removal of foreign body from tonsil and adenoid by incision**

  Excludes *that without incision (98.13)*

✖ **28.92 Excision of lesion of tonsil and adenoid**

  Excludes *biopsy of tonsil and adenoid (28.11)*

✖ **28.99 Other**

● **29 Operations on pharynx**

  Includes: operations on:
  hypopharynx
  nasopharynx
  oropharynx
  pharyngeal pouch
  pyriform sinus

✖ **29.0 Pharyngotomy**
  Drainage of pharyngeal bursa

  Excludes *incision and drainage of retropharyngeal abscess (28.0)*
  removal of foreign body (without incision) (98.13)

● **29.1 Diagnostic procedures on pharynx**

  29.11 Pharyngoscopy

  29.12 Pharyngeal biopsy
  Biopsy of supraglottic mass

  29.19 Other diagnostic procedures on pharynx

  Excludes *x-ray of nasopharynx:*
  contrast (87.06)
  other (87.09)

✖ **29.2 Excision of branchial cleft cyst or vestige**

  Excludes *branchial cleft fistulectomy (29.52)*

● **29.3 Excision or destruction of lesion or tissue of pharynx**

✖ **29.31 Cricopharyngeal myotomy**

  Excludes *that with pharyngeal diverticulectomy (29.32)*

✖ **29.32 Pharyngeal diverticulectomy**

✖ **29.33 Pharyngectomy (partial)**
> **Excludes** *laryngopharyngectomy (30.3)*

✖ **29.39 Other excision or destruction of lesion or tissue of pharynx**

✖ **29.4 Plastic operation on pharynx**
Correction of nasopharyngeal atresia
> **Excludes** *pharyngoplasty associated with cleft palate repair (27.62–27.63)*

● **29.5 Other repair of pharynx**

✖ **29.51 Suture of laceration of pharynx**

✖ **29.52 Closure of branchial cleft fistula**

✖ **29.53 Closure of other fistula of pharynx**
Pharyngoesophageal fistulectomy

✖ **29.54 Lysis of pharyngeal adhesions**

✖ **29.59 Other**

● **29.9 Other operations on pharynx**

29.91 Dilation of pharynx
Dilation of nasopharynx

✖ **29.92 Division of glossopharyngeal nerve**

✖ **29.99 Other**
> **Excludes** *insertion of radium into pharynx and nasopharynx (92.27)*
> *removal of intraluminal foreign body (98.13)*

6.   OPERATIONS ON THE RESPIRATORY SYSTEM (30–34)

● **30   Excision of larynx**

  ● **30.0   Excision or destruction of lesion or tissue of larynx**

   ✖ **30.01   Marsupialization of laryngeal cyst**

   ✖ **30.09   Other excision or destruction of lesion or tissue of larynx**
        Stripping of vocal cords
        Excludes   *biopsy of larynx (31.43)*
                    laryngeal fistulectomy (31.62)
                    laryngotracheal fistulectomy (31.62)

  ✖ **30.1   Hemilaryngectomy**

  ● **30.2   Other partial laryngectomy**

   ✖ **30.21   Epiglottidectomy**

   ✖ **30.22   Vocal cordectomy**
        Excision of vocal cords

   ✖ **30.29   Other partial laryngectomy**
        Excision of laryngeal cartilage

  ✖ **30.3   Complete laryngectomy**
        Block dissection of larynx (with thyroidectomy) (with synchronous tracheostomy)
        Laryngopharyngectomy
        Excludes   *that with radical neck dissection (30.4)*

  ✖ **30.4   Radical laryngectomy**
        Complete [total] laryngectomy with radical neck dissection (with thyroidectomy) (with synchronous tracheostomy)

● **31   Other operations on larynx and trachea**

  31.0   Injection of larynx
        Injection of inert material into larynx or vocal cords

  31.1   Temporary tracheostomy
        Tracheotomy for assistance in breathing

  ● **31.2   Permanent tracheostomy**

   ✖ **31.21   Mediastinal tracheostomy**

   ✖ **31.29   Other permanent tracheostomy**
        Excludes   *that with laryngectomy (30.3–30.4)*

  ✖ **31.3   Other incision of larynx or trachea**
        Excludes   *that for assistance in breathing (31.1–31.29)*

  ● **31.4   Diagnostic procedures on larynx and trachea**

   31.41   Tracheoscopy through artificial stoma
        Excludes   *that with biopsy (31.43–31.44)*

   31.42   Laryngoscopy and other tracheoscopy
        Excludes   *that with biopsy (31.43–31.44)*

   31.43   Closed [endoscopic] biopsy of larynx

   31.44   Closed [endoscopic] biopsy of trachea

   ✖ **31.45   Open biopsy of larynx or trachea**

   31.48   Other diagnostic procedures on larynx
        Excludes   *contrast laryngogram (87.07)*
                    microscopic examination of specimen from larynx (90.31–90.39)
                    soft tissue x-ray of larynx NEC (87.09)

   31.49   Other diagnostic procedures on trachea
        Excludes   *microscopic examination of specimen from trachea (90.41–90.49)*
                    x-ray of trachea (87.49)

  ✖ **31.5   Local excision or destruction of lesion or tissue of trachea**
        Excludes   *biopsy of trachea (31.44–31.45)*
                    laryngotracheal fistulectomy (31.62)
                    tracheoesophageal fistulectomy (31.73)

  ● **31.6   Repair of larynx**

   ✖ **31.61   Suture of laceration of larynx**

   ✖ **31.62   Closure of fistula of larynx**
        Laryngotracheal fistulectomy
        Take-down of laryngostomy

   ✖ **31.63   Revision of laryngostomy**

   ✖ **31.64   Repair of laryngeal fracture**

   ✖ **31.69   Other repair of larynx**
        Arytenoidopexy
        Graft of larynx
        Transposition of vocal cords
        Excludes   *construction of artificial larynx (31.75)*

  ● **31.7   Repair and plastic operations on trachea**

   ✖ **31.71   Suture of laceration of trachea**

   ✖ **31.72   Closure of external fistula of trachea**
        Closure of tracheotomy

   ✖ **31.73   Closure of other fistula of trachea**
        Tracheoesophageal fistulectomy
        Excludes   *laryngotracheal fistulectomy (31.62)*

   ✖ **31.74   Revision of tracheostomy**

   ✖ **31.75   Reconstruction of trachea and construction of artificial larynx**
        Tracheoplasty with artificial larynx

   ✖ **31.79   Other repair and plastic operations on trachea**

  ● **31.9   Other operations on larynx and trachea**

   ✖ **31.91   Division of laryngeal nerve**

   ✖ **31.92   Lysis of adhesions of trachea or larynx**

   31.93   Replacement of laryngeal or tracheal stent

   31.94   Injection of locally-acting therapeutic substance into trachea

   31.95   Tracheoesophageal fistulization

   ✖ **31.98   Other operations on larynx**
        Dilation of larynx
        Division of congenital web of larynx
        Removal of keel or stent of larynx
        Excludes   *removal of intraluminal foreign body from larynx without incision (98.14)*

   ✖ **31.99   Other operations on trachea**
        Excludes   *removal of:*
                    intraluminal foreign body from trachea without incision (98.15)
                    tracheostomy tube (97.37)
                    replacement of tracheostomy tube (97.23)
                    tracheostomy toilette (96.55)

● **32   Excision of lung and bronchus**

  Includes: rib resection as operative approach
            sternotomy as operative approach
            sternum-splitting incision as operative approach
            thoracotomy as operative approach

  Code also any synchronous bronchoplasty (33.48)

  ● **32.0   Local excision or destruction of lesion or tissue of bronchus**
        Excludes   *biopsy of bronchus (33.24–33.25)*
                    bronchial fistulectomy (33.42)

32.01   Endoscopic excision or destruction of lesion or tissue of bronchus

✖ **32.09   Other local excision or destruction of lesion or tissue of bronchus**

> **Excludes**   *that by endoscopic approach (32.01)*

✖ **32.1   Other excision of bronchus**
Resection (wide sleeve) of bronchus

> **Excludes**   *radical dissection [excision] of bronchus (32.6)*

● **32.2   Local excision or destruction of lesion or tissue of lung**

✖ **32.21   Plication of emphysematous bleb**

✖ **32.22   Lung volume reduction surgery**

32.28   Endoscopic excision or destruction of lesion or tissue of lung

> **Excludes**   *biopsy of lung (33.26–33.27)*

✖ **32.29   Other local excision or destruction of lesion or tissue of lung**
Resection of lung:
    NOS
    wedge

> **Excludes**   *biopsy of lung (33.26–33.27)*
> *that by endoscopic approach (32.28)*
> *wide excision of lesion of lung (32.3)*

✖ **32.3   Segmental resection of lung**
Partial lobectomy

✖ **32.4   Lobectomy of lung**
Lobectomy with segmental resection of adjacent lobes of lung

> **Excludes**   *that with radical dissection [excision] of thoracic structures (32.6)*

✖ **32.5   Complete pneumonectomy**
Excision of lung NOS
Pneumonectomy (with mediastinal dissection)

✖ **32.6   Radical dissection of thoracic structures**
Block [en bloc] dissection of bronchus, lobe of lung, brachial plexus, intercostal structure, ribs (transverse process), and sympathetic nerves

✖ **32.9   Other excision of lung**

> **Excludes**   *biopsy of lung and bronchus (33.24–33.27)*
> *pulmonary decortication (34.51)*

● **33   Other operations on lung and bronchus**

> **Includes:**   rib resection as operative approach
> sternotomy as operative approach
> sternum-splitting incision as operative approach
> thoracotomy as operative approach

✖ **33.0   Incision of bronchus**

✖ **33.1   Incision of lung**

> **Excludes**   *puncture of lung (33.93)*

● **33.2   Diagnostic procedures on lung and bronchus**

33.21   Bronchoscopy through artificial stoma

> **Excludes**   *that with biopsy (33.24, 33.27)*

33.22   Fiber-optic bronchoscopy

> **Excludes**   *that with biopsy (33.24, 33.27)*

33.23   Other bronchoscopy

> **Excludes**   *that for:*
> *aspiration (96.05)*
> *biopsy (33.24, 33.27)*

✖ **33.24   Closed [endoscopic] biopsy of bronchus**
Bronchoscopy (fiberoptic) (rigid) with:
    brush biopsy of "lung"
    brushing or washing for specimen collection
    excision (bite) biopsy

> **Excludes**   *closed biopsy of lung, other than brush biopsy of "lung" (33.26, 33.27)*

✖ **33.25   Open biopsy of bronchus**

> **Excludes**   *open biopsy of lung (33.28)*

33.26   Closed [percutaneous] [needle] biopsy of lung

> **Excludes**   *endoscopic biopsy of lung (33.27)*

✖ **33.27   Closed endoscopic biopsy of lung**
Fiber-optic (flexible) bronchoscopy with fluoroscopic guidance with biopsy
Transbronchial lung biopsy

> **Excludes**   *brush biopsy of "lung" (33.24)*
> *percutaneous biopsy of lung (33.26)*

✖ **33.28   Open biopsy of lung**

✖ **33.29   Other diagnostic procedures on lung and bronchus**

> **Excludes**   *contrast bronchogram:*
> *endotracheal (87.31)*
> *other (87.32)*
> *lung scan (92.15)*
> *magnetic resonance imaging (88.92)*
> *microscopic examination of specimen from bronchus or lung (90.41–90.49)*
> *routine chest x-ray (87.44)*
> *ultrasonography of lung (88.73)*
> *vital capacity determination (89.37)*
> *x-ray of bronchus or lung NOS (87.49)*

● **33.3   Surgical collapse of lung**

33.31   Destruction of phrenic nerve for collapse of lung

33.32   Artificial pneumothorax for collapse of lung
Thoracotomy for collapse of lung

33.33   Pneumoperitoneum for collapse of lung

✖ **33.34   Thoracoplasty**

✖ **33.39   Other surgical collapse of lung**
Collapse of lung NOS

● **33.4   Repair and plastic operation on lung and bronchus**

✖ **33.41   Suture of laceration of bronchus**

✖ **33.42   Closure of bronchial fistula**
Closure of bronchostomy
Fistulectomy:
    bronchocutaneous
    bronchoesophageal
    bronchovisceral

> **Excludes**   *closure of fistula:*
> *bronchomediastinal (34.73)*
> *bronchopleural (34.73)*
> *bronchopleuromediastinal (34.73)*

✖ **33.43   Closure of laceration of lung**

✖ **33.48   Other repair and plastic operations on bronchus**

✖ **33.49   Other repair and plastic operations on lung**

> **Excludes**   *closure of pleural fistula (34.73)*

✖ **33.5   Lung transplant**

> **Excludes**   *combined heart-lung transplantation (33.6)*

Code also cardiopulmonary bypass [extracorporeal circulation] [heart-lung machine] (39.61)

✖ **33.50   Lung transplantation, not otherwise specified**

✖ **33.51   Unilateral lung transplantation**

✖ **33.52 Bilateral lung transplantation**
    Double-lung transplantation
    En bloc transplantation

    Code also cardiopulmonary bypass [extracorporeal circulation] [heart-lung machine] (39.61)

✖ **33.6 Combined heart-lung transplantation**

    Code also cardiopulmonary bypass [extracorporeal circulation] [heart-lung machine] (39.61)

● **33.9 Other operations on lung and bronchus**

    33.91 Bronchial dilation

✖ **33.92 Ligation of bronchus**

✖ **33.93 Puncture of lung**
    | Excludes | *needle biopsy (33.26)*

✖ **33.98 Other operations on bronchus**
    | Excludes | *bronchial lavage (96.56)*
    removal of intraluminal foreign body from bronchus without incision (98.15)

✖ **33.99 Other operations on lung**
    | Excludes | *other continuous mechanical ventilation (96.70–96.72)*
    respiratory therapy (93.90–93.99)

● **34 Operations on chest wall, pleura, mediastinum, and diaphragm**
    | Excludes | *operations on breast (85.0–85.99)*

● **34.0 Incision of chest wall and pleura**
    | Excludes | *that as operative approach—omit code*

    34.01 Incision of chest wall
    Extrapleural drainage
    | Excludes | *incision of pleura (34.09)*

✖ **34.02 Exploratory thoracotomy**

✖ **34.03 Reopening of recent thoracotomy site**

    34.04 Insertion of intercostal catheter for drainage
    Chest tube
    Closed chest drainage
    Revision of intercostal catheter (chest tube) (with lysis of adhesions)

    34.05 Creation of pleuroperitoneal shunt

    34.09 Other incision of pleura
    Creation of pleural window for drainage
    Intercostal stab
    Open chest drainage
    | Excludes | *thoracoscopy (34.21)*
    thoracotomy for collapse of lung (33.32)

✖ **34.1 Incision of mediastinum**
    | Excludes | *mediastinoscopy (34.22)*
    mediastinotomy associated with pneumonectomy (32.5)

● **34.2 Diagnostic procedures on chest wall, pleura, mediastinum, and diaphragm**

    34.21 Transpleural thoracoscopy

✖ **34.22 Mediastinoscopy**

    Code also any lymph node biopsy (40.11)

    34.23 Biopsy of chest wall

    34.24 Pleural biopsy

    34.25 Closed [percutaneous] [needle] biopsy of mediastinum

✖ **34.26 Open mediastinal biopsy**

✖ **34.27 Biopsy of diaphragm**

✖ **34.28 Other diagnostic procedures on chest wall, pleura, and diaphragm**
    | Excludes | *angiocardiography (88.50–88.58)*
    aortography (88.42)
    arteriography of:
      intrathoracic vessels NEC (88.44)
      pulmonary arteries (88.43)
    microscopic examination of specimen from chest wall, pleura, and diaphragm (90.41–90.49)
    phlebography of:
      intrathoracic vessels NEC (88.63)
      pulmonary veins (88.62)
    radiological examinations of thorax:
      C.A.T. scan (87.41)
      diaphragmatic x-ray (87.49)
      intrathoracic lymphangiogram (87.34)
      routine chest x-ray (87.44)
      sinogram of chest wall (87.38)
      soft tissue x-ray of chest wall NEC (87.39)
      tomogram of thorax NEC (87.42)
      ultrasonography of thorax 88.73)

✖ **34.29 Other diagnostic procedures on mediastinum**
    | Excludes | *mediastinal:*
      pneumogram (87.33)
      x-ray NEC (87.49)

✖ **34.3 Excision or destruction of lesion or tissue of mediastinum**
    | Excludes | *biopsy of mediastinum (34.25–34.26)*
    mediastinal fistulectomy (34.73)

✖ **34.4 Excision or destruction of lesion of chest wall**
    Excision of lesion of chest wall NOS (with excision of ribs)
    | Excludes | *biopsy of chest wall (34.23)*
    costectomy not incidental to thoracic procedure (77.91)
    excision of lesion of:
      breast (85.20–85.25)
      cartilage (80.89)
      skin (86.2–86.3)
    fistulectomy (34.73)

● **34.5 Pleurectomy**

✖ **34.51 Decortication of lung**

✖ **34.59 Other excision of pleura**
    Excision of pleural lesion
    | Excludes | *biopsy of pleura (34.24)*
    pleural fistulectomy (34.73)

✖ **34.6 Scarification of pleura**
    Pleurosclerosis
    | Excludes | *injection of sclerosing agent (34.92)*

● **34.7 Repair of chest wall**

    34.71 Suture of laceration of chest wall
    | Excludes | *suture of skin and subcutaneous tissue alone (86.59)*

    34.72 Closure of thoracostomy

✖ **34.73 Closure of other fistula of thorax**
    Closure of:
      bronchopleural fistula
      bronchopleurocutaneous fistula
      bronchopleuromediastinal fistula

✖ **34.74 Repair of pectus deformity**
    Repair of:
      pectus carinatum (with implant)
      pectus excavatum (with implant)

✖ **34.79 Other repair of chest wall**
    Repair of chest wall NOS

● **34.8 Operations on diaphragm**

✖ **34.81 Excision of lesion or tissue of diaphragm**

    Excludes *biopsy of diaphragm (34.27)*

✖ **34.82 Suture of laceration of diaphragm**

✖ **34.83 Closure of fistula of diaphragm**
    Thoracicoabdominal fistulectomy
    Thoracicogastric fistulectomy
    Thoracicointestinal fistulectomy

✖ **34.84 Other repair of diaphragm**

    Excludes *repair of diaphragmatic hernia (53.7–53.82)*

✖ **34.85 Implantation of diaphragmatic pacemaker**

✖ **34.89 Other operations on diaphragm**

● **34.9 Other operations on thorax**

  34.91 Thoracentesis

  34.92 Injection into thoracic cavity
    Chemical pleurodesis
    Injection of cytotoxic agent or tetracycline
    Requires additional code for any cancer
      chemotherapeutic substance (99.25)

    Excludes *that for collapse of lung (33.32)*

✖ **34.93 Repair of pleura**

✖ **34.99 Other**

    Excludes *removal of:*
      mediastinal drain (97.42)
      sutures (97.43)
      thoracotomy tube (97.41)

7. OPERATIONS ON THE CARDIOVASCULAR SYSTEM (35–39)

● **35 Operations on valves and septa of heart**

Includes: sternotomy (median) (transverse) as operative
approach
thoracotomy as operative approach

Code also cardiopulmonary bypass [extracorporeal circulation] [heart-lung machine] (39.61)

● **35.0 Closed heart valvotomy**

Excludes *percutaneous (balloon) valvuloplasty (35.96)*

✖ **35.00 Closed heart valvotomy, unspecified valve**

✖ **35.01 Closed heart valvotomy, aortic valve**

✖ **35.02 Closed heart valvotomy, mitral valve**

✖ **35.03 Closed heart valvotomy, pulmonary valve**

✖ **35.04 Closed heart valvotomy, tricuspid valve**

● **35.1 Open heart valvuloplasty without replacement**

Includes: open heart valvotomy

Excludes *that associated with repair of:*
endocardial cushion defect (35.54, 35.63, 35.73)
valvular defect associated with atrial and ventricular septal defects (35.54, 35.63, 35.73)
percutaneous (balloon) valvuloplasty (35.96)

Code also cardiopulmonary bypass if performed [extracorporeal circulation] [heart-lung machine] (39.61)

✖ **35.10 Open heart valvuloplasty without replacement, unspecified valve**

✖ **35.11 Open heart valvuloplasty of aortic valve without replacement**

✖ **35.12 Open heart valvuloplasty of mitral valve without replacement**

✖ **35.13 Open heart valvuloplasty of pulmonary valve without replacement**

✖ **35.14 Open heart valvuloplasty of tricuspid valve without replacement**

● **35.2 Replacement of heart valve**

Includes: excision of heart valve with replacement

Code also cardiopulmonary bypass [extracorporeal circulation] [heart-lung machine] (39.61)

Excludes *that associated with repair of:*
endocardial cushion defect (35.54, 35.63, 35.73)
valvular defect associated with atrial and ventricular septal defects (35.54, 35.63, 35.73)

✖ **35.20 Replacement of unspecified heart valve**
Repair of unspecified heart valve with tissue graft or prosthetic implant

✖ **35.21 Replacement of aortic valve with tissue graft**
Repair of aortic valve with tissue graft (autograft) (heterograft) (homograft)

✖ **35.22 Other replacement of aortic valve**
Repair of aortic valve with replacement:
NOS
prosthetic (partial) (synthetic) (total)

✖ **35.23 Replacement of mitral valve with tissue graft**
Repair of mitral valve with tissue graft (autograft) (heterograft) (homograft)

✖ **35.24 Other replacement of mitral valve**
Repair of mitral valve with replacement:
NOS
prosthetic (partial) (synthetic) (total)

✖ **35.25 Replacement of pulmonary valve with tissue graft**
Repair of pulmonary valve with tissue graft (autograft) (heterograft) (homograft)

✖ **35.26 Other replacement of pulmonary valve**
Repair of pulmonary valve with replacement:
NOS
prosthetic (partial) (synthetic) (total)

✖ **35.27 Replacement of tricuspid valve with tissue graft**
Repair of tricuspid valve with tissue graft (autograft) (heterograft) (homograft)

✖ **35.28 Other replacement of tricuspid valve**
Repair of tricuspid valve with replacement:
NOS
prosthetic (partial) (synthetic) (total)

● **35.3 Operations on structures adjacent to heart valves**

Code also cardiopulmonary bypass [extracorporeal circulation] [heart-lung machine] (39.61)

✖ **35.31 Operations on papillary muscle**
Division of papillary muscle
Reattachment of papillary muscle
Repair of papillary muscle

✖ **35.32 Operations on chordae tendineae**
Division of chordae tendineae
Repair of chordae tendineae

✖ **35.33 Annuloplasty**
Plication of annulus

✖ **35.34 Infundibulectomy**
Right ventricular infundibulectomy

✖ **35.35 Operations on trabeculae carneae cordis**
Division of trabeculae carneae cordis
Excision of trabeculae carneae cordis
Excision of aortic subvalvular ring

✖ **35.39 Operations on other structures adjacent to valves of heart**
Repair of sinus of Valsalva (aneurysm)

● **35.4 Production of septal defect in heart**

35.41 Enlargement of existing atrial septal defect
Rashkind procedure
Septostomy (atrial) (balloon)

✖ **35.42 Creation of septal defect in heart**
Blalock-Hanlon operation

● **35.5 Repair of atrial and ventricular septa with prosthesis**

Includes: repair of septa with synthetic implant or patch

Code also cardiopulmonary bypass [extracorporeal circulation] [heart-lung machine] (39.61)

✖ **35.50 Repair of unspecified septal defect of heart with prosthesis**

Excludes *that associated with repair of:*
endocardial cushion defect (35.54)
septal defect associated with valvular defect (35.54)

✖ **35.51 Repair of atrial septal defect with prosthesis, open technique**
Atrioseptoplasty with prosthesis
Correction of atrial septal defect with prosthesis
Repair:
foramen ovale (patent)
with prosthesis ostium secundum defect with prosthesis

Excludes *that associated with repair of:*
atrial septal defect associated with valvular and ventricular septal defects (35.54)
endocardial cushion defect (35.54)

ICD-9-CM

001–099

Vol. 3

✖ **35.52 Repair of atrial septal defect with prosthesis, closed technique**
Insertion of atrial septal umbrella [King-Mills]

✖ **35.53 Repair of ventricular septal defect with prosthesis**
Correction of ventricular septal defect with prosthesis
Repair of supracristal defect with prosthesis

| Excludes | *that associated with repair of:*
endocardial cushion defect (35.54)
ventricular defect associated with valvular and atrial septal defects (35.54)

✖ **35.54 Repair of endocardial cushion defect with prosthesis**
Repair:
atrioventricular canal with prosthesis (grafted to septa)
ostium primum defect with prosthesis (grafted to septa)
valvular defect associated with atrial and ventricular septal defects with prosthesis (grafted to septa)

| Excludes | *repair of isolated:*
atrial septal defect (35.51–35.52)
valvular defect (35.20, 35.22, 35.24, 35.26, 35.28)
ventricular septal defect (35.53)

● **35.6 Repair of atrial and ventricular septa with tissue graft**

Code also cardiopulmonary bypass [extracorporeal circulation] [heart-lung machine] (39.61)

✖ **35.60 Repair of unspecified septal defect of heart with tissue graft**

| Excludes | *that associated with repair of:*
endocardial cushion defect (35.63)
septal defect associated withvalvular defect (35.63)

✖ **35.61 Repair of atrial septal defect with tissue graft**
Atrioseptoplasty with tissue graft
Correction of atrial septal defect with tissue graft
Repair:
foramen ovale (patent) with tissue graft
ostium secundum defect with tissue graft

| Excludes | *that associated with repair of:*
atrial septal defect associated with valvular and ventricular septal defects (35.63)
endocardial cushion defect (35.63)

✖ **35.62 Repair of ventricular septal defect with tissue graft**
Correction of ventricular septal defect with tissue graft
Repair of supracristal defect with tissue graft

| Excludes | *that associated with repair of:*
endocardial cushion defect(35.63)
ventricular defect associate with valvular and atrial septal defects (35.63)

✖ **35.63 Repair of endocardial cushion defect with tissue graft**
Repair of:
atrioventricular canal with tissue graft
ostium primum defect with tissue graft
valvular defect associated with atrial and ventricular septal defects with tissue graft

| Excludes | *repair of isolated:*
atrial septal defect (35.61)
valvular defect (35.20–35.21, 35.23, 35.25, 35.27)
ventricular septal defect (35.62)

● **35.7 Other and unspecified repair of atrial and ventricular septa**

Code also cardiopulmonary bypass [extracorporeal circulation] [heart-lung machine] (39.61)

✖ **35.70 Other and unspecified repair of unspecified septal defect of heart**
Repair of septal defect NOS

| Excludes | *that associated with repair of:*
endocardial cushion defect (35.73)
septal defect associated with valvular defect (35.73)

✖ **35.71 Other and unspecified repair of atrial septal defect**
Repair NOS:
atrial septum
foramen ovale (patent)
ostium secundum defect

| Excludes | *that associated with repair of:*
atrial septal defect associated with valvular ventricular septal defects (35.73)
endocardial cushion defect (35.73)

✖ **35.72 Other and unspecified repair of ventricular septal defect**
Repair NOS:
supracristal defect
ventricular septum

| Excludes | *that associated with repair of:*
endocardial cushion defect (35.73)
ventricular septal defect associated with valvular and atrial septal defects (35.73)

✖ **35.73 Other and unspecified repair of endocardial cushion defect**
Repair NOS:
atrioventricular canal
ostium primum defect
valvular defect associated with atrial and ventricular septal defects

| Excludes | *repair of isolated:*
atrial septal defect (35.71)
valvular defect (35.20, 35.22, 35.24, 35.26, 35.28)
ventricular septal defect (35.72)

● **35.8 Total repair of certain congenital cardiac anomalies**

Note: For partial repair of defect [e.g. repair of atrial septal defect in tetralogy of Fallot]—code to specific procedure

✖ **35.81 Total repair of tetralogy of Fallot**
One-stage total correction of tetralogy of Fallot with or without:
commissurotomy of pulmonary valve
infundibulectomy
outflow tract prosthesis
patch graft of outflow tract
prosthetic tube for pulmonary artery
repair of ventricular septal defect (with prosthesis)
take-down of previous systemic-pulmonary artery anastomosis

✖ 35.82 Total repair of total anomalous pulmonary venous connection
One-stage total correction of total anomalous pulmonary venous connection with or without:
anastomosis between (horizontal) common pulmonary trunk and posterior wall of left atrium (side-to-side)
enlargement of foramen ovale
incision [excision] of common wall between posterior left atrium and coronary sinus and roofing of resultant defect with patch graft (synthetic)
ligation of venous connection (descending anomalous vein) (to left innominate vein) (to superior vena cava)
repair of atrial septal defect (with prosthesis)

✖ 35.83 Total repair of truncus arteriosus
One-stage total correction of truncus arteriosus with or without:
construction (with aortic homograft) (with prosthesis) of a pulmonary artery placed from right ventricle to arteries supplying the lung
ligation of connections between aorta and pulmonary artery
repair of ventricular septal defect (with prosthesis)

✖ 35.84 Total correction of transposition of great vessels, not elsewhere classified
Arterial switch operation [Jatene]
Total correction of transposition of great arteries at the arterial level by switching the great arteries, including the left or both coronary arteries, implanted in the wall of the pulmonary artery

Excludes *baffle operation [Mustard] [Senning] (35.91)*
creation of shunt between right ventricle and pulmonary artery [Rastelli] (35.92)

● 35.9 Other operations on valves and septa of heart

Code also cardiopulmonary bypass, if performed [extracorporeal circulation] [heart-lung machine] (39.61)

✖ 35.91 Interatrial transposition of venous return
Baffle:
atrial
interatrial
Mustard's operation
Resection of atrial septum and insertion of patch to direct systemic venous return to tricuspid valve and pulmonary venous return to mitral valve

✖ 35.92 Creation of conduit between right ventricle and pulmonary artery
Creation of shunt between right ventricle and (distal) pulmonary artery

Excludes *that associated with total repair of truncus arteriosus (35.83)*

✖ 35.93 Creation of conduit between left ventricle and aorta
Creation of apicoaortic shunt
Shunt between apex of left ventricle and aorta

✖ 35.94 Creation of conduit between atrium and pulmonary artery
Fontan procedure

✖ 35.95 Revision of corrective procedure on heart
Replacement of prosthetic heart valve poppet
Resuture of prosthesis of:
septum
valve

Excludes *complete revision—code to specific procedure*
replacement of prosthesis or graft of:
septum (35.50–35.63)
valve (35.20–35.28)

✖ 35.96 Percutaneous valvuloplasty
Percutaneous balloon valvuloplasty

✖ 35.98 Other operations on septa of heart

✖ 35.99 Other operations on valves of heart

● 36 Operations on vessels of heart

Includes: sternotomy (median) (transverse) as operative approach
thoracotomy as operative approach

Code also cardiopulmonary bypass, if performed [extracorporeal circulation] [heart-lung machine] (39.61)

Code also any injection or infusion of platelet inhibitor (99.20) ◄

● 36.0 Removal of coronary artery obstruction and insertion of stent(s)

✖ 36.01 Single vessel percutaneous transluminal coronary angioplasty [PTCA] or coronary atherectomy without mention of thrombolytic agent
Balloon angioplasty of coronary artery
Coronary atherectomy
Percutaneous coronary angioplasty NOS
PTCA NOS

Excludes *multiple vessel percutaneous transluminal coronary angioplasty [PTCA] or coronary atherectomy performed during the same operation (36.05)*

Code also any insertion of coronary stent(s)(36.06)

✖ 36.02 Single vessel percutaneous transluminal coronary angioplasty [PTCA] or coronary atherectomy with mention of thrombolytic agent
Balloon angioplasty of coronary artery with infusion of thrombolytic agent [streptokinase]
Coronary atherectomy

Excludes *multiple vessel percutaneous transluminal coronary angioplasty [PTCA] or coronary atherectomy performed during the same operation (36.05)*
single vessel PTCA or coronary atherectomy without mention of thrombolytic agent (36.01)

Code also any insertion of coronary stent(s) (36.06)

✖ 36.03 Open chest coronary artery angioplasty
Coronary (artery):
endarterectomy (with patch graft)
thromboendarterectomy (with patch graft)
Open surgery for direct relief of coronary artery obstruction

Excludes *that with coronary artery bypass graft (36.10–36.19)*

Code also any insertion of coronary stent(s) (36.06)

36.04 Intracoronary artery thrombolytic infusion
That by direct coronary artery injection, infusion, or catheterization
enzyme infusion
platelet inhibitor

Excludes *infusion of platelet inhibitor (99.20)* ◄
infusion of thrombolytic agent (99.10) ◄

   ● **Use Additional Digit(s)**   ✖ **Valid O.R. Procedure**   ◄▶ **New Code**   ◀▬ ▬▶ **Revised Code**

✖ 36.05 Multiple vessel percutaneous transluminal coronary angioplasty [PTCA] or coronary atherectomy performed during the same operation, with or without mention of thrombolytic agent
Balloon angioplasty of multiple coronary arteries
Coronary atherectomy

Code also any:
intracoronary artery thrombolytic infusion (36.04)
insertion of coronary stent(s) (36.06)

> **Excludes** *single vessel PTCA or coronary atherectomy*
> *without mention of thrombolytic agent (36.01)*
> *with mention of thrombolytic agent (36.02)*

✖ 36.06 Insertion of coronary artety stent(s)
Stent graft

Code also any:
open chest coronary artery angioplasty (36.03)
percutaneous transluminal coronary angioplasty [PTCA] or coronary atherectomy (36.01, 36.02, 36.05)

✖ 36.09 Other removal of coronary artery obstruction
Coronary angioplasty NOS

> **Excludes** *that by open angioplasty (36.03)*
> *that by percutaneous transluminal coronary angioplasty [PTCA] or coronary atherectomy (36.01–36.02, 36.05)*

● 36.1 Bypass anastomosis for heart revascularization

Code also cardiopulmonary bypass [extracorporeal circulation] [heart-lung machine] (39.61)

✖ 36.10 Aortocoronary bypass for heart revascularization, not otherwise specified
Direct revascularization:
cardiac with catheter stent, prosthesis, or vein graft
coronary with catheter stent, prosthesis, or vein graft
heart muscle with catheter stent, prosthesis, or vein graft
myocardial with catheter stent, prosthesis, or vein graft
Heart revascularization NOS

✖ 36.11 Aortocoronary bypass of one coronary artery

✖ 36.12 Aortocoronary bypass of two coronary arteries

✖ 36.13 Aortocoronary bypass of three coronary arteries

✖ 36.14 Aortocoronary bypass of four or more coronary arteries

✖ 36.15 Single internal mammary-coronary artery bypass
Anastomosis (single):
mammary artery to coronary artery
thoracic artery to coronary artery

✖ 36.16 Double internal mammary-coronary artery bypass
Anastomosis, double:
mammary artery to coronary artery
thoracic artery to coronary artery

✖ 36.17 Abdominal-coronary artery bypass
Anastomosis:
Gastroepiploic-coronary artery

✖ 36.19 Other bypass anastomosis for heart revascularization

✖ 36.2 Heart revascularization by arterial implant
Implantation of:
aortic branches [ascending aortic branches] into heart muscle
blood vessels into myocardium
internal mammary artery [internal thoracic artery] into:
heart muscle
myocardium
ventricle
ventricular wall
indirect heart revascularization NOS

● 36.3 Other heart revascularization ◀▦

✖ 36.31 Open chest transmyocardial revascularization ◀

✖ 36.32 Other transmyocardial revascularization ◀
Percutaneous transmyocardial revascularization ◀
Thoracoscopic transmyocardial revascularization ◀

✖ 36.39 Other heart revascularization ◀
Abrasion of epicardium ◀
Cardio-omentopexy ◀
Intrapericardial poudrage ◀
Myocardial graft: ◀
mediastinal fat ◀
omentum ◀
pectoral muscles ◀

● 36.9 Other operations on vessels of heart

Code also cardiopulmonary bypass [extracorporeal circulation] [heart-lung machine] (39.61)

✖ 36.91 Repair of aneurysm of coronary vessel

✖ 36.99 Other operations on vessels of heart
Exploration of coronary artery
Incision of coronary artery
Ligation of coronary artery
Repair of arteriovenous fistula

● 37 Other operations on heart and pericardium

Code also any injection or infusion of platelet inhibitor (99.20) ◀▶

37.0 Pericardiocentesis

● 37.1 Cardiotomy and pericardiotomy

Code also cardiopulmonary bypass [extracorporeal circulation] [heart-lung machine] (39.61)

✖ 37.10 Incision of heart, not otherwise specified
Cardiolysis NOS

✖ 37.11 Cardiotomy
Incision of:
atrium
endocardium
myocardium
ventricle

✖ 37.12 Pericardiotomy
Pericardial window operation
Pericardiolysis
Pericardiotomy

● 37.2 Diagnostic procedures on heart and pericardium

37.21 Right heart cardiac catheterization
Cardiac catheterization NOS

> **Excludes** *that with catheterization of left heart (37.23)*

37.22 Left heart cardiac catheterization

> **Excludes** *that with catheterization of right heart (37.23)*

37.23 Combined right and left heart cardiac catheterization

✖ 37.24 Biopsy of pericardium

● Use Additional Digit(s)   **✖ Valid O.R. Procedure**   **◀▶ New Code**   **◀▦ ▦▶ Revised Code**

37.25 Biopsy of heart

**37.26 Cardiac electrophysiologic stimulation and re-
cording studies**

    Electrophysiologic studies [EPS]
    Programmed electrical stimulation

    Code also any concomitant procedure

    Excludes   *His bundle recording (37.29)*

37.27 Cardiac mapping

    Code also any concomitant procedure

    Excludes   *electrocardiogram (89.52)*
        His bundle recording (37.29)

**37.29 Other diagnostic procedures on heart and peri-
cardium**

    Excludes   *angiocardiography (88.50–88.58)*
        cardiac function tests (89.41–89.69)
        *cardiovascular radioisotopic scan and function
          study (92.05)*
        coronary arteriography (88.55–88.57)
        diagnostic pericardiocentesis (37.0)
        diagnostic ultrasound of heart (88.72)
        x-ray of heart (87.49)

● **37.3 Pericardiectomy and excision of lesion of heart**

    Code also cardiopulmonary bypass [extracorporeal cir-
culation] [heart-lung machine] (39.61)

  ✖ **37.31 Pericardiectomy**

      Excision of:
        adhesions of pericardium
        constricting scar of:
          epicardium
          pericardium

  ✖ **37.32 Excision of aneurysm of heart**

  Includes: repair of aneurysm of heart   ◀

  ✖ **37.33 Excision or destruction of other lesion or tissue of heart**

    Excludes   *catheter ablation of lesion or tissues of heart
        (37.34)*

  ✖ **37.34 Catheter ablation of lesion or tissues of heart**
      Cryoablation of lesion or tissues of heart
      Electrocurrent of lesion or tissues of heart
      Resection of lesion or tissues of heart

  ✖ **37.35 Partial ventriculectomy**
      Ventricular reduction surgery
      Ventricular remodeling
      Code also any synchronous:
        mitral valve repair (35.02, 35.12)
        mitral valve replacement (35.23–35.24)

✖ **37.4 Repair of heart and pericardium**

✖ **37.5 Heart transplantation**

    Excludes   *combined heart-lung transplantation (33.6)*

● **37.6 Implantation of heart assist system**

  ✖ **37.61 Implant of pulsation balloon**

  ✖ **37.62 Implant of other heart assist system**
      Insertion of centrifugal pump
      Insertion of heart pump
      Insertion of heart assist system, not specified
        as pulsatile
      Insertion of heart assist system, NOS

  ✖ **37.63 Replacement and repair of heart assist system**

  ✖ **37.64 Removal of heart assist system**

    Excludes   *that with replacement of implant (37.63)*

  ✖ **37.65 Implant of external, pulsatile heart assist system**

    Note: Device not implantable (outside the body
        but connected to heart) with external cir-
        culation and pump.

    Excludes   *Implant of pulsation balloon (37.61)*

  ✖ **37.66 Implant of an implantable, pulsatile heart assist system**

    Note: Device directly connected to the heart and
        implanted in the upper left quadrant of
        peritoneal cavity.
      Transportable, implantable heart assist sys-
        tem.

    Excludes   *Implant of pulsation balloon (37.61)*

  ✖ **37.67 Implantation of cardiomyostimulation system**   ◀

    Note: Two-step open procedure consisting of transfer
        of one end of the latissimus dorsi muscle; wrap-
        ping it around the heart; rib resection; implanta-
        tion of epicardial cardiac pacing leads into the
        right ventricle; tunneling and pocket creation
        for the cardiomyostimulator.   ◀

● **37.7 Insertion, revision, replacement, and removal of
pacemaker leads; insertion of temporary pacemaker
system; or revision of pocket**

    Code also any insertion and replacement of pacemaker
device (37.80–37.87)

  **37.70 Initial insertion of lead [electrode], not other-
wise specified**

    Excludes   *insertion of temporary transvenous pacemaker
        system (37.78)*
        *replacement of atrial and/or ventricular lead(s)
        (37.76)*

  **37.71 Initial insertion of transvenous lead [electrode]
into ventricle**

    Excludes   *insertion of temporary transvenous pacemaker
        system (37.78)*
        *replacement of atrial and/or ventricular lead(s)
        (37.76)*

  **37.72 Initial insertion of transvenous leads [elec-
trodes] into atrium and ventricle**

    Excludes   *insertion of temporary transvenous pacemaker
        system (37.78)*
        *replacement of atrial and/or ventricular lead(s)
        (37.76)*

  **37.73 Initial insertion of transvenous lead [electrode]
into atrium**

    Excludes   *insertion of temporary transvenous pacemaker
        system (37.78)*
        *replacement of atrial and/or ventricular lead(s)
        (37.76)*

  ✖ **37.74 Insertion or replacement of epicardial lead
[electrode] into epicardium**
      Insertion or replacement of epicardial by:
        sternotomy
        thoracotomy

    Excludes   *replacement of atrial and/or ventricular lead(s)
        (37.76)*

  ✖ **37.75 Revision of lead [electrode]**
      Repair of electrode [removal with re-insertion]
      Repositioning of lead [electrode]
      Revision of lead NOS

    Excludes   *repositioning of temporary transvenous pace-
        maker system—omit code*

✖**37.76 Replacement of transvenous atrial and/or ventricular lead(s) [electrode]**
Removal or abandonment of existing transvenous or epicardial lead(s) with transvenous lead(s) replacement

Excludes *replacement of epicardial lead [electrode] (37.74)*

✖**37.77 Removal of lead(s) [electrode] without replacement**
Removal:
epicardial lead (transthoracic approach)
transvenous lead(s)

Excludes *removal of temporary transvenous pacemaker system—omit code*
that with replacement of:
atrial and/or ventricular lead(s) [electrode] (37.76)
epicardial lead [electrode] (37.74)

37.78 Insertion of temporary transvenous pacemaker system

Excludes *intraoperative cardiac pacemaker (39.64)*

✖**37.79 Revision or relocation of pacemaker pocket**
Debridement and reforming pocket (skin and subcutaneous tissue)
Relocation of pocket [creation of new pocket]

●**37.8 Insertion, replacement, removal, and revision of pacemaker device**

Code also any lead insertion, lead replacement, lead removal and/or lead revision (37.70–37.77)

✖**37.80 Insertion of permanent pacemaker, initial or replacement, type of device not specified**

37.81 Initial insertion of single-chamber device, not specified as rate responsive

Excludes *replacement of existing pacemaker device (37.85-37.87)*

37.82 Initial insertion of single-chamber device, rate responsive
Rate responsive to physiologic stimuli other than atrial rate

Excludes *replacement of existing pacemaker device (37.85-37.87)*

37.83 Initial insertion of dual-chamber device
Atrial ventricular sequential device

Excludes *replacement of existing pacemaker device (37.85-37.87)*

✖**37.85 Replacement of any type pacemaker device with single-chamber device, not specified as rate responsive**

✖**37.86 Replacement of any type of pacemaker device with single-chamber device, rate responsive**
Rate responsive to physiologic stimuli other than atrial rate

✖**37.87 Replacement of any type pacemaker device with dual-chamber device**
Atrial ventricular sequential device

✖**37.89 Revision or removal of pacemaker device**
Repair of pacemaker device

Excludes *removal of temporary transvenous pacemaker system—omit code*
replacement of existing pacemaker device (37.85–37.87)

●**37.9 Other operations on heart and pericardium**

✖**37.91 Open chest cardiac massage**

Excludes *closed chest cardiac massage (99.63)*

37.92 Injection of therapeutic substance into heart

37.93 Injection of therapeutic substance into pericardium

✖**37.94 Implantation or replacement of automatic cardioverter/defibrillator, total system [AICD]**
Implantation of defibrillator with leads (epicardial patches), formation of pocket (abdominal fascia) (subcutaneous), any transvenous leads, intraoperative procedures for evaluation of lead signals, and obtaining defibrillator threshold measurements
Techniques:
lateral thoracotomy
medial sternotomy
subxiphoid procedure

Code also extracorporeal circulation, if performed (39.61)

Code also any concomitant procedure [e.g., coronary bypass] (36.00–36.19)

✖**37.95 Implantation of automatic cardioverter/defibrillator lead(s) only**

✖**37.96 Implantation of automatic cardioverter/defibrillator pulse generator only**

✖**37.97 Replacement of automatic cardioverter/defibrillator lead(s) only**

✖**37.98 Replacement of automatic cardioverter/defibrillator pulse generator only**

✖**37.99 Other**
Removal of cardioverter/defibrillator pulse generator only without replacement
Repositioning of lead(s) (sensing) (pacing) [electrode]
Repositioning of pulse generator
Revision of cardioverter/defibrillator (automatic) pocket

Excludes *cardiac retraining (93.36)*
conversion of cardiac rhythm (99.60–99.69)

● **Use Additional Digit(s)**   ✖ **Valid O.R. Procedure**   ◀▶ **New Code**   ⬅➡ **Revised Code**

● **38 Incision, excision, and occlusion of vessels**

Code also cardiopulmonary bypass [extracorporeal circulation] [heart-lung machine] (39.61)

Excludes *that of coronary vessels (36.01–36.99)*

The following fourth-digit subclassification is for use with appropriate categories in section 38.0, 38.1, 38.3, 38.5, 38.6, 38.8, and 38.9 according to site. Valid fourth-digits are in [brackets] at the end of each code/description.

0 unspecified site
1 intracranial vessels
  Cerebral (anterior) (middle)
  Circle of Willis
  Posterior communicating artery
2 other vessels of head and neck
  Carotid artery (common) (external) (internal)
  Jugular vein (external) (internal)
3 upper limb vessels
  Axillary
  Brachial
  Radial
  Ulnar
4 aorta
5 other thoracic vessels
  Innominate
  Pulmonary (artery) (vein)
  Subclavian
  Vena cava, superior
6 abdominal arteries
  Celiac
  Gastric
  Hepatic
  Iliac
  Mesenteric
  Renal
  Splenic
  Umbilical

  Excludes *abdominal aorta (4)*

7 abdominal veins
  Iliac
  Portal
  Renal
  Splenic
  Vena cava (inferior)
8 lower limb arteries
  Femoral (common) (superficial)
  Popliteal
  Tibial
9 lower limb veins
  Femoral
  Popliteal
  Saphenous
  Tibial

✖ ● **38.0 Incision of vessel**
[0–9]   Embolectomy
         Thrombectomy

  Excludes *puncture or catheterization of any:*
         artery (38.91, 38.98)
         vein (38.92–38.95, 38.99)

✖ ● **38.1 Endarterectomy**
[0–6, 8]   Endarterectomy with:
         embolectomy
         patch graft
         temporary bypass during procedure
         thrombectomy

● **38.2 Diagnostic procedures on blood vessels**

  ✖ **38.21 Biopsy of blood vessel**

  38.22 Percutaneous angioscopy
  Excludes *angioscopy of eye (95.12)*

✖ **38.29 Other diagnostic procedures on blood vessels**
  Excludes *blood vessel thermography (88.86)*
         circulatory monitoring (89.61–89.69)
         contrast:
           angiocardiography (88.50–88.58)
           arteriography (88.40–88.49)
           phlebography (88.60–88.67)
         impedance phlebography (88.68)
         peripheral vascular ultrasonography (88.77)
         plethysmogram (89.58)

✖ ● **38.3 Resection of vessel with anastomosis**
[0–9]   Angiectomy
         Excision of:
           aneurysm (arteriovenous) with anastomosis
           blood vessel (lesion) with anastomosis

✖ **38.4 Resection of vessel with replacement**
[0–9]   Angiectomy
         Excision of:
           aneurysm (arteriovenous) or blood vessel (lesion) with replacement

Requires the use of one of the following fourth-digit subclassifications to identify site:

0 unspecified site
1 intracranial vessels
  Cerebral (anterior) (middle)
  Circle of Willis
  Posterior communicating artery
2 other vessels of head and neck
  Carotid artery (common) (external) (internal)
  Jugular vein (external) (internal)
3 upper limb vessels
  Axillary
  Brachial
  Radial
  Ulnar
4 aorta, abdominal
  Code also any thoracic vessel involvement (thoracoabdominal procedure) (38.45)
5 thoracic vessels
  Aorta (thoracic)
  Innominate
  Pulmonary (artery) (vein)
  Subclavian
  Vena cava, superior
  Code also any abdominal aorta involvement (thoracoabdominal procedure) (38.44)
6 abdominal arteries
  Celiac
  Gastric
  Hepatic
  Iliac
  Mesenteric
  Renal
  Splenic
  Umbilical

  Excludes *abdominal aorta (4)*

7 abdominal veins
  Iliac
  Portal
  Renal
  Splenic
  Vena cava (inferior)
8 lower limb arteries
  Femoral (common) (superficial)
  Popliteal
  Tibial
9 lower limb veins
  Femoral
  Popliteal
  Saphenous
  Tibial

✖ ● **38.5 Ligation and stripping of varicose veins**
[0–3, 5, 7, 9]

> **Excludes** *ligation of varices:*
>   *esophageal (42.91)*
>   *gastric (44.91)*

✖ ● **38.6 Other excision of vessel**
  [0–9]   Excision of blood vessel (lesion) NOS

> **Excludes** *excision of vessel for aortocoronary bypass*
>   *(36.10–36.14)*
>   *excision with:*
>   *anastomosis (38.30–38.39)*
>   *graft replacement (38.40–38.49)*
>   *implant (38.40–38.49)*

38.7 Interruption of the vena cava
    Insertion of implant or sieve in vena cava
    Ligation of vena cava (inferior) (superior)
    Plication of vena cava

✖ ● **38.8 Other surgical occlusion of vessels**
  [0–9]   Clamping of blood vessel
         Division of blood vessel
         Ligation of blood vessel
         Occlusion of blood vessel

> **Excludes** *adrenal vessels (07.43)*
>   *esophageal varices (42.91)*
>   *gastric or duodenal vessel for ulcer (44.40–*
>   *44.49)*
>   *gastric varices (44.91)*
>   *meningeal vessel (02.13)*
>   *spermatic vein for varicocele (63.1)*
>   *surgical occlusion of vena cava (38.7)*
>   *that for chemoembolization (99.25)*
>   *that for control of (postoperative) hemorrhage:*
>   *anus (49.95)*
>   *bladder (57.93)*
>   *following vascular procedure (39.41)*
>   *nose (21.00–21.09)*
>   *prostate (60.94)*
>   *tonsil (28.7)*
>   *thyroid vessel (06.92)*

● **38.9 Puncture of vessel**

> **Excludes** *that for circulatory monitoring (89.61–89.69)*

38.91 Arterial catheterization

38.92 Umbilical vein catheterization

38.93 Venous catheterization, not elsewhere classified

> **Excludes** *that for cardiac catheterization (37.21–37.23)*
>   *that for renal dialysis (38.95)*

38.94 Venous cutdown

38.95 Venous catheterization for renal dialysis

> **Excludes** *insertion of totally implantable vascular access*
>   *device [VAD] (86.07)*

38.98 Other puncture of artery

> **Excludes** *that for:*
>   *arteriography (88.40–88.49)*
>   *coronary arteriography (88.55–88.57)*

38.99 Other puncture of vein
    Phlebotomy

> **Excludes** *that for:*
>   *angiography (88.60–88.69)*
>   *extracorporeal circulation (39.61, 50.92)*
>   *injection or infusion of:*
>   *sclerosing solution (39.92)*
>   *therapeutic or prophylactic substance*
>   *(99.11–99.29)*
>   *perfusion (39.96–39.97)*
>   *phlebography (88.60–88.69)*
>   *transfusion (99.01–99.09)*

● **39 Other operations on vessels**

> **Excludes** *those on coronary vessels (36.00–36.99)*

✖ **39.0 Systemic to pulmonary artery shunt**
    Descending aorta-pulmonary artery anastomosis
      (graft)
    Left to right anastomosis (graft)
    Subclavian-pulmonary anastomosis (graft)

    Code also cardiopulmonary bypass [extracorporeal circulation] [heart-lung machine] (39.61)

✖ **39.1 Intra-abdominal venous shunt**
    Anastomosis:
      mesocaval
      portacaval
      portal vein to inferior vena cava
      splenic and renal veins
      transjugular intrahepatic portosystemic shunt
      (TIPS)

> **Excludes** *peritoneovenous shunt (54.94)*

● **39.2 Other shunt or vascular bypass**

✖ **39.21 Caval-pulmonary artery anastomosis**

    Code also cardiopulmonary bypass (39.61)

✖ **39.22 Aorta-subclavian-carotid bypass**
    Bypass (arterial):
      aorta to carotid and brachial
      aorta to subclavian and carotid
      carotid to subclavian

✖ **39.23 Other intrathoracic vascular shunt or bypass**
    Intrathoracic (arterial) bypass graft NOS

> **Excludes** *coronary artery bypass (36.10–36.19)*

✖ **39.24 Aorta-renal bypass**

✖ **39.25 Aorta-iliac-femoral bypass**
    Bypass:
      aortofemoral
      aortoiliac
      aortoiliac to popliteal
      aortopopliteal
      iliofemoral [iliac-femoral]

✖ **39.26 Other intra-abdominal vascular shunt or bypass**
    Bypass:
      aortoceliac
      aortic-superior mesenteric
      common hepatic-common iliac-renal
    Intra-abdominal arterial bypass graft NOS

> **Excludes** *peritoneovenous shunt (54.94)*

✖ **39.27 Arteriovenostomy for renal dialysis**
    Anastomosis for renal dialysis
    Formation of (peripheral) arteriovenous
      fistula for renal [kidney] dialysis

    Code also any renal dialysis (39.95)

✖ **39.28 Extracranial-intracranial (EC-IC) vascular bypass**

✖ **39.29 Other (peripheral) vascular shunt or bypass**
    Bypass (graft):
      axillary-brachial
      axillary-femoral [axillofemoral] (superficial)
      brachial
      femoral-femoral
      femoroperoneal
      femoropopliteal (arteries)
      femorotibial (anterior) (posterior)
      popliteal
      vascular NOS

> **Excludes** *peritoneovenous shunt (54.94)*

● **39.3 Suture of vessel**
    Repair of laceration of blood vessel
    Excludes *any other vascular puncture closure device-omit*
            code
        suture of aneurysm (39.52)
        that for control of hemorrhage (postoperative):
            anus (49.95)
            bladder (57.93)
            following vascular procedure (39.41)
            nose (21.00–21.09)
            prostate (60.94)
            tonsil (28.7)

✖ **39.30 Suture of unspecified blood vessel**

✖ **39.31 Suture of artery**

✖ **39.32 Suture of vein**

● **39.4 Revision of vascular procedure**

✖ **39.41 Control of hemorrhage following vascular sur-
        gery**
    Excludes *that for control of hemorrhage (post operative):*
            anus (49.95)
            bladder (57.93)
            nose (21.00–21.09)
            prostate (60.94)
            tonsil (28.7)

✖ **39.42 Revision of arteriovenous shunt for renal dial-
        ysis**
        Conversion of renal dialysis:
            end-to-end anastomosis to end-to-side
            end-to-side anastomosis to end-to-end
            vessel-to-vessel cannula to arteriovenous
                shunt
        Removal of old arteriovenous shunt and cre-
            ation of new shunt
    Excludes *replacement of vessel-to-vessel cannula (39.94)*

✖ **39.43 Removal of arteriovenous shunt for renal dial-
        ysis**
    Excludes *that with replacement [revision] of shunt (39.42)*

✖ **39.49 Other revision of vascular procedure**
        Declotting (graft)
        Revision of:
            anastomosis of blood vessel
            vascular procedure (previous)

● **39.5 Other repair of vessels**

✖ **39.50 Angioplasty or atherectomy of non-coronary
        vessel**
        Percutaneous transluminal angioplasty (PTA)
            of non-coronary vessels:
            Head and neck arteries:
                basilar
                carotid
                vertebral
            Lower extremity vessels
            Mesenteric artery
            Renal artery
            Upper extremity vessels
        Code also any:
            injection or infusion of thrombolytic agent
                (99.10)
            insertion of non-coronary stent(s) or stent
                grafts(s) (39.90)

✖ **39.51 Clipping of aneurysm**
    Excludes *clipping of arteriovenous fistula (39.53)*

✖ **39.52 Other repair of aneurysm**
        Repair of aneurysm by:
            coagulation
            electrocoagulation
            filipuncture
            methyl methacrylate
            suture
            wiring
            wrapping
    Excludes *re-entry operation (aorta) (39.54)*
        that with:
            graft replacement (38.40–38.49)
            resection (38.30–38.49, 38.60–38.69)

✖ **39.53 Repair of arteriovenous fistula**
        Embolization of carotid cavernous fistula
        Repair of arteriovenous fistula by:
            clipping
            coagulation
            ligation and division
    Excludes *repair of arteriovenous shunt for renal dialysis*
            (39.42)
        that with:
            graft replacement (38.40–38.49)
            resection (38.30–38.49, 38.60–38.69)

✖ **39.54 Re-entry operation (aorta)**
        Fenestration of dissecting aneurysm of tho-
            racic aorta
        Code also cardiopulmonary bypass [extracorpo-
        real circulation] [heart-lung machine] (39.61)

✖ **39.55 Reimplantation of aberrant renal vessel**

✖ **39.56 Repair of blood vessel with tissue patch graft**
    Excludes *that with resection (38.40–38.49)*

✖ **39.57 Repair of blood vessel with synthetic patch
        graft**
    Excludes *that with resection (38.40–38.49)*

✖ **39.58 Repair of blood vessel with unspecified type
        of patch graft**
    Excludes *that with resection (38.40–38.49)*

✖ **39.59 Other repair of vessel**
        Aorticopulmonary window operation
        Arterioplasty NOS
        Construction of venous valves (peripheral)
        Plication of vein (peripheral)
        Reimplantation of artery
        Code also cardiopulmonary bypass [extracorpo-
        real circulation] [heart-lung machine] (39.61)
    Excludes *interruption of the vena cava (38.7)*
        reimplantation of renal artery (39.55)
        that with:
            graft (39.56–39.58)
            resection (38.30–38.49, 38.60–38.69)

● **39.6 Extracorporeal circulation and procedures auxiliary to
    heart surgery**

    **39.61 Extracorporeal circulation auxiliary to open
        heart surgery**
        Artificial heart and lung
        Cardiopulmonary bypass
        Pump oxygenator
    Excludes *extracorporeal hepatic assistance (50.92)*
        extracorporeal membrane oxygenation [ECMO]
            (39.65)
        hemodialysis (39.95)
        percutaneous cardiopulmonary bypass (39.66)

    **39.62 Hypothermia (systemic) incidental to open heart
        surgery**

39.63 Cardioplegia
Arrest:
  anoxic
  circulatory

39.64 Intraoperative cardiac pacemaker
Temporary pacemaker used during and immediately following cardiac surgery

39.65 Extracorporeal membrane oxygenation [ECMO]
Excludes *extracorporeal circulation auxiliary to open heart surgery (39.61)*
percutaneous cardiopulmonary bypass (39.66)

39.66 Percutaneous cardiopulmonary bypass
Closed chest
Excludes *extracorporeal circulation auxiliary to open heart surgery (39.61)*
extracorporeal hepatic assistance (50.92)
extracorporeal membrane oxygenation [ECMO] (39.65)
hemodialysis (39.95)

✖ **39.8 Operations on carotid body and other vascular bodies**
Chemodectomy
Denervation of:
  aortic body
  carotid body
Glomectomy, carotid
Implantation into carotid body:
  electronic stimulator
  pacemaker
Excludes *excision of glomus jugulare (20.51)*

● **39.9 Other operations on vessels**

39.90 Insertion of non-coronary artery stent or stents
Endovascular recanalization techniques
Stent graft(s)

Code also any non-coronary angioplasty or atherectomy (39.50)

✖ **39.91 Freeing of vessel**
Dissection and freeing of adherent tissue:
  artery-vein-nerve bundle
  vascular bundle

✖ **39.92 Injection of sclerosing agent into vein**
Excludes *injection:*
  esophageal varices (42.33)
  hemorrhoids (49.42)

✖ **39.93 Insertion of vessel-to-vessel cannula**
Formation of:
  arteriovenous:
    fistula by external cannula
    shunt by external cannula

Code also any renal dialysis (39.95)

✖ **39.94 Replacement of vessel-to-vessel cannula**
Revision of vessel-to-vessel cannula

39.95 Hemodialysis
Artificial kidney
Hemodiafiltration
Hemofiltration
Renal dialysis
Excludes *peritoneal dialysis (54.98)*

39.96 Total body perfusion

Code also substance perfused (99.21–99.29)

39.97 Other perfusion
Perfusion NOS
Perfusion, local [regional] of:
  carotid artery
  coronary artery
  head
  lower limb
  neck
  upper limb

Code also substance perfused (99.21–99.29)
Excludes *perfusion of:*
  kidney (55.95)
  large intestine (46.96)
  liver (50.93)
  small intestine (46.95)

✖ **39.98 Control of hemorrhage, not otherwise specified**
Angiotripsy
Control of postoperative hemorrhage NOS
Venotripsy
Excludes *control of hemorrhage (postoperative):*
  anus (49.95)
  bladder (57.93)
  following vascular procedure (39.41)
  nose (21.00–21.09)
  prostate (60.94)
  tonsil (28.7)
  that by:
    ligation (38.80–38.89)
    suture (39.30–39.32)

✖ **39.99 Other operations on vessels**
Excludes *injection or infusion of therapeutic or prophylactic substance (99.11–99.29)*
transfusion of blood and blood components (99.01–99.09)

8.   OPERATIONS ON THE HEMIC AND LYMPHATIC SYSTEM (40–41)

● **40   Operations on lymphatic system**

✖ **40.0   Incision of lymphatic structures**

● **40.1   Diagnostic procedures on lymphatic structures**

✖ **40.11   Biopsy of lymphatic structure**

✖ **40.19   Other diagnostic procedures on lymphatic structures**

Excludes *lymphangiogram:*
abdominal (88.04)
cervical (87.08)
intrathoracic (87.34)
lower limb (88.36)
upper limb (88.34)
microscopic examination of specimen (90.71–90.79)
radioisotope scan (92.16)
thermography (88.89)

● **40.2   Simple excision of lymphatic structure**

Excludes *biopsy of lymphatic structure (40.11)*

✖ **40.21   Excision of deep cervical lymph node**

✖ **40.22   Excision of internal mammary lymph node**

✖ **40.23   Excision of axillary lymph node**

✖ **40.24   Excision of inguinal lymph node**

✖ **40.29   Simple excision of other lymphatic structure**
Excision of:
cystic hygroma
lymphangioma
Simple lymphadenectomy

✖ **40.3   Regional lymph node excision**
Extended regional lymph node excision
Regional lymph node excision with excision of lymphatic drainage area including skin, subcutaneous tissue, and fat

● **40.4   Radical excision of cervical lymph nodes**
Resection of cervical lymph nodes down to muscle and deep fascia

Excludes *that associated with radical laryngectomy (30.4)*

✖ **40.40   Radical neck dissection, not otherwise specified**

✖ **40.41   Radical neck dissection, unilateral**

✖ **40.42   Radical neck dissection, bilateral**

● **40.5   Radical excision of other lymph nodes**

Excludes *that associated with radical mastectomy (85.45–85.48)*

✖ **40.50   Radical excision of lymph nodes, not otherwise specified**
Radical (lymph) node dissection NOS

✖ **40.51   Radical excision of axillary lymph nodes**

✖ **40.52   Radical excision of periaortic lymph nodes**

✖ **40.53   Radical excision of iliac lymph nodes**

✖ **40.54   Radical groin dissection**

✖ **40.59   Radical excision of other lymph nodes**

Excludes *radical neck dissection (40.40–40.42)*

● **40.6   Operations on thoracic duct**

✖ **40.61   Cannulation of thoracic duct**

✖ **40.62   Fistulization of thoracic duct**

✖ **40.63   Closure of fistula of thoracic duct**

✖ **40.64   Ligation of thoracic duct**

✖ **40.69   Other operations on thoracic duct**

✖ **40.9   Other operations on lymphatic structures**
Anastomosis of peripheral lymphatics
Dilation of peripheral lymphatics
Ligation of peripheral lymphatics
Obliteration of peripheral lymphatics
Reconstruction of peripheral lymphatics
Repair of peripheral lymphatics
Transplantation of peripheral lymphatics
Correction of lymphedema of limb, NOS

Excludes *reduction of elephantiasis of scrotum (61.3)*

● **41   Operations on bone marrow and spleen**

● **41.0   Bone marrow or hematopoietic stem cell transplant**

Excludes *aspiration of bone marrow from donor (41.91)*

✖ **41.00   Bone marrow transplant, not otherwise specified**

✖ **41.01   Autologous bone marrow transplant**
With extracorporeal purging of malignant cells from marrow
Autograft of bone marrow NOS

✖ **41.02   Allogeneic bone marrow transplant with purging**
Allograft of bone marrow with in vitro removal (purging) of T-cells

✖ **41.03   Allogeneic bone marrow transplant without purging**
Allograft of bone marrow NOS

41.04   Autologous hematopoietic stem cell transplant

41.05   Allogeneic hematopoietic stem cell transplant

41.06   Cord blood stem cell transplant

41.1   Puncture of spleen

Excludes *aspiration biopsy of spleen (41.32)*

✖ **41.2   Splenotomy**

● **41.3   Diagnostic procedures on bone marrow and spleen**

41.31   Biopsy of bone marrow

41.32   Closed [aspiration] [percutaneous] biopsy of spleen

✖ **41.33   Open biopsy of spleen**

41.38   Other diagnostic procedures on bone marrow

Excludes *microscopic examination of specimen from bone marrow (90.61–90.69)*
radioisotope scan (92.05)

41.39   Other diagnostic procedures on spleen

Excludes *microscopic examination of specimen from spleen (90.61–90.69)*
radioisotope scan (92.05)

● **41.4   Excision or destruction of lesion or tissue of spleen**

Excludes *excision of accessory spleen (41.93)*

✖ **41.41　Marsupialization of splenic cyst**

✖ **41.42　Excision of lesion or tissue of spleen**

　Excludes *biopsy of spleen (41.32–41.33)*

✖ **41.43　Partial splenectomy**

✖ **41.5　Total splenectomy**
　　　Splenectomy NOS

● **41.9　Other operations on spleen and bone marrow**

　41.91　Aspiration of bone marrow from donor for transplant

　Excludes *biopsy of bone marrow (41.31)*

　41.92　Injection into bone marrow

　Excludes *bone marrow transplant (41.00–41.03)*

✖ **41.93　Excision of accessory spleen**

✖ **41.94　Transplantation of spleen**

✖ **41.95　Repair and plastic operations on spleen**

　41.98　Other operations on bone marrow

✖ **41.99　Other operations on spleen**

● **Use Additional Digit(s)**　　✖ **Valid O.R. Procedure**　　◀▶ **New Code**　　◀▥▥▶ **Revised Code**　　1127

9.   OPERATIONS ON THE DIGESTIVE SYSTEM (42–54)

● 42 Operations on esophagus

  ● 42.0 Esophagotomy

    ✖ 42.01 Incision of esophageal web

    ✖ 42.09 Other incision of esophagus
        Esophagotomy NOS

    Excludes *esophagomyotomy (42.7)*
        esophagostomy (42.10–42.19)

  ● 42.1 Esophagostomy

    ✖ 42.10 Esophagostomy, not otherwise specified

    ✖ 42.11 Cervical esophagostomy

    ✖ 42.12 Exteriorization of esophageal pouch

    ✖ 42.19 Other external fistulization of esophagus
        Thoracic esophagostomy

        Code also any resection (42.40–42.42)

  ● 42.2 Diagnostic procedures on esophagus

    ✖ 42.21 Operative esophagoscopy by incision

    42.22 Esophagoscopy through artificial stoma
    Excludes *that with biopsy (42.24)*

    42.23 Other esophagoscopy
    Excludes *that with biopsy (42.24)*

    42.24 Closed [endoscopic] biopsy of esophagus
        Brushing or washing for specimen collection
        Esophagoscopy with biopsy
        Suction biopsy of the esophagus
    Excludes *esophagogastroduodenoscopy [EGD] with closed biopsy (45.16)*

    ✖ 42.25 Open biopsy of esophagus

    42.29 Other diagnostic procedures on esophagus
    Excludes *barium swallow (87.61)*
        esophageal manometry (89.32)
        microscopic examination of specimen from esophagus (90.81–90.89)

  ● 42.3 Local excision or destruction of lesion or tissue of esophagus

    ✖ 42.31 Local excision of esophageal diverticulum

    ✖ 42.32 Local excision of other lesion or tissue of esophagus
    Excludes *biopsy of esophagus (42.24–42.25)*
        esophageal fistulectomy (42.84)

    42.33 Endoscopic excision or destruction of lesion or tissue of esophagus
        Ablation of esophageal neoplasm by endoscopic approach
        Control of esophageal bleeding by endoscopic approach
        Esophageal polypectomy by endoscopic approach
        Esophageal varices by endoscopic approach
        Injection of esophageal varices by endoscopic approach
    Excludes *biopsy of esophagus (42.24–42.25)*
        fistulectomy (42.84)
        open ligation of esophageal varices (42.91)

    ✖ 42.39 Other destruction of lesion or tissue of esophagus
    Excludes *that by endoscopic approach (42.33)*

  ● 42.4 Excision of esophagus
    Excludes *esophagogastrectomy NOS (43.99)*

    ✖ 42.40 Esophagectomy, not otherwise specified

    ✖ 42.41 Partial esophagectomy

        Code also any synchronous:
          anastomosis other than end-to-end (42.51–42.69)
          esophagostomy (42.10–42.19)
          gastrostomy (43.11–43.19)

    ✖ 42.42 Total esophagectomy

        Code also any synchronous:
          gastrostomy (43.11–43.19)
          interposition or anastomosis other than end-to-end (42.51–42.69)

    Excludes *esophagogastrectomy (43.99)*

  ● 42.5 Intrathoracic anastomosis of esophagus

    Code also any synchronous:
      esophagectomy (42.40–42.42)
      gastrostomy (43.1)

    ✖ 42.51 Intrathoracic esophagoesophagostomy

    ✖ 42.52 Intrathoracic esophagogastrostomy

    ✖ 42.53 Intrathoracic esophageal anastomosis with interposition of small bowel

    ✖ 42.54 Other intrathoracic esophagoenterostomy
        Anastomosis of esophagus to intestinal segment NOS

    ✖ 42.55 Intrathoracic esophageal anastomosis with interposition of colon

    ✖ 42.56 Other intrathoracic esophagocolostomy
        Esophagocolostomy NOS

    ✖ 42.58 Intrathoracic esophageal anastomosis with other interposition
        Construction of artificial esophagus
        Retrosternal formation of reversed gastric tube

    ✖ 42.59 Other intrathoracic anastomosis of esophagus

  ● 42.6 Antesternal anastomosis of esophagus

    Code also any synchronous:
      esophagectomy (42.40–42.42)
      gastrostomy (43.1)

    ✖ 42.61 Antesternal esophagoesophagostomy

    ✖ 42.62 Antesternal esophagogastrostomy

    ✖ 42.63 Antesternal esophageal anastomosis with interposition of small bowel

    ✖ 42.64 Other antesternal esophagoenterostomy
        Antethoracic:
          esophagoenterostomy
          esophagoileostomy
          esophagojejunostomy

    ✖ 42.65 Antesternal esophageal anastomosis with interposition of colon

    ✖ 42.66 Other antesternal esophagocolostomy
        Antethoracic esophagocolostomy

    ✖ 42.68 Other antesternal esophageal anastomosis with interposition

    ✖ 42.69 Other antesternal anastomosis of esophagus

  ✖ 42.7 Esophagomyotomy

  ● 42.8 Other repair of esophagus

    42.81 Insertion of permanent tube into esophagus

    ✖ 42.82 Suture of laceration of esophagus

    ✖ 42.83 Closure of esophagostomy

✖ **42.84 Repair of esophageal fistula, not elsewhere classified**

> **Excludes**   *repair of fistula:*
> *bronchoesophageal (33.42)*
> *esophagopleurocutaneous (34.73)*
> *pharyngoesophageal (29.53)*
> *tracheoesophageal (31.73)*

✖ **42.85 Repair of esophageal stricture**

✖ **42.86 Production of subcutaneous tunnel without esophageal anastomosis**

✖ **42.87 Other graft of esophagus**

> **Excludes**   *antesternal esophageal anastomosis with interposition of:*
>   *colon (42.65)*
>   *small bowel (42.63)*
> *antesternal esophageal anastomosis with other interposition (42.68)*
> *intrathoracic esophageal anastomosis with interposition of:*
>   *colon (42.55)*
>   *small bowel (42.53)*
> *intrathoracic esophageal anastomosis with other interposition (42.58)*

✖ **42.89 Other repair of esophagus**

● **42.9 Other operations on esophagus**

✖ **42.91 Ligation of esophageal varices**

> **Excludes**   *that by endoscopic approach (42.33)*

42.92 Dilation of esophagus
Dilation of cardiac sphincter

> **Excludes**   *intubation of esophagus (96.03, 96.06–96.08)*

42.99 Other

> **Excludes**   *insertion of Sengstaken tube (96.06)*
> *intubation of esophagus (96.03, 96.06–96.08)*
> *removal of intraluminal foreign body from esophagus without incision (98.02)*
> *tamponade of esophagus (96.06)*

● **43 Incision and excision of stomach**

✖ **43.0 Gastrotomy**

> **Excludes**   *gastrostomy (43.11–43.19)*
> *that for control of hemorrhage (44.49)*

● **43.1 Gastrostomy**

43.11 Percutaneous [endoscopic] gastrostomy [PEG]
Percutaneous transabdominal gastrostomy

43.19 Other gastrostomy

> **Excludes**   *percutaneous [endoscopic] gastrostomy [PEG] (43.11)*

✖ **43.3 Pyloromyotomy**

● **43.4 Local excision or destruction of lesion or tissue of stomach**

43.41 Endoscopic excision or destruction of lesion or tissue of stomach
Gastric polypectomy by endoscopic approach
Gastric varices by endoscopic approach

> **Excludes**   *biopsy of stomach (44.14–44.15)*
> *control of hemorrhage (44.43)*
> *open ligation of gastric varices (44.91)*

✖ **43.42 Local excision of other lesion or tissue of stomach**

> **Excludes**   *biopsy of stomach (44.14–44.15)*
> *gastric fistulectomy (44.62–44.63)*
> *partial gastrectomy (43.5–43.89)*

✖ **43.49 Other destruction of lesion or tissue of stomach**

> **Excludes**   *that by endoscopic approach (43.41)*

✖ **43.5 Partial gastrectomy with anastomosis to esophagus**
Proximal gastrectomy

✖ **43.6 Partial gastrectomy with anastomosis to duodenum**
Billroth I operation
Distal gastrectomy
Gastropylorectomy

✖ **43.7 Partial gastrectomy with anastomosis to jejunum**
Billroth II operation

● **43.8 Other partial gastrectomy**

✖ **43.81 Partial gastrectomy with jejunal transposition**
Henley jejunal transposition operation

Code also any synchronous intestinal resection (45.51)

✖ **43.89 Other**
Partial gastrectomy with bypass gastrogastrostomy
Sleeve resection of stomach

● **43.9 Total gastrectomy**

✖ **43.91 Total gastrectomy with intestinal interposition**

✖ **43.99 Other total gastrectomy**
Complete gastroduodenectomy
Esophagoduodenostomy with complete gastrectomy
Esophagogastrectomy NOS
Esophagojejunostomy with complete gastrectomy
Radical gastrectomy

● **44 Other operations on stomach**

● **44.0 Vagotomy**

✖ **44.00 Vagotomy, not otherwise specified**
Division of vagus nerve NOS

✖ **44.01 Truncal vagotomy**

✖ **44.02 Highly selective vagotomy**
Parietal cell vagotomy
Selective proximal vagotomy

✖ **44.03 Other selective vagotomy**

● **44.1 Diagnostic procedures on stomach**

✖ **44.11 Transabdominal gastroscopy**
Intraoperative gastroscopy

> **Excludes**   *that with biopsy (44.14)*

44.12 Gastroscopy through artificial stoma

> **Excludes**   *that with biopsy (44.14)*

44.13 Other gastroscopy

> **Excludes**   *that with biopsy (44.14)*

44.14 Closed [endoscopic] biopsy of stomach
Brushing or washing for specimen collection

> **Excludes**   *esophagogastroduodenoscopy [EGD] with closed biopsy (45.16)*

✖ **44.15 Open biopsy of stomach**

44.19 Other diagnostic procedures on stomach

> **Excludes**   *gastric lavage (96.33)*
> *microscopic examination of specimen from stomach (90.81–90.89)*
> *upper GI series (87.62)*

● **44.2 Pyloroplasty**

✖ **44.21 Dilation of pylorus by incision**

44.22 Endoscopic dilation of pylorus
Dilation with balloon endoscope
Endoscopic dilation of gastrojejunostomy site

✖ **44.29 Other pyloroplasty**
Pyloroplasty NOS
Revision of pylorus

● **44.3　Gastroenterostomy without gastrectomy**

✖ **44.31　High gastric bypass**
　　Printen and Mason gastric bypass

✖ **44.39　Other gastroenterostomy**
　　Bypass:
　　　gastroduodenostomy
　　　gastroenterostomy
　　　gastrogastrostomy
　　Gastrojejunostomy without gastrectomy NOS

● **44.4　Control of hemorrhage and suture of ulcer of stomach or duodenum**

✖ **44.40　Suture of peptic ulcer, not otherwise specified**

✖ **44.41　Suture of gastric ulcer site**

　　Excludes　*ligation of gastric varices (44.91)*

✖ **44.42　Suture of duodenal ulcer site**

　　44.43　Endoscopic control of gastric or duodenal bleeding

　　44.44　Transcatheter embolization for gastric or duodenal bleeding

　　Excludes　*surgical occlusion of abdominal vessels (38.86–38.87)*

　　44.49　Other control of hemorrhage of stomach or duodenum
　　　That with gastrotomy

✖ **44.5　Revision of gastric anastomosis**
　　Closure of:
　　　gastric anastomosis
　　　gastroduodenostomy
　　　gastrojejunostomy
　　Pantaloon operation

● **44.6　Other repair of stomach**

✖ **44.61　Suture of laceration of stomach**

　　Excludes　*that of ulcer site (44.41)*

　　44.62　Closure of gastrostomy

✖ **44.63　Closure of other gastric fistula**
　　Closure of:
　　　gastrocolic fistula
　　　gastrojejunocolic fistula

✖ **44.64　Gastropexy**

✖ **44.65　Esophagogastroplasty**
　　Belsey operation
　　Esophagus and stomach cardioplasty

✖ **44.66　Other procedures for creation of esophagogastric sphincteric competence**
　　Fundoplication
　　Gastric cardioplasty
　　Nissen's fundoplication
　　Restoration of cardio-esophageal angle

✖ **44.69　Other**
　　Inversion of gastric diverticulum
　　Repair of stomach NOS

● **44.9　Other operations on stomach**

✖ **44.91　Ligation of gastric varices**

　　Excludes　*that by endoscopic approach (43.41)*

✖ **44.92　Intraoperative manipulation of stomach**
　　Reduction of gastric volvulus

　　44.93　Insertion of gastric bubble (balloon)

　　44.94　Removal of gastric bubble (balloon)

✖ **44.99　Other**

　　Excludes　*change of gastrostomy tube (97.02)*
　　　dilation of cardiac sphincter (42.92)
　　　gastric:
　　　　cooling (96.31)
　　　　freezing (96.32)
　　　　gavage (96.35)
　　　　hypothermia (96.31)
　　　　lavage (96.33)
　　　insertion of nasogastric tube (96.07)
　　　irrigation of gastrostomy (96.36)
　　　irrigation of nasogastric tube (96.34)
　　　removal of:
　　　　gastrostomy tube (97.51)
　　　　intraluminal foreign body from stomach without incision (98.03)
　　　replacement of:
　　　　gastrostomy tube (97.02)
　　　　(naso-)gastric tube (97.01)

● **45　Incision, excision, and anastomosis of intestine**

● **45.0　Enterotomy**

　　Excludes　*duodenocholedochotomy (51.41–51.42, 51.51)*
　　　that for destruction of lesion (45.30–45.34)
　　　that of exteriorized intestine (46.14, 46.24, 46.31)

✖ **45.00　Incision of intestine, not otherwise specified**

✖ **45.01　Incision of duodenum**

✖ **45.02　Other incision of small intestine**

✖ **45.03　Incision of large intestine**

　　Excludes　*proctotomy (48.0)*

● **45.1　Diagnostic procedures on small intestine**

　　Code also any laparotomy (54.11–54.19)

✖ **45.11　Transabdominal endoscopy of small intestine**
　　Intraoperative endoscopy of small intestine

　　Excludes　*that with biopsy (45.14)*

　　45.12　Endoscopy of small intestine through artificial stoma

　　Excludes　*that with biopsy (45.14)*

　　45.13　Other endoscopy of small intestine
　　Esophagogastroduodenoscopy [EGD]

　　Excludes　*that with biopsy (45.14, 45.16)*

　　45.14　Closed [endoscopic] biopsy of small intestine
　　Brushing or washing for specimen collection

　　Excludes　*esophagogastroduodenoscopy [EGD] with closed biopsy (45.16)*

✖ **45.15　Open biopsy of small intestine**

　　45.16　Esophagogastroduodenoscopy [EGD] with closed biopsy
　　Biopsy of one or more sites involving esophagus, stomach, and/or duodenum

　　45.19　Other diagnostic procedures on small intestine

　　Excludes　*microscopic examination of specimen from small intestine (90.91–90.99)*
　　　radioisotope scan (92.04)
　　　ultrasonography (88.74)
　　　x-ray (87.61–87.69)

● **45.2　Diagnostic procedures on large intestine**

　　Code also any laparotomy (54.11–54.19)

✖ **45.21　Transabdominal endoscopy of large intestine**
　　Intraoperative endoscopy of large intestine

　　Excludes　*that with biopsy (45.25)*

　　45.22　Endoscopy of large intestine through artificial stoma

　　Excludes　*that with biopsy (45.25)*

45.23 Colonoscopy

Flexible fiberoptic colonoscopy

Excludes *endoscopy of large intestine through artificial stoma (45.22)*
flexible sigmoidoscopy (45.24)
rigid proctosigmoidoscopy (48.23)
transabdominal endoscopy of large intestine (45.21)

45.24 Flexible sigmoidoscopy

Endoscopy of descending colon

Excludes *rigid proctosigmoidoscopy (48.23)*

45.25 Closed [endoscopic] biopsy of large intestine

Biopsy, closed, of unspecified intestinal site
Brushing or washing for specimen collection
Colonoscopy with biopsy

Excludes *proctosigmoidoscopy with biopsy (48.24)*

✖ **45.26 Open biopsy of large intestine**

45.27 Intestinal biopsy, site unspecified

45.28 Other diagnostic procedures on large intestine

45.29 Other diagnostic procedures on intestine, site unspecified

Excludes *microscopic examination of specimen (90.91–90.99)*
scan and radioisotope function study (92.04)
ultrasonography (88.74)
x-ray (87.61–87.69)

● **45.3 Local excision or destruction of lesion or tissue of small intestine**

45.30 Endoscopic excision or destruction of lesion of duodenum

Excludes *biopsy of duodenum (45.14–45.15)*
control of hemorrhage (44.43)
fistulectomy (46.72)

✖ **45.31 Other local excision of lesion of duodenum**

Excludes *biopsy of duodenum (45.14–45.15)*
fistulectomy (46.72)
multiple segmental resection (45.61)
that by endoscopic approach (45.30)

✖ **45.32 Other destruction of lesion of duodenum**

Excludes *that by endoscopic approach (45.30)*

✖ **45.33 Local excision of lesion or tissue of small intestine, except duodenum**

Excision of redundant mucosa of ileostomy

Excludes *biopsy of small intestine (45.14–45.15)*
fistulectomy (46.74)
multiple segmental resection (45.61)

✖ **45.34 Other destruction of lesion of small intestine, except duodenum**

● **45.4 Local excision or destruction of lesion or tissue of large intestine**

✖ **45.41 Excision of lesion or tissue of large intestine**

Excision of redundant mucosa of colostomy

Excludes *biopsy of large intestine (45.25–45.27)*
endoscopic polypectomy of large intestine (45.42)
fistulectomy (46.76)
multiple segmental resection (45.71)
that by endoscopic approach (45.42–45.43)

45.42 Endoscopic polypectomy of large intestine

Excludes *that by open approach (45.41)*

45.43 Endoscopic destruction of other lesion or tissue of large intestine

Endoscopic ablation of tumor of large intestine
Endoscopic control of colonic bleeding

Excludes *endoscopic polypectomy of large intestine (45.42)*

✖ **45.49 Other destruction of lesion of large intestine**

Excludes *that by endoscopic approach (45.43)*

● **45.5 Isolation of intestinal segment**

Code also any synchronous:
anastomosis other than end-to-end (45.90–45.94)
enterostomy (46.10–46.39)

✖ **45.50 Isolation of intestinal segment, not otherwise specified**

Isolation of intestinal pedicle flap
Reversal of intestinal segment

✖ **45.51 Isolation of segment of small intestine**

Isolation of ileal loop
Resection of small intestine for interposition

✖ **45.52 Isolation of segment of large intestine**

Resection of colon for interposition

● **45.6 Other excision of small intestine**

Code also any synchronous:
anastomosis other than end-to-end (45.90–45.93, 45.95)
colostomy (46.10–46.13)
enterostomy (46.10–46.39)

Excludes *cecectomy (45.72)*
enterocolectomy (45.79)
gastroduodenectomy (43.6–43.99)
ileocolectomy (45.73)
pancreatoduodenectomy (52.51–52.7)

✖ **45.61 Multiple segmental resection of small intestine**

Segmental resection for multiple traumatic lesions of small intestine

✖ **45.62 Other partial resection of small intestine**

Duodenectomy
Ileectomy
Jejunectomy

Excludes *duodenectomy with synchronous pancreatectomy (52.51–52.7)*
resection of cecum and terminal ileum (45.72)

✖ **45.63 Total removal of small intestine**

● **45.7 Partial excision of large intestine**

Code also any synchronous:
anastomosis other than end-to-end (45.92–45.94)
enterostomy (46.10–46.39)

✖ **45.71 Multiple segmental resection of large intestine**

Segmental resection for multiple traumatic lesions of large intestine

✖ **45.72 Cecectomy**

Resection of cecum and terminal ileum

✖ **45.73 Right hemicolectomy**

Ileocolectomy
Right radical colectomy

✖ **45.74 Resection of transverse colon**

✖ **45.75 Left hemicolectomy**

Excludes *proctosigmoidectomy (48.41–48.69)*
second stage Mikulicz operation (46.04)

✖ **45.76 Sigmoidectomy**

✖ **45.79 Other partial excision of large intestine**

Enterocolectomy NEC

✖ **45.8 Total intra-abdominal colectomy**

Excision of cecum, colon, and sigmoid

Excludes *coloproctectomy (48.41–48.69)*

● **45.9 Intestinal anastomosis**

Code also any synchronous resection (45.31–45.8, 48.41–48.69)

Excludes *end-to-end anastomosis—omit code*

● **Use Additional Digit(s)**   ✖ **Valid O.R. Procedure**   ◀▶ **New Code**   ⬅▦➡ **Revised Code**   **1131**

✖ 45.90 Intestinal anastomosis, not otherwise specified

✖ 45.91 Small-to-small intestinal anastomosis

✖ 45.92 Anastomosis of small intestine to rectal stump
Hampton procedure

✖ 45.93 Other small-to-large intestinal anastomosis

✖ 45.94 Large-to-large intestinal anastomosis

> **Excludes** *rectorectostomy (48.74)*

✖ 45.95 Anastomosis to anus
Formation of endorectal ileal pouch (H-pouch) (J-pouch) (S-pouch) with anastomosis of small intestine to anus

● **46 Other operations on intestine**

● **46.0 Exteriorization of intestine**

> **Includes:** loop enterostomy
> multiple stage resection of intestine

✖ 46.01 Exteriorization of small intestine
Loop ileostomy

✖ 46.02 Resection of exteriorized segment of small intestine

✖ 46.03 Exteriorization of large intestine
Exteriorization of intestine NOS
First stage Mikulicz exteriorization of intestine
Loop colostomy

✖ 46.04 Resection of exteriorized segment of large intestine
Resection of exteriorized segment of intestine NOS
Second stage Mikulicz operation

● **46.1 Colostomy**

Code also any synchronous resection (45.49, 45.71–45.79, 45.8)

> **Excludes** *loop colostomy (46.03)*
> *that with abdominoperineal resection of rectum (48.5)*
> *that with synchronous anterior rectal resection (48.62)*

✖ 46.10 Colostomy, not otherwise specified

✖ 46.11 Temporary colostomy

✖ 46.13 Permanent colostomy

46.14 Delayed opening of colostomy

● **46.2 Ileostomy**

Code also any synchronous resection (45.34, 45.61–45.63)

> **Excludes** *loop ileostomy (46.01)*

✖ 46.20 Ileostomy, not otherwise specified

✖ 46.21 Temporary ileostomy

✖ 46.22 Continent ileostomy

✖ 46.23 Other permanent ileostomy

46.24 Delayed opening of ileostomy

● **46.3 Other enterostomy**

Code also any synchronous resection (45.61–45.8)

46.31 Delayed opening of other enterostomy

46.32 Percutaneous (endoscopic) jejunostomy [PEJ]
Endoscopic conversion of gastrostomy to junostomy

46.39 Other
Duodenostomy
Feeding enterostomy

● **46.4 Revision of intestinal stoma**

✖ 46.40 Revision of intestinal stoma, not otherwise specified
Plastic enlargement of intestinal stoma
Reconstruction of stoma of intestine
Release of scar tissue of intestinal stoma

> **Excludes** *excision of redundant mucosa (45.41)*

✖ 46.41 Revision of stoma of small intestine

> **Excludes** *excision of redundant mucosa (45.33)*

✖ 46.42 Repair of pericolostomy hernia

✖ 46.43 Other revision of stoma of large intestine

> **Excludes** *excision of redundant mucosa (45.41)*

● **46.5 Closure of intestinal stoma**

Code also any synchronous resection (45.34, 45.49, 45.61–45.8)

✖ 46.50 Closure of intestinal stoma, not otherwise specified

✖ 46.51 Closure of stoma of small intestine

✖ 46.52 Closure of stoma of large intestine
Closure or take-down of:
cecostomy
colostomy
sigmoidostomy

● **46.6 Fixation of intestine**

✖ 46.60 Fixation of intestine, not otherwise specified
Fixation of intestine to abdominal wall

✖ 46.61 Fixation of small intestine to abdominal wall
Ileopexy

✖ 46.62 Other fixation of small intestine
Noble plication of small intestine
Plication of jejunum

✖ 46.63 Fixation of large intestine to abdominal wall
Cecocoloplicopexy
Sigmoidopexy (Moschowitz)

✖ 46.64 Other fixation of large intestine
Cecofixation
Colofixation

● **46.7 Other repair of intestine**

> **Excludes** *closure of:*
> *ulcer of duodenum (44.42)*
> *vesicoenteric fistula (57.83)*

✖ 46.71 Suture of laceration of duodenum

✖ 46.72 Closure of fistula of duodenum

✖ 46.73 Suture of laceration of small intestine, except duodenum

✖ 46.74 Closure of fistula of small intestine, except duodenum

> **Excludes** *closure of:*
> *artificial stoma (46.51)*
> *vaginal fistula (70.74)*
> *repair of gastrojejunocolic fistula (44.63)*

✖ 46.75 Suture of laceration of large intestine

✖ 46.76 Closure of fistula of large intestine

> **Excludes** *closure of:*
> *gastrocolic fistula (44.63)*
> *rectal fistula (48.73)*
> *sigmoidovesical fistula (57.83)*
> *stoma (46.52)*
> *vaginal fistula (70.72–70.73)*
> *vesicocolic fistula (57.83)*
> *vesicosigmoidovaginal fistula (57.83)*

✖ 46.79 Other repair of intestine

● **46.8 Dilation and manipulation of intestine**

   ● **Use Additional Digit(s)**   ✖ **Valid O.R. Procedure**   ◀▶ **New Code**   ⬅⬛⬛▶ **Revised Code**

✖ **46.80 Intra-abdominal manipulation of intestine, not otherwise specified**
Correction of intestinal malrotation
Reduction of:
    intestinal torsion
    intestinal volvulus
    intussusception

> **Excludes** *reduction of intussusception with:* ◄
>   *fluoroscopy (96.29)* ◄
>   *ionizing radiation enema (96.29)* ◄
>   *ultrasonography guidance (96.29)* ◄

✖ **46.81 Intra-abdominal manipulation of small intestine**

✖ **46.82 Intra-abdominal manipulation of large intestine**

46.85 Dilation of intestine
Dilation (balloon) of duodenum
Dilation (balloon) of jejunum
Endoscopic dilation (balloon) of large intestine
That through rectum or colostomy

● **46.9 Other operations on intestines**

✖ **46.91 Myotomy of sigmoid colon**

✖ **46.92 Myotomy of other parts of colon**

✖ **46.93 Revision of anastomosis of small intestine**

✖ **46.94 Revision of anastomosis of large intestine**

46.95 Local perfusion of small intestine
Code also substance perfused (99.21–99.29)

46.96 Local perfusion of large intestine
Code also substance perfused (99.21–99.29)

✖ **46.99 Other**
Ileoentectropy

> **Excludes** *diagnostic procedures on intestine (45.11–45.29)*
> *dilation of enterostomy stoma (96.24)*
> *intestinal intubation (96.08)*
> *removal of:*
>   *intraluminal foreign body from large intestine*
>   *without incision (98.04)*
>   *intraluminal foreign body from small intestine*
>   *without incision (98.03)*
>   *tube from large intestine (97.53)*
>   *tube from small intestine (97.52)*
> *replacement of:*
>   *large intestine tube or enterostomy device*
>   *(97.04)*
>   *small intestine tube or enterostomy device*
>   *(97.03)*

● **47 Operations on appendix**

Includes: appendiceal stump

✖ **47.0 Appendectomy**

> **Excludes** *incidental appendectomy, so described*
>   *laparoscopic (47.11)*
>   *other (47.19)*

47.01 Laparoscopic appendectomy

47.09 Other appendectomy

✖ **47.1 Incidental appendectomy**

47.11 Laparoscopic incidental appendectomy

47.19 Other incidental appendectomy

✖ **47.2 Drainage of appendiceal abscess**

> **Excludes** *that with appendectomy (47.0)*

● **47.9 Other operations on appendix**

✖ **47.91 Appendicostomy**

✖ **47.92 Closure of appendiceal fistula**

✖ **47.99 Other**
Anastomosis of appendix

> **Excludes** *diagnostic procedures on appendix (45.21–45.29)*

● **48 Operations on rectum, rectosigmoid and perirectal tissue**

✖ **48.0 Proctotomy**
Decompression of imperforate anus
Panas' operation [linear proctotomy]

> **Excludes** *incision of perirectal tissue (48.81)*

✖ **48.1 Proctostomy**

● **48.2 Diagnostic procedures on rectum, rectosigmoid and perirectal tissue**

✖ **48.21 Transabdominal proctosigmoidoscopy**
Intraoperative proctosigmoidoscopy

> **Excludes** *that with biopsy (48.24)*

48.22 Proctosigmoidoscopy through artificial stoma

> **Excludes** *that with biopsy (48.24)*

48.23 Rigid proctosigmoidoscopy

> **Excludes** *flexible sigmoidoscopy (45.24)*

48.24 Closed [endoscopic] biopsy of rectum
Brushing or washing for specimen collection
Proctosigmoidoscopy with biopsy

✖ **48.25 Open biopsy of rectum**

48.26 Biopsy of perirectal tissue

48.29 Other diagnostic procedures on rectum, rectosigmoid and perirectal tissue

> **Excludes** *digital examination of rectum (89.34)*
> *lower GI series (87.64)*
> *microscopic examination of specimen from rectum (90.91–90.99)*

● **48.3 Local excision or destruction of lesion or tissue of rectum**

48.31 Radical electrocoagulation of rectal lesion or tissue

48.32 Other electrocoagulation of rectal lesion or tissue

48.33 Destruction of rectal lesion or tissue by laser

48.34 Destruction of rectal lesion or tissue by cryosurgery

✖ **48.35 Local excision of rectal lesion or tissue**

> **Excludes** *biopsy of rectum (48.24–48.25)*
> *excision of perirectal tissue (48.82)*
> *hemorrhoidectomy (49.46)*
> *[endoscopic] polypectomy of rectum (48.36)*
> *rectal fistulectomy (48.73)*

48.36 [Endoscopic] polypectomy of rectum

● **48.4 Pull-through resection of rectum**
Code also any synchronous anastomosis other than end-to-end (45.90, 45.92–45.95)

✖ **48.41 Save submucosal resection of rectum**
Endorectal pull-through operation

✖ **48.49 Other pull-through resection of rectum**
Abdominoperineal pull-through
Altemeier operation
Swenson proctectomy

> **Excludes** *Duhamel abdominoperineal pull-through (48.65)*

✖ 48.5 Abdominoperineal resection of rectum

Includes: with synchronous colostomy
Combined abdominoendorectal resection
Complete proctectomy

Code also any synchronous anastomosis other than end-to-end (45.90, 45.92–45.95)

Excludes *Duhamel abdominoperineal pull-through (48.65)*
that as part of pelvic exenteration (68.8)

● 48.6 Other resection of rectum

Code also any synchronous anastomosis other than end-to-end (45.90, 45.92–45.95)

✖ 48.61 Transsacral rectosigmoidectomy

✖ 48.62 Anterior resection of rectum with synchronous colostomy

✖ 48.63 Other anterior resection of rectum

Excludes *that with synchronous colostomy (48.62)*

✖ 48.64 Posterior resection of rectum

✖ 48.65 Duhamel resection of rectum
Duhamel abdominoperineal pull-through

✖ 48.69 Other
Partial proctectomy
Rectal resection NOS

● 48.7 Repair of rectum

Excludes *repair of:*
current obstetric laceration (75.62)
vaginal rectocele (70.50, 70.52)

✖ 48.71 Suture of laceration of rectum

✖ 48.72 Closure of proctostomy

✖ 48.73 Closure of other rectal fistula

Excludes *fistulectomy:*
perirectal (48.93)
rectourethral (58.43)
rectovaginal (70.73)
rectovesical (57.83)
rectovesicovaginal (57.83)

✖ 48.74 Rectorectostomy
Rectal anastomosis NOS

✖ 48.75 Abdominal proctopexy
Frickman procedure
Ripstein repair of rectal prolapse

✖ 48.76 Other proctopexy
Delorme repair of prolapsed rectum
Proctosigmoidopexy
Puborectalis sling operation

Excludes *manual reduction of rectal prolapse (96.26)*

✖ 48.79 Other repair of rectum
Repair of old obstetric laceration of rectum

Excludes *anastomosis to:*
large intestine (45.94)
small intestine (45.92–45.93)
repair of:
current obstetric laceration (75.62)
vaginal rectocele (70.50, 70.52)

● 48.8 Incision or excision of perirectal tissue or lesion

Includes: pelvirectal tissue
rectovaginal septum

✖ 48.81 Incision of perirectal tissue
Incision of rectovaginal septum

✖ 48.82 Excision of perirectal tissue

Excludes *perirectal biopsy (48.26)*
perirectofistulectomy (48.93)
rectal fistulectomy (48.73)

● 48.9 Other operations on rectum and perirectal tissue

✖ 48.91 Incision of rectal stricture

✖ 48.92 Anorectal myectomy

✖ 48.93 Repair of perirectal fistula

Excludes *that opening into rectum (48.73)*

✖ 48.99 Other

Excludes *digital examination of rectum (89.34)*
dilation of rectum (96.22)
insertion of rectal tube (96.09)
irrigation of rectum (96.38–96.39)
manual reduction of rectal prolapse (96.26)
proctoclysis (96.37)
rectal massage (99.93)
rectal packing (96.19)
removal of:
impacted feces (96.38)
intraluminal foreign body from rectum without incision (98.05)
rectal packing (97.59)
transanal enema (96.39)

● 49 Operations on anus

● 49.0 Incision or excision of perianal tissue

✖ 49.01 Incision of perianal abscess

✖ 49.02 Other incision of perianal tissue
Undercutting of perianal tissue

Excludes *anal fistulotomy (49.11)*

49.03 Excision of perianal skin tags

✖ 49.04 Other excision of perianal tissue

Excludes *anal fistulectomy (49.12)*
biopsy of perianal tissue (49.22)

● 49.1 Incision or excision of anal fistula

Excludes *closure of anal fistula (49.73)*

✖ 49.11 Anal fistulotomy

✖ 49.12 Anal fistulectomy

● 49.2 Diagnostic procedures on anus and perianal tissue

49.21 Anoscopy

49.22 Biopsy of perianal tissue

49.23 Biopsy of anus

49.29 Other diagnostic procedures on anus and perianal tissue

Excludes *microscopic examination of specimen from anus (90.91–90.99)*

● 49.3 Local excision or destruction of other lesion or tissue of anus
Anal cryptotomy
Cauterization of lesion of anus

Excludes *biopsy of anus (49.23)*
control of (postoperative) hemorrhage of anus (49.95)
hemorrhoidectomy (49.46)

49.31 Endoscopic excision or destruction of lesion or tissue of anus

✖ 49.39 Other local excision or destruction of lesion or tissue of anus

Excludes *that by endoscopic approach (49.31)*

● 49.4 Procedures on hemorrhoids

49.41 Reduction of hemorrhoids

49.42 Injection of hemorrhoids

49.43 Cauterization of hemorrhoids
Clamp and cautery of hemorrhoids

× 49.44　Destruction of hemorrhoids by cryotherapy

× 49.45　Ligation of hemorrhoids

× 49.46　Excision of hemorrhoids
　　　Hemorrhoidectomy NOS

49.47　Evacuation of thrombosed hemorrhoids

× 49.49　Other procedures on hemorrhoids
　　　Lord procedure

● **49.5　Division of anal sphincter**

× 49.51　Left lateral anal sphincterotomy

× 49.52　Posterior anal sphincterotomy

× 49.59　Other anal sphincterotomy
　　　Division of sphincter NOS

× 49.6　Excision of anus

● **49.7　Repair of anus**

　Excludes　*repair of current obstetric laceration (75.62)*

× 49.71　Suture of laceration of anus

× 49.72　Anal cerclage

× 49.73　Closure of anal fistula

　Excludes　*excision of anal fistula (49.12)*

× 49.74　Gracilis muscle transplant for anal incontinence

× 49.79　Other repair of anal sphincter
　　　Repair of old obstetric laceration of anus

　Excludes　*anoplasty with synchronous hemorrhoidectomy (49.46)*
　　　　repair of current obstetric laceration (75.62)

● **49.9　Other operations on anus**

　Excludes　*dilation of anus (sphincter) (96.23)*

× 49.91　Incision of anal septum

× 49.92　Insertion of subcutaneous electrical anal stimulator

× 49.93　Other incision of anus
　　　Removal of:
　　　　foreign body from anus with incision
　　　　seton from anus

　Excludes　*anal fistulotomy (49.11)*
　　　　removal of intraluminal foreign body without incision (98.05)

× 49.94　Reduction of anal prolapse

　Excludes　*manual reduction of rectal prolapse (96.26)*

× 49.95　Control of (postoperative) hemorrhage of anus

× 49.99　Other

● **50　Operations on liver**

× 50.0　Hepatotomy
　　　Incision of abscess of liver
　　　Removal of gallstones from liver
　　　Stromeyer-Little operation

● **50.1　Diagnostic procedures on liver**

50.11　Closed (percutaneous) [needle] biopsy of liver
　　　Diagnostic aspiration of liver

× 50.12　Open biopsy of liver
　　　Wedge biopsy

× 50.19　Other diagnostic procedures on liver

　Excludes　*liver scan and radioisotope function study (92.02)*
　　　　microscopic examination of specimen from liver (91.01–91.09)

● **50.2　Local excision or destruction of liver tissue or lesion**

× 50.21　Marsupialization of lesion of liver

× 50.22　Partial hepatectomy
　　　Wedge resection of liver

　Excludes　*biopsy of liver (50.11–50.12)*
　　　　hepatic lobectomy (50.3)

× 50.29　Other destruction of lesion of liver
　　　Cauterization of hepatic lesion
　　　Enucleation of hepatic lesion
　　　Evacuation of hepatic lesion

　Excludes　*percutaneous aspiration of lesion (50.91)*

× 50.3　Lobectomy of liver
　　　Total hepatic lobectomy with partial excision of other lobe

× 50.4　Total hepatectomy

● **50.5　Liver transplant**

× 50.51　Auxiliary liver transplant
　　　Auxiliary hepatic transplantation leaving patient's own liver in situ

× 50.59　Other transplant of liver

● **50.6　Repair of liver**

× 50.61　Closure of laceration of liver

× 50.69　Other repair of liver
　　　Hepatopexy

● **50.9　Other operations on liver**

　Excludes　*lysis of adhesions (54.5)*

50.91　Percutaneous aspiration of liver

　Excludes　*percutaneous biopsy (50.11)*

50.92　Extracorporeal hepatic assistance

50.93　Localized perfusion of liver

50.94　Other injection of therapeutic substance into liver

50.99　Other

● **51　Operations on gallbladder and biliary tract**

　Includes:　operations on:
　　　　ampulla of Vater
　　　　common bile duct
　　　　cystic duct
　　　　hepatic duct
　　　　intrahepatic bile duct
　　　　sphincter of Oddi

● **51.0　Cholecystotomy and cholecystostomy**

51.01　Percutaneous aspiration of gallbladder

　Excludes　*needle biopsy (51.12)*

× 51.02　Trocar cholecystostomy

× 51.03　Other cholecystostomy

× 51.04　Other cholecystotomy
　　　Cholelithotomy NOS

● **51.1　Diagnostic procedures on biliary tract**

　Excludes　*that for endoscopic procedures classifiable to 51.64, 51.84–51.88, 52.14, 52.21, 52.93–52.94, 52.97–52.98*

51.10　Endoscopic retrograde cholangiopancreatography [ERCP]

　Excludes　*endoscopic retrograde:*
　　　cholangiography [ERC] (51.11)
　　　pancreatography [ERP] (52.13)

51.11　Endoscopic retrograde cholangiography [ERC]

　Excludes　*endoscopic retrograde:*
　　　cholangiopancreatography [ERCP] (51.10)
　　　pancreatography [ERP] (52.13)

51.12　Percutaneous biopsy of gallbladder or bile ducts
　　　Needle biopsy of gallbladder

✖ **51.13   Open biopsy of gallbladder or bile ducts**

51.14   Other closed [endoscopic] biopsy of biliary duct or sphincter of Oddi
Brushing or washing for specimen collection
Closed biopsy of biliary duct or sphincter of Oddi by procedures classifiable to 51.10–51.11, 52.13

51.15   Pressure measurement of sphincter of Oddi
Pressure measurement of sphincter by procedures classifiable to 51.10–51.11, 52.13

✖ **51.19   Other diagnostic procedures on biliary tract**
> Excludes   *biliary tract x-ray (87.51–87.59)*
> *microscopic examination of specimen from biliary tract (91.01–91.09)*

● **51.2   Cholecystectomy**

✖ **51.21   Other partial cholecystectomy**
Revision of prior cholecystectomy
> Excludes   *that by laparoscope (51.24)*

✖ **51.22   Cholecystectomy**
> Excludes   *laparoscopic cholecystectomy (51.23)*

✖ **51.23   Laparoscopic cholecystectomy**
That by laser

✖ **51.24   Laparoscopic partial cholecystectomy**

● **51.3   Anastomosis of gallbladder or bile duct**
> Excludes   *resection with end-to-end anastomosis (51.61–51.69)*

✖ **51.31   Anastomosis of gallbladder to hepatic ducts**

✖ **51.32   Anastomosis of gallbladder to intestine**

✖ **51.33   Anastomosis of gallbladder to pancreas**

✖ **51.34   Anastomosis of gallbladder to stomach**

✖ **51.35   Other gallbladder anastomosis**
Gallbladder anastomosis NOS

✖ **51.36   Choledochoenterostomy**

✖ **51.37   Anastomosis of hepatic duct to gastrointestinal tract**

✖ **51.39   Other bile duct anastomosis**
Anastomosis of bile duct NOS
Anastomosis of unspecified bile duct to:
    intestine
    liver
    pancreas
    stomach

● **51.4   Incision of bile duct for relief of obstruction**

✖ **51.41   Common duct exploration for removal of calculus**
> Excludes   *percutaneous extraction (51.96)*

✖ **51.42   Common duct exploration for relief of other obstruction**

✖ **51.43   Insertion of choledochohepatic tube for decompression**
Hepatocholedochostomy

✖ **51.49   Incision of other bile ducts for relief of obstruction**

● **51.5   Other incision of bile duct**
> Excludes   *that for relief of obstruction (51.41–51.49)*

✖ **51.51   Exploration of common duct**
Incision of common bile duct

✖ **51.59   Incision of other bile duct**

● **51.6   Local excision or destruction of lesion or tissue of biliary ducts and sphincter of Oddi**
Code also anastomosis other than end-to-end (51.31, 51.36–51.39)
> Excludes   *biopsy of bile duct (51.12–51.13)*

✖ **51.61   Excision of cystic duct remnant**

✖ **51.62   Excision of ampulla of Vater (with reimplantation of common duct)**

✖ **51.63   Other excision of common duct**
Choledochectomy
> Excludes   *fistulectomy (51.72)*

51.64   Endoscopic excision or destruction of lesion of biliary ducts or sphincter of Oddi
Excision or destruction of lesion of biliary duct by procedures classifiable to 51.10–51.11, 52.13

✖ **51.69   Excision of other bile duct**
Excision of lesion of bile duct NOS
> Excludes   *fistulectomy (51.79)*

● **51.7   Repair of bile ducts**

✖ **51.71   Simple suture of common bile duct**

✖ **51.72   Choledochoplasty**
Repair of fistula of common bile duct

✖ **51.79   Repair of other bile ducts**
Closure of artificial opening of bile duct NOS
Suture of bile duct NOS
> Excludes   *operative removal of prosthetic device (51.95)*

● **51.8   Other operations on biliary ducts and sphincter of Oddi**

✖ **51.81   Dilation of sphincter of Oddi**
Dilation of ampulla of Vater
> Excludes   *that by endoscopic approach (51.84)*

✖ **51.82   Pancreatic sphincterotomy**
Incision of pancreatic sphincter
Transduodenal ampullary sphincterotomy
> Excludes   *that by endoscopic approach (51.85)*

✖ **51.83   Pancreatic sphincteroplasty**

51.84   Endoscopic dilation of ampulla and biliary duct
Dilation of ampulla and biliary duct by procedures classifiable to 51.10–51.11, 52.13

51.85   Endoscopic sphincterotomy and papillotomy
Sphincterotomy and papillotomy by procedures classifiable to 51.10–51.11, 52.13

51.86   Endoscopic insertion of nasobiliary drainage tube
Insertion of nasobiliary tube by procedures classifiable to 51.10–51.11, 52.13

51.87   Endoscopic insertion of stent (tube) into bile duct
Endoprosthesis of bile duct
Insertion of stent into bile duct by procedures classifiable to 51.10–51.11, 52.13
> Excludes   *nasobiliary drainage tube (51.86)*
> *replacement of stent (tube) (97.05)*

51.88   Endoscopic removal of stone(s) from biliary tract
Laparoscopic removal of stone(s) from biliary tract
Removal of biliary tract stone(s) by procedures classifiable to 51.10–51.11, 52.13
> Excludes   *percutaneous extraction of common duct stones (51.96)*

✖ **51.89** Other operations on sphincter of Oddi

● **51.9** Other operations on biliary tract

    ✖ **51.91** Repair of laceration of gallbladder

    ✖ **51.92** Closure of cholecystostomy

    ✖ **51.93** Closure of other biliary fistula
       Cholecystogastroenteric fistulectomy

    ✖ **51.94** Revision of anastomosis of biliary tract

    ✖ **51.95** Removal of prosthetic device from bile duct
       Excludes *nonoperative removal (97.55)*

    51.96 Percutaneous extraction of common duct stones

    51.98 Other percutaneous procedures on biliary tract
       Percutaneous biliary endoscopy via existing
          T-tube or other tract for:
       dilation of biliary duct stricture
       removal of stone(s) except common duct
          stone
       exploration (postoperative)
       Percutaneous transhepatic biliary drainage
       Excludes *percutaneous aspiration of gallbladder (51.01)*
          percutaneous biopsy and/or collection of specimen
             by brushing or washing (51.12)
          percutaneous removal of common duct stone(s)
             (51.96)

    ✖ **51.99** Other
       Insertion or replacement of biliary tract pros-
          thesis
       Excludes *biopsy of gallbladder (51.12–51.13)*
          irrigation of cholecystostomy and other biliary
             tube (96.41)
          lysis of peritoneal adhesions (54.5)
          nonoperative removal of:
             cholecystostomy tube (97.54)
             tube from biliary tract or liver (97.55)

● **52** Operations on pancreas

    Includes: operations on pancreatic duct

    ● **52.0** Pancreatotomy

       ✖ **52.01** Drainage of pancreatic cyst by catheter

       ✖ **52.09** Other pancreatotomy
          Pancreatolithotomy
          Excludes *drainage by anastomosis (52.4, 52.96)*
             incision of pancreatic sphincter (51.82)
             marsupialization of cyst (52.3)

    ● **52.1** Diagnostic procedures on pancreas

       52.11 Closed [aspiration] [needle] [percutaneous] bi-
          opsy of pancreas

       ✖ **52.12** Open biopsy of pancreas

       52.13 Endoscopic retrograde pancreatography [ERP]
       Excludes *endoscopic retrograde:*
          cholangiography [ERC] (51.11)
          cholangiopancreatography [ERCP] (51.10)
          that for procedures classifiable to 51.14–51.15,
             51.64, 51.84–51.88, 52.14, 52.21,
             52.92–52.94, 52.97–52.98

       52.14 Closed [endoscopic] biopsy of pancreatic duct
          Closed biopsy of pancreatic duct by proce-
             dures classifiable to 51.10–51.11, 52.13

       ✖ **52.19** Other diagnostic procedures on pancreas
       Excludes *contrast pancreatogram (87.66)*

          endoscopic retrograde pancreatography [ERP]
             (52.13)
          microscopic examination of specimen from pan-
             creas (91.01–91.09)

● **52.2** Local excision or destruction of pancreas and pancre-
    atic duct
    Excludes *biopsy of pancreas (52.11–52.12, 52.14)*
          pancreatic fistulectomy (52.95)

       52.21 Endoscopic excision or destruction of lesion or
          tissue of pancreatic duct
          Excision or destruction of lesion or tissue of
             pancreatic duct by procedures classifiable
             to 51.10–51.11, 52.13

       ✖ **52.22** Other excision or destruction of lesion or tis-
          sue of pancreas or pancreatic duct

    ✖ **52.3** Marsupialization of pancreatic cyst
    Excludes *drainage of cyst by catheter (52.01)*

    ✖ **52.4** Internal drainage of pancreatic cyst
       Pancreaticocystoduodenostomy
       Pancreaticocystogastrostomy
       Pancreaticocystojejunostomy

    ● **52.5** Partial pancreatectomy
    Excludes *pancreatic fistulectomy (52.95)*

       ✖ **52.51** Proximal pancreatectomy
          Excision of head of pancreas (with part of
             body)
          Proximal pancreatectomy with synchronous
             duodenectomy

       ✖ **52.52** Distal pancreatectomy
          Excision of tail of pancreas (with part of body)

       ✖ **52.53** Radical subtotal pancreatectomy

       ✖ **52.59** Other partial pancreatectomy

    ✖ **52.6** Total pancreatectomy
       Pancreatectomy with synchronous duodenectomy

    ✖ **52.7** Radical pancreaticoduodenectomy
       One-stage pancreaticoduodenal resection with chole-
          dochojejunal anastomosis, pancreaticojejunal an-
          astomosis, and gastrojejunostomy
       Two-stage pancreaticoduodenal resection (first stage)
          (second stage)
       Radical resection of the pancreas
       Whipple procedure
       Excludes *radical subtotal pancreatectomy (52.53)*

    ● **52.8** Transplant of pancreas

       ✖ **52.80** Pancreatic transplant, not otherwise specified

       ✖ **52.81** Reimplantation of pancreatic tissue

       ✖ **52.82** Homotransplant of pancreas

       ✖ **52.83** Heterotransplant of pancreas

       52.84 Autotransplantation of cells of Islets of Lan-
          gerhans
          Homotransplantation of islet cells of pancreas

       ✖ **52.85** Allotransplantation of cells of Islets of Langer-
          hans
          Heterotransplantation of islet cells of pancreas

       ✖ **52.86** Transplantation of cells of Islets of Langer-
          hans, not otherwise specified

    ● **52.9** Other operations on pancreas

       ✖ **52.92** Cannulation of pancreatic duct
       Excludes *that by endoscopic approach (52.93)*

       52.93 Endoscopic insertion of stent (tube) into pan-
          creatic duct
          Insertion of cannula or stent into pancreatic
             duct by procedures classifiable to 51.10–
             51.11, 52.13
       Excludes *endoscopic insertion of nasopancreatic drainage*
             tube (52.97)
          replacement of stent (tube) (97.05)

● **Use Additional Digit(s)**   ✖ **Valid O.R. Procedure**   ◄► **New Code**   ⇚ ⇛ **Revised Code**

52.94 Endoscopic removal of stone(s) from pancreatic duct
Removal of stone(s) from pancreatic duct by procedures classifiable to 51.10–51.11, 52.13

✖ **52.95 Other repair of pancreas**
Fistulectomy of pancreas
Simple suture of pancreas

✖ **52.96 Anastomosis of pancreas**
Anastomosis of pancreas (duct) to:
intestine
jejunum
stomach
Excludes anastomosis to:
    bile duct (51.39)
    gallbladder (51.33)

52.97 Endoscopic insertion of nasopancreatic drainage tube
Insertion of nasopancreatic drainage tube by procedures classifiable to 51.10–51.11, 52.13
Excludes drainage of pancreatic cyst by catheter (52.01)
    replacement of stent (tube) (97.05)

52.98 Endoscopic dilation of pancreatic duct
Dilation of Wirsung's duct by procedures classifiable to 51.10–51.11, 52.13

52.99 Other
Dilation of pancreatic [Wirsung's] duct by open approach
Repair of pancreatic [Wirsung's] duct by open approach
Excludes irrigation of pancreatic tube (96.42)
    removal of pancreatic tube (97.56)

● **53 Repair of hernia**
Includes: hernioplasty
herniorrhaphy
Excludes manual reduction of hernia (96.27)

● **53.0 Unilateral repair of inguinal hernia**

✖ **53.00 Unilateral repair of inguinal hernia, not otherwise specified**
Inguinal herniorrhaphy NOS

✖ **53.01 Repair of direct inguinal hernia**

✖ **53.02 Repair of indirect inguinal hernia**

✖ **53.03 Repair of direct inguinal hernia with graft or prosthesis**

✖ **53.04 Repair of indirect inguinal hernia with graft or prosthesis**

✖ **53.05 Repair of inguinal hernia with graft or prosthesis, not otherwise specified**

● **53.1 Bilateral repair of inguinal hernia**

✖ **53.10 Bilateral repair of inguinal hernia, not otherwise specified**

✖ **53.11 Bilateral repair of direct inguinal hernia**

✖ **53.12 Bilateral repair of indirect inguinal hernia**

✖ **53.13 Bilateral repair of inguinal hernia, one direct and one indirect**

✖ **53.14 Bilateral repair of direct inguinal hernia with graft or prosthesis**

✖ **53.15 Bilateral repair of indirect inguinal hernia with graft or prosthesis**

✖ **53.16 Bilateral repair of inguinal hernia, one direct and one indirect, with graft or prosthesis**

✖ **53.17 Bilateral inguinal hernia repair with graft or prosthesis, not otherwise specified**

● **53.2 Unilateral repair of femoral hernia**

✖ **53.21 Unilateral repair of femoral hernia with graft or prosthesis**

✖ **53.29 Other unilateral femoral herniorrhaphy**

● **53.3 Bilateral repair of femoral hernia**

✖ **53.31 Bilateral repair of femoral hernia with graft or prosthesis**

✖ **53.39 Other bilateral femoral herniorrhaphy**

● **53.4 Repair of umbilical hernia**
Excludes repair of gastroschisis (54.71)

✖ **53.41 Repair of umbilical hernia with prosthesis**

✖ **53.49 Other umbilical herniorrhaphy**

● **53.5 Repair of other hernia of anterior abdominal wall (without graft or prosthesis)**

✖ **53.51 Incisional hernia repair**

✖ **53.59 Repair of other hernia of anterior abdominal wall**
Repair of hernia:
epigastric
hypogastric
spigelian
ventral

● **53.6 Repair of other hernia of anterior abdominal wall with graft or prosthesis**

✖ **53.61 Incisional hernia repair with prosthesis**

✖ **53.69 Repair of other hernia of anterior abdominal wall with prosthesis**

✖ **53.7 Repair of diaphragmatic hernia, abdominal approach**

● **53.8 Repair of diaphragmatic hernia, thoracic approach**

✖ **53.80 Repair of diaphragmatic hernia with thoracic approach, not otherwise specified**
Thoracoabdominal repair of diaphragmatic hernia

✖ **53.81 Plication of the diaphragm**

✖ **53.82 Repair of parasternal hernia**

✖ **53.9 Other hernia repair**
Repair of hernia:
ischiatic
ischiorectal
lumbar
obturator
omental
retroperitoneal
sciatic
Excludes relief of strangulated hernia with exteriorization of intestine (46.01, 46.03)
    repair of pericolostomy hernia (46.42)
    repair of vaginal enterocele (70.92)

   ● **Use Additional Digit(s)**   ✖ **Valid O.R. Procedure**   ◄► **New Code**   ⬅⬆➡ **Revised Code**

● **54 Other operations on abdominal region**

Incudes: operations on:
  epigastric region
  flank
  groin region
  hypochondrium
  inguinal region
  loin region
  male pelvic cavity
  mesentery
  omentum
  peritoneum
  retroperitoneal tissue space

  Excludes *female pelvic cavity (69.01–70.92)*
  hernia repair (53.00–53.9)
  obliteration of cul-de-sac (70.92)
  retroperitoneal tissue dissection (59.00–59.09)
  skin and subcutaneous tissue of abdominal wall (86.01–86.99)

✖ **54.0 Incision of abdominal wall**
  Drainage of:
  abdominal wall
  extraperitoneal abscess
  retroperitoneal abscess

  Excludes *incision of peritoneum (54.95)*
  laparotomy (54.11–54.19)

● **54.1 Laparotomy**

  ✖ **54.11 Exploratory laparotomy**

  Excludes *exploration incidental to intra- abdominal surgery—omit code*

  ✖ **54.12 Reopening of recent laparotomy site**
  Reopening of recent laparotomy site for:
  control of hemorrhage
  exploration
  incision of hematoma

  ✖ **54.19 Other laparotomy**
  Drainage of intraperitoneal abscess or hematoma

  Excludes *culdocentesis (70.0)*
  drainage of appendiceal abscess (47.2)
  exploration incidental to intra-abdominal surgery—omit code
  Ladd operation (54.95)
  removal of foreign body (54.92)

● **54.2 Diagnostic procedures of abdominal region**

  ✖ **54.21 Laparoscopy**
  Peritoneoscopy

  Excludes *laparoscopic cholecystectomy (51.23)*
  that incidental to destruction of fallopian tubes (66.21–66.29)

  ✖ **54.22 Biopsy of abdominal wall or umbilicus**

  ✖ **54.23 Biopsy of peritoneum**
  Biopsy of:
  mesentery
  omentum
  peritoneal implant

  Excludes *closed biopsy of:* ◀
  omentum (54.24) ◀
  peritoneum (54.24) ◀

  54.24 Closed [percutaneous] [needle] biopsy of intra-abdominal mass
  Closed biopsy of: ◀
  omentum ◀
  peritoneum ◀

  Excludes *that of:*
  fallopian tube (66.11)
  ovary (65.11)
  uterine ligaments (68.15)
  uterus (68.16)

54.25 Peritoneal lavage
  Diagnostic peritoneal lavage

  Excludes *peritoneal dialysis (54.98)*

✖ **54.29 Other diagnostic procedures on abdominal region**

  Excludes *abdominal lymphangiogram (88.04)*
  abdominal x-ray NEC (88.19)
  angiocardiography of venae cava (88.51)
  C.A.T. scan of abdomen (88.01)
  contrast x-ray of abdominal cavity (88.11–88.15)
  intra-abdominal arteriography NEC (88.47)
  microscopic examination of peritoneal and retroperitoneal specimen (91.11–91.19)
  phlebography of:
  intra-abdominal vessels NEC (88.65)
  portal venous system (88.64)
  sinogram of abdominal wall (88.03)
  soft tissue x-ray of abdominal wall NEC (88.09)
  tomography of abdomen NEC (88.02)
  ultrasonography of abdomen and retroperitoneum (88.76)

✖ **54.3 Excision or destruction of lesion or tissue of abdominal wall or umbilicus**
  Debridement of abdominal wall
  Omphalectomy

  Excludes *biopsy of abdominal wall or umbilicus (54.22)*
  size reduction operation (86.83)
  that of skin of abdominal wall (86.22, 86.26, 86.3)

✖ **54.4 Excision or destruction of peritoneal tissue**
  Excision of:
  appendices epiploicae
  falciform ligament
  gastrocolic ligament
  lesion of:
  mesentery
  omentum
  peritoneum
  presacral lesion NOS
  retroperitoneal lesion NOS

  Excludes *biopsy of peritoneum (54.23)*
  endometrectomy of cul-de-sac (70.32)

✖ **54.5 Lysis of peritoneal adhesions**
  Freeing of adhesions of:
  biliary tract
  intestines
  liver
  pelvic peritoneum
  peritoneum
  spleen
  uterus

  Excludes *lysis of adhesions of:*
  bladder (59.11)
  fallopian tube and ovary
  laparoscopic (65.81)
  other (65.89)
  kidney (59.02)
  ureter (59.02)

  ✖ **54.51 Laparoscopic lysis of peritoneal adhesions**

  ✖ **54.59 Other lysis of peritoneal adhesions**

● **54.6 Suture of abdominal wall and peritoneum**

  ✖ **54.61 Reclosure of postoperative disruption of abdominal wall**

  ✖ **54.62 Delayed closure of granulating abdominal wound**
  Tertiary subcutaneous wound closure

  ✖ **54.63 Other suture of abdominal wall**
  Suture of laceration of abdominal wall

  Excludes *closure of operative wound—omit code*

● **Use Additional Digit(s)** ✖ **Valid O.R. Procedure** ◀▶ **New Code** ⟵⟶ **Revised Code**

✖ 54.64   Suture of peritoneum
Secondary suture of peritoneum

> **Excludes**   *closure of operative wound—omit code*

● 54.7   Other repair of abdominal wall and peritoneum

✖ 54.71   Repair of gastroschisis

✖ 54.72   Other repair of abdominal wall

✖ 54.73   Other repair of peritoneum
Suture of gastrocolic ligament

✖ 54.74   Other repair of omentum
Epiplorrhaphy
Graft of omentum
Omentopexy
Reduction of torsion of omentum

> **Excludes**   *cardio-omentopexy (36.39)*   ⬅

✖ 54.75   Other repair of mesentery
Mesenteric plication
Mesenteropexy

● 54.9   Other operations of abdominal region

> **Excludes**   *removal of ectopic pregnancy (74.3)*

54.91   Percutaneous abdominal drainage
Paracentesis

> **Excludes**   *creation of cutaneoperitoneal fistula (54.93)*

✖ 54.92   Removal of foreign body from peritoneal cavity

✖ 54.93   Creation of cutaneoperitoneal fistula

✖ 54.94   Creation of peritoneovascular shunt
Peritoneovenous shunt

✖ 54.95   Incision of peritoneum
Ladd operation
Revision of distal catheter of ventricular shunt
Revision of ventriculoperitoneal shunt at peritoneal site

> **Excludes**   *that incidental to laparotomy (54.11–54.19)*

54.96   Injection of air into peritoneal cavity
Pneumoperitoneum

> **Excludes**   *that for:*
>   *collapse of lung (33.33)*
>   *radiography (88.12–88.13, 88.15)*

54.97   Injection of locally-acting therapeutic substance into peritoneal cavity

> **Excludes**   *peritoneal dialysis (54.98)*

54.98   Peritoneal dialysis

> **Excludes**   *peritoneal lavage (diagnostic) (54.25)*

54.99   Other

> **Excludes**   *removal of:*
>   *abdominal wall suture (97.83)*
>   *peritoneal drainage device (97.82)*
>   *retroperitoneal drainage device (97.81)*

10. OPERATIONS ON THE URINARY SYSTEM (55–59)

● **55 Operations on kidney**

Includes: operations on renal pelvis

Excludes *perirenal tissue (59.00–59.09, 59.21–59.29, 59.91–59.92)*

● **55.0 Nephrotomy and nephrostomy**

Excludes *drainage by:*
anastomosis (55.86)
aspiration (55.92)
incision of kidney pelvis (55.11–55.12)

✖ **55.01 Nephrotomy**
Evacuation of renal cyst
Exploration of kidney
Nephrolithotomy

✖ **55.02 Nephrostomy**

✖ **55.03 Percutaneous nephrostomy without fragmentation**
Nephrostolithotomy, percutaneous (nephroscopic)
Percutaneous removal of kidney stone(s) by:
basket extraction
forceps extraction (nephroscopic)
Pyelostolithotomy, percutaneous (nephroscopic)
With placement of catheter down ureter

Excludes *percutaneous removal by fragmentation (55.04)*
repeat nephroscopic removal during current episode (55.92)

✖ **55.04 Percutaneous nephrostomy with fragmentation**
Percutaneous nephrostomy with disruption of kidney stone by ultrasonic energy and extraction (suction) through endoscope
With placement of catheter down ureter
With fluoroscopic guidance

Excludes *repeat fragmentation during current episode (59.95)*

● **55.1 Pyelotomy and pyelostomy**

Excludes *drainage by anastomosis (55.86)*
percutaneous pyelostolithotomy (55.03)
removal of calculus without incision (56.0)

✖ **55.11 Pyelotomy**
Exploration of renal pelvis
Pyelolithotomy

✖ **55.12 Pyelostomy**
Insertion of drainage tube into renal pelvis

● **55.2 Diagnostic procedures on kidney**

55.21 Nephroscopy

55.22 Pyeloscopy

55.23 Closed [percutaneous] [needle] biopsy of kidney
Endoscopic biopsy via existing nephrostomy, nephrotomy, pyelostomy, or pyelotomy

✖ **55.24 Open biopsy of kidney**

✖ **55.29 Other diagnostic procedures on kidney**

Excludes *microscopic examination of specimen from kidney (91.21–91.29)*
pyelogram:
intravenous (87.73)
percutaneous (87.75)
retrograde (87.74)
radioisotope scan (92.03)
renal arteriography (88.45)
tomography:
C.A.T. scan (87.71)
other (87.72)

● **55.3 Local excision or destruction of lesion or tissue of kidney**

✖ **55.31 Marsupialization of kidney lesion**

✖ **55.39 Other local destruction or excision of renal lesion or tissue**
Obliteration of calyceal diverticulum

Excludes *biopsy of kidney (55.23–55.24)*
partial nephrectomy (55.4)
percutaneous aspiration of kidney (55.92)
wedge resection of kidney (55.4)

✖ **55.4 Partial nephrectomy**
Calycectomy
Wedge resection of kidney

Code also any synchronous resection of ureter (56.40–56.42)

● **55.5 Complete nephrectomy**

Code also any synchronous excision of:
bladder segment (57.6)
lymph nodes (40.3, 40.52–40.59)

✖ **55.51 Nephroureterectomy**
Nephroureterectomy with bladder cuff
Total nephrectomy (unilateral)

Excludes *removal of transplanted kidney (55.53)*

✖ **55.52 Nephrectomy of remaining kidney**
Removal of solitary kidney

Excludes *removal of transplanted kidney (55.53)*

✖ **55.53 Removal of transplanted or rejected kidney**

✖ **55.54 Bilateral nephrectomy**

Excludes *complete nephrectomy NOS (55.51)*

● **55.6 Transplant of kidney**

✖ **55.61 Renal autotransplantation**

✖ **55.69 Other kidney transplantation**

✖ **55.7 Nephropexy**
Fixation or suspension of movable [floating] kidney

● **55.8 Other repair of kidney**

✖ **55.81 Suture of laceration of kidney**

✖ **55.82 Closure of nephrostomy and pyelostomy**

✖ **55.83 Closure of other fistula of kidney**

✖ **55.84 Reduction of torsion of renal pedicle**

✖ **55.85 Symphysiotomy for horseshoe kidney**

✖ **55.86 Anastomosis of kidney**
Nephropyeloureterostomy
Pyeloureterovesical anastomosis
Ureterocalyceal anastomosis

Excludes *nephrocystanastomosis NOS (56.73)*

✖ **55.87 Correction of ureteropelvic junction**

✖ **55.89 Other**

● **55.9 Other operations on kidney**

Excludes *lysis of perirenal adhesions (59.02)*

✖ **55.91 Decapsulation of kidney**
Capsulectomy of kidney
Decortication of kidney

55.92 Percutaneous aspiration of kidney (pelvis)
Aspiration of renal cyst
Renipuncture

Excludes *percutaneous biopsy of kidney (55.23)*

55.93 Replacement of nephrostomy tube

55.94 Replacement of pyelostomy tube

55.95 Local perfusion of kidney

55.96 Other injection of therapeutic substance into kidney
Injection into renal cyst

✖ **55.97 Implantation or replacement of mechanical kidney**

✖ **55.98 Removal of mechanical kidney**

✖ **55.99 Other**
| Excludes | removal of pyelostomy or nephrostomy tube (97.61)

● **56 Operations on ureter**

✖ **56.0 Transurethral removal of obstruction from ureter and renal pelvis**
Removal of:
blood clot from ureter or renal pelvis without incision
calculus from ureter or renal pelvis without incision
foreign body from ureter or renal pelvis without incision
| Excludes | manipulation without removal of obstruction (59.8)
that by incision (55.11, 56.2)
transurethral insertion of ureteral stent for passage of calculus (59.8)

✖ **56.1 Ureteral meatotomy**

✖ **56.2 Ureterotomy**
Incision of ureter for:
drainage
exploration
removal of calculus
| Excludes | cutting of ureterovesical orifice (56.1)
removal of calculus without incision (56.0)
transurethral insertion of ureteral stent for passage of calculus (59.8)
urinary diversion (56.51–56.79)

● **56.3 Diagnostic procedures on ureter**

56.31 Ureteroscopy

56.32 Closed percutaneous biopsy of ureter
| Excludes | endoscopic biopsy of ureter (56.33)

56.33 Closed endoscopic biopsy of ureter
Cystourethroscopy with ureteral biopsy
Transurethral biopsy of ureter
Ureteral endoscopy with biopsy through ureterotomy
Ureteroscopy with biopsy
| Excludes | percutaneous biopsy of ureter (56.32)

✖ **56.34 Open biopsy of ureter**

56.35 Endoscopy (cystoscopy) (looposcopy) of ileal conduit

✖ **56.39 Other diagnostic procedures on ureter**
| Excludes | microscopic examination of specimen from ureter (91.21–91.29)

● **56.4 Ureterectomy**
Code also anastomosis other than end-to-end (56.51–56.79)
| Excludes | fistulectomy (56.84)
nephroureterectomy (55.51–55.54)

✖ **56.40 Ureterectomy, not otherwise specified**

✖ **56.41 Partial ureterectomy**
Excision of lesion of ureter
Shortening of ureter with reimplantation
| Excludes | biopsy of ureter (56.32–56.34)

✖ **56.42 Total ureterectomy**

● **56.5 Cutaneous uretero-ileostomy**

✖ **56.51 Formation of cutaneous uretero-ileostomy**
Construction of ileal conduit
External ureteral ileostomy
Formation of open ileal bladder
Ileal loop operation
Ileoureterostomy (Bricker's) (ileal bladder)
Transplantation of ureter into ileum with external diversion
| Excludes | closed ileal bladder (57.87)
replacement of ureteral defect by ileal segment (56.89)

✖ **56.52 Revision of cutaneous uretero-ileostomy**

● **56.6 Other external urinary diversion**

✖ **56.61 Formation of other cutaneous ureterostomy**
Anastomosis of ureter to skin
Ureterostomy NOS

✖ **56.62 Revision of other cutaneous ureterostomy**
Revision of ureterostomy stoma
| Excludes | nonoperative removal of ureterostomy tube (97.62)

● **56.7 Other anastomosis or bypass of ureter**
| Excludes | ureteropyelostomy (55.86)

✖ **56.71 Urinary diversion to intestine**
Anastomosis of ureter to intestine
Internal urinary diversion NOS
Code also any synchronous colostomy (46.10–46.13)
| Excludes | external ureteral ileostomy (56.51)

✖ **56.72 Revision of ureterointestinal anastomosis**
| Excludes | revision of external ureteral ileostomy (56.52)

✖ **56.73 Nephrocystanastomosis, not otherwise specified**

✖ **56.74 Ureteroneocystostomy**
Replacement of ureter with bladder flap
Ureterovesical anastomosis

✖ **56.75 Transureteroureterostomy**
| Excludes | ureteroureterostomy associated with partial resection (56.41)

✖ **56.79 Other**

● **56.8 Repair of ureter**

✖ **56.81 Lysis of intraluminal adhesions of ureter**
| Excludes | lysis of periureteral adhesions (59.01–59.02)
ureterolysis (59.01–59.02)

✖ **56.82 Suture of laceration of ureter**

✖ **56.83 Closure of ureterostomy**

✖ **56.84 Closure of other fistula of ureter**

✖ **56.85 Ureteropexy**

✖ **56.86 Removal of ligature from ureter**

✖ **56.89 Other repair of ureter**
Graft of ureter
Replacement of ureter with ileal segment implanted into bladder
Ureteroplication

● **56.9 Other operations on ureter**

56.91 Dilation of ureteral meatus

✖ **56.92 Implantation of electronic ureteral stimulator**

✖ **56.93 Replacement of electronic ureteral stimulator**

✖ **56.94 Removal of electronic ureteral stimulator**
| Excludes | that with synchronous replacement (56.93)

✖ **56.95 Ligation of ureter**

✖ **56.99 Other**

> Excludes *removal of ureterostomy tube and ureteral cathe-*
> *ter (97.62)*
> *ureteral catheterization (59.8)*

● **57 Operations on urinary bladder**

> Excludes *perivesical tissue (59.11–59.29, 59.91–59.92)*
> *ureterovesical orifice (56.0–56.99)*

57.0 Transurethral clearance of bladder
Drainage of bladder without incision
Removal of:
    blood clots from bladder without incision
    calculus from bladder without incision
    foreign body from bladder without incision

> Excludes *that by incision (57.19)*

● **57.1 Cystotomy and cystostomy**

> Excludes *cystotomy and cystostomy as operative ap-*
> *proach—omit code*

57.11 Percutaneous aspiration of bladder

57.12 Lysis of intraluminal adhesions with incision into bladder

> Excludes *transurethral lysis of intraluminal adhesions*
> *(57.41)*

57.17 Percutaneous cystostomy
Closed cystostomy
Percutaneous suprapubic cystostomy

> Excludes *removal of cystostomy tube (97.63)*
> *replacement of cystostomy tube (59.94)*

✖ **57.18 Other suprapubic cystostomy**

> Excludes *percutaneous cystostomy (57.17)*
> *removal of cystostomy tube (97.63)*
> *replacement of cystostomy tube (59.94)*

✖ **57.19 Other cystotomy**
Cystolithotomy

> Excludes *percutaneous cystostomy (57.17)*
> *suprapubic cystostomy (57.18)*

● **57.2 Vesicostomy**

> Excludes *percutaneous cystostomy (57.17)*
> *suprapubic cystostomy (57.18)*

✖ **57.21 Vesicostomy**
Creation of permanent opening from bladder
to skin using a bladder flap

✖ **57.22 Revision or closure of vesicostomy**

> Excludes *closure of cystostomy (57.82)*

● **57.3 Diagnostic procedures on bladder**

57.31 Cystoscopy through artificial stoma

57.32 Other cystoscopy
Transurethral cystoscopy

> Excludes *cystourethroscopy with ureteral biopsy (56.33)*
> *retrograde pyelogram (87.74)*
> *that for control of hemorrhage (postoperative):*
> *bladder (57.93)*
> *prostate (60.94)*

✖ **57.33 Closed [transurethral] biopsy of bladder**

✖ **57.34 Open biopsy of bladder**

✖ **57.39 Other diagnostic procedures on bladder**

> Excludes *cystogram NEC (87.77)*
> *microscopic examination of specimen from blad-*
> *der (91.31–91.39)*
> *retrograde cystourethrogram (87.76)*

● **57.4 Transurethral excision or destruction of bladder tissue**

✖ **57.41 Transurethral lysis of intraluminal adhesions**

✖ **57.49 Other transurethral excision or destruction of lesion or tissue of bladder**
Endoscopic resection of bladder lesion

> Excludes *transurethral biopsy of bladder (57.33)*
> *transurethral fistulectomy (57.83–57.84)*

● **57.5 Other excision or destruction of bladder tissue**

> Excludes *that with transurethral approach (57.41–57.49)*

✖ **57.51 Excision of urachus**
Excision of urachal sinus of bladder

> Excludes *excision of urachal cyst of abdominal wall (54.3)*

✖ **57.59 Open excision or destruction of other lesion or tissue of bladder**
Endometrectomy of bladder
Suprapubic excision of bladder lesion

> Excludes *biopsy of bladder (57.33–57.34)*
> *fistulectomy of bladder (57.83–57.84)*

✖ **57.6 Partial cystectomy**
Excision of bladder dome
Trigonectomy
Wedge resection of bladder

● **57.7 Total cystectomy**

> **Includes:** total cystectomy with urethrectomy

✖ **57.71 Radical cystectomy**
Pelvic exenteration in male
Removal of bladder, prostate, seminal vesi-
    cles, and fat
Removal of bladder, urethra, and fat in a fe-
    male
Code also any:
    lymph node dissection (40.3, 40.5)
    urinary diversion (56.51–56.79)

> Excludes *that as part of pelvic exenteration in female*
> *(68.8)*

✖ **57.79 Other total cystectomy**

● **57.8 Other repair of urinary bladder**

> Excludes *repair of:*
> *current obstetric laceration (75.61)*
> *cystocele (70.50–70.51)*
> *that for stress incontinence (59.3–59.79)*

✖ **57.81 Suture of laceration of bladder**

✖ **57.82 Closure of cystostomy**

✖ **57.83 Repair of fistula involving bladder and intes-tine**
Rectovesicovaginal fistulectomy
Vesicosigmoidovaginal fistulectomy

✖ **57.84 Repair of other fistula of bladder**
Cervicovesical fistulectomy
Urethroperineovesical fistulectomy
Uterovesical fistulectomy
Vaginovesical fistulectomy

> Excludes *vesicoureterovaginal fistulectomy (56.84)*

✖ **57.85 Cystourethroplasty and plastic repair of blad-der neck**
Plication of sphincter of urinary bladder
V-Y plasty of bladder neck

✖ **57.86 Repair of bladder exstrophy**

✖ **57.87 Reconstruction of urinary bladder**
Anastomosis of bladder with isolated segment
    of ileum
Augmentation of bladder
Replacement of bladder with ileum or sig-
    moid [closed ileal bladder]

Code also resection of intestine (45.50–45.52)

● **Use Additional Digit(s)**   ✖ **Valid O.R. Procedure**   ◀▶ **New Code**   ⬅➡ **Revised Code**

✖ 57.88 Other anastomosis of bladder
Anastomosis of bladder to intestine NOS
Cystocolic anastomosis
> **Excludes** *formation of closed ileal bladder (57.87)*

✖ 57.89 Other repair of bladder
Bladder suspension, not elsewhere classified
Cystopexy NOS
Repair of old obstetric laceration of bladder
> **Excludes** *repair of current obstetric laceration (75.61)*

● 57.9 Other operations on bladder

✖ 57.91 Sphincterotomy of bladder
Division of bladder neck

57.92 Dilation of bladder neck

✖ 57.93 Control of (postoperative) hemorrhage of bladder

57.94 Insertion of indwelling urinary catheter

57.95 Replacement of indwelling urinary catheter

✖ 57.96 Implantation of electronic bladder stimulator

✖ 57.97 Replacement of electronic bladder stimulator

✖ 57.98 Removal of electronic bladder stimulator
> **Excludes** *that with synchronous replacement (57.97)*

✖ 57.99 Other
> **Excludes** *irrigation of:*
>   *cystostomy (96.47)*
>   *other indwelling urinary catheter (96.48)*
> *lysis of external adhesions (59.11)*
> *removal of:*
>   *cystostomy tube (97.63)*
>   *other urinary drainage device (97.64)*
> *therapeutic distention of bladder (96.25)*

● 58 Operations on urethra

Includes: operations on:
    bulbourethral gland [Cowper'sgland]
    periurethral tissue

✖ 58.0 Urethrotomy
Excision of urethral septum
Formation of urethrovaginal fistula
Perineal urethrostomy
Removal of calculus from urethra by incision
> **Excludes** *drainage of bulbourethral gland or periurethral tissue (58.91)*
> *internal urethral meatotomy (58.5)*
> *removal of urethral calculus without incision (58.6)*

✖ 58.1 Urethral meatotomy
> **Excludes** *internal urethral meatotomy (58.5)*

● 58.2 Diagnostic procedures on urethra

58.21 Perineal urethroscopy

58.22 Other urethroscopy

58.23 Biopsy of urethra

58.24 Biopsy of periurethral tissue

58.29 Other diagnostic procedures on urethra and periurethral tissue
> **Excludes** *microscopic examination of specimen from urethra (91.31–91.39)*
> *retrograde cystourethrogram (87.76)*
> *urethral pressure profile (89.25)*
> *urethral sphincter electromyogram (89.23)*

● 58.3 Excision or destruction of lesion or tissue of urethra
> **Excludes** *biopsy of urethra (58.23)*
> *excision of bulbourethral gland (58.92)*
> *fistulectomy (58.43)*
> *urethrectomy as part of:*
>   *complete cystectomy (57.79)*
>   *pelvic evisceration (68.8)*
>   *radical cystectomy (57.71)*

58.31 Endoscopic excision or destruction of lesion or tissue of urethra
Fulguration of urethral lesion

58.39 Other local excision or destruction of lesion or tissue of urethra
Excision of:
    congenital valve of urethra
    lesion of urethra
    stricture of urethra
Urethrectomy
> **Excludes** *that by endoscopic approach (58.31)*

● 58.4 Repair of urethra
> **Excludes** *repair of current obstetric laceration (75.61)*

✖ 58.41 Suture of laceration of urethra

✖ 58.42 Closure of urethrostomy

✖ 58.43 Closure of other fistula of urethra
> **Excludes** *repair of urethroperineovesical fistula (57.84)*

✖ 58.44 Reanastomosis of urethra
Anastomosis of urethra

✖ 58.45 Repair of hypospadias or epispadias

✖ 58.46 Other reconstruction of urethra
Urethral construction

✖ 58.47 Urethral meatoplasty

✖ 58.49 Other repair of urethra
Benenenti rotation of bulbous urethra
Repair of old obstetric laceration of urethra
Urethral plication
> **Excludes** *repair of:*
>   *current obstetric laceration (75.61)*
>   *urethrocele (70.50–70.51)*

✖ 58.5 Release of urethral stricture
Cutting of urethral sphincter
Internal urethral meatotomy
Urethrolysis

58.6 Dilation of urethra
Dilation of urethrovesical junction
Passage of sounds through urethra
Removal of calculus from urethra without incision
> **Excludes** *urethral calibration (89.29)*

● 58.9 Other operations on urethra and periurethral tissue

✖ 58.91 Incision of periurethral tissue
Drainage of bulbourethral gland

✖ 58.92 Excision of periurethral tissue
> **Excludes** *biopsy of periurethral tissue (58.24)*
> *lysis of periurethral adhesions*
>   *laparoscopic (59.12)*
>   *other (59.11)*

✖ 58.93 Implantation of artificial urinary sphincter [AUS]
Placement of inflatable:
    bladder sphincter
    urethral sphincter
Removal with replacement of sphincter device [AUS]
With pump and/or reservoir

     ● **Use Additional Digit(s)**   ✖ **Valid O.R. Procedure**   ◀▶ **New Code**   ⬅⬛ ⬛➡ **Revised Code**

✖ 58.99 Other
Removal of inflatable urinary sphincter without replacement
Repair of inflatable sphincter pump and/or reservoir
Surgical correction of hydraulic pressure of inflatable sphincter device

> **Excludes** *removal of:*
> *intraluminal foreign body from urethra without incision (98.19)*
> *urethral stent (97.65)*

● 59 Other operations on urinary tract

● 59.0 Dissection of retroperitoneal tissue

✖ 59.00 Retroperitoneal dissection, not otherwise specified

✖ 59.02 Other lysis of perirenal or periureteral adhesions

> **Excludes** *that by laparoscope (59.03)*

✖ 59.03 Laparoscopic lysis of perirenal or periureteral adhesions

✖ 59.09 Other incision of perirenal or periureteral tissue
Exploration of perinephric area
Incision of perirenal abscess

● 59.1 Incision of perivesical tissue

✖ 59.11 Other lysis of perivesical adhesions

✖ 59.12 Laparoscopic lysis of perivesical adhesions

✖ 59.19 Other incision of perivesical tissue
Exploration of perivesical tissue
Incision of hematoma of space of Retzius
Retropubic exploration

● 59.2 Diagnostic procedures on perirenal and perivesical tissue

✖ 59.21 Biopsy of perirenal or perivesical tissue

✖ 59.29 Other diagnostic procedures on perirenal tissue, perivesical tissue, and retroperitoneum

> **Excludes** *microscopic examination of specimen from:*
> *perirenal tissue (91.21–91.29)*
> *perivesical tissue (91.31–91.39)*
> *retroperitoneum NEC (91.11–91.19)*
> *retroperitoneal x-ray (88.14–88.16)*

✖ 59.3 Plication of urethrovesical junction
Kelly-Kennedy operation on urethra
Kelly-Stoeckel urethral plication

✖ 59.4 Suprapubic sling operation
Goebel-Frangenheim-Stoeckel urethrovesical suspension
Millin-Read urethrovesical suspension
Oxford operation for urinary incontinence
Urethrocystopexy by suprapubic suspension

✖ 59.5 Retropubic urethral suspension
Burch procedure
Marshall-Marchetti-Krantz operation
Suture of periurethral tissue to symphysis pubis
Urethral suspension NOS

✖ 59.6 Paraurethral suspension
Pereyra paraurethral suspension
Periurethral suspension

● 59.7 Other repair of urinary stress incontinence

✖ 59.71 Levator muscle operation for urethrovesical suspension
Cystourethropexy with levator muscle sling
Gracilis muscle transplant for urethrovesical suspension
Pubococcygeal sling

59.72 Injection of implant into urethra and/or bladder neck
Collagen implant
Endoscopic injection of implant
Fat implant
Polytef implant

✖ 59.79 Other
Anterior urethropexy
Repair of stress incontinence NOS
Tudor "rabbit ear" urethropexy

59.8 Ureteral catheterization
Drainage of kidney by catheter
Insertion of ureteral stent
Ureterovesical orifice dilation

Code also any ureterotomy (56.2)

> **Excludes** *that for:*
> *retrograde pyelogram (87.74)*
> *transurethral removal of calculus or clot from ureter and renal pelvis (56.0)*

● 59.9 Other operations on urinary system

> **Excludes** *nonoperative removal of therapeutic device (97.61–97.69)*

✖ 59.91 Excision of perirenal or perivesical tissue

> **Excludes** *biopsy of perirenal or perivesical tissue (59.21)*

✖ 59.92 Other operations on perirenal or perivesical tissue

59.93 Replacement of ureterostomy tube
Change of ureterostomy tube
Reinsertion of ureterostomy tube

> **Excludes** *nonoperative removal of ureterostomy tube (97.62)*

59.94 Replacement of cystostomy tube

> **Excludes** *nonoperative removal of cystostomy tube (97.63)*

59.95 Ultrasonic fragmentation of urinary stones
Shattered urinary stones

> **Excludes** *percutaneous nephrostomy with fragmentation (55.04)*
> *shock-wave disintegration (98.51)*

59.99 Other

> **Excludes** *instillation of medication into urinary tract (96.49)*
> *irrigation of urinary tract (96.45–96.48)*

11.　OPERATIONS ON THE MALE GENITAL ORGANS (60–64)

● **60　Operations on prostate and seminal vesicles**

　　Includes: operations on periprostatic tissue

　　　Excludes　*that associated with radical cystectomy (57.71)*

✖ **60.0　Incision of prostate**
　　Drainage of prostatic abscess
　　Prostatolithotomy

　　Excludes　*drainage of periprostatic tissue only (60.81)*

● **60.1　Diagnostic procedures on prostate and seminal vesicles**

　　60.11　Closed [percutaneous] [needle] biopsy of prostate
　　　Approach:
　　　　transrectal
　　　　transurethral
　　　Punch biopsy

✖ **60.12　Open biopsy of prostate**

　　60.13　Closed [percutaneous] biopsy of seminal vesicles
　　　Needle biopsy of seminal vesicles

✖ **60.14　Open biopsy of seminal vesicles**

✖ **60.15　Biopsy of periprostatic tissue**

✖ **60.18　Other diagnostic procedures on prostate and periprostatic tissue**

　　Excludes　*microscopic examination of specimen from prostate (91.31–91.39)*
　　　　x-ray of prostate (87.92)

✖ **60.19　Other diagnostic procedures on seminal vesicles**

　　Excludes　*microscopic examination of specimen from seminal vesicles (91.31–91.39)*
　　　　x-ray:
　　　　　contrast seminal vesiculogram (87.91)
　　　　　other (87.92)

● **60.2　Transurethral prostatectomy**

　　Excludes　*local excision of lesion of prostate (60.61)*

　　✖ **60.21　Transurethral (ultrasound) guided laser induced prostatectomy (TULIP)**
　　　Ablation (contact) (noncontact) by laser

　　✖ **60.29　Other transurethral prostatectomy**
　　　Excision of median bar by transurethral approach
　　　Transurethral electrovaporization of prostrate (TEVAP)
　　　Transurethral enucleative procedure
　　　Transurethral prostatectomy NOS
　　　Transurethral resection of prostate (TURP)

✖ **60.3　Suprapubic prostatectomy**
　　Transvesical prostatectomy

　　Excludes　*local excision of lesion of prostate (60.61)*
　　　　radical prostatectomy (60.5)

✖ **60.4　Retropubic prostatectomy**

　　Excludes　*local excision of lesion of prostate (60.61)*
　　　　radical prostatectomy (60.5)

✖ **60.5　Radical prostatectomy**
　　Prostatovesiculectomy
　　Radical prostatectomy by any approach

　　Excludes　*cystoprostatectomy (57.71)*

● **60.6　Other prostatectomy**

✖ **60.61　Local excision of lesion of prostate**
　　Excision of prostatic lesion by any approach

　　Excludes　*biopsy of prostate (60.11–60.12)*

✖ **60.62　Perineal prostatectomy**
　　Cryoablation of prostate
　　Cryoprostatectomy
　　Cryosurgery of prostate
　　Radical cryosurgical ablation of prostate (RCSA)

　　Excludes　*local excision of lesion of prostate (60.61)*

✖ **60.69　Other**

● **60.7　Operations on seminal vesicles**

　　60.71　Percutaneous aspiration of seminal vesicle

　　Excludes　*needle biopsy of seminal vesicle (60.13)*

✖ **60.72　Incision of seminal vesicle**

✖ **60.73　Excision of seminal vesicle**
　　Excision of Müllerian duct cyst
　　Spermatocystectomy

　　Excludes　*biopsy of seminal vesicle (60.13–60.14)*
　　　　prostatovesiculectomy (60.5)

✖ **60.79　Other operations on seminal vesicles**

● **60.8　Incision or excision of periprostatic tissue**

✖ **60.81　Incision of periprostatic tissue**
　　Drainage of periprostatic abscess

✖ **60.82　Excision of periprostatic tissue**
　　Excision of lesion of periprostatic tissue

　　Excludes　*biopsy of periprostatic tissue (60.15)*

● **60.9　Other operations on prostate**

　　60.91　Percutaneous aspiration of prostate

　　Excludes　*needle biopsy of prostate (60.11)*

　　60.92　Injection into prostate

✖ **60.93　Repair of prostate**

✖ **60.94　Control of (postoperative) hemorrhage of prostate**
　　Coagulation of prostatic bed
　　Cystoscopy for control of prostatic hemorrhage

✖ **60.95　Transurethral balloon dilation of the prostatic urethra**

✖ **60.99　Other**

　　Excludes　*prostatic massage (99.94)*

● **61　Operations on scrotum and tunica vaginalis**

　　61.0　Incision and drainage of scrotum and tunica vaginalis

　　Excludes　*percutaneous aspiration of hydrocele (61.91)*

● **61.1　Diagnostic procedures on scrotum and tunica vaginalis**

　　61.11　Biopsy of scrotum or tunica vaginalis

　　61.19　Other diagnostic procedures on scrotum and tunica vaginalis

✖ **61.2　Excision of hydrocele (of tunica vaginalis)**
　　Bottle repair of hydrocele of tunica vaginalis

　　Excludes　*percutaneous aspiration of hydrocele (61.91)*

　　61.3　Excision or destruction of lesion or tissue of scrotum
　　Fulguration of lesion of scrotum
　　Reduction of elephantiasis of scrotum
　　Partial scrotectomy of scrotum

　　Excludes　*biopsy of scrotum (61.11)*
　　　　scrotal fistulectomy (61.42)

● **61.4 Repair of scrotum and tunica vaginalis**

    61.41 Suture of laceration of scrotum and tunica vaginalis

    ✖ **61.42 Repair of scrotal fistula**

    ✖ **61.49 Other repair of scrotum and tunica vaginalis**
       Reconstruction with rotational or pedicle flaps

● **61.9 Other operations on scrotum and tunica vaginalis**

    61.91 Percutaneous aspiration of tunica vaginalis
       Aspiration of hydrocele of tunica vaginalis

    ✖ **61.92 Excision of lesion of tunica vaginalis other than hydrocele**
       Excision of hematocele of tunica vaginalis

    ✖ **61.99 Other**
       Excludes *removal of foreign body from scrotum without incision (98.24)*

● **62 Operations on testes**

    ✖ **62.0 Incision of testis**

● **62.1 Diagnostic procedures on testes**

    62.11 Closed [percutaneous] [needle] biopsy of testis

    ✖ **62.12 Open biopsy of testis**

    ✖ **62.19 Other diagnostic procedures on testes**

✖ **62.2 Excision or destruction of testicular lesion**
    Excision of appendix testis
    Excision of cyst of Morgagni in the male
    Excludes *biopsy of testis (62.11–62.12)*

✖ **62.3 Unilateral orchiectomy**
    Orchidectomy (with epididymectomy) NOS

● **62.4 Bilateral orchiectomy**
    Male castration
    Radical bilateral orchiectomy (with epididymectomy)

    Code also any synchronous lymph node dissection (40.3, 40.5)

    ✖ **62.41 Removal of both testes at same operative episode**
       Bilateral orchidectomy NOS

    ✖ **62.42 Removal of remaining testis**
       Removal of solitary testis

✖ **62.5 Orchiopexy**
    Mobilization and replacement of testis in scrotum
    Orchiopexy with detorsion of testis
    Torek (-Bevan) operation (orchidopexy) (first stage) (second stage)
    Transplantation to and fixation of testis in scrotum

● **62.6 Repair of testes**
    Excludes *reduction of torsion (63.52)*

    ✖ **62.61 Suture of laceration of testis**

    ✖ **62.69 Other repair of testis**
       Testicular graft

✖ **62.7 Insertion of testicular prosthesis**

● **62.9 Other operations on testes**

    62.91 Aspiration of testis
    Excludes *percutaneous biopsy of testis (62.11)*

    62.92 Injection of therapeutic substance into testis

    ✖ **62.99 Other**

● **63 Operations on spermatic cord, epididymis, and vas deferens**

● **63.0 Diagnostic procedures on spermatic cord, epididymis, and vas deferens**

    63.01 Biopsy of spermatic cord, epididymis, or vas deferens

    ✖ **63.09 Other diagnostic procedures on spermatic cord, epididymis, and vas deferens**
       Excludes *contrast epididymogram (87.93)*
       contrast vasogram (87.94)
       other x-ray of epididymis and vas deferens (87.95)

✖ **63.1 Excision of varicocele and hydrocele of spermatic cord**
    High ligation of spermatic vein
    Hydrocelectomy of canal of Nuck

✖ **63.2 Excision of cyst of epididymis**
    Spermatocelectomy

✖ **63.3 Excision of other lesion or tissue of spermatic cord and epididymis**
    Excision of appendix epididymis
    Excludes *biopsy of spermatic cord or epididymis (63.01)*

✖ **63.4 Epididymectomy**
    Excludes *that synchronous with orchiectomy (62.3–62.42)*

● **63.5 Repair of spermatic cord and epididymis**

    ✖ **63.51 Suture of laceration of spermatic cord and epididymis**

    63.52 Reduction of torsion of testis or spermatic cord
    Excludes *that associated with orchiopexy (62.5)*

    ✖ **63.53 Transplantation of spermatic cord**

    ✖ **63.59 Other repair of spermatic cord and epididymis**

63.6 Vasotomy
    Vasostomy

● **63.7 Vasectomy and ligation of vas deferens**

    63.70 Male sterilization procedure, not otherwise specified

    63.71 Ligation of vas deferens
       Crushing of vas deferens
       Division of vas deferens

    63.72 Ligation of spermatic cord

    63.73 Vasectomy

● **63.8 Repair of vas deferens and epididymis**

    ✖ **63.81 Suture of laceration of vas deferens and epididymis**

    ✖ **63.82 Reconstruction of surgically divided vas deferens**

    ✖ **63.83 Epididymovasostomy**

    63.84 Removal of ligature from vas deferens

    ✖ **63.85 Removal of valve from vas deferens**

    ✖ **63.89 Other repair of vas deferens and epididymis**

● **63.9 Other operations on spermatic cord, epididymis, and vas deferens**

    63.91 Aspiration of spermatocele

    ✖ **63.92 Epididymotomy**

    ✖ **63.93 Incision of spermatic cord**

    ✖ **63.94 Lysis of adhesions of spermatic cord**

    ✖ **63.95 Insertion of valve in vas deferens**

    ✖ **63.99 Other**

● **64 Operations on penis**

    Includes: operations on:
       corpora cavernosa
       glans penis
       prepuce

✖ **64.0　Circumcision**

● **64.1　Diagnostic procedures on the penis**

  ✖ **64.11　Biopsy of penis**

  64.19　Other diagnostic procedures on penis

✖ **64.2　Local excision or destruction of lesion of penis**

  Excludes *biopsy of penis (64.11)*

✖ **64.3　Amputation of penis**

● **64.4　Repair and plastic operation on penis**

  ✖ **64.41　Suture of laceration of penis**

  ✖ **64.42　Release of chordee**

  ✖ **64.43　Construction of penis**

  ✖ **64.44　Reconstruction of penis**

  ✖ **64.45　Replantation of penis**
    Reattachment of amputated penis

  ✖ **64.49　Other repair of penis**

  Excludes *repair of epispadias and hypospadias (58.45)*

✖ **64.5　Operations for sex transformation, not elsewhere classified**

● **64.9　Other operations on male genital organs**

  64.91　Dorsal or lateral slit of prepuce

  ✖ **64.92　Incision of penis**

  ✖ **64.93　Division of penile adhesions**

  64.94　Fitting of external prosthesis of penis
    Penile prosthesis NOS

  ✖ **64.95　Insertion or replacement of non-inflatable penile prosthesis**
    Insertion of semi-rigid rod prosthesis into shaft of penis

  Excludes *external penile prosthesis (64.94)*
    inflatable penile prosthesis (64.97)
    plastic repair, penis (64.43–64.49)
    that associated with:
      construction (64.43)
      reconstruction (64.44)

✖ **64.96　Removal of internal prosthesis of penis**
  Removal without replacement of non-inflatable or inflatable penile prosthesis

✖ **64.97　Insertion or replacement of inflatable penile prosthesis**
  Insertion of cylinders into shaft of penis and placement of pump and reservoir

  Excludes *external penile prosthesis (64.94)*
    non-inflatable penile prosthesis (64.95)
    plastic repair, penis (64.43–64.49)

✖ **64.98　Other operations on penis**
  Corpora cavernosa-corpus spongiosum shunt
  Corpora-saphenous shunt
  Irrigation of corpus cavernosum

  Excludes *removal of foreign body:*
    intraluminal (98.19)
    without incision (98.24)
    stretching of foreskin (99.95)

✖ **64.99　Other**

  Excludes *collection of sperm for artificial insemination (99.96)*

12.   OPERATIONS ON THE FEMALE GENITAL ORGANS (65–71)

● **65**   **Operations on ovary**

● **65.0**   **Oophorotomy**
     Salpingo-oophorotomy

   ✖ **65.01**   **Laparoscopic oophorotomy**

   ✖ **65.09**   **Other oophorotomy**

● **65.1**   **Diagnostic procedures on ovaries**

   ✖ **65.11**   **Aspiration biopsy of ovary**

   ✖ **65.12**   **Other biopsy of ovary**

   ✖ **65.13**   **Laparoscopic biopsy of ovary**

   ✖ **65.14**   **Other laparoscopic diagnostic procedures on ovaries**

   ✖ **65.19**   **Other diagnostic procedures on ovaries**
     | Excludes | *microscopic examination of specimen from ovary (91.41–91.49)*

● **65.2**   **Local excision or destruction of ovarian lesion or tissue**

   ✖ **65.21**   **Marsupialization of ovarian cyst**
     | Excludes | *that by laparoscope (65.23)*

   ✖ **65.22**   **Wedge resection of ovary**
     | Excludes | *that by laparoscope (65.24)*

   ✖ **65.23**   **Laparoscopic marsupialization of ovarian cyst**

   ✖ **65.24**   **Laparoscopic wedge resection of ovary**

   ✖ **65.25**   **Other laparoscopic local excision or destruction of ovary**

   ✖ **65.29**   **Other local excision or destruction of ovary**
     Bisection of ovary
     Cauterization of ovary
     Partial excision of ovary
     | Excludes | *biopsy of ovary (65.11–65.13)*
     that by laparoscope (65.25)

● **65.3**   **Unilateral oophorectomy**

   ✖ **65.31**   **Laparoscopic unilateral oophorectomy**

   ✖ **65.39**   **Other unilateral oophorectomy**
     | Excludes | *that by laparoscope (65.31)*

● **65.4**   **Unilateral salpingo-oophorectomy**

   ✖ **65.41**   **Laparoscopic unilateral salpingo-oophorectomy**

   ✖ **65.49**   **Other unilateral salpingo-oophorectomy**

● **65.5**   **Bilateral oophorectomy**

   ✖ **65.51**   **Other removal of both ovaries at same operative episode**
     Female castration
     | Excludes | *that by laparoscope (65.53)*

   ✖ **65.52**   **Other removal of remaining ovary**
     Removal of solitary ovary
     | Excludes | *that by laparoscope (65.54)*

   ✖ **65.53**   **Laparoscopic removal of both ovaries at same operative episode**

   ✖ **65.54**   **Laparoscopic removal of remaining ovary**

● **65.6**   **Bilateral salpingo-oophorectomy**

   ✖ **65.61**   **Other removal of both ovaries and tubes at same operative episode**
     | Excludes | *that by laparoscope (65.63)*

   ✖ **65.62**   **Other removal of remaining ovary and tube**
     Removal of solitary ovary and tube
     | Excludes | *that by laparoscope (65.64)*

   ✖ **65.63**   **Laparoscopic removal of both ovaries and tubes at same operative episode**

   ✖ **65.64**   **Laparoscopic removal of remaining ovary and tube**

● **65.7**   **Repair of ovary**
     | Excludes | *salpingo-oophorostomy (66.72)*

   ✖ **65.71**   **Other simple suture of ovary**
     | Excludes | *that by laparoscope (65.74)*

   ✖ **65.72**   **Other reimplantation of ovary**
     | Excludes | *that by laparoscope (65.75)*

   ✖ **65.73**   **Other salpingo-oophoroplasty**
     | Excludes | *that by laparoscope (65.76)*

   ✖ **65.74**   **Laparoscopic simple suture of ovary**

   ✖ **65.75**   **Laparoscopic reimplantation of ovary**

   ✖ **65.76**   **Laparoscopic salpingo-oophoroplasty**

   ✖ **65.79**   **Other repair of ovary**
     Oophoropexy

● **65.8**   **Lysis of adhesions of ovary and fallopian tube**

   ✖ **65.81**   **Laparoscopic lysis of adhesions of ovary and fallopian tube**

   ✖ **65.89**   **Other lysis of adhesions of ovary and fallopian tube**
     | Excludes | *that by laparoscope (65.81)*

● **65.9**   **Other operations on ovary**

   ✖ **65.91**   **Aspiration of ovary**
     | Excludes | *aspiration biopsy of ovary (65.11)*

   ✖ **65.92**   **Transplantation of ovary**
     | Excludes | *reimplantation of ovary*
     laparoscopic (65.75))
     other (65.72)

   ✖ **65.93**   **Manual rupture of ovarian cyst**

   ✖ **65.94**   **Ovarian denervation**

   ✖ **65.95**   **Release of torsion of ovary**

   ✖ **65.99**   **Other**

● **66**   **Operations on fallopian tubes**

● **66.0**   **Salpingotomy and salpingostomy**

   ✖ **66.01**   **Salpingotomy**

   ✖ **66.02**   **Salpingostomy**

● **66.1**   **Diagnostic procedures on fallopian tubes**

   ✖ **66.11**   **Biopsy of fallopian tube**

   ✖ **66.19**   **Other diagnostic procedures on fallopian tubes**
     | Excludes | *microscopic examination of specimen from fallopian tubes (91.41–91.49)*
     radiography of fallopian tubes (87.82–87.83, 87.85)
     Rubin's test (66.8)

● **66.2**   **Bilateral endoscopic destruction or occlusion of fallopian tubes**

     Includes: bilateral endoscopic destruction or occlusion of fallopian tubes by:
       culdoscopy
       endoscopy
       hysteroscopy
       laparoscopy
       peritoneoscopy
     endoscopic destruction of solitary fallopian tube

   ✖ **66.21**   **Bilateral endoscopic ligation and crushing of fallopian tubes**

✖ **66.22 Bilateral endoscopic ligation and division of fallopian tubes**

✖ **66.29 Other bilateral endoscopic destruction or occlusion of fallopian tubes**

● **66.3 Other bilateral destruction or occlusion of fallopian tubes**

   Includes: destruction of solitary fallopian tube

   Excludes *endoscopic destruction or occlusion of fallopian tubes (66.21–66.29)*

✖ **66.31 Other bilateral ligation and crushing of fallopian tubes**

✖ **66.32 Other bilateral ligation and division of fallopian tubes**
   Pomeroy operation

✖ **66.39 Other bilateral destruction or occlusion of fallopian tubes**
   Female sterilization operation NOS

✖ **66.4 Total unilateral salpingectomy**

● **66.5 Total bilateral salpingectomy**

   Excludes *bilateral partial salpingectomy for sterilization (66.39)*
   that with oophorectomy (65.61–65.64)

✖ **66.51 Removal of both fallopian tubes at same operative episode**

✖ **66.52 Removal of remaining fallopian tube**
   Removal of solitary fallopian tube

● **66.6 Other salpingectomy**

   Includes: salpingectomy by:
     cauterization
     coagulation
     electrocoagulation
     excision

   Excludes *fistulectomy (66.73)*

✖ **66.61 Excision or destruction of lesion of fallopian tube**

   Excludes *biopsy of fallopian tube (66.11)*

✖ **66.62 Salpingectomy with removal of tubal pregnancy**

   Code also any synchronous oophorectomy (65.31, 65.39)

✖ **66.63 Bilateral partial salpingectomy, not otherwise specified**

✖ **66.69 Other partial salpingectomy**

● **66.7 Repair of fallopian tube**

✖ **66.71 Simple suture of fallopian tube**

✖ **66.72 Salpingo-oophorostomy**

✖ **66.73 Salpingo-salpingostomy**

✖ **66.74 Salpingo-uterostomy**

✖ **66.79 Other repair of fallopian tube**
   Graft of fallopian tube
   Reopening of divided fallopian tube
   Salpingoplasty

66.8 Insufflation of fallopian tube
   Insufflation of fallopian tube with:
     air
     dye
     gas
     saline
     Rubin's test

   Excludes *insufflation of therapeutic agent (66.95)*
   that for hysterosalpingography (87.82–87.83)

● **66.9 Other operations on fallopian tubes**

   66.91 Aspiration of fallopian tube

✖ **66.92 Unilateral destruction or occlusion of fallopian tube**

   Excludes *that of solitary tube (66.21–66.39)*

✖ **66.93 Implantation or replacement of prosthesis of fallopian tube**

✖ **66.94 Removal of prosthesis of fallopian tube**

✖ **66.95 Insufflation of therapeutic agent into fallopian tubes**

✖ **66.96 Dilation of fallopian tube**

✖ **66.97 Burying of fimbriae in uterine wall**

✖ **66.99 Other**

   Excludes *lysis of adhesions of ovary and tube*
   laparoscopic (65.81)
   other (65.89)

● **67 Operations on cervix**

   67.0 Dilation of cervical canal

   Excludes *dilation and curettage (69.01–69.09)*
   that for induction of labor (73.1)

● **67.1 Diagnostic procedures on cervix**

✖ **67.11 Endocervical biopsy**

   Excludes *conization of cervix (67.2)*

✖ **67.12 Other cervical biopsy**
   Punch biopsy of cervix NOS

   Excludes *conization of cervix (67.2)*

✖ **67.19 Other diagnostic procedures on cervix**

   Excludes *microscopic examination of specimen from cervix (91.41–91.49)*

✖ **67.2 Conization of cervix**

   Excludes *that by:*
   cryosurgery (67.33)
   electrosurgery (67.32)

● **67.3 Other excision or destruction of lesion or tissue of cervix**

✖ **67.31 Marsupialization of cervical cyst**

✖ **67.32 Destruction of lesion of cervix by cauterization**
   Electroconization of cervix
   LEEP (loop electrosurgical excision procedure) ◀
   LLETZ (large loop excision of the transformation zone) ◀

✖ **67.33 Destruction of lesion of cervix by cryosurgery**
   Cryoconization of cervix

✖ **67.39 Other excision or destruction of lesion or tissue of cervix**

   Excludes *biopsy of cervix (67.11–67.12)*
   cervical fistulectomy (67.62)
   conization of cervix (67.2)

✖ **67.4 Amputation of cervix**
   Cervicectomy with synchronous colporrhaphy

✖ **67.5 Repair of internal cervical os**
   Cerclage of isthmus uteri
   Shirodkar operation

● **67.6 Other repair of cervix**

   Excludes *repair of current obstetric laceration (75.51)*

✖ **67.61 Suture of laceration of cervix**

✖ **67.62 Repair of fistula of cervix**
Cervicosigmoidal fistulectomy

Excludes *fistulectomy:*
cervicovesical (57.84)
ureterocervical (56.84)
vesicocervicovaginal (57.84)

✖ **67.69 Other repair of cervix**
Repair of old obstetric laceration of cervix

● **68 Other incision and excision of uterus**

✖ **68.0 Hysterotomy**
Hysterotomy with removal of hydatidiform mole

Excludes *hysterotomy for termination of pregnancy (74.91)*

● **68.1 Diagnostic procedures on uterus and supporting structures**

68.11 Digital examination of uterus

Excludes *pelvic examination, so described (89.26)*
postpartal manual exploration of uterine cavity (75.7)

68.12 Hysteroscopy

Excludes *that with biopsy (68.16)*

✖ **68.13 Open biopsy of uterus**

Excludes *closed biopsy of uterus(68.16)*

✖ **68.14 Open biopsy of uterine ligaments**

Excludes *closed biopsy of uterine ligaments (68.15)*

✖ **68.15 Closed biopsy of uterine ligaments**
Endoscopic (laparoscopy) biopsy of uterine
adnexa, except ovary and fallopian tube

✖ **68.16 Closed biopsy of uterus**
Endoscopic (laparoscopy) (hysteroscopy) biopsy of uterus

Excludes *open biopsy of uterus (68.13)*

✖ **68.19 Other diagnostic procedures on uterus and
supporting structures**

Excludes *diagnostic:*
aspiration curettage (69.59)
dilation and curettage (69.09)
*microscopic examination of specimen from uterus
(91.41–91.49)*
pelvic examination (89.26)
radioisotope scan of:
placenta (92.17)
uterus (92.19)
ultrasonography of uterus (88.78–88.79)
x-ray of uterus (87.81–87.89)

● **68.2 Excision or destruction of lesion or tissue of uterus**

✖ **68.21 Division of endometrial synechiae**
Lysis of intraluminal uterine adhesions

✖ **68.22 Incision or excision of congenital septum of
uterus**

✖ **68.23 Endometrial ablation**
Dilation and curettage
Hysteroscopic endometrial ablation

✖ **68.29 Other excision or destruction of lesion of
uterus**
Uterine myomectomy

Excludes *biopsy of uterus (68.13)*
uterine fistulectomy (69.42)

✖ **68.3 Subtotal abdominal hysterectomy**
Supracervical hysterectomy

✖ **68.4 Total abdominal hysterectomy**
Hysterectomy:
extended

Code also any synchronous removal of tubes and
ovaries (65.3–65.6)

● **68.5 Vaginal hysterectomy**

Code also any synchronous:
removal of tubes and ovaries (65.31–65.64)
repair of cystocele or rectocele (70.50–70.52)
repair of pelvic floor (70.79)

✖ **68.51 Laparoscopically assisted vaginal hysterectomy (LAVH)**

✖ **68.59 Other vaginal hysterectomy**

Excludes *laparoscopically assisted vaginal hysterectomy
(LAVH) (68.51)*
radical vaginal hysterectomy (68.7)

✖ **68.6 Radical abdominal hysterectomy**
Modified radical hysterectomy
Wertheim's operation

Code also any synchronous:
lymph gland dissection (40.3, 40.5)
removal of tubes and ovaries (65.61–65.64)

Excludes *pelvic evisceration (68.8)*

✖ **68.7 Radical vaginal hysterectomy**
Schauta operation

Code also any synchronous:
lymph gland dissection (40.3, 40.5)
removal of tubes and ovaries (65.61–65.64)

✖ **68.8 Pelvic evisceration**
Removal of ovaries, tubes, uterus, vagina, bladder,
and urethra (with removal of sigmoid colon
and rectum)

Code also any synchronous:
colostomy (46.12–46.13)
lymph gland dissection (40.3, 40.5)
urinary diversion (56.51–56.79)

✖ **68.9 Other and unspecified hysterectomy**
Hysterectomy NOS

Excludes *abdominal hysterectomy, any approach (68.3,
68.4, 68.6)*
*vaginal hysterectomy, any approach (68.51,
68.59, 68.7)*

● **69 Other operations on uterus and supporting structures**

● **69.0 Dilation and curettage of uterus**

Excludes *aspiration curettage of uterus (69.51–69.59)*

✖ **69.01 Dilation and curettage for termination of pregnancy**

✖ **69.02 Dilation and curettage following delivery or
abortion**

✖ **69.09 Other dilation and curettage**
Diagnostic D and C

● **69.1 Excision or destruction of lesion or tissue of uterus
and supporting structures**

✖ **69.19 Other excision or destruction of uterus and
supporting structures**

Excludes *biopsy of uterine ligament (68.14)*

● **69.2 Repair of uterine supporting structures**

✖ **69.21 Interposition operation**
Watkins procedure

✖ **69.22 Other uterine suspension**
Hysteropexy
Manchester operation
Plication of uterine ligament

✖ **69.23 Vaginal repair of chronic inversion of uterus**

✖ **69.29 Other repair of uterus and supporting structures**

✖ **69.3 Paracervical uterine denervation**

● **Use Additional Digit(s)**   ✖ **Valid O.R. Procedure**   ◀▶ **New Code**   ⬅➡ **Revised Code**

● **69.4 Uterine repair**

   Excludes | *repair of current obstetric laceration (75.50–75.52)*

   ✖ **69.41 Suture of laceration of uterus**

   ✖ **69.42 Closure of fistula of uterus**
   Excludes | *uterovesical fistulectomy (57.84)*

   ✖ **69.49 Other repair of uterus**
   Repair of old obstetric laceration of uterus

● **69.5 Aspiration curettage of uterus**
   Excludes | *menstrual extraction (69.6)*

   ✖ **69.51 Aspiration curettage of uterus for termination of pregnancy**
   Therapeutic abortion NOS

   ✖ **69.52 Aspiration curettage following delivery or abortion**

   69.59 Other aspiration curettage of uterus

69.6 Menstrual extraction or regulation

69.7 Insertion of intrauterine contraceptive device

● **69.9 Other operations on uterus, cervix, and supporting structures**
   Excludes | *obstetric dilation or incision of cervix (73.1, 73.93)*

   69.91 Insertion of therapeutic device into uterus
   Excludes | *insertion of:*
   intrauterine contraceptive device (69.7)
   laminaria (69.93)
   obstetric insertion of bag, bougie, or pack (73.1)

   69.92 Artificial insemination

   69.93 Insertion of laminaria

   69.94 Manual replacement of inverted uterus
   Excludes | *that in immediate postpartal period (75.94)*

   ✖ **69.95 Incision of cervix**
   Excludes | *that to assist delivery (73.93)*

   69.96 Removal of cerclage material from cervix

   ✖ **69.97 Removal of other penetrating foreign body from cervix**
   Excludes | *removal of intraluminal foreign body from cervix (98.16)*

   ✖ **69.98 Other operations on supporting structures of uterus**
   Excludes | *biopsy of uterine ligament (68.14)*

   ✖ **69.99 Other operations on cervix and uterus**
   Excludes | *removal of:*
   foreign body (98.16)
   intrauterine contraceptive device (97.71)
   obstetric bag, bougie, or pack (97.72)
   packing (97.72)

● **70 Operations on vagina and cul-de-sac**

70.0 Culdocentesis

● **70.1 Incision of vagina and cul-de-sac**

   70.11 Hymenotomy

   ✖ **70.12 Culdotomy**

   ✖ **70.13 Lysis of intraluminal adhesions of vagina**

   ✖ **70.14 Other vaginotomy**
   Division of vaginal septum
   Drainage of hematoma of vaginal cuff

● **70.2 Diagnostic procedures on vagina and cul-de-sac**

   70.21 Vaginoscopy

   70.22 Culdoscopy

   ✖ **70.23 Biopsy of cul-de-sac**

   ✖ **70.24 Vaginal biopsy**

   ✖ **70.29 Other diagnostic procedures on vagina and cul-de-sac**

● **70.3 Local excision or destruction of vagina and cul-de-sac**

   ✖ **70.31 Hymenectomy**

   ✖ **70.32 Excision or destruction of lesion of cul-de-sac**
   Endometrectomy of cul-de-sac
   Excludes | *biopsy of cul-de-sac (70.23)*

   ✖ **70.33 Excision or destruction of lesion of vagina**
   Excludes | *biopsy of vagina (70.24)*
   vaginal fistulectomy (70.72–70.75)

✖ **70.4 Obliteration and total excision of vagina**
   Vaginectomy
   Excludes | *obliteration of vaginal vault (70.8)*

● **70.5 Repair of cystocele and rectocele**

   ✖ **70.50 Repair of cystocele and rectocele**

   ✖ **70.51 Repair of cystocele**
   Anterior colporrhaphy (with urethrocele repair)

   ✖ **70.52 Repair of rectocele**
   Posterior colporrhaphy

● **70.6 Vaginal construction and reconstruction**

   ✖ **70.61 Vaginal construction**

   ✖ **70.62 Vaginal reconstruction**

● **70.7 Other repair of vagina**
   Excludes | *lysis of intraluminal adhesions (70.13)*
   repair of current obstetric laceration (75.69)
   that associated with cervical amputation (67.4)

   ✖ **70.71 Suture of laceration of vagina**

   ✖ **70.72 Repair of colovaginal fistula**

   ✖ **70.73 Repair of rectovaginal fistula**

   ✖ **70.74 Repair of other vaginoenteric fistula**

   ✖ **70.75 Repair of other fistula of vagina**
   Excludes | *repair of fistula:*
   rectovesicovaginal (57.83)
   ureterovaginal (56.84)
   urethrovaginal (58.43)
   uterovaginal (69.42)
   vesicocervicovaginal (57.84)
   vesicosigmoidovaginal (57.83)
   vesicoureterovaginal (56.84)
   vesicovaginal (57.84)

   ✖ **70.76 Hymenorrhaphy**

   ✖ **70.77 Vaginal suspension and fixation**

   ✖ **70.79 Other repair of vagina**
   Colpoperineoplasty
   Repair of old obstetric laceration of vagina

✖ **70.8 Obliteration of vaginal vault**
   LeFort operation

● **70.9 Other operations on vagina and cul-de-sac**

✖ **70.91   Other operations on vagina**

> **Excludes**   *insertion of:*
> *diaphragm (96.17)*
> *mold (96.15)*
> *pack (96.14)*
> *pessary (96.18)*
> *suppository (96.49)*
> *removal of:*
> *diaphragm (97.73)*
> *foreign body (98.17)*
> *pack (97.75)*
> *pessary (97.74)*
> *replacement of:*
> *diaphragm (97.24)*
> *pack (97.26)*
> *pessary (97.25)*
> *vaginal dilation (96.16)*
> *vaginal douche (96.44)*

✖ **70.92   Other operations on cul-de-sac**
Obliteration of cul-de-sac
Repair of vaginal enterocele

● **71   Operations on vulva and perineum**

● **71.0   Incision of vulva and perineum**

✖ **71.01   Lysis of vulvar adhesions**

✖ **71.09   Other incision of vulva and perineum**
Enlargement of introitus NOS

> **Excludes**   *removal of foreign body without incision (98.23)*

● **71.1   Diagnostic procedures on vulva**

✖ **71.11   Biopsy of vulva**

✖ **71.19   Other diagnostic procedures on vulva**

● **71.2   Operations on Bartholin's gland**

71.21   Percutaneous aspiration of Bartholin's gland (cyst)

✖ **71.22   Incision of Bartholin's gland (cyst)**

✖ **71.23   Marsupialization of Bartholin's gland (cyst)**

✖ **71.24   Excision or other destruction of Bartholin's gland (cyst)**

✖ **71.29   Other operations on Bartholin's gland**

✖ **71.3   Other local excision or destruction of vulva and perineum**
Division of Skene's gland

> **Excludes**   *biopsy of vulva (71.11)*
> *vulvar fistulectomy (71.72)*

✖ **71.4   Operations on clitoris**
Amputation of clitoris
Clitoridotomy
Female circumcision

✖ **71.5   Radical vulvectomy**

Code also any synchronous lymph gland dissection (40.3, 40.5)

● **71.6   Other vulvectomy**

✖ **71.61   Unilateral vulvectomy**

✖ **71.62   Bilateral vulvectomy**
Vulvectomy NOS

● **71.7   Repair of vulva and perineum**

> **Excludes**   *repair of current obstetric laceration (75.69)*

✖ **71.71   Suture of laceration of vulva or perineum**

✖ **71.72   Repair of fistula of vulva or perineum**

> **Excludes**   *repair of fistula:*
> *urethroperineal (58.43)*
> *urethroperineovesical (57.84)*
> *vaginoperineal (70.75)*

✖ **71.79   Other repair of vulva and perineum**
Repair of old obstetric laceration of vulva or perineum

✖ **71.8   Other operations on vulva**

> **Excludes**   *removal of:*
> *foreign body without incision (98.23)*
> *packing (97.75)*
> *replacement of packing (97.26)*

✖ **71.9   Other operations on female genital organs**

13.   OBSTETRICAL PROCEDURES (72–75)

● **72   Forceps, vacuum, and breech delivery**

72.0   Low forceps operation
Outlet forceps operation

72.1   Low forceps operation with episiotomy
Outlet forceps operation with episiotomy

● **72.2   Mid forceps operation**

72.21   Mid forceps operation with episiotomy

72.29   Other mid forceps operation

● **72.3   High forceps operation**

72.31   High forceps operation with episiotomy

72.39   Other high forceps operation

72.4   Forceps rotation of fetal head
De Lee maneuver
Key-in-lock rotation
Kielland rotation
Scanzoni's maneuver

Code also any associated forceps extraction (72.0–72.39)

● **72.5   Breech extraction**

72.51   Partial breech extraction with forceps to aftercoming head

72.52   Other partial breech extraction

72.53   Total breech extraction with forceps to aftercoming head

72.54   Other total breech extraction

72.6   Forceps application to aftercoming head
Piper forceps operation

> **Excludes**   *partial breech extraction with forceps to aftercoming head (72.51)*
> *total breech extraction with forceps to aftercoming head (72.53)*

● **72.7   Vacuum extraction**

Includes: Malström's extraction

72.71   Vacuum extraction with episiotomy

72.79   Other vacuum extraction

72.8   Other specified instrumental delivery

72.9   Unspecified instrumental delivery

● **73   Other procedures inducing or assisting delivery**

● **73.0   Artificial rupture of membranes**

73.01   Induction of labor by artificial rupture of membranes
Surgical induction NOS

> **Excludes**   *artificial rupture of membranes after onset of labor (73.09)*

73.09   Other artificial rupture of membranes
Artificial rupture of membranes at time of delivery

73.1 Other surgical induction of labor
Induction by cervical dilation

> Excludes | *injection for abortion (75.0)*
> *insertion of suppository for abortion (96.49)*

● **73.2 Internal and combined version and extraction**

73.21 Internal and combined version without extraction
Version NOS

73.22 Internal and combined version with extraction

73.3 Failed forceps
Application of forceps without delivery
Trial forceps

73.4 Medical induction of labor

> Excludes | *medication to augment active labor— omit code*

● **73.5 Manually assisted delivery**

73.51 Manual rotation of fetal head

73.59 Other manually assisted delivery
Assisted spontaneous delivery
Credé maneuver

73.6 Episiotomy
Episioproctotomy
Episiotomy with subsequent episiorrhaphy

> Excludes | *that with:*
> *high forceps (72.31)*
> *low forceps (72.1)*
> *mid forceps (72.21)*
> *outlet forceps (72.1)*
> *vacuum extraction (72.71)*

73.8 Operations on fetus to facilitate delivery
Clavicotomy on fetus
Destruction of fetus
Needling of hydrocephalic head

● **73.9 Other operations assisting delivery**

73.91 External version

73.92 Replacement of prolapsed umbilical cord

73.93 Incision of cervix to assist delivery
Dührssen's incisions

✖ **73.94 Pubiotomy to assist delivery**
Obstetric symphysiotomy

✖ **73.99 Other**

> Excludes | *dilation of cervix, obstetrical to induce labor (73.1)*
> *insertion of bag or bougie to induce labor (73.1)*
> *removal of cerclage material (69.96)*

● **74 Cesarean section and removal of fetus**

Code also any synchronous:
hysterectomy (68.3–68.4, 68.6, 68.8)
myomectomy (68.29)
sterilization (66.31–66.39, 66.63)

✖ **74.0 Classical cesarean section**
Transperitoneal classical cesarean section

✖ **74.1 Low cervical cesarean section**
Lower uterine segment cesarean section

✖ **74.2 Extraperitoneal cesarean section**
Supravesical cesarean section

✖ **74.3 Removal of extratubal ectopic pregnancy**
Removal of:
ectopic abdominal pregnancy
fetus from peritoneal or extraperitoneal cavity following uterine or tubal rupture

> Excludes | *that by salpingostomy (66.02)*
> *that by salpingotomy (66.01)*
> *that with synchronous salpingectomy (66.62)*

✖ **74.4 Cesarean section of other specified type**
Peritoneal exclusion cesarean section
Transperitoneal cesarean section NOS
Vaginal cesarean section

● **74.9 Cesarean section of unspecified type**

✖ **74.91 Hysterotomy to terminate pregnancy**
Therapeutic abortion by hysterotomy

✖ **74.99 Other cesarean section of unspecified type**
Cesarean section NOS
Obstetrical abdominouterotomy
Obstetrical hysterotomy

● **75 Other obstetric operations**

75.0 Intra-amniotic injection for abortion
Injection of:
prostaglandin for induction of abortion
saline for induction of abortion
Termination of pregnancy by intrauterine injection

> Excludes | *insertion of prostaglandin suppository for abortion (96.49)*

75.1 Diagnostic amniocentesis

75.2 Intrauterine transfusion
Exchange transfusion in utero
Insertion of catheter into abdomen of fetus for transfusion

Code also any hysterotomy approach (68.0)

● **75.3 Other intrauterine operations on fetus and amnion**

Code also any hysterotomy approach (68.0)

75.31 Amnioscopy
Fetoscopy
Laparoamnioscopy

75.32 Fetal EKG (scalp)

75.33 Fetal blood sampling and biopsy

75.34 Fetal monitoring, not otherwise specified

75.35 Other diagnostic procedures on fetus and amnion
Intrauterine pressure determination

> Excludes | *amniocentesis (75.1)*
> *diagnostic procedures on gravid uterus and placenta (87.81, 88.46, 88.78, 92.17)*

✖ **75.36 Correction of fetal defect**

75.37 Amnioinfusion ◀
Code also injection of antibiotic (99.21) ◀

75.4 Manual removal of retained placenta

> Excludes | *aspiration curettage (69.52)*
> *dilation and curettage (69.02)*

● **75.5 Repair of current obstetric laceration of uterus**

✖ **75.50 Repair of current obstetric laceration of uterus, not otherwise specified**

✖ **75.51 Repair of current obstetric laceration of cervix**

75.52 Repair of current obstetric laceration of corpus uteri

● **75.6 Repair of other current obstetric laceration**

✖ **75.61 Repair of current obstetric laceration of bladder and urethra**

75.62 Repair of current obstetric laceration of rectum and sphincter ani

75.69 Repair of other current obstetric laceration
Episioperineorrhaphy
Repair of:
   pelvic floor
   perineum
   vagina
   vulva
Secondary repair of episiotomy

   | Excludes | *repair of routine episiotomy (73.6)*

75.7 Manual exploration of uterine cavity, postpartum

75.8 Obstetric tamponade of uterus or vagina

   | Excludes | *antepartum tamponade (73.1)*

● **75.9 Other obstetric operations**

75.91 Evacuation of obstetric incisional hematoma of perineum
Evacuation of hematoma of:
   episiotomy
   perineorrhaphy

75.92 Evacuation of other hematoma of vulva or vagina

✖ **75.93 Surgical correction of inverted uterus**
Spintelli operation

   | Excludes | *vaginal repair of chronic inversion of uterus (69.23)*

75.94 Manual replacement of inverted uterus

✖ **75.99 Other**

14. OPERATIONS ON THE MUSCULOSKELETAL SYSTEM (76–84)

● **76   Operations on facial bones and joints**

> | **Excludes** | accessory sinuses (22.00–22.9)
> nasal bones (21.00–21.99)
> skull (01.01–02.99)

● **76.0   Incision of facial bone without division**

✖ **76.01   Sequestrectomy of facial bone**
Removal of necrotic bone chip from facial bone

✖ **76.09   Other incision of facial bone**
Reopening of osteotomy site of facial bone

> | **Excludes** | osteotomy associated with orthognathic surgery
> (76.61–76.69)
> removal of internal fixation device (76.97)

● **76.1   Diagnostic procedures on facial bones and joints**

✖ **76.11   Biopsy of facial bone**

✖ **76.19   Other diagnostic procedures on facial bones and joints**

> | **Excludes** | contrast arthrogram of temporomandibular joint
> (87.13)
> other x-ray (87.11–87.12, 87.14–87.16)

✖ **76.2   Local excision or destruction of lesion of facial bone**

> | **Excludes** | biopsy of facial bone (76.11)
> excision of odontogenic lesion (24.4)

● **76.3   Partial ostectomy of facial bone**

✖ **76.31   Partial mandibulectomy**
Hemimandibulectomy

> | **Excludes** | that associated with temporomandibular arthro-
> plasty (76.5)

✖ **76.39   Partial ostectomy of other facial bone**
Hemimaxillectomy (with bone graft or prosthesis)

● **76.4   Excision and reconstruction of facial bones**

✖ **76.41   Total mandibulectomy with synchronous reconstruction**

✖ **76.42   Other total mandibulectomy**

✖ **76.43   Other reconstruction of mandible**

> | **Excludes** | genioplasty (76.67–76.68)
> that with synchronous total mandibulectomy
> (76.41)

✖ **76.44   Total ostectomy of other facial bone with synchronous reconstruction**

✖ **76.45   Other total ostectomy of other facial bone**

✖ **76.46   Other reconstruction of other facial bone**

> | **Excludes** | that with synchronous total ostectomy (76.44)

✖ **76.5   Temporomandibular arthroplasty**

● **76.6   Other facial bone repair and orthognathic surgery**

Code also any synchronous:
bone graft (76.91)
synthetic implant (76.92)

> | **Excludes** | reconstruction of facial bones (76.41–76.46)

✖ **76.61   Closed osteoplasty [osteotomy] of mandibular ramus**
Gigli saw osteotomy

✖ **76.62   Open osteoplasty [osteotomy] of mandibular ramus**

✖ **76.63   Osteoplasty [osteotomy] of body of mandible**

✖ **76.64   Other orthognathic surgery on mandible**
Mandibular osteoplasty NOS
Segmental or subapical osteotomy

✖ **76.65   Segmental osteoplasty [osteotomy] of maxilla**
Maxillary osteoplasty NOS

✖ **76.66   Total osteoplasty [osteotomy] of maxilla**

✖ **76.67   Reduction genioplasty**
Reduction mentoplasty

✖ **76.68   Augmentation genioplasty**
Mentoplasty:
NOS
with graft or implant

✖ **76.69   Other facial bone repair**
Osteoplasty of facial bone NOS

● **76.7   Reduction of facial fracture**

Includes: internal fixation

Code also any synchronous:
bone graft (76.91)
synthetic implant (76.92)

> | **Excludes** | that of nasal bones (21.71–21.72)

✖ **76.70   Reduction of facial fracture, not otherwise specified**

76.71   Closed reduction of malar and zygomatic fracture

✖ **76.72   Open reduction of malar and zygomatic fracture**

76.73   Closed reduction of maxillary fracture

✖ **76.74   Open reduction of maxillary fracture**

76.75   Closed reduction of mandibular fracture

✖ **76.76   Open reduction of mandibular fracture**

✖ **76.77   Open reduction of alveolar fracture**
Reduction of alveolar fracture with stabilization of teeth

76.78   Other closed reduction of facial fracture
Closed reduction of orbital fracture

> | **Excludes** | nasal bone (21.71)

✖ **76.79   Other open reduction of facial fracture**
Open reduction of orbit rim or wall

> | **Excludes** | nasal bone (21.72)

● **76.9   Other operations on facial bones and joints**

✖ **76.91   Bone graft to facial bone**
Autogenous graft to facial bone
Bone bank graft to facial bone
Heterogenous graft to facial bone

✖ **76.92   Insertion of synthetic implant in facial bone**
Alloplastic implant to facial bone

76.93   Closed reduction of temporomandibular dislocation

✖ **76.94   Open reduction of temporomandibular dislocation**

76.95   Other manipulation of temporomandibular joint

76.96   Injection of therapeutic substance into temporomandibular joint

✖ **76.97   Removal of internal fixation device from facial bone**

> | **Excludes** | removal of:
> dental wiring (97.33)
> external mandibular fixation device NEC
> (97.36)

✖ **76.99   Other**

● **77 Incision, excision, and division of other bones**

> **Excludes** *laminectomy for decompression (03.09)*
> *operations on:*
> *accessory sinuses (22.00–22.9)*
> *ear ossicles (19.0–19.55)*
> *facial bones (76.01–76.99)*
> *joint structures (80.00–81.99)*
> *mastoid (19.9–20.99)*
> *nasal bones (21.00–21.99)*
> *skull (01.01–02.99)*

The following fourth-digit subclassification is for use with appropriate categories in section 77 to identify the site. Valid fourth-digit categories are in brackets under each code.

  0 unspecified site
  1 scapula, clavicle, and thorax [ribs and sternum]
  2 humerus
  3 radius and ulna
  4 carpals and metacarpals
  5 femur
  6 patella
  7 tibia and fibula
  8 tarsals and metatarsals
  9 other
    Pelvic bones
    Phalanges (of foot) (of hand)
    Vertebrae

✖ ● **77.0 Sequestrectomy**
  [0–9]

✖ ● **77.1 Other incision of bone without division**
  [0–9]   Reopening of osteotomy site

> **Excludes** *aspiration of bone marrow (41.31, 41.91)*
> *removal of internal fixation device (78.60–78.69)*

✖ ● **77.2 Wedge osteotomy**
  [0–9]

> **Excludes** *that for hallux valgus (77.51)*

✖ ● **77.3 Other division of bone**
  [0–9]   Osteoarthrotomy

> **Excludes** *clavicotomy of fetus (73.8)*
> *laminotomy or incision of vertebra (03.01–03.09)*
> *pubiotomy to assist delivery (73.94)*
> *sternotomy incidental to thoracic operation—*
> *omit code*

✖ ● **77.4 Biopsy of bone**
  [0–9]

● **77.5 Excision and repair of bunion and other toe deformities**

  ✖ **77.51 Bunionectomy with soft tissue correction and osteotomy of the first metatarsal**

  ✖ **77.52 Bunionectomy with soft tissue correction and arthrodesis**

  ✖ **77.53 Other bunionectomy with soft tissue correction**

  ✖ **77.54 Excision or correction of bunionette**
    That with osteotomy

  ✖ **77.56 Repair of hammer toe**
    Filleting of hammer toe
    Fusion of hammer toe
    Phalangectomy (partial) of hammer toe

  ✖ **77.57 Repair of claw toe**
    Capsulotomy of claw toe
    Fusion of claw toe
    Phalangectomy (partial) of claw toe
    Tendon lengthening of claw toe

  ✖ **77.58 Other excision, fusion and repair of toes**
    Cockup toe repair
    Overlapping toe repair
    That with use of prosthetic materials

  ✖ **77.59 Other bunionectomy**
    Resection of hallux valgus joint with insertion of prosthesis

✖ ● **77.6 Local excision of lesion or tissue of bone**
  [0–9]

> **Excludes** *biopsy of bone (77.40–77.49)*
> *debridement of compound fracture (79.60–79.69)*

✖ ● **77.7 Excision of bone for graft**
  [0–9]

✖ ● **77.8 Other partial ostectomy**
  [0–9]   Condylectomy

> **Excludes** *amputation (84.00–84.19, 84.91)*
> *arthrectomy (80.90–80.99)*
> *excision of bone ends associated with:*
> *arthrodesis (81.00–81.29)*
> *arthroplasty (81.31–81.87)*
> *excision of cartilage (80.5–80.6, 80.80–80.99)*
> *excision of head of femur with synchronous re-*
> *placement (81.51–81.53)*
> *hemilaminectomy (03.01–03.09)*
> *laminectomy (03.01–03.09)*
> *ostectomy for hallux valgus (77.51–77.59)*
> *partial amputation:*
> *finger (84.01)*
> *thumb (84.02)*
> *toe (84.11)*
> *resection of ribs incidental to thoracic opera-*
> *tion—omit code*
> *that incidental to other operation—omit code*

✖ ● **77.9 Total ostectomy**
  [0–9]

> **Excludes** *amputation of limb (84.00–84.19, 84.91)*
> *that incidental to other operation—omit code*

● **78 Other operations on bones, except facial bones**

> **Excludes** *operations on:*
> *accessory sinuses (22.00–22.9)*
> *facial bones (76.01–76.99)*
> *joint structures (80.00–81.99)*
> *nasal bones (21.00–21.99)*
> *skull (01.01–02.99)*

The following fourth-digit subclassification is for use with categories in section 78 to identify the site. Valid fourth-digit categories are in [brackets] under each code.

  0 unspecified site
  1 scapula, clavicle, and thorax [ribs and sternum]
  2 humerus
  3 radius and ulna
  4 carpals and metacarpals
  5 femur
  6 patella
  7 tibia and fibula
  8 tarsals and metatarsals
  9 other
    Pelvic bones
    Phalanges (of foot) (of hand)
    Vertebrae

✖ ● **78.0 Bone graft**
  [0–9]   Bone:
    bank graft
    graft (autogenous) (heterogenous)
   That with debridement of bone graft site (removal of sclerosed, fibrous or necrotic bone or tissue)
   Transplantation of bone

   Code also any excision of bone for graft (77.70–77.79)

> **Excludes** *that for bone lengthening (78.30–78.39)*

✖ ● 78.1 Application of external fixation device
[0–9]   Minifixator with insertion of pins/wires/screws into bone

> **Excludes** *other immobilization, pressure, and attention to wound (93.51–93.59)*

✖ ● 78.2 Limb shortening procedures
[0, 2–5, 7–9] Epiphyseal stapling
      Open epiphysiodesis
      Percutaneous epiphysiodesis
      Resection/osteotomy

✖ ● 78.3 Limb lengthening procedures
[0, 2–5, 7–9] Bone graft with or without internal fixation devices or osteotomy
      Distraction technique with or without corticotomy/osteotomy

      Code also any application of an external fixation device (78.10–78.19)

✖ ● 78.4 Other repair or plastic operations on bone
[0–9]   Other operation on bone NEC
      Repair of malunion or nonunion fracture NEC

> **Excludes** *application of external fixation device (78.10–78.19)*
> *limb lengthening procedures (78.30–78.39)*
> *limb shortening procedures (78.20–78.29)*
> *osteotomy (77.3)*
> *reconstruction of thumb (82.61–82.69)*
> *repair of pectus deformity (34.74)*
> *repair with bone graft (78.00–78.09)*

✖ ● 78.5 Internal fixation of bone without fracture reduction
[0–9]   Internal fixation of bone (prophylactic)
      Reinsertion of internal fixation device
      Revision of displaced or broken fixation device

> **Excludes** *arthroplasty and arthrodesis (81.00–81.87)*
> *bone graft (78.00–78.09)*
> *limb shortening procedures (78.20–78.29)*
> *that for fracture reduction (79.10–79.19, 79.30–79.59)*

✖ ● 78.6 Removal of implanted devices from bone
[0–9]   External fixator device (invasive)
      Internal fixation device
      Removal of bone growth stimulator (invasive)

> **Excludes** *removal of cast, splint, and traction device (Kirschner wire) (Steinmann pin) (97.88)*
> *removal of skull tongs or halo traction device (02.95)*

✖ ● 78.7 Osteoclasis
[0–9]

✖ ● 78.8 Diagnostic procedures on bone, not elsewhere classified
[0–9]

> **Excludes** *biopsy of bone (77.40–77.49)*
> *magnetic resonance imaging (88.94)*
> *microscopic examination of specimen from bone (91.51–91.59)*
> *radioisotope scan (92.14)*
> *skeletal x-ray (87.21–87.29, 87.43, 88.21–88.33)*
> *thermography (88.83)*

✖ ● 78.9 Insertion of bone growth stimulator
[0–9]   Insertion of:
      bone stimulator (electrical) to aid bone healing
      osteogenic electrodes for bone growth stimulation
      totally implanted device (invasive)

> **Excludes** *non-invasive (transcutaneous) (surface) stimulator (99.86)*

● 79 Reduction of fracture and dislocation

Includes: application of cast or splint
      Reduction with insertion of traction device (Kirschner wire) (Steinmann pin)

Code also any application of external fixation device (78.10–78.19)

> **Excludes** *external fixation alone for immobilization of fracture (93.51–93.56, 93.59)*
> *internal fixation without reduction of fracture (78.50–78.59)*
> *operations on:*
>   *facial bones (76.70–76.79)*
>   *nasal bones (21.71–21.72)*
>   *orbit (76.78–76.79)*
>   *skull (02.02)*
>   *vertebrae (03.53)*
> *removal of cast or splint (97.88)*
> *replacement of cast or splint (97.11–97.14)*
> *traction alone for reduction of fracture (93.41–93.46)*

The following fourth-digit subclassification is for use with appropriate categories in section 79 to identify the site. Valid fourth-digit categories are in [brackets] under each code.
      0 unspecified site
      1 humerus
      2 radius and ulna
      Arm NOS
      3 carpals and metacarpals
      Hand NOS
      4 phalanges of hand
      5 femur
      6 tibia and fibula
      Leg NOS
      7 tarsals and metatarsals
      Foot NOS
      8 phalanges of foot
      9 other specified bone

● 79.0 Closed reduction of fracture without internal fixation
> **Excludes** *that for separation of epiphysis (79.40–79.49)*

✖ ● 79.1 Closed reduction of fracture with internal fixation
> **Excludes** *that for separation of epiphysis (79.40–79.49)*

✖ ● 79.2 Open reduction of fracture without internal fixation
[0–9]
> **Excludes** *that for separation of epiphysis (79.50–79.59)*

✖ ● 79.3 Open reduction of fracture with internal fixation
[0–9]
> **Excludes** *that for separation of epiphysis (79.50–79.59)*

✖ ● 79.4 Closed reduction of separated epiphysis
[0–2, 5, 6, 9] Reduction with or without internal fixation

✖ ● 79.5 Open reduction of separated epiphysis
[0–2, 5, 6, 9] Reduction with or without internal fixation

✖ ● 79.6 Debridement of open fracture site
[0–9]   Debridement of compound fracture

● 79.7 Closed reduction of dislocation

Includes: closed reduction (with external traction device)

> **Excludes** *closed reduction of dislocation of temporomandibular joint (76.93)*

      79.70 Closed reduction of dislocation of unspecified site

      79.71 Closed reduction of dislocation of shoulder

      79.72 Closed reduction of dislocation of elbow

      79.73 Closed reduction of dislocation of wrist

      79.74 Closed reduction of dislocation of hand and finger

79.75   Closed reduction of dislocation of hip

79.76   Closed reduction of dislocation of knee

79.77   Closed reduction of dislocation of ankle

79.78   Closed reduction of dislocation of foot and toe

79.79   Closed reduction of dislocation of other specified sites

● **79.8   Open reduction of dislocation**

> **Includes:** open reduction (with internal and external fixation devices)
>
> | **Excludes** | *open reduction of dislocation of temporomandibular joint (76.94)* |

✖ **79.80   Open reduction of dislocation of unspecified site**

✖ **79.81   Open reduction of dislocation of shoulder**

✖ **79.82   Open reduction of dislocation of elbow**

✖ **79.83   Open reduction of dislocation of wrist**

✖ **79.84   Open reduction of dislocation of hand and finger**

✖ **79.85   Open reduction of dislocation of hip**

✖ **79.86   Open reduction of dislocation of knee**

✖ **79.87   Open reduction of dislocation of ankle**

✖ **79.88   Open reduction of dislocation of foot and toe**

✖ **79.89   Open reduction of dislocation of other specified sites**

✖ ● **79.9   Unspecified operation on bone injury**
[0–9]

● **80   Incision and excision of joint structures**

> **Includes:** operations on:
> capsule of joint
> cartilage
> ligament
> meniscus
> synovial membrane
>
> | **Excludes** | *cartilage of temporomandibular joint (76.01–76.99)* |

The following fourth-digit subclassification is for use with appropriate categories in section 80 to identify the site:
0 unspecified site
1 shoulder
2 elbow
3 wrist
4 hand and finger
5 hip
6 knee
7 ankle
8 foot and toe
9 other specified sites
   Spine

✖ ● **80.0   Arthrotomy for removal of prosthesis**
Includes: cement spacer

✖ ● **80.1   Other arthrotomy**
Arthrostomy

> | **Excludes** | *that for:* |
> *arthrography (88.32)*
> *arthroscopy (80.20–80.29)*
> *injection of drug (81.92)*
> *operative approach—omit code*

✖ ● **80.2   Arthroscopy**

● **80.3   Biopsy of joint structure**
Aspiration biopsy

✖ ● **80.4   Division of joint capsule, ligament, or cartilage**
Goldner clubfoot release
Heyman-Herndon(-Strong) correction of metatarsus varus
Release of:
   adherent or constrictive joint capsule
   joint
   ligament

> | **Excludes** | *symphysiotomy to assist delivery (73.94)* |
> *that for:*
> *carpal tunnel syndrome (04.43)*
> *tarsal tunnel syndrome (04.44)*

● **80.5   Excision or destruction of intervertebral disc**

✖ **80.50   Excision or destruction of intervertebral disc, unspecified**
Unspecified as to excision or destruction

✖ **80.51   Excision of intervertebral disc**
Diskectomy
Removal of herniated nucleus pulposus
Level:
   cervical
   thoracic
   lumbar (lumbosacral)
That by laminotomy or hemilaminectomy
That with decompression of spinal nerve root at same level
Requires additional code for any concomitant decompression of spinal nerve root at different level from excision site

Code also any concurrent spinal fusion (81.00–81.09)

> | **Excludes** | *intervertebral chemonucleolysis (80.52)* |
> *laminectomy for exploration of intraspinal canal (03.09)*
> *laminotomy for decompression of spinal nerve root only (03.09)*

80.52   Intervertebral chemonucleolysis
With aspiration of disc fragments
With diskography
Injection of proteolytic enzyme into intervertebral space (chymopapain)

> | **Excludes** | *injection of anesthetic substance (03.91)* |
> *injection of other substances (03.92)*

✖ **80.59   Other destruction of intervertebral disc**
Destruction NEC
That by laser

✖ **80.6   Excision of semilunar cartilage of knee**
Excision of meniscus of knee

✖ ● **80.7   Synovectomy**
Complete or partial resection of synovial membrane

> | **Excludes** | *excision of Baker's cyst (83.39)* |

✖ ● **80.8   Other local excision or destruction of lesion of joint**

✖ ● **80.9   Other excision of joint**

> | **Excludes** | *cheilectomy of joint (77.80–77.89)* |
> *excision of bone ends (77.80–77.89)*

● **81   Repair and plastic operations on joint structures**

● **81.0   Spinal fusion**

> **Includes:** arthrodesis of spine with:
> bone graft
> internal fixation

✖ **81.00   Spinal fusion, not otherwise specified**

✖ **81.01 Atlas-axis spinal fusion**
Craniocervical fusion by anterior, transoral, or posterior technique
C1-C2 fusion by anterior, transoral, or posterior technique
Occiput C2 fusion by anterior, transoral, or posterior technique
> **Excludes** *that for pseudarthrosis (81.09)*

✖ **81.02 Other cervical fusion, anterior technique**
Arthrodesis of C2 level or below:
anterior (interbody) technique
anterolateral technique
> **Excludes** *that for pseudarthrosis (81.09)*

✖ **81.03 Other cervical fusion, posterior technique**
Arthrodesis of C2 level or below:
posterior (interbody) technique
posterolateral technique
> **Excludes** *that for pseudarthrosis (81.09)*

✖ **81.04 Dorsal and dorsolumbar fusion, anterior technique**
Arthrodesis of thoracic or thoracolumbar region:
anterior (interbody) technique
anterolateral technique
> **Excludes** *that for pseudarthrosis (81.09)*

✖ **81.05 Dorsal and dorsolumbar fusion, posterior technique**
Arthrodesis of thoracic or thoracolumbar region:
posterior (interbody) technique
posterolateral technique
> **Excludes** *that for pseudarthrosis (81.09)*

✖ **81.06 Lumbar and lumbosacral fusion, anterior technique**
Arthrodesis of lumbar or lumbosacral region:
anterior (interbody) technique
anterolateral technique
> **Excludes** *that for pseudarthrosis (81.09)*

✖ **81.07 Lumbar and lumbosacral fusion, lateral transverse process technique**
> **Excludes** *that for pseudarthrosis (81.09)*

✖ **81.08 Lumbar and lumbosacral fusion, posterior technique**
Arthrodesis of lumbar or lumbosacral region:
posterior (interbody) technique
posterolateral technique

✖ **81.09 Refusion of spine, any level or technique**
Correction of pseudarthrosis of spine

● **81.1 Arthrodesis of foot and ankle**

Includes: arthrodesis of foot and ankle with:
bone graft
external fixation device

✖ **81.11 Ankle fusion**
Tibiotalar fusion

✖ **81.12 Triple arthrodesis**
Talus to calcaneus and calcaneus to cuboid and navicular

✖ **81.13 Subtalar fusion**

✖ **81.14 Midtarsal fusion**

✖ **81.15 Tarsometatarsal fusion**

✖ **81.16 Metatarsophalangeal fusion**

✖ **81.17 Other fusion of foot**

● **81.2 Arthrodesis of other joint**

Includes: arthrodesis with:
bone graft
external fixation device
excision of bone ends and compression

✖ **81.20 Arthrodesis of unspecified joint**

✖ **81.21 Arthrodesis of hip**

✖ **81.22 Arthrodesis of knee**

✖ **81.23 Arthrodesis of shoulder**

✖ **81.24 Arthrodesis of elbow**

✖ **81.25 Carporadial fusion**

✖ **81.26 Metacarpocarpal fusion**

✖ **81.27 Metacarpophalangeal fusion**

✖ **81.28 Interphalangeal fusion**

✖ **81.29 Arthrodesis of other specified joints**

● **81.4 Other repair of joint of lower extremity**

Includes: arthroplasty of lower extremity with:
external traction or fixation
graft of bone (chips) or cartilage
internal fixation device

✖ **81.40 Repair of hip, not elsewhere classified**

✖ **81.42 Five-in-one repair of knee**
Medial meniscectomy, medial collateral ligament repair, vastus medialis advancement, semitendinosus advancement, and pes anserinus transfer

✖ **81.43 Triad knee repair**
Medial meniscectomy with repair of the anterior cruciate ligament and the medial collateral ligament
O'Donoghue procedure

✖ **81.44 Patellar stabilization**
Roux-Goldthwait operation for recurrent dislocation of patella

✖ **81.45 Other repair of the cruciate ligaments**

✖ **81.46 Other repair of the collateral ligaments**

✖ **81.47 Other repair of knee**

✖ **81.49 Other repair of ankle**

● **81.5 Joint replacement of lower extremity**

Includes: arthroplasty of lower extremity with:
external traction or fixation
graft of bone (chips) or cartilage
internal fixation device or prosthesis
removal of cement spacer

✖ **81.51 Total hip replacement**
Replacement of both femoral head and acetabulum by prosthesis
Total reconstruction of hip

✖ **81.52 Partial hip replacement**
Bipolar endoprosthesis

✖ **81.53 Revision of hip replacement**
Partial
Total

✖ **81.54 Total knee replacement**
Bicompartmental
Tricompartmental
Unicompartmental (hemijoint)

✖ **81.55 Revision of knee replacement**
> **Excludes** *arthrodesis of knee (81.22)*

✖ **81.56 Total ankle replacement**

✖ **81.57 Replacement of joint of foot and toe**

✖ **81.59 Revision of joint replacement of lower extremity, not elsewhere classified**

● **81.7 Arthroplasty and repair of hand, fingers and wrist**

Includes: arthroplasty of hand and finger with:
external traction or fixation
graft of bone (chips) or cartilage
internal fixation device or prosthesis

Excludes *operations on muscle, tendon and fascia of hand (82.01–82.99)*

✖ **81.71 Arthroplasty of metacarpophalangeal and interphalangeal joint with implant**

✖ **81.72 Arthroplasty of metacarpophalangeal and interphalangeal joint without implant**

✖ **81.73 Total wrist replacement**

✖ **81.74 Arthroplasty of carpocarpal or carpometacarpal joint with implant**

✖ **81.75 Arthroplasty of carpocarpal or carpometacarpal joint without implant**

✖ **81.79 Other repair of hand, fingers and wrist**

● **81.8 Arthroplasty and repair of shoulder and elbow**

Includes: arthroplasty of upper limb NEC with:
external traction or fixation
graft of bone (chips) or cartilage
internal fixation device or prosthesis

✖ **81.80 Total shoulder replacement**

✖ **81.81 Partial shoulder replacement**

✖ **81.82 Repair of recurrent dislocation of shoulder**

✖ **81.83 Other repair of shoulder**
Revision of arthroplasty of shoulder

✖ **81.84 Total elbow replacement**

✖ **81.85 Other repair of elbow**

● **81.9 Other operations on joint structures**

81.91 Arthrocentesis
Joint aspiration

Excludes *that for:*
arthrography (88.32)
biopsy of joint structure (80.30–80.39)
injection of drug (81.92)

81.92 Injection of therapeutic substance into joint or ligament

✖ **81.93 Suture of capsule or ligament of upper extremity**

Excludes *that associated with arthroplasty (81.71–81.75, 81.80–81.81, 81.84)*

✖ **81.94 Suture of capsule or ligament of ankle and foot**

Excludes *that associated with arthroplasty (81.56–81.59)*

✖ **81.95 Suture of capsule or ligament of other lower extremity**

Excludes *that associated with arthroplasty (81.51–81.55, 81.59)*

✖ **81.96 Other repair of joint**

✖ **81.97 Revision of joint replacement of upper extremity**

Includes: Partial
Removal of cement spacer
Total

✖ **81.98 Other diagnostic procedures on joint structures**

Excludes *arthroscopy (80.20–80.29)*
biopsy of joint structure (80.30–80.39)
microscopic examination of specimen from joint (91.51–91.59)
thermography (88.83)
x-ray (87.21–87.29, 88.21–88.33)

✖ **81.99 Other**

● **82 Operations on muscle, tendon, and fascia of hand**

Includes: operations on:
aponeurosis
synovial membrane (tendon sheath)
tendon sheath

● **82.0 Incision of muscle, tendon, fascia, and bursa of hand**

✖ **82.01 Exploration of tendon sheath of hand**
Incision of tendon sheath of hand
Removal of rice bodies in tendon sheath of hand

Excludes *division of tendon (82.11)*

✖ **82.02 Myotomy of hand**

Excludes *myotomy for division (82.19)*

✖ **82.03 Bursotomy of hand**

82.04 Incision and drainage of palmar or thenar space

✖ **82.09 Other incision of soft tissue of hand**

Excludes *incision of skin and subcutaneous tissue alone (86.01–86.09)*

● **82.1 Division of muscle, tendon, and fascia of hand**

✖ **82.11 Tenotomy of hand**
Division of tendon of hand

✖ **82.12 Fasciotomy of hand**
Division of fascia of hand

✖ **82.19 Other division of soft tissue of hand**
Division of muscle of hand

● **82.2 Excision of lesion of muscle, tendon, and fascia of hand**

✖ **82.21 Excision of lesion of tendon sheath of hand**
Ganglionectomy of tendon sheath (wrist)

✖ **82.22 Excision of lesion of muscle of hand**

✖ **82.29 Excision of other lesion of soft tissue of hand**

Excludes *excision of lesion of skin and subcutaneous tissue (86.21–86.3)*

● **82.3 Other excision of soft tissue of hand**

Code also any skin graft (86.61–86.62, 86.73)

Excludes *excision of skin and subcutaneous tissue (86.21–86.3)*

✖ **82.31 Bursectomy of hand**

✖ **82.32 Excision of tendon of hand for graft**

✖ **82.33 Other tenonectomy of hand**
Tenosynovectomy of hand

Excludes *excision of lesion of:*
tendon (82.29)
sheath (82.21)

✖ **82.34 Excision of muscle or fascia of hand for graft**

✖ **82.35 Other fasciectomy of hand**
Release of Dupuytren's contracture

Excludes *excision of lesion of fascia (82.29)*

✖ **82.36 Other myectomy of hand**

Excludes *excision of lesion of muscle (82.22)*

✖ **82.39 Other excision of soft tissue of hand**

Excludes *excision of skin (86.21–86.3)*
excision of soft tissue lesion (82.29)

● **82.4 Suture of muscle, tendon, and fascia of hand**

✖ **82.41 Suture of tendon sheath of hand**

✖ **82.42 Delayed suture of flexor tendon of hand**

✖ **82.43 Delayed suture of other tendon of hand**

✖ **82.44 Other suture of flexor tendon of hand**
  Excludes *delayed suture of flexor tendon of hand (82.42)*

✖ **82.45 Other suture of other tendon of hand**
  Excludes *delayed suture of other tendon of hand (82.43)*

✖ **82.46 Suture of muscle or fascia of hand**

● **82.5 Transplantation of muscle and tendon of hand**

✖ **82.51 Advancement of tendon of hand**

✖ **82.52 Recession of tendon of hand**

✖ **82.53 Reattachment of tendon of hand**

✖ **82.54 Reattachment of muscle of hand**

✖ **82.55 Other change in hand muscle or tendon length**

✖ **82.56 Other hand tendon transfer or transplantation**
  Excludes *pollicization of thumb (82.61)*
            transfer of finger, except thumb (82.81)

✖ **82.57 Other hand tendon transposition**

✖ **82.58 Other hand muscle transfer or transplantation**

✖ **82.59 Other hand muscle transposition**

● **82.6 Reconstruction of thumb**

  Includes: digital transfer to act as thumb

    Code also any amputation for digital transfer (84.01, 84.11)

✖ **82.61 Pollicization operation carrying over nerves and blood supply**

✖ **82.69 Other reconstruction of thumb**
        "Cocked-hat" procedure [skin flap and bone]
    Grafts:
        bone to thumb skin (pedicle) to thumb

● **82.7 Plastic operation on hand with graft or implant**

✖ **82.71 Tendon pulley reconstruction**
        Reconstruction for opponensplasty

✖ **82.72 Plastic operation on hand with graft of muscle or fascia**

✖ **82.79 Plastic operation on hand with other graft or implant**
        Tendon graft to hand

● **82.8 Other plastic operations on hand**

✖ **82.81 Transfer of finger, except thumb**
  Excludes *pollicization of thumb (82.61)*

✖ **82.82 Repair of cleft hand**

✖ **82.83 Repair of macrodactyly**

✖ **82.84 Repair of mallet finger**

✖ **82.85 Other tenodesis of hand**
        Tendon fixation of hand NOS

✖ **82.86 Other tenoplasty of hand**
        Myotenoplasty of hand

✖ **82.89 Other plastic operations on hand**
        Plication of fascia
        Repair of fascial hernia
  Excludes *that with graft or implant (82.71–82.79)*

● **82.9 Other operations on muscle, tendon, and fascia of hand**
  Excludes *diagnostic procedures on soft tissue of hand (83.21–83.29)*

✖ **82.91 Lysis of adhesions of hand**
        Freeing of adhesions of fascia, muscle, and tendon of hand
  Excludes *decompression of carpal tunnel (04.43)*
            that by stretching or manipulation only (93.26)

82.92 Aspiration of bursa of hand

82.93 Aspiration of other soft tissue of hand
  Excludes *skin and subcutaneous tissue (86.01)*

82.94 Injection of therapeutic substance into bursa of hand

82.95 Injection of therapeutic substance into tendon of hand

82.96 Other injection of locally-acting therapeutic substance into soft tissue of hand
  Excludes *subcutaneous or intramuscular injection (99.11–99.29)*

✖ **82.99 Other operations on muscle, tendon, and fascia of hand**

● **83 Operations on muscle, tendon, fascia, and bursa, except hand**

  Includes: operations on:
        aponeurosis
        synovial membrane of bursa and tendon sheaths
        tendon sheaths
  Excludes *diaphragm (34.81–34.89)*
            hand (82.01–82.99)
            muscles of eye (15.01–15.9)

● **83.0 Incision of muscle, tendon, fascia, and bursa**

✖ **83.01 Exploration of tendon sheath**
        Incision of tendon sheath
        Removal of rice bodies from tendon sheath

✖ **83.02 Myotomy**
  Excludes *cricopharyngeal myotomy (29.31)*

✖ **83.03 Bursotomy**
        Removal of calcareous deposit of bursa
  Excludes *aspiration of bursa (percutaneous) (83.94)*

✖ **83.09 Other incision of soft tissue**
        Incision of fascia
  Excludes *incision of skin and subcutaneous tissue alone (86.01–86.09)*

● **83.1 Division of muscle, tendon, and fascia**

✖ **83.11 Achillotenotomy**

✖ **83.12 Adductor tenotomy of hip**

✖ **83.13 Other tenotomy**
        Aponeurotomy
        Division of tendon
        Tendon release
        Tendon transection
        Tenotomy for thoracic outlet decompression

✖ **83.14 Fasciotomy**
        Division of fascia
        Division of iliotibial band
        Fascia stripping
        Release of Volkmann's contracture by fasciotomy

✖ **83.19 Other division of soft tissue**
        Division of muscle
        Muscle release
        Myotomy for thoracic outlet decompression
        Myotomy with division
        Scalenotomy
        Transection of muscle

● **83.2 Diagnostic procedures on muscle, tendon, fascia, and bursa, including that of hand**

✖ **83.21 Biopsy of soft tissue**
  Excludes *biopsy of chest wall (34.23)*
            biopsy of skin and subcutaneous tissue (86.11)

✖ 83.29 Other diagnostic procedures on muscle, tendon, fascia, and bursa, including that of hand

> **Excludes** *microscopic examination of specimen (91.51–91.59)*
> *soft tissue x-ray (87.09, 87.38–87.39, 88.09, 88.35, 88.37)*
> *thermography of muscle (88.84)*

● 83.3 Excision of lesion of muscle, tendon, fascia, and bursa

> **Excludes** *biopsy of soft tissue (83.21)*

✖ 83.31 Excision of lesion of tendon sheath
Excision of ganglion of tendon sheath, except of hand

✖ 83.32 Excision of lesion of muscle
Excision of:
    heterotopic bone
    muscle scar for release of Volkmann's contracture
    myositis ossificans

✖ 83.39 Excision of lesion of other soft tissue
Excision of Baker's cyst

> **Excludes** *bursectomy (83.5)*
> *excision of lesion of skin and subcutaneous tissue (86.3)*
> *synovectomy (80.70–80.79)*

● 83.4 Other excision of muscle, tendon, and fascia

✖ 83.41 Excision of tendon for graft

✖ 83.42 Other tenonectomy
Excision of:
    aponeurosis
    tendon sheath
    Tenosynovectomy

✖ 83.43 Excision of muscle or fascia for graft

✖ 83.44 Other fasciectomy

✖ 83.45 Other myectomy
Debridement of muscle NOS
Scalenectomy

✖ 83.49 Other excision of soft tissue

✖ 83.5 Bursectomy

● 83.6 Suture of muscle, tendon, and fascia

✖ 83.61 Suture of tendon sheath

✖ 83.62 Delayed suture of tendon

✖ 83.63 Rotator cuff repair

✖ 83.64 Other suture of tendon
Achillorrhaphy
Aponeurorrhaphy

> **Excludes** *delayed suture of tendon (83.62)*

✖ 83.65 Other suture of muscle or fascia
Repair of diastasis recti

● 83.7 Reconstruction of muscle and tendon

> **Excludes** *reconstruction of muscle and tendon associated with arthroplasty*

✖ 83.71 Advancement of tendon

✖ 83.72 Recession of tendon

✖ 83.73 Reattachment of tendon

✖ 83.74 Reattachment of muscle

✖ 83.75 Tendon transfer or transplantation

✖ 83.76 Other tendon transposition

✖ 83.77 Muscle transfer or transplantation
Release of Volkmann's contracture by muscle transplantation

✖ 83.79 Other muscle transposition

● 83.8 Other plastic operations on muscle, tendon, and fascia

> **Excludes** *plastic operations on muscle, tendon, and fascia associated with arthroplasty*

✖ 83.81 Tendon graft

✖ 83.82 Graft of muscle or fascia

✖ 83.83 Tendon pulley reconstruction

✖ 83.84 Release of clubfoot, not elsewhere classified
Evans operation on clubfoot

✖ 83.85 Other change in muscle or tendon length
Hamstring lengthening
Heel cord shortening
Plastic achillotenotomy
Tendon plication

✖ 83.86 Quadricepsplasty

✖ 83.87 Other plastic operations on muscle
Musculoplasty
Myoplasty

✖ 83.88 Other plastic operations on tendon
Myotenoplasty
Tendon fixation
Tenodesis
Tenoplasty

✖ 83.89 Other plastic operations on fascia
Fascia lengthening
Fascioplasty
Plication of fascia

● 83.9 Other operations on muscle, tendon, fascia, and bursa

> **Excludes** *nonoperative:*
> *manipulation (93.25–93.29)*
> *stretching (93.27–93.29)*

✖ 83.91 Lysis of adhesions of muscle, tendon, fascia, and bursa

> **Excludes** *that for tarsal tunnel syndrome (04.44)*

✖ 83.92 Insertion or replacement of skeletal muscle stimulator

✖ 83.93 Removal of skeletal muscle stimulator

83.94 Aspiration of bursa

83.95 Aspiration of other soft tissue

> **Excludes** *that of skin and subcutaneous tissue (86.01)*

83.96 Injection of therapeutic substance into bursa

83.97 Injection of therapeutic substance into tendon

83.98 Injection of locally-acting therapeutic substance into other soft tissue

> **Excludes** *subcutaneous or intramuscular injection (99.11–99.29)*

✖ 83.99 Other operations on muscle, tendon, fascia, and bursa
Suture of bursa

● 84 Other procedures on musculoskeletal system

● 84.0 Amputation of upper limb

> **Excludes** *revision of amputation stump (84.3)*

✖ 84.00 Upper limb amputation, not otherwise specified
Closed flap amputation of upper limb NOS
Kineplastic amputation of upper limb NOS
Open or guillotine amputation of upper limb NOS
Revision of current traumatic amputation of upper limb NOS

●   **Use Additional Digit(s)**   ✖   **Valid O.R. Procedure**   ◀▶   **New Code**   ⬅▦➡   **Revised Code**

✖ **84.01 Amputation and disarticulation of finger**

 Excludes *ligation of supernumerary finger (86.26)*

✖ **84.02 Amputation and disarticulation of thumb**

✖ **84.03 Amputation through hand**
  Amputation through carpals

✖ **84.04 Disarticulation of wrist**

✖ **84.05 Amputation through forearm**
  Forearm amputation

✖ **84.06 Disarticulation of elbow**

✖ **84.07 Amputation through humerus**
  Upper arm amputation

✖ **84.08 Disarticulation of shoulder**

✖ **84.09 Interthoracoscapular amputation**
  Forequarter amputation

● **84.1 Amputation of lower limb**

 Excludes *revision of amputation stump (84.3)*

✖ **84.10 Lower limb amputation, not otherwise specified**
  Closed flap amputation of lower limb NOS
  Kineplastic amputation of lower limb NOS
  Open or guillotine amputation of lower limb
   NOS
  Revision of current traumatic amputation of
   lower limb NOS

✖ **84.11 Amputation of toe**
  Amputation through metatarsophalangeal joint
  Disarticulation of toe

 Excludes *ligation of supernumerary toe (86.26)*

✖ **84.12 Amputation through foot**
  Amputation of forefoot
  Amputation through middle of foot
  Chopart's amputation
  Midtarsal amputation
  Transmetatarsal amputation

✖ **84.13 Disarticulation of ankle**

✖ **84.14 Amputation of ankle through malleoli of tibia and fibula**

✖ **84.15 Other amputation below knee**
  Amputation of leg through tibia and fibula
   NOS

✖ **84.16 Disarticulation of knee**
  Batch, Spitler, and McFaddin amputation
  Mazet amputation
  S.P. Roger's amputation

✖ **84.17 Amputation above knee**
  Amputation of leg through femur
  Amputation of thigh
  Conversion of below-knee amputation into
   above-knee amputation
  Supracondylar above-knee amputation

✖ **84.18 Disarticulation of hip**

✖ **84.19 Abdominopelvic amputation**
  Hemipelvectomy
  Hindquarter amputation

● **84.2 Reattachment of extremity**

✖ **84.21 Thumb reattachment**

✖ **84.22 Finger reattachment**

✖ **84.23 Forearm, wrist, or hand reattachment**

✖ **84.24 Upper arm reattachment**
  Reattachment of arm NOS

✖ **84.25 Toe reattachment**

✖ **84.26 Foot reattachment**

✖ **84.27 Lower leg or ankle reattachment**
  Reattachment of leg NOS

✖ **84.28 Thigh reattachment**

✖ **84.29 Other reattachment**

✖ **84.3 Revision of amputation stump**
  Reamputation of stump
  Secondary closure of stump
  Trimming of stump

 Excludes *revision of current traumatic amputation [revision by further amputation of current injury] (84.00–84.19, 84.91)*

● **84.4 Implantation or fitting of prosthetic limb device**

✖ **84.40 Implantation or fitting of prosthetic limb device, not otherwise specified**

 84.41 Fitting of prosthesis of upper arm and shoulder

 84.42 Fitting of prosthesis of lower arm and hand

 84.43 Fitting of prosthesis of arm, not otherwise specified

✖ **84.44 Implantation of prosthetic device of arm**

 84.45 Fitting of prosthesis above knee

 84.46 Fitting of prosthesis below knee

 84.47 Fitting of prosthesis of leg, not otherwise specified

✖ **84.48 Implantation of prosthetic device of leg**

● **84.9 Other operations on musculoskeletal system**

 Excludes *nonoperative manipulation (93.25–93.29)*

✖ **84.91 Amputation, not otherwise specified**

✖ **84.92 Separation of equal conjoined twins**

✖ **84.93 Separation of unequal conjoined twins**
  Separation of conjoined twins NOS

✖ **84.99 Other**

15.   OPERATIONS ON THE INTEGUMENTARY SYSTEM (85–86)

● **85   Operations on the breast**

> **Includes:** operations on the skin and subcutaneous tissue of:
> breast female or male
> previous mastectomy site female or male
> revision of previous mastectomy site

85.0   Mastotomy
Incision of breast (skin)
Mammotomy

> **Excludes**   *aspiration of breast (85.91)*
> *removal of implant (85.94)*

● **85.1   Diagnostic procedures on breast**

85.11   Closed [percutaneous] [needle] biopsy of breast

✖ **85.12   Open biopsy of breast**

85.19   Other diagnostic procedures on breast

> **Excludes**   *mammary ductogram (87.35)*
> *mammography NEC (87.37)*
> *manual examination (89.36)*
> *microscopic examination of specimen (91.61–91.69)*
> *thermography (88.85)*
> *ultrasonography (88.73)*
> *xerography (87.36)*

● **85.2   Excision or destruction of breast tissue**

> **Excludes**   *mastectomy (85.41–85.48)*
> *reduction mammoplasty (85.31–85.32)*

✖ **85.20   Excision or destruction of breast tissue, not otherwise specified**

✖ **85.21   Local excision of lesion of breast**
Lumpectomy
Removal of area of fibrosis from breast

> **Excludes**   *biopsy of breast (85.11–85.12)*

✖ **85.22   Resection of quadrant of breast**

✖ **85.23   Subtotal mastectomy**

> **Excludes**   *quadrant resection (85.22)*

✖ **85.24   Excision of ectopic breast tissue**
Excision of accessory nipple

✖ **85.25   Excision of nipple**

> **Excludes**   *excision of accessory nipple (85.24)*

● **85.3   Reduction mammoplasty and subcutaneous mammectomy**

✖ **85.31   Unilateral reduction mammoplasty**
Unilateral:
amputative mammoplasty
size reduction mammoplasty

✖ **85.32   Bilateral reduction mammoplasty**
Amputative mammoplasty
Reduction mammoplasty (for gynecomastia)

✖ **85.33   Unilateral subcutaneous mammectomy with synchronous implant**

> **Excludes**   *that without synchronous implant (85.34)*

✖ **85.34   Other unilateral subcutaneous mammectomy**
Removal of breast tissue with preservation of skin and nipple
Subcutaneous mammectomy NOS

✖ **85.35   Bilateral subcutaneous mammectomy with synchronous implant**

> **Excludes**   *that without synchronous implant (85.36)*

✖ **85.36   Other bilateral subcutaneous mammectomy**

● **85.4   Mastectomy**

✖ **85.41   Unilateral simple mastectomy**
Mastectomy:
NOS
complete

✖ **85.42   Bilateral simple mastectomy**
Bilateral complete mastectomy

✖ **85.43   Unilateral extended simple mastectomy**
Extended simple mastectomy NOS
Modified radical mastectomy
Simple mastectomy with excision of regional lymph nodes

✖ **85.44   Bilateral extended simple mastectomy**

✖ **85.45   Unilateral radical mastectomy**
Excision of breast, pectoral muscles, and regional lymph nodes [axillary, clavicular, supraclavicular]
Radical mastectomy NOS

✖ **85.46   Bilateral radical mastectomy**

✖ **85.47   Unilateral extended radical mastectomy**
Excision of breast, muscles, and lymph nodes [axillary, clavicular, supraclavicular, internal mammary, and mediastinal]
Extended radical mastectomy NOS

✖ **85.48   Bilateral extended radical mastectomy**

● **85.5   Augmentation mammoplasty**

> **Excludes**   *that associated with subcutaneous mammectomy (85.33, 85.35)*

✖ **85.50   Augmentation mammoplasty, not otherwise specified**

85.51   Unilateral injection into breast for augmentation

85.52   Bilateral injection into breast for augmentation
Injection into breast for augmentation NOS

✖ **85.53   Unilateral breast implant**

✖ **85.54   Bilateral breast implant**
Breast implant NOS

✖ **85.6   Mastopexy**

✖ **85.7   Total reconstruction of breast**

● **85.8   Other repair and plastic operations on breast**

> **Excludes**   *that for:*
> *augmentation (85.50–85.54)*
> *reconstruction (85.7)*
> *reduction (85.31–85.32)*

85.81   Suture of laceration of breast

✖ **85.82   Split-thickness graft to breast**

✖ **85.83   Full-thickness graft to breast**

✖ **85.84   Pedicle graft to breast**

✖ **85.85   Muscle flap graft to breast**

✖ **85.86   Transposition of nipple**

✖ **85.87   Other repair or reconstruction of nipple**

✖ **85.89   Other mammoplasty**

● **85.9   Other operations on the breast**

85.91   Aspiration of breast

> **Excludes**   *percutaneous biopsy of breast (85.11)*

85.92   Injection of therapeutic agent into breast

> **Excludes**   *that for augmentation of breast (85.51–85.52)*

✖ **85.93   Revision of implant of breast**

✖ **85.94   Removal of implant of breast**

✖ **85.95   Insertion of breast tissue expander**
Insertion (soft tissue) of tissue expander (one or more) under muscle or platysma to develop skin flaps for donor use

✖ **85.96**   **Removal of breast tissue expander(s)**

✖ **85.99**   **Other**

● **86**   **Operations on skin and subcutaneous tissue**

     Includes: operations on:
         hair follicles
         male perineum
         nails
         sebaceous glands
         subcutaneous fat pads
         sudoriferous glands
         superficial fossae

     Excludes   *those on skin of:*
         anus (49.01–49.99)
         breast (mastectomy site) (85.0–85.99)
         ear (18.01–18.9)
         eyebrow (08.01–08.99)
         eyelid (08.01–08.99)
         female perineum (71.01–71.9)
         lips (27.0–27.99)
         nose (21.00–21.99)
         penis (64.0–64.99)
         scrotum (61.0–61.99)
         vulva (71.01–71.9)

● **86.0**   **Incision of skin and subcutaneous tissue**

     86.01   **Aspiration of skin and subcutaneous tissue**
         Aspiration of:
             abscess of nail, skin, or subcutaneous tissue
             hematoma of nail, skin, or subcutaneous tissue
             seroma of nail, skin, or subcutaneous tissue

     86.02   **Injection or tattooing of skin lesion or defect**
         Injection of filling material
         Insertion of filling material
         Pigmenting of skin of filling material

     86.03   **Incision of pilonidal sinus or cyst**

     Excludes   *marsupialization (86.21)*

     86.04   **Other incision with drainage of skin and subcutaneous tissue**

     Excludes   *drainage of:*
         fascial compartments of face and mouth (27.0)
         palmar or thenar space 82.04)
         pilonidal sinus or cyst 86.03)

     86.05   **Incision with removal of foreign body from skin and subcutaneous tissue**
         Removal of tissue expander(s) from skin or soft tissue other than breast tissue

     Excludes   *removal of foreign body without incision (98.20–98.29)*

✖   **86.06**   **Insertion of totally implantable infusion pump**

         Code also any associated catheterization

     Excludes   *insertion of totally implantable vascular access device (86.07)*

     86.07   **Insertion of totally implantable vascular access device [VAD]**
         Totally implanted port

     Excludes   *insertion of totally implantable infusion pump (86.06)*

     86.09   **Other incision of skin and subcutaneous tissue**
         Creation of thalamic stimulator pulse generator pocket, new site
         Exploration:
             sinus tract, skin
             superficial fossa
         Undercutting of hair follicle

     Excludes   *that of:*
         cardiac pacemaker pocket, new site (37.79)
         fascial compartments of face and mouth (27.0)

● **86.1**   **Diagnostic procedures on skin and subcutaneous tissue**

     86.11   **Biopsy of skin and subcutaneous tissue**

     86.19   **Other diagnostic procedures on skin and subcutaneous tissue**

     Excludes   *microscopic examination of specimen from skin and subcutaneous tissue (91.61–91.79)*

● **86.2**   **Excision or destruction of lesion or tissue of skin and subcutaneous tissue**

     ✖ **86.21**   **Excision of pilonidal cyst or sinus**
         Marsupialization of cyst

     Excludes   *incision of pilonidal cyst or sinus (86.03)*

     ✖ **86.22**   **Excisional debridement of wound, infection, or burn**
         Removal by excision of:
             devitalized tissue
             necrosis
             slough

     Excludes   *debridement of:*
         abdominal wall (wound) (54.3)
         bone (77.60–77.69)
         muscle (83.45)
         of hand (82.36)
         nail (bed) (fold) (86.27)
         nonexcisional debridement of wound, infection, or burn (86.28)
         open fracture site (79.60–79.69)
         pedicle or flap graft (86.75)

     86.23   **Removal of nail, nail bed, or nail fold**

     86.24   **Chemosurgery of skin**
         Chemical peel of skin

     ✖ **86.25**   **Dermabrasion**
         That with laser

     Excludes   *dermabrasion of wound to remove embedded debris (86.28)*

     86.26   **Ligation of dermal appendage**

     Excludes   *excision of preauricular appendage (18.29)*

     86.27   **Debridement of nail, nail bed, or nail fold**
         Removal of:
             necrosis
             slough

     Excludes   *removal of nail, nail bed, or nail fold (86.23)*

     86.28   **Nonexcisional debridement of wound, infection or burn**
         Debridement NOS
         Removal of devitalized tissue, necrosis and slough by such methods as:
             brushing
             irrigation (under pressure)
             scrubbing
             washing

● **86.3**   **Other local excision or destruction of lesion or tissue of skin and subcutaneous tissue**
         Destruction of skin by:
             cauterization cryosurgery
             fulguration
             laser beam
         That with Z-plasty

     Excludes   *adipectomy (86.83)*
         biopsy of skin (86.11)
         wide or radical excision of skin (86.4)
         Z-plasty without excision (86.84)

● ✖ **86.4**   **Radical excision of skin lesion**
         Wide excision of skin lesion involving underlying or adjacent structure

     Code also any lymph node dissection (40.3–40.5)

● **86.5   Suture of skin and subcutaneous tissue**

     86.51   Replantation of scalp

     86.59   Suture of skin and subcutaneous tissue of other sites

● **86.6   Free skin graft**

     Includes: excision of skin for autogenous graft

     | Excludes | *construction or reconstruction of:*
         penis (64.43–64.44)
         trachea (31.75)
         vagina (70.61–70.62)

     ✖ **86.60   Free skin graft, not otherwise specified**

     ✖ **86.61   Full-thickness skin graft to hand**

     | Excludes | *heterograft (86.65)*
         homograft (86.66)

     ✖ **86.62   Other skin graft to hand**

     | Excludes | *heterograft (86.65)*
         homograft (86.66)

     ✖ **86.63   Full-thickness skin graft to other sites**

     | Excludes | *heterograft (86.65)*
         homograft (86.66)

     86.64   Hair transplant

     | Excludes | *hair follicle transplant to eyebrow or eyelash (08.63)*

     ✖ **86.65   Heterograft to skin**
         Pigskin graft
         Porcine graft

     ✖ **86.66   Homograft to skin**
         Graft to skin of:
         amnionic membrane from donor skin from donor

     86.67   Dermal regenerative graft ◀
         Artificial skin, NOS ◀
         Creation of "neodermis" ◀
         Decellularized allodermis ◀
         Integumentary matrix implants ◀
         Prosthetic implant of dermal layer of skin ◀
         Regenerate dermal layer of skin ◀

     | Excludes | *heterograft to skin (86.65)* ◀
         homograft to skin (86.66) ◀

     ✖ **86.69   Other skin graft to other sites**

     | Excludes | *heterograft (86.65)*
         homograft (86.66)

● **86.7   Pedicle grafts or flaps**

     | Excludes | *construction or reconstruction of:*
         penis (64.43–64.44)
         trachea (31.75)
         vagina (70.61–70.62)

     ✖ **86.70   Pedicle or flap graft, not otherwise specified**

     ✖ **86.71   Cutting and preparation of pedicle grafts or flaps**
         Elevation of pedicle from its bed
         Flap design and raising
         Partial cutting of pedicle or tube
         Pedicle delay

     | Excludes | *pollicization or digital transfer (82.61, 82.81)*
         revision of pedicle (86.75)

     ✖ **86.72   Advancement of pedicle graft**

     ✖ **86.73   Attachment of pedicle or flap graft to hand**

     | Excludes | *pollicization or digital transfer (82.61, 82.81)*

     ✖ **86.74   Attachment of pedicle or flap graft to other sites**
         Attachment by:
         advanced flap
         double pedicled flap
         pedicle graft
         rotating flap
         sliding flap
         tube graft

     ✖ **86.75   Revision of pedicle or flap graft**
         Debridement of pedicle or flap graft
         Defatting of pedicle or flap graft

● **86.8   Other repair and reconstruction of skin and subcutaneous tissue**

     ✖ **86.81   Repair for facial weakness**

     ✖ **86.82   Facial rhytidectomy**
         Face lift

     | Excludes | *rhytidectomy of eyelid (08.86–08.87)*

     ✖ **86.83   Size reduction plastic operation**
         Reduction of adipose tissue of:
         abdominal wall (pendulous)
         arms (batwing)
         buttock
         liposuction ◀
         thighs (trochanteric lipomatosis)

     | Excludes | *breast (85.31–85.32)*

     ✖ **86.84   Relaxation of scar or web contracture of skin**
         Z-plasty of skin

     | Excludes | *Z-plasty with excision of lesion (86.3)*

     ✖ **86.85   Correction of syndactyly**

     ✖ **86.86   Onychoplasty**

     ✖ **86.89   Other repair and reconstruction of skin and subcutaneous tissue**

     | Excludes | *mentoplasty (76.67–76.68)*

● **86.9   Other operations on skin and subcutaneous tissue**

     ✖ **86.91   Excision of skin for graft**
         Excision of skin with closure of donor site

     | Excludes | *that with graft at same operative episode (86.60-86.69)*

     86.92   Electrolysis and other epilation of skin

     | Excludes | *epilation of eyelid (08.91–08.93)*

     ✖ **86.93   Insertion of tissue expander**
         Insertion (subcutaneous) (soft tissue) of expander (one or more) in scalp (subgaleal space), face, neck, trunk except breast, and upper and lower extremities for development of skin flaps for donor use

     | Excludes | *flap graft preparation (86.71)*
         tissue expander, breast (85.95)

     86.99   Other

     | Excludes | *removal of sutures from:*
         abdomen (97.83)
         head and neck (97.38)
         thorax (97.43)
         trunk NEC (97.84)
         wound catheter:
         irrigation (96.58)
         replacement (97.15)

16.   MISCELLANEOUS DIAGNOSTIC AND THERAPEUTIC PROCEDURES (87–99)

● **87   Diagnostic Radiology**

● **87.0   Soft tissue x-ray of face, head, and neck**

  Excludes *angiography (88.40–88.68)*

  87.01   Pneumoencephalogram

  87.02   Other contrast radiogram of brain and skull
  Pneumocisternogram
  Pneumoventriculogram
  Posterior fossa myelogram

  87.03   Computerized axial tomography of head
  C.A.T. scan of head

  87.04   Other tomography of head

  87.05   Contrast dacryocystogram

  87.06   Contrast radiogram of nasopharynx

  87.07   Contrast laryngogram

  87.08   Cervical lymphangiogram

  87.09   Other soft tissue x-ray of face, head, and neck
  Noncontrast x-ray of:
  adenoid
  larynx
  nasolacrimal duct
  nasopharynx
  salivary gland
  thyroid region
  uvula

  Excludes *x-ray study of eye (95.14)*

● **87.1   Other x-ray of face, head, and neck**

  Excludes *angiography (88.40–88.68)*

  87.11   Full-mouth x-ray of teeth

  87.12   Other dental x-ray
  Orthodontic cephalogram or cephalometrics
  Panorex examination of mandible
  Root canal x-ray

  87.13   Temporomandibular contrast arthrogram

  87.14   Contrast radiogram of orbit

  87.15   Contrast radiogram of sinus

  87.16   Other x-ray of facial bones
  X-ray of:
  frontal area
  mandible
  maxilla
  nasal sinuses
  nose
  orbit
  supraorbital area
  symphysis menti
  zygomaticomaxillary complex

  87.17   Other x-ray of skull
  Lateral projection of skull
  Sagittal projection of skull
  Tangential projection of skull

● **87.2   X-ray of spine**

  87.21   Contrast myelogram

  87.22   Other x-ray of cervical spine

  87.23   Other x-ray of thoracic spine

  87.24   Other x-ray of lumbosacral spine
  Sacrococcygeal x-ray

  87.29   Other x-ray of spine
  Spinal x-ray NOS

● **87.3   Soft tissue x-ray of thorax**

  Excludes *angiocardiography (88.50–88.58)*
  angiography (88.40–88.68)

  87.31   Endotracheal bronchogram

  87.32   Other contrast bronchogram
  Transcricoid bronchogram

  87.33   Mediastinal pneumogram

  87.34   Intrathoracic lymphangiogram

  87.35   Contrast radiogram of mammary ducts

  87.36   Xerography of breast

  87.37   Other mammography

  87.38   Sinogram of chest wall
  Fistulogram of chest wall

  87.39   Other soft tissue x-ray of chest wall

● **87.4   Other x-ray of thorax**

  Excludes *angiocardiography (88.50–88.58)*
  angiography (88.40–88.68)

  87.41   Computerized axial tomography of thorax
  C.A.T. scan of thorax
  Crystal linear scan of x-ray beam of thorax
  Electronic subtraction of thorax
  Photoelectric response of thorax
  Tomography with use of computer, x-rays,
  and camera of thorax

  87.42   Other tomography of thorax
  Cardiac tomogram

  87.43   X-ray of ribs, sternum, and clavicle
  Examination for:
  cervical rib
  fracture

  87.44   Routine chest x-ray, so described
  X-ray of chest NOS

  87.49   Other chest x-ray
  X-ray of:
  bronchus NOS
  diaphragm NOS
  heart NOS
  lung NOS
  mediastinum NOS
  trachea NOS

● **87.5   Biliary tract x-ray**

  87.51   Percutaneous hepatic cholangiogram

  87.52   Intravenous cholangiogram

  87.53   Intraoperative cholangiogram

  87.54   Other cholangiogram

  87.59   Other biliary tract x-ray
  Cholecystogram

● **87.6   Other x-ray of digestive system**

  87.61   Barium swallow

  87.62   Upper GI series

  87.63   Small bowel series

  87.64   Lower GI series

  87.65   Other x-ray of intestine

  87.66   Contrast pancreatogram

  87.69   Other digestive tract x-ray

● **87.7   X-ray of urinary system**

  Excludes *angiography of renal vessels (88.45, 88.65)*

  87.71   Computerized axial tomography of kidney
  C.A.T. scan of kidney

  87.72   Other nephrotomogram

    ● **Use Additional Digit(s)**   ✖ **Valid O.R. Procedure**   ◀▶ **New Code**   ⬅ ➡ **Revised Code**

87.73 Intravenous pyelogram
Diuretic infusion pyelogram

87.74 Retrograde pyelogram

87.75 Percutaneous pyelogram

87.76 Retrograde cystourethrogram

87.77 Other cystogram

87.78 Ileal conduitogram

87.79 Other x-ray of the urinary system
KUB x-ray

● **87.8 X-ray of female genital organs**

87.81 X-ray of gravid uterus
Intrauterine cephalometry by x-ray

87.82 Gas contrast hysterosalpingogram

87.83 Opaque dye contrast hysterosalpingogram

87.84 Percutaneous hysterogram

87.85 Other x-ray of fallopian tubes and uterus

87.89 Other x-ray of female genital organs

● **87.9 X-ray of male genital organs**

87.91 Contrast seminal vesiculogram

87.92 Other x-ray of prostate and seminal vesicles

87.93 Contrast epididymogram

87.94 Contrast vasogram

87.95 Other x-ray of epididymis and vas deferens

87.99 Other x-ray of male genital organs

● **88 Other diagnostic radiology and related techniques**

● **88.0 Soft tissue x-ray of abdomen**

Excludes	*angiography (88.40–88.68)*

88.01 Computerized axial tomography of abdomen
C.A.T. scan of abdomen

Excludes	*C.A.T. scan of kidney (87.71)*

88.02 Other abdomen tomography

Excludes	*nephrotomogram (87.72)*

88.03 Sinogram of abdominal wall
Fistulogram of abdominal wall

88.04 Abdominal lymphangiogram

88.09 Other soft tissue x-ray of abdominal wall

● **88.1 Other x-ray of abdomen**

88.11 Pelvic opaque dye contrast radiography

88.12 Pelvic gas contrast radiography
Pelvic pneumoperitoneum

88.13 Other peritoneal pneumogram

88.14 Retroperitoneal fistulogram

88.15 Retroperitoneal pneumogram

88.16 Other retroperitoneal x-ray

88.19 Other x-ray of abdomen
Flat plate of abdomen

● **88.2 Skeletal x-ray of extremities and pelvis**

Excludes	*contrast radiogram of joint (88.32)*

88.21 Skeletal x-ray of shoulder and upper arm

88.22 Skeletal x-ray of elbow and forearm

88.23 Skeletal x-ray of wrist and hand

88.24 Skeletal x-ray of upper limb, not otherwise specified

88.25 Pelvimetry

88.26 Other skeletal x-ray of pelvis and hip

88.27 Skeletal x-ray of thigh, knee, and lower leg

88.28 Skeletal x-ray of ankle and foot

88.29 Skeletal x-ray of lower limb, not otherwise specified

● **88.3 Other x-ray**

88.31 Skeletal series
X-ray of whole skeleton

88.32 Contrast arthrogram

Excludes	*that of temporomandibular joint (87.13)*

88.33 Other skeletal x-ray

Excludes	*skeletal x-ray of:* *extremities and pelvis 88.21–88.29)* *face, head, and neck (87.11–87.17)* *spine (87.21–87.29)* *thorax (87.43)*

88.34 Lymphangiogram of upper limb

88.35 Other soft tissue x-ray of upper limb

88.36 Lymphangiogram of lower limb

88.37 Other soft tissue x-ray of lower limb

Excludes	*femoral angiography (88.48, 88.66)*

88.38 Other computerized axial tomography
C.A.T. scan NOS

Excludes	*C.A.T. scan of:* *abdomen (88.01)* *head (87.03)* *kidney (87.71)* *thorax (87.41)*

88.39 X-ray, other and unspecified

● **88.4 Arteriography using contrast material**

Includes: angiography of arteries
arterial puncture for injection of contrast material
radiography of arteries (by fluoroscopy)
retrograde arteriography

Note: The fourth-digit subclassification identifies the site to be viewed, not the site of injection.

Excludes	*arteriography using:* *radioisotopes or radionuclides (92.01–92.19)* *ultrasound (88.71–88.79)* *fluorescein angiography of eye (95.12)*

88.40 Arteriography using contrast material, unspecified site

88.41 Arteriography of cerebral arteries
Angiography of:
basilar artery
carotid (internal)
posterior cerebral circulation
vertebral artery

88.42 Aortography
Arteriography of aorta and aortic arch

88.43 Arteriography of pulmonary arteries

88.44 Arteriography of other intrathoracic vessels

Excludes	*angiocardiography (88.50–88.58)* *arteriography of coronary arteries (88.55–88.57)*

88.45 Arteriography of renal arteries

88.46 Arteriography of placenta
Placentogram using contrast material

88.47 Arteriography of other intra-abdominal arteries

88.48 Arteriography of femoral and other lower extremity arteries

88.49 Arteriography of other specified sites

● **88.5 Angiocardiography using contrast material**

Includes: arterial puncture and insertion of arterial
catheter for injection of contrast material
cineangiocardiography
selective angiocardiography

Code also synchronous cardiac catheterization (37.21–
37.23)

| **Excludes** | *angiography of pulmonary vessels (88.43, 88.62)* |

88.50 Angiocardiography, not otherwise specified

88.51 Angiocardiography of venae cavae
Inferior vena cavography
Phlebography of vena cava (inferior) (supe-
rior)

88.52 Angiocardiography of right heart structures
Angiocardiography of:
pulmonary valve
right atrium
right ventricle (outflow tract)

| **Excludes** | *that combined with left heart angiocardiography (88.54)* |

88.53 Angiocardiography of left heart structures
Angiocardiography of:
aortic valve
left atrium
left ventricle (outflow tract)

| **Excludes** | *that combined with right heart angiocardiography (88.54)* |

88.54 Combined right and left heart angiocardiography

88.55 Coronary arteriography using a single catheter
Coronary arteriography by Sones technique
Direct selective coronary arteriography
using a single catheter

88.56 Coronary arteriography using two catheters
Coronary arteriography by:
Judkins technique
Ricketts and Abrams technique
Direct selective coronary arteriography using
two catheters

88.57 Other and unspecified coronary arteriography
Coronary arteriography NOS

88.58 Negative-contrast cardiac roentgenography
Cardiac roentgenography with injection of
carbon dioxide

● **88.6 Phlebography**

Includes: angiography of veins
radiography of veins (by fluoroscopy)
retrograde phlebography
venipuncture for injection of contrast material
venography using contrast material

Note: The fourth-digit subclassification (88.60–88.67)
identifies the site to be viewed, not the site of
injection.

Excludes	*angiography using:*
	radioisotopes or radionuclides (92.01–92.19)
	ultrasound (88.71–88.79)
	fluorescein angiography of eye (95.12)

**88.60 Phlebography using contrast material, unspeci-
fied site**

**88.61 Phlebography of veins of head and neck using
contrast material**

**88.62 Phlebography of pulmonary veins using con-
trast material**

**88.63 Phlebography of other intrathoracic veins us-
ing contrast material**

**88.64 Phlebography of the portal venous system us-
ing contrast material**
Splenoportogram (by splenic arteriography)

**88.65 Phlebography of other intra-abdominal veins
using contrast material**

**88.66 Phlebography of femoral and other lower ex-
tremity veins using contrast material**

**88.67 Phlebography of other specified sites using
contrast material**

88.68 Impedance phlebography

● **88.7 Diagnostic ultrasound**

Includes: echography
ultrasonic angiography
ultrasonography

88.71 Diagnostic ultrasound of head and neck
Determination of midline shift of brain
Echoencephalography

| **Excludes** | *eye (95.13)* |

88.72 Diagnostic ultrasound of heart
Echocardiography

88.73 Diagnostic ultrasound of other sites of thorax
Aortic arch ultrasonography
Breast ultrasonography
Lung ultrasonography

88.74 Diagnostic ultrasound of digestive system

88.75 Diagnostic ultrasound of urinary system

**88.76 Diagnostic ultrasound of abdomen and retro-
peritoneum**

**88.77 Diagnostic ultrasound of peripheral vascular sys-
tem**
Deep vein thrombosis ultrasonic scanning

88.78 Diagnostic ultrasound of gravid uterus
Intrauterine cephalometry:
echo
ultrasonic
Placental localization by ultrasound

88.79 Other diagnostic ultrasound
Ultrasonography of:
multiple sites
nongravid uterus
total body

● **88.8 Thermography**

88.81 Cerebral thermography

88.82 Ocular thermography

88.83 Bone thermography
Osteoarticular thermography

88.84 Muscle thermography

88.85 Breast thermography

88.86 Blood vessel thermography
Deep vein thermography

88.89 Thermography of other sites
Lymph gland thermography
Thermography NOS

● **88.9 Other diagnostic imaging**

88.90 Diagnostic imaging, not elsewhere classified

**88.91 Magnetic resonance imaging of brain and
brain stem**

**88.92 Magnetic resonance imaging of chest and myo-
cardium**
For evaluation of hilar and mediastinal lymphadenopathy

88.93   Magnetic resonance imaging of spinal canal
Spinal cord levels:
    cervical
    thoracic
    lumbar (lumbosacral)
Spinal cord
Spine

88.94   Magnetic resonance imaging of musculoskeletal
Bone marrow blood supply
Extremities (upper) (lower)

88.95   Magnetic resonance imaging of pelvis, prostate, and bladder

88.97   Magnetic resonance imaging of other and unspecified sites
Abdomen
Eye orbit
Face
Neck

88.98   Bone mineral density studies
Dual photon absorptiometry
Quantitative computed tomography (CT) studies
Radiographic densitometry
Single photon absorptiometry

● **89   Interview, evaluation, consultation, and examination**

● **89.0   Diagnostic interview, consultation, and evaluation**
| Excludes | *psychiatric diagnostic interview (94.11–94.19)* |

89.01   Interview and evaluation, described as brief
Abbreviated history and evaluation

89.02   Interview and evaluation, described as limited
Interval history and evaluation

89.03   Interview and evaluation, described as comprehensive
History and evaluation of new problem

89.04   Other interview and evaluation

89.05   Diagnostic interview and evaluation, not otherwise specified

89.06   Consultation, described as limited
Consultation on a single organ system

89.07   Consultation, described as comprehensive

89.08   Other consultation

89.09   Consultation, not otherwise specified

● **89.1   Anatomic and physiologic measurements and manual examinations—nervous system and sense organs**
Excludes	*ear examination (95.41–95.49)*
	eye examination (95.01–95.26)
	the listed procedures when done as part of a general physical examination (89.7)

89.10   Intracarotid amobarbital test
Wada test

89.11   Tonometry

89.12   Nasal function study
Rhinomanometry

89.13   Neurologic examination

89.14   Electroencephalogram
| Excludes | *that with polysomnogram (89.17)* |

89.15   Other nonoperative neurologic function tests

89.16   Transillumination of newborn skull

89.17   Polysomnogram
Sleep recording

89.18   Other sleep disorder function tests
Multiple sleep latency test [MSLT]

89.19   Video and radio-telemetered electroencephalographic monitoring
Radiographic EEG monitoring
Video EEG monitoring

● **89.2   Anatomic and physiologic measurements and manual examinations—genitourinary system**
| Excludes | *the listed procedures when done as part of a general physical examination (89.7)* |

89.21   Urinary manometry
Manometry through:
    indwelling ureteral catheter
    nephrostomy
    pyelostomy
    ureterostomy

89.22   Cystometrogram

89.23   Urethral sphincter electromyogram

89.24   Uroflowmetry [UFR]

89.25   Urethral pressure profile [UPP]

89.26   Gynecological examination
Pelvic examination

89.29   Other nonoperative genitourinary system measurements
Bioassay of urine
Renal clearance
Urine chemistry

● **89.3   Other anatomic and physiologic measurements and manual examinations**
| Excludes | *the listed procedures when done as part of a general physical examination (89.7)* |

89.31   Dental examination
Oral mucosal survey
Periodontal survey

89.32   Esophageal manometry

89.33   Digital examination of enterostomy stoma
Digital examination of colostomy stoma

89.34   Digital examination of rectum

89.35   Transillumination of nasal sinuses

89.36   Manual examination of breast

89.37   Vital capacity determination

89.38   Other nonoperative respiratory measurements
Plethysmography for measurement of respiratory function
Thoracic impedance plethysmography

89.39   Other nonoperative measurements and examinations
14 C-Urea breath test
Basal metabolic rate [BMR]
Gastric:
    analysis
    function NEC
Excludes	*body measurement (93.07)*
	cardiac tests (89.41–89.69)
	fundus photography (95.11)
	limb length measurement (93.06)

● **89.4   Cardiac stress tests and pacemaker checks**

89.41   Cardiovascular stress test using treadmill

89.42   Masters' two-step stress test

89.43   Cardiovascular stress test using bicycle ergometer

89.44   Other cardiovascular stress test
Thallium stress test with or without transesophageal pacing

89.45   Artificial pacemaker rate check
Artificial pacemaker function check NOS

89.46　Artificial pacemaker artifact wave form check

89.47　Artificial pacemaker electrode impedance check

89.48　Artificial pacemaker voltage or amperage threshold check

● **89.5　Other nonoperative cardiac and vascular diagnostic procedures**

> **Excludes** *fetal EKG (75.32)*

89.50　Ambulatory cardiac monitoring
Analog devices [Holter-type]

89.51　Rhythm electrocardiogram
Rhythm EKG (with one to three leads)

89.52　Electrocardiogram
ECG NOS
EKG (with 12 or more leads)

89.53　Vectorcardiogram (with ECG)

89.54　Electrographic monitoring
Telemetry

> **Excludes** *ambulatory cardiac monitoring (89.50)*
> *electrographic monitoring during surgery—omit code*

89.55　Phonocardiogram with ECG lead

89.56　Carotid pulse tracing with ECG lead

> **Excludes** *oculoplethysmography (89.58)*

89.57　Apexcardiogram (with ECG lead)

89.58　Plethysmogram

> **Excludes** *plethysmography (for):*
> *measurement of respiratory function (89.38)*
> *thoracic impedance (89.38)*

89.59　Other nonoperative cardiac and vascular measurements

● **89.6　Circulatory monitoring**

> **Excludes** *electrocardiographic monitoring during surgery—omit code*

89.61　Systemic arterial pressure monitoring

89.62　Central venous pressure monitoring

89.63　Pulmonary artery pressure monitoring

> **Excludes** *pulmonary artery wedge monitoring (89.64)*

89.64　Pulmonary artery wedge monitoring
Pulmonary capillary wedge [PCW] monitoring
Swan-Ganz catheterization

89.65　Measurement of systemic arterial blood gases

89.66　Measurement of mixed venous blood gases

89.67　Monitoring of cardiac output by oxygen consumption technique
Fick method

89.68　Monitoring of cardiac output by other technique
Cardiac output monitor by thermodilution indicator

89.69　Monitoring of coronary blood flow
Coronary blood flow monitoring by coincidence counting technique

89.7　General physical examination

89.8　Autopsy

● **90　Microscopic examination-I**

The following fourth-digit subclassification is for use with categories in section 90 to identify type of examination:
1 bacterial smear
2 culture
3 culture and sensitivity
4 parasitology
5 toxicology
6 cell block and Papanicolaou smear
9 other microscopic examination

● **90.0　Microscopic examination of specimen from nervous system and of spinal fluid**

● **90.1　Microscopic examination of specimen from endocrine gland, not elsewhere classified**

● **90.2　Microscopic examination of specimen from eye**

● **90.3　Microscopic examination of specimen from ear, nose, throat, and larynx**

● **90.4　Microscopic examination of specimen from trachea, bronchus, pleura, lung, and other thoracic specimen, and of sputum**

● **90.5　Microscopic examination of blood**

● **90.6　Microscopic examination of specimen from spleen and of bone marrow**

● **90.7　Microscopic examination of specimen from lymph node and of lymph**

● **90.8　Microscopic examination of specimen from upper gastrointestinal tract and of vomitus**

● **90.9　Microscopic examination of specimen from lower gastrointestinal tract and of stool**

● **91　Microscopic examination-II**

The following fourth-digit subclassification is for use with categories in section 91 to identify type of examination
1 bacterial smear
2 culture
3 culture and sensitivity
4 parasitology
5 toxicology
6 cell block and Papanicolaou smear
9 other microscopic examination

● **91.0　Microscopic examination of specimen from liver, biliary tract, and pancreas**

● **91.1　Microscopic examination of peritoneal and retroperitoneal specimen**

● **91.2　Microscopic examination of specimen from kidney, ureter, perirenal and periureteral tissue**

● **91.3　Microscopic examination of specimen from bladder, urethra, prostate, seminal vesicle, perivesical tissue, and of urine and semen**

● **91.4　Microscopic examination of specimen from female genital tract**
Amnionic sac
Fetus

● **91.5　Microscopic examination of specimen from musculoskeletal system and of joint fluid**
Microscopic examination of:
bone
bursa
cartilage
fascia
ligament
muscle
synovial membrane
tendon

● **91.6 Microscopic examination of specimen from skin and other integument**
    Microscopic examination of:
      hair
      nails
      skin
    | **Excludes** | *mucous membrane—code to organ site that of operative wound (91.70–91.79)* |

● **91.7 Microscopic examination of specimen from operative wound**

● **91.8 Microscopic examination of specimen from other site**

● **91.9 Microscopic examination of specimen from unspecified site**

● **92 Nuclear medicine**

  ● **92.0 Radioisotope scan and function study**

    92.01 Thyroid scan and radioisotope function studies
      Iodine-131 uptake
      Protein-bound iodine
      Radio-iodine uptake

    92.02 Liver scan and radioisotope function study

    92.03 Renal scan and radioisotope function study
      Renal clearance study

    92.04 Gastrointestinal scan and radioisotope function study
      Radio-cobalt B12 Schilling test
      Radio-iodinated triolein study

    92.05 Cardiovascular and hematopoietic scan and radioisotope function study
      Bone marrow scan or function study
      Cardiac output scan or function study
      Circulation time scan or function study
      Radionuclide cardiac ventriculogram scan or function study
      Spleen scan or function study

    92.09 Other radioisotope function studies

  ● **92.1 Other radioisotope scan**

    92.11 Cerebral scan
      Pituitary

    92.12 Scan of other sites of head
    | **Excludes** | *eye (95.16)* |

    92.13 Parathyroid scan

    92.14 Bone scan

    92.15 Pulmonary scan

    92.16 Scan of lymphatic system

    92.17 Placental scan

    92.18 Total body scan

    92.19 Scan of other sites

  ● **92.2 Therapeutic radiology and nuclear medicine**
    | **Excludes** | *that for:* |
        ablation of pituitary gland (07.64–07.69)
        destruction of chorioretinal lesion (14.26–14.27)

    92.21 Superficial radiation
      Contact radiation [up to 150 KVP]

    92.22 Orthovoltage radiation
      Deep radiation [200–300 KVP]

    92.23 Radioisotopic teleradiotherapy
      Teleradiotherapy using:
        Cobalt-60
        Iodine-125
        radioactive cesium

    92.24 Teleradiotherapy using photons
      Megavoltage NOS
      Supervoltage NOS
      Use of:
        Betatron
        linear accelerator

    92.25 Teleradiotherapy using electrons
      Beta particles

    92.26 Teleradiotherapy of other particulate radiation
      Neutrons
      Protons NOS

    ✖ **92.27 Implantation or insertion of radioactive elements**
      Code also incision of site

    92.28 Injection or instillation of radioisotopes
      Intracavitary injection or instillation
      Intravenous injection or instillation

    92.29 Other radiotherapeutic procedure

  ● **92.3 Stereotactic radiosurgery**   ⬅▥
    | **Excludes** | *stereotactic biopsy* |
    Code also stereotactic head frame application (93.59)

    92.30 Stereotactic radiosurgery, not otherwise specified ◄

    92.31 Single source photon radiosurgery ◄
      High energy x-rays ◄
      Linear accelerator (LINAC) ◄

    92.32 Multi-source photon radiosurgery ◄
      Cobalt 60 radiation ◄
      Gamma irradiation ◄

    92.33 Particulate radiosurgery ◄
      Particle beam radiation (cyclotron) ◄
      Proton accelerator ◄

    92.39 Stereotactic radiosurgery, not elsewhere classified ◄

● **93 Physical therapy, respiratory therapy, rehabilitation, and related procedures**

  ● **93.0 Diagnostic physical therapy**

    93.01 Functional evaluation

    93.02 Orthotic evaluation

    93.03 Prosthetic evaluation

    93.04 Manual testing of muscle function

    93.05 Range of motion testing

    93.06 Measurement of limb length

    93.07 Body measurement
      Girth measurement
      Measurement of skull circumference

    93.08 Electromyography
    | **Excludes** | *eye EMG (95.25)* |
        that with polysomnogram (89.17)
        urethral sphincter EMG (89.23)

    93.09 Other diagnostic physical therapy procedure

  ● **93.1 Physical therapy exercises**

    93.11 Assisting exercise
    | **Excludes** | *assisted exercise in pool (93.31)* |

    93.12 Other active musculoskeletal exercise

    93.13 Resistive exercise

    93.14 Training in joint movements

    93.15 Mobilization of spine

    93.16 Mobilization of other joints
    | **Excludes** | *manipulation of temporomandibular joint (76.95)* |

93.17 Other passive musculoskeletal exercise

93.18 Breathing exercise

93.19 Exercise, not elsewhere classified

● **93.2 Other physical therapy musculoskeletal manipulation**

93.21 Manual and mechanical traction

> **Excludes** *skeletal traction (93.43–93.44)*
> *skin traction (93.45–93.46)*
> *spinal traction (93.41–93.42)*

93.22 Ambulation and gait training

93.23 Fitting of orthotic device

93.24 Training in use of prosthetic or orthotic device
Training in crutch walking

93.25 Forced extension of limb

93.26 Manual rupture of joint adhesions

93.27 Stretching of muscle or tendon

93.28 Stretching of fascia

93.29 Other forcible correction of deformity

● **93.3 Other physical therapy therapeutic procedures**

93.31 Assisted exercise in pool

93.32 Whirlpool treatment

93.33 Other hydrotherapy

93.34 Diathermy

93.35 Other heat therapy
Acupuncture with smoldering moxa
Hot packs
Hyperthermia NEC
Infrared irradiation
Moxibustion
Paraffin bath

> **Excludes** *hyperthermia for treatment of cancer (99.85)*

93.36 Cardiac retraining

93.37 Prenatal training
Training for natural childbirth

93.38 Combined physical therapy without mention of the components

93.39 Other physical therapy

● **93.4 Skeletal traction and other traction**

93.41 Spinal traction using skull device
Traction using:
caliper tongs
Crutchfield tongs
halo device
Vinke tongs

> **Excludes** *insertion of tongs or halo traction device (02.94)*

93.42 Other spinal traction
Cotrel's traction

> **Excludes** *cervical collar (93.52)*

93.43 Intermittent skeletal traction

93.44 Other skeletal traction
Bryant's traction
Dunlop's traction
Lyman Smith traction
Russell's traction

93.45 Thomas' splint traction

93.46 Other skin traction of limbs
Adhesive tape traction
Boot traction
Buck's traction
Gallows traction

● **93.5 Other immobilization, pressure, and attention to wound**

> **Excludes** *wound cleansing (96.58–96.59)*

93.51 Application of plaster jacket

> **Excludes** *Minerva jacket (93.52)*

93.52 Application of neck support
Application of:
cervical collar
Minerva jacket
molded neck support

93.53 Application of other cast

93.54 Application of splint
Plaster splint
Tray splint

> **Excludes** *periodontal splint (24.7)*

93.55 Dental wiring

> **Excludes** *that for orthodontia (24.7)*

93.56 Application of pressure dressing
Application of:
Gibney bandage
Robert Jones' bandage
Shanz dressing

93.57 Application of other wound dressing

93.58 Application of pressure trousers
Application of:
anti-shock trousers
MAST trousers
vasopneumatic device

93.59 Other immobilization, pressure, and attention to wound
Elastic stockings
Electronic gaiter
Intermittent pressure device
Oxygenation of wound (hyperbaric)
Stereotactic head frame application
Velpeau dressing

● **93.6 Osteopathic manipulative treatment**

93.61 Osteopathic manipulative treatment for general mobilization
General articulatory treatment

93.62 Osteopathic manipulative treatment using high- velocity, low-amplitude forces
Thrusting forces

93.63 Osteopathic manipulative treatment using low-velocity, high-amplitude forces
Springing forces

93.64 Osteopathic manipulative treatment using isotonic, isometric forces

93.65 Osteopathic manipulative treatment using indirect forces

93.66 Osteopathic manipulative treatment to move tissue fluids
Lymphatic pump

93.67 Other specified osteopathic manipulative treatment

● **93.7 Speech and reading rehabilitation and rehabilitation of the blind**

93.71 Dyslexia training

93.72 Dysphasia training

93.73 Esophageal speech training

93.74 Speech defect training

93.75 Other speech training and therapy

93.76 Training in use of lead dog for the blind

93.77 Training in braille or Moon

93.78 Other rehabilitation for the blind

● **93.8 Other rehabilitation therapy**

93.81 Recreation therapy
Diversional therapy
Play therapy
Excludes *play psychotherapy (94.36)*

93.82 Educational therapy
Education of bed-bound children
Special schooling for the handicapped

93.83 Occupational therapy
Daily living activities therapy
Excludes *training in activities of daily living for the blind (93.78)*

93.84 Music therapy

93.85 Vocational rehabilitation
Sheltered employment
Vocational:
assessment
retraining
training

93.89 Rehabilitation, not elsewhere classified

● **93.9 Respiratory therapy**
Excludes *insertion of airway (96.01–96.05)*
other continuous mechanical ventilation (96.70–96.72)

93.90 Continuous positive airway pressure [CPAP]

93.91 Intermittent positive pressure breathing [IPPB]

93.93 Nonmechanical methods of resuscitation
Artificial respiration
Manual resuscitation
Mouth-to-mouth resuscitation

93.94 Respiratory medication administered by nebulizer
Mist therapy

93.95 Hyperbaric oxygenation
Excludes *oxygenation of wound (93.59)*

93.96 Other oxygen enrichment
Catalytic oxygen therapy
Cytoreductive effect
Oxygenators
Oxygen therapy
Excludes *oxygenation of wound (93.59)*

93.97 Decompression chamber

93.98 Other control of atmospheric pressure and composition
Antigen-free air conditioning
Helium therapy

93.99 Other respiratory procedures
Continuous negative pressure ventilation [CNP]
Postural drainage

● **94 Procedures related to the psyche**

● **94.0 Psychologic evaluation and testing**

94.01 Administration of intelligence test
Administration of:
Stanford-Binet
Wechsler Adult Intelligence Scale
Wechsler Intelligence Scale for Children

94.02 Administration of psychologic test
Administration of:
Bender Visual-Motor Gestalt Test
Benton Visual Retention Test
Minnesota Multiphasic Personality Inventory
Wechsler Memory Scale

94.03 Character analysis

94.08 Other psychologic evaluation and testing

94.09 Psychologic mental status determination, not otherwise specified

● **94.1 Psychiatric interviews, consultations, and evaluations**

94.11 Psychiatric mental status determination
Clinical psychiatric mental status determination
Evaluation for criminal responsibility
Evaluation for testimentary capacity
Medicolegal mental status determination
Mental status determination NOS

94.12 Routine psychiatric visit, not otherwise specified

94.13 Psychiatric commitment evaluation
Pre-commitment interview

94.19 Other psychiatric interview and evaluation
Follow-up psychiatric interview NOS

● **94.2 Psychiatric somatotherapy**

94.21 Narcoanalysis
Narcosynthesis

94.22 Lithium therapy

94.23 Neuroleptic therapy

94.24 Chemical shock therapy

94.25 Other psychiatric drug therapy

94.26 Subconvulsive electroshock therapy

94.27 Other electroshock therapy
Electroconvulsive therapy (ECT)
EST

94.29 Other psychiatric somatotherapy

● **94.3 Individual psychotherapy**

94.31 Psychoanalysis

94.32 Hypnotherapy
Hypnodrome
Hypnosis

94.33 Behavior therapy
Aversion therapy
Behavior modification
Desensitization therapy
Extinction therapy
Relaxation training
Token economy

94.34 Individual therapy for psychosexual dysfunction
Excludes *that performed in group setting (94.41)*

94.35 Crisis intervention

94.36 Play psychotherapy

94.37 Exploratory verbal psychotherapy

94.38 Supportive verbal psychotherapy

94.39 Other individual psychotherapy
Biofeedback

● **94.4 Other psychotherapy and counselling**

94.41 Group therapy for psychosexual dysfunction

94.42 Family therapy

94.43 Psychodrama

94.44 Other group therapy

94.45 Drug addiction counselling

94.46 Alcoholism counselling

94.49 Other counselling

● **94.5 Referral for psychologic rehabilitation**

94.51 Referral for psychotherapy

94.52 Referral for psychiatric aftercare:
That in:
    halfway house
    outpatient (clinic) facility

94.53 Referral for alcoholism rehabilitation

94.54 Referral for drug addiction rehabilitation

94.55 Referral for vocational rehabilitation

94.59 Referral for other psychologic rehabilitation

● **94.6 Alcohol and drug rehabilitation and detoxification**

94.61 Alcohol rehabilitation

94.62 Alcohol detoxification

94.63 Alcohol rehabilitation and detoxification

94.64 Drug rehabilitation

94.65 Drug detoxification

94.66 Drug rehabilitation and detoxification

94.67 Combined alcohol and drug rehabilitation

94.68 Combined alcohol and drug detoxification

94.69 Combined alcohol and drug rehabilitation and detoxification

● **95 Ophthalmologic and otologic diagnosis and treatment**

● **95.0 General and subjective eye examination**

95.01 Limited eye examination
Eye examination with prescription of spectacles

95.02 Comprehensive eye examination
Eye examination covering all aspects of the visual system

95.03 Extended ophthalmologic work-up
Examination (for):
    glaucoma
    neuro-ophthalmology
    retinal disease

95.04 Eye examination under anesthesia
Code also type of examination

95.05 Visual field study

95.06 Color vision study

95.07 Dark adaptation study

95.09 Eye examination, not otherwise specified
Vision check NOS

● **95.1 Examinations of form and structure of eye**

95.11 Fundus photography

95.12 Fluorescein angiography or angioscopy of eye

95.13 Ultrasound study of eye

95.14 X-ray study of eye

95.15 Ocular motility study

95.16 P32 and other tracer studies of eye

● **95.2 Objective functional tests of eye**
| Excludes | *that with polysomnogram (89.17)* |

95.21 Electroretinogram [ERG]

95.22 Electro-oculogram [EOG]

95.23 Visual evoked potential [VEP]

95.24 Electronystagmogram [ENG]

95.25 Electromyogram of eye [EMG]

95.26 Tonography, provocative tests, and other glaucoma testing

● **95.3 Special vision services**

95.31 Fitting and dispensing of spectacles

95.32 Prescription, fitting, and dispensing of contact lens

95.33 Dispensing of other low vision aids

95.34 Ocular prosthetics

95.35 Orthoptic training

95.36 Ophthalmologic counselling and instruction
Counselling in:
    adaptation to visual loss
    use of low vision aids

● **95.4 Nonoperative procedures related to hearing**

95.41 Audiometry
Békésy 5-tone audiometry
Impedance audiometry
Stapedial reflex response
Subjective audiometry
Tympanogram

95.42 Clinical test of hearing
Tuning fork test
Whispered speech test

95.43 Audiological evaluation
Audiological evaluation by:
    Bárány noise machine
    blindfold test
    delayed feedback
    masking
    Weber lateralization

95.44 Clinical vestibular function tests
Thermal test of vestibular function

95.45 Rotation tests
Bárány chair

95.46 Other auditory and vestibular function tests

95.47 Hearing examination, not otherwise specified

95.48 Fitting of hearing aid
| Excludes | *implantation of electromagnetic hearing device (20.95)* |

95.49 Other nonoperative procedures related to hearing
Adjustment (external components) of cochlear prosthetic device

● **96 Nonoperative intubation and irrigation**

● **96.0 Nonoperative intubation of gastrointestinal and respiratory tracts**

96.01 Insertion of nasopharyngeal airway

96.02 Insertion of oropharyngeal airway

96.03 Insertion of esophageal obturator airway

96.04 Insertion of endotracheal tube

96.05 Other intubation of respiratory tract

96.06 Insertion of Sengstaken tube
Esophageal tamponade

96.07 Insertion of other (naso-)gastric tube
Intubation for decompression
| Excludes | *that for enteral infusion of nutritional substance (96.6)* |

96.08 Insertion of (naso-)intestinal tube
Miller-Abbott tube (for decompression)

96.09 Insertion of rectal tube
Replacement of rectal tube

● **96.1 Other nonoperative insertion**
| Excludes | *nasolacrimal intubation (09.44)* |

96.11 Packing of external auditory canal

96.14 Vaginal packing

96.15 Insertion of vaginal mold

96.16 Other vaginal dilation

96.17 Insertion of vaginal diaphragm

96.18 Insertion of other vaginal pessary

96.19 Rectal packing

● **96.2 Nonoperative dilation and manipulation**

96.21 Dilation of frontonasal duct

96.22 Dilation of rectum

96.23 Dilation of anal sphincter

96.24 Dilation and manipulation of enterostomy stoma

96.25 Therapeutic distention of bladder
    Intermittent distention of bladder

96.26 Manual reduction of rectal prolapse

96.27 Manual reduction of hernia

96.28 Manual reduction of enterostomy prolapse

96.29 Reduction of intussusception of alimentary tract ◄
    With: ◄
       Fluoroscopy ◄
       Ionizing radiation enema ◄
       Ultrasonography guidance ◄
    Hydrostatic reduction ◄
    Pneumatic reduction ◄

> **Excludes** *Intra-abdominal manipulation of intestine, not otherwise specified (46.80)* ◄

● **96.3 Nonoperative alimentary tract irrigation, cleaning, and local instillation**

96.31 Gastric cooling
    Gastric hypothermia

96.32 Gastric freezing

96.33 Gastric lavage

96.34 Other irrigation of (naso-)gastric tube

96.35 Gastric gavage

96.36 Irrigation of gastrostomy or enterostomy

96.37 Proctoclysis

96.38 Removal of impacted feces
    Removal of impaction:
       by flushing
       manually

96.39 Other transanal enema
    Rectal irrigation

> **Excludes** *reduction of intussusception of alimentary tract by ionizing radiation enema (96.29)* ◄

● **96.4 Nonoperative irrigation, cleaning, and local instillation of other digestive and genitourinary organs**

96.41 Irrigation of cholecystostomy and other biliary tube

96.42 Irrigation of pancreatic tube

96.43 Digestive tract instillation, except gastric gavage

96.44 Vaginal douche

96.45 Irrigation of nephrostomy and pyelostomy

96.46 Irrigation of ureterostomy and ureteral catheter

96.47 Irrigation of cystostomy

96.48 Irrigation of other indwelling urinary catheter

96.49 Other genitourinary instillation
    Insertion of prostaglandin suppository

● **96.5 Other nonoperative irrigation and cleaning**

96.51 Irrigation of eye
    Irrigation of cornea

> **Excludes** *irrigation with removal of foreign body (98.21)*

96.52 Irrigation of ear
    Irrigation with removal of cerumen

96.53 Irrigation of nasal passages

96.54 Dental scaling, polishing, and debridement
    Dental prophylaxis
    Plaque removal

96.55 Tracheostomy toilette

96.56 Other lavage of bronchus and trachea

96.57 Irrigation of vascular catheter

96.58 Irrigation of wound catheter

96.59 Other irrigation of wound
    Wound cleaning NOS

> **Excludes** *debridement (86.22, 86.27–86.28)*

96.6 Enteral infusion of concentrated nutritional substances

● **96.7   Other continuous mechanical ventilation**

> **Includes:** Endotracheal respiratory assistance
> Intermittent mandatory ventilation [IMV]
> Positive end expiratory pressure [PEEP]
> Pressure support ventilation [PSV]
> That by tracheostomy
> Weaning of an intubated (endotracheal tube)
>   patient

> **Excludes**   *bi-level airway pressure (93.90)*
> *continuous negative pressure ventilation [CNP]*
> *   (iron lung) (cuirass) (93.99)*
> *continuous positive airway pressure [CPAP]*
> *   (93.90)*
> *intermittent positive pressure breathing [IPPB]*
> *   (93.91)*
> *that by face mask (93.90–93.99)*
> *that by nasal cannula (93.90–93.99)*
> *that by nasal catheter (93.90–93.99)*

> Code also any associated:
> endotracheal tube insertion (96.04)
> tracheostomy (31.1–31.29)

> Note: Endotracheal Intubation

> To calculate the number of hours (duration) of continuous mechanical ventilation during a hospitalization, begin the count from the start of the (endotracheal) intubation. The duration ends with (endotracheal) extubation.

> If a patient is intubated prior to admission, begin counting the duration from the time of the admission. If a patient is transferred (discharged) while intubated, the duration would end at the time of transfer (discharge).

> For patients who begin on (endotracheal) intubation and subsequently have a tracheostomy performed for mechanical ventilation, the duration begins with the (endotracheal) intubation and ends when the mechanical ventilation is turned off (after the weaning period).

> Tracheostomy

> To calculate the number of hours of continuous mechanical ventilation during a hospitalization, begin counting the duration when mechanical ventilation is started. The duration ends when the mechanical ventilator is turned off (after the weaning period).

> If a patient has received a tracheostomy prior to admission and is on mechanical ventilation at the time of admission, begin counting the duration from the time of admission. If a patient is transferred (discharged) while still on mechanical ventilation via tracheostomy, the duration would end at the time of the transfer (discharge).

    96.70   Continuous mechanical ventilation of unspecified duration
       Mechanical ventilation NOS

    96.71   Continuous mechanical ventilation for less than 96 consecutive hours

    96.72   Continuous mechanical ventilation for 96 consecutive hours or more

● **97   Replacement and removal of therapeutic appliances**

   ● **97.0   Nonoperative replacement of gastrointestinal appliance**

    97.01   Replacement of (naso-)gastric or esophagostomy tube

    97.02   Replacement of gastrostomy tube

    97.03   Replacement of tube or enterostomy device of small intestine

    97.04   Replacement of tube or enterostomy device of large intestine

    97.05   Replacement of stent (tube) in biliary or pancreatic duct

   ● **97.1   Nonoperative replacement of musculoskeletal and integumentary system appliance**

    97.11   Replacement of cast on upper limb

    97.12   Replacement of cast on lower limb

    97.13   Replacement of other cast

    97.14   Replacement of other device for musculoskeletal immobilization

    97.15   Replacement of wound catheter

    97.16   Replacement of wound packing or drain

> **Excludes**   *repacking of:*
> *dental wound (97.22)*
> *vulvar wound (97.26)*

   ● **97.2   Other nonoperative replacement**

    97.21   Replacement of nasal packing

    97.22   Replacement of dental packing

    97.23   Replacement of tracheostomy tube

    97.24   Replacement and refitting of vaginal diaphragm

    97.25   Replacement of other vaginal pessary

    97.26   Replacement of vaginal or vulvar packing or drain

    97.29   Other nonoperative replacements

   ● **97.3   Nonoperative removal of therapeutic device from head and neck**

    97.31   Removal of eye prosthesis

> **Excludes**   *removal of ocular implant (16.71)*
> *removal of orbital implant (16.72)*

    97.32   Removal of nasal packing

    97.33   Removal of dental wiring

    97.34   Removal of dental packing

    97.35   Removal of dental prosthesis

    97.36   Removal of other external mandibular fixation device

    97.37   Removal of tracheostomy tube

    97.38   Removal of sutures from head and neck

    97.39   Removal of other therapeutic device from head and neck

> **Excludes**   *removal of skull tongs (02.94)*

   ● **97.4   Nonoperative removal of therapeutic device from thorax**

    97.41   Removal of thoracotomy tube or pleural cavity drain

    97.42   Removal of mediastinal drain

    97.43   Removal of sutures from thorax

    97.49   Removal of other device from thorax

   ● **97.5   Nonoperative removal of therapeutic device from digestive system**

    97.51   Removal of gastrostomy tube

97.52   **Removal of tube from small intestine**

97.53   **Removal of tube from large intestine or appendix**

97.54   **Removal of cholecystostomy tube**

97.55   **Removal of T-tube, other bile duct tube, or liver tube**

97.56   **Removal of pancreatic tube or drain**

97.59   **Removal of other device from digestive system**
Removal of rectal packing

● **97.6**   **Nonoperative removal of therapeutic device from urinary system**

97.61   **Removal of pyelostomy and nephrostomy tube**

97.62   **Removal of ureterostomy tube and ureteral catheter**

97.63   **Removal of cystostomy tube**

97.64   **Removal of other urinary drainage device**
Removal of indwelling urinary catheter

97.65   **Removal of urethral stent**

97.69   **Removal of other device from urinary system**

● **97.7**   **Nonoperative removal of therapeutic device from genital system**

97.71   **Removal of intrauterine contraceptive device**

97.72   **Removal of intrauterine pack**

97.73   **Removal of vaginal diaphragm**

97.74   **Removal of other vaginal pessary**

97.75   **Removal of vaginal or vulvar packing**

97.79   **Removal of other device from genital tract**
Removal of sutures

● **97.8**   **Other nonoperative removal of therapeutic device**

97.81   **Removal of retroperitoneal drainage device**

97.82   **Removal of peritoneal drainage device**

97.83   **Removal of abdominal wall sutures**

97.84   **Removal of sutures from trunk, not elsewhere classified**

97.85   **Removal of packing from trunk, not elsewhere classified**

97.86   **Removal of other device from abdomen**

97.87   **Removal of other device from trunk**

97.88   **Removal of external immobilization device**
Removal of:
   brace
   cast
   splint

97.89   **Removal of other therapeutic device**

● **98**   **Nonoperative removal of foreign body or calculus**

● **98.0**   **Removal of intraluminal foreign body from digestive system without incision**

> **Excludes**   *removal of therapeutic device (97.51–97.59)*

98.01   **Removal of intraluminal foreign body from mouth without incision**

98.02   **Removal of intraluminal foreign body from esophagus without incision**

98.03   **Removal of intraluminal foreign body from stomach and small intestine without incision**

98.04   **Removal of intraluminal foreign body from large intestine without incision**

98.05   **Removal of intraluminal foreign body from rectum and anus without incision**

● 98.1   **Removal of intraluminal foreign body from other sites without incision**

> **Excludes**   *removal of therapeutic device (97.31–97.49, 97.61–97.89)*

98.11   **Removal of intraluminal foreign body from ear without incision**

98.12   **Removal of intraluminal foreign body from nose without incision**

98.13   **Removal of intraluminal foreign body from pharynx without incision**

98.14   **Removal of intraluminal foreign body from larynx without incision**

98.15   **Removal of intraluminal foreign body from trachea and bronchus without incision**

98.16   **Removal of intraluminal foreign body from uterus without incision**

> **Excludes**   *removal of intrauterine contraceptive device (97.71)*

98.17   **Removal of intraluminal foreign body from vagina without incision**

98.18   **Removal of intraluminal foreign body from artificial stoma without incision**

98.19   **Removal of intraluminal foreign body from urethra without incision**

● 98.2   **Removal of other foreign body without incision**

> **Excludes**   *removal of intraluminal foreign body (98.01–98.19)*

98.20   **Removal of foreign body, not otherwise specified**

98.21   **Removal of superficial foreign body from eye without incision**

98.22   **Removal of other foreign body without incision from head and neck**
Removal of embedded foreign body from eyelid or conjunctiva without incision

98.23   **Removal of foreign body from vulva without incision**

98.24   **Removal of foreign body from scrotum or penis without incision**

98.25   **Removal of other foreign body without incision from trunk except scrotum, penis, or vulva**

98.26   **Removal of foreign body from hand without incision**

98.27   **Removal of foreign body without incision from upper limb, except hand**

98.28   **Removal of foreign body from foot without incision**

98.29   **Removal of foreign body without incision from lower limb, except foot**

● 98.5   **Extracorporeal shockwave lithotripsy [ESWL]**
Lithotriptor tank procedure
Disintegration of stones by extracorporeal induced shockwaves
That with insertion of stent

98.51   **Extracorporeal shockwave lithotripsy [ESWL] of the kidney, ureter and/or bladder**

98.52   **Extracorporeal shockwave lithotripsy [ESWL] of the gallbladder and/or bile duct**

98.59   **Extracorporeal shockwave lithotripsy of other sites**

●   **Use Additional Digit(s)**   ✖   **Valid O.R. Procedure**   ◀▶   **New Code**   ◀▬▬▶   **Revised Code**

● **99 Other nonoperative procedures**

● **99.0 Transfusion of blood and blood components**
Use additional code for that done via catheter or cut-down (38.92–38.94)

99.00 Perioperative autologous transfusion of whole blood or blood components
Intraoperative blood collection
Postoperative blood collection
Salvage

99.01 Exchange transfusion
Transfusion:
exsanguination
replacement

99.02 Transfusion of previously collected autologous blood
Blood component

99.03 Other transfusion of whole blood
Transfusion:
blood NOS
hemodilution
NOS

99.04 Transfusion of packed cells

99.05 Transfusion of platelets
Transfusion of thrombocytes

99.06 Transfusion of coagulation factors
Transfusion of antihemophilic factor

99.07 Transfusion of other serum
Transfusion of plasma
Excludes *injection [transfusion] of:*
antivenin (99.16)
gamma globulin (99.14)

99.08 Transfusion of blood expander
Transfusion of Dextran

99.09 Transfusion of other substance
Transfusion of:
blood surrogate
granulocytes
Excludes *transplantation [transfusion] of bone marrow (41.0)*

● **99.1 Injection or infusion of therapeutic or prophylactic substance**

Includes: injection or infusion given:
hypodermically acting locally or systemically
intramuscularly acting locally or systemically
intravenously acting locally or systemically

99.10 Injection or infusion of thrombolytic agent ◄
Streptokinase ◄
Tissue plasminogen activator (TPA) ◄
Urokinase ◄
Excludes *aspirin—omit code* ◄
GP IIB/IIIa platelet inhibitors (99.20) ◄
heparin (99.29) ◄
single vessel percutaneous transluminal coronary angioplasty [PTCA] or coronary atherectomy with mention of thrombolytic agent (36.02) ◄
warfarin—omit code ◄

99.11 Injection of Rh immune globulin
Injection of:
Anti-D (Rhesus) globulin
RhoGAM

99.12 Immunization for allergy
Desensitization

99.13 Immunization for autoimmune disease

99.14 Injection of gamma globulin
Injection of immune sera

99.15 Parenteral infusion of concentrated nutritional substances
Hyperalimentation
Total parenteral nutrition [TPN]
Peripheral parenteral nutrition [PPN]

99.16 Injection of antidote
Injection of:
antivenin
heavy metal antagonist

99.17 Injection of insulin

99.18 Injection or infusion of electrolytes

99.19 Injection of anticoagulant

● **99.2 Injection or infusion of other therapeutic or prophylactic substance**

Includes: injection or infusion given:
hypodermically acting locally or systemically
intramuscularly acting locally or systemically
intravenously acting locally or systemically

Use additional code for:
injection (into):
breast (85.92)
bursa (82.94, 83.96)
intraperitoneal (cavity) (54.97)
intrathecal (03.92)
joint (76.96, 81.92)
kidney (55.96)
liver (50.94)
orbit (16.91)
other sites—see Alphabetic Index
perfusion:
NOS (39.97)
intestine (46.95, 46.96)
kidney (55.95)
liver (50.93)
total body (39.96)

99.20 Injection or infusion of platelet inhibitor ◄
Glycoprotein IIB/IIIa inhibitor ◄
GP IIB/IIIa inhibitor ◄
GP IIB/IIa inhibitor ◄
Excludes *infusion of heparin (99.29)*
injection or infusion of thrombolytic agent (99.10) ◄

99.21 Injection of antibiotic

99.22 Injection of other anti-infective

99.23 Injection of steroid
Injection of cortisone
Subdermal implantation of progesterone

99.24 Injection of other hormone

99.25 Injection or infusion of cancer chemotherapeutic substance
Chemoembolization
Injection or infusion of antineoplastic agent
Excludes *immunotherapy, antineoplastic (99.28)*
injection of radioisotope (92.28)
injection or infusion of biological response modifier [BRM] as an antineoplastic agent (99.28)

99.26 Injection of tranquilizer

99.27 Iontophoresis

99.28 Injection or infusion of biological response modifier [BRM] as an antineoplastic agent
Immunotherapy, antineoplastic
Tumor vaccine ◄

  ● **Use Additional Digit(s)**   ✖ **Valid O.R. Procedure**   ◄► **New Code**   ◄▬ ▬► **Revised Code**

99.29 Injection or infusion of other therapeutic or prophylactic substance

Excludes	immunization (99.31–99.59)

          injection of sclerosing agent into:
             esophageal varices (42.33)
             hemorrhoids (49.42)
             veins (39.92)
          injection or infusion of platelet inhibitor (99.20) ◄
          injection or infusion of thrombolytic agent (99.10) ◄

● **99.3 Prophylactic vaccination and inoculation against certain bacterial diseases**

99.31 Vaccination against cholera

99.32 Vaccination against typhoid and paratyphoid fever
      Administration of TAB vaccine

99.33 Vaccination against tuberculosis
      Administration of BCG vaccine

99.34 Vaccination against plague

99.35 Vaccination against tularemia

99.36 Administration of diphtheria toxoid

Excludes	administration of:

          diphtheria antitoxin (99.58)
          diphtheria-tetanus-pertussis, combined (99.39)

99.37 Vaccination against pertussis

Excludes	administration of diphtheria-tetanus-pertussis, combined (99.39)

99.38 Administration of tetanus toxoid

Excludes	administration of:

          diphtheria-tetanus-pertussis, combined (99.39)
          tetanus antitoxin (99.56)

99.39 Administration of diphtheria-tetanus-pertussis, combined

● **99.4 Prophylactic vaccination and inoculation against certain viral diseases**

99.41 Administration of poliomyelitis vaccine

99.42 Vaccination against smallpox

99.43 Vaccination against yellow fever

99.44 Vaccination against rabies

99.45 Vaccination against measles

Excludes	administration of measles-mumps-rubella vaccine (99.48)

99.46 Vaccination against mumps

Excludes	administration of measles-mumps-rubella vaccine (99.48)

99.47 Vaccination against rubella

Excludes	administration of measles-mumps-rubella vaccine (99.48)

99.48 Administration of measles-mumps-rubella vaccine

● **99.5 Other vaccination and inoculation**

99.51 Prophylactic vaccination against the common cold

99.52 Prophylactic vaccination against influenza

99.53 Prophylactic vaccination against arthropod-borne viral encephalitis

99.54 Prophylactic vaccination against other arthropod-borne viral diseases

99.55 Prophylactic administration of vaccine against other diseases
      Vaccination against:
         anthrax
         brucellosis
         Rocky Mountain spotted fever
         Staphylococcus
         Streptococcus
         typhus

99.56 Administration of tetanus antitoxin

99.57 Administration of botulism antitoxin

99.58 Administration of other antitoxins
      Administration of:
         diphtheria antitoxin
         gas gangrene antitoxin
         scarlet fever antitoxin

99.59 Other vaccination and inoculation
      Vaccination NOS

Excludes	injection of:

          gamma globulin (99.14)
          Rh immune globulin (99.11)
       immunization for:
          allergy (99.12)
          autoimmune disease (99.13)

● **99.6 Conversion of cardiac rhythm**

Excludes	open chest cardiac:

          electric stimulation (37.91)
          massage (37.91)

99.60 Cardiopulmonary resuscitation, not otherwise specified

99.61 Atrial cardioversion

99.62 Other electric countershock of heart
      Cardioversion:
         NOS
         external
      Conversion to sinus rhythm
      Defibrillation
      External electrode stimulation

99.63 Closed chest cardiac massage
      Cardiac massage NOS
      Manual external cardiac massage

99.64 Carotid sinus stimulation

99.69 Other conversion of cardiac rhythm

● **99.7 Therapeutic apheresis**

99.71 Therapeutic plasmapheresis

99.72 Therapeutic leukopheresis
      Therapeutic leukocytapheresis

99.73 Therapeutic erythrocytapheresis
      Therapeutic erythropheresis

99.74 Therapeutic plateletpheresis

99.79 Other
      Apheresis (harvest) of stem cells

● **99.8 Miscellaneous physical procedures**

99.81 Hypothermia (central) (local)

Excludes	gastric cooling (96.31)

          gastric freezing (96.32)
          that incidental to open heart surgery (39.62)

99.82 Ultraviolet light therapy
      Actinotherapy

99.83 Other phototherapy
      Phototherapy of the newborn

Excludes	extracorporeal photochemotherapy (99.88)

          photocoagulation of retinal lesion (14.23–14.25, 14.33–14.35, 14.53–14.55)

99.84 Isolation
     Isolation after contact with infectious disease
     Protection of individual from his surroundings
     Protection of surroundings from individual

99.85 Hyperthermia for treatment of cancer
     Hyperthermia (adjunct therapy) induced by microwave, ultrasound, low energy radio frequency, probes (interstitial), or other means in the treatment of cancer

     Code also any concurrent chemotherapy or radiation therapy

99.86 Non-invasive placement of bone growth stimulator
     Transcutaneous (surface) placement of pads or patches for stimulation to aid bone healing

     Excludes   *insertion of invasive or semi-invasive bone growth stimulators (device) (percutaneous electrodes) (78.90–78.99)*

99.88 Therapeutic photopheresis
     Extracorporeal photochemotherapy
     Extracorporeal photopheresis

     Excludes   *other phototherapy (99.83)*
     ultraviolet light therapy (99.82)

● **99.9   Other miscellaneous procedures**

99.91 Acupuncture for anesthesia

99.92 Other acupuncture

     Excludes   *that with smoldering moxa (93.35)*

99.93 Rectal massage (for levator spasm)

99.94 Prostatic massage

99.95 Stretching of foreskin

99.96 Collection of sperm for artificial insemination

99.97 Fitting of denture

99.98 Extraction of milk from lactating breast

99.99 Other

HCPCS 2000: LEVEL II NATIONAL CODES

PART I

Introduction

The Health Care Financing Administration (HCFA) Common Procedure Coding System (HCPCS) is a collection of codes and descriptors that represent procedures, supplies, products, and services which may be provided to Medicare beneficiaries and to individuals enrolled in private health insurance programs. The codes are divided into three levels (or groups), as described below:

Level I - Codes and descriptors copyrighted by the American Medical Association's Current Procedural Terminology, fourth edition (CPT-4). These are 5-position numeric codes primarily representing physician services.

Level II - These are 5-position alpha-numeric codes representing primarily items and nonphysician services that are not represented in the Level I codes. Included are codes and descriptors copyrighted by the American Dental Association's Current Dental Terminology, second edition (CDT-2). These are 5-position alpha-numeric codes comprising the D series. This book does not contain codes D0100 through D9999. They can be purchased from the American Dental Association, Department of Salable Material, 211 East Chicago Avenue, Chicago, IL 60611-2678, (800) 947-4748. All other Level II codes and descriptors are approved and maintained jointly by the Alpha-Numeric Editorial Panel (consisting of HCFA, the Health Insurance Association of America, and the Blue Cross and Blue Shield Association).

Level III - Codes and descriptors developed by Medicare carriers for use at the local (carrier) level. These are 5-position alpha-numeric codes in the W, X, Y, or Z series representing physician and non-physician services that are not repre-sented in the Level I or II codes. This book does not contain Level III codes. They are available as a supplement to this book from the Health Care Financing Administration, Bureau of Data Management and Strategy, Room N3-09-16, 7500 Security Boulevard, Baltimore, MD 21244-1850, ATTN: Division of Provider Data.

Headings are provided as a means of grouping similar or closely related items. The placement of a code under a heading does not indicate additional means of classification, nor does it relate to any health insurance coverage categories.

HCPCS also contains modifiers, which are 2-position codes and descriptors used to indicate that a service or procedure that has been performed has been altered by some specific circumstance but not changed in its definition or code. Modifiers are grouped by the three levels described above. Level I modifiers and descriptors are copyrighted by the American Medical Association. Modifiers in the D series are copyrighted by the American Dental Association. This book does not contain D series modifiers. They are available directly from the American Dental Association at the address listed above. Modifiers in the WA through ZZ range are reserved for local (Level III) assignment. This book does not contain Level III modifiers. They are available from the HCFA, as described above.

HCPCS is designed to promote uniform reporting and statistical data collection of medical procedures, supplies, products, and services.

HCPCS Disclaimer

Inclusion or exclusion of a procedure, supply, product, or service does not imply any health insurance coverage or reimbursement policy.

While HCPCS makes as much use as possible of generic descriptions, the inclusion of brand names to describe devices or drugs is intended only for indexing purposes; it is not meant to convey endorsement of any particular product or drug.

Updating HCPCS

The primary updates are made annually.

Legend

✿ Special coverage instructions
◆ Not covered by or valid for Medicare
✻ Carrier discretion
◀▶ New code
◀▥▥▶ Revised code

LEVEL II NATIONAL MODIFIERS

AA	Anesthesia services performed personally by anesthesiologist
AB	(Deleted 12/31/99)
AC	(Deleted 12/31/99)
AD	Medical supervision by a physician: more than four concurrent anesthesia procedures
AE	(Deleted 12/31/99)
AF	(Deleted 12/31/99)
AG	(Deleted 12/31/99)
AH	Clinical psychologist
AJ	Clinical social worker
AK	(Deleted 12/31/98)
AL	(Deleted 12/31/98)
AM	Physician, team member service
AN	(Deleted 12/31/98)
AP	Determination of refractive state was not performed in the course of diagnostic ophthalmological examination
AS	Physician assistant, nurse practitioner, or clinical nurse specialist services for assistant at surgery
AT	Acute treatment (this modifier should be used when reporting service for chiropractic manipulation.)
AU	(Deleted 12/31/98)
AV	(Deleted 12/31/98)
AW	(Deleted 12/31/98)
AY	(Deleted 12/31/98)
BP	The beneficiary has been informed of the purchase and rental options and has elected to purchase the item
BR	The beneficiary has been informed of the purchase and rental options and has elected to rent the item
BU	The beneficiary has been informed of the purchase and rental options and after 30 days has not informed the supplier of his/her decision

CC	Procedure code change. Use CC when the procedure code submitted was changed either for administrative reasons or because an incorrect code was filed
E1	Upper left eyelid
E2	Lower left eyelid
E3	Upper right eyelid
E4	Lower right eyelid
➡ EJ	Subsequent claim for a defined course of therapy, eg, EPO, sodium
EM	Emergency reserve supply (for ESRD benefit only)
EP	Service provided as part of Medicaid early periodic screening diagnosis and treatment (EPSDT) program
ET	Emergency treatment (dental procedures performed in emergency situations should show the modifier ET)
F1	Left hand, second digit
F2	Left hand, third digit
F3	Left hand, fourth digit
F4	Left hand, fifth digit
F5	Right hand, thumb
F6	Right hand, second digit
F7	Right hand, third digit
F8	Right hand, fourth digit
F9	Right hand, fifth digit
FA	Left hand, thumb
FP	Service provided as part of Medicaid Family Planning Program
G1	Most recent URR reading of less than 60
G2	Most recent URR reading of 60 to 64.9
G3	Most recent URR reading of 65 to 69.9
G4	Most recent URR reading of 70 to 74.9
G5	Most recent URR reading of 75 or greater
G6	ESRD patient for whom less than six dialysis sessions have been provided in a month
▶ G7	Pregnancy resulted from rape or incest or pregnancy certified by physician as life threatening
▶ G8	Monitored anesthesia care (MAC) for deep complex, complicated, or markedly invasive surgical procedure
▶ G9	Monitored anesthesia care patient who has history of severe cardiopulmonary condition
GA	Waiver of liability statement on file
GC	This service has been performed in part by a resident under the direction of a teaching physician

GE   This service has been performed by a resident without the presence of a teaching physician under the primary care exception

GH   Diagnostic mammogram converted from screening mammogram on same day

GJ   "Opt out" physician or practitioner emergency or urgent service

GN   Service delivered personally by a speech-language pathologist or under an outpatient speech-language pathology plan of care

GO   Service delivered personally by an occupational therapist or under an outpatient occupational therapy plan of care

GP   Service delivered personally by a physical therapist or under an outpatient physical therapy plan of care

GT   Via interactive audio and video telecommunication systems

GX   Service not covered by Medicare

K0   Lower extremity prosthesis functional Level 0—does not have the ability or potential to ambulate or transfer safely with or without assistance and a prosthesis does not enhance their quality of life or mobility.

K1   Lower extremity prosthesis functional Level 1—has the ability or potential to use a prosthesis for transfers or ambulation on level surfaces at fixed cadence. Typical of the limited and unlimited household ambulator.

K2   Lower extremity prosthesis functional Level 2—has the ability or potential for ambulation with the ability to traverse low level environmental barriers such as curbs, stairs or uneven surfaces. Typical of the limited community ambulator.

K3   Lower extremity prosthesis functional Level 3—has the ability or potential for ambulation with variable cadence. Typical of the community ambulator who has the ability to traverse most environmental barriers and may have vocational, therapeutic, or exercise activity that demands prosthetic utilization beyond simple locomotion.

K4   Lower extremity prosthesis functional Level 4—has the ability or potential for prosthetic ambulation that exceeds the basic ambulation skills, exhibiting high impact, stress, or energy levels, typical of the prosthetic demands of the child, active adult, or athlete.

KA   Add on option/accessory for wheelchair

KH   Durable medical equipment prosthetics and orthotics supplies (DMEPOS) item, initial claim, purchase or first month rental

KI   Durable medical equipment prosthetics and orthotics supplies (DMEPOS) item, second or third month rental

KJ   Durable medical equipment prosthetics and orthotics supplies (DMEPOS) item, parenteral enteral nutrition (PEN) pump or capped rental, months four to fifteen

KK   Inhalation solution compounded from an FDA approved formulation

KL   Product characteristics defined in medical policy are met

KM   Replacement of facial prosthesis including new impression/moulage

KN   Replacement of facial prosthesis using previous master model

KO   Single drug unit dose formulation

KP   First of a multiple drug unit dose formulation

KQ   Second or subsequent drug of a multiple drug unit dose formulation

KS   Glucose monitor supply for diabetic beneficiary not treated with insulin

LC   Left circumflex coronary artery

LD   Left anterior descending coronary artery

LL   Lease/rental (use the LL modifier when DME equipment rental is to be applied against the purchase price)

LR   Laboratory round trip

LS   FDA-monitored intraocular lens implant

LT   Left side (used to identify procedures performed on the left side of the body)

MS   Six month maintenance and servicing fee for reasonable and necessary parts and labor which are not covered under any manufacturer or supplier warranty

NR   New when rented (use the 'NR' modifier when DME which was new at the time of rental is subsequently purchased)

NU   New equipment

PL   Progressive addition lenses

Q1   (Deleted 9/30/97)

Q2   HCFA/ORD demonstration project procedure/service

Q3   Live kidney donor: Services associated with postoperative medical complications directly related to the donation

Q4	Service for ordering/referring physician qualifies as a service exemption
Q5	Service furnished by a substitute physician under a reciprocal billing arrangement
Q6	Service furnished by a locum tenens physician
Q7	One Class A finding
Q8	Two Class B findings
Q9	One Class B and two Class C findings
QA	FDA investigational device exemption
QB	Physician providing service in a rural HPSA
QC	Single channel monitoring
QD	Recording and storage in solid state memory by a digital recorder
QE	Prescribed amount of oxygen is less than 1 liter per minute (LPM)
QF	Prescribed amount of oxygen exceeds 4 liters per minute (LPM) and portable oxygen is prescribed
QG	Prescribed amount of oxygen is greater than 4 liters per minute (LPM)
QH	Oxygen conserving device is being used with an oxygen delivery system
QK	Medical direction of two, three, or four concurrent anesthesia procedures involving qualified individuals
QL	Patient pronounced dead after ambulance called
QM	Ambulance service provided under arrangement by a provider of services
QN	Ambulance service furnished directly by a provider of services
QP	Documentation is on file showing that the laboratory test(s) was ordered individually or ordered as a CPT-recognized panel other than automated profile codes or G0058, G0059, and G0060.
QR	(Deleted 12/31/99)
◆ QS	Monitored anesthesia care service
QT	Recording and storage on tape by an analog tape recorder
QU	Physician providing service in an urban HPSA (health professional shortage area)
QW	CLIA waived test
QX	CRNA service: with medical direction by a physician
QY	Anesthesiologist medically directs one CRNA
QZ	CRNA service: without medical direction by a physician
RC	Right coronary artery
RP	Replacement and repair. 'RP' may be used to indicate replacement of DME, orthotic and prosthetic devices which have been in use for sometime. The claim shows the code for the part, followed by the 'RP' modifier and the charge for the part.
RR	Rental (use the 'RR' modifier when DME is to be rented)
RT	Right side (used to identify procedures performed on the right side of the body
SF	Second opinion ordered by a professional review organization (PRO) per Section 9401, P.L. 99-272 (100% reimbursement—no Medicare deductible or coinsurance)
SG	Ambulatory surgical center (ASC) facility service
T1	Left foot, second digit
T2	Left foot, third digit
T3	Left foot, fourth digit
T4	Left foot, fifth digit
T5	Right foot, great toe
T6	Right foot, second digit
T7	Right foot, third digit
T8	Right foot, fourth digit
T9	Right foot, fifth digit
TA	Left foot, great toe
TC	Technical component. Under certain circumstances, a charge may be made for the technical component alone. Under those circumstances the technical component charge is identified by adding modifier 'TC' to the usual procedure number. Technical component charges are institutional charges and not billed separately by physicians. However, portable x-ray suppliers only bill for technical component and should utilize modifier 'TC'. The charge data from portable x-ray suppliers will then be used to build customary and prevailing profiles.
UE	Used durable medical equipment
VP	Aphakic patient

Ambulance Modifiers

Modifiers that are used on claims for ambulance services are created by combining two alpha characters. Each alpha character, with the exception of X, represents an origin (source) code or a destination code. The pair of alpha codes creates one modifier. The first position alpha-code=origin; the second position alpha-code=destination. On form HCFA-1491 (which is used to report ambulance services), Item 12 should contain the origin code and Item 13 should contain the destination code.

Origin and destination codes and their descriptions are listed below:

D Diagnostic or therapeutic site other than 'P' or 'H' when these are used as origin codes

E Residential, domiciliary, custodial facility (other than an 1819 facility)

G Hospital based dialysis facility (hospital or hospital related)

H Hospital

I Site of transfer (e.g., airport or helicopter pad) between modes of ambulance transport

J Non-hospital based dialysis facility

N Skilled nursing facility (SNF) (1819 facility)

P Physician's office (includes HMO non-hospital facility, clinic, etc.)

R Residence

S Scene of accident or acute event

X (Destination code only.) Intermediate stop at physician's office enroute to the hospital (includes non-hospital facility, clinic, etc.)

PET Scan Code Modifiers

Modifiers that are used on claims for PET myocardial perfusion imaging are created by combining two alpha characters. Each alpha character represents the results of the PET scan and the previous test, with the first letter indicating the results of the PET scan, while the second letter indicates the results of the test done prior to the PET scan.

The test result codes and their descriptions are listed below:

Code

N Negative

E Equivocal

P Positive, but not suggestive of extensive ischemia

S Positive and suggestive of extensive ischemia (greater than 20% of the left ventricle)

TRANSPORT SERVICES INCLUDING AMBULANCE A0000-A0999

◆ A0021 Ambulance service, outside state per mile, transport (Medicaid only)
Cross Reference A0030

✺ A0030 Ambulance service, conventional air service, transport, one way
MCM 2120.4

✺ A0040 Ambulance service, air, helicopter service, transport
MCM 2120.4

✺ A0050 Ambulance service, emergency, water, special transportation services
MCM 2120.1, MCM 2125

◆ A0080 Non-emergency transportation: per mile—volunteer, with no vested or personal interest

◆ A0090 Non-emergency transportation, per mile, volunteer, interested individual, neighbor

◆ A0100 Non-emergency transportation: taxi—intra city

◆ A0110 Non-emergency transportation and bus, intra or inter state carrier

◆ A0120 Non-emergency transportation: mini-bus, mountain area transports, other non-profit transportation systems

◆ A0130 Non-emergency transportation: wheel-chair van

◆ A0140 Non-emergency transportation and air travel (private or commercial), intra or inter state

◆ A0160 Non-emergency transportation: per mile—caseworker or social worker

◆ A0170 Non-emergency transportation: ancillary: parking fees, tolls, other

◆ A0180 Non-emergency transportation: ancillary: lodging—recipient

◆ A0190 Non-emergency transportation: ancillary: meals—recipient

◆ A0210 Non-emergency transportation: ancillary: meals—escort

✳ A0225 Ambulance service, neonatal transport, base rate, emergency transport, one way

✳ A0300 Ambulance service, basic life support (BLS), non-emergency transport, all inclusive (mileage and supplies)

✳ A0302 Ambulance service, BLS, emergency transport, all inclusive (mileage and supplies)

✳ A0304 Ambulance service, advanced life support (ALS), non-emergency transport, no specialized ALS services rendered, all inclusive (mileage and supplies)

✳ A0306 Ambulance services, ALS, non-emergency transport, specialized ALS services rendered, all inclusive (mileage and supplies)

✳ A0308 Ambulance service, ALS, emergency transport, no specialized ALS services rendered, all inclusive (mileage and supplies)

✳ A0310 Ambulance service, ALS, emergency transport, specialized ALS services rendered, all inclusive (mileage and supplies)

✳ A0320 Ambulance service, BLS, non-emergency transport, supplies included, mileage separately billed

✳ A0322 Ambulance service, BLS, emergency transport, supplies included, mileage separately billed

* A0324   Ambulance service, ALS, non-emergency transport, no specialized ALS services rendered, supplies included, mileage separately billed

* A0326   Ambulance service, ALS, non-emergency transport, specialized ALS services rendered, supplies included, mileage separately billed

* A0328   Ambulance service, ALS, emergency transport, no specialized ALS services rendered, supplies included, mileage separately billed

* A0330   Ambulance service, ALS, emergency transport, specialized ALS services rendered, supplies included, mileage separately billed

* A0340   Ambulance service, BLS, non-emergency transport, mileage included, disposable supplies separately billed

* A0342   Ambulance service, BLS, emergency transport, mileage included, disposable supplies separately billed

* A0344   Ambulance service, ALS, non-emergency transport, no specialized ALS services rendered, mileage included, disposable supplies separately billed

* A0346   Ambulance service, ALS, non-emergency transport, specialized ALS services rendered, mileage included, disposable supplies separately billed

* A0348   Ambulance service, ALS, emergency transport, no specialized ALS services rendered, mileage included, disposable supplies separately billed

* A0350   Ambulance service, ALS, emergency transport, specialized ALS services rendered, mileage included, disposable supplies separately billed

* A0360   Ambulance service, BLS, non-emergency transport, mileage and disposable supplies separately billed

* A0362   Ambulance service, BLS, emergency transport, mileage and disposable supplies separately billed

* A0364   Ambulance service, ALS, non-emergency transport, no specialized ALS services rendered, mileage and disposable supplies separately billed

* A0366   Ambulance service, ALS, non-emergency transport, specialized ALS services rendered, mileage and disposable supplies separately billed

* A0368   Ambulance service, ALS, emergency transport, no specialized ALS services rendered, mileage and disposable supplies separately billed

* A0370   Ambulance service, ALS, emergency transport, specialized ALS services rendered, mileage and disposable supplies separately billed

* A0380   BLS mileage (per mile)

* A0382   BLS routine disposable supplies

* A0384   BLS specialized service disposable supplies; defibrillation (used by ALS ambulances and BLS ambulances in jurisdictions where defibrillation is permitted in BLS ambulances)

* A0390   ALS mileage (per mile)

* A0392   ALS specialized service disposable supplies; defibrillation (to be used only in jurisdictions where defibrillation cannot be performed in BLS ambulances)

* A0394   ALS specialized service disposable supplies; IV drug therapy

* A0396   ALS specialized service disposable supplies; esophageal intubation

* A0398   ALS routine disposable supplies

* A0420   Ambulance waiting time (ALS or BLS), one half (½) hour increments

Waiting Time Table

Units	Time	Units	Time
1	½ to 1 hrs.	6	3 to 3½ hrs.
2	1 to 1½ hrs.	7	3½ to 4 hrs.
3	1½ to 2 hrs	8	4 to 4½ hrs.
4	2 to 2½ hrs.	9	4½ to 5 hrs.
5	2½ to 3 hrs.	10	5 to 5½ hrs.

* A0422   Ambulance (ALS or BLS) oxygen and oxygen supplies, life sustaining situation

* A0424   Extra ambulance attendant, ALS or BLS (requires medical review)

◆ A0888   Noncovered ambulance mileage, per mile (e.g., for miles traveled beyond closest appropriate facility) MCM 2125

✪ A0999   Unlisted ambulance service MCM 2120.1, MCM 2125

CHIROPRACTIC A2000-A2999

A2000   (Deleted 12/31/97, Cross Reference CPT)

MEDICAL AND SURGICAL SUPPLIES A4000-A8999

⇒ ◆ A4206   Syringe with needle, sterile 1 cc, each

⇒ ◆ A4207   Syringe with needle, sterile 2 cc, each

⇒ ◆ A4208   Syringe with needle, sterile 3 cc, each

⇒◆ A4209   Syringe with needle, sterile 5 cc or greater, each
◆ A4210   Needle-free injection device, each
CIM 60-9
✪ A4211   Supplies for self-administered injections
MCM 2049
✳ A4212   Non-coring needle or stylet with or without catheter
⇒◆ A4213   Syringe, sterile, 20 cc or greater, each
✳ A4214   Sterile saline or water, 30 cc vial
⇒◆ A4215   Needles only, sterile, any size, each
✪ A4220   Refill kit for implantable infusion pump
CIM 60-14
✳ A4221   Supplies for maintenance of drug infusion catheter, per week (list drug separately)
✳ A4222   Supplies for external drug infusion pump, per cassette or bag (list drug separately)
⇒✪ A4230   Infusion set for external insulin pump, non-needle cannula type
CIM 60-14
⇒✪ A4231   Infusion set for external insulin pump, needle type
CIM 60-14
⇒✪ A4232   Syringe with needle for external insulin pump, sterile, 3 cc
CIM 60-14
⇒◆ A4244   Alcohol or peroxide, per pint
⇒◆ A4245   Alcohol wipes, per box
⇒◆ A4246   Betadine or pHisoHex solution, per pint
⇒◆ A4247   Betadine or iodine swabs/wipes, per box
◆ A4250   Urine test or reagent strips or tablets (100 tablets or strips)
MCM 2100
✪ A4253   Blood glucose test or reagent strips for home blood glucose monitor, per 50 strips
CIM 60-11
✪ A4254   Replacement battery, any type, for use with medically necessary home blood glucose monitor owned by patient, each
CIM 60-11
◆ A4245   Alcohol wipes, per box
✳ A4256   Normal, low and high calibrator solution/chips
✳ A4258   Spring-powered device for lancet, each
✪ A4259   Lancets, per box of 100
CIM 60-11
◆ A4260   Levonorgestrel (contraceptive) implants system, including implants and supplies
Medicare Statute 1862a 1

◆ A4261   Cervical cap for contraceptive use
Medicare Statute 1862a 1
✪ A4262   Temporary, absorbable lacrimal duct implant, each
✪ A4263   Permanent, long-term, non-dissolvable lacrimal duct implant, each
MCM 15030
✳ A4265   Paraffin, per pound
✳ A4270   Disposable endoscope sheath, each
▶✳ A4280   Adhesive skin support attachment for use with external breast prosthesis, each

Vascular Catheters

✪ A4300   Implantable access catheter (venous, arterial, epidural or peritoneal), external access
MCM 2130
✳ A4301   Implantable access total system; catheter, port/reservoir (venous, arterial or epidural), percutaneous access
✳ A4305   Disposable drug delivery system, flow rate of 50 ml or greater per hour
✳ A4306   Disposable drug delivery system, flow rate of 5 ml or less per hour

Incontinence Appliances and Care Supplies

✪ A4310   Insertion tray without drainage bag and without catheter (accessories only)
MCM 2130
✪ A4311   Insertion tray without drainage bag with indwelling catheter, Foley type, two-way latex with coating (Teflon, silicone, silicone elastomer or hydrophilic, etc.)
MCM 2130
✪ A4312   Insertion tray without drainage bag with indwelling catheter, Foley type, two-way, all silicone
MCM 2130
✪ A4313   Insertion tray without drainage bag with indwelling catheter, Foley type, three-way, for continuous irrigation
MCM 2130
✪ A4314   Insertion tray with drainage bag with indwelling catheter, Foley type, two-way latex with coating (Teflon, silicone, silicone elastomer or hydrophilic, etc.)
MCM 2130
✪ A4315   Insertion tray with drainage bag with indwelling catheter, Foley type, two-way, all silicone
MCM 2130

✹ A4316   Insertion tray with drainage bag with indwelling catheter, Foley type, three-way, for continuous irrigation
MCM 2130

✹ A4320   Irrigation tray with bulb or piston syringe, any purpose
MCM 2130

∗ A4321   Therapeutic agent for urinary catheter irrigation

✹ A4322   Irrigation syringe, bulb or piston, each
MCM 2130

✹ A4323   Sterile saline irrigation solution, 1000 ml
MCM 2130

✹ A4326   Male external catheter specialty type, e.g., inflatable, faceplate, etc., each
MCM 2130

✹ A4327   Female external urinary collection device; metal cup, each
MCM 2130

✹ A4328   Female external urinary collection device; pouch, each
MCM 2130

✹ A4329   External catheter starter set, male/female, includes catheters/urinary collection device, bag/pouch and accessories (tubing, clamps, etc.), 7-day supply
MCM 2130

✹ A4330   Perianal fecal collection pouch with adhesive, each
MCM 2130

✹ A4335   Incontinence supply; miscellaneous
MCM 2130

✹ A4338   Indwelling catheter; Foley type, two-way latex with coating (Teflon, silicone, silicone elastomer, or hydrophilic, etc.), each
MCM 2130

✹ A4340   Indwelling catheter; specialty type, e.g., coudé, mushroom, wing, etc.), each
MCM 2130A

✹ A4344   Indwelling catheter, Foley type, two-way, all silicone, each
MCM 2130A

✹ A4346   Indwelling catheter; Foley type, three-way for continuous irrigation, each
MCM 2130

✹ A4347   Male external catheter with or without adhesive, with or without anti-reflux device; per dozen
MCM 2130

✹ A4351   Intermittent urinary catheter; straight tip, each
MCM 2130

✹ A4352   Intermittent urinary catheter; coudé (curved) tip, each
MCM 2130

∗ A4353   Intermittent urinary catheter, with insertion supplies

✹ A4354   Insertion tray with drainage bag but without catheter
MCM 2130

✹ A4355   Irrigation tubing set for continuous bladder irrigation through a three-way indwelling Foley catheter, each
MCM 2130

External Urinary Supplies

✹ A4356   External urethral clamp or compression device (not to be used for catheter clamp), each
MCM 2130

✹ A4357   Bedside drainage bag, day or night, with or without anti-reflux device, with or without tube, each
MCM 2130

✹ A4358   Urinary leg bag; vinyl, with or without tube, each
MCM 2130

✹ A4359   Urinary suspensory without leg bag, each
MCM 2130

Ostomy Supplies

✹ A4361   Ostomy faceplate, each
MCM 2130A

✹ A4362   Skin barrier; solid, 4 × 4 or equivalent; each
MCM 2130

  A4363   (Deleted 12/31/99)

✹ A4364   Adhesive for ostomy or catheter; liquid (spray, brush, etc.), cement, powder or paste; any composition (e.g., silicone, latex, etc.); per oz
MCM 2130

∗ A4365   Ostomy adhesive remover wipes, 50 per box

✹ A4367   Ostomy belt, each
MCM 2130A

∗ A4368   Ostomy filter, any type, each

▶∗ A4369   Ostomy skin barrier, liquid (spray, brush, etc.), per oz

▶∗ A4370   Ostomy skin barrier, paste, per oz

▶∗ A4371   Ostomy skin barrier, powder, per oz

▶∗ A4372   Ostomy skin barrier, solid 4 × 4 or equivalent, standard wear, with built-in convexity, each

▶∗ A4373   Ostomy skin barrier, with flange (solid, flexible, or accordion), standard wear, with built-in convexity, any size, each

---

▶∗ A4374 Ostomy skin barrier, with flange (solid, flexible, or accordion), extended wear, with built-in convexity, any size, each

▶∗ A4375 Ostomy pouch, drainable, with faceplate attached, plastic, each

▶∗ A4376 Ostomy pouch, drainable, with faceplate attached, rubber, each

▶∗ A4377 Ostomy pouch, drainable, for use on faceplate, plastic, each

▶∗ A4378 Ostomy pouch, drainable, for use on faceplate, rubber, each

▶∗ A4379 Ostomy pouch, urinary, with faceplate attached, plastic, each

▶∗ A4380 Ostomy pouch, urinary, with faceplate attached, rubber, each

▶∗ A4381 Ostomy pouch, urinary, with faceplate attached, rubber, each

▶∗ A4382 Ostomy pouch, urinary, for use on faceplate, heavy plastic, each

▶∗ A4383 Ostomy pouch, urinary, for use on faceplate, rubber, each

▶∗ A4384 Ostomy faceplate equivalent, silicone ring, each

▶∗ A4385 Ostomy skin barrier, solid 4 × 4 or equivalent, extended wear, without built-in convexity, each

▶∗ A4386 Ostomy skin barrier, with flange (solid, flexible, or accordion), extended wear, without built-in convexity, any size, each

▶∗ A4387 Ostomy pouch closed, with standard wear barrier attached, with built-in convexity (1 piece), each

▶∗ A4388 Ostomy pouch, drainable, with extended wear barrier attached, without built-in convexity (1 piece), each

▶∗ A4389 Ostomy pouch, drainable, with standard wear barrier attached, with built-in convexity (1 piece), each

▶∗ A4390 Ostomy pouch, drainable, with extended wear barrier attached, with built-in convexity (1 piece), each

▶∗ A4391 Ostomy pouch, urinary, with extended wear barrier attached, without built-in convexity (1 piece), each

▶∗ A4392 Ostomy pouch, urinary, with standard wear barrier attached, with built-in convexity (1 piece), each

▶∗ A4393 Ostomy pouch, urinary, with extended wear barrier attached, with built-in convexity (1 piece), each

▶∗ A4394 Ostomy deodorant for use in ostomy pouch, liquid, per fluid ounce

▶∗ A4395 Ostomy deodorant for use in ostomy pouch, solid, per tablet

✪ A4397 Irrigation supply; sleeve, each
MCM 2130

✪ A4398 Ostomy irrigation supply; bag, each
MCM 2130A

✪ A4399 Ostomy irrigation supply; cone/catheter, including brush
MCM 2130A

✪ A4400 Ostomy irrigation set
MCM 2130

✪ A4402 Lubricant, per ounce
MCM 2130

✪ A4404 Ostomy ring, each
MCM 2130

✪ A4421 Ostomy supply; miscellaneous
MCM 2130

Miscellaneous Supplies

✪ A4454 Tape, all types, all sizes
MCM 2130

✪ A4455 Adhesive remover or solvent (for tape, cement or other adhesive), per ounce
MCM 2130

✪ A4460 Elastic bandage, per roll (e.g., compression bandage)
MCM 2079

∗ A4462 Abdominal dressing holder/binder, each

∗ A4465 Non-elastic binder for extremity

✪ A4470 Gravlee jet washer
CIM 50-4

✪ A4480 VABRA aspirator
CIM 50-10

∗ A4481 Tracheostoma filter, any type, any size, each

∗ A4483 Moisture exchanger, disposable, for use with invasive mechanical ventilation

◆ A4490 Surgical stockings above knee length, each
MCM 2079, MCM 2133, CIM 60-9

◆ A4495 Surgical stockings thigh length, each
MCM 2079, MCM 2133, CIM 60-9

◆ A4500 Surgical stockings below knee length, each
MCM 2079, MCM 2133, CIM 60-9

◆ A4510 Surgical stockings full length, each
MCM 2079, MCM 2133, CIM 60-9

⟾✪ A4550 Surgical trays
MCM 15030

◆ A4554 Disposable underpads, all sizes, (e.g., Chux's)
MCM 2130, CIM 60-9

⟾∗ A4556 Electrodes, (e.g., apnea monitor), per pair

⟾∗ A4557 Lead wires, (e.g., apnea monitor), per pair

∗ A4558 Conductive paste or gel

∗ A4560 Pessary

∗ A4565 Slings

✪ A4570 Splint
MCM 2079

∗ A4572 Rib belt

✪ **Special coverage instructions**   ◆ **Not covered by or valid for Medicare**   ∗ **Carrier discretion**   ◀▶ **New code**   ⟸⟾ **Revised code**

◆ A4575   Topical hyperbaric oxygen chamber, disposable
CIM 35-10

✪ A4580   Cast supplies (e.g., plaster)
MCM 2079

✱ A4590   Special casting material (e.g., fiberglass)

✱ A4595   TENS supplies, 2 lead, per month

Supplies for Respiratory and Oxygen Equipment

✱ A4611   Battery, heavy duty; replacement for patient-owned ventilator

✱ A4612   Battery cables; replacement for patient-owned ventilator

✱ A4613   Battery charger; replacement for patient-owned ventilator

✱ A4614   Peak expiratory flow rate meter, hand held

✪ A4615   Cannula, nasal
MCM 3312, CIM 60-4

✪ A4616   Tubing (oxygen), per foot
MCM 3312, CIM 60-4

✪ A4617   Mouth piece
MCM 3312, CIM 60-4

✪ A4618   Breathing circuits
MCM 3312, CIM 60-4

✪ A4619   Face tent
MCM 3312, CIM 60-4

✪ A4620   Variable concentration mask
MCM 3312, CIM 60-4

✱ A4621   Tracheotomy mask or collar

✪ A4622   Tracheostomy or laryngectomy tube
CIM 65-16

✪ A4623   Tracheostomy, inner cannula (replacement only)
CIM 65-16

✱ A4624   Tracheal suction catheter, any type, each

✱ A4625   Tracheostomy care kit for new tracheostomy

✱ A4626   Tracheostomy cleaning brush, each

◆ A4627   Spacer, bag or reservoir, with or without mask, for use with metered dose inhaler
MCM 2100

✱ A4628   Oropharyngeal suction catheter, each

✱ A4629   Tracheostomy care kit for established tracheostomy

Supplies for Other Durable Medical Equipment

✪ A4630   Replacement batteries. Medically necessary TENS owned by patient
CIM 65-8

✪ A4631   Replacement batteries for medically necessary electronic wheelchair owned by patient
CIM 60-9

✪ A4635   Underarm pad, crutch, replacement, each
CIM 60-9

✪ A4636   Replacement, handgrip, cane, crutch, or walker, each
CIM 60-9

✪ A4637   Replacement, tip, cane, crutch, walker, each
CIM 60-9

✪ A4640   Replacement pad for use with medically necessary alternating pressure pad owned by patient
MCM 4107.6, CIM 60-9

Supplies for Radiological Procedures

✱ A4641   Supply of radiopharmaceutical diagnostic imaging agent, not otherwise classified
MCM 15030

✱ A4642   Supply of satumomab pendetide, radiopharmaceutical diagnostic imaging agent, per dose
MCM 15030

✱ A4643   Supply of additional high dose contrast material(s) during magnetic resonance imaging, e.g., gadoteridol injection
MCM 15030

✪ A4644   Supply of low osmolar contrast material (100–199 mg of iodine)
MCM 15022, MCM 15030

✪ A4645   Supply of low osmolar contrast material (200–299 mg of iodine)
MCM 15022, MCM 15030

✪ A4646   Supply of low osmolar contrast material (300–399 mg of iodine)
MCM 15022, MCM 15030

✪ A4647   Supply of paramagnetic contrast material, e.g., gadolinium
MCM 15022, MCM 15030

✱ A4649   Surgical supply, miscellaneous

Supplies for ESRD

Note: For DME items for ESRD see procedures codes E1510–E1699. For dialysis procedures, see M0900–M0999.

✪ A4650   Centrifuge (includes calibrated microcapillary tubes and sealease)

✪ A4655   Needles and syringes for dialysis

✪ A4660   Sphygmomanometer/blood pressure apparatus with cuff and stethoscope

✪ A4663   Blood pressure cuff only

◆ A4670   Automatic blood pressure monitor
CIM 50-42

⊕ A4680   Activated carbon filters for dialysis
CIM 55-1
⊕ A4690   Dialyzers (artificial kidneys) all brands, all sizes per unit
⊕ A4700   Standard dialysate solution, each
⊕ A4705   Bicarbonate dialysate solution, each
⊕ A4712   Water, sterile
⊕ A4714   Treated water (deionized, distilled, reverse osmosis) for use in dialysis system
CIM 55-1
⊕ A4730   Fistula cannulation set for dialysis only
⊕ A4735   Local/topical anesthetics for dialysis only
⊕ A4740   Shunt accessories for dialysis only
⊕ A4750   Blood tubing, arterial or venous, each
⊕ A4755   Blood tubing, arterial and venous combined
⊕ A4760   Dialysate standard testing solution, supplies
⊕ A4765   Dialysate concentrate additives, each
⊕ A4770   Blood testing supplies (e.g., vacutainers and tubes)
⊕ A4771   Serum clotting time tube, per box
⊕ A4772   Dextrostick or glucose test strips, per box
⊕ A4773   Hemostix, per bottle
⊕ A4774   Ammonia test paper, per box
⊕ A4780   Sterilizing agent for dialysis equipment, per gallon
⊕ A4790   Cleansing agents for equipment for dialysis only
⊕ A4800   Heparin for dialysis and antidote, any strength, porcine or beef, up to 1000 units, 10–30 ml (for parenteral use see B4216)
⊕ A4820   Hemodialysis kit supplies
⊕ A4850   Hemostats with rubber tips for dialysis
⊕ A4860   Disposable catheter caps
⊕ A4870   Plumbing and/or electrical work for home dialysis equipment (Medicaid suspend for medical review)
⊕ A4880   Storage tanks utilized in connection with water purification system, replacement tanks for dialysis
CIM 55-1
⊕ A4890   Contracts, repair and maintenance, for home dialysis equipment (non-covered)
MCM 2100.4
⊕ A4900   Continuous ambulatory peritoneal dialysis (CAPD) supply kit
⊕ A4901   Continuous cycling peritoneal dialysis (CCPD) supply kit
⊕ A4905   Intermittent peritoneal dialysis (IPD) supply kit

⊕ A4910   Non-medical supplies for dialysis (i.e., scale, scissors, stopwatch, etc.)

Note: The above procedures (A4910) 'Non-medical supplies' includes the following: scale, scissors, stopwatch, surgical brush, thermometer, tool kit, tourniquet, and tube occluding forceps/clamps.
⊕ A4912   Gomco drain bottle
⊕ A4913   Miscellaneous dialysis supplies, not identified elsewhere, by report
⊕ A4914   Preparation kits
⊕ A4918   Venous pressure clamps, each
⊕ A4919   Dialyzer holder, each
⊕ A4920   Harvard pressure clamp, each
⊕ A4921   Measuring cylinder, any size, each
⊕ A4927   Gloves, sterile or non-sterile, per pair

Additional Ostomy Supplies

⊕ A5051   Pouch, closed; with barrier attached (1 piece)
MCM 2130
⊕ A5052   Pouch, closed; without barrier attached (1 piece)
MCM 2130
⊕ A5053   Pouch, closed; for use on faceplate
MCM 2130
⊕ A5054   Pouch, closed; for use on barrier with flange (2 piece)
MCM 2130
⊕ A5055   Stoma cap
MCM 2130
⊕ A5061   Pouch, drainable; with barrier attached (1 piece)
MCM 2130
⊕ A5062   Pouch, drainable; without barrier attached (1 piece)
MCM 2130
⊕ A5063   Pouch, drainable; for use on barrier with flange (2 piece system)
MCM 2130
◆ A5064   Pouch, drainable, with faceplate attached; plastic or rubber
MCM 2130
◆ A5065   Pouch, drainable, for use on faceplate; plastic or rubber
MCM 2130
⊕ A5071   Pouch, urinary; with barrier attached (1 piece)
MCM 2130
⊕ A5072   Pouch, urinary; without barrier attached (1 piece)
MCM 2130
⊕ A5073   Pouch, urinary; for use on barrier with flange (2 piece)
MCM 2130

◆ A5074   Pouch, urinary, with faceplate attached; plastic or rubber
MCM 2130

◆ A5075   Pouch, urinary, for use on faceplate; plastic or rubber
MCM 2130

✪ A5081   Continent device; plug for continent stoma
MCM 2130

✪ A5082   Continent device; catheter for continent stoma
MCM 2130

✪ A5093   Ostomy accessory; convex insert
MCM 2130

Additional Incontinence Appliances/Supplies

✪ A5102   Bedside drainage bottle with or without tubing, rigid or expandable, each
MCM 2130

✪ A5105   Urinary suspensory; with leg bag, with or without tube
MCM 2130

✪ A5112   Urinary leg bag; latex
MCM 2130

✪ A5113   Leg strap; latex, per set
MCM 2130

✪ A5114   Leg strap; foam or fabric, per set
MCM 2130

Supplies for Either Incontinence or Ostomy Appliances

✪ A5119   Skin barrier; wipes, box per 50
MCM 2130

✪ A5121   Skin barrier; solid, 6 × 6 or equivalent, each
MCM 2130

✪ A5122   Skin barrier; solid, 8 × 8 or equivalent, each
MCM 2130

✪ A5123   Skin barrier; with flange (solid, flexible or accordion), any size, each
MCM 2130

➠ ✪ A5126   Adhesive or non-adhesive; disc or foam pad
MCM 2130

✪ A5131   Appliance cleaner, incontinence and ostomy appliances, per 16 oz
MCM 2130

✪ A5149   Incontinence/ostomy supply; miscellaneous
MCM 2130

✳ A5200   Percutaneous catheter/tube anchoring device, adhesive skin attachment

Diabetic Shoes, Fitting and Modifications

✪ A5500   For diabetics only, fitting (including follow-up), custom preparation and supply of off-the-shelf depth-inlay shoe manufactured to accommodate multi-density insert(s), per shoe
MCM 2134

✪ A5501   For diabetics only, fitting (including follow-up), custom preparation and supply of shoe molded from cast(s) of patient's foot (custom molded shoe), per shoe
MCM 2134

✪ A5502   For diabetics only, multiple density insert(s), per shoe
MCM 2134

✪ A5503   For diabetics only, modification (including fitting) of off-the-shelf depth-inlay shoe or custom-molded shoe with roller or rigid rocker bottom, per shoe
MCM 2134

✪ A5504   For diabetics only, modification (including fitting) of off-the-shelf depth-inlay shoe or custom-molded shoe with wedge(s), per shoe
MCM 2134

✪ A5505   For diabetics only, modification (including fitting) of off-the-shelf depth-inlay shoe or custom-molded shoe with metatarsal bar, per shoe
MCM 2134

✪ A5506   For diabetics only, modification (including fitting) of off-the-shelf depth-inlay shoe or custom-molded shoe with off-set heel(s), per shoe
MCM 2134

✪ A5507   For diabetics only, not otherwise specified modification (including fitting) of off-the-shelf depth-inlay shoe or custom-molded shoe, per shoe
MCM 2134

▶✳ A5508   For diabetics only, deluxe feature of off-the-shelf depth-inlay shoe or custom-molded shoe, per shoe

Dressings

✳ A6020   Collagen based wound dressing, each dressing

◆ A6025   Silicone gel sheet, each

✳ A6154   Wound pouch, each

✳ A6196   Alginate dressing, wound cover, pad size 16 sq in or less, each dressing

✳ A6197   Alginate dressing, wound cover, pad size more than 16 sq in but less than or equal to 48 sq in, each dressing

* A6198 Alginate dressing, wound cover, pad size more than 48 sq in, each dressing

* A6199 Alginate dressing, wound filler, per 6 inches

* A6200 Composite dressing, pad size 16 sq in or less, without adhesive border, each dressing

* A6201 Composite dressing, pad size more than 16 sq in but less than or equal to 48 sq in, without adhesive border, each dressing

* A6202 Composite dressing, pad size more than 48 sq in, without adhesive border, each dressing

* A6203 Composite dressing, pad size 16 sq in or less, with any size adhesive border, each dressing

* A6204 Composite dressing, pad size more than 16 sq in but less than or equal to 48 in, with any size adhesive border, each dressing

* A6205 Composite dressing, pad size more than 48 sq in, with any size adhesive, each dressing

* A6206 Contact layer, 16 sq in or less, each dressing

* A6207 Contact layer, more than 16 sq in but less than or equal to 48 sq in, each dressing

* A6208 Contact layer, more than 48 sq in, each dressing

* A6209 Foam dressing, wound cover, pad size 16 sq in or less, without adhesive border, each dressing

* A6210 Foam dressing, wound cover, pad size more than 16 sq in but less than or equal to 48 sq in, without adhesive border, each dressing

* A6211 Foam dressing, wound cover, pad size more than 48 sq in, without adhesive border, each dressing

* A6212 Foam dressing, wound cover, pad size 16 sq in or less, with any size adhesive border, each dressing

* A6213 Foam dressing, wound cover, pad size more than 16 sq in but less than or equal to 48 sq in, with any size adhesive border, each dressing

* A6214 Foam dressing, wound cover, pad size more than 48 sq in, with any size adhesive border, each dressing

* A6215 Foam dressing, wound filler, per gram

* A6216 Gauze, non-impregnated, non-sterile, pad size 16 sq in or less, without adhesive border, each dressing

* A6217 Gauze, non-impregnated, non-sterile, pad size more than 16 sq in but less than or equal to 48 sq in, without adhesive border, each dressing

* A6218 Gauze, non-impregnated, non-sterile, pad size more than 48 sq in, without adhesive border, each dressing

* A6219 Gauze, non-impregnated, pad size 16 sq in or less, with any size adhesive border, each dressing

* A6220 Gauze, non-impregnated, pad size more than 16 sq in but less than or equal to 48 sq in, with any size adhesive border, each dressing

* A6221 Gauze, non-impregnated, pad size more than 48 sq in, with any size adhesive border, each dressing

* A6222 Gauze, impregnated, other than water or normal saline, pad size 16 sq in or less, without adhesive border, each dressing

* A6223 Gauze, impregnated, other than water or normal saline, pad size more than 16 sq in but less than or equal to 48 sq in, without adhesive border, each dressing

* A6224 Gauze, impregnated, other than water or normal saline, pad size more than 48 sq in, without adhesive border, each dressing

* A6228 Gauze, impregnated, water or normal saline, pad size 16 sq in or less, without adhesive border, each dressing

* A6229 Gauze, impregnated, water or normal saline, pad size more than 16 sq in but less than or equal to 48 sq in, without adhesive border, each dressing

* A6230 Gauze, impregnated, water or normal saline, pad size more than 48 sq in, without adhesive border, each dressing

* A6234 Hydrocolloid dressing, wound cover, pad size 16 sq in or less, without adhesive border, each dressing

* A6235 Hydrocolloid dressing, wound cover, pad size more than 16 sq in but less than or equal to 48 sq in, without adhesive border, each dressing

* A6236 Hydrocolloid dressing, wound cover, pad size more than 48 sq in, without adhesive border, each dressing

* A6237 Hydrocolloid dressing, wound cover, pad size 16 sq in or less, with any size adhesive border, each dressing

* A6238 Hydrocolloid dressing, wound cover, pad size more than 16 sq in but less than or equal to 48 sq in, with any size adhesive border, each dressing

* A6239 Hydrocolloid dressing, wound cover, pad size more than 48 sq in, with any size adhesive border, each dressing
* A6240 Hydrocolloid dressing, wound filler, paste, per fluid ounce
* A6241 Hydrocolloid dressing, wound filler, dry form, per gram
* A6242 Hydrogel dressing, wound cover, pad size 16 sq in or less, without adhesive border, each dressing
* A6243 Hydrogel dressing, wound cover, pad size more than 16 sq in but less than or equal to 48 sq in, without adhesive border, each dressing
* A6244 Hydrogel dressing, wound cover, pad size more than 48 sq in, without adhesive border, each dressing
* A6245 Hydrogel dressing, wound cover, pad size 16 sq in or less, with any size adhesive border, each dressing
* A6246 Hydrogel dressing, wound cover, pad size more than 16 sq in but less than or equal to 48 sq in, with any size adhesive border, each dressing
* A6247 Hydrogel dressing, wound cover, pad size more than 48 sq in, with any size adhesive border, each dressing
* A6248 Hydrogel dressing, wound filler, gel, per fluid ounce
* A6250 Skin sealants, protectants, moisturizers, ointments, any type, any size
* A6251 Specialty absorptive dressing, wound cover, pad size 16 sq in or less, without adhesive border, each dressing
* A6252 Specialty absorptive dressing, wound cover, pad size more than 16 sq in but less than or equal to 48 sq in, without adhesive border, each dressing
* A6253 Specialty absorptive dressing, wound cover, pad size more than 48 sq in, without adhesive border, each dressing
* A6254 Specialty absorptive dressing, wound cover, pad size 16 sq in or less, with any size adhesive border, each dressing
* A6255 Specialty absorptive dressing, wound cover, pad size more than 16 sq in but less than or equal to 48 sq in, with any size adhesive border, each dressing
* A6256 Specialty absorptive dressing, wound cover, pad size more than 48 sq in, with any size adhesive border, each dressing
* A6257 Transparent film, 16 sq in or less, each dressing

* A6258 Transparent film, more than 16 sq in but less than or equal to 48 sq in, each dressing
* A6259 Transparent film, more than 48 sq in, each dressing
* A6260 Wound cleansers, any type, any size
* A6261 Wound filler, not elsewhere classified, gel/paste, per fluid ounce
* A6262 Wound filler, not elsewhere classified, dry form, per gram
* A6263 Gauze, elastic, non-sterile, all types, per linear yard
* A6264 Gauze, non-elastic, non-sterile, per linear yard
* A6265 Tape, all types, per 18 sq in
* A6266 Gauze, impregnated, other than water or normal saline, any width, per linear yard
* A6402 Gauze, non-impregnated, sterile, pad size 16 sq in or less, without adhesive border, each dressing
* A6403 Gauze, non-impregnated, sterile, pad size more than 16 sq in, less than or equal to 48 sq in, without adhesive border, each dressing
* A6404 Gauze, non-impregnated, sterile, pad size more than 48 sq in, without adhesive border, each dressing
* A6405 Gauze, elastic, sterile, all types, per linear yard
* A6406 Gauze, non-elastic, sterile, all types, per linear yard

RESPIRATORY DME, INEXPENSIVE AND ROUTINELY PURCHASED (A7700–A7017)

▶* A7700 Canister, disposable, used with suction pump, each
▶* A7001 Canister, non-disposable, used with suction pump, each
▶* A7002 Tubing, used with suction pump, each
▶* A7003 Administration set, with small volume nonfiltered pneumatic nebulizer, disposable
▶* A7004 Small volume nonfiltered pneumatic nebulizer, disposable
▶* A7005 Administration set, with small volume nonfiltered pneumatic nebulizer, non-disposable
▶* A7006 Administration set, with small volume filtered pneumatic nebulizer
▶* A7007 Large volume nebulizer, disposable, unfilled, used with aerosol compressor
▶* A7008 Large volume nebulizer, disposable, prefilled, used with aerosol compressor

▶ * A7009   Reservoir bottle, nondisposable, used with large volume ultrasonic nebulizer

▶ * A7010   Corrugated tubing, disposable, used with large volume nebulizer, 100 feet

▶ * A7011   Corrugated tubing, non-disposable, used with large volume nebulizer, 10 feet

▶ * A7012   Water collection device, used with large volume nebulizer

▶ * A7013   Filter, disposable, used with aerosol compressor

▶ * A7014   Filter, non-disposable, used with aerosol compressor or ultrasonic generator

▶ * A7015   Aerosol mask, used with DME nebulizer

▶ * A7016   Dome and mouthpiece, used with small volume ultrasonic nebulizer

▶ ✪ A7017   Nebulizer, durable, glass or autoclavable plastic, bottle type, not used with oxygen

ADMINISTRATIVE, MISCELLANEOUS AND INVESTIGATIONAL A9000-A9999

Note: The following codes do not imply that codes in other sections are necessarily covered.

✪ A9150   Non-prescription drugs
MCM 2050.5

◆ A9160   Non-covered service by podiatrist
Medicare Statute 1861R3

◆ A9170   Non-covered service by chiropractor
Medicare Statute 1861R5

◆ A9190   Personal comfort item
Medicare Statute 1861A6

◆ A9270   Non-covered item or service
MCM 2303

◆ A9300   Exercise equipment
MCM 2100.1, CIM 60-9

Supplies for Radiology Procedures

✪ A9500   Supply of radiopharmaceutical diagnostic imaging agent, technetium Tc 99M sestamibi, per dose
MCM 15022

⇒ ✪ A9502   Supply of radiopharmaceutical diagnostic imaging agent, technetium Tc 99M tetrofosmin, per unit dose
MCM 15022

✪ A9503   Supply of radiopharmaceutical diagnostic imaging agent, technetium Tc 99M, medronate, up to 30 MCI
MCM 15022

▶ * A9504   Supply of radiopharmaceutical diagnostic imaging agent, technetium Tc99M apticide
MCM 15022

✪ A9505   Supply of radiopharmaceutical diagnostic imaging agent, thallous chloride Tl 201, per MCI

* A9507   Supply of radiopharmaceutical diagnostic imaging agent, indium In 111 capromab pendetide, per dose
MCM 15022

* A9600   Supply of therapeutic radiopharmaceutical, strontium-89 chloride, per MCI

* A9605   Supply of therapeutic radiopharmaceutical, samarium Sm 153 lexidronam, 50 mCi

Miscellaneous Service Component

▶ * A9900   Miscellaneous supply, accessory, and/or service component of another HCPCS code

▶ * A9901   Delivery, set up, and/or dispensing service component of another HCPCS code

ENTERAL AND PARENTERAL THERAPY (B4000–B9999)

Enteral Formulae and Enteral Medical Supplies

✪ B4034   Enteral feeding supply kit; syringe, per day
MCM 2130, MCM 4450, CIM 65-10

✪ B4035   Enteral feeding supply kit; pump fed, per day
MCM 2130, MCM 4450, CIM 65-10

✪ B4036   Enteral feeding supply kit; gravity fed, per day
MCM 2130, MCM 4450, CIM 65-10

✪ B4081   Nasogastric tubing with stylet, per day
MCM 2130, MCM 4450, CIM 65-10

✪ B4082   Nasogastric tubing without stylet
MCM 2130, MCM 4450, CIM 65-10

✪ B4083   Stomach tube, Levine type, per day
MCM 2130, MCM 4450, CIM 65-10

✪ B4084   Gastrostomy/jejunostomy tubing, per day
MCM 2130, MCM 4450, CIM 65-10

* B4085   Gastrostomy tube, silicone with sliding ring, each

✪ B4150   Enteral formulae; category I; semisynthetic intact protein/protein isolates, 100 calories = 1 unit
MCM 2130, MCM 4450, CIM 65-10

✪   **Special coverage instructions**   ◆   **Not covered by or valid for Medicare**   *   **Carrier discretion**   ◀▶   **New code**   ◀▬▬▶   **Revised code**

⊗ B4151   Enteral formulae; category I: natural intact protein/protein isolates, 100 calories = 1 unit
MCM 2130, MCM 4450, CIM 65-10

⊗ B4152   Enteral formulae; category II: intact protein/protein isolates (calorically dense), 100 calories = 1 unit
MCM 2130, MCM 4450, CIM 65-10

⊗ B4153   Enteral formulae; category III: hydrolized protein/amino acids, 100 calories = 1 unit
MCM 2130, MCM 4450, CIM 65-10

⊗ B4154   Enteral formulae; category IV: defined formula for special metabolic need, 100 calories = 1 unit
MCM 2130, MCM 4450, CIM 65-10

⊗ B4155   Enteral formulae; category V: modular components (protein, carbohydrates, fat), 100 calories = 1 unit
MCM 2130, MCM 4450, CIM 65-10

⊗ B4156   Enteral formulae; category VI: standardized nutrients, 100 calories = 1 unit
MCM 2130, MCM 4450, CIM 65-10

Parenteral Nutritional Solutions and Supplies

⊗ B4164   Parenteral nutrition solution: carbohydrates (dextrose), 50% or less (500 ml = 1 unit)—home mix
MCM 2130, MCM 4450, CIM 65-10

⊗ B4168   Parenteral nutrition solution; amino acid, 3.5% (500 ml = 1 unit)—home mix
MCM 2130, MCM 4450, CIM 65-10

⊗ B4172   Parenteral nutrition solution; amino acid, 5.5% through 7% (500 ml = 1 unit)—home mix
MCM 2130, MCM 4450, CIM 65-10

⊗ B4176   Parenteral nutrition solution; amino acid, 7% through 8.5% (500 ml = 1 unit)—home mix
MCM 2130, MCM 4450, CIM 65-10

⊗ B4178   Parenteral nutrition solution: amino acid, greater than 8.5% (500 ml = 1 unit)—home mix
MCM 2130, MCM 4450, CIM 65-10

⊗ B4180   Parenteral nutrition solution; carbohydrates (dextrose), greater than 50% (500 ml = 1 unit)—home mix
MCM 2130, MCM 4450, CIM 65-10

⊗ B4184   Parenteral nutrition solution; lipids, 10% with administration set (500 ml = 1 unit)
MCM 2120, MCM 4450, CIM 65-10

⊗ B4186   Parenteral nutrition solution, lipids, 20% with administration set (500 ml = 1 unit)
MCM 2130, MCM 4450, CIM 65-10

⊗ B4189   Parenteral nutrition solution; compounded amino acid and carbohydrates with electrolytes, trace elements, and vitamins, including preparation, any strength, 10 to 51 gm of protein—premix
MCM 2130, MCM 4450, CIM 65-10

⊗ B4193   Parenteral nutrition solution; compounded amino acid and carbohydrates with electrolytes, trace elements, and vitamins, including preparation, any strength, 52 to 73 gm of protein—premix
MCM 2130, MCM 4450, CIM 65-10

⊗ B4197   Parenteral nutrition solution; compounded amino acid and carbohydrates with electrolytes, trace elements and vitamins, including preparation, any strength, 74 to 100 gm of protein—premix
MCM 2130, MCM 4450, CIM 65-10

⊗ B4199   Parenteral nutrition solution; compounded amino acid and carbohydrates with electrolytes, trace elements and vitamins, including preparation, any strength, over 100 gm of protein—premix
MCM 2130, MCM 4450, CIM 65-10

⊗ B4216   Parenteral nutrition additives (vitamins, trace elements, heparin, electrolytes) home mix, per day
MCM 2130, MCM 4450, CIM 65-10

⊗ B4220   Parenteral nutrition supply kit; premix, per day
MCM 2130, MCM 4450, CIM 65-10

⊗ B4222   Parenteral nutrition supply kit; home mix, per day
MCM 2130, MCM 4450, CIM 65-10

⊗ B4224   Parenteral nutrition administration kit, per day
MCM 2130, MCM 4450, CIM 65-10

⊗ B5000   Parenteral nutrition solution; compounded amino acid and carbohydrates with electrolytes, trace elements, and vitamins, including preparation, any strength, renal—Amirosyn-RF, Nephr-Amine, Ren-Amine—premix
MCM 2130, MCM 4450, CIM 65-10

⊗ B5100   Parenteral nutrition solution; compounded amino acid and carbohydrates with electrolytes, trace elements, and vitamins, including preparation, any strength, hepatic—FreAmine HBC, HepatAmine—premix
MCM 2130, MCM 4450, CIM 65-10

⊕ B5200   Parenteral nutrition solution; compounded amino acid and carbohydrates with electrolytes, trace elements, and vitamins, including preparation, any strength, stress— branch chain amino acids—premix
MCM 2130, MCM 4450, CIM 65-10

Enteral and Parenteral Pumps

⊕ B9000   Enteral nutrition infusion pump, without alarm
MCM 2130, MCM 4450, CIM 65-10

⊕ B9002   Enteral nutrition infusion pump, with alarm
MCM 2130, MCM 4450, CIM 65-10

⊕ B9004   Parenteral nutrition infusion pump, portable
MCM 2130, MCM 4450, CIM 65-10

⊕ B9006   Parenteral nutrition infusion pump, stationary
MCM 2130, MCM 4450, CIM 65-10

⊕ B9998   NOC for enteral supplies
MCM 2130, MCM 4450, CIM 65-10

⊕ B9999   NOC for parenteral supplies
MCM 2130, MCM 4450, CIM 65-10

DENTAL PROCEDURES D0100—D9999

Codes D0100—D9999 are dental codes copyrighted to the American Dental Association. A copy of the Current Dental Terminology which contains all of the dental codes can be purchased from the American Dental Association.

DURABLE MEDICAL EQUIPMENT E0100—E9999

Canes

⊕ E0100   Cane, includes canes of all materials, adjustable or fixed, with tip
MCM 2100.1, CIM 60-3, CIM 60-9

⊕ E0105   Cane, quad or three prong, includes canes of all materials, adjustable or fixed, with tips
MCM 2100.1, CIM 60-9, CIM 60-15

Crutches

⊕ E0110   Crutches, forearm, includes crutches of various materials, adjustable or fixed, pair, complete with tips and handgrips
MCM 2100.1, CIM 60-9

⊕ E0111   Crutches, forearm, includes crutches of various materials, adjustable or fixed, each, with tips and handgrips
MCM 2100.1, CIM 60-9

⊕ E0112   Crutches, underarm, wood, adjustable or fixed, pair, with pads, tips and handgrips
MCM 2100.1, CIM 60-9

⊕ E0113   Crutches, underarm, wood, adjustable or fixed, each, with pads, tips and handgrip
MCM 2100.1, CIM 60-9

⊕ E0114   Crutches, underarm, other than wood, adjustable or fixed, pair, with pads, tips and handgrips
MCM 2100.1, CIM 60-9

⊕ E0116   Crutches, underarm, other than wood, adjustable or fixed, each, with pads, tips and handgrips
MCM 2100.1, CIM 60-9

Walkers

⊕ E0130   Walker, rigid (pickup), adjustable or fixed height
MCM 2100.1, CIM 60-9

⊕ E0135   Walker, folding (pickup), adjustable or fixed height
MCM 2100.1, CIM 60-9

⊕ E0141   Rigid walker, wheeled, without seat
MCM 2100.1, CIM 60-9

⊕ E0142   Rigid walker, wheeled, with seat
MCM 2100.1, CIM 60-9

⊕ E0143   Folding walker, wheeled, without seat
MCM 2100.1, CIM 60-9

▶⊕ E0144   Enclosed, framed folding walker, wheeled, with posterior seat
MCM 2100.1, CIM 60-9

⊕ E0145   Walker, wheeled, with seat and crutch attachments
MCM 2100.1, CIM 60-9

⊕ E0146   Folding walker, wheeled, with seat
MCM 2100.1, CIM 60-9

⊕ E0147   Heavy duty, multiple breaking system, variable wheel resistance walker
MCM 2100.1, CIM 60-9

∗ E0153   Platform attachment, forearm crutch, each

∗ E0154   Platform attachment, walker, each

⇒∗ E0155   Wheel attachment, rigid pick-up walker, per pair

Attachments

∗ E0156   Seat attachment, walker

∗ E0157   Crutch attachment, walker, each

⊕ **Special coverage instructions**   ◆ **Not covered by or valid for Medicare**   ∗ **Carrier discretion**   ◀▶ **New code**    **Revised code**

➡ * E0158   Leg extensions for a walker, per set of four (4)

* E0159   Brake attachment for wheeled walker, replacement, each

Commodes

✪ E0160   Sitz type bath or equipment, portable, used with or without commode
CIM 60-9

✪ E0161   Sitz type bath or equipment, portable, used with or without commode, with faucet attachment/s
CIM 60-9

✪ E0162   Sitz bath chair
CIM 60-9

✪ E0163   Commode chair, stationary, with fixed arms
MCM 2100.1, CIM 60-9

✪ E0164   Commode chair, mobile, with fixed arms
MCM 2100.1, CIM 60-9

✪ E0165   Commode chair, stationary, with detachable arms
MCM 2100.1, CIM 60-9

✪ E0166   Commode chair, mobile, with detachable arms
MCM 2100.1, CIM 60-9

✪ E0167   Pail or pan for use with commode chair
CIM 60-9

* E0175   Foot rest, for use with commode chair, each

Decubitus Care Equipment

✪ E0176   Air pressure pad or cushion, nonpositioning
CIM 60-9

✪ E0177   Water pressure pad or cushion, nonpositioning
CIM 60-9

✪ E0178   Gel or gel-like pressure pad or cushion, nonpositioning
CIM 60-9

✪ E0179   Dry pressure pad or cushion, nonpositioning
CIM 60-9

✪ E0180   Pressure pad, alternating with pump
MCM 4107.6, CIM 60-9

✪ E0181   Pressure pad, alternating with pump, heavy duty
MCM 4107.6, CIM 60-9

✪ E0182   Pump for alternating pressure pad
MCM 4107.6, CIM 60-9

✪ E0184   Dry pressure mattress
MCM 4107.6, CIM 60-9

✪ E0185   Gel or gel-like pressure pad for mattress, standard mattress length and width
MCM 4107.6, CIM 60-9

✪ E0186   Air pressure mattress
CIM 60-9

✪ E0187   Water pressure mattress
CIM 60-9

✪ E0188   Synthetic sheepskin pad
MCM 4107.6, CIM 60-9

✪ E0189   Lambswool sheepskin pad, any size
MCM 4107.6, CIM 60-9

* E0191   Heel or elbow protector, each

✪ E0192   Low pressure and positioning equalization pad, for wheelchair
MCM 4107.6, CIM 60-9

* E0193   Powered air flotation bed (low air loss therapy)

✪ E0194   Air fluidized bed
CIM 60-9, Cross Reference Q0049

✪ E0196   Gel pressure mattress
CIM 60-9

✪ E0197   Air pressure pad for mattress, standard mattress length and width
CIM 60-9

✪ E0198   Water pressure pad for mattress, standard mattress length and width
CIM 60-9

✪ E0199   Dry pressure pad for mattress, standard mattress length and width
CIM 60-9

Heat/Cold Application

✪ E0200   Heat lamp, without stand (table model), includes bulb, or infrared element
MCM 2100.1, CIM 60-9

* E0202   Phototherapy (bilirubin) light with photometer

✪ E0205   Heat lamp, with stand, includes bulb, or infrared element
MCM 2100.1, CIM 60-9

✪ E0210   Electric heat pad, standard
CIM 60-9

✪ E0215   Electric heat pad, moist
CIM 60-9

✪ E0217   Water circulating heat pad with pump
CIM 60-9

✪ E0218   Water circulating cold pad with pump
CIM 60-9

* E0220   Hot water bottle

✪ E0225   Hydrocollator unit, includes pads
MCM 2210.3, CIM 60-9

* E0230   Ice cap or collar

✪ E0235　Paraffin bath unit, portable (see medical supply code A4265 for paraffin)
MCM 2210.3, CIM 60-9

✪ E0236　Pump for water circulating pad
CIM 60-9

✪ E0238　Non-electric heat pad, moist
CIM 60-9

✪ E0239　Hydrocollator unit, portable
MCM 2210.3, CIM 60-9

Bath and Toilet Aids

◆ E0241　Bath tub wall rail, each
MCM 2100.1, CIM 60-9

◆ E0242　Bath tub rail, floor base
MCM 2100.1, CIM 60-9

◆ E0243　Toilet rail, each
MCM 2100.1, CIM 60-9

◆ E0244　Raised toilet seat
CIM 60-9

◆ E0245　Tub stool or bench
CIM 60-9

✻ E0246　Transfer tub rail attachment

✪ E0249　Pad for water circulating heat unit
CIM 60-9

Hospital Beds and Accessories

✪ E0250　Hospital bed, fixed height, with any type side rails, with mattress
MCM 2100.1, CIM 60-18

✪ E0251　Hospital bed, fixed height, with any type side rails, without mattress
MCM 2100.1, CIM 60-18

✪ E0255　Hospital bed, variable height, hi-lo, with any type side rails, with mattress
MCM 2100.1, CIM 60-18

✪ E0256　Hospital bed, variable height, hi-lo, with any type side rails, without mattress
MCM 2100.1, CIM 60-18

✪ E0260　Hospital bed, semi-electric (head and foot adjustment), with any type side rails, with mattress
MCM 2100.1, CIM 60-18

✪ E0261　Hospital bed, semi-electric (head and foot adjustment), with any type side rails, without mattress
MCM 2100.1, CIM 60-18

✪ E0265　Hospital bed, total electric (head, foot and height adjustments), with any type side rails, with mattress
MCM 2100.1, CIM 60-18

✪ E0266　Hospital bed, total electric (head, foot and height adjustments), with any type side rails, without mattress
MCM 2100.1, CIM 60-18

◆ E0270　Hospital bed, institutional type includes: oscillating, circulating and Stryker frame, with mattress
CIM 60-9

✪ E0271　Mattress, innerspring
CIM 60-9, CIM 60-18

✪ E0272　Mattress, foam rubber
CIM 60-9, CIM 60-18

◆ E0273　Bed board
CIM 60-9

◆ E0274　Over-bed table
CIM 60-9

✪ E0275　Bed pan, standard, metal or plastic
CIM 60-9

✪ E0276　Bed pan, fracture, metal or plastic
CIM 60-9

✪ E0277　Powered pressure-reducing air mattress
CIM 60-9

✻ E0280　Bed cradle, any type

✪ E0290　Hospital bed, fixed height, without side rails, with mattress
MCM 2100.1, CIM 60-18

✪ E0291　Hospital bed, fixed height, without side rails, without mattress
MCM 2100.1, CIM 60-18

✪ E0292　Hospital bed, variable height, hi-lo, without side rails, with mattress
MCM 2100.1, CIM 60-18

✪ E0293　Hospital bed, variable height, hi-lo, without side rails, without mattress
MCM 2100.1, CIM 60-18

✪ E0294　Hospital bed, semi-electric (head and foot adjustment), without side rails, with mattress
MCM 2100.1, CIM 60-18

✪ E0295　Hospital bed, semi-electric (head and foot adjustment), without side rails, without mattress
MCM 2100.1, CIM 60-18

✪ E0296　Hospital bed, total electric (head, foot and height adjustments), without side rails, with mattress
MCM 2100.1, CIM 60-18

✪ E0297　Hospital bed, total electric (head, foot and height adjustments), without side rails, without mattress
MCM 2100.1, CIM 60-18

Bed Accessories

✪ E0305　Bed side rails, half length
CIM 60-18

✪ E0310　Bed side rails, full length
CIM 60-18

◆ E0315　Bed accessory: board, table, or support device, any type
CIM 60-9

✪ E0325　Urinal; male, jug-type, any material
CIM 60-9

✪ Special coverage instructions　◆ Not covered by or valid for Medicare　✻ Carrier discretion　◀▶ New code　◀┅┅▶ Revised code

✪ E0326   Urinal; female, jug-type, any material
CIM 60-9

✳ E0350   Control unit for electronic bowel irrigation/evacuation system

✳ E0352   Disposable pack (water reservoir bag, speculum, valving mechanism and collection bag/box) for use with the electronic bowel irrigation/evacuation system

Other Decubitus Care Equipment

✳ E0370   Air pressure elevator for heel

✳ E0371   Non-powered advanced pressure-reducing overlay for mattress, standard mattress length and width

✳ E0372   Powered air overlay for mattress, standard mattress length and width

✳ E0373   Non-powered advanced pressure-reducing mattress

Oxygen and Related Respiratory Equipment

✪ E0424   Stationary compressed gaseous oxygen system, rental; includes contents (per unit), regulator, flowmeter, humidifier, nebulizer, cannula or mask, and tubing; unit = 50 cu ft
MCM 4107.9, CIM 60-4

✪ E0425   Stationary compressed gas system, purchase; includes regulator, flowmeter, humidifier, nebulizer, cannula or mask, and tubing
MCM 4107.9, CIM 60-4

✪ E0430   Portable gaseous oxygen system, purchase; includes regulator, flowmeter, humidifier, cannula or mask, and tubing
MCM 4107.9, CIM 60-4

✪ E0431   Portable gaseous oxygen system, rental; includes regulator, flowmeter, humidifier, cannula or mask, and tubing
MCM 4107.9, CIM 60-4

✪ E0434   Portable liquid oxygen system, rental; includes portable container, supply reservoir, humidifier, flowmeter, refill adaptor, contents gauge, cannula or mask, and tubing
MCM 4107.9, CIM 60-4

✪ E0435   Portable liquid oxygen system, purchase; includes portable container, supply reservoir, flowmeter, humidifier, contents gauge, cannula or mask, tubing and refill adaptor
MCM 4107.9, CIM 60-4

✪ E0439   Stationary liquid oxygen system, rental; includes use of reservoir, contents (per unit), regulator, flowmeter, humidifier, nebulizer, cannula or mask, and tubing; 1 unit = 10 lb
MCM 4107.9, CIM 60-4

✪ E0440   Stationary liquid oxygen system, purchase; includes use of reservoir, contents indicator, regulator, flowmeter, humidifier, nebulizer, cannula or mask, and tubing
MCM 4107.9, CIM 60-4

✪ E0441   Oxygen contents, gaseous, per unit (for use with owned gaseous stationary systems or when both a stationary and portable gaseous system are owned; 1 unit = 50 cu ft)
MCM 4107.9, CIM 60-4

✪ E0442   Oxygen contents, liquid, per unit (for use with owned liquid stationary systems or when both a stationary and portable liquid system are owned; 1 unit = 10 lb)
MCM 4107.9, CIM 60-4

✪ E0443   Portable oxygen contents, gaseous, per unit (for use only with portable gaseous systems when no stationary gas or liquid system is used; 1 unit = 5 cu ft)
MCM 4107.9, CIM 60-4

✪ E0444   Portable oxygen contents, liquid, per unit (for use only with portable liquid systems when no stationary gas or liquid system is used; 1 unit = 1 lb)
MCM 4107.9, CIM 60-4

➠ ✪ E0450   Volume ventilator, stationary or portable, with backup rate feature, used with invasive interface (e.g., tracheostomy tube)
CIM 60-9

E0452   (Deleted 12/31/99)

E0453   (Deleted 12/31/99)

✪ E0455   Oxygen tent, excluding croup or pediatric tents
MCM 4107.9, CIM 60-4

✳ E0457   Chest shell (cuirass)

✳ E0459   Chest wrap

✪ E0460   Negative pressure ventilator, portable or stationary
CIM 60-9

✳ E0462   Rocking bed, with or without side rails

✪ E0480   Percussor, electric or pneumatic, home model
CIM 60-9

IPPB Machines

✿ E0500   IPPB machine, all types, with built-in nebulization; manual or automatic valves; internal or external power source
CIM 60-9

Humidifiers/Nebulizers/Compressors for Use with Oxygen IPPB Equipment

✿ E0550   Humidifier, durable for extensive supplemental humidification during IPPB treatments or oxygen delivery
CIM 60-9

✿ E0555   Humidifier, durable, glass or autoclavable plastic bottle type, for use with regulator or flowmeter
MCM 4107.9, CIM 60-9

✿ E0560   Humidifier, durable for supplemental humidification during IPPB treatment or oxygen delivery
CIM 60-9

✳ E0565   Compressor, air power source for equipment which is not self-contained or cylinder driven

✿ E0570   Nebulizer, with compressor
MCM 4107.9, CIM 60-9

✿ E0575   Nebulizer, ultrasonic
CIM 60-9

✿ E0580   Nebulizer, durable, glass or autoclavable plastic, bottle type, for use with regulator or flowmeter
MCM 4107.9, CIM 60-9

✿ E0585   Nebulizer, with compressor and heater
MCM 4107.9, CIM 60-9

➟ ✳ E0590   Dispensing fee for covered drug administered through DME nebulizer

Suction Pump/Room Vaporizers

✿ E0600   Suction pump, home model, portable
CIM 60-9

✿ E0601   Continuous airway pressure (CPAP) device
CIM 60-17

➟ ◆ E0602   Breast pump, all types

✿ E0605   Vaporizer, room type
CIM 60-9

✿ E0606   Postural drainage board
CIM 60-9

Monitoring Equipment

✿ E0607   Home blood glucose monitor
CIM 60-11

✿ E0608   Apnea monitor
CIM 60-17

✿ E0609   Blood glucose monitor with special features (e.g., voice synthesizers, automatic timers, etc.)
CIM 60-11

Pacemaker Monitor

✿ E0610   Pacemaker monitor, self-contained (checks battery depletion, includes audible and visible check systems)
CIM 50-1, CIM 60-17

✿ E0615   Pacemaker monitor, self-contained (checks battery depletion and other pacemaker components, includes digital/visible check systems)
CIM 50-1, CIM 60-7

➟ ✳ E0616   Implantable cardiac event recorder with memory, activator, and programmer

Patient Lifts

✿ E0621   Sling or seat, patient lift, canvas or nylon
CIM 60-9

◆ E0625   Patient lift, Kartop, bathroom or toilet
CIM 60-9

✿ E0627   Seat lift mechanism incorporated into a combination lift-chair mechanism
MCM 4107.8, CIM 60-8, Cross Reference Q0080

✿ E0628   Separate seat lift mechanism for use with patient owned furniture—electric
MCM 4107.8, CIM 60-8, Cross Reference Q0078

✿ E0629   Separate seat lift mechanism for use with patient owned furniture—non-electric
MCM 4107.8, Cross Reference Q0079

✿ E0630   Patient lift, hydraulic, with seat or sling
CIM 60-9

✿ E0635   Patient lift, electric, with seat or sling
CIM 60-9

Pneumatic Compressor and Appliances

✿ E0650   Pneumatic compressor, non-segmental home model
CIM 60-16

✿ E0651   Pneumatic compressor, segmental home model without calibrated gradient pressure
CIM 60-16

⊛ E0652   Pneumatic compressor, segmental home model with calibrated gradient pressure
CIM 60-16

⊛ E0655   Non-segmental pneumatic appliance for use with pneumatic compressor, half arm
CIM 60-16

⊛ E0660   Non-segmental pneumatic appliance for use with pneumatic compressor, full leg
CIM 60-16

⊛ E0665   Non-segmental pneumatic appliance for use with pneumatic compressor, full arm
CIM 60-16

⊛ E0666   Non-segmental pneumatic appliance for use with pneumatic compressor, half leg
CIM 60-16

⊛ E0667   Segmental pneumatic appliance for use with pneumatic compressor, full leg
CIM 60-16

⊛ E0668   Segmental pneumatic appliance for use with pneumatic compressor, full arm
CIM 60-16

⊛ E0669   Segmental pneumatic appliance for use with pneumatic compressor, half leg
CIM 60-16

⊛ E0671   Segmental gradient pressure pneumatic appliance, full leg
CIM 60-16

⊛ E0672   Segmental gradient pressure pneumatic appliance, full arm
CIM 60-16

⊛ E0673   Segmental gradient pressure pneumatic appliance, half leg
CIM 60-16

Ultraviolet Cabinet

⊛ E0690   Ultraviolet cabinet, appropriate for home use
CIM 60-9

Safety Equipment

✳ E0700   Safety equipment (e.g., belt, harness or vest)

Restraints

✳ E0710   Restraints, any type (body, chest, wrist or ankle)

Trancutaneous and/or Neuromuscular Electrical Nerve Stimulators—TENS

⊛ E0720   TENS, two lead, localized stimulation
MCM 4107.6, CIM 35-20, CIM 35-46

⊛ E0730   TENS, four lead, larger area/multiple nerve stimulation
MCM 4107.6, CIM 35-20, CIM 35-46

⊛ E0731   Form fitting conductive garment for delivery of TENS or NMES (with conductive fibers separated from the patient's skin by layers of fabric)
CIM 45-25

◆ E0740   Incontinence treatment system, pelvic floor stimulator, monitor, sensor and/or trainer
CIM 65-11

✳ E0744   Neuromuscular stimulator for scoliosis

⊛ E0745   Neuromuscular stimulator, electronic shock unit
CIM 35-27

⊛ E0746   Electromyography (EMG), biofeedback device
CIM 35-27

⊛ E0747   Osteogenesis stimulator, electrical, non-invasive, other than spinal applications
CIM 35-48

⊛ E0748   Osteogensis stimulator, electrical, non-invasive, spinal applications
CIM 35-48

⊛ E0749   Osteogenesis stimulator, electrical, surgically implanted
CIM 35-48

⊛ E0751   Implantable neurostimulator pulse generator, or combination of external transmitter with implantable receiver (includes extension)
CIM 65-8

⊛ E0753   Implantable neurostimulator electrodes/leads, per group of 4
CIM 65-8

✳ E0755   Electronic salivary reflex stimulator (intra-oral/non-invasive)

◆ E0760   Ostogenesis stimulator, low intensity ultrasound, non-invasive
CIM 35-48

Infusion Supplies

✳ E0776   IV pole

▶✳ E0779   Ambulatory infusion pump, mechanical, reusable, for infusion 8 hours or greater

▶✳ E0780   Ambulatory infusion pump, mechanical, reusable, for infusion less than 8 hours

✢ E0781   Ambulatory infusion pump, single or multiple channels, electric or battery operated with administrative equipment, worn by patient
CIM 60-14

✢ E0782   Infusion pump, implantable, non-programmable
CIM 60-14

✢ E0783   Infusion pump system, implantable, programmable (includes all components, e.g., pump, catheter, connectors, etc.)
CIM 60-14

✢ E0784   External ambulatory infusion pump, insulin
CIM 60-14

✢ E0785   Implantable intraspinal (epidural/intrathecal) catheter used with implantable infusion pump, replacement
CIM 60-14

✢ E0791   Parenteral infusion pump, stationary, single or multi-channel
MCM 2130, MCM 4450, CIM 65-10

Traction Equipment — Cervical

✢ E0840   Traction frame, attached to headboard, cervical traction
CIM 60-9

✢ E0850   Traction stand, free-standing, cervical traction
CIM 60-9

* E0855   Cervical traction equipment not requiring additional stand or frame

Traction — Overdoor

✢ E0860   Traction equipment, overdoor, cervical
CIM 60-9

Traction — Extremity

✢ E0870   Traction frame, attached to footboard, extremity traction (e.g., Buck's)
CIM 60-9

✢ E0880   Traction stand, free-standing, extremity traction (e.g., Buck's)
CIM 60-9

Traction — Pelvic

✢ E0890   Traction frame, attached to footboard, pelvic traction
CIM 60-9

✢ E0900   Traction stand, free-standing, pelvic traction (e.g., Buck's)
CIM 60-9

Trapeze Equipment, Fracture Frame and Other Orthopedic Devices

✢ E0910   Trapeze bars, also known as patient helper, attached to bed, with grab bar
CIM 60-9

✢ E0920   Fracture frame, attached to bed, includes weights
CIM 60-9

✢ E0930   Fracture frame, free-standing, includes weights
CIM 60-9

✢ E0935   Passive motion exercise device
CIM 60-9

✢ E0940   Trapeze bar, free-standing, complete with grab bar
CIM 60-9

✢ E0941   Gravity assisted traction device, any type
CIM 60-9

* E0942   Cervical head harness/halter

* E0943   Cervical pillow

* E0944   Pelvic belt/harness/boot

* E0945   Extremity belt/harness

✢ E0946   Fracture, frame, dual with cross bars, attached to bed, (e.g., Balken, Four Poster)
CIM 60-9

✢ E0947   Fracture frame, attachments for complex pelvic traction
CIM 60-9

✢ E0948   Fracture frame, attachments for complex cervical traction
CIM 60-9

Wheelchairs

* E0950   Tray

* E0951   Loop heel, each

* E0952   Loop toe, each

✢ E0953   Pneumatic tire, each
CIM 60-9

✢ E0954   Semi-pneumatic caster, each
CIM 60-9

Wheelchair Accessories

✢ E0958   Wheelchair attachment to convert any wheelchair to one arm drive
CIM 60-9

✢   Special coverage instructions   ◆   Not covered by or valid for Medicare   *   Carrier discretion   ◀▶   New code   ⭠⭢   Revised code

✪ E0959   Amputee adapter (device used to compensate for transfer of weight due to lost limbs to maintain proper balance)
CIM 60-9

✪ E0961   Brake extension, for wheelchair
CIM 60-9

✪ E0962   1" cushion, for wheelchair
CIM 60-9

✪ E0963   2" cushion, for wheelchair
CIM 60-9

✪ E0964   3" cushion, for wheelchair
CIM 60-9

✪ E0965   4" cushion, for wheelchair
CIM 60-9

✪ E0966   Hook-on head rest extension
CIM 60-9

✪ E0967   Wheelchair hand rims with eight vertical rubber-tipped projections, pair
CIM 60-9

✪ E0968   Commode seat, wheelchair
CIM 60-9

✪ E0969   Narrowing device, wheelchair
CIM 60-9

✪ E0970   No. 2 footplates, except for elevating leg rest
CIM 60-9

✪ E0971   Anti-tipping device wheelchair
CIM 60-9

✱ E0972   Transfer board or device

✪ E0973   Adjustable-height detachable arms, desk or full length, wheelchair
CIM 60-9

✱ E0974   "Grade-aid" (device to prevent rolling back on an incline) for wheelchair

✪ E0975   Reinforced seat upholstery, wheelchair
CIM 60-9

✪ E0976   Reinforced back, wheelchair, upholstery or other material
CIM 60-9

✱ E0977   Wedge cushion, wheelchair

✱ E0978   Belt, safety with airplane buckle, wheelchair

✱ E0979   Belt, safety with velcro closure, wheelchair

✱ E0980   Safety vest, wheelchair

✪ E0990   Elevating leg rest, each
CIM 60-9

✪ E0991   Upholstery seat
CIM 60-9

✪ E0992   Solid seat insert
CIM 60-9

✪ E0993   Back, upholstery
CIM 60-9

✪ E0994   Arm rest, each
CIM 60-9

✪ E0995   Calf rest, each
CIM 60-9

✪ E0996   Tire, solid, each
CIM 60-9

✪ E0997   Caster with a fork
CIM 60-9

✪ E0998   Caster without fork
CIM 60-9

✪ E0999   Pneumatic tire with wheel
CIM 60-9

✪ E1000   Tire, pneumatic caster
CIM 60-9

✪ E1001   Wheel, single
CIM 60-9

Rollabout Chair

✪ E1031   Rollabout chair, any and all types with castors 5 in or greater
CIM 60-9

Wheelchair—Fully Reclining

✪ E1050   Fully reclining wheelchair, fixed full-length arms, swing-away detachable elevating leg rests
CIM 60-9

✪ E1060   Fully reclining wheelchair, detachable arms, desk or full-length, swing-away detachable elevating leg rests
CIM 60-9

✪ E1065   Power attachment (to convert any wheelchair to motorized wheelchair, e.g., Solo)
CIM 60-9

✪ E1066   Battery charger
CIM 60-9

✪ E1069   Deep cycle battery
CIM 60-9

✪ E1070   Fully reclining wheelchair, detachable arms (desk or full-length), swing-away detachable foot rest
CIM 60-9

✪ E1083   Hemi-wheelchair, fixed full-length arms, swing-away detachable elevating leg rest
CIM 60-9

✪ E1084   Hemi-wheelchair, detachable arms (desk or full-length) arms, swing-away detachable elevating leg rests
CIM 60-9

✪ E1085   Hemi-wheelchair, fixed full-length arms, swing-away detachable foot rests
CIM 60-9

✪ E1086   Hemi-wheelchair, detachable arms (desk or full-length), swing-away detachable foot rests
CIM 60-9

❂ E1087   High-strength lightweight wheelchair, fixed full-length arms, swing-
away detachable elevating leg rests
CIM 60-9

❂ E1088   High-strength lightweight wheelchair, detachable arms (desk or full-
length), swing-away detachable elevating leg rests
CIM 60-9

❂ E1089   High-strength lightweight wheelchair, fixed-length arms, swing-
away detachable foot rest
CIM 60-9

❂ E1090   High-strength lightweight wheelchair, detachable arms (desk or full-
length), swing-away detachable foot
rests
CIM 60-9

❂ E1091   Youth wheelchair, any type
CIM 60-9

❂ E1092   Wide, heavy duty wheelchair, detachable arms (desk or full-length), swing-
away detachable elevating leg rests
CIM 60-9

❂ E1093   Wide, heavy duty wheelchair, detachable arms (desk or full-length)
swing-away detachable foot rests
CIM 60-9

Wheelchair — Semi-reclining

❂ E1100   Semi-reclining wheelchair, fixed full-
length arms, swing-away detachable
elevating leg rests
CIM 60-9

❂ E1110   Semi-reclining wheelchair, detachable arms (desk or full-length), elevating leg rest
CIM 60-9

Wheelchair — Standard

❂ E1130   Standard wheelchair, fixed full-
length arms, fixed or swing-away
detachable foot rests
CIM 60-9

❂ E1140   Wheelchair, detachable arms (desk
or full-length), swing-away detachable foot rests
CIM 60-9

❂ E1150   Wheelchair, detachable arms (desk
or full-length), swing-away detachable elevating leg rests
CIM 60-9

❂ E1160   Wheelchair, fixed full-length arms,
swing-away detachable elevating leg
rests
CIM 60-9

Wheelchair — Amputee

❂ E1170   Amputee wheelchair, fixed full-
length arms, swing-away detachable
elevating leg rests
CIM 60-9

❂ E1171   Amputee wheelchair, fixed full-
length arms, without foot rests or
leg rests
CIM 60-9

❂ E1172   Amputee wheelchair, detachable
arms (desk or full-length), without
foot rests or leg rests
CIM 60-9

❂ E1180   Amputee wheelchair, detachable
arms (desk or full-length) swing-
away detachable foot rests
CIM 60-9

❂ E1190   Amputee wheelchair, detachable
arms (desk or full-length), swing-
away detachable elevating leg rests
CIM 60-9

❂ E1195   Heavy duty wheelchair, fixed full-
length arms, swing-away detachable
elevating leg rests
CIM 60-9

❂ E1200   Amputee wheelchair, fixed full-
length arms, swing-away detachable
foot rest
CIM 60-9

Wheelchair — Power

❂ E1210   Motorized wheelchair, fixed full-
length arms, swing-away detachable
elevating leg rests
CIM 60-5, CIM 60-9

❂ E1211   Motorized wheelchair, detachable
arms (desk or full-length) swing-
away, detachable elevating leg rest
CIM 60-5, CIM 60-9

❂ E1212   Motorized wheelchair, fixed full-
length arms, swing-away detachable
foot rests
CIM 60-5, CIM 60-9

❂ E1213   Motorized wheelchair, detachable
arms (desk or full-length), swing-
away detachable foot rests
CIM 60-5, CIM 60-9

Wheelchair — Special Size

❂ E1220   Wheelchair; specially sized or constructed (indicate brand name,
model number, if any) and justification
CIM 60-6

❂ **Special coverage instructions**   ◆ **Not covered by or valid for Medicare**   ✳ **Carrier discretion**   ◀▶ **New code**   ◀▦▶ **Revised code**

⊕ E1221   Wheelchair with fixed arm, foot
          rests
          CIM 60-6
⊕ E1222   Wheelchair with fixed arm, elevat-
          ing leg rests
          CIM 60-6
⊕ E1223   Wheelchair with detachable arms,
          foot rests
          CIM 60-6
⊕ E1224   Wheelchair with detachable arms,
          elevating leg rests
          CIM 60-6
⊕ E1225   Semi-reclining back for customized
          wheelchair
          CIM 60-6
⊕ E1226   Full-reclining back for customized
          wheelchair
          CIM 60-6
⊕ E1227   Special height arms for wheelchair
          CIM 60-6
⊕ E1228   Special back height for wheelchair
          CIM 60-6
⊕ E1230   Power operated vehicle (three- or
          four-wheel non-highway); specify
          brand name and model number
          MCM 4107.6, CIM 60-5

Wheelchair—Lightweight

⊕ E1240   Lightweight wheelchair, detachable
          arms (desk or full-length), swing-
          away detachable, elevating leg rest
          CIM 60-9
⊕ E1250   Lightweight wheelchair, fixed full-
          length arms, swing-away detachable
          foot rest
          CIM 60-9
⊕ E1260   Lightweight wheelchair, detachable
          arms (desk or full-length), swing-
          away detachable foot rest
          CIM 60-9
⊕ E1270   Lightweight wheelchair, fixed full-
          length arms, swing-away detachable
          elevating leg rests
          CIM 60-9

Wheelchair—Heavy Duty

⊕ E1280   Heavy duty wheelchair, detachable
          arms (desk or full-length), elevating
          leg rests
          CIM 60-9
⊕ E1285   Heavy duty wheelchair, fixed full-
          length arms, swing-away detachable
          foot rest
          CIM 60-9

⊕ E1290   Heavy duty wheelchair, detachable
          arms (desk or full-length), swing-
          away detachable foot rest
          CIM 60-9
⊕ E1295   Heavy duty wheelchair, fixed full-
          length arms, elevating leg rest
          CIM 60-9
⊕ E1296   Special wheelchair seat, height from
          floor
          CIM 60-6
⊕ E1297   Special wheelchair seat depth, by
          upholstery
          CIM 60-6
⊕ E1298   Special wheelchair seat depth and/
          or width, by construction
          CIM 60-6

Whirlpool Equipment

◆ E1300   Whirlpool, portable (overtub type)
          CIM 60-9
⊕ E1310   Whirlpool, non-portable (built-in
          type)
          CIM 60-9

Repairs and Replacement Parts

⊕ E1340   Repair or nonroutine service for du-
          rable medical equipment requiring
          the skill of a technician, labor com-
          ponent, per 15 minutes
          MCM 2100.4

Additional Oxygen Related Equipment

⊕ E1353   Regulator
          MCM 4107.9, CIM 60-4
⊕ E1355   Stand/rack
          CIM 60-4
⊕ E1372   Immersion external heater for nebu-
          lizer
          CIM 60-4
⊕ E1375   Nebulizer, portable, with small com-
          pressor, with limited flow
          CIM 60-4, CIM 60-9
⊕ E1377   Oxygen concentrator, high humidity
          system equivalent to 244 cu ft
          MCM 4107.9, CIM 60-4, Cross Refer-
          ence Q0036
⊕ E1378   Oxygen concentrator, high humidity
          system equivalent to 488 cu ft
          MCM 4107.9, CIM 60-4, Cross Refer-
          ence Q0036
⊕ E1379   Oxygen concentrator, high humidity
          system equivalent to 732 cu ft
          MCM 4107.9, CIM 60-4, Cross Refer-
          ence Q0036

⊛ E1380 Oxygen concentrator, high humidity system equivalent to 976 cu ft
MCM 4107.9, CIM 60-4, Cross Reference Q0036

⊛ E1381 Oxygen concentrator, high humidity system equivalent to 1220 cu ft
MCM 4107.9, CIM 60-4, Cross Reference Q0036

⊛ E1382 Oxygen concentrator, high humidity system equivalent to 1464 cu ft
MCM 4107.9, CIM 60-4, Cross Reference Q0036

⊛ E1383 Oxygen concentrator, high humidity system equivalent to 1708 cu ft
MCM 4107.9, CIM 60-4, Cross Reference Q0036

⊛ E1384 Oxygen concentrator, high humidity system equivalent to 1952 cu ft
MCM 4107.9, CIM 60-4, Cross Reference Q0036

⊛ E1385 Oxygen concentrator, high humidity system equivalent to over 1952 cu ft
MCM 4107.9, CIM 60-4, Cross Reference Q0036

▶ ⊛ E1390 Oxygen concentrator, capable of delivering 85 percent or greater oxygen concentration at the prescribed flow rate
CIM 60-4

✳ E1399 Durable medical equipment, miscellaneous

E1400 (Deleted 12/31/99)
E1401 (Deleted 12/31/99)
E1402 (Deleted 12/31/99)
E1403 (Deleted 12/31/99)
E1404 (Deleted 12/31/99)

⊛ E1405 Oxygen and water vapor enriching system with heated delivery
MCM 4107, CIM 60-4

⊛ E1406 Oxygen and water vapor enriching system without heated delivery
MCM 4107, CIM 60-4

Artificial Kidney Machines and Accessories

⊛ E1510 Kidney, dialysate delivery system, kidney machine, pump recirculating, air removal system, flow rate meter, power off, heater and temperature control with alarm, IV poles, pressure gauge, concentrate container

⊛ E1520 Heparin infusion pump for dialysis

Note: For supplies for ESRD, see codes A4650–A 4999.

⊛ E1530 Air bubble detector for dialysis
⊛ E1540 Pressure alarm for dialysis
⊛ E1550 Bath conductivity meter for dialysis

⊛ E1560 Blood leak detector for dialysis
⊛ E1570 Adjustable chair, for ESRD patients
⊛ E1575 Transducer protectors/fluid barriers, any size, each
⊛ E1580 Unipuncture control system for dialysis
⊛ E1590 Hemodialysis machine
⊛ E1592 Automatic intermittent peritoneal dialysis system
⊛ E1594 Cycler dialysis machine for peritoneal dialysis
⊛ E1600 Delivery and/or installation charges for renal dialysis equipment
⊛ E1610 Reverse osmosis water purification system
CIM 55-1A
⊛ E1615 Deionizer water purification system
CIM 55-1A
⊛ E1620 Blood pump for dialysis
⊛ E1625 Water softening system
CIM 55-1B
✳ E1630 Reciprocating peritoneal dialysis system
⊛ E1632 Wearable artificial kidney
⊛ E1635 Compact (portable) travel hemodialyzer system
⊛ E1636 Sorbent cartridges, per case
⊛ E1640 Replacement components for hemodialysis and/or peritoneal dialysis machines that are owned or being purchased by the patient
⊛ E1699 Dialysis equipment, unspecified, by report

Jaw Motion Rehabilitation System and Accessories

✳ E1700 Jaw motion rehabilitation system
✳ E1701 Replacement cushions for jaw motion rehabilitation system, package of 6
✳ E1702 Replacement measuring scales for jaw motion rehabilitation system, package of 200

Other Orthopedic Devices

✳ E1800 Dynamic adjustable elbow extension/flexion device
✳ E1805 Dynamic adjustable wrist extension/flexion device
✳ E1810 Dynamic adjustable knee extension/flexion device
✳ E1815 Dynamic adjustable ankle extension/flexion device
✳ E1820 Soft interface material, dynamic adjustable extension/flexion device

---

⊛ Special coverage instructions   ◆ Not covered by or valid for Medicare   ✳ Carrier discretion    New code    Revised code

* E1825   Dynamic adjustable finger extension/flexion device
* E1830   Dynamic adjustable toe extension/flexion device
▶ ⊛ E1900   Synthesized speech augmentative communication device with dynamic display
CIM 60-9

Procedures/Professional Services (Temporary) G0000–G9999

Note: This section contains national codes assigned by HCFA on a temporary basis to identify procedures/professional services.

PET Scan Code Modifiers

Modifiers that are used on claims for PET myocardial perfusion imaging are created by combining two alpha characters. Each alpha character represents the results of the PET scan and the previous test, with the first letter indicating the results of the PET scan, while the second letter indicates the test done prior to the PET scan.

The test result codes and their descriptions are listed below:

Code

N   Negative
E   Equivocal
P   Positive, but not suggestive of extensive ischemia
S   Positive and suggestive of extensive ischemia (greater than 20% of the left ventricle)

* G0001   Routine venipuncture for collection of specimen(s)
* G0002   Office procedure, insertion of temporary indwelling catheter, Foley type (separate procedure)
⊛ G0004   Patient demand single or multiple event recording with pre-symptom memory loop and 24 hour attended monitoring, per 30 day period; includes transmission, physician review and interpretation
CIM 50-15
⊛ G0005   Patient demand single or multiple event recording with pre-symptom memory loop and 24 hour attended monitoring, per 30 day period; recording (includes hookup, recording and disconnection)
CIM 50-15

⊛ G0006   Patient demand single or multiple event recording with pre-symptom memory loop and 24 hour attended monitoring, per 30 day period; 24 hour attended monitoring, receipt of transmissions, and analysis
CIM 50-15
⊛ G0007   Patient demand single or multiple event recording with pre-sympton memory loop and 24 hour attended monitoring, per 30 day period; physician review and interpretation only
CIM 50-15
* G0008   Administration of influenza virus vaccine
* G0009   Administration of pneumococcal vaccine
* G0010   Administration of hepatitis B vaccine
⊛ G0015   Post-symptom telephonic transmission of electrocardiogram rhythm strip(s) and 24 hour attended monitoring, per 30 day period; tracing only
CIM 50-15
⊛ G0016   Post-symptom telephonic transmission of electrocardiogram rhythm strips(s) and 24 hour attended monitoring, per 30 day period; physician review and interpretation only
CIM 50-15
⊛ G0025   Collagen skin test kit
CIM 65-9
* G0026   Fecal leukocyte examination
* G0027   Semen analysis; presence and/or motility of sperm excluding Huhner
⊛ G0030   PET myocardial perfusion imaging (following previous PET, G0030–G0047); single study, rest or stress (exercise and/or pharmacologic)
CIM 50-36
⊛ G0031   PET myocardial perfusion imaging (following previous PET, G0030–G0047); multiple studies, rest or stress (exercise and/or pharmacologic)
CIM 50-36
⊛ G0032   PET myocardial perfusion imaging (following rest SPECT); single study, rest or stress (exercise and/or pharmacologic)
CIM 50-36
⊛ G0033   PET myocardial perfusion imaging (following rest SPECT); multiple studies, rest or stress (exercise and/or pharmacologic)
CIM 50-36
⊛ G0034   PET myocardial perfusion imaging (following stress SPECT); single study, rest or stress (exercise and/or pharmacologic)
CIM 50-36

✪ G0035   PET myocardial perfusion imaging (following stress SPECT); multiple studies, rest or stress (exercise and/or pharmacologic)
CIM 50-36

✪ G0036   PET myocardial perfusion imaging (following coronary angiography); single study, rest or stress (exercise and/or pharmacologic)
CIM 50-36

✪ G0037   PET myocardial perfusion imaging (following coronary angiography); multiple studies, rest or stress (exercise and/or pharmacologic)
CIM 50-36

✪ G0038   PET myocardial perfusion imaging, (following stress planar myocardial perfusion); single study, rest or stress (exercise and/or pharmacologic)
CIM 50-36

✪ G0039   PET myocardial perfusion imaging (following stress planar myocardial perfusion); multiple studies, rest or stress (exercise and/or pharmacologic)
CIM 50-36

✪ G0040   PET myocardial perfusion imaging (following stress echocardiogram); single study, rest or stress (exercise and/or pharmacologic)
CIM 50-36

✪ G0041   PET myocardial perfusion imaging (following stress echocardiogram); multiple studies, rest or stress (exercise and/or pharmacologic)
CIM 50-36

✪ G0042   PET myocardial perfusion imaging (following stress nuclear ventriculogram); single study, rest or stress (exercise and/or pharmacologic)
CIM 50-36

✪ G0043   PET myocardial perfusion imaging, (following stress nuclear ventriculogram); multiple studies, rest or stress (exercise and/or pharmacologic)
CIM 50-36

✪ G0044   PET myocardial perfusion imaging (following rest ECG); single study, rest or stress (exercise and/or pharmacologic)
CIM 50-36

✪ G0045   PET myocardial perfusion imaging (following rest ECG); multiple studies, rest or stress (exercise and/or pharmacologic)
CIM 50-36

✪ G0046   PET myocardial perfusion imaging (following stress ECG); single study, rest or stress (exercise and/or pharmacologic)
CIM 50-36

✪ G0047   PET myocardial perfusion imaging, (following stress ECG); multiple studies, rest or stress (exercise and/or pharmacologic)
CIM 50-36

✱ G0050   Measurement of post-voiding residual urine and/or bladder capacity by ultrasound

✪ G0101   Cervical or vaginal cancer screening; pelvic and clinical breast examination

▶✪ G0102   Prostate cancer screening; digital rectal examination
MCM 4182, CIM 50-55

▶✪ G0103   Prostate cancer screening; prostate specific antigen test (PSA), total
MCM 4182, CIM 50-55

✪ G0104   Colorectal cancer screening; flexible sigmoidoscopy

✪ G0105   Colorectal cancer screening; colonoscopy on individual at high risk

✪ G0106   Colorectal cancer screening; alternative to G0104, screening sigmoidoscopy, barium enema

✪ G0107   Colorectal cancer screening; fecal-occult blood test, 1-3 simultaneous determinations

✪ G0108   Diabetes outpatient self-management training services, individual, per session

✪ G0109   Diabetes self-management training services, group session, per individual

✪ G0110   NETT pulmonary-rehabilitation; education/skills training, individual

✪ G0111   NETT pulmonary-rehabilation; education/skills training, group

✪ G0112   NETT pulmonary-rehabilation; nutritional guidance, initial

✪ G0113   NETT pulmonary-rehabilation; nutritional guidance, subsequent

✪ G0114   NETT pulmonary-rehabilation; psychosocial consultation

✪ G0115   NETT pulmonary-rehabilation; psychological testing

✪ G0116   NETT pulmonary-rehabilation; psychosocial counselling

✪ G0120   Colorectal cancer screening; alternative to G0105, screening colonoscopy, barium enema

◆ G0121   Colorectal cancer screening; colonoscopy on individual not meeting criteria for high risk

◆ G0122   Colorectal cancer screening; barium enema

⊛ G0123   Screening cytopathology, cervical or vaginal (any reporting system); collected in preservative fluid, automated thin layer preparation, screening by cytotechnologist under physician supervision
CIM 50-20, Laboratory Certification: cytology

⊛ G0124   Screening cytopathology, cervical or vaginal (any reporting system); in preservative fluid, automated thin layer preparation, requiring interpretation by physician
CIM 50-20, Laboratory Certification: cytology

⊛ G0125   PET lung imaging of solitary pulmonary nodules, using 2-(fluorine-18)-fluoro-2-deoxy-d-glucose (FDG), following CT with or without contrast
MCM 4173, CIM 50-36

⊛ G0126   PET lung imaging of solitary pulmonary nodules, using 2-(fluorine-18)-fluoro-2-deoxy-d-glucose (FDG), following CT with or without contrast; initial staging of pathologically diagnosed non–small cell lung cancer
MCM 4173, CIM 50-36

⊛ G0127   Trimming of dystrophic nails, any number
MCM 2323, MCM 4120

⊛ G0128   Direct (face-to-face with patient) skilled nursing services of a registered nurse provided in a comprehensive outpatient rehabilitation facility, each 10 minutes beyond the first 5 minutes
Medicare Statute 1833a

▶✶ G0129   Therapist, furnished as a component of a partial hospitalization treatment program, per day

⊛ G0130   Single energy x-ray absorptiometry (SEXA) bone density study, one or more sites; appendicular skeleton (peripheral) (e.g., radius, wrist, heel)
CIM 50-44

⊛ G0131   CT bone mineral density study, one or more sites; axial skeleton (e.g., hips, pelvis, spine)
CIM 50-44

⊛ G0132   CT bone mineral density study, one or more sites; appendicular skeleton (peripheral) (e.g., radius, wrist, heel)
CIM 50-44

G0133   (Deleted 12/31/98) Cross Reference CPT

✶ G0141   Screening cytopathology smears, cervical or vaginal, performed by automated system, with manual rescreening requiring interpretation by physician
Lab Certification: cytology

✶ G0143   Screening cytopathology, cervical or vaginal (any reporting system); collected in preservative fluid, automated thin layer preparation, with manual screening and rescreening by cytotechnologist under physician supervision
Lab Certification: cytology

✶ G0144   Screening cytopathology, cervical or vaginal (any reporting system); collected in preservative fluid, automated thin layer preparation, with manual screening and computer-assisted rescreening by cytotechnologist under physician supervision
Lab Certification: cytology

✶ G0145   Screening cytopathology, cervical or vaginal (any reporting system); collected in preservative fluid, automated thin layer preparation, with manual screening and computer-assisted rescreening using cell selection and review under physician supervision
Lab Certification: cytology

✶ G0147   Screening cytopathology smears, cervical or vaginal; performed by automated system under physician supervision
Lab Certification: cytology

✶ G0148   Screening cytopathology smears, cervical or vaginal; performed by automated system with manual rescreening
Lab Certification: cytology

▶✶ G0151   Services of physical therapist in home health setting, each 15 minutes

▶✶ G0152   Services of occupational therapist in home health setting, each 15 minutes

▶✶ G0153   Services of speech and language pathologist in home health setting, each 15 minutes

▶✶ G0154   Services of skilled nurse in home health setting, each 15 minutes

▶✶ G0155   Services of clinical social worker in home health setting, each 15 minutes

▶✶ G0156   Services of home health aide in home health setting, each 15 minutes

▶✶ G0159   Percutaneous thrombectomy and/or revision, arteriovenous fistula, autogenous or nonautogenous dialysis graft

▶⊛ G0160   Cryosurgical ablation of localized prostate cancer, primary treatment only (postoperative irrigations and aspiration of sloughing tissue included)
CIM 35-96

▶ ⊕ G0161   Ultrasonic guidance for interstitial placement of cryosurgical probes
CIM 35-96

▶ ⊕ G0163   Positron emission tomography (pet), whole body, for recurrence of colorectal metastatic cancer
MCM 4173, CIM 50-36

▶ ⊕ G0164   Positron emission tomography (pet), whole body, for staging and characterization of lymphoma
MCM 4173, CIM 50-36

▶ ⊕ G0165   Positron emission tomography (pet), whole body, for recurrence of melanoma or melanoma metastatic cancer
MCM 4173, CIM 50-36

▶ ⊕ G0166   External counterpulsation, per treatment session
CIM 35-74

▶ ⊕ G0167   Hyperbaric oxygen treatment not requiring physician attendance, per treatment session
CIM 35-70

▶ ✱ G0168   Wound closure utilizing tissue adhesive(s) only

▶ ✱ G0169   Removal of devitalized tissue, without use of anesthesia (conscious sedation, local, regional, general)

▶ ✱ G0170   Application of tissue cultured skin grafts, including Bilaminate skin substitutes or Neodermis, including site preparation, initial 25 sq cms

▶ ✱ G0171   Application of tissue cultured skin grafts, including Bilaminate skin substitutes or Neodermis, including site preparation, each additional 25 sq cms

▶ ✱ G0172   Training and educational services furnished as a component of a partial hospitalization treatment program, per day

DRUGS OTHER THAN CHEMOTHERAPY
J0000–J8999

⊕ J0120   Injection, tetracycline, up to 250 mg
MCM 2049

⊕ J0130   Injection abciximab, 10 mg
MCM 2049

⊕ J0150   Injection, adenosine, 6 mg (not to be used to report any adenosine phosphate compounds; instead use A9270)
MCM 2049

⊕ J0151   Injection, adenosine, 90 mg (not to be used to report any adenosine phosphate compounds; instead use A9270)
MCM 2049

⊕ J0170   Injection, adrenalin, epinephrine, up to 1 ml ampule
MCM 2049

⊕ J0190   Injection, biperiden lactate, per 5 mg
MCM 2049

▶ ⊕ J0200   Injection, alatrofloxacin mesylate, 100 mg
MCM 2049.5

⊕ J0205   Injection, alglucerase, per 10 units
MCM 2049

⊕ J0207   Injection, amifostine, 500 mg
MCM 2049

⊕ J0210   Injection, methyldopate HCl, up to 250 mg
MCM 2049

⊕ J0256   Injection, alpha-1-proteinase inhibitor (human), 10 mg
MCM 2049

⇒ ⊕ J0270   Injection, alprostadil, per 1.25 mcg (Code may be used for Medicare when drug administered under the direct supervision of a physician, not for use when drug is self-administered.)
MCM 2049

⇒ ⊕ J0275   Alprostadil urethral suppository (Code may be used for Medicare when drug administered under the direct supervision of a physician, not for use when drug is self-administered.)
MCM 2049

⊕ J0280   Injection, aminophylline, up to 250 mg
MCM 2049

⊕ J0285   Injection, amphotericin B, 50 mg
MCM 2049

⊕ J0286   Injection, amphotericin B, any lipid formulation, 50 mg
MCM 2049

⇒ ⊕ J0290   Injection, ampicillin sodium, 500 mg
MCM 2049

⊕ J0295   Injection, ampicillin sodium/sulbactam sodium, per 1.5 gm
MCM 2049

⊕ J0300   Injection, amobarbital, up to 125 mg
MCM 2049

⊕ J0330   Injection, succinylcholine chloride, up to 20 mg
MCM 2049

⊕ J0340   Injection, nandrolone phenpropionate, up to 50 mg
MCM 2049

⊕ J0350   Injection, anistreplase, per 30 units
MCM 2049

⊕ J0360   Injection, hydralazine HCl, up to 20 mg
MCM 2049

⊕ J0380   Injection, metaraminol bitartrate, per 10 mg

⊕ **Special coverage instructions**   ◆ **Not covered by or valid for Medicare**   ✱ **Carrier discretion**   ◀▶ **New code**   ⇐⇒ **Revised code**

J0390   Injection, chloroquine HCl, up to 250 mg
MCM 2049

J0395   Injection, abutamine HCl, 1 mg
MCM 2049

J0400   Injection, trimethaphan camsylate, up to 500 mg
MCM 2049

J0460   Injection, atropine sulfate, up to 0.3 mg
MCM 2049

J0470   Injection, dimercaprol, per 100 mg
MCM 2049

J0475   Injection, baclofen, 10 mg
MCM 2049

▶ J0456   Injection, azithromycin, 500 mg
MCM 2049.5

J0476   Injection, baclofen 50 mcg for intrathecal trial
MCM 2049

J0500   Injection, dicyclomine HCl, up to 20 mg
MCM 2049

J0510   Injection, benzquinamide HCl, up to 50 mg
MCM 2049

J0515   Injection, benztropine mesylate, per 1 mg
MCM 2049

J0520   Injection, bethanechol chloride, myotonachol or urecholine, up to 5 mg
MCM 2049

J0530   Injection, penicillin G benzathine and penicillin G procaine, up to 600,000 units
MCM 2049

J0540   Injection, penicillin G benzathine and penicillin G procaine, up to 1,200,000 units
MCM 2049

J0550   Injection, penicillin G benzathine and penicillin G procaine, up to 2,400,000 units
MCM 2049

J0560   Injection, penicillin G benzathine, up to 600,000 units
MCM 2049

J0570   Injection, penicillin G benzathine, up to 1,200,000 units
MCM 2049

J0580   Injection, penicillin G benzathine, up to 2,400,000 units
MCM 2049

J0585   Botulinum toxin type A, per unit
MCM 2049

J0590   Injection, ethylnorepinephrine HCl, 1 ml
MCM 2049

J0600   Injection, edetate calcium disodium, up to 1000 mg
MCM 2049

J0610   Injection, calcium gluconate, per 10 ml
MCM 2049

J0620   Injection, calcium glycerophosphate and calcium lactate, per 10 ml
MCM 2049

J0630   Injection, calcitonin (salmon), up to 400 units
MCM 2049

J0635   Injection, calcitriol, 1 mcg ampule
MCM 2049, Cross Reference Q0088

J0640   Injection, leucovorin calcium, per 50 mg
MCM 2049

J0670   Injection, mepivacaine HCl, per 10 ml
MCM 2049

➡ J0690   Injection, cefazolin sodium, 500 mg
MCM 2049

J0694   Injection, cefoxitin sodium, 1 gm
MCM 2049, Cross Reference Q0090

J0695   Injection, cefonicid sodium, 1 gm
MCM 2049

J0696   Injection, ceftriaxone sodium, per 250 mg
MCM 2049

J0697   Injection, sterile cefuroxime sodium, per 750 mg
MCM 2049

➡ J0698   Injection, cefotaxime sodium, per gm
MCM 2049

J0702   Injection, betamethasone acetate and betamethasone sodium phosphate, per 3 mg
MCM 2049

J0704   Injection, betamethasone sodium phosphate, per 4 mg
MCM 2049

J0710   Injection, cephapirin sodium, up to 1 gm
MCM 2049

J0713   Injection, ceftazidime, per 500 mg
MCM 2049

J0715   Injection, ceftizoxime sodium, per 500 mg
MCM 2049

J0720   Injection, chloramphenicol sodium succinate, up to 1 gm
MCM 2049

J0725   Injection, chorionic gonadotropin, per 1,000 USP units
MCM 2049

J0730   Injection, chlorpheniramine maleate, per 10 mg
MCM 2049

J0735   Injection, clonidine HCl, 1 mg
MCM 2049

J0740   Injection, cidofovir, 375 mg
MCM 2049

✪ J0743   Injection, cilastatin sodium; imipenem, per 250 mg
MCM 2049

✪ J0745   Injection, codeine phosphate, per 30 mg
MCM 2049

✪ J0760   Injection, colchicine, per 1 mg
MCM 2049

✪ J0770   Injection, colistimethate sodium, up to 150 mg
MCM 2049

✪ J0780   Injection, prochlorperazine, up to 10 mg
MCM 2049

✪ J0800   Injection, corticotropin, up to 40 units
MCM 2049

✪ J0810   Injection, cortisone, up to 50 mg
MCM 2049

✪ J0835   Injection, cosyntropin, per 0.25 mg
MCM 2049

✪ J0850   Injection, cytomegalovirus immune globulin intravenous (human), per vial
MCM 2049

✪ J0895   Injection, deferoxamine mesylate, 500 mg per 5 cc
MCM 2049, Cross Reference Q0087

✪ J0900   Injection, testosterone enanthate and estradiol valerate, up to 1 cc
MCM 2049

✪ J0945   Injection, brompheniramine maleate, per 10 mg
MCM 2049

✪ J0970   Injection, estradiol valerate, up to 40 mg
MCM 2049

✪ J1000   Injection, depo-estradiol cypionate, up to 5 mg
MCM 2049

✪ J1020   Injection, methylprednisolone acetate, 20 mg
MCM 2049

✪ J1030   Injection, methylprednisolone acetate, 40 mg
MCM 2049

✪ J1040   Injection, methylprednisolone acetate, 80 mg
MCM 2049

✪ J1050   Injection, medroxyprogesterone acetate, 100 mg
MCM 2049

◆ J1055   Injection, medroxyprogesterone acetate for contraceptive use, 150 mg
Medicare Statute 1862A1

✪ J1060   Injection, testosterone cypionate and estradiol cypionate, up to 1 ml
MCM 2049

✪ J1070   Injection, testosterone cypionate, up to 100 mg
MCM 2049

✪ J1080   Injection, testosterone cypionate, 1 cc, 200 mg
MCM 2049

✪ J1090   Injection, testosterone cypionate, 1 cc, 50 mg
MCM 2049

✪ J1095   Injection, dexamethasone acetate, per 8 mg
MCM 2049

⇒ ✪ J1100   Injection, dexamethasone sodium phosphate, up to 4 mg/ml
MCM 2049

✪ J1110   Injection, dihydroergotamine mesylate, per 1 mg
MCM 2049

✪ J1120   Injection, acetazolamide sodium, up to 500 mg
MCM 2049

✪ J1160   Injection, digoxin, up to 0.5 mg
MCM 2049

✪ J1165   Injection, phenytoin sodium, per 50 mg
MCM 2049

✪ J1170   Injection, hydromorphone, up to 4 mg
MCM 2049

✪ J1180   Injection, dyphylline, up to 500 mg
MCM 2049

✪ J1190   Injection, dexrazoxane HCl, per 250 mg
MCM 2049

✪ J1200   Injection, diphenhydramine HCl, up to 50 mg
MCM 2049

✪ J1205   Injection, chlorothiazide sodium, per 500 mg
MCM 2049

✪ J1212   Injection, dimethyl sulfoxide, DMSO, 50%, 50 ml
MCM 2049, CIM 45-23

✪ J1230   Injection, methadone HCl, up to 10 mg
MCM 2049

✪ J1240   Injection, Dimenhydrinate, up to 50 mg
MCM 2049

✪ J1245   Injection, dipyridamole, per 10 mg
MCM 2049, MCM 15030

✪ J1250   Injection, dobutamine HCl, per 250 mg
MCM 2049

⇒ ✪ J1260   Injection, dolasetron mesylate, 10 mg
MCM 2049

✪ J1320   Injection, amitriptyline HCl, up to 20 mg
MCM 2049

✪ J1325   Injection, epoprostenol, 0.5 mg
MCM 2049

▶ ✪ J1327   Injection, eptifibatide, 5 mg
MCM 2049

✪ **Special coverage instructions**   ◆ **Not covered by or valid for Medicare**   ✱ **Carrier discretion**   ◀▶ **New code**   ⇐⇒ **Revised code**

J1330   Injection, ergonovine maleate, up to 0.2 mg
MCM 2049

J1362   Injection, erythromycin gluceptate, per 250 mg
MCM 2049

J1364   Injection, erythromycin lactobionate, per 500 mg
MCM 2049

J1380   Injection, estradiol valerate, up to 10 mg
MCM 2049

J1390   Injection, estradiol valerate, up to 20 mg
MCM 2049

J1410   Injection, estrogen conjugated, per 25 mg
MCM 2049

J1435   Injection, estrone, per 1 mg
MCM 2049

J1436   Injection, etidronate disodium, per 300 mg
MCM 2049

▶ J1438   Injection, etanercept, 25 mg (Code may be used for Medicare when drug administered under the direct supervision of a physician, not for use when drug is self-administered.)

J1440   Injection, filgrastim (G-CSF), 300 mcg
MCM 2049

J1441   Injection, filgrastim (G-CSF), 480 mcg
MCM 2049

▶ J1450   Injection, fluconazole, 200 mg
MCM 2049.5

J1455   Injection, foscarnet sodium, per 1000 mg
MCM 2049

J1460   Injection, gamma globulin, intra-muscular, 1 cc
MCM 2049

J1470   Injection, gamma globulin, intra-muscular, 2 cc
MCM 2049

J1480   Injection, gamma globulin, intra-muscular, 3 cc
MCM 2049

J1490   Injection, gamma globulin, intra-muscular, 4 cc
MCM 2049

J1500   Injection, gamma globulin, intra-muscular, 5 cc
MCM 2049

J1510   Injection, gamma globulin, intra-muscular, 6 cc
MCM 2049

J1520   Injection, gamma globulin, intra-muscular, 7 cc
MCM 2049

J1530   Injection, gamma globulin, intra-muscular, 8 cc
MCM 2049

J1540   Injection, gamma globulin, intra-muscular, 9 cc
MCM 2049

J1550   Injection, gamma globulin, intra-muscular, 10 cc
MCM 2049

J1560   Injection, gamma globulin, intra-muscular, over 10 cc
MCM 2049

J1561   Injection, immune globulin, intrave-nous, 500 mg
MCM 2049

J1562   Injection, immune globulin, intrave-nous, 5 gm
MCM 2049

J1565   Injection, respiratory syncytial virus immune globulin, intravenous, 50 mg
MCM 2049

J1570   Injection, ganciclovir sodium, 500 mg
MCM 2049

J1580   Injection, Garamycin, gentamicin, up to 80 mg
MCM 2049

J1600   Injection, gold sodium thiomalate, up to 50 mg
MCM 2049

J1610   Injection, glucagon HCl, per 1 mg
MCM 2049

J1620   Injection, gonadorelin HCl, per 100 mcg
MCM 2049

J1626   Injection, granisetron HCl, 100 mcg
MCM 2049

J1630   Injection, haloperidol, up to 5 mg
MCM 2049

J1631   Injection, haloperidol decanoate, per 50 mg
MCM 2049

J1642   Injection, heparin sodium, (Heparin Lock Flush), per 10 units
MCM 2049

J1644   Injection, heparin sodium, per 1000 units
MCM 2049

J1645   Injection, dalteparin sodium, per 2500 IU
MCM 2049

J1650   Injection, enoxaparin sodium, 10 mg
MCM 2049

J1670   Injection, tetanus immune globulin (human), up to 250 units
MCM 2049

J1690   Injection, prednisolone tebutate, up to 20 mg
MCM 2049

J1700   Injection, hydrocortisone acetate, up to 25 mg
MCM 2049

J1710   Injection, hydrocortisone sodium phosphate, up to 50 mg
MCM 2049

✪ **Special coverage instructions**   ◆ **Not covered by or valid for Medicare**   ✳ **Carrier discretion**   ◀▶ **New code**   ◀▥▥▶ **Revised code**

✪ J1720 Injection, hydrocortisone sodium succinate, up to 100 mg
MCM 2049

✪ J1730 Injection, diazoxide, up to 300 mg
MCM 2049

✪ J1739 Injection, hydroxyprogesterone caproate, 125 mg/ml
MCM 2049

✪ J1741 Injection, hydroxyprogesterone caproate, 250 mg/ml
MCM 2049

✪ J1742 Injection, ibutilide fumarate, 1 mg
MCM 2049

▶ ✪ J1745 Injection, infliximab, 10 mg
MCM 2049

▶ ✪ J1750 Injection, iron dextran, 50 mg
MCM 2049.5

J1760 (Deleted 12/31/99)

J1770 (Deleted 12/31/99)

J1780 (Deleted 12/31/99)

✪ J1785 Injection, imiglucerase, per unit
MCM 2049

✪ J1790 Injection, droperidol, up to 5 mg
MCM 2049

✪ J1800 Injection, propranolol HCl, up to 1 mg
MCM 2049

✪ J1810 Injection, droperidol and fentanyl citrate, up to 2 ml ampule
MCM 2049

➠ ✪ J1820 Injection, insulin, up to 100 units
MCM 2049, CIM 60-14

➠ ✪ J1825 Injection, interferon beta-1a, 33 mcg (Code may be used for Medicare when drug administered under the direct supervision of a physician, not for use when drug is self-administered.)
MCM 2049

➠ ✪ J1830 Injection interferon beta-1b, per 0.25 mg (Code may be used for Medicare when drug administered under the direct supervision of a physician, not for use when drug is self-administered.)
MCM 2049

✪ J1840 Injection, kanamycin sulfate, up to 500 mg
MCM 2049

✪ J1850 Injection, kanamycin sulfate, up to 75 mg
MCM 2049

✪ J1885 Injection, ketorolac tromethamine, per 15 mg
MCM 2049

✪ J1890 Injection, cephalothin sodium, up to 1 gm
MCM 2049

✪ J1910 Injection, Kutapressin, up to 2 ml
MCM 2049

✪ J1930 Injection, propiomazine HCl, up to 20 mg
MCM 2049

✪ J1940 Injection, furosemide, up to 20 mg
MCM 2049

✪ J1950 Injection, leuprolide acetate (for depot suspension), per 3.75 mg
MCM 2049

✪ J1955 Injection, levocarnitine, per 1 gm
MCM 2049

✪ J1956 Injection, levofloxacin, 250 mg
MCM 2049

✪ J1960 Injection, levorphanol tartrate, up to 2 mg
MCM 2049

✪ J1970 Injection, methotrimeprazine, up to 20 mg
MCM 2049

✪ J1980 Injection, hyoscyamine sulfate, up to 0.25 mg
MCM 2049

✪ J1990 Injection, chlordiazepoxide HCl, up to 100 mg
MCM 2049

✪ J2000 Injection, lidocaine HCl, 50 cc
MCM 2049

✪ J2010 Injection, lincomycin HCl, up to 300 mg
MCM 2049

✪ J2060 Injection, lorazepam, 2 mg
MCM 2049

✪ J2150 Injection, mannitol, 25% in 50 ml
MCM 2049

✪ J2175 Injection, meperidine HCl, per 100 mg
MCM 2049

✪ J2180 Injection, meperidine and promethazine HCl, up to 50 mg
MCM 2049

✪ J2210 Injection, methylergonovine maleate, up to 0.2 mg
MCM 2049

✪ J2240 Injection, metocurine iodide, up to 2 mg
MCM 2049

✪ J2250 Injection, midazolam HCl, per 1 mg
MCM 2049

✪ J2260 Injection milrinone lactate, per 5 ml
MCM 2049

✪ J2270 Injection, morphine sulfate, up to 10 mg
MCM 2049

✪ J2271 Injection, morphine sulfate, 100 mg
MCM 2049, CIM 60-14

✪ J2275 Injection, morphine sulfate (preservative-free sterile solution), per 10 mg
MCM 2049

✪ J2300 Injection, nalbuphine HCl, per 10 mg
MCM 2049

✪ J2310 Injection, naloxone HCl, per 1 mg
MCM 2049

✪ J2320   Injection, nandrolone decanoate, up to 50 mg
MCM 2049

✪ J2321   Injection, nandrolone decanoate, up to 100 mg
MCM 2049

✪ J2322   Injection, nandrolone decanoate, up to 200 mg
MCM 2049

✪ J2330   Injection, thiothixene, up to 4 mg
MCM 2049

✪ J2350   Injection, niacinamide, niacin, up to 100 mg
MCM 2049

▶✪ J2352   Injection, octreotide acetate, 1 mg
MCM 2049

✪ J2355   Injection, oprelvekin, 5 mg
MCM 2049

✪ J2360   Injection, orphenadrine citrate, up to 60 mg
MCM 2049

✪ J2370   Injection, phenylephrine HCl, up to 1 ml
MCM 2049

✪ J2400   Injection, chloroprocaine HCl, per 30 ml
MCM 2049

✪ J2405   Injection, ondansetron HCl, per 1 mg
MCM 2049

✪ J2410   Injection, oxymorphone HCl, up to 1 mg
MCM 2049

✪ J2430   Injection, pamidronate disodium, per 30 mg
MCM 2049

✪ J2440   Injection, papaverine HCl, up to 60 mg
MCM 2049

✪ J2460   Injection, oxytetracycline HCl, up to 50 mg
MCM 2049

✪ J2480   Injection, hydrochlorides of opium alkaloids, up to 20 mg
MCM 2049

▶✪ J2500   Injection, paricalcitol, 5 mcg
MCM 2049

✪ J2510   Injection, penicillin G procaine, aqueous, up to 600,000 units
MCM 2049

✪ J2512   Injection, pentagastrin, per 2 ml
MCM 2049

✪ J2515   Injection, pentobarbital sodium, per 50 mg
MCM 2049

✪ J2540   Injection, penicillin G potassium, up to 600,000 units
MCM 2049

▶✪ J2543   Injection, piperacillin sodium/tazo-bactam sodium, 1 gram 0.125 grams (1.125 grams)
MCM 2049

✪ J2545   Pentamidine isethionate, inhalation solution, per 300 mg, administered through a DME
MCM 2049, Cross Reference Q0077

✪ J2550   Injection, promethazine HCl, up to 50 mg
MCM 2049

✪ J2560   Injection, phenobarbital sodium, up to 120 mg
MCM 2049

✪ J2590   Injection, oxytocin, up to 10 units
MCM 2049

✪ J2597   Injection, desmopressin acetate, per 1 mcg
MCM 2049

✪ J2640   Injection, prednisolone sodium phosphate, to 20 mg
MCM 2049

✪ J2650   Injection, prednisolone acetate, up to 1 ml
MCM 2049

✪ J2670   Injection, tolazoline HCl, up to 25 mg
MCM 2049

✪ J2675   Injection, progesterone, per 50 mg
MCM 2049

✪ J2680   Injection, fluphenazine decanoate, up to 25 mg
MCM 2049

✪ J2690   Injection, procainamide HCl, up to 1 gm
MCM 2049

✪ J2700   Injection, oxacillin sodium, up to 250 mg
MCM 2049

✪ J2710   Injection, neostigmine methylsulfate, up to 0.5 mg
MCM 2049

✪ J2720   Injection, protamine sulfate, per 10 mg
MCM 2049

✪ J2725   Injection, protirelin, per 250 mcg
MCM 2049

✪ J2730   Injection, pralidoxime chloride, up to 1 gm
MCM 2049

✪ J2760   Injection, phentolamine mesylate, up to 5 mg
MCM 2049

✪ J2765   Injection, metoclopramide HCl, up to 10 mg
MCM 2049

▶✪ J2780   Injection, ranitidine hydrochloride, 25 mg
MCM 2049

✪ J2790   Injection, Rho(D) immune globulin, human, one dose package
MCM 2049

✪ J2792   Injection, Rho(D) immune globulin (human), IV, solvent detergent, 100 IU
MDC 2049

⊛ J2800   Injection, methocarbamol, up to 10 ml
MCM 2049

⊛ J2810   Injection, theophylline, per 40 mg
MCM 2049

⊛ J2820   Injection, sargramostim (GM-CSF), 50 mcg
MCM 2049

⊛ J2860   Injection, secobarbital sodium, up to 250 mg
MCM 2049

⊛ J2910   Injection, aurothioglucose, up to 50 mg
MCM 2049

⊛ J2912   Injection, sodium chloride, 0.9%, per 2 ml
MCM 2049

⊛ J2920   Injection, methylprednisolone sodium succinate, up to 40 mg
MCM 2049

⊛ J2930   Injection, methylprednisolone sodium succinate, up to 125 mg
MCM 2049

⊛ J2950   Injection, promazine HCl, up to 25 mg
MCM 2049

⊛ J2970   Injection, methicillin sodium, up to 1 gm
MCM 2049

⊛ J2994   Injection, reteplase, 37.6 mg, two single-use vials
MCM 2049

⊛ J2995   Injection, streptokinase, per 250,000 IU
MCM 2049

⊛ J2996   Injection, alteplase recombinant, per 10 mg
MCM 2049

⊛ J3000   Injection, streptomycin, up to 1 gm
MCM 2049

⊛ J3010   Injection, fentanyl citrate, up to 2 ml
MCM 2049

➠ ⊛ J3030   Injection, sumatriptan succinate, 6 mg (Code may be used for Medicare when drug administered under the direct supervision of a physician, not for use when drug is self-administered.)
MCM 2049

⊛ J3070   Injection, pentazocine HCl, up to 30 mg
MCM 2049

⊛ J3080   Injection, chlorprothixene, up to 50 mg
MCM 2049

⊛ J3105   Injection, terbutaline sulfate, up to 1 mg
MCM 2049

⊛ J3120   Injection, testosterone enanthate, up to 100 mg
MCM 2049

⊛ J3130   Injection, testosterone enanthate, up to 200 mg
MCM 2049

⊛ J3140   Injection, testosterone suspension, up to 50 mg
MCM 2049

⊛ J3150   Injection, testosterone propionate, up to 100 mg
MCM 2049

⊛ J3230   Injection, chlorpromazine HCl, up to 50 mg
MCM 2049

➠ ⊛ J3240   Injection, thyrotropin, 0.9 mg
MCM 2049

▶ ⊛ J3245   Injection, tirofiban hydrochloride, 12.5 mg
MCM 2049

⊛ J3250   Injection, trimethobenzamide HCl, up to 200 mg
MCM 2049

⊛ J3260   Injection, tobramycin sulfate, up to 80 mg
MCM 2049

⊛ J3265   Injection, torsemide, 10 mg/ml
MCM 2049

⊛ J3270   Injection, imipramine HCl, up to 25 mg
MCM 2049

⊛ J3280   Injection, thiethylperazine maleate, up to 10 mg
MCM 2049

⊛ J3301   Injection triamcinolone acetonide, per 10 mg
MCM 2049

⊛ J3302   Injection triamcinolone diacetate, per 5 mg
MCM 2049

⊛ J3303   Injection triamcinolone hexacetonide, per 5 mg
MCM 2049

⊛ J3305   Injection, trimetrexate glucuronate, per 25 mg
MCM 2049

⊛ J3310   Injection, perphenazine, up to 5 mg
MCM 2049

⊛ J3320   Injection, spectinomycin dihydrochloride, up to 2 gm
MCM 2049

⊛ J3350   Injection, urea, up to 40 gm
MCM 2049

⊛ J3360   Injection, diazepam, up to 5 mg
MCM 2049

⊛ J3364   Injection, urokinase, 5000 IU vial
MCM 2049

⊛ J3365   Injection, IV, urokinase, 250,000 IU vial
MCM 2049, Cross Reference Q0089

➠ ⊛ J3370   Injection, vancomycin HCl, 500 mg
MCM 2049, CIM 60-14

⊛ **Special coverage instructions**   ◆ **Not covered by or valid for Medicare**   ✳ **Carrier discretion**   ◀▶ **New code**   ⬅➠ **Revised code**

- ✪ J3390 Injection, methoxamine HCl, up to 20 mg
  MCM 2049
- ✪ J3400 Injection, triflupromazine HCl, up to 20 mg
  MCM 2049
- ✪ J3410 Injection, hydroxyzine HCl, up to 25 mg
  MCM 2049
- ✪ J3420 Injection, vitamin B-12 cyanocobalamin, up to 1000 mcg
  MCM 2049, CIM 45-4
- ✪ J3430 Injection, phytonadione (vitamin K), per 1 mg
  MCM 2049
- ✪ J3450 Injection, mephentermine sulfate, up to 30 mg
  MCM 2049
- ✪ J3470 Injection, hyaluronidase, up to 150 units
  MCM 2049
- ✪ J3475 Injection, magnesium sulfate, per 500 mg
  MCM 2049
- ✪ J3480 Injection, potassium chloride, per 2 mEq
  MCM 2049
- ✪ J3490 Unclassified drugs
  MCM 2049
- ◆ J3520 Edetate disodium, per 150 mg
  CIM 35-64, CIM 45-20
- ✪ J3530 Nasal vaccine inhalation
  MCM 2049
- ◆ J3535 Drug administered through a metered dose inhaler
  MCM 2050.5
- ◆ J3570 Laetrile, amygdalin, vitamin B-17
  CIM 45-10

Miscellaneous Drugs and Solutions

- ✪ J7030 Infusion, normal saline solution, 1000 cc
  MCM 2049
- ✪ J7040 Infusion, normal saline solution, sterile (500 ml = 1 unit)
  MCM 2049
- ✪ J7042 5% dextrose/normal saline (500 ml = 1 unit)
  MCM 2049
- ✪ J7050 Infusion, normal saline solution, 250 cc
  MCM 2049
- ✪ J7051 Sterile saline or water, up to 5 cc
  MCM 2049
- ✪ J7060 5% dextrose/water (500 ml = 1 unit)
  MCM 2049
- ✪ J7070 Infusion, D-5-W, 1000 cc
  MCM 2049

- ✪ J7100 Infusion, dextran 40, 500 ml
  MCM 2049
- ✪ J7110 Infusion, dextran 75, 500 ml
  MCM 2049
- ✪ J7120 Ringer's lactate infusion, up to 1000 cc
  MCM 2049
- ✪ J7130 Hypertonic saline solution, 50 or 100 mEq, 20 cc vial
  MCM 2049
- ✪ J7190 Factor VIII, anti-hemophilic factor (human), per IU
  MCM 2049
- ✪ J7191 Factor VIII, anti-hemophilic factor (porcine), per IU
  MCM 2049
- ✪ J7192 Factor VIII (anti-hemophilic factor recombinant), per IU
  MCM 2049
- ✪ J7194 Factor IX, complex, per IU
  MCM 2049
-   J7196 (Deleted 12/31/99)
- ✪ J7197 Antithrombin III (human), per IU
  MCM 2049
- ▶ ✪ J7198 Anti-inhibitor, per IU
  MCM 2049, CIM 45-24
- ▶ ✪ J7199 Hemophilia clotting factor, not otherwise classified
  MCM 2049, CIM 45-24
- ◆ J7300 Intrauterine copper contraceptive
  Medicare Statute 1862A1
- ✪ J7310 Ganciclovir, 4.5 mg, long-acting implant
  MCM 2049
- ✳ J7315 Sodium hyaluronae, 20 mg, for intra-articular injection
- ✳ J7320 Hylan G-F 20, 16 mg, for intra-articular injection

Immunosuppressive Drugs (Includes Non-injectibles)

- ⇒ ✪ J7500 Azathioprine, oral, 50 mg
  MCM 2049.5
- ⇒ ✪ J7501 Azathioprine, parenteral, 100 mg
  MCM 2049
- ▶ ✪ J7502 Cyclosporine, oral, 100 mg
  MCM 4029.5
-   J7503 (Deleted 1/1/00) Cross Reference J7516
- ⇒ ✪ J7504 Lymphocyte immune globulin, antithymocyte globulin, parenteral 250 mg
  MCM 2049, CIM 45-22
- ✪ J7505 Monoclonal antibodies, parenteral, 5 mg
  MCM 2049
- ✪ J7506 Prednisone, oral, per 5 mg
  MCM 2049.5

✪ **Special coverage instructions**   ◆ **Not covered by or valid for Medicare**   ✳ **Carrier discretion**   ◀▶ **New code**   ⇐⇒ **Revised code**

✪ J7507 Tacrolimus, oral, per 1 mg
MCM 2049.5

✪ J7508 Tacrolimus, oral, per 5 mg
MCM 2049.5

✪ J7509 Methylprednisolone oral, per 4 mg
MCM 2049.5

✪ J7510 Prednisolone oral, per 5 mg
MCM 2049.5

✪ J7513 Daclizumab, parenteral, 25 mg
MCM 2049.5

▶✳ J7515 Cyclosporine, oral, 25 mg

▶✳ J7516 Cyclosporin, parenteral, 250 mg

▶✳ J7517 Mycophenolate mofetil, oral, 250 mg

✪ J7599 Immunosuppressive drug, not otherwise classified
MCM 2049.5

Inhalation Solutions

▶✪ J7608 Acetylcysteine, inhalation solution administered through DME, unit dose form, per gram
MCM 2100.5

✪ J7610 Acetylcysteine, 10%, per ml, inhalation solution administered through DME
MCM 2100.5

✪ J7615 Acetylcysteine, 20%, per ml, inhalation solution administered through DME
MCM 2100.5

▶✪ J7618 Albuterol, inhalation solution administered through DME, concentrated form, per milligram
MCM 2100.5

▶✪ J7619 Albuterol, inhalation solution administered through DME, unit dose form, per milligram
MCM 2100.5

✪ J7620 Albuterol sulfate, 0.083%, per ml, inhalation solution administered through DME
MCM 2100.5, MCM 2049

✪ J7625 Albuterol sulfate, 0.5%, per ml, inhalation solution administered through DME
MCM 2100.5, MCM 2049

✳ J7627 Bitolterol mesylate, 0.2%, per 10 ml, inhalation solution administered through DME

▶✪ J7628 Bitolterol mesylate, inhalation solution administered through DME, concentrated form, per milligram
MCM 2100.5

▶✪ J7629 Bitolterol mesylate, inhalation solution administered through DME, unit dose form, per milligram
MCM 2100.5

✪ J7630 Cromolyn sodium, per 20 mg, inhalation solution administered through DME
MCM 2100.5, MCM 2049

▶✪ J7631 Cromolyn sodium, inhalation solution administered through DME, unit dose form, per 10 milligrams
MCM 2100.5

▶✪ J7635 Atropine, inhalation solution administered through DME, concentrated form, per milligram
MCM 2100.5

▶✪ J7636 Atropine, inhalation solution administered through DME, unit dose form, per milligram
MCM 2100.5

▶✪ J7637 Dexamethasone, inhalation solution administered through DME, concentrated form, per milligram
MCM 2100.5

▶✪ J7638 Dexamethasone, inhalation solution administered through DME, unit dose form, per milligram
MCM 2100.5

▶✪ J7639 Dornase alpha, inhalation solution administered through DME, unit dose form, per milligram
MCM 2100.5

✪ J7640 Epinephrine, 2.25%, per ml, inhalation solution administered through DME
MCM 2100.5

▶✪ J7642 Glycopyrrolate, inhalation solution administered through DME, concentrated form, per milligram
MCM 2100.5

▶✪ J7643 Glycopyrrolate, inhalation solution administered through DME, unit dose form, per milligram
MCM 2100.5

▶✪ J7644 Ipratropium bromide, inhalation solution administered through DME, unit dose form, per milligram
MCM 2100.5

✪ J7645 Ipratropium bromide 0.02%, per ml, inhalation solution, administered through a DME
MCM 2100.5

▶✪ J7648 Isoetharine HCl, inhalation solution administered through DME, concentrated form, per milligram
MCM 2100.5

▶✪ J7649 Isoetharine HCl, inhalation solution administered through DME, unit dose form, per milligram
MCM 2100.5

✪ J7650 Isoetharine HCl, 0.1%, per ml, inhalation solution administered through DME
MCM 2100.5, MCM 2049

✪ **Special coverage instructions** ◆ **Not covered by or valid for Medicare** ✳ **Carrier discretion** ◀▶ **New code** ◀▬▬▶ **Revised code**

✪ J7651   Isoetharine HCl, 0.125%, per ml, inhalation solution administered through DME
MCM 2100.5, MCM 2049

✪ J7652   Isoetharine HCl, 0.167%, per ml, inhalation solution administered through DME
MCM 2100.5, MCM 2049

✪ J7653   Isoetharine HCl, 0.2%, per ml, inhalation solution administered through DME
MCM 2100.5, MCM 2049

✪ J7654   Isoetharine HCl, 0.25%, per ml, inhalation solution administered through DME
MCM 2100.5, MCM 2049

✪ J7655   Isoetharine HCl, 1.0%, per ml, inhalation solution administered through DME
MCM 2100.5, MCM 2049

▶✪ J7658   Isoproterenol HCl, inhalation solution administered through DME, concentrated form, per milligram
MCM 2100.5

▶✪ J7659   Isoproterenol HCl, inhalation solution administered through DME, unit dose form, per milligram
MCM 2100.5

✪ J7660   Isoproterenol HCl, 0.5%, per ml, inhalation solution administered through DME
MCM 2100.5

✪ J7665   Isoproterenol HCl, 1.0%, per ml, inhalation solution administered through DME
MCM 2100.5

▶✪ J7668   Metaproterenol sulfate, inhalation solution administered through DME, concentrated form, per 10 milligrams
MCM 2100.5

▶✪ J7669   Metaproterenol sulfate, inhalation solution administered through DME, unit dose form, per 10 milligrams
MCM 2100.5

✪ J7670   Metaproterenol sulfate, 0.4%, per 2.5 ml, inhalation solution administered through DME
MCM 2049, MCM 2100.5

✪ J7672   Metaproterenol sulfate, 0.6%, per 2.5 ml, inhalation solution administered through DME
MCM 2049, MCM 2100.5

✪ J7675   Metaproterenol sulfate, 5.0%, per ml, inhalation solution administered through DME
MCM 2049, MCM 2100.5

▶✪ J7680   Terbutaline sulfate, inhalation solution administered through DME, concentrated form, per milligram
MCM 2100.5

▶✪ J7681   Terbutaline sulfate, inhalation solution administered through DME, unit dose form, per milligram
MCM 2100.5

▶✪ J7682   Tobramycin, unit dose form, 300 mg, inhalation solution, administered through DME
MCM 2100.5

▶✪ J7683   Triamcinolone, inhalation solution administered through DME, concentrated form, per milligram
MCM 2100.5

▶✪ J7684   Triamcinolone, inhalation solution administered through DME, unit dose form, per milligram
MCM 2100.5

✪ J7699   NOC drugs, inhalation solution administered through DME
MCM 2100.5

✪ J7799   NOC drugs, other than inhalation drugs, administered through DME
MCM 2100.5

◆ J8499   Prescription drug, oral, non-chemotherapeutic, NOS
MCM 2049

▶✪ J8510   Busulfan; oral, 2 mg
MCM 2049.5

▶✪ J8520   Capecitabine, oral, 150 mg
MCM 2049.5

▶✪ J8521   Capecitabine, oral, 500 mg
MCM 2049.5

✪ J8530   Cyclophosphamide, oral, 25 mg
MCM 2049.5

✪ J8560   Etoposide, oral, 50 mg
MCM 2049.5

✪ J8600   Melphalan, oral, 2 mg
MCM 2049.5

✪ J8610   Methotrexate, oral, 2.5 mg
MCM 2049.5

✪ J8999   Prescription drug, oral, chemotherapeutic, NOS
MCM 2049.5

CHEMOTHERAPY DRUGS J9000–J9999

Note: The cost of the chemotherapy drug only, not to include the administration

✪ J9000   Doxorubicin HCl, 10 mg
MCM 2049

▶✪ J9001   Doxorubicin hydrochloride, all lipid formulations, 10 mg
MCM 2049

✪ J9015   Aldesleukin, per single use vial
MCM 2049

✪ J9020   Asparaginase, 10,000 units
MCM 2049

✪ J9031   BCG (intravesical), per instillation
MCM 2049

✪ J9040   Bleomycin sulfate, 15 units
MCM 2049

✪ J9045   Carboplatin, 50 mg
MCM 2049

✪ J9050   Carmustine, 100 mg
MCM 2049

✪ J9060   Cisplatin, powder or solution, per
10 mg
MCM 2049

✪ J9062   Cisplatin, 50 mg
MCM 2049

✪ J9065   Injection, cladribine, per 1 mg
MCM 2049

✪ J9070   Cyclophosphamide, 100 mg
MCM 2049

✪ J9080   Cyclophosphamide, 200 mg
MCM 2049

✪ J9090   Cyclophosphamide, 500 mg
MCM 2049

✪ J9091   Cyclophosphamide, 1.0 gm
MCM 2049

✪ J9092   Cyclophosphamide, 2.0 gm
MCM 2049

✪ J9093   Cyclophosphamide, lyophilized,
100 mg
MCM 2049

✪ J9094   Cyclophosphamide, lyophilized,
200 mg
MCM 2049

✪ J9095   Cyclophosphamide, lyophilized,
500 mg
MCM 2049

✪ J9096   Cyclophosphamide, lyophilized,
1.0 gm
MCM 2049

✪ J9097   Cyclophosphamide, lyophilized,
2.0 gm
MCM 2049

✪ J9100   Cytarabine 100 mg
MCM 2049

✪ J9110   Cytarabine, 500 mg
MCM 2049

✪ J9120   Dactinomycin, 0.5 mg
MCM 2049

✪ J9130   Dacarbazine, 100 mg
MCM 2049

✪ J9140   Dacarbazine, 200 mg
MCM 2049

✪ J9150   Daunorubicin, HCl, 10 mg
MCM 2049

✪ J9151   Daunorubicin citrate liposomal formulation, 10 mg
MCM 2049

✪ J9165   Diethylstilbestrol diphosphate,
250 mg
MCM 2049

✪ J9170   Docetaxel, 20 mg
MCM 2049

✪ J9181   Etoposide, 10 mg
MCM 2049

✪ J9182   Etoposide, 100 mg
MCM 2049

✪ J9185   Fludarabine phosphate, 50 mg
MCM 2049

✪ J9190   Fluorouracil, 500 mg
MCM 2049

✪ J9200   Floxuridine, 500 mg
MCM 2049

✪ J9201   Gemcitabine HCl, 200 mg
MCM 2049

✪ J9202   Goserelin acetate implant, per
3.6 mg
MCM 2049

✪ J9206   Irinotecan, 20 mg
MCM 2049

✪ J9208   Ifosfamide, 1 gm
MCM 2049

✪ J9209   Mesna, 200 mg
MCM 2049

✪ J9211   Idarubicin HCl, 5 mg
MCM 2049

✪ J9212   Injection, interferon alfacon-1, recombinant, 1 mcg
MCM 2049

✪ J9213   Interferon, alfa-2a, recombinant,
3 million units
MCM 2049

✪ J9214   Interferon, alfa-2b, recombinant,
1 million units
MCM 2049

✪ J9215   Interferon, alfa-n3 (human leukocyte
derived), 250,000 IU
MCM 2049

✪ J9216   Interferon, gamma-1B, 3 million units
MCM 2049

✪ J9217   Leuprolide acetate (for depot suspension), 7.5 mg
MCM 2049

✪ J9218   Leuprolide acetate, per 1 mg
MCM 2049

✪ J9230   Mechlorethamine HCl (nitrogen
mustard), 10 mg
MCM 2049

✪ J9245   Injection, melphalan HCl, 50 mg
MCM 2049

✪ J9250   Methotrexate sodium, 5 mg
MCM 2049

✪ J9260   Methotrexate sodium, 50 mg
MCM 2049

✪ J9265   Paclitaxel, 30 mg
MCM 2049

✪ J9266   Pegaspargase, per single dose vial
MCM 2049

✪ J9268   Pentostatin, per 10 mg
MCM 2049

✪ J9270   Plicamycin, 2.5 mg
MCM 2049

✪ J9280   Mitomycin, 5 mg
MCM 2049

✪ J9290   Mitomycin, 20 mg
MCM 2049

⊛ J9291   Mitomycin, 40 mg
MCM 2049

⊛ J9293   Injection, mitoxantrone HCl, per
5 mg
MCM 2049

⊛ J9310   Rituximab, 100 mg
MCM 2049

⊛ J9320   Streptozocin, 1 gm
MCM 2049

⊛ J9340   Thiotepa, 15 mg
MCM 2049

⊛ J9350   Topotecan, 4 mg
MCM 2049

▶ * J9355   Trastuzumab, 10 mg

▶ ⊛ J9357   Valrubicin, intravesical, 200 mg
MCM 2049

⊛ J9360   Vinblastine sulfate, 1 mg
MCM 2049

⊛ J9370   Vincristine sulfate, 1 mg
MCM 2049

⊛ J9375   Vincristine sulfate, 2 mg
MCM 2049

⊛ J9380   Vincristine sulfate, 5 mg
MCM 2049

⊛ J9390   Vinorelbine tartrate, per 10 mg
MCM 2049

⊛ J9600   Porfimer sodium, 75 mg
MCM 2049

⊛ J9999   Not otherwise classified, antineoplastic drugs
MCM 2049, CIM 45-16

K CODES DURABLE MEDICAL EQUIPMENT— TEMPORARY CODES—K0000–K9999

Wheelchairs

Note: This section contains national codes assigned by HCFA on a temporary basis and are for the exclusive use of the durable medical equipment regional carriers (DMERC).

* K0001   Standard wheelchair
* K0002   Standard hemi (low seat) wheelchair
* K0003   Lightweight wheelchair
* K0004   High-strength, lightweight wheelchair
* K0005   Ultralightweight wheelchair
* K0006   Heavy-duty wheelchair
* K0007   Extra heavy-duty wheelchair
* K0008   Custom manual wheelchair/base
* K0009   Other manual wheelchair/base
* K0010   Standard-weight frame motorized/power wheelchair
* K0011   Standard-weight frame motorized/power wheelchair, with programmable control parameters for speed adjustment, tremor dampening, acceleration control and braking

* K0012   Lightweight portable motorized/power wheelchair
* K0013   Custom motorized/power wheelchair base
* K0014   Other motorized/power wheelchair base
* K0015   Detachable, non-adjustable height arm rest, each
* K0016   Detachable, adjustable height arm rest, complete assembly, each
* K0017   Detachable, adjustable height arm rest, base, each
* K0018   Detachable, adjustable height arm rest, upper portion, each
* K0019   Arm pad, each
* K0020   Fixed, adjustable height arm rest, pair
* K0021   Anti-tipping device, each
* K0022   Reinforced back upholstery
* K0023   Solid back insert, planar back, single density foam, attached with straps
* K0024   Solid back insert, planar back, single density form, with adjustable hook-on hardware
* K0025   Hook-on head rest extension
* K0026   Back upholstery for ultralightweight or high-strength lightweight wheelchair
* K0027   Back upholstery for wheelchair type other than ultralightweight or high-strength lightweight wheelchair
⇒ * K0028   Manual, fully reclining back
* K0029   Reinforced seat upholstery
* K0030   Solid seat insert, planar seat, single density foam
⇒ * K0031   Safety belt/pelvic strap, each
* K0032   Seat upholstery for ultralightweight or high-strength lightweight wheelchair
* K0033   Seat upholstery for wheelchair type other than ultralightweight or high-strength lightweight wheelchair
* K0034   Heel loop, each
* K0035   Heel loop with ankle strap, each
* K0036   Toe loop, each
* K0037   High mount flip-up foot rest, each
* K0038   Leg strap, each
* K0039   Leg strap, H-style, each
* K0040   Adjustable angle footplate, each
* K0041   Large size footplate, each
* K0042   Standard size footplate, each
* K0043   Foot rest, lower extension tube, each
* K0044   Foot rest, upper hanger bracket, each
* K0045   Foot rest, complete assembly
* K0046   Elevating leg rest, lower extension tube, each
* K0047   Elevating leg rest, upper hanger bracket, each
* K0048   Elevating leg rest, complete assembly
* K0049   Calf pad, each

* K0050   Ratchet assembly
* K0051   Cam release assembly, foot rest or leg rest, each
* K0052   Swing-away, detachable foot rests, each
* K0053   Elevating foot rests, articulating (telescoping), each
* K0054   Seat width of 10", 11", 12", 15", 17", or 20" for a high-strength, lightweight or ultralightweight wheelchair
* K0055   Seat depth of 15", 17", or 18" for a high-strength, lightweight or ultra-lightweight wheelchair
* K0056   Seat height less than 17" or equal to or greater than 21" for a high-strength, lightweight, or ultralight-weight wheelchair
* K0057   Seat width 19" or 20" for heavy duty or extra heavy duty chair
* K0058   Seat depth 17" or 18" for motorized/power wheelchair
* K0059   Plastic coated hand rim, each
* K0060   Steel hand rim, each
* K0061   Aluminum hand rim, each
* K0062   Hand rim with 8 to 10 vertical or oblique projections, each
* K0063   Hand rim with 12 to 16 vertical or olbique projections, each
* K0064   Zero pressure tube (flat-free inserts), any size, each
➡ * K0065   Spoke protectors, each
* K0066   Solid tire, any size, each
* K0067   Pneumatic tire, any size, each
* K0068   Pneumatic tire tube, each
* K0069   Rear wheel assembly, complete, with solid tire, spokes or molded, each
* K0070   Rear wheel assembly, complete, with pneumatic tire, spokes or molded, each
* K0071   Front caster assembly, complete, with pneumatic tire, each
* K0072   Front caster assembly, complete, with semi-pneumatic tire, each
* K0073   Caster pin lock, each
* K0074   Pneumatic caster tire, any size, each
* K0075   Semi-pneumatic caster tire, any size, each
* K0076   Solid caster tire, any size, each
* K0077   Front caster assembly, complete, with solid tire, each
* K0078   Pneumatic caster tire tube, each
* K0079   Wheel lock extension, pair
* K0080   Anti-rollback device, pair
* K0081   Wheel lock assembly, complete, each
* K0082   22 NF deep cycle lead acid battery, each
* K0083   22 NF gel cell battery, each

* K0084   Group 24 deep cycle lead acid battery, each
* K0085   Group 24 gel cell battery, each
* K0086   U-1 lead acid battery, each
* K0087   U-1 gel cell battery, each
* K0088   Battery charger, lead acid or gel cell
* K0089   Battery charger, dual mode
* K0090   Rear wheel tire for power wheelchair, any size, each
* K0091   Rear wheel tire tube other than zero pressure for power wheelchair, any size, each
* K0092   Rear wheel assembly for power wheelchair, complete each
* K0093   Rear wheel, zero pressure tire tube (flat-free insert) for power wheelchair, any size, each
* K0094   Wheel tire for power base, any size, each
* K0095   Wheel tire tube other than zero pressure for each base, any size, each
* K0096   Wheel assembly for power base, complete, each
* K0097   Wheel zero pressure tire tube (flat-free insert) for power base, any size, each
* K0098   Drive belt for power wheelchair
➡ * K0099   Front caster for power wheelchair, each
➡ * K0100   Wheelchair adapter for amputee, pair (device used to compensate for transfer of weight due to lost limbs to maintain proper balance)
➡ * K0101   One-arm drive attachment, each
➡ * K0102   Crutch and cane holder, each
* K0103   Transfer board, less than 25"
➡ * K0104   Cylinder tank carrier, each
➡ * K0105   IV hanger, each
* K0106   Arm trough, each
* K0107   Wheelchair tray
➡ * K0108   Wheelchair component or accessory, not otherwise specified
* K0109   Customization of wheelchair base frame, options or accessories

Spinal Orthotics

* K0112   Trunk support device, vest type, with inner frame, prefabricated
* K0113   Trunk support device, vest type, without inner frame, prefabricated
* K0114   Back support system for use with a wheelchair, with inner frame, prefabricated
* K0115   Seating system, back module, posterior-lateral control, with or without lateral supports, custom fabricated for attachment to wheelchair base

---

* K0116   Seating system, combined back and seat module, custom fabricated for attachment to wheelchair base

Immunosuppressive Drugs

K0119   (Deleted 12/31/99)
K0120   (Deleted 12/31/99)
K0122   (Deleted 12/31/99)
K0123   (Deleted 12/31/99)

Incontinence Supplies/Appliances

K0137   (Deleted 12/31/99)
K0138   (Deleted 12/31/99)
K0139   (Deleted 12/31/99)

Other

K0168   (Deleted 12/31/99)
K0169   (Deleted 12/31/99)
K0170   (Deleted 12/31/99)
K0171   (Deleted 12/31/99)
K0172   (Deleted 12/31/99)
K0173   (Deleted 12/31/99)
K0174   (Deleted 12/31/99)
K0175   (Deleted 12/31/99)
K0176   (Deleted 12/31/99)
K0177   (Deleted 12/31/99)
K0178   (Deleted 12/31/99)
K0179   (Deleted 12/31/99)
K0180   (Deleted 12/31/99)
K0181   (Deleted 12/31/99)
* K0182   Water, distilled, used with large volume nebulizer, 1000 ml
* K0183   Nasal application device, used with positive airway pressure device
* K0184   Nasal pillows/seals, replacement for nasal application device, pair
* K0185   Head gear, used with positive airway pressure device
* K0186   Chin strap, used with positive airway pressure device
* K0187   Tubing, used with positive airway pressure device
* K0188   Filter, disposable, used with positive airway pressure device
* K0189   Filter, non-disposable, used with positive airway pressure device
K0190   (Deleted 12/31/99)
K0191   (Deleted 12/31/99)
K0192   (Deleted 12/31/99)
K0193   (Deleted 9/30/99)
K0194   (Deleted 9/30/99)
⊛ K0195   Elevating leg rests, pair (for use with capped rental wheelchair base) CIM 60-9

* K0268   Humidifier, non-heated, used with positive airway pressure device
* K0269   Aerosol compressor, adjustable pressure, light duty for intermittent use
* K0270   Ultrasonic generator with small-volume ultrasonic nebulizer
K0277   (Deleted 12/31/99)
K0278   (Deleted 12/31/99)
K0279   (Deleted 12/31/99)
* K0280   Extension drainage tubing, any type, any length, with connector/adaptor, for use with urinary leg bag or urostomy pouch, each
* K0281   Lubricant, individual sterile packet, for insertion of urinary catheter, each
* K0283   Saline solution, per 10 ml, metered dose dispenser, for use with inhalation drugs
K0284   (Deleted 12/31/99)
K0400   (Deleted 12/31/99)
K0401   (Deleted 12/31/99)
* K0407   Urinary catheter anchoring device, adhesive skin attachment
* K0408   Urinary catheter anchoring device, leg strap
* K0409   Sterile water irrigation solution, 1000 ml
* K0410   Male external catheter, with adhesive coating, each
* K0411   Male external catheter, with adhesive strip, each
K0412   (Deleted 12/31/99)
⊛ K0415   Prescription antiemetic drug, oral, per 1 mg, for use in conjunction with oral anti-cancer drug, not otherwise specified MCM 2049.5C
⊛ K0416   Prescription antiemetic drug, rectal, per 1 mg, for use in conjunction with oral anti-cancer drug, not otherwise specified MCM 2049.5C
K0417   (Deleted 12/31/99)
K0418   (Deleted 12/31/99)
K0419   (Deleted 12/31/99)
K0420   (Deleted 12/31/99)
K0421   (Deleted 12/31/99)
K0422   (Deleted 12/31/99)
K0423   (Deleted 12/31/99)
K0424   (Deleted 12/31/99)
K0425   (Deleted 12/31/99)
K0426   (Deleted 12/31/99)
K0427   (Deleted 12/31/99)
K0428   (Deleted 12/31/99)
K0429   (Deleted 12/31/99)
K0430   (Deleted 12/31/99)
K0431   (Deleted 12/31/99)
K0432   (Deleted 12/31/99)
K0433   (Deleted 12/31/99)

	K0434	(Deleted 12/31/99)
	K0435	(Deleted 12/31/99)
	K0436	(Deleted 12/31/99)
	K0437	(Deleted 12/31/99)
	K0438	(Deleted 12/31/99)
	K0439	(Deleted 12/31/99)

* K0440   Nasal prosthesis—provided by a non-physician

* K0441   Midfacial prosthesis—provided by a non-physician

* K0442   Orbital prosthesis—provided by a non-physician

* K0443   Upper facial prosthesis—provided by a non-physician

* K0444   Hemi-facial prosthesis—provided by a non-physician

* K0445   Auricular prosthesis—provided by a non-physician

* K0446   Partial facial prosthesis—provided by a non-physician

* K0447   Nasal septal prosthesis—provided by a non-physician

* K0448   Unspecified maxillofacial prosthesis, by report—provided by a non-physician

* K0449   Repair or modification of maxillofacial prosthesis, labor component, 15 minute increments—provided by a non-physician

* K0450   Adhesive, liquid, for use with facial prosthesis only, per ounce

* K0451   Adhesive remover, wipes, for use with facial prosthesis, per box of 50

* K0452   Wheelchair bearings, any type

K0453   (Deleted 12/31/98)
Cross Reference J0285

⊛ K0455   Infusion pump used for uninterrupted administration of epoprostenol
CIM 60-14

* K0456   Hospital bed, heavy duty, extra wide, with any type side rails, with mattress

* K0457   Extra wide, heavy duty commode chair, each

* K0458   Heavy duty walker, without wheels, each

* K0459   Heavy duty wheeled walker, each

* K0460   Power add-on, to convert manual wheelchair to motorized wheelchair, joystick control

* K0461   Power add-on, to convert manual wheelchair to power operated vehicle, tiller control

▶⊛ K0462   Temporary replacement for patient owed equipment being repaired, any type
MCM 5102.3

⊛ K0501   Aerosol compressor, battery powered, for use with small volume nebulizer
CIM 60-9

K0503   (Deleted 12/31/99)

	K0504	(Deleted 12/31/99)
	K0505	(Deleted 12/31/99)
	K0506	(Deleted 12/31/99)
	K0507	(Deleted 12/31/99)
	K0508	(Deleted 12/31/99)
	K0509	(Deleted 12/31/99)
	K0511	(Deleted 12/31/99)
	K0512	(Deleted 12/31/99)
	K0513	(Deleted 12/31/99)
	K0514	(Deleted 12/31/99)
	K0515	(Deleted 12/31/99)
	K0516	(Deleted 12/31/99)
	K0518	(Deleted 12/31/99)
	K0519	(Deleted 12/31/99)
	K0520	(Deleted 12/31/99)
	K0521	(Deleted 12/31/99)
	K0522	(Deleted 12/31/99)
	K0523	(Deleted 12/31/99)
	K0524	(Deleted 12/31/99)
	K0525	(Deleted 12/31/99)
	K0526	(Deleted 12/31/99)
	K0527	(Deleted 12/31/99)
	K0528	(Deleted 12/31/99)

* K0529   Sterile water or sterile saline, 1000 ml, used with large volume nebulizer
MCM 2049

K0530   (Deleted 12/31/99)

▶⊛ K0531   Humidifier, heated, used with positive airway pressure device
CIM 60-9

▶⊛ K0532   Respiratory assist device, bi-level pressure capability, without backup rate feature, used with noninvasive interface, e.g., nasal or facial mask (intermittent assist device with continuous positive airway pressure device)
CIM 60-9

▶⊛ K0533   Respiratory assist device, bi-level pressure capability, with backup rate feature, used with noninvasive interface, e.g., nasal or facial mask (intermittent assist device with continuous positive airway pressure device)
CIM 60-9

▶⊛ K0534   Respiratory assist device, bi-level pressure capability, with backup rate feature, used with invasive interface, e.g., tracheostomy tube (intermittent assist device with continuous positive airway pressure device)
CIM 60-9

ORTHOTIC PROCEDURES—L0100–L4999

Orthotic Devices—Spinal

Cervical

* L0100   Cervical, craniostenosis, helmet molded to patient model

---

⊛ **Special coverage instructions**   ◆ **Not covered by or valid for Medicare**   * **Carrier discretion**   ◀▶ **New code**   ⬅▬▬➡ **Revised code**

* L0110   Cervical, craniostenosis, helmet, non-molded
* L0120   Cervical, flexible, non-adjustable (foam collar)
* L0130   Cervical, flexible, thermoplastic collar, molded to patient
* L0140   Cervical, semi-rigid, adjustable (plastic collar)
* L0150   Cervical, semi-rigid, adjustable molded chin cup (plastic collar with mandibular/occipital piece)
* L0160   Cervical, semi-rigid, wire frame occipital/mandibular support
* L0170   Cervical, collar, molded to patient model
* L0172   Cervical, collar, semi-rigid thermoplastic foam, two piece
* L0174   Cervical, collar, semi-rigid, thermoplastic foam, two piece with thoracic extension

Multiple Post Collar

* L0180   Cervical, multiple post collar, occipital/mandibular supports, adjustable
* L0190   Cervical, multiple post collar, occipital/mandibular supports, adjustable cervical bars (SOMI, Guilford, Taylor types)
* L0200   Cervical, multiple post collar, occipital/mandibular supports, adjustable cervical bars, and thoracic extension

Thoracic

* L0210   Thoracic, rib belt
* L0220   Thoracic, rib belt, custom fabricated

Thoracic—Lumbar—Sacral

Flexible

* L0300   Thoracic-lumbar-sacral-orthosis (TLSO), flexible (dorso-lumbar surgical support)
* L0310   TLSO, flexible (dorso-lumbar surgical support), custom fabricated
* L0315   TLSO, flexible dorso-lumbar surgical support, elastic type, with rigid posterior panel
* L0317   TLSO, flexible dorso-lumbar surgical support, hyperextension, elastic type, with rigid posterior panel

Anterior-Posterior Control

* L0320   TLSO, anterior-posterior control (Taylor type), with apron front

* L0330   TLSO, anterior-posterior-lateral control (Knight-Taylor type), with apron front

Anterior-Posterior-Lateral Rotary-Control

* L0340   TLSO, anterior-posterior-lateral-rotary control (Arnold, Magnuson, Steindler types), with apron front
* L0350   TLSO, anterior-posterior-lateral-rotary control, flexion compression jacket, custom fitted
* L0360   TLSO, anterior-posterior-lateral-rotary control, flexion compression jacket molded to patient model
* L0370   TLSO, anterior-posterior-lateral-rotary control, hyperextension (Jewett, Lennox, Baker, Cash types)
* L0380   TLSO, anterior-posterior-lateral-rotary control, with extensions
* L0390   TLSO, anterior-posterior-lateral control molded to patient model
* L0400   TLSO, anterior-posterior-lateral control molded to patient model, with interface material
* L0410   TLSO, anterior-posterior-lateral control, two-piece construction molded to patient model
* L0420   TLSO, anterior-posterior-lateral control, two piece construction molded to patient model, with interface material
* L0430   TLSO, anterior-posterior-lateral control, with interface material custom fitted
* L0440   TLSO, anterior-posterior-lateral control, with overlapping front section, spring steel front, custom fitted

Lumbar—Sacral

Flexible

* L0500   Lumbar-sacral-orthosis (LSO), flexible, (lumbar-sacral surgical support)
* L0510   LSO, flexible (lumbar-sacral surgical support), custom fabricated
* L0515   LSO, flexible, lumbar-sacral surgical support elastic type, with rigid posterior panel

Anterior-Posterior-Lateral Control

* L0520   LSO, anterior-posterior-lateral control (Knight, Wilcox types), with apron front

Anterior-Posterior Control

* L0530   LSO, anterior-posterior control (Macausland type), with apron front

Lumbar-Flexion

* L0540   LSO, lumbar flexion (Williams flexion type)

Anterior-Posterior-Lateral Control (Body Jacket)

* L0550   LSO, anterior-posterior-lateral control, molded to patient model
* L0560   LSO, anterior-posterior lateral control, molded to patient model, with interface material
* L0565   LSO, anterior-posterior-lateral control, custom fitted

Sacroiliac

Flexible

* L0600   Sacroiliac, flexible (sacroiliac surgical support)
* L0610   Sacroiliac, flexible (sacroiliac surgical support), custom fabricated

Semi-rigid

* L0620   Sacroiliac, semi-rigid (Goldthwaite, Osgood types), with apron front

Cervical-Thoracic-Lumbar-Sacral

Anterior-Posterior-Lateral Control

* L0700   Cervical-thoracic-lumbar-sacral-orthoses (CTLSO), anterior-posterior-lateral control, molded to patient model (Minerva type)
* L0710   CTLSO, anterior-posterior-lateral control, molded to patient model, with interface material (Minerva type)

HALO Procedure

* L0810   HALO procedure, cervical halo incorporated into jacket vest
* L0820   HALO procedure, cervical halo incorporated into plaster body jacket
* L0830   HALO procedure, cervical halo incorporated into Milwaukee type orthosis
* L0860   Addition to HALO procedures, magnetic resonance image compatible system

Torso Supports

Ptosis Supports

* L0900   Torso support, ptosis support
* L0910   Torso support, ptosis support, custom fabricated

Pendulous Abdomen Supports

* L0920   Torso support, pendulous abdomen support
* L0930   Torso support, pendulous abdomen support, custom fabricated

Postsurgical Supports

* L0940   Torso support, postsurgical support
* L0950   Torso support, postsurgical support, custom fabricated
* L0960   Torso support, postsurgical support, pads for postsurgical support

Additions to Spinal Orthoses

* L0970   TLSO, corset front
* L0972   LSO, corset front
* L0974   TLSO, full corset
* L0976   LSO, full corset
* L0978   Axillary crutch extension
* L0980   Peroneal straps, pair
* L0982   Stocking supporter grips, set of four (4)
* L0984   Protective body sock, each
* L0999   Addition to spinal orthosis, not otherwise specified

Orthotic Devices—Scoliosis Procedures—L1000–L1499

Note: Orthotic care of scoliosis differs from other orthotic care in that the treatment is more dynamic in nature and utilizes ongoing continual modification of the orthosis to the patient's changing condition.

This coding structure uses the proper names—or eponyms—of the procedures because they have historic and universal acceptance in the profession. It should be recognized that variations to the basic procedures described by the founders/developers are accepted in various medical and orthotic practices throughout the country. All procedures include a model of patient when indicated.

Scoliosis—Cervical—Thoracic—Lumbar—Sacral (Milwaukee)

* L1000   Cervical-thoracic-lumbar-sacral orthosis (CTLSO) (Milwaukee), inclusive of furnishing initial orthosis, including model
* L1010   Addition to cervical-thoracic-lumbar-sacral orthosis (CTLSO) or scoliosis orthosis, axilla sling

Correction Pads

* L1020   Addition to CTLSO or scoliosis orthosis, kyphosis pad

* L1025 Addition to CTLSO or scoliosis orthosis, kyphosis pad, floating
* L1030 Addition to CTLSO or scoliosis orthosis, lumbar bolster pad
* L1040 Addition to CTLSO or scoliosis orthosis, lumbar or lumbar rib pad
* L1050 Addition to CTLSO or scoliosis orthosis, sternal pad
* L1060 Addition to CTLSO or scoliosis orthosis, thoracic pad
* L1070 Addition to CTLSO or scoliosis orthosis, trapezius sling
* L1080 Addition to CTLSO or scoliosis orthosis, outrigger
* L1085 Addition to CTLSO or scoliosis orthosis, outrigger, bilateral with vertical extensions
* L1090 Addition to CTLSO or scoliosis orthosis, lumbar sling
* L1100 Addition to CTLSO or scoliosis orthosis, ring flange, plastic or leather
* L1110 Addition to CTLSO or scoliosis orthosis, ring flange, plastic or leather, molded to patient model
* L1120 Addition to CTLSO, scoliosis orthosis, cover for upright, each

Scoliosis—Cervical—Thoracic—Lumbar—Sacral (Low Profile)

* L1200 Thoracic-lumbar-sacral-orthosis (TLSO), inclusive of furnishing initial orthosis only
* L1210 Addition to TLSO, (low profile), lateral thoracic extension
* L1220 Addition to TLSO (low profile), anterior thoracic extension
* L1230 Addition to TLSO (low profile), milwaukee type superstructure
* L1240 Addition to TLSO (low profile), lumbar derotation pad
* L1250 Addition to TLSO (low profile), anterior ASIS pad
* L1260 Addition to TLSO (low profile), anterior thoracic derotation pad
* L1270 Addition to TLSO (low profile), abdominal pad
* L1280 Addition to TLSO (low profile), rib gusset (elastic), each
* L1290 Addition to TLSO (low profile), lateral trochanteric pad

Other Scoliosis Procedures

* L1300 Other scoliosis procedure, body jacket molded to patient model
* L1310 Other scoliosis procedure, postoperative body jacket
* L1499 Spinal orthosis, NOS

Thoracic—Hip—Knee—Ankle

* L1500 Thoracic-hip-knee-ankle orthosis (THKAO), mobility frame (Newington, Parapodium types)
* L1510 THKAO, standing frame
* L1520 THKAO, swivel walker

Orthotic Devices—Lower Limb

Note: the procedures in L1600-L2999 are considered as 'base' or 'basic procedures' and may be modified by listing procedure from the 'additions sections' and adding them to the base procedure.

Hip—Flexible

* L1600 Hip orthosis (HO), abduction control of hip joints, flexible, Frejka type with cover
* L1610 HO, abduction control of hip joints, flexible, Frejka cover only
* L1620 HO, abduction control of hip joints, flexible, Pavlik harness
* L1630 HO, abduction control of hip joints, semi-flexible (Von Rosen type)
* L1640 HO, abduction control of hip joints, static, pelvic band or spreader bar, thigh cuffs
* L1650 HO, abduction control of hip joints, static, adjustable, (Ilfled type)
* L1660 HO, abduction control of hip joints, static, plastic
* L1680 HO, abduction control of hip joints, dynamic, pelvic control, adjustable hip motion control, thigh cuffs (Rancho hip action type)
* L1685 HO, abduction control of hip joint, postoperative hip abduction type, custom fabricated
* L1686 HO, abduction control of hip joint, postoperative hip abduction type
* L1690 Combination, bilateral, lumbar-sacral, hip, femur orthosis providing adduction and internal rotation control

Legg-Perthes

* L1700 Legg-Perthes orthosis (Toronto type)
* L1710 Legg-Perthes orthosis (Newington type)
* L1720 Legg-Perthes orthosis, trilateral (Tachdijan type)
* L1730 Legg-Perthes orthosis (Scottish Rite type)
* L1750 Legg-Perthes orthosis, Legg Perthes sling (Sam Browne type)
* L1755 Legg-Perthes orthosis (Patten bottom type)

Knee

* L1800   Knee orthosis (KO), elastic with stays
* L1810   KO, elastic with joints
* L1815   KO, elastic or other elastic type material with condylar pads
* L1820   KO, elastic with condylar pads and joints
* L1825   KO, elastic knee cap
* L1830   KO, immobilizer, canvas longitudinal
* L1832   KO, adjustable knee joints, positional orthosis, rigid support
* L1834   KO, without knee joint, rigid, molded to patient model
* L1840   KO, derotation, medial-lateral, anterior cruciate ligament, custom fabricated to patient model
* L1843   KO, single upright, thigh and calf, with adjustable flexion and extension joint, medial-lateral and rotation control custom fitted
* L1844   KO, single upright, thigh and calf, with adjustable flexion and extension joint, medial-lateral and rotation control, molded to patient model
* L1845   KO, double upright, thigh and calf, with adjustable flexion and extension joint, medial-lateral and rotation control, custom fitted
* L1846   KO, double upright, thigh and calf, with adjustable flexion and extension joint, medial-lateral and rotation control, molded to patient model
* L1847   Knee orthosis, double upright with adjustable joint, with inflatable air support chambers
* L1850   KO, Swedish type
* L1855   KO, molded plastic, thigh and calf sections, with double upright knee joints, molded to patient model
* L1858   KO, molded plastic, polycentric knee joints, pneumatic knee pads (CTI)
* L1860   KO, modification of supracondylar prosthetic socket, molded to patient model (SK)
* L1870   KO, double upright, thigh and calf lacers, molded to patient model with knee joints
* L1880   KO, double upright, non-molded thigh and calf cuffs/lacers with knee joints
* L1885   KO, single or double upright, thigh and calf, with functional active resistance control

Ankle—Foot

* L1900   Ankle-foot orthosis (AFO), spring wire, dorsiflexion assist calf band
* L1902   AFO, ankle gauntlet

* L1904   AFO, molded ankle gauntlet, molded to patient model
* L1906   AFO, multiligamentus ankle support
* L1910   AFO, posterior, single bar, clasp attachment to shoe counter
* L1920   AFO, single upright with static or adjustable stop (Phelps or Perlstein type)
* L1930   AFO, plastic
* L1940   AFO, molded to patient model, plastic
* L1945   AFO, molded to patient model, plastic, rigid anterior tibial section (floor reaction)
* L1950   AFO, spiral, molded to patient model (IRM type), plastic
* L1960   AFO, posterior solid ankle, molded to patient model, plastic
* L1970   AFO, plastic molded to patient model, with ankle joint
* L1980   AFO, single upright free plantar dorsiflexion, solid stirrup, calf band/cuff (single bar 'BK' orthosis)
* L1990   AFO, double upright free plantar dorsiflexion, solid stirrup, calf band/cuff (double bar 'BK' orthosis)

Hip-Knee-Ankle-Foot (or Any Combination)

Note: L2000, L2020, and L2036 are base procedures to be used with any knee joint. L2010 and L2030 are to be used only with no knee joint.

* L2000   Knee-ankle-foot-orthosis (KAFO), single upright, free knee, free ankle, solid stirrup, thigh and calf bands/cuffs (single bar 'AK' orthosis)
* L2010   KAFO, single upright, free ankle, solid stirrup, thigh and calf bands/cuffs (single bar 'AK' orthosis), without knee joint
* L2020   KAFO, double upright, free knee, free ankle, solid stirrup, thigh and calf bands/cuffs (double bar 'AK' orthosis)
* L2030   KAFO, double upright, free ankle, solid stirrup, thigh and calf bands/cuffs (double bar 'AK' orthosis), without knee joint
* L2035   KAFO, full plastic, static, prefabricated (pediatric size)
* L2036   KAFO, full plastic, double upright, free knee, molded to patient model
* L2037   KAFO, full plastic, single upright, free knee, molded to patient model
* L2038   KAFO, full plastic, without knee joint, multi-axis ankle, molded to patient model (Lively orthosis or equal)

* L2039   KAFO, full plastic, single upright, polyaxial hinge, medial-lateral rotation control, molded to patient model

Torsion Control

* L2040   Hip-knee-ankle-foot orthosis (HKAFO), torsion control, bilateral rotation straps, pelvic band/belt

* L2050   HKAFO, torsion control, bilateral torsion cables, hip joint, pelvic band/belt

* L2060   HKAFO, torsion control, bilateral torsion cables, ball bearing hip joint, pelvic band/belt

* L2070   HKAFO, torsion control, unilateral rotation straps, pelvic band/belt

* L2080   HKAFO, torsion control, unilateral torsion cable, hip joint, pelvic band/belt

* L2090   HKAFO, torsion control, unilateral torsion cable, ball bearing hip joint, pelvic band/belt

Fracture Orthoses

* L2102   Ankle-foot-orthosis (AFO), fracture orthosis, tibial fracture cast orthosis, plaster type casting material, molded to patient

* L2104   AFO, fracture orthosis, tibial fracture cast orthosis, synthetic type casting material, molded to patient

* L2106   AFO, fracture orthosis, tibial fracture cast orthosis, thermoplastic type casting material, molded to patient

* L2108   AFO, fracture orthosis, tibial fracture cast orthosis, molded to patient model

* L2112   AFO, fracture orthosis, tibial fracture orthosis, soft

* L2114   AFO, fracture orthosis, tibial fracture orthosis, semi-rigid

* L2116   AFO, fracture orthosis, tibial fracture orthosis, rigid

* L2122   Knee-ankle-foot-orthosis, (KAFO), fracture orthosis, femoral fracture cast orthosis, plaster type casting material, molded to patient

* L2124   KAFO, fracture orthosis, femoral fracture cast orthosis, synthetic type casting material, molded to patient

* L2126   KAFO, fracture orthosis, femoral fracture cast orthosis, thermoplastic type casting material, molded to patient

* L2128   KAFO, fracture orthosis, femoral fracture cast orthosis, molded to patient model

* L2132   KAFO, fracture orthosis, femoral fracture cast orthosis, soft

* L2134   KAFO, fracture orthosis, femoral fracture cast orthosis, semi-rigid

* L2136   KAFO, fracture orthosis, femoral fracture cast orthosis, rigid

Additions to Fracture Orthosis

* L2180   Addition to lower extremity fracture orthosis, plastic shoe insert with ankle joints

* L2182   Addition to lower extremity fracture orthosis, drop lock knee joint

* L2184   Addition to lower extremity fracture orthosis, limited motion knee joint

* L2186   Addition to lower extremity fracture orthosis, adjustable motion knee joint (Lerman type)

* L2188   Addition to lower extremity fracture orthosis, quadrilateral brim

* L2190   Addition to lower extremity fracture orthosis, waist belt

* L2192   Addition to lower extremity fracture orthosis, hip joint, pelvic band, thigh flange, and pelvic belt

Additions to Lower Extremity Orthosis

Additions—Shoe—Ankle—Shin—Knee

* L2200   Addition to lower extremity, limited ankle motion, each joint

* L2210   Addition to lower extremity, dorsiflexion assist (plantar flexion resist), each joint

* L2220   Addition to lower extremity, dorsiflexion and plantar flexion assist/resist, each joint

* L2230   Addition to lower extremity, split flat caliper stirrups and plate attachment

* L2240   Addition to lower extremity, round caliper and plate attachment

* L2250   Addition to lower extremity, footplate, molded to patient model, stirrup attachment

* L2260   Addition to lower extremity, reinforced solid stirrup (Scott-Craig type)

* L2265   Addition to lower extremity, long tongue stirrup

* L2270   Addition to lower extremity, varus/valgus correction ('T') strap, padded/lined or malleolus pad

* L2275   Addition to lower extremity, varus/valgus correction, plastic modification, padded/lined

* L2280   Addition to lower extremity, molded inner boot

* L2300 Addition to lower extremity, abduction bar (bilateral hip involvement), jointed, adjustable
* L2310 Addition to lower extremity, abduction bar, straight
* L2320 Addition to lower extremity, non-molded lacer
* L2330 Addition to lower extremity, lacer molded to patient model
* L2335 Addition to lower extremity, anterior swing band
* L2340 Addition to lower extremity, pre-tibial shell, molded to patient model
* L2350 Addition to lower extremity, prosthetic type, (BK) socket, molded to patient model, (used for 'PTB' 'AFO' orthoses)
* L2360 Addition to lower extremity, extended steel shank
* L2370 Addition to lower extremity, Patten bottom
* L2375 Addition to lower extremity, torsion control, ankle joint and half solid stirrup
* L2380 Addition to lower extremity, torsion control, straight knee joint, each joint
* L2385 Addition to lower extremity, straight knee joint, heavy duty, each joint
* L2390 Addition to lower extremity, offset knee joint, each joint
* L2395 Addition to lower extremity, offset knee joint, heavy duty, each joint
* L2397 Addition to lower extremity orthosis, suspension sleeve

Additions to Straight Knee or Offset Knee Joints

* L2405 Addition to knee joint, drop lock, each joint
* L2415 Addition to knee joint, cam lock (Swiss, French, Bail types), each joint
* L2425 Addition to knee joint, disc or dial lock for adjustable knee flexion, each joint
* L2430 Addition to knee joint, ratchet lock for active and progressive knee extension, each joint
* L2435 Addition to knee joint, polycentric joint, each joint
* L2492 Addition to knee joint, lift loop for drop lock ring

Additions—Thigh/Weight Bearing

Gluteal/Ischial Weight

* L2500 Addition to lower extremity, thigh/weight bearing, gluteal/ischial weight bearing, ring

* L2510 Addition to lower extremity, thigh/weight bearing, quadri-lateral brim, molded to patient model
* L2520 Addition to lower extremity, thigh/weight bearing, quadri-lateral brim, custom fitted
* L2525 Addition to lower extremity, thigh/weight bearing, ischial containment/narrow M-L brim molded to patient model
* L2526 Addition to lower extremity, thigh/weight bearing, ischial containment/narrow M-L brim, custom fitted
* L2530 Addition to lower extremity, thigh-weight bearing, lacer, non-molded
* L2540 Addition to lower extremity, thigh/weight bearing, lacer, molded to patient model
* L2550 Addition to lower extremity, thigh/weight bearing, high roll cuff

Additions—Pelvic and Thoracic Control

* L2570 Addition to lower extremity, pelvic control, hip joint, Clevis type two position joint, each
* L2580 Addition to lower extremity, pelvic control, pelvic sling
* L2600 Addition to lower extremity, pelvic control, hip joint, Clevis type, or thrust bearing, free, each
* L2610 Addition to lower extremity, pelvic control, hip joint, Clevis or thrust bearing, lock, each
* L2620 Addition to lower extremity, pelvic control, hip joint, heavy duty, each
* L2622 Addition to lower extremity, pelvic control, hip joint, adjustable flexion, each
* L2624 Addition to lower extremity, pelvic control, hip joint, adjustable flexion, extension, abduction control, each
* L2627 Addition to lower extremity, pelvic control, plastic, molded to patient model, reciprocating hip joint and cables
* L2628 Addition to lower extremity, pelvic control, metal frame, reciprocating hip joint and cables
* L2630 Addition to lower extremity, pelvic control, band and belt, unilateral
* L2640 Addition to lower extremity, pelvic control, band and belt, bilateral
* L2650 Addition to lower extremity, pelvic and thoracic control, gluteal pad, each
* L2660 Addition to lower extremity, thoracic control, thoracic band
* L2670 Addition to lower extremity, thoracic control, paraspinal uprights

---

⊘ Special coverage instructions   ◆ Not covered by or valid for Medicare   * Carrier discretion   ◀▶ New code   ⬅▥▥▷ Revised code

* L2680   Addition to lower extremity, thoracic control, lateral support uprights

Additions—General

* L2750   Addition to lower extremity orthosis, plating chrome or nickel, per bar
* L2755   Addition to lower extremity orthosis, carbon graphite lamination
* L2760   Addition to lower extremity orthosis, extension, per extension, per bar (for lineal adjustment for growth)
* L2770   Addition to lower extremity orthosis, any material—per bar or joint
* L2780   Addition to lower extremity orthosis, non-corrosive finish, per bar
* L2785   Addition to lower extremity orthosis, drop lock retainer, each
* L2795   Addition to lower extremity orthosis, knee control, full kneecap
* L2800   Addition to lower extremity orthosis, knee control, knee cap, medial or lateral pull
* L2810   Addition to lower extremity orthosis, knee control, condylar pad
* L2820   Addition to lower extremity orthosis, soft interface for molded plastic, below knee section
* L2830   Addition to lower extremity orthosis, soft interface for molded plastic, above knee section
* L2840   Addition to lower extremity orthosis, tibial length sock, fracture or equal, each
* L2850   Addition to lower extremity orthosis, femoral length sock, fracture or equal, each
* L2860   Addition to lower extremity joint, knee or ankle, concentric adjustable torsion style mechanism, each
* L2999   Lower extremity orthoses, not otherwise specified

Foot (Orthopedic Shoes)

Insert, Removable, Molded to Patient Model

⊛ L3000   Foot, insert, removable, molded to patient model, 'UCB' type, Berkeley shell, each
    MCM 2323
⊛ L3001   Foot, insert, removable, molded to patient model, Spenco, each
    MCM 2323
⊛ L3002   Foot, insert, removable, molded to patient model, Plastazote or equal, each
    MCM 2323

⊛ L3003   Foot, insert, removable, molded to patient model, silicone gel, each
    MCM 2323
⊛ L3010   Foot, insert, removable, molded to patient model, longitudinal arch support, each
    MCM 2323
⊛ L3020   Foot, insert, removable, molded to patient model, longitudinal/metatarsal support, each
    MCM 2323
⊛ L3030   Foot, insert, removable, formed to patient foot, each
    MCM 2323

Arch Support, Removable, Premolded

⊛ L3040   Foot, arch support, removable, premolded, longitudinal, each
    MCM 2323
⊛ L3050   Foot, arch support, removable, premolded, metatarsal, each
    MCM 2323
⊛ L3060   Foot, arch support, removable, premolded, longitudinal/metatarsal, each
    MCM 2323

Arch Support, Non-removable, Attached to Shoe

⊛ L3070   Foot, arch support, non-removable attached to shoe, longitudinal, each
    MCM 2323
⊛ L3080   Foot, arch support, non-removable attached to shoe, metatarsal, each
    MCM 2323
⊛ L3090   Foot, arch support, non-removable attached to shoe, longitudinal/metatarsal, each
    MCM 2323
⊛ L3100   Hallus-valgus night dynamic splint
    MCM 2323

Abduction and Rotation Bars

⊛ L3140   Foot, abduction rotation bar, including shoes
    MCM 2323
⊛ L3150   Foot, abduction rotation bar, without shoes
    MCM 2323
* L3160   Foot, adjustable shoe-styled positioning device
⊛ L3170   Foot, plastic heel stabilizer
    MCM 2323

Orthopedic Footwear

✳ L3201 Orthopedic shoe, oxford with supinator or pronator, infant
MCM 2323

✳ L3202 Orthopedic shoe, oxford with supinator or pronator, child
MCM 2323

✳ L3203 Orthopedic shoe, oxford with supinator or pronator, junior
MCM 2323

✳ L3204 Orthopedic shoe, hightop with supinator or pronator, infant
MCM 2323

✳ L3206 Orthopedic shoe, hightop with supinator or pronator, child
MCM 2323

✳ L3207 Orthopedic shoe, hightop with supinator or pronator, junior
MCM 2323

✳ L3208 Surgical boot, infant, each
MCM 2079

✳ L3209 Surgical boot, each, child
MCM 2079

✳ L3211 Surgical boot, each, junior
MCM 2079

✳ L3212 Benesch boot, pair, infant
MCM 2079

✳ L3213 Benesch boot, pair, child
MCM 2079

✳ L3214 Benesch boot, pair, junior
MCM 2079

◆ L3215 Orthopedic footwear, ladies' shoes, oxford
Medicare Statute 1862A8

◆ L3216 Orthopedic footwear, ladies' shoes, depth inlay
Medicare Statute 1862A8

◆ L3217 Orthopedic footwear, ladies' shoes, hightop, depth inlay
Medicare Statute 1862A8

✳ L3218 Orthopedic footwear, ladies' surgical boot, each
MCM 2323

◆ L3219 Orthopedic footwear, men's shoes, oxford
Medicare Statute 1862A8

◆ L3221 Orthopedic footwear, men's shoes, depth inlay
Medicare Statute 1862A8

◆ L3222 Orthopedic footwear, men's shoes, hightop, depth inlay
Medicare Statute 1862A8

✳ L3223 Orthopedic footwear, men's surgical boot, each
MCM 2323

✳ L3224 Orthopedic footwear, ladies' shoe, oxford, used as an integral part of a brace (orthosis)
MCM 2323D

✳ L3225 Orthopedic footwear, men's shoe, oxford, used as an integral part of a brace (orthosis)
MCM 2323D

✳ L3230 Orthopedic footwear, custom shoes, depth inlay
MCM 2323

✳ L3250 Orthopedic footwear, custom molded shoe, removable inner mold, prosthetic shoe, each
MCM 2323

✳ L3251 Foot, shoe molded to patient model, silicone shoe, each
MCM 2323

✳ L3252 Foot, shoe molded to patient model, Plastazote (or similar), custom fabricated, each
MCM 2323

✳ L3253 Foot, molded shoe Plastazote (or similar), custom fitted, each
MCM 2323

✳ L3254 Non-standard size or width
MCM 2323

✳ L3255 Non-standard size or length
MCM 2323

✳ L3257 Orthopedic footwear, additional charge for split size
MCM 2323

✳ L3260 Ambulatory surgical boot, each
MCM 2079

✱ L3265 Plastazote sandal, each

Shoe Modifications

Lifts

✳ L3300 Lift, elevation, heel, tapered to metatarsals, per inch
MCM 2323

✳ L3310 Lift, elevation, heel and sole, Neoprene, per inch
MCM 2323

✳ L3320 Lift, elevation, heel and sole, cork, per inch
MCM 2323

✳ L3330 Lift, elevation, metal extension (skate)
MCM 2323

✳ L3332 Lift, elevation, inside shoe, tapered, up to ½ in
MCM 2323

✳ L3334 Lift, elevation, heel, per inch
MCM 2323

Wedges

✳ L3340 Heel wedge, SACH
MCM 2323

✳ L3350 Heel wedge
MCM 2323

✳ **Special coverage instructions**   ◆ **Not covered by or valid for Medicare**   ✱ **Carrier discretion**   ◀▶ **New code**   ◀▬ ▬▶ **Revised code**

⊛ L3360　Sole wedge, outside sole
　　　　　MCM 2323
⊛ L3370　Sole wedge, between sole
　　　　　MCM 2323
⊛ L3380　Clubfoot wedge
　　　　　MCM 2323
⊛ L3390　Outflare wedge
　　　　　MCM 2323
⊛ L3400　Metatarsal bar wedge, rocker
　　　　　MCM 2323
⊛ L3410　Metatarsal bar wedge, between sole
　　　　　MCM 2323
⊛ L3420　Full sole and heel wedge, between
　　　　　sole
　　　　　MCM 2323

Heels

⊛ L3430　Heel, counter, plastic reinforced
　　　　　MCM 2323
⊛ L3440　Heel, counter, leather reinforced
　　　　　MCM 2323
⊛ L3450　Heel, SACH cushion type
　　　　　MCM 2323
⊛ L3455　Heel, new leather, standard
　　　　　MCM 2323
⊛ L3460　Heel, new rubber, standard
　　　　　MCM 2323
⊛ L3465　Heel, Thomas with wedge
　　　　　MCM 2323
⊛ L3470　Heel, Thomas extended to ball
　　　　　MCM 2323
⊛ L3480　Heel, pad and depression for spur
　　　　　MCM 2323
⊛ L3485　Heel, pad, removable for spur
　　　　　MCM 2323

Orthopedic Shoe Additions

⊛ L3500　Orthopedic shoe addition, insole,
　　　　　leather
　　　　　MCM 2323
⊛ L3510　Orthopedic shoe addition, insole,
　　　　　rubber
　　　　　MCM 2323
⊛ L3520　Orthopedic shoe addition, insole,
　　　　　felt covered with leather
　　　　　MCM 2323
⊛ L3530　Orthopedic shoe addition, sole, half
　　　　　MCM 2323
⊛ L3540　Orthopedic shoe addition, sole, full
　　　　　MCM 2323
⊛ L3550　Orthopedic shoe addition, toe tap,
　　　　　standard
　　　　　MCM 2323
⊛ L3560　Orthopedic shoe addition, toe tap,
　　　　　horseshoe
　　　　　MCM 2323

⊛ L3570　Orthopedic shoe addition, special
　　　　　extension to instep (leather with
　　　　　eyelets)
　　　　　MCM 2323
⊛ L3580　Orthopedic shoe addition, convert
　　　　　instep to Velcro closure
　　　　　MCM 2323
⊛ L3590　Orthopedic shoe addition, convert
　　　　　firm shoe counter to soft counter
　　　　　MCM 2323
⊛ L3595　Orthopedic shoe addition, March bar
　　　　　MCM 2323

Transfer or Replacement

⊛ L3600　Transfer of an orthosis from one shoe
　　　　　to another, caliper plate, existing
　　　　　MCM 2323
⊛ L3610　Transfer of an orthosis from one
　　　　　shoe to another, caliper plate, new
　　　　　MCM 2323
⊛ L3620　Transfer of an orthosis from one shoe
　　　　　to another, solid stirrup, existing
　　　　　MCM 2323
⊛ L3630　Transfer of an orthosis from one
　　　　　shoe to another, solid stirrup, new
　　　　　MCM 2323
⊛ L3640　Transfer of an orthosis from one
　　　　　shoe to another, Dennis Browne
　　　　　splint (Riveton), both shoes
　　　　　MCM 2323
⊛ L3649　Orthopedic shoe, modification, addi-
　　　　　tion or transfer, not otherwise speci-
　　　　　fied
　　　　　MCM 2323

Orthotic Devices—Upper Limb

Note: The procedures in this section are considered
as "base" or "basic procedures" and may be modified by listing procedures from the Additions section
and adding them to the base procedure.

Shoulder

∗ L3650　Shoulder orthosis, (SO), figure of '8'
　　　　　design abduction restrainer
∗ L3660　SO, figure of '8' design abduction
　　　　　restrainer, canvas and webbing
∗ L3670　SO, acromio/clavicular (canvas and
　　　　　webbing type)
∗ L3675　SO, vest type abduction restrainer,
　　　　　canvas webbing type, or equal

Elbow

∗ L3700　Elbow orthoses (EO), elastic with
　　　　　stays

⊛ **Special coverage instructions**　◆ **Not covered by or valid for Medicare**　∗ **Carrier discretion**　◀▶ **New code**　◀▥ ▥▶ **Revised code**

HCPCS
Introduction

* L3710   EO, elastic with metal joints
* L3720   EO, double upright with forearm/arm cuffs, free motion
* L3730   EO, double upright with forearm/arm cuffs, extension/flexion assist
* L3740   EO, double upright with forearm/arm cuffs, adjustable position lock with active control

Wrist—Hand—Finger

* L3800   Wrist-hand-finger-orthoses (WHFO), short opponens, no attachments
* L3805   WHFO, long opponens, no attachment
▶ * L3807   Wrist-hand-finger-orthoses (WHFO), extension assist, with inflatable Palmer air support, with or without thumb extension

Additions

* L3810   WHFO, addition to short and long opponens, thumb abduction ('C') bar
* L3815   WHFO, addition to short and long opponens, second MP abduction assist
* L3820   WHFO, addition to short and long opponens, IP extension assist, with MP extension stop
* L3825   WHFO, addition to short and long opponens, MP extension stop
* L3830   WHFO, addition to short and long opponens, MP extension assist
* L3835   WHFO, addition to short and long opponens, MP spring extension assist
* L3840   WHFO, addition to short and long opponens, spring swivel thumb
* L3845   WHFO, addition to short and long opponens, thumb IP extension assist, with MP stop
* L3850   WHO, addition to short and long opponens, action wrist, with dorsiflexion assist
* L3855   WHFO, addition to short and long opponens, adjustable MP flexion control
* L3860   WHFO, addition to short and long opponens, adjustable MP flexion control and IP
* L3890   Addition to upper extremity joint, wrist or elbow, concentric adjustable torsion style mechanism, each
* L3900   WHFO, dynamic flexor hinge, reciprocal wrist extension/flexion, finger flexion/extension, wrist or finger driven

* L3901   WHFO, dynamic flexor hinge, reciprocal wrist extension/flexion, finger flexion/extension, cable driven

External Power

* L3902   WHFO, external powered, compressed gas
* L3904   WHFO, external powered, electric

Other Wrist-Hand-Finger Orthoses—Custom Fitted

* L3906   WHO, wrist gauntlet, molded to patient model
* L3907   WHFO, wrist gauntlet with thumb spica, molded to patient model
* L3908   WHO, wrist extension control cock-up, non-molded
* L3910   WHFO, Swanson design
* L3912   HFO, flexion glove with elastic finger control
* L3914   WHO, wrist extension cock-up
* L3916   WHFO, wrist extension cock-up, with outrigger
* L3918   HFO, knuckle bender
* L3920   HFO, knuckle bender, with outrigger
* L3922   HFO, knuckle bender, two segment to flex joints
* L3924   WHFO, Oppenheimer
* L3926   WHFO, Thomas suspension
* L3928   HFO, finger extension, with clock spring
* L3930   WHFO, finger extension, with wrist support
* L3932   FO, safety pin, spring wire
* L3934   FO, safety pin, modified
* L3936   WHFO, Palmar
* L3938   WHFO, dorsal wrist
* L3940   WHFO, dorsal wrist, with outrigger attachment
* L3942   HFO, reverse knuckle bender
* L3944   HFO, reverse knuckle bender, with outrigger
* L3946   HFO, composite elastic
* L3948   FO, finger knuckle bender
* L3950   WHFO, combination Oppenheimer, with knuckle bender and two attachments
* L3952   WHFO, combination Oppenheimer, with reverse knuckle and two attachments
* L3954   HFO, spreading hand
* L3956   Addition of joint to upper extremity orthosis, any material, per joint

Shoulder—Elbow—Wrist—Hand

Abduction Positioning—Custom Fitted

* L3960   Shoulder-elbow-wrist-hand orthosis, (SEWHO), abduction positioning, airplane design
* L3962   SEWHO, abduction positioning, Erb's palsy design
* L3963   SEWHO, molded shoulder, arm, forearm, and wrist, with articulating elbow joint
* L3964   SEO, mobile arm support attached to wheelchair, balanced, adjustable
* L3965   SEO, mobile arm support attached to wheelchair, balanced, adjustable Rancho type
* L3966   SEO, mobile arm support attached to wheelchair, balanced, reclining
* L3968   SEO, mobile arm support attached to wheelchair, balanced, friction arm support (friction dampening to proximal and distal joints)
* L3969   SEO, mobile arm support, monosuspension arm and hand support, overhead elbow forearm hand sling support, yoke type arm suspension support

Additions to Mobile Arm Supports

* L3970   SEO, addition to mobile arm support, elevating proximal arm
* L3972   SEO, addition to mobile arm support, offset or lateral rocker arm with elastic balance control
* L3974   SEO, addition to mobile arm support, supinator

Fracture Orthoses

* L3980   Upper extremity fracture orthosis, humeral
* L3982   Upper extremity fracture orthosis, radius/ulnar
* L3984   Upper extremity fracture orthosis, wrist
* L3985   Upper extremity fracture orthosis, forearm, hand with wrist hinge
* L3986   Upper extremity fracture orthosis, combination of humeral, radius/ulnar, wrist, (example—Colles' fracture)
* L3995   Addition to upper extremity orthosis, sock, fracture or equal, each
* L3999   Upper limb orthosis, not otherwise specified

Specific Repair

* L4000   Replace girdle for Milwaukee orthosis
* L4010   Replace trilateral socket brim
* L4020   Replace quadrilateral socket brim, molded to patient model
* L4030   Replace quadrilateral socket brim, custom fitted
* L4040   Replace molded thigh lacer
* L4045   Replace non-molded thigh lacer
* L4050   Replace molded calf lacer
* L4055   Replace non-molded calf lacer
* L4060   Replace high roll cuff
* L4070   Replace proximal and distal upright for KAFO
* L4080   Replace metal bands, KAFO, proximal thigh
* L4090   Replace metal bands, KAFO-AFO, calf or distal thigh
* L4100   Replace leather cuff, KAFO, proximal thigh
* L4110   Replace leather cuff, KAFO-AFO, calf or distal thigh
* L4130   Replace pretibial shell

Repairs

☼ L4205   Repair of orthotic device, labor component, per 15 minutes
MCM 2100.4
☼ L4210   Repair of orthotic device, repair or replace minor parts
MCM 2100.4, MCM 2130D, MCM 2133

Ancillary Orthotic Services

   L4310   (Deleted 12/31/98)
Cross Reference L4396
   L4320   (Deleted 12/31/98)
Cross Reference L4396
* L4350   Pneumatic ankle control splint (e.g., air cast)
* L4360   Pneumatic walking splint (e.g., air cast)
* L4370   Pneumatic full leg splint (e.g., air cast)
* L4380   Pneumatic knee splint (e.g., air cast)
   L4390   (Deleted 12/31/98)
Cross Reference L4396
➠ * L4392   Replace soft interface material, ankle contracture splint
➠ * L4394   Replace soft interface material, static AFO
➠ * L4396   Static AFO for positioning, pressure reduction, may be used for minimal ambulation
* L4398   Foot drop spint, recumbent positioning device

PROSTHETIC PROCEDURES—L5000–L9999

Lower Limb L5000–L5999

Note: The procedures in this sections are considered as "base" or "basic procedures" and may be modified by listing items/procedures or special materials from the "additions section" and adding them to the base procedure.

Partial Foot

  ⊛ L5000   Partial foot, shoe insert with longitudinal arch, toe filler
MCM 2323

  ⊛ L5010   Partial foot, molded socket, ankle height, with toe filler
MCM 2323

  ⊛ L5020   Partial foot, molded socket, tibial tubercle height, with toe filler
MCM 2323

Ankle

  ✳ L5050   Ankle, Symes, molded socket, SACH foot

  ✳ L5060   Ankle, Symes, metal frame, molded leather socket, articulated ankle/foot

Below Knee

  ✳ L5100   Below knee, molded socket, shin, SACH foot

  ✳ L5105   Below knee, plastic socket, joints and thigh lacer, SACH foot

Knee Disarticulation

  ✳ L5150   Knee disarticulation (or through knee), molded socket, external knee joints, shin, SACH foot

  ✳ L5160   Knee disarticulation (or through knee), molded socket, bent knee configuration, external knee joints, shin, SACH foot

Above Knee

  ✳ L5200   Above knee, molded socket, single axis constant friction knee, shin, SACH foot

  ✳ L5210   Above knee, short prosthesis, no knee joint ('stubbies'), with foot blocks, no ankle joints, each

  ✳ L5220   Above knee, short prosthesis, no knee joint ('stubbies'), with articulated ankle/foot, dynamically aligned, each

  ✳ L5230   Above knee, for proximal femoral focal deficiency, constant friction knee, shin, SACH foot

Hip Disarticulation

  ✳ L5250   Hip disarticulation, Canadian type; molded socket, hip joint, single axis constant friction knee, shin, SACH foot

  ✳ L5270   Hip disarticulation, tilt table type; molded socket, locking hip joint, single axis constant friction knee, shin, SACH foot

Hemipelvectomy

  ✳ L5280   Hemipelvectomy, Canadian type; molded socket, hip joint, single axis constant friction knee, shin, SACH foot

Endoskeleton—Below Knee

  ✳ L5300   Below knee, molded socket, SACH foot, endoskeletal system, including soft cover and finishing

Endoskeletal—Knee Disarticulation

  ✳ L5310   Knee disarticulation (or through knee), molded socket, SACH foot endoskeletal system, including soft cover and finishing

Endoskeletal—Above Knee

  ✳ L5320   Above knee, molded socket, open end, SACH foot, endoskeletal system, single axis knee, including soft cover and finishing

Endoskeletal—Hip Disarticulation

  ✳ L5330   Hip disarticulation, Canadian type; molded socket, endoskeletal system, hip joint, single axis knee, SACH foot, including soft cover and finishing

Endoskeletal—Hemipelvectomy

  ✳ L5340   Hemipelvectomy, Canadian type; molded socket, endoskeletal system, hip joint, single axis knee, SACH foot, including soft cover and finishing

---

⊛ **Special coverage instructions**   ◆ **Not covered by or valid for Medicare**   ✳ **Carrier discretion**    **New code**   **Revised code**

Immediate Postsurgical or Early Fitting Procedures

* L5400   Immediate postsurgical or early fitting, application of initial rigid dressing, including fitting, alignment, suspension, and one cast change, below knee

* L5410   Immediate post surgical or early fitting, application of initial rigid dressing, including fitting, alignment and suspension, below knee, each additional cast change and realignment

* L5420   Immediate postsurgical or early fitting, application of initial rigid dressing, including fitting, alignment and suspension and one cast change 'AK' or knee disarticulation

* L5430   Immediate postsurgical or early fitting, application of initial rigid dressing, including fitting, alignment and suspension, 'AK' or knee disarticulation, each additional cast change and realignment

* L5450   Immediate postsurgical or early fitting, application of non-weight bearing rigid dressing, below knee

* L5460   Immediate postsurgical or early fitting, application of non-weight bearing rigid dressing, above knee

Initial Prosthesis

* L5500   Initial, below knee 'PTB' type socket, non-alignable system, pylon, no cover, SACH foot, plaster socket, direct formed

* L5505   Initial, above knee—knee disarticulation, ischial level socket, non-alignable system, pylon, no cover, SACH foot, plaster socket, direct formed

Preparatory Prosthesis

* L5510   Preparatory, below knee 'PTB' type socket, non-alignable system, pylon, no cover, SACH foot, plaster socket, molded to model

* L5520   Preparatory, below knee 'PTB' type socket, non-alignable system, pylon, no cover, sach foot, thermoplastic or equal, direct formed

* L5530   Preparatory, below knee 'PTB' type socket, non-alignable system, pylon, no cover, SACH foot, thermoplastic or equal, molded to model

* L5535   Preparatory, below knee 'PTB' type socket, non-alignable system, no cover, SACH foot, prefabricated, adjustable open end socket

* L5540   Preparatory, below knee 'PTB' type socket, non-alignable system, pylon, no cover, SACH foot, laminated socket, molded to model

* L5560   Preparatory, above knee–knee disarticulation, ischial level socket, non-alignable system, pylon, no cover, SACH foot, plaster socket, molded to model

* L5570   Preparatory, above knee–knee disarticulation, ischial level socket, non-alignable system, pylon, no cover, SACH foot, thermoplastic or equal, direct formed

* L5580   Preparatory, above knee–knee disarticulation, ischial level socket, non-alignable system, pylon, no cover, SACH foot, thermoplastic or equal, molded to model

* L5585   Preparatory, above knee–knee disarticulation, ischial level socket, non-alignable system, pylon, no cover, SACH foot, prefabricated adjustable open end socket

* L5590   Preparatory, above knee–knee disarticulation, ischial level socket, non-alignable system, pylon, no cover, SACH foot, laminated socket, molded to model

* L5595   Preparatory, hip disarticulation–hemipelvectomy, pylon, no cover, SACH foot, thermoplastic or equal, molded to patient model

Additions to Lower Extremity

* L5600   Preparatory, hip disarticulation–hemipelvectomy, pylon, no cover, SACH foot, laminated socket, molded to patient model

* L5610   Addition to lower extremity, endoskeletal system, above knee, hydra-cadence system

* L5611   Addition to lower extremity, endoskeletal system, above knee–knee disarticulation, 4-bar linkage, with friction swing phase control

* L5613   Addition to lower extremity, endoskeletal system, above knee–knee disarticulation, 4-bar linkage, with hydraulic swing phase control

* L5614   Addition to lower extremity, exoskeletal system, above knee–knee disarticulation, 4-bar linkage, with pneumatic swing phase control

* L5616   Addition to lower extremity, endoskeletal system, above knee, universal multiplex system, friction swing phase control

* L5617   Addition to lower extremity, quick change self-aligning unit, above knee or below knee, each

Additions—Test Sockets

* L5618   Addition to lower extremity, test socket, Symes
* L5620   Addition to lower extremity, test socket, below knee
* L5622   Addition to lower extremity, test socket, knee disarticulation
* L5624   Addition to lower extremity, test socket, above knee
* L5626   Addition to lower extremity, test socket, hip disarticulation
* L5628   Addition to lower extremity, test socket, hemipelvectomy
* L5629   Addition to lower extremity, below knee, acrylic socket

Additions—Socket Variations

* L5630   Addition to lower extremity, Symes type, expandable wall socket
* L5631   Addition to lower extremity, above knee or knee disarticulation, acrylic socket
* L5632   Addition to lower extremity, Symes type, 'PTB' brim design socket
* L5634   Addition to lower extremity, Symes type, posterior opening (Canadian) socket
* L5636   Addition to lower extremity, Symes type, medial opening socket
* L5637   Addition to lower extremity, below knee, total contact
* L5638   Addition to lower extremity, below knee, leather socket
* L5639   Addition to lower extremity, below knee, wood socket
* L5640   Addition to lower extremity, knee disarticulation, leather socket
* L5642   Addition to lower extremity, above knee, leather socket
* L5643   Addition to lower extremity, hip disarticulation, flexible inner socket, external frame
* L5644   Addition to lower extremity, above knee, wood socket
* L5645   Addition to lower extremity, below knee, flexible inner socket, external frame
* L5646   Addition to lower extremity, below knee, air cushion socket
* L5647   Addition to lower extremity, below knee, suction socket
* L5648   Addition to lower extremity, above knee, air cushion socket

* L5649   Addition to lower extremity, ischial containment/narrow M-L socket
* L5650   Additions to lower extremity, total contact, above knee or knee disarticulation socket
* L5651   Addition to lower extremity, above knee, flexible inner socket, external frame
* L5652   Addition to lower extremity, suction suspension, above knee or knee disarticulation socket
* L5653   Addition to lower extremity, knee disarticulation, expandable wall socket

Additions—Socket Insert and Suspension

* L5654   Addition to lower extremity, socket insert, Symes, (Kemblo, Pelite, Aliplast, Plastazote or equal)
* L5655   Addition to lower extremity, socket insert, below knee (Kemblo, Pelite, Aliplast, Plastazote or equal)
* L5656   Addition to lower extremity, socket insert, knee disarticulation (Kemblo, Pelite, Aliplast, Plastazote or equal)
* L5658   Addition to lower extremity, socket insert, above knee (Kemblo, Pelite, Aliplast, Plastazote or equal)
* L5660   Addition to lower extremity, socket insert, Symes, silicone gel or equal
* L5661   Addition to lower extremity, socket insert, multi-durometer Symes
* L5662   Addition to lower extremity, socket insert, below knee, silicone gel or equal
* L5663   Addition to lower extremity, socket insert, knee disarticulation, silicone gel or equal
* L5664   Addition to lower extremity, socket insert, above knee, silicone gel or equal
* L5665   Addition to lower extremity, socket insert, multi-durometer, below knee
* L5666   Addition to lower extremity, below knee, cuff suspension
* L5667   Addition to lower extremity, below knee/above knee, socket insert, suction suspension with locking mechanism
* L5668   Addition to lower extremity, below knee, molded distal cushion
* L5669   Addition to lower extremity, below knee/above knee, socket insert, suction suspension without locking mechanism
* L5670   Addition to lower extremity, below knee, molded supracondylar suspension ('PTS' or similar)

---

* L5672   Addition to lower extremity, below knee, removable medial brim suspension

* L5674   Addition to lower extremity, below knee, latex sleeve suspension or equal, each

* L5675   Addition to lower extremity, below knee, latex sleeve suspension or equal, heavy duty, each

* L5676   Addition to lower extremity, below knee, knee joints, single axis, pair

* L5677   Addition to lower extremity, below knee, knee joints, polycentric, pair

* L5678   Addition to lower extremity, below knee, joint covers, pair

* L5680   Addition to lower extremity, below knee, thigh lacer, non-molded

* L5682   Addition to lower extremity, below knee, thigh lacer, gluteal/ischial, molded

* L5684   Addition to lower extremity, below knee, fork strap

* L5686   Addition to lower extremity, below knee, back check (extension control)

* L5688   Addition to lower extremity, below knee, waist belt, webbing

* L5690   Addition to lower extremity, below knee, waist belt, padded and lined

* L5692   Addition to lower extremity, above knee, pelvic control belt, light

* L5694   Addition to lower extremity, above knee, pelvic control belt, padded and lined

* L5695   Addition to lower extremity, above knee, pelvic control, sleeve suspension, neoprene or equal, each

* L5696   Addition to lower extremity, above knee or knee disarticulation, pelvic joint

* L5697   Addition to lower extremity, above knee or knee disarticulation, pelvic band

* L5698   Addition to lower extremity, above knee or knee disarticulation, Silesian bandage

* L5699   All lower extremity prostheses, shoulder harness

Additions—Feet—Ankle Units

* L5700   Replacement, socket, below knee, molded to patient model

* L5701   Replacement, socket, above knee–knee disarticulation, including attachment plate, molded to patient model

* L5702   Replacement, socket, hip disarticulation, including hip joint, molded to patient model

* L5704   Replacement, custom shaped protective cover, below knee

* L5705   Replacement, custom shaped protective cover, above knee

* L5706   Replacement, custom shaped protective cover, knee disarticulation

* L5707   Replacement, custom shaped protective cover, hip disarticulation

Additions—Exoskeletal—Knee–Shin System

* L5710   Addition, exoskeletal knee-shin system, single axis, manual lock

* L5711   Addition, exoskeletal knee-shin system, single axis, manual lock, ultra-light material

* L5712   Addition, exoskeletal knee-shin system, single axis, friction swing and stance phase control (safety knee)

* L5714   Addition, exoskeletal knee-shin system, single axis, variable friction swing phase control

* L5716   Addition, exoskeletal knee-shin system, polycentric, mechanical stance phase lock

* L5718   Addition, exoskeletal knee-shin system, polycentric, friction swing and stance phase control

* L5722   Addition, exoskeletal knee-shin system, single axis, pneumatic swing, friction stance phase control

* L5724   Addition, exoskeletal knee-shin system, single axis, fluid swing phase control

* L5726   Addition, exoskeletal knee-shin system, single axis, external joints, fluid swing phase control

* L5728   Addition, exoskeletal knee-shin system, single axis, fluid swing and stance phase control

* L5780   Addition, exoskeletal knee-shin system, single axis, pneumatic/hydra pneumatic swing phase control

Component Modification

* L5785   Addition, exoskeletal system, below knee, ultra-light material (titanium, carbon fiber or equal)

* L5790   Addition, exoskeletal system, above knee, ultra-light material (titanium, carbon fiber or equal)

* L5795   Addition, exoskeletal system, hip disarticulation, ultra-light material (titanium, carbon fiber or equal)

Endoskeletal

* L5810   Addition, endoskeletal knee-shin system, single axis, manual lock

* L5811   Addition, endoskeletal knee-shin system, single axis, manual lock, ultralight material
* L5812   Addition, endoskeletal knee-shin system, single axis, friction swing and stance phase control (safety knee)
* L5814   Addition, endoskeletal knee-shin system, polycentric, hydraulic swing phase control, mechanical stance phase lock
* L5816   Addition, endoskeletal knee-shin system, polycentric, mechanical stance phase lock
* L5818   Addition, endoskeletal knee-shin system, polycentric, friction swing, and stance phase control
* L5822   Addition, endoskeletal knee-shin system, single axis, pneumatic swing, friction stance phase control
* L5824   Addition, endoskeletal knee-shin system, single axis, fluid swing phase control
* L5826   Addition, endoskeletal knee-shin system, single axis, hydraulic swing phase control, with miniature high activity frame
* L5828   Addition, endoskeletal knee-shin system, single axis, fluid swing and stance phase control
* L5830   Addition, endoskeletal knee-shin system, single axis, pneumatic/ swing phase control
* L5840   Addition, endoskeletal knee-shin system, four-bar linkage or multiaxial, pneumatic swing phase control
* L5845   Addition, endoskeletal, knee-shin system, stance flexion feature, adjustable
* L5846   Addition, endoskeletal, knee-shin system, microprocessor control feature, swing phase only
* L5850   Addition, endoskeletal system, above knee or hip disarticulation, knee extension assist
* L5855   Addition, endoskeletal system, hip disarticulation, mechanical hip extension assist
* L5910   Addition, endoskeletal system, below knee, alignable system
* L5920   Addition, endoskeletal system, above knee or hip disarticulation, alignable system
➠ * L5925   Addition, endoskeletal system, above knee, knee disarticulation or hip disarticulation, manual lock
* L5930   Addition, endoskeletal system, high activity knee control frame
* L5940   Addition, endoskeletal system, below knee, ultralight material (titanium, carbon fiber or equal)

* L5950   Addition, endoskeletal system, above knee, ultralight material (titanium, carbon fiber or equal)
* L5960   Addition, endoskeletal system, hip disarticulation, ultralight material (titanium, carbon fiber or equal)
* L5962   Addition, endoskeletal system, below knee, flexible protective outer surface covering system
* L5964   Addition, endoskeletal system, above knee, flexible protective outer surface covering system
* L5966   Addition, endoskeletal system, hip disarticulation, flexible protective outer surface covering system
➠ * L5968   Addition to lower limb prosthesis, multiaxial ankle with swing phase active dorsiflexion feature
* L5970   All lower extremity prostheses, foot, external heel, SACH foot
* L5972   All lower extremity prostheses, flexible heel foot (Safe, Sten, Bock Dynamic or equal)
* L5974   All lower extremity prostheses, foot, single axis ankle/foot
* L5975   All lower extremity prostheses, combination single axis ankle and flexible heel foot
* L5976   All lower extremity prostheses, energy storing foot (Seattle Carbon Copy II or equal)
* L5978   All lower extremity prostheses, foot, multiaxial ankle/foot
* L5979   All lower extremity prostheses, multiaxial ankle/foot, dynamic response
* L5980   All lower extremity prostheses, flex foot system
* L5981   All lower extremity prostheses, flexwalk system or equal
* L5982   All exoskeletal lower extremity prostheses, axial rotation unit
* L5984   All endoskeletal lower extremity prostheses, axial rotation unit
* L5985   All endoskeletal lower extremity prostheses, dynamic prosthetic pylon
* L5986   All lower extremity prostheses, multiaxial rotation unit ('MCP' or equal)
* L5987   All lower extremity prostheses, shank foot system with vertical loading pylon
➠ * L5988   Addition to lower limb prosthesis, vertical shock reducing pylon feature
* L5999   Unlisted procedures for lower extremity prosthesis

Upper Limb

Note: The procedures in L6000–L6599 are considered as base or basic procedures and may be modified by listing procedures from the additions sections. The base procedures include only standard friction wrist and control cable system unless otherwise specified.

Partial Hand

* L6000   Partial hand, Robin-Aids, thumb remaining (or equal)
* L6010   Partial hand, Robin-Aids, little and/or ring finger remaining (or equal)
* L6020   Partial hand, Robin-Aids, no finger remaining (or equal)

Wrist Disarticulation

* L6050   Wrist disarticulation, molded socket, flexible elbow hinges, triceps pad
* L6055   Wrist disarticulation, molded socket with expandable interface, flexible elbow hinges, triceps pad

Below Elbow

* L6100   Below elbow, molded socket, flexible elbow hinge, triceps pad
* L6110   Below elbow, molded socket, (Muenster or Northwestern suspension types)
* L6120   Below elbow, molded double wall split socket, step-up hinges, half cuff
* L6130   Below elbow, molded double wall split socket, stump activated locking hinge, half cuff

Elbow Disarticulation

* L6200   Elbow disarticulation, molded socket, outside locking hinge, forearm
* L6205   Elbow disarticulation, molded socket with expandable interface, outside locking hinges, forearm

Above Elbow

* L6250   Above elbow, molded double wall socket, internal locking elbow, forearm

Shoulder Disarticulation

* L6300   Shoulder disarticulation, molded socket, shoulder bulkhead, humeral section, internal locking elbow, forearm
* L6310   Shoulder disarticulation, passive restoration (complete prosthesis)
* L6320   Shoulder disarticulation, passive restoration (shoulder cap only)

Interscapular Thoracic

* L6350   Interscapular thoracic, molded socket, shoulder bulkhead, humeral section, internal locking elbow, forearm
* L6360   Interscapular thoracic, passive restoration (complete prosthesis)
* L6370   Interscapular thoracic, passive restoration (shoulder cap only)

Immediate and Early Postsurgical Procedures

* L6380   Immediate postsurgical or early fitting, application of initial rigid dressing, including fitting alignment and suspension of components, and one cast change, wrist disarticulation or below elbow
* L6382   Immediate postsurgical or early fitting, application of initial rigid dressing including fitting alignment and suspension of components, and one cast change, elbow disarticulation or above elbow
* L6384   Immediate postsurgical or early fitting, application of initial rigid dressing including fitting alignment and suspension of components, and one cast change, shoulder disarticulation or interscapular thoracic
* L6386   Immediate postsurgical or early fitting, each additional cast change and realignment
* L6388   Immediate postsurgical or early fitting, application of rigid dressing only

Endoskeletal—Below Elbow

* L6400   Below elbow, molded socket, endoskeletal system, including soft prosthetic tissue shaping

Endoskeletal—Elbow Disarticulation

* L6450   Elbow disarticulation, molded socket, endoskeletal system, including soft prosthetic tissue shaping

Endoskeletal—Above Elbow

* L6500   Above elbow, molded socket, endoskeletal system, including soft prosthetic tissue shaping

Endoskeletal—Shoulder Disarticulation

* L6550   Shoulder disarticulation, molded socket, endoskeletal system, including soft prosthetic tissue shaping

Endoskeletal—Interscapular Thoracic

* L6570   Interscapular thoracic, molded socket, endoskeletal system, including soft prosthetic tissue shaping
* L6580   Preparatory, wrist disarticulation or below elbow, single wall plastic socket, friction wrist, flexible elbow hinges, figure of eight harness, humeral cuff, Bowden cable control, USMC or equal pylon, no cover, molded to patient model
* L6582   Preparatory, wrist disarticulation or below elbow, single wall socket, friction wrist, flexible elbow hinges, figure of eight harness, humeral cuff, Bowden cable control, USMC or equal pylon, no cover, direct formed
* L6584   Preparatory, elbow disarticulation or above elbow, single wall plastic socket, friction wrist, locking elbow, figure of eight harness, fair lead cable control, USMC or equal pylon, no cover, molded to patient model
* L6586   Preparatory, elbow disarticulation or above elbow, single wall socket, friction wrist, locking elbow, figure of eight harness, fair lead cable control, USMC or equal pylon, no cover, direct formed
* L6588   Preparatory, shoulder disarticulation or interscapular thoracic, single wall plastic socket, shoulder joint, locking elbow, friction wrist, chest strap, fair lead cable control, USMC or equal pylon, no cover, molded to patient model
* L6590   Preparatory, shoulder disarticulation or interscapular thoracic, single wall socket, shoulder joint, locking elbow, friction wrist, chest strap, fair lead cable control, USMC or equal pylon, no cover, direct formed

Additions—Upper Limb

Note: The following procedures/modifications/components may be added to other base procedures. The items in this section should reflect the additional complexity of each modification procedure, in addition to base procedure, at the time of the original order.

* L6600   Upper extremity addition, polycentric hinge, pair

* L6605   Upper extremity addition, single pivot hinge, pair
* L6610   Upper extremity addition, flexible metal hinge, pair
* L6615   Upper extremity addition, disconnect locking wrist unit
* L6616   Upper extremity addition, additional disconnect insert for locking wrist unit, each
* L6620   Upper extremity addition, flexion-friction wrist unit
* L6623   Upper extremity addition, spring assisted rotational wrist unit with latch release
* L6625   Upper extremity addition, rotation wrist unit with cable lock
* L6628   Upper extremity addition, quick disconnect hook adapter, Otto Bock or equal
* L6629   Upper extremity addition, quick disconnect lamination collar with coupling piece, Otto Bock or equal
* L6630   Upper extremity addition, stainless steel, any wrist
* L6632   Upper extremity addition, latex suspension sleeve, each
* L6635   Upper extremity addition, lift assist for elbow
* L6637   Upper extremity addition, nudge control elbow lock
* L6640   Upper extremity additions, shoulder abduction joint, pair
* L6641   Upper extremity addition, excursion amplifier, pulley type
* L6642   Upper extremity addition, excursion amplifier, lever type
* L6645   Upper extremity addition, shoulder flexion-abduction joint, each
* L6650   Upper extremity addition, shoulder universal joint, each
* L6655   Upper extremity addition, standard control cable, extra
* L6660   Upper extremity addition, heavy duty control cable
* L6665   Upper extremity addition, Teflon, or equal, cable lining
* L6670   Upper extremity addition, hook to hand, cable adapter
* L6672   Upper extremity addition, harness, chest or shoulder, saddle type
* L6675   Upper extremity addition, harness, figure of ('8') eight type, for single control
* L6676   Upper extremity addition, harness, figure of ('8') eight type, for dual control
* L6680   Upper extremity addition, test socket, wrist disarticulation or below elbow

✳ L6682   Upper extremity addition, test socket, elbow disarticulation or above elbow

✳ L6684   Upper extremity addition, test socket, shoulder disarticulation or interscapular thoracic

✳ L6686   Upper extremity addition, suction socket

✳ L6687   Upper extremity addition, frame type socket, below elbow or wrist disarticulation

✳ L6688   Upper extremity addition, frame type socket, above elbow or elbow disarticulation

✳ L6689   Upper extremity addition, frame type socket, shoulder disarticulation

✳ L6690   Upper extremity addition, frame type socket, interscapular-thoracic

✳ L6691   Upper extremity addition, removable insert, each

✳ L6692   Upper extremity addition, silicone gel insert or equal, each

➡ ✳ L6693   Upper extremity addition, locking elbow, forearm counterbalance

Terminal Devices

Hooks

❂ L6700   Terminal device, hook, Dorrance, or equal, model #3
MCM 2133

❂ L6705   Terminal device, hook, Dorrance, or equal, model #5
MCM 2133

❂ L6710   Terminal device, hook, Dorrance, or equal, model #5X
MCM 2133

❂ L6715   Terminal device, hook, Dorrance, or equal, model #5XA
MCM 2133

❂ L6720   Terminal device, hook, Dorrance, or equal, model #6
MCM 2133

❂ L6725   Terminal device, hook, Dorrance, or equal, model #7
MCM 2133

❂ L6730   Terminal device, hook, Dorrance, or equal, model #7LO
MCM 2133

❂ L6735   Terminal device, hook, Dorrance, or equal, model #8
MCM 2133

❂ L6740   Terminal device, hook, Dorrance, or equal, model #8X
MCM 2133

❂ L6745   Terminal device, hook, Dorrance, or equal, model #88X
MCM 2133

❂ L6750   Terminal device, hook, Dorrance, or equal, model #10P
MCM 2133

❂ L6755   Terminal device, hook, Dorrance, or equal, model #10X
MCM 2133

❂ L6765   Terminal device, hook, Dorrance, or equal, model #12P
MCM 2133

❂ L6770   Terminal device, hook, Dorrance, or equal, model #99X
MCM 2133

❂ L6775   Terminal device, hook, Dorrance, or equal, model #555
MCM 2133

❂ L6780   Terminal device, hook, Dorrance, or equal, model #SS555
MCM 2133

❂ L6790   Terminal device, hook, Accu hook, or equal
MCM 2133

❂ L6795   Terminal device, hook, 2 load, or equal
MCM 2133

❂ L6800   Terminal device, hook, APRL VC, or equal
MCM 2133

❂ L6805   Terminal device, modifier wrist flexion unit
MCM 2133

❂ L6806   Terminal device, hook, TRS Grip, Grip III, VC, or equal
MCM 2133

❂ L6807   Terminal device, hook, Grip I, Grip II, VC, or equal
MCM 2133

❂ L6808   Terminal device, hook, TRS Adept, infant or child, VC, or equal
MCM 2133

❂ L6809   Terminal device, hook, TRS Super Sport, passive
MCM 2133

❂ L6810   Terminal device, pincher tool, Otto Bock or equal
MCM 2133

Hands

❂ L6825   Terminal device, hand, Dorrance, VO
MCM 2133

❂ L6830   Terminal device, hand, APRL, VC
MCM 2133

❂ L6835   Terminal device, hand, Sierra, VO
MCM 2133

❂ L6840   Terminal device, hand, Becker Imperial
MCM 2133

❂ L6845   Terminal device, hand, Becker Lock Grip
MCM 2133

❂ L6850   Terminal device, hand, Becker Plylite
MCM 2133

❂ **Special coverage instructions**   ◆ **Not covered by or valid for Medicare**   ✳ **Carrier discretion**   ◀▶ **New code**   ⬅▦➡ **Revised code**

✪ L6855   Terminal device, hand, Robin-Aids,
VO
MCM 2133

✪ L6860   Terminal device, hand, Robin-Aids,
VO soft
MCM 2133

✪ L6865   Terminal device, hand, passive hand
MCM 2133

✪ L6867   Terminal device, hand, detroit infant
hand (mechanical)
MCM 2133

✪ L6868   Terminal device, hand, passive infant
hand, (Steeper, Hosmer or equal)
MCM 2133

✪ L6870   Terminal device, hand, child MITT
MCM 2133

✪ L6872   Terminal device, hand, NYU child
hand
MCM 2133

✪ L6873   Terminal device, hand, mechanical
infant hand, Steeper or equal
MCM 2133

✪ L6875   Terminal device, hand, Bock, VC
MCM 2133

✪ L6880   Terminal device, hand, Bock, VO
MCM 2133

Gloves for Above Hands

✳ L6890   Terminal device, glove for above
hands, production glove

✳ L6895   Terminal device, glove for above
hands, custom glove

Hand Restoration

✳ L6900   Hand restoration (casts, shading and
measurements included), partial
hand, with glove, thumb or one finger remaining

✳ L6905   Hand restoration (casts, shading and
measurements included), partial
hand, with glove, multiple fingers
remaining

✳ L6910   Hand restoration (casts, shading and
measurements included), partial hand,
with glove, no fingers remaining

✳ L6915   Hand restoration (shading, and
measurements included), replacement glove for above

External Power

Base Devices

✳ L6920   Wrist disarticulation, external
power, self-suspended inner socket,
removable forearm shell, Otto Bock
or equal, switch, cables, two batteries and one charger, switch control
of terminal device

✳ L6925   Wrist disarticulation, external
power, self-suspended inner socket,
removable forearm shell, Otto Bock
or equal, electrodes, cables, two batteries and one charger, myoelectronic control of terminal device

✳ L6930   Below elbow, external power, self-
suspended inner socket, removable
forearm shell, Otto Bock or equal,
switch, cables, two batteries and one
charger, switch control of terminal
device

✳ L6935   Below elbow, external power, self-
suspended inner socket, removable
forearm shell, Otto Bock or equal,
electrodes, cables, two batteries and
one charger, myoelectronic control
of terminal device

✳ L6940   Elbow disarticulation, external
power, molded inner socket, removable humeral shell, outside locking
hinges, forearm, Otto Bock or equal,
switch, cables, two batteries and one
charger, switch control of terminal
device

✳ L6945   Elbow disarticulation, external
power, molded inner socket, removable humeral shell, outside locking
hinges, forearm, Otto Bock or equal,
electrodes, cables, two batteries and
one charger, myoelectronic control
of terminal device

✳ L6950   Above elbow, external power,
molded inner socket, removable humeral shell, internal locking elbow,
forearm, Otto Bock or equal, switch,
cables, two batteries and one
charger, switch control of terminal
device

✳ L6955   Above elbow, external power,
molded inner socket, removable humeral shell, internal locking elbow,
forearm, Otto Bock or equal, electrodes, cables, two batteries and one
charger, myoelectronic control of
terminal device

* L6960   Shoulder disarticulation, external power, molded inner socket, removable shoulder shell, shoulder bulkhead, humeral section, mechanical elbow, forearm, Otto Bock or equal, switch, cables, two batteries and one charger, switch control of terminal device

* L6965   Shoulder disarticulation, external power, molded inner socket, removable shoulder shell, shoulder bulkhead, humeral section, mechanical elbow, forearm, Otto Bock or equal, electrodes, cables, two batteries and one charger, myoelectronic control of terminal device

* L6970   Interscapular-thoracic, external power, molded inner socket, removable shoulder shell, shoulder bulkhead, humeral section, mechanical elbow, forearm, Otto Bock or equal, switch, cables, two batteries and one charger, switch control of terminal device

* L6975   Interscapular-thoracic, external power, molded inner socket, removable shoulder shell, shoulder bulkhead, humeral section, mechanical elbow, forearm, Otto Bock or equal, electrodes, cables, two batteries and one charger, myoelectronic control of terminal device

Terminal Devices

* L7010   Electronic hand, Otto Bock, Steeper or equal, switch controlled

* L7015   Electronic hand, System Teknik, Variety Village or equal, switch controlled

* L7020   Electronic greifer, Otto Bock or equal, switch controlled

* L7025   Electronic hand, Otto Bock or equal, myoelectronically controlled

* L7030   Electronic hand, System Teknik, Variety Village or equal, myoelectronically controlled

* L7035   Electronic greifer, Otto Bock or equal, myoelectronically controlled

* L7040   Prehensile actuator, Hosmer or equal, switch controlled

* L7045   Electronic hook, child, Michigan or equal, switch controlled

Elbow

* L7170   Electronic elbow, Hosmer or equal, switch controlled

* L7180   Electronic elbow, Boston, Utah or equal, myoelectronically controlled

* L7185   Electronic elbow, adolescent, Variety Village or equal, switch controlled

* L7186   Electronic elbow, child, Variety Village or equal, switch controlled

* L7190   Electronic elbow, adolescent, Variety Village or equal, myoelectronically controlled

* L7191   Electronic elbow, child, Variety Village or equal, myoelectronically controlled

* L7260   Electronic wrist rotator, Otto Bock or equal

* L7261   Electronic wrist rotator, for Utah arm

* L7266   Servo control, Steeper or equal

* L7272   Analogue control, UNB or equal

* L7274   Proportional control, 6-12 volt, Liberty, Utah or equal

Battery Components

* L7360   Six volt battery, Otto Bock or equal, each

* L7362   Battery charger, six volt, Otto Bock or equal

* L7364   Twelve volt battery, Utah or equal, each

* L7366   Battery charger, Twelve volt, Utah or equal

* L7499   Upper extremity prosthesis, not otherwise specified

Repairs

⊗ L7500   Repair of prosthetic device, hourly rate (excludes V5335 repair of oral or laryngeal prosthesis or artifical larynx)
MCM 2100.4, MCM 2130D, MCM 2133

⊗ L7510   Repair of prosthetic device, repair or replace minor parts (excludes V5335 repair of oral or laryngeal prosthesis or artificial larynx)
MCM 2100.4, MCM 2130D, MCM 2133

* L7520   Repair prosthetic device, labor component, per 15 minutes

* L7900   Vacuum erection system

Breast Prostheses

⊗ L8000   Breast prosthesis, mastectomy bra
MCM 2130A

⊗ L8010   Breast prosthesis, mastectomy sleeve
MCM 2130A

⊗ L8015   External breast prosthesis garment, with mastectomy form, post mastectomy
MCM 2130

⊗ **Special coverage instructions**   ◆ **Not covered by or valid for Medicare**   * **Carrier discretion**   ◀▶ **New code**   ◀▦ ▦▶ **Revised code**

⚙ L8020   Breast prosthesis, mastectomy form
MCM 2130A

⚙ L8030   Breast prosthesis, silicone or equal
MCM 2130A

⚙ L8035   Custom breast prosthesis, post mastectomy, molded to patient model
MCM 2130

✳ L8039   Breast prosthesis, not otherwise
specified

Elastic Supports

◆ L8100   Gradient compression stocking, below knee, 18–30 mm Hg, each
MCM 2133, CIM 60-9

◆ L8110   Gradient compression stocking, below knee, 30–40 mm Hg, each
MCM 2133, CIM 60-9

◆ L8120   Gradient compression stocking, below knee, 40–50 mm Hg, each
MCM 2133, CIM 60-9

◆ L8130   Gradient compression stocking,
thigh length, 18–30 mm Hg, each
MCM 2133, CIM 60-9

◆ L8140   Gradient compression stocking,
thigh length, 30–40 mm Hg, each
MCM 2133, CIM 60-9

◆ L8150   Gradient compression stocking,
thigh length, 40–50 mm Hg, each
MCM 2133, CIM 60-9

◆ L8160   Gradient compression stocking, full
length/chap style, 18–30 mm Hg,
each
MCM 2133, CIM 60-9

◆ L8170   Gradient compression stocking, full
length/chap style, 30–40 mm Hg,
each
MCM 2133, CIM 60-9

◆ L8180   Gradient compression stocking, full
length/chap style, 40–50 mm Hg,
each
MCM 2133, CIM 60-9

◆ L8190   Gradient compression stocking,
waist length, 18–30 mm Hg, each
MCM 2133, CIM 60-9

◆ L8195   Gradient compression stocking,
waist length, 30–40 mm Hg, each
MCM 2133, CIM 60-9

◆ L8200   Gradient compression stocking,
waist length, 40–50 mm Hg, each
MCM 2133, CIM 60-9

◆ L8210   Gradient compression stocking, custom made
MCM 2133, CIM 60-9

◆ L8220   Gradient compression stocking,
lymphedema
MCM 2133, CIM 60-9

◆ L8230   Gradient compression stocking, garter belt
MCM 2133, CIM 60-9

✳ L8239   Gradient compression stocking, not
otherwise specified

Trusses

⚙ L8300   Truss, single with standard pad
MCM 2133, CIM 70-1, CIM 70-2

⚙ L8310   Truss, double with standard pads
MCM 2133, CIM 70-1, CIM 70-2

⚙ L8320   Truss, addition to standard pad, water pad
MCM 2133, CIM 70-1, CIM 70-2

⚙ L8330   Truss, addition to standard pad,
scrotal pad
MCM 2133, CIM 70-1, CIM 70-2

Prosthetic Socks

⚙ L8400   Prosthetic sheath, below knee, each
MCM 2133

⚙ L8410   Prosthetic sheath, above knee, each
MCM 2133

⚙ L8415   Prosthetic sheath, upper limb, each
MCM 2133

✳ L8417   Prosthetic sheath/sock, including a
gel cushion layer, below knee or
above knee, each

⚙ L8420   Prosthetic sock, multiple ply, below
knee, each
MCM 2133

⚙ L8430   Prosthetic sock, multiple ply, above
knee, each
MCM 2133

➡ ⚙ L8435   Prosthetic sock, multiple ply, upper
limb, each
MCM 2133

⚙ L8440   Prosthetic shrinker, below knee,
each
MCM 2133

⚙ L8460   Prosthetic shrinker, above knee,
each
MCM 2133

⚙ L8465   Prosthetic shrinker, upper limb,
each
MCM 2133

⚙ L8470   Prosthetic sock, single ply, fitting,
below knee, each
MCM 2133

⚙ L8480   Prosthetic sock, single ply, fitting,
above knee, each
MCM 2133

⚙ L8485   Prosthetic sock, single ply, fitting,
upper limb, each
MCM 2133

✳ L8490   Addition to prosthetic sheath/sock,
air seal suction retention system

✳ L8499   Unlisted procedure for miscellaneous prosthetic services

---

⚙ **Special coverage instructions**   ◆ **Not covered by or valid for Medicare**   ✳ **Carrier discretion**    **New code**   ⬅▥▥ ▥▥➡ **Revised code**

Prosthetic Implants

Integumentary System

✿ L8500   Artificial larynx, any type
MCM 2130, CIM 65-5

✿ L8501   Tracheostomy speaking valve
CIM 65-16

✿ L8600   Implantable breast prosthesis, silicone or equal
MCM 2130, CIM 35-47

✿ L8603   Collagen implant, urinary tract, per 2.5 cc syringe, includes shipping and necessary supplies
CIM 65-9

Head (Skull, Facial Bones, and Temporomandibular Joint)

✿ L8610   Ocular implant
MCM 2130

✿ L8612   Aqueous shunt
MCM 2130, Cross Reference Q0074

✿ L8613   Ossicula implant
MCM 2130

✿ L8614   Cochlear device/system
MCM 2130, CIM 65-14

✿ L8619   Cochlear implant external speech processor, replacement
CIM 65-14

Upper Extremity

✿ L8630   Metacarpophalangeal joint implant
MCM 2130

Lower Extremity (Joint: Knee, Ankle, Toe)

✿ L8641   Metatarsal joint implant
MCM 2130

✿ L8642   Hallux implant
MCM 2130, Cross Reference Q0073

Miscellaneous Muscular-Skeletal

✿ L8658   Interphalangeal joint implant
MCM 2130

Cardiovascular System

✿ L8670   Vascular graft material, synthetic, implant
MCM 2130

Genital

✳ L8699   Prosthetic implant, not otherwise specified

▶✳ L9900   Orthotic and prosthetic supply, accessory, and/or service component of another HCPCS "L" code

MEDICAL SERVICES M0000–M0009

Other Medical Services

✿ M0064   Brief office visit for the sole purpose of monitoring or changing drug prescriptions used in the treatment of mental psychoneurotic and personality disorders
MCM 2476.3

◆ M0075   Cellular therapy
CIM 35-5

◆ M0076   Prolotherapy
CIM 35-13

◆ M0100   Intragastric hypothermia using gastric freezing (MNP)
CIM 35-65

M0101   (Deleted 12/31/98) Cross Reference CPT

Cardiovascular Services

◆ M0300   IV chelation therapy (chemical endarterectomy)
CIM 35-64

◆ M0301   Fabric wrapping of abdominal aneurysm (MNP)
CIM 35-34

◆ M0302   Assessment of cardiac output by electrical bioimpedance
CIM 50-54, Cross Reference Q0066

LABORATORY TESTS (P2000–P2999)

Chemistry and Toxicology Tests

✿ P2028   Cephalin flocculation, blood
CIM 50-34

✿ P2029   Congo red, blood
CIM 50-34

◆ P2031   Hair analysis (excluding arsenic)
CIM 50-24

✿ P2033   Thymol turbidity, blood
CIM 50-34

✿ P2038   Mucoprotein, blood (seromucoid) (medical necessity procedure)
CIM 50-34

Pathology Screening Tests

✸ P3000 Screening Papanicolaou smear, cervical or vaginal, up to three smears, by technician under physician supervision
CIM 50-20, Laboratory Certification: cytology

✸ P3001 Screening Papanicolaou smear, cervical or vaginal, up to three smears, requiring interpretation by physician
CIM 50-20, Laboratory Certification: cytology

Microbiology Tests

◆ P7001 Culture, bacterial, urine; quantitative, sensitivity study
Cross Reference CPT, Laboratory Certification: bacteriology

Miscellaneous Pathology

✸ P9010 Blood (whole), for transfusion, per unit
MCM 2455A

✸ P9011 Blood (split unit), specify amount
MCM 2455A

✸ P9012 Cryoprecipitate, each unit
MCM 2455B

✸ P9013 Fibrinogen unit
MCM 2455B

P9014 (Deleted 12/31/98) Cross Reference J1460

P9015 (Deleted 12/31/98) Cross Reference J1561

✸ P9016 Leukocyte-poor blood, each unit
MCM 2455B

✸ P9017 Plasma, single donor, fresh frozen, each unit
MCM 2455B

✸ P9018 Plasma protein fraction, each unit
MCM 2455B

✸ P9019 Platelet concentrate, each unit
MCM 2455B

✸ P9020 Platelet rich plasma, each unit
MCM 2455B

✸ P9021 Red blood cells, each unit
MCM 2455A

✸ P9022 Washed red blood cells, each unit
MCM 2455A

▶✸ P9023 Plasma, pooled multiple donor, solvent/detergent treated, frozen, each unit
MCM 2455B

✸ P9603 Travel allowance one way in connection with medically necessary laboratory specimen collection drawn from home bound or nursing home bound patient; prorated miles actually traveled.
MCM 5114.1K

✸ P9604 Travel allowance one way in connection with medically necessary laboratory specimen collection drawn from home bound or nursing home bound patient; prorated trip charge
MCM 5114.1K

P9610 (Deleted 12/31/98) Cross Reference P9612

✸ P9612 Catheterization for collection of specimen, single patient, all places of service
MCM 5114.1D

✸ P9615 Catheterization for collection of specimen(s) (multiple patients)
MCM 5114.1D

Q CODES—TEMPORARY CODES—Q0000–Q9999

✳ Q0034 Administration of influenza vaccine to Medicare beneficiaries by participating demonstration sites

✸ Q0035 Cardiokymography
CIM 50-50

Q0068 (Deleted 12/31/99)

✸ Q0081 Infusion therapy, using other than chemotherapeutic drugs, per visit
CIM 60-14

✳ Q0082 Activity therapy furnished in connection with partial hospitalization (e.g., music, dance, art or play therapies that are not primarily recreational), per visit

✳ Q0083 Chemotherapy administration by other than infusion technique only (e.g., subcutaneous, intramuscular, push), per visit

✸ Q0084 Chemotherapy administration by infusion technique only, per visit
CIM 60-14

✳ Q0085 Chemotherapy administration by both infusion technique and other technique(s) (e.g., subcutaneous, intramuscular, push), per visit

✸ Q0086 Physical therapy evaluation/treatment, per visit
MCM 2210

☻ Q0091   Screening Papanicolaou smear; obtaining, preparing and conveyance of cervical or vaginal smear to laboratory
CIM 50-20

☻ Q0092   Setup portable X-ray equipment
MCM 2070.4

✳ Q0111   Wet mounts, including preparations of vaginal, cervical or skin specimens
Laboratory Certification: bacteriology, mycology, parasitology

✳ Q0112   All potassium hydroxide (KOH) preparations
Laboratory Certification: mycology

✳ Q0113   Pinworm examinations
Laboratory Certification: parasitology

✳ Q0114   Fern test
Laboratory certification: routine chemistry

✳ Q0115   Post-coital direct, qualitative examinations of vaginal or cervical mucus
Laboratory certification: hematology

Q0132   (Deleted 12/31/99)

☻ Q0136   Injection, epoetin alfa, (for non-ESRD use), per 1000 units
MCM 2049

◆ Q0144   Azithromycin dihydrate, oral, capsules/powder, 1 gm

✳ Q0156   Infusion, albumin (human), 5%, 500 ml

✳ Q0157   Infusion, albumin (human), 25%, 50 ml

Q0159   (Deleted 12/31/98) Cross Reference J0151

☻ Q0160   Factor IX (anti-hemophilic factor, purified, non-recombinant) per IU
MCM 2049

☻ Q0161   Factor IX (anti-hemophilic factor, recombinant) per IU
MCM 2049

Q0162   (Deleted 12/31/98) Cross Reference P9612

☻ Q0163   Diphenhydramine HCl, 50 mg, oral, FDA approved prescription antiemetic, for use as a complete therapeutic substitute for an IV antiemetic at time of chemotherapy treatment not to exceed a 48 hour dosage regimen
Medicare Statute 4557

☻ Q0164   Prochlorperazine maleate, 5 mg, oral, FDA approved prescription antiemetic, for use as a complete therapeutic substitute for an IV antiemetic at the time of chemotherapy treatment, not to exceed a 48 hour dosage regimen
Medicare Statute 4557

☻ Q0165   Prochlorperazine maleate, 10 mg, oral, FDA approved prescription antiemetic, for use as a complete therapeutic substitute for an IV antiemetic at the time of chemotherapy treatment, not to exceed a 48 hour dosage regimen
Medicare Statute 4557

☻ Q0166   Granisetron HCl, 1 mg, oral, FDA approved prescription antiemetic, for use as a complete therapeutic substitute for an IV antiemetic at the time of chemotherapy treatment, not to exceed a 24 hour dosage regimen
Medicare Statute 4557

☻ Q0167   Dronabinol, 2.5 mg, oral, FDA approved prescription antiemetic, for use as a complete therapeutic substitute for an IV antiemetic at the time of chemotherapy treatment, not to exceed a 48 hour dosage regimen
Medicare Statute 4557

☻ Q0168   Dronabinol, 5 mg, oral, FDA approved prescription antiemetic, for use as a complete therapeutic substitute for an IV antiemetic at the time of chemotherapy treatment, not to exceed a 48 hour dosage regimen
Medicare Statute 4557

☻ Q0169   Promethazine HCl, 12.5 mg, oral, FDA approved prescription antiemetic, for use as a complete therapeutic substitute for an IV antiemetic at the time of chemotherapy treatment, not to exceed a 48 hour dosage regimen
Medicare Statute 4557

☻ Q0170   Promethazine HCl, 25 mg, oral, FDA approved prescription antiemetic, for use as a complete therapeutic substitute for an IV antiemetic at the time of chemotherapy treatment, not to exceed a 48 hour dosage regimen
Medicare Statute 4557

☻ Q0171   Chlorpromazine HCl, 10 mg, oral, FDA approved prescription antiemetic, for use as a complete therapeutic substitute for an IV antiemetic at the time of chemotherapy treatment, not to exceed a 48 hour dosage regimen
Medicare Statute 4557

☻ Q0172   Chlorpromazine HCl, 25 mg, oral, FDA approved prescription antiemetic, for use as a complete therapeutic substitute for an IV antiemetic at the time of chemotherapy treatment, not to exceed a 48 hour dosage regimen
Medicare Statute 4557

✪ Q0173   Trimethobenzamide HCl, 250 mg, oral, FDA approved prescription antiemetic, for use as a complete therapeutic substitute for an IV antiemetic at the time of chemotherapy treatment, not to exceed a 48 hour dosage regimen
Medicare Statute 4557

✪ Q0174   Thiethylperazine maleate, 10 mg, oral, FDA approved prescription antiemetic, for use as a complete therapeutic substitute for an IV antiemetic at the time of chemotherapy treatment, not to exceed a 48 hour dosage regimen
Medicare Statute 4557

✪ Q0175   Perphenazine, 4 mg, oral, FDA approved prescription antiemetic, for use as a complete therapeutic substitute for an IV antiemetic at the time of chemotherapy treatment, not to exceed a 48 hour dosage regimen
Medicare Statute 4557

✪ Q0176   Perphenazine, 8 mg, oral, FDA approved prescription antiemetic, for use as a complete therapeutic substitute for an IV antiemetic at the time of chemotherapy treatment, not to exceed a 48 hour dosage regimen
Medicare Statute 4557

✪ Q0177   Hydroxyzine pamoate, 25 mg, oral, FDA approved prescription antiemetic, for use as a complete therapeutic substitute for an IV antiemetic at the time of chemotherapy treatment, not to exceed a 48 hour dosage regimen
Medicare Statute 4557

✪ Q0178   Hydroxyzine pamoate, 50 mg, oral, FDA approved prescription antiemetic, for use as a complete therapeutic substitute for an IV antiemetic at the time of chemotherapy treatment, not to exceed a 48 hour dosage regimen
Medicare Statute 4557

✪ Q0179   Ondansetron HCl, 8 mg, oral, FDA approved prescription antiemetic, for use as a complete therapeutic substitute for an IV antiemetic at the time of chemotherapy treatment, not to exceed a 48 hour dosage regimen
Medicare Statute 4557

✪ Q0180   Dolasetron mesylate, 100 mg, oral, FDA approved prescription antiemetic, for use as a complete therapeutic substitute for an IV antiemetic at the time of chemotherapy treatment, not to exceed a 24 hour dosage regimen
Medicare Statute 4557

✪ Q0181   Unspecified oral dosage form, FDA approved prescription antiemetic, for use as a complete therapeutic substitute for a IV antiemetic at the time of chemotherapy treatment, not to exceed a 48 hour dosage regimen
Medicare Statute 4557

Q0182   (Deleted 12/31/98) Cross Reference J0275

✱ Q0183   Dermal tissue, of human origin, with and without other bioengineered or processed elements, but without metabolically active elements, per square centimeter

✱ Q0184   Dermal tissue, of human origin, with or without other bioengineered or processed elements, with metabolically active elements, per square centimeter

✱ Q0185   Dermal and epidermal tissue of human origin, with or without bioengineered or processed elements, with metabolically active elements, per square centimeter.

▶ ✪ Q0186   Paramedic intercept, rural area, transport furnished by a volunteer ambulance company which is prohibited by state law from billing third party payers

▶ ✪ Q0187   Factor VIIA (coagulation factor, recombinant) per 1.2 mg
MCM 2049

▶ ✪ Q1001   New technology intraocular lens category 1 as defined in Federal Register notice

▶ ✪ Q1002   New technology intraocular lens category 2 as defined in Federal Register notice

▶ ✪ Q1003   New technology intraocular lens category 3 as defined in Federal Register notice

▶ ✪ Q1004   New technology intraocular lens category 4 as defined in Federal Register notice

▶ ✪ Q1005   New technology intraocular lens category 5 as defined in Federal Register notice

Injection Codes for Epocetin Alfa (EPO)

✪ Q9920   Injection of EPO, per 1000 units, at patient HCT of 20 or less
MCM 4273.1

✪ Q9921   Injection of EPO, per 1000 units, at patient HCT of 21
MCM 4273.1

✪ Q9922   Injection of EPO, per 1000 units, at patient HCT of 22
MCM 4273.1

✪ Q9923   Injection of EPO, per 1000 units, at patient HCT of 23
MCM 4273.1

✪ Q9924   Injection of EPO, per 1000 units, at patient HCT of 24
MCM 4273.1

✪ Q9925   Injection of EPO, per 1000 units, at patient HCT of 25
MCM 4273.1

✪ Q9926   Injection of EPO, per 1000 units, at patient HCT of 26
MCM 4273.1

✪ Q9927   Injection of EPO, per 1000 units, at patient HCT of 27
MCM 4273.1

✪ Q9928   Injection of EPO, per 1000 units, at patient HCT of 28
MCM 4273.1

✪ Q9929   Injection of EPO, per 1000 units, at patient HCT of 29
MCM 4273.1

✪ Q9930   Injection of EPO, per 1000 units, at patient HCT of 30
MCM 4273.1

✪ Q9931   Injection of EPO, per 1000 units, at patient HCT of 31
MCM 4273.1

✪ Q9932   Injection of EPO, per 1000 units, at patient HCT of 32
MCM 4273.1

✪ Q9933   Injection of EPO, per 1000 units, at patient HCT of 33
MCM 4273.1

✪ Q9934   Injection of EPO, per 1000 units, at patient HCT of 34
MCM 4273.1

✪ Q9935   Injection of EPO, per 1000 units, at patient HCT of 35
MCM 4273.1

✪ Q9936   Injection of EPO, per 1000 units, at patient HCT of 36
MCM 4273.1

✪ Q9937   Injection of EPO, per 1000 units, at patient HCT of 37
MCM 4273.1

✪ Q9938   Injection of EPO, per 1000 units, at patient HCT of 38
MCM 4273.1

✪ Q9939   Injection of EPO, per 1000 units, at patient HCT of 39
MCM 4273.1

✪ Q9940   Injection of EPO, per 1000 units, at patient HCT of 40 or above
MCM 4273.1

DOMESTIC RADIOLOGY SERVICES R0000–R5999

Transportation/Setup of Portable X-Ray Equipment

✪ R0070   Transportation of portable X-ray equipment and personnel to home or nursing home, per trip to facility or location, one patient seen
MCM 2070.4, MCM 5244B

✪ R0075   Transportation of portable X-ray equipment and personnel to home or nursing home, per trip to facility or location, more than one patient seen, per patient
MCM 2070.4, MCM 5244B

✪ R0076   Transportation of portable EKG to facility or location, per patient
MCM 2070.1, MCM 2070.4, CIM 50-15

TEMPORARY NATIONAL CODES S0009–S9999

▶◆ S0009   Injection, butorphanol tartrate, 1 mg
▶◆ S0010   Injection, somatrem, 5 mg
▶◆ S0011   Injection, somatropin, 5 mg
▶◆ S0012   Butorphanol tartrate, nasal spray, 25 mg
▶◆ S0014   Tacrine hydrochloride, 10 mg
▶◆ S0016   Injection, amikacin sulfate, 500 mg
▶◆ S0017   Injection, aminocaproic acid, 5 grams
▶◆ S0020   Injection, bupivacaine hydrochloride, 30 ml
▶◆ S0021   Injection, ceftoperazone sodium, 1 gram
▶◆ S0023   Injection, cimetidine hydrochloride, 300 mg
▶◆ S0024   Injection, ciprofloxacin, 200 mg
▶◆ S0028   Injection, famotidine, 20 mg
▶◆ S0029   Injection, fluconazole, 400 mg
▶◆ S0030   Injection, metronidazole, 500 mg
▶◆ S0032   Injection, nafcillin sodium, 2 grams
▶◆ S0034   Injection, ofloxacin, 400 mg
▶◆ S0039   Injection, sulfamethoxazole and trimethoprim, 10 ml
▶◆ S0040   Injection, ticarcillin disodium and clavulanate potassium, 3.1 grams
▶◆ S0071   Injection, acyclovir sodium, 50 mg
▶◆ S0072   Injection, amikacin sulfate, 100 mg
▶◆ S0073   Injection, aztreonam, 500 mg
▶◆ S0074   Injection, cefotetan disodium, 500 mg
▶◆ S0077   Injection, clindamycin phosphate, 300 mg

▶◆ S0078   Injection, fosphenytoin sodium, 750 mg
▶◆ S0080   Injection, pentamidine isethionate, 300 mg
▶◆ S0081   Injection, piperacillin sodium, 500 mg
▶◆ S0090   Sildenafil citrate, 25 mg
▶◆ S0096   Injection, itraconazole, 200 mg
▶◆ S0097   Injection, ibutilide fumarate, 1 mg
▶◆ S0098   Injection, sodium ferric gluconate complex in sucrose, 62.5 mg
▶◆ S0601   Screening proctoscopy
▶◆ S0605   Digital rectal examination, annual
▶◆ S0610   Annual gynecological examination, new patient
▶◆ S0612   Annual gynecological examination, established patient
▶◆ S0620   Routine ophthalmological examination including refraction; new patient
▶◆ S0621   Routine ophthalmological examination including refraction; established patient
▶◆ S0800   Laser in situ keratomileusis (lasik)
▶◆ S0810   Photorefractive keratectomy (prk)
▶◆ S2050   Donor enterectomy, with preparation and maintenance of allograft; from cadaver
▶◆ S2052   Transplantation of small intestine allograft
▶◆ S2053   Transplantation of small intestine and liver allografts
▶◆ S2054   Transplantation of multivisceral organs
▶◆ S2055   Harvesting of donor multivisceral organs, with preparation and maintenance of allografts; from cadaver donor
▶◆ S2109   Autologous chondrocyte transplantation (preparation of autologous cultured chondrocytes)
▶◆ S2190   Subcutaneous implantation of medication pellet(s)
▶◆ S2204   Transmyocardial laser revascularization
▶◆ S2205   Minimally invasive direct coronary artery bypass surgery involving mini-thoracotomy or mini-sternotomy surgery, performed under direct vision; using arterial graft(s), single coronary arterial graft
▶◆ S2206   Minimally invasive direct coronary artery bypass surgery involving mini-thoracotomy or mini-sternotomy surgery, performed under direct vision; using arterial graft(s), two coronary arterial grafts

▶◆ S2207   Minimally invasive direct coronary artery bypass surgery involving mini-thoracotomy or mini-sternotomy surgery, performed under direct vision; using venous graft only, single coronary venous graft
▶◆ S2208   Minimally invasive direct coronary artery bypass surgery involving mini-thoracotomy or mini-sternotomy surgery, performed under direct vision; using single arterial and venous graft(s), single venous graft
▶◆ S2209   Minimally invasive direct coronary artery bypass surgery involving mini-thoracotomy or mini-sternotomy surgery, performed under direct vision; using two arterial grafts and single venous graft
▶◆ S2210   Cryosurgical ablation (in situ destruction) of tumorous tissue, one or more lesions; liver
▶◆ S2300   Arthroscopy, shoulder, surgical; with thermally induced capsulorrhaphy
▶◆ S2350   Diskectomy, anterior, with decompression of spinal cord and/or nerve root(s) including osteophytectomy; lumbar, single interspace
▶◆ S2351   Diskectomy, anterior, with decompression of spinal cord and/or nerve root(s) including osteophytectomy; lumbar, each additional interspace (list separately in addition to code for primary procedure)
▶◆ S3645   HIV-1 antibody testing of oral mucosal transudate
▶◆ S3650   Saliva test, hormone level; during menopause
▶◆ S3652   Saliva test, hormone level; to assess preterm labor risk
▶◆ S8035   Magnetic source imaging
▶◆ S8040   Topographic brain mapping
▶◆ S8048   Isolated limb perfusion
▶◆ S8049   Intraoperative radiation therapy (single administration)
▶◆ S8060   Supply of contrast material for use in echocardiography (use in addition to echocardiography code)
▶◆ S8092   Electron beam computed tomography (also known as ultrafast CT, cine CT)
▶◆ S8095   Wig (for medically induced hair loss)
▶◆ S8096   Portable peak flow meter
▶◆ S8110   Peak expiratory flow rate (physician services)
▶◆ S8200   Chest compression vest
▶◆ S8205   Chest compression system generator and hoses (for use with chest compression vest—S8200)
▶◆ S8260   Oral orthotic for treatment of sleep apnea, includes fitting, fabrication, and materials

---

▶◆ S8300   Sacral nerve stimulation test lead kit
▶◆ S8950   Complex lymphedema therapy, each 15 minutes
▶◆ S9001   Home uterine monitor with or without associated nursing services
▶◆ S9022   Digital subtraction angiography (use in addition to cpt code for the procedure for further identification)
▶◆ S9023   Xenon regional cerebral blood flow studies
▶◆ S9024   Paranasal sinus ultrasound
▶◆ S9033   Gait analysis
▶◆ S9055   Procuren or other growth factor preparation to promote wound healing
▶◆ S9056   Coma stimulation per diem
▶◆ S9075   Smoking cessation treatment
▶◆ S9085   Meniscal allograft transplantation
▶◆ S9090   Vertebral axial decompression, per session
▶◆ S9122   Home health aide or certified nurse assistant, providing care in the home; per hour
▶◆ S9123   Nursing care, in the home; by registered nurse, per hour
▶◆ S9124   Nursing care, in the home; by licensed practical nurse, per hour
▶◆ S9125   Respite care, in the home, per diem
▶◆ S9126   Hospice care, in the home, per diem
▶◆ S9127   Social work visit, in the home, per diem
▶◆ S9128   Speech therapy, in the home, per diem
▶◆ S9129   Occupational therapy, in the home, per diem
▶◆ S9140   Diabetic management program, follow-up visit to non-MD provider
▶◆ S9141   Diabetic management program, follow-up visit to MD provider
▶◆ S9455   Diabetic management program, group session
▶◆ S9460   Diabetic management program, nurse visit
▶◆ S9465   Diabetic management program, dietitian visit
▶◆ S9470   Nutritional counseling, dietitian visit
▶◆ S9472   Cardiac rehabilitation program, non-physician provider, per diem
▶◆ S9473   Pulmonary rehabilitation program, non-physician provider, per diem
▶◆ S9474   Enterostomal therapy by a registered nurse certified in enterostomal therapy, per diem
▶◆ S9475   Ambulatory setting substance abuse treatment or detoxification services, per diem
▶◆ S9480   Intensive outpatient psychiatric services, per diem
▶◆ S9485   Crisis intervention mental health services, per diem
▶◆ S9524   Nursing services related to home iv therapy, per diem

▶◆ S9527   Insertion of a peripherally inserted central venous catheter (picc), including nursing services and all supplies
▶◆ S9528   Insertion of midline central venous catheter, including nursing services and all supplies
▶◆ S9543   Administration of medication, intramuscularly, epidurally or subcutaneously, in the home setting, including all nursing care, equipment, and supplies; per diem
▶◆ S9990   Services provided as part of a phase II clinical trial
▶◆ S9991   Services provided as part of a phase III clinical trial
▶◆ S9992   Transportation costs to and from trial location and local transportation costs (e.g., fares for taxicab or bus) for clinical trial participant and one caregiver/companion
▶◆ S9994   Lodging costs (e.g., hotel charges) for clinical trial participant and one caregiver/companion
▶◆ S9996   Meals for clinical trial participant and one caregiver/companion
▶◆ S9999   Sales tax

VISION SERVICES (V0000—V2799)

Frames

✸ V2020   Frames, purchases
        MCM 2130
◆ V2025   Deluxe frame
        MCM 3045.4

Spectacle Lenses

Note: If a CPT procedure code for supply of spectacles or a permanent prosthesis is reported, recode with the specific lens type listed below. For aphakic temporary spectacle correction, see CPT.

Single Vision, Glass or Plastic

✱ V2100   Sphere, single vision, plano to plus or minus 4.00, per lens
✱ V2101   Sphere, single vision, plus or minus 4.12 to plus or minus 7.00d, per lens
✱ V2102   Sphere, single vision, plus or minus 7.12 to plus or minus 20.00d, per lens
✱ V2103   Spherocylinder, single vision, plano to plus or minus 4.00d sphere, .12 to 2.00d cylinder, per lens

* V2104   Spherocylinder, single vision, plano to plus or minus 4.00d sphere, 2.12 to 4.00d cylinder, per lens
* V2105   Spherocylinder, single vision, plano to plus or minus 4.00d sphere, 4.25 to 6.00d cylinder, per lens
* V2106   Spherocylinder, single vision, plano to plus or minus 4.00d sphere, over 6.00d cylinder, per lens
* V2107   Spherocylinder, single vision, plus or minus 4.25 to plus or minus 7.00 sphere, .12 to 2.00d cylinder, per lens
* V2108   Spherocylinder, single vision, plus or minus 4.25d to plus or minus 7.00d sphere, 2.12 to 4.00d cylinder, per lens
* V2109   Spherocylinder, single vision, plus or minus 4.25 to plus or minus 7.00d sphere, 4.25 to 6.00d cylinder, per lens
* V2110   Sperocylinder, single vision, plus or minus 4.25 to 7.00d sphere, over 6.00d cylinder, per lens
* V2111   Spherocylinder, single vision, plus or minus 7.25 to plus or minus 12.00d sphere, .25 to 2.25d cylinder, per lens
* V2112   Spherocylinder, single vision, plus or minus 7.25 to plus or minus 12.00d sphere, 2.25d to 4.00d cylinder, per lens
* V2113   Spherocylinder, single vision, plus or minus 7.25 to plus or minus 12.00d sphere, 4.25 to 6.00d cylinder, per lens
* V2114   Spherocylinder, single vision, sphere over plus or minus 12.00d, per lens
* V2115   Lenticular (myodisc), per lens, single vision
* V2116   Lenticular lens, nonaspheric, per lens, single vision
* V2117   Lenticular, aspheric, per lens, single vision
* V2118   Aniseikonic lens, single vision
* V2199   Not otherwise classified, single vision lens

Bifocal, Glass or Plastic

* V2200   Sphere, bifocal, plano to plus or minus 4.00d, per lens
* V2201   Sphere, bifocal, plus or minus 4.12 to plus or minus 7.00d, per lens
* V2202   Sphere, bifocal, plus or minus 7.12 to plus or minus 20.00d, per lens
* V2203   Spherocylinder, bifocal, plano to plus or minus 4.00d sphere, .12 to 2.00d cylinder, per lens
* V2204   Spherocylinder, bifocal, plano to plus or minus 4.00d sphere, 2.12 to 4.00d cylinder, per lens

* V2205   Spherocylinder, bifocal, plano to plus or minus 4.00d sphere, 4.25 to 6.00d cylinder, per lens
* V2206   Spherocylinder, bifocal, plano to plus or minus 4.00d sphere, over 6.00d cylinder, per lens
* V2207   Spherocylinder, bifocal, plus or minus 4.25 to plus or minus 7.00d sphere, .12 to 2.00d cylinder, per lens
* V2208   Spherocylinder, bifocal, plus or minus 4.25 to plus or minus 7.00d sphere, 2.12 to 4.00d cylinder, per lens
* V2209   Spherocylinder, bifocal, plus or minus 4.25 to plus or minus 7.00d sphere, 4.25 to 6.00d cylinder, per lens
* V2210   Spherocylinder, bifocal, plus or minus 4.25 to plus or minus 7.00d sphere, over 6.00d cylinder, per lens
* V2211   Spherocylinder, bifocal, plus or minus 7.25 to plus or minus 12.00d sphere, .25 to 2.25d cylinder, per lens
* V2212   Spherocylinder, bifocal, plus or minus 7.25 to plus or minus 12.00d sphere, 2.25 to 4.00d cylinder, per lens
* V2213   Spherocylinder, bifocal, plus or minus 7.25 to plus or minus 12.00d sphere, 4.25 to 6.00d cylinder, per lens
* V2214   Spherocylinder, bifocal, sphere over plus or minus 12.00d, per lens
* V2215   Lenticular (myodisc), per lens, bifocal
* V2216   Lenticular, nonaspheric, per lens, bifocal
* V2217   Lenticular, aspheric lens, bifocal
* V2218   Aniseikonic, per lens, bifocal
* V2219   Bifocal seg width over 28 mm
* V2220   Bifocal add over 3.25d
* V2299   Specialty bifocal (by report)

Trifocal, Glass or Plastic

* V2300   Sphere, trifocal, plano to plus or minus 4.00d, per lens
* V2301   Sphere, trifocal, plus or minus 4.12 to plus or minus 7.00d per lens
* V2302   Sphere, trifocal, plus or minus 7.12 to plus or minus 20.00, per lens
* V2303   Spherocylinder, trifocal, plano to plus or minus 4.00d sphere, .12 to 2.00d cylinder, per lens
* V2304   Spherocylinder, trifocal, plano to plus or minus 4.00d sphere, 2.25 to 4.00d cylinder, per lens
* V2305   Spherocylinder, trifocal, plano to plus or minus 4.00d sphere, 4.25 to 6.00 cylinder, per lens
* V2306   Spherocylinder, trifocal, plano to plus or minus 4.00d sphere, over 6.00d cylinder, per lens

* V2307   Spherocylinder, trifocal, plus or minus 4.25 to plus or minus 7.00d sphere, .12 to 2.00d cylinder, per lens

* V2308   Spherocylinder, trifocal, plus or minus 4.25 to plus or minus 7.00d sphere, 2.12 to 4.00d cylinder, per lens

* V2309   Spherocylinder, trifocal, plus or minus 4.25 to plus or minus 7.00d sphere, 4.25 to 6.00d cylinder, per lens

* V2310   Spherocylinder, trifocal, plus or minus 4.25 to plus or minus 7.00d sphere, over 6.00d cylinder, per lens

* V2311   Spherocylinder, trifocal, plus or minus 7.25 to plus or minus 12.00d sphere, .25 to 2.25d cylinder, per lens

* V2312   Spherocylinder, trifocal, plus or minus 7.25 to plus or minus 12.00d sphere, 2.25 to 4.00d cylinder, per lens

* V2313   Spherocylinder, trifocal, plus or minus 7.25 to plus or minus 12.00d sphere, 4.25 to 6.00d cylinder, per lens

* V2314   Spherocylinder, trifocal, sphere over plus or minus 12.00d, per lens

* V2315   Lenticular (myodisc), per lens, trifocal

* V2316   Lenticular nonaspheric, per lens, trifocal

* V2317   Lenticular, aspheric lens, trifocal

* V2318   Aniseikonic lens, trifocal

* V2319   Trifocal seg width over 28 mm

* V2320   Trifocal add over 3.25d

* V2399   Specialty trifocal (by report)

Variable Asphericity

* V2410   Variable asphericity lens, single vision, full field, glass or plastic, per lens

* V2430   Variable asphericity lens, bifocal, full field, glass or plastic, per lens

* V2499   Variable sphericity lens, other type

Contact Lenses

If a CPT procedure code for supply of contact lens is reported, recode with specific lens type listed below (per lens).

* V2500   Contact lens, PMMA, spherical, per lens

* V2501   Contact lens, PMMA, toric or prism ballast, per lens

* V2502   Contact lens PMMA, bifocal, per lens

* V2503   Contact lens PMMA, color vision deficiency, per lens

* V2510   Contact lens, gas permeable, spherical, per lens

* V2511   Contact lens, gas permeable, toric, prism ballast, per lens

* V2512   Contact lens, gas permeable, bifocal, per lens

* V2513   Contact lens, gas permeable, extended wear, per lens

☼ V2520   Contact lens, hydrophilic, spherical, per lens
CIM 45-7, CIM 65-1

☼ V2521   Contact lens, hydrophilic, toric, or prism ballast, per lens
CIM 45-7, CIM 65-1

☼ V2522   Contact lens, hydrophilic, bifocal, per lens
CIM 45-7, CIM 65-1

☼ V2523   Contact lens, hydrophilic, extended wear, per lens
CIM 45-7, CIM 65-1

* V2530   Contact lens, scleral, gas impermeable, per lens (for modification, see CPT)

☼ V2531   Contact lens, scleral, gas permeable, per lens (for contact lens modification, see CPT)
CIM 65-3

* V2599   Contact lens, other type

Low Vision Aids

If a CPT procedure code for supply of low vision aid is reported, recode with specific systems listed below.

* V2600   Hand-held low vision aids and other nonspectacle mounted aids

* V2610   Single lens spectacle mounted low vision aids

* V2615   Telescopic and other compound lens system, including distance vision telescopic, near vision telescopes and compound microscopic lens system

Prosthetic Eye

☼ V2623   Prosthetic eye, plastic, custom
MCM 2133

* V2624   Polishing/resurfacing of ocular prosthesis

* V2625   Enlargement of ocular prosthesis

* V2626   Reduction of ocular prosthesis

☼ V2627   Scleral cover shell
CIM 65-3

* V2628   Fabrication and fitting of ocular conformer

* V2629   Prosthetic eye, other type

Intraocular Lenses

☼ V2630   Anterior chamber intraocular lens
MCM 2130

○ V2631   Iris supported intraocular lens
           MCM 2130
○ V2632   Posterior chamber intraocular lens
           MCM 2130

Miscellaneous

* V2700   Balance lens, per lens
* V2710   Slab off prism, glass or plastic, per
           lens
* V2715   Prism, per lens
* V2718   Press-on lens, Fresnel prism, per lens
* V2730   Special base curve, glass or plastic,
           per lens
○ V2740   Tint, plastic, rose 1 or 2 per lens
           MCM 2130B
○ V2741   Tint, plastic, other than rose 1-2, per
           lens
           MCM 2130B
○ V2742   Tint, glass, rose, 1 or 2, per lens
           MCM 2130B
○ V2743   Tint, glass, other than rose, 1 or 2
           per lens
           MCM 2130B
○ V2744   Tint, photochromatic, per lens
           MCM 2130B
○ V2750   Anti-reflective coating, per lens
           MCM 2130B
○ V2755   U-V lens, per lens
           MCM 2130B
* V2760   Scratch resistant coating, per lens
* V2770   Occluder lens, per lens
* V2780   Oversize lens, per lens
* V2781   Progressive lens, per lens
* V2785   Processing, preserving and trans-
           porting corneal tissue
* V2799   Vision service, miscellaneous

HEARING SERVICES V5000—V5299

Note: These codes are for non-physician services.

◆ V5008   Hearing screening
           MCM 2320
◆ V5010   Assessment for hearing aid
           Medicare Statute 1862A7
◆ V5011   Fitting/orientation/checking of
           hearing aid
           Medicare Statute 1862A7
◆ V5014   Repair/modification of a hearing aid
           Medicare Statute 1862A7
◆ V5020   Conformity evaluation
           Medicare Statute 1862A7
◆ V5030   Hearing aid, monaural, body worn,
           air conduction
           Medicare Statute 1862A7
◆ V5040   Hearing aid, monaural, body worn,
           bone conduction
           Medicare Statute 1862A7

◆ V5050   Hearing aid, monaural, in the ear
           Medicare Statute 1862A7
◆ V5060   Hearing aid, monaural, behind the
           ear
           Medicare Statute 1862A7
◆ V5070   Glasses, air conduction
           Medicare Statute 1862A7
◆ V5080   Glasses, bone conduction
           Medicare Statute 1862A7
◆ V5090   Dispensing fee, unspecified hearing
           aid
           Medicare Statute 1862A7
◆ V5100   Hearing aid, bilateral, body worn
           Medicare Statute 1862A7
◆ V5110   Dispensing fee, bilateral
           Medicare Statute 1862A7
◆ V5120   Binaural, body
           Medicare Statute 1862A7
◆ V5130   Binaural, in the ear
           Medicare Statute 1862A7
◆ V5140   Binaural, behind the ear
           Medicare Statute 1862A7
◆ V5150   Binaural, glasses
           Medicare Statute 1862A7
◆ V5160   Dispensing fee, binaural
           Medicare Statute 1862A7
◆ V5170   Hearing aid, CROS, in the ear
           Medicare Statute 1862A7
◆ V5180   Hearing aid, CROS, behind the ear
           Medicare Statute 1862A7
◆ V5190   Hearing aid, CROS, glasses
           Medicare Statute 1862A7
◆ V5200   Dispensing fee, CROS
           Medicare Statute 1862A7
◆ V5210   Hearing aid, BICROS, in the ear
           Medicare Statute 1862A7
◆ V5220   Hearing aid, BICROS, behind the
           ear
           Medicare Statute 1862A7
◆ V5230   Hearing aid, BICROS, glasses
           Medicare Statute 1862A7
◆ V5240   Dispensing fee, BICROS
           Medicare Statute 1862A7
○ V5299   Hearing service, miscellaneous
           MCM 2320

Speech-Language Pathology Services

Note: These codes are for non-physician services.

◆ V5336   Repair/modification of augmenta-
           tive communicative system or de-
           vice (excludes adaptive hearing aid)
           Medicare Statute 1862A7
○ V5362   Speech screening
           MCM 2320
○ V5363   Language screening
           MCM 2320
○ V5364   Dysphagia screening
           MCM 2320

○ **Special coverage instructions**   ◆ **Not covered by or valid for Medicare**   * **Carrier discretion**   ◆▶ **New code**   ◀▦▦▶ **Revised code**

IA—Intra-arterial administration
IV—Intravenous administration
IM—Intramuscular administration
IT—Intrathecal
SC—Subcutaneous administration
INH—Administration by inhaled solution
VAR—Various routes of administration
OTH—Other routes of administration
ORAL—Administered orally

Intravenous administration includes all methods, such as gravity infusion, injections, and timed pushes. The "VAR" posting denotes various routes of administration and is used for drugs that are commonly administered into joints, cavities, tissues, or topical applications, in addition to other parenteral administrations. Listings posted with "OTH" indicate other administration methods, such as suppositories or catheter injections.

A

Drug	Dose	Route	Code
Abbokinase, *see* Urokinase			
Abbokinase, Open Cath, *see* Urokinase			
Abciximab	10 mg	IV	J0130
Abelcet, *see* Amphotericin B lipid complex			
ABLC, *see* Amphotericin B			
Acetazolamide sodium	up to 500 mg	IM, IV	J1120
Acetylcysteine	10%, per ml	INH	J7610
	20%, per ml	INH	J7615
Acetylcysteine, unit dose form	per gram	INH	J7608
Achromycin, *see* Tetracycline			
ACTH, *see* Corticotropin			
Acthar, *see* Corticotropin			
Actimmune, *see* Interferon gamma-1b			
Activase, *see* Alteplase recombinant			
Adenocard, *see* Adenosine			
Adenosine	6 mg	IV	J0150
Adenosine	90 mg	IV	J0151
Adrenalin Chloride, *see* Adrenalin, epinephrine			
Adrenalin, epinephrine	up to 1 ml ampule	SC, IM	J0170
Adriamycin PFS, *see* Doxorubicin HCl			
Adriamycin RDF, *see* Doxorubicin HCl			
Adrucil, *see* Fluorouracil			
Aggrastat, *see* Tirofiban hydrochloride			
A-hydroCort, *see* Hydrocortisone sodium phosphate			
Akineton, *see* Biperiden			
Alatrofloxacin mesylate, injection 100 mg		IV	J0200
Albumin (human)	500 ml, 5%	IV	Q0156
	50 ml, 25%	IV	Q0157
Albuterol sulfate	0.083%, per ml	INH	J7620
	0.5%, per ml	INH	J7625
Albuterol, concentrated form	per mg	INH	J7618
Albuterol, unit dose form	per mg	INH	J7619
Aldesleukin	per single use vial	IM, IV	J9015
Aldomet, *see* Methyldopa HCl			
Alferon N, *see* Interferon alfa-n3			
Alglucerase	per 10 units	IV	J0205
Alkaban-AQ, *see* Vinblastine sulfate			
Alkeran, *see* Melphalan, oral			
Alpha-1-proteinase inhibitor (human)	per 10 mg	IV	J0256
Alprostadil, injection	1.25 mcg	OTH injection	J0270 J0275
Alprostadil, urethral suppository		OTH	
Alteplase recombinant	per 10 mg	IV	J2996
Alupent, *see* Metaproterenol sulfate or Metaproterenol, compounded			
Amcort, *see* Triamcinolone diacetate			
A-Methapred, *see* Methylprednisolone sodium succinate			
Amgen, *see* Interferon alpha-con-1			
Amifostine	500 mg	IV	J0207
Aminophylline/Aminophyllin	up to 250 mg	IV	J0280
Amitriptyline HCl	up to 20 mg	IM	J1320
Amobarbital	up to 125 mg	IM, IV	J0300
Amphocin, *see* Amphotericin B			
Amphotericin B	50 mg	IV	J0285
Amphotericin B lipid complex	50 mg	IV	J0286
Ampicillin sodium	up to 500 mg	IM, IV	J0290
Ampicillin sodium/sulbactam sodium	per 1.5 gm	IM, IV	J0295
Amygdalin, *see* Laetrile, Amygdalin, vitamin B-17			
Amytal, *see* Amobarbital			
Anabolin LA 100, *see* Nandrolone decanoate			
Ancef, *see* Cefazolin sodium			
Andrest 90-4, *see* Testosterone enanthate and estradiol valerate			
Andro-Cyp, *see* Testosterone cypionate			
Andro-Cyp 200, *see* Testosterone cypionate			
Andro L.A. 200, *see* Testosterone enanthate			
Andro-Estro 90-4, *see* Testosterone enanthate and estradiol valerate			
Andro/Fem, *see* Testosterone cypionate and estradiol cypionate			
Androgyn L.A., *see* Testosterone enanthate and estradiol valerate			
Androlone-50, *see* Nandrolone phenpropionate			
Androlone-D 100, *see* Nandrolone decanoate			
Andronaq-50, *see* Testosterone suspension			
Andronaq-LA, *see* Testosterone cypionate			
Andronate-200, *see* Testosterone cypionate			

Andronate-100, *see* Testosterone cypionate

Andropository 100, *see* Testosterone enanthate

Andryl 200, *see* Testosterone enanthate

Anectine, *see* Succinylcholine chloride

Anergan 25, *see* Promethazine HCl

Anergan 50, *see* Promethazine HCl

Anistreplase	30 units	IV	J0350
Anti-Inhibitor	per IU	IV	J7198

Antispas, *see* Dicyclomine HCl

Antithrombin III (human)	per IU	IV	J7197

A.P.L., *see* Chorionic gonadotropin

Apresoline, *see* Hydralazine HCl

AquaMEPHYTON, *see* Vitamin K

Aralen, *see* Chloroquine HCl

Aramine, *see* Metaraminol

Arbutamine	1 mg	IV	J0395

Aredia, *see* Pamidronate disodium

Arfonad, *see* Trimethaphan camsylate

Aristocort Forte, *see* Triamcinolone diacetate

Aristocort Intralesional, *see* Triamcinolone diacetate

Aristospan Intra-Articular, *see* Triamcinolone hexacetonide

Aristospan Intralesional, *see* Triamcinolone hexacetonide

Arrestin, *see* Trimethobenzamide HCl

Asparaginase	10,000 units	IV, IM	J9020

Astramorph PF, *see* Morphine sulfate

Atgam, *see* Lymphocyte immune globulin

Ativan, *see* Lorazepam

Atropine, concentrated form	per mg	INH	J7635
Atropine, unit dose form	per mg	INH	J7636
Atropine sulfate	up to 0.3 mg	IV, IM, SC	J0460

Atrovent, *see* Ipratropium bromide

Aurothioglucose	up to 50 mg	IM	J2910

Autoplex T, *see* Hemophilia clotting factors

Avonex, *see* Interferon beta-1a

Azathioprine	50 mg	ORAL	J7500
Azathioprine, parenteral	100 mg	IV	J7501
Azithromycin dihydrate	1 gm	ORAL	Q0144
Azithromycin, injection	500 mg	IV	J0456

B

Baclofen	10 mg	IT	J0475
Baclofen for intrathecal trial	50 mcg	OTH	J0476

Bactocill, *see* Oxacillin sodium

BAL in oil, *see* Dimercaprol

Banflex, *see* Orphenadrine citrate

BCG (Bacillus Calmette and Guérin), live	per vial instillation	IV	J9031

Bena-D 10, *see* Diphenhydramine HCl

Bena-D 50, *see* Diphenhydramine HCl

Benadryl, *see* Diphenhydramine HCl

Benahist 10, *see* Diphenhydramine HCl

Benahist 50, *see* Diphenhydramine HCl

Ben-Allergin-50, *see* Diphenhydramine HCl

Benefix, *see* Factor IX, recombinant

Benoject-10, *see* Diphenhydramine HCl

Benoject-50, *see* Diphenhydramine HCl

Bentyl, *see* Dicyclomine

Benzquinamide HCl	up to 50 mg	IM, IV	J0510
Benztropine mesylate	per 1 mg	IM, IV	J0515

Berubigen, *see* Vitamin B-12, cyanocobalamin

Betalin 12, *see* Vitamin B-12, cyanocobalamin

Betameth, *see* Betamethasone sodium phosphate

Betamethasone acetate & betamethasone sodium phosphate	3 mg of ea	IM	J0702
Betamethasone sodium phosphate	4 mg	IM, IV	J0704

Betaseron, *see* Interferon beta-1b

Bethanechol chloride	up to 5 mg	SC	J0520

Bicillin L-A, *see* Penicillin G benzathine

Bicillin C-R 900/300, *see* Penicillin G procaine and penicillin G benzathine

Bicillin C-R, *see* Penicillin G benzathine and penicillin G procaine

BiCNU, *see* Carmustine

Biperiden lactate	per 5 mg	IM, IV	J0190
Bitolterol mesylate, 0.2%	per 10 ml	INH	J7627
Bitolterol mesylate, concentrated form	per mg	INH	J7628
Bitolterol mesylate, unit dose form	per mg	INH	J7629

Blenoxane, *see* Bleomycin sulfate

Bleomycin sulfate	15 units	IM, IV, SC	J9040
Botulinum toxin type A	per 100 units	IM	J0585

Brethine, *see* Terbutaline sulfate or Terbutaline, compounded

Bricanyl Subcutaneous, *see* Terbutaline sulfate

Brompheniramine maleate	per 10 mg	IM, SC, IV	J0945

Bronkephrine, *see* Ethylnorepinephrine HCl

Bronkosol, *see* Isoetharine HCl

Busulfan	2 mg	ORAL	J8510

C

Caine-1, *see* Lidocaine HCl

Caine-2, *see* Lidocaine HCl

Calcijex, *see* Calcitriol

Calcimar, *see* Calcitonin-salmon

Calcitonin-salmon	up to 400 units	SC, IM	J0630
Calcitriol	1 mcg ampule	IM	J0635

Calcium Disodium Versenate, *see* Edetate calcium disodium			
Calcium gluconate	per 10 ml	IV	J0610
Calcium glycerophosphate & calcium lactate	per 10 ml	IM, SC	J0620
Calphosan, *see* Calcium glycerophosphate & calcium lactate			
Camptosar, *see* Irinotecan			
Capecitabine	150 mg	ORAL	J8520
	500 mg	ORAL	J8521
Carbocaine with Neo-Cobefrin, *see* Mepivacaine			
Carbocaine, *see* Mepivacaine			
Carboplatin	50 mg	IV	J9045
Carmustine	100 mg	IV	J9050
Carnitor, *see* Levocarnitine			
Cefadyl, *see* Cephapirin sodium			
Cefazolin sodium	up to 500 mg	IV, IM	J0690
Cefizox, *see* Ceftizoxime sodium			
Cefonicid sodium	1 g	IV	J0695
Cefotaxime sodium	per 1 g	IV, IM	J0698
Cefoxitin sodium	1 g	IV, IM	J0694
Ceftazidime	per 500 mg	IM, IV	J0713
Ceftizoxime sodium	per 500 mg	IV, IM	J0715
Ceftriaxone sodium	per 250 mg	IV, IM	J0696
Cefuroxime sodium, sterile	per 750 mg	IM, IV	J0697
Celestone Phosphate, *see* Betamethasone sodium phosphate			
Celestone Soluspan, *see* Betamethasone acetate and betamethasone sodium phosphate			
CellCept, *see* Mycophenolate mofetil			
Cel-U-Jec, *see* Betamethasone sodium phosphate			
Cenacort Forte, *see* Triamcinolone diacetate			
Cenacort A-40, *see* Triamcinolone acetonide			
Cephalothin sodium	up to 1 g	IM, IV	J1890
Cephapirin sodium	up to 1 g	IV, IM	J0710
Ceredase, *see* Alglucerase			
Cerezyme, *see* Imiglucerase			
Cerubidine, *see* Daunorubicin HCl			
Chealamide, *see* Endrate ethylenediamine-tetra-/acetic acid			
Chlor-100, *see* Chlorpheniramine maleate			
Chloramphenicol sodium succinate	up to 1 g	IV	J0720
Chlordiazepoxide HCl	up to 100 mg	IM, IV	J1990
Chloromycetin Sodium Succinate, *see* Chloramphenicol sodium succinate			
Chlor-Pro, *see* Chlorpheniramine maleate			
Chlor-Pro 10, *see* Chlorpheniramine maleate			
Chloroprocaine HCl	per 30 ml	VAR	J2400
Chlorpromazine HCl, oral	10 mg	ORAL	Q0171
	25 mg	ORAL	Q0172
Chloroquine HCl	up to 250 mg	IM	J0390
Chlorothiazide sodium	per 500 mg	IV	J1205
Chlorpheniramine maleate	per 10 mg	IV, IM, SC	J0730
Chlorpromazine HCl	up to 50 mg	IM, IV	J3230
Chlorprothixene	up to 50 mg	IM	J3080
Chlor-Trimeton, *see* Chlorpheniramine maleate			
Chorex-5, *see* Chorionic gonadotropin			
Chorex-10, *see* Chorionic gonadotropin			
Chorignon, *see* Chorionic gonadotropin			
Chorionic gonadotropin	per 1,000 USP units	IM	J0725
Choron-10, *see* Chorionic gonadotropin			
Cidofovir	375 mg	IV	J0740
Cilastatin sodium, imipenem	per 250 mg	IV, IM	J0743
Cisplatin, powder or solution	per 10 mg	IV	J9060
Cisplatin	50 mg	IV	J9062
Cladribine	per mg	IV	J9065
Claforan, *see* Cefotaxime sodium			
Clonidine HCl	1 mg	epidural	J0735
Cobex, *see* Vitamin B-12, cyanocobalamin			
Codeine phosphate	per 30 mg	IM, IV, SC	J0745
Codimal-A, *see* Brompheniramine maleate			
Cogentin, *see* Benztropine mesylate			
Colchicine	per 1 mg	IV	J0760
Colistimethate sodium	up to 150 mg	IM, IV	J0770
Coly-Mycin M, *see* Colistimethate sodium			
Compa-Z, *see* Prochlorperazine			
Compazine, *see* Prochlorperazine			
Cophene-B, *see* Brompheniramine maleate			
Copper contraceptive, intrauterine	—	OTH	J7300
Corgonject-5, *see* Chorionic gonadotropin			
Corticotropin	up to 40 units	IV, IM, SC	J0800
Cortisone acetate, *see* Cortisone			
Cortisone	up to 50 mg	IM	J0810
Cortone Acetate, *see* Cortisone			
Cortrosyn, *see* Cosyntropin			
Cosmegen, *see* Dactinomycin			
Cosyntropin	per 0.25 mg	IM, IV	J0835
Cotranzine, *see* Prochlorperazine			
Cromolyn sodium	per 20 mg	INH	J7630
Cromolyn sodium, unit dose form	per 10 mg	INH	J7631
Crysticillin 300 A.S., *see* Penicillin G procaine			
Crysticillin 600 A.S., *see* Penicillin G procaine			
Cyclophosphamide	100 mg	IV	J9070
	200 mg	IV	J9080
	500 mg	IV	J9090
	1 g	IV	J9091
	2 g	IV	J9092
Cyclophosphamide, lyophilized	100 mg	IV	J9093
	200 mg	IV	J9094
	500 mg	IV	J9095
	1 g	IV	J9096
	2 g	IV	J9097
Cyclophosphamide, oral	25 mg	ORAL	J8530
Cyclosporine, oral	25 mg	ORAL	J7515

Cyclosporine, parenteral	100 mg	ORAL	J7502
	250 mg	IV	J7516
Cytarabine	100 mg	SC, IV	J9100
	500 mg	SC, IV	J9110
Cytomegalovirus immune globulin intravenous (human)	per vial	IV	J0850
Cytosar-U, *see* Cytarabine			
Cytovene, *see* Ganciclovir sodium			
Cytoxan, *see* Cyclophosphamide; cyclophosphamide, lyophilized; and cyclophosphamide, oral			

D

D-5-W, infusion	1000 cc	IV	J7070
Dacarbazine	100 mg	IV	J9130
	200 mg	IV	J9140
Daclizumab	25 mg	IV	J7513
Dactinomycin	0.5 mg	IV	J9120
Dalalone, *see* Dexamethasone sodium phosphate			
Dalalone L.A., *see* Dexamethasone acetate			
Dalteparin sodium	per 2500 IU	SC	J1645
Daunorubicin citrate, liposomal formulation	10 mg	IV	J9151
Daunorubicin HCl	10 mg	IV	J9150
DaunoXome, (*see* Daunorubicin citrate, liposomal formulation			
DDAVP, *see* Desmopressin acetate			
Decadron Phosphate, *see* Dexamethasone sodium phosphate			
Decadron, *see* Dexamethasone sodium phosphate			
Decadron-LA, *see* Dexamethasone acetate			
Deca-Durabolin, *see* Nandrolone decanoate			
Decaject, *see* Dexamethasone sodium phosphate			
Decaject-L.A., *see* Dexamethasone acetate			
Decolone-50, *see* Nandrolone decanoate			
Decolone-100, *see* Nandrolone decanoate			
De-Comberol, *see* Testosterone cypionate and estradiol cypionate			
Deferoxamine mesylate	500 mg per 5 cc	IM, SC, IV	J0895
Dehist, *see* Brompheniramine maleate			
Deladumone, *see* Testosterone enanthate and estradiol valerate			
Deladumone OB, *see* Testosterone enanthate and estradiol valerate			
Delatest, *see* Testosterone enanthate			
Delatestadiol, *see* Testosterone enanthate and estradiol valerate			
Delatestryl, *see* Testosterone enanthate			
Delta-Cortef, *see* Prednisolone, oral			

Delestrogen, *see* Estradiol valerate			
Demadex, *see* Torsemide			
Demerol HCl, *see* Meperidine HCl			
DepAndro 100, *see* Testosterone cypionate			
DepAndro 200, *see* Testosterone cypionate			
DepAndrogyn, *see* Testosterone cypionate and estradiol cypionate			
DepGynogen, *see* Depo-estradiol cypionate			
DepMedalone 40, *see* Methylprednisolone acetate			
DepMedalone 80, *see* Methylprednisolone acetate			
Depo-estradiol cypionate	up to 5 mg	IM	J1000
Depogen, *see* Depo-estradiol cypionate			
Depoject, *see* Methylprednisolone acetate			
Depo-Medrol, *see* Methylprednisolone acetate			
Depopred-40, *see* Methylprednisolone acetate			
Depopred-80, *see* Methylprednisolone acetate			
Depo-Provera, *see* Medroxyprogesterone acetate			
Depotest, *see* Testosterone cypionate			
Depo-Testadiol, *see* Testosterone cypionate and estradiol cypionate			
Depotestogen, *see* Testosterone cypionate and estradiol cypionate			
Depo-Testosterone, *see* Testosterone cypionate			
Desferal Mesylate, *see* Deferoxamine mesylate			
Desmopressin acetate	1 mcg	IV, SC	J2597
Dexacen LA-8, *see* Dexamethasone acetate			
Dexacen-4, *see* Dexamethasone sodium phosphate			
Dexamethasone, concentrated form	per mg	INH	J7637
Dexamethasone, unit form	per mg	INH	J7638
Dexamethasone acetate	per 8 mg	IM	J1095
Dexamethasone sodium phosphate	up to 4 mg/ml	IM, IV, OTH	J1100
Dexasone, *see* Dexamethasone sodium phosphate			
Dexasone L.A., *see* Dexamethasone acetate			
Dexferrum, *see* Iron dextran			
Dexone, *see* Dexamethasone sodium phosphate			
Dexone LA, *see* Dexamethasone acetate			
Dexrazoxane HCl	250 mg	IV	J1190
Dextran 40	500 ml	IV	J7100
Dextran 75	500 ml	IV	J7110
Dextrose 5%/normal saline solution	500 ml = 1 unit	IV	J7042
Dextrose/water (5%)	500 ml = 1 unit	IV	J7060
D.H.E. 45, *see* Dihydroergotamine			
Diamox, *see* Acetazolamide sodium			

Estra-D, *see* Depo-estradiol cypionate			
Estra-L 20, *see* Estradiol valerate			
Estra-L 40, *see* Estradiol valerate			
Estra-Testrin, *see* Testosterone enanthate and estradiol valerate			
Estradiol Cypionate, *see* Depo-estradiol cypionate			
Estradiol L.A., *see* Estradiol valerate			
Estradiol L.A. 20, *see* Estradiol valerate			
Estradiol L.A. 40, *see* Estradiol valerate			
Estradiol valerate	up to 10 mg	IM	J1380
	up to 20 mg	IM	J1390
	up to 40 mg	IM	J0970
Estro-Cyp, *see* Depo-estradiol cypionate			
Estrogen, conjugated	per 25 mg	IV, IM	J1410
Estroject L.A., *see* Depo-estradiol cypionate			
Estrone	per 1 mg	IM	J1435
Estrone 5, *see* Estrone			
Estrone Aqueous, *see* Estrone			
Estronol, *see* Estrone			
Estronol-L.A., *see* Depo-estradiol cypionate			
Etanercept, injection	25 mg	IM, IV	J1438
Ethylnorepinephrine HCl	1 ml	SC, IM	J0590
Ethyol, *see* Amifostine			
Etidronate disodium	per 300 mg	IV	J1436
Etopophos, *see* Etoposide			
Etoposide	10 mg	IV	J9181
	100 mg	IV	J9182
Etoposide, oral	50 mg	ORAL	J8560
Everone, *see* Testosterone enanthate			

F

Factor VIIa (coagulation factor, recombinant)	per mg	IV	Q0187
Factor VIII (anti-hemophilic factor, human)	per IU	IV	J7190
Factor VIII (anti-hemophilic factor, porcine)	per IU	IV	J7191
Factor VIII, (anti-hemophilic factor, recombinant)	per IU	IV	J7192
Factor IX (anti-hemophilic factor, purified, non-recombinant)	per IU	IV	Q0160
Factor IX (anti-hemophilic factor, recombinant)	per IU	IV	Q0161
Factor IX, complex	per IU	IV	J7194
Factors, other hemophilia clotting	per IU	IV	J7196
Factrel, *see* Gonadorelin HCl			
Feiba VH Immuno, *see* Factors, other hemophilia clotting			
Fentanyl citrate	up to 2 ml	IM, IV	J3010
Filgrastim (G-CSF)	300 mcg	SC, IV	J1440
	480 mcg	SC, IV	J1441
Flexoject, *see* Orphenadrine citrate			
Flexon, *see* Orphenadrine citrate			
Flolan, *see* Epoprostenol			
Floxuridine	500 mg	IV	J9200
Fluconazole	200 mg	IV	J1450
Fludara, *see* Fludarabine phosphate			

Fludarabine phosphate	50 mg	IV	J9185
Fluorouracil	500 mg	IV	J9190
Fluphenazine decanoate	up to 25 mg	IM, SC	J2680
Folex, *see* Methotrexate sodium			
Folex PFS, *see* Methotrexate sodium			
Follutein, *see* Chorionic gonadotropin			
Fortaz, *see* Ceftazidime			
Foscarnet sodium	per 1,000 mg	IV	J1455
Foscavir, *see* Foscarnet sodium			
FUDR, *see* Floxuridine			
Fungizone Intravenous, *see* Amphotericin B			
Furomide M.D., *see* Furosemide			
Furosemide	up to 20 mg	IM, IV	J1940

G

Gamastan, *see* Gamma globulin and Immune globulin			
Gamma globulin	1 cc	IM	J1460
	2 cc	IM	J1470
	3 cc	IM	J1480
	4 cc	IM	J1490
	5 cc	IM	J1500
	6 cc	IM	J1510
	7 cc	IM	J1520
	8 cc	IM	J1530
	9 cc	IM	J1540
	10 cc	IM	J1550
	over 10 cc	IM	J1560
Gammar, *see* Gamma globulin and immune globulin			
Gammar-IV, *see* Immune globulin intravenous (human)			
Gamulin RH, *see* Rho(D) immune globulin			
Ganciclovir, implant	4.5 mg	OTH	J7310
Ganciclovir sodium	500 mg	IV	J1570
Garamycin, gentamicin	up to 80 mg	IM, IV	J1580
Gemcitabine HCl	200 mg	IV	J9201
Gemsar, *see* Gemcitabine HCl			
Gentamicin Sulfate, *see* Garamycin, gentamicin			
Gentran, *see* Dextran 40			
Gentran 75, *see* Dextran 75			
Gesterol 50, *see* Progesterone			
Gesterol L.A. 250, *see* Hydroxyprogesterone Caproate			
Glucagon HCl	per 1 mg	SC, IM, IV	J1610
Glukor, *see* Chorionic gonadotropin			
Glycopyrrolate, concentrated form	per 1 mg	INH	J7642
Glycopyrrolate, unit dose form	per 1 mg	INH	J7643
Gold sodium thiomalate	up to 50 mg	IM	J1600
Gonadorelin HCl	per 100 mcg	SC, IV	J1620
Gonic, *see* Chorionic gonadotropin			
Goserelin acetate implant	per 3.6 mg	SC	J9202
Granisetron HCl, injection	100 mcg	IV	J1626
Granisetron HCl, oral	1 mg	ORAL	Q0166
Gynogen L.A. "10," *see* Estradiol valerate			
Gynogen L.A. "20," *see* Estradiol valerate			
Gynogen L.A. "40," *see* Estradiol valerate			

H

Haldol, *see* Haloperidol			
Haloperidol	up to 5 mg	IM, IV	J1630
Haloperidol decanoate	per 50 mg	IM	J1631
Hemofil M, *see* Factor VIII			
Hemophilia clotting factors (e.g., anti-inhibitors)	per IU	IV	J7198
Hemophilia clotting factors, NOC	per IU	IV	J7199
Hep-Lock, *see* Heparin sodium (heparin lock flush)			
Hep-Lock U/P, *see* Heparin sodium (heparin lock flush)			
Heparin sodium	1,000 units	IV, SC	J1644
Heparin sodium (heparin lock flush)	10 units	IV	J1642
Herceptin, *see* Trastuzumab			
Hexadrol Phosphate, *see* Dexamethasone sodium phosphate			
Histaject, *see* Brompheniramine maleate			
Histerone 50, *see* Testosterone suspension			
Histerone 100, *see* Testosterone suspension			
Hyalgan, *see* Hyaluronate sodium			
Hyaluronidase	up to 150 units	SC, IV	J3470
Hyate:C, *see* Factor VIII (anti-hemophilic factor)			
Hybolin Improved, *see* Nandrolone phenpropionate			
Hybolin Decanoate, *see* Nandrolone decanoate			
Hycamtin, *see* Topotecan			
Hydeltra-T.B.A., *see* Prednisolone tebutate			
Hydeltrasol, *see* Prednisolone sodium phosphate			
Hydralazine HCl	up to 20 mg	IV, IM	J0360
Hydrate, *see* Dimenhydrinate			
Hydrochlorides of opium alkaloids	up to 20 mg	IM, SC	J2480
Hydrocortisone acetate	up to 25 mg	IV, IM, SC	J1700
Hydrocortisone sodium phosphate	up to 50 mg	IV, IM, SC	J1710
Hydrocortisone succinate sodium	up to 100 mg	IV, IM, SC	J1720
Hydrocortone Acetate, *see* Hydrocortisone acetate			
Hydrocortone Phosphate, *see* Hydrocortisone sodium phosphate			
Hydromorphone HCl	up to 4 mg	SC, IM, IV	J1170
Hydroxyprogesterone Caproate	25 mg/ml	IM	J1739
Hydroxyprogesterone Caproate	250 mg/ml	IM	J1741
Hydroxyzine HCl	up to 25 mg	IM	J3410
Hydroxyzine pamoate	25 mg	ORAL	Q0177
	50 mg	ORAL	Q0178
Hylan G-F 20	16 mg	OTH	J7320
Hylutin, *see* Hydroxyprogesterone Caproate			
Hyoscyamine sulfate	up to 0.25 mg	SC, IM, IV	J1980
Hyperstat IV, *see* Diazoxide			
Hyper-Tet, *see* Tetanus immune globulin, human			
HypRho-D, *see* Rho(D) immune globulin			

Hyprogest 250, *see* Hydroxyprogesterone Caproate			
Hyrexin-50, *see* Diphenhydramine HCl			
Hyzine-50, *see* Hydroxyzine HCl			

I

Ibutilide fumarate	1 mg	IV	J1742
Idamycin, *see* Idarubicin HCl			
Idarubicin HCl	5 mg	IV	J9211
Ifex, *see* Ifosfamide			
Ifosfamide	per 1 g	IV	J9208
Ilotycin, *see* Erythromycin gluceptate			
Imferon, *see* Iron dextran			
Imiglucerase	per unit	IV	J1785
Imipramine HCl	up to 25 mg	IM	J3270
Imitrex, *see* Sumatriptan succinate			
Immune globulin	per 500 mg	IV	J1561
Immune globulin, anti-thymocyte globulin	25 mg	IV	J7504
Immune globulin intravenous	5 gm	IV	J1562
Immunosuppressive drug, not otherwise classified			J7599
Imuran, *see* Azathioprine			
Inapsine, *see* Droperidol			
Inderal, *see* Propranolol HCl			
Infed, *see* Iron dextran			
Infergen, *see* Interferon alfa-1			
Infliximab, injection	10 mg	IM, IV	J1745
Innovar, *see* Droperidol with fentanyl citrate			
Insulin	up to 100 units	SC	J1820
Intal, *see* Cromolyn sodium or Cromolyn sodium, compounded			
Integrilin, injection, *see* Eptifibatide			
Interferon alphacon-1, recombinant	1 mcg	SC	J9212
Interferon alfa-2a, recombinant	3 million units	SC, IM	J9213
Interferon alfa-2b, recombinant	1 million units	SC, IM	J9214
Interferon alfa-n3 (human leukocyte derived)	250,000 IU	IM	J9215
Interferon beta-1a	33 mcg	IM	J1825
Interferon beta-1b	0.25 mg	SC	J1830
Interferon gamma-1b	3 million units	SC	J9216
Intrauterine copper contraceptive, *see* Copper contraceptive, intrauterine			
Ipratropium bromide 0.2%	per ml	INH	J7645
Ipratropium bromide, unit dose form	per mg	INH	J7644
Irinotecan	20 mg	IV	J9206
Iron dextran	50 mg	IV, IM	J1750
Isocaine HCl, *see* Mepivacaine			
Isoetharine HCl	0.1% per ml	INH	J7650
	0.125% per ml	INH	J7651
	0.167% per ml	INH	J7652
	0.2% per ml	INH	J7653
	0.25% per ml	INH	J7654
	1.0% per ml	INH	J7655
Isoetharine HCl, concentrated form	per mg	INH	J7648
Isoetharine HCl, unit dose form	per mg	INH	J7649

Isoproterenol HCl	0.5% per ml	INH	J7660
	1.0%, per ml	INH	J7665
Isoproterenol HCl, concentrated form	per mg	INH	J7658
Isoproterenol HCl, unit dose form	per mg	INH	J7659
Isuprel, *see* Isoproterenol HCl or Isoproterenol HCl, compounded			

J

Jenamicin, *see* Garamycin, gentamicin			

K

Kabikinase, *see* Streptokinase			
Kaleinate, *see* Calcium gluconate			
Kanamycin sulfate	up to 75 mg	IM, IV	J1850
Kanamycin sulfate	up to 500 mg	IM, IV	J1840
Kantrex, *see* Kanamycin sulfate			
Keflin, *see* Cephalothin sodium			
Kefurox, *see* Cufuroxime sodium			
Kefzol, *see* Cefazolin sodium			
Kenaject-40, *see* Triamcinolone acetonide			
Kenalog-10, *see* Triamcinolone acetonide			
Kenalog-40, *see* Triamcinolone acetonide			
Kestrone 5, *see* Estrone			
Ketorolac tromethamine	per 15 mg	IM, IV	J1885
Key-Pred 25, *see* Prednisolone acetate			
Key-Pred 50, *see* Prednisolone acetate			
Key-Pred-SP, *see* Prednisolone sodium phosphate			
K-Flex, *see* Orphenadrine citrate			
Klebcil, *see* Kanamycin sulfate			
Koāte-HP, *see* Factor VIII			
Kogenate, *see* Factor VIII			
Konakion, *see* Vitamin K, phytonadione, etc.			
Konȳne 80, *see* Factor IX, complex			
Kutapressin	up to 2 ml	SC, IM	J1910
Kytril, *see* Granisetron HCl			

L

L.A.E. 20, *see* Estradiol valerate			
Laetrile, Amygdalin, vitamin B-17			J3570
Lanoxin, *see* Digoxin			
Largon, *see* Propiomazine HCl			
Lasix, *see* Furosemide			
L-Caine, *see* Lidocaine HCl			
Leucovorin calcium	per 50 mg	IM, IV	J0640
Leukine, *see* Sargramostim (GM-CSF)			
Leuprolide acetate (for depot suspension)	3.75 mg	IM	J1950
	7.5 mg	IM	J9217
Leuprolide acetate	per 1 mg	IM	J9218
Leustatin, *see* Cladribine			
Levaquin I.U., *see* Levofloxacin			
Levocarnitine	per 1 gm	IV	J1955
Levo-Dromoran, *see* Levorphanol tartrate			

Levofloxacin	250 mg	IV	J1956
Levoprome, *see* Methotrimeprazine			
Levorphanol tartrate	up to 2 mg	SC, IV	J1960
Levsin, *see* Hyoscyamine sulfate			
Librium, *see* Chlordiazepoxide HCl			
Lidocaine HCl	50 cc	VAR	J2000
Lidoject-1, *see* Lidocaine HCl			
Lidoject-2, *see* Lidocaine HCl			
Lincocin, *see* Lincomycin HCl			
Lincomycin HCl	up to 300 mg	IV	J2010
Liquaemin Sodium, *see* Heparin sodium			
Lioresal, *see* Baclofen			
LMD (10%), *see* Dextran 40			
Lovenox, *see* Enoxaparin sodium			
Lorazepam	2 mg	IM, IV	J2060
Lufyllin, *see* Dyphylline			
Luminal Sodium, *see* Phenobarbitol sodium			
Lupron, *see* Leuprolide acetate			
Lymphocyte immune globulin, anti-thymocyte globulin	250 mg	IV	J7504
Lyophilized, *see* Cyclophosphamide, lyophilized			

M

Magnesium sulfate	500 mg		J3475
Mannitol	25% in 50 ml	IV	J2150
Marmine, *see* Dimenhydrinate			
Mechlorethamine HCl (nitrogen mustard), HN_2	10 mg	IV	J9230
Medralone 40, *see* Methylprednisolone acetate			
Medralone 80, *see* Methylprednisolone acetate			
Medrol, *see* Methylprednisolone			
Medroxyprogesterone acetate	100 mg	IM	J1050
	150 mg	IM	J1055
Mefoxin, *see* Cefoxitin sodium			
Melphalan HCl	50 mg	IV	J9245
Melphalan, oral	2 mg	ORAL	J8600
Menoject LA, *see* Testosterone cypionate and estradiol cypionate			
Mepergan Injection, *see* Meperdine and promethazine HCl			
Meperidine HCl	per 100 mg	IM, IV, SC	J2175
Meperidine and promethazine HCl	up to 50 mg	IM, IV	J2180
Mephentermine sulfate	up to 30 mg	IM, IV	J3450
Mepivacaine HCL	per 10 ml	VAR	J0670
Mesna	200 mg	IV	J9209
Mesnex, *see* Mesna			
Metaprel, *see* Metaproterenol sulfate			
Metaproterenol sulfate	0.4%, per 2.5 ml	INH	J7670
	0.6%, per 2.5 ml	INH	J7672
	5.0%, per ml	INH	J7675
Metaproterenol sulfate, concentrated form	per 10 mg	INH	J7668
Metaproterenol sulfate, unit dose form	per 10 mg	INH	J7669
Metaraminol bitartrate	per 10 mg	IV, IM, SC	J0380

Metastron, *see* Strontium-89 chloride			
Methadone HCl	up to 10 mg	IM, SC	J1230
Methergine, *see* Methylergonovine maleate			
Methicillin sodium	up to 1 g	IM, IV	J2970
Methocarbamol	up to 10 ml	IV, IM	J2800
Methotrexate, oral	2.5 mg	ORAL	J8610
Methotrexate sodium	5 mg	IV, IM, IT, IA	J9250
	50 mg	IV, IM, IT, IA	J9260
Methotrexate LPF, *see* Methotrexate sodium			
Methotrimeprazine	up to 20 mg	IM	J1970
Methoxamine HCl	up to 20 mg	IM, IV	J3390
Methylergonovine maleate	up to 0.2 mg	IM, IV	J2210
Methyldopate HCl	up to 250 mg	IV	J0210
Methylergonovine maleate	up to 0.2 mg		J2210
Methylprednisolone, oral	per 4 mg	ORAL	J7509
Methylprednisolone acetate	20 mg	IM	J1020
	40 mg	IM	J1030
	80 mg	IM	J1040
Methylprednisolone sodium succinate	up to 40 mg	IM, IV	J2920
	up to 125 mg	IM, IV	J2930
Metoclopramide HCl	up to 10 mg	IV	J2765
Metocurine iodide	up to 2 mg	IV	J2240
Miacalcin, *see* Calcitonin-salmon			
Midazolam HCl	per 1 mg	IM, IV	J2250
Milrinone lactate	per 5 ml	IV	J2260
Mithracin, *see* Plicamycin			
Mitomycin	5 mg	IV	J9280
	20 mg	IV	J9290
	40 mg	IV	J9291
Mitoxantrone HCl	per 5 mg	IV	J9293
Monocid, *see* Cefonicic sodium			
Monoclate-P, *see* Factor VIII			
Monoclonal antibodies, parenteral	5 mg	IV	J7505
Mononine, *see* Factor IX, purified, non-recombinant			
Morphine sulfate	up to 10 mg	IM, IV, SC	J2270
	100 mg	IM, IV, SC	J2271
Morphine sulfate, preservative-free	per 10 mg	IM, IV, SC	J2275
M-Prednisol-40, *see* Methylprednisolone acetate			
M-Prednisol-80, *see* Methylprednisolone acetate			
Mucomyst, *see* Acetylcysteine or Acetylcysteine, compounded			
Mucosol, *see* Acetylcysteine			
Muse, *see* Alprostadil			
Mustargen, *see* Mechlorethamine HCl			
Mutamycin, *see* Mitomycin			
Myleran, *see* Busulfan			
Mycophenolate mofetil	250 mg	ORAL	J7517
Myochrysine, *see* Gold sodium thiomalate			
Myolin, *see* Orphenadrine citrate			
N			
Nalbuphine HCl	per 10 mg	IM, IV, SC	J2300
Naloxone HCl	per 1 mg	IM, IV, SC	J2310
Nandrobolic, *see* Nandrolone phenpropionate			
Nandrobolic L.A., *see* Nandrolone decanoate			
Nandrolone decanoate	up to 50 mg	IM	J2320

	up to 100 mg	IM	J2321
	up to 200 mg	IM	J2322
Nandrolone phenpropionate	up to 50 mg	IM	J0340
Narcan, *see* Naloxone HCl			
Nasahist B, *see* Brompheniramine maleate			
Nasal vaccine inhalation		INH	J3530
Navane, *see* Thiothixene			
Navelbine, *see* Vinorelbine tartrate			
ND Stat, *see* Brompheniramine maleate			
Nebcin, *see* Tobramycin sulfate			
NebuPent, *see* Pentamidine isethionate			
Nembutal Sodium Solution, *see* Pentobarbital sodium			
Neocyten, *see* Orphenadrine citrate			
Neo-Durabolic, *see* Nandrolone decanoate			
Neoquess, *see* Dicyclomine HCl			
Neosar, *see* Cyclophosphamide			
Neostigmine methylsulfate	up to 0.5 mg	IM, IV, SC	J2710
Neo-Synephrine, *see* Phenylephrine HCl			
Neumega, *see* Oprelvekin			
Neupogen, *see* Filgrastim (G-CSF)			
Neutrexin, *see* Trimetrexate glucuronate			
Nervocaine 1%, *see* Lidocaine HCl			
Nervocaine 2%, *see* Lidocaine HCl			
Nesacaine, *see* Chloroprocaine HCl			
Nesacaine-MPF, *see* Chloroprocaine HCl			
Niacinamide, niacin	up to 100 mg	IV, SC, IM	J2350
Nicotinic Acid, *see* Niacinamide, niacin			
Nicotinamide, *see* Niacinamide, niacin			
Nipent, *see* Pentostatin			
Nordryl, *see* Diphenhydramine HCl			
Norflex, *see* Orphenadrine citrate			
Norzine, *see* Thiethylperazine maleate			
Not otherwise classified drugs			J3490
Not otherwise classified drugs		other than INH, administered thru DME	J7799
Not otherwise classified drugs		INH, administered thru DME	J7699
Not otherwise classified drugs, anti-neoplastic		—	J9999
Not otherwise classified drugs, chemotherapeutic		ORAL	J8999
Not otherwise classified drugs, immunosuppressive		—	J7599

Not otherwise classified drugs, nonchemotherapeutic		ORAL	J8499
Novantrone, *see* Mitoxantrone HCl			
Novo Seven, *see* Factor VIIa			
NPH, *see* Insulin			
Nubain, *see* Nalbuphine HCl			
Nulicaine, *see* Lidocaine HCl			
Numorphan, *see* Oxymorphone HCl			
Numorphan H.P., *see* Oxymorphone HCl			
O			
Octreotide Acetate, injection	1 mg	IM, IV	J2352
Oculinum, *see* Botulinum toxin type A			
O-Flex, *see* Orphenadrine citrate			
Omnipen-N, *see* Ampicillin			
Oncaspar, *see* Pegaspargase			
Oncovin, *see* Vincristine sulfate			
Ondansetron HCl	1 mg	IV	J2405
Ondansetron HCl, oral	8 mg	ORAL	Q0179
Oprelvekin	5 mg	SC	J2355
Oraminic II, *see* Brompheniramine maleate			
Ormazine, *see* Chlorpromazine HCl			
Orphenadrine citrate	up to 60 mg	IV, IM	J2360
Orphenate, *see* Orphenadrine citrate			
Or-Tyl, *see* Dicyclomine			
Oxacillin sodium	up to 250 mg	IM, IV	J2700
Oxymorphone HCl	up to 1 mg	IV, SC, IM	J2410
Oxytetracycline HCl	up to 50 mg	IM	J2460
Oxytocin	up to 10 units	IV, IM	J2590
P			
Paclitaxel	30 mg	IV	J9265
Pamidronate disodium	per 30 mg	IV	J2430
Pantopon, *see* Hydrochlorides of opium alkaloids			
Papaverine HCl	up to 60 mg	IV, IM	J2440
Paragard T 380 A, *see* Copper contraceptive, intrauterine			
Paraplatin, *see* Carboplatin			
Paricalcitol, injection	5 mcg	IV, IM	J2500
Pegaspargase	per single dose vial	IM, IV	J9266
Penicillin G benzathine	up to 600,000 units	IM	J0560
	up to 1,200,000 units	IM	J0570
	up to 2,400,000 units	IM	J0580
Penicillin G benzathine and penicillin G procaine	up to 600,000 units	IM	J0530
	up to 1,200,000 units	IM	J0540
	up to 2,400,000 units	IM	J0550
Penicillin G potassium	up to 600,000 units	IM, IV	J2540
Penicillin G procaine, aqueous	up to 600,000 units	IM, IV	J2510
Pentagastrin	per 2 ml	SC	J2512
Pentamidine isethionate	per 300 mg	INH	J2545
Pentazocine HCl	up to 30 mg	IM, SC, IV	J3070
Pentobarbital sodium	per 50 mg	IM, IV, OTH	J2515
Pentostatin	per 10 mg	IV	J9268
Peptavlon, *see* Pentagastrin			
Permapen, *see* Penicillin G benzathine			
Perphenazine, injection	up to 5 mg	IM, IV	J3310
Perphenazine, tablets	4 mg	ORAL	Q0175
	8 mg	ORAL	Q0176
Persantine IV, *see* Dipyridamole			
Pfizerpen, *see* Penicillin G potassium			
Pfizerpen A.S., *see* Penicillin G procaine			
Phenazine 25, *see* Promethazine HCl			
Phenazine 50, *see* Promethazine HCl			
Phenergan, *see* Promethazine HCl			
Phenobarbital sodium	up to 120 mg	IM, IV	J2560
Phentolamine mesylate	up to 5 mg	IM, IV	J2760
Phenylephrine HCl	up to 1 ml	SC, IM, IV	J2370
Phenytoin sodium	per 50 mg	IM, IV	J1165
Photofrin, *see* Porfimer sodium			
Phytonadione (Vitamin K)	per 1 mg	IM, SC, IV	J3430
Piperacillin/Tazobactam Sodium, injection	1.125 g	IV	J2543
Pitocin, *see* Oxytocin			
Plantinol AQ, *see* Cisplatin			
Plas + SD, *see* Plasma, pooled multiple donor			
Plasma, pooled multiple donor, frozen, each unit		IV	P9023
Platinol, *see* Cisplatin			
Plicamycin	2,500 mcg	IV	J9270
Polocaine, *see* Mepivacaine			
Polycillin-N, *see* Ampicillin			
Porfimer Sodium	75 mg	IV	J9600
Potassium chloride	per 2 mEq	IV	J3480
Pralidoxime chloride	up to 1 g	IV, IM, SC	J2730
Predalone T.B.A., *see* Prednisolone tebutate			
Predalone-50, *see* Prednisolone acetate			
Predcor-25, *see* Prednisolone acetate			
Predcor-50, *see* Prednisolone acetate			
Predicort-50, *see* Prednisolone acetate			
Prednisone	per 5 mg	ORAL	J7506
Prednisol TBA, *see* Prednisolone tebutate			
Prednisolone, oral	5 mg	ORAL	J7510
Prednisolone acetate	up to 1 ml	IM	J2650
Prednisolone sodium phosphate	up to 20 mg	IV, IM	J2640
Prednisolone tebutate	up to 20 mg	VAR	J1690
Predoject-50, *see* Prednisolone acetate			
Pregnyl, *see* Chorionic gonadotropin			
Premarin Intravenous, *see* Estrogen, conjugated			
Prescription, chemotherapeutic, not otherwise specified		ORAL	J8999
Prescription, nonchemotherapeutic, not otherwise specified		ORAL	J8499

Primacor, *see* Milrinone lactate

Primaxin I.M., *see* Cilastatin sodium, imipenem

Primaxin I.V., *see* Cilastatin sodium, imipenem

Priscoline HCl, *see* Tolazoline HCl

Pro-Depo, *see* Hydroxyprogesterone Caproate

Procainamide HCl	up to 1 g	IM, IV	J2690
Prochlorperazine	up to 10 mg	IM, IV	J0780
Prochlorperazine maleate, oral	5 mg	ORAL	Q0164
	10 mg	ORAL	Q0165

Profasi HP, *see* Chorionic gonadotropin

Profilnine Heat-Treated, *see* Factor IX

Progestaject, *see* Progesterone

Progesterone	per 50 mg	IM	J2675

Prograf, *see* Tacrolimus, oral

Prokine, *see* Sargramostim (GM-CSF)

Prolastin, *see* Alpha 1-proteinase inhibitor (human)

Proleukin, *see* Aldesleukin

Prolixin Decanoate, *see* Fluphenazine decanoate

Promazine HCl	up to 25 mg	IM	J2950
Promethazine HCl, injection	up to 50 mg	IM, IV	J2550
Promethazine HCl, oral	12.5 mg	ORAL	Q0169
	25 mg	ORAL	Q0170

Pronestyl, *see* Procainamide HCl

Propiomazine HCl	up to 20 mg	IV, IM	J1930

Proplex T, *see* Factor IX

Proplex SX-T, *see* Factor IX

Propranolol HCl	up to 1 mg	IV	J1800

Prorex-25, *see* Promethazine HCl

Prorex-50, *see* Promethazine HCl

Prostaphlin, *see* Procainamide HCl

Prostigmin, *see* Neostigmine methylsulfate

Protamine sulfate	per 10 mg	IV	J2720
Protirelin	per 250 mcg	IV	J2725

Prothazine, *see* Promethazine HCl

Protopam Chloride, *see* Pralidoxime chloride

Proventil, *see* Albuterol sulfate, compounded

Prozine-50, *see* Promazine HCl

Q

Quelicin, *see* Succinylcholine chloride

R

Ranitidine HCl, injection	25 mg	IV, IM	J2780

Recombinate, *see* Factor VIII

Redisol, *see* Vitamin B-12 cyanocobalamin

Regitine, *see* Phentolamine mesylate

Reglan, *see* Metoclopramide HCl

Regular, *see* Insulin

Relefact TRH, *see* Protirelin

Remicade, *see* Infliximab, injection

Reo Pro, *see* Abciximab

Rep-Pred 40, *see* Methylprednisolone acetate

Rep-Pred 80, *see* Methylprednisolone acetate

RespiGam, *see* Respiratory Syncytial Virus

Respiratory Syncytial Virus Immune-globulin	50 mg	IV	J1565

Retavase, *see* Reteplase

Reteplase	37.6 mg	IV	J2994

Rheomacrodex, *see* Dextran 40

Rhesonativ, *see* Rho(D) immune globulin, human

Rheumatrex Dose Pack, *see* Methotrexate, oral

Rho(D) immune globulin, human	1 dose package	IM	J2790
Rho(D)immune globulin (human), solvent detergent	100 IU	IV	J2792

RhoGAM, *see* Rho(D) immune globulin, human

Ringer's lactate infusion	up to 1,000 cc	IV	J7120

Rituxan, *see* Rituximab

Rituximab	100 mg	IU	J9310

Robaxin, *see* Methocarbamol

Rocephin, *see* Ceftriaxone sodium

Roferon-A, *see* Interferon alfa-2A, recombinant

Rubex, *see* Doxorubicin HCl

Rubramin PC, *see* Vitamin B-12 cyanocobalamin

S

Saline solution	5% dextrose, 500 ml	IV	J7042
	infusion, 250 cc	IV	J7050
	infusion, 1,000 cc	IV	J7030
Saline solution, sterile	500 ml = 1 unit	IV, OTH	J7040
	up to 5 cc	IV, OTH	J7051

Sandimmune, *see* Cyclosporine

Sandoglobulin, *see* Immune globulin intravenous (human)

Sandostatin Lar Depot, *see* Octreotide

Sargramostim (GM-CSF)	50 mcg	IV	J2820
Secobarbital sodium	up to 250 mg	IM, IV	J2860

Seconal, *see* Secobarbital sodium

Selestoject, *see* Betamethasone sodium phosphate

Sinusol-B, *see* Brompheniramine maleate

Sodium chloride, 0.9%	per 2 ml		J2912
Sodium hyaluronate	20 mg	OTH	J7315

Solganal, *see* Aurothioglucose

Solu-Cortef, *see* Hydrocortisone sodium phosphate			J1710

Solu-Medrol, *see* Methylprednisolone sodium succinate

Solurex, *see* Dexamethasone sodium phosphate

Solurex LA, *see* Dexamethasone acetate

Sparine, *see* Promazine HCl

Spasmoject, *see* Dicyclomine HCl

Spectinomycin HCl	up to 2 g	IM	J3320

Drug	Dose	Route	Code
Staphcillin, *see* Methicillin sodium			
Stilphostrol, *see* Diethylstilbestrol diphosphate			
Streptase, *see* Streptokinase			
Streptokinase	per 250,000 IU	IV	J2995
Streptomycin Sulfate, *see* Streptomycin			
Streptomycin	up to 1 g	IM	J3000
Streptozocin	1 gm	IV	J9320
Strontium-89 chloride	per 10 ml	IV	J3005
Sublimaze, *see* Fentanyl citrate			
Succinylcholine chloride	up to 20 mg	IV, IM	J0330
Sumatriptan succinate	6 mg	SC	J3030
Surostrin, *see* Succinycholine chloride			
Sus-Phrine, *see* Adrenalin, epinephrine			
Synkavite, *see* Vitamin K, phytonadione, etc.			
Syntocinon, *see* Oxytocin			
Synvisc, *see* Hylan G-F 20			
Sytobex, *see* Vitamin B-12 cyanocobalamin			
T			
Tacrolimus, oral	per 1 mg	ORAL	J7507
	per 5 mg	ORAL	J7508
Talwin, *see* Pentazocine HCl			
Taractan, *see* Chlorprothixene			
Taxol, *see* Paclitaxel			
Taxotere, *see* Docetaxel			
Tazidime, *see* Ceftazidime			
Technetium TC Sestamibi	per dose		A9500
TEEV, *see* Testosterone enanthate and estradiol valerate			
Terbutaline sulfate	up to 1 mg	SC, IV	J3105
Terbutaline sulfate, concentrated form	per 1 mg	INH	J7680
Terbutaline sulfate, unit dose form	per 1 mg	INH	J7681
Terramycin IM, *see* Oxytetracycline HCl			
Testa-C, *see* Testosterone cypionate			
Testadiate, *see* Testosterone enanthate and estradiol valerate			
Testadiate-Depo, *see* Testosterone cypionate			
Testaject-LA, *see* Testosterone cypionate			
Testaqua, *see* Testosterone suspension			
Test-Estro Cypionates, *see* Testosterone cypionate and estradiol cypionate			
Test-Estro-C, *see* Testosterone cypionate and estradiol cypionate			
Testex, *see* Testosterone propionate			
Testoject-50, *see* Testosterone suspension			
Testoject-LA, *see* Testosterone cypionate			
Testone LA 200, *see* Testosterone enanthate			
Testone LA 100, *see* Testosterone enanthate			
Testosterone Aqueous, *see* Testosterone suspension			
Testosterone enanthate and estradiol valerate	up to 1 cc	IM	J0900
Testosterone enanthate	up to 100 mg	IM	J3120
	up to 200 mg	IM	J3130
Testosterone cypionate	1 cc, 50 mg	IM	J1090
	up to 100 mg	IM	J1070
	1 cc, 200 mg	IM	J1080
Testosterone cypionate and estradiol cypionate	up to 1 ml	IM	J1060
Testosterone propionate	up to 100 mg	IM	J3150
Testosterone suspension	up to 50 mg	IM	J3140
Testradiol 90/4, *see* Testosterone enanthate and estradiol valerate			
Testrin PA, *see* Testosterone enanthate			
Tetanus immune globulin, human	up to 250 units	IM	J1670
Tetracycline	up to 250 mg	IM, IV	J0120
Thallous Chloride TL 201	per MCI		A9505
Theelin Aqueous, *see* Estrone			
Theophylline	per 40 mg	IV	J2810
TheraCys, *see* BCG live			
Thiethylperazine maleate, injection	up to 10 mg	IM	J3280
Thiethylperazine maleate, oral	10 mg	ORAL	Q0174
Thiotepa	15 mg	IV	J9340
Thiothixene	up to 4 mg	IM	J2330
Thorazine, *see* Chlorpromazine HCl			
Thymoglobulin, *see* Immune globulin, anti-thymocyte			
Thypinone, *see* Protirelin			
Thyrogen, *see* Thyrotropin Alfa			
Thyrotropin Alpha, injection	up to 10 IU	IM, SC	J3240
Tice BCG, *see* BCG live			
Ticon, *see* Trimethobenzamide HCl			
Tigan, *see* Trimethobenzamide HCl			
Tiject-20, *see* Trimethobenzamide HCl			
Tirofiban hydrochloride, injection	12.5 mg	IM, IV	J3245
Tobi, *see* Tobramycin, inhalation solution			
Tobramycin, inhalation solution	300 mg	INH	J7682
Tobramycin sulfate	up to 80 mg	IM, IV	J3260
Tofranil, *see* Imipramine HCl			
Tolazoline HCl	up to 25 mg	IV	J2670
Topotecan	4 mg	IV	J9350
Toradol, *see* Ketorolac tromethamine			
Torecan, *see* Thiethylperazine maleate			
Tornalate, *see* Bitolterol mesylate			
Torsemide	10 mg/ml	IV	J3265
Totacillin-N, *see* Ampicillin			
Trastuzumab	10 mg	ORAL	J9355
Tri-Kort, *see* Triamcinolone acetonide			
Triam-A, *see* Triamcinolone acetonide			
Triamcinolone, concentrated form	per 1 mg	INH	J7683
Triamcinolone, unit dose	per 1 mg	INH	J7684
Triamcinolone acetonide	per 10 mg	IM	J3301
Triamcinolone diacetate	per 5 mg	IM	J3302
Triamcinolone hexacetonide	per 5 mg	VAR	J3303
Triflupromazine HCl	up to 20 mg	IM, IV	J3400
Trilafon, *see* Perphenazine			

Trilog, *see* Triamcinolone acetonide

Trilone, *see* Triamcinolone diacetate

Trimethaphan camsylate	up to 500 mg	IV	J0400
Trimethobenzamide HCl, injection	up to 200 mg	IM	J3250
Trimethobenzamide HCl, oral	250 mg	ORAL	Q0173
Trimetrexate glucuronate	per 25 mg	IV	J3305

Trobicin, *see* Spectinomycin HCl

Trovan, *see* Alatrofloxacin mesylate

U

Ultrazine-10, *see* Prochlorperazine

Unasyn, *see* Ampicillin sodium/sulbactam sodium

Unclassified drugs (*see also* Not otherwise classified)			J3490
Unspecified oral antiemetic			Q0181
Urea	up to 40 gm	IV	J3350

Ureaphil, *see* Urea

Urecholine, *see* Bethanechol chloride

Urokinase	5,000 IU vial	IV	J3364
	250,000 IU vial	IV	J3365

V

V-Gan 25, *see* Promethazine HCl

V-Gan 50, *see* Promethazine HCl

Valergen 10, *see* Estradiol valerate

Valergen 20, *see* Estradiol valerate

Valergen 40, *see* Estradiol valerate

Valertest No. 1, *see* Testosterone enanthate and estradiol valerate

Valertest No. 2, *see* Testosterone enanthate and estradiol valerate

Valium, *see* Diazepam

Valrubicin, intravesical	200 mg	OTH	J9357

Valstar, *see* Valrubicin

Vancocin, *see* Vancomycin HCl

Vancoled, *see* Vancomycin HCl

Vancomycin HCl	up to 500 mg	IV, IM	J3370

Vasoxyl, *see* Methoxamine HCl

Velban, *see* Vinblastine sulfate

Velsar, *see* Vinblastine sulfate

Ventolin, *see* Albuterol sulfate

VePesid, *see* Etoposide and Etoposide, oral

Versed, *see* Midazolam HCl

Vesprin, *see* Triflupromazine HCl

Vinblastine sulfate	1 mg	IV	J9360

Vincasar PFS, *see* Vincristine sulfate

Vincristine sulfate	1 mg	IV	J9370
	2 mg	IV	J9375
	5 mg	IV	J9380
Vinorelbine tartrate	per 10 mg	IV	J9390

Vistaject-25, *see* Hydroxyzine HCl

Vistaril, *see* Hydroxyzine HCl

Vistide, *see* Cidofovir

Vitamin K, phytonadione, menadione, menadiol sodium diphosphate	per 1 mg	IM, SC, IV	J3430
Vitamin B-12 cyanocobalamin	up to 1,000 mcg	IM, SC	J3420

W

Wehamine, *see* Dimenhydrinate

Wehdryl, *see* Diphenhydramine HCl

Wellcovorin, *see* Leucovorin calcium

Win Rho SD, *see* Rho(D)immune globulin (human), solvent detergent

Wyamine Sulfate, *see* Mephentermine sulfate

Wycillin, *see* Penicillin G procaine

Wydase, *see* Hyaluronidase

X

Xeloda, *see* Capecitabine

Xylocaine HCl, *see* Lidocaine HCl

Z

Zanosar, *see* Streptozocin

Zantac, *see* Ranitidine HCl

Zemplar, *see* Paricalcitol

Zenapax, *see* Daclizumab

Zetran, *see* Diazepam

Zinacef, *see* Cefuroxime sodium

Zithromax, *see* Azithromycin dihydrate

Zithromax I.V., *see* Azithromycin, injection

Zofran, *see* Ondansetron HCl

Zoladex, *see* Goserelin acetate implant

Zolicef, *see* Cefazolin sodium

Zosyn, *see* Piperacillin

A

B

C

Caine (-1, -2), J2000
Calcijex, J0635
Calcimar, J0630
Calcitriol, J0635
Calcitonin-salmon, J0630
Calcium disodium edetate, J0600
Calcium Disodium Versenate, J0600
Calcium gluconate, J0610
Calcium glycerophosphate and calcium lactate, J0620
Calcium lactate and calcium glycerophosphate, J0620
Calcium leucovorin, J0640
Calibrator solution, A4256
Calphosan, J0620
Camptosar, *see* Irinotecan
Cane, E0100, E0105
    accessory, A4636, A4637
Canister, disposable, used with suction pump, A7000
Canister, non-disposable, used with suction pump, A7001
Cannula, nasal, A4615
Capecitabine, oral, J8520, J8521
Carbocaine with Neo-Cobefrin, J0670
Carbon filter, A4680
Carboplatin, J9045
Cardia Event, recorder, implantable, E0616
Cardiokymography, Q0035
Cardiovascular services, M0300–M0302
Carmustine, J9050
Carnitor, J1955
Cast
    hand restoration, L6900–L6915
    materials, special, A4590
    plaster, L2102, L2122
    supplies, A4580, A4590
    synthetic, L2104, L2124
    thermoplastic, L2106, L2126
Caster, front, for power wheelchair, K0099
Caster, wheelchair, E0997, E0998
Catheter, A4300–A4365
    anchoring device, A5200, K0407, K0408
    cap, disposable (dialysis), A4860
    external collection device, A4327–A4330, A4347, K0410, K0411
    indwelling, A4338–A4346
    indwelling, insertion of, G0002
    insertion tray, A4354
    intermittent with insertion supplies, A4353
    irrigation supplies, A4355, K0409
    male external, K0410, K0411
    oropharyngeal suction, A4628
    starter set, A4329
    trachea (suction), A4624
Catheterization, specimen collection, P9610, P9615
Cefadyl, J0710
Cefazolin sodium, J0690
Cefizox, J0715
Cefonicid sodium, J0695
Cefotaxime sodium, J0698
Cefoxitin, J0694
Ceftazidime, J0713
Ceftizoxime sodium, J0715
Ceftriaxone sodium, J0696
Cefuroxime sodium, J0697
Celestone Phosphate, J0704
CellCept, K0412
Cellular therapy, M0075
Cel-U-Jec, J0704
Cement, ostomy, A4364

Cenacort A-40, J3301
Cenacort Forte, J3302
Centrifuge, A4650
Cephalin Flocculation, blood, P2028
Cephalothin sodium, J1890
Cephapirin sodium, J0710
Ceredase, J0205
Cerezyme, J1785
Cerubidine, J9150
Cervical
    halo, L0810–L0830
    head harness/halter, E0942
    orthosis, L0100–L0200
    pillow, E0943
    traction, E0855
Cervical cap contraceptive, A4261
Cervical-thoracic-lumbar-sacral orthosis (CTLSO), L0700, L0710
Chair
    adjustable, dialysis, E1570
    lift, E0627
    rollabout, E1031
    sitz bath, E0160–E0162
Chealamide, J3520
Chelation therapy, M0300
Chemical endarterectomy, M0300
Chemistry and toxicology tests, P2028–P3001
Chemotherapy
    administration, Q0083–Q0085 (hospital reporting only)
    drug, oral, not otherwise classified, J8999
    drugs (*see also* drug by name), J9000–J9999
Chest shell (cuirass), E0457
Chest wrap, E0459
Chin cup, cervical, L0150
Chin strap (for positive airway pressure device), K0186
Chlor-100, J0730
Chloramphenicol sodium succinate, J0720
Chlordiazepoxide HCl, J1990
Chloromycetin Sodium Succinate, J0720
Chloroprocaine HCl, J2400
Chloroquine HCl, J0390
Chlorothiazide sodium, J1205
Chlorpheniramine maleate, J0730
Chlor-Pro (10), J0730
Chlorpromazine HCl, J3230
Chlorprothixene, J3080
Chlor-Trimeton, J0730
Chorex (-5, -10), J0725
Chorignon, J0725
Chorionic gonadotropin, J0725
Choron 10, J0725
Cidofovir, J0740
Cilastatin sodium, imipenem, J0743
Cisplatin, J9060, J9062
Cladribine, J9065
Claforan, J0698
Clamp
    dialysis, A4910, A4918, A4920
    external urethral, A4356
Cleanser, wound, A6260
Cleansing agent, dialysis equipment, A4790
Clonidine, J0735
Clotting time tube, A4771
Clubfoot wedge, L3380
Cobex, J3420
Cochlear prosthetic implant, L8614
    replacement, L8619
Codeine phosphate, J0745
Codimal-A, J0945
Cogentin, J0515

Colchicine, J0760
Colistimethate sodium, J0770
Collagen
    skin test, G0025
    urinary tract implant, L8603
    wound dressing, A6020
Collar, cervical
    multiple post, L0180–L0200
    nonadjust (foam), L0120
Collection device for nebulizer, K0177
Coly-Mycin M, J0770
Comfort items, A9190
Commode, E0160–E0175, K0457
    lift, E0625
    pail, E0167
    seat, wheelchair, E0968
Compa-Z, J0780
Compazine, J0780
Composite dressing, A6200–A6205
Compressed gas system, E0424–E0480, L3902
Compression bandage, A4460
Compression stockings, L8100–L8239
Compressor, E0565, E0570, E0650–E0652, E1375, K0269
    filter, aerosol, K0178–K0179
Concentrator, oxygen, E1377–E1385
Conductivity meter, bath, dialysis, E1550
Congo red, blood, P2029
Contact layer, A6206–A6208
Contact lens, V2500–V2599
Continent device, A5081, A5082
Continuous positive airway pressure (CPAP) device, E0601
    compressor, K0269
    intermittent assist, E0452
    nasal application accessories, K0184
Contraceptive
    cervical cap, A4261
    intrauterine, copper, J7300
    Levonorgestrel, implants and supplies, A4260
Contracts, maintenance, ESRD, A4890
Contrast material
    injection during MRI, A4643
    low osmolar, A4644–A4646
Cophene-B, J0945
Corgonject-5, J0725
Corneal tissue processing, V2785
Corrugated tubing, used with nebulizer, K0175, K0176
Corset, spinal orthosis, L0970–L0976
Corticotropin, J0800
Cortisone acetate, J0810
Cortone Acetate, J0810
Cortrosyn, J0835
Corvert, *see* Ibutilide fumarate
Cosmegen, J9120
Cosyntropin, J0835
Cotranzine, J0780
Cover, wound
    alginate dressing, A6196–A6198
    collagen dressing, A6020
    foam dressing, A6209–A6214
    hydrocolloid dressing, K0234–K0239
    hydrogel dressing, A0242–A0248
    specialty absorptive dressing, A6251–A6256
CPAP (continuous positive airway pressure) device, E0601
    chin strap, K0186
    compressor, K0269
    filter, K0188, K0189
    headgear, K0185

D

E

Edetate calcium disodium, J0600
Edetate disodium, J3520
Eggcrate dry pressure pad/mattress,
     E0179, E0184, E0199
Elastic
   bandage, A4460
   gauze, A6263–A6405
   support, L8100–L8230
Elavil, J1320
Elbow
   disarticulation, endoskeletal, L6450
   orthosis (EO), E1800, L3700–L3740
   protector, E0191
Electrical work, dialysis equipment,
     A4870
Electrocardiogram strips,
   monitoring, G0004–G0007
   physician interpretation, G0016
   tracing, G0015
   transmission, G0015, G0016
Electrodes, per pair A4556
Elevating leg rest, K0195
Elspar, J9020
Emergency transportation, A0050,
     A0225, A0302, A0308, A0310, A0322,
     A0328, A0330, A0342, A0348, A0350,
     A0362, A0368, A0370
Emete-Con, J0510
EMG, E0746
Eminase, J0350

Enbrel, J1438
Endarterectomy, chemical, M0300
Endoscope sheath, A4270
Endoskeletal system, addition, L5925
Enovil, J1320
Enoxaparin sodium, J1650
Enteral
   feeding supply kit (syringe) (pump)
     (gravity), B4034–B4036
   formulae, B4150–B4156
   nutrition infusion pump (with alarm)
     (without), B9000, B9002
Epinephrine, J0170, J7640
Epoetin alpha, for non-ESRD use,
     Q0136
Epoprostenol, J1325
Ergonovine maleate, J1330
Erythromycin gluceptate, J1362
Erythromycin lactobionate, J1364
ESRD (end stage renal disease; *see also*
     Dialysis)
   machines and accessories, E1510–
     E1699
   plumbing, A4870
   services, E1510–E1699
   supplies, A4650–A4927
Estra-D, J1000
Estradiol, J1060, J1000
   cypionate and testosterone cypionate,
     J1060
   L.A., J0970, J1380, J1390
   L.A. 20, J0970, J1380, J1390

   L.A. 40, J0970, J1380, J1390
   valerate and testosterone enanthate,
     J0900
Estra-L (20, 40), J0970, J1380, J1390
Estra-Testrin, J0900
Estro-Cyp, J1000
Estrogen conjugated, J1410
Estroject L.A., J1000
Estrone (5, Aqueous), J1435
Estronol, J1435
   -L.A., J1000
Ethylnorepinephrine HCl, J0590
Ethyol, *see* Amifostine
Etidronate disodium, J1436
Etopophos, *see* Etoposide
Etoposide, J9181, J9182
Etoposide, oral, J8560
Everone, J3120, J3130
Exercise equipment, A9300
External
   ambulatory infusion pump, E0781,
     E0784
   power, battery components, L7360–
     L7499
   power, elbow, L7160–L7191
   urinary supplies, A4356–A4359
Extremity belt/harness, E0945
Eye
   lens (contact) (spectacle), V2100–V2615
   prosthetic, V2623, V2629
   service (miscellaneous), V2700–V2799

F

Faceplate, ostomy, A4361, K0428
Face tent, oxygen, A4619
Factor VIII, anti-hemophilic factor,
     J7190–J7192
Factor IX, J7194, Q0160, Q0161
Factrel, J1620
Fecal leukocyte examination, G0026
Feiba VH Immuno, J7196
Fentanyl citrate, J3010
Fentanyl citrate and droperidol, J1810
Fern test, Q0114
Fibrinogen unit, P9013
Filgrastim (G-CSF), J1440, J1441
Filler, wound
   alginate dressing, A6199
   foam dressing, A6215
   hydrocolloid dressing, A6240, A6241
   hydrogel dressing, A6248
   not otherwise classified, A6261,
     A6262
Film, transparent (for dressing), A6257–
     A6259

Filter
   aerosol compressor, K0178, K0179
   CPAP device, K0188, K0189
   dialysis carbon, A4680
   ostomy, A4368
   tracheostoma, A4481
   ultrasonic generator, K0179
Fistula cannulation set, A4730
Flexoject, J2360
Flexon, J2360
Flolan, *see* Epoprostenol
Flowmeter, E0440, E0555, E0580
Floxuridine, J9200
Fluconazole, injection, J1450
Fludara, J9185
Fludarabine phosphate, J9185
Fluid barrier, dialysis, E1575
Fluorouracil, J9190
Fluphenazine decanoate, J2680
Foam dressing, A6209–A6215
Foam pad adhesive, A5126
Folding walker, E0135, E0143
Folex, J9260
   PFS, J9260

Foley catheter, A4312–A4316, A4338–
     A4346
Follutein, J0725
Footdrop splint, L4398
Footplate, E0175, E0970
Footwear, orthopedic, L3201–L3265
Forceps, dialysis, A4910
Forearm crutches, E0110, E0111
Foscarnet sodium, J1455
Foscavir, J1455
Fracture
   bedpan, E0276
   frame, E0920, E0930, E0946–E0948
   orthosis, L2102–L2136, L3980–L3986
   orthotic additions, L2180–L2192, L3995
Fragmin, *see* Dalteparin sodium
Frames (spectacles), V2020, V2025
FUDR, J9200
Fungizone, intravenous, *see* Amphoteri-
     cin B
Furomide MD, J1940
Furosemide, J1940

G

Gadolinium, A4647
Gamastan, J1460–J1561
Gamma globulin, J1460–J1561
Gammar, J1460–J1561
Gamulin RH, J2790
Ganciclovir, implant, J7310
Ganciclovir sodium, J1570
Garamycin, J1580
Gas system
  compressed, E0424, E0425
  gaseous, E0430, E0431, E0441, E0443
  liquid, E0434–E0440, E0442, E0444
Gastrostomy/jejunostomy tubing, B4084
Gastrostomy tube, B4085
Gauze (*see also* Bandage)
  elastic, A6263, A6405
  impregnated, A6222–A6230, A6266
  nonelastic, A6264, A6406
  nonimpregnated, A6216–A6221,
    A6402–A6404

Gel
  conductive, A4558
  pressure pad, E0178, E0185, E0196
Gemcitabine HCl, J9201
Gemzar, *see* Gemcitabine HCl
Generator
  implantable neurostimulator, E0751
  ultrasonic with nebulizer, K0270
Gentamicin (Sulfate), J1580
Gentran, J7100, J7110
Gesterol 50, J2675
  L.A. 250, J1741
Glasses
  air conduction, V5070
  binaural, V5120–V5150
  bone conduction, V5080
  frames, V2020, V2025
  hearing aid, V5230
Gloves, dialysis, A4927
Glucagon HCl, J1610

Glucose test strips, A4253, A4772
Glukor, J0725
Gluteal pad, L2650
Glycopyrrolate, inhalation solution concentrated, J7642
Glycopyrrolate, inhalation solution, unit dose, J7643
Gold sodium thiomalate, J1600
Gomco drain bottle, A4912
Gonadorelin HCl, J1620
Gonic, J0725
Goserelin acetate implant (*see also* Implant), J9202
Grab bar, trapeze, E0910, E0940
Grade-aid, wheelchair, E0974
Granisetron HCl, J1626
Gravity traction device, E0941
Gravlee jet washer, A4470
Gynogen, J1380, J1390
  L.A. (10, 20, 40), J0970, J1380, J1390

H

Hair analysis (excluding arsenic), P2031
Haldol, J1630
  Decanoate (-50, -100), J1631
Hallus-Valgus dynamic splint, L3100
Hallux prosthetic implant, L8642
Haloperidol, J1630
  decanoate, J1631
Halo procedures, L0810–L0860
Halter, cervical head, E0942
Hand restoration, L6900–L6915
  partial prosthesis, L6000–L6020
  orthosis (WHFO), E1805, E1825,
    L3800–L3805, L3900–L3954
  rims, wheelchair, E0967
Handgrip (cane, crutch, walker), A4636
Harness, E0942, E0944, E0945
Harvard pressure clamp, dialysis, A4920
Headgear (for positive airway pressure device), K0185
Hearing devices, V5000–V5299, L8614
Heat
  application, E0200–E0239
  lamp, E0200, E0205
  pad, E0210, E0215, E0237, E0238, E0249
Heater (nebulizer), E1372
Heel
  elevator, air, E0370
  protector, E0191
  shoe, L3430–L3485
  stabilizer, L3170
Helicopter, ambulance (*see also* Ambulance), A0040
Helmet, cervical, L0100, L0110
Hemi-wheelchair, E1083–E1086

Hemipelvectomy prosthesis, L5280, L5340
Hemodialysis
  kit, A4820
  machine, E1590
Hemodialyzer, portable, E1635
Hemofil M, J7190
Hemoglobin, Q0116
Hemophilia clotting factor, J7190–J7198
Hemophilia clotting factor, NOC, J7199
Hemostats, A4850
Hemostix, A4773
Heparin infusion pump, dialysis, E1520
Heparin lock flush, J1642
Heparin sodium, A4800, J1644
Hep-Lock (U/P), J1642
Herceptin, J9355
Hexadrol Phosphate, J1100
Hexalite, A4590
Hip
  disarticulation prosthesis, L5250,
    L5270, L5330
  orthosis (HO), L1600–1690
Hip-knee-ankle-foot orthosis (HKAFO),
  L2040–L2090
Histaject, J0945
Histerone (-50, -100), J3140
HKAFO, L2040–L2090
HN₂, J9230
Hot water bottle, E0220
Humidifier, E0550–E0560, K0268
Hyalgan, J7315
Hyaluronidase, J3470
Hyate, J7191
Hybolin Decanoate, J2321
  improved, J0340

Hycamtin, *see* Topotecan
Hydeltra-TBA, J1690
Hydeltrasol, J2640
Hydralazine HCl, J0360
Hydrate, J1240
Hydraulic patient lift, E0630
Hydrochlorides of opium alkaloids, J2480
Hydrocollator, E0225, E0239
Hydrocolloid dressing, A6234–A6241
Hydrocortisone
  acetate, J1700
  sodium phosphate, J1710
  sodium succinate, J1720
Hydrocortone
  acetate, J1700
  phosphate, J1710
Hydrogel dressing, A6242–A6248
Hydromorphone, J1170
Hydroxyprogesterone caproate, J1739, J1741
Hydroxyzine HCl, J3410
Hylan G-F 20, J7320
Hylutin, J1741
Hyoscyamine sulfate, J1980
Hyperbaric oxygen chamber, topical, A4575
Hyperstat IV, J1730
Hyper-Tet, J1670
Hypertonic saline solution, J7130
HypRho-D, J2790
Hyprogest 250, J1741
Hyrexin-50, J1200
Hyzine-50, J3410

M

N

Nalbuphine HCl, J2300
Naloxone HCl, J2310
Nandrobolic, J0340
  L.A., J2321
Nandrolone
  decanoate, J2320–J2322
  phenpropionate, J0340
Narrowing device, wheelchair, E0969
Nasahist B, J0945
Nasal application device, K0183
Nasal pillows/seals (for nasal application device), K0184
Nasal vaccine inhalation, J3530
Nasogastric tubing, B4081, B4082
Navane, J2330
ND Stat, J0945
Nebcin, J3260
Nebulizer, E0570–E0585
  aerosol compressor, K0501
  aerosol mask, A7015
  corrugated tubing, disposable, A7010
  corrugated tubing, non-disposable, A7011
  distilled water, K0182
  drug dispensing fee, E0590
  filter, disposable, A7013
  filter, non-disposable, A7014
  heater, E1372
  large volume, disposable, prefilled, A7008
  large volume, disposable, unfilled, A7007
  not used with oxygen, durable, glass, A7017
  pneumatic, administration set, A7003, A7005, A7006
  pneumatic, nonfiltered, A7004
  portable, E1375
  small volume, K0168–K0171, K0270
  ultrasonic, dome and mouthpiece, A7016
  ultrasonic, reservoir bottle, non-disposable, A7009
  water collection device, large volume nebulizer, A7012
NebuPent, J2545
Needle, A4215
  dialysis, A4655
  non-coring, A4212
  with syringe, A4206–A4209
Nembutal Sodium Solution, J2515
Neocyten, J2360
Neo-Durabolic, J2320–J2322
Neonatal transport, ambulance, base rate, A0225
Neoquess, J0500
Neosar, J9070–J9092
Neostigmine methylsulfate, J2710
Neo-Synephrine, J2370
Nervocaine (1%, 2%), J2000
Nesacaine MPF, J2400
Neumega, J2355
Neuromuscular stimulator, E0745
Neurostimulator electrodes, E0753
  pulse generator, E0751
  receiver, E0751
Neutrexin, J3305
Niacin, J2350
Niacinamide, J2350
Nicotinamide, J2350

Nicotinic acid, J2350
Nipent, J9268
Nitrogen mustard, J9230
Nonchemotherapy drug, oral, J8499
Noncovered services, A9160, A9170, A9270
Nonelastic gauze, A6264, A6406
Nonemergency transportation, A0080–A0210
Nonimpregnated gauze dressing, A6216–A6221, A6402–A6404
Nonmetabolic active tissue, Q0183
Nonprescription drug, A9150
Nordryl, J1200
Norflex, J2360
Norzine, J3280
Not otherwise classified drug, J3490, J7599, J7699, J7799, J8499, J8999, J9999, Q0181
Novantrone, J9293
Novo Seven, Q0187
NPH, J1820
NITOL category 1, Q1001
NITOL category 2, Q1002
NITOL category 3, Q1003
NITOL category 4, Q1004
NITOL category 5, Q1005
Nulicaine, J2000
Numorphan H.P., J2410
Nutrition
  enteral infusion pump, B9000, B9002
  parenteral infusion pump, B9004, B9006
  parenteral solution, B4164–B5200

O

Occipital/mandibular support, cervical, L0160
Ocular prosthetic implant, L8610
Oculinum, J0585
O-Flex, J2360
Omnipen-N, J0290
Oncaspar, J9266
Oncovin, J9370
Ondansetron HCl, J2405
One arm, drive attachment, K0101
Opium alkaloids, hydrochlorides of, J2480
Oprelvekin, J2355
O & P supply/accessory/service, L9900
Oraminic II, J0945
Ormazine, J3230
Oropharyngeal suction catheter, A4628
Orphenadrine, J2360
Orphenate, J2360
Orthopedic shoes
  arch support, L3040–L3100
  footwear, L3201–L3265
  insert, L3000–L3030
  lift, L3300–L3334
  miscellaneous additions, L3500–L3595
  positioning device, L3140–L3170
  transfer, L3600–L3649
  wedge, L3340–L3420
Orthotic additions
  carbon graphite lamination, L2755
  fracture, L2180–L2192, L3995
  halo, L0860
  lower extremity, L2200–L2999, L4320
  ratchet lock, L2430
  scoliosis, L1010–L1120, L1210–L1290
  shoe, L3300–L3595, L3649
  spinal, L0970–L0984
  upper extremity joint, L3956
  upper limb, L3810–L3890, L3970–L3974, L3995

Orthotic devices
  ankle-foot (AFO; *see also* Orthopedic shoes), E1815, E1830, L1900–L1990, L2102–L2116, L3160
  anterior-posterior, L0320, L0330, L0530
  anterior-posterior-lateral, L0520, L0550–L0565, L0700, L0710
  anterior-posterior-lateral-rotary, L0340–L0440
  cervical, L0100–L0200
  cervical-thoracic-lumbar-sacral (CTLSO), L0700, L0710
  elbow (EO), E1800, L3700–L3740
  fracture, L2102–L2136, L3980–L3986
  halo, L0810–L0830
  hand (WHFO), E1805, E1825, L3800, L3805, L3900–L3954
  hip (HO), L1600–L1690
  hip-knee-ankle-foot (HKAFO), L2040–L2090
  interface material, E1820
  knee (KO), E1810, L1800–L1885
  knee-ankle-foot (KAFO; *see also* Orthopedic shoes), L2000–L2038, L2122–L2136
  Legg-Perthes, L1700–L1755
  lumbar flexion, L0540
  lumbar-sacral (LSO), L0500–L0565
  multiple post collar, L0180–L0200
  not otherwise specified, L0999, L1499, L2999, L3999, L5999, L7499, L8039, L8239
  pneumatic splint, L4350–L4380
  repair or replacement, L4000–L4210
  replace soft interface material, L4390–L4394
  sacroiliac, L0600–L0620
  scoliosis, L1000–L1499
  shoe, *see* Orthopedic shoes
  shoulder (SO), L3650–L3675
  shoulder-elbow-wrist-hand (SEWHO), L3960–L3969

  spinal, cervical, L0100–L0200
  spinal, DME, K0112–K0116
  thoracic, L0210
  thoracic-hip-knee-ankle (THKO), L1500–L1520
  thoracic-lumbar-sacral (TLSO), L0300–L0440
  toe, E1830
  torso supports, L0900–L0960
  wrist-hand-finger (WHFO), E1805, E1825, L3800, L3805, L3900–L3954
Or-Tyl, J0500
Ossicular prosthetic implant, L8613
Osteogenesis stimulator, E0747–E0749, E0760
Ostomy
  accessories, A5093
  supplies, A4361–A4421, A5051–A5149
Oxacillin sodium, J2700
Oxygen
  ambulance, A0422
  chamber, hyperbaric, topical, A4575
  concentrator, E1390
  concentrator, high humidity system, E1377–E1385
  mask, A4620, A4621
  medication supplies, A4611–A4627
  rack/stand, E1355
  regulator, E1353
  respiratory equipment/supplies, A4611–A4627, E0424–E0480
  supplies and equipment, E0425–E0444, E0455
  tent, E0455
  tubing, A4616
  water vapor enriching system, E1405, E1406
Oxymorphone HCl, J2410
Oxytetracycline HCl, J2460
Oxytocin, J2590

Q

Quad cane, E0105
Quelicin, J0330

R

Rack/stand, oxygen, E1355
Radial head, prosthetic implant, L8620
Radiology service, R0070–R0076
Radiopharmaceutical diagnostic imaging agent, A4641, A4642, A9500, A9502, A9503, A9505, A9507
Radiopharmaceutical diagnostic imaging agent, Technetium Tc 99m Apticide, A9504
Radiopharmaceutical, therapeutic, A9600, A9605
Rail
  bathtub, E0241, E0242, E0246
  bed, E0305, E0310
  toilet, E0243
Reciprocating peritoneal dialysis system, E1630
Red blood cells, P9021, P9022
Redisol, J3420
Reduction pneumoplasty, G0061
Regitine, J2760
Reglan, J2765
Regular insulin, J1820
Regulator, oxygen, E1353

Relefact TRH, J2725
Remicade, J1745
Reo Pro, J0130
Repair
  contract, ESRD, A4890
  durable medical equipment, E1340
  orthosis, L4000–L4130
  prosthetic, L7500, L7510, K0285
Replacement
  battery, A4254, A4630, A4631
  components, ESRD machine, E1640
  pad (alternating pressure), A4640
  tanks, dialysis, A4880
  tip for cane, crutches, walker, A4637
  underarm pad for crutches, A4635
Rep-Pred 40, J1030
  80, J1040
Reservoir bottle (for ultrasonic nebulizer), K0174
RespiGam, *see* Respiratory syncytial virus immune globulin
Respiratory
  Heated humidifier used with PAP, K0531
  Invasive assist with backup, K0534

  Noninvasive assist with backup, K0533
  Noninvasive assist without backup, K0532
Respiratory syncytial virus immune globulin, J1565
Restraint, any type, E0710
Retavase, J2994
Reteplase, J2994
Rhesonativ, J2790
Rho(D) immune globulin, (human), J2790, J2792
Rho-GAM, J2790
Rib belt, thoracic, A4572, L0210, L0220
Ringer's lactate infusion, J7120
Ring, ostomy, A4404
Rituxan, J9310
Rituximab, J9310
Robaxin, J2800
Robin-Aids, L6000, L6010, L6020, L6855, L6860
Rocephin, J0696
Rocking bed, E0462
Rollabout chair, E1031
Rubex, J9000
Rubramin PC, J3420

S

MEDICARE CARRIERS MANUAL (MCM), SELECT

2005 WHEN PART B EXPENSES ARE INCURRED

2005.1 Physicians' Expense for Surgery, Childbirth, and Treatment for Infertility

A. Surgery and Childbirth.—Skilled medical management is appropriate throughout the events of pregnancy, beginning with diagnosis, continuing through delivery and ending after the necessary postnatal care. Similarly, in the event of termination of pregnancy, regardless of whether terminated spontaneously or for therapeutic reasons (i.e., where the life of the mother would be endangered if the fetus were brought to term), the need for skilled medical management and/or medical services is equally important as in those cases carried to full term. After the infant is delivered and is a separate individual, items and services furnished to the infant are not covered on the basis of the mother's eligibility.

Most surgeons and obstetricians bill patients an all inclusive package charge intended to cover all services associated with the surgical procedure or delivery of the child. All expenses for surgical and obstetrical care, including preoperative/prenatal examinations and tests and postoperative/postnatal services are considered incurred on the date of surgery or delivery, as appropriate. This policy applies whether the physician bills on a package charge basis, or itemizes his/her bill separately for these items.

Occasionally, a physician's bill may include charges for additional services not directly related to the surgical procedure or the delivery. Such charges are considered incurred on the date the additional services are furnished.

The above policy applies only where the charges are imposed by one physician or by a clinic on behalf of a group of physicians. Where charges are imposed by more than one physician for surgical or obstetrical services, all preoperative/prenatal and postoperative/postnatal services performed by the physician who performed the surgery or delivery are considered incurred on the date of the surgery or delivery. Expenses for services rendered by other physicians are considered incurred on the date they were performed.

B. Treatment for Infertility.—Reasonable and necessary services associated with treatment for infertility are covered under Medicare. Infertility is a condition sufficiently at variance with the usual state of health to make it appropriate for a person who normally is expected to be fertile to seek medical consultation and treatment. Coordinate with PROs to see that utilization guidelines are established for this treatment if inappropriate utilization or abuse is suspected.

2049 DRUGS AND BIOLOGICALS

Generally, drugs and biologicals are covered only if all of the following requirements are met:

- They meet the definition of drugs or biologicals (see section 2049.1);
- They are of the type that cannot be self-administered (see section 2049.2);
- They meet all the general requirements for coverage of items as incident to a physician's services (see section 2050.1 and 2050.3);
- They are reasonable and necessary for the diagnosis or treatment of the illness or injury for which they are administered according to accepted standards of medical practice (see section 2049.4);
- They are not excluded as immunizations (see section 2049.4.B); and
- They have not been determined by the FDA to be less than effective. (See section 2049.4D.)

Drugs that can be self-administered, such as those in pill form, or are used for self-injection, are generally not covered by Part B. However, the statute provides for the coverage of some self-administered drugs. Examples of self-administered drugs that are covered include blood clotting factors, drugs used in immunosuppressive therapy, erythropoietin for dialysis patients, osteoporosis drugs for certain homebound patients, and certain oral cancer drugs. (See section 2100.5 and 2130D for coverage of drugs which are necessary to the effective use of DME or prosthetic devices.)

2049.1 Definition of Drug or Biological.

—Drugs and biologicals must be determined to meet the statutory definition. Under the statute, payment may be made for a drug or biological only where it is included, or approved for inclusion, in the latest official edition of the United States Pharmacopoeia, the National Formulary, or the United States Homeopathic Pharmacopoeia, except for those unfavorably evaluated in AMA Drug Evaluations (successor publication to New Drugs) or Accepted Dental Therapeutics (successor publication to Accepted Dental Remedies). Combination drugs are also included in the definition of drugs if the combination itself or all of the therapeutic ingredients of the combination are included, or approved for inclusion, in any of the above drug compendia.

Drugs and biologicals are considered approved for inclusion in a compendium if approved under the established procedure by the professional organization responsible for revision of the compendium.

2049.2 Determining Self-Administration of Drug or Biological.

—Whether a drug or biological is of a type which cannot be self-administered is based on the usual method of administration of the form of that drug or biological as furnished by the physician. Thus, where a physician gives a patient pills or other oral medication, these are excluded from coverage since the form of the drug given to the patient is usually self-administered. Similarly, if a physician gives a patient an injection which is usually self-injected (e.g., insulin or calcitonin), this drug is excluded from coverage, unless administered to the patient in an emergency situation (e.g., diabetic coma). Where, however, a physician injects a drug which is not usually self-injected, this drug is not subject to the self-administrable drug exclusion (regardless of whether the drug may also be available in oral form) since it is not self-administrable in the form in which it was furnished to the patient.

Whole blood is a biological which cannot be self-administered and is covered when furnished incident to a physician's services. Payment may also be made for blood fractions if all coverage requirements are satisfied. (See section 2455 on Part B blood deductible.)

2049.3 Incident-to Requirements.

—In order to meet all the general requirements for coverage under the incident-to provision, an FDA approved drug or biological must be of a form that cannot be self-administered and must be furnished by a physician and administered by him/her or by auxiliary personnel employed by him/her under his/her personal supervision. The charge, if any, for the drug or biological must be included in the physician's bill, and the cost of the drug or biological must represent an expense to the physician. Drugs and biologicals furnished by other health professionals may also meet these requirements. (See section 2154, 2156, 2158 and 2160 for specific instructions.)

2049.4 Reasonableness and Necessity.

—Use of the drug or biological must be safe and effective and otherwise reasonable and necessary. (See section 2303.) Drugs or biologicals approved for marketing by the Food and Drug Administration (FDA) are considered safe and effective for purposes of this requirement when used for indications specified on the labeling. Therefore, you may pay for the use of an FDA approved drug or biological, if:

- It was injected on or after the date of the FDA's approval;
- It is reasonable and necessary for the individual patient; and
- All other applicable coverage requirements are met.

Deny coverage for drugs and biologicals which have not received final marketing approval by the FDA unless you receive instructions from HCFA to the contrary. For specific guidelines on coverage of Group C cancer drugs, see the Coverage Issues Manual.

If there is reason to question whether the FDA has approved a drug or biological for marketing, obtain satisfactory evidence of FDA's approval. Acceptable evidence includes a copy of the FDA's letter to the drug's manufacturer approving the new drug application (NDA); or listing of the drug or biological in the FDA's Approved Drug Products or FDA Drug and Device Product Approvals; or a copy of the manufacturer's package insert, approved by the FDA as part of the labeling of the drug, containing its recommended uses and dosage, as well as possible adverse reactions and recommended precautions in using it. When necessary, the RO may be able to help in obtaining information.

An unlabeled use of a drug is a use that is not included as an indication on the drug's label as approved by the FDA. FDA approved drugs used for indications other than what is indicated on the official label may be covered under Medicare if the carrier determines the use to be medically accepted, taking into consideration the major drug compendia, authoritative medical literature and/or accepted standards of medical practice. In the case of drugs used in an anti-cancer chemotherapeutic regimen, unlabeled uses are covered for a medically accepted indication as defined in section 2049.4.C.

Determinations as to whether medication is reasonable and necessary for an individual patient should be made on the same basis as all other such determinations (i.e., with the advice of medical consultants and with reference to accepted standards of medical practice and the medical circumstances of the individual case). The following guidelines identify three categories with specific examples of situations in which medications would not be reasonable and necessary according to accepted standards of medical practice.

1. Not for Particular Illness.—Medications given for a purpose other than the treatment of a particular condition, illness, or injury are not covered (except for certain immunizations). Exclude the charge for medications, e.g., vitamins, given simply for the general good and welfare of the patient and not as accepted therapy for a particular illness.

2. Injection Method Not Indicated.—Medication given by injection (parenterally) is not covered if standard medical practice indicates that the administration of the medication by mouth (orally) is effective and is an accepted or preferred method of administration. For example, the accepted standards of medical practice for the treatment of certain diseases is to initiate therapy with parenteral penicillin and to complete therapy with oral penicillin. Exclude the entire charge for penicillin injections given after the initiation of therapy if oral penicillin is indicated unless there are special medical circumstances which justify additional injections.

3. Excessive Medications.—Medications administered for treatment of a disease which exceed the frequency or duration of injections indicated by accepted standards of medical practice are not covered. For example, the accepted standard of medical practice in the maintenance treatment of pernicious anemia is one vitamin B-12 injection per month. Exclude the entire charge for injections given in excess of this frequency unless there are special medical circumstances which justify additional injections.

Supplement the guidelines as necessary with guidelines concerning appropriate use of specific injections in other situations. Use the guidelines to screen out questionable cases for special review, further development or denial when the injection billed for would not be reasonable and necessary. Coordinate any type of drug treatment review with the PRO.

If a medication is determined not to be reasonable and necessary for diagnosis or treatment of an illness or injury according to these guidelines, exclude the entire charge (i.e., for both the drug and its administration). Also exclude from payment any charges for other services (such as office visits) which were primarily for the purpose of administering a noncovered injection (i.e., an injection that is not reasonable and necessary for the diagnosis or treatment of an illness or injury).

A. Antigens.—Payment may be made for a reasonable supply of antigens that have been prepared for a particular patient if: (1) the antigens are prepared by a physician who is a doctor of medicine or osteopathy, and (2) the physician who prepared the antigens has examined the patient and has determined a plan of treatment and a dosage regimen. Antigens must be administered in accordance with the plan of treatment and by a doctor of medicine or osteopathy or by a properly instructed person (who could be the patient) under the supervision of the doctor. The associations of allergists that HCFA consulted advised that a reasonable supply of antigens is considered to be not more than a 12-week supply of antigens that has been prepared for a particular patient at any one time. The purpose of the reasonable supply limitation is to assure that the antigens retain their potency and effectiveness over the period in which they are to be administered to the patient. (See section 2005.2 and 2050.2.)

B. Immunizations.—Vaccinations or inoculations are excluded as immunizations unless they are directly related to the treatment of an injury or direct exposure to a disease or condition, such as antirabies treatment, tetanus antitoxin or booster vaccine, botulin antitoxin, antivenin sera, or immune globulin. In the absence of injury or direct exposure, preventive immunization (vaccination or inoculation) against such diseases as smallpox, polio, diphtheria, etc., is not covered. However, pneumococcal, hepatitis B, and influenza virus vaccines are exceptions to this rule. (See items 1, 2 and 3.) In cases where a vaccination or inoculation is excluded from coverage, deny the entire charge.

1. Pneumococcal Pneumonia Vaccinations.—Part B of Medicare pays 100 percent of the reasonable charge for pneumococcal pneumonia vaccine and its administration to a patient if it is ordered by a physician who is a doctor of medicine or osteopathy. This includes revaccination of patients at highest risk of pneumococcal infection.

A physician does not have to be present to meet the physician order requirement if a previously written physician order (standing order) is on hand and it specifies that for any person receiving the vaccine (1) the person's age, health, and vaccination status must be determined; (2) a signed consent must be obtained; (3) an initial vaccine may be administered only to persons at high risk (see below) of pneumococcal disease; (4) revaccination may be administered only to persons at highest risk of serious pneumococcal infection and those likely to have a rapid decline in pneumococcal antibody levels, provided that at least 5 years have passed since receipt of a previous dose of pneumococcal vaccine; and (5) a record indicating the date the vaccine was given must be presented to each patient.

Persons at high risk for whom an initial vaccine may be administered include all people age 65 and older; immunocompetent adults who are at increased risk of pneumococcal disease or its complications because of chronic illness (e.g., cardiovascular disease, pulmonary disease, diabetes mellitus, alcoholism, cirrhosis, or cerebrospinal fluid leaks); and individuals with compromised immune systems (e.g., splenic dysfunction or anatomic asplenia, Hodgkin's disease, lymphoma, multiple myeloma, chronic renal failure, HIV infection, nephrotic syndrome, sickle cell disease, or organ transplantation).

Persons at highest risk and those most likely to have rapid declines in antibody levels are those for whom revaccination may be appropriate. This group includes persons with functional or anatomic asplenia (e.g., sickle cell disease, splenectomy), HIV infection, leukemia, lymphoma, Hodgkin's disease, multiple myeloma, generalized malignancy, chronic renal failure, nephrotic syndrome, or other conditions associated with immunosuppression such as organ or bone marrow transplantation, and those receiving immunosuppressive chemotherapy. Routine revaccination of people age 65 or older who are not at highest risk is not appropriate.

To help avoid potentially unnecessary doses, every patient should be given a record of their vaccination. Nevertheless, those administering the vaccine should not require the patient to present an immunization record prior to administering the pneumococcal vaccine, nor should they feel compelled to review the patient's complete medical record if it is not available. Instead, provided that the patient is competent, it is acceptable for them to rely on the patient's verbal history to determine prior vaccination status. If the patient is uncertain about their vaccination history in the past 5 years, the vaccine should be given. However, if the patient is certain he/she was vaccinated in the last 5 years, the vaccine should not be given. If the patient is certain that the vaccine was given and that more than 5 years have passed since receipt of the previous dose, revaccination is not appropriate unless the patient is at highest risk.

2. Hepatitis B Vaccine.—With the enactment of P.L. 98-369, coverage under Part B was extended to hepatitis B vaccine and its administration, furnished to a Medicare beneficiary who is at high or intermediate risk of contracting hepatitis B. This coverage is effective for services furnished on or after September 1, 1984.

High-risk groups currently identified include (see exception below):

- End stage renal disease (ESRD) patients;
- Hemophiliacs who receive Factor VIII or IX concentrates;
- Clients of institutions for the mentally retarded;
- Persons who live in the same household as a hepatitis B virus (HBV) carrier;
- Homosexual men; and
- Illicit injectable drug abusers.

Intermediate risk groups currently identified include:

- Staff in institutions for the mentally retarded; and
- Workers in health care professions who have frequent contact with blood or blood-derived body fluids during routine work.

EXCEPTION: Persons in the above-listed groups would not be considered at high or intermediate risk of contracting hepatitis B, however, if there is laboratory evidence positive for antibodies to hepatitis B. (ESRD patients are routinely tested for hepatitis B antibodies as part of their continuing monitoring and therapy.)

For Medicare program purposes, the vaccine may be administered upon the order of a doctor of medicine or osteopathy by home health agencies, skilled nursing facilities, ESRD facilities, hospital outpatient departments, persons recognized under the incident to physicians' services provision of law, and doctors of medicine and osteopathy.

A charge separate from the ESRD composite rate will be recognized and paid for administration of the vaccine to ESRD patients.

For ESRD laboratory tests, see Coverage Issues Manual, section 50-17.

3. Influenza Virus Vaccine.—Effective for services furnished on or after May 1, 1993, the Medicare Part B program covers influenza virus vaccine and its administration when furnished in compliance with any applicable State law by any provider of services or any entity or individual with a supplier number. Typically, these vaccines are administered once a year in the fall or winter. Medicare does not require for coverage purposes that the vaccine must be ordered by a doctor of medicine or osteopathy. Therefore, the beneficiary may receive the vaccine upon request without a physician's order and without physician supervision.

C. Unlabeled Use For Anti-Cancer Drugs.—Effective January 1, 1994, unlabeled uses of FDA approved drugs and biologicals used in an anti-cancer chemotherapeutic regimen for a medically accepted indication are evaluated under the conditions described in this paragraph. A regimen is a combination of anti-cancer agents which has been clinically recognized for the treatment of a specific type of cancer. An example of a drug regimen is: Cyclophosphamide + vincristine + prednisone (CVP) for non-Hodgkin's lymphoma.

In addition to listing the combination of drugs for a type of cancer, there may be a different regimen or combinations which are used at different times in the history of the cancer (induction, prophylaxis of CNS involvement, post remission, and relapsed or refractory disease). A protocol may specify the combination of drugs, doses, and schedules for administration of the drugs. For purposes of this provision, a cancer treatment regimen includes drugs used to treat toxicities or side effects of the cancer treatment regimen when the drug is administered incident to a chemotherapy treatment. Contractors must not deny coverage based solely on the absence of FDA approved labeling for the use, if the use is supported by one of the following and the use is not listed as "not indicated" in any of the three compendia. (See note at the end of this subsection.)

1. American Hospital Formulary Service Drug Information.—Drug monographs are arranged in alphabetical order within therapeutic classifications. Within the text of the monograph, information concerning indications is provided, including both labeled and unlabeled uses. Unlabeled uses are identified with daggers. The text must be analyzed to make a determination whether a particular use is supported.

2. American Medical Association Drug Evaluations.—Drug evaluations are organized into sections and chapters that are based on therapeutic classifications. The evaluation of a drug provides information concerning indications, including both labeled and unlabeled uses. Unlabeled uses are not specifically identified as such. The text must be analyzed to make a determination whether a particular use is supported. In making these determinations, also refer to the AMA Drug Evaluations Subscription, Volume III, section 17 (Oncolytic Drugs), chapter 1 (Principles of Cancer Chemotherapy), tables 1 and 2.

Table 1, Specific Agents Used in Cancer Chemotherapy, lists the anti-neoplastic agents which are currently available for use in various cancers. The indications presented in this table for a particular anti-cancer drug include labeled and unlabeled uses (although they are not identified as such). Any indication appearing in this table is considered to be a medically accepted use.

Table 2, Clinical Responses to Chemotherapy, lists some of the currently preferred regimens for various cancers. The table headings include (1) type of cancer, (2) drugs or regimens currently preferred, (3) alternative or secondary drugs or regimens, and (4) other drugs or regimens with reported activity.

A regimen appearing under the preferred or alternative/secondary headings is considered to be a medically accepted use.

A regimen appearing under the heading "Other Drugs or Regimens with Reported Activity" is considered to be for a medically accepted use provided:

- The preferred and alternative/secondary drugs or regimens are contraindicated; or
- A preferred and/or alternative/secondary drug or regimen was used but was not tolerated or was ineffective; or
- There was tumor progression or recurrence after an initial response.

3. United States Pharmacopoeia Drug Information (USPDI).—Monographs are arranged in alphabetical order by generic or family name. Indications for use appear as accepted, unaccepted, or insufficient data. An indication is considered to be a medically accepted use only if the indication is listed as accepted. Unlabeled uses are identified with brackets. A separate indications index lists all indications included in USPDI along with the medically accepted drugs used in treatment or diagnosis.

4. A Use Supported by Clinical Research That Appears in Peer Reviewed Medical Literature.—This applies only when an unlabeled use does not appear in any of the compendia or is listed as insufficient data or investigational. If an unlabeled use of a drug meets these criteria, contact the compendia to see if a report regarding this use is forthcoming. If a report is forthcoming, use this information as a basis for your decision making. The compendium process for making decisions concerning unlabeled uses is very thorough and continuously updated. Peer reviewed medical literature includes scientific, medical, and pharmaceutical publications in which original manuscripts are published, only

after having been critically reviewed for scientific accuracy, validity, and reliability by unbiased independent experts. This does not include in-house publications of pharmaceutical manufacturing companies or abstracts (including meeting abstracts).

In determining whether there is supportive clinical evidence for a particular use of a drug, your medical staff (in consultation with local medical specialty groups) must evaluate the quality of the evidence in published peer reviewed medical literature. When evaluating this literature, consider (among other things) the following:

• The prevalence and life history of the disease when evaluating the adequacy of the number of subjects and the response rate. While a 20 percent response rate may be adequate for highly prevalent disease states, a lower rate may be adequate for rare diseases or highly unresponsive conditions.
• The effect on the patient's well-being and other responses to therapy that indicate effectiveness, e.g., a significant increase in survival rate or life expectancy or an objective and significant decrease in the size of the tumor or a reduction in symptoms related to the tumor. Stabilization is not considered a response to therapy.
• The appropriateness of the study design. Consider:

1. Whether the experimental design in light of the drugs and conditions under investigation is appropriate to address the investigative question. (For example, in some clinical studies, it may be unnecessary or not feasible to use randomization, double blind trials, placebos, or crossover.);

2. That nonrandomized clinical trials with a significant number of subjects may be a basis for supportive clinical evidence for determining accepted uses of drugs; and

3. That case reports are generally considered uncontrolled and anecdotal information and do not provide adequate supportive clinical evidence for determining accepted uses of drugs.

Use peer reviewed medical literature appearing in the following publications:

• American Journal of Medicine;
• Annals of Internal Medicine;
• The Journal of the American Medical Association;
• Journal of Clinical Oncology;
• Blood;
• Journal of the National Cancer Institute;
• The New England Journal of Medicine;
• British Journal of Cancer;
• British Journal of Hematology;
• British Medical Journal;
• Cancer;
• Drugs;
• European Journal of Cancer (formerly the European Journal of Cancer and Clinical Oncology);
• Lancet; or
• Leukemia.

You are not required to maintain copies of these publications. If a claim raises a question about the use of a drug for a purpose not included in the FDA approved labeling or the compendia, ask the physician to submit copies of relevant supporting literature.

4. Unlabeled uses may also be considered medically accepted if determined by you to be medically accepted generally as safe and effective for the particular use.

NOTE: If a use is identified as not indicated by HCFA or the FDA or if a use is specifically identified as not indicated in one or more of the three compendia mentioned or if you determine based on peer reviewed medical literature that a particular use of a drug is not safe and effective, the off-label usage is not supported and, therefore, the drug is not covered.

5. Less Than Effective Drug.—This is a drug that has been determined by the Food and Drug Administration (FDA) to lack substantial evidence of effectiveness for all labeled indications. Also, a drug that has been the subject of a Notice of an Opportu-

nity for a Hearing (NOOH) published in the Federal Register before being withdrawn from the market, and for which the Secretary has not determined there is a compelling justification for its medical need, is considered less than effective. This includes any other drug product that is identical, similar, or related. Payment may not be made for a less than effective drug.

Because the FDA has not yet completed its identification of drug products that are still on the market, existing FDA efficacy decisions must be applied to all similar products once they are identified.

6. Denial of Medicare Payment for Compounded Drugs Produced in Violation of Federal Food, Drug, and Cosmetic Act.— The Food and Drug Administration (FDA) has found that, from time to time, firms established as retail pharmacies engage in mass production of compounded drugs, beyond the normal scope of pharmaceutical practice, in violation of the Federal Food, Drug, and Cosmetic Act (FFDCA). By compounding drugs on a large scale, a company may be operating as a drug manufacturer within the meaning of the FFDCA, without complying with requirements of that law. Such companies may be manufacturing drugs which are subject to the new drug application (NDA) requirements of the FFDCA, but for which FDA has not approved an NDA or which are misbranded or adulterated. If the manufacturing and processing procedures used by these facilities have not been approved by the FDA, the FDA has no assurance that the drugs these companies are producing are safe and effective. The safety and effectiveness issues pertain to such factors as chemical stability, purity, strength, bioequivalency, and biovailability.

Section 1862(a)(1)(A) of the Act requires that drugs must be reasonable and necessary in order to be covered under Medicare. This means, in the case of drugs, they must have been approved for marketing by the FDA. Section 2049.4 instructs carriers to deny coverage for drugs that have not received final marketing approval by the FDA, unless instructed otherwise by HCFA. Section 2300.1 instructs carriers to deny coverage of services related to the use of noncovered drugs as well. Hence, if DME or a prosthetic device is used to administer a noncovered drug, coverage is denied for both the nonapproved drug and the DME or prosthetic device.

In those cases in which the FDA has determined that a company is producing compounded drugs in violation of the FFDCA, Medicare does not pay for the drugs because they do not meet the FDA approval requirements of the Medicare program. In addition, Medicare does not pay for the DME or prosthetic device used to administer such a drug if FDA determines that a required NDA has not been approved or that the drug is misbranded or adulterated.

HCFA will notify you when the FDA has determined that compounded drugs are being produced in violation of the FFDCA. Do not stop Medicare payment for such a drug unless you are notified that it is appropriate to do so through a subsequent instruction. In addition, if you or ROs become aware that other companies are possibly operating in violation of the FFDCA, notify:

Health Care Financing Administration
Bureau of Policy Development
Office of Physician and Ambulatory Care Policy
7500 Security Blvd.
Baltimore, MD 21244-1850

2049.5 Self-Administered Drugs and Biologicals.—Drugs that are self-administered are not covered by Medicare Part B unless the statute provides for such coverage. This includes blood clotting factors, drugs used in immunosuppressive therapy, erythropoietin for dialysis patients, certain oral anti-cancer drugs, and oral anti-nausea drugs when used in certain situations.

A. Immunosuppressive Drugs.—Until January 1, 1995, immunosuppressive drugs are covered under Part B for a period of 1 year following discharge from a hospital for a Medicare covered organ transplant. HCFA interprets the 1-year period after the date of the transplant procedure to mean 365 days from the day on which an inpatient is discharged from the hospital. Beneficiaries are eligible to receive additional Part B coverage within 18 months after the discharge date for drugs furnished in 1995; within 24 months for drugs furnished in 1996; within 30 months for drugs furnished in 1997; and within 36 months for drugs furnished after 1997.

Covered drugs include those immunosuppressive drugs that have been specifically labeled as such and approved for marketing by the FDA, as well as those prescription drugs, such as prednisone, that are used in conjunction with immunosuppressive drugs as part of a therapeutic regimen reflected in FDA approved labeling for immunosuppressive drugs. Therefore, antibiotics, hypertensives, and other drugs that are not directly related to rejection are not covered. The FDA had identified and approved for marketing five specifically labeled immunosuppressive drugs. They are Sandimmune (cyclosporine), Sandoz Pharmaceutical; Imuran (azathioprine), Burroughs Wellcome; Atgam (antithymocyte globulin), Upjohn; and Orthoclone OKT3 (Muromonab-CD3), Ortho Pharmaceutical, and Prograf (tacrolimus), Fujisawa USA, Inc. You are expected to keep informed of FDA additions to the list of the immunosuppressive drugs.

B. Erythropoietin (EPO).—The statute provides that EPO is covered for the treatment of anemia for patients with chronic renal failure who are on dialysis. Coverage is available regardless of whether the drug is administered by the patient or the patient's caregiver. EPO is a biologically engineered protein which stimulates the bone marrow to make new red blood cells.

NOTE: Non-ESRD patients who are receiving EPO to treat anemia induced by other conditions such as chemotherapy or the drug zidovudine (commonly called AZT) must meet the coverage requirements in section 2049.

EPO is covered for the treatment of anemia for patients with chronic renal failure who are on dialysis when:

- It is administered in the renal dialysis facility; or
- It is self-administered in the home by any dialysis patient (or patient caregiver) who is determined competent to use the drug and meets the other conditions detailed below.

NOTE: Payment may not be made for EPO under the incident to provision when EPO is administered in the renal dialysis facility. (See section 5202.4.)

Medicare covers EPO and items related to its administration for dialysis patients who use EPO in the home when the following conditions are met.

1. Patient Care Plan.—A dialysis patient who uses EPO in the home must have a current care plan (a copy of which must be maintained by the designated back-up facility for Method II patients) for monitoring home use of EPO which includes the following:

a. Review of diet and fluid intake for aberrations as indicated by hyperkalemia and elevated blood pressure secondary to volume overload;

b. Review of medications to ensure adequate provision of supplemental iron;

c. Ongoing evaluations of hematocrit and iron stores;

d. Reevaluation of the dialysis prescription taking into account the patient's increased appetite and red blood cell volume;

e. Method for physician and facility (including back-up facility for Method II patients) follow-up on blood tests and a mechanism (such as a patient log) for keeping the physician informed of the results;

f. Training of the patient to identify the signs and symptoms of hypotension and hypertension; and

g. The decrease or discontinuance of EPO if hypertension is uncontrollable.

2. Patient Selection.—The dialysis facility, or the physician responsible for all dialysis-related services furnished to the patient, must make a comprehensive assessment that includes the following:

a. Pre-selection monitoring. The patient's hematocrit (or hemoglobin), serum iron, transferrin saturation, serum ferritin, and blood pressure must be measured.

b. Conditions the patient must meet. The assessment must find that the patient meets the following conditions:

(1) Is a dialysis patient;

(2) Has a hematocrit (or comparable hemoglobin level) that is as follows:

(a) For a patient who is initiating EPO treatment, no higher than 30 percent unless there is medical documentation showing the need for EPO despite a hematocrit (or comparable hemoglobin level) higher than 30 percent. Patients with severe angina, severe pulmonary distress, or severe hypotension may require EPO to prevent adverse symptoms even if they have higher hematocrit or hemoglobin levels.

(b) For a patient who has been receiving EPO from the facility or the physician, between 30 and 36 percent; and

(3) Is under the care of:

(a) A physician who is responsible for all dialysis-related services and who prescribes the EPO and follows the drug labeling instructions when monitoring the EPO home therapy; and

(b) A renal dialysis facility that establishes the plan of care and monitors the progress of the home EPO therapy.

c. The assessment must find that the patient or a caregiver meets the following conditions:

(1) Is trained by the facility to inject EPO and is capable of carrying out the procedure;

(2) Is capable of reading and understanding the drug labeling; and

(3) Is trained in, and capable of observing, aseptic techniques.

d. Care and storage of drug. The assessment must find that EPO can be stored in the patient's residence under refrigeration and that the patient is aware of the potential hazard of a child's having access to the drug and syringes.

3. Responsibilities of Physician or Dialysis Facility.—The patient's physician or dialysis facility must:

a. Develop a protocol that follows the drug label instructions;

b. Make the protocol available to the patient to ensure safe and effective home use of EPO;

c. Through the amounts prescribed, ensure that the drug on hand at any time does not exceed a 2-month supply; and

d. Maintain adequate records to allow quality assurance for review by the network and State survey agencies. For Method II patients, current records must be provided to and maintained by the designated back-up facility.

See section 5202.4 for information on EPO payment.

Submit claims for EPO in accordance with section 4273.1 and 4273.2.

C. Oral Anti-Cancer Drugs.—Effective January 1, 1994, Medicare Part B coverage is extended to include oral anti-cancer drugs that are prescribed as anti-cancer chemotherapeutic agents providing they have the same active ingredients and are used for the same indications as anti-cancer chemotherapeutic agents which would be covered if they were not self-administered and they were furnished incident to a physician's service as drugs and biologicals.

This provision applies only to the coverage of anti-neoplastic chemotherapeutic agents. It does not apply to oral drugs and/or biologicals used to treat toxicity or side effects such as nausea or bone marrow depression. Medicare will cover anti-neoplastic chemotherapeutic agents, the primary drugs which directly fight the cancer, and self-administered antiemetics which are necessary for the administration and absorption of the anti-neoplastic chemotherapeutic agents when a high likelihood of vomiting exists. The substitution of an oral form of an anti-neoplastic drug requires that the drug be retained for absorption. The antiemetic drug is covered as a necessary means for administration of the oral drug (similar to a syringe and needle necessary for injectable administration). Oral drugs prescribed for use with the primary drug which enhance the anti-neoplastic effect of the primary drug or permit the patient to tolerate the primary anti-neoplastic drug in higher doses for longer periods are not covered. Self-administered antiemetics to reduce the side effects of nausea and vomiting brought on by the primary drug are not included beyond the administration necessary to achieve drug absorption.

In order to assure uniform coverage policy, regional carriers and FIs must be apprised of local carriers' anti-cancer drug medical review policies which may impact on future medical review policy development. Local carrier's current and proposed anti-cancer drug medical review polices should be provided by local carrier medical directors to regional carrier or FI medical directors, upon request.

For an oral anti-cancer drug to be covered under Part B, it must:

- Be prescribed by a physician or other practitioner licensed under State law to prescribe such drugs as anti-cancer chemotherapeutic agents;
- Be a drug or biological that has been approved by the Food and Drug Administration (FDA);
- Have the same active ingredients as a non-self-administrable anti-cancer chemotherapeutic drug or biological that is covered when furnished incident to a physician's service. The oral anti-cancer drug and the non-self-administrable drug must have the same chemical/generic name as indicated by the FDA's Approved Drug Products (Orange Book), Physician's Desk Reference (PDR), or an authoritative drug compendium;
- Be used for the same indications, including unlabeled uses, as the non-self-administrable version of the drug; and
- Be reasonable and necessary for the individual patient.

D. *Oral Anti-Nausea Drugs.*—Section 4557 of the Balanced Budget Act of 1997 amends section 1861(s)(2) by extending the coverage of oral anti-emetic drugs under the following conditions:

- Coverage is provided only for oral drugs approved by the Food and Drug Administration (FDA) for use as anti-emetics;
- The oral anti-emetic must either be administered by the treating physician or in accordance with a written order from the physician as part of a cancer chemotherapy regimen;
- Oral anti-emetic drugs administered with a particular chemotherapy treatment must be initiated within 2 hours of the administration of the chemotherapeutic agent and may be continued for a period not to exceed 48 hours from that time; and
- The oral anti-emetic drugs provided must be used as a full therapeutic replacement for the intravenous anti-emetic drugs that would have otherwise been administered at the time of the chemotherapy treatment.

Only drugs pursuant to a physician's order at the time of the chemotherapy treatment qualify for this benefit. The dispensed number of dosage units may not exceed a loading dose administered within 2 hours of that treatment, plus a supply of additional dosage units not to exceed 48 hours of therapy.

Oral drugs that are not approved by the FDA for use as anti-emetics and which are used by treating physicians adjunctively in a manner incidental to cancer chemotherapy are not covered by this benefit and are not reimbursable within the scope of this benefit.

It is recognized that a limited number of patients will fail on oral anti-emetic drugs. Intravenous anti-emetics may be covered (subject to the rules of medical necessity) when furnished to patients who fail on oral anti-emetic therapy.

This coverage, effective for services on or after January 1, 1998, is subject to regular Medicare Part B coinsurance and deductible provisions.

NOTE: Existing coverage policies authorizing the administration of suppositories to prevent vomiting when oral cancer drugs are used are unchanged by this new coverage.

E. Hemophilia Clotting Factors.—Section 1861(s)(2)(I) of the Act provides Medicare coverage of blood clotting factors for hemophilia patients competent to use such factors to control bleeding without medical supervision, and items related to the administration of such factors. Hemophilia, a blood disorder characterized by prolonged coagulation time, is caused by deficiency of a factor in plasma necessary for blood to clot. (The discovery in 1964 of a cryoprecipitate rich in antihemophilic factor activity facilitated management of acute bleeding episodes.) For purposes of Medicare Part B coverage, hemophilia encompasses the following conditions:

- Factor VIII deficiency (classic hemophilia);
- Factor IX deficiency (also termed plasma thromboplastin component (PTC) or Christmas factor deficiency); and
- Von Willebrand's disease.

Claims for blood clotting factors for hemophilia patients with these diagnoses may be covered if the patient is competent to use such factors without medical supervision.

The amount of clotting factors determined to be necessary to have on hand and thus covered under this provision is based on the historical utilization pattern or profile developed by the carrier for each patient. It is expected that the treating source; e.g., a family physician or comprehensive hemophilia diagnostic and treatment center, has such information. From this data, the contractor is able to make reasonable projections concerning the quantity of clotting factors anticipated to be needed by the patient over a specific period of time. Unanticipated occurrences involving extraordinary events, such as automobile accidents of inpatient hospital stays, will change this base line data and should be appropriately considered. In addition, changes in a patient's medical needs over a period of time require adjustments in the profile. (See section 5245 for payment policies.)

2050 SERVICES AND SUPPLIES

Services and supplies (including drugs and biologicals which cannot be self-administered) are those furnished incident to a physician's professional services. (Certain hospital services may also be covered as incident to physicians' services when rendered to hospital outpatients. Payment for these services is made under Part B to a hospital by the hospital's intermediary.)

To be covered incident to the services of a physician, services and supplies must be:

- An integral, although incidental, part of the physician's professional service (see section 2050.1);
- Commonly rendered without charge or included in the physician's bill (see section 2050.1A);
- Of a type that are commonly furnished in physician's offices or clinics (see section 2050.1A);
- Furnished under the physician's direct personal supervision (see section 2050.1B); and
- Furnished by the physician or by an individual who qualifies as an employee of the physician. (See section 2050.1C.)

2050.1 Incident to Physician's Professional Services.—Incident to a physician's professional services means that the services or supplies are furnished as an integral, although incidental, part of the physician's personal professional services in the course of diagnosis or treatment of an injury or illness.

A. Commonly Furnished in Physicians' Offices.—Services and supplies commonly furnished in physicians' offices are covered under the incident to provision. Where supplies are clearly of a type a physician is not expected to have on hand in his/her office or where services are of a type not considered medically appropriate to provide in the office setting, they would not be covered under the incident to provision.

Supplies usually furnished by the physician in the course of performing his/her services, e.g., gauze, ointments, bandages, and oxygen, are also covered. Charges for such services and supplies must be included in the physicians' bills. (See section 2049 regarding coverage of drugs and biologicals under this provision.) To be covered, supplies, including drugs and biologicals, must represent an expense to the physician. For example, where a patient purchases a drug and the physician administers it, the cost of the drug is not covered.

B. Direct Personal Supervision.—Coverage of services and supplies incident to the professional services of a physician in private practice is limited to situations in which there is direct personal physician supervision. This applies to services of auxiliary personnel employed by the physician and working under his/her supervision, such as nurses, nonphysician anesthetists, psychologists, technicians, therapists, including physical therapists, and other aides. Thus, where a physician employs auxiliary personnel to assist him/her in rendering services to patients and includes the charges for their services in his/her own bills, the services of such personnel are considered incident to the physician's service if there is a physician's service rendered to which the services of such personnel are an incidental part and there is direct personal supervision by the physician.

This does not mean, however, that to be considered incident to each occasion of service by a nonphysician (or the furnishing of a supply) need also always be the occasion of the actual rendition of a personal professional service by the physician. Such a service or supply could be considered to be incident to when furnished during a course of treatment where the physician performs an initial service and subsequent services of a frequency which reflect his/her active participation in and management of the course of treatment. (However, the direct personal supervision requirement must still be met with respect to every nonphysician service.)

Direct personal supervision in the office setting does not mean that the physician must be present in the same room with his or her aide. However, the physician must be present in the office suite and immediately available to provide assistance and direction throughout the time the aide is performing services.

If auxiliary personnel perform services outside the office setting, e.g., in a patient's home or in an institution, their services are covered incident to a physician's service only if there is direct personal supervision by the physician. For example, if a nurse accompanied the physician on house calls and administered an injection, the nurse's services are covered. If the same nurse made the calls alone and administered the injection, the services are not covered (even when billed by the physician) since the physician is not providing direct personal supervision. Services provided by auxiliary personnel in an institution (e.g., skilled nursing facility, nursing, or convalescent home) present a special problem in determining whether direct physician supervision exists. The availability of the physician by telephone and the presence of the physician somewhere in the institution does not constitute direct personal supervision. (See section 45-15 of the Coverage Issues Manual for instructions used if a physician maintains an office in an institution.) For hospital patients, there is no Medicare coverage of the services of physician-employed auxiliary personnel as services incident to physicians' services under section 1861(s) (2)(A) of the Social Security Act. Such services can be covered only under the hospital outpatient or inpatient benefit and payment for such services can be made to only the hospital by a Medicare intermediary. For services in a hospital, see section 2390. (See section 2070 concerning physician supervision of technicians performing diagnostic X-ray procedures in a physician's office.)

C. Employment.—To be considered an employee for purposes of this section, the nonphysician performing an incident to service may be a part-time, full-time, or leased employee of the supervising physician, physician group practice, or of the legal entity that employs the physician (hereafter referred to collectively as the physician or other entity) who provides direct personal supervision (as described below). A leased employee is a nonphysician working under a written employee leasing agreement which provides that:

• The nonphysician, although employed by the leasing company, provides services as the leased employee of the physician or other entity; and

• The physician or other entity exercises control over all actions taken by the leased employee with regard to the rendering of medical services to the same extent as the physician or other entity would exercise such control if the leased employee were directly employed by the physician or other entity.

In order to satisfy the employment requirement, the nonphysician (either leased or directly employed) must be considered an employee of the supervising physician or other entity under the common law test of an employer/employee relationship specified in section 210(j)(2) of the Act, 20 CFR404.1007, and section RS 2101.020 of the Retirement and Survivors Insurance part of the Social Security Program Operations Manual System.

Services provided by auxiliary personnel not in the employ of the physician, physician group practice, or other legal entity, even if provided on the physician's order or included in the physician's bill, are not covered as incident to a physician's service since the law requires that the services be of kinds commonly furnished in physicians' offices and commonly either rendered without charge or included in physicians' bills. As with the physicians' personal professional service, the patient's financial liability for the incidental services is to the physician, physician group practice, or other legal entity. Therefore, the incidental service must represent an expense incurred by the physician, physician group practice, or other legal entity responsible for providing the professional service.

2050.2 Services of Nonphysician Personnel Furnished Incident to Physician's Services.—In addition to coverage being available for the services of such nonphysician personnel as nurses, technicians, and therapists when furnished incident to the professional services of a physician (as discussed in section 2050.1), a physician may also have the services of certain nonphysician practitioners covered as services incident to a physician's professional services. These nonphysician practitioners, who are being licensed by the States under various programs to assist or act in the place of the physician, include, for example, certified nurse midwives, certified registered nurse anesthetists, clinical psychologists, clinical social workers, physician assistants, nurse practitioners, and clinical nurse specialists. (See sections 2150 through 2160 for coverage instructions for various allied health/nonphysician practitioners' services.)

Services performed by these nonphysician practitioners incident to a physician's professional services include not only services ordinarily rendered by a physician's office staff person (e.g., medical services such as taking blood pressures and temperatures, giving injections, and changing dressings) but also services ordinarily performed by the physician himself or herself such as minor surgery, setting casts or simple fractures, reading x-rays, and other activities that involve evaluation or treatment of a patient's condition.

Nonetheless, in order for services of a nonphysician practitioner to be covered as incident to the services of a physician, the services must meet all of the requirements for coverage specified in section 2050 through 2050.1. For example, the services must be an integral, although incidental, part of the physician's personal professional services, and they must be performed under the physician's direct personal supervision.

A nonphysician practitioner such as a physician assistant or a nurse practitioner may be licensed under State law to perform a specific medical procedure and may be able (see section 2156 or 2158, respectively) to perform the procedure without physician supervision and have the service separately covered and paid for by Medicare as a physician assistant's or nurse practitioner's service. However, in order to have that same service covered as incident to the services of a physician, it must be performed under the direct personal supervision of the physician as an integral part of the physician's personal in-office service. As explained in section 2050.1, this does not mean that each occasion of an incidental service performed by a nonphysician practitioner must always be the occasion of a service actually rendered by the physician. It does mean that there must have been a direct, personal, professional service furnished by the physician to initiate the course of treatment of which the service being performed by the nonphysician practitioner is an incidental part, and there must be subsequent services by the physician of a frequency that reflects his or her continuing active participation in and management of the course of treatment. In addition, the physician must be physically present in the same office suite and be immediately available to render assistance if that becomes necessary.

Note also that a physician might render a physician's service that can be covered even though another service furnished by a nonphysician practitioner as incident to the physician's service might not be covered. For example, an office visit during which the physician diagnoses a medical problem and established a course of treatment could be covered even if, during the same visit, a nonphysician practitioner performs a noncovered service such as an acupuncture.

2050.3 Incident to Physician's Service in Clinic.—Services and supplies incident to a physician's service in a physician directed clinic or group association are generally the same as those described above.

A physician directed clinic is one where (a) a physician (or a number of physicians) is present to perform medical (rather than administrative) services at all times the clinic is open; (b) each patient is under the care of a clinic physician; and (c) the non-physician services are under medical supervision.

In highly organized clinics, particularly those that are departmentalized, direct personal physician supervision may be the responsibility of several physicians as opposed to an individual attending physician. In this situation, medical management of all services provided in the clinic is assured. The physician ordering a particular service need not be the physician who is supervising the service. Therefore, services performed by therapists and other aides are covered even though they are performed in another department of the clinic.

Supplies provided by the clinic during the course of treatment are also covered. When the auxiliary personnel perform services outside the clinic premises, the services are covered only if performed under the direct personal supervision of a clinic physician. If the clinic refers a patient for auxiliary services performed by personnel who are not employed by the clinic, such services are not incident to a physician's service.

2051 SERVICES INCIDENT TO A PHYSICIAN'S SERVICE TO HOMEBOUND PATIENTS UNDER GENERAL PHYSICIAN SUPERVISION

A. When Covered.—In some medically underserved areas, there are only a few physicians available to provide services over broad geographic areas or to a large patient population. The lack of medical personnel (and, in many instances, a home health agency servicing the area) significantly reduces the availability of certain medical services to homebound patients. Some physicians and physician-directed clinics, therefore, call upon nurses and other paramedical personnel to provide these services under general (rather than direct) supervision. In some areas, such practice has tended to become the accepted method of delivery of these services.

The Senate Finance Committee Report accompanying the 1972 Amendments to the Social Security Act recommended that the direct supervision requirement of the "incident to" provision be modified to provide coverage for services provided in this manner. Accordingly, to permit coverage of certain of these services, the direct supervision criterion in section 2050.2 above is not applicable to individual or intermittent services outlined in section 2051B when they are performed by personnel meeting any pertinent State requirements (e.g., a nurse, technician, or physician extender) and where the criteria listed below also are met:

1. The patient is homebound, i.e., confined to his/her home (see section 2051.1 for the definition of a "homebound" patient and section 2100.3 for the definition of patient's "place of residence").

2. The service is an integral part of the physician's service to the patient (thus, the patient must be one the physician is treat-

ing) and is performed under general physician supervision by employees of the physician or clinic. General supervision means that the physician need not be physically present at the patient's place of residence when the service is performed; however, the service must be performed under his/her overall supervision and control.

The physician orders the service(s) to be performed, and contact is maintained between the nurse or other employee and the physician, e.g., the employee contacts the physician directly if additional instructions are needed, and the physician must retain professional responsibility for the service. All other "incident to" requirements must be met. (See section 2050 to 2050.5.)

3. The services are included in the physician's/clinic's bill and he/she (or it) has incurred an expense for them. (See section 2050.2.)

4. The services of the paramedical are required for the patient's care; that is, they are reasonable and necessary as defined in section 2303.

5. When the service can be furnished by an HHA in the local area, it cannot be covered when furnished by a physician/clinic to a homebound patient under this provision, except as described in section 2051C.

B. Covered Services.—Where the requirements in section 2051.A are met, the direct supervision requirement in section 2050.2 is not applicable to the following services:

1. Injections;

2. Venipuncture;

3. EKGs;

4. Therapeutic exercises;

5. Insertion and sterile irrigation of a catheter;

6. Changing of catheters and collection of catheterized specimen for urinalysis and culture;

7. Dressing changes, e.g., the most common chronic conditions which may need dressing changes are decubitus care and gangrene;

8. Replacement and/or insertion of nasogastric tubes;

9. Removal of fecal impaction, including enemas;

10. Sputum collection for gram stain and culture, and possible acid-fast and/or fungal stain and culture;

11. Paraffin bath therapy for hands and/or feet in rheumatoid arthritis or osteoarthritis; and

12. Teaching and training the patient for:

a. the care of colostomy and ileostomy;

b. the care of permanent tracheostomy;

c. testing urine and care of the feet (diabetic patients only); and

d. blood pressure monitoring.

Teaching and training services (also referred to as educational services) can be covered only where they provide knowledge essential for the chronically ill patient's participation in his own treatment and only where they can be reasonably related to such treatment or diagnosis. Educational services that provide more elaborate instruction than is necessary to achieve the required level of patient education are not covered. After essential information has been provided, the patient should be relied upon to obtain additional information for himself.

2070 DIAGNOSTIC X-RAY, DIAGNOSTIC LABORATORY, AND OTHER DIAGNOSTIC TESTS

2070.1 Independent Laboratories.—Diagnostic laboratory services furnished by an independent laboratory are covered under medical insurance if the laboratory is an approved Independent Clinical Laboratory. (However, as is the case of all diagnostic services, in order to be covered these services must be related to a patient's illness or injury (or symptom or complaint) and ordered by a physician. See section 2020.1 for the definition of a "physician".)

A. Definition of Independent.—An independent laboratory is one which is independent both of an attending or consulting physician's office and of a hospital which meets at least the requirements to qualify as an emergency hospital as defined in section 1861(e) of the Act. (A consulting physician is one whose services include history taking, examination of the patient, and, in each case, furnishing to the attending physician an opinion regarding diagnosis or treatment. A physician providing clinical laboratory services for patients of other physicians is not considered to be a consulting physician.)

A laboratory which is operated by or under the supervision of a hospital (or the organized medical staff of the hospital) which does not meet at least the definition of an emergency hospital is considered to be an independent laboratory. However, a laboratory serving hospital patients and operated on the premises of a hospital which meets the definition of an emergency hospital is presumed to be subject to the supervision of the hospital or its organized medical staff and is not an independent laboratory. A laboratory which a physician or group of physicians maintains for performing diagnostic tests in connection with his own or the group practice is also not considered to be an independent laboratory.

An out-of-hospital laboratory is ordinarily presumed to be independent unless there is written evidence establishing that it is operated by or under the supervision of a hospital which meets at least the definition of an emergency hospital or of the organized medical staff of such a hospital.

Where a laboratory operated on hospital premises is claimed to be independent or where an out-of-hospital facility is designated as a hospital laboratory, the RO makes the determination concerning the laboratory's status.

B. Clinical Defined.—A clinical laboratory is a laboratory where microbiological, serological, chemical, hematological, radio-bioassay, cytological, immunohematological, or pathological examinations are performed on materials derived from the human body, to provide information for the diagnosis, prevention, or treatment of a disease or assessment of a medical condition.

C. Approval of Laboratories.—An approved independent clinical laboratory is one which is approved by the Secretary of Health, Education, and Welfare as meeting the specific conditions for coverage under the program. These require that: (1) where State or applicable local law provides for licensing of independent clinical laboratories, the laboratory is either licensed under such law or it is approved as meeting the requirements for licensing laboratories; and (2) such laboratories also meet the health and safety requirements prescribed by the Secretary of Health, Education, and Welfare. See "Conditions for Coverage of Services of Independent Laboratories." (HIRM 1 Subpart M)

Diagnostic laboratory tests performed by a laboratory of a nonparticipating hospital which meet the statutory definition of an emergency hospital are covered only if the laboratory meets the requirements set forth in the regulations for hospital laboratories.

Services rendered by an independent clinical laboratory are covered under medical insurance only if the laboratory has been approved under the program. Carriers are furnished lists of approved laboratories and their approved specialties by HCFA. If you have any reason to question the lists concerning additions or deletions of particular laboratories or specialties, clarifying information should be requested from the RO.

Laboratory Certification and Decertification

You must notify your physicians of the initial certification of the laboratories in your service areas and also furnished certification information about laboratories outside your service area upon request from individual physicians or clinics. This information is available from the RO (see section 2070.1D below). Where there are any changes in the certification of a laboratory, i.e., addition or deletion of tests for which the laboratory is certified, notify the physicians in your service areas of these changes.

When some or all of the services of an independent laboratory no longer meet the conditions for coverage, inform all physicians having an interest in the laboratory's certification status of the effective date of decertification, reasons for the decertification, and the applicability of the determination to the various categories of diagnostic tests performed by the independent laboratory. Notification to the physicians must be made prior to the termination date since you cannot honor any bill for services performed after the termination date.

If you issue a monthly bulletin or newsletter to physicians in your service area you may wish to use this vehicle to inform the physicians involved. If, in a particular instance, timely notification cannot be made by use of the regular monthly bulletin or newsletter, a special bulletin will be necessary. In cases where there are a limited number of physicians in a remote area, a notification to all physicians in your service area may not be necessary. In these situations, you may wish to limit the scope of the notification and use means other than the monthly newsletter. You must secure the prior approval of the regional office for limited notification.

For notices of decertification, you will receive a copy of the decertification letter to the laboratory from the RO. Language suitable for use in the carrier notices to physicians concerning the reasons for the decertification will also be supplied. The following information will be included in the notification:

1. Name and address of laboratory;
2. Effective date of decertification;
3. Which services are not covered (all or particular specialty(ies); and
4. Reason for decertification.

Your notification to the physicians should contain a statement that no payment can be made under title XVIII on behalf of Medicare patients receiving these services from the laboratory on or after the effective decertification dates.

A copy of all notifications to physicians concerning laboratory decertifications, whether by regular monthly newsletter or by a special bulletin, should be sent to the RO Contractor Operations Staff on the date of issuance.

NOTE: The notification to physicians also applies to services performed by suppliers of portable X-ray services (see section 2070.4B).

D. The Specialty Provision.—One of the conditions for coverage of services of independent laboratories is that the laboratory agrees to perform tests for Medicare beneficiaries only in the specialties for which it is certified. Clinical laboratory services rendered in a specialty for which an independent laboratory is not certified are not covered and claims for payment of benefits for these services must be denied.

HCFA furnishes lists to the carriers showing specialties and subspecialties in which each laboratory has been certified. The lists are updated quarterly. Each carrier receives two lists showing the independent laboratories located in its service area: one list by provider number and the other list alphabetical. For information on laboratories not located within a carrier's service area, the RO maintains national lists showing all approved laboratories. A key is furnished for interpreting the codes on the lists. See section 4110ff. for additional information.

2070.2 Psychological Tests.—The diagnostic testing services performed by a psychologist (who is not a clinical psychologist as defined in section 2150.A) practicing independently of an institution, agency, or physician's office are covered as other diagnostic tests if a physician orders such testing. Medicare covers this type of testing as an outpatient service if furnished by any psychologist who is licensed or certified to practice psychology in the State or jurisdiction where he or she is furnishing services or, if the jurisdiction does not issue licenses, if provided by any practicing psychologist. (It is HCFA's understanding that all States, the District of Columbia, and Puerto Rico license psychologists, but that some trust territories do not. Examples of psychologists, other than clinical psychologists, whose services are covered under this provision include, but are not limited to, educational psychologists and counseling psychologists.)

To determine whether the diagnostic psychological testing services of a particular independent psychologist are covered under Part B in States which have statutory licensure or certification, secure from the appropriate State agency a current listing of psychologists holding the required credentials. In States or territories which lack statutory licensing and certification, check individual qualifications as claims are submitted. Possible reference sources are the national directory of membership of the American Psychological Association, which provides data about the educational background of individuals and indicates which members are board-certified, and records and directories of the State or territorial psychological association. If qualification is dependent on a doctoral degree from a currently accredited program, verify the date of accreditation of the school involved, since such accreditation is not retroactive. If the reference sources listed above do not provide enough information (e.g., the psychologist is not a member of the association), contact the psychologist personally for the required information. You may wish to maintain a continuing list of psychologists whose qualifications have been verified.

NOTE: Diagnostic psychological testing services performed by persons who meet these requirements are covered as other diagnostic tests. When, however, the psychologist is not practicing independently, but is on the staff of an institution, agency, or clinic, that entity bills for the diagnostic services.

Expenses for such testing are not subject to the payment limitation on treatment for mental, psychoneurotic, and personality disorders. (See section 2470ff.) Independent psychologists are not required by law to accept assignment when performing psychological tests. However, regardless of whether the psychologist accepts assignment, he or she must report on the claim form the name and address of the physician who ordered the test.

Consider psychologists as practicing independently when:

- They render services on their own responsibility, free of the administrative and professional control of an employer such as a physician, institution, agency;
- The persons they treat are their own patients; and
- They have the right to bill directly, collect and retain the fee for their services.

A psychologist practicing in an office located in an institution may be considered an independently practicing psychologist when both of the following conditions exist:

- The office is confined to a separately identified part of the facility which is used solely as the psychologist's office and cannot be construed as extending throughout the entire institution; and
- The psychologist conducts a private practice, i.e., services are rendered to patients from outside the institution as well as to institutional patients.

2070.4 Coverage of Portable X-ray Services Not Under the Direct Supervision of a Physician.—

A. Diagnostic X-ray Tests.—Diagnostic x-ray services furnished by a portable x-ray supplier are covered under Part B when furnished in a place or residence used as the patient's home and in nonparticipating institutions. These services must be performed under the general supervision of a physician and certain conditions relating to health and safety (as prescribed by the Secretary) must be met.

Diagnostic portable x-ray services are also covered under Part B when provided in participating SNFs and hospitals, under circumstances in which they cannot be covered under hospital insurance, i.e., the services are not furnished by the participating institution either directly or under arrangements that provide for the institution to bill for the services. (See section 2255 for reimbursement for Part B services furnished to inpatients of participating and nonparticipating institutions.)

B. Applicability of Health and Safety Standards.—The health and safety standards apply to all suppliers of portable x-ray services, except physicians who provide immediate personal supervision during the administration of diagnostic x-ray services. Payment is made only for services of approved suppliers who have been found to meet the standards. Notice of the coverage dates for services of approved suppliers are given to carriers by the RO.

When the services of a supplier of portable x-ray services no longer meet the conditions of coverage, physicians having an interest in the supplier's certification status must be notified. The notification action regarding suppliers of portable x-ray equipment is the same as required for decertification of independent laboratories, and the procedures explained in section 2070.1C should be followed.

C. Scope of Portable X-Ray Benefit.—In order to avoid payment for services which are inadequate or hazardous to the patient, the scope of the covered portable X-ray benefit is defined as:

- skeletal films involving arms and legs, pelvis, vertebral column, and skull;
- chest films which do not involve the use of contrast media (except routine screening procedures and tests in connection with routine physical examinations); and
- abdominal films which do not involve the use of contrast media.

D. Exclusions from Coverage as Portable X-Ray Services.—Procedures and examinations which are not covered under the portable X-ray provision include the following:

- procedures involving fluoroscopy;
- procedures involving the use of contrast media;
- procedures requiring the administration of a substance to the patient or injection of a substance into the patient and/or special manipulation of the patient;
- procedures which require special medical skill or knowledge possessed by a doctor of medicine or doctor of osteopathy or which require that medical judgment be exercised;
- procedures requiring special technical competency and/or special equipment or materials;
- routine screening procedures; and
- procedures which are not of a diagnostic nature.

E. Reimbursement Procedure.—

1. Name of Ordering Physician.—Assure that portable X-ray tests have been provided on the written order of a physician. Accordingly, if a bill does not include the name of the physician who ordered the service, that information must be obtained before payment may be made.

2. Reason Chest X-Ray Ordered.—Because all routine screening procedures and tests in connection with routine physical examinations are excluded from coverage under Medicare, all bills for portable X-ray services involving the chest contain, in addition to the name of the physician who ordered the service, the reason an X-ray test was required. If this information is not shown, it is obtained from either the supplier or the physician. If the test was for an excluded routine service, no payment may be made.

See also section 4110 ff. for additional instructions on reviewing bills involving portable X-ray.

F. Electrocardiograms.—The taking of an electrocardiogram tracing by an approved supplier of portable X-ray services may be covered as an "other diagnostic test." The health and safety standards referred to in section 2070.4B are thus also applicable to such diagnostic EKG services, e.g., the technician must meet the personnel qualification requirements in the Conditions for

Coverage of Portable X-ray Services. (See section 50-15 (Electrocardiographic Services) in the Coverage Issues Manual.)

2079 SURGICAL DRESSINGS, AND SPLINTS, CASTS, AND OTHER DEVICES USED FOR REDUCTIONS OF FRACTURES AND DISLOCATIONS

Surgical dressings are limited to primary and secondary dressings required for the treatment of a wound caused by, or treated by, a surgical procedure that has been performed by a physician or other health care professional to the extent permissible under State law. In addition, surgical dressings required after debridement of a wound are also covered, irrespective of the type of debridement, as long as the debridement was reasonable and necessary and was performed by a health care professional who was acting within the scope of his or her legal authority when performing this function. Surgical dressings are covered for as long as they are medically necessary.

Primary dressings are therapeutic or protective coverings applied directly to wounds or lesions either on the skin or caused by an opening to the skin. Secondary dressing materials that serve a therapeutic or protective function and that are needed to secure a primary dressing are also covered. Items such as adhesive tape, roll gauze, bandages, and disposable compression material are examples of secondary dressings. Elastic stockings, support hose, foot coverings, leotards, knee supports, surgical leggings, gauntlets, and pressure garments for the arms and hands are examples of items that are not ordinarily covered as surgical dressings. Some items, such as transparent film, may be used as a primary or secondary dressing.

If a physician, certified nurse midwife, physician assistant, nurse practitioner, or clinical nurse specialist applies surgical dressings as part of a professional service that is billed to Medicare, the surgical dressings are considered incident to the professional services of the health care practitioner. (See section 2050.1, 2154, 2156, 2158, and 2160.) When surgical dressings are not covered incident to the services of a health care practitioner and are obtained by the patient from a supplier (e.g., a drugstore, physician, or other health care practitioner that qualifies as a supplier) on an order from a physician or other health care professional authorized under State law or regulation to make such an order, the surgical dressings are covered separately under Part B.

Splints and casts, etc., include dental splints.

2100 DURABLE MEDICAL EQUIPMENT—GENERAL

Expenses incurred by a beneficiary for the rental or purchase of durable medical equipment (DME) are reimbursable if the following three requirements are met. The decision whether to rent or purchase an item of equipment resides with the beneficiary.

A. The equipment meets the definition of DME (section 2100.1); and

B. The equipment is necessary and reasonable for the treatment of the patient's illness or injury or to improve the functioning of his malformed body member (section 2100.2); and

C. The equipment is used in the patient's home (section 2100.3).

Payment may also be made under this provision for repairs, maintenance, and delivery of equipment as well as for expendable and nonreusable items essential to the effective use of the equipment subject to the conditions in section 2100.4.

See section 2105 and its appendix for coverage guidelines and screening list of DME. See section 4105.3 for models of payment: decisions as to rental or purchase, lump sum and periodic payments, etc. Where covered DME is furnished to a beneficiary by a supplier of services other than a provider of services, reimbursement is made by the carrier on the basis of the reasonable charge. If the equipment is furnished by a provider of services, reimbursement is made to the provider by the intermediary on a reasonable cost basis; see Coverage Issues Appendix 25-1 for hemodialysis equipment and supplies.

2100.1 Definition of Durable Medical Equipment.—Durable medical equipment is equipment which (a) can withstand repeated use, (b) is primarily and customarily used to serve a medical purpose, (c) generally is not useful to a person in the absence of an illness or injury; and (d) is appropriate for use in the home.

All requirements of the definition must be met before an item can be considered to be durable medical equipment.

A. Durability.—An item is considered durable if it can withstand repeated use, i.e., the type of item which could normally be rented. Medical supplies of an expendable nature, such as incontinent pads, lambs wool pads, catheters, Ace bandages, elastic stockings, surgical face masks, irrigating kits, sheets and bags are not considered "durable" within the meaning of the definition. There are other items which, although durable in nature, may fall into other coverage categories such as braces, prosthetic devices, artificial arms, legs, and eyes.

B. Medical Equipment.—Medical equipment is equipment which is primarily and customarily used for medical purposes and is not generally useful in the absence of illness or injury. In most instances, no development will be needed to determine whether a specific item of equipment is medical in nature. However, some cases will require development to determine whether the item constitutes medical equipment. This development would include the advice of local medical organizations (hospitals, medical schools, medical societies) and specialists in the field of physical medicine and rehabilitation. If the equipment is new on the market, it may be necessary, prior to seeking professional advice, to obtain information from the supplier or manufacturer explaining the design, purpose, effectiveness and method of using the equipment in the home as well as the results of any tests or clinical studies that have been conducted.

1. Equipment Presumptively Medical.—Items such as hospital beds, wheelchairs, hemodialysis equipment, iron lungs, respirators, intermittent positive pressure breathing machines, medical regulators, oxygen tents, crutches, canes, trapeze bars, walkers, inhalators, nebulizers, commodes, suction machines and traction equipment presumptively constitute medical equipment. (Although hemodialysis equipment is a prosthetic device (section 2130), it also meets the definition of DME, and reimbursement for the rental or purchase of such equipment for use in the beneficiary's home will be made only under the provisions for payment applicable to DME. See sections 25-1 and 25-2 of the Coverage Issues Appendix for coverage of home use of hemodialysis.)

NOTE: There is a wide variety in type of respirators and suction machines. The carrier's medical staff should determine whether the apparatus specified in the claim is appropriate for home use.

2. Equipment Presumptively Nonmedical.—Equipment which is primarily and customarily used for a nonmedical purpose may not be considered "medical" equipment for which payment can be made under the medical insurance program. This is true even though the item has some remote medically related use. For example, in the case of a cardiac patient, an air conditioner might possibly be used to lower room temperature to reduce fluid loss in the patient and to restore an environment conducive to maintenance of the proper fluid balance. Nevertheless, because the primary and customary use of an air conditioner is a nonmedical one, the air conditioner cannot be deemed to be medical equipment for which payment can be made.

Other devices and equipment used for environmental control or to enhance the environmental setting in which the beneficiary is placed are not considered covered DME. These include, for example, room heaters, humidifiers, dehumidifiers, and electric air cleaners. Equipment which basically serves comfort or convenience functions or is primarily for the convenience of a person caring for the patient, such as elevators, stairway elevators, and posture chairs do not constitute medical equipment. Similarly, physical fitness equipment, e.g., an exercycle; first-aid or precautionary-type equipment, e.g., present portable oxygen units; self-help devices, e.g., safety grab bars; and training equipment, e.g., speech teaching machines and Braille training texts, are considered nonmedical in nature.

3. Special Exception Items.—Specified items of equipment may be covered under certain conditions even though they do not meet the definition of DME because they are not primarily and customarily used to serve a medical purpose and/or are generally useful in the absence of illness or injury. These items would be covered when it is clearly established that they serve a therapeutic purpose in an individual case and would include:

a. Gel pads and pressure and water mattresses (which generally serve a preventive purpose) when prescribed for a patient who had bed sores or there is medical evidence indicating that he is highly susceptible to such ulceration; and

b. Heat lamps for a medical rather than a soothing or cosmetic purpose, e.g., where the need for heat therapy has been established.

In establishing medical necessity (section 2100.2) for the above items, the evidence must show that the item is included in the physician's course of treatment and a physician is supervising its use. (See also Appendix to section 2105.)

NOTE: The above items represent special exceptions and no extension of coverage to other items should be inferred.

2100.2 Necessary and Reasonable.—Although an item may be classified as DME, it may not be covered in every instance. Coverage in a particular case is subject to the requirement that the equipment be necessary and reasonable for treatment of an illness or injury, or to improve the functioning of a malformed body member. These considerations will bar payment for equipment which cannot reasonably be expected to perform a therapeutic function in an individual case or will permit only partial therapeutic function in an individual case or will permit only partial payment when the type of equipment furnished substantially exceeds that required for the treatment of the illness or injury involved. See section 4105.2 for required evidence of medical necessity and determination of period of medical necessity.

A. Necessity for the Equipment.—Equipment is necessary when it can be expected to make a meaningful contribution to the treatment of the patient's illness or injury or to the improvement of his malformed body member. In most cases the physician's prescription for the equipment and other medical information available to the carrier will be sufficient to establish that the equipment serves this purpose.

B. Reasonableness of the Equipment.—Even though an item of DME may serve a useful medical purpose, the carrier must also consider to what extent, if any, it would be reasonable for the Medicare program to pay for the item prescribed. The following considerations should enter into the determination of reasonableness:

1. Would the expense of the item to the program be clearly disproportionate to the therapeutic benefits which could ordinarily be derived from use of the equipment?

2. Is the item substantially more costly than a medically appropriate and realistically feasible alternative pattern of care?

3. Does the item serve essentially the same purpose as equipment already available to the beneficiary?

Claims for payment for the relatively few billed items of equipment found to be out of line with tests of "reasonableness" should be denied in full except in the following case: Where it is determined that there exists a medically appropriate and realistically feasible alternative pattern of care for which payment could be made, payment should be based on the reasonable charge for this alternative.

The following example points up the need to take account of the reasonableness of the services rendered.

Example: The median price of standard whirlpool bath equipment is about $600 plus plumbing expenses necessary to install it in the patient's home. Program coverage of such equipment in the patient's home should be limited to those cases where it is prescribed for conditions where the whirlpool bath can be expected to provide a substantial therapeutic benefit justifying its costs. For example, bursitis or chronic osteoarthritis would not generally justify Medicare payment for whirlpool bath equipment in the home since it would not be reasonable to expect that a whirlpool bath would be significantly more beneficial than a normal warm bath. Moreover, where the patient is not homebound, payment for this item in the patient's home should be restricted to the cost of providing the service elsewhere, e.g., an outpatient department of a participating hospital, if that alternative is less costly.

C. Payment Consistent with What Is Necessary and Reasonable.—Where a claim is filed for equipment containing features of an aesthetic nature or features of a medical nature which are not required by the patient's condition or where there exists a reasonably feasible and medically appropriate alternative pattern of care which is less costly than the equipment furnished, the amount payable is based on the reasonable charge for the equipment or alternative treatment which meets the patient's medical needs. See section 5107 for reasonable charge determination.

The acceptance of an assignment binds the supplier-assignee to accept the reasonable charge for the medically required equipment or service as the full charge and he cannot charge the beneficiary the differential attributable to the equipment actually furnished. (See section 3045.3 for effect of assignment when more expensive equipment is furnished.)

2100.3 Definition of Beneficiary's Home.—For purposes of rental and purchase of DME a beneficiary's home may be his own dwelling, an apartment, a relative's home, a home for the aged, or some other type of institution. However, an institution may not be considered a beneficiary's home if it:

A. Meets at least the basic requirement in the definition of a hospital, i.e., it is primarily engaged in providing by or under the supervision of physicians, to inpatients, diagnostic and therapeutic services for medical diagnosis, treatment, and care of injured, disabled, and sick persons, or rehabilitation services for the rehabilitation of injured, disabled, or sick persons; or

B. Meets at least the basic requirement in the definition of a skilled nursing facility, i.e., it is primarily engaged in providing to inpatients skilled nursing care and related services for patients who require medical or nursing care, or rehabilitation services for the rehabilitation of injured, disabled or sick persons.

Thus, if an individual is a patient in an institution or distinct part of an institution which provides the services described in subsection A or B, he is not entitled to have payment made for rental or purchase of DME since such an institution may not be considered his home. (See section 4105.4 when beneficiary is in an institution for part of a month.)

See section 4105.1 for claims processing where the beneficiary's residence is in question.

2100.4 Repairs, Maintenance, Replacement, and Delivery.—Under the circumstances specified below, payment may be made for repair, maintenance, and replacement of medically required DME which the beneficiary owns or is purchasing, including equipment which had been in use before the user enrolled in Part B of the program. Since renters of equipment usually recover from the rental charge the expenses they incur in maintaining in working order the equipment they rent out, separately itemized charges for repair, maintenance and replacement of rented equipment are not covered, except in the case set out in subsection E.

However, payment generally is not made for repair, maintenance, and replacement of purchased equipment that requires frequent and substantial servicing, capped rental equipment, or oxygen equipment. See section 5102.3 for exceptions.

A. Repairs.—Repairs to equipment which a beneficiary is purchasing or already owns are covered when necessary to make the equipment serviceable. If the expense for repairs exceeds the estimated expense of purchasing or renting another item of equipment for the remaining period of medical need, no payment can be made for the amount of the excess. (See subsection C where claims for repairs suggest malicious damage or culpable neglect.)

B. Maintenance.—Routine periodic servicing, such as testing, cleaning, regulating and checking of the beneficiary's equipment is not covered. Such routine maintenance is generally expected to be done by the owner rather than by a retailer or some other person who charges the beneficiary. Normally, purchasers of DME are given operating manuals which describe the type of servicing an owner may perform to properly maintain the equipment. Thus, hiring a third party to do such work is for the convenience of the beneficiary and is not covered.

However, more extensive maintenance which, based on the manufacturers' recommendations, is to be performed by authorized technicians, is covered as repairs. This might include, for example, breaking down sealed components and performing tests which require specialized testing equipment not available to the beneficiary.

C. Replacement.—Replacement of equipment which the beneficiary owns or is purchasing is covered in cases of loss or irreparable damage or wear and when required because of a change in the patient's condition. Expenses for replacement required because of loss or irreparable damage may be reimbursed without a physician's order when in the judgment of the carrier the equipment as originally ordered, considering the age of the order, still fills the patient's medical needs. However, claims involving replacement equipment necessitated because of wear or a change in the patient's condition must be supported by a current physician's order. (See section 2306D in regard to payment for equipment replaced under a warranty.)

Cases suggesting malicious damage, culpable neglect or wrongful disposition of equipment as discussed in section 2100.6 should be investigated and denied where the carrier determines that it is unreasonable to make program payment under the circumstances. Refer such cases to the program integrity specialist in the RO.

D. Delivery.—Reasonable charges for delivery of DME whether rented or purchased are covered if the supplier customarily makes separate charges for delivery and this is a common practice among the other local suppliers. See section 5105 for the rules that apply for making reimbursement for such charges.

E. Leased Renal Dialysis Equipment.—Generally, where renal dialysis equipment is leased directly from the manufacturer, the rental charge is closely related to the manufacturer's cost of the equipment which means it does not include a margin for recovering the cost of repairs beyond the initial warranty period. In view of physical distance and other factors which may make it impractical for the manufacturer to perform repairs, it is not feasible to make the manufacturer responsible for all repairs and include a margin for the additional costs. Therefore, reimbursement may be made for the repair and maintenance of home dialysis equipment leased directly from the manufacturer (or other party acting essentially as an intermediary between the patient and the manufacturer for the purpose of assuming the financial risk) if the rental charge does not include a margin to recover these costs, and then only when the patient is free to secure repairs locally in the most economical manner.

Where, on the other hand, a third party is in the business of medical equipment retail supply and rental, the presumption that there is a margin in the rental charge for dialysis equipment to cover the costs of repair services will be retained. The exclusion from coverage of separately itemized repair charges will, therefore, continue to be applied in these situations, and the patient must look to the supplier to perform (or cover the cost of) necessary repairs, maintenance, and replacement of the home dialysis equipment.

In all cases, whether the dialysis equipment is being purchased, is owned outright, or is being leased, Medicare payment is to be made only after the initial warranty period has expired. Generally, reimbursement for repairs, maintenance, and replacement parts for medically necessary home dialysis equipment may be made in a lump-sum payment. However, where extensive repairs are required and the charge for repairing the item represents a substantial proportion of the purchase price of a replacement system, exercise judgment with respect to a possible need to make periodic payments, instead of a lump-sum payment, for repair of such equipment.

As in the case of the maintenance of purchased DME, routine periodic servicing of leased dialysis equipment, including most testing and cleaning, is not covered. While reimbursement will be made for more extensive maintenance and necessary repairs of leased dialysis equipment, the patient or family member is expected to perform those services for which the training for home or self-dialysis would have qualified them, e.g., replacement of a light bulb.

Reasonable charges for travel expenses related to the repair of leased dialysis equipment are covered if the repairman customarily charges for travel and this is a common practice among other repairmen in the area. When a repair charge includes an element for travel, however, the location of other suitably qualified repairmen will be considered in determining the allowance for travel.

NOTE: The above coverage instructions pertain to a special case and no extension of such coverage with respect to other items should be inferred.

2100.5 Coverage of Supplies and Accessories.—Reimbursement may be made for supplies, e.g., oxygen (see section 60-4 in the Coverage Issues Manual for the coverage of oxygen in the home), that are necessary for the effective use of durable medical equipment. Such supplies include those drugs and biologicals which must be put directly into the equipment in order to achieve the therapeutic benefit of the durable medical equipment or to assure the proper functioning of the equipment, e.g., tumor chemotherapy agents used with an infusion pump or heparin used with a home dialysis system. However, the coverage of such drugs or biologicals does not preclude the need for a determination that the drug or biological itself is reasonable and necessary for treatment of the illness or injury or to improve the functioning of a malformed body member.

In the case of prescription drugs, other than oxygen, used in conjunction with durable medical equipment, prosthetic, orthotics, and supplies (DMEPOS) or prosthetic devices, the entity that dispenses the drug must furnish it directly to the patient for whom a prescription is written. The entity that dispenses the drugs must have a Medicare supplier number, must possess a current license to dispense prescription drugs in the State in which the drug is dispensed, and must bill and receive payment in its own name. A supplier that is not the entity that dispenses the drugs cannot purchase the drugs used in conjunction with DME for resale to the beneficiary. Payments made for drugs provided on or after December 1, 1996 to suppliers not having a valid pharmacy license to dispense prescription drugs must be recouped.

Reimbursement may be made for replacement of essential accessories such as hoses, tubes, mouth pieces, etc., for necessary DME, only if the beneficiary owns or is purchasing the equipment.

2105 COVERAGE GUIDELINES FOR DURABLE MEDICAL EQUIPMENT CLAIMS

Reimbursement may be made for expenses incurred by a patient for the rental or purchase of durable medical equipment (DME) for use in his/her home provided that all the conditions in column A have been met. Column B indicates the actions to be taken to establish that the conditions have been met.

The patient, not the carrier, decides whether an item is to be rented or purchased. The patient may elect to rent even though purchase is more economical.

Column A Conditions	Column B Review Action
Payment may be made for the following:	
Items DME (section 2100.1) that are medically necessary (section 2100.2).	Appendix shows coverage status of items of equipment. If item is not listed in appendix, refer to supervisor, who will determine whether item is covered in accordance with section 2100ff.
Separate charges for repairs, maintenance, and delivery. (See sections 2100.4 and 5105.)	*Repairs*—only if DME is being purchased or is already owned by patient and repair is necessary to make the equipment serviceable. If expense for repairs exceeds the estimated expense to purchase or rent another item for the remaining period of medical need, deny the excess. (See special exception in section 2100.4E for repair of dialysis delivery system.)

Refer to supervisor any claim suggesting deliberate or malicious damage or destruction, for handling in accordance with section 2100.4C.

	Maintenance—only if the equipment is being purchased or is already owned by the patient and if the maintenance is extensive amounting to repairs, i.e., requiring the services of skilled technicians. (Deny claims for *routine* maintenance and periodic servicing, e.g., testing, cleaning, checking, oiling, etc.) (See special exception in section 2100.4E for maintenance of dialysis delivery system.)
	Delivery—of rented or purchased equipment only if (a) the supplier customarily makes a separate charge for delivery, and (b) this is a common practice of the local suppliers.
Separate charges for disposable, e.g., oxygen, if essential to the effective use of medically necessary durable medical equipment. Separate charges for replacement of essential accessories such as hoses, tubes, mouthpieces, etc., only if the beneficiary owns or is purchasing durable medical equipment (section 2100.5). (Medications used in connection with durable medical equipment are covered under certain conditions—see section 2100.5.)	Claim must indicate that (a) the patient has the DME for which item is intended; (b) the DME continues to be medically necessary; and (c) the items are readily identifiable as the type customarily used with such equipment.

If the quantity of accessories and/or supplies included in a claim seems excessive or if claims for such items are received from the same claimant with undue frequency, refer to supervisor for handling in accordance with section 2100.6.

DME must be for use in patient's residence other than a health care institution. (sections 2100.3 and 4105.1)	Payment cannot be made for equipment for use in an institution whose provider number in the current edition of the *Directory of Medical Facilities* classifies as a participating hospital, an emergency hospital, meets 1861(e)(1), a participating SNF or meets 1819(a). If one of these institutions has a distinct part which does not meet either 1861(e)(1) or 1819(a), the patient may be considered in his/her residence if he/she was physically located in such distinct part during the use period.
Physician's prescription required. (See section 4105.2.)	For DME claims other than home oxygen, review the prescription and other information in the claim to determine medical necessity and to establish the duration of medical need. If DME is necessary, accept the physician's estimate of the duration of its need when it does not exceed 6 months. When the physician's estimate exceeds 6 months, is indefinite, or is lacking, refer the claim to your supervisor. The prescription should include the patient's diagnosis and prognosis, the reason the equipment is required, and an estimate (in months) of the duration of its need; if the prescription lacks this information, refer to your supervisor. (See section 4105.2.) A prescription for home dialysis delivery systems does not require an estimate of duration of its need. For home oxygen claims, the attending physician must complete and sign Form HCFA-484 (Attending Physician's Certification of Medical Necessity for Home Oxygen Therapy), or the physician's employee may complete the form for the physician's review and signature. (See sections 3312 and 3399.) For all certifications accompanying initial claims and for some recertifications, the results of the most recent arterial blood gas or arterial oxygen saturation test(s) on the patient must be included to establish whether the coverage criteria in Medicare Coverage Issues Manual, section 60-4 are met. (See section 4105.6.)

2105.1 New Supplier Effective Billing Date—A supplier of durable medical equipment, prosthetic, orthotics, and supplies (DME-POS) may begin to submit claims for services provided to Medicare beneficiaries on or after the date that the National Supplier Clearinghouse (NSC) issues a number to the supplier. This date will determine the effective date for billing Medicare. Any services provided by a supplier prior to its effective date may not be reimbursed.

2120 AMBULANCE SERVICE

Reimbursement may be for expenses incurred for ambulance service provided the conditions specified in the following subsections are met. (See sections 4115 and 2125 concerning instructions for processing ambulance service claims.)

2120.4 Air Ambulance Services.—Medically appropriate air ambulance transportation is a covered service regardless of the State or region in which it is rendered. However, approve claims only if the beneficiary's medical condition is such that transportation by either basic or advanced life support land ambulance is not appropriate.

A. Coverage Requirements.—Air ambulance transportation services, either by means of a helicopter or fixed wing aircraft, may be determined to be covered only if—

• The vehicle and crew requirements described in section 2120.1 are met;
• The beneficiary's medical condition required immediate and rapid ambulance transportation that could not have been provided by land ambulance; and either
  — The point of pickup is inaccessible by land vehicle (this condition could be met in Hawaii, Alaska, and in other remote or sparsely populated areas of the continental United States), or
  — Great distances or other obstacles (for example, heavy traffic) are involved in getting the patient to the nearest hospital with appropriate facilities as described in subsection D.

B. Medical Appropriateness.—Medical appropriateness is only established when the beneficiary's condition is such that the time needed to transport a beneficiary by land, or the instability of transportation by land, poses a threat to the beneficiary's survival or seriously endangers the beneficiary's health. Following is an advisory list of examples of cases for which air ambulance could be justified. The list is not inclusive of all situations that justify air transportation, nor is it intended to justify air transportation in all locales in the circumstances listed.

• Intracranial bleeding requiring neurosurgical intervention;
• Cardiogenic shock;
• Burns requiring treatment in a Burn Center;
• Conditions requiring treatment in a Hyperbaric Oxygen Unit;
• Multiple severe injuries; or
• Life-threatening trauma.

C. Time Needed for Land Transport.—Differing Statewide Emergency Medical Services (EMS) systems determine the amount and level of basic and advanced life support land transportation available. However, there are very limited emergency cases where land transportation is available but the time required to transport the patient by land as opposed to air endangers the beneficiary's life or health. As a general guideline, when it would take a land ambulance 30 to 60 minutes or more to transport an emergency patient, consider air transportation appropriate.

D. Appropriate Facility.—It is required that the beneficiary be transported to the nearest hospital with appropriate facilities for treatment. The term "appropriate facilities" refers to units or components of a hospital that are capable of providing the required level and type of care for the patient's illness and that have available the type of physician or physician specialist needed to treat the beneficiary's condition. In determining whether a particular hospital has appropriate facilities, take into account whether there are beds or a specialized treatment unit immediately available and whether the necessary physicians and other relevant medical personnel are available in the hospital at the time the patient is being transported. The fact that a more distant hospital is better equipped does not in and of itself warrant a finding that a closer hospital does not have appropriate facilities. Such a finding is warranted, however, if the beneficiary's condition requires a higher level of trauma care or other specialized service available only at the more distant hospital.

E. Hospital to Hospital Transport.—Air ambulance transport is covered for transfer of a patient from one hospital to another if the medical appropriateness criteria are met, that is, transportation by ground ambulance would endanger the beneficiary's health and the transferring hospital does not have adequate facilities to provide the medical services needed by the patient. Examples of such services include burn units, cardiac care units, and trauma units. A patient transported from one hospital to another hospital is covered only if the hospital to which the patient is transferred is the nearest one with appropriate facilities. Coverage is not available for transport from a hospital capable of treating the patient because the patient and/or his or her family prefers a specific hospital or physician.

F. Special Coverage Rule.—Air ambulance services are not covered for transport to a facility that is not an acute care hospital, such as a nursing facility, physician's office or a beneficiary's home.

G. Special Payment Limitations.—If a determination is made that transport by ambulance was necessary, but land ambulance service would have sufficed, payment for the air ambulance service is based on the amount payable for land transport, if less costly.

If the air transport was medically appropriate (that is, land transportation was contraindicated and the beneficiary required air transport to a hospital), but the beneficiary could have been treated at a nearer hospital than the one to which he or she was transported, the air transport payment is limited to the rate for the distance from the point of pickup to that nearer hospital.

H. Documentation.—Obtain adequate documentation of the determination of medical appropriateness for the air ambulance service. All claims for air ambulance services are to be reviewed by your medical staff.

2125 COVERAGE GUIDELINES FOR AMBULANCE SERVICE CLAIMS

Reimbursement may be made for expenses incurred by a patient for ambulance service provided conditions 1, 2, and 3 in the left-hand column have been met. The right-hand column indicates the documentation needed to establish that the condition has been met.

Conditions	Review Action
1. Patient was transported by an approved supplier of ambulance services.	1. Ambulance supplier is listed in the carrier's table of approved ambulance companies. (section 2120.1C)
2. The patient was suffering from an illness or injury which contraindicated transportation by other means. (section 2120.2A)	2. (a) Presume the requirement was met if file shows the patient: (i) Was transported in an emergency situation, e.g., as a result of an accident, injury, or acute illness, or (ii) Needed to be restrained, or (iii) Was unconscious or in shock, or (iv) Required oxygen or other emergency treatment on the way to his destination, or (v) Had to remain immobile because of a fracture that had not been set or the possibility of a fracture, or (vi) Sustained an acute stroke or myocardial infarction, (vii) Was experiencing severe hemorrhage, or (viii) Was bed confined before and after the ambulance trip, or (ix) Could be moved only by stretcher.

(b) In the absence of any of the conditions listed in (a) above additional documentation should be obtained to establish medical need where the evidence indicates the existence of the circumstances listed below:

(i) Patient's condition would not ordinarily require movement by stretcher, or

(ii) The individual was not admitted as a hospital inpatient (except in accident cases), or

(iii) The ambulance was used solely because other means of transportation were unavailable, or

(iv) The individual merely needed assistance in getting from his room or home to a vehicle.

(c) Where the information indicates a situation not listed in 2(a) or 2(b) above, refer the case to your supervisor.

3. The patient was transported from and to points listed below. (section 2120.3)

(a) From patient's residence (or other place where need arose) to hospital or skilled nursing home.

3. Claims should show points of pickup and destination.

(a) (i) Condition met if trip began within the institution's service area as shown in the carrier's locality guide.

(ii) Condition met where the trip began outside the institution's service area if the institution was the nearest one with appropriate facilities. Refer to supervisor for determination.

NOTE: A patient's residence is the place where he makes his home and dwells permanently, or for an extended period of time. A skilled nursing home is one which is listed in the Directory of Medical Facilities as a participating SNF or as an institution which meets section 1861(j)(1) of the law.

NOTE: A claim for ambulance service to a participating hospital or skilled nursing facility should not be denied on the grounds that there is a nearer nonparticipating institution having appropriate facilities.

(b) Skilled nursing home to a hospital or hospital to a skilled nursing home.

(b) (i) Condition met if pickup point is within the service area of the destination as shown in the carrier's locality guide.

(ii) Condition met where the pickup point is outside the service area of the destination if the destination institution was the nearest one with appropriate facilities. Refer to supervisor for determination.

(c) Hospital to hospital or skilled nursing home to skilled nursing home.

(c) Condition met if the discharging institution was not an appropriate facility and the admitting institution was the nearest one with appropriate facilities.

(d) From a hospital or skilled nursing home to patient's residence

(d) (i) Condition met if patient's residence is within the institution's service area as shown in the carrier's locality guide.

(ii) Condition met where the patient's residence is outside the institution's service area if the institution was the nearest one with appropriate facilities. Refer to supervisor for determination.

(e) Round trip for hospital or participating skilled nursing facility inpatients to the nearest hospital or nonhospital treatment facility where the beneficiary is an inpatient.

(e) Condition met if the necessary diagnostic or therapeutic service required by the patient's condition is not available at the institution.

NOTE: Ambulance service to a physician's office or a physician-directed clinic is not covered. (See section 2120.3G where a stop is made at a physician's office enroute to a hospital and 2120.3C for additional exceptions.)

4. Ambulance services involving hospital admissions in Canada or Mexico are covered (section 2312 ff.) if the following conditions are met:

a. The foreign hospitalization has been determined to be covered; and

b. The ambulance service meets the coverage requirements set forth in sections 2120 to 2120.3. If the foreign hospitalization has been determined to be covered on the basis of emergency services (section 2312.2A) the necessity requirement (section 2120.2) and the destination requirement (section 2120.3) are considered met.

5. Make partial payment for otherwise covered ambulance service which exceeded limits defined in item 3. (Claims supervisors are to make all partial payment determinations.) Base the payment on the amount payable had the patient been transported: (1) from the pickup point to the nearest appropriate facility, or (2) from the nearest appropriate facility to his/her residence where he/she is being returned home from a distant institution. (See section 5215.2.)

2130 PROSTHETIC DEVICES

A. General.—Prosthetic devices (other than dental) which replace all or part of an internal body organ (including contiguous tissue), or replace all or part of the function of a permanently inoperative or malfunctioning internal body organ are covered when furnished on a physician's order. This does not require a determination that there is no possibility that the patient's condition may improve sometime in the future. If the medical record, including the judgment of the attending physician, indicates the condition is of long and indefinite duration, the test of permanence is considered met. (Such a device may also be covered under section 2050.1 as a supply when furnished incident to a physician's service.)

Examples of prosthetic devices include cardiac pacemakers, prosthetic lenses (see subsection B), breast prostheses (including a surgical brassiere) for postmastectomy patients, maxillofacial devices and devices which replace all or part of the ear or nose. A urinary collection and retention system with or without a tube is a prosthetic device replacing bladder function in case of permanent urinary incontinence. The Foley catheter is also considered a prosthetic device when ordered for a patient with permanent urinary incontinence. However, Chux, diapers, rubber sheets, etc., are supplies that are not covered under this provision. (Although hemodialysis equipment is a prosthetic device, payment for the rental or purchase of such equipment for use in the home is made only under the provisions for payment applicable to durable medical equipment (see section 4105ff) or the special rules that apply to the ESRD program.)

NOTE: Medicare does not cover a prosthetic device dispensed to a patient prior to the time at which the patient undergoes the procedure that makes necessary the use of the device. For example, do not make a separate Part B payment for an intraocular lens (IOL) or pacemaker that a physician, during an office visit prior to the actual surgery, dispenses to the patient for his/her use. Dispensing a prosthetic device in this manner raises health and safety issues. Moreover, the need for the device cannot be clearly established until the procedure that makes its use possible is successfully performed. Therefore, dispensing a prosthetic device in this manner is not considered reasonable and necessary for the treatment of the patient's condition.

Colostomy (and other ostomy) bags and necessary accouterments required for attachment are covered as prosthetic devices. This coverage also includes irrigation and flushing equipment and other items and supplies directly related to ostomy care, whether the attachment of a bag is required.

Accessories and/or supplies which are used directly with an enteral or parenteral device to achieve the therapeutic benefit of the prosthesis or to assure the proper functioning of the device are covered under the prosthetic device benefit subject to the additional guidelines in the Coverage Issues Manual section 65-10 to 65-10.3.

Covered items include catheters, filters, extension tubing, infusion bottles, pumps (either food or infusion), intravenous (IV) pole, needles, syringes, dressings, tape, heparin sodium (parenteral only), volumetric monitors (parenteral only), and parenteral and enteral nutrient solutions. Baby food and other regular grocery products that can be blenderized and used with the enteral system are not covered. Note that some of these items, e.g., a food pump and an IV pole, qualify as DME. Although coverage of the enteral and parenteral nutritional therapy systems is provided on the basis of the prosthetic device benefit, the payment rules relating to rental or purchase of DME apply to such items. (See section 4105.3.) Code claims in accordance with the HCFA Common Procedure Coding System (HCPCS).

The coverage of prosthetic devices includes replacement of and repairs to such devices as explained in subsection D.

B. Prosthetic Lenses.—The term "internal body organ" includes the lens of an eye. Prostheses replacing the lens of an eye include postsurgical lenses customarily used during convalescence from eye surgery in which the lens of the eye was removed. In addition, permanent lenses are also covered when required by an individual lacking the organic lens of the eye because of surgical removal or congenital absence. Prosthetic lenses obtained on or after the beneficiary's date of entitlement to supplementary medical insurance benefits may be covered even though the surgical removal of the crystalline lens occurred before entitlement.

1. Prosthetic Cataract Lenses.—Make payment for one of the following prosthetic lenses or combinations of prosthetic lenses when determined to be medically necessary by a physician (see section 2020.25 for coverage of prosthetic lenses prescribed by a doctor of optometry) to restore essentially the vision provided by the crystalline lens of the eye:

- prosthetic bifocal lenses in frames;
- prosthetic lenses in frames for far vision, and prosthetic lenses in frames for near vision; or
- when a prosthetic contact lens(es) for far vision is prescribed (including cases of binocular and monocular aphakia), make payment for the contact lens(es) and prosthetic lenses in frames for near vision to be worn at the same time as the contact lens(es), and prosthetic lenses in frames to be worn when the contacts have been removed.

Make payment for lenses which have ultraviolet absorbing or reflecting properties, in lieu of payment for regular (untinted) lenses, if it has been determined that such lenses are medically reasonable and necessary for the individual patient.

Do not make payment for cataract sunglasses obtained in addition to the regular (untinted) prosthetic lenses since the sunglasses duplicate the restoration of vision function performed by the regular prosthetic lenses.

2. Payment for IOLs Furnished in Ambulatory Surgical Centers (ASCs). Effective for services furnished on or after March 12, 1990, payment for IOLs inserted during or subsequent to cataract surgery in a Medicare certified ASC is included with the payment for facility services that are furnished in connection with the covered surgery. Section 5243.3 explains payment procedures for ASC facility services and the IOL allowance.

3. Limitation on Coverage of Conventional Lenses.—Make payment for no more than one pair of conventional eyeglasses or conventional contact lenses furnished after each cataract surgery with insertion of an IOL.

C. Dentures.—Dentures are excluded from coverage. However, when a denture or a portion thereof is an integral part (built-in) of a covered prosthesis (e.g., an obturator to fill an opening in the palate), it is covered as part of that prosthesis.

D. Supplies, Repairs, Adjustments, and Replacement.—Make payment for supplies that are necessary for the effective use of a prosthetic device (e.g., the batteries needed to operate an artificial larynx). Adjustment of prosthetic devices required by wear or by a change in the patient's condition is covered when ordered by a physician. To the extent applicable, follow the provisions relating to the repair and replacement of durable medical equipment in section 2100.4 for the repair and replacement of prosthetic devices. (See section 2306.D in regard to payment for devices replaced under a warranty.) Regardless of the date that the original eyewear was furnished (i.e., whether before, on, or after January 1, 1991), do not pay for replacement of conventional eyeglasses or contact lenses covered under subsection B.3.

Necessary supplies, adjustments, repairs, and replacements are covered even when the device had been in use before the user enrolled in Part B of the program, so long as the device continues to be medically required.

2133 LEG, ARM, BACK, AND NECK BRACES, TRUSSES, AND ARTIFICIAL LEGS, ARMS, AND EYES

These appliances are covered when furnished incident to physicians' services or on a physician's order. A brace includes rigid and semi-rigid devices which are used for the purpose of supporting a weak or deformed body member or restricting or eliminating motion in a diseased or injured part of the body. Elastic stockings, garter belts, and similar devices do not come within the scope of the definition of a brace. Back braces include, but are not limited to, special corsets, e.g., sacroiliac, sacrolumbar, dorsolumbar corsets and belts. A terminal device (e.g., hand or hook) is covered under this provision whether an artificial limb is required by the patient. (See section 2323.) Stump stockings and harnesses (including replacements) are also covered when these appliances are essential to the effective use of the artificial limb.

Adjustments to an artificial limb or other appliance required by wear or by a change in the patient's condition are covered when ordered by a physician. To the extent applicable, follow the provisions in section 2100.4 relating to the repair and replacement of durable medical equipment for the repair and replacement of artificial limbs, braces, etc. Adjustments, repairs and replacements are covered even when the item had been in use before the user enrolled in Part B of the program so long as the device continues to be medically required.

2134 THERAPEUTIC SHOES FOR INDIVIDUALS WITH DIABETES

Coverage of therapeutic shoes (depth or custom-molded) along with inserts for individuals with diabetes is available as of May 1, 1993. These diabetic shoes are covered if the requirements as specified in this section concerning certification and prescription are fulfilled. In addition, this benefit provides for a pair of diabetic shoes even if only one foot suffers from diabetic foot disease. Each shoe is equally equipped so that the affected limb, as well as the remaining limb, is protected.

Claims for therapeutic shoes for diabetics are processed by the Durable Medical Equipment Regional Carriers (DMERCs.)

A. Definitions.—The following items may be covered under the diabetic shoe benefit:

1. Custom-Molded Shoes.—Custom-molded shoes are shoes that are:

- Constructed over a positive model of the patient's foot;
- Made from leather or other suitable material of equal quality;
- Have removable inserts that can be altered or replaced as the patient's condition warrants; and
- Have some form of shoe closure.

2. Depth Shoes.—Depth shoes are shoes that:

- Have a full length, heel-to-toe filler that, when removed, provides a minimum of 3/16 inch of additional depth used to accommodate custom-molded or customized inserts;
- Are made from leather or other suitable material of equal quality;
- Have some form of shoe closure; and
- Are available in full and half sizes with a minimum of 3 widths so that the sole is graded to the size and width of the upper portions of the shoes according to the American standard last sizing schedule or its equivalent. (The American standard last sizing schedule is the numerical shoe sizing system used for shoes sold in the United States.)

3. Inserts.—Inserts are total contact, multiple density, removable inlays that are directly molded to the patient's foot or a model of the patient's foot and that are made of a suitable material with regard to the patient's condition.

B. Coverage.—

1. Limitations.—For each individual, coverage of the footwear and inserts is limited to one of the following within one calendar year:

- No more than one pair of custom-molded shoes (including inserts provided with such shoes) and two additional pairs of inserts; or
- No more than one pair of depth shoes and three pairs of inserts (not including the non-customized removable inserts provided with such shoes).

2. Coverage of Diabetic Shoes and Brace.—Orthopedic shoes, as stated in section 2323.D, generally are not covered. This exclusion does not apply to orthopedic shoes that are an integral part of a leg brace. In situations in which an individual qualifies for both diabetic shoes and a leg brace, these items are covered separately. Thus, the diabetic shoes may be covered if the requirements for this section are met, while the brace may be covered if the requirements of section 2133 are met.

3. Substitution of Modifications for Inserts.—An individual may substitute modification(s) of custom-molded or depth shoes instead of obtaining a pair(s) of inserts in any combination. Payment for the modification(s) may not exceed the limit set for the inserts for which the individual is entitled. The following is a list of the most common shoe modifications available, but it is not meant as an exhaustive list of the modifications available for diabetic shoes:

- Rigid Rocker Bottoms.—These are exterior elevations with apex positions for 51 percent to 75 percent distance measured from the back end of the heel. The apex is a narrowed or pointed end of an anatomical structure. The apex must be positioned behind the metatarsal heads and tapering off sharply to the front tip of the sole. Apex height helps to eliminate pressure at the metatarsal heads. Rigidity is ensured by the steel in the shoe. The heel of the shoe tapers off in the back in order to cause the heel to strike in the middle of the heel.
- Roller Bottoms (Sole or Bar).—These are the same as rocker bottoms, but the heel is tapered from the apex to the front tip of the sole.
- Metatarsal Bars.—An exterior bar is placed behind the metatarsal heads in order to remove pressure from the metatarsal heads. The bars are of various shapes, heights, and construction depending on the exact purpose.

- Wedges (Posting).—Wedges are either of hind foot, fore foot, or both and may be in the middle or to the side. The function is to shift or transfer weight bearing upon standing or during ambulation to the opposite side for added support, stabilization, equalized weight distribution, or balance.
- Offset Heels.—This is a heel flanged at its base either in the middle, to the side, or a combination, that is then extended upward to the shoe in order to stabilize extreme positions of the hind foot.

Other modifications to diabetic shoes include, but are not limited to:

- Flared heels;
- Velcro closures; and
- Inserts for missing toes.

4. Separate Inserts.—Inserts may be covered and dispensed independently of diabetic shoes if the supplier of the shoes verifies in writing that the patient has appropriate footwear into which the insert can be placed. This footwear must meet the definitions found above for depth shoes and custom-molded shoes.

C. Certification.—The need for diabetic shoes must be certified by a physician who is a doctor of medicine or a doctor of osteopathy and who is responsible for diagnosing and treating the patient's diabetic systemic condition through a comprehensive plan of care. This managing physician must:

- Document in the patient's medical record that the patient has diabetes;
- Certify that the patient is being treated under a comprehensive plan of care for his or her diabetes, and that he or she needs diabetic shoes; and
- Document in the patient's record that the patient has one or more of the following conditions:
  - Peripheral neuropathy with evidence of callus formation;
  - History of pre-ulcerative calluses;
  - History of previous ulceration;
  - Foot deformity;
  - Previous amputation of the foot or part of the foot; or
  - Poor circulation.

D. Prescription.—Following certification by the physician managing the patient's systemic diabetic condition, a podiatrist or other qualified physician who is knowledgeable in the fitting of diabetic shoes and inserts may prescribe the particular type of footwear necessary.

E. Furnishing Footwear.—The footwear must be fitted and furnished by a podiatrist or other qualified individual such as a pedorthist, an orthotist, or a prosthetist. The certifying physician may not furnish the diabetic shoes unless he or she is the only qualified individual in the area. It is left to the discretion of each carrier to determine the meaning of "in the area."

F. Payment.—For 1994, payment for diabetic shoes and inserts is limited to 80 percent of the reasonable charge, up to a limit of $348 for one pair of custom-molded shoes including any initial inserts, $59 for each additional pair of custom-molded shoe inserts, $116 for one pair of depth shoes, and $59 for each pair of depth shoe inserts. These limits are based on 1988 amounts that were set forth in section 1833(o) of the Act and then adjusted by the same percentage increases allowed for DME for fee screen limits by applying the same update factor that is applied to DME fees, except that if the updated limit is not a multiple of $1, it is rounded to the nearest multiple of $1. Although percentage increases in payment for diabetic shoes are the same percentage increases that are used for payment of DME through the DME fee schedule, the shoes are not subject to DME coverage rules or the DME fee schedule. In addition, diabetic shoes are neither considered DME nor orthotics, but a separate category of coverage under Medicare Part B. (See section 1861(s)(12) and section 1833(o) of the Act.)

Payment for the certification of diabetic shoes and for the prescription of the shoes is considered to be included in the payment for the visit or consultation during which these services are provided. If the sole purpose of an encounter with the beneficiary is to dispense or fit the shoes, then no payment may be made for a visit or consultation provided on the same day by the same physician. Thus, a separate payment is not made for certification of the need for diabetic shoes, the prescribing of diabetic shoes, or the fitting of diabetic shoes unless the physician documents that these services were not the sole purpose of the visit or consultation.

2150 CLINICAL PSYCHOLOGIST SERVICES

Section 6113(a) of OBRA 1989 (P.L. 101-239) eliminates the restriction on clinical psychologist (CP) services imposed by prior law, which required that, to be paid for directly, the services be furnished at community mental health centers (CMHCs) or offsite of a CMHC for those who are institutionalized or are physically or mentally impaired.

A CMHC is an institution that provides the mental health services required by section 1916(c)(4) of the PHS Act and is certified by the appropriate State authorities as meeting such requirements.

Services furnished by a CP and services furnished incident to the services of a CP to hospital patients during the period July 1, 1990, through December 31, 1990, were bundled. Therefore, Medicare made payment to the hospital for these services. However, as a result of the enactment of section 4157 of OBRA 1990, effective January 1, 1991, clinical psychologist services furnished to hospital patients are no longer bundled under 42 CFR 411.15(m). Section 4157 amended section 1862(a)(14) of the Act to unbundle and permit direct payment to CPs for such services under Medicare Part B.

The diagnostic services of psychologists who are not clinical psychologists, and who are practicing independently, are discussed in section 2070.2.

A. Clinical Psychologist Defined.—To qualify as a CP, a practitioner must meet the following requirements:

- Hold a doctoral degree in psychology from a program in clinical psychology of an educational institution that is accredited by an organization recognized by the Council on Post-Secondary Accreditation;
- Meet licensing or certification standards for psychologists in independent practice in the State in which he or she practices; and
- Possess 2 years of supervised clinical experience, at least one of which is postdegree.

B. Qualified Clinical Psychologist Services Defined.—Effective July 1, 1990, the diagnostic and therapeutic services of CPs and services and supplies furnished incident to such services are covered as the services furnished by a physician or as incident to physician's services are covered. However, the CP must be legally authorized to perform the services under applicable licensure laws of the State in which they are furnished.

C. Types of Clinical Psychologist Services That May Be Covered.—CPs may provide the following services:

- Diagnostic and therapeutic services that the CP is legally authorized to perform in accordance with State law and/or regulation. Pay all qualified CPs based on the fee schedule for their diagnostic and therapeutic services. Continue to pay those practitioners who do not meet the requirements for a CP on a reasonable charge basis for the provision of diagnostic services under section 2070.2.
- Services and supplies furnished incident to a CP's services are covered if the requirements that apply to services incident to a physician's services, as described in section 2050.1 are met. These services must be:
  — Mental health services that are commonly furnished in CPs' offices;
  — An integral, although incidental, part of professional services performed by the CP;
  — Performed under the direct personal supervision of the CP, i.e., the CP must be physically present and immediately available; and
  — Furnished without charge or included in the CP's bill.

Any person involved in performing the service must be an employee of the CP (or an employee of the legal entity that employs the supervising CP) under the common law control test of the Act, as set forth in 20 CFR 404.1007 and section RS 2101.020 of the Retirement and Survivors Insurance part of the Social Security Program Operations Manual System.

Be familiar with appropriate State laws and/or regulations governing a CP's scope of practice. The development of lists of appropriate services may prove useful.

D. Noncovered Services.—The services of CPs are not covered if they are otherwise excluded from Medicare coverage even though a clinical psychologist is authorized by State law to perform them. For example, section 1862(a)(1)(A) of the Act excludes from coverage services that are not "reasonable and necessary for the diagnosis or treatment of an illness or injury or to improve the functioning of a malformed body member." Therefore, even though the services are authorized by State law, the services of a CP that are determined to be not reasonable and necessary are not covered.

E. Requirement for Consultation.—When applying for a Medicare provider number, a CP must submit to the carrier an attestation agreement to the effect that, contingent upon the patient's consent, he or she will attempt to consult with the patient's attending or primary care physician in accordance with accepted professional ethical norms, taking into consideration patient confidentiality.

Section 6113(c) of Public Law 101-239 requires the Secretary to develop criteria to pay for qualified psychologist services directly to the clinical psychologist under Part B. These criteria must address the circumstances under which the psychologist consults with the patient's attending physician. HCFA plans to develop these criteria through rulemaking.

The conferees discuss the consultation requirement in the conference report. That report stipulates that:

- The CP has informed the patient of the desirability of conferring with the patient's primary care or attending physician to consider potential medical conditions contributing to the patient's condition; and
- The CP has provided written notification to the patient's designated attending or primary care physician that services are being provided to the patient, or has consulted directly with the physician to consider medical conditions that may be contributing to the patient's symptoms, unless the patient specifically requests that such notice or consultation not be made.

See H.R. Conf. Rep. No. 386, 101st Cong., 1st Sess. 789 (1989).

F. Payment Limitation.—Payment for the services of CPs is made on the basis of a fee schedule or the actual charge, whichever is less, and only on the basis of assignment.

G. Outpatient Mental Health Services Limitation.—All covered therapeutic services furnished by qualified CPs are subject to the outpatient mental health services limitation in section 2470ff (i.e., only $62\frac{1}{2}$ percent of expenses for these services are considered incurred expenses for Medicare purposes). The limitation does not apply to diagnostic services. (See section 2476.5).

H. Assignment Requirement.—Make all claims for covered services rendered by CPs on an assignment basis.

2152 CLINICAL SOCIAL WORKER SERVICES

Medical and other health services include the services provided by a clinical social worker (CSW). Payment is made only under assignment. The amount payable cannot exceed 80 percent of the lesser of the actual charge for the services or 75 percent of the amount paid to a psychologist for the same service. See section 5112 for the payment guidelines and subsection F for application of the mental health payment limitation.

A. Clinical Social Worker Defined.—Section 1861(hh) of the Act defines a "clinical social worker" as an individual who:

- Possesses a master's or doctor's degree in social work;
- Has performed at least 2 years of supervised clinical social work; and
- Either
  — Is licensed or certified as a clinical social worker by the State in which the services are performed; or
  — In the case of an individual in a State that does not provide for licensure or certification, has completed at least 2 years or 3,000 hours of post master's degree supervised clinical social work practice under the supervision of a master's level social worker in an appropriate setting such as a hospital, SNF, or clinic.

B. Clinical Social Worker Services Defined.—Section 1861(hh)(2) of the Act defines "clinical social worker services" as those services that the CSW is legally authorized to perform under State law (or the State regulatory mechanism provided by State law) of the State in which such services are performed for the diagnosis and treatment of mental illnesses. Services furnished to an inpatient of a hospital or an inpatient of an SNF that the SNF is required to provide as a requirement for participation are not included. The services that are covered are those that are otherwise covered if furnished by a physician or as incident to a physician's professional service.

C. Covered Services.—Coverage is limited to the services a CSW is legally authorized to perform in accordance with State law (or State regulatory mechanism established by State law). The services of a CSW may be covered under Part B if they are:

- The type of services that are otherwise covered if furnished by a physician, or as incident to a physician's service. (See section 2020 for a description of physicians' services and section 2020.2 for the definition of a physician.);
- Performed by a person who meets the definition of a CSW (see subsection A.); and
- Not otherwise excluded from coverage.

Become familiar with the State law or regulatory mechanism governing a CSW's scope of practice in your service area. The development of a list of services within the scope of practice may prove useful.

D. Noncovered Services.—Services of a CSW are not covered when furnished to inpatients of a hospital or to inpatients of a SNF if the services furnished in the SNF are those that the SNF is required to furnish as a condition of participation in Medicare. In addition, CSW services are not covered if they are otherwise excluded from Medicare coverage even though a CSW is authorized by State law to perform them. For example, the Medicare law excludes from coverage services that are not "reasonable and necessary for the diagnosis or treatment of an illness or injury or to improve the functioning of a malformed body member."

F. Outpatient Mental Health Services Limitation.—All covered therapeutic services furnished by qualified CSWs are subject to the outpatient psychiatric services limitation in section 2470ff. (i.e., only 62 1/2 percent of expenses for these services are considered incurred expenses for Medicare purposes). The limitation does not apply to diagnostic services. (See section 2476.5.)

2210 PAYABLE PHYSICAL THERAPY (PT)

A. General.—To be covered PT services, the services must relate directly and specifically to an active written treatment regimen established by the physician after any needed consultation with the qualified physical therapist and must be reasonable and necessary to the treatment of the individual's illness or injury. Effective July 18, 1984, a plan of treatment for OPT services may be established by either the physician or the qualified physical therapist providing such services. Services related to activities for the general good and welfare of patients, e.g., general exercises to promote overall fitness and flexibility and activities to provide diversion or general motivation, do not constitute PT services for Medicare purposes.

Services furnished beneficiaries must constitute PT where entitlement to benefits is at issue. Since the OPT benefit under Part B

provides coverage only of PT services, payment can be made only for those services which constitute PT.

B. Reasonable and Necessary.—To be considered reasonable and necessary the following conditions must be met:

- The services must be considered under accepted standards of medical practice to be a specific and effective treatment for the patient's condition.
- The services must be of such a level of complexity and sophistication or the condition of the patient must be such that the services required can be safely and effectively performed only by a qualified physical therapist or under his supervision. Services which do not require the performance or supervision of a physical therapist are not considered reasonable or necessary PT services, even if they are performed or supervised by a physical therapist. (When you determine the services furnished were of a type that could have been safely and effectively performed only by a qualified physical therapist or under his supervision, presume that such services were properly supervised. However, this assumption is rebuttable, and, if in the course of processing claims you find that PT services are not being furnished under proper supervision, deny the claim and bring this matter to the attention of the Division of Survey and Certification of the RO.)
- The development, implementation, management, and evaluation of a patient care plan constitute skilled physical therapy services when, because of the beneficiary's condition, those activities require the skills of a physical therapist to meet the beneficiary's needs, promote recovery, and ensure medical safety. Where the skills of a physical therapist are needed to manage and periodically reevaluate the appropriateness of a maintenance program because of an identified danger to the patient, those reasonable and necessary management and evaluation services could be covered, even if the skills of a therapist are not needed to carry out the activities performed as part of the maintenance program.
- While a beneficiary's particular medical condition is a valid factor in deciding if skilled physical therapy services are needed, a beneficiary's diagnosis or prognosis should never be the sole factor in deciding that a service is or is not skilled. The key issue is whether the skills of a physical therapist are needed to treat the illness or injury, or whether the services can be carried out by nonskilled personnel.
- A service that ordinarily would be performed by nonskilled personnel could be considered a skilled physical therapy service in cases in which there is clear documentation that, because of special medical complications, a skilled physical therapist is required to perform or supervise the service. However, the importance of a particular service to a beneficiary or the frequency with which it must be performed does not, by itself, make a nonskilled service into a skilled service.
- There must be an expectation that the patient's condition will improve significantly in a reasonable (and generally predictable) period of time, or the services must be necessary for the establishment of a safe and effective maintenance program required in connection with a specific disease state.
- The amount, frequency, and duration of the services must be reasonable.

NOTE: Claims for PT services denied because they are not considered reasonable and necessary are excluded by section 1862(a)(1) of the Act and are thus subject to consideration under the waiver of liability provision in section 1879 of the Act. (See section 7300.10.)

2210.1 Restorative Therapy.—To constitute physical therapy a service must, among other things, be reasonable and necessary to the treatment of the individual's illness. If an individual's expected restoration potential would be insignificant in relation to the extent and duration of physical therapy services required to achieve such potential, the physical therapy would not be considered reasonable and necessary. In addition, there must be an expectation that the patient's condition will improve significantly in a reasonable (and generally predictable) period of time. However, if at any point in the treatment of an illness it is determined that the expectations will not materialize the services will no longer be considered reasonable and necessary; and they, therefore, should be excluded from coverage under section l862(a)(1) of the Act.

Skilled physical therapy may be needed, and improvement in a patient's condition may occur, even where a patient's full or partial recovery is not possible. For example, a terminally ill patient may begin to exhibit self-care, mobility, and/or safety dependence requiring skilled physical therapy services. The fact that full or partial recovery is not possible does not necessarily mean that skilled physical therapy is not needed to improve the patient's condition. The deciding factors are always whether the services are considered reasonable, effective treatments for the patient's condition and require the skills of a physical therapist, or whether they can be safely and effectively carried out by nonskilled personnel without physical therapy supervision.

2210.2 Maintenance Programs.—The repetitive services required to maintain function generally do not involve complex and sophisticated physical therapy procedures, and, consequently, the judgment and skill of a qualified physical therapist are not required for safety and effectiveness.

However, in certain instances, the specialized knowledge and judgment of a qualified physical therapist may be required to establish a maintenance program intended to prevent or minimize deterioration caused by a medical condition, if the program is to be safely carried out and the treatment aims of the physician achieved. Establishing such a program is a skilled service. For example, a Parkinson patient who has not been under a restorative physical therapy program may require the services of a physical therapist to determine what type of exercises will contribute the most to maintain the patient's present functional level. In such situations, the initial evaluation of the patient's needs, the designing by the qualified physical therapist of a maintenance program which is appropriate to the capacity and tolerance of the patient and the treatment objectives of the physician, the instruction of the patient or family members in carrying out the program, and such infrequent reevaluations as may be required would constitute physical therapy.

While a patient is under a restorative physical therapy program, the physical therapist should reevaluate his/her condition when necessary and adjust any exercise program the patient is expected to carry out himself/herself or with the aid of supportive personnel to maintain the function being restored. Consequently, by the time it is determined that no further restoration is possible, i.e., by the end of the last restorative session, the physical therapist will have already designed the maintenance program required and instructed the patient or supportive personnel in the carrying out of the program. Therefore, where a maintenance program is not established until after the restorative physical therapy program has been completed, it would not be considered reasonable and necessary for the treatment of the patient's condition and would be excluded from coverage under section l862(a)(1) of the Act.

The repetitive services required to maintain function sometimes involve the use of complex and sophisticated therapy procedures, and, consequently, the judgment and skill of a physical therapist might be required for the safe and effective rendition of such services.

Example: Where there is an unhealed, unstable fracture which requires regular exercise to maintain function until the fracture heals, the skills of a physical therapist would be needed to ensure that the fractured extremity is maintained in proper position and alignment during maintenance range of motion exercises.

2210.3 Application of Guidelines.—The following discussion illustrates the application of the above guidelines to some of the more common physical therapy modalities and procedures utilized in the treatment of patients:

    1. Hot Pack, Hydrocollator, Infra-Red Treatments, Paraffin Baths and Whirlpool Baths.—Heat treatments of this type and whirlpool baths do not ordinarily require the skills of a qualified physical therapist. However, in a particular case the skills, knowledge, and judgment of a qualified physical therapist might be required in such treatments or baths, e.g., where the patient's condition is complicated by circulatory deficiency, areas of desensitization, open wounds, or other complications. Also, if such treatments are given prior to but as an integral part of a skilled physical therapy procedure, they would be considered part of the physical therapy service.

    2. Gait Training.—Gait evaluation and training furnished a patient whose ability to walk has been impaired by neurological, muscular, or skeletal abnormality require the skills of a qualified physical therapist. However, if gait evaluation and training cannot reasonably be expected to improve significantly the patient's ability to walk, such services would not be considered reasonable and necessary. Repetitive exercises to improve gait or maintain strength and endurance, and assistive walking, such as provided in support for feeble or unstable patients, are appropriately provided by supportive personnel, e.g., aides or nursing personnel and do not require the skills of a qualified physical therapist.

    3. Ultrasound, Shortwave, and Microwave Diathermy Treatments.—These modalities must always be performed by or under the supervision of a qualified physical therapist, and therefore, such treatments constitute physical therapy.

    4. Range of Motion Tests.—Only the qualified physical therapist may perform range of motion tests and, therefore, such tests would constitute physical therapy.

    5. Therapeutic Exercises.—Therapeutic exercises which must be performed by or under the supervision of a qualified physical therapist due either to the type of exercise employed or to the condition of the patient would constitute physical therapy. Range of motion exercises require the skills of a qualified physical therapist only when they are part of the active treatment of a specific disease which has resulted in a loss or restriction of mobility (as evidenced by physical therapy notes showing the degree of motion lost and the degree to be restored) and such exercises, either because of their nature or the condition of the patient, may only be performed safely and effectively by or under the supervision of a qualified physical therapist. Generally, range of motion exercises which are not related to the restoration of a specific loss of function but rather are related to the maintenance of function (see section 2210.2) do not require the skills of a qualified physical therapist.

2215 SERVICES FURNISHED BY A PHYSICAL OR OCCUPATIONAL THERAPIST IN INDEPENDENT PRACTICE

Coverage of outpatient physical therapy, and occupational therapy under Part B includes the services of a qualified therapist in independent practice when furnished in the therapist's office or the beneficiary's home. (For coverage guidelines, see section 2210 for physical therapy, and section 2217 for occupational therapy.) Medicare payment is based on the Medicare physician fee schedule less coinsurance and any deductible amounts due. (See chapter 15 of Medicare Carriers Manual for discussion of the Medicare physician fee schedule and its applicability to outpatient physical therapy and occupational therapy services.) The limit on incurred expenses that is recognized for payment purposes, for each type of therapy in a calendar year, is $900. (For years 1990 through 1993, the limit is $750, and for years prior to 1990, the limit is $500.) Thus, if the beneficiary has already satisfied the Part B deductible, the maximum amount presently payable under each of these benefits is $720, i.e., 80 percent of $900. (See section 2480.)

NOTE: The limit on expenses applies only to items and services covered under the therapy benefit. It does not apply to items covered under a separate benefit, e.g., braces, that are furnished and billed by an occupational therapist.

NOTE: Services furnished by a therapist in the therapist's office under arrangements with hospitals in rural communities and public health agencies (or services provided in the beneficiary's home under arrangements with a provider of outpatient physical or occupational therapy services) are not covered under this provision.

A. Qualified Physical Therapist Defined.—A qualified physical therapist for program coverage purposes is an individual who is licensed as a physical therapist by the State in which practicing and meeds one of the following requirements:

• Has graduated from a physical therapy curriculum approved by the American Physical Therapy Association, or by the Council on Medical Education and Hospitals of the American Medical Association, or jointly by the Council on Medical Education of the American Medical Association and the American Physical Therapy Association;
• Prior to January 1, 1966, was admitted to membership by the American Physical Therapy Association, or was admitted to registration by the American Registry of Physical Therapists, or has graduated from a physical therapy curriculum in a 4-year college or university approved by a State department of education:
• Has 2 years of appropriate experience as a physical therapist and has achieved a satisfactory grade on proficiency examination approved by the Secretary except that such determinations of proficiency do not apply with respect to persons initially licensed by a State as a physical therapist after December 31, 1977, or seeking qualification as a physical therapist after that data;
• Was licensed or registered prior to January 1, 1966, and prior to January 1, 1970, had 15 years of full-time experience in the treatment of illness or injury through the practice of physical therapy in which services were rendered under the order and direction of attending and referring physicians;
• If trained outside the United States, was graduated since 1928 from a physical therapy curriculum approved in the country in which the curriculum was located and in which there is a member organization of the World Confederation for Physical Therapy, meets the requirements for membership in a member organization of the World Confederation for Physical Therapy, has 1 year of experience under the supervision of an active member of the American Physical Therapy Association, and has successfully completed a qualifying examination as prescribed by the American Physical Therapy Association.

The RO advises you of those physical therapists who are qualified.

B. Qualified Occupational Therapist Defined.—A qualified occupational therapist for program coverage purposes is an individual who is licensed as an occupational therapist by the State in which practicing and meets one of the following requirements:

• Is a graduate of an occupational therapy curriculum accredited jointly by the Council on Medical Education of the American Medical Association and the American Occupational Therapy Association;
• Is eligible for certification by or for the National Registration Examination of the American Occupational Therapy Association; or
• Has 2 years of appropriate experience as an occupational therapist, and has achieved a satisfactory grade on a proficiency examination conducted, approved, or sponsored by the U.S. Public Health Service, except that such determinations of proficiency do not apply with respect to persons initially licensed by a State or seeking initial qualification as an occupational therapist after December 31, 1977.

The RO advises you which occupational therapists are qualified.

C. Independent Practice Defined.—Consider a qualified therapist to be in independent practice if:

• The therapist renders services free of the administrative and professional control of an employer such as a physician, institution, agency;
• The therapist maintains office space at his/her own expense and furnishes services only in that space or the patient's home;
• The patients treated are the therapist's own patients; and
• The therapist has the right to collect fees for the services rendered.

The therapist need not be in full-time private practice but must be engaged in private practice on a regular basis, i.e., the therapist is recognized as a private practitioner and for that purpose has access to the necessary equipment to provide an adequate program of therapy.

A therapist in independent practice ordinarily is responsible for the expenses of an office and maintains hours of such frequency and duration that the patients treated can receive services as medically indicated. However, certain therapists, usually a therapist primarily engaged in teaching therapy in a university, may be considered independent for purposes of services furnished to patients in their home even though the therapist has no office outside the university. When a therapist does not maintain an office, the bonafides of the therapist's independence and access to appropriate equipment should be reviewed carefully.

D. Setting for Covered Services.—Coverage of services furnished by a qualified therapist in independent practice is limited to those services performed in the therapist's office or the beneficiary's home. (See section 2100.3.) A therapist with an office in a teaching institution may not provide covered services in that setting as an independent practitioner. Such services are covered as part of the institution's services.

E. Other Conditions for Coverage of Services.—In addition to the requirements described in subsections A to D, the services must be furnished in accordance with health and safety requirements set forth in regulations at 42 CFR 405, subpart Q, and must meet the following conditions:

1. Patient Must Be Under Care of Physician.—The attending physician may be the patient's private physician or a physician associated with an institution. There must be evidence in the clinical record maintained by the therapist that the patient has been seen by the physician at least every 30 days and the therapist must indicate on the bill the name of the physician and the date the patient was last seen by the physician. (See section 4161.)

2. Services Must Be Furnished Under Plan of Treatment.—The therapy must be furnished under a written plan of treatment established by the physician or therapist caring for the patient. The plan must be established (i.e., reduced to writing either by the physician who makes the plan available to the therapist or by the therapist himself/herself) before treatment is begun. The plan must be promptly signed by the physician or therapist and incorporated into the therapist's permanent record for the patient.

The plan must relate the type, amount, frequency, and duration of the therapy services that are to be furnished the patient and indicate the diagnosis and anticipated goals. Any changes are made in writing and signed by the physician or by the therapist. Changes made pursuant to oral orders given by the attending physician must be immediately recorded in the patient"s records and signed by the therapist receiving the orders. While the physician may change a plan of treatment established by the therapist providing such services, the therapist may not alter a plan of treatment established by a physician.

The plan must be reviewed by the physician, in consultation with the therapist at such intervals as the severity of the patient's condition requires, but at least every 30 days. Each review of the plan contains the initials of the physician and the date of review. The patient's plan normally is not forwarded to you for review. The plan of treatment and the therapist's clinical records concerning the beneficiary are retained by the therapist but must be available to you. The therapist must certify on the billing form that the plan is on file and was in effect at the time the services were rendered.

2217 COVERED OCCUPATIONAL THERAPY

A. General.—Covered occupational therapy services must relate directly and specifically to a written treatment regimen established by the physician, after any needed consultation with the qualified occupational therapist, or by the occupational therapist providing the services.

Occupational therapy is medically prescribed treatment concerned with improving or restoring functions which have been impaired by illness or injury or, where function has been permanently lost or reduced by illness or injury, to improve the individual's ability to perform those tasks required for independent functioning. Such therapy may involve:

- The evaluation, and reevaluation as required, of a patient's level of function by administering diagnostic and prognostic tests;
- The selection and teaching of task-oriented therapeutic activities designed to restore physical function, e.g., use of woodworking activities on an inclined table to restore shoulder, elbow and wrist range of motion lost as a result of burns;
- The planning, implementing, and supervising of individualized therapeutic activity programs as part of an overall "active treatment" program for a patient with a diagnosed psychiatric illness, e.g., the use of sewing activities which require following a pattern to reduce confusion and restore reality orientation in a schizophrenic patient;
- The planning and implementing of therapeutic tasks and activities to restore sensory-integrative function, e.g., providing motor and tactile activities to increase sensory input and improve response for a stroke patient with functional loss resulting in a distorted body image;
- The teaching of compensatory technique to improve the level of independence in the activities of daily living, for example:
  — Teaching a patient who has lost the use of an arm how to pare potatoes and chop vegetables with one hand;
  — Teaching an upper extremity amputee how to functionally utilize a prosthesis;
  — Teaching a stroke patient new techniques to enable him to perform feeding, dressing and other activities as independently as possible; or
  — Teaching a hip fracture/hip replacement patient techniques of standing tolerance and balance to enable him or her to perform such functional activities as dressing and home-making tasks.
- The designing, fabricating, and fitting of orthotic and self-help devices, e.g., making a hand splint for a patient with rheumatoid arthritis to maintain the hand in a functional position or constructing a device which would enable an individual to hold a utensil and feed himself independently; or
- Vocational and prevocational assessment and training, subject to the limitations specified in section 2217.B.

Only a qualified occupational therapist has the knowledge, training, and experience required to evaluate and, as necessary, reevaluate a patient's level of function, determine whether an occupational therapy program could reasonably be expected to improve, restore, or compensate for lost function and, where appropriate, recommend to the physician a plan of treatment.

 B. Coverage Criteria.—Occupational therapy designed to improve function is considered reasonable and necessary for the treatment of the individual's illness or injury only where an expectation exists that the therapy will result in a significant practical improvement in the individual's level of functioning within a reasonable period of time. Where an individual's improvement potential is insignificant in relation to the extent and duration of occupational therapy services required to achieve improvement, such services would not be considered reasonable and necessary and thus are not covered. If a valid expectation of improvement exists at the time the occupational therapy program is instituted, the services would be covered even though the expectation may not be realized. However, in such situations the services would be covered only up to the time at which it would have been reasonable to conclude that the patient is not going to improve. Once a patient has reached the point where no further significant practical improvement can be expected, the skills of an occupational therapist will not be required in the carrying out of any activity and/or exercise program required to maintain function at the level to which it has been restored. Consequently, while the services of an occupational therapist in designing a maintenance program and making infrequent but periodic evaluation of its effectiveness would be covered, carrying out the program is not considered reasonable and necessary for the treatment of illness or injury and such services are not covered.

Generally speaking, occupational therapy is not required to effect improvement or restoration of function where a patient suffers a temporary loss or reduction of function (e.g., temporary weakness which may follow prolonged bed rest following major abdominal surgery) which could reasonably be expected to improve spontaneously as the patient gradually resumes normal activities. Accordingly, occupational therapy furnished in such situations is not considered reasonable and necessary for the treatment of the individual's illness or injury and the services are not covered.

Occupational therapy may also be required for a patient with a specific diagnosed psychiatric illness. If such services are required they are covered assuming the coverage criteria are met. However, where an individual's motivational needs are not related to a specific diagnosed psychiatric illness, the meeting of such needs does not usually require an individualized therapeutic program. Such needs can be met through general activity programs or the efforts of other professional personnel involved in the care of the patient, because patient motivation is an appropriate and inherent function of all health disciplines which is interwoven with other functions performed by such personnel for the patient. Accordingly, since the special skills of an occupational therapist are not required, an occupational therapy program for individuals who do not have a specific diagnosed psychiatric illness is not considered reasonable and necessary for the treatment of an illness or injury. Services furnished under such a program are not covered.

Occupational therapy may include vocational and prevocational assessment and training. When services provided by an occupational therapist are related solely to specific employment opportunities, work skills, or work settings, they are not reasonable or necessary for the diagnosis or treatment of an illness or injury and are not covered. However, exercise care in applying this exclusion, because the assessment of level of function and the teaching of compensatory techniques to improve the level of function, especially in activities of daily living, are services which occupational therapists provide for both vocational and nonvocational purposes. For example, an assessment of sitting and standing tolerance might be nonvocational for a mother of young children or a retired individual living alone, but would be a vocational test for a sales clerk. Training an amputee in the use of a prosthesis for telephoning is necessary for everyday activities as well as for employment purposes. Major changes in life style may be mandatory for an individual with a substantial disability. The techniques of adjustment cannot be considered exclusively vocational or nonvocational.

Services of support personnel (e.g., occupational therapy assistants) and supplies used in furnishing covered therapy (e.g., looms, ceramic tiles, or leather) are included as part of the covered service. These items and services cannot be billed separately; they must be included in the therapist's bill. The restriction on a separate coverage and billing does not apply to items which meet the definition of brace in section 2133.

2251 COVERAGE OF CHIROPRACTIC SERVICES

2251.1 Manual Manipulation.—Coverage of chiropractic service is specifically limited to treatment by means of manual manipulation, i.e., by use of hands. No other diagnostic or therapeutic service furnished by a chiropractor or under his or her order is covered. This means that if a chiropractor orders, takes, or interprets an X-ray to demonstrate a subluxation of the spine, the X-ray can be used for claims processing purposes (see section 4118.C.2(d)), but Medicare coverage and payment is not available for those services. (Of course, this prohibition does not affect the coverage of X-rays furnished by other practitioners under the program. For example, an X-ray taken for the purpose of determining or demonstrating the existence of a subluxation of the spine is a diagnostic X-ray test covered under section 1861(s)(3) of the Act if ordered, taken, and interpreted by a physician who is a doctor of medicine or osteopathy.)

Additionally, manual devices (i.e., those that are hand-held with the thrust of the force of the device being controlled manually) may be used by chiropractors in performing manual manipulation of the spine. However, no additional payment is available for use of the device, nor does Medicare recognize an extra charge for the device itself.

The word "correction" may be used in lieu of "treatment." Also, a number of different terms composed of the following words may be used to describe manual manipulation as defined above:

• Spine or spinal adjustment by manual means;
• Spine or spinal manipulation;
• Manual adjustment; and
• Vertebral manipulation or adjustment.

In any case in which the term(s) used to describe the service performed suggests that it may not have been treatment by means of manual manipulation, refer the claim for professional review and interpretation.

2251.2 Subluxation Demonstrated by X-Ray.—The manual manipulation must be directed to the spine for the purpose of correcting a subluxation demonstrated by X-ray to exist. Differing meanings have been assigned to the word "subluxation," but for Medicare purposes it means an incomplete dislocation, off-centering, misalignment, fixation, or abnormal spacing of the vertebrae anatomically that must be demonstrable on an X-ray film to individuals trained in the reading of X-rays.

The documenting X-ray must have been taken at a time reasonably proximate to the initiation of a course of treatment. Unless you conclude that more specific X-ray evidence is warranted, an X-ray is considered reasonably proximate if it was taken no more than 12 months prior to or 3 months following the initiation of a course of chiropractic treatment. In certain cases of chronic subluxation (e.g., scoliosis), an older X-ray may be accepted provided the beneficiary's health record indicates the condition has existed longer than 12 months and there is a reasonable basis for concluding that the condition is permanent.

2251.3 Necessity for Treatment.—The patient must have a significant health problem in the form of a neuromusculoskeletal condition necessitating treatment, and the manipulative services rendered must have a direct therapeutic relationship to the patient's condition. Spinal axis aches, strains, sprains, nerve pains, and functional mechanical disabilities of the spine are considered to provide therapeutic grounds for chiropractic manipulative treatment. Most other diseases and pathological disorders do not provide therapeutic grounds for chiropractic manipulative treatment. Examples of these are rheumatoid arthritis, muscular dystrophy, multiple sclerosis, pneumonia, and emphysema.

Most spinal joint problems fall into the following categories:

• Acute subluxation-type (strains or sprains);
• Chronic subluxation-type (loss of joint mobility or other joint problems); or
• Nerve root problems (e.g., pinching) that may accompany conditions in either of the above conditions in either of the above categories.

2303 SERVICES NOT REASONABLE AND NECESSARY

Items and services which are not reasonable and necessary for the diagnosis or treatment of illness or injury, or to improve the functioning of a malformed body member; e.g., payment *cannot* be made for the rental of a special hospital bed to be used by the patient in his home unless it was a reasonable and necessary part of the patient's treatment. See also section 2318.

2320 ROUTINE SERVICES AND APPLIANCES

Routine physical checkups; eyeglasses, contact lenses, and eye examinations for the purpose of prescribing, fitting or changing eyeglasses; eye refractions; hearing aids and examinations for hearing aids; and immunizations are not covered.

The routine physical checkup exclusion applies to (a) examinations performed without relationship to treatment or diagnosis for a specific illness, symptom, complaint, or injury, and (b) examinations required by third parties such as insurance companies, business establishments, or Government agencies.

(If the claim is for a diagnostic test or examination performed solely for the purpose of establishing a claim under title IV of Public Law 91-173 (Black Lung Benefits), advise the claimant to contact his/her Social Security office regarding the filing of a claim for reimbursement under that program.)

The exclusions apply to eyeglasses or contact lenses and eye examinations for the purpose of prescribing, fitting, or changing eyeglasses or contact lenses for refractive errors. The exclusions do not apply to physician services (and services incident to a physician's service) performed in conjunction with an eye disease (e.g., glaucoma or cataracts) or to postsurgical prosthetic lenses which are customarily used during convalescence from eye surgery in which the lens of the eye was removed or to permanent prosthetic lenses required by an individual lacking the organic lens of the eye, whether by surgical removal or congenital disease. Such prosthetic lens is a replacement for an internal body organ (the lens of the eye). (See section 2130.)

The coverage of services rendered by an ophthalmologist is dependent on the purpose of the examination rather than on the ultimate diagnosis of the patient's condition. When a beneficiary goes to an ophthalmologist with a complaint or symptoms of an eye disease or injury, the ophthalmologist's services (except for eye refractions) are covered regardless of the fact that only eyeglasses were prescribed. However, when a beneficiary goes to his/her ophthalmologist for an eye examination with no specific complaint, the expenses for the examination are not covered even though as a result of such examination the doctor discovered a pathologic condition.

In the absence of evidence to the contrary, assume that an eye examination performed by an ophthalmologist on the basis of a complaint by the beneficiary or symptoms of an eye disease was not for the purpose of prescribing, fitting, or changing eyeglasses.

Expenses for all refractive procedures, whether performed by an ophthalmologist (or any other physician) or an optometrist and without regard to the reason for performance of the refraction, are excluded from coverage. (See sections 4125 and 5217 for claims review and reimbursement instructions concerning refractive services.)

With the exception of vaccinations for pneumococcal pneumonia, hepatitis B, and influenza, which are specifically covered under the law, vaccinations or inoculations are generally excluded as immunizations unless they are directly related to the treatment of an injury or direct exposure such as antirabies treatment, tetanus antitoxin or booster vaccine, botulin antitoxin, antivenin, or immune globulin.

2323 FOOT CARE AND SUPPORTIVE DEVICES FOR FEET

A. Exclusion of Coverage.—The following foot care services are generally excluded from coverage under both Part A and Part B. Exceptions to this general exclusion for limited treatment of routine foot care services are described in subsections A.2 and B. (See section 4120 for procedural instructions in applying foot care exclusions.)

1. Treatment of Flat Foot.—The term "flat foot" is defined as a condition in which one or more arches of the foot have flattened out. Services or devices directed toward the care or correction of such conditions, including the prescription of supportive devices, are not covered.

2. Treatment of Subluxation of Foot.—Subluxations of the foot are defined as partial dislocations or displacements of joint surfaces, tendons, ligaments, or muscles of the foot. Surgical or nonsurgical treatments undertaken for the sole purpose of correcting a subluxated structure in the foot as an isolated entity are not covered.

This exclusion does not apply to medical or surgical treatment of subluxation of the ankle joint (talo-crural joint). In addition, reasonable and necessary medical or surgical services, diagnosis, or treatment for medical conditions that have resulted from or are associated with partial displacement of structures is covered. For example, if a patient has osteoarthritis that has resulted in a partial displacement of joints in the foot, and the primary treatment is for the osteoarthritis, coverage is provided.

3. Routine Foot Care.—Except as provided in subsection B, routine foot care is excluded from coverage. Services that normally are considered routine and not covered by Medicare include the following:

- The cutting or removal of corns and calluses;
- The trimming, cutting, clipping, or debriding of nails; and
- Other hygenic and preventive maintenance care, such as cleaning and soaking the feet, the use of skin creams to maintain skin tone of either ambulatory or bedfast patients, and any other service performed in the absence of localized illness, injury, or symptoms involving the foot.

B. Exceptions to Routine Foot Care Exclusion

1. Necessary and Integral Part of Otherwise Covered Services.—In certain circumstances, services ordinarily considered to be routine may be covered if they are performed as a necessary and integral part of otherwise covered services, such as diagnosis and treatment of ulcers, wounds, or infections.

2. Treatment of Warts on Foot.—The treatment of warts (including plantar warts) on the foot is covered to the same extent as services provided for the treatment of warts located elsewhere on the body.

3. Presence of Systemic Condition.—The presence of a systemic condition such as metabolic, neurologic, or peripheral vascular disease may require scrupulous foot care by a professional that in the absence of such condition(s) would be considered routine (and, therefore, excluded from coverage). Accordingly, foot care that would otherwise be considered routine may be covered when systemic condition(s) result in severe circulatory embarrassment or areas of diminished sensation in the individual's legs or feet. (See subsection C.)

In these instances, certain foot care procedures that otherwise are considered routine (e.g., cutting or removing corns and calluses, or trimming, cutting, clipping, or debriding nails) may pose a hazard when performed by a nonprofessional person on patients with such systemic conditions. (See section 4120 for procedural instructions.)

4. Mycotic Nails.—In the absence of a systemic condition, treatment of mycotic nails may be covered.

The treatment of mycotic nails for an ambulatory patient is covered only when the physician attending the patient's mycotic condition documents that (1) there is clinical evidence of mycosis of the toenail, and (2) the patient has marked limitation of ambulation, pain, or secondary infection resulting from the thickening and dystrophy of the infected toenail plate.

The treatment of mycotic nails for a nonambulatory patient is covered only when the physician attending the patient's mycotic condition documents that (1) there is clinical evidence of mycosis of the toenail, and (2) the patient suffers from pain or secondary infection resulting from the thickening and dystrophy of the infected toenail plate.

For the purpose of these requirements, documentation means any written information that is required by the carrier in order for services to be covered. Thus, the information submitted with claims must be substantiated by information found in the patient's medical record. Any information, including that contained in a form letter, used for documentation purposes is subject to carrier verification in order to ensure that the information adequately justifies coverage of the treatment of mycotic nails. (See section 4120 for claims processing criteria.)

C. Systemic Conditions.—Although not intended as a comprehensive list, the following metabolic, neurologic, and peripheral vascular diseases (with synonyms in parentheses) most commonly represent the underlying conditions that might justify coverage for routine foot care.

*Diabetes mellitus
*Arteriosclerosis obliterans (ASO, arteriosclerosis of the extremities, occlusive peripheral arteriosclerosis)
*Buerger's disease (thromboangiitis obliterans)
*Chronic thrombophlebitis

*Peripheral neuropathies involving the feet
  *Associated with malnutrition and vitamin deficiency
    Malnutrition (general, pellagra)
    Alcoholism
    Malabsorption (celiac disease, tropical sprue)
    Pernicious anemia
  *Associated with carcinoma
  *Associated with diabetes mellitus
  *Associated with drugs and toxins
  *Associated with multiple sclerosis
  *Associated with uremia (chronic renal disease)
  *Associated with traumatic injury
  *Associated with leprosy or neurosyphilis
  *Associated with hereditary disorders
  *Hereditary sensory radicular neuropathy
  *Angiokeratoma corporis diffusum (Fabry's)
  *Amyloid neuropathy

When the patient's condition is one of those designated by an asterisk (*), routine procedures are covered only if the patient is under the active care of a doctor of medicine or osteopathy who documents the condition.

D. Supportive Devices for Feet.—Orthopedic shoes and other supportive devices for the feet generally are not covered. However, this exclusion does not apply to such a shoe if it is an integral part of a leg brace (see section 2133), and its expense is included as part of the cost of the brace. Also, this exclusion does not apply to therapeutic shoes furnished to diabetics. (See section 2134.)

E. Coding.—You are responsible for informing all medical specialties that codes and policies for routine foot care and supportive devices for the feet are not exclusively for the use of podiatrists. These codes must be used to report foot care services regardless of the specialty of the physician who furnishes the services. Instruct physicians to use the most appropriate code available when billing for routine foot care.

2329 COSMETIC SURGERY

Cosmetic surgery or expenses incurred in connection with such surgery are not covered. Cosmetic surgery includes any surgical procedure directed at improving appearance, except when required for the prompt (i.e., as soon as medically feasible) repair of accidental injury or for the improvement of the functioning of a malformed body member. For example, this exclusion does not apply to surgery in connection with treatment of severe burns or repair of the face following a serious automobile accident or to surgery for therapeutic purposes which coincidentally also serves some cosmetic purpose.

2455 MEDICAL INSURANCE BLOOD DEDUCTIBLE

A. General.—Program payment under Part B may not be made for the first three units of whole blood, or packed red cells, received by a beneficiary in a calendar year. For purpose of the blood deductible, a unit of whole blood means a pint of whole blood. The term whole blood means human blood from which none of the liquid or cellular components has been removed. Where packed red cells are furnished, a unit of packed red cells is considered equivalent to a pint of whole blood. After the three unit deductible has been satisfied, payment may be made for all blood charges, subject to the normal coverage and reasonable charge criteria.

NOTE: Blood is a biological and can be covered under Part B only when furnished incident to a physician's services. (See sections 2050.1ff. for a more complete explanation of services rendered "incident to a physician's services.")

B. Application of the Blood Deductible.—The blood deductible applies only to whole blood or packed red cells. Other components of blood such as platelets, fibrinogen, plasma, gamma globulin, and serum albumin are not subject to the blood deductible. These components of blood are covered biologicals.

The blood deductible involves only the charges for the blood (or packed red cells). Charges for the administration of blood or packed cells are not subject to the blood deductible. Accordingly, although payment may not be made for the first three pints of blood and/or units of packed red cells furnished to a beneficiary in a calendar year, payment may be made (subject to the cash deductible) for the administration charges for all covered pints or units including the first three furnished in a calendar year.

The blood deductible applies only to the first three pints and/or units furnished in a calendar year, even though more than one physician or clinic furnished blood. Furthermore, to count toward the deductible, the blood must be covered with respect to all applicable criteria (i.e., it must be medically necessary, it must be furnished incident to a physician's services, etc.). (See section 2050.5.)

2470 OUTPATIENT MENTAL HEALTH TREATMENT LIMITATION

Regardless of the actual expenses a beneficiary incurs for treatment of mental, psychoneurotic, and personality disorders while the beneficiary is not an inpatient of a hospital at the time such expenses are incurred, the amount of those expenses that may be recognized for Part B deductible and payment purposes is limited to 62.5 percent of the Medicare allowed amount for those services. This limitation is called the outpatient mental health treatment limitation. Expenses for diagnostic services (e.g., psychiatric testing and evaluation to diagnose the patient's illness) are not subject to this limitation. This limitation applies only to therapeutic services and to services performed to evaluate the progress of a course of treatment for a diagnosed condition, as described in section 2472.3.

3045 FILING THE REQUEST - ASSIGNMENTS

3045.4 Effect of Assignment upon Purchase of Cataract Glasses from Participating Physician or Supplier.—A pair of cataract glasses is comprised of two distinct products: a professional product (the prescribed lenses) and a retail commercial product (the frames). The frames serve not only as a holder of lenses but also as an article of personal apparel. As such, they are usually selected on the basis of personal taste and style. Although Medicare will pay only for standard frames, most patients want deluxe frames. Participating physicians and suppliers cannot profitably furnish such deluxe frames unless they can make an extra (non-covered) charge for the frames even though they accept assignment.

Therefore, a participating physician or supplier (whether an ophthalmologist, optometrist, or optician) who accepts assignment on cataract glasses with deluxe frames may charge the Medicare patient the difference between his usual charge to private pay patients for glasses with standard frames and his usual charge to such patients for glasses with deluxe frames, in addition to the applicable deductible and coinsurance on glasses with standard frames, if all of the following requirements are met:

A. The participating physician or supplier has standard frames available, offers them for sale to the patient, and explains to the patient the price and other differences between standard and deluxe frames.

B. The participating physician or supplier obtains from the patient (or his representative) and keeps on file the following signed and dated statement:

Name of Patient   Medicare Claim Number

Having been informed that an extra charge is being made by the physician or supplier for deluxe frames, that this extra charge is not covered by Medicare, and that standard frames are available for purchase from the physician or supplier at no extra charge, I have chosen to purchase deluxe frames.

____

Signature   Date

C. The participating physician or supplier itemizes on his claim his actual charge for the lenses, his actual charge for the standard frames, and his actual extra charge for the deluxe frames (charge differential).

Once the assigned claim for deluxe frames has been processed, the carrier will explain the extra charge for the deluxe frames on the EOMB, as indicated in the following example.

		BILLED	APPROVED
CATARACT LENSES	JULY 20, 1985	$200.00	$175.00

APPROVED AMOUNT LIMITED BY ITEM 5C ON BACK

STANDARD FRAMES	JULY 20, 1985	$ 20.00	$ 15.00

APPROVED AMOUNT LIMITED BY ITEM 5C ON BACK

DR. JONES AGREED TO CHARGE NO MORE FOR THE ABOVE SERVICES THAN THE AMOUNT APPROVED BY MEDICARE.

EXTRA CHARGE DE-LUXE	JULY 20, 1985	$ 35.00	$ 00.00

MEDICARE DOES NOT PAY THE EXTRA CHARGE FOR DE-LUXE FRAMES.

TOTAL APPROVED AMOUNT	$190.00
MEDICARE PAYMENT (80% OF THE AP-PROVED AMOUNT)	$152.00

WE ARE PAYING A TOTAL OF $152.00 TO DR. JONES FOR THE ABOVE SERVICES. YOU ARE RESPONSIBLE FOR THE DIFFERENCE OF $38.00 BETWEEN THE APPROVED AMOUNT AND THE MEDICARE PAYMENT, PLUS THE EXTRA CHARGE OF $35.00 FOR DELUXE FRAMES.

3045.7 Mandatory Assignment and Other Requirements for Home Dialysis Supplies and Equipment Paid Under Method II.

A. General.—Effective for services furnished on or after February 1, 1990, pay only on an assignment basis for home dialysis supplies and equipment furnished a beneficiary who has selected Method II. There is also a monthly payment limitation: $2,080 for continuous cycling peritoneal dialysis (CCPD) and $1,600 for all other methods of dialysis. (Note, however, that beneficiaries are permitted to have on hand one month's emergency reserve supplies.) This payment may be made to only one supplier per beneficiary. (See sections 4270-4271.)

B. Billing Instructions.—Claims for these supplies must be completed as follows:

• You may allow suppliers to bill for more than one month's supplies at a time. However, the date of service field must identify the month for which the supplies are purchased, so that you can apply the monthly payment limit. This may be accomplished by using a separate line for each month's supplies or by using inclusive service dates and the units field.

Example: In July 1990, a supplier bills for 2 CCPD supply kits. The first kit was supplied for the patient's use in June, and the second for use in July.

If the supplier lists both kits on the same line, that item must include the following information:
— Date of service: From: 060190 To 073190
— Procedure Code: A4900
— Units: 2

If the supplier lists each month's supplies on a separate line, the inclusive dates of service for each month are the first to the last date of each month (e.g., 060190 to 063090).

• Modifier "QR" must be used to designate the one month's emergency reserve supplies. This allows you to identify situations in which the payment limit for a given month may be exceeded if an emergency reserve is billed for in addition to regular monthly supplies. It also allows you to ensure that emergency supplies are not purchased more frequently than required.

• HCPCS code A4901 identifies CCPD supplies.

C. Processing Claims.—The monthly limit applies to all home dialysis supplies and equipment furnished the beneficiary. Since more than one supply or piece of equipment may be furnished for a given month, apply the limit to the supplies in the order in which they are billed by the sole supplier. For example, if the allowable charge for the first code billed does not exceed the limit, apply the limit to the subsequent code(s) in order of billing until the limit is met.

If a claim identifies the beneficiary as a CCPD patient by use of HCPCS code A4901, apply the higher monthly limit.

If two different suppliers submit bills for the same month for the same beneficiary, pay only the first supplier that submits a bill.

Deny payment for supplies and equipment if any of the following conditions are met:

- The supplier has not accepted assignment (use EOMB message no. 4.9);
- The supplies were furnished by a second supplier (use EOMB message 4.10); or
- The monthly limit has been paid (use EOMB message 4.11.)

(See section 7012 for EOMB messages.); or

- The claim is marked as non-assigned and evidence clearly shows that the supplier intends not to accept assignment. (Refer to sections 3040.3 and 3040.4 for processing instructions for claims inadvertently submitted as unassigned.)

3060 CLAIMS, FILING, JURISDICTION AND DEVELOPMENT PROCEDURES

3060.6 Payment Under Reciprocal Billing Arrangements

A. General.—The patient's regular physician may submit the claim, and (if assignment is accepted) receive the Part B payment, for covered visit services (including emergency visits and related services) which the regular physician arranges to be provided by a substitute physician on an occasional reciprocal basis, if:

- The regular physician is unavailable to provide the visit services;
- The Medicare patient has arranged or seeks to receive the visit services from the regular physician;
- The substitute physician does not provide the visit services to Medicare patients over a continuous period of longer than 60 days; and
- The regular physician identifies the services as substitute physician services meeting the requirements of this section by entering in item 24d of Form HCFA-1500 HCPCS Q5 modifier (service furnished by a substitute physician under a reciprocal billing arrangement) after the procedure code. When Form HCFA-1500 is next revised, provision will be made to identify the substitute physician by entering his/her unique physician identification number (UPIN) on the form and cross-referring the entry to the appropriate service line item(s) by number(s). Until further notice, the regular physician must keep in file a record of each service provided by the substitute physician, associated with the substitute physician's UPIN, and make this record available to you upon request.

If the only substitution services a physician performs in connection with an operation are postoperative services furnished during the period covered by the global fee, these services need not be identified on the claim as substitution services.

A physician may have reciprocal arrangements with more than one physician. The arrangements need not be in writing.

B. Definitions

1. Covered Visit Service.—The term "covered visit service" includes not only those services ordinarily characterized as a covered physician visit, but also any other covered items and services furnished by the substitute physician or by others as incident to his/her services.

Items and services furnished by the staff of the substitute physician covered as incident to his/her services if billed by him/her are still covered if billed by the regular physician under this section.

Items and services furnished by the staff of the regular physician covered as incident to his/her services if furnished under his/her supervision are still covered if furnished under the supervision of the substitute physician.

2. Continuous Period of Covered Visit Services.—A continuous period of covered visit services begins with the first day on which the substitute physician provides covered visit services to Medicare Part B patients of the regular physician, and it ends with the last day on which the substitute physician provides these services to these patients before the regular physician returns to work. This period continues without interruption on days on which no covered visit services are provided to patients on behalf of the regular physician or are furnished by some other substitute physician on behalf of the regular physician. A new period of covered visit services can begin after the regular physician has returned to work.

Example: The regular physician goes on vacation on June 30, 1992, and returns to work on September 4, 1992. A substitute physician provides services to Medicare Part B patients of the regular physician on July 2, 1992, and at various times thereafter, including August 30th and September 2, 1992. The continuous period of covered visit services begins on July 2nd and runs through September 2nd, a period of 63 days. Since the September 2nd services are furnished after the expiration of 60 days of the period, the regular physician is not entitled to bill and receive direct payment for them. The substitute physician must bill for these services in his/her own name. The regular physician may, however, bill and receive payment for the services which the substitute physician provides on his/her behalf in the period July 2nd through August 30th.

C. Unassigned Claims Under Reciprocal Billing Arrangements.—The requirements for the submission of claims under reciprocal billing arrangements are the same for assigned and unassigned claims.

D. Medical Group Claims Under Reciprocal Billing Arrangements.—The requirements of this section do not apply to the substitution arrangements among physicians in the same medical group where claims are submitted in the name of the group. On claims submitted by the group, the group physician who actually performed the service must be identified in the manner described in section 3060.9.

For a medical group to submit assigned and unassigned claims for the covered visit services of a substitute physician who is not a member of the group, the requirements of subsection A must be met. The medical group must enter in item 24d of Form HCFA-1500 the HCPCS modifier Q5 after the procedure code. Until further notice, the medical group must keep in file a record of each service provided by the substitute physician, associated with the substitute physician's UPIN, and make this record available to you upon request. In addition, the medical group physician for whom the substitution services are furnished must be identified by his/her provider identification number (PIN) in block 24k of the appropriate line item.

For an independent physician to submit assigned and unassigned claims for the substitution services of a physician who is a member of a medical group, the requirements of subsection A must be met. The independent physician must enter in item 24 of Form HCFA-1500 HCPCS modifier Q5 after the procedure code. Until further notice, the independent physician must keep in file a record of each service provided by the substitute medical group physician, associated with the substitute physician's UPIN, and make this record available to you upon request.

Physicians who are members of a group but who bill in their own names are treated as independent physicians for purposes of applying the requirements of this section.

E. Guidance to Physicians.—Inform physicians of the requirements of this section. Advise physicians and, if necessary, remind them that, in entering the code Q5 modifier, the regular physician (or the medical group, where applicable) is certifying that the services are covered visit services furnished by the substitute physician identified in a record of the regular physician which is available for inspection, and are services for which the regular physician (or group) is entitled under this section to submit the claim. Mention the possible penalties under subsection F for false certifications.

F. Penalties.—A physician or other person who falsely certifies that the requirements of this section are met may be subject to possible civil and criminal penalties for fraud. Also, the physician's right to receive payment or to submit claims under this section or even to accept any assignments may be revoked. The revocation procedures are set forth in section 14025.

G. Claims Review.—If a line item includes the code Q5 certification, assume that the claim meets the requirements of this section in the absence of evidence to the contrary. You need not track the 60-day period or validate the billing arrangement on a prepayment basis, absent postpayment findings which indicate that the certifications by a particular physician may not be valid.

H. Payment Amount.—When you make Part B payment under this section, you determine the payment amount as though the regular physician or his/her staff provided the services. The identification of the substitute physician is primarily for purposes of providing an audit trail to verify that the services were furnished, not for purposes of the payment or the limiting charge. Also, notices of noncoverage under section 7300ff. and 7330ff. are to be given in the name of the regular physician.

3060.7 Payment Under Locum Tenens Arrangements

A. Background.—It is a longstanding and widespread practice for physicians to retain substitute physicians to take over their professional practices when the regular physicians are absent for reasons such as illness, pregnancy, vacation, or continuing medical education, and for the regular physician to bill and receive payment for the substitute physician's services as though he/she performed them himself/herself. The substitute physician generally has no practice of his/her own and moves from area to area as needed. The regular physician generally pays the substitute physician a fixed amount per diem, with the substitute physician having the status of an independent contractor rather than of an employee. These substitute physicians are generally called "locum tenens" physicians.

Honor such billing and payment arrangements with respect to locum tenens physician's services furnished before January 1, 1994. Discontinue doing so with respect to services furnished after December 31, 1993 (unless the locum tenens physician is an employee of the regular physician, in which case section 3060.1 applies, or all services of the locum tenens physician for patients of the regular physician are performed in the offices of the regular physician, in which case section 3060.3C applies).

B. Interim Payment Procedure—For services furnished before January 1, 1994, the patient's regular physician may submit the claim, and (if assignment is accepted) receive the Part B payment, for covered visit services (including emergency visits and related services) of a locum tenens physician who is not an employee of the regular physician and whose services for patients of the regular physician are not restricted to the regular physician's offices, if:

- The regular physician is unavailable to provide the visit services;
- The Medicare beneficiary has arranged or seeks to receive the visit services from the regular physician;
- The regular physician pays the locum tenens for his/her services on a per diem or similar fee-for-time basis;
- The substitute physician does not provide the visit services to Medicare patients over a continuous period of longer than 60 days; and
- The regular physician identifies the services as substitute physician services meeting the requirements of this section by entering HCPCS Q6 modifier (service furnished by a locum tenens physician) after the procedure code. When Form HCFA-1500 is next revised, provision will be made to identify the substitute physician by entering his/her unique physician identification number (UPIN) on the form and cross-referring the entry to the appropriate service line item(s) by number(s). Until further no-

tice, the regular physician must keep in file a record of each service provided by the substitute physician, associated with the substitute physician's UPIN, and make this record available to you upon request.

See section 3060.6B for definitions of covered visit services and continuous period of covered visit services.

If the only substitution services a physician performs in connection with an operation are postoperative services furnished during the period covered by the global fee, these services need not be identified on the claim as substitution services.

C. Unassigned Claims Under Locum Tenens Arrangements.— The requirements for the submission of claims under reciprocal billing arrangements are the same for assigned and unassigned claims.

D. Medical Group Claims Under Locum Tenens Arrangements.—For a medical group to submit assigned and unassigned claims for the services a locum tenens physician provides for patients of the regular physician who is a member of the group, the requirements of subsection B must be met. For purposes of these requirements, per diem or similar fee-for-time compensation which the group pays the locum tenens physician is considered paid by the regular physician. Also, a physician who has left the group and for whom the group has engaged a locum tenens physician as a temporary replacement may still be considered a member of the group until a permanent replacement is obtained. The group must enter in item 24d of Form HCFA-1500 the HCPCS Q6 modifier after the procedure code. Until further notice, the group must keep in file a record of each service provided by the substitute physician, associated with the substitute physician's UPIN, and make this record available to you upon request. In addition, the medical group physician for whom the substitution services are furnished must be identified by his/her provider identification number (PIN) on block 24k of the appropriate line item.

3312 EVIDENCE OF MEDICAL NECESSITY FOR DURABLE MEDICAL EQUIPMENT

For certain items or services billed to the DME Regional Carrier (DMERC), the supplier must receive a signed Certificate of Medical Necessity (CMN) from the treating physician. The supplier must retain the original copy of the signed CMN in their records. CMNs communicate, either on paper or in an electronic record, required medical necessity information and have a DMERC form number (e.g., 01, 02, 03) and a revision number (e.g., .01, .02). Some DMERC forms also have an alpha suffix (e.g., A, B, C).

All CMNs have a HCFA form number in addition to the DMERC form number. (See the following listing of CMN form numbers.) The HCFA form number is in the bottom left corner of the form. CMNs are referred to by their HCFA form numbers. DMERC form numbers identify the CMN on electronic claims submitted to the DMERC in the National Standard Format (NSF). Form HCFA-484 serves as the CMN for home oxygen therapy.

The original CMN must be retained in the supplier's file and be available to the DMERCs on request. When CMNs are submitted on hard copy, the supplier must include a copy of only the front side. When CMNs are submitted electronically, only information from sections A, B, and D is required.

The following is a list of the currently approved CMNs:

DMERC FORM	HCFA FORM	ITEMS ADDRESSED
484.2	484	Home oxygen therapy
01.02A	841	Hospital beds
01.02B	842	Support surfaces
02.02A	843	Motorized wheelchairs
02.02B	844	Manual wheelchairs
03.02	845	Continuous positive airway pressure (CPAP) devices
04.02B	846	Lymphedema pumps (pneumatic compression devices)
04.02C	847	Osteogenesis stimulators

Table continued on following page

DMERC FORM	HCFA FORM	ITEMS ADDRESSED
06.02	848	Transcutaneous electrical nerve stimulators (TENS)
07.02A	849	Seat lift mechanisms
07.02B	850	Power operated vehicles
09.02	851	Infusion pumps
10.02A	852	Parenteral nutrition
10.02B	853	Enteral nutrition
11.01	854	Section C continuation (manual and motorized wheelchairs—ONLY)

The CMN sent to the physician must be two-sided with instructions on the back. Because these forms have been approved by the Office of Management and Budget (OMB), when a CMN is submitted with a paper claim, the hard copy must be an **exact** reproduction of the HCFA form. However, when the CMN is submitted electronically, the font on the hard copy CMN, which the supplier retains in their files, may be modified as follows:

- Pitch may vary from 10 characters per inch (cpi) to 17.7 cpi;
- Line spacing must be 6 lines per inch;
- Each CMN must have a minimum 1/4 inch margin on all four sides;
- Without exception, these modified hard copy forms must contain identical questions/wording to the HCFA forms, in the same sequence, with the same pagination, and identical instructions/definitions printed on the back; and
- CMN question sets may not be combined.

The CMN can serve as the physician order if the narrative description is sufficiently detailed. This would include quantities needed and frequency of replacement on accessories, supplies, nutrients, and drugs. For items requiring a written order on hand prior to delivery (air fluidized beds, TENS, POVs, seat lift mechanisms), suppliers may utilize a completed and physician-signed CMN for this purpose. Otherwise, a separate order in addition to a subsequently completed and signed CMN is necessary.

The information in section B of the CMN may not be completed by the supplier. A supplier who knowingly and willfully completes section B of the form is subject to a civil money penalty up to $1,000 for each form or document so distributed. Any supplier who remains in noncompliance after repeated attempts by the contractor to get the supplier into compliance, refer to your RO as a potential civil money penalty case.

The information in section C of the CMN (fee schedule amount and the supplier's charge for the medical equipment or supplies being furnished) must be completed on the form by the supplier prior to it being furnished to the physician. A supplier who knowingly and willfully fails to include this information may be subject to a civil money penalty up to $1,000 for each form or document so distributed. Any supplier who remains in non-compliance, after repeated attempts by the contractor to get the supplier into compliance, refer to your RO as a potential civil money penalty case.

Do not modify the language or content when reprinted. Also, do not accept any CMN that has been modified in any way by any other party. In addition, do not accept any other certifications of medical necessity by other insurers or government agencies.

A. Completion of Certificate of Medical Necessity Forms

1. SECTION A: (This may be completed by supplier.)

a. Certification Type/Date.—If this is an initial certification for this patient, the date (MM/DD/YY) is indicated in the space marked "INITIAL." If this is a revised certification (to be completed when the physician changes the order, based on the patient's changing clinical needs), the initial date is indicated in the space marked "INITIAL," and the revision date is indicated in the space marked "REVISED." If this is a recertification, the initial date is indicated in the space marked "INITIAL," and the recertification date is indicated in the space marked "RECERTIFICATION." Whether a REVISED or RECERTIFIED CMN is submitted, the INITIAL date as well as the REVISED or RECERTIFICATION date is always furnished.

b. Patient Information.—This indicates the patient's name, permanent legal address, telephone number, and his/her health insurance claim number (HICN) as it appears on his/her Medicare card and on the claim form.

c. Supplier Information.—This indicates the name of the company (supplier name), address, telephone number, and the Medicare supplier number assigned by the National Supplier Clearinghouse (NSC).

d. Place of Service.—This indicates the place in which the item is being used, i.e., patient's home is 12, skilled nursing facility (SNF) is 31, or end stage renal disease (ESRD) facility is 65. See section 4030.5 for a complete list.

e. Facility Name.— This indicates the name and complete address of the facility, if the place of service is a facility.

f. HCPCS Codes.— This is a list of all HCPCS procedure codes for items ordered that require a CMN. Procedure codes that do not require certification are not listed on the CMN.

g. Patient Date of Birth (DOB), Height, Weight, and Sex.— This indicates patient's DOB (MM/DD/YY), height in inches, weight in pounds, and sex (male or female).

h. Physician Name and Address.—This indicates the treating physician's name and complete mailing address.

i. UPIN.—This indicates the treating physician's unique physician identification number (UPIN).

j. Physician's Telephone Number.—This indicates the telephone number where the treating physician can be contacted (preferably where records would be accessible pertaining to this patient) if additional information is needed.

2. SECTION B: (This may not be completed by the supplier. While this section may be completed by a nonphysician clinician, or a physician employee, it must be reviewed by the treating physician. Publish this requirement about section B in your bulletins at least annually.)

a. Estimated Length of Need.—This indicates the estimated length of need (the length of time (in months) the physician expects the patient to require use of the ordered item). If the treating physician expects that the patient will require the item for the duration of his/her life, 99 is entered. For recertification and revision CMNs, the cumulative length of need (the total length of time in months from the initial date of need) is entered.

b. Diagnosis Codes.—Listed in the first space is the ICD-9 code that represents the primary reason for ordering this item. Additional ICD-9 codes that would further describe the medical need for the item (up to 3 codes) are also listed. A given CMN may have more than one item billed, and for each item, the primary reason for ordering may be different. For example, a CMN is submitted for a manual wheelchair (K0001) and elevating leg rests (K0195). The primary reason for K0001 is stroke, and the primary reason for K0195 is edema.

c. Question Section.—This section is used to gather clinical information regarding the patient's condition, the need for the DME, and supplies.

d. Name of Person Answering Section B Questions.—If a clinical professional other than the treating physician (e.g., home health nurse, physical therapist, dietitian, or a physician employee) answers the questions in section B, he/she must print his/her name, give his/her professional title, and the name of his/her employer, where indicated. If the treating physician answered the questions, this space may be left blank.

3. SECTION C: (This is completed by the supplier.)

a. Narrative Description of Equipment and Cost.—The supplier indicates (1) a narrative description of the item(s) ordered, as well as all options, accessories, supplies, and drugs; (2) the supplier's charge for each item, option, accessory, supply, and drug; and (3) the Medicare fee schedule allowance for each item, option, accessory, supply, or drug, if applicable.

4. SECTION D: (This is completed by the treating physician.)

a. Physician Attestation.—The treating physician's signature certifies the CMN which he/she is reviewing includes sections A, B, C, and D, the answers in section B are correct, and the self-identifying information in section A is correct.

b. Physician Signature and Date.—After completion and/or review by the treating physician of sections A, B, and C, the treating physician must sign and date the CMN in section D, verifying the attestation appearing in this section. The treating physician's signature also certifies the items ordered are medically necessary for this patient. Signature and date stamps are not acceptable.

B. Development of Incomplete Data.—Claims that require development for missing or incomplete information are nonclean claims for purposes of processing timeliness standards. Develop the missing information directly with the DME supplier.

When written development is necessary, advise the supplier (or in nonassigned claims, the beneficiary) and stress to the claimant that no payment can be made unless the treating physician provides satisfactory evidence of medical necessity within 45 days.

4105.2 Evidence of Medical Necessity.—A physician prescription (order) which has been signed and dated by the treating physician is required to be kept on file by the supplier for all Durable Medical Equipment, Prosthetic, and Orthotic Supplies (DMEPOS) items. Prescriptions (orders) must include:

- Beneficiary's name and full address;
- Physician's signature (not a stamped signature);
- Date physician signed order;
- Description of the items including all options or additional features which will be billed separately or will require an upgraded code;
- Start date of order (if appropriate); and
- Diagnosis (if specified in policies);

It should also include where appropriate:

- Any other information such as medical necessity;
- Length of medical necessity (for rental items that do not have a Certificate of Medical Necessity (CMN) or supplies with ongoing use); and
- Explanation of how item(s) is/are to be used.

For certain items of DME (as described in section 3312), a CMN is required to be submitted with the claim. Other items may require the prescription to be filed with the claim. Carriers must regularly notify the supplier community which items need a CMN and which items need a prescription filed with the claim.

If replacement supplies are needed for the therapeutic use of purchased DMEPOS, the treating physician must specify on the prescription, or on the CMN, the type of supplies needed and the frequency with which they must be replaced, used, or consumed. Evaluate supply utilization information as part of your medical necessity determination for DMEPOS. Do not accept "PRN" or "as needed" utilization estimates for supply replacement, use, or consumption.

Absent a State law to the contrary *or* a supply utilization problem, the prescription or physician's certification submitted for the DMEPOS may also serve as medical evidence for supply replacement claims. However, when a prescription for DMEPOS is renewed or revised, supply utilization information must be specified or updated by the physician on the CMN. Assess the continuing medical necessity.

Establish procedures for monitoring the utilization of replacement supplies. Inform suppliers of the need to submit updated medical information if the patient's condition materially changes the equipment, device, or supply utilization requirements. Absent such notification, do not allow bills for unexplained increases in supply utilization above the usage level you previously determined as medically necessary. Suppliers must provide this information with the claim where indicated in published policy or to make it available to the DMERC on request.

If necessary or appropriate for your medical necessity determination, ask the supplier to obtain documentation from the treating physician, establishing the severity of the patient's condition and the immediate and long term need for the equipment and the therapeutic benefits the patient is expected to realize from its use. Do not accept a claim of therapeutic effectiveness or benefit based on speculation or theory alone. When restoration of function is cited as a reason for use of DMEPOS, the exact nature of the deformity or medical problem should be clear from the medical evidence submitted. Also, the manner in which the equipment or device will restore or improve the bodily function should be explained by the treating physician.

If you are unsuccessful in obtaining medical information from the supplier for non-assigned claims, give the beneficiary the opportunity to obtain the desired information from the supplier. If, after obtaining the requested information, a question of medical necessity remains, have your medical staff resolve the issue.

Also, be alert to certifications signed by physicians who are under sanction. In addition, be alert to claims submitted for referring physicians identified in the SADMERC abstract.

A. Period of Medical Necessity.—Your file must be documented to show how the period of medical necessity was established. You need not develop the period of medical necessity in the case of inexpensive purchased equipment.

The period of medical necessity for *home dialysis equipment* must be specified, e.g., "at least x months." Situations may occur causing temporary nonuse of equipment:

- Beneficiary requires in-facility treatment for restabilization or as a result of some acute condition. The beneficiary is expected to return to home dialysis.
- Beneficiary is temporarily without a suitable home dialysis assistant.
- Beneficiary is away from home but expects to return.
- Beneficiary is a transplant candidate and is taken off home dialysis preparatory to transplant. (If the transplant cannot occur, or if the transplant is not successful, the patient will very likely resume home dialysis and an evaluation can be made whether it will be within the immediate or foreseeable future.)

Under such circumstances, determine that medical necessity exists and pay for a period of up to 3 months after the month home dialysis equipment was last used. This does not eliminate the necessity for periodic reevaluation of medical necessity. It provides a tolerance to avoid frequent reevaluation in renal dialysis situations and provides for continuity of payments where economically advantageous.

B. Safeguards in Making Monthly Payments.—Establish appropriate safeguards to assure that payments are not made beyond the last month of medical necessity. Develop appropriate safeguards to identify and investigate the following:

- Multiple claims for rental of the same or similar equipment from the same supplier within the same rental month (e.g., rental claims with different start dates but within the same rental period);
- Contraindicated items of rented or purchased equipment;
- Incompatible claims information (e.g., liquid oxygen contents billed for a purchased gas delivery system);
- Medical equipment rentals or purchases after a beneficiary's death;
- Rental start dates on or after the purchase of the same or comparable equipment (absent evidence that the beneficiary has disposed of purchased equipment);
- Rental claims for the same or similar equipment from different suppliers for the same or overlapping rental months; and
- Equipment rental start dates within periods of confinement in an institution that cannot be considered a patient's home.

Resolve these situations on a prepayment bases. Development, if necessary, may be via written or telephone contact per section

3311, subject to any other documentation or development guidelines specified in section 4105ff.

To the extent possible, give beneficiaries and supplier-assignees advance notice of the date and reason that payments are scheduled to stop. (See section 7012ff. for EOMB language.)

4107 DURABLE MEDICAL EQUIPMENT BILLING AND PAYMENT CONSIDERATIONS UNDER THE FEE SCHEDULE

The Omnibus Budget Reconciliation Act of 1987 requires that payment for DME, prosthetics and orthotics be made under fee schedules effective January 1, 1989. The allowable charge is limited to the lower of the actual charge for the equipment, or the fee schedule amount. The equipment is categorized into one of six classes:

- Inexpensive or other routinely purchased DME;
- Items requiring frequent and substantial servicing;
- Customized items;
- Prosthetic and orthotic devices;
- Capped rental items; or
- Oxygen and oxygen equipment.

The fee schedule allowances for each class are determined in accord with section 5102ff.

4107.1 General Billing and Claims Processing—Subject to some of the specific billing and processing requirements, bills are to be submitted, processed and paid in accordance with section 4105ff. and 5102ff.

You are responsible for processing outpatient and noninstitutional claims for DME and oxygen previously paid by fiscal intermediaries to hospitals, CORFs, SNFs, and OPT providers. Prosthetic, orthotic, and inpatient DME and oxygen claims, however, continue to be billed by these providers to their FIs. You will not receive any claims from HHAs which have transferred to regional home health intermediaries (RHHIs). Issue billing numbers as necessary and pay the appropriate fee schedule amounts. If the item billed is in the capped rental category, develop with the beneficiary or assignee, as appropriate, to determine the length of time the beneficiary has continuously rented the item. Process in accordance with section 4107.4.

Payable bills or claims must specify whether equipment is rented or purchased. For purchased equipment, the itemized bill or claim must also indicate whether equipment is new or used. If the supplier fails to indicate on an assigned claim whether equipment was new or used, assume purchased equipment is used and process the claim accordingly, i.e., pay on the basis of the used purchase fee. If an unassigned purchase claim does not specify whether the item was new or used, develop the claim in accordance with section 3311.

4107.2 Rent/Purchase Decisions.—For services provided on or after October 1, 1988, discontinue making rent/purchase decisions on rental claims. (See section 5101.2.) For purchase claims with dates of service before January 1, 1989, continue to make rent/purchase decisions. Discontinue making rent/purchase decisions for purchase claims with dates of service on or after January 1, 1989. Do not pay for oxygen delivery systems, items requiring frequent and substantial servicing or capped rental items that were purchased on or after June 1, 1989.

4107.3 Comparability and Inherent Reasonableness Limitations.—For services provided on or after January 1, 1989, do not apply the comparable circumstances provision in section 5026. Also, for services provided between January 1, 1989 and December 31, 1990, do not apply the special payment limitation provisions in section 5246 to DME and orthotics/prosthetics subject to the fee schedules in section 5102ff.

4107.4 15 Month Ceiling on Capped Rental Items.—Ensure that your system accurately computes the 15 month period for capped rental items. (See section 5102.1E3 and 5102.3C1 and 2.)

4107.5 Transcutaneous Electrical Nerve Stimulator (TENS).—To permit an attending physician time to determine whether purchase of a TENS unit is medically appropriate, ensure that your system allows no more than 10 percent of the fee schedule purchase amount for up to 2 months of rental prior to purchase. Do not apply the rentals toward the purchase allowance.

4107.6 Written Order Prior to Delivery.—Ensure that your system will pay for the equipment listed below only when the supplier has a written order in hand prior to delivery. Otherwise, do not pay for that item even if a written order is subsequently furnished. However, you can pay for a similar item if it is subsequently provided by an unrelated supplier which has a written order in hand prior to delivery. The HCPCS codes for the equipment requiring a written order are:

• E0180	• E0190
• E0181	• E0192
• E0182	• E0195
• E0183	• E0620
• E0184	• E0720
• E0185	• E0730
• E0188	• E1230
• E0189	

4107.7 Special Requirements for Oxygen Claims.—There are a number of billing considerations for oxygen claims. The chart in section 4107.9 indicates what is payable under which situation.

A. Monthly Billing.—Fee schedule payments for stationary oxygen system rentals are all inclusive and represent a monthly allowance per beneficiary. Accordingly, a supplier must bill on a monthly basis for stationary oxygen equipment and contents furnished during a rental month.

A portable equipment add-on is also payable when portable oxygen is prescribed and you determine it to be medically necessary in accordance with Medicare coverage requirements. The portable add-on must be claimed in order to be paid. (See section 4107.10.)

Claims may be submitted when expenses are incurred for initial rentals of oxygen systems, or no sooner than the monthly anniversary date in the case of an established oxygen patient. In the latter situation, suppliers must indicate the monthly volume of oxygen contents delivered, rounded in accordance with subsection D3,

Where the beneficiary has purchased a stationary system (other than a concentrator and/or a portable delivery system), oxygen contents must be billed and paid on a monthly basis, except for unassigned oxygen contents claims submitted by a beneficiary. For beneficiary filed claims, allow, on a claim-by-claim basis, the submitted charge until the applicable monthly fee for oxygen contents has been met.

B. Reduced Number of HCPCS Codes.—The number of HCPCS codes for billing of oxygen claims have been reduced. See section 4107.9 for the codes and their definitions.

C. Use of Payment Modifiers.—The monthly payment amount for stationary oxygen is subject to adjustment depending on the amount of oxygen prescribed (liters per minute (LPM)), and whether or not portable oxygen is also prescribed. (See section 5102.1.) To make proper payment adjustments, supplier claims must indicate the appropriate HCPCS modifier described below, if applicable. On unassigned claims, suppliers should indicate this information on the itemized bill.

- If the prescribed amount of oxygen is less than 1 LPM, the modifier is "QE". Reduce the monthly payment amount for stationary oxygen by 50 percent.
- If the prescribed amount of oxygen is greater than 4 LPM, the modifier is "QG". Increase the monthly payment amount for stationary oxygen by 50 percent. Conduct prepayment medical review of these claims.
- If the prescribed amount of oxygen exceeds 4 LPM and portable oxygen is prescribed, the modifier is "QF". Increase the monthly

payment for stationary oxygen by the higher of 50 percent of the monthly stationary oxygen payment amount, or the fee schedule amount for the portable oxygen add-on. (See section 5102.1.F2j.) Conduct a prepayment medical review of these claims.

D. Units Required.—Excluding concentrators, suppliers must furnish units of oxygen contents in Item 24F of their HCFA-1500 claims, or the itemized bill furnished to the beneficiary for unassigned claims.

1. Initial Oxygen Claims.—When submitting an initial claim for rental of a gaseous or liquid oxygen delivery system, units of oxygen contents furnished for the first month need not be indicated. Base your payment upon the lower of the actual charge for the initial rental month or the monthly payment amount.

2. Subsequent Oxygen Claims.—For dates of service subsequent to the initial rental month, suppliers should indicate actual content usage for the month billed or, if billed prospectively, the actual content usage during the previous rental month, rounded in accordance with subsection D3. Base your payment determination on the lower of the actual charge submitted or the monthly payment amount.

For applying these instructions, treat claims submitted under recertifications of continuing and uninterrupted need for oxygen therapy as subsequent claims if a change in suppliers is not involved.

If a change in suppliers has occurred, apply the initial rule in subsection D.1 above for specifying oxygen contents delivered for the initial rental month by the new supplier.

Develop subsequent rental claims for gaseous or liquid oxygen delivery systems that do not include "unit" information. (See section 3311.)

3. Rounding of Oxygen Contents.—For stationary gas system rentals, suppliers should indicate, in item 24F of the HCFA-1500, oxygen contents in unit multiples of 50 cubic feet, rounded to the nearest increment of 50. For example, if 73 cubic feet of oxygen was delivered during the rental month, the item 24F unit entry "01" indicates the nearest 50 cubic foot increment. For stationary liquid systems, units of contents should be specified in multiples of 10 pounds of liquid contents delivered, rounded to the nearest 10 pound increment. For example, if 63 pounds of liquid oxygen were delivered during the applicable rental month billed, the unit entry "06" is made in Item 24F. For units of portable contents only (i.e., no stationary gas or liquid system used), round to the nearest five cubic feet or one liquid pound, respectively.

Periodically audit supplier records to verify that gaseous and liquid content usage is reported correctly.

E. Conserving Device Modifier.—Suppliers must indicate if an oxygen conserving device is being used with an oxygen delivery system by using HCPCS modifier "QH".

4107.8 EOMB Messages.—The following EOMB messages are suggested: (See section 7012ff. for other applicable messages.)

A. General

- "This is the maximum approved amount for this item." (Use when payment is reduced for a line item.)

B. Inexpensive/Frequently Purchased Equipment

- "The total approved amount for this item is ________ whether this item is purchased or rented." (Use in first month.)
- "This is your next to last rental payment."
- "This is your last rental payment."
- "This item has been rented up to the Medicare payment limit."
- "The approved amount has been reduced by the previously approved rental amounts."

C. Items Requiring Frequent and Substantial Servicing.—Use the general rental messages in section 4107.8A, if applicable. If the beneficiary has purchased the item prior to June 1, 1989, follow section 7014.6. If the beneficiary purchased an item in this category on or after June 1, 1989, use the following message:

- "This equipment can only be paid for on a rental basis."

D. Customized Items and Other Prosthetic and Orthotic Devices

- "The total approved amount for this item is ________."

E. Capped Rental Items

- "Under a provision of Medicare law, monthly rental payments for this item can continue for up to 15 months from the first rental month or until the equipment is no longer needed, whichever comes first."
- "If you no longer are using this equipment or have recently moved and will rent this item from a different supplier, please contact our office." (Use on beneficiary's EOMB.)
- "This is your next to last rental payment."
- "This is your last rental payment."
- "This item has been rented up to the 15 month Medicare payment limit."
- "Your equipment supplier must supply and service this item for as long as you continue to need it."
- "Medicare cannot pay for maintenance and/or servicing of this item until 6 months have elapsed since the end of the 15th paid rental month."

If the beneficiary purchased a capped rental item prior to June 1, 1989, follow section 7014.6. If the beneficiary purchased a capped rental item on or after June 1, 1989, use the following denial message:

- "This equipment can only be paid for on a rental basis."

F. Oxygen and Oxygen Equipment

- "The monthly allowance includes payment for all covered oxygen contents and supplies."
- "Payment for the amount of oxygen supplied has been reduced or denied based on the patient's medical condition." (To supplier after medical review.)
- "The approved amount has been reduced to the amount allowable for medically necessary oxygen therapy." (To beneficiary.)
- "Payment denied because the allowance for this item is included in the monthly payment amount."
- "Payment denied because Medicare oxygen coverage requirements are not met."

If the beneficiary purchased an oxygen system prior to June 1, 1989, follow section 7014.6. If the beneficiary purchased an oxygen system on or after June 1, 1989, use the following denial message:

- "This item can only be paid for on a rental basis."

G. Items Requiring a Written Order Prior to Delivery

- "Payment is denied because the supplier did not obtain a written order from your doctor prior to the delivery of this item."

4107.9 Oxygen HCPCS Codes Effective 1/1/89

NEW	OLD	DEFINITION
Q0036 See notes (1) and (8)	E1377–E1385, E1397	Oxygen concentrator, high humidity
Q0038 See note (2)	E0400, E0405	Oxygen contents, gaseous, per unit (for use with owned gaseous stationary systems or when both a stationary and portable gaseous system are owned; 1 unit = 50 cu ft)
Q0039 See note (2)	E0410, E04150	Oxygen contents, liquid, per unit (for use with owned stationary liquid systems or when both a stationary and portable liquid system are owned; 1 unit = 10 lb)

Table continued on following page

NEW	OLD	DEFINITION
Q0040 See note (2)	E0416	Portable oxygen contents, per unit (for use only with portable gaseous systems when no stationary gas system is used; 1 unit = 5 cu ft)
Q0041 See note (2)	None	Portable oxygen contents, liquid, per unit (for use only with portable liquid systems when no stationary liquid system is used; 1 unit = 1 lb)
Q0042 See note (3)	E0425	Stationary compressed, gas system rental, includes contents (per unit), regulator with flow gauge, humidifier, nebulizer, cannula or mask and tubing; 1 unit = 50 cu ft
E0425 See notes (4) and (8)	Same	No change
E0430 See notes (8) and (9)	Same	No change
E0435 See notes (7) and (8)	Same	No change in terminology, but see note (7).
Q0043 See note (3)	E0440	Stationary liquid oxygen system rental, includes contents (per unit), use of reservoir, contents indicator, flowmeter, humidifier, nebulizer, cannula or mask and tubing; 1 unit of contents = 10 lb
0440 See note (4)	Same	No change
E0455 See note (6)	Same	No change
E0555 See note (6)	Same	No change
E0580 See note (6)	Same	No change
E1351 See note (6)	Same	No change
E1352 See note (6)	Same	No change
E1353 See notes (6) and (8)	Same	No change
E1354 See note (6)	Same	No change
E1371 See note (6)	Same	No change
E1374 See note (6)	Same	No change
E1400 See notes (1) and (8)	E1388–E1396	Same as Q0014
E1401 See notes (1) and (8)	E1388–E1396	Same as Q0015
E1402	Same	No change
E1403	Same	No change
E1404	Same	No change
E1405 See note (10)	Q0037	Combine the fee schedule amounts for the stationary oxygen system and the nebulizer with a compressor and heater (code E0585) to determine the fee schedule amount to apply to oxygen enrichers with a heater (code E1405)
E1406	Q0037	Combine the fee schedule amounts for the stationary oxygen system and the nebulizer with only a compressor (i.e., without a heater, code E0570) to determine the fee schedule amount to apply to oxygen enrichers without a heater (code E1406)

NOTES:

(1) For billing concentrator rentals or purchases

(2) For monthly billing of contents used with purchased gas or liquid oxygen delivery systems (i.e., no stationary system is being rented)

(3) For billing gas or liquid system rentals only

(4) For billing of purchased stationary gas or liquid systems

(5) For billing the portable add-on for liquid systems

(6) For billing of replacement items for oxygen delivery systems purchased prior to 6/1/89

(7) For services furnished on or after 6/1/89, use E0435 when only portable liquid is prescribed (i.e., no stationary liquid system prescribed) or both stationary and portable oxygen were prescribed but the patient uses a stationary system other than a liquid system (e.g., stationary system is concentrator)

(8) Do not pay for oxygen systems purchased on or after 6/1/89

(9) For billing the portable add-on for gas systems

(10) For billing of rental oxygen and water vapor enriching systems only.

4118 CHIROPRACTIC SERVICES

A. Verification of Chiropractor's Qualifications.—Establish a reference file of chiropractors eligible for payment as physicians under the criteria in section 2020.26. Pay only chiropractors on file. Information needed to establish such files is furnished by the RO.

The RO is notified by the appropriate State agency by which chiropractors are licensed and whether each meets the national uniform standards.

B. Documentation.—In addition to a statement of the diagnosis and symptoms and other pertinent information required to process a claim for a physician's services, the claim and/or attachments involving chiropractic treatment must:

- Specify the precise spinal level of subluxation (see section 2251.4A) giving rise to the diagnosis and symptoms;
- Contain a certification on all bills by the treating chiropractor that an X-ray film (including the date of the film) is available for your review demonstrating the existence of a subluxation at the specified level of the spine. If the beneficiary refuses to have the X-ray, the chiropractor should bill using HCPCS code A9170, Noncovered Service by a Chiropractor, and the claim should be denied as a technical denial; and
- Include identification of the treatment phase and adjustment, e.g., second, fifth, tenth treatment.

The following Medicare Summary Notice (MSN)/Explanation of Medicare Benefits (EOMB) message should be generated:

"This service is covered only when recent x-rays support the need for the service."# (MSN message 3.1.)

"Medicare pays for the services of a chiropractor only when "recent"# x-rays support the need for the services. Recent means the x-rays were taken within the last 12 months."# (EOMB message 3.1.)

On the provider remittance, use existing American National Standard Institute (ANSI) X12-835 claims adjustment reason code 96, noncovered charges. In addition, install and include the following new line level remark code M111, "We do not pay for chiropractic manipulative treatment when the beneficiary refuses to have an x-ray taken."#

EFFECTIVE FOR CLAIMS WITH DATES OF SERVICE ON AND AFTER JANUARY 1, 2000, THE X-RAY IS NO LONGER REQUIRED.

C. Claims Review

1. Condition Consistent with Treatment

a. Do not pay for manual manipulation of the spine in treating conditions other than those indicated in sections 2251.3 and 2251.4.

b. Deny claims for treatment of any condition not reasonable related to a subluxation involving vertebrae at the spinal level specified.

c. Claims for treatment exceeding the carrier's utilization parameters established per section 2251.5 should be questioned or denied in accordance with established procedures.

2. X-ray Review

a. Carriers should conduct postpayment reviews of X-rays on a sample basis. Prepayment review should be undertaken in all questionable cases.

b. It is the responsibility of the treating chiropractor to make the documenting X-ray(s) available to the carrier's review staff. If X-rays are not made available, or suggest a pattern in failing to demonstrate subluxations for any reason, including unacceptable technical quality, the carrier should conduct prepayment review of X-rays in 100 percent of the subsequent claims for treatments by the practitioner involved until satisfied the deficiency will no longer occur. Where there is no X-ray documentation of subluxation on prepayment review, the claims, of course, should be denied.

c. The X-ray film(s) must have been taken at a time reasonably proximate to the initiation of the course of treatment and must demonstrate a subluxation at the level of the spine specified by the treating chiropractor on the claim (section 2251.4)

d. An X-ray obtained by the chiropractor for his own diagnostic purposes before commencing treatment should suffice for claims documentation purposes. However, when subluxations were for treatment purposes diagnosed by some other means and X-rays are taken to satisfy Medicare's documentation requirement, carriers should ask chiropractors to cone in on the site of the subluxation in producing X-rays. Such a practice would not only minimize the exposure of the patient but should result in a film more clearly portraying the subluxation.

e. An X-ray will be considered of acceptable technical quality if any individual trained in the reading of X-rays could recognize a subluxation if present.

f. When claims have been denied because the X-ray(s) initially offered failed to document the existence of a subluxation requiring treatment, no review of these decisions should be undertaken on the basis of X-ray(s) subsequently taken. Permitting such reviews could be an inducement to excessive exposure of patients to radiation in cases where the decision to treat was made despite X-rays that did not show a subluxation.

4120 FOOT CARE

4120.1 Application of Foot Care Exclusions to Physicians' Services.—The exclusion of foot care is determined by the nature of the service (section 2323). Thus, reimbursement for an excluded service should be denied whether performed by a podiatrist, osteopath, or a doctor of medicine, and without regard to the difficulty or complexity of the procedure.

When an itemized bill shows both covered services and noncovered services not integrally related to the covered service, the portion of charges attributable to the noncovered services should be denied. (For example, if an itemized bill shows surgery for an ingrown toenail and also removal of calluses not necessary for the performance of toe surgery, any additional charge attributable to removal of the calluses should be denied.)

In reviewing claims involving foot care, the carrier should be alert to the following exceptional situations:

1. Payment may be made for incidental noncovered services performed as a necessary and integral part of, and secondary to, a covered procedure. For example, if trimming of toenails is required for application of a cast to a fractured foot, the carrier need not allocate and deny a portion of the charge for the trimming of the nails. However, a separately itemized charge for such excluded service should be disallowed. When the primary procedure is covered the administration of anesthesia necessary for the performance of such procedure is also covered.

2. Payment may be made for initial diagnostic services performed in connection with a specific symptom or complaint if it seems likely that its treatment would be covered even though the resulting diagnosis may be one requiring only noncovered care.

3. Payment may be made for routine-type foot care such as cutting or removal of corns, calluses, or nails when the patient has a systemic disease of sufficient severity that unskilled performance of such procedure would be hazardous (section 2323C).

a. Claims for such routine services would show in item 7D of the SSA-1490 the complicating systemic disease. Where these services were rendered by a podiatrist this item should also include the name of the MD or DO who diagnosed the complicating condition. In those cases where active care is required, the approximate date the beneficiary was last seen by such physician must also be indicated.

NOTE: Section 939 of P.L. 96-499 removed "warts" from the routine foot care exclusion effective July 1, 1981.

b. Relatively few claims for routine-type care are anticipated considering the severity of conditions contemplated as the basis for this exception. Claims for this type of foot care should not be paid in the absence of convincing evidence that nonprofessional performance of the service would have been hazardous for the beneficiary because of an underlying systemic disease. The mere statement of a diagnosis such as those mentioned in section 2323C does not of itself indicate the severity of the condition. Where development is indicated to verify diagnosis and/or severity the carrier should follow existing claims processing practices which may include review of carrier's history and medical consultation as well as physician contacts.

c. A presumption of coverage may be made by the carrier where the claim or other evidence available discloses certain physical and/or clinical findings consistent with the diagnosis and indicative of severe peripheral involvement. For purposes of applying this presumption, the following findings are pertinent:

Class A Findings
—Nontraumatic amputation of foot or integral skeletal portion thereof
Class B Findings
—Absent posterior tibial pulse
—Advanced trophic changes as (three required): hair growth (decrease or absence); nail changes (thickening); pigmentary changes (discoloration); skin texture (thin, shiny); skin color (rubor or redness)
—Absent dorsalis pedis pulse

Class C Findings
—Claudication
—Temperature changes (e.g., cold feet)
—Edema
—Paresthesia (abnormal spontaneous sensations in the feet)
—Burning

The presumption of coverage may be applied when the physician rendering the routine foot care has identified: (1) a Class A finding; (2) two of the Class B findings; or (3) one Class B and two Class C findings. Case evidencing findings falling short of these alternatives may involve podiatric treatment that may constitute covered care and should be reviewed by the carrier's medical staff and developed as necessary.

For purposes of applying the coverage presumption where the routine services have been rendered by a podiatrist, the carrier may deem the active care requirement met if the claim or other evidence available discloses that the patient has seen an MD or DO for treatment and/or evaluation of the complicating disease process during the 6-month period prior to the rendition of the routine-type service or had come under such care shortly after the services were furnished usually as a result of a referral.

4120.2 Application of the "Reasonable and Necessary" Limitation to Foot Care Services.—In evaluating claims for foot care services, in addition to determining whether any of the other statutory limitations apply, carriers should assure that payment is made only for services which are "reasonable and necessary" for diagnosis or treatment of an illness or injury or to improve the functioning of a malformed body member. (See section 2303.) Determinations as to whether a foot care service is reasonable and necessary should be made on the same basis as all other such determinations—that is, with the advice of medical consultants and with reference to accepted standards of medical practice and the circumstances of the individual case. With appropriate professional consultation, guidelines should be established concerning the scope, frequency, and duration of services which would constitute reasonable and necessary utilization of services for various foot conditions; these guidelines should be used to screen out for denial, claims in which the services billed would clearly not be reasonable and necessary and to screen out questionable cases for special review or further development.

For example, infections of the feet and toenails which cause pain or deformity of sufficient degree to markedly limit ambulation may require a variety of medical services such as physical examination, and laboratory tests for the purpose of diagnosing the existence and type of infectious condition (and differentiating it from other types of dermatoses), prescription of a regimen of treatment, periodic examinations throughout the course of treatment to evaluate the status of the lesion and watch for complicating factors, and active treatment by one or a combination of the following modalities:

(1) surgical excision (avulsion) of the affected nail(s);
(2) mechanical debridement of the lesion;
(3) topical treatment; or
(4) systemic treatment.

With the appropriate advice from physicians who treat foot infections (e.g., dermatologists, podiatrists and surgeons), guidelines should be developed concerning accepted standards of medical practice with respect to appropriate utilization of the above types of services for different types of infectious conditions, taking into account such factors as the indications for various modalities of treatment, the required duration of different courses of therapy, and the required frequency of follow-up evaluation examinations. For example, when a physician prescribes a topical medication for an infection, patients are usually expected to perform most of the treatment by themselves at home (or if residing in nursing homes or skilled nursing facilities, etc., the staff of the facility is expected to perform most of the treatment), with perhaps occasional follow-up visits to (or by) the physician for eval-uation of the status of the lesion. As part of the initial diagnostic and follow-up evaluation visits, the physician may cleanse the lesion and apply medication and these services would, of course, be covered where they are an accepted integral component of such visits; however, if the patient regularly comes to the physician to receive the care which he is expected to perform himself at home and there are no special medical circumstances relating to the infection warranting such special care, this would represent excessive utilization of physicians' services and should be excluded.

Carriers' utilization guidelines should enable them to identify where a course of therapy involves more frequent follow-up visits than are the accepted standards of physician care for that modality of therapy and to deny payment for such excessive visits unless there is documentation of special medical circumstances relating to the infection justifying the extra visits. For instance, in the case of claims for patients whose initial course of treatment includes a medically necessary visit to the physician for mechanical debridement of a mycotic lesion of the toenail, carriers must use a 60-day claims processing screen for identifying excessive follow-up services for the patient (i.e., the presumption would be that only one follow-up visit is covered every 60 days following the end of the initial treatment period unless medical documentation is submitted that supports more frequent visits). Similarly, utilization guidelines should identify when visits extend beyond the period of follow-up evaluation which is the accepted standard for a particular course of treatment for an infection and to deny payment for visits beyond the period unless development reveals complications in the infectious condition necessitating more prolonged treatment.

4172.6 Exempt CRNAs at Rural Hospitals.—Recent legislation provides for continuation of the nonphysician anesthetist pass-through in certain hospitals located in rural areas beginning January 1, 1989, and continuing through the end of calendar year 1991. Hospitals have until April 1, 1989 to establish to the Fiscal Intermediary's satisfaction that they meet specific qualifying criteria for this exemption. FIs will inform you of the names of CRNAs, AAs, and the hospitals who qualify or are in the process of qualifying for the exemption. During the qualifying period, and once the exemption is granted, FIs will continue reimbursement under the pass-through method. Institute appropriate edits to detect duplicate billings in these situations. In the event a hospital's attempt to qualify for the exemption is ultimately denied, the hospital, CRNA, or AA may then bill you for services retroactive to January 1, 1989, in accordance with the procedures in section 4172ff.

4182 PROSTATE CANCER SCREENING TESTS AND PROCEDURES

The following sections summarize coverage requirements and detail claims processing procedures for prostate cancer screening tests and procedures.

4182.1 Coverage Summary.—Sections 1861(s)(2)(P) and 1861(oo) of the Social Security Act (as added by section 4103 of the Balanced Budget Act of 1997), provide for coverage of certain prostate cancer screening tests and procedures subject to certain coverage, frequency, and payment limitations. Effective for services furnished on or after January 1, 2000, Medicare will cover prostate cancer screening tests and procedures for the early detection of prostate cancer. Coverage currently consists of the following tests and procedures furnished to an individual for the early detection of prostate cancer:

A. Screening Digital Rectal Examination.—This test is a clinical examination of an individual's prostate for nodules or other abnormalities of the prostate; and

B. Screening Prostate Specific Antigen (PSA) Blood Test.—This test detects the marker for adenocarcinoma of the prostate.

For more information regarding coverage of prostate cancer screening tests and procedures, refer to section 50-55 of the *Coverage Issues Manual.*

HCPCS Code; Type of Service (TOS)	Description	Payment	
		Requirements	Methodology/Fee Schedule
G0102; TOS = 1	Prostate cancer screening; digital rectal examination	1. Performed on a male Medicare beneficiary aged 50 or older 2. Performed by one of the following: a. Doctor of medicine or osteopathy b. Qualified physician assistant c. Qualified nurse practitioner d. Qualified clinical nurse specialist e. Qualified certified nurse midwife 3. Performed at a frequency no greater than once every 12 months (See section 4182.4).	1. Refer to the physician's fee schedule. 2. Apply deductible and coinsurance. 3. Claims from physicians for these examinations where assignment was not taken are subject to the Medicare limiting charge. (See section 7555).
G0103; TOS = 5	Prostate cancer screening; PSA test	1. Performed on a male Medicare beneficiary aged 50 or older 2. Ordered by the beneficiary's attending: a. Physician (doctor of medicine or osteopathy) b. Qualified physician assistant c. Qualified nurse practitioner d. Qualified clinical nurse specialist e. Qualified certified nurse midwife 3. Performed at a frequency no greater than once every 12 months. (See section 4182.4.)	1. Refer to the clinical laboratory fee schedule; payment for this test is the same as for code "84153, PSA; total." 2. Do not apply deductible and co-insurance.

4182.2 Requirements for Submitting Claims.—Submit claims for prostate cancer screening tests on Health Insurance Claim Form HCFA-1500 or electronic equivalent. Follow the general instructions in section 2010, Purpose of Health Insurance Claim Form HCFA-1500, *Medicare Carriers Manual*, Part 4, Chapter 2.

4182.3 HCPCS Codes and Payment Requirements.—The following table lists coverable codes and services for prostate cancer screening tests and procedures. Pay for these services according to the appropriate fee schedule when all of the requirements noted are met.

4182.4 Calculating the Frequency.—Once a beneficiary has received any (or all) of the covered prostate cancer screening test/procedures, he may receive another (or all) of such test/procedures after 11 full months have passed. To determine the 11-month period, start your count beginning with the month after the month in which any (or all) of the previous covered screening test/procedures was performed.

Example: The beneficiary received a screening PSA test in January 2000. Start your count beginning February 2000. The beneficiary is eligible to receive another screening PSA test in January 2001 (the month after 11 months have passed.)

4182.5 CWF Edits.—Effective for dates of service January 1, 2000, and later, CWF will edit prostate cancer screening tests and procedures for age, frequency, sex, and valid HCPCS code.

4273 CLAIMS FOR PAYMENT FOR EPOETIN ALFA (EPO)

Effective June 1, 1989, the drug EPO is covered under Part B if administered incident to a physician's services. EPO is used to treat anemia associated with chronic renal failure, including patients on dialysis and those who are not on dialysis.

4273.2 Completion of Subsequent Claims for EPO.—Subsequent claims include the following:

A. Diagnoses

B. Hematocrit or Hemoglobin.—This is indicated by the appropriate Q code. Claims include an EJ modifier to the Q code. This allows you to identify subsequent claims which do not require as much information as initial claims and prevent unnecessary development.

C. Number of Units Administered.—See section 4273.1 for a description of these items. Subsequent claims may be submitted electronically. See section 3023.7 for including the number of units in standard format EMC claims.

5102.2 Other Issues.—

A. Minimum Data Requirements for Fee Schedule.—

1. For items with fees calculated under the methodology of section 5102.1.A, B, or D.

a. If you have data for at least four suppliers who have at least three charges each, accept the fee schedule calculated on that data.

b. If you have charge data, but less than the threshold level, establish the fee schedule amounts at 1.017 times the average of the adjusted prevailing charges (including gap-filled prevailing charges) in effect on January 1, 1987 and December 21, 1986.

c. If you have no charge data, establish the fee schedule amounts at 1.017 times the average of gap-filled prevailing charge amounts in effect on December 31, 1986 and January 1, 1987, if calculated.

2. Gap-fill the fee schedule for items for which charge data were unavailable during the 1986–87 data base period using the fee schedule amounts for comparable equipment, using properly calculated fee schedule amounts from a neighboring carrier, or using supplier price lists with prices in effect during the data base year, adjusted by a factor of 1.017 to approximate the original fee schedule amount. Mail order catalogs are particularly suitable sources of price information for items such as urological and ostomy supplies which require constant replacement. If the only available price information is from a period other than the base period, apply the following deflation factors against current pricing in order to approximate the base year price for gap-filling purposes:

Price In Effect Date	Oxygen	Deflation Factors Equipment Category Prosthetics and Orthotics, Items that Require Frequent Servicing, and Inexpensive Capped Rental	and Routinely Purchased Items
June 1987	.965	.971	.973
June 1988	.971	.934	.936
June 1989	.882	.888	.890
June 1990	.843	.848	.851

After deflation, the result must be increased by 1.7 percent and by the cumulative covered item update to complete the gap-filling (i.e., an additional 3.7 percent for a 1991 DME fee).

Note that when gap-filling for capped rental items, it is necessary to first gap-fill the purchase price, then compute the base period fee schedule at 10 percent of the base period purchase price.

For used equipment, establish fee schedule amounts at 75 percent of the fee schedule amount for new equipment.

3. When gap-filling, for those carrier areas where a sales tax was imposed in the base period, add the applicable sales tax, e.g., 5 percent, to the gap-filled amount where the gap-filled amount does not take into account the sales tax, e.g., where the gap-filled amount is computed from pre-tax price lists or from another carrier area without a sales tax. Likewise, if the gap-filled amount is calculated from another carrier's fees where a sales tax is imposed, adjust the gap-filled amount to reflect the applicable local sales tax circumstances.

B. Replacement.—Replacement of equipment which the beneficiary owns or is purchasing or is a capped rental item is covered in cases of loss or irreparable damage or wear and when required because of a change in the patient's condition subject to the following provisions. Expenses for replacement required because of loss or irreparable damage may be reimbursed without a physician's order when in your judgment the equipment as originally ordered, considering the age of the order, still fills the patient's medical needs. However, support claims involving replacement equipment necessitated because of wear or a change in the patient's condition by a current physician's order. (See section 2306.D in regard to payment for equipment replaced under a warranty.)

Investigate and deny cases suggesting malicious damage, culpable neglect or wrongful disposition of equipment as discussed in section 2100.6 where you determine that it is unreasonable to make program payment under the circumstances. Refer such cases to the program integrity specialist in the RO.

Do not pay for replacement of rented equipment except capped rental items. (See section 5102.1.E.7.) However, pay for replacement of purchased equipment in the following classes: inexpensive or routinely purchased, customized items, capped rental, and other prosthetic and orthotic devices. Do not pay for purchase or replacement of items that require frequent and substantial servicing or oxygen equipment.

C. Transcutaneous Electrical Nerve Stimulator (TENS).—In order to permit an attending physician time to determine whether the purchase of a TENS is medically appropriate for a particular patient, pay 10 percent of the purchase price of the item for each of 2 months. Determine the purchase price and payment for maintenance and servicing under the same rules in section 5102.1.A.

D. Written Order Prior to Delivery.—Pay for certain types of equipment only when the supplier has a written order in hand prior to delivery. You will be provided with a listing of the equipment subject to this restriction. If the written order is not in hand prior to delivery, payment may never be made for that item even if a written order is subsequently furnished. If a similar item is subsequently provided by an unrelated supplier pursuant to a written order in hand prior to delivery, payment may be made.

E. Railroad Claims.—Exclude any railroad retirement claims in computing the fee schedules.

F. Coordination Between Intermediaries and Carriers.—Furnish copies of fee schedules, maintenance and service fees, and updates to Medicare fiscal intermediaries and to the Railroad Retirement Board carrier. Provide schedule updates at least 30 days prior to the scheduled implementation. Fiscal intermediaries use the fee schedules to pay for covered items supplied by hospitals, home health agencies, and other providers. Fiscal intermediaries consult with carriers on filling gaps in fee schedules. You make the final decision on gap-filling amounts.

G. Maintenance and Servicing.—Pay the reasonable and necessary charges for maintenance and servicing of purchased equipment in the following classes: inexpensive or frequently purchased, customized items, other prosthetic and orthotic devices, and capped rental items purchased in accordance with section 5102.1.E.5 or 6. Do not pay for maintenance and servicing of purchased items that require frequent and substantial servicing, or oxygen equipment. Reasonable and necessary charges include only those made for parts and labor that are not otherwise covered under a manufacturer's or supplier's warranty. Pay on a lump-sum, as needed basis based on your individual consideration for that item. Payment may not be made for maintenance and servicing of rented equipment other than the maintenance and servicing fee established for capped rental items in section 5102.1.E.4.

1. Maintenance.—Routine periodic servicing, such as testing, cleaning, regulating, and checking of the beneficiary's equipment, is not covered. Such routine maintenance is generally expected to be done by the owner rather than by a retailer or some other person who charges the beneficiary. Normally, purchasers of DME are given operating manuals which describe the type of servicing an owner may perform to properly maintain the equipment. It is reasonable to expect that beneficiaries will perform this maintenance. Thus, hiring a third party to do such work is for the convenience of the beneficiary and is not covered.

However, more extensive maintenance which, based on the manufacturers' recommendations, is performed by authorized technicians, is covered. This might include, e.g., breaking down sealed components and performing tests which required specialized testing equipment not available to the beneficiary.

2. Servicing.—Servicing of equipment which a beneficiary is purchasing or already owns is covered when necessary to make the equipment serviceable. The service charge may include the use of "loaner" equipment where this is required. If the expense for servicing exceeds the estimated expense of purchasing or renting another item of equipment for the remaining period of medical need, no payment can be made for the amount of the excess. Investigate and deny cases suggesting malicious damage, culpable neglect, or wrongful disposition of equipment as discussed in section 2100.6 where you determine that it is unreasonable to make program payment under the circumstances. Refer such cases to the program integrity specialist in the RO.

5102.3 Transition to Fee Schedule-Relationship to Prior Rules.—

A. Comparability and Inherent Reasonableness Limitations.—Effective January 1, 1989, until further notice, you may no longer apply the comparable circumstances provision contained in section 5026. Between January 1, 1989 and December 31, 1990, you may not apply the special limitations provision contained in section 5246.

B. Purchase of Items Requiring Frequent and Substantial Servicing or Capped Rental Items.—

1. Purchase Prior to January 1, 1989.—If the beneficiary purchased an item of equipment in either of these two categories (see section 5102.1.B or E) prior to January 1, 1989, pay the reasonable and necessary charges for maintenance and servicing of this equipment. In the event the item of equipment needs to be replaced on or after June 1, 1989, pay on a rental basis according to the instructions in section 5102.1.B. or E.

If the beneficiary purchased the equipment even though you determined that rental was more economical under the rent/purchase guidelines, or if the beneficiary made an approved purchase on an installment plan, make payment on an installment basis until the purchase price has been reached or medical necessity terminated. If the purchase price has not been reached by January 1, 1989, continue paying on an installment basis but at the monthly fee schedule amount until the purchase price is reached, the purchase price fee schedule calculated under prior instructions is reached, or the medical necessity ends, whichever occurs first. The limitation on total payments to 15 months rental (as described in section 5102.1.E) does not apply.

2. Purchase on or After June 1, 1989.—If a beneficiary purchased an item of equipment that requires frequent and substantial servicing on or after June 1, 1989, do not make payment. Also, do not make payment for maintenance and servicing or for replacement of items in either category that are purchased on or after June 1, 1989. If a beneficiary purchased an item of equipment in the capped rental category between June 1, 1989 and April 30, 1991, do not make payment. Also, do not make payment for maintenance and servicing. However, see section 5102.1.E.5 or 6 for payment of purchase options after April 30, 1991 and for payment of replacement of items purchased between June 1, 1989 and April 30, 1991.

3. Purchase Between January 1, 1989 and June 1, 1989.—If a beneficiary purchased an item of equipment in either category after December 31, 1988, but before June 1, 1989, pay monthly installments equivalent to the rental fee schedule amounts until the medical necessity ends, the purchase price fee schedule calculated under prior instructions is reached, or the actual purchase charge has been reached, whichever occurs first. Pay the reasonable and necessary charges for maintenance and servicing of this equipment. In the event the item of equipment needs to be replaced on or after June 1, 1989, pay on a rental basis according to the instructions in section 5102.1.B. or E. Payment may be made for purchase even if the purchase was preceded by a period of rental. However, total payments for rental plus purchase of capped rental items may not exceed the amount that would have been paid had the equipment been continuously rented for 15 months. (Therefore, if a purchase occurs during a period of continuous use after 15 months of rentals have been paid, no payment may be made other than the reasonable and necessary charges for servicing as described in section 5102.1.E.4.)

C. Purchase of Oxygen Equipment.—

1. Purchase Prior to June 1, 1989.—If the beneficiary purchased stationary or portable oxygen equipment (see section 5102.1.F) prior to June 1, 1989, pay the reasonable and necessary charges for maintenance and servicing of this equipment. In the event the item of equipment needs to be replaced on or after June 1, 1989, pay on a rental basis according to the instructions in section 5102.1.F.

If the beneficiary purchased the equipment even though you determined that rental was more economical under the rent/purchase guidelines, or if the beneficiary made an approved purchase on an installment plan, make payment on an installment basis until the purchase price had been reached or medical necessity terminated. If the purchase price has not been reached by June 1, 1989, continue paying on an installment basis (see section 5102.1.F.9) but at the monthly fee schedule amount until the purchase price is reached or the medical necessity ends, whichever occurs first.

2. Purchase on or After June 1, 1989.—If a beneficiary purchased stationary or portable oxygen equipment on or after June 1, 1989, do not make payment for the equipment. However, make payment for the contents in accordance with section 5102.1.F.4 or 5. Also, do not make payment for maintenance and servicing or for replacement of oxygen equipment that is purchased on or after June 1, 1989.

D. 15-Month Ceiling.—For purposes of computing the 10-month purchase option or the 15-month period for capped rental items, begin counting the first month that the beneficiary continu-

ously rented the equipment. For example, if the beneficiary began renting the equipment in July 1988, the rental month which begins in January 1989 is counted as the beneficiary's 7th month of rental. Therefore, if the equipment has been continuously rented prior to October 2, 1987, no further rental payments are made since the 15-month period is terminated before January 1, 1989. The maintenance and service provision in section 5102.1.E.4 begins July 1, 1989.

If the beneficiary has reached (on a date of service prior to January 1989) the purchase price limitation on a rental claim, do not make any further purchase or rental payments until the useful life has elapsed according to the instructions in section 5102.1.E.7. However, for capped rental items previously rented that have reached the purchase cap under the rent/purchase rules, pay claims for maintenance and servicing fees in accordance with section 5102.1.E.4 effective July 1, 1989.

E. Oxygen.—Claims for oxygen contents provided after May 31, 1989, but prior to the start of the June equipment rental month, may be paid in either of the following two ways. Either continue paying the reasonable charge payment amount for contents through the end of the May monthly rental period; or pay the reasonable charge payment amount for contents through the end of May and pay the actual charge for contents up to the fee schedule allowance for oxygen contents only as prorated for the period June 1 through the end of the May rental period. Begin paying the appropriate full fee schedule amount at the beginning of the new rental period. For example, a beneficiary's rental period began May 15, 1989. Pay on a reasonable charge basis from May 15 through June 14; or pay on a reasonable charge basis from May 15 through May 31, 1989 and pay the actual charge up to 14/31 of the oxygen contents fee (established in section 5102.1.F.4) from June 1 through June 14, 1989. Pay the lesser of the full fee schedule amount or actual charge beginning June 15, 1989.

F. Purchase Options for Capped Rental Items.—

1. Electric Wheelchairs.—If the beneficiary purchases an electric wheelchair prior to May 1, 1991, pay for the wheelchair as a routinely purchased item in accordance with section 5102.1.A. If the beneficiary elects to rent an electric wheelchair prior to May 1, 1991, pay the rental fee schedule amount not to exceed the purchase price in accordance with section 5102.1.A. If, on May 1, 1991, the purchase price has not been reached, convert the monthly fee schedule amount from routinely purchased to capped rental. As such, each month's rental before and after conversion must be counted toward the 10 month purchase option in section 5102.1.E.6 and the 15 month rental cap in section 5102.1.E.2.

2. All Other Capped Rental Items.—If the beneficiary purchased a capped rental item prior to May 1, 1991, do not make payment. If the beneficiary rented a capped rental item prior to May 1, 1991, pay the rental fee schedule amount not to exceed the 15 month rental cap in accordance with section 5102.1.E.2. Each month's rental must be counted toward the 10 month purchase option in section 5102.1.E.6 and the 15 month rental cap in section 5102.1.E.2.

5102.3 Transition to Fee Schedule-Relationship to Prior Rules.—

A. Comparability and Inherent Reasonableness Limitations.—Effective January 1, 1989, until further notice, you may no longer apply the comparable circumstances provision contained in section 5026. Between January 1, 1989 and December 31, 1990, you may not apply the special limitations provision contained in section 5246.

B. Purchase of Items Requiring Frequent and Substantial Servicing or Capped Rental Items.—

1. Purchase Prior to January 1, 1989.—If the beneficiary purchased an item of equipment in either of these two categories (see section 5102.1.B or E) prior to January 1, 1989, pay the reasonable and necessary charges for maintenance and servicing of this equipment. In the event the item of equipment needs to be re-

placed on or after June 1, 1989, pay on a rental basis according to the instructions in section 5102.1.B. or E.

If the beneficiary purchased the equipment even though you determined that rental was more economical under the rent/purchase guidelines, or if the beneficiary made an approved purchase on an installment plan, make payment on an installment basis until the purchase price has been reached or medical necessity terminated. If the purchase price has not been reached by January 1, 1989, continue paying on an installment basis but at the monthly fee schedule amount until the purchase price is reached, the purchase price fee schedule calculated under prior instructions is reached, or the medical necessity ends, whichever occurs first. The limitation on total payments to 15 months rental (as described in section 5102.1.E) does not apply.

2. Purchase on or After June 1, 1989.—If a beneficiary purchased an item of equipment that requires frequent and substantial servicing on or after June 1, 1989, do not make payment. Also, do not make payment for maintenance and servicing or for replacement of items in either category that are purchased on or after June 1, 1989. If a beneficiary purchased an item of equipment in the capped rental category between June 1, 1989 and April 30, 1991, do not make payment. Also, do not make payment for maintenance and servicing. However, see section 5102.1.E.5 or 6 for payment of purchase options after April 30, 1991 and for payment of replacement of items purchased between June 1, 1989 and April 30, 1991.

3. Purchase Between January 1, 1989 and June 1, 1989—If a beneficiary purchased an item of equipment in either category after December 31, 1988, but before June 1, 1989, pay monthly installments equivalent to the rental fee schedule amounts until the medical necessity ends, the purchase price fee schedule calculated under prior instructions is reached, or the actual purchase charge has been reached, whichever occurs first. Pay the reasonable and necessary charges for maintenance and servicing of this equipment. In the event the item of equipment needs to be replaced on or after June 1, 1989, pay on a rental basis according to the instructions in section 5102.1.B. or E. Payment may be made for purchase even if the purchase was preceded by a period of rental. However, total payments for rental plus purchase of capped rental items may not exceed the amount that would have been paid had the equipment been continuously rented for 15 months. (Therefore, if a purchase occurs during a period of continuous use after 15 months of rentals have been paid, no payment may be made other than the reasonable and necessary charges for servicing as described in section 5102.1.E.4.)

C. Purchase of Oxygen Equipment—

1. Purchase Prior to June 1, 1989.—If the beneficiary purchased stationary or portable oxygen equipment (see section 5102.1.F) prior to June 1, 1989, pay the reasonable and necessary charges for maintenance and servicing of this equipment. In the event the item of equipment needs to be replaced on or after June 1, 1989, pay on a rental basis according to the instructions in section 5102.1.F.

If the beneficiary purchased the equipment even though you determined that rental was more economical under the rent/purchase guidelines, or if the beneficiary made an approved purchase on an installment plan, make payment on an installment basis until the purchase price has been reached or medical necessity terminated. If the purchase price has not been reached by June 1, 1989, continue paying on an installment basis (see section 5102.1.F.9) but at the monthly fee schedule amount until the purchase price is reached or the medical necessity ends, whichever occurs first.

2. Purchase on or After June 1, 1989.—If a beneficiary purchased stationary or portable oxygen equipment on or after June 1, 1989, do not make payment for the equipment. However, make payment for the contents in accordance with section 5102.1.F.4 or 5. Also, do not make payment for maintenance and servicing or for replacement of oxygen equipment that is purchased on or after June 1, 1989.

D. 15-Month Ceiling.—For purposes of computing the 10-month purchase option or the 15-month period for capped rental

items, begin counting the first month that the beneficiary continuously rented the equipment. For example, if the beneficiary began renting the equipment in July 1988, the rental month which begins in January 1989 is counted as the beneficiary's 7th month of rental. Therefore, if the equipment has been continuously rented prior to October 2, 1987, no further rental payments are made since the 15-month period is terminated before January 1, 1989. The maintenance and service provision in section 5102.1.E.4 begins July 1, 1989.

If the beneficiary has reached (on a date of service prior to January 1989) the purchase price limitation on a rental claim, do not make any further purchase or rental payments until the useful life has elapsed according to the instructions in section 5102.1.E.7. However, for capped rental items previously rented that have reached the purchase cap under the rent/purchase rules, pay claims for maintenance and servicing fees in accordance with section 5102.1.E.4 effective July 1, 1989.

E. Oxygen.—Claims for oxygen contents provided after May 31, 1989, but prior to the start of the June equipment rental month, may be paid in either of the following two ways. Either continue paying the reasonable charge payment amount for contents through the end of the May monthly rental period; or pay the reasonable charge payment amount for contents through the end of May and pay the actual charge for contents up to the fee schedule allowance for oxygen contents only, as prorated for the period June 1 through the end of the May rental period. Begin paying the appropriate full fee schedule amount at the beginning of the new rental period. For example, a beneficiary's rental period began May 15, 1989. Pay on a reasonable charge basis from May 15 through June 14; or pay on a reasonable charge basis from May 15 through May 31, 1989 and pay the actual charge up to 14/31 of the oxygen contents fee (established in section 5102.1.F.4) from June 1 through June 14, 1989. Pay the lesser of the full fee schedule amount or actual charge beginning June 15, 1989.

F. Purchase Options for Capped Rental Items.—

1. Electric Wheelchairs.—If the beneficiary purchases an electric wheelchair prior to May 1, 1991, pay for the wheelchair as a routinely purchased item in accordance with section 5102.1.A. If the beneficiary elects to rent an electric wheelchair prior to May 1, 1991, pay the rental fee schedule amount not to exceed the purchase price in accordance with section 5102.1.A. If, on May 1, 1991, the purchase price has not been reached, convert the monthly fee schedule amount from routinely purchased to capped rental. As such, each month's rental before and after conversion must be counted toward the 10 month purchase option in section 5102.1.E.6 and the 15 month rental cap in section 5102.1.E.2.

2. All Other Capped Rental Items.—If the beneficiary purchased a capped rental item prior to May 1, 1991, do not make payment. If the beneficiary rented a capped rental item prior to May 1, 1991, pay the rental fee schedule amount not to exceed the 15 month rental cap in accordance with section 5102.1.E.2. Each month's rental must be counted toward the 10 month purchase option in section 5102.1.E.6 and the 15 month rental cap in section 5102.1.E.2.

5107 ADDITIONAL EXPENSES FOR DELUXE FEATURES

The payment amount for a given service or item, whether rented or purchased, must be consistent with what is reasonable and medically necessary to serve the intended purpose. Additional expenses for "deluxe" features or items which are rented or purchased for aesthetic reasons or added convenience do not meet the reasonableness test. Thus, where a service or item is medically necessary and covered under the Medicare program, and the patient wishes to obtain such deluxe features, the payment is based upon the payment amount for the kind of service or item normally used to meet the intended purpose (i.e., the standard item). Usually this is the least costly item. You may, of course, determine that the payment amount for a more expensive service or item is reasonable when the additional expense is for an added feature which is medically necessary in a given case. For example, a more expensive item may be medically necessary where a patient in a weakened condition needs a power-operated wheelchair or a power-operated vehicle that may be appropriately used as a wheelchair since the patient is not strong enough to operate a manual wheelchair.

5107.1 Payment for Power-Operated Vehicles That May Be Appropriately Used as Wheelchair

(See section 25-5, Chapter II, Coverage Issues Manual.)—The fee schedule amount for a power-operated vehicle that may be appropriately used as wheelchair, including all medically necessary accessories, is the *lowest* of the:

• Actual charge for the power-operated vehicle, or
• Fee schedule amount for the power-operated vehicle.

5205 CHARGES FOR RARE OR UNUSUAL PROCEDURES

You will occasionally be confronted with situations in which a new or rare procedure is performed and for which it is difficult to obtain information on customary and prevailing charges.

In such situations, in order to make the reasonable charge determination, (a) obtain data, if possible, on the charges made for the unusual or rare procedure in other areas similar to the locality in which the service was rendered; or (b) consult with the local medical society regarding the appropriate charge to be made for this procedure. A relative value scale may be used together with available information about the physician's customary charges and about the prevailing charges for more frequently performed services in the locality in order to fill gaps in the data available to you.

Where you cannot obtain sufficient information through your knowledge of medical care charges in other localities, consult with any medical authority that you would consider helpful, such as the medical personnel on your staff, the local or state medical society, or hospital medical personnel. In assessing the value of the procedure, the medical personnel should take into consideration: (a) its complexity; (b) the surgical skill required; (c) the time needed to perform the procedure; and (d) the prevailing charges in the locality for other procedures of comparable complexity. You should then base your judgment as to the reasonable charge for a given service on the best available medical opinion and information on customary and prevailing charges.

5114.1 Reasonable Charges

D. Specimen Collection Fee.—Separate charges made by physicians (except for services furnished to dialysis patients as indicated below), independent laboratories (except for services furnished to dialysis patients as indicated below), or hospital laboratories for drawing or collecting specimens are allowed up to $3 whether the specimens are referred to physicians or other laboratories for testing. This fee is not paid to anyone who has not actually extracted the specimen from the patient. Only one collection fee is allowed for each patient encounter, regardless of the number of specimens drawn. When a series of specimens is required to complete a single text (e.g., glucose tolerance test), the series is treated as a single encounter. A specimen collection fee is allowed in circumstances such as drawing a blood sample through venipuncture (i.e., inserting into a vein a needle with syringe or Vacutainer to draw the specimen) or collecting a urine sample by catheterization.

A specimen collection fee for physicians is allowed *only* when (1) it is the accepted and prevailing practice among physicians in the locality to make separate charges for drawing or collecting a specimen, *and* (2) it is the customary practice of the physician performing such services to bill separate charges for them.

A specimen collection fee is not allowed when the cost of collecting the specimen is minimal, such as a throat culture or a routine capillary puncture for clotting or bleeding time. Stool specimen collection for an occult blood test is usually done by the patient at home, and a fee for such collection is not allowed. When a stool specimen is collected during a rectal examination, the collection is an incidental byproduct of that examination. Costs such as gloves are related to the rectal examination and compensated for in the payment for the visit. Payment for performing the test is separate from the specimen collection fee. Costs such as media (e.g., the slides) and labor are included in the payment for the test.

You no longer have authority to make payment for routine handling charges where a specimen is referred by one laboratory to another. Preparatory services, e.g., where a referring laboratory prepares a specimen before transfer to a reference laboratory, are considered an integral part of the testing process, and the costs of such services are included in the charge for the total testing service.

A specimen collection fee is allowed when it is medically necessary for a laboratory technician to draw a specimen from either a nursing home patient or homebound patient. The technician must personally draw the specimen, e.g., venipuncture or urine sample by catheterization. A specimen collection fee is not allowed in situations where a patient is not in a nursing facility or confined to his home. When a laboratory performs the specimen collection, it may receive payment both for the draw and for the associated travel to obtain the specimen(s) for testing. Payment may be made to the laboratory even if the nursing facility has on-duty personnel qualified to perform the specimen collection. When the nursing home performs the specimen collection, it may only receive payment for the draw. Specimen collection performed by nursing home personnel for patients covered under Part A is paid for as part of the facility's payment for its reasonable costs, not on the basis of the specimen collection fee.

Special rules apply when services are furnished to dialysis patients. ESRD facilities are only paid by intermediaries. Therefore, never pay a specimen collection fee to an ESRD facility. The specimen collection fee is not allowed when a physician or one of the physician's employees draws the specimen from the dialysis patient because it is included in the Monthly Capitation Payment (MCP). (See section 5037.) Independent laboratories are not paid the specimen collection fee for specimens collected that are used in performing a laboratory test reimbursed under the composite rate. If a home dialysis patient selects reimbursement Method II (see section 4271) and all other criteria for payment are met, pay an independent laboratory the specimen collection fee for specimens collected from the patient.

The coinsurance and deductible provisions do not apply to the specimen collection fee where 100 percent of the fee schedule amount is payable on the basis of an assignment to the persons or entities drawing the specimen. For services (including specimen collection) rendered on or after January 1, 1987, payment to laboratories or physicians is only made on the basis of an assignment. For services rendered prior to January 1, 1987, acceptance of an assignment is optional for physicians. However, the coinsurance and deductible is applied to the specimen collection fee where a physician collects the specimen and does not accept assignment.

Complex vascular injection procedures, such as arterial punctures and venesections, are not subject either to this specimen collection policy or to the assignment provisions.

K. Travel Allowance.—In addition to a specimen collection fee allowed under section 5114.1D, a travel allowance can also be made to cover the costs of travel to collect a specimen from a nursing home or homebound patient. The additional allowance can be made only where a specimen collection fee is also payable, i.e., no travel allowance is made where the technician merely performs a messenger service to pick up a specimen drawn by a physician or nursing home personnel. The travel allowance may not be paid to a physician unless the trip to the home or nursing home was solely for the purpose of drawing a specimen. Otherwise travel costs are considered to be associated with the other purposes of the trip. Since a travel allowance can now be paid routinely, the differential specimen collection amount formerly allowed when a specimen is collected from a single patient rather than multiple patients (i.e., $5 rather than $3) is discontinued.

The allowance is intended to cover the estimated travel costs of collecting a specimen and is an allowance reflecting the technician's salary and travel costs. The following HCPCS codes are used for travel allowances:

P9603—Travel allowance-one way, in connection with medically necessary laboratory specimen collection drawn from homebound or nursing home bound patient; prorated miles actually traveled (carrier allowance on per mile basis); or

P9604—Travel allowance-one way, in connection with medically necessary laboratory specimen collection drawn from homebound or nursing home bound patient; prorated trip charge (carrier allowance on flat fee basis).

Identify round trip travel by use of modifier LR.

If you determine that it results in equitable payment, you may extend your former payment allowances for additional travel (such as to a distant rural nursing home) to all circumstances where travel is required. This might be appropriate, for example, if your former payment allowance was on a per mile basis. Otherwise you must establish an appropriate allowance. If you decide to establish a new allowance, one method is to consider developing a travel allowance consisting of:

- The current Federal mileage allowance for operating personal automobiles, plus
- A personnel allowance per mile to cover personnel costs based on an estimate of average hourly wages and average driving speed.

Four your convenience, a chronology of mileage rates from July 1, 1984 to date is listed below:

Mileage Rate	From	To
20.5 cents	July 1, 1984	July 31, 1987
21 cents	August 1, 1987	August 13, 1988
22.5 cents	August 14, 1988	September 16, 1989
24 cents	September 17, 1989	June 29, 1991
25 cents	June 30, 1991	

Travel allowance amounts claimed by suppliers are prorated by the total number of patients (including Medicare and non-Medicare patients) from whom specimens are drawn or picked up on a given trip.

Example 1: On October 1, 1989, a carrier determines that the average technician is paid $9 per hour and estimates 45 miles per hour as the average speed driven or $.20 per mile. This amount plus the Federal mileage allowance of $0.24 per mile results in a total allowance of $0.44 per mile. A laboratory technician makes a trip to two nursing homes involving a total mileage of 20 miles and draws specimens from three patients, Medicare as well as non-Medicare patients. In addition, specimens that were not drawn by the technician are picked up from two patients. A travel allowance per Medicare claim of $1.76 can be made (20 miles round trip × $0.44 per mile divided by 5). The supplier bills 4 miles (20 miles ÷ 5) under code P9603LR.

Example 2: The carrier, through a review of the laboratory records, estimates that on average four specimens are drawn or picked up each trip, and that the average trip is 30 miles including both round trips and one way trips. Assuming the same facts as Example 1 (i.e., $9 per hour and 45 miles per hour), the carrier establishes a flat travel allowance of $3.30. Suppliers bill code P9604 and are paid 3.30 regardless of actual distance or number of patients served.

In keeping with the principles of section 5024 and section 5200, a payment in addition to the routine travel allowance determined under this section may be allowed to cover the additional costs of travel to collect a specimen from a nursing home or homebound patient when clinical diagnostic laboratory tests are needed on an emergency basis outside the general business hours of the laboratory making the collection.

15030 SUPPLIES

Make a separate payment for supplies furnished in connection with a procedure only when one of the two following conditions exists:

A. HCPCS codes A4550, A4200, and A4263 are billed in conjunction with the appropriate procedure in the Medicare Physician Fee Schedule Data Base (place of service is physician's office); or

B. The supply is a pharmaceutical or radiopharmaceutical diagnostic imaging agent (including codes A4641 through A4647); pharmacologic stressing agent (code J1245); or therapeutic radionuclide (CPT code 79900). The procedures performed are:

- Diagnostic radiologic procedures (including diagostic nuclear medicine) requiring pharmaceutical or radiopharmaceutical contrast media and/or pharmacological stressing agent,
- Other diagnostic tests requiring a pharmacological stressing agent,
- Clinical brachytherapy procedures (other than remote afterloading high intensity brachytherapy procedures (CPT codes 77781 through 77784) for which the expendable source is included in the TC RVUs), or
- Therapeutic nuclear medicine procedures.

7517.1 Laboratory Claims.—In performing medical review, deny claims for any tests for which a laboratory cannot provide adequate information to support payment. Generally, you may assume the medical necessity of a laboratory test if there is documentation that each test performed was individually ordered by a physician. This includes claims for automated chemistry profiles where documentation includes evidence that each test is ordered individually (i.e., not ordered as part of a profile or custom panel).

NOTE: For these purposes, an order for a disease or organ panel (as defined in the Current Procedural Terminology— Fourth Edition (CPT-4) is considered an individually ordered test. Medical necessity can be reevaluated if an aberrant pattern of utilization is uncovered. In such cases, additional information can be required. (See section 7517.2.)

Where laboratory tests are not ordered individually (i.e., these are ordered in an automated profile or custom panel), your determination of whether a test is reasonable and necessary should include consideration of:

- Whether the test provides additional needed information;
- Whether the information could be obtained through another test which has a lower price; and
- Whether the test is ordered at an unusually high frequency.

Each of the tests ordered must be reasonable and necessary. Follow-up tests repeated because of compromised specimens, inadequate specimens, incorrect specimens, or incorrect test ordering should be denied unless adequate documentation is provided to justify payment. The laboratory must explain why follow-up tests are repeated.

APPENDIX B

COVERAGE ISSUES MANUAL (CIM), SELECT

35-5 CELLULAR THERAPY—NOT COVERED

Cellular therapy involves the practice of injecting humans with foreign proteins like the placenta or lungs of unborn lambs. Cellular therapy is without scientific or statistical evidence to document its therapeutic efficacy and, in fact, is considered a potentially dangerous practice. Accordingly, cellular therapy is not considered reasonable and necessary within the meaning of section 1862(a)(1) of the law.

35-10 HYPERBARIC OXYGEN THERAPY

For purposes of coverage under Medicare, hyperbaric oxygen (HBO) therapy is a modality in which the entire body is exposed to oxygen under increased atmospheric pressure.

A. Covered Conditions.—Program reimbursement for HBO therapy will be limited to that which is administered in a chamber (including the one man unit) and is limited to the following conditions:

1. Acute carbon monoxide intoxication.

2. Decompression illness.

3. Gas embolism.

4. Gas gangrene.

5. Acute traumatic peripheral ischemia. HBO therapy is a valuable adjunctive treatment to be used in combination with accepted standard therapeutic measures when loss of function, limb, or life is threatened.

6. Crush injuries and suturing of severed limbs. As in the previous conditions, HBO therapy would be an adjunctive treatment when loss of function, limb, or life is threatened.

7. Progressive necrotizing infections (necrotizing fasciitis, Meleney ulcer).

8. Acute peripheral arterial insufficiency.

9. Preparation and preservation of compromised skin grafts.

10. Chronic refractory osteomyelitis, unresponsive to conventional medical and surgical management.

11. Osteoradionecrosis as an adjunct to conventional treatment.

The following uses of HBO are covered for services rendered on and after 10/1/82.

12. Soft tissue radionecrosis as an adjunct to conventional treatment.

13. Cyanide poisoning.

The following use of HBO is covered for services rendered on or after 2/22/84.

14. Actinomycosis, only as an adjunct to conventional therapy when the disease process is refractory to antibiotics and surgical treatment.

B. Noncovered Conditions.—All other indications not specified under section 35-10 (A) are not covered under the Medicare program. No program payment may be made for any conditions other than those listed in section 35-10 (A).

C. Reasonable Utilization Parameters.—Make payment where HBO therapy is clinically practical. HBO therapy should not be a replacement for other standard successful therapeutic measures. Depending on the response of the individual patient and the severity of the original problem, treatment may range from less than 1 week to several months' duration, the average being 2 to 4 weeks. Review and document the medical necessity for use of hyperbaric oxygen for more than 2 months, regardless of the condition of the patient, before further reimbursement is made.

D. Topical Application of Oxygen.—This method of administering oxygen does not meet the definition of HBO therapy as stated above. Also, its clinical efficacy has not been established. Therefore, no Medicare reimbursement may be made for the topical application of oxygen. (Cross refer: section 35-31.)

E. Physician Supervision Requirement.—For HBO therapy to be covered under the Medicare program, the physician must be in constant attendance during the entire treatment. This is a professional activity that cannot be delegated in that it requires independent medical judgment by the physician. The physician must be present, carefully monitoring the patient during the hyperbaric oxygen therapy session and be immediately available should a complication occur. This requirement applies in all settings: no payment will be made under Part A or Part B, unless the physician is in constant attendance during the HBO therapy procedure.

F. Credentials.—A physician qualified in HBO therapy treatment is defined by Medicare for this purpose to be credentialed by the hospital in which HBO therapy is being performed specifically in hyperbaric medicine and the management of acute cardiopulmonary emergencies, including placement of chest tube. Credentialing includes, at a minimun, the following:

• Training, experience, and privileges within the institution to manage acute cardiopulmonary emergencies, including advanced cardiac life support, and emergency myringotomy;
• Completion of a recognized hyperbaric medicine training program as established by either the American College of Hyperbaric Medicine or the Undersea and Hyperbaric Medical Society (UHMS) with a minimum of 60 hours of training and documented by a certificate of completion or an equivalent program; and
• Continuing medical education in hyperbaric medicine of a minimum of 16 hours every 2 years after initial credentialing.

An additional requirement that must be met for Medicare's payment for hyperbaric medical therapy is that cardiopulmonary resuscitation team coverage must be immediately available during the hours of the hyperbaric chamber operations.

35-13 PROLOTHERAPY, JOINT SCLEROTHERAPY, AND LIGAMENTOUS INJECTIONS WITH SCLEROSING AGENTS—NOT COVERED

The medical effectiveness of the above therapies has not been verified by scientifically controlled studies. Accordingly, reimbursement for these modalities should be denied on the ground that they are not reasonable and necessary as required by section 1862(a)(1) of the law.

35-20 TREATMENT OF MOTOR FUNCTION DISORDERS WITH ELECTRIC NERVE STIMULATION—NOT COVERED

While electric nerve stimulation has been employed to control chronic intractable pain for some time, its use in the treatment of motor function disorders, such as multiple sclerosis, is a recent innovation, and the medical effectiveness of such therapy has not been verified by scientifically controlled studies. Therefore, where electric nerve stimulation is employed to treat motor function disorders, no reimbursement may be made for the stimulator or for the services related to its implantation since this treatment cannot be considered reasonable and necessary.

See sections 35-27 and 65-8.

NOTE: Medicare coverage of deep brain stimulation by implantation of a stimulator device is not prohibited. Therefore, coverage of deep brain stimulation provided by an implanted deep brain stimulator is at the carrier's discretion.

35-27 BIOFEEDBACK THERAPY

Biofeedback therapy provides visual, auditory or other evidence of the status of certain body functions so that a person can exert voluntary control over the functions, and thereby alleviate an abnormal bodily condition. Biofeedback therapy often uses electrical devices to transform bodily signals indicative of such functions as heart rate, blood pressure, skin temperature, salivation, peripheral vasomotor activity, and gross muscle tone into a tone or light, the loudness or brightness of which shows the extent of activity in the function being measured.

Biofeedback therapy differs from electromyography, which is a diagnostic procedure used to record and study the electrical properties of skeletal muscle. An electromyography device may be used to provide feedback with certain types of biofeedback.

Biofeedback therapy is covered under Medicare only when it is reasonable and necessary for the individual patient for muscle re-education of specific muscle groups or for treating pathological muscle abnormalities of spasticity, incapacitating muscle spasm, or weakness, and more conventional treatments (heat, cold, massage, exercise, support) have not been successful. This therapy is not covered for treatment of ordinary muscle tension states or for psychosomatic conditions.

(See HCFA-Pub. 14-3, sections 2200ff., 2215, and 4161; HCFA-Pub. 13-3, section 3133.3, 3148, and 3149; HCFA-Pub. 10, section 242 and 242.5 for special physical therapy requirements. See also sections 35-20 and 65-8.)

35-31 TREATMENT OF DECUBITUS ULCERS

An accepted procedure for healing decubitus ulcers is to remove dead tissue from the lesions and to keep them clean to promote the growth of new tissue. This may be accomplished by hydrotherapy (whirlpool) treatments. Hydrotherapy (whirlpool) treatment for decubitus ulcers is a covered service under Medicare for patients when treatment is reasonable and necessary. Some other methods of treating decubitus ulcers, the safety and effectiveness of which have not been established, are not covered under the Medicare program. Some examples of these types of treatments are: ultraviolet light, low intensity direct current, topical application of oxygen, and topical dressings with Balsam of Peru in castor oil.

35-34 FABRIC WRAPPING OF ABDOMINAL ANEURYSMS— NOT COVERED

Fabric wrapping of abdominal aneurysms is not a covered Medicare procedure. This is a treatment for abdominal aneurysms which involves wrapping aneurysms with cellophane or fascia lata. This procedure has not been shown to prevent eventual rupture. In extremely rare instances, external wall reinforcement may be indicated when the current accepted treatment (excision of the aneurysm and reconstruction with synthetic materials) is not a viable alternative, but external wall reinforcement is not fabric wrapping. Accordingly, fabric wrapping of abdominal aneurysms is not considered reasonable and necessary within the meaning of section 1862(a)(1) of the Act.

35-46 ASSESSING PATIENT'S SUITABILITY FOR ELECTRICAL NERVE STIMULATION THERAPY

Electrical nerve stimulation is an accepted modality for assessing a patient's suitability for ongoing treatment with a transcutaneous or an implanted nerve stimulator. Accordingly, program payment may be made for the following techniques when used to determine the potential therapeutic usefulness of an electrical nerve stimulator:

A. Transcutaneous Electrical Nerve Stimulation (TENS).—This technique involves attachment of a transcutaneous nerve stimulator to the surface of the skin over the peripheral nerve to be stimulated. It is used by the patient on a trial basis and its effectiveness in modulating pain is monitored by the physician, or physical therapist. Generally, the physician or physical therapist is able to determine whether the patient is likely to derive a significant therapeutic benefit from continuous use of a transcutaneous stimulator within a trial period of 1 month; in a few cases this determination may take longer to make. Document the medical necessity for such services which are furnished beyond the first month. (See section 45-25 for an explanation of coverage of medically necessary supplies for the effective use of TENS.)

If TENS significantly alleviates pain, it may be considered as primary treatment; if it produces no relief or greater discomfort than the original pain, electrical nerve stimulation therapy is ruled out. However, where TENS produces incomplete relief, further evaluation with percutaneous electrical nerve stimulation may be considered to determine whether an implanted peripheral nerve stimulator would provide significant relief from pain. (See section 35-46B.)

Usually, the physician or physical therapist providing the services will furnish the equipment necessary for assessment. Where the physician or physical therapist advises the patient to rent the TENS from a supplier during the trial period rather than supplying it himself/herself, program payment may be made for rental of the TENS as well as for the services of the physician or physical therapist who is evaluating its use. However, the combined program payment which is made for the physician's or physical therapist's services and the rental of the stimulator from a supplier should not exceed the amount which would be payable for the total service, including the stimulator, furnished by the physician or physical therapist alone.

B. Percutaneous Electrical Nerve Stimulation (PENS).—This diagnostic procedure which involves stimulation of peripheral nerves by a needle electrode inserted through the skin is performed only in a physician's office, clinic, or hospital outpatient department. Therefore, it is covered only when performed by a physician or incident to physician's service. If pain is effectively controlled by percutaneous stimulation, implantation of electrodes is warranted.

As in the case of TENS (described in subsection A), generally the physician should be able to determine whether the patient is likely to derive a significant therapeutic benefit from continuing use of an implanted nerve stimulator within a trial period of 1 month. In a few cases, this determination may take longer to make. The medical necessity for such diagnostic services which are furnished beyond the first month must be documented.

NOTE: Electrical nerve stimulators do not prevent pain but only alleviate pain as it occurs. A patient can be taught how to employ the stimulator, and once this is done, can use it safely and effectively without direct physician supervision. Consequently, it is inappropriate for a patient to visit his physician, physical therapist or an outpatient clinic on a continuing basis for treatment of pain with electrical nerve stimulation. Once it is determined that electrical nerve stimulation should be continued as therapy and the patient has been trained to use the stimulator, it is expected that a stimulator will be implanted or the patient will employ the TENS on a continual basis in his home. Electrical nerve stimulation treatments furnished by a physician in his office, by a physical therapist or outpatient clinic are excluded from coverage by section 1862(a)(1) of the law. (See section 65-8 for an explanation of coverage of the therapeutic use of implanted peripheral nerve stimulators under the prosthetic devices benefit. See section 60-20 for an explanation of coverage of the therapeutic use of TENS under the durable medical equipment benefit.)

35-47 BREAST RECONSTRUCTION FOLLOWING MASTECTOMY

During recent years there has been a considerable change in the treatment of diseases of the breast such as fibrocystic disease, and cancer. While extirpation of the disease remains of primary importance, the quality of life following initial treatment is increasingly recognized as of great concern. The increased use of breast reconstruction procedures is due to several factors:

- A change in epidemiology of breast cancer, including an apparent increase in incidence;
- Improved surgical skills and techniques;
- The continuing development of better prostheses; and
- Increasing awareness by physicians of the importance of post-surgical psychological adjustment.

Reconstruction of the affected and the contralateral unaffected breast following a medically necessary mastectomy is considered a relatively safe and effective noncosmetic procedure. Accordingly, program payment may be made for breast reconstruction surgery following removal of a breast for any medical reason.

Program payment may not be made for breast reconstruction for cosmetic reasons. (Cosmetic surgery is excluded from coverage under section 1862(a)(10) of the Social Security Act.)

35-48 OSTEOGENIC STIMULATION

Electrical stimulation to augment bone repair can be attained either invasively or noninvasively. Invasive devices provide electrical stimulation directly at the fracture site either through percutaneously placed cathodes or by implantation of a coiled cathode wire into the fracture site. The power pack for the latter device is implanted into soft tissue near the fracture site and subcutaneously connected to the cathode, creating a self-contained system with no external components. The power supply for the former device is externally placed and the leads connected to the inserted cathodes. With the noninvasive device, opposing pads, wired to an external power supply, are placed over the cast. An electromagnetic field is created between the pads at the fracture site.

1. Noninvasive Stimulator.—The noninvasive stimulator device is covered only for the following indications:

- Nonunion of long bone fractures;
- Failed fusion, where a minimum of 9 months has elapsed since the last surgery;
- Congenital pseudarthroses; and
- As an adjunct to spinal fusion surgery for patients at high risk of pseudarthrosis due to previously failed spinal fusion at the same site or for those undergoing multiple level fusion. A multiple level fusion involves 3 or more vertebrae (e.g., L3-L5, L4-S1, etc).

2. Invasive (Implantable) Stimulator.—The invasive stimulator device is covered only for the following indications:

- Nonunion of long bone fractures;
- As an adjunct to spinal fusion surgery for patients at high risk of pseudarthrosis due to previously failed spinal fusion at the same site or for those undergoing muliple level fusion. A multiple level fusion involves 3 or more vertebrae (e.g., L3-L5, L4-S1, etc).

Nonunion, for all types of devices, is considered to exist only after six or more months have elapsed without healing of the fracture.

3. Ultrasonic Osteogenic Stimulators.—An ultrasonic osteogenic stimulator is a non-invasive device that emits low intensity, pulsed ultrasound. The ultrasound signal is applied to the skin surface at the fracture location via ultrasound, conductive coupling gel in order to accelerate the healing time of the fracture. The device is intended for use with cast immobilization.

There is insufficient evidence to support the medical necessity of using an ultrasonic osteogenic stimulator. Therefore, the device is not covered, because it is not considered reasonable and necessary.

35-50 COCHLEOSTOMY WITH NEUROVASCULAR TRANSPLANT FOR MENIERE'S DISEASE—NOT COVERED

Meniere's disease (or syndrome) is a common cause of paroxysmal vertigo. Meniere's syndrome is usually treated medically. When medical treatment fails, surgical treatment may be required.

While there are two recognized surgical procedures used in treating Meniere's disease (decompression of the endolymphatic hydrops and labyrinthectomy), there is no scientific evidence supporting the safety and effectiveness of cochleostomy with neurovascular transplant in treatment of Meniere's syndrome. Accordingly, Medicare does not cover cochleostomy with neurovascular transplant for treatment of Meniere's disease.

35-61 TRANSSEXUAL SURGERY

Transsexual surgery, also known as sex reassignment surgery or intersex surgery, is the culmination of a series of procedures designed to change the anatomy of transsexuals to conform to their gender identity. Transsexuals are persons with an overwhelming desire to change anatomic sex because of their fixed conviction that they are members of the opposite sex. For the male-to-female, transsexual surgery entails castration, penectomy and vulva-vaginal construction. Surgery for the female-to-male transsexual consists of bilateral mammectomy, hysterectomy and salpingo-oophorectomy, which may be followed by phalloplasty and the insertion of testicular prostheses.

Transsexual surgery for sex reassignment of transsexuals is controversial. Because of the lack of well-controlled, long-term studies of the safety and effectiveness of the surgical procedures and attendant therapies for transsexualism, the treatment is considered experimental. Moreover, there is a high rate of serious complications for these surgical procedures. For these reasons, transsexual surgery is not covered.

35-64 CHELATION THERAPY FOR TREATMENT OF ATHEROSCLEROSIS

Chelation therapy is the application of chelation techniques for the therapeutic or preventive effects of removing unwanted metal ions from the body. The application of chelation therapy using ethylenediamine-tetra-acetic acid (EDTA) for the treatment and prevention of atherosclerosis is controversial. There is no widely accepted rationale to explain the beneficial effects attributed to this therapy. Its safety is questioned and its clinical effectiveness has never been established by well designed, controlled clinical trials. It is not widely accepted and practiced by American physicians. EDTA chelation therapy for atherosclerosis is considered experimental. For these reasons, EDTA chelation therapy for the treatment or prevention of atherosclerosis is not covered.

Some practitioners refer to this therapy as chemoendarterectomy and may also show a diagnosis other than atherosclerosis, such as arteriosclerosis or calcinosis. Claims employing such variant terms should also be denied under this section.

Cross-refer: section 45-20

35-65 GASTRIC FREEZING

Gastric freezing for chronic peptic ulcer disease is a non-surgical treatment which was popular about 20 years ago but now is seldom done. It has been abandoned due to a high complication rate, only temporary improvement experienced by patients, and lack of effectiveness when tested by double-blind, controlled clinical trials. Since the procedure is now considered obsolete, it is not covered.

35-74 ENHANCED EXTERNAL COUNTERPULSATION (EECP) FOR SEVERE ANGINA—COVERED (Effective for services performed on or after July 1, 1999).

Enhanced external counterpulsation (EECP) is a non-invasive outpatient treatment for coronary artery disease refractory to medical and/or surgical therapy. Although these and similiar devices are cleared by the Food and Drug Administration (FDA) for use in treating a variety of conditions, including stable or unstable angina pectoris, acute myocardial infarction, and cardiogenic shock. Medicare coverage is limited to its use in patients with stable angina pectoris, since only that use has developed sufficient evidence to demonstrate its medical effectiveness. Other uses of this device and similar devices remain non-covered. In addition, the non-coverage of hydraulic versions of these types of devices remains in force.

Coverage is further limited to those enhanced external counterpulsation systems that have sufficiently demonstrated their medical effectiveness in treating patients with severe angina in well-designed clinical trials. Note that a 510(k) clearance by the Food and Drug Administration does not, by itself, satisfy this requirement.

Coverage is provided for the use of EECP for patients who have been diagnosed with disabling angina (Class III or Class IV, Canadian Cardiovascular Society Classification or equivalent classification) who, in the opinion of a cardiologist or cardiothoracic surgeon, are not readily amenable to surgical intervention, such as PTCA or cardiac bypass because: (1) their condition is inoperable, or at high risk of operative complications or post-operative failure; (2) their coronary anatomy is not readily amenable to such procedures; or (3) they have co-morbid states which create excessive risk.

A full course of therapy usually consists of 35 one-hour treatments which may be offered once or twice daily, usually 5 days per week. The patient is placed on a treatment table where the lower extremities are wrapped in a series of three compressive air cuffs which inflate and deflate in synchronization with the patient's cardiac cycle.

During diastole the three sets of air cuffs are inflated sequentially (distal to proximal) compressing the vascular beds within the muscles of the calves, lower thighs, and upper thighs. This action results in an increase in diastolic pressure, generation of retrograde arterial blood flow, and an increase in venous return. The cuffs are deflated simultaneously just prior to systole, which produces a rapid drop in vascular impedance, a decrease in ventricular workload, and an increase in cardiac output.

The augmented diastolic pressure and retrograde aortic flow appear to improve myocardial perfusion, while systolic unloading appears to reduce cardiac workload and oxygen requirements. The increased venous return coupled with enhanced systolic flow appears to increase cardiac output. As a result of this treatment, most patients experience increased time until onset of ischemia, increased exercise tolerance, and a reduction in the number and severity of anginal episodes. Evidence was presented that this effect lasted well beyond the immediate post-treatment phase, with patients symptom-free for several months to two years.

This procedure must be done under direct supervision of a physician.

35-77 NEUROMUSCULAR ELECTRICAL STIMULATION (NMES) IN THE TREATMENT OF DISUSE ATROPHY

Neuromuscular electrical stimulation (NMES) involves the use of a device which transmits an electrical impulse to the skin over selected muscle groups by way of electrodes. Coverage of NMES is limited to the treatment of disuse atrophy where nerve supply to the muscle is intact, including brain, spinal cord and peripheral nerves, and other non-neurological reasons for disuse are causing atrophy. Some examples would be casting or splinting of a limb, contracture due to scarring of soft tissue as in burn lesions, and hip replacement surgery (until orthotic training begins). (See section 45-25 for an explanation of coverage of medically necessary supplies for the effective use of NMES.)

35-90 EXTRACORPOREAL IMMUNOADSORPTION (ECI) USING PROTEIN A COLUMNS FOR THE TREATMENT OF PATIENTS WITH IDIOPATHIC THROMBOCYTOPENIA PURPURA (ITP) FAILING OTHER TREATMENTS

Extracorporeal immunoadsorption (ECI), using protein A columns, has been developed for the purpose of selectively removing circulating immune complexes (CIC) and immunoglobulins (IgG) from patients in whom these substances are associated with their diseases. The technique involves pumping the patient's anti-coagulated venous blood through a cell separator from which 1 to 3 liters of plasma are collected and perfused over adsorbent columns, after which the plasma rejoins the separated, unprocessed cells and is retransfused to the patient.

The use of protein A columns is covered by Medicare only for the treatment of ITP failing other treatments. Other uses of these columns are currently considered to be investigational and, therefore, not reasonable and necessary under the Medicare law (section 1862(a)(1)(A) of the Act).

Until a national code is issued, use the following Q code (temporary code):

> Q0068   Extracorporeal plasmapheresis; immunoadsorption with staphylococcal protein A columns.

This code will facilitate data keeping in order to help evaluate this new technology.

35-93 LUNG VOLUME REDUCTION SURGERY (REDUCTION PNEUMOPLASTY, ALSO CALLED LUNG SHAVING OR LUNG CONTOURING) UNILATERAL OR BILATERAL BY OPEN OR THORACOSCOPIC APPROACH FOR TREATMENT OF EMPHYSEMA OR CHRONIC OBSTRUCTIVE PULMONARY DISEASE—NOT GENERALLY COVERED

Lung volume reduction surgery (LVRS) or reduction pneumoplasty, also referred to as lung shaving or lung contouring, is performed on patients with emphysema and chronic obstructive pulmonary disease (COPD) in order to allow the underlying compressed lung to expand, and thus, establish improved respiratory function. The goal of this procedure is to offer a better quality of life for patients with emphysema and COPD. In addition, LVRS may be offered as a "bridge to transplant" for patients who otherwise may not have been considered candidates for lung transplantation.

Unilateral or bilateral LVRS by open or thoracoscopic approach is not generally covered, because there is insufficient medical evidence available to base a determination that this procedure is generally safe and effective. Therefore, LVRS generally cannot be considered reasonable and necessary under section 1862(a)(1)(A) of the Act in most cases.

When this policy was first established in December 1995, HCFA committed Medicare to reviewing the scientific literature as it was published in order to modify coverage policy as clinical data were developed. HCFA has reviewed data that suggest the need for a randomized clinical trial regarding the safety and effectiveness of LVRS. On April 24, 1996, the Health Care Financing Administration (HCFA) and the National Heart, Lung and Blood Institute (NHLBI) of the National Institutes of Health announced their intention to collaborate on a multi-center, randomized clinical study evaluating the effectiveness of LVRS. On December 20, 1996, HCFA and NHLBI announced the clinical centers and the data coordinating center that will be participating in the study. HCFA has determined that LVRS is reasonable and necessary when it is provided under the conditions detailed by the protocol of the HCFA/NHLBI clinical study. Therefore, Medicare will cover LVRS in those limited circumstances when it is provided to a Medicare beneficiary under the protocols established for the study. Coverage will be provided where the care is furnished in facilities that are approved as meeting the criteria established by HCFA and NHLBI for this study.

This study will consist of a registry of all patients referred to the participating clinical centers for LVRS. In addition, a subset of patients from the registry who meet specific inclusion criteria will be invited to participate in the randomized trial. All randomized patients will receive intensive medical therapy and pulmonary rehabilitation. Half will be selected randomly to undergo LVRS, which will be performed via median sternotomy or video-assisted thoracoscopy.

Medicare will provide coverage to those beneficiaries who may participate in the randomized trial for all services integral to the study and for which the Medicare statute does not prohibit. This includes tests performed to determine whether a beneficiary qualifies for randomization, LVRS, and follow-up tests that are necessary during participation in the randomized study. However, Medicare will not provide coverage for those services that are prohibited by the Act. For example, Medicare will provide coverage for pulmonary rehabilitation and pulmonary function testing, but will not provide coverage for oral steroids provided as part of a physician's service under section 1862(S)(2) of the Act because they are self-administrable and thus statutorily excluded from coverage.

Payment for these services will be provided under the usual payment systems. For example, Part A services will be paid for according to the DRG system, and Part B physician services will be paid for according to the physician fee schedule.

The data from the randomized phase of the study will be analyzed and monitored continuously in order to determine any appropriate changes in Medicare coverage. These determinations will include if and how coverage will be continued.

35-96 CRYOSURGERY OF PROSTATE (Effective for services performed on or after July 1, 1999)

Cryosurgery of the prostate gland, also known as cryosurgical ablation of the prostate (CSAP), destroys prostate tissue by applying extremely cold temperatures in order to reduce the size of the prostate gland. It is safe and effective, as well as medically necessary and appropriate, as primary treatment for patients with clinically localized prostate cancer, Stages T1–T3.

35-99 ABORTION

Abortions are not covered Medicare procedures except

1. if the pregnancy is the result of an act of rape or incest; or

2. in the case where a woman suffers from a physical disorder, physical injury, or physical illness, including a life-endangering physical condition caused by or arising from the pregnancy itself, that would, as certified by a physician, place the woman in danger of death unless an abortion is performed.

45-4 VITAMIN B12 INJECTIONS TO STRENGTHEN TENDONS, LIGAMENTS, ETC., OF THE FOOT—NOT COVERED

Vitamin B12 injections to strengthen tendons, ligaments, etc., of the foot are not covered under Medicare because (1) there is no evidence that vitamin B12 injections are effective for the purpose of strengthening weakened tendons and ligaments, and (2) this is nonsurgical treatment under the subluxation exclusion. Accordingly, vitamin B12 injections are not considered reasonable and necessary within the meaning of section 1862(a)(1) of the Act.

See Intermediary Manual sections 3101.3 and 3158, and Carriers Manual, sections 2050.5 and 2323.

45-7 HYDROPHILIC CONTACT LENS FOR CORNEAL BANDAGE

Some hydrophilic contact lenses are used as moist corneal bandages for the treatment of acute or chronic corneal pathology, such as bullous keratopathy, dry eyes, corneal ulcers and erosion, keratitis, corneal edema, descemetocele, corneal ectasis, Mooren's ulcer, anterior corneal dystrophy, neurotrophic keratoconjunctivitis, and for other therapeutic reasons.

Payment may be made under section 1861(s)(2) of the Act for a hydrophilic contact lens approved by the Food and Drug Administration (FDA) and used as a supply incident to a physician's service. Payment for the lens is included in the payment for the physician's service to which the lens is incident. Contractors are authorized to accept an FDA letter of approval or other FDA published material as evidence of FDA approval. (See section 65-1 for coverage of a hydrophilic contact lens as a prosthetic device.)

See Intermediary Manual, section 3112.4 and Carriers Manual, sections 2050.1 and 15010.

45-10 LAETRILE AND RELATED SUBSTANCES—NOT COVERED

Laetrile (and the other drugs called by the various terms mentioned below) have been used primarily in the treatment or control of cancer. Although the terms "Laetrile," "laetrile," "amygdalin," "Sarcarcinase," "vitamin B-17," and "nitriloside" have been used interchangeably, the chemical identity of the substances to which these terms refer has varied.

The FDA has determined that neither Laetrile nor any other drug called by the various terms mentioned above, nor any other product which might be characterized as a "nitriloside" is generally recognized (by experts qualified by scientific training and experience to evaluate the safety and effectiveness of drugs) to be safe and effective for any therapeutic use. Therefore, use of this drug cannot be considered to be reasonable and necessary within the meaning of section 1862(a)(1) of the Act and program payment may not be made for its use or any services furnished in connection with its administration.

A hospital stay only for the purpose of having laetrile (or any other drug called by the terms mentioned above) administered is not covered. Also, program payment may not be made for laetrile (or other drug noted above) when it is used during the course of an otherwise covered hospital stay, since the FDA has found such drugs to not be safe and effective for any therapeutic purpose.

45-16 CERTAIN DRUGS DISTRIBUTED BY THE NATIONAL CANCER INSTITUTE

Under its Cancer Therapy Evaluation, the Division of Cancer Treatment of the National Cancer Institute (NCI), in cooperation with the Food and Drug Administration, approves and distributes certain drugs for use in treating terminally ill cancer patients. One group of these drugs, designated as Group C drugs, unlike other drugs distributed by the NCI, are not limited to use in clinical trials for the purpose of testing their efficacy. Drugs are classified as Group C drugs only if there is sufficient evidence demonstrating their efficacy within a tumor type and that they can be safely administered.

A physician is eligible to receive Group C drugs from the Divison of Cancer Treatment only if the following requirements are met:

- A physician must be registered with the NCI as an investigator by having completed an FD-Form 1573;
- A written request for the drug, indicating the disease to be treated, must be submitted to the NCI;
- The use of the drug must be limited to indications outlined in the NCI's guidelines; and
- All adverse reactions must be reported to the Investigational Drug Branch of the Division of Cancer Treatment.

In view of these NCI controls on distribution and use of Group C drugs, intermediaries may assume, in the absence of evidence to the contrary, that a Group C drug and the related hospital stay are covered if all other applicable coverage requirements are satisfied.

If there is reason to question coverage in a particular case, the matter should be resolved with the assistance of the local PSRO, or if there is none, the assistance of your medical consultants.

Information regarding those drugs which are classified as Group C drugs may be obtained from:

Office of the Chief, Investigational Drug Branch
Division of Cancer Treatment, CTEP, Landow Building
Room 4C09, National Cancer Institute
Bethesda, Maryland 20205

45-20 ETHYLENEDIAMINE-TETRA-ACETIC (EDTA) CHELATION THERAPY FOR TREATMENT OF ATHEROSCLEROSIS

The use of EDTA as a chelating agent to treat atherosclerosis, arteriosclerosis, calcinosis, or similar generalized condition not listed by the FDA as an approved use is not covered. Any such use of EDTA is considered experimental.

See section 35-64 for an explanation of this conclusion.

45-22 LYMPHOCYTE IMMUNE GLOBULIN, ANTI-THYMOCYTE GLOBULIN (EQUINE)

The lymphocyte immune globulin preparations are biologic drugs not previously approved or licensed for use in the management of renal allograft rejection. A number of other lymphocyte immune globulin products of equine, lapine, and murine origin are currently under investigation for their potential usefulness in controlling allograft rejections in human transplantation. These biologic drugs are viewed as adjunctive to traditional immunosuppressive products such as steroids and anti-metabolic drugs. At present, lymphocyte immune globulin preparations are not recommended to replace conventional immunosuppressive drugs, but to supplement them and to be used as alternatives to elevated or accelerated dosing with conventional immunosuppressive agents.

The FDA has approved one lymphocyte immune globulin preparation for marketing, lymphocyte immune globulin, anti-thymocyte globulin (equine). This drug is indicated for the management of allograft rejection episodes in renal transplantation. It is covered under Medicare when used for this purpose. Other forms of lymphocyte globulin preparation which the FDA approves for this indication in the future may be covered under Medicare.

45-23 DIMETHYL SULFOXIDE (DMSO)

DMSO is an industrial solvent produced as a chemical byproduct of paper production from wood pulp. The Food and Drug Administration has determined that the only purpose for which DMSO is safe and effective for humans is in the treatment of the bladder condition, interstitial cystitis. Therefore, the use of DMSO for all other indications is not considered to be reasonable and necessary. Payment may be made for its use only when reasonable and necessary for a patient in the treatment of interstitial cystitis.

45-24 ANTI-INHIBITOR COAGULANT COMPLEX (AICC)

Anti-inhibitor coagulant complex, AICC, is a drug used to treat hemophilia in patients with factor VIII inhibitor antibodies. AICC has been shown to be safe and effective and has Medicare coverage when furnished to patients with hemophilia A and inhibitor antibodies to factor VIII who have major bleeding episodes and who fail to respond to other, less expensive therapies.

45-25 SUPPLIES USED IN THE DELIVERY OF TRANSCUTANEOUS ELECTRICAL NERVE STIMULATION (TENS) AND NEUROMUSCULAR ELECTRICAL STIMULATION (NMES)—

Transcutaneous Electrical Nerve Stimulation (TENS) and/or Neuromuscular Electrical Stimulation (NMES) can ordinarily be delivered to patients through the use of conventional electrodes, adhesive tapes and lead wires. There may be times, however, where it might be medically necessary for certain patients receiving TENS or NMES treatment to use, as an alternative to conventional electrodes, adhesive tapes and lead wires, a form-fitting conductive garment (i.e., a garment with conductive fibers which are separated from the patients' skin by layers of fabric).

A form-fitting conductive garment (and medically necessary related supplies) may be covered under the program only when:

1. It has received permission or approval for marketing by the Food and Drug Administration;

2. It has been prescribed by a physician for use in delivering covered TENS or NMES treatment; and

3. One of the medical indications outlined below is met:

- The patient cannot manage without the conductive garment because there is such a large area or so many sites to be stimulated and the stimulation would have to be delivered so frequently that it is not feasible to use conventional electrodes, adhesive tapes and lead wires;
- The patient cannot manage without the conductive garment for the treatment of chronic intractable pain because the areas or sites to be stimulated are inaccessible with the use of conventional electrodes, adhesive tapes and lead wires;

- The patient has a documented medical condition such as skin problems that preclude the application of conventional electrodes, adhesive tapes and lead wires;
- The patient requires electrical stimulation beneath a cast either to treat disuse atrophy, where the nerve supply to the muscle is intact, or to treat chronic intractable pain; or
- The patient has a medical need for rehabilitation strengthening (pursuant to a written plan of rehabilitation) following an injury where the nerve supply to the muscle is intact.

A conductive garment is not covered for use with a TENS device during the trial period specified in section 35-46 unless:

4. The patient has a documented skin problem prior to the start of the trial period; and

5. The carrier's medical consultants are satisfied that use of such an item is medically necessary for the patient.

(See conditions for coverage of the use of TENS in the diagnosis and treatment of chronic intractable pain in sections 35-46 and 60-20 and the use of NMES in the treatment of disuse atrophy in section 35-77.)

50 DIAGNOSTIC SERVICES

50-1 Cardiac Pacemaker Evaluation Services

Medicare covers a variety of services for the post-implant follow-up and evaluation of implanted cardiac pacemakers. The following guidelines are designed to assist contractors in identifying and processing claims for such services.

NOTE: These new guidelines are limited to lithium battery-powered pacemakers, because mercury-zinc battery-powered pacemakers are no longer being manufactured and virtually all have been replaced by lithium units. Contractors still receiving claims for monitoring such units should continue to apply the guidelines published in 1980 to those units until they are replaced.

There are two general types of pacemakers in current use—single-chamber pacemakers, which sense and pace the ventricles of the heart, and dual-chamber pacemakers which sense and pace both the atria and the ventricles. These differences require different monitoring patterns over the expected life of the units involved. One fact of which contractors should be aware is that many dual-chamber units may be programmed to pace only the ventricles; this may be done either at the time the device is implanted or at some time afterward. In such cases, a dual-chamber unit, when programmed or reprogrammed for ventricular pacing, should be treated as a single-chamber pacemaker in applying screening guidelines.

The decision as to how often any patient's pacemaker should be monitored is the responsibility of the patient's physician who is best able to take into account the condition and circumstances of the individual patient. These may vary over time, requiring modifications of the frequency with which the patient should be monitored. In cases where monitoring is done by some entity other than the patient's physician, such as a commercial monitoring service or hospital outpatient department, the physician's prescription for monitoring is required and should be periodically renewed (at least annually) to assure that the frequency of monitoring is proper for the patient. Where a patient is monitored both during clinic visits and transtelephonically, the contractor should be sure to include frequency data on both types of monitoring in evaluating the reasonableness of the frequency of monitoring services received by the patient.

Since there are over 200 pacemaker models in service at any given point, and a variety of patient conditions that give rise to the need for pacemakers, the question of the appropriate frequency of monitorings is a complex one. Nevertheless, it is possible to develop guidelines within which the vast majority of pacemaker monitorings will fall and contractors should do this, using their own data and experience, as well as the frequency guidelines which follow, in order to limit extensive claims development to those cases requiring special attention.

Guidelines for Transtelephonic Monitoring of Cardiac Pacemakers

A. General.—Transtelephonic monitoring of pacemakers is coming into increasingly widespread use, with the services being furnished by commercial suppliers, hospital outpatient departments and physicians' offices.

Telephone monitoring of cardiac pacemakers as described below is medically efficacious in identifying early signs of possible pacemaker failure, thus reducing the number of sudden pacemaker failures requiring emergency replacement. All systems which monitor the pacemaker rate (bpm) in both the free-running and/or magnetic mode are effective in detecting subclinical pacemaker failure due to battery depletion. More sophisticated systems are also capable of detecting internal electronic problems within the pulse generator itself and other potential problems. In the case of dual chamber pacemakers in particular, such monitoring may detect failure of synchronization of the atria and ventricles, and the need for adjustment and reprogramming of the device.

NOTE: The transmitting device furnished to the patient is simply one component of the diagnostic system, and is not covered as durable medical equipment. Those engaged in transtelephonic pacemaker monitoring should reflect the costs of the transmitters in setting their charges for monitoring.

B. Definition of Transtelephonic Monitoring.—In order for transtelephonic monitoring services to be covered, the services must consist of the following elements:

1. A minimum 30-second readable strip of the pacemaker in the free-running mode;

2. Unless contraindicated, a minimum 30-second readable strip of the pacemaker in the magnetic mode; and

3. A minimum 30 seconds of readable ECG strip.

C. Frequency Guidelines for Transtelephonic Monitoring.—The guidelines below constitute a system which contractors should use, in conjunction with their knowledge of local medical practices, to screen claims for transtelephonic monitoring prior to payment. It is important to note that they are not recommendations with respect to a minimum frequency for such monitorings, but rather a maximum frequency (within which payment may be made without further claims development). As with previous guidelines, more frequent monitorings may be covered in cases where contractors are satisfied that such monitorings are medically necessary; e.g., based on the condition of the patient, or with respect to pacemakers exhibiting unexpected defects or premature failure. Contractors should seek written justification for more frequent monitorings from the patient's physician and/or any monitoring service involved.

These guidelines are divided into two broad categories—Guideline I, which will apply to the majority of pacemakers now in use, and Guideline II, which will apply only to pacemaker systems (pacemaker and leads) for which sufficient long-term clinical information exists to assure that they meet the standards of the Inter-Society Commission for Heart Disease Resources (ICHD) for longevity and end-of-life decay. (The ICHD standards are: (1) 90 percent cumulative survival at 5 years following implant; and (2) an end-of-life decay of less than a 50 percent drop of output voltage and less than 20 percent deviation of magnet rate, or a drop of 5 beats per minute or less, over a period of 3 months or more.) Contractors should consult with their medical advisers and other appropriate individuals and organizations (such as the North American Society of Pacing and Electrophysiology, which publishes product reliability information) should questions arise over whether a pacemaker system meets the ICHD standards.

The two groups of guidelines are then further broken down into two general categories—single chamber and dual-chamber pacemakers. Contractors should be aware that the frequency with which a patient is monitored may be changed from time to time for a number of reasons, such as a change in the patient's overall condition, a reprogramming of the patient's pacemaker, the development of better information on the pacemaker's longevity or failure mode, etc. Consequently, changes in the proper

set of guidelines may be required. Contractors should inform physicians and monitoring services to alert contractors to any changes in the patient's monitoring prescription that might necessitate changes in the screening guidelines applied to that patient. (Of particular importance is the reprogramming of a dual-chamber pacemaker to a single-chamber mode of operation. Such reprogramming would shift the patient from the appropriate dual-chamber guideline to the appropriate single-chamber guideline.)

Guideline I

1. Single-chamber pacemakers:
   1st month—every 2 weeks.
   2nd through 36th month—every 8 weeks.
   37th month to failure—every 4 weeks.

2. Dual-chamber pacemaker:
   1st month—every 2 weeks.
   2nd through 6th month—every 4 weeks.
   7th through 36th month—every 8 weeks.
   37th month to failure—every 4 weeks.

Guideline II

1. Single-chamber pacemakers:
   1st month—every 2 weeks.
   2nd through 48th month—every 12 weeks.
   49th through 72nd month—every 8 weeks.
   Thereafter—every 4 weeks.

2. Dual-chamber pacemaker:
   1st month—every 2 weeks.
   2nd through 30th month—every 12 weeks.
   31st through 48th month—every 8 weeks.
   Thereafter—every 4 weeks.

D. Pacemaker Clinic Services

1. General—Pacemaker monitoring is also covered when done by pacemaker clinics. Clinic visits may be done in conjunction with transtelephonic monitoring or as a separate service; however, the services rendered by a pacemaker clinic are more extensive than those currently possible by telephone. They include, for example, physical examination of patients and reprogramming of pacemakers. Thus, the use of one of these types of monitoring does not preclude concurrent use of the other.

2. Frequency Guidelines—As with transtelephonic pacemaker monitoring, the frequency of clinic visits is the decision of the patient's physician, taking into account, among other things, the medical condition of the patient. However, contractors can develop monitoring guidelines that will prove useful in screening claims. The following are recommendations for monitoring guidelines on lithium-battery pacemakers:

a. For single-chamber pacemakers—twice in the first 6 months following implant, then once every 12 months.

b. For dual-chamber pacemakers—twice in the first 6 months, then once every 6 months.

50-4 GRAVLEE JET WASHER

The Gravlee Jet Washer is a sterile, disposable, diagnostic device for detecting endometrial cancer. The use of this device is indicated where the patient exhibits clinical symptoms or signs suggestive of endometrial disease, such as irregular or heavy vaginal bleeding.

Program payment cannot be made for the washer or the related diagnostic services when furnished in connection with the examination of an asymptomatic patient. Payment for routine physical checkups is precluded under the statute. (See section 1862(a)(7) of the Act.)

(See Intermediary Manual, section 3157 and Carriers Manual, section 2320.)

50-15 ELECTROCARDIOGRAPHIC SERVICES

Reimbursement may be made under Part B for electrocardiographic (EKG) services rendered by a physician or incident to his/her services or by an approved laboratory or an approved supplier of portable X-ray services. Since there is no coverage for EKG services of any type rendered on a screening basis or as part of a routine examination, the claim must indicate the signs and symptoms or other clinical reason necessitating the services.

A separate charge by an attending or consulting physician for EKG interpretation is allowed only when it is the normal practice to make such charge in addition to the regular office visit charge. No payment is made for EKG interpretations by individuals other than physicians.

On a claim involving EKG services furnished by a laboratory or a portable X-ray supplier, identify the physician ordering the service and, when the charge includes both the taking of the tracing and its interpretation, include the identity of the physician making the interpretation. No separate bill for the services of a physician is paid unless it is clear that he/she was the patient's attending physician or was acting as a consulting physician. The taking of an EKG in an emergency, i.e., when the patient is or may be experiencing what is commonly referred to as a heart attack, is covered as a laboratory service or a diagnostic service by a portable X-ray supplier only when the evidence shows that a physician was in attendance at the time the service was performed or immediately thereafter.

Where EKG services are rendered in the patient's home and the laboratory's or portable X-ray supplier's charge is higher than that imposed for the same service when performed in the laboratory or portable X-ray supplier's office, the medical need for home service should be documented. In the absence of such justification, reimbursement for the service if otherwise medically necessary should be based on the reasonable charge applicable when performed in the laboratory or X-ray supplier's office.

The documentation required in the various situations mentioned above must be furnished not only when the laboratory or portable X-ray supplier bills the patient or carrier for its service, but also when such a facility bills the attending physician who, in turn, bills the patient or carrier for the EKG services. (In addition to the evidence required to document the claim, the laboratory or portable X-ray supplier must maintain in its records the referring physician's written order and the identity of the employee taking the tracing.)

Long Term EKG Monitoring, also referred to as long-term EKG recording, Holter recording, or dynamic electrocardiography, is a diagnostic procedure which provides a continuous record of the electrocardiographic activity of a patient's heart while he is engaged in his daily activities.

The basic components of the long-term EKG monitoring systems are a sensing element, the design of which may provide either for the recording of electrocardiographic information on magnetic tape or for detecting significant variations in rate or rhythm as they occur, and a component for either graphically recording the electrocardiographic data or for visual or computer assisted analysis of the information recorded on magnetic tape. The long-term EKG permits the examination in the ambulant or potentially ambulant patient of as many as 70,000 heartbeats in a 12-hour recording while the standard EKG which is obtained in the recumbent position, yields information on only 50 to 60 cardiac cycles and provides only a limited data base on which diagnostic judgments may be made.

Many patients with cardiac arrhythmias are unaware of the presence of an irregularity in heart rhythm. Due to the transient nature of many arrhythmias and the short intervals in which the rhythm of the heart is observed by conventional standard EKG techniques, the offending arrhythmias can go undetected. With the extended examination provided by the long-term EKG, the physician is able not only to detect but also to classify various types of rhythm disturbances and waveform abnormalities and note the frequency of their occurrence. The knowledge of the reaction of the heart to daily activities with respect to rhythm, rate, conduction disturbances, and ischemic changes are of great assistance in directing proper therapy and rehabilitation.

This modality is valuable in both inpatient and outpatient diagnosis and therapy. Long-term monitoring of ambulant or potentially ambulant inpatients provides significant potential for reducing the length of stay for post-coronary infarct patients in the intensive care setting and may result in earlier discharge from the hospital with greater assurance of safety to the patients. The indications for the use of this technique, noted below, are similar for both inpatients and outpatients.

The long-term EKG has proven effective in detecting transient episodes of cardiac dysrhythmia and in permitting the correlation of these episodes with cardiovascular symptomatology. It is also useful for patients who have symptoms of obscure etiology suggestive of cardiac arrhythmia. Examples of such symptoms include palpitations, chest pain, dizziness, light-headedness, near syncope, syncope, transient ischemic episodes, dyspnea, and shortness of breath.

This technique would also be appropriate at the time of institution of any arrhythmic drug therapy and may be performed during the course of therapy to evaluate response. It is also appropriate for evaluating a change of dosage and may be indicated shortly before and after the discontinuation of anti-arrhythemic medication. The therapeutic response to a drug whose duration of action and peak of effectiveness is defined in hours cannot be properly assessed by examining 30 to 40 cycles on a standard EKG rhythm strip. The knowledge that all patients placed on anti-arrhythmic medication do not respond to therapy and the known toxicity of anti-arrhythmic agents clearly indicate that proper assessment should be made on an individual basis to determine whether medication should be continued and at what dosage level.

The long-term EKG is also valuable in the assessment of patients with coronary artery disease. It enables the documentation of etiology of such symptoms as chest pain and shortness of breath. Since the standard EKG is often normal during the intervals between the episodes of precordial pain, it is essential to obtain EKG information while the symptoms are occurring. The long-term EKG has enabled the correlation of chest symptoms with the objective evidence of ST-segment abnormalities. It is appropriate for patients who are recovering from an acute mycardial infarction or coronary insufficiency before and after discharge from the hospital, since it is impossible to predict which of these patients is subject to ventricular arrhythmias on the basis of the presence or absence of rhythm disturbances during the period of initial coronary care. The long-term EKG enables the physician to identify patients who are at a higher risk of dying suddenly in the period following an acute myocardial infarction. It may also be reasonable and necessary where the high-risk patient with known cardiovascular disease advances to a substantially higher level of activity which might trigger increased or new types of arrhythmias necessitating treatment. Such a high-risk case would be one in which there is documentation that acute phase arrhythmias have not totally disappeared during the period of convalescence.

In view of recent developments in cardiac pacemaker monitoring techniques (see CIA 50-1), the use of the long-term EKG for routine assessment of pacemaker function can no longer be justified. Its use for the patient with an internal pacemaker would be covered only when he has symptoms suggestive of arrhythmia not revealed by the standard EKG or rhythm strip.

These guidelines are intended as a general outline of the circumstances under which the use of this diagnostic procedure would be warranted. Each patient receiving a long-term EKG should be evaluated completely, prior to performance of this diagnostic study. A complete history and physical examination should be obtained and the indications for use of the long-term EKG should be reviewed by the referring physician.

The performance of a long-term EKG does not necessarily require the prior performance of a standard EKG. Nor does the demonstration of a normal standard EKG preclude the need for a long-term EKG. Finally, the demonstration of an abnormal standard EKG does not obviate the need for a long-term EKG if there is suspicion that the dysrhythmia is transient in nature.

A period of recording of up to 24 hours would normally be adequate to detect most transient arrhythmias and provide essential diagnostic information. The medical necessity for longer periods of monitoring must be documented.

Medical documentation for adjudicating claims for the use of the long-term EKG should be similar to other EKG services, X-ray services, and laboratory procedures. Generally, a statement of the diagnostic impression of the referring physician with an indication of the patient's relevant signs and symptoms should be sufficient for purposes of making a determination regarding the reasonableness and medical necessity for the use of this procedure. However, the intermediaries or carriers should require whatever additional documentation their medical consultants deem necessary to properly adjudicate the individual claim where the information submitted is not adequate.

It should be noted that the recording device furnished to the patient is simply one component of the diagnostic system and a separate charge for it will not be recognized under the durable medical equipment benefit.

Patient-Activated EKG Recorders, distributed under a variety of brand names, permit the patient to record an EKG upon manifestation of symptoms, or in response to a physician's order (e.g., immediately following strong exertion). Most such devices also permit the patient to simultaneously voice-record in order to describe symptoms and/or activity. In addition, some of these devices permit transtelephonic transmission of the recording to a physician's office, clinic, hospital, etc., having a decoder/recorder for review and analysis, thus eliminating the need to physically transport the tape. Some of these devices also permit a "time sampling" mode of operation. However, the "time sampling" mode is not covered—only the patient-activated mode of operation, when used for the indications described below, is covered at this time.

Services in connection with patient-activated EKG recorders are covered when used as an alternative to the long-term EKG monitoring (described above) for similar indications—detecting and characterizing symptomatic arrhythmias, regulation of anti-arrhythmic drug therapy, etc. Like long-term EKG monitoring, use of these devices is covered for evaluating patients with symptoms of obscure etiology suggestive of cardiac arrhythmia such as palpitations, chest pain, dizziness, lightheadedness, near syncope, syncope, transient ischemic episodes, dyspnea and shortness of breath.

As with long-term EKG monitors, patient-activated EKG recorders may be useful for both inpatient and outpatient diagnosis and therapy. While useful for assessing some post-coronary infarct patients in the hospital setting, these devices should not, however, be covered for outpatient monitoring of recently discharged post-infarct patients.

Computer Analyzed Electrocardiograms.—Computer interpretation of EKGs is recognized as a valid and effective technique which will improve the quality and availability of cardiology services. Reimbursement may be made for such computer service when furnished in the setting and under the circumstances required for coverage of other electrocardiographic services. Where either a laboratory's or a portable x-ray supplier's charge for EKG services includes the physician review and certification of the printout as well as the computer interpretation, the certifying physician must be identified on the HCFA-1490 before the entire charge can be considered a reimbursable charge. Where the laboratory's (or portable x-ray supplier's) reviewing physician is not identified, the carrier should conclude that no professional component is involved and make its charge determination accordingly. If the supplying laboratory (or portable x-ray supplier when supplied by such a facility) does not include professional review and certification of the hard copy, a charge by the patient's physician may be recognized for the service. In any case the charge for the physician component should be substantially less than that for physician interpretation of the conventional EKG tracing in view of markedly reduced demand on the physician's time where computer interpretation is involved. Considering the unit cost reduction expected of this innovation, the total charge for the complete EKG service (taking of tracing and interpretation) when computer interpretation is employed should never exceed that considered reasonable for the service when physician interpretation is involved.

Transtelephonic Electrocardiographic Transmissions (Formerly Referred to as EKG Telephone Reporter Systems).—Effective for services furnished on and after March 1, 1980, coverage is extended to include the use of transtelephonic electrocardiographic (EKG) transmissions as a diagnostic service for the indications described below, when performed with equipment meeting the standards described below, subject to the limitations and conditions specified below. Coverage is further limited to the amounts payable with respect to the physician's service in interpreting the results of such transmissions, including charges for rental of the equipment. The device used by the beneficiary is part of a total diagnostic system and is not considered durable medical equipment.

1. Covered Uses.—The use of transtelephonic EKGs is covered for the following uses:

a. To detect, characterize, and document symptomatic transient arrhythmias;

b. To overcome problems in regulating antiarrhythmic drug dosage;

c. To carry out early posthospital monitoring of patients discharged after myocardial infarction; (only if 24-hour coverage is provided, see 4. below).

Since cardiology is a rapidly changing field, some uses other than those specified above may be covered if, in the judgment of the contractor's medical consultants, such a use was justifiable in the particular case. The enumerated uses above represent uses for which a firm coverage determination has been made, and for which contractors may make payment without extensive claims development or review.

2. Specifications for Devices.—The devices used by the patient are highly portable (usually pocket-sized) and detect and convert the normal EKG signal so that it can be transmitted via ordinary telephone apparatus to a receiving station. At the receiving end, the signal is decoded and transcribed into a conventional EKG. There are numerous devices available which transmit EKG readings in this fashion. For purposes of Medicare coverage, however, the transmitting devices must meet at least the following criteria:

a. They must be capable of transmitting EKG Leads, I, II, or III;

b. These lead transmissions must be sufficiently comparable to readings obtained by a conventional EKG to permit proper interpretation of abnormal cardiac rhythms.

3. Potential for Abuse—Need for Screening Guidelines.—While the use of these devices may often compare favorably with more costly alternatives, this is the case only where the information they contribute is actively utilized by a knowledgeable practitioner as part of overall medical management of the patient. Consequently, it is vital that contractors be aware of the potential for abuse of these devices, and adopt necessary screening and physician education policies to detect and halt potentially abusive situations. For example, use of these devices to diagnose and treat suspected arrhythmias as a routine substitute for more conventional methods of diagnosis, such as a careful history, physical examination, and standard EKG and rhythm strip would not be appropriate. Moreover, contractors should require written justification for use of such devices in excess of 30 consecutive days in cases involving detection of transient arrhythmias.

Contractors may find it useful to review claims for these devices with a view toward detecting patterns of practice which may be useful in developing schedules which may be adopted for screening such claims in the future.

4. Twenty-four Hour Coverage.—No payment may be made for the use of these devices to carry out early posthospital monitoring of patients discharged after myocardial infarction unless provision is made for 24 hour coverage in the manner described below.

Twenty-four hour coverage means that there must be, at the monitoring site (or sites) an experienced EKG technician receiving calls; tape recording devices do not meet this requirement. Further, such technicians should have immediate access to a physician, and have been instructed in when and how to contact available facilities to assist the patient in case of emergencies.

Cross-refer: HCFA-Pub. 13-3, sections 3101.5, 3110, 3112.3, HCFA-Pub. 14-3, sections 2070, 2255, 2050.1

50-20 DIAGNOSTIC PAP SMEARS

A diagnostic Pap smear and related medically necessary services are covered under Medicare Part B when ordered by a physician under one of the following conditions:

- Previous cancer of the cervix, uterus, or vagina that has been or is presently being treated;
- Previous abnormal Pap smear;
- Any abnormal findings of the vagina, cervix, uterus, ovaries, or adnexa;
- Any significant complaint by the patient referrable to the female reproductive system; or
- Any signs or symptoms that might in the physician's judgment reasonably be related to a gynecologic disorder.

In respect to the last bullet, the contractor's medical staff must determine whether in a particular case a previous malignancy at another site is an indication for a diagnositic Pap smear or whether the test must be considered a screening Pap smear as described in section 50-20.1.

50-20.1 Screening PAP Smears and Pelvic Examinations for Early Detection of Cervical or Vaginal Cancer
(For screening Pap smears, effective for services performed on or after July 1, 1990. For pelvic examinations including clinical breast examination, effective for services furnished on or after January 1, 1998.)

A screening Pap smear (use HCPCS code P3000 Screening Papanicolaou smear, cervical or vaginal, up to three smears; by technician under physician supervision *or* P3001 Screening Papanicolaou smear, cervical or vaginal, up to three smears requiring interpretation by physician). (Use HCPCS codes G0123 Screening Cytopathology, cervical or vaginal (any reporting system), collected in preservation fluid, automated thin layer preparation, screening by cytotechnologist under physician supervision *or* G0124 Screening Cytopathology, cervical or vaginal (any reporting system) collected in preservative fluid, automated thin layer preparation, requiring interpretation by physician) and related medically necessary services provided to a woman for the early detection of cervical cancer (including collection of the sample of cells and a physician's interpretation of the test results) and pelvic examination (including clinical breast examination) (use HCPCS code G0101 cervical or vaginal cancer screening; pelvic and clinical breast examination) are covered under Medicare Part B when ordered by a physician (or authorized practitioner) under one of the following conditions:

- She has not had such a test during the preceding 3 years or is a woman of childbearing age (section 1861(nn) of the Act).
- There is evidence (on the basis of her medical history or other findings) that she is at high risk of developing cervical cancer and her physician (or authorized practitioner) recommends that she have the test performed more frequently than every 3 years.

High risk factors for cervical and vaginal cancer are:

- Early onset of sexual activity (under 16 years of age)
- Multiple sexual partners (five or more in a lifetime)
- History of sexually transmitted disease (including HIV infection)
- Fewer than three negative or any Pap smears within the previous 7 years; and
- DES (diethylstilbestrol)-exposed daughters of women who took DES during pregnancy.

NOTE: Claims for Pap smears must indicate the beneficiary's low or high risk status by including the appropriate ICD-9-CM on the line item (Item 24E of the HCFA-1500).

- V76.2, special screening for malignant neoplasms of the cervix, indicates low risk; and

- V15.89, other specified personal history presenting hazards to health, indicates high risk.

If Pap smear or pelvic exam claims do not point to one of these diagnosis codes, the claim will reject in the Common Working File. Claims can contain up to four diagnosis codes, but the one pointed to on the line item must be either V76.2 or V15.89.

Definitions:

A woman as described in section 1861(nn) of the Act is a woman who is of childbearing age and has had a Pap smear test during any of the preceding 3 years that indicated the presence of cervical or vaginal cancer or other abnormality, or is at high risk of developing cervical or vaginal cancer.

A woman of childbearing age is one who is premenopausal and has been determined by a physician or other qualified practitioner to be of childbearing age, based upon the medical history or other findings.

"Other qualified practitioner," as defined in 42 CFR 410.56(a) includes a certified nurse midwife (as defined in section 1861(gg) of the Act), or a physician assistant, nurse practitioner, or clinical nurse specialist (as defined in section 1861(aa) of the Act) who is authorized under State law to perform the examination.

Screening Pelvic Examination:

Section 4102 of the Balanced Budget Act of 1997 provides for coverage of screening pelvic examinations (including a clinical breast examination) for all female beneficiaries, effective January 1, 1998, subject to certain frequency and other limitations. A screening pelvic examination (including a clinical breast examination) should include at least seven of the following eleven elements:

- Inspection and palpation of breasts for masses or lumps, tenderness, symmetry, or nipple discharge.
- Digital rectal examination including sphincter tone, presence of hemorrhoids, and rectal masses. Pelvic examination (with or without specimen collection for smears and cultures) including:
- External genitalia (e.g., general appearance, hair distribution, or lesions).
- Urethral meatus (e.g., size, location, lesions, or prolapse).
- Urethra (e.g., masses, tenderness, or scarring).
- Bladder (e.g., fullness, masses, or tenderness).
- Vagina (e.g., general appearance, estrogen effect, discharge lesions, pelvic support, cystocele, or rectocele).
- Cervix (e.g., general appearance, lesions, or discharge).
- Uterus (e.g., size, contour, position, mobility, tenderness, consistency, descent, or support).
- Adnexa/parametria (e.g., masses, tenderness, organomegaly, or nodularity).
- Anus and perineum.

This description is from Documentation Guidelines for Evaluation and Management Services, published in May 1997 and was developed by the Health Care Financing Administration and the American Medical Association.

50-24 HAIR ANALYSIS—NOT COVERED

Hair analysis to detect mineral traces as an aid in diagnosing human disease is not a covered service under Medicare.

The correlation of hair analysis to the chemical state of the whole body is not possible at this time, and therefore this diagnostic procedure cannot be considered to be reasonable and necessary under section 1862(a)(1) of the law.

50-34 OBSOLETE OR UNRELIABLE DIAGNOSTIC TESTS

   A. Diagnostic Tests (Effective for Services Performed on or after May 15, 1980.—Do not routinely pay for the following diagnostic tests because they are obsolete and have been replaced by more advanced procedures. The listed tests may be paid for only if the medical need for the procedure is satisfactorily justified by the physician who performs it. When the services are subject to PRO review, the PRO is responsible for determining that satisfactory medical justification exists. When the services are not subject to

PRO review, the intermediary or carrier is responsible for determining that satisfactory medical justification exists. This includes:

- Amylase, blood isoenzymes, electrophoretic,
- Chromium, blood,
- Guanase, blood,
- Zinc sulphate turbidity, blood,
- Skin test, cat scratch fever,
- Skin test, lymphopathia venereum,
- Circulation time, one test,
- Cephalin flocculation,
- Congo red, blood,
- Hormones, adrenocorticotropin quantitative animal tests,
- Hormones, adrenocorticotropin quantitative bioassay,
- Thymol turbidity, blood,
- Skin test, actinomycosis,
- Skin test, brucellosis,
- Skin test, psittacosis,
- Skin test, trichinosis,
- Calcium, feces, 24-hour quantitative,
- Starch, feces, screening,
- Chymotrypsin, duodenal contents,
- Gastric analysis, pepsin,
- Gastric analysis, tubeless,
- Calcium saturation clotting time,
- Capillary fragility test (Rumpel-Leede),
- Colloidal gold,
- Bendien's test for cancer and tuberculosis,
- Bolen's test for cancer,
- Rehfuss test for gastric acidity, and
- Serum seromucoid assay for cancer and other diseases.

B. Cardiovascular Tests (Effective For Services Performed On or After January 1, 1997).—Do not pay for the following phonocardiography and vectorcardiography diagnostic tests because they have been determined to be outmoded and of little clinical value. They include:

- Phonocardiogram with or without ECG lead; with supervision during recording with interpretation and report (when equipment is supplied by the physician),
- Phonocardiogram; tracing only, without interpretation and report (e.g., when equipment is supplied by the hospital, clinic),
- Phonocardiogram; interpretation and report,
- Phonocardiogram with EKG lead, with indirect carotid artery and/or jugular vein tracing, and/or apex cardiogram; with interpretation and report,
- Phonocardiogram; without interpretation and report;
- Phonocardiogram; interpretation and report only;
- Intracardiac;
- Vectorcardiogram (VCG), with or without ECG; with interpretation and report;
- Vectorcardiogram; tracing only, without interpretation and report; and
- Vectorcardiogram; interpretation and report only.

50-36　POSITRON EMISSION TOMOGRAPHY (PET or PETT) SCANS (EFFECTIVE FOR SERVICES PERFORMED ON OR AFTER MARCH 14, 1995)

I. General Description

Positron emission tomography (PET), also known as positron emission transverse tomography (PETT), is a noninvasive imaging procedure that assesses perfusion and the level of metabolic activity in various organ systems of the human body. A positron camera (tomograph) is used to produce cross-sectional tomographic images by detecting radioactivity from a radioactive tracer substance (radiopharmaceutical) that is injected into the patient.

Medicare has been continuously reviewing the scientific literature regarding PET scans, and has established coverage for three uses—one in 1995 and two in 1998 (see below). As with other new or evolving technologies, we will continue to review the progress of this technology, with a view toward modifying our policy, based upon the best evidence available as to the medical effectiveness of such scans. This instruction adds coverage of PET for evaluation of recurrent colorectal cancer in patients with rising levels of carcino-

embryonic antigen (CEA), for staging of lymphoma (both Hodgkins and non-Hodgkins) when the PET scan substitutes for a Gallium scan, and for the detection of recurrent melanoma. All other uses of PET scans remain not covered by Medicare.

II. Conditions Applicable to All Covered Uses of PET Scans:

Regardless of any other terms or conditions, all uses of PET scans, in order to be covered by the Medicare program, must meet the following conditions:

1. Such scans must be performed using a camera that has either been approved or cleared for marketing by the FDA to image radionuclides in the body.

2. Submission of claims for payment must include any information Medicare requires to assure that the PET scans performed were: (a) medically necessary; (b) did not unnecessarily duplicate other covered diagnostic tests, and (c) did not involve investigational drugs or procedures using investigational drugs, as determined by the Food and Drug Administration (FDA).

3. The PET scan entity submitting claims for payment must keep such patient records as Medicare requires on file for each patient for whom a PET scan claim is made.

III. Coverage of PET Scans Using Rubidium 82 (Rb 82) and Related Tests—Effective for Services Performed on or After March 14, 1995:

PET scans done at rest or with pharmacological stress used for noninvasive imaging of the perfusion of the heart for the diagnosis and management of patients with known or suspected coronary artery disease using the FDA-approved radiopharmaceutical Rubidium 82 (Rb 82) are covered, provided such scans meet either one of the two following conditions:

1. The PET scan, whether rest alone or rest with stress, is used in place of, but not in addition to, a single photon emission computed tomography (SPECT); or

2. The PET scan, whether rest alone or rest with stress, is used following a SPECT that was found inconclusive. In these cases, the PET scan must have been considered necessary in order to determine what medical or surgical intervention is required to treat the patient. (For purposes of this requirement, an inconclusive test is a test(s) whose results are equivocal, technically uninterpretable, or discordant with a patient's other clinical data.)

NOTE: PET scans using rubidium 82, whether rest or stress, are not covered by Medicare for routine screening or asymptomatic patients, regardless of the level of risk factors applicable to such patients.

C. Submission of Claims Data.—Claims for PET scans must include the following information. Failure to submit this information may result in denial of a claim.

The PET center must, for any PET scan for which payment is claimed, complete all required information on the claim form (including proper codes and modifiers) to indicate the results of the PET scan, as well as information as to whether the PET scan was done after an inconclusive noninvasive cardiac test. The information submitted with respect to the previous cardiac test must specify the type of test done prior to the PET scan and whether it was inconclusive or unsatisfactory. These explanations are in the form of special G codes used for billing PET scans.

D. Maintenance of Patient Record Data Onsite.—In view of these limitations on coverage, HCFA may decide to conduct some postpayment reviews to determine that the use of PET scans is consistent with this instruction. PET centers must keep patient record information on file for each Medicare patient for whom a PET scan claim is made. These medical records will be used in any postpayment reviews and must include the information necessary to substantiate the need for the PET scan. The records must include standard information (e.g., age, sex, and height) along with any annotations regarding body size or type which indicated a need for a PET scan to determine that patient's condition (i.e., any reason the nature of the patient's body size or type mandated the use of a PET scan in order to continue treatment).

50-42 AMBULATORY BLOOD PRESSURE MONITORING WITH FULLY AND SEMI-AUTOMATIC (PATIENT-ACTIVATED) PORTABLE MONITORS—NOT COVERED

While ambulatory blood pressure monitoring in hypertensive patients using fully and semi-automatic (patient-activated) portable monitors is a safe and accurate means of measuring blood pressure, the clinical usefulness of the data obtained from such devices is not clearly established. Researchers and clinicians cite the need for standardization of instrumentation and further study of this technology to better ascertain its role in hypertensive therapy. Accordingly, program payment may not be made for the use of such devices at this time.

50-44 BONE (MINERAL) DENSITY STUDIES

Bone (mineral) density studies are used to evaluate diseases of bone and/or the responses of bone diseases to treatment. The studies assess bone mass or density associated with such diseases as osteoporosis, osteomalacia, and renal osteodystrophy. Various single or combined methods of measurement may be required to: (a) diagnose bone disease, (b) monitor the course of bone changes with disease progression, or (c) monitor the course of bone changes with therapy. Bone density is usually studied by using photodensitometry, single or dual photon absorptiometry, or bone biopsy. The following bone (mineral) density studies are covered under Medicare:

A. Single Photon Absorptiometry.—A non-invasive radiological technique that measures absorption of a monochromatic photon beam by bone material. The device is placed directly on the patient, uses a low dose of radionuclide, and measures the mass absorption efficiency of the energy used. It provides a quantitative measurement of the bone mineral of cortical and trabecular bone, and is used in assessing an individual's treatment response at appropriate intervals.

Single photon absorptiometry is covered under Medicare when used in assessing changes in bone density of patients with osteodystrophy or osteoporosis when performed on the same individual at intervals of 6 to 12 months.

B. Bone Biopsy.—A physiologic test which is a surgical, invasive procedure. A small sample of bone (usually from the ilium) is removed, generally by a biopsy needle. The biopsy sample is then examined histologically, and provides a qualitative measurement of the bone mineral of trabecular bone. This procedure is used in ascertaining a differential diagnosis of bone disorders and is used primarily to differentiate osteomalacia from osteoporosis.

Bone biopsy is covered under Medicare when used for the qualitative evaluation of bone no more than four times per patient, unless there is special justification given. When used more than four times on a patient, bone biopsy leaves a defect in the pelvis and may produce some patient discomfort.

C. Photodensitometry (Radiographic Absorptiometry).—A non-invasive radiological procedure that attempts to assess bone mass by measuring the optical density of extremity radiographs with a photodensitometer, usually with a reference to a standard density wedge placed on the film at the time of exposure. This procedure provides a quantitative measurement of the bone mineral of cortical bone, and is used for monitoring gross bone change.

The following bone (mineral) density study is not covered under Medicare: dual photon absorptiometry. A noninvasive radiological technique that measures absorption of a dichromatic beam by bone material. This procedure is not covered under Medicare because it is still considered to be in the investigational stage.

50-50 DISPLACEMENT CARDIOGRAPHY

Displacement cardiography, including cardiokymography and photokymography, is a noninvasive diagnostic test used in evaluating coronary artery disease.

A. Cardiokymography.—(Effective for Services Rendered on or after October 12, 1988).

Cardiokymography is a covered service only when it is used as an adjunct to electrocardiographic stress testing in evaluating coronary artery disease and only when the following clinical indications are present:

• For male patients, atypical angina pectoris or nonischemic chest pain; or
• For female patients, angina, either typical or atypical.

B. Photokymography.—not covered. Photokymography remains excluded from coverage.

50-54 CARDIAC OUTPUT MONITORING BY ELECTRICAL BIOIMPEDANCE—NOT COVERED (Effective for services performed on or after July 1, 1999)

Cardiac monitoring using electrical bioimpedance, a form of plethysmography, is covered, effective for services furnished on or after July 1, 1999, for the uses and conditions described below. Contractors should be aware that this technology is in the process of being proven for additional uses. Therefore, the uses below represent the current situation. Contractors may cover additional uses when they believe there is sufficient evidence of the medical effectiveness of such uses.

These devices utilize electrical bioimpedance to noninvasively produce hemodynamic measurements of cardiac output, specifically, stroke volume, contractility, systemic vascular resistance, and thoracic fluid content. These devices are covered for the following uses:

1. Noninvasive diagnosis or monitoring of hemodynamics in patients with suspected or known cardiovascular disease;

2. Differentiation of cardiogenic from pulmonary causes of acute dyspnea;

3. Optimization of atrioventricular interval for patient with A/V sequential cardiac pacemakers;

4. Patients with need of determination for intravenous inotropic therapy;

5. Post heart transplant myocardial biopsy patients; and,

6. Patients with a need for fluid management.

Not covered at this time are the use of such devices for any monitoring of patients with proven or suspected disease involving severe regurgitation of the aorta, or for patients with minute ventilation (MV) sensor function pacemakers, since the device may adversely affect the functioning of that type of pacemaker. Also, these devices do not render accurate measurements in cardiac bypass patients while on a cardiopulmonary bypass machine, but do provide accurate measurements prior to and post bypass pump.

Covered uses of cardiac output monitoring by electrical bioimpedance should be billed using HCPCS code M0302.

50-55 PROSTATE CANCER SCREENING TESTS—COVERED (Effective for services furnished on or after January 1, 2000)

A. General—Section 4103 of the Balanced Budget Act of 1997 provides for coverage of certain prostate cancer screening tests subject to certain coverage, frequency, and payment limitations. Effective for services furnished on or after January 1, 2000. Medicare will cover prostate cancer screening tests/procedures for the early detection of prostate cancer.

Coverage of prostate cancer screening tests includes the following procedures furnished to an individual for the early detection of prostate cancer:

• Screening digital rectal examination; and
• Screening prostate specific antigen blood test.

B. Screening Digital Rectal Examinations—Screening digital rectal examinations (HCPCS code G0102) are covered at a frequency of once every 12 months for men who have attained age 50 (at least 11 months have passed following the month in which the last Medicare-covered screening digital rectal examination was performed). Screening digital rectal examination means a clinical examination of an individual's prostate for nodules or other abnormalities of the prostate. This screening must be performed by a doctor of medicine or osteopathy (as defined in section 1861(r)(1) of the Act), or by a physician assistant, nurse practitioner, clinical nurse specialist, or certified nurse midwife (as defined in section 1861(aa) and section 1861(gg) of the Act) who is authorized under State law to perform the examination, fully knowledgeable about the beneficiary's medical condition, and would be responsible for using the results of any examination performed in the overall management of the beneficiary's specific medical problem.

C. Screening Prostate Specific Antigen Tests.—Screening prostate specific antigen tests (code G0103) are covered at a frequency of once every 12 months for men who have attained age 50 (at least 11 months have passed following the month in which the last Medicare-covered screening prostate specific antigen test was performed). Screening prostate specific antigen tests (PSA) means a test to detect the marker for adenocarcinoma of prostate. PSA is a reliable immunocytochemical marker for primary and metastatic adenocarcinoma of prostate. This screening must be ordered by the beneficiary's physician or by the beneficiary's physician assistant, nurse practitioner, clinical nurse specialist, or certified nurse midwife (the term "attending physician" is defined in section 1861(r)(1) of the Act to mean a doctor of medicine or osteopathy and the terms "physician assistant, nurse practitioner, clinical nurse specialist, or certified nurse midwife" are defined in section 1861(aa) and section 1861(gg) of the Act) who is fully knowledgeable about the beneficiary's medical condition, and who would be responsible for using the results of any examination (test) performed in the overall management of the beneficiary's specific medical problem.

55 DIALYSIS EQUIPMENT

55-1 WATER PURIFICATION AND SOFTENING SYSTEMS USED IN CONJUNCTION WITH HOME DIALYSIS

A. Water Purification Systems.—Water used for home dialysis should be chemically free of heavy trace metals and/or organic contaminants which could be hazardous to the patient. It should also be as free of bacteria as possible but need not be biologically sterile. Since the characteristics of natural water supplies in most areas of the country are such that some type of water purification system is needed, such a system used in conjunction with a home dialysis (either peritoneal or hemodialysis) unit is covered under Medicare.

There are two types of water purification systems which will satisfy these requirements:

Deionization—The removal of organic substances, mineral salts of magnesium and calcium (causing hardness), compounds of fluoride and chloride from tap water using the process of filtration and ion exchange; or

Reverse Osmosis—The process used to remove impurities from tap water utilizing pressure to force water through a porous membrane.

Use of both a deionization unit and reverse osmosis unit in series, theoretically to provide the advantages of both systems, has been determined medically unnecessary since either system can provide water which is both chemically and bacteriologically pure enough for acceptable use in home dialysis. In addition, spare deionization tanks are not covered since they are essentially a precautionary supply rather than a current requirement for treatment of the patient.

Activated carbon filters used as a component of water purification systems to remove unsafe concentrations of chlorine and chloramines are covered when prescribed by a physician.

B. Water Softening System.—Except as indicated below, a water softening system used in conjunction with home dialysis is excluded from coverage under Medicare as not being reasonable and necessary within the meaning of section 1862(a)(1) of the law. Such a system, in conjunction with a home dialysis unit, does not

adequately remove the hazardous heavy metal contaminants (such as arsenic) which may be present in trace amounts.

A water softening system may be covered when used to pretreat water to be purified by a reverse osmosis (RO) unit for home dialysis where:

- The manufacturer of the RO unit has set standards for the quality of water entering the RO (e.g., the water to be purified by the RO must be of a certain quality if the unit is to perform as intended);
- The patient's water is demonstrated to be of a lesser quality than required; and
- The softener is used only to soften water entering the RO unit, and thus, used only for dialysis. (The softener need not actually be built into the RO unit, but must be an integral part of the dialysis system.)

C. Developing Need When a Water Softening System Is Replaced with a Water Purification Unit in an Existing Home Dialysis System.—The medical necessity of water purification units must be carefully developed when they replace water softening systems in existing home dialysis systems. A purification system may be ordered under these circumstances for a number of reasons. For example, changes in the medical community's opinions regarding the quality of water necessary for safe dialysis may lead the physician to decide the quality of water previously used should be improved, or the water quality itself may have deteriorated. Patients may have dialyzed using only an existing water softener previous to Medicare ESRD coverage because of inability to pay for a purification system. On the other hand, in some cases, the installation of a purification system is not medically necessary. Thus, when such a case comes to your attention, ask the physician to furnish the reason for the changes. Supporting documentation, such as the supplier's recommendations or water analysis, may be required. All such cases should be reviewed by your medical consultants.

Cross-refer: Intermediary Manual, sections 3113, 3643 (item 1c); Carriers Manual, sections 2100, 2100.2 2130, 2105 (item 1c); Hospital Manual, section 235.

60 DURABLE MEDICAL EQUIPMENT

60-3 WHITE CANE FOR USE BY A BLIND PERSON—NOT COVERED

A white cane for use by a blind person is more an identifying and self-help device rather than an item which makes a meaningful contribution in the treatment of an illness or injury.

60-4 HOME USE OF OXYGEN

A. General.—Medicare coverage of home oxygen and oxygen equipment under the durable medical equipment (DME) benefit (see section 1861(s)(6) of the Act) is considered reasonable and necessary only for patients with significant hypoxemia who meet the medical documentation, laboratory evidence, and health conditions specified in subsections B, C, and D. This section also includes special coverage criteria for portable oxygen systems. Finally, a statement on the absence of coverage of the professional services of a respiratory therapist under the DME benefit is included in subsection G.

B. Medical Documentation.—Initial claims for oxygen services must include a completed Form HCFA-484 Certification of Medical Necessity: Oxygen Therapy) to establish whether coverage criteria are met and to ensure that the oxygen services provided are consistent with the physician's prescription or other medical documentation. The treating physician's prescription or other medical documentation must indicate that the other forms of treatment (e.g., medical and physical therapy directed at secretions, bronchospasm and infection) have been tried, have not been sufficiently successful, and oxygen therapy is still required. While there is no substitute for oxygen therapy, each patient must receive optimum therapy before long-term home oxygen therapy is ordered. Use Form HCFA-484 for recertifications. (See Medicare Carriers Manual section 3312 for completion of Form HCFA-484.)

The medical and prescription information in section B of Form HCFA-484 can be completed only by the treating physician, the physician's employee, or another clinician (e.g., nurse, respiratory therapist, etc.) as long as that person is not the DME supplier. Although hospital discharge coordinators and medical social workers may assist in arranging for physician-prescribed home oxygen, they have no authority to prescribe the services. Suppliers may not enter this information. While this section may be completed by a nonphysician clinician or a physician employee, it must be reviewed and the form HCFA-484 signed by the attending physician.

A physician's certification of medical necessity for oxygen equipment must include the results of specific testing before coverage can be determined.

Claims for oxygen must also be supported by medical documentation. Separate documentation is used with electronic billing. (See Medicare Carriers Manual, Part 3, section 4105.6.) This documentation may be in the form of a prescription written by the patient's attending physician who has recently examined the patient (normally within a month of the start of therapy) and must specify:

- A diagnosis of the disease requiring home use of oxygen;
- The oxygen flow rate; and
- An estimate of the frequency, duration of use (e.g., 2 liters per minute, 10 minutes per hour, 12 hours per day), and duration of need (e.g., 6 months or lifetime).

NOTE: A prescription for "Oxygen PRN" or "Oxygen as needed" does not meet this last requirement. Neither provides any basis for determining if the amount of oxygen is reasonable and necessary for the patient.

A member of the carrier's medical staff should review all claims with oxygen flow rates of more than 4 liters per minute before payment can be made.

The attending physician specifies the type of oxygen delivery system to be used (i.e., gas, liquid, or concentrator) by signing the completed form HCFA-484. In addition the supplier or physician may use the space in section C for written confirmation of additional details of the physician's order. The additional order information contained in section C may include the means of oxygen delivery (mask, nasal, cannula, etc.), the specifics of varying flow rates, and/or the noncontinuous use of oxygen as appropriate. The physician confirms this order information with his or her signature in section D.

New medical documentation written by the patient's attending physician must be submitted to the carrier in support of revised oxygen requirements when there has been a change in the patient's condition and need for oxygen therapy.

Carriers are required to conduct periodic, continuing medical necessity reviews on patients whose conditions warrant these reviews and on patients with indefinite or extended periods of necessity as described in Medicare Carriers Manual, Part 3, section 4105.5. When indicated, carriers may also request documentation of the results of a repeat arterial blood gas or oximetry study.

NOTE: Section 4152 of OBRA 1990 requires earlier recertification and retesting of oxygen patients who begin coverage with an arterial blood gas result at or above a partial pressure of 55 or an arterial oxygen saturation percentage at or above 89. (See Medicare Carriers Manual, section 4105.5 for certifications and retesting schedules.)

   C. Laboratory Evidence.—Initial claims for oxygen therapy must also include the results of a blood gas study that has been ordered and evaluated by the attending physician. This is usually in the form of a measurement of the partial pressure of oxygen (PO_2) in arterial blood. (See Medicare Carriers Manual, Part 3, section 2070.1 for instructions on clinical laboratory tests.) A measurement of arterial oxygen saturation obtained by ear or pulse oximetry, however, is also acceptable when ordered and evaluated by the attending physician and performed under his or her supervision or when performed by a qualified provider or supplier of laboratory services. When the arterial blood gas and the oximetry studies are both used to document the need for home oxygen therapy and the results are conflicting, the arterial blood gas study is the preferred source of documenting medical need. A DME supplier is not considered a qualified provider or supplier of laboratory services for purposes of these guidelines. This prohibition does not extend to the results of a blood gas test conducted by a hospital certified to do such tests. The conditions under which the laboratory tests are performed must be specified in writing and submitted with the initial claim, i.e., at rest, during exercise, or during sleep.

The preferred sources of laboratory evidence are existing physician and/or hospital records that reflect the patient's medical condition. Since it is expected that virtually all patients who qualify for home oxygen coverage for the first time under these guidelines have recently been discharged from a hospital where they submitted to arterial blood gas tests, the carrier needs to request that such test results be submitted in support of their initial claims for home oxygen. If more than one arterial blood gas test is performed during the patient's hospital stay, the test result obtained closest to, but no earlier than 2 days prior to, the hospital discharge date is required as evidence of the need for home oxygen therapy.

For those patients whose initial oxygen prescription did not originate during a hospital stay, blood gas studies should be done while the patient is in the chronic stable state, i.e., not during a period of an acute illness or an exacerbation of their underlying disease.

Carriers may accept an attending physician's statement of recent hospital test results for a particular patient, when appropriate, in lieu of copies of actual hospital records.

A repeat arterial blood gas or oximetry study is normally appropriate when evidence indicates that an oxygen recipient has undergone a major change relevant to home use of oxygen. If the carrier has reason to believe that there has been a major change in the patient's physical condition, it may ask for documentation of the results of another blood gas or oximetry study.

   D. Health Conditions.—Coverage is available for patients with significant hypoxemia in the chronic stable state if: (1) the attending physician has determined that the patient has a health condition outlined in subsection D1, (2) the patient meets the blood gas evidence requirements specified in subsection D3, and (3) the patient has appropriately tried other alternative treatment measures without complete success. (See subsection B.)

   1. Conditions for Which Oxygen Therapy May Be Covered.—

- A severe lung disease, such as chronic obstructive pulmonary disease, diffuse interstitial lung disease, whether of known or unknown etiology; cystic fibrosis bronchiectasis; widespread pulmonary neoplasm; or
- Hypoxia-related symptoms or findings that might be expected to improve with oxygen therapy. Examples of these symptoms and findings are pulmonary hypertension, recurring congestive heart failure due to chronic cor pulmonale, erythrocytosis, impairment of the cognitive process, nocturnal restlessness, and morning headache.

   2. Conditions for Which Oxygen Therapy Is Not Covered.—

- Angina pectoris in the absence of hypoxemia. This condition is generally not the result of a low oxygen level in the blood, and there are other preferred treatments;
- Breathlessness without cor pulmonale or evidence of hypoxemia. Although intermittent oxygen use is sometimes prescribed to relieve this condition, it is potentially harmful and psychologically addicting;
- Severe peripheral vascular disease resulting in clinically evident desaturation in one or more extremities. There is no evidence that increased PO_2 improves the oxygenation of tissues with impaired circulation; or
- Terminal illnesses that do not affect the lungs.

3. Covered Blood Gas Values.—If the patient has a condition specified in subsection D1, the carrier must review the medical documentation and laboratory evidence that has been submitted for a particular patient (see subsections B and C) and determine if coverage is available under one of the three group categories outlined below.

a. Group I.—Except as modified in subsection D, coverage is provided for patients with significant hypoxemia evidenced by any of the following:

(1) An arterial PO_2 at or below 55 mm Hg, or an arterial oxygen saturation at or below 88 percent, taken at rest, breathing room air.

(2) An arterial PO_2 at or below 55 mm Hg, or an arterial oxygen saturation at or below 88 percent, taken during sleep for a patient who demonstrates an arterial PO_2 at or above 56 mm Hg, or an arterial oxygen saturation at or above 89 percent, while awake; or a greater than normal fall in oxygen level during sleep (a decrease in arterial PO_2 more than 10 mm Hg, or decrease in arterial oxygen saturation more than 5 percent) associated with symptoms or signs reasonably attributable to hypoxemia (e.g., impairment of cognitive processes and nocturnal restlessness or insomnia). In either of these cases, coverage is provided only for use of oxygen during sleep, and then only one type of unit will be covered. Portable oxygen, therefore, would not be covered in this situation.

(3) An arterial PO_2 at or below 55 mm Hg or an arterial oxygen saturation at or below 88 percent, taken during exercise for a patient who demonstrates an arterial PO_2 at or above 56 mm Hg, or an arterial oxygen saturation at or above 89 percent, during the day while at rest. In this case, supplemental oxygen is provided for during exercise if there is evidence the use of oxygen improves the hypoxemia that was demonstrated during exercise when the patient was breathing room air.

b. Group II.—Except as modified in subsection D, coverage is available for patients whose arterial PO_2 is 56 to 59 mm Hg or whose arterial blood oxygen saturation is 89 percent, if there is evidence of:

(1) Dependent edema suggesting congestive heart failure;

(2) Pulmonary hypertension or cor pulmonale, determined by measurement of pulmonary artery pressure, gated blood pool scan, echocardiogram, or "P" pulmonale on EKG (P wave greater than 3 mm in standard leads II, III, or AVF); or

(3) Erythrocythemia with a hematocrit greater than 56 percent.

c. Group III.—Except as modified in subsection D, carriers must apply a rebuttable presumption that a home program of oxygen use is not medically necessary for patients with arterial PO_2 levels at or above 60 mm Hg, or arterial blood oxygen saturation at or above 90 percent. In order for claims in this category to be reimbursed, the carrier's reviewing physician needs to review any documentation submitted in rebuttal of this presumption and grant specific approval of the claims. HCFA expects few claims to be approved for coverage in this category.

d. Variable Factors That May Affect Blood Gas Values.— In reviewing the arterial PO_2 levels and the arterial oxygen saturation percentages specified in subsections D3A, B and C, the carrier's medical staff must take into account variations in oxygen measurements that may result from such factors as the patient's age, the altitude level, or the patient's decreased oxygen carrying capacity.

E. Portable Oxygen Systems.—A patient meeting the requirements specified below may qualify for coverage of a portable oxygen system either (1) by itself or (2) to use in addition to a stationary oxygen system. Portable oxygen is not covered when it is provided only as a backup to a stationary oxygen system. A portable oxygen system is covered for a particular patient if:

• The claim meets the requirements specified in subsections A to D, as appropriate; and

• The medical documentation indicates that the patient is mobile in the home and would benefit from the use of a portable oxygen system in the home. Portable oxygen systems are not covered for patients who qualify for oxygen solely based on blood gas studies obtained during sleep.

F. Respiratory Therapists.—Respiratory therapists' services are not covered under the provisions for coverage of oxygen services under the Part B durable medical equipment benefit as outlined above. This benefit provides for coverage of home use of oxygen and oxygen equipment, but does not include a professional component in the delivery of such services.

(See section 60-9; Intermediary Manual, Part 3, section 3113ff; and Medicare Carriers Manual, Part 3, section 2100ff.)

60-5 POWER-OPERATED VEHICLES THAT MAY BE USED AS WHEELCHAIRS

Power-operated vehicles that may be appropriately used as wheelchairs are covered under the durable medical equipment provision.

These vehicles have been appropriately used in the home setting for vocational rehabilitation and to improve the ability of chronically disabled persons to cope with normal domestic, vocational and social activities. They may be covered if a wheelchair is medically necessary and the patient is unable to operate a wheelchair manually.

A specialist in physical medicine, orthopedic surgery, neurology, or rheumatology must provide an evaluation of the patient's medical and physical condition and a prescription for the vehicle to assure that the patient requires the vehicle and is capable of using it safely. When an intermediary determines that such a specialist is not reasonably accessible, e.g., more than 1 day's round trip from the beneficiary's home, or the patient's condition precludes such travel, a prescription from the beneficiary's physician is acceptable.

The intermediary's medical staff reviews all claims for a power-operated vehicle, including the specialists' or other physicians' prescriptions and evaluations of the patient's medical and physical conditions, to insure that all coverage requirements are met. (See section 60-9 and Intermediary Manual, Part 3, section 3629.)

60-6 SPECIALLY SIZED WHEELCHAIRS

Payment may be made for a specially sized wheelchair even though it is more expensive than a standard wheelchair. For example, a narrow wheelchair may be required because of the narrow doorways of a patient's home or because of a patient's slender build. Such difference in the size of the wheelchair from the standard model is not considered a deluxe feature.

A physician's certification or prescription that a special size is needed is not required where you can determine from the information in file or other sources that a specially sized wheelchair (rather than a standard one) is needed to accommodate the wheelchair to the place of use or the physical size of the patient.

To determine the reasonable charge in these cases, use the criteria set out in Carriers Manual, sections 5022, 5022.1, 5200, and 5205, as necessary.

Cross-refer: Intermediary Manual, sections 3113.2C, 3642.1, 3643 (item 3); Carriers Manual, sections 2100.2c, 2105, 4105.2, 5107; Hospital Manual, sections 235.2c, 420.1 (item 13).

60-7 SELF-CONTAINED PACEMAKER MONITORS

Self-contained pacemaker monitors are accepted devices for monitoring cardiac pacemakers. Accordingly, program payment may be made for the rental or purchase of either of the following pacemaker monitors when it is prescribed by a physician for a patient with a cardiac pacemaker:

A. Digital Electronic Pacemaker Monitor.—This device provides the patient with an instantaneous digital readout of his pacemaker pulse rate. Use of this device does not involve professional services until there has been a change of five pulses (or more) per minute above or below the initial rate of the pacemaker; when such change occurs, the patient contacts his physician.

B. Audible/Visible Signal Pacemaker Monitor.—This device produces an audible and visible signal which indicates the pacemaker rate. Use of this device does not involve professional services until a change occurs in these signals; at such time, the patient contacts his physician.

NOTE: The design of the self-contained pacemaker monitor makes it possible for the patient to monitor his pacemaker periodically and minimizes the need for regular visits to the outpatient department of the provider.

Therefore, documentation of the medical necessity for pacemaker evaluation in the outpatient department of the provider should be obtained where such evaluation is employed in addition to the self-contained pacemaker monitor used by the patient in his home.

Cross-refer: section 50-1

60-8 SEAT LIFT

Reimbursement may be made for the rental or purchase of a medically necessary seat lift when prescribed by a physician for a patient with severe arthritis of the hip or knee and patients with muscular dystrophy or other neuromuscular diseases when it has been determined the patient can benefit therapeutically from use of the device. In establishing medical necessity for the seat lift, the evidence must show that the item is included in the physician's course of treatment, that it is likely to effect improvement, or arrest or retard deterioration in the patient's condition, and that the severity of the condition is such that the alternative would be chair or bed confinement.

Coverage of seat lifts is limited to those types which operate smoothly, can be controlled by the patient, and effectively assist a patient in standing up and sitting down without other assistance. Excluded from coverage is the type of lift which operates by a spring release mechanism with a sudden, catapult-like motion and jolts the patient from a seated to a standing position. Limit the payment for units which incorporate a recliner feature along with the seat lift to the amount payable for a seat lift without this feature.

Cross-refer: Carriers Manual, section 5107

60-9 DURABLE MEDICAL EQUIPMENT REFERENCE LIST

The durable medical equipment (DME) list which follows is designed to facilitate your processing of DME claims. This section is designed to be used as a quick reference tool for determining the coverage status of certain pieces of DME and especially for those items which are commonly referred to by both brand and generic names. The information contained herein is applicable (where appropriate) to all DME coverage determinations discussed in the DME portion of this manual. The list is organized into two columns. The first column lists alphabetically various generic categories of equipment on which national coverage decisions have been made by HCFA; and the second column notes the coverage status of each equipment category.

In the case of equipment categories that have been determined by HCFA to be covered under the DME benefit, the list outlines the conditions of coverage that must be met if payment is to be allowed for the rental or purchase of the DME by a particular patient, or cross-refers to another section of the manual where the applicable coverage criteria are described in more detail. With respect to equipment categories that cannot be covered as DME, the list includes a brief explanation of why the equipment is not covered. This DME list will be updated periodically to reflect any additional national coverage decisions that HCFA may make with regard to other categories of equipment.

When you receive a claim for an item of equipment which does not appear to fall logically into any of the generic categories listed, you have the authority and responsibility for deciding whether those items are covered under the DME benefit. These decisions must be made by each contractor based on the advice of its medical consultants, taking into account:

- The general DME coverage instructions in the Carriers Manual, section 2100ff and Intermediary Manual, section 3113ff (see below for brief summary);
- Whether the item has been approved for marketing by the Food and Drug Administration (FDA) (see Carriers Manual, section 2303.1 and Intermediary Manual, section 3151.1) and is otherwise generally considered to be safe and effective for the purpose intended; and
- Whether the item is reasonable and necessary for the individual patient.

As provided in the Carriers Manual, section 2100.1, and Intermediary Manual, section 3113.1, the term DME is defined as equipment which

- Can withstand repeated use; i.e., could normally be rented, and used by successive patients;
- Is primarily and customarily used to serve a medical purpose;
- Generally is not useful to a person in the absence of illness or injury; and
- Is appropriate for use in a patient's home.

Durable Medical Equipment Reference List

Air Cleaners—deny—environmental control equipment; not primarily medical in nature (section 1861(n) of the Act)

Air Conditioners—deny—environmental control equipment; not primarily medical in nature (section 1861(n) of the Act)

Air-Fluidized Bed—(*See* section 60-19.)

Alternating Pressure Pads—covered if patient has, or is highly susceptible to, and matresses and decubitus ulcers and patient's physician has Lambs Wool Pads specified that he will be supervising its use in connection with his course of treatment.

Audible/Visible Signal—(*See* Self-Contained Pacemaker Monitor.) Pacemaker Monitor

Augmentative Communication—(*See* Communicator.) Device

Bathtub Lifts—deny—convenience item; not primarily medical in nature (section 1861(n) of the Act)

Bathtub Seats—deny—comfort or convenience item; hygienic equipment; not primarily medical in nature (section 1861(n) of the Act)

Bead Bed—(*See* section 60-19.)

Bed Baths (home type)—deny—hygienic equipment; not primarily medical in nature (section 1861(n) of the Act)

Bed Lifter (bed elevator)—deny—not primarily medical in nature (section 1861(n) of the Act).

Bedboards—deny—not primarily medical in nature (section 1861(n) of the Act)

Bed Pans (autoclavable hospital type)—covered if patient is bed confined

Bed Side Rails—(*See* Hospital Beds, section 60-18.)

Beds—Lounge (power or manual)—deny—not a hospital bed; comfort or convenience item; not primarily medical in nature (section 1861(n) of the Act)

Beds—Oscillating—deny—institutional equipment; inappropriate for home use

Bidet Toilet Seat—(*See* Toilet Seats.)

Blood Glucose Analyzer—deny—unsuitable for home use (*See* section 60-11.)

Blood Glucose Monitor—covered if patient meets certain conditions (*See* section 60-11.)

Braille Teaching Texts—deny—educational equipment; not primarily medical in nature (section 1861(n) of the Act)

Canes—covered if patient's condition impairs ambulation (*See* section 1861(m).)

Carafes—deny—convenience item; not primarily medical in nature (section 1861(n) of the Act)

Catheters—deny—nonreusable disposable supply (section 1861(n) of the Act)

Commodes—covered if patient is confined to bed or room

NOTE: The term "room confined" means that the patient's condition is such that leaving the room is medically contraindicated. The accessibility of bathroom facilities generally would not be a factor in this determination. However, confinement of a patient to his home in a case where there are no toilet facilities in the home may be equated to room confinement. Moreover, payment may also be made if a patient's medical condition confines him to a floor of his home and there is no bathroom located on that floor (*See* Hospital Beds in section 60-18 for definition of "bed confinement".)

Communicator—deny—convenience item; not primarily medical in nature (section 1861(n) of the Act)

Continuous Passive Motion—Continuous Passive Motion (CPM) devices are covered for patients who have received a total knee replacement. To qualify for coverage, use of the device must commence within two days following surgery. In addition, coverage is limited to that portion of the three week period following surgery during which the device is used in the patient's home.

There is insufficient evidence to justify coverage of these devices for longer periods of time or for other applications.

Continuous Positive Airway Pressure (CPAP)—(*See* section 60-17.)

Crutches—covered if patient's condition impairs ambulation

Cushion Lift Power Seat—(*See* Seat Lifts.)

Dehumidifiers (room or central heating system type)—deny—environmental control equipment; not primarily medical in nature (section 1861(n) of the Act)

Diathermy Machines (standard and pulses wave types)—deny—inappropriate for home use (*See* section 35-41.)

Digital Electronic—(*See* Self-Contained Pacemaker Monitor.) Pacemaker Monitor

Disposable Sheets and Bags—deny—nonreusable disposable supplies (section 1861(n) of the Act)

Elastic Stockings—deny—nonreusable supply; not rental-type items (section 1861(n) of the Act)

Electric Air Cleaners—deny—(See Air Cleaners.) (section 1861(n) of the Act)

Electric Hospital Beds—(*See* Hospital Beds section 60-18.)

Electrostatic Machines—deny—(*See* Air Cleaners and Air Conditioners.) (section 1861(n) of the Act)

Elevators—deny—convenience item; not primarily medical in nature (section 1861(n) of the Act)

Emesis Basins—deny—convenience item; not primarily medical in nature (section 1861(n) of the Act)

Esophageal Dilator—deny—physician instrument; inappropriate for patient use

Exercise Equipment—deny—not primarily medical in nature (section 1861(n) of the Act)

Fabric Supports—deny—nonreusable supplies; not rental-type item (section 1861(n) of the Act)

Face Masks (oxygen)—covered if oxygen is covered (*See* section 60-4.)

Face Masks (surgical)—deny—nonreusable disposable items (section 1861(n) of the Act)

Flowmeter—(*See* Medical Oxygen Regulators)

Fluidic Breathing Assister—(*See* IPPB Machines.)

Fomentation Device—(*See* Heating Pads.)

Gel Flotation Pads and Mattresses—(*See* Alternating Pressure Pads.)

Grab Bars—deny—self-help device; not primarily medical in nature (section 1861(n) of the Act)

Heat and Massage Foam Cushion Pad—deny—not primarily medical in nature; personal comfort item (section 1861(n) and 1862(a)(6) of the Act)

Heating and Cooling Plants—deny—environmental control equipment; not primarily medical in nature (section 1861(n) of the Act)

Heating Pads—covered if the contractor's medical staff determines patient's medical condition is one for which the application of heat in the form of a heating pad is therapeutically effective.

Heat Lamps—covered if the contractor's medical staff determines patient's medical condition is one for which the application of heat in the form of a heat lamp is therapeutically effective.

Hospital Beds—(*See* section 60-18.)

Hot Packs—(*See* Heating Pads.)

Humidifiers (oxygen)—(*See* Oxygen Humidifiers.)

Humidifiers (room or central heating system types)—deny—environmental control equipment; not medical in nature (section 1861(n) of the Act)

Hydraulic Lift—(*See* Patient Lifts.)

Incontinent Pads—deny—non-reusable supply; hygienic item (section 1861(n) of the Act.)

Infusion Pumps—For external and implantable pumps, see section 60-14. If the pump is used with an enteral or parenteral malnutritional therapy system, *see* section 65-10 to 65.10.2 0.2 for special coverage rules.

Injectors (hypodermic jet pressure powered devices for injection of insulin)—deny—noncovered self-administered drug supply; section 1861(s)(2)(A) of the Act)

IPPB Machines—covered if patient's ability to breathe is severely impaired

Iron Lungs—(*See* Ventilators.)

Irrigating Kit—deny—nonreusable supply; hygienic equipment (section 1861(n) of the Act)

Lambs Wool Pads—covered under same conditions as alternating pressure pads and mattresses

Leotards—deny—(*See* Pressure Leotards.) (section 1861(n) of the Act)

Lymphedema Pumps (segmental and non-segmental therapy types)—covered (*See* section 60-16.)

Massage Devices—deny—personal comfort items; not primarily medical in nature (section 1861(n) and 1862(a)(6) of the Act)

Mattress—covered only where hospital bed is medically necessary (Separate charge for replacement mattress should not be allowed where a hospital bed with mattress is rented.) (*See* section 60-18.)

Medical Oxygen Regulators—covered if patient's ability to breathe is severely impaired (*See* section 60-4.)

Mobile Geriatric Chair—(*See* Rolling Chairs.)

Motorized Wheelchairs—(*See* Wheelchairs (power operated).)

Muscle Stimulators—Covered for certain conditions (*See* section 35-77.)

Nebulizers—covered if patient's ability to breathe is severely impaired

Oscillating Beds—deny—institutional equipment—inappropriate for home use

Overbed Tables—deny—convenience item; not primarily medical in nature (section 1861(n) of the Act)

Oxygen—covered if the oxygen has been prescribed for use in connection with medically necessary durable medical equipment (*See* section 60-4.)

Oxygen Humidifiers—covered if a medical humidifier has been prescribed for use in connection with medically necessary durable medical equipment for purposes of moisturizing oxygen (*See* section 60-4.)

Oxygen Regulators (Medical)—(*See* Medical Oxygen Regulators.)

Oxygen Tents—(*See* section 60-4.)

Paraffin Bath Units (Portable)—(*See* Paraffin Bath Units [Portable].)

Paraffin Bath Units (Standard)—deny—institutional equipment; inappropriate for home use

Parallel Bars—deny—support exercise equipment; primarily for institutional use; in the home setting other devices (e.g., a walker) satisfy the patient's need

Patient Lifts—covered if contractor's medical staff determines patient's condition is such that periodic movement is necessary to effect improvement or to arrest or retard deterioration in his condition.

Percussors—covered for mobilizing respiratory tract secretions in patients with chronic obstructive lung disease, chronic bronchitis, or emphysema, when patient or operator of powered percussor has received appropriate training by a physician or therapist, and no one competent to administer manual therapy is available.

Portable Oxygen Systems:

1. Regulated (adjustable—covered under conditions specified in flow rate) section 60-4. Refer all claims to medical staff for this determination.

2. Preset (flow rate—deny—emergency, first-aid, or not adjustable) precautionary equipment; essentially not therapeutic in nature.

Portable Paraffin Bath Units—covered when the patient has undergone a successful trial period of paraffin therapy ordered by a physician and the patient's condition is expected to be relieved by long term use of this modality.

Portable Room Heaters—deny—environmental control equipment; not primarily medical in nature (section 1861(n) of the Act)

Portable Whirlpool Pumps—deny—not primarily medical in nature; personal comfort items (section 1861(n) and 1862(a)(6) of the Act)

Postural Drainage Boards—covered if patient has a chronic pulmonary condition

Preset Portable Oxygen Units—deny—emergency, first-aid, or precautionary equipment; essentially not therapeutic in nature

Pressure Leotards—deny—nonreusable supply, not rental-type item (section 1861(n) of the Act)

Pulse Tachometer—deny—not reasonable or necessary for monitoring pulse of homebound patient with or without a cardiac pacemaker

Quad-Canes—(*See* Walkers.)

Raised Toilet Seats—deny—convenience item; hygienic equipment; not primarily medical in nature (section 1861(n) of the Act)

Reflectance Colorimeters—(*See* Blood Glucose Analyzer.)

Respirators—(*See* Ventilators.)

Rolling Chairs—covered if the contractor's medical staff determines that the patient's condition is such that there is a medical need for this item and it has been prescribed by the patient's physician in lieu of a wheelchair. Coverage is limited to those roll about chairs having casters of at least 5 inches in diameter and specifically designed to meet the needs of ill, injured, or otherwise impaired individuals. Coverage is denied for the wide range of chairs with smaller casters as are found in general use in

homes, offices, and institutions for many purposes not related to the care or treatment of ill or injured persons. This type is not primarily medical in nature. (section 1861(n) of the Act)

Safety Roller—(*See* section 60-15.)

Sauna Baths—deny—not primarily medical in nature; personal comfort items (section 1861(n) and (1862(a)(6) of the Act)

Seat Lift—covered under the conditions specified in section 60-8. Refer all to medical staff for this determination.

Self-Contained Pacemaker—covered when prescribed by a physician. Monitor for a patient with a cardiac pacemaker (*See* section 50-1C and 60-7.)

Sitz Bath—covered if the contractor's medical staff determines patient has an infection or injury of the perineal area and the item has been prescribed by the patient's physician as a part of his planned regimen of treatment in the patient's home.

Spare Tanks of Oxygen—deny—convenience or precautionary supply

Speech Teaching Machine—deny—education equipment; not primarily medical in nature (section 1861(n) of the Act)

Stairway Elevators—deny—(*See* Elevators.) (section l861(n) of the Act)

Standing Table—deny—convenience item; not primarily medical in nature (section 1861(n) of the Act)

Steam Packs—these packs are covered under the same condition as a heating pad (*See* Heating Pads.)

Suction Machine—covered if the contractor's medical staff determines that the machine specified in the claim is medically required and appropriate for home use without technical or professional supervision.

Support Hose—deny (*See* Fabric Supports.) (section 1861(n) of the Act)

Surgical Leggings—deny—nonreusable supply; not rental-type item (section 1861(n) of the Act)

Telephone Alert Systems—deny—these are emergency communications systems and do not serve a diagnostic or therapeutic purpose

Telephone Arms—deny—convenience item; not medical in nature (section 1861(n) of the Act)

Toilet Seats—deny—not medical equipment (section 1861(n) of the Act)

Traction Equipment—covered if patient has orthopedic impairment requiring traction equipment which prevents ambulation during the period of use. (Consider covering devices usable during ambulation; e.g., cervical traction collar, under the brace provision.)

Trapeze Bars—covered if patient is bed confined and the patient needs a trapeze bar to sit up because of respiratory condition, to change body position for other medical reasons, or to get in and out of bed.

Treadmill Exerciser—deny—exercise equipment; not primarily medical in nature (section 1861(n) of the Act)

Ultraviolet Cabinet—covered for selected patients with generalized intractable psoriasis. Using appropriate consultation, the contractor should determine whether medical and other factors justify treatment at home rather than at alternative sites, e.g., outpatient department of a hospital.

Urinals (autoclavable hospital type)—covered if patient is bed confined

Vaporizers—covered if patient has a respiratory illness

Ventilators—covered for treatment of neuromuscular diseases, thoracic restrictive diseases, and chronic respiratory failure consequent to chronic obstructive pulmonary disease. Includes both positive and negative pressure types.

Walkers—covered if patient's condition impairs ambulation (*See* also section 60-15.)

Water and Pressure Pads and Mattresses—(*See* Alternating Pressure Pads and Mattresses.)

Wheelchairs—covered if patient's condition is such that without the use of a wheelchair he would otherwise be bed or chair confined. An individual may qualify for a wheelchair and still be considered bed confined.

Wheelchairs (power operated) and wheelchairs with other special features—covered if patient's condition is such that a wheelchair is medically necessary and the patient is unable to operate the wheelchair manually. Any claim involving a power wheelchair or a wheelchair with other special features should be referred for medical consultation since payment for the special features is limited to those which are medically required because of the patient's condition. (See section 60-5 for power operated and section 60-6 for specially sized wheelchairs.)

NOTE: A power-operated vehicle that may appropriately be used as a wheelchair can be covered. (*See* section 60-5 for coverage details.)

Whirlpool Bath Equipment—covered if patient is homebound and has a (standard) condition for which the whirlpool bath can be expected to provide substantial therapeutic benefit justifying its cost. Where patient is not homebound but has such a condition, payment is restricted to the cost of providing the services elsewhere; e.g., an outpatient department of a participating hospital, if that alternative is less costly. In all cases, refer claim to medical staff for a determination.

Whirlpool Pumps—deny—(*See* Portable Whirlpool Pumps.) (section 1861(n) of the Act)

White Cane—deny—(*See* section 60-3.)

60-11 HOME BLOOD GLUCOSE MONITORS

There are several different types of blood glucose monitors which use reflectance meters to determine blood glucose levels. Medicare coverage of these devices varies, both with respect to the type of device and the medical condition of the patient for whom the device is prescribed.

Reflectance colorimeter devices used for measuring blood glucose levels in clinical settings are not covered as durable medical equipment for use in the home because their need for frequent professional recalibration makes them unsuitable for home use. However, some types of blood glucose monitors which use a reflectance meter specifically designed for home use by diabetic patients may be covered as durable medical equipment, subject to the conditions and limitations described below.

Blood glucose monitors are meter devices which read color changes produced on specially treated reagent strips by glucose concentrations in the patient's blood. The patient, using a disposable sterile lancet, draws a drop of blood, places it on a reagent strip and, following instructions which may vary with the device used, inserts it into the device to obtain a reading. Lancets, reagent strips, and other supplies necessary for the proper functioning of the device are also covered for patients for whom the device is indicated. Home blood glucose monitors enable certain patients to better control their blood glucose levels by frequently checking and appropriately contacting their attending physician for advice and treatment. Studies indicate that the patient's ability to carefully follow proper procedures is critical to obtaining satisfactory results with these devices. In addition, the cost of the devices, with their supplies, limits economical use to patients who must make frequent checks of their blood glucose levels. Accordingly, coverage of home blood glucose monitors is limited to patients meeting the following conditions:

• The patient must be an insulin-treated diabetic;
• The patient's physician states that the patient is capable of being trained to use the particular device prescribed in an appropriate manner. In some cases, the patient may not be able to perform this function, but a responsible individual can be trained to use the equipment and monitor the patient to assure that the intended effect is achieved. This is permissible if the record is properly documented by the patient's physician; and
• The device is designed for home rather than clinical use.

There is also a blood glucose monitoring system designed especially for use by those with visual impairments. The monitors used in such systems are identical in terms of reliability and sensitivity to the standard blood glucose monitors described above. They differ by having such features as voice synthesizers, automatic timers, and specially designed arrangements of supplies and materials to enable the visually impaired to use the equipment without assistance.

These special blood glucose monitoring systems are covered under Medicare if the following conditions are met:

• The patient and device meet the four conditions listed above for coverage of standard home blood glucose monitors; and
• The patient's physician certifies that he or she has a visual impairment severe enough to require use of this special monitoring system.

The additional features and equipment of these special systems justify a higher reimbursement amount than allowed for standard blood glucose monitors. Separately identify claims for such devices and establish a separate reimbursement amount for them. For those carriers using HCPCS, the procedure code and definition is: EO609—Blood Glucose Monitor—with special features (e.g., voice synthesizers, automatic timer).

60-14 INFUSION PUMPS

The following indications for treatment using infusion pumps are covered under medicare:

A. External Infusion Pumps.—

1. Iron Poisoning (Effective for Services Performed On or After 9/26/84).—When used in the administration of deferoxamine for the treatment of acute iron poisoning and iron overload, only external infusion pumps are covered.

2. Thromboembolic Disease (Effective for Services Performed On or After 9/26/84).—When used in the administration of heparin for the treatment of thromboembolic disease and/or pulmonary embolism, only external infusion pumps used in an institutional setting are covered.

3. Chemotherapy for Liver Cancer (Effective for Services Performed On or After 1/29/85).—The external chemotherapy infusion pump is covered when used in the treatment of primary hepatocellular carcinoma or colorectal cancer where this disease is unresectable or where the patient refuses surgical excision of the tumor.

4. Morphine for Intractable Cancer Pain (Effective for Services Performed On or After 4/22/85).—Morphine infusion via an external infusion pump is covered when used in the treatment of intractable pain caused by cancer (in either an inpatient or outpatient setting, including a hospice).

Other uses of external infusion pumps are covered if the contractor's medical staff verifies the appropriateness of the therapy and of the prescribed pump for the individual patient.

NOTE: Payment may also be made for drugs necessary for the effective use of an external infusion pump as long as the drug being used with the pump is itself reasonable and necessary for the patient's treatment.

B. Implantable Infusion Pumps.—

1. Chemotherapy for Liver Cancer (Effective for Services Performed On or After 9/26/84).—The implantable infusion pump is covered for intra-arterial infusion of 5-FUdR for the treatment of liver cancer for patients with primary hepatocellular carcinoma or Duke's Class D colorectal cancer, in whom the metastases are limited to the liver, and where (1) the disease is unresectable or (2) where the patient refuses surgical excision of the tumor.

2. Anti-Spasmodic Drugs for Severe Spasticity.—An implantable infusion pump is covered when used to administer anti-spasmodic drugs intrathecally (e.g., baclofen) to treat chronic intractable spasticity in patients who have proven unresponsive to less invasive medical therapy as determined by the following criteria:

- As indicated by at least a 6-week trial, the patient cannot be maintained on noninvasive methods of spasm control, such as oral anti-spasmodic drugs, either because these methods fail to control adequately the spasticity or produce intolerable side effects, and
- Prior to pump implantation, the patient must have responded favorably to a trial intrathecal dose of the anti-spasmodic drug.

3. Opioid Drugs for Treatment of Chronic Intractable Pain.—An implantable infusion pump is covered when used to administer opioid drugs (e.g., morphine) intrathecally or epidurally for treatment of severe chronic intractable pain of malignant or non-malignant origin in patients who have a life expectancy of at least 3 months and who have proven unresponsive to less invasive medical therapy as determined by the following criteria:

- The patient's history must indicate that he/she would not respond adequately to noninvasive methods of pain control, such as systemic opioids (including attempts to eliminate physical and behavioral abnormalities which may cause an exaggerated reaction to pain); and
- A preliminary trial of intraspinal opioid drug administration must be undertaken with a temporary intrathecal/epidural catheter to substantiate adequately acceptable pain relief and degree of side effects (including effects on the activities of daily living) and patient acceptance.

4. Coverage of Other Uses of Implanted Infusion Pumps.—Determinations may be made on coverage of other uses of implanted infusion pumps if the contractor's medical staff verifies that:

- The drug is reasonable and necessary for the treatment of the individual patient;
- It is medically necessary that the drug be administered by an implanted infusion pump; and
- The FDA approved labeling for the pump must specify that the drug being administered and the purpose for which it is administered is an indicated use for the pump.

5. Implantation of Infusion Pump Is Contraindicated.—The implantation of an infusion pump is contraindicated in the following patients:

- Patients with a known allergy or hypersensitivity to the drug being used (e.g., oral baclofen, morphine, etc.);
- Patients who have an infection;
- Patients whose body size is insufficient to support the weight and bulk of the device; and
- Patients with other implanted programmable devices since crosstalk between devices may inadvertently change the prescription.

NOTE: Payment may also be made for drugs necessary for the effective use of an implantable infusion pump as long as the drug being used with the pump is itself reasonable and necessary for the patient's treatment.

The following indications for treatment using infusion pumps are not covered under Medicare:

A. External Infusion Pumps.—

1. Diabetes (Effective for Services Performed On or After 1/29/85).—The use of an external infusion pump for the subcutaneous infusion of insulin in the treatment of diabetes is not covered.

2. Vancomycin (Effective for Services Beginning On or After September 1, 1996).—Medicare coverage of vancomycin as a durable medical equipment infusion pump benefit is not covered. There is insufficient evidence to support the necessity of using an external infusion pump, instead of a disposable elastomeric pump or the gravity drip method, to administer vancomycin in a safe and appropriate manner.

B. Implantable Infusion Pump.—

1. Thromboembolic Disease (Effective for Services Performed On or After 9/26/84).—According to the Public Health Service, there is insufficient published clinical data to support the safety and effectiveness of the heparin implantable pump. Therefore, the use of an implantable infusion pump for infusion of heparin in the treatment of recurrent thromboembolic disease is not covered.

2. Diabetes—Implanted infusion pumps for the infusion of insulin to treat diabetes is not covered. The data do not demonstrate that the pump provides effective administration of insulin.

60-15 SAFETY ROLLER

"Safety roller" is the generic name applied to devices for patients who cannot use standard wheeled walkers. They may be appropriate, and therefore covered, for some patients who are obese, have severe neurological disorders, or restricted use of one hand, which makes it impossible to use a wheeled walker that does not have the sophisticated braking system found on safety rollers.

In order to assure that payment is not made for a safety roller when a less expensive standard wheeled walker would satisfy the patient's medical needs, carriers refer safety roller claims to their medical consultants. The medical consultant determines whether some or all of the features provided in a safety roller are necessary, and therefore covered and reimbursable. If it is determined that the patient could use a standard wheeled walker, the charge for the safety roller is reduced to the charge of a standard wheeled walker.

Some obese patients who could use a standard wheeled walker if their weight did not exceed the walker's strength and stability limits can have it reinforced and its wheel base expanded. Such modifications are routine mechanical adjustments and justify a moderate surcharge. In these cases the carrier reduces the charge for the safety roller to the charge for the standard wheeled walker plus the surcharge for modifications.

In the case of patients with medical documentation showing severe neurological disorders or restricted use of one hand which makes it impossible for them to use a wheeled walker that does not have a sophisticated braking system, a reasonable charge for the safety roller may be determined without relating it to the reasonable charge for a standard wheeled walker. (Such reasonable charge should be developed in accordance with the instructions in Medicare Carriers Manual, sections 5010 and 5205.)

Cross Refer: Carriers Manual, sections 2100ff., section 60-9.

60-16 PNEUMATIC COMPRESSION DEVICES (USED FOR LYMPHEDEMA)

Lymphedema is the swelling of subcutaneous tissues due to the accumulation of excessive lymph fluid. The accumulation of lymph fluid results from an impairment to the normal clearing function of the lymphatic system and/or from an excessive production of lymph. It is a relatively uncommon, chronic condition which may be due to many causes, e.g., surgical removal of lymph nodes, post radiation fibrosis, scarring of lymphatic channel, onset of puberty (Milroy's disease), and congenital anomalies. In the home setting, both the segmental and nonsegmental pneumatic compression devices are covered only for the treatment of generalized, refractory lymphedema.

Pneumatic compression devices are only covered as a treatment of last resort, i.e., other less intensive treatments must have been tried first and found inadequate. Such treatments would include leg or arm elevation and custom fabricated gradient pressure stockings or sleeves. Pneumatic compression devices may be covered only when prescribed by a physician and when they are used with appropriate physician oversight, i.e., physician evaluation of the patient's condition to determine medical necessity of the device, suitable instruction in the operation of the machine, a treatment plan defining the pressure to be used and the frequency and duration of use, and ongoing monitoring of use and response to treatment.

The determination by the physician of the medical necessity of a pneumatic compression device must include (1) the patient's diagnosis and prognosis; (2) symptoms and objective findings, including measurements which establish the severity of the condition; (3) the reason the device is required, including the treatments which have been tried and failed; and (4) the clinical response to an initial treatment with the device. The clinical response includes the change in pre-treatment measurements, ability to tolerate the treatment session and parameters, and ability of the patient (or caregiver) to apply the device for continued use in the home.

In general, the nonsegmented (HCPCS code E0650) or segmented (HCPCS code E0651) compression device without manual control of pressure in each chamber is considered the least costly alternative that meets the clinical needs of the individual. Therefore, when a claim for a segmented pneumatic compression device which allows for manual control in each chamber is received, payment must be made for the least expensive medically appropriate device. If the patient medically needs a segmented device but does not need manual controls, payment must be made for HCPCS code E0651. The segmented device with manual control (HCPCS code E0652) is covered only when there are unique characteristics that prevent the individual from receiving satisfactory pneumatic treatment using a less costly device, e.g., significant sensitive skin scars or the presence of contracture or pain caused by a clinical condition that requires the more costly manual control device.

The use of pneumatic compression devices may be medically appropriate only for those patients with generalized, refractory edema from venous insufficiency with lymphatic obstruction (i.e., recurrent cellulitis with secondary scarring of the lymphatic system) with significant ulceration of the lower extremity(ies) who have received repeated, standard treatment from a physician using such methods as a compression bandage system or its equivalent, but fail to heal after 6 months of continuous treatment. The exact nature of the medical problem must be clear from the medical evidence submitted. If, after obtaining this information, a question of medical necessity remains, the contractor's medical staff resolves the issue.

Cross Refer: section 60-9.

60-17 CONTINUOUS POSITIVE AIRWAY PRESSURE (CPAP)

CPAP is a noninvasive technique for providing low levels of air pressure from a flow generator, via a nose mask, through the nares. The purpose is to prevent the collapse of the oropharyngeal walls and the obstruction of airflow during sleep, which occurs in obstructive sleep apnea (OSA). The diagnosis of OSA requires documentation of at least 30 episodes of apnea, each lasting a minimum of 10 seconds, during 6 to 7 hours of recorded sleep. The use of CPAP is covered under Medicare when used in adult patients with moderate or severe OSA for whom surgery is a likely alternative to CPAP.

Initial claims must be supported by medical documentation (separate documentation where electronic billing is used), such as a prescription written by the patient's attending physician, that specifies:

- a diagnosis of moderate or severe obstructive sleep apnea, and
- surgery is a likely alternative.

The claim must also certify that the documentation supporting a diagnosis of OSA (described above) is available.

Cross Refer: section 60-9.

60-18 HOSPITAL BEDS

A. General Requirements for Coverage of Hospital Beds.—A physician's prescription, and such additional documentation as the contractors' medical staffs may consider necessary, including medical records and physicians' reports, must establish the medical necessity for a hospital bed due to one of the following reasons:

- The patient's condition requires positioning of the body; e.g., to alleviate pain, promote good body alignment, prevent contractures, avoid respiratory infections, in ways not feasible in an ordinary bed; or
- The patient's condition requires special attachments that cannot be fixed and used on an ordinary bed.

B. Physician's Prescription.—The physician's prescription, which must accompany the initial claim, and supplementing documentation when required, must establish that a hospital bed is medically necessary. If the stated reason for the need for a hospi-

tal bed is the patient's condition requires positioning, the prescription or other documentation must describe the medical condition, e.g., cardiac disease, chronic obstructive pulmonary disease, quadriplegia or paraplegia, and also the severity and frequency of the symptoms of the condition, that necessitates a hospital bed for positioning.

If the stated reason for requiring a hospital bed is the patient's condition requires special attachments, the prescription must describe the patient's condition and specify the attachments that require a hospital bed.

C. Variable Height Feature.—In well documented cases, the contractors' medical staffs may determine that a variable height feature of a hospital bed, approved for coverage under subsection A above, is medically necessary and, therefore, covered, for one of the following conditions:

- Severe arthritis and other injuries to lower extremities; e.g., fractured hip. The condition requires the variable height feature to assist the patient to ambulate by enabling the patient to place his or her feet on the floor while sitting on the edge of the bed;
- Severe cardiac conditions. For those cardiac patients who are able to leave bed, but who must avoid the strain of "jumping" up or down;
- Spinal cord injuries, including quadriplegic and paraplegic patients, multiple limb amputee and stroke patients. For those patients who are able to transfer from bed to a wheelchair, with or without help; or
- Other severely debilitating diseases and conditions, if the variable height feature is required to assist the patient to ambulate.

D. Electric Powered Hospital Bed Adjustments.—Electric powered adjustments to lower and raise head and foot may be covered when the contractor's medical staff determines that the patient's condition requires frequent change in body position and/or there may be an immediate need for a change in body position (i.e., no delay can be tolerated) and the patient can operate the controls and cause the adjustments. Exceptions may be made to this last requirement in cases of spinal cord injury and brain damaged patients.

E. Side Rails.—If the patient's condition requires bed side rails, they can be covered when an integral part of, or an accessory to, a hospital bed.

Cross refer: Carriers Manual, section 5015.4

60-19 AIR-FLUIDIZED BED

An air-fluidized bed uses warm air under pressure to set small ceramic beads in motion which simulate the movement of fluid. When the patient is placed in the bed, his body weight is evenly distributed over a large surface area which creates a sensation of "floating." Medicare payment for home use of the air-fluidized bed for treatment of pressure sores can be made if such use is reasonable and necessary for the individual patient.

A decision that use of an air-fluidized bed is reasonable and necessary requires that:

- The patient has a stage 3 (full thickness tissue loss) or stage 4 (deep tissue destruction) pressure sore;
- The patient is bedridden or chair bound as a result of severely limited mobility;
- In the absence of an air-fluidized bed, the patient would require institutionalization;
- The air-fluidized bed is ordered in writing by the patient's attending physician based upon a comprehensive assessment and evaluation of the patient after conservative treatment has been tried without success;
- A trained adult caregiver is available to assist the patient with activities of daily living, fluid balance, dry skin care, repositioning, recognition and management of altered mental status, dietary needs, prescribed treatments, and management and support of the air-fluidized bed system and its problems such as leakage;
- A physician directs the home treatment regimen, and reevaluates and recertifies the need for the air-fluidized bed on a monthly basis; and

- All other alternative equipment has been considered and ruled out.

Home use of the air-fluidized bed is not covered under any of the following circumstances:

- The patient has coexisting pulmonary disease (the lack of firm back support makes coughing ineffective and dry air inhalation thickens pulmonary secretions);
- The patient requires treatment with wet soaks or moist wound dressings that are not protected with an impervious covering such as plastic wrap or other occlusive material;
- The caregiver is unwilling or unable to provide the type of care required by the patient on an air-fluidized bed;
- Structural support is inadequate to support the weight of the air-fluidized bed system (it generally weighs 1600 pounds or more);
- Electrical system is insufficient for the anticipated increase in energy consumption; or
- Other known contraindications exist.

Coverage of an air-fluidized bed is limited to the equipment itself. Payment for this covered item may only be made if the written order from the attending physician is furnished to the supplier prior to the delivery of the equipment. Payment is not included for the caregiver or for architectural adjustments such as electrical or structural improvement.

Cross refer: Carriers Manual, section 5102.2

60-20 TRANSCUTANEOUS ELECTRICAL NERVE STIMULATORS (TENS)

TENS is a type of electrical nerve stimulator that is employed to treat chronic intractable pain. This stimulator is attached to the surface of the patient's skin over the peripheral nerve to be stimulated. It may be applied in a variety of settings (in the patient's home, a physician's office, or in an outpatient clinic). Payment for TENS may be made under the durable medical equipment benefit. (See section 45-25 for an explanation of coverage of medically necessary supplies for the effective use of TENS and section 45-19 for an explanation of coverage of TENS for acute postoperative pain.)

65 PROSTHETIC DEVICES

65-1 HYDROPHILIC CONTACT LENSES

Hydrophilic contact lenses are eyeglasses within the meaning of the exclusion in section 1862(a)(7) of the law and are not covered when used in the treatment of nondiseased eyes with spherical ametrophia, refractive astigmatism, and/or corneal astigmatism. Payment may be made under the prosthetic device benefit, however, for hydrophilic contact lenses when prescribed for an aphakic patient.

Contractors are authorized to accept an FDA letter of approval or other FDA published material as evidence of FDA approval.

(*See* section 45-7 for coverage of a hydrophilic lens as a corneal bandage.)

Cross-refer: Intermediary Manual, sections 3110.3, 3110.4, 3151, and 3157; Carriers Manual, sections 2130, 2320; Hospital Manual, sections 228.3, 228.4, 260.1 and 260.7.

65-3 SCLERAL SHELL

Scleral shell (or shield) is a catch-all term for different types of hard scleral contact lenses.

A scleral shell fits over the entire exposed surface of the eye as opposed to a corneal contact lens which covers only the central non-white area encompassing the pupil and iris. Where an eye has been rendered sightless and shrunken by inflammatory disease, a scleral shell may, among other things, obviate the need for surgical enucleation and prosthetic implant and act to support the surrounding orbital tissue.

In such a case, the device serves essentially as an artificial eye. In this situation, payment may be made for a scleral shell under section 1861(s)(8) of the law.

Scleral shells are occasionally used in combination with artificial tears in the treatment of "dry eye" of diverse etiology. Tears ordinarily dry at a rapid rate, and are continually replaced by the lacrimal gland. When the lacrimal gland fails, the half-life of artificial tears may be greatly prolonged by the use of the scleral contact lens as a protective barrier against the drying action of the atmosphere. Thus, the difficult and sometimes hazardous process of frequent instillation of artificial tears may be avoided. The lens acts in this instance to substitute, in part, for the functioning of the diseased lacrimal gland and would be covered as a prosthetic device in the rare case when it is used in the treatment of "dry eye."

Cross-refer: HCFA-Pub. 13-3, sections 3110.4, 3110.5; HCFA-Pub. 14-3, sections 2130, 2133; HCFA-Pub. 10, sections 210.4, 211

65-5 ELECTRONIC SPEECH AIDS

Electronic speech aids are covered under Part B as prosthetic devices when the patient has had a laryngectomy or his larynx is permanently inoperative. There are two types of speech aids. One operates by placing a vibrating head against the throat; the other amplifies sound waves through a tube which is inserted into the user's mouth. A patient who has had radical neck surgery and/or extensive radiation to the anterior part of the neck would generally be able to use only the "oral tube" model or one of the more sensitive and more expensive "throat contact" devices.

Cross-refer: HCFA-Pub. 13-3, section 3110.4; HCFA-Pub. 14-3, section 2130; HCFA-Pub. 10, section 228.4

65-7 INTRAOCULAR LENSES (IOLs)

An intraocular lens, or pseudophakos, is an artificial lens which may be implanted to replace the natural lens after cataract surgery. Intraocular lens implantation services, as well as the lens itself, may be covered if reasonable and necessary for the individual. Implantation services may include hospital, surgical, and other medical services, including pre-implantation ultrasound (A-scan) eye measurement of one or both eyes.

Cross-refer: HCFA-Pub. 13-3, sections 3110.4, 3151, 3157; HCFA-Pub.14-3, section 2130; HCFA-Pub. 10, section 228.4

65-8 ELECTRICAL NERVE STIMULATORS

Two general classifications of electrical nerve stimulators are employed to treat chronic intractable pain: peripheral nerve stimulators and central nervous system stimulators.

A. Implanted Peripheral Nerve Stimulators.—Payment may be made under the prosthetic device benefit for implanted peripheral nerve stimulators. Use of this stimulator involves implantation of electrodes around a selected peripheral nerve. The stimulating electrode is connected by an insulated lead to a receiver unit which is implanted under the skin at a depth not greater than 1/2 inch. Stimulation is induced by a generator connected to an antenna unit which is attached to the skin surface over the receiver unit. Implantation of electrodes requires surgery and usually necessitates an operating room.

NOTE: Peripheral nerve stimulators may also be employed to assess a patient's suitability for continued treatment with an electric nerve stimulator. As explained in section 35-46, such use of the stimulator is covered as part of the total diagnostic service furnished to the beneficiary rather than as a prosthesis.

B. Central Nervous System Stimulators (Dorsal Column and Depth Brain Stimulators).—The implantation of central nervous system stimulators may be covered as therapies for the relief of chronic intractable pain, subject to the following conditions:

1. Types of Implantations.—There are two types of implantations covered by this instruction:

a. Dorsal Column (Spinal Cord) Neurostimulation.—The surgical implantation of neurostimulator electrodes within the dura mater (endodural) or the percutaneous insertion of electrodes in the epidural space is covered.

b. Depth Brain Neurostimulation.—The stereotactic implantation of electrodes in the deep brain (e.g., thalamus and periaqueductal gray matter) is covered.

2. Conditions for Coverage.—No payment may be made for the implantation of dorsal column or depth brain stimulators or services and supplies related to such implantation, unless all of the conditions listed below have been met:

a. The implantation of the stimulator is used only as a late resort (if not a last resort) for patients with chronic intractable pain;

b. With respect to item a, other treatment modalities (pharmacological, surgical, physical, or psychological therapies) have been tried and did not prove satisfactory, or are judged to be unsuitable or contraindicated for the given patient;

c. Patients have undergone careful screening, evaluation and diagnosis by a multidisciplinary team prior to implantation. (Such screening must include psychological, as well as physical evaluation);

d. All the facilities, equipment, and professional and support personnel required for the proper diagnosis, treatment training, and followup of the patient (including that required to satisfy item c must be available; and

e. Demonstration of pain relief with a temporarily implanted electrode precedes permanent implantation.

Contractors may find it helpful to work with PROs to obtain the information needed to apply these conditions to claims.

See Intermediary Manual, section 3110.4 and section 35-20 and 35-27.

65-9 INCONTINENCE CONTROL DEVICES

A. Mechanical/Hydraulic Incontinence Control Devices.—Mechanical/hydraulic incontinence control devices are accepted as safe and effective in the management of urinary incontinence in patients with permanent anatomic and neurologic dysfunctions of the bladder. This class of devices achieves control of urination by compression of the urethra. The materials used and the success rate may vary somewhat from device to device. Such a device is covered when its use is reasonable and necessary for the individual patient.

B. Collagen Implant.—A collagen implant, which is injected into the submucosal tissues of the urethra and/or the bladder neck and into tissues adjacent to the urethra, is a prosthetic device used in the treatment of stress urinary incontinence resulting from intrinsic sphincter deficiency (ISD). ISD is a cause of stress urinary incontinence in which the urethral sphincter is unable to contract and generate sufficient resistance in the bladder, especially during stress maneuvers.

Prior to collagen implant therapy, a skin test for collagen sensitivity must be administered and evaluated over a 4 week period.

In male patients, the evaluation must include a complete history and physical examination and a simple cystometrogram to determine that the bladder fills and stores properly. The patient then is asked to stand upright with a full bladder and to cough or otherwise exert abdominal pressure on his bladder. If the patient leaks, the diagnosis of ISD is established.

In female patients, the evaluation must include a complete history and physical examination (including a pelvic exam) and a simple cystometrogram to rule out abnormalities of bladder compliance and abnormalities of urethral support. Following that determination, an abdominal leak point pressure (ALLP) test is performed. Leak point pressure, stated in cm H_2O, is defined as the intra-abdominal pressure at which leakage occurs from the bladder (around a catheter) when the bladder has been filled with a minimum of 150 cc fluid. If the patient has an ALLP of less than 100 cm H_2O, the diagnosis of ISD is established.

To use a collagen implant, physicians must have urology training in the use of a cystoscope and must complete a collagen implant training program.

Coverage of a collagen implant, and the procedure to inject it, is limited to the following types of patients with stress urinary incontinence due to ISD:

- Male or female patients with congenital sphincter weakness secondary to conditions such as myelomeningocele or epispadias;
- Male or female patients with acquired sphincter weakness secondary to spinal cord lesions;
- Male patients following trauma, including prostatectomy and/or radiation; and
- Female patients without urethral hypermobility and with abdominal leak point pressures of 100 cm H_2O or less.

Patients whose incontinence does not improve with 5 injection procedures (5 separate treatment sessions) are considered treatment failures, and no further treatment of urinary incontinence by collagen implant is covered. Patients who have a reoccurrence of incontinence following successful treatment with collagen implants in the past (e.g., 6 to 12 months previously) may benefit from additional treatment sessions. Coverage of additional sessions may be allowed but must be supported by medical justification.

C. Electronic Stimulators.—Pelvic floor electrical stimulators, whether inserted into the vaginal canal or rectum or implanted in the pelvic area, used as a treatment for urinary incontinence, e.g., as a bladder pacer or a retraining mechanism, are not covered. The effectiveness of these devices is unproven. (See section 65-11.)

See Intermediary Manual, section 3110.4.

65-10 ENTERAL AND PARENTERAL NUTRITIONAL THERAPY COVERED AS PROSTHETIC DEVICE

There are patients who, because of chronic illness or trauma, cannot be sustained through oral feeding. These people must rely on either enteral or parenteral nutritional therapy, depending upon the particular nature of their medical condition.

Coverage of nutritional therapy as a Part B benefit is provided under the prosthetic device benefit provision, which requires that the patient must have a permanently inoperative internal body organ or function thereof. (See Intermediary Manual, section 3110.4.) Therefore, enteral and parenteral nutritional therapy are not covered under Part B in situations involving temporary impairments. Coverage of such therapy, however, does not require a medical judgment that the impairment giving rise to the therapy will persist throughout the patient's remaining years. If the medical record, including the judgment of the attending physician, indicates that the impairment will be of long and indefinite duration, the test of permanence is considered met.

If the coverage requirements for enteral or parenteral nutritional therapy are met under the prosthetic device benefit provision, related supplies, equipment and nutrients are also covered under the conditions in the following paragraphs and Intermediary Manual, section 3110.4.

65-10.1 Parenteral Nutrition Therapy.—Daily parenteral nutrition is considered reasonable and necessary for a patient with severe pathology of the alimentary tract which does not allow absorption of sufficient nutrients to maintain weight and strength commensurate with the patient's general condition.

Since the alimentary tract of such a patient does not function adequately, an indwelling catheter is placed percutaneously in the subclavian vein and then advanced into the superior vena cava where intravenous infusion of nutrients is given for part of the day. The catheter is then plugged by the patient until the next infusion. Following a period of hospitalization, which is required to initiate parenteral nutrition and to train the patient in catheter care, solution preparation, and infusion technique, the parenteral nutrition can be provided safely and effectively in the patient's home by nonprofessional persons who have undergone special training. However, such persons cannot be paid for their services, nor is payment available for any services furnished by nonphysician professionals except as services furnished incident to a physician's service.

For parenteral nutrition therapy to be covered under Part B, the claim must contain a physician's written order or prescription and sufficient medical documentation to permit an independent conclusion that the requirements of the prosthetic device benefit are met and that parenteral nutrition therapy is medically necessary. An example of a condition that typically qualifies for coverage is a massive small bowel resection resulting in severe nutritional deficiency in spite of adequate oral intake. However, coverage of parenteral nutrition therapy for this and any other condition must be approved on an individual, case-by-case basis initially and at periodic intervals of no more than 3 months by the carrier's medical consultant or specially trained staff, relying on such medical and other documentation as the carrier may require. If the claim involves an infusion pump, sufficient evidence must be provided to support a determination of medical necessity for the pump. Program payment for the pump is based on the reasonable charge for the simplest model that meets the medical needs of the patient as established by medical documentation.

Nutrient solutions for parenteral therapy are routinely covered. However, Medicare pays for no more than 1 month's supply of nutrients at any one time. Payment for the nutrients is based on the reasonable charge for the solution components unless the medical record, including a signed statement from the attending physician, establishes that the beneficiary, due to his/her physical or mental state, is unable to safely or effectively mix the solution and there is no family member or other person who can do so. Payment will be on the basis of the reasonable charge for more expensive pre-mixed solutions only under the latter circumstances.

65-10.2 Enteral Nutrition Therapy.—Enteral nutrition is considered reasonable and necessary for a patient with a functioning gastrointestinal tract who, due to pathology to or nonfunction of the structures that normally permit food to reach the digestive tract, cannot maintain weight and strength commensurate with his or her general condition. Enteral therapy may be given by nasogastric, jejunostomy, or gastrostomy tubes and can be provided safely and effectively in the home by nonprofessional persons who have undergone special training. However, such persons cannot be paid for their services, nor is payment available for any services furnished by nonphysician professionals except as services furnished incident to a physician's service.

Typical examples of conditions that qualify for coverage are head and neck cancer with reconstructive surgery and central nervous system disease leading to interference with the neuromuscular mechanisms of ingestion of such severity that the beneficiary cannot be maintained with oral feeding. However, claims for Part B coverage of enteral nutrition therapy for these and any other conditions must be approved on an individual, case-by-case basis. Each claim must contain a physician's written order or prescription and sufficient medical documentation (e.g., hospital records, clinical findings from the attending physician) to permit an independent conclusion that the patient's condition meets the requirements of the prosthetic device benefit and that enteral nutrition therapy is medically necessary. Allowed claims are to be reviewed at periodic intervals of no more than 3 months by the contractor's medical consultant or specially trained staff, and additional medical documentation considered necessary is to be obtained as part of this review.

Medicare pays for no more than 1 month's supply of enteral nutrients at any one time.

If the claim involves a pump, it must be supported by sufficient medical documentation to establish that the pump is medically necessary, i.e., gravity feeding is not satisfactory due to aspiration, diarrhea, dumping syndrome, etc. Program payment for the pump is based on the reasonable charge for the simplest model that meets the medical needs of the patient as established by medical documentation.

65-10.3 Nutritional Supplementation

Some patients require supplementation of their daily protein and caloric intake. Nutritional supplements are often given as a medicine between meals to boost protein-caloric intake or the mainstay of a daily nutritional plan. Nutritional supplementation is not covered under Medicare Part B.

65-11 BLADDER STIMULATORS (PACEMAKERS)—NOT COVERED

There are a number of devices available to induce emptying of the urinary bladder by using electrical current which forces the muscles of the bladder to contract. These devices (commonly known as bladder stimulators or pacemakers) are characterized by the implantation of electrodes in the wall of the bladder, the rectal cones, or the spinal cord. While these treatments may effectively empty the bladder, the issue of safety involving the initiation of infection, erosion, placement, and material selection has not been resolved. Further, some facilities previously using electronic emptying have stopped using this method due to the pain experienced by the patient.

The use of spinal cord electrical stimulators, rectal electrical stimulators, and bladder wall stimulators is not considered reasonable and necessary. Therefore, no program payment may be made for these devices or for their implantation

65-14 COCHLEAR IMPLANTATION

A cochlear implant device is an electronic instrument, part of which is implanted surgically to stimulate auditory nerve fibers, and part of which is worn or carried by the individual to capture, amplify, and code sound. Cochlear implant devices are available in single channel and multi-channel models. The purpose of implanting the device is to provide an awareness and identification of sounds and to facilitate communication for persons who are profoundly hearing impaired.

Medicare coverage is provided only for those patients who meet all of the following selection guidelines.

A. General.—

- Diagnosis of bilateral severe-to-profound sensorineural hearing impairment with limited benefit from appropriate hearing (or vibrotactile) aids;
- Cognitive ability to use auditory clues and a willingness to undergo an extended program of rehabilitation;
- Freedom from middle ear infection, an accessible cochlear lumen that is structurally suited to implantation, and freedom from lesions in the auditory nerve and acoustic areas of the central nervous system;
- No contraindications to surgery; and
- The device must be used in accordance with the FDA-approved labeling.

B. Adults.—Cochlear implants may be covered for adults (over age 18) for prelinguistically, perilinguistically, and postlinguistically deafened adults. Postlinguistically deafened adults must demonstrate test scores of 30 percent or less on sentence recognition scores from tape recorded tests in the patient's best listening condition.

C. Children.—Cochlear implants may be covered for prelinguistically and postlinguistically deafened children aged 2 through 17. Bilateral profound sensorineural deafness must be demonstrated by the inability to improve on age appropriate closed-set word identification tasks with amplification.

65-16 TRACHEOSTOMY SPEAKING VALVE

A trachea tube has been determined to satisfy the definition of a prosthetic device, and the tracheostomy speaking valve is an add-on to the trachea tube which may be considered a medically necessary accessory that enhances the function of the tube. In other words, it makes the system a better prosthesis. As such, a tracheostomy speaking valve is covered as an element of the trachea tube which makes the tube more effective.

70 BRACES—TRUSSES—ARTIFICIAL LIMBS AND EYES

70-1 CORSET USED AS HERNIA SUPPORT

A hernia support (whether in the form of a corset or truss) which meets the definition of a brace is covered under Part B under section 1861(s)(9) of the Act.

See Intermediary Manual, section 3110.5; Medicare Carriers Manual, section 2133; and Hospital Manual, section 228.5.

70-2 SYKES HERNIA CONTROL

Based on professional advice, it has been determined that the Sykes hernia control (a spring-type, U-shaped, strapless truss) is not functionally more beneficial than a conventional truss. Make program reimbursement for this device only when an ordinary truss would be covered. (Like all trusses, it is only of benefit when dealing with a reducible hernia). Thus, when a charge for this item is substantially in excess of that which would be reasonable for a conventional truss used for the same condition, base reimbursement on the reasonable charges for the conventional truss.

See Intermediary Manual, section 3110.5; Medicare Carriers Manual, section 2133; and Hospital Manual, section 228.5.